NTA UGC NET/JRF/SET

PAPER - 2

English

NTA UGC NET/JRF/SET

PAPER - 2

English

Author

Mridula Sharma *(MA, M.Ed)*
Ajeet Singh Jadaun *(MA, B.Ed)*
Anjali Singh Chauhan *(MA, UGC NET English)*
Tanveen Kaur *(MA, Asst Prof Delhi University)*
Dr. Chakreswari Dixit *(MA, Ph.D)*
Chhavi Kumar *(MA (English, History), B.Ed, M.Ed)*

ARIHANT PUBLICATION (INDIA) LIMITED

卐 **Administrative & Production Offices**

Regd. Office

'Ramchhaya' 4577/15, Agarwal Road, Darya Ganj, New Delhi -110002
Tele: 011- 47630600, 43518550

卐 **Head Office**

Kalindi, TP Nagar, Meerut (UP) - 250002
Tel: 0121-7156203, 7156204

卐 **Sales & Support Offices**

Agra, Ahmedabad, Bengaluru, Bareilly, Chennai, Delhi, Guwahati, Hyderabad, Jaipur, Jhansi, Kolkata, Lucknow, Nagpur & Pune.

卐 **PRICE** ₹835.00

Published by Arihant Publications (India) Ltd.

For further information about the books published by Arihant, log on to www.arihantbooks.com or e-mail at info@arihantbooks.com

PREFACE

On behalf of UGC (NTA) National Testing Agency has been assigned to conduct a National Eligibility Test for Indian Nationals for the post of Assistant Professors or Junior Research Fellowship. NTA has been established as a premier specialist autonomous testing organisation to conduct entrance examinations for recruitment in higher educational institutions. The aspirants appearing in UGC Net Examination have to face two challenges at present one is lack of really good book and study material in the market, second an updated syllabus in all subject (including English Literature) with very little micro frame work.

Arihant Publications has always aimed at providing the most useful and updated books to the aspirants. We are glad to present this book in a totally new format. It has been divided in Ten (10) Units with 29 Chapters as per the latest syllabus guideline provided by N.T.A (National Testing Agency). Efforts have been made to present chapters under different units with comprehensive information under various headings. Each chapter contains substantial amount of questions related to a particular topic or genre with new pattern and types of questions which are being asked in the exam. Utmost care has been taken to keep the language effective but simple and presentation very systematic and lucid. Socio-historical backgrounds of all the literary period right from Anglo Saxon Period to Contemporary Period has been included. Required information about different writers of a particular genre incorporated (like drama, poetry or fiction) has been provided. It includes all the major and minor writers their biographical sketch, their literary works and analysis of their prominent works. Previous years' questions have also been included along with three sample papers to help the students to crack the exam.

This book is an endeavour to match the expectations of the aspirants and readers. As the book has been designed to according to the latest syllabus, valuable suggestions from the readers are solicited. A team of expert authors of ARIHANT has strived hard to present this book in this new format.

We are highly thankful to ARIHANT PUBLICATION, MEERUT, Management and other people associated with bringing out this new book.

At the end, we would like to say 'Best of Luck' to our READERS!

Authors

SYLLABUS

Unit I	Drama
Unit II	Poetry
Unit III	Fiction, Short Stories
Unit IV	Non-Fictional Prose
Unit V	Language: Basic Concepts, Theories and Pedagogy
Unit VI	English in India: History, Evolution and Futures
Unit VII	Cultural Studies
Unit VIII	Literary Criticism
Unit IX	Literary Theory Post World War II
Unit X	Research Methods and Materials in English

NOTE

The first four units must also be tested through comprehension passages to assess critical reading, critical thinking and writing skills. These four units will cover all literatures in English.

CONTENTS

Solved Papers 2024-23

English (Paper-2)

Solved Paper, August 2024

General Instructions

1. There are total one hundred questions in this paper. Each question carries 2 marks.
2. All questions are compulsory.

---

1. Who among the following wrote 'Plan of a Novel'?

(1) EM Forster (2) DH Lawrance
(3) Jane Austen (4) Thomas Hardy

2. Which one of the following English novels received Sahitya Akademi Awards for the year 2023?

(1) *Requiem in Raga Janki* by Neelum Saran Gour
(2) *All the Lives We Never Lived* by Anuradha Roy
(3) *The Blind Lady's Descendants* by Anees Salim
(4) *Chronicles of a Corpse Bearer* by Cyrus Mistry

3. Match List-I with List-II.

	List-I (Events)		List-II (Years)
A.	International Year of the World's Indigenous People	I.	1998
B.	Australian Parliament formally apologised to the stolen generation	II.	1993
C.	Formal end of White Australian Policy	III.	1973
D.	The First National Sorry Day	IV.	2008

Choose the correct answer from the options given below.

	A	B	C	D
(1)	I	III	IV	II
(2)	III	I	II	IV
(3)	IV	II	I	III
(4)	II	IV	III	I

4. Who among the following women writers wrote the first female Dalit autobiography?

(1) Sharmila Rege
(2) Urmila Pawar
(3) Shantabai Krushnaji Kamble
(4) Meena Kandasamy

5. MH Abram's *'The Mirror and the Lamp : Romantic Theory and the Critical Tradition'*

A. describes 18th century English Literature as 'mirror'.
B. describes 19th century English Literature as 'lamp'.
C. describes 19th century English Literature as 'mirror'.
D. the metaphor of 'mirror' is used to describe literature as a cool intellectual reflection of outward realities.
E. the metaphor of 'mirror' is used to describe literature as an illumination shed by artists upon their inner and outer worlds.

Choose the correct answer from the options given below.

(1) C, D and E
(2) C, D and A
(3) A, B and D
(4) A, B and E

6. Which one of the following novels by EM Forster is about 'homosexual love'?
(1) *Howard End*
(2) *A Room with a View*
(3) *Maurice*
(4) *Where Angels Fear to Tread*

7. Three satirical stories by WM Thackeray portraying unhappy marriage and exploitation of one partner by the other, are titled as
(1) *Men's Wives*
(2) *Wive's Husbands*
(3) *Wife and Husband*
(4) *Wife without a Husband*

8. Which of the following assertions/assumptions are not true regarding cultures of space?
A. Space is about power to control access, representation and use.
B. Space is simply land or built-up area.
C. The Space influences social relations and communities.
D. Space is socially constructed through social relations.
E. Space has nothing to do with everyday activities of people.

Choose the correct answer from the options given below.
(1) A, B and C only (2) E and D only
(3) B and E only (4) A and E only

9. Who said that an author has no claim to original thought but only to apt presentation of what was already being thought by others?
(1) Alexander Pope (2) Ezra Pound
(3) Max Muller (4) Harold Bloom

10. John Dryden's *Of Dramatic Poesy : An Essay* is written in the form of a dialogue between Eugenius, Crites, Lisideius and Neander, where Neander represents
(1) Alexander Pope (2) John Dryden
(3) Sir Robert Howard (4) Charles Sackville

11. Arrange the following plays by Shakespeare in order of their production/publication.
A. *Twelfth Night*
B. *The Taming of the Shrew*
C. *Much Ado About Nothing*
D. *Romeo and Juliet*
E. *The Winter's Tale*

Choose the correct answer from the options given below.
(1) D, C, B, A, E (2) B, D, A, E, C
(3) A, D, C, B, E (4) B, D, C, A, E

12. Which one of the following plays mock the Restoration drama of Dryden and Thomas Otway?
(1) *The Beggar's Opera* by John Gay
(2) *Tom Thumb* by Henry Fielding
(3) *The Critic* by RB Sheridan
(4) *The Rehearsal* by George Villiers

13. Match List-I with List-II.

List-I (Australian Aboriginal Texts)		List-II (Authors)
A. *Wahngin Country*	I.	Alexis Wright
B. *Plains of Promise*	II.	Jack Davis
C. *My Place*	III.	Anita Heiss
D. *Not Meeting Mr. Right*	IV.	Sally Morgan

Choose the correct answer from the options given below.

	A	B	C	D		A	B	C	D
(1)	IV	III	II	I	(2)	I	IV	III	II
(3)	II	I	IV	III	(4)	III	II	I	IV

14. Who among the following wrote that
"Poetry is not a branch of authorship: it is 'the stuff of which one life is made'. The rest is 'mere oblivion', a dead letter: for all that is worth remembering in life, is the poetry of it?"
(1) Mary Shelley (2) Charles Lamb
(3) William Hazlitt (4) ST Coleridge

15. In *Long Revolution*, Raymond Williams conducted a long-range study of 350 canonical writers drawn from the *Oxford Introduction to English Literature* for the period
(1) 1789-1950 (2) 1764-1939
(3) 1450-1914 (4) 1470-1920

16. Terms 'social fact' and 'collective consciousness' in the context of language were used by
A. Franz Boas B. Bloomfield
C. Emile Durkheim D. Noam Chomsky
E. Saussure

Choose the correct answer from the options given below.
(1) C and E
(2) A and B
(3) B and C
(4) D and B

17. The key principles of research design brought together in material on measurement principles, sampling and case study, survey and experimentation is termed as
(1) Research methodology
(2) Research methods
(3) Research techniques

(4) Research designs

18. Place the following works in ascending order of their publication year.

A. *Diamond Dust* by Anita Desai

B. *Breast-Giver* by Mahashweta Devi

C. *Death and the King's Horseman* by Wole Soyinka

D. *Dream on Monkey Mountain* by Derek Walcott

E. *Exile and the Kingdom* by Albert Camus

Choose the correct answer from the options given below.

(1) A, B, C, D, E (2) E, D, C, B, A
(3) D, B, C, A, E (4) B, C, A, D, E

19. Neo-Platonism was founded by

A. Plato B. Plotinus
C. Porphyry D. Aristotle
E. Pythagoras

Choose the correct answer from the options given below.

(1) A and B (2) C and D
(3) B and C (4) D and E

20. Which of the following assumption is not true with regard to Lacan's concept/theory of standpoint?

A. It assumes that social position can provide privileged perspective on some relations and knowledge.

B. It argues that those who are marginalised or oppressed may have access to insights and perceptions that dominant group lacks.

C. It refers to a situation in which the oppressed class is destined to lose the class consciousness.

D. It suggests that the perspectives of those on the margins of society cannot help to understand social dynamics.

E. The theory is based on the idea that social contradictions and political struggle can shape counter-hegemonic norms.

Choose the correct answer from the options given below.

(1) A and C
(2) D and E
(3) B and C
(4) C and D

21. Phonetics refers to

A. production of speech sounds
B. reception of speech sounds
C. transmission of speech sounds
D. pattern of speech sounds
E. word formation

Choose the correct answer from the options given below.

(1) A and C (2) B and D
(3) D and E (4) A and D

22. Chronologically arrange the following in order of their publication/occurrence.

A. Caxton printed Malory's *Morte D'Arthur*

B. Establishment of Caxton's printing press

C. Gutenberg printed Bible in Mainz, Germany

D. Caxton's *History of Troy,* first book printed in English

E. First translation of the Christian Bible into English by John Wycliff.

Choose the correct answer from the options given below.

(1) B, E, D, C, A (2) C, B, E, A, D
(3) E, C, D, B, A (4) D, A, B, C, E

23. Who said that language is a system of signs whose parts can and must be considered in their synchronic solidarity?

(1) Saussure (2) Bloomfield
(3) Roman Jakobson (4) Sigmund Freud

24. Arrange the works of Toni Morrison in the order of chronology of their publication.

A *Jazz*
B. *Beloved*
C. *In Bluest Eye*
D. *Song of Solomon*
E. *Tar Baby*

Choose the correct answer from the options given below.

(1) A, E, C, D, B (2) D, C, E, B, A
(3) C, D, E, B, A (4) E, D, A, B, C

25. Who wrote the poem *Poem in Praise of Menstruation*?

(1) Gloria Steinem (2) Seamus Heaney
(3) Francis Thompson (4) Lucille Clifton

26. Match List-I with List-II.

	List-I (Authors)		List-II (Nobel Prize Years)
A.	Wole Soyinka	I.	1991
B.	Nadine Gordimer	II.	1993
C.	Derek Walcott	III.	2003
D.	JM Coetzee	IV.	1986

Codes

	A	B	C	D
(1)	II	IV	III	I
(2)	III	II	IV	I
(3)	IV	I	II	III
(4)	I	III	IV	II

27. Chronologically arrange the following works in order of their publication.

A. Ariosto's *Orlando Furioso*

B. Martin Luther King's *95 Theses at Wittenberg*

C. *The first Book of Common Prayer* by Thomas Cranmer

D. Thomas More's *Utopia*

E. Machieavelli's *The Prince*

Choose the correct answer from the options given below.

(1) E, D, B, A, C
(2) A, C, B, E, D
(3) E, B, C, A, D
(4) D, A, B, C, E

28. In *The Post Modern Condition Lyotard* announced the eclipse of all grand narratives. The one whose death he above all sought to declare was

(1) Hegelian Spirit
(2) Christian Redemption
(3) Keynesian Equilibrium
(4) Classical Socialism

29. Match List-I with List-II.

	List-I		List-II
A.	Heteroglossia	I.	Deliberate foolishness/ non-sense for effect
B.	Homosociality	II.	Diversity of languages used in Epics
C.	Mathanavi	III.	Same-sex relationships which are not necessarily sexual
D.	Morology	IV.	Long narrative epic or heroic poem in rhyming couplets

Choose the correct answer from the options given below.

	A	B	C	D		A	B	C	D
(1)	IV	I	III	II	(2)	III	IV	I	II
(3)	II	III	IV	I	(4)	I	II	III	IV

30. Who among the following are writers of wordless graphic narratives?

A. Roy Fuller

B. Orijit Sen

C. Anthony Hecht

D. George Mathew Appupen

E. George Monbiot

Choose the correct answer from the options given below.

(1) A and C
(2) B and C
(3) B and D
(4) D and E

31. Match List-I with List-II.

	List-I		List-II
A.	The Language Instinct	I.	Steven Pinker
B.	Reflections of Language	II.	Noam Chomsky
C.	Variety of language serving a specialised function in a multi-lingual community	III.	Creole/ Creolisation
D.	Existence of a common variety of language for people from different cultures	IV.	Diglossia

Choose the correct answer from the options given below.

	A	B	C	D		A	B	C	D
(1)	I	II	IV	III	(2)	III	IV	II	I
(3)	I	II	III	IV	(4)	IV	III	I	II

32. Which research treats physical and social world as objects based on standardised data?

(1) Empirical (2) Action
(3) Quantitative (4) Qualitative

33. Which among the following texts are not written by Mary Wollstonecraft?

A. *The Wrongs of Man*

B. *Vindication of the Rights of Man*

C. *Thoughts on the Education of Sons*

D. *Vindication of the Rights of Woman*

E. *The Wrongs of Women*

Choose the correct answer from the options given below.

(1) B and D
(2) B and E
(3) D and E
(4) A and C

34. The term 'Collective Unconsciousness'

A. was introduced by Sigmund Freud.

B. was introduced by Carl Jung.

C. contains archetypes or universal primordial images and ideas.

D. contains stereotypes and individual experiences stored in unconscious.

E. is used to describe the unconscious common to humanity as a whole that originates in the inherited structures of the brain.

Choose the correct answer from the options given below.

(1) A, C and E
(2) B, C and E
(3) B, D and E
(4) C, D and E

35. Identify the name of the essayist who made the following assertion

"If a man will begin with certainties, he shall end in doubts, but if will be content to begin with doubts, he shall end in certainties."

(1) Richard Hooker (2) Sir Francis Bacon
(3) Sir Richard Steele (4) Joseph Addison

36. Which of the following is not a Dalit narrative written by Perumal Murugan?

(1) *Tirukkural : The Book of Desire*
(2) *Poonachi*
(3) *One Part Woman*
(4) *Pyre*

37. Big Daddy is a fictional character in

(1) the novel *Ninety Eighty Four* by George Orwell
(2) the play *Cat on a Hot Tin Roof* by Tennessee William
(3) the play *Look Back in Anger* by John Osborne
(4) the novel *Brave New World* by Aldous Huxley

38. Greek word 'Polis' refers to

A. social structure B. political structure
C. legal structure D. city state
E. barbarians

Choose the correct answer from the options given below.

(1) B and D (2) A and B
(3) B and C (4) D and E

39. The property of research to replicate the same results using the same technique is termed as

(1) Validity (2) Reliability
(3) Relevance (4) Coherence

40. Match List-I with List-II.

List-I (Terms)	List-II (Meanings)
A. Catastrophe	I. The introductory part of a play or narrative poem.
B. Epitasis	II. The final action that completes the unravelling of the plot in a play, especially a tragedy.
C. Protasis	III. The dramatic complication that immediately precedes the climax of the play.
D. Catastasis	IV. The part of the play that develops the main action and that lends to the catastrophe

Choose the correct answer from the options given below.

	A	B	C	D
(1)	IV	II	III	I
(2)	IV	II	I	III
(3)	II	IV	I	III
(4)	II	I	IV	III

41. Arrange the following Black American writers chronologically (in order of their birth).

A. Maya Angelou B. Toni Morrison
C. Alice Walker D. Langston Hughes
E. James Baldwin

Choose the correct answer from the options given below.

(1) D, A, E, C, B (2) D, E, A, B, C
(3) E, A, D, B, C (4) E, A, B, C, D

42. Match List-I with List-II

List-I	List-II
A. Langue	I. Meaning conveyed
B. Parole	II. Socially shared language
C. Signifier	III. Speech
D. Signified	IV. Word

Choose the correct answer from the options given below.

	A	B	C	D
(1)	II	III	IV	I
(2)	I	IV	III	II
(3)	III	II	I	IV
(4)	IV	III	II	I

43. Which text is considered to be the first book of poetry published by an Aboriginal author?

(1) Tracey Moffatt's *Night Cries : A Rural Tragedy*
(2) David Unaipon's *Native Legends*
(3) Oodgeroo Noonuccal's *We Are Going*
(4) Doris Pilkington Garimara's *Caprice : A Stockman's Daughter*

44. In his work, *The Dialogic Imagination,* Mikhail Bakhtin

A. develops theory of Polyphony.
B. postulates that language is imaginary.
C. postulates that language evolves dynamically.
D. argues that language gets affected by the culture that produces it as it helps to shape that culture.
E. develops theory of imaginative language.

Choose the correct answer from the options given below.

(1) B, D and E (2) A, C and D
(3) A, B and D (4) C, D and E

45. From which book of John Milton's poem *Paradise Lost* the epigraph of Mary Shelley's novel *Frankenstein* taken when Adam asks God

"Did I request thee, maker from my clay to mould me man? Did I solicit thee, from darkness to promote me?"

(1) Book I (2) Book II
(3) Book X (4) Book XII

46. Chronologically arrange the Rudiom playwrights in order of their birth.

A. Asif Currimbhoy B. Nissim Ezekiel

C. Cyrus Mistry D. Mahesh Dattani

E. Gurcharan Das

Choose the correct answer from the options given below.

(1) A, D, E, C, B (2) D, B, C, E, A

(3) A, E, D, B, C (4) B, A, E, C, D

47. *Kai Po Che!* is the screen adaptation of which one of the following novels by Chetan Bhagat?

(1) *The 3 Mistakes of My Life*

(2) *Five Point Someone*

(3) *Half Girlfriend*

(4) *Two States*

48. Which of the following assertions is not true with respect to 'cultural intermediaries'?

(1) The term 'cultural intermediaries' was introduced by the French cultural theorist Pierre Bourdieu.

(2) Cultural intermediaries mediate between the production of cultural events and its consumers.

(3) Promotional materials do not constitute cultural intermediaries.

(4) Fan clubs are cultural intermediaries.

49. Which one of the following plays by Henrik Ibsen was described as 'an open sewer'?

(1) *A Doll's House*

(2) *An Enemy of the People*

(3) *Ghosts*

(4) *The Wild Duck*

50. Who among the following were associated with Metaphysical Society founded in 1869 by Sir James Knowles?

A. Robert Browning

B. TH Huxley

C. Alfred Tennyson

D. Mathew Arnold

E. William Gladstone

Choose the correct answer from the options given below.

(1) A, B and C

(2) B, D and E

(3) C, D and E

(4) B, C and E

51. *Women in Love* is a sequel to which one of the following novels by DH Lawrance?

(1) *Lady Chatterley's Lover*

(2) *The White Peacock*

(3) *Sons and Lovers*

(4) *The Rainbow*

52. Who among the following is not associated with lesbian and gay studies?

A. Jane Rule

B. Jonathan Dollimore

C. John Wain

D. Elizabeth Jennings

E. Richard Dyer

Choose the correct answer from the options given below.

(1) A and E (2) C and D

(3) B and C (4) D and E

53. A manuscript having an overlap with earlier papers by the same authors or by some of the present authors is termed as.

(1) Plagiarism (2) Self-plagiarism

(3) Intertextuality (4) Multiple references

54. Sequence the following works of Dostoyevsky in the order of their publication

A. *Notes from Underground*

B. *Crime and Punishment*

C. *The Idiot*

D. *The Brothers Karamazov*

E. *Poor Folk*

Choose the correct answer from the options given below.

(1) B, C, E, A D

(2) E, A, B, C, D

(3) A, B, C, D, E

(4) C, A, D, B, E

55. Sherlock Holmes, the greatest of all fictional detectives, made his first appearance in which one of the following novels by Sir Arthur Conan Doyle.

(1) *Strand Magazine*

(2) *A Study in Scarlet*

(3) *The Adventures of Sherlock Holmes*

(4) *The Case-Book of Sherlock Holmes*

56. Which one of the following is not a screen adaptation of Shakespeare's *The Comedy of Errors*?

(1) *The Boys from Syracuse*

(2) *Angoor*

(3) *Do Dooni Chaar*

(4) *Love in a Wood*

57. Chronologically arrange the novels of Salman Rushdie in order of their publication.

A. *Fury*

B. *Midnight's Children*

C. *The Ground Beneath Her Feet*

D. *The Moor's Last Sigh*

E. *Grimus*

Choose the correct answer from the options given below.

(1) B, C, A, D, E (2) E, B, D, C, A
(3) A, E, B, C, D (4) D, C, B, E, A

58. Wittgenstein's statement, 'Limits of language defines limits of thought', means,

A. the structure of language defines its meaning.
B. tntended meaning defines structure of language.
C. that which can be defined meaningfully, can be thought.
D. structure and meaning are independent of each other.
E. thought precedes language.

Choose the correct answer from the options given below.

(1) A and C (2) A and B
(3) D and E (4) C and D

59. The term 'Post-modernism' was used in 1917 by German philosopher Rudolf Pannwitz to describe

(1) Nihilism of 20th century's Western culture
(2) Communism as a system of governance
(3) Decline of oligarchies
(4) Epistemic violence

60. Plato viewed poetry as

A. an imitation of reality
B. self-subsistent entity
C. distant from reality
D. manifestation of reality
E. life as experience in reality

Choose the correct answer from the options given below.

(1) A and C (2) B and D (3) D and E (4) A and E

61. Match List-I with List-II.

List-I (Novel)	List-II (Novelist)
A. *Delinquent Chacha*	I. Rohinton Mistry
B. *Tales from Firozsha Baag*	II. Ved Prakash Mehta
C. *Beethoven Among the Cows*	III. Gita Hariharan
D. *A Thousand Faces of Night*	IV. Rukun Advani

Choose the correct answer from the options given below.

	A	B	C	D
(1)	I	III	II	IV
(2)	II	I	IV	III
(3)	IV	II	III	I
(4)	III	IV	II	I

62. Who among the following were not associated with Kit-Cat Club?

A. George Etherege
B. Richard Steele
C. Samuel Johnson
D. William Congreve
E. Joseph Addison

Choose the correct answer from the options given below.

(1) B and D (2) B and E
(3) A and C (4) D and E

63. Who made the following statements in defense of *Santarasa* "the eight rasas are like eight gods and the santa is like their highest centre Siva"?

(1) Bharat (2) Anandavardhan
(3) Dandin (4) Abhinavagupta

64. Match List-I with List-II.

List-I (Works)	List-II (Authors)
A. *On a Muggy Night in Mumbai*	I. R. Raj Rao
B. *The Golden Gate*	II. Mahesh Duttani
C. *The Boyfriend*	III. Vikram Chandra
D. *Love and Longing in Bombay*	IV. Vikram Seth

Choose the correct answer from the options given below.

	A	B	C	D
(1)	II	IV	I	III
(2)	IV	III	II	I
(3)	I	II	IV	III
(4)	III	I	II	IV

65. Who wrote the book *The History of European Languages*?

(1) Alexander Murrey
(2) AS Diamond
(3) William Jones
(4) Bloomfield

66. Chronologically arrange the fictional writings of RK Narayan in order of their publication.

A. *The Vendor of Sweets*
B. *The Bachelor of Arts*
C. *The English Teacher*
D. *The Guide*
E. *The Financial Expert*

Choose the correct answer from the options given below.

(1) A, D, B, E, C
(2) C, B, D, A, E
(3) B, C, E, D, A
(4) E, A, B, C, D

67. Match List-I with List-II.

List-I (Texts)	List-II (Authors)
A. *Critique of Judgement*	I. Martin Heidegger
B. *The Phenomenology of Spirit*	II. Sigmund Freud
C. *Group Pyschology and the Analysis of the Ego*	III. Immanuel Kant
D. *The Role of the University in the New Reich*	IV. GWF Hegel

Choose the correct answer from the options given below.

	A	B	C	D		A	B	C	D
(1)	III	I	IV	II	(2)	I	II	III	IV
(3)	II	III	IV	I	(4)	III	IV	II	I

68. Match List-I with List-II.

List-I (Poems)	List-II (Indian Poets)
A. *Night of the Scorpion*	I. Kamala Das
B. *Unfinished Poem*	II. AK Ramanujan
C. *The Looking Glass*	III. Eunice de Souza
D. *To a Friend Far Away*	IV. Nissim Ezekiel

Choose the correct answer from the options given below.

	A	B	C	D		A	B	C	D
(1)	III	II	IV	I	(2)	II	I	III	IV
(3)	IV	III	I	II	(4)	II	IV	I	III

69. Which of the following is considered to be the first Indian novel in English?

(1) Bankimchandra Chatterjee's *Rajamohan's Wife*
(2) Toru Dutt's *The Young Zamindar*
(3) KK Sinha's *Sanjogita*
(4) KK Sinha's *The Star of Sikri*

70. Arrange the following plays in order of their publication.

A. *Death of a Salesman* by Arthur Miller
B. *The Glass Menagerie* by Tennessee Williams
C. *Who is Afraid of Virginia Wolf?* by Edward Albee
D. *The Iceman Cometh* by Eugene O' Neil
E. *Twelve Angry Man* by Reginald Rose

Choose the correct answer from the options given below.

(1) A, D, E, B, C
(2) A, C, B, E, D
(3) D, C, B, A, E
(4) D, B, A, E, C

71. Match List-I with List-II.

List-I (Concepts/Theories)	List-II (Developed by)
A. Poly-system Theory	I. Ernst-August Gutt
B. Relevance Theory	II. Hans J. Vermeer
C. Skopos Theory	III. Itamar Enen-Zohar
D. Covert Translation	IV. Juliane House

Choose the correct answer from the options given below.

	A	B	C	D		A	B	C	D
(1)	II	III	IV	I	(2)	III	I	II	IV
(3)	I	IV	III	II	(4)	IV	II	I	III

72. Match List-I with List-II.

List-I (Rhymes)	List-II (Authors)
A. Twinkle, Twinkle Little Star	I. William Miller
B. Wee Willie Winkie	II. Jane and Ann Taylor
C. Mary had a Little Lamb	III. Sarah Catherine Martin
D. Old Mother Hubbard	IV. Sarah Josepha Hale

Choose the correct answer from the options given below.

	A	B	C	D		A	B	C	D
(1)	I	III	II	IV	(2)	II	IV	III	I
(3)	III	II	I	IV	(4)	II	I	IV	III

73. Chronologically arrange the fictional writings of Margaret Atwood.

A. *Edible Woman*
B. *The Handmaid's Tale*
C. *The Blind Assassin*
D. *Lady Oracle*
E. *The Robbers Bride*

Choose the correct answer from the options given below.

(1) B, C, A, E, D
(2) D, B, C, A, E
(3) E, A, D, C, B
(4) A, D, B, E, C

74. *The Birth of Tragedy from the Spirit of Music* by Friedrich Nietzsche

A. examines the origins and development of poetry, specifically Greek tragedy.
B. argues that Socratic rationalism and optimism led to the death of Greek tragedy.
C. examines the origin of music and dance in ancient Greece.
D. argues that Greek tragedy arose out of the fusion of Apollonian and Dionysian elements.

E. argues that the music is the spirit of tragedy.

Choose the correct answer from the options given below.

(1) A, B and D (2) A, C and E
(3) B, D and E (4) B, C and D

75. Which one of the following statements about 'Booker Prize' is not correct?

(1) A prestigious British award given annually to a full-length novel.
(2) Eligible writers shall belong to the United Kingdom and the Commonwealth countries.
(3) It was established in 1968 by Booker McDonald, a multi-national company.
(4) It was established to provide a counterpart to the Prix Goncourt in France.

76. *Absalom, Absalom!* is

(1) a novel by William Faulkner
(2) a satirical poem by John Dryden
(3) a drama by GB Shaw
(4) a poem by PB Shelley

77. Arrange the following partitions based film in order of their release/production.

A. *Garm Hava* B. *Tamas*
C. *Khamosh Pani* D. *Chinnamul*
E. *Subarnarekha*

Choose the correct answer from the options given below.

(1) D, E, A, B, C (2) E, D, B, A, C
(3) A, B, D, E, C (4) A, D, E, B, C

78. The Latin epic *Aenid* by Virgil

A. incorporates various legends of Aeneas and makes him the founder of Roman greatness.
B. relates the story of the legendary founding of Rome.
C. relates the story of the legendary founding of Lavinium.
D. recounts the story of Aeneas' journey in the first six books of the epic and these six books are patterned after *Homer's Odyssey*.
E. recounts the story of Aeneas' journey in the last 6 books of the epic and these 6 books are patterned after *Homer's Odyssey*

Choose the correct answer from the options given below.

(1) A, C and D
(2) A, B and D
(3) A , D and E
(4) A, C and E

79. Match List-I with List-II.

List-I (Post-Colonial Terms)	List-II (Coined/Employed by)
A. Othering	I. The term employed by Robert Young
B. Ecological Imperialism	II. Coined by Gayatri Spivak
C. Colonial Desire	III. Coined by Alfred W. Crosby
D. Third Space	IV. Coined by Homi K. Bhabha

Choose the correct answer from the options given below.

	A	B	C	D		A	B	C	D
(1)	IV	II	I	III	(2)	III	I	IV	II
(3)	I	III	II	IV	(4)	II	III	I	IV

80. The term 'abstract poem'

A. was coined by Edith Sitwell.
B. refers to a poem in which words are chosen for their aural quality.
C. refers to a poem in which words are chosen for imagery and symbolism.
D. was coined by WH Auden.
E. refers to a poem in which words are not specifically used for their sense/meaning.

Choose the correct answer from the options given below.

(1) B, C and D (2) A, B and E
(3) A, C and E (4) C, D and E

81. The salient tendencies of Hellenistic Philosophy are

A. Cynicism
B. Epicureanism
C. Stoicism
D. Surrealism
E. Expressionism

Choose the correct answer from the options given below.

(1) A, B and D (2) A, B and C
(3) A, D and E (4) A, B and E

82. *Akkarmashi (The Outcaste)* is an autobiography of which one of the following Dalit writers?

(1) Annabhau Sathe
(2) Sharankumar Limbale
(3) Anand Teltumbde
(4) Baby Kamble

83. Arrange the following novels by Chinua Achebe in order of their publication.

A. *A Man of the People*
B. *Things Fall Apart*
C. *Arrow of God*
D. *Anthills of Savannah*
E. *No Longer at Ease*

Choose the correct answer from the options given below.

(1) C, B, E, D, A
(2) B, C, E, A, D
(3) B, E, C, A, D
(4) A, B, D, E, C

84. Hypothesis made during or after the research work is over, is known as

(1) Inductive hypothesis
(2) Deductive hypothesis
(3) Null hypothesis
(4) Internal hypothesis

85. Who among the following American writers was the first Black American to become the US Poet Laureate and Consultant in Poetry at the Library of Congress?

(1) Kyra Davis
(2) Meri Nana-Ama Donquah
(3) Rita Francis Dove
(4) Lucille Clifton

86. *Things as They Are* or *The Adventure of Caleb Williams* was written as a call to end

(1) the abuse of workers by the industrialists.
(2) the abuse of masses by the Church.
(3) the abuse of power by a tyrannical government.
(4) the abuse of tenants by the landlords.

87. Chronologically arrange the Anglo-Indian writer's in order of their birth.

A. Sarojini Naidu
B. Michael Madhusudan Dutta
C. Manmohan Ghose
D. Henry Derozio
E. Toru Datt

Choose the correct answer from the options given below.

(1) C, E, A, B, D
(2) D, B, E, C, A
(3) B, D, C, E, A
(4) A, E, B, D, E

88. Which among the following is said to be the first fiction magazine (created by Hugo Gernsback)?

(1) Time and the Conways
(2) Henceforward
(3) New Worlds
(4) Amazing Stories

89. *Friendship's Garland* (1871) is a sequel to which one of the following works by Mathew Arnold?

(1) *Culture and Anarchy*
(2) *Essays in Criticism*
(3) *On the Study of Celtic Literature*
(4) *Literature and Dogma*

90. Match List-I with List-II.

	List-I (Disability Narratives)		List-II (Writers)
A.	*A Room Called Earth*	I.	Won-pyung Sohn
B.	*Tomorrow, and Tomorrow and Tomorrow*	II.	Padma Venkatraman
C.	*A Time to Dance*	III.	Medeleine Ryan
D.	*Almond : A Novel*	IV.	Gabrielle Zevin

Choose the correct answer from the options given below.

	A	B	C	D
(1)	II	III	I	IV
(2)	IV	II	I	III
(3)	III	IV	II	I
(4)	I	II	IV	III

Directions (Q. Nos. 91-95) *Read the passage carefully and answer the questions that follows.*

Leaning into the afternoons, I cast my sad nets towards your oceanic eyes.

There in the highest blaze my solitude lengthens and flames, its aims turning a drowning man's.

I send out red signals across your absent eyes that smell like the sea or the beach by a lighthouse.

You keep only darkness, my distant female from your regard sometimes the coast of dread emerges. Leaning into the afternoons, I fling my sad nets to that sea that thrashed by your oceanic eyes.

The birds of night peck at the first stars that flash like my soul when I love you.

The night gallops on its shadowy mare shedding blue tassels over the land.

91. What is the central theme of the poem?
(1) Search for self
(2) Love and longing
(3) Self-fulfilment
(4) Fate and destiny

92. Identify the mood of the poem.
(1) Sombre
(2) Sarcastic
(3) Exhilarating
(4) Nostalgic

93. The phrases 'oceanic eyes' and 'absent eyes' are the examples of
(1) Parallelism
(2) Consonance
(3) Anaphora
(4) Dissonance

94. What does the phrase 'red signals sent out' signify?
(1) Passion/zest for life
(2) Distress and desperation of speaker
(3) Threatening signals
(4) Hopefulness and warmth

95. Identify the type of imagery used in the poem.
(1) Natural imagery
(2) War imagery
(3) Urban imagery
(4) Metaphysical imagery

Directions (Q. Nos. 96-100) *Read the passage carefully and answer the questions that follows.*

Suspicion amongst thoughts are like bats amongst birds, they ever fly by twilight. Certainly, they are to be repressed, or at the least well guarded : for they cloud the mind; they lease friends. And they check with business, whereby business cannot go on currently. They dispose kings to tyranny, husbands to jealously, wise men to irresolution and melancholy. They are defects, not in the heart, but in the brain; for they take place in the stoutest natures; as in the example of Henry the seventh of England. There was not a more suspicious man, nor a more stout. And in such a composition, they do small hurt. For commonly, they are not admitted. But with examination, whether they be likely or not. But in fearful natures, they gain ground too fast. There is nothing that makes a man suspect much, more than to know little; and therefore men should remedy suspicion by procuring to know more, and not to keep their suspicions in smother. What would men have? Do they not think they will have their own ends, and be truer to themselves than to them? Therefore there is no better way to moderate suspicions, than to account upon such suspicions as true, and yet to bridle them as false. For so far a man ought to make use of suspicions, as to provide, as if that should true that he suspects, yet it may do him no hurt. Suspicions that the mind of itself gathers are but buzzes; but suspicions: that are artificially nourished, and put into men's heads by the tales and whisperings of others, have strings. Certainly, the best mean to clear the way in this same wood of suspicion, is frankly to communicate them with the party that he suspects. For thereby, he shall be sure to know more of the truth of them than he did before; and withal shall make that party more circumspect not to give further cease of suspicion. But this would not be done to men of base natures; for they, if they find themselves once suspected, will never be true. The situation says, suspicion gives license to faith; as if suspicion did give a passport to faith; but it ought rather to kindle it to discharge itself.

96. What tone does the passage predominantly convey?
(1) Nostalgic and sentimental
(2) Urgent and alarmed
(3) Detached and reflective
(4) Suspenseful and dramatic

97. What is the primary theme of the paragraph?
(1) The challenges of maintaining supremacy
(2) The importance of personal relationships
(3) Perspectivising suspicion
(4) To contrast between fearful and stout people

98. What does the word 'guarded' signify?
(1) To protect
(2) To possess
(3) To keep under control
(4) Militaristic exercise

99. What helps in eliminating suspicion?
(1) Stout physique
(2) Discussion and knowledge
(3) Observation
(4) Eternal alliance

100. Which among the following is true in the context of given paragraph?
(1) Henry the Seventh ruled ruthlessly for long time.
(2) Suspicion is a stepping stone to faith.
(3) Suspicion kills the layer of human spirit.
(4) Rulers should supress suspicion of all forms.

ANSWERS

1	(3)	2	(1)	3	(4)	4	(3)	5	(3)	6	(3)	7	(1)	8	(3)	9	(1)	10	(2)
11	(4)	12	(4)	13	(3)	14	(3)	15	(4)	16	(1)	17	(2)	18	(2)	19	(3)	20	(4)
21	(1)	22	(3)	23	(1)	24	(3)	25	(4)	26	(*)	27	(1)	28	(4)	29	(3)	30	(3)
31	(1)	32	(3)	33	(4)	34	(2)	35	(2)	36	(1)	37	(2)	38	(1)	39	(2)	40	(3)
41	(2)	42	(1)	43	(3)	44	(2)	45	(3)	46	(4)	47	(1)	48	(1 & 3)	49	(3)	50	(4)
51	(4)	52	(2)	53	(2)	54	(2)	55	(2)	56	(4)	57	(2)	58	(1)	59	(1)	60	(1)
61	(2)	62	(3)	63	(4)	64	(1)	65	(1)	66	(3)	67	(4)	68	(3)	69	(1)	70	(*)
71	(2)	72	(4)	73	(4)	74	(1)	75	(2 & 3)	76	(1)	77	(1)	78	(1)	79	(4)	80	(2)
81	(2)	82	(2)	83	(3)	84	(2)	85	(3)	86	(3)	87	(2)	88	(4)	89	(1)	90	(3)
91	(2)	92	(1)	93	(1)	94	(2)	95	(1)	96	(3)	97	(3)	98	(3)	99	(2)	100	(2)

English (Paper-2)

Solved Paper, December 2023

General Instructions

1. There are total one hundred questions in this paper. Each question carries 2 marks.
2. All questions are compulsory.

---

1. Which among the following is not written by RR Leavis?

(1) *Education and the University (1943)*
(2) *Culture and Practical Reason (1976)*
(3) *English Literature in Our Time and the University (1969)*
(4) *Revaluation (1936)*

2. Which among the following texts is not based on the theme of disability?

(1) Madeleine Ryan's *A Room Called Earth*
(2) Gabrielle Zevin's *Tomorrow and Tomorrow and Tomorrow*
(3) GB Shaw's *Mrs. Warren's Profession*
(4) Julia Heaberlin's *We are All the Same in the Dark*

3. Which statement among the following defines Pidgin?

(1) A language that is used as a kind of lingua franca among speakers, though it is not a native language of anyone.
(2) A language which has large number of varieties and dialects used across the world.
(3) An African language used by the natives to showcase their culture and customs.
(4) A language with structured grammar and sound system spoken in Australia.

4. What is the appropriate term for the study of language across time (e.g., the history of the changes in a language)?

(1) Diachronic
(2) Synchronic
(3) Syntagmatic
(4) Paradigmatic

5. Which among the following rightly defines 'homonyms'?

(1) Morphemes which sound different but have the same meanings.
(2) Morphemes which sound the same but have different meanings.
(3) Morphemes which are added to other morphemes.
(4) Morphemes which sound the same but have different spellings.

6. What among the following rightly defines Pragmatics?

(1) Study of the units of meaning in a language and their pattern of occurrence
(2) The study of meaning
(3) The study of meaning in context
(4) The study of the sounds

7. Which among the following does not relate to Universal Grammar?

(1) It is based on the idea that certain aspects of syntactic structure are the universal.

(2) It suggests that all languages possess the same set of categories and relations.

(3) Universal grammar is a theoretical concept proposed by Edward Sapir.

(4) It is based on the postulate that the human brain contains an innate mental grammar.

8. Which statement among the following rightly defines 'inversion'?

(1) A structure in which an auxiliary or other verb comes at the end of the sentence.

(2) A structure in which an auxiliary or other verb comes before its subject.

(3) A structure in which an auxiliary may be omitted without affecting the meaning.

(4) A structure in which an auxiliary is considered essential.

9. Which statement rightly defines split infinitive?

(1) A structure in which an adverb comes between 'to' and the rest of the infinitive.

(2) A structure in which an adjective comes between 'to' and the rest of the infinitive.

(3) A structure in which an adjective comes before bare infinitive.

(4) A structure in which an adverb follows to-infinitive.

10. Which statement among the following is not true about *Ferdinand de Saussure's Course in General Linguistics*?

(1) It was published posthumously in 1915.

(2) It discusses the concepts of 'langue' and 'parole'.

(3) 'Langue' denotes actual oral and written communication by member(s) of a particular speech community.

(4) Saussure advocated a synchronic examination of language.

11. Which of the following texts is not based on transgender issues?

(1) *Myself Mona Ahmed* by Dayanita Singh

(2) *The Ministry of Utmost Happiness* by Arundhati Rọy

(3) *The Beast with Nine Billion Feet* by Anil Menon

(4) *The Man Who Would be Queen* by Hoshang Merchant

12. "Neo-colonialism is the worst form of imperialism for those who practice it, it means power without responsibility and for those who suffer from it, it means exploitation without redress". Identify the author.

(1) Robert JC Young

(2) Edward W Said

(3) Kwame Nkrumah

(4) Ngugi wa Thiong'O

13. Which among the following statements is not true about NEP, 2020?

(1) The policy recommends establishment of Indian Institute of English Literature and Interpretation.

(2) It recommends high quality programmes and degrees in translation and interpretation.

(3) It recommends establishment of academies for each of the scheduled languages listed in the eighth schedule of the Constitution.

(4) It recommends that proficiency in Indian languages be included as part of qualification parameters for employment opportunities.

14. Who among the following wrote Art of Rhetoric?

(1) Cleanth Brooks (2) Sir Thomas Wilson

(3) Sir John Cheke (4) Raymond Williams

15. Identify the poet who has said that "poetry has fallen from its pedestal as the highest estimation of learning... to be the laughing stock of children"?

(1) William Wordsworth

(2) Sir Philip Sidney

(3) William Blake

(4) George Gascoigne

16. What does 'bricolage' mean in the Derridean usage?

(1) Borrowing concepts from different sources and reshaping them to suit one's needs

(2) Endless play of signifiers

(3) Deconstructing the given concept to arrive at truth

(4) Difference

17. Paul J. Crutzen describes 'Anthropocene' as

(1) a new world order.

(2) post-political zeitgeist.

(3) decisive human impact upon earth's environment and biosphere.

(4) aporia of grand narratives in the post-globalised world shaping human subjectivities.

18. Who among the following is the recipient of Noble Prize in Literature for the year 2021?

(1) Louise Gluck (2) Annie Ernaux

(3) Abdulrazak Gurnah (4) Peter Handke

19. Who has defined defamiliarisation (ostranenie) as an aesthetic technique implying the renewal of preception?

(1) Viktor Shklovsky (2) Roman Jakobson

(3) Jacques Derrida (4) Vladimir Propp

20. Which is the thrust of Jean Paul Sartre's impassioned response to Camus' *The Rebel*?
(1) Rejection of spiritualistic elements
(2) Renunciation of historical responsibility and commitment
(3) Ethic of narrative
(4) Problem of bad faith

21. Name the poet who has composed the following poems.
A. *A Hymn to God the Father*
B. *Elegy on Mistress Bulstrode*
C. *Hymn to God My God, in My Sickness*
D. *A Valediction of Weeping*
Choose the correct answer from the options given below.
(1) William Shakespeare (2) Christopher Marlowe
(3) John Donne (4) Ben Jonson

22. Who among the following coined the term 'Speculative Fiction'?
(1) Hugo Gernsback (2) Robert A. Heinlein
(3) Dan Bloom (4) John Stuart Mill

23. My love is of a birth as rare
As, tis, for object, strange and high;
It was forgotten by despair
Upon impossibility. (Andrew Marvell)
Name the poem from which these lines have been taken.
(1) *The Garden*
(2) *The Horatian Ode*
(3) *The Definition of Love*
(4) *To His Coy Mistress*

24. Who is the author of the pandemic fiction *The Last Man*?
(1) Mary Shelley
(2) Jose Saramago
(3) Ahmad Ali
(4) Gabriel Garcia Marquez

25. Who has composed *A Red Rose*?
(1) Joanna Ballie
(2) Robert Burns
(3) William Wordsworth
(4) Samuel Taylor Coleridge

26. In which year *She Walks in Beauty*, a poem by Lord Byron, was composed?
(1) 1788 (2) 1824 (3) 1815 (4) 1814

27. Who composed the poem *The Phoenix and the Turtle*?
(1) William Blake (2) William Shakespeare
(3) William Cowper (4) Robert Burns

28. *A Vindication of the Rights of Women* was written by Mary Wollstonecraft. Who wrote *A Vidication of the Rights of Man*?
(1) JS Mill
(2) Thomas Paine
(3) John Braine
(4) Amis Kingsley

29. Who said about Northrop Frye that he did not lock literature into an ivory tower, instead he emphasised its centrality to the development of a civilised humane society?
(1) Philip Wheelwright
(2) Margaret Atwood
(3) Ernst Jones
(4) Richard Chase

30. Which of the following is not included in the positive evils of Scott as a novelist?
(1) His great haste in the composition of his stories
(2) His haphazard financial methods which tended to over production
(3) Haste in the constructibn of his plots
(4) He had sensitive ear for rhythm and melody

31. According to Lev Manovich, 'Cultural analytics' refers to
(1) the study of culture to decipher the prevalent power relation in the society.
(2) the use of computational methods to examine contemporary digital media.
(3) schizoanalysis of culture to locate the contestation among multiple ideological formations.
(4) archeological approach td the study of power and knowledge.

32. In Michel Foucault's words, 'Panopticon' refers to
(1) the metaphor for the modern disciplinary society.
(2) the example of a totalitarian society.
(3) the metaphor for a pre-modern society marked by equality.
(4) the device for administering corporal punishment.

33. The goal of Schizoanalysis is
(1) to study schizophrenia in the light of neoliberal theories.
(2) to reassess the impact of materialist thought in human actions.
(3) to analyse the unconscious from a transcendentalist perspective.
(4) To scrutinise the specific nature of libidinal investments in the economic and political sphere.

34. Which of the following is not correct about tribal narratives and the writers?

(1) *Escaping the Land* is written by Mamang Dai.
(2) *Kocharethi* is written by Narayan.
(3) *Amrutara Sanatana* is written by Pratibha Ray.
(4) *A Motherland Being Deserted* is written by Salge Hansda.

35. "A little learning is a dangerous thing, drink deep, or taste not the Pierian spring". Which literary critic has expressed the above given thought?

(1) De Quincey (2) Alexander Pope
(3) William Shakespeare (4) Samuel Johnson

36. Who among the following denounced literary works as the works of devil?

(1) FR Leavis (2) TS Eliot
(3) Stephen Gosson (4) William Ponsonby

37. Who has defined a poet in the following words? "The poet, described in ideal perfection, brings the whole soul of man into activity, with the subordination of its faculties to each other according to their relative worth and dignity".

(1) William Wordsworth
(2) John Keats
(3) Samuel Taylor Coleridge
(4) PB Shelley

38. A modern philosophical tendency which stresses the perceiver's role in determining meaning is known as

(1) Ontology (2) Epistemology
(3) Phenomenology (4) Facticity

39. Who wrote the book *Subculture: The Meaning of Style* (1979)?

(1) Stephen Greenblatt (2) Stuart Hall
(3) Dick Hebdige (4) Max Weber

40. The famous text *The Empire Writes Back* came out in the year

(1) 1989 (2) 1988 (3) 1987 (4) 1990

41. Which of the following statements are true in the context of Rudyard Kipling?

A. Kipling was born on 30th December, 1865 in Bombay, India.
B. Kipling was awarded Noble Prize in 1907.
C. *The Jungle Books* consist of four collections of stories.
D. Kipling originally used Shivalik hills as the background of *The Jungle Book*.
E. *The Jungle Book* was published in 1894.

Choose the correct answer from the options given below.

(1) A, B and C (2) B, C and D
(3) C, D and E (4) A, B and E

42. Which of the following statements are true about Ngugi wa Thiong 'O's *Decolonising the Mind*?

A. The complete title of the text is Decolonising the Mind: *The Politics of Language in Africa Literature*.
B. The text was originally published in 1886 while he was on a short visit to London to attend a conference.
C. It discusses that the choice of language and the use to which language is put is central to people's definition of themselves.
D. Through this text the Nigerian author defends the use of English as a tool to progress
E. Ngugi observed that in a school in a colonial setup, the language of his education was no longer the language of his cultute.

Choose the correct answer from the options given below.

(1) A, B and C (2) B, C and D
(3) C, D and E (4) A, C and E

43. Which of the following statements are true with regard to Postcolonial theory and literature?

A. *The Empire Writes Back* is a non-fictional text on post-colonialism
B. *Black Skin White Masks* is a fictional text narrating multi-disciplinary analysis of the effects of colonialism on the protagonist.
C. *A Critique of Post-colonial Reason* is a work written by Gayatri Chakravorty Spivak.
D. Edward W. Said wrote his autobiography titled *In Place* to reflect the love-hate relationship with the West.
E. Post-colonialism addresses those questions that emerge in the wake of the departure of colonial masters.

Choose the correct answer from the options given below.

(1) A, C and E (2) B, C and D
(3) A, D and E (4) C, D and E

44. Which among the following is/are not true about Negritude?

A. The movement was started by French speaking African and Caribbean writers living in Paris.
B. The movement aimed at examining Western values critically and to reassess African culture.
C. The movement was against British colonial rule and the policy of colonisation.
D. The leading figure of the movement was Leopold Sedar Senghor.
E. The movement was influenced by the creed of Art for Art's Sake.

Choose the correct answer from the options given below.

(1) A and B (2) B and C
(3) C and E (4) D and E

45. Which among the following are not true about Feminist Movement?

A. Mary Wollstonecraft's *A Vindication of the Rights of Women* challenges the notion that women exist only to please men.

B. Issue of women's suffrage dominated international feminism for more than fifty years.

C. *The Female Eunuch* was written and published by an African writer named Sarah Millin.

D. Kate Millet's *Sexual Politics* broadened the term 'politics' to include all 'power-structured relationship'.

E. The second wave of feminism was led by Generation Xers.

Choose the correct answer from the options given below.

(1) A and B (2) B and C
(3) C and E (4) D and E

46. Which among the following are not true about the Booker Prize?

A. The winner of The International Booker Prize 2023 is *Tomb of Sand* written by Geetanjali Shree and translated by Daisy Rockwell.

B. Each year, the prize is awarded to the best sustained work of fiction written in english.

C. *The International Booker Prize was instituted* in 2002.

D. The Booker Prize is awarded to the best sustained work of fiction written in English and published in the UK and Ireland.

E. The International Booker Prize is awarded for the finest single work of fiction, translated into English, from around the world.

Choose the correct answer from the options given below.

(1) B and D (2) A and C
(3) C and E (4) D and E

47. Harlem Renaissance manifests blossoming of African-American culture. Which among the following are the key features of the movement?

A. It advocated freedom from Victorian moral values.

B. The movement emerged in the early 19th century.

C. The movement started from Harlem district of New York city.

D. The magazines such as *The Crisis, Opportunity* and *The Messengers* were crucial for the movement.

E. Harlem was formerly a Black residential district that gradually became virtually a White city.

Choose the correct answer from the options given below.

(1) A, B and C (2) B, C and D
(3) C, D and E (4) A, C and D

48. Which among the following are not the slave narratives?

A. *Black Boy* by Richard Wright

B. *An Untamed State* by Roxane Gay

C. *Behind the Scenes* by Elizabeth Keckley

D. *The Nature of Blood* by Caryl Phillips

E. *Up From Slavery* by Booker T. Washington

Choose the correct answer from the options given below.

(1) B and D (2) C and E
(3) A and B (4) B and C

49. Which of the following definitions are wrong?

A. A fricative sound involves the close approximation of two articulators.

B. Stops involve closure of the ariculators to obstruct the air-stream.

C. Raising of the front of the tongue to form a secondary articulation is called velarisation.

D. A trill occurs when an articulator is held loosely fairly close to another articulator so that it sets into vibration.

E. Raising of the back of the tongue while making another articulation elsewhere is called palatalisation.

Choose the correct answer from the options given below.

(1) A and B (2) B and C
(3) C and E (4) D and E

50. Which among the following are the Australian Aboriginal texts?

A. *Their Eyes were Watching God* by Hurston

B. *Terra Nullius* by Claire G. Coleman

C. *My Place* by Sally Morgan

D. *The Bandwoman's Narrative* by Hannah Bond

E. *Follow the Rabbit-Proof Fence* by Doris Pilkington.

Choose the correct answer from the options given below.

(1) A, B and C (2) B, C and E
(3) C, D and E (4) A, C and D

51. Which among the following texts are not written by an Indian Diaspora Novelist?

A. *Darkness*
B. *Moth Smoke*
C. *Whereabouts*
D. *The Reluctant Fundamentalist*
E. *Clear Light of Day*

Choose the correct answer from the options given below.

(1) A and B (2) B and C
(3) B and D (4) D and E

52. Which among the following are not true about *The Defense of Poesie by Philip Sidney*?

A. The text was published posthumously in 1595.
B. It is also titled as *An Apology for Poetry*.
C. Philip Sidney criticises Geoffrey Chaucer's *Troilus and Criseyde* and Spenser's *The Shepheades Calendar*.
D. The text is the first major piece of literary criticism in English
E. The text defends Plato for his decision to ban poets from the ideal state as described in Republic

Choose the correct answer from the options given below.

(1) A and B (2) B and C
(3) C and D (4) C and E

53. Which statements among the following are not relevant to *Biographia Literaria*?

A. The first volume of the text recounts the author's friendship with Robert Southey and William Blake
B. Another edition of the text was published later in 1847 with his daughter Sara's appended notes
C. It is a work by ST Coleridge in two volumes
D. In this work, Coleridge discusses the difference between fancy and imagination
E. In the first volume, Coleridge acknowledges his teachers and philosophers including Aristotle and Plato

Choose the correct answer from the options given below.

(1) A and B
(2) B and C
(3) A and E
(4) D and E

54. Which among the following statements do not relate to William Empson's *Seven Types of Ambiguity*?

A. Empson uses the term 'ambiguity' to refer to any verbal nuance which may give room for alternative reaction to the same piece of literature
B. The first type of ambiguity is simple metaphor which may be effective in several ways at once
C. The third type of ambiguity consists of two apparently disconnected meaning given simultaneously
D. Empson calls the fifth type of ambiguity as 'unfortunate confusion' with examples from Shelley and Swinburne
E. Seventh type of ambiguity refers to the division in the reader's mind

Choose the correct answer from the options given below.

(1) A and B (2) B and C
(3) C and D (4) D and E

55. Which of the following assumptions are not true with reference to post-feminism?

A. Post-feminism is based on the postulates of feminism laid down by Elaine Showalter
B. A discourse popularised by the mass media in 1990s reflecting a reaction against the feminist theories of 1970s and 1980s
C. Post-feminism establishes the relevance of fender binary where man is essentially powerful
D. Post-feminism is characterised by emphasis on femininity as well as on 'the career women'
E. Post-feminis discourse extends into other areas such as eco-feminism and cyber feminism

Choose the correct answer from the options given below.

(1) A and C (2) B and C
(3) C and D (4) D and E

56. Which of these are true about New historicism?

A. New Historicists do not use thick descriptions for the examination of cultural production
B. Literary works are not autonomous and timeless
C. History is always narrated. History is a matter of interpretation
D. All historical analysis is objective
E. History is neither progressive nor linear

Choose the correct answer from the options given below.

(1) A and E (2) A and C
(3) C and E (4) A and B

57. Which among the following assumptions are not true in the context of diasporic identities?

A. Migrancy constructs modes of existence and ways of seeing that go beyond actual journey between countries.
B. Migrancy can expose the migrants and their children to displacement and fragmentation.
C. The dominant narratives of belonging and identify can accommodate those who live in-between.
D. Living in-between can be a pleasurable experience.
E. Home is a problematic concept.

Choose the correct answer from the options given below

(1) A and B (2) C and A
(3) C and B (4) C and D

58. Which assertions are not true in the context of Cultural Studies?

A. Popular culture means the set of practices, beliefs and objects that embody the most broadly shared meanings of a social system.
B. Dominant culture signifies the invisible aspects of our practices and attitudes.
C. Residual culture is that part of the old cultural practices that remain in traces in modern culture.
D. The discipline is comparatively new and is opposed to rigid methods associated with traditional Marxist approaches.
E. It discourages that audibility of women in public spaces.

Choose the correct answer from the options given below.

(1) E and B (2) A and E
(3) B and C (4) C and E

59. Which among the following is not true about EP Thompson's *The Making of the Working Class*?

A. Studies the development of working class consciousness.
B. Defines class as a relationship not as a social structure.
C. It is the first systematic study of the history of working class.
D. It critiques Virginia Woolf's *A Room of One's Own*.
E. Reinforces the idea that race and ethnicity are the forms of collective identity.

Choose the correct answer from the options given below.

(1) A and B (2) C and D
(3) E and D (4) B and D

60. 'Discordia Concors', a phrase used by Johnson in his Life of Cowley, implies

A. a term used to refer to ironic inversion of residual ideology in a text
B. a combination of two philosophically similar discourses
C. a term used to refer diminishing metaphor
D. a combination of dissimilar images
E. a combination of contradictory ideas and concepts

Choose the correct answer from the options given below.

(1) D and E (2) C and D
(3) A and E (4) B and D

61. Which of the following options cover the basic issues related to feminist literary criticism?

A. Women are caught up in a prison house of language that is male specific.
B. Gender equality is just an idea and largely unachievable.
C. Human society is largely entrenched in patriarchal ideology.
C. Sex and Gender can not be treated as two distinct categories.
D. One universal feminism will be the remedy to the historical subjugation.

Choose the correct answer from the options given below.

(1) A and D (2) A and E
(3) A and C (4) B and D

62. Choose two statements which aptly describe renaissance humanism.

A. It prepared man for an eternal life.
B. It was anthropocentric.
C. It was a more theological philosophy.
D. It rejected the distinction between neumenal and phenomenal world.
E. It brought immense revival of interest in classical literature and thought.

Choose the correct answer from the options given below.

(1) B and E
(2) A and B
(3) B and D
(4) C and E

63. What statements are true about liberal humanism?

A. Language is not constitutive.
B. There is no fixed and absolute truth. No unalterable essences at all.
C. Our mind is an empty state and all enquiry into the artistic phenomenon is objective.

D. It is language that shapes the reality and not the other way round.
E. Truth is not provisional.

Choose the correct answer from the options given below.

(1) D and E (2) C and D
(3) C and E (4) A and E

64. Which two of the following statements are true about concept of contrapuntal reading?

A. It locates the anxiety of influence in the text.
B. It decodes the political unconscious of the author.
C. It unveils how some literary texts are complicit in justifying the ideologies of imperialism.
D. It shows how the author can consciously structure the meaning of the text.
E. It decodes the intertextual element in the text which shape the rendering of characters as heroes of villains.

Choose the correct answer from the options given below.

(1) D and A (2) C and E
(3) B and C (4) C and D

65. Which of the following societal attributes are not accepted by feminist critics regarding objectification of woman's body?

A. Beauty contests commodify the woman's body for the men's gaze.
B. All women suffer from 'penis-envy'.
C. Cosmetic surgery and body adornment become 'feminine' modes.
D. The country is itself imaged as a woman's body that demands protection by men.
E. Men have traditionally been projected as rational and women as 'irrational' or emotional.

Choose the correct answer from the options given below.

(1) D and E (2) B and E
(3) C and E (4) B and D

66. Match List-I with List-II.

	List-I (Authors)		List-II (Works)
A.	Nigel Dennis	I.	*Technique as Discovery*
B.	George Orwell	II.	*The Gay Science*
C.	Mark Schorer	III.	*Cards of Identify*
D.	Nietzsche	IV.	*Down and Out in Paris and London*

Choose the correct answer from the options given below.

	A	B	C	D		A	B	C	D
(1)	III	IV	I	II	(2)	III	IV	II	I
(3)	IV	III	II	I	(4)	IV	III	I	II

67. Match List-I with List-II.

	List-I (Works)		List-II (Characters)
A.	Charles Dickens' *Martin Chuzzlewit*	I.	Abraham Durbeyfield
B.	GB Shaw's *The Doctor's Dilemma*	II.	Harry
C.	Thomas Hardy's *Tess of d'Urbervilles*	III.	Sir Ralph Bloomfield Bonnington
D.	TS Eliot's *The Family Reunion*	IV.	Mrs Gamp

Choose the correct answer from the options given below.

	A	B	C	D		A	B	C	D
(1)	IV	III	II	I	(2)	III	II	IV	I
(3)	III	II	I	IV	(4)	IV	III	I	II

68. Match List-I with List-II.

	List-I (Writers)		List-II (Concepts)
A.	Hugo Gernsback	I.	Biopolitics
B.	Edmund Husserl	II.	Phenomenology
C.	JC Ransom	III.	Science Fiction Novel
D.	Michel Foucault	IV.	New Criticism

Choose the correct answer from the options given below.

	A	B	C	D		A	B	C	D
(1)	IV	II	III	I	(2)	III	II	IV	I
(3)	III	II	I	IV	(4)	IV	I	II	III

69. Match List-I with List-II.

	List-I (Authors)		List-II (Works)
A.	Ann Radcliff	I.	*The Deserted Village*
B.	Oliver Goldsmith	II.	*The Romance of the Forest*
C.	Swinburne	III.	*The Vision of Judgement*
D.	Lord Byron	IV.	*The Sisters*

Choose the correct answer from the options given below.

	A	B	C	D		A	B	C	D
(1)	III	II	I	IV	(2)	III	IV	I	II
(3)	II	IV	III	I	(4)	II	I	IV	III

70. Match List-I with List-II.

List-I (Autobiographies)	List-II (Writers)
A. *My Second Innings*	I. TN Seshan
B. *Justice for the Judge: An Autobiography*	II. LK Advani
C. *My Country My Life*	III. Ranjan Gogoi
D. *Through the Broken Glass*	IV. Shanti Bhushan

Choose the correct answer from the options given below.

	A	B	C	D		A	B	C	D
(1)	III	II	I	IV	(2)	IV	III	II	I
(3)	I	IV	III	II	(4)	II	I	IV	III

71. Match List-I with List-II.

List-I (Works)	List-II (Authors)
A. *Aadha Gaon (Half a Village)*	I. Attia Hosain
B. *Aag Ka Darya (River of Fire)*	II. Rahi Masoom Raza
C. *Sunlight on A Broken Column*	III. Intizar Husain
D. *Basti*	IV. Qurrutulain Hyder

Choose the correct answer from the options given below.

	A	B	C	D		A	B	C	D
(1)	IV	II	III	I	(2)	I	III	II	IV
(3)	II	IV	I	III	(4)	III	I	IV	II

72. Match List-I with List-II.

List-I (Works)	List-II (Authors)
A. *The English Comic Writers*	I. David Hume
B. *Essays Moral and Political*	II. William Hazlitt
C. *The Second Sex*	III. Robert Wilson Lynd
D. *The Pleasures of Ignorance*	IV. Simone de Beauvoir

Choose the correct answer from the options given below.

	A	B	C	D		A	B	C	D
(1)	II	I	IV	III	(2)	I	III	II	IV
(3)	IV	II	I	III	(4)	III	I	II	IV

73. Match List-I with List-II.

List-I (Movies)	List-II (Inspired by/Adaptation of)
A. Kai Po Che!	I. *Macbeth* by William Shakespeare
B. Slumdog Millionaire	II. *Romeo and Juliet* by William Shakespeare
C. Maqbool	III. *The 3 Mistakes of My Life* by Chetan Bhagat
D. Ishaqzaade	IV. *Q & A* by Vikas Swarup

Choose the correct answer from the options given below.

	A	B	C	D		A	B	C	D
(1)	I	II	III	IV	(2)	II	I	IV	III
(3)	III	IV	I	II	(4)	IV	III	II	I

74. Match List-I with List-II.

List-I (Works)	List-II (Authors)
A. *The Nutmeg's Curse: Parables for a Planet in Crisis*	I. Amitav Kumar
B. *Victor City*	II. Amitav Ghosh
C. A Time Outside This Time: A Novel	III. Jhumppa Lahiri
D. *Translating Myself and Others*	IV. Salman Rushdie

Choose the correct answer from the options given below.

	A	B	C	D		A	B	C	D
(1)	I	III	II	IV	(2)	III	II	IV	I
(3)	IV	I	III	II	(4)	II	IV	I	III

75. Match List-I with List-II.

List I (Terms)	List II (Definitions)
A. *Malbe ka Malik* (His Heap of Rubble)	I. Bhisham Sahni
B. *Amritsar Aa Gaya Hai* (We Have Arrived in Amritsar)	II. Ismat Chughtai
C. *Jadein* (Roots)	III. Rajendra Singh Bedi
D. *Lajwanti*	IV. Mohan Rakesh

Choose the correct answer from the options given below.

	A	B	C	D		A	B	C	D
(1)	I	III	IV	II	(2)	II	IV	III	I
(3)	III	II	I	IV	(4)	IV	I	II	III

76. **Arrange the following texts chronologically on the basis of their publication.**

A. *A Literature of Their Own: British Women Novelists from Bronte to Lessing* by Elaine Showalter

B. *In Search of Our Mother's Gardens* by Alice Walker

C. *The Mad Women in the Attic: The Women Writer and the Nineteenth Century Imagination* by Sandra Gilbert and Susan Guban

D. *Sexual Politics* by Kate Millett

E. *The Second Sex* by Simone De Beauvoir

Choose the correct answer from the options given below.

(1) E, C, B, D, A (2) E, C, B, A, D
(3) E, D, B, A, C (4) E, D, B, C, A

77. Arrange the following critial texts chronologically on the basis of their publication.

A. *The Historical Novel* (George Lukacs)
B. *The New Criticism* (TS Eliot)
C. *The Business of Criticism* (Helen Gardner)
D. *The Political Unconscious* (Frederic Jameson)
E. *Essays on Ideology* (Louis Althusser)

Choose the correct answer from the options given below.

(1) B, E, D, A, C (2) B, C, A, D, E
(3) B, C, D, A, E (4) B, E, A, D, C

78. Arrange the following texts chronologically on the basis of the date of publication.

A. *Frankenstein* by Mary Shelley
B. *A Room of One's Own* by Virginia Woolf
C. *Maria* by Mary Wollstonecraft
D. *The Female Eunuch* by Germaine Greer
E. *The Return of the Soldier* by Rebecca West

Choose the correct answer from the options given below.

(1) C, B, A, D, E (2) C, A, E, D, B
(3) C, B, E, A, D (4) A, E, B, C, D

79. Arrange the following in chronologically order of the date/year of publication.

A. JG Ballard's *The Atrocity Exhibition*
B. Donna Haraway's *When Species Meet*
C. Thomas Friedman's *The World is Flat*
D. Francis Fukuyama's *End of History*
E. William Gibson's *Neuromancer*

Choose the correct answer from the options given below.

(1) C, D, B, A, E (2) A, E, D, C, B
(3) E, C, D, A, B (4) D, E, C, B, A

80. Chronologically arrange the following works on literary criticism in order of their publication

A. An Apologie for Poetrie
B. The Art of Rhetorique
C. Preface to lyrical Ballads
D. Essays in Criticism
E. The Metaphysical Poets

Choose the correct answer from the options given below.

(1) E, A, B, C, D (2) B, A, C, D, E
(3) C, D, B, A, E (4) A, C, E, D, B

81. Arrange the following philosophers/literary critics of Indian origin, chronologically.

A. Bhoja B. Lollata
C. Udbhata D. Dandin
E. Bhamah

Choose the correct answer from the options given below.

(1) D, C, B, A, E (2) E, D, C, B, A
(3) C, A, B, E, D (4) A, E, C, B, D

82. Identify the correct order of the publication of DH Lawrence's works'.

A. Rainbow
B. Kangaroo
C. Women in Love
D. Sons and Lovers
E. The Widowing of Mrs. Holroyd

Choose the correct answer from the options given below.

(1) D, E, A, C, B (2) B, C, D, E, A
(3) A, B, C, D, E (4) A, E, C, B, D

83. Choose the correct order of publication of Thomas Carlyle's works.

A. *History of the French Revolution*
B. *Signs of the Times*
C. *Chartism*
D. *Occasional Discourse on the Nigger Question*
E. *Heros and Hero Worship*

Choose the correct answer from the options given below.

(1) D, E, B, C, A (2) B, A, C, E, D
(3) B, C, D, E, A (4) A, B, C, D, E

84. Arrange the following literary texts in the chronological sequence.

A. *Middlemarch*
B. *The Good Soldier*
C. *Night and Day*
D. *A Passage to India*
E. *Heart of Darkness*

Choose the correct answer from the options given below.

(1) A, E, D, B, C (2) A, C, D, B, E
(3) A, B, C, D, E (4) A, D, B, C, E

85. Arrange the following works of VS Naipaul in the chronological sequence.

A. *A House for Mr. Biswas*
B. *The Mimic Men*
C. *The Mystic Masseur*
D. *Half A Life*
E. *Magic Seeds*

Choose the correct answer from the options given below.

(1) A, D, C, B, E
(2) E, B, A, C, D
(3) C, A, B, D, E
(4) D, E, A, C, B

86. Given below are two statements, one is labelled as Assertion (A) and the other is labelled as Reason (R).

Assertion (A) Marxism makes no claim to universality.

Reason (R) Post-modernism jettisons totalising frameworks.

In the light of the above statements, choose the correct answer from the options given below.

(1) Both A and R are true and R is the correct explanation of A.
(2) Both A and R are true, but R is not the correct explanation of A.
(3) A is true, but R is false.
(4) A is false, but R is true.

87. Given below are two statements, one is labelled as Assertion A and the other is labelled as Reason (R).

Assertion (A) Aphorism is a concise expression of doctrine conveyed in a pithy and memorable statement

Reason (R) The term 'aphoria' is gradually applied to any statement generally accepted as true, so that is now roughly synonymous with maxim

In the light of the above statements, choose the correct answer from the options given below.

(1) Both A and R are true and R is the correct explanation of A.
(2) Both A and R are true but R is not the correct explanation of A.
(3) A is true, but R is false.
(4) A is false, but R is true.

88. Given below are two statements, one is labelled as Assertion (A) and the other is labelled as Reason (R).

Assertion (A) Michel do Montaigne established the term 'essay' as a new literary form in his text Essays.

Reason (R) Francis Bacon is generally considered as the father of English essay.

In the light of the above statements, choose the correct answer from the options given below.

(1) Both A and R are true and R is the correct explanation of A.
(2) Both A and R are true but R is not the correct explanation of A.
(3) A is true, but R is false.
(4) A is false, but R is true.

89. Given below are two statements.

Statement (I) Doris Pilkington's *Follow the Rabbit-Proof Fence* is based on the experiences of the 'Stolen Generation'.

Statement (II) Nadine Gordimer's *My Son's Story* deals with coloured or mixed-race protagonists in the backdrop of apartheid.

In the light of the above statements, choose the correct answer from the options given below.

(1) Both Statement I and Statement II are correct.
(2) Both Statement I and Statement II are incorrect.
(3) Statement I is correct, but Statement II is incorrect.
(4) Statement I is incorrect, but Statement II is correct.

90. Given below are two statements.

Statement (I) Toni Morrison's *Beloved* is based on true story of a black slave woman.

Statement (II) *Beloved* is a novel about the trauma of apartheid.

In the light of the above statements, choose the correct answer from the options given below.

(1) Both Statement I and Statement II are correct.
(2) Both Statement I and Statement II are incorrect.
(3) Statement I is correct, but Statement II is incorrect.
(4) Statement I is incorrect, but Statement II is correct.

Directions (Q. Nos. 91-95) *Read the passage carefully and answer the questions that follows.*

Studies serve for delight, for omament and for ability. Their chief use for delight is in privateness and retiring for amament, is in discourse, and for ability is in the judgement and disposition of business. For expert man can execute, and perhaps judge of particulars, one by one; but the general counsels, and the plots and marshaling of affairs come best form those that are leamed. To spend too much time in studies is sloth to use them too much for omament is affectation, to make judgment wholly by their rules, is the humour of a scholar. They perfect nature, and are perfected by experience for natural abilities are like natural plants, that need pruning, by study and themselves do given about them won by observation Read not to contradict and confute, not to believe and take for granted not to find talk and discourse, but to wight and consider. Some books are to be tasted, others to be swallowed and some few to be read wholly and with diligence and attention, Some books also may be read by deputy, and extracts made of them by other, but that would be only in less important arguments, and the meaner sort of books, else distilled books are like common distilled water fieshy things. Reading maketh a full man conference a ready man and writing an exact man. And therefore if man writes little he had need have great memorym, if he confers little he had need have a present wit. and he reads little, he had need have much cunning to seem to know that the doth not. Histories make men wise, poets witty, the mathematics subtle, natural philosophy deep, moral gave, logic and rhetoric able to contend.

91. Why should a man read books?
(1) To contradict and conflict
(2) To weigh and consider
(3) To find discourse
(4) To take for granted

92. How many categories the author has suggest for the purpose of reading?
(1) One (2) Three
(3) Four (4) Two

93. What according to the author makes a man wise, witty, subtle and morally and philosophically deep?
(1) Thinking deep and loud
(2) Contemplation
(3) Interaction
(4) Reading

94. How does reading became perfect?
(1) Through personal experience
(2) Through social experience
(3) Through practical experience
(4) Through cultural experience

95. What are the advantages of studying books?
(1) Delight
(2) Ornament
(3) Ability to success
(4) Delight, ornament and ability

Directions (Q. Nos. 96-100) *Read the paggage carefully and answer the questions that follows.*

When she rises in the morning
I linger to watch her
She spreads the both cloth her Glistening white on the shoulders,
While down her sides the mellow
Golden shadow glows as
She stoops to the sponge, and her swung breasts
Sway like full-blown yellow
Gloire de Dijon roses.
She drips herself with water and her shoulders
Glisten as silver, they crumble up Like wet and falling roses and I listen
For the sluicing of their rain-dishevelled petals In the window full of sunlight concentrates her golden shadow
Fold on fold, unit it glows as Mellow as the glory roses.

96. Which dominant rasa is there in the poem?
(1) Karuna rasa
(2) Adbhuta rasa
(3) Shringara rasa
(4) Hasya rasa

97. What is the central symbol in the poem?
(1) Woman as morning
(2) Woman as rose
(3) Shoulders as sodden rose petals
(4) Shadow as flower head

98. What is the women doing in the poem?
(1) She watching in the looking glass
(2) She is peeping out of the window of her room
(3) She is taking bath
(4) She is collecting roses in the morning

99. What are the objects which come in contact with the woman's body?
(1) Flower, sunbeam, shadow and water
(2) Shadow and sunbeams
(3) Sunbeams, shadow and water
(4) Sunbeams, water and flower

100. The first two lines of the poem
(1) act as a framing device for the rest of the poem
(2) give the setting of the poem
(3) have confirmation of life
(4) show unceasing life

ANSWERS

1 (2)	2 (3)	3 (1)	4 (1)	5 (2)	6 (3)	7 (3)	8 (2)	9 (1)	10 (3)
11 (3)	12 (3)	13 (1)	14 (2)	15 (2)	16 (1)	17 (3)	18 (3)	19 (1)	20 (2)
21 (3)	22 (2)	23 (3)	24 (1)	25 (2)	26 (4)	27 (2)	28 (2)	29 (2)	30 (4)
31 (2)	32 (1)	33 (4)	34 (3)	35 (2)	36 (3)	37 (3)	38 (3)	39 (3)	40 (1)
41 (4)	42 (4)	43 (1)	44 (3)	45 (3)	46 (2)	47 (4)	48 (1)	49 (3)	50 (2)
51 (3)	52 (4)	53 (3)	54 (4)	55 (1)	56 (3)	57 (4)	58 (1)	59 (3)	60 (1)
61 (3)	62 (1)	63 (3)	64 (3)	65 (2)	66 (1)	67 (4)	68 (2)	69 (4)	70 (2)
71 (3)	72 (1)	73 (3)	74 (4)	75 (4)	76 (3)	77 (2)	78 (2)	79 (2)	80 (2)
81 (2)	82 (1)	83 (2)	84 (3)	85 (3)	86 (2)	87 (1)	88 (2)	89 (1)	90 (3)
91 (2)	92 (2)	93 (4)	94 (3)	95 (4)	96 (3)	97 (2)	98 (3)	99 (3)	100 (1)

Solved Paper

2022

English (Paper-2)

Solved Paper, October 2022

General Instructions

1. There are total one hundred questions in this paper. Each question carries 2 marks.
2. All questions are compulsory.

---

1. Besides being a playwright, who among the following has translated homer?

(1) Ben Johnson (2) Thomas Dekker
(3) Thomas Heywood (4) George Chapman

2. Which of the following is not true about 'Lyrical ballads'?

(1) It is a manifesto of romantic poetry.
(2) It turns English poetry away from the social and intellectual sophistication of the seventeenth and the eighteenth-century poetry.
(3) It takes poetry out of the confines of reason and intellect to the unravished and unspoilt beauties of nature.
(4) It is very particular about the form and structure of a poem.

3. Which of the following observations are true about Roland Barthes' contributions to literary theory?

A. He rejected the model for structural analysis of narratives.
B. He perceived 'meaning' as an effect of various interconnections among linguistic codes.
C. He identified the various codes found in the process of structuration.
D. He played a significant role in the development of 'semiology'.
E. He questioned the concept of literary criticism as an act of uncovering some hidden truth intended by the 'author'.

Choose the correct answer from the options given below.

(1) A, B and C (2) C,D and E
(3) B, C, D and E (4) A, B, C,D and E

4. The writer and the world by V.S.Naipaul is a

(1) Novel
(2) Travelogue
(3) Collection of essays
(4) Non-fiction

5. Given below are two statements. One is labelled as Assertion (A) and the other is labelled as Reason (R).

Assertion (A) The Marxists represent Marxism as a scientific account of social change.

Reason (R) The Marxist ideology believes that culture is a mirror of social life and the artist is an engineer of the human soul educating the working classes.

In the light of the above statements, choose the most appropriate answer from the options given below.

(1) Both A and R are correct and R is the correct explanation of A.
(2) Both A and R are correct, but R is not the correct explanation of A.
(3) A is correct, but R is not correct.
(4) A is not correct, but R is correct.

6. The 'ancient and modern quarrel' in western literary criticism appears during

(1) 100BC (2) Fifth century AD
(3) Sixteenth century AD (4) Twentieth century AD

7. Given below are two statements, one is labelled as Assertion (A) and the other is labelled as Reason (R).

Assertion (A) In so far as we are taught how to read, what we engage are not texts but paradigms.

Reason (R) We appropriate meaning from a text according to what we need or desire or, in other words, according to the critical assumptions of the predispositions that we bring to it.

In the light of the above statements, choose the most appropriate answer from the options given below.

(1) Both A and R are correct and R is the correct explanation of A.
(2) Both A and R are correct, but R is not the correct explanation of A.
(3) A is correct, but R is not correct.
(4) A is not correct, but R is correct.

8. Which of the following critics is associated with the term 'contrapuntal reading'?

(1) Mikhail Bakhtin (2) Edward Said
(3) Roland Barthes (4) Jacques Derrida

9. Match List I with List II.

List I	List II
A. Hamlet	I. 1606
B. Macbeth	II. 1599
C. Julius Caesar	III. 1604
D. Othello	IV. 1600

Choose the correct answer from the options given below.

	A	B	C	D
(1)	III	IV	II	I
(2)	I	II	IV	III
(3)	II	I	III	IV
(4)	IV	I	II	III

10. Match List I with List II.

List I	List II
A. "Faces along the bar/cling to their average day."	I. Wilfred Owen
B. "The awful daring of a moments surrender."	II. TS Eliot
C. "Bent double, like old beggars under sacks."	III. Allen Ginsberg
D. "I saw the best minds of my generation destroyed by madness."	IV. WH Anden

Choose the correct answer from the options given below.

	A	B	C	D
(1)	IV	II	I	III
(2)	III	I	IV	II
(3)	I	IV	II	III
(4)	II	IV	I	III

11. Given below are two statements.

Statement I The teaching of non-native literature to the students of English language teaching is arid.

Statement II The negative responses in ELT classroom can create an interesting classroom situation.

In the light of the above statements, choose the most appropriate answer from the options given below.

(1) Both statement I and statement II are correct.
(2) Both statement I and statement II are incorrect.
(3) Statement I is correct, but statement II is incorrect.
(4) Statement I is incorrect, but statement II is correct.

12. Which of these statements are true in the context of neuro-linguistic programming?

A. 'Neuro' in NLP means that our behaviour is determined by our sensory experiences.
B. Grammatical knowledge is a matter of practice.
C. NLP was developed by Richard Bandler and John Grinder in the 1970s.
D. Neuro covers "invisible thoughts and visible physiological reactions".
E. All of the above.

Choose the most appropriate answer from the options given below.

(1) Only E (2) A, C and D
(3) A and D (4) B, C and D

13. Identify the combination(s) that belong to the genre of sci-fi/speculative fiction.

A. Vandana Singh - The Woman Who Thought She was a Planet : And Other Stories

B. Tehmina Durrani - Blasphemy

C. Salman Rushdie - The Satanic Verses

D. Priya Sarukkai Chabria - Generation 14

E. Gautam Bhatia - The Wall

Choose the most appropriate answer from the options given below.

(1) A, B and D
(2) A, D and E
(3) A, C and D
(4) D, A and C

14. Given below are two statements, one is labelled as Assertion (A) and the other is labelled as Reason (R).

Assertion (A) Jacques Lacan was radically critical of the esistium psychoanalytical theory.

Reason (R) Lacan was expelled from the international psychoanalytical association in 1959.

In the light of the above statements, choose the most appropriate answer from the options given below.

(1) Both A and R are true and R is the correct explanation of A.
(2) Both A and R are true, but R is not the correct explanation of A.
(3) A is true, but R is false.
(4) A is false, but R is true.

15. When was Haruki Murakami's men without women published?

(1) 2017 (2) 2018
(3) 2014 (4) 2019

16. Given below are two statements.

Statement I Hannah Arendt's 'defactualisation' is very close to the concept of 'post-truth'.

Statement II Post-truth relies on absolute lies.

In the light of the above statements, choose the most appropriate answer from the options given below.

(1) Both statement I and statement II are correct.
(2) Both statement I and statement II are incorrect.
(3) Statement I is correct, but statement II is incorrect.
(4) Statement I is incorrect, but statement II is correct.

17. Match List I with List II

List I	List II
A. Donald Davie	I. Against Romanticism
B. Philip Larkin	II. Hurry on Down
C. Kingsley Amis	III. The Shires
D. John Wain	IV. The North Ship

Choose the correct answer from the options given below.

	A	B	C	D		A	B	C	D
(1)	IV	I	II	III	(2)	I	III	IV	II
(3)	II	I	III	IV	(4)	III	IV	I	II

18. Which of the following are Plato's main objections against poetry?

A. The poet is an imitator.

B. The poet is incapable of bravery.

C. The poet, by fueling passions and emotions, weakens the reasoning capacity of the citizens.

D. The poet is less responsible.

E. The poet has no knowledge of the world.

Choose the correct answer from the options given below.

(1) A, C and E
(2) A and B
(3) B and D
(4) E and D

19. Match List I with List II.

List I	List II
A. To the Light House	I. 1913
B. Sons and Lovers	II. 1927
C. Finnegans Wake	III. 1939
D. The Waste Land	IV. 1922

Choose the correct answer from the options given below.

	A	B	C	D		A	B	C	D
(1)	I	II	IV	III	(2)	IV	II	I	III
(3)	III	IV	I	II	(4)	II	I	III	IV

20. Given below are two statements.

Statement I Comparative literature is a study of different cultures, nations and genres and it explores the inherent relationship between literature and other forms of cultural exploration.

Statement II In the study of literature and culture, the importance of methodology is secondary.

In the light of the above statements, choose the correct answer from the options given below.

(1) Both statement I and statement II are true.
(2) Both statement I and statement II are false.
(3) Statement I is true, but statement II is false.
(4) Statement I is false, but statement II is true.

21. Which among the following is an incomplete poem by PB Shelley?
(1) The Triumph of Life
(2) Ode to The West-Wind
(3) Queen Mab
(4) The Daemon of the World

22. Who said, "there is, there can be and there ought to be the difference between the language of prose and metrical composition"?
(1) John Dryden (2) William Wordsworth
(3) ST Coleridge (4) TS Eliot

23. Which of the following is not a part of Amitav Ghosh's Ibis trilogy?
(1) Sea of poppies
(2) River of smoke
(3) Flood of fire
(4) The Calcutta chromosome

24. Which among the following are true about Harold Printer?
A. Harold Printer was born in the year 1925.
B. He was influenced by Samuel Beckett and the theatre of the absurd.
C. The caretaker and the alchemist are his famous plays.
D. Stanley is a character in the birthday party.
E. Betrayal is a story of a married couple.

Choose the correct answer from the options given below.
(1) A, D and E (2) B, D and E
(3) B, C and D (4) A, C and D

25. Which of the following concepts are associated with Bhartrhari's theory of 'Śphota'?
A. Rasa B. Alankara C. Dhvani D. Vakrokti E. Shabda Brahman

Choose the most appropriate answer from the options given below.
(1) A and E (2) C and E (3) D and B (4) A and C

26. Who is the author of a literature of their own?
(1) Sandra Gilbert and Susan Gubar
(2) Elaine Showalter
(3) Virginia Woolf
(4) Sylvia Plath

27. The deserted village by Oliver Goldsmith
(1) Critiques the rural institutions.
(2) Voices revolt of the individual man against institutions.
(3) Reflects upon different views on the human soul.
(4) Advocates urbanism over rural backwardness.

28. Match List I with List II.

	List I	List II
A.	Malcolm Bradbury	I. Masters
B.	David Lodge	II. Lucky Jim
C.	Kingsley Amis	III. The History Man
D.	CP Snow	IV. Changing Places

Choose the correct answer from the options given below.

	A	B	C	D		A	B	C	D
(A)	I	II	III	IV	(B)	III	IV	II	I
(C)	II	III	IV	I	(D)	IV	III	I	II

29. Under the net (1954) is written by
(1) John Fowles
(2) Iris Murdoch
(3) Edmund Goose
(4) William Cooper

30. Who among the following has authored 'The Revenger's Tragedie'?
(1) Cyril Tourneur (2) John Webster
(3) John Fletcher (4) Thomas Heywood

31. What is the correct sequence of the following feminist texts?
A. Sexual Politics
B. A World of Difference
C. The Female Imagination
D. Thinking About Women
E. A Room of One's Own

Choose the correct answer from the options given below.
(1) A, B, C, D, E (2) E, B, D, A, C
(3) E, D, A, C, B (4) B, C, D, E, A

32. Given below are two statements.

Statement I "……… he who discovers no god whatever, how shall he discover heroes the visible temples of God" is a statement by Thomas Carlyle.

Statement II "It is not that men are ill fed, but that they have no pleasure in the work by which they make their bread and therefore look to wealth as the only means of pleasure" is a statement made by John Ruskin.

In the light of the above statements, choose the correct answer from the options given below.

(1) Both statement I and statement II are true.
(2) Both statement I and statement II are false.
(3) Statement I is true, but statement II is false.
(4) Statement I is false, but statement II is true.

33. Which of the following articles of the Indian Constitution made the provision for use of English, alongside Hindi, for official purposes, for fifteen years?

(1) Article 351 (2) Article 344
(3) Article 343 (4) Article 348

34. Kimberle Crenshaw's term 'intersectionality' is widely used for

A. academic deterioration
B. racial justice
C. peace formation
D. complex construction of power
E. identity politics

Choose the most appropriate answer from the options given below.

(1) B, D and E (2) A, C and E
(3) B, D and C (4) C, D and E

35. The heroic couplet is a pair of

(1) twelve-syllable lines that rhyme.
(2) ten-syllable lines that rhyme.
(3) eight-syllable lines that do not rhyme.
(4) eight-syllable lines that rhyme.

36. Given below are two statements, one is labelled as Assertion (A) and the other is labelled as Reason (R).

Assertion (A) Roland Barthes describes two basic categories of text as 'the readerly' and 'the writerly.'

Reason (R) Language is the window through which one sees the world.

In the light of the above statements, choose the most appropriate answer from the options given below.

(1) Both A and R are correct and R is the correct explanation of A.
(2) Both A and R are correct, but R is not the correct explanation of A.
(3) A is correct, but R is not correct.
(4) A is not correct, but R is correct.

37. Given below are two statements, one is labelled as Assertion (A) and the other is labelled as Reason (R).

Assertion (A) In 19th century, Charlotte Perkins Gilman asserted economic independence over voting rights.

Reason (R) The representation of women as power-seekers was not socially acceptable in 19th century America.

In the light of the above statements, choose the most appropriate answer from the options given below.

(1) Both A and R are correct and R is the correct explanation of A.
(2) Both A and R are correct, but R is not the correct explanation of A.
(3) A is correct, but R is not correct.
(4) A is not correct, but R is correct.

38. AL Tennyson in the following lines.

"Yet I doubt not through the ages one increasing purpose runs.
And the thoughts of men are widen'd with the process of the suns".

(1) Reflects upon secularism
(2) Reflects upon evolutionary faith
(3) Reflects upon utilitarianism
(4) Reflects upon materialism

39. Given below are two statements.

Statement I According to WH Auden. The importance of being earnest is the purest example in English literature of a 'verbal opera'.

Statement II Oscar Wilde possessed profound insight into the range of the arts that in a combined form make theatre performance possible.

In the light of the above statement, choose the correct answer from the options given below.

(1) Both statement I and statement II are true.
(2) Both statement I and statement II are false.
(3) Statement I is true, but statement II is false.
(4) Statement I is false, but statement II is true.

40. Canadian Multiculturalism Act was passed in the year.

(1) 1958 (2) 1968 (3) 1978 (4) 1988

41. Who among the following attached himself to the Earl of Nottingham's theatrical company?

(1) William Shakespeare (2) Christopher Marlowe
(3) George Peele (4) Ben Johnson

42. Consumerism is a major theme in which of the following works?

A. Loyalties
B. Saint Joan of stockyards
C. Death of a salesman
D. Candida
E. Waiting for Godot

Choose the most appropriate answer from the options given below.

(1) A and B (2) D and A (3) B and C (4) A and E

43. Which of the following theorists identifies 'metonymy' and 'metaphor' as two fundamental structures of language?

(1) Ferdinand de Sassure (2) Roland Barthes
(3) JL Austin (4) Roman Jacobson

44. Who is the author of the essay "Three Women's Texts and a Critique of Imperialism" (1985)?

(1) Ania Loomba
(2) Meenakshi Mukherjee
(3) Susan Meyer
(4) Gayatri Chakravorty Spivak

45. What is meant by 'corporate author' in research?

(1) A writer who belongs to a corporate company.
(2) A writer who writes on matters of corporate affairs.
(3) A work produced by an institution, an association or a government agency.
(4) A renowned author.

46. Which among the following are appropriate about Latin American literature?

A. There has been racial coherence and unity in literary representations of Latin America.
B. The Latin American literary tradition draws analogy between plant growth and human movement.
C. Dzul Poot's stories depict the geography of the chilam balam towns.
D. Quechua had a wider popularity and presence across different nations.
E. The Latin American literature is unitary and refrains from intextuality of any kind.

Choose the most appropriate answer from the options given below.

(1) A, D and E (2) C, B and E
(3) B, C and E (4) B, C and D

47. Identify the correct combination among the following.

A. Spondee–It consists of three stressed syllables.
B. Pyrrhic–It consists of two unstressed syllables.
C. Amphimacer–It is a metrical foot of three syllables.
D. Choriambus–It is a foot of verse consisting of two stressed syllables enclosing two unstressed syllables.
E. Trochaic–It has a stressed syllable followed by an unstressed one.

Choose the most appropriate answer from the options given below.

(1) A, B and C (2) B, C and E
(3) B, C and D (4) C, D and E

48. Who among the following in the article, 'Fleshly School of Poetry'. Attacked the pre-Raphaelites, especially DG Rossetti?

(1) Robert Browning
(2) William Holeman Hunt
(3) Robert Buchanan
(4) Christina Rossetti

49. Subramani's Fantasy Eaters (1988) is a

(1) Novel (2) Collection of short stories
(3) Collection of essays (4) Poem

50. Identify the correct combinations.

A. Dadaism - Tristan Tzara
B. Super realism - Guillanne Apollinaire
C. Surrealism - Filipo Marinetti
D. Futurism - Andre Breton
E. Nihilism - Ivan Sergeyevich Turgenev

Choose the correct answer from the options given below.

(1) A, C and E (2) A, B and E
(3) B, C and D (4) C, D and E

51. Tolkappiyam is a book of grammar and poetics written in the .... language.

(1) Telugu (2) Tamil
(3) Kannada (4) Malayalam

52. Identify the correct pairs.

A. The Boyfriend - Juliette Banerjee
B. Nude Therapy - Margaret Chatterjee
C. The Other Woman and Other Stories - Dina Mehta
D. The Yankee and The Yogi - BG Siddharth
E. Prejudice of Ages - Vera Sharma

Choose the correct answer from the options given below.

(1) A, B and C (2) A, C and D
(3) B, C and E (4) C, D and E

53. "It is significant that the productive capacities of this third space have a colonial or post colonial provenance". The above lines have been written by

(1) Salman Rushdie (2) Edward Said
(3) Benedict Anderson (4) Homi K Bhabha

54. In which year Miles Coverdale translated The Old Testament of the Bible?

(1) 1533 (2) 1534 (3) 1535 (4) 1536

55. Who among the following is not a recipient of the Nobel prize for literature?

(1) Winston Churchill
(2) TS Eliot
(3) WH Auden
(4) Madam Curie

56. Match List I with List II.

	List I	List II
A.	"Willing to wound, and yet afraid to strike."	I. Irony
B.	"It is a truth universally acknowledged that a single man in possession of good fortune must be in want of a wife."	II. Simile
C.	"Thou still unravished bride of quietness. Thou foster child of silence and slow time."	III. Antithesis
D.	"And ice, mast-high, come floating by, as green as emerald."	IV. Assonance

Codes

	A	B	C	D		A	B	C	D
(1)	II	III	I	IV	(2)	III	I	IV	II
(3)	III	II	IV	I	(4)	I	IV	II	III

57. Anglo-Irish relations in the 20th century have been represented in which of the following novels?

A. Elizabeth Bowen—The Last September
B. May Sinclair—The Divine Fire
C. JG Farewell—Troubles
D. J F Farewell—The Siege of Krishnapur
E. Jeffery Farnol—Black Bartlemy's Treasure

Choose the most appropriate answer from the options given below.

(1) A, B and C (2) A and C
(3) D, E and B (4) B, C and A

58. Match List I with List II.

	List-I	List-II
A.	The Poetics of Prose	I. Stanley Fish
B.	Problems of Dostoevsky's Poetics	II. Tzvetan Todrov
C.	Surprised by Sin	III. Mikhail Bakhtin
D.	The Way Women Write	IV. Mary Hiatt

Choose the correct answer from the options given below.

	A	B	C	D		A	B	C	D
(1)	IV	II	I	III	(2)	III	IV	II	I
(3)	II	III	I	IV	(4)	II	IV	III	I

59. Stuart hall belongs to .... schools of cultural studies.

(1) Oxford (2) Cambridge
(3) Birmingham (4) American

60. Match List I with List II.

	List I	List II
A.	Salim Ali	I. Wild Beauty
B.	Jim Corbett	II. The Fall of a Sparrow
C.	Kailash Sankhala	III. Night and Days: My Book of Indian Wildlife
D.	M Krishnan	IV. My India

Choose the correct answer from the options given below.

	A	B	C	D		A	B	C	D
(1)	II	IV	I	III	(2)	III	II	IV	I
(3)	I	III	IV	II	(4)	II	III	IV	I

61. Which of the collections of poems are not written by Meena Alexander?

A. River and Bride B. Articulate Silence
C. Raw Silk D. Stone Roots
E. A Time to Change

Codes

(1) A and B (2) B and D (3) C and E (4) B and E

62. Find out the correct sequence of the publications of the following books.

(1) India–An Area of Darkness, India–A wounded Civilisation, India–A Million Mutinies Now, A House for Mr. Biswas
(2) A House for Mr. Biswas, India–A Million Mutinies Now, India–An Area of Darkness, India–A Wounded Civilisation
(3) A House for Mr. Biswas, India–An Area of Darkness, India–A Wounded Civilisation, India–A Million Mutinies Now
(4) India-A Wounded Civilisation, A House for Mr. Biswas, India-An Area of Darkness, India-A Million Mutinies Now

63. Choose the right chronological sequence of publication of the following novels by Margaret Atwood.

A. Lady Oracle B. The Blind Assassin
C. The Handmaid's Tale D. The Testaments

E. Alias Grace

Codes

(1) A, B, C, D, E (2) A, C, E, B, D
(3) E, A, D, B, C (4) C, A, D, E, B

64. According to Roland Barthes, which of the following 'codes' are common to all narratives?

A. Synthetic code B. Proairctic code
C. Semic code D. Hermencutic code
E. Symbolic code

Choose the correct answer from the options given below.

(1) A and B (2) B and C
(3) A, B and C (4) B, C, D and E

65. J Hillis Miller, one of the leading exponents of deconstruction, makes a deconstructionist reading of which of the following poems of PB Shelley?

(1) The Triumph of Life
(2) Ode to The West Wind
(3) Revolt of Islam
(4) The Witch of Atlas

66. Who is the author of the poem 'House of Fame'?

(1) William Langland (2) Geoffrey Chaucer
(3) Thomas Moore (4) Philip Sidney

67. Which of these are correct combination of the works by Doris Lessing and their respective themes?

A. The Golden Notebook—deals with Johor travelling to Rohonda.
B. The Good Terrorist—is about a doomed love affair.
C. Shikasta—is about a planet, which is cut-off due to the advanced influence of civilisation.
D. Alfred and Emily—explores the life of her parents.
E. The Grass is Singing—draws from her experiences in Africa.

Codes

(1) B, A and D (2) A, B and E
(3) C, D and E (4) A and B

68. Which of these graphic narratives depict political crisis?

A. Amruta Patil	Kari
B. Joe Sacco	Footnotes in Gaza
C. Art Spiegelman	Maus
D. Sarnath Banerjee	Corridor
E. Phoebe Gloeckner	The Dairy of a Teenage Girl

Choose the most appropriate answer from the options given below.

(1) A, B and C (2) C, D and E
(3) B and C (4) B, C and D

69. Identify the poems termed as 'pastoral elegies'.

A. Lycidas B. In memory of WB Yeats
C. Adonais D. Thyrsis
E. In Memoriam

Choose the most appropriate answer from the options given below.

(1) A, B and C (2) B, C and E
(3) A, C and D (4) C, D and E

70. The book Women Beware Women was published in the year

(1) 1612 (2) 1620 (3) 1621 (4) 1622

71. Who among the following were poet laureates of England?

A. Alfred Austin B. Robert Bridges
C. Watts Dunton D. Oscar Wilde

Choose the correct answer from the options given below.

(1) A and C (2) A and D
(3) B, C and D (4) A, B and C

72. Find the correct explanation of the term 'Aporia'.

(1) It denotes a speaker's or character's deliberation on an irresolvable question.
(2) It is an address to something inanimate.
(3) It is applied to a work of art fraught with inherent tension.
(4) It refers to a form of denial of existence.

73. Which among the following is appropriate about Ngugi wa Thiong'o's article 'literature in schools'?

A. The article discusses the relevance and adequacy of the present education system.
B. It advocates teaching of European texts and literature to the students of the third world countries.
C. It reflects negatively upon the literature taught to the Kenyan students in national schools.
D. It argues that cultural imperialism distorts people's vision of history.
E. It observes that European teachers are better equipped to teach literature to the Kenyan students.

Choose the most appropriate answer from the options given below.

(1) A, B and C (2) C, D and E
(3) B, C and D (4) A, C and D

74. Identify the correct ones among the following.

A. Arun Kolatkar uses colloquial speech in his poems.

B. Kolatkar envisions abstract qualities to paint a picture of life of his own kind.

C. The poem boatride by Kolatkar talks about a ride in the Ganges.

D. Private poems in public garden is composed by Dilip Chitre.

E. 'In Ethiopia' is a poem on Africa by Arun Kolatkar.

Choose the most appropriate answer from the options given below.

(1) A, B and C (2) B, D and E

(3) A, B and D (4) C, B and E

75. Identify the one that has not been paired correctly.

(1)	Criticism in Wilderness	Geoffrey Hartman
(2)	Madness and Civilisation	Roland Barthes
(3)	Poetry and Repression	Harold bloom
(4)	Strangers to Ourselves	Julia Kristeva

76. Match List I with List II.

List I	List II
A. O' Henry	I. The Last Suttee
B. Rudyard Kipling	II. Beauty
C. Oscar Wilde	III. At Verona
D. Ralph Waldo Emerson	IV. Hard to Forget

Choose the correct answer from the options given below.

	A	B	C	D
(1)	III	I	IV	II
(2)	II	IV	III	I
(3)	IV	I	III	II
(4)	I	III	II	IV

77. Who among the following critics appropriates the following statement by Karl Marx?

"They cannot represent themselves: the must be represented".

(1) Ruth Vanita

(2) Kamla Bhasin

(3) Flaria Agnes

(4) Chandra Talpade Mohanty

78. Which writer does not belong to the Angry Young Men movement?

(1) John Osborne (2) Kingsley Amis

(3) Seamus Heaney (4) Philip Larkin

79. What does Aristotle mean by the phrase 'language with pleasurable accessories' in his definition of tragedy?

A. A language full of pompous vocabulary

B. An embellished language

C. A language full of rhythm and harmony

D. A language superadded with song

E. Emotive language

Choose the correct answer from the options given below.

(1) A and B (2) B and E

(3) C and D (4) A, B and D

80. Match the following works of Edward Braithwaite according to their year of publication.

List I	List II
A. Rights of passage	I. 1973
B. Islands	II. 1969
C. Masks	III. 1967
D. The Arrivants	IV. 1968

Codes

	A	B	C	D
(1)	II	I	III	IV
(2)	I	III	IV	II
(3)	IV	II	I	III
(4)	III	IV	II	I

81. 'A man can be destroyed but not defeated'. Which of the following texts glorifies this as its predominant theme?

(1) The Old Man and the Sea

(2) War and Peace

(3) A Farewell to Arms

(4) For Whom the Bell Tolls

82. Which of these are not forms of flash fiction?

A. Drabble B. Postcard fiction

C. Novelette D. Short story

E. Nanofiction

Choose the most appropriate answer from the options given below.

(1) A and E (2) A, B and E

(3) D and E (4) C, D and E

83. Identify the correct combination among the following.

A. Demons—Novel

B. Landlady—Novella

C. The Crocodile—Short-story

D. A Writer's Diary—Essay

E. Mary Stuart—Translation

Choose the most appropriate answer from the options given below.

(1) A, B and E (2) C, D and E
(3) B, C and E (4) B, C and D

84. Should poets' bicycle-pump the human heart or squash it flat?

'Man's love is of man's life a thing apart:
Girls aren't like that'

The above lines are written by

(1) Philip Larkin (2) Kingsley Amis
(3) Donald Davie (4) John Wain

85. Gaiutra Bahadur wrote an autobiographic novel titled

(1) An Era of Darkness (2) Dauka Puran
(3) The Collie Woman (4) Rama's Banishment

86. Philip Sidney's Arcadia was influenced by

(1) the Spanish Romance of Montemayor
(2) the Italian Paintings of Veronese
(3) the Arthurian Legends
(4) the Metaphysical Poetry

87. Which among the following is true about the Tractarian Movement?

A. It was widespread across the world.
B. The other leaders of the movement were Paul Newman and RH Fronde.
C. The movement began with a sermon by John Keble in 1833.
D. Pusey gave the movement cohesion, fame and a name.
E. The ideal of the Christian church was praised by oxford convocation.

Choose the most appropriate answer from the options given below.

(1) A, B and C (2) A, C and E
(3) C, D and E (4) B, C and D

88. Match List I with List II.

List I	List II
A. Gender and Nation	I. Catherine Belsey
B. Greek Homosexuality	II. KJ Dover
C. The Subject of Tragedy	III. WEB Du Bois
D. The Souls of Black Folk	IV. Nira Yuval-Davis

Codes

	A	B	C	D		A	B	C	D
(1)	I	IV	III	II	(2)	III	II	IV	I
(3)	II	IV	III	I	(4)	IV	II	I	III

89. Identify the novels that were published in the 1980s and the 1990s.

A. Red Earth and Pouring Rain
B. The Circle of Reason
C. The Ghosts of Vasu Master
D. Miguel Street
E. The Siege of Babylon

Choose the correct answer from the options given below.

(1) B, C, D and E (2) A, B and C
(3) B, A and D (4) A, C and E

90. Which of the following denote the three phases of literary feminism according to Elain Showalter?

A. Feminine B. Gynie
C. Womanish D. Feminist
E. Female

Choose the most appropriate answer from the options given below.

(1) A, B and C (2) A, D and E
(3) A, B and E (4) B, C and D

Directions (Q.Nos. 91-95) *Read the following passage and answer the questions that follow.*

However, faced with this world of faithful and complicated objects, the child can only identify himself as owner. As user, never as creator, he does not invent the world. He uses it: there are, prepared for him, actions without adventure, without wonder, without joy. He is turned into a little stay-at-home householder who does not even have to invent the mainsprings of adult causality, they are supplied to him ready-made, he has only to help himself. He is never allowed to discover anything from start to finish. The merest set of blocks, provided it is not too refined, implies a very different learning of the world. Then the child does not in any way create meaningful objects, it matters little to him whether they have an adult name. The actions he performs are not those of a user but those of a demiurge. He creates forms which walk, which roll, he creates life, not property. Objects now act by themselves, they are no longer an inert and complicated material in the palm of his hand.

Roland Barthes 'Toys' (Excerpt from Mythologies)

91. Which of the following is a correct interpretation?

(1) The child claims the object as his property.
(2) The objects that the child holds are obscure and useless.
(3) The child cannot understand the design of the object.
(4) In touching the object, the child creates dynamic forms of life.

92. In the context of the above passage, which is the closest to being true.
(1) Children actively learn while playing.
(2) Children are objects for toy makers.
(3) Toys affect the cognitive abilities of the children.
(4) Children recreate meaning from the toys.

93. The adult causality is about
(1) sensual and sexual knowledge of the world.
(2) cognitive and logical structure of the world.
(3) nihilistic recreation of the world.
(4) linguistic structure of the objects.

94. The word 'demiurge' connotes
(1) cognitive inactiveness of the children.
(2) their sensational realisation of the objects.
(3) their creative abilities.
(4) their sudden discovery.

95. The world of objects makes the child
(1) imaginative (2) inventor
(3) actant (4) creator

Directions (Q.Nos. 96-100) *Read the following poem and answer the question that follow.*

'This was Mr bleaney's room he stayed
The whole time he was at the bodies, till
They moved him, 'flowered curtains, thin and frayed,
Fall to within five inches of the sill.
Whose window shows a strip of building land,
Tussocky littered. 'Mr Bleaney's took
My bit of garden properly in hand.'
Bed, upright chair, sixty-watt bulb, no book
Behind the door, no room for books or bags
'I'll take it. 'So it happens that I lie
Where Mr Bleaney lay, and stub my fags
On the same saucer-souvenir, and try
Stuffing my ears with cotton, wool, to drown
The jabbering set he egged her on yo buy,
I know his habits .... what time he came down'
His preference for sauce to gravy, why
He kept on plugging at the four aways___
Likewise their yearly frame: the Frinton folk
Who put him up for summer holidays
And Christmas at his sister's house in stoke
But if he stood and watched the frigid wind
Tousling the clouds, lay on the fusty bed
Telling himself that this was home, and grinned,
And shivered, without shaking off the dread
That how we live measures our own nature,
And at his age having no more to show
Than one hired box should make him pretty sure
He warranted no better, I don't know.
Philip Larkin

96. The poem, 'Mr Bleaney', is written in a .... form.
(1) satirical (2) lyrical
(3) dramatic (4) philosophical

97. In the third line 'They refers to'
(1) workers (2) owners
(3) master (4) manufacturers

98. Mr. Bleaney was the .... of the house.
(1) owner (2) tenant (3) master (4) possessor

99. According to the speaker Mr. Bleany was
(1) a humorous person
(2) a social and fun-loving person
(3) a hard working person
(4) a sad and dull person

100. The poem 'Mr. Bleaney' deals with the portrayal of his
(1) richness (2) extravagance
(3) luxuriousness (4) ordinariness

ANSWERS

1 (4)	2 (4)	3 (3)	4 (3, 4)	5 (1)	6 (3)	7 (1)	8 (2)	9 (*)	10 (1)
11 (1)	12 (2)	13 (2)	14 (2)	15 (3)	16 (3)	17 (4)	18 (1)	19 (4)	20 (3)
21 (1)	22 (*)*	23 (4)	24 (2)	25 (2)	26 (2)	27 (2)	28 (2)	29 (2)	30 (1)
31 (3)	32 (1)	33 (3)	34 (1)	35 (2)	36 (2)	37 (1)	38 (2)	39 (1)	40 (4)
41 (2)	42 (3)	43 (4)	44 (4)	45 (3)	46 (4)	47 (*)	48 (3)	49 (2)	50 (2)
51 (2)	52 (2)	53 (4)	54 (3)	55 (3)	56 (2)	57 (2)	58 (3)	59 (3)	60 (1)
61 (1)	62 (3)	63 (2)	64 (2)	65 (1)	66 (2)	67 (3)	68 (3)	69 (3)	70 (*)
71 (*)	72 (*)	73 (4)	74 (4)	75 (2)	76 (3)	77 (4)	78 (4)	79 (3)	80 (*)
81 (1)	82 (*)	83 (*)	84 (2)	85 (3)	86 (1)	87 (4)	88 (4)	89 (2)	90 (2)
91 (4)	92 (3)	93 (2)	94 (3)	95 (3, 4)	96 (3)	97 (*)	98 (2)	99 (4)	100 (4)

English (Paper-2)
Solved Paper, December 2021

General Instructions

1. There are total one hundred questions in this paper. Each question carries 2 marks.
2. All questions are compulsory.

Directions (Q. Nos. 1-3) *Read the following passage and answer the questions that follow :*

What can be the use of a poetry that has no true subject except the poet's own selfhood? The traditional use of poetry in the Western world has been instruction through delight, where teaching has meant the common truths or common deceptions of societal tradition, and where esthetic pleasure has meant a fulfillment of expectations founded upon past joys of the same design.

But an individual psyche has its own accidents, which it needs to call truths, and its own necessity for self-recognition, which requires the pleasures of originality, even if those pleasures depend upon a kind of lying against time, and against the achievements of the past. The use of such poetry demands to be seen in a deidealised way, if it is to be seen more truly.

—Harold Bloom, 'The Use of Poetry'

1. In the context of the above which is closest to being true?
(a) There can be no use of poetry.
(b) Man may be the true subject of poetry.
(c) Poetry can have no true subject.
(d) The poet himself may be the subject.

2. If 'selfhood' of a poet is the subject of poetry, then 'originality' shall spring from
(a) creating ideal pleasures
(b) re-living the past joys
(c) some truth of untruths
(d) truth of self-recognition

3. What is meant by 'traditional use of poetry'?
(a) Promoting doubtful pleasure
(b) Promoting joyous expectations
(c) Promoting serious ideas
(d) Promoting social honesty in life

Directions (Q.Nos. 4-6) *Read the following poem and answer the questions that follow :*

No worst, there is none.
No worst, there is none. Pitched past pitch of grief,
More pangs will, schooled at forepangs, wilder wring.
Comforter, where, where is your comforting?
Mary, mother of us, where is your relief?
My cries heave, herds-long; huddle in a main, a chief
Woe, world-sorrow; on an age-old anvil wince and sing—
Then lull, then leave off. Fury had shrieked 'No lingering!
Let me be fell: force I must be brief."
O the mind, mind has mountains; cliffs of fall
Frightful, sheer, no-man-fathomed. Hold them cheap
May who ne'er hung there. Nor does long our small
Durance deal with that steep or deep. Here! creep,
Wretch, under a comfort serves in a whirlwind: all
Life death does end and each day dies with sleep.

—Gerard Manley Hopkins

4. Which of the following best describes the meaning of the title of the poem, 'No worst, there is none.'?
(a) It is not worst because there is nothing.
(b) It is very bad as no one is there.
(c) No it is worst as nothing is there.
(d) Nothing can be so much bad as this.

5. Which two of the following are true?
   1. Not all know the intensity or depth of suffering.
   2. Death does not put an end to our sufferings.
   3. Suffering is seen as winds that hinder comfort.
   4. Suffering's intensity or depth is in the mind.

   Choose the correct answer from the options given below :

   (a) 1 and 4 (b) 1 and 2
   (c) 2 and 4 (d) 3 and 4

6. Beyond the intensity of known grief, there can be
   (a) no grief than being experienced
   (b) only a new pain more painful
   (c) only the twisted known pains
   (d) the griefs beyond limits of pain

Directions (Q.Nos. 7-8) *Read the following extract and answer the questions that follow :*

'Justice' was done, and the President of the Immortals, in Aeschylean phrase, had ended his sport with Tess. And the D'Urberville knights and dames slept on in their tombs unknowing. The two speechless gazers bent themselves down to the earth, as if in prayer, and remained thus a long time, absolutely motionless; the flag continued to wave silently. As soon as they had enough strength they arose, joined hands again, and went on.

—Thomas Hardy, Tess of the D'Urbervilles

7. How did the 'sport with Tess' end?
   (a) She was hanged.
   (b) She died an untimely death.
   (c) She was expelled from Wintoncester.
   (d) The tormentor married her.

8. Who are the 'two speechless gazers'?
   (a) Liza-Lu and Angel Clare
   (b) Parson Tringham and Mrs. d'Urberville
   (c) Reverend James Clare and Mrs. Brooks
   (d) Tess's two parents

Directions (Q.Nos. 9-10) *Read the following extract and answer the questions that follow:*

The solemn temples, the great globe itself,
Yea, all which it inherit, shall dissolve
And, like this insubstantial pageant faded,
Leave not a rack behind. We are such stuff
As dreams are made on, and our little life
Is rounded with a sleep. — Shakespeare The Tempest

9. 'This insubstantial pageant' refers to
   (a) a non-real performance.
   (b) enactment with support structure.
   (c) the destroyed mother earth.
   (d) the shutdown of Globe theatre.

10. 'We are such stuff as dreams are made on' means
    (a) Human life is full of imaginary colours.
    (b) Our life is a text of what happened.
    (c) There is no substance to human life.
    (d) We are a bundle of past reality.

11. Who is the author of the essay, 'What Isn't Literature?'
    (a) E. D. Hirsch Jr.
    (b) Hans-Georg Gadamer
    (c) Paul Ricoeur
    (d) Terry Eagleton

12. Given below are two statements

    Statement I In 'Waiting for Godot', it is Vladimir who questions the Boy who comes from Godot towards the end of the two Acts.

    Statement II In 'Waiting for Godot', it is Estragon who says, "Nothing happens, nobody comes, nobody goes, it's awful."

    In light of the above statements, choose the correct answer from the options given below

    (a) Both Statement I and Statement II are false
    (b) Both Statement I and Statement II are true
    (c) Statement I is false but Statement II is true
    (d) Statement I is true but Statement II is false

13. Who is the author of the essay 'Lear, Tolstoy and the Fool'?
    (a) Aldous Huxley
    (b) George Orwell
    (c) Somerset Maugham
    (d) Virginia Woolf

14. Which two of the following stage directions are from Harold Pinter's 'The Birthday Party'?
    1. The living-room of a house on a seaside town.
    2. A garbage pail on the ground next to the porch steps.
    3. A light shows from upstairs bedroom, lower floor windows being dark.
    4. He hangs the drum around his neck, taps it gently with the sticks, then marches round the table, beating it regularly.

    Choose the correct answer from the options given below:

    (a) 1 and 3 (b) 1 and 4
    (c) 2 and 3 (d) 3 and 4

15. Who among the following is said to have believed that the Persian Gulf War (1990-91) never happened?
    (a) Jacques Derrida
    (b) Jean Baudrillard
    (c) Jurgen Habermas
    (d) Zygmunt Bauman

16. Which two of the following conform to liberal humanist thought?

1. Literature transcends the limits of the age of its origin and so is timeless.
2. Literature is untouched by the essential human nature which is unchanging.
3. Literature is devoid of any purpose to enhance life or promote human values.
4. Identity is a unique essence unaffected by environment and society.

Choose the correct answer from the options given below:

(a) 1 and 3 (b) 1 and 4
(c) 2 and 3 (d) 2 and 4

17. Who among the following Dickens characters appears as a ghost?

(a) Daniel Quilp (b) Dora Spenlow
(c) Esther Summerson (d) Jacob Marley

18. Match List I with List II.

List I (Playwright)	List II (Play)
A. Bertolt Brecht	1. Cat on a Hot Tin Roof
B. Tennessee Williams	2. Life of Galileo
C. Vaclav Havel	3. Miss Julie
D. August Strindberg	4. Temptation

Choose the correct answer from the options given below:

	A	B	C	D
(a)	1	2	4	3
(b)	2	1	4	3
(c)	3	2	1	4
(d)	4	3	1	2

19. Match List I with List II

List I (Text)	List II (Author)
A. Modernity at Large	1. J. Urry
B. The Tourist Gaze	2. E.W Said
C. Culture and Imperialism	3. C.L.R. James
D. The Black Jacobins	4. A. Appadurai

Choose the correct answer from the options given below:

	A	B	C	D
(a)	2	3	4	1
(b)	3	4	2	1
(c)	4	1	2	3
(d)	4	3	2	1

20. Who, among the following, played the most significant role in mobilising the concept of 'cultural intermediaries'?

(a) Karl Marx
(b) Luis Althusser
(c) Pierre Bourdieu
(d) Jurgen Habermas

21. Given below are two statements

Statement I Linguists, being primarily interested in the scientific study of language, approach language dispassionately.

Statement II Linguists are necessarily polyglots who bring their own biases to language study.

In the light of the above statements, choose the most appropriate answer from the options given below

(a) Both Statement I and Statement II are incorrect.
(b) Both Statement I and Statement II are correct.
(c) Statement I is correct but Statement II is incorrect.
(d) Statement I is incorrect but Statement II is correct.

22. Which of the following clusters is associated with what Julia Kristeva terms the 'semiotic'?

(a) Authority, order and patriarchy
(b) Displacement, slippage and condensation
(c) Logic, reason and power
(d) Repression, control and normalcy

23. Match List I with List II.

List I (Writer)	List II (Book)
A. Bankimchandra Chatterjee	1. Untouchable
B. Mulk Raj Anand	2. Rajmohan's Wife
C. Panchkouree Khan	3. Stories from Indian Christian Life
D. Kamala Sathianathan	4. The Revelations of an Orderly

Choose the correct answer from the options given below :

Codes

	A	B	C	D
(a)	1	3	2	4
(b)	2	1	4	3
(c)	3	4	2	1
(d)	4	1	2	3

24. Which of the following are novels by Ian McEwan?

1. Atonement
2. The Man with Two Left Feet
3. The Child in Time
4. The Rachel Papers

Choose the correct answer from the options given below :

(a) 1 and 3 (b) 2 and 4
(c) 3 and 4 (d) 4 and 1

25. Given below are two statements

Statement I New Historicism stipulates that teleological connotations of history have to be eschewed.

Statement II New Historicism neither denies nor accepts totalizing explanations of historical events.

In light of the above statements, choose the correct answer from the options given below

(a) Both Statement I and Statement II are false
(b) Both Statement I and Statement II are true
(c) Statement I is false but Statement II is true
(d) Statement I is true but Statement II is false

26. In 'Mr Bennett and Mrs Brown' Virginia Woolf

(a) analyses the state of modern fiction by contrasting two generations of writers.
(b) criticises book buying preferences of the educated English class.
(c) presents modernity as a stable and coherent project uniting all artists.
(d) responds to E.M Forster's remarks on character in fiction.

27. Arrange the following texts in the chronological order of publication.

1. This Bridge Called My Back
2. Sexual Politics
3. Gender Trouble
4. The Feminine Mystique

Choose the correct answer from the options given below :

(a) 2, 4, 1, 3 (b) 2, 4, 3, 1
(c) 4, 1, 2, 3 (d) 4, 2, 1, 3

28. Which two works in the following list are written by Aphra Behn?

1. Rover
2. Oroonoko
3. Soldier's Fortune
4. The Princess of Cleve

Choose the correct answer from the options given below :

(a) 1 and 2 (b) 1 and 3
(c) 2 and 3 (d) 2 and 4

29. Which two of the following are works by Gustave Flaubert?

1. The Temptation of Saint Anthony
2. Old Goriot
3. Therese Raquin
4. Sentimental Education

Choose the correct answer from the options given below :

(a) 1 and 3 (b) 1 and 4
(c) 2 and 3 (d) 2 and 4

30. Which of these best describes Shyam Selvadurai's novel, 'Funny Boy'?

(a) Coming-of-age novel
(b) Novel of manners
(c) Picaresque novel
(d) Sentimental novel

31. In 'The Function of Criticism' T.S. Eliot attacked J.Middleton Murry and similar critics for being devotees of what he called

(a) the Inner Voice
(b) the Muse's Mystery
(c) the Romantic Impulse
(d) the Symbol Hunt

32. In 'Politics and the English Language' which two of the following 'tricks' are mentioned by George Orwell as 'bad habits' of English use?

1. obsolete words
2. pretentious diction
3. dying metaphors
4. false modifiers

Choose the correct answer from the options given below :

(a) 1 and 2 (b) 2 and 3
(c) 2 and 4 (d) 3 and 4

33. What was poor Yorick in Hamlet?

(a) Actor (b) Gravedigger
(c) Jester (d) Soldier

34. Which two of the following conform to Northrop Frye's typology of literature?

1. Mythos of spring: Comedy
2. Mythos of summer: Satire
3. Mythos of autumn: Tragedy
4. Mythos of winter: Romance

Choose the correct answer from the options given below :

(a) 1 and 2 (b) 1 and 3
(c) 2 and 4 (d) 3 and 4

35. With which of these is Ngugi wa Thiongo generally associated?

(a) Decolonising the Body
(b) Decolonising the Mind
(c) Decolonising the Polity
(d) Decolonising the State

36. Choose the right chronological sequence of the publication of the following books:

1. Margaret Atwood, 'The Handmaid's Tale'
2. Alice Walker, 'The Color Purple'
3. Doris Lessing, 'The Golden Notebook'
4. Toni Morrison, 'The Bluest Eye'

Choose the correct answer from the options given below :

(a) 1, 2, 4, 3 (b) 2, 1, 4, 3
(c) 3, 4, 2, 1 (d) 4, 3, 2, 1

37. Which of these poets wrote a poem that served to inspire WB Yeats to write his own poem, 'When you are Old'?

(a) Francois Villon (b) Edmund Spencer
(c) Heinrich Heine (d) Pierre de Ronsard

38. What was the name of the journal published from Bowling Green University beginning 1969, which carried essays on amusement parks, comics and detective films?

(a) Journal of Culture Studies
(b) Journal of Mass Culture
(c) Journal of Popular Culture
(d) Journal of Public Culture

39. Arrange the following language areas of the human brain in the order in which they involve in hearing, understanding and saying a word:

1. arcuate fasciculus
2. anterior speech cortex
3. motor cortex
4. posterior speech cortex

Choose the correct answer from the options given below :

(a) 1, 3, 4, 2
(b) 2, 1, 4, 3
(c) 3, 2, 1, 4
(d) 4, 1, 2, 3

40. Which of these does Meenakshi Mukherjee propose as the possible target readership of early Indian English novel?

1. A pan-Indian readership
2. A localized Indian readership
3. A British readership
4. The colonial administrator in India

Choose the correct answer from the options given below :

(a) 3 and 4 (b) 1 and 2
(c) 1 and 4 (d) 2 and 3

41. Arrange the following terms in the chronological order of their use in literary theory:

1. gynesis 2. scriptible
3. negritude 4. paratext

Choose the correct answer from the options given below :

(a) 1, 2, 3, 4 (b) 2, 3, 4, 1
(c) 3, 1, 4, 2 (d) 4, 1, 3, 2

42. Which of the following statements is true of the working group set up by the University Grants Commission in 1978 to study the medium of instruction in higher education?

(a) It argued that English as a highly developed language was best suited for India's industrial and scientific progress.
(b) It asserted that English had the potential to further polarize an already-divided nation along socio- economic and intellectual fault lines.
(c) It observed that English need not be displaced as the medium of instruction although regional languages were quite ready to take over its functions.
(d) It recommended a quicker switchover of the medium of instruction from English to Indian languages.

43. Match List I with List II.

List I (Poet)	List II (Language)
A. Charles Baudelaire	1. French
B. Heinrich Heine	2. German
C. Sylvia Path	3. English
D. Jose Marti	4. Spanish

Choose the correct answer from the options given below :

Codes

	A	B	C	D
(a)	1	2	3	4
(b)	2	3	4	1
(c)	3	4	1	2
(d)	4	1	2	3

44. Who among the following represents the global spread of English diagrammatically as three concentric circles?

(a) Braj B. Kachru
(b) David Crystal
(c) Jenny Cheshire
(d) Salikoko Mufwene

45. Arrange the following plays in their chronological sequence:

1. Sergeant Musgrave's Dance
2. The Playboy of the Western World
3. Look Back in Anger
4. Man and Superman

Choose the correct answer from the options given below :

(a) 2, 4, 1, 3 (b) 2, 4, 3, 1
(c) 4, 2, 1, 3 (d) 4, 2, 3, 1

46. Who, among the following, is known to have used elements from the Yakshagana tradition in his theatre?
(a) Mahesh Dattani
(b) Badal Sircar
(c) Girish Karnad
(d) Mohan Rakesh

47. In 'An Apology for Poetry' Sidney discusses the didactic function of poetry by comparing it to philosophy and
(a) aesthetics (b) ethics
(c) history (d) religion

48. Who is the author of the short story, 'Beethoven Was One-Sixteenth Black'?
(a) Andre Brink
(b) Bessie Head
(c) J M Coetzee
(d) Nadine Gordimer

49. Arrange the following essays in the chronological order of publication.
1. T. S. Eliot, 'The Function of Criticism'
2. Edgar Allan Poe, 'The Philosophy of Composition'
3. Henry James, 'The Art of Fiction'
4. Virginia Woolf, 'Modern Fiction'

Choose the correct answer from the options given below :
(a) 2, 3, 1, 4 (b) 2, 3, 4, 1
(c) 3, 2, 1, 4 (d) 3, 2, 4, 1

50. Who among the following considered paraphrase as 'a heresy'?
(a) Cleanth Brooks
(b) Edmund Wilson
(c) I.A. Richards
(d) Percy Lubbock

51. Who among the following edited 'The Cornhill Magazine'?
(a) Anthony Trollope
(b) Charles Dickens
(c) Lewis Carroll
(d) William Makepeace Thackeray

52. Which two of the following writers does AD Hope address through his poetic responses in 'A Book of Answers'?
1. Tolstoy 2. Dostoevsky
3. Mallarme 4. Goethe

Choose the correct answer from the options given below :
(a) 1 and 3 (b) 1 and 4
(c) 2 and 3 (d) 2 and 4

53. Match List I with List II.

List I (Novel)	List II (Author)
A. Don Quixote	1. Machado de Assis
B. Sorrows of Young Werther	2. Honore de Balzac
C. Lost Illusions	3. Goethe
D. Epitaph of a Small Winner	4. Miguel de

Choose the correct answer from the options given below :

	A	B	C	D		A	B	C	D
(a)	1	3	2	4	(b)	2	1	3	4
(c)	3	1	4	2	(d)	4	3	2	1

54. Which of these plays by Girish Karnad shares its theme with Thomas Mann's 'The Transposed Heads'?
(a) Tale Danda (b) Yayati
(c) Nagamandala (d) Hayavadana

55. Virginia Woolf's 'Orlando' opens in 1588 and Orlando, a sixteen-year-old boy, writes a poem called
(a) The Evergreen Tree
(b) The Magic Tree
(c) The Oak Tree
(d) The Poison Tree

56. Who among the following compared 'the mind in creation' to 'a fading coal'?
(a) Coleridge (b) Keats
(c) Shelley (d) Wordsworth

57. Empiricist linguistics is concerned with
(a) directly observable sense-data
(b) innate language knowledge
(c) investigation of the human mind
(d) reason as a determinant of enquiry

58. Which of the following are true of 'performance', as used in linguistic theory?
1. It is analogous to the Saussurean concept of langue.
2. It refers to the specific utterances of individual native speakers in actual situations.
3. It is an innate grammar that suggests humans' universal ability to use language.
4. It includes hesitations and unfinished structures arising out of psychological difficulties acting upon the speaker.

Choose the correct answer from the options given below :
(a) 1 and 2 (b) 1 and 3
(c) 2 and 3 (d) 2 and 4

59. Given below are two statements, one is labelled as Assertion (A) and the other is labelled as Reason (R).

Assertion (A) Postmodern narratives focus on the indeterminate and unstable nature of textuality and subjectivity.

Reason (R) Postmodern narrative acts regard narratives and characters as tentative representations of writing and identity.

In light of the above statements, choose the correct answer from the options given below

(a) (A) is false but (R) is true
(b) (A) is true but (R) is false
(c) Both (A) and (R) are true and (R) is the correct explanation of (A)
(d) Both (A) and (R) are true but (R) is not the correct explanation of (A)

60. Which of the following poems contains John Donne's famous conceit bringing a parallel between lovers and the hands of a compass?

(a) A Valediction: Forbidding Mourning
(b) A Valediction: Of Weeping
(c) Lovers Infinitenesse
(d) Negative Love

61. Which of these UK universities saw the first institutional incorporation of Cultural Studies?

(a) Bath Spa University
(b) Cambridge University
(c) Oxford University
(d) University of Birmingham

62. Which of the following words refers to a sound that is associated with a particular meaning?

(a) phoneme (b) phonemoid
(c) phonestheme (d) phonic substance

63. Arrange the following characters in their chronological sequence of appearance

1. Mirabell
2. Shylock
3. Jimmy Porter
4. Sir Epicure Mammon

Choose the correct answer from the options given below :

(a) 4, 2, 1, 3 (b) 2, 4, 1, 3
(c) 2, 4, 3, 1 (d) 4, 2, 3, 1

64. Match List I with List II.

List I (First line)	**List II** (Poet)
A. "Courage!" he said, and pointed toward the land...	1. G.M. Hopkins
B. I am poor brother Lippo, by your leave!	2. Alfred Tennyson
C. I caught this morning morning's minion...	3. D.G. Rossetti
D. Look in my face; my name is Mighthave-been	4. Mathew Arnold
E. The sea is calm tonight	5. Robert Browning

Choose the correct answer from the options given below :

	A	B	C	D	E
(a)	2	3	1	5	4
(b)	2	5	1	3	4
(c)	3	4	5	1	2
(d)	4	5	1	3	2

65. Which of the following statements best describes Terry Eagleton's views on literature?

(a) It is closely allied to religion in its significance and seriousness.
(b) It is involved in the reproduction of the dominant social order.
(c) Its primary purpose is to produce beauty and pleasure.
(d) Its raison d'etre is to reflect social reality directly.

66. According to Longinus which two of the following qualities apply to 'great poetry'?

1. It must be the work of genius, an inspired person.
2. It must cause a feeling of melancholy in the reader.
3. It must employ devices of rhetoric.
4. It must please selectively and on special occasions.

Choose the correct answer from the options given below :

(a) 1 and 3
(b) 1 and 2
(c) 2 and 4
(d) 3 and 4

67. Who among the following is the founder of the Survey of English Usage (SEU)?

(a) Bryan Garner
(b) Henry Watson Fowler
(c) Michael Swan
(d) Randolph Quirk

68. What 19th-century philosophical term of Russian origin did Friedrich Nietzsche use to describe the disintegration of traditional morality in western society?

(a) absolutism
(b) anarchism
(c) cynicism
(d) nihilism

69. Given below are two statements

Statement I Unlike scientific research, literary research does not have specific materials for investigation and scientific tools for reaching a conclusion and formulating a theory.

Statement II Literary research consists of critical interpretations of an author's work to the exclusion of biography and editing of texts.

In the light of the above statements, choose the most appropriate answer from the options given below :

(a) Both Statement I and Statement II are correct.
(b) Both Statement I and Statement II are incorrect.
(c) Statement I is correct but Statement II is incorrect.
(d) Statement I is incorrect but Statement II is correct.

70. Which two of the following are true according to the documentation style prescribed by the eighth edition of the MLA Handbook?

1. If the title page of a book contains an imprint as well as the publisher's name, omit the imprint and use the publisher's name.
2. While giving a URL copy it from the Web browser but omit http:// or https://.
3. If a quotation extends to more than five lines set it off from the text as block indented an inch from the left margin.
4. Long titles should be abbreviated using the first letter of key words typed in upper case without intervening space.

Choose the correct answer from the options given below :

(a) 1 and 2
(b) 1 and 3
(c) 2 and 3
(d) 2 and 4

71. Which of these questions would Cultural Studies be most interested in asking?

1. Who decides what is to be produced?
2. Who can afford the artifact?
3. How is the artifact marketed?
4. What is the register of speech in the artifact?

Choose the correct answer from the options given below :

(a) 1, 2 and 4
(b) 1, 2 and 3
(c) 1, 3 and 4
(d) 2, 3 and 4

72. Which of the following does the Subaltern Studies project contend?

1. Traditional historiography celebrated the role of the subalterns.
2. Traditional history of India's freedom movement celebrates the contribution of select icons.
3. Traditional historiography highlights the dominant strands of India's freedom struggle.
4. Subaltern Studies historiography highlights the dominant strands of India's freedom struggle.

Choose the correct answer from the options given below :

(a) 1 and 2 (b) 1 and 3
(c) 2 and 3 (d) 2 and 4

73. Arrange the following periodicals in the chronological order in which they started publication:

1. The Spectator
2. The Tatler
3. The Rambler
4. The Critical Review

Choose the correct answer from the options given below :

(a) 1, 2, 3, 4 (b) 1, 4, 2, 3
(c) 2, 1, 3, 4 (d) 2, 3, 4, 1

74. Who, among these, does Gabriel Garcia Marquez name right in the beginning of his Nobel Prize address?

1. Ferdinand Magellan
2. Christopher Columbus
3. Marco Polo
4. Antonio Pigafetta

Choose the correct answer from the options given below :

(a) 1 and 4 (b) 1 and 2
(c) 2 and 3 (d) 3 and 4

75. Arrange the following lines of poetry in their chronological sequence:

1. "An aged man is but a paltry thing."
2. "The world is too much with us."
3. "Daddy, I have had to kill you."
4. "After great pain, a formal feeling comes"

Choose the correct answer from the options given below :

(a) 2, 4, 1, 3 (b) 2, 4, 3, 1
(c) 4, 2, 1, 3 (d) 4, 2, 3, 1

76. Erich Auerbach's 'Mimesis' (1946) ends with a chapter on
(a) George Eliot's 'Middlemarch'
(b) James Joyce's 'Ulysses'
(c) Virginia Woolf 's 'To the Lighthouse'
(d) Wyndham Lewis's 'The Apes of God'

77. From whom does Gayatri Chakravorty Spivak borrow the term 'subaltern'?
(a) Friedrich Engels
(b) Karl Marx
(c) Louis Althusser
(d) Antonio Gramsci

78. Match List I with List II.

List I (Author)	List II (Text)
A. Sean O'Casey	1. I'm Talking About Jerusalem
B. Dylan Thomas	2. The Winslow Boy
C. Terence Rattigan	3. Juno and the Paycock
D. Arnold Wesker	4. In the Shadow of the Glen
E. J.M. Synge	5. Under Milk Wood

Choose the correct answer from the options given below :

	A	B	C	D	E
(a)	2	1	3	5	4
(b)	3	5	2	1	4
(c)	4	2	3	5	1
(d)	5	4	2	1	3

79. Match List I with List II.

List I (Character)	List II (Novel)
A. Winston Smith	1. Sons and Lovers
B. Paul Morel	2. Ulysses
C. Whiskey Priest	3. Nineteen Eighty-four
D. Leopold Bloom	4. Decline and Fall
E. Paul Pennyfeather	5. The Power and the Glory

Choose the correct answer from the options given below :

	A	B	C	D	E
(a)	1	5	2	3	4
(b)	3	1	5	2	4
(c)	4	3	5	2	1
(d)	5	1	4	2	3

80. Which two of the following concepts are deployed in the work of Frederic Jameson?
1. Pastiche 2. Hyperreal
3. Schizophrenia 4. Habitus

Choose the correct answer from the options given below :
(a) 1 and 2 (b) 1 and 3
(c) 2 and 4 (d) 3 and 4

81. Which of the following are features of the 'Theatre of the Absurd'?
1. emphasis on the central role of God in the universe
2. presentation of futile actions devoid of any goal
3. portrayal of situations that point to the meaningfulness of life
4. lacking in conflicts and dramatic tensions
5. presenting players in a stasis or drift without definite roles

Choose the correct answer from the options given below :
(a) 1, 2 and 4 (b) 1, 3 and 5
(c) 2, 3 and 4 (d) 2, 4 and 5

82. Match List I with List II

List I (Author)	List II (Form)
A. Pindar	1. Epinicia
B. Menander	2. Old Comedy
C. Sappho	3. Lyric poetry
D. Aristophanes	4. New Comedy

Choose the correct answer from the options given below :

	A	B	C	D
(a)	1	3	2	4
(b)	1	4	3	2
(c)	2	1	4	3
(d)	3	4	1	2

83. What might the speaker mean when he addresses 'Time' in a Shakespearean sonnet and declares that "I will be true, despite thy scythe and thee "?
1. Time preserves human life.
2. With time comes change.
3. Time creates opportunities.
4. Time removes human life.

Choose the correct answer from the options given below :
(a) 1 and 2 (b) 1 and 3
(c) 2 and 4 (d) 3 and 4

84. Charles Lamb used the pseudonym Elia for writing in which of the following periodicals?
(a) Athenaeum
(b) London Magazine
(c) The Edinburg Review
(d) The Quarterly Review

85. Which two of the following are highlighted in relation to specific historical moments by Stephen Greenblatt?

1. crisis of meaning
2. circulation of meaning
3. production of meaning
4. deferral of meaning

Choose the correct answer from the options given below :

(a) 1 and 2 (b) 2 and 3
(c) 2 and 4 (d) 3 and 4

86. Which of these does the book 'How to read Donald Duck' identify as an important element in its analysis of imperialist ideology in the Walt Disney comicbook?

(a) heartless civilisation
(b) impoverished royalty
(c) noble savage
(d) scientific magic

87. Which among the following are the works of George Gissing?

1. New Grub Street
2. Agnes Grey
3. The Odd Women
4. Mary Barton

Choose the correct answer from the options given below :

(a) 1 and 2 (b) 1 and 3
(c) 2 and 4 (d) 3 and 4

88. Which of the following poems by Robert Browning contains the lines, "Our interest's on the dangerous edge of things. The honest thief, the tender murderer/The superstitious atheist......" ?

(a) A Death in the Desert
(b) Bishop Blougram's Apology
(c) Count Gismond
(d) Love Among the Ruins

89. Which of these constitute the preoccupations of the protagonist of Upamanyu Chatterjee's 'English, August'?

1. Marijuana
2. Magic
3. Monotheism
4. Marcus Aurelius

Choose the correct answer from the options given below :

(a) 1 and 4 (b) 1 and 2
(c) 2 and 3 (d) 2 and 4

90. In comparative philology and sometimes in modern phonology, what is the term used to refer to the deletion of a vowel within a word?

(a) Aphaeresis (b) Equi-deletion
(c) Paradigm (d) Syncope

91. Which of the following novels has its epigraph taken from the Katha Upanishad?

(a) 'A Room with a View' by E. M. Forster
(b) 'Point Counter Point' by Aldous Huxley
(c) 'The Island of Doctor Moreau' by H. G. Wells
(d) 'The Razor's Edge' by Somerset Maugham

92. 'Potato' is a sixteenth-century borrowing into English from

(a) French (b) German
(c) Norwegian (d) Spanish

93. What function of English is exemplified by the use of English in India as a 'link language' along with a first language by stable bilinguals in well-defined social contexts?

(a) auxiliary
(b) complementary
(c) equative
(d) supplementary

94. In Noam Chomsky's definition of grammar which two features are drawn from mathematics ?

1. complexity 2. abstraction
3. transformation 4. generation

Choose the correct answer from the options given below :

(a) 1 and 2
(b) 1 and 3
(c) 2 and 4
(d) 3 and 4

95. Which of these constitutes the only extant trilogy from ancient Greek tragedy?

(a) Agamemnon, Choephori, The Eumenides
(b) Agamemnon, Orestes, The Eumenides
(c) King Oedipus, Oedipus at Colonus, Antigone
(d) King Oedipus, Orestes, Antigone

96. Who among the following belong to the Chicago School of critics?

1. R. S. Crane
2. E. M.W. Tillyard
3. Elder Olson
4. Allen Tate

Choose the correct answer from the options given below :

(a) 1 and 3 (b) 1 and 4
(c) 2 and 3 (d) 2 and 4

97. Which of these did the Wood's Despatch (1854) seek to propagate?

1. Impart Western knowledge to Indians
2. Restrict access to English learning in India
3. Educate British officers in Sanskrit and Persian
4. Create a class of public servants

Choose the correct answer from the options given below :

(a) 1 and 2 (b) 1 and 3
(c) 1 and 4 (d) 2 and 3

98. Arrange the following journals in the chronological order in which they started publication.

1. The Tatler 2. The Examiner
3. The Review 4. The Spectator

Choose the correct answer from the options given below :

(a) 1, 4, 3, 2 (b) 2, 1, 4, 3
(c) 3, 1, 2, 4 (d) 3, 1, 4, 2

99. Which of the following are poems by Nissim Ezekiel that make fun of Indians' use of English?

1. 'Goodbye Party for Miss Pushpa T.S.'
2. 'Philosophy'
3. 'Very Indian Poem in Indian English'
4. 'Jewish Wedding in Bombay'
5. 'Poet, Lover, Birdwatcher'

Choose the correct answer from the options given below:

(a) 1 and 3 (b) 1, 2 and 4
(c) 1, 3 and 5 (d) 2 and 4

100. Match List I with List II.

	List I (Essay)		List II (Essayist)
A.	'The Tory Fox-Hunter'	1.	Francis Bacon
B.	'What I Believe'	2.	Joseph Addison
C.	'The Death of the Moth'	3.	E.M. Forster
D.	'Of Ambition'	4.	Virginia Woolf

Choose the correct answer from the options given below :

	A	B	C	D
(a)	1	3	4	2
(b)	2	3	4	1
(c)	3	4	2	1
(d)	4	1	2	3

ANSWERS

1	(d)	2	(c)	3	(b)	4	(d)	5	(a)	6	(c)	7	(a)	8	(a)	9	(a)	10	(c)
11	(a)	12	(b)	13	(b)	14	(b)	15	(b)	16	(b)	17	(d)	18	(b)	19	(c)	20	(c)
21	(c)	22	(b)	23	(b)	24	(a)	25	(d)	26	(a)	27	(d)	28	(a)	29	(b)	30	(a)
31	(a)	32	(b)	33	(c)	34	(b)	35	(b)	36	(c)	37	(d)	38	(c)	39	(d)	40	(a)
41	(*)	42	(a)	43	(a)	44	(a)	45	(d)	46	(c)	47	(c)	48	(d)	49	(b)	50	(a)
51	(d)	52	(a)	53	(d)	54	(d)	55	(c)	56	(c)	57	(a)	58	(d)	59	(c)	60	(a)
61	(d)	62	(c)	63	(b)	64	(b)	65	(b)	66	(a)	67	(d)	68	(d)	69	(b)	70	(a)
71	(b)	72	(c)	73	(c)	74	(a)	75	(a)	76	(c)	77	(d)	78	(b)	79	(b)	80	(b)
81	(d)	82	(b)	83	(c)	84	(b)	85	(b)	86	(c)	87	(b)	88	(b)	89	(a)	90	(d)
91	(d)	92	(d)	93	(b)	94	(d)	95	(a)	96	(a)	97	(c)	98	(c,d)	99	(a)	100	(b)

English (Paper-2)
Solved Paper, October 2020

General Instructions

1. There are total one hundred questions in this paper. Each question carries 2 marks.
2. All questions are compulsory.

1. The deductive method differs from the inductive method in drawing its conclusions from:
(a) verification
(b) particular instances
(c) applications
(d) general truths

2. Which one of the following journals publishes articles related to critical theory exclusively?
(a) Salmagundi
(b) Diacritics
(c) Callaloo
(d) Grand Street

3. Which one of the following assumptions best expresses the position of Post-Structuralist Criticism?
(a) Definite structures underlie empirical events.
(b) Language is representational.
(c) Apprehension of reality is a construct.
(d) Knowledge operates according to procedures that are axiomatic.

4. Which one of the following is correct about Saussure's analysis of language?
(a) La langue is the system of a language.
(b) Parole focuses on language as a system at a particular time.
(c) La langue is the particular instance of speech and writing.
(d) Parole is the study of language over a period of time.

5. Who among the following theorists particularly emphasised the social and historical dimensions of a text's reception?
(a) Wolfgang Iser
(b) Stanley Fish
(c) Hans Robert Jauss
(d) Pierre Bourdieu

6. Which one among the following is a set of the Metaphysical Poets?
(a) John Dryden, George Herbert and Alexander Pope
(b) Henry Vaughan, John Dryden and John Donne
(c) John Donne, Henry Vaughan and Andrew Marvell
(d) Samuel Johnson, TS Eliot and Herbert Grierson

7. Which one of the following statements is true about Aristotle's poetics?
(a) He asserted the value of poetry by integrating rhetoric and imitation (mimesis).
(b) He asserted the value of poetry by focusing on both rhetoric and imitation (mimesis).
(c) He asserted the value of poetry by giving preference to rhetoric over imitation (mimesis).
(d) He asserted the value of poetry by focusing on imitation (mimesis) rather than rhetoric.

8. Who said of the blank verse, quoting an unnamed critic, that it is "...verse only to the eye", adding flurther that it "has neither the easiness of prose, nor the melody of numbers"?
(a) John Dryden
(b) Alexander Pope
(c) Samuel Taylor Coleridge
(d) Samuel Johnson

9. Poetry according to Sir Philip Sidney is of three kinds. They are:
(a) religious, dramatic, romantic
(b) classical, romantic, neo-classical
(c) philosophical, imaginative, narrative
(d) religious, philosophical, imaginative

10. In Anxiety of Influence which of the following definitions is given by Harold Bloom to explain the term, 'clinamen'?

(a) Poetic hyperbole (b) Poetic misprision
(c) Poetic sublime (d) Poetic supplement

11. Who among the following is known to have popularised the term 'glocalisation'?

(a) Ronald Robertson (b) Francis Fukuyama
(c) John Urry (d) John Tomlinson

12. Who among the following coined the dictum, "the medium is the message"?

(a) Raymond Williams
(b) Erving Goffman
(c) Marshall McLuhan
(d) John Fiske

13. Who among the following presented the concept of 'multi-accentuality' of the sign, saying that signs possess an 'inner dialectical quality' and 'evaluative accent'?

(a) Roland Barthes
(b) Stuart Hall
(c) Jacques Derrida
(d) Valentin Voloshinov

14. On 11th December, 1823, Ram Mohan Roy addressed a letter to the British authority which pleaded for modern western education and is considered historically important for the introduction of English education in India. Who was the letter addressed to?

(a) Lord Amherst (b) Lord Minto
(c) Lord Macaulay (d) Lord Bentick

15. Which British adminsitrator sought "to make everything as English as possible in a country which resembles England in nothing", as recorded by Sir Thomas Munro?

(a) Lord Bentick (b) Lord Hastings
(c) Lord Cornwallis (d) Lord Wellesley

16. Who among the following was the first Director of the Central Institute of English and Foreign Languages, Hyderabad (now EFL University)?

(a) Prof VK Gokak (b) Prof CD Narasimhaiah
(c) Prof CJ Daswani (d) Prof KRS Iyengar

17. Which one of the following best explains the term 'paralanguage'?

(a) The ways in which people mask what they mean by the words they use.
(b) The ways in which people show what they mean other than by the words they use.
(c) The ways in which words carry meanings unintended by the speaker.
(d) The ways in which the silence underlying speech communicates wrong meanings.

18. Which two of the following oppositions are best evoked by Hamlet's utterance-"To be or not to be"?

1. Between life and death
2. Between action and emotion
3. Between affirmation and confirmation
4. Between doing and abstaining from doing

Chose the correct answer from the options given below.

(a) 1 and 4 only (b) 2 and 4 only
(c) 3 and 1 only (d) 4 and 3 only

19. Who among the following linguists proposed the terms, 'competence' and 'performance'?

(a) Noah Webster (b) Steven Pinker
(c) Roman Jakobson (d) Noam Chomsky

20. Which one of these statements defines the scope of semiotics?

(a) Semiotics studies the sound systems of a language.
(b) Semiotics is a study of sign systems.
(c) Semiotics studies human sign system only.
(d) Semiotics is a study of non-human sign systems only.

21. Which according to Thomas Hobbes is the only 'science' God has bestowed on mankind, that informs the structure of his monumental work, Leviathan?

(a) Astronomy (b) Architecture
(c) Occult sciences (d) Geometry

22. As mentioned in "My First Acquaintance with Poets". which poet does William Hazlitt describe as the "only person I ever knew who answered the idea of a man of genius"?

(a) Coleridge (b) Wordsworth
(c) Byron (d) Shelley

23. Which one of the following essays holds that "As a method, realism is a complete failure"?

(a) Virginia Woolf, 'The Mark on the Wall'
(b) Oscar Wilde, 'The Decay of Lying'
(c) D.H Lawrence, 'Why the Novel Matters'
(d) Mary McCarthy, 'My Confession'

24. Which of the following novels is structured into a poem of 999 lines, preceded by a foreword, followed by a Commentary and an Index?

(a) Ragtime
(b) Pale Fire
(c) The Inner Side of the Wind
(d) Hourglass

25. Which among the following novels includes a questionnaire for the reader such as 'Do you like the story so far? Yes () No ()'?

(a) Mantissa by John Fowles
(b) Waterland by Graham Swift
(c) Snow White by Donald Barthelme
(d) If on a Winter's Night a Traveller by Italo Calvino

26. What is the subject of Ivan's controversial essay in Brothers Karamazov?
(a) Transubstantiation (b) The evils of clergy
(c) The Eucharist (d) Ecclesiastical courts

27. Which one of the following Sherlock Holmes' stories refers to a significant event in English history?
(a) The Musgrove Ritual (b) The Speckled Band
(c) The Solitary Cyclist (d) The Red-Headed League

28. Harold Skimpole is a character in
(a) Bleak House (b) Dombey and Son
(c) Great Expectations (d) Oliver Twist

29. Who is the author of 'A Fragment' (1819), one of the earliest vampire stories in English?
(a) PB Shelley (b) Lord Byron
(c) Bram Stoker (d) Mary Shelley

30. Lala Kanshi Ram is a character in:
(a) Arun Joshi's The Apprentice
(b) Chaman Nahal's Azadi
(c) Anita Desai's Fire on the Mountain
(d) Kamala Markhandaya's A Handful of Rice

31. Which of the following poems by Philip Larkin deals with the trauma of a rape victim who says "Even so distant, I can taste the grief"?
(a) Deceptions (b) Faith Healing
(c) Sad Steps (d) Wild Oats

32. In which of the Bog poems does Seamus Heaney speak about the 'perishable treasure' of a body 'Murdered, forgotten, nameless, terrible'?
(a) Bog Queen (b) Grauballe Man
(c) Punishment (d) Strange Fruit

33. Which book of Paradise Lost incorporates the speech rhythms of Adam and Eve's marital quarrel?
(a) Book 4 (b) Book 6
(c) Book 7 (d) Book 9

34. Who among the following wrote Mazeppa, a long narrative poem about a seventeenth-century military leader of Ukraine?
(a) William Cowper (b) Lord Byron
(c) PB Shelley (d) ST Coleridge

35. Which one of the following statements is appropriately true of Harold Pinter's plays?
(a) Menace is in the air and it leads to bloody violence.
(b) Menace is in the air and it is realised through the female characters.
(c) Menace is in the air, but it is not pinned down, or explained.
(d) Menace is in the air and anarchy follows in a systematic manner.

36. To which mythological character is Faustus compared in the Prologue of Dr. Faustus?
(a) Perseus (b) Theseus
(c) Icarus (d) Achilles

37. Who makes the following speech in Samuel Beckett's Waiting for Godot?
"Astride of a grave and a difficult birth. Down in the hole, lingeringly, the grave-digger puts on the forceps."
(a) Estragon (b) Lucky
(c) Vladimir (d) Pozzo

38. Which of the following are the major themes in William Congreve's The Way of the World?
(a) Jealousy and revenge (b) Love and intrigue
(c) Intrigue and death (d) Love and loyalty

39. What game do the characters play in Act II of Harold Pinter's The Birthday Party?
(a) A game of chess (b) A game of cards
(c) Blind man's buff (d) Musical chairs

40. The Duchess of Malfi is based on
(a) a French romance (b) an Italian novella
(c) a Geman fable (d) a Scottish chronicle

41. Which two of the following strictly follow the parameters of documentation prescribed by the eighth edition of the MLA Handbook?
1. Nunberg, Geoffrey, editor. The Future of the Book. U of California P, 1996.
2. Puig, Manuel. Kiss of the Spider Woman. Trans. Thomas Colchie, London: Vintage, 1991.
3. Nunberg, Geoffrey, ed. The Future of the Book. Berkeley: U of California P, 1996.
4. Puig, Manuel. Kiss of the Spider Woman. Translated by Thomas Colchie, Vintage Books, 1991.

Choose the correct answer from the options given below.
(a) 1 and 2 only (b) 1 and 3 only
(c) 1 and 4 only (d) 2 and 3 only

42. A research hypothesis is:
1. a proposition which is always true.
2. a provisional explanation of anything.
3. a theory which will be disproved by evidence.
4. a statement which is assumed to be true for the sake of argument.

Choose the most appropriate answer from the options given below:
(a) 1 and 2 only (b) 2 and 3 only
(c) 2 and 4 only (d) 1 and 3 only

43. Which two of the following aspects are to be scrupulously followed to avoid the trap of plagiarism?
1. Subjectivity 2. Acknowledgement
3. Citation 4. Interpretation

Choose the most appropriate answer from the options given below.
(a) 1 and 2 only (b) 1 and 3 only
(c) 3 and 4 only (d) 2 and 3 only

44. Which two texts among the following are linked to literary feminism?

1. A Small Place
2. The Yellow Wallpaper
3. Emma
4. A Room of One's Own

Choose the correct answer from the options given below:

(a) 1 and 4 only (b) 3 and 4 only
(c) 2 and 4 only (d) 1 and 3 only

45. Who among the following feminist theorists posited a separate realm of female experience captured in a style of writing different from men's?

1. Elaine Showalter
2. Luce Irigaray
3. Kate Millett
4. Simone de Beauvoir
5. Helene Cixous

Choose the correct answer fromthe options given below:

(a) 1, 3 and 4 only (b) 2 and 4 only
(c) 3, 4 and 5 only (d) 2 and 5 only

46. Which of these statements describe correctly the basic assumption of Structuralism?

1. Structuralism is concerned with signs and signification.
2. A structuralist theory considers only verbal conventions and codes.
3. Structuralism began in the works of Jacques Derrida that influenced the 20th century literary criticism.
4. Structuralism challenges the long-standing belief that literature reflects a given reality.
5. All signs are arbitrary but without them we cannot comprehend reality.

Choose the correct answer from the options given below:

(a) 1, 3 and 5 only (b) 1, 4 and 5 only
(c) 1, 2 and 3 only (d) 1, 2 and 5 only

47. Which two terms among the following are associated with formalist criticism?

1. Aura
2. Actant
3. Narratee
4. Defamiliarisation
5. Foregrounding

Choose the correct answer from the options given below.

(a) 1 and 3 only (b) 2 and 4 only
(c) 2 and 3 only (d) 4 and 5 only

48. Who among the following believed that rhyme is not an integral part of poetry?

1. William Wordsworth
2. Horace
3. Samuel Daniel
4. Philip Sidney

Choose the most appropriate answer from the options given below

(a) 1 and 3 only (b) 2 and 4 only
(c) 1 and 4 only (d) 4 and 3 only

49. Who among the following are the two great masters of the French language that T S Eliot contrasts with Dryden and Milton in 'The Metaphysical Poets'?

1. Francois Villon
2. Jean Racine
3. Charles Baudelaire
4. Arthur Rimbaud

Choose the correct answer from the options given below:

(a) 1 and 3 only (b) 1 and 4 only
(c) 2 and 3 only (d) 2 and 4 only

50. Which two terms from among the following are specifically linked to the work of Pierre Bourdieu?

1. Habitus
2. Consciousness
3. Desire
4. Distinction

Choose the correct answer from the options given below:

(a) 1 and 3 only (b) 1 and 4 only
(c) 2 and 4 only (d) 3 and 4 only

51. Macaulay's Minute of 1835 sought to

1. promote European literature and science among the natives.
2. impart knowledge of English literature and science through translated texts.
3. encourage branches of native learning by more useful studies.
4. stop expenditure on the publication of oriental works and spend funds only on English education.

Choose the correct answer from the options given below.

(a) 1 and 4 only (b) 2 and 4 only
(c) 1 and 3 only (d) 2 and 3 only

52. Which two of the following statements are applicable to 'metalanguage'?

It is

1. a technical language which describes the properties of language.
2. known as a 'first-order' language.
3. a 'second-order' language that replaces a first-order' language with metaphors.
4. a 'second-order' language.

Choose the correct answer from the options given below:

(a) 1 and 2 only (b) 3 and 4 only
(c) 1 and 4 only (d) 2 and 3 only

53. 'Hari wrote a poem on the mountains'. Which two of the following are admissible statements about the above sentence?

1. The sentence is an example of lexical ambiguity.
2. The sentence is an example of structural ambiguity.
3. The sentence involves two deep structures.
4. The sentence involves two surface structures.

Choose the correct answer from the options given below:

(a) 1 and 2 only (b) 2 and 3 only
(c) 2 and 4 only (d) 3 and 4 only

54. Which two of the following events are described in Samuels Pepys's Diary?

1. The Plague in London
2. The Great Fire of London
3. The War of Spanish Succession
4. Essex Rebellion

Choose the correct answer from the given below:

(a) 1 and 2 only (b) 1 and 3 only
(c) 2 and 3 only (d) 2 and 4 only

55. Which two of the following inspired the rise of the periodical essay?

1. Robert Burton
2. Francois Rabelais
3. Francis Bacon
4. Michel de Montaigne

Choose the correct answer from the options given below.

(a) 3 and 1 only (b) 1 and 2 only
(c) 3 and 4 only (d) 2 and 4 only

56. Which two of the following works does Walter Pater regard as examples of 'great art' in his essay 'Style'?

1. Iliad 2. The Divine Comedy
3. Les Miserables 4. Faust

Choose the most appropriate answer from the options given below.

(a) 1 and 2 only (b) 1 and 4 only
(c) 2 and 3 only (d) 2 and 4 only

57. According to his essay 'Civil Disobedience', what two things did Thoreau learn from the night he spent in jail?

1. He concluded that the State is ultimately weak.
2. He realised that captivity inspires courage.
3. He realised that the neighbours are only friends during good times.
4. He concluded that captivity brings wisdom about human affairs.

Choose the correct answer from the options given below.

(a) 1 and 2 only (b) 1 and 3 only
(c) 1 and 4 only (d) 3 and 4 only

58. Which two of the following are the titles of the sections in Thomas De Quincey's 'The English Mail-Coach'?

1. The Glory of Mobility
2. The Vision of Sudden Death
3. The Glory of Motion
4. The Vision of Unexpected Truth

Choose the correct answer from the options given below.

(a) 1 and 2 only (b) 1 and 4 only
(c) 2 and 3 only (d) 2 and 4 only

59. Which two of the following books are explorations of the art of the novel by novelists?

1. The Brief Compass
2. The Naive and the Sentimental Novelist
3. The Visionary Company
4. Testaments Betrayed

Choose the most appropriate answer from the options given below.

(a) 1 and 2 only (b) 1 and 3 only
(c) 2 and 3 only (d) 2 and 4 only

60. The lives of which of the following writers have been the subject matter of novels by Anthony Burgess?

1. Milton 2. Marlowe
3. Shelley 4. Keats

Choose the correct answer from the options given below:

(a) 1 and 2 only (b) 1 and 4 only
(c) 2 and 3 only (d) 2 and 4 only

61. Which two rivers are mentioned by Andrew Marvell at the beginning of 'To His Coy Mistress'?

1. The Ganges 2. Thames
3. Humber 4. The Jhelum

Choose the correct answer from the options given below:

(a) 1 and 4 only (b) 1 and 2 only
(c) 1 and 3 only (d) 2 and 3 only

62. Which two poems in the following list are examples of dramatic monologue?

1. Alfred Tennyson's 'Ulysses'
2. Philip Larkin's 'Church Going'
3. Carol Ann Duffy's 'Medusa'
4. Katherine Philip's 'A Married State'

Choose the correct answer from the options given below.

(a) 1 and 4 only (b) 2 and 3 only
(c) 3 and 4 only (d) 1 and 3 only

63. Which two of the following poems are by Robert Browning?

1. 'Locksley Hall'
2. 'The Pied Piper of Hamelin'
3. 'The Lady of Shalott'
4. 'Two in the Campagna'

Choose the correct answer from the options given below:

(a) 1 and 4 only (b) 2 and 3 only
(c) 1 and 3 only (d) 2 and 4 only

64. Which two of the following dramatists are associated with the Epic Theatre?

1. Fernando Arrabal 2. Bertolt Brecht
3. Arnolt Bronnen 4. James Saunders

Choose the correct answer from the options given below.

(a) 1 and 2 only (b) 2 and 3 only
(c) 1 and 4 only (d) 2 and 4 only

65. Which two characters/speakers among the following exhibit the studious abstraction of scholars? I

1. Shylock 2. Hamlet
3. Il Penseroso 4. Mosca

Choose the correct answer from the options given below:

(a) 1 and 4 only (b) 2 and 3 only
(c) 3 and 4 only (d) 1 and 3 only

66. Match List I with List II.

List I (Terms)	List II (Theorists)
A. Arche-ecriture	1. Julia Kristeva
B. Cyborg	2. Donna Haraway
C. Genotext	3. Friedrich Schleiermacher
D. Hermeneutic circle	4. Jacques Derrida

Choose the correct answer from the options given below.

	A	B	C	D
(a)	4	2	1	3
(b)	3	1	2	4
(c)	3	2	4	1
(d)	4	1	2	3

67. Match List I with List II.

List I (Terms)	List II (Theorists)
A. Superreader	1. Michel Foucault
B. Biopower	2. Mikhail Bakhtin
C. Bricolage	3. Michael Riffaterre
D. Chronotope	4. Claude Levi-Strauss

Choose the correct answer from the options given below.

	A	B	C	D
)	3	2	4	1
(b)	3	1	4	2
	4	1	3	2
(d)	2	1	4	3

68. Match List I with List II.

List I (Critics)	List II (Texts)
A. Horace	1. A Defence of Rhyme
B. John Dryden	2. Timber: or, Discoveries
C. Samuel Daniel	3. Ars Poetica
D. Ben Jonson	4. Of Dramatic Poesy

Choose the correct answer from the options given below.

	A	B	C	D
(a)	2	1	4	3
(b)	3	4	2	1
(c)	3	4	1	2
(d)	2	4	1	3

69. Match List I with List II.

List I (Authors)	List II (Texts)
A. Michel de Certeau	1. Distinction
B. John Fiske	2. Reading the Romance
C. Pierre Bourdieu	3. Understanding Popular Culture
D. Janice Radway	4. The Practice of Everyday Life

Choose the correct answer from the options given below.

	A	B	C	D
(a)	4	1	2	3
(b)	3	4	1	2
(c)	4	3	1	2
(d)	3	1	4	2

70. Match List I with List II.

List I (Linguists)	List II (Concepts)
A. Paul Grice	1. language death
B. Edward Sapir	2. linguistic signs
C. Ferdinand de Saussure	3. linguistic relativity
D. Nancy Dorian	4. cooperative principle

Choose the correct answer from the options given below.

	A	B	C	D
(a)	1	3	4	2
(b)	4	3	2	1
(c)	3	4	1	2
(d)	3	4	2	1

71. Match List I with List II.

List I (Word Borrowed)	List II (Source Indian Language)
A. Mongoose	1. Tamil
B. Loot	2. Malayalam
C. Curry	3. Hindi/Urdu
D. Betel	4. Marathi

Choose the correct answer from the options given below.

	A	B	C	D
(a)	4	3	1	2
(b)	4	2	1	3
(c)	2	3	4	1
(d)	2	1	4	3

72. Match List I with List II.

List I (Essayists)	List II (Essays)
A. George Orwell	1. 'On the Artificial Comedy of the Last Century'
B. Michel de Montaigne	2. 'Why I Write'
C. Charles Lamb	3. 'A Modest Proposal'
D. Jonathan Swift	4. 'On the Cannibals'

Choose the correct answer from the options given below.

	A	B	C	D
(a)	3	4	2	1
(b)	2	4	1	3
(c)	4	3	2	1
(d)	2	3	1	4

73. Match List I with List II.

List I (Authors)	List II (Texts)
A. Thomas Pynchon	1. G.
B. Howard Jacobson	2. V
C. Anthony Burgess	3. J
D. John Berger	4. M/F

Choose the correct answer from the options given below.

	A	B	C	D
(a)	2	4	1	3
(b)	2	3	4	1
(c)	2	3	1	4
(d)	4	3	1	2

74. Match List I with List II.

List I (Lines)	List II (Poems)
A. 'Monuments of unaging intellect'	1. 'Leda and the Swan'
B. 'In the foul rag-and-bone shop of the heart'	2. 'Adam's Curse'
C. 'So mastered by the, brute blood of the air'	3. 'Sailing to Byzantium'
D. 'As weary-hearted as that hollow moon'	4. 'The Circus Animals' Desertion'

Choose the correct answer from the options given below.

	A	B	C	D
(a)	3	4	2	1
(b)	3	1	4	2
(c)	3	4	1	2
(d)	2	1	4	3

75. Match List I with List II

List I (Authors)	List II (Works)
A. John Keats	1. Alastor
B. William Wordsworth	2. Songs of Experience
C. P.B. Shelley	3. Lamia
D. William Blake	4. The Excursion

Choose the correct answer from the options given below.

	A	B	C	D
(a)	3	1	4	2
(b)	3	4	1	2
(c)	1	4	3	2
(d)	4	2	1	3

76. Arrange the following terms in the chronological order of emergence:

1. Heresy of Paraphrase
2. Stream of Consciousness
3. Practical Criticism
4. Defamiliarisation

Choose the correct answer from the options given below.

(a) 4, 2, 3, 1 (b) 2, 4, 1, 3 (c) 2, 4 , 3, 1 (d) 4, 3, 2, 1

77. Arrange the following critical works in their chronological order of publication

1. Preface to Lyrical Ballads
2. A Defence of Rhyme
3. Life of Cowley
4. The frontiers of Criticism

Choose the correct answer from the options given below.

(a) 1, 3, 2 and 4 (b) 2, 1 , 3 and 4
(c) 2, 3, 1 and 4 (d) 3, 1, 4 and 2

78. Arrange the following in the chronological order of publication:

1. Aspects of the Theory of Syntax
2. Course in General Linguistics
3. Semiotics and the Philosophy of Language
4. How to Do Things with Words

Choose the correct answer from the options given below:

(a) 4, 2, 1, 3 (b) 3, 2, 1, 4 (c) 2, 4, 1, 3 (d) 2, 1, 4, 3

79. Arrange the following in the chronological order of publication:

1. Advancement of Learning
2. The Origin of Species
3. On Heroes and Hero Worship
4. The Lives of the Poets

Choose the correct answer from the options given below:

(a) 4, 1, 3, 2 (b) 4, 1, 2, 3 (c) 1, 4, 3, 2 (d) 1, 4, 2, 3

80. Arrange the following 18th century magazines in the chronological order of publication:

1. The Critical Review 2. The Monthly Review
3. The Gentleman's Magazine
4. The Rambler

Choose the correct answer from the options given below.

(a) 1, 4, 2, 3 (b) 4, 1, 2, 3
(c) 2, 1, 3, 4 (d) 3, 2, 4, 1

81. Arrange the following in the chronological order of publication:

1. Crome Yellow
2. Sons and Lovers
3. Mrs Dalloway
4. A Portrait of the Artist as a Young Man

Choose the correct answer from the options given below.

(a) 2, 1, 4, 3 (b) 1, 2, 4, 3
(c) 1, 3, 2, 4 (d) 2, 4, 1, 3

82. Arrange the following women novelists in the chronological order (by date of birth):

1. Anne Bronte 2. Jane Austen
2. Ann Radcliffe 4. Fanny Burney
5. Maria Edgeworth

Choose the correct answer from the options given below.

(a) 2, 1, 4, 3, 5 (b) 3, 4, 2, 5, 1
(c) 4, 3, 5, 2, 1 (d) 1, 2, 3, 5, 4

83. Arrange the following authors in the chronological order of their birth:

1. Oscar Wilde 2. William Langland
3. Geoffrey Chaucer 4. John Dryden
5. Alexander Pope

Choose the correct answer from the options given below:

(a) 2, 3, 4, 5, 1 (b) 1, 2, 3, 5, 4
(c) 2, 3, 4, 1, 5 (d) 3, 2, 1, 4, 5

84. Arrange the following plays in their chronological order:

1. The Country Wife 2. Cymbeline
3. The Spanish Tragedy
4. The Rivals

Choose the correct answer from the options given below:

(a) 2, 1, 3, 4 (b) 2, 3, 4, 1
(c) 3, 2, 1, 4 (d) 3, 1, 2, 4

85. Arrange the following plays in the chronological order of publication:

1. All for Love 2. Venice Preserved
3. The School for Scandal
4. The Country Wife

Choose the correct answer from the options given below.

(a) 2, 3, 1, 4 (b) 4, 1, 2, 3
(c) 3, 2, 4, 1 (d) 1, 4, 3, 2

86. Given below are two statements, one is labelled as Assertion (A) and the other is labelled as Reason (R).

Assertion (A) Research methods are a range oftools that are used for different types of inquiry.

Reason (R) The tools used in research are products of the situations in which they are applied.

In light of the above statements, choose the correct answer from the options given below:

(a) Both A and R are true and R is the correct explanation of A
(b) Both A and R are true, but R is not the correct explanation of A
(c) A is true, but R is false
(d) A is false, but R is true

87. Given below are two statements, one is labelled as Assertion (A) and the other is labelled as Reason (R).

Assertion (A) Signs are never neutral or innocent.

Reason (R) In all cases, signs are organised into systems that convey some meaning.

In light of the above statements, choose the correct answer from the options given below:

(a) Both A and R are true and R is the correct explanation of A
(b) Both A and R are true, but R is not the correct explanation of A
(c) A is true, but R is false
(d) A is false, but R is true

88. Given below are two statements:

Statement I Consumption is an outcome of self-interest and a maximisation of personal pleasure.

Statement II There are strong correlations between social status and such things as housing styles, musical tastes and food preferences.

In light of the above statements, choose the correct answer from the options given below:

(a) Both Statement I and Statement II are true
(b) Both Statement I and Statement II are false
(c) Statement I is correct, but Statement II is false
(d) Statement I is false, but Statement II is true

89. Given below are two statements:

Statement I The Orientalists in British India were not sympathetic towards India's ancient learning.

Statement II William Jones thought that in 'imagination', 'ratiocination', and philosophy, Indians were by no means inferior to Europeans.

In light of the above statement, choose the correct answer from the options given below

(a) Both Statement I and Statement II are true
(b) Both Statement I and Statement II are false
(c) Statement I is correct, but Statement II is false
(d) Statement I is false, but Statement II is true

90. Given below are two statements, one is labelled as Assertion (A) and the other is labelled as Reason (R).

Assertion (A) The introduction of English in India was primarily for the benefit and consolidation of British power.

Reason (R) English catered to the social and economic aspirations of the emerging middle class and urban elites in India.

In light of the above statements, choose the correct answer from the options given below:

(a) Both A and R are true and R is the correct explanation of A
(b) Both A and R are true, but R is not the correct explanation of A
(c) A is true, but R is false
(d) A is false, but R is true

Directions *(Q. Nos. 91-93) Read the following paragraph and answer the five questions which as follows :*

Daybreak

At dawn she lay with her profile at that angle Which, sleeping, seems the stone face of an angel; Her hair a harp the hand of a breeze follows To play, against the white cloud of the pillows. Then in a flush of rose she woke, and her eyes were open, Swimming with blue through the rose flesh of dawn. From her dew of lips, the drop of one word Fell, from a dawn of fountains, when she murmured 'Darling,'–upon my heart the song of the first bird.

'My dream glides in my dream,' she said, 'come true. I waken from you to my dream of you.' O, then my waking dream dared to assume The audacity of her sleep. Our dreams Flowed into each other's arms, like streams.

91. Which among the following best describes the lady's face as "At dawn she lay..." asleep?

(a) Her face appears to be that of a stone sculpture's.
(b) The side-view of her face appears to be that of a sculpted angel's.
(c) Her face appears to be that of a stone-angel.
(d) The side-view of her face appears to be taht of an angel's.

92. Match List I with List II

List I (The Item)	List II (What it is an example of)
A. 'Her hair'	1. player
B. 'pillows'	2. 'a harp'
C. 'breeze'	3. 'rose'
D. 'cheeks'	4. 'cloud'

Choose the correct answer from the options given below.

	A	B	C	D
(a)	1	2	4	3
(b)	3	1	2	4
(c)	2	4	1	3
(d)	4	3	1	2

93. Match List I with List II.

List I (Item)	List II (What it is an example of)
A. 'Her hair a harp'	1. Simile
B. 'the hand of a breeze'	2. Metaphor
C. 'seems the stone face'	3. Oxymoron
D. 'my waking dream'	4. Synecdoche

Choose the correct answer from the options given below:

	A	B	C	D
(a)	2	4	1	3
(b)	4	2	3	1
(c)	4	3	2	1
(d)	1	4	2	3

Directions *(Q. Nos. 94-95) Read the following paragraph and answer the five questions which as follows :*

Logic cannot have any empirical part; that is, a part in which the universal and necessary laws of thought should rest on grounds taken from experience; otherwise it would not be logic, i.e., a canon for the understanding or the reason, valid for all thought, and capable of demonstration. Natural and moral philosophy, on the contrary, can each have their empirical part, since the former has to determine the laws of nature as an object of experience; the latter, the laws of the human will, so far as it is affected by nature: the former, however, being laws according to which everything does happen; the latter, laws according to which everything ought to happen. Etics, however, must also consider the conditions under which what ought to happen frequently does not. Immanuel Kant.

94. Logic cannot have any empirical part', because:

1. laws of thought are subjective.
2. it propounds laws whose applicability can be shown.
3. its laws are valid for all thought.
4. its laws are valid for everyone's experience.

Choose the most appropriate answer from the options given below:

(a) 1 and 4 only (b) 2 and 3 only
(c) 1 and 3 only (d) 2 and 4 only

95. Based on the given passage, which two of the following statements are correct?

1. For natural philosophy, nature influences the laws.
2. For moral philosophy, nature is to be experienced.
3. Natural philosphy does not describe how things actually do happen.
4. Moral philosophy accounts for what should be.

Choose the correct answer from the options given below:

(a) 1 and 3 only (b) 2 and 4 only
(c) 3 and 4 only (d) 1 and 4 only

Directions *(Q. Nos. 96-98) Read the following paragraph and answer the five questions which as follow :*

And the creature run from the cur? There thou mightst behold the great image of authority : a dog's obeyed in office–Thou rascal beadle, hold thy bloody hand! Why dost thou lash that whore? Strip thine own back; Thou hotly lust'st to use her in that kind. For which thou whipp'st her. The usurer hangs the cozener. Thraugh tatter'd clothes small vices do appear; Robes and furr'd gowns hide all. Plate sin with gold, And the strong lance of justice hurtless breaks; Arm it in rags, a pigmy's straw doth pierce it. King Lear

96. Who speaks these lines and to whom?

(a) Edgar to Lear
(b) Goneril to Edgar
(c) Lear to Gloucester
(d) Gloucester to Lear

97. In the passage, the chrch officer is asked to whip his own back rather than the prostitute's because:

(a) as a religious man he should punish himself for others' sins.
(b) he at one time had lusted after her.
(c) men like him make them prostitutes.
(d) he does not have the authority to whip a woman.

98. The two sentences in the lines from 'Through tatter'd clothes....' to "...straw doth pierce it" deal with two foibles, (i) vice and (ii) sin. About these two, the speaker says that

(a) Vice afflicts all but sin afflicts only the weak.
(b) Sin afflicts all but vice afflicts only the strong.
(c) Sin and vice are seen in both the weak and the strong.
(d) Sin and vice are palpable in the weak and impalpable in the strong.

Directions *(Q. Nos. 99-100) Read the following paragraph and answer the five questions which as follow :*

The surgeon deposited it in her arms. She imprinted her cold, white lips passionately on its forehead; passed her hands over her face; gazed wildly around; shuddered; fell back and died. They chafed her breast, hands, temples; but the blood had stopped forever. They talked of hope and comfort. They had been strangers too long. 'It's all over, Mrs. Thingummy!', said the surgeon at last.

Dickens, Oliver Twist

99. In the expression, "passed her hands over her face", the 'face' is of:

(a) the lady surgeon
(b) the child
(c) the nurse
(d) the patient

100. The implication of "they had been strangers too long" is

(a) Those who spoke of 'hope and comfort' had been strangers too long.
(b) 'Hope' had been stranger to 'comfort' for too long.
(c) 'Hope and comfort' had been stranger to the patient too long.
(d) 'Hope and comfort' had been strangers to the surgeon, nurse and the patient too long.

ANSWERS

1	(d)	2	(b)	3	(c)	4	(a)	5	(c)	6	(c)	7	(d)	8	(d)	9	(d)	10	(b)
11	(a)	12	(c)	13	(d)	14	(a)	15	(c)	16	(a)	17	(b)	18	(a)	19	(d)	20	(b)
21	(d)	22	(a)	23	(b)	24	(b)	25	(c)	26	(d)	27	(a)	28	(a)	29	(b)	30	(b)
31	(a)	32	(d)	33	(d)	34	(b)	35	(c)	36	(c)	37	(c)	38	(b)	39	(c)	40	(b)
41	(c)	42	(c)	43	(d)	44	(b)	45	(d)	46	(b)	47	(d)	48	(b)	49	(c)	50	(b)
51	(a)	52	(c)	53	(b)	54	(a)	55	(c)	56	(c)	57	(b)	58	(c)	59	(d)	60	(d)
61	(c)	62	(d)	63	(d)	64	(b)	65	(b)	66	(a)	67	(b)	68	(c)	69	(c)	70	(b)
71	(a)	72	(b)	73	(b)	74	(c)	75	(b)	76	(c)	77	(c)	78	(c)	79	(c)	80	(d)
81	(d)	82	(c)	83	(a)	84	(c)	85	(b)	86	(b)	87	(a)	88	(a)	89	(d)	90	(b)
91	(b)	92	(c)	93	(a)	94	(b)	95	(d)	96	(c)	97	(c)	98	(d)	99	(d)	100	(c)

English (Paper-2)
Solved Paper, June 2019

General Instructions

1. There are total one hundred questions in this paper. Each question carries 2 marks.
2. All questions are compulsory.

1. Which of the following poems by Thomas Hardy was originally titled By the Century's Deathbed?
   (a) The Minute Before Meeting
   (b) Neutral Tones
   (c) The Darkling Thrush
   (d) The Oxen
2. Which of the following descriptions fits the unit of verse, Dactyl?
   (a) One stressed syllable followed by three unstressed syllables
   (b) One stressed syllable followed by two unstressed syllables
   (c) Two stressed syllables followed by one unstressed syllable
   (d) Two stressed syllables followed by two unstressed syllables
3. Who wrote a guide called How to Write a Doctoral Thesis: The Humanistic Subjects, considered equal in standard to the American MLS Handbook or The Chicago Manual of Style?
   (a) Alain Robbe-Grillet (b) Cesare Pavese
   (c) Umberto Eco (d) Leo Spitzer
4. Who of the following are being talked about in the following lines?

   "... you seem to understand me,
   By each at once her choppy finger laying
   Upon her skinny lips : you should be women,
   And yet your beards forbid me to interpret
   That you are so."

   (a) The plebeians in Coriolanus
   (b) The sisters in King Lear
   (c) The witches in Macbeth
   (d) The players in Hamlet
5. What is the meaning of 'langue' in Saussurean linguistics?
   (a) Individual speech acts
   (b) An organised system of differences
   (c) The dialectic between thought and speech
   (d) Language in the abstract sense
6. Who is the author of the Short story, 'The Ghost of Firozsha Baag'?
   (a) Vikram Seth (b) VS Naipaul
   (c) Kiran Desai (d) Rohinton Mistry

All in the world know the beauty of the beautiful and in doing this they have (the idea of) what ugliness is; they all know the skill of the skillful and in doing this they have (the idea of) what the want of the skill is.

So it is that existence and non-existence gave birth to (the idea of) the other, that difficulty and ease produce (the idea of) the other, that the length and shortness fashion out the one figure of the other, that (the idea of) height and lowness arise from the contrast of one with the other, that the musical notes and tones become harmonious through the relation of one with another; and that being before and behind give the idea of one following another.

7. Which one of the following is the correct meaning of the ominous little phrase 'the idea of' in the first sentence of the passage?
(a) Prior knowledge
(b) Prior imagination
(c) Prior confirmation
(d) Prior rejection

8. From which Greek word does the term 'comedy' derive and what does it mean?
(a) Comedia, largeness of heart
(b) Komoidia, revel-song
(c) Commodios, commodious
(d) Komedieon, light foolery

9. What is the meaning of Ziauddin Sardar's statement?
"Cultural studies started as a dissenting intellectual tradition outside academia, dedicated to exposing power in all its cultural forms. But it has now become a discipline and a part of the academic establishment and its power structure."
(a) Devolution (b) Displacement
(c) Institutionalisation (d) Dissension

10. Which of the following works is reviewed in George Orwell's essay, Inside the Whale?
(a) Henry Miller's Tropic of Cancer
(b) James Joyce's Ulysses
(c) D. H. Lawrence's Lady Chatterley's Lover
(d) Anais Nin's Delta of Venus

11. Why did T. S. Eliot assert that Virgil, not Homer, is the poet of Europe?
(a) There are some initial moral concerns in Virgil
(b) Virgil belongs to the Roman period
(c) Homer was a pagan who was a renegade
(d) Virgil wrote in Latin while Homer wrote in Greek

12. Which edition of the Lyrical Ballads was the first one to have the Preface by Wordsworth?
(a) 1798 (b) 1800
(c) 1802 (d) 1804

13. In Eliot's Love Song of J.Alfred Prufrock who among the following painters is the object of conversation among the perambulating women?
(a) da Vinci (b) Raphael
(c) Michelangelo (d) Donatello

14. Which type of textual copy is concerned with an assessment of the physical details of the books and their exact relationship to the condition in which the book was planned to appear at the time of its initial publication?
(a) Real copy (b) Ideal copy
(c) Initial copy (d) Base copy

15. Which one of the following novels of Jane Austen was abandoned unfinished?
(a) Northanger Abbey (b) Persuasion
(c) The Watsons (d) Emma

16. Which novel by JG Farrell describes the experiences of a polio victim?
(a) Troubles (b) The Singapore Grip
(c) The Lung (d) The Hill Station

17. Who speaks the following lines and to whom?
"O, look upon me, sir,
And hold your hands in benediction o'er me.
No, sir, you must not kneel."
(a) Kent to Lear (b) Cordelia to Lear
(c) Goneril to Lear (d) Regan to Kent

18. "He that is not with us is against us. He that is not against us is with us." Who said this?
(a) Charles Lamb (b) Francis Bacon
(c) Samuel Johnson (d) R. W. Emerson

19. Match the character with the novel.

Characters	Novels
A. Kate	1. Great Expectations
B. Florence	2. Nicholas Nickleby
C. Miss Havisham	3. David Copperfield
D. Agnes	4. Dombey and Son

Choose the correct option from those given below:

	A	B	C	D
(a)	1	3	4	2
(b)	2	4	1	3
(c)	3	1	2	4
(d)	4	2	3	1

20. Which of the following two points were emphasised by 'Wood's Despatch of 1854'?
1. Teaching of the English language along with the study of vernacular language
2. Compulsory inclusion of Christianity in the curriculum
3. The gradual withdrawal of government patronage from Indian languages
4. The importance of female education

Choose the correct option
(a) 1 and 4 (b) 1 and 2
(c) 1 and 3 (d) 2 and 3

21. What is the Priest's entreaty to Oedipus in the opening scene of Oedipus Rex?
(a) To liberate Thebes from the domination of the Sphinx
(b) To rid Thebes of the plague that afflicts its people
(c) To afford the Thebans the luxury of newer forms of worship
(d) To send Creon to seek advice from the oracle of Delphi oracle

22. "The last temptation is the greatest treason
To do the right deed for the wrong reason."
(T. S. Eliot, Murder in the Cathedral)
Why is the 'temptation', 'treason' for the speaker of the lines?
(a) It is only self-serving (b) It is not intended
(c) It violates a norm (d) It is conspiratorial

23. Which one of the following groups of novelists has, in the given order, Captain Ahab, Hester Prynne, Roderick Usher and Daisy Miller as characters in their novels?

(a) Henry James, Edgar A. Poe, Nathaniel Hawthorne, Herman Melville
(b) Herman Melville, Nathaniel Hawthorne, Edgar A. Poe, Henry James
(c) Edgar A. Poe, Henry James, Nathaniel Hawthorne, Herman Melville
(d) Nathaniel Hawthorne, Edgar A. Poe, Henry James, Herman Melville

24. Match each of the following concepts/objects with the corresponding description:

List I		List II
A. Farce	1.	Articles and objects used on the stage
B. Props	2.	Drama written to be read rather than acted
C. Music hall	3.	Characterized by broad humour, wild antics, slapsticks etc.
D. Closet drama	4.	Variety entertainment of songs, comic turns that flourished in England through the late 19th Century

Choose the correct option from those given below:

	A	B	C	D		A	B	C	D
(a)	4	2	1	3	(b)	3	1	4	2
(c)	1	3	2	4	(d)	2	4	3	1

25. Which of the following combinations correctly defines the phonological system of Indian English in relation to Standard English?

1. Absence of aspirated consonants
2. Simplified vowel system
3. Similar international pattern
4. Presence of voiced aspirated consonants

Choose the correct option:

(a) 1 and 2 (b) 2 and 4
(c) 3 and 1 (d) 2 and 3

26. What is 'euphuism'?

(a) Eulogical and adulatory style of writing
(b) Discursive and hortatory style of writing
(c) Pompous and affected style of writing
(d) Exalted and grand style of writing

27. Which one of the following paired terms is correct in its explication?

(a) Phonology—Sound system
(b) Semiology—Ordering of speech sounds
(c) Etymology—Sign system
(d) Morphology—Evolution of words

28. Which of the following statements best describes TS Eliot's assertion that Shakespeare's Hamlet is an 'artistic failure'?

(a) Hamlet's emotion is not adequately objectified
(b) Hamlet's feelings far outweigh the release of his emotions
(c) Hamlet's obsession should have been within representational limits
(d) Hamlet's indecisiveness slows the steady progress of action

29. Who among the following explored the shifting and contested power-relations, knowledge and the human body?

(a) Louis Althusser (b) Clifford Geertz
(c) Jacques Lacan (d) Michel Foucault

30. Match the works with authors.

Works		Authors
A. Image-Music-Text	1.	M. H. Abrams
B. Why Marx was Right	2.	Raymond Williams
C. The Mirror and the Lamp	3.	Roland Barthes
D. Culture and Society	4.	Terry Eagleton

Choose the correct option from those given below:

	A	B	C	D		A	B	C	D
(a)	1	2	4	3	(b)	4	3	2	1
(c)	2	1	3	4	(d)	3	4	1	2

31. From among the following, identify the two correct statements in Johnson's criticism of Shakespeare :

1. His Athenians are not sufficiently Greek and his kings not completely royal.
2. He sacrifices virtue to convenience and is more careful to please than to instruct.
3. He adheres to strict chronology and gives to one age or nation only its own customs and opinions.
4. He sacrifices reason, property and truth to pursue even a poor and barren quibble.

Choose the correct option:

(a) 1 and 2 (b) 1 and 3
(c) 3 and 4 (d) 2 and 4

32. Who among the following is celebrated in John Keats's Lines on the Mermaid Tavern?

(a) Jack, the Ripper (b) Bryson of the Park
(c) Jack, the Giant-Killer (d) Robin Hood

33. Who among the following analysed the naturalisation of connotative meanings into myths?

(a) Michel Foucault (b) Roman Ingarden
(c) J. Hillis Miller (d) Ronald Barthes

34. Read the following lines :

IN A STATION OF THE METRO

The apparition of these faces in the crowd:

Petals on a wet, black bough.

Which of the following poetic programmes is illustrated by the above lines?

(a) The Movement (b) Naturalism
(c) Symbolism (d) Imagism

35. Identify the author in whose works the character Ashenden appears many times :

(a) Dorothy Sayers
(b) Daniel Defoe
(c) D.H. Lawrence
(d) Somerset Maugham

36. In which of the following paired terms, the relationship between the active and passive forms of a sentence can be best established?

(a) Deep structure—Surface structure
(b) Signifier—Signified
(c) Metaphor—Metonymy
(d) Syntagmatic—Paradigmatic

37. By which two of the following processes, according to Michel Foucault, does power operate?

1. By right rather than technique
2. By normalization rather than law
3. By control rather than punishment
4. By repression rather than agreement

Choose the correct option:

(a) 1 and 3 (b) 2 and 3
(c) 2 and 4 (d) 1 and 4

38. "The great English novelists are Jane Austen, George Eliot, Henry James and Joseph Conrad." Which one of the following critical texts begins with the above assertion?

(a) Walter Allen, The English Novel
(b) Terry Eagleton, The English Novel
(c) FR Leavis, The Great Tradition
(d) Ian Watt, Rise of the Novel

39. Match the following journals with their distinguishing aims and methods of scholarship.

List I	List II
A. Obsidian	1. Literature, history and the philosophy of history
B. Clio	2. Literature and arts in the African diaspora
C. Interventions	3. Feminist writing
D. Signs	4. Postcolonial writing

Choose the correct option from those given below:

	A	B	C	D		A	B	C	D
(a)	2	1	4	3	(b)	4	3	1	2
(c)	2	4	1	3	(d)	3	1	4	2

40. Identify the two names from the following who are associated with Hermeneutics :

1. Edmund Husserl
2. ED Hirsch
3. Martin Heidegger
4. Stephen Greenblatt

Choose the correct option:

(a) 1 and 3 (b) 1 and 2
(c) 2 and 3 (d) 2 and 4

41. Match the Novelist with the Publisher.

List I	List II
A. Laurence Sterne	1. Thomas Lowndes
B. Henry Fielding	2. Andrew Millar
C. Frances Burney	3. William Taylor
D. Daniel Defoe	4. Robert Dodsley

Choose the correct option from those given below :

	A	B	C	D		A	B	C	D
(a)	3	1	2	4	(b)	2	4	1	3
(c)	4	2	1	3	(d)	2	3	4	1

42. Which two writers have written essays on the defence of poetry?

1. Sir Philip Sidney
2. P. B. Shelley
3. Dr. Mathew Arnold
4. T. S. Eliot

Choose the correct option:

(a) 1 and 4 (b) 1 and 3
(c) 3 and 4 (d) 1 and 2

43. Which of the following is the accurate description of 'dramatic irony'?

(a) A character's knowledge or expectation is contradicted by what the audience knows, or by the outcome of events
(b) An audience knows or expects something to happen but the events on stage turn out to be different
(c) Ironic events and expectations of actual actions and results converge in drama and the audience feels rewarded
(d) A dramatist's irony reinforces his actors' performance, thereby fulfilling audience's expectations

44. Given below are two statements, one is labelled as Assertion (A) and the other is labelled as Reason (R) :

Assertion (A) Instances of beliefs triggering action are present in social life and may give rise to problems in determining 'causality'.

Reason (R) Beliefs may not be accompanied by or give rise to logically appropriate actions and actions may occur which are consistent with motivations and intentions, but they often, if not usually, also have unanticipated outcomes.

In the light of the above two statements choose the correct option:

(a) Both A and R are true and R is the correct explanation of A
(b) Both A and R are true, but R is not the correct explanation of A
(c) A is true, but R is false
(d) A is false, but R is true

45. Who says the following lines and to whom?

"If it be aught toward the general good,
Set honor in one eye and death i' th' other,
And I will look on both indifferently."

(a) Octavius to Antony
(b) Hamlet to Claudius
(c) Brutus to Cassius
(d) Casca to Calpurnia

46. Which one of the following correctly describes the meaning of Macbeth's words '...life is but a walking shadow'?

(a) Life is just devoid of light
(b) Life is just devoid of substance
(c) Life is just devoid of spirit
(d) Life is just devoid of stability

47. Which of the following poets does William Hazlitt call 'Don Quixote-like' in his essay, My First Acquaintance with Poets?

(a) William Wordsworth
(b) Samuel Taylor Coleridge
(c) William Cowper
(d) Lord Byron

48. For which one of the following reasons, in Oscar Wilde's novel, The Picture of Dorian Gray, Gray breaks down when he sees his finished portrait?

(a) Overwhelmed by the beauty of the portrait
(b) Overjoyed by the feeling that his beauty will be known to all
(c) Distraught by the fact that his beauty will fade while the portrait stays beautiful
(d) Distraught by the badly drawn portrait

49. Match the critics and their works.

Critics	Works
A. Edward Said	1. The Illusions of Postmodernism
B. Terry Eagleton	2. Contemporary Marxist Criticism
C. Francis Mulhern	3. Theory into Practice
D. KM Newton	4. Culture and Imperialism

Choose the correct option from those given below:

	A	B	C	D
(a)	4	1	2	3
(b)	4	1	3	2
(c)	2	1	4	3
(d)	1	2	3	4

50. Which of the following sociologists' ideas on the practice of receiving and giving gifts are used by J. Hillis Miller to reinforce her arguments in the essay, Critic as Host?

(a) Emile Durkheim (b) Max Weber
(c) Marcel Mauss (d) Daniel Benll

51. Which of the following books is written by an Englishman in universal Latin, is further added to by the Flemish Peter Giles, is revised by the Dutch Erasmus, is printed at Louvain in 1516, later at Paris, still later at Basle, where it was illustrated by two woodcuts from the hand of the German Holbein?

(a) The Golden Legend (b) Confessio Amantis
(c) Utopia (d) Erewhon

52. The Sadler Commission Report (1917-1919) was critical of the quality of students graduating from the university and had very perceptive remarks on English and the use of mother tongue in Indian education.

What was this Commission appointed for?

(a) To examine the functioning of the Directorate of Public Instruction in Delhi
(b) To study the problems of Calcutta University
(c) To investigate and recommend teaching methods of languages generally
(d) To evolve a three-language formula for the Indian schools

53. Match the books with the writers.

List I	List II
A. The Madwoman in the Attic	1. Frantz Fanon
B. The Wretched of the Earth	2. Stephen Greenblatt
C. Shakespearean Negotiations	3. Stanley Fish
D. Is There a Text in This Class?	4 Sandra M. Gilbert and Susan Gubar

Choose the correct option from those given below:

	A	B	C	D
(a)	3	4	1	2
(b)	1	2	3	4
(c)	4	1	2	3
(d)	2	3	4	1

54. Who among the following established and popularised the concept of 'Cardinal Vowels'?

(a) A. S. Hornby (b) E. V. Lucas
(c) Daniel Jones (d) C. J. Dodson

55. Which writer applied the term 'cultural poetics' to his own critical contribution to make literature and arts as part of social practice?

(a) Stephen Greenblatt
(b) Mikhail Bakhtin
(c) Jonathan Dollimore
(d) Raymond Williams

56. Which one of the following is the right definition of 'peer review'?

(a) A post-publication process in which the work is submitted to a panel of reviewers for ascertaining quality
(b) A pre-publication process in which work submitted for publication is evaluated for quality by experts in the field
(c) A pre-publication process in which work submitted for publication is accompanied by recommendation of other experts in the field
(d) A post-publication process in which the work is submitted for a professional review

57. What, according to Raymond Williams, is the right description of the term 'Cultural Materialism'?

(a) The cultural effect that religion has in social life
(b) The political effect that matter has in social lives
(c) The material effect that culture has in wider social life
(d) The effect of social life in cultural situations of uncertainty

58. Which one of the following of Plato's beliefs/acts was Shelley countering by saying that 'pets are the unacknowledged legislators of mankind'?

(a) Banishment of poets from the republic
(b) Distrust of value of poetry for mankind
(c) Preference for legislators over poets
(d) Description of poets as mad men

59. Which of the following propositions refers to the recommendations of Charles Grant?

(a) The introduction of English as the medium of instruction in an Indian system of education that included literature, art and craft
(b) The introduction of English as the medium of instruction from lower levels in a few states as an experiment
(c) The introduction of English as the medium of instruction in a Western system of education that included literature, natural sciences and mechanical inventions
(d) The introduction of English as the medium of instruction in regional medium institutions that included only literature

60. "To see him act is like reading Shakespeare by flashes of lighting." About which Shakespearean actor Coleridge wrote the above line?

(a) David Garrick
(b) Richard Burbage
(c) John Philip Kemble
(d) Edmund Kean

61.* Identify the stage that falls between the imaginary and symbolic stages according to Jacques Lacan :

(a) Middle stage (b) Minor st ge
(c) Medieval stage (d) Intermediate stage

* Answer not given in official answer key.

62. Who is the author of the essay, 'The Rationale of the Copy-Text'?

(a) Fredson Burns (b) WW Greg
(c) RB McKerrow (d) Paul Maas

63. Which among the following clusters matches the prose style that came to be known as 'Carlylese'?

(a) Capital letters, exclamation marks, phrases in German
(b) Question marks, long sentences, phrases in French
(c) Frequent ellipses, Latin sayings, comic non-sequitors
(d) Biblical phrases, capital letters, missing letters

64. Which of the following aptly names the language resulting from the contact of two mutually unintelligible language systems?

(a) Creole (b) Dialect (c) Colloquial (d) Pidgin

65. Which one of the following arrangements of poets is in the correct chronological order?

(a) William Langland, William Dunbar, Layamon
(b) William Langland, Layamon, William Dunbar
(c) Layamon, William Langland, William Dunbar
(d) William Dunbar, Layamon, William Langland

66. Match the following items/ideas with the writers who first used/popularized them:

List I	List II
A. The Frontier Thesis	1. Raymond Williams
B. The Lost Generation	2. Homi Bhabha
C. Third Space	3. F. J. Turner
D. Structure of Feeling	4. Gertrude Stein

Choose the correct option from those given below:

	A	B	C	D
(a)	4	1	2	3
(b)	3	1	4	2
(c)	3	4	2	1
(d)	1	3	4	2

67. What is being described by Wordsworth in the following lines from his poem, 'The Thorn'?

I've measured it from side to side;
'Tis three feet long and two feet wide.

(a) Fallen bough (b) A cradle
(c) A small cot (d) An Infant's grave

68. What is the name of the poetic style characterized by short staccato rhymed lines, as shown below?

What can it avayle
To dryve forth a snayle,
Or to make a sayle
Of a heryngės tayle?

(a) Cranmerish (b) Wolseyan
(c) Chaucerian (d) Skeltonic

69. Which of the following statements is true in terms of distribution of metrical feet?

(a) Anapaestic is to Dactylic as Trochaic is to Iambic
(b) Trochaic is to Anapaestic as Dactylic is to Iambic.
(c) Iambic is to Trochaic as Anapaestic is to Dactylic
(d) Dactylic is to Trochaic as Iambic is to Anapaestic

70. What term used by Ferdinand de Saussure corresponds to Noam Chomsky's term 'performance'?
(a) Difference (b) Parole
(c) Paradigm (d) Langue

71. In which of Anita Desai's novels does an insane wife kill her husband?
(a) Voices in the City (b) In Custody
(c) Cry, The Peacock (d) Baumgartner's Bombay

72. Which of the following novels by Iris Murdoch tells the story of an ageing theatre celebrity who withdraws into a life of seclusion and writes a diary/journal/novel?
(a) The Sandcastle
(b) Under the Net
(c) The Sea, the Sea
(d) Flight from the Enchanter

73. Which of the following correctly describes 'black humour' as a morbid and provocative treatment of
(a) old age and disease (b) youth and passionate love
(c) death and disease (d) childhood and accident

74. In which play, other than Julius Caesar, has Shakespeare depicted the Romans better than the Roman writers themselves have done?
(a) Troilus and Cressida (b) Coriolanus
(c) Romeo and Juliet (d) Two Gentlemen of Verona

75. What was Gramsci's term for cultural consensus supporting capitalism?
(a) Monopoly (b) Ideology
(c) Discourse (d) Hegemony

76. Considering the story of the novel, what does the title 'Dombey and Son' stand for?
(a) It suggests the choice between a son and a daughter
(b) It suggests the commercial aspect of life
(c) It suggests the opposition between a father and a son
(d) It suggests the importance of a dynasty

77. While looking for publication details of a book, a researcher may consult the book's copyright page, which may appear
(a) just after the cover
(b) usually the reverse of the title page
(c) invariably the reverse of the title page
(d) just before the title page

78. Which one of the following is the source of the passage given below?
"I have observed with growing anxiety the career of this word culture during the past six of seven years. We may find it natural, and significant, that during a period of unparalleled destructiveness, this word should come to have an important role ... "
(a) F. R. Leavis, Mass Civilization and Minority Culture
(b) T. S. Eliot, Notes Towards the Definition of Culture
(c) Raymond Williams, Culture and Society
(d) Stuart Hall, Cultural Representations and Signifying Practices

79. What does 'Harlem Renaissance' refer to?
(a) A scientific and rational ethos, including freedom from superstition, in 18th century Europe
(b) The flourishing of African American literature in the 1920s and 1930s
(c) A church system, overseen by a governing hierarchy of four courts, championed by the English Puritans
(d) The revelation of Christ to the Gentiles in the persons of the Magi

80. Who is referred to as 'beast' in the quote 'Kill the beast! Cut his throat! Spill his blood' in William Golding's Lord of the Flies?
(a) Ralph (b) Piggy
(c) Simon (d) Roger

81. Which of the following plays is characterized by the exclusivity of a single character talking to himself?
(a) A Streetcar Named Desire
(b) Equus
(c) The Misanthrope
(d) Krapp's Last Tape

82. Given below are two statements, one is labelled as Assertion (A) and the other is labelled as Reason (R).

Assertion (A) The dialects of English that have resulted from the regional separation of English-speaking communities have not acquired the status of language.

Reason (R) The Germanic dialects that are now Dutch, English, German, Swedish etc., have become distinct owing to geographical dispersion.

In the light of the above two statements choose the correct option:
(a) Both A and R are true and R is the correct explanation of A
(b) Both A and R are true, but R is not the correct explanation of A
(c) A is true, but R is false
(d) A is false, but R is true

83. The medieval English university organized its studies based on the seven liberal arts. Three of these, the trivium, referred to the study of
(a) arithmetic, geometry, music
(b) astronomy, music, logic
(c) geometry, grammar, music
(d) grammar, logic, rhetoric

84. "Culture is ordinary : that is the first fact." Which one of the following is the source of this statement?
(a) The Country and the City (b) Resources of Hope
(c) The Long Revolution (d) Keywords

85. Who among the following is mourned in Walt Whitman's O Captain! My Captain!?
(a) R. W. Emerson (b) John Keats
(c) P. B. Shelley (d) Abraham Lincoln

86. Which artistic technique best describes the interplay of light and shade in the following lines?
"I have looked at it so long
I think it is part of my heart. But it flickers.
Faces and darkness separate us over and over
A woman bends over me,
Searching my reaches for what she really is
Then she turns to those liars, the candles or the moon.
I see her back, and reflect it faithfully."
(a) Collage (b) Flashback
(c) Montage (d) Chiaroscuro

87. Which two titles from among the following deal with Lssues related to the institutionalisation of English in post-independence India?
1. Provocations 2. Professing Literature
3. The Lie of the Land 4. The Muse Unchained
The right combination according to the code is
(a) 1 and 4 (b) 1 and 3
(c) 2 and 3 (d) 3 and 4

88. What, in sum, is Sidney's point in the following?
"Nature never set forth the earth in so rich tapestry as divers poets have done; neither with pleasant rivers, fruitful trees, sweet-smelling flowers, nor what so ever else may make the too-much-loved earth more lovely. Her world is brazen, the poets only deliver a golden." (Philip Sidney)
(a) Works of art are superior to the natural world they represent
(b) Works of art can often compete with the natural world represented by them
(c) Neither the poets nor the natural world they set forth equal nature's rich tapestry
(d) The natural world is far superior to the works of art that represent it

It is an axiom in mental philosophy, that we can think of nothing which we have not perceived. When I say that we can think of nothing, I mean we can imagine nothing, we can reason of nothing, we can remember nothing, we can foresee nothing.

The most astonishing combinations of poetry, the subtlest deductions of logic and mathematics, are no other than combinations which the intellect makes of sensations according to its own laws. A catalogue of all the thoughts of the mind, and of all their possible modifications, is a cyclopaedic history of the universe.

89. According to the writer, perception is the basic epistemology. Which one of the following is the other accepted epistemology?
(a) Language (b) Experience
(c) Inference (d) Simile

90. According to the passage given, which of the following correctly captures the meaning of 'a cylopaedic history of the universe'?
(a) The knowledge about the universe from its beginning to its possible end
(b) A catalogue of rivers, mountains and continents
(c) Statements about the universe based on logic and mathematics
(d) A published encyclopaedia of the universe

91. Which one of the following words best describes the heroes of Cervantes' Don Quixote, Mark Twain's The Adventures of Tom Sawyer and Thomas Mann's The Confessions of Felix Krull?
(a) Ficelle (b) Picaro
(c) Mannequin (d) Philanderer

92. In the study of Anglo-American literatures, certain distinguished names in critical/editorial scholarship become synonymous with famous writers and periods of literary history.
Match the following names with their respective areas of scholarship:

List I	List II
A. Edward Mendelson	1. John Milton
B. Jerome McGann	2. Ezra Pound
C. Stanley Fish	3. W. H. Auden
D. Hugh Kenner	4. Textual Scholarship

Choose the correct option from those given below:

	A	B	C	D
(a)	2	1	4	3
(b)	3	4	1	2
(c)	4	3	2	1
(d)	3	2	4	1

93. Which of the following correctly list the two novels figuring the writer as a public figure, as a celebrity and as grist for the academic mill?
(a) Rabbit Redux and Rabbit, Run
(b) Rabbit is Rich and The Coup
(c) Of the Farm and The Centaur
(d) Bech : A Book and Bech is Back

94. Who among the following is one of the University Wits?
(a) Thomas Hooker (b) Thomas Nashe
(c) Michael Drayton (d) William Harvey

95. Given below are two statements, one is labelled as Assertion (A) and the other is labelled as Reason (R) :

Assertion (A) Language constructs meaning.

Reason (R) Language structures meanings depending on the speaking subjects' perception, context and auditor(s).

In the light of the above two statements, choose the correct option:

(a) Both A and R are true and R is the correct explanation of A
(b) Both A and R are true, but R is not the correct explanation of A
(c) A is true, but R is false
(d) A is false, but R is true

96. Match the play with the subject matter of the play:

List I	List II
A. The Doctor's Dilemma	1. Flouting of stage conventions
B. You Never Can Tell	2. Satire on military heroes
C. Candida	3. Devaluation of social traditions
D. Arms and the Man	4. Mockery of physicians' ignorance

Choose the correct option from those given below:

	A	B	C	D
(a)	2	3	4	1
(b)	3	1	4	2
(c)	1	2	3	4
(d)	4	3	1	2

THE GROCER'S CHILDREN
The grocer's children
eat day-old bread,
moldy cakes and cheese,
soft black bananas
on stale shredded wheat,
weeviled rice, their plates
heaped high with wilted
greens, bruised fruit,
surprise treats
from unlabelled cans,
tainted meat.
The grocer's children
never go hungry.

97. Which of the following words best describes the last sentence of the poem?

(a) Ironic (b) Paradoxical
(c) Pathetic (d) Disdainful

98. What is suggested by the word 'tainted' in line 11?

(a) Tinctured (b) Cooked (c) Spoiled (d) Boiled

99. How does the poem achieve its effect?

(a) It lists a number of grocery items which do not have any tangible nutritive benefit
(b) It presents a series of inedible fare in the face of the basic need to eat
(c) It strays away from the tongue-in-cheek beginning to state the obvious
(d) It posits the circumspect existence of a reasonable plan to alleviate hunger

100. Whose point of view seems to have been stated in the poem?

(a) The gorcer's (b) The children's
(c) The narrator's (d) The poet's

ANSWERS

1	*(c)*	2	*(b)*	3	*(c)*	4	*(c)*	5	*(b)*	6	*(d)*	7	*(a)*	8	*(b)*	9	*(c)*	10	*(a)*
11	*(a)*	12	*(b)*	13	*(c)*	14	*(b)*	15	*(c)*	16	*(c)*	17	*(b)*	18	*(b)*	19	*(b)*	20	*(a)*
21	*(b)*	22	*(a)*	23	*(b)*	24	*(b)*	25	*(b)*	26	*(c)*	27	*(a)*	28	*(a)*	29	*(d)*	30	*(d)*
31	*(d)*	32	*(d)*	33	*(d)*	34	*(d)*	35	*(d)*	36	*(a)*	37	*(b)*	38	*(c)*	39	*(a)*	40	*(a)*
41	*(c)*	42	*(d)*	43	*(a)*	44	*(a)*	45	*(c)*	46	*(b)*	47	*(a)*	48	*(c)*	49	*(a)*	50	*(c)*
51	*(c)*	52	*(b)*	53	*(c)*	54	*(c)*	55	*(a)*	56	*(b)*	57	*(c)*	58	*(c)*	59	*(c)*	60	*(d)*
61	*(*)*	62	*(b)*	63	*(a)*	64	*(d)*	65	*(c)*	66	*(c)*	67	*(d)*	68	*(d)*	69	*(c)*	70	*(b)*
71	*(c)*	72	*(c)*	73	*(c)*	74	*(b)*	75	*(d)*	76	*(a)*	77	*(b)*	78	*(b)*	79	*(b)*	80	*(c)*
81	*(d)*	82	*(b)*	83	*(d)*	84	*(b)*	85	*(d)*	86	*(d)*	87	*(b)*	88	*(a)*	89	*(c)*	90	*(a)*
91	*(b)*	92	*(b)*	93	*(d)*	94	*(b)*	95	*(a)*	96	*(d)*	97	*(a)*	98	*(c)*	99	*(b)*	100	*(c)*

SOLVED PAPERS

ENGLISH

Solved Paper, December 2018

General Instructions

1. There are total one hundred questions in this paper. Each question carries 2 marks.
2. All questions are compulsory.

1 'The chapter on the fall of the Rupee you may omit. It is somewhat too sensational. Even these metallic problems have their melodramatic side.' The fall of the Indian rupee in the final decades of 19th century is referred to in one of Oscar Wilde's plays. Identify the play.

(a) A Woman of No Importance
(b) Lady Windermere's Fan
(c) An Ideal Husband
(d) The Importance of Being Earnest

2 Who viewed Wordsworth, Southey and Coleridge as representatives of a "sect of poets.... dissenters from the established systems in poetry and criticism" who constituted "the most formidable conspiracy against sound judgement in matters political"?

(a) Henry Vaughan (b) Francis Jeffrey
(c) Francisco Franco (d) Ralph Vaughan

3 This poet was of the Auden generation and was only briefly a member of the communist party. In his poem, 'The Pylons', he averred that the Pylons are "Bare like nude giant girls that have no secrets". This prompted the label, Pylon poets, for the new generation of poets who were happy to use the gas works or pistons of a steam-engine as poetic imagery. (Name this poet).

(a) Louis Mac Neice (b) Stephen Spender
(c) Christopher Isherwood (d) Cecil Day Lewis

4 In the spring of 1941, Nikos Kazantzakis embarked on one of his most ambitious projects, a play known as *Yangtze*, What English/Greek title is it now known as?

(a) Zorba (b) Zoroaster
(c) Buddha (d) Brobdingnag

5 The term 'Digger' is associated with a group of agrarian communists who flourished in England in 1649-50 and were led by

(a) Laurence Clarkson (b) George Fox
(c) John Lilburne (d) Gerrard Winstanley

6 Who among the following exemplified the role of the 'peasant poet'?

(i) John Clare (ii) John Keats'
(iii) William Cobbett (iv) Robert Burns

The right combination according to the code is

Codes

(a) (ii) and (iii)
(b) (i) and (ii)
(c) (i) and (iv)
(d) (iii) and (iv)

7 Arnold Wesker is associated with 'kitchen-sink drama', a rather condescending title applied to the then new-wave realistic drama depicting the family lives of working class characters, on stage and in broadcast plays. Two of the following plays begin with one character doing the dishes in a kitchen sink. Identify the pair.

(i) The Kitchen
(ii) Chicken Soup with Barley
(iii) Roots
(iv) Menace

The right combination according to the code is

Codes

(a) (i) and (iv) (b) (ii) and (iv)
(c) (ii) and (iii) (d) (i) and (ii)

8 In imitation of which classical poet did Samuel Johnson writer his *London* and *The Vanity of Human Wishes*?

(a) Homer (b) Juvenal
(c) Tasso (d) Horace

9 There are helpers and harmers among fellow-pilgrim's in Christian's journey in Pilgrim's Progress. Who among the following is not a helper?

(a) The Evangelist (b) Mr. Worldly Wiseman
(c) Goodwill (d) The Interpreter

10 The following epitaph was written by Rudyard Kipling during the War of 1914-18.

HINDU SEPOY IN FRANCE

This man is his own country prayed we know not to what powers.

We pray them to reward him for his bravery in ours. 'Powers' here refers to .... 'them' to .... and 'ours' to ....

(a) authorities, his compatriots, our country
(b) the divine, powers, our country
(c) the military, the Hindu sepoys, powers
(d) the Hindus, the French, the British

11 Which Walter Scott novel in set in France is the 15th century?

(a) The Antiquarry (b) Redgauntlet
(c) Quentin Durward (d) Ivanhoe

12 Match the Character with the Play.

	Character	Play
(a)	Dorimant	1. The Plain Dealer
(b)	Lady Fidget	2. The Man of Mode
(c)	Malevole	3. The Country Wife
(d)	Vernish	4. The Malcontent

Codes

	A	B	C	D		A	B	C	D
(a)	4	3	1	2	(b)	2	3	4	1
(c)	4	1	3	2	(d)	2	4	3	1

13 "What is honour? A word.What is that word honour? Air. A trim reckoning! Who hath it? He that died o' Wednesday. Doth he feel it ? No. Doth he hear it? No. Is it insensible, then? Yea, to the dead. But will it not live with the living? No, Why? Detraction will not suffer it. Therefore, I'II none of it. Honour is a mere scutcheon and so ends my catechism."

Which character in the following Shakespeare's dramas made this statement about honour?

(a) Hamlet in Hamlet, the Prince of Denmark
(b) Hotspur in King Henry IV-Part I
(c) Falstaff in King Henry IV-Part I
(d) Claudius in Hamlet, the Prince of Denmark

14 Allen Tate once made a useful distinction between structure and texture. The distinction referred to

(a) the devices employed to enlighten objects and materials in a narrative, and the objects and material themselves, respectively.
(b) the main line of a narrative, argument, etc, and the rhetorical, stylistic, metaphorical and other devices respectively.
(c) the rhetorical, stylistic, metaphorical and other devices, and the main line of a narrative, argument, etc, respectively.
(d) objects and materials on which a narrative casts light, and the devices employed to enlighten them respectively.

15 *Evelina* was published in 1778.

(a) using the name Fanny Burney
(b) anonymously
(c) posthumously
(d) under a pseudonym

16 The title of Dylan Thomas's Deaths and entrances was taken from

(a) Rudyard Kipling's '*A Death Bed*'
(b) John Donne's '*Death's Duell*'
(c) William Shakespeare's '*Macbeth*'
(d) T.S. Eliot's '*Murder in the Cathedral*'

17 Jonathan Swift arrived in London in 1710 and confronted a rapidly changing world in the new Tory ministry. His reactions to this world are vividly recorded in this *Journal of Stella*, a series of letters addressed to

(i) Hester Vanhomrigh
(ii) Esther Johnson
(iii) Rebecca Dingley
(iv) Lady Mary Montagu

The right combination according to the code is.

Codes

(a) (i) and (ii) (b) (ii) and (iv)
(c) (ii) and (iii) (d) (iii) and (iv)

18 The fault of Cowley and perhaps of all the writers of the metaphysical race is that of pursuing his thoughts to their ramifications, by which he loses the grandeur of generality: for of the greatest things the parts are little; what is little can be but pretty, and by claiming dignity becomes ridiculous. Thus all the power of description is destroyed by a scrupulous enumeration; and the force of metaphors is lost, when the mind by the mention of particulars is turned more upon the original than the secondary sense, more upon that form which the illustration is drawn than that to which it is applied.

(Life of Cowley, 1779)

What Dr. Johnson actually faults here is

(a) the force of metaphors that blunts description.
(b) the metaphysical poets tendency to saunter away.
(c) the metaphysical insistence on the particular than the general.
(d) the mind that goes a stray toward the original.

19 Which of the following is the most accurate statement by W.E.B. Du Bois's famous articulation of the 'twoness' of black Americans?

(a) "It is a peculiar sensation, this double-consciousness, this sense of always looking at one's self through the eyes of others".
(b) "Through the eyes of others, is sense of always looking at one's self, we acquire the double-consciousness. "
(c) "This double consciousness, this sense of always looking at one's self through the eyes of others, is a peculiar sensation".
(d) "This sense of always looking at one's self, a peculiar sensation through the eyes of others, is double-consciousness"

20 Allan Sealy's *The Trotter-Nama* traces the history of the Anglo-Indian community in a chronicle of seven generations of the Trotter family, told by the seventh Trotter. This narrator is

(a) a collector of rare manuscripts.
(b) a quack in the Indian outback.
(c) an accountant in the Indian army.
(d) a forger of Indian miniatures.

21 Match the plays to their setting.

(a) Krapp's Last Tape	1. A country road; A tree.
(b) Happy Days	2. Bare interior; Two small windows high up; grey light.
(c) Waiting for Godot	3. Expanse of scorched grass forming a low mound; blinding light.
(d) Endgame	4. A late evening in future; white light.

Codes

	A	B	C	D		A	B	C	D
(a)	2	4	3	1	(b)	3	4	1	2
(c)	4	3	1	2	(d)	2	3	1	4

22 The en-ending to denote the plural nouns (as in oxen, children, brethren) has survived from the

(a) Anglo-Norman case of making plural nouns
(b) Middle English hymnals and chants in English parishes
(c) Old Middle English pronouncing custom of plurals
(d) Old English practice of making plural nouns

23 "Tomorrow, and tomorrow, and tomorrow, ... in this petty pace from day to day, To the last .... of recorded time;
And all our yesterdays have lighted fools,
The way to dusty death. Out, out, brief candle!
Life's but a walking shadow, a poor player, That .... and frets his hour upon the stage, And then is .... no more, it is a tale. Told by an idiot, full of sound and fury, Signifying nothing."

Fill in the blanks. Choose the set that carries the correct words.

(a) Walks, breath, creeps, shown
(b) Moves, syllable, frowns, heard
(c) Creeps, moment, struts, seen
(d) Creeps, syllable, struts, heard

24 "Full many a lady
I have eye'd with best regard; and many a time
The harmony of their tongues hath into bondage
Brought my too diligent ear; for several virtues
Have I liked several women; never any
With so full soul, but some defect in her
Did quarrel with the noblest grace she ow'd,
And put it to the foil. But you, o you,
So perfect and so peerless , are created of every creature's best".

This passage admiring the perfect matching of inner and outward beauty of a woman is taken from

(a) Thomas Middleton's Women Beware Women
(b) Marlowe's Dr. Faustus
(c) Shakespeare's Tempest
(d) John Webster's The Duchess of Malfi

25 Adherents of the 14th century religious movement associated with vernacular preaching, translation of New Testament into English, and challenges to the authority of priests and bishops were called

(a) Levellers (b) Agnostics (c) Deists (d) Lollards

26 Early African-American texts like slave narratives were often described as told to narratives as their 'authors' dictated their experiences. The persons who noted down theses experiences are

(a) Amanuenses (b) Translators
(c) Abolitionists (d) Slave-drivers

27 What is the delicate balancing act of Andrew Marvell's 'Horatian Ode'?

(a) Praising Roman virtues while endorsing Christian beliefs.
(b) Celebrating the Restoration while regretting the frivolity of the new regime.
(c) Praising feminine virtues while mocking the fixation on chastity.
(d) Celebrating Cromwell's victories while inviting sympathy for the executed king.

28 What attitude towards death would you find in such poems as Tennyson's 'Crossing the Bar', Whitman's 'Death Carol' and Kiplings 'L' Envoi'?

(a) Hope (b) Protest
(c) Resignation (d) Despair

29 In an ode, William Collins lamented the passing of a contemporary poet. The ode began with the line "In yonder grave a Druid lies." Name the poet whose passing Collins laments.

(a) William Cowper (b) Thomas Gray
(c) James Thomson (d) Alexander Pope

30 In his essay 'The Function of Criticism at the Present Time' (1864) Matthew Arnold contended that

(a) Creative power should be ranked higher than critical power
(b) Creative and critical powers are not comparable in any way
(c) Critical power should be ranked higher than creative power
(d) Creative and critical powers should be ranked equally

31 Deconstructionist critics argue that texts are never free from

(a) the equivocal and ironically unstable worldview of the author
(b) the interpretations bestowed by the totalizing critic
(c) distortions inherent in the rhetoricity of language
(d) the material conditions the determine that production and reception

32 It was the first narrative on the life of a black woman slave to be published in England. in 1831. It has profound influence on the abolition movement in Britain. Identify the book and its author.

(a) Elizabeth-*Memoir of Old Elizabeth*, a Coloured Woman
(b) Mattie Jane Jackson -*The Story of Mattie J Jackson*
(c) Mary Prince-*The History of Mary Prince*
(d) Harriet Jacobs-*Incidents in the Life of a Slave Girl*

33 Ah, what a trifle is a heart,
If once into love's hands it come!
All other griefs allow a part
To other griefs, and ask themselves but some;
They come to us, but us love draws;
He swallows us and never chaws;
By him, as by chain'd shot, whole ranks do die;
He is the tyrant pike, our hearts the fry.
-John Donne, 1633

Which sentence best paraphrases line five of the passage above?

(a) Emotions can damage us, but none as severely as love.
(b) Love tends to grab us and never let go.
(c) Unbidden pain afflicts us, but we are lured by love.
(d) Distress comes in many forms, but none lasts as long as heartache.

34 The 'grammar bullies'-you read them in places like *the New York Times*-and they tell you what is correct.

You must never use 'hopefully'. Hopefully, we will be going there on Thursday. "That is incorrect and wrong and you are basically an ignorant pig if you say it.

This is judgementalism. The game that is being played there is a game of social class. It has nothing do with the morality of writing and speaking and thinking clearly, of which George Orwell, for instance, talked so well.

To which famous essay of Orwell does the author refer here?

(a) 'Inside the Whale'
(b) 'Reflections on Gandhi'
(c) 'Politics and the English Language'
(d) 'Why I Write'

35 In which of his novels does Italo Calvino construct his narrative through a tarot pack of cards and re-interpret the Western canon providing new versions of Oedipus Rex, Faust, Hamlet, Macbeth and King Lear?

(a) Invisible Cities
(b) The Castle of Crossed Destnies
(c) The Path to the Nest of Spiders
(d) Our Ancestors

36 "The good thing about words, "Hanif Kureishi remarks in "Loose Tongues", "is that their final effect is incalculable. [.....] You can never know what your words might turn out to mean for yourself or for someone else; or what the world they make will be like. Anything could happen. The problem with silence is that we know exactly what it will be like."

Kureishi, in some, suggests.

(i) There is always some risk involved in writing/speaking.
(ii) It is better to avoid using words than to risk miscommunication.
(iii) Words being predictable, are always open to misinterpretation.
(iv) The unpredictable, in deed, is the strength of words.

Determine the correct combination according to the code.

(a) (i) and (iv) (b) (ii) and (iii)
(c) (ii) and (iv) (d) (i) and (iii)

37 Identify the Fireside poets of the US.

(a) Amy Lowell, Emily Dickinson, Phillis Wheatley
(b) T.S. Eliot, Wallace, Stevens, William Carlos
(c) Marianne Moore, Elizabeth Bishop, Anne Seaton
(d) William Cullen Bryant, H.W. Longfellow, Oliver Wendell Holmes

38 **S.T. Coleridge's 'Dejection An Ode' opens with an epigraph which is a reference to a ballad. Identify the ballad.**

(a) 'La Belle Dame Sans Merci'
(b) 'Ballad of Sir Patrick Spence'
(c) 'Ballad of the Gibbet' (d) 'Ballad of the Goodly Fere'

39 **Which of the following statements is true of *The Way of the World*?**

(a) *The Way of the World* presents a heroine pretending to love an older man.
(b) Millamant and Mirabell fail to obtain the consent of Millamant's aunt for their marriage.
(c) *The Way of the World* was performed and published in 1702.
(d) *The Way of the World* failed on stage.

40 **In his *Practical Criticism* I.A.Richards suggests that there are several kinds of meanings and that the 'total meaning' is a blend of contributory meanings which are of different types. He identified four kinds of meaning, or the total meaning of a word depends upon four factors. Choose the right combination as proposed by Richards.**

(a) Image, Feeling, Tone and Intention
(b) Sound, Sense, Tone and Matter
(c) Sense, Feeling, Tone and Matter
(d) Sense, Feeling Tone and Intention

41 **What is peculiar about the reference in the following to some poets' names in the plural?**

"It is a freezing, bleak day in January, and I am looking for poetry. I see a few Chaucers, a few Shakespeares, and a hardcover, three-dollar *History of Modern Poetry* published in 1987."

(a) Unusual; awkward metaphors no longer in use.
(b) Usually refer to biographies of the poets in question.
(c) Synecdochic use; names for their respective works.
(d) Standard reference to more texts of one poet/author.

42 **In Thomas Moore's *Utopia* (Book II), the reader is told that in this new world there are few mistakes in marriage because**

(a) prospective husbands and wives see one another naked before agreeing to the match.
(b) The family Gods are invoked before finalising the nuptials.
(c) there is a community get together where prospective husbands and wives announce wedding plans endorsed by elders.
(d) there is an extensive courtship period preceding the actual wedding.

43 **During the Raj, the British viewed their rule in terms of a thankless duty to uplift the downtrodden and inculcate order into Oriental minds. The mission to civilize the 'silent, sullen peoples' of the East was a burden imposed upon them by destiny.**

The last observation in a fairly obvious allusion to

(a) Rudyard Kipling's 'The White Man's Burden'
(b) Maud Diver's 'The Englishwoman in India'
(c) J.R. Ackerley's Hindoo Holiday 'An Indian Journal'
(d) Flora Annie Steel's 'The Garden of Fidelity'

44 **The titular figure of Federico Garcia Lorca's elegy 'Lament for Ignacio Sanchez Mejias' was**

(a) a revolutionary who was associated with Che Guevara
(b) a popular priest and poet
(c) a popular matador and writer
(d) a say who helped the revolutionaries during the Spanish Civil War

45 **Thomas Nashe's *The Unfortunate Traveller* is narrated by**

(a) Philip Foxe, an English highwayman
(b) Jack Wilton, an English page
(c) Ben Lyte, a coarse Papist
(d) Peter Marston, a sworn Calvinist

46 **Match the character with the work.**

Characters	Name of work
(a) Rupert Birkin	1. Sons and Lovers
(b) Lydia Lensky	2. Kangaroo
(c) Miriam Leivers	3. Women in Love
(d) Richard Somers	4. The Rainbow

Codes

	A	B	C	D
(a)	4	1	2	3
(b)	2	3	4	1
(c)	3	4	1	2
(d)	1	2	4	3

47 **Which post-war British poet ends a poem with the line, "Get Stewed Books are a load of crap"?**

(a) Thom Gunn
(b) Ted Hughes
(c) Philip Larkin
(d) Craig Raine

48 **Which of the following had the alternative title *Things as They Are*?**

(a) William Godwin's Caleb *Williams*
(b) Mary Shelley's *Frankenstein*
(c) Horace Walpole's *The Castle of Otranto*
(d) Sir Walter Scott's *Waverley*

49 **The Norman Conquest was a significant landmark in English, history. What French did the Normans speak and what was it known as?**

(a) They spoke Norman French (Anglo-Norman). Their was certainly not ther standard French.
(b) They spoke a dialectal French (also called Anglo-Frisian), somewhat closer to the Parisian.
(c) They spoke standard French (of mainland France). Their French was very sweet and musical.
(d) They spoke normal French, rather distinct from Anglo-Norman, another standard language.

50 Which of the following is the most accurate description of *Butler English*?

(a) A pidgin, also called "Kitchen English" spoken by South Asians in Europe
(b) A minimal pidgin that emerged during colonial times in the Madras Presidency.
(c) Any non-grammatical variety of English used by menials in Commonwealth countries.
(d) A dialect of English spoken by the descendants of Anglo-Indians.

51 Which of the following would not be invoked to describe a form of new Historicist Criticism?

(a) Cultural materialism
(b) Post-structural recovery of authorial intent
(c) Geneology of patriarchal discourse
(d) Archaeology of social constructs

52 Why did Plato banish the poet from his ideal state?

(a) Poetry makes an artificial distinction between form and content.
(b) Poetry deals with form, to the neglect of content.
(c) The poet can never produce a completely accurate replica of the reality it seeks to represent, and (moreover) the purpose of art is not to describe reality but to change it.
(d) In representing the sensual aspects, of reality, the poet fails to discern the transcendent reality behind mere appearance.

53 Which of the following themes was not common to the works of Cavalier poets such as Thomas Carew, Sir John Denham, Edmund Waller, Sir John Suckling, James Shirley, Richard Lovelace, and Robert Herrick?

(a) Loyalty to the king
(b) Courtly ideals of the good life
(c) Pious devotion to religious virtues
(d) Carpe diem

54 The Romantic period produced a fair amount of dramatic criticism. A notable example is "On the Knocking at the Gate in *Macbeth*".

Who is the author?

(a) William Charles Macready (b) Thomas de Quincey
(c) William Hazlitt (d) Edmund Kean

55 As a boy growing up in Squire Allworthy's estate, Tom get one of the following characters into trouble. Identify the character.

(a) Nightingale (b) Partridge
(c) Blifil (d) Black George

56 .... read *Adam Bede* with such pleasure that she not only keenly recommended it to her relatives but also commissioned two paintings of scenes from the novel.

(a) Queen Victoria
(b) Margaret Cavendish
(c) George Eliot
(d) Horace Nightingale

57 One of the most flexible metres, ... is a five foot line. It was introduced by Geoffrey Chaucer in the 14th century and has since then become the commonest of metres in English poetry. (Fill in the blank)

(a) Iambic (b) Hexameter (c) Pentameter (d) Trochaic

58 *Mango Souffle*, India's first major gay themed film, is an adaptation of Mahesh Dattani play.

(a) Do the Needful
(b) On a Muggy Night in Mumbai
(c) Dance like a Man
(d) Bravely Fought the Queen

59 In this novel by Graham Greene a double agent uses classic works of fiction to encode secret information. "He put Clarissa Harlowe back in the bookcase" is the first clue to his treachery. Then he draws on War and Peace and The Way We Live Now as matrices for secretly transmitting information. Identify the novel.

(a) The Human Factor (b) The Man Within
(c) Our Man in Havana (d) The Confidential Agent

60 Match the Term with the Theorist.

Term	Theorist
(a) Negritude	1. Alice Walker
(b) Womanism	2. Jurgen Habermas
(c) Interpellation	3. Aime Cesaire
(d) Public Sphere	4. Louis Althusser

Codes

	A	B	C	D
(a)	1	2	4	3
(b)	3	2	4	1
(c)	2	1	4	3
(d)	3	1	4	2

61 Which of the following is not indebted to the Gothic genre?

(a) Matthew Lewis's *The Monk*
(b) Ann Radcliffe's *The Italian*
(c) William Beckford's *Vathek*
(d) Tobias Smollett's *Roderick Random*

62 In Marlow's *Doctor Faustus*, what books does Valdes counsel Faustus of study in preparation for conjuring up spirits ?

(i) The works of Bacon and Abanus
(ii) The Hebrew psalter and New Testament
(iii) The works of Ovid and Homer
(iv) The works of Baxter and Horst

The right combination according to the code is:

(a) (i) and (iv) (b) (ii) and (iii)
(c) (i) and (iii) (d) (i) and (ii)

63 In traditional ELT methods and materials, the native speaker is elevated and idealized against stereotyped non-native speakers. This tendency is dubbed .... by Adrian Holliday.

(a) Native speakerism (b) The non-native fallacy
(c) The near-native fallacy (d) The native-speaker bias

64 **Match the poem with the opening lines.**

(a) 'Ode to Psyche'	1. "My heart aches, and a drowsy numbness pains, My sense, as through of hemlock I had drunk",
(b) 'Ode on a Grecian'	2. "No, no, go not to Lethe, neither twist Woolf's"-bane, tight-rooted, for its poisonous wine",
(c) 'Ode to a Nightingale'	3. "Thou still unravish'd bride of quietness, Thou foster-child of silence and slow time",
(d) 'Ode on Melancholy'	4. "O Goddess ! hear these tuneless numbers, wrong, By sweet enforcement and remembrance dear,"

Codes

	A	B	C	D		A	B	C	D
(a)	1	3	2	4	(b)	4	1	3	2
(c)	4	3	1	2	(d)	3	4	2	1

65 **Match the following authors with the novels.**

Name of Author	Name of Novel
A. Chitra Banerjee Divakaruni	1. Inheritance
B. Anita Rau Badami	2. Listening Now
C. Anajana Appachana	3. Sister of My Heart
D. Indira Ganesan	4. The Hero's Walk

Codes

	A	B	C	D		A	B	C	D
(a)	1	3	2	4	(b)	4	2	1	3
(c)	3	4	2	1	(d)	4	1	3	2

66 **Match the author with the title.**

Author	Title
A. Alan Paton	1. Open City
B. Ngugi wa Thiong'o	2. Cry, the Beloved Country
C. Teju Cole	3. A Grain of Wheat
D. Wole Soyinka	4. The Interpreters

Codes

	A	B	C	D		A	B	C	D
(a)	1	3	4	2	(b)	3	2	4	1
(c)	2	3	1	4	(d)	3	1	4	2

67 **Herr God, Herr Lucifer**
Beware
Beware.
Out of the ash
I rise with my red hair
And I eat men like air.
Lines 4 and 5 in the above evoke.

(a) Christ's resurrection
(b) The legend of the Lady of the Lake
(c) The myth of the phoenix
(d) The fairy-tale of a girl in the woods

68 **Match the following concepts with their definitions.**

Concepts	Definitions
A. Collocation	1. A semantic relationship of one-to-many
B. Corpus	2. A grid used in lexical analysis
C. Hyponymy	3. A combination of two lexical items in a grammatical pattern
D. Matrix	4. A large body of texts

Codes

	A	B	C	D
(a)	4	2	3	1
(b)	1	3	4	2
(c)	3	4	1	2
(d)	3	1	2	4

69 **Identify the character, a black-eyed dwarf who "constantly revealed a few discoloured fangs that were yet scattered in his mouth, and gave him the aspect of a panting dog".**

(a) Rigand in *Little Dorrit*
(b) Mulberry Hawk in *Nicholas Nickleby*
(c) Daniel Quilp in *The Old Curiosity Shop*
(d) Mr. Crook in *Bleak House*

70 **The following lines are W.B Yeats's metaphor for an old man.**
A tattered coat upon a stick, unless
Soul clap its hands and sing, and louder sing
For every tatter in its mortal dress.
Here, the aged man is .... and his "soul .... in its mortal dress," is ....

(a) tenor, vehicle
(b) analogy, analogue
(c) point, counterpoint
(d) vehicle tenor

71 **Alas ! what boots it with uncessant care**
To tend the homely, slighted Shepherd's trade,
And strictly meditate the thankless Muse?
Were it not better done, as others use,
To sport with Amaryllis in the shade,
Or with the tangles of Neaera's hair?
Who are Amaryllis and Neaera in the above extract from John Milton's 'Lycidas'?

(a) Both were one-time lovers of Lycidas, the dead shepherd.
(b) Both were goddesses of love and war respectively appearing in Greek pastoral poetry.
(c) Amaryllis is a shepherdess mentioned in Shakespeare's romantic comedies Neaera, a minor character in *Love's Labour's Lost*.
(d) Amaryllis is a shepherdess mentioned in ancient pastoral poetry, notably in Virgil's Eclogues; Neaera, a nymph who appears in Virgil's Eclogues.

72 1992 demolition of the disputed structure in Ayodya produced two controversial literary responses. Identify them.

(a) Annals and Antiquities, between Sunlight and Shadows
(b) The Moor's Last Sigh, Lajja
(c) Chronicles of a Riot Foretold, Shame
(d) Out of Place, The Algebra of Infinite Justice

73 "Why don't we have a little game? Let's pretend that were human beings, and that we are actually alive."

This passage forms part of

(a) Harold Pinter's the Birthday Party
(b) Samuel Beckett's Waiting for Godot
(c) Agatha Christie's The Mousetrap
(d) John Osborne's Look Back in Anger

74 David Malouf's novel *'Ransom'* is based

(a) an episode in the *Trojan War*
(b) an episode in the *Mahabharata*
(c) a war memoir by Edmund Blunden
(d) a war poem by Yevgeny Yevtushenko

75 Which of the following statements on *Rajmohan's Wife* is not true?

(a) By common consent, Rajmohan's Wife is the firs novel in English published by an Indian.
(b) His vivid descriptions of the routine of Bengali households reveal a lot about the 19 th century.
(c) Bankim Chandra published it soon after serialisation and was related in seeing its first copy.
(d) The novel was serialised in 1864 in a short-lived magazine in Calcutta.

76 One of the less noticed and acknowledged distinction to *The Canterbury Tales* is that

(a) instead of revealing England's divisions, it revelled in its diversity.
(b) it alerted us to the term auctor, someone who is both 'an originator, or one who gives increase', the best description for Chaucer himself.
(c) it upheld the idea that we cannot divorce poetry from knowledge because poetry itself is an object of knowledge.
(d) it married domesticity to divinity, the baker's loaf with the bread of life.

77 In which work does William Blake say that Milton was "a true poet and of devil' s party without knowing it"?

(a) 'The Marriage of Heaven and Hell'
(b) 'The Chimney Sweeper'
(c) 'London'
(d) ' Songs of Innocence'

78 I have carried the manuscript of these translations about with me for days, reading it in railway trains, or on the top of omnibuses and in restaurants, and I have often had to close it lest some stranger would see how much it moved me. These lyrics which are in the original, my.... (Indian friends) tell me , full of subtlety of rhythm, of untranslatable delicacies of colour, of metrical invention display in their thought a world I have dreamed of all my life long. The work of a supreme culture, they yet appear as much a growth of the common soil as the grass and the rushes. A tradition, where poetry and religion are the same thing, has passed through the centuries, gathering from learned and unlearned metaphor and emotion, and carried back again to the multitude the thought of the scholar and the noble. If the civilisation of Bengal remains unbroken, if that common mind which as one divines runs through all, is not, a with us, broken into a dozen minds that know nothing of each other, something even of what is most subtle in these verses will have come, in a few generations, to the beggar on the roads.

—W.B. Yeats, from Introduction to Rabindranath Tagore's Gitanjali

In this passage, Yeats praises Indian culture primarily because it

(a) embodies values and gives rise to art that can be shared by people of all classes.
(b) reflects a marvellous eclecticism in drawing from many disparate cultures.
(c) is accessible to Westerners though it is rooted in different religious tradition.
(d) has been flexible enough to survive a transition into the modern world.

79 "Reality is that nothing happens. How many of the events of history have occurred, ask yourselves, for this and for that reason, but for no other reason fundamentally, than the desire to make things happen ? I present to you History, the fabrication, the diversion, the reality obscuring drama".

Which postmodern novel thus subverts the truth claims of traditional historiography?

(a) Graham Swift's *Waterland*
(b) A.S. Byatt's *Possession*
(c) John Fowles's *The French Lieutenant's Woman*
(d) Michael Ondaatje's *The English Patient*

80 What comes 'After great pain' in the famous Emily Dickinson poem?

(a) A concrete simplicity
(b) The letting go
(c) A formal feeling
(d) Substantial light

81 What type of writing did Walter Pater define as "The special and opportune art to the modern world"?

(a) Nonfiction Prose (b) Comic drama
(c) The lyric (d) The novel

82 Which ancient Greek writer's name is directly mentioned in Lord Byron's poem 'The Isles of Greece'?

(a) Sophocles (b) Euripides (c) Sappho (d) Aeschylus

83 Braj Kachru has observed a tendency among Indian-English speakers and writers to use hybridised lexical items. One example of this is

(a) Lathi-charge (b) Jugarh
(c) Ping-pong (d) Chaywallah

84 Nicholas Nickleby firmly established Charles Dickens as a dominant novelist of his time and the book as an unrivalled literary phenomenon. To celebrate the completion of the book, a painter noted that there had been nothing comparable to him since the days of Samuel Richardson. Identefy the painter.

(a) David Wilkie (b) John Cruickshank
(c) Ernest Dawson (d) Leonard Woolf

85 Who among the following are referred to as the "Scottish Chaucerians"?

(i) Thomas Hoccleve (ii) Robert Henryson
(iii) John Lydgate (iv) William Dunbar

The right combination according to the code is.

Codes

(a) (i) and (ii) (b) (iii) and (iv)
(c) (ii) and (iii) (d) (ii) and (iv)

86 Match the writer with the work.

Writer	Name of work
A. George Puttenham	1. Leviathan
B. Thomas Sprat	2. The Practice of Piety
C. Lewis Bayly	3. The Art of English Poesy
D. Thomas Hobbes	4. The History of the Royal Society

Codes

	A	B	C	D		A	B	C	D
(a)	4	3	2	1	(b)	3	4	2	1
(c)	3	2	4	1	(d)	3	4	1	2

87 Which of the following poems is quoted as the epigraph to A Raisin in the Sun by Lorraine Hansberry?

(a) 'The Big Sea'
(b) 'The Negro Speaks of Rivers'
(c) 'Harlem (A Dream Deferred)'
(d) 'I, too, Sing America'

88 Given below are two statements, one labelled as Assertion (A) and the other labelled as Reason (R). Read the statements and choose the correct answer using the code given below.

Assertion (A) Gender studies do not see an urgent need to help us navigate the various pitfalls of racism, ethnocentrism, cultural relativism, and plain ignorance that flow form using "culture" as an explanatory tool.

Reason (R) Issues relating to women's rights, gender roles, sexuality and family obligations are centrally implicated in the so-called clash or civilisations between Christianity of Secularism, and Islam.

Codes

(a) (R) is (A) and vice versa
(b) (R) does not follow logically from (A)
(c) (A) is only partly addressed in (R)
(d) (A) and (R) are most logically related

89 "We know now that a text is not a line of words releasing a single 'theological' meaning (the 'message' of the Author- God) but a multidimensional space in which a variety of writings, none of them original, blend and clash .... literature .... be refusing to assign a 'secret', an ultimate meaning, to the text (and to the world as text) liberates what may by called an anti-theological activity, an activity that is truly revolutionary since to refuse to fix meaning is, in the end to refuse God and his hypostases reason, science, law".

The passage comes from which of the following essays?

(a) 'What is an Author?' by Michel Foucault
(b) 'Tradition and Individual Talent' by TS Eliot
(c) 'The Death of the Author' by Roland Barthes
(d) 'Discourse in the Novel' by Mikhail Bakhtin

90 The enigmatic castle which K attempts to reach in vain in Franz Kafka's *The Castle* belongs to

(a) Count Aloofwest
(b) Count Strangewest
(c) Count Westwest
(d) Count Eastwest

91 Who among the ancients prescribed that poetry should both instruct and delight?

(a) Longinus (b) Aristotle (c) Plotinus (d) Horace

92 Albert Camus borrows the following epigraph to his novel 'The Plague' from............. .

"It is as reasonable to represent one kind of imprisonment by another, as it is to represent anything the really exists by that which exists not."

(a) Deniel Defoe's Robinson Crusoe
(b) Robert Burton's The Anatomy of Melancholy
(c) Jeremy Bentham's The Principles of Morals and Legislation
(d) James Hogg's The Confessions of a Justified Sinner

93 Which of the following acts were not passed during the Victorian Era?

(a) The Married Women's Property Rights Act
(b) The Women's Suffrage Act
(c) The Custody Act
(d) A Series of Factory Acts

94 What tone will be best suited to the following poem?

THE COMING OF WISDOM WITH AGE

Though leaves are many, the root is one;
Through all the lying days of my youth
I swayed my leaves and flowers in the sun;
Now I may wither into the truth.

(a) Exultation
(b) Revulsion
(c) Regret
(d) Excitement

95 What is an 'implied reader'?

(a) The ideal reader of a work of literature which is approximated over time by successive responses of generations of actual readers.
(b) The ideal audience envisioned by the author and to whom the work of literature is supposedly addressed.
(c) The ideal 'average' reader who can approach a work of literature with no preconceived ideas about the author's life, the time of composition, etc.
(d) A reader who embodies all those predispositions necessary for a literary work to exercise its effect.

96 "Search the heads of the greatest rivers in the world, you shall find them but bubbles of water."

Who is the author of this line?

(a) Oscar Wilde
(b) John Webster
(c) R.B. Sheridan
(d) Francis Bacon

97 Which interpretation of Keats' 'Beauty is truth, truth beauty' best represents the mimetic perspective?

(a) A work of literature is "beautiful" insofar as it offers an accurate representation of its subject matter, with fully realised characters and vivid description of events.
(b) Those aspects of reality which we perceive to be "beautiful" are the only worthy subject matter of the artist, and it is the artist's job to observe closely and isolate those sublime elements from the flux of the mundane.
(c) The author's arbitrary imposition of order upon the chaotic impressions of reality constitutes the only "truth" in a work of art.
(d) The line is an ironic quotation, the equation of "beauty" and "truth" as "all we know on earth" suggests that reality is an illusory concept and that the primary function of art is to construct a world within an aesthetic reality of its own.

Comprehension

The following is an extract from a famous play. Read it carefully to answer questions that follow.

Maid [From the hall doorway,] Ma'am, a lady to see you
Nora All right, let her come in.
[........The Maid shows in Mrs. Linde, dressed in travelling clothes, and shuts the door after her.]
Mrs. Linde: [In a dispirited and somewhat hesitant voice.] Hello, Nora.
Nora: [Uncertain] Hello
Mrs. Linde: You don't recognize me.
Nora: No, I don't know but wait, I think—[Exclaiming.] What! What! What Is it really you?
Mrs. Linde; Yes, It's me.
Nora: Kristine! To think I didn't recognize you. But then, how could I? (More quietly).
How you' ve changed, Kristine!
Mrs. Linde: Yes, no doubt I have. In nine—ten long years.
Nora It is so long since we met! Yes, it's all of that. Oh these last eight years have been a happy time, believe me. And so now you've come in to town, too. Made the long trip in the winter. That took courage.
Mrs. Linde: I just got here by ship this morning.
Nora: To enjoy yourself over Christmas, Of course, Oh, how lovely! Yes, enjoy ourselves, we'll do that. But take your coat off. You're not still cold? (Helping her.) There now' let's get cozy here by the stove. No, the easy chair there ! I'll take the rocker here. (Seizing her hands.) Yes, now you have your old look again it was only in that first moment. You're a bit more pale, Kristine and maybe a bit thinner.
Mrs Linde And much, much older, Nora.
Nora: Yes, perhaps a bit older; a tiny, thiny bit; not much at all [Stopping short suddenly serious] Oh, but thoughtless me, to sit here, chattering away. Sweet, good Kristine, can you forgive me?
Mrs. Linde: What do you mean, Nora?
Nora: (Softly.) Poor Kristine, you've become a widow.
Mrs. Linde : Yes, three years ago .
Nora : Oh, I knew it, Of course; I read it in the papers, Oh, Kristine, you must believe me; I often thought of writing you then, but kept postponing it, and something always interfered.
Mrs. Linde: Nora dear, I understand completely
Nora: No, it was awful of me, Kristine, You poor thing, how much you have gone through. And he left you nothing?
Mrs.Linde: No
Nora : And no children?
Mrs. Linde: No.
Nora: Nothing at all, then?
Mrs. Linde: Not even a sense of loss to feed on.
Nora: (Looking incredulously at her). But Kristine, how could that be?
Mrs. Linde: (Smiling wearily and smoothing her hair.) Oh, sometimes it happens, Nora.
Nora: So completely alone. How terribly hard that must be for you. I have three lovely children. You can't see them now; they're out with the maid.

98 Which of the following descriptions best applies to the above extract?

(a) A chance meeting between old friends which leaves one puzzling over the inexplicable losses the other suffered.
(b) Friends comparing notes and counting losses in a meeting sudden and unanticipated.
(c) The sense of loss inevitable with the passage of time and the imperceptible dissolution of the conventional marriage.
(d) A meeting of two friends-one married, the other unmarried after a gap of years.

Comprehension

The following is an extract from a famous play. Read it carefully to answer questions that follow.

Maid: [From the hall doorway,] Ma'am, a lady to see you—

Nora: All right, let her come in.

[........The Maid shows in Mrs. Linde, dressed in travelling clothes, and shuts the door after her.]

Mrs. Linde: [In a dispirited and somewhat hesitant voice.] Hello, Nora.

Nora: [Uncertain.] Hello—

Mrs. Linde: You don't recognize me.

Nora: No, I don't know—but wait, I think—[Exclaiming.] What! What! Is it really you?

Mrs. Linde; Yes, It's me.

Nora: Kristine! To think I didn't recognize you. But then, how could I? (More quietly).

How you' ve changed, Kristine!

Mrs. Linds: Yes, no doubt I have. In nine—ten long years.

Nora: It is so long since we met! Yes, it's all of that. Oh, these last eight years have been a happy time, believe me. And so now you've come in to town, too. Made the long trip in the winter. That took courage.

Mrs. Linde: I just got here by ship this morning.

Nora: To enjoy yourself over Christmas, of course, Oh, how lovely! Yes, enjoy ourselves, we'll do that. But take your coat off. You're not still cold? (Helping her.) There now let's get cozy here by the stove. No, the easy chair there ! I'II take the rocker here. (Seizing her hands.) Yes, now you have your old look again; it was only in that first moment. You're a bit more pale, Kristine-and maybe a bit thinner.

Mrs: Linde: And much much older, Nora.

Nora: Yes, perhaps a bit older; a tiny, tiny bit, not much at all [Stopping short suddenly serious.] Oh, but thoughtless me, to sit here, chattering away, Sweet, good Kristine, can you forgive me?

Mrs. Linde: What do you mean, Nora?

Nora: (Softly). Poor Kristine, you've become a widow.

Mrs. Linde : Yes, three years ago .

Nora : Oh, I knew it, of course; I read it in the papers, Oh, Kristine, you must believe me; I often thought of writing you then, but kept postponing it, and something always interfered.

Mrs. Linde: Nora dear, I understand completely.

Nora: No, it was awful of me, Kristine, You poor thing, how much you have gone through. And he left you nothing?

Mrs.Linde: No

Nora : And no children?

Mrs. Linde: No.

Nora: Nothing at all, then?

Mrs. Linde: Not even a sense of loss to feed on.

Nora: (Looking incredulously at her.) But Kristine, how could that be?

Mrs. Linde: (Smiling wearily and smoothing her hair.) Oh, sometimes it happens, Nora.

Nora: So completely alone. How terribly hard that must be for you. I have three lovely children. You can't see them now; they're out with the maid.

99 Identify the play of which this section is an excerpt.

(a) Wit by Margaret Edson
(b) The Cherry Orchard by Anton Chekhov
(c) The Importance of Being Earnest by Oscar Wilde
(d) A Doll's House by Henrik Ibsen

The following is an extract from a famous play. Read it carefully to answer questions that follow.

Maid: [From the hall doorway,] Ma'am, a lady to see you—

Nora: All right, let her come in.

[........The Maid shows in Mrs. Linde, dressed in travelling clothes, and shuts the door after her.]

Mrs. Linde: [In a dispirited and somewhat hesitant voice.] Hello, Nora.

Nora: [Uncertain.] Hello—

Mrs. Linde: You don't recognize me.

Nora: No, I don't know—but wait, I think—[Exclaiming.] What! What! Is it really you?

Mrs. Linde; Yes, It's me.

Nora: Kristine! To think I didn't recognize you. But then, how could I? (More quietly).

How you' ve changed, Kristine!

Mrs. Linds: Yes, no doubt I have. In nine—ten long years.

Nora: It is so long since we met! Yes, it's all of that. Oh, these last eight years have been a happy time, believe me. And so now you've come in to town, too. Made the long trip in the winter. That took courage.

Mrs. Linde: I just got here by ship this morning.

Nora: To enjoy yourself over Christmas, Of course, Oh, how lovely! Yes, enjoy ourselves, we'll do that. But take your coat off. you're not still cold? (Helping her.) There now let's get cozy here by the stove. No, the easy chair there ! I'II take the rocker here. (Seizing her hands.) Yes, now you have your old look again; it was only in that first moment. You're a bit more pale, Kristine-and maybe a bit thinner.

Mrs: Linde: And much, much older, Nora.

Nora: Yes, perhaps a bit older; a tiny, tiny bit, not much at all [Stopping short suddenly serious.] Oh, but thoughtless me, to sit here, chattering away. Sweet, good Kristine, can you forgive me?

Mrs. Linde: What do you mean, Nora?

Nora: (Softly). 1 Poor Kristine, you've become a widow.

Mrs. Linde : Yes, three years ago .

Nora : Oh, I knew it, of course; I read it in the papers, Oh, Kristine, you must believe me; I often thought of writing you then, but kept postponing it, and something always interfered.

Mrs. Linde: Nora dear, I understand completely

Nora: No, it was awful of me, Kristine, You poor thing, how much you have gone through. And he left you nothing?

Mrs.Linde: No

Nora : And no children?

Mrs. Linde: No.

Nora: Nothing at all, then?

Mrs. Linde: Not even a sense of loss to feed on.

Nora: (Looking incredulously at her.) But Kristine, how could that be?
Mrs. Linde: (Smiling wearily and smoothing her hair.) Oh, sometimes it happens, Nora.
Nora: So completely alone. How terribly hard that must be for you I have three lovely children. You can't see them now; they're out with the maid.

100 'Not even a sense of loss to feed on' implies that

(a) Mrs. Linde is sentimentally attached to an irretrievable past
(b) Mrs. Linde is given over to feeding on sorrow.
(c) Mrs. Linde's severance from her tragic pair is total.
(d) Mrs. Linde is completely devoid of all feeling.

ANSWERS

1. *(c)*	2. *(b)*	3. *(b)*	4. *(a)*	5. *(c)*	6. *(d)*	7. *(c)*	8. *(d)*	9. *(b)*	10. *(b)*
11. *(d)*	12. *(c)*	13. *(a)*	14. *(b)*	15. *(b)*	16. *(c)*	17. *(c)*	18. *(b)*	19. *(d)*	20. *(a)*
21. *(c)*	22. *(c)*	23. *(d)*	24. *(b)*	25. *(d)*	26. *(a)*	27. *(c)*	28. *(a)*	29. *(a)*	30. *(c)*
31. *(d)*	32. *(d)*	33. *(c)*	34. *(d)*	35. *(d)*	36. *(d)*	37. *(a)*	38. *(a)*	39. *(c)*	40. *(c)*
41. *(c)*	42. *(a)*	43. *(a)*	44. *(b)*	45. *(b)*	46. *(c)*	47. *(a)*	48. *(a)*	49. *(a)*	50. *(a)*
51. *(d)*	52. *(c)*	53. *(c)*	54. *(b)*	55. *(c)*	56. *(a)*	57. *(c)*	58. *(b)*	59. *(d)*	60. *(a)*
61. *(d)*	62. *(b)*	63. *(a)*	64. *(c)*	65. *(c)*	66. *(c)*	67. *(c)*	68. *(b)*	69. *(d)*	70. *(d)*
71. *(d)*	72. *(b)*	73. *(d)*	74. *(b)*	75. *(a)*	76. *(d)*	77. *(a)*	78. *(a)*	79. *(c)*	80. *(d)*
81. *(d)*	82. *(c)*	83. *(a)*	84. *(c)*	85. *(b)*	86. *(c)*	87. *(d)*	88. *(b)*	89. *(c)*	90. *(c)*
91. *(b)*	92. *(d)*	93. *(a)*	94. *(d)*	95. *(c)*	96. *(d)*	97. *(b)*	98. *(a)*	99. *(c)*	100. *(a)*

ENGLISH

Solved Paper, July 2018

General Instructions

1. There are total one hundred questions in this paper. Each question carries 2 marks.
2. All questions are compulsory.

---

1 **Which narrative poem by Lord Tennyson presents the story of a fisherman turned merchantsailor who, after a shipwreck, is marooned on a desert island ?**

(a) 'Crossing the Bar' (b) 'Tithonus'
(c) 'Enoch Arden' (d) 'Maud'

2 **In "Memorial Verses" Matthew Arnold pays tribute to three great poets. Who are they ?**

(a) Goethe, Shakespeare, Wordsworth
(b) Goethe, Shakespeare, Milton
(c) Shakespeare, Milton, Wordsworth
(d) Goethe, Wordsworth, Byron

3 **Who among the following English playwrights wrote screenplays on novels such as Marcel Proust's In Search of Lost Time, John Fowles's French Lieutenant's Woman, and Margaret Atwood's Handmaid's Tale ?**

(a) John Arden (b) Edward Bond
(c) Harold Pinter (d) David Hare

4 **The years in English literary history between 1649 and 1660 are known as ....**

(a) the Neo-classical period (b) the Commonwealth period
(c) the Stuart period (d) the Jacobean period

5 **In RK Narayan's Swami and Friends, which game offers Swami the best kind of emotional release from the strains and pressures of disagreeable circumstances ?**

(a) cricket (b) football (c) tennis (d) hockey

6 **William Blake expressed the importance of the particular when he said that "To Generalize is to be .... To particularize is the alone Distinction of Merit." Fill in the blank.**

(a) an idiot (b) a poet
(c) a dreamer (d) a skunk

7 **Which of the following was not a dialect of Old English ?**

(a) Irish
(b) Northumbrian
(c) Mercian
(d) Kentish

8 **Anthony Burgess's last novel, published in 1993, is called A Dead Man in Deptford. Who is the central character to whom the title refers?**

(a) Sir Walter Raleigh (b) Sir Philip Sidney
(c) Christopher Marlowe (d) Earl of Southampton

9 **Choose the correct chronological order :**

(a) William Caxton prints the first English book - William Shakespeare's First Folio - John Milton's Areopagitica - 'Tottel's Miscellany' (Songs and Sonnets).
(b) 'Tottel's Miscellany' (Songs and Sonnets) - William Shakespeare's First Folio - William Caxton prints the first English book - John Milton's Areopagitica.
(c) William Caxton prints the first English book - 'Tottel's Miscellany' (Songs and Sonnets)- William Shakespeare's First Folio - John Milton's Areopagitica.
(d) William Shakespeare's First Folio - John Milton's Areopagitica - William Caxton prints the first English book - 'Tottel's Miscellany' (Songs and Sonnets).

10 What does the phrase ut pictura poesis from Horace's Art of Poetry mean ?

(a) "as in painting, so in poetry"
(b) "poetry beggars pictorial description"
(c) "as in poetry, so in painting"
(d) "picture above all poetry"

11 Who among the following is the author of Account of the Augustan Age in England (1759) ?

(a) John Gay (b) William Hazlitt
(c) Oliver Goldsmith (d) Samuel Johnson

12 In how many parts did Cervantes publish his novel, Don Quixote ?

(a) three (b) five (c) two (d) twelve

13 Lytton Strachey's Eminent Victorians carries biographical sketches of writers and public figures. Identify the list below that correctly mentions those Eminent Victorians.

(a) Cardinal Manning, Florence Nightingale, Thomas Arnold and General Gordon
(b) A.E.W. Mason, Sir Arthur Quiller Couch, Matthew Arnold, Robert Bridges
(c) E.F. Benson, Cardinal Manning, Lord Tennyson, Beatrice Webb
(d) George Harding, General Gordon, Robert Browning, Mrs Humphrey Ward

14 One of the following statements about the eponymous saint of Dryden's "Song for St. Cecilia's Day" is incorrect. Identify that statement.

(a) St Cecilia was a Roman lady, an early Christian martyr
(b) St Cecilia was an Armenian devotee of the Christian faith
(c) St. Cecilia's festival is celebrated on 22 November in England
(d) St Cecilia was a patroness of music who was fabled to have invented the organ

15 Which of the statements on Michael Roberts's Faber Book of Modern Verse (1936) is not true ?

(a) His anthology canonized modern poetry and poets for quite some decades
(b) The collection begins with the poems of Robert Bridges
(c) Roberts omitted the Georgian poets in his anthology
(d) Yeats, Eliot and Pound find a place in the Faber Book of 1936

16 Who among the following proposed that the First Gulf War had never taken place, it was simply a hyperreal, media-generated spectacle ?

(a) Richard Rorty (b) Jean-Francois Lyotard
(c) Jean Baudrillard (d) Umberto Eco

17 Sir Thomas Browne's Urn Burial was prompted by ....

(a) the discovery of ancient burial-urns near Norwich
(b) the contemporary researches on burial rites in Norway
(c) the death of St Francis of Assissi and his burial
(d) the publication of the English Book of Common Prayer

18 Identify from among the following list those that cannot be called War Fiction.

1. A Modern Instance
2. Catch - 22
3. The Age of Innocence
4. The Naked and the Dead

Codes

(a) 1 and 4
(b) 2 and 3
(c) 1 and 3
(d) 2 and 4

19 Who among the following writers was not the one identified with The Movement of the 1950's England ?

(a) Roy Fuller
(b) Kingsley Amis
(c) Philip Larkin
(d) Donald Davie

20 Which of the following novels does not belong to Nuruddin Farah's Blood In the Sun Trilogy ?

(a) Maps (b) Knots
(c) Gifts (d) Secrets

21 In the following series, which one has all the poets correctly matched with their poems ?

(a) Ezekiel, 'Poet, Lover, Birdwatcher'; Ramanujan, 'Small-scale Reflections on a Great House'; Dutt, 'Sunset at Puri'; Mahapatra, 'Our Casuarina Tree'.
(b) Ezekiel, 'Sunset at Puri'; Ramanujan, 'Small-scale Reflections on a Great House'; Dutt, 'Our Casuarina Tree'; Mahapatra, 'Poet, Lover, Birdwatcher'.
(c) Ezekiel, 'Poet, Lover, Birdwatcher'; Ramanujan, 'Sunset at Puri'; Dutt, 'Our Casuarina Tree'; Mahapatra, 'Small-scale Reflections on a Great House'.
(d) Ezekiel, 'Poet, Lover, Birdwatcher'; Ramanujan, 'Small-scale Reflections on a Great House'; Dutt, 'Our Casuarina Tree'; Mahapatra, 'Sunset at Puri'.

22 From among the following, identify the incorrect observation regarding Ferdinand de Saussure's seminal distinction between langue and parole.

(a) Parole is the particular language system, the elements of which we learn as children, and which is codified in our grammars and dictionaries, whereas langue is the language-occasion (what A says to B).
(b) A language consists in the interrelationship between langue and parole.
(c) Saussure made this crucial distinction in a study called A Course in General Linguistics (1916).
(d) Langue is the particular language-system, the elements of which we learn as children, and which is codified in our grammars and dictionaries, whereas parole is the language-occasion (what A says to B).

23 John Heywood wrote a farcical interlude called The Four P's. Who were the Four P's ?

(a) a Palmer, a Pedlar, a Pothecary, a Packer
(b) a Printer, a Pedlar, a Pothecary, a Palmer
(c) a Pedlar, a Parson, a Palmer, a Pothecary
(d) a Palmer, a Pardoner, a Pothecary, a Pedlar

24 In the mechanical drill method of second language acquisition

1. The learner has the freedom to choose from many responses.
2. The learner's response is totally controlled.
3. Comprehension of the item by the learner is not required.
4. Comprehension of the item by the learner is obligatory.

The right combination according to the code is

(a) 1 and 4 (b) 1 and 3
(c) 2 and 3 (d) 2 and 4

25 Thou wilt not wake
Till I thy fate shall overtake;
Till age, or grief, or sickness must
Marry my body to that dust
It so much loves; and fill the room
My heart keeps empty in thy Tomb.
Stay for me there; I will not fail
To meet thee in that hollow Vale.
And think not much of my delay;
I am already on the way.
Which of the following readings do you find appropriate to the spirit of the lines above ?

(a) In that interspace between the lines, the ending of one and the beginning of another, there is a silent internal language, the poem'89s language-within-language, tacitly signalled through the deployment of rhymed space.
(b) Ageing and dying are of course helplessly passive; but here love makes them as though they were now also willing things in the husband eager to join his dead wife. Through simple intimate tones of their shared earthly life - stay for me, wait for me, I will not fail - he not only imagines her but imagines her thinking of him.
(c) The lyric voice here can feel the poem speaking back to him - in the cold lineal stare of 'there was nothing in my belief' - even as his dead wife did not. It is as though the poem itself then demands his response, in order to be able to move from one line to another. To attempt that movement in keeping the poem's space alive, the lyric voice asserts, "I will not fail/To meet there in that hollow Vale."
(d) My whole nature was so penetrated with grief and humiliation of such considerations, that, even now, famous and caressed and happy as I am, I often forget in my dream that I have a dear wife who died, leaving me alone in this world. Even that I am a man, and now I wander desolately back to that time of our lives when my wife and I shared moments of bliss.

26 Match the characters with the novels

(a) Arthur Seaton	(i) Top Girls
(b) Marlene	(ii) The Golden Notebook
(c) Anna Wulf	(iii) The Swimming Pool Library
(d) Beckwith	(iv) Saturday Night and Sunday Morning

Codes

	(a)	(b)	(c)	(d)
(a)	(ii)	(iii)	(i)	(iv)
(b)	(iv)	(i)	(ii)	(iii)
(c)	(iii)	(iv)	(ii)	(i)
(d)	(ii)	(iv)	(iii)	(i)

27 The very last passage of a novel is given below. Identify the novel. "Welcome, O life, I go to encounter for the millionth time the reality of experience and to forge in the smithy of my soul the uncreated conscience of my race. April 27. Old father, old artificer, stand me now and ever in good stead."

(a) To the light house
(b) A Portrait of the Artist as a Young Man
(c) Maurice
(d) Almayer's Folly

28 Francis Bacon's New Atlantis is about a utopian state called ....

(a) Asgard (b) Avalon
(c) Bensalem (d) Baltia

29 The 1950's saw the rise of backlash against modernism and against New Romanticism that became known as The Movement. Which of the following little magazines came to be associated with The Movement ?

1. Departure
2. New Verse
3. London Mercury
4. New Poems

The right combination according to the code is

(a) 1 and 2 (b) 3 and 4
(c) 1 and 4 (c) 2 and 4

30 The error of interpreting a literary work by referring to evidence outside of itself, such as the design and purpose of the author is called ....

(a) Affective fallacy (b) Intentional fallacy
(c) Authorial fallacy (d) Synecdochic fallacy

31 A.R. Ammons parodies a famous poem in his "Swoggled" I'd rather be suckled by an outworn pagan than get my horn wreathed in an old triton. Which poet, which poem ?

(a) John Keats, 'On First Looking into Chapman's Homer'
(b) John Milton, 'On His Blindness'
(c) William Wordsworth, 'The World is Too Much with Us'
(d) Elizabeth B. Browning, 'How do I Love Thee... ?'

32 Fanny Burney's Evelina carries the subtitle

(a) or a Naive Lady's Entrance into the World
(b) or a Young Lady's Entrance into the World
(c) or a Young Lady's Exit from the World
(d) or a Bold Lady's Entrance into the Hall

33 What does Philip Sidney call poet-haters in his Defence of Poesie ?

(a) Misogynists (b) Misanthropes
(c) Misnomers (d) Mysomousoi

34 Who, among the following, raises the following painful question of longing and belonging ?
"Where shall I turn, divided to the vein ?
I who have cursed
The drunken officer of British rule, how choose
Between this Africa and the English tongue I love?"

(a) Derek Walcott (b) Louise Bennett
(c) Kamau Brathwaite (d) Wole Soyinka

35 In the 1940's, a critic and a philosopher produced two influential and controversial papers called 'The Intentional Fallacy' and 'The Affective Fallacy'. Identify them.

1. Cleanth Brooks
2. Monroe C. Beardsley
3. William K. Wimsalt Jr.
4. R.P. Blackmur

The right combination according to the code is :

(a) 1 and 2 (b) 2 and 4
(c) 2 and 3 (d) 3 and 4

36 Philip Larkin's 'Sad Steps' notices "The way the moon dashes through clouds that blow Loosely as cannon-smoke to stand apart...." The poem alludes to

(a) Coleridge's 'Dejection : An Ode'
(b) The moonlit scenes in A Midsummer Night's Dream
(c) Philip Sidney's Astrophel and Stella
(d) T.S. Eliot's 'Morning at the Window'

37 Match the following opening lines with their respective titles :

(a) "I leant upon a coppice gate"	(i) "Thirteen Blackbirds"
(b) "A sudden blow : the great wings beating still...."	(ii) "Sympathy"
(c) "Among twenty snowy mountains"	(iii) "The Darkling Thrush"
(d) "I know what the caged bird feels, alas..."	(iv) "Leda and the Swan"

Codes

(a) (b) (c) (d)
(a) (iv) (iii) (ii) (i)
(b) (iii) (iv) (i) (ii)
(c) (ii) (i) (iii) (iv)
(d) (i) (ii) (iv) (iii)

38 Identify the titles that were published in the 1920's.

(a) Look, Stranger (b) The Tower
(c) The Waste Land (d) The Road to Wigan Pier

Codes

(a) 1 and 3 (b) 2 and 3
(c) 2 and 4 (d) 3 and 4

39 This novel is dedicated 'To the railroad of bones' and has as its epigraph the line, "I am the woman they give dead women's clothes to" from Christine Gelineau's 'Inheritance'. Identify the novel.

(a) African Psycho by Alain Mabanckou
(b) The Chibok Girls by Helon Habila
(c) The Underground Railroad by Colson Whitehead
(d) The Book of Night Women by Marlon James

40 An English poet couldn't help the excitement that an historical event caused in his life-time :
Bliss was it in that dawn to be alive,
But to be young was very heaven.
Which poet ? What 'dawn'?

(a) W.H. Auden ; the Spanish Civil War
(b) Lord Tennyson ; the Jubilee of Queen Victoria's reign
(c) William Wordsworth ; the French Revolution
(d) William Blake ; the Industrial Revolution

41 Which novel by John Banville tells the story of a group of travellers who arrive on a small island and stumble upon the house of Prof. Kreutznaer whose relationship to a painting entitled The Golden World by a fictional Dutch artist named Vaublin plays a central role ?

(a) Ghosts (b) The Sea (c) The Ark (d) Eclipse

42 Identify the two plays, usually paired for their critique of the politics of language and acts of police interrogation.

(a) Earthly Powers, The Wanting Seed
(b) Chicken Soup with Barley, Roots
(c) Left-handed Liberty, The Hero Rises
(d) One for the Road, Mountain Language

43 Semiotics originated mainly in the works of two theorists. They are :

1. Charles Sanders Peirce
2. Mikhail Bakhtin
3. Ferdinand de Saussure
4. Valentin Voloshinov

The right combination according to the code is

(a) 1 and 2 (b) 2 and 3
(c) 1 and 3 (d) 2 and 4

44 Burton's Anatomy of Melancholy was published in 1621 and expanded and altered in .... subsequent editions.

(a) two (b) four
(c) six (d) five

45 Which of the following magazines self-consciously created an identity for Vorticists, a group of painters, sculptors and writers?

(a) Blast (b) The Egoist
(c) The Criterion (d) New Age

46 "In every cry of every Man,
In every Infant's cry of fear,
In every voice, in every ban..."
The figure of speech characterized by repetition of words or group of words at the beginning of consecutive sentences is called ....

(a) apostrophe (b) anaphora
(c) incremental repetition (d) alliteration

47 **At whose behest does the Redcrosse Knight undertake his quest in The Faerie Queene ?**

(a) Gloriana's (b) Una's
(c) Duessa's (d) Prosperine's

48 **In which city did John Ruskin see a paradigm for Victorian Britain?**

(a) Vienna (b) Venice
(c) Rome (d) Paris

49 **Which novel of Kazuo Ishiguro is narrated by a Japanese widow living in England and draws on the destruction and rehabilitation of Nagasaki ?**

(a) An Artist of the Floating World
(b) The Unconsoled
(c) A Pale View of Hills
(d) When We Were Orphans

50 **Which novel opens thus : "Whether I shall turn out to be the hero of my own life, or whether that station will be held by anyone else, these pages must show."**

(a) Tristram Shandy (b) Lady Audley's Secret
(c) David Copperfield (d) Fitz-Boodle's Confessions

51 **Traces of the Morality plays are discernible in a play like Dr Faustus, traces such as ....**

(a) vernacular songs adapting secular themes
(b) its soliloquizing protagonist, Good and Bad Angels and its final moral
(c) its refrains from the Corpus Christi Carol, the complaint of Christ, the lover of mankind
(d) its rhythmical prose, and the presence of a larger narrative rhythm in the Morality plays

52 **The branch of philosophy that asks the question, "How do we know what we know ?" is ....**

(a) ontology (b) epistemology
(c) eschatology (d) phenomenology

53 **The eighteenth century practice in England of bookselling was midway between direct patronage and impersonal sales. A patron paid half the cost of a book before publication and half on delivery. The author of the book received these payments directly. The patron's name appeared in the preface for the book published in this manner. This practice was known as ....**

(a) Subscription (b) Contribution
(c) Pre-publication (d) Remaindering

54 **Oxford India has published a volume of Premchand translations in English, The Oxford India Premchand. Who among the following is not one of the translators ?**

(a) David Rubin (b) Alok Rai
(c) Gillian Wright (d) Christopher King

55 **Which of the two novels of Jane Austen have the spa town of Bath as a primary location ?**

1. Emma
2. Pride and Prejudice
3. Northanger Abbey
4. Persuasion

The right combination according to the code is

(a) 1 and 4 (b) 2 and 3
(c) 3 and 4 (d) 1 and 2

56 **In the communicative approach to ELT, the development of language learning or teaching involves a shift :**

1. from form-based to a meaning-based approach.
2. from an eclectic approach to a rigid method.
3. from teacher-centred to learner-centred classes.
4. from broad-based competence to specific needs.

The right combination, according to the code is

(a) 1 and 4 (b) 1 and 4
(c) 3 and 3 (d) 1 and 3

57 **The four Moral Essays of Alexander Pope are addressed to carefully selected figures. Identify the correct group.**

(a) Timons, Newton, Martha Blount, Wellington
(b) Lord Cobham, Robert Walpole, Houghton Hall, Chandos
(c) Martha Blount, Lord Cobham, Bathurst, Burlington
(d) William III, John Haydn, Joseph Addison, John Dennis

58 **Bertolt Brecht's Mother Courage and Her Children presents the war-torn Europe as its protagonist as she follows troops with her canteenwagon.**
What is the real name of Mother Courage ?

(a) Paula Danckert (b) Anna Fierling
(c) Jane Vanstone (d) Jani Lauzon

59 **From among the following, identify the journal that publishes articles on English language teaching and learning.**

(a) University of Toronto Quarterly
(b) Agenda
(c) TESOL Quarterly (d) English Language Notes

60 **Arrange the following elegies in English in chronological order.**

(a) 'Elegy Written in a Country Churchyard' - 'Adonais' - 'Thyrsis' - 'In Memoriam'
(b) 'Elegy Written in a Country Churchyard' - 'Adonais' - 'In Memoriam' - 'Thyrsis'
(c) 'Elegy Written in a Country Churchyard' - 'In Memoriam' - 'Adonais' - 'Thyrsis'
(d) 'Adonais' - 'Elegy Written in a Country Churchyard' - 'In Memoriam' - 'Thyrsis'

61 **Who is the only one of Milton's contemporaries to be mentioned by name in Paradise Lost ?**

(a) Francis Bacon
(b) Johannes Vermeer
(c) Gallileo
(d) King Charles 1

62 K.S. Maniam is a major writer of Indian origin, writing in English, born and living in Malaysia. Identify two of his novels from the following list.

1. The Rice Mother 2. The Return
3. Touching Earth 4. Between Lives

The right combination according to the code is

(a) 1 and 4 (b) 2 and 3 (c) 3 and 4 (d) 2 and 4

63 What did Thomas Percy collect in his Reliques?

(a) medieval folklore and lyrics of the Midlands
(b) old songs, ballads, and romances in English and Scots
(c) Highland lore, mostly oral wisdom of the Scots
(d) Romantic idylls, sonnets and odes

64 Nirad Chaudhuri's Autobiography of an Unknown Indian concludes with an essay on the course of Indian history. But in the penultimate chapter Chaudhuri concludes the account of events in his life. How does this narrative end ?

(a) Chaudhuri ties the knot with his childhood sweetheart and moves from Calcutta to Delhi
(b) Chaudhuri obtains a job in the military accounts department and gives it up because he finds it soul-destroying
(c) Chaudhuri joins the editorial team of a Calcutta newspaper and is upset over the drudgery of a reporter's life
(d) Chaudhuri rushes to his ancestral village Bangram on receiving the news of the death of his uncle and recalls his past life

65 In John Gower's Confessio Amantis, Amans, the lover makes his confession to the priest named ....

(a) Verito (b) Genius (c) Amor (d) Phoebe

66 In Eugene Ionesco's Chairs, the absurdity is not so much in the banal words that are uttered as ....

(a) in the large scale use of frightening stage props and lightning effects
(b) in the absurdist interpretation of them by character after character
(c) in the fact that they are spoken to an ever-growing number of empty chairs
(d) in the fact that they are spoken time and again by members of the audience

67 A half-sentence in Purchas his Pilgrimage triggered off 'Kubla Khan'. Whose work was Purchas his Pilgrimage ?

(a) Robert Herrick, the poet's
(b) John Hakluyt's, the collector of traveller's tales
(c) Samuel Purchas, the London Parson's
(d) Edward Purchas, the globe-trotter's

68 Based on the life of a thirteenth-century troubadour, from among the following identify the work, that marked a catastrophic failure in Robert Browning's poetic career, earning him a reputation for impenetrable difficulty ?

(a) Paracelsus (b) Sordello
(c) The Ring and The Book (d) Pauline

69 In Tristram Shandy, the Author's preface ....

(a) is hawked to the highest bidder.
(b) appears in-between chapters 13 and 14 in Volume II.
(c) is printed in italics in all editions.
(d) appears in-between chapters 10 and 11 in Volume I.

70 Evelyn Waugh once complained that TS Eliot's Poems, 1909-1925 was "marvellously good, but very hard to understand." The most pessimistic novel Waugh wrote was called .... and he owed the title to ....

(a) Black Mischief - 'Sweeney among the Nightingales'
(b) Scoop - 'Morning At the Window'
(c) Prancing Nigger - 'Ash Wednesday'
(d) A Handful of Dust - 'The Waste Land'

71 During the years 1830 to 1850, the illusion of peace in Victorian England was broken by such incidents as ....

(a) the Revolution in France and the Chartist Movement in England
(b) the General Strike of 1835 and the Rail Tragedy of 1847
(c) the visionary libertarianism of poets and the lawless embodiment of revolution
(d) the disaster of the Indian Mutiny and the incompetent bungling of the Crimean War

72 Gulliver receives the following response when he boasts about his countrymen : "... the most pernicious race of little odious vermin that nature ever suffered to crawl upon the face of the earth." Whose response?

(a) The King of Lilliput's (b) The King of Brobdingnag's
(c) The Governor of Glubbdubrib's
(d) The first of the Houyhnhnms's he meets

73 In the Inferno Dante, as he travels through the various circles of the hell finds Judas who is unable to speak. What is the reason behind this ?

(a) His tongue is transformed into a coiled snake.
(b) His head is battered and so he cannot open his mouth.
(c) Lucifer is chewing on his head.
(d) His tongue is pulled out and nailed on the tree of sin.

74 **Assertion** (A) Our reality is linguistic, a language mediated reality.
Reason (R) Our perception and understanding of reality are largely constructed by the words and other signs we use.

In the light of the statements above,

Codes

(a) Both A and R are true and R is the correct explanation of A
(b) Both A and R are true, but R is not the correct explanation of A
(c) A is true but R is false
(d) A is false but R is true

75 In his book, In Theory, Aijaz Ahmed works out the relations between the three entities

(a) Classes, Nations, Literatures
(b) Regions, Nation, Languages
(c) State, Religions, Gender
(d) Literature, Print, Theory

76 In 1660, a group of 12 people including Robert Boyle and Christopher Wren formed what they called the Royal Society. In 1663, it became The Royal Society of London for Improving Natural Knowledge. What was the Society's motto?

(a) 'In Him we trust' (b) 'In the words of no one'
(c) 'Lighted to lighten' (d) 'Love conquers all'

77 Of whom did W.B. Yeats say that "We were the last Romantics"?

(a) The Pre-Raphaelite Brotherhood
(b) The Imagiste poets
(c) His Friends in the Irish Literary Revival
(d) Himself and his lady love, Maud Gonne

78 Who wrote The Wandering Jew, a poem in four cantos and the short lyric, "The Wandering Jew's Soliloquy" ?

(a) ST Coleridge (b) Lord Byron
(c) Thomas Gray (d) PB Shelley

79 Where, according to TS Eliot, are we likely to only the best, but the most individual parts of a poet's work" ?

(a) in the poet's juvenilia or rejected drafts
(b) in the best anthologies and scrap-books
(c) in those parts where the dead poets assert their immortality
(d) in those parts where the living poets depart from their ancestors

80 Which of the following is true of The Canterbury Tales ?

(a) Chaucer, the pilgrim, narrates Sir Thopas' Tale only
(b) Chaucer, the pilgrim, narrates The Tale of Melibee only
(c) Chaucer, the pilgrim, narrates both Sir Thopas' Tale and The Tale of Melibee
(d) Chaucer, the pilgrim does attempt to narrate an unnamed tale but abruptly stops due to the intervention of the other pilgrims

81 During the reign of Norman Kings, it was fashionable to speak .... in upper-class circles in England.

(a) Norse (b) Latin
(c) Danish (d) French

82 Who, among the following, collaborated with Purohit Swami in translating the Ten Principal Upanishads into English ?

(a) Christopher Fry (b) Aldous Huxley
(c) Lawrence Durrell (d) WB Yeats

83 What unique distinction does Ben Jonson's 'To Penshurst' have in the English literary canon ?

(a) It is the only distinguished poem in English addressed to the Lords of Penshurst.
(b) It celebrates Philip Sidney's elevation to knighthood, Sidney being the youngest scion of the family.
(c) It is one of the first English poems celebrating a specific place, a forerunner to Cooper's Hill and Windsor-Forest.
(d) It is the first poem in an elegiac series that late Elizabethan poets began on the demise of the Lord of Penshurst.

84 It is well known that in many of his plays, Tom Stoppard has consciously drawn upon earlier, often reputed, works. Match the following Stoppard plays with earlier works whose spirit seems to have informed them.

(a) Rosencrantz and (i) Hamlet Guildenstern Are Dead
(b) Indian Ink (ii) A Passage to India
(c) Inspector Hound (iii) The Mousetrap
(d) Travesties (iv) Importance of Being Earnest

Codes

	(a)	(b)	(c)	(d)		(a)	(b)	(c)	(d)
(a)	(iii)	(ii)	(i)	(iv)	(b)	(i)	(ii)	(iv)	(iii)
(c)	(iv)	(iii)	(i)	(ii)	(d)	(ii)	(i)	(iv)	(iii)

85 After discovering the truth about his heinous crimes committed in the past, what does Oedipus request as his punishment ?

(a) exile
(b) castration
(c) decapitation
(d) blindness

86 How does Women in Love open ?

(a) Rupert Birkin, Lawrence's alter ego, is taking a walk in the English Countryside.
(b) The Brangwen sisters, Ursula and Gudrun, are 'working and talking.'
(c) The wedding party gathers at shortlands, the Criches's home.
(d) The last lesson is in progress, 'peaceful and still' in Ursula's classroom.

87 Samuel Johnson has the following to say about an English poet : "These images are marked by glittering accumulations of ungraceful ornaments: they strike, rather than please. The images are magnified by affectation : the language is laboured into harshness. The mind of the writer seems to work with unnatural violence - 'Double, double, toil and trouble'. He has a kind of strutting dignity, and is tall by walking on tiptoe. His art and his struggle are too visible, and there is too little appearance of ease and nature." Identify the poet.

(a) Thomas Gray (b) John Dryden
(c) John Milton (d) Thomas Wyatt

88 "Take the smoking disclaimer issue" begins Vishal Bharadwaj. "Putting a disclaimer every time somebody smokes on screen is not an answer. If MF Hussain had painted a man with a cigar, would you have asked him to put the disclaimer, "Cigarette smoking is injurious to health' on the painting" ? The point Bharadwaj makes with his rhetorical question is the following :

(a) The smoking disclaimer is ineffectual because MF Hussain's painting wouldn't have carried it.
(b) The smoking disclaimer on objects perceived as 'art' is simply superfluous.
(c) The smoking disclaimer is ineffectual because 'art' entertains but does not instruct.
(d) The smoking disclaimer on screen or on an MF Hussain painting distracts us from enjoying art.

89 According to ...., certain verbs actually 'perform' an act when they are uttered.

(a) Speech Act theorists such as Austin and Searle
(b) Russian Formalists such as Shklovsky and Propp
(c) Language theorists such as Sapir and Whorf
(d) Cognitive linguists such as Lakoff and Johnson

90 Haunted castles, strange noises, and an acceptance of the supernatural with all its trappings mark ....

(a) metafiction (b) fantasy fiction
(c) epistolary fiction (d) gothic fiction

91 .... sure it waits upon
Some god o' th' island. Sitting on a bank,
Weeping again the King my father's wrack,
This music crept by me upon the waters,
Allaying both their fury and my passion
With its sweet air. Thence I have followed it,
Or it hath drawn me rather....

1. These lines, spoken by Edgar in King Lear, are part of a long speech delivered on the heath.
2. These lines, spoken by Ferdinand in The Tempest, describe Ariel's music.
3. The passage reappears in an altered and ironic version in T.S. Eliot's Waste Land.
4. The passage reappears verbatim in W.H. Auden's Sea and the Mirror.

Which of the following statements on this passage are true?

(a) 1 and 4 (b) 2 and 3
(c) 3 and 4 (d) 1 and 3

92 Arrange the following plays of Shakespeare according to their periods (early, middle, late...) of composition.

(a) As You Like It, Love's Labours Lost, Antony and Cleopatra, The Tempest, Midsummer Night's Dream
(b) Antony and Cleopatra, The Tempest, Midsummer Night's Dream, Love's Labours Lost, As You Like It
(c) Love's Labours Lost, Midsummer Night's Dream, As You Like It, Antony and Cleopatra, The Tempest
(d) Midsummer Night's Dream, Antony and Cleopatra, The Tempest, As You Like It, Love's Labours Lost

93 Who among the following is not a reader-response critic ?

(a) Maud Bodkin
(b) Hans-Robert Jauss
(c) Stanley Fish
(d) Wolfgang Iser

94 Leo Tolstoy's Anna Karenina's closing lines present...

(a) a sad reflection on the unfortunate suicide of Anna which should have been averted
(b) the enlivening freshness of a rain which has been threatening to break out
(c) Levin's affirmation that whatever happens to him, life is not meaningless but unquestionably meaningful
(d) Vronsky's lament over the death of Anna which ends on a positive note, affirming the human tendency to pass over the tragic events with hope

95 Which of the following novels begins with a Prologue under the title 'The Storming of Seringapatam', saying 'I address these lines written in India - to my relatives in England'?

(a) The Siege of Krishnapur by JG Farell
(b) The Moonstone by Wilkie Collins
(c) The Sign of Four by Sir Arthur Conan Doyle
(d) The Jewel in the Crown by Paul Scott

96 In "Gerontion", T.S. Eliot says : "............ has many cunning passages, contrived corridors / And issues, deceives with whispering ambitions, / Guides us by vanities." What is Eliot's subject ?

(a) History (b) Politics (c) State (d) Religion

Directions (Q. Nos. 97-100) *Read the following poem and answer the questions that follow*

The Mountain
My students look at me expectantly.
I explain to them that the life of art is a life
of endless labor. Their expressions
hardly change; they need to know
a little more about endless labor.
So I tell them the story of Sisyphus,
how he was doomed to push
a rock up a mountain, knowing nothing
would come of this effort
but that he would repeat it
indefinitely. I tell them
there is joy in this, in the artist's life,
that one eludes
judgment, and as I speak
I am secretly pushing a rock myself,
slyly pushing it up the steep
face of a mountain. Why do I lie
to these children? They aren't listening,
they aren't deceived, their fingers

tapping at the wooden desks -
So I retract
the myth; I tell them it occurs
in hell, and that the artist lies
because he is obsessed with attainment,
that he perceives the summit
as that place where he will live for ever,
a place about to be
transformed by his burden: with every breath,
I am standing at the top of the mountain.
Both my hands are free. And the rock has added
height to the mountain.
(Louise Gluck)

97 Whose poetic voice is triggered right from the beginning ?
(a) of student's
(b) of teacher's
(c) of critics'
(d) of an observer's

98 The speaker brings up the story of Sisyphus specifically by way of glossing ....
(a) art in life (b) life in art
(c) endless labor (d) poetic expectation

99 In its context, the words 'their fingers / tapping at the wooden desks', best represent the students' ....
(a) lack of protest (b) lack of interest
(c) show of disrespect (d) show of impatience

100 Why does the speaker say that "the rock has added height to the mountain" ?
(a) because the speaker is already on the top of the mountain.
(b) because both the hands of the speaker are now free.
(c) because the mountain now seems largely incomprehensible.
(d) because she feels that the immensity of the problem has grown.

ANSWERS

1. (c)	2. (d)	3. (c)	4. (b)	5. (a)	6. (a)	7. (a)	8. (c)	9. (c)	10. (a)
11. (c)	12. (c)	13. (a)	14. (b)	15. (b)	16. (c)	17. (a)	18. (c)	19. (a)	20. (b)
21. (d)	22. (a)	23. (d)	24. (c)	25. (b)	26. (b)	27. (b)	28. (c)	29. (c)	30. (b)
31. (c)	32. (b)	33. (d)	34. (a)	35. (c)	36. (c)	37. (b)	38. (b)	39. (d)	40. (c)
41. (a)	42. (d)	43. (c)	44. (d)	45. (a)	46. (b)	47. (*)	48. (b)	49. (c)	50. (c)
51. (b)	52. (b)	53. (a)	54. (c)	55. (c)	56. (d)	57. (c)	58. (b)	59. (c)	60. (b)
61. (c)	62. (d)	63. (b)	64. (b)	65. (b)	66. (c)	67. (c)	68. (b)	69. (*)	70. (d)
71. (d)	72. (b)	73. (c)	74. (a)	75. (a)	76. (b)	77. (c)	78. (d)	79. (c)	80. (c)
81. (d)	82. (d)	83. (c)	84. (*)	85. (a)	86. (b)	87. (a)	88. (b)	89. (a)	90. (d)
91. (b)	92. (c)	93. (a)	94. (c)	95. (b)	96. (a)	97. (b)	98. (c)	99. (d)	100. (d)

NTA
UGC
NET/JRF/SET

ENGLISH

CHAPTER 01

Ancient, Medieval and Anglo-Norman Drama

Drama is believed to have started its journey as early as 5th century BC. The main function of drama is to reflect society and its current culture. Modes of drama keep changing from time to time. Mystery and Morality plays were the most popular form during the Anglo-Norman and the Revival Age. *Everyman* is considered to be the best morality play of the said age.

In this Chapter

- Drama : An Introduction
- Ancient and Medieval Drama
- Anglo-Norman Literature
- Drama of the Age of Revival
- Important Dramatists of the Age of Revival

Drama: An Introduction

The word 'drama' is derived from the Greek word 'chan' which means to do or to perform. Technically it means a deed or action on the stage. Drama has a particular relation with action. A cursory glance at its history clearly shows that since its inception, action has been an integral part of drama. Drama is neither the name of statements in dialogue nor just a collection of characters as well as events nor is it just entertainment and philosophy. Somewhere it is meant for purification of hearts and sometimes for salvation. Its elements on the one hand include characterisation, plot and dialogue and on the other hand stillness, sound and light. So, it is difficult to define drama in brief.

In literature, a drama is the portrayal of fictional or non-fictional events through the performance of written dialogue (either prose or poetry). Drama can be performed on stage, on film, or the radio. Drama is typically called *play*, and its creators are known as *Playwrights* or *Dramatists*. Drama depends heavily on spoken dialogue to keep the audience informed about the characters' feelings, personalities, motivations and plans.

Origin, Growth and Development of Drama

The origin of the drama is deeply rooted in the instincts of mankind. This is true of the Greek, Indian, Chinese, Egyptian and of the modern Christian drama.

The ancient Greek drama shows close kinship with the religious ceremonies of people. Greek drama is acclaimed to be the earliest recorded form of drama (5th century BC). It is said to have originated from the Dionysian religious rites, and also remained a communal rite during the classical period. Dionysus, God of life and death, God of wine and of fertile Earth was the father of Greek comedy and tragedy. The dramatists of this age gave insight into the philosophy and religious beliefs of the ancient Greece. These early Greek plays treated life's basic problems with utmost honesty and attacked social ills using legendary and mythological themes. This helped to ensure sanity and balance in the society.

In the Medieval period, drama was used to clarify the message of the gospel through the re-enactment of the biblical stories during mass gatherings. It was later expanded to include the dramatisation of the lives of the saints and other notable stories of the Bible that did not form part of the Sunday's lessons. It was therefore used for the spiritual and moral growth of the people.

Drama and theatre also played important roles in the social lives of the people in the ancient Roman Empire, England, Germany and France. Playwrights like Shakespeare, Brecht, Goethe, Moliere and others in varying degrees used their works to enable their respective countries to carve out and affirm a unique identity for themselves.

The American industrial sector was radically but positively affected through the intervention of one play, Arthur Miller's *Death of a Salesman.* This play is regarded as being responsible for the spirit of industrial revolution in America.

In Africa, Kenya to be precise, a playwright, Ngugi wa Thiong'o was arrested and detained because of the political and social consciousness which his play, *I Will Marry When I Want,* aroused in the audience after the production. The play was written and presented in his Kikuyu language; this enabled the audience, to assimilate its message immediately and to react accordingly. Ngugi was forced into exile.

The drama of any society, therefore, reflects the problems, aspirations, philosophy and cultural background of the people. In fact, the themes have transcended through many dramatic periods. Also, the fact that these plays were performed by professional actors makes them a transition between the classical drama and the plays we see today.

Functions of Drama

It presents a story realistically through the actors to the audience. Drama is therefore used to entertain, inform and educate people. We can see that it is the most effective tool for mass mobilisation by the Government and Private Agencies. For instance, most campaigns against AIDS, Drug Abuse, Child Abuse and so on, are presented in the form of drama to educate, enlighten, while at the same time to entertain people.

Of all the creative artists, the dramatist is in the best position to reflect his society and to cause social reforms. This is because his work has a unique characteristic of presenting events in a vivid, picturesque and realistic manner. This helps to stamp social conditions, realistically in the minds of the audience. Its message is therefore immediate. The rich and the poor, the young and the old, the literate and the illiterate enjoy and grasp the message of drama once it is presented in the appropriate language.

Types of Drama

Dramatic performances are generally classified into specific categories according to the mood, tone and actions depicted in the plot.

Some popular types of drama include

Comedy

Lighter in tone, comedies are intended to make the audience laugh and usually have happy endings. Comedies place off-beat characters in unusual situations causing them to do and say funny things. Comedy can also be sarcastic in nature, poking fun at serious topics. There are also several sub-genres of comedy, including romantic comedy, sentimental comedy, a comedy of manners and tragic comedy.

Tragedy

Based on darker themes, tragedies portray serious subjects like death, disaster and human suffering in a dignified and thought-provoking way. Rarely enjoying happy endings, characters in tragedies, like Shakespeare's *Hamlet*, are often burdened by tragic character flaws that ultimately lead to their demise.

Melodrama

The word melodrama is coined from melo (music) and dran (drama). It is, therefore, a play that utilises music extensively. But the utilisation of music is not the only factor in melodrama, what really makes it melodrama, is its portrayal of the protagonist and the antagonist. The protagonist suffers a lot, but triumphs in the end, while the antagonist suffers, so melodrama can be defined as a play that has serious action caused by a villain and a destruction of the villain which brings about a happy resolution in the play.

Tragic-Comedy

We have seen that tragedy is a serious play that ends on a sad note while comedy ends happily. In traditional tragedy, playwrights were not allowed to bring in any comic action. In *Oedipus Rex*, for instance, we will observe that the atmosphere is tense from the beginning to the end. As time went on, even from the Elizabethan period, comic characters were included in tragic plays. This is called 'comic relief'.

Tragic-comedy is a play that mixes both comic and tragic elements in equal proportion. It therefore elicits both tragic and comic emotions. In these plays, the characters take on tragedy with humour in bringing serious situations to happy endings.

Farce

Farce which is referred to as comedy of situation, is a humorous play on a trivial theme usually one that is familiar to the audience. The themes that are treated in farce include mistaken identity, elaborate misunderstanding, switched costume (men in women's clothes) heroes forced under tables, misheard instructions, discoveries, disappearances and many such situations. it presents physical activities that grow out of situations. Farce does not treat serious social issues.

Opera

This versatile genre of drama combines theatre, dialogue, music and dance to tell grand stories of tragedy or comedy. Since characters express their feelings and intentions through song rather than dialogue, performers must be both skilled actors and singers. The decidedly tragic *La Boheme* by Giacomo Puccini and the bawdy comedy *Falstaff* by Giuseppe Verdi are classic examples of opera.

Elements of Drama

According to the Aristotelian conventions, six basic elements are followed in any drama across eras. *These are*

Dianoia

The theme of the play, is the central idea around which the story is built. It is either expressed through dialogue or action or inferred after the entire performance.

Mythos

The order of events occurring in a play is the plot. What the characters do, what happens to them in the end, constitutes the plot. The unfolding of the story through the series of incidents, the sequencing, the background and the climax constitute the plot.

Ethos

The characters of a play are essentially the persons who perform the drama. They are interwoven with the plot and bring out the theme of the play.

Lexis

The diction or the language used in the most important aspect of a play. It is only through the language, the dialogues that the playwright communicates with the audience and brings his characters alive. The wit, accent, tone, soliloquies are a few techniques which say a lot about a character. Language may include both verbal and non-verbal techniques. There are many famous dialogues and monologues which have lent an eternal life to a drama e.g. 'To be or not to be .....' the famous soliloquy is still fresh in the minds of the readers.

Melos

The music compositions, the sounds and rhythm of dialogues, the background score and sound effects is the melos element of the drama. The right kind of music, placed at the right points in the story, elevates the drama to another level. In Greek plays, melos would also consist of the utterances by the chorus.

Opsis

The visual elements like costumes, special effects, stage props and make-up accentuate the visual elements of the play and highlight the characters.

Ancient and Medieval Drama

Ancient Greek Drama was the first seed which was sowed and became a base for all later dramas. The Roman Drama was an offshoot of the Greek but was soon degraded and corrupted in later empires. With the coming of Christianity as the state religion, theatre was considered lowly and frowned upon. Very soon the Church itself was utilising the tendencies, earlier endeavoured to be crushed. The 'cradle of the drama' 'rested on the altar'.

Drama arose in 10th century in monasteries when modifications were being done in mass. Religion could be explained to the illiterate using the plays which depicted scenes from the Master's life. Often symbolic objects were used to convey the tales' meanings and even the priests used Pantomime to explain the events of Christian ritual celebrations. These performances developed into liturgical dramas, the earliest is *Whom do You Seek* Easter Trope, dating ca. 925. Liturgical drama was sung by two groups and no actors were involved. However, between 965 and 975 Ethelwold of Winchester composed *Regularis Concordia* (Monastic Agreement)' which contains a playlet complete with directions for performance, the liturgical plays were performed near a Church, with incidental music and not as essential parts of a standard church service.

Anglo-Norman Literature

Also known as the Norman French literature includes old French language writings as used in medieval England. After the Norman Conquest in 1066, this dialect became the vernacular of court, the law, the church, schools, universities, and other areas of trade. Anglo-Norman was an acquired tongue and a mark of gentleness used in wales and Ireland and to a certain limit in Scotland.

Norman conquest is also known as the *Battle of Hastings.* The most obvious change after this battle was the introduction of Anglo-Norman as the language of ruling classes in England, displacing old English.

The Hundred Years' War alienation towards France resulted in increased use of English, with French only surviving in Parliament and law. The earliest play entirely in French, *Le Mystere D' Adam* is Anglo-Norman.

A Few other plays belonging to Anglo-Norman literature are given below

Le Jeu d'Adam (The Play of Adam)

It is an Anglo-Norman play composed around 11th-12th century. This semi liturgical play is written in old French. Like the English Mystery Plays (or Cycle Plays), it is a dramatic representation of stories from the Bible (both old and new Testaments). The play is based on the Latin responses of the Septuagesima mass, which recount the Creation, Temptation and Fall of Adam and Eve and the story of Cain and Abel. It dramatises the fall of Adam and Eve in the garden of Eden and the story of their sons, Cain and Abel. The play has also been seen as a precursor to old French farce.

Seinte Resurrection (Resurrection of the Saviour)

It is a 12th century incomplete play written in the Anglo-Norman dialect. The play deals with the burial and Resurrection of Christ. The play's style is related to the historical realism of late medieval passion plays. Only 522 lines of the play remain with us as a fragment.

Le Jeu de Saint Nicholas (The Play of St Nicholas)

It is a Miracle Play by Jean Bodel. It was performed in 1201. It is an important transitional work, which combines elements of traditional miracle play with secular elements. The play concerns a pagan Saracen King, who hears that Christians have invaded his land. The King then consults his idol, Tervagan about his future. In response, Tervagan both laughs and cries. The king, then wages war with the Christians and massacres them.

The lone survivor, Preudom is imprisoned. He prays before the statue of St Nicholas. The King questions Preudom about the powers of his idol. In reply, Preudom claims that the saint's powers can help in recovering one's lost possessions.

The King, then, wishes to test the power of the claim and keeps the statue in his treasure. Three thieves, however, steal the King's treasure. Enraged at Preudom, the King sentences him to death. Preudom, then prays to the saint, who, in turn, visits the thieves and persuades them to return the treasure.

On finding his lost treasure, the pagan King releases Preudom from captivity and converts himself to Christianity. The idol of Tervagan is smashed and the entire court gets converted to Christianity. *Le Jeu de Saint Nicolas* is also of importance for its introduction of comic scenes based on contemporary life and is one of the first Latin school dramas to be translated into the vernacular.

Drama of the Age of Revival

Mystery Plays

Mystery Plays dramatised stories from the Bible. They included dramatisations of the *Fall of Lucifer, Cain and Abel, Noah and the Flood, The Nativity and The Passion of Christ*. The mystery plays were long cyclic dramas of the creation, fall and redemption of human kind, based on biblical narratives, concentrating mainly on the life and passion of Jesus Christ. They always ended with the Last Judgement.

Texts of cycles staged at York, Chester and Wakefield and at an unstated location in East Anglia (the N Town plays) have survived together with fragments from Coventry, Newcastle and Norwich. The plays are thus known by these names. They were traditionally performed on 'Corpus Christi Day', one of the many festival days of the Christian calendar and so were also known as the *Corpus Christi Plays. Some of these plays are*

The Wakefield Cycle

The Wakefield cycle has several brilliant plays, attributed to the anonymous Wakefield Master. This cycle consists of thirty two plays commencing with the creation, and the *Second Shepherds Play*, is one of the masterpieces of medieval English literature. The usual series the plays follow Noah, Abraham and Isaac.,. the last Supper, and the other important plays like the Hanging of Judas.

Second Shepherds' Play

The Second Shepherd's play was written in the late 15th century. It is part of the Wakefield mystery play cycle. The title of the play refers not to a second shepherd, but to the fact that this play was the second of two plays that dealt with the Biblical nativity story.

The play begins with a conversation between three shepherds, Coll, Gib and Daw (a boy, who works for them), as they watch over their sheep. They complain about such problems as the weather and their poverty. Another character Mak arrives, pretending to be a messenger from a Southern lord, but the shepherds recognise him and suspect that he plans to steal their sheep.

As the shepherds settle down for a night on the Moons, Mak takes advantage of their exhausted slumber to make off with a prized sheep. Mak and his wife Gill devise a scheme to put the sheep in a cradle and pretend it's her newborn son. When the shepherds wake and find the sheep gone, they immediately say Mak to visit.

The shepherds discover the couple's ruse and Mak is brought to justice, with a merciful twist. They punish Mak by tossing him in a blanket and then return to the fields. An angel arrives and calls to the shepherds, telling them to find the child born in Bethlehem. They enter the stable and discover Mary and the Christ-child. The story thus mingles sacred and profane. The play's dual plot is designed to remind the audience of the two-fold nature of man's existence-the real world on Earth and the spiritual world of the after-life.

The Chester Plays

The 25 Chester plays are more serious and didactic, acted on Monday, Tuesday and Wednesday in Whitsun week from 1268 to 1577, then in 1600. Important plays of this cycle are *Fall of Lucifer* and *The Creation and The Fall*. Using strange animals and a flight of pigeons added interest and made these more realistic.

The Conventry Plays

These plays were said to be acted at conventry on the festival of Corpus Christi. The forty-two plays are preserved, and it is known that not all the plays were acted in one year, the custom was to perform the first twenty-eight in one year and the remainder the next year.

Miracle Plays

Miracle plays were representations of lives of different saints. They specially re-enacted miraculous interventions by the saints. Although many scholars consider the term 'Miracle play' to include the genre of mystery play, others distinguish miracle plays from mystery plays by way of their source material. Whereas mystery plays are based upon scripture, miracle plays are not recognised as miracle plays since, they resemble miracles more than any other dramatic form. Examples of Miracle plays are *The Conversion of St Paul*, *Mary Magdalene* and *The Play of the Sacrament*.

The Conversation of St Paul

The Digby Conversion of Saint Paul is a middle English miracle play of the late 15th century. The play's dominant motif is conversion, which it explores through the biblical figure of Saul, who, thanks to a miraculous encounter, is changed from an avowed persecutor of Christians to a steadfast advocate for the faith. The stanzaic form of the play is a very regular rhyme royal.

The Play of the Sacrament

Play of the Sacrament is the only host Miracle play to survive in English. It was written in the East Midland dialect of Middle English not long after 1461, *Play of the Sacrament* tells the story of a miracle, in which a rich Jewish merchant and his companions purchase the consecrated host from a Christian merchant and subject it to a series of tests in order to determine the truth of the Christian claim that Christ is present in it.

At the end of the play, he is converted and promises to repeat his story for the moral instruction of others susceptible to the blandishments of covetousness. The play's central scene, the staging of the bloody torture of consecrated bread, is consistent with widespread reports of host desecration that circulated in chronicles and sermons throughout Europe beginning at the end of the 13th century.

Morality Plays

Morality plays, evolving from the medieval sermon, conveyed a moral truth or lesson using allegorical terms. They personified moral qualities (such as charity or vice) or abstractions (such as death or youth).

They were dramatised allegories of the life of man, his temptation and sinning, his quest for salvation and his confrontation by death. The purpose of the morality play was didactic; its object was to instruct the audience on the application of Christian doctrine to everyday life and the cultivation of character. The earliest complete extant morality play is *The Castle of Perseverance*, which was written around 1425. *Everyman* written around 1500 is perhaps the best known morality play. It depicts Everyman's journey in the face of death.

The Castle of Perseverance

It is a 15th century morality play of 3649 lines. The play describes the whole ontology of man, opening before his birth and ending after his death and his judgement before the throne of God. The protagonist is Humanum Genus or Man. Mankind's traditional three enemies, the world, the flesh and the devil speak from his own scaffold, introducing his followers, the Seven Deadly Sins.

World points out his chief henchman, greed (avarice, or covetousness), whose central importance in the seduction of mankind is signalled by his placement on his own scaffold. Flesh is accompanied by sloth, gluttony and lechery; the Devil by pride, wrath and envy.

Mankind is born, perhaps from the bed, which lies at the base of the castle. He points out his ignorance and helplessness, asking for God's grace; he introduces his two companions, the good and bad Angels, noting that every man has such a pair of advisors, one good and one evil. There is a comical debate between man's Bonus Angelus (Good Angel) and Malus Angelus (Bad Angel).

Mankind opts for the pleasures of the world. He sins first by becoming a servant of the World, who sends him to avarice and the other deadly sins. When penance pierces him with a lance, he confesses to shrift, receives absolution and enters the castle of perseverance. But mankind's enemies, alerted by backbiter, summon the sins to a siege against the castle. Although six of the sins are repelled by their opposing virtues, avarice succeeds in enticing the aging mankind back to worldly goods.

Mankind's pleasure in his newfound wealth is interrupted by the figure of death, who stabs mankind with his lance. With the coming of death, he realises that his treasure will go to an unknown heir and he dies calling on God for mercy. The soul reproaches the body and cries again for mercy. However, since mankind died in a state of sin, the good angel is unable to help his soul and it is carried off to hell by the bad angel.

But mankind's last request for mercy has summoned the four daughters of God; Truth, Justice, Peace and Mercy, who then debate his case before God. God judges in favour of mankind and directs the daughters to remove the soul from hell.

The Somonyng Everyman

The Somonyng of Everyman (*The Summoning of Everyman*), usually referred to simply as *Everyman*, is a late 15th century English morality play. A short play of some 900 lines, it portrays a complacent Everyman, who is informed by death of his approaching end.

It is speculated that the play is based upon a *Dutch* (Flemish) morality play of the same period called *Elckerlijc*. The play centers on Everyman's plea for companionship on his journey to his grave. He realises during the course of his journey that in the end, he can only fall back on his moral and religious values. The play is an allegory of life, in which the only thing that will save Everyman from certain damnation is good deeds alone.

Skelton's Magnificence

It was written by John Skelton, often referred as a 'Goodly Interlude. it is considered to be the first extant political morality play. The play was designed to be acted in the hall of Court of Henry VIII. Composed of 2500 lines, the play was printed around 1530. The play shows how Magnificence is deceived by vices, but finally redeemed by good hope and perseverance.

According to Tai-Won Kim, "with its primary focus on Magnificence's financial mismanagement and the political and economic consequences of his willful conduct, Skelton's play calls for a royal balance between extravagance and parsimony and thereby links the arts of political and personal government." It is a veiled attack on Cardinal Wolsey.

Interludes

The term denotes a short play or playlet actually performed between the courses of a cycle of plays. It can be applied to a variety of short entertainments, including secular farces and witty dialogues with a religious or political point. The Interlude developed out of the morality and the two cannot always be distinguished. John Heywood is a popular writer of interludes in this period.

The manuscripts of medieval English plays were usually ephemeral performance scripts, with even fewer numbers surviving. Hrotsvitha of Gandersheim was the first person to compose drama in the Latin West. She was a 10th century German secular canoness, dramatist and poet who wrote the classical imitations of Terence.

Important Dramatists of the Age of Revival

Henry Medwall (1462-1502)

Henry Medwall is popular as the first known English vernacular dramatist. He was educated at Eton College and the University of Cambridge and participated in dramatic performances there. He served as a chaplain in the household of Cardinal John Norton, the Archbishop of Canterbury under Henry VII.

Literary Career and Works

He wrote a morality play, *Nature,* but is mostly known for *Fulgens and Lucrece* (1497) the first secular play surviving in English. This play appears to have been written for performance at Christmas time between the courses of a banquet at which Morton entertained ambassadors from abroad. Medwall died in 1502.

Medwall's Fulgens and Lucrece

- The play is based upon a Ciceronian declamation on true nobility *De Vera Nobilitate* (1428).
- It is the first vernacular play to be printed in England.
- It is the first play to show the influence of classical antiquity.
- It is the first, in which a woman is the central character. The heroine has to choose between two rival suitors.
- The play is a debate on the origins of true nobility, enlivened by the interruptions of household servants.

John Rastell (1475-1536)

English printer and author John Rastell was the son of a leading Coventry citizen and Warwickshire justice of the peace. He is said to have been born in London. Rastell's first press was at 'the Abbot of Winchcombe's place' by the Fleet bridge.

Literary Career and Works

After 1526, Rastell started printing works of his own authorship, which give him an important place in the history of Tudor drama. Two plays, *Of gentylnes and nobylyte* and *The Nature of the Four Elements* may with fair certainty be attributed to him, while a third, *Calisto and Melibea*, shows signs of his workmanship.

The Nature of the Four Elements portrays the benefits of a humanistic education in a not very dramatic allegory, where the hero Humanity is led away from his books and into a tavern by the vice-figure ignorance and the cheerful sensual appetite. The purpose of this play is to awaken interest in natural science and discovery. In *Of gentylnes and nobylyte*, largely a dialogue between a ploughman and a knight, the evils of inheritance are attacked and it is argued that nobility is not a matter of birth. Both plays present the notion of the 'commonweal', and the third, *Calisto and Melibea*, concludes with a moralising address on the theme, that natural knowledge and reason are aids to religion.

Rastell's best-known work is *The Pastyme of People, the Chronydes of dyvers Realmys and most specially of the Realme of England* (1529), a chronicle dealing with English history from the earliest times to the reign of Richard III.

John Bale (1495-1563)

John Bale was an English theologian, historian, playwright, literary historian and Bishop of Ossory. He was born at the little village of Cove, near Dunwich in Suffolk, on 21st November, 1495.

Literary Career and Works

Bale is said to have attracted Cromwell's attention by his dramas, which were morality plays or scriptural plays setting forth the reformed opinions. Bale's propagandist play *King Johan* was first acted on 2nd January, 1539. *King Johan* tells the history of King John's defeat and death at the hands of the Roman powers in a morality-play framework of allegorical figures. Apart from this play, Bale is known for *The Image of Both Churches*, which is a thorough commentary on the Book of Revelation.

The 8 years of Bale's exile were his most productive period as a writer. When pro-Protestant Edward VI came to the English throne in 1548, it prompted an outpouring of twelve works from Bale, including *A Comedy Concerning Three Laws* and *The Image of Both Churches.* Bale subsequently returned to England and resumed his ecclesiastical duties. In 1552, despite Bale's reluctance, Edward appointed him to the Bishopric of Ossory. Bale chronicled his experiences in this turbulent and staunchly Catholic diocese in his *Vocacyon of Johan Bale to the Bishoprick of Ossorie in Irelande* (1553). He died in November 1563 in Canterbury.

Niccolo Machiavelli (1469-1527)

Italian author and statesman Niccolo di Bernardo dei Machiavelli, was born at Florence on 3rd May, 1469. At an early age, he became a pupil of a renowned Latin teacher, Paolo da Ronciglione. He is believed to have attended the University of Florence and received an excellent humanist education. Not much is known about his biographical history.

Literary Career and Works

In 1500, he was sent on his first assignment to France to obtain terms from Louis XII for continuing the war against Pisa: it is this king, who in his conduct of affairs in Italy, committed the five capital errors in statecraft summarised in *The Prince* and was consequently driven out.

His visits to courts of various Kings and experience in foreign policy would later form the basis of many of the principles he expresses in *The Prince* and the great personages that he met form the examples from which he draws his lessons.

Machiavelli's historical writings comprise

- *Florentine Histories,*
- *Discourses on the First Decade of Titus Livius,* (commonly known as *The Discourses*), *a Life of Castruccio Castrancani* (unfinished) and *History of the Affairs of Lucca*.

His literary works comprise an imitation of *The Golden Ass* by Apuleius, an essay on the Italian language, the play *Mandragola* and several minor compositions. He also wrote Seven books on *The Art of War*. His greatest known work is the political treatise, *The Prince* (1532). The book gives a set of rules for establishment and preservation of authority and advocates adoption of any means, fair or unfair. Machiavelli died in San Casciano in 1527, just a few miles outside his beloved Florence.

Machiavelli's Mandragola

Machiavelli portrays fortuna and virtu in *Mandragola* to demonstrate that immorality is acceptable. He makes the protagonist boast virtue and his leading lady encompass fortuna the protagonist. Callimaco is the virtuous prince that Machiavelli alludes to in the prince, with fervent aspirations, willing to endanger his life, thus worthy of his love Lucrezia and worthy of authority. The antagonist Nicia, holds power, like an inherited prince but loses Fortuna because of his passiveness. Each character is a representative political figurehead, reiterating ideas from the Prince, with the help of marks and stock figures.

Theatre is a cautious means of exposing truths as the audience connects with the action, but is removed enough from the stage that there is no looming fear.

EXAM BASED QUESTIONS

1 What was the change noticed in 'Literature' after Battle of Hastings?
(a) Completely new revolution in the field of literature
(b) Completely transformed the sentiments and tastes of English rulers
(c) Innovation of new poems and ballads
(d) New sentiments of French people were introduced

2 Which among the following is not the feature of French literature that Normans imported to England?
(a) Clarity of expression
(b) Clarity of language
(c) Varied moods and themes
(d) Gloom and other worldly attitude

3 The first official document written in Anglo-Norman was
(a) Chancellor's Speech (b) Statute Promulgated
(c) Magna Carta (d) None of these

4 Example of Manuscript, which gives us an excellent picture of the literature in the Norman period?
(a) Ballads (b) Advocate's Library
(c) Seven Wise Masters (d) None of these

5 Which of these plays is written in Old French?
(a) The Play of Adam
(b) Resussection of the Saviors
(c) The Play of St Nicholas
(d) Otuel

6 What does Adam's name mean?
(a) First (b) Foolish (c) Father (d) Man

7 From which part of Adam's body did God make Eve?
(a) Finger (b) Rib (c) Vertebra (d) Shoulder

8 What tree were Adam and Eve forbidden to eat from?
(a) An Apple Tree
(b) The Tree of Life
(c) The Tree of Knowledge of Good and Evil
(d) The Tree of Death

9 What kind of fruit did Adam and Eve eat?
(a) The Bible doesn't say (b) A pomegranate
(c) An apple (d) Grapes

10 When Adam and Eve realised they were naked, what did they use to cover themselves?
(a) Fig leaves (b) Tree bark
(c) Animal furs (d) Feathers

11 How many years did Adam live?
(a) 305 years (b) 777 years
(c) 608 years (d) 930 years

12 Eve's third son was the ancestor of Noah and therefore the ancestor of all living humans (since all of humanity except Noah's family perished in the Flood). What was his name?
(a) Lamech (b) Cain
(c) Seth (d) Abel

13 Where did Adam and Eve live?
(a) Israel (b) Sodom (c) Zion (d) Eden

14 Which two trees grew in the midst of the garden?
(a) The tree of life and the tree of knowledge of good and evil
(b) The tree of death and the tree of joy and despair
(c) The tree of life and the tree of death
(d) The tree of knowledge of good and evil and the tree of joy and despair

15 Which tree bore fruit that God forbade Adam and Eve to partake of?
(a) The tree of life
(b) The tree of knowledge of good and evil
(c) The tree of joy and despair
(d) The tree of death

16 What would not happen to anyone who would partake of such fruit?
(a) They would know for themselves the difference between right and wrong
(b) They would become all-knowing
(c) They would be able to bear children
(d) They would die

17 What animal deceived Eve?
(a) A wolf (b) A crow
(c) A fox (d) A serpent

18 The animal who deceived Eve represents
(a) Lucifer
(b) The spirits of Eve's unborn children
(c) Jesus
(d) Adam

19 What did the deceptive animal convince Eve to do?
(a) Partake of the forbidden fruit
(b) Blaspheme against the Lord
(c) Kill an animal
(d) Leave Adam

20 What did Adam do after Eve obeyed the animal and transgressed against the Lord's commandment?
(a) He condemned her
(b) He forgave her
(c) He exiled her
(d) He also transgressed against the Lord's commandment

21 **Why did Adam hide himself from the Lord?**
(a) He was embarrassed because he realised he was naked
(b) He wanted the Lord to prove to him that he can see all
(c) He was ashamed of his wife's transgression
(d) He wanted to see if he could outwit the Lord

22 **What did the Lord not do as a result of the disobedience of Adam and Eve?**
(a) Cause them to work the ground for food
(b) Cast them out of Eden and his presence
(c) Kill them instantly
(d) Give them the ability to feel emotion

23 **How did God curse the animal that deceived Eve?**
(a) He sent it to live under the ground and never see light
(b) He forced it to live on the ground and in the dust
(c) He caused it to be constantly hunted by all other animals
(d) He bound it to the skies and forbade it to ever perch and rest

24 **What does Eve's name mean?**
(a) Mother of all living
(b) Blessed mother
(c) Mother of knowledge
(d) Mother of death

25 **How did God say mankind was similar to him?**
(a) They could create life
(b) They would live forever
(c) They could feel joy and sorrow
(d) They could know good from evil

26 **Why did God protect the tree of life?**
(a) So that man would live forever
(b) So that Adam and Eve would not lose the ability to bear children
(c) To ensure that he could never be destroyed
(d) So that man couldn't obtain a means to live forever

27 **What did God place at the East of the garden of Eden to guard the tree of life?**
(a) A dragon with seven heads
(b) Cherubims and a flaming sword
(c) A seraph with six wings
(d) A pit of poisonous serpents

28 **What did the Lord do for Adam and Eve before he exiled them?**
(a) He armed them with weapons
(b) He allowed them to rest
(c) He fed them
(d) He clothed them

29 **Where did the term 'Xmas' come from?**
(a) Newspaper editors first used it to save space in headlines
(b) It was created as a derogatory term for Christmas
(c) It was first used by department stores for 'Xmas Sale' signs
(d) The Greek letter 'X'

30 **Which of the following is true about the origin of candy canes?**
(a) The red stripes were intended to represent the blood of Christ
(b) The mint flavouring was purposely derived from hyssop, a biblical herb
(c) They were intentionally made in the shape of a J for Jesus
(d) They were first made to keep children quiet at church

31 **What is Santa called in France?**
(a) Pere Noel
(b) Pere Fouettard
(c) Hans Trapp
(d) Pere Frost

32 **Which of the following is not another name for the gift-giving spirit of Saint Nick?**
(a) Burklaas
(b) Beelzebub
(c) Belsnickel
(d) Befana

33 **Why is the day after Christmas also known as 'Boxing Day'?**
(a) Unwanted presents are traditionally boxed up and returned to the store
(b) Because boxes of solicited money were opened
(c) Professional Boxing matches were frequently scheduled for the day for entertainment
(d) Because of the fisticuffs that frequently break out between siblings over who gets to play with which toys by this time

34 **When Mary Magdalene first saw Jesus after his resurrection, who did she think he was?**
(a) Soldier
(b) Gardener
(c) Angel
(d) Lost

35 **Two followers of Jesus were walking to a village when the risen Christ appeared to them. At first they didn't recognise him, and they explained to him what had been happening in Jerusalem; they then recognised him when he broke bread with them. What was the name of the village?**
(a) Capernaum
(b) Emmaus
(c) Tiberias
(d) Salamis

36 **Which word is applied to denote the whole translation from the Middle Ages to the modern world, is more correctly applied to the revival of art resulting from the discovery and imitation of classic models in the 14th century?**
(a) Renaissance
(b) Reformation
(c) Restoration
(d) Humanism

37 **Where did a new literature arise in the world, the first modern literature?**
(a) Italy
(b) Germany
(c) France
(d) All of these

38 **Which culture was at its height when the revival of learning started?**
(a) Asian Culture
(b) African Culture
(c) Australian Culture
(d) European Culture

39 Which of the following plays gained notoriety for its caricature of the philosopher Socrates?
(a) The Birds (b) The Wasps
(c) The Clouds (d) The Frogs

40 On which day, mystery plays traditionally performed?
(a) Corpus Christi Day (b) St. Valentines Day
(c) St. Patricks Day (d) None of these

41 Name some mystery plays of 15th century?
(a) Fall of Lucifer, Cain and Abel
(b) Fall of Lucifer, The Play of the Sacrament, Everyman
(c) Fall of Lucifer, Cain and Abel, The Castle of Preservance
(d) Fall of Lucifer, Cain and Abel, The Nativity and the Passion of Christ

42 Second Shepherds' play is
(a) morality play of 14th century
(b) mystery play of 15th century
(c) miracle play of 15th century
(d) an interlude of 14th to 15th century

43 What was the theme of the Second Shepherds' play?
(a) The play refers to a Second Shepherd
(b) Play talks about Three Shepherds
(c) Play was the second of two plays that dealt with the biblical native story
(d) The play was about Mary and Christ

44 The dual plot of Second Shepherd's play was designed to remind the audience
(a) The three shepherd's named Coll, Gib and Daw
(b) People take advantage of the sheep
(c) Virgin Mary gave birth to Christ
(d) The two fold nature of man's existence

45 Miracle plays were the representations of
(a) lives of saints (b) lives of angels
(c) lives of devils (d) All of these

46 Names of some miracle plays of 15th century.
(a) Second Shepherd's Play, The Conversion of St. Paul, The Play of the Sacrament
(b) The Conversion of St. Paul, Mary Magdalene, Everyman
(c) The Conversion of St. Paul, Mary Magdalene, The Play of the Sacrament
(d) The Conversion of St. Paul, The Castle of Preservance, Everyman

47 Morality plays conveyed a
(a) dramatised allegory (b) moral truth
(c) miracles (d) lessons from the Bible

48 The early religious drama is associated with
(a) superstitions and beliefs
(b) mysteries and histories
(c) interludes and mysteries
(d) miracles and morality

49 'Everyman' (1490) is an important extant example of
(a) religious play (b) morality play
(c) interlude (d) artistic drama

50 'Hero Humanity' and 'Villain Ignorance' belong to an allegory.
(a) The Pastimes of People
(b) The Four Elements
(c) King Johan
(d) The Castle of Perseverance

51 The best of John Heywood's interludes was
(a) The Four P's
(b) Ralph Roister Doister
(c) Gammer Gurton's Needle
(d) King Johan

52 The famous Dutch scholar, who is known for Wolloquis and in Praise of Folly
(a) Shakespeare (b) Erasmus
(c) John Marston (d) Boccaccio

53 Who wrote the play 'The Prince'?
(a) Erasmus (b) John Bale
(c) Henry Medwell (d) Machiavelli

54 According to Machiavelli, which of the following statements about hereditary states is not valid?
(a) Subjects naturally love the ruling family
(b) They should retain traditional institutions
(c) Their traditional institutions should be adapted to current events
(d) They are more difficult to control than new states

55 Which of the following is a course of action that should not be taken by a prince of a new principality?
(a) Change the laws and taxes
(b) Punish insurrection
(c) Destroy the family of the former prince
(d) Establish settlements

56 Machiavelli was a great figure and a writer during the renaissance period in Italian history, he was greatly influenced by great figures before him, he was influenced by?
(a) Dante Alighieri (b) Plato
(c) Leonardo da Vinci (d) All of these

57 One of Machiavelli's sayings, 'If an injury has to be done to a man it should be so severe that his vengeance needs to be feared', he was often called the father of modern?
(a) Mathematics (b) Political science
(c) Economics (d) Renaissance movement

58 Machiavelli wrote a lot of books on different subjects during his long life and career, however, he wrote a play titled?
(a) Candid (b) Human Happiness
(c) The Prince (d) Mandrake

59 **Machiavelli hoped to land an advisory position within the Florentine government and so he dedicated The Prince to the then Florence Governor named?**
(a) Henry Thoreau (b) Waldo Emerson
(c) Florenzo de' Medici (d) Cicero

60 **Countless of literary work was credited to his name in the various field he plunged during his lifetime, the most famous of his to date is?**
(a) The Prince (b) Discourses on Livy
(c) Florentine Histories (d) The Art of War

61 **Machiavelli is most famous for his short political treatise 'The Prince' written in 1513 and not published until later, five years later after his death, when was the Prince published**
(a) 1533 (b) 1532
(c) 1534 (d) 1530

62 **Name the play that deals with the burial and resurrection of the Christ.**
(a) The Play of Adam
(b) The Play of St. Nicholas
(c) Resurrection of the Saviour
(d) Oresteia

63 **Which miracle play concerns a pagan Saracen king, who hears that Christians have invaded his land?**
(a) Oresteia
(b) The Play of St Nicholas
(c) The Play of Adam
(d) Resurrection of the Saviour

64 **Which of the following plays is seen as a precursor to old French Farce?**
(a) The Play of Adam
(b) The Play of St Nicholas
(c) Resurrection of the Saviour
(d) Oresteia

65 **Which play out of the given is part of the wake field mystery play cycle?**
(a) The Conversion of St Paul
(b) The Play of the Sacrament
(c) The Castle of Perseverance
(d) Second Shephards Play

66 **Under which category does the Play 'The Conversion of St. Paul' fall?**
(a) Miracle Plays
(b) Mystery Plays
(c) Morality Plays
(d) Heroic Plays

67 **Which kind of plays always ended with the last Judgement?**
(a) Miracle Plays
(b) Mystery Plays
(c) Morality Plays
(d) Heroic Plays

68 **The earliest complete extant morality play which was written around 1425 is**
(a) Mary Magdalene
(b) Everyman
(c) The Castle of Perseverance
(d) Magnificence

69 **Which play centres on People's plea for companionship on their journey to their grave?**
(a) The Castle of Perseverance
(b) Magnificence
(c) Mary Magdalene
(d) Everyman

70 **Which play is considered to be the first extant political morality play?**
(a) Magnificence
(b) The Castle of Perseverance
(c) Everyman
(d) Mary Magdalene

71 **Name the play which was first vernacular play to be printed in England besides showing the influence of classical antiquity.**
(a) Mandragola (Mandrake) (b) Fulgens and Lucrece
(c) Everyman (d) Magnificence

72 **Which of the following pairs is incorrectly matched?**
(a) Simeon : Chronicle
(b) Layamon : History
(c) Reginald : Poetry
(d) Marie de France : Drama

73 **Which of the following pairs is incorrectly matched?**
(a) Romance : King Horn
(b) Didactic : Emare
(c) Lay : Equitan
(d) Drama : The Play of St Nicholas

74 **Which of the following is not correctly matched?**
(a) The Second Shephards' : Mystery Play
(b) Mary Magdalene : Miracle Play
(c) The Castle of Perseverance : Morality Play
(d) Skelton's Magnificence : Interlude

75 **Which of the following is incorrectly matched?**
(a) Henry Medwall : Nature
(b) Desiderius Erasmus : The Praise of Folly
(c) Machiavelli : The Partyme of People
(d) John Rastell : Calisto and Melibea

76 **Which of the following is not correctly matched?**
(a) Fulgens and Lucree : Erasmus
(b) Prince : Niccolo Machiavelli
(c) The Nature of Four Elements : John Rastell
(d) King Johan : John Bale

77 Which of the following is in chronological order?
(a) Erasmus John Rastell, John Bale, Henry Medwall
(b) John Rastell, John Bale, Henry Medwall, Erasmus
(c) Henry Medwall, Erasmus, John Rastell, John Bale
(d) John Bale, Henry Medwall, Erasmus, John Rastell

78 Which of the following is in chronological order?
(a) De Vera Nobilitate, Fulgens and Lucree, Prince, King Johan
(b) Prince, De Vera Nobilitate, King Johan, Fulgens and Lucree
(c) King Johan, Prince, Fulgens and Lucree, De Vera Nobilitate
(d) Fulgens and Lucree, De Vera Nobilitate, Prince, King Johan

79 Which of the following is in chronological order?
(a) The Play of the St. Nicholas, Resurrection of the Saviour, The Play of Adam, The Image of Both Churches
(b) The Play of Adam, Resurrection of the Saviour, The Play of St. Nicholas, The Image of Both Churches
(c) Resurrection of the Saviour, The Play of Adam, The Play of St. Nicholas, The Image of Both Churches
(d) The Play of Adam, The Play of St. Nicholas, Resurrection of the Saviour, The Image of Both Churches

80 In the following series, which set of authors and their works is correctly matched?
(a) John Barbour-Account of the Lives of Eminenturiters; John Bale-The Floure of Curtesye; John Skelton-Bruce; John Lydgate-Garlande of Laurell
(b) John Barbour-The Floure of Curtesye; John Bale-Account or the Lives of Eminenturiters; John Skelton-Bruce; John Lydgate-Garlande of Laurell
(c) John Barbour-Garlande of Laurell; John Bale-The Floure of Curtesye; John Skelton-Bruce; John Lydgate-Account of the Lives of Eminenturiters
(d) John Barbour-Bruce; John Bale-Account of the Lives of Eminenturiters; John Skelton-Garlande of Laurell; John Lydgate-The Floure of Curtesye

81 Match the following.

List I	List II
A. Mandragola	1. John Bale
B. Nature	2. John Rastell
C. Calisto and Melibea	3. Henry Medwall
D. King Johan	4. Niccolo Machiavelli

Codes

	A	B	C	D		A	B	C	D
(a)	1	2	3	4	(b)	4	3	2	1
(c)	2	3	4	1	(d)	3	4	1	2

82 What is common to all of them?
1. Henry Medwall 2. John Rastell
3. John Bale
Codes
(a) All of them were important dramatists of the Age of Revival
(b) All of them wrote miracle and morality plays
(c) All of them were important poets of the Age of Revival
(d) All of them edited Shakespeare's works

83 Consider the following works.
1. The Testament of Cressied
2. Garmont of Gud Ladeis
3. Peblis to the Play
4. Magnificience
Which of the following works does/do not belong to Henryson?
(a) 1 and 2 (b) Only 4 (c) 3 and 4 (d) Only 3

84 Which of the following is not a miracle play?
1. The Conversion of St. Paul
2. The Play of Sacrament
3. Mary Magdalene 4. Everyman
Select the correct answer using given codes given below.
(a) Both 1 and 2 (b) Only 2 (c) Both 3 and 4 (d) Only 4

85 Consider the following statements about 'Fulgens and Lucrece.'
1. The play is based upon a Ciceronian declamation.
2. It is the first vernacular play to be printed in England.
3. It is the first play to show the influence of classical antiquity.
4. It is the first play, in which man is the central character.
Which of the statements given above is/are incorrect?
(a) Only 1 (b) Only 2 (c) Only 3 (d) Only 4

86 Consider the following statements regarding 'Second Shepherd's Play'.
1. It was written in late 15th century.
2. It is a part of Wakefield's cycle of mystery plays.
3. An angel arrives and tells the Shepherd that a child is born in Bethlehem.
4. But the child is not born.
Which of the statements given above is correct?
(a) Only 1 (b) Only 2 (c) Only 3 (d) Only 4

87 According to Tai-Won-Kim, "With its primary focus on magnificence's financial mismanagement and the political and economic consequences of his willful conduct, his play calls for a royal balance between extravagance and parsimony and thereby links the arts of political and personal government."
Who wrote the above mentioned play 'Magnificence'?
(a) William Caxton (b) Erasmus
(c) Skelton (d) Heywood

Directions (Q. Nos. 88-90) *In the questions given below are two statements labelled as Assertion (A) and Reason (R). In the context of these two statements, which one of the following is correct?*

Codes

(a) Both A and R are true and R is the correct explanation of A
(b) Both A and R are true but R is not the correct explanation of A
(c) A is true but R is false
(d) A is false but R is true

88 **Assertion** (A) Romance became a popular literary form in the Anglo-Norman Period.
Reason (R) Anglo-Saxon Versification gave way to regular meter and rhyme.

89 **Assertion** (A) Henry VIII's reign marked England's transition from a medieval to modern nation.
Reason (R) This was particularly evident in the political changes resulting from Henry's policies during and after his break with the Roman Catholic Church.

90 **Assertion** (A) Education and ideas of the Renaissance spread during the age of revival.
Reason (R) In 1476, the first printing press in England was established.

Directions (Q. Nos. 91-95) *Read the following passage carefully and answer questions that follow*

The literary distaste for politics, however, seems to be focused not so much on the largely murky practice of politics in itself as a subject of literary representation but rather more on how it is often depicted in literature, i.e., on the very politics of such representation. A political novel often turns out to be not merely a novel about politics but a novel with a politics of its own, for it seeks not merely to show us how things are but has fairly definite ideas about how things should be, and precisely what one should think and do in order to make things move in that desired direction. In short, it seeks to convert and enlist the reader to a particular cause or ideology; it often is (in an only too familiar phrase) not literature but propaganda. This is said to violate the very spirit of literature which is to broaden our understanding of the world and the range of our sympathies rather than to narrow them down through partisan commitment. As John Keats said, 'We hate poetry that has a palpable design upon us'.

Another reason why politics does not seem amenable to the highest kind of literary representation seems to arise from the fact that politics by its very nature is constituted of ideas and ideologies. If political situations do not lend themselves to happy literary treatment, political ideas present perhaps an even greater problem in this regard. Literature, it is argued, is about human experiences rather than about intellectual abstractions; it deals in what is called the 'felt reality' of human flesh and blood, and in sap and savour (rasa) rather than in lifeless ideas. In an extensive discussion of the matter in her book Ideas and the Novel, the American novelist Mary McCarthy observed that ideas are still today felt to be unsightly in the novel though that was not so in 'former days', i.e., in the 18th and 19th centuries. Her formulation of the precise nature of the incompatibility between ideas on the one hand and the novel on the other betrays perhaps a divided conscience in the matter and a sense of dilemma shared by many writers and readers: "An idea cannot have Loose ends, but a novel, I almost think, needs them. Nevertheless, there is enough in common for the novelists to feel. the attraction of ideas while taking up arms against them - most often with weapons of mockery."

91 According to the passage, a political novel often turns out to be a

(a) literary distaste for politics
(b) literary representation of politics
(c) novel with its own politics
(d) depiction of murky practice of politics

92 A political novel reveals

(a) reality of the things
(b) writer's perception
(c) particular ideology of the readers
(d) the spirit of literature

93 The constructs of politics by its nature is

(a) prevalent political situation
(b) ideas and ideologies
(c) political propaganda
(d) understanding of human nature

94 Literature deals with

(a) human experiences in politics
(b) intellectual abstractions
(c) dry and empty ideas
(d) felt reality of human life

95 The observation of the novelist, Mary McCarthy reveals

(a) unseen felt ideas of today in the novel
(b) dichotomy of conscience on political ideas and novels
(c) compatibility between idea and novel
(d) endless ideas and novels

PREVIOUS YEARS' QUESTIONS

July 2018

1 Traces of the Morality plays are discernible in a play like Dr. Faustus, traces such as
(a) Vernacular songs adapting secular themes
(b) Its soliloquising protagonist, good and bad angels and its final moral
(c) Its refrains from the Corpus Christi Carol, the complaint of Christ, the lover of mankind
(d) Its rhythmical prose arid the presence or a larger narrative rhythm in the morality plays.

July 2016

2 Which of the following is not an allegorical character in the play Everyman?
(a) Kindred (b) Strength
(c) Christian (d) Discretion

December 2014

3 Mystery and Miracle play in English were based on ....
(a) English folklore (b) English legends
(c) Biblical stories (d) Anglo-Saxon myths

4 'The old order changeth, yielding place to new' is from
(a) Morte d' Arthur
(b) Idylls of the King
(c) Paracelsus
(d) Asolando

5 There are some characteristics of morality plays.
1. They are dramatised allegories of the life of man.
2. They depict man's temptation and sinning, his quest for salvation and his confrontation with death.
3. Though the hero represents mankind, the other characters are by no means personifications of virtues, vices and death.
4. A character known as the vice often plays the role of the hero, a predecessor of the Villain-hero in Elizabethan drama.

Codes
(a) 1 and 2 (b) 1 and 3
(c) 1 and 4 (d) 2 and 3

ANSWERS

Objective Questions

1. *(b)*	2. *(d)*	3. *(b)*	4. *(b)*	5. *(a)*	6. *(d)*	7. *(b)*	8. *(c)*	9. *(a)*	10. *(a)*
11. *(a)*	12. *(c)*	13. *(d)*	14. *(a)*	15. *(b)*	16. *(c)*	17. *(d)*	18. *(a)*	19. *(a)*	20. *(d)*
21. *(a)*	22. *(c)*	23. *(b)*	24. *(a)*	25. *(d)*	26. *(d)*	27. *(b)*	28. *(d)*	29. *(d)*	30. *(d)*
31. *(a)*	32. *(b)*	33. *(b)*	34. *(b)*	35. *(b)*	36. *(a)*	37. *(c)*	38. *(d)*	39. *(c)*	40. *(a)*
41. *(d)*	42. *(b)*	43. *(c)*	44. *(d)*	45. *(a)*	46. *(c)*	47. *(b)*	48. *(d)*	49. *(b)*	50. *(b)*
51. *(a)*	52. *(b)*	53. *(d)*	54. *(d)*	55. *(a)*	56. *(d)*	57. *(b)*	58. *(d)*	59. *(c)*	60. *(a)*
61. *(b)*	62. *(c)*	63. *(b)*	64. *(a)*	65. *(d)*	66. *(a)*	67. *(b)*	68. *(c)*	69. *(d)*	70. *(a)*
71. *(b)*	72. *(d)*	73. *(b)*	74. *(d)*	75. *(c)*	76. *(a)*	77. *(c)*	78. *(a)*	79. *(b)*	80. *(d)*
81. *(b)*	82. *(a)*	83. *(c)*	84. *(d)*	85. *(d)*	86. *(d)*	87. *(c)*	88. *(b)*	89. *(b)*	90. *(a)*
91. *(c)*	92. *(b)*	93. *(b)*	94. *(d)*	95. *(a)*					

Previous Years' Questions

1. *(b)*	2. *(c)*	3. *(c)*	4. *(a)*	5. *(a)*

Elizabethan to Jacobean Drama (1550-1625)

The most important characteristics of the Elizabethan Age were the comparative religious tolerance, social contentment, intellectual liberty, unbounded patriotism and peace at home and abroad. The Age appealed to the imagination and the intellect and literature instinctively turned to the drama.

Elizabethan Age

Elizabethan Age is named after the reign of the last Tudor Monarch of England, Queen Elizabeth I who ruled from 1558 to 1603. However, the age is not just limited to the period when Elizabeth ruled. There are certain literary characteristics, which developed during Elizabeth's reign and continued for some years after her death in 1603.

According to WH Hudson, we call Elizabethan all the years from the beginning of the Queen's reign to the period of James I's death in 1625. However, the period of James's reign from 1603 to 1625 is sometimes taken as a different period called the Jacobean period. Elizabeth I's 45 years reign is generally considered to be one of the most glorious and golden periods in English history.

Her reign saw a rise in the concept of nationalism in England and this is reflected in the increased interest that writers had in writing literary and dramatic works in the English language. As a result, Elizabethan England saw a significant growth in cultural developments. The Queen herself was a great patron of arts and her actions, image and court atmosphere led to the flourishing of arts and literature in the period.

In this Chapter

During this period, England made significant advances in the realm of navigation and exploration. It began colonisation of the Americans with Walter Raleigh's excursions to the Atlantic shore and establishment of the Roanoke colony. Its most important accomplishment was the circumnavigation of the world by Sir Francis Drake between 1577 and 1580.

Literature of the Elizabethan Age

Elizabethan England saw a remarkable blossoming of arts and literature. Renaissance humanism, protestant zeal, geographical and scientific discovery all contributed to this upsurge of creative power. Drama was the dominant genre in Elizabethan Age. William Shakespeare was the most significant playwright of the age. Shakespeare's oeuvre includes a wide variety of comedies, tragedies, tragicomedies and sonnets. Owing to the influence he wielded, the age is also sometimes named after him as 'The Age of Shakespeare'.

This age saw the appearance of the first English comedy and the first blank verse tragedy in the 1550-60s. These ultimately gave rise to art forms that remain heavily studied even today. In *Ralph Roister Doister*, a comic play by Nicholas Udall is generally regarded as the first comedy to be written in the English language around 1553. In 1562, one of the earliest of blank verse plays, *Gorboduc*, was performed for the Queen. It is considered to be the first English blank verse tragedy.

Elizabethan Age also witnessed the establishment of 'The Theatre' in 1576, the earliest theatre ever built. Following 'The Theatre' closely were theatres such as 'The Rose', 'The Swan' and most popular of all, 'The Globe', created in 1599. Elizabethan drama broke away from religious domination, which was the major focus of medieval mystery and morality plays. Elizabethan drama often used poetical metre (rhythm) for its dialogue, especially the five-foot iambic pentameter (pairs of syllables unstressed followed by stressed).

Apart from drama, Elizabethan age also saw flowering of poetry (the sonnet, the Spenserian stanza) and inspired a wide variety of splendid prose by writers such as Francis Bacon.

The literature of the Elizabethan Age flourished in various forms such as tragedy, comedy, poetry, drama and chronicles etc. *These are described below*

Tragedy

Tragedy, branch of drama that treats in a serious and dignified style the sorrowful or terrible events encountered or caused by a heroic individual. By extension the term may be applied to other literary works, such as the novel.

Although, the word tragedy is often used loosely to describe any sort of disaster or misfortune, it more precisely refers to a work of art that probes with high seriousness of questions concerning the role of man in the universe. The Greeks of Attica, the ancient state whose chief city was Athens, first used the word in the 5th century BCE to describe a specific kind of play, which was presented at festivals in Greece.

Historically, tragedy of a high order has been created in only four periods and locales: Attica, in Greece, in the 5th century BCE; England in the reigns of Elizabeth I and James I, from 1558 to 1625; 17th-century France and Europe and America during the second half of the 19th century and the first half of the 20th century.

Each period saw the development of a special orientation and emphasis, a characteristic style of theatre. In the modern period, roughly from the middle of the 19th century, tragedy has found some place in few novels.

First English Tragedy : Gorboduc

- *Gorboduc or The Tragedy of Ferrex and Porrex* is considered to be the first tragedy written in English. It is also believed to be the earliest English tragic play in blank verse. It was written by Thomas Norton (1532-1584) and Thomas Sackville (1536-1608) and was first performed in 1561. Norton wrote the first three acts of *Gorboduc* while Sackville the last two.
- The story of the play is derived from Geoffrey of Monmouth's *Historia Regum Britanniae* (1135-38; *History of the Kings of Britain*), which relates the dispute between Gorboduc's (King of Britain) two sons, Ferrex and Porrex, over the issue of succession.
- The play follows the sophisticated tragic models of Seneca. Significant imitations of *Gorboduc* include Gascoigne and Kinwelmersh's *Jocasta* and *Gismond* of *Salern*, written by five gentlemen of the Inner Temple.

Comedy

Comedy is a literary genre and a type of dramatic work that is amusing and satirical in its tone, mostly having a cheerful ending. The motif of this dramatic work is triumph over unpleasant circumstances by creating comic effects, resulting in a happy or successful conclusion.

Thus, the purpose of comedy is to amuse the audience. Comedy has multiple sub-genres depending upon the source of the humour, context in which an author delivers dialogues and delivery methods which include farce, satire and burlesque. Tragedy is opposite to comedy, as tragedy deals with sorrowful and tragic events in a story.

First English Comedy : Ralph Roister Doister

- *Ralph Roister Doister* is considered to be the first English comedy. It was written by the English playwright, Nicholas Udall, probably between 1551 and 1553.
- The protagonist of this play, Ralph Roister Doister is a well-to-do, doltish young man, who brags about his bravery, but acts like a coward whenever he is called to action. Ralph's attempts to woo a rich widow Christian Custance, do not attain success. The play shows the influence of the classical playwrights Plautus and Terence.

Poetry

Elizabethan age was a great age of English literature. During this time the writing of poetry was the part of education among the educated people. That is why many books of poetry by different writers appeared during this age.

Drama

Drama was the chief literary glory of the Elizabethan Age. In the beginning, these dramas were not so well-written though the comedies were better than the tragedies. *Ralph Roister Doister* is taken as the first regular English comedy. It was a kind of farce in rough verse written by Nicholas Udall.

Another comedy was Gammer Gurton's *Needle* acted at Cambridge University in 1566. Lyly improved the comedy in his prose comedy *Compaspe* and *Edymion. Gorboduc*, written by Thomas Norton and Thomas Sackville, was the first regular tragedy. It was very dull and written in poor blank verse. Thomas Kyd improved the tragedy by writing *The Spanish Tragedy*. It is a tragedy of blood and revenge.

Main Dramastists of Elizabethan Age

The Elizabethan period was a great one for the theatre and performing arts. There were numerous playwrights who contributed a lot of great works. A lot of the wonderful plays that are performed today came from this period. William Shakespeare was the most renowned writer from this period. This era can be characterised as pre-Shakespearean era and Shakespearean era.

University Wits

'University Wits' is a group of English dramatists, who wrote in the 16th century and were educated at the universities Oxford or Cambridge. They significantly influenced the development of Elizabethan literature. The group includes - John Lyly, George Peele, Robert Greene, Christopher Marlowe, Thomas Lodge, Thomas Nashe and Thomas Kyd (he was also a part although he had studied at the Merchant Taylor's School, an excellent place in itself).

According to Edward Albert, the plays of University Wits had certain common features-. there was a fascination towards heroic themes, style and treatment was also heroic and the themes were tragic in nature.

Brief description of the dramatists of the group, called 'University Wits'

John Lyly (1554-1606)

John Lyly was born in Kent in 1554. His father, Peter Lyly was the Registrar of Canterbury and his grandfather William Lyly was a well-known grammarian. He received his education at Magdalen College, Oxford, from where he graduated in 1573 and completed MA in 1575.

In 1583, Lyly married Beatrice Browne, a Yorkshire heiress. The same year he came in control of the first Blackfriars Theatre. He also served as an MP three times, the first of which was for Hindon in Wiltshire, in 1589.

Literary Career and Works

Lyly is best known for his prose romance, *Euphues, or the Anatomy of Wit* (1578) and its sequel *Euphues and His England* (1580).

The name Euphues literally means a person well-endowed with wit. In Lyly's work, Euphues is a young gentleman of Athens, who is graced by nature with great personal beauty and by fortune with a large patrimony. But he uses his brilliant wit to enjoy the pleasures of wickedness rather than the honours of virtue. Euphues exemplifies the demoralised state of Italian society.

Major Works

- Euphues, or the Anatomy of Wit (1578)
- Euphues and His England (1580)
- Campaspe (1584)
- Sappho and Phao (1584)
- Mother Bombie (1589)
- Midas (1589)
- Love's Metamorphosis (1589)
- Endymion (1591)
- Gallathea (1592)
- Woman on the Moon (1597)

George Peele (1558-1596)

George Peele was born in London in 1558. His father, James Peele, was a clerk and teacher of book-keeping, writing and arithmetic, who wrote textbooks on accountancy. In 1565, Peele became a free scholar at Christ's Hospital, of which his father was clerk.

Christ's Hospital was a charitable institution administered by the Corporation of London, where Peele was taught writing and arithmetic. In 1571, Peele went to Oxford. He was a student first at Broadgates Hall (now Pembroke College) and later at Christ Church, whence he graduated in 1577 and completed MA in 1579.

Literary Career and Works

In 1585, he was employed to write the *Device of the Pageant* born before Woolston Dixie and in 1591, he devised the pageant in honour of another Lord Mayor, Sir William Webbe. Peele's The *Arraignment of Paris* (1584) was a courtly mythological pastoral play, which paid tribute to Queen Elizabeth. His *The Battle of Alcazar* (1594) was a semi-historical play, while *The Old Wives' Tale* (1595) was a romantic satire on the current dramatic taste.

Major Works

- The Arraignment of Paris (1584)
- The Famous Chronicle of King Edward, the First (1593)
- The Battle of Alcazar (1594)
- The Old Wives' Tale (1595)
- The Love of King David and Fair Bathseba (1599)

Robert Greene (1558-1592)

English dramatist Robert Greene is considered to be the founder of Romantic Comedy. Greene was born in Norwich in 1558. He studied at St John's College, Cambridge, in 1575 and graduated in 1578.

Literary Career and Works

Greene's literary career began with the romance *Mamillia* in 1583. His *Honourable History of Friar Bungay and Friar Bacon*, a play written in 1591 and published in 1594 is considered to be one of the first romantic comedies. This play deals with Bacon's proof of his magical powers before King Henry III. His short romances, written in the manner of Lyly's *Euphues*, include *Pandosto: The Triumph of Wit* (1588), from which Shakespeare drew the plot for *A Winter's Tale*.

Greene also wrote pamphlets related to urban low life such as *A Notable Discovery of Coosnage* (1592). He also wrote an autobiographical pamphlet- *A Groatsworth of Wit Bought with a Million of Repentance* (1592). Greene died in 1592 in the house of a poor shoemaker.

Major Works

- Mamillia (1583)
- Euphues: His Censure to Philautus (1587)
- Pandosto: The Triumph of Wit (1588)
- The History of Orlando Furioso (1590)
- A Looking Glass for London and England (with Thomas Lodge) (1590)
- The Scottish History of James the Fourth (1590)
- The Comical History of Alphonsus, King of Aragon (1590)
- A Groatsworth of Wit Bought with a Million of Repentance (1592)
- Philomela (1592)
- A Quip for an Upstart Courtier (1592)
- Honourable History of Friar Bacon and Friar Bungay (1594)

Thomas Lodge (1557-1625)

Thomas Lodge was probably born in London in 1557. His father, Sir Thomas Lodge, served as Lord Mayor of London for the 1562-63 term and his mother, Lady Anne Lodge, was the stepdaughter of William Laxton, who had been Lord Mayor of London from 1544 to 1545. However, their high social position soon weakened as a result of his father's bankruptcy.

Lodge made his first appearance at the University of Oxford about the year 1573, and was afterwards a scholar under the learned Mr Edward Hobye of Trinity College. In 1578, he joined Lincoln's Inn, London for a study of law. However, he left it midway, went against the wishes of his family and took up literature.

Literary Career and Works

He first came to attention in literary circles for his *Defence of Plays* in 1580. This pamphlet was written in reply to Stephen Gosson's attack on stage plays. Lodge's best known play is his prose romance *Rosalynde,* which provided the plot for Shakespeare's *As You Like It*. His other plays include *An Alarum Against Usurers* (1584), *Scillaes Metamorphosis* (1589), *The Wounds of Civil War* (1594) and *A Margarite of America* (1596). Lodge also collaborated with Robert Greene on the play *A Looking Glass for London and England.* While Lodge gained some success for his literary endeavours, he gradually became convinced about its lack of monetary potential.

To escape poverty, he took several long sea voyages and also worked on medicines to make his living. In 1597, he became a Roman Catholic and he graduated in medicine from the University of *Avignon* in 1598. He received another MD degree from Oxford in 1602 and thereafter practised medicine in London and in Brussels. Lodge died in 1626.

Major Works

- An Alarum Against Usurers (1584)
- Scillaes Metamorphosis (1589)
- Rosalynde: Euphues Golden Legacie (1590)
- The Wounds of Civil War (1594)
- A Looking Glass for London and England (1594, with Robert Greene)
- A Margarite of America (1596)
- A Treatise of the Plague (1603)

Thomas Nashe (1567-1601)

Thomas Nashe was born in November 1567 at Lowestoft, a fishing port in Eastern England. He was the third son of a clergyman called William Nashe. His father later became a minister. Nashe studied at St John's College, Cambridge and gained his bachelor's degree in 1586. After his father's death, Nashe could not continue his education and left Cambridge for London. There, he involved himself in the Martin Marprelate controversy, a religious and literary argument which arose as a result of Archbishop Whitgift's strict censorship policies.

Literary Career and Works

Martin Marprelate was the pseudonym, under which appeared several Puritan pamphlets (1588-89) satirising the authoritarianism of the Church of England under Archbishop John Whitgift. Nashe is believed to have written several satiric pamphlets, of which *An Almond for a Parrot* (1590) can be attributed to him with conviction.

Nashe's most significant work is his picaresque tale *The Unfortunate Traveller or The Life of Jack Wilton* (1594). It is an account of the wild overseas adventures of a youngster called Jack Wilton. This work is considered to be the precursor of the picaresque novel and is also sometimes known as the first English historical novel. His other works are *Pierce Penniless: His Supplication to the Devil* (1592), *The Terrors of the Night* (1594) and *Summer's Last Will and Testament* (1600).

Nashe was involved in a bitter pamphlet war with Gabriel Harvey, whom he also abuses in *Pierce Penniless.* Harvey further attacked Nashe's *Pierce Penniless* in *Pierce's Supererogation* (1593), which Nashe in turn countered with *Have with You to Saffron Walden* (1596). This 'war' controversy finally ended in June 1599, when Archbishop Whitgift and Bishop Bancroft decreed that "All Nashe's books and Doctor Harveye's books be taken away wheresoever they may be found and that none of their books be ever printed thereafter." Nashe died at the age of 34, in 1601.

Major Works

- The Anatomy of Absurdity (1589)
- Preface to Greene's Menaphon (1589)
- An Almond for a Parrot (1590)
- Pierce Penniless (1592)
- Summer's Last Will and Testament (play performed 1592, published 1600)
- Christ's Tears over Jerusalem (1593)
- Terrors of the Night (1594)
- The Unfortunate Traveller (1594)
- Have with You to Saffron-Walden (1596)
- Isle of Dogs (1597)

Thomas Kyd (1557-1594)

Thomas Kyd was born in 1558 probably in London. He was educated at the Merchant Taylors School in London. It is believed that Kyd did not proceed to the universities; he apparently followed, soon after leaving school, his father's business as a scrivener.

Literary Career and Works

Kyd probably began his career as a popular playwright about 1583 and produced his most significant work; *The Spanish Tragedy or Hironimo is Mad Again*, sometime around 1589-92. It was based on the tragedies written by the Roman playwright Seneca, whose plays focused on murder and revenge. Kyd's play established on the Elizabethan stage the revenge tragedy, a genre which included William Shakespeare's *Hamlet*.

Other works by Kyd are his translations of Torquato Tasso's *Padre di Famiglia*, published as *The Householder's Philosophy* (1588) and translation of Robert Garnier's *Cornelia* (1594). In 1590, Kyd seems to have given up writing for the stage and entered the service of an unnamed lord, who employed a troop of players.

Kyd was probably the private secretary of this nobleman. Kyd's lord patronised a company of players for which Christopher Marlowe (1564-1593) also most likely wrote. This brought Kyd and Marlowe into close acquaintance. In early May 1593, Kyd was arrested by the Queen's Privy Council for possession of heretical and blasphemous papers.

His papers were found shuffled with some of Marlowe's, who was imprisoned a week later. Kyd was imprisoned and interrogated thoroughly about the origins of his papers. Kyd confessed that he had received the papers from Marlowe. Though he was later released, his patron refused to take him back into service. He therefore died of poverty in 1594.

Kyd's Spanish Tragedy

- Kyd's *Spanish Tragedy* was written between 1582 and 1589.
- It was the first example of a revenge tragedy, a type of play that was to become extremely popular on the Elizabethan stage during the last decade of the 16th century.
- It was modeled on Seneca's revenge tragedies.
- The central motif of the play is the revenge of Hironimo, Marshal of the Spain for the murder of his son Horatio.
- Horatio, in love with the beautiful Belimperia, was murdered by the Prince of Portugal and by Belimperia's brother Lorenzo, who wanted her to marry the Prince.
- Kyd's play introduced a new kind of character in drama an obsessive, brooding and mistrustful plotter.

Christopher Marlowe (1564-1593)

The most talented of Shakespeare's contemporaries, Christopher Marlowe was born in Canterbury around 26th February, 1564. He was the second child and eldest son of John Marlowe, a Canterbury shoemaker. Marlowe received a scholarship from Matthew Parker, Archbishop of Canterbury to study music, religion, Latin and literature and entered King's School, Canterbury. Later, he joined Corpus Christi College, Cambridge, from late 1580 until 1587. During his later Cambridge years, Marlowe translated Ovid's *Amores* (The Loves) and the first book of Lucan's *Pharsalia* from Latin.

Literary Career and Works

After his education, Marlowe went to London where he started writing for the stage. His first play, *Dido, Queen of Carthage*, was also written while he was still a student at Cambridge, but it was not published until 1594. His second play, *Tamburlaine the Great,* about a Scythian shepherd and his thirst for power was published in 1590.

Marlowe's famous 'mighty lines' first came into focus in this play and also established blank verse as the staple medium for later Elizabethan and Jacobean dramatic writing. His other famous plays are *Dr Faustus* (1604), about a scholar, who in his quest for infinite knowledge and power, sells his soul to the Devil and *The Jew of Malta* (1633), which is a dramatic presentation of a Machiavellian man-Barabas.

Apart from his dramatic works, Marlowe also succeeded in non-dramatic verse. His *Hero and Leander* is a mythological poem consisting of 818 lines. This unfinished poem was completed after his death by George Chapman.

Marlowe died of a stab wound in a possible government safe house in Deptford on 30th May, 1593. He was buried on the 1st of June in the churchyard of St Nicholas at Deptford.

Major Works

- Tamburlaine (1590)
- The Massacre at Paris (1593)
- Dido, Queen of Carthage (1594)
- Edward II (1594)
- Doctor Faustus (1604)
- The Jew of Malta (1633)

Poetry

- Translation of Book One of Lucan's Pharsalia (date unknown)
- Translation of Ovid's Elegies (1580s)
- The Passionate Shepherd to His Love (pre-1593)
- Hero and Leander (1593, unfinished; completed by George Chapman, 1598)

Francis Bacon (1561-1626)

Philosopher and statesman Francis Bacon was born in London on 22nd January, 1561. His father, Sir Nicholas Bacon, was the Lord Keeper of the Great Seal under Queen Elizabeth I. His mother, Lady Anne Cooke Bacon, was his father's second wife and daughter to Sir Anthony Cooke, a humanist, who was Edward VI's tutor.

Political and Literary Career

Bacon composed his first political memorandum *A Letter of Advice to Queen Elizabeth*, which earned him instant attention.

Bacon's political career flourished under the reign of King James I. He was knighted in 1603 and further went on to receive a number of appointments, including Solicitor General, Attorney General, Lord Chancellor and his father's old position, Lord Keeper of the Great Seal. He also became a member of the Privy Council and received two titles, Baron Verulam and Viscount St Albans.

His political career came to an abrupt end in 1621, when he was impeached for taking bribes. Bacon pleaded guilty and spent four days in prison at the Tower of London. Because of this, he lost his position at the court. He devoted the remaining years of his life to writing and produced some of his most significant works such as *The History of the Reign of King Henry VII* (1622), six essays on natural history called *The History of Winds* (1622) and *De Augmentis Scientiarum* (1623). Francis Bacon died at Highgate, in the Earl of Arundel's house on 9th April, 1626, due to complications arising from bronchitis.

Major Works

- Essays: Religious Meditations (1597)
- The Elements of the Common Law of England (1597)
- A Declaration of the Practises and Treasons attempted and committed by Robert, late Earl of Essex and his complices (1601)
- Sir Francis Bacon his Apology, in certain Imputations Concerning the Late Earl of Essex (1604)
- Certain considerations touching the Better Pacification and Edification of the Church of England (1604)
- The Proficience and Advancement of Learning (1605)
- De Sapientia Veterum Liber (1609)
- The Charge of Sir Francis Bacon, Knight, the King's Attorney-General, Touching Duels (1614)
- The Wisdom of the Ancients (1619)
- Novum Organum (1620)
- The History of the Reign of King Henry VII (1622)
- The History of Winds (1622)
- Apophthegms, New and Old (1625)
- The New Atlantis (1626)

Important Quotes of Bacon

- "If a man will begin with certainties, he shall end in doubts; but if he will be content to begin with doubts, he shall end in certainties."
- 'Knowledge is power'.
- "Fame is like a river that beareth up things light and swollen and drowns things weighty and solid."
- "Reading make a full man; conference a ready man; and writing an exact man."
- "Imagination was given to man to compensate him for what he is not; a sense of humour to console him for what he is."
- "Wives are young men's mistresses, companions for middle age and old men's nurses."

William Shakespeare (1564-1616): The Bard of Avon

William Shakespeare was considered to be the greatest writer of the Elizabethan Age. Shakespearean age changed the face of drama in England. The Elizabethan period was so much dominated by him that many literary figures started calling 'The Elizabethan Age' itself as 'The Shakespearean Age'.

Actually, it was the later part of the Elizabethan Age i.e. 1590-1613 where Shakespeare had a major role to play alongwith some of his contemporaries.

In the meantime, influenced and motivated by the growing popularity of the English Literature, many other authors, besides Shakespeare took the centre-stage to give rise to a sort of new era, called the Jacobean period (1603-1625).

To sum up, the period from 1590 to 1625, witnessing the rise of William Shakespeare and his contemporaries including the Jacobean writers, can be aptly termed as 'The Age of Shakespeare and His Contemporaries' or 'The Later Elizabethan Period'.

It was this period when English Literature scaled new peaks in all forms of writings especially 'drama' and mainly owing to William Shakespeare.

English poet and playwright William Shakespeare was born and raised in Stratford-upon-Avon. He was baptized on 26th April, 1564. His father, John Shakespeare was a burgess of the recently constituted corporation of Stratford. His mother, Mary Arden was a local landed heiress. William Shakespeare had two older sisters, Joan and Judith and three younger brothers, Gilbert, Richard and Edmund.

Not much is known of Shakespeare's education. It is generally assumed that he attended the local grammar school, the King's New School. At the age of 18, Shakespeare married 26 years old Anne Hathaway, with whom he had three children- Susanna, Hamnet and Judith. Hamnet died at the age of eleven, by which time Shakespeare was already a successful playwright.

Shakespeare's literary career started around 1590. By this time, he started earning a living as an actor and a playwright in London and possibly had several plays produced. Two years later, he became a leading member of the Lord Chamberlain's Men, an acting company in London. Shakespeare with his company also built the 'Glove Theater' in 1599. His fame started with it. After the crowning of King James I, in 1603, the company changed its name to the King's Men.

Shakespeare produced most of his known work between 1589 and 1613. Most of his plays were written as 'quarto texts', on a sheet of paper folded four ways. A few of his plays were printed in his lifetime, though they appeared more voluminously after his death. His first collection of works was printed in 1623.

Shakespeare retired to Stratford a few years before his death. After 1606-1607, Shakespeare wrote fewer plays and none are attributed to him after 1613. His last three plays were collaborations, probably with John Fletcher, who succeeded him as the house playwright for the King's Men. Shakespeare died on the 23rd of April, 1616.

Shakespeare's Literary Life

Shakespeare's literary life can be divided into four main periods

(i) Pre-1594 (*King Richard III, The Comedy of Errors* etc),
(ii) 1594-1600 (*King Henry V, A Midsummer Night's Dream* etc),
(iii) 1601-1608 (*Macbeth, King Lear* etc.)
(iv) Post-1608 (*Cymbeline, The Tempest* etc).

First Literary Period (1585-1594)

In his first literary period, Shakespeare wrote 26 sonnets and 7 plays. Reuben Post Halleck states that this was a period, 'Showing the exuberance of youthful love and imagination'. Plays of this period also show the influence of Christopher Marlowe. *Henry VI* (Part I, II and III), *Richard III, Titus Andronicus, Comedy of Errors, Taming of the Shrew* and Shakespeare's poems *Venus and Adonis* and *Rape of Lucrece* were all written during this period.

Second Literary Period (1594-1600)

To Shakespeare's second period is attributed to his chronicle-history plays and joyous comedies. This period constitutes historical plays such as *Richard II*, *Henry IV*, (Part I and II) and *Henry V* and comedies such as *Midsummer Night's Dream, The Merchant of Venice, Much Ado about Nothing, As You Like It* and *Twelfth Night*. This period shows progress in Shakespeare's dramatic art.

Third Literary Period (1601-1608)

In the third period of his literary life, Shakespeare mostly wrote tragedies or romances with tragic resonances. Some of Shakespeare's most famous tragedies were written in this period: *Hamlet, Othello, King Lear, Macbeth, Antony and Cleopatra*.

His bitter comedies such as *All's Well that Ends Well* and *Measure for Measure* also belong to this period. The darkness/bitterness/sadness that characterises the works of this period was perhaps influenced by events in Shakespeare's own life: his father's death in 1601, execution of Earl of Essex by Elizabeth and distressful state of his friends' lives.

Fourth Literary Period (1609-1613)

During the late years of his life, Shakespeare wrote three plays: *Winter's Tale, Cymbeline* and *The Tempest*. Plays of this period are characterised by a grave cynicism and resignation. This period also includes works in collaboration such as Henry VIII and The Two *Noble Kinsmen.*The *Tempest* was Shakespeare's last written play.

Shakespearean Plays

The plays written by English poet, playwright and actor William Shakespeare have the reputation of being among the greatest in the English language and in Western literature. Traditionally, the plays are divided into the genres of comedy, tragedy and history, they have been translated into every major living language, in addition to being continually performed all around the world.

Many of his plays appeared in print as a series of quartos, but approximately half of them remained unpublished until 1623, when the posthumous first folio was published. The traditonal division of his plays into tragedies, comedies, and histories follows the categories used in the first Folio.

However modern criticism has labelled some of these plays 'problem plays' that elude easy categorisation or perhaps purposely break generic conventions and has introduced the term romances for what scholars believe to be his later comedies.

Shakespearean Genres

A literary genre is a classification which includes all those written works which have similar characteristics in terms of form, style or content. Genres can be as broad as novels, drama and poetry or can be further classified as in the breakup of drama into tragedy, comedy, melodrama etc.

When we speak of Shakespearean genres we indicate that Shakespeare's literary output can be classified in various ways and this clarification helps us to understand his work better. For example when a play by Shakespeare is categorised as tragedy, it will have certain features

- Protagonist will usually be of high stature.
- There will be personal and may-be state related problems.
- Eventually the play will end in a number of deaths including those of the main characters.

Shakespear's plays were printed individually before 1623 from his manuscripts or playscripts for performance called quartos.

The *First Folio* was brought out in 1623, its editors were Johan Heminges and Henry Condell (Shakespeas's fellows in The King's Men). Other editions brought out during 17th century were called Second, Third, Fourth and Fifth Folios.

In 1623, John Heminges and Henry Condell included only dramatic works in the compilation, entitled Master William Sakespeare's comedies, histories and tragedies published according to the true original copies, the sonnets of Shakespeare or his longer poems such as the *Rape of Lucrece*. In addition in the intervening years many scholars have disputed the exclusion of certain plays which did not appear in the First Folio but are held to be written by Shakespeare for example, *The Two Noble Kinsmen*.

It is generally accepted that William Shakespeare wrote 38 plays (Some of which were collaborative efforts), a sequence of 154 sonnets, two long narrative poems and various other short poems. The two plays which were not included in the First Folio were *Pericles*, *Prince of Tyre* and *The Two Noble Kinsmen*.

Shakespeare's plays can be classified into the following broad categories

- Romantic Comedy
- Shakespearean Tragedies
- Historical Plays
- Problem Plays
- Shakespearean Roman Plays

Shakespearean Comedy

Shakespeare perfected the genre of Romantic comedy. Most of his comedies are of the romantic type. The main theme of Shakespeare's comedy is love.

However, even though love is the main ingredient, Shakespeare's conception of love is never of the Petrarchan kind. In fact, in comedies such as *As You Like It*, he imparts a realistic touch to love and criticises the Petrarchan idea of love. In his comedies, lovers usually experience a set of obstacles before they get united in a harmonious manner. The play frequently ends with a marriage or a celebration. All conflicts get resolved at the end.

Shakespeare's romantic comedies are all set in an imaginative world far away from the dull and dreary world of everyday life. Examples of these are the magical forest in *The Midsummer Night's Dream* or the Forest of Arden in *As You Like it.* However, even when the characters depart to a newer fanciful world, Shakespeare adds touches of realism.

Allardyce Nicoll states in this regard that: "There are contemporary figures and contemporary fashions in *Love's Labour Lost;* Bottom and his companions mingle with the fairies; Sir Toby Belch and Sir Andrew Aguecheek are companions of Viola and Olivia, Dogberry and Verges of Hero and Beatrice. This is the cardinal characteristic of Shakespeare's romantic world the union of realism and fantasy.

In most of Shakespeare's mature comedies, there is always addition of a philosophical insight. Through the use of humour, Shakespeare deals with serious issues *e.g. As You Like It. It* takes up the issue of power, court politics and issue of cross-dressing, while *Comedy of Errors* takes up the issue of insanity.

Works of Shakespearean Comedy

- As You Like It
- Cymbeline
- The Merchant of Venice
- Taming of the Shrew
- Twelfth Night
- Comedy of Errors
- Love's Labour's Lost
- Pericles, Prince of Tyre
- The Tempest
- The Merry Wives of Windsor
- A Midsummer Night's Dream
- Much Ado About Nothing
- The Two Gentlemen of Verona
- The Winter's Tale

Shakespearean Tragedy

According to AC Bradley, a Shakespearean tragedy can be divided into three parts

1. An exposition of the state of affairs.
2. The beginning, growth and vicissitudes of the conflict.
3. The final catvastrophe or tragic outcome.

Shakespearean tragedy is primarily concerned with one person the tragic hero. The tragic hero is a person of high social estate, raised above the rest. It is he who undergoes suffering as a result of his tragic flaw or error of judgement. In case of Shakespeare's *Othello* for instance, tragedy occurs as a result of *Othello*'s tragic flaw-sexual jealousy.

The tragedy ends with the death of the tragic hero. However, even though the hero dies, moral order is eventually restored at the end. Shakespeare's tragedies developed out of earlier 16th century tragedies, which had antecedents in the 'tragedies' of medieval poetry—verse accounts of disaster, suffering and death, usually of mighty rulers.

Works of Shakespearean Tragedy

- Romeo and Juliet
- King Lear
- Othello
- Julius Caesar
- Coriolanus
- Macbeth
- Hamlet
- Titus Andronicus
- Antony and Cleopatra
- Timon of Athens

Shakespeare's Historical Plays

Although, there is no uniform consensus about what exactly constitutes a Shakespearean history play, yet the term generally refers to the ten plays that cover English history from the 12th to 16th centuries and each named after and focusing on a reigning monarch.

According to Michael Hattaway, Shakespeare's historical plays are "Related to history mainly by offering representations of historical figures and the creation of theatre out of historical events". Shakespeare's primary source for his history plays was Raphael Holinshed's *Chronicles of England, Scotland and Ireland.*

John M Mercer identifies some significant features of Shakespeare's historical plays

- Shakespeare's history plays usually have episodic plots "Unified primarily by their presentation of significant events from the reign of one monarch".
- They "Reflect the political ideology of the chronicle history books as well as the personal bias of the playwright".
- They may usually contain elements of both tragedy and comedy or exhibit the traits of just one of these genres. For instance, in addition to being history plays, Shakespeare's *Richard II* and *Richard III* are tragedies and *Henry IV*, *Part I* and *Henry V* are comedies.

Historical Plays of Shakespeare

- King John
- Richard II
- Henry IV, Part 2
- Henry VI, Part 1
- Edward III
- Henry IV, Part 1
- Henry V
- Henry VI, Part 2
- Henry VI, Part 3
- Richard III (also considered a tragedy)
- Henry VIII

Shakespeare's Problem Plays

While most of Shakespeare's plays fall into the above cited categories of tragedies, comedies or histories, there are some plays of his, which defy the conventions of these genres. These plays of Shakespeare do not neatly fit into any of these categories.

It was the critic Frederick S Boas who first used the term 'problem plays' for some of Shakespeare's plays in 1896, though the term was not his coinage and was already in use before for writers like Ibsen and Shaw. Boas borrowed and adapted the term for Shakespearean use. The three plays that are usually categorised as problem plays are *All's Well That Ends Well, Measure for Measure and Troilus and Cressida.* All three of these plays were written between 1599 and 1605.

According to Edward Dowden, these three plays of Shakespeare marked a change from Shakespeare's previous comedy works *All's Well that Ends Well* was 'grave and earnest'; *Measure for Measure* was 'dark and bitter'; while *Troilus and Cressida* was 'strange and difficult'. However, Frederick S Boas thought that this group of difficult plays/problem plays should also include *Hamlet*.

He remarked that this play was "Distinguished from the others by its tragic ending, but it was akin to them in its general temper and atmosphere."

Boas believed that these four plays presented problems of classification not just for the critics, but also for the audience. They centered on problems, which demanded attention and broke the conventions of genre.

There is no uniform consensus on *Hamlet* as a problem play. While critics such as Boas and Tillyard argued that *Hamlet* was a problem play, others like WW Lawrence and Peter Ure rejected this argument.

Shakespeare's Roman Plays

Though *Julius Caesar, Antony and Cleopatra* and *Coriolanus* are included under tragedies, yet they are also sometimes considered by critics in a separate category known as Roman plays of Shakespeare.

All these plays are set in Rome, deal with similar subjects and make use of the same source- North's translation of Plutarch's Lives. Dominika Klenova states that Shakespeare uses his source material as a framework, which helps him develop his own conception of creating drama out of biography. He also develops his idea of the Roman character and elaborates on him at both 'national' and individual level.

Peter J Leithart cites certain common features of Shakespeare's Roman plays

- They are all set in ancient Rome and were staged in Roman costume and Roman sets.
- Blood, violence and mayhem are important features of these plays.
- Suicide is depicted as an important Roman custom. Brutus and Cassius, Antony and Portia all commit suicide and Coriolanus also submits to death at the hands of the Volscians.
- Shakespeare depicts the Romans as self-conscious, theatrical and historically aware characters.

Soliloquies in Plays

Shakespeare's plays are also notable for their use of soliloquies, in which a character makes a speech to himself or herself so the audience can understand the character's inner motivations and conflict.

Source Material of the Shakespearean Plays

As was common in the period, Shakespeare based many of his plays on the work of other playwrights and recycled older stories and historical material. His dependence on earlier sources was a natural consequence of the speed at which playwrights of his era wrote; in addition, plays based on already popular stories appear to have been seen as more likely to draw large crowds.

There were also aesthetic reasons: Renaissance aesthetic theory too seriously the dictum that tragic plots should be grounded in history. For example, *King Lear* is probably an adaptation of an older play, *King Leir* and the *Henriad* probably derived from the famous victories of Henry V.

Shakespeare's Plays and Their Sources

Play	Source
The Comedy of Errors	Platus' Menaechmi
The Two Gentlemen of Verona	Jorge de Montemajor's pastoral romance Diana Enamorada
As You Like It	Thomas Lodge's Rosalynde
Romeo and Juliet	Arthur Brooke's verse poem The Tragical History of Romeo and Juliet
Julius Caesar and other Roman plays	Thomas North's Translation of Plutarch's Lives of the Noble Grecians and Romans
Hamlet	Saxo Grammaticus' Historia Danica
Othello	Cinthio's Hecatommithi
Macbeth	Stories from Holinshed's Chronicles of Scotland
All's Well that Ends Well	William Painter's Palace of Pleasure
Pericles	John Gower's Confessio Amantis
Cymbeline	Boccaccio's Decameron
The Winter's Tale	Robert Greene's pastoral romance Pandosto or The Triumph of Time

Shakespeare's Style of Writing

While many passages in Shakespeare's plays are written in prose, he almost always wrote a large proportion of his plays and poems in iambic pentameter. In some of his early works (like Romeo and Juliet), he even added punctuation at the end of these iambic pentameter lines to make the rhythm even stronger.

He and many dramatists of this period used the form of blank verse extensively in character dialogue, thus heightening poetic effects. To end many scenes in his plays he used a rhyming couplet to give a sense of conclusion, or completion. A typical example is provided in *Macbeth*: as Macbeth leaves the stage to murder Duncan (to the sound of a chiming clock), he says,

"Hear it is not Duncan; for it is a knell
That summons thee to heaven or to hell."

Shakespeare's writing (especially his plays) also feature extensive wordplay in which double entendres and rhetorical flourishes are repeatedly used. Humour is a key element in all of Shakespeare's plays.

Although a large amount of his comical talent is evident in his comedies, some of the most entertaining scenes and characters are found in tragedies such as Hamlet and histories such as Henry IV, Part I. Shakespeare's humour was largely influenced by Plautus.

Shakespeare's Contemporaries

Though the best known playwright of the Renaissance is, of course, William Shakespeare, it cannot be disputed that several others have an eminent place in the history of English Drama and theatre.

Brief description of a few important contemporaries is given below

George Chapman (1559-1634)

George Chapman was born in Hitchin, a town in Hertfordshire some thirty miles from London. It is believed that he studied at Oxford. He spent a few years in the household of a nobleman and sometime later got engaged in military service.

Literary Career and Works

Chapman's first published work was *The Shadow of Night* (1594). This long poem was divided into two parts, the *Hymnus in Noctem* and the *Hymnus in Cynthiam*. These contained hymns dedicated to Night and Cynthia, the Greek Goddess of Moon. His second work, *Ovid's Banquet of Sense* (1595) parodied the genre of the erotic narrative poem such as Shakespeare's *Venus and Adonis*.

Chapman's reputation was further cemented by his continuation of Christopher Marlowe's *Hero and Leander* (1598) and his translations of Homer. John Keats effusively praised Chapman's translation of Homer in his famous poem *On First Looking into Chapman's Homer*. Apart from *Homer*, Chapman also translated the *Georgics of Virgil* and the works of Hesiod. Chapman began writing for the stage around 1595. His first extant play, *The Blind Beggar of Alexandria* was produced in 1596. His most famous comedy was *All Fools*, based on two classical Roman comedies by Terence, the *Heauton Timorumenos* and the *Adelphoe*.

His best known tragedy was *Bussy D'Ambois*, based on the career of a protégé of brother of Henry III of France. Bussy is portrayed as a malcontent in a world of courtly intrigue. Despite his success as a dramatist, Chapman lived in dire financial straits. He was imprisoned for debt in 1600. He died in poverty in London around 1634.

Major Works

- The Shadow of Night (1594)
- Ovid's Banquet of Sense (1595)
- The Blind Beggar of Alexandria (1596)
- A Humorous Day's Mirth (1597)
- All Fools (1605)
- Bussy D'Ambois (1607)
- The Revenge of Bussy D'Ambois (1610)
- The Iliads of Homer (1611)
- Caesar and Pompey (1613)
- The Whole Works of Homer (1616)
- The Crown of All Homer's Works (1624)

Ben Jonson (1572-1637)

Ben Jonson was born in 1572 in London. His father, a clergyman died before he was born and his mother remarried a bricklayer named Robert Brett. Jonson was educated at Westminster School by the great classical scholar William Camden. For a brief period, Jonson joined his stepfather's trade-bricklaying, but soon became dissatisfied and later joined the army. He returned to London about 1594 and married Anne Lewis on 14th November, 1594.

Literary Career and Works

In London, Jonson joined a theatrical company and established himself as an actor and playwright. He was charged for sedition for a satirical play, he wrote alongwith Thomas Nashe, entitled *The Isle of Dogs* (1597). A year later, he gained recognition with his first major success, *Every Man In His Humour*. This play and its sequel *Every Man Out of His Humour*, elaborated his famous theory of humours.

Jonson was also involved in the famous War of Theatres with playwrights; John Marston and Thomas Dekker. Marston had presented a satirical portrait of Jonson in his *Histrio-mastix* in 1599.

In reply, Jonson critiqued Marston's style as 'fustian' in his *Every Man Out of His Humour*. Marston believed Jonson attacked him in his *Cynthia's Revels* and in turn, Marston satirised Jonson as Lampatho Doria in his play *What You Will*. Later, Jonson wrote *The Poetaster* in which he mocked both Marston's and Dekker's style of writing. Apart from his humour plays, Jonson's most well-known plays are his comedies *Epicoene* or *The Silent Woman*, *Volpone*, *The Alchemist* and *Bartholomew Fair*. Jonson's two tragedies on Roman themes are *Sejanus* and *Catiline*.

In his Essay of *Dramatic Poesy*, Dryden praised Jonson as "The most learned and judicious writer, which any theatre ever had". He compared Jonson with Shakespeare and called him 'the more correct poet'. According to Dryden, if Shakespeare was Homer, Jonson was Virgil. Jonson died on 6th August, 1637 and was buried in Westminster Abbey under a plain slab, on which was later carved the words, 'O Rare Ben Jonson!'

Major Works

Comedies

- A Tale of A Tub (1596)
- The Isle of Dogs, (1597 with Thomas Nashe)
- Every Man in His Humour (1598)
- Every Man Out of His Humour (1599)
- Cynthia's Revels (1600)
- The Poetaster (1601)
- Eastward Ho(1605), a collaboration with John Marston and Georage Chapman
- Volpone (1606)
- Epicoene, or the Silent Woman (1609)
- The Alchemist, Comedy (1610)
- Bartholomew Fair, Comedy (1614)

Tragedies

- Sejanus (1603)
- Catiline (1611)

Masques

- The Coronation Triumph, or The King's Entertainment (1604)
- The Masque of Beauty (1608)
- The Hue and Cry After Cupid, or The Masque at Lord Haddington's Marriage (1608)
- The Masque of Queens (1609)
- The King's Entertainment at Welbeck in Nottinghamshire (1633)
- Love's Welcome at Bolsover (1634)

Thomas Heywood (1570-1641)

Thomas Heywood was probably born in Lincolnshire in 1570. He was educated at Cambridge, but left without a degree, when his father died in 1593 and became a fellow of Peterhouse. After this, he moved to London and wrote a play for the Admiral's Men an acting company, in October, 1596.

Literary Career and Works

Heywood's first play was perhaps *The Four Prentices of London*, a tale of four apprentices, who become knights and travel to Jerusalem. Most of Heywood's significant plays were written between 1600 and 1620. In 1633, in the preface to his play *The English Traveller*, Heywood claimed to have written 220 plays.

Heywood's most popular play was a domestic tragedy *A Woman Killed with Kindness*. It is the story of a happy marriage broken when Anne, the wife is seduced by her husband's friend.

The title of the play is taken from a proverb in Shakespeare's *The Taming of a Shrew*. Heywood also wrote a number of pamphlets and poems. During the late years of his career, he devoted himself to writing non-dramatic works. He was called 'Prose Shakespeare' by Charles Lamb. He died in 1641 and was buried in St James's Church in the Clerkenwell section of London.

Major Works

- A Woman Killed with Kindness (1602-03)
- An Apology for Actors, Containing Three Brief Treatises (1612)
- The Royal King and the Loyal Subject (1615-18)
- The English Traveller (1623)
- A Mayden-Head Well Lost (1634)
- A Challenge for Beautie (1636)
- Loves Maistresse or The Queens Masque (1636)

Thomas Dekker (1572-1632)

Thomas Dekker was born in London in 1572. There is no biographical information available about Dekker like his upbringing or education. He might have acquired some knowledge of Latin, French and Dutch and he may have been in military service in his early years.

Literary Career and Works

Dekker started his literary career in the 1590s. In the year 1599, Dekker produced two plays, *Old Fortunatus* (1599), a morality play based on German legend and *The Shoemaker's Holiday* (1599), a comedy centered on Simon Eyre, a shoemaker. The plot of the second play derives from Thomas Deloney's story.

Dekker's most famous and successful play was *The Honest Whore* (1604-1605). It is the story of a prostitute Bellafront, who redeems herself.

Dekker also wrote successful pamphlets such as *The Wonderful Year* (1603), a graphic account of London beset by plague. He further provided accounts of London underworld in pamphlets, *The Seven Deadly Sins of London* (1606) and *The Belman of London* (1608). *The Gull's Hornbook* (1609), *the Roaring girl* (1610) written with Thomas Middleton. Thomas Dekker died in 1632, being heavily in debt.

Major Works

- Old Fortunatus (1599)
- The Shoemaker's Holiday (1599)
- The Honest Whore (1604-05)
- The Wonderful Year (1603)
- The Seven Deadly Sins of London (1606)
- The Belman of London (1608)
- The Gull's Hornbook (1609)
- The Roaring Girl (1610)

John Marston (1576-1634)

John Marston was born in Oxfordshire, England on 7th October, 1576. He was the son of an English lawyer and his Italian wife. Marston attended Brasenose College, Oxford in 1592 and received his BA in 1594. He entered the Middle Temple to study law and remained there until 1608, but did not complete his legal education.

Literary Career and Works

Marston's literary career began as a poet in 1598. His first known works are *Books of Ovidian eroticism and poetic satire, The Metamorphosis of Pigmalion's Image* and *The Scourge of Villanie* A year later, Marston began working as a playwright for Philip Henslowe. He wrote all his plays before taking holy orders in 1609. *Histriomastix* is considered as his first play.

His other popular plays are *Antonio and Mellida* (which deals with the 'comic crosses of true love' faced by Antonio, son of the good Duke Andrugio, and Mellida, daughter of the wicked Duke Piero), *Malcontent* (a satirical comedy which is centered on a supplanted Duke who returns to his Dukedom in disguise) and *The Dutch Courtesan* (story of two friends, Freevill and Puritan Malheureux, and their turbulent relationship with the passionate Dutch Courtesan Franceschina).

Probably under the influence of his father-in-law, Marston became a reader at the Bodleian library at Oxford in 1609 and was made a deacon on 24th September and a priest on 24th December, 1609. A few years later, he was assigned the living of Christchurch, Hampshire. Marston died on 24th June, 1634 in London.

Major Works

- The Metamorphosis of Pigmalions Image. And Certaine Satyres (1598)
- The Scourge of Villanie. Three Bookes of Satyres (1599)
- Histriomastix (1599)
- Antonio and Mellida (1599-1600)
- Antonio's Revenge (1600)
- Jacke Drums Entertainment: Or, The Comedie of Pasquill and Katherine (1600-01)
- What You Will (1601)
- The Malcontent (1604)
- Parasitaster, or The Fawn (1604)
- Eastward Ho (by Marston, George Chapman, and Ben Jonson, 1604-1605)
- The Dutch Courtesan (1605)
- The Spectacle presented to the Sacred Majesties of Great Britain, and Denmark as They Passed through London (1606)
- The Entertainment of the Dowager-Countess of Darby (1607)

Thomas Middleton (1580-1627)

Thomas Middleton was born in London in 1580. He was the son of a London master bricklayer, who was later elevated to the status of a gentleman. He studied at Queen's College, Oxford and Gray's Inn. By 1600, Middleton had already published three books of verse and also began writing for the stage.

Literary Career and Works

Middleton's comedies deal with London life in the tradition of Dekker and Heywood. His earliest surviving independent play, *Blurt, Master Constable* was printed in 1602. As a playwright, he was frequently commissioned to write pageants and civic entertainments. His famous comedies of intrigue were, *A Trick to Catch the Old One* (1605), *A Mad World, My Masters* (1605) and *A Chaste Maid in Cheapside* (1611). His play *A Game at Chess* (1625), an allegory about England and Spain's political tension was anti-Spanish in tone. It drew the ire of the Spanish ambassador and prompted James I to suppress the play.

His most famous tragedy was *Women Beware Women* (1625), which depicts the degeneration of Bianca, wife of Leantio, after the Duke of Florence seduces her in presence of her husband. Middleton also wrote a highly successful tragedy in collaboration with William Rowley in 1622, titled *The Changeling*. The heroine of this play was Beatrice Joanna, who in her quest to escape marriage to a man she dislikes, ends up getting entangled in the vicious schemes of her servant De Flores (who also loves her). Middleton died of natural causes at Newington Butts and was buried there on 4th July, 1627.

Major Works

- The Phoenix (1603–04)
- The Honest Whore, Part 1 (1604), co-written with Thomas Dekker
- Michaelmas Term (1604)
- A Trick to Catch the Old One (1605)
- A Mad World, My Masters (1605)
- The Bloody Banquet (1608–09); co-written with Thomas Dekker.
- A Chaste Maid in Cheapside (1611)
- More Dissemblers Besides Women (1614)
- A Fair Quarrel (1616). Co-written with William Rowley.
- The Old Law (1618–19). Co-written with William Rowley and perhaps a third collaborator, who may have been Philip Massinger or Thomas Heywood.
- Anything for a Quiet Life (1621). Co-written with John Webster.
- The Changeling (1622). Co-written with William Rowley.
- Women Beware Women (1625)
- A Game at Chess (1625)

John Webster (1578-1634)

John Webster was probably born in London in 1578. He was the son of a coach-maker and a member of the Merchant Taylors' Company. It is believed that Webster studied at the Merchant Taylors' School. He later married Sara Peniall.

Literary Career and Works

Webster was employed as a playwright in the theatre company of Phillip Henslowe. His literary career began with collaborative works with writers such as Dekker, Rowley, Ford and Heywood. Between 1602 and 1605, he collaborated on 5 plays, including *Caesar's Fall*, *Lady Jane*, *Westward Ho!* and *Northward Ho!*. Webster's first individually written play was *The Devil's Law Case*, a tragicomedy.

This was followed by his two most famous plays, *The White Devil* and *The Duchess of Malfi*, among the finest of all Jacobean tragedies. Both of them are revenge tragedies. *The White Devil* is centered on Vittoria Corombona and the Duke of Brachiano, who are in an adulterous relationship. The Duke murders Vittoria's husband and his own wife. After the murders, both of them get married. However, justice is restored at the end with both the Duke and Vittoria getting killed at the hands of Isabella's (Duke's slain wife) avengers. *The Duchess of Malfi*, on the other hand, revolves around a widowed Duchess, who marries her steward, *Antonio* Bologna secretly without her brothers' knowledge.

When the Duchess' brothers, Cardinal and Ferdinand become aware of her secret marriage, they both get her and Antonio killed. However, here too justice prevails with the death and downfall of the evil characters at the end of the play. Webster died sometime around November, 1634. Elizabethan theatre rapidly declined after his death.

Major Works

- Caesar's Fall (1602, collaboration with Michael Drayton, Thomas Dekker, Thomas Middleton and Anthony Munday)
- Lady Jane (1602, collaboration with Heywood and other)
- Westward Ho (1604, collaboration with Thomas Dekker)
- Northward Ho (1605, collaboration with Dekker)
- The White Devil (1608-09)
- The Devil's Law Case (1610)
- The Duchess of Malfi (1613)
- Anything For a Quiet Life (1621, collaboration with Middleton)
- The Fair Maid of the Inn (1625, collaboration with Massinger and Ford)
- A Cure for a Cuckold (1625, collaboration with Heywood)

Philip Massinger (1583-1640)

Philip Massinger was born in Salisbury, Southern England in 1583. He was the son of Anne and Arthur Massinger. His father was servant to the prominent Herbert family and at one time a fellow of Merton College, Oxford. Massinger studied at St Alban Hall, Oxford, but left without a degree. Massinger's career as a playwright began around 1613. He became John Fletcher's primary collaborator when Beaumont got married and retired from the theatre.

Literary Career and Works

His collaboration with Fletcher, began around 1613 and ended at Fletcher's death in 1625, spanning some 20 plays, including *The Custom of the Country* (1619), *The False One* (1619–23), *The Beggar's Bush* (1612-1615), and *The Spanish Curate* (1622). He also collaborated with Thomas Middleton and William Rowley on *The Old Law* and with Nathan Field in *The Fatal Dowry*.

Massinger began writing independently from 1620 onwards. His most important individual works are his comedies *A New Way to Pay Old Debts* (1625), *The City Madam* (1632), both of which probed economic and social issues and the historical tragedy.

The Roman Actor (1626) *A New Way to Pay Old Debts* relied for its plot on Middleton's *A Trick to Catch the Old One*. It is a comedy of an extortioner, Sir Giles Overreach, who is tricked into restoring his nephew Willborn's fortunes. *The City Madam* mocks the social pretensions of Lady Frugal, who is obsessed about class. *The Roman Actor*, on the other hand is a tragedy based on the life of the Roman emperor Domitian, who was murdered in AD 96. It carries suggestions of Jonson's *Sejanus*. Massinger died in London, where he had spent most of his adult life, early in 1640.

Major Works

- The Maid of Honour (1621)
- The Duke of Milan (1621–1623)
- The Unnatural Combat (1621)
- The Bondman (1623)
- The Renegado (1624)
- The Parliament of Love (1624)
- A New Way to Pay Old Debts (1625)
- The Roman Actor (1626)
- The Great Duke of Florence (1627)
- The Picture (1629)
- Believe as You List (1631)
- The City Madam (1632)
- The Guardian (1633)
- The Bashful Lover (1636)

John Ford (1586-1639)

John Ford was born in Ilsington, Devon in 1586. He studied at Exeter College, Oxford, in 1601 and entered the Middle Temple in November 1602.

Literary Career and Works

Ford's first published work was an elegy, he wrote on the Earl of Devonshire in *Fame's Memorial* (1606). Before he started writing dramatic works, Ford wrote poems such as *Christ's Bloody Sweat* (1613), and two prose essays published as pamphlets, *The Golden Mean* (1613) and *A Line of Life* (1620).

His first venture in dramatic work may well have been in the writing or revising of *A Bad Beginning Makes a Good Ending*, which was acted by the King's Men at court in 1612-1613. However, he came to limelight with his collaborative work with Thomas Dekker and William Rowley, *The Witch of Edmonton* in 1621.

His reputation as a playwright rests on the plays *Tis Pity She's a Whore* (1624) and *The Broken Heart*; *The Lover's Melancholy* (1628). Revolving around the theme of incest, *Tis Pity She's a Whore* centers on the siblings Giovanni and Annabella, who insist on the rightness of their incestuous passion for each other, regardless of structures of religion, family and society. *The Broken Heart*, on the other hand, depicts Penthea, a noble and virtuous heroine, who is forced by her brother to leave her love, Orgilus and marry Bassanes. Ford died in 1639.

Major Works

- Christ's Bloody Sweat (1613)
- The Witch of Edmonton (1621), with Thomas Dekker and William Rowley
- The Sun's Darling (1624), with Dekker
- Tis Pity She's a Whore (1624)
- The Lover's Melancholy (1628)
- The Broken Heart (1628)
- Love's Sacrifice (1632)
- Perkin Warbeck (1629–34)
- The Fancies Chaste and Noble (1635-36)
- The Lady's Trial (1638)

Beaumont and Fletcher

Collaboration between playwrights Francis Beaumont (1584-1616) and John Fletcher (1579-1625) was so successful that they are often named together as a group. Beaumont was the son of a chief justice, and Fletcher the son of a clergyman who later became Lord Bishop of London. While Beaumont was born in Leicestershire and educated at Oxford and the Inner Temple, Fletcher was born in Sussex and studied at Corpus Christi, Cambridge.

Beaumont's first published verses were prefaced to his brother John Beaumont's *The Metamorphosis of Tobacco* (1602). The same year, his *Salmacis* and *Hermaphroditus* was also published. While both Beaumont and Fletcher wrote solo plays, their works in collaboration are better known.

Literary Career and Works

It is unclear how or where both these playwrights met or how their association started. However, their collaboration started in 1607 and lasted until Beaumont's death in 1616. They worked together on more than fifty plays. They appear to have replaced Shakespeare around 1609 as chief dramatists of the King's Men. They wrote *Philaster, The Maid's Tragedy, Cupid's Revenge* and *A King* and *No King* all in a span of two years. The first collected edition of the plays of Beaumont and Fletcher came out in 1647.

According to Martha Fletcher Bellinger, in the combined works of Beaumont and Fletcher, there is 'sureness of touch, humor, pathos and intensity'.

"Fletcher was more brilliant of the two, with the ability to create witty, graceful dialogue; while tragic intensity and genial humri were the special gifts of Beaumont.

In their joint plays their talents are so organically combined, so completely merged into one, that the hand of Beaumont cannot be clearly distinguished from that of Fletcher."

While Beaumont had died of fever in 1616 and was buried at Westminster Abbey, Fletcher died in 1625 and was buried at St. Saviour's, Southwark.

Major Works

Beaumont's Works

- Salmacis and Hermaphroditus (1602).
- The Woman Hater (1605).
- The Masque of The Inner-Temple and Gray's Inn (1612).

Fletcher's Works

- The Faithful Shepherdess (1609).
- The Tragedy of Valentinian (1610-14).
- The Woman's Prize; or, The Tamer Tamed (1611).
- The Mad Lover (1616).
- The Wild-Goose Chase (1621).
- Rule a Wife and Have a Wife (1624).

Beaumont and Fletcher Plays in Collaboration

- Philaster; or, Love Lies A-Bleeding (1610)
- The Coxcomb (1608-1610)
- The Maid's Tragedy (1610)
- The Captain (1609-1612)
- A King and No King (1611)
- Cupid's Revenge (1611)
- The Noble Gentleman (1613)
- Love's Pilgrimage (1615-16)
- The Scornful Lady (1616)

Important Points

- The fact that so many plays survive from the Elizabethan and Jacobean times is itself an indication of the popularity of both, the theatre and the plays written for the theatre.
- If we keep Shakespeare at the Centre of English Renaissance drama, he had two sets of contemporaries or 'fellow dramatists' The first included the University Wits and the second set of colleagues included Chapman, Jonson, Marston, Middleton, Heywood etc and towards the end Beaumont, Fletcher and Webster. Thus Renaissance drama can be neatly, if artificially divided into two segments. Shakespeare bridging them and uniting them.
- The closure of theatres in 1642 by order of Parliament brought an end to renaissance English drama as it is known understood today and when the theatres re-opened in 1660. It was a new era that dawned.

EXAM BASED QUESTIONS

1 What form of fine art is the Elizabethan Era most famous for?
(a) Literature (b) Painting
(c) Ballet (d) Theatre

2 What type of plays were performed at the English theatre ?
(a) History plays (b) Comedies
(c) Tragedies (d) All of these

3 The first complete tragedy of the Senecan type, which was written by Thomas Morton and Thomas Sackville?
(a) Ralph Roister Doister (b) Needle
(c) Jocasta (d) Gorboduc

4 John Lyly's plays are
(a) Campaspe, Endymion and Gallathea
(b) Tamburlaine the Great, The Jew of Malta and Edward, The Second
(c) The Battle of Alcazar, The 'Old Wives' Tale and the Arraignment of Paris.
(d) The Spanish Tragedy and Gorboduc

5 Who calls Elizabeth age of England as a noble and puissant nation, rousing herself, like a strong man after sleep and shaking her invincible locks?
(a) Spenser (b) Johnson
(c) Lyly (d) John Milton

6 Who was known for his work, prose romance Euphues?
(a) Robert Greene (b) John Lyly
(c) Thomas Kyd (d) Christopher Marlowe

7 With whom is 'Endymion' is related?
(a) Drayton (b) Lyly
(c) Greene (d) Peele

8 Name the dramatist of Campuses, Edition, Love's Metamorphosis.
(a) John Lyly (b) Robert Greene
(c) Thomas Lodge (d) Thomas Nashe

9 George Peele plays are
(a) The Spanish Tragedy and Gorboduc
(b) The Jew of Malta, Doctor Faustus and Edward the Second
(c) The Battle of Alcazar, The 'Old Wives' Tales and the Arraignment of Paris
(d) The Unfortunate Traveller and The Life of Jack Wilton

10 The dramatist known for his musical ability?
(a) John Lyly (b) Robert Greene
(c) George Peele (d) Thomas Kyd

11 Which play of George Peele was a pastoral play?
(a) The Battle of Alcazar
(b) The Arraignment of Paris
(c) The Famous Chronicle of King Edward
(d) The Old Wives Tale

12 Which of these is a kind of mystery play of George Peele?
(a) The Battle of Alcazar
(b) The Arraignment of Paris
(c) The Old Wives Tale
(d) The Love of King David and Fair Bethsheba

13 Which of these is a romantic satire on the current dramatic taste of George Peele?
(a) The Arraignment of Paris (b) The Old Wives' Tale
(c) The Battle of Alcazar (d) None of these

14 The Old Wives' Tale was written by
(a) George Peele (b) John Lyly
(c) Thomas Kyd (d) Edward

15 Which play of Robert Greene was written jointly with Lodge ?
(a) The Comical History of Alphonsus King of Aragon
(b) The Honourable History of Friar Bacon and Friar Bungay
(c) The History of Orlando Furioso
(d) A Looking Glass for London and England

16 Christopher Marlowe's plays are
(a) The Comical History of Alphonsus King of Aragon, The History of Orlando, Furioso and The Scottish History of James, The Fourth
(b) The Spanish Tragedy and Gorboduc
(c) The Jew of Malta, Tamburlaine, The Great and Doctor Faustus
(d) The Unfortunate Traveller and The Life of Jack Wilton

17 In the first three plays of Marlowe each of the heroes is consumed by a burning passion which leads to his doom. In The Jew of Malta, it is the greed for riches, in Dr Faustus it is inordinate thirst for knowledge. Which passion is depicted in his Tamburlaine?
(a) Thirst for bloodshed (b) Homicidal instinct
(c) Lust (d) Thirst for power

18 Barabbas is ruined by Christians. He plans a revenge by resorting to incredible cruelties until he falls into a cauldron of boiling water prepared for his enemies. This is in short, the story of a play by Marlowe. Identify the play.
(a) Edward II (b) The Jew of Malta
(c) The Massacre of Paris (d) Dido

19 Who among the following Marlovian characters is consumed by greed?
(a) Barabbas (b) Tamburlaine
(c) Doctor Faustus (d) Mephistopheles

20 Which among the following plays by Christopher Marlowe has epic features?
(a) Doctor Faustus (b) Edward II
(c) Hero and Leander (d) Tamburlaine

21 The hero of Marlowe's Tamburlaine was born as a
(a) carpenter (b) goldmith
(c) shepherd (d) fisherman

22 Which of the following is not a revenge tragedy?
(a) The White Devil (b) The Duchess of Malfi
(c) Doctor Faustus (d) The Spanish Tragedy

23 The immediate source of Christopher Marlowe's Doctor Faustus is
(a) a French narrative (b) a Dutch narrative
(c) a German narrative (d) None of these

24 Thomas Nashe's plays are
(a) The Unfortunate Traveller and The Life of Jack Wilton
(b) The Spanish Tragedy and Gorboduc
(c) The Jew of Malta, Doctor Faustus and Edward the Second
(d) None of the above

25 Which is correct for the work of Nashe?
(a) Defense of Plays (b) The Jew of Malta
(c) The Spanish Tragedy (d) Pierce Penniless

26 'The Unfortunate Traveller' has been authored by
(a) Robert Greene (b) Thomas Deloney
(c) Thomas Nashe (d) Thomas Lodge

27 Thomas Kyd's plays are
(a) The Spanish Tragedy and Gorboduc
(b) The Jew of Malta, Tamburlaine the Great and Doctor Faustus
(c) The Unfortunate Traveller and The Life of Jack Wilton
(d) None of the above

28 Who among the following is included in University Wits but did not study at University?
(a) John Lyly (b) Thomas Nashe
(c) George Peele (d) Thomas Kyd

29 Thomas Kyd's 'The Spanish Tragedy' was influenced by
(a) Seneca (b) Tertullian (c) Virgil (d) Plautus

30 Given below are some of early tragedies. Out of these one was full of 'horror'. However, it became popular and remained so till the end of the century. Ben Jonson refers to it in his 'Everyman in his Humor ' Identify it.
(a) Dr. Faustus by Marlowe
(b) The Jew of Malta by Marlowe
(c) Spanish Tragedy by Kyd
(d) Gorboduc by Thomas Morton and Thomas Sackville

31 Which one of them is not from the University Wits?
(a) Thomas Lodge (b) Robert Greene
(c) Thomas Kyd (d) Thomas North

32 'The plays of the University Wits and certain common features-treatment was heroic and themes were tragic' was said by
(a) Lyly (b) Edward Albert
(c) Peele (d) Lodge

33 Who worked in active manner regarding Queen Elizabeth's safety?
(a) Bacon (b) Spenser
(c) Webbe (d) Hooker

34 'Novum Organum' is the book written by
(a) Thomas Deloney (b) Thomas Watson
(c) Bacon (d) Watson

35 When was Bacon made Attorney-General?
(a) 1600 (b) 1607 (c) 1601 (d) 1612

36 'A letter of advice to Queen Elizabeth' earned instant attention to which of these authors?
(a) Hooker (b) Robert Greene
(c) Bacon (d) Thomas Kyd

37 'I have taken all knowledge for my province' was said by
(a) Ben Johnson (b) John Heywood
(c) Bacon (d) Raleigh

38 When did Bacon publish his 10 essays?
(a) 1597 (b) 1612
(c) 1625 (d) 1607

39 How many acts are there in William Shakespeare's plays?
(a) Three (b) Four
(c) Five (d) Six

40 When was Romeo and Juliet written?
(a) First period (b) Second period
(c) Third period (d) Fourth period

41 Macbeth hires assassins to murder Banquo's son, named
(a) Angus (b) Ross
(c) Fleance (d) Lennox

42 Macbeth from Shakespeare's play was
(a) great general (b) good commander
(c) a scholar (d) a ripe old king

43 Othello was
(a) great general (b) good commander
(c) a scholar prime (d) a ripe old king

44 Hamlet was
(a) good commander (b) great general
(c) a scholar prince (d) a ripe old king

45 Who was the childhood friend of Helena in 'A Midsummer Night's Dream'?
(a) Thesus (b) Hermia (c) Lysander (d) Demetrius

46 Which character of Shakespeare describes thoughtful love?
(a) Orlando and Rosalind (b) Celia and Oliver
(c) Phebo and Silvius (d) Helena and Oberon

47 Which character of Shakespeare describes love at first sight?
(a) Orlando and Rosalind (b) Celia and Oliver
(c) Phebo and Silvius (d) Helena and Oberon

48 In which play does Shakespeare introduced us to the world of fairies, with the roguish imp of folklore, Puck?
(a) The Tempest
(b) As You Like It
(c) Twelfth Night
(d) A Midsummer Night's Dream

49 Who is travelling with Macbeth when he first encounters the three witches?
(a) Macduff (b) Mercutio
(c) Lady Macbeth (d) Banquo

50 The mature comedy by Shakespeare is
(a) The Comedy of Errors (b) Twelfth Night
(c) All's Well That Ends Well (d) Love's Labour's Lost

51 Which of these is the romantic comedy of Shakespeare?
(a) Twelfth Night (b) The Comedy of Errors
(c) The Taming of the Shrew (d) Love's Labour's Lost

52 Which of these is the dark comedies/problem comedies?
(a) Measure for Measure (b) As You Like It
(c) Much Ado About Nothing (d) None of these

53 Which play is called as the dramatic romances/tragic comedies/reconciliation plays?
(a) The Merchant of Venice (b) Hamlet
(c) Pericles
(d) The Training of the Shrew

54 Helena is the character belongs to whose play?
(a) Spenser (b) John Lyly
(c) Thomas Nashe (d) Shakespeare

55 Who was known for his tragedies?
(a) Shakespeare (b) Thomas Kyd
(c) John Lyly (d) Spenser

56 The tragic comedy among these is
(a) The Twelfth (b) As You Like It
(c) Cymbeline (d) Love's Labour's Lost

57 Great tragedies of Shakespeare is/are
(a) Macbeth (b) Othello
(c) Hamlet (d) All of these

58 Which is the Shakespeare's master piece of pictorial art?
(a) The Passionate Pilgrim and the Phoenix and the Turtle
(b) A Lover's Complaint
(c) The Rape of Lucrece
(d) Venus and Adonis

59 Queen Elizabeth, it is said, desired to see Falstaff in Love, so at her behest Shakespeare wrote a comedy entitled.
(a) Taming of the Shrew (b) Comedy of Errors
(c) Merry Wives of Windsor (d) Measure for Measure

60 Who wrote the romance Rosalinda which supplied the plot for Shakespeare's 'As You Like It'?
(a) Greene (b) Lodge (c) Lyly (d) Nashe

61 Shakespeare depended primarily on two sources for his legendary and historical plays. Which is the most important one?
(a) King Arthur's legend (b) Holinshed's Chronicles
(c) Plutarch's Lives (d) Legends of Charlemagne

62 How many plays are attributed to Shakespeare in toot?
(a) 37 (b) 36
(c) 21 (d) 154

63 Which is the last play written by William Shakespeare?
(a) As You Like It
(b) Two Gentlemen from Verona
(c) Henry V
(d) The Tempest

64 How are Polonius and Laertes related?
(a) Father/Son (b) Uncle/Nephew
(c) Cousin/Cousin (d) Brother/Brother

65 Who tells Macbeth, 'The queen, my lord, is dead'?
(a) Seyton (b) Siward
(c) The Doctor (d) Caithness

66 What is the name of the playlet Hamlet stages for Claudius?
(a) Slings and Arrows (b) Vice of Kings
(c) The Murder of Gonzago (d) The Slaying of Lucianus

67 How does Lady Macbeth explain her husband's wild behaviour at the banquet?
(a) She tells the guests that Banquo's ghost is haunting Macbeth
(b) She tells the guests that Macbeth has had too much to drink
(c) She informs the guests that Macbeth is ill
(d) She reveals that Macbeth is overcome with grief over the death of Duncan

68 What poison does Claudius pour into the ear of Hamlet's father, causing his death?
(a) Burdock (b) Hebenon
(c) Baneberry (d) Hemlock

69 How many soliloquies does Hamlet deliver?
(a) 2 (b) 4 (c) 7 (d) 9

70 Name the theatre in which Shakespeare had shares.
(a) The Black Friars (b) The Theatre
(c) The Universe (d) The Rose

71 In which year, Shakespeare and others from his company built the 'Globe Theatre' and he got the name and fame in the theatrical life?
(a) 1599 (b) 1597 (c) 1610 (d) 1601

72 The first printed collection of William Shakespeare's plays was brought out by Heming and Condell who asserted that they did the work "in order to keep the memory of so worthy a friend and fellow alive." What is this first edition now called?
(a) Heming and Condell's Edition
(b) Everyman's Shakespeare
(c) First Folio
(d) Authentic Shakespeare

73 Which of the following books marks the beginning of Shakespeare's success?
(a) Love's Labour's Lost (b) The Merchant of Venice
(c) Venus and Adonis (d) Sonnets

74 Who is the Shrew in the play 'The Taming of the Shrew'?
(a) Bianca (b) Cleopatra (c) Katherine (d) Matilda

75 Who was appreciated for his psychological realism?
(a) Thomas Nashe (b) Christopher Marlowe
(c) Spenser (d) Shakespeare

76 Who in Shakespeare's Hamlet mambles a song from the 'Book of Songs and Sonnets' known as Total's Miscellany?
(a) Hamlet himself
(b) One of the two clowns, a grave-digger
(c) Polonius
(d) Gertrude

77 Name the play in which Shakespeare and Fletcher collaborated.
(a) Henry VIII
(b) Griselda
(c) The Two Noble Kinsmen
(d) The Maid's Tragedy

78 How would you classify The Knight of the Burning Pestle by Beaumont and Fletcher?
(a) Comedy (b) Tragedy
(c) Tragic-Comedy (d) Farce

79 This public place was made famous and immortal by Shakespeare, Seldon, Donne, Beaumont, Fletcher and Ben Jonson. Name it.
(a) The Friday Street Club (b) Mermaid Tavern
(c) Bread Street Tavern (d) Will's Coffee House

80 Who wrote the book England from Noah to Elizabeth?
(a) Daniel
(b) Michael Drayton
(c) William Warner
(d) Christopher Marlowe

81 Name the writer of the Elizabethan period who completed Marlowe's 'Hero and Leander' and collaborated with Jonson and Marston in Eastward Ho I.
(a) Thomas Dekker (b) George Chapman
(c) John Webster (d) Thomas Heywood

82 One contemporary of Jonson had a bitter and extravagant style. In his Poetaster Jonson gives him a purge which makes him vomit his learned and bombastic words.
(a) George Chapman (b) Thomas Dekker
(c) Marston (d) Fournier

83 Arcadia, a pastoral romance, was written by its author to entertain
(a) the queen
(b) his friend Spenser
(c) his daughter
(d) his sister, the Countess of Pembroke

84 Philoclea and Pamela in 'The Arcadia' are the daughters of
(a) Proclus (b) Basilisk (c) Musidorus (d) Earaches

85 Name the picaresque romance which is considered by some critics as the first Elizabethan novel.
(a) Rosalinda by Lodge
(b) Euphuism's Golden Legacy by Lodge
(c) Jack of Newbury by Deloney
(d) Jack Wilton or The Unfortunate Traveller by Nashe

86 Who among the following is not a 'University Wit'?
(a) Christopher Marlowe (b) George Peele
(c) Robert Greene (d) Ben Jonson

87 Ben Jonson is tragedy 'Sejanus' was published in
(a) 1610 (b) 1611 (c) 1603 (d) 1602

88 What all did Ben write?
(a) Comedies (b) Historical tragedies
(c) Court masques (d) All of these

89 In which century Ben's influence reappeared?
(a) 16th (b) 18th (c) 19th (d) 20th

90 Ben's first play was
(a) Every Man in his Humour
(b) The Poetaster's
(c) Every Man Out of his Humour, Cynthia's Revels
(d) Volpone, The Fox

91 A classical influence on Ben Jonson's Volpone is
(a) Juvenal (b) Aristophanes
(c) Plautus (d) Terence

92 Ben Jonson's comedies are
(a) Volpone, Bartholomew Fair, The Shoemaker's Holiday
(b) Volpone, The Alchemist, Epicoene
(c) Volpone, The Alchemist, The Knight of the Burning Pestle
(d) Volpone, Epicoene, The Shoemaker's Holiday

93 After considering the characters from Shakespeare's play tell, who was the elder/younger both in Edward the 'Second'.
(a) Mortimer (b) Spenser
(c) Both (a) and (b) (d) None of these

94 Who wrote the comedy, 'The Case is Altered'?
(a) Shakespeare (b) Nicholas Udall
(c) Ben Jonson (d) Robert Greene

95 Who was known for his Senecan plays of blood?
(a) Ben Jonson (b) George Chapman's
(c) John Webster (d) John Lyly

96 Who belonged to the School of Seneca?
(a) Chapman and Lyly (b) Marston and Dekker
(c) Chapman and Marston (d) Lyly and Dekker

97 Whose work is melodramatic and sensational?
(a) George Chapman's (b) John Webster's
(c) Ben Jonson's (d) Shakespeare's

98 When was John Webster's 'The White Devil' Published?
(a) 1601 (b) 1609 (c) 1599 (d) 1612

99 Some of John Webster's famous works are
(a) The White Devil (b) Duchess of Malfi
(c) The Devil's Law Case (d) All of these

100 'Black Book' and 'Mother Hubbard's Tale' is written by
(a) Thomas Heywood (b) Nashe
(c) Middleton (d) Dekker

101 'Where the bee sucks' is a song from which of the plays of Shakespeare?
(a) Othello (b) The Tempest
(c) Twelfth Night (d) As You Like It

102 Sexual possessiveness is a theme of Shakespeare's
(a) Coriolanus
(b) Julius Caesar
(c) Henry IV Part-I
(d) A Midsummer Night's Dream

103 Sexual jealousy is a theme is a Shakespeare's
(a) The Merchant of Venice (b) The Tempest
(c) Othello (d) King Lear

104 Who, among the following, is not a practitioner Jacobean tragedy?
(a) George Villiers (b) John Marston
(c) John Webster (d) Thomas Middleton

105 Which of the following is a major Jacobean play ?
(a) Everyman (b) Gorboduc
(c) Romeo and Juliet (d) The Duchess of Malfi

106 Some of the Jacobean playwrights were prolific. One of them claimed to have written 200 plays. The playwright is
(a) John Ford (b) Thomas Dekker
(c) Philip Massinger (d) Thomas Heywood

107 He was a musician in the court of Henry VIII. His aim was to amuse and not moralise. His interludes were hillarious and they paved the way for comedy. Name the writer and his work.
(a) Bishop Bale-King John
(b) John Heywood-The Four 'P' s
(c) John Skelton-Magnificence
(d) Lindsay-Satire of the Three Estates

108 What is Chatillon's message to John in the play 'King John' by Shakespeare ?
(a) Abdicate or Philip will attack
(b) Agree to marry Blanche or it will be war
(c) Give up Ireland or the Danes will attack
(d) Knight the Bastard or suffer the consequences

109 What is Falconbridge's complaint in the play 'King John'?
(a) His older brother, a bastard, has claimed his inheritance
(b) His father willed it to him
(c) He wants the inheritance even though he is his mother's younger son
(d) All of the above

110 What happens to John in the play 'King John'?
(a) He drowns
(b) He dies of old age
(c) He is poisoned by a monk
(d) He abdicates in favour of Louis

111 Which of these is correct about the Spanish Tragedy?
(a) It is not example of revenge tragedy
(b) It was modelled on Spenser's revenge tragedies
(c) The play did not introduce a new kind of character obsessive, blooding and mistrustful plotter
(d) It was not written between 1582 and 1589

112 Which of the following statements about 'As you Like It' is correct?
(a) It is based on the Forest of Arden
(b) It is a tragedy
(c) It is written by Ben Jonson
(d) It carries a pastoral and other poems

113 Which of the following is incorrect for 'Hamlet'?
(a) Polonius (b) Gertrude
(c) Claudius (d) Miranda

114 Which of the following is not true for Shakespeare's plays?
(a) Titus Andronicus (b) The Tempest
(c) Cymbeline (d) Shakespeare in Love

115 Which of the following is correct for a problem play?
(a) Macbeth (b) King John
(c) As You Like it (d) All's Well that Ends Well

116 ...... was the first master of the art of plot construction in English drama.
(a) George Peele (b) Robert Greene
(c) Thomas Kyd (d) John Lyly

117 ...... wrote comical history of Alphonsus.
(a) George Peele (b) John Lyly
(c) Thomas Kyd (d) Robert Greene

118 ...... is the first tragic dramatist who used the device of Nemesis in an artistic and psychological manner.
(a) George Peele (b) Robert Greene
(c) Christopher Marlowe (d) Thomas Kyd

119 ......took the characters and many of the incidents for three great Roman Plays from Plutarch's lives.
(a) Samuel Purchas (b) Shakespeare
(c) Thomas North (d) Sir Walter Raleigh

120 Shakespeare has portrayed sufferings in ...... plays.
(a) romantic (b) problem
(c) comedies (d) dramatic romances

121 William Shakespeare's Julius Caesar Antony and Cleopatra and Coriolanus are based on ....
(a) Holinshed's Chronicles (b) Folk-tales and Legends
(c) Older Roman Plays (d) Plutarch's Lives

122 ...... was the legendary queen of the Amazons, engaged to Theseus in 'A Midsummer Night's Dream'.
(a) Helena (b) Hermia (c) Hippolyta (d) Puck

123 ...... was Hermia's father who brought a complaint against his daughter to Theseus in 'A Midsummer Night's Dream'.
(a) Oberon (b) Egeus (c) Puck (d) Lysander

124 ......in 'A Midsummer Night's Dream' is a young man of Athens, in love with Hermia ?
(a) Thesus (b) Oberon
(c) Titania (d) Lysander

125 ...... of Shakespeare describes pastoral love.
(a) Orlando and Rosalind (b) Celia and Oliver
(c) Phoebe and Silvius (d) Helena and Oberon

126 Which of the following pairs is correctly matched ?
(a) As You Like It : Forest of Arden
(b) Dr Faustus : Quest for infinite Knowledge
(c) The Jew of Malta : Machiavellian man Barabas
(d) Romeo and Juliet : Magical forest

127 Which of the following pairs is correctly matched ?
(a) Romantic comedy : King Lear
(b) Problem play : Hamlet
(c) Tragedy : Venus and Adonis
(d) Poem : As You Like It

128 Which of the following pairs is incorrectly matched ?
(a) Roman play : Julius Caesar
(b) Problem play : Measure for Measure
(c) History play : Antony and Cleopatra
(d) Tragedy : Othello

129 Which of the following pairs is correctly matched ?
(a) Tottel : Chronicles
(b) Holinshed : Duchess of Malfi
(c) Webster : Miscellany
(d) Ben Jonson : Alchemist

130 Which of the following pairs is correctly matched ?
(a) King Lear : 1616
(b) Sonnets : 1609
(c) The King James Bible : 1611
(d) Image of the Globe Theatre : 1608

131 Which is the correct historical chronological order?
(a) John Milton is born, Globe Theatre Burned, Death of Shakespeare, Defeat of Spanish Armada
(b) Defeat of Spanish Armada, John Milton is born, Globe Theatre burned, Death of Shakespeare
(c) Globe Theatre burned, Death of Shakespeare, Defeat of Spanish Armada, John Milton is born
(d) Death of Shakespeare, John Milton is born, Globe Theatre burned, Defeat of Spanish Armada

132 Which of the following is in the correct sequence?
(a) Greene, Shakespeare, Nashe, Lyly
(b) Shakespeare, Nashe, Lyly, Greene
(c) Lyly, Greene, Shakespeare, Nashe
(d) Nashe, Lyly, Greene, Shakespeare

133 Which of the following is in chronological order?
(a) Romeo and Juliet, Julius Caesar, The Winter's Tale, The Tempest
(b) The Tempest, Romeo and Juliet, Julius Caesar, The Winter's Tale
(c) The Winter's Tale, Romeo and Juliet, Julius Caesar, The Tempest
(d) Julius Caesar, The Tempest, The Winter's Tale, Romeo and Juliet

134 Which is the correct sequence of the works of Shakespeare ?
(a) Comedy of Errors, Hamlet, As You Like It, Macbeth
(b) Comedy of Errors, As You Like It, Hamlet, Macbeth
(c) Hamlet, Macbeth, Comedy of Errors, As You Like It
(d) Hamlet, Macbeth, As You Like It, Comedy of Errors

135 Which of the following is in the correct sequence? The Pre-Raphaelite Brotherhood, The University Wits, The Rhymers 'Club, The transitional Poets, The Scottish Chaucerians.
(a) The Scottish Chaucerians, The University, Wits, The Transitional Poets, The Pre-Raphaelite Brotherhood, Te Rhymers' Club
(b) The Rhymers' Club, The University Wits, The Scottish Chaucerians, The Transitional Poets, The Pre-Raphaelite Brotherhood
(c) The Pre-Raphaelite Brotherhood, The Rhymers' Club, The Transitional Poets, The Scottish Chaucerians, The University Wits
(d) The University Wits, The Scottish Chaucerians, The Pre-Raphaelite Brotherhood, The Transitional Poets, The Rhymers' Club

136 Match the following.

	List I (Writers)		List II (Songs)
A.	Shakespeare's	1.	Drink to me only with thine eyes
B.	Marlowe's	2.	Cupid and my canpaspe played
C.	Lyly's	3.	Is this the face
D.	Jonson's	4.	Under the greenwood tree

Codes

	A	B	C	D
(a)	3	4	2	1
(b)	3	2	4	1
(c)	4	3	2	1
(d)	2	3	4	1

137 Match the following.

	List I		List II
A.	Romantic Comedy	1.	King Lear
B.	Problem Play	2.	Venus and Adonis
C.	Tragedy	3.	Twelfth Night
D.	Poem	4.	Hamlet

Codes

	A	B	C	D		A	B	C	D
(a)	2	1	4	3	(b)	3	4	1	2
(c)	3	1	4	2	(d)	2	4	1	3

138 Match the following.

	List I (Writers)		List II (Works)
A.	Shakespeare	1.	Abbicen's England
B.	Warner	2.	Venus and Adonis
C.	Thomas Heywood	3.	The Spanish Tragedy
D	Thomas Kyd	4	Supposes

Codes

	A	B	C	D		A	B	C	D
(a)	2	1	4	3	(b)	3	2	4	1
(c)	4	1	2	3	(d)	3	2	1	4

139 Match the following.

	List I		List II
A.	George Peele, Robert Greene, Thomas Lodge, Thomas Kyd	1.	The Rhymers Club/The Decadence of the 1890's
B.	William Congreve, William Wycherley, George Etherege, George Farquhar	2.	The Pre-Raphaelite Brotherhood
C.	John Everett Milais, James Collinson, Ford Madox Brown, Dante Gabriel Rossetti	3.	The University Wits
D.	Ernest Dowson, Lionel Johnson, WB Yeats	4	The Restoration Playwrights

Codes

	A	B	C	D		A	B	C	D
(a)	3	2	1	4	(b)	1	4	3	2
(c)	2	1	4	3	(d)	3	4	2	1

140 Match the following.

	List I		List II
A.	The Woman Hater	1.	1605
B.	The Maid's Tragedy	2.	1610
C.	Cupid's Revenge	3.	1611
D.	The Mad Lover	4.	1616

Codes

	A	B	C	D		A	B	C	D
(a)	3	4	2	1	(b)	1	2	3	4
(c)	4	3	2	1	(d)	2	1	4	3

141 In the following series, which one has all the works correctly matched with their periods?

(a) King John- First Period, Twelfth Night - Second Period, Cressida - Third Period, Timon of Athens - Fourth Period
(b) King John- Second Period, Twelfth Night-First Period, Cressida- Fourth Period, Timon of Athens- Third Period
(c) King John- Fourth Period, Twelfth Night- Third Period, Cressida- Second Period, Timon of Athens- First Period
(d) King John- First Period, Twelfth Night- Third Period, Cressida- Second Period, Timon of Athens- Fourth Period

142 In the following series, which one has all the plays correctly matched with their types.

(a) Othello-Comedy Play, Henry V-Tragedy Play, Measure for Measure- Historical Play, The Merchant of Venice-Problem Play
(b) Othello-Tragedy Play, Henry V-Historical Play, Measure for Measure- Problem Play, The Merchant of Venice-Comedy Play
(c) Othello-Problem Play, Henry V-Historical Play, Measure for Measure- Comedy Play, The Merchant of Venice-Tragedy Play
(d) Othello-Tragedy Play, Henry V-Comedy Play, Measure for Measure-Problem Play, The Merchant of Venice-Historical Play

143 In the following series, which one has all the works correctly matched with the year of their publication?

(a) Pericles-1609, Cymbeline-1607, The Tempest-1608, Antony and Cleopatra-1611
(b) Pericles-1611, Cymbeline-1608, The Tempest-1607, Antony and Cleopatra-1609
(c) Pericles-1608, Cymbeline- 1609, The Tempest-1611, Antony and Cleopatra-1607
(d) Pericles-1607, Cymbeline - 1608, The Tempest-1609, Antony and Cleopatra-1611

144 In the following series, which one has all the works correctly matched with their writers?

(a) Troilus and Cressida- George Chapman, All Fools- Ben Jonson, Sejanus-John Heywood, The English Traveller-Shakespeare
(b) Troilus and Cressida-John Heywood, All Fools-George Chapman, Sejanus-Shakespeare, The English Traveller-Ben Jonson

(c) Troilus and Cressida-Shakespeare, All Fools- John Heywood, Sejanus-John Heywood, The English Traveller-Ben Jonson
(d) Troilus and Cressida-Shakespeare, All Fools-George Chapman, Sejanus-Ben Jonson, The English Traveller-John Heywood

145 In the following series, which one has all the songs correctly matched with their composers?
(a) Or Scorn, or Pity on Me Take- Dekker, Cold's the Wind-Lodge, Fair is Foul and Foul is Fair- Ben Jonson, Love in My Bosom Like a Bee- Shakespeare
(b) Or Scorn, or Pity on Me Take- Shakespeare, Cold's the Wind-Ben Jonson, Fair is Foul and Foul is Fair-Dekker, Love in My Bosom Like a Bee-Lodge
(c) Or Scorn, or Pity on Me Take- Ben Jonson, Cold's the Wind-Dekker, Fair is Foul and Foul is Fair-Shakespeare, Love in My Bosom Like a Bee- Lodge
(d) Or Scorn, or Pity on Me Take- Shakespeare, Cold's the Wind-Dekker, Fair is Foul and Foul is Fair-Ben Jonson, Love in My Bosom Like a Bee- Lodge

146 Consider the following statements.
The Spanish Tragedy
1. the first example of revenge tragedy.
2. was not modelled on Seneca's revenge tragedies.
3. was not written between 1582 and 1589.
4. was written by Thomas Kyd.

Which of the statements given above are correct?
(a) 1 and 2 (b) 1 and 4 (c) 3 and 2 (d) 3 and 4

147 Consider the following statements.
1. Marlowe's contribution is remarkable for the age and English literature.
2. His plays are full of passion and energy.
3. There seems to be a desire to do something which is charming in itself portrayal.

Which of the statements given above are correct?
(a) 1 and 2 (b) 1 and 3 (c) 2 and 3 (d) All of these

148 Consider the following statements.
1. John Lyly's plays are allegorical and mythical in tone.
2. John Lyly's plays display realistic features.
3. John Lyly is known for his musical ability.

Which of the statements given above are correct?
(a) 1 and 3 (b) 2 and 3 (c) 1 and 2 (d) 1, 2 and 3

149 What is common to the following works? Identify to correct description below.
1. Tamburlaine 2. Edward II
3. Doctor Faustus 4. The Jew of Malta

Codes
(a) All are works of Marlowe
(b) All are comedies of Shakespeare
(c) All are history plays of Shakespeare
(d) All are masques of Ben Jonson

150 Consider the following statements.
1. The Advancement of Learning Bacon's book published and meant to teach the English readers, how to think of knowledge and how to make use of it.
2. Bacon denoted to three subjects; the discovery of truth, the welfare of his country and the reform of religion.

Which of the statements given above is/are correct?
(a) Only 1 (b) Only 2
(c) Both 1 and 2 (d) Neither 1 nor 2

151 What is common to following works? Identify to correct description below.
1. Essay
2. Novum Organum
3. The History of Winds the New Atlantis

Codes
(a) All of them are works by John Foxers
(b) All of them are written by Camdern
(c) All of them are works by Francis Bacon
(d) All of them are names of sonnet sequences

152 Consider the following statements according to Allardyce Nicoll, Shakespearean comedy
1. is the union of realism and fantasy.
2. addition of a philosophical insight.
3. is not set in imaginative world.
4. does not frequently end with a marriage celebration.

Which of the statements given above are correct?
(a) 1 and 2 (b) 1 and 4
(c) 3 and 2 (d) 3 and 4

153 What is common to the following works? Identify the correct description below.
1. The Tempest
2. As You Like It
3. Cymbeline
4. Twelfth Night

Codes
(a) All are Shakespeare's comedies
(b) All are Shakespeare's History plays
(c) All are Shakespeare's Problem plays
(d) All are works by Ben Jonson

154 What is common to the following plays? Identify the correct description below.
1. King Lear 2. Othello
3. Macbeth 4. Hamlet

Codes
(a) All are works of Spenser
(b) All are works of Christopher Marlowe
(c) All are tragedies of Shakespeare
(d) All are restoration works of different playwrights

155 Consider the following statements.

1. Shakespeare is employed sources for his plays are North's translation of Plutarch's lives of the Noble Grecians and Romans.
2. Shakespeare made changes in the history of the Roman.

Which of the statements given above is/are correct?

(a) Both 1 and 2 (b) Only 1
(c) Only 2 (d) Neither 1 nor 2

156 Consider the following statements according to John M Murcer, significant features of Shakespeare's play are

1. They usually have episodic plots.
2. They reflect the political ideology of the chronicle history books.
3. They usually do not contain elements of tragedy and comedy.
4. They do not reflect the personal bias of the playwright.

Which of the statements given above are correct?

(a) 1 and 2 (b) 1 and 4
(c) 3 and 2 (d) 3 and 4

157 Consider the following statements, according to AC Bradley, Shakespeare's tragedies

1. can be divided into three parts exposition, conflict, catastrophe.
2. are concerned primarily with one person the tragic hero.
3. does not end with the death of the tragic hero.
4. does not under go suffering as a result of his tragic flaw.

Which of the statements given above are correct?

(a) 1 and 2 (b) 1 and 4 (c) 3 and 2 (d) 3 and 4

158 Consider the following statements according of Peter J Laihart, Shakespeare's Roman plays have certain common features.

1. They are not set in ancient Rome.
2. Blood, mayhem and violence are not important features of this play.
3. Suicide is depicted as an important Roman custom.
4. Romans are deputed as self conscious, theatrical and historically.

Which of the statements given above are correct?

(a) 1 and 2 (b) 1 and 4
(c) 3 and 2 (d) 3 and 4

159 Consider the following statements.

1. Shakespeare and his company built the globe theatre.
2. He got the name and fame in theatrical life.

Which of the statements given above are correct?

(a) Only 1 (b) Only 2
(c) Both 1 and 2 (d) Neither 1 nor 2

160 What is common to the following works? Identify the correct description below.

1. A Tale of a Tub
2. Every Man in His Humour
3. The Alchemist
4. Volpone

Codes

(a) All are comedies of Ben Jonson
(b) All are masques of Ben Jonson
(c) All are tragedies of Shakespeare
(d) All are essays of Bacon

161 Which of all these belong to 'Major Tetralogy'?

1. Richard II 2. King John
3. Henry V 4. Henry VIII

Codes

(a) Only 1 (b) Only 2 (c) 3 and 4 (d) 1 and 3

162 Which of these works belong to Shakespeare?

1. The Witch
2. The Merry Wives of Windsor
3. Measure for Measure
4. Caesar and Pompey

Codes

(a) 2 and 3 (b) 3 and 4 (c) 2 and 4 (d) 1 and 4

163 Which of these is/are Roman plays of Shakespeare?

1. Julius Caesar 2. Antony and Cleopatra
3. Henry V 4. Merry Wives of Windsor

Codes

(a) Only 1 (b) 1 and 2 (c) 3 and 4 (d) Only 4

164 Which of these works is/are collaboration of Beaumont and Fletcher?

1. The Woman Hater 2. The Mad Lover
3. Cupid's Revenge 4. The Scornful Lady

Codes

(a) Only 1 (b) Only 2 (c) 2 and 3 (d) 3 and 4

165 Whose collaborations are the following works? The False one, The Knight of Malta The Double Marriage, The Honest Man's Forture

1. Fletcher and Beaumont
2. Massinger and Fletcher
3. Massinger, Fletcher and Nathan Field
4. Massinger and Beaumont

Codes

(a) Only 1 (b) Only 2 (c) 2 and 3 (d) 2 and 4

166 Which famous play does the quote, "When shall we three meet again in thunder, lightning or in rain?" Come from

(a) The Taming of the Shrew (b) King Lear
(c) The Tempest (d) Macbeth

167 "The fault, dear Brutus, is not in our stars, but in ourselves that we are underlings." Who said this and in which play?
(a) Cassius in Julius Caesar
(b) Antony in Julius Caesar
(c) Caliban in the Tempest
(d) Antony in Antony and Cleoparta

168 "Farewell! Othello's occupation's gone", What does this cry signify?
(a) There were no dramatists left after Ben Jonson
(b) The dramatists were taking other occupations
(c) The British Parliament closed the theatre as Puritans came to power
(d) People preferred poetry

169 In which of Shakespeare's plays the following lines appear:
"Blow, blow, thou winter wind Thou art not so unkind As man's ingratitude.."?
(a) All's Well That Ends Well
(b) As You Like It
(c) Antony and Cleopatra
(d) King Lear

170 In 1609, an unusual event took place which gave a theme to Shakespeare for one of his enchanting plays. An English ship disappeared and all aboard were given up for lost. However, a year later the sailors came back. They had been ship-wrecked on the unknown Bermudas and were terrified by mysterious noises which they thought came from the devils. This account was used by Shakespeare in
(a) The Tempest
(b) The Winter's Tale
(c) The Hamlet
(d) As You Like It

171 Which famous Shakespeare's play does the quote, "My salad days, when I was green in judgment." come from?
(a) Antony and Cleopatra
(b) Hamlet, Prince of Denmark
(c) The Winters Tale
(d) The Merry Wives of Windsor

172 Which famous Shakespeare's play does the quote, "Neither a borrower nor a lender be" come from?
(a) Cymbeline
(b) Hamlet
(c) Titus Andronicus
(d) Pericles, Prince of Tyre

173 Which famous Shakespeare's is play does the quote, "How sharper than a serpent's tooth it is to have a thankless child!" come from?
(a) King Lear
(b) As You Like It
(c) The Famous History of the Life of King Henry VIII
(d) The Life and Death of King John

174 Which famous Shakespeare's play does the quote, "The first thing we do, let's kill all the lawyers" come from?
(a) The Merry Wives of Windsor
(b) Othello, the Moor of Venice
(c) Pericles, Prince of Tyre
(d) King Henry the Sixth, Part II

175 Who says, "Good night, sweet prince/And flights of angels sing thee to thy rest."?
(a) Fortinbras (b) Marcellus (c) Chorus (d) Horatio

176 "My bounty is as boundless as the sea, ..." Name the work from which the above line has been taken.
(a) Women Beware Women (b) A Challenge for Beauty
(c) Romeo and Juliet (d) Hamlet

177 "Let me not to the marriage of true minds." Name the work and the author of the above line.
(a) Caesar and Pompey-George Chapman
(b) A Tale of a Tub-Ben Jonson
(c) Caesar's Fall-John Webster
(d) Sonnet 116-William Shakespeare

178 "All the world's a stage, and all the men and women merely players; they have their exits and their entrances, and one man in his time plays many parts, his acts being seven ages." Who quoted the above lines?
(a) Ben Jonson (b) Thomas Dekker
(c) William Shakespeare (d) Thomas Middleton

179 "I know death hath ten thousand several doors
For men to take their exits; and t'is found
They go on such strange geometrical hinges,
You may open them both ways: any way, for heaven-sake"
Name the author and the work from which the above lines have taken.
(a) Shakespeare, Othello
(b) John Webster, The Duchess of Malfi
(c) Ben Jonson, Catiline
(d) John Marston, Antonio and Mellida

180 There is a tide in the affairs of men,
Which taken at the flood, leads on to fortune.
Omitted, all the voyage of their life is bound in shallows and in miseries.
On such a full sea are we now afloat. And we must take the current when it serves,
or lose our ventures.
(a) John Webster (b) John Ford
(c) Philip Massinger (d) William Shakespeare

181 "Drink to me only with thine eyes,
And I will pledge with mine;
or leave a kiss but in the cup
And I'll not look for wine.'
(a) Ben Jonson (b) Shakespeare
(c) Walter Raleigh (d) Thomas Heywood

182 "Shall I compare thee to a summer's day? Thou art more lovely and more temperate. Rough winds do shake the darling buds of May. And summer's lease hath all too short a date."

(a) This is Shakespeare in Sonnet 18
(b) This is Philip Sidney in Astrophel and Stella
(c) This is Samuel Daniel in Dalia
(d) This is Michael Drayton in Idea

183 About whom these words are uttered "Cover her face; mine eyes dazzle: She died young."

(a) Juliet in Romeo and Juliet (Shakespeare)
(b) Duchess in the Duchess of Malfi (Webster)
(c) Cordelier in King Lear (Shakespeare)
(d) Anne in A Woman Killed with Kindness (Thomas Heywood)

184 'Ripeness is all' is a line from

(a) Hamlet (b) King Lear
(c) Othello (d) Macbeth

185 Which of the following characters of Webster's The White Devil utters the memorable words
Oft gay and honour'd robes those tortures try we think cag'd birds sing, when indeed they cry?

(a) Vittoria Corombona
(b) Bracciano
(c) The Cardinal
(d) Flamineo

186 Hamlet, lying wounded, says to his friend, 'Horatio, I am dead.' This is an example of

(a) protasis (b) anacrusis
(c) prolepsis (d) pun

187 "His life was gentle; and the elements/So mixed in him, that nature might stand up/And say to all the world" 'This was a man!'

(a) Enobarbus on Antony
(b) Brutus on Caesar
(c) Cleopatra on Antony
(d) Marc Antony on Caesar

188 Whom would you assign the line "Drink to me only with thine eyes"?

(a) John Lyly
(b) William Shakespeare
(c) Ben Jonson
(d) Thomas Nashe

189 "Castiza:" False! I defy you both!
I have endured you with an ear of fire;
Your tongues have struck hot irons on my face!
Mother, come from that poisonous woman there."
Gratiana: "Where?"
Castiza: "Do you not see her? She's too inward then."
From which work of an author have the above lines been taken?

(a) Thomas Middleton, The Revenger's Tragedy
(b) John Ford, Tis Pity She's A Whore
(c) John Webster, The White Devil
(d) Philip Massinger, The City Madam

Direction (Q. No. 190) *On the basis of extract given below answer the given question.*

"Lost, I am Lost! My fates have doomed my death.
The more I strive, I love; the more I love,
The less I hope. I see my ruin, certain.
What judgement or endeavors could apply
To my incurable and restless wounds
I throughly have examined, but in vain.
Oh, that it were not in religion sin
To make our love a God and worship it!
I have even wearied heaven with prayers, dried up
The spring of my continual tears, even starved
My veins with daily fasts; what wit or art
Could counsel, I have practiced. But, alas,
I find all these but dreams and old men's tales
To fright unsteady youth; I'm still the same.
Or I must speak or burst. Tis not, I know,
My lust, but tis my fate that leads me on.
Keep fear and low fainthearted shame with slaves!
I'll tell her that I love her, through my heart
Were rated at the price of that attempt."

190 From which work of an author have the above lines been taken?

(a) Thomas Middleton, The Revenger's Tragedy
(b) John Ford, Tis Pity She's A Whore
(c) John Webster, The White Devil
(d) Philip Massinger, The City Madam

Directions (Q.Nos. 191-192) *In the questions given below are two statements labelled as Assertion (A) and Reason (R). In the context of the two statements, which one of the following is correct?*

Codes

(a) A is true, but R is false (b) A is false, but R is true
(c) Both A and R are true, but R is not the correct explanation of A
(d) Both A and R are true and R is the correct explanation of A

191 **Assertion** (A) 'Group of English dramatists were called University Wits'.
Reason (R) They were educated at the University Oxford or Cambridge.

192 **Assertion** (A) Kyd was released by the Queen's Privy Council.
Reason (R) Kyd possessed heretical and blasphemous papers.

Directions (Q. Nos. 193-195) *In the questions given below are two statements labelled as Assertion (A) and Reason (R). In the context of the two statements, which one of the following is correct?*

Codes

(a) Both A and R are true and R is the correct explanation of A
(b) Both A and R are true, but R is not the correct explanation of A
(c) A is true, but R is false
(d) A is false, but R is true

193 **Assertion** (A) In the Shakespeare's tragedies, the hero is always from the higher strata of the society and the entire society witness his fall and finally the hero dies.

Reason (R) Just because of his own decision or fault.

194 **Assertion** (A) The life of Jack Wilton by Nashe sometimes known as the First English Historical novel.

Reason (R) It is an account of the wild oversee adventures of a youngster called Jack Wilton.

195 **Assertion** (A) Most of Shakespeare's plays were written as Quarto texts.

Reason (R) The plays were not written on a sheet of paper folded four ways.

Directions (Q.Nos. 196-200) *Read the Passage carefully and answer the questions that follow. Adapted from "The Cask of Amontillado" by Edgar Allan Poe (1846)*

The thousand injuries of Fortunato to I had borne as I best could, but when he ventured upon insult I vowed revenge. You, who so well know the nature of my soul, will not suppose, however, that I gave utterance to a threat. At length I would be avenged; this was a point definitively settled - but the very definitiveness with which it was resolved precluded-the idea of risk. I must not only punish but punish with impunity. A wrong is unredressed when retribution overtakes its redresser. It is equally unredressed when the avenger fails to make himself felt as such to him who has done the wrong.

It must be understood that neither by word nor deed had I given Fortunato cause to doubt my good will. I continued, as was my wont, to smile in his face, and he did not perceive that my smile now was at the thought of his immolation.

He had a weak point - this Fortunato - although in other regards he was a man to be respected and even feared. He prided himself upon his connoisseurship in wine. Few Italians have the true virtuoso spirit. For the most part their enthusiasm is adopted to suit the time and opportunity, to practice imposture upon the British and Austrian millionaires. In painting and gemmary, Fortunato, like his countrymen, was a quack, but in the matter of old wines he was sincere. In this respect I did not differ from him materially; - I was skillful in the Italian vintages myself, and bought largely whenever I could.

It was about dusk, one evening during the supreme madness of the carnival season, that I encountered my friend. He accosted me with excessive warmth, for he had been drinking much. The man wore motley. He had on a tight-fitting parti-striped dress, and his head was surmounted by the conical cap and bells. I was so pleased to see him that I thought I should never have done wringing his hand.

I said to him - "My dear Fortunato, you are luckily met. How remarkably well you are looking to-day. But I have received a pipe of what passes for Amontillado, and I have my doubts."

"How?" said he. "Amontillado? A pipe? Impossible! And in the middle of the carnival"

"I have my doubts," I replied; and I was silly enough to pay the full Amontillado price without consulting you in the matter. You were not to be found, and I was fearful of losing a bargain."

"Amontillado !"

"I have my doubts."

"Amontillado!"

"And I must satisfy them."

"Amontillado!"

"As you are engaged, I am on my way to Luchresi. If anyone has a critical turn it is he. He will tell me -"

"Luchresi cannot tell Amontillado from Sherry."

"And yet some fools will have it that his taste is a match for your own."

"Come, let us go."

"Whither?"

"To your vaults."

196 **"A wrong is equally unredressed when the avenger fails to make himself felt as such to him who has done the wrong" In this line, the narrator indicates that he wants what to happen?**

(a) He wants to avenge a harm done to Fortunato
(b) He wants Fortunato to know why he is being punished
(c) He wants to understand how Fortunato feels about having offended him
(d) He wants to make Fortunato apologise

197 **In the line "I continued, as was my wont, to smile in his face, and he did not perceive that my smile now was at the thought of his immolation," the word immolation is closest in meaning to what?**

(a) Sacrifice
(b) Punishment
(c) Chastisement
(d) Burning oneself

198 **In the line, "I must not only punish but punish with impunity," the word 'impunity' is closest in meaning to what?**

(a) freedom from punishment or consequences
(b) disputation of the truth
(c) the taking on of responsibility for something
(d) exemption from legal action

199 **In the line, "I continued, as was my wont, to smile in his face, and he did not perceive that my smile now was at the thought of his immolation," the word wont is closest in meaning to what?**

(a) A habitual way of doing something
(b) A desire for something
(c) A distaste for something
(d) A need for something

200 **According to the first line, what causes the narrator to decide to vow revenge on Fortunato?**

(a) Fortunato has injured him in a thousand ways.
(b) Fortunato has become friends with Luchresi.
(c) Fortunato has claimed to be a connoisseur of wine.
(d) Fortunato has insulted him somehow.

PREVIOUS YEARS' QUESTIONS

December 2018

1 Thomas Nashe's The Unfortunate Traveller is narrated by

(a) Ben Lyte, a coarse Papist
(b) Jack Wilton, an English page
(c) Peter Marston, a sworn Calvinist
(d) Philip Foxe, an English highwayman

2 What is honour? A word. What is that word honour? Air. A trim reckoning! Who hath it? He that died 0' Wednesday. Doth he feel it? No. Doth he hear it? No. is it insensible, then? Yea, to the dead. But will it not live with the living? No. why? Detraction will not suffer it. - therefore, I'll none of it: Honour is a mere scutcheon; and so ends my catechism."
Which character in the following Shakespeare's dramas made this statement about honour?

(a) Claudius in Hamlet, the Prince of Denmark
(b) Falstaff in King Henry IV-Part 1
(c) Hotspur in King Henry IV-Part 1
(d) Hamlet in Hamlet, the Prince of Denmark

3 "Search the heads of the greatest rivers in the world, you shall find them but bubbles of water". Who is the author of this line?

(a) Oscar Wilde (b) Francis Bacon
(c) John Webster (d) RB Sheridan

4 In Marlowe's Doctor Faustus, what books does Valdes council Faustus to study in preparation for conjuring up spirits?

1. the works of Bacon and Abanus
2. the Hebrew Psalter and New Testament
3. the works of Ovid and Homer
4. the works of Baxter and Horst

The right combination according to the code is:

(a) 1 and 2 (b) 2 and 3
(c) 1 and 4 (d) 1 and 3

5 Read the passage given below

"Full many a lady
I have eye'd with best regard: and many a time
The harmony of their tongues hath into bondage
Brought my too diligent ear; for several virtues
Have I liked several women; never any
With so full soul, but some defect in her
Did quarrel with the noblest grace she ow'd,
And put it to the foil. But you, O you,
So perfect and so peerless, are created
Of every creature's best."

This passage admiring the perfect matching of inner and outward beauty of a woman is taken from

(a) Marlowe's Dr. Faustus
(b) John Webster's The Duchess of Malfi
(c) Thomas Middleton's Women Beware Women
(d) Shakespeare's Tempest

July 2018

6 John Heywood wrote a farcical interlude called The Four 'P's.

(a) a Palmer, a Pedlar, a Pothecary, a Packer
(b) a Printer, a Pedlar, a Pothecary, a Palmer
(c) a Pedlar, a Parson, a Palmer, a Pothecary
(d) a Palmer, a Pardoner, a Pothecary, a Pedlar

7 Traces of the morality plays are discernible in a play like Dr. Faustus, traces such as

(a) vernacular songs adapting secular themes
(b) its soliloquising protagonist, good and bad angels and its final moral
(c) its refrains from the Corpus Christi Carol, the complaint of christi, the lover of mankind
(d) its rhythmical prose and the presence of a larger narrative rhythm in the morality plays

8 Arrange the following plays of Shakespeare according to their periods (early, middle, late....) of composition.

(a) As You Like It, Love's Labour's Lost, Antony and Cleopatra, The Tempest, A Midsummer Night's Dream
(b) Antony and Cleopatra, The Tempest, A Midsummer Night's Dream, Love's Labour's Lost, As You Like It
(c) Love's Labour's Lost, A Midsummer Night's Dream, As You Like It, Antony and Cleopatra, The Tempest
(d) A Midsummer Night's Dream, Antony and Cleopatra, The Tempest, As You Like It, Love's Labour's Lost

9 ...sure it waits upon
Some God o the island. Sitting on a bank
Weeping again the King my father's wrack
This music crept by me upon the waters,
Allaying both their fury and my passion
With its sweet air. Thence I have followed it,
Or it hath drawn me rather...

Which of the following statements in this passage are true?

1. These lines, spoken by Edgar in King Lear, are part of a long speech delivered on the heath
2. These lines, spoken by Ferdinand in The Tempest, Describe Ariel's music
3. The passage reappears in an altered and ironic version in T.S Eliot's Waste Land

4. The Passage reappears verbatim in W.H Auden's Sea and the Mirror

The correct answer according to the codes is

(a) 1 and 4 (b) 2 and 3 (c) 3 and 4 (d) 1 and 3

December 2017

10 There is a play on the name of Machiavelli in the prologue to Christopher Marlowe's

(a) Doctor Faustus (b) The Jew of Malta
(c) Tamburlaine, The Great (d) Edward II

11 Which of the following lines by Shakespeare is repeated several times in Virginia Woolf's novel Mrs. Dalloway?

(a) If music be the food of love, play on
(b) Fear no more the heat of the Sun, Nor the furious winter's rages
(c) Those are pearls that were his eyes
(d) There is a tide in the affairs of man

12 "All the world's a stage,
And all the men and women merely players",
occurs in Shakespeare's' As You Like It.' Which character says the line?

(a) Jacques (b) Celia (c) Rosalind (d) Touchstone

13 In An Essay of Dramatic Poesy whom does John Dr[illegible] refer to as "the most learned and jud[illegible]ous wr[illegible]ich any theater ever had"?

(a) John Webster (b) Christopher Marlowe
(c) Ben Jonson (d) William Shakespeare

14 The first instance of female cross-dressing with the disconcerting nuances of a boy actor dressing as a boy while playing the role of a woman in the dramatic world of Shakespeare occurs in ……

(a) The Two Gentlemen of Verona
(b) As You Like It
(b) Twelfth Night
(d) A Midsummer Night's Dream

15 In this Jacobean play the Black King and his men, representing Spain and the Jesuits, are checkmated by the White knight, Prince Charles. This political satire drew crowds to the Globe Theater until the Spanish ambassador protested and James I suppressed the play.
Identify the play.

(a) The Wonderfull Yeare
(b) A Game at Chess
(c) A King and No King
(d) The Knight of the Burning Pestle

16 Identify the important theatres of the Elizabethan period.

1. Peacock 2. Globe
3. Swan 4. Grand

The right combination according to the codes is

(a) 1 and 2 (b) 2 and 3 (c) 2 and 4 (d) 1 and 4

January 2017

17 In Shakespeare's Macbeth who was 'untimely ripped' from his mother's womb?

(a) Macbeth (b) Macduff (c) Duncan (d) Malcolm

18 Feste is a clown in

(a) Twelfth Night (b) As You Like It
(c) The Taming of the Shrew (d) Much Ado About Nothing

19 Identify Falstaff's first words in Henry IV, Part I.

(a) Now, Harry, what time of day is it, led?
(b) Now, Hal, what time of day is it, led?
(c) Now, Harry, what time of night is it, led?
(d) Now, Hal, what time of night is it, led?

20 Identify from the following list two plays written by John Webster.

1. A Woman Killed with Kindness
2. The Revenger's Tragedy
3. The White Devil
4. The Duchess of Malfi

The right combination according to the codes is

(a) 1 and 4 (b) 2 and 4 (c) 3 and 4 (d) 1 and 3

July 2016

21 In King Lear for what reason does Kent assume a disguise?

(a) To continue to serve Lear, thought Lear has banished him
(b) To spy on Edmund
(c) To antagonise Goneril and Regan
(d) To revenge upon Lear for banishing him

22 In An Essay of Dramatic Poesy to whom does Dryden refer with the phrase "he needed not the spectacles of books to read nature"?

(a) Ben Jonson (b) Ovid
(c) William Shakespeare (d) Geoffrey Chaucer

23 Why does Love wit in Ben Jonson's play the Alchemist leave his house, setting the stage for his servant face, alongwith subtle, a fake alchemist to fleece people?

(a) To visit his father who left him long ago
(b) To find out new sources of minting money
(c) Because of an epidemic of plague
(d) To make a pilgrimage

24 Shakespeare famously neglects to observe Aristotle's rules concerning the three dramatic unities and Samuel Johnson undertakes to defend Shakespeare from these criticisms in his preface to Shakespeare. Which of the Aristotelian dramatic unities does Jonson believe Shakespeare to observe most successfully?

(a) Time (b) Place (c) Action
(d) Jonson does not feel that the Aristotelian dramatic unities are important

December 2015

25 "How all their plays be neither right tragedies, nor right comedies, mingling kings and clowns, not because the matter so carrieth it, but trust in the down by head and shoulders to play a part in majestical matters."
What term does Philip Sidney use to characterise such plays and which of the unities of Aristotle do they violate?
(a) Mongrel tragicomedy; unity of action
(b) Mixed tragedies; unity of action
(c) Multi-plot drama; unity of time
(d) Mingled yarn; unity of place

26 This revenge tragedy opens with the long soliloquy of the protagonist carrying the skull of his poisoned fiance and swearing vengeance for the old Duke. Who has committed the vicious act? Identify the play.
(a) The Spanish Tragedy (b) The Revenger's Tragedey
(c) The Duchess of Malfi (d) The Changeling

27 Christopher Marlowe was one of the first major writers to affirm what can be identified as a clearly homosexual sensibility. Which drama of his deals with it?
(a) Edward II (b) The Jew of Malta
(c) Doctor Faustus (d) Dido, Queen of Carthage

28 Which of the following plays of William Shakespeare is not directly referred to in TS Eliot's 'The Waste Land'?
(a) Hamlet (b) King Lear
(c) Coriolanus (d) The Tempest

29 In Shakespeare's time who owned the rights to a theatrical script?
(a) The playwright(s)
(b) The patron of the acting company
(c) The printer
(d) The acting company

30 If you cannot understand an argument and remark, 'It's Greek to me', you are quoting...
(a) John Milton (b) Samuel Johnson
(c) William Shakespeare (d) John Donne

31 Match the following.

	List I (Phrases)		List II (Characters)
A.	Motiveless malignity	1.	Macbeth
B.	Reason in Madness	2.	Hamlet
C.	Supp'd full of horrors	3.	Lear
D.	To be, or not to be	4.	Iago

Codes

	A	B	C	D		A	B	C	D
(a)	1	3	2	4	(b)	4	2	3	1
(c)	4	3	1	2	(d)	3	1	2	4

32 Thomas and Henrietta Bowdler's edition of The Family Shakespeare give rise to the word 'Bowdlerize'. What does it mean?
(a) The expurgation of indelicate language
(b) The modernisation of archaic vocabulary
(c) The insertion of bawdy songs
(d) The expansion of female characters

June 2015

33 To whom does Francis Bacon offer the following piece of advice?
"Let him sequester himself from the Company of his Countrymen and diet in such places, where there is good company of the Nation .... let him upon his Removes .... Procure Recommendation, to some person of Quality, residing in the place, whether he remove ...."
(a) The Beaux (b) The Peddler
(c) The Traveller (d) The Stationer

34 Christopher Marlowe's heroes are said to be larger than life, exaggerated both in their faults and in their qualities. They have a desire for everything in extreme. In one of his plays the hero wants to conquer the whole world. The name of the play is ....
(a) The Jew of Malta
(b) Doctor Faustus
(c) Tamburlaine the Great
(d) Edward II

35 The ascension of King James I in .... inaugurated the Jacobean age.
(a) 1600 (b) 1601 (c) 1603 (d) 1609

36 Which of the following pair best describes the characteristic features of Marlowe's portrait of Tamburlaine?
1. Ambition 2. Apathy
3. Cruelty 4. Sympathy
Select the correct answer using the codes given below.
(a) 1 and 2 (b) 1 and 4 (c) 1 and 3 (d) 2 and 3

37 Falstaff is a character in ....
1. Henry IV Part I
2. The Merry Wives of Windsor
3. The Comedy of Errors 4. Titus Andronicus
Select the correct answer using the codes given below.
(a) 1 and 2 (b) 1 and 3 (c) 3 and 4 (d) 1 and 4

December 2014

38 In King Lear who among the following speaks in the voice of Poor Tom?
(a) Kent (b) Edgar (c) Edmund (d) Gloucester

39 Who among Shakespeare's contemporaries did not write tragedies?
(a) Thomas Kyd (b) John Lyly
(c) Christopher Marlowe (d) Ben Jonson

40 Identify the person who sets himself up as the 'Knight' with a pestle rather than a sword in the play. The Knight of the Burning Pestle.
(a) Ralph (b) Tim (c) George (d) Squire

41 Match the following.

List I (Shakespearean Actors)	List II (Periods)
A. David Garrick	1. The 19th century
B. John Gielgud	2. The 18th century
C. Henry Irving	3. The Restoration
D. Thomas Betterton	4. The 20th century

Codes

	A	B	C	D		A	B	C	D
(a)	2	4	1	3	(b)	4	2	1	3
(c)	3	4	1	2	(d)	2	3	4	1

June 2014

42 Act V of Marlow's Edward the Second shows, the murder of the king. Where does it take place?
(a) Westminster, a room in the palace
(b) A room in Berkeley Castle
(c) A room in Kilingworth Castle
(d) Within the Abbey of Neath

43 The separation of styles in accordance with class appears more consistently in ....than in medieval works of literature and art.
(a) Ben Jonson (b) Shakespeare
(c) Philip Sidney (d) Edmund Spenser

44 "Keep up your bright swords, for the dew will rust them. Good Signior, you shall more command with years. Than with your weapons." The above lines are addressed by Othello to
(a) Roderigo and Officers
(b) Brabantio, Roderigo and Officers
(c) The Duke and Senators
(d) Montano and Cassio

45 The centre of his plays is a proud character on Marlowe's model, with a bold licence in speech and action, full of elaborate metaphors, phrase tumbling after phrase, as he asserts himself in the French Court. Dryden unjustly described his style as 'a dwarfish thought, dressed up in gigantic words'.
Who is this Jacobean playwright?
(a) John Fletcher
(b) John Webster
(c) George Chapman
(d) John Marston

46 What is Johnson's opinion regarding the 'Violation' of the three unities in the plays of Shakespeare?
1. Shakespeare should have followed the unities.
2. Shakespeare followed the important unity of action satisfactorily.
3. Shakespeare's plays suffered because they did not follow the unities.
4. Unity of time and place arise from false assumptions.

Codes
(a) 1 and 2 (b) 2 and 4
(c) 3 and 4 (d) 1 and 3

47 "But deeds and language, such as men do use,
"And persons, such as comedy would choose,
when she would show an image of the time,
and sport with human follies, not with crime."
In the above lines, Jonson
1. opposes the artificiality of the romantic tragic comedy.
2. initiates the use of realism.
3. considers analysis of moral shortcomings more important.
4. encourages the use of farce with melodrama.

Codes
(a) 1, 2 and 3
(b) 1, 2 and 4
(c) 1, 3 and 4
(d) 2, 3 and 4

ANSWERS

Objective Questions

1. *(d)*	2. *(d)*	3. *(d)*	4. *(a)*	5. *(c)*	6. *(b)*	7. *(b)*	8. *(a)*	9. *(c)*	10. *(c)*
11. *(b)*	12. *(d)*	13. *(b)*	14. *(a)*	15. *(a)*	16. *(c)*	17. *(d)*	18. *(b)*	19. *(a)*	20. *(d)*
21. *(c)*	22. *(c)*	23. *(c)*	24. *(a)*	25. *(d)*	26. *(c)*	27. *(a)*	28. *(d)*	29. *(a)*	30. *(c)*
31. *(d)*	32. *(b)*	33. *(a)*	34. *(c)*	35. *(d)*	36. *(c)*	37. *(c)*	38. *(a)*	39. *(c)*	40. *(a)*
41. *(c)*	42. *(a)*	43. *(b)*	44. *(c)*	45. *(b)*	46. *(a)*	47. *(b)*	48. *(d)*	49. *(d)*	50. *(b)*
51. *(a)*	52. *(a)*	53. *(c)*	54. *(d)*	55. *(a)*	56. *(c)*	57. *(d)*	58. *(d)*	59. *(c)*	60. *(b)*
61. *(b)*	62. *(a)*	63. *(d)*	64. *(a)*	65. *(a)*	66. *(c)*	67. *(c)*	68. *(b)*	69. *(c)*	70. *(a)*
71. *(a)*	72. *(c)*	73. *(c)*	74. *(c)*	75. *(d)*	76. *(b)*	77. *(a)*	78. *(d)*	79. *(b)*	80. *(c)*
81. *(b)*	82. *(c)*	83. *(d)*	84. *(b)*	85. *(d)*	86. *(d)*	87. *(c)*	88. *(d)*	89. *(c)*	90. *(a)*
91. *(b)*	92. *(b)*	93. *(c)*	94. *(c)*	95. *(c)*	96. *(c)*	97. *(b)*	98. *(d)*	99. *(d)*	100. *(c)*
101. *(b)*	102. *(d)*	103. *(c)*	104. *(a)*	105. *(d)*	106. *(d)*	107. *(b)*	108. *(a)*	109. *(d)*	110. *(c)*
111. *(b)*	112. *(a)*	113. *(d)*	114. *(d)*	115. *(d)*	116. *(d)*	117. *(b)*	118. *(c)*	119. *(b)*	120. *(d)*
121. *(d)*	122. *(c)*	123. *(b)*	124. *(d)*	125. *(c)*	126. *(d)*	127. *(b)*	128. *(c)*	129. *(d)*	130. *(c)*
131. *(b)*	132. *(c)*	133. *(a)*	134. *(b)*	135. *(a)*	136. *(c)*	137. *(b)*	138. *(a)*	139. *(d)*	140. *(b)*
141. *(a)*	142. *(b)*	143. *(c)*	144. *(d)*	145. *(c)*	146. *(b)*	147. *(d)*	148. *(c)*	149. *(a)*	150. *(c)*
151. *(c)*	152. *(a)*	153. *(a)*	154. *(c)*	155. *(a)*	156. *(a)*	157. *(a)*	158. *(d)*	159. *(c)*	160. *(a)*
161. *(d)*	162. *(a)*	163. *(b)*	164. *(d)*	165. *(c)*	166. *(d)*	167. *(a)*	168. *(c)*	169. *(b)*	170. *(a)*
171. *(a)*	172. *(b)*	173. *(a)*	174. *(d)*	175. *(d)*	176. *(c)*	177. *(d)*	178. *(c)*	179. *(b)*	180. *(d)*
181. *(a)*	182. *(a)*	183. *(b)*	184. *(b)*	185. *(d)*	186. *(c)*	187. *(d)*	188. *(c)*	189. *(a)*	190. *(b)*
191. *(d)*	192. *(b)*	193. *(a)*	194. *(a)*	195. *(a)*	196. *(a)*	197. *(c)*	198. *(b)*	199. *(d)*	200. *(a)*

Previous Years' Questions

1. *(b)*	2. *(b)*	3. *(c)*	4. *(a)*	5. *(d)*	6. *(d)*	7. *(b)*	8. *(c)*	9. *(b)*	10. *(b)*
11. *(b)*	12. *(a)*	13. *(c)*	14. *(a)*	15. *(b)*	16. *(b)*	17. *(a)*	18. *(b)*	19. *(b)*	20. *(c)*
21. *(a)*	22. *(c)*	23. *(c)*	24. *(c)*	25. *(a)*	26. *(b)*	27. *(a)*	28. *(b)*	29. *(d)*	30. *(c)*
31. *(c)*	32. *(a)*	33. *(c)*	34. *(c)*	35. *(c)*	36. *(c)*	37. *(a)*	38. *(b)*	39. *(b)*	40. *(a)*
41. *(a)*	42. *(b)*	43. *(b)*	44. *(b)*	45. *(c)*	46. *(b)*	47. *(a)*			

Restoration to Neo-Classical Age Drama

Drama was the most popular trend in the Restoration period. The Heroic Drama and the Comedy of Manners were the two most popular genre of the drama of this age. John Dryden was the main exponent of heroic drama. The Augustan Drama witnessed its decline due to economic reasons besides Licensing Act 1737. With Samuel Johnson, Age of Sensibility or Neo-Sensibility or Neo-Classical drama came to an end.

Restoration Age

The period between 1660 (which marked the end of the English Civil Wars, (1642-1649) and the year 1780 is often referred with several names: The 'Augustan Age', 'The Neo-classical Age' and 'The Age of Sensibility'.

The term 'Restoration' is also used for initial decades because of the restoration of Monarchy under Charles II in 1660. After a period of major social and political turmoil and a short lived. 'Protectorate' under Oliver Cromwell's reign, England was looking for peace.

Even after restoring the monarchy in 1660, with Charles II, the country soon slid into chaos. The Holland Wars (1665-1667) worsened the economic situation. But now England had Parliamentary system that could check the King's actions. Protestantism became the dominant religious system, except during James II's reign (1685-1688).

In 1688, exasperated with the continued incompetence of their kings, the English. Parliamentarians invited William of Orange to take over as England's ruler. William and his wife Mary came to occupy the Throne of England without even a minor battle-an event celebrated as the 'Glorious Revolution' or the bloodless revolution. It marked the domination of Hanoverian dynasty over England and the end of the Stuart line of rulers.

In this Chapter

In 1707, an Act was signed that United Scotland, England and Wales, even though Scotland remained rebellion and unhappy with its union with England throughout this period.

- The term 'Augustan' captures the fascination of the writers of this period with the Roman period of Augustus Caesar (27BC-AD10).
- The 'Age of Enlightenment' indicates the intellectual changes where rationalism and the scientific approach were seen as the most valuable features of the human race, with producing and popularising various kinds of knowledge in botany or in language.
- The term 'The Age of Sensibility' denotes the renewed interest in the senses where intellectuals and writers debated the two 'opposites' of Reason and Sentiment, Mind and Feeling.
- The term 'Neo-classical' refers to the interest many writers and artists had in Classical-Greek, Roman and Latin literatures and arts. Translations and adaptations from the ancient forms marked a revival of interest in the classical arts and the age in hence termed, 'Neo-classical'.
- Neo-classical literature was written between 1660 and 1798.

This time period can be broken down into three parts

1. The Restoration period
2. The Augustan period
3. The Age of Johnson (The Age of Sensibility)

Drama of the Restoration Age

The writers of Restoration age drove out the moral earnestness and seriousness, which had characterised the Puritan writers and replaced it with a spirit of joy and cheerfulness. Because of the French influence on English court, the literature of the age was influenced by French models. Comedies of Molière, the tragedies of Corneille and Racine and the satires, epistles and versified essays of Boileau were taken as inspiration.

In the literature of this age, one sees a change from fancy to wit and from poetry to prose. Pamphlet literature also came into trend. Two great diarists, John Evelyn and Samuel Pepys belong to this period. One of the most popular texts of the time was Butler's *Hudibras* which ridiculed the Puritans. According to JE Luebering, "Many of the literary forms, considered typical of the modern world including the novel, biography, history, travel writing and journalism, were either invented or reached their maturity during this period".

Drama was the most popular genre in the Restoration period. Two types of plays ruled the drama of this period. The first were heroic plays, which presented characters of almost superhuman stature and their predominant themes were exalted ideals of love, honour and courage.

The second was Restoration comedy of manners which satirised the ideals, mannerisms and behaviour of the upper class in society. John Dryden was the best representative writer of the Restoration age since he wrote in every popular form prevalent during the time like comedy, tragedy, heroic plays, odes, satires, translations of classical works etc.

Literary Trends

The main trends prevalent during the restoration period in the field of literature were heroic drama and comedy of manners.

The brief description of the two trends is mentioned below

Heroic Drama

Heroic drama, also known as heroic tragedy was a popular literary form during the Restoration period. Heroic drama had larger than life heroes and heroines, highly rhetorical dialogue and exotic locales. Like heroic poems or epics, it was written in heroic couplets. Dryden defined heroic play as 'an imitation of a heroic poem'. The plot of the play involved the fate of an empire. Love and valour were the subjects of the heroic plays. They were influenced by French classical tragedy and its dramatic unities.

Though Dryden was the main exponent of heroic drama, it was Sir William D'Avenant who first established the mode. A playwright during the reign of Charles I and later the manager of the theatrical troupe, The Duke's Company-William D'Avenant wrote what is considered the first heroic drama, *The Siege of Rhodes.* Cazamian terms the play as 'The germ transmitted from France to both of English opera and heroic tragedy'.

The play deals with the siege of Rhodes (an island off Greece) by the Turkish king Soleiman, the Magnificent. The valour of the Sultan is matched by the conjugal devotion of Lanthe, wife of the Sicilian Duke Alphonso, who succeeds in saving her husband and those who are defending the island from the Turkish hordes.

Dryden's first heroic drama, *The Indian Queen* (1664), was a joint effort with Robert Howard. His other heroic plays were *Tyrannic Love* (1669), *The Conquest of Granada* (1670), *Amboyna* (1673) and *Aureng-Zebe* (1675). Other practitioners of heroic drama include Elkanah Settle, Nathaniel Lee and Thomas Otway.

Criticism of Heroic Drama

Heroic Drama also received its share of criticism. Blamires in his *A History of the English Literature* states that "The heroic drama of this period too often sacrifices naturalness and artistic discipline to supposed force of impact; and it fails to purchase sympathy through over-selling of astonishment." Dryden and his genre of heroic plays were also mocked by Buckingham's burlesque *The Rehearsal* (1671).

Comedy of Manners

Comedy of manners is a style of dramatic comedy that reflects the life, ideals and manners of upper class society. It depicts the relations and intrigues of men and women belonging to polished sections of society.

According to Dr Tracey Sanders, "Main characteristics of Restoration comedy of manners include a flamboyant display of witty, blunt sexual dialogue, bedroom intrigues, sensual hints and bold and flashy behaviour."

Restoration comedy of manners was influenced by Ben Jonson's comedy of humours. Deriving inspiration from Jonson's comedies, the 'Comedy of Manners' takes a completely new coloration combining a humour and a critical trait that the English theatre had never known before. A reading of historical context of the time is essential for understanding the development of this genre.

English audiences, who were starved of entertainment during the Puritan regime, demanded a new style of drama, which was free of sexual restraints and moral seriousness. Also, the carefree lifestyle of Charles II and his court influenced this style of comedy.

According to Julia Stefanova and Lubomir Terziev, the Comedy of Manners depicts a small world which has a distinct territory of its own, the fashionable parts of the London of Charles II's time.

Its main activities take place in the public gardens like Hyde Park, St James's Park, Mulberry Garden, fashionable clubs, houses and drawing-rooms of the aristocratic and leisured classes. Its inhabitants seldom move out of this charming world unless it is in search of adventure. Main dramatists who practised this form of comedy are William Congreve, George Etherege, Wycherley and Aphra Behn.

The theatres which were closed in 1642, were opened during the Restoration. They became the riotous haunt of the upper classes. Consequently, the plays written for the play houses were distinctly calculated by the authors to appeal to a courtly and Cavalier audience. It is that explains the rise of the heroic tragedy, which dealt with themes of epic magnitude and the development of the Comedy of Manners, which portrayed the sophisticated life of the dominant class of society-its gaity, foppery, insolence and intrigue.

Impact of Comedy of Manners

According to Muhammad Naeem, main impact of Comedy of Manners was

- Restoration comedy held a mirror to the high society of the Restoration Age. It depicted a society in full transition, a society in which the bourgeoisie take an increasing role and women a newfound liberty.
- The persistent attack on the sanctity of the marital bond made by the comedy writers and the parallel advocacy of free love (mainly to cater to the needs of the libido) imparts to the comedy of manners a pronounced immoral note.
- Most comedy writers relished the presentation of scenes and acts suggestive or even clearly indicative of sexual licentiousness.
- The comic dialogue was bristling with salacious innuendoes.
- Due to its sexual frankness and openness, Restoration comedy of manners has also been criticised for being immoral. Jeremy Collier, for instance attacked major Restoration playwrights such as Dryden, Congreve, Wycherley for bringing debauchery and profanity on stage in his anti-theatre pamphlet, A Short View of the Immorality and Profaneness of the English Stage.

Dramatists of the Restoration Age

Main dramatists of the Restoration Age were George Etherege, William Wycherley, William Congreve, Aphra Behn, John Vanbrugh and George Farguhar. *Brief description of the above mentioned dramatists is given below*

George Etherege (1635-1691)

Restoration playwright George Etherege was born in Maidenhead, South England in 1635. His mother was Mary Powney. Etherege studied at Lord Williams's School and later studied law at Clement' Inn, London.

Literary Career and Works

Etherege's first play, *The Comical Revenge or Love in a Tub* (1664) premiered at the Duke's theatre in 1664. This play introduced a style of wit hitherto unknown upon the English stage. In 1668, he brought out *She Would If She Could* (1668), a comedy in many respects admirable, full of action, wit and spirit, and immoral at the same time. His last play, *The Man of Mode* (1676), is famous for its creation of the great fop, Sir Fopling Flutter.

It is believed that it was Etherege who introduced the comedy of manners to the English theatre. Etherege was knighted in 1680 and married a rich widow. He was sent by Charles II on a mission to the Hague and in March 1685, was appointed resident minister in the imperial German court at Regensburg. His years spent as English minister to Ratisbon (1685–89) are recorded in his *Letterbook*. Etherege died in Paris, probably in 1691.

William Wycherley (1640-1715)

English dramatist William Wycherley was born in Clive in the English county of Shropshire. His father, Daniel was High Steward in the household of the Marquess of Winchester and his mother, Bethia was a lady-in-waiting to the Marchioness.

At the age of fifteen, Wycherley was sent to be educated in France, where he was brought up in the household of the Duke of Montausier. Here, he also became a Roman Catholic. In 1660, Wycherley entered Oxford but soon left without taking a degree.

Literary Career and Works

His first play, *Love in a Wood* was performed by the King's Men at Theatre Royal, in 1671. The play was an instant success and established him as a fashionable and witty writer. His two greatest and most successful comedies were *The Country Wife*, acted in 1675 and *The Plain Dealer*, in 1677. *The Country Wife* was centered on an inexperienced young country wife, Mrs Margery Pinchwife. *The Plain Dealer* was based on Moliere's *Le Misanthrope* and featured mainly, a misanthrope disgusted with the hypocrisies of ordinary social behaviour. *The Gentleman Dancing Master* (1672) was also written by him. He died in 1715.

William Congreve (1670-1729)

English poet and playwright William Congreve was born in Yorkshire, England in 1670. His father was **William Congreve** (1637–1708) and mother, Mary nee Browning.

Since, his father was an officer in the army and the commander of a Garrison near Cork in Ireland, Congreve was educated at Kilkenny and then at Trinity College, Dublin with Jonathan Swift. In 1691, he studied law in Middle Temple, London. Though he entered Law College, Congreve felt the pull towards literature and started writing.

Literary Career and Works

At the age of 17, Congreve wrote his first book, *Incognito*, a romantic novel published few years later, in 1692. His first play, *The Old Bachelor*, was first acted in January, 1693 and was so successful that it soon established him as a playwright of repute. The old bachelor of the title was Heartwell. This play was followed by other plays such as *The Double-Dealer, Love for Love, The Mourning Bride,* and *The Way of the World*.

His best known play was *The Way of the World*, which was based on the love story of Mirabell and Millamant. However, even though the play earned him critical acclaim, it did not prove to be successful on stage. After this, Congreve wrote no more plays.

He became embroiled in a controversy with Jeremy Collier on the morality of the stage. He suffered from gout and bad sight. Finally, at the age of thirty, he became an elder statesman of letters. Congreve died at the age of 58, on 19th January, 1729.

Aphra Behn (1640-1689)

Early Life

Aphra Behn was born in Wye, near Canterbury in 1640. Considered to be the first professional woman writer, nothing conclusive is known of her parentage or education. It is surmised that she was born to Bartholomew Johnson, a barber and Elizabeth Denham. It is believed that Behn had a Catholic upbringing. She is supposed to have married a merchant named Behn in 1664, who might have died early.

Literary Career and Works

Her first play, *The Forc'd Marriage* appeared in 1670. This was followed by *The Amorous Prince* and her sole tragedy, *Abdelazer*. After this, she turned to writing witty comedies of sexual intrigue such as *The Town Fop*, (1676), *The Debauchee*, (1677), and *The Counterfeit Bridegroom*. Her best known play, *The Rover* was so famous that King Charles II's mistress and famous actress Nell Gwyn came out of retirement to play the role of the whore, Angelica Bianca. The play centers around two pairs of lovers, Helena and Willmore, Florinda and Belvile.

Apart from writing numerous plays at a time, when women were censured for taking up writing as a career, Behn also wrote a short novel, *Oroonoko*. It is about an African prince, Oroonoko who falls in love with a young woman, Imoinda. When their love is discovered, Imoinda is sold into slavery to Suriname. One day, Oroonoko, who is a slave owner himself, is lured by the captain of an English ship and taken as a slave to Guiana. Here, he is united with his beloved. He tries to attain freedom but is caught and badly beaten. Realising that there is no way out, he kills his love and their unborn child. As soon as he is about to kill himself, he is captured and later executed.

Aphra Behn is a radical writer, who championed the cause of women and their sexual desire at a time when it was believed that women should be seen and not heard. Women such as Behn who wrote or acted on the stage were seen as whores. Undeterred by this stereotypical typecasting, Behn manages to break new ground. Acknowledging her importance, Virginia Woolf had stated, "All women together, ought to let flowers fall upon the grave of Aphra Behn... for it was she who earned them the right to speak their minds." Behn died on 16th April, 1689.

Major Works

Plays

- The Forced Marriage (1670)
- The Amorous Prince (1671)
- The Dutch Lover (1673)
- Abdelazer (1676)
- The Town Fop (1676)
- The Rover, Part 1 (1677) and Part 2 (1681)
- Sir Patient Fancy (1678)
- The Feigned Courtesans (1679)
- The Young King (1679)
- The Roundheads (1681)
- The City Heiress (1682)
- Like Father, Like Son (1682)
- The Emperor of the Moon (1687)

Novels

- Love-Letters between a Nobleman and His Sister (1684)
- Oroonoko (1688)

Short Stories

- The History of the Nun: or, the Fair Vow-Breaker (1688)
- The Dumb Virgin: or, The Force of Imagination (1700)

Poetry

- Poems upon Several Occasions, with A Voyage to the Island of Love (1684)
- Lycidus; or, The Lover in Fashion (1688)

John Vanbrugh (1664-1726)

English dramatist and architect John Vanbrugh was born in the parish of St Nicolas Acons in the City of London in 1664. His father, Giles was a businessman in Chester, while his mother was Elizabeth Carleton. He studied at King's School, Chester and later travelled to France to study arts.

Literary Career and Works

It was during his imprisonment that he wrote first comedy, *The Relapse: Or Virtue in Danger*- sequel to Colley Cibber's *Love's Last Shift*. This was followed by another play, *The Provok'd Wife*, which was criticised for its immorality. After his stint as a playwright, Vanbrugh changed his career and turned to architecture. The reasons for this remain unclear. In the words of Jonathan Swift, Vanbrugh's genius "without thought or lecture ... hugely turned to architecture". Vanbrugh was not a trained architect, but had a natural talent for it. In 1699, he began designing Castle Howard, Yorkshire, for the Earl of Carlisle and later the Blenheim Palace. Vanbrugh is considered to be a leading exponent of the English Baroque style.

He again wrote for the stage for a short while during his later years. Vanbrugh died on 26th March, 1726.

Major Works

- The Relapse: Or Virtue in Danger (1696)
- The Provok'd Wife (1697)
- Aesop (1697)
- The False Friend (1702)
- The Confederacy (1705)
- The Mistake (1705)

George Farquhar (1677-1707)

Irish playwright George Farquhar was born in Londonderry, Ireland, in 1677. His father was an Irish clergyman. Farquhar entered Trinity College, Dublin, as a sizar or servitor, a class of poor scholars who received a college allowance in return for performing menial duties. He did not remain there for long and soon started acting on the Dublin stage through the acquaintance of the actor Robert Wilks.

Literary Career and Works

On encouragement of Wilks, he went off to London to write comedy. His first comedy, *Love and a Bottle* (1698) was performed at Drury Lane in 1699. This was followed by other plays such as *The Constant Couple* (1699), *Sir Harry Wildair* (1701), *The Inconstant* (1702) and *The Twin Rivals* (1702).

Later, he joined the military as a lieutenant and secured a scanty income by helping to recruit men and raise troops. Three years later, he returned to playwriting with the hugely successful *The Recruiting Officer* (1706). On his deathbed, he completed his masterpiece, *The Beaux' Stratagem* (1707), a witty, realistic comedy set in the country. Farquhar died on 29th April, 1707, a few days after his last play opened to great success.

John Dryden (1631-1700)

John Dryden was one of the greatest prose writers of this period. His prefaces and his famous 'Essay on Dramatic Poesy' make him–the leader of the modern prose in which the style is plain, simple and free from all exaggerations.

John Dryden was not only an acclaimed prose writer or just a poet, but also the greatest literary figure of the Restoration Age. In fact, he was a perfect and true representative of the Restoration Age.

English poet, playwright and critic John Dryden was born in Aldwinkle, Northamptonshire in 1631. He was the eldest of 14th children of Erasmus Dryden and Mary Pickering. He studied at King's School at Westminster as a king's scholar under Richard Busby. Dryden married the daughter of the Earl of Berkshire, Lady Elizabeth Howard (1638–1714), who bore him three sons.

Literary Career and Works

It was at Westminster that Dryden wrote his first verse, an elegy *Upon the Death of Lord Hastings* and contributed it for *Lachrymae Musarum* (1649). After Westminster, Dryden entered Trinity College, Cambridge and graduated in 1654. His father died in the same year. Dryden obtained work with Cromwell's Secretary of State, John Thurloe. On the death of Cromwell, he published his first important work, *Heroic Stanzas*.

After the Restoration, he wrote a royalist panegyric celebrating the return of Charles II, titled *Astraea Redux* (1660). He also wrote *To His Sacred Majesty A Panegyric* for the King's coronation. Dryden's poetry celebrating the restoration pleased Charles II so much that he was named Poet Laureate in 1668 and two years later, royal historiographer. After the Restoration, Dryden devoted himself to writing plays as the theatres had reopened. His first play, *A Wild Gallant* appeared in 1663. This was followed by other plays such as *The Rival Ladies* (1664) and *The Indian Queen* (1664).

In the 1660s, Dryden also started writing works, which established him as a critic of repute. Dr Johnson called him 'the father of English criticism'. His first major critical work was the *Essay of Dramatic Poesy* (1668), followed by *A Defence of an Essay* (1668) and *Essay of Heroic Plays* (1672).

Dryden is today best known for his satirical works, *Absalom and Achitophel* (1681) and *Mac Flecknoe* (1682). Both these works established his eminence as a verse satirist. To this era also belong the didactic poem *Religio Laici* (1682), which argues the case for Anglicanism and *The Hind and the Panther* (1687), marking his conversion to Catholicism.

After the Revolution of 1688, Dryden lost his Laureateship with the accession of William III. Because of his refusal to take an oath of allegiance, Dryden became out of favour with the court. Writing became his sole source of income. He also translated Virgil's *Aeneid*, Homer's *Iliad*, Ovid's *Epistles* and *Metamorphosis*. Dryden died on 12th May, 1700 due to an inflammation caused by Gout.

An Essay of Dramatic Poesy

Dryden's *An Essay of Dramatic Poesy* was probably written in 1666 during the closure of London theatres due to plague. It was published in 1688, the essay can be seen as a defence of drama as an art form. The essay is structured as a dialogue/debate between four speakers- Eugenius, Crites, Lisideius and Neander.

These stand for William Davenant, Robert Howard, Roger Boyle and Dryden respectively. The essay begins with a reference to a naval battle between the British and Dutch on 3rd June, 1665, in the English Channel.

Four speakers named above observe this battle from a barge floating on Thames. After the battle gets over and the English navy wins, the four speakers begin discussing English drama. Eugenius literally means 'a well-born genius'. He favours the moderns over the ancients, arguing that the moderns have excelled over the ancients because of having learned and profited from their example. The name Crites comes from the Greek word 'critic' or one who is able to express a reasoned judgement on something. He argues in favour of the ancients and applauds the observance of the three unities in drama. He considers Ben Jonson as the greatest English playwright because he followed the ancients' example by adhering to the unities.

Lisideius' name is probably based on the royal emblem of France, the fleur-delis. He argues in favour of the modern day French playwrights. He believes that French drama is superior to English drama because of their adherence to the classical unities, because of their focus on one plot and one character and because of their use of narration.

The name Neander literally means 'the new man'. He favours the moderns, but does not disparage the ancients. He states that English are best at 'The lively imitation of nature' (human nature), conceding that while French poesy is beautiful, it is also lifeless like a 'statue'. He critiques 'the barrenness of the French plots' and praises the 'variety and copiousness of the English plays'. Neander also goes on to defend the genre of tragicomedy since it increases the effectiveness of both tragic and comic elements by way of contrast. He indicates his preference for Shakespeare over Ben Jonson.

Shakespeare "had the largest and most comprehensive soul," while Jonson was "The most learned and judicious writer which any theater ever had." Before Dryden, the English had no native criticism on drama.

Dryden's essay thus breaks new ground and makes serious efforts to develop a theory of drama by discussing ancient, contemporary French and English drama and by comparing the works of various individual English dramatists and the foreign dramatists.

Major Works

- The Indian Emperor (tragedy, 1665)
- Annus Mirabilis (poem, 1667)
- The Enchanted Island (comedy), 1667, an adaptation with William D'Avenant of Shakespeare's The Tempest
- Secret Love, or The Maiden Queen (1667)
- An Essay of Dramatick Poesie (1668)
- An Evening's Love (comedy, 1668)
- Tyrannick Love (tragedy, 1669)
- The Conquest of Granada (1670)
- Marriage à La Mode (1672)
- Aureng-zebe (1675)
- All for Love (1678)
- Oedipus (heroic drama), 1679, an adaptation with Nathaniel Lee of Sophocles' Oedipus
- Absalom and Achitophel (1681)
- The Medal (1682)
- Threnodia Augustalis (1685)
- A Song for St Cecilia's Day (1687)
- Amphitryon (1690)
- Don Sebastian (1690)
- Love Triumphant (1694)
- The Works of Virgil (1697)
- Alexander's Feast (1697)
- Fables, Ancient and Modern (1700)

Short Description of Dryden's Works

Work	Description
Astraea Redux	Royalist Panegyric written in heroic couplets, in which Dryden welcomes the new regime of Charles II.
Threnodia Augustalis	517 line poem written to commemorate the death of Charles II. Title –A Reference to Threnody, a poem of mourning. Subtitled 'A Funeral Pindarique Poem Sacred to the Memory of King Charles II'.
Religio Laici or A Layman's Faith	A verse essay that represents Dryden's tentative and candid examination of major religious issues of his day, and expresses his adherence to Church of England. Published as a premise to The Hind and the Panther.
The Hind and the Panther	Allegorical poem in heroic couplets written after Dryden's conversion to Catholicism in 1685. Adopts the framework of a beast fable, with Roman Catholics represented as Hinds, Anglicans as Panthers, Quakers as Hares, Presbyterians as Wolves, Independents as Bears, Anabaptists as Boar and Free Thinkers as Apes.
Alexander's Feast Or, The Power of Music, an Ode in Honour of St Cecilia's Day	Second of Dryden's odes honouring Saint Cecilia, the patron saint of music. The other being 'A Song for St Cecilia's Day'. Describes the feast given by Alexander the Great at Persepolis after the victory of Greeks over the Persian King Darius.
To The Memory of Mr Oldham (1684)	Elegy written on the death of the poet John Oldham.
All for Love or the World Well Lost	Heroic drama written in blank verse, which is an adaptation of Shakespeare's Antony and Cleopatra.

Neo-Classical Drama

Augustan drama can refer to the dramas of ancient Rome during the reign of Caesar Augustus, but it most commonly refers to the plays of Great Britain in the early 18th century, a subset of 18th-century Augustan (Neo-classical) literature. King George I referred to himself as 'Augustus', and the poets of the era took this reference as apropos, as the literature of Rome during Augustus moved from historical and didactic literature to the literature of highly finished and sophisticated epics and satire.

In drama, it was an age in transition between the highly witty and sexually playful Restoration comedy, the pathetic tragedy or she-tragedy of the turn of the 18th century and any later plots of middle-class anxiety. The Augustan stage retreated from the Restoration's focus on cuckoldry, marriage for fortune and a life of leisure. Instead, Augustan drama reflected questions that the mercantile class had about itself and what it meant to be gentry; what it meant to be a good merchant, how to achieve wealth with morality and the proper role of those who serve.

Augustan drama has a reputation as an era of decline. One reason for this is that there were few dominant figures of the Augustan stage. Instead of a single genius, a number of playwrights worked steadily to find subject matter that would appeal to a new audience. In addition to this, playhouses began to dispense with playwrights altogether or to hire playwrights to match assigned subjects, and this made to produce the master of the script. When the public got tired of anonymously authored, low-content plays and a new generation of wits made the stage political and aggressive again, the Whig ministry stepped in and began official censorship that put an end to daring and innovative content. This conspired with the public's taste for special effects to reduce theatrical output and promote the novel.

Augustan-era drama ended definitively in 1737 with the Licensing Act. Prior to 1737, the English stage was changing rapidly from Restoration comedy and Restoration drama and their noble subjects to the quickly developing melodrama. George Lillo and Richard Steele wrote the trend-setting plays of the early Augustan period. Lillo's plays consciously turned from heroes and kings toward shopkeepers and apprentices. They emphasied drama on a household scale rather than a national scale, and the hamartia (tragic flaw) and agon (conflict) in his tragedies are the common flaws of yielding to temptation and the commission of Christian sin. The plots are resolved with Christian forgiveness and repentance. Steele's *The Conscious Lovers* (1722) hinges upon his young hero avoiding fighting a duel. These plays set up a new set of values for the stage. Instead of amusing or inspiring the audience, they sought to instruct the audience and ennoble it. Further, the plays were popular precisely because they seemed to reflect the audience's own lives and concerns.

As during the Restoration, economic reality drove the stage during the Augustan period. Under Charles II court patronage meant economic success, and therefore the Restoration stage featured plays that would suit the monarch and/or court. The drama that celebrated kings and told the history of Britain's monarchs was fit fare for the crown and courtiers. Charles II was a philanderer and so Restoration comedy featured a highly sexualised set of plays. However, after the reign of William III and Mary II, the court and crown stopped taking a great interest in the playhouse.

Theaters had to get their money from the audience of city dwellers, therefore and consequently plays that reflected city anxieties and celebrated the lives of citizens were the ones to draw crowds. The aristocratic material from the Restoration continued to be mounted, and adaptations of Tudor plays were made and run, but the new plays that were authored and staged were the domestic and middle-class dramas. The other dramatic innovation was 'spectacle'. Plays that had little or no next, but emphasised novel special effects.

During the 18th century, drama steadily declined. Only remarkable dramatists shone out during this age. Goldsmith, Joseph Addison and Richard Steele were a few prominent figures who continued to enrich dramatic literature, otherwise, there was hardly any dramatist of the status of the Restoration or the Elizabethan dramatists during the age.

Oliver Goldsmith (1730-1774)

Anglo-Irish poet, playwright and novelist Oliver Goldsmith was born in Kilkenny West, Ireland in 1730. Goldsmith studied at Trinity College, Dublin. He coursed through a variety of professions, finally settling on medicine in 1752.

Literary Career and Works

For some years, he worked as an apothecary's assistant, school usher, physician and as a hack writer. However, he soon rose to fame with his *Enquiry into the Present State of Polite Learning in Europe.* Goldsmith also came to the notice of Samuel Johnson's, who invited Goldsmith to join his exclusive Turk's Head Club. Through Johnson's patronage, Goldsmith began to publish his first master works, including the novel *The Vicar of Wakefield*.

His other works include *The Citizen of the World* (a collection of essays, 1762), *An Elegy on the Death of a Mad Dog* (ironic poem, 1766), *The Good-Natur'd Man* (comic play, 1768), *She Stoops to Conquer* (a farce, 1773) and *The Deserted Village* (a poem on rural population and the Enclosure Movement, 1770). Goldsmith died on 4th April, 1774, after suffering from kidney disease.

She Stoops to Conquer

- Goldsmith's Comedy, *She Stoops to Conquer or Mistakes of a Night* was first performed in London in 1773.
- The play opens with a prologue in which an actor mourns the death of the classical low comedy.
- The play's heroine and the 'she' of the title is Kate Hardcastle, daughter of Mr Hardcastle who falls in love with Charles Marlow.
- Marlow is extremely shy around refined ladies of upper class but comfortable with women of humble birth. He mistakes Kate for a woman of the lower class and she allows him to continue to mistake her identity. She poses as a maid so that he becomes comfortable.
- The subplot revolves around the romance between Marlow's friend, George Hastings and Constance Neville, niece of Mrs Hardcastle.
- The play ends with the two couples, Marlow and Kate and Hastings and Constance- united and ready to wed.
- The play deals with the theme of social class.

Henry Fielding (1707-1754)

English novelist and playwright Henry Fielding was born in Sharpham park, England in 1707. He received his education at Eton Cottege and the University of Leiden.

Literary Career and Works

When Fielding returned to England, he started writing theatrical comedies. He also became manager of the Little Theatre in the Haymarket in 1736. *The Author's Farce* and *Rape upon Rape* were some of his famous plays. However, the passing of Theatrical Licensing Act in 1737, put an end to his career as a playwright. He became editor of *The Champion*. He was prompted to turn to fiction after reading Richardon's *Pamela*. He not only wrote *Shamela*, a parody of the novel, but followed it up with *Joseph Andrews* in 1742.

In 1743, Fielding published three volumes of *Miscellanies*, which included the famous work, *The Life of Mr Jonathan Wild the Great*, based on the life of a notorious criminal. His most popular novel, *The History of Tom Jones, A Foundling* established him as leading exponent of the English novel. Fielding had married Charlotte Cradock in 1734, on whom he later modeled the heroines of both Tom Jones and Amelia. Fielding got afflicted with health problems such as asthma, dropsy and severe gout, which forced him to retire in 1754. He also wrote an account of his journey, *The Journal of a Voyage to Lisbon*, in which he chronicled the slowness of travel, the incompetence of doctors and his own courage in overcoming these obstacles. He died in Lisbon in 1754.

Joseph Addison (1672-1719)

English essayist, playwright and politician Joseph Addison was born in Milston, Wiltshire in 1672. He studied at Charterhouse, where he was a classmate of Richard Steele and at The Queen's College, Oxford. Two years later, Addison became a Fellow of Magdalen College.

Literary Career and Works

In 1693, Addison addressed a poem to John Dryden, the former Poet Laureate, and his first major work, *An Account of the Greatest English Poets*, a book about the lives of English poets, was published in 1694. This was followed by *An Address to King William* (1695) and a Latin poem entitled *Pax Gulielmi* (1697), on the peace of Ryswick.

Addison rose to fame with *The Campaign* (1704), an epic celebrating the victory of Marlborough at Blenheim. The poem was commissioned by Lord Halifax, and its great success resulted in Addison's appointment in 1705 as undersecretary of state.

Addison is more famous today as an essayist. In 1710, he began contributing essays to *The Tatler*, which Richard Steele had founded in 1709. In 1771, both of them brought out the first number of *The Spectator*, another periodical. In 1713, Addison's *Cato*, a play with political overtones was performed with much success on the stage. Besides these, he also wrote *a Dialogue on Medals* and left unfinished a work on the evidences of Christianity. Addison died at Holland House on the 17th June, 1719.

Richard Steele (1672-1729)

Irish writer and politician Richard Steele was born in Dublin, Ireland in 1672. He studied at Christ Church, Oxford. Steele joined the army and rose to the rank of captain within two years. However, he left it in 1705 to turn his attention towards a career in writing.

Literary Career and Works

In 1701, Steele's *The Christian Hero*, a moralistic tract was published. His first play, the comedy *The Funeral or Grief a-la-mode*, was performed successfully at Drury Lane Theatre in 1701. This play was a satire on the new profession of undertaking. This was followed by *The Lying Lover or The Ladies's Friendship* in 1703. His third comedy, *The Tender Husband or The Accomplished Fools*, produced in 1705, achieved some success.

The *Dear Prue* of a series of delightful letters had been addressed to the second wife of Steele, Mary Scurlock, by him. Later he became governor of Drury Lane Theatre, where he produced *The Conscious Lovers* (1723), a popular play. Steele died at Carmarthen, Wales in 1729.

The Age of Johnson

The age of Johnson is also often referred as the age of sensibility which ranged from the middle of the eighteenth century until 1798. Ending the age of Johnson, the Romantic period arrived in 1798 with the publication of *Lyrical Ballads* by poets William Wordsworth and Samuel Taylor Coleridge.

Samuel Johnson (1709-1784)

Born in Lichfield, Staffordshire, Johnson attended Pembroke College, Oxford for just over a year, but lack of funds forced him to leave.

He worked as a teacher and then moved to London where he wrote for *The Gentleman's Magazine*.

Literary Career and Works

Johnson was the most famous poet, critic and playwright and fictional writer. He wielded considerable influence over this era with works that focussed on Neo-classical aesthetics (the study of natural and artistic beauty with an eye toward the great classical writers).

Writers of the age of Johnson focussed on qualities of intellect, reason, balance and order. Notable publications of the age of Johnson include Burke's *A Philosophical Inquiry into the Origins of Our Ideas on the Sublime and Beautiful* (1757), Johnson's *The Rambler* (1750-52) and Goldsmith's *The Vicar of Wakefield* (1766).

About a hundred papers of Dr Johnson were contributed to the Idler, which appeared between 1758 and 1760, which were shorter and lighter than the essays of the *Rambler*. The Rambler appeared twice a week, between 1750 and 1752. These essays were serious with ponderous English, lack of humour and unrelieved gravity, making it a heavy reading therefore not very popular.

His greatest contribution as a prose writer is his *Preface to his Dictionary*, various periodicals, his philosophical novel *Rasselas* and his critical works *Lives of the Poets and Preface to Shakespeare*. Dr Johnson has to his credit the making of the English Dictionary with witty meanings and comments that he added to 40,000 words in 1755. His style though vigorous and direct is heavy and learned with a name called. 'Johnsonese' which Chamber's dictionary defines as "Johnsonion style of idiom, diction or an imitation of it-ponderous English, full of antithesis, balanced triads and words of classical origin."

Johnson's only play *Irene* is a Neo-classical Tragedy written between 1726 and 1749, and was first performed on 6th February, 1749 in a production by his friend and former pupil, David Garrick. The play was a commercial success and earned Johnson more money than anything else he had written up to that point. However, it was never revived during his lifetime or any time later, making it one of the most unsuccessful plays ever written by a major author and considered his greatest failure by Johnson himself.

After creating an indellible mark and a prestigious place for himself in English Literature. Johnson died on 13th December, 1784 and was buried at Westminster Abbey.

Important Points

- Drama remains the most well known literary genre from the age. Within drama the best work from the 1660-1700 period is in comedy, even though a large number of tragedies were also written and staged. Among the tragedians are Thomas Otway, George Lillo Nicholas Rowe and John Dryden. The main type of Restoration tragedy was the heroic drama. The tragic play was characterised by a high level of melodrama and dramatic speeches.
- Restoration comedy, mostly set in and around London, dealt with follies, eccentricities and attitudes of the upper classes. Three main forces of Restoration comedy were : comedy of manner, of humour and of intrigue.
- The 'Big Five' of Restoration Comedy were George Etherege, William Congreve, William Wycherley, George Farquhar, and Sir John Vanburgh exposed the hypocrisies of upper class society by showing how the mask of virtue concealed envy, corruption and immorality. The comedies are full of intrigues, regarding marriage and morals. Cuckoldry and amorous pursuits are standard devices here. Adultery is a common theme and gossip is a major subject of condensation.

EXAM BASED QUESTIONS

1 What is the term for a highly sexualised, womanising male protagonist found in a Restoration comedy?
(a) A knave (b) A rake
(c) A gadabout (d) A silver fox

2 What marked the beginning of the period of Restoration comedies in English theatrical history?
(a) Oliver Cromwell retaking the throne of England
(b) An increased interest in social critique
(c) Charles II retaking the throne of England
(d) Women becoming professional playwrights for the first time

3 What is a major trait of Restoration comedy?
(a) Plays were full of a variety of scene types
(b) Professional actresses take the stage for the first time
(c) An emphasis on highly sexual situations
(d) All of the above are true

4 In what year did the Restoration period begin?
(a) 1760 (b) 1694
(c) 1660 (d) 1770

5 Who was king during the Restoration period?
(a) James II (b) Charles II
(c) Edward V (d) Charles I

6 What was the effect of the Restoration of 1660?
(a) The return of Charles Stuart to England
(b) The trial and execution of Mary, Queen of Scots
(c) The resignation of Robert Walpole
(d) The succession of George II

7 Which of the following is not a example of Restoration comedy?
(a) Etherege's The Man of Mode
(b) Whycherley's The Country Wife
(c) Behn's The Rover
(d) Marlowe's Doctor Faustus

8 Who ascended the British throne during the Glorious or Bloodless, Revolution in 1688?
(a) Elizabeth I (b) William and Mary
(c) George II (d) James II

9 Who among the following is not a Restoration playwright?
(a) William Congreve
(b) William Wycherley
(c) Ben Jonson
(d) George Etherege

10 What year was the play 'The Man of Mode' written and staged?
(a) 1700 (b) 1676
(c) 1976 (d) 1670

11 Who is the protagonist of the play 'The Man of Mode'?
(a) Young Bellair (b) Dorimant
(c) Medley (d) Sir Fopling Flutter

12 In the play 'The Man of Mode, 'Sir Fopling Flutter is a
(a) Villain (b) Hero (c) Lothario (d) Fop

13 Who is Lady Townley in the Play 'The Man of Mode'?
(a) Dorimant's lover (b) Emilia's mother
(c) Old Bellair's sister (d) Harriet's mother

14 Who is attracted to Emilia in the play 'The Man of Mode'?
(a) Sir Fopling Flutter (b) Old Bellair
(c) Medley (d) Dorimant

15 What is Belinda's 'plot' in the play 'The Man of Mode'?
(a) To seduce Medley
(b) To make Mrs. Loveit jealous
(c) To break up Emilia and young Bellair
(d) To befriend Harriet

16 Which was the third play by Wycherley, a capital play?
(a) The Relapse
(b) Love in a Tub
(c) Love for All
(d) The Holy War

17 In which theatre did William Wycherley produce in his works?
(a) Jija Bai Lane (b) Alexander Street
(c) Drury Lane (d) Chaucer Lane

18 Which of the following plays by William Wycherley is in part an adaptation of Moliere's Le Misanthrope?
(a) The Plain Dealer
(b) The Country Wife
(c) Love in a Wood
(d) The Gentleman Dancing Master

19 Identify the work which is based on Moliere's Le Misanthrope and follows the relationship problems of a sea captain?
(a) The Church Porch (b) The Gifts of God
(c) Paradise Lost (d) The Plain Dealer

20 One of the most popular and vulgar examples of Restoration comedy is William Wycherley's play
(a) The Country Wife
(b) Romeo and Juliet
(c) To His Mistress Going to Bed
(d) The Rover

21 Whom has Horner employed to spread the rumor of his impotence in the play 'The Country Wife'?
(a) Sir Jasper Fidget (b) Mr. Sparkish
(c) The Quack (d) Jack Pinchwife

22 Who has supposedly deprived Horner of his sexual potency in the play 'The Country Wife'?
(a) A French Prostitute (b) An English Surgeon
(c) A French Surgeon (d) An English Prostitute

23 Why does Sir Jasper want his wife to spend time with the 'eunuch' Horner in the play 'The Country Wife'?
(a) Horner has money, which he might lose to lady fidget at cards
(b) Sir Jasper dislikes horner and wants to punish him with lady fidget's company
(c) Horner has been pestering Sir Jasper for this opportunity
(d) Horner will provide safe companionship while Sir Jasper tends to his business

24 How does Horner convince Sir Jasper's encourage that the rumors of his impotence are true in the play 'The Country Wife?
(a) By feigning envy of other men
(b) By showing them a note from the quack
(c) By feigning an aversion to women
(d) By breaking down in tears

25 What, in Horner's opinion, is a 'lasting, rational, and manly pleasure' in the play 'The Country Wife'?
(a) Shooting parties (b) The theater
(c) Same-sex friendship (d) Boating

26 Who is known as the finest writer of the Comedy of Manners?
(a) George Etherege (b) William Black
(c) William Congreve (d) John Sucking

27 The Restoration comedy, The Double Dealer was written by
(a) John Dryden (b) William Wycherley
(c) William Congreve (d) George Etherege

28 Congreve's character Mirabell is a master
(a) of all trades (b) schemer (c) planner (d) lover

29 Why is Fainall upset with Mrs. Marwood at the end of Act, Scene 3?
(a) Because she spoiled his plans to get Mrs. Millamant's fortune
(b) Because she is clearly not in love with him
(c) Because he loves Millamant
(d) Because his wife shouldn't be having an affair with Mirabell, so he is angry at the world

30 What genre of play is 'The Way of the World'?
(a) Comedy (b) Tragedy
(c) Commedia dell'arte
(d) Restoration comedy/comedy of manners

31 Who is the play "The Way of the World' dedicated to?
(a) Charles II (b) William Shakespeare
(c) Ralph, earl of montague (d) Romeo, earl of montague

32 Who does Mirabell wish to marry in the play 'The Way of the World'?
(a) Ms. Millamant (b) Ms. Marwood
(c) Mrs. Fainall (d) Lady Wishfort

33 Who stands in the way of Mirabell marrying the women he desires in the play 'The Way of the World'?
(a) Mrs. Fainall (b) Mrs. Millamant
(c) Ms. Marwood (d) Lady Wishfort

34 What qualities are rooted in the proposed marriage between Sir Rowland and Lady Wishfort in the play 'The Way of the World'?
(a) Falsehood, deceit and conformity with society's expectations
(b) Adultery, deceit and pretentiousness
(c) Vanity, greed and lies
(d) Society's conception of marriage, illicit sex and lies

35 What does Ms. Millamant achieve when she renounces Mirabell in the play 'The Way of the World'?
(a) She pleases Lady Wishfort and retains her fortune
(b) She frustrates Mrs. Marwood and pleases Fainall
(c) She creates an out for Mirabell and destroys Lady Wishfort's plan to marry sir Rowland
(d) She angers Sir Wilfull Witwoud and Fainall

36 Why does Congreve say these critics should be the subject of on stage satire?
(a) Because they would retaliate
(b) Because this would inflate their sense of self-importance
(c) Because they are not important enough to bother with
(d) Because critics should not be made fun of since they hold a lot of power with the public

37 Why did Congreve use the epilogue in the play 'The Way of the World'?
(a) It satisfied his need for self-justification
(b) To urge the critics to praise his play
(c) It provided the opportunity for a pre-planned response to his critics
(d) To defy the critics by ranting against their analysis

38 What kind of person is Sir Wilfull Witwoud in the play 'The Way of the World'?
(a) Happy-go-lucky (b) Genuine but uncultured
(c) Rude and pretentious (d) Youthful and crude

39 Aphra Behn is noted as being
(a) the first professional black playwright
(b) the most risque of all Restoration authors
(c) the first professional female playwright
(d) a Puritan who hated the theater

40 In the play 'Oroonoko' the narrator compares the natives to
(a) Eloisa and Abelard (b) Spark and Finn
(c) Adam and Eve (d) Romeo and Juliet

41 In the play 'Oroonoko' the country from which the slaves originate is
(a) China (b) Coramantien
(c) Holland (d) Uganda

42 How does a plantation owner go about getting slaves in the play 'Oroonoko'?
(a) Orders them like merchandise
(b) Sends an overseer to personally apprehend the slaves
(c) Hires a ship
(d) None of the above

43 Because Belvile can see how much the duel with her brother is upsetting Florinda, what unexpected thing does he do in the play 'Rover'?
(a) He wounds Pedro
(b) He lays his sword at Florinda's feet
(c) He calls upon his friends to help fight
(d) He flees the scene

44 Why doesn't Pedro know who the Englishmen were he fought off with his sword after the attack on Florinda in the play 'Rover'?
(a) They were wearing masks
(b) They ran away too quickly
(c) They have never met
(d) They were too drunk

45 Who, disguised as man , still hides when she sees Pedro coming her way in the play 'Rover'?
(a) Valeria (b) Florinda (c) Hellena (d) Angellica

46 What does Florinda do to test Belvile's love for her as they are standing around with Frederica and Valeria in the play 'Rover'?
(a) She removes her disguise and offers him a ring as a token of her affection
(b) While still in disguise, she offers him a ring as a token of her affection
(c) She gives him a complicated quiz
(d) While still in disguise, she offers him a lock of her hair as a token of her affection

47 According to Blunt, what kind of things could Lucetta teach the prostitutes of England in the play 'Rover'?
(a) A lesson in generosity (b) A love song about France
(c) A song about ltaly (d) A lesson in love

48 What does the masked woman demand that Willmore tell her as she reveals who she is in the play 'Rover'?
(a) To know if he will marry her
(b) To know how much money he has
(c) To know how many other women he's betrayed
(d) To know his true love

49 As they are flirting with each other out on the street, how does Florinda reveal her true identity to Belvile in the play 'Rover'?
(a) Florinda gives Belvile a good kick and then leaves
(b) Florinda gives Belvile a picture of herself and then leaves
(c) Florinda gives Belvile a kiss and then leaves
(d) Florinda gives Belvile back the ring he gave her

50 Who was the hero of the Rover?
(a) Belville (b) Angelica
(c) Horner (d) Willmore

51 Identify a remarkably modern style divorce, due to the couple failing to make each other happy?
(a) The Comus
(b) Comus
(c) The Recruiting Officer
(d) The Beau's Stratagem

52 Which of the following women exposed themselves to scandal by writing racy stories for the popular press?
(a) Charlotte Perkins Gillman, Mary Wroth and Elizabeth Cary
(b) Aphra Behn, Delarivier Manley and Eliza Haywood
(c) Anne Finch, Anne Killigrew and Lady Mary Wortley Montagu
(d) Rachel Speght, Katherine Philips and Frances Burney

53 Who is considered to have brought England a modern literature between 1660 and 1700 that combined a cosmopolitan outlook on the latest European trends with some of the richness of Chaucer and Shakespeare?
(a) Addison (b) Bunyan
(c) Crabbe (d) Dryden

54 Heroic couplet is written by
(a) Dryden (b) Shakespeare
(c) Bunyan (d) Milton

55 In the era of John Dryden the Roman church is a symbol for
(a) Wolf (b) Anglican Church
(c) Hind (d) Panther

56 Which of the following uses blank verse?
(a) Donne's The Flea
(b) Dryden's All For Love
(c) Shelley's A Defence of Poetry
(d) Congreve's The Way of the World

57 In which of his works does Dryden leave his cherished heroic couplet for the blank verse of Marlowe and Shakespeare?
(a) Antony and Cleopatra
(b) Duke of Monmouth
(c) The Hind and Panther
(d) All for Love

58 Who is the greatest literary figure of the Restoration and in his work we have an excellent reflection age of both the good and the evil tendencies of the age, in which he lived?
(a) Goldsmith (b) John Dryden
(c) Waller (d) Congreve

59 The English satirist who used the sharp edge of praise to attack his victims was
(a) Ben Jonson (b) John Donne
(c) John Dryden (d) Samuel Butler

60 Why does Mark Antony initially mistrust his estranged best friend, Dolabella in the play 'All for Love'?
(a) Mark Antony secretly has strong feelings for Dolabella
(b) Ventidius, who strongly wishes Mark Antony would leave Egypt, has invited Dolabella
(c) Dolabella is too loyal to Caesar Octavius to intercede on Mark Antony's behalf
(d) Dolabella admits he is attracted to Cleopatra

61 What is the structural principle John Dryden used while choosing the setting of the play 'All for Love'?
(a) Unity of time, place, and action
(b) French Neo-classicism
(c) Decorum
(d) A thrust stage

62 Which is the most significant objection to Mark Antony and Cleopatra's love in the play 'All for Love'?
(a) Their love makes the Roman Empire and Egypt sociopolitically vulnerable
(b) They have not produced an heir
(c) They are fickle
(d) Their love is adulterous

63 How does Cleopatra characterise her death in the play 'All for love'?
(a) She calls it the winter of her life
(b) She calls it her lover
(c) She calls it a shadow looming over her life
(d) She calls it her wedding to Mark Antony

64 Who is the the protagonist in the play 'All for Love?
(a) Cleopatra, because she is the emotional center of the play
(b) Mark Antony, because his actions move the plot forward
(c) Cleopatra, because she never changes her mind about how much she loves Mark Antony
(d) Mark Antony, because he is the noblest character in the play

65 To whom does Octavia say she will give the love she previously reserved for Mark Antony in the play 'All for Love'?
(a) Agrippina and Antonia (b) Herself
(c) Ventidius and Alexas (d) Dolabella

66 Which theme does the tension between the lovers and their advisers best illustrate in the play 'All for Love'?
(a) Sometimes one is manipulated by those who claim to love him/her/z
(b) Love weakens one's reason
(c) Civic duty is more important than personal desire
(d) Love makes one only attend to one's own desires

67 What is decorum in terms of drama?
(a) Decorum is the moral standard of seventeenth century England
(b) Decorum is a term indicating noble character
(c) Decorum is a seventeenth century standard for dramatic characters, who are expected to behave as befits their role, rank age, personal character, and gender
(d) Decorum is a form of theater popular in France and England

68 What does Mr. Hardcastle disdain most of all in the play 'She Stoops to Conquer?
(a) Town manners (b) Country manners
(c) Money (d) Arranged marriages

69 Why does Mrs. Hardcastle defend Tony in the play 'She Stoops to Conquer?
(a) She hates Hardcastle (b) He blackmails her
(c) She's his mother (d) She does not defend him

70 Who does Mrs. Hardcastle hope Tony will marry in the play 'She stoops to Conquer'?
(a) Constance Neville
(b) She does not want him married
(c) Kate hardcastle
(d) The landlady at the inn

71 Which character is the best example of moderation in the play 'She Stoops to Conquer?
(a) Tony Lumpkin (b) Kate
(c) Mr. Hardcastle (d) Mrs. Hardcastle

72 What is Mrs. Hardcastle's great vice in the play 'She Stoops to Conquer'?
(a) Lust (b) Vanity
(c) Thievery (d) Depression

73 What is Constance's inheritance ?
(a) She is destitute (b) A set of gowns
(c) Jewels (d) A dowry

74 Which character has a complicated relationship with his or her mother in the play 'She Stoops to Conquer'?
(a) Tony (b) Hastings
(c) Kate (d) Mr. Hardcastle

75 What is Mrs. Hardcastle's complaint with her husband in the play 'She Stoops to Conquer'?
(a) He doesn't dress for dinner
(b) He has no taste in furniture
(c) They never have company come to the house
(d) They do not travel to town now and then

76 What is Mr. Hardcastle's response to Mrs. Hardcastle's complaining that he only likes old things in the play 'She Stoops to Conquer?
(a) He says she thinks anything bought last month is old
(b) He says she will have to own that he is pretty fond of an old wife
(c) He says she known he just bought a new horse
(d) He says she just does not know the value of antiques

77 The good vicar kept insisting upon one name for each of his daughters, but was overruled each time by the fancies of romantic female whims: Olivia was named to please her mother and Sophia at the insistence of a rich relation in the play 'The Vicar of Wakefield'. What name had he held dear to his heart?
(a) Harriet (b) Agatha
(c) Grissel (d) Ermengarde

78 Mrs. Primrose and her daughters were skilled at the manufacture of a certain libation, which they offered proudly to all of their company in the play 'The Vicar of Wakefield'. What was this beverage?
(a) Hard Cider
(b) Rosewater Cordial
(c) Brown Ale
(d) Gooseberry Wine

79 George, the eldest son, was in love with the daughter of a neighbouring gentleman. As their fortunes were well-suited, the match was certain to take place in the play 'The Vicar of Wakefield'. What was the name of the lovely young lady?
(a) Miss Rosamund Carteret (b) Miss Catherine Spriggs
(c) Miss Elizabeth Darby. (d) Miss Arabella Wilmot

80 The family moved to a less expensive lodging where Dr. Primrose could earn a little money by managing a farm. On their first night on the road, the owner of the inn told them of the character of their new landlord, Squire Thornhill. What, in the opinion of the innkeeper, was the principal fault of their new landlord?
(a) He was exceptionally harsh to the poor
(b) He drank to excess
(c) He was selfish about the hunting rights on his lands
(d) He ruined the daughters of the neighbours

81 Mr. Burchell set out upon the road with them the next day, and endeared himself to the family by performing and important service, saving a member of the family from certain peril in the play 'The Vicar of Wakefield'. Who did he save, and from what?
(a) Moses/choking
(b) Olivia /galloping horse
(c) Sophia /drowning
(d) George/a ruffian

82 The girls lost their places in town through the intercession of someone who wrote a scathing letter decrying 'the intrusion of vice and baseness amongst so much innocence.' The family was angry that anyone would so falsely accuse their girls in this manner in the play 'The Vicar of Wakefield'. Who wrote the offensive note to the ladies in town?
(a) Mr. Thornhill (b) Mr. Jenkinson
(c) Mr. Flamberough (d) Mr. Burchell

83 Dr. Primrose met with a great joy and a terrible calamity upon his journey from town. Amazingly, he encountered his lost child Olivia in an inn in the play 'The Vicar of Wakefield', but what misfortune befell the family upon his return home?
(a) Fire (b) Robbers (c) Flood (d) Illness

84 The reunited Primrose family discovered that someone of their acquaintance had been playing a masquerade on them, and was in reality the great philanthropist Sir William Thornhill. Who had been hiding his real identity?
(a) IC Squire Thornhill (b) Mr. Tyburn
(c) Mr. Jenkinson (d) Mr. Burchell

85 Who teamed with Joseph Addison to form the famous literary partnership that put out the news sheet 'The Tatler' and the daily paper 'The Spectator'?
(a) Richard Steele (b) John Barrington
(c) Samuel Richards (d) Albert Samuel

86 The attempt to exclude James from the throne during the Restoration age was termed as...... .
(a) The Exclusion Crisis (b) The Inclusion Crisis
(c) The Glorious Revolution (d) The Orange Revolution

87 The main trends prevalent during the Restoration age in the field of literature were ....
(a) satires (b) odes (c) heroic drama (d) tragedy

88 .... called himself a eunuch or impotent in the play 'The Country Wife'.
(a) Josper (b) Horner (c) Alithea (d) Harcourt

89 ...... attacked major Restoration play-wrights such as Dryden, Congreve and Wycherley for bringing debauchery and profanity on stage, in his anti-theatre pamphlet, A short view of the immortality and profaneness of the English stage.
(a) George Etherege (b) Jeremy Collier
(c) Samuel Pepys (d) John Locke

90 Considered to be the first professional woman writer, Aphra Behn's first play, ... appeared in 1670.
(a) The Amorous Prince (b) Abdelazer
(c) The Rover (d) The Forc'd Marriage

91 In William Congreve's 'The Way of the World' though Mrs. Millamant doesn't act it, Mrs. Millamant actually .... Mirabell.

(a) dislikes (b) bores (c) loves (d) frustrates

92 John Vanbrugh's .... was a sequel to Colley Cibeer's Love's Last Shift.

(a) The Relapse : or the Virtue in Danger
(b) The Provok'd Wife
(c) The False Friend
(d) The Mistake

93 .... is a heroic drama written in blank verse which is an adaption of Shakespeare's Antony and Cleopatra.

(a) The Hind and the Panther
(b) To the Memory of Mr. Oldham
(c) Religio Laici
(d) All for Love or The World Well Lost

94 The play 'The Man of Mode' is an example of .... literature.

(a) Colonial (b) Puritan (c) Restoration (d) Victorian

95 The natives are particularly adept at... in the play 'Oroonoko',

(a) Scuba diving
(b) Climbing trees and fishing
(c) Growing plants (d) Hunting tigers

96 Which of these statements about 'Comedy of Manners' is incorrect?

(a) It is a style of dramatic comedy that reflects the life, ideals and manners of upper class society
(b) A flamboyant display of wity, blunt sexual dialogue
(c) It depicts the relations and intrigues of men and women belonging to polished sections of society
(d) It did not include intrigues, sexual innuendos and rakish behaviour

97 Which of the following statements is correct? The main characteristic of 'An Essay of Dramatic Poesy'

(a) It was published in 1666
(b) It defends drama as an art form
(c) It is written by John Dryden
(d) The essay is structured as a dialogue between ten speakers

98 Which of the following is incorrect?

(a) Heroic drama was a popular literary trend during the restoration period
(b) Comedy of manners was the second most popular genre during restoration period
(c) Blamires' A History of English Literature applauded heroic drama of restoration period
(d) Dryden was the main exponent of heroic drama

99 Which of the following is not correct?

(a) Restoration comedy of manners was influenced by Ben Johnson's comedy of humours
(b) Joseph Addison was one of the dramatists who practised comedy of manners
(c) Most comedy writers relished the presentation of scenes and acts suggestive or even clearly indicative of sexual licentiousness
(d) Dryden and his genre of heroic plays were mocked by Buckingham's burlesque 'The Rehearsal'

100 Which of the following is not true?

(a) 'She would if she could' was written by Dryden
(b) 'The Plain Dealer' was written by William Wycherly
(c) 'The Double Dealer' was written by William Congreve
(d) 'The Forc'd Marriage was written by Aphra Behn

101 Which of the following pairs is incorrectly matched?

(a) She Would If She Could : George Etherege
(b) The Plain Dealer : William Wycherley
(c) The Double Dealer : William Congreve
(d) Sir Harry Wildair : Aphra Behn

102 Which of the following is correctly matched?

(a) Abdelazer : John Vanbrugh
(b) The Recruiting Officer : George Farquhar
(c) Essay of Dramatic Poesy : John Locke
(d) Reprobation Asserted : John Dryden

103 Which of the following pairs is incorrectly matched?

(a) Aphra Behn : Like Father Like Son
(b) William Congreve : The Country Wife
(c) John Dryden : The Indian Queen
(d) John Bunyan : Saved by Grace

104 Which of the following dramatists sequence is in correct chronological order?

(a) Aphra Behn, William Congreve, George Etherege, John Vanbrugh
(b) George Etherege, Aphra Behn, John Vanbrugh, William Congreve
(c) William Congreve, George Etherege, Aphra Behn, John Vanbrugh
(d) William Congreve, Aphra Behn, George Etherege, John Vanbrugh

105 Which of the following lists of plays is incorrect chronological order?

(a) An Evening's Love, Love in a Wood, The Dutch Lover, The Old Bachelor
(b) Love in a Wood, The Dutch Lover, The Old Bachelor, An Evening's Love
(c) The Dutch Lover, The Old Bachelor, An Evening's Love, Love in a Wood
(d) The Old Bachelor, An Evening's Love, Love in a Wood, The Dutch Lover

106 Match the following.

List I	List II
A. The Mourning Bride	1. William Wycherley
B. The Gentleman Dancing Master	2. Thomas Otway
C. The Sullen Lovers	3. William Congreve
D. Don Carlos	4. Thomas Shadwell

Codes

	A	B	C	D		A	B	C	D
(a)	1	2	3	4	(b)	2	3	1	4
(c)	3	1	4	2	(d)	3	2	1	4

107 Match the following.

List I	List II
A. The Man of Mode, or Sir Fopling Flutter	1. George Farquhar
B. Love for Love	2. George Etherege
C. Aurengzeb	3. William Congreve
D. The Beaux Stratagem	4. John Dryden

Codes

	A	B	C	D		A	B	C	D
(a)	2	1	3	4	(b)	2	3	4	1
(c)	4	1	2	3	(d)	1	3	4	2

108 In the following series, which one has all the dramatists matched correctly with their works?

(a) George Etherege-The Old bachelor, William Congreve-The Counterfeit Bridegroom, Aphra Behn-The Enchanted Island, John Dryden-The Man of Mode

(b) George Etherege-The Enchanted Island, William Congreve-The Man of Mode, Aphra Behn-The Old Bachelor, John Dryden-The Counterfeit Bridegroom

(c) George Etherege-The Counterfeit Bridegroom, William Congreve-The Man of Mode, Aphra, Behn-The Old Bachelor John Dryden-The Enchanted Island

(d) George Etherege-The Man of Mode, Aphra Behn-The Counterfeit Bridegroom. William Congreve-The Old Bachelor, John Dryden-the Enchanted Island

109 In the following series, which one has all the writers correctly matched with their works?

(a) William Wycherley-The Plain Dealer, John Vanbrugh-The Provoked Wife, George Farquhar- The Twin Rivals, John Bunyan-The Holy City or the New Jerusalem

(b) William Wycherley-The Twin Rivals, John Vanbrugh-The Plain Dealer, George Farquhar-The Plain Dealer, John Bunyan-The Holy City or the New Jerusalem

(c) William Wycherley- The Holy City or the New Jerusalem, John Vanbrugh- The Twin Rivals, George Farquhar- The Provoked Wife, John Bunyan-The Plain Dealer

(d) William Wycherley-The Holy City or the New Jerusalem, John Vanbrugh-the Plain Dealer, George Farquhar-The Provoked Wife, John Bunyan-The Twin Rivals

110 In the following series, which one has all the plays matched correctly with their composers?

(a) The Indian Emperor-John Dryden, The Inconstant-Aphra Behn, The Town Fop-William Congreve, The Way of the World-George Farquhar

(b) The Indian Emperor-John Dryden, The Inconstant-George Farquhar, The Town Fop-Aphra Behn, The Way of the World-William Congreve

(c) The Indian Emperor-William Congreve, The Inconstant-Aphra Behn, The Town Fop - John Dryden, The Way of the World - George Farquhar

(d) The Indian Emperor- George Farquhar, The Inconstant- John Dryden, The Town Fop - William Congreve, The Way of the World-Aphra Behn

111 Match the dramatists with their plays.

List I (Dramatist)	List II (Play)
A. George Etherege	1. The Comical Revenge or Love in a Tub
B. William Wycherley	2. The Gentleman Dancing Master
C. William Congreve	3. The Mourning Bride
D. Aphra Behn	4. The Amorous Prince

	A	B	C	D		A	B	C	D
(a)	1	2	3	4	(b	2	3	4	1
(c)	3	4	1	2	(d)	4	1	2	3

112 Match the plays with their playwrights.

List I (Play)	List II (Play wright)
A. The Relapse	1. George Farquhar
B. Love for Love	2. John Dryden
C. Secret Love	3. John Vanbrugh
D. The Constant Couple	4. William Congreve

Codes

	A	B	C	D		A	B	C	D
(a)	1	2	3	4	(b)	3	4	2	1
(c)	4	3	2	1	(d)	2	4	1	3

113 Match the dramatists with their works.

List I (Dramatist)	List II (Work)
A. John Dryden	1. The Campaign
B. Oliver Goldsmith	2. Rape Upon Rape
C. Henry Fielding	3. The Vicar of Wakefield
D. Joseph Addition	4. The Indian Emperor

Codes

	A	B	C	D		A	B	C	D
(a)	2	1	4	3	(b)	1	2	3	4
(c)	4	3	2	1	(d)	3	4	2	1

114 Match the works with their playwrights.

List I (Work)	List II (Dramatist)
A. The Way of the World	1. George Farquhar
B. The Beaux Stratagen	2. Aphra Behn
C. The Lying Lover	3. William Congreve
D. The Rover	4. Richard Steele

Codes

	A	B	C	D
(a)	1	2	3	4
(b)	4	3	2	1
(c)	1	4	2	3
(d)	3	1	4	2

115 Match the characters with their plays.

	List I (Character)		List II (Plays)
A.	Dr. Primrose	1.	The Man of Mode
B.	Mirabell	2.	The Country Wife
C.	Dorimant	3.	The Vicar of the Wakefield
D.	Horner	4.	The Way of the World

Codes

	A	B	C	D		A	B	C	D
(a)	3	4	1	2	(b)	2	1	4	3
(c)	1	2	3	4	(d)	4	3	2	1

116 Consider the following statements, 'The main, Comedy of Manners' are

1. the comic dialogue bristled with salacious innuendos.
2. the comic dialogue did not bristle with salacious innuendos.
3. it did not hold a mirror to the high society.
4. there was a pronounced immoral note and scenes and acts suggested sexual licentiousness.

Which of the statements given above are correct?

(a) 1 and 2 (b) 1 and 4
(c) 3 and 4 (d) 3 and 2

117 Which comedy is also known as Comedy of Manners?

1. Restoration comedy 2. Jacobean comedy
3. Spenserian comedy 4. Elizabethan comedy

Select the correct answer using the codes given below.

(a) 2 and 4 (b) Only 1
(c) 2 and 3 (d) Only 2

118 What is common to the following writers?

1. William Congreve 2. George Etherege
3. Wycherley 4. Aphra Behn

Identify the correct description below.

(a) All of them were prose writers of the Neo-classical Age
(b) All of them were proponents of Caribbean Literature
(c) All of them practised Comedy of Manners
(d) All of them wrote Ballads

119 Which of the following is/are John Dryden's Heroic drama/s?

1. All For Love
2. Pepys
3. The Conquest of Granada
4. Oedipus

Select the correct answer using the codes given below.

(a) 1 and 2 (b) 2 and 3
(c) 2 and 4 (d) 3 and 4

120 Which of the following are dramatists of the comedy of the manners of the Restoration Age?

1. Samuel Butler 2. Samuel Pepys
3. William Wycherley 4. Aphra Behn

Select the correct answer using the codes give below.

(a) 1 and 2
(b) 2 and 3
(c) 3 and 4
(d) Only 3

121 "Love gilds us over and makes us show fine things to one another for a time, but soon the gold wears off and then again the native brass appears."
From which work of an author have these lines been taken?

(a) Love in a Wood, William Wycherley
(b) The Man of Mode, George Etherege
(c) The Double-Dealer, William Congreve
(d) The Forc'd Marriage, Aphra Behn

122 "Tis my maxim, he's a fool that marries, but he's a greater that does not marry a fool."
From which work of an author have these lines been taken?

(a) She would If She could, George Etherege
(b) The Old Bachelor, William Congreve
(c) The Country Wife, William Wycherley
(d) The Forc'd Marriage, Aphra Behn

123 "But say what you will, 'tis better to be left than never to have been loved. To pass our youth in dull indifference, to refuse the sweets of life because they once must leave us, is as preposterous as to wish to have been born old, because we one day must be old."
From which work of an author have these lines been taken?

(a) Letterbook, George Etherege
(b) The Plain-Dealer, William Wycherley
(c) The Amorous Prince, Aphra Behn
(d) The Way of the World, William Congreve

124 "Music has charms to soothe a savage breast, to soften rocks, or bend a knotted oak. I've read that things inanimate have moved, and as with living sould, have been inform'd, by magic numbers and persuasive sound."
Which restoration age writer's lines are these?

(a) John Bunyan
(b) William Congreve
(c) Aphra Behn
(d) John Dryden

125 "How I should despise such a thing if I were a man. What a nose she has! what a chin! what a neck! Then her eyes-and the worst kissing lips in the universe."
From which work of an author have these lines been taken?

(a) The Provoked Wife, John Vanbrugh
(b) Love for Love, William Congreve
(c) The Country Wife, William Wycherley
(d) The Debauchee, Aphra Behn

126 "We are the men of intrinsic value, who can strike our fortunes out of ourselves, whose worth is independent of accidents in life, or revolutions in government: we have heads to get money, and hearts to spend it"
From which Composer's work have these lines been taken?
(a) John Vanbrugh, The Relapse
(b) George Farquhar, The Beaux' Stratagem
(c) John Dryden, Heroic Stanzas
(d) John Bunyan, Grace Abounding

127 "Nature well drawn, and wit, must now give place
To gaudy non-sense and to dull grimace:
Nor is it strange that you should like so much
That kind of wit, for most of yours is such."
Which of the following dramatists in which of his/her works has had the above lines?
(a) George Etherege, The Man of Mode
(b) William Wycherley, The Country Wife
(c) William Congreve, Love For Love
(d) Aphra Behn, Oroonoko

128 "Marrying to increase love is like gaming to become rich; alas, you only lose what little stock you had before"
Which of the following dramatists in which of his/her works has had the above lines?
(a) George Etherege, The Man of Mode
(b) William Wycherley, The Country Wife
(c) William Congreve, Love For Love
(d) Aphra Behn, Oroonoko

129 "All well bred persons lie – Besides, you are a woman; you must never speak what you think..."
Which of the following dramatists in which of his/her works has had the above lines?
(a) George Etherege, The Man of Mode
(b) William Wycherley, The Country Wife
(c) William Congreve, Love For Love
(d) Aphra Behn, Oroonoko

130 "A poet is a painter in his way, he draws to the life, but in another kind; we draw the nobler part, the soul and the mind; the pictures of the pen shall outlast those of the pencil, and even worlds themselves."
Which of the following dramatists in which of his/her works has had the above lines?
(a) George Etherege, The Man of Mode
(b) William Wycherley, The Country Wife
(c) William Congreve, Love For Love
(d) Aphra Behn, Oroonoko

131 "WILLMORE: Nay, if we part so, let me die like a Bird upon a Bough, at the Sheriff's Charge. By Heaven, both the Indies shall not buy thee from me. I adore thy Humour and will marry thee, and we are so of one Humour, it must be a Bargain - give me thy Hand - [Kisses her hand.] And now let the blind ones (Love and Fortune) do their worst."
Which of the following dramatists in which of his/her works has had the above lines?
(a) Aphra Behn, The Rover
(b) John Vanbrugh, The Provoked Wife
(c) George Farquhar, The constant couple; or, a trip to the Jubilee
(d) John Dryden, Aureng-Zebe

132 "Fantastic fortune thou deceitful light,
That cheats the weary traveller by night,
Though on a precipice each step you tread,
I am resolved to follow where you lead."
Which of the following dramatists in which of his/her works has had the above lines?
(a) Aphra Behn, The Rover
(b) John Dryden, All for Love
(c) Oliver Goldsmith, She Stoops to Conquer
(d) Henry Fielding, The History of Tom Jones, a Foundling

133 "Shield me, kind heaven, what an inundation of impertinence is here coming upon us!"
Which of the following dramatists in which of his/her works has had the above lines?
(a) Aphra Behn, The Rover
(b) John Vanbrugh, The Provoked Wife
(c) George Farquhar , The constant couple; or, a trip to the Jubilee
(d) John Dryden, Aureng-Zebe

134 "I have told my passion, my eyes have spoke it, my tongue pronounced it, and my pen declared it; I have sighed it, wrote it, and subscribed it, now my heart is full of you, my head raves of you and my hand writes to you but all in vain."
Which of the following dramatists in which of his/her works has had the above lines?
(a) Aphra Behn, The Rover
(b) John Vanbrugh, The Provoked Wife
(c) George Farquhar , The constant couple; or, a trip to the Jubilee
(d) John Dryden, Aureng-Zebe

135 "When I consider Life, 'tis all a cheat;
Yet, fooled with hope, men favour the deceit;
Trust on, and think to-morrow will repay:
To-morrow's falser than the former day;
Lies worse; and while it says, we shall be blest
With some new joys, cuts off what we possesst."
Which of the following dramatists in which of his/her works has had the above lines?
(a) Aphra Behn, The Rover
(b) John Vanbrugh, The Provoked Wife
(c) George Farquhar , The constant couple; or, a trip to the Jubilee
(d) John Dryden, Aureng-Zebe

136 "All is not gold that glitters,
Pleasure seems sweet, but proves a glass of bitters"

Which of the following dramatists in which of his/her works has used the above lines?
(a) Oliver Goldsmith, She Stoops to Conquer
(b) Oliver Goldsmith, The Good-Natured Man
(c) Joseph Addison, Cato
(d) Richard Steele, The Lying Lover

137 "Modesty seldom resides in a breast that is not enriched with nobler virtues."
(a) Oliver Goldsmith, She Stoops to Conquer
(b) Oliver Goldsmith, The Good-Natured Man
(c) Joseph Addison, Cato
(d) Richard Steele, The Lying Lover

138 Friendship is a disinterested commerce between equals; love, an abject intercourse between tyrants and slaves.

Which of the following dramatists in which of his/her works has used the above lines?
(a) Oliver Goldsmith, She Stoops to Conquer
(b) Oliver Goldsmith, The Good-Natured Man
(c) Joseph Addison, Cato
(d) Richard Steele, The Lying Lover

139 Don't let us make imaginary evils, when you know we have so many real ones to encounter.

Which of the following dramatists in which of his/her works has used the above lines?
(a) Oliver Goldsmith, She Stoops to Conquer
(b) Oliver Goldsmith, The Good-Natured Man
(c) Joseph Addison, Cato
(d) Richard Steele, The Lying Lover

140 "He who hesitates is lost."

Which of the following dramatists in which of his/her works has used the above lines?
(a) Oliver Goldsmith, She Stoops to Conquer
(b) Oliver Goldsmith, The Good-Natured Man
(c) Joseph Addison, Cato
(d) Richard Steele, The Lying Lover

Directions (Q. Nos. 141-145) *In the questions given below are two statements labelled as Assertion (A) and Reason (R). In the context of the two statements, which one of the following is correct?*

Codes
(a) Both A and R are true and R is the correct explanation of A
(b) Both A and R are true, but R is not the correct explanation of A
(c) A is true, but R is false
(d) A is false, but R is true

141 **Assertion** (A) When women were censured for taking up writing as a career, Aphra Behn wrote a short novel, Oroonoko besides numerous plays.
Reason (R) It is about an African prince, Oroonoko, who falls in love with a young woman, Imoinda.

142 **Assertion** (A) Dryden and his genre of heroic plays were mocked by Buckingham's Burlesque: The Rehearsal.
Reason (R) Dryden was the main exponent of heroic drama.

143 **Assertion** (A) Dolabella describes that 'Her soul's too great, after such injuries'.
Reason (R) Octavia's love is spiritual for Antony.

144 **Assertion** (A) Octavia describes that. 'I have lost my honour, lost my fame'.
Reason (R) 'She is the beloved of Antony not his wife'.

145 **Assertion** (A) Dryden is best known for his Satirical works, Absalom and Achitophel and Mac Flecknoe.
Reason (R) Dryden won fame through his prose work, Grace Abounding.

Directions (Q. Nos. 146-150) *Read the given passage and answer the questions that follows.*

A Chocolate-house

Mirabell and Fainall Rising form Cards

Mirabell: You are a fortunate Man, Mr. Fainall.

Fainall: Have we done?

Mirabell: What you please. I'll play on to entertain you.

Fainall: No, I'll give you your revenge another time, when your are not so indifferent; your are thinking of something esle now, and play too negligently; the Coldness of a losing Gamester lessense the Pleasure of the Winner: I'd no more play with a Man that slighted his ill Fortune, than I'd make Love to a Woman who undervalu'd the Loss of her Reputation.

Mirabell: You have a Taste extreamely delicate, and are for refining on your Pleasures.

Fainall: Prithee, why so reserved? Something has put you out of humour.

Mirabell: Not at all. I happen to be grave today, and you are gay; that's all

Fainall: Confess, Millamant and your quarreled last night.The discovery of your sham Addresses to [My Lady Wishfort], to conceal your Love to her Niece, has provok'd this Separation: Had you dissembl'd better, Things might have continu'd in the state of Nature.

Mirabell: I did as much as Man cou'd, with any reasonable Conscience; I proceeded to the very last Act of Flattery with her, and was guilty of a Song in her Commendation: Nay, I got a Friend to pur her into a Lampoon, and compliment her with the Imputation of an Affair with a young Fellow, which I carry'd so far, that I told her the malicious Town took notice that she was grown fat of a suddain; and when she lay in of a Dropsie, persuaded he she was reported to be in Labour, The Devil's in't, if an old Woman is to be flatter'd further, unless a man shou'd endeavour downright personally to debauch her; and that my Virtue forbad me.

146 The dialogue comes from which of the following plays?

(a) The Way of the World
(b) The Man of Mode
(c) The Rover
(d) The Country Wife

147 Which of the following most accurately explains Fainall's remarks about gambling and lovemaking (lines 5-12)?

(a) Fainall wishes to be loved by all: he therefore chooses companions, at cards and in romance, who will not too deeply question his motives
(b) Fainall plays for hight stakes: the pleasure he takes in cards and women is dependent on the thrill of great risk
(c) Fainall is addicated to both cards and women: although he knows he should be more disciplined and discreet in both areas, he cannot help himself
(d) Fainall expresses a cynical and libertine pleasure in the pain of other: for him to enjoy winning at cards, the loser has to be unhappy; for him to enjoy seducing a woman, she has to regret the consequences

148 Which of the following best describes line 28-34 'Nay ....Labour'?

(a) Mirabell has flattered Lady Wishfort by telling her that she is the subject of scandalous rumors
(b) Mirabell has complimented a friend for defending Lady Wishfort's reputation
(c) Mirabell has spread a rumour to cover up the true cause of Lady Wishfort's illness
(d) Mirabell has criticised fashionable society for lampooning a former beauty who is now aging

149 When Mirabell refers to his 'Conscience' (line 26) and his 'Virtue' (line 38), he expects Fainall to understand that he is

(a) a sincere Christian whose faith prevents him from breaking the Commandments
(b) an atheist disdainful fo any societal standards, which he disparages by invoking 'the Devil'
(c) a wit who makes 'Sham Addresses' by verbal rather than by physical means
(d) a man who is fearful of venereal disease and therefore reluctant to engage in promiscuous sex

150 A parallel between a card game and the battle of the sexes is also developed in which of the following eighteenth-century works?

(a) A tale of a Tub
(b) Rape of the Lock
(c) Joseph Andrews
(d) The Vanity of Human Wishes

PREVIOUS YEARS' QUESTIONS

December 2018

1 Which of the following statements is true of The Way of the World?

(a) The Way of the World failed on stage
(b) Millamant and Mirabell fail to obtain the consent of Millamant's aunt for their marriage
(c) The Way of the World presents a heroine pretending to love an older man
(d) The Way of the World was performed and published in 1702

2 Match the character with the play.

Character	Play
A. Dorimant	1. The Plain Dealer
B. Lady Fidget	2. The Man of Mode
C. Malevole	3. The Country Wife
D. Vernish	4. The Malcontent

Codes

	A	B	C	D
(a)	4	3	1	2
(b)	2	3	4	1
(c)	2	4	3	1
(d)	4	1	3	2

November 2017

3 Aphra Behn's Oroonoko is set in

(a) Surinam
(b) Abyssinia
(c) Egypt
(d) Assyria

4 In the epilogue to Congreve's Way of the World there is a warning.

Others there are whose malice we'd prevent,
Such, who watch plays, whit scurrilous intent
To mark out who by characters are meant.

....

These, with false glosses feed their own ill-nature, And turn to libel, what was meant a satire, What does this warning mean?

(a) Critics should not be ill-natured and malicious
(b) Critics should not look for portrait of real people in the play's characters and remember that the play is a social satire
(c) Critics should avoid writing malicious reviews, lest they be charged with libel
(d) Critics should try to identify the real-life equivalent for each character

January 2017

5 In Restoration comedies the following is true except

(a) the London life of hedonistic young men is portrayed
(b) names encapsulate traits
(c) unchaste women, widows and cuckolds scarcely make an appearance
(d) the heroines seek a say in the choice of a marriage partner

6 In William Congreve's 'The Way of the World' Fainall is Lady Wishfort's

(a) son (b) son-in-law
(c) nephew (d) servant

7 1692 William Congreve published Incognita, a work of fiction which is dubbed a 'novel' on its title-page. What is the sub-title?

(a) Love and Duty Reconcil'd
(b) Beauty in Distress
(c) Virtue Rewarded
(d) Love in Excess

July 2016

8 In William Congreve's 'The Way of the World' Identify the speaker of the line "One's cruelty is one's power, and when one parts with ones cruelty, one part with one's power".

(a) Mirabell (b) Witwoud (c) Millamant (d) Mincing

9 At the beginning of the Restoration period, there was a seismic shift in the social, political and religious attitudes of the English. Which of the following statement best describes that shift?

(a) England shifted from an aristocratic Catholic monarchy to a parliamentary democracy
(b) England shifted from an atheistic oligarchy to a desistic squirearchy
(c) England shifted from a Republican Puritan Commonwealth to an aristocratic Anglican monarchy
(d) England shifted from a parliamentary democracy to an aristocratic Catholic tyranny

December 2015

10 Who,among the following, advanced the theory-that the mind is a tabula rasa at birth and acquires all ideas by experience?

(a) John Locke (b) John Wesley
(c) Isaac Watts (d) Denis Diderot

11 John Dryden described a major English poet as "a rough diamond and must first be polished ere he shine..." Identify him .

(a) Geoffrey Chaucer (b) John Gower
(c) George Herbert (d) Robert Herrick

June 2015

12 In John Dryden's Essay on Dramatic Poesy Neander defends the English invention of

(a) romantic comedy (b) action tragedy
(c) tragi-comedy (d) morality plays

13 In 1668, Dryden wrote of Dramaic Poesie: An Essay which uses .... separate characters to dramatise the conflicting viewpoints which new theatrical activity had produced.

(a) three (b) two
(c) four (d) six

14 A significant developement in 1662 was the establishment of The Royal Society in England. The main purpose of the society was ....

(a) to set the rules for the royal court and governance
(b) to guide and promote the development of science and scientific exploration
(c) the set norms for civil society
(d) to promote theatre

15 Choose the right chronological sequence below.

(a) Victorian period, Jacobean period, Tudor period, Restoration period
(b) Edwardian period, Tudor period, Jacobean period, Victorian period
(c) Tudor period. Jacobean period, Restoration period, Edwardian period
(d) Jacobean period, Tudor period, Restoration period, Edwardian period

December 2014

16 In Aphra Behn's Oronooko, how does the Titular character die?

(a) He disembowels himself (b) He is whipped to death
(c) He is hanged in the public square
(d) He is cut to pieces slowly by the executioner

17 In Jeremy Collier's 1698 pamphlet attacking the immorality and profaneness of the English stage, who among the following was the principal target?

(a) William Congreve (b) John Dryden
(c) John Vanbrugh (d) William Wycherley

18 The first official royal Poet Laureate in English literary history was

(a) Ben Jonson (b) William Davenant
(c) Jonn Dryden (d) Thomas Shadwell

19 "Heav'n has no rage, like love to hatred turn'd/Nor Hell a fury, like a woman scorn 'd."

Identify the text in which the above quote occurs

(a) The Double-Dealer (b) The Way of the World
(c) The Mourning Bride (d) Love for Love

June 2014

20 Whom does Mirabell deceive into believing that he loves her in 'The Way of the World'?

(a) Millamant (b) Lady Wishfort
(c) Mrs Marwood (d) Mrs Fainall

21 Why did Phaedra, wife of Theseus, commit suicide by hanging herself?

(a) Theseus hated her
(b) Her stepson, Hippolytus rejected her love
(c) Hippolytus wanted to marry her
(d) She was lonely and depressed

22 Match the following.

List I (Dramatist)	List II (Play)
A. Thomas Otway	1. The Provok'd Husband
B. William Wycherley	2. The Recruiting Officer
C. Colley Cibber	3. The Country Wife
D. George Farquhar	4. The Orphan or the Unhappy Marriage

Codes

	A	B	C	D		A	B	C	D
(a)	4	3	1	2	(b)	3	2	1	2
(c)	4	2	3	1	(d)	3	1	2	4

ANSWERS

Objective Questions

1 (b)	2 (c)	3 (d)	4 (c)	5 (a)	6 (a)	7 (d)	8 (b)	9 (c)	10 (b)
11 (b)	12 (d)	13 (b)	14 (b)	15 (b)	16 (a)	17 (c)	18 (a)	19 (d)	20 (a)
21 (c)	22 (c)	23 (d)	24 (c)	25 (c)	26 (c)	27 (c)	28 (b)	29 (a)	30 (d)
31 (c)	32 (a)	33 (d)	34 (a)	35 (a)	36 (b)	37 (c)	38 (b)	39 (c)	40 (c)
41 (b)	42 (a)	43 (b)	44 (a)	45 (a)	46 (b)	47 (a)	48 (c)	49 (b)	50 (d)
51 (d)	52 (b)	53 (d)	54 (a)	55 (c)	56 (b)	57 (d)	58 (b)	59 (c)	60 (d)
61 (a)	62 (a)	63 (d)	64 (b)	65 (a)	66 (c)	67 (c)	68 (a)	69 (c)	70 (a)
71 (b)	72 (b)	73 (c)	74 (a)	75 (d)	76 (b)	77 (c)	78 (d)	79 (d)	80 (d)
81 (c)	82 (d)	83 (a)	84 (d)	85 (a)	86 (a)	87 (c)	88 (b)	89 (b)	90 (d)
91 (c)	92 (a)	93 (d)	94 (c)	95 (b)	96 (d)	97 (d)	98 (c)	99 (b)	100 (a)
101 (d)	102 (b)	103 (b)	104 (b)	105 (a)	106 (c)	107 (b)	108 (d)	109 (a)	110 (b)
111 (a)	112 (b)	113 (c)	114 (d)	115 (a)	116 (b)	117 (b)	118 (c)	119 (d)	120 (c)
121 (b)	122 (c)	123 (d)	124 (b)	125 (a)	126 (b)	127 (a)	128 (b)	129 (c)	130 (d)
131 (a)	132 (a)	133 (b)	134 (c)	135 (d)	136 (c)	137 (b)	138 (c)	139 (d)	140 (d)
141 (b)	142 (a)	143 (a)	144 (a)	145 (c)	146 (a)	147 (d)	148 (a)	149 (c)	150 (b)

Previous Years' Questions

1 (a)	2 (b)	3 (a)	4 (b)	5 (c)	6 (b)	7 (a)	8 (c)	9 (c)	10 (a)
11 (a)	12 (c)	13 (c)	14 (b)	15 (c)	16 (d)	17 (c)	18 (c)	19 (c)	20 (b)
21 (d)	22 (a)								

Victorian Age to Modern Age Drama

The Victorian drama witnesses a downtrend during this period due to rise of other literary forms, particularly novel, and other social changes like Industrialisation taking place. Oscar Wilde was the most important playwright of this age. But the Modern Age sets the revival of drama with playwrights like Ibsen, GB Shaw, TS Eliot etc.

The Victorian Drama

The Victorian era stretches from 1837 tp 1901, the period during which Queen Victoria ruled. Most historians of Victorian life and art have not given sustained and serious attention to the drama and the theatrical environment in which it was produced.

During this age, the theatre takes the back seat due to other important issues like growth of the industry, labour legislation and political enfranchisement. The drama written during the bulk of the century is generally looked upon as the black sheep of Victorian literature. Indeed, even historians of theatrical art tend to treat the nineteenth-century English theatre with overtones of derision, while most surveys of British drama seem to suggest that the genre underwent a nearly total eclipse between the plays of Sheridan and Shaw. Yet the Victorian theatre was one of the most vitally active in the long history of dramatic art. Particularly after the well-reported attendance of the newly ascended Queen Victoria made it unquestionably respectable, the Theatre was a part of the lives of Londoners of all classes.

That the Victorian drama is, to the serious critic, little more than a minor adjunct to the literature of the century is perhaps implicit in the absence from the roster of successful dramatists of those authors whom we typically thing of in connection with the other fields of Victorian literature. Most of the important novelists of the century followed Thackeray's example and abjured the stage completely; those who, like Dickens, had an abiding love for the theatre more often than not confined their dramatic efforts to amateur theatricals.

In this Chapter

- *The Victorian Drama*
- *Modern Age Drama*
- *Major Dramatists of the Modern Age*

Oscar Wilde as Victorian Era Playwright

Oscar Wilde is one of the most prominent playwrights of the Victorian era. Wilde's easy wit insured an immediate success for the brilliant series of dramas that he wrote in the early nineties. In early 1892 *Lady Windermere's Fan* appeared at the St James' Theatre and was at once popular. The same year *Wilde* also wrote *Salome*. It was followed the next year by *A Woman of No Importance, An Ideal Husband* and *The Importance of Being Earnest*, both filled with wit and brilliant paradoxes, appeared in 1895. They were the last things that Oscar Wilde was to write before he developed meningitis and suffered his untimely death. Other plays include *Vera*; or *The Nihilists* (1880), *The Duchess of Padua* (1883), *A Florentine Tragedy (La Sainte Courtisane 1893)*.

Wilde's work has inspired many other fellow writers. His work has been translated into many languages and has been on the stage over and over again. Oscar Wilde was certainly the most outstanding representative of the poetry of the Aesthetic movement, but he is better known for his activity as a playwright. He gave fantasy, vivacity and a breath of new life to drama. His comedies, full of humour, intrigued and fascinated the audience.

Other Victorian Age Playwrights

Other important writers include John Millington Synge, whose plays include *Riders to the Sea* and *The Playboy of the Western World* (1907). Dion Boucicault was another famous playwright of the Victorian era. His famous plays include *The Colleen Bawn,* and *The Shaughraun.*

Modern Age Drama

The drama which had suffered steep decline during the Victorian Age was revived with great force at the beginning of the 20th century and the course of six decades has witnessed many trends and currents in the 20th century drama. Modern drama, which developed around the turn of the twentieth century, focused on alienation and disconnection. These themes can be seen in some of the most famous plays of playwrights such as Henrik Ibsen, George Bernard Shaw and Eugene O'Neill.

Main Characteristics of Modern Drama

The important characteristics of Modern Drama are discussed below

Realism

Realism is the most significant and outstanding quality of the Modern English Drama. The dramatists of the earlier years of the 20th century were interested in naturalism and it was their endeavour to deal with real problems of life in a realistic technique to their plays.

It was Henrik Ibsen, the Norwegian dramatist who popularised realism in Modern Drama. He dealt with the problems of real life in a realistic manner in his play. His example was followed by Robertson Arthur Jones, Galsworthy and GB Shaw in their plays. Modern Drama has developed the problem play and there are many modern dramatists who have written a number of problem plays. They dealt with the problems of marriage, justice, law, administration and strife between capital and labour in their dramas.

They used theatre as a means for bringing about reforms in the conditions of society prevailing in their days. Henrik Ibsen's play *A Doll's House* is a good example of a problem play. The problem play was a new experiment in the form and technique and dispensed with the conventional devices and expedients of theatre.

Play of Ideas

Modern Drama is essentially a drama of ideas rather than action. The stage is used by dramatists to give expression to certain ideas which they want to spread in the society. The Modern Drama dealing with the problems of life has become far more intelligent than ever it was in the history of drama before the present age. With the treatment of actual life, the drama became more and more a drama of ideas, sometimes veiled in the main action, sometimes didactically act forth.

Romanticism

The earlier dramatists of the 20th century were realists at the core, but the passage of time brought in a new trend in Modern Drama. Romanticism, which had been very dear to Elizabethan dramatists found its way in Modern Drama and it was mainly due to Sir JM Barrie's effort that the new wave of Romanticism swept over Modern Drama for some years of the 20th century. Barrie kept aloof from realities of life and made excursion into the world of romance.

Poetic Drama

16th and 17th centuries were great ages of poetic drama in various parts of Europe which declined in 18th and 19th centuries (except in Germany) the earlier dramatists like: Ibsen, Henry Arthur Jones, Arthur Wing Pinero, Shaw etc had been dealing with melodramatic romanticism displaying it with aristocratic existence first, followed by middle class lives and finally of labour-class conditions. Realism had spent itself and it began to be generally recognised that the naturalistic conversation cultivated from 1890 to 1920 was insufficient, that the terms of life could never be the terms of art.

Dramatists were aiming at a profounder view of life than was introduced by the majority of the Realists and a different medium of expression.

The poetic dramatists believed that imagination may be more intensely stirred by what is remote in time and place than by what is near and familiar.

Poetic drama while aiming at the poetic in atmosphere or theme, is naturalistic in characterisation and dialogue. But the dissatisfaction with naturalistic dialogue led to attempts to bring back poetry into the speech of the theatre.

The Poetic verse drama gained importance in the 30s with dramatists such as TS Eliot and Christopher Fry.

Significant playwrights of English poetic drama in 20th century included WH Auden and Christopher Isherwood who collaborated for two poetic dramas *The Dog Beneath The Skin* and *The Ascent of F6: A Tragedy in Two Acts* (1936).

Christopher Fry's *The Lady's Not for Burning* made him a major force in theatre in the 1940s and 1950s. It is a wry comedy set in the Middle Ages in which love overcomes prejudice and hypocrisy. An English gentlewoman is accused of witchcraft in a small English town around the year 1400. Jennet Jourdemayne, the lady, will die as a matter of course and bureaucrat convenience. Thomas Mendip-whom she has just met-is determined to save her and then discovers to his dismay that he has also fallen in love with her. Written in blank verse, the play is a comedy, but the danger suggested by the title is real.

History and Biographical Plays

Another trend, visible in the Modern English Drama is in the direction of using history and biography for dramatic technique. There are many beautiful historical and biographical plays in modern dramatic literature. Shaw's *Caesar and Cleopatra* are historical plays of great importance. John Drinkwater's *Abraham Lincoln* and *Mary Stuart* are also historical plays.

Irish Movement

A new trend in the Modern English Drama was introduced by the Irish dramatists who brought about the Celtic Revival in the literature.

In the hands of the Irish dramatists like Yeats, JM Synge, TC Murrey etc drama ceased to be realistic in character and became an expression of the hopes and aspirations of the Irish people from remote ways to their own times.

Comedy of Manners

There is a revival of Comedy of Manners in Modern Dramatic Literature. Oscar Wilde, Maugham, N Coward etc have done much to revive the comedy of wit in our days. The drama after the second world war has not exhibited a love for comedy and the social conditions of the period after the war were not very favourable for the development of the artificial comedy of the Restoration Age.

Impressionism

It is a movement that shows the effects of things and events on the mind of the artist and the attempt of the artist to express his expressions. Impressionism constitutes another important feature of modern drama. In the impressionistic plays of WB Yeats, the main effort is in the direction of recreating the experience of the artist and his impressions about reality rather than in presenting reality as it is. The impressionistic drama of the modern age seeks to suggest the impressions on the artist rather than making an explicit statement about the objective characteristics of things or objects.

Expressionism

It is a movement that tries to express the feelings and emotions of the people rather than objects and events. Expressionism is another important feature of modern drama. It marks an extreme reaction against the naturalism. The movement which had started early in Germany made its way in England drama and several modern dramatists like JB Priestly, Sean O' Casey, CK Munro and Elmer Rice have made experiments in the expressionistic tendency in modern drama.

Major Dramatists of the Modern Age

Henrik Johan Ibsen (1828-1906)

Ibsen was born to Knud Ibsen and Marichen Altenburg, into a well-to-do merchant family, in the small port town of Skien in Telemark county, a city which was noted for shipping timber.

At fifteen, Ibsen was forced to leave school. He moved to the small town of Grimstad to become an apprentice pharmacist and began writing plays. In 1846, when Ibsen was 18, he had a liaison with Else Sophie Jensdatter Birkedalen which produced a son, Hans Jacob Hendrichsen Birkedalen, whose upbringing Ibsen paid for until the boy was fourteen, though Ibsen never saw Hans Jacob.

Literary Career and Works

His first play, the tragedy *Catilina* (1850), was published under the pseudonym 'Brynjolf Bjarme', when he was only 22, but it was not performed. His first play to be staged, *The Burial Mound* (1850), received little attention. Still, Ibsen was determined to be a playwright, although the numerous plays he wrote in the following years remained unsuccessful. Ibsen's main inspiration in the early period, right up to Peer Gynt, was apparently the Norwegian author Henrik Wergeland and the Norwegian folk tales as collected by Peter Christen Asbjornsen and Jorgen Moe. In Ibsen's youth, Wergeland was the most acclaimed and by far the most read Norwegian poet and playwright.

His next play, *Brand* (1865), brought him the critical acclaim he sought, along with a measure of financial success, as did the following play, *Peer Gynt* (1867). With success, Ibsen became more confident and began to introduce more and more of his own beliefs and judgements into the drama, exploring what he termed the 'drama of ideas'. His next series of plays are often considered his Golden Age, when he entered the height of his power and influence, becoming the centre of dramatic controversy across Europe.

Ibsen moved from Italy to Dresden, Germany, in 1868, where he spent years writing the play he regarded as his main work, *Emperor and Galilean* (1873), dramatising the life and times of the Roman emperor Julian the Apostate. Ibsen moved to Munich in 1875 and began work on his first contemporary realist drama *The Pillars of Society*, first published and performed in 1877. *A Doll's House* followed in 1879. This play is a scathing criticism of the marital roles accepted by men and women which characterised Ibsen's society.

Late in his career, Ibsen turned to a more introspective drama that had much less to do with denunciations of society's moral values and more to do with the problems of individuals. In such later plays as *Hedda Gabler* (1890) and *The Master Builder* (1892), Ibsen explored psychological conflicts that transcended a simple rejection of current conventions.

Henrik Ibsen is famously known as the father of Modern Drama and it is worth recognising how literal an assessment that is. The Norwegian playwright was not merely one of a wave of new writers to experiment with dramatic form, nor did he make small improvements that were built upon by successors. Ibsen rose to prominence in large part because of his refusal to follow the rules of theatre at the time. His determination to forge his own style of drama coincided with a rising demand by the new intelligentsia for a serious 'thinking' theatre, contrary to the frivolous entertainment on mainstream stages. Ibsen's realist plays, such as *A Doll's House, Ghosts*, and *An Enemy of the People*, were championed by this class of society upon their publication. He died on 23rd May, 1906.

Major Works

- *Ghosts* followed in 1881, another scathing commentary on the morality of Ibsen's society, in which a widow reveals to her pastor that she had hidden the evils of her marriage for its duration.
- In *An Enemy of the People* (1882), Ibsen went even further. In earlier plays, controversial elements were important and even pivotal components of the action, but they were on the small scale of individual households. In *An Enemy*, controversy became the primary focus and the antagonist was the entire community. One primary message of the play is that the individual, who stands alone, is more often 'right' than the mass of people, who are portrayed as ignorant and sheeplike.
- *The Wild Duck* (1884) is, by many, considered Ibsen's finest work and it is certainly the most complex. It tells the story of Gregers Werle, a young man who returns to his hometown after an extended exile and is reunited with his boyhood friend Hjalmar Ekdal. Over the course of the play, the many secrets that lie behind the Ekdal's apparently happy home are revealed to Gregers, who insists on pursuing the absolute truth or the 'Summons of the Ideal'. Among these truths: Gregers' father impregnated his servant Gina, then married her off to Hjalmar to legitimise the child. Another man has been disgraced and imprisoned for a crime, the elder Werle committed. Furthermore, while Hjalmar spends his days working on a wholly imaginary 'invention', his wife is earning the household income.

Lady Gregory (1852-1932)

Lady Gregory was born as Isabella Augusta Persse on 15th March, 1852 at Roxborough, County Galway, Ireland. Along with Yeats and Edward Martyn, she helped found the Irish National Theater Society and served as manager of the Abbey Theater in Dublin.

Literary Career and Works

In 1896, she met WB Yeats and served as his lifelong patron. She collaborated with Yeats on *The Pot of Broth* in 1902, the year she wrote her own first plays, *The Jackdaw and A Losing Game*. Her first performed play was *Twenty-Five*, which was produced in 1903. Lady Gregory rewrote ancient

Irish legends in her plays, *Cuchulain of Muirthemne* (1902), *Gods and Fighting Men* (1904) and *The Book of Saints and Wonders* (1906). Her work for the Abbey Theatre, played a considerable part in the late 19th century Irish literary revival. She died in Coole, Ireland on 22nd May, 1932.

George Bernard Shaw (1856-1950)

The youngest child of a civil servant, George Bernard Shaw was born in Dublin, Ireland. Shaw was an Irish dramatist and literary critic. He is considered to be the first modern dramatist to establish his plays as literature. Shaw is the only person to have been awarded both the Nobel Prize in Literature and an Oscar for his work on the film adaptation of his plays, *Pygmalion*.

Literary Career and Works

Shaw worked as a junior clerk in a Dublin estate agency for sometime, before moving to London in 1876. There, he established himself as a leading theatre and music critic writing reviews for the *Saturday Review, Dramatic Review* (1885-86), *Our Corner* (1885-86), *The Pall Mall Gazette* (1885-88), *The World* (1886-94) and *The Star* (1888-90). He also became a prominent member of the Fabian Society (British Socialist Organisation) and wrote many speeches for it.

Shaw began his literary career by writing novels, but all five of his novels proved unsuccessful.

His early plays, *Widowers' Houses* (1892), *The Philanderer* (1898) and *Mrs Warren's Profession* (1893) have been characterised as 'unpleasant plays' because "their dramatic power is used to force the spectator to face unpleasant facts." These plays were followed by his 'pleasant plays' written to amuse the audience.

These included *Arms and the Man* (1894), *Candida* (1898), *You Never Can Tell* (1897) and *The Man of Destiny* (1895). *Arms and the Man* was Shaw's first commercial success. It debunks romantic heroism associated with war and deals with the futility of war. After the interruption of his dramatic output caused by World War I, Shaw returned to the stage with his last works, including his ambitious *Back to Methuselah* (1921), a five-play cycle on what he called the 'creative evolution' and *Saint Joan* (1923), a play based on the life and trial of Joan of Arc. He died of kidney failure on 2nd November, 1950, at the age of 94, precipitated by injuries incurred by falling while pruning trees.

Major Works

Drama

- Plays Unpleasant (Published 1898)
- Widowers' Houses (1892)
- The Philanderer (1898)
- Mrs Warren's Profession (1893)
- Plays Pleasant (Published 1898)
- Arms and the Man (1894)
- Candida (1894)
- The Man of Destiny (1895)
- You Never Can Tell (1897)
- Three Plays for Puritans (Published 1901)
- The Devil's Disciple (1897)
- Caesar and Cleopatra (1898)
- Captain Brassbound's Conversion (1899)
- Man and Superman (1902-03)
- Major Barbara (1905)
- The Doctor's Dilemma (1906)
- Pygmalion (1912-13)
- Back to Methuselah (1921)
- In the Beginning
- The Gospel of the Brothers Barnabas
- The Thing Happens
- Tragedy of an Elderly Gentleman
- As Far As Thought Can Reach
- Saint Joan (1923)

Essays

- Quintessence of Ibsenism (1891)
- The Perfect Wagnerite, Commentary on the Ring (1898)
- The Intelligent Woman's Guide to Socialism and Capitalism (1928)

James Matthew Barrie (1860-1937)

Scottish author and dramatist James Barrie was born on 9th May, 1860, in Forfarshire, Scotland. He is best remembered as the creator of Peter Pan. Barrie studied at the University of Edinburgh and spent 2 years on the Nottingham Journal before settling in London as a freelance writer in 1885.

Literary Career and Works

His first successful book, *Auld Licht Idylls* (1888), contained sketches of life in Kirriemuir, Scotland. Barrie soon wrote a string of popular novels set in Scotland, including *A Window in Thrums* (1889). After achieving success with fiction, Barrie turned to drama. In 1894, he married actress Mary Ansell. Their marriage was childless. In 1897, he formed an attachment to Sylvia Llewellyn Davies and it was to her sons, through whom he began to live again the experience of childhood, that he told in his first *Peter Pan stories*.

The famous character of Peter Pan first appeared in *The Little White Bird* (1902). In 1904, the play *Peter Pan, the Boy Who Wouldn't Grow Up,* premiered on stage.

The creation of this boy hero added a touch of romanticism to the whole world of childhood. Barrie died on 19th June, 1937, in London, England. As a part of his will, he gave the copyright of Peter Pan to a children's hospital in London.

Major Works

- Auld Licht Idylls (1888)
- Better Dead (1888)
- When a Man's Single (1888)
- A Window in Thrums (1889)
- My Lady Nicotine (1890)
- The Little Minister (1891)
- Richard Savage (1891)
- Quality Street (1901)
- The Admirable Crichton (1902)
- The Little White Bird or Adventures in Kensington Gardens (1902)
- Little Mary (1903)
- Peter Pan (staged 1904)
- Peter Pan in Kensington Gardens (1906)
- What Every Woman Knows (1908)
- When Wendy Grew Up - An Afterthought (1908)
- Peter and Wendy (novel) (1911)
- A Kiss for Cinderella (1912)
- Mary Rose (1920)

John Galsworthy (1867-1933)

English novelist and playwright John Galsworthy was born in Surrey, England in 1867. He was educated at Harrow School and studied law at New College, Oxford. He was called to the bar at Lincoln's Inn in 1890. However, Galsworthy soon became dissatisfied with law and turned to writing.

Literary Career and Works

His first collection of short stories, *From the Four Winds* (1897) and the novel *Jocelyn* (1898) was written under the pseudonym John Sinjohn. *The Island Pharisees* (1904) was the first book to appear under his own name.

Galsworthy is best known for his series of three novels and *Two Forsyte Interludes*. It chronicles the Life of an upper class British family and includes the works, *The Man of Property* (1906), *Indian Summer of a Forsyt* (1918), *In Chancery* (1920), *Awakening* (1920) and *To Let* (1921).

Galsworthy was also a successful dramatist. His famous plays include *The Silver Box* (1906), which shows how law discriminates between the rich and the poor; *Strife* (1909), a study of labour rights and industrial relations; *Justice* (1910), a realistic portrayal of prison life and institutionalism and *Loyalties* (1922), dealing with anti-Semitism Galsworthy was awarded the Belgian Palmes d'Or in 1919 and the Order of Merit in 1929. John Galsworthy died of a stroke at his home in London, 'Grove Lodge'.

Major Works

- From the Four Winds 1897)
- Jocelyn (1898)
- Villa Rubein (1900)
- A Man of Devon (1901)
- The Island Pharisees (1904)
- The Silver Box (1906)
- The Forsyte Saga (1906-21)
- The Man of Property (1906)
- (Interlude) Indian Summer of a Forsyte (1918)
- In Chancery (1920)
- (Interlude) Awakening (1920)
- To Let (1921)
- Strife (1909)
- Fraternity (1909)
- Joy (1909)
- Justice (1910)
- The Skin Game (1920)
- Loyalties (1922)
- A Modern Comedy (1924-1928)
- The White Monkey, 1921
- (Interlude) A Silent Wooing (1927)
- The Silver Spoon (1926)
- (Interlude) Passers By (1927)
- Swan Song (1928)
- On Forsyte Change (1930)
- Over the River (1933)

Sean O' Casey (1880-1964)

Born as John Casey in Dublin, Ireland, O' Casey was the last of the major 20th century playwrights associated with the Abbey Theatre. He was born in a poor, Irish Protestant family and his works give a realistic picture of Irish tenement life. O'Casey became the General Secretary for the Irish Citizen Army (ICA). He also wrote the Constitution for the ICA and his time in this organisation later provided the material for his first published work, *The Story of the Irish Citizen Army*, 1913-1916.

Literary Career and Works

O'Casey is known for his Dublin Trilogy of plays *The Shadow of a Gunman* (1923), *Juno and the Paycock* (1924) and *The Plough and the Stars* (1926). *The Shadow of a Gunman* deals with the impact of revolutionary politics on the inhabitants of the Dublin slums. It is set in Mountjoy Square, where O'Casey himself had lived.

Juno and the Paycock deals with the effects of the Irish civil war on the poor people living in Dublin. *The Plough and the Stars* is also set in the Dublin tenements in the year 1916 and centres on a young married couple called Jack and Nora Clitheroe. O'Casey is considered to be the first noted playwright to write about Dublin working classes. O'Casey died of a heart attack, in England at the age of 84.

Juno and the Paycock

Juno and the Paycock is the second play of the Dublin trilogy that deals with contemporary historical events in Ireland. The play was first staged at the Abbey Theatre in Dublin in 1924. It is set in the apartment of a two-room Tenancy belonging to the Boyle Family within a tenement house in Dublin.

O'Casey has taken the characters of Juno and the Paycock from Greek mythology. Juno is the name of a Roman Goddess; the protector of suppliants and the jealous wife of Jupiter. However, Juno Boyle in the play is a Dublin housewife, an Earthly human figure, who struggles for hard life.

Juno's husband, Captain Boyle, has aristocratic airs about him. He hates manual work. He enjoys the company of courtiers like companion and of some sycophant who adores him in flattery and always praises him. He is drawn from Shakespeare's *Captain Jack Falstaff*. Boyle's family consists of four persons; Captain Boyle, Juno Boyle, their son Johnny and their daughter Mary.

The play examines man's relationship to his environment primarily in terms of money. It has been labelled as a 'tragi-comedy'.

Major Works

- Lament for Thomas Ashe (1917), as Sean O'Cathasaigh
- The Story of Thomas Ashe (1917), as Sean O'Cathasaigh
- The Shadow of a Gunman (1923)
- Juno and the Paycock (1924)
- The Plough and the Stars (1926)
- The Silver Tassie (1927)
- The End of the Beginning (1937)
- Red Roses for Me (1942)
- Cock-a-Doodle Dandy (1949)
- Behind the Green Curtains (1961)

Autobiography (6 Volumes)

- I Knock at the Door
- Pictures in the Hallway
- Drums Under the Window
- Inishfallen, Fare Thee Well
- Rose and Crown
- Sunset and Evening Star

Thomas Sterns Eliot

He was born to a wealthy and respectable family of merchants in St Louis, Missouri, USA on 26th September, 1888. Eliot entered Harvard University in 1906 and graduated in three years and received his master's degree in his fourth year, Being deeply interested in literature, religion and philosophy he began to write. His first efforts were largely poetic. After graduation he continued his study of philosophy and French literature.

Literary Career and Works

TS Eliot's early volumes of poetry include *Prufrock and Other Observations* (1917) and *Power* (1919). His famous poem *The Waste Land* portrayed the beginning of Eliot's search for his own religious faith. Another volume of poems *The Hollow Man* was published in 1925.

From 1930 to 1960, Eliot published a variety of literary works. *Ash Wednesday* (1930) and *Four Quartets* (1943) were two major poems. In 1934, he wrote *The Rock* and in 1935, *Murder in Cathedral* both were religious dramas. *The Family Reunion* (1939), *The Cocktail Party* (1959).

The Confidential Clerk (1955) and the *Elder Statesman* (1959) are his other well known plays. His essays like *Tradition and Individual Talent* brought him repute as a literary critic. In 1932, he was appointed the Charles Eiot Norton Professor of poetry at Harvard. In 1948, Eliot was awarded the Nobel Prize for literature. He died in 1965.

Murder in the Cathedral is a play in verse about the dangers of temptations on the way to sainthood or power.

Thomas Becket resisted several temptations coupled with cajolery and threat. He is offered a return to political power alongside king Henry while at the same time, he is accused of disloyalty to the nation and his ecclesiastical office, and threatened physically. Though tempted by sainthood and lured by power, Thomas sees martyrdom and pleasure as human weaknesses.

Major Works

- Sweeney Agnoistes (1926)
- The Rock (1934)
- Murder in the Cathedral (1935)
- The Family Reunion (1939)
- The Cocktail Party (1949)
- The Confidential Clerk (1953)
- The Elder Statesman (1958)

Noel Coward (1899-1973)

English playwright, composer, actor and director Noel Coward was born on 16th December, 1899 in Teddington, a quiet suburban village near London. He studied at the Royal Chapel School in London. Coward launched his professional acting career at the age of 12, making his London debut as Prince Mussel in a children's show called *The Goldfish*. After this, he starred in several productions with Sir Charles Hawtrey, an actor and comedian.

Literary Career and Works

Coward's acting career suffered when he was called for military duty in 1918. During the war, he suffered a minor head injury which made him hospitalised for several months. After discharge from the hospital, Noel found that the demand for his acting talents had decreased.

Thereafter, he devoted time to play writing. His first effort as a playwright, *Rat Trap*, was a realistic study of its characters' emotions. It was written in 1917, but was not published until 1926. This was followed by the success of *I' Leave It To You* (1920), *The Vortex* (1924) *Hay Fever, Fallen Angels* (both 1925) and *Easy Virtue* (1926). Noel Coward died in 1973. He is buried in Firefly Hill, Jamaica.

Major Works

- The Rat Trap (1918)
- The Young Idea (1922)
- The Better Half (1922)
- The Queen Was in the Parlour (1922)
- Weatherwise (1923)
- The Vortex (1924)
- Easy Virtue (1925)
- Semi-Monde Originally Ritz Bar (1926)
- This Was A Man (1926)
- Private Lives (1930)
- Cavalcade (1931)
- Blithe Spirit (1941)
- Quadrille (1952)
- Waiting in the Wings (1960)
- I'll Leave It To You (1920)
- Sirocco (1921)
- Fallen Angels (1925)
- Hay Fever (1925)
- The Marquise (1927)
- Post Mortem (1932)
- Design For Living (1933)
- Peace In Our Time (1947)
- Nude With Violin (1956)

Samuel Beckett (1906-1989)

Samuel Beckett was an Irish novelist, playwright,and poet. He was born near Dublin and educated at Trinity College, but moved permanently to Paris in 1937.

Literary Career and Works

Beckett started his literary career by writing short stories and novels. His first short story collection *More Pricks than Kicks* was published in 1934. His first novel *Murphy* is about an Irishman's escape from a girl, he is about to marry to a life of contemplation as a nurse in a mental institution.

Although, this novel did not manage to win critical acclaim, Beckett's trilogy of novels- *Molloy, Malone Dies* and *The Unnamable* established his reputation as an influential avant-garde writer. However, it is largely his modernist plays that cemented his reputation. Beckett's play *Waiting for Godot*, originally written in French, premiered in a Paris theatre on 5th January, 1953.

Waiting for Godot has been defined as a play in which Nothing happens, nobody comes, nobody goes.

This play established Beckett as a leading figure of The Theatre of Absurd, a form of theatre that emphasises the absurdity of human existence through meaningless dialogue, purposeless situations, lack of logical development and mindless repetition of lines and action.

Beckett was awarded the Nobel Prize in Literature in 1969. He died on 22nd December, 1989.

Waiting For Godot

Initially written in French in 1948 as En Attendant Godot. Beckett's play was published in French in October of 1952 before its first stage production in Paris in January of 1953. Later translated into English by Beckett himself as *Waiting for Godot*, the play was produced in London in 1955 and in the United States in 1956.

In his play *Waiting for Godot*, Samuel Beckett presents before us a highly absurd situation of two tramps-Vladimir and Estragon waiting for someone called Godot, who doesn't come.

Both the tramps follow the same routine everyday; come and stand under a tree, wait for Godot, indulge in senseless activities, keep on waiting the whole day, decide to begin afresh the next day. They wait for Godot, try to pass their time but he never arrives. Estragon and Vladimir symbolise the human condition as a period of waiting. Act II of the play is a mere replication of the first act with only one or two changes. Lucky accompanied by his master Pozzo comes in the first act, but in the second the situation is reversed - Lucky is the master, Pozzo is his slave, who is blind now.

Waiting for Godot is part of the 'Theatre of the Absurd'. This implies that it is meant to be irrational and meaningless. Absurd theatre does not have the concepts of drama, chronological plot, logical language, themes and recognisable settings.

Major Works

Theatre

- Waiting for Godot (1953)
- Act Without Words I (1956)
- Act Without Words II (1956)
- Endgame (1957)
- Krapp's Last Tape (1958)
- Happy Days (1961)

Novels

- Dream of Fair to Middling Women (1932; published 1992)
- Murphy (1938)
- Watt (1945; published 1953)
- Molloy (1951)
- Malone Dies (1951)
- The Unnamable (1953)
- How It Is (1961)

Eugene Ionesco (1909-1994)

Eugene Ionesco was born in Slatina, Romania to a Romanian father and French mother. He was one of the foremost playwrights of the Theatre of the Absurd. He studied French literature at the University of Bucharest.

Literary Career and Works

Ionesco had not intended to write plays. He wrote plays almost by accident after having learnt English at the age of forty. His first play *The Bald Soprano* (1950; English translation, 1958), satirises the deadliness and idiocy of the daily life of a bourgeois society frozen in meaningless formalities. Surprised by the success of the play, Ionesco embarked on a career as a writer. His plays have been characterised as 'anti-plays', which characteristically combine a dream or nightmare atmosphere with grotesque, bizarre and whimsical humour. These plays break the conventions of naturalistic theatre and present parodies of human condition. Ionesco's other well-known plays are *The Chairs* (a tragic farce that represents the meaninglessness of life) and *Rhinoceros* (a response to the upsurge of forces of Fascism, Nazism and Communism). Eugene Ionesco died at the age of 84 on 28th March, 1994.

Major Works

- The Bold Soprano (1950)
- Salutations (1950)
- The Lesson (1951)
- The Motor Show (1951)
- The Chairs (1952)
- The Leader (1953)
- Victims of Duty (1953)
- Maid to Marry (1953)
- Amedee or How to Get Rid of it (1954)
- Jack, or The Submission (1955)
- The New Tenant (1955)
- The Picture (1955)
- Improvisation (1956)
- The Foot of the Wall (1956)
- The Future is in Eggs, or It Takes All Sorts to Make a World (1957)
- The Killer (1958)
- Foursome (1959)
- Rhinoceros (1959)
- Learning to Walk (1960)
- Frenzy for Two, or More (1962)
- Exit the King (1962)
- Stroll in the Air (1962)
- Hunger and Thirst (1964)
- The Hard Boiled Egg (1960)
- The Overnight (1966)
- The Mire (1966)
- The Killing Game (1970)
- The Duel (1971)
- Double Act (1971)
- Macbett (1972)
- On What a Bloody Circus (1973)
- Man with Bags (1977)
- Journeys Among the Dead (1980)
- The Viscount (unfinished)

EXAM BASED QUESTIONS

1 Who played Torvald Helmer in the 1973 film of 'The Doll's House'?
(a) Anthony Hopkins (b) Laurence Olivier
(c) Burt Reynolds (d) Marlon Brando

2 Right before his death, Ibsen's nurse remarked that he seemed better. What was Ibsen's reply?
(a) "Tell my wife you're wrong."
(b) "I know not seems!"
(c) "I will be dead inside of the hour."
(d) "On the contrary!."

3 In what country were most of Ibsen's plays set?
(a) Holland (b) Sweden (c) Norway (d) Finland

4 In what language did Ibsen write his plays?
(a) Danish (b) Finnish
(c) Swedish (d) English

5 Which of Ibsen's plays holds the distinction of being the world's 'most performed'?
(a) Hedda Gabler (b) Peer Gynt
(c) A Doll's House (d) An Enemy of the People

6 What genre did Ibsen help found in the theatre arts?
(a) Surrealism (b) Psycho-realism
(c) Modernism (d) Confessionalism

7 For whom did the Nurse work for before taking care of Nora's children in the play 'The Doll's House'?
(a) Mrs Linde and Her Children
(b) Nora's Father and Little Nora
(c) Dr Skein and Little Helmer
(d) None of the above

8 What is the sweet that Nora is forbidden to eat in the play 'The Doll's House'?
(a) Fruit Cakes
(b) Candy Canes
(c) Marzipan
(d) Macaroons

9 Which of the following events is the subject of discussion at the very beginning of the play 'The Doll's House'?
(a) Nora's Deal with Krogstad
(b) Torvald and Nora's Trip to Italy
(c) Krogstad and Christine's Marriage
(d) Torvald's Promotion to Manager of The Bank

10 Which of the following is not a part of Nora's dilemma stemming from her loan from Krogstad in the play 'The Doll's House'?
(a) She is afraid her father will find out
(b) She never told Torvald
(c) She can't convince Torvald not to fire Krogstad
(d) She forged a signature to obtain the loan

11 Nora flirts with Dr Rank, showing him what in the play 'The Doll's House'?
(a) Her new dress (b) Her silk stockings
(c) Her silk gloves (d) Her silk slip

12 In the play 'The Doll's House' according to Torvald, it would be impossible to work with Krogstad because
(a) Nora would object
(b) Torvald becomes physically ill in Krogstad's presence
(c) Krogstad has physically threatened Torvald
(d) Torvald is too jealous of Krogstad

13 How does Dr Rank inform Nora that he has reached the final stages of his illness in the play 'The Doll's House'?
(a) He asks Torvald to tell her
(b) He sends her a note
(c) He leaves a black cross on his visiting card
(d) He tells her while they are dancing

14 In the play 'The Doll's House' Krogstad has gotten a bad reputation because of a scandal in which he allegedly
(a) stole money from the bank
(b) forged a signature
(c) destroyed valuable bank documents
(d) blackmailed a coworker at the bank

15 Which of the following best symbolises the character that Nora plays in her marriage with Torvald in the play 'The Doll's House'?
(a) Her cat
(b) The dress she wears to the party
(c) The tarantella (d) Her new boots

16 Mrs Linde's character in the play 'The Doll's House' symbolises all of the following except
(a) the pitfalls of marrying for money
(b) Nora's potential future
(c) the potential emptiness of motherhood
(d) moral perfection

17 In the play 'The Doll's House' the tarantella symbolises all of the following except
(a) Nora's role as performer for Torvald
(b) The equality of Nora and Torvald's marriage
(c) Nora's desire to rid herself of the poison that has developed out of her transaction with Krogstad
(d) Nora's desire to retain Torvald's attention

18 The entire play 'Hedda Gabler' takes place in the drawing room of the Tesman's home, which is dominated by a large portrait of General Gabler. What was his relationship to Hedda?
(a) Twin Brother (b) Father
(c) First Husband (d) Great-Grandfather

19 Tesman has a close relationship with his maiden aunt Juliana, who has been like a mother to him following the early deaths of his parents. Hedda clearly finds her company and her fawning over her nephew quite tiresome, and carelessly (or so it seems) disparages this article of her clothing, possibly in an attempt to keep her at a distance.

(a) Her bonnet (b) Her shawl
(c) Her gloves (d) Her parasol

20 Shortly after Aunt Juliana leaves, the Tesmans receive a visit from Mrs. Thea Elvsted (nee Rysing) a former schoolmate of Hedda's and an old flame of George's. Hedda had never liked Thea and found a particular physical feature of hers to be especially irritating; what was it?

(a) Her eyes (b) Her fingernails
(c) Her teeth (d) Her hair

21 Hedda contrives to have a private interview with Mrs. Elvsted, during which she learns a number of extraordinary things concerning her relationship with Eilert Lovborg, who had previously had an intimate friendship with Hedda herself. Which of these does Mrs. Elvsted not reveal to Hedda?

(a) That she has left her husband for Lovborg
(b) That Lovborg has told her about his past relationship with Hedda
(c) That she has been helping Lovborg in his work
(d) That she has helped to rehabilitate Lovborg

22 At the beginning of Act II, Hedda is called upon by Judge Brack, a friend of hers who had arranged the purchase of the villa in which she and George now live. In what extraordinary way does she greet him upon his arrival?

(a) She kisses him passionately
(b) She fires a pistol at him
(c) She slaps his face
(d) She throws a vase at him

23 During her conversation with Judge Brack, Hedda offers numerous reasons for her marriage to the tedious and conventional Tesman. Which of these is not a reason she offers for accepting his proposal?

(a) He was unquestionably respectable
(b) She had 'danced herself tired'
(c) She was in love with him
(d) He offered to provide for her

24 Midway through Act II, the much talked-about Eilert Lovborg finally makes his appearance. After exchanging pleasantries with Tesman and Judge Brack, he and Hedda contrive to have a private talk about their past relationship. It is revealed that Hedda ended the relationship; what, according to her, was her reason for doing so?

(a) She had become bored with him
(b) Her father refused to let her see him
(c) He fell in love with Thea
(d) It threatened to develop into something more serious

25 Lovborg recalls that at the end of their relationship, Hedda had threatened to shoot him. What reason does she give for her failure to do so?

(a) She had only been joking
(b) She loved him too much to do it
(c) She was afraid of scandal
(d) She was afraid of firearms

26 Lovborg at first resolutely refuses to drink any alcohol during his visit to the Tesmans' villa. However a certain statement of Hedda's angers him, and he retaliates by downing two glasses of punch. What is it that Hedda reveals?

(a) That Tesman had spoken disparagingly of his book
(b) That Thea was planning to return to her husband
(c) That Thea had been terrified of losing him to another woman
(d) That Judge Brack is mocking him

27 At the end of Act II, much to Mrs. Elvsted's dismay, Lovborg changes his mind and decides to accept Judge Brack's invitation to a dinner party at his home. Hedda 'comforts' Thea by assuring her that Lovborg will return at ten o'clock. In what fanciful manner, suggestive of a certain God from pagan antiquity, does Hedda imagine Lovborg returning?

(a) With wings at his feet
(b) With a trident in his hand
(c) With thunder in his eyes
(d) With vine leaves in his hair

28 Act III takes place early the following morning when, to Mrs. Elvsted's dismay, Lovborg has not yet returned from the party at Judge Brack's. Tesman eventually returns and informs Hedda of a number of things which occurred at the dinner party concerning Lovborg. Which of these does he not tell her about Lovborg?

(a) That he had dropped his manuscript on the way home
(b) That he had behaved with a complete lack of self-control
(c) That he had read part of his book aloud
(d) That Lovborg had despaired over losing his manuscript

29 Tesman reads a letter sent to him from Aunt Juliana summoning him to the bedside of her sister, Aunt Rina, who is near death. Hedda refuses to accompany him on his final visit to his aunt; what reason does she give for doing so?

(a) She refuses to look upon sickness and death
(b) She is afraid of catching an infection
(c) She had never liked Aunt Rina
(d) She is too ill to accompany him

30 After Tesman's departure, Judge Brack arrives and provides Hedda with further details of Lovborg's drunken debauch on the previous evening. In particular, he informs her of an occurrence which he is certain will destroy Lovborg's reputation and cause him to be turned away from any respectable household. What was it?

(a) Lovborg had ended up in bed with a married woman
(b) Lovborg had made a pass at a man
(c) Lovborg had fatally assaulted someone
(d) Lovborg had been arrested at Mademoiselle Diana's

31 One of the most memorable scenes of the play- or indeed of any play- is the conclusion of Act III. Alone, Hedda produces the manuscript and, opening the door of the stove, feeds it to the flames. What memorable line does she utter while destroying the manuscript?
(a) "I am burning your child."
(b) "Rome is burning."
(c) "I am burning your soul."
(d) "I am setting fire to your heart."

32 Mrs. Elvsted appears, in a state of terrible anxiety, having heard some disquieting rumors about Lovborg being hospitalised. Judge Brack soon appears and confirms her worst fears: Lovborg has shot himself in the breast and lies in a hospital, near death. Thea and Tesman are dismayed by the news, but Hedda regards it as a beautiful act of renunciation. Brack, however, takes her aside and informs her that Lovborg's death was far from the courageous, noble act she has envisioned. Which of the following does he not tell her about Lovborg's death?
(a) That it was not a suicide
(b) That the shooting took place at Mlle Diana's
(c) That Lovborg was shot in the bowels, not the breast
(d) That it was, in fact, a murder-suicide

33 Act IV ends with Hedda taking her own life after realising that her illusion of Eilert Lovborg ending his life 'beautifully' has gone sordidly wrong, that Tesman and Thea will reproduce the work of Lovborg's that she had exultantly destroyed, and that she is now under the power of Judge Brack. To whom does she address her final line in the play, before shooting herself?
(a) Judge Brack (b) George Tesman
(c) Mrs. Elvsted (d) Eilert Lovborg

34 Who fathered Regina in the play 'Ghosts'?
(a) Captain Alving (b) Pastor Manders
(c) Oswald (d) Jakob Engstrand

35 Before she married Captain Alving, in whom was Mrs. Alving most interested in the play 'Ghosts'?
(a) Jakob Engstrand (b) Pastor Manders
(c) Krogstad (d) Tesman

36 What sort of memorial is Mrs. Alving building to honour the late Captain in the play 'Ghosts'?
(a) A school
(b) An orphans asylum
(c) An establishment for sailors
(d) A garden

37 Who is Johanna in the play 'Ghosts'?
(a) A ghost
(b) The patron saint of a Norwegian port city
(c) A former lover of Oswald
(d) A former servant

38 Whose daughter does Engstrand believe Regina to be in the play 'Ghosts'?
(a) A Chamberlain's
(b) A yachtsman's
(c) A common sailor's
(d) His own

39 Why is Regina hesitant to join Mrs. Alving and Oswald for champagne in the play 'Ghosts'?
(a) Her father is an alcoholic
(b) She knows Pastor Manders will catch her
(c) She is always careful not to follow in her mother's footsteps
(d) She doesn't want to forget her place as a servant

40 Why does Oswald return home in the play 'Ghosts'?
(a) He wants to honour his father, and his father's ghost has instructed him to come
(b) He feels ill, and he wants to marry a Norwegian wife
(c) The 'joy of life' compels him to make his mother happy
(d) He feels ill and wants to honour his father's memorial

41 In which way does Oswald differ from his father in the play 'Ghosts'?
(a) He drinks
(b) He flirts with the maid
(c) He has a compromised reputation
(d) He smokes

42 At the start of the play 'Ghosts', Pastor Manders realises which of the following facts?
(a) Captain Alving continued his debauchery even after his wife returned to him
(b) Mrs. Alving was once interested in him romantically
(c) Regina is Captain Alving's daughter
(d) Mrs. Alving is a freethinker and supports the idea of couples living together unmarried

43 What is Jakob Engstrand by profession in the play 'Ghosts'?
(a) A bartender
(b) An asylum patient
(c) A carpenter working on an asylum
(d) A doctor in an asylum

44 Who is the last person to leave the ruins of the asylum in the play 'Ghosts'?
(a) Mrs Alving (b) Pastor Manders
(c) Captain Alving (d) Oswald

45 How does Mrs Alving first learn that Oswald is flirting with Regina in the play 'Ghosts'?
(a) Engstrand tells Pastor Manders
(b) She catches them in the garden
(c) She hears Regina resisting him in the dinning room
(d) She hears Oswald talking about her in a drunken delirium

46 At the beginning of the play, Mrs Alving expects Oswald to receive which of the following in the play 'Ghosts'?
(a) Mander's blessing
(b) His father's inheritance
(c) Engstrand's blessing as Regina's husband
(d) Her own inheritance

47 How does Oswald first appear in the play 'Ghosts'?
(a) Smoking a pipe (b) Smoking a cigar
(c) Drinking chilled punch (d) Drinking champagne

48 How is the play 'Ghosts' structured?
(a) Into three acts, of two scenes each
(b) Into four scenes
(c) Into three acts
(d) Into five acts of three scenes each

49 What does Oswald carry in order to be ready for emergencies in the play 'Ghosts'?
(a) His father's pistols (b) Morphine pills
(c) A picture of Regina (d) A silver cross

50 Which of the following plays by Shaw was used as the basis for the film 'My Fair Lady'?
(a) Major Barbara (b) Saint Joan
(c) Heartbreak House (d) Pygmalion

51 Which writer said of Shaw, "He hasn't an enemy in the world, and none of his friends like him"?
(a) Oscar Wilde (b) HG Wells
(c) Saki (d) GK Chesterton

52 Which of Shaw's plays has the Don Juan legend as its underlying theme?
(a) Anthony and Cleopatra (b) Man and Superman
(c) Candida (d) The Devil's Disciple

53 Which nationality did George Bernard Shaw describe as '...99 per cent an idiot'?
(a) American (b) English
(c) French (d) Irish

54 Which fellow writer caustically said of Shaw, "(his) work makes me admire the magnificent tolerance and broadmindedness of the English"?
(a) Hilaire Belloc (b) WH Auden
(c) Edgar Allan Poe (d) James Joyce

55 From what cause did Shaw die in 1950?
(a) Suffered a heart attack and drowned on a long distance swim.
(b) Due to kidney failure after falling from a tree
(c) He caught pneumonia while ice swimming
(d) Suffered a stroke in a sauna

56 'The Dedication' begins with a letter written by which author?
(a) Mark Twain (b) James Joyce
(c) Franz Kafka (d) George Bernard Shaw

57 Which topic does Shaw claim to have failed when writing a play?
(a) Himself (b) Superheroes
(c) God (d) Relationships

58 Shaw does not believe one of the following is a great writer:
(a) Keats (b) Shakespeare
(c) Byron (d) Joyce

59 Shaw says that women no longer ask for
(a) trifles (b) forgiveness
(c) pity (d) permission

60 According to Shaw, who is uniquely absent from the complicated actions of ordinary men and women?
(a) Man (b) God (c) Lucifer (d) Artist

61 According to Shaw, most writers portray men as
(a) Repressed (b) Fearful
(c) The sexual initiator (d) Godlike

62 When Pozzo first enters, what does he reveal he is on his way to do in the play 'Waiting for Godot'?
(a) Meet Godot (b) Kill someone
(c) Meet a lover (d) Sell his slave

63 What has happened to Pozzo when he and Lucky return on the second night in the play 'Waiting for Godot'?
(a) He is blind
(b) His leg is broken
(c) He can't speak
(d) He's a different person

64 Which character is addressed by the most names in the play 'Waiting for Godot'?
(a) Vladimir (b) Estragon (c) Pozzo (d) Lucky

65 Which is not one of Estragon's characteristics in the play 'Waiting for Godot'?
(a) Weakness (b) Poor memory
(c) Egotistical (d) Helplessness

66 What is Godot's name thought to refer to in the play 'Waiting for Godot'?
(a) Mankind (b) The universe
(c) The Earth (d) God

67 The two main characters in 'Waiting for Godot' are
(a) The boy and Lucky (b) Pozzo and Lucky
(c) Estragon and Lucky (d) Estragon and Vladimir

68 The main characters in the play 'Waiting for Godot' call each other
(a) Pozzo and Lucky (b) Estragon and Vladimir
(c) Gogo and Didi (d) Boy and Lucky

69 When Act I opens in the play 'Waiting for Godot' Estragon is
(a) Making castles in the dirt (b) Staring off into space
(c) Asleep (d) Trying to pull his boot off

70 The first time Pozzo and Lucky meet Estragon and Vladimir in Act I, Pozzo tells Estragon and Vladimir that Lucky
(a) taught him beautiful things
(b) wants to escape
(c) told him many secrets
(d) doesn't want to stay there

71 Finally, toward the end of the play, Vladimir tells Estragon they will hang themselves tomorrow unless
(a) Godot comes
(b) they find enough money to live better
(c) Lucky and Pozzo come back
(d) the boy comes back

72 When Estragon tries to make Lucky feel better in the way Pozzo suggested, Lucky
(a) is grateful and shows his great appreciation
(b) Is confused and doesn't understand why Estragon is helping him
(c) kicks him violently in the shins and gives the handkerchief back to Pozzo
(d) puts down his packages, lies down, and falls asleep

73 What does Estragon do as soon as his leg feels good enough to walk again in Act I?
(a) He walks over to Lucky and hugs him again
(b) He walks over to Lucky and spits on him
(c) He entertains the others by dancing
(d) He hugs Vladimir

74 In the beginning of the play 'Rhinoceros', Berenger thinks that Daisy loves
(a) Jean (b) Mr Papillon
(c) Dudard (d) Berenger

75 The Grocer's wife offers the Housewife in the play 'Rhinoceros'
(a) a drink
(b) another cat to replace her dead one
(c) a job (d) a loaf of bread

76 In the office, who at first does not believe the rhinoceros exists?
(a) Dudard (b) MR. Papillon (c) Botard (d) Daisy

77 When Botard sees the rhinoceros at the office, he
(a) jumps out the window to join it
(b) claims to understand how it happened and why
(c) becomes a rhinoceros himself
(d) runs away, terrified

78 When Mr. Papillon understands that Mr. Boeuf has become a rhinoceros, he
(a) cannot speak
(b) sees it as an excuse to fire him
(c) feels sympathy for Mrs. Boeuf and offers her money
(d) orders dinner

79 What indicates that Jean will turn into a rhinoceros?
(a) His choice of meat for dinner
(b) His hoarse voice and migraine headache
(c) His bewildering hallucinations
(d) His angry shouting and long tail

80 What does Girl-Friend do when Young Lover says, "It means that between us there is a basis of understanding on which we can build the edifice of our future" in the play 'The Future is in Eggs'?
(a) Embraces him (b) Laughs
(c) Begins to leave (d) Kisses him

81 After the death of the Queen Victoria .... ascended the throne.
(a) George V (b) George III
(c) Edward VII (d) Edward VI

82 'The Intelligent Woman's Guide to Socialism' has been written by ....
(a) Rudyard Kipling (b) GB Shaw
(c) George Gissing (d) George Moore

83 Ionesco shows emptiness of existence by representing .... in the play 'Chairs'.
(a) empty Chairs (b) two Chairs
(c) legless Chairs (d) two People on a Chair

84 'The Countess Cathleen' the Green Helmet, A Full Moon in March' are the famous plays of
(a) Coleridge (b) Yeats
(c) Spenser (d) Shaw

85 The play 'Waiting For Godot' established .... as a leading figure of the Theatre of Absurd.
(a) Sean O' Casey (b) Noel Coward
(c) Eugene Ionesco (d) Samuel Beckett

86 Which of the following statements is incorrect about GB Shaw?
(a) He wrote 'Arms and the Man'
(b) He won the Nobel Prize in Literature
(c) He won an Oscar for adaptation of his play 'Pygmalion'
(d) He was a successful novelist

87 Which of the following statements is correct about Eugene Ionesco?
(a) He was one of the play wright of the 'Theatre of The Absurd'
(b) His plays have not been characterised as 'anti-plays'
(c) His plays do not break the conventions of naturalistic theatre
(d) His plays do not present parodies of human condition

88 Which of the following statements is incorrect?
(a) Oscar Wilde is one of the most prominent playwrights of the Victorian Era
(b) The play Lady Windermere's Fan was written by Oscar Wilde in 1892

(c) The play boy of the Western World was written by Oscar Wilde in 1907
(d) Oscar Wilde also wrote the play 'Salome'

89 **Which of the following is not true?**
(a) 'Catilina' was Henrik Ibsen's First play
(b) Ibsen wrote all his plays under the pseudonym 'Brynjolf Bjarme'
(c) Ibsen was highly inspired by Henrik Wergeland
(d) Ibsen's next play 'Brand won him the critical acclaim'

90 **Which of the following is not correct?**
(a) Sean O' Casey launched his professional acting career at the age of 12, making his London debut as 'Prince Mussel'
(b) 'The Rat Trap' was Noel Coward's first composition as a play wright
(c) John Galsworthy wrote his first collection of stories under the pseudonym 'John Sinjohn
(d) The Famous character of Peter Pan first appeared in 'The Little White Bird'

91 **Which of the following pairs is correctly matched?**
(a) GB Shaw : Pygmalion
(b) Lady Gregory : Deaths and Entravels
(c) John Masefield : The Jackdaw
(d) Dylan Thomas : The Midnight Folk

92 **Which of the following pairs is correctly matched?**
(a) Samuel Beckett : Waiting for Godot
(b) Harold Pinter : The Bald Soprano
(c) John Osborne : The Birthday Party
(d) Eugene Ionesco : Look Back in Anger

93 **Which of the following pairs is incorrectly matched?**
(a) The Silver Box : John Galsworthy
(b) The Shadow of Gunman : Sean O' Casey
(c) The Bald Soprano : Samuel Beckett
(d) Fallen Angels : Noel Coward

94 **Which of the following alternatives has modern age playwrights in chronological order?**
(a) GB Shaw, John Galsworthy, Eugene Ionesco, Henrik Ibsen
(b) Henrik Ibsen, GB Shaw, John Galsworthy, Eugene Ionesco
(c) John Galsworthy, Henrik Ibsen, Eugene Ionesco, GB Shaw.
(d) Eugene Ionesco, John Galsworthy, GB Shaw, Henrik Ibsen

95 **Which of the following has plays in correct chronological order?**
(a) Juno and the Paycock, I Leave It To You, Gods and Fighting Men, Hedda Gabler
(b) I Leave It To you, Gods and Fighting Men, Hedda Gabler, Juno and the Paycock
(c) Gods and Fighting Men, Hedda Gabler, Juno and the Paycock, I Leave It To You
(d) Hedda Gabler, Gods and Fighting Men, I Leave It To You, Juno and The Paycock

96 **Match the following dramatists with their plays.**

(Dramatist)	(Play)
1. Oscar Wilde	A. A Woman of No Importance
2. JM Synge	B. Riders to the Sea
3. Dion Boucicault	C. The Colleen Bawn
4. Henrik Ibsen	D. An Enemy of the People

Codes
(a) 1–A, 2–B, 3–C, 4–D (b) 1–B, 2–C, 3–D, 4–A
(c) 1–C, 2–D, 3–A, 4–B (d) 1–D, 2–A, 3–B, 4–C

97 **Match the following plays with their playwrights.**

(Play)	(Playwright)
1. A Losing Game	A. John Galsworthy
2. Saint Joan	B. JM Barrie
3. What Every Woman Knows	C. GB Shaw
4. Justice	D. Lady Gregory

Codes
(a) 1–A, 2–B, 3–C, 4–D (b) 1–D, 2–C, 3–B, 4–A
(c) 1–B, 2–D, 3–A, 4–C (d) 1–C, 2–B, 3–D, 4–A

98 **Match the following characters with their plays.**

(Character)	(Play)
1. Nora	A. Hedda Gabler
2. Tesman	B. A Enemy of the People
3. Regina	C. A Doll's House
4. Dr. Thomas Stockmann	D. Ghosts

Codes
(a) 1–A, 2–B, 3–C, 4–D (b) 1–D, 2–C, 3–B, 4–A
(c) 1–C, 2–A, 3–D, 4–B (d) 1–A, 2–C, 3–B, 4–D

99 **Match the following plays with their character.**

(Character)	(Play)
1. Raina Petkoff	A. Rhinoceros
2. John Barthwick	B. Arms and the Man
3. Pozzo	C. Waiting for Godot
4. Berenger	D. The Silver–Box

Codes
(a) 1–A, 2–B, 3–C, 4–D
(b) 1–D, 2–C, 3–B, 4–A
(c) 1–C, 2–A, 3–D, 4–B
(d) 1–B, 2–D, 3–C, 4–A

100 **Match the following playwrights with their plays.**

(Playwright)	(Play)
1. Sean O' Casey	A. The Plough and the Stars
2. Noel Coward	B. Hay Fever
3. Samuel Beckett	C. Happy Days
4. Eugene Ionesco	D. The Chairs

Codes
(a) 1–A, 2–B, 3–C, 4–D (b) 1–D, 2–C, 3–B, 4–A
(c) 1–C, 2–A, 3–D, 4–B (d) 1–B, 2–D, 3–A, 4–C

101 Match the following.

List I	List II
1. Major Barbara	A. John Galsworthy
2. An Ideal Husband	B. Lady Gregory
3. The Jackdaw	C. Oscar Wilde
4. The Country House	D. G. B Shaw

Codes
(a) 1–A, 2B, 3–C, 4–D (b) 1–D, 2–C, 3–B, 4–A
(c) 1–B, 2–D, 3–A, 4–C (d) 1–C, 2–A, 3–D, 4–B

102 Match the following.

List I	List II
1. JM Barrie	A. The Vortex
2. Sean O' Casey	B. A Kiss for Cinderella
3. Noel Coward	C. Rhinoceros
4. Eugene Ionesco	D. The Shadow of a Gunman

Codes
(a) 1–A, 2–B, 3–C, 4–D (b) 1–D, 2–C, 3–B, 4–A
(c) 1–B, 2–D, 3–A, 4–C (d) 1–C, 2–A, 3–D, 4–B

103 Match the following

List I	List II
1. Dr. Rank	A. Hedda Gabler
2. Eilert Lovborg	B. Waiting for Godot
3. Oswald	C. A Doll's House
4. Vladimir	D. Ghosts

Codes
(a) 1–A, 2B, 3–C, 4–D (b) 1–D, 2–C, 3–B, 4–A
(c) 1–B, 2–D, 3–A, 4–C (d) 1–C, 2–A, 3–D, 4–B

104 In the given series, which one has playwrights matched correctly with their plays?
(a) Henrik Ibsen–The Wild Duck, GB Shaw–Candida, JM Barrie–Peter Pan, John Galsworthy-Strife
(b) Henrik Ibsen–Strife, GB Shaw–Peter Pan, JM Barrie–Candida, John Galsworthy-The Wild Duck
(c) Henrik Ibsen–Candida, GB Shaw-Strife, JM Barrie-The Wild Duck, John Galsworthy-Peter Pan
(d) Henrik Ibsen–Peter Pan, GB Shaw-The Wild Duck, JM Barrie–Strife, John Galsworthy-Candida

105 In the given series, which one has characters matched correctly with their works?
(a) Donal Davoran–The Shadow of a Gunman, Napolean Bonapart–Rat Trap, Edla Willmansson–A Woman of No Importance, Mrs. Rachel Arbuthnot–The Man of Destiny
(b) Donal Davoran–The Shadow of a Gunman, Napolean Bonapart-The Man of Destiny, Edla Willmansson-Rat Trap, Mrs. Rachel Arbuthnot-A Woman of No Importance.
(c) Donal Davoran–The Man of Destiny, Napolean Bonapart-The Shadow of a Gunman, Edla Willmansson–Rat Trap, Mrs. Rachel Arbuthnot–A Woman of No Importance.
(d) Donal Davoran–The Man of Destiny, Napolean Bonapart–The Shadow of a Gunman, Edla Willmansson–A Woman of No Importance, Mrs. Rachel Arbuthnot–Rat Trap.

106 Consider the following statements.
1. Bernard Shaw belong the period of 1856-1950.
2. Bernard Shaw was born in Dublin.
3. He wrote 'You Never Can Tell'.

Which of the statements given above is/are correct?
(a) 1 and 2 (b) 2 and 3 (c) 1 and 3 (d) All of these

107 Consider the following statements.
1. John Galsworthy belonged to 1867–1933.
2. Galsworthy wrote 'The Philanderer'.
3. He wrote 'The Man of Property'.

Which of the statements given above is/are not correct?
(a) 1 and 2 (b) 2 and 3 (c) Only 2 (d) Only 3

108 What is common to all of the writer? Identify to correct description below.
1. Eugene Ionesco 2. Arthur Adamov
3. Samuel Beckett

Codes
(a) All of them wrote Anti-Fascist dramas in verse
(b) All of them were leading figures of the theatre of the Absurd
(c) All of them died by committing suicide
(d) All of them forerunners of Dadaism

109 Consider the following statements.
1. Henrik Ibsen used the pseudonym 'Brynjolf Bjarme' for his first play 'Catilina'
2. Henrik Ibsen was famously known as Father of Modern Drama.
3. His First play 'Catilina' was performed with great success.
4. Pygmalion was one of his famous plays.

Which of the statements given above is/are true for Henrik Ibsen?
(a) 1 and 2 (b) 2 and 3 (c) 3 and 4 (d) 1, 2 and 3

110 Consider the following statements.
1. Lady Gregory collaborated with Yeats on The Pot of Broth in 1902.
2. WB Yeats served as Lady Gregory's Life–long Patron.
3. Lady Gregory's first performed play was 'Twenty-Five'.
4. Lady Gregory re–wrote ancient Greek legends in her plays.

Which of the statement(s) given above is/are true for Lady Gregory?
(a) 1 and 2 (b) 1 and 3 (c) 2 and 3 (d) 1, 2, 3 and 4

111 Consider the following statements.
1. JM Barrie started his career with drama.
2. He is best remembered as the creator of Peter Pan.

3. JM Barrie passed a childless married life.
4. 'Awakening' was written by JM Barrie.

Which of the statement(s) given above is/are true for James Matthew Barrie?

(a) 1 and 2 (b) 1 and 4 (c) 2 and 3 (d) 2 and 4

112 Consider the following statements.

1. Sean O' Casey became the General Secretary of the Irish Citizen Army (ICA) in 1914.
2. He wrote 'the Foryste Saga' for the people of Dublin.
3. He was one of the first 20th century major playwrights.
4. He is known for his Dublin Trilogy of Plays. 'The Shadow of a Gunman', 'Juno and the Paycock' and 'The Plough and the Stars'.

Which of the statement(s) given above is/are true for Sean O' Casey?

(a) 1 and 2 (b) 1 and 3 (c) 2 and 3 (d) 1 and 4

113 Consider the following statements.

1. Coward launched his professional acting career at the age of 12.
2. He made his debut as Prince Mussel in a children's show 'The Goldfish'.
3. He later wrote 'To Let' in 1921.
4. He also wrote 'Over the River' in 1933.

Which of the statement(s) given above is/are true For Noel Coward?

(a) 1 and 2 (b) 2 and 3 (c) 3 and 4 (d) 1, 2 and 3

114 Consider the following works

1. Easy Virtue 2. Murphy
3. Waiting for Godot 4. The Rat Trap

Which of the works given above belong to Samuel Beckett?

(a) 1 and 2 (b) 2 and 3 (c) 3 and 4 (d) 1 and 3

115 Consider the following dramatists.

1. Eugene Ionesco 2. GB Shaw
3. Oscar Wilde 4. Millington Synge

Which of the dramatists given above belong to the Victorian Age?

(a) 1 and 2 (b) 2 and 3 (c) 2, 3 and 4 (d) 1 and 3

116 "Helmer: But this is disgraceful. Is this the way you neglect your most sacred duties?
Nora: What do you consider is my most sacred duty?
Helmer: Do I have to tell you that? Isn't it your duty to your husband and children?
Nora: I have another duty, just as sacred.
Helmer: You can't have. What duty do you mean?
Nora: My duty to myself."

Which of the following dramatists in which of his/her works has had the above lines?

(a) Henrik Ibsen, A Doll's House
(b) Lady Augusta Gregory, Gods and Fighting Men
(c) George Bernard Shaw, Man and Superman
(d) JM Barrie, Peter Pan

117 "You have never loved me. You have only thought it pleasant to be in love with me."

Which of the following dramatists in which of his/her works has had the above lines?

(a) Henrik Ibsen, A Doll's House
(b) Lady Augusta Gregory, Gods and Fighting Men
(c) George Bernard Shaw, Man and Superman
(d) JM Barrie, Peter Pan

118 "It's not only what we have inherited from our father and mother that walks in us. It's all sorts of dead ideas, and lifeless old beliefs, and so forth. They have no vitality, but they cling to us all the same, and we can't get rid of them."

Which of the following dramatists in which of his/her works has had the above lines?

(a) Ibsen Henrik, Ghosts
(b) Lady Augusta Gregory, Gods and Fighting Men
(c) George Bernard Shaw, Mrs. Warren's Profession
(d) JM Barrie, The Little Minister

119 "You should never wear your best trousers when you go out to fight for freedom and truth."

Which of the following dramatists in which of his/her works has had the above lines?

(a) Henrik Ibsen, An Enemy of the People
(b) George Bernard Shaw, Back to Methuselah
(c) JM Barrie, The Little White Bird
(d) John Galsworthy, The Forsyte Saga

120 "He sat beside me pleasantly and played his sweet music to me, and in the end he foretold things that put drunkenness on my wits."

Which of the following dramatists in which of his/her works has had the above lines?

(a) Ibsen Henrik, Ghosts
(b) Lady Augusta Gregory, Gods and Fighting Men
(c) George Bernard Shaw, Mrs. Warren's Profession
(d) JM Barrie, The Little Minister

121 "And while they were in the same place, there came a great mist about them and a darkness, so that they could not know what way they were going, and they heard the noise of a rider coming towards them. 'It would be a great grief to us,' said Conn, to be brought away into a strange country."

Which of the following dramatists in which of his/her works has had the above lines?

(a) Henrik Ibsen, A Doll's House
(b) Lady Augusta Gregory, Gods and Fighting Men
(c) George Bernard Shaw, Man and Superman
(d) JM Barrie, Peter Pan

122 "The reasonable man adapts himself to the world: the unreasonable one persists in trying to adapt the world to himself. Therefore all progress depends on the unreasonable man."

Which of the following dramatists in which of his/her works has had the above lines?
(a) Henrik Ibsen, A Doll's House
(b) Lady Augusta Gregory, Gods and Fighting Men
(c) George Bernard Shaw, Man and Superman
(d) JM Barrie, Peter Pan

123 "People are always blaming their circumstances for what they are. I don't believe in circumstances. The people who get on in this world are the people who get up and look for the circumstances they want, and if they can't find them, make them."
Which of the following dramatists in which of his/her works has had the above lines?
(a) Ibsen Henrik, Ghosts
(b) Lady Augusta Gregory, Gods and Fighting Men
(c) George Bernard Shaw, Mrs. Warren's Profession
(d) JM Barrie, The Little Minister

124 "You use a glass mirror to see your face; you use works of art to see your soul."
Which of the following dramatists in which of his/her works has had the above lines?
(a) Henrik Ibsen, An Enemy of the People
(b) George Bernard Shaw, Back to Methuselah
(c) JM Barrie, The Little White Bird
(d) John Galsworthy, The Forsyte Saga

125 "He knows nothing; and he thinks he knows everything. That points clearly to a political career."
Which of the following dramatists in which of his/her works has had the above lines?
(a) George Bernard Shaw, Major Barbara
(b) JM Barrie, Peter Pan
(c) John Galsworthy, The White Monkey
(d) Seán O'Casey, The Shadow of A Gunman

126 "When the first baby laughed for the first time, its laugh broke into a thousand pieces, and they all went skipping about, and that was the beginning of fairies."
Which of the following dramatists in which of his/her works has had the above lines?
(a) Henrik Ibsen, A Doll's House
(b) Lady Augusta Gregory, Gods and Fighting Men
(c) George Bernard Shaw, Man and Superman
(d) JM Barrie, Peter Pan

127 "The reason birds can fly and we can't is simply because they have perfect faith, for to have faith is to have wings."
Which of the following dramatists in which of his/her works has had the above lines?
(a) Henrik Ibsen, An Enemy of the People
(b) George Bernard Shaw, Back to Methuselah
(c) JM Barrie, The Little White Bird
(d) John Galsworthy, The Forsyte Saga

128 "Let no one who loves be called altogether unhappy. Even love unreturned has its rainbow."
Which of the following dramatists in which of his/her works has had the above lines?
(a) Ibsen Henrik, Ghosts
(b) Lady Augusta Gregory, Gods and Fighting Men
(c) George Bernard Shaw, Mrs Warren's Profession
(d) JM Barrie, The Little Minister

129 "You know that place between sleep and awake, that place where you still remember dreaming? That's where I'll always love you. That's where I'll be waiting."
Which of the following dramatists in which of his/her works has had the above lines?
(a) George Bernard Shaw, Major Barbara
(b) JM Barrie, Peter Pan
(c) John Galsworthy, The White Monkey
(d) Seán O'Casey, The Shadow of A Gunman

130 "Love is not a hot-house flower, but a wild plant, born of a wet night, born of an hour of sunshine; sprung from wild seed, blown along the road by a wild wind. A wild plant that, when it blooms by chance within the hedge of our gardens, we call a flower; and when it blooms outside we call a weed; but, flower or weed, whose scent and colour are always, wild!
Which of the following dramatists in which of his/her works has had the above lines?
(a) Henrik Ibsen, An Enemy of the People
(b) George Bernard Shaw, Back to Methuselah
(c) JM Barrie, The Little White Bird
(d) John Galsworthy, The Forsyte Saga

131 "Light-heartedness always made Soames suspicious - there was generally some reason for it."
Which of the following dramatists in which of his/her works has had the above lines?
(a) John Galsworthy, The White Monkey
(b) Sean O'Casey, Red Roses for Me
(c) Eugene Ionesco, Rhinoceros
(d) Samuel Beckett, Waiting for Godot

132 "That tendency...to lie awake between the hours of two and four, when the chrysalis of faint misgiving becomes so readily the butterfly of panic."
Which of the following dramatists in which of his/her works has had the above lines?
(a) George Bernard Shaw, Major Barbara
(b) JM Barrie, Peter Pan
(c) John Galsworthy, The White Monkey
(d) Seán O'Casey, The Shadow of A Gunman

133 "She stood for a moment looking up at the stars, so far, so many, bright and cold. And with a faint smile she thought: 'I wonder which is my lucky star!"
Which of the following dramatists in which of his/her works has had the above lines?
(a) John Galsworthy, Flowering Wilderness
(b) Samuel Beckett, Krapp's Last Tape and Embers
(c) Noël Coward, Blithe Spirit
(d) Eugène Ionesco, The Bald Soprano

134 "That's the Irish People all over - they treat a serious thing as a joke and a joke as a serious thing."
Which of the following dramatists in which of his/her works has had the above lines?
(a) George Bernard Shaw, Major Barbara
(b) JM Barrie, Peter Pan
(c) John Galsworthy, The White Monkey
(d) Seán O'Casey, The Shadow of A Gunman

135 "It's I who know that well: when it was dark, you always carried the Sun in your hand for me."
Which of the following dramatists in which of his/her works has had the above lines?
(a) John Galsworthy, The White Monkey
(b) Sean O'Casey, Red Roses for Me
(c) Eugene Ionesco, Rhinoceros
(d) Samuel Beckett, Waiting for Godot

136 "It's a sad reflection on society how many people are shocked by honesty... and how few by dishonesty."
Which of the following dramatists in which of his/her works has had the above lines?
(a) John Galsworthy, Flowering Wilderness
(b) Samuel Beckett, Krapp's Last Tape and Embers
(c) Noël Coward, Blithe Spirit
(d) Eugène Ionesco, The Bald Soprano

137 "The tears of the world are a constant quantity. For each one who begins to weep somewhere else another stops. The same is true of the laugh."
Which of the following dramatists in which of his/her works has had the above lines?
(a) John Galsworthy, The White Monkey
(b) Sean O'Casey, Red Roses for Me
(c) Eugene Ionesco, Rhinoceros
(d) Samuel Beckett, Waiting for Godot

138 "Perhaps my best years are gone. When there was a chance of happiness. But I wouldn't want them back. Not with the fire in me now. No, I wouldn't want them back."
Which of the following dramatists in which of his/her works has had the above lines?
(a) John Galsworthy, Flowering Wilderness
(b) Samuel Beckett, Krapp's Last Tape and Embers
(c) Noël Coward, Blithe Spirit
(d) Eugène Ionesco, The Bald Soprano

139 "Daisy: I never knew you were such a realist-I thought you were more poetic. Where's your imagination? There are many sides to reality. Choose the one that's best for you. Escape into the world of imagination."
Which of the following dramatists in which of his/her works has had the above lines?
(a) John Galsworthy, The White Monkey
(b) Sean O'Casey, Red Roses for Me
(c) Eugene Ionesco, Rhinoceros
(d) Samuel Beckett, Waiting for Godot

140 "I'd rather lay an egg in a box than go and steal an ox."
Which of the following dramatists in which of his/her works has had the above lines?
(a) John Galsworthy, Flowering Wilderness
(b) Samuel Beckett, Krapp's Last Tape and Embers
(c) Noel Coward, Blithe Spirit
(d) Eugene Ionesco, The Bald Soprano

141 **Assertion** (A) Arms and the Man was GB Shaw's first commercial success.
Reason (R) It debunks romantic Recorism associated with war and deals with the futility of war.
Codes
(a) A is true, but R is false
(b) A is false, but R is true
(c) Both A and R are true, but R is not the correct explanation of A
(d) Both A and R are true and R is the correct explanation of A

Directions (Q. Nos 142-145) *In the questions given below are the statements labelled as Assertion (A) and Reason (R). In the context of the two statements, which one of the following is appropriate?*
Codes
(a) Both A and R are true and R is the correct explanation of A.
(b) Both A and R are true but R is not the correct explanation of A.
(c) A is true but R is false.
(d) A is false but R is true.

142 **Assertion** (A) Oscar Wilde is better known for his activity as a playwright.
Reason (R) He gave fantasy, vivacity and a breath of new life to drama.

143 **Assertion** (A) Realism is the most significant and outstanding quality of modern English drama.
Reason (R) TS Eliot was the main dramatist who gave importance to poetic plays.

144 **Assertion** (A) Henrik Ibsen introduced more and more of his own beliefs and judgements into the drama, exploring what he termed the 'drama of ideas'.
Reason (R) Ibsen's 'An Enemy was devoid of any controversy.'

145 **Assertion** (A) Eugene Ionesco had intended to write plays from the beginning of his career.
Reason (R) His plays have been characterised as 'anti–plays' which characteristically combine a dream or nightmare atmosphere with grotesque, bizarre and whimisical humour.

Directions (Q. Nos. 146-150) *Read the following passage and answer the questions that follow*

Now they have all gone,' said Louis. 'I am alone. They have gone into the house for breakfast, and I am left standing by the wall among the flowers. It is very early, before lessons. Flower after flower is specked on the depths of green. The petals are harlequins. Stalks rise from the black hollows beneath. The flowers swim like fish made of light upon the dark, green waters. I hold a stalk in my hand. I am the stalk. My roots go down to the depths of the world, tremors shake me, and the weight of the earth is pressed to my ribs. Up here my eyes are green leaves, unseeing. I am a boy in grey flannels with a belt fastened by a brass snake up here. Down there my eyes are the lidless eyes of a stone figure in a desert by the Nile. I see women passing with red pitchers to the river; I see camels swaying and men in turbans. I hear tramplings, tremblings, stirrings round me.

'Up here Bernard, Neville, Jinny and Susan (but not Rhoda) skim the flower-beds with their nets. They skim the butterflies from the nodding tops of the flowers. They brush the surface of the world. Their nets are full of fluttering wings. "Louis! Louis! Louis!" they shout. But they cannot see me. I am on the other side of the hedge. There are only little eye-holes among the leaves.'

146 The characters Bernard, Neville, Jinny and Susan belong to which novel of Virginia Woolf?
(a) Mrs Dalloway (b) Jacob's Room
(c) The Waves (d) To the Lighthouse

147 Who cannot be seen?
(a) Bernard (b) Louis (c) Neville (d) Jinny

148 What does fluttering wings imply?
(a) Butterflies (b) Birds (c) Flowers (d) Net

149 What is a possible reading to *The Waves*?
(a) All the characters are still children
(b) All the characters are speaking from beyond the grave
(c) All the characters are Tyler Durden
(d) All the characters are one person

150 When did 'The Waves' publish?
(a) 1916 (b) 1925
(c) 1931 (d) 1941

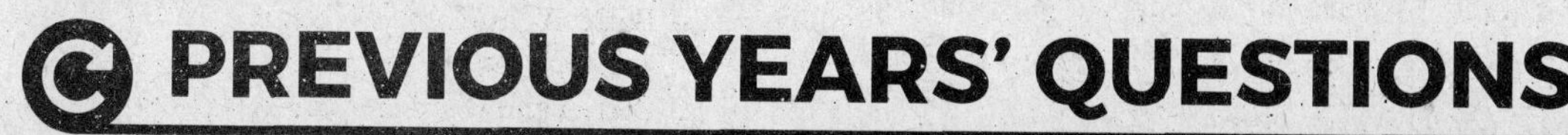

PREVIOUS YEARS' QUESTIONS

December 2018

1 In the spring of 1941, Nikos Kazantzakis embarked on one of the his most ambitious projects, a play known as Yangtze. What English/Greek title is it now known as?
(a) Buddha (b) Brobdingnag
(c) Zoroaster (d) Zorba

November 2017

2 In which play by Eugene Ionesco do you find the grotesque image of the leg of a corpse thrusting onto the stage, and, which begins to grow larger as the play progresses in a menacing manner?
(a) The Bald Soprano
(b) Amede or How to Get Rid of It
(c) Exit the King
(d) The Lesson

July 2016

3 Which character of Henrik Ibsen speaks the following lines. "The life of a normally constituted idea is generally about seventeen or eighteen years, at the most twenty"?
(a) Nora in A Doll's House
(b) Dr. Thomas Stockman in An Enemy of the People
(c) John Rosmer in Rosmersholm
(d) Oswald in Ghosts

December 2015

4 In Beckett's waiting for Godot the characters often use dislocated, repetitious and cliched speech primarily to
(a) illustrate the essentially illogical, purposeless nature of the human condition
(b) re-create the workings of the sub-conscious
(c) mock the exaggerated dignity and wisdom of modern self-professed intellectuals
(d) reinforce the comic action of farcical plots

December 2014

5 Who are Didi and Gogo?
(a) They are two characters in Endgame
(b) They are nicknames, respectively, for Lucky and Pozzo
(c) They are nicknames, respectively, for Vladimir and Estragon
(d) They are two characters in Breath

6 Samuel Beckett's trilogy published together in London, in 1959 under the English titles is
(a) More Pricks than Kicks, Murphy, Molloy
(b) B Molloy, Malone Dies, The Unnamable
(c) Molloy, Murphy, Malone Dies
(d) The Unnamable, More Pricks than Kicks, Murphy

7 The following is an exchange between two characters, husband and wife, in a famous play. The lines appear at the very end of an emotionally-charged sequence of the last scene
"...I've stopped believing in miracles."
"But I'll believe. Tell me ! Transform ourselves to the point that ......?"
"That our living together could be a true marriage."
(She goes out down the hall)
Which play? Name the characters.
(a) Othello Othello, Desdemona
(b) Sure Thing Bill, Betty
(c) A Doll's House Helmer, Nora
(d) Death of a Salesman Willy, Linda

8 One of the following texts was published earlier than 1955. Identify the text
(a) William Golding, The Inheritors
(b) Philip Larkin, The Less Deceived
(c) William Empson, Collected Poems
(d) Samuel Beckett, Waiting for Godot

9 Which of the following can be best described as: (i) the first statement Bernard Shaw's idea of Life Force; a play dealing with a woman's pursuit of her mate; and (ii) a play whose third act called 'Don Juan in Hell' is both conventional and hilarious?
(a) The Devil's Disciple
(b) Man and Superman
(c) Candida
(d) Arms and the Man

ANSWERS

Objective Questions

1. *(a)*	2. *(d)*	3. *(c)*	4. *(a)*	5. *(c)*	6. *(c)*	7. *(b)*	8. *(d)*	9. *(d)*	10. *(a)*
11. *(b)*	12. *(b)*	13. *(c)*	14. *(b)*	15. *(b)*	16. *(d)*	17. *(b)*	18. *(b)*	19. *(a)*	20. *(d)*
21. *(b)*	22. *(b)*	23. *(c)*	24. *(c)*	25. *(c)*	26. *(c)*	27. *(d)*	28. *(d)*	29. *(a)*	30. *(d)*
31. *(a)*	32. *(d)*	33. *(a)*	34. *(a)*	35. *(b)*	36. *(b)*	37. *(d)*	38. *(b)*	39. *(d)*	40. *(d)*
41. *(c)*	42. *(b)*	43. *(c)*	44. *(d)*	45. *(c)*	46. *(d)*	47. *(a)*	48. *(c)*	49. *(b)*	50. *(d)*
51. *(a)*	52. *(b)*	53. *(a)*	54. *(d)*	55. *(b)*	56. *(d)*	57. *(d)*	58. *(c)*	59. *(c)*	60. *(d)*
61. *(c)*	62. *(d)*	63. *(a)*	64. *(a)*	65. *(c)*	66. *(d)*	67. *(d)*	68. *(c)*	69. *(d)*	70. *(a)*
71. *(a)*	72. *(c)*	73. *(b)*	74. *(c)*	75. *(b)*	76. *(c)*	77. *(b)*	78. *(b)*	79. *(b)*	80. *(c)*
81. *(c)*	82. *(b)*	83. *(a)*	84. *(b)*	85. *(d)*	86. *(d)*	87. *(a)*	88. *(c)*	89. *(b)*	90. *(a)*
91. *(a)*	92. *(a)*	93. *(c)*	94. *(b)*	95. *(d)*	96. *(a)*	97. *(b)*	98. *(c)*	99. *(d)*	100. *(a)*
101. *(b)*	102. *(c)*	103. *(d)*	104. *(a)*	105. *(b)*	106. *(d)*	107. *(c)*	108. *(b)*	109. *(a)*	110. *(b)*
111. *(c)*	112. *(d)*	113. *(a)*	114. *(b)*	115. *(c)*	116. *(a)*	117. *(a)*	118. *(a)*	119. *(a)*	120. *(b)*
121. *(b)*	122. *(c)*	123. *(c)*	124. *(b)*	125. *(a)*	126. *(d)*	127. *(c)*	128. *(d)*	129. *(b)*	130. *(d)*
131. *(a)*	132. *(c)*	133. *(a)*	134. *(d)*	135. *(b)*	136. *(b)*	137. *(d)*	138. *(c)*	139. *(c)*	140. *(d)*
141. *(d)*	142. *(a)*	143. *(b)*	144. *(c)*	145. *(d)*	146. *(c)*	147. *(b)*	148. *(a)*	149. *(d)*	150. *(c)*

Previous Years' Questions

1. *(a)*	2. *(b)*	3. *(b)*	4. *(a)*	5. *(c)*	6. *(b)*	7. *(c)*	8. *(d)*	9. *(b)*

The Contemporary Drama

The Contemporary Drama began with rejection of 19th century reaslist model in the later-half of the 20th century. Epic theater, theatre of cruelty and the theatre of the absurd took the centre-stage. Bertolt Brecht, Harold Pinter, and Eugene O' Neill were a few of the greatest playwrights of the Contemporary age. Brecht's *Mother Courage and Her Children* was written against the backdrop of the rise of Hitler.

Drama in Contemporary Period

Inspired by the changes in the literary and art world in the 20th century, in which numerous new artistic movements like Cubism, Surrealism and Futurism took place. A number of theatrical movements arose which rejected the 19th century realist model, choosing instead to play with the language and elements of dramatic convention which had previously been dominant. All this together formed the drama of the contemporary age. These included the Brechtian Epic theater, Artaud's Theatre of Cruelty and the so called Theatre of the Absurd. *These can be understood under the following heads*

Epic Theatre

Epic theatre arose in the early to mid-twentieth century from the theories and practice of a number of theatre practitioners, including Erwin Piscator, Vladimir Mayakovsky, Vsevolod Meyerhold and most famously, Bertolt Brecht. Epic theatre rejects the core tenants of realism and naturalism, asserting that the purpose of a play, more than entertainment or the imitation of reality, is to present ideas and invite the audience to make judgements on them. Characters are not intended to mimic real people but to represent opposing sides of an argument, archetypes or stereotypes.

The audience should always be aware that it is watching a play and should remain at an emotional distance from the action; Brecht described this ideal as the Verfremdungseffekt-variously translated as 'alienation effect', 'defamiliarisation effect', or 'estrangement effect'. It is the opposite of the suspension of disbelief.

In this Chapter

- *Drama in Contemporary Period*
- *Contemporary Dramatists*

Common production techniques in epic theatre include simplified, non-realistic set designs and announcements or visual captions, that interrupt and summarise the action. Brecht used comedy to distance his audiences from emotional or serious events and was heavily influenced by musicals and fairground performers, putting music and song in his plays. Acting in epic theatre requires actors to play characters believably without convincing either the audience or themselves that they are truly the characters.

Theatre of Cruelty

Brecht's own social and political focus departed also from surrealism and the Theatre of Cruelty, as developed in the writings and dramaturgy of Antonin Artaud, who sought to affect audiences viscerally, psychologically, physically and irrationally.

Artaud had pessimistic view of the world but he believed that theatre could affect change. His approach tried to remove the audience from the everyday chores and use symbolic objects to work with the emotions and soul of the audience. The goal was to attack the audience's senses through an array of technical methods and acting so that they would be brought out of their desensitisation and have to confront themselves through the use of the grotesque, the ugly and pain.

Theatre of the Absurd

Theatre of the Absurd is a designation for particular plays written by a number of primarily European playwrights in the late 1940s, 1950s and 1960s as well as to the style of theatre which has evolved from their work.

The term was coined by the critic Martin Esslin based on Albert Camus' philosophy that life is inherently without meaning as illustrated in his work *The Myth of Sisyphus*. Though the term is applied to a wide range of plays, some characteristics coincide in many of the plays: broad comedy, often similar to Vaudeville, mixed with horrific or tragic images; characters caught in hopeless situations forced to do repetitive or meaningless actions; dialogue full of cliches, wordplay and nonsense; plots that are cyclical or absurdly expensive; either a parody or dismissal of realism and the concept of the 'well-made play'.

In the first (1961) edition, Esslin presented the four defining playwrights of the movement as Samuel Beckett, Arthur Adamov, Eugene Lonesco, and Jean Genet, and in subsequent editions he added a fifth playwright, Harold Pinter - although each of these writers has unique preoccupations and techniques that go beyond the term 'absurd'. Other writers whom Esslin associated with this group include Tom Stoppard, Friedrich Durrenmatt, Fernando Arrabal, Edward Albee and Jean Tardieu.

Contemporary Dramatists

Bertolt Brecht (1898-1956)

He was born in 1898. He was a German poet and playwright. He is known for his anti-Aristotlean epic theatre. Brecht believed in arousing the spectators capacity for action through his plays and transforming them from spectators to actors. His first play was *Baal* in 1922. This was followed by *Drums in the Night, Jungle of the Cities, Man Equals Man* and *A Respectable Wedding*.

His play *Mother Courage and Her Children* was written against the backdrop of the rise of Hitler. He opposed the Nazi Movement, Fled from Germany in 1933 and emigrated to America. In 1940s, he was accused by the House of the Un-American Activities Committee for holding left wing views. He later left America and settled in East Germany. He died in 1956 in East Berlin.

Major Works

Saint Joan of the Stockyards

The play was written between 1922-1931 and published in 1959. In this version of the story of Joan of Arc, Brecht transforms her into 'Joan Dark', a member of the 'Black Straw Hats' in 20th century Chicago. The play charts Joan's battle with Pierpont Mauler, the sycophantic owner of the meat-packing plant. Like her predecessor, Joan is doomed woman, a martyr and an innocent in a world of strike-breakers, fat cats and penniless workers. Like many of Brecht's plays it is laced with humour and songs as part of its epic dramaturgical structure. The play, which was never staged in Brecht's lifetime.

Mother Courage and Her Children (1939)

Mother Courage is one of the plays that Brecht wrote in resistance to the rise of Fascism and Nazism. In response to the invasion of Poland by German Armies of Adolf Hitler in 1939, Brecht wrote this play.

Following Brecht's own principles for political drama, the play is not set in modern times but during the Thirty Years' War of 1618-1648. It involved all the European states.

It follows the fortune of Anna Fierling, nicknamed 'Mother Courage', a wily canteen woman with the Swedish Army. She is determined to make her living from the war. Over the course of the play, she loses all three of her children, Eilif, Kattrin and Swiss Cheese, to the very war from which she tried to profit.

Major Works

- Happy End (1929)
- Fear and Misery of the Third Reich (1938)
- The Trial of Lucullus (1940)
- The Days of the Commune (1956)
- Trumpets and Drums (1955)

John Arden (1930-2012)

He was a British Marxist playwright. He was born in 1930. In royal court theatre, he got success with this play, *Live Like Pigs* (1958). In this play, he deals with the resettlement of gypsies in a housing estate which explores anti-social behaviour. John Arden was typical of a new generation of dramatists who started their careers at royal court. He was impressed with Bertolt Brecht. His play *The Happy Haven* (1960) was a farcical play with masks.

Serjeant Musgrave's Dance

Arden's most celebrated and a short play is based on anti-militaristic theme with a combination of music, song and symbolism. In this play, he deals with very real people, who are involved in a complex situation and seeking for principles to guide them. In *Armstrong's Last Goodnight* (1964) and *Left Handed Liberty* (1965), he used historical events as settings for the evaluation of morality. Arden has written many experimental plays for young people with his wife, Margaretta D'Areys.

Arnold Wesker (1932 - Present)

He was a British dramatist born in 1932. Among the dramatists of World War II, he is one of the most notable. He wrote three plays in the beginning of his career. *Chicken Soup with Barley* (1958), *Roots* (1959)and *I'm talking about Jerusalem* (1960). He describes in these plays East End's Jews search for security, principles and happiness. Though he tries to show the working class for about 30 years, he has to admit that there is lack of progress and purpose because the welfare state has brought comfort and destroyed causes. He often clearly searches for pseudo-culture or a return to 19th century socialism.

Major Works

- *Chips with Everything* was written in 1962. It has the combination of comedy, satire and a tragic allegory coloured with mysticism.
- *Their Very Own and Golden City* was written in 1965. It is a long and detailed study of socialism and social progress. Arnold Wesker shows that his thoughts on society are old fashioned and he becomes a pessimist.
- *The Friends* was written in 1970. In this play, Wesker is again, pessimist. He is responsible for founding centre 42, which is to take arts to neglected places.

David Storey (1933-2017)

He is an English playwright, novelist and rugby player. He was born in 1933, in Yorkshire. He was trained as an artist at the Slade School. After doing many jobs, he turned to writing.

Works of Storey

The Restoration of Arnold Middleton (1966), *The Contractor* (1969), *The Changing Room* (1971) and *Life Class* (1974), In all his plays, the writer sees madness or craziness as only defense, but these comedies are written in a more unnatural form.

Tom Stoppard (1937- Present)

Sir Tom Stoppard, born in 1937, is a Czech-born British playwright and screenwriter. He has written prolifically for TV, radio, film and stage, finding prominence with plays such as Arcadia, The Coast of Utopia, Every Good Boy Deserves Favour etc. His works cover the themes of human rights, censorship and political freedom, often delving into the deeper philosophical thematic of society. Stoppard has been a key playwright of the National Theatre and is one of the most internationally performed dramatists of his generation.

Major Works

Rosencrantz and Guildenstern Are Dead

Rosencrantz and Guildenstern Are Dead is an absurdist, existential tragicomedy by Tom Stoppard, first staged at the Edinburgh Festival Fringe in 1966. The play expands upon the exploits of two minor characters from Shakespeare's Hamlet, the courtiers Rosencrantz and Guildenstern.

Comparisons have also been drawn with Samuel Beckett's Waiting for Godot, for the presence of two central characters who almost appear to be two halves of a single character. Many plot features are similar as well: the characters pass time by playing questions, impersonating other characters, and interrupting each other or remaining silent for long periods of time.

The Real Inspector Hound

The play was written between 1961 and 1962, drawing on Stoppard's experiences as a Bristol theatre critic. *The Real Inspector Hound* is a short, one-act play by Tom Stoppard. The plot follows two theatre critics named Moon and Birdboot who are watching a ludicrous setup of a country house murder mystery, in the style of a whodunit. By chance, they become involved in the action causing a series of events that parallel the play they are watching.

Every Good Boy Deserves Favour

Every Good Boy Deserves Favour is a stage play by Tom Stoppard. It was first performed in 1977. The play criticises the Soviet practice of treating political dissidence as a form of mental illness. Its title derives from the popular mnemonic used by music students to remember the notes on the lines of the treble clef. The cast comprises six actors, but also a full orchestra, which not only provides music throughtout the play but also forms an essential part of the action. A chamber-orchestra version also exists. The play is dedicated to Viktor Fainberg and Vladimir Bukovsky, two Soviet dissidents expelled to the West.

John Clifford Mortimer (1923-2009)

He was an English dramatist and barrister born in 1923. He learnt his methods from radio and television and became famous. He is best known for his *Rumpole of the Bailey* plays.

Dock Brief was written in 1957 from a TV script. In the *Wrong Side of the Park* (1960) and *Two Stars for Comfort* (1972), he wrote sympathetically about the lonely, the neglected and the unsuccessful.

He struggled against the established rules. *Collaboration* (1973) and *The Bells of Hell* (1977) are his more successful comedies.. These are full-length plays in which he uses sharpness and understanding of the subtle difference in the feeling and meaning of the character. A Voyage Round My Father (1970) is a tender autobiography and review of an era. He died in 2009.

Major Works

Rumpole of the Bailey (1978)

Rumpole of the Bailey is a British television series created and written by the British writer and barrister John Mortimer. It stars, Leo Mckern as Horace Rumpole, an ageing London barrister who defends any and all clients. The original show has been spun off into a series of short stories, novels and radio programmes.

Edward Bond (1935)

He is an English poet and playwright born in 1935. He was one of those writers, who wanted a direct attack on the audience through horrifying, shocking even disgusting situations. His imagery is violent. His language is concise and clear. His plays depict man in social, political and mental chains and portray the world to be full of hopelessness.

Major Works

Saved (1965) and *Pope's Wedding* are his first plays. Bond sees anger and violence as the only means of self-expression, open to the socially deprived.

Bingo was written in 1974. The play shows Shakespeare in his self-satisfied retirement and complicit in the economic oppression of the poor but silent when it comes to effective social protest. His other plays are *Narrow Road to the Deep North* (1968), *Lear* (1971) and *The Fool* (1975). All these plays have imaginatively different expression of his philosophy. *Early Morning*, an excellent example of blank farce was written in 1968.

Peter Nichols (1927)

He is an English writer born in 1927. He was versatile and imaginative. He left acting to become a playwright. His plays are quite autobiographical in nature.

A Day in the Death of Joe Egg (1967) describes a marriage and a child sensitively.

Forget Me - Not - Lane (1971) This play recollects the war period through the eyes of young people. It is a comedy with music. It has personal recollections, disguise and moments of history.

The National Health (1969) and *Chez Nous* (1974) Both plays have biting satires in a language, which forces a man to listen even when it hurts.

John Osborne (1929-1994)

John Osborne was an English playwright, born in London on 12th December, 1929. He obtained his education from a private boarding school, Belmont College. Osborne did not receive a college/university education. He began work in the theatre as an actor and writer.

Literary Career and Works

His play *Look Back in Anger*, which opened on 8th May, 1956 at the Royal Court Theatre in London, revolutionised English theatre. This play became a representative text of the Angry Young Men Movement. Its protagonist-Jimmy Porter captured the angry and rebellious nature of the postwar generation. The Angry Young Men Movement consisted of a group of British novelists and playwrights in the 1950s, who expressed their dissatisfaction with the prevailing sociopolitical order of their country.

This group of intellectuals, who had grown up after the World War II, belonged to lower middle class or working class backgrounds. They revolted against the hypocrisy of the upper classes and rebelled against unfair treatment meted out to them. Apart from Osborne, other writers that belonged to this movement were John Wain, Kingsley Amis, Alan Sillitoe and John Braine. Osborne's next play *The Entertainer* (1957) examined the decline of post-war Britain through the decline of the once powerful art of English music hall. Osborne used theatre as a weapon to revolt against accepted norms and ideals.

He once remarked, "I do not like the kind of society, in which I find myself. I like it less and less. I love the theatre more and more because I know that it is what I always dreamed it might be: a weapon. I am sure that it can be one of the decisive weapons of our time". Apart from plays, Osborne also ventured into writing screenplays, television adaptations and autobiography. He died as a result of complications from diabetes on 24th December, 1994, in Shropshire, England.

Major Work

Look Back in Anger

Look Back in Anger opened at the Royal Court Theatre on 8th May, 1956. The play is set in a one-room attic apartment in the Midlands of England. This large room is the home of Jimmy Porter, his wife Alison and his business partner and friend Cliff Lewis, who has a separate bedroom across the hall. The cultural backdrop to the play is the rise and fall of the British Empire. The beginning of the 20th century saw the peak of power and influence of British colonialism. By the 1950's, World War II, which devastated the British economy. The rise of the United States as the new world military and political power meant that the British Empire had entered a steep decline. Jimmy Porter is representative of an entire culture that remained nostalgic for this past glory.

Jimmy Porter, the play's main character, became the model for the 'Angry Young Man,' a nickname given to an entire generation of artists and working class young men in post World War II British society. Jimmy is angry at the social and political structures that he believes has kept him from achieving his dreams and aspirations. He directs this anger towards his friends and, most notably, his wife Alison. The play is also the first well-known example of 'Kitchen Sink' drama, a term used to denote plays that rely on realism to explore domestic social relations. *Look Back in Anger* was adapted in 1958, as a film by John Osborne and Nigel Kneale. A second film was made in 1980, directed by Lindsay Anderson.

His Major Works

Plays

- The Devil Inside (1950, with Stella Linden)
- Look Back in Anger (1956)
- The Entertainer (1957)
- Luther (1961)
- Inadmissible Evidence (1964)
- A Patriot for Me (1965)

Autobiography

- A Better Class of Person (autobiography, 1981)
- Almost a Gentleman (Sequel to A Better Class of Person, 1991)

Shelagh Delaney (1939-2011)

Shelagh Delaney was an English dramatist and screen writer. She was born in Broughton in 1939. She was associated with the theatre of Royal Court. She died of breast cancer in 2011.

A Taste of Honey

It was published in 1958. It is a beautiful combination of solid realism and romantic dream fantasy. In this play, on one hand, she shows the innocence of young love. On the other hand, she describes the conflicts of mother-daughter relationship and homosexuality. She got success with this play.

Harold Pinter (1930-2008)

Harold Pinter was a renowned English playwright, screenwriter and director. He was born to a Jewish Tailor in London in 1930. Pinter studied acting at the Royal Academy of Dramatic Art and the Central School of Speech and Drama, but soon left to undertake an acting career under the stage name David Baron.

Literary Career and Works

Pinter started writing plays in 1957. He wrote a short play, *The Room*, in 1957 and went on to create his first full-length drama, *The Birthday Party*. This play tasted little commercial success. It was with *The Caretaker* in 1960s, that Pinter achieved a measure of success. The play concerns two brothers- Aston and Mick and a tramp-Davies. *The Homecoming* is considered to be a turning point in Pinter's literary career. The play explores the life of a predominantly male working class family. Set in North London, the play begins with the homecoming of Teddy and his wife, Ruth. After 6 years of marriage and living in America with their three sons, Ruth finally meets Teddy's family. His father, uncle and two brothers, all live in the same house. Competition among the men increases with the coming of Ruth to draw her attention.

Pinter's plays fall under the category of Comedy of Menace. The term was first applied to Pinter's plays by the theatre critic Irving Wardle, but was also the subtitle of David Campton's *The Lunatic View*.

Comedy of Menace denotes a kind of play, in which the characters feel threatened by some overpowering or frightening force. This fear and menace becomes a source of comedy. Pinter also wrote screenplays for *The French Lieutenant's Woman, The Last Tycoon,* and *The Handmaid's Tale*. He received the Nobel Prize for Literature in 2005. Pinter died from liver cancer on 24th December, 2008.

Major Works

- The Room (1957)
- The Dumb Waiter (1957)
- The Dwarfs (1960)
- The Basement (1966)
- Family Voices (1980)
- The New World Order (1991)
- Party Time (1991)
- Betrayal
- Ashes to Ashes
- The Birthday Party (1957)
- The Caretaker (1959)
- The Homecoming (1964)
- Monologue (1972)
- Celebration (1999)
- No Man's Land

Arthur Miller (1915-2005)

Arthur Miller is counted as one of the three great dramatists of the modern American drama. He was born in a Jewish family in New York in 1915. His family belonged to middle class, His family was suffering from financial crisis so he had to search for a job to meet his family needs and continue his studies. He worked as an assistant in a shop for 2 years. He joined the Michigan University in 1934-1938 and studied journalism and writing plays.

Literary Career and Works

He got many prizes for his dramatic talent during his university education. He wrote his first play *Honours at Dawn*. This play won the university's *Avery Hopwood Award* for him. In 1983, he wrote his play *No Villain Later*, it was renamed *They Too Arise.* This play also won the same award for him. It also won the prize of Theatre Guild Bureau of New Plays. He wrote many plays during the World War II. He wrote *The Man, who Had All the Luck* in NewYork in 1944.

He wrote a book of report age *Situation Normal* and the screen play *The Story of G L. In 1945,* he wrote a novel *Focus*. His play *All My Sons* won for him the Donald Son award and the New York Drama, Critics Circle Award. He has written about his second wife 'Marilyn Monroe' who was a celebrity. He has written about ten major plays, short stories, film scripts, critical essays and a novel. He wrote his play *Death of a Salesman* in 1949 at the Morosco, New York.

Situation Normal is a volume of sketches pertaining to life in the army *The Man who had All The Luck* is his first novelistic play. *The Crucible* is a kind of modern parable. *Memory of Two Mondays* and *A View from the Bridge* are focussed on the commonman.

The Misfits is the effect of maladjustment in a matrimonial alliance. *After the fall* is based on the stream of consciousness technique. 'The Prince' describes family quarrel between two brothers. He died in 2005.

Major Works

Plays

- The Crucible (1953)
- After the Fall (1963)
- Incident at Vichy (1964)
- The Prince (1968)
- Playing for Time (1981)
- Two-way Mirror (1985)
- The American Clock (1980)
- A View from the Bridge (1955)
- The Archbishop's Ceiling (1977)
- A Memory of Two Mondays (1955)

Novel

- The Misfits

Autobiography

- Time Bounds (1987)

Short Story

- I Don't Need You Anymore

Tennessee Williams (1911-1983)

He was born on 26th March, 1911, Palm Sunday in the rectory of Dr Walter Edward, who was his maternal grandfather in Columbus. Palm Sunday is considered holy because on this day Jesus Christ entered Jerusalem. It is the Sunday before Easter. His father had Cornelius Coffin Williams was a man of ancestry.

His mother Edwina Darkin belonged to the Quakers. His father was a travelling salesman for the international shoe company. So, his family lived at Episcapal rectories in Mississippi with his wife's parents.

In 1918, his father got promotion as a sales manager so the family moved to St Louis. This transfer affected both the children because they had lost carefree and natural environment of the rectories. At St Louis, they were ridiculed for their Southern ways and manners. These things brought him and his sister Rose closer to each other. When his brother Darkin was born, he was sent to his maternal grandfather for a year in Clarksdale, Mississippi.

During his study, he studied the books of Dickens, Shakespeare and other writers from his grandfather's library.

When he returned home in St Louis, he found that his family atmosphere had become worse because his father went on quarrelling with his mother continuously. He found solace in the books and type writer of $ 10, which was gifted to him by his mother on his 11th birthday. Soon, he (Nickname-Tom) began to write from his typewriter. He wrote many poems, vignettes, sketches and short stories.

Literary Career and Works

At the University of Missouri, his grandfather Dakin Ralph helped him in admission. He met Hazel Kramer. She had been his intimate friend since his grammar school days in St Louis. At the university, he was the first youngman, who won an honourable mention from the Dramatic Arts Club for his play named *'Beauty is the World'*. He failed in the reserved Officers Training Corps. Being angry his father pulled him out of the school and got him a job at the international shoe company as clerk-cum-typist. He hated this job.

He wrote a comedy named *Cairo, Shanghai, Bombay* to be played in the theatre. This play got some success. At the Washington University in St Louis, he made friendship with Clarkmills Mc Burney. During this period, he wrote a play called *The Magic Tower*. In a play writing contest conducted by the theatre Guild of Webster Grooves, Missouri, he won the first prize for this play. He was introduced to Mummers, a little theatre group of St Louis. He continued to write plays in college.

After years of obseurity Williams got great success with his play *The Glass Menagerie*. He continued to write until his death on 25th February, 1983, by accidental choking.

Major Works

- A Street Care Named Desire (1947)
- Summer and Smoke (1948)
- Eccentricities of a Nightingale (1964)
- The Rose Tattoo (1951)
- Camino Real (1953)
- Cat on a Hot Tin Roof (1955)
- Garden District (1958)
- Sweet Bird of Youth (1959)
- Period of Adjustment (1960)
- Night of the Iguana (1961)
- The Milk Train Doesn't Stop Here Anymore (1962)
- Slapstick Tragedy (1965)
- The Seven Descendants of Myrtle (1968)
- In the Bar of a Toky Hotel (1969)
- Small craft Warnings (1972)
- The Red Devil Sattery Sign (1975)
- Vieux Carree (1977)
- Creve Coeur (1978)
- Clothes for a Summer Hotel (1980).

Eugene O' Neill (1888-1953)

Eugene O' Neill was the greatest dramatist in America. He was born on 16th October, 1888 in an up-town family hotel named Barrett House on Broadway at 43, Street New York.

His father James O' Neill was a famous actor. His mother Ella Quinlan was a beautiful lady, who was a fan of music. Eugene O' Neill would go with his father on his acting tours. He got his early education from Catholic Boarding School. For 6 years, he studied at the Betts Academy. In 1902, he went to Princeton. He took admission in the university, but studied only a year.

Literary Career and Works

Eugene decided to devote himself full-time to writing plays (the events immediately prior to going to the sanatorium are dramatised in his masterpiece, *Long Day's Journey into Night*). O'Neill had previously been employed by the New London Telegraph, writing poetry as well as reporting. O'Neill's first play, *Bound East for Cardiff*, premiered at this theatre on a wharf in Province town Massachusetts.

O'Neill's first published play, *Beyond the Horizon*, opened on Broadway in 1920 to great acclaim, and was awarded the Pulitzer Prize for Drama. His first major hit was *The Emperor Jones*, which ran on Broadway in 1920 and obliquely commented on the US occupation of Haiti that was a topic of debate in that year's presidential election. In the Hairy Ape, the Hero Yank is different from the Aristotlean theory of tragic heroes because he has no tragic flaw yet he meets a sad end. His best-known plays include *Anna Christie* (Pulitzer Prize 1922), *Desire Under the Elms* (1924), *Strange Interlude* (Pulitzer Prize 1928), *Mourning Becomes Electra* (1931), and his only well-known comedy, *Ah, Wilderness!*, a wistful re-imagining of his youth as he wished it had been. In 1936, he received the Nobel Prize for Literature after he had been nominated that year by Henrik Schuck, member of the Swedish Academy. After a ten-years pause, O'Neill's now-renowned play *The Iceman Cometh* was produced in 1946. The following year's *A Moon for the Misbegotten* failed, and it was decades before coming to be considered as among his best works.

He was also part of the modern movement to partially revive the classical heroic mask from ancient Greek theatre and Japanese Noh theatre in some of his plays, such as *The Great God Brown* and *Lazarus Laughed*.

Major Works

- The Iceman Cometh
- Beyond the Horizon (1918)
- Anna Christie (1920)
- The Hairy Ape (1921)
- Desire Under the Elms (1924)
- The Great God Brown (1925)
- Strange Interlude (1926).

Other Dramatists of Contemporary Period

Name	Time Period	Major Works
Christopher Fry	18th December, 1907 - 30th June, 2005	The Boy with a Cart (1939) A Phoenix Too Frequent (1946) The Lady's Not for Burning (1948) Venus Observed (1950) A Sleep of Prisoners (1951) A Yard of Sun (1970) A Ringing of Bells (2001)
Sir Terence Rattigan	10th June, 1911-30th November, 1977	French Without Tears (1936) After the Dance (1939) The Winslow Boy (1946) The Browning Version (1948) The Deep Blue Sea (1952) Separate Tables (1954)
Peter Ustinov	16th April, 1921-28th March, 2004	The Love of Four Colonels (1951) We're No Angles (1955) Romanoff and Juliet (1956)
Peter Levin Shaffer	15th May, 1926-6th June, 2016	The Salt Land (1954) Five Finger Exercise (1958) The Private Ear, The Public Eye (1962) The Royal Hunt of the Sun (1964) Black Comedy (1965) Lettice and Lovage (1986)
John Whiting	15th November, 1917 - 16th June, 1963	No More A - Roving (1947) A Penny for a Song. (1951) The Gates of Summer. (1956) No Why (1957) The Devils. A play (1960)
Robert Oxton Bolt	15th August, 1924 - 21st February, 1995	The Critic and the Heart (1957) The Tiger and the Horse (1960) Gentle Jack (1963) Vivat ! Vivat Regina ! (1971) State of Revolution (1977)
Ann Jellicoe	15th July, 1927 - 31st August, 2017	The Sport of My Mad Mother (1956) The Knack (1961)
Norman Frederick Simpson	29th January, 1919 - 27th August, 2011	A Resounding Tinkle (1957) One Way Pendulum (1959) The Cresta Run (1965)
Brendan Behan	9th February, 1923 - 20th March, 1964	The Quare Fellow (1954) An Giall (The Hostage) (1958) Richard's Cork Leg (1972)
Bernard Kops	28th November, 1926 - Present	The Dream of Peter Mann (1960) Enter Solly Gold (1962) Ezra (1981, about Ezra Pound), Playing Sinatra (1991)
Henry Livings	20th September, 1929 - 20th February, 1998	Big Soft Nellie (1961) Kelly's Eye (1963) Eh? (1964) The Little Mrs Foster Show (1966) The Finest Family in the Land (1970) The Public (1988) Stop The Children's Laughter (1990)
David Mercer	27th June, 1928 - 8th August, 1980	Ride a Cock Horse (1965) Belcher's Luck (1966) A Suitable Case for Treatment (1966) After Haggerty (1970)
Giles Cooper	9th August, 1918 - 2nd December, 1966	Everything In The Garden (1962) The Other Man (1964) Happy Family (1966)
Charles Dyer	17th July, 1928 - Present	The Rattle of a Simple Man (1963) Stair Case (1966) Mother Adam (1970)
David Halliwell	31st July, 1936 - 16th March, 2006	A Who's Who of Flapland (1967) The Three Angles (1970) Bleats from a Brighouse Pleasure Ground (1971)
Joe Orton	1st January, 1933 - 9th August, 1967	Entertaining Mr Sloane (1964) Loot (1966) The Ruffian on the Stair (1967) The Erpingham Camp (1967) What the Butler Saw (1969)
EA Whitehead	3rd April, 1933 - Present	The Foursome (1971) Alpha Beta (1972) The Sea Anchor (1975) Old Flames (1975) Mecca (1977)
Frank Marcus	30th June, 1928 - 5th August, 1996	The Formation Dancers (1964) The Killing of Sister George (1965) Mrs. Mouse, Are You Within ? (1968) Notes On a Love Affair (1972)
Alan Bennett	9th May, 1934 - Present	Forty Years On (1968) Getting On (1971) Habeas Corpus (1973)
Christopher Hampton	26th January, 1946 - Present	When Did You Last See My Mother? (1964) The Philanthropist (1969) White Chameleon (1991) The Talking Cure (2002)
William Douglas Home	3rd June, 1912 - 28th September, 1992	The Chiltern Hundreds (1947) The Reluctant Debutante (1955) The Cigarette Girl (1962) Lloyd George Knew My Father (1972)
Alan Ayckbourn	12th April, 1939 - Present	Relatively Speaking (1967) The Other Half Loves (1970) The Norman Conquests Trilogy (1973) Absurd Person Singular (1975)

EXAM BASED QUESTIONS

1 Where was Brecht when he wrote 'Mother Courage and Her Children'?
(a) Switzerland (b) Sweden
(c) Austria (d) Germany

2 What was the theatre form that Brecht founded?
(a) Post-war theatre (b) Dramatic theatre
(c) In-yer-face theatre (d) Epic theatre

3 What is Mother Courage's real name?
(a) Anna Fierling (b) Adolf Hitler
(c) Anne Doubtfire (d) Kattrin Haupt

4 What is the name of Mother Courage's only daughter in the play 'Mother Courage and Her Children'?
(a) Kattrin (b) Doris Lessing
(c) Eilif (d) Swiss Cheese

5 How did the protagonist get the nickname 'Mother Courage' in the play 'Mother Courage and Her Children'?
(a) By driving through a bombardment to sell some moldy bread
(b) By selling her cart to save her son
(c) By being the only woman to help fight off a catholic invasion
(d) By singing numerous difficult songs in public

6 Which child is Mother Courage's favourite in the play 'Mother Courage and Her Children'?
(a) Kattrin (b) Swiss Cheese
(c) Eilif (d) The Cook

7 How does Mother Courage predict the Sergeant's death in the play's first scene in the play 'Mother Courage and Her Children'?
(a) By making him draw a black cross on a piece of paper
(b) By finding a mystic symbol drawn on his uniform
(c) By reading his tea leaves
(d) By seeing into the future

8 Which of Mother Courage's children works as a paymaster in the play 'Mother Courage and Her Children'?
(a) The Chaplain (b) Kattrin
(c) Eilif (d) Swiss Cheese

9 How many of Mother Courage's children die by the end of the play?
(a) Eilif and Swiss Cheese (2)
(b) Only Eilif (1)
(c) Swiss Cheese and Kattrin (2)
(d) All of them (3)

10 Who finds their fortune through the war in the play 'Mother Courage and Her Children'?
(a) Yvette (b) Eilif
(c) The Cook (d) Swiss Cheese

11 What is Yvette Pottier's occupation in the play 'Mother Courage and Her Children'?
(a) Cook (b) Seamstress
(c) Prostitute (d) Chaplain

12 What does Yvette Pottier wear that Kattrin later steals in the play 'Mother Courage and Her Children'?
(a) Scarf
(b) Hat and red high-heeled boots
(c) Soldier's uniform (d) Lederhosen

13 How does Kattrin attempt to awake the townsfolk in the play 'Mother Courage and Her Children'?
(a) Shooting a harquebus
(b) Banging a drum
(c) Shouting loudly
(d) Chopping a tree with an axe

14 How does courage protect her children in the play 'Mother Courage and Her Children'?
(a) By running away in her cart
(b) By lying about their places of birth
(c) By drawing a knife on the soldiers
(d) By pretending to be a soldier

15 What disability does Kattrin have in the play 'Mother Courage and Her Children'?
(a) She can not walk (b) She is blind
(c) She is dumb (d) She is deaf

16 What does Yvette sing to Mother Courage and Kattrin?
(a) The Song of the Great Souls of the Earth
(b) The Fraternisation Song
(c) The Song of the Great Capitulation
(d) The Song of the House

17 Who does Socrates represent in "The Song of the Great Souls of the Earth" in the play 'Mother Courage and Her Children'?
(a) Swiss Cheese (b) Mother Courage
(c) Eilif (d) Kattrin

18 Why does the Chaplain join the Wagon in the play 'Mother Courage and Her Children'?
(a) Because the Swedish Commander fires him
(b) Because he loves Mother Courage
(c) Because the Catholics launch a surprise attack
(d) Because he is jealous of the Cook

19 How does Mother Courage plan to buy her Wagon out of hock in the play 'Mother Courage and Her Children'?
(a) She will take a loan from Yvette
(b) She will haggle with the One-Eyed Man
(c) She will raise her prices
(d) She will use the money from Swiss Cheese's cashbox

20 Why does the young peasant at Halle finally agree to serve as the enemy soldiers' guide?
(a) Because they threaten his cattle
(b) Because they threaten his family
(c) Because they threaten Kattrin
(d) Because they threaten the wagon

21 With what object does Mother Courage tell her children's fortune in the play 'Mother Courage and Her Children'?
(a) A drum (b) A helmet (c) A bag (d) A bowl

22 Why can the Cook and Mother Courage not bring Kattrin to Utrecht in the play 'Mother Courage and Her Children'?
(a) They have no room for her
(b) They cannot afford to support her
(c) Their customers would not stand the sight of her
(d) All of the above

23 Why is there a momentary declaration of peace in the play 'Mother Courage and Her Children'?
(a) The Kaiser falls (b) The Swedish King falls
(c) Commander Tilly falls (d) The Pope falls

24 How does Mother Courage lose her officers' shirts?
(a) Kattrin uses them to swaddle a baby
(b) The Chaplain uses them to bandage the wounded
(c) Mother Courage uses them to bandage Kattrin
(d) Eilif takes them for his new Lieutenant's uniform

25 What epithet causes Mother Courage to sever ties with the Chaplain in the play 'Mother Courage and Her Children'?
(a) A vulture (b) A whore
(c) A hyena (d) A lice bug

26 What does Mother Courage give Kattrin after she has been disfigured in the play 'Mother Courage and Her Children'?
(a) The drum (b) The red boots
(c) The hedgehog (d) The baby

27 Where do Mother Courage, the Cook, and the Chaplain discuss the politics of the war in the play 'Mother Courage and Her Children'?
(a) Inside the Wagon (b) In front of the Wagon
(c) On the Highway (d) Behind the Wagon

28 Why won't they ring bells for the commander's funeral in the play 'Mother Courage and Her Children'?
(a) Bells sound too celebratory
(b) They destroyed the bells
(c) He hated bells
(d) He doesn't deserve them

29 Why is Mother Courage encouraged to leave the farmhouse quickly and not stay with Kattrin's body?
(a) Soldiers are coming (b) The peasants are angry
(c) She is very rude (d) It's getting dark

30 Why is the cook angry with the Chaplain when he returns?
(a) He told Mother Courage to buy supplies
(b) He is a thief
(c) He is trying to marry Kattrin
(d) He is flirting with Mother Courage

31 Why doesn't Mother Courage have any bandages to help the peasants with?
(a) She sold them all to soldiers
(b) She was robbed
(c) She used them herself
(d) They are impossible to find

32 Why does Mother Courage sing 'The Song of Great Capitulation' in the play 'Mother Courage and Her Children'?
(a) To pass the time
(b) To get money
(c) To calm the soldier
(d) To tell a story

33 Why is Eilif being killed in the play 'Mother Courage and Her Children'?
(a) He's a traitor (b) He attacked peasants
(c) He stole the Chief's wife (d) He is a lazy soldier

34 Verfremdungseffekt is an integral aspect of Brechtian theatre. How would you translate this German term, a device that makes the audience insistently aware that what they're watching is a fiction?
(a) Alienation-effect (b) Audience-effect
(c) Special-effect (d) Equality-effect

35 Who wrote the haunting, wisecracking music for Brecht's The Threepenny Opera (1928), adapted from John Gay's 18th-century The Beggar's Opera?
(a) Kurt Weill (b) Friedrich Holländer
(c) Anton Webern (d) Ralph Vaughan Williams

36 In 1949, Brecht and his second wife Helene Weigel set up their own theatre company, which still exists today. Can you name it?
(a) Berliner Ensemble (b) Deutsche Ensemble
(c) Brecht Ensemble (d) Jelly-Donut Ensemble

37 In Brecht's The Resistible Rise of Arturo Ui – an anti-fascist parable starring Chicago gangsters – a trust named after which vegetable plays a prominent role?
(a) Broccoli
(b) Cauliflower
(c) Broad bean
(d) Artichoke

38 Brecht's Life of Galileo exists in two different versions – the first from 1938, the second revised by the author following the atomic explosions that brought an end to the Second World War. What is the key change he made to the play's conclusion?

(a) Instead of successfully outwitting the inquisition, Galileo recants
(b) Instead of recanting, Galileo successfully outwits the inquisition
(c) The stage is suddenly illuminated by a blinding flash, a reference to Hiroshima
(d) Confronted with the inquisition's torture instruments, he launches into a version of Mack the Knife

39 While in America, Brecht wrote the screenplay for a film directed by Fritz Lang. Can you name it?
(a) The Hangman Must Die
(b) American Guerrilla in the Philippines
(c) Hangmen Also Die!
(d) American Werewolf

40 Brecht's Der gute Mensch von Sezuan (often translated as 'The Good Person of Szechwan') originally went under which title?
(a) Die Ware Liebe (Product Love) .
(b) Die Ware Leben (Product Life)
(c) Der gute Mensch von Birmingham (The Good Person of Birmingham)
(d) Der gute Mensch von Berlin (The Good Person of Berlin)

41 After being blacklisted by Hollywood, Brecht was called before the House Un-American Activities Committee in 1947. What happened at the hearing?
(a) He performed a revolutionary ballad of his own composition
(b) He admitted being a member of the Communist party and asked to be deported from the US
(c) He jumped on top of a desk and cried: 'Long live Lenin!'
(d) He denied being a member of the Communist party, anxious about catching a flight back to Europe

42 Who does McCann and Goldberg accuse Stanley of killing in the play 'The Birthday Party'?
(a) His wife (b) His brother (c) His child (d) His mother

43 At whose deathbed does Goldberg recall being at when talking with McCann?
(a) His wife's (b) His father's
(c) His child's (d) His mother's

44 What does McCann sing for Meg in Act 2, Part 3 in the play 'The Birthday Party'?
(a) An Irish folk song (b) A rap
(c) A hymn (d) An opera

45 As Lenny joins the conversation that Ruth, Lenny, and Teddy have been engaged in after lunch, what subject does Lenny ask Teddy about in the play 'The Homecoming'?
(a) Lenny asks if Teddy makes enough money to support his family
(b) Lenny asks if Teddy is a good father
(c) Lenny asks Teddy why it's taken him so long to visit
(d) Lenny asks a question about being a doctor of philosophy

46 What does Lenny want Max to tell him in the play 'The Homecoming'?
(a) If he was going to inherit the house someday
(b) Why he gets blamed for everything that happens
(c) If his parents were trying to have a baby or if his conception was an accident .
(d) Why no one would ever loan him any money

47 When Teddy comes downstairs while Ruth and Lenny are talking together, what does Lenny do in the play 'The Homecoming'?
(a) He picks up the newspaper and begins reading
(b) He tells Teddy not to interrupt their conversation
(c) He turns on the radio
(d) He asks Teddy to stay for a few more days

48 What does Max ask Teddy in response to the conversation about Ruth and Joey in bed together in the play 'The Homecoming'?
(a) If Ruth has had any affairs since they've been married
(b) If Ruth is a whore
(c) If Ruth cooks or just has sex
(d) If Ruth is a tease to him

49 What does Max give Teddy at the end of the play 'The Homecoming'?
(a) Some advice
(b) A family bible
(c) A picture of his grandfather
(d) A bottle of whiskey

50 When Teddy and Ruth are left alone in the living room, how does he try to convince her to go home with him in the play 'The Homecoming'?
(a) He tells her that she could get her old job back
(b) He says she is making a poor impression on his family
(c) He tells her he wants to leave
(d) He reminds her about her sons

51 Why does Joey protest against the plan for Ruth to become a prostitute?
(a) He doesn't want to share her with a bunch of slobs
(b) She could easily make a lot more money
(c) It won't give her enough time to clean the house
(d) She isn't well

52 What does Ruth tell Lenny about her life before she married Teddy in the play 'The Homecoming'?
(a) She says she was a school teacher
(b) She says she used to always go out in the evenings
(c) She says she used to think she would never marry
(d) She says she was a photographic model

53 When Max and Sam enter as the brothers are discussing Joey's time upstairs with Ruth, what is the first thing Max asks in the play 'The Homecoming'?
(a) If anyone has seen the newspaper
(b) If Teddy is finally leaving
(c) If Joey and Lenny have cleaned up the house
(d) If "the whore is still in bed"

54 What is the last thing Ruth tells Teddy as he leaves at the end of the play 'The Homecoming'?
(a) She tells him he's making a mistake by leaving
(b) She tells him to give her back the money for her ticket
(c) She tells him she will miss him
(d) She tells him not to be a stranger

55 What sound is heard before the curtain rises in the play 'The Death of a Salesman'?
(a) A melody played on a flute
(b) Bagpipes playing a highland lament
(c) Fiddle music reminiscent of the countryside
(d) Stage hands moving sets about

56 What is Willy Loman carrying as he enters the stage in the play 'The Death of a Salesman'?
(a) An attache case and a large sample case
(b) Two large sample cases
(c) A very large sample bag
(d) Take-out meals

57 Why is Happy Loman perhaps less self-assured than Biff in the play 'The Death of a Salesman'?
(a) Happy has never been as loved by their father as Biff
(b) Happy has never had the gratifying social life that Biff has
(c) Happy has never risked failure
(d) Happy has never tasted the success that Biff has

58 'Fearless creatures' populate which place, according to Charley in the play 'The Death of a Salesman'?
(a) White house (b) Stock exchange
(c) Jail cells (d) Colorado ranches

59 Why did Biff not keep in contact with his parents when he was out West in the play 'The Death of a Salesman'?
(a) He was homeless, living on the streets in Oklahoma city
(b) He was moving from place to place without a concrete address
(c) He was in jail
(d) He did not want to have any contact with his father

60 Which is not a sign of the Loman sons' arrested adolescence in the play 'The Death of a Salesman'?
(a) Both men remain in their old bedroom at home
(b) Happy believes that since he can outfight any man he works for, he should be boss
(c) Both men rely on their mother for meals and for laundry
(d) Biff still plays with his football

61 What causes the rift between Biff and Willy Loman in the play 'The Death of a Salesman'?
(a) Biff has unrealistic expectations about his father's success.
(b) Willy finds that Biff has been stealing
(c) Biff finds that Willy is having an affair
(d) Willy is disappointed that Biff refuses to go to college

62 Why does Bernard not help Biff cheat on the Regents exam in the play 'The Death of a Salesman'?
(a) Biff does not show up to the exam at all out of bitterness toward Willy
(b) Bernard neither admires nor respects Biff
(c) It is a state exam, and Bernard could be arrested
(d) Bernard thinks that Biff should do his own work

63 "A man is not a bird to come and go with the springtime." Which character makes this statement in the play 'The Death of a Salesman'?
(a) Charley (b) Biff (c) Linda (d) Happy

64 What does Biff steal from Bill Oliver's office as an adult in the play 'The Death of a Salesman'?
(a) A trophy (b) Seeds
(c) Money (d) A pen

65 What is Bernard's adult occupation in the play 'The Death of a Salesman'?
(a) Police Officer (b) Lawyer
(c) Doctor (d) Writer

66 What Shakespearean play do the main characters of the play 'Rosencrantz and Guildenstern Are Dead' appear in?
(a) King Lear (b) Hamlet
(c) Romeo and Juliet (d) Richard III

67 What is puzzling about the game in the play 'Rosencrantz and Guildenstern Are Dead'?
(a) They do not fully understand the rules
(b) The coin lands on the same side and highly improbable number of times
(c) Rosencrantz is cheating, Unbeknownst to Guildenstern
(d) It requires a minimum of four players, but they are playing with two

68 Who is Ophelia in the play 'Rosencrantz and Guildenstern Are Dead'?
(a) Hamlet's daughter
(b) Rosencrantz's love interest
(c) A young woman in love with Hamlet
(d) Guildenstern's love interest

69 Which of the following is not a reason for Hamlet's strange behaviour in the play 'Rosencrantz and Guildenstern Are Dead'?
(a) Claudius married Hamlet's mother
(b) Claudius killed Hamlet's father
(c) Claudius took Hamlet's throne
(d) Claudius is planning to kill Gertrude

70 Why have Rosencrantz and Guildenstern been sent for in the play 'Rosencrantz and Guildenstern Are Dead'?
(a) To overthrow Claudius
(b) To kill Hamlet
(c) To learn why Hamlet is disturbed
(d) To bring Hamlet back to england to be institutionalised

71 What is the object of the game 'Questions' in the play 'Rosencrantz and Guildenstern Are Dead'?
(a) To ask your opponent as many questions as possible before they fall asleep
(b) To have a conversation entirely composed of questions
(c) All of the above
(d) None of the above

72 How does Hamlet know that Claudius killed his father in the play 'Rosencrantz and Guildenstern Are Dead'?
(a) Hamlet overheard claudius confess to polonius
(b) Gertrude told him
(c) Rosencrantz and Guildenstern told him
(d) His father's angry ghost told him .

73 What is one of the reasons Guildenstern is disturbed about their predicament in the play 'Rosencrantz and Guildenstern Are Dead'?
(a) They cannot remember their past
(b) Nobody will tell them why they have been sent for
(c) Hamlet will not speak to them
(d) All of the above

74 Why are Rosencrantz and Guildenstern sent to apprehend Hamlet?
(a) We are never told
(b) Hamlet has gone mad
(c) Hamlet has killed polonius
(d) All of the above

75 What genre does the play Rosencrantz and Guildenstern Are Dead belong to?
(a) Tragedy (b) Comedy (c) History (d) Morality

76 Which play was written against the backdrop of the rise of Hitler ?
(a) Mother Courage and Her Children
(b) Man Equals Man
(c) Happy End (d) Drums in the Night

77 Which of the following works of Brecht is the version of story of Joan Arc and never staged in his lifetime ?
(a) The Life of Edward II of England
(b) The Duchess of Malfi
(c) Saint Joan of the Stockyards
(d) Downfall of the Egotist Johann Fatzer

78 In which of the following plays, John Arden addressed its antimilitaristic theme with a combination of Brechtian exposition and music hall routines?
(a) Crow (b) Lupercal
(c) Serjeant Musgrave's Dance
(d) None of these

79 Identify from the following the author of 'Live Like Pigs', a play about the settlement of Gypsies in a housing estate, which explores anti-social behaviour?
(a) John Arden (b) Joe Orton
(c) Philip Larkin (d) None of these

80 Harold Pinter's first four plays are
(a) The Caretaker, The Room, The Homecoming, The Birthday Party
(b) The Room, The Dumb Waiter, The Birthday Party, The Caretaker
(c) The Homecoming, The Caretaker, Old Times, Betrayal
(d) The Dumb Waiter, The Caretaker, No Man's Land, Betrayal

81 Which of the following works, which does not belong to Harold Pinter ?
(a) The Dumb Waiter (b) The Last September
(c) Betrayal (d) One for the Road

82 Identify the work which does not belong to 'John Osborne'?
(a) Collected Poems (b) Waiting for Godot
(c) The Lord of the Rings (d) All of these

83 Which play of Osborne focuses on the life and marital struggles of an intelligent and educated but disaffect young man of working class origin, Jimmy Porter, and his equally competent yet impassive upper middle class wife Alison ? It takes inspiration from John's personal life experiences.
(a) The Devil Inside Him (b) Look Back in Anger
(c) Under Plain Cover (d) Watch It Come Down

84 This play is a part of trilogy by Arnold Wesker which describes East End's Jews' search for security, principles and happiness.
(a) Chicken Soup with Barley
(b) Chips with Everything
(c) The Old Ones
(d) Their Very Own and Golden City.

85 Which play of Tom Stoppard is an absurdist, existential tragicomedy and expands upon two minor characters from Hamlet ?
(a) The Real Inspector Hound
(b) Every Good Boy Deserves Favour
(c) Rosencrantz and Guildenstern Are Dead
(d) The Coast of Utopia

86 According to epic theatre, the purpose of a play is ....
(a) to present ideas and invite the audience to make judgement on them
(b) to entertain the audience
(c) to educate the audience
(d) to arouse the spirit of excitement and motivation in the audience

87 The term 'theatre of the absurd' was coined by.......... .
(a) Samuel Beckett (b) Martin Esslin
(c) Antonin Artaud (d) Arthur Adamov

88 ......is known for his anti-Aristotlean epic theatre.
(a) Antonin Artaud (b) Arthur Adamov
(c) Bertolt Brecht (d) Martin Esslin

89 ......is one of Bertolt Brecht's plays which was never staged during his life-time
(a) Mother Courage and Her Children
(b) The Days of the Commune
(c) Trumpets and Drums
(d) Saint Joan of the Stockyards

90 Mother Courage says that she still has ......, which gives her hope to carry on.
(a) Eilif
(b) A husband
(c) Money
(d) Swiss Cheese

91 Which of the following statements is incorrect ?
(a) John Arden was a British marxist playwright
(b) Arden rose to fame with his play, 'Live Like Pigs'.
(c) Arden's wife, Margaretta D'Areys also supported him in his writings
(d) Arden was a critic of Bertolt Brecht for writings

92 Which of the following statements is not true ?
(a) Shelagh Delaney was associated with the theatre of Royal Court.
(b) Her play 'A Taste of Honey' is a beautiful combination of solid realism and romantic dream fantasy.
(c) She also wrote 'Left Handed Liberty'.
(d) The Play 'A Taste of Honey' also discussed 'homosexuality'.

93 Which of the following statements is not correct?
(a) Sir Tom Stoppard is a Czeck-born British Playwright.
(b) His works mainly covered themes of suspense, thrill and vulgarity.
(c) He had been a key playwright of the National Theatre.
(d) 'Every Good Boy Deserves Favour' is a stage play written by Tom Stoppard.

94 Which of the following pairs is incorrectly matched?
(a) The Happy Haven : Arnold Wesker
(b) The Changing Room : David Storey
(c) Rumpole of the Bailey : John Clifford Mortimer
(d) Bingo : Edward Bond

95 Which of the following pairs of play wrights is not matched correctly with its plays ?
(a) Christopher Fry : A Yard of Sun
(b) Sir Terence Rattigan : The Love of Four Colonels
(c) Peter Levin Shaffer : Black Comedy
(d) JohnWhiting : The Devils

Directions (Q. Nos. 96-98) *In the questions given below are two statements labelled as Assertion (A) and Reason (R). In the context of the two statements, which one of the following is correct?*

Codes
(a) Both A and R are true and R is the correct explanation of A
(b) Both A and R are true but R is not the correct explanation of A
(c) A is true but R is false
(d) A is false but R is true

96 **Assertion** (A) A number of theatrical movements arose which rejected the 19th century realist model, choosing instead to play with the language and elements of dramatic convention which had previously been dominant.
Reason (R) These included the Brechtian Epic Theatre, Artaud's Theatre of Cruelty and the so called Theatre of the Absurd.

97 **Assertion** (A) John Arden was typical of a new generation of dramatists who started their careers at royal court.
Reason (R) He used historical events as settings for the evaluation of morality.

98 **Assertion** (A) Tom Stoppard wrote prolifically for TV, Radio, Film and Stage.
Reason (R) He wrote 'The Real Inspector Hound'.

99 Which of the following alternatives has contemporary dramatists in the correct chronological order ?
(a) Ann Jellicoe, Robert Oxton Bolt, Brendan Behan, Norman Frederick Simpson.
(b) Robert Oxton Bolt, Brendan Behan, Norman Frederick Simpson, Ann Jellicoe.
(c) Brendan Behan, Norman Frederick Simpson, Ann Jellicoe, Robert Oxton Bolt.
(d) Norman Frederick Simpson, Brendan Behan, Robert Oxton Bolt, Ann Jellicoe.

100 Which of the following lists of works is in chronological order ?
(a) Forty Years On, The Other Half Loves, The Sea Anchor, The Talking Cure.
(b) The Other Half Loves, The Sea Anchor, The Talking Cure, Forty Years On.
(c) The Sea Anchor, The Talking Cure, Forty Years On, The Other Half Loves.
(d) The Talking Cure, Forty Years On, The Other Half Loves, The Sea Anchor.

101 Match the plays with their dramatists.

List I (Play)	List II (Dramatist)
1. Man Equals Man	A. Bertolt Brecht
2. Serjeant Musgrave's Dance	B. John Arden
3. Chicken Soup With Barley	C. Arnold Wesker
4. The Contracter	D David Storey

Codes
(a) 1-A, 2-B, 3-C, 4-D
(b) 1-D, 2-C, 3-B, 4-A
(c) 1-B, 2-D, 3-A, 4-C
(d) 1-C, 2-A, 3-D, 4-B

102 Match the playwrights with their plays.

List I (Playwright)	List II (Play)
1. Tom Stoppard	A. Forget Me Not Lane
2. John Clifford Mortimer	B. Early Morning
3. Edward Bond	C. Wrong Side of the Park
4. Peter Nichols	D. The Real Inspector Hound

Codes
(a) 1-A, 2-B, 3-C, 4-D (b) 1-D, 2-C, 3-B, 4-A
(c) 1-B, 2-D, 3-A, 4-C (d) 1-C, 2-A, 3-D, 4-B

103 Match the characters with their plays.

List I (Character)	List II (Plays)
1. Kattrin	A. The Home-Coming
2. Stanley	B. Mother Courage and Her Children
3. Ruth	C. The Death of a Salesman
4. Willy Loman	D. The Birthday Party

Codes
(a) 1-A, 2-B, 3-C, 4-D (b) 1-D, 2-C, 3-B, 4-A
(c) 1-B, 2-D, 3-A, 4-C (d) 1-C, 2-A, 3-D, 4-B

104 Match the plays with their playwrights :

List I (Play)	List II (Playwright)
1. Indmissible evidence	A. Harold Pinter
2. The Room	B. Tennessee Williams
3. They Too Arise	C. John Orborne
4. The Magic Tower	D. Arthur Miller

Codes
(a) 1-A, 2-B, 3-C, 4-D (b) 1-D, 2-C, 3-B, 4-A
(c) 1-B, 2-D, 3-A, 4-C (d) 1-C, 2-A, 3-D, 4-B

105 Match the playwrights with their works.

List I (Playwright)	List II (Work)
1. Eugene O' Neill	A. Anna Christie
2. Bernard Kops	B. The Dream of Peter Mann
3. Henry Living	C. Honour and Offer
4. David Mercer	D. A Suitable Case for Treatment

Codes
(a) 1-A, 2-B, 3-C, 4-D (b) 1-D, 2-C, 3-B, 4-A
(c) 1-B, 2-D, 3-A, 4-C (d) 1-C, 2-A, 3-D, 4-B

106 Match the following.

List I (Character)	List II (Play)
1. Ophelia	A. Mother Courage and Her Children
2. Linda	B. The Home-Coming
3. Teddy	C. The Death of a Salesman
4. Yvette	D. Rosencrantz and Guildenstern Are Dead

Codes
(a) 1-A, 2-B, 3-C, 4-D (b) 1-D, 2-C, 3-B, 4-A
(c) 1-B, 2-D, 3-A, 4-C (d) 1-C, 2-A, 3-D, 4-B

107 Match the following.

List I (Play)	List II (Dramatist)
1. The Other Man	A. Joe Orton
2. Stair Case	B. Giles Cooper
3. Who is Who of Flapland	C. Charles Dyer
4. The Ruffian on the Stair	D. David Helliwell

Codes
(a) 1-A, 2-B, 3-C, 4-D (b) 1-D, 2-C, 3-B, 4-A
(c) 1-B, 2-C, 3-A, 4-D (d) 1-C, 2-A, 3-D, 4-B

108 Match the following.

List I (Playwright)	List II (Work)
1. Frank Marcus	A. Getting On
2. Alan Bennet	B. The Cigarette Girl
3. Christopher Hampton	C. Notes On a Love Affair
4. William Douglas Home	D. When Did You Last See My Mother?

Codes
(a) 1-A, 2-B, 3-C, 4-D (b) 1-D, 2-C, 3-B, 4-A
(c) 1-B, 2-D, 3-A, 4-C (d) 1-C, 2-A; 3-D, 4-B

109 In the given series, which one has characters, matched correctly with their plays
(a) Claudius-Rosencrantz and Guildenstern Are Dead,Bernard–The Death of a Salesman, Joey–The Home-Coming, Lulu-The Birthday Party
(b) Claudius– The Death of a Salesman, Bernard–The Home-Coming, Joey–The Birthday Party, Lulu–Rosencrantz and Guildenstern Are Dead.
(c) Claudius– The Home-Coming, Bernard The Birthday Party, Joey-Rosencrantz and Guildenstern Are Dead, Lulu–The Death of a Salesman.
(d) Claudius– The Birthday Party, Bernard–Rosencrantz and Guildenstern Are Dead, Joey–The Death of a Salesman, Lulu–The Home-Coming.

110 In the given series, which one has all the plays matched correctly with their playwrights ?
(a) The Foursome-Eugene O'Neill, Bound East for Cardiff-Arthur Miller, Honours at Down John Osborne, The Entertainer- E.A White Head.
(b) The Foursome–. E.A. White Head, Bound East for Cardiff–Eugene O'Neill, Honours at Dawn-Arthur Miller, The Entertainer-John Osborne.
(c) The Foursome-Arthur Miller, Bound East for Cardiff-John Osborne, Honours at Dawn-Eugene O'Neill, The Entertainer-E.A. White Head.
(d) The Foursome–E.A. White Head, Bound East for Cardiff–Eugene O'Neill, Honours at Dawn– John Osborne, The Entertainer-Arthur Miller.

111 Consider the following statements.
1. Bertolt Brecht was a German Playwright and poet.
2. His first play was Baal.
3. He supported Nazi Movement.
4. 'State' of Revolution was written by him.

Which of the above given are true for Bertolt Brecht?
(a) 1 and 2 (b) 1 and 3
(c) 2 and 3 (d) 3 and 4

112 Consider the following statements.
1. Tom Stoppard is an American playwright.
2. His works cover the themes of human rights, censorship and political freedom.
3. His play 'Rosencrantz and Guidenstern Are Dead has been drawn with Samuel Beckett's Waiting for Godot'.

4. The Play 'Rosencrantz and Guildenstern Are Dead' is dedicated to Viktor Fainberg and Vladimir Bukovsky, two Soviet dissidents expelled to the West.

Which of the above given are correct?

(a) 1 and 2 (b) 2 and 3
(c) 3 and 4 (d) 1 and 3

113 Consider the following statements.

1. Harold Pinter started writing plays in 1947.
2. 'The Room' was his first play.
3. His plays fall under the category of comedy of menace.
4. He received the Nobel Prize for Literature in 2005.

Which of the above given are true ?

(a) 1 and 2 (b) 2 and 3
(c) 3 and 4 (d) 2, 3 and 4

114 Consider the following statements.

1. Arthur Miller is considered one of the greatest American Dramatists.
2. He belonged to a prosperous family of high class.
3. His first play 'Honours at Dawn' won him the University's 'Avery Hopwood Award'.
4. 'Summer and Smoke' was written by him.

Which of the above given is correct?

(a) 1 and 2 (b) 2 and 3
(c) 1 and 3 (d) 3 and 4

115 Consider the following plays.

1. The Emperor Jones
2. Desire under the Elms
3. The Lady's Not For Burning
4. The Sport of My Mad Mother

Which of these belong(s) to Eugene O' Neill?

(a) 1 and 2 (b) 2 and 3
(c) 3 and 4 (d) Only 1

116 "The aim of science is not to open the door to infinite wisdom, but to set a limit to infinite error."

Which of the following dramatists in which of his/her works has had the above lines?

(a) Bertolt Brecht, Life of Galileo
(b) John B. Arden, Rewire Your Brain: Think Your Way to a Better Life
(c) Shelagh Delaney, The Lion in Love
(d) David Storey, Saville

117 "Thousands of years ago, when our ancestors encountered a predatory animal like a lion, it was best to react immediately and not stand around thinking about the lion, admiring its beauty or wondering why it was bothering them instead of tracking down some tasty antelope. Thus, the fast track to the amygdala kept our ancestors alive."

Which of the following dramatists in which of his/her works has had the above lines?

(a) Bertolt Brecht, Life of Galileo
(b) John B. Arden, Rewire Your Brain: Think Your Way to a Better Life
(c) Shelagh Delaney, The Lion in Love
(d) David Storey, Saville

118 "Anything's hard to find if you go around looking for it with your eyes shut."

Which of the following dramatists in which of his/her works has had the above lines?

(a) Bertolt Brecht, Life of Galileo
(b) John B. Arden, Rewire Your Brain: Think Your Way to a Better Life
(c) Shelagh Delaney, The Lion in Love
(d) David Storey, Saville

119 "I dreamt about you last night. Fell out of bed twice"

Which of the following dramatists in which of his/her works has had the above lines?

(a) Shelagh Delaney, A Taste of Honey: A Play
(b) Tom Stoppard, Rosencrantz and Guildenstern Are Dead
(c) John Mortimer, The Summer of a Dormouse
(d) Peter Nichols, A Voyage for Madmen

120 JO: As I was going up Pippin Hill,
Pippin Hill was dirty.
And there I met a pretty miss,
And she dropped me a curtsy.
Little miss, pretty miss,
Blessings light upon you.
If I had half a crown a day,
I'd gladly spend it on you.

Which of the following dramatists in which of his/her works has had the above lines?

(a) Shelagh Delaney, A Taste of Honey: A Play
(b) Tom Stoppard, Rosencrantz and Guildenstern Are Dead
(c) John Mortimer, Paradise Postponed
(d) Peter Nichols, The Rocks

121 "Bletchley said, sweating freshly in the heat of the bus. 'Some of the species adapt, others don't. In effect, when coal is acquired by wholly mechanical means or perhaps isn't even needed at all, people like Batty and his brothers, and Stringer, won't have a function. And when the function ceases so does the species, or those parts of it that can't recognize or create a further function."

Which of the following dramatists in which of his/her works has had the above lines?

(a) Bertolt Brecht, Life of Galileo
(b) John B. Arden, Rewire Your Brain: Think Your Way to a Better Life
(c) Shelagh Delaney, The Lion in Love
(d) David Storey, Saville

122 "We cross our bridges when we come to them and burn them behind us, with nothing to show for our progress except a memory of the smell of smoke, and a presumption that once our eyes watered."

Which of the following dramatists in which of his/her works has had the above lines?

(a) Shelagh Delaney, A Taste of Honey: A Play
(b) Tom Stoppard, Rosencrantz and Guildenstern Are Dead
(c) John Mortimer, The Summer of a Dormouse
(d) Peter Nichols, A Voyage for Madmen

123 "We're more of the love, blood, and rhetoric school. Well, we can do you blood and love without the rhetoric, and we can do you blood and rhetoric without the love, and we can do you all three concurrent or consecutive. But we can't give you love and rhetoric without the blood. Blood is compulsory. They're all blood, you see."

Which of the following dramatists in which of his/her works has had the above lines?

(a) Shelagh Delaney, A Taste of Honey: A Play
(b) Tom Stoppard, Rosencrantz and Guildenstern Are Dead
(c) John Mortimer, Paradise Postponed
(d) Peter Nichols, The Rocks

124 "The ordinary-sized stuff which is our lives, the things people write poetry about—clouds—daffodils—waterfalls—what happens in a cup of coffee when the cream goes in—these things are full of mystery, as mysterious to us as the heavens were to the Greeks."

Which of the following dramatists in which of his/her works has had the above lines?

(a) Tom Stoppard, Arcadia
(b) John Mortimer, Paradise Postponed
(c) John Osborne, Look Back in Anger
(d) Harold Pinter, The Homecoming

125 "Writing about the indignities of old age: the daunting stairway to the restaurant restroom, the benefits of a wheelchair in airports and its disadvantages at cocktail parties, giving the user what he described as a child's-eye view of the party and a crotch-level view of the guests. Dying is a matter of slapstick and pratfalls. The ageing process is not gradual or gentle. It rushes up, pushes you over and runs off laughing. No one should grow old who isn't ready to appear ridiculous."

Which of the following dramatists in which of his/her works has had the above lines?

(a) Shelagh Delaney, A Taste of Honey: A Play
(b) Tom Stoppard, Rosencrantz and Guildenstern are Dead
(c) John Mortimer, The Summer of a Dormouse
(d) Peter Nichols, A Voyage for Madmen

126 "She felt a tightness in her chest and sent for Dr Simcox.
'What's the trouble?'
"Look out there, that's the trouble! It's so green and quiet and it's always bloody raining."
'That's England, Mrs Mallard-Greene. I'm afraid there's no known cure for it."

Which of the following dramatists in which of his/her works has had the above lines?

(a) Shelagh Delaney, A Taste of Honey: A Play
(b) Tom Stoppard, Rosencrantz and Guildenstern Are Dead
(c) John Mortimer, Paradise Postponed
(d) Peter Nichols, The Rocks

127 "Take sex, for instance."
'What do you want me to do with it?'
'Try to be serious for a moment. Take the sex life of our father.'
Even after a couple of brandies he felt extremely reluctant to discuss sex and his father. 'It's something I'd rather not think about,' he said. 'We all come into existence as a result of a momentary embrace by our parents which find impossible to imagine. [...] We all assume we're the result of our own particular immaculate conception."

Which of the following dramatists in which of his/her works has had the above lines?

(a) Tom Stoppard, Arcadia
(b) John Mortimer, Paradise Postponed
(c) John Osborne, Look Back in Anger
(d) Harold Pinter, The Homecoming

128 "One day a Japanese guard came into the 20-year-old Moitessier's cell intending to kill him. He raised his pistol, but they locked eyes until, inexplicably, the guard lowered the pistol and walked away. Now, years later, tenderised by solitude, Moitessier wished he had spared the rat."

Which of the following dramatists in which of his/her works has had the above lines?

(a) Shelagh Delaney, A Taste of Honey: A Play
(b) Tom Stoppard, Rosencrantz and Guildenstern Are Dead
(c) John Mortimer, The Summer of a Dormouse
(d) Peter Nichols, A Voyage for Madmen

129 "Keep Ithaka always in your mind. Arriving there is what you are destined for. But do not hurry the journey at all. Better if it lasts for years, so you are old by the time you reach the island, wealthy with all you have gained on the way, not expecting Ithaka to make you rich. Ithaka gave you the marvelous journey. Without her you would not have set out. . ."

Which of the following dramatists in which of his/her works has had the above lines?

(a) Shelagh Delaney, A Taste of Honey: A Play
(b) Tom Stoppard, Rosencrantz and Guildenstern Are Dead
(c) John Mortimer, Paradise Postponed
(d) Peter Nichols, The Rocks

130 "Jimmy: The injustice of it is almost perfect! The wrong people going
hungry, the wrong people being loved, the wrong people dying!"
Which of the following dramatists in which of his/her works has had the above lines?
(a) Tom Stoppard, Arcadia
(b) John Mortimer, Paradise Postponed
(c) John Osborne, Look Back in Anger
(d) Harold Pinter, The Homecoming

131 "You wouldn't understand my works. You wouldn't have the faintest idea of what they were about. You wouldn't appreciate the points of reference. You're way behind. All of you. There's no point in sending you my works. You'd be lost. It's nothing to do with a question of intelligence. It's a way of being able to look at the world. It's a question of how far you can operate on things and not in things. I mean it's a question of your capacity to ally the two, to relate the two, to balance the two. To see, to be able to see! I'm the one who can see. That's why I can write my critical works. Might do you good...have a look at them...see how certain people can view...things... how certain people can maintain...intellectual equilibrium. Intellectual equilibrium. You're just objects. You just...move about. I can observe it. I can see what you do. It's the same as I do. But you're lost in it. You won't get me being...I won't be lost in it."
Which of the following dramatists in which of his/her works has had the above lines?
(a) Tom Stoppard, Arcadia
(b) John Mortimer, Paradise Postponed
(c) John Osborne, Look Back in Anger
(d) Harold Pinter, The Homecoming

132 "EMMA: We're lovers.
ROBERT: Ah, yes. I thought it might be something like that. Something along those lines.
EMMA: When?
ROBERT: What?
EMMA: When did you think?
ROBERT: Yesterday. Only yesterday. When I saw his handwriting on the letter. Before yesterday I was quite ignorant.
EMMA: Ah. (pause) I'm sorry.
ROBERT: Sorry? (silence) How long?
EMMA: Sometime.
ROBERT: Yes, but how long exactly?
EMMA: Five years.
ROBERT: Five years?"
Which of the following dramatists in which of his/her works has had the above lines?
(a) Harold Pinter, Betrayal
(b) Arthur Miller, Death of a Salesman
(c) Tennessee Williams, Cat on a Hot Tin Roof
(d) Eugene O'Neill, The Great God Brown

133 "JERRY: Look at the way you're looking at me. I can't wait for you. I'm bowled over, I'm totally knocked out, you dazzle me, you jewel, my jewel, I can't ever sleep again, no, listen, it's the truth, I won't walk, I'll be a cripple, I'll descend, I'll diminish, into total paralysis, my life is in your hands, that's what you're banishing me to, a state of catatonia, do you know the state of catatonia? do you? do you? the state of...where the reigning prince is the prince of emptiness, the prince of absence, the prince of desolation. I love you.
EMMA: My husband is at the other side of that door.
JERRY: Everyone knows. The world knows. It knows. But they'll never know, they'll never know, they're in a different world. I adore you. I'm madly in love with you. I can't believe that what anyone is at this moment saying, has ever happened. Nothing has ever happened. Nothing. Your eyes kill me. I'm lost. You're wonderful."
Which of the following dramatists in which of his/her works has had the above lines?
(a) Harold Pinter, Betrayal
(b) Eugene O'Neill, Beyond the Horizon
(c) John Mortimer, Rumpole and the Penge Bungalow Murders
(d) John Osborne, Look Back in Anger

134 "Listen. You know what it's like when you're in a room with the light on and then suddenly the light goes out? I'll show you. It's like this."
He turns out the light.
BLACKOUT"
Which of the following dramatists in which of his/her works has had the above lines?
(a) Harold Pinter, No Man's Land
(b) Arthur Miller, The Crucible
(c) Tennessee Williams, A Streetcar Named Desire
(d) Eugene O'Neill, The Iceman Cometh

135 "When you lead a life of scholarship you can't be bothered with the humorous realities, you know, tits, that kind of thing."
Which of the following dramatists in which of his/her works has had the above lines?
(a) Harold Pinter, Ashes to Ashes
(b) Arthur Miller, A View from the Bridge: A Play in Two Acts
(c) Tennessee Williams, The Milk Train Doesn't Stop Here Anymore
(d) Eugene O'Neill, Long Day's Journey into Night

136 "I don't say he's a great man. Willie Loman never made a lot of money. His name was never in the paper. He's not the finest character that ever lived. But he's a human being, and a terrible thing is happening to him. So, attention must be paid. He's not to be allowed to fall in his grave like an old dog. Attention, attention must finally be paid to such a person."

Which of the following dramatists in which of his/her works has had the above lines?
(a) Harold Pinter, Betrayal
(b) Arthur Miller, Death of a Salesman
(c) Tennessee Williams, Cat on a Hot Tin Roof
(d) Eugene O'Neill, The Great God Brown

137 "Life, woman, life is God's most precious gift; no principle, however glorious, may justify the taking of it."
Which of the following dramatists in which of his/her works has had the above lines?
(a) Harold Pinter, No Man's Land
(b) Arthur Miller, The Crucible
(c) Tennessee Williams, A Streetcar Named Desire
(d) Eugene O'Neill, The Iceman Cometh

138 "Just remember, kid, you can quicker get back a million dollars that was stolen than a word that you gave away."
Which of the following dramatists in which of his/her works has had the above lines?
(a) Harold Pinter, Ashes to Ashes
(b) Arthur Miller, A View from the Bridge: A Play in Two Acts
(c) Tennessee Williams, The Milk Train Doesn't Stop Here Anymore
(d) Eugene O'Neill, Long Day's Journey into Night

139 "I've got the guts to die. What I want to know is, have you got the guts to live?"
Which of the following dramatists in which of his/her works has had the above lines?
(a) Harold Pinter, Betrayal
(b) Arthur Miller, Death of a Salesman
(c) Tennessee Williams, Cat on a Hot Tin Roof
(d) Eugene O'Neill, The Great God Brown

140 "I don't want realism. I want magic! Yes, yes, magic! I try to give that to people. I misrepresent things to them. I don't tell the truth, I tell what ought to be the truth. And it that's sinful, then let me be damned for it!"
Which of the following dramatists in which of his/her works has had the above lines?
(a) Harold Pinter, No Man's Land
(b) Arthur Miller, The Crucible
(c) Tennessee Williams, A Streetcar Named Desire
(d) Eugene O'Neill, The Iceman Cometh

141 "We all live in a house on fire, no fire department to call; no way out, just the upstairs window to look out of while the fire burns the house down with us trapped, locked in it."
Which of the following dramatists in which of his/her works has had the above lines?
(a) Harold Pinter, Ashes to Ashes
(b) Arthur Miller, A View from the Bridge: A Play in Two Acts
(c) Tennessee Williams, The Milk Train Doesn't Stop Here Anymore
(d) Eugene O'Neill, Long Day's Journey into Night

142 "Why am I afraid to dance, I, who love music and rhythm and grace and song and laughter? Why am I afraid to live, I who love life and the beauty of flesh and the living colours of the Earth and sky and sea? Why am I afraid to love, I who love love?"
Which of the following dramatists in which of his/her works has had the above lines?
(a) Harold Pinter, Betrayal
(b) Arthur Miller, Death of a Salesman
(c) Tennessee Williams, Cat on a Hot Tin Roof
(d) Eugene O'Neill, The Great God Brown

143 "Suppose I was to tell you that it's just beauty that's calling me, the beauty of the far off and unknown, the mystery and spell which lures me, the need of freedom of great wide spaces, the joy of wandering on and on----in quest of the secret which is hidden over there----beyond the horizon?"
Which of the following dramatists in which of his/her works has had the above lines?
(a) Harold Pinter, Betrayal
(b) Eugene O'Neill, Beyond the Horizon
(c) John Mortimer, Rumpole and the Penge Bungalow Murders
(d) John Osborne, Look Back in Anger

144 "To hell with the truth! As the history of the world proves, the truth has no bearing on anything. It's irrelevant and immaterial, as the lawyers say. The lie of a pipe dream is what gives life to the whole misbegotten mad lot of us, drunk or sober."
Which of the following dramatists in which of his/her works has had the above lines?
(a) Harold Pinter, No Man's Land
(b) Arthur Miller, The Crucible
(c) Tennessee Williams, A Streetcar Named Desire
(d) Eugene O'Neill, The Iceman Cometh

145 "It wasn'the fog I minded, Cathleen. I really love fog..... It hides you from the world and the world from you. You feel that everything has changed, and nothing is what it seemed to be. No one can find or touch you any more."
Which of the following dramatists in which of his/her works has had the above lines?
(a) Harold Pinter, Ashes to Ashes
(b) Arthur Miller, A View from the Bridge: A Play in Two Acts
(c) Tennessee Williams, The Milk Train Doesn't Stop Here Anymore
(d) Eugene O'Neill, Long Day's Journey into Night

Directions (Q. Nos. 146-150) *Read the passage and answer the questions that follow*

American Heritage

By the beginning of the twentieth century, far fewer Native Americans lived in New England than had inhabited the region three centuries earlier. Many of these people lived in small groups on portions of the vast lands that their ancestors had long occupied.

Though, fewer in number, they honoured their tribal identities, cherished their ancestral homelands, and wanted to keep what they had. To help ensure the survival of their heritage, Native Americans eventually turned to the US legal system.

Leading the way, were two Maine tribes, the Penobscots and the Passamaquoddies, whose histories differed little from that of most other Native Americans in the region. Like other tribes, their populations had decreased markedly over the centuries; so had the amount of land they controlled. After the American Revolution, state governments had imposed treaties that transferred much of the Native Americans' land to state and private ownership. With the loss of their land base and its resources, tribal populations tended to disperse as individuals sought opportunities elsewhere. In Maine, the Penobscots and Passamaquoddies held only two small reservations by the early twentieth century.

Thus matters stood for the next half century. Then, in 1957, a federal program designed to encourage the assimilation of Native American peoples threatened to terminate the Penobscot and Passamaquoddy tribal governments. Tribal leaders resisted. With the help of other Native American activists, they thwarted the attempt and in the process strengthened tribal authority. It was a small victory, but one that encouraged them to seek other ways of asserting their rights.

The changing social and political climate of the 1960s and 1970s prompted many Native American groups to insist that the federal government live up to its treaty commitments. Alert to the claims being made by other Native Americans, Penobscot and Passamaquoddy leaders saw their opportunity. The two tribes had fought for the colonists in the American Revolution, and in return the Continental Congress had promised protection of their hunting grounds. By the twentieth century, those vast tracts had become extremely valuable. The two tribes decided to sue the federal government for the return of about two-thirds of the state of Maine.

The land, they claimed, had been taken illegally, first by Massachusetts (of which Maine formed a part unit 1820) and then by Maine. They based their case on the Indian Trade and Intercourse Act of 1790. That law, which made the federal government a trustee of Native American property, declared that no transfers of Indian land were valid unless approved by Congress. Since the tribes could demonstrate that state treaties involving more than 1,200,000 acres of land taken from them had never been submitted to Congress, they had a strong case. Much to the surprise and chagrin of many observers, the suit was successful. In 1980, the Maine Indian Settlement Act awarded the tribes a substantial monetary settlement that enabled them to buy land, develop tribal businesses, and provide employment for tribal members.

In winning the case, the Penobscots and passamaquoddies had established an important legal precedent. Other New England tribes would soon use that precedent to assert their own rights and to reassert the full dimensions of the cultural heritage their forebearers had handed down to them.

146 **Which of the following statements from the first paragraph of the passage best expresses the main idea of that paragraph?**

(a) By the beginning of the twentieth century, far fewer Native Americans lived in New England than had inhabited the region three centuries earlier
(b) Many of these people lived in small groups on portions of the vast lands that their ancestors had long occupied
(c) Though fewer in number, they honored their tribal identities, cherished their ancestral homelands, and wanted to keep what they had
(d) To help insure the survival of their heritage, Native Americans eventually turned to the U.S. legal system

147 **Which of the following statements best expresses the author's point of view?**

(a) The author has tremendous respect for the basic fairness of the US legal system
(b) The author is surprised that the Native Americans of New England took so long to assert their rights
(c) The author admires what the Penobscots and Passamaquoddies were able to accomplish
(d) The author believes that the lawsuits brought by the Penobscots and Passamaquoddies had little merit

148 **According to information presented in the passage, which of the following most influenced Penobscot and Passamaquoddy leaders to sue the federal government?**

(a) Their continuing opposition to federal efforts to encourage the assimilation of Native American groups
(b) Changes in the federal law governing the transfer of tribally owned lands
(c) Demands by other Native American groups during the 1960s and 1970s that the government honour its treaty commitments
(d) The tribes' contributions to the patriot cause during the American Revolution

149 **Which of the following statements provides the best evaluation of the author's credibility?**

(a) The author's misconceptions about Native American history strongly detract from the credibility of the passage
(b) Despite confusion about how the U.S. legal system works, the author presents an informed accounts of the lawsuits discussed in the passage
(c) The author's bias against the federal government strongly detracts from the credibility of the passage
(d) Although clearly sympathetic to Native Americans, the author presents a balanced accounts of their efforts to assert their rights

150 Which of the following statements best summarises the main points of the passage?

(a) After centuries of population decline and land loss, Native Americans in New England employed the legal system to assert their rights and strengthen the economic bases of their communities

(b) The 1960s and 1970s marked an important turning point in Native American history, particularly in New England, where major tribes reclaimed lands they had lost centuries earlier

(c) Even though the Penobscots' and Passamaquoddies' lands had been reduced to two small reservations, the tribes assumed an important leadership role among the Native Americans of New England

(d) The legal initiatives of the Penobscots and Passamaquoddies made the state of Maine a leading center of Native American activism throughout the closing decades of the 20th century

PREVIOUS YEARS' QUESTIONS

December 2018

Directions (Q. Nos. 1-3) *The following is an extract from a famous play. Read it carefully to answer questions that follow.*

Maid: [from the hall doorway] ma'am; a lady to see you -

Nora: all right, let her come in.

...the maid shows in MRS LINDE, dressed in travelling clothes, and shuts the door after her.]

Mrs. Linde: [in a dispirited and somewhat hesitant voice Hello, Nora.

Nora: hello

Mrs Linde: you don't recognise me.

Nora: no, I don't know - but wait, I think - what! what! is it really you?

Mrs Linde: Yes its me

Nora: Kristine! to think I didn't recognise you. But then, how could I?

How you've changed, Kristine!

Mrs. Linde: Yes, no doubt I have. In nine - ten long years.

Nora: It is so long since we met! yes, it's all of that. Oh, these last eight years have been a happy time, believe me. And so now you've come in to town, too. Made the long trip in the winter. That took courage.

Mrs Linde : I just got here by ship this morning.

Nora: To enjoy yourself over Christmas, of course. Oh,how lovely !yes, enjoy ourselves we'll do that but take your coat off. You are not still cold? There now, lets get cozy here by the stove. No, the easy chair there! I will take the rocker here. Yes, now you have your old look again; it was only in that first moment. You are a bit more pale, Kristine - and may be a bit thinner.

Mrs Linde: And much, much older Nora.

Nora: Yes, perhaps a bit older; a tiny, tiny bit; not much at all. Oh, but thoughtless me, to sit here, chattering away. Sweet, can u forgive me?

Mrs Linde: What do you mean?

Nora: You have become a widow.

Mrs Linde: Yes, three years ago.

Nora: I knew it, of course; I read it in the papers. Oh, Kristine, you must believe me; I often thought of writing you then, but kept postponing it, and something always interfered.

Mrs Linde: Nora, dear, I understand completely.

Nora: It was awful of me. You poor thing, how much you have gone through. And he
left you nothing?

Mrs Linde: No

Nora: And no children?

Mrs Linde: No.

Nora: Nothing at all then?

Mrs Linde: Not even a sense of loss to feed on.

Nora: But how could that be?

Mrs Linde: Oh, sometimes it happens, Nora.

Nora: So completely alone. How terribly hard that must be for you. I have three lovely children. You can't see them now; they are out with the maid.

1 "Not even a sense of loss to feed on" implies that

(a) Mrs Linde is given over to feeding on sorrow
(b) Mrs Linde is completely devoid of all feeling
(c) Mrs Linde is sentimentally attached to an irretrievable past
(d) Mrs Linde's severance from her tragic pair is total

2 Identify the play of which this section is an excerpt.

(a) A Doll's House by Henrik Ibsen
(b) The Cherry Orchard by Anton Chekhov
(c) Wit by Margaret Edson
(d) The importance of Being Earnest by Oscar Wilde

3 Which of the following description best applies to the above extract?

(a) Friends comparing notes and counting losses in a meeting sudden and unanticipated.
(b) the sense of loss inevitable with the passage of time and the imperceptible dissolution of the conventional marriage.
(c) A chance meeting between old friends which leaves one puzzling over the inexplicable losses the other suffered.
(d) A meeting of two friends - one married, the other unmarried after a gap of years.

4 Match the plays to their setting:

A. Krapp's last tape	1. a country road;a tree
B. Happy days	2. bare interior; two small windows high up; grey light
C. Waiting for Godot	3. expanse of scorched grass forming a low mound; blinding light
D. Endgame	4. a laze evening in future, white light.

Codes
(a) A-3, B-4, C-1 D-2
(b) A-2, B-3, C-1, D-4
(c) A-4, B-3, C-1, D-2
(d) A-2, B-4, C-3, D-1

5 Arnold Wesker is associated with 'kitchen-sink drama', a rather condescending title applied to the then new-wave realistic drama depicting the family lives of working-class characters on stage and in broadcast plays. Two of the following plays begin with one character doing the dishes in a kitchen sink. Identify the pair.
1. the Kitchen
2. chicken soup with barley
3. roots
4. menace

The right combination according to the codes is
(a) 2 and 4 (b) 1 and 4 (c) 1 and 2 (d) 2 and 3

July 2018

6 Bertolt Brecht's Mother Courage and Her Children presents the war-torn Europe as its protagonist as she follows troops with her canteenwagon. What is the real name of Mother Courage?
(a) Paula Danckert
(b) Anna Fierling
(c) Lane Vanstone
(d) Jani Lauzon

November 2017

7 Pinter once admitted that he first became aware of the dramatic power of the pause from seeing a popular American comedian. Which one?
(a) Bob Hope
(b) W. C. Fields
(c) Jack Benny
(d) Charlie Chaplin

8 In Pinter's Birthday Party Stanley is terrorised by two visitors to a seaside boarding house. Identify the two
1. McGrath 2. Goldberg
3. McCann 4. Robinson

The right combination according to the codes is
(a) 1 and 2 (b) 2 and 3
(c) 1 and 4 (d) 2 and 4

9 Which pair of plays belongs to the early career of Harold Pinter?
I. The Caretaker II. One for the Road
III. Celebration IV. The Room

The right combination according to the codes is
(a) I and III (b) II and III
(c) I and IV (d) II and IV

January 2017

10 In Bertolt Brecht's Mother Courage and Her Children, which song does Yvette sing to Mother Courage and Kattrin?
(a) "The Song of the Great Souls of the Earth"
(b) "The Fraternisation Song"
(c) "The Song of the Great Capitulation"
(d) "The Memorial Song"

11 Which play by Tom Stoppard set in Zurich during the First World War presents a character's interactions with James Joyce as he was writing Ulysses, Tristran Zara during the rise of Dadaism, and Lenin leading up to the Russian Revolution, all of whom were living in Zurich at that time?
(a) After Magritte
(b) Dirty Linen
(c) Artist Descending a Staircase
(d) Travesties

12 Which play by Tom Stoppard has a play within the play?
(a) Enter a Free Man
(b) The Real Inspector Hound
(c) Jumpers (d) Night and Day

13 What is occupation of Max's son, Lenny, in Harold Pinter's The Home coming?
(a) Boxer (b) Butcher (c) Pimp (d) Cab driver

July 2016

14 Bertolt Brecht's concept of alienation was a rejection of the idea that realism was the only mode of art a critique of capitalist society should produce. Alienation is best described as
(a) making the audience feel that they do not belong
(b) distancing artistic conventions to prevent an emotional catharsis
(c) scripting unnatural behaviour on stage
(d) a rejection of capitalism or the market

15 Identify two of the following written by Christopher Fry.
I. French Without Tears
II. The Lady's Not For Burning
III. Venus Observed
IV. The Deep Blue Sea

The right combination according to the codes is
(a) II and III (b) I and III (c) II and IV (d) I and IV

December 2015

16 Which of the modern plays by a British playwright actually puts Shakespeare as character on stage?
(a) Edward Bond's Bingo
(b) Harold Pinter's Mountain Language
(c) Terence Rattigan's Inspector Calls
(d) Joe Orton's Loot

July 2015

17 Who among the following playwrights was the son of a gardener?
(a) Harold Pinter (b) Joe Orton
(c) Tom Stoppard (d) Edward Bond

June 2014

18 Match the following.

	List I (Dramatist)		List II (Play)
A.	Arnold Wesker	1.	Jumpers
B.	Harold Pinter	2.	What the Butler Saw
C.	Joe Orton	3.	The Room
D.	Tom Stoppard	4.	Roots

Codes

	A	B	C	D
(a)	3	2	4	1
(b)	1	2	4	3
(c)	4	3	2	1
(d)	4	3	1	2

ANSWERS

Objective Questions

1. (b)	2. (d)	3. (a)	4. (a)	5. (a)	6. (c)	7. (a)	8. (d)	9. (d)	10. (a)
11. (c)	12. (b)	13. (b)	14. (c)	15. (c)	16. (b)	17. (a)	18. (c)	19. (d)	20. (a)
21. (b)	22. (d)	23. (b)	24. (b)	25. (c)	26. (b)	27. (d)	28. (b)	29. (a)	30. (a)
31. (a)	32. (c)	33. (b)	34. (a)	35. (a)	36. (a)	37. (b)	38. (a)	39. (c)	40. (a)
41. (d)	42. (a)	43. (b)	44. (a)	45. (d)	46. (c)	47. (c)	48. (d)	49. (c)	50. (d)
51. (a)	52. (d)	53. (d)	54. (d)	55. (a)	56. (b)	57. (c)	58. (c)	59. (c)	60. (c)
61. (c)	62. (c)	63. (c)	64. (d)	65. (a)	66. (b)	67. (b)	68. (c)	69. (d)	70. (c)
71. (c)	72. (d)	73. (a)	74. (c)	75. (b)	76. (a)	77. (c)	78. (c)	79. (a)	80. (b)
81. (b)	82. (d)	83. (b)	84. (a)	85. (c)	86. (a)	87. (b)	88. (c)	89. (d)	90. (a)
91. (d)	92. (c)	93. (b)	94. (a)	95. (b)	96. (a)	97. (b)	98. (c)	99. (d)	100. (a)
101. (a)	102. (b)	103. (c)	104. (d)	105. (a)	106. (b)	107. (c)	108. (d)	109. (a)	110. (b)
111. (a)	112. (b)	113. (d)	114. (c)	115. (a)	116. (a)	117. (b)	118. (c)	119. (a)	120. (a)
121. (d)	122. (b)	123. (b)	124. (a)	125. (c)	126. (c)	127. (b)	128. (d)	129. (d)	130. (c)
131. (d)	132. (a)	133. (a)	134. (a)	135. (a)	136. (b)	137. (b)	138. (b)	139. (c)	140. (c)
141. (c)	142. (d)	143. (b)	144. (d)	145. (d)	146. (c)	147. (c)	148. (c)	149. (d)	150. (a)

Previous Years' Questions

1. (d)	2. (a)	3. (c)	4. (c)	5. (d)	6. (b)	7. (c)	8. (b)	9. (c)	10. (b)
11. (d)	12. (b)	13. (c)	14. (b)	15. (a)	16. (a)	17. (b)	18. (c)		

CHAPTER 06

Pre-Chaucerian and The Age of Chaucer Poetry

Poetry is vast with various forms, features and elements. 'Beowulf' is considered to be the oldest example of poetry dating back to eighth century. Romances in poetic verse form were popular during the Anglo-Norman period. Chaucer is called the father of English poetry. His most acclaimed collection of poems 'The Canterbury Tales' narrates various pilgrimage tales.

English Poetry

Poetry is a form of writing that uses not only words, but also form, patterns of sound, imagery and figurative language to convey the message. In general, poetry deals with particular things in concrete language, since our emotions most readily respond to these things. From the poem's particular situation, the reader may then generalise; the generalities arise by implication from the particular. In other words, a poem is most often concrete and particular; the 'message,' if there is any, is general and abstract; it's implied by the images. Images, in turn, suggest meanings beyond the mere identity of the specific object. Poetry 'plays' with meaning when it identifies resemblances or makes comparisons between things.

Elements of Poetry

Elements of poetry can be classified into following types

Rhythm

It is a literary device which demonstrates the long and short patterns through stressed and unstressed syllables particularly in verse form.Rhythm in writing acts as beat does in music. The use of rhythm in poetry arises from the need that some words are to be produced more strongly than others. They might be stressed for longer period of time. For example from *Romeo Juliet* by Shakespeare

"Two households, both alike in dignity,
In fair Verona, where we lay our scene,
From ancient grudge break to new mutiny,
where civil blood makes civil hands unclean.
From forth the fatal loins of these two foes,
A pair of star-cross'd lovers take their life; "

In this Chapter

- *English Poetry*
- *Pre-Chaucerian Age*
- *Anglo-Norman Poets*
- *Age of Chaucer*
- *Alliterative Revival*
- *Other Poets of the Age of Chaucer*

Rhyme

A rhyme is a repetition of similar sounding words occurring at the end of lines in poems or songs. A rhyme is a tool utilising repeating patterns that brings rhythm or musicality in poems which differentiate them from prose which is plain. A rhyme is employed for the specific purpose of rendering a pleasing effect to a poem which makes its recital an enjoyable experience. For example

> Had we but world enough, and time,
> "This coyness, lady, were no crime.
> We would sit down and think which way,
> To walk and pars our long love's day."

Alliteration

Alliteration is derived from Latin's 'Latira'. It means 'letters of alphabet'. It is a stylistic device in which a number of words, having the same first consonant sound, occur close together in a series. For example from Samuel Taylor Coleridge's *The Rime of the Ancient Mariner*

> "*The fair breeze blew, the white foam flew,*
> The furrow followed free.
> We were the first that ever burst
> Into the silent sea."

In the above lines we see alliteration ('b', 'f' and 's') in the phrases 'breeze blew', 'foam flew', 'furrow followed', and 'silent sea'.

Assonance

Assonance takes place when two or more words close to one another repeat the same vowel sound but start with different consonant sounds. Assonance is primarily used in poetry in order to add rhythm and music, by adding an internal rhyme to a poem. For example William Wordsworth employs assonance to create an internal rhyme in his poem *Daffodils*:

> "I wandered lonely as a cloud
> That floats on high o'er vales and hills,
> When all at once I saw a crowd,
> A host, of golden daffodils;
> Beside the lake, beneath the trees,
> Fluttering and dancing in the breeze..."

Stanza

In poetry, a stanza is a division of four or more lines having a fixed length, meter or rhyming scheme. Stanza divides a poem in such a way that does not harm its balance but rather it adds beauty to the symmetry of a poem. Moreover, it allows poets to shift their moods and present different subject matters in their poems. Stanzas are a series of lines grouped together and separated by an empty line from other stanzas. They are the equivalent of a paragraph in an essay. One way to identify a stanza is to count the number of lines.

Traditional English language poems have the following kinds of stanzas

(i) **Couplet** It consists of two rhyming lines having the same meter.

(ii) **Tercet** A tercet comprises three lines following a same rhyming scheme a a a or have a rhyming pattern a b a. Sir Thomas Wyatt introduced tercet in 16th century.

(iii) **Quatrain** It is a form of stanza having four lines popularised by a Persian poet, Omar Khayyam, who called it a Rubai. It has common rhyming schemes a a a a, a a b b, a b a b.

(iv) **Quintain** It also referred to as cinquain is a stanza of five lines which may be rhymed or unrhymed and has a typical stress pattern. Its invention is attributed to Crapsey.

(v) **Sestet** It is a kind of stanza that consists of six lines. It is the second division of Italian or sonnets of Petrarch following an octave or the first division comprising eight lines.

Imagery

It means to use figurative language to represent objects, actions and ideas in such a way that it appeals to our physical senses. For example Imagery of light and darkness is repeated many times in Shakespeare's *Romeo* and *Juliet*

> "O, she doth teach the torches to burn bright!
> It seems she hangs upon the cheek of night
> Like a rich jewel in an Ethiope's ear;"

Romeo praises Juliet by saying that she appears more radiant than the brightly lit torches in the hall. He says that at night her face glows like a bright jewel shining against the dark skin of an African. Through the contrasting images of light and dark, Romeo portrays Juliet's beauty.

Diction

It can be defined as style of speaking or writing determined by the choice of words by a speaker or a writer. For example Keats in his *Ode to the Grecian Urn* uses formal diction to achieve a certain effect.

> 'Heard melodies are sweet, but those unheard Are sweeter:
> therefore, ye soft pipes, play on'

Notice the use of formal 'ye' instead of informal 'you'. The formality here is due to the respect the urn inspires in Keats. In the same poem he says:

> 'Ah, happy, happy boughs! that cannot shed.
> Your leaves, nor ever bid the spring adieu.'

It is more formal to use 'adieu' than to say 'goodbye'.

Kinds (Genres) of Poetry

There are three types of poetry

1. **Narrative Poetry** A poem that tells a story, and has the elements of a story. Often narrative poems have a rhyme scheme. For example: *The Raven* by Edgar Allen Poe
2. **Dramatic Poetry** A poem where the speaker is someone other than the poet himself. A dramatic poem often includes characters and dialogue. A dramatic monologue is often from a fictional character's point of view. For example: *Meeting At Night* by Robert Browning.
3. **Lyrical Poetry** It is any poem with one speaker (not necessarily the poet) who expresses strong thoughts and feelings. Most poems, especially modern ones, are lyric poems.

Other Forms of Poetry

Other than three types of poetry, there are some other forms of poetry. *These are*

Sonnet

The word sonnet is derived from the Italian word 'sonetto'. It means a small or little song or lyric. In poetry, a sonnet has 14 lines. Each line has 10 syllables. It has a specific rhyme scheme. Generally, sonnets are divided into different groups based on the rhyme scheme they follow. The Italian, or petrarchan sonnet, named after Francesco petrarch, the Italian poet was introduced into English poetry in the early 16th century by Sir Thomas Wyatt. Its fourteen lines break into an octane which usually rhymes abbaabba, and a sestet which may rhyme xyzxyz or xyxyxy or any multiple variations possible using or two or three rhyme sounds. The English sonnet, developed by Henry Howard, Earl of Surrey, consists of three quatrains and a couplet i.e. it rhymes abab cdcd efefgg, also popularised by Shakespeare and now known as Shakespearean sonnet.

Ode

It is a literary technique that is lyrical in nature, but not very lengthy. You have often read odes in which poets praise people, natural scenes and abstract ideas. It is highly solemn and serious in its tone and subject matter and usually is used with elaborate patterns of stanzas. However, the tone is often formal. For example Ode to the Confederate Dead by Allen Tate

"Row after row with strict impunity
The headstones yield their names to the element,
The wind whirrs without recollection;
In the riven troughs the splayed leaves. Pile up, of nature the casual sacramen
To the seasonal eternity of death..."

Epic

An epic poem is a long, usually book length that has a heroic or adventurous theme, can sometimes be related to mythology. For example Homer's *Odyssey*, John Milton's Paradise Lost.

Elegy

A melancholic poem in which poet laments the death of a subject, however, consoles towards the end is called elegy. For example Gary R. Hess', *1983*

In 1983
On the day of changes, a child was born
This child did not see the world...

Epitaph

A small poem used as an inscription on tombstone of a dead person. For example Ben Jonson's *On My First Sonne*

"Farewell, thou child of my right hand, and joy,
My sin was too much hope of thee, loved boy..."

Free Verse

It consists of non-rhyming lines, without any metrical pattern, but follows a natural rhythm. For example *Come Slowly, Eden* by Emily Dickinson

Come slowly, Eden
Lips unused to thee.
Bashful, sip thy Jessamines,
As the fainting Bee,
Reaching late his flower,
Round her chamber hums, Counts his nectars
Enters, And is lost in balms!

Ballad

It is a type of narrative poem that narrates a story, often talks about folk or legendary tales. It may take a form of moral lesson or a song.For example *Tam Lin* is an example of a popular (traditional) ballad.

'O I forbid you, maiden all, That wears gold in your hair,
To come or go by Carterhaugh
For young Tam Lin is there.

Limerick

This is a type of humorous poem with five anapestic lines in which first, second and fifth lines have three feet and third and fourth have two feet with a strict rhyme scheme of aabba. For example *From To Miss Vera Beringer* by Lewis Carroll

"There was a young lady of station
'I love man' was her sole exclamation
But when men cried, 'You flatter'
She replied, 'Oh! no matter
Isle of Man is the true explanation."

Figurative/Connotative Devices

Figurative devices are certain words or the phrases that add essence and clarity to poem. *Some of the important figurative devices are discussed below*

Simile It is the rhetorical term used to designate the most elementary form of resemblances: most similes are introduced by 'like' or 'as.' These comparisons are usually between dissimilar situations or objects that have something in common, such as 'My love is like a red, red rose.'

Metaphor A metaphor leaves out 'like' or 'as' and implies a direct comparison between objects or situations. 'All flesh is grass.'

Synecdoche It is a form of metaphor, which in mentioning an important (and attached) part signifies the whole (e.g. 'hands' for labour).

Metonymy It is similar to synecdoche; it's a form of metaphor allowing an object closely associated (but unattached) with an object or situation to stand for the thing itself (e.g. the crown or throne for a king or the bench for the judicial system).

Symbol A symbol is like a simile or metaphor with the first term left out. 'My love is like a red, red rose' is a simile, if through persistent identification of the rose with the beloved woman, we may come to associate the rose with her and her particular virtues. At this point, the rose would become a symbol.

Allegory It can be defined as a one to one correspondence between a series of abstract ideas and a series of images or pictures presented in the form of a story or a narrative. For example, George Orwell's Animal Farm is an extended allegory that represents the Russian Revolution through a fable of a farm and its rebellious animals.

Personification It occurs when you treat abstractions or inanimate objects as human, that is, giving them human attributes, powers, or feelings (e.g., 'nature wept' or 'the wind whispered many truths to me.)'

Irony It takes many forms. Most basically, irony is a figure of speech in which actual intent is expressed through words that carry the opposite meaning.

Paradox It is usually a literal contradiction of terms or situations.

History of Poetry in English

English poetry has witnessed a long and worthy history. Poets began writing in Old English as early as the seventh century, but the most famous Old English poem, *Beowulf*, has been dated to the eighth century. *Beowulf* deals with the adventures of a brave warrior in Pre-Christian Europe. He kills two monsters, becomes a king and then kills a dragon before dying of his wounds. *Beowulf* is an example of a heroic epic, a long narrative poem that mixes history and legend. There were other heroic epics written at this time, but only parts of them have survived. Poetry from this time, very rarely rhymed, but often used alliteration, in which a sound is repeated throughout each line.

Poetry in English has witnessed various stages in different periods. *These are*

The Middle Ages

There were many poets writing in English during the Middle Ages. Poetry from this time was often religious or romantic in nature. The long poem *Sir Gawain and the Green Knight* is about a quest taken up by one of the knights of King Arthur's court. It deals with the common romantic themes of honour and chivalry. *Piers Plowman*, a poem written by William Langland, is an allegory about the search for a religious life. Perhaps the most famous poet from this period is Geoffrey Chaucer, whose collection of poetic stories, *The Canterbury Tales*, are still taught to children in schools.

Renaissance Effect

After the Renaissance, English poets began experimenting with new styles of writing. The poet Thomas Wyatt wrote sonnets, an Italian style of poetry in which each poem consists of fourteen rhyming lines. Other poets, such as Thomas Campion, wrote songs in which their poetry was set to music. Edmund Spenser returned to the old, heroic style when he wrote *The Faerie Queene*, a long poem dealing with the adventures of several questing knights. John Donne, who is considered one of the Metaphysical Poets, wrote intelligent poetry in which themes such as love and death were explored through metaphors.

The Romantic

At the end of the eighteenth century, English poetry went through a Golden Age. Many poets from this time belonged to the Romantic movement, in which creative expression was given absolute importance and many of the constraints and rules of earlier poetry were done away with. Lord Byron was a poet and adventurer. He wrote masterpieces such as *Don Juan* and *Childe Harold's* Pilgrimage before he died in Greece fighting against the Ottoman Empire. John Keats wrote some of the most beautiful love poems in the English language and died when he was only twenty-five.

William Wordsworth, the 'harbinger of nature' wrote a lot of poetry of nature and brought a turn-around in the style and the thought process of his successors.

Samuel Taylor Coleridge suffered from poor health and depression and was addicted to opium, but wrote astonishingly complex and captivating poems such as the famous *Rime of the Ancient Mariner*.

Percy Bysshe Shelley wrote poetry influenced by classical mythology and was an early advocate of pacifism and vegetarianism. He died in a storm at sea before he was thirty years old. The lives of many Romantic poets were characterised by tragedy, but they wrote some of the most enduring and popular poems in the English language.

The Victorian Poetry

The Victorian poets and the Pre-Raphaelites followed the Romantic poets. Alfred, Lord Tennyson was the Poet Laureate of England for many years, and wrote lyrical poems characterised by perfect and precise use of the English language. Elizabeth Barrett Browning wrote religious poetry with a modern bent. William Butler Yeats was an Irish poet whose poems were full of symbolism as well as beautiful imagery. His poems were often inspired by Irish legends, and he was awarded the Nobel Prize in Literature in 1923.

Modern Age

The twentieth century saw the birth of the Modernist movement in English poetry. TS Eliot wrote shockingly original poems that dealt with bleak and existential themes, but were still strangely beautiful and compelling. Ezra Pound was a friend of TS Eliot and another prominent poet who was concerned with the clarity and precision of the English language. Perhaps the most famous poet from this period was Dylan Thomas. He wrote at the same time as the Modernists, but isn't considered a Modernist poet. His poems are known for their unique imagery and virtuosic use of words and rhythm.

The appeal of poetry is universal and for people who are learning English as a second language, English poetry can be easier to read than novels, and more interesting than articles or essays. Epic poems such as *Beowulf* and *The Faerie Queene* are probably not a good place to start, but poems by the Romantic and Victorian poets are often simple and easy to understand, while still being examples of beautiful and refined English.

Pre-Chaucerian Age

With the Norman conquest of England, beginning in 1111, the Norman language predominantly replaced the Anglo-Saxon language as a written literary language. The new aristocracy spoke mainly Norman, and this became the standard language of courts, parliament and polite society. Therefore this age is also called Anglo-Norman period. As the invaders integrated, their language and literature mingled with that of the natives: the Oil dialect of the upper classes became Anglo-Norman and Anglo-Saxon underwent a gradual transition into Middle English.

While Anglo-Norman or Latin was preferred for high culture, English literature did not completely die out and a number of important works illustrate the development of the language. Around the turn of the 13th century, Layamon wrote his *Brut*, based on *Roman de Brut* by Wace's 12th century Anglo-Norman epic of the same name; Layamon's language is recognisably Middle English, though his prosody shows a strong Anglo-Saxon influence. Other transitional works were preserved as popular entertainment, including a variety of lyrics, romances, lais and religious writings. With time, the English language regained prestige, and in 1362 it replaced French and Latin in Parliament and courts of law.

It was with the 14th century that major works of English literature began to appear once again; these include the so-called Pearl Poet's Pearl, Patience, Cleanness, and Sir Gawain and the Green Knight; Langland's political and religious allegory Piers Plowman; Gower's Confessio Amantis; and the works of Chaucer who is the most highly regarded English poet of the Middle Ages and was seen by his contemporaries as a successor to the great tradition of Virgil and Dante. Chaucer established himself as the greatest poet of the period and came to be known as the father of English poetry in the later stages.

Literature of the Anglo-Norman Period

During the Anglo-Norman period, old English poetry totally disappeared. English began to be discarded in favour of French and Latin. Writings in the English vernacular began to be disregarded and French became established as the natural speech of the cultivated and the high-born.

In contrast with the strength and somberness of Anglo-Saxon poetry, the Normans brought to England, bright and romantic tales of love and adventure. English literature inevitably felt the influence of the Norman French. In poetry, e.g. the Anglo-Saxon versification gave way to regular meter and rhyme. In subject matter, too, the change was great.

The French had developed the chivalric system to a point of brilliance and elaborateness unknown in England. Romance became a popular literary form, indicating the age to be a chivalric rather than heroic one. Breton lays were developed by writers like Marie de France and Chrétien de Troyes into the form known as 'romance.' Romance was the most popular narrative genre for late medieval readers. These romances were mostly borrowed from Latin and French sources. They deal with the stories of King Arthur, The War of Troy and The Mythical Doings of Charlemagne and of Alexander the Great.

Apart from romances, other principal genres were the chronicles, and other moral literature. Historical writing was popular both in Normandy and in the rest of the Continent and although, after the Norman Conquest, Latin replaced English for use in documents and chronicles, examples of both are found in Anglo-Norman. Religious houses caused lives of native saints to be written and The Fourth Lateran Council of 1215 led to the compilation of moral and instructive works. Thus, social and political differences between the two countries prevented Anglo-Norman literature from being a mere provincial imitation of French.

Romance in Anglo-Norman Period

Romance denotes a type of literature that flourished from the 12th to the 14th centuries. Romance was a popular genre in the Anglo-Norman period. It replaced Anglo-Saxon heroic poetry to become one of the most thriving modes in the Anglo-Norman period. Medieval romances signified a style of heroic prose and verse narrative that was popular in the aristocratic circles. The romances usually involved stories about marvel-filled adventures, often of a knight errant portrayed as having heroic qualities, who goes on a quest.

Jean Bodel, author of the Chanson des Saisnes (Song of the Saxons) classified medieval romances into three main categories: The Matter of France, The Matter of Britain and The Matter of Rome.

The Matter of France

Stories from the Matter of France deal with the legendary adventures of Charlemagne, the 9th century. Christian emperor of the West. French *Chansons de Geste* (Song of deeds) are a group of epic poems composed by trouvères and produced in Northern France. These are concerned with war and heroism. One of the most famous stories from the Matter of France is the *Chanson de Roland*, which tells the story of Roland's courageous fight against hopeless odds, ending with the hero's death.

Jane Anderson Jones divides the matter of France romances into two broad groups. The first group, concerning the story of Otuel, contains such romances as *Otuel, The Sege of Melayne* and *Roland and Vernagu*, while the second group, concerned with the story of Ferumbras, contains such romances as *The Sowdone of Babylone* and *Sir Ferumbras*.

Few important romances of France are as follows

- Otuel
- The Sege of Melayne
- Roland and Vernagu
- Sir Ferumbras
- The Sowdone of Babylone

Otuel

Otuel was composed around 1330 in East Midlands. .The main theme of this romance is the battles fought between Christians and Saracens. It is a Saracen knight, who arrives at Charlemagne's court in Paris with a message from the powerful Saracen Emperor Garcy. The Emperor demands that Charlemagne surrender France and abandon Christianity.

The French however refuse, as a result of which Otuel and Roland agree to fight a duel. Both of them fight fiercely. Roland realises his opponent could be a valuable ally and offers him to adopt Christianity and marry Charlemagne's daughter Belisant. Suddenly, a miracle happens and a white dove appears on Otuel's helmet. Interpreting it as a good omen, Otuel accepts the offer.

He joins Charlemagne's army and they travel to Lombardy to attack Garcy. Garcy laments Otuel's treachery and tries to capture him. However, with God's help, the French knights' achieve victory and many Saracens overcome and flee. At the end, Garcy is captured and later surrenders before Charlemagne.

The Sege of Melayne

It is considered part of the Otuel group of Charlemagne romances. It was written in 12-line rhyming stanzas. Central figure of this romance is Bishop Turpin. According to Alan Lupack, "Turpin is pictured as an unswerving defender of the faith. He demands high standards and correct action from those around him and even more from himself. Nor is he afraid to use the spiritual or political power of his religious position." The main story concerns how Lombardy was conquered by the Saracens.

The Matter of Britain

The Matter of Britain romances are the most famous category of romance. Stories from the matter of Britain are mainly based on the life of King Arthur and his Knights of the Round Table. They derive from French Arthurian legends. The characters of the Matter of Britain are heroic Knights, whose superiority is reflected not only in their physical strength and in the defence of values, but especially in the fidelity to their own individual destiny: Famous Arthurian romances include Robert Wace's Geste des Bretons (Deeds of the Britons) and Chretien de Troyes' and The Knight of the Cart.

Few important romances of Britain are as follows

- Sir Degare
- Sir Orfeo
- The Earl of Toulouse
- Emare
- Geste des Bretons
- The Knight of the Cart

Sir Degare

Sir Degare is a 14th century verse romance. It carries features of a Briton Lay. According to some scholars, the poem is supposed to be based upon a lost Breton lay, Lai d'Esgaré.

The story concerns Degare, who becomes a proficient knight after being abandoned at birth. Degare goes in search of his parents and unwittingly marries his mother. Degare fights with his father until he reveals the truth about himself. At the end, Degare's parents marry and he marries the daughter of widowed King of Litel Bretaygn.

Sir Orfeo

Sir Orfeo is a 13th century romance composed by an unknown Celtic author. It is a reworking of the classical myth of the great musician Orpheus and his wife Eurydice. The romance narrates the tale of King Orfeo, a harp player without equals among the contemporary harp players. His wife, Heurodis, is abducted by the fairy King, but Orfeo, through his harp playing, manages to bring her back to the land of mortals.

The poem was probably translated from a French romance of the kind called a Breton lay. " Few features of the story suggest that the source story had been Anglicised. *e.g.,* Orpheus becomes Orfeo, an English king although he's a harpist. The Gods Pluto and Juno become humanised to serve as parents. Traciens becomes Winchester and Orfeo favours the election of a successor by Parliament". The poem contains authentic fairy lore, including the strong traditional association of fairies with the dead.

The Matter of Rome

The Matter of Rome deals with classical stories, the mighty exploits of Alexander, the Great, the Trojan War, the Siege of Thebes, the Siege of Troy, the Adventures of Aeneas etc. It represents the ancient classical culture, as seen through medieval eyes and was primarily aimed at instruction. These romances were derived from conventions of courtly love, which began in the love lyrics of Provence.

Examples of Matter of Rome include Benoit de Sainte-Maure's Roman de Troie.

Few important romances of Rome are as follows

- Roman de Troie
- Roman de Eneais
- Roman de Thebes
- Roman de Alexander

Roman de Eneias

- It is a French romance written by an anonymous Norman poet probably between 1155 and 1160.
- According to Kathryn Talarico, it is "One of the earliest 'romances' in the 12th century meaning of the term and is one of the most curious admixtures of influences of both Virgil and Ovid".
- The story taken from Virgil's Aeneid concerns Eneas, shipwrecked and stranded, who lands in Carthage-an extraordinary city ruled by Dido, an extraordinary woman.

Roman de Thebes

- It is believed to be an adaptation of the epic Thebais by the late Latin poet Statius. It is composed in the 12th century, the poem consists of around 10000 lines. Its main theme is fratricidal combat.
- The story describes how the curse of Oedipus was passed on to his two sons, Etiocles and Polynices, who fight war with each other over who shall rule Thebes.

Miscellaneous Romances

There are many romances, which fall outside the purview of the above mentioned categories. This category of miscellaneous romances is based on various themes and of varying quality.

Few important miscellaneous romances are as follow

- Floris and Blancheflour
- Chevalere Assigne
- Sir Cleges
- Roberd of Cisyle
- King Edward and the Shepherd

Floris and Blancheflour

Floris and Blancheflour is a verse romance composed around 1250. It was probably adapted from a 12th century French original. This romance tells the story of a Christian lady, who has been captured by the Saracens. The Saracens, recognising her nobility make her a lady-in-waiting to their queen. Both the lady and the queen bear children on the same day, during a festival of flowers: A daughter Blancheflour is born to the lady, while the queen bears a son, Floris. Both the children are brought up together and eventually fall in love.

Fearing that they will marry, the king decides to execute Blancheflour. His queen persuades him to send Floris away instead, hoping that the separation will dull their love. The king gets a false tomb erected to convince Floris that Blancheflour has died. When Floris tries to kill himself, the queen finally reveals the truth. Floris goes in search to seek Blancheflour, while his parents give him a cup and a magic ring for protection. Both are united at Babylon and eventually married.

Sir Cleges

It was written in the 14th century, *Sir Cleges* is a chivalric verse romance. It is composed in 12-line tail-rhyme stanzas. The plot concerns Sir Cleges, one of Uther Pendragon's knights and his wife, Clarys. Both of them give alms generously and hold annual feasts.

However, after some years, their wealth depletes and they sell off their property. On Christmas eve, Cleges discovers that one of his cherry trees is miraculously covered in fruit. He worries that it is a bad omen, but Clarys urges him to take the fruit to Uther's court in Cardiff. At the court, none of the ushers or stewards let him enter. However, on seeing the cherries, they agree, in return for one a third of whatever reward is offered by the king.

As his reward, Cleges asks the king to administer twelve blows with his staff. The king reluctantly agrees and Cleges divides his 'reward' between the porter, the usher and the steward. When the reason for his strange request is eventually revealed, the king and his court are delighted. King Uther gives Cardiff Castle and other goods to Cleges, makes him his steward and his son a squire.

Anglo-Norman Poets

Philippe de Thaun

Philippe de Thaun was an Anglo-Norman poet, possibly from the area around Caen in Normandy, who was active in the early 13th century. He is considered to be the earliest Anglo-Norman poet of the period. From one of his works, we get the information that he was patronised by Adelaide of Louvaine, Queen of Henry I.

He is known for two poems. The first is *Livre des Creatures*, which is a treatise on astronomy. It was probably written around 1119. It is a treatise on 'creatures' in the sense of being about created things. The text is also called the 'Comput' from its focus on numbers; it deals with numbers in the calendar and in astronomy, as well as numbers of religious or mystical significance. His second work, which is more popular is the allegorical *Bestiaire*. It is believed to have been written after 1121. Composed of some 1570 lines, the poem is written in the Anglo-Norman dialect. It is a book of natural history containing descriptions of various animals alongwith brief moralisations.

Benoit de Sainte Maur

Benoit de Sainte-Maure was a 12th century French poet. He was patronised by Henry II. His *Roman de Troie* (The Romance of Troy), was a source for later works set during the Trojan War, such as Chaucer's Troilus and Criseyde. Consisting of around 30000 lines, this work is mainly a paraphrase of the history of the Phyrgian Dares.

Another major work, by Benoit, is a long verse *Chronique des ducs de Normandie.* A large portion of it is a paraphrase of the Latin histories of Dudo St Quentin and Guillaume de Jumieges. Composed of around 44000 lines, it begins with the creation of the world and ends with the death of Henry I.

Jordan Fantosme

Jordan Fantosme was an Anglo-Norman poet and chronicler. He was probably an Italian (named Giordano Fantasma), who came to England in the train of Henry of Blois. He is believed to have been the spiritual chancellor of the diocese of Winchester.

He is known for the historical poem *La Chronique de Jordan Fantosme* (Chronicle of the War between the English and the Scots in 1173 and 1174). Written in Latin, the poem describes the barons' revolt against King Henry II and William the Lion's Scottish incursions into Northern England in 1173-1174. Matthew Strickland refers to this poem as of "Primary importance for the study of war, diplomacy and knighthood, in the Anglo-Norman world."

Chretien de Troyes

Chretien de Troyes was a French poet, who is known for the five Arthurian romances he wrote in the 12th century. Information about Chretien comes almost solely from indirect evidence in his works and scholarly speculation has led to much controversy on this subject. Chretien was a court poet, probably attached to the court of the count and countess of Champagne.

Chretien's tales, written in the vernacular, followed the appearance in France of Wace's *Roman de Brut* (1155), a translation of Geoffrey of Monmouth's *Historia regum Britanniae,* which in.troduced Britain and the Arthurian legend to continental Europe.

Chretien's romances were probably composed between 1160 and 1180. They were imitated by other French poets and were translated and adapted frequently during the next few centuries as the romance continued to develop as a narrative form.

His five romances are *Erec; Cliges; Lancelot* (ou Le Chevalier a la Charrette); *Yvain* (ou Le Chevalier au lion) and *Perceval* (ou Le Conte du Graal). *Erec* is about an Arthurian knight, who is put to various trials to claim the love of Enide. *Cliges* is about the knight Cliges and his love for his uncle's wife, Fenice. *Lancelot* deals for the first time with the love affair of Guinevere and Lancelot. *Yvain* centers on a knight, who is exiled from the favours of his lady and required to perform a number of heroic deeds before regaining her. His last unfinished romance *Perceval* is dedicated to his patron Philip, Count of Flanders. It narrates the adventures and growing pains of the young knight Perceval. *Chretien de Troyes* might also have written a non-Arthurian tale Guillaume d'Angleterre, based on the legend of St Eustace.

Marie de France

Marie de France was the earliest French poet of the 12th century. Her actual birth date is not known. She was born in Normandy, France. The exact city of her birth is not known, but the area of Normandy is about 50 miles outside of Paris. Marie de France later moved to England. She was perhaps a half-sister of Henry II (r 1154-1189). She is considered by many to be Marie, daughter of Geoffrey IV of Anjou, who was the father of Henry II. De France wrote in Anglo-Norman, the dialect spoken among the aristocracy of England and large parts of Northern France.

She was part of a generation of writers (notable among them *Chretien de Troyes*), who were in the process of inventing the French verse romance.

She is best known for her *Lais*, which are short narrative or lyrical poems, usually in octosyllabic couplets, intended to be sung. This poetic and musical form was popular among the poets (trouveres) of Northern France. Marie's lays are written in eight-syllable rhyming couplets. The *Lais* range from 118-1184 lines in length.

Marie is known for her fables. She has written 103 short fables with a prologue and epilogue. Half of the fables written by Marie are derived from Aesop's fables. 63 of the fables came originally from Marie herself. Most of Marie's fables are about beasts. Only one-third of her fables include human characters. Marie de France's fables tell a moral lesson. Her fables are meant to set examples.

Lais of Marie de France

The Lais of Marie de France is a collection of 12 narrative poems that were written sometime in the 12th century. The subject of the Lais is love and courtliness. De France's *Lais* have been considered by many to be the first significant collection of medieval courtly romance. The *Lais* begins with a 'Prologue', in which Marie states her reason for composing the lais and confesses her hope that her audience will enjoy the work.

Marie de France's Lais

- Guigemar
- Equitan
- Le Fresne (The Ash Tree)
- Bisclaveret (The Were Wolf)
- Lanval
- Les Deus Amanz (The two lovers)
- Yonec
- The Nightingale
- Milum
- Chaitivel (The Unfortunate One)
- Chevrifoil (Honey Suckle)
- Eliduc

Notable Anglo-Norman Poems

The Owl and the Nightingale

The Owl and the Nightingale is a popular medieval English poem written probably in the 13th century. It takes the form of a spirited dispute between two birds on the subject of the relative beauty and merit of their songs. It is composed of approximately 2000 lines of verse in rhymed, octosyllabic couplets, this allegorical and didactic poem is usually ascribed to Master Nicholas of Guildford, about whom little is known.

The Owl and the Nightingale is the earliest example in Middle English of a literary form known as debate poetry. The Nightingale opens the debate, chiding the Owl as a creature of the night, a bird that loves the dark and hence is evil. After the Owl's successful retort, she accuses the latter of singing only of woe.

Cursor Mundi

Cursor Mundi (Runner of the world) is an anonymous Middle English poem written in North of England around 13-14th century. containing 30000 lines, this poem relates the history of the world as recorded in the Old and New Testaments. It is written in form of eight-syllabled couplets.

The poem begins with a Prologue, in which the poet provides the rationale behind his undertaking. Men desire to read old romances of Alexander, Julius Caesar, Greece, Troy, Brut, Arthur, of Tristram, Sweet Ysoude and others. But better than tales of love is the story of the Virgin. He states that all men take delight in their *paramours*; but the best lady of all is the Virgin Mary. Whoever devotes himself to her, finds true and lasting love. Therefore, the poet will compose a work in her honour.

Religious and Moral Writing in the Anglo-Norman Period

According to AR Waller and AW Ward, "The religious writings of the time may be divided into 4 sections, according to the aims, which they severally have in view. The purport of the first is to teach Biblical history; the second to exhort to holier living; the third is connected with the religious life of women; the last with the Virgin cult and mysticism." The earliest translation of a book of Bible was by Sanson de Nanteuil, who translated into verse the proverbs of Solomon, with commentary. Nanteuil devoted 11000 lines of verse to the Proverbs of Solomon for Lady Adelaide de Condé, wife of a Lincolnshire baron.

An anonymous author wrote *The Poema Morale*, a sermon in the South-Eastern dialect around the year 1170. Concerned with the sins of the people, the sermon was very popular for a long time. Composed in the form of a poem, it stands in the homiletic tradition of the period, but it reveals at the same time a sincere personal element in that the persona, a wise old man, wishes others to profit from his experience. The *Ormulum or Orrmulum* was a popular outlay of the Holy Book, written by an English monk named Orm (or Ormin). It was a collection of homilies on the Gospels consisting of almost 19000 lines of Middle English verse. Though of little literary interest, the work is invaluable to philologists studying Middle English phonology and tracing the development of English through the Norman conquests.

The Fourth Lateran Council (1215) made acquisition of theological knowledge necessary for the laymen and clergy. The Fourth Lateran Council was summoned on 19th April, 1213 to meet in November 1215. It was attended by numerous bishops and abbots of the church as well as priors and even chapters of churches and of religious orders namely Cistercians, Premonstratensians, Hospitallers and Templars and the kings and civil authorities throughout Europe. At this council, it was decided that annual confessions should be made obligatory and bishops should be more attentive towards their teaching.

To fulfill these conditions, a large number of religious works that discussed the basic elements of Christianity were published. St Edmund of Abingdon wrote *Speculum Ecclesiae* ('Mirror of Holy Church'), widely read in England and elsewhere in the 13th and 14th centuries. The work provides a comprehensive plan for achieving spiritual perfection.

Love Rune by Thomas of Hales is one of the earliest successful religious poems of the period. The work was probably composed for a girl, who devoted herself to God. In this poem, a Maid of Christ chooses her lover the Heavenly Bridegroom. The work elevates love of Christ above earthly love.

Age of Chaucer

The Age of Chaucer covers the period from 1340 to 1400. It was a period of transition and turbulence. This age was a meeting ground of two divergent periods—the old and the new, the Medieval and the Renaissance. Though the spirit of the middle ages had not yet passed away, the seeds of modernity were being sown. This period witnessed remarkable social, religious and political changes.

It was in this period that the crucial Hundred Years War between England and France took place. This war awakened English nationalism and gave rise to a national consciousness. The victories of Edward and the Black Prince on French soil during the Hundred Years War gave a feeling of national pride and self-respect to the people of England. This period marked the beginning of a new language and literature. English came to its own because of the great works done by Chaucer, William Langland and Wycliffe, who wrote in English. The various dialects of Middle English spoken in the 14th century were similar to Modern English. In 1362, a statute ordained that English would be the language of law courts.

There was also growth of trade and commerce. Feudalism was beginning to break down and features of money economy came into being. There was rise of the 'burgesses' who organised themselves into craft guilds. The church's authority began to be questioned with reformers like Wycliffe. Wycliffe voiced the discontent of common people and tried to awaken the conscience of society. The 14th century was marked by widespread protests and rebellions against Feudal institutions and royal authority.The way was prepared by the wars of kings, which depleted the royal treasury and led to unjust taxation on common people.

In general, the Age of Chaucer witnessed a series of uprisings and agitations, which led to a churning of the society and paved the way for a new society.

Characteristics of Chaucerian Age

Edward Albert sums up the main characteristics of Chaucerian age, According to him, "A curious modern note begins to be apparent at this period. There is a sharper spirit of criticism, a more searching interest in man's affairs and a less child like whinl and a less complacent acceptance of the established order. The vogue of the romance, though it has by no means gone, is passing and in Chaucer it is derided. The freshness of the romantic ideal is being superseded by the more acute spirit of drama, which even at this early time is faintly foreshadowed.

Another more modern feature that at once strikes the observer is that the age of anonymity is passing away. Though many of the texts still lack named authors, the greater number of books can be definitely ascribed. Moreover, we have for the first time a figure of outstanding literary importance, who gives to the age the form and pressure of his genius."

Social and Cultural Aspects

14th century society was still very much divided into the three traditional estates, those who pray (the Church), those who fight (the nobility) and those who work (everyone else). The church was the most powerful institution and owned a third of the property. Taken together, the crown, the nobility and the church owned about 75% of English land.

The three estates lasted until the middle of the 14th century, when new classes based solely on professions began to rise. The mercantile class was introduced, which consisted of merchants and was considered an urban middle-class. The rise of this middle class, in turn, led to the disintegration of French cultural hegemony. Another new class was the intellectuals, which broke off from the first estate, the church.

Economic Aspects

The economy of medieval England was overwhelmingly agricultural. Chaucer's age was a period of continuous economic upheaval. Due to the Black Plague, population had reduced and the economy had declined. The Hundred Years' War also contributed to depleting the national treasury and had an adverse impact on the economy of that time.

During the 14th century, towns began to function as commercial centres, but long distance trade was still undeveloped. There was rise of the merchant class and formation of trade guilds. Craftsmen, artisans and merchants formed organisations that regulated most aspects of its members businesses.

Wool industry became an important sector. The woolen industry moved into rural areas, where raw material for processing was available. Instead of exporting wool to Flanders, the English began to make cloth themselves on a large scale. The town of bath was important in this respect, since it had a developing wool industry.

During Chaucer's age, peasants began to realise their worth and started demanding better wages and reforms. The Peasants Revolt is a manifestation of that. Money began to replace labour services.

Religious Aspects

The office of the pope was still extremely powerful and the church was a major social and cultural force of the period. Papacy had the power to appoint bishops. People had to resort to the services of the priests to communicate with God. Priests had to be paid to say masses or release souls from Purgatory. The king, too employed clerical ministers and paid them by church preferments.

However, The Black Death disorganised the church by thinning the ranks of the clergy. In Chaucer's Age, the position of church began to be gradually undermined and people for the first time began to show signs of discontent against the churchmen. The laity questioned the special privileges and the vast amount of wealth available to the clergy.

The Heresy or religious revolt appeared in England. Unlike earlier heresies, this time it was led by a prominent member of the establishment: John Wycliffe, an Oxford scholar, a theologian of the first rank. Wycliffe became a big threat to the church in the last decades of the century. Lollardy, a movement instigated by John Wycliffe, began to question the church's claim to be the sole authority on matters of religion. Lollardy posed a serious problem for the church because a number of nobles took Wycliffe's ideas from the confines of Oxford University out into the political world.

Important Events of the Age of Chaucer

The Hundred Years' War (1337-1453)

The accession of Edward III marked the beginning of that struggle with France popularly known as "The Hundred Years' War" a title which explains itself.

The Hundred Years' War was a series of wars between England and France. The main cause of the Hundred Year's War was a dynastic struggle for the French throne. Following the death of Philip IV and his sons, Louis X, Philip V and Charles IV, the Capetian Dynasty came to an end. Since, no direct male heir existed, Edward III of England, Philip IV's grandson by his daughter Isabella, asserted his claim to the throne. This was rejected by the French nobility, who preferred Philip IV's nephew, Philip of Valois.

The war is commonly divided into three phases separated by truces: the Edwardian Era War (1337-1360), the Caroline War (1369-1389) and the Lancastrian War (1415-1453).

Edwardian Era

The Edwardian War was the first phase of the Hundred Years' War lasting from 1337 to 1360, from the outbreak of hostilities until the signing of the Treaty of Bretigny. During this phase, Edward III's army defeated the French at the Battle of Crecy in 1346 and again in 1356 at the Battle at Poitiers.

Caroline War

The Caroline War was the second phase of the Hundred Years' War between France and England, following the Edwardian War. It was named after Charles V of France, who resumed the war after the Treaty of Bretigny was signed in 1360. He wanted to get back everything that France had lost and his attempts proved successful. He defeated the English several times because of civil crisis and internal conflicts in England.

Lancastrian War

The Lancastrian War was the third phase of the Anglo-French Hundred Years War. It lasted from 1415, when Henry V of England invaded Normandy, to 1429, when English successes were reversed by the arrival of Joan of Arc. The phase was so-named because it had its beginnings in the plans of Henry IV, the first of the House of Lancaster to sit on the English throne.

Result of the War Though, France is believed to have won the last major battle of the Hundred Years' War, both France and England emerged as major nation states.

Effect of the War The increased expenditure on war meant increased taxes on common people. This led to social unrest in England. It is estimated that 40% of England's priests died in the epidemic. This left a large gap, which was hastily filled with underqualified and poorly trained applicants, which accelerated the decline in church power and influence that culminated in the English Reformation.

The Black Death (1348-50)

Black Death or the Bubonic Plague was one of the most devastating pandemic in human history. It spread across Europe in 1347 and killed more than four million people. It was caused by the bacterium Yersinia pestis that circulates among wild rodents, where they live in great numbers and density. The first outbreak of plague swept across England in 1348-49. The plague killed between 30-40% of the entire population of England. Peasants fled their fields. Livestock were left to fend for themselves and crops left to rot.

Effect of Black Death

Black Death resulted in many social changes. Since population decreased, labour too became less. The remaining peasants and labourers, who had survived started demanding increased wages. Therefore, peasants benefitted through increased employment options and higher wages. Society became more mobile, as peasants moved to accept work, where they could command a good wage. In some cases, market towns disappeared, or suffered a decline despite the economic boom in rural areas.

The Peasants' Revolt (1381)

The Peasants' Revolt was one of a number of popular revolts in late medieval Europe. The immediate cause of the uprising was imposition of a third poll tax. It was the third time in 4 years that such a tax had been imposed. This crippling tax meant that everyone over the age of 15 had to pay one shilling. Since the people were already reeling under social and economic difficulties as a result of the Black Death, they refused to pay this tax. Non-payment of taxes led to a series of official investigations. The revolt began, when locals reacted to the poll-tax collector and threw him out. From this village, resistance to tax collectors spread to neighbouring villages.

On 7th June, 1381, Wat Tyler joined the uprising in Maidstone and assumed leadership of the Kentish rebels. Led by Tyler, the rebels marched to London. On 14th June, 1381 Richard II agreed to meet Wat Tyler and the rebels. In the meeting, Wat Tyler explained to the king the demands of the rebels. The demands were met by the king.

Unfortunately, these concessions sparked further outbreaks of violence. Another meeting was arranged between Tyler and the king, this time at Smithfield, on 15th June. During this meeting, an argument broke out, during which Tyler was killed, probably by one of the king's servants and loyalists. This resulted in the end of the revolt in London.

Geoffrey Chaucer (1343-1400)

The 'father of English poetry' and the greatest narrative of England was Geoffrey Chaucer. With his emergence, a new era of English poetry started. Geoffrey Chaucer was born about 1343 in the Vintry, the wine merchant's street. At a young age, Chaucer served as a page attendent to Elizabeth, Countess of Ulster and wife of Lionel, Edward III's third son. Chaucer primarily obtained his education at the Court and learnt French and Latin there.

In 1359, at the age of 19, he accompanied Lionel, the Duke of Clarence on a military campaign to France, where he was taken prisoner. Chaucer's value in the royal family can be ascertained from the fact that the English King Edward III (1312-1377) paid a ransom for his release. After his release, Chaucer was transferred to the king's own service and promoted to the rank of esquire. Edward III later sent him on diplomatic missions to France, Genoa and Florence. His travels exposed him to the work of authors such as Dante, Boccaccio and Froissart.

Around 1366, Chaucer married Philippa de Roet, daughter of the Flemish Sir Gilles de Roet. Philippa received an annuity from the queen consort of Edward III. Her sister, Katharine was for many years the mistress and later the third wife of John of Gaunt, another sons of Edward III and a powerful patron. Through this connection, Chaucer became John of Gaunt's kinsman. He enjoyed Gaunt's patronage throughout his life. He was granted a royal annuity for life of 20 pounds.

Literary Career and Works

In 1369, Chaucer was asked by John of Gaunt to compose a memorial poem, written in English, to be recited at the Mass for his deceased wife Blanche, Duchess of Lancaster. The result was Chaucer's first work, *the Book of the Duchess*. During the 1370s, Chaucer went on several journeys abroad on diplomatic and commercial missions. He visited France and Northern Italy as a member of the embassy to Bernabo Visconti, the ruler of Milan. After his return from Italy, he wrote *The Parliament of Fowls*, *The Legend of Good Women* and *Troilus and Creseide*, the first of his works to be widely admired.

Chaucer held a number of royal posts during his lifetime. In 1374, he was appointed Comptroller of the lucrative London customs. In 1382, he was made controller of taxes on wine and other goods with the right to employ a deputy.

Around 1385, Chaucer lost all his offices at the overthrow of the faction of his patron, Duke John of Gaunt (uncle of the young king, Richard II, who had succeeded his grandfather, Edward III, some years before).

After losing office, he moved to a residence in Kent, England. Chaucer was soon restored to power and in 1386; he was elected Member of Parliament for Kent. A year later, Chaucer's wife, Philippa died. In 1389, Chaucer was made clerk of the king's works, overseeing royal building projects.

It was during the fag end of his life that Chaucer composed *The Canterbury Tales*, a collection of 24 tales narrated by 29 pilgrims. Chaucer retired to a house in the gardens of St. Mary's in Westminster in December 1398. It was here that he died two years later at the age of 60. He was buried in Westminster Abbey, the first of the men of letters to be laid in the nook which has, since become the Poets' Corner.

Historical Chronology of Chaucer's Life

Year	Event
1340-1345	Birth of Geoffrey Chaucer
1357	Chaucer appointed page in the household of Elizabeth de Burgh, Countess of Ulster.
1359	Chaucer served in the retinue of Lionel in the war in France.
1360	Chaucer captured by the French at the siege of Reims, Edward III pays ransom for release.
1367	Chaucer becomes an esquire in the household of Edward III, Birth of Chaucer's son-Thomas.
1367-1370	Chaucer translates parts of Romaunt of the Rose
1368	Chaucer writes the book of the Duchess
1369	Chaucer travels to Northern France and serves in the army of John of Gaunt.
1374	Chaucer appointed Controller of the Customs for hides, skins and wool in the port of London
1378	Chaucer travels to Italy Milan on a diplomatic mission
1378-1381	Chaucer writes Saint Cecelia, The House of Fame, Anelida and Arcite and Palamon and Arcite
1380	Accused, and acquited of the 'raptus or rape' of Cecily Champain. Chaucer writes The Parliament of Fowls.
1381-86	Chaucer writes Boece, and .
1385	Chaucer granted a permanent deputy in the Customs.
1385-1389	Chaucer serves as Justice of the Peace for Kent.
1386	Chaucer becomes a Member of Parliament for Kent, Retires from Controllership of Customs. writes The Legend of Good Women
1387-1392	Chaucer begins The Canterbury Tales.
1389	Appointed clerk of the Works at Westminster, Tower of London.
1390	Appointed Commissioner of Walls and Ditches.
1391	Chaucer retires from Clerkship of the King's works, appointed Deputy Forester of the Royal Forest of North Petherton, Somerset.
1391-1392	Writes The Treatise of the Astrolabe
1392-1395	Most of the Canterbury Tales written.
1394	Chaucer is granted an annuity for life of 20 pounds by the King.
1399	Henry IV confirms Chaucer's financial rights and privileges granted by Richard II, with an additional annuity of 40 pounds. Chaucer retires to Westminster.
1400	Chaucer's Death on 25th October.

Three Period of Chaucer's Life

First Period (French Period)

Chaucer's first period was of French influence. It includes his early work, which is based largely on French models, especially the Roman de la Rose and the poems of Guillaume de Machaut. Chaucer's chief works during this time were the *Book of the Duchess,* an allegorical elegy written in 1369 on the death of Blanche, wife of John of Gaunt and a partial translation of the *Roman de la Rose*.

Second Period (Italian Period)

This was Chaucer's period of Italian influence. During this time, his works were modeled primarily on Dante and Boccaccio. Major works of the second period include. *The House of Fame,* recounting the adventures of Aeneas after the *Fall of Troy; The Parliament of Fowls*, which talks about the mating of fowls on *St Valentine's Day* and a prose translation of Boethius' *De consolation philosophiae.*

Third Period (English Period)

Chaucer's third period was a period of mature strength and originality, in which he pursued the bent of his own genius. During this period, he wrote *The Legend of Good Women,* a series of biographies of famous women from myth and history. Chaucer's masterpiece, the 17000 lines *Canterbury Tales* (written mostly after 1387) also belongs to this period.

Linguistic Importance of Chaucer

In Chaucer's age, English was not the language of high culture. Even though ordinary people spoke English, French was the language of power, spoken by royalty, aristocrats and high-powered officials.

Most literature in England was also not written in English. Chaucer however gave impetus to the development of English as a literary language by deciding to write in English.

He added new words from Romance languages-Latin, French, Italian and Spanish and enriched the language of English.

English literature before Chaucer had not used much of rhyme. Chaucer took the idea of rhyme from French literature and introduced it into English.

Chaucer is known for his metrical innovations and new verse forms. He invented the rhyme royal and was one of the first English poets to use the five-stress line, a decasyllabic cousin to the iambic pentameter in his work. According to the American poet Lowell, Chaucer "found his native tongue a dialect and left it a language."

Literary Importance of Chaucer

Matthew Arnold called Chaucer "the father of our splendid English poetry". According to him, Chaucer was founder of a new tradition. His superiority existed both in the substance of poetry and in the style of his poetry.

"For Arnold, Chaucer's major contribution towards poetry was his adherence to realism. His was a 'large, free, sound representation of things, that had 'truth of substance'.

Long called Chaucer's Prologue to the Canterbury Tales as 'the prologue to modern fiction'. Its vivid characterisation is one of the hallmarks of fiction. The Canterbury Tales contains so many miniature novels in itself. Chaucer's Troilus and Criseyde has been called 'a novel in verse'. SD Neil remarks, had Chaucer written in prose, it is possible that his 'Troilus and Criseyde' and not Richardson's 'Pamela' would be celebrated as the first English novel'.

Major Works

The Book of the Duchess (1368-69)

The Book of the Duchess is the first of Chaucer's major poems. This is an elegy written on the death of Blanche, *Duchess of Lancaster*. It is written in the form of a dream allegory. It carries influences from Guillaume Lorris's *Roman de la Rose*. The poem begins with a sleepless poet, who lies on bed reading a book. He reads a story about Ceyx and Alcione and wanders around in his thoughts.

Suddenly, the poet falls asleep and dreams a wonderful story. In his dream, he sees a 'man in black', a knight, who tells him about his courtship of a beautiful lady and his mourning for her death. When the poet awakes, he decides that this dream should be preserved in rhyme. The poem serves twin purposes of elegy and eulogy. It is composed of more than 1300 lines in octosyllables.

The House of Fame (1379-80)

It is an autobiographical poem composed in three books. It is written in the form of a dream allegory. Book I begins with the narrator falling asleep and dreaming about a temple dedicated to the Goddess Venus. Inside the temple, he finds inscriptions that depict the story of Virgil's Aeneid. Rest of the book portrays Dido's betrayal by Aeneas. In Book II, the narrator is carried by an eagle, which speaks to him in a human voice and assures him that Jove has decided to reward him by sending him to the House of Fame.

In Book III, he reaches the House of Fame and meets the Goddess Fame. The allegorical description of this house and its inhabitants is left unfinished. The poem carries influences of Boccaccio, Ovid, Virgil's *Aeneid* and Dante's *Divine Comedy*. Main themes of the poem are process of poetic creation and operations of the capricious Goddess Fame.

The Parliament of Fowls (1380s)

The Parliament of Fowls is a poem written to celebrate the marriage of King Richard II to Anne of Bohemia in 1382. It is written in the form of a dream vision in rhyme royal stanza form. It relies upon the beast fable tradition.

It presents a vision of birds gathered to choose their mates on St. Valentine's Day. The poem begins with the narrator reading Cicero's Dream of Scipio and his reading is awarded by the appearance of a visionary guide. He is led to Venus' temple where a Parliament of birds is being held. The birds conduct a debate about how to choose a mate. While the debate remains unresolved, the bottom line that emerges is that the nobler the bird, the more formal are the rituals of courtship associated with it.

Troilus and Criseyde (1378-85)

Troilus and Criseyde is Chaucer's longest poem of about 8000 lines. It is divided into five books. Giovanni Boccaccio's *Filostrato* (written in 1330s) is the source of this poem.

Chaucer transforms Boccaccio's story into a psychological novel in verse. He creates the character of Pandarus, Criseyde's uncle. Historical backdrop of the poem is Trojan War. The poem is about the tragic love affair of a Trojan prince, Troilus and a young beautiful widow, Criseyde. Criseyde's father has abandoned Troy and shifted loyalty to the Greek side. Through an exchange of prisoners, Criseyde goes over to her father in the Greek camp and leaves swearing loyalty to Troilus. However, she meets a Greek escort, Diomede, changes her mind and proves unfaithful.

Chaucer does not condemn Criseyde's character. He is sympathetic to the cause of women, understands the plight of women in a male dominated society and gives us reasons behind Criseyde's decision to desert Troilus. Criseyde's character is complex. She is beautiful and mysterious. She is also a practical woman, who thinks before she acts. Troilus is a brave warrior. He is emotional and reticent. He displays the qualities of an ideal courtly lover.

The Legend of Good Women (1380s)

It is written in the form of a dream vision. It contains a Prologue and nine stories. The Prologue to the book cites reasons behind Chaucer's collection of stories about good women. Cupid, The God of Love accuses Chaucer of defaming women by writing works, which are critical of romantic love and women.

Cupid is accompanied by a mysterious Queen, who is revealed to be Alcestis, Queen of Thrace. This Queen offers recommendations to Chaucer to make amends for what he has written so far. As a penance, he is asked to write a book about women, who have proved loving and faithful, unlike Criseyde. The narrator accepts the instructions and begins work on his book about legendary 'good' women. It recounts the stories of women from history and myth, who were martyrs to love, such as Dido, Thisbe, Medea, Cleopatra, Hypsipyle, Ariadne, Lucrece, Phillis , Philomela and Hypermnestra. This book is Chaucer's take on the 'woman question'. Considered to be an attack on anti-feminism. *The Legend of Good Women* is Chaucer's unfinished work.

The Canterbury Tales (1386-95)

Chaucer's most acclaimed work; *The Canterbury Tales* is a collection of stories narrated by twenty-nine pilgrims on their way to the shrine of martyr Saint Thomas Becket in Canterbury. All the pilgrims gather at Tabard Inn, Southwark in preparation for their pilgrimage. Harry Bailly, the Host of the Inn suggests a story telling contest, according to which the pilgrim with the best story would be awarded an elegant dinner at the end of the trip. The Host, Harry Bailey, himself becomes the judge of the contest. These is a narrator, who is both a pilgrim and recorder of all events. Chaucer originally planned that each character should narrate four tales. But out of the original 120, only 24 tales got written. The book also contains a General Prologue, which provides the characterisation of the pilgrims.

Pilgrims of Canterbury Tales

The pilgrims represent all sections of society from gentry to humble craftsmen (the only absentees are the labouring poor, unable to afford a pilgrimage of this kind). There are respectable people from the various classes such as the knight, the parson and the yeoman but the emphasis falls mainly on characters, who are pretentious, abusive, deceitful, greedy or corrupt.

Portrait of The Knight

The highest in social hierarchy and therefore the first story-teller. Brave, worthy and honourable, the knight has fought crusades for the sake of Christianity. The Knight represents the values of chivalry, truth, honour and justice.

The Knight's Tale : A Romance

The Knight begins his tale with the story of Theseus, a prince, who married Hippolyta, the Queen of Scythia and brought her sister, Emily, back to Athens with him after conquering her kingdom of Amazons. Outside Athens, he meets a band of weeping women and learns that the tyrant Creon has murdered their husbands and dishonours the dead by leaving them unburied. Incensed, Theseus quickly overthrows Creon and restores the Theban dead to the women for ceremonial burying. After the destruction of

Creon's forces, booty hunters find two young knights (Palamon and Arcite), who are not quite dead. Theseus decides against executing the knights and instead imprisons them with no hope of ransom.

The prisoners are cousins and sworn brothers. Both live in the prison tower for several years until they see Emily in a nearby garden. Both fall immediately in love with her. Palamon compares her to Venus and prays for an escape from the prison. Similarly, Arcite claims that he would rather be dead than not have Emily. The two fight over her, each calling the other a traitor. Eventually, Theseus proposes a formal tournament in one year with each knight supported by one hundred knights. The winner of the contest would get the hand of Emily. On the evening before the battle, Palamon, Emily and Arcite pray. Palamon prays to Venus, Goddess of love; Emily prays to Diana, Goddess of chastity and Arcite prays to Mars, God of war.

All receive a vision indicating that their prayers will be answered. The three prayers and resulting promises cause confusion in heaven until Saturn, God of destiny, promises that Palamon will win his love and Arcite will win the battle. In this way, the Knight's story finishes on a happy note. The Knight's Tale perfectly fits the Knight himself: i.e. he chooses a story filled with knights, love, honour, chivalry and adventure. It adheres to traditional values of chivalric, knightly honour, in which there are strict codes of behaviour, which one must follow. The tale is a Chivalric romance, with elements of epic and satire.

Portrait of the Squire

The Knight's son, he is youthful, handsome and curly-haired. In contrast to the Knight, he is a vain, lusty young man. He enjoys singing, writing poetry and horse-riding and considers himself a lady's man.

Portrait of the Yeoman

The Yeoman is the servant, who accompanies the Knight and the Squire. His dress (coat and a hood of green) and weapons (bow and sword) suggest that he might have been a forester. He is incharge of the Knight's woodlands and appears to be the ideal simple, loyal peasant; yet he is so well-equipped with elaborate weapons and perfect arrows that his simplicity is suspected. The narrator also suggests that Yeoman is profiting in some way as he manages forests, which are not his.

Portrait of the Miller

Chaucer pays great attention to the physical appearance of the Miller. He is big, stout, brawny, broad and strong; short shouldered and has a red beard. His nose has a hairy wart. He has a large mouth and large nostrils. He wears a blue hood and a white coat. He is an expert at wrestling, has animal-like instincts and steals corn.

The Miller's Tale: A Fabliau

When the Knight concludes his tale, everybody approves it and considers it a noble story worth remembering. The Host then jovially calls upon the Monk to tell a tale that would surpass the Knight's.

However, the Miller, who is very drunk, protests that he has a splendid tale for the occasion and one that can match the Knight's. Nobody is able to stop the Miller from telling his vulgar tale. Chaucer apologises to the readers for including this tale in his book, but reminds the reader that he is bound to tell all the stories, since a prize is involved. In the Prologue to the Miller's Tale, we noticed social tension between different classes for the first time.

Miller's Tale

The Miller's Tale is about a carpenter at Oxford, who was rich and miserly. To make extra money, the carpenter rented a room in his house to a poor student, Nicholas. The carpenter had recently wedded a wife, only 18 years old, whom he protected fiercely - because, as she was young and he was old, he knew that he might well be cuckolded. However, eventually, Nicholas and the carpenter's young and beautiful wife, Alisoun, started scheming about how they could have an affair without the carpenter finding out.

One day, when the old carpenter has gone to Ossney on some work Alisoun and Nicholas hatch a plan to sleep together at night. Nicholas carries enough food and drinks to last him two days and instructs Alisoun to tell the carpenter, if he should ask for him that she hasn't the faintest idea where he is. The carpenter notices Nicholas's absence and surmises that something might be wrong with him and even fears that Nicholas might have died. The carpenter's servant goes to check on Nicholas and finds him sitting bolt upright and motionless with a gaping mouth on his bed.

Thinking that Nicholas has had an attack of fit, the carpenter shakes him hard by the shoulders to bring him to his senses. Nicholas then pretends to come out of his stupor and tricks the carpenter into believing that he has had a vision that Noah's flood is about to recur in less than an hour's time.

Nicholas advises the carpenter to hang three boat-like tubs by the rafters and to stow them with a day's provisions and an axe for cutting the ropes to allow the tubs to float in the flood. Further, the tubs are to be hung far apart from each other and nobody is to talk or look at each other during the flood.

The foolish carpenter does as directed and fastens the three tubs to the rafters. At night, the carpenter, Old John, his wife and Nicholas enter into their respective tubs and pray to God. In a short while, the carpenter falls asleep. Soon Alisoun and Nicholas get out of their tubs and quietly go to bed.

In the meanwhile, an amourish parish clerk Absolon passes by. Hoping to get a kiss from Alisoun, he sidles up to the window and calls to her. She harshly replies that she loves another. After Absolon persists, Alisoun puts her naked ass out of the window, which he kisses.

Determined to avenge Alisoun's prank, Absolon hurries back into town to the blacksmith and obtains a red-hot iron poker. He returns with it to the window and knocks again, asking for a kiss and promising Alisoun a golden ring. This time Nicholas, having gotten up to relieve himself anyway, sticks his rear out the window and farts thunderously in **Absolon's** face. Absolon brands Nicholas's buttocks with the poker.

Nicholas leaps up and cries out, Help! Water! Water!. John, still hanging from the roof, wakes up and assumes Nicholas's cries mean that the flood has come. He grabs the axe, cuts free the tub and comes crashing to the ground, breaking his arm. The noise attracts many of the townspeople. The carpenter tells the story of the predicted flood, but Nicholas and Alisoun pretend ignorance, telling everyone that the carpenter is mad. The town's people laugh that all have received their dues and the Miller merrily asks that God save the company.

The *Miller's Tale* responds to the Knight's by turning the Knight's courtly love into a burlesque farce. The Miller places his lovers' intrigues in a lower-class context, satirising the pretensions of long-suffering courtly lovers by portraying Nicholas and Alisoun in a frank and sexually graphic manner.

Portrait of the Reeve

He works as a steward on an estate. He is an old, choleric, thin man with shaved head and lean legs. He wears a blue overcoat and carries a rusty blade. He was earlier a carpenter and resents the Miller's tale about a stupid carpenter. He distrusts people and keeps a check on everyone. He is a part of the feudal system and therefore makes sure that nobody cheats him.

The Reeve's Tale : A Fabliau

The company of pilgrims laughs at the story of Nicholas and Absolon, which the miller has narrated. Only Oswald, the Reeve is angry because he was a carpenter, like John, the butt of the joke in the Miller's Tale.

The Reeve promises to 'answere' and to some extent 'sette [the Miller's] howve' ('set his hood' make a fool out of him). The Miller has scornfully told a tale, the Reeve continues, about how a carpenter was tricked. The Reeve resolves to 'quit' the Miller's Tale.

The Reeve's Tale

The Reeve narrates a story about a Miller, who lives in Trumpington, near Cambridge. He and his wife have a beautiful 20 years old daughter and a 6 months old baby boy. He is very proud of the fact that he can fish, wrestle and shoot. He carries several kinds of knives with him and is extremely skilled in their use. However, this Miller is in reality a thief. His nickname is Simkin. He never loses a chance to steal and even steals the corn or meal that comes to him for grinding.

Two Cambridge students, John and Aleyn, receive permission from the master of their college to see the corn ground at the mill and resolve not to let the dishonest Miller cheats them out of even half a grain of corn. The two clerks arrive at the mill and greet Simkin, telling him they are there to grind their corn and take it back to the college. While they grind the corn in the mill, Simkin creeps outside, finds the clerks' horse and sets it loose.

The clerks step outside to discover that their horse has run away; Aleyn, almost out of his mind with frustration, forgets all about the corn.

The two gullible clerks run off towards the fen. With them out of the picture, the Miller takes out half a bushel of their flour and tells his wife to go and make a loaf of bread out of it, satisfied with himself for outwitting the clerks. Meanwhile, the two clerks run up and down, spending hours chasing their horse, until, at almost night-time, they catch him in a ditch. The two of them realise that the Miller had tricked them. They beg the Miller to provide them lodging for the night since, they cannot travel in the dark and offer to pay him money.

The Miller puts up a bed for them in his only bedroom. The Miller and his wife sleep on one bed, they sleep on another and the Miller's daughter sleeps alone on another bed. The baby boy sleeps in a cradle at the foot of the Miller's bed.

Aleyn and John are unable to sleep because of the miller's snoring. Aleyn then resolves to have sex with the miller's daughter, in revenge for the corn that he felt sure that miller has stolen from them.

Aleyn, proceeds straight to the daughter's bed, where he very quickly achieves his aim.

John, alone in his bed, feels jealous of Aleyn (still having sex with the Miller's daughter) and decides to get some of the action for himself taking the baby's cradle from the foot of the miller's bed and placing it at the foot of his own. Shortly thereafter, the Miller's wife gets up to answer nature's call and comes back to her bed. She looks around for the baby and not finding it anywhere thinks that she has got into the wrong bed. She then goes over to John's bed and finding the baby, slips in. John seizes the chance and has intercourse with the Miller's wife.

As dawn approaches, Aleyn bids farewell to the Miller's daughter who tells him to take the cake lying outside the door, which has been baked out of the stolen flour before they left the Miller. He then goes to the Miller's bed thinking that his companion John was in it and boasts about how he has had the Miller's daughter three times that night. The furious Miller gets up cursing. The Miller's wife thinks that she is on bed with the Miller and accidentally hits him on the head mistaking him for Aleyn. The students further beat the Miller and escape with their retrieved flour baked into a cake.

As the Knight's Tale was 'repaid' and 'replayed' in the Miller's Tale (both about two men in love with the same woman) on a different status level and as the Miller parodied and highlighted the idealised nature of the Knight's tale by replacing its romance setting with gritty realism, so the Reeve's tale performs a similar treatment on the Miller's.

Portrait of the Wife of Bath

She is one of the most famous characters in literature. Her name is Alisoun. She is a professional weaver. She is gap-toothed, somewhat deaf and wears bright scarlet red stockings. She has been married five times and had many other affairs in her youth, making her an expert in the art of love. She enjoys talking and wearing ornate clothes. She likes to live life on her own terms.

She makes a great show of being religious, takes part in charities, but in reality, is concerned more with the appearance of it. Reportedly good-humoured and full of life, the Wife of Bath is going to Canterbury to find her sixth husband.

The Wife of Bath's Tale : An Arthurian Romance

The wife of Bath begins her lengthy prologue by announcing that she has always followed the rule of experience rather than authority. The Wife of Bath uses the prologue to explain the basis of her theories about experience versus authority and to introduce the point that she illustrates in her tale: The thing, women most desire is complete control ('sovereignty') over their husbands. Because she has had 5 husbands, the wife feels that she can speak with authority from this experience and, in the prologue, she tells how she got the upper hand with each of them.

Wife of Bath's Tale

In the days of King Arthur, a young Knight rides out from the court one day. There he spies a beautiful and solitary maiden and ravishes her. The girl's outraged family appeals to King Arthur for justice and he condemns the youth to death. However, the Queen and her ladies take pity on the tragic young Knight and persuade the king to leave the youth to their judgment. The Queen commands the youth to spend a year travelling all across the country interviewing women. At the end of the year, he is to return to court and be able to tell the Queen, what it is that women most desire. If he cannot provide the correct response, he will forfeit his life.

After a year of searching for this knowledge, the young knight has received so many different answers that he despairs of surviving his trial. As he sadly and reluctantly begins his journey back to the court, he sees an exceedingly ugly old woman. When he tells her of his sad state, the old woman promises to give him the answer he is seeking, if he will swear to grant her anything she wishes. The young Knight eagerly gives his word in exchange for which the old hag confides to him the proper answer to the question proposed by the Queen. The old woman accompanies the youth back to the court. When they are ushered into the presence of the Queen, she asks, if he has learned, what it is that women most desire. He gives her the answer supplied by the old woman; that women wish to have complete control over their husbands, their love affairs and to be the master of their men.

After this answer turns out correct, the old hag claims her wish. She asks the knight to marry her. On their wedding night, the old woman proceeds to lecture him on the trivial nature of appearance. Then, she gives the Knight two choices: she can be either ugly by day, but loyal and faithful for the rest of the time; or beautiful by day, but disgraceful and unfaithful for the rest of the time. The knight, truly perplexed by his entire situation, leaves the choice to her and asks her to decide. The woman pleased rewards him both.

The Wife of Bath's Tale is referred to technically as an exemplum, a story told to illustrate an intellectual idea. In this case, the tale is to provide an answer to the question "What do women most desire?" The answer provided is: the man must give the woman the upper hand in marriage, if he wishes to be happy.

Portrait of the Clerk of Oxford

A sincere, devout student of philosophy at Oxford University, who loves learning. Much of his study is devoted to the works of Aristotle. He is poor and spends all his money on books. He speaks little, but when he does, his words are full of wisdom and moral virtue.

The Clerk's Tale : A Folk Tale

The jovial host teases the young Cleric for his quiet, demure behaviour, but begs him to tell them a merry story with no preaching and no rhetoric. This gentler clergyman, in contrast with the two, who preceded him, mildly agrees to relate a tale first written by Francis Petrarch, an Italian poet whom the Cleric revered.

The Clerk's Tale

The Clerk's Tale begins with a description of Walter, The Marquis of Saluzzo, who was wise, noble and honourable, but whose mind was always seeking immediate pleasures. Walter loves his freedom and has refused to be bound by marriage; his subjects, however, long for an heir to the throne.

One day, a delegation of lords of the kingdom humbly beseeches Walter to seek a wife. The king is so impressed with their petition that he agrees to marry. To confirm the agreement, the lords ask him to set a wedding date. Walter grants the lords the right to choose the wedding day and he will choose his own bride.

Walter surprises everyone by choosing a peasant girl for his bride. She is beautiful and virtuous. Walter had noticed her many times as he rode through his domain. The maiden was named Griselda. She was the daughter of Janicula, the poorest of all the Marquis' farmers. Shortly before the wedding, Walter asks Janicula for permission to marry his daughter; the old man agrees. Then Walter wins Griselda's consent. He makes one condition for their marriage: that Griselda promise to obey his will and to do so cheerfully, even, if it causes her pain. Griselda assents to these conditions and they are married.

He tested her thrice : First by taking away her daughter, then son and lastly Walter pretends to divorce Griselda and marry again. Griselda did not utter a single word of objection in all the instances. Seeing this, Walter could no longer stand his cruelty.

He confesses that the cruel tests had been perfectly met by Griselda and that he could find no more patient and steadfast woman. They live the rest of their lives in bliss and when Walter dies, his son succeeds to the throne. Many elements of the story of Griselda come from Petrach and much of it is modelled from a tale in Boccaccio's Decameron. The structure of this story grows out of the nature of the two main characters. Walter seems to be as determined to be cruel and wanton in his testing of Griselda as Griselda is in being submissive to Walter's perverted demands. Each then possesses a single quality and these are seen pitted against each other. But because Griselda tolerates everything, she brings about a happy conclusion for both of them.

Portrait of the Franklin

He is a wealthy landowner, who lives for his own sensual pleasure. He is a connoisseur of food and wine. He is compared to Epicurus and St Julian because he is jovial and hospitable. He has a white beard and a ruddy complexion and carries a dagger and a trinket-bag of silk in his girdle. As an aside, the reader is told that he has served as a justice of the peace and a member of Parliament, but these are only incidental as far as he is concerned.

A frankelyn was in his compaignye.
Whit was his berd as is the dayesye;
Of his complexioun he was sangwyn.
Wel loved he by the morwe a sop in wyn;
To lyven in delit was evere his wone,
For he was Epicurus owene sone,
That heeld opinioun that pleyn delit
Was verray felicitee parfit.
An housholdere, and that a greet, was he;
Seint Julian he was in his contree.
His breed, his ale, was alweys after oon;
A bettre envyned man was nowher noon.

The Franklin's Tale : A Breton Lay

The Franklin tells the assembled company of pilgrims that he will relate an old Breton Lay as best as he can. He asks the pilgrims to excuse his homely style and speech, since he is a plain blunt man. He has no feeling for the colours of rhetoric and speech, since the only colours that he has seen are those that are used for paint and the flowers that grow in the meadows.

Franklin's Tale

The Franklin's Tale begins with the courtship of the Breton Knight Arviragus and Dorigen, who eventually got married happily. Their marriage was one of equality, in which neither of the two was master or servant; and the narrator comments specifically that when "maistrie" (the desire of the Wife of Bath and the women in her tale) enters into a marriage, love flaps its wings and flies away.

After an year of marriage, Arviragus decided to go to Britain for 2 years to seek training in arms. Dorigen laments his absence and often sits on the shore looking at the bare rocks. One day when she went on a picnic, a squire named Aurelius confesses his love to Dorigen. She first refuses and then puts forward a condition to consent to his love. She asked Aurelius to remove all the rocks from the coast of Britanny to make her husband's return voyage safe, which was an impossible task. Aurelius then prays to Apollo to entreat his sister Lucina, Goddess of the sea, to send such a massive tide that it would drown all the rocks on the coast of Britanny. He then faints and falls sick for 2 years. Afterwards, Aurelius brother finds a student magician who can decipher codes of magic found in rare books. Aurelius promises him to pay 1000 pound if he could remove the rocks. The magician performs the deal and is successful. Aurelius then asks Dorigen to keep her promise. Horrified Dorigen attempts suicide rather than disgracing herself.

In the meanwhile, Arviragus returns and Dorigen confides to him about the problem. He asks her to keep her promise and go to Aurelius. On hearing this, Aurelius sets Dorigen free from his promise, seeing her husband's generosity and Dorigen's reluctance.

When Aurelius tells the whole story to the student magician, he also sets Aurelius free of debt and goes away.

The Franklin ends the story by asking the listeners to decide, which of the three men was more generous. The Franklin's Tale is a Breton lay, a brief romance supposedly descending from Celtic origins and usually dealing with themes of romance, love and usually containing some sort of supernatural ingredient.

The tale seems to offer the solution to the problem raised and complicated in the other 'Marriage Group' tales in its initial comments that 'maistrie' has no place in love. It emphasises the idea that love, patience and forbearance are the essence of love and marriage.

Portrait of the Doctor/Physician

The physician is well educated, articulate and thrifty. He is fond of gold and makes a lot of money during the plague season. Though, the Physician keeps himself in perfect physical health, the narrator calls into question his spiritual health.

For all his great learning, the Physician has not studied the Bible, the implication being that he lacks the concern and mercy of the true healer. He also studies the influence of stars on human beings.

Portrait of the Pardoner

He sells pardons and indulgences-reprieves from penance in exchange for charitable donations to the church. He has yellow hair, bulging eye balls, a goat-like voice and wears a small hat.

He fools people to make money and carries a bag full of fake relics. He is greedy and a hypocrite. He has an ambiguous sexuality. He is good at singing and preaching.

The Pardoner's Tale: A Moral Exemplum

After the Physician's Tale, the Host is deeply affected and wishes to hear a cheerful tale. The more genteel members of the company, fearing that the Pardoner will tell a vulgar story, ask the Pardoner for a tale with a moral. In the Prologue, the Pardoner then goes on to explain the methods that he employs in his preaching. He always starts with the text 'Radix malorum est cupiditas' *i.e.*, 'Love of money is the root of all evil'. He then shows his official certificates; his license and says a few words in Latin. The Pardoner says that although he is a vicious fellow he can tell a tale with a moral and asks the pilgrims to listen.

Pardoner's Tale

There once lived in Flanders a company of three rioters, who did nothing, but engage in sinful behaviour. The three drunkards hear a bell tolling a funeral and a boy tells them that a friend of theirs, killed by a thief called Death, is about to be burried. The tavern keeper says this fellow, Death, has slain a whole village about a mile from there. The three drunkards swear an oath to find Death and slay him before nightfall. They head out for the town. Shortly, they meet a very old man, who points them to an oak tree, where he says they will meet death. The three men rush to the spot and to their surprise, find eight bushels of gold coins. They decide to move the treasure at night to avoid being accused of robbery.

They draw straws to decide, who would go to the town to buy food provisions and wine for them, while the other two would guard the gold. The youngest of the men draws the shortest straw and set off towards the town. As soon as he departs to the town, the other two hatch a conspiracy to kill him when he returns and divide his share amongst them.

In the meanwhile, the youngest man also grows greedy and desires to keep the entire treasure for himself. He brings a strong rat poison and three bottles of wine. He mixes the poison in two bottles and keeps the third one clean. When he returns to the spot, the other two men kill him and then sit down to drink their wine that has been poisoned. They also meet death on the spot. Thus, all of them die through trickery and treachery born of their greed.

He calls upon the Pilgrims to buy his relics and pardons and immediately get absolution. He suggests that the Host, who is the most sinful should make his offering first. The Host becomes extremely angry at this suggestion and hints that the Pardoner is a eunuch. The Pardoner becomes so enraged that he does not utter a single word in response. The worthy Knight then resolves the quarrel and restores normalcy.

Portrait of The Shipman

The shipman is a huge, uncouth man, who is an expert sailor. He rides his horse so poorly that it is obvious, the man is much more comfortable on the sea than on the land. His skin has turned brown from years of sailing. He steals wine, while the ship's captain sleeps. In Chaucer's time, shipmen were issued royal license to protect English trade.

Portrait of the Prioress

Her name is Madame Eglantyne. She is modest, coy, and courteous. She wears a gold brooch with 'Love conquers all' inscribed in Latin. She pretends to be of a higher aristocratic class, speaks French, sings and has acquired manners that are above someone of her station. She is hypocritical and cares more about animals than people. The Prioress is accompanied by the Nun, who is her chaplain. The reader is told nothing about the Nun or about the Priest, who is also with the Prioress.

The Prioress' Tale : A Miracle of the Virgin

After jesting rather coarsely about the monk in the Shipman's Tale and monks in general the Host switches to a tone of exaggerated politeness in inviting the Prioress to tell her tale. The Prioress' Prologue comes in the form of a prayer, especially to the Virgin Mary and also establishes her theoretical tics and the pose. She extols Mary, the mother of Jesus as the 'whitest Lily-flower.' This hymn acts as a preview of the tale to follow.

The Prioress' Tale

Once in a Christian town in Asia, there was a Jewish ghetto at the end of a street, in which usury and other things hateful to Christ occurred. The Christian minority in the town opened a school for their children in this city at the other end of the same street. Among the children attending this school was a widow's son, an angelic 7 years old who was, even at his young age, deeply devoted to his faith. Everyday, the child would walk along the Jewish street boldly and clearly singing the song Ave Marie and Alma redemptoris, praising the Virgin Mary and pay reverence to Christ. Satan makes Jewish feel insulted by his singing and they plan a conspiracy to kill the child. The hired killer slits the boy's throat and throws his body into a drain. The boy's mother asks everyone about his whereabouts but everyone lies and does not tell anything.

Then Jesus himself puts in her thoughts the direction to the alley, where the child had been murdered and the pit, where his body was cast away. As the widow nears the place, the child's voice breaks forth singing, 'O Alma Redemptoris'. The Christian people gather around in astonishment. The provost of the city is called; upon seeing the child, he bids all the Jews to be fettered, bound and confined. Later, they are drawn by wild horses and hanged.

The child continues to sing during the mass. The abbot sprinkles holy water over him and questions the boy about his ability to sing even when his throat has been slit. The child answers that Jesus had willed him to sing until his death and when his death came near, the Virgin commanded him to sing the anthem even in death and laid a pearl upon his tongue.

The Virgin has assured him that she will take him away to heaven after the removal of the pearl. The saintly Abbot then takes away the pearl and the child dies peacefully. The whole congregation falls prostrate to the ground in praise of the Virgin. A shining tomb of marble is erected in honour of the young boy.

> 'The Prioress' Tale shows the power of the meek and the poor, who trust in Christ. The Prioress is a devoted and meek Christian lady and she begins by offering a prayer to Christ and especially to the Virgin Mary, the gist, of which is that, because the Prioress is herself like a child, the Virgin must help her with this story in her honour.

Portrait of the Monk

The monk's character is in complete contrast to his religious vocation. He cares little for the rule, devotes time to hunting and eating.

Loves good food and wine. He finds the inn more to his liking than the cold severe monastery. He is large, loud and well clad in hunting boots and furs. Like the Prioress, Chaucer gives him an ironic treatment.

The Monk's Tale : A Tragedy

After the Tale of Melibeus narrated by Chaucer, the Host turns to the Monk. He comments on the Monk's well-fed and sturdy appearance, remarks that he would make a fine breeder. He feels that the church is taking all the best men and leaving only weaklings among the laity, who are fathering inferior offspring. He then demands a merry tale from the Monk.

The Monk bears all this taunting and disrespect patiently. He vows to tell some tragedies, which he defines as stories relating to persons of high station and prosperity, who fall from power into misery and poverty.

The Monk's Tale

The Monk catalogues the fickleness of Fortune through a series of abbreviated tales about such people as Lucifer, Adam, Hercules, Samson, Nero and so on all, who were initially favoured, but eventually abandoned by Fortune. He begins by narrating the story of Lucifer, the brightest angel, who fell from his high station to become Satan. He then accounts the unfortunate fall of Adam by his act of disobedience. He then narrates the mighty Samson's tale at greater length, explaining how he falls from grace, when he admits his secret to his wife, who betrays it to his enemies and then takes another lover. The Monk then moralises that tragedy serves to warn all husbands not to confide life-endangering secrets to their wives.

The Monk then recites the tragic story of Hercules, the paragon of strength. Hercules preferred to throw himself on burning hot coals rather than die by poison sent by his lover Dejanira by dipping his shirt into it. The Monk draws the moral that men should always beware of fortune, who loves to overthrow her victims in a manner that they least expect.

The next story is about Nabugodonosor (also spelled Nebuchadnezzar), who was the king of Babylon, who had twice defeated Israel. The proud king constructed a large gold statue that he demanded his subjects pray to or else be cast into a pit of flames. Yet, when Daniel disobeyed the king, Nebuchadnezzar lost all dignity, acting like a great beast until God relieved him of his insanity. The Monk then moralises that power and authority do not insure one against fate.

The Monk then continues with the tale of Zenobia, the Queen of Palmyria, who was beautiful and victorious in war. She was captivated by Aurelius along with her sons after the death of her husband Idenathus.

He took them through a victory procession in Rome, where the mobs gaped at her humiliation.

The Monk then warns everybody to beware of treachery and narrates a few stories in support. He talks about King Pedro of Spain, subject of the next story, who was cast from his kingdom by his brother. When attempting to regain his throne, Pedro was murdered by this brother. The Monk's next example is Peter, King of Cyprus; who brought ruin on his kingdom and was thus, murdered. Other tragedies that he narrates include Bernabo Visconti, who wrongly imprisoned his nephew. Ugolini of Pisa, a count, was imprisoned in a tower in Pisa with his three young children after Ruggieri, the bishop of Pisa, had led a rebellion against him. His youngest son died of starvation and out of his misery Ugolini gnawed on his own arms. The two children that remained, thought that Ugolini was chewing himself out of hunger and offered themselves as meals for him.

The Monk then relates the story of the vicious Nero, who held a mighty empire under his sway. His every wish became a law.

However, power corrupted with cruelty does not last long. The people rebelled against him and he had to flee to escape their wrath. Nobody offered him shelter and even spurned his request to kill him. Finally, he had to kill himself. Fortune thus overthrew Nero's overweening pride.

The Monk next tells of Antiochus. Epiphanes, who was punished by God for attacks on the Jews. God make Antiochus infested with loathsom maggots. The Monk then admits that most have heared of Alexander the Great, poisoned by his very own offspring. He follows with the tale of Julius Caesar, who had pompey murdered but was himself assassinated by Brutus.

The final story is of Croesus, King of Lydia. He was taken captive and sentenced to be burnt to death. But a sudden heavy downpour put out the fire and let him escape. He became convinced that he could not be killed by anybody and once again started waging wars. One night he had a strange dream, which his daughter interpreted as a warning that he would be hanged to death. And the proud king indeed met his death by hanging.

The Monk's series of little tragedies report the gloomy news that all wealth and position in the world are pure illusion and nothing can prevent the fall of the proud.

The Nun's Priest's Tale : A Mock Heroic Beast Fable

Prologue to the Nun's Priest's Tale The Knight interrupts the listing of tragedies by the Monk, saying that such dismal tales of woe and sorrow are making everyone sad. The Host immediately agrees, commenting that the long narration has almost put everyone to sleep. He begs the Monk to tell them something different. When the Monk declines, Harry calls upon the Nun's priest to tell a happy story. The Priest laughingly agrees, seeing that the clever Monk has revenged himself on Harry Bailley by nearly boring him to death.

The Nun's Priest's Tale

The tale is about an old widow, who lives along with her two daughters in a small cottage near a meadow. The widow leads a very simple life, since her income is very frugal. She owned a cock who was the best in the area. There was no other cock as handsome, strong and heroic than him. This cock has seven hens at his disposal. The hen with the brightest feathered throat is the lovely and gracious Lady Pertelote. Her social poise and gentility has captivated Chaunticleer's heart.

One morning Chaunticleer dreamt of being hunted by a fox and got scared. Hearing this, Lady Pertelote call him a coward and he diverted the talk somehow. He then tells the stories of people who ignored the prophecies seen in dream and met their fate because of it.

One day, Chaunticleer was delightedly watching a butterfly as it glided over the cabbage patch, when he suddenly noticed the fox, who was hiding there. His natural instinct bade him to flee from his arch enemy, but the fox restrains him by praising his excellent voice.

As soon as Chaunticleer stands on his tiptoes, stretches out his neck, closes his eyes and, begins to sing, the fox grabs him by the throat and runs off to the wood with him.

However, there is a reversal of fortune. Chaunticleer goads the fox into hurling curses at the crowd chasing him. The foolish fox is enchanted by this suggestion and when he opens his mouth, Chaunticleer breaks free and flows to a high perch on a tree. The fox realises that God sends ill luck to those, who talk, when they should keep quiet; while Chaunticleer realises that fortune doesn't favour those, who shut their eyes when they are required to look. Thus, the Nun's priest ends his tale with a moral. At the end of the tale, both have learned survival strategies.

Portrait of The Merchant

He is shrewd and arrogant. He would never let others become aware of his true financial status. The merchant talks of nothing, but business and thinks himself an expert on all matters related to trade. He trades in furs and other clothes, mostly from Flanders. He represents the rising middle class.

Portrait of the Friar

His name is Hubert. He is a sensual, licentious man, who seduces young girls and then arranges their marriages. He spends most of his time at bars and carries knives and pins in his sleeves. He accepts bribes, readily gives absolutions to people in exchange for money and avoids sick and poor people because they have no money to give him. He is wanton, merry and quite irreligious.

Portrait of Sergeant of Law

A successful lawyer commissioned by the king. He is cautious and wise. He upholds justice in every dispute. He knows every statute of England's law by heart. He projects an image of himself as busy and successful.

Portrait of the Guildsmen

The five guildsmen are the Haberdasher, the Carpenter, the Weaver, the Dyer and the Tapestry Maker. Though, they have different trades, they appear as a unit. They represent the rising new middle classes, who have newly earned money and desire to flaunt it. All of these men carry favour with their wives, who would have been highly unpleasant, had not their husbands prospered.

Portrait of the Cook

He works for the Guildsmen and is known for his culinary skills. He is quite able and experienced. The only detail provided about him, is a crusty sore on his leg. To medieval observers, such an affliction rendered a person unclean and to be avoided.

Portrait of the Parson

The Parson is a very poor, but holy and virtuous man. He is benign, diligent and patient in adversity. He preaches the Gospel and practices, what he preaches. Whatever little money he has, he gives to his poor parishioners and tries to set an ideal for others. Chaucer is full of admiration for this sole devout Churchman in the entire company.

Portrait of the Plowman

Brother of the parson, the plowman is an honest worker. Like his brother, he is also a virtuous man. A member of the peasant class, he pays his tithes to the Church and leads a good Christian life. He wears a tabbard smock that reflects his poverty.

Portrait of the Manciple

He works at Inns of Court. He is incharge of getting provisions for the court. Though illiterate, he is smart and frugal. He is smarter than the thirty lawyers he feeds. The Manciple has tricked his employers by embezzling profits in his shady deals for them, leaving them to live frugally as he spends the money he stole from them.

Portrait of the Summoner

He is an officer of the church, who calls people for a church trial. He is extremely unattractive, with his red complexion, pimples, boils and skin infected with scales. He loves garlic and leeks, has a bad breath and often gets drunk. He is lecherous and morally corrupt.

Summary of Canterbury Tales

Tale	Genre	Verse Form	Summary
The Knight's Tale	Romance	Iambic Pentameter	An English Romance, in which Palamon and Arcite contend for the love of King Theseus' sister-in-law Emily. Arcite dies and Palamon wins Emily's hand.
The Miller's Tale	Fabliau	Iambic Pentameter	A farce, in which an older husband, John is cuckolded by his young wife, Alisoun and her lover, Nicholas.
The Reeve's Tale	Fabliau	Rhyming Couplets	Tale about Simkin, a miller, cuckolded by John and Aleyn, two clerks.
The Wife of Bath's Tale	Arthurian Romance	Iambic Pentameter	A young, lusty knight rapes a beautiful maiden and is sentenced to death by the king. The Queen intercedes on his behalf and gives him a chance to save his life, if he can find out what is it that women desires the most. The answer is sovereignty.
The Clerk's Tale	Folk Tale/Moral Tale	Rime Royal	About Walter, a marquis of Saluzzo in Italy, who is asked by his subjects to marry in order to provide a heir. He decides to marry a peasant, named Griselda. After marriage, he tests her loyalty and she turns successful.
The Franklin's Tale	Breton Lay	Iambic Pentameter	About marriage of Breton knight Arviragus and Dorigen, proves that 'maistrie' has no place in love.
The Pardoner's Tale	Moral Exemplum	Iambic Pentameter	About three drunken and debauched men, who set out to find and kill Death. On their way, they find a large amount of gold coins and forget about their quest to kill Death. Consumed by greed, all of them kill each other.
The Prioress' Tale	Miracle Of The Virgin, Subset Of Medieval Saint' Legend	Rime Royal	In a Jewish ghetto, a 7 year old boy sings a hymn to the Virgin. Jews, offended by his singing in their ghetto, kill him and hide the body in a latrine. The boy continues to sing even after death and is ultimately restored to Heaven.
The Monk's Tale	Tragedy	Monk's Tale Stanza: Eight Four-Stress Lines Rhyming ababbcbc.	Collection of tragedies, designed to advise men not to trust in blind prosperity, but to be aware that Fortune is fickle and ever-changing.
The Nun's Priest's Tale	Mock-Heroic Beast Fable	Iambic Pentameter	About a braggart rooster, Chaunticleer and his practical wife, Pertelote.

Alliterative Revival

14th century witnessed a revival of alliterative poetry, which culminated in the major masterpieces of *Sir Gawain and the Green Knight, Pearl* and *Piers Plowman.* These works breathed new life into the traditional, native English form inherited from the Anglo-Saxons.

The resurgence of alliterative verse during the so-called Alliterative Revival suggests that alliterative poetry in English had been composed more or less continuously as part of an on-going oral tradition outside the court milieu.

Besides the Gawain-poet's works, the Alliterative Revival includes such works as William Langland's *Piers Plowman*, John Clerk of Whaley's *Destruction of Troy,* the anonymous political satire *Winner and Waster, the Parliament of the Three Ages and the Alliterative Morte Arthure* (*like Sir Gawain and the Green Knight*, an Arthurian Tale). The poems of the Alliterative Revival were all written by well educated and possibly clerical poets, share themes of high moral seriousness and use Northern and Western English dialects. All were the works of provincial poets, living far from Chaucer's cosmopolitan London. The Alliterative Revival's use of native English poetic forms suggests an appeal to English patriotism and national identity, as well as an attempt to distinguish English poetry from its more influential French competitors.

Rich description of natural settings and the use of vivid, realistic detail are two other distinguishing features of the Alliterative Revival, and Sir Gawain and the Green Knight is a prime example of both. All of the Gawain-poet's works are notable for their extreme attention to detail, whether of settings or of activities. In general, the Gawain-poet's works are more elegant and polished than the rest of the Alliterative Revival, indicating that they were intended for a cultured and refined audience.

The Pearl Poet

The 'Pearl Poet' or the 'Gawain Poet', is the name given to the author of Pearl, an alliterative poem written in 14th century Middle English. Its author appears also to have written the poems *Sir Gawain* and the *Green Knight, Patience, Cleanness* and possibly *Saint Erkenwald*.

The Pearl Poet remains unidentified. Some scholars have argued to assign the poem to one John Massey, a member of the landed gentry from Cheshire. The poet was well read in English romances and probably in French ones, too; he drew extensively on the Vulgate in three of his poems and had a general awareness of Christian exegesis and of sermons, though specific debts have not been established.

The only book he cites by name is Jean de Meun's *Roman de la rose* in Cleanness, in which he also makes use of Mandeville's Travels (in perhaps the English as well as the French text. His extensive command of the technical vocabularies of courtesy (Gawain and Pearl), hunting and armour (Gawain), feasts (Gawain and Cleanness), mysticism (Pearl) and ships (Patience) is compatible with Dante.

The 'Pearl' or the 'Gawain' poet wrote in the ancient (and often beautiful) alliterative tradition of Old English narrative poetry. This tradition gave way to the pattern, set by Chaucer and Gower, of accentual-syllabic verse. While Chaucer wrote in the English of London, the Gawain-poet wrote in the dialect of Cheshire a county in the North-West Midlands of England on the border with Wales some 190 miles North-West from London. Because of these reasons, the several masterpieces of the Gawain Poet have languished.

Symbolism in the Pearl Poem

In his epigraph to The Pearl, Steinbeck writes, "If this story is a parable, perhaps everyone takes his own meaning from it and reads his own life into it." The epigraph emphasises the fact that the significance of the pearl as a symbol varies with different readers. Some critics believe that Pearl stands for the soul of the poem's narrator. Pearl is also taken to stand for the Eucharist and the Blessed Virgin. The Pearl image is not static, but dynamic.

Works of Pearl Poet

The Pearl

It is an elegy in about 1200 lines on the death of a little girl. It is a mystical poem of much beauty, in which a bereaved father sees a vision of his daughter among the glorified. It is believed to have been written by the same author as that of Cleanness and Patience.

The Pearl is written in the form of a dream vision. In this poem, the despairing narrator wanders through a garden containing the grave of his infant daughter. He has a vision of Paradise lying beyond a river and recognises the adult woman seated there as his daughter.

As she scolds him for his extended grief, she describes her present situation. Married to the Lord of Heaven, she has a status equal to that of other blessed souls (many of whom led long and exemplary Christian lives), which she explains by relating the Parable of the Workers in the Vineyard; the heavenly souls endless bliss she equates to the pearl of great price of another biblical parable.

In answer to his questions, the narrator is allowed to see the New Jerusalem, through which the Lamb of God leads a procession that includes the dreamer's daughter. He tries to join her by crossing the river, but awakens to find himself back in his garden, consoled by his vision and resolved to accept his lot in life.

Sir Gawain and the Green Knight (1350-1400)

The alliterative poem *Sir Gawain and the Green Knight*, likely written in the mid 14th century, survives in a late 14th century manuscript with three other poems Pearl, Purity and Patience by the same author. Gawain is typical of Middle English alliterative poems, in that it is written in alliterative long lines; Following the basic metrical principles of Old English verse.

A larger story that frames the narrative is that of Morgan le Faye's traditional hatred for Arthur and his court, called Camelot. Morgan, Arthur's half sister and a powerful sorceress, usually appears in legend as an enemy of the Round Table. Indeed, medieval readers knew of Morgans role in the destined fall of Camelot, the perfect world depicted in Sir Gawain and the Green Knight. The poems second frame is a historical one.

The poem begins and ends with references to the myth of Britain's lineage from the ancient city of Troy, by way of Britain's Trojan founder, Brutus. Sir Gawain and the Green Knight makes use of most of the conventions and ideals of the Arthurian romance, yet also points out its contradictions and failings.

Religious Pieces of Poetry such as cleanness (purity) and patience existed in the age of Chaucer. 'Cleanness' and 'Patience' are Middle English alliterative poems written in the late 14th century. These retell Biblical stories and discuss moral virtues.

Ballads in the Age of Chaucer

"Towards the latter part of the 14th century, popular songs, particularly traditional ballads had become an important source of entertainment. The ballads were constantly appearing among the common people, but they were seldom written and found no standing in polite literature.

The ballad is a French form built entirely on three rhyming sounds consisting of three 8 line stanzas and a 4 line or 5 line Envoy. The ballad usually tells a story on subjects that concern the commons and attract their attention such as love, war, faithfulness, treachery, the supernatural world. Among the most notable ballads are those of Robin Hood Ballad, Chevy Chace and Sir Patrick Spens and the Nutbrown Maid.

Guillaume de Machaut was the leading French poet and composer of the 14th century. A large number of ballads were composed on the life and adventures of Robin Hood and in the green wood. *Chevy Chase* is one of the oldest and finest epical ballads on the 'border' matter. It lets the story of the fight between Percy of Northumberland and Douglas of Scotland.

Nut brown Maid is a ballad in the strictest term. The nut brown maid, a Baron's daughter loves a man whom she believes to be a squire.'

Romances of the Age of Chaucer

The Tale of Gamelyn (1350)

The Tale of Gamelyn is an English metrical romance of some 900 lines, written in the East Midland dialect of *Middle English,* in rhymed couplets. It is the story of a younger son, left at his father's death in the care of a wicked elder brother, who seeks to cheat him out of his inheritance. The tale opens with the old knight Sir Johan of Boundys on his death bed. He knows his end is near and he has called his neighbours so that in their presence, he may divide his lands among his three sons. He knows that his neighbours will try to cheat the young Gamelyn of his share, but the old man is determined to have his own way.

He divides all his lands; gives five ploughlands to the eldest son, five more to the second, and all that remains to the share of Gamelyn. After Sir Johans death, *Gamelyn* is deprived of his inheritance by his brothers and becomes an outlaw in the forest. Eventually, he is able to regain his estates and the sheriff who had helped his brothers is hanged. The poem was added to a version of *The Canterbury Tales,* where it follows the unfinished Cook's Tale.

William and the Werewolf

Translated into Middle English by a poet we know only as 'William' sometimes between 1350s and 1360s, this is a retelling of the much older *Roman de Guillaume de Palerne.*

The romance was translated into Middle English in the mid 14th century at the instigation of one Humphrey de Bohun, 6th Earl of Hereford and nephew to King Edward II of England. This is the first work of fiction to feature a benevolent werewolf.

Religious Writing in the Age of Chaucer

Ayenbite of Inwyt (Remorse of Conscience) Written in 1340, The Ayenbite is a translation of the French Somme le Roi (also known as the Book of Vices and Virtues), a late 13th century treatise on Christian morality. It is a confessional prose work written in a Kentish dialect of Middle English.

Pricke of Conscience (1340) The Pricke of Conscience is one of the most popular literary texts of the time. It was once attributed to Richard Rolle, a mystic but is now ascribed to an anonymous 14th century author. The poem comprises about 10000 lines set into four-stressed rhyming couplets and is divided into seven parts and a prologue. It deals with the miserable state of mankind, worldly life, death, Purgatory, Doomsday, the torments of hell and the joys of heaven.

Revelations of Divine Love (1390s) Written by Julian of Norwich, it is a book of Christian mystical devotions. It is believed to be the first published book in the English language to be written by a woman. The subject of the Revelations is love God's love for mankind shown in the Passion, suffering and death of Jesus Christ and the response of man towards God, his maker, keeper and preserver. The book describes a series of wonderful 'Revelations' or 'Showings' that Julian experienced after a period of ill health.

Other Poets of the Age of Chaucer

William Langland (1330-1386)

English poet Wlliam Langland is generally regarded as the single author of the remarkable 14th century poem Piers Plowman. Little is known about Langland's life and history. Inferences about his life have been mostly drawn from what seem to be autobiographical references in the poem, Piers Plowman.

Langland was probably born in Ledbury, Herefordshire in about 1332. He was probably educated at a Benedictine monastery in the Malvern Hills. He was educated for a career in the Church, but appears to have married and never proceeded beyond minor orders. He later moved to London, where he earned a living by singing masses and copying documents. Langland had a deep knowledge of medieval theology and was fully committed to all the implications of Christian doctrine. He is believed to have died in London in 1386.

Major Works

Piers the Plowman

- The full title of the poem is *The Vision of William* concerning Piers the Plowman.
- Composed around 1379, the poem survives in three distinct versions. None of the versions can be assembled into any progressive series of evolution.
- It is an allegorical poem in unrhymed alliterative verse.
- The lead character, Piers is a hardworking, sincere and honest plowman. The poem describes his spiritual quest.
- The poem employs the common medieval form of the dream vision, in which the author presents the story under the guise of having dreamt it.
- The poem is both a social satire and a vision of the simple Christian life. The poet describes 14th century English society in terms of its failure to represent an ideal society living in accord with Christian principles. This failure springs from the corruption of the ecclesiastical order.
- The text has been thought to be subversive and rebellious, possibly encouraging the Peasant's Revolt of 1381. It condemns the practices of the religious classes, sympathises with the sufferings of the poor and espouses the virtue of honest labour.

Three Dreams of the Poem

The poem consists of three dream visions

- In which Holy Church and Lady Meed (representing the temptation of riches), woo the dreamer;
- In which Piers leads a crowd of penitents in search of St Truth; and
- The vision of Do-well (the practice of the virtues), Do-bet (in which Piers becomes the Good Samaritan practicing charity) and Do-best, (in which the simple plowman is identified with Christ himself).

Piers the Plowman

In a somer seson, whan softe was the sonne,
I shoop me into shroudes as I a sheep were,
In habite as an heremite unholy of werkes,
Wente wide in this world wondres to here.
Ac on a May morwenynge on Malverne hilles
Me bifel a ferly, of Fairye me thoghte.
I was wery forwandred and wente me to reste
Under a brood bank by a bourne syde;
And as I lay and lenede and loked on the watres,
I slombred into a slepyng, it sweyed so murye.
Thanne gan I meten a merveillous swevene
That I was in a wildernesse, wiste I nevere where.
A[c] as I biheeld into the eest an heigh to the sonne,
I seigh a tour on a toft trieliche ymaked,
A deep dale bynethe, a dongeon therinne,
With depe diches and derke and dredfulle of sighte.
A fair feeld ful of folk fond I ther bitwene
Of alle manere of men, the meene and the riche,
Werchynge and wandrynge as the world asketh.
Somme putten hem to the plough, pleiden ful selde,
In settynge and sowynge swonken ful harde,
And wonnen that thise wastours with glotonye destruyeth.

John Gower (1330-1408)

English poet John Gower was one of the major court poets of the 14th century. According to David Daiches, Gower was "a more typical representative of his age and class than Chaucer could claim to be".

There is little biographical information available about him. He was probably born into a prominent Yorkshire family. He may have held a legal office of some kind, perhaps in Westminster.

Liferary Career and Works

Gower's first major work, probably begun about 1376, was in French. It is called Miroir de l'Omme or Speculum meditantis. It describes the development of sin, vices and virtues, as also the remedy of repentance available to man, with a special appeal to the Blessed Virgin Mary. Gower's next work is the long Latin poem Vox clamantis (the voice of one crying out) written in 1385. It is a dream allegory that deals with the Peasants Revolt. It develops a moral analysis of social decay in England under Richard II.

Gower's most well-known work is the 33000 line Middle English poem, *Confessio Amantis* ('The Lover's Confession'). It was written at the request of King Richard II, who had asked Gower for 'som newe thing' to read. The first version of the poem was dedicated to Richard. In a later version, Gower dedicated his poem to Henry of Derby, the son of John of Gaunt and the future King Henry IV.

Confessio Amantis is a collection of exemplary tales of love. It is written in octosyllabic couplets. The work records the confession made by an ageing lover, Amans to Genius, the priest of the Goddess Venus as a frame story for a collection of shorter narrative poems. At the end of the poem, Gower is cured of his affectation and recovers his reason. At the end of his life, Gower wrote some Latin poems and some of his French ballads. He married late in life in 1398. He is believed to have died around 1408.

Confessio Amantis

I may noght strecche up to the hevene
Min hand, ne setten al in evene
This world, which evere is in balance:
It stant noght in my sufficance
So grete thinges to compasse,
Bot I mot lete it overpasse
And treten upon othre thinges.
Forthi the stile of my writinges
Fro this day forth I thenke change
And speke of thing is noght so strange,
Which every kinde hath upon honde,
And wherupon the world mot stonde,
And hath don sithen it began,
And schal whil ther is any man;
And that is love, of which I mene
To trete, as after schal be sene.

EXAM BASED QUESTIONS

1 'The Romance Cycle of Rome' talks about
(a) Heroism of Chanson de Roland
(b) Deeds of Alexander and Fall of Troy
(c) Arthur Legendary
(d) Knights of Round Table

2 The Romance stories during Anglo-Norman period were influenced by
(a) English and French sources
(b) English and Norman sources
(c) Latin and English sources
(d) Latin and French sources

3 Which of the following is/are from the romance period?
(a) King Arthur
(b) The War of Troy
(c) Alexander the great
(d) All of these

4 What is the collection of French literature 'Oriental Tales' called?
(a) Historical Regum Britanniae
(b) Meri Greenwood Men
(c) The Seven Wise Masters
(d) None of the above

5 Which is the only epic preserved in the Anglo-Norman script in the British Museum.
(a) Ipomedon
(b) Pelerinage de Charlemagne
(c) Romance of Horn
(d) None of the above

6 Name the ballad, which is gradually collected into the Geste of Robin Hood?
(a) Land of Cockagne
(b) Merrie Greenwood Man
(c) The Owl and the Nightingale
(d) Luxury Land

7 Identify the poem, in which a lover sends to his mistress a love-greeting composed in three languages.
(a) Garly English Lyrics
(b) Plainte 'd' armour
(c) Seventy-one Ballads
(d) None of these

8 Identify out of the following, which is not covered in the satire 'Bounte' des Femmes'?
(a) Political Ambitions
(b) Humility
(c) Courtesy
(d) None of the above

9 The most popular collection of fables in the middle ages was written by
(a) Marie de France
(b) Thomas Malory
(c) William Caxton
(d) Shakespeare

10 Which of these works can be attributed to Christian de Troyes?
(a) The Nightingale
(b) Yonec
(c) Lancelot
(d) The Owl and the Nightingale

11 What form of writing is 'Merri Green wood men'?
(a) English Prose
(b) Ballads
(c) Metrical Romance
(d) Lyrics

12 Which melodious song was written at the end of 13th century?
(a) Love Rune
(b) Cleanness
(c) Alysoun
(d) Patience

13 What is not a part of Fableause, fables written during Anglo-Norman Period.
(a) La Gageure
(b) La Belle Dame Sans Merci
(c) La Trois Dames
(d) None of the above

14 What is Orm's Ormulum?
(a) It is a ballad of the gospel lessons
(b) It is a morality play of the gospel lessons
(c) It is a lyric of the gospel lessons
(d) It is a paraphrase of the gospel lessons

15 Which poem takes the form of a spirited dispute between two birds on the subject of the relative beauty and merit of their songs?
(a) The Frog and the Nightingale
(b) The Owl and the Nightingale
(c) Livere des Creatures
(d) Bestiaire

16 To whom is the poem 'The Owl and the Nightingale' usually ascribed?
(a) Philipple de thaun
(b) Jordan Fantosme
(c) Nicholas of Guild Ford
(d) Hilarious

17 Name the earliest example of a debate poetry in the middle English ages.
(a) Cursor Mundi
(b) Roman de Troie
(c) The Owl and the Nightingale
(d) The Legend of St. Malchus

18 "The debate is opened by chiding the other as a creature of night a bird that loves dark and hence is evil".
To which poem do the above lines refer to?
(a) Cursor Mundi
(b) Bestiaire
(c) The Frog and the Nightingale
(d) The Owl and the Nightingale

19 Which poem written in form of eight syllabled couplets, containing 30,000 lines, relates the history of the world as recorded in the old and new Testaments.
(a) Cursor Mundi
(b) The Owl and the Nightingale
(c) Roman de Troie
(d) Livre des Creatures

20 What does the title 'Cursor Mundi' mean?
(a) Preserver of the World (b) Runner of the World
(c) Destroyer of the World (d) Saviour of the World

21 The poet of which poem states that 'All men take delight in their 'Paramours'; but the best lady of all is the Virgin Mary'. Therefore, he will compose a work in her honour.
(a) The Legend of St. Malchus
(b) Bestiaire
(c) Cursor Mundi
(d) The Owl and the Nightinagle

22 Which poem begins with a prologue in which the poet provides the rationale behind his undertaking?
(a) Roman de Troie (b) Bestiaire
(c) The Legend of St. Malchus
(d) Cursor Mundi

23 The poet of which poem purports to tell about the old and the new law the trinity, the fall of angels, Adam, Abraham and the Patriarchs, then of christ's coming, his birth and three kings of his public life and passion and finally crucifixion and the 'Harrowing of Hell'.
(a) Cursor Mundi
(b) The Legend of st. Malchus
(c) La Chronique de Jordan Fantosme
(d) Bestiaire

24 Identify the one out of the four chief dialects that flourished in the pre-Chaucerian period that became the standard English in Chaucer's time.
(a) The West Midland (b) The East Midland
(c) The Southern Midland (d) None of the above

25 Which of the following, features of French literature did the Normans import to England?
(a) Varied verification
(b) Gloom and other worldly attitude
(c) Varied moods and themes
(d) Variety of language

26 What is the significance of (1st May, 1380) in Chaucer's life?
(a) He became the great author of English literature
(b) He got the name as the father of English literature
(c) He is released from Culpability in the raptus
(d) He is put under supervision for his activities

27 In Chaucer's times the Peasants' Revolts resulted in the
(a) dethronement of the king
(b) demolition of church as an institution
(c) end of serfdom
(d) rise of nationalism

28 Who wrote the 'Romance of the Rose'?
(a) John Gower and John Barbour
(b) William Langland and John Gaunt
(c) Boccaccio and Dante
(d) Guillaeme de Lorris and Jean de Meung

29 A dreary allegorical poem, in which love is represented as a queen rose in a garden, surrounded by her court and ministers
(a) Canterbury Tales (b) The Prologue
(c) Complaint to his Empty Purse
(d) Roman de la Rose

30 In which of the following works did Chaucer use ottava rima, the eight syllabic line rhyming in couplets?
(a) The Canterbury Tales (b) The Prologue
(c) The Book of the Duchess (d) None of these

31 The first published work of Chaucer
(a) The Canterbury Tales (b) Roman de La Rose
(c) The Book of the Duchess (d) The House of Fame

32 The major work of Chaucer during appointment as Comptroller was
(a) The Canterbury Tales (b) The House of Fame
(c) Legend of Good Woman (d) Complaint of the Lady

33 Chaucer wrote a poem on the marriage of Richard II with Anne of Bohemia. Which of the following is this?
(a) Yeoman (b) The House of Fame
(c) The Parlement of Foules (d) The ABC

34 The myth generated by the poem 'Parlement of Foules' is
(a) people assemble and call the vampire by their own will
(b) woman gather before the Goddess nature to show their mates
(c) monkeys assemble before the Goddess to show their power
(d) birds gather before the Goddess nature to show their mates

35 What is done by Pandarus in Troilus and Criseyde?
(a) Learn the secrets and bring the young people together
(b) Allows the marriage of Troilus and Criseyde
(c) Fight the war till the last breath
(d) United the two nations and brought peace and harmony

36 Cressida promised to herself that
(a) she will be happily live with her father
(b) she will be true to Troilus
(c) she will be true to Diomede
(d) she will be true to the Country

37 Which of the following tales is in prose?
(a) The Parliament of Foules
(b) The Legend of Good Women
(c) The House of Fame
(d) The Book of Duchess

38 The poem by Chaucer, known to be the first attempt in English to use the Heroic Couplet is
(a) The Complaint unto Pity
(b) The Romance of the Rose
(c) The Legend of Good Women
(d) Troilus and Criseyde

39 In the 'Doctor of Physique', Chaucer was heavily dependent upon
(a) modern science (b) church
(c) astrology (d) All of the above

40 Who among the following has been named as 'The Morning Star of the Renaissance'?
(a) Shakespeare (b) Alexander
(c) Marlowe (d) Chaucer

41 The Book of the Duchess by Chaucer is
(a) lengthy allegory on the death of his patron's wife
(b) short lyrical story of the Duchess of Wales
(c) long narrative story of an adulterous
(d) tribute to his beloved and her beauty

42 Chaucer has been criticised for presenting an incomplete picture of his times, because
(a) he overemphasises the rights of the lower class
(b) he exaggerates the courtly benevolence
(c) he writes for the court and cultivated classes and neglects the suffering of the poor
(d) he supports the Lollardy and the Peasant Revolution too fervently

43 In the 'Canterbury Tales', the varieties of pilgrims are going to
(a) The Tomb of Saint John Walter
(b) The Tomb of Saint Thomas Becket
(c) To the Tomb of Sir Joseph
(d) To the Canterbury Cathedral homage

44 In Prologue and Canterbury Tales, Chaucer employed the
(a) Ottava Rhyma (b) Rhyma Royal
(c) Heroic Couplet (d) Both (a) and (c)

45 Who was the most jovial host in the Canterbury Tales?
(a) Miller (b) Knight
(c) Harry Bailey (d) John

46 The Fictional Inn, where the pilgrims meet in the Canterbury Tales is
(a) Canterbury (b) Tabard
(c) Princetown (d) None of these

47 The gist of the 'Canterbury Tales' has been taken from
(a) Filostrato (b) Decamerone
(c) Polychronicon (d) None of these

48 Which out of the following is in prose only, in the Canterbury Tales?
(a) Squire's Tale
(b) Chaucer's Tales of Melibee
(c) Knight's Tale
(d) None of these

49 The Tale that tells managing several husbands by making lives miserable
(a) Roman de La Rose (b) The House of Fame
(c) Complaint to his Lady (d) Wife of Bath

50 A lively mix of the variety of genres told by travellers from all aspects of society is
(a) Book of the Leone
(b) The Canterbury Tales
(c) Troilus and Criseyde
(d) The House of Fame

51 The names of two Cambridge students in the Miller's tale were
(a) Miller and John (b) Synkyn and Aleyn
(c) Miller and Synakyn (d) Aleyn and John

52 The pilgrims laughed heartily at the tale by Miller, but who took the offence thinking that the Miller meant to disparage carpenters
(a) The Knight (b) Oswald the Reeve
(c) Aleyn (d) Alison

53 What is being told by Chaucer's Monk's Tale, which is subtitled as 'De Casibus Virorum illustrian'?
(a) It tells about the story of pilgrims going to St. Johns Cathedral
(b) It tells about the unhappy ends of famous men
(c) It tells about the illustration of happy men out of the pilgrims
(d) It tells about the tale of monk who goes for meditation

54 In the Prologue to the Canterbury Tales, the fading chivalry of Middle Ages is represented by the aged knight, while the budding chivalry of Chaucerian times is represented by
(a) The Friar (b) The Squire
(c) The Parson (d) Wycliffe

55 What is the true import of the clerk's tale in the Canterbury Tales?
(a) That man can make his own fortune
(b) That adversity is the best teacher
(c) As you sow, so you reap
(d) That man must learn to endure adversity with courage and understanding

56 What is common to the following characters? Identify the description below correct.
1. The Knight
2. The Manciple
3. The Summoner
4. The Prioress

Codes
(a) All of them have been created by Langland
(b) All of them have been portrayed by Mandeville
(c) All of them are part of Canterbury Tales
(d) All of them are works of Gower

57 Name the famous poets, Chaucer met in the wedding of Lionel of Antwerp.
(a) Dante (b) John Hawkwood
(c) Jean Froissart and Petrarch
(d) Dante and Petrarch

58 What was the most significant aspect of the growing apocrypha?

(a) With Thynne's edition, it began to include medieval texts that made Chaucer appear as a proto-protestant Lollard

(b) It began to exclude medieval texts that made Chaucer appear as a proto-protestant

(c) It began to include and exclude texts that made Chaucer appear as a proto-protestant

(d) It began to improvise......?

59 What is common to these poems? Identify the correct description below.

1. The Pearl
2. Patience
3. Cleanness

Codes

(a) All of them are works of the Gawain poet
(b) All of them are written in iambic pentameter
(c) All of them are beast fables
(d) All of them are religious and didactive writing

60 What is common to these works? Identify the correct description below.

1. Robin Hood Ballad
2. Chevy Chace
3. Sir Patrick Spens and the Nutbrown Maid

Codes

(a) All of them are part of the Pearl poem
(b) All of them are part of Canterbury Tales
(c) All of them are names of Ballads written in the Age of Chaucer
(d) All of them are dream allegories

61 What is common to the following works? Identify the correct description below.

1. The Tale of Gamelyn
2. William and the Werewolf
3. Sir Gawain and the Green Knight

Codes

(a) All of these are romances written in the Age of Chaucer
(b) All of them are works of Chaucer
(c) All of them have been edited by Langland
(d) All of them have been written by Gower

62 In Langland's 'Piers the Plowman' the final appearance of piers is as

(a) Jesus (b) The Holy Trinity
(c) Charity (d) The Good Samaritan

63 'Piers Plowman' has a subtitle. It is

(a) Pilgrim (b) The Truth
(c) A Vision (d) None of these

64 Which is the poem written in Saxon manner, with accent and alliteration, a powerful poem aiming at social reform and vividly portraying the life of the common people?

(a) Hind Horn (b) Mary Hamilton
(c) The Nutbrown Mayde (d) Piers Plowman

65 Who is the author of 'A treatise on the Astrolable'?

(a) Chaucer (b) Langland
(c) Barbour (d) Gower

66 'Confessio Amantis' written by Gower is based on

(a) Moral Teachings (b) Adventure
(c) Love (d) Both (b) and (c)

67 In which language did Lollards preach common people?

(a) French (b) English
(c) Italian (d) Spanish

68 The translation of Bible was carried out by Nicholas of Hereford and

(a) Wycliffe (b) John Menderille
(c) John Purvey (d) William

69 Identify the poet from the following who was known for 'Bruce' the supreme national poem of Scotland?

(a) Langland (b) Wycliffe
(c) Chaucer (d) Barbour

70 Who called himself as a 'Nettle in Chaucer's garden of poetry'?

(a) Eustache Deschamps (b) John Gower
(c) John Gaunt (d) Thomas Usk

71 The poem 'Troilus and Criseyde' is based on .... work.

(a) Boccaccio (b) Dante (c) Petrarch (d) Barbour

72 During the Italian Period, the reward of a gallon of wine was awarded to/for ....

(a) getting married to a queen
(b) for outstanding work in foreign country
(c) for artistic achievement
(d) for ending Hundred Years' War

73 'House of Fame' is based on .... form.

(a) realistic
(b) virtual imagination
(c) dream vision
(d) religious

74 'The Parliament of foules' was written to celebrate .... second marriage.

(a) Richard's (b) Henry's
(c) John of Gaint's (d) None of these

75 .... is the longest tale in the 'Canterbury Tales.'

(a) The Cook's Tale (b) The Franklin's Tale
(c) The Knight's Tale (d) Both (a) and (c)

76 About .... lines are in verse in 'The Canterbury Tales'.

(a) 16500 (b) 13400
(c) 17000 (d) 18100

77 .... poem talks about the story of the son of the 'Trojan King Priam'.

(a) The Complaint of Woman (b) Canterbury Tales
(c) Troilus and Criseyde (d) The House of Fame

78 .... is the longest and finest poem of the Italian Period of the Chaucer.

(a) The Complaint of Woman
(b) Canterbury Tales
(c) Troilus and Criseyde (d) The House of Fame

79 .... is a Chaucer's Book, which hints that the grants of Chaucer might not have been paid.

(a) The Canterbury Tales
(b) The Book of Duchess
(c) The Complaint of Chaucer to his Purse
(d) The Knight's Tale

80 The works of Pearl Poet include ....

(a) Cleanness
(b) Patience
(c) Sir Gawain and the green Knight
(d) All of the above

81 Which of the following statements about the genres during Anglo-Norman period is incorrect?

(a) Chronicles recorded the history of kings
(b) Works of early writers were mostly romances
(c) Religious writing portrayed the religious life of women
(d) Romances dealt with marvel filled adventures

82 Which of these points is incorrect about the 'Lais'?

(a) They are lyrical poems
(b) They are written by Anselm
(c) They are usually in octosyllabic couplets
(d) They are intended to be sung

83 Which of these about Geoffrey Chaucer is incorrect?

(a) Chaucer's first period was of French influence
(b) The second period was of Italian influence
(c) The third period is also known as the English period
(d) There was also a fourth period

84 Which of the following statements about 'The House of Fame' is correct?

(a) It is an autobiographical poem composed in ten books
(b) In Book III the narrator meets the Goddess Venus
(c) It is not in the form of a dream allegory
(d) The poem carries influences of Dante's 'Divine Comedy'

85 Which of the following about the 'Parliament of Fowls', is incorrect?

(a) It relies upon the beast table tradition
(b) It is written in rhyme royal
(c) It is written to celebrate the marriage of King Richard II to Anne of Bohemia
(d) It presents a vision of animals gathered on Martyrs Day

86 Which of these historical events chronology pairs is correctly matched with their period?

(a) Hundred years' war	:	1337-1453
(b) Edwardian era war	:	1415-1453
(c) Caroline war	:	1337-1360
(d) Lancastrian war	:	1369-1389

87 Which of these books with their contents is incorrectly matched?

(a) The Book of the Duchess	:	Elegy on the death of Blanche
(b) The Parliament of Fowls	:	Marriage of King Richard II to Anne
(c) Troilus and Criseyde	:	Trojan War
(d) The House of Fame	:	Pilgrims on their way to a shrine

88 Which of the following profession is correctly matched with their description?

(a) The Knight	:	Madame Eglantyne
(b) The Squire	:	Highest in social hierarchy
(c) The Prioress	:	Knight's son
(d) The Nun	:	The Priosess's chaplain

89 Which of the following pairs is not correctly matched?

(a) John Wycliffe	:	Lollard Movement
(b) John Mandville	:	Canterbury Tales
(c) John Gower	:	Vox Clamantis
(d) William Langland	:	Piers Plowman

90 Which of these authors is correctly matched with works?

(a) William Langland	:	Canterbury Tales
(b) Wycliffe	:	Destruction of Troy
(c) Geoffrey Chaucer	:	Piers Plowman
(d) Julian of Norwich	:	Revelation of Divine Love

Directions (Q. Nos. 91-95) *In the questions given below are two statements labelled as Assertion (A) and Reason (R). In the context of two statements, which one of the following is correct?*

Codes

(a) Both A and R are true and R is the correct explanation of A
(b) Both A and R are true, but R is not the correct explanation of A
(c) A is true, but R is false
(d) A is false, but R is true

91 **Assertion** (A) 'The Owl and the Nightingale' is a popular medieval English poem.
Reason (R) The poem relates the history of the world as recorded in the old and new testaments.

92 **Assertion** (A) De France's Lais have been considered by many to be the first significant collection of medieval courtly romance.
Reason (R) The subject of the lais is love and courtliness.

93 **Assertion** (A) Chaucer's Canterbury Tales say 'There was corruption in the church'.
Reason (R) This is because the hierarchy of the religious people didn't let the other people know the reality of the theology. They kept the scriptures away from the common people and advantage themselves.

94 **Assertion** (A) 'The Pearl' is an elegy in about 1200 lines.
Reason (R) 'The Pearl' is written in the form of a dream vision.

95 Given below are two statements, one labelled as Assertion (A) and the other labelled as Reason (R).
Assertion (A) Chaucer describes 'Madame Eglentyne' thus 'She was so charitable and so pitous, She wolde wepe, if that she sawe a mous caught in atrappe'
Reason (R) On her 'broche of gold full shene' was written 'Amor Vincit Omnia'.
In the context of the two statements, which one of the following is correct?

96 Which of the following is in correct sequence?
(a) Hundred Years' War, Peasants Revolt, Black Death
(b) Hundred Years' War, Black Death, Peasants Revolt
(c) Peasants Revolt, Black Death, Hundred Years' War
(d) Black Death, Peasants Revolt, Hundred Years' War

97 Which of the following is in chronological order according to Chaucer' life?
(a) Fought in France, Appointed as Comptroller, Elected in Parliament
(b) Appointed as Comptroller, Elected in Parliament, Fought in France
(c) Fought in France, Elected in Parliament, Appointed as a Comptroller
(d) Elected in Parliament, Fought in France, Appointed as a Comptroller

98 Which of the following is in chronological order of years it was completed?
(a) The House of Fame, The Parliament of Fowls, The Legend of Good Women
(b) The Parliament of Fowls, The House of Fame, The Legend of Good Women
(c) The Parliament of Fowls, The Legend of Good Women, The House of Fame
(d) The House of Fame, The Legend of Good Women, The Parliament of Fowls

99 Which of the following is in correct sequence?
(a) Troilus and Criseyde, The Legend of Good Women, The Canterbury Tales
(b) The Canterbury Tales, The Legend of Good Women, Troilus and Criseyde
(c) The Legend of Good Women, Troilus and Criseyde, The Canterbury Tales
(d) Troilus and Criseyde, The Canterbury Tales, The Legend of Good Women

100 Which of the following is in correct sequence?
(a) Pearl Poet, Chaucer, Wycliffe
(b) Pearl Poet, Wycliffe, Chaucer
(c) Chaucer, Wycliffe, Pearl Poet
(d) Wycliffe, Chaucer, Pearl Poet

101 Consider the following statements.
1. 'The Owl and the Nightingale' is a spiritual dispute between two birds.
2. 'Cursor Mundi' contains 30000 lines.
3. 'The Owl and The Nightingale' consists of 5000 lines of use.
4. 'Cursor Mundi' relates the history of the world as recorded in Iuluis Calsas.

Which of the statements given above is/are correct?
(a) 1 and 3
(b) Only 4
(c) Only 3
(d) 2 and 4

102 Consider the following statements. Cursor Mundi
1. is an anonymous middle English poem.
2. contains 5000 lines.
3. is written in form of ten syllabled couplets.
4. relates the history of the world as recorded in the old and new testaments.

Which of the statements given above are correct?
(a) 1 and 2 (b) 1 and 4
(c) 3 and 2 (d) 3 and 4

103 Consider the following statements.
The Lay of the Nightingale
1. is about two knights, who live next door to each other.
2. is a short narrative or lyrical poem.
3. is not poetic and musical in form.
4. does not belong to the Breton cycle.

Which of the statements given above are correct?
(a) 1 and 2 (b) 1 and 4
(c) 3 and 2 (d) 3 and 4

104 Consider the following statements.
The owl and the Nightingale
1. is a medieval English poem written in the 13th century.
2. it takes the form of an amiable discussion between the two birds.
3. It consists of 5000 lines.
4. It is not ascribed to Master Nicholas of Guildford.

Which of the statements given above are correct?
(a) 1 and 2 (b) 1 and 4
(c) 3 and 2 (d) 3 and 4

105 Whose impact was reflected in Chaucer's work after going to Italy?
1. Dante
2. Petrarch
3. Boccacio

Select the correct answer using the codes given below.
(a) 1 and 2 (b) 1 and 3
(c) 2 and 3 (d) All of these

106 Which of the following are works of the Italian Period?

1. Roman de La Rose
2. The Legend of Good Women
3. Troilus and Criseyde
4. Canterbury Tales

Select the correct answer using the codes given below.

(a) 1 and 2 (b) 2 and 3
(c) 3 and 4 (d) 1, 2 and 3

107 Which of the given are translated by Chaucer?

1. The Canterbury Tales
2. Boethius Consolation of Philosophy Consolation
3. The Romance of the Rose

Select the correct answer using the codes given below.

(a) 1 and 2 (b) 2 and 3
(c) 3 and 1 (d) All of these

108 Chaucer's Parlement of Foules is in part

1. puzzle 2. debate
3. threnody 4. beast fable

The correct combination for the above statement, according to the codes is

(a) 1, 2 and 4 (b) 2, 3 and 4
(c) 1 and 4 (d) 2 and 4

109 What Chaucer talked about in the poem Troilus and Criseyde, which become a central theme in the Tale of Troy?

1. Sentiment and Tragedy of love
2. The Psychology of the heroine
3. Famous saint biography from Cathedral

Select the correct answer using the codes given below.

(a) 1 and 2 (b) 1 and 3
(c) 2 and 3 (d) All of these

110 Who accompanied the knight in the Canterbury Tales?

1. The Yeoman 2. The Squire 3. The Nun

Select the correct answer using the codes given below.

(a) 1 and 2 (b) 2 and 3
(c) 1 and 3 (d) Only 1

111 The Prioress Tale was about the

1. Virgin Mary
2. Chaunticleer
3. Walter

Select the correct answer using the codes given below.

(a) Only 2 (b) Only 3 (c) Only 1 (d) 1 and 3

112 Which pilgrim was sincere, poor and spent all money on books?

1. The Merchant
2. The Prioress
3. The Clerk of Oxford

Select the correct answer using the codes given below.

(a) Only 2 (b) Only 3 (c) 1 and 3 (d) 2 and 3

113 The dream visions of the poem 'Piers the Plowman' are

1. in which Holy Church and Lady Meed woo the dreamer
2. in which Piers lead a crowd of penitents in search of St. Thomas
3. the vision of Do-well, Do-bet and Do-best

Select the correct answer using the codes given below.

(a) Only 1
(b) 2 and 3
(c) 1 and 3
(d) Only 3

114 Romances in the age of Chaucer include

1. William and the Werewolf
2. Purity
3. The Tale of Gamelyn

Select the correct answer using the codes given below.

(a) 1 and 2 (b) 1 and 3
(c) 2 and 3 (d) All of these

115 The religious writings in the age of Chaucer include

1. Ayenbite of Inwyt
2. Revelation of Divine Love
3. The Pearl
4. Pricke of Conscience

Select the correct answer using the codes given below.

(a) 1, 3 and 4 (b) 1, 2 and 3
(c) 2, 3 and 4 (d) 1, 2 and 4

116 Match the following poems with their category of nature:

Poem	Category of Nature
1. The Owl and the Nightingale	A. Religious and Didactic
2. Lanval	B. Romance
3. Sir Degare	C. Lais
4. Love Rune	D. Debate

Codes

(a) 1-A, 2-B, 3-C, 4-D
(b) 1-D, 2-C, 3-B, 4-A
(c) 1-B, 2-D, 3-A, 4-C
(d) 1-C, 2-A, 3-D, 4-B

117 Match the following pilgrims with their profession traits.

Pilgrim	Profession Trait
1. The Yeoman	A. Servant
2. The Knight	B. Code of Behaviour
3. The Manciple	C. Expert in Buying
4. The Summoner	D. Morally corrupt

Codes

(a) 1-A, 2-B, 3-C, 4-D
(b) 1-D, 2-C, 3-B, 4-A
(c) 1-B, 2-D, 3-A, 4-C
(d) 1-C, 2-A, 3-D, 4-B

118 Match the following pilgrims of 'The Canterbury Tales' by Chaucer with their activities.

Pilgrim	Activity
1. The Wife of Bath	A. Hunting to pass time
2. The Monk	B. Devoted to studies
3. The Clerk of Oxford	C. Enjoying life on own terms
4. The Shipman	D. Expert sailor

Codes
(a) 1-A, 2-B, 3-C, 4-D
(b) 1-D, 2-C, 3-B, 4-A
(c) 1-C, 2-A, 3-B, 4-D
(d) 1-C, 2-A, 3-D, 4-B

119 Match the main characteristics with the pilgrims of the canterbury Tales.

Characteristics	Pilgrim
1. Miser	A. The Parson
2. Man of Learning	B. The Reeve
3. Ill tempered	C. The Doctor of Physics
4. Gay	D. The Friar

Codes
(a) 1-A, 2-B, 3-C, 4-D
(b) 1-D, 2-C, 3-B, 4-A
(c) 1-B, 2-D, 3-A, 4-C
(d) 1-C, 2-A, 3-D, 4-B

120 Match the following characters of the Canterbury Tales with their 'Tales'.

Character	Tale
1. Knight	A. Palamon and Arcite
2. Peasant - Griselda	B. The Clerk's Tale
3. Chaunticleer	C. Nun's Priest's Tale
4. Madam Eglantyne	D. Portrait of the Prioress

Codes
(a) 1-A, 2-B, 3-C, 4-D
(b) 1-D, 2-C, 3-B, 4-A
(c) 1-B, 2-D, 3-A, 4-C
(d) 1-C, 2-A, 3-D, 4-B

121 Match the following.

List I (Books)	List II (Years)
A. The House of Fame	1. 1386
B. The Parliament of Foules	2. 1379
C. The Legend of Good women	3. 1382
D. Chaucer began writing (The Canterbury Tales)	4. 1380

Codes

	A	B	C	D
(a)	2	3	4	1
(b)	1	2	3	4
(c)	4	3	2	1
(d)	4	1	2	3

122 Match the following.

List I (Pilgrims)	List II (Profession)
A. The Knight	1. King Theseus
B. The Miller	2. Aleyn
C. The Clerk	3. Absolom
D. The Reeve	4. King's Business

Codes

	A	B	C	D
(a)	1	2	3	4
(b)	1	4	3	2
(c)	2	3	4	1
(d)	4	3	2	1

123 Match the personalities and their relations.

List I	List II
A. Troilus	1. Son of Priam
B. Criseyde	2. Lover of Troilus
C. Calchas	3. Father of Criseyde
D. Pandarus	4. Uncle of Criseyde

Codes

	A	B	C	D
(a)	2	4	1	3
(b)	3	2	4	1
(c)	1	2	3	4
(d)	4	3	2	1

124 Match the novels with their years.

List I	List II
A. Cleanness	1. 1382-87
B. Piers Plowman	2. 1385
C. Troilus and Criseyde	3. 1389
D. Confessio Amantis	4. 1375

Codes

	A	B	C	D
(a)	4	3	2	1
(b)	1	2	3	4
(c)	2	3	4	1
(d)	4	1	2	3

125 Match the works with their writers.

List I	List II
A. Piers the Plowman	1. The Canterbury Tales
B. Old Testament	2. John Gower
C. Vox Clamantis	3. John Wycliffe
D. Geoffrey Chaucer	4. Willam Langland

Codes

(a)	4	3	2	1
(b)	1	2	3	4
(c)	2	4	3	1
(d)	2	3	4	1

126 In the following series, which one has all the poets correctly matched in the poems?
(a) 'Polychronican'- John of Trevisa; 'Vox Clamantis'- Anonymous; 'Piers the Plowman'- Gower; 'Sir Gawain and the Green Knight'- Langland
(b) 'Polychronican'- Gower; 'Vox Clamantis'- John Gower; 'Piers the Plowman'- Langland; 'Sir Gawain and the Green Knight-Anonymous'
(c) 'Polychronican'- Langland; 'Vox Clamantis'- Anonymous; 'Piers the Plowman'- John of Trevisa; 'Sir Gawain and the Green Knight'- Gower
(d) 'Polychronican'- Langland; 'Vox Clamantis'- Gower; 'Piers the Plowman'- Anonymous; 'Sir Gawain and the Green Knight'- John of Trevisa

127 In the following series, which one has all the poets correctly matched with the poems?

(a) Langland-'A Treatise on the Astrolable'; Gower-'Speculum Meditantis'; Chaucer- 'The Romaunt of the Roses'; Barbour- 'Bruce'
(b) Langland-'Bruce'; Gower- 'Speculum Meditantis'; Chaucer-'A Treatise on the Astrolable'; Barbour- 'The Romaunt of the Roses'
(c) Langland-'The Romaunt of the Roses'; Gower- 'Treatise on the Astrolable'; Chaucer- 'Speculum Meditantis'; Barbour-'Bruce'
(d) Langland-'The Romaunt of the Roses'; Gower- 'Bruce'; Chaucer-'Speculum Meditantis'; Barbour- 'A Treatise on the Astrolable'

128 In the following series, which one has the correctly matched writers with their works?

(a) Wycliffe-Translated Bible into Vernacular; Chaucer-Piers the Plowman; Langland- Vox Clamantis; John Gower- The Canterbury Tales
(b) Wycliffe- Vox Clamantis; Chaucer- Translated Bible into Vernacular; Langland- Piers the Plowman; John Gower- The Canterbury Tales
(c) Wycliffe- Transtated Bible into Vernacular; Chaucer-The Canterbury Tales; Langland- Piers the Plowman; John Gower- Vox Clamantis
(d) Wycliffe- The Canterbury Tales; Chaucer-Translated Bible into Vernacular; Langland- Piers the Plowman; John Gower- Vox Clamantis

129 In the following series, which one has the correctly matched events with their years of occurrences?

(a) Accession of Henry IV-1399; The Peasants' Revolt-1377; Death of Chaucer- 1400; Reformation by Wycliffe-1381
(b) Accession of Henry IV-1399; The Peasants' Revolt-1381; Death of Chaucer-1400; Reformation by Wycliffe-1377.
(c) Accession of Henry IV- 1399; The Peasants' Revolt-1400; Death of Chaucer-1381; Reformation by Wycliffe-1377
(d) Accession of Henry IV-1381; The Peasants' Revolt-1400; Death of Chaucer-1377; Reformation by Wycliffe- 1399

130 In the following series, which one has the correctly matched personalities with their relations?

(a) Lewis- Chaucer's son; Elizabeth- Chaucer's daughter; Alice- the Duchess of Suffolk; Edward III- the son of Edward II
(b) Lewis- Chaucer's daughter; Elizabeth- the Duchess of Suffolk; Alice- the son of Edward II; Edward III-Chaucer's son
(c) Lewis- The son of Edward II; Elizabeth- Chaucer's son; Alice-Chaucer's daughter; Edward III- The Duchess of Suffolk
(d) Lewis- The son of Edward II; Elizabeth- The Duchess of Suffolk; Alice- Chaucer's daughter; Edward III-Chaucer's son

131 "A curious modern note begins to be apparent at this period. There is a sharper spirit of criticism, a more searching interest in men's affairs and a less child like whin and a less complacent acceptance, of the established order. The vogue of the romance, though it has by no means gone, is being superseded by the more acute spirit of drama, which even at this early time is faintly foreshadowed.

Another more modern feature that at one strikes the observer is that the age of anonymity is passing away. Though many of the tests still lack named authors, the greater number of books can be definitely ascribed. Moreover, we have for the first time a figure of outstanding literary importance, who gives to the age the form and pressure of his genius.

The above extract is said by whom and for whom?

(a) Edward Albert for Chaucer
(d) Edward Spenser for Chaucerian Age
(c) Edward Albert for Chaucerian Age
(d) William Langland for Chaucer

132 "Sir John of Boundes was his name
He coude of norture and of mochel game
Thre sones the knyght had and with his body he won The eldest was a moche schrewe and sone bygan."

Name the poem above extract has been taken from?

(a) Sir Gawain and the Green Knight
(b) The Tale of Gamelyn
(c) William and the Werewolf
(d) The Knight's Tale

133 This was the tale: There was a king
That highte seys and hadde a wyf,
The beste that mighte bere lyf; And this quene highte Alcyone

Name the poem and the event for which it is written?

(a) The Parliament of Fowls; St. Valentine's Day
(b) The Canterbury Tales; Pilgrimage to St. Thomas Becket
(c) The Book of the Duchess; Death of Blanche-Duchess of Lancaster
(d) None of the above

134 Ruskin speaks of the "Necessity to all high imagination that it should point straight from life".

Whom did he praise in these lines?

(a) Wycliffe
(b) Boccaccio
(c) Dante
(d) Chaucer

135 "O hateful harm ! Condicion of poverte! With thrust, with cold, with hunger so confounde (d)"
In which poem of Chaucer, do these lines appear?
(a) The Parson's Tale
(b) The Pardoner's Tale
(c) Of the Mannes Tale of Lawe
(d) The Priest's Tale

136 The lines, "She was a worthy woman al hir lyve/Housbondes at cherche dore she hadde five", are an example of
(a) blank verse (b) clerihew
(c) heroic couplet (d) free verse

137 Both Hocdeve and Lydgate praise him for his style 'as a flower of eloquence'. Who is praised in the above line?
(a) Geoffrey Chaucer (b) John Gower
(c) The Pearl Poet (d) William Langland

138 Thomson, in his 'Later Louards say that', 'by the time the Roman establishment was succeeded by the Anglican, lollardy was developing into puritanism'?
Who was the pioneer of the Lollards Movement mentioned in the above lines?
(a) Langland (b) Chaucer
(c) Wycliffe (d) Gower

139 "As smale children doon in hire childhede
Among thise children was a wydwes sone
A little clergeon, seven year of age
That day by day to scole was his wene
And eek also, Where as he saugh the ymage
Of Cristes mooder, hadde he in usage.
Which song did the seven year old boy mentioned in the above extract used to sing on his way to his school?
(a) Ave Marie and Alma redemptoris
(b) Tribute to Jesus Christ
(c) Hymn to virgin Mary (d) None of the above

140 A lovyere and a lusty bacheler,
With lokkes crulleas they were leyd in presse.
Of twenty year of age he was, I gesse.
Of his stature he was of evene lengthe,
And wonderly delyvere and of greet strengthe.
And he hadde been somtyme in chyvachie.
In Flaundres, in Artoys and Pycardie,
And born hym weel, as of so litel space,
In hope to stonded in his lady grace.
Embrouded was he, as it were a meede
Al ful of freehe floures, whyte and reede.
Which pilgrim of Chaucer's 'Canterbury Tales' is described in the above extract?
(a) The Squire (b) The Friar
(c) The Merchant (d) The Yeoman

141 "My theme is alwey onn and evere was
"Radix malorum est cupiditas"
What is the meaning of "Radix Malorum est cupiditas" in the above lines?
(a) Healing powers for all ailments
(b) Greed is the root of all evil
(c) The parishioners always love pardoner
(d) The Pardoner believes in collecting money

142 "I wol biwaille in manere of tragedie
The harm of hem that stoode in heigh degree
And fillen so that ther has no remedie
To brynge hem out of hir adversitee
For certain, whan that fortune list to flee
Ther may no man the cours of hire withholde".
What is the theme of the Monk's tale as explained in the above extract?
(a) Downfall of persons of high power and prosperity
(b) Downfall of man because of woman
(c) Tragedies are realistic
(d) Greed is the root cause of all evil

143 "When that Aprille with his shoures soote,
The droghte of March hath perced to the roote,
And bathed every veyne in switch licour
Of which vertu engendered is the flour;"
The above extract is the prologue of which of the following poem?
(a) The House of Fame (b) Confessio Amantis
(c) The Canterbury Tales (d) The Book of the Duchess

144 A thousand tymes have I herd men telle
That there is Joye in heaven, and peyne in helle:
The above extract is the beginning of prologue of a which of the following works of Chaucer?
(a) Parliament of Foules
(b) The Book of the Duchess
(c) The Canterbury Tales
(d) Legend of Good Women

145 "Patience herself, what goddess e'er she be. Doth lesserblench at suff'rance than I do".
For whom these lines were said by Troilus in Act I Scene 1 of Troilus and Criseyde?
(a) The Squire (b) Pandarus (c) Calchas (d) Helen

146 According to an American poet, "Chaucer found his native tongue a dialect and left it a language."
Who was the American poet?
(a) Mathew Arnold (b) Lowell
(c) Edward Albert (d) Steinbeck

147 According to Mathew Arnold, "this contribution was a large free' sound representation of things, that had truth of substance."
Who is referred to in the above lines?
(a) John Gower (b) William Langland
(c) John Wycliffe (d) Geoffrey Chaucer

148 "What sholde we won men werche the while?'
Somme Shul sowe the sak, quod piers, for
shedyin of the whete;
The above extract has been taken from
(a) Vox Clamantis
(b) Piers the Plowman
(c) Old Testament
(d) Canterbury Tales

149 "The sea sal ryse, als the buke says Abouten the heght of ilka mountayne"
What is the meaning of above lines taken from 'Pricke of Conscience'?
(a) The sea rises
(b) The sea took the height of mountain
(c) The sea rises and overflows
(d) None of the above

150 Steinbeck writes, "If this story is a parable, perhaps everyone takes his own meaning from it and reads his own life into it."
Which poem is referred to in the above lines?
(a) Sir Gawain and the Green Knight
(b) The Pearl
(c) Revelation of Divine love
(d) Confessio Amantis

151 "In a somer seson, whan softe was the sonne,
I shoop me into shroudes as I a sheep were,
In habite as an heremite unholy of werkes,
Wente wide in this world wondres to here
Ac on a May morwenynge on Malverne hilles
Me bifel a ferly, of Fairye me thoghte.
I was were forwandred and wente me to reste
Under a brood bank by a bourne syde;
And as I lay and lenede and loked on the watres,
I slombred into a slepyng, it sweyed so murye.
Thanne gan I meten a merveillous swevene
That I was in a wildernesse, wiste I nevere
where."
The above extract is the beginning of which poem?
(a) Confessio Amantis
(b) The Canterbury Tales
(c) Speculum Meditantis
(d) Piers the Plowman

152 According to David Daiches, "Gower was a more typical representative of his age and class than Chaucer could claim to be".
Why did David said so about Gower?
(a) Because Gower was one of the major court poets of the 14th century
(b) Because Gower was a personal friend of Geoffrey Chaucer
(c) Both (a) and (b)
(d) None of the above

153 "O worthi noble kyng, Henry the ferthe,
In whom the glade fortune is befalle
The people to governe uppon this earthe,
God hath thee chose, in comforts of ous alle:
The worschipe of this lond, which was down
falle, Now stant upriht thurgh grace of the
goodnesse, Which every man is holde forto
blesse."
Name the poem and the poet of the above extract.
(a) Confessio Amantis by John Gower
(b) Piers the Plowman by William Langland
(c) In Praise of Peace by John Gower
(d) The House of fame by Geoffrey Chaucer

154 The line 'He loved gold in special for, gold in physic is a cordial'.
(a) Gower (b) Chaucer (c) Malory (d) Mandeville

155 "Forthi the stile of my writinges
Fro this day foth I thenke change
And speke of thing is noght so strange,
Which every kinde hath upon honde, And
wherupon the world mot stonde,
And hath don sithen it began,
And schal whil ther is any man;
And that is love, of which I mene
To trete, as after schal be sene."
The above extract has been taken from confessio Amantis by John Gower. What is the theme of the given extract and poem in whole?
(a) Confessions made by priest Genius to an aging lover.
(b) Confessions made by an ageing lover to the priest Genius.
(c) One sided love
(d) Confession of hatred by priest Genius for the aging lover.

Directions (Q. Nos. 156-160) *Read the following poem and answer the questions.*

Old and alone, she sits at nights.
Nodding before the television.
The house is quiet now. She knits,
rises to put the kettle on,
watches a cowboy's killing, reads
the local Births and Deaths and falls
asleep at 'growing stock-piles of war-heads'
A world that threatens worse ills
fades. She dreams of life spent
in the one house: suffers again
poverty, sickness, abandonment,
a child's death, a brother's brain
melting to madness. Seventy years
of common trouble; the kettle sings.
At midnight she says her silly prayers,
And takes her teeth out and collects her night-things.

156 How was the past of the lady is described in the poem?

1. Poverty stricken
2. Sickness
3. Child's death
4. Abandonment

Select the correct answer using the codes given below.

(a) Only 2
(b) 2, 3 and 4
(c) 1, 2 and 3
(d) All of the above

157 What is the theme of the poem?

(a) Hopelessness and universality of mortality
(b) Good times will come soon
(c) Distressing routine of the lady
(d) Distressing past of the lady

158 Which of the following part of the poem shows personification?

(a) Collects her night things
(b) Says her silly prayers
(c) The kettle sings
(d) A world that threatens worse ills fades

159 What is the symbolic meaning of war heads?

(a) Explosives
(b) The woman has experienced world war
(c) People are killing each other
(d) People had been beheaded

160 What does 'brother's brain melting to madness' mean?

(a) The brain of woman's brother has started melting
(b) Woman's brother is not with her
(c) The mental health of woman's brother is deteriorating
(d) None of the above

PREVIOUS YEARS' QUESTIONS

December 2018

1 One of the less noticed and acknowledged distinction of The Canterbury Tales is that

(a) instead of revealing England's divisions, it reveled in its diversity.
(b) it upheld the idea that we cannot divorce poetry from knowledge because poetry itself is an object ok knowledge
(c) it alerted us to the term auctor, someone who is both 'an originator, or one who gives increase', the best description for Chaucer himself.
(d) it married domesticity to divinity, the baker's loaf with the bread of life.

2 One of the most flexible metres, ... is a five foot line. It was introduced by Geoffrey Chaucer in the fourteenth century and has since then become the commonest of metres in English poetry.

(a) Iambic (b) Trochaic (c) Hexameter (d) Pentameter

June 2018

3 In the Inferno Dante, as he travels through the various circles of the hell finds Judas who is unable to speak. What is the reason behind this?

(a) His tongue is transformed into a coiled snake
(b) His head is battered and so he cannot open his mouth
(c) Lucifer is chewing on his head
(d) His tongue is pulled out and nailed on the tree of sin.

4 In John Gower's confessio Amantis, Amans the lover makes his confession ot the priest named

(a) Verito (b) Genius
(c) Amor (d) Phoebe

5 Which of the following is true of The Canterbury Tales?

(a) Chaucer, the pilgrim, narrates Sir Thomas Tale only
(b) Chaucer, the pilgrim, narrates The Tale of Melibee only
(c) Chaucer, the pilgrim, narrates Sir Thomas Tale and the of Melibee
(d) Chaucer, the pilgrim does attempt ot narrate an unnamed tale but abruptly stops due to the intervention of the other pilgrims

6 During the reign of Norman kings, it was fashionable to speak..... in upper-class circles in England.

(a) Norse (b) Latin (c) Danish (d) French

November 2017

7 In Canterbury Tales who has a red face full of sores?

(a) The Summoner (b) The shipman
(c) The Yeoman (d) The Reeve

8 The metrical form of Gower's Confessio Amantis is

(a) iambic pentameter (b) anapestic trimeter
(c) octosyllabic couplets (d) trochaic tetrameter

January 2017

9 In the general Prologue to 'The Canterbury Tales' which two characters are examples of deep Christian goodness?

1 The Summoner 2. The Parson
3. The Ploughman 4. The Pardoner

The right combination according to the code is

(a) 1 and 2 (b) 2 and 4 (c) 2 and 3 (d) 3 and 4

10 Two of the following words were borrowed from French after the Norman Conquest.

1 Mutton
2. Pork
3. Sheep
4. Swine

The right combination according to the code is:

(a) 1 and 2
(b) 1 and 3
(c) 2 and 4
(d) 2 and 4

July 2016

11 In Geoffrey Chaucer's Canterbury Tales, the pilgrims, like the medieval society of which they are a part, are made up of three social groups or 'estates'. What are the three estates?

(a) Nobility, church and commoners
(b) Royalty, nobility and peasantry
(c) Royalists, republicans and peasants
(d) Country, city and commons

12 Name the dominant meter of the following quatrain: The curfew tolls the knell of parting day,
The lowing herd winds slowly o'er the lea,
The plowman homeward plods his weary way,
And leaves the world to darkness and to me.

(a) Iambic Hexameter
(b) Trochaic Pentameter
(c) Iambic Pentameter
(d) Terza Rima

13 During the middle English period, many words were borrowed from two languages

1 Celtic
2. Latin
3. French
4. Old Norse

The right combination according to the code is:

(a) 1 and 2
(b) 2 and 3
(c) 2 and 4
(d) 3 and 4

December 2015

14 Chaucer satirises the Monk because the Monk

(a) is to concerned with courtesy and metters of etiquette
(b) cheats the poor peasants by selling them false religious relics
(c) courts favour of wealthy people but spends no time with poor people
(d) spends too much time on hunting and too little time on religious duty

June 2015

15 Which Canterbury pilgrim carries a brooch inscribed with the Latin words meaning 'Love Conquers All'?

(a) The Prioress
(b) The Monk
(c) The wife of Bath
(d) The Squire

16 What is the moral of 'The Nun's Priest's Tale'?

(a) Slow and steady wins the race
(b) Greed is the root of all evil
(c) Beauty lies within
(d) Never trust a flatterer

17 The direct French influence on the English language during the middle English period was in the form of..... .

(a) loss of inflections
(b) intake of French words into English
(c) both the loss of inflections and intake of French words into English
(d) addition of inflections

18 Chaucer's first work, 'The Book of the Duchess' is dream poem on the death of..... .

(a) Duchess of Malfi
(b) Duchess of Lancaster
(c) Duchess of Scotland
(d) Duchess of Paris

December 2014

19 From the Canterbury pilgrims, which group would qualify as the 'upper class'?

(a) The Pardoner, the Miller, The Nun's Priest
(b) Franklin, Parson, Wife of Bath
(c) The Knight, The Squire, The Prioress
(d) The Reeve, The Manciple, The Clerk

20 How did Chaucer's pardoner make his living?

(a) By selling stolen cattle from the neighbourhood ottery
(b) By selling indulgences to those who committed sins
(c) By pardoning those who stole property or committed other crimes
(d) By assisting the Friar in Church services

June 2014

21 Modern English emerged from the

(a) South Midland dialect
(b) East Midland dialect
(c) French Language
(d) Northumbrian dialect

22 Most culinary terms in English are derived from

(a) Exotic cooking
(b) French cooking
(c) Native sources
(d) Arabic cooking

23 How many legends of good women could Chaucer complete in his 'The Legend of Good Women'?

(a) Six
(b) Seven
(c) Eight
(d) Nine

ANSWERS

Objective Questions

1. *(b)*	2. *(d)*	3. *(d)*	4. *(c)*	5. *(b)*	6. *(b)*	7. *(b)*	8. *(a)*	9. *(a)*	10. *(c)*
11. *(d)*	12. *(c)*	13. *(b)*	14. *(d)*	15. *(b)*	16. *(c)*	17. *(c)*	18. *(d)*	19. *(a)*	20. *(b)*
21. *(c)*	22. *(d)*	23. *(a)*	24. *(b)*	25. *(a)*	26. *(c)*	27. *(c)*	28. *(d)*	29. *(d)*	30. *(c)*
31. *(c)*	32. *(b)*	33. *(c)*	34. *(d)*	35. *(a)*	36. *(c)*	37. *(b)*	38. *(c)*	39. *(c)*	40. *(d)*
41. *(a)*	42. *(c)*	43. *(b)*	44. *(c)*	45. *(c)*	46. *(b)*	47. *(b)*	48. *(b)*	49. *(d)*	50. *(b)*
51. *(d)*	52. *(b)*	53. *(c)*	54. *(b)*	55. *(d)*	56. *(c)*	57. *(c)*	58. *(a)*	59. *(a)*	60. *(c)*
61. *(a)*	62. *(d)*	63. *(c)*	64. *(d)*	65. *(b)*	66. *(c)*	67. *(b)*	68. *(c)*	69. *(d)*	70. *(a)*
71. *(a)*	72. *(c)*	73. *(c)*	74. *(a)*	75. *(c)*	76. *(c)*	77. *(c)*	78. *(c)*	79. *(c)*	80. *(d)*
81. *(b)*	82. *(b)*	83. *(d)*	84. *(d)*	85. *(d)*	86. *(a)*	87. *(d)*	88. *(d)*	89. *(b)*	90. *(d)*
91. *(a)*	92. *(c)*	93. *(a)*	94. *(b)*	95. *(a)*	96. *(b)*	97. *(a)*	98. *(a)*	99. *(a)*	100. *(a)*
101. *(a)*	102. *(b)*	103. *(a)*	104. *(a)*	105. *(a)*	106. *(c)*	107. *(b)*	108. *(a)*	109. *(b)*	110. *(a)*
111. *(c)*	112. *(b)*	113. *(c)*	114. *(b)*	115. *(d)*	116. *(b)*	117. *(a)*	118. *(c)*	119. *(d)*	120. *(a)*
121. *(a)*	122. *(b)*	123. *(c)*	124. *(d)*	125. *(a)*	126. *(b)*	127. *(a)*	128. *(c)*	129. *(b)*	130. *(a)*
131. *(c)*	132. *(b)*	133. *(c)*	134. *(c)*	135. *(c)*	136. *(c)*	137. *(a)*	138. *(c)*	139. *(a)*	140. *(a)*
141. *(b)*	142. *(a)*	143. *(c)*	144. *(d)*	145. *(a)*	146. *(b)*	147. *(d)*	148. *(b)*	149. *(c)*	150. *(b)*
151. *(d)*	152. *(a)*	153. *(c)*	154. *(a)*	155. *(b)*	156. *(d)*	157. *(a)*	158. *(c)*	159. *(b)*	160. *(c)*

Pervious Years' Questions

1. *(a)*	2. *(d)*	3. *(c)*	4. *(b)*	5. *(c)*	6. *(d)*	7. *(a)*	8. *(c)*	9. *(c)*	10. *(a)*
11. *(a)*	12. *(c)*	13. *(b)*	14. *(d)*	15. *(a)*	16. *(d)*	17. *(b)*	18. *(d)*	19. *(c)*	20. *(b)*
21. *(b)*	22. *(b)*	23. *(d)*							

Poetry in the Age of Revival (1400-1550)

The Revival age poetry witnessed the introduction of the sonnet by Wyatt and Surrey. The pastoral poetry, allegory, ballads, satire and didactic poems were the new trends of this age. The poets of the age were divided in the category of English Chaucerians, Scottish Chaucerians and the New Court poets.

The Age of Revival

The Age of Revival witnessed rebellions like, The Wars of the Roses and Cade's rebellion. English Chaucerians and Scottish Chaucerian poets influenced by Chaucer made significant contributions. Wyatt and Surrey introduced the sonnet with its metrical rhyme scheme.

The period following the death of Geoffrey Chaucer witnessed a wide range of political changes. Henry V was crowned as the King in 1413. Soon, after his accession in April 1413, Henry V resolved to revive the war against France and stake his claim to the French throne.

In August 1415, Henry's army landed at France and surrounded the port town of Harfleur. The English army achieved a major victory at the Battle of Agincourt in 1415. By November 1415, Henry's army returned to a rousing welcome in England. Five years later, by the Treaty of Troyes, France accepted all the demands of the English King. Henry V was recognised as an heir to the French throne and Catherine, the daughter of Charles VI, King of France became his wife.

However, Henry V could not live long enough and died in Bois de Vincennes on 31st August, 1922. After his death, his son, Henry VI became the King, but he was not strong enough to maintain a powerful hold on the English Empire. Soon after, the French under the magic leadership of Joan of Arc regained all their possessions.

During the Middle Ages, a period that took place between the fall of ancient Rome in 476 AD and the beginning of the 14th century, Europeans made few advances in science and art. It is also known as the 'Dark Ages', the era is often branded as a

In this Chapter

time of war, ignorance, famine and pandemics. The Renaissance started in Florence, Italy, a place with a rich cultural history. Great Italian writers, artists, politicians and others declared that they were participating in an intellectual and artistic revolution that would be much different from what they had experienced during the Dark Ages. The movement first expanded to other Italian city-states. Then, during the 15th century, Renaissance ideas spread from Italy to France and then throughout Western and Northern Europe.

Although other European countries experienced their Renaissance later than Italy, the impacts were still revolutionary. Humanism encouraged Europeans to question the role of the Roman Catholic Church during the Renaissance. As more people learned how to read, write and interpret ideas, they began to closely examine and critique religion as they knew it. Also the printing press allowed for texts, including the Bible, to be easily reproduced and widely read by the people themselves, for the first time.

Scholars believe that the demise of the Renaissance was the result of several compounding factors. By the end of the 15th century, numerous wars had plagued the Italian peninsula. Spanish, French and German invaders battling for Italian territories caused disruption and instability in the region.

Also, changing trade routes led to a period of economic decline and limited the amount of money that wealthy contributors could spend on the arts. Later, in a movement known as the Counter-Reformation, the Catholic church censored artists and writers in response to the Protestant Reformation. Many Renaissance thinkers feared being too bold, which stifled creativity. Furthermore, in 1545, the Council of Trent established the Roman Inquisition, which made humanism and any views that challenged the Catholic church as an act of heresy dissidence, punishable by death. By the early 17th century, the Renaissance movement had died out, giving way to the Age of Enlightenment.

Literature of the Age of Revival

The period following the death of Chaucer was largely a barren period that did not produce any work of note. In the Age of Revival, the focus was more on classical learning. The interest in classical literature prevented the growth of native literature. Metrical romances continued to be translated from the French homilies and saints' legends and rhyming chronicles were still manufactured.

According to William J Long, "The 15th century was an age of preparation, of learning the beginnings of science and of getting acquainted with the great ideals, the stern law, the profound philosophy, the suggestive mythology and the noble poetry of the Greeks and Romans. So, the mind was furnished with ideas for a new literature."

Poetic Trends in the Age of Revival

Following are the types of poetry prevalent in the age of revival

The Pastoral

- During this age, the pastoral mode became an important vehicle for satire of court and urban life.
- Alexander Barclay produced five eclogues, three of which were translated from Pope Pius II's *Miserae Curialium* and two from Italian poet Baptista Mantuanus' poetry. Barclay was the first to use this mode in the 14th century and it was later developed by Spenser in the 16th century.

Allegory

- Chaucer's allegorical poetry was imitated by the English and Scottish Chaucerians.
- Chaucer's works, which had the most influence on his successors were *The Parlement of Foules, The Book of the Duchess* and *The House of Fame.*
- William Dunbar's *The Golden Targe*, Stephen Hawes' *Example of Virtue* and Lydgate's *Temple of Glas* are examples of this kind.

Ballads

- Narrative poems of usually folk origin, Ballads became popular during 15th century.
- Ballads about Robin Hood were being sung from the late 14th century and Wynkyn de Worde's collection of Robin Hood ballads was printed around 1495.
- Some of the popular ballads of this age were *Lamkin*, *The Wife of Usher's Well*, *Chevy Chase* and *Lord Randal*.
- Two main characteristics of the ballads of this age were
  - (i) they sprang from the unlettered common people and
  - (ii) they were objective, dealing not with a poet's thought or feeling but with a man or a deed.

Satire and Didacticism

- Both Alexander Barclay and John Skelton had a sense of outrage at the contemporary scene. Their works reflect this satirist's outrage.
- Barclay's *Ship of Fools* saw the world as a collection of fools.
- Skelton's *Bowge of Court* satirised contemporary court life. Dunbar's satire, as seen in *The Dance of the Seven Deadly Sins*, is in nature of a jovial invective.

Categorisation of the Poets of the Age of Revival

The poets of the Age of Revival are described into three categories

1. English Chaucerians
2. Scottish Chaucerians
3. New Court Poets

English Chaucerians

English Chaucerians were a group of 15th and 16th century poets, whose works were influenced by Geoffrey Chaucer. They used Chaucerian diction and phraseology or poetic forms.

Thomas Hoccleve (1369-1426)

Thomas Hoccleve was a contemporary of Chaucer. He was probably born in London around 1369. There is little biographical information available about him. He has been grouped together with John Lydgate and others as one of the 'English Chaucerians'. Hoccleve might have died around 1426-27 in Southwick, England.

Literary Career and Works

Hoccleve's first work for which a date is known with certainty is *Letter of Cupid,* which was published in 1402. A translation and adaptation of the popular French poet Christine de Pisan's *Epistre au Dieu d'Amours* (1399), the poem was one of Hoccleve's most popular works. It was an example of courtly poetry in the manner of the lines of the *Roman de la Rose.*

His next poem was *La Mâle Règle* ('The Male Regimen'; 1406'). In this autobiographical poem, Hoccleve complains of the hardships of his life, many of which, he confesses, he brought on himself. He describes his physical ailments, financial strains and moral failings quite accurately. Hoccleve's principal work, *De Regimine Principum* (*The Regiment of Princes,* 1411-12) was written for the future King Henry V, when he was Prince of Wales. This homily is written in the form of a seven-line stanza. Consisting of advice to the prince on the proper conduct of a monarch, the poem was Hoccleve's most successful work. The poem's prologue includes a lengthy dialogue between Hoccleve and a beggar and an address to Chaucer.

Hoccleve's poem was written at a time, when England was still feeling the consequences of the deposition of Richard II, which haunted the usurper's reign by raising questions about the legitimacy of the Lancastrian line. It was dedicated to Prince Henry, who ceased to be a prince, when he ascended the throne on 21st March, 1413, as Henry V. The poem begins with a 2000-line prologue, which sets the poem in the context of a complaint about the author's overdue annuity. Hoccleve reminds the Prince of delinquent payments due to him and therefore the poem can also be considered as a personal petition, a critique of the current regime or even a work of propaganda.

Hoccleve cites three sources for his poem. The first is Aristotle's letter to Alexander the Great known as the *Secreta Secretorum*, the second is Aegidius Romanus's (c. 1247-1316) *De regimine principum* and the third Jacob de Cessolis' *Chessbook.*

Letter of Cupid

Cupido, unto whos commandement
The gentil kinrede of goddes on hy
And peple infernal been obedient,
And the mortel folk seruen bisyly,
Of goddesse Sitheree sone oonly,
To alle tho that to our deitee
Been sogettes greetinges senden we.
In general, we wole that yee knowe
That ladies of honour and reverence
And other gentil wommen han ysowe
Swich seed of complainte in our audience
Of men that doon hem outrage and offense
That it our eres greeveth for to heere,
So, pitous is th' effect of hir mateere;
And passing alle londes on this yle
That clept is Albioun they moost complaine;
They sayn that ther is croppe and roote of guile,
So, can tho men dissimulen and faine
With standing dropes in hir eyen twaine,
Whan that hir herte feeleth no distresse.

John Lydgate (1370-1449)

John Lydgate was a Benedictine monk belonging to the ancient and prestigious abbey of Bury St Edmunds in Suffolk. He was born at Lydgate, Suffolk, about 1370. He may have been educated at the School of the Benedictine monks and later at the Benedictine house of studies at Oxford. He became a subdeacon in 1389, a deacon in 1393 and in 1397, he was ordained a priest. He is believed to have founded a school of rhetoric at Bury Saint Edmunds, where he taught the sons of noble families.

Literary Career and Works

Lydgate's only prose work, *The Serpent of Division* was written in 1422. His three most important works are the long poems, *The Troy Book* (1412-20), *The Siege of Thebes*

(1420-22) and *The Fall of Princes* (1431-38). *The Troy Book* was written at the behest of The Prince of Wales, later King Henry V. It is an attempt to recount the story of the Trojan War. Lydgate's poem is a translation and expansion of Guido delle Colonne's *Historia destructionis Troiae*, a Latin prose account written in 1287.

The Siege of Thebes falls about midway in Lydgate's career and was completed before the death of Henry V. The work is based on some version of the French *Roman de Thèbes* (c. 1175). The main body of the work is an elaborate 4540-line exemplum chronicling the disastrous careers of a series of deeply flawed kings: Oedipus, his sons Eteocles and Polynices and finally Creon.

The work is also related to Chaucer's *Canterbury Tales*. Lydgate imagines himself joining Chaucer's pilgrims in Canterbury and narrates a tale that is meant to be a companion piece to *The Knight's Tale*. *The Falle of Princes* charts the rise and fall of the fortunes of famous people.

The text is based on a similar work by Boccaccio. It begins with the Fall of Adam and Eve and ends eight books later, with the account of the capture of King John of France at the Battle of Poitiers in 1356. Containing 36365 lines, this is Lydgate's longest work. In addition to these works, Lydgate also wrote courtly poems. *The Complaint of the Black Knight, The Floure of Courtesye* and *The Temple of Glas* (1403), *Saints' Lives* (The Man of Law's Tale), devotional poems (The Life of Our Lady and The Dance of Death) and occasional pieces. He probably died at the monastery of Bury St Edmunds.

The Floure of Curtesye

In Feverier, whan the frosty moone
Was horned, ful of Phebus firy lyght
And that she gan to reyse her streames sone,
Saynt Valentyne, upon thy blisful nyght
Of dutie whan glad is every wight,
And foules chese, to voyde her olde sorowe,
Everyche his make, upon the next morowe,
The same tyme, I herde a larke synge
Ful lustely, agayne the morowe gray:
"Awake, ye lovers, out of your slombringe,
This glad morowe, in al the haste ye may"
Some observaunce dothe unto this day,
Your choyse agen of herte to renewe,
In confyrmyng forever to be trewe.
"And ye that be, of chosyng, at your large
This lusty day, by custome of nature,
Take upon you the blisful holy charge
To serve love, whyle your lyfe may dure,
With herte, body and al your besy cure,
Forevermore, as Venus and Cipride
For you disposeth and the God Cupyde.'

Stephen Hawes (1475-1525)

Stephen Hawes was a poet and courtier, who served King Henry VII of England. He was probably born about 1475 in Suffolk. He was educated at Oxford and travelled in England, Scotland and France. He was Groom of the Chamber to Henry VII. He was known for his sharp memory and could repeat by heart the works of most of the English poets, especially the poems of John Lydgate, whom he called his master.

Literary Career and Works

Hawes' most popular work was the long allegorical poem, *The Passetyme of Pleasure* (1509). The main theme of the poem was the education and pilgrimage of the knight Graunde Amoure. The poem was written in rime royal and contained about 5800 lines, divided into forty-five chapters.

His other notable work was the allegorical *The Example of Vertu*. It was mostly written in the seven-line Chaucerian stanza, except the description of the arming of the hero, where decasyllabic couplets are used and it was divided into 14 chapters. Hawes can be labelled as a Chaucerian only in prosody and not in content.

Like Chaucer, he employed rime royal and decasyllabic couplets in his work. According to A C Ward, "Hawes looked upon himself as a follower of Chaucer, though he was in fact a belated medievalist using verse as a medium for sermonical allegories uneasily wedded to chivalrous romance."

The Passetyme of Pleasure

The good Dame Mercy with Dame Charyte
My body buryed full ryght humbly
In a fayre temple of olde antyquyte,
Where was for me a dyryge devoutely
And with many a masse full right solempnely;
And over my grave, to be in memory,
Remembraunce made this lytell epytaphy:
"O erthe, on erthe it is a wonders cace
That thou arte blynde and wyll not the knowe.
Though upon erthe thou hast thy dwellynge-place,
Yet erthe at laste must nedes the overthrowe.
Thou thynkest the to be none erthe I trowe;
For yf thou dydest, thou woldest than apply
To forsake pleasure and to lerne to dy.
"O erthe, of erthe why arte thou so proude?
Now what thou arte call to remembraunce.
Open thyn eres unto my songe aloude.
Is not thy beauté, strength and puyssaunce,
Though it be cladde with clothes of plesaunce,
Very erthe and also worms fode,

Whan erthe to erthe shall so tourne the blode?
"The vyle carkes set upon a fyre
Dooth often haunte the synne of lechery,
Fulfyllynge the foule carnall desyre.
Thus erthe with erthe is corrupte mervaylously;
And erthe on erthe wyll nothynge puryfye
Tyll erthe to erthe be nere subverted.
For erthe with erthe is so perverted.
"O mortall folke! you may beholde and se
Howe I lye here, sometyme a myghty knyght;
The end of joye and all prosperyte
Is dethe at last, through his course and myght;
After the day there cometh the derke night;
For though the day be never so longe,
At last the belles ryngeth to evensonge.

John Skelton (1460-1529)

John Skelton was one of the most prominent of early Tudor poets and satirists. Erasmus called Skelton 'the one light and glory of British letters,' mainly because of his translations of the classics and his Latin verses. Skelton was probably born in Dist Norfolk, around 1460. He studied at Oxford University, where he gained a Laureate-a degree in rhetoric. In 1493, Skelton received the same honour at Cambridge and also at Leuven.

Literary Career and Works

Skelton found a patron in the learned Countess of Richmond, Henry VII's mother, for whom he wrote *of Mannes Lyfe the Peregrynacioun,* a translation, a lost translation of Guillaume de Deguilleville's *Pèlerinage de la vie humaine.* He also wrote an elegy *Of the death of the noble prince Kynge Edwarde the forth.*

John Skelton also served as the tutor to Henry VIII for five years. Based on his experiences, he wrote a satire of court life entitled *Bowge of Courte,* which was published in 1499. His other famous works include *Colin Clout* (1521) which was directed against the power of Cardinal Wolsey, *Phyllyp Sparrow* (1505) the lament of a Norwich school girl for her pet bird killed by a cat and *Ballade of the Scottysshe Kynge* (1513), a celebration of the victory at Flodden.

Skelton's famous *Magnificence* (1516), is an allegory in which the generous prince Magnificence is first destroyed by his own ill-advised generosity then restored by Goodhope, Perseverance and related virtues. Skelton's repetition of short two beat lines with accents became known as the skeltonic meter.

The Bowge of Court

Bowge of Court is Skelton's earliest surviving major work. It falls into the category of political and historical allegory. *Bowge of Court* is written in seven line stanzas and Drede, the narrator of the poem, encounters seven different people, while on his journey on the boat. It is a dream allegory satirising court life.

Bowge of Court

In Autumpne when the sonne in vyrgyne
By radyante hete enryped hath our corne
Whan luna full of mutabylyte
As Emperes the dyademe hath worne
Of our pole artyke smylynge halfe in scorne
At our foly and our vnstedfastnesse
The tyme whan Mars to werre hym dyd dres
I callynge to mynde the great auctoryte
Of poetes olde whyche full craftely
Under as couerte termes as coude be
Can touche a troughte and cloke it subtylly
Wyth fresshe vtteraunce full sentencyously
Dyuerse in style some spared not vyce to wrythe
Some of moralyte nobly dyde endyte
Wherby I rede theyr renome and theyr fame
Maye neuer dye bute euermore endure
I was sore moued to a force the same
But Ignoraunce full soone dyde me dyscure
And shewed that in this arte I was not sure
For to Illumyne she sayde I was to dulle
Auysynge me my penne awaye to pulle
And not to wrythe/ for he so wyll atteyne
Excedynge ferther than his connynge is
His hede maye be harde but feble is his brayne
Yet haue I knowen suche er this
But of reproche surely he maye not mys
That clymmeth hyer than he may fotynge haue
What and he slyde downe who shall hym saue
Thus vp and down my mynde was drawen and cast
That I ne wyste what to do was beste
Soo sore enwered that I was at the laste
Enforsed to slepe and for to take some reste
And to lye downe as soone as I me dreste
At harwyche porte slumbrynge as I laye
In myne hostes house called powers keye.

Alexander Barclay (1474-1552)

Poet and priest, Alexander Barclay was born around 1474. A Scotsman by descent, he probably came to England very early. He studied in Oxford and perhaps, also in Cambridge.

Literary Career and Works

Barclay started his literary career with a translation of Pierre Gringore's *Le chasteau de labour,* published by Antoine Verard (*c.* 1503) and reprinted by Pynson (*c.* 1505) and Wynkyn de Worde (1506 and *c.* 1510).

Though, most of Barclay's writings are translations, his writing style allowed him to keep the spirit of the original work, while successfully adapting each piece to incorporate his own ideas concerning English society.

Barclay's most well-known work *The Ship of Fools* (1509), is an adaptation of a popular German satire, Das Narrenschiff, by Sebastian Brant. It looks forward to Erasmus' *Praise of Folly*. The work describes a ship laden with fools setting sail for the fool's paradise of Narragonia. The author identifies the many varying examples of folly separately, including the corrupt judge, the drunkard and the untrained physician. Barclay adapted Brant's story to his own view of English society. He also wrote the first formal eclogues in English, filled with entertaining pictures of rural life. In 1552, Barclay became rector of All Hallows, Lombard Street, in the city of London. Soon afterwards, he died at Croydon, where he had passed part of his youth and there he was buried.

The Ship of Fools

Who that is besy to mesure and compace
The heuyn and erth and all the worlde large
Describynge the clymatis and folke of euery place
He is a fole and hath a greuous charge
Without auauntage, wherfore let hym discharge
Hym selfe, of that fole whicle in his necke doth syt
About suche folyes dullynge his mynde and wyt.

That fole, of wysdome and reason doth fayle
And also discression labowrynge for nought.
And in this shyp shall helpe to drawe the sayle
Which day and nyght infixeth all his thought
To haue the hole worlde within his body brought
Measurynge the costes of euery royalme and landne
And clymatis, with his compace, in his hande

George Ashby (1390 – 1475)

George Ashby was an English civil servant and poet. He is better known as a writer of political verse. Ashby was born about 1390 and was from Warwickshire. He acted as clerk of the Signet Office under Henry VI and his queen, Margaret of Anjou.

Literary Career and Works

Ashby was perhaps confined in the Fleet Prison by the Yorkist conquerors of Henry VI, who was deposed in 1461. He also wrote a poem on the same theme titled, *George Ashby, Complaint of a Prisoner in the Fleet 1463*. He also wrote a longer poem on the *Active Policy of a Prince*, intended to instruct the ill-fated son of Margaret and Henry. Ashby's *Dicts and Sayings of Various Philosophers* is a collection of versified proverbial material in Latin translated into 1263 lines of rime royal verse.

Osbern Bokenham (1393-1463)

Osbern Bokenham was an English poet and friar. His birthplace was near 'an old pryory of Blake canons,'.

Bokenham is best known as the author of a verse collection entitled *Legends of Holy Women*. It is composed of 10000 lines, the poem is written in the Middle English Suffolk dialect. It is written entirely in Chaucerian decasyllabic verse. It consists of thirteen legends of holy maidens and women.

The women included in this series are St Margaret Virgin, St Anne Mother of St Mary, St Christine, St Faith, St Agnes, St Dorothy, Mary Magdalen, St Katherine, St Cecelia, St Agatha, St Lucy, St Elizabeth and Eleven Thousand Virgins of Saint Ursula.

George Ripley (1415-1490)

George Ripley was an English writer and alchemist. He was Canon regular of the Angustiman priory at Bridlington. Ripley travelled worldwide in his search for alchemical knowledge. He studied in Italy for 20 years, becoming a great favourite of Pope Innocent VIII.

He returned to England in 1477 and wrote his work *The Compound of Alchymy or the 12 Gates leading to the Discovery of the Philosopher's Stone (Liber Duodecim Portarum),* dedicated to King Edward IV.

Thomas Norton (1433-1513)

Thomas Norton was an English poet and alchemist born in Bristol, England, towards the end of the 14th century. Norton himself does not appear to have reaped monetary benefit at any time from his erudition, but is believed to have been a comparatively poor man throughout the whole of his life. Norton died around 1513.

Norton is best known for his work, *Ordinall of Alchemy* written about 1477.

Henry Bradshaw (1450-1513)

Henry Bradshaw was an English poet born in Chester. He entered the Benedictine monastery of Saint Werburgh.

He wrote a Latin treatise *De antiquitate et magnificentia Urbis Cestricie*, which is lost and *An Other Balade To Saynt Werburge*, a life of the patron saint of his monastery in English seven-lined stanza.

Scottish Chaucerians

Scottish Chaucerians were a group of Scottish poets of 15th and early 16th century whose work was indebted to Chaucer. They differed in tone, style and subject matter from their English counterparts. Recent critics have brought to notice that Chaucer's influence on these poets was slight and they also relied on other sources apart from Chaucer.

James I of Scotland (1394-1437)

James I was a Stuart King, who was renowned for being a poet as well as a prince. He was born at Dunfermline in July, 1394. He was sent to France in 1406 and there he was captured by pirates of Flamborough Head. Soon, James became a prisoner of the English King Henry IV. The English kept him imprisoned in the Tower of London for 18 years, but gave him a good education.

Literary Career and Works

It was during his imprisonment that James was exposed to English writing. His love poem *The Kingis Quair* (The King's Book, 1435) owes a lot to Chaucer and makes use of the rhyme royal. The poem focuses on 'James' love for a woman whom, he had first seen during his captivity (historically Joan Beaufort, a relation of the English king, Henry Bolingbroke), but he reveals nothing explicit about the lady or his courtship of her; instead he follows Boethian conventions in portraying his sufferings and his attempts to obtain immortal assistance.

According to Linne R Mooney and Mary Jo Arn, "Chaucer's influence on James is pervasive: James' fictional frame - the reading of a book to overcome sleeplessness and then having a dream, which is related to the contents of the book probably derives from Chaucer's framing of *The Book of the Duchess*; his falling in love at first sight with a woman he sees from his prison tower may derive from Chaucer's Knight's Tale; his description of the sudden onset of lovesickness, from Chaucer's *Troilus and Criseyde* and his descriptions of dream landscapes and goddesses, from *The Book of the Duchess*, *The House of Fame* and *The Parlement of Foules.*"

After the death of King Henry V of England in 1422, James was eventually released under the Treaty of London for a sizeable ransom and after a marriage had been arranged, on 12th February, 1424, to Joan Beaufort, daughter of the Duke of Somerset. James then returned to be crowned at Scone on 2nd May, 1424. He ruled for sometime before being murdered in Perth on 20th February, 1437.

Robert Henryson (1425-1500)

Robert Henryson was a significant writer of 15th century Scotland. Along with Gavin Douglas and William Dunbar, Henryson is one of the Scotland's major medieval 'makars' or poetic 'makers'. There is very little biographical information available about Henryson's life.

Literary Career and Works

Henryson's main works include a version of *Aesop's Fables* (usually entitled *The Morall fabillis of Esope the Phrygian*), *The Testament of Cresseid*, a follow-on to Chaucer's *Troilus and Criseyde*, (but also seen as his own, a poem in its own right), *Robene and Makyne* and *Orpheus and Eurydice*, a version of the classic tale.

In *The Testament of Cresseid*, Henryson takes up the story of Chaucer's heroine in *Troilus and Criseyde* and decides to provide his own interpretation to the story. He purports to describe, "the fatal desteny of fair Cresseid, that ended wretchedly."

The poem is made up of three basic parts, the prologue, tale and the epilogue. The prologue begins with an account of the weather by the poet himself, who decides to pass the time on a miserable day by reading Chaucer's *Troilus and Criseyde*. The author then decides to occupy himself by writing his own tale.

The *Tale of Cresseid* describes her exclusion after her betrayal of Troilus and abandonment by the lustful Diomede. She blasphemes both Venus and Cupid and rails against them for her ruin.

The God punishes her with leprosy, which destroys her looks and condemns her to penury. She is forced to lead life as a leper and beg for alms. During one of her begging encounters, she meets Troilus. She then laments her infidelity and bequeaths her body to the toads and worms and her royal ring to Troilus.

In contrast to Chaucer's poem, Henryson's poem ends with Cresseid's death. Chaucer, by the end of his tale, destroys any confidence the audience might have in courtly love. But Henryson rearranges fate to suit his purposes: his Troilus lives rather than dies and his Cresseid dies due to her infidelity.

The Testament of Cresseid

Thus chydand with her drerie destenye,
Weiping, scho woik the nicht fra end to end;
Bot all in vane; hir dule, hir cairfull cry,
Micht not remeid, nor yit hir murning mend.
Ane lipper lady rais and till hir wend,
And said, "Quhy spurnis thow aganis the wall,
To sla thyself and mend nathing at all?
"Sen thy weiping dowbillis bot thy wo,
I counsall the mak vertew of ane neid;
To leir to clap thy clapper to and fro,
And leir efter the law of lipper leid."
Thair was na buit, bot furth with thame scho yeid,
Fra place to place, quhill cauld and hounger sair
Compellit hir to be ane rank beggair.
That samin tyme of Troy the garnisoun,
Quhilk had to chiftane worthie Troylus,
Throw jeopardie of weir had strikken down
Knichtis of Grece in number marvellous:
With greit tryumphe and laude victorious
Agane to Troy richt royallie they raid,
The way quhair Cresseid with the lipper baid.
Seing that companie, thai come all with ane stevin;
Thay gaif ane cry and schuik coppis gude speid;
Said, "Worthie lordis, for Goddis lufe of hevin,
To us lipper part of your almous deid."
Than to thair cry nobill Troylus tuik heid,
Having pietie, neir by the place can pas
Quhair Cresseid sat, not witting quhat scho was.
Than upon him scho kest up baith her ene,
And with ane blenk it come into his thocht
That he sumtime hir face befoir had sene;
But scho was in sic plye he knew hir nocht;
Yit than hir luik into his mynd it brocht
The sweit visage and amorous blenking
Of fair Cresseid, sumtyme his awin darling.
Na wonder was, suppois in mynd that he
Tuik hir figure sa sone, and lo! now quhy!
The idole of ane thing in cace may be
Sa deip imprentit in the fantasy,
That it deludis the wittis outwardly,
And sa appeiris in forme and lyke estait
Within the mynd, as it was figurait.

William Dunbar (1460-1520)

Scottish poet William Dunbar is often referred to as the 'Chaucer of Scotland'. He was probably born around 1460 in East Lothian.

Literary Career and Works

Dunbar's chief allegorical poems are *The Goldyn Targe*, a courtly dream-vision poem that celebrates the victory of love over the golden shield of reason and *The Thrissil* and *the Rois*, a prothalamium celebrating the marriage of James IV and Margaret Tudor. Dunbar's most well-known work is *Lament for the Makers*, an elegy dedicated to the distinguished writers who had preceded him, including Geoffrey Chaucer, John Gower and John Lydgate. Although written in a ballad form, the poem is actually a meditation on serious moral and religious issues. It focuses on death as a great leveler and comments on the transience of human nature.

Lament for the Makers

I THAT in heill was and gladness
Am trublit now with great sickness
And feblit with infirmitie:
Timor Mortis conturbat me.
Our plesance here is all vain glory,
This fals world is, but transitory,
The flesh is bruckle, the Feynd is slee:
Timor Mortis conturbat me.
The state of man does change and vary,
Now sound, now sick, now blyth, now sary,
Now dansand mirry, now like to die:
Timor Mortis conturbat me.
No state in Erd here standis sicker;
As with the wynd wavis the wicker
So, wannis this world's vanitie:
Timor Mortis conturbat me.

Dunbar also wrote a number of biting satires. Examples of these are *The Satire on Edinburgh*, *The General Satire*, the *Epitaph on Donald Owre* and the powerful vision of *The Dance of the Sevin Deidlie Synnis*.

Gavin Douglas (1475-1522)

Scottish bishop, poet and translator, Gavin Douglas is best known for his vigorous translation of Virgil's *Aeneid* into Scot, the English of the lowlands of Scotland. Douglas was born around 1475, at Tantallon Castle, East Lothian. He died in London in the year 1522 suffering from plague.

Literary Career and Works

Douglas was appointed provost of St Giles Church, Edinburgh, about 1501. About this time he wrote *The Palace of Honor*, a poem dedicated to James IV. The poem is written in Older Scots, the linguistic descendant of the language spoken by the 12th century English immigrants to the burghs of Southern and Eastern Scotland. It is in the form of a dream vision. The dream shows a way to approach the heavenly ideal, ascending from a chaotic and infernal beginning. The poem itself is based upon a distinction between earthly and heavenly.

Douglas' most significant literary achievement is his translation of Virgil's *Aeneid* in July 1513. It included not only the original 12 books of the *Aeneid*, but also the 13th book, composed by Mapheus Vegius in 1428. Douglas' *Aeneid* is written in decasyllabic rhyming couplets and is divided into several chapters for each individual book. Douglas not only intends to make Virgil available to non-Latinists, but to 'bring the Scots language confidently into play'.

Conscience

Quhen halie Kirk first fluris t in 'outhheid,
Prelatis wer chosin of all perfectioun;
For Conscience than the brydill had to leid,
And Conscience maid the hale electioun,
Syne eftir that come schrewit correctioun,
And thocht that Conscience had our large ane weid,
And of his habite out cuttit thay ane skreid.
And fra Conscience the Con thay clip away,
And maid of Conscience Science and na mair;
Bot it the Kirk stude weill, full mony day
For it wes rewlit be mene of wit and layre;
Syn eftir that Sciens began to payr,
And thocht at Sciens was our lang ane jaip,
The Sci away fast can thay rub and scraip;
And fra Sci of Science wes adew,
Than left thai nocht bot this sillab Ens,
Quhilk in our language singnifies that schrew
Riches and geir, that gart all grace go hens;
For Sciens baith and faythfull Consciens
Sa corruptit ar with this warldis gude,
That falset joukis in everie clerkis hude.
O hungrie Ens! cursit with cairis calde,
All kynd of folk constrenis thow to wirk;
For thé that thief Judas his Maister said;
For thé Symon infectit Halie Kirk;
To poysoun Justice thow dois nevir irk;
Thow fals Ens, go hens, thou monsture peralous,
God send Defens with Conscience in till ws!

Sir David Lyndsay (1490-1555)

Scottish poet and courtier David Lyndsay is the last of Scottish Chaucerians. Little is known of his biographical history. Lyndsay's death has been recorded in the Register of the Privy Seal in April, 1555.

Literary Career and Works

Lyndsay composed his most famous work, *A Pleasant Satyre of the Thrie Estaits,* the only fully preserved Scottish play in the genre of morality, which boldly interpreted the main religious and political problems of the era. His other works include *The Dream of Schir David Lyndesay*. The most Chaucerian of Lyndsay' poems, *Monarchy (Monarche)* a serious poetic overview of world history, beginning with Genesis and ending with the fifth empire and *History and Testament of Squire Meldrum*, poetic biography of a squire.

New Court Poets

The court poets are the poets appointed for life as an officer of the royal household, formerly expected to write poems in celebration of court and national events. Some of the renowned court poets of the age of revival are discussed below

Thomas Wyatt (1503-1542)

Thomas Wyatt is often called the pioneer of the new English poetry. It was he who introduced the sonnet form in English. Wyatt was born at Allington near Maidstone Kent in 1503. As a boy, he made the acquaintance of a lady Sir Thomas Boleyn's daughter Anne with whom, he was rumoured to have close relations. However, Boleyn and King Henry VIII married in 1533.

Wyatt, devastated, sat down and wrote his famous sonnet *Whose List To Hunt*

Whoso List To Hunt

Whose list to hunt ? I know where is an hind
But as for me, alas ! I may no more,
The vain travail hath wearied me so sore ;
I am of them that furthest come behind.
Yet may, I by no means my wearied mind
Draw from the deer, but as she fleeth afore
Fainting I follow, I leave off therefore,
Since, in a net, I seek to hold the wind.
Who list her hunt, I put him out of doubt
As well as I, may spend his time in vain !
And graven with diamonds in letters plain,
There is written her fair neck round about ;
'Noli me tangere ; for Caesar's I am,
And wild for to hold, though I seem tame.

During Wyatt's lifetime, none of his poems had been published except for *The Court of Venus.* His first published work was *Certain Psalms*, which were metrical translations of penitential psalms. He died on 11th October 1542.

Wyatt's Contribution to English Poetry

Wyatt's frequent travels to Italy made him acquainted with the sonnets of Petrarch. It was from Italy that he drew ideas through, which English poetry was rejuvenated. Wyatt translated several of Petrarch's sonnets and brought the Petrarchan sonnet form into English. However, Wyatt was not a mere translator or imitator of the works of an already great writer. Wyatt took Petrarch's form and words as a basis to represent his own culture and his own world.

He used artificial love-themes and Petrarchan conceits in his poetry, but departed from Petrarch in his rhyme schemes. Petrarch's sonnets consisted of an 'octave', rhyming *abba abba*, followed, after a turn by a 'sestet' with various rhyme schemes. However, his poems never ended in a rhyming couplet. Wyatt employed the Petrarchan octave, but his most common sestet scheme was *cddc ee*. This marked the beginning of an exclusively 'English' contribution to sonnet structure, that is 3 quatrains and a closing couplet.

In addition to imitations of works by the classical writers Seneca and Horace, he experimented in stanza forms including the rondeau, epigrams, terza rima, ottava rima songs, satires and also with monorime, triplets with refrains, quatrains with different length of line and rhyme schemes, quatrains with codes and the French forms of douzaine and treizaine. According to Claude Rawson, Wyatt adapted and invented new modes-both formal and intellectual and helped in renovation of poetry. In words of David Daiches, "it is with Thomas Wyatt that modern English poetry can be seen to begin".

Earl of Surrey, Henry Howard (1516-1547)

English poet Henry Howard, Earl of Surrey was born in Hunsdon, Hertfordshire, England. The eldest son of Lord Thomas Howard, Henry took the courtesy title of Earl of Surrey in 1524, when his father succeeded as 3rd Duke of Norfolk. Educated by tutors, he lived an eventful life as a soldier and a courtier, eventually marrying Lady Frances de Vere, daughter of the Earl of Oxford.

Literary Career and Works

Most of Surrey's poetry was published after his death. His name is often cited together with Wyatt as both of them are considered to have fathered the English sonnet form. Surrey was the first to develop the sonnet form used by William Shakespeare and also translated Books II in Virgil's *The Aeneid*, marking the first use of Blank verse in English.

One of Surrey's sonnets, *Love that doth reign,* which is a translation of a Petrarchan sonnet, is given below to provide a deeper understanding of his poetry.

Love that Doth Reign

Love that doth reign and live within my thought .
And built his seat within my captive breast,
Clad in arms wherein with me he fought,
Oft in my face he doth his banner rest.
But, she that taught me love and suffer pain,
My doubtful hope and eke my hot desire
With shamefaced look to shadow and refrain,
Her smiling grace converteth straight to ire.
And coward Love, then, to the heart apace
Taketh his flight, where he doth lurk and 'plain,
His purpose lost and dare not show his face.
For my lord's guilt thus faultless bide I pain,
Yet from my lord shall not my foot remove;
Sweet is the death that taketh end by love

Surrey's Contribution to English Poetry

Earl of Surrey improved on the versification of Wyatt's sonnets, securing fluency and smoothness. While, Wyatt introduced the sonnet into English, it was Surrey, who gave them the rhyming meter and the division into quatrains that now characterises the sonnets variously named English, Elizabethan or Shakespearean sonnets.

Surrey was also the first English poet to publish in blank verse, in his translation of Books II and IV in *Virgil's Aeneid*. Book 4 was published in 1554 and Book 2 in 1557. Apart from the sonnet and blank verse, Surrey also experimented with a variety of meters. He showed a particular fondness for the poulter's measure, using it in several of his love poems and in his translations from the Psalms and Ecclesiastes.

According to Frederick Morgan Padelford, "Surrey's outstanding contribution to prosody was his insistence that metrical accent should be coincident with sentence stress and word accent, that is, that the metrical accent should fall upon the words, which are naturally stressed because of their importance and upon the accented, rather than upon the unaccented, syllables of such words."

EXAM BASED QUESTIONS

1 Which word is applied to denote the whole translation from the Middle Ages to the modern world, is more correctly applied to the revival of art resulting from the discovery and imitation of classic models in the 14th century?
(a) Renaissance (b) Reformation
(c) Restoration (d) Humanism

2 Which culture was at its height when the revival of learning started?
(a) Asian Culture (b) African Culture
(c) Australian Culture (d) European Culture

3 A Ballad is always
(a) Narrative (b) Analytical
(c) Narrative or Analytical (d) Non-Narrative

4 'Border Ballads' deal with
(a) the English Scottish Skirmishes
(b) the English France Skirmishes
(c) the English Italy Skirmishes
(d) the English Norman Skirmishes

5 'The Nut Brown Maid' is known as
(a) epic (b) sonnet
(c) ballad (d) an essay

6 The most remarkable Ballads of the 15th century include
(a) The Nut Brown Maid (b) Chevy - Chase
(c) Morte d' Arthur (d) Both 'a' and 'b'

7 'The Paston Letters' is an important work of the 15th century because
(a) of its literary merit
(b) of its valuable and reliable social chronicles
(c) of its innovative style and form
(d) of poverty of the age in prose writing

8 'The Love Poetry' and 'The Sonnet' were together brought from
(a) Italy (b) France
(c) Belgium (d) None of these

9 Who were called the Post Chaucerians?
(a) James I, John Barbour, Robert Henryson
(b) Thomas Hoccleve, Stephen Hawes, John Lydgate
(c) William Dunbar, Thomas Malory, Caxton
(d) Robert Fabyan, Edward Hall, Henry VII

10 What is common to all of them?
1. Thomas Hoccleve 2. John Lydgate
3. Stephen Hawes 4. John Skelton

Codes
(a) All of them were playwrights of the Age of Revival
(b) All of them were English Chaucerians a group of poets influenced by Geoffrey Chaucer
(c) All of them were University Wits
(d) All of them were poets, who wrote in rime royal

11 Thomas Hoccleve's first book is a translation of the French poet Christine de Pisan's Epistre au Dieu d' Amours. This book is
(a) The Regiment of Princes
(b) The Complaint of our Lady
(c) Hoccleve's Complaint
(d) The Letter of Cupid

12 Hoccleve's Complaint is composed by
(a) Hoccleve (b) Lydgate
(c) Henryson (d) Hawes

13 AC Ward calls one of England's earliest biographers to
(a) Alexander Barclay (b) Thomas Malory
(c) John Lydgate (d) Thomas Hoccleve

14 The most voluminous of Chaucerians, who has written more than 140000 lines is
(a) Hawes (b) Barclay
(c) Skelton (d) Lydgate

15 "The Fall of Princess', 'The Troy Book', 'The Story of Thebes' ', The Pilgrimage of the Life of Man' and 'The Complaint of the Black Knight' are chief works of
(a) Stephen Hawes (b) John Lydgate
(c) John Skelton (d) William Shakespeare

16 Who declared himself as a follower of Chaucer?
(a) Lydgate (b) Hawes (c) Hoccleve (d) Skelton

17 'A Joyful Medytacyon' is a creation of
(a) Barclay (b) Hawes
(c) Spenser (d) Lydgate

18 Which of the following is not the work of Stephen Hawes?
(a) The Pastime of Pleasure
(b) The History of Graunde Amoure
(c) La Belle Pucel
(d) Story of Thebes

19 A consistent follower of Chaucer is
(a) James I of Scotland (b) Thomas Hoccleve
(c) John Lydgate (d) None of these

20 Who is known for his pungent satire in the 15th century?
(a) John Skelton (b) Langland
(c) Alexander Barclay (d) Gower

21 Who was the tutor to Henry VIII?
(a) Stephen Hawes (b) John Lydgate
(c) John Barbour (d) John Skelton

22 'Why come ye not to court' and 'Dirge on Edward IVth' is composed by
(a) Skelton (b) Lydgate
(c) Hoccleve (d) Gower

23 **Which among the following is not written by Skelton?**
(a) Morte d' Arthur (b) Bowge of Court
(c) Adagia (d) Erasmus

24 **Philip Sparrow is a creation of**
(a) Skelton (b) Lydgate (c) Hoccleve (d) Caxton

25 **'Book of Philip Sparrow' was written for a pet bird. The bird belonged to**
(a) John Skelton (b) James I (c) Wolsey (d) Jane Scrope

26 **What type of satire is 'The Bowge of Court'?**
(a) Pungent Satire Prosodic Satire
(b) Allegorical Satire
(c) Both (a) and (b) (d) None of the above

27 **The difference between two English Chaucerians, John Skelton and Alexander Barclay is**
(a) John used eclogues whereas Barclay does not
(b) John's satires were ragged, tattered and jagged
(c) Alexander satirises the vices of common people and clergy
(d) Both (b) and (c)

28 **'The Ship of the Fools' is composed by**
(a) Hoccleve (b) Alexander Barclay
(c) Skelton (d) Lydgate

29 **'The Ship of the Fools' is the translation of the work of the German poet, Sebastian Brant. This translation was done by**
(a) Chaucer (b) Alexander Barclay
(c) Sebastian Brant (d) Mantuanus

30 **The invention of the genre, the eclogues is attributed to**
(a) Stephen Hawes (b) William Dunbar
(c) Alexander Barclay (d) Gavin Douglas

31 **Alexander Barclay's eclogues is**
(a) tragedies (b) love stories
(c) moral satires (d) melancholy stories

32 **'Certayne Eclogues is composed by**
(a) Alexander Barclay (b) Hoccleve
(c) Hawes (d) Dunbar

33 **'Complaint of a Prisoner in a Fleet' is written by**
(a) George Ashby (b) Benet
(c) Henry Bradshaw (d) Thomas Norton

34 **'Legends of Holy Women' was written by**
(a) Thomas Norton (b) George Ripley
(c) Osbern Bokenham (d) Henry Bradshaw

35 **What is common to all of them?**
1. James I of Scotland 2. Robert Henryson
3. William Dunbar 4. Gavin Douglas
Codes
(a) All of them were English Chaucerians
(b) All of them wrote Sonnets
(c) All of them were Scottish Chaucerians
(d) All of them wrote their works in French and Latin

36 **Scottish Chaucerians and their poetry is**
(a) retrogressive (b) progressive
(c) Both (a) and (b) (d) spiritual

37 **Which English/Scottish Chaucerian faced captivity and for how long?**
(a) Robert Henryson , 12 years
(b) John Lydgate, 18 years
(c) Stephen Hawes, 18 years
(d) James I of Scotland, 18 years

38 **'Christ is Kirk on the Grene' is written by**
(a) James I (b) Lydsay
(c) John Gower (d) Henryson

39 **What does James I of Scotland commemorate during his captivity of the English?**
(a) Romantic incident (b) Sad incident
(c) Strange incident (d) Happy incident

40 **Who is known for Testament of Cresseid, in which he recast the conclusion of Chaucer's Troilus and Criseyde?**
(a) Robert Henryson (b) Malory
(c) Caxton (d) William Dunbar

41 **Why did Chaucer's Troilus die heart broken?**
(a) Because Criseyde left a ring in his remembrance
(b) Because Criseyde betrayed him for Diomede
(c) Because Troilus built a tomb in Criseyde's remembrance
(d) None of the above

42 **'Testament of Cresseid' is a work done by**
(a) Robert Henryson (b) John Skeleton
(c) Thomas Hoccleve (d) William Dunbar

43 **The difference between Chaucer's 'Troilus' and Robert Henryson's 'Troilus' is**
(a) Chaucer's Troilus begs and Henryson's does not
(b) Chaucer's Troilus remains alive, but on the other hand Robert Henryson's Troilus dies
(c) There is no difference
(d) Chaucers Troilus dies whereas Robert's remain alive

44 **When Criseyde was begging at the time of her death whom did she leave a ring for?**
(a) Priam (b) Pandarus (c) Troilus (d) Calcha

45 **Which of the following is not written by Henryson?**
(a) Testament of Cresseid
(b) Orpheus and Eurydice
(c) Peblis to the Play
(d) Robene and Makyne

46 **'Garmond of Gude Ladies' is written by**
(a) Lyndsay (b) Henryson
(c) Lydgate (d) None of these

47 **Name the British poet, who was the successor of Chaucer, but predecessor of Spenser.**
(a) Robert Henryson (b) William Dunbar
(c) James I of Scotland (d) Criseyde

48 Who is the author of the 'Thrissel and the Rois'?
(a) Gavin Douglas (b) John Lydgate
(c) Thomas Hoccleve (d) William Dunbar

49 Which work do we find Dunbar dealing with in the union of the countries England and Scotland?
(a) The Golden Targe
(b) The Thistle and the Rose
(c) The Two Married Women
(d) The House of Fame

50 The two allegories — 'The Thistle' and 'The Rose' and 'The Golden Targe' are written by
(a) Gavin Douglas (b) Robert Henryson
(c) William Dunbar (d) Thomas Hoccleve

51 From the given, identify which is not a work of first category written by William Dunbar?
(a) Hymns (b) The Rois (c) Bewty (d) The Prisoner

52 On the basis of style of versification Dunbar's work is divided among
(a) formal allegory (b) comic and satiric verse
(c) religious poetry (d) All of these

53 The first translator of Virgil into English was
(a) Chaucer (b) Lydgate
(c) Douglas (d) Gower

54 'The Palace of Honour' 'King Hart', 'Conscience' and 'Aeneid' (translation of Virgil) are written by
(a) David Lyndsay (b) Gavin Douglas
(c) Thomas Malory (d) Edward Hall

55 Which of the following is not implemented by Gavin Douglas?
(a) Allegorical Technique (b) Eight line stanza
(c) Nine line stanza (d) Formal allegory

56 The satire of the three estates, a remarkable one known for its reformist zeal, was composed by
(a) John Bales (b) Sir David Lyndsay
(c) Thomas Sackville (d) Thomas Norton

57 'The Dreame', 'The Testament of Squire Meldram', 'The Testament and Compleynt of Papyngo' and 'A Pleasant Satyre of the Thrie Estaitis' are the chief works of
(a) Alexander Barclay (b) John Skelton
(c) William Dunbar (d) Sir David Lyndsay

58 Who among the following is not a Scottish Chaucerian?
(a) John Skelton (b) William Dunbar
(c) Robert Henryson (d) James I of Scotland

59 The first man, who wrote lyrics in English was
(a) Sir Thomas Wyatt (b) Earl of Surrey
(c) Sir Philip Sidney (d) Shakespeare

60 'Vogue of the lyric' was inaugurated by
(a) Wyatt (b) Earl of Surrey
(c) Thomas Sackville (d) Sir Thomas Moore

61 Thomas Wyatt used Petrarchan sonnet form for his poems. But he changed its select (last six lines) while octave (first eight lines) were the same. The rhyme scheme of his select is
(a) cde, cde (b) cd, cd, ee (c) cdd, cee (d) cd, ef, gg

62 He was born in 1517. He was more courageous than his friend and master. He excelled his master as a metrist in case and assurances. Who was this disciple and his master?
(a) Surrey and Wyatt (b) Erasmus and Moor
(c) Henryson and Chaucer (d) Hawes and Chaucer

63 Who among the following were famous for 'drunk deep of Italian Poetry'?
(a) Henry Howard and Earl of Surrey
(b) Thomas Wyatt and Henry Howard
(c) Thomas Wyatt, Henry Howard and Earl of Surrey
(d) None of the above

64 Surrey is noted for
(a) translation of Dante's work
(b) translation of two books of Virgil in strange meter
(c) translation of Homer's work
(d) translation of Chaucer's work

65 Why was Henry Howard sentenced to execution by Henry VIII?
(a) Adultery (b) Treason (c) Alchemy (d) Blasphemy

66 Who of the following was not part of the group of 'High' Renaissance poets?
(a) Sir Thomas Wyatt (b) Philip Sidney
(c) Edmund Spenser (d) William Shakespeare

67 What is the name of a sonnet series linked by repeating the last verse of one sonnet in the first verse of the next, until the circle is closed by using the first verse of the first sonnet as the last verse of the last sonnet?
(a) A sonnet band (b) A sonnet crown
(c) A sonnet throne (d) A sonnet cap

68 Henry Howard and Sir Thomas Wyatt both based sonnets on which of Petrach's poems about unrequited love?
(a) Rime 110 (b) Rime 120 (c) Rime 130 (d) Rime 140

69 Wyatt frequently used an exaggerated figure of speech in which intellectual cleverness figured at least as largely as real emotion. What is the name of this device?
(a) Conceit (b) Conceal
(c) Concave (d) Comparison

70 Words from which semantic field can be found in the fourth verse of Wyatt's The long love that in my thought doth harbour?
(a) Mythological (b) Animal
(c) Military (d) Religious

71 Sweet is the death that taketh end by love is the last verse of which of the following sonnets?
(a) Sir Thomas Wyatt's "The long love that in my thought doth harbour"
(b) Henry Howard's "Love, that doth reign and live within my thought"
(c) Edmund Spenser's "Lyke as a ship that through the Ocean wyde"
(d) Philip Sidney's "Loving in truth, and fain in verse my love to show"

72 What do Wyatt's following verses refer to? Into my face presseth with bold presseth with bold pretense And therein campeth, spreading his banner.
(a) A blush (b) A punch (c) A rash (d) A kiss

73 In which year were Wyatt's The long love that in my thought doth harbour and Howard's Love, that doth reign and live within my thought both published?
(a) 1556 (b) 1557
(c) 1558 (d) 1559

74 What is the division of Henry Howard, Earl of Surrey's sonnet?
(a) Three quatrains and a couplet
(b) An octave and a sestet
(c) Three quatrains and a sestet
(d) An octave and two couplets

75 Earl of Surrey wrote sonnets, but he changed its rhyming scheme. What was it?
(a) ab, ab, cdcd, efef, gg (b) abba, abba, cde, cde
(c) abab, cdcd, eg, eg, ff (d) abba, abba, cdc, dee

76 During the 15th century, Renaissance ideas spread from ...... to ....
(a) Italy to China (b) India to Italy
(c) Italy of Europe (d) Italy to France

77 Abolition of Pope's authority took place in ....
(a) 1530 (b) 1532 (c) 1534 (d) 1536

78 During the Age of Revival, ...became an important vehicle for satire of court and urban life.
(a) pastoral (b) allegory
(c) ballads (d) sonnets

79 Thomas Hoccleve believed in............. .
(a) autobiographical work (b) mortality
(c) confessional Tone (d) didacticism

80 John Lydgate's least dull work is ....
(a) The Fall of Princes (b) The Troy Book
(c) London Lack penny (d) None of these

81 The tradition of allegorical and dream poetry employs the works of ....
(a) Hoccleve (b) Stephen Hawes
(c) John Lydgate (d) John Skelton

82 Stephen Hawes' most popular work was the long allegorial poem....... .
(a) The Example of Vertu
(b) The Conversion of Swereers
(c) A Joyfidi Medytenon to all Englonde
(d) The Passtyme of Pleasure

83 'Garlande of Laurell' was written by .... in ....
(a) Lydgate, 1623 (b) Lydgate, 1523
(c) Skelton, 1523 (d) Skelton, 1623

84 Barclay wrote the first formal ....in English filled with entertaing pictures of rural life.
(a) epilogues (b) eclogues
(c) ecologues (d) epochs

85 Norton is best known for his work ....
(a) Ordinal of Alchemy
(b) The Compound of Alchemy
(c) An Other Balade to Saynt Werburge
(d) Dicts and Sayings of Various Philosphers

86 Which of the following statements about 'The Regiment of Princes' is correct?
(a) It was not dedicated to Prince Henry
(b) The poem begins with a 2000 lines prologue
(c) It was written by John Lydgate
(d) The poet cites five sources for his poem

87 Which of the following statements about 'The Fall of Princes' is correct?
(a) It is written by Thomas Hoccleve
(b) It is based on a similar work by Boccaccio
(c) It begins with the creation of the world by God
(d) It is the poet's shortest work

88 Which of the following statements about 'The Pastimes of Pleasure' is correct?
(a) It is written by John Lydgate
(b) It was written in 1600 lines
(c) The main theme of the poem was the education and pilgrimage of the Knight Graunde Amoure
(d) The poem was written in iambic pentameter

89 Which of the following about 'The Bowge of Courte' is not correct?
(a) It is written by John Skelton
(b) It is a political and historical allegory
(c) It is written in seven line stanzas
(d) The narrator of the poem encounters seven different people while on his journey on the train

90 Which of the following statements about 'The Ship of Fools' is not correct?
(a) It is written by Alexander Barclay
(b) It was written by 1509
(c) It is an adaptation of a popular German satire by Sebastian Brant
(d) The work describes a ship laden with tools setting sail for the Garden of Eden

91 Which of the following pairs is correctly matched?

	Genre		Author
(a)	Satire and Didacticism	:	John Skelton
(b)	Ballads	:	Barclay
(c)	Allegory	:	Lord Randal
(d)	The pastoral	:	William Dunbar

92 Which of the following pairs is correctly matched?

	Work		Genre
(a)	The Pastoral	:	Lamkin
(b)	Allegory	:	Translation from Pope Puis' II's Miserae Curialiun
(c)	Ballad	:	Lydgate's Temple of Glas
(d)	Satire and Didacticism	:	Ship of Fools

93 Which of the following pairs is correctly matched?

(a)	Skelton	:	Bowge of Courte
(b)	Elyot	:	The Kingis Quair
(c)	Cranmer	:	Philip Sparrow
(d)	Douglas	:	Garlande of Laurell

94 Which of the following pairs is incorrectly matched?

	Author		Work
(a)	Hoccleve	:	Letter of Cupid
(b)	John Lydgate	:	The Seige of Thebes
(c)	John Skelton	:	Castle of Labour
(d)	Alexander Barclay	:	The Ship of Fools

95 Which of the following pairs is correctly matched?

(a)	John Skelton	:	Colin Clouts
(b)	Thomas Norton	:	King Hart
(c)	William Dunbar	:	Ordinal of Alchemy
(d)	Gawin Douglas	:	Lament for the Makers

Directions (Q. Nos. 96-100) *In the questions given below are two statements labelled as Assertion (A) and Reason (R). In the context of these two statements, which one of the following is correct.*

(a) Both A and R are true and R is the correct explanation of A
(b) Both A and R are true but R is not the correct explanation of A
(c) A is true but R is False
(d) A is false but R is true

96 **Assertion** (A) The Renaissance started in Florence, Italy, a place with a rich cultural history.
Reason (R) Great Italian writers, artistes, politicians and others declared that they were participating in an intellectual and artistic revolution that would be much different from what they experienced during the Dark Ages.

97 **Assertion** (A) In the Age of Revival, the Focus was more on classical learning.
Reason (R) Metrical romances continued to be translated from the French, homilies and saint's legends.

98 **Assertion** (A) During the Age of Revival, pastoral mode of poetry became an important vehicle for satire of court and urban life.
Reason (R) Barclay was the first to use this mode in 14th Century and produced Five eclogues.

99 **Assertion** (A) Ballads became popular during 15th century.
Reason (R) William Dunnbar's 'The Golden Targe' was an example of popular Ballads.

100 **Assertion** (A) John Skelton was one of the Scottish Chaucerians.
Reason (R) Skelton's 'Bawge of Court' satirised contemporary court life during the Age of Revival.

101 According to their birth, which is the correct chronological order?
(a) Hoccleve, Lydgate, Hawes, Skelton
(b) Hoccleve, Lydgate, Skelton, Hawes
(c) Hoccleve, Lydgate, Skelton, Lydgate
(d) Skelton, Hawes, Lydgate, Hoccleve

102 Which of the following is in chronological order?
(a) Act of Supremacy, Introduction of the Blank verse by Wyatt, The Great Bible
(b) Act of Supremacy, The Great Bible, Introduction of the Blank Verse by Wyatt
(c) The Great Bible, Introduction of the Blank Verse by Wyatt, Act of Supremacy
(d) Introduction of the Blank Verse by Wyatt, The Great Bible, Act of Supremacy

103 Which of the following is in chronological order according to their creative year written by Alexander Barclay?
(a) The Mirror of Good Manners, Eclogues, The Ship of Fools, Castle of Labour
(b) Eclogues, The Ship of Fools, The Mirror of Good Manners, Castle of Labour
(c) The Ship of Fools, Castle of Labour, Eclogues, The Mirror of Good Manners
(d) Castle of Labour, The Ship of Fools, Eclogues, The Mirror of Good Manners

104 Which of the following has the English Chaucerian poets in the correct chronological order?
(a) George Ashby, Osbern Bokenham, Thomas Norton, Henry Bradshaw
(b) Henry Bradshaw, Thomas Norton, Osbern Bokenham, George Ashby
(c) Thomas Norton, Osbern Bokenham, George Ashby, Henry Bradshaw
(d) Osbern Bokenham, George Ashby, Thomas Norton, Henry Bradshaw

105 Which of the following has Scottish Chaucerians in the correct chronological order?
(a) Sir David Lindsay, William Dunbar, Robert Henryson, James I
(b) James I, William Dunbar, Robert Henryson, Sir David Lindsay
(c) James I, Robert Henryson, William Dunbar, Sir David Lindsay
(d) William Dunbar, Robert Henryson, Sir David Lindsay, James I

106 Consider the following statements.
1. Ballad is a simple, spirited short poem narrating some popular story.
2. Joseph Addison commented, 'The darling songs the common place'.
3. Usual Ballads consists of five lines having six and eight accented syllables.

Which of the statements given above is/are incorrect?
(a) All of these (b) 1 and 2
(c) Only 3 (d) None of these

107 Which of the following is not a part of Allegorical /Dream Poetry?
1. Border Ballads.
2. The Parliament of Fowls.
3. The Book of the Duchess
4. The House of Fame.

Codes
(a) Only 1 (b) Only 2
(c) Only 3 (d) None of these

108 Consider the following statements regarding 'La Male Regle' written by Thomas Hoccleve.
1. It is an autobiographical poem.
2. He complains of the hardships of his life.
3. He describes his diseases, financial strains and moral failings.
4. He wrote this book in 1506.

Which of the statements given above is/are correct?
(a) 1 and 2 (b) 2 and 4 (c) Only 3 (d) Only 4

109 Consider the following statements:
1. The Falle of Princess is the longest work of Lydgate containing 36365 lines.
2. The main theme of Pastime of Pleasure is the education and pilgrimage of the Knight Graunde Amoure
3. Skelton's Ballad of the Scottysshe Kynge was directed against the power of Cardinal Wolsey.

Which of the statements given above is/are incorrect?
(a) Only 2 (b) Only 3 (c) 1 and 2 (d) 2 and 3

110 Consider the following statements.
1. Barclay wrote the first formal ecologues in English.
2. Ashby's Dicts and Sayings of various Philosophers is in English.
3. Norton's Ordinall of Alchemy was written about 1477.

Which of the statements given above is/are correct?
(a) Only 1 (b) 1 and 3
(c) Only 2 (d) 1 and 3

111 Consider the following statements about James I.
1. James I was arrested by the English in 1406.
2. He remained in prison for 18 years.
3. He married Joan Beaufort the cousin of Henry V.
4. He wrote 'Lament for the Makaris'.

Which one of the statements given above is correct?
(a) 1 and 2 (b) 2 and 3
(c) 1, 2 and 3 (d) None of these

112 Consider the following works.
1. The Testament of Cressied
2. Garmont of Gud Ladeis
3. Peblis to the Play
4. Magnificience

Which of the following works does/do not belong to Henryson?
(a) 1 and 2 (b) Only 4 (c) 3 and 4 (d) Only 3

113 Consider the following statements regarding 'The Golden Targe' written by William Dunbar.
1. In this work the poet gave the traditional metre.
2. It is a Chaucerian type of allegory.
3. It is colourful like a rainbow.
4. He used seven line stanza with two rhymes.

Which of the statements given above is correct?
(a) 1 and 3 (b) 1 and 2
(c) Only 3 (d) Only 4

114 Consider the following statements about Gavin Douglas' works.
1. The Palice of Honour is dedicated to James IV.
2. Douglas' most singnificant literary achievement is translation of Virgil's Aeneid.
3. King Hart is a moral allegory.

Which of the following statements given above are correct?
(a) 1 and 3 (b) 2 and 3
(c) 1 and 2 (d) All of these

115 Consider the following statements.
1. Henry Howard was the person to use the unrimed and ten syllable verse and it is called 'The Blank Verse'.
2. He collaborated with Wyatt in bringing out 'Songs' and Sonnets.'
3. 'Songs and Sonnets' is popularly known as Tottel's Miscellany.

Which of the statements given above is/are correct?
(a) Only 1 (b) 1 and 3
(c) Only 2 (d) All of these

116 Match the following English Chaucerian poems with their poets.

Poem	Poet
1. Letter of Cupid	A. Thomas Hoccleve
2. The Troy Book	B. John Lydgate
3. The Conversyon of Swerers	C. Stephen Hawes
4. Colin Clout	D. John Skeleton

Codes

(a) 1–A, 2–B, 3–C, 4–D (b) 1–D, 2–C, 3–B, 4–A
(c) 1–B, 2–D, 3–A, 4–C (d) 1–C, 2–A, 3–D, 4–B

117 Match the following Scottish Chaucerian poets with their poems.

Scottish Chaucerian Poet	Poem
1. James I	A. The Dreme
2. Robert Henryson	B. The Eneados
3. Gavin Douglas	C. The Testament of Cresseid
4. Sir David Lindsay	D. The Kingis Quair

Codes

(a) 1–A, 2–B, 3–C, 4–D (b) 1–D, 2–C, 3–B, 4–A
(c) 1–B, 2–D, 3–A, 4–C (d) 1–C, 2–A, 3–D, 4–B

118 Match the following poets with their poems.

Poet	Poem
1. Benedict Burgh	A. Legends of Holy Women
2. George Ripley	B. A Poem in Praise of Lydgate
3. Osbern Bokenham	C. Whose List to Hunt
4. Thomas Wyatt	D. The Mistery of Alchemists

Codes

(a) 1–A, 2–B, 3–C, 4–D (b) 1–D, 2–C, 3–B, 4–A
(c) 1–B, 2–D, 3–A, 4–C (d) 1–C, 2–A, 3–D, 4–B

119 Match the following poems with their correct description.

Poem	Description
1. Complaint of a Prisoner in the Fleet	A. It describes Alchemy as an unholy art.
2. Ordinall of Alchemy	B. It is a meditation serious moral and religious issues.
3. Legends of Holy Women	C. It describes the poet's predicament of being thrown into prison and the sufferings, he underwent.
4. Lament for the Makers	D. Virtuous maidens are described here.

Codes

(a) 1–A, 2–B, 3–C, 4–D (b) 1–D, 2–C, 3–B, 4–A
(c) 1–C, 2–A, 3–D, 4–B (d) 1–B, 2–D, 3–A, 4–C

120 Match the following.

A. Lydgate	1. The Fall of Princes
B. Hoccleve	2. The Pastime of Pleasure
C. Hawes	3. The Regiment of Princess
D. Norton	4. Ordinal of Alchemy

Codes

	A	B	C	D		A	B	C	D
(a)	1	3	2	4	(b)	1	2	3	4
(c)	4	1	3	2	(d)	3	4	2	1

121 Match the following.

A. Barclay	1. Legends of Holy women
B. John Skelton	2. The Ship of Fools
C. Dunbar	3. Phillip Sparrow
D. Bokenham	4. The Thrissil and the Rois

Codes

	A	B	C	D		A	B	C	D
(a)	1	3	2	4	(b)	2	3	4	1
(c)	2	4	1	3	(d)	4	1	3	2

122 Match the following.

List I	List II
A. Love That Doth Reign and Live	1. William Dunbar
B. Farewell Love And All Thy Laws For Ever	2. George Ashby
C. Of James Dog	3. Henry Howard
D. Complaint of a Prisoner in the fleet	4. Thomas Wyatt

Codes

A B C D
(a) A–1, B–2, C–3, D–4
(b) A–4, B–3, C–2, D–1
(c) A–3, B–1, C–4, D–2
(d) A–3, B–4, C–1, D–2

123 In the following series, which set of poets and their works is correctly matched?

(a) Lament for the Makers-Dunbar; Garlande of Laurell-Hawes; The Example of Vertu-Skelton; The Ship of Fools-Barclay
(b) Lament for the Makers-Hawes;Garlende of Laurell-Skelton; The Example of Vertu-Barclay; The Ship of Fools-Dunbar
(c) Lament for the Makers-Dunbar; Garlande of Laurell-Skelton; The Example of Vertu-Hawes; The Ship of Fools-Barclay
(d) Lament for the Makers-Barclay; Garlande of Laurell-Dunbar; The Example of Vertu-Skelton; The Ship of Fools-Hawes

124 In the following series, which set of poems and poets is correctly matched?

(a) Certain Psalms-Hoccleve, La male Regle-Thomas Wyatt London Lick Penny-Ashby, Complaint of a Prisoner in the Fleet-Ldgate.
(b) Certain Psalms-Ashby; La Male Regle-Lydgate; London Lick Penny-Hoccleve; Complaint of Prisoner in the Fleet-Thomas Wyatt.
(c) Certain Psalms-Thomas Wyatt; La Male Regle-Lydgate; London Lick Penny-Ashby; Complaint of a Prisoner in the Fleet-Hoccleve.
(d) Certain Psalms-Thomas Wyatt; La Male Regle-Hoccleve; London Lick Penny-Lydgate; Complaint of a Prisoner in the Fleet-Ashby.

125 In the following series, which set of authors and their works is correctly matched?

(a) Dunbar-The Goldyn Targe; Douglas-The Palice of Honour; Skelton-Bowge of Courte; Pecock-The Book of Faith
(b) Dunbar-The Book of Faith; Douglas-The Goldyn Targe; Skelton-The Palice of Honour; Pecock-Bowge of Courte
(c) Dunbar-Bowge of Courte; Douglas-The Book of Faith; Skelton-The Goldyn Targe; Pecock-The Palice of Honour
(d) Dunbar-The Palice of Honour; Douglas-Bowge of Courte; Skelton-The Book of Faith; Pecock-The Goldyn Targe

126 According to William J Long, "the 15th century was an age of preparation of learning and the beginnings of Science and of getting acquainted with the great ideals, the stern law, the profound philosophy, the suggestive mythology and the noble poetry of the Greeks and Romans". So the mind was furnished with ideas for a new literature.
Which period does 15th century refer to?

(a) The Age of Chaucer
(b) The Age of Elizabeth
(c) The Age of Revival (d) The Shakespearean Age

127 "Cupido, unto whose commandement
The gentil kinrede of Goddess on hy
And people internal been obedient,
And the mortel folk seruen bisyly,
Of goddesse Sitheree sone oonly"
Name the poem and poet of the above extract.

(a) The Regiment of Princess, Hoccleve
(b) The floure of Curtesye, Lydgate
(c) The Example of Vertu, Hawers
(d) Letter of Cupid, Hoccleve

128 "Simple is my goste and sears my letterure,
Unto youre excellence for the write
Mine inward love and yit in aventure
Wol I me put, thogh I can, but lyte."
Who wrote these lines, for whom?

(a) James Stewart for Joan Beaufort
(b) Thomas Hoccleve for Chaucer
(c) Thomas Malory for Caxton
(d) Robert Henryson for Chaucer

129 Who declared himself 'a stupid student of an excellent master'?

(a) Thomas Hoccleve
(b) Stephen Hawes
(c) Alexander Barclay
(d) None of these

130 'The stupid scholar of an excellent master'. This line was once said by

(a) Robert Henryson
(b) Hoccleve
(c) John Lydgate
(d) Stephen Hawes

131 Compton Rickett says, 'There is no duller dog in literature than Hoccleve.' The critic wants to say that

(a) Hoccleve is a duller dog in literature
(b) We get too much of dry reasoning in his works
(c) Hoccleve has no interest in literature
(d) Hoccleve describes dog in literature

132 The statement 'But I was dulle and learned leyte or naught' was said by

(a) Robert Henryson (b) John Lydgate
(c) Thomas Hoccleve (d) Alexander Barclay

133 "First the Pylgrimes sothly everichon,
At the Tabbard assembled on be on,
And the Suthwerk shortly forto seye
To Canterbury ridyng on her weie
Tellynge a tale as I reherce can"
The above extract is the prologue of Lydgate's work. Identify the work.

(a) The Fall of Princess (b) The Floure of Curteyse
(c) The Seige of Thebes (d) The Temple of Glas

134 "In feverier, whan the frostymoone
Was horned, ful of Phebus firy nyght,
And that she gan toreyse her streames sone,
Saynt Valentyne, upon this blisful nyght
The above work of Lydgate relates to which of the following Chaucer's work?

(a) The Canterbury Tales (b) The House of Fame
(c) The Hook of Duchess (d) The Parliament of Foules

135 "Be the day weary, or be the day long, At length it draweth to Evensong." The poet of these lines had a gift for phrases, which lightens up his lengthy poetry. Who is the poet?

(a) Thomas Hoccleve (b) Robert Henryson
(c) Stephen Hawes (d) James I

136 According to AC Ward, "He looked upon himself as a followers of Chaucer, though he was in fact a belated medievalist using verse as a medium for sermonical allegories uneasily nedded to chivalrous romance.
Who is talked about in the above lines?

(a) John Lydgate (b) Stephen Hawes
(c) Thomas Hoccleve (d) John Skelton

137 "The good Dame Mery with Dame Charyte
My body buryed full ryght humbly
In a fayre temple of olde antyquyte,
Where was for me dyryge solempnely;
And overy my grave, to be in memory"
The above extract has been taken from 'The Passetyme of Pleasure'. What is the main theme of the poem?

(a) Education and pilgrimage of knight Grande Amoure
(b) Education of Henry VII
(c)) Pilgrimage of the Prince
(d) None of the above

138 "In Septembre in fallynge of the lefe
When phebus made his declynacyon
And all the whete gadred was in the shefe
By radyaunt hete and operayon"
Name the poem and the poet of the above extract.

(a) The Fall of Princes, John Lydgate
(b) The Example of vertu, Stephen Hawes
(c) The Lyf of our Lady, John Skelton
(d) The Pastime of Pleasure, Stephen Hawes

139 "For tho' my rime be ragged
Tattered and Jagged
Rudely rain-beaten
Rusty and moth-eaten
It hath in it some pith"
These lines are written by

(a) James I
(b) John Barbour
(c) John Skelton
(d) Stephen Hawes

140 Whom John Skelton attacked in, 'Why come ye not to court'?

(a) Henry V (b) Henry VI
(c) Richard III (d) Wolsey

141 "In Autumpne when the Sonne in Vyrgyne
By radyante hate enryped hath our corne
When luna fall of mutabylyte
As Emperes the dyademe hate worne"
Who is the narrator of the above poem?

(a) Sauncepere (b) Daunger
(c) Drede (d) Fortune

142 "Afore Myghelmas, that tyme of season,
I was commyttyd geynst ryght and reason,
Into a pryson, whose name the flete hight,
By a gret commaundment of a lord
To whom I must obey for hys gret myght"
Identify the poem, and from which the above extract
has been taken (?)

(a) Dicts and Sayings of various Philosophers
(b) The 12 Gates leading to the Discovery of the Philosopher's Stone
(c) The Ordinall of Alchemy
(d) Complaint of a Prisoner in the Fleet

143 "Heigh in the hevynnis figure circulere
The rody sterres twynklyng as fyre,
And in Aqary, citherea the clere
Rynsid hir tressis like the goldin wyre"
Identify the poem and the poet of the above extract.

(a) Christis kirk on the Grene, James I
(b) The kings Quair, James I
(c) Legends of Holy women, Bokenham
(d) Peblis to the Play, James I

144 "The lipper folk to Cresseyde than can draw
To Se the equall distribution."
of all almous; but quhan the gold they saw
Ilk one to uther prevelie can roun."
These lines have been taken from

(a) Chaucer's Troilus and Criseyde
(b) Henryson's The Testament of Cressyde
(c) Shakespeare's Troilus and Cressyde
(d) None of the above

145 Legouis said, 'He dazzles the eyes and ravishes the ears.' For whom he is saying and which quality he describes?

(a) Robert Henryson, Painting rustic scenes and dialogues
(b) William Dunbar, Colorful painting and melody
(c) Hoccleve, Humour and Reasoning
(d) Lydgate, Description Rustic

146 "I That is heill was and gladness
Am trublit now with great sickness
And fblit with infirmitee:
Timor mortis conturbat me."
The above extract has been taken from 'Lament for the Makers'. Which is a/an

(a) elegy dedicated to preceding poets of Dunbar including Chaucer, Gower and Lydgate
(b) dream allegory dedicated to preceding poets of Dunbar including Chaucer, Gower and Lydgate
(c) elegy dedicated to the king James IV
(d) None of the above

147 "Quhen halie kirk first flurist in outhheid,
Prelatis were chosin of all perfection;
For conscience than the brydill had to leid,
And Conscience Maid the hale election"
Identify the poem, and from which the above extract has been taken?

(a) The Palice of Honour (b) King Hart
(c) The Aenid (d) Conscience

148 "Love that both reign and live within my thought
And built his seat within my captive breast"
The above lines have been taken from 'Love that Doth Reign' which is a

(a) sonnet by Surrey
(b) ballad by Surrey
(c) dream allegory by Surrey
(d) pastoral by Surrey

149 "Lovers beware and take good heed to whom
You give your love, for whom you suffer pain.
I tell you there are few enough among them
To be trusted to give true love back again.
Make proof, your effort will be proved in vain.
Therefore I urge you, take them as you find,
For their constancy's like weathercocks in wind."
Which of the following poets in which of his/her works has had the above lines?

(a) Robert Henryson, The Testament of Cresseid and Seven Fables
(b) William Dunbar, The Merle and the Nightingale
(c) David Lindsay, A Voyage to Arcturus
(d) Thomas Wyatt, Sir Thomas Wyatt, the Complete Poems

150 "All love is lost but God alone."
Which of the following poets in which of his/her works has had the above line?
(a) Robert Henryson, The Testament of Cresseid and Seven Fables
(b) William Dunbar, The Merle and the Nightingale
(c) Daavid Lindsay, A Voyage to Arcturus
(d) Thomas Wyatt, Sir Thomas Wyatt, the Complete Poems

151 London, thou art the flower of cities all !
Gemme of all joy, jasper of jocunditie.
Which of the following poets in which of his/her works has had the above lines?
(a) William Dunbar, London
(b) Sir Thomas Wyatt, Selected Poems
(c) David Lindsay, A Voyage to Arcturus
(d) Henry Howard, 'A Lady Complains of Her Lover's Absence' found in "Poems of Love and Chivalry"

152 "Someone has described love to you. You have had it described to you. You have head that it is a small, fearful, selfish joy. It is not that–it is wild, and scornful, and sportive, and bloody…… How should you know."
Which of the following poets in which of his/her works has had the above lines?
(a) Robert Henryson, The Testament of Cresseid and Seven Fables
(b) William Dunbar, The Merle and the Nightingale
(c) David Lindsay, A Voyage to Arcturus
(d) Thomas Wyatt, Sir Thomas Wyatt, the Complete Poems

153 "These bloody days have broken my heart.
My lust, my youth did them depart,
And blind desire of estate.
Who hastes to climb seeks to revert.
Of truth, circa Regna tonat."
Which of the following poets in which of his/her works has had the above lines?
(a) Robert henryson, The Testament of Cresseid and Seven Fables
(b) William Dunbar, The Merle and the Nightingale
(c) David Lindsay, A Voyage to Arcturus
(d) Thomas Wyatt, Sir Thomas Wyatt, the Complete Poems

154 "I find no peace, and all my war is done,
I fear and hope; I burn and freeze like ice;
I fly above the wind yet can I not arise;
And naught I have and all the world I seize on.
That looseth nor locketh holdeth me in prison,
And holdeth me not, yet can I scape nowise;
Nor letteth me live nor die at my devise,
And yet of death it giveth none occasion.
Without eyen I see, and without tongue I plain;
I desire to perish, and yet I ask health;
I love another, and thus I hate myself;
I feed me in sorrow, and laugh in all my pain.
Likewise displeaseth me both death and life
And my delight is causer of this strife."
(a) William Dunbar, London
(b) Sir Thomas Wyatt, Selected Poems
(c) David Lindsay, A Voyage to Arcturus
(d) Henry Howard, 'A Lady Complains of Her Lover's Absence' found in "Poems of Love and Chivalry"

155 "When other lovers, in arms across,
Rejoice their chief delight,
Drowned in tears, to mourn my loss,
I stand the bitter night
In my window, where I may see
Before the winds how the clouds flee:
Lo, what a mariner love that made of me!
Which of the following poets in which of his/her works has had the above lines?
(a) WILLIAM DUNBAR, London
(b) Sir Thomas Wyatt, Selected Poems
(c) David Lindsay, A Voyage to Arcturus
(d) Henry Howard, 'A Lady Complains of Her Lover's Absence' found in "Poems of Love and Chivalry"

Directions (Q. Nos. 156-160) *Read the following poem and answer the questions that follow.*

Piping down the valleys wild
Piping songs of pleasant glee
On a cloud I saw a child.
And he laughing said to me.

Pipe a song about a Lamb;
So I piped with merry chear,
Piper pipe that song again–
So I piped, he wept to hear.

Drop thy pipe thy happy pipe
Sing thy songs of happy chear,
So I sung the same again
While he wept with joy to hear

Piper sit thee down and write
In a book that all may read–
So he vanish'd from my sight.
And I pluck'd a hollow reed.

And I made a rural pen,
And I stain'd the water clear,
And I wrote my happy songs
Every child may joy to hear

156 What did the child do after listening to the song about the lamb?
(a) Started crying (b) Weeping with joy
(c) The child vanished in the sky
(d) The child started laughing

157 'Lamb' here refers to
(a) Young one of sheep
(b) God
(c) Author
(d) None of the above

158 What is the rhyming scheme of the 5th quatrain?
(a) Abab (b) Abcd
(c) Abba (d) Abcb

159 What do hollow reed and stained water signify?
(a) Pen and ink (b) Grass and water
(c) Pen and water (d) None of these

160 What was the purpose of writing advice?
(a) The child wants poet to write about God
(b) The child wants to read the verse again and again
(c) So that all could read it later
(d) The child wants to keep the shepherd busy

PREVIOUS YEARS' QUESTIONS

December 2018

1 Who among the following are referred to as the 'Scottish Chaucerians'?
1. Thomas Hoccleve 2. Robert Henryson
3. John Lydgate 4. William Dunbar
The right combination according to the codes is
(a) 1 and 2 (b) 3 and 4
(c) 2 and 3 (d) 2 and 4

November 2017

2 John Lydgate begins his Siege of Thebes with a prologue of 176 lines in which he imagines himself joining Chaucer's pilgrims in Canterbury, where he speaks with the Host and agrees to tell the first tale on homeward journey. The story that Lydgate tells as the pilgrims depart from Canterbury is meant to be a companion piece to.
(a) the Pardoner's Tale (b) the Wife of Bath's Tale
(c) the Knight's Tale (d) the Miller's Tale

January 2017

3 Identify the correct chronological sequence of the following early English texts.
(a) Troilus and Criseyde–the Owl and the Nightingale–Utopia–Morte d'Arthur
(b) Troilus and Criseyde–Utopia–Morte d'Arthur–The Owl and the Nightingale
(c) The Owl and the Nightingale–Troilus and Criseyde–Morte d'Arthur–Utopia
(d) The Owl and the Nightingale–Morte d'Arthur–Troilus and Criseyde–Utopia

July 2016

4 Select the right chronological sequence of the date of Bible translations.
(a) King James Version–Tyndale–Revised Standard Version–Holman Christian Standard Bible
(b) Revised Standard Version–King James Version–Tyndale–Holman Christian Standard Bible
(c) Tyndale–King James Version–Revised Standard Version–Holman Christian Standard Version
(d) Revised Standard Version–Holman Christian Standard Bible–King James Version–Tyndale

December 2015

5 William Dunbar's Lament for the makers is about
(a) kings (b) priests
(c) poets (d) peasants

June 2014

6 Where Sir Thomas Wyatt adapted Petrarch and Petrarchanism to English sounds and metres, Surrey's verse tends to look back beyond Petrarch to the
(a) French verse (b) Italian verse
(c) Spanish verse (d) Latin verse

June 2013

7 Sir Thomas Wyatt and the Earl of Surrey jointly brought out Tottel's Miscellany during the Renaissance. Identify the name of the Earl of Surrey from the following.
(a) Thomas Lodge (b) Thomas Nashe
(c) Thomas Sackville (d) Henry Howard

ANSWERS

Objective Questions

1. *(a)*	2. *(d)*	3. *(a)*	4. *(a)*	5. *(c)*	6. *(d)*	7. *(b)*	8. *(a)*	9. *(b)*	10. *(b)*
11. *(d)*	12. *(a)*	13. *(c)*	14. *(d)*	15. *(b)*	16. *(b)*	17. *(b)*	18. *(d)*	19. *(d)*	20. *(a)*
21. *(d)*	22. *(a)*	23. *(a)*	24. *(a)*	25. *(d)*	26. *(b)*	27. *(a)*	28. *(b)*	29. *(b)*	30. *(c)*
31. *(c)*	32. *(a)*	33. *(a)*	34. *(c)*	35. *(c)*	36. *(b)*	37. *(d)*	38. *(a)*	39. *(a)*	40. *(a)*
41. *(b)*	42. *(a)*	43. *(d)*	44. *(c)*	45. *(c)*	46. *(b)*	47. *(b)*	48. *(d)*	49. *(b)*	50. *(c)*
51. *(a)*	52. *(d)*	53. *(c)*	54. *(b)*	55. *(d)*	56. *(b)*	57. *(d)*	58. *(a)*	59. *(a)*	60. *(a)*
61. *(c)*	62. *(a)*	63. *(b)*	64. *(b)*	65. *(b)*	66. *(a)*	67. *(b)*	68. *(d)*	69. *(a)*	70. *(c)*
71. *(b)*	72. *(a)*	73. *(b)*	74. *(a)*	75. *(a)*	76. *(d)*	77. *(c)*	78. *(a)*	79. *(d)*	80. *(c)*
81. *(c)*	82. *(d)*	83. *(c)*	84. *(b)*	85. *(a)*	86. *(b)*	87. *(b)*	88. *(c)*	89. *(d)*	90. *(d)*
91. *(a)*	92. *(d)*	93. *(a)*	94. *(c)*	95. *(a)*	96. *(a)*	97. *(b)*	98. *(a)*	99. *(c)*	100. *(d)*
101. *(b)*	102. *(b)*	103. *(d)*	104. *(a)*	105. *(c)*	106. *(a)*	107. *(a)*	108. *(d)*	109. *(b)*	110. *(d)*
111. *(c)*	112. *(c)*	113. *(d)*	114. *(d)*	115. *(d)*	116. *(a)*	117. *(b)*	118. *(c)*	119. *(c)*	120. *(a)*
121. *(b)*	122. *(d)*	123. *(c)*	124. *(d)*	125. *(a)*	126. *(c)*	127. *(d)*	128. *(b)*	129. *(a)*	130. *(b)*
131. *(b)*	132. *(b)*	133. *(c)*	134. *(d)*	135. *(c)*	136. *(b)*	137. *(a)*	138. *(b)*	139. *(c)*	140. *(d)*
141. *(c)*	142. *(d)*	143. *(b)*	144. *(b)*	145. *(b)*	146. *(a)*	147. *(d)*	148. *(a)*	149. *(a)*	150. *(b)*
151. *(a)*	152. *(c)*	153. *(d)*	154. *(b)*	155. *(d)*	156. *(b)*	157. *(b)*	158. *(d)*	159. *(a)*	160. *(c)*

Previous Years' Questions

1. *(d)*	2. *(c)*	3. *(c)*	4. *(c)*	5. *(c)*	6. *(d)*	7. *(d)*

The Elizabethan Poetry

The Elizabethan song tradition began with the era. Consolidating power of the Queen gave rise to courtly poetry also with Spenser's 'Faerie Queene' being the prime example. Shakespeare came out with a new form of the sonnet; the English sonnet. Philip Sydney was also equally important poet of the Elizabethan Age.

The Elizabethan Poetry: An Introduction

The Elizabethan period (1558 to 1603) in poetry is characterised by a number of frequently overlapping developments. The introduction and adaptation of themes, models and verse forms from other European traditions and classical literature, the Elizabethan song tradition, the emergence of a courtly poetry often centred around the figure of the monarch and the growth of a verse-based drama are among the most important of these developments.

Popular Form during Elizabethan Poetry

The Elizabethan Song

A wide range of Elizabethan poets wrote songs, including Nicholas Grimald, Thomas Nashe and Robert Southwell. There are also a large number of extant anonymous songs from the period. Perhaps the greatest of all the songwriters was Thomas Campion. Campion is also notable because of his experiments with metres based on counting syllables rather than stresses. These quantitative metres were based on classical models and should be viewed as part of the wider Renaissance revival of Greek and Roman artistic methods.

The songs were generally printed either in miscellanies or anthologies such as Richard Tottel's 1557 Songs and Sonnets or in songbooks that included printed music to enable performance. These performances formed an integral part of both public and private entertainment. By the end of the 16th century, a new generation of composers, including John Dowland, William Byrd, Orlando Gibbons, Thomas Weelkes and Thomas Morley were helping to bring the art of Elizabethan song to an extremely high musical level.

In this Chapter

- *The Elizabethan Poetry: An Introduction*
- *Main Poets of the Elizabethan Age*
- *Literary Criticism in Elizabethan Age*
- *Shakespearean Poetry*

Elizabethan poems and plays were often written in iambic meters, based on a metrical foot of two syllables, one unstressed and one stressed. However, much metrical experimentation took place during the period, and many of the songs, in particular, departed widely from the iambic norm.

The Elizabethan Courtly Poetry

With the consolidation of Elizabeth's power, the courtly poetry flourished as there seemed to be a race among the poets to impress upon the queen and win her loyalty. This encouraged the emergence of a poetry aimed at and often set in an idealised version of the courtly world.

Among the best known examples of this kind of poetry are Edmund Spenser's *The Faerie Queene*, which is effectively an extended hymn of praise to the queen, and Philip Sidney's *Arcadia*. This courtly trend can also be seen in Spenser's *Shepheardes Calender*. This poem marks the introduction into an English context of the classical pastoral, a mode of poetry that assumes an aristocratic audience with a certain kind of attitude to the land and peasants. The explorations of love found in the sonnets of William Shakespeare and the poetry of Walter Raleigh and others also imply a courtly audience.

The Elizabethan Classicism

Virgil's *Aeneid*, Thomas Campion's metrical experiments, and Spenser's *Shepheardes Calender* and plays like Shakespeare's *Antony and Cleopatra* are all examples of the influence of classicism on Elizabethan poetry. It remained common for poets of the period to write on themes from classical mythology; Shakespeare's *Venus and Adonis* and the Christopher Marlowe/George Chapman's *Hero and Leander* are examples of this kind of work.

Translations of classical poetry also became more widespread, with the versions of *Ovid's Metamorphoses* by Arthur Golding (1565–67) and George Sandys (1626), and Chapman's translations of Homer's *Iliad* (1611) and *Odyssey* (c.1615), among the outstanding examples.

Literature of the Elizabethan Age

Elizabethan England saw a remarkable flourishing of arts and literature. Renaissance humanism, Protestant zeal, geographical and scientific discovery all contributed to this upsurge of creative power. Drama was the dominant genre in Elizabethan Age.

Poetry was also quite popular and did not lag far behind drama in the Elizabethan Age.

Elizabethan Poetry

Elizabethan age was a great age of English literature. During this time the writing of poetry was the part of education among the educated people. That is why many books of poetry by different writers appeared during this age.

The proper Elizabethan literary age began in 1579, but before that year, Sir Thomas Wyatt and Earl of Surrey made their poetic contributions. Sir Wyatt brought the sonnet from Italy and made it popular in England. He followed the tradition of the Petrarchan sonnet with octave and sestet. They were later changed into English sonnet style by Shakespeare, who divided the sonnet into three quatrains summed up by a couplet. The Earl of Surrey wrote the first blank verse in English. The Elizabethan Age produced many beautiful lyrics. One of the finest lyricists was Sir Philip Sidney.

Elizabethan Lyric

Lyric poetry was the second most important literary genre in the Elizabethan period. After the repressive religious restraint of the middle ages, Elizabethan England experienced abandon and spontaneity. These qualities provided an atmosphere conducive for the creation of lyric poetry. Lyric poetry in the Elizabethan Age was usually identified as relatively short poems about personal, romantic topics or poems set to the tune of a musical instrument. Fluency, sweetness and melody were some of the characteristics of Elizabethan lyric poetry. The Elizabethan lyric owes its first inspiration almost exclusively to the influence of Italian poetry. The lyrical expressions first began with the efforts of Wyatt and Surrey, whose work mostly derives from and imitates the Italian lyrics of Petrarch.

However, with Spenser, the Elizabethan lyric comes into its own and acquires a singular character. Spenser's *The Faerie Queene* is the only long Elizabethan lyric poem of very high rank. Almost every Elizabethan poet tried his hand at the lyric. Elizabethan lyric varied in form, theme and expression. It consisted of forms such as the sonnet, song, pastoral, ode, elegy and epithalamion.

Famous Lyrical Verse Collections

- The Paradise of Dainty Devices (1576)
- A Gorgeous Gallery of Gallant Inventions (1578)
- A Handful of Pleasant Delights (1584)
- The Phoenix Nest (1593)
- The Passionate Pilgrim (1599)
- England's Helicon (1600)
- England's Parnassus (1600)

Elizabethan Sonnets

A sonnet is a lyric poem consisting of 14 lines of iambic pentameter, with an intricate rhyme scheme. Elizabethan sonnets were of two main types: Italian or Petrarchan sonnet and Shakespearean sonnet and apart from them other was Spenserian sonnet.

Italian or Petrarchan Sonnet

Petrarchan sonnet consists of an octave followed by a sestet. The most common rhyme scheme of this sonnet is abba abba cde cde or abba abba cdc cdc. The Petrarchan sonnet form was brought to England by Sir Thomas Wyatt, who wrote in the Petrarchan form in iambic pentameter and used Petrarch's typical rhyming patterns.

Shakespearean Sonnet

Unlike the Italian form, Shakespearean sonnet is considered as the quintessentially English sonnet. It is made up of three quatrains and ends in a rhymed couplet. The couplet is the defining feature of this sonnet. The rhyme scheme of this sonnet is abab cdcd efef gg. The Shakespearean sonnet is often used to develop a sequence of metaphors or ideas, one in each quatrain, while the couplet offers either a summary or a new take on the preceeding images or ideas.

Shakespeare also popularised the English sonnet, which made significant changes to Petrarch's model. A collection of 154 sonnets, dealing with themes such as the passage of time, love, beauty and mortality, were first published in a 1609 quarto.

Spenserian Sonnet

Apart from the two forms discussed above, there is a third variant called the Spenserian sonnet. Developed by Edmund Spenser, this is a sonnet form composed of three quatrains and a couplet in iambic pentameter. It was an outgrowth of the stanza pattern that Spenser used in *The Faerie Queene*. The rhyme scheme of Spenserian sonnet is abab bcbc cdcd ee.

Important Sonnet Sequences in Elizabethan Age

- Sir Philip Sidney's *Astrophel and Stella* (1591, 108 sonnets and 11 songs to Penelope Rich)
- Edmund Spenser's *Amoretti* (1594, 88 sonnets and an Epithalamion to Elizabeth Boyle)
- Samuel Daniel's *Delia* (1592, 50 sonnets)
- Michael Drayton's *Idea's Mirror* (1594, 64 sonnets to Phoebe), later reworked as *Idea* (1619, 73 sonnets)
- Fulke Greville's *Caelica* (1633, 109 sonnets)
- Shakespeare's sonnets (1609, 154 sonnets, first 126 addressed to a 'fair youth, next addressed to a 'Dark Lady').
- Lady Mary Wroth's *Pamphilia* to *Amphilanthus* (1621, 48 sonnets, included in Urania. The only notable sonnet sequence during the English Renaissance to be written by a woman).

Main Poets of the Elizabethan Age

The famous poets of the Elizabethan Age were Edmund Spenser, Philip Sidney and Michael Drayton. Fulke Greville, Samuel Daniel, and Thomas Campion also played an important role in the poetry of Elizabethan Age besides the legendary Shakespeare. Their brief description is given below

Edmund Spenser (1552-1599)

Edmund Spenser was born in East Smithfield, London to John Spenser, a cloth-maker. He was educated at Merchant Taylor's School and at Pembroke Hall, Cambridge, a Puritan College. After taking his BA in 1573 and MA in 1576, Spenser left Cambridge for Kent, where he acted as secretary to Dr John Young, former master of Pembroke College and newly appointed Bishop of Rochester.

Literary Career and Works

It was at Kent that he published his first publicly-released (1579) poetic work, *The Shepheardes Calendar (1579)*, to positive reviews. It was dedicated to Philip Sidney. In imitation of the classical poet Virgil, the *Shepheardes Calendar* (1579) consists of a series of eclogues (short poems usually cast as pastoral dialogues), in which various characters, in the guise of innocent and simple shepherds, discuss life and love, formulating weighty and often satirical opinions on questions of the day. The twelve eclogues correspond to twelve months of English calendar.

Through his poetry, Spenser hoped to secure a place at court, which he visited in Walter Raleigh's company to deliver his most famous work, *The Faerie Queene* (Book 1-3, 1590; Book 4-6, 1596). He offered Elizabeth *The Faerie Queene* in an attempt to gain her favour. In recognition for his poem, Elizabeth awarded Spenser £100. However, he earned the ire of Lord Burghley, who he lampooned in the text of Mother Hubbard's Tale for preventing the payment of the sum promised by the Queen. As a result of this, he had to return to Ireland in early 1591 without further preferment.

In 1596, Spenser wrote a prose pamphlet titled, *A View of the Present State of Ireland*. It was written in dialogue form from the standpoint of the Anglo-Irish chronicles, the pamphlet argued that Ireland would never be totally 'pacified' by the English until its indigenous language and customs had been destroyed, if necessary by violence. Two years later, in September 1598, Spenser was appointed Sheriff of Cork, but his tenure was short-lived. He was driven from his home by the native Irish forces during the Nine Years War. He took up lodging in King's Street and it was here that he died in January 1599. He was buried in Westminster Abbey.

Philip Sidney (1554-1586)

Philip Sidney was born at Penshurst, in Kent, on the 29th November, 1554. He was the eldest son of Sir Henry Sidney and Lady Mary Dudley. His father was a close companion of the young King Edward VI and continued to serve his country under Queen Mary and later, Queen Elizabeth. His mother was the daughter of John Dudley, the 1st Duke of Northumberland and the sister of Robert Dudley, the 1st Earl of Leicester.

Sidney was named after his Godfather, King Philip II of Spain. Sidney attended Shrewsbury school with his lifelong friend Fulke Greville. He later studied at Christ Church, Oxford but left without taking a degree in order to travel the continent and complete his education in an alternative way. He travelled through France (narrowly escaping the horrors of the Saint Bartholomew Massacre in Paris), Germany, Italy and Austria.

Literary Career and Works

In 1575, Sidney returned to England and became a courtier at the court of Queen Elizabeth. It was here that he first made the acquaintance of Penelope Devereux, the eldest daughter of Lord Essex-a girl of only 12 years of age. It was to her that Sidney dedicated his sonnet sequence *Astrophel and Stella*. In 1583, Sidney received the title of knighthood.

When, news of the projected marriage of Queen Elizabeth to the Duke of Anjou-the Roman Catholic heir to the French throne became known, this roused Sidney to take action. He wrote an extremely bold letter to the Queen expressing his opposition to the match and as a result, he swiftly became the object of her severe displeasure. Retiring from court to avoid the Queen's wrath, Sidney spent several months living on the estate of his sister, Mary Herbert, Countess of Pembroke and writing the pastoral romance *Arcadia*.

Major Works

- The Countess of Pembroke's Arcadia (1590)
- Astrophel and Stella (1591)
- An Apology for Poetry (also known as 'A Defence of Poesie' and 'The Defence of Poetry' (1595)

Michael Drayton (1563-1631)

English poet Michael Drayton was born at Hartshill in Warwickshire in 1563. From an early age, Drayton wanted to be a poet. About Drayton's life, we have little biographical details. Very little is known about Michael Drayton and it is that he was in service of Sir Henry Goodeere of Polesworth, who also provided for Drayton's education.

Literary Career and Works

Drayton's first work was a verse paraphrase of parts of the Old Testament and Apocrypha, *The Harmony of the Church* (1591).

His next work, *Idea, the Shepherd's Garland* (1593), was written in pastoral form and consisted of nine eclogues. His other works were *Ideas Mirror* (1594) a collection of love sonnets, *Endymion and Phoebe* (1595) -an erotic epyllion and historical poems *Robert, Duke of Normandy* (1596) *Mortimeriados* (1596) amd *Matilda* (1594).

While in his early versions of the Idea poems, Drayton identified *Mary Sidney Herbert, Countess of Pembroke* and *Lucy*, as Idea and celebrated them as ideal patrons; in his later versions, he identifies Anne Goodyer Rainsford (daughter of his patron) as "Modest Idea, flowre of Womanhood, / That Rowland hath so highly Deifide."

One of Drayton's finest works, *England's Heroical Epistles* (1597), a collection of verse letters by lovers, earned Drayton the title of 'our English Ovid'. This was written in imitation of Ovid's *Heroides*.

His *Polyolbion*, completed in 1622 and ten years in the writing, is one of the longest poems in English, a varied topographical and historical celebration of England's glories. Drayton died in London on 2nd December, 1631. He was buried in Westminster Abbey under a monument with an epitaph by Ben Johnson commissioned by the Countess of Dorset.

Fulke Greville (1554-1628)

Fulke Greville, 1st Baron Brooke was born in Beauchamp Court, Warwickshire, in 1554. He belonged to an influential family with aristocratic connections. He was the only son of Sir Fulke Greville (1536-1606) and Anne Neville, the daughter of Ralph Neville (4th Earl of West Morland). In 1564, Greville joined Philip Sidney at the newly founded school at Shrewsbury. In 1568, he entered Jesus College, Cambridge.

Literary Career and Works

After completing his education, Greville was offered a post connected with the court of the Welsh Marches by Sir Henry Sidney, Philip Sidney's father, but he gave it up in order to follow Sidney to the court of Queen Elizabeth I. He soon became a great favourite with Queen Elizabeth I. Greville, Philip Sidney and Sir Edward Dyer became members of the Areopagus club, the literary clique which, under the leadership of Gabriel Harvey, supported the introduction of classical meters into English verse.

Greville and Sidney had also tried to sail with Sir Francis Drake in 1585 in his expedition against the Spanish West Indies, but Elizabeth forbade Drake to take them with him. A year later, Elizabeth also refused Greville's request to join the Earl of Leicester in his campaign in the Netherlands but permitted Sidney. Sidney died of a musket shot at this campaign.

Greville wrote an elegy on the death of Sidney to *The Phoenix Nest* (1593) and a biography of his friend, *Life of the Renowned Sir Philip Sidney.*

Major Works

- An Elegy on the Death of Sir Philip Sidney (1593)
- Mustapha (1609)
- Alaham (1633)
- Caelica (1633)
- A Treatie of Humane Learning (1633)
- The Life of the Renowned Sir Philip Sidney (1652)
- Of Monarchy (1670)
- A Treatise of Religion (1670)

Samuel Daniel (1562-1619)

English poet, critic and dramatist Samuel Daniel was born in Somersetshire in 1562. His father was a master of music, and his younger brother was also a musician of note. Daniel entered Magdalen College, Oxford University in 1579 and remained there until 1581. It was here that he met John Florio who is remembered mainly for his later translation of Montaigne.

Literary Career and Works

After his education, Daniel appears to have travelled widely and developed knowledge of French and Italian Literature. His first published work, *The Worthy Tract of Paulus Jovius*- a translation of *Paulus Jovius,* was printed in 1585. By 1590s, Daniel attained the patronage of Mary, Countess of Pembroke and dedicated his next volume *Delia,* containing certain sonnets: *With the Complaint of Rosamond* (1592) to her. This contained fifty sonnets and the romance called *The Complaint of Rosamond.* Daniel was appointed inspector of Kirkham's children of the queen's revels. In this capacity, he wrote several dramatic works, including a masque *The Vision of the Twelve Goddesses.* In his later years, Daniel retired to a farm called *The Ridge,* which he rented at Beckington, near Devizes in Wiltshire. He died here in 1619.

Major Works

- The Worthy Tract of Paulus Jovius, Contayning a Discourse of Rare Inuentions, Called Imprese (1595)
- Delia, Contayning Certayne Sonnets: With the Complaint of Rosamond (1592)
- Delia and Rosamond Augmented, Cleopatra (1602)
- A Panegyrike Congratulatorie to the Kings Majestie. Also Certaine Epistles (1603)
- The Vision of the 12 Goddesses (1604)
- A Funeral Poem upon the Death of the Late Noble Earl of Devonshyre (1606)
- The Queens Arcadia (1606)
- The Tragedie of Philotas (1607)

Thomas Campion (1567-1620)

Poet and composer Thomas Campion was born in London on 12th February, 1567. He was the son of Lucy and John Campion, a clerk of the Court of Chancery. Both his parents died early. Campion entered Peterhouse, Cambridge in 1584. Although, he left without taking a degree, it was here he made some of his most significant acquaintances: Abraham Fraunce, Gabriel Harvey and Thomas Nashe. In 1586, he joined Gray's Inn as a law student.

Literary Career and Works

Campion's first published work as a poet appeared in 1591. Five of his songs appeared in Newman's unauthorised edition of Sir Philip Sidney's Astrophel and Stella. His first individual collection *Poemata,* which contained Latin panegyrics, elegies and epigrams, was published in 1595.

Campion's next published work was in Latin, *Thomae Campiani Poemata* (1595) and included the incomplete epic *Ad Thamesin,* celebrating the defeat of the Spanish Armada. In 1602, Campion also wrote a treatise on poetry titled *Observations in the Art of English Poesie.*

Campion also achieved reputation as a composer. He wrote over one hundred lute songs in the Books of Airs, with the first collection (co-written with Philip Rosseter) appearing in 1601 and four more following throughout the 1610s. Campion is also known for his famous book on music theory - *A New Way of Making Fowre Parts in Counterpoint.* Campion died on 1st March, 1620 and was buried on the day of his death at St. Dunstan's-in-the-West, Fleet Street.

Major Works

- Thomae Campiani Poemata. Ad Thamesin. Fragmentum Vmbre. Liber Elegiarum. Liber Epigrammatum (1595)
- A Book of Airs (1602)
- Observations in the Art of English Poesie (1602)
- The Description of a Maske, presented before the King's Majestie at White-Hall, on Twelfth Night Last, in Honour of the Lord Hayes (1607)
- Two Books of Ayres. The First Contayning Divine and Morall Songs: The Second, Light Conceits of Lovers (1613)
- Songs of Mourning: Bewailing the Untimely Death of Prince Henry (1613)
- The Description of a Maske: Presented in the Banqueting Roome at Whitehall, on Saint Stephens Night Last, At the Mariage of the Right Honourable the Earle of Somerset (1614)
- The Third and Fourth Booke of Ayres (1617)

Literary Criticism in Elizabethan Age

Many writers worked on the critical analysis of the literature during the Elizabethan period. A few of such significant works have been described in brief below

George Gascoigne's: Certayne Notes of Instruction (1575)

Gascoigne's *Certayne Notes of Instruction* first appeared in his work *The Posies of George Gascoigne, Esquire, corrected, perfected, and augmented by the Author* in 1575. It is considered to be the first English manual of versification. These notes were written at the request of Master Eduardo Donati. As the intent on the title page indicates, the work concerns, 'The making of verse or hyme in English'. It discusses English verse and meter. Michael Mack states that the book is almost a "Handbook written by a poet for other poets, offering practical advice for keeping audiences entertained". Gascoigne also emphasises ingenuity and invention as qualities of a good poet. Mere rhetorical figures and figures of speech are not enough, unless the poem reflects the poet's originality and invention.

He states, "The first and most necessary point that ever I found need to be considered in making of a delectable poeme is this, to ground it upon some fine invention. For it is not inough to roll in pleasant woordes, nor yet to thunder in Rym, Ram, Ruff, by letter (quoth my master Chaucer) nor yet to abounde in apt vocables, or epythetes, unlesse the Invention have in it also a liquid salis. By this aliquid salis, I meane some good and fine devise, strewing the quicke capacitie of a writer: and where I say some good and fine invention, I meane that I would have it both fine and good."

William Webbe's: Discourse of English Poetry (1586)

Webbe's *Discourse of English Poetry Together with the Author's Judgment Touching the Reformation of Our English Verse* was written and published in 1586. The work was dedicated to his patron, Edward Sulyard.

Webbe attempts a historical survey of poetry and also reviews poetry of his day. He also applauds the poetic skills of the lords and gentlemen in the Queen's court. Webbe argues that the scarcity of good English poetry since Chaucer's day was not due to lack of poetic ability, or to the poverty of the language, but to the lack of a proper system of prosody.

He abuses "This tinkerly verse, which we call hyme," as of barbarous origin and comments on the works of his contemporaries, displaying enthusiasm for Spenser's *Shepheardes Calendar* and admiration for Phaer's translation of *Virgil.*

George Puttenham's: The Arte of English Poesie (1589)

The Arte of English Poesie was written by English writer and critic George Puttenham in 1589. The book first appeared anonymous and was later ascribed to Puttenham. It was addressed to the Queen, with a publisher's dedication to Lord Burghley. It is considered to be "The most ambitious and comprehensive undertaking in Elizabethan criticism".

According to Charles M Willis, Puttenham had to conceal his name as a writer because his Catholic family was involved in a bitter religious conflict with Protestant and Puritan Church leaders, which reached a climax in 1584 when his Catholic nephew Francis Throckmorton was executed for treason. *The Arte of English Poesie* has been divided into three books. The *First* book contains a history of poetry and discusses diverse kinds of poetry. Puttenham specially mentions Sir Thomas Wyatt and Henry, Earl of Surrey, as 'The first reformers of our English metre and style'. The *second* book discusses prosody and contains an account of five types of English verse structures: the *Staffe, the Measure, Concord or Symphony, Situation* and *Figure.* The *third* book discusses figures of speech.

Philip Sidney's: An Apology for Poetry (1595)

According to Sidney, poetry is not only the most ancient form of learning, which the earliest thinkers used as a means of introducing difficult ideas to the unlearned, but both philosophers like Plato himself and historians make use of the devices of poetry in order to effectively communicate their message. Sidney's *Apology* is the first serious attempt to apply the classical rules to English poetry.

Sidney's *An Apology for Poetry* is a spirited defense of poetry against all the charges laid against it. It was originally published under two different titles, *The Defence of Poesie* and *An Apology for Poetry*. The reason for the two titles of this critical treatise derives from its complicated publishing history: three editions in 1595 and a fourth in 1598. The first appearance in 1595 was William Ponsonby's *The Defence of Poesie*; this was followed shortly by Henry Olney's publication of *An Apology for Poetry*.

A third edition was brought out by Ponsonby in 1595 with his title page and fourth edition was brought out by Sidney's sister, who collected his works. *An Apology for Poetry* was written partly as a response to Stephen Gosson's *School of Abuse*. Gosson had stated that a man could employ his time more usefully than in poetry, that it is the 'mother of lies', it is immoral and that Plato was right in banishing poets from his ideal commonwealth.

In poetry's defense, Sidney states that poetry alone teaches and moves to virtue and therefore a man cannot better spend his time than in it. Poetry is even capable of making the unpleasant like war and horror pleasant in terms of the means through, which it is presented.

Thomas Campion's: Observations in the Art of English Poesie (1602)

Campion's *Observations in the Art of English Poesie* was published in 1602. The main purpose of the book is set down by Campion on the title page as, "Wherein it is demonstratively proved and by example confirmed that the English tongue will receive several kinds of numbers, proper to itself, which are all in this book set forth and were never before this time by any man attempted".

In this work, Campion argued that verse written in English should emulate classical meters. He believed that classical meters fitted the English tongue better than the 'Vulgar and unartificial custom of rhyming'.

Elise Bickford Jorgens states that Campion offended many lyric poets of the time by declaring that, "The facility and popularity of rhyme creates as many poets as a hot summer flies". Most lyric poets of Campion's time were regular users of rhyme. Campion also discussed types of verse forms, which are best suited to English and outlined a method for establishing the number of syllables in lines of English poetry.

Samuel Daniel's: A Defence of Rime/Rhyme (1603)

Daniel's *A Defence of Rhyme* was printed in 1603. It was written in reply to Thomas Campion's *Observations on the Art of English Poesie*, which argued that rhyme was not suited to the genius of the English language. Through his work, Daniel wanted to demonstrate that rhyme was 'The fittest harmonie of words that comports agrees with our language'. He argued that rhyme did not check poetic imagination, but imparted an outline to the poet's ideas.

Daniel's prose essay rejected blindly following classical models, emphasised individuality of English mode of writing and plurality of kinds of eloquence. He argued, "All our understandings are not to be built by the square of Greece and Italic. We are the children of nature as well as they. All their Poesie, all their Philosophie is nothing, unless we bring the discerning light of concept with us to apply it to use. It is not bookes, but only that great booke of the world and the all overspreading grace of heaven that makes men truely Judicial."

Shakespearean Poetry

Apart from his large repertoire of plays, Shakespeare also dabbled in poetry. His five poems known to us are: *Venus and Adonis* (1593), *Rape of Lucrece* (1594), *Passionate Pilgrim* (1598) *Phoenix and the Turtle* (1601) and the *Lover's Complaint* (1609). *Venus and Adonis* and *Rape of Lucrece* are Shakespeare's well known narrative poems, which are dedicated to Henry Wriothesley, Earl of Southampton.

The story of *Venus and Adonis* is taken from Ovid's *Metamorphosis*. It describes the unsuccessful seduction of a handsome young man Adonis by Venus, the Goddess of Love. According to Sanders, the poem contrasts a passive male sexuality with an active female one. Venus tries to woo Adonis, forces a sally of kisses upon him, boasts about her own charms, yet fails to win him. In the end, Adonis is killed by a wild boar. His body melts away leaving behind a flower, which Venus then wears in her bosom.

The story of *Rape of Lucrece* is derived from Ovid's *Fasti*, Livy's *History of Rome* and perhaps Chaucer's *The Legend of Good Women*. It describes the rape of a virtuous noblewoman Lucrece by the son of King Tarquin, Sextus Tarquinius. Lucrece is the wife of Tarquinius' friend. When Lucrece's father and husband arrive, she tells them about the rape and asks for vengeance. After this, she stabs herself to death. At the end, the entire Tarquin family is rooted out, deposed and banished.

His poem *Passionate Pilgrim* is a collection of poems by Shakespeare. However, only a few of these poems are today accepted as Shakespeare's. *Phoenix and the Turtle* is an allegorical poem, in which birds die and become one in their love for each other. *Lover's Complaint* narrates the story of a young woman, who laments over her seduction by a persuasive, womanising young man. He eventually leaves her and breaks her heart.

Shakespeare's Poetry

- Venus and Adonis (1593)
- Rape of Lucrece (1594)
- Shakespeare's Sonnets (1594)
- Passionate Pilgrim (1598)
- Phoenix and the Turtle (1601)
- Lover's Complaint (1609)

Shakespearean Sonnets

Shakespeare's sonnets are poems that William Shakespeare wrote on a variety of themes. When discussing or referring to Shakepeare's sonnets, it is almost always a reference to the 154 sonnets that were first published all together in a quarto in 1609; however there are six additional sonnets that Shakespeare wrote and included in the plays Romeo and Juliet, Henry V and Love's Labour's Lost.

Shakespeare's sonnets are considered as a continuation of the sonnet tradition that swept through the Renaissance, from Petrarch in 14th century Italy and was finally intoduced in 16th century England by Thomas Wyatt. With few exceptions, Shakespeare's sonnets observe the stylistic form of the English sonnet—the rhyme scheme, the 14 lines and the meter. But Shakespeare's sonnets introduce such significant departures of content that they seem to be rebelling against well-worn 200 years old traditions. Instead of expressing worshipful love for an almost godess-like yet unobtainable female love-object, as Petrarch, Dante and Philip Sidney had done, Shakespeare introduces a young man. He also introduces the Dark Lady, who is not a goddess. Shakespeare explores themes such as just, homoeroticism, misogyny, infidelity and acrimony in ways that may challenge, but which also open new terrain for the sonnet form.

The Quarto : The Source of Shakespearean Sonnets

The primary source of Shakespeare's sonnets is a Quarto published in 1609 titled Shakespeare's sonnets. It contains 154 sonnets, which are followed by the long poem *A Lover's Complaint*. Thirteen copies of the quarto have survived in fairly good shape from the 1609 edition, which is the only edition, there were no other printings. There is evidence in a note on the title page of one of the extant copies that the great Elizabethan actor Edward Alleyn bought a copy in June 1609 for one shilling.

The sonnets cover such themes as the passage of time, love, infidelity, jealousy, beauty and mortality. The first 126 are addressed to a young man,; the last 28 are either addressed to, or refer to a woman. (Sonnets 138 and 144 had previously been published in the 1599 miscellany The Passionate Pilgrim).

The first 17 poems, traditionally called the procreation sonnets, are addressed to the young man–urging him to marry and have children in order to immortalise his beauty by passing it to the next generation. Other sonnets express the speaker's love for the young man; brood upon loneliness, death and the transience of life; seem to criticise the young man for preferring a rival poet; express ambiguous feelings for the speaker's mistress; and pun on the poet's name. The final two sonnets are allegorical treatments of Greek epigrams referring to the 'little love-god' cupid.

EXAM BASED QUESTIONS

1 Which dynasty brought political stability to England from 1485 to 1603?
(a) Stuart (b) Tudor (c) Hannover (d) Windsor

2 Who was the publisher of the first printed anthology of English poetry, Miscellany (1557)?
(a) Richard Bottel (b) Richard Tottel
(c) Richard Mottel (d) Richard Pottel

3 During the reign of which monarch did 'High' Renaissance Poetry flourish?
(a) Henry VII (b) Mary I
(c) Henry VIII (d) Elizabeth I

4 Which is the title of the first work ever written in Spenserian stanza?
(a) The Faerie Countesse (b) The Faerie Princesse
(c) The Faerie Godmothere (d) The Faerie Queene

5 The first verse of Edmund Spenser's Sonnet 34 (Lyke as a ship that through the Ocean wyde) is an example of which rhetorical device?
(a) Simile (b) Metaphor (c) Epithet (d) Allusion

6 What would be a modern translation of the word 'carefull', which appears in the penultimate verse of Spenser's sonnet 34?
(a) Angry (b) Cautious (c) Worried (d) Sad

7 In which of the verses of Spenser's sonnet 34 is the problem of unrequited love resolved?
(a) Final couplet (b) Final quintet
(c) Final octet (d) Final sestet

8 What does the reference to a storm in verse 9 of Spenser's Sonnet 34 show us?
(a) Rage (b) Pessimism
(c) Optimism (d) Destruction

9 In which of the following sonnets is the female protagonist given a voice?
(a) Edmund Spenser's sonnet 75
(b) Philip Sidney's Astrophil and Stella 7
(c) Edmund Spenser's sonnet 34
(d) Philip Sidney's Astrophil and Stella 1

10 In sonnet 75, the woman's name is written upon the 'strand'. What is a 'strand'?
(a) Parchment (b) Stone
(c) Shore (d) Tree bark

11 Edmund Spenser's Sonnets 34 and 75 were published in 1595 as part of which collection?
(a) Amoretto (b) Amaretto
(c) Amoretti (d) Amaretti

12 What was the name of Edmund Spenser's second wife, who inspired many of his sonnets?
(a) Elizabeth Doyle (b) Elizabeth Boyle
(c) Elizabeth Coyle (d) Elizabeth Foyle

13 Spenser's sonnet 75 demonstrates the influence of which philosophy in Renaissance poetry?
(a) Neonomianism (b) Nominalism
(c) Neovitalism (d) Neoplatonism

14 Who wrote the introductory sonnet to Spenser's Faerie Queene?
(a) Spencer himself (b) Sir Philip Sidney
(c) Sir Walter Raleigh (d) Leicester

15 Which of the following is a typical rhyme scheme of the Petrarchan sonnet?
(a) A sestet (aba aba) and octet (cddc cddc)
(b) An octet (abba abba) and sestet (cde cde)
(c) Abab cdcd efef gg
(d) Abab bcbc cdcd ee

16 Petrarchan sonnets consists of
(a) The octave (b) The sestet
(c) Both (a) and (b) (d) None of these

17 The Petrarchan sonnet's sestet consists of
(a) Five lines (b) Six lines
(c) Seven lines (d) Eight lines

18 What is the typical rhyme scheme of the Spenserian sonnet?
(a) Abab cdcd efef gg (b) Abab bcbc cdcd aa
(c) Abab bcbc cdcd ee (d) Abba cddc effe ff

19 What is the name of an extended poetic treatment of a single theme?
(a) A sonnet circle (b) A sonnet round
(c) A sonnet series (d) A sonnet cycle

20 What is the name of a sonnet series linked by repeating the last verse of one sonnet in the first verse of the next, until the circle is closed by using the first verse of the first sonnet as the last verse of the last sonnet?
(a) A sonnet band
(b) A sonnet crown
(c) A sonnet throne
(d) A sonnet cap

21 Which of the following is said to have had an important influence on Edmund Spenser's works?
(a) Ovid's Metamorphoses
(b) Ariosto's Orlando Furioso
(c) Heroic epic tales of Charlemagne
(d) All of the above

22 The final couplet of Spenser's sonnet 75 makes reference to what?
(a) The author's secret sorrow
(b) The apocalypse
(c) A summer's day
(d) The woman's beauty

23 How does Spenser's use of the 'volta' differ from that of the Italian sonneteers, who tended to introduce a new idea in verse 9?
(a) Although he often starts verse 9 with 'But' or 'Yet', the real turn normally occurs in the final couplet
(b) Although he often starts verse 9 with 'But' or 'Yet', the real turn normally occurs in the final quintet
(c) Although he often starts verse 9 with 'But' or 'Yet', the real turn normally occurs in the final verse
(d) Although he often starts verse 9 with 'But' or 'Yet', the real turn normally occurs in the final quartet

24 In the following verse from Spenser's Sonnet 75, what does the word 'rare' mean? My verse your virtues rare shall eternise.
(a) Strange (b) Never
(c) Extraordinary (d) Bizarre

25 Edmund Spenser is considered the best poet of Elizabethan age. Identify his period.
(a) 1551-1560 (b) 1552-1599
(c) 1557-1590 (d) 1552-1596

26 Which work records Spenser's experiences of his first visit to England in 1589-90 when he was introduced by Sir Walter Raleigh to the Queen?
(a) Strophes
(b) Colin Clout's Come Home Again
(c) Prothalamion (d) Amoretti

27 Spenser portrayed Elizabeth in many of his works. In which of his famous work, he also portrays her?
(a) Holiness (b) Faerie Queene
(c) Chastity (d) Friendship

28 The Elizabethan master of Arcadian or Pastoral poetry.
(a) Spenser (b) Thomas Nashe
(c) Thomas Kyd (d) John Foxe

29 Edmund Spenser grew acquainted with the classics and the Italian poets at
(a) Australia (b) Stanford
(c) Lancaster (d) Cambridge

30 Spenser's Shepheardes Calender was published in
(a) 1564 (b) 1590 (c) 1616 (d) 1579

31 Edmund Spenser was made secretary to Lord Grey in
(a) 1578 (b) 1579 (c) 1580 (d) 1581

32 Name the castle where Spenser lived and finished the first three books of Faerie Queene.
(a) Leicester House (b) Kilcolman
(c) Lord Grey's Castle (d) Harvey House

33 Which poem of Spenser was praised by Coleridge for its 'Swan-Like Movement'?
(a) Epithalamion (b) Prothalamion
(c) Amoretti (d) Strophe

34 Who is known for his Amoretti?
(a) Shakespeare (b) Sidney (c) Chapman (d) Spenser

35 The figure of the Warrior Virgin in Spenser's Faerie Queene is represented by the character
(a) Britomart (b) Gloriana
(c) Cynthia (d) Duessa

36 Who was known as the English Petrarch?
(a) Sidney (b) Spenser
(c) Drayton (d) None of these

37 'Astorphel and Stella' consisted of
(a) 108 sonnets and 11 songs (b) 108 sonnets
(c) 11 songs (d) None of these

38 Which among these is the masterpiece of Philip Sidney?
(a) Astrophel and Stella (b) The Arcadia
(c) The Defense of Poesie (d) None of these

39 Which of the following poems is a Pastoral romance?
(a) Astrophel and Stella (b) Arcadia
(c) The Battle of Agincourt (d) Endymion and Pholbe

40 Philip Sidney wrote 'An Apology for Poetry' in immediate response to
(a) Plato's Republic
(b) Aristotle's Poetics
(c) Stephen Gosson's The School of Abuse
(d) Jeremy Collier's Immorality and Profaneness of the English Stage

41 The Defence of Poesie, by Sir Philip Sidney, is considered the first work of literary criticism in English literature. What is the text also known as?
(a) An Apology for Poetry (b) A Vindication of Poetry
(c) In Support of Poetry (d) An Excuse for Poetry

42 In the following phrase from The Defence of Poesie, who or what is the referent of 'her'? Her world is brazen, the poets only deliver a golden
(a) The moon
(b) The Poet's Lover
(c) Nature
(d) Artemis, the Greek Goddess of the Hunt

43 In The Defence of Poesie, Sidney states that literature communicates deep and important truths through what?
(a) Lies (b) Paradoxes
(c) Biblical references (d) Facts and figures

44 What is Sidney's standpoint in the debate over whether art needs social commitment?
(a) Art exists solely for art's sake
(b) Aesthetic contemplation should be balanced with morality in art
(c) Art should provide moral grounding and disregard aesthetics
(d) None of the above

45 Who is thought to be the inspiration for 'Stella' of Sidney's Astrophel and Stella sonnet sequence?
(a) Penelope Devereux, Lady Rich
(b) Penelope Debereux, Lady Rich
(c) Penelope Depereux, Lady Rich
(d) Penelope Delereux, Lady Rich

46 In which year was Astrophel and Stella published?
(a) 1430 (b) 1591
(c) 1600 (d) 1491

47 In the second stanza of Astrophel and Stella 1, what does the reference to 'turning others' leaves' mean?
(a) Starting a fresh
(b) Getting inspiration from others
(c) Gathering leaves in the autumn
(d) Stealing books

48 The term 'feet' in the verse 'And others feet still seemed but strangers in my way' from the third stanza of Astrophel and Stella 1, is an example of what?
(a) Simile (b) Paradox
(c) Homonym (d) Chiasmus

49 What is paradoxical about the poet's frustrations in Astrophel and Stella 1?
(a) The poet describes his difficulties to express himself using Italian conventions ('others' feet'), even though the poem itself follows a classical Italianate structure.
(b) The poet knows that his love will never be requited so his efforts to get the woman's attention are all in vain
(c) The poet makes reference to a 'muse', when Renaissance poets did not believe in inspiration from external sources
(d) Although words come flooding to the poet, their meaning is not clear to him

50 In the final couplet of Astrophel and Stella 7, what reason is given for the black colour of Stella's eyes?
(a) For aesthetic effect (her black eyes complement her fair skin)
(b) To protect her from the dazzling sunlight
(c) To show nature's great power by making black seem beautiful
(d) To honour the deaths of the men who have died for her love

51 Michael Drayton brought out his 'The Morrimeriados' in how many line stanza?
(a) 8-line stanzas
(b) 3-line stanzas
(c) 7-line stanzas
(d) 4-line stanzas

52 Whose poetry is full of patriotism?
(a) Sidney (b) Spenser
(c) Drayton (d) Shakespeare

53 Which of these is a known work of Michael Drayton?
(a) Poly-Olbion (b) The Baron's War
(c) England's Heroic Epistles (d) The Battle of Agincourt

54 The first example of songs and sonnets might be quoted as
(a) Mero and Leader (b) Venus and Adonis
(c) As you Like It (d) Tottel's Miscellany

55 The master of closet lyric during Elizabeth period
(a) George Wither (b) William Browne
(c) Shakespeare (d) Samuel Daniel

56 Song writers or lyricist of the period were
(a) Thomas Campion (b) William Byrd
(c) John Dowland (d) All of these

57 Which is a collection of critical and literary principles?
(a) Arcadia (b) Apology for Poetry
(c) Calendar (d) Needle

58 What is called as a nest of singing birds about the composition of poetry?
(a) Chaucer age (b) Elizabethan age
(c) Puritan age (d) Jacobean age

59 Shakespeare's sonnets
(a) do not carry a dedication
(b) are dedicated to James I of England
(c) are dedicated to Mary Arden
(d) are dedicated to an unknown 'Mr WH'

60 How many sonnets has Shakespeare written in total?
(a) 150 (b) 154 (c) 120 (d) 130

61 The primary source of Shakespeare's sonnets is
(a) Petrarch (b) Quarto
(c) Chaucer's poems (d) Philip Sidney's work

62 The first 126 sonnets of Shakespeare refer to
(a) the God (b) a young woman
(c) a young man (d) the queen

63 Which Shakespeare sonnets refer to the 'Little Love-God' cupid?
(a) The first 126 sonnets
(b) The last 28 sonnets
(c) Sonnet 138 and 144
(d) The final two sonnets

64 The sonnets were written in the style of Petrarch and other in the style of
(a) Marlowe's (b) Johnson's
(c) Lyly's (d) Shakespeare

65 Which of Ben Jonson's work is a scathing satire on false poets of the age?
(a) Volpone, The Fox (b) Poetaster
(c) Cynthia's Revel
(d) Epicene or The Silent Woman

66 What is the typical rhyme scheme of the English or Shakespearian sonnet?
(a) Abab bcbc cdcd ee (b) Abab cdcd efef gg
(c) Abba cddc effe gg (d) Abbc cdde effg aa

67 Who in Shakespeare's Hamlet mumbles a song from the 'Book of Songs and Sonnets' known as Tottel's Miscellany?
(a) Hamlet himself
(b) One of the two clowns, a grave-digger
(c) Polonius
(d) Gertrude

68 Which of the following books marks the beginning of Shakespeare's success?
(a) Love's Labor Lost (b) The Merchant of Venice
(c) Venus and Adonis (d) Sonnets

69 He was a musician in the court of Henry VIII. His aim was to amuse and not moralise. His interludes were hilarious and they paved the way for comedy. Name the writer and his work.
(a) Bishop Bale-King John
(b) John Heywood-The Four Ps
(c) Skelton-Magnificence
(d) Lindsay-Satire of the Three Estates

70 One contemporary of Jonson had a bitter and extravagant style. In his Poetaster Jonson gives him a purge which makes him vomit his learned and bombastic words. Who is this poet?
(a) George Chapman (b) Thomas Dekker
(c) Marston (d) Fournier

71 Elizabethan lyrical was wearied in form and mainly comprised ....
(a) sonnet (b) song
(c) pastoral form (d) All of these

72 .... were given the credit to introduce the sonnet in England.
(a) Camden and Knox (b) Hakluyt and Purchas
(c) Wyatt and Surrey (d) None of these

73 Spenser referred .... as his master in English.
(a) Thomas Kyd (b) Drayton
(c) Dryden (d) Shakespeare

74 .... for his 'Astrophel and Stella' Love is the chief element in these sonnets.
(a) Daniel (b) Sidney (c) Spenser (d) Drayton

75 .... is a sumptuous allegorical entertainment combining poetry, music, dance, scenery and extravagant costumes.
(a) Mosque (b) Ballad
(c) Satinse (d) Lyric

76 .... sonnet sequence known as idea represents platonic idea of beauty.
(a) Edmund Spenser (b) William Shakespeare
(c) Drayton (d) Thomas Wyatt

77 Shakespeare has written several poems and .... sonnets.
(a) 130 (b) 160 (c) 180 (d) 154

78 .... was the Golden Age of sonnet.
(a) Elizabethan Age (b) Jacobean Age
(c) Puritan Age (d) Shakespearean Age

79 The fourth part of sonnet is known as .... in Shakespearean sonnet.
(a) Couplet (b) Octane
(c) Sestet (d) Quatrains

80 Edmund Spenser and .... offered hints for the perpetration of Spenser's The Faerie Queene indicating a plan of 12 books in all that was never completed?
(a) Bacon (b) Daniel
(c) Drayton (d) Raleigh

81 Which is not correct for the poets of Elizabethan Age?
(a) John Knox (b) Philip Sidney
(c) Michael Drayton (d) Spenser

82 Which is not correct for Edmund Spenser?
(a) He wrote Shepheardes calendar
(b) He offered Faerie Queen to Elizabeth to gain her favour
(c) Queen Elizabeth was rather infuriated by Faerie Queen.
(d) In 1598, he was appointed sheriff of cork.

83 Which is not true for Philip Sydney?
(a) Astrophell and Stella (b) Caelica
(c) An Apology For Poetry (d) Arcadia

84 Which of the following pairs is correctly matched?

(a)	Nicholas Udall	:	Ralph Roister Doister
(b)	Shakespeare	:	Gorboduc
(c)	Spenser	:	Astrophel and Stella
(d)	Sidney	:	Faerie Queene

85 Which of the following pairs is incorrectly matched?

(a)	Sidney	:	Astrophel and Stella
(b)	Spenser	:	Shepheardes Calendar
(c)	Nicholas Udall	:	Ralph Roister Doister
(d)	Drayton	:	Amoretti

Directions (Q. Nos. 86-88) *In the questions given below are two statements labelled as Assertion (A) and Reason (R). In the context of these two statements, which one of the following is correct?*

Codes
(a) Both A and R are true and R is the correct explanation of A
(b) Both A and R are true but R is not the correct explanation of A
(c) A is true but R is false
(d) A is false but R is true

86 Assertion (A) Drayton was given the title of 'Our English Ovid'.
Reason (R) Drayton wrote a beautiful collection of verse letters by lovers.

87 Assertion (A) Lyric poetry was the second most important literary genre in the Elizabethan period.
Reason (R) Fluency, sweetness and melody were some of the characteristics of Elizabethan lyric poetry.

88 Assertion (A) The twelve eclogues in 'The Shepheardes Calendar' correspond to twelve months of English calendar.
Reason (R) Edmund Spenser offered The Shepheardes Calendar to queen Elizabeth to win her favour.

89 Which of the following is in correct sequence of Spenser's works?
(a) The Shepheardes Calendar, The Faerie Queene, Epithalamion, Prothalamion
(b) Epithalamion, Prothalamion, The Faerie Queene, The Shepheardes Calendar
(c) Protholamion, Epithalamion, The Shepheardes Calendar, The Faerie Queene
(d) The Faerie Queene, The Shepheardes Calendar, Prothalamion, Epithalamion

90 Which of the following is in correct sonnet sequence of the Elizabethan Age?
(a) Delia, Astrophel and Stella, Shakespeare's Sonnets, Amoretti
(b) Astrophel and Stella, Delia, Amoretti, Shakespeare's Sonnets
(c) Amoretti, Delia, Astrophel and Stella, Shakespeare's Sonnets
(d) Shakespeare's Sonnets, Amoretti, Delia, Astrophel and Stella

91 Spenser completed six books about
1. Holiness
2. Chastity
3. Temperance
4. Friendship
5. Courtesy
6. Justice

Select the correct answer using the codes given below.
(a) 1, 2 and 4
(b) 1, 3 and 2
(c) 1, 4 and 5
(d) All of these

92 Consider the following statements about Faerie Queene
1. It is written by Edmund Spenser.
2. It is an allegorical poem.
3. The immediate model was not Ariosto's Orlando Furioso.
4. It does not tell the story of several knights each respresenting a particular virtue.

Which of the statements given above are correct?
(a) 1 and 2
(b) 1 and 4
(c) 3 and 2
(d) 3 and 4

93 What is common to the following works? Identify the correct description below.
1. The Shepheardes Calendar
2. The Faerie Queene
3. Epithalamion
4. Prothalamion

Codes
(a) All of them were written by Ben Jonson
(b) All of these are sonnets
(c) All of these are chronicles
(d) All of these were written by Edmund Spenser

94 Michael Drayton was interested in reading
1. Greek authors
2. French sonneteers
3. Italian poets

Select the correct answer using the codes given below.
(a) 1 and 2
(b) 2 and 3
(c) 1 and 3
(d) 1, 2 and 3

95 Consider the following statements about Philip Sydney.
1. He was named after his Godfather, King Philip II of Spain.
2. He dedicated his sonnet sequence Astrophel and Stella to his Godfather.
3. He received the title of Knighthood in 1853.
4. He wrote a letter of appreciation to Queen Elizabeth expressing his support to marry the Duke of Anjou. The Roman catholic heir to the French Throne.

Which of the statements given above are correct?
(a) 1 and 2
(b) 1 and 3
(c) 2 and 3
(d) 3 and 4

96 Consider the following statements about Michael Drayton.
1. His first work was a verse para-phrase of parts of the Old Testament and Apocrypha, The Harmony of the Church.
2. One of his works 'Idea, The Shephard's Garland' consisted of 12 eclogues.
3. Ideas Mirror written by him is an erotic epyllion.
4. He earned the title of 'Our English Ovid' after his work 'England's Heroical Epistles.

Which of the statements given above are correct?
(a) 1 and 2
(b) 2 and 3
(c) 1 and 4
(d) 2 and 4

97 Consider the following statements about Fulke Greville.

1. He sailed with Sir Francis Drake in his expedition to the Spanish West Indies in 1585.
2. He joined the Earl of Leicester against the wishes of Queen Elizabeth in 1586.
3. He wrote an elegy 'The Phoenix Nest' on the death of Philip Sydney.
4. He wrote a biography of his friend 'Life of the Renowned Sir Philip Sydney.

Which of the statements given above are correct?

(a) 1 and 2 (b) 2 and 3 (c) 1 and 4 (d) 3 and 4

98 Consider the following statements about Samuel Daniel

1. 'The Worthy Tract of Paulus Jovius' was his published work.
2. He dedicated 'Delia, containing certain sonnets with the complaint of Rosamond to Mary, counters of Penulsroke.
3. In his later years, he retired to a farm called 'the ridge'.
4. He died in 1599.

Which of the sentences given above are correct?

(a) 1, 2 and 3 (b) 1, 2 and 4 (c) 1 and 2 (d) 2 and 3

99 Consider the following statements about Thomas Campion.

1. His first individual collection 'Poemata' was published in 1595.
2. His incomplete epic 'Ad Thamesin' celebrated the victory of the Spanish Armada.
3. He wrote a Treatise on poetry titled 'observations in the Art of English Poesie'.
4. 'He is also known for his famous book 'The Tragedie of Philotas'.

Which of the following statements are correct?

(a) 1 and 2 (b) 1 and 3 (c) 2 and 3 (d) 3 and 4

100 Consider the following works of Shakespeare.

1. Cymbeline
2. The Winter's Tale
3. Rape of Lucree
4. Phoenix and The Turtle

Which of the works given above are correct?

(a) 1 and 2 (b) 2 and 3 (c) 3 and 4 (d) 1 and 4

101 Match the following.

List I	List II
A. Amoretti	1. A collection of eighty Petrarchan sonnets
B. Prothalamion	2. An ode on Marriage
C. Astrophel	3. An elegy on the death of Sir Phillip
D. Four Hymns	4. Written to Glorify love and humour

Codes

	A	B	C	D		A	B	C	D
(a)	1	2	3	4	(b)	2	3	4	1
(c)	3	4	2	1	(d)	4	3	1	2

102 Match the following.

List I (Writers)	List II (Workers)
A. Sidney	1. Hero and Leander
B. Spenser	2. Delia
C. Daniel	3. Astrophel and Stella
D. Marlowe	4. Amoretti

Codes

	A	B	C	D		A	B	C	D
(a)	1	2	3	4	(b)	3	4	2	1
(c)	2	4	1	3	(d)	3	4	1	2

103 Match the following.

List I	List II
A. Poly-Olbion	1. Thomas Campion
B. Caelica	2. Fulk Greville
C. Poemata	3. Shakespeare
D. Lover's Complain	4. Michael Drayton

Codes

	A	B	C	D		A	B	C	D
(a)	1	2	3	4	(b)	4	3	2	1
(c)	4	2	1	3	(d)	3	1	4	2

104 Match the following poets with their poems.

List I (Poet)	List II (Poem)
A. Edmund Spenser	1. The Shepheardes Calendar
B. Philip Sidney	2. Astrophell and Stella
C. Michael Drayton	3. Endymion and Phoebe
D. Fulke Greville	4. The Phoenix Nest

Codes

	A	B	C	D		A	B	C	D
(a)	1	2	3	4	(b)	4	3	2	1
(c)	3	1	4	2	(d)	2	4	1	3

105 Match the following poems with their poets.

List I (Poem)	List II (Poet)
A. Robert, Duke of Normandy	1. Samuel Daniel
B. The Complaint of Rosamond	2. Shakespeare
C. Songs of Mourning	3. Michael Drayton
D. Venus and Adonis	4. Thomas Campion

Codes

	A	B	C	D		A	B	C	D
(a)	1	2	3	4	(b)	4	3	2	1
(c)	3	1	4	2	(d)	2	4	1	3

106 "Loving in truth and rain in verse my tone to show that the clear
She might take some pleasure of my pain
Pleasure might cause her read, reading might make her know
Knowledge might pity win and pity grace obtain."

(a) This is Sidney in Astrophel and Stella
(b) This is Spenser in Faerie Queene
(c) This is Drayton in Idea
(d) This is Garcoigne in a Hundreth Sundrie Flowers

107 "One day I wrote her name upon the strand
But came the waves and washed it away
Again I wrote it with a second hand
But came the tide and made my pairs his prey."

(a) This is Spenser in Amoretti (Sonnet 75)
(b) This is Daniel in Delia
(c) This is Shakespeare (Sonnet 19)
(d) This is Drayton in Idea

108 'Holds my young braine captivated Golden Age' The sonnet tells the readers that the lover is passing sleepless nights, but he wants his beloved to sleep and have rest.

(a) This is the correct explanation of sonnet
(b) This is not the correct explanation of the sonnet
(c) The sonnet is not correct
(d) None of the above

109 Edmund Spenser dedicated his Shepherd's Calendar to his friend describing him as "the distinguished and virtuous gentleman most worthy of all titles both of learning and chivalry." Who was this friend?

(a) Sir Walter Raleigh (b) Leicester
(c) Harvey (d) Sir Philip Sidney

110 "The Long Love that in my heart doth harbour And in Mine heart doth keep his residence" is a sonnet by

(a) Wyatt (b) Shakespeare
(c) Philip Sidney (d) Spenser

111 "For whatsoever from one place doth fall,
Is with the tide unto an other brought:
For there is nothing lost, that may be found, if sought."

Which of the following poets in which of his/her works has had the above lines?

(a) Edmund Spenser, The Faerie Queene
(b) Philip Sidney, Astrophel and Stella
(c) Fulke Greville, Baron Brooke
(d) Thomas Campion, Book of Airs

112 "Ah! when will this long weary day have end,
And lende me leave to come unto may love?

Which of the following poets in which of his/her works has had the above lines?

(a) Edmund Spenser, Amoretti and Epithalamion
(b) Sir Philip Sidney, A Defence of Poetry
(c) Fulke Greville, Poems by Fulke Greville
(d) Thomas Campion, Observations in the Art of English Poesie

113 "For love is celestial harmony
Of likely hearts compos'd of stars' concent,
Which join together in sweet sympathy,
To work each other's joy and true content,
Which they have harbour'd since their first descent
Out of their heavenly bowers, where they did see
And know each other here belov'd to be."

Which of the following poets in which of his/her works has had the above lines?

(a) Edmund Spenser, Fowre Hymnes
(b) Philip Sidney, Astrophel and Stella
(c) Michael Drayton, The Barrons' Wars
(d) Thomas Campion, Book of Airs

114 "I hate the day, because it lendeth light
To see all things, but not my love to see."

Which of the following poets in which of his/her works has had the above lines?

(a) Edmund Spenser, Daphna
(b) Philip Sidney, A Defence of Poetry
(c) Michael Dryton, England's Heroical Epistles
(d) Fulke Greville, Baron Brooke

115 "Biting my truant pen, beating myself for spite:
"Fool!" said my muse to me, "look in thy heart, and write."

Which of the following poets in which of his/her works has had the above lines?

(a) Edmund Spenser, The Faerie Queene
(b) Philip Sidney, Astrophel and Stella
(c) Fulke Greville, Baron Brooke
(d) Thomas Campion, Book of Airs

116 "Come, Sleep; O Sleep! the certain knot of peace,
The baiting-place of wit, the balm of woe,
The poor man's wealth, the prisoner's release,
Th' indifferent judge between the high and low;
With shield of proof shield me from out the prease
Of those fierce darts Despair at me doth throw."

Which of the following poets in which of his/her works has had the above lines?

(a) Edmund Spenser, Fowre Hymnes
(b) Philip Sidney, Astrophel and Stella
(c) Michael Drayton, The Barron's Wars
(d) Thomas Campion, Book of Airs

117 "If you have so Earth-creeping a mind that it cannot lift itself up to look to the sky of poetry...thus much curse I must send you, in the behalf of all poets, that while you live, you live in love, and never get favour for lacking skill of a sonnet; and, when you die, your memory die from the Earth for want of an epitaph."

Which of the following poets in which of his/her works has had the above lines?

(a) Edmund Spenser, Amoretti and Epithalamion
(b) Sir Philip Sidney, A Defence of Poetry
(c) Fulke Greville, Poems by Fulke Greville
(d) Thomas Campion, Observations in the Art of English Poesie

118 "So, then, the best of the historian is subject to the poet; for whatsoever action or faction, whatsoever counsel, policy, or war-stratagem the historian is bound to recite, that may the poet, if he list, with his imitation make his own, beautifying it both for further teaching and more delighting, as it pleaseth him; having all, from Dante's Heaven to his Hell, under the authority of his pen."

Which of the following poets in which of his/her works has had the above lines?

(a) Edmund Spenser, Daphna
(b) Philip Sidney, A Defence of Poetry
(c) Michael Drayton, England's Heroical Epistles
(d) Fulke Greville, Baron Brooke

119 "You that seek what life is in death,
Now find it air that once was breath.
New names unknown, old names gone:
Till time end bodies, but souls none.
Reader! then make time, while you be,
But steps to your eternity."

Which of the following poets in which of his/her works has had the above lines?

(a) Edmund Spenser, The Faerie Queene
(b) Philip Sidney, Astrophel and Stella
(c) Fulke Greville, Baron Brooke
(d) Thomas Campion, Book of Airs

120 "Oh, wearisome conditions of humanity!
Born under one law, to another bound,
Vainly begot and yet forbidden vanity:
Created sick, commanded to be sound.
What meaneth Nature by these diverse laws—
Passion and reason, self-division's cause?

Which of the following poets in which of his/her works has had the above lines?

(a) Edmund Spenser, Amoretti and Epithalamion
(b) Sir Philip Sidney, A Defence of Poetry
(c) Fulke Greville, Poems by Fulke Greville
(d) Thomas Campion, Observations in the Art of English Poesie

121 Lost is our freedom,
When we submit to women so:
Why do we need them,
When in their best they work our woe.

Which of the following poets in which of his/her works has had the above lines?

(a) Edmund Spenser, The Faerie Queene
(b) Philip Sidney, Astrophel and Stella
(c) Fulke Greville, Baron Brooke
(d) Thomas Campion, Book of Airs

122 Lovely forms do flow
From conceit divinely framed;
Heaven is music, and thy beauty's
Birth is heavenly.

Which of the following poets in which of his/her works has had the above lines?

(a) Edmund Spenser, Amoretti and Epithalamion
(b) Sir Philip Sidney, A Defence of Poetry
(c) Fulke Greville, Poems by Fulke Greville
(d) Thomas Campion, Observations in the Art of English Poesie.

123 ILL news hath wings, and with the wind doth go,
Comfort's a cripple and comes ever slow.

Which of the following poets in which of his/her works has had the above lines?

(a) Edmund Spenser, Fowre Hymnes
(b) Philip Sidney, Astrophel and Stella
(c) Michael Drayton, The Barrons' Wars
(d) Thomas Campion, Book of Airs

124 Care draws on care, woe comforts woe again,
Sorrow breeds sorrow, on grief brings forth twain.

Which of the following poets in which of his/her works has had the above lines?

(a) Edmund Spenser, Daphna
(b) Philip Sidney, A Defence of Poetry
(c) Michael Drayton, England's Heroical Epistles
(d) Fulke Greville, Baron Brooke

125 Our floods queen, Thames, for ships and swans is crowned.

Which of the following poets in which of his/her works has had the above lines?

(a) Michael Drayton, "To the River Ankor"
(b) Thomas Campion, Book of Airs
(c) Edmund Spenser, Daphna
(d) Philip Sidney, A Defence of Poetry

126 The mind is free, whate'er afflict the man,
A King's a King, do Fortune what she can.

Which of the following poets in which of his/her works has had the above lines?

(a) Edmund Spenser, Fowre Hymnes
(b) Philip Sidney, Astrophel and Stella
(c) Thomas Campion, Book of Airs
(d) Michael Drayton, The Barrons' Wars

127 Which of the following poets referred to the 'dark lady' sonnet sequence as 'abominably harsh, obscure and worthless'?

(a) Miguel de Cervantes (b) Thomas Campion
(c) Ben Johnson (d) William Wordsworth

128 Which Latin concept explored by Shakespeare in his sonnets refers to a state which lies between eternity and the temporal existence of material beings.

(a) Aelus (b) Aegae (c) Aevum (d) Aedivum

129 The first seventeen sonnets of Shakespeare's collection are traditionally called what?

(a) The procreation sonnets
(b) The procrastination sonnets
(c) The propagation sonnets
(d) The promulgation sonnets

130 With Sonnet 18 'shall I compare thee to a summer's day' the tone of the sonnets changes towards.

(a) Indifference (b) Joviality
(c) Light heartedness (d) Romantic Intimacy

131 Which of the following is a theme dealt with is Shakespeare's sonnets

(a) Love (b) Mortality
(c) The passage of time (d) All of these

132 In the following verse from sonnet 18, what are possible interpretations of the word 'untrimmed'
By chance or natures changing course untrimmed.

(a) With a lack of decoration and fails
(b) Like the sails on a ship which have not been adjusted to catch the wind properly.
(c) unruly or disorganised
(d) All of the Above

133 What is the meaning of 'eternal summer' in the ninth verse of sonnet 18?
But they eternal summer shall not fade

(a) Confidence (b) Love
(c) Youth (d) Happiness

134 "And Time that gave doth now his gift confound (Sonnet 60), Shakespeare highlights the fact that time both gives and kills. This seemingly self contradictory statement in example of which rhetorical device?

(a) Simile (b) Paradox
(c) Hyperbole (d) Eponym

135 The beginning of which quartrain normally marks the 'Volta' in Shakespeare's sonnets?

(a) The fourth (b) The second
(c) The first (d) The third

Directions (Q. Nos. 136-140) *Read the poem and answer the questions that follow*

All the world's a stage
And all the men and women merely players:
They have their exits and their entrances;
And one man in his time plays many parts,
His acts being seven ages.
At first the infant,
Mewling and puking in the nurse's arms.
Then the whining schoolboy, with his satchel
And shining morning face, creeping like snail
Unwillingly to school.
And then the lover,
Sighing like furnace, with a woeful ballad
Made to his mistress' eyebrow.
Then a solider.
Full of strange oaths, and bearded like the pard,
Jealous in honour, sudden and quick in quarrel,
Seeking the bubble reputation.
Even in the cannon's mouth.
And then the justice,
In fair round belly with good capon lined,
With eyes severe on beard of formed cut,
Full of wise saws and modern instances;
And so he plays his part.
The sixth age shifts
Into the lean and slippered pantaloon,
With spectacles and nose and pouch on side,
His youthful hose, well saved, a world too wide
For his shrunk shank; and his big manly voice,
Turning again toward childish treble, pipes
And whistles in his sound.
Last scene of all,
That ends this strange eventful history,
Is second childishness and mere oblivion,
Sans teeth, sans eyes, sans taste, sans everything.

136 What is being described in the poem from the beginning?

(a) Various stages of life of a person
(b) Importance of life of a person
(c) Challenges of life faced by a person
(d) The power of nature to mould one's life

137 Which figure of speech is being used in the lines 'Even in the cannon's mouth?

(a) Metaphor (b) Alliteration
(c) Personification (d) Oxymoron

138 In the given context, the phrase 'seeking the bubble reputation' means

(a) a youth yearning for false fame
(b) a youth wishing for fame at the earliest with quickly changing motives
(c) a youth longing for instant fame
(d) a youth hankering after everlasting fame

139 Why does the poet compare the lover with a furnace?

(a) A lover destroys everything like a burning furnace
(b) A lover is helpless like a burning furnace
(c) A lover is as active as a burning furnace
(d) A lover's heart is burning out of pain of his beloved's separation like a burning furnace

140 What is the theme of the poem?

(a) The world is a stage where people have to perform different roles at different times
(b) Life is wonderful but the fourth stage of justice is the best
(c) The last stage repeats the second stage of life towards the end
(d) We should be sincere and serious during our first stage as that governs the rest of life

PREVIOUS YEARS' QUESTIONS

January 2017

1 As Sidney argues in 'A Defence of Poesy' which discipline is more useful and praiseworthy-history or poetry?

(a) History 'being captivated to truth' is more useful than poetry
(b) Poetry where man can see 'virtue exalted and vice punished' is more useful than history
(c) History is more useful for poetry is 'an encouragement to unbridled wickedness'
(d) History and poetry are synonymous and so both are useful

July 2016

2 Two cantos from the seventh book of 'The Faerie Queene' appeared posthumously. They are known as

(a) Mutability cantos
(b) Friendship cantos
(c) Justice cantos
(d) Courtesy cantos

3 In his Defence of Poesy what is the 'best and most accomplished kind of poetry' in Sidney estimation?

(a) Heroical, or Epic poetry
(b) Lyric poetry
(c) Pastoral poetry
(d) Elegiac poetry

4 In his 'Defence of Poesy' which of the following works does Sidney command as good examples of English Poesy?

1. The Mirror of Magistrates
2. The Shepheardes Calendar
3. Lament for the Makers
4. Ballad of Scottish King

The right combination according to the code is

(a) 1 and 3
(b) 1 and 4
(c) 1 and 2
(d) 2 and 3

5 What metaphor does Edmund Spenser employ (Faerie Queene Book 1 Canto 12) to frame his tale and to describe the relationship between the tale and its readers?

(a) That of a caravan of lost souls, traversing a desert
(b) That of a stagecoach, which picks up diverse passengers along the way
(c) That of a ship filled with jolly mariners
(d) That of a riderless horse, following his own direction

June 2015

6 Philip Sidney defended poetry against such descriptions of it as 'the mother of lies' and 'the nurse of abuse.' His main argument here is ....

(a) the poet is no conjuror of illusionist and represents a world
(b) the poet cannot lie because he is not claiming to tell us the truth
(c) the poet cannot speak the truth because he is not representing the real world
(d) the poet is a philosopher for whom truth is a lie and lie truth, in an imaginary world

June 2014

7 A Spenserian stanza has

(a) 4 iambic pentameters
(b) 2 iambic pentameters
(c) 8 iambic pentameters
(d) 10 iambic pentameters

8 In Spenser's Re Faerie Queene, there are the allegorised moral and religious virtues with the counterparts in the vices. Identify the correctly matched set.

(a)	Una	:	Truth
	Guyon	:	Temperance
	Duessa	:	Deceit
	Orgoglio	:	Pride
(b)	Una	:	Pride
	Guyon	:	Deceit
	Duessa	:	Temperance
	Orgoglio	:	Truth
(c)	Una	:	Deceit
	Guyon	:	Pride
	Duessa	:	Temperance
	Orgoglio	:	Truth
(d)	Una	:	Temperance
	Guyon	:	Truth
	Duessa	:	Pride
	Orgoglio	:	Deceit

9 In the 'Defence of Poesy', what did Sidney attribute to poetry?

(a) A magical power whereby poetry plays tricks on the reader
(b) A divine power whereby poetry transmits a message from God to the reader
(c) A moral power whereby poetry encourages the reader to evaluate virtuous models
(d) A realistic power that cannot be made to seem like mere illusion and trickery

10 In relation to Spenser's Faerie Queene which of the following character virtue link is rightly matched.

(a) Justice-Artegall; Courtsey-Guyon; Temperance-Calidore
(b) Chasity-Britomart; Justice-Guyon; Temperance-Talus
(c) Courtsey-Calidore; Temperance-Guyon; Justice- Artegall
(d) Courtsey-Calidore; Temperance-Artegall; Justice-Britomart

June 2012

11 Which statements below on the Spenserian stanza is/are accurate ?

1. A quatrain, unrhymed, but alliterative.
2. A stanza of four lines in iambic pentameter.
3. An eight-line stanza in iambic pentameter followed by a ninth in sixth iambic feet.
4. An eight-line stanza with sixth iambic feet followed by a ninth in iambic pentameter.

Select the correct answer using the codes given below.

(a) 1 and 2 (b) Only 2
(c) Only 3 (d) Only 4

12 ...... was the first sonnet sequence in English.

(a) Edmund Spenser's Amoretti
(b) Philip Sidney's Astrophel and Stella
(c) Samuel Daniel's Delia
(d) Michael Drayton's Idea's Mirror

13 Which of the following statements is correct?

(a) Gorboduc is a comedy, while Ralph Roister Doister and Gammer Gurton's Needle are tragedies
(b) Gorboduc is a tragedy, while Ralph Roister Doister and Gammer Gurton's Needle are comedies
(c) All of them are problem plays
(d) All of them are farces

14 'The grey-eyed morn smiles on the frowning night,
Check' ring the Eastern clouds with streaks of light;
And flecked darkness like a drunkard reels
From 4th day's path and Titan's burning wheels.'
The speaker describes

(a) The Setting Sun
(b) The Return Home of a Drunkard
(c) The Drawing of a New Day (d) The Rising Sun

December 2012

15 Shakespeare's sonnets

(a) do not carry a dedication
(b) are dedicated to James I of England
(c) are dedicated to Mary Arden
(d) are dedicated to an unknown 'Mr WH'

ANSWERS

Objective Questions

1. (b)	2. (b)	3. (d)	4. (d)	5. (a)	6. (c)	7. (d)	8. (c)	9. (a)	10. (c)
11. (c)	12. (b)	13. (d)	14. (c)	15. (b)	16. (c)	17. (b)	18. (c)	19. (d)	20. (b)
21. (d)	22. (b)	23. (a)	24. (c)	25. (b)	26. (b)	27. (b)	28. (a)	29. (d)	30. (d)
31. (c)	32. (b)	33. (b)	34. (d)	35. (a)	36. (a)	37. (a)	38. (a)	39. (b)	40. (c)
41. (a)	42. (c)	43. (a)	44. (b)	45. (a)	46. (b)	47. (b)	48. (c)	49. (a)	50. (d)
51. (c)	52. (c)	53. (a)	54. (d)	55. (d)	56. (d)	57. (b)	58. (b)	59. (d)	60. (b)
61. (b)	62. (c)	63. (d)	64. (d)	65. (b)	66. (b)	67. (b)	68. (c)	69. (b)	70. (c)
71. (d)	72. (c)	73. (c)	74. (b)	75. (a)	76. (c)	77. (d)	78. (d)	79. (a)	80. (d)
81. (a)	82. (c)	83. (b)	84. (a)	85. (d)	86. (a)	87. (b)	88. (c)	89. (a)	90. (b)
91. (d)	92. (a)	93. (d)	94. (d)	95. (b)	96. (c)	97. (d)	98. (a)	99. (b)	100. (c)
101. (a)	102. (b)	103. (c)	104. (a)	105. (d)	106. (a)	107. (a)	108. (a)	109. (d)	110. (a)
111. (a)	112. (a)	113. (a)	114. (a)	115. (b)	116. (b)	117. (b)	118. (b)	119. (c)	120. (c)
121. (d)	122. (d)	123. (c)	124. (c)	125. (a)	126. (d)	127. (d)	128. (c)	129. (a)	130. (d)
131. (d)	132. (d)	133. (c)	134. (b)	135. (d)	136. (a)	137. (c)	138. (b)	139. (d)	140. (a)

Previous Years' Questions

1. (b)	2. (a)	3. (a)	4. (c)	5. (c)	6. (b)	7. (a)	8. (a)	9. (c)	10. (c)
11. (d)	12. (a)	13. (b)	14. (c)	15. (d)					

The Puritan and Restoration Age Poetry

The Puritan poetry mainly focused on religion and devotion to God. The poetry of this age can be categorised into three kinds; Spenserian, Metaphysical and Cavalier poetry. The Restoration Age poetry witnessed the introduction of heroic couplets by John Dryden. John Milton along with Dryden is considered to be the greatest literary figure of this era.

English Renaissance Poetry

After the Elizabethan era, English Renaissance poetry can be seen as belonging to one of three strains; the Metaphysical poets, the Cavalier poets and the school of Spenser. However, the boundaries between these three groups are not always very clear and an individual poet could write in more than one manner. All these strains of poetry together fell under the ambit of Puritan and Caroline Poetry.

The Puritan Age

The Puritan Age is named after the rise of the Puritan movement in England in the 17th century. Puritans were a group of English speaking protestants who were dissatisfied with the religious reformation movement carried out during the reign of Elizabeth. They wanted a complete purification of Church of England and removal of practices such as hierarchical leadership, clerical vestments and the various rituals of the church, which were associated with Rome. They stood for what they believed was pure Christianity (hence, the name Puritan), untainted by the many historical changes that other denominations had introduced.

The Puritans emerged as a strong political force during the English Civil War (1642-1651). The English Civil War was a series of conflicts between Charles I and his supporters called the Cavaliers on one hand and the Parliamentarians or the Roundheads on other hand. The Roundheads mainly comprised the Puritan middle classes. The war ended in 1651 with the victory of the Parliamentarians. Charles I was executed while his son, Charles II fled to France. Any hopes of monarchy were

In this Chapter

demolished and the monarchical rule was replaced first with the Commonwealth of England (1649-53) and then with a Protectorate (1653-59), under Oliver Cromwell's personal rule. The establishment of a Protectorate under Cromwell was a victory for the Puritans. The Puritans remained in ascendancy till 1660, when Charles II was restored to the throne.

Though, the Puritans as a group are often denounced as narrow-minded and repressive, yet in reality they also aimed for religious and civil liberty. According to WH Hudson, the Puritans 'had strict rules regarding life and conduct' and 'an uncompromising spirit', which sought to 'confine literature within the circumscribed field of its own particular interests'. Defending the outlook of the Puritans, WJ Long states that the enactment of severe laws under Cromwell and the prohibition of simple pleasures during the age should not blind us to the fact that it was "The intensity of the struggle against despotism" that had made Puritans 'narrow and hard'.

Literature of the Puritan Age

Literature of the Puritan age was characterised by a spirit of sombreness and pensiveness. In keeping with the religious ideals and political standards of the Puritans; religious verse, theological tracts and political treatises replaced romantic poetry.

According to John Richard Green, a great 'moral change' came over the people of England. "England became the people of a book and that book was the Bible." With the outbreak of the Civil War, theatres were closed down. In 1642, under the influence of the Puritans, the English Parliament issued an ordinance suppressing all stage plays in the theatres. The strict religious views of the Puritans spread to encompass many social activities within England. Therefore, these years around 1642, saw very little theatrical activity in England as the Puritans considered theatre as 'immoral' and 'depraved'. In 1644, the Globe Theatre was demolished by the Puritans.

While the earlier spirit of the Elizabethan age still remained in a lesser form in the Spenserian poets of the age, poetry also took new and until then unseen forms and expression in the new class of metaphysical poets. The values and beliefs of the Puritans found their strongest voice in John Milton. Milton is considered to be the greatest representative of the Puritan Age. WJ Long identifies three main characteristics, in which Puritan literature differs from that of the preceding age.

First, even though Elizabethan literature was diverse in form, it had a "Marked unity in spirit, resulting from the patriotism of all classes and their devotion to a queen who, with all her faults, sought first the nation's welfare". However, with the Puritan age, no such devotion to the crown could be seen, since the monarch ruled in despotic manner earning the ire of the masses. England became 'divided by the struggle for political and religious liberty'; and the literature also became 'divided in spirit'.

Second, while Elizabethan literature was full of youth and vitality; the literature of Puritan age is characterised by sadness and pessimism.

The last feature, which separates Puritan literature from the literature, that preceded it is that unlike Elizabethan literature which was intensely romantic, Puritan age literature lacks romantic fervour. Even in love poems such as those of Donne, an intellectual spirit replaces the spontaneous emotion of love and passion.

Poetry of the Puritan Age

Puritan poetry was exclusively focused around the devotion of God, and that all his acts were a mark of his love or wrath. This is just like the literature, yet it follows a generally poetic structure. By a poetic structure, they used stricter form than later years, with more usage of rhyme schemes, stricter stanzas. Poems were often written in response to life events, like when Anne Bradstreet's husband went to England, she decided to write a poem wishing for his safe return, and hoping that the Lord would keep her safe. Another example was the poem that she wrote after fainting, asking the Lord for salvation, as fainting was seen as an evil thing. Poems of this period were too different from the previous era. They seemed to be full of depression besides being devoted to Church.

Classification of the Poets of the Puritan Age

Poets of the Puritan age can be divided into three main groups according to the tradition of poetry they followed

These three groups of poets are

1. Spenserian Poets
2. Cavalier Poets
3. Metaphysical Poets

Spenserian Poets

Even after the Elizabethan age, Edmund Spenser continued to cast his influence on some of the poets. Some of the important poets, who styled themselves after the school of Spenser were Phineas Fletcher and Giles Fletcher, William Browne, George Wither and William Drummond. The works of these poets imitate the style and themes of Spenser's poetry.

Certain Common features in the poetry of the Spenserian poets are

- Spenserian stanza, verse form that consists of eight iambic pentameter lines followed by a ninth line of six iambic feet (an alexandrine); the rhyme scheme is ababbcbcc.
- The first eight lines produce an effect of formal unity, while the hexameter completes the thought of the stanza.
- Invented by Edmund Spenser for his poem *The Faerie Queene* (1590-1609), the Spenserian stanza has origins in the Old French ballad (eight-lines stanzas, rhyming, ababbcbc), the Italian Ottava rima (eight iambic pentameter lines with a rhyme scheme of abababcc) and the stanza form used by Chaucer in his *Monk's Tale* (eight lines rhyming ababbcbc).
- A revolutionary innovation in its day, the Spenserian stanza fell into general disuse during the 17th and 18th centuries. It was revived in the 19th century by the Romantic poets e.g. Byron in *Childe Harold's Pilgrimage*, Keats in *The Eve of St. Agnes*, and Shelley in *Adonais*

Some of the important Spenserian poets are Phineas Fletcher, Giles Fletcher, George Wither, William Browne and William Drummond.

Phineas Fletcher (1582-1650)

Phineas Fletcher was born at Cranbrook, Kent in 1582. He was the son of Dr Giles Fletcher and brother of Giles the younger. He attended Eton and King's College, Cambridge. He graduated in 1604 and completed MA in 1608.

Literary Career and Works

Fletcher's earliest work appeared in *Sorrowes Joy*, a poetical miscellany, compiled at the university in 1603. Fletcher took holy orders in 1621 and obtained the living of Helgay, Norfolk. Fletcher's best known poem, *The Purple Island* (1633), an allegorical description of man, in the style of Spenser was published in 1633.

Written in twelve cantos, the poem describes the 'corporeal and intellectual functions of man' (Nathan Drake). It was dedicated to his friend Edward Benlowes and included his *Piscatorie Eclogues* and other *Poetical Miscellanies*. His other works are *The Locusts* (1627) or *Apollyonist*- a satire against the Jesuits, Sicelides (1631)-a pastoral play and an erotic poem *Britain's Ida* (1628), *The way to Blessedness* (1632), *Joy in Tribulation* (1632).

Fletcher died at Helgay in 1650.

Giles Fletcher (1588-1623)

English poet Giles Fletcher was born in London about 1588. He was the brother of the poet Phineas Fletcher and cousin of the dramatist John Fletcher. He was educated at Westminster School and Trinity College, Cambridge. He became reader in Greek Grammar in 1615 and reader in Greek Language in 1618. Like his elder brother, he too took the holy orders and became Rector of Alderton in Suffolk.

Literary Career and Works

Fletcher is best known for his poem *Christs Victorie* and *Triumph in Heaven and Earth over and after death.* The poem is written in eight-line stanzas deriving from Edmund Spenser. According to WJ Courthope, the poem is divided into four parts: "The action of the first, *Christ's Victory in Heaven*, begins towards the close of Christ's actual life on Earth... *Christ's Victory on Earth* is a fanciful version of the incidents of the *Temptation; Christ's Triumph over Death* relates (as far as it can be called narrative at all) the Saviour's *Crucifixion and Burial*; Christ's *Triumph after Death* is a description of the *Resurrection and Ascension."*

Edmund Gosse states that Giles excels among the Spenserian school of poets and he even aims at "higher majesties of melody and imagination than Spenser attempted".

Gosse considers *Christ's Victory* as 'undoubtedly the most coherent and the best of all the works' 'written in direct discipleship of Spenser.' Fletcher's other works include *Canto upon the Death of Eliza, An Elegy upon Prince Henry's Death* and a short poem in riming couplets *A Description of Encolpius.*

Fletcher died in Suffolk in 1623.

George Wither (1588-1667)

English poet George Wither was born at Bentworth in Hampshire. He was sent to Oxford in 1603, but left the university without completing his graduation. Thereafter, he went to London, where he entered one of the Inns of Chancery to study law.

Literary Career and Works

Wither's earliest works probably include an elegy (1612) he wrote on the death of Prince Henry and a volume of Congratulatory poems (1613) on the marriage of the princess Elizabeth. In 1612-13, his satirical work, *Abuses Stript and Whipt* was published, which included a poem called *The Scourge*, in which the then Lord Chancellor was attacked. As a result of this, Wither was confined to the Marshalsea prison. After his release, Wither published the pastoral eclogues *The Shepherd's Hunting* (1615) and *Fidelia*, a love elegy (1617).

Wither returned to the satiric vein with the publication of *Wither's Motto* in 1621, which again earned him the ire of the authorities. Wither was arrested for the second time. His other works are *Fair Virtue* (1622), *Juvenilia* (1622), a collection of love and pastoral poetry.

His later work was religious in tone after his conversion to Puritanism. His *Hymns and Songs of the Church* (1623) are written in a more sober vein.

Wither also fought under Cromwell as a Major General during the English Civil War and was arrested after the Restoration when the poet, Sir John Denham, interceded on his behalf. He died in London in 1667.

William Browne (1590-1645)

William Browne was born at Tavistock, in Devonsire in 1590. He studied at Exeter College, Oxford but later entered the Inner Temple, one of the four inns of the Court.

Literary Career and Works

Browne however, was more interested in poetry than law. He returned to Oxford, in middle life, as tutor to the Earl of Caernarvon. After this, the Earl of Pembroke appointed him in office. He received the patronage and lived with the family of the Earl of Pembroke. Browne died at Ottery-St-Mary in 1645.

Browne's chief works are *Britannia's Pastorals I* (1613), *Britannia's Pastorals II* (1616) and *The Shepherd's Pipe* (1614). *Britannia's Pastorals* are written in heroic couplets and contain vivid descriptions of nature. Calling Browne, "One of the sweetest pastoral writers in the world", the critic Henry Neele lists his merits and states that Browne's scenery is 'English'. "He takes us to the leafy shores of Devon and the fertile banks of Tamar and describes their beauties with the ardour of a lover and the truth of a painter." Neele further adds that Browne's works are rich in 'poetry and imagination'.

William Drummond (1585-1649)

Scottish poet William Drummond was born at Hawthornden Castle, Midlothian in 1585. He was the son of John Drummond, first Laird owner of a large, long established scottish estate of Hawthornden and his wife, Susannah Fowler Drummond. He attended Edinburgh's High School and did his masters from Edinburgh University. Fond of reading, Drummond had a huge collection of books. Drummond died in 1649.

Literary Career and Works

Drummond's first volume of verse, a pastoral elegy, *Teares on the Death of Moeliades* was published in 1613. His next poem *Forth Feasting: A Panegyricke to the King's Most Excellent Majestie* (1617) was written in heroic couplets and celebrated King James's visit to Scotland.

His prose works include an essay on death-*A Cypresse Grove* (1623) and *The History of Scotland* (1655). Drummond married Elizabeth Logan in 1632. He also wrote for an entertainment staged for the coronation of Charles I.

Cavalier Poets

Cavalier poets were a group of English gentlemen poets, who gathered at the court of Charles I. Because of their loyalty and support for Charles I, these poets were called 'cavaliers'. They were also cavaliers in their style of life and believed in the ideal of the Renaissance man - who was a lover, a soldier, a gallant, a man of affairs, a musician and a poet all at once.

Certain common features in the poetry of the Cavalier Poets are

- The Cavalier Poets use "Direct and colloquial (conversational) language expressive of a highly individual personality".
- According to Dr Munib Ayoub, "Cavalier poets reflect the lighter side of life and literature in the 17th century the gay, hopeful, passionate and amorous kind of poetry".
- Important themes in their poetry include the theme of honour and the theme of carpe diem or seize the day i.e. live the moment at a time.
- Their poetry aims to entertain rather than provoke the audience.

Some of the important Cavalier poets are Robert Herrick, Thomas Carew, John Suckling and Richard Lovelace.

Robert Herrick (1591-1674)

Robert Herrick was born to Julia Stone and Nicholas Herrick in London in 1591. Herrick's father died, when he was only fourteen months old. It is not clear whether Herrick obtained his schooling. In 1607, he became apprenticed to his uncle Sir William Herrick as a goldsmith. Later, he graduated from Saint John's College, Cambridge in 1617. Herrick died at the age of 83 in 1674.

Literary Career and Works

Herrick became a disciple of the famous playwright Ben Jonson. In 1623, Herrick took holy orders and later became vicar of Dean Prior in Devonshire. He acted as chaplain to Buckingham on the expedition to the Île de Ré. In 1629, he was appointed by Charles I to the living of Dean Prior in the diocese of Exeter. Herrick spent the rest of his life in Exeter. His main work is *Hesperides; or, the Works Both Humane and Divine of Robert Herrick, Esq* (1648). A group of religious poems with the title *Noble Numbers* was included separately in *Hesperides.*

Thomas Carew (1594-1640)

Thomas Carew was born at West Wickham in Kent in 1594-95. His father Matthew Carew was a lawyer and descended from a prominent Cornish gentry. Carew's family moved to London about 1598.

Carew was educated at Merton College, Oxford and the Middle Temple in London. In 1613, Carew was appointed as secretary to Sir Dudley Carleton on embassies to Italy and the Netherlands. However, he was fired few years later for making insulting remarks about Carleton and his wife. In 1619, he became part of an entourage of Sir Edward Herbert on an embassy to Paris.

Carew died in 1640 and was buried in Saint Dunstan's in the West, Westminster.

Literary Career and Works

According to Michael P Parker, Carew's first essay in the genre of the country-house poem was *To Saxham*. It imitated Ben Jonson's praise of the Sidney family in his most famous country house poem, *To Penshurst*. His first published poem was verses prefixed to Thomas May's comedy *The Heir*.

Carew is mostly known for his amorous and sensuous lyrics such as 'Ask me no more where love bestows' and 'He that loves a rosy cheek'. His erotic poem *A Rapture* is considered to be the best and longest of his poems.

John Suckling (1609-1642)

John Suckling was born at Whitton, Middlesex, on 10th February, 1609. His father, Sir John Suckling was Secretary of State under James I and Comptroller of the Household of Charles I and his mother, Elizabeth Cranfield was the sister of Sir Lionel Cranfield, 1st Earl of Middlesex. Suckling inherited his family estate at the age of 18. He was educated at Westminster School, Trinity College Cambridge and Grays Inn.

Literary Career and Works

Suckling's prose work *Account of Religion by Reason* was written in 1637. It was dedicated to Edward Sackville, fourth Earl of Dorset. His play, *Aglaura* was published in 1638. His poems include *Ballade upon a Wedding, I Prithee, Send me Back My Heart* and *Why So Pale and Wan, Fond Lover?'*. *Goblins* (1646) is another important work of Suckling.

It is rumoured that Suckling committed suicide in Paris in 1642.

Richard Lovelace (1618-1657)

Richard Lovelace was born at Woolwich, London in 1618. He was the oldest son of Sir William Lovelace and Anne Barne Lovelace. His father was a soldier, who was killed during the war with Spain and Holland in 1627. Lovelace was educated at Charterhouse School and at Gloucester Hall, Oxford. Lovelace died in poverty in 1658.

Literary Career and Works

At Oxford, Lovelace wrote a comedy, *The Scholars* and a tragedy called *The Soldiers*. King Charles I and Queen Henrietta Maria were so impressed by Lovelace's works and demeanor that they honoured him with degree of MA, though he was only in his second year at the university.

Lovelace was an important figure at court. He accompanied Charles I on his expedition to quell the Scots' rebellion of 1639-40. After the failure of this campaign, he withdrew to his estates in Kent where he remained until 1642. He was imprisoned at Petre house in Aldersgate for suspected involvement in disturbances at Kent. During his time in prison, Lovelace collected and revised for the press a volume of occasional poems. This was published in 1649 under the title of *Lucasta*.

Metaphysical Poets

The term 'metaphysical' is loosely applied to a group of 17th century poets such as John Donne, Andrew Marvell, Henry Vaughan, George Herbert and Richard Crashaw. These poets did not belong to a school of poetry, but were united by "Common characteristics of wit, inventiveness and a love of elaborate stylistic manoeuvres". Their poetry was rich in intellectual complexity.

John Dryden was the first to use the term 'metaphysic' in his criticism of Donne. In his *Discourse Concerning Satire,* Dryden had stated that Donne in his poetry "affects the Metaphysics... in his amorous verses, where nature only should reign; and perplex the minds of the fair sex with nice speculations of philosophy, when he should engage their hearts." While Dryden had used the term in reference to Donne, Samuel Johnson extended it to a group of poets. In *The Lives of the Poets*, Johnson stated that "about the beginning of the 17th century appeared a race of writers that may be termed as the metaphysical poets". Both Dryden and Johnson had used the term 'metaphysical' in a negative sense to criticise the excesses of this group of poets. Johnson believed that metaphysical poets only wanted to 'show their learning'. In their poetry, "The most heterogeneous ideas were yoked together with violence".

Common features of metaphysical poetry are

- Metaphysical poetry is characterised by a subtle, complex and concentrated thought.
- It is intellectually rigorous.
- It employs bold and ingenious conceits, also called metaphysical conceits. Johnson called it "A combination of dissimilar images". e.g., in his poem *A Valediction: Forbidding Mourning*, Donne compares the two lovers to a compass.
  "If they be two, they are two so
  As stiff twin compasses are two,
  Thy soul the fixed foot, makes no show
  To move, but doth, if th'other do."
- It employs unusual images taken from different fields of knowledge history, geography, astronomy, alchemy, mathematics, etc.
- It has a dramatic quality to it and often has an abrupt aggressive opening.
- It frequently makes use of paradox. For instance, in his poem, 'Batter my Heart', the speaker appeals to God,
  "Take me to you, imprison me, for I
  Except you enthral me, never shall be free,
  Nor ever chaste, except you ravish me."

The elevation of Metaphysical poets owes a great deal to HC Grierson's *Introduction* to *Metaphysical Lyrics and Poems of the Seventeenth Century* published in 1912. After this, the reputation of metaphysical soared as a result of TS Eliot's path breaking critical essay *The Metaphysical Poets*. According to him, metaphysical poets like Donne fused thought and emotion.

One finds an 'association of sensibility' in their poetry, which later changed to a 'dissociation of sensibility' in the Victorian poets. Comparing Donne with the Victorian poets, Tennyson and Browning, Eliot states, "Tennyson and Browning are poets and they think; but they do not feel their thought as immediately as the odour of a rose. A thought to Donne was an experience; it modified his sensibility."

Some of the important metaphysical poets are John Donne, George Herbert, Richard Crashaw, Henry Vaughan and Andrew Marvell.

John Donne (1572-1631)

English poet, cleric and lawyer John Donne was born in Bread Street, London in 1572. He belonged to a prominent Roman Catholic family, but converted to Anglicanism during the 1590s. He was educated at the University of Oxford. His next three years were spent at the University of Cambridge, but he received no degree at either university because he refused to take the Oath of Supremacy required at graduation. After this, Donne began the study of law at Lincoln's Inn, London, in 1592 and seemed destined for a legal or diplomatic career.

Literary Career and Works

Donne was appointed as Chief Secretary to the Lord Keeper of the Great Seal, Sir Thomas Egerton. Egerton's London home, York House, was considered to be the most influential social centre in England at that time. During these years, he fell in love with Egerton's niece, Anne More and secretly married her without his patron's permission in 1601.

This earned him the ire of Egerton , resulting in his dismissal from the position of Chief Secretary and a brief imprisonment. After his release, Donne accepted a country life in Pyrford, Surrey and a meagre living as a lawyer. Donne wrote many of his significant works such as *Divine Poems* (1607) and *Biathanatos* (1607), which contained a defence of suicide during this period.

He wrote the two Anniversaries, *An Anatomy of the World* (1611) and *Of the Progress of the Soul* (1612) for his chief patron MP Sir Robert Drury. In 1610 and 1611, he wrote two anti-Catholic polemics *Pseudo-Martyr* and *Ignatius his Conclave*. Jesus Cora Alonso divided Donne's poetry into three main groups: "one, satires and cynically anti-petrarchan love poems; two, sincere, deeply-felt neoplatonic amatory poems and philosophical complimentary verses to influential female friends and three, his devotional poems."

Donne's *Devotions upon Emergent Occassions* (1624) was a prose work dedicated to Charles I. It was written after he recovered from a serious bout of illness. His last sermon was *Death's Duell or A Consolation to the Soul*. Donne became a priest of the Anglican Church in 1615 and was appointed royal chaplain later that year. In 1621, Donne was made Dean of St Paul's Cathedral.

He died on 31st March, 1631 and was buried at St Paul's Cathedral.

Donne's Famous Poems

- 'The Flea'
- 'The Good-Morrow'
- 'The Sun Rising'
- 'The Canonisation'
- 'A Valediction Forbidding Mourning'
- 'The Ecstacy'
- 'Elegy XX To His Mistress Going to Bed'
- 'Holy Sonnet X Death Be Not Proud'
- 'Holy Sonnet XIV Batter my heart-three-person'd God'
- 'Hymn to God, My God, In My Sickness'
- 'Good Friday, 1613. Riding Westward'

A Valediction : Forbidding Mourning

As virtuous men pass mildly away,
And whisper to their souls, to go,
Whilst some of their sad friends do say,
'The breath goes now,' and some say, 'No'
So let us melt, and make no noise,
No tear-floods, nor sigh-tempests move;
'Twere profanation of our joys
To tell the laity our love.
Moving of th' Earth brings harms and fears;
Men reckon what it did, and meant;
But trepidation of the spheres,
Though greater far, is innocent.
Dull sublunary lovers' love
(Whose soul is sense) cannot admit
Absence, because it doth remove
Those things which elemented it.
But we by a love so much refin'd,
That ourselves know not what it is,
Inter-assured of the mind,
Care less, eyes, lips, and hands to miss.
Our two souls therefore, which are one,
Though I must go, endure not yet
A breach, but an expansion,
Like gold to airy thinness beat.
If they be two, they are two so
As stiff twin compasses are two;
Thy soul, the fix'd foot, makes no show
To move, but doth, if the' other do.
And though it in the center sit,
Yet when the other for doth roam,
It leans, and hearkens after it,
And grows erect, as that comes home,
Such wilt thou be to me, who must,
Like the otherfoot, obliquely run;
Thy firmness makes my circle just,
And makes me end where I begun.

'A Valediction : Forbidding Mourning': Summary

A Valediction : Forbidding Mourning is one of Donne's most famous and simplest poems and also probably his most direct statement of his ideal of spiritual love. For all his erotic carnality in poems, such as *The Flea*, Donne professed a devotion to a kind of spiritual love that transcended the merely physical. Here, anticipating a physical separation from his beloved, he invoked the nature of that spiritual love to ward off the 'tear-floods' and 'sigh-tempests' that might otherwise attend on their farewell. The poem is essentially a sequence of metaphors and comparisons, each describing a way of looking at their separation that will help them to avoid the mourning forbidden by the poem's title.

The poet begins by comparing the love between his beloved and himself with the passing away of virtuous men. Such men expire so peacefully that their friends cannot determine when they are truly dead. Likewise, his beloved should let the two of them depart in peace, not revealing their love to the laity (ordinary people).

The speaker explains that he is forced to spend time apart from his lover, but before he leaves, he tells her that their farewell should not be the occasion for mourning and sorrow. In the same way that virtuous men die mildly and without complaint.

Though he must go, their souls are still one and therefore, they are not enduring a breach, they are rather experiencing an expansion. If their souls are physically separate for the time being, they are still like the feet of a compass i.e., His lover's soul is the fixed foot in the centre and his soul is the foot that moves around the other. The firmness of the centre foot makes a perfect circle which the outer foot draws.

The nine stanzas of this *Valediction* are quite simple compared to many of Donne's poems, which utilise strange metrical patterns overlaid jarringly on regular rhyme schemes. Here, each four-line stanza is quite unadorned, with an ABAB rhyme scheme and an iambic tetrameter.

George Herbert (1593-1633)

The son of Richard and Magdalen Newport Herbert, George Herbert was born in Montgomery, Wales in 1593. His mother, Magdalen Newport, was patron to distinguished literary figures such as John Donne, who also dedicated his *Holy Sonnets* to her.

His father died when he was only 3 years old and thereafter he was raised by his mother. Herbert was educated at Westminster School and Trinity College, Cambridge.

Literary Career and Works

After his college graduation, he was appointed reader in Rhetoric at Cambridge and in 1620 he was elected public orator, a position of great eminence. In 1629, Herbert married Jane Danvers and the following year, he became an Anglican priest. He served the rural parishes of Fugglestone St Peter and Bemerton in Wiltshire until his death. Herbert's well known works are *The Temple* (a collection of religious poems) and *A Priest to the Temple* (a prose tract that offers practical wisdom to clergy). He was considered to be the most important British devotional lyricist of his time. Herbert died of constipation in 1633 at the age of forty.

The Affliction (I)

When first thou didst entice to thee my heart,
I thought the service brave;
So many joys I writ down for my part,
Besides what I might have
Out of my stock of natural delights,
Augmented with thy gracious benefits.
I looked on thy furniture so fine,
And made it fine to me;
Thy glorious household-stuff did me entwine,
And 'tice me unto thee.
Such stars I counted mine: both heav'n and earth;
Paid me my wages in a world of mirth.
What pleasures could I want, whose King I serv'd,
Where joys my fellows were?
Thus argu'd into hopes, my thoughts reserv'd
No place for grief or fear.
Therefore my sudden soul caught at the place,
And made her youth and fierceness seek thy face.
At first thou gav'st me milk and sweetnesses,
I had my wish and way;
My days were straw'd with flow'rs and happiness;
There was no month but May.
But with my years sorrow did twist and grow,
And made a party unawares for woe.
My flesh began unto my soul in pain,
"Sicknesses cleave my bones;
Consuming agues dwell in ev'ry vein,
And tune my breath to groans."
Sorrow was all my soul; I scarce believ'd,
Till grief did tell me roundly, that I liv'd.
When I got health, thou took'st away my life,
And more, for my friends die;
My mirth and edge was lost, a blunted knife
Was of more use than I.
Thus thin and lean without a fence or friend,
I was blown through with ev'ry storm and wind.
Whereas my birth and spirit rather took
The way that takes the town;
Thou didst betray me to a ling'ring book,
And wrap me in a gown.
I was entangled in the world of strife,
Before I had the power to change my life.
Yet, for I threaten'd oft the siege to raise,
Not simp'ring all mine age,
Thou often didst with academic praise
Melt and dissolve my rage.
I took thy sweet'ned pill, till I came where
I could not go away, nor persevere.
Yet lest perchance I should too happy be
In my unhappiness,
Turning my purge to food, thou throwest me
Into more sicknesses.
Thus doth thy power cross-bias me, not making
Thine own gift good, yet me from my ways taking.
Now I am here, what thou wilt do with me
None of my books will show;
I read, and sigh, and wish I were a tree,
For sure then I should grow
To fruit or shade at least some bird would trust
Her household to me, and I should be just.

The Affliction (I) Summary

This is the first of a series of five poems which Herbert wrote under the heading of *Affliction*. The poet here gives us first hand account of his sufferings, physical and mental; and then expresses in the final stanza his feelings of submission and humility towards God. When the poet first felt the urge to devote his life to God by becoming a priest, he thought it to be a noble mission. He imagined that, through his devotion of God, he would be blessed with many Joys.

At first, the poet was blessed by God with all kinds of delight and joys. But, with the passing of time, he was afflicted by misfortunes and found himself in miserable state. Other misfortunes also befell him. Many of his friends and well-wishers died and he lost his zest for life. He felt that he had become even more useless than a blunted knife.

The poet at this stage felt that in view of his aristocratic birth and breeding, he should have taken up a courtier's career in London but that, under God's influence, he had wrongly decided to become a priest.

Now the poet does not know what God intends to do with him. The poet is feeling disillusioned with his vocation of a priest. He wishes that he were a tree instead of a human being. As a tree, he could have served a more useful purpose. Despite God's unkindness, however, the poet feels that he must remain submissive to God. Though he thinks that he should give up the life of a priest and should serve under some master other than God, the poet cannot really decide to leave God.

This is one of Herbert's most autobiographical poems, written presumably before he became a clergyman, but at a point in his life when he was not sure what he was going to do. The poem is actually an account of his spiritual life up to the present. The poem is entitled *Affliction* because, although his early experiences were joyful and believing in God came easily, his life has subsequently been overshadowed by suffering.

In the final stanza it seems that Herbert is tempted to turn away but the last line offers the possibility of a different conclusion. In Herbert's collection of his poetry, this is the first of no fewer than five poems entitled Affliction.

Richard Crashaw (1613-1649)

English poet Richard Crashaw was the son of William Crashaw, a Puritan preacher in London. Crashaw's exact date of birth is not known. He was probably born in London. Crashaw attended High Church College at Cambridge, Pembroke.

Literary Career and Works

It was during his graduation that he published *Epigrammatum Sacrorum Liber* ('A Book of Sacred Epigrams'), a collection of Latin verse on scriptural subjects. Going against his father's religious views, Crashaw became a fellow of Peterhouse College where he was also ordained. He was forced to resign from his post because of his Catholic leanings influences.

England was not a safe heaven for Catholics like Crashaw and the Civil War altered his life. Crashaw fled to France and spent the rest of his life in exile at Little Gidding and Oxford and on the Continent. The Civil War deprived him of a successful career as preacher and probably of continued participation in the Anglican Church. Crashaw became a Roman Catholic around 1645. Abraham Cowley, his friend saw him living in conditions of utter poverty and introduced him to Queen Henrietta Maria of England. The Queen further recommended him to the Pope and he got the position of sub-canon of the Cathedral of Santa Casa in Loreto. However, just 4 months after attaining this position, Crashaw died. Crashaw's major poetry appeared in *Steps to the Temple* in 1646. The title indicates Crashaw's debt to George Herbert. Crashaw's style reflected a 17th century movement called Marinism or Secentismo.

This movement was popularised by the Italian poet Giambattista Marino. It was a reaction against classicism, marked by extravagant metaphors, hyperbole, fantastic word play and original myths, all written with great sonority and sensuality and with the aim to startle.

Major Works

- Epigrammatum Sacrorum Liber (1634).
- Steps to the Temple, Sacred Poems, With other Delights of the Muses (1646)
- Carmen Deo Nostro, Te Decet Hymns Sacred Poems (1652)
- A Letter from Mr Crashaw to the Countess of Denbigh Against Irresolution and Delay in matters of Religion (1653).
- Richard Crashaw Poem at a Epigrammata (1670).

Henry Vaughan (1621-1695)

Son of Thomas Vaughan and Denise, Henry Vaughan was born in Newton-upon-Usk in Breconshire, Wales in 1621. Vaughan attended Jesus College, Oxford. However, due to family pressure, he had to abandon an Oxford degree for a career in law. Vaughan's studies were disrupted again due to the outbreak of the Civil War in 1642. He was called back home and served on the Royalist side.

Literary Career and Works

In 1646, Vaughan's *Poems, with the Tenth Satire of Juvenal Englished* was published, followed by a second volume in 1647. In 1650, his collection of religious poems, *Silex Scintillans*, meaning *The Fiery Flint* or *The Flashing Flint* was published.

In his poems on several occasions and in the preface to his volume, Vaughan referred to George Herbert as 'the blessed man whose holy life and verse gained many pious converts'. Vaughan died on 23rd April, 1695, at the age of 73.

Major Works

- Olor Iscanus: A Collection of Some Select Poems, and Translations (1651)
- The Mount of Olives: Or, Solitary Devotions (1652)
- Hermetical Physick: Or, The right way to preserve, and to restore Health, By That famous and faithful Chymist, Henry Nollivs, Englished by Henry Vaughan, Gent (1655)
- Thalia Rediviva: The Pass-Times and Diversions of a Country (1678)

The Retreat

HAPPY those early days, when I
Shin'd in my angel-infancy !
Before I understood this place
Appointed for my second race,
Or taught my soul to fancy ought
But a white, celestial thought ;
When yet I had not walk'd above
A mile or two from my first love,
And looking back—at that short space—
Could see a glimpse of His bright face ;
When on some gilded cloud, or flow'r,
My gazing soul would dwell an hour,
And in those weaker glories spy
Some shadows of eternity ;
Before I taught my tongue to wound
My conscience with a sinful sound,
Or had the black art to dispense
A sev'ral sin to ev'ry sense,
But felt through all this fleshly dress
Bright shoots of everlastingness.
O how I long to travel back,
And tread again that ancient track !
That I might once more reach that plain,
Where first I left my glorious train ;
From whence th' enlighten'd spirit sees
That shady City of palm-trees.
But ah ! my soul with too much stay
Is drunk, and staggers in the way !
Some men a forward motion love,
But I by backward steps would move ;
And when this dust falls to the urn,
In that state I came, return.

The Retreat: Summary

Henry Vaughan's poem *The Retreat* is about the loss of heavenly innocence experienced during childhood and a desire to regain this lost state of 'angel infancy'.

The Retreat focuses on the double meaning of the word, 'retreat': both a place of refuge and the act of withdrawal. Childhood is viewed by Vaughan as a happy place, a world of innocence and bliss which the adult Vaughan has lost sight of. Vaughan talks of his mortal life as his second race. Suggesting that our life on Earth follows on from a previous, heavenly existence which we enjoyed before our birth. Vaughan talks of Christ as his first love. Vaughan says that he longs to travel back to those childhood years when he felt closer to God. Throughout *The Retreat*, Henry Vaughan refers to our (short) time on Earth, contrasting it with the eternity of heaven:

A metaphysical poem *The Retreat* is full with short and suggestive conceits, homily images and compressed sentences essentially belonging to metaphysical poetry.

Rhetorically, a paradox is a statement which apparently seems self-contradictory or absurd, but in reality carries a sound sense. Here, too, the poet makes a paradoxical statement that backward motion would be better for him. This is because forward motion is morally backward as it leads on to sin, on the other hand, backward motion in time leads to innocence and so morally forward.

In rhyming 'flower' with 'hour', Vaughan reminds us that everything has its moment in the Sun and then withers and dies like a flower. Our childhood is but an hour; our lives scarcely longer. Before he had grown a bit older and started sinning, Vaughan tells us, he felt the bright shoots of everlastingness. These 'bright shoots' are to be contrasted with the flower which will not wither away and die.

Vaughan concludes *The Retreat* by saying that whereas many people prefer to think in terms of progress, looking forward to the future, he prefers to look back to his earlier time when he was in touch with heaven and glimpsed the eternity of the afterlife.

Andrew Marvell (1621-1678)

Son of the Reverend Andrew Marvell and Anne Pease Marvell, Andrew Marvell was born in Winestead-in-Holderness, East Riding of Yorkshire, near the city of Kingston upon Hull.

His father was a lecturer at Holy Trinity Church and master of the Charterhouse in Hull. Marvell was educated at Trinity College, Cambridge. After his graduation, Marvell travelled widely abroad in France, Holland, Switzerland, Spain, and Italy.

Literary Career and Works

In 1650, he became the tutor of 20-year-old Mary Fairfax (later Duchess of Buckingham), daughter of Sir Thomas Fairfax, retired Lord General of the parliamentary forces. It was at the seat of his patron- Nun Appleton House that Marvell wrote many of his poems.

His poem *Upon Appleton House: To My Lord Fairfax* was a country house poem in manner of Jonson's *To Penshurst*. Marvell was also a well-known politician.

He held office in Cromwell's government and represented Hull to Parliament during the Restoration. He also paid tribute to Cromwell in his famous ode *An Horatian Ode Upon Cromwell's Return from Ireland*.

Marvell died on 16th August, 1678.

Marvell's Poems

Nature Poems

- Upon Appleton House
- The Garden
- Bermudas

The Mower Poems

- 'The Mower, against Gardens
- Damon the Mower
- The Mower to the Glo-Worms
- The Mower's Song

Religious Poems

- A Dialogue, between The Resolved Soul, and Created Pleasure
- A Dialogue between the Soul and Body
- The Coronet
- Eyes and Fears

Love Poems

- The Nymph Complaining for the Death of her Fawn
- Young Love
- To his Coy Mistress
- The unfortunate Lover
- Daphnis and Chloe
- The Definition of Love

Political Poems During Cromwellian Era

- An Horatian Ode upon Cromwell's Return from Ireland
- The Character of Holland
- The First Anniversary of the Government Under His Highness The Lord Protector
- A Poem upon the Death of His late Highnesse the Lord Protector

To His Coy Mistress

Had we but World enough, and Time,
This coyness Lady were no crime.
We would sit down and think which way
To walk and pass our long Loves Day.
Thou by the Indian Ganges side.
Should'st Rubies find: I by the Tide
Of Humber would complain. I would
Love you ten years before the Flood:
And you should if you please refuse
Till the Conversion of the Jews.
My vegetable Love should grow
Vaster then Empires, and more slow.
An hundred years should go to praise
Thine Eyes, and on thy Forehead Gaze.
Two hundred to adore each Breast.
But thirty thousand to the rest.
An Age at least to every part,
And the last Age should show your Heart.
For Lady you deserve this State;
Nor would I love at lower rate.
But at my back I alwaies hear
Times winged Charriot hurrying near:
And yonder all before us lye
Desarts of vast Eternity.
Thy Beauty shall no more be found;
Nor, in thy marble Vault, shall sound
My ecchoing Song: then Worms shall try
That long preserv'd Virginity:
And your quaint Honour turn to durst;
And into ashes all my Lust.
The Grave's a fine and private place,
But none I think do there embrace.
Now therefore, while the youthful hew
Sits on thy skin like morning glew,
And while thy willing Soul transpires
At every pore with instant Fires,
Now let us sport us while we may;
And now, like am'rous birds of prey,
Rather at once our Time devour,
Than languish in his slow-chapt pow'r.
Let us roll all our Strength, and all
Our sweetness, up into one Ball:
And tear our Pleasures with rough strife,
Thorough the Iron gates of Life.
Thus, though we cannot make our Sun
Stand still, yet we will make him run.

To His Coy Mistress : Summary

To His Coy Mistress is one of the most famous poems of the 17th century. It's a classic seduction poem, which sees Marvell endeavouring to persuade his would-be-lover, or 'mistress', to go to bed with him.

Besides being a seduction lyric, *To His Coy Mistress* is also a carpe diem poem, which argues that we should seize the day because life is short.

To His Coy Mistress is divided into three sections, each forming a distinct stage of an argument. In the first section, Marvell, addressing his sweetheart, says that the woman's reluctance to have sex with him would be fine, if life wasn't too short. In Hull, England, Marvell complains about his absent love as he sits by the River Humber and his mistress in India by the Ganges, finding rubies.

Marvell would spend thousands of years praising the woman's eyes and breasts, because she deserves such praise and attention. But such a plan is a fantasy, because in reality, time is short.

What lies before Marvell and his mistress is not a full and rich succession of days upon days of lived existence, but instead long deserts of eternity-the eternity of death, rather than an eternal life of praise and courtship.

In future the woman's honour and virginity will mean nothing and turn to dust, while Marvell's desire for her will, like his body, be 'ashes'. After all, people can't make love in the grave.

In the third and final section of *To His Coy Mistress*, Marvell says that, in light of what he's just said, the only sensible thing to do is to enjoy themselves and go to bed together. Marvell ends his poem by exhorting his mistress to join him in rushing headlong at the gates barring them from full enjoyment of life, using his strength and her sweetness to create a 'ball', like a cannonball, which can be used to bombard and destroy the 'iron gates of life'.

This poem is a philosophical poem mixed with the feeling of love. It is a fine lyric with beautiful style. The theme of love has been expressed in a very intelligent way in this poem.

Other Poets of the Puritan Age

The Puritan Age witnessed the rise of many other poets who could not be placed in any of the above mentioned categories. Some of such poets are John Milton, Edmund Waller, William Davenant, Sir, John Denham and Abraham Cowley. All these poets had a great role to play in this era. John Milton, in particular, influenced the literature of the said time a lot. He is rightly considered to be the greatest literary figure of the Puritan Age.

John Milton (1608-1674)

English poet and polemicist John Milton was born in London in 1608. He was the son of John Milton and Sarah Jeffrey. Milton's father was a scrivener and a music composer.

He studied at Paul's School and Christ's College, Cambridge. At Cambridge, Milton was known as 'The Lady of Christ's'. During his Cambridge years, Milton became friends with Edward King, to whom he later dedicated an elegy, *Lycidas*.

Literary Career and Works

At Cambridge, Milton wrote a number of poems such as *On the Morning of Christ's Nativity*, his *Epitaph on the admirable Dramatick Poet, W. Shakespeare*. Perhaps during the Cambridge period were also written his companion poems, *L'Allegro* and Il *Penseroso*.

L'Allegro meant 'the happy man' while *Il Penseroso* meant 'the melancholy man'. In these companion pieces, Milton compares and contrasts two impulses in human nature: "the active and contemplative, the social and solitary, the mirthful and melancholic, the cheerful and meditative, the erotic and Platonic". After completing his masters, Milton retired to Hammersmith, his father's new home.

In 1638, he embarked on a tour to France and Italy. Four years later, he married Mary Powell, who was almost half his age. Their relationship did not succeed and gave Milton inspiration to write his divorce tracts, which argued for separation on grounds of incompatibility.

Milton later married twice again: Katherine Woodcock in 1656, who died giving birth in 1658 and Elizabeth Minshull in 1662. Milton was appointed Secretary for Foreign Tongues by the Council of State in March 1649. During this period, he wrote *Eikonoklastes* and *Defensio pro populo Anglicano.* The year 1652 was a dark period for Milton, since he lost his eyesight completely and his first wife Mary died. After the Restoration of Charles II to the throne in 1660, Milton was arrested as a defender of the Commonwealth, fined and soon released. He spent the rest of his life writing his most famous works, *Paradise Lost*, *Paradise Regained* and *Samson Agonistes*.

Milton died of gout in November, 1674 and was buried in the church of St Giles, Cripplegate.

Lycidas

- *Lycidas* was a pastoral elegy written by Milton and published in 1638. The poem is also labeled as a 'monody' a lyrical lament for one voice.
- The poem first appeared in a 1638 collection of elegies entitled *justa Edourdo King Naufrago.*
- It was dedicated to the memory of Edward King, Milton's fellow student and friend during his Cambridge years. King had died by drowning.
- The name *Lycidas* is derived from Theocritus' Idylls, where Lycidas was a poet and goatherd.
- The poem can be divided into six sections: a prologue, four main parts and an epilogue.
- The poem begins with Milton invoking the Muse and explaining the reasons for writing the poem. Milton laments the death of Lycidas in the manner of traditional elegiac poets and asks the Muse where she had been when her Lycidas was dying. After this, he turns to general reflections on life and death.
- The poem's speaker, a persona for Milton's own voice, is a fellow shepherd who mourns the loss of a friend with whom he shared duties in tending sheep.
- The poem concludes with Lycidas rising from the dead, entering Heaven and being entertained by saints.

- It is mostly written in iambic pentameter, with irregularly appearing short lines of six syllables. The poem's 193 lines are divided into verse paragraphs of irregular length and changing rhyme schemes.
- Milton transforms King into a symbolic pastoral character. King is seen as the lost shepherd Lycidas.

Paradise Lost

- Milton's epic poem *Paradise Lost* was originally published in ten books in 1667.
- The second edition of the poem came out with twelve books in 1674. It is based on the Biblical story of the fall of Adam or Eve. It begins in hell, where Satan and his followers are recovering from defeat in a war they had waged against God. All of them plan to take revenge against God by seducing Man, his favourite creation.
- Satan transforms into the form of a serpent and successfully seduces Eve in the Garden of Eden. Satan's eloquent rhetoric forces Eve to partake the fruit of the forbidden tree.
- Adam, resigned to join in her fate, also eats the fruit. As a result of it, their innocence is lost and they become aware of their nakedness.
- Adam and Eve are exiled from Paradise because of the sin of disobedience to the word of God.
- Milton announces his main subject as 'Man's Disobedience' and the overall theme of his epic poem as 'Justifying the ways of God to men'.

Paradise Lost Book I

Of Mans First Disobedience, and the Fruit
Of that Forbidden Tree, whose mortal tast
Brought Death into the World, and all our woe,
With loss of Eden, till one greater Man
Restore us, and regain the blissful Seat,
Sing Heav'nly Muse,that on the secret top
Of Oreb, or of Sinai, didst inspire
That Shepherd, who first taught the chosen Seed,
In the Beginning how the Heav'ns and Earth
Rose out of Chaos: Or if Sion Hill
Delight thee more, and Siloa's Brook that flow'd
Fast by the Oracle of God; I thence
Invoke thy aid to my adventurous Song,
That with no middle flight intends to soar
Above th' Aonian Mount, while it pursues
Things unattempted yet in Prose or Rhime.
And chiefly Thou O Spirit, that dost prefer
Before all Temples th' upright heart and pure,
Instruct me, for Thou know'st; Thou from the first
Wast present, and with mighty wings outspread
Dove-like satst brooding on the vast Abyss
And mad'st it pregnant: What in me is dark
Illumin, what is low raise and support;
That to the highth of this great Argument
I may assert Eternal Providence,
And justifie the wayes of God to men.

Paradise Lost (Book I) : Summary

Greek epics involved heroes, ware, and heroic acts. They usually began with the writer invoking a muse as his guide. By invoking a muse that inspired Moses, Milton places *Paradise Lost* in the same epic category as religious texts and signals that he is writing an epic in the tradition of the ancient Greeks. His lengthy introduction and naming of all of the fallen angels in Hell resembles an epic catalogue, a long list of soldiers found in epics like *The Illiad* and *The Odyssey*. Further, Milton portrays Satan as a military leader who assembles and commands his troop of fallen angels. Milton opens *Paradise Lost* by formally declaring his poem's subject:humankind's first act of disobedience towards God and the consequences that followed from it.

The act is Adam and Eve's eating of the forbidden fruit of the Tree of Knowledge, as told in Genesis, the first book of the Bible. In the first line, Milton refers to the outcome of Adam and Eve's sin as the 'fruit' of the forbidden tree, punning on the actual apple and the figurative fruits of their actions. Milton asserts that this original sin brought death to human beings for the first time, causing us to lose our home in paradise until Jesus comes to restore humankind to its former position of purity. Milton's speaker announces that he wants to be inspired with this sacred knowledge because he wants to show his fellow man that the fall of humankind into sin and death was part of God's greater plan, and the God's plan is justified. John Milton was not only the greatest poet of the Puritan age but he was equally capable of composing prose literature. His prose works have magnificent passages, which shows the power and harmony of our English speech. His prose works are mainly focussed at politics, philosophy and religion.

Other Works of John Milton

Poems

- L'Allegro (1631)
- Il Penseroso (1631)
- A Mask Presented at Ludlow Castle, 1632 commonly known as Comus (a masque, 1634)
- Lycidas (1637)
- Poems of Mr John Milton, Both English and Latin (1645)
- When I consider how my light spent (commonly referred to as 'On his Blindness')
- On the Late Massacre in Piedmont (1655).

- Paradise Lost (1667)
- Paradise Regained (1671)
- Samson Agonistes (1671)
- Poems, and c, Upon Several Occasions (1673)
- Arcadas: A Masque (Date is unknown)

Prose

- Of Reformation (1641)
- Of Prelatical Episcopacy (1641)
- Animadversions (1641)
- The Reason of Church-Government Urged against Prelaty (1642)
- Apology for Smectymnuus (1642)
- Doctrine and Discipline of Divorce (1643)
- Judgement of Martin Bucer Concerning Divorce (1644)
- Of Education (1644)
- Areopagitica (1644)
- Tetrachordon (1645)
- Colasterion (1645)
- The Tenure of Kings and Magistrates (1649)
- Eikonoklastes (1649)
- Defensio pro Populo Anglicano [First Defence] (1651)
- Defensio Secunda [Second Defence] (1654)
- A Treatise of Civil Power (1659)
- The Likeliest Means to Remove Hirelings from the Church (1659)
- The Ready and Easy Way to Establish a Free Commonwealth (1660)
- Brief Notes Upon a Late Sermon (1660)
- Accedence Commenced Grammar (1669)
- History of Britain (1670)
- Artis logicae plenior institutio (Art of Logic 1672)
- Of True Religion (1673)
- Epistolae Familiares (1674)
- Prolusiones (1674)
- A brief History of Moscovia and other less known countries lying Eastward of Russia as far as Cathay, gathered from the writings of several Eye-witnesses (1682)
- De Doctrina Christiana (1823)

Edmund Waller (1606-1687)

English poet and politician Edmund Waller was born in Coleshill, Hertfordshire in 1606. He was the eldest son of Robert Waller and Anne Hampden. He was educated at Eton College and the University of Cambridge. Waller was elected to Parliament at the young age of 16 and gained reputation as a skillful orator. In 1631, he married Anne Banks, a London heiress, who died just three years after their marriage. He married Mary Bracey for a second time in 1644.

Literary Career and Works

In 1655, he published *A Panegyric to my Lord Protector* and was made a Commissioner for Trade'. After the restoration of monarchy, he wrote another glowing tribute *To the King, upon his Majesty's Happy Return. Being challenged by Charles II.*

The first edition of Waller's poems appeared much later in 1664. His later works include *Divine Poems* (1685) and *The Second Part of Mr Waller's Poems* (1690). Waller is considered to be a pioneer, who refined the classical couplet in English verse. He is best known for his lyrics, *Go Lovely Rose* and *On a Girdle*.

Waller died at Hall Barn in 1687.

Go, Lovely Rose

Go, lovely rose!
Tell her that wastes her time and me
That now she knows,
When I resemble her to thee,
How sweet and fair she seems to be.
Tell her that's young,
And shuns to have her graces spied,
That hadst thou sprung
In deserts, where no men abide,
Thou must have uncommended died.
Small is the worth
Of beauty from the light retired;
Bid her come forth,
Suffer herself to be desired,
And not blush so to be admired.
Then die! that she
The common fate of all things rare
May read in thee;
How small a part of time they share
That are so wondrous sweet and fair!

Go, Lovely Rose : Summary

Go, Lovely Rose is Edmund Waller's most notable work. Waller was a prominent figure in 17th century England, and his poems circulated widely before they were published in a collected edition in 1645.

Go, Lovely Rose conveys a carpe diem (seize the day) theme similar to that of two other famous poems of the same era. *To the Virgins, to Make Much of Time* (1648) by Robert Herrick and *To his Coy Mistress* (1681) by Andrew Marvell. The poem, which contains four stanzas, each with five lines, has symmetry in theme as well as form. The lines are composed primarily of iambic feet-every other syllable is stressed.

The short lines of each stanza rhyme, as do the longer lines (2, 4 and 5), forming an ababb rhyme scheme. The rose, addressed in the first line, serves as the unifying image, symbolising the brevity of youth and beauty. The poem opens with a conversation of sorts between the speaker and a rose. The rose serves as a metaphor for an attractive woman. The speaker hopes that the lesson provided by the rose will prompt the maiden to yield to his advances. There is a sense of impatience in the speaker's tone.

In the second stanza, Waller reveals that the woman is shy. The image of a delicate rosebud withering in the heat of the desert sun reinforces the speaker's directive that time is short. Therefore, the woman must not hide her beauty. If she waits too long, it may be too late and like the rose in the desert, her 'bloom' will be lost. The focus of a central image continues in the third stanza, when the speaker amplifies the mission of the rose. She must abandon what the speaker hints is a false modesty and let herself be admired and desired without a blush. Like an unseen rose in the wilderness, her beauty is worthless if it remains hidden.

The object lesson concludes in the final stanza. The rose must die at the completion of its message so that the woman will see for herself. The rose serves as both messenger and metaphor. Its fragile petals and transient beauty may convince the reluctant woman in a way that an impatient suitor could not.

William Davenant (1606-1668)

English poet and playwright William Davenant was born at the Crown Inn, Oxford in 1606. He was the son of Jane Shepherd Davenant and John Davenant. His father was proprietor of the Crown Inn and later Mayor of Oxford. It is rumoured that William Shakespeare was Davenant's Godfather. Davenant was educated in Oxford at St Paul's Parish under Edward Sylvester, 'a noted Latinist and Grecian'. He did not complete his degree, but was later employed at court as a page, in the retinue of the Duchess of Richmond.

Literary Career and Works

He began serving the famed literary courtier Fulke Greville and remained in his service until Greville's death. Davenant's first play, the tragedy of *Albovine* appeared in 1629. His other works were *King of the Lombards*, a revenge tragedy completed in 1627 and *The Cruel Brother*, another tragedy of the same year which was acted in Blackfriars; also *The Colonel*, a tragicomedy that was retitled *The Siege* when it was published in 1673 and *The Just Italian*, both were acted in 1629. In 1638, Davenant produced a collection of his lyrical verses titled *Madagascar and other Poems*. His collected *Poems on Several Occasions* were published posthumously in the 1673 edition of his works.

During the 1640s, Davenant was accused of being part of an army plot to overthrow the House of Commons. He was imprisoned but later acquitted. As a supporter of Charles I during the Civil War, Davenant was knighted by the king in 1643. Davenant died in London on 7th April, 1668.

Major Works

Poetry

- Ieffereidos (1630)
- Madagascar, with other Poems (1638)
- London, King Charles his Augusta, or, City Royal, of the founders, the names, and oldest honours of that City (1648)
- A Discourse upon Gondibert, an heroick poem (1650)

Plays, Masques and Operas

- Albovine, tragedy (1629)
- The Cruel Brother, tragedy (1630)
- The Just Italian, comedy (1630)
- The Temple of Love, masque (1635)
- The Wits, comedy (1636)
- The Platonick Lovers, comedy (1636)
- The Triumphs of the Prince D'Amour, masque (1636)
- Britannia Triumphans, masque, with Inigo Jones (1638)
- Salmacida Spolia, masque (1640)
- The Unfortunate Lovers, tragedy (1643)
- Love and Honour, tragicomedy (1649)
- The Siege of Rhodes, Part I, tragicomedy (1656)
- The Cruelty of the Spaniards in Peru, opera (1658)
- The History of Sir Francis Drake, history (1659)
- The Siege of Rhodes, Part II, tragicomedy (1663)
- The Man's the Master, comedy (1669)
- News from Plymouth, comedy (1673)
- The Spanish Lovers, or The Distresses, comedy (1673)
- The Playhouse to Be Let, comedy (1673)

Sir John Denham (1615-1669)

English poet and courtier Sir John Denham was born in Dublin, Ireland in 1615. He was the son of John Denham the Elder and Eleanor Moore. Denham's father was Lord Chief Justice of the King's Bench in Ireland. In 1617, his father became Baron of the Exchequer in England and moved to London with his family. Denham studied at Trinity College, Oxford and later studied law at Lincoln's Inn in London. He was admitted to the bar in 1639.

Literary Career and Works

Denham started his literary career with a paraphrase of the second book of the *Aeneid*. He also wrote a prose tract against gambling, *The Anatomy of Play*. He gained reputation as a literary figure with *The Sophy*, (a blank-verse historical tragedy) acted in 1641 and with *Coopers Hill* a poem published in 1642. Denham's last years were spent in a mental asylum since he was suffering from dementia.

He died in London in 1669.

Major Works

- A Letter Sent to William Laud (1641)
- The Sophy (1641)
- Coopers Hill (1642)
- Mr. Hampton's speech (1643)
- Second advice to the painter (1667)
- The Anatomy of Play (1651)
- The Destruction of Troy (1656)
- Panegyrick on Monck (1659)
- A Relation of a Quaker (1659)
- Prologue to his Majesty at the first play at the Cock-pit (1661)
- The True Presbyterian without disguise (1661)
- Poems and translations, with The Sophy (1668)
- Cato Major, of old age, A poem (1669)
- Version of the psalms (1714)

Abraham Cowley (1618-1667)

Poet and essayist Abraham Cowley was born in London in 1618. He was the posthumous son of a wealthy London stationer. Cowley received his education at Westminster school and the University of Cambridge.

Literary Career and Works

Cowley began studying medicine and became an MD in 1657. Cowley first published his volume of verse, *Poetical Blossoms* (1633), which appeared when he was only fifteen. His other works include the poetic collection *The Mistress*, an unfinished epic *Davideis* and a stage comedy *The Guardian*. During his late years, Cowley obtained a property near Chertsey, retired to the country and devoted himself to botany and books. He also wrote a pamphlet on *The Advancement of Experimental Philosophy*. Cowley died in the Porch House, in Chertsey in 1667 and was buried in Westminster Abbey.

Restoration Age

John Milton's *Paradise Lost* (1667), a story of fallen pride, was the first major poem to appear in England during the Restoration Age. The court of Charles II had, in its years in France, learned a worldliness and sophistication that marked it as distinctively different from the monarchies that preceded the Republic. Even if Charles had wanted to reassert the divine right of kingship, the Protestantism and taste for power of the intervening years would have rendered it impossible.

One of the greatest English poets, John Milton (1608–74), wrote during this period of religious and political instability. He is generally seen as the last major poet of the English Renaissance, though his major epic poems were written in the Restoration period. Some of Milton's important poems, were written before the Restoration Era. Among the important poems Milton wrote during this period are *L'Allegro*, 1631; *Il Penseroso*, 1634; *Comus* (a masque), 1638; and *Lycidas* (1638). His later major works include *Paradise Lost* (1667), *Paradise Regained*, 1671 and *Samson Agonistes*, 1671. Milton's works reflect deep personal convictions, a passion for freedom and self-determination and the urgent issues and political turbulence of his day. Writing in English, Latin and Italian, he achieved international fame during his lifetime and his celebrated *Areopagitica* (1644), written in condemnation of pre-publication censorship, is among history's most influential and passionate defences of free speech and freedom of the press. William Hayley's 1796 biography called him the 'greatest English author' and he remains generally regarded 'as one of the pre-eminent writers in the English language'.

John Dryden (1631 to 1700) was a highly influential English poet during the Restoration period in England. His first published poem; *Heroique Stanzas* (1658), was the eulogy for the Lord Protector of England, Oliver Cromwell. His poems often contained factual information and sought to express his thoughts in a precise way. His other published poems include: *Hidden Flame, Mac Flecknoe, One Happy Moment, A Song for St. Cecelia's Day, Song for Amphitryon, Song to a Fair Young Lady, Going Out of the Town in the Spring* and *To the Memory of Mr. Oldham*.

Poetry of the Restoration Age

The main poets of this age were John Dryden and Samuel Butler. The poetry of the Restoration period was formal, intellecutal, satirical, realistic and written in heroic couplet, of which Dryden was the supreme master. Dryden is the dominating figure of this age. He laid the foundation of the classical school of poetry in England. His poetry can be conveniently divided under three heads:

1. **Political Satires** Absalom and Achitophel and The Medal.
2. **Doctrinal Poems** Religio Laici and The Hindi and the Panther
3. **The Fables** The Palamon and Arcite.

Satire

Satire was born and encouraged out of the world of fashion and scepticism. All the major poets of the Puritan and Restoration Age and Augustan period like Samuel Butler and John Dryden wrote satirical verse. Their satire was often written in defence of public order and the established church and government

John Dryden (1631-1700)

John Dryden was not only an acclaimed prose writer or just a poet, but also the greatest literary figure of the Restoration Age. In fact, he was a perfect and true representative of the Restoration Age.

English poet, playwright and critic John Dryden was born in Aldwinkle, Northamptonshire in 1631. He was the eldest of 14th children of Erasmus Dryden and Mary Pickering. He studied at King's School at Westminster as a king's scholar under Richard Busby. Dryden married the daughter of the Earl of Berkshire, Lady Elizabeth Howard (1638–1714), who bore him three sons.

Literary Career and Works

It was at Westminster that Dryden wrote his first verse, an elegy *Upon the Death of Lord Hastings* and contributed it for *Lachrymae Musarum* (1649). After Westminster, Dryden entered Trinity College, Cambridge and graduated in 1654. His father died in the same year. Dryden obtained work with Cromwell's Secretary of State, John Thurloe. On the death of Cromwell, he published his first important work, *Heroic Stanzas*.

After the Restoration, he wrote a royalist panegyric celebrating the return of Charles II, titled *Astraea Redux (1660)*. He also wrote *To His Sacred Majesty A Panegyric* for the King's coronation. Dryden's poetry celebrating the restoration pleased Charles II, so much that he was named Poet Laureate in 1668 and two years later, royal historiographer.

Dryden is today best known for his satirical works, *Absalom and Achitophel* (1681) and *Mac Flecknoe* (1682). Both these works established his eminence as a verse satirist. To this era also belong the didactic poem *Religio Laici* (1682), which argues the case for Anglicanism and *The Hind and the Panther* (1687), marking his conversion to Catholicism.

After the Revolution of 1688, Dryden lost his Laureateship with the accession of William III. Because of his refusal to take an oath of allegiance, Dryden became out of favour with the court. Writing became his sole source of income. He also translated Virgil's *Aeneid*, Homer's *Iliad*, Ovid's *Epistles* and *Metamorphosis*. Dryden died on 12th May, 1700,due to an inflammation caused by gout.

Major Works

- The Indian Emperor (tragedy, 1665)
- Annus Mirabilis (poem, 1667)
- The Enchanted Island (comedy), 1667, an adaptation with William D'Avenant of Shakespeare's The Tempest
- Secret Love, or The Maiden Queen (1667)
- An Essay of Dramatick Poesie (1668)
- An Essay of Dramatic Poesy
- An Evening's Love (comedy, 1668)
- Tyrannick Love (tragedy, 1669)
- The Conquest of Granada (1670)
- Marriage à la mode (1672)
- Aureng-zebe (1675)
- All for Love (1678)
- Oedipus (heroic drama), 1679, an adaptation with Nathaniel Lee of Sophocles' Oedipus
- Absalom and Achitophel (1681)
- The Medal (1682)
- Threnodia Augustalis (1685)
- A Song for St Cecilia's Day (1687)
- Amphitryon (1690)
- Don Sebastian (1690)
- Love Triumphant (1694)
- The Works of Virgil (1697)
- Alexander's Feast (1697)
- Fables, Ancient and Modern (1700)

Short Description of Dryden's Works

Work	Description
Astraea Redux	Royalist Panegyric written in heroic couplets, in which Dryden welcomes the new regime of Charles II.
Threnodia Augustalis	517 line poem written to commemorate the death of Charles II. Title –a reference to threnody, a poem of mourning. Subtitled 'A Funeral Pindarique Poem Sacred to the Memory of King Charles II'.
Religio Laici or A Layman's Faith	A Verse essay that represents Dryden's tentative and candid examination of major religious issues of his day, and expresses his adherence to Church of England. Published as a premise to The Hind and the Panther.
The Hind and the Panther	Allegorical poem in heroic couplets written after Dryden's conversion to Catholicism in 1685. Adopts the framework of a beast fable, with Roman Catholics represented as Hinds, Anglicans as Panthers, Quakers as Hares, Presbyterians as Wolves, Independents as Bears, Anabaptists as Boar and Free Thinkers as Apes.
Alexander's Feast Or, The Power of Music, an Ode in Honor of St Cecilia's Day	Second of Dryden's odes honoring Saint Cecilia, the patron saint of music. The other being 'A Song for St Cecilia's Day'. Describes the feast given by Alexander the Great at Persepolis after the victory of Greeks over the Persian King Darius.
To The Memory of Mr Oldham (1684)	Elegy written on the death of the poet John Oldham

Absalom and Achitophel

In pious times, ere priestcraft did begin,
Before polygamy was made a sin;
When man on many multiplied his kind,
Ere one to one was cursedly confined;
When nature prompted, and no law denied,
Promiscuous use of concubine and bride;
Then Israel's monarch 1 after heaven's own heart,
His vigorous warmth did variously impart
To wives and slaves; and, wide as his command,
Scattered his Maker's image through the land.
Michal, 2 of royal blood, the crown did wear,
A soil ungrateful to the tiller's care:
Not so the rest; for several mothers bore
To godlike David several sons before.
But since like slaves his bed they did ascend,
No true succession could their seed attend.
Of all the numerous progeny was none
So beautiful, so brave, as Absalom;
Whether inspired by some diviner lust,
His father got him with a greater gust;
Or that his conscious destiny made way
By manly beauty, to imperials way.

Absalom and Achitophel : Summary

It was published in 1681, *Absalom and Achitophel* is a political satire in heroic couplets. The political background of the poem revolves around the Popish Plot (1678 an alleged plot by Catholics to kill the king and make England Catholic again), the Exclusion Crisis (to keep Charles' Catholic brother, James, from inheriting the throne after Charles' death) and the Monmouth Rebellion (1685: an attempt to put the king's illegitimate son James, Duke of Monmouth on the throne).

According to Dr William Tarvin, the poem was "Written for Charles II and was published a few days before judgement was to be pronounced in the trial of the Earl of Shaftesbury, the Ashley of the Cabal".

Dryden adopts a Biblical framework for this political story. The story of Absalom's revolt against King David in the Old Testament is taken as framework to narrate the contemporary political events of his time. David stands for King Charles II, Absalom for James, Duke of Monmouth, Charles II's illegitimate son, Achitophel for Anthony Ashley Cooper, the first Earl of Shaftesbury, who encouraged Monmouth to rebel and Zimri stands for the second Duke of Buckingham. The poem opens with a depiction of the Jews beset by fears and rumours of plots against King David by a discredited sect. Achitophel, leader of the King's opponents, inflames the crowd against their monarch with a view toward replacing the rightful heir with Absalom, the king's illegitimate son. The poem bears resemblance to Milton's *Paradise Lost*. Achitophel is structured as Satan. Like Satan, he uses flattery and persuasive rhetoric to tempt Absalom. David is structured as God while Absalom becomes Adam or the fallen Man. A second part of *Absalom and Achitophel* largely composed by Nahum Tate, playwright and poet laureate of Britain, but containing 200 lines by Dryden that were directed at his literary rivals Thomas Shadwell and Elkanah Settle was published in 1682.

Mac Flecknoe

All human things are subject to decay,
And, when Fate summons, monarchs must obey
This Flecknoe found, who, like Augustus, young
Was call'd to empire, and had govern'd long:
In prose and verse, was own'd, without dispute
Through all the realms of Non-sense, absolute.
This aged prince now flourishing in peace,
And blest with issue of a large increase,
Worn out with business, did at length debate
To settle the succession of the State:
And pond'ring which of all his sons was fit
To reign and wage immortal war with wit;
Cry'd, 'tis resolv'd; for nature pleads that he
Should only rule, who most resembles me:
Shadwell alone my perfect image bears,
Mature in dullness from his tender years.
Shadwell alone, of all my sons, is he
Who stands confirm'd in full stupidity.
The rest to some faint meaning make pretence,
But Shadwell never deviates into sense.
Some beams of wit on other souls may fall,
Strike through and make a lucid interval;
But Shadwell's genuine night admits no ray,
His rising fogs prevail upon the day
Besides his goodly fabric fills the eye,
And seems design'd for thoughtless majesty:
Thoughtless as monarch oaks, that shade the plain,
And spread in solemn state, supinely reign.
Heywood and Shirley were but types of thee,
Thou last great prophet of tautology
Even I, a dunce of more renown than they,
Was sent before but to prepare thy way;
And coarsely clad in Norwich drugget came
To teach the nations in thy greater name.

- Dryden's *Mac Flecknoe; or, A satyr upon the True-Blew-Protestant Poet, TS* is a mock heroic poem published in 1682.
- The poem is an attack on Thomas Shadwell, a well-known playwight and an indifferent poet.

- There were several reasons for enemity between Shadwell and Dryden. Both had different political affiliations-Dryden was a Tory and Shadwell was a Whig, both had different religious affiliations- Shadwell satirised Catholic and Anglican priests in a play entitled *The lancashire-Witches, and Tegue o Divelly the Irish-Priest* and offended Dryden at a time, when he was considering conversion to Catholicism. Both also had different literary ideals and preferences. While Dryden preferred Shakespeare; Shadwell idolised Jonson. Dryden preferred comedy of wit while Shadwell comedy of humours.
- Dryden had criticised Shaftesbury in his satirical poem entitled *The Medal*, which provoked Dryden's opponent, Thomas Shadwell to write *The Medal of John Bayes* as the answer for the satire. This was followed by the publication of *Mac Flecknoe* in answer.
- In his poem, Dryden portrays Shadwell as 'Mac' (the son of Flecknoe) Richard Flecknoe having been an even less accomplished poet than Shadwell. He is the dullest son of Flecknoe who 'never deviates into sense'.
- Flecknoe chooses Shadwell as his heir to the throne of dullness and expresses the hope that his son will 'advance in new impudence, new ignorance'.
- Shadwell's enormous stupidity is highlighted throughout the poem. His corpulence, his mountain belly and his addicion to opium are referred to.
- The poem ends by drawing a parallel to the Biblical story of the mantle of Elijah falling on the shoulders of Elisha giving him a double portion of his sire's prophetic spirit.

Samuel Butler (1613-1680)

English poet and satirist Samuel Butler was born at Strensham, Worcestershire in 1613. He was the son of a yeoman. Butler studied at the King's School, Worcester. Butler held several clerical posts.

Literary Career and Works

Butler is best known for his mock heroic poem, *Hudibras*, a satire on the Cromwellians and on the Presbyterian Church. The poem was published after the Restoration in 1663. Sir Hudibras of Butler's poem is a Presbyterian knight, one of those who rode out against the monarchy during England's civil war.

The name Hudibras is derived from the rash, hardy, 'melancholy' knight in Spenser's *The Faerie Queene*. After the publication of *Hudibras*, Butler is said to have received a gift of £300 from Charles II. However, despite the popularity of the work, Butler failed to get a position at court.

Two years after the publication of the third part of *Hudibras* he died, on the 25th, September 1680 and was buried by his friend Longueville, a bencher of the Middle Temple, in the churchyard of St Paul's, Covent Garden.

Major Works

- The Lord Roos his answer to the Marquess of Dorchester's letter (1660)
- Hudibras: the first part (1663)
- Hudibras: the second part (1664)
- To the memory of the most renowned Du-Vall (1671)
- Two letters (1672)
- Hudibras: the third and last part (1678)
- Characters (1759)

EXAM BASED QUESTIONS

1 **In the 17th century, which age is known as the awakening of Europe.**
(a) The Jacobean age (b) The Restoration age
(c) The Elizabethan age (d) The Puritan age

2 **What was the reason for the end of the reign of Elizabeth, which was marked by an outburst of English songs as remarkable in its sudden development as the rise of the drama?**
(a) The increasing influence of French instead of Italian verse
(b) The increasing influence of English instead of Italian verse
(c) The decreasing influence of French instead of Italian verse
(d) The decreasing influence of English instead of Italian verse

3 **Which out of these stood like a rock for religious tolerance in Puritan age?**
(a) John Eliot (b) Cromwell
(c) Thomas Hooker (d) Hampden

4 **After the Elizabethan age, four poets fall in the group of allegorical and pastoral**
(a) Giles Fletcher, George Wither, Phineas Fletcher and William Brown
(b) Spenser, Galileo, Bacon, Browning
(c) Both 'a' and 'b'
(d) None of the above

5 **The age of Caroline is an age of poetry of three kinds. Which is not of this age?**
(a) Puritan age (b) Spenserian age
(c) Metaphysical age (d) Cavalier age

6 **Which poetry uses the straight forward expression and direct language instead of using metaphors and unrealistic imagery?**
(a) Metaphysical poetry (b) Postal poetry
(c) Cavalier poetry (d) Transition poetry

7 **The poets who got inspiration from Ben Jonson under the banner of the Cavalier poets are**
(a) Robert Herrick and Thomas Carew
(b) Ben Jonson and Robert Browning
(c) Alexander Pope and Robert Herrick
(d) Thomas Carew and Alexander Pope

8 **Among the following who was the fourth son born to London goldsmith, Nicholas?**
(a) Robert Herrick (b) Andrew Marwell
(c) Milton (d) Thomas Carew

9 **Whose poetry is divided into three groups like anatomy poems, religious poems and epigrams?**
(a) Ben Jonson (b) Thomas Carew
(c) Spenser (d) Robert Herrick

10 **'To Daffodils' is a poem written by**
(a) Robert Herrick (b) William Wordsworth
(c) John Keats (d) PB Shelley

11 **Which out of the following poetic masters have been followed by 'Thomas Carew"?**
(a) Hazlitt and Herrick (b) Milton and John Donne
(c) John Donne and Wither (d) Ben Jonson and Donne

12 **"Carew, it seems to have more distinction than that he is commonly accorde(d)" is a statement by**
(a) Edmund Waller (b) Henry Vaughan
(c) Robert Herrick (d) FR Leavis

13 **Which poet wrote of both 'A Divine Mistress' and 'A Cruel Mistress'?**
(a) John Donne (b) Richard Crashaw
(c) Henry Vaughan (d) Thomas Carew

14 **In which book does, 'Sir John Suckling' try to express his feelings and experience?**
(a) My Dearest Rival
(b) Ballad upon a wedding
(c) Struck from wild life like spark from his rapier
(d) Urn Burial

15 **Who among the following is a Cavalier poet?**
(a) Henry Vaughan (b) Richard Crashaw
(c) John Suckling (d) Anne Finch

16 **We have an Italian glimpse in the poem 'To Althea, from Prison' which refers to**
(a) Richard Lovelace (b) Richard Bord
(c) Professor Grierson (d) Thomas Hooker

17 **In which poem of Richard Lovelace's do we have an 'Italian glimpse'?**
(a) To Lucasta (b) To Althea, from prison
(c) Going beyond the seas (d) Going to the Warnes

18 **Who is known as a group of English poets associated with Charles I and his exiled son, most of their work between 1637 and 1660 are**
(a) Metaphysical Poet (b) Chaucerian Poet
(c) Spenserian Poet (d) Cavalier Poet

19 **Metaphysical poetry is concerned with the exposition of philosophical concept of the life of the universe.**
(a) The given statement is true
(b) The given statement is false
(c) The given statement belongs to Humour
(d) The given statement is wit

20 **The metaphysical poets employed many extended comparisons, also known as**
(a) gargantuan similes (b) conceits
(c) splendid comparisons (d) paradoxes

21 John Donne was on the path to success. He was private secretary to a high court official, Sir Thomas Egerton. How did he ruin his career?
(a) He wrote a private, critical poem about Queen Elizabeth
(b) He eloped with Egerton's niece
(c) It was discovered that he was a Catholic
(d) He basically made a pass at Egerton's wife

22 In what poem does John Donne try to convince a woman to have sex with him?
(a) The Apparition
(b) The Flea
(c) To His Mistress Going to Bed
(d) All of the above

23 In 'Lovers' Infiniteness,' what does the speaker demand?
(a) That he be Heard
(b) That God Listen to his Prayer
(c) All of his Lady's Love
(d) A Song

24 What is the significance of going West in 'Good Friday, 1613. Riding Westward'?
(a) The Poet is Riding West But Concerned With The East
(b) The Poet is Eager To Reach Wales
(c) The Poet is Worried About Leaving England
(d) The Setting Sun Reminds Him of Nature's Wonders

25 Which poem of John Donne is a play on Marlowe's 'Passionate Shepherd to His Love'?
(a) Song (b) The Ecstasy
(c) The Bait (d) The Funeral

26 Name the poem by John Donne which was probably about his wife's death.
(a) XVII Holy Sonnet
(b) The Flea
(c) A Valediction: Forbiding Mourning
(d) The Funeral

27 John Donne dedicated his holy sonnets to whose mother?
(a) Richard Crashaw's
(b) His Own
(c) Andrew Marvell's
(d) George Herbert's

28 Which of the following poems uses 'metaphysical conceits?
(a) PB Shelley's Ode to the West Wind
(b) John Donne's 'A Valediction Forbidding Mourning'
(c) John Milton's 'Paradise Lost'
(d) Thomas Hobbes, 'Leviathan'

29 Who developed the interest in suicide and an obsession with death?
(a) John Donne
(b) John Bunyan
(c) John Milton
(d) Thomas Fuller

30 George Herbert wrote a poem in which he insisted that even simple, uncomplicated verse can be beautiful if it plainly states the truth. In it, he says, "Nor let them punish me with loose of ryme,/Who plainly say, My God, My King." What is the name of this poem?
(a) Sinne (I) (b) Love (I)
(c) Jordan (I) (d) Affliction (II)

31 In Herbert's 'The Pulley', what alone among the blessing does God withhold from man?
(a) Pleasure (b) rest (c) wisdom (d) truth

32 Richard Crashaw wrote a poem called 'Non Vi' that contained a picture of a heart. What is this picture called?
(a) Concrete Poetry (b) A Symbol
(c) An emblem (d) A Coat of Arms

33 Richard Crashaw wrote a poem about which other metaphysical poet's book?
(a) His own (b) John Donne's
(c) George Herbert's (d) Andrew Marvell's

34 Who spoke face to face with God for the first time in English poetry?
(a) Henry Vaughan (b) John Donne
(c) George Herbert (d) Edmund Spenser

35 Who was called at heart a mystic?
(a) Richard Crashaw (b) George Herbert
(c) Henry Vaughan (d) Abraham Cowley

36 In which poem does Vaughan treat death in lovely terms?
(a) Regeneration (b) Cock-crowing
(c) Ascension-Hymn (d) The Night

37 Which metaphysical poet wrote a poem encouraging Christians to honour Christmas piously, and not by emulating heathen customs of decoration and reveling?
(a) George Herbert (b) Henry Vaughan
(c) John Donne (d) Andrew Marvell

38 Henry Vaughan experienced a spiritual awakening inspired by the poems of which metaphysical poet?
(a) His own (b) George Herbert
(c) Thomas Carew (d) John Donne

39 What does Vaughan refer to as a Sweet, sacred hill?
(a) Calvary (b) The Mount of Olives
(c) Mount Sinai (d) Golgotha

40 Andrew Marvell wrote an Horation Ode upon this man's return from Ireland.
(a) Jonathan Swift (b) Bonnie Prince Charles
(c) Cromwell (d) John Milton

41 Who is not a metaphysical poet from the following?
(a) Donne (b) Herbert (c) Waller (d) Fletcher

42 **Who is responsible for the Puritan spirit and finds its noblest expression?**
(a) Burton (b) Donne
(c) Herbert (d) Milton

43 **Pick out the pastoral elegy from the following.**
(a) The Holy War (b) Lycidas
(c) Comus (d) Il Penserosa

44 **In which year was the book 'Paradise Lost' completed?**
(a) 1667 (b) 1664 (c) 1661 (d) 1668

45 **Which out of these portrays Christ's resistance to Satan's temptation and his victory over them?**
(a) Paradise Lost (b) Lycidas
(c) L' Allegro (d) Paradise Regained

46 **What does Milton describe about in the book in Paradise Lost?**
(a) Transports upto heaven again
(b) Description of the council of evil spirit
(c) Paradise and the innocent state of man
(d) Fall of Man

47 **In which great epic, Adam fell to the first temptation by Satan and exile from the Heaven?**
(a) Paradise Lost (b) Paradise Regained
(c) Divine Commedia (d) On His Blindness

48 **Who utters those words 'Milton is the God-gifted organ voice of England'?**
(a) Tennyson (b) Paine
(c) Boyle (d) Fuller

49 **Which of the following poems uses 'Monody'?**
(a) Alfred Tenyson's 'Ulysses'
(b) John Milton's 'Lycidas'
(c) Henry Vaughan's 'The Retreat'
(d) John Donne's 'The Flea'

50 **Mainly four poets are the link between Spenser and Milton.**
(a) Phineas Fletcher, Giles Fletcher, George Wither, William Browne
(b) William Browne, Robert Herrick, John Donne, John Lock
(c) Evelyn, John Dryden, Izzak Walton, John Bunyan
(d) Galileo, Isaac Newton, John Suckling, George Wither

51 **What is 'L' Allegro's companion piece called?**
(a) Lamia (b) Hyperion
(c) II Penseroso (d) Thyrsis

52 **Which is like an excursion into the English fields at sunrise?**
(a) Paradise Regained (b) L' Allegro
(c) John Grower (d) Robert Herrick

53 **In which great epic the person of Christ withstands the temper and is established once more in the divine favour?**
(a) Masque of Comus (b) Arcadis
(c) L' Allegro (d) Paradise Regained

54 **Identify the father of 'Couplet'?**
(a) Greene (b) Waller (c) Pope (d) Goldsmith

55 **Who was the first poet to use consistently the close couplet which dominates poetry of next century?**
(a) Henry Vaughan (b) Edmund Waller
(c) Abraham Cowley (d) Andrew Marvell

56 **Which of the following poems uses heroic couplets?**
(a) William Browne's Britannia's Pastorals
(b) John Donne's The Good Morrow
(c) Geroge Herbert's The Affliction
(d) Henry Vaughan's The Retreat

57 **In the Poem, Ode: of wit, he presents wit in a different manner. The poet is**
(a) Richard Crashaw (b) George Herbert
(c) Abraham Cowley (d) Henry Vaughan

58 **A curious combination of scientific and credulous research in the matter of popular superstition is**
(a) Religio Medici (b) Pilgrim's Progress
(c) Vulgar Errors (d) Urn Burial

59 **Who was called The Shakespeare of Divines?**
(a) Jeremy Taylor (b) Thomas Fuller
(c) Robert Burton (d) Richard Bater

60 **'The Saints Everlasting Rest' was written by**
(a) Izaak Walton (b) Richard Baxter
(c) Jeremy Taylor (d) Thomas Fuller

61 **What is called genuine poetic feeling harsh meters and these strained and whimsical images and turns of speech?**
(a) Octanes (b) Ballad (c) Satire (d) Conceits

62 **Who did not belong to the Puritan age?**
(a) Eliot (b) Milton
(c) John Heywood (d) Camden

63 **Which book of Milton is the most widely read literary work of the Puritan age?**
(a) Lycidas (b) The Paradise Lost
(c) The Paradise Regained (d) Samson Agonistes

64 **In the era of John Dryden the Roman church is a symbol for**
(a) Wolf (b) Anglican Church
(c) Hind (d) Panther

65 **Which of the following uses blank verse?**
(a) Donne's The Flea
(b) Dryden's All For Love
(c) Shelley's A Defence of Poetry
(d) Congrev's the Way of the World

66 **Who is the greatest literary figure of the Restoration and in his work we have an excellent reflection both the good and the evil tendencies of the age. In which he lived?**
(a) Goldsmith (b) John Dryden
(c) Waller (d) Congreve

67 The English satirist who used the sharp edge praise to attack his victims was
(a) Ben Johnson (b) John Donne
(c) John Dryden (d) Samuel Buttler

68 Mac Flecknoe is an attack on Dryden's literary rival,
(a) Richard Flecknoe (b) Thomas Shadwell
(c) John Wilmot (d) Mathew Prior

69 Which poet, critic and translator brought England and modern literature between 1660 and 1700?
(a) Addison (b) Bunyan
(c) Crabbe (d) Dryden

70 What literary work best captures a sense of the political turmoil, particularly regarding the issue of religion, just after the Restoration?
(a) Gay's Beggar's Opera
(b) Butler's Hudibras
(c) Fielding's Jonathan Wild
(d) Dryden's Absalom and Achitophel

71 Who said "A thought to Donne was an experience. It modified his sensibility?"
(a) FR Leavis (b) TS Elot
(c) Samuel Johnson (d) IA Richards

72 After becoming a Catholic which famous religious poem John Dryden wrote
(a) Religio Laici (b) All for Love
(c) The Hind and the Panther (d) Annus Mirabillis

73 In 'Absalom and Achitophel' The King David was
(a) Duke of Monmouth (b) Charles II
(c) Charles III (d) Duke of Buckingham

74 Who is known as the father of literary criticism?
(a) John Dryden (b) Izaak Walton
(c) John Eliot (d) Cromwell

75 In whose poem is 'Achitophel' structured as Satan of Paradise Lost, who uses flattery and persuasive rhetoric to tempt Absalom?
(a) Samell Butler (b) John Dryden
(c) George Farquhar (d) John Vanbrugh

76 ....'s earliest work appeared is sorrow's joys.
(a) Phineas Fletcher (b) Giles Fletcher
(c) George Whither (d) William Drummond

77 .... poets use 'Direct and collogial language expressive of highly individual personality.'
(a) Spenserian (b) Cavalier
(c) Metaphysical (d) Pre-Augustan

78 Lovelace wrote a comedy called...... .
(a) The Soldiers (b) To Althea
(c) The Scholars (d) Lucasta

79 Poetry of the .... poets was rich in intellectual complexity.
(a) Spenserian (b) Cavalier
(c) Pre-Augustan (d) Metaphysical

80 .... is a Tribute to 'Cromwell' by Andrew Marvell.
(a) Bermudas (b) An Horatian ode
(c) Damon the Mower (d) Young Love

81 'Albovine Tragedy' is a work by ....
(a) Edmund Waller (b) Sir John Denham
(c) William Davenant (d) Abraham Cowly

82 .... and Cromwell's sword were the two outward bullworks of Puritanism.
(a) John Donne's Pen (b) John Dryden's Pen
(c) John Ckling's Pen (d) John Milton's Pen

83 John Donne was born into a family that was .... but he became a(n) .... priest.
(a) Agnostic, Anglican (b) Anglican, Roman Catholic
(c) Roman Catholic, Anglican
(d) Puritan, Lutheran, Anglican

84 In "The Canonization", Donne says, "The .... riddle hath more wit/By us: we two being one, are it. /So, to one neutral thing both sexes fit./We die and rise the same, and prove/Mysterious by this love." What's missing from the blank?
(a) Sphinx (b) Giant's (c) Twisted (d) Phoenix

85 George Herbert ends his poem 'The Collar' with these lines: "Methought I heard one calling, Childe:/And I reply'd, ..."
(a) Forgive me (b) My Lord (c) I Am (d) By Christ

86 Which of the following statements is incorrect?
(a) The poet who got inspiration from Ben Jonson come under the banner of the Cavalier poets
(b) The Cavalier poets were Royalists
(c) The period of Cavalier poets is mainly known for their sermons
(d) Robert Herrick is a true Cavalier

87 Which of the following statements is true about Thomas Fuller?
(a) Fuller was a person who devoted his life to being a clergy
(b) He was called the Shakespeare of divines
(c) Fuller was known as the busiest man of his age
(d) Fuller was a clergyman and Royalist

88 Which of the following statements is correct?
(a) Metaphysical poetry is wit or conceit
(b) Metaphysical poets deal with the subjects like love, death and religion
(c) Metaphysical poets love emotional experience
(d) Metaphysical has meanings like philosophical, involved and fantastic

89 Which of the following statements on John Donne's 'Forbidding Mourning' is not true?
(a) His love for his wife is spiritual
(b) Their souls have been connected with each other
(c) She should not feel disappointment because death can't separate them
(d) Both 'a' and 'c'

90 Which of the following statements is true?
(a) Bible says that to hoard and hide money is a sin and therefore is punished by God
(b) The God was very pleased when Adam and Eve at the forbidden fruit of knowledge
(c) The first time the Goddess of poetry was sitting on the secret top of Mount Horeb
(d Both 'a' and 'c'

91 Which of the following pairs is correctly matched?
(a) 1643 Battle of Stratton
(b) 1647 Oliver Cromwell defeats Charles II
(c) 1649 Charles imprisoned
(d) 1951 King Charles tried for treason

92 Which of the following pairs is incorrectly matched?
(a) Marvell : To His Coy Mistress
(b) Crashaw : The Ecstasy
(c) Donne : The Canonisation
(d) Milton : Paradise Lost

93 Which of the following pairs is correctly matched?
(a) 1647 : Mount of Olives
(b) 1649 : The Mistress
(c) 1952 : Lucasta
(d) 1638 : Lycidas

94 Which of the following pairs is incorrectly matched?
(a) Phenias Fletcher : Spenserian Poet
(b) Robert Herrick : Cavalier Poet
(c) John Donne : Metaphysical Poet
(d) Thomas Çarew : Restoration Poet

95 Which of the following is incorrectly matched?
(a) Samson Agonistes : John Milton
(b) Mac Flecknoe : John Dryden
(c) On a Girdle : William Davenante
(d) Hudibras : Samuel Butler

Directions (Q. Nos. 96-99) *In the questions given below are two statements labelled as Assertion (A) and Reason (R). In the context of these two statements, which of the following is correct?*
(a) A is true, but R is false
(d) A is false, but R is true
(c) Both A and R are true, but R is not the correct explanation of A
(d) Both A and R are true and R is the correct explanation of A

96 **Assertion** (A) Very little theatrical activity was seen in England during the Puritan Age.
Reason (R) With the outbreak of the Civil War, theatres were closed down.

97 **Assertion** (A) Literature of the Puritan Age was somber and pensive.
Reason (R) This was in keeping with the religious ideals and political standards of the Puritans.

98 **Assertion** (A) Cavalier poets were a group of English gentleman poets who gathered at The Court of Charles I.
Reason (R) Because of their loyalty and support for Charles I, these poets were called as 'Cavaliers'

99 **Assertion** (A) The poetry of the metaphysical poets was rich in intellectual complexity.
Reason (R) The metaphysical did not employ unusual images and conceits.

100 **Assertion** (A) Dryden is best known for his Satirical works, Absalom and Achitophel and Mac Flecknoe.
Reason (R) Dryden won fame through his prose work, Grace Abounding.
Code
(a) Both A and R are true and R is the correct explanation of A
(b) Both A and R are true, but R is not the correct explanation of A
(c) A is true, but R is false
(d) A is false, but R is true

101 Which of the following is in chronological order?
(a) L'Allegro, Paradise Lost, Lycidas, Paradise Regained
(b) Paradise Lost, Lycidas, L'Allegro, Paradise Regained
(c) Lycidas, Paradise Lost, L'Allegro, Paradise Regained
(d) L'Allegro, Lycidas, Paradise Lost, Paradise Regained

102 Which of the following is in chronological order?
(a) Richard Lovelace, Thomas Carew, Robert Herrick, Henry Vaughan
(b) Thomas Carew, Robert Herrick, Richard Lovelace, Henry Vaughan
(c) Robert Herrick, Thomas Carew, Richard Lovelace, Henry Vaughan
(d) Richard Lovelace, Robert Herrick, Thomas Carew, Henry Vaughan

103 Which of the following works are in chronological order?
(a) A Canto upon the Death of Eliza, The Shepherd's Hunting, Forth Feasting, The Purple Island
(b) The Purple Island, A Canto upon the Death of Eliza, The Shepherd's Hunting, Forth Feasting,
(c) The Shephard's Hunting, Forth Feasting, A Canto upon the Death of Eliza, The Shepherd's Hunting
(d) Forth Feasting, A Canto upon the Death of Eliza, The Shepherd's Hunting, The Purple Island

104 Which of the following is in chronological order?
(a) The Rival Ladies, Religio Laici, The Hind and the Panther
(b) Religio Laici, The Hind and the Panther, The Rival Ladies
(c) The Hind and the Panther, Religio Laici, The Rival Ladies
(d) The Rival Ladies, The Hind and the Panther, Religio Laici

105 Which of the following is in chronological order?
(a) A Defence of an Essay, Mac Flecknoe, Absalom and Achitophel
(b) Absalom and Achitophel, Mac Flecknoe, A Defence of an Essay
(c) A Defence of an Essay, Absalom and Achitophel, Mac Flecknoe
(d) Mac Flecknoe, A Defence of an Essay, Absalom and Achitophel

106 What is common to the following writers? Identify the correct description below
1. Phineas Fletcher 2. Giles Fletcher
3. George Whither 4. William Browne
Codes
(a) All of them were Spenserian poets of the Puritan Age
(b) All of them wrote tragedies in the same age
(c) All of them wrote comedies in the same age
(d) All of them were critics of Cromwell's regime

107 What is common to the following writers? Identify the correct description below
1. Robert Herrick 2. Thomas Carew
3. John Suckling 4. Richard Lovelace
Codes
(a) All of these were Restoration playwrights
(b) All of them were Elizabethan poets
(c) All of them were Cavalier poets of the Puritan Age
(d) All of them edited Donne's Poems

108 What is common to the following writers? Identify the correct description below
1. John Donne
2. George Herbert
3. Richard Crashaw
4. Henry Vaughan
Codes
(a) All of them were prose writers of the Puritan Age
(b) All of them were metaphysical poets of the Puritan Age
(c) All of them wrote Shakespearean tragedies
(d) All of them edited poems of the Elizabethan Age

109 The following works are mentioned with their composers written against them
1. The Mower's song- Andrew Marvell
2. The Good Morrow- Richard Crashaw
3. The Temple- George Herbert
4. Britain's Ida-Giles Fletcher
Which of the following is/are correct?
Codes
(a) 1 and 2 (b) 2 and 3
(c) 1 and 3 (d) 2 and 4

110 A list of the Puritan works is given below
1. L'Allegro 2. Lycidas
3. Juvinilia 4. The Reformed Pastor
Which of these is/are not the work/s of John Milton?
Codes
(a) 1 and 3 (b) 1 and 4
(c) Only 3 (d) 3 and 4

111 Poets of the Puritan Age are mentioned below
1. William Browne 2. George Herbert
3. Richard Crashaw 4. Robert Herrick
Which of the above is/are metaphysical poet/s?
Codes
(a) 1 and 2 (b) 2 and 3 (c) 2 and 4 (d) only 4

112 Poems of the Puritan Age are mentioned below
1. Sorrows Joy
2. Epithalamia Encomia
3. Britannia's Pastorals
4. Upon Appleton House
Which of these poems are compositions of the Spenserian poets of the Puritan Age?
Codes
(a) 1 and 2 (b) 1 and 3 (c) 2 and 3 (d) 3 and 4

113 Themes of some parts of the 'Paradise Lost' by Milton are mentioned below
1. Divine judgement upon Adam and Eve
2. Story of the temptation by Satan
3. Michael's vision continues
4. Almighty accepts Adam's repentance
Which of the above are themes of Book X and IX of the 'Paradise Lost' respectively?
Codes
(a) 1 and 2 (b) 2 and 3
(c) 2 and 4 (d) 1 and 4

114 A set of poems are given below
1. The Retreat 2. Go Lovely Rose
3. A Valediction 4. To His Coy Mistress
Which poems are centred around convincing one's beloved for love and romance leaving behind the hesitation and modesty?
Codes
(a) 1 and 2 (b) 2 and 3
(c) 2 and 4 (d) 3 and 4

115 A few poets of the Puritan age are mentioned below
1. William Drummond 2. John Suckling
3. Richard Lovelace 4. Henry Vaughan
Which of the above is/are Cavalier poets of the Puritan Age?
Codes
(a) 1 and 2 (b) 2 and 3
(c) 1 and 4 (d) 2 and 4

116 Match the following Spenserian poets with their poems.

Spenserian Poet	Poem
1. Phineas Fletcher	A. Purple Island
2. Giles Fletcher	B. Christs's Victorie
3. George Whither	C. The Scourage
4. William Browne	D. The Shephard's Pipe

Codes
(a) 1–A, 2–B, 3–C, 4–D (b) 1–D, 2–C, 3–B, 4–A
(c) 1–B, 2–D, 3–A, 4–C (d) 1–C, 2–A, 3–D, 4–B

117 Match the following poems with their Cavalier poets.

Poem		Cavalier Poet
1. To the Virgins, to Make Much of Time	A.	Richard Lovelace
2. A Rapture	B.	John Suckling
3. The Constant Lover	C.	Thomas Carew
4. The Rose	D.	Robert Herrick

Codes

(a) 1–A, 2–B, 3–C, 4–D (b) 1–D, 2–C, 3–B, 4–A
(c) 1–B, 2–D, 3–A, 4–C (d) 1–C, 2–A, 3–D, 4–B

118 Match the following metaphysical poets with their poems.

Metaphysical Poet		Poem
1. John Donne	A.	I Walk'd the Other Day
2. George Herbert	B.	The Dream
3. Henry Vaughan	C.	The Unfortunate Lover
4. Andrew Marvell	D.	The Pulley

Codes

(a) 1–A, 2–B, 3–C, 4–D (b) 1–D, 2–C, 3–B, 4–A
(c) 1–B, 2–D, 3–A, 4–C (d) 1–C, 2–A, 3–D, 4–B

119 Match the following poems with their Puritan and Restoration Age poets.

Poem		Age Poet
1. Summons To Love	A.	Richard Crashaw
2. An Epitaph upon Husband and Wife	B.	Sir John Denham
3. To a Very Young Lady	C.	William Drummond
4. Friendship and single Life against Love and Marriage	D.	Edmund Waller

Codes

(a) 1–A, 2–B, 3–C, 4–D (b) 1–D, 2–C, 3–B, 4–A
(c) 1–B, 2–D, 3–A, 4–C (d) 1–C, 2–A, 3–D, 4–B

120 Match the following.

List I	List II
A. The Relique	1. Richard Crashaw
B. The Shepherd's Hunting	2. Thomas Traherne
C. The Delights of Muse	3. John Donne
D. Roman Forgeries	4. Wither

Codes

	A	B	C	D		A	B	C	D
(a)	4	1	3	2	(b)	3	4	1	2
(c)	2	1	4	3	(d)	3	1	4	2

121 Match the following.

List I	List II
A. Book I	1. Fall of Man
B. Book II	2. Description of the Council of Evil Spirt
C. Book III	3. Transports upto Heaven Again
D. Book IV	4. Paradise and Innocent State of Man

Codes

	A	B	C	D		A	B	C	D
(a)	2	3	1	4	(b)	4	1	3	2
(c)	1	2	3	4	(d)	2	1	3	4

122 Match the following works with their authors correctly.

List I	List II
A. Phineas Fletcher	1. Coopers Hills
B. Edmund Waller	2. Poetical Blossoms
C. Sir John Denham	3. Go Lovely Rose
D. Abraham Cowley	4. The Locusts

Codes

	A	B	C	D		A	B	C	D
(a)	4	1	2	3	(b)	1	2	4	3
(c)	3	2	4	1	(d)	4	3	1	2

123 In the following series, which one has all the poets matched correctly with their category?

(a) George Wither-Spenserian, Thomas Carew-Cavalier Richard Crashaw-Metaphysical, Milton-Pre Augustan
(b) Millton-Pre Augustan, Richard Crashaw-Metaphysical, Thomas Carew-Spenserian, George Wither-Cavalier.
(c) George Wither-Pre Augustan, Thomas Carew-Cavalier Richard Crashaw-Spenserian, Milton-Metaphysical.
(d) George Wither-Metaphysical, Thomas Carew-Spenserian Richard Crashaw-Cavalier, Milton-Pre Augustan.

124 In the following series, which one has all the poems matched correctly with their poets?

(a) A Valediction-Henry Vaughan, The Affliction-George Herbert, The Retreat-Andrew Marvell, To His Coy Mistress-John Donne
(b) A Valediction-Andrew Marvell, The Affliction-John Donne, The Retreat-George Herbert, To His Coy Mistress-Henry Vaughan
(c) A Valediction-John Donne, The Affliction-George Herbert, The Retreat-Henry Vaughan, To His Coy Mistress-Andrew Marvell
(d) A Valediction-John Donne, The Affliction-Henry Vaughan, The Retreat-George Herbert, To His Coy Mistress-Andrew Marvell.

125 In the following series, which one has all the works correctly matched with their composers?

(a) Juvenilia- Richard Lovelace, to Althea-George Whither The Flea- Jeremy Taylor, The Rule and Exercises of Holy Living- John Donne.
(b) Juvenilia- Jeremy Taylor, to Althea-John Donne The Flea- Richard Lovelace, The Rule and Exercises of Holy Living- George Whither
(c) Juvenilia-George Whither, To Althea-Richard Lovelace, The Flea- Jeremy Taylor, The Rule and Exercises of Holy Living- John Donne
(d) Juvenilia-George Whiter, To Althea- Richard Lovelace, The Flea- John Donne, The Rule and Exercises of Holy Living- Jeremy Taylor

126 "If little labour, little are our gains:
Man's fortunes are according to his pains."
Which of the following poets in which of his/her works has used the above lines?
(a) Robert Herrick, Hesperides.
(b) Thomas Carew, Disdain Returned
(c) Sir John Suckling, Why so pale and wan, Fond lover?
(d) Richard Lovelace, To Althea, from Prison

127 Bid Me to live and I will live' is the statement about
(a) Thomas Carew (b) FR Leavis
(c) Robert Herrick (d) Lovelace

128 He that loves a rosy cheek,
Or a coral lip admires,
Or, from star-like eyes, doth seek
Fuel to maintain his fires;
As old Time makes these decay,
So his flames must waste away.
Which of the following poets in which of his/her works has used the above lines?
(a) Robert Herrick, Hesperides
(b) Thomas Carew, Disdain Returned.
(c) Sir John Suckling, Why so pale and wan, Fond lover?
(d) Richard Lovelace, To Althea, from Prison

129 Wise poets that wrapt Truth in tales,
Knew her themselves through all her veils.
Which of the following poets in which of his/her works has used the above lines?
(a) Thomas Carew, Ingrateful Beauty Threatened
(b) Richard Lovelace, The Lucasta Poems
(c) John Donne, The Good Morrow
(d) george Herbert,The Temple

130 "Out upon it, I have loved
Three whole days together!
And am like to love three more,
If it prove fair weather.
Time shall moult away his wings
Ere he shall discover
In the whole wide world again
Such a constant lover"
Which of the following poets in which of his/her works has used the above lines?
(a) Robert Herrick, Hesperides
(b) Thomas Carew, Disdain Returned
(c) Sir John Suckling, Why so pale and wan, Fond lover?
(d) Richard Lovelace, To Althea, from Prison

131 "Stone walls do not a prison make,
Nor iron bars a cage;
Minds innocent and quiet take
That for an hermitage;
If I have freedom in my love
And in my soul am free,
Angels alone, that soar above,
Enjoy such liberty."
Which of the following poets in which of his/her works has used the above lines?
(a) Robert Herrick, Hesperides
(b) Thomas Carew, Disdain Returned
(c) Sir John Suckling, Why so pale and wan, Fond lover?
(d) Richard Lovelace, To Althea, from Prison

132 "I could not love thee, Dear, so much,
Loved I not Honour more."
Which of the following poets in which of his/her works has used the above lines?
(a) Thomas Carew, Ingrateful Beauty Threatened
(b) Richard Lovelace, The Lucasta Poems .
(c) John Donne, The Good Morrow
(d) George Herbert,The Temple

133 "My face in thine eye, thine in mine appeares,
And true plaine hearts doe in the faces rest,
Where can we finde two better hemispheares
Without sharpe North, without declining West?
What ever dyes, was not mixt equally;
If our two loves be one, or, thou and I
Love so alike, that none doe slacken, none can die."
Which of the following poets in which of his/her works has used the above lines?
(a) Thomas Carew, Ingrateful Beauty Threatened
(b) Richard Lovelace, The Lucasta Poems
(c) John Donne, The Good Morrow
(d) George Herbert,The Temple

134 For those, whom thou think'st thou dost overthrow,
Die not, poor Death, nor yet canst thou kill me.
From rest and sleep, which but thy picture[s] be,
Much pleasure, then from thee much more must flow,
And soonest our best men with thee do go,
Rest of their bones, and soul's delivery.
Which of the following poets in which of his/her works has used the above lines?
(a) John Donne, Death Be Not Proud .
(b) Richard Crashaw, The Complete Poetry Of Richard Crashaw
(c) Henry Vaughan, The dawning
(d) Abraham Cowley, The Poems of Abraham Cowley

135 He must pull out his own eyes and see no creature, before he can say, he sees no God; He must be no man and quench his reasonable soul, before he can say to himself, there is no God."
(a) John Milton
(b) John Donne
(c) Thomas Hobbes
(d) Andrew Marvell

136 Which metaphysical poet utters "Do not kill the flee, their bloods have been united together."
(a) Henry Vaughan
(b) John Donne
(c) Richard Crashaw
(d) Andrew Marvell

137 "Great wits are sure to madness near allied
And thin partitions do their bounds divide". The above line appears in...

(a) Mac Flecknoe (b) Absalom and Achitophel
(c) Essay on Man (d) Alexander's Feast

138 Many, affecting wit beyond their power,
Have got to be a dear fool for an hour.

Which of the following poets in which of his/her works has used the above lines?

(a) Thomas carew, Ingrateful Beauty Threatened
(b) Richard Lovelace, The Lucasta Poems
(c) John Donne, The Good Morrow
(d) George Herbert, The Temple.

139 "Let me not love thee, if I love thee not, He has no right to receive, love if he could not love others." Which Puritan age poet's lines are these?

(a) George Herbert (b) John Donne
(c) Andrew Marvell (d) John Suckling

140 My lines and life are free, as the road is the statement of

(a) George Herbert (b) William Black
(c) John Donne (d) Robert Herrick

141 "Tis not the work of force but skill
To find the way into man's will.
Tis love alone can hearts unlock.
Who knows the WORD, he needs not knock."

Which of the following poets in which of his/her works has used the above lines?

(a) John Donne, Death Be Not Proud
(b) Richard Crashaw, The Complete Poetry Of Richard Crashaw
(c) Henry Vaughan, The dawning
(d) Abraham Cowley, The Poems of Abraham Cowley

142 Yet let my course, my aim, my love,
And chief acquaintance be above;
So when that day and hour shall come,
In which Thyself will be the sun,
Thou'lt find me drest and on my way,
Watching the break of Thy great day."

Which of the following poets in which of his/her works has used the above lines?

(a) John Donne, Death Be Not Proud
(b) Richard Crashaw, The Complete Poetry Of Richard Crashaw
(c) Henry Vaughan, The dawning .
(d) Abraham Cowley, The Poems of Abraham Cowley

143 "Some men a forward motion love, But I by backward steps would move and when this dust falls to the urn in that state I came, return." From which poem of the Puritan Age have these lines been taken?

(a) Henry Vaughan's 'Retreat'
(b) Andrew Marvell's 'The Definition of Love'
(c) John Donne's 'The Sun Rising'
(d) Edmund Waller's 'Go Lovely Rose'

144 "Had we but world enough and time,
This coyness, Lady, were no crime.
We would sit down and think which way
To walk and pass our long love's day."
To which Puritan age work do these lines belong?

(a) John Milton's 'Paradise Regained'
(b) John Donne's 'The Good Morrow'
(c) Andrew Marvell's 'To his Coy Mistress'
(d) Richard Lovelace's 'Lucasta'

145 "A mighty pain to love it is,
And 't is a pain that pain to miss;
But of all pains, the greatest pain
It is to love, but love in vain."

Which of the following poets in which of his/her works has used the above lines?

(a) John Donne, Death Be Not Proud
(b) Richard Crashaw, The Complete Poetry Of Richard Crashaw
(c) Henry Vaughan, The dawning
(d) Abraham Cowley, The Poems of Abraham Cowley

146 "For you may palm upon us new for old:
All, as they say, that glitters, is not gold."

Which of the following poets in which of his/her works has used the above lines?

(a) John Dryden, The Hind and the Panther
(b) Andrew Marvell, To His Coy Mistress
(c) Thomas Carew, A Song
(d) Robert Herrick, The Poems of Robert Herrick

147 "His knowledge was not far behind
The knight's, but of another kind,
And he another way came by't;
Some call it Gifts and some New Light.
A lib'ral art, that costs no pains
of study, industry, or brains."

From which work of an author of the Restoration age have these lines been taken?

(a) Hudibras, Samuel Butler
(b) The Comical Revenge, George Etherege
(c) The Country Wife, William Wycherley
(d) The Mourning Bride, William Congreve

148 'The beauty shall no more be found' this statement wants to convey the message that

(a) Beauty is not stronger than a flower
(b) Time can snatch the charm of beauty
(c) Time is more powerful
(d) Time is very powerful and the days of beauty are numbered

149 As virtuous men pass mildly away and whisper to their souls to go whilst some of their sad friends say, the breath goes now and some says no; which statements are true?

(a) When the virtuous die, some of their friends say the breath pass away now and some others say 'no'
(b) When virtuous die we should not shed tears and pass them silently

(c) To cover a wide range of feelings from physical to spiritual and intellectual
(d) Both 'a' and 'b'

150 'Invoke thy aid to my adventures song', here the word 'aid' refers to
(a) The poet wants help from the muse to write the poem
(b) The poet treated his songs adventures
(c) Satan makes it clear that their defeat is physical
(d) Both 'a' and 'c'

151 'Farewell happy fields, where joy ever dwells'. Which statements is true?
(a) Satan is bidding farewell to the blessed Heaven
(b) Adam and Eve tasted the forbidden fruit and they are living happily
(c) God is very disappointed after this
(d) Both 'a' and 'b'

152 'Or that sea beast leviathan'. Which statement justifies the statement?
(a) The sea is very large in which Adam and Eve has fallen
(b) As sailors report, the captain of the ship fixes the anchor in Leviathan's body
(c) Satan was monstrous like the sea beast 'Leviathan'
(d) All of the above

153 "To be blind is not miserable; not to be able to bear blindness, that is miserable." Whose famous quote is this?
(a) John Milton (b) John Donne
(c) George Herbert (d) Andrew Marvell

154 "He is invoking the muse to remove the darkness of ignorance." Whose lines are these?
(a) Edmund Waller (b) William Davenant
(c) John Milton (d) Abraham Cowley

155 In which work of John Milton, a character states that "He has been defeated but not his will. He has not given up his endeavour to take the revenge."
(a) 'L'Allegro' (b) Lycidas
(c) Samson Agonistes (d) Paradise Lost

Directions (Q. Nos. 156-160) *Read the following poem and answer the questions given below.*

The Flea by JOHN DONNE

Mark but his flea and mark in this,
How little that which thou deniest me is;
It sucked me first and now sucks thee,
And in this flea our two bloods mingled be;
thou know'st that this cannot be said
A sin, nor shame, nor loss of maidenhead,
Yet this enjoys before it woo,
And pampered swells with one blood made of two,
And this, alas, is more than we would do.
Oh stay, three lives in one flea spare,
where we almost, nay more than married are.
this flea is you and I and this
Our marriage bed and marriage temple is;
Though parents grudge and you, w'are met,
And cloistered in these living walls of het.
Though use make you apt to kill me,
Let not to that, self-murder added be,
And sacrilege, three sins in killing three.
Cruel and sudden, hast thou since
Purpled thy nail, in blood of innocence?
Wherein could this flea guilty be,
Except in that drop which it sucked from thee?
Yet thou triumph'st and say'st that thou
Find'st not thy self, nor me the weaker now;
Tis true; then learn how false, fears be:
Just so much honor, when thou yield'st to me,
Will waste, as this flea's death took life form thee.

156 What does the 'Flea' symbolise in the poem?
(a) The Marriage bed
(b) The bride
(c) The groom
(d) Disturbing element

157 What is the theme of the poem?
(a) To convey the message of love for animals
(b) To Persuade 'the would be lover' for sex
(c) To liken females to the insects
(d) To demonstrate the kindness of males towards insects

158 Why does the poet stop the woman from killing the Flea?
(a) The poet has Fallen in love with the flea
(b) The poet wants to impress his beloved by being an animal lover
(c) Killing a Flea, which has sucked their blood, may amount to a suicide and thus guilty of sacrilege
(d) The poet feels the flea is harmless

159 What does the word 'maiden head' in para mean?
(a) Adolescent
(b) Princess
(c) The head of a castle
(d) Virgin

160 What is the rhyme scheme of the poem?
(a) aa bb cc ddd
(b) aa bb cc dd
(c) aa bb aa bb
(d) aa bb ab cde

PREVIOUS YEARS' QUESTIONS

December 2018

1 Which of the following themes was not common to the works of Cavelier poets such as Thomas Carew, Sir John Denham, Edmund Waller, Sir John Suckling, James Shirley, Richard Lovelace, and Robert Herrick?

(a) Loyalty to the King
(b) Country ideals of the good life
(c) Pious devotion to religious virtues
(d) Carpe diem

2 What is the delicate balancing act of Andrew Marvell's 'Horation Ode'?

(a) Praising Roman virtues while endorsing Christian beliefs.
(b) Celebrating the Restoration while regretting the frivolity of the new regime.
(c) Praising feminine virtues while mocking the fixation on chastity.
(d) Celebrating Cromwell's victories while inviting sympathy for the executed King.

3 Read the passage given below
Ah, what a trifle is a heart,
If once into love's hands it come!
All other griefs, allow a part
To other griefs, and ask themselves but some;
They come to us, but us love draws;
He swallowsus and never chaws;
By him, as by chain'd shot, whole ranks do die;
He is the tyrant pike, our hearts the fry.
-John Donnem, 1633

Which sentence best paraphrases line of the passage above?

(a) Love tends to grab us and never let go.
(b) Distress comes in many forms, but none lasts as long as heartache.
(c) Unbidden pain afflicts us, but we are lured by love.
(d) Emotions can damage us, but none as severely as love.

4 Read the lines from the poem
Alas! what boots it with uncessant care
To tend the homely, slighted Shepherd's trade,
And strictly meditate the thankless Muse?
Were it not better done, as others use,
To sport with Amaryllis in the shade,
Or with the tangles of Neaera's hair?

Who are Amaryllis and Neaera in the above extract from john Milton's 'Lycidas'?

(a) Both were goddesses of love and war respectively appearing in Greek pastoral poetry.
(b) Amaryllis is a shepherdess mentioned in Shakespearce's romantic comedies; Neaera, a minor character in love's Labour's lost
(c) Amaryllis is a shepherdess mentioned in ancient pastoral poetry, notably in Virgil's eculogues; Neaera, a nymph who appears in Virgil's Eclogues.
(d) Both were one-time lovers of Lycidas, the dead shepherd.

July 2018

5 Who is the only one of Milton's contemporaries to be mentioned by name in Paradise Lost?

(a) Francis Bacon (b) Johannes Vermeer
(c) Galileo (d) King Charles

6 Robert Burton's Anatomy of Melancholy was published in 1621 and expanded and altered in .... subsequent editions.

(a) two (b) four (c) six (d) five

7 One of the following statements about the eponymous saint of Dryden's 'Song for St. Cecilia's Day' is incorrect. Identify that Statement.

(a) St. Cecilia's was a Roman Lady, an early Christian martyr
(b) St. Cecilia's was an Armenian devotee of the Christian Faith
(c) St. Cecilia's festival is celebrated on 22nd November in England
(d) St. Cecilia's was a patroness of music who was fabled to have invented the organ

November 2017

8 Who/Which among the following gave the expression, "a leopard can't change its spot," to English language?

(a) The King James Bible (b) Geoffrey Chaucer
(c) Shakespeare (d) The Royal Society

9 Who among the following is the author of Steps of the Temple?

(a) John Donne
(b) Richard Crashaw
(c) George Herbert
(d) Henry Vaughan

10 Which of the following rivers are mentioned in Andrew Marvell's poem 'To His Coy Mistress'?

(a) Thames and Rhine
(b) Thames and Ganges
(c) Ganges and Humber
(d) Thames and Humber

11 Samuel Johnson denounced the metaphysical poets saying, "About the beginning of the seventeenth century appeared a race of writers that may be termed the metaphysical poets". In the biography of which of the following poets in his Lives of Poets did Johnson make this remark?

(a) John Dryden (b) Thomas Parnell
(c) Abraham Cowley (d) Alexander Pope

January 2017

12 **8.** Who among the following contemporaries of John Donne wrote the following lines on his death: " Here lies a king, that ruled as he thought fit/the universal monarch of wit"?

(a) George Herbert (b) Henry King
(c) Thomas Carew (d) Henry Crashaw

13 The term, 'poetic justice,' to designate the idea the good are rewarded and the evil punished, devised by

(a) Aristotle (b) John Dryden
(c) Thomas Rhymer (d) Ben Jonson

14 The medall, a poem written by John Dryden in 1681, is sub-titled

(a) a satire against Sedition (b) a satire against Tyranny
(c) a satire against Greed (d) a satire against Apostasy

July 2016

15 Thomas Carew's poems appeared in print in 1640 and contain a variety of amorous addresses to and reflections on, a fictional mistress known as

(a) Celia (b) Julia (c) Anne (d) Melanie

16 Who of the following is a Cavalier poet?

(a) George Herbert (b) John Donne
(c) Robert Herrick (d) Andrew Marvell

17 Which of the following phrases is not found in Thomas Gray's Elegy written in a Country Churchyard?

(a) For from the madding crowed
(b) A youth to fortune and fame unknown
(c) Full many a flower is born to blush unseen
(d) All nature is but art unknown to thee

18 John Milton's description of gold as a 'precious bane' (Paradise Lost, book II) is best described as

(a) a dactyl (b) an oxymoron
(c) enjambment (d) zeugma

19 In Paradise Lost which character narrates the story of the making of Eve from a rib in Adam's side?

(a) Adam (b) Eve
(c) Raphael (d) God

20 As Adam and Eve leave Paradise, "hand in hand with wand ring steps and slow" (Book XII, Paradise Lost) what is their consolation?

(a) They are comforted by their love for one another
(b) They are comforted by their fore knowledge of the coming of Christ as redeemer of mankind
(c) They are comforted by God, who travels before them in the form of a pillar of fire
(d) They are comforted by the angel, who holds each to\f them by the hand

21 John's Dryden's two philosophic religious poems are

1. Absalom and Achitophel
2. A Layman's faith
3. Annus Mirabilis
4. The Hind and the Panther

The right combination according to the code is

(a) 1 and 2 (b) 3 and 1
(c) 2 and 3 (d) 2 and 4

December 2015

22 What is the name of the angel, who of those who owed allegeance to Satan, dared to protest against him impious doctrine and left his company to return to God (Paradise Lost, Book V)

(a) Michael (b) Abdiel (c) Uriel (d) Gabriel

23 The famous sonnet of John Milton beginning "When I consider how my light is spent.." ends with..

(a) Before me stares a wolfish eye, behind me creeps a groan or sigh
(b) They also serve who only stand and wait
(c) And - which is more you'll be a Man, my son
(d) And bless him for the sake of him that's gone

24 "Where there is leisure for fiction, there is little grief", was Samuel Johnson's criticism of a famous poem. Which poem was it?

(a) P B Shelley's 'Adonais'
(b) Philip Sidney's 'Astrophel and Stella'
(c) Thomas Gray's 'Elegy Written on a Country Churchyard'
(d) John Milton's 'Lycidas'

25 Match the following

List I	List II
A. Robert Burton	1. Urn Burial
B. Richard Hooker	2. The Unfortunate Traveller
C. Thomas Browne	3. The Anatomy of Melancholy
D. Thomas Nashe	4. Of the Laws of Ecclesiastical Politie

Codes

	A	B	C	D
(a)	3	1	2	4
(b)	4	2	1	3
(c)	3	4	1	2
(d)	1	3	4	2

26 John Dryden described a major English poet as "a rough diamond and must first be polished ere he shines… ." Identify him.

(a) Geoffrey Chaucer (b) John Gower
(c) George Herbert (d) Robert Herrick

27 "So when the last and dreadful hour
This crumbling pageant shall devour,
The trumpet shall be heard on high,
The dead shall live, the living die,
And music shall untune the sky"
These are the closing lines of a famous poem. Identify the poem.

(a) II Penseroso
(b) Song for St Cecilia's Day
(c) The Good–Morrow
(d) Song: The Year's at the Spring

June 2016

28 Who among the following poets compared human tears to 'love's wine?

(a) Ben Jonson
(b) John Donne
(c) Andrew Marvell
(d) John Suckling

29 Who among the following was a contemporary of John Milton and wrote *The Worthy communicant*? It is aid that his prose can be read easily, when Milton's must be studied.

(a) Jeremy Taylor (b) John Bunyan
(c) Andrew Marvell (d) George Herbert

30 The opening sixteen lines of Paradise Lost comprise

(a) One sentence (b) Two sentences
(c) Three sentences (d) Four sentences

31 In Paradise Lost Milton presents the action of man in two stages in Books.... .

(a) IV and IX (b) IV and VIII
(c) III and IX (d) V and X

32 In tracing the history of English poetry, Thomas Gray's "Progress of Poesy" invokes a major poet as follows
"Nor second He, that rode sublime
Upon the seraph-wigs of Extasy,
The secrets of Th' Abyss to spy."
Who is 'He'?

(a) William Shakespeare
(b) Edmund Spenser
(c) John Milton
(d) John Dryden

33 "In the seventeenth century", writes TS Eliot in "The Metaphysical Poets", "a dissociation of sensibility set in, from which we have never recovered; and this dissociation, as is a natural, was aggravated by the influence of the two most powerful poets of the century, ...and....

(a) Ben Jonson and Abraham Cowley
(b) George Herbert and Henry Vaughan
(c) John Donne and Andrew Marvell
(d) John Milton and John Dryden

34 The term 'Poetic justice' was coined by……. .

(a) Samuel Taylor Coleridge (b) Thomas Rymer
(c) Samuel Johnson (d) William Wordsworth

December 2014

35 Who among the following wrote a poem comparing a lover's heart to a hand grenade?

(a) John Donne (b) Abraham Cowley
(c) Wilfred Owen (d) Robert Graves

36 "My lute, be as thou wert when thou didst grow
With thy green mother in some shady groove".
-William Drummond
The above quote is an example of..... .

(a) end-stopped rhyme (b) alliteration
(c) run-on line (d) tercet

37 The first official royal Poet Laureate in English literary history was… .

(a) Ben Jonson (b) William Davenant
(c) John Dryden (d) Thomas Shadwell

June 2014

38 In which poem of Donne's is the lover's face reflected in the eyes of his beloved?

(a) The Good Morrow
(b) The Canonisation
(c) The Apparition
(d) A Valediction: Forbidding Mourning

39 In Paradise Lost BK IX Milton writes that Adam was overcome with '...' and so ate the forbidden fruit against his 'better knowledge'.

(a) 'female charm' (b) 'exceeding love'
(c) 'faithful love' (d) 'taste so divine'

40 "That glory never shall his wrath or might extort me." (Paradise Lost, Book I)
What 'glory' is being referred to by Satan?

(a) The courage never to submit or yield
(b) To reign in hell
(c) To defeat God
(d) To spread evil

ANSWERS

Objective Questions

1. (d)	2. (a)	3. (b)	4. (a)	5. (b)	6. (c)	7. (a)	8. (a)	9. (d)	10. (a)
11. (d)	12. (d)	13. (d)	14. (a)	15. (c)	16. (a)	17. (a)	18. (d)	19. (a)	20. (b)
21. (b)	22. (d)	23. (c)	24. (a)	25. (c)	26. (a)	27. (d)	28. (b)	29. (a)	30. (c)
31. (b)	32. (c)	33. (c)	34. (c)	35. (c)	36. (c)	37. (b)	38. (b)	39. (b)	40. (c)
41. (d)	42. (d)	43. (b)	44. (b)	45. (d)	46. (d)	47. (a)	48. (a)	49. (b)	50. (a)
51. (c)	52. (b)	53. (d)	54. (b)	55. (b)	56. (a)	57. (c)	58. (c)	59. (a)	60. (b)
61. (a)	62. (c)	63. (b)	64. (c)	65. (b)	66. (b)	67. (c)	68. (b)	69. (d)	70. (d)
71. (b)	72. (c)	73. (b)	74. (a)	75. (b)	76. (a)	77. (b)	78. (c)	79. (d)	80. (b)
81. (c)	82. (d)	83. (b)	84. (d)	85. (b)	86. (c)	87. (d)	88. (c)	89. (c)	90. (d)
91. (a)	92. (b)	93. (d)	94. (d)	95. (c)	96. (c)	97. (d)	98. (d)	99. (a)	100. (c)
101. (d)	102. (c)	103. (a)	104. (a)	105. (c)	106. (a)	107. (c)	108. (b)	109. (c)	110. (d)
111. (b)	112. (b)	113. (a)	114. (c)	115. (b)	116. (a)	117. (b)	118. (c)	119. (d)	120. (b)
121. (c)	122. (d)	123. (a)	124. (c)	125. (d)	126. (a)	127. (c)	128. (b)	129. (a)	130. (c)
131. (d)	132. (b)	133. (c)	134. (a)	135. (b)	136. (b)	137. (b)	138. (d)	139. (a)	140. (a)
141. (b)	142. (c)	143. (a)	144. (c)	145. (d)	146. (a)	147. (a)	148. (d)	149. (b)	150. (a)
151. (a)	152. (c)	153. (a)	154. (c)	155. (d)	156. (a)	157. (b)	158. (c)	159. (d)	160. (a)

Previous Year's Questions

1. (c)	2. (d)	3. (c)	4. (c)	5. (c)	6. (d)	7. (b)	8. (a)	9. (b)	10. (c)
11. (c)	12. (c)	13. (c)	14. (a)	15. (a)	16. (c)	17. (d)	18. (b)	19. (a)	20. (b)
21. (d)	22. (b)	23. (b)	24. (d)	25. (c)	26. (a)	27. (b)	28. (b)	29. (a)	30. (a)
31. (a)	32. (c)	33. (d)	34. (b)	35. (b)	36. (c)	37. (c)	38. (a)	39. (a)	40. (a)

Neo-Classical/Augustan Age (1700-1798)

The spirit of the Neo-classical/Augustan poetry was the imagination and emotion. The poetry of this age also differed in subject matter and the form from the earlier age poetry. Graveyard poetry and odes became the poetic trend of the age. Alexander Pope, Edward Gay, James Thomson and Dr Samuel Johnson were a few notable poets of the age.

Augustan Age: An Introduction

The term 'Augustan Age' comes from the self-conscious imitation of the original Augustan writers, Virgil, Horace and by many writers of the period. The literature of this period, which conformed to Pope's aesthetic principles is distinguished by its striving for harmony and precision, its urbanity and its imitation of classical models.

The 18th century is sometimes called the Augustan age and contemporary admiration for the classical world extended to the poetry of the time. Not only did the poets aim for a polished style in emulation of the Roman ideal, they also translated and imitated Greek and Latin verses resulting in measured rationalised elegant verses. Pope produced versions of the two Homeric epics: *Iliad* and *Odyssey*.

A number of notable women poets emerged during the period of the Restoration, including Aphra Behn, Margaret Cavendish, Mary Chudleigh, Anne Finch, Anne Killigrew and Katherine Philips. Nevertheless, print publication by women poets was still relatively scarce when compared to that of men, though manuscript evidence indicates that many more women poets were practising than was previously thought. Disapproval of feminine 'forwardness', however, kept many out of print in the early part of the period and even as the century progressed women authors still felt the need to justify their inclusion into the public sphere by claiming economic necessity or the pressure of friends. Women writers were increasingly active in all genres throughout the 18th century and by the 1790s women's poetry was flourishing.

In this Chapter

Notable poets, later in the period include Anna Laetitia Barbauld, Joanna Baillie, Susanna Blamire, Felicia Hemans, Mary Leapor, Lady Mary Wortley Montagu, Hannah More and Mary Robinson.

The Late 18th Century Poetry

Towards the end of the 18th century, poetry began to move away from the strict Augustan ideals and a new emphasis on the sentiments and feelings of the poet was established. This trend can perhaps be most clearly seen in the handling of nature, with a move away from poems about formal gardens and landscapes by urban poets and towards poems about nature as lived in. The leading exponents of this new trend include Thomas Gray, George Crabbe, Christopher Smart and Robert Burns as well as the Irish poet Oliver Goldsmith. These poets can be seen as paving the way for the Romantic Movement.

Poetry in the Augustan Age

The poetry of the 18th century differs entirely from that of another period in English literature. It differs alike in subject-matter, in spirit and in form. Matthew Arnold calls Pope and Dryden classics not of poetry, but of prose, he says that they are great is in the regions of half poetry.

There was rhetoric style of poetry which was very much different from the poetry of Shakespeare and Wordsworth. Their poetry was deeper and had a more imaginative perception of life and nature expressed in the language and rhythm of restrained emotions. On the other hand, rhetoric expresses feeling which is not deep and not quite sincere, and tries to strike and influence the reader instead of being satisfied with expressing itself and for that purpose, relies mainly on tricks of language such as antithesis, epigram etc.

Eighteenth-century poetry differs from ordinary poetry, in subject-matter, in spirit and in form. The spirit of ordinary poetry is one of the imagination and feeling, that is to say imaginative and emotional; that of 18th-century poetry is one of the commonsense and reason, that is to say intellectual and rational.

There were four very important limitations of subject-matter

(i) The exclusion of the supernatural form of poetry.

(ii) The exclusion of rural life and restriction to the life of the town and of good society.

(iii) The exclusion of external nature.

(iv) The exclusion of human emotions.

Lastly, the poetry of the 18th century differs widely in form, i.e. in language and metre, from that of preceding and subsequent poetry. This difference proceeds from a revolt against the poetical language of the 17th century.

Poetic Trends of the Augustan Age

Poetic trends of the age of Augustan can be classified under the following heads

Graveyard Poetry

Graveyard School of Poets refers to a group of 18th century poets, whose works dealt with the themes of death, sorrow and mortality. Often set in a graveyard, the poems of the Graveyard School mused on the alterations of life, the solitude of death and the grave and the anguish of bereavement. Much of the poetry of the Graveyard School can be seen as a response to and development from the disease of the 17th century melancholy. Graveyard school not only incorporates melancholy, but expands the range of emotional responses to death to include grief, tenderness, tearfulness, nostalgia and other states of mind.

Eric Parisot defines the term 'Graveyard Poetry' as "a relatively modern term used by critics to denote poetry that meditated on the 'Transience of life', the imminence of death and the consolation accorded by a Christian after-life".

Parisot further adds that the term at its narrowest specifically applies to four poems Thomas Parnell's *'A Night Piece on Death'* (1721), Robert Blair's *The Grave* (1743), Edward Young's *Night Thoughts* (1742-45) and Thomas Gray's *Elegy Written in a Country Churchyard* (1751). The Graveyard school, with its depictions of graves, churchyards, night, death and ghosts, has also been seen as laying the groundwork for Gothic literature.

The Ode

There are two important forms of the Ode (i) Pindaric Ode (ii) Horatian Ode

Pindaric Ode

Pindarics was a term for a class of loose and irregular odes greatly in fashion in England during the close of the 17th and the beginning of the 18th century. This ode was named after an ancient Greek poet, Pindar, who began writing choral poems that were meant to be sung at public events. It contains three triads; strophe, antistrophe and final stanza as epode, with irregular rhyme patterns and lengths of lines.

Horatian Ode

Horatian ode is a short lyric poem written in stanzas of two or four lines in the manner of the 1st-century-BC Latin poet Horace. In contrast to the lofty, heroic odes of the Greek poet Pindar (compare epinicion), most of Horace's odes are intimate and reflective; they are often addressed to a friend and deal with friendship, love, and the practice of poetry. In the early 18th century, Jonathan Swift, and Samuel Johnson revived the Horatian spirit.

Major Poets of the Augustan Age

Alexander Pope (1688-1744)

English poet, critic and satirist Alexander Pope was born in Lombard Street, London in 1688. He was the only child of Alexander Pope Senior, a linen draper and Edith Turner Pope. Both his parents were born Catholics and as a result, Pope's education was affected by the penal law in force at the time, which upheld the status of the established Church of England and banned Catholics from teaching on pain of perpetual imprisonment. Since, he was excluded from a public education, Pope was educated largely at home. He learned Greek and Latin under the tutelage of a local priest and later at Catholic school.

Literary Career and Works

He composed his *Pastorals* at Binfield. *The Pastorals* were published in the 6th part of Tonson's *Poetical Miscellanies*. This was followed by *An Essay on Criticism* published in May 1711, which was well received and established his literary reputation. His well known mock-heroic epic *The Rape of the Lock* was first published in 1712. It was based on a family quarrel between the Petres and Fermors, when the 7th Lord Petre cut off a lock of Miss Arabella Fermor's hair.

Around 1713, Pope alongwith Jonathan Swift, John Gay, John Arbuthnot and Thomas Parnell founded a literary club called the Scriblerus Club to satirise *All the false tastes in learning*. The character of *Martinus Scriblerus* was originally conceived as a focus for the club's satire against current trends in culture and scholarship. The name Martin was taken from John Dryden's comic character Sir Martin Mar-all, whose name had become synonymous with absurd error; Scriblerus was a reference to scribler, the contemporary term of contempt for a talentless writer.

The club's major production, *Memoirs of Martinus Scriblerus* was a collaboration of its members.

Pope's fame also rests on his translations of Homer. He translated Homer's *The Iliad* (1720), which took him six years to complete and later also undertook a translation of *The Odyssey* (1726). His other important works are *Windsor Forest, The Dunciad* and his *Epistles*.

During his late years, Pope moved to Twickenham. He died on the 30th of May, 1744 and he was buried in the parish church of Twickenham.

Short Description of Pope's Works

Work	Description
Pastorals	Pope's Pastorals were among his first published poems, appearing in the 6th part of Jacob Tonson's Poetical Miscellanies. It offered an idealised view of country life modeled on Virgil's pastorals.
Messiah	Poem which deals with Virgil's Fourth Eclogue, which was said to predict the birth of Christ.
Windsor Forest	Pope's first political poem, which celebrated the rule of Queen Anne and the Peace Treaty of Utrecht. Windsor Forest-a famous royal hunting ground, functions as a metaphor for political life of the nation. Poem dedicated to George Granville, Secretary of War in Queen Anne' government.
The Dunciad	Poem celebrates the Goddess Dullness and the progress of her agents across Britain. In the 1st version, Pope's target of attack was Lewis Theobald, who was replaced by Colly Cibber in 1742-43.
An Essay on Man	Philosophical essay written in heroic couplets, *i.e.,* concerned with vindicating ways of God to Man. Pope's arguments in the Essay derive in part from Bolingbroke' fragmentary philosophical writings. It comprises four epistles addressed to Lord Bolingbroke..These are: 1) Of the Nature and State of Man, with Respect to the Universe 2) Of the Nature and State of Man, with Respect to Himself as an Individual 3) Of the Nature and State of Man, with Respect to Society 4) Of the Nature and State of Man, with Respect to Happiness.
Epistle to a Lady	Verse letter written in heroic couplets, which is addressed to Martha Blount. It is a Horatian Epistle in form. Pope is critical of women, who live a public aristocratic life, while he celebrates Martha, a woman who shines in the private life.

An Essay on Criticism

'Tis hard to say, if greater want of skill
Appear in writing or in judging ill;
But, of the two, less dang'rous is th' offence
To tire our patience, than mislead our sense.
Some few in that, but numbers err in this,
Ten censure wrong for one who writes amiss;
A fool might once himself alone expose,
Now one in verse makes many more in prose.
'Tis with our judgments as our watches, none
Go just alike, yet each believes his own.
In poets as true genius is but rare,
True taste as seldom is the critic' share;
Both must alike from Heav'n derive their light,
These born to judge, as well as those to write.
Let such teach others who themselves excel,
And censure freely who have written well.
Authors are partial to their wit, 'tis true,
But are not critics to their judgment too?
Yet if we look more closely we shall find
Most have the seeds of judgment in their mind;
Nature affords at least a glimm'ring light;
The lines, tho' touch'd but faintly, are drawn right.

An Essay on Criticism: Summary

- Pope's *Essay on Criticism* is a didactic poem in heroic couplets, which was published in 1711. It is the nearest thing in 18th century English writing, to what might be called a 'Neo-classical manifesto'. It contains a thumbnail history of criticism from Aristotle to William Walsh. David Cody states that, "the essay was in part an attempt on Pope's part to identify and refine his own positions as poet and critic and his response to an ongoing critical debate, which centered on the question of whether poetry should be 'natural' or written according to predetermined 'artificial' rules inherited from the classical past."
- *The essay is divided into three sections, which deals with*
  - (i) The need of studying the principles of taste and improving out judgement by studying the ancients and holding them in high esteem.
  - (ii) Causes that hinder correct judgement.
  - (iii) Functions of a critic.
- According to Walter Jackson Bate "Pope lists three main characteristics essential for a good critic: awareness of his own limitations, knowledge of nature in its general forms and imitation of the ancients." Pope states that an ideal critic needs to possess taste, judgement and learning.

The Rape of the Lock

What dire Offence from am'rous Causes springs,
What mighty Contests rise from trivial Things,
I sing-This verse to CARYL, Muse! is due;
This, ev'n Belinda may vouchsafe to view:
Slight is the Subject, but not so the Praise,
If She inspire and He approve, my Lays.
Say what strange Motive, Goddess! cou'd compel
A well-bred Lord t'assault a gentle Belle?
Oh say what stranger Cause, yet unexplor'd,
Coud make a gentle Belle reject a Lord?
In tasks so bold, can little Men engage,
And in soft Bosoms, dwell such mighty Rage.
Sol thro' white Curtains shot a tim'rous Ray,
And ope'd those Eyes that must eclipse the Day:
Now Lap-dogs give themselves the rouzing Shake,
And sleepless Lovers, just at Twelve, awake:
Thrice rung the Bell, the Slipper knock'd the Ground,
And the press'd Watch return'd a silver sound,
Belinda still her downy Pillow prest,
Her guardian Sylph prolong'd the balmy rest.
'Twas he had summon'd to her silent Bed
The Morning Dream that hover'd o'er her Head.

The Rape of the Lock

This mock heroic epic was first published in 1712 with two cantos and later expanded into five cantos in 1714. It was dedicated to John Caryll. It was based on Lord Petre's cutting of a lock of hair of Arabella Fermor. In Pope's poem, Belinda is based on the historical Arabella Fermor and the Baron is the pseudonym for the historical Robert, Lord Petre.

The action of the poem begins with the rising Sun awakening the residents of a wealthy household. Though everyone, including the lapdogs, has risen, Belinda remains asleep. She dreams of a handsome youth, who informs her that she is protected by a 'Thousand bright inhabitants of air spirits' that were once human women, who now protect virgins. Belinda's guardian sylph is Ariel and her lapdog is named as Shock. The poem from the beginning acquaints us with the idleness, late rising and fondness for domestic pets of the aristocratic ladies. Pope criticises the frivolous aspect of femininity.

At a social gathering attended by many young and wealthy socialites where they play cards over coffee, the Baron takes up a pair of scissors and cuts off a lock of Belinda's hair. Belinda flies in rage. Clarissa who has aided the Baron in his crime urges Belinda to drop her anger in favour of good sense.

A battle then ensues between the ladies and the gentlemen, which Pope compares to a battle amidst the confusion, the lock is lost. In the concluding part of the poem, Pope assures Belinda that her lock has been immortalised in the heavens as a constellation.

Pope's mock-heroic treatment underscores the ridiculousness of a society in which values have lost all proportions and the trivial is handled with the gravity and solemnity that ought to be accorded to truly important issues. The poem is a reflection of artificial and hollow life of 18th century society.

Edward Young (1683-1765)

Edward Young was born at his father's rectory at Upham, near Winchester, where he was baptised on 3rd July, 1683. He was one of the most prominent English poets of 18th century, a dramatist and a literary critic also.

Literary Career and Works

Edward Young's first publication was an *Epistle to.... Lord Lansdoune* written in 1713, followed by a *Poem on the Last Day*, dedicated to Queen Anne. In 1714, he published *The Force of Religion: or Vanquished Love* which was dedicated to the Countess of Salisbury. It was about the execution of Lady

Jane Grey and her husband. He wrote an epistle to Joseph Addison *On the late Queen's Death and His Majestly's Accession to the Throne* in 1714, in which he hurried to shower praise on the new king. He met Philip, Duke of Wharton, whom he accompanied to Dublin in 1717. In the following years, he produced the play, *Busiris*. His play *Revenge* was dedicated to Wharton.

From 1725 to 1728, he published a series of seven satires on *The Universal Passion* dedicated to the Duke of Dorset, George Bubb Dodington, Sir Spencer Compton, Lady Elizabeth Germain and Sir Robert Walpole. In 1728, his satires were compiled into the collection, *Love of Fame, the Universal passion*. In the late 1720s and 1730s, he published a number of works including *The Instalment, The Foreign Address* etc.

Young was known for seeking patronage for his poetry, his theatrical works, and his career in the church. However, he failed mainly because he picked patrons whose fortunes were declining.

Night-Thoughts, considered among his most important works, was written in memory of his wife and step-daughter who died within year of each other. It is a long poem written in blank verse and published in nine parts in the years starting from 1742 to 1745.

An excerpt from the Poem 'Night Thoughts' also known as The Complaint : or Night Thoughts on Life, Death, and Immortality is given below

Night Thoughts

By Nature's law, what may be, may be now;
There's no prerogative in human hours:
In human hearts what bolder thought can rise,
Than man's presumption on to-morrow's dawn?
Where is tomorrow? In another world.
For numbers this is certain; the reverse
Is sure to none; and yet on this perhaps,
This peradventure, infamous for lies,
As on a rock of adamant we build
Our mountain hopes; spin out eternal schemes,
As we the fatal sisters would outspin,
And, big with life's futurities, expire.

In 1759, he published the critical prose. *Conjectures on Original Composition*, in which he emphasised the importance of originality being more valuable than classic indoctrination or imitation.He died at the age of 81 in Welwyn on 5th April, 1765.

John Gay (1685-1732)

John Gay, the English poet, was a highly prolific and respected writer in the 18th century London. He was born into an ancient Devonshire family in England as the youngest son of William Gay and his wife on 30th June, 1685.

Literary Career and Works

Gay had a deep love for literature and began his career as a poet and ballad-lyric writer. He had a quirky sense of humour and a talent for writing satirical and ironic pieces. His first published poem was a parody, *Wine*. His first play was *The Mohawks* which was never produced. His second play, *The Wife of Bath*, was produced at Drury Lane, a prominent theatre, in 1713. His poem *Rural Sports* first appeared in 1713. It was an evocative work that described in detail the country side and dealt with hunting and fishing. This poem was dedicated to Alexander Pope who was his lifelong supporter and a close friend.

He found his first big success in 1714 with the play, *The Shepherd Week*, a series of six mock classical poems drawn from rural English life. The purpose of writing this was to ridicule the Arcadian pastorals of Ambrose Philips. In 1716 his poem *Trivia* or, *The Art of Walking on the Streets of London*, was published. This poem was highly appreciated for its vivid descriptions of London and is considered to be his finest poem.

Though he produced many great works of literature over his long and productive career, his ballad opera *The Beggar's Opera* is the best known of his works. The ballad opera parodied the King's government and his Chief Minister, Robert Walpole. He used the symbols of highwaymen and thieves to depict the moral degradation of the society.

He died at the age of 47 on 4th December, 1732 in London.

James Thomson (1700-1748)

Scottish poet, James Thomson was born on 11th September, 1700, in Ednam, Roxburgh, Scotland. Taught at first by Robert Riccaltoun, Thomson then attended school at Jedburgh. In 1715, he matriculated at the University of Edinburgh, where he became a divinity student.

Literary Career and Works

Thomson went to London in 1725 where he earned his living as a tutor. He published his masterpiece, a long blank verse poem in four parts, called *The Season*. The first part *Winter* appeared in 1726, but its dedication procured only 20 guineas, not a patron. The poem was very well received, however, and it was followed by *Summer* (1727) and *Spring* (1728). The poems were applauded and imitated. Thomson's belief that the scientist and poet must collaborate in the service of God, as revealed through nature, found its best expression in *To the Memory of Sir Isaac Newton* (1727). The whole poem *The Seasons* including *Autumn*, was published in 1730.

Thomson's tragedy *Sophonisba* was produced at Drury Lane Theatre in 1730 with moderate success. He then sold the copyright of this play and that of *Spring*. He wrote a long poem based on his travels, *Liberty*, which was publilshed in five parts (1734-1736) and was a failure. After his patron Talbot's death in 1737, Thomson lost his sinecure. He retrieved his fortunes, however, with his tragedy *Agamemnon*, produced in 1738. Thomson's next tragedy, *Edward* and *Eleanora*, published in 1739, was banned for political reasons.

With his friends David Mallet, Thomson wrote in 1740, the masque *Alfred*, with music by Thomas Arne, for which he created the song *Rule, Britannia*. In 1744 Thomson's new patron, George Lyttleton, a lord commissioner of the Teasury, appointed him surveyor general of the Leeward Island, and in 1745 *Tancred* and *Sigismunda*, Thomson's most successful play, was produced. *The Castle of Indolence*, a poem written in imitation of Edmund Spenser and reflecting Thomson's love of idleness, appeared in 1748. He died in that year on 27th of August .

The Season

- The *Season* was the first sustained nature poem in English and concludes with a *Hymn to Nature*.
- The work was a revolutionary departure; its novelty lay not only in subject matter but in structure.
- What was most striking to Thomson's earliest readers was his audacity in unifying his poem without a 'plot' or other narrative device, thereby defying the Aristotelian criteria revered by the Neo-classicist critics.

Dr Samuel Johnson (1709-1784)

English poet, biographer, critic and lexicographer Dr Samuel Johnson was born in the country town of Lichfield in Staffordshire in 1709. As a child, Johnson was taken ill when he contracted scrofula (a tubercular infection of the lymph glands) from his nurse. Plagued by physical difficulties, Johnson found comfort in the written world.

He obtained his early education at Lichfield Grammar School and later attended Pembroke College, Oxford.

Literary Career and Works

At Oxford, Johnson translated Pope's *Messiah* in Latin, which was published in 1731. In 1734, he managed to complete a translation of Father Jeronymo Lobo's *Account of Abyssinia,* which became his first published book. In May 1738, Johnson's first major work, the poem *'London'-Imitation of the Third Satire of Juvenal,* was published anonymously. This was followed by his works, *Life of Mr Richard Savage, The Vanity of Human* Wishes (Imitation of The Tenth Satire of juvenal) and the play *Irene*.

Johnson's most monumental work, *A Dictionary of the English Language* was begun in 1746, when a group of publishers approached him to create a dictionary of English language. He worked for 9 years on this work, which was finally published in 1755. This work established his literary reputation.

Johnson's other important works are his satirical *Rasselas, Prince of Abyssinia, The Life of Ascham, Notes to Shakespeare and The Fountains: A Fairy Tale.* He is also known for his essays for the periodicals, The Rambler (1750-52) and *The Idler* (1758-60) and *The Lives of the Poets* (1779-81). In 1762, when George III came to the throne, Johnson was provided with a pension of £300 per year. During his late years, Johnson published his *A Journey to the Western Islands of Scotland* and *Prayers* and *Meditations*.

He died in 1784 at the age of 75 and was buried in Westminster Abbey.

London

Imitation of the Third Satire of Juveual

- The full title of the Poem is *London–Imitation of the Third Satire of Juvenal*.
- Johnson transforms Juvenal's cultural satire into a political one with its focus on the corruption in the court of King George II.
- It is a satire which addresses the condition of 18th century England, marked by various changes on the personal and public front.
- Johnson utilises the figure of Thales to develop his socio-political critique of the metropolitan space, represented by London. The poem begins with Thales leaving London for the countryside.

Johnson's Preface to the Plays of William Shakespeare

- Published in 1765, Johnson's *Preface to The Plays of William Shakespeare* is considered as a classic document of English literary criticism.
- According to Johnson, a great work of art is that which subsists through a long time and remains a classic despite variations of taste and change of manners. Shakespeare's works are such works, which have passed down from generation to generation.
- Johnson describes Shakespeare as the 'poet of nature', one who 'Holds up to his readers a faithful mirror of manners and of life'.

- Shakespeare's drama is peopled with characters that are not exaggerated, but men who speak and act as readers do.
- Johnson then goes on to describe the intermingling of comedy and tragedy in Shakespeare's plays. His plays are neither tragedies nor comedies, but compositions of a different kind; exhibiting the real state of nature, which consists of both good and evil, joy and sorrow.
- After listing Shakespeare's positive points and merits as a playwright, Johnson critically examines his faults. *Shakespeare's faults as a playwright* are
  - (i) He sacrifices virtue to convenience and writes without any moral purpose.
  - (ii) His plots are loosely constructed.
  - (iii) He pays no attention to unities of time or place.
  - (iv) He is imperfect in comic scenes, which become usually gross.
  - (v) His diction is pompous and his catastrophe is imperfectly produced.
  - (vi) His fondness for quibbles.
- However, Johnson also states that Shakespeare's faults owe more to the careless manner of their publication.
- Arthur Sherbo calls Johnson's *Preface* as 'His greatest single critical pronouncement' and 'a landmark in Shakespearean criticism'.

Lives of the Poets

- Johnson's *Lives of the Most Eminent English Poets* consists of short biographies and critical appraisals of 52 poets.
- It was originally written as 'Introductions' to a trade edition of the works of poets whom the booksellers selected for re-publication.
- The lives are ordered chronologically by date of death, not birth and range in length from a few pages to an entire volume.
- The poets described mostly belong to the 17th and 18th centuries.
- Poets covered in the volume range from Abraham Cowley, John Milton, John Dryden, Joseph Addison, and Alexander Pope to minor poets such as William Collins and William Shenstone.
- Poet's biographies are divided into three distinct parts: a narrative of the poet's life, a presentation of his character and a critical assessment of his main poems.
- Johnson himself stated about this work, "I know that I have not written anything more generally commended than the *Lives of the Poets*".

A Dictionary of the English Language

Samuel Johnson's *A Dictionary of the English Language* is one of the most famous dictionaries in history which contained 40000 words.

It included a history of the language, a grammar and an extensive list of words representing basic general vocabulary, based on the best conversation of contemporary London and the normal usage of respected writers. Its strong point was that each word was defined in detail and definitions illustrated with quotations covering every branch of learning.

According to Walter Jackson Bate, Johnson's Dictionary 'easily ranks as one of the greatest single achievements of scholarship and probably the greatest ever performed by one individual, who laboured under anything like the disadvantages in a comparable length of time'.

Thomas Gray (1716-1771)

English poet Thomas Gray was born in Cornhill, London in 1716. Gray owned his education and upbringing to his mother. He was educated at Eton and Cambridge. It was at Eton that Gray became friends with Horace Walpole, Richard West and Thomas Ashton. This group was termed as 'the Quadruple Alliance'.

Literary Career and Works

In 1739, Gray went on a continental tour with Walpole where they had a disagreement. However, they were reconciled in 1745 and Walpole later published Gray's *The Progress of Poetry* and *The Bard*. Gray was closely attached to Richard West and his death in 1742 dealt a grievous blow to Gray. It also inspired a *Sonnet on the Death of Richard West*. His *Elegy on a Country Churchyard,* on which he had probably been working intermittently from 1742, also perhaps owes something to West's death. A visit to the Lake District during 1760s led to the production of his *Journey among the English Lakes,* based on notes taken at that time.

He died on 30th July, 1771 in Cambridge.

Works of Gray

An Elegy Written in a Country Churchyard

The curfew tolls the knell of parting day,
The lowing herd winds slowly o'er the lea,
The ploughman homeward plods his weary way,
And leaves the world to darkness and to me.
Now fades the glimmering landscape on the sight,
And all the air a solemn stillness holds,
Save where the beetle wheels his droning flight
And drowsy tinklings lull the distant folds:
Save that from yonder ivy-mantled tower
The moping owl does to the moon complain
Of such as, wandering near her secret bower,

Molest her ancient solitary reign.
Beneath those rugged elms, that yew-tree' shade,
Where heaves the turf in many a mouldering heap,
Each in his narrow cell for ever laid,
The rude Forefathers of the hamlet sleep.
The breezy call of incense-breathing morn,
The swallow twittering from the straw-built shed,
The cock' shrill clarion, or the echoing horn,
No more shall rouse them from their lowly bed.
For them no more the blazing hearth shall burn,
Or busy housewife ply her evening care:
No children run to lisp their sire' return,
Or climb his knees the envied kiss to share,
Oft did the harvest to their sickle yield,
Their furrow oft the stubborn glebe has broke;
How jocund did they drive their team afield!
How bow'd the woods beneath their sturdy stroke!
Let not Ambition mock their useful toil,
Their homely joys and destiny obscure;
Nor Grandeur hear with a disdainful smile
The short and simple annals of the Poor.
Another came; nor yet beside the rill,
Nor up the lawn, nor at the wood was he;
'The next with dirges due in sad array
Slow through the church-way path we saw him borne,-
Approach and read (for thou canst read) the lay
Graved on the stone beneath yon aged thorn'.

An Elegy Written in a Country Churchyard

- Thomas Gray's *Elegy Written in a Country Churchyard* was first published in 1751.
- The Elegy is usually said to have been inspired by the death of Gray's friend, Richard West in 1742.
- The poem consists of 128 lines divided into 32 quatrains including three stanzas devoted to *the epitaph*.
- The poem invokes the classical idea of *memento mori*, a Latin phrase, which states plainly to all mankind, 'remember that you must die.'
- The speaker of the poem sees a country churchyard at sunset, which impels him to meditate on the nature of human mortality. The speaker muses on the inevitability of death.
- The speaker also deals with the futility of all human ambitions and aspirations since 'the paths of glory lead but to the grave.
- Both the rich and the poor desire to be remembered after death. The dying man desires some dear person to shed tears on his death as a mark of mourning.
- According to WV Moody and RM Lovett, "the Elegy is the finest flower of that literature of melancholy which Gray may be said to be haunted by a Hamlet like melancholy and sense of frustration."

William Collins (1721-1759)

English poet William Collins was born in Chichester, England in 1721, where his father served as Mayor. Collins was educated at Winchester College and at Magdalen College, Oxford.

Literary Career and Works

His first verses were published in a six penny pamphlet on *The Royal Nuptials. His Persian Eclogues* (1742) were published when he was only 17. This was followed by *Verses Humbly Address'd to Sir Thomas Hanmer* in 1743. In 1749, he also published the *Elegy on Thomson, and the Dirge in Cymbeline*. In the beginning of 1750, he composed the *Ode on the Popular Superstitions of the Highlands. Collins is also well-known for his twelve odes- Ode to Fear, Ode to Pity, Ode on the Poetical Character, Ode for Music, Ode to Evening, Ode to Mercy, Ode to Simplicity, Ode Written In The Beginning Of The Year 1746, Ode to Liberty, Ode to a Lady on the Death of Colonel Ross, Ode to Peace and The Manners An Ode.*

Collins died on 12th June 1759.

Oliver Goldsmith (1730-1774)

Anglo-Irish poet, playwright and novelist Oliver Goldsmith was born in Kilkenny West, Ireland in 1730. Goldsmith studied at Trinity College, Dublin. He coursed through a variety of professions, finally settling on medicine in 1752.

Literary Career and Works

For some years, he worked as an apothecary's assistant, school usher, physician and as a hack writer. However, he soon rose to fame with his *Enquiry into the Present State of Polite Learning in Europe.* Goldsmith also came to the notice of Samuel Johnson's, who invited Goldsmith to join his exclusive Turk's Head Club. Through Johnson's patronage, Goldsmith began to publish his first master works, including the novel *The Vicar of Wakefield*.

His other works include *The Citizen of the World* (a collection of essays, 1762), *An Elegy on the Death of a Mad Dog* (ironic poem, 1766), *The Good-Natur'd Man* (comic play, 1768), *She Stoops to Conquer* (a farce, 1773) and *The Deserted Village* (a poem on rural population and the Enclosure Movement, 1770).

Goldsmith died on 4th April, 1774, after suffering from kidney disease.

The Deserted Village

Sweet Auburn! loveliest village of the plain,
Where health and plenty cheer'd the labouring swain,
Where smiling spring its earliest visit paid,
And parting summer' lingering blooms delay'd:
Dear lovely bowers of innocence and ease,
Seats of my youth, when every sport could please:
How often have I loiter'd o'er thy green,
Where humble happiness endear'd each scene!
How often have I paused on every charm,
The shelter'd cot, the cultivated farm,
The never failing brook, the busy mill,
The decent church that topp'd the neighbouring hill,
The hawthorn bush, with seats beneath the shade,
For talking age and whispering lovers made!
How often have I bless'd the coming day,
When toil remitting lent its turn to play,
And all the village train, from labour free,
Led up their sports beneath the spreading tree:
While many a pastime circled in the shade,
The young contending as the old survey'd;
And many a gambol frolick'd o'er the ground,
And sleights of art and feats of strength went round.
And still, as each repeated pleasure tired,
Succeeding sports the mirthful band inspired;
The dancing pair that simply sought renown,
By holding out to tire each other down;
The swain mistrustless of his smutted face,
While secret laughter titter'd round the place;
The bashful virgin' sidelong looks of love,
The matron' glance that would those looks reprove.

The Deserted Village: Summary

- Consisting of 430 lines in heroic couplets, Goldsmith's poem *The Deserted Village* was published in 1770.
- The poem arose as a result of the Enclosure Movement, in which landowners closed off public lands in order to better organise and keep track of land and animals. The land that was previously shared with peasants, was now closed off. The movement had a negative impact on peasant farmers. It caused massive urbanisation as many farmers were forced to give up their shares of the land to wealthy landowners and move into the cities in search of work.
- The poem describes the desertion of rural areas and movement of population from rural to urban.
- Goldsmith is saddened at the sight of the depopulated village, whose natural innocence has been usurped by the artificiality of industrialisation against the topography of Auburn.
- He laments the loss of the simple, idyllic rural way of life that has disappeared due to changing economic conditions in 18th century England.
- According to RS Crane, "The lament over the ruin of Auburn must be regarded as simply the most memorable of a long series of pamphlets called forth in the sixties and seventies of the 18th century by the English agricultural revolution".

William Cowper (1731-1800)

English poet William Cowper was born in the rectory of Great Berkhampstead, Hertfordshire in 1731. After his mother's death, Cowper was sent to Dr Pittman's Boarding School. In 1748, he enrolled in the Middle Temple to pursue a Law degree.

Literary Career and Works

It was in 1779 that Cowper made his first appearance as an author by the *Olney Hymns,* written in conjunction with Newton.

This was followed by *John Gilpin*- a comic ballad, *The Task*- a poem in six books with poems such as *The Winter Evening, The Winter Morning Walk* and *The Winter Walk at Noon* and *The Castaway*-his last poem describing a sailor washed aboard. Cowper died of dropsy in the spring of 1800.

George Crabbe (1754-1832)

English poet and clergyman George Crabbe was born in Aldeburgh, Suffolk, England in 1754. Crabbe became a surgeon-apothecary in 1775. After 4 years, he abandoned his medical career to pursue a career in writing.

Literary Career and Works

In 1780, he travelled to London to gain a foothold in the literary establishment. After months of virtual destitution, he wrote a pleading letter to the highly influential statesman and philosopher, Edmund Burke, who, admiring Crabbe's writing, helped him have his long poem, *The Library* published. Burke helped him greatly in advancing his literary career and guiding his career in the church. Burke introduced him to the literary and artistic society of London, including Sir Joshua Reynolds and Samuel Johnson.

Crabbe is best known for his poem, *The Village,* written as a protest against Oliver Goldsmith's *The Deserted Village*. The poem concentrated on the poverty and bleakness of life in the region of Suffolk, a fishing village.

His other poems include *Poems* (1807), *The Borough* (1810), *Tales in Verse* (1812), *Tales of the Hall* (1819), and *Posthumous Tale* (1834) In 1814, Crabbe became Vicar of Trowbridge in Wiltshire, where he remained till his death. He died on 3rd February, 1832.

© The Village

The village life and every care that reigns
O'er youthful peasants and declining swains;
What labour yields and what, that labour past,
Age, in its hour of languor, finds at last;
What forms the real picture of the poor,
Demands a song-the Muse can give no more.
Fled are those times, if e'er such times were seen,
When rustic poets praised their native green;
No shepherds now, in smooth alternate verse,
Their country' beauty or their nymphs' rehearse;
Yet still for these we frame the tender strain,
Still in our lays fond Corydons complain,
And shepherds' boys their amorous pains reveal,
The only pains, alas! they never feel.
On Mincio' banks, in Caesar' bounteous reign,
If Tityrus found the Golden Age again,
Must sleepy bards the flattering dream prolong,
Mechanic echoes of the Mantuan song?
From truth and nature shall we widely stray,
Where Virgil, not where Fancy, leads the way?
Yes, thus the Muses sing of happy swains,
Because the Muses never knew their pains.
They boast their peasants' pipes, but peasants now
Resign their pipes and plod behind the plough;
And few amid the rural tribe have time
To number syllables and play with rhyme;
Save honest Duck, what son of verse could share
The poet' rapture and the peasant' care?
Or the great labours of the field degrade
With the new peril of a poorer trade?
From one chief cause these idle praises spring,
That themes so easy few forbear to sing;
They ask no thought, require no deep design,
But swell the song and liquefy the line;
The gentle lover takes the rural strain,
A nymph his mistress and himself a swain;
With no sad scenes he clouds his tuneful prayer,
But all, to look like her, is painted fair.

Robert Burns (1759-1796)

Scottish poet Robert Burns known as the Bard of Ayrshire was born in the village of Alloway, Ayrshire of South West Scotland in 1759. Despite their poverty, Burns's parents ensured that their son would have a good education. His father hired a tutor for him and also taught him himself.

Literary Career and Works

Most of Burns' early poetry was written in song form to well-known Scottish tunes, the first being *Handsome Nell,* a tribute to Nelly Kirkpatrick of Dalrymple. Burns' first published work of poetry was *Poems, Chiefly in the Scottish Dialect* in 1786.

This is also known as Burns's *Kilmarnock Volume*. This was intended to raise money for his emigration to West Indies, but it became so successful that Burns cancelled his plans of moving there. The *Kilmarnock Volume* was a mixture of several poems, Scots poems such as *The Twa Dogs, Scotch Drink, The Holy Fair, An Address to the Deil, The Death* and *Dying Words of Poor Maillie, To a Mouse* and *To a Louse*; six gloomy and histrionic poems in English and verse letters addressed to friends.

According to Mary Ellen Brown, *"The Kilmarnock* edition shows Burns' penchant for self-presentation and his ability to choose variable poses to fit the expectations of the intended receiver. Burns presents himself as an untutored rhymer, who wrote to counteract life's woes; he simulates anxiety over the reception of his poems; he pays tribute to the genius of the Scotch Poets Ramsay and Fergusson and he requests the reader's indulgence".

It also showcases Burns as a "local poet, turning life to verse in slight, spur-of-the-moment pieces, occasional rhymes made on local personages, often to the gratification of their enemies". Burns' other important work was *Tam O's Shanter,* a verse tale that depicted Tam's escape from witches. Written in eight-syllable couplets, the poem was based on a folk legend. During his later years, Burns worked as an Exciseman for the Excise Division in Dumfries. In addition to his duties as exciseman, he wrote numerous 'occasional' poems and did an immense amount of work for the two song collections.

Burns died on 21st July, 1796, at the age of 37.

EXAM BASED QUESTIONS

1 What name is given to the English literary period that emulated the Rome of Virgil, Horace, and Ovid?

(a) Augustan (b) Metaphysical
(c) Romantic (d) Neo-Romantic

2 Which of the following is not a common feature of neoclassical poetry?

(a) Imitation of classical forms and allusion to mythology
(b) An effort to represent human nature
(c) Use of the rhymed couplet
(d) Fantastic comparisons

3 Most neoclassical poets viewed the world in terms of a strictly ordered hierarchy. What was this hierarchy called?

(a) The Way of the World
(b) The Foundational Ladder
(c) The Order of Angels
(d) The Great Chain of Being

4 What literary work best captures a sense of the political turmoil, particularly regarding the issue of religion, just after the Restoration?

(a) Gay's Beggar's Opera
(b) Butler's Hudibras
(c) Fielding's Jonathan Wild
(d) Pope's Dunciad

5 Which metrical form was Pope said to have brought to perfection?

(a) the heroic couplet
(b) blank verse
(c) free verse
(d) the ode

6 Which work exposes the frivolity of fashionable London?

(a) Defoe's Robinson Crusoe
(b) Swift's Gulliver's Travels
(c) Richardson's Clarissa
(d) Pope's The Rape of the Lock

7 What mock epic begins: "What dire offence from am'rous causes springs, / What mighty contests rise from trivial things"?

(a) Dryden's 'Mac Flecknoe'
(b) Pope's 'The Rape of the Lock'.
(c) Pope's 'The Dunciad'
(d) Dryden's 'Absalom and Achitophel'

8 Why didn't Alexander Pope attend an English university?

(a) He lived in Italy until the age of 27
(b) Asthma, headaches, and spinal deformity made him an invalid
(c) He was a Catholic, and therefore forbidden from attending
(d) He just wasn't bright enough

9 Alexander Pope coined many a modern day cliché. Which of the following did not originate with him?

(a) To err is human, to forgive divine
(b) Let not the sun go down upon your wrath
(c) A little learning is a dangerous thing
(d) Fools rush in where angels fear to tread

10 What Pope poem begins, "In these deep solitudes and awful cells,/Where heav'nly-pensive contemplation dwells,/And ever-musing melancholy reigns;/What means this tumult in a vestal's veins?"

(a) The Rape of the Lock (b) Solitude: An Ode
(c) The Dunciad (d) Eloisa to Abelard

11 Pope made money by selling subscriptions to his translation of this classical epic.

(a) The Bhagavad Gita (b) The Odyssey
(c) The Illiad (d) The Aeneid

12 The Rape of the Lock is a parody of which epic poem?

(a) Paradise Lost (b) The Odyssey
(c) The Iliad (d) The Aeneid

13 Arabella Fermor was the historical inspiration for which character in the poem 'Rape of the Lock'?

(a) Clarissa (b) Ariel (c) Belinda (d) Thalestris

14 Robert, Lord Petre was the historical inspiration for which character in the poem 'Rape of the Lock'?

(a) The Baron (b) Sir Plume (c) Dapperwit (d) Sir Fopling

15 Who asked Pope to write a comic poem about the historical incident between Arabella Fermor and Lord Petre in order to reconcile their families?

(a) Joseph Addison (b) John Caryll
(c) Henry St. John, Lord Bolingbroke
(d) Jonathan Swift

16 Which character is named for an Amazonian Queen in Greek mythology in the poem 'Rape of the Lock'?

(a) Thalestris (b) Umbriel (c) Belinda (d) Clarissa

17 In Canto I of the poem 'Rape of the Lock', which character warns Belinda in a dream that some dire disaster will befall her that day'?

(a) Thalestris (b) Clarissa (c) Ariel (d) Umbriel

18 According to Pope's depiction of the supernatural sprites, what do indecisive women become in the poem 'Rape of the Lock'?

(a) Sylphs (b) Nymphs
(c) Gnomes (d) Salamanders

19 According to Pope's depiction of the supernatural sprites, what do coquettes become in the poem 'Rape of the Lock'?
(a) Nymphs (b) Salamanders (c) Sylphs (d) Gnomes

20 With what are the four types of sprites associated in the poem 'Rape of the Lock'
(a) The four nations governed by the British crown.
(b) The four phases of life
(c) The four elements
(d) The four points on a compass

21 During Belinda's dream, Ariel explains that the Sylphs are charged with protecting which type of woman?
(a) All Women (b) Virgins
(c) Young Wives (d) Old Women

22 Pope's reference to 'mighty rage' is an allusion to the fury of which epic hero in Homer's The Iliad?
(a) Menelaus (b) Achilles
(c) Agamemnon (d) Hector

23 The 'goddess' for whom Belinda performs her sacred rites is actually who or what?
(a) Belinda's accessories and cosmetics
(b) The Goddess of spleen
(c) Belinda's maid
(d) Belinda's reflection in the mirror

24 How does Belinda's toilette function within the poem?
(a) It does not serve a larger purpose within the poem.
(b) It explains Belinda's beauty.
(c) It establishes the poem's mock-heroic motifs.
(d) It protects her from any harm during the day.

25 Why does the Baron get up early in the poem 'Rape of the Lock'?
(a) To arrive at the party first
(b) To build an altar to love
(c) To get ready for the party
(d) To steal Belinda's hair

26 What does Pope specify is the primary function of Belinda's ringlets?
(a) To occasion poetry (b) To be beautiful
(c) To be objects of worship (d) To attract men

27 To where does Ariel deploy most of his army of Sylphs?
(a) Belinda's petticoat (b) Belinda's lapdog
(c) Belinda's earrings (d) Belinda's hair

28 Who arms the Baron with a pair of scissors in the poem 'Rape of the Lock'?
(a) Belinda (b) Sir Plume (c) Lord Petre (d) Clarissa

29 What does Thalestris think the Baron will do with the lock in the poem 'Rape of the Lock'?
(a) Show it off to all their friends
(b) Have it set into a ring
(c) Neither of the above
(d) Both of these

30 What happens to the lock of hair at the end of the poem?
(a) It is returned to its rightful owner
(b) It is set into a ring
(c) It is offered to the poet as a token of gratitude
(d) It is turned into a constellation

31 According to Samuel Johnson, 'No man but a blockhead ever wrote except for...:
(a) love' (b) honour' (c) money' (d) fun'

32 Whose great Dictionary, published in 1755, included more than 114,000 quotations?
(a) William Hogarth (b) Jonathan Swift
(c) Samuel Johnson (d) Ben Jonson

33 This famous neoclassical poet wrote on profound themes such as death, but he also had a lighter side. He once wrote an ode to a cat drowned in a tub of gold fishes.
(a) Alexander Pope (b) William Collins
(c) Thomas Gray (d) Ben Jonson

34 Whom does Alexander Pope satirise in the portrait of Sporus?
(a) Lady Wortley Montague (b) Joseph Addison
(c) Lord Shaftsbury (d) Lord Harvey

35 The expression 'Thy hand' great Anarch' occurs in a satire by
(a) Dryden (b) Pope (c) Johnson (d) Swift

36 Pope's The Rape of the Lock was published in 1712 in
(a) three cantos (b) four cantos
(c) five cantos (d) two cantos

37 Which among the following are not Pope's work?
(a) Journal (b) The Fatal Sisters
(c) Windsor Forest (d) Both (a) and (b)

38 Pope writes a scathing expose of the bad writers and pseudo-intellectuals of his day in
(a) Frankenstein (b) The Fatal Revenge
(c) Moral Epistler (d) Dunciad

39 The main idea of Pope 'The Dunciad' was taken from
(a) Absalom and Achitophel
(b) Mac Flecknoe
(c) The Medal
(d) An Epistle to Dr Arbuthnot

40 'Elegy to the Memory of an 'Unfortunate Lady' was written by
(a) William Collins (b) Alexander Pope
(c) William Blake (d) James Thomson

41 Pope's 'Essay on Man' can best be read as a poem of
(a) classical understanding of nature
(b) anti-romantic view of life
(c) sociological estimate of man
(d) philosophical apprehension of life

42 The famous poem 'Four Pastorals' describes
(a) festivals (b) the shepherds
(c) seasons (d) None of these

43 The year 1728 is important for two authors. Identify the correct combination.
(a) For Pope's 'The Dunciad' and John Gay's 'The Beggar's Opera'
(b) For Johnson's 'London' and fielding's 'Joseph Andrews'
(c) For Addison's 'Cato, A Tragedy' and Defoe's 'Robinson Crusoe'
(d) For Pope's Essay on Man and Richardson's Clarissa

44 In 'The Rape of the Lock' Pope repeatedly compares Belinda to
(a) the sun (b) the moon
(c) the North Star (d) the rose

45 Identify from the following. Which was the first publication of Edward Young?
(a) The Installment
(b) The Foreign Address
(c) Epistle to .... Lord Lansdowne
(d) Love of Fame, the Universal Passion

46 Which of the following work is considered as the most important work of Young?
(a) Night Thoughts
(b) Conjectures on Original Composition
(c) The Forced Religion on Vanquished Love
(d) Busiris

47 Which is the best known ballad work of John Gay?
(a) Trivia, or The Art of Walking in the Streets of London
(b) The Beggar's Opera
(c) Wine
(d) Rural Sports

48 Which of the following work of Thomson was banned for political reasons?
(a) Agamemnon (b) The Season
(c) Edward and Eleonara
(d) The Castle of Indolence

49 Dr Johnson's 'The Vanity of Human Wishes' expresses
(a) Epicureanism (b) Humanism
(c) Stoicism (d) Cynicism

50 The most obvious feature of Johnson's The Lives of the Poets is the euipoise between
(a) language and form (b) style and content
(c) biography and criticism (d) myth and archetype

51 With whom was Dr Johnson intimately associated in his personal life?
(a) Boswell (b) Dryden
(c) Alexander Pope (d) Lord Bolingbroke

52 Samuel Johnson's Lives of Poets (1781) was originally a series of introductions to the poets he wrote for a group of London publishers. They were collected as
(a) Lives of English Poets' Critical and Biographical Essays
(b) Prefaces, Biographical and Critical, to the Works of English Poets
(c) Notes, Biographical and Critical, on the Works of English Poets
(d) Lives of English Poets Biographical and Critical Notes

53 A journey to the Western Islands of Scotland was written by
(a) Samuel Johnson (b) Samuel Richardson
(c) Lawrence Sterne (d) Joseph Addison

54 Johnson's Dictionary of the English language published in the year
(a) 1719 (b) 1755 (c) 1739 (d) 1759

55 Which among the following literary work does not belong to 'Thomas Gray'?
(a) The Bard (b) Odes
(c) The Progress of Poetry (d) The Tiger

56 What is the source of inspiration behind Gray's 'An Elegy Written in a Country Churchyard'?
(a) Human nature (b) Death of Gray's friend
(c) Political tensions (d) None of these

57 'Ode to Evening' was written by
(a) William Blake (b) Jonathan Swift
(c) Alexander Pope (d) William Collins

58 Which work among the following is romantic in nature, but has been written in the prevailing mechanical couplets by William Collins?
(a) Oriental Eclogues (b) Rule Britannia
(c) The Seasons (d) The Castle of Indolence

59 Collins is well known for his
(a) Epistle to Sir Thomas Hanmer on his edition of Shakespeare's works
(b) Dirge in Cymbeline
(c) Twelve Odes
(d) Elegy on Thomson

60 Who invited Goldsmith to join Turk's Head Club?
(a) Thomas Gray (b) Johnson
(c) Collins (d) John Gay

61 Goldsmith's poem 'The Deserted Village' describes
(a) desertion of rural areas (b) desertion of urban areas
(c) decline in necessary supply (d) the condition of labourers

62 'The Winter Morning' forms part of a longer poem by
(a) Cowper (b) Blake (c) Burns (d) Byron

63 Which work among the following does not belong to 'William Cowper'?
(a) Female Orators
(b) On the Receipt of my Mother's Picture
(c) Stage Realism (d) Both 'a' and 'c'

64 **Burns' poetry 'Poems, chiefly in the Scottish Dailect' is also known as**
(a) Kilmarnock Volume (b) Tam O's Shanter
(c) The Twa Dogs (d) The Holy Fair

65 **Tale of a Tub is about**
(a) warring political factions
(b) struggling lower-class people
(c) controversial philosophical documents
(d) contending religious parties

66 **.......is the masterpiece of Pope.**
(a) To Spring (b) The Rape of the Lock
(c) Mosaic of Quotations, Parodies and Allusions
(d) Both 'b' and 'c'

67 **'The Lives of the Poets' is the masterpiece of ..... .**
(a) Thomas Gray (b) Oliver Goldsmith
(c) Samuel Johnson (c) Henry Fielding

68 **'The Village' written as a protest against 'The Deserted Village' is a famous poem of .... .**
(a) William Cowper (b) Oliver Goldsmith
(c) George Crabbe (d) Robert Burns

69 **The Poem 'Ode on the Poetical Character' was written by.......**
(a) Thomas Gray
(b) William Collins
(c) Samuel Johnson
(d) Oliver Goldsmith

70 **The .... edition shows Burn's penchant for self presentation and his ability to choose variable poses to fit the expectations of the intended receiver.**
(a) The Kilmarnock
(b) Tam O's Shanter
(c) Posthumous Tale
(d) The Castaway

71 **Which of the following statements about' Alexander Pope' is incorrect?**
(a) Pope translated half of the 'Odyssey' and Elijah Frenton and John Milton finished the work
(b) 'Dunciad' satire of Pope was begun originally as a controversy concerning Shakespeare
(c) 'Essay on Man' of Pope was to indicate the way of God to man
(d) Pope wrote Moral Epistles

72 **Which of these statements about 'Graveyard Poetry' is correct?**
(a) It refers to a group of 16th century poets
(b) These works dealt with the themes of death, sorrow and mortality
(c) These poems were often set in a graveyard
(d) These poems were a response to and development from the disease of melancholy

73 **Which of these statements about 'Lives of the Poets' is correct?**
(a) It is written by Daniel Defoe
(b) It describes poets belonging to the 20th century
(c) It consists of short biographies and critical appraisals of 100 poets
(d) The poets biographies are divided into three distinct parts

74 **Which of the following statements is incorrect?**
(a) Pope's 'Messiah' was translated in latin by Samuel Johnson
(b) The famous poem 'Season' was originally written by Samuel Johnson
(c) 'A Dictionary of the English Language', published in 1755, was the most monumental work of Samuel Johnson
(d) The poem 'London' by Samuel Johnson was a satire on the 18th century England

75 **Which of the following statements is incorrect?**
(a) The poem 'The Deserted Village' was written as a protest against George Crabbe's poem 'The Village'
(b) 'The Deserted Village' describes the desertion of rural areas due to industrialisation
(c) 'The Village' concentrated on the poverty and bleakness of life in a Fishing Village.
(d) Oliver Goldsmith used 430 lines in heroic couplets for the poem 'The Deserted Village'

76 **Which of the following pairs is correctly matched?**
(a) The Battle of the Books : Quarrel between ancient and modern authors
(b) The Rape of the lock : Tribute to 'The rude forefathers of the Hamlet'
(c) Gray's Elegy : Accumulation of wealth and the consequent loss of human lives.
(d) The Deserted Village : Quarrel between two families caused by Lord Petre

77 **Which of these author-text pairs is correctly matched?**
(a) Alexander Pope : She Stoops to Conquer
(b) Henry Fielding : Essay on Man
(c) Richard Sheridan : The Rivals
(d) Oliver Goldsmith : Joseph Andrews

78 **Which of the following pairs is incorrectly matched?**
(a) Thomas Paine : The Age of Reason
(b) William Cowper : The Task
(c) Oliver Goldsmith : The Female Quixote
(d) Richard Sheridan : The School for Scandal

79 **Which of the following pairs is correctly matched?**
(a) Pope : The Winter Morning Walk
(b) Johnson : The Winds or Forest
(c) Burns : Songs of Innocence
(d) Cowper : The Winter Evening

80 **Which of the following pairs is not matched correctly?**
(a) A Poem on The Last Day : Edward Young
(b) The Seasons : Thomas Gray
(c) Ode to Fear : William Collins
(d) Handsome Nell : Robert Burns

Directions (Q. No.s 82-83) *In the questions given below are two statements labelled as Assertion (A) and Reason (R). In the context of two statements, which one of the following is correct?*

Codes

(a) Both A and R are correct, and R is the correct explanation of A
(b) Both A and R are correct but R is not the correct explanation of A
(d) Both A and R are correct
(d) Neither A nor R is correct

81 **Assertion** (A) 'The essence of poetry is the invention, which produces surprises and delights.
Reason (R) Poetry is always full of delights.

82 **Assertion** (A) In 'The Rape of the Lock', Pope talks about the vanity of life of the upper class youth.
Reason (R) Youth are busy in partying, playing cards and insulting each other.

83 **Assertion** (A) Henry Fielding has been acclaimed. with the 'Father of the English Novel'.
Reason (R) His works showed major development like the decline of the drama and rise of the novel.

84 Which of the following is in correct chronological order about the publication of works?

(a) Tale of a Tub, Rape of the Lock, Peace of Ryswick
(b) Peace of Ryswick, Tale of Tub, Rape of the Lock
(c) Peace of Ryswick, Rape of the Lock, Tale of the Tub
(d) Rape of the Lock, Peace of Ryswick, Tale of a Tub

85 Which of the following is in chronological order according to the publication of works?

(a) Elegy in a Country Churchyard, The Descent of Odin, Northern Antiquities
(b) The Descent of Odin, Elegy is Country Churchyard, Northern Antiquities
(c) The Descent of Odin, Northern Antiquities, Elegy in a Country Churchyard
(d) Elegy in Country Churchyard, Northern Antiquities, The Descent of Odin

86 Consider the following statements
The Rape of the Lock is

1. a mock heroic epic, first published in 1712.
2. the poem is a reflection of the artificial and hollow life of 18th century society.
3. a ballad, first published in 1705.
4. not a reflection of artificial and hollow life of 18th century society.

Which of the statements given above are correct?

(a) 1 and 4 (b) 1 and 2
(c) 3 and 2 (d) 3 and 2

87 Consider the following statements.

1. Johnson received three hundred pounds as yearly pension granted by George III.
2. Johnson founded literary club with Joshua Reynolds.
3. Bunyan belongs to the Augustan Age.

Which of the statements given above are correct?

(a) 1 and 2 (b) 1 and 3
(c) 2 and 3 (d) All of these

88 Consider the following statements, 'London' is

1. written by Samuel Richardson.
2. written in heroic couplets and published in 1738.
3. socio-political critique of the metropolitan space represented by London.
4. not a socio-political critique of the metropolitan space represented by London.

Which of the statements given above are correct?

(a) 1 and 4 (b) 1 and 2
(c) 3 and 4 (d) 3 and 2

89 'An Elegy written in a Country Churchyard' is

1. written by Thomas Gray and published in 1751.
2. the elegy has been inspired by the death of Gray's wife in 1745.
3. the poem does not deal with the futility of all human ambitions and aspirations.
4. the poem invokes the classical idea of memento moria.

Which of the statements given above are correct?

(a) 1 and 4 (b) 1 and 2
(c) 3 and 4 (d) 3 and 2

90 Consider the following statements.
'The Deserted Village' is

1. written by Oliver Goldsmith and published in 1830.
2. consists of 800 lines in iambic pentameter.
3. arose as a result of the Enclosure Movement.
4. the poem which describes the desertion of rural areas and movement of population from rural to urban.

Which of the statements given above are correct?

(a) 1 and 4 (b) 1 and 2 (c) 3 and 4 (d) 3 and 2

91 What is common to the following works? Identify the correct description below.

1. Night Piece of Death
2. The Grave
3. Night Thoughts
4. Elegy Written in a Country Churchyard

Codes

(a) All belong to the oeuvre of works by the University Wits
(b) All are examples of 'Graveyard Poetry'
(c) All are examples of 'Literature of Sensibility'
(d) All are examples of Romantic poetry

92 What is common to the following poets? Identify the correct description below.

1. Thomas Parnell
2. Robert Blair
3. Edward Young
4. Thomas Gray

Codes

(a) All are poets, who belong to the group of 18th century poets known as Graveyard School of poets
(b) All of them, wrote 'Literature of Sensibility'
(c) All of them wrote periodical essays
(d) All of them wrote farces and pantomimes

93 What is common in the following poets? Identify the correct description below? .

1. Dr Samuel Johnson
2. Thomas Gray
3. William Collins
4. Oliver Goldsmith

Codes

(a) All were important poets of the Augustan Age
(b) All were important novelists of the Augustan Age
(c) All were famous dramatists of the Elizabethan Age
(d) All were famous dramatists of the Modern Age

94 Consider the following poems

1. The Art of walking on the streets of London
2. The Force of Religion: Or Vanquished Love
3. To the Memory of Sir Issac Newton
4. Night Thoughts

Which of the above given are the poems of Edward Young?

(a) 1 and 2
(b) 2 and 3
(c) 2 and 4
(d) 3 and 4

95 Consider the following poetic works

1. An Elegy on the Death of a Mad Dog
2. John Gilpin
3. The Borough
4. Posthumous Tale

Which of the above poems belong to George Crabbe?

(a) 1 and 2 (b) 2 and 3
(c) 1 and 3 (d) 3 and 4

96 Match the following poems with their Augustan Poets.

Poem	Augustan Poet
1. Pastorals	A. Alexander Pope
2. Love of Fame, The Universal Passion	B. Edward Young
3. Wine	C. John Gay
4. The Seasons	D. James Thomson

Codes

(a) 1-A, 2-B, 3-C, 4-D
(b) 1-D, 2-C, 3-B, 4-A
(c) 1-B, 2-D, 3-A, 4-C
(d) 1-C, 2-A, 3-D, 4-B

97 Match the following Neo-classical poets with their poems.

Neo-classical Poet	Poem
1. Dr. Samuel Johnson	A. The Deserted Village
2. Thomas Gray	B. Ode to Mercy
3. William Collins	C. The Progress of Poetry
4. Oliver Goldsmith	D. London-Imitation of the Third Satire of Juvenal

Codes

(a) 1-a, 2-B, 3-C, 4-D (b) 1-D, 2-C, 3-B, 4-A
(c) 1-B, 2-D, 3-A, 4-C (d) 1-C, 2-A, 3-D, 4-B

98 Match the following poetical works with their poets.

Poetical Work	Poet
1. The Task	A. William Collins
2. Tales in Verse	B. William Cowper
3. Ode to Peace	C. Robert Burns
4. The Holy Fair	D. George Crabbe

Codes

(a) 1-A, 2-B, 3-C, 4-D (b) 1-D, 2-C, 3-B, 4-A
(c) 1-B, 2-D, 3-A, 4-C (d) 1-C, 2-A, 3-D, 4-B

99 Match the following poets with their works.

(Poet)	(Work)
1. Alexander Pope	A. The Beggar's Opera
2. John Gay	B. The Castaway
3. William Collins	C. Messiah
4. William Cowper	D. Ode to Simplicity

Codes

(a) 1-A, 2-B, 3-C, 4-D (b) 1-D, 2-C, 3-B, 4-A
(c) 1-B, 2-D, 3-A, 4-C (d) 1-C, 2-A, 3-D, 4-B

100 Match the following works with their authors.

List I	List II
A. The Good Natured Man	1. Thomas Gray
B. The Vanity of Human Wishes	2. Alexander Pope
C. The Fatal Sisters	3. Oliver Goldsmith
D. Essay on Man	4 Samuel Johnson

Codes

	A	B	C	D		A	B	C	D
(a)	1	3	2	4	(b)	4	2	3	1
(c)	3	4	1	2	(d)	1	3	4	2

101 Match the following works with their authors.

List I	List II
A. The Progress of Error	1. Joseph Addison
B. Stage Realism	2. Edward Gibbon
C. Roderick	3. William Cowper
D. History	4. Tobias Smollett

Codes

	A	B	C	D		A	B	C	D
(a)	3	1	4	2	(b)	4	3	2	1
(c)	1	2	3	4	(d)	1	3	2	4

102 Match the following.

List I (Books)	List II (Authors)
A. Windsor Forest	1. Adam Smith
B. Wealth of Nations	2. Thomas Gray
C. The Progress of Poetry	3. Alexander Pope
D. The Vanity of Human Wishes	4. Samuel Johnson

Codes

	A	B	C	D		A	B	C	D
(a)	1	2	3	4	(b)	3	1	2	4
(c)	4	3	2	1	(d)	1	3	2	4

103 In the following series, which of the set is correctly matched?

(a) Shakespeare- The Fatal Sisters, Thomas Gray-An Address to King William, Joseph Addison- Macbeth, William Cowper- The Progress of Error

(b) Shakespeare- The Progress of Error, Thomas Gray, Macbeth, Joseph Addison- An Address to King William William Cowper- The Fatal Sisters

(c) Shakespeare- Macbeth, Thomas Gray- The Fatal Sisters Joseph Addison- An Address to King William, William Cowper- The Progress of Error

(d) Shakespeare- Macbeth, Thomas Gray- An Address to King William, Joseph Addison- The Fatal Sisters, William Cowper - The Progress of Error

104 In the given series, which set has all the alternatives matched correctly?

(a) Windsor Forest-Alexander Pope, The Castle of Indolence-James Thomson, The Bard-Thomas Gray, A Marriage Ring-George Crabbe

(b) Windsor Forest-George Crabbe, The Castle of Indolence-Thomas Gray, The Bard James Thomson, A Marriage Ring-Alexander Pope.

(c) Windsor Forest-Thomas Gray, The Castle of Indolence-James Thomson, The Bard-Alexander Pope, A Marriage Ring-George Crabbe

(d) Windsor Forest-James Thomson, The Castle of Indolence-George Crabbe, The Bard-Alexander Pope, A Marriage Ring-Thomas Gray

105 In the given series, which one has all the neo-classical poets matched correctly with their poems?

(a) John Gay-A Red Red Rose, Dr. Samuel Johnson-The Manners An Ode William Collins From the Vanity of Human Wishes, Robert Burns-To a Young Lady, With some Lampreys.

(b) John Gay-To a Young Lady, With some Lampreys, Dr. Samuel Johnson-From The Vanity of Human Wishes, William Collins. The Manners An Ode, Robert Burns-A Red, Red Rose.

(c) John Gay-From the Vanity of Human Wishes, Dr. Samuel Johnson-A Red, Red Rose, William Collins-To a Young Lady, With some Lampreys, Robert Burns-The Manners An Ode.

(d) John Gay-The Manners An ode, Dr. Samuel Johnson-To a Young Lady, With Some Lampreys, William Collins-A Red, Red Rose, Robert Burns-From 'he Vanity of Human Wishes.

106 Alexander Pope stated, 'First follow Nature and your judgement frame by her just standard, which is still, i.e., always the same.'

In which essay did Pope state the above lines?

(a) An Essay on Man (b) Essay on Criticism
(c) The Dunciad (d) None of these

107 Eric Parisot defines the term 'Graveyard Poetry' as "a relatively modern term used by critics to denote poetry that meditated on the Transience of life, the imminence of death and the consolation accorded by a Christian after-life". The Graveyard school, with its depictions of graves, churchyards, night, death and ghosts, has also been seen as laying the groundwork for

(a) Romantic Literature
(b) Modern Literature
(c) Gothic Literature
(d) None of these

108 Who commented, 'Order is Heaven's First law'?

(a) William Blake (b) John Donne
(c) William Shakespeare (d)Alexander Pope

109 David Cody states that the essay was "in part an attempt on Pope's part to identify and refine his own positions as poet and critic and his response to an ongoing critical debate, which centered on the question of whether poetry should be 'natural' or written according to predetermined 'artificial' rules inherited from the classical past."

Which essay of Pope is referred to in the above statement?

(a) An Essay on Man (b) Messiah
(c) Essay on Criticism (d) The Rape of the Lock

110 Thrice rung the Bell, the Slipper knock'd the Ground, And the press'd Watch return'd a silver sound, Belinda still her downy Pillow prest, Her guardian Sylph proln'gd the balmy rest. Twas he had summon'd to her silent Bed The Morning Dream that hover'd o'er her Head'. Name the poem and the poet of the above lines.

(a) Poem on the Last Day, Edward Young
(b) The Rape of the Lock, Alexander Pope
(c) The Season, James Thomson
(d) The Vanity of Human Wishes, Samuel Johnson

111 "These satyrs have been favourably received at home and abroad. I am not conscious of the least malevolence to any particular person through all the characters: though some persons may be selfish as to engross a general application to themselves." The above lines are a preface from Edward Young's work which is a series of seven satires. Identify the work.

(a) Love of Fame, the Universal Passion
(b) London-lmitation of the Third Satire of Juvenal
(c) Night Thoughts on Life, Death and Immortality
(d) The Art of Walking on the Streets of London

112 'I wake-How happy they, who wake no more Yet that were vain. if dreams infest the grave.' The above lines have been taken from Young's Night Thought's which was written in the memory of his dead .

(a) Wife and step-daughter (b) Mother and wife
(c) Wife and daughter (d) Wife and step-sister

113 'Through winter streets to your course aright;
How to walk clean by day, and safe by night;
How Jostling crowds, with prudence, to decline;
When to assert the wall, and when resign'
Name the poem of the above lines.

(a) The Beggar's Opera (b) Trivia
(c) The Castle of Indolence (d) The Season

114 'See, Winter comes to rule the varied year,
Sullen and sad, With all his rising train
Vapours, clouds, and storms Be these my theme'
The above lines have been taken from Thomson's work. Identify the work.

(a) The Seasons: Spring
(b) To the Memory of sir Isaac Newton
(c) The Seasons: Winter
(d) Agamemnon

115 "Shakespeare has written without rules and he neglected the laws of propriety". Whose words are these?

(a) Steele (b) Samuel Johnson
(c) Samuel Richardson (d) None of these

116 "Poetry is the art of uniting pleasure with truth by calling imagination to the help of reason". Whose statement is this? '

(a) Johnson
(b) George Lillo
(c) Steele
(d) None of the above

117 According to WV Moody and RM Lovett, "the Elegy is the finest flower of that literature of Melancholy "which Gray may be said to be haunted by a Hamlet, like Melancholy and sense of frustration."

Which work of Gray is referred to in the above line?

(a) Poems by Mr Gray
(b) An Elegy written in a Country Churchyard
(c) An Ode on a Distant Prospect of Eton College
(d) Ode Performed in the Senate-House at Cambridge

118 "Beauties in vain their pretty eyes may roll;
Charms strike the sight, but merit wins the soul."

Which of the following poets in which of his/her works has used the above lines?

(a) Alexander Pope, The Rape of the Lock .
(b) Edward Young, Night Thoughts: Or, The Complaint And The Consolation
(c) John Gay, The Beggar's Opera
(d) James Thomson, The City of Dreadful Night

119 "How happy is the blameless vestal's lot!
The world forgetting, by the world forgot.
Eternal sunshine of the spotless mind!
Each pray'r accepted, and each wish resign'd"

Which of the following poets in which of his/her works has used the above lines?

(a) Alexander Pope, Eloisa to Abelard
(b) Edward Young, Poetical Works of the Rev. Dr. Edward Young
(c) John Gay, The Mad Dog
(d) Thomas Gray, An Elegy Written In A Country Churchyard

120 "Hope springs eternal in the human breast;
Man never Is, but always To be blest.
The soul, uneasy, and confin'd from home,
Rests and expatiates in a life to come."

Which of the following poets in which of his/her works has used the above lines?

(a) Alexander Pope, An Essay on Man .
(b) John Gay, 'The Poet and the Rose', Fables
(c) Thomas Gray, Ode on the Death of a Favourite Cat, Drowned in a Tub of Goldfishes
(d) William Cowper, The Complete Poetical Works of William Cowper

121 "At thirty a man suspects himself a fool;
Knows it at forty; and reforms his plan;
At fifty chides his infamous delay,
Pushes his prudent purpose to resolve;
In all the magnanimity of thought
Resolves; and re-resolves; then dies the same."

Which of the following poets in which of his/her works has used the above lines?

(a) Alexander Pope, The Rape of the Lock
(b) Edward Young, Night Thoughts: Or, The Complaint And The Consolation
(c) John Gay, The Beggar's Opera
(d) James Thomson, The City of Dreadful Night

122 "For her own breakfast she'll project a scheme,
Nor take her tea without a stratagem."

Which of the following poets in which of his/her works has used the above lines?

(a) Alexander Pope, Eloisa to Abelard
(b) Edward Young, Poetical Works of the Rev. Dr. Edward Young
(c) John Gay, The Mad Dog
(d) Thomas Gray, An Elegy Written In A Country Churchyard

123 Who takes a woman must be undone,
That basilisk is sure to kill.
The fly that sips treacle is lost in the sweets,
So he that tastes woman, woman, woman,
He that tastes woman, ruin meets.

Which of the following poets in which of his/her works has used the above lines?

(a) Alexander Pope, The Rape of the Lock
(b) Edward Young, Night Thoughts: Or, The Complaint And The Consolation

(c) John Gay, The Beggar's Opera
(d) James Thomson, The City of Dreadful Night

124 And though you duck them ne'er so long,
Not one salt drop e'er wets their tongue;
'Tis hence they scandal have at will,
And that this member ne'er lies still.

Which of the following poets in which of his/her works has used the above lines?

(a) Alexander Pope, Eloisa to Abelard
(b) Edward Young, Poetical Works of the Rev. Dr. Edward Young
(c) John Gay, The Mad Dog
(d) Thomas Gray, An Elegy Written In A Country Churchyard

125 I hate the man who builds his name
On ruins of another's fame.
Thus prudes, by characters o'erthrown,
Imagine that they raise their own.
Thus Scribblers, covetous of praise,
Think slander can transplant the bays.

Which of the following poets in which of his/her works has used the above lines?

(a) Alexander Pope, An Essay on Man
(b) John Gay, "The Poet and the Rose", Fables
(c) Thomas Gray, Ode on the Death of a Favourite Cat, Drowned in a Tub of Goldfishes
(d) William Cowper, The Complete Poetical Works of William Cowper

126 Woman's mind
Oft' shifts her passions, like th'inconstant wind;
Sudden she rages, like the troubled main,
Now sinks the storm, and all is calm again.

Which of the following poets in which of his/her works has used the above lines?

(a) Alexander Pope, Moral Essays
(b) John Gay, Dione
(c) Thomas Gray, The complete English poems of Thomas Gray
(d) William Cowper, The Task and Other Poems

127 "Your woe hath been my anguish; yea, I quail
And perish in your perishing unblest.
And I have searched the highths and depths, the scope
Of all our universe, with desperate hope
To find some solace for your wild unrest."

Which of the following poets in which of his/her works has used the above lines?

(a) Alexander Pope, The Rape of the Lock
(b) Edward Young, Night Thoughts: Or, The Complaint And The Consolation
(c) John Gay, The Beggar's Opera
(d) James Thomson, The City of Dreadful Night

128 "Full many a gem of purest ray serene
The dark unfathom'd caves of ocean bear:
Full many a flower is born to blush unseen,
And waste its sweetness on the desert air."

Which of the following poets in which of his/her works has used the above lines?

(a) Alexander Pope, Eloisa to Abelard
(b) Edward Young, Poetical Works of the Rev. Dr. Edward Young
(c) John Gay, The Mad Dog
(d) Thomas Gray, An Elegy Written In A Country Churchyard

129 'From hence, ye Beauties, undeceiv'd,
Know one false step is ne'er retriev'd,
And be with caution bold.
Not all that tempts your wand'ring eyes
And heedless hearts, is lawful prize;
Nor all, that glisters, gold.'

Which of the following poets in which of his/her works has used the above lines?

(a) Alexander Pope, An Essay on Man
(b) John Gay, "The Poet and the Rose", Fables
(c) Thomas Gray, Ode on the Death of a Favourite Cat, Drowned in a Tub of Goldfishes
(d) William Cowper, The Complete Poetical Works of William Cowper

130 "Yet, ah! why should they know their fate,
Since sorrow never comes too late,
And happiness too swiftly flies?
Thought would destroy their Paradise.
No more;-where ignorance is bliss,
'Tis folly to be wise."

Which of the following poets in which of his/her works has used the above lines?

(a) Alexander Pope, Moral Essays
(b) John Gay, Dione
(c) Thomas Gray, The complete English poems of Thomas Gray
(d) William Cowper, The Task and Other Poems

131 'Now stir the fire, and close the shutters fast,
Let fall the curtains, wheel the sofa round,
And, while the bubbling and loud hissing urn
Throws up a steamy column and the cups
That cheer but not inebriate, wait on each,
So let us welcome peaceful ev'ning in.'

Which of the following poets in which of his/her works has used the above lines?

(a) Alexander Pope, An Essay on Man
(b) John Gay, "The Poet and the Rose", Fables
(c) Thomas Gray, Ode on the Death of a Favourite Cat, Drowned in a Tub of Goldfishes
(d) William Cowper, The Complete Poetical Works of William Cowper

132 'Eternity for bubbles proves at last a senseless bargain.'

Which of the following poets in which of his/her works has used the above lines?

(a) Alexander Pope, Moral Essays
(b) John Gay, Dione
(c) Thomas Gray, The complete English poems of Thomas Gray
(d) William Cowper, The Task and Other Poems

133 "I am monarch of all I survey,
My right there is none to dispute,
From the centre all round to the sea,
I am lord of the fowl and the brute.
o solitude! Where are the charms
That sages have seen in thy face?
Better dwell in the midst of alarms,
Than reign in this horrible place."

Which of the following poets in which of his/her works has used the above lines?

(a) Alexander Pope, An Essay on Criticism
(b) William Cowper, The Poetical Works Of William Cowper
(c) William Blake, Songs of Experience
(d) Robert Burns, The Complete Poetical Works of Robert Burns

134 "O, wad some Power the giftie gie us
To see oursels as others see us!
It wad frae monie a blunder free us,
An' foolish notion."

Which of the following poets in which of his/her works has used the above lines?

(a) Alexander Pope, An Essay on Criticism
(b) William Cowper, The Poetical Works Of William Cowper
(c) William Blake, Songs of Experience
(d) Robert Burns, The Complete Poetical Works of Robert Burns

135 'But pleasures are like poppies spread,
You seize the flower, it's bloom is shed;
Or, like the snow-fall in the river,
A moment white, then melts forever.'

Which of the following poets in which of his/her works has used the above lines?

(a) William Blake, "Barren Blossom"
(b) Robert Burns, Tam O'Shanter
(c) Alexander Pope, An Essay on Criticism
(d) William Cowper, The Poetical Works Of William Cowper

Directions (Q. Nos. 136-140) *Read the given poem and answer the questions that follow.*

A Bird Came Down

A Bird, came down the Walk -
He did not know I saw
He bit an Angle Worm in halves
And ate the fellow, raw,
And then, he drank a Dew
From a convenient Grass -
And then hopped sidewise to the Wall
To let a Beetle pass -
He glanced with rapid eyes,
That hurried all abroad -
They looked like frightened Beads, I thought,
He stirred his Velvet Head. -
Like one in danger, Cautious,
I offered him a Crumb,
And he unrolled his feathers,
And rowed him softer Home-
Than Oars divide the Ocean,
Too silver for a seam,
Or Butterflies, off Banks of Noon,
Leap, plashless as they swim.

136 What is the poem about?

(a) A normal occurrence in nature of a bird searching for its food and its interaction with a human.
(b) A fight between a bird and a poet.
(c) A bird eating a beetle.
(d) A bird teaching others how to eat a worm.

137 Why has the poet called the grass 'convenient'?

(a) Because the bird could see the beetle in the grass.
(b) Because grass is greener on the other side.
(c) Because it was easy for the bird to have dew from it.
(d) Because the bird could see the worm in the grass.

138 How do you explain the 'plashless' in the last line?

(a) The poet tells us that the bird cannot swim.
(b) Since the bird does not have oars it could not splash in the water.
(c) Since dew was on the grass the bird did not make a splash.
(d) The poet compares the flight of the bird as though it was a 'swim' in the air without the accompanying splashes on water.

139 The bird did not do which of the following?

(a) Cook the worm and eat it.
(b) Let the beetle pass.
(c) Unroll his feathers.
(d) Glance with rapid eyes.

140 How does the poet describe the eyes of the bird?

(a) Watery like dew.
(b) Like grass.
(c) Like frightened beads.
(d) Like butterflies.

PREVIOUS YEARS' QUESTIONS

December 2018

1 In imitation of which classical poet did Samuel Johnson write his London and The Vanity of Human Wishes?

(a) Horace (b) Homer
(c) Juvenal (d) Tasso

2 Who among the ancients prescribed that poetry should both instruct and delight?

(a) Longinus
(b) Plotinus
(c) Aristotle
(d) Horace

3 Who among the following examplified the role of the 'peasant poet'?

1. John Clare 2. John Keats
3. William Cobbett 4. Robert Burns

The right combination according to the code is:

(a) 1 and 2 (b) 3 and 4
(c) 2 and 3 (d) 1 and 4

December 2018

4 What is the delicate balancing act of Andrew Marvell's Horation ode?

(a) Praising Roman virtues while endorsing christian beliefs
(b) Celebrating the Restoration while regretting the frivolity of the new regine
(c) Praising feminine virtues which mocking the fixation on chastity.
(d) Celebrating Cromwells' victories while inviting sympathy for the executed king

5 The Fault of Cowley and perhaps of all the writers of the metaphysical race is that of pursuing his thoughts to their ramifications, by which he loses the grandeur of generatity; for of the greatest things the parts are little; what is little can be but pretty, and by claiming dignity becomes ridiculous. Thus all the power of description is destroyed by a scrupulous enumeration; and the force of scrupulous enumeration; and the force of metaphors is lost when the mind by the mintion of particulars is turned more upon the original than the secondary sense, more upon that from which the illustration is drawn than that to which it is applied.
What Dr Johnson actually faults here is

(a) The metaphysical insistence on the particular than the general.
(b) The force of metaphors that blunts description
(c) the mind that goes astray towards the original
(d) the metaphysical poets' tendency to saunter away.

6 In an ode, William Collins lamented the passing of a contemporary poet. The ode began with the line; "In Yonder Grave a Druid Lies."
Name the poet whose passing Collins laments

(a) James Thomson (b) Alexander Pope
(c) William Cowper (d) Thomas Gray

July 2018

7 The four moral essays of Alexander Pope are addressed to carefully selected figures, Identify,

(a) Timons Newton, Martha Blount, Willington
(b) Lord Cobham, Robert Walpole, Houghton Hall, Chandos
(c) Martha Blount, Lord Cobham Bathurst, Burlington
(d) William III, John Haydn, Joseph Addison, John Dennis

8 William Blake expressed the importance of the particular when he said that "To generalise is to be........, To particularise is the alone distinction of merit." Fill in the blank.

(a) an Idiot (b) a Poet
(c) a Dreamer (d) a Skunk

9 "In every cry of every Man,
In every Infant's cry of fear
In every voice, in every ban"
The figure of speech characterised by repetition of words or group of words at the beginning of consecutive sentence is called ....

(a) Apostrophe (b) Anaphora
(c) Incremental Repetition (d) Alliteration

10 Samuel Johnson has the following to say about an English poet:
"These images are marked by glittering accumulations of ungraceful ornaments: they strike, rather than please. The images are magnified by affectation: the language is laboured into harshness. 'The mind of the writer seems to work with unnatural violence-Double, double, toil and trouble'. He has a kind of strutting dignity and is tall by walking on tiptoe. His art and his struggle are too visible and there is too little appearance of ease and nature." Identify the poet.

(a) Thomas Gray (b) John Dryden
(c) John Milton (d) Thomas Wyatt

November 2017

11 What happens to the lock of hair at the end of Alexander Pope's 'The Rape of the Lock'?

(a) It is given back to its rightful owner
(b) It Is preserved in a monument
(c) It turns into a star
(d) It Is presented to the poet as a token of gratitude

January 2017

12 Samuel Johnson denounced the metaphysical poets saying, "About the beginning of the 17th century appeared a race of writers that may be termed the metaphysical poets.'; In the biography of which of the following poets in his Lives of Poets did Johnson Make this remark?

(a) John Dryden (b) Thomas Parnell
(c) Abraham Cowley (d) Alexander Pope

13 Samuel Johnson's Lives of the English Poets combines the following except

(a) analytical (b) literary.history
(c) personal biography (d) socratic dialogue

14 William Blake has a rare elan to provide telling images in arresting phrases. Match the phrases with the poems they belong to

A. 'mind forg' manacles'	1. 'The Tyger'
B. 'eternal winter'	2. 'The Sick Rose'
C. 'fearful symmetry'	3. 'London'
D. 'crimson joy'	4. 'Holy Thursday'

Codes

	A	B	C	D		A	B	C	D
(a)	2	4	1	3	(b)	3	1	4	2
(c)	3	4	1	2	(d)	4	1	2	3

15 Alexander Pope revised 'The Rape of the Lock' three times. In the final revision of the poem in 1717 he inserted a speech by

(a) Belinda (b) Clarissa (c) Betty (d) Thalestris

16 James Thomson's long poem, 'The Seasons', revised rand expanded all his life, began in the first instance as a poem entitled

(a) Spring (b) Summer (c) Winter (d) Autumn

July 2016

17 Which of the following phrases is not found in Thomas Gray's 'Elegy Written in a Country Churchyard'?

(a) Far from the madding crowd
(b) A youth to Fortune and Fame unknown
(c) Full many a flower is born to blush unseen
(d) All nature is but art, unknown to thee

18 Who among the following was praised and patronised as a 'Ploughman Poet'?

(a) John Clare (b) George Crabbe
(c) Robert Burns (d) Walter Scott

19 In John Gay's Beggar's Opera, what is Peachum's occupation?

1. Pimp
2. Lawyer
3. Fencer of stolen goods and master of a gang of thieves
4. Impleader of less powerful criminals

The right combination according to the code is

(a) 3 and 4 (b) 2 and 3
(c) 1 and 4 (d) 2 and 4

20 In particular William Blake was influenced by the religious writings of

1. Martin Luther
2. Jacob Boehme
3. Emanuel Swedenborg
4. Confucius

The right combination according to the code is

(a) 1 and 4 (b) 1 and 2 (c) 1 and 3 (d) 3 and 4

December 2015

21 Samuel Johnson's 'Dissertation upon Poetry' is part of which of his following works? .

(a) The final section of his preface to Shakespeare
(b) A chapter of his novel Rasselas
(c) The epilogue of his Lives of Poets
(d) One of his Rambler essays

22 "Where there is leisure for fiction, there is little grief", was Samuel Johnson's criticism of a famous poem. Which poem was it? .

(a) PB Shelley's 'Adonais'
(b) Philip Sidney's 'Astrophel and Stella'
(c) Thomas Gray's 'Elegy Written in a Country Churchyard'
(d) John Milton's 'Lycidas'

July 2015

23 In tracing the history of English poetry, Thomas Gray's 'Progress of Poesy' invokes a major poet as follows:

"Nor second He, that rode sublime
Upon the seraph-wings of Extasy,
The secrets of th' Abyss to spy."

Who is 'He'?

(a) William Shakespeare (b) Edmund Spenser
(c) John Milton (d) John Dryden

24 William Cowper wrote in The Task (IV. 681-82) about those who "build factories with blood, conducting trade/ At the sword's point..." These lines allude to

(a) Turkish militant traders across Europe
(b) Nordic conquerors across East Asia
(c) West India slave-plantation owners and the East India Company 'nabobs'
(d) Exploiters of child labour in the London suburbs

25 While compiling what sort of book did Samuel Richardson conceive of the idea for his Pamela Virtue Rewarded?

(a) An account of the plague In London
(b) An instruction manual for manners
(c) A book of devotion
(d) A book of model letters

26 "Nature and Nature's Laws lay hid in Night, God said Let Newton be! and all was Light." Alexander Pope's famous couplet impressive captures..... .
(a) Newton's confirmation of the Genesis passage where God ordains Light
(b) Newton's empirical observations of Philosophiae Naturalis Principal Mathematica
(c) Newton's application of principles of motion to account for many natural phenomena
(d) Newton's discovery that all colours are contained in white light

27 Samuel Johnson wrote London in imitation of?
(a) Horace (b) Ovid (c) Juvenal (d) Moschus

28 Samuel Johnson's use at the term 'metaphysical' piece of criticism was ..... .
(a) approving (b) disapproving
(c) positive (d) accidental

29 In Gulliver's Tavels Struldbruggs are...... .
(a) people replete with abstract learning
(b) people exempt from natural death
(c) People persecuted by pets and servants
(d) People lured by a new idea

December 2014

30 William Blake developed the ideas of 'Prolifics' and 'Devourers' in
(a) Jerusalem
(b) Milton
(c) Marriage of Heaven and Hell
(d) Songs of Innocence and Songs of Experience

31 Who does Alexander Pope refer to in the following lines)
"Born to no pride; inheriting no strife,
or marrying discord in a noble wife,
Stranger to civil and religious rage,
The good man walked innoxious through his age."
(a) Pope's father
(b) Pope himself
(c) Dr Arbothnot
(d) The Duke of Marlborough

June 2014

32 "Where ignorance is Bliss
Tis folly to be wise." Who wrote these lines?
(a) Pope
(b) Gray
(c) Collins
(d) Southey

33 In Blake's 'The Human Abstract', the fragmented world of experience is symbolised in the image of the
(a) caterpillar
(b) fly
(c) reven
(d) fruit of deceit

34 "Love seeketh only self to please, To bind another to its delight." This selfish and possessive nature of love is illustrated in Blake's
(a) 'The Clod and the Peble' (b) 'The Sick Rose'
(c) 'A Poision Tree' (d) 'A Sunflower'

ANSWERS

Objective Questions

1. (a)	2. (d)	3. (d)	4. (d)	5. (a)	6. (d)	7. (b)	8. (c)	9. (b)	10. (d)
11. (c)	12. (c)	13. (c)	14. (a)	15. (b)	16. (a)	17. (c)	18. (b)	19. (c)	20. (c)
21. (b)	22. (b)	23. (d)	24. (c)	25. (b)	26. (d)	27. (a)	28. (d)	29. (d)	30. (d)
31. (c)	32. (c)	33. (c)	34. (d)	35. (b)	36. (d)	37. (d)	38. (d)	39. (b)	40. (b)
41. (d)	42. (c)	43. (a)	44. (a)	45. (c)	46. (a)	47. (a)	48. (c)	49. (d)	50. (c)
51. (a)	52. (b)	53. (a)	54. (b)	55. (d)	56. (c)	57. (d)	58. (a)	59. (c)	60. (b)
61. (a)	62. (a)	63. (d)	64. (a)	65. (d)	66. (b)	67. (c)	68. (c)	69. (b)	70. (a)
71. (a)	72. (a)	73. (d)	74. (b)	75. (a)	76. (a)	77. (c)	78. (c)	79. (d)	80. (b)
81. (b)	82. (a)	83. (c)	84. (b)	85. (a)	86. (b)	87. (b)	88. (d)	89. (a)	90. (c)
91. (b)	92. (a)	93. (a)	94. (c)	95. (d)	96. (a)	97. (b)	98. (c)	99. (d)	100. (c)
101. (a)	102. (b)	103. (c)	104. (a)	105. (b)	106. (b)	107. (c)	108. (d)	109. (c)	110. (b)
111. (a)	112. (a)	113. (b)	114. (c)	115. (b)	116. (a)	117. (b)	118. (a)	119. (a)	120. (a)
121. (b)	122. (b)	123. (c)	124. (c)	125. (b)	126. (b)	127. (d)	128. (d)	129. (c)	130. (c)
131. (d)	132. (d)	133. (b)	134. (d)	135. (b)	136. (a)	137. (c)	138. (d)	139. (a)	140. (c)

Previous Years' Questions

1. (c)	2. (d)	3. (d)	4. (d)	5. (d)	6. (a)	7. (c)	8. (a)	9. (b)	10. (a)
11. (c)	12. (c)	13. (d)	14. (c)	15. (b)	16. (c)	17. (d)	18. (c)	19. (a)	20. (c)
21. (b)	22. (d)	23. (c)	24. (c)	25. (d)	26. (d)	27. (c)	28. (b)	29. (b)	30. (c)
31. (a)	32. (b)	33. (d)	34. (a)						

The Romantic Age Poetry (1798-1837)

The Romantic Age poetry is characterised by a shift from structure, intellect and reason towards freedom of thoughts and expressions besides idealisation of nature. Individuality and passion were valued by the Romantic poets. William Blake, William Wordsworth, Samuel Taylor Coleridge, PB Shelly and John Keats were a few important poets of the age.

Background to the Romantic Age

Towards the end of the 18th century, major changes in agriculture, manufacturing, mining, transport and technology in England took place. These major technological and socio-economic changes, resulted from the replacement of an economy based on manual labour to one dominated by industry and machine manufacturing. The first phase of Industrial Revolution was from about 1750 to 1850. Coal and the steam engines were the main driving forces of this phase.

By 1800, steam power had become a practical reality. It radically improved Britain's core industries, namely the production of textiles, metalwork and other manufactured goods and the mining of coal and other raw materials. By 1820, the potential of the steam engine as a viable source of power for ships and railway locomotives had been realised.

While, England was being radically transformed by the Industrial Revolution and turned into the most industrialised nation, it also led to social unrest among the working class. It generated a violent class conflict between employers and workers, most notably in the Luddite Riots of 1811-12, when textile workers in the North of England attacked the new mills and machinery, which had put them out of work.

In August 1819, The Peterloo Massacre (or Battle of Peterloo) occurred at St Peter's Field, Manchester, England, when cavalry charged into a crowd of 60000-80000 gathered at a meeting to demand the reforms of parliamentary representation. Graham Milner states that the "massacre was one outcome of an extraordinarily powerful and determined agitation for social and political justice in England, which at times approached pre-revolutionary proportions. The primary social force behind this mass agitation was the new working class." This new working class was born out of the Industrial Revolution.

In this Chapter

- *Background to the Romantic Age*
- *Major Poets of the Romantic Age*

Literary Background to the Romantic Age

The German poet Friedrich Schlegel is given credit for using the term 'romantic' to describe literature for the first time. He defined it as, "literature depicting emotional matter in an imaginative form." F L Lucas in his book, *The Decline and Fall of the Romantic Ideal* (1948) gave around 11396 definitions of 'romanticism'. The American Scholar A O Lovejoy stated that the word 'romantic' has come to mean, so many things that, by itself, it means nothing at all.

However, generally speaking, the Romantic movement in literature is characterised by a shift from the structured, intellectual, reasoned approach of the 1700's to use of the imagination, freedom of thought and expression and an idealisation of nature. While, Enlightenment thinkers of the 18th century had valued reason and rationality, Romantics valued emotion, passion and individuality. They turned from impersonal works to works of a more subjective, personal nature.

William Long states that "the essence of Romanticism was, it must be remembered, that literature must reflect all that is spontaneous and unaffected in nature and in man and be free to follow its own fancy in its own way." Poetry was the dominant genre in the Romantic period. The Romantic poets such as Wordsworth and Coleridge withdrew into an inner world and were less concerned with the outer public world. They also turned to the nature and devoted themselves to recording its beauty as a counterpart to the wide ugliness of the industrial towns.

Characteristics of Romanticism

Harley Henry sums up the main characteristics of Romanticism as

- "Romanticism turned away from the 18th century emphasis on reason and artifice. Instead, the Romantics embraced imagination and naturalness." Coleridge defined imagination, as a creative power, which colours objects of sense with the mind's own light.
- "Romantic era poets rejected the public, formal and witty works of the previous century. They preferred poetry that spoke of personal experiences and emotions, often in simple, unadorned language." Romantic poets believed that feelings and emotions could create poetry. Wordsworth himself defined good poetry as 'the spontaneous overflow of powerful feelings'.
- The artist or the individual self gained primacy in this period. The poet or artist was seen as a creator of a piece of work, which reflected his individuality and inner mind.
- "Many Romantics turned to a past or an inner dream world that they felt was more picturesque and magical than the ugly Industrial Age they lived in. These mysterious and supernatural elements can be seen in Coleridge's, *Kubla Khan* and in Keats' poem *La Belle Dame Sans Merci*.
- "Most Romantics believed in individual liberty and sympathised with those who rebelled against tyranny."
- The Romantics thought of nature as transformative; they were fascinated by the ways; nature and the human mind mirrored the others creative properties.
- The Romantics each used the lyric as the form best suited to expressions of feeling, self-revelation and the imagination.

Major Poets of the Romantic Age

Romantic Poets are divided into two major groups i.e. First Generation Romantics and Second Generation Romantics

First Generation Romantic Poets

The first generation's writings were inspired by the Battle of Bastille and the French Revolution. They wrote at a time of revolutionary fervour. The main poets belonging to this generation were William Blake, William Wordsworth, Coleridge and Southey.

William Blake (1757-1827)

English poet, engraver and painter William Blake was born in London, England, on 28th November, 1757. From his earliest years, he saw visions. When his parents did observe that he was different from his peers they did not force him to attend conventional school. He learned to read and write at home. At age of fourteen he began a seven-year apprenticeship to an engraver. After he was twenty-one, Blake studied for a time at the Royal Academy of Arts.

Literary Career and Works

Blake's first printed work, *Poetical Sketches* (1783), is a collection of apprentice verse, mostly imitating classical models. The poems protest against war, tyranny and King George III's treatment of the American colonies.

In 1787 Blake produced *Songs of Innocence* (1789), as the first major work in his new process, followed by *Songs of Experience* (1794). The magnificent lyrics in these two collections carefully compare the openness of innocence with the bitterness of experience. They are a milestone because they are a rare instance of the successful union of two art forms by one man.

Works such as *The French Revolution* (1791), *America, a Prophecy* (1793), *Visions of the Daughters of Albion* (1793) and *Europe, a Prophecy* (1794) express his opposition to the English monarchy and to 18th-century political and social tyranny in general. Theological tyranny is the subject of *The Book of Urizen* (1794). In the prose work *The Marriage of Heaven and Hell* (1790-93), he satirised oppressive authority in church and state.

In Felpham, he experienced profound spiritual insights that prepared him for his mature works, the great visionary epics written and etched between 1804 and 1820. *Milton* (1804-08), *Vala*, or *The Four Zoas* (1797; rewritten after 1800), and *Jerusalem* (1804-20) have neither traditional plots, characters, rhyme nor meter. They envision a new and higher kind of innocence, the human spirit triumphant over reason. *The Four Zoas* was a mystical story predicting the future showing how evil is rooted in man's basic faculties-reason, passion, instinct and imagination. Imagination was the hero.

His last six years of life were spent at Foundation Courts, surrounded by a group of admiring young artists. Blake did some of his best pictorial works: the *Illustrations to the Book of Job* and his unfinished *Dante*. In 1824, his health began to weaken and he died singing in London, England, on 12th August, 1827.

Among his best known lyrics today are *The Lamb*, *The Tyger* and *London*. Lyrics of Blake's *The Lamb* from *Songs of Innocence is given below*

The Lamb

Little Lamb, who make thee
Dost thou know who made three,
Gave thee life, and bid thee feed
By the steam and o'er the mead;
Gave thee clothing of delight,
Softest clothing, wooly, bright;
Gave thee such a tender voice,
Making all the vales rejoice!
Little Lamb, who made thee
Dost thou know who made thee
Little Lamb, I'll tell thee,
Little Lamb, I'll tell thee:
He is called by thy name,
For he calls himself a Lamb
He is meek, and he is mild,
He bacame a little child.
I a child, and thou a lamb,
We are called by His name.
Little Lamb; God bless thee!
Little Lamb; God bless thee!

William Wordsworth (1770-1850)

British poet William Wordsworth was born at Cockermouth, in Cumberland in 1770. After his mother's death, Wordsworth was sent to Hawkshead Grammar School, near Windermere. Later, he was sent to St John's College, Cambridge, where he developed radical political views.

Literary Career

He made his debut as a writer in 1787, when he published a sonnet in *The European Magazine.*

Wordsworth was reunited with his sister Dorothy in 1794. He moved with his sister to Racedown Lodge on the Devon / Somerset border and it was here that he met the poet Samuel Taylor Coleridge. He moved closer to Coleridge at Alfoxden House and they collaborated on and published *Lyrical Ballads* (1798), which began with Coleridge's *Rime of the Ancient Mariner* and ended with Wordsworth's *Tintern Abbey*. Around 1798, Wordsworth began writing a large and philosophical autobiographical poem, completed in 1805 and published posthumously in 1850 under the title *The Prelude.*

His other collections are *Poems in Two Volumes,* which included the poems: *Ode to Duty, Resolution and Independence and Intimations of Immortality*; *The Excursion* and *Laodamia.* In 1843, Wordsworth succeeded Robert Southey (1774-1843) as England's poet laureate.

He died in 1850 and was buried in Grasmere Churchyard.

Major Works

The Preface to the Lyrical Ballads

- The *Lyrical Ballads* were first published in 1798, but it was only in the second edition published in 1800, that a Preface was added. *Lyrical Ballads* consisted of 23 poems, four by Coleridge and the rest by Wordsworth.
- The *Preface to the Lyrical Ballads* is regarded as a Romantic manifesto, wherein Wordsworth sets out the rules for a new kind of poetry and poetic theory.
- It declares the dawn of the English Romantic Movement. Wordsworth and Coleridge, with the publication of the *Lyrical Ballads*, break away with the Neo-classical tendencies in poetry.
- Wordsworth claims to be breaking away from the 'artificiality', 'triviality' or 'over-elaborate' and 'contrived quality' of 18th century poetry and charting a new course.

- He states that he has chosen 'incidents and situations from common life' and described them in a simple and natural language 'really used by men'.
- The subject matter of his poetry is not the rich or the powerful, but humble and rustic folk.
- He describes poet as 'a man speaking to men': a man endowed with more lively sensibility, more enthusiasm and tenderness, who has a greater knowledge of human nature, and a more comprehensive soul, than one supposed to be common among mankind.
- Dr William Tarvin describes the different stages of Wordsworth's theory of poetic creation. "First, the poet encounters a commonplace incident, which for reasons unknown at the time arouses powerful feelings in his mind. At a later time, when he is far away from the incident and can 'see' it only in his mind, the poet looks back calmly on the feelings aroused by this incident. Suddenly his mind becomes agitated to the point that it calls forth a facsimile of the original feelings he had experienced. At this point, having proceeded through three sequences of (i) powerful feelings, (ii) tranquil assessment and (iii) a recreation of the powerful feelings in his mind, the poet is ready to write."

The Prelude

- Wordsworth's autobiographical poem, *The Prelude* was begun in 1799 and was completed in 1805. However, it was published only after his death in 1850.
- The first version containing two books was published in 1799. The second version with 13 books was published in 1805 and the final revised version came out in 1850 with 14 books.
- The poem is subtitled *Growth of a Poet's Mind; An Autobiographical Poem.* It is an account of Wordsworth's growth and development as a poet.
- Wordsworth begins the poem by describing the impact, the natural world had on his childhood by describing, its beauty and richness, as he states, "To more than infant softness, giving me, /Among the fretful dwelling of mankind. /A knowledge, a dim earnest of the calm/Which nature breathes among the fields and groves?"
- He describes his passage from childhood animal pleasures, through adolescent, sensual passion for the wild and gloomy, to the adult awareness of the relation of our perception of the natural world and finally to our sense of the human and moral world.
- The influence of French Revolution also forms a major part of the poem. Wordsworth describes his early days of political disinterestedness towards the cause of the French people to his days of active involvement in the cause and finally growing disenchantment towards the cause as a result of the failure of ideals associated with the revolution.
- A key concept of Wordsworth's *Prelude* is 'the spots of time'. These are epiphanic moments where "Ordinary, everyday events and entities appear extraordinary and transcendent, become charged through the creative imagination with enormous physical, emotional and spiritual meanings." (Arthur Clements)
- These 'spots of time' have a 'renovating virtues'; they nourish our minds and enhance pleasure. They are intense emotional experiences in life that could be recalled by the imagination to revitalise and renew poetic strength. Examples of these are the boat-stealing episode in the opening book and ascent of mount snowdon.

According to *Algy Pug*, "*The Prelude* is the first major narrative poem in European literature which deals solely with the spiritual journey of the author. In this respect, the only predecessor to, which it can be compared is Dante's *Divine Comedy*, which is similarly a journey from personal confusion to certitude, from ignorance to realisation.

However, Dante starts his journey at the age of 35 and through a lengthy rite of passage, involving both moral and intellectual purification, arrives at a state of illumination, that he is not really able to describe. In *The Prelude*, on the other hand, illumination appears as the background on which the story is inscribed."

Samuel Taylor Coleridge (1772-1834)

English poet and literary critic Samuel Taylor Coleridge or ST Coleridge was born in Ottery St Mary, Devonshire in 1772. Coleridge was educated at Christ's Hospital and Jesus College, Cambridge with the intention of becoming a church minister. In 1793, Coleridge got enlisted in the 15th Light Dragoons as Silus Tomkyn Comberbache, but his brother got him discharged by reason of insanity. He then returned to Cambridge, but left his studies again in 1794, without a degree to tour Wales. Coleridge met Robert Southey in Bristol in 1794 and both proposed a utopian community that would fulfill the idealistic goals of the revolutionaries without degenerating into the violence of the Terror, a community to be called 'pantisocracy' and to be established in the New World at Susquehanna river in Pennsylvania.

Literary Career

His first volume of poetry, *Poems on Various Subjects* was published in 1796. It was during this time that he also began an intimate friendship with Wordsworth and Dorothy. Collaboration with Wordsworth produced the *Lyrical Ballads* in 1798. In 1799, Coleridge joined the Wordsworth, who was staying at the Hutchinson farm in Durham. There he fell in love with Sara, sister of Wordsworth's fiancée- Mary Hutchinson. Sara appears in Coleridge's journals and poems as *Asra*.

In 1817, he published *Biographia Literaria*, which contained his finest literary criticism. He continued to publish poetry and prose, notably *Sibylline Leaves* (1817), *Aids to Reflection* (1825) and *Church and State* (1830). His best known poems are *The Rime of the Ancient Mariner* and *Kubla Khan*, the latter of which was reportedly written under the influence of opium. Coleridge was elected a fellow of the Royal Society of Literature in 1824.

He died at Highgate, near London on 25th July, 1834.

Major Works

Biographia Literaria

- In his *Biographia Literaria*, Coleridge makes a distinction between fancy and imagination. Fancy for Coleridge is a lower faculty that is employed for tasks that are 'passive' and 'mechanical'. Imagination, on the other hand, extracts 'hidden ideas and meaning' from such data and is a creative power.
- According to Coleridge, Fancy brings together images and even when brought together, they continue to retain their individual properties.
- He then further divides imagination into two kinds: primary and secondary. The primary imagination is defined as 'the living power and prime agent of all human perception' whereas the secondary imagination is 'an echo of the former'.
- The primary imagination is merely the power of receiving impressions of the external world through the senses. It is possessed by everyone.
- The secondary imagination works upon what is perceived by the primary imagination. Its raw material is the sensation and impressions supplied to it by the primary imagination.

An excerpt from Biographia Literaria, in which Coleridge explains his concepts of Fancy and Imagination is given below

The imagination, then I consider either as primary or secondary. The primary imagination I hold to be the living power and prime agent of all human perception and as a repetition in the finite mind of the eternal act of creation in the infinite I AM. The secondary I consider as an echo of the former, co-existing with the conscious will, yet still as identical with the primary in the kind of its agency and differing only in degree and in the mode of its operation. It dissolves, diffuses, dissipates, in order to re-create or where this process is rendered impossible, yet still, at all events, it struggles to idealise and to unify.

It is essentially vital, even as all objects (as objects) are essentially fixed and dead. Fancy, on the contrary, has no other counters to play with, but fixities and definites. The fancy is indeed no other than a mode of memory emancipated from the order of time and space and blended with and modified, by that empirical phenomenon of the will, which we express by the word choice . But equally with the ordinary memory it must receive all its materials ready made from the law of association.

"Good Sense is the Body of poetic genius, Fancy its Drapery, Motion its Life and Imagination the Soul that is everywhere and in each and forms all into one graceful and intelligent whole."

Kubla Khan

In Xanadu did Kubla Khan
A stately pleasure-dome decree:
Where Alph, the sacred river, ran
Through caverns measureless to man
Down to a sunless sea.
So, twice five miles of fertile ground
With walls and towers were girdled round;
And there were gardens bright with sinuous rills,
Where blossomed many an incense-bearing tree;
And here were forests ancient as the hills,
Enfolding sunny spots of greenery.
But oh! that deep romantic chasm which slanted
Down the green hill athwart a cedarn cover!
A savage place! as holy and enchanted
As e'er beneath a waning moon was haunted
By woman wailing for her demon-lover!
And from this chasm, with ceaseless turmoil seething,
As if this earth in fast thick pants were breathing,
A mighty fountain momently was forced:
Amid whose swift half-intermitted burst
Huge fragments vaulted like rebounding hail,
Or chaffy grain beneath the thresher's flail:
And mid these dancing rocks at once and ever
It flung up momently the sacred river.

Kubla Khan: Summary

- Coleridge's poem *Kubla Khan,* was published in 1816. It is subtitled as *A Vision in a Dream : A Fragment.*
- According to Coleridge's Preface to *Kubla Khan*, he was living in ill health during the summer of 1797 in a lonely farm-house between Porlock and Linton, on the Exmoor confines of Somerset and Devonshire. Having taken an 'anodyne,' he fell asleep immediately upon reading a 16th century travel book by Samuel Purchas.
- 'Purchas, *His Pilgrimage*', the work described Xanadu, the summer palace of the Mongol ruler and Emperor of China Kubla Khan. While, sleeping for three hours, Coleridge composed 200 to 300 lines, "If that indeed can be called composition, in which all the images rose up before him as things, with a parallel production of the correspondent expressions, without any sensation or consciousness of effort". Upon waking, he set about writing lines of poetry that came to him from the dream until he was interrupted by a person from Porlock. Returning to the poem, Coleridge could recall only 'some 8 or 10 scattered lines and images'.
- Coleridge's poem describes Xanadu, the Palace of Kubla Khan, a Mongol Emperor. The poem's speaker starts by describing the setting of the Emperor's palace, which he calls a 'pleasure dome' in contrast to the structured dome. Its gardens, the landscape surrounding Kubla's domain are wild and untamed, covered by ancient forests and cut by a majestic river.
- In the latter part of the poem, the speaker talks about another vision of his dream where a woman is calling to her daemonic (a supernatural being between gods and humans) lover. The speaker believes that her song would transport him to a dream world, in which he could 'build that dome in air' and in which he can drink 'the milk of Paradise'.
- John Spencer Hill states that *Kubla Khan* is a poem about poetry and poetic process. Under this reading, "*Kubla Khan*, who causes a pleasure-dome and elaborate gardens to be constructed in Xanadu, is a type of the artist, whose glorious creation, as the ancestral voices from the deep caverns warn, is a precariously balanced reconciliation of the natural and the artificial." The birth of the sacred river and its passage through the garden of *Kubla Khan* symbolises "the sudden eruption of the subconscious into the realm of the conscious mind and its eventual inevitable recession back into the deep well of the unconscious."
- David Daiches states that the building of a palace dedicated to pleasure in a place, which is 'sacred' directly symbolises the combination of pleasure and sacredness which, for Coleridge, was the sign of true art.
- The second stanza, he says, explores the kind of passionate and marvelous experience with which poetry deals. He goes on to suggest the way in which the creative imagination operates and the end, where *Kubla Khan* hears ancestral voices prophesying war, indicates that art is always under threat from the violence of the external world.
- The third stanza, which begins: 'The shadow of the dome of pleasure', brings together images of pleasure and the sacred river, and of coldness, of Sun and of ice, which again symbolises Art or Poetry.
- The final stanza recollects and describes a moment of poetic inspiration and expresses the wish that the poet could revive and prolong the moment so that he could build the palace of art and dwell there in continued poetic ecstasy.

Robert Southey (1774-1843)

English poet and biographer Robert Southey was born in Bristol, England in 1774. His early years were spent at Bath. Southey was educated at Westminster School in London, but was later expelled for writing an essay condemning excessive corporal punishment, which he published in the school magazine.

Literary Career and Works

In 1792, he got admitted to Oxford. In 1794, he met Samuel Taylor Coleridge, who shared both his literary aspirations and his radical political views and together that same year, the two wrote a verse drama, *The Fall of Robespierre*. Southey published his first collection of poems in 1795. Between 1796 and 1798, he wrote many ballads, including *The Inchcape Rock* and *The Battle of Blenheim*. His first published prose work, *Letters Written During a Short Residence in Spain and Portugal* was also written during this period.

Southey was appointed as the poet laureate in 1813. Writing for the Quarterly Review and other publications, he became increasingly identified with Tory politics. He wrote *A Vision of Judgement* commemorating the death of George III, which was later mocked by Byron in his *The Vision of Judgement.*

Along with Wordsworth and Coleridge, Southey formed part of the Lake School of Poets, named, so because they lived in the English Lake District of Cumberland and Westmorland. The term was first used derogatorily, when critic Francis Jeffrey conferred this designation on the three poets in an article published in *The Edinburgh Review* in 1817.

Apart from his poetry, Southey also had a talent as a biographer. He is known for his biographies, *The Life of Nelson* and *Life of Wesley.*

Southey died in Cumberland in 1843.

Works of Southey

The Fall of Robespierre

- The Fall of Robespierre is a three-act written by Robert Southey and Samuel Coleridge in 1794.
- It follows the events in France after the downfall of Maximilien Robespierre. Robespierre is portrayed as a tyrant, but Southey's contributions praise him as a destroyer of despotism.
- The play does not operate as an effective drama for the stage, but rather as a sort of dramatic poem with each act being a different scene.
- According to Coleridge, "my sole aim is to imitate the impassioned and highly figurative language of the French Orators and develop the characters of the chief actors on a vast stage of horrors."
- The play is filled with various speeches on the topic of liberty. The first scene is set in the Tuileries, in which Bertrand Barere, Jean-Lambert Tallien and Louis Legendre, opponents of Robespierre discuss their plans to challenge the 'tyrant'. Their conversation comprises highly rhetorical speeches as if they were part of a public meeting.
- The third act, originally written by Lovell, was rewritten by Southey. Within the act, the opponents of Robespierre compare themselves to the assassins of Julius Caesar who are restoring the republic. In the final speech, Bertrand Barere discusses the history of French Revolution and lists the various would-be despots who have attempted to usurp liberty for Louis XVI to Robespierre himself, concluding that France will be a Beacon of liberation to the world.

The Inchcape Rock

Nor stir in the air, no stir in the sea,
The ship was still as she could be;
Her sails from heaven received no motion,
Her keel was steady in the ocean.
Without either sign or sound of their shock,
The waves flow'd over the Inchcape Rock;
So little they rose, so little they fell,
They did not move the Inchcape Bell.
The Abbot of Aberbrothok
Had placed that bell on the Inchcape Rock;
On a buoy in the storm it floated and swung,
And over the waves its warning rung.
When the Rock was hid by the surge's swell,
The Mariners heard the warning Bell;
And then they knew the perilous Rock,
And blest the Abbot of Aberbrothok

The Inchcape Rock: Summary

- *The Inchcape Rock* is a ballad written by English poet Robert Southey.
- Published in 1802, it tells the story of a 14th-century attempt by the Abbot of Arbroath (Aberbrothock) to install a warning bell on Inchcape, a notorious sandstone reef about 11 miles (18 km) off the East coast of Scotland.
- The poem tells how the bell was removed by a pirate, who subsequently perished on the reef while returning to Scotland in bad weather some time later.
- Like many of Southey's ballads *The Inchcape Rock* describes a supernatural event, but its main theme is that those who do bad things will ultimately be punished accordingly and poetic justice done.

Second Generation Romantics

When the second generation of Romantics started writing, war had already ended. But Britain was beset by different social and political tensions, which led to the Peterloo Massacre.

According to Stephen Bygrave in his book, *Romantic Writings*, another major difference between the two generations was that the second generation of Romantic poets died at a relatively young age. Also, the social backgrounds of the two generation of writers were different. Wordsworth and Coleridge came from a Cambridge background, Southey from Oxford, while Blake was a Londoner, who trained as an artisan. All three of them had contact with radical groups, who met to discuss the revolutionary ideas of Godwin and Paine. Among the second generation Romantics, Byron and Shelley lived in exile, while Keats was attacked in terms of class.

George Gordon Byron or Lord Byron (1788-1824)

British Romantic poet, Lord Byron was born in London in 1788. Born with a club-foot, Byron spent the first 10 years in his mother's lodgings in Aberdeen.

Literary Career and Works

Byron attended Harrow School, London and Trinity College, Cambridge. At Cambridge, he engaged in many sexual escapades and also fell in debt. He fell in love with his distant cousin, Mary Chaworth and this unrequited not reciprocated passion found expression in several poems, including *Hills of Annesley* and *The Adieu*. Byron's first collection of poetry, *Hours of Idleness* appeared in 1807. The poems were savagely attacked by Henry Brougham in the *Edinburgh Review.* Byron replied with the publication of his satire, *English Bards and Scotch Reviewers* (1809).

Along with his close friend, John Cam Hobhouse, Byron went on a grand tour to Greece, Albania, Spain, Portugal and Malta in 1809. Byron returned to England in the summer of 1811, having completed the opening cantos of *Childe Harold's Pilgrimage,* a poetic travelogue of picturesque lands.

This poem instantly catapulted Byron to fame so much that he himself remarked that 'I awoke and found myself famous. Byron was rumoured to have had affairs with several women. The agitation of these affairs and the sense of mingled guilt and exultation they aroused in his mind are reflected in the Oriental tales he wrote during the period, such as *The Giaour*, *The Bride of Abydos* and *The Corsair*.

After divorcing his wife Annabella Milbanke in 1816, Byron was criticised and hounded by the press. As a result, Byron fled England and settled in Italy. He began writing his masterpiece, *Don Juan,* an epic-satire novel-in-verse loosely based on a legendary hero. In 1822 Byron, Leigh Hunt and Percy Bysshe Shelley travelled to Italy, where the three men published the political journal, *The Liberal*. By publishing in Italy they remained free from the fear of being prosecuted by the British authorities. In 1823, Byron was elected to the Greek committee of liberation against the Turks and sailed for Greece. However, his health deteriorated soon after.

Byron died from a bad fever in Greece on 19th April, 1824 at Messolonghi.

Major Works

English Bards and Scotch Reviewers

- Published anonymously in 1809, *English Bards and Scotch Reviewers* was Byron's first major work after his volume *Hours of Idleness*.
- It was a satirical poem written in heroic couplets.
- It was modeled on Alexander Pope's satirical verse.
- The foundation for *English Bards* was a poem called *British Bards*, written by Byron in October 1807. In January 1808, after the *Edinburgh Review* published a scathing review of Byron's book of poems *Hours of Idleness*; Byron was, so incensed that he revised his original satire and renamed it *English Bards and Scotch Reviewers*.
- The work is an attack on contemporary writers and critics.
- The poem is a vindication of the Augustan ideals of wit, reason and propriety, which Byron felt had been devalued by his contemporaries.
- Byron draws a contrast between past and present and argues that modern writers, with few exceptions, have neglected their great heritage from Shakespeare, Milton, Dryden and Pope. It is an attack on the excesses of the contemporary writers: Wordsworth, Coleridge, Southey, Mrs Radcliff and others.
- CH Herford called Byron's *English Bards* as "The last angry reverberation of the literary satire of Dryden and Pope". He termed it an *Inverted Dunciad* where the "novice falls upon the masters of his day, as the Augustan master upon the nonentities of his and emulates Pope's stiletto with a vigorous bludgeon".

Canto I: Childe Harold's Pilgrimage

Oh, thou, in Hellas deemed of heavenly birth,
Muse, formed or fabled at the minstrel's will!
Since, shamed full oft by later lyres on Earth,
Mine dares not call thee from thy sacred hill:
Yet there I've wandered by thy vaunted rill;
Yes! sighed o'er Delphi's long-deserted shrine
Where, save that feeble fountain, all is still;
Nor mote my shell awake the weary nine
To grace so plain a tale–this lowly lay of mine.
Whilome in Albion's isle there dwelt a youth,
Who ne in virtue's ways did take delight;
But spent his days in riot most uncouth,
And vexed with mirth the drowsy ear of night.
Ah, me! in sooth he was a shameless wight,
Sore given to revel and ungodly glee;
Few earthly things found favour in his sight
Save concubines and carnal companie,
And flaunting wassailers of high and low degree.
Childe Harold was he hight, but whence his name
And lineage long, it suits me not to say;
Suffice it, that perchance they were of fame,
And had been glorious in another day:
But one sad losel soils a name for aye,
However, mighty in the olden time;
Nor all that heralds rake from coffined clay,
Nor florid prose, nor honeyed lines of rhyme,
Can blazon evil deeds, or consecrate a crime.
Childe Harold basked him in the noontide Sun,
Disporting there like any other fly,
Nor deemed before his little day was done
One blast might chill him into misery.

Childe Harold's Pilgrimage: Summary

- Byron's *Childe Harold's Pilgrimage* written in four cantos was published between 1812 and 1818.
- It is a semi-autobiographical poem that focuses on a nobleman disillusioned with sensory pleasures and embarking on a search for entity.
- The *Childe* of the poem's title is a medieval title for a young man, who is eligible for knighthood.
- It is this poem, which introduced the concept of the Byronic hero- a brooding, solitary man, who is an outcast or outlaw.
- Byron envisioned *Childe Harold's Pilgrimage* as a poetic travelogue of his experiences in Portugal, Spain, Greece and Albania. In his 'Preface' to the poem, Byron stated that the poem "was written, for the most part, amidst the scenes which it attempts to describe. It was begun in Albania and the parts relative to Spain and Portugal were composed from the author's observations in those countries. Thus, it may be necessary to state for the correctness of the descriptions".
- The poem also reflects Byron's political views, particularly his support for Greek independence from Turkey and the Convention of Cintra in which the English politicians allowed enemy French soldiers captured in battle to return to France with their loot intact.
- The poem is written in Spenserian stanzas.

© *Canto I: Don Juan*

I want a hero: an uncommon want,
When every year and month sends forth a new one,
Till, after cloying the gazettes with cant,
The age discovers he is not the true one;
Of such as these I should not care to vaunt,
I'll therefore take our ancient friend Don Juan–
We all have seen him, in the pantomime,
Sent to the devil somewhat ere his time.
Vernon, the butcher Cumberland, Wolfe, Hawke,
Prince Ferdinand, Granby, Burgoyne, Keppel, Howe,
Evil and good, have had their tithe of talk,
And fill'd their sign posts then, like Wellesley now;
Each in their turn like Banquo's monarchs stalk,
Followers of fame, 'nine farrow' of that sow
France, too, had Buonaparté and Dumourier
Recorded in the Moniteur and Courier.

Don Juan

- Byron's *Don Juan* is an unfinished poem written between 1819 and 1824. Consisting of 16 cantos, this satirical mock-epic details the life and adventures of a young Spaniard, Don Juan.
- The poem is regarded as largely autobiographical in nature. Don Juan's encounters are viewed as poetic reconstructions of Byron's own life and his affairs with several women in his life.
- Byron reverses the European legend of Don Juan (where Juan was a libertine) and makes his protagonist a naïve young man seduced by women.
- In Byron's poem, Juan becomes the passive recipient of the erotic attentions of a succession of aggressive and powerful women. The poem begins with a dedication to Robert Southey and William Wordsworth. The narrator distances himself from these 'great' men by insisting that his own muse is of a lesser nature and so his verse will be lesser as well.
- The narrative of the poem begins with Juan's birth to Don Jose and Donna Inez, his education and his early love affair with Julia, wife of Don Alfonso of Seville. Juan then goes through a range of experiences and encounters with different women.
- The poem is written in the Italian ottava rima or eight-line stanza, the poetic form favoured by the Italian satirical writers of mock-heroic romances.

Percy Bysshe Shelley (1792-1822)

English poet PB Shelley was born at Field Place near Horsham, England in 1792. Shelley attended Sion House Academy from 1802-1804 and later joined Eton College. In 1810, Shelley entered University College, Oxford. However, both he and his friend, Thomas Jefferson Hogg, were expelled after a year for suspected authorship of a pamphlet entitled *The Necessity of Atheism*.

Literary Career and Works

Shelley's first publication was a Gothic Novel, *Zastrozzi* (1810). He eloped and married 16 years old Harriet Westbrook in 1811 in Scotland. When his marriage did not go well he became interested in a woman named Elizabeth Hitckener, a school teacher who inspired his first major poem, *Queen Mab*. Shelley continued to be involved in politics and in 1817 wrote the pamphlet *A Proposal for Putting Reform to the Vote Throughout the United Kingdom*. In 1817, Shelley produced *Laon and Cythna*, a long narrative poem that was withdrawn after only a few copies were published because of its references to incest, as well as attacks on religion. It was later edited and reissued as *The Revolt of Islam* (1818).

He also wrote 'Preface' to his wife's novel, *Frankenstein*. Shelley's pastoral elegy on the death of Keats, *Adonais* appeared in 1821. By 1820, the Shelley finally settled in Pisa, Italy, where Shelley extended his literary circle to include Byron, Leigh Hunt, Edward Trelawny, Edward Williams,

Thomas Jefferson Hogg and the young John Keats. On 8th July, 1822, Percy Shelley and Edward Williams set sail from Leghorn en route to Lerici. They both drowned during this journey.

Major Works

A Defence of Poetry

- Shelley's *A Defence of Poetry* was originally written in 1821 in response to Thomas Love Peacock's *The Four Ages of Poetry*.
- Shelley begins his essay by distinguishing between reason and imagination. He defines reason as logical thought and imagination as perception, arguing that "Reason respects the differences and imagination the similitudes of things".
- Shelley states that Poetry is the 'expression of the imagination' of the poet. Poets, using their imagination, 'imagine and express' the 'indestructible order'.
- A poem, for him is, "The very image of life expressed in its eternal truth . . . the creation of actions according to the unchangeable forms of human nature, as existing in the mind of the Creator"; while Poetry is 'a mirror which makes beautiful that which is distorted'.
- Poets, for Shelley, are "not only the authors of language and of music...they are the institutors of laws and the founders of Civil Society." They are the 'unacknowledged legislators of the world'. Poets have the power to transform society.
- Gerald Lucas states that Shelley believes poetry to be divine, since it "Provides the seed for all of humanity's creations: religions, institutions, politics, philosophy and technology."
- Shelley says that poetry both pleases and instructs. It gives both pleasure and wisdom.
- Poetry as a whole, he argues, 'is ever-accompanied with pleasure' and it 'lifts the veil from the hidden beauty of the world'. Poetry's primary purpose is to focus on revealing the beauty in the world that is apparently hidden from people.

Ode to the West Wind

O wild West Wind, thou breath of Autumn's being,
Thou, from whose unseen presence the leaves dead
Are driven, like ghosts from an enchanter fleeing,
Yellow and black and pale and hectic red,
Pestilence-stricken multitudes: O thou,
Who chariotest to their dark wintry bed
The wingèd seeds, where they lie cold and low,
Each like a corpse within its grave,until
Thine azure sister of the Spring shall blow
Her clarion o'er the dreaming earth, and fill
(Driving sweet buds like flocks to feed in air)
With living hues and odours plain and hill:
Wild Spirit, which art moving everywhere;
Destroyer and Preserver; hear, O hear!
Thou on whose stream, 'mid the steep sky's commotion,
Loose clouds like Earth's decaying leaves are shed,
Shook from the tangled boughs of Heaven and Ocean,
Angels of rain and lightning: there are spread
On the blue surface of thine airy surge,
Like the bright hair uplifted from the head
Of some fierce Maenad, even from the dim verge
Of the horizon to the zenith's height,
The locks of the approaching storm.

Ode to the West Wind: Summary

- Shelley's *Ode to the West Wind* was written in 1819 and published in the *Prometheus Unbound* volume in 1820.
- The poem is written in terza rima a verse form consisting of stanzas of three lines (tercets); the first and third lines rhyming with one another and the second rhyming with the first and third of the following tercet.
- In his note to the poem, Shelley wrote, "This poem was conceived and chiefly written in a wood that skirts the Arno, near Florence and on a day when that tempestuous wind, whose temperature is at once mild and animating, was collecting the vapours, which pour down the autumnal rains. They began, as I foresaw, at sunset with a violent tempest of hail and rain, attended by that magnificent thunder and lightning peculiar to the Cisalpine regions".
- The poem is addressed to the West Wind. The speaker of the poem appeals to the West Wind to infuse him with a new spirit and a new power to spread his ideas.
- The West Wind is personified both as a 'Preserver' and a 'Destroyer'.
- The speaker describes the effects of the West Wind on land, air and water.
- The speaker wants to be like the wind's lyre and implores the wind to blow his thoughts over the universe so that they might become seeds to cause a new birth. He wants to be an agent of change and spread his revolutionary ideas.
- Ian Lancashire states that in this poem, Shelley invokes Zephirus, the West Wind, to free his 'dead thoughts' and words, "As from an unextinguished hearth / Ashes and sparks", in order to prophesy a renaissance among humanity, 'to quicken a new birth'. He hopes that his 'spark-like, potentially fiery thoughts and words' will 'enlighten humanity and liberate it from intellectual and moral imprisonment'.

John Keats (1795-1821)

English Romantic poet John Keats was born in Moorgate, London in 1795. Keats studied for sometime at the Clarke School, Enfield, but had to withdraw to apprentice with an apothecary-surgeon and study medicine in a London hospital. He became a licensed apothecary in 1816, but never really practised medicine.

Literary Career and Works

He soon got acquainted with celebrated artists of his time such as Leigh Hunt, Shelley and Benjamin Robert Haydon. In May 1816, Hunt helped him publish his first poem *On Solitude* in a magazine called the *Examiner*. The first volume of his poetry, *Poems* by John Keats, was eventually published in 1817.

Keats' first long poem, *Endymion* appeared in 1818. This poem begins with the famous lines, 'A thing of beauty is a joy for ever'. Based on the Greek myth of Endymion, a shepherd loved by the Moon Goddess Selene, the poem is written in heroic couplets. Keats called this poem 'a test, a trial' of his 'powers of imagination' and of his 'invention'.

The poem was dedicated to Thomas Chatterton. The year 1819 was the most productive year of Keats's life. It is also called his annus mirabilis as he wrote most of his important poems such as *The Eve of St Agnes, La Belle Dame Sans Merci* and his great odes *To Melancholy, To a Nightingale, To Psyche* and *To a Grecian Urn* during this period.

He arrived in Naples in late 1820 and then moved to Rome, when he was in the last stages of tuberculosis. Keats died on 23rd February, 1821. He was buried in the Protestant Cemetery in Rome. On his tombstone appears, at his own request, the words 'Here lies one whose name was writ in water'.

Keats and Negative Capability

- In a letter to his brothers, George and Thomas Keats, on 21st December, 1817, Keats introduced the concept of Negative Capability.
- He described the term as "when a man is capable of being in uncertainties, mysteries, doubts, without any irritable reaching after fact and reason".
- Keats stated that great poets should have the willingness to remain in doubt or not to resolve conflicts or ambiguities. Some uncertainties were best left open to imagination and that the element of doubt and ambiguity added romanticism.
- According to the Bedford Glossary of Literary and Critical Terms, in order for a poet to 'perceive reality in all its manifold complexity', "He or she must remain open-minded...to embrace the unsure and ambiguous, to avoid the temptation to rationalise all uncertainties, to negate one's own personality and prejudices" Keats believed that Shakespeare possessed the quality of negative capability.

Ⓒ *Ode to a Nightingale*

My heart aches and a drowsy numbness pains
My sense, as though of hemlock I had drunk,
Or emptied some dull opiate to the drains
One minute past and Lethe-wards had sunk:
'Tis not through envy of thy happy lot,
But being too happy in thine happiness,-
That thou, light-winged Dryad of the trees,
In some melodious plot
Of beechen green and shadows numberless,
Singest of summer in full-throated ease.
O, for a draught of vintage! that hath been
Cool'd a long age in the deep-delved Earth,
Tasting of Flora and the country green,
Dance and Provencal song and sunburnt mirth!
O for a beaker full of the warm South,
Full of the true, the blushful Hippocrene,
With beaded bubbles winking at the brim,
And purple-stained mouth;
That I might drink and leave the world unseen,
And with thee fade away into the forest dim:
Fade far away, dissolve and quite forget
What thou among the leaves hast never known,
The weariness, the fever and the fret
Here, where men sit and hear each other groan;
Where palsy shakes a few, sad, last gray hairs,
Where youth grows pale and spectre-thin and dies;
Where but to think is to be full of sorrow
And leaden-eyed despairs,
Where Beauty cannot keep her lustrous eyes,
Or new Love pine at them beyond tomorrow.

Ode to a Nightingale

- Keats' *Ode to a Nightingale* was composed in 1819.
- Charles Brown, a friend with whom Keats was living when he composed this poem, wrote about its composition: "In the spring of 1819 a nightingale had built her nest near my house. Keats felt a tranquil and continual joy in her song and one morning he took his chair from the breakfast table to the grass-plot under a plum-tree, where he sat for two or

three hours. When he came into the house, I perceived he had some scraps of paper in his hand and these he was quietly thrusting behind the books. On inquiry, I found those scraps, four or five in number, contained his poetic feeling on the song of our nightingale".

- The speaker begins with a declaration of his heartache. So, exquisite is the song of the nightingale in the shadowy forest that it makes the speaker's heart ache with joy and numbs his senses like a drug. The singing kindles in him a desire for a draught of wine, greenery, country dances, the music of Southern France and days spent in the Sunshine.
- He longs to disappear into the dim forest with the nightingale and fade away. In the world of the nightingale, he would forget about the afflictions of the world-weariness, fever, worries, old age.
- The speaker tells the nightingale to fly away and says that he will follow, not through alcohol (Not charioted by Bacchus and his pards), but through poetry, which will give him 'viewless wings'.
- Surrounded by the nightingale's song, the speaker thinks that the idea of death seems richer than ever and he longs to 'cease upon the midnight with no pain.' By the end of the poem, the speaker realises that the nightingale is immortal. The song of the nightingale that he is listening to was also heard in ancient times by emperors and peasants.
- He comes back to a realisation of his own state and consciousness. He realises that he cannot escape even with the help of his imagination. At the end of the poem, the speaker wonders whether he has had a true insight or experience or whether he has been daydreaming.
- In Keats' ode, the song of the nightingale is a symbol of art that outlasts mortal life.

EXAM BASED QUESTIONS

1 Which book is subtitled "Showing the Two Contrary States of the Human Soul"?
(a) The Marriage of Heaven and Hell
(b) Songs of Innocence and Experience
(c) Poetical Sketches
(d) Jerusalem

2 Whose mother died when he 'was very young,' and who was sold before his 'tongue/Could scarcely cry' in the poem 'London'?
(a) The School-Boy (b) The Little Black Boy
(c) The Chimney Sweeper (d) The Little Boy Lost

3 Blake once pushed a soldier out of his garden and all the way to a nearby inn, where the soldier was quartered. The soldier then charged Blake with what?
(a) Blasphemy (b) Assault
(c) Sedition (d) Battery

4 Which work contains a title page depicting a naked man throwing himself upon a scantily clad woman, while another woman looks on?
(a) The Book of Thel
(b) Visions of the Daughters of Albion
(c) The Marriage of Heaven and Hell
(d) The Four Zoas

5 Whose sigh 'runs in blood down palace walls' in the poem 'London'?
(a) The Little Black Boy's (b) The Happless Soldier's
(c) The Little Vagabond's (d) The Chimney Sweep's

6 Which of the following books, according to Blake, contained all he knew?
(a) The Inferno (b) The Bible
(c) The Talmud (d) The Canterbury Tales

7 Identify Blake's first printed work.
(a) Song of Innocence (b) Poetical Sketches
(c) The Book of Urizen (d) The French Revolution

8 Which of the following work is considered as a milestone in Blake's literary career?
(a) America, a Prophecy
(b) The Marriage of Heaven and Hell
(c) Songs of Innocence and Experience
(d) The Four Zoos

9 'William Blake' famous poems such as 'London', 'The Sick Rose', and 'The Tyger' appear in
(a) Songs of Innocence
(b) Songs of Experience
(c) The Marriage of Heaven and Hell
(d) Vision of the Daughters of Albion

10 When were the Lyrical Ballads published?
(a) 1797 (b) 1798
(c) 1800 (d) 1801

11 The Lyrical Ballads opens with
(a) Kubla Khan
(b) Ode to Duty
(c) Rime of the Ancient Mariner
(d) Immortality Ode

12 The Lyrical Ballads closes with
(a) Kubla Khan
(b) Immortality Ode
(c) Cristobel
(d) Lines Written above Tin tern Abbey

13 Who was the third person with Coleridge and Wordsworth at Quantico Hills when the Lyrical Ballads were composed?
(a) Robert Southey (b) Walter Scott
(c) Dorothy Wordsworth (d) Mary Lamb

14 Who wrote the famous Preface to the Lyrical Ballads?
(a) Coleridge (b) Southey
(c) Wordsworth (d) Byron

15 What was Wordsworth's professed aim in the Lyrical Ballads?
(a) Purge poetry of all conceit
(b) Simplicity of diction
(c) Make it intelligible to common people
(d) All of the above

16 Who was hailed by critics as the first living poet and one of the greatest that England had ever produced?
(a) Scott (b) Donne (c) Wordsworth
(d) Dryden

17 Which romantic poet coined the famous phrase 'Spots of Time'?
(a) John Keats (b) William Wordsworth
(c) ST Coleridge (d) Lord Byron

18 In which of the following spiritual appeal of nature is expressed in almost every line?
(a) To a Highland Girl (b) Stepping Westward
(c) Tintern Abbey (d) Solitary Reaper

19 Who wrote 'Lines Written a Few Miles Above Tintern Abbey'?
(a) Wordsworth (b) Coleridge
(c) Byron (d) John Wilson

20 Which of the Wordsworth's works records his impressions of a manufacturing district of Northern England?
(a) The Excursion (b) The Ruined Cottage
(c) Prelude (d) None of these

21 Who wrote Lucy poems?
(a) Wordsworth (b) Southey
(c) Scott (d) Donne

22 The concept of Pantheism believes in
(a) objectivity
(b) healing power in nature
(c) confession
(d) natural calamity

23 Wordsworth believed in the concept of
(a) hellenism
(b) pantheism
(c) negative capability
(d) willing suspension of disbelief

24 Who amongst the following was reforming poetry or upholding the moral law?
(a) Scott (b) Wordsworth
(c) Keats (d) Byron

25 'Aids to Reflection' is written by
(a) Wordsworth (b) Coleridge
(c) Blake (d) Porter

26 Who wrote 'Religious Musings?'
(a) Wordsworth (b) Coleridge
(c) John Gibson (d) Francis Jeffrey

27 'The Fall of Robespierre' is written by
(a) Coleridge (b) John Gibson
(c) Francis Jeffrey (d) Jane Porter

28 'Daydream' of Coleridge reminds of which poem in past
(a) The Devil's Thought (b) Highland Girl
(c) Songs of Innocence (d) Suicide Argument

29 Who wrote 'Fears in Solitude'?
(a) John Gibson (b) Francis Jeffrey
(c) Jane Porter (d) Coleridge

30 'The Rime of Ancient Mariner' is about
(a) a perilous adventure in the sea
(b) the accidental killing of an octopus
(c) the curse of a sea God
(d) the guilt and expiation of the Ancient Mariner

31 Which bird is killed by the Mariner in 'The Ancient Mariner'?
(a) Penguin (b) Flamingo (c) Albatross (d) Swan

32 Who among the following wrote' Ode to France' under the influence of the French Revolution?
(a) Wordsworth (b) Shelley
(c) Coleridge (d) Blake

33 Which among the following is a fragment, painting a gorgeous oriental dream picture such as in October sunset?
(a) The Fall of Robespierre (b) Christabel
(c) Day Dream (d) Kubla Khan

34 Which among the following is a fragment, which seems to have planned as the story of a pure young girl, who fell under the spell of a sorcerer, in the shape of a woman Geraldine?
(a) Day Dream (b) The Devil Thought
(c) Christabel (d) Kubla Khan

35 What was on the banks of the Susquehanna, which was to be an ideal community, in which the citizens combined farming and literature?
(a) The Fall of Robespierre (b) Kubla Khan
(c) Pantisocracy (d) Day Dream

36 The phrase 'The willing suspension of disbelief' occurs in
(a) Biographia Literaria
(b) Preface to Lyrical Ballads
(c) In Defence of Poetry
(d) Poetics

37 Coleridge's 'Kubla Khan' remains 'a fragment' because
(a) he was called by Wordsworth who was living in Porlock at that time
(b) Dorothy Wordsworth was upset over their love affair
(c) he was interrupted by a called, a person on business from Porlock
(d) he ran out of his stock of opium

38 Which among the following is a poem composed by two enthusiasts, which is full of the two revolutionaries spirit?
(a) To a Highland Girl (b) The Fall of Robespierre
(c) Kubla Khan (d) Day Dream

39 Who wrote the ambitious poem 'Thalaba'?
(a) Wordsworth (b) Southey
(c) John Gibson (d) Francis Jeffrey

40 Which among the following is a tale of Arabian enchantment?
(a) Madoc (b) Roderick
(c) Thalaba (d) The Curse of Kehama

41 'Auld Cloots' was written by
(a) Southey (b) John Gibson
(c) Francis Jeffrey (d) Jane Porter

42 'The Well of St Keyne' was written by
(a) Wordsworth (b) Francis Jeffrey
(c) Jane Porter (d) Southey

43 In his 1817 review of Coleridge's Biographia Literaria, Francis Jeffery grouped the following poets together as the 'Lake School of Poets'.
(a) Keats, Wordsworth and Coleridge
(b) Wordsworth, Byron and Coleridge
(c) Blake, Wordsworth and Coleridge
(d) Wordsworth, Coleridge and Southey

44 Byron's 'The Vision of Judgement' is a satire directed against
(a) Charles Lamb (b) John Keats
(c) Henry Hallam (d) Robert Southey

45 Who pretends to know the secret, unwhole some side of Europe, which generally hides itself in the dark?
(a) Scott (b) Blake
(c) Byron (d) Wordsworth

46 Which out of these is the first volume published by Byron?
(a) English Bards (b) Dunciad
(c) Hours of Idleness (d) Talisman

47 Who among the following is not called 'Lake Poets'?
(a) Byron (b) Coleridge
(c) Southey (d) Wordsworth

48 Who said that the poet was a 'mere babbler'?
(a) Scott (b) Byron (c) Wordsworth
(d) Gibson

49 In which poem do we meet these characters? Don Alfonso, Julia, Sultana?
(a) Lara (b) Don Juan
(c) Childe Harold (d) Beppo

50 Who is Halide in Don Juan?
(a) Wife of Don Alfonso (b) Daughter of an old pirate
(c) Princess of Constantinople (d) A Duchess

51 The verse form of Byron's Childe Harold was influenced by
(a) Milton (b) Spenser
(c) Shakespeare (d) Pope

52 Which canon of Childe Harold was more frequently read than any other work of Byron?
(a) Last two canons (b) First two canons
(c) Third and fourth canons (d) Mid canons

53 Who wrote the 'Witch of Atlas'?
(a) Scott (b) Wordsworth (c) Blake (d) Shelley

54 Who wrote Adonais?
(a) Scott (b) Shelley (c) Blake (d) Gibson

55 Who among the following is far different in character in Shelley's 'Adonais'?
(a) Beatrice (b) Hellas
(c) Epipsychidion (d) Emilia Viviani

56 Who among the following is like a wanderer following a vague, beautiful vision forever sad and forever unsatisfied?
(a) Shelley (b) Scott (c) Gibson (d) Blake

57 The 'Pansies' as the symbol of sad thoughts and 'violets' as the symbol of modesty and innocence was used by
(a) John Keats (b) PB Shelley
(c) ST Coleridge (d) William Wordsworth

58 Identify from the following, who had called Wordsworth, a 'Moral Eunuch'.
(a) Byron (b) Shelley
(c) Coleridge (d) Browning

59 Shelley was expelled from the Oxford University due to the publication of
(a) The Revolt of Islam (b) The Necessity of Atheism
(c) The Triumph of Life (d) The Masque of Anarchy

60 Which among the following is a wonderful threnody, or a song of grief over the death of the poet Keats?
(a) Kubla Khan (b) Queen Mab
(c) Adonais (d) Hellas

61 Which out of the following is the poet's confession not simply of failure, but of undying hope in some better thing that is to come?
(a) Prometheus Unbound (b) Talisman
(c) Adonais (d) Alastor

62 We meet characters such as Asia, Hercules, Jupiter in
(a) Hellas (b) Prometheus unbound
(c) Adonais (d) Queen Mab

63 Which character was the only one of Shelley's character, who seems to be entirely human?
(a) Prometheus (b) Hellas
(c) Emilia (d) Beatrice

64 Who brought the concept of negative capability?
(a) Wordsworth (b) Coleridge
(c) Keats (d) Shelley

65 Who has been labelled as an Escapist?
(a) Coleridge (b) Keats (c) Blake (d) Gibson

66 Which is the most perfect of Keats' medieval poems, which is not a story after the manner of the metrical romances, but rather a vivid painting of a romantic mood?
(a) Endymion (b) Isabella
(c) Hyperion (d) The Eve of St Agnes

67 Identify the poem from the following, in which Keats bears the mark of Hellenism?
(a) Lamia and Grecian Urn (b) Ode to Nightingale
(c) Endymion and Hyperion (d) All of these

68 Which of the following poets has been said to be endowed with 'Organic Sensibility'?
(a) Coleridge (b) Keats
(c) Blake (d) Byron

69 Which is the story written by Keats, of a young Shepherd beloved by a Moon Goddess?
(a) Isabella (b) Endymion
(c) The Eve of St Agnes (d) Faerie Queene

70 Who wrote the 'Eve of St Agnes'?
(a) Scott (b) Keats
(c) Wordsworth (d) Blake

71 Who of the following is known for his Hel-lenic Spirit?
(a) Lord Byron (b) PB Shelley
(c) Southey (d) John Keats

72 Which is the pair of lovers Endymion does not meet in Keat's Endymion?
(a) Venus and Adonis (b) Romeo and Juliet
(c) Glaucus and Scylla (d) Arcthusa and Alpheus

73 Who is Adonais of the poem Adonais?
(a) Lord Byron (b) John Keats
(c) Shelley himself (d) None of these

74 This patriotic song is often prescribed for school anthologies in India:
"Breathes there the man, with soul so dead who never to himself hath said, this is my own, my native land." Who is the poet?
(a) Robert Southey (b) Walter Scott
(c) Lord Byron (d) William Wordsworth

75 Who wrote a poem by the name *The Shepherd's Calendar*, that was published in 1827?
(a) William Cobett (b) Robert Bloomfield
(c) John Clare (d) Hopkins

76 Keats called .... as 'the Egotistical Sublime.'
(a) Shelley (b) Blake
(c) Wordsworth (d) Coleridge

77 Wordsworth in his poem .... tells the scholar to do away with books and make nature his teacher.
(a) The Prelude (b) Tables Turned
(c)Tintern Abbey (d) None of these

78 These lines about French Revolution, 'Liberty the soul of life shall reign /Shall throb in every pulse, shall flow through every vein' were written by ....
(a) Southey (b) Godwin (c) Coleridge (d) Blake

79 The poetry of Wordsworth and Coleridge was notably influenced by.......... .
(a) the Napoleonic Wars (b) the Glorious Revolution
(c) the French Revolution (d) Poor Laws

80 'The Book of the Church' and 'Sir Thomas Moore' was written by ....
(a) Coleridge (b) Blake (c) Southey (d) Keats

81 .... wrote blank-verse tragedies such as Cain, Manfred, Marino Faliero and 'The Deformed Transformed'.
(a) Scott (b) Byron (c) Godwin (d) Coleridge

82 In Shelley's work 'Hymn of Pan', the Greek God Pan fights with ....
(a) Zeus (b) Titans (c) Apollo (d) All of these

83 .... is a Rhaphsody celebrating Platonic love, the most impalpable and so one of the most characteristic of all Shelley's works ?
(a) Hellas (b) Emilia Viviani
(c) Episychidion (d) Beatrice

84 .... lived apart from men and from all political measures, worshipping beauty like a devotee, perfectly content to write what was in his own heart or to reflect some splendor of the natural world as he saw or dreamed it to be?
(a) Wordsworth (b) John Keats
(c) Shelley (d) Byron

85 .... has expressed his dislike for poetry 'that has a palpable design upon us' in one of his letters.
(a) Wordsworth
(b) Keats
(c) Coleridge (d) Shelley

86 Which of the following is not true for William Wordsworth periods?
(a) His childhood and youth in the Cumberland hills from 1770 to 1787
(b) A period of uncertainty, of storms and stress, including his University life at Cambridge, his travels abroad and his revolutionary experience from 1787 to 1800
(c) A short, but significant period fo finding himself and his work from 1797 to 1799
(d) A long period of retirement in the Northern Lake region, where he was born and where for a full half century he lived, so close to nature that her influence is reflected in all his poetry

87 Which of the following statements about Don Juan is not true?
(a) The poem begins with a dedication to Robert Southey and William Wordsworth
(b) The poem is written in the Italian ottava rima
(c) The poem consists of 16 cantos
(d) It is a ballad

88 Which of these statements about 'Kubla Khan' is not correct?
(a) The poem describes Xanadu, the palace of Kubla Khan, a Mongol emperor
(b) It is a poem about poetry and poetic process
(c) The speaker talks about a vision of his a woman calling to her demonic lover
(d) The poem's speaker starts by describing the setting of the emperor's garden

89 Which of these statements about Childe Harold's Pilgrimage is true?
(a) It is a lyric which focusses on illusion
(b) It is written in ten cantos
(c) It introduced the concept of the Byronic hero
(d) It does not reflect Byron's political views

90 Which of the following statements about 'Ode to a Nightingale' is true?
(a) It was composed in 1800
(b) The speaker begins with a declaration of his Heartache
(c) The speaker realises that the nightingale is mortal at the end of the poem
(d) In the poem, the song of the nightingale is a symbol of art that outlasts mortal life

91 Which of the following pairs is correctly matched?

	Authors		Books
(a)	William Wordsworth	:	Don Juan
(b)	Samuel Taylor Coleridge	:	Kubla Khan
(c)	John Keats	:	Ode to the West Wind
(d)	Shelley	:	Rime of the Ancient Mariner

92 Which of the following pairs is correctly matched?

	Authors		Books
(a)	William Blake	:	Don Juan
(b)	William Wordsworth	:	The Marriage of Heaven and Hell
(c)	Lord Byron	:	The Prelude
(d)	Robert Southey	:	The Inchcape Rock

93 Which of the following pairs is correctly matched?

	Authors		Works
(a)	William Blake	:	Songs of Experience
(b)	PB Shelley	:	Don Juan
(c)	Samuel Taylor Coleridge	:	Christabel
(d)	William Wordsworth	:	The Inchcape Rock

94 Which of the following pairs is incorrectly matched?

	Authors		Works
(a)	Samuel Taylor Coleridge	:	Kubla Khan
(b)	PB Shelley	:	Ode to the West Wind
(c)	John Keats	:	To a Nightingale
(d)	Byron	:	To a Grecianurn

95 Which of the following pairs is correctly matched?

	Authors		Works
(a)	Robert Southey	:	Adonais
(b)	Lord Byron	:	The Fall of Robespierre
(c)	PB Shelley	:	Childe Harold's Pilgrimage
(d)	John Keats	:	Ode to a Nightingale

96 **Assertion** (A) Literary and historical periodisation often has nothing to do with the lifetime of writers. Thus, we see two writers born in the same year belonging to two separate periods.

Reason (R) Thomas Carlyle and John Keats were born in 1795. In standard literary histories, Keats is a Romantic and Carlyle, a Victorian.

Codes

(a) A and R are correct (b) A is correct R is incorrect
(c) A and R are incorrect (d) R does not follow A

97 **Assertion** (A) Romanticism as a literary and artistic movement started in reaction against the age of Enlightenment.

Reason (R) The Age of Enlightenment focussed on reason and empirical thought.

Codes

(a) A is true, but R is false
(b) A is false, but R is true
(c) Both A and R are true, but R is not the correct explanation of A
(d) Both A and R are true and R is the correct explanation of A

98 **Assertion** (A) At the beginning of the Romantic period, there was a turmoil in the society.

Reason (R) The reason behind the turmoil was due to the political and economic problems.

Codes

(a) A is true, but R is false (b) Both A and R are true
(c) A is false, but R is true (d) Both A and R are false

99 **Assertion** (A) Romantic period is also known as the age of revolutions.

Reason (R) The Romantic period coincided with the revolution in France and America.

Codes

(a) A is true, but R is false
(b) A is false, but R is true
(c) Both A and R are true, but R is not the correct explanation of A
(d) Both A and R are true and R is the correct explanation of A

100 **Assertion** (A) The first generation romantic age poets were inspired by the Battle of Bastille and the French Revolution.

Reason (R) The second generation romantic age poets were inspired by the second World War.

(a) Both A and R are correct and R is the correct explanation of A
(b) Both A and R are correct but R is not the correct explanation of A
(c) A is true but R is false
(d) A is false but R is True

101 Which of the following is in a proper sequence?

(a) Queen Mab, Mont Blanc, Mansfield Park
(b) Queen Mab, Mansfield Park, Mont Blanc
(c) Mansfield Park, Mont Blanc, Queen Mab
(d) Mont Blanc, Mansfield Park, Queen Mab

102 Which of the following is in correct sequence?

(a) Keats, Byron, Shelley (b) Byron, Shelley, Keats
(c) Keats Shelley, Byron (d) Shelley, Byron, Keats

103 Which of the following is in correct sequence?

(a) Ode to the West Wind, To a Skylark, A Defence of Poetry
(b) A Defence of Poetry, To a Skylark, Ode to the West Wind
(c) To a Skylark, A Defence of Poetry, Ode to the West Wind
(d) A Defence of Poetry, Ode to the West Wind, To a Skylark

104 Which of the following is in correct sequence?

(a) Don Juan, Weiner, Childe Harold's Pilgrimage
(b) Weiner, Don Juan, Childe Harold's Pilgrimage
(c) Childe Harold's Pilgrimage, Don Juan, Weiner
(d) Don Juan, Childe Harold's Pilgrimage, Weiner

105 Which of the following is in correct sequence?
(a) The Inchcape Rock, After Blenheim, The Fall of Robespierre
(b) After Blenheim, The Inchcape Rock, The Fall of Robespierre
(c) The Fall of Robespierre, After Blenheim, The Inchcape Rock
(d) After Blenheim, The Fall of Robespierre, The Inchcape Rock

106 Consider the following statements correctly. The Romantics were characterised by
1. a belief in individual liberty and sympathy with those who rebelled against tyranny.
2. the Romantic thought of nature as permanent.
3. a disbelief in individual liberty and sympathy with those, who rebelled against by tyranny.
4. the Romantics thought of nature as transformative.

Which of the statements given above are correct?
(a) 1 and 2 (b) 1 and 4 (c) 3 and 4 (d) 3 and 2

107 Combine the statements correctly.
The main characteristics of 'spots of time' are
1. epiphanic moments where ordinary events appears transcendent.
2. intense physical experiences.
3. epiphanic moments, which derange one mind and reduce pleasure.
4. intense emotional experience in life.

Which of the statements given above are correct?
(a) 1 and 4 (b) 1 and 2 (c) 3 and 4 (d) 3 and 2

108 Which of the following statements is not correct for William Wordsworth?
1. Poet of Common Man and Lover of Nature.
2. Loved to write on Love and Mankind.
3. Employed day-to-day language in his poems.

Select the correct answer using the codes given below.
(a) Only 2 (b) Only 1
(c) 1 and 2 (d) None of the above

109 Combine the statements correctly. The main characteristics of Coleridge's 'Biographia Literaria' are
1. the primary imagination is merely the power of receiving impressions of the external world through the senses.
2. the secondary imagination works up on what is perceived by the primary imagination.
3. the primary imagination is not possessed by everyone.
4. the secondary imagination represented an inferior faculty.

Which of the statements given above are correct?
(a) 1 and 4 (b) 1 and 2 (c) 3 and 4 (d) 3 and 2

110 Which of the following is true about Kubla Khan?
1. It was a complete dream.
2. It was a dream segment.
3. It was a reality.
4. It was a sensational achievement.

Select the correct answer using the codes given below.
(a) 2 and 3 (b) Only 3
(c) Only 2 (d) Only 1

111 Combine the statements correctly. The main characteristics of Don Juan are
1. It is a finished poem by Byron.
2. It consists of sixteen cantos.
3. It is a satirical mock epic.
4. The poem is written in French Ottava Rima.

Which of the statements given above are correct?
(a) 1 and 4 (b) 1 and 2
(c) 3 and 4 (d) 3 and 2

112 Combine the statements correctly.
The main characteristics of 'Childe Harold's Pilgrimage' are
1. It is written in six cantos published between 1812 and 1818.
2. The poem's title is a medieval title for an old man, who is eligible for knighthood.
3. It is a semi-autobiographical poem that focusses on a nobleman.
4. The poem also reflects Byron's political view.

Which of the statements given above are correct?
(a) 1 and 4 (b) 1 and 2 (c) 3 and 4 (d) 3 and 2

113 In his distinction between Reason and Imagination, Shelley identifies the following.
1. It is the enumeration of qualities already known.
2. It is the perception of the value of those qualities, both separately and as a whole.
3. It respects the differences.
4. It respects the similitudes of things. The correct combination reads.

Which of the statements given above is/are correct?
(a) 1 and 3 for reason; 2 and 4 for imagination
(b) 1 and 2 for reason 3 and 4 for imagination
(c) 2 and 3 for reason; 1 and 4 for imagination
(d) 3 and 4 for reason; 1 and 2 for imagination

114 Which of the following is not true for John Keats?
1. He was a lover of beauty.
2. Labelled as an escapist.
3. Lost his parents during the childhood.

Select the correct answer using the codes given below
(a) Only 1 (b) All of these
(c) None of these (d) Only 2

115 Consider the following statements about 'Ode to the West Wind'.

1. It is written by PB Shelley
2. It was published in 1820.
3. It is not written in terza rima.
4. It is not addressed to the West Wind.

Which of the statements given above are correct?

(a) 1 and 2 (b) 1 and 4
(c) 3 and 2 (d) 3 and 4

116 Match the following first generation romantic poets with their poems.

First Generation Romantic Poet
1. William Blake
2. William Wordsworth
3. Samuel Taylor Côleridge
4. Robert Southey

Poem
A. A Poison Tree B. The Prelude
C. Kubla khan D. Joan of Arc

(a) 1-A, 2-B, 3-C, 4-D (b) 1-D, 2-C, 3-B, 4-A
(c) 1-B, 2-D, 3-A, 4-C (d) 1-C, 2-A, 3-D, 4-B

117 Match the following poems with their first generation romantic poets.

1. The Lamb 2. The Solitary Reaper
3. Frost at Midnight 4. Thalaba the Destroyer

First Generation Romantic Poet
A. Robert Southey B. Samuel Taylor Coleridge
C. William WordsworthD. William Blake

(a) 1-A, 2-B, 3-C, 4-D (b) 1-D, 2-C, 3-B, 4-A
(c) 1-B, 2-D, 3-A, 4-C (d) 1-C, 2-A, 3-D, 4-B

118 Match the following opening lines with the poems of Romantic Age:

Opening Lines of the Poem
1. Nor stir in the air, nor stir in the sea.
2. Oh, thou, in Hellas deemed of Heavenly birth...
3. I want a hero, an uncommon want.....
4. My heart aches and a drowry numbness pains......

Romantic Age Poem
A. Don Juan B. The Inckcape Rock
C. Ode to a Nightingale
D. Childe Harold's Pilgrimage

(a) 1-A, 2-B, 3-C, 4-D (b) 1-D, 2-C, 3-B, 4-A
(c) 1-B, 2-D, 3-A, 4-C (d) 1-C, 2-A, 3-D, 4-B

119 Match the following romantic age poets with the year of their birth.

Romantic Age Poet
1. Robert Southey 2. Lord Bryon
3. PB Shelly 4. John Keats

Birth Year
A. 1788 B. 1795 C. 1774 D. 1792

(a) 1-A, 2-B, 3-C, 4-D (b) 1-D, 2-C, 3-B, 4-A
(c) 1-B, 2-D, 3-A, 4-C (d) 1-C, 2-A, 3-D, 4-B

120 Match the following romantic age poets with their poems.

List I	List II
A. William Wordsworth	1. After Blenheim
B. Samuel Taylor Coleridge	2. London
C. William Blake	3. Christabel
D. Robert Southey	4. A Slumber did my spirit seal

(a) A-1, B-2, C-3, D-4 (b) A-4, B-3, C-2, D-1
(c) A-2, B-4, C-1, D-3 (d) A-3, B-1, C-4, D-2

121 Match the following poems with their poets.

List I	List II
A. Ozymandias	1. John Keats
B. Shl Walks in Beauty	2. William Wordsworth
C. Ode on a Grecian Urn	3. PB Shelley
D. Composed upon Westminster	4. Lord Bryon Bridge,

(a) A-1, B-2, C-3, D-4 (b) A-4, B-3, C-2, D-1
(c) A-2, B-4, C-1, D-3 (d) A-3, B-4, C-1, D-2

122 Match the following works with their years.

List I	List II
A. The Excursion	1. 1814
B. Lyrical Ballads	2. 1798
C. The Duddon Sonnets	3. 1820
D. The Devil's Walk	3. 1830

Codes

	A	B	C	D		A	B	C	D
(a)	1	2	3	4	(b)	4	3	2	1
(c)	2	3	4	1	(d)	1	3	2	4

123 In the following series, which set of author and work is correctly matched?

(a) Wordsworth-The Revolt of Islam, Coleridge-The Bride of Abydos, Byron-Aids to Reflection, PB Shelley-Ode to Duty
(b) Wordsworth-The Revolt of Islam, Coleridge-Ode to Duty, Byron-Aids to Reflection, PB Shelley-The Bride of Abydos
(c) Wordsworth-Ode to Duty, Coleridge-Aids to Reflection, Byron-The Bride of Abydos, PB Shelley-The Revolt of Islam
(d) Wordsworth-Aids to Reflection, Coleridge-Ode to Duty, Byron-The Bride of Abydos, PB Shelley-The Revolt of Islam

124 In the following series, which set of author and their work is correctly matched?

(a) Coleridge-The Eve of St Agnes, Southey-The Rime of the Ancient Mariner, Byron-The Inchcape Rock, Keats-Childe Harold's Pilgrimage
(b) Coleridge-Childe Harold's Pilgrimage, Sothey- The Eve of ST Agnes, Byron-The Rime of the Ancient Mariner, Keats-The Inchcape Rock

(c) Coleridge-The Inchcape Rock, Southey-Childe Harold's Pilgrimage, Byron-The Eve of St Agnes, Keats-The Rime of the Ancient Mariner
(d) Coleridge-The Rime of the Ancient Mariner, Southey-The Inchcape Rock, Byron-Childe Harold's Pilgrimage, Keats-The Eve of St Agnes

125 In the given series, which one has all the romantic age poems matched correctly with the year of their publication?
(a) The Tyger-1794, Lucy Gray-1800, To a Skylark-1820, Endymion-1818
(b) The Tyger-1818, Lucy Gray-1820, To a Skylark 1794, Endymion-1800
(c) The Tyger-1794, Lucy Gray-1800, To a Skylark-1818, Endymion-1820.
(d) The Tyger-1820 Lucy Gray-1818 To a Skylark-1860, Endymion-1794.

126 It appears that in Paradise Lost Book I 'Milton belongs to the Devil's party without knowing it'.
Who among the following made this statement?
(a) Frank Kermode (b) William Empson
(c) CS Lewis (d) William Blake

127 Which are the figures of speech used in the following lines by Blake?
"Tyger, tyger, burning bright
In the forest of the night,
What immortal hand or eye
Could frame thy fearful symmetry?"
(a) Simile and personification
(b) Irony and synecdoche
(c) Apostrophe and synecdoche
(d) Metonymy and apostrophe

128 The Holy Word
That walked among the ancient trees,
Calling the lapsed soul,
And weeping in the evening dew,
That might control The starry pole
And fallen, fallen light renew
Which of the following poets in which of his/her works has used the above lines?
(a) Alexander Pope, An Essay on Criticism
(b) William Cowper, The Poetical Works of William Cowper
(c) William Blake, Songs of Experience.
(d) Robert Burns, The Complete Poetical Works of Robert Burns

129 I feared the fury of my wind
Would blight all blossoms fair and true;
And my Sun it shined and shined,
And my wind it never blew; But a blossom fair and true
Was not found on any tree,
For all blossoms grew and grew Faithless, false, though fair to see.
Which of the following poets in which of his/her works has used the above lines?
(a) William Blake, "Barren Blossom".
(b) Robert Burns, Tam O'Shanter
(c) Alexander Pope, An Essay on Criticism
(d) William Cowper, The Poetical Works of William Cowper

130 I wander thro' each chartered street Near where the chartered Thames doth flow.
Which of the following poets in which of his/her works has used the above lines?
(a) William Blake, London.
(b) Robert Burns, Tam O'Shanter
(c) Alexander Pope, An Essay on Criticism
(d) William Cowper, The Poetical works of William Cowper.

131 Which of the following poems features the phrase, 'The still, sad music of humanity'?
(a) "Ode: Intimations of Immortality from Recollections of Early Childhood"
(b) 'Michael: A Pastoral Poem'
(c) 'The Solitary Reaper'
(d) 'Tintern Abbey'

132 "But Europe at that time was thrilled up with joy France standing on the top of golden hours and human nature seeming born again".
These lines regarding the French Revolution are of
(a) De Quincey
(b) Shelley
(c) Wordsworth (d) Sir Walter Raleigh

133 He is not fully recognised at home, he is not recognised at all abroad. Yet I firmly believe that the poetical performance of .... is, after that of Shakespeare and Milton, Undoubtedly most considerable in our language.
To Whom does Matthew Arnold refer in the above statement?
(a) Edmund Spenser (b) John Keats
(c) William Wordsworth (d) ST Coleridge

134 "Bliss was it in that dawn to be alive/but to be young was very heaven?"
(a) Keats
(b) Coleridge
(c) Wordsworth
(d) Blake

135 William Long stated, "The essence of the literature was to be remembered, that literature must reflect all that is spontaneous and unaffected in nature and in man and be free to follow its own fancy in its own way."
Which literature is referred to in the above statement?
(a) Romantic
(b) Neo-Classic
(c) Victorian
(d) Modern

136 Who wrote "Hymn before Sunrise in the vale of Chamoceni?"
(a) Wordsworth (b) Blake
(c) Coleridge (d) Porter

137 Who said about Coleridge's poetry "All that he did excellently might be bound up in twenty pages, but it should be bound in pure gold"?
(a) Stafford Broke (b) John Gibson
(c) Francis Jeffrey (d) Jane Porter

138 In which poem Coleridge starts with "My eyes make pictures when they are shut............. ."
(a) The Devil Thought (b) Day Dream
(c) Songs of Innocence (d) Suicide Argument

139 "Liberty the soul of life shall reign I shall throb in every pulse, shall flow through every vein". Who wrote the above lines regarding the French Revolution?
(a) Thomas Paine (b) ST Coleridge
(c) William Godwin (d) Robert Southey

140 "O Lady! We receive but we give,
And in our life alone does Nature live:
Ours is her wedding garment, ours her shroud!
And would we ought behold, of higher work,
Than that inanimate cold world allowed"
The above extract has been taken from Coleridge's.........
(a) Christabel (b) Kubla Khan
(c) The Dejection Ode (d) The Ancient Mariner

141 "In Xanadu, did Kubla Khan a stately pleasure – dome decree .. where Alph, the sacred river, ran through caverns measureless to man."
(a) This is Coleridge in 'Kubla Khan'
(b) This is Shelley in 'Adonais'
(c) This is Southey in 'Inchcape Rock'
(d) This is Byron in 'Don Juan'

142 Day after day, day after day,
We stuck, nor breath nor motion;
As idle as a painted ship
Upon a painted ocean
Water, water, everywhere,
And all the boards did shrink;
Water, water, everywhere,
Nor any drop to drink."
Identify the poem and the poet of the above lines.
(a) Coleridge's 'The Rime of the Ancient Mariner'
(b) Byron's 'Don Juan'
(c) Keat's 'Ode to Autum'
(d) Shelley's 'Adonais'

143 "Man's love is of man's life a thing apart, "Tis woman's whole existence"
These lines have been taken from?
(a) Lara
(b) Don Juan
(c) Childe Harold
(d) None of these

144 In a letter of his brother George in September 1819, John Keats had this to say about a fellow romantic poet: "He describes what he sees I describe what I imagine: Mine is the hardest task". The poet under references is
(a) Wordsworth (b) Coleridge
(c) Byron (d) Southey

145 Are driven like ghosts from an enchanter fleeing, yellow and black and Pale and hectic red, Pestilence — Stricken multitudes".
These lines have been taken from the famous
(a) The Night of the Scorpion
(b) Ode to the West Wind
(c) The Mirror
(d) The Rime of the Ancient Mariner

146 The famous quote "Our sweetest songs are those that tell our saddest thoughts" is by
(a) Robert Southey (b) Rudyard Kipling
(c) PB Shelley (d) ST Coleridge

147 "Men of England, Wherefore plough, for the lords, who day ye low? Wherefore weave with toil and care, the rich robes you tyrants wear"?
These revolutionary thoughts hailed from
(a) Byron (b) Shelley
(c) De Quincey (d) Walter Scott

148 O wild West wind, thou breath of Autumn's being Thou from whose unseen presence the leaves dead
Are driven, like ghosts from an enchanter fleeing...
(a) This is Shelley in 'Ode to the West Wind'
(b) This is Keats in 'To a Nightingale'
(c) This is Byron in 'La Belle Dame Sans Merci'
(d) This is Coleridge in 'Kubla Khan'

149 "Men of England, wherefore plough
For the lords who day ye low?
Wherefore weave with toil and case
the rich robes you tyrants wear?"
These revolutionary thoughts hailed from
(a) Coleridge (b) Blake (c) Shelley (d) Scott

150 'Life, like a dome of many-coloured glass,
Stains the white radiance of Eternity,
Until Death tramples it into fragments'
The above lines occur in
(a) 'Dejection: An Ode (b) Adonais
(c) In Memoriam (d) Thyrsis

151 My heart aches and a drowsy numbness pains My sense, as though of hemlock I had drunk or emptied some dull opiate to the drains one minute part, and Lethe – wards had sunk: 'This not through every of thy happy, lot
(a) This is Shelley in 'Adonais'
(b) This is Keats in 'Ode to a Nightingale'
(c) This is Byron in 'Childe Harold'
(d) This is Blake in 'Songs of Innocence'

152 Whose epitaph contains "here lies one whose name was written in water"?
(a) Coleridge (b) Blake
(c) John Keats (d) William Wordsworth

153 Which famous Romantic poem begins with the line : "Hail to thee, blithe spirit ! / Bird thou never wert"?
(a) 'Ode to a Nightingale' (b) 'To the Cuckoo'
(c) 'To a Skylark' (d) 'To the Daisy'

154 "A portion of the loveliness
Which once he made more lovely"?
Who does 'he' refer to in these lines by Shelley?
(a) Coleridge
(b) Shelley himself
(c) Blake
(d) Keats

155 The words 'where are the songs of spring? Ay, where are they?' occcur in:
(a) Ode to the West Wind
(b) The Seasons
(c) Ode to Autumn
(d) Resolution and Independence

Directions (Q. Nos. 156-160) *Read the following poem and answer the questions.*

Behold her, single in the field,
Yon solitary Highland Lass!
Reaping and singing by herself;
Stop here, or gently pass!
Alone she suts and binds the grain,
And sings a melancholy strain;
O listen! for the Vale profound
Is overflowing with the sound.
No Nightingale did ever chaunt
More welcome notes to weary bands
Of travellers in some shady haunt,
Among Arabian sands:
A voice so thrilling ne'er was heard
In spring-time from the Cuckoo-bird,
Breaking the silence of the seas
Among the farthest Hebrides.

156 How does the poet know that the song is melancholy when he cannot understand the words?
(a) From the girl's expression
(b) From the words of the song
(c) From the tune
(d) From her dress

157 What effect does the girl's song have over the surroundings?
(a) Has no effect
(b) All people desert the valley
(c) The valley echoes with the song
(d) The valey is indifferent

158 What is cuckoo bird famous for?
(a) Cheerfulne
(b) Thrill
(c) Driving away tiredness
(d) Welcoming the spring

159 Hebrides means:
(a) a group of trees
(b) far off valleys
(c) sea
(d) a group of islands off near Scotland

160 The singing of the Solitary Reaper is compared to the
(a) nightingale and robin (b) cuckoo and peacock
(c) nightingale and cuckoo (d) cuckoo and owl

PREVIOUS YEARS' QUESTIONS

December 2018

1 In which work does William Blake say that Milton was "a true poet and of devil's party without knowing it"?
(a) 'London'
(b) 'Songs of Innocence'
(c) 'The Marriage of Heaven and Hell'
(d) 'The Chimney Sweeper'

2 Which ancient writer's name is directly mentioned in Lord Byron's poem 'the Isles of Greece'?
(a) Euripides
(b) Sophocles
(c) Aeschylus
(d) Sappho

3 Match the poem with the opening lines:
(a) 'Ode to Psyche'
(b) 'Ode on a Grecian Urn'
(c) 'Ode to a Nightingale'
(d) 'Ode on Melancholy'
1. "My heart aches, and a drowsy numbness pains my sense, as though of Hemlock I had drunk,"
2. "No, no, go not to Lethe, neither twist Wolf's-bane, tight-rooted, for its Poisonous wine,"
3. "Thou still unravish'd bride of quietness, Thou foster-child of silence and slow time,"
4. "O Goddess! hear these tuneless numbers, by sweet enforcement and Remembrance dear,"

Codes
(a) (a)-(4), (b)-(1), (c)-(3), (d)-(2)
(b) (a)-(3), (b)-(4), (c)-(2), (d)-(1)
(c) (a)-(4), (b)-(3), (c)-(1), (d)-(2)
(d) (a)-(1), (b)-(3), (c)-(2), (d)-(4)

4 Who viewed Wordsworth, Southey and Coleridge as representatives of a "sect of poets...... Dissenters from the established systems in poetry and criticism" who constituted "the most formidable conspiracy against sound judgement is malters political"?
(a) Henry Vaughan (b) Francisco Franco
(c) Ralph Vaughan (d) Francis Jeffrey

5 S.T. Coleridge's 'Dejection: An Ode' opens with an epigraph which is a reference to a ballad. Identify the ballad.
(a) Ballad of Goodly Fere (b) La Belle Dame Sans Merci
(c) Ballad of Sir Patrick Spence
(d) Ballad of the Gibbet

6 Which interpretation of Keats, 'Beauty is truth, truth beauty' best represents the mimetic perspective.
(a) The line is an ironic quotation, the equation of "beauty" and "truth" as "all we know on earth" suggests that reality is an illusory concept and that the primary function of art is to construct a world within an aesthetic reality of its own.
(b) Those aspects of reality which we perceive to be "beautiful" are the only worthy subject matter of the artist and it is the artist's job to observe closely and isolate those sublime elements from the flux of the mundane.
(c) The authors arbitrary imposition of order upon the chaotic impressions of reality constitutes the only 'truth' is a work of art.
(d) A work of literature is 'beautiful' in so far as it offers and acurate representation of its subject matter, with fully realized characters and vivid description of events.

July 2018

7 A half-sentence in Purchas his Pilgrimage triggered off 'Kubla Khan'. Whose work was Purchas his Pilgrimage?
(a) Robert Herrick, the Poet's
(b) John Hakluyt's, the collector of traveller's tales
(c) Samuel Purchas, the London Parson's
(d) Edward Purchas, the globe-trotter's

8 An English poet couldn't help the excitement that an historical event caused in his life-time.
Bliss was it in that dawn to be alive,
But to be young was very heaven
Which poet? What 'dawn'?
(a) WH Auden; the Spanish Civil War
(b) Lord Tennyson; The Jubilee of Queen Victoria's reign
(c) William Wordsworth, The French Revolution
(d) William Blake; The Industrial Revolution

November 2017

9 For Coleridge, our power to perceive symbols gleaned from the world about us is related to the category of
(a) primary imagination (b) secondary imagination
(c) fancy (d) intuition

10 This Byron work revolves around a wife whose husband is presumed lost at sea and she takes a lover in his absence. Everybody behaves agreeably on the husband's return. Byron's technical skills in verse is in display here as the work counterpoints the colloquial and the formal. Identify the work.
(a) Manfred (b) Don Juan
(c) Beppo (d) The Bride of Abydos

11 William Blake has a rare elan to provide telling images in arresting phrases. Match the phrases with the poems they belong to:

List I	List II
A. 'mind forg manacles'	1. 'The Tyger'
B. 'eternal winter'	2. 'The Sick Rose'
C. 'fearful symmetry'	3. 'London'
D. 'crimson joy'	4. 'Holy Thursday'

Codes

	A	B	C	D		A	B	C	D
(a)	3	4	1	2	(b)	3	1	4	2
(c)	3	2	4	1	(d)	4	1	2	3

12 The opening lines of Wordsworth's 'Immortality Ode':
"There was a time when meadow, grove, and stream,
The Earth, and every common sight,
To me did seem
Apparelled in celestial light
The glory and freshness of a dream",
closely resembles Coleridge's lines:
"There was a time when earth, and sea and skies,
The bright green vale, and the forest' dark recess,
In steady loveliness"
Identify the Coleridge poem.
(a) 'Fears In Solitude' (b) 'The Mad Monk'
(c) 'To William Wordsworth' (d) 'Dejection : An Ode'

13 Which character created by Coleridge makes the following account of her harrowing experience?
"Five warriors seized me yestermorn,
Me, even me, a maid forlorn
They choked my cries with force and fright,
And tied me on a palfrey white".
(a) Geraldine (b) Christabel (c) Christabel's mother
(d) The maid who appeared in Christabel's dream

14 Which Byron work begins thus
"I want a hero : an uncommon want, when every year and month sends forth a new ne ...."?
(a) Beppo (b) Cain (c) Manfred (d) Don Juan

15 In the opening book of *The Prelude* Wordsworth mentions famously that he was "fostered alike by........and....".
Pick out the right pair.
1. nature 2. fear 3. imagination 4. beauty
The right combination according to the code is
(a) 1 and 3 (b) 4 and 2 (c) 4 and 3 (d) 1 and 4

January 2017

16 Which statement best expresses the theme of Coleridge's 'The Rime of the Ancient Mariner'?
(a) To kill a living creature is immoral
(b) People should honour and respect all living things
(c) Prayer can accomplish miracles
(d) True harmony is achieved only through cooperative effort

17 Who among the following Greek Philosophers has a bearing on the composition of Shelley's 'Adonais'?
(a) Miletus (b) Socrates (c) Plato (d) Aristotle

18 What would help a reader recognise Keats's 'To Autumn' as a poem from the Romantic Period?
(a) Its logical succession of images
(b) Its concise use of couplets
(c) Its lavish natural imagery
(d) Its use of iambic pentameter

19 Which Byron poem begins in the following manner
"I want a hero : an uncommon want, when every year and month sends forth a new one"?
(a) Beppo
(b) Childe Harold's Pilgrimage
(c) Don Juan
(d) The Vision of Judgement

20 "O, for a draught of vintage that hath been
Cooled a long age in the deep-delved Earth,
Tasting of Flora and the country green,
Dance, and Provencal song, and sunburnt mirth!"
The above description is an example of
(a) Paronomasia (b) Synaesthesia
(c) Aphaeresis (d) Synecdoche

21 In the Fall of Hyperion : A Dream, Keats sees a ladder leading upwards and is addressed by a prophetess in the following words: "None can usurp this height ...../ But those to whom the miseries of the world / Are misery, and will not let them rest." Who is the prophetess?
(a) Urania (b) Moneta
(c) Melete (d) Mneme

22 Keats's "La Belle Dame Sans Merci" combines two poetic forms
1. Lyric
2. Dramatic Monologue
3. Ballad
4. Sonnet
The right combination according to the code is
(a) 2 and 3 (b) 1 and 4
(c) 1 and 3 (d) 2 and 4

July 2016

23 Which British University figures in William Wordsworth's Prelude?
(a) Durham (b) Glasgow
(c) Cambridge (d) Oxford

24 Childe Harold's Pilgrimage is a
(a) religious allegory (b) fairy tale
(c) long poem (d) utopian novel

25 Antagonised by what he considered to be the provinciality of the Lake Poets, Byron wrote the preface to which of his works as a rebuke to Wordworth's own introduction to 'The Thorn'?
(a) The Prisoner of Chillon
(b) Don Juan
(c) Childe Harold's Pilgrimage
(d) The Vision of Judgement

26 PB Shelley's Julian and Maddalo is conversation between Julian and Count Maddalo.
Who do these characters represent?
(a) Julian represents Keats and Count Maddalo, Byron
(b) Julian represents Shelley and Count Maddalo, Byron
(c) Julian represents Shelley and Count Maddalo, William Godwin
(d) Julian represents Mary Shelley and Count Maddalo, William Godwin

27 In Biographia Literaria ST Coleridge defines the imagination as the faculty by which
(a) the soul perceives the phenomenal diversity of the universe.
(b) the soul perceives the spiritual unity of the universe.
(c) the mind acquires images by its associative power.
(d) the mind separates images by its discriminatory power.

28 Which writer of the Romantic period makes the following comment. "The poet is far from dealing only with these subtle and analogical truths. Truths of every kind belongs to him, provided it can bud into any kind of beauty or is capable of being illustrated and impressed by poetic faculty"?
(a) Wordsworth in Preface to the Lyrical Ballads
(b) William Hazlitt in 'On the Feeling of Immortality in Youth'
(c) Leigh Hunt in What is Poetry
(d) Keats in one of his letters to his brother

29 Match the work with author.

List I	List II
A. The Excursion	1. ST Coleridge
B. Christabel' BP	2. Shelley
C. Milton	3. William Wordsworth
D. Queen Mab	4. William Blake

Codes

	A	B	C	D		A	B	C	D
(a)	3	1	2	4	(b)	3	1	4	2
(c)	2	3	1	4	(d)	2	1	3	4

December 2015

30 In Which of the following does Robert Southey detail the Indian superstitions as an idolatry to be suppressed by a civilising protestant form of colonialism?
(a) Thalaba (b) The Curse of Kehama
(c) Pitying the wolves (d) Country Horrors

31 Which of the following is not a school associate with Romantic period in English literature?
(a) The Cockney School (b) The Fireside School
(c) The Lake School (d) The Satanic School

32 According to Coleridge, the "secondary imagination dissolves, diffuses, ...in order to recreate.."
Choose the right word for the blank.
(a) disintegrates (b) dissipates (c) displaces (d) dissociates

33 These beauteous forms,
Through a long absence, have been to me
As is a landscape to a blind man's eye.... (Tintern Abbey Lines) Which of the following rhetorical term best suits these lines?
(a) Apostrophe (b) Litotes
(c) Hyperbole (d) Catachresis

34 Sweet is the lore which nature brings;
Our meddling intellect
Mis-shapes the beauteous forms of things:
We murder to dissect.
Which of the following best summarises the speaker's position?
(a) Nature is incomplete without a human witness to attes to its beauty
(b) Human endeavours will succeed only if the laws of nature are taken into account
(c) Nature yields a pleasure superior to that derived from intrusive human inquiry
(d) The flaws inherent in human nature are also evident in the natural world

35 "Humble and rustic life was generally chosen, because, in that condition, the essential passions of the heart find a better soil in which they can attain their maturity, are less under restraint, and speak a plainer and more emphatic language.. The language, too, of these men has been adopted..
because such men hourly communicate with the best objects from which the best part of language is originally derived".
Which of the following groups of the authors's poems in the Lyrical ballads (1800) contradict this statement in the 'Preface to the Lyrical Ballads", as pointed out by ST Coleridge?
(a) 'Ode on the Intimations of Immortality', Prelude
(b) 'The Tasks,' Seasons
(c) 'Michael', 'Ruth', The Brothers'
(d) 'Elegy Written in a Country Churchyard', 'Ode on the Popular Superstitions of the Highlands'

36 One of the most quoted statements on poetry by John Keats is reproduced with blanks below complete the statement with correct words.
"If Poetry....as naturally as the leaves to a tree, it ....at all".
(a) does not come, had better not come
(b) comes not, might come not
(c) come not, had better not come
(d) come not, did not come

July 2015

37 In 'The Rime of the Ancient Mariner' what disaster befalls the ship and the crew?
(a) The ship is caught in ice and breaks into pieces
(b) A fierce storm batters the ship and drowns the crew
(c) 'Slimy things with legs' attack the ship and kill many of the crew
(d) The ship is becalmed and the crew dies of thirst

38 Which of the following is not true of the Byronic hero?
(a) Moody (b) Passionate
(c) Repentant (d) Remorse-torn

39 With what does the speaker claim to be half in love in 'Ode to a Nightingale'?
(a) The nightingale's haunting melody
(b) The scented flavour of early summer
(c) The night sky and all the star
(d) The peace that comes with death

40 In his famous letter to Benjamin Bailey (22nd November, 1817) John Keats wrote: "I am certain of nothing but the holiness of the Heart's affections and the truth of Imagination - What the imagination seizes as beauty must be truth."Which of the following sentences follows this passage?
(a) Now I am sensible all this is a mere sophistication, however it may neighbour to any truths, to excuse my own indolence
(b) The imagination may be compared to Adam's dream he woke and found it true

(c) This however I am persuaded of, that nothing beside imagination can give us sweet sensations and pleasurable thoughts
(d) My pains at last some respite shall afford, while I behold the battles imagination maintains

December 2014

41 In Wordsworth's *Prelude* the Boy of Winander is affected by
(a) blindness (b) deafness
(c) muteness (d) lameness

42 From among the following, identify Coleridge's companion in a fanciful scheme to establish an Utopian community of free love on the banks of the Susquehaina river?
(a) Lord Byron (b) Robert Southey
(c) William Hazlitt (d) William Wordsworth

43 This work was satire in Ottava Rima, attacking George III and Robert Southey. Identify the poem.
(a) Dunciad
(b) The Vision of Judgement
(c) Childe Harold's Pilgrimage
(d) Alastor

44 What superstition the Eve of St Agnes is crucial to an understanding John Keat's famous poem?
(a) If a virgin performed the proper ritual on St Agnes' Eve, she would dream of her future husband
(b) If a virgin performed the proper ritual on St Agnes' Eve, she would marry her lover
(c) If a married woman performed the proper ritual on St Agnes' Eve, she would be reunited with her husband
(d) If a woman performed the proper ritual on St Agnes' Eve, she would dream of her future lover

45 What a mockery this.
Of history, the past and that to come
Now do I feel how all men are deceived, Reading of
nations and their, in faith,
Faith given to vanity and emptiness...*The prelude*
the above extract is form
(a) Book 9 Residence in France
(b) Book 7 Residence in Loddon
(c) Book 3 Residence in Cambridge
(d) Book 4 Summer Vacations

June 2014

46 The prelude although begun as early as 1799 and finished in its first version in 1805, was not published until
(a) 1815 (b) 1820
(c) 1830 (d) 1850

47 Coleridge's 'The Rime of the Ancient Mariner' is a poem in...
(a) 8 parts
(b) 9 parts
(c) 7 parts
(d) 6 parts

48 "A rosy sanctuary will I dress with the wreathed trellis of a working brain."
(a) Adonais
(b) Ode to Psyche
(c) Eve of St Agnes
(d) Endymion

49 Though Coleridge refers to 'Motive-hunting of a motiveless malignity', the 'human villain' Iago is far from 'motiveless'. His motives are:
1. He has been disappointed of military promotion.
2. He suspects Othello of cuckolding him.
3. He has been in love with Desdemona.
4. He wants to become Othello.

Codes
(a) 1 and 2
(b) 1 and 3
(c) 2 and 4
(d) 2 and 4

50 'Thou wast no born for death immortal Bird.' In what sense is the Bird 'immortal' as compared to mortal man?
1. Here man as an individual is unfairly compared to a bird as a species.
2. The word 'Bird' stands for the Nightingale's song.
3. When considered as a species man is equally 'Immortal' as the 'Bird'.
4. The 'Bird' is 'Immortal' because songs of birds have given pleasure to man through the ages.

Codes
(a) 1 and 3 (b) Only 4
(c) 2 and 4 (d) 1 and 4

ANSWERS

Objective Questions

1. (b)	2. (c)	3. (c)	4. (a)	5. (b)	6. (b)	7. (b)	8. (c)	9. (b)	10. (b)
11. (c)	12. (d)	13. (c)	14. (c)	15. (d)	16. (c)	17. (b)	18. (c)	19. (a)	20. (a)
21. (a)	22. (b)	23. (b)	24. (b)	25. (b)	26. (b)	27. (a)	28. (c)	29. (d)	30. (d)
31. (c)	32. (c)	33. (d)	34. (c)	35. (c)	36. (a)	37. (c)	38. (b)	39. (b)	40. (c)
41. (a)	42. (d)	43. (d)	44. (d)	45. (c)	46. (c)	47. (a)	48. (b)	49. (b)	50. (b)
51. (b)	52. (b)	53. (d)	54. (b)	55. (c)	56. (a)	57. (b)	58. (b)	59. (b)	60. (c)
61. (d)	62. (b)	63. (d)	64. (c)	65. (b)	66. (d)	67. (d)	68. (b)	69. (b)	70. (b)
71. (d)	72. (b)	73. (b)	74. (b)	75. (c)	76. (c)	77. (b)	78. (c)	79. (c)	80. (c)
81. (b)	82. (d)	83. (c)	84. (b)	85. (b)	86. (b)	87. (d)	88. (d)	89. (c)	90. (d)
91. (b)	92. (d)	93. (b)	94. (d)	95. (d)	96. (a)	97. (c)	98. (b)	99. (d)	100. (c)
101. (b)	102. (b)	103. (a)	104. (c)	105. (c)	106. (b)	107. (a)	108. (a)	109. (b)	110. (c)
111. (d)	112. (c)	113. (a)	114. (c)	115. (a)	116. (a)	117. (b)	118. (c)	119. (d)	120. (b)
121. (d)	122. (a)	123. (c)	124. (d)	125. (a)	126. (d)	127. (c)	128. (c)	129. (a)	130. (a)
131. (d)	132. (c)	133. (c)	134. (c)	135. (a)	136. (c)	137. (a)	138. (b)	139. (b)	140. (c)
141. (a)	142. (a)	143. (b)	144. (c)	145. (b)	146. (c)	147. (b)	148. (a)	149. (c)	150. (b)
151. (b)	152. (c)	153. (c)	154. (d)	155. (c)	156. (c)	157. (c)	158. (d)	159. (d)	160. (c)

Pervious Years' Questions

1. (c)	2. (d)	3. (c)	4. (d)	5. (c)	6. (d)	7. (c)	8. (c)	9. (a)	10. (c)
11. (a)	12. (b)	13. (a)	14. (d)	15. (b)	16. (b)	17. (c)	18. (c)	19. (c)	20. (b)
21. (b)	22. (c)	23. (c)	24. (c)	25. (b)	26. (b)	27. (b)	28. (c)	29. (b)	30. (b)
31. (b)	32. (b)	33. (b)	34. (c)	35. (c)	36. (c)	37. (d)	38. (c)	39. (d)	40. (b)
41. (c)	42. (b)	43. (b)	44. (a)	45. (a)	46. (d)	47. (c)	48. (b)	49. (a)	50. (c)

The Victorian Poetry (1837-1901)

The Victorian Age poetry witnessed varied forms like realism, pessimism, morality, sentimentality, humour, a sense of responsibility, dramatic monologue, advancement of science and scepticism. The Victorian poetry can be divided into the High Victorian poetry and the Pre-Raphaelite Poetry. Tennyson, Robert Browning, Matthew Arnold and DG Rossetti were a few important poets of the age.

The Victorian Age

The Victorian (1837-1901) Age is named after the reign of Queen Victoria, who ruled from 1837 to 1901. She was the first English monarch to see her name given to the period of her reign while still living. Vast social, political and technological changes occurred during this age. It was one of the most prosperous periods in the history of England, a period of industrial development and colonial expansion. It is also sometimes known as the Age of Reform because of the plethora of reforms, which took place during this period.

It was an age of democracy. The major democratic movement in Britain during Queen Victoria's reign was directed towards expanding the voting population for parliamentary elections. Victoria came to the throne 5 years after the passage of the 1832 Reform Bill, which reduced property requirements for voting and holding office in Britain and increased the number of individuals entitled to vote. However, the 1832 Reform Act still failed to extend the vote beyond those owning property. As a result of this, People's Charter was drawn up for the London Working Men's Association (LWMA) by Thomas Lovett and Francis Place in 1838, which demanded votes for all men, equal electoral districts; abolition of the requirement that Members of Parliament be property owners; payment for MPs; annual general elections and the secret ballot. This movement known as the Chartist Movement of 1838, became important for working class agitators for social reform.

The 1867 Reform Bill (extended right to vote to all settled male tenants) and 1884 Reform Bill (which gave working men in rural England the same rights as those in the boroughs) achieved further democratisation of British politics and by the end of

In this Chapter

- *The Victorian Age*
- *Poets of the Victorian Age*
- *Pre-Raphaelite Poets*

the 19th century universal male suffrage became almost a reality. However, women were still deprived of the right to vote.

Apart from social and political reforms, reforms also took place on the economic front. The most important of these was the repeal of the Corn Laws in 1846. The Corn Laws were a series of statutes enacted between 1815 and 1846, which kept corn prices at a high level to protect British farming from foreign competition. These laws were repealed by Prime Minister Robert Peel in 1846.

The Victorian age was also characterised by the triumph of the middle classes, with their belief in progress, their opposition to governmental interference in trade and economics, their moral prudery, their religious faith and their observance of external superficial norms for behaviour.

Several movement and reforms took place during this period, which influenced the literature. There was tremendous growth in publication of periodicals and also the emergence of children's literature as a genere. Dramatic monologue emerged as a poetic form in the poems of Robert Browning. Charles Dickens, George Eliot, the Bronte sisters were storytellers and their novels reflected the Victorian period.

Literary Movements of the Victorian Age

Apart from social, political and economic reforms, Victorian age also witnessed a few literary movements.
A notable few are described in brief below

Oxford Movement

Oxford movement was a 19th century movement centred at the University of Oxford that sought renewal of Roman Catholic thought and practice within the Church of England. Immediate cause of the movement was the change that took place in the relationship between the State and the Church of England.

The igniting factor was the proposal of the Whig government to suppress half the Anglican bishoprics and to re-dispose their incomes, without first consulting the church. This created a wave of opposition, spearheaded by John Keble, John Henry Newman and others.

John Henry Newman dated the beginning of the Oxford movement to Keble's Assize Sermon of July 1833, on National Apostasy. Other figures associated with this movement were Richard Hurrell Froude, Frederick Faber, Isaac Williams, Charles Marriott, Bernard Dalgairns, William Ward and Edward Bouverie Pusey. Although, it was primarily a religious movement, its main connection with literature was the series of doctrinal papers setting forth the aims and teachings of the movement. These were named as the Tracts for the Times.

Aesthetic Movement

The Aesthetic movement was launched during the later part of the 19th century and emphasised aesthetic values over moral or social themes in literature and other arts. It was a reaction against utilitarian philosophies, predominance of scientific thinking and the widespread belief of the middle classes that art should have a moral purpose. The movement drew upon the formula of 'l'art pour l 'art'-Art for art's sake-articulated most memorably by the French novelist Théophile Gautier in his 1836 preface to *Mademoiselle de Maupin.* Gautier was one of a number of French writers and artists of the period, who argued that art should be evaluated with reference to its own criteria.

While, the historical roots of the movement can be traced back to Immanuel Kant's *Critique of Judgement* (1790), the movement was brought into England by Walter Pater, who in The *Renaissance* (1873) remarked that 'The love of art for its own sake'. He believed that art produced pleasurable sensations that added up to an impression of beauty.

The most important and the most known writer of late Victorian period associated with this movement was Oscar Wilde. Wilde felt very strongly about elegance and richness and it was this very coherence of philosophy that held the Aesthetic Movement together and gave it a lasting influence.

Pre-Raphaelite Movement/Brotherhood

Pre-raphaelites were a group of artists, poets and painters first formed in 1848, who rejected the dramatic, artificial mannerist painting styles succeeding Raphael and Michelangelo (hence the term 'Pre-Raphaelite') and aimed to create more genuine, humble representations of their subjects.

The Pre-Raphaelite Brotherhood was formed by three Royal Academy students Dante Gabriel Rossetti, who was a gifted poet as well as a painter, William Holman Hunt and John Everett Millais. They were later joined by William Michael Rossetti, James Collinson, Thomas Woolner and FG Stephens.

The Pre-Raphaelite/Brotherhood was based on the following principles

- To have genuine ideas to express.
- To study nature attentively.
- To sympathise with what is direct and serious and heartfelt in previous art.
- To defy all conventions of art.

The ideals of this group of painters and artists were taken over by a literary movement, which included Dante Gabriel Rossetti, Christina Rossetti, William Morris and Algernon Charles Swinburne. In poetry, the movement came in the shape of a revolt against contemporary poetry of the kind of Tennyson's, which was full of tradition and involved in the immediate, mundane problems of contemporary society. The Pre-Raphaelites also started a periodical called *The Germ* (1850), which outlined their aesthetic theories. The most famous literary work associated with the Pre-Raphaelites was DG Rossetti's poem, *The Blessed Damozel.*

The Scottish poet and critic Robert Buchanan criticised the Pre-Raphaelite school of poetry and termed it as fleshly school of poetry. It was a term of abuse coined by him to attack the explicit nature of subject matter as well as erotic imagery in the poetry of poets such as Rossetti, Swinburne and William Morris.

Buchanan identified Rossetti as the leader of this group whose followers had taken a vow. "To appreciate fleshliness as the distinct and supreme end of poetic and pictorial art; to state that poetic expression is greater than poetic thought and by inference that the body is greater than the soul and sound superior to sense and that the poet, properly to develop his poetic faculty, must be an intellectual hermaphrodite, to whom the very facts of day and night are lost in a whirl of aesthetic terminology."

Conflict Between Science and Religion in the Victorian Age

During, the early part of the 19th century, science and religion existed in harmony with each other. Science was believed to be in the interest of divine revelation. However, as new scientific developments and the development of Biblical criticism came into being, man's faith in God and religion began to be questioned leading to a crisis of faith. In 1859, Charles Darwin published his book, *The Origin of Species,* in which he laid out the theory of evolution. Darwin's proposition 'that instead of being created by some higher power, man actually evolved from a lower species' was seen as contrary to the teachings of the Bible (which taught that man was created in God's image).

Darwin also argued that species with useful adaptations to the environment are more likely to survive and produce progeny than those with less useful adaptations. Darwinian theories contradicted the notion, central to Christianity and many other faiths, that man had a special God given place in the natural order.

Instead, proponents of evolution pointed to signs in human anatomy - remnants of a tailbone, for instance showing common ancestry with other mammals.

According to Dr Andrzej Diniejko, "Darwin's theory of evolution thereby undermined the value of traditional religion and morality, which had been accepted for centuries as the guiding principle of mankind, because it implied that man was no more than a 'talking monkey' and no God was necessary to create him. It revolutionalised man's conception of himself. Darwin thus started a new anthropocentrism that deprived man of his unique position in the world. In the light of Darwin's theory, man appears left alone in the universe without any divine power, which should or could protect him".

The Darwinian thesis was further built upon with the publication of Huxley's *Man's Place in Nature* (1863), Lyell's *The Antiquity of Man* (1863) and by Darwin himself in *The Descent of Man* (1871). Huxley articulated the religious conflict of his age and questioned, "Does God exist? How can we know Him? Why isn't He revealed more unambiguously in the scriptures? Why would He create evil and why would He allow the good to suffer and the wicked to flourish? Does He intervene miraculously in this world?"

He coined the term agnosticism to express his religious scepticism and stated that the essence of it lay in following reason. He further added that every man should be able to give a reason for the faith i.e. in him and if there is no tangible reason, there can be no faith.

Apart from new scientific discoveries, a new range of Biblical critics also appeared, who delved into the Bible only to raise question marks about several of its aspects. One of these was David Frederick Strauss, who in his *Life of Jesus* (1835), doubts about the reliability of the New Testament. Feuerbach's *Essence of Christianity* (1854) argued that the idea of God was created by man to express the divine within himself. Doubt became the order of the day in Victorian England. It was no longer a religious sin; it became a necessity, keeping in mind the rapid developments of the age.

Victorian Poetry

Poetry written in England during the reign of Queen Victoria (1837-1901) may be referred to as Victorian poetry. England, during this time, was undergoing a tremendous cultural upheaval; the accepted forms of literature, art and music had undergone a radical change. The Romantic Movement, which preceded the Victorian Renaissance, had often portrayed the human pursuit of knowledge and power as a beautiful thing.

Following Romanticism, Victorian poets continued many of the previous era's main themes, such as religious skepticism and valorisation of the artist as genius; but Victorian poets also developed a distinct sensibility. Most of the Victorian poets used imagery and the senses to convey the scenes of struggles between religion and science and ideas about nature and romance, which transport the reader into the minds and hearts of the people of the Victorian age, even today.

The reclaiming of the past was a major part of Victorian literature with an interest in both classical and medieval literature of England. The Victorians loved the heroic, chivalrous stories of knights of old and they hoped to regain some of that noble, courtly behaviour and impress it upon the people both at home and in the wider empire.

There was a lot of radical social change and as such many poets of this time didn't like the romanticised version of society. The Victorian poetry is, thus, divided into two main groups of poetry: The high Victorian poetry and the Pre-Raphaelite poetry.

Comic verse abounded in the Victorian era. Magazines such as Punch magazine and Fun magazine teemed with the humorous invention and were aimed at a well-educated readership. The most famous collection of Victorian comic verse is the Bad ballads.

The writers of this period are known for their interest in verbal embellishment, mystical interrogation, brooding skepticism, and whimsical nonsense. The most prolific and well-regarded poets of the age include Alfred Lord Tennyson, Robert Browning, Elizabeth Barret Browning, Matthew Arnold and Oscar Wilde.

One of the most significant accomplishments of the Victorian era is the appearance of female poets. There were few female poets before, as poetry was considered to be predominantly male occupation. Despite these views, works of such poets as Elizabeth Browning, Christina Rossetti and the Bronte sisters became famous during the Victorian age.

Victorian poetry, thus, marks an important era in the history of poetry, providing the link between the Romantic Movement and the Modernist Movement (Pre-Raphaelitism) of the 20th century.

Three Phases of the Victorian Age

The Victorian period is often divided into three main phases- early (1837-1848); mid (1848-1870) and late (1870-1901).

Early Victorian Phase

The Early Victorian period was a period of turbulence, marked by economic, political and social difficulties.

Important events during this phase were the Chartist Movement and Repeal of the Corn Laws. This period also saw large scale expansion of railways. Literature of this period focused on the concerns of the new emerging middle and working class. JS Mill and Thomas Carlyle are writers that belong to this phase.

Mid Victorian Phase

The second phase of Victorian age was a period of economic prosperity and colonial expansion. Contrary to the first phase, this was a much stable stage. This phase witnessed the Great Exhibition of 1851, the first international exhibition of manufactured products.

It was organised by Henry Cole and Prince Albert and held in a purpose-built Crystal Palace in Hyde Park, London. This phase of Victorian age saw the appearance of scientific works such as Charles Darwin's *The Origin of Species* (1859) and *The Descent of Man* (1871) which challenged long held religious assumptions. Works of Charles Dickens and George Eliot belong to this phase.

Late Victorian Phase

The third phase of Victorian period was a period of scepticism, when people began to question Britain's Empire building activities. An important topic of debate during this phase was the proposed Home Rule for Ireland.

Literature of this period was marked by the Decadent Movement, who aspired to set literature and art free from the materialistic pre-occupations of industrialised society. Writers associated with this movement were Oscar Wilde, Arthur Symons and Ernest Dowson. These writers took a cue from French writers such as Baudelaire and Gautier and showed interest in perversity, ennui boredom art for art's sake, transgressive modes of sexuality, artificiality and decay.

Characteristics of Victorian Poetry

The main characteristics of Victorian age can be understood under the following heads

Realism

The Victorian poetry was quite realistic in nature and quite less idealised as compared to the Romanic poets who were idealists and believed in Art for the Art's Sake. Nature, that was everything for the Romantics, lost that idealised position in the Victorian era and became just a source of leisure and inspiration for the poets.

Focus on Masses

The Romantic poetry mainly focused on rural an rustic life. It is no way related to the city life. On the other hand, Victorian poets used language as well as themes common to the city life and thus wrote about the masses and for the masses.

Pessimism

As already discussed, Victorians were quite realistic and thus were more concerned about the reality rather than the ideal world. Due to industrial revolution and advancement in science and technology, there was a drastic increase in the city population that gave rise to slums, poverty, unemployment, corruption diseases, deaths etc. Thus, Victorian Poetry which focused on the pains and sufferings of commoners had a note of pessimism.

Science and Technology

The advancement in Science and inventions was welcomed by the Victorian poets. It made them believe that a man can find all solutions to his problems and sufferings. They made their readers believe that they should use science for their betterment.

Questioning to God

It was an important feature of Victorian poetry. The development of empirical science, rationalism and radicalism led the people to give up the religious thoughts and be more sceptic. Moreover, corruption in the Church, defining the morality of Priests, etc also led the people to question the religious institutions.

A Sense of Responsibility

The Romantics believed in 'return to nature'. A number of the Romantics did not like the city life and instead of giving voice to the victims of industrialisation, they left the city life. On the other hand, Victorian poets took the responsibility of social reform and gave voice to the commoners by living with them.

Morality

Though morality saw a steep decline in Victoran era, a number of poets tried to retain it by encouraging the people to be honest and noble.

Interest in Medieval Myths and Folklore

The Victorians showed great favour towards Medieval Literature. They loved mythical and chivalrous anecdotes of Medieval Knights, Courtly Love etc. This interest is contrary to that of Romantics as the latter loved classical myths and legends.

Use of Sensory Devices and Imagery

The poets of the preceding era used imagery vividly. However, the Victorians also used sensory devices to describe the abstract scenes of chaos between religion and science.

Sentimentality

The Victorians wrote about artistic creations thus giving way to deeper imaginations through emotions and sentiments.

Humour

A number of poets wrote humorous and whimsical verses. e.g. *Bad Ballads*.

Dramatic Monologue

A dramatic monologue is a long speech by a single person. It differs from soliloquy which means the expression of ideas by a character in a play. On the other hand, dramatic monologue is a kind of lyric which was used and improved by Robert Browning.

Poets of the Victorian Age

Alfred Lord Tennyson (1809-1892)

English poet Alfred Tennyson was born in Somersby, Lincolnshire, England in 1809. He was the fourth of twelve children of a clergyman George and his wife, Elizabeth Tennyson. Tennyson's father had a family history of mental illness. Tennyson studied at Louth Grammar School and later joined Trinity College, Cambridge. It was at Cambridge that he developed an intense friendship with Arthur Hallam.

Literary Career and Works

Tennyson and Hallam were part of a literary group called the apostles. This group provided Tennyson the confidence he needed as a young poet. Tennyson's first collection of poems *Chiefly Lyrical* was published in 1830. This was followed by a second volume called the *Poems* in 1832. This volume received unfavourable reviews, though his friend Hallam continued to promote it. Hallam's sudden death in 1833 jolted Tennyson and he began writing the *In Memoriam,* an elegy for his lost friend. Besides being his closest friend, Hallam was engaged to his sister Emily Tennyson. Tennyson did not publish anything for 10 years, since Hallam's death.

Poems, Two Volumes (1842), marked a change in Tennyson's fortunes. The success of this volume established him as a popular poet and he also started receiving a government pension few years later. His poem, *The Princess,* a *Medley* Dealing with the subject of women's higher education was published in 1847. In 1850, his most well known poem, *In Memoriam* got published.

It brought him to the notice of Queen Victoria and he succeeded Wordsworth as the Poet Laureate of England. The same year, he also got married to Emily Sellwood, to whom he had been engaged earlier. In 1884, Tennyson accepted a peerage and became Alfred Lord Tennyson.

His other works include *Maud and Other Poems* (his first Laureate volume, which included two of his famous public utterances- *Ode on the Death of the Duke of Wellington* and *Charge of the Light Brigade,* 1855), *The Idylls of the King* (retelling of *Malory's Le Morte d'Arthur* , 1859) and the plays; *Queen Mary* (1875), *Harold* (1876) and *Becket* (1879). *Ulyesses* is also one of his main poems.

Tennyson died in Haslemere, England on 6th October, 1892 and was buried in Westminster Abbey.

Major Works

- Poems, Chiefly Lyrical (1830)
- Poems (1832)
- Poems, 2 volumes (1842)
- The Princess: A Medley (1847)
- In Memoriam (1850)
- Ode on the Death of the Duke of Wellington (1852)
- Maud and Other Poems (1855)
- Idylls of the King (1859)
- Enoch Arden etc (1864)
- The Holy Grail and Other Poems (1869)
- Queen Mary: A Drama (1875)
- Harold (1876)
- Becket (1879)
- Demeter and Other Poems (1889)
- The Death of Oenone, Akbar's Dream and Other Poems (1892)

In Memoriam

- Tennyson's poem, *In Memoriam* is an elegiac tribute to his friend Arthur Henry Hallam, who died in 1833 at the age of 22.
- The poem was written over the course of 17 years (1833-1849) and was finally published in 1850.
- *In Memoriam* is a mammoth work that includes 133 poems (including the prologue and the epilogue).
- The poem shows Tennyson battling with the issue of mortality, trying to come to terms with his friend's death and gradually accepting it.
- The poem concludes with an epilogue, an epithalamion on the occasion of the wedding of Tennyson's sister Emilia in 1842.

Robert Browning (1812-1889)

Victorian poet Robert Browning, considered the master of dramatic monologue, was born in Camberwell, England in 1812. Browning's father was a well-paid clerk for the Bank of England, while his mother Sarah was an accomplished pianist. Browning was mostly self-taught and utilised his father's huge library which contained more than 6000 books. At the age of 16, he attended the University College in London, but a year later he grew dissatisfied and left it to pursue learning at his own pace.

Literary Career and Works

Browning started writing poetry at the age of 12. In 1833, Browning anonymously published his first major work, *Pauline* and in 1840 he published *Sordello*. On encouragement by the actor William Macready, Browning tried writing for the stage, but did not prove successful. However, writing for the stage helped him develop his form of the dramatic monologue-a literary form in which a character, addressing a silent audience at a critical moment, reveals his own character.

In 1844, Browning read Elizabeth Barrett's *Poems* and finally met her in 1845. She was an invalid suffering from a lung ailment since her adolescence and living in the care of an extremely protective father. Despite her health issues they got married in 1846, against the wishes of Barrett's father and settled in Florence. Browning wrote little during his married life. After Elizabeth Barrett's death in 1861, he moved to London with his son and began to publish his poetry.

Browning's most famous works are his *Dramatic Lyrics* (containing his popular poems *My Last Duchess* and *Porphyria's Lover*; 1842), *Dramatic Romances* (containing *The Lost Leader* and *The Laboratory*; 1845), *Dramatis Personae* (containing *Caliban upon Setebos* and *Rabbi Ben Ezra*; 1864) and *Men and Women* (containing *Fra Lippo Lippi* and *The Last Ride Together, 1855).* Some of his famous poems from various poetic works are. *My last Duchess, Soliloque of the Spanish Cloister, HomeThoughts*, from *Abroad, The Bishop orders* his *Tomb, Fra-Lippo Lippy*, A *Toccata of Galluppi's* and *Memorabilia* etc.

The Ring and the Book (1868) is considered to be Browning's most celebrated achievement that established his popularity. It is a verse novel that is based on a sensational Roman murder trial in 1698. It is centred on Pompilia- a beautiful young woman, who is so unhappy in her marriage to Count Franceschini, an older and cruel nobleman, that she prevails upon a young priest to help her return to her parents' home.

The count finds them, has Pompilia sent to a convent and banishes the priest. When Pompilia returns to her parents, the count arranges for the assassination of Pompilia and her parents. The count is arrested, tried and executed.

Browning's influences grew during the late 60s and 70s and finally lead to the founding of the Browning society in 1881. He was awarded honorary degrees by Oxford University in 1882 and the University of Edinburgh in 1884. Browning died in Venice on 12th December, 1889.

Major Works

- Pauline; A Fragment of a Confession (1833)
- Paracelsus (1835)
- Strafford (play) (1837)
- Sordello (1840)
- Bells and Pomegranates Number I: Pippa Passes (play) (1841)
- Bells and Pomegranates Number II: King Victor and King Charles (play) (1842)
- Bells and Pomegranates Number III: Dramatic Lyrics (1842)
- Bells and Pomegranates Number IV: The Return of the Druses (play) (1843)
- Bells and Pomegranates Number V: A Blot in the Scutcheon (play) (1843)
- Bells and Pomegranates Number VI: Colombe's Birthday (play) (1844)
- Bells and Pomegranates Number VII: Dramatic Romances and Lyrics (1845)
- Men and Women (1855)
- Dramatic Personae (1864)
- The Ring and the Book (1868-69)

My Last Duchess

Ferrara
That's my last Duchess painted on the wall,
Looking as if she were alive. I call
That piece a wonder, now: Fr Pandolf's hands
Worked busily a day and there she stands.
Will't please you sit and look at her? I said
"Fra Pandolf" by design, for never read
Strangers like you that pictured countenance,
The depth and passion of its earnest glance,
But to myself they turned (since none puts by
The curtain I have drawn for you, but I)
And seemed as they would ask me, if they durst,
How such a glance came there; so, not the first
Are you to turn and ask thus. Sir, twas not
Her husband's presence only, called that spot
Of joy into the Duchess' cheek: perhaps
Fra Pandolf chanced to say "Her mantle laps
"Over my lady's wrist too much," or "Paint
Must never hope to reproduce the faint
"Half-flush that dies along her throat:" Such stuff
Was courtesy, she thought and cause enough
For calling up that spot of joy. She had
A heart--how shall I say?--too soon made glad,
Too easily impressed; she liked whate'er
She looked on and her looks went everywhere.
Sir, 'twas all one! My favour at her breast,
The dropping of the daylight in the West,
The bough of cherries some officious fool
Broke in the orchard for her, the white mule
She rode with round the terrace--all and each
Would draw from her alike the approving speech,
Or blush, at least. She thanked men,--good! but thanked
Somehow--I know not how--as if she ranked
My gift of a nine-hundred-years-old name
With anybody's gift. Who'd stoop to blame
This sort of trifling? Even had you skill
In speech--(which I have not)--to make your will
Quite clear to such an one and say, "Just this
"Or that in you disgusts me; here you miss,
"Or there exceed the mark"--and if she let
Herself be lessoned so, nor plainly set
Her wits to yours, forsooth and made excuse,
--E'en then would be some stooping; and I choose
Never to stoop.

My Last Duchess (1842): Summary

This poem is based on historical events involving Alfonso, the Duke of Ferrara, who lived in the 16th century. The Duke is the speaker of the poem. He tells us he is entertaining an emissary who has come to negotiate the Duke's marriage (he has recently been widowed) to the daughter of another powerful family. As he shows the visitor through his palace, he stops before a portrait of the late Duchess, apparently a young and lovely girl. The Duke begins reminiscing about the portrait sessions, then about the Duchess herself. His musings give way to a diatribe tirade on her disgraceful behaviour: he claims she flirted with everyone and did not appreciate his 'gift of a nine-hundred-years-old name'. As his monologue continues, the reader realises with ever-more chilling certainty that the Duke in fact caused the Duchess' early demise.

My Last Duchess comprises rhyming pentameter lines. The lines do not employ end-stops; rather, they use enjambment-that is, sentences and other grammatical units do not necessarily conclude at the end of lines. Consequently, the rhymes do not create a sense of closure when they come, but rather remain a subtle driving force behind the Duke's compulsive revelations.

The Duke is quite a performer: he mimics other's voices, creates hypothetical situations and uses the force of his personality to make horrifying information seem merely colorful. Indeed, the poem provides a classic example of a dramatic monologue: the speaker is clearly distinct from the poet and audience is suggested but never appears in the poem and the revelation of the Duke's character is the poem's primary aim.

Browning and the Dramatic Monologue

- The dramatic monologue as a poetic form achieved its first distinction in the works of Robert Browning.
- Browning's poems- *My Last Duchess* and *Porphyria's Lover* are considered to be the models for this form.
- In *My Last Duchess*, the Duke is negotiating with an emissary for a second wife. Even though, it is the duke who is talking about the character of his last wife, the duchess to the messenger, one can derive lots of facts about his own character through the manner, in which he speaks and the way in which he describes his wife. He is revealed to be an emotionally cold, calculating, materialistic and haughty man.
- In *Porphyria's Lover*, the speaker describes the act of murdering the woman he loved. During the course of explaining his reasons for the crime, the speaker reveals himself to be a jealous, possessive and psychopathic lover.
- According to David Daiches, Browning's dramatic monologues are written to "Project with an almost quizzical violence, a certain kind of personality, a certain temperament, a way of looking at life, even a moment of history realised in the self-revelation of a type". They are 'set pieces in which a fully known character' is 'set sharply before the reader'.

Matthew Arnold (1822-1888)

British poet and critic Matthew Arnold was born at Laleham on the Thames in London in 1822. He was the son of Thomas Arnold, the famous headmaster of Rugby School, who was celebrated in the novel *Tom Brown's Schooldays*. His mother, Mary Penrose Arnold was the daughter of an Anglican clergyman.

As a child, Arnold attended the Reverend John Buckland's Preparatory School. Later, he studied at Rugby School and Balliol College, Oxford. After completing his graduation at Oxford, he returned to the Rugby School and worked as a teacher of classics. In 1845, he was honoured with a Fellowship at Oriel College, Oxford. He pursued his studies there with John Keble and John Henry Newman.

Literary Career and Works

Arnold was appointed as private secretary to Lord Lansdowne in 1847. Lansdowne helped him in securing an inspectorship of schools in 1851. This new position provided him with a measure of financial security and enabled him to marry Fanny Lucy Wightman, the daughter of a judge. Arnold's first book of poetry, *The Strayed Reveller: And Other Poems*, was published anonymously in 1849. This was followed by *Empedocles on Etna* (1852) and *Poems* (1853), which established his reputation as a poet. Some of his famous poems from various poetic works are: *Desire, Dream, A Summer Night, Consolation, The Scholar* Gipsy and *Dover Beach etc*. In 1857, Arnold was appointed as 'Professor of Poetry' at Oxford and served this position for two consecutive terms of 5 years.

He was the first professor to deliver lectures in English instead of Latin. Arnold's career as a literary critic began in the late sixties. He published his *Lectures on Translating Homer* in 1861, followed by *Last Words on Translating Homer* in 1862, *Essays on Criticism* in 1865 and *Culture and Anarchy* in 1869. Arnold died on 15th April, 1888, at the age of 65, in Liverpool, England.

Major Works

Poetry

- Alaric at Rome: A Prize Poem (1840)
- Cromwell: A Prize Poem (1843)
- The Strayed Reveller and Other Poems (1849)
- Empedocles on Etna and Other Poems (1852)
- Poems: A New Edition (1853)
- Poems: Second Series (1855)
- Merope: A Tragedy (1858)
- New Poems (1867)
- A Empedocles on Etna: A Dramatic Poem (1900)

Prose

- England and the Italian Question (1859)
- On Translating Homer: Three Lectures Given at Oxford (1861)
- Essays in Criticism (1865)
- Culture and Anarchy: An Essay in Political and Social Criticism (1869)
- On the Modern Element in Literature (1869)
- Literature and Dogma: An Essay towards a Better Apprehension of the Bible (1873)
- The Hundred Greatest Men: Portraits of the One Hundred Greatest Men of History (1879)
- On the Study of Celtic Literature (1883)
- Discourses in America (1885)
- Education Department (1886)

Brief Description of Arnold's Famous Poems

Poem	Description
Rugby Chapel	This poem was written over 20 years after the death of his father, Thomas Arnold. This poem demonstrates Arnold's regard for his father.
Dover Beach	Published in 1867, this poem deals with the Victorian problem of loss of faith. It was probably written shortly after a visit he and his wife made to the Dover region of South-Eastern England, the setting of the poem, in 1851.
The Scholar Gypsy	It is about a 17 year old Oxford student, who had disappeared among the gypsies. It is a meditative pastoral poem that owes much to the classical poet Theocritus.
Thyrsis	It is an elegy on the death of Arnold's friend, Arthur Hugh Clough. It was first published in Macmillan's Magazine in 1866. Clough, in this poem, is portrayed as Thyrsis-a shepherd poet.
Sohrab and Rustum	First published in 1853, it is a narrative poem based on the heroic legend of Rustum, a Hercules figure from Persian mythology and his killing of his long-lost son Sohrab in single combat.

Dover Beach

The sea is calm tonight,
The tide is full, the moon lies fair
Upon the straits; on the French coast the light
Gleams and is gone; the cliffs of England stand,
Glimmering and vast, out in the tranquil bay.
Come to the window, sweet is the night air!
Only, from the long line of spray
Where the sea meets the moon-blanched land,
Listen! you hear the grating roar
Of pebbles which the waves draw back, and fling,
At their return, up the high strand,
Begin, and cease and then again begin,
With tremulous cadence slow and bring
The eternal note of sadness in.
Sophocles long ago
Heard it on the A (E)gean and it brought
Into his mind the turbid ebb and flow
Of human misery; we
Find also in the sound a thought,
Hearing it by this distant northern sea.
The Sea of Faith
Was once, too, at the full and round Earth's shore
Lay like the folds of a bright girdle furled.
But now I only hear
Its melancholy, long, withdrawing roar,
Retreating, to the breath
Of the night wind, down the vast edges drear
And naked shingles of the world.

Dover Beach (1867): Summary

Arguably Matthews Arnold's most famous peom, *Dover Beach* manages to comment on his most recurring themes despite its relatively short length. Its message like many of his other poems is that the world's mystery has declined in the face of modernity. However, that decline is here painted as particularly uncertain, dark and volatile. One night, the speaker of *Dover Beach* sits with a woman inside a house, looking out over the English Channel near the town of Dover. They see the lights on the coast of France just twenty miles away and the sea is quiet and calm.

When the light in France suddenly extinguishes, the speaker focuses on the English side, which remains tranquil. He trades visual imagery for aural imagery, describing the 'grating roar' of the pebbles being pulled out by the waves. He finishes the first stanza by calling the music of the world an 'eternal note of sadness.' The next stanza flashes back to ancient Greece, where Sophocles heard this same sound on the Aegean Sea and was insipired by it to write his plays about human misery.

Stanza three introduces the poem's main metaphor, with: "The Sea of Faith/Was once, too, at the full, and round Earth's shore." The Phrases suggests that faith is fading from society like the tide is from the shore. The speaker laments this decline of faith through melancholy diction. In the final stanza, the speaker directly addresses his beloved who sits next to him, asking that they always be true to one another and to the world that is laid out before them. He warns, however, that the world beauty is only an illusion, since it is in fact a battlefield full of people fighting in absolute darknenss.

What also makes the poem particularly powerful is that his romantic streak has almost no tinge of the religious. Instead, he speaks of the 'Sea of Faith' without linking it to any deity or heaven. This 'faith' has a definite humanist tinge-it seems to have once guided decisions and smoothed over the world' problems, tying everyone together in a meaningful way. It is no accident that the sight inspiring such reflection is that of untouched nature, almost entirely absent from any human involvement. In fact, the speaker's true reflection begins once the only sign of life the light over France extinguishes. What Arnold is expressing is an innate quality, a natural drive towards beauty.

Arnold's Famous Critical Work Culture and Anarchy

It was first published in 1869, Arnold's philosophical essay argues for a restructuring of England's social ideology. Arnold contrasts culture, which he defines as 'the study of perfection,' with anarchy, the prevalent mood of England's then new democracy. Culture is inspired by 'right reason,' the reason that comes from the 'best self' rather than the 'ordinary self.' It seeks to cultivate the 'free play' of thought, the 'sheer desire to see things as they are.'

He divides human society into three main classes: Barbarians, Philistines and the Populace. The Barbarians represent the aristocrats, the Philistines represent the middle class and the populace are the working classes. The Barbarians are confident of their place and are characterised by individualism. However, they have lost touch with the rest of society of which they were once an integral part. The Philistines are associated with business and money-making and are oblivious to culture. The word Philistine is derived from German. The third class, the Populace is raw and still not fully developed. This class is mostly exploited by the Barbarians and Philistines. *Culture and Anarchy* is also famous for its popularisation of the phrase 'sweetness and light', first coined by Jonathan Swift in *The Battle of the Books*. Sweetness and Light stands for beauty and wisdom that culture adds to life.

Elizabeth Barrett Browning (1806-1861)

English poet Elizabeth Barrett Browning was born at Coxhoe Hall, Durham, England in 1806. She was the eldest of twelve children born to Edward Moulton Barrett and Mary Graham Clarke. Her father made most of his considerable fortune from Jamaican sugar plantations and in 1809 he bought Hope End, a 500-acre estate near the Malvern Hills. Elizabeth Barrett led a privileged life in the country. She did not receive any formal education and was educated at home with her siblings. Barrett read voraciously and by the age of 8 had learned to read Homer in the original Greek.

Literary Career and Works

Her first narrative poem *The Battle of Marathon* was printed in 1820. However, at the age of 15, Barrett was struck with a nervous ailment, which plagued her for the rest of her life. This was believed to have arisen from a fall she had while saddling a pony. Barrett's second collection *An Essay on Mind and Other Poems* was published anonymously in 1826. Her first major collection of poems was entitled *The Seraphim and Other Poems*, which was published in 1838. Her first collected edition appeared under the title *Poems* in 1844. It was this collection that attracted the attention of fellow poet Robert Browning. This led to the beginning of a literary love affair, which culminated in marriage in 1846.

Barrett's *Sonnets from the Portuguese* were written during their courtship and expressed her love for Browning. 'Portuguese' of the title was a reference to 16th century. Portuguese poet Camoens and to Browning's nickname for his wife. Elizabeth Barrett's most known work is her long blank verse novel, *Aurora Leigh* (1856). This work is considered to be a woman's version of Wordsworth's *The Prelude* (1850) and tells the story of the young poet, Aurora Leigh, who lives in England with an unsympathetic aunt after the death of her Italian mother and English father. Barrett shows her heroine thwarted by the male dominance of her age. Barrett's poems also dealt with the theme of social injustice. Two of her poems, *Casa Guidi Windows* and *Poems Before Congress*, dealt with the Italian fight for independence.

Elizabeth Barrett Browning died in Florence on 29th June, 1861.

Sonnets from the Portuguese

How do I love thee? Let me count the ways.
I love thee to the depth and breadth and height
My soul can reach, when feeling out of sight
For the ends of being and ideal grace.
I love thee to the level of every day's
Most quiet need, by sun and candle-light.
I love thee freely, as men strive for right;
I love thee purely, as they turn from praise.
I love thee with the passion put to use
In my old griefs and with my childhood's faith.
I love thee with a love I seemed to lose
With my lost saints. I love thee with the breath,
Smiles, tears, of all my life; ands if God choose,
I shall but love thee better after death.

Major Works

- The Battle of Marathon; A Poem (1820)
- An Essay on Mind, with Other Poems (1826)
- Miscellaneous Poems (1833)
- The Seraphim and Other Poems (1838)
- Poems (1844)
- A Drama of Exile; and other Poems (1845)
- Poems: New Edition (1850)
- The Poems of Elizabeth Barrett Browning (1850)
- Sonnets from the Portuguese (1850)
- Casa Guidi Windows: A Poem (1851)
- Two Poems (1854)
- Aurora Leigh (1857)
- Napoleon III in Italy and Other Poems (1860)
- Poems before Congress (1860)
- Last Poems (1862)

Arthur Hugh Clough (1819-1861)

English poet Arthur Hugh Clough was born in Liverpool in 1819. He was the son of James Clough and Anne Perfect. Clough's father was a Liverpool cotton merchant, who immigrated with his family to America.

In 1828, Clough was sent back to England to be educated. He entered Rugby School, where he formed a great admiration for the headmaster, Thomas Arnold and developed a close friendship with Thomas' son, Matthew Arnold.

Hugh won a scholarship to Balliol College, Oxford and later became a fellow of Oriel College. In 1850, Clough became professor of English Literature at University College. In 1852, Clough travelled to Boston and met Waldo Emerson. Inspired by his friendship with Emerson, he went to Harvard and lectured. On his return to England in 1854, Clough married Blanche Smith. He pursued a civil service career until his health failed in 1860.

Literary Career and Works

Clough's first published work, *The Bothie of Tober-na-Vuolich,* a narrative in hexameters, appeared in 1848. This poem, which is the most popular of his works, tells the story of Claude, a supercilious Oxford graduate, who is initially contemptuous of Rome and of a young English woman he meets on the grand tour, Mary Trevellyn.

This work was followed by *Ambarvalia,* a collection of lyrics, in 1849. His posthumous poems include *Amours de Voyage*, the dialogues *Dypsichus* and the tales *Mari Magno*.

Clough died in Florence in 1861.

Pre-Rephaelite Poets

The Pre-Raphaelites were a loose and baggy collective of Victorian poets, painters, illustrators and designers whose tenure lasted from 1848 to roughly the turn of the century. Drawing inspiration from visual art and literature, their works privileged atmosphere and mood over narrative, focusing on medieval subjects, artists introspection, female beauty, sexual yearning and altered states of mid-century, the Pre-Raphaelites helped to popularise the notion of 'art for art's sake'.

Generally devoid of the political edge that characterised much Victorian art and literature, Pre-Raphaelite work nevertheless incorporated elements of 19th century realism in its attention to detail and its close observation of the natural world. The groups's intention was to reform art by rejecting what it considered the mechanistic approach first adopted by Mannerist artists who succeeded Raphael and Michelangelo. Its members believed the classical poses and elegant compositions of Raphael in particular had been a corrupting influence on the academic teaching of art. The major Pre-Raphaelite poets were Dante Gabriel Rossetti, Christina Rossetti, William Morris and Algernon Charles Swinburne.

Dante Gabriel Rossetti (1828-1882)

Victorian poet and painter Dante Gabriel Rossetti was born as Gabriel Charles Dante Rossetti in London in 1828. He later changed his name to Dante Gabriel Rossetti to signify how Dante Alighieri served as a continuous source of inspiration for his work. His father, Gabriele Pasquale Giuseppe Rossetti was an Italian political refugee, a poet and a professor at King's College, while his mother Frances Polidori was half Italian and half English and worked as a private teacher. Rossetti did his schooling from Mr Paul's Day School in Portland Place and later attended King's College School. In 1842, Rossetti enrolled in the art school Cary's Academy. He furthered his artistic education by attending the royal Academy Antique School in 1846. However, he grew dissatisfied and left it in 1847 to concentrate on his art.

Literary Career and Works

In 1848, when the Pre-Raphaelite movement was founded, Rossetti produced his first important painting. His translation of Dante's *Vita Nuova* was also finished in October 1848. He exhibited his first major oil painting, *The Girlhood of Mary Virgin* at the Free Exhibition in March 1849. Around this time, Rossetti met Elizabeth Eleanor Siddal, a milliner's assistant, who became a model for many of his paintings and sketches. They were engaged in 1851, but did not marry until 1860.

Rossetti's most well known poem is *The Blessed Damozel.* It narrates the story of a young woman, who dies unexpectedly at a very young age. Even after attaining heavenly bliss, she longs for the love of her Earthly companion. The poem unites the physical and the spiritual and illustrates Rossetti's belief in human love being one of life's greatest values. Rossetti's other works include: *The Early Italian Poets, Poems, A Sonnet Sequence and House of Life.* From the mid-1860s, Rossetti began suffering from eye trouble and insomnia and showed signs of paranoia. He began to spend more time at the country home of his close friend William Morris and lived and worked there.

He died at Burchington, Kent on 9th April, 1882.

Major Works

- Sir Hugh the Heron: A Legendary Tale in Four Parts (1843)
- The Early Italian Poets (1861)
- Poems (1869)
- Ballads and Sonnets (1881)
- Sonnets and Lyrical Poems (1894)
- My Sister's Sleep (1870)

The Blessed Damozel

The blessed damozel leaned out
From the gold bar of Heaven;
Her eyes were deeper than the depth
Of waters stilled at even;
She had three lilies in her hand,
And the stars in her hair were seven.
Her robe, ungirt from clasp to hem,
No wrought flowers did adorn,
But a white rose of Mary's gift,
For service meetly worn;
Her hair that lay along her back
Was yellow like ripe corn.
Herseemed she scarce had been a day
One of God's choristers;
The wonder was not yet quite gone
From that still look of hers;
Albeit, to them she left, her day
Had counted as ten years.
(To one, it is ten years of years.
. . . Yet now and in this place,
Surely she leaned o'er me - her hair
Fell all about my face. . . .
Nothing: the autumn-fall of leaves.
The whole year sets apace.)
It was the rampart of God's house
That she was standing on;
By God built over the sheer depth
The which is Space begun;
So high, that looking downward thence
She scarce could see the Sun.
It lies in Heaven, across the flood
Of ether, as a bridge.
Beneath, the tides of day and night
With flame and darkness ridge
The void, as low as where this Earth
Spins like a fretful midge.
Around her, lovers, newly met
'Mid deathless love's acclaims,
Spoke evermore among themselves
Their heart-remembered names;
And the souls mounting up to God
Went by her like thin flames.

Blassed Damozel: Summary

The Blessed Damozel was first published in 1850. It is a dramatic lyric poem consisting of 24 stanzas of six lines each. The tone of the poem is romantic yet depressing. After reading Poem's *The Raven* about a person who mourns the passing of his beloved, a woman named Lenore and going through Dante's *Divine Comedy* in which the writer's first romantic endeavour takes him all through purgatory and also heaven during his imaginary course through the realm, Rossetti conceived the idea for his poem.

The theme of the poem is undying love. Even though the death of one woman has separated her from the man she loves, the love between them as well as the hope that one day they will reunite in heaven lives on. 'Damozel' is an archaic word and the poetic version of 'damsel' which refers to a young unmarried lady.

The woman in the poem feels that since she cannot reach her lover, her lover needs to reach her. She says that she has prayed for their union and then stops for a while and worries that her lover has not prayed yet. She asks God and wants to learn whether it is true that the strength of two lovers is perfect. If it is true, then she feels afraid that something terrible has haappened to her lover, or that her lover has forgotten her or is no longer in love with her.

The Blessed Damozel presents the expression of an ancient and well-known theme; the desire of an isolated separated lover to achieve unity with the beloved. Rossetti has framed this vision as a reverie, a daydream, a wish-fulfilling dream in the mind of a lover. The heart of the poem is the ironic conflict between the earthly bodily desire and the tradition that heaven is a place of disembodied souls, comforted and joyful in the presence of God. This irony is emphasised by the poem's religious framework.

Christina Rossetti (1830-1894)

One of the most important of English woman poets in the Victorian age, Christina Rossetti was born in London in 1830. She was the sister of the famous poet and painter Dante Gabriel Rossetti. Christina was educated at home by her mother, who was a teacher and committed to the cause of intellectual excellence.

At the age of 15, Christina suffered a nervous breakdown and remained an invalid for few years. At the age of 17, she fell in love with and got engaged to James Collinson, one of the first members of the Pre-Raphaelite Brotherhood. However, she broke this engagement, when he decided to become a Roman Catholic and formally resigned his membership of the Pre-Raphaelite Brotherhood.

Literary Career and Works

Christina's first poems were written in 1842 and printed in the private press of her grandfather. In 1850, under the pseudonym Ellen Alleyne, she contributed seven poems to the Pre-Raphaelite journal *The Germ*. In 1853, when the Rossetti family was in financial difficulties, Christina helped her mother keep a day school at Frome, Somerset, but this venture did not succeed.

Christina and her mother returned to London, where Christina's father died in 1854. Christina Rossetti's best-known work, *Goblin Market and Other Poems,* was published in 1862. Her other works include poetry collections. *A Pageant and Other Poems* (1881) and *The Face of the Deep* (1892) and religious prose works such as *Seek and Find* (1879) and *Called To Be Saints* (1881).

Christina developed breast cancer in 1893 and died on 29th December, 1894.

Major Works

Poetry

- Goblin Market and Other Poems (1862)
- Prince's Progress and Other Poems (1866)
- Sing-Song: A Nursery-Rhyme Book (1872)
- A Pageant and Other Poems (1881)
- The Face of the Deep (1892)
- Verses (1893)
- New Poems (1896)

Prose

- Commonplace and Other Short Stories (1870)
- Seek and Find (1879)
- Called To Be Saints: The Minor Festivals (1881)
- Time Flies: A Reading Diary (1888)

William Morris (1834-1896)

English artist and writer William Morris was born in Walthamstow, London in 1834. He was the son of William and Emma Morris. Morris attended Marlborough School and later, Exeter College at Oxford University. After graduating from Oxford, he worked in the architectural offices of George Street, who specialised in the Gothic Revival style, but soon left to pursue painting under the tutelage of Dante Gabriel Rossetti.

Literary Career and Works

Morris began writing poetry in the 1850s and his book *The Defence of Guenevere and Other Poems* was published in 1858. The book was dedicated to Dante Gabriel Rossetti. With its vivid portraits of Arthurian figures, the work reflected Morris' poetic interest in the aesthetic principles and techniques of the Pre-Raphaelite painters. His other works include *The Earthly Paradise* (1868-1870), *A Dream of John Ball* (1888) and the utopian *News from Nowhere* (1890).

In 1884, Morris, alongwith Walter Crane, Eleanor Marx, Ernest Belfort Bax and Edward Aveling formed the Socialist League. The League had a journal called the Commonweal, which was financed and edited by Morris. He wrote a number of works on socialism such as *Art and Socialism, Chants for Socialists* and *Signs of Change.*

Morris founded the Kelmscott Press at Hammersmith in 1891. He was also offered the post of Poet laureate after Tennyson but declined it. Morris died at Kelmscott House in 1896.

Major Works

- The Hollow Land (1856)
- The Defence of Guenevere and other Poems (1858)
- The Life and Death of Jason (1867)
- The Earthly Paradise (1868–1870)
- Love is Enough, or The Freeing of Pharamond: A Morality (1872)
- The Story of Sigurd the Volsung and the Fall of the Niblungs (1877)
- Hopes and Fears For Art (1882)
- The Pilgrims of Hope (1885)
- A Dream of John Ball (1888)
- A Tale of the House of the Wolfings and All the Kindreds of the Mark Written in Prose and in Verse (1889)
- The Roots of the Mountains (1890)
- Poems By the Way (1891)
- News from Nowhere (or, An Epoch of Rest) (1890)
- The Story of the Glittering Plain (1891)
- The Wood Beyond the World (1894)
- Child Christopher and Goldilind the Fair (1895)
- The Well at the World's End (1896)
- The Water of the Wondrous Isles (1897)
- The Sundering Flood (1897) (published posthumously)

Algernon Charles Swinburne (1837-1909)

Victorian poet, novelist and critic Algernon Charles Swinburne or AC Swinburne was born in London in 1837. He was the son of an admiral, Captain Charles Henry Swinburne and Lady Henrietta Swinburne-.daughter of the 3rd Earl of Ashburnham. Swinburne studied at Eton College and Balliol College, Oxford. He left university without taking a degree in 1860.

Literary Career and Works

Swinburne was a member. of an undergraduate group of intellectuals, writers, artists, thinkers, who called themselves the 'Old Mortality' and published a short-lived journal *Undergraduate Papers*. His first two published works were plays, *The Queen Mother* and *Rosamond*, which were dedicated to Dante Gabriel Rossetti and appeared in 1861.

Swinburne published two more works in 1865: *Atalanta in Calydon,* a lyrical drama modelled on Greek tragedy with blank verse dialogue and rhymed, lyrical choruses and *Chastelard,* the first in Swinburne's trilogy of dramas on the subject of Mary Stuart. This was followed by the first series of *Poems and Ballads* in 1866.

This poetical volume contained *Dolores, Hymn to Proserpine, Faustine* and *A Dozen Other Dark*, exquisitely musical poems. Other collections of his poems are *Song of Italy* (1867), *Songs before Sunrise* (1871), *Erechtheus* (1876), *Poems and Ballads, Tristram of Lyonesse* (1882), *A Century of Roundels* (1883), *A Midsummer Holiday* (1884), *Marino Faliero* (1885), *Locrine* (1887),*The Sisters* (1892), *Astrophel* (1894), *The Tale of Balen* (1896), *Rosamund, Queen of the Lombards* (1899), *A Channel Passage* (1904) *and The Duke of Gandia* (1908).

Swinburne was also a noted critic and his critical acumen is demonstrated in works such as Essays and Studies (1875) and his monographs on *William Shakespeare* (1880), *Victor Hugo* (1886) and *Ben Jonson* (1889). Swinburne died at the Pines on 10th April, 1909 at the age of 72.

Major Works

Verse Drama

- The Queen Mother (1860)
- Rosamond (1860)
- Chastelard (1865)
- Bothwell (1874)
- Mary Stuart (1881)
- Marino Faliero (1885)
- Locrine (1887)
- The Sisters (1892)
- Rosamund, Queen of the Lombards (1899)

Poetry

- Atalanta in Calydon (1865)
- Poems and Ballads (1866)
- Songs Before Sunrise (1871)
- Songs of Two Nations (1875)
- Erecthus (1876)
- Poems and Ballads, Second Series (1878)
- Songs of the Springtides (1880)
- Studies in Song (1880)
- The Heptalogia, or the Seven against Sense. A Cap with Seven Bells (1880)
- Tristam of Lyonesse (1882)
- A Century of Roundels (1883)
- A Midsummer Holiday and Other Poems (1884)
- Poems and Ballads, Third Series (1889)
- Astrophel and Other Poems (1894)
- The Tale of Balen (1896)

Criticism

- William Blake: A Critical Essay (1868)
- Under the Microscope (1872)
- George Chapman: A Critical Essay (1875)
- Essays and Studies (1875)
- A Note on Charlotte Brontë (1877)
- A Study of Shakespeare (1880)
- A Study of Victor Hugo (1886)
- A Study of Ben Johnson (1889)
- Studies in Prose and Poetry (1894)
- The Age of Shakespeare (1908)
- Shakespeare (1909)

Rudyard Kipling (1865-1936)

Rudyard Kipling was born in Bombay, India, in 1865. His father, John Lockwood Kipling, was principal of the Jeejeebyhoy School of Art, an architect and artist who had come to the colony. Kipling spent the first years of his life in India, remembering it in later years as almost a paradise. 'My first impression,' he wrote in his posthumously published autobiography *Something of Myself for My Friends Known and Unknown*, "is of daybreak, light and colour and golden and purple fruits at the level of my shoulder."

In 1871,. however, his parents sent him and his sister Beatric-called 'Trix'-to England, partly to avoid health problems, but also so that the children could begin their schooling.

Literary Career and Works

Rudyard Kipling is one of the best-known of the late Victorian poets and story-tellers. Although, he was awarded the Nobel Prize for literature in 1907, his unpopular political views caused his work to be neglected shortly after his death. Critics, however, recognise the power of his work.

The young writer's reputation soared after he settled in London.'Kipling's official biographer, CE Carrington,' declares cantalupo 'calls 1890 'Rudyard Kipling's year. There had been nothing like his sudden rise to fame since Byron.' 'His poems and stories,' writes O Toole, "elicited strong reactions of love and hate from the start-almost none of his advocates and detractors were temperate in praise or in blame. Ordinary readers liked the rhythms, the cockney speech, and the imperialist sentiments of his poems and short stories; critics generally damned the works for the same reasons." Many of his works were originally published in periodicals and later collected in various editions as Barrack-Room Ballads; famus poems such as '*The Ballad of East and West*,' *Danny Deever*, *Tommy*, and *The Road to Mandalay* date from this time. Kipling wrote many other works during the periods that he produceed his children's classics.

Major Works

- The Bell Buoy
- The Benefactors
- The Children
- The City of Sleep
- Danny Deever
- A Death-Bed
- Epitaphs of the War
- For All We Have And Are
- Gethsemane
- Gunga Din
- Harp Song of the Dane Women
- Justice
- The Long Trail
- Mesopotamia
- A Pict Song
- Recessional
- The Secret of the Machines
- Sestina of the Tramp-Royal
- The Song of the Banjo
- Song of the Galley-Slaves
- Tin Fish
- The Trade
- The Verdicts
- L' Envoi
- If

EXAM BASED QUESTIONS

1 What was the relationship between Victorian poets and the Romantics?

(a) The Romantics remained largely forgotten until their rediscovery by T. S. Eliot in the 1920s.
(b) The Victorians were disgusted by the immorality and narcissism of the Romantics.
(c) The Romantics were seen as gifted but crude artists belonging to a distant, semi-barbarous age.
(d) The Victorians were strongly influenced by the Romantics and experienced a sense of belatedness.

2 Experimentation in which of the following areas of poetic expression characterise Victorian poetry and allow Victorian poets to represent psychology in a different way?

(a) the use of pictorial description to construct visual images to represent the emotion or situation of the poem
(b) sound as a means to express meaning
(c) perspective, as in the dramatic monologue
(d) All of the above

3 Which of the following would not have been an appropriate topic of a Victorian poem?

(a) heroisms from the distant past
(b) events only in the contemporary age
(c) amorous romance depicted in epistolary form
(d) All of the above

4 Which best describes the general feeling expressed in literature during the last decade of the Victorian era?

(a) melancholic languor and comic self-criticism
(b) sincere earnestness
(c) raucous celebration mixed with self-congratulatory sophistication
(d) boredom mixed with a desire for enlivening innovation

5 Which of the following contributed to the growing awareness in the Late Victorian Period of the immense human, economic, and political costs of running an empire?

(a) the Boer War in the South of Africa
(b) the Jamaica Rebellion in 1865
(c) the Irish Question
(d) All of the above

6 Which genres seemed particularly amenable to Victorians in instructing the public about social matters and promoting partisan viewpoints?

(a) the novel
(b) non-fiction prose
(c) the religious tract
(d) All of the above

7 What does it mean if women are called 'surplus' or "redundant" in the Victorian era?

(a) They remained unmarried due to a population imbalance between the sexes.
(b) The unfair labor conditions resulted in a surplus of textiles, causing them to drop in price.
(c) They were women writers who wrote frequently about similar topics.
(d) They prostituted themselves as a way to make money in a market economy that didn't provide extensive job opportunities to women.

8 What was common amongst DG Rossetti, Christina Rossetti, Morris and Swinburne?

(a) They all belonged to the Lake School
(b) They all belonged to the Raphaelite School
(c) They all belonged to the Pre-Raphaelite School
(d) They all belonged to the Romantic School

9 Which one of the following best describes the general feeling expressed in literature during the last decade of the Victorian era?

(a) Studied melancholy and aestheticism
(b) The triumph of science and morbidity
(c) Sincere earnestness and Protestant zeal
(d) Raucous celebration combined with paranoid interpretation

10 It is unimaginable that all the following events happened in one year.

1. Arthur Evans discovered the first European civilisation; his excavations in Crete revealed a culture that was far older than either Attic Greece or Ancient Rome.
2. Sir Arthur Quiller-Couch published the 'Oxford Book of English Verse'.
3. Pablo Picasso stepped off the Barcelona train at Gare'd Orsay, Paris.
4. Max Planck unveiled the Quantum Theory.
5. Hugo de Vries identified what would later come to be called genes.
6. Sigmund Freud published "The Interpretation of Dreams'.
7. Coca-cola arrived in Britain.

Identify the year.

(a) 1899 (b) 1900 (c) 1901 (d) 1903

11 The period of Queen Victoria's reign is

(a) 1830-1900 (b) 1837-1901
(c) 1830-1901 (d) 1837-1900

12 In how many phases was Victorian age divided?

(a) Two (b) Three (c) Four (d) FiIve

13 First phase of the Victorian age was of how many years?
(a) 10 (b) 11 (c) 12 (d) 14

14 First phase period was between
(a) 1832-1846 (b) 1846-1869
(c) 1869-1876 (d) 1876-1889

15 Tennyson became Poet Laureate in
(a) 1850 (b)1855 (c) 1876 (d) 1833

16 'Two Brothers' a poem by Alfred Tennyson appeared in
(a) 1827 (b) 1855 (c) 1876 (d) 1875

17 The plan of Arthurian stories has influenced the composition of Tennyson's
(a) In Memoriam (b) Idylls
(c) Maud (d) Locksley Hall

18 'In Memoriam' was published in
(a) 1855 (b) 1850 (c) 1875 (d) 1876

19 Which of the following Tennyson poems is a dramatic monologue?
(a) In Memoriam
(b) The Charge of the Light Brigade
(c) Crossing the Bar
(d) Tithonus

20 Which poem was published by Tennyson after winning the award of Chancellor Medal?
(a) Timbuctoo (b) Lyrical Ballad
(c) Poems Chiefly Lyrical (d) The Princess

21 Which poem of Tennyson was a long poem of over three thousand lines of blank verse?
(a) Wages (b) The Princess
(c) The Higher Pantheism (d) Maud

22 Which poem by Tennyson was an answer to the question of woman's rights and woman's sphere. Which was then, as in our own day, strongly agitating the public mind?
(a) Wages (b) The Higher Pantheism
(c) The Princess (d) Maud

23 Which poem is called in literature a mono drama, telling the story of a lover, who passes from morbidness to ecstasy, then to anger and murder, followed by insanity and recovery?
(a) Wages (b) The Higher Pantheism
(c) Maud (d) The Princess

24 Which of the following poems by Tennyson does not speak of old age and death?
(a) The Beggar Maid (b) The Lotus-Eaters
(c) Ulysses (d) 'Tithonus'

25 Which contemporary discussions on women's rights did Tennyson's The Princess address?
(a) the grueling working conditions for women in textile factories
(b) the debate on women's suffrage
(c) the need to enlarge and improve educational opportunities for women, resulting in the establishment of the first women's college in London .
(d) the question of monarchical succession and if a woman should hold royal power

26 Which poem gives us the soul of an Arab, vain and proud of his fast horse, which was never beaten in a race?
(a) Abt Vogler
(b) The Bishop Orders his Tomb
(c) Muleykeh
(d) My Last Duchess

27 Which poem is the study of a musician's soul by Browning?
(a) Abt Vogler
(b) The Bishop Orders his Tomb
(c) Muleykeh
(d) My Last Duchess

28 Which poem is an interesting revelation of the mind of a vain and worldly man, this time a churchman, whose words tell you far more than Browning's dreams about his own character?
(a) Abt Vogler (b) Muleykeh
(c) My Last Duchess
(d) The Bishop Orders his Tomb

29 Which poetic work is the strength and weakness of the perfect painter, whose love for soulless woman with a pretty face saddens Browning's life and hampers Browning's best work?
(a) Abt Vogler (b) Andrea del Sarto
(c) My Last Duchess (d) Muleykeh

30 An immense poem, twice as long a 'Paradise Lost' and longer by some two thousand lines than the Iliad by Browning.
(a) Pippa Passes (b) The Ring and the Book
(c) Saul (d) Cleon

31 Which of these poems uses dramatic monologue as a poetic form?
(a) Wordsworth's 'The Prelude'
(b) Robert Browning's 'My Last Duchess'
(c) Tennyson's 'In Memoriam'
(d) Shelley's 'Adonais'

32 Who is regarded as the poet, who has spoken the strongest word of faith to an age of doubt?
(a) Browning
(b) Tennyson
(c) Blake
(d) Scott

33 Which literary work contains the best expression of Browning's own faith in life both here and hereafter?
(a) A Toccata of Galuppi's
(b) Rabbi Ben Ezra
(c) A Grammarian's Funeral
(d) Fra Lippo Lippi

34 Which literary work by Browning is an exquisite tribute to his dead wife?
(a) My Star (b) Prospice
(c) One Word More (d) Meeting at Night

35 What bothered the Duke about the Duchess' smile?
(a) It was false
(b) It was easily given to anyone
(c) It was never reserved for him
(d) It was crooked

36 What is the rhyme scheme of My Last Duchess?
(a) Enjambed blank verse
(b) Enjambed ryhming couplets
(c) End-stopped rhyming couplets
(d) End-stopped blank verse

37 How is Porphyria killed in the Last Duchess?
(a) She is stabbed (b) She is shot
(c) She is drowned (d) She is strangled

38 What makes Soliloquy of the Spanish Cloister a soliloquy?
(a) A speaker who is distinct from the poet, has no implied audience
(b) A speaker who is distinct from the poet, who has an audience before him
(c) The poet is the speaker and is talking to himself
(d) The poet is the speaker and is addressing a pretend audience

39 Who is the speaker's primary adversary in 'Soliloquy of the Spanish Cloister'?
(a) The Prior (b) The Pope
(c) Brother Lawrence (d) Fra Lippo Lippi

40 What season does the poet describe in 'Home-Thoughts from Abroad'?
(a) Spring (b) Summer (c) Fall (d) Winter

41 In "The Bishop Orders His Tomb…" where does the Bishop say the lapis for the tomb is hidden?
(a) In the catacombs beneath the church
(b) Buried in a vineyard
(c) At his mistress's home
(d) Buried beneath the altar

42 Why is the Bishop so concerned with his tomb?
(a) He wants to outdo his predecessor
(b) He believes it will ensure his immortality
(c) He has done nothing to ensure either his earthly reputation or his salvation
(d) All of the above

43 What kind of art does 'Fra Lippo Lippi' by Robert Browning produce?
(a) Abstract art (b) Nebulous religious art
(c) Landscapes (d) Portraits of real people

44 Which of the following painters is not someone to whom Andrea compares himself?
(a) Raphael (b) Michelangelo
(c) Leonardo da Vinci (d) Titian

45 Which city is described in 'A Toccata of Galuppi's'?
(a) London (b) Rome
(c) Florence (d) Venice

46 What does the poet find in his walk across the moor in 'Memorabilia'?
(a) A bird's nest (b) A robin's egg
(c) A dead sparrow (d) An eagle's feather

47 Which late poet has the stranger in 'Memorabilia' met?
(a) Shelley (b) Keats
(c) Wordsworth (d) Milton

48 What crime has Andrea del Sarto committed?
(a) Murder (b) Adultery
(c) Theft (d) Blasphemy

49 What was the name of Arnold's first book of poetry?
(a) New poems (b) Empedocles on etna
(c) The strayed reveler (d) The scholar-gipsy

50 Which is not a common theme throughout Arnold's poetry?
(a) Faith (b) Anti-modernism
(c) Money (d) Love

51 In 'Desire,' what does Arnold wish that humans be saved from?
(a) A life lived only for pleasure
(b) Belief in God and devils
(c) The temptations of life
(d) The terrible apocalypse that was soon coming

52 Which two entities are personified in 'Desire' by Matthew Arnold?
(a) The soul and pride (b) Time and destiny
(c) Light and darkness (d) Water and fire

53 In 'To Marguerite: Continued,' Arnold compares humans to what?
(a) Storms (b)Monkeys
(c) Islands (d) Stones

54 In 'Dream,' what is the name of the speaker's friends?
(a) Arthur (b) Matthew
(c) Andrew (d) Martin

55 What are the names of the woman in 'A Dream'?
(a) Margaret and Emily (b) Marguerite and Olivia
(c) Dorothy and Lenore (d) Laura and Mary

56 Which two elements does Arnold juxtapose in 'A Dream'?
(a) Water and fire
(b) Earth and air
(c) Earth and fire
(d) Air and water

57 What does the speaker of 'A Summer Night' speak to?
(a) The Sun (b) A cloud (c) A star (d) The moon

58 What important message does 'Consolation' relay about time?
(a) Time drags on forever (b) Time is relative
(c) We are in control of our time
(d) Humans will never use their time wisely

59 Which characters in 'Consolation' beg for their time to be extended?
(a) Two world leaders
(b) A pair of sick brothers
(c) The goddess of destiny and the God of time
(d) The couple

60 Why does Arnold refer to different corners of the globe in 'Consolation'?
(a) To suggest the futility of life
(b) To express the universality of time
(c) Because some place do not experience time
(d) Because he has travelled to all these places

61 The Scholar-Gipsy is
(a) a former Oxford student
(b) Matthew Arnold' friend
(c) Matthew Arnold himself
(d) a native-born Gipsy

62 What does the Scholar-Gipsy take from the gypsies?
(a) Their Children
(b) Their ability to see the future
(c) Their jewellery and precious gems
(d) Their secrets of learning and imagination

63 Why does the speaker believe that the Scholar-Gipsy is still alive?
(a) Because the Scholar-Gipsy did not live like everyone else
(b) Because the Scholar-Gipsy is only an idea
(c) Because the Scholar-Gipsy was secretly a God
(d) Because he himself is the Scholar-Gipsy

64 Matthew Arnold classified human society into three main classes
(a) Barbarians, Philistines and Populace
(b) High, Middle, Low
(c) Aristocracy, Genteel, Workers
(d) Upper, Middle, Lower

65 One of the follwing poems in Men and Women is addressed to Elizabeth Barrett Browning by the poet. Identify it.
(a) In Three Days (b) By the Fireside
(c) One Way of Love (d) One Word More

66 Elizabeth Barrett's poem the Cry of the Children is concerned with which major issue attendant on the Time of Troubles during the 1830s and 1840s?
(a) Women's rights and suffrage
(b) Child labour
(c) Chartism
(d) The prudishness and old-fashioned ideals of her fellow Victorians

67 A noble and inspiring book of love poem by Miss Barrett
(a) The Cry of the Children
(b) Sonnets from the Portuguese
(c) Lady Geraldine's Courtship
(d) Casa Guidi Windows

68 A novel in verse, having for its hero a young social reformer and for its heroine a young woman, poetical and enthusiastic by Barrett.
(a) Casa Guidi Windows (b) Aurora Leigh
(c) Poems Before Congress (d) The Princess

69 Who among the following Victorian poets disliked his middle name?
(a) Arthur Hugh Clough
(b) Dante Gabriel Rossetti
(c) Gerard Manley Hopkins
(d) Algernon Charles Swinburne

70 'Amours de Voyage' is written by
(a) Elizabeth Barrett Browning (b) John Ruskin
(c) Arthur Hugh Clough (d) Charles Dickens

71 The term, 'curtal sonnet', was coined by
(a) John Milton (b) William Blake
(c) Gerald Manley Hopkins (d) Matthew Arnold

72 'Invictus' is the work of
(a) WE Henley (b) William Morris
(c) DG Rossetti (d) AC Swinburne

73 Who had talent of both a painter and a poet?
(a) Tennyson (b) Browning
(c) Matthew Arnold (d) DG Rossetti

74 Who led the Pre Raphaelite Movement?
(a) Tennyson (b) Browning
(c) Matthew Arnold (d) DG Rossetti

75 What was founded on a medieval superstition by Rossetti?
(a) The Confession
(b) The Ballad of Sister Helen
(c) The King's Tragedy
(d) The House of Life

76 For ...... poem Tennyson got Chancellor's Medal.
(a) Lyrical Ballad (b) Timbuctoo
(c) Merlin and the Glean (d) The Princess

77 ..... is the symbolic name for poetry and thought.
(a) Pauline (b) Paracelsus
(c) Bells and Pomegranates (d) Poems by Two Brothers

78 ...... was modeled after Browning by Rossetti.
(a) The Confession
(b) The Ballad of Sister Helen
(c) The King's Tragedy
(d) The House of Life

79 ...... was the son of an exiled Italian painter and scholar, was distinguished both as a painter and as a poet.
(a) Rossetti (b) Tennyson (c) Browning (d) Blake

80 ...... is an epic founded upon one of the old sagas and Morris prose romance.

(a) Sigurd the Volsung
(b) The Earthly Paradise
(c) The House of the Wolfings
(d) The Roots of the Mountains

81 The speaker of 'A Summer Night' is best described as ....

(a) Jilted (b) Angry
(c) Restless (d) Confused

82 'Sigurd the Volsung is out of an old saga' is the work of ....

(a) John Ruskin (b) William Morris
(c) AC Swinburne (d) Charles Dickens

83 'The House of the Wolfings' and 'The Roots of the Mountains' are the works of ....

(a) John Davidson (b) HW Longfellow
(c) William Morris (d) None of these

84 ...... modeled his lyrical drama 'Atlanta in Calydon'.

(a) William Morris
(b) AC Swinburne
(c) John Ruskin
(d) DG Rossetti

85 Fill in the blanks from Tennyson's The Princess
Man for the field and Woman for the ....
Man for the sword and for the .... she:
Man with the head and woman with the........... .
Man to command and woman to ....

(a) Crop: scabbard; foot; agree
(b) throne; scepter; soul; decree
(c) school ; scalpel; pen; set free
(d) hearth: needle: heart; obey

86 Which of these statements about 'Dramatic Monologue' is incorrect?

(a) A single person, who is clearly not the poet utters the speech
(b) The person addresses and interacts with one or more people
(c) The main purpose of the lyric is to reveal the speaker's temperament and character
(d) The dramatic monologue as a poetic form achieved its first distinction in the works of Tennyson

87 Which of these statements about 'In Memoriam' is true?

(a) It is not an elegiac tribute to Arthur Henry Hallam
(b) It is not written by Lord Tennyson
(c) The poem was written over the course of 20 years
(d) The poem concludes with an epithalamion

88 Which of these statements about Culture and Anarchy is true?

(a) It was not written by Matthew Arnold
(b) It was not published in 1869
(c) The author divides human society into four main classes
(d) The book is famous for its popularisation of the phrase 'sweetness and light'

89 Which of the following is incorrect?

(a) Elizabeth Barret Browning was a Victorian poetess
(b) DG Rossettiwa a pre-Raphaelite poet
(c) Aesthetic Movement emphasised on moral and social theme over physical beauty or nature
(d) Oscar Wilde was the most important and the most known of the late Victorian Age

90 Which of the following statements is not true of Dante Gabriel Rossetti?

(a) DG Rossetti was a Londoner, the son of an Italian refugee, who taught Italian at King's college
(b) Rossetti formed the Pre-Raphaelite brotherhood with Holman Hunt, Ford Madox Brown and Painter Millais
(c) He married Christina Georgina, who was a poet in her right
(d) Rossetti's 'Blessed Damozel' displays his remarkable gifts as a poet and painter

91 Which of the follwoing pairs is incorrectly matched?

(a) Robert Browning : Victorian Poet
(b) Matthew Arnold : Pre-Raphaelite Poet
(c) Elizabeth Barret Browning : Victorian Poetess
(d) Christina Rossetti : Pre-Raphaelite Poetess

92 Which of the following pairs is correctly matched?

(a) The Ring and the Book : Arthur Hugh Clough
(b) Culture and Anarchy : DG Rossetti
(c) Songs of Two Nations : Algernon Charles Swinburne
(d) Ballads and Sonnets : Christina Rossetti

93 Which of the following pairs is incorrectly matched?

(a) The Hollow Land : William Morris
(b) Pauline : Alfred Lord Tennyson
(c) Dramatic Romances and Lyrics : Robert Browning
(d) Sohrab and Rustam : Matthew Arnold

94 Which of the following pairs is correctly matched?

(a) Walter Pater : Messes-The Epicurean
(b) Oscar Wilde : The Coral Island
(c) Anthony Trollope : The Importance of Being Earnest
(d) RM Ballantyne : Barchester Towers

95 Which of the following pairs is incorrectly matched?

(a) 1837 : Queen Victoria ascends the throne
(b) 1853 : Outbreak of Crimean war
(c) 1846 : Repeal of Corn Laws
(d) 1845 : Death of Prince Albert

Directions (Q. Nos. 96-100) *In the questions given below are two statements labelled as Assertion (A) and Reason (R). In the context of the two statements, which one of the following is correct?*

Codes

(a) A is true, but R is false
(b) A is false, but R is true
(c) Both A and R are true, and R is the correct explanation of A
(d) Both A and R are true but R is not the correct explanation of A

96 **Assertion** (A) The Victorian Age is sometimes known as the Age of Reform.
Reason (R) A plethora of reforms was planned, but not executed during this period.

97 **Assertion** (A) Doubt became the order of the day in Victorian England.
Reason (R) Doubt was no longer a religious sin ; it became a necessity, keeping in mind the rapid developments of the Age.

98 **Assertion** (A) Robert Buchanan criticised the Pre- Raphaelite school of poetry.
Reason (R) He attacked the explicit nature of subject matter as well as erotic imagery in the poetry of different poets.

99 **Assertion** (A) The readers find wit and humour throughout Arthur Hugh Clough's work.
Reason (R) Arthur Hugh Clough has given satirical and humorous works to his readers.

100 **Assertion** (A) The readers, who read about AC Swinburne deeply know his love for sea and childhood.
Reason (R) AC Swinburne's music was appealing and makes the readers read his works again and again.

101 Which of the following is the correct chronological sequence?
(a) A Poison Tree, The Deserted Village, The Blessed Damozel, Ozymandias
(b) The Deserted Village, A Poison Tree, Ozymandias, The Blessed Damozel
(c) The Blessed Damozel, A Poison Tree, The Deserted Village, Ozymandias
(d) The Deserted Village, The Blessed Damozel, Ozymandias, A Poison Tree

102 Arrange the following in correct chronological order as per their publishing year.
1. The Ring and the Book
2. Sordello
3. Men and Women

Codes
(a) 2, 1, 3 (b) 2, 3, 1 (c) 3, 2, 1 (d) 1, 3, 2

103 Which of the following works of Tennyson are in correct chronological order?
(a) Poems; Chiefly Lyrical, The Princess, Maud and other Poems, Idylls of the King
(b) The Princess, Idylls of the King, Maud and other Poems, Poems; Chiefly Lyrical
(c) Idylls of the King, The Princess, Maud and the other Poems, Poems, Chiefly Lyrical
(d) Maud and the other Poems, Poems; Chiefly Lyrical, Idylls of the King, The Princess

104 Which of the following poets are in correct chronological order as per their birth?
(a) Matthew Arnold, DG Rossetti, Alfred Tennyson, Swinburne
(b) DG Rossetti, Matthew Arnold, Swinburne, Alfred Tennyson
(c) Alfred Tennyson, Swinburne, Matthew Arnold, DG Rossetti
(d) Alfred Tennyson, Matthew Arnold, DG Rossetti, Swinburne

105 Which of the following Victorian poetry is in correct chronological order?
(a) The Blessed Damozel, Goblin Market and Other Poems, Dover Beach, My Last Duchess
(b) My Last Duchess, Dover Beach, Goblin Market and Other Poems, The Blessed Damozel
(c) Dover Beach, The Blessed Damozel, Goblin Market and Other Poems, My Last Duchess
(d) My Last Duchess, The Blessed Damozel, Dover Beach, Goblin Market and Other Poems

106 Consider the following statements about the Victorian Age. The Victorian Age
1. is sometimes known as the Age of Reform.
2. was an age of democracy.
3. was characterised by the triumph of the aristocracy.
4. did not allow colonial expansion.

Which of the statements given above are correct?
(a) 1 and 2
(b) 1 and 4
(c) 3 and 2
(d) 3 and 4

107 Tennyson's Ulysses is
1. a poem expressing the need for going forward and braving the struggles of life
2. a dramatic monologue
3. a morbid poem
4. a poem making extensive use of satire

The right combination for the above statement, according to the code is
(a) 1 and 4
(b) 2 and 3
(c) 3 and 4
(d) 1 and 2

108 Consider the following statements.

1. Browning is one of the famous poets of the Victorian Age.
2. Browning is known for his dramatic monologue.
3. Browning is called the Victorian Donne.

Which of the statements given above is/are correct?

(a) Only 1 (b) Only 2
(c) Only 3 (d) All of these

109 Consider the following statements.

1. Strafford was written by Browning.
2. Men and Women was published in 1853.
3. Talism is not a work by Browning.

Which of the statements given above is/are correct?

(a) 1 and 2 (b) 2 and 3
(c) 1 and 3 (d) None of these

110 Consider the following statements.

1. Arnold has employed the classical themes.
2. Arnold's poetry appeals to the reader's mind.
3. He is known for his work like 'Men and Women.'

Which of the statements given above is/are correct?

(a) Only 1 (b) Only 2
(c) 1 and 3 (d) 1 and 2

111 Consider the following statements.
Matthew Arnold's 'Culture and Anarchy'

1. was first published in 1869.
2. does not argue for a restructuring of England's social ideology.
3. does not contrast culture with anarchy.
4. culture seeks to cultivate the 'Free Play' of thought.

Which of the statements given above are correct?

(a) 1 and 2
(b) 1 and 4
(c) 3 and 2
(d) 3 and 4

112 Consider the following statements.

1. Arthur Clough has given satirical and humorous works to his readers.
2. Clough has voiced the Victorian concern of Science and Religion.

Which of the statements given above is/are correct?

(a) Only 1
(b) Only 2
(c) Both 1 and 2
(d) None of these

113 What is common to the following writers? Identify the correct description below.

1. Dante Gabriel Rossetti
2. Christina Rossetti
3. William Morris
4. AC Swinburne

Codes

(a) All of them are University Wits
(b) All of them are Lake Poets
(c) All of them are Pre–Raphaelite poets
(d) All of them wrote tragedies of the Victorian Age

114 Consider the following statements.

1. The Seraphim and other poems was written by Elizabeth Barrett.
2. Dante Gabriel Rossetti's period was 1828-1882.
3. The Blessed Damozel was written by Browning.

Which of the statements given above is/are incorrect?

(a) 1 and 2 (b) 2 and 3
(c) 1 and 3 (d) Only 3

115 Consider the following statements.

1. Swinburne had knowledge of verse and had interest in trying new things.
2. The readers, who read about him deeply know his love for sea and childhood.

Which of the statements given above is/are correct?

(a) Only 1 (b) Only 2
(c) Both 1 and 2 (d) None of the above

116 Match the following Victorian poets with their poems.

Victorian Poet

1. Alfred Lord Tennyson
2. Robert Browning
3. Mathew Arnold
4. Elizabeth Barrett Browning

Poem

A. Charge of the Light Brigade
B. Porphyria's Lover
C. The Strayed Reveller and other Poems
D. The Battle of Marathon

(a) 1-A, 2-B, 3-C, 4-D
(b) 1-D, 2-C, 3-B, 4-A
(c) 1-B, 2-D, 3-A, 4-C
(d) 1-C, 2-A, 3-D, 4-B

117 Match the following poems with their Pre-Raphaelite Poets.

Poem

1. My Sister's Sleep
2. A Pageant and other Poems
3. The Defence of Guenevere and other Poems
4. Song of Italy

Pre-Raphaelite Poet

A. Algernon Charles Swinburne
B. William Morris
C. Christina Rossetti
D. Dante Gabriel Rossetti

(a) 1-A, 2-B, 3-C, 4-D (b) 1-D, 2-C, 3-B, 4-A
(c) 1-B, 2-D, 3-A, 4-C (d) 1-C, 2-A, 3-D, 4-B

118 Match the following Victorian age poems with the year of their publication.

Victorian Age Poem
1. In Memorium
2. Cromwell: A Prize Poem
3. Prince's Progress and Other Poems
4. A Mid Summer Holiday

Year of Publication
A - 1866
B - 1850
C - 1884
D - 1843

Codes
(a) 1-A, 2-B, 3-C, 4-D (b) 1-D, 2-B, 3-C, 4-A
(c) 1-B, 2-D, 3-C, 4-A (d) 1-C, 2-A, 3-D, 4-B

119 Match the following poems with their Victorian poets:

Poem
1. Sohrab and Rustam
2. Casa Guidi Windows
3. House of Life
4. Love is Enough

Victorian Poet
A. Elizabeth Barrett Browning
B. Willaim Morris
C. Mathew Arnold
D. D.G. Rossetti

Codes
(a) 1-A, 2-B, 3-C, 4-D (b) 1-D, 2-C, 3-B, 4-A
(c) 1-B, 2-D, 3-A, 4-C (d) 1-C, 2-A, 3-D, 4-B

120 Match the following.

List I (Line)	List II (Poem)
A. That's My Last Duches painted on the wall	1. The Blessed Damozel
B. How do I love thee? Let me count the ways	2. Dover Beach
C. The sea is calm tonight	3. Sonnet No 43
D. The blessed damozel learned out	4. My Last Duchess

Codes

	A	B	C	D		A	B	C	D
(a)	4	3	2	1	(b)	3	2	1	4
(c)	1	2	3	4	(d)	2	4	3	1

121 Match the following.

List I (Poets)	List II (Works)
A. William Morris	1. Chasteland
B. AC Swinburne	2. Paracelsus
C. Robert Browninge	3. A Dream of John Bull
D. Arthur Hugh Clough	4. Amours de Voyage

Codes

	A	B	C	D		A	B	C	D
(a)	4	3	2	1	(b)	3	2	4	1
(c)	3	1	2	4	(d)	2	1	4	3

122 Match the following:

List I (Poem)	List II (Poet)
A. Idylls of the King	1. Christina Rossetti
B. Consolation	2. Elizabeth Barrett Browning
C. Sonnets from the Portuguese	3. Matthew Arnold
D. Goblin Market and other Poems	4. Tennyson

Codes
(a) 1-A, 2-B, 3-C, 4-D
(b) 1-D, 2-C, 3-B, 4-A
(c) 1-B, 2-D, 3-A, 4-C
(d) 1-C, 2-A, 3-D, 4-B

123 In the series given below, which one has all the poets correctly matched with their works?
(a) Alfred Tennyson-Thyrsis, Robert Browning-Ave, Matthew Arnold-The Princess, DG Rossetti-Strafford
(b) Alfred Tennyson-The Princess, Robert Browning-Strafford Matthew Arnold-Thyrsis, DG Rossetti-Ave
(c) Alfred Tennyson-Thyrsis, Robert Browning-The Princess Matthew Arnold-Ave, DG Rossetti-Strafford
(d) Alfred Tennyson-Ave, Robert Browning-Thyrsis, Matthew Arnold-The Princess, DG Rossetti-Strafford

124 The following series, which one has all the works matched correctly with their publishing years?
(a) Dramatic Personal-1850, Men and Women-1854, Pauline-1836, Sordello-1855
(b) Dramatic Personal-1850, Men and Women-1854, Pauline-1855, Sordello-1836
(c) Dramatic Personal-1854, Men and Women-1850, Pauline 1836, Sordello-1855
(d) Dramatic Personal-1854, Men and Women-1855 Pauline-1836, Sordello-1850

125 In the series given below, which one has all the works matched correctly with their composers?
(a) Songs before Sunrise-William Morris, The Earthly Paradise-Christina Rossetti, The Face of the Deep-Arthur Hugh Clough, Ambarvalia-Swinburne
(b) Songs before Sunrise-Swinburne, The Earthly Paradise-William Morris, The Face of the Deep-Christina Rossetti, Ambarvalia-Arthur Hugh Clough
(c) Songs before Sunrise-Arthur Hugh Clough, The Earthly Paradise-William Morris, The Face of the Deep-Christina Rossetti, Ambarvalia-Swinburne
(d) Songs before Sunrise-Christina Rossetti, The Earthly Paradise-Arthur Hugh Clough, The Face of the Deep-Swinburne, Ambarvalia-William Morris

126 Half the night I waste in sighs,
Half in dreams I sorrow after
The delight of early skies;
In a wakeful dose I sorrow
For the hand, the lips, the eyes,
For the meeting of the morrow,
The delight of happy laughter,
The delight of low replies."

From which work of a Victorian poet have these lines been taken?
(a) Maud and other poems-Alfred Tennyson
(b) Dover Beach-Matthew Arnold
(c) My Last Duchess-Robert Browning
(d) The Blessed Damozel-DG Rossetti

127 "I hold it true, whate'er befall;
I feel it when I sorrow most;
'Tis better to have loved and lost
Than never to have loved at all."

Which of the following poets in which of his/her works has used the above lines?
(a) Alfred Lord Tennyson, In Memoriam
(b) Robert Browning, Men and Women and Other Poems
(c) Matthew Arnold, Dover Beach and Other Poems
(d) Elizabeth Barrett Browning, Sonnets from the Portuguese

128 'Though much is taken, much abides; and though
We are not now that strength which in old days
Moved earth and heaven, that which we are, we are;
One equal temper of heroic hearts,
Made weak by time and fate, but strong in will
To strive, to seek, to find, and not to yield."

Which of the following poets in which of his/her works has used the above lines?
(a) Alfred Lord Tennyson, Idylls of the King and a Selection of Poems
(b) Robert Browning, Paracelsus
(c) Matthew Arnold, 'The Forsaken Merman'
(d) Elizabeth Barrett Browning, Sonnets from the Portuguese and Other Love Poems

129 "Cover her face; mine eyes dazzle; she died young
...... She and I were twins: And should I die this
instant, I had liv'd her time to a minute"

In the light of the above quotation which of the following interpretations is not correct?
(a) The beauty and youth of the Duchess become obvious to Ferdinand when he sees her dead body
(b) Only when he identifies himself with her does he realise the anormity of his crime
(c) When he compares the age of the Duchess with his own and puts himself in her position does he realise his guilt
(d) He wants her face to be covered because it reminds him of her infidelity

130 "The year's at the spring
And day's at the morn;
Morning's at seven;
The hill-side' dew-pearled;
The lark's on the wing;
The snail's on the thorn;
God's in his heaven
All's right with the world!"

From which work of a Victorian poet have these lines been taken?
(a) Amours de Voyage-Arthur Hugh Clough
(b) Rugby Chapel-Matthew Arnold
(c) Pippa Passes-Robert Browning
(d) The death of Oenone-Alfred Lord Tennyson

131 "Ah, but a man's reach should exceed his grasp,
Or what's a heaven for?"

Which of the following poets in which of his/her works has used the above lines?
(a) Alfred Lord Tennyson, In Memoriam
(b) Robert Browning, Men and Women and Other Poems
(c) Matthew Arnold, Dover Beach and Other Poems
(d) Elizabeth Barrett Browning, Sonnets from the Portuguese

132 "At times I almost dream
I too have spent a life the sages' way,
And tread once more familiar paths. Perchance
I perished in an arrogant self-reliance
Ages ago; and in that act a prayer
For one more chance went up so earnest, so
Instinct with better light let in by death,
That life was blotted out - not so completely
But scattered wrecks enough of it remain,
Dim memories, as now, when once more seems
The goal in sight again."

Which of the following poets in which of his/her works has used the above lines?
(a) Alfred Lord Tennyson, Idylls of the King and a Selection of Poems
(b) Robert Browning, Paracelsus .
(c) Matthew Arnold, 'The Forsaken Merman'
(d) Elizabeth Barrett Browning, Sonnets from the Portuguese and Other Love Poems

133 "Ah, love, let us be true
To one another! for the world, which seems
To lie before us like a land of dreams,
So various, so beautiful, so new,
Hath really neither joy, nor love, nor light,
Nor certitude, nor peace, nor help for pain;
And we are here as on a darkling plain
Swept with confused alarms of struggle and flight,
Where ignorant armies clash by night."

Which of the following poets in which of his/her works has used the above lines?
(a) Alfred Lord Tennyson, In Memoriam
(b) Robert Browning, Men and Women and Other Poems
(c) Matthew Arnold, Dover Beach and Other Poems .
(d) Elizabeth Barrett Browning, Sonnets from the Portuguese

134 No, no thou hast not felt the lapse of hours!
For what wears out the life of mortal men?
'Tis that repeated shocks, again, again,
Exhaust the energy of strongest souls
And numb the elastic powers...

Who does the poet address here?
(a) The Scholar Gipsy
(b) Telemachus
(c) The Nightingale
(d) The Poet's sister Dorothy

135 "The sea is calm tonight
The tide is full, the moon lies fair
upon the straits, on the French coast the light
Gleams and is gone, the cliffs of England stand,
Glimmering and vast, out in the tranquil bay
Come to the window, sweet is the night air".

(a) This is DG Rossetti in House of Life
(b) This is Christina Rossetti in Goblin Market and other Poems
(c) This is Swinburne in Songs of Italy
(d) This is Matthew Arnold in Dover Beach

136 "Up the still, glistening beaches,
Up the creeks we will hie,
Over banks of bright seaweed
The ebb-tide leaves dry.
We will gaze, from the sand-hills,
At the white, sleeping town;
At the church on the hill-side-
And then come back down.
Singing:" There dwells a loved one,
But cruel is she!
She left lonely for ever
The kings of the sea.

Which of the following poets in which of his/her works has used the above lines?

(a) Alfred Lord Tennyson, Idylls of the King and a Selection of Poems
(b) Robert Browning, Paracelsus
(c) Matthew Arnold, 'The Forsaken Merman' .
(d) Elizabeth Barrett Browning, Sonnets from the Portuguese and Other Love Poems

137 "But love me for love's sake, that evermore
Thou may'st love on through love' eternity".

Which of the following poets in which of his/her works has used the above lines?

(a) Alfred Lord Tennyson, In Memoriam
(b) Robert Browning Men and Women and Other Poems
(c) Matthew Arnold, Dover Beach and Other Poems
(d) Elizabeth Barrett Browning, Sonnets from the Portuguese

138 "The widest land
Doom takes to part us, leaves thy heart in mine
With pulses that beat double. What I do
And what I dream include thee, as the wine
Must taste of its own grapes."

Which of the following poets in which of his/her works has used the above lines?

(a) Elizabeth Barrett Browning, Sonnets from the Portuguese and Other Love Poems
(b) Arthur Hugh Clough, Say not the Struggle Naught Availeth
(c) Dante Gabriel Rossetti, The House of Life
(d) William Morris, Poems By The Way & Love Is Enough

139 "A harmless life, she called a virtuous life,
A quiet life, which was not life at a" ... "

Which of the following poets in which of his/her works has used the above lines?

(a) Elizabeth Barrett Browning, Aurora Leigh and Other Poems.
(b) Dante Gabriel Rossetti, Pre-Raphaelite Poetry: An Anthology
(c) Christina Rossetti, Complete Poems
(d) Algernon Charles Swinburne, The Garden of Proserpine

140 "The chances are that, being a woman, young,
And pure, with such a pair of large, calm eyes,
You write as well" ...and ill ...upon the whole,
As other women. if as we", what then?
If even a little better, ..still, what then?
We want the Best in art now, or no art."

Which of the following poets in which of his/her works has used the above lines?

(a) Elizabeth Barrett Browning, Aurora Leigh and Other Poems
(b) William Morris, The House of the Wolfings
(c) Christina Rossetti, Complete Poems
(d) Algernon Charles Swinburne, The Garden of Proserpine

141 "How do I love thee? Let me count the ways
I love thee to the depth and breadth and height.
My soul can reach, when feeling out of sight
For the ends of being and ideal grace".

(a) This is Robert Browning in 'Fra Lappo Lippi'
(b) This is Matthew Arnold in Rugby Chapel
(c) This is Elizabeth Barrettt Browning in Love Sonnet 43 in Sonnets from the Portuguese
(d) This is William Morris in The Earthly Paradise

142 "Girls blush, sometimes, because they are alive,
Half wishing they were dead to save the shame.
The sudden blush devours them, neck and brow;
They have drawn too near the fire of life, like gnats,
And flare up bodily, wings and all. What then?
Who's sorry for a gnat ... or a girl?"

Which of the following poets in which of his/her works has used the above lines?

(a) Dante Gabriel Rossetti, Pre-Raphaelite Poetry: An Anthology
(b) Christina Rossetti, Complete Poems
(c) Algernon Charles Swinburne, The Garden of Proserpine
(d) Elizabeth Barrett Browning, A Little Book Of Love Poems

143 "Better a crust of black bread than a mountain of paper confections,
Better a daisy in Earth than a dahlia cut and gathered,
Better a cowslip with toot than a prize carnation without it"

From which work of a Victorian poet have these lines been taken?

(a) The Bothie of Tober-na-Vuolich-Arthur Hugh Clough
(b) Hopes and Fears for Art-William Morris
(c) In Memoriam-Alfred Lord Tennyson
(d) A Pageant and Other Poems-Christina Rossetti

144 And not by eastern windows only,
When daylight comes, comes in the light;
In front the sun climbs slow, how slowly!
But westward, look, the land is bright!"

Which of the following poets in which of his/her works has used the above lines?

(a) Elizabeth Barrett Browning, Sonnets from the Portuguese and Other Love Poems
(b) Arthur Hugh Clough, Say not the Struggle Naught Availeth
(c) Dante Gabriel Rossetti, The House of Life
(d) William Morris, Poems By The Way & Love Is Enough

145 "Look in my face; my name is Might-have-been;
I am also call'd No-more, Too-late, Farewell"

Which of the following poets in which of his/her works has used the above lines?

(a) Elizabeth Barrett Browning, Sonnets from the Portuguese and Other Love Poems
(b) Arthur Hugh Clough, Say not the Struggle Naught Availeth
(c) Dante Gabriel Rossetti, The House of Life
(d) William Morris, Poems By The Way & Love Is Enough

146 "Love, which is quickly kindled in the gentle heart, seized this man for the fair form that was taken from me, the manner still hurts me. Love which absolves no beloved one from loving, seized me so strongly with his charm that, as thou seest, it does not leave me yet"

Which of the following poets in which of his/her works has used the above lines?

(a) Elizabeth Barrett Browning, Aurora Leigh and Other Poems
(b) Dante Gabriel Rossetti, Pre-Raphaelite Poetry: An Anthology
(c) Christina Rossetti, Complete Poems
(d) Algernon Charles Swinburne, The Garden of Proserpine

147 "Around her, lovers, newly met
'Mid deathless love's acclaims,
Spoke evermore among themselves
Their heart-remember'd names;
And the souls mounting up to God
Went by her like thin flames"

From which work of a Pre-Raphaelite poet have these lines been taken?

(a) Poems by the Way-William Morris
(b) The Blessed Damozel-DG Rossetti
(c) Prince's Progress and other Poems-Christina Rossetti
(d) Atalanta in Calydon-Algernon Charless Swinburne

148 "For there is no friend like a sister
In calm or stormy weather;
To cheer one on the tedious way,
To fetch one if one goes astray,
To lift one if one totters down,
To strengthen whilst one stands"

From which work of a Pre-Raphaelite poet have these lines been taken?

(a) House of Life-DG Rossetti
(b) The Life and Death of Jason-William Morris
(c) Goblin Market and Other Poems-Christina Rossetti
(d) Poems and Ballads-Swinburne

149 "Sometimes I said: It is an empty name
I long for; to a name why should I give
The peace of all the days I have to live?--
Yet gave it all the same.
Alas, thou foolish one! alike unfit
For healthy joy and salutary pain:
Thou knowest the chase useless, and again
Turnest to follow it."

Which of the following poets in which of his/her works has used the above lines?

(a) Elizabeth Barrett Browning, Aurora Leigh and Other Poems
(b) Dante Gabriel Rossetti, Pre-Raphaelite Poetry: An Anthology
(c) Christina Rossetti, A Pause for Thought, Complete Poems
(d) Algernon Charles Swinburne, The Garden of Proserpine

150 "Now let us go, love, down the winding stair,
With fingers intertwined..."

From which work of a Victorian poet have these lines been taken?

(a) The Holy Grail and Other Poems-Alfred Lord Tennyson
(b) The Battle of Marathon-Elizabeth Barrett Browning
(c) The Early Italian Poets-DG Rossetti
(d) The Defence of Guenevere and Other Poems-William Morris

151 "With the arrogance of youth, I determined to do no less than to transform the world with Beauty. If I have succeeded in some small way, if only in one small corner of the world, amongst the men and women I love, then I love, then I shall count myself blessed and blessed and blessed and the work goes on."

From which work of a Pre-Raphaelite poet have these lines been taken?

(a) The Well At The World's End-William Morris
(b) Sing-Song: A Nursery-Rhyme-Christina Rossetti
(c) Songs of the Springtides-AC Swinburne
(d) Vita Nuova-DG Rossetti

152 "E'en so the world of men may turn
At even of some hurried day
And see the ancient glimmer burn
Across the waste that hath no way;
Then with that faint light in its eyes
A while I bid it linger near
And nurse in wavering memories
The bitter-sweet of days that were."

Which of the following poets in which of his/her works has used the above lines?

(a) Elizabeth Barrett Browning, Aurora Leigh and Other Poems
(b) William Morris, The House of the Wolfings
(c) Christina Rossetti, Complete Poems
(d) Algernon Charles Swinburne, The Garden of Proserpine

153 "Love makes clear the eyes that else would never see: "Love makes blind the eyes to all but me and thee."

Which of the following poets in which of his/her works has used the above lines?

(a) Elizabeth Barrett Browning, Sonnets from the Portuguese and Other Love Poems
(b) Arthur Hugh Clough, Say not the Struggle Naught Availeth
(c) Dante Gabriel Rossetti, The House of Life
(d) William Morris, Poems By The Way & Love Is Enough

154 "I dare not always touch her, lest the kiss
Leave my lips charred. Yea, Lord, a little bliss,
Brief, bitter bliss, one hath for a great sin;
Nathless thou knowest how sweet a thing it is".

From which work of a Pre-Raphaelite poet have these lines been taken?

(a) The story of Glittering Pain-William Morris
(b) Laus Veneris And Other Poems and Ballads-Algernon Charles Swinburne
(c) Seek and Find-Christina Rossetti
(d) Sonnets and Lyrical Poems-DG Rossetti

155 "From too much love of living
From hope and fear set free,
We thank with brief thanksgiving
Whatever gods may be
That no life lives for ever;
That dead men rise up never;
That even the weariest river
Winds somewhere safe to sea."

Which of the following poets in which of his/her works has used the above lines?

(a) Elizabeth Barrett Browning, Aurora Leigh and Other Poems
(b) Dante Gabriel Rossetti, Pre-Raphaelite Poetry: An Anthology
(c) Christina Rossetti, Complete Poems
(d) Algernon Charles Swinburne, The Garden of Proserpine .

Directions (Q.Nos. 156-160) *Read the passage and answer the following questions.*

My Last Duchess

That's my last Duchess painted on the wall,
Looking as if she were alive. I call
That piece a wonder, now: Fra Pandolf's hands
Worked busily a day and there she stands.
Will't please you sit and look at her? I said
'Fra Pandolf' by design, for never read
Strangers like you that pictured countenances,
The depth and passion of its earnest glance,
But to myself they turned (since none puts by
The curtain I have drawn for you, but I)
And seemed as they would ask me, if they durst,
How such a glance came there; so, not the first
Are you to turn and ask thus. Sir, twas not
Her husband's presence only, called that spot
Of joy into the Duchess' cheek: perhaps
Fra Pandolf chanced to say "Her mantle laps
Over my lady's wrist too much", or "Paint
Half-flush that dies along her throat": such stuff
Was courtesy, she thought and cause enough
For calling up that spot of joy. She had
A heart-how shall I say?–Too soon made glad,
Too easily impressed; she liked whate'er
She looked on and her looks went everywhere.

156 What is the word mantle as used in the poem? "Her mantle laps over my lady's wrist too much."

(a) A shelf or counter (b) A bracelet
(c) A cloak (d) An exotic fruit

157 What is meant by the phrase 'a spot of joy' (lines 14-15)?

(a) A brightness in the eye (b) A blush
(c) A time of merriment (d) A tear

158 What does the Duke mean by "Her (the Duchess's) looks went everywhere"?

(a) She was too easily distracted by things and therefore, did not pay enough attention to the Duke
(b) She suffered from Amblyopia causing her eyes to look in different directions of each other and cause the Duke to see her as unattractive
(c) She was tempted by other men and very unfaithful to the Duke
(d) She was overly cautious and her eyes were constantly scanning for danger

159 What is the structure of this poem?

(a) Rhymed Iambic pentameter
(b) Un-rhymed Iambic pentameter
(c) Un-rhymed Iambic tetrameter
(d) Rhymed Iambic tetrameter

160 How would the tone of this poem best be described?

(a) Mischievous (b) Ironic (c) Unsettling (d) Pompous

PREVIOUS YEARS' QUESTIONS

December 2018

1 During the Raj, the British viewed their rule in terms of a thankless duty to uplift the downtrodden and inclucate order into Oriental minds. The mission to civilise the 'silent, sullen peoples' of the east was a burden imposed upon them by destiny.
The last observation is a fairly obvious allusion to

(a) JR Ackerley's 'Hindoo Holiday: An Indian Journal'
(b) Flora Annie Steel's 'The Garden of Fidelty'
(c) Maud Diver's 'the Englishwoman in India'
(d) Rudyard Kipling's 'the White Man's Burden'

2 What attitude towards death would you find in such poems as Tennyson's 'crossing the bar,' Whitman's 'Death Carol,' and Kipling's 'L'Envoi'?

(a) Resignation (b) Despair (c) Hope (d) Protest

July 2018

3 Which narrative poem by Lord Tennyson presents the story of a fisherman turned Merchant sailor who, after a shipwreck, is marooned on a desert island?

(a) Crossing the Bar (b) Tithonus
(c) Enoch Arden (d) Maud

4 Based on the life of a 13th century troubadour from among the following identify the work, that market a catastropic failure in Robert Browning's poetic career, earning him a reputation for impenetrable difficulty?

(a) Paracelsus (b) Sordello
(c) The Ring and the Book (d) Pauline

5 In 'Memorial Verses' Matthew Arnold pays tribute to three great poets. Who are they?

(a) Goethe, Shakespeare, Wordsworth
(b) Goethe, Shakespeare, Milton
(c) Shakespeare, Milton, Wordsworth
(d) Goethe, Wordsworth, Byron

6 Arrange the following Elegies in English in chronological order.

(a) Elegy Written in a Country Churchyard-Adonais-Thyrsis-In Memoriam
(b) Elegy Written in a Country Churchyard-Adonais-In Memoriam-Thyrsis
(c) Elegy Written in a Country Churchyard-In Memoriam-Adonais-Thyrsis
(d) Adonais-Elegy Written in a Country Churchyard-In Memoriam- Thyrsis

November 2017

7 Which of the following historical events does Tennyson's poem 'The Charge of the Light Brigade' describe?

(a) The Battle of Hastings (b) The Wars of the Roses
(c) The Battle of Waterloo (d) The Crimean War

8 In Robert Browning's 'Andrea del Sarto', with which of the following painters does Andrea not compare himself with?

(a) Michelangelo (b) Leonardo da Vinci
(c) Rembrandt (d) Raphael

9 In which poem does Matthew Arnold express the dilemma of:
"Wandering between two worlds, one dead, the other powerless to be born"?

(a) Self-Dependence
(b) Stanzas from the Grande Chartreuse
(c) To a Republican Friend
(d) Dover Beach

10 Which Victorian poet is the author of the following lines?
"God himself is the best Poet,
And the Real is His song."

(a) Lord Tennyson (b) Robert Browning
(c) Matthew Arnold (d) Elizabeth Barrett Browning

11 Who published the first collected edition of Gerard Manley Hopkins's poems in 1918?

(a) Robert Bridges
(b) Coventry Patmore
(c) John Betjeman
(d) Stephen Spender

12 Arrange the following in the chronological order of publication.

(a) In Memoriam - A Christmas Carol - Men and Women - Henry Esmond
(b) A Christmas Carol - In Memoriam - Men and Women - Henry Esmond
(c) A Christmas Carol - In Memoriam - Henry Esmond - Men and Women
(d) In Memoriam - A Christmas Carol- Henry Esmond - Men and Women

January 2017

13 Who is the author of the poem 'The Defence of Lucknow' dealing with the siege of Lucknow, one of the terrible incidents of the Indian Mutiny?

(a) Rudyard Kipling
(b) Edward Lear
(c) Alfred Lord Tennyson
(d) Robert Browning

14 In 'My Last Duchess' which of the following is not one of the Duchess's misdemeanours, according to the Duke?
(a) She was flattered by compliments from Fra Pandolf
(b) She enjoyed the sunset as much as she enjoyed her husband's favour
(c) She wouldn't listen to her husband when he tried to correct her behaviour
(d) She was equally grateful for all acts of kindness, regardless of their source

15 Elizabeth Barrett Browning's sonnets from the Portuguese is
1. a sequence of forty four Petrarchan sonnets.
2. a rewriting of Popean didactic verse.
3. a depiction of a contemporary setting and small events of ordinary life.
4. a scathing criticism of the British colonial enterprise

The right combination according to the code is
(a) 1 and 2 (b) 1 and 3 (c) 2 and 4 (d) 1 and 4

16 Dante Gabriel Rossetti founded the Pre-Rephaelite Brotherhood which included
1. Holman Hunt 2. Arthur Hugh Clough
3. Gerald Manley Hopkings
4. John Millais

(a) 2 and 3 (b) 1 and 4 (c) 1 and 3 (d) 2 and 4

17 In the second ending of John Fowles's The French Lieutenant's Woman Charles Smithson's lawyer finds that Sarah has been living in the house of
(a) William Morris (b) William Holman Hunt
(c) DG Rossetti (d) James Collinson

July 2016

18 Which of the following is another term to describe 'art for art's sake'?
(a) Aestheticism (b) Didacticism
(c) Realism (d) Neo-realism

19 In which year did the Great Exhibition take place?
(a) 1851 (b) 1857 (c) 1861 (d)1871

20 In which of the following poems does Tennyson describe and condemn the spirit of aestheticism whose sole religion is the worship of beauty and of knowledge for their own sake and which ignores human responsibility and obligations of one's fellowmen?
(a) The Princess (b) The Lady of Shalott
(c) The Place of Art (d) Tithonus

21 Robert Browning's Rabbi Ben Ezra is a defence of
(a) youth against old age (b) old age against youth
(c) power against knowledge (d) knowledge against power

22 In the opening stanza of 'Song of Myself', Whitman begins his spiritual awakening at the age of
(a) 37 (b) 15 (c) 24 (d) 61

23 Who narrates Heart of Darkness?
(a) Marlow
(b) Director of companies
(c) Kurtz
(d) An unnamed narrator

December 2015

24 Which of the following is described by Robert Browning as 'A Child's Story'?
(a) Bells and Pomegranates
(b) Pauline
(c) Fifine at the Fair
(d) The Pied Piper of Hamelin

25 In Robert Browning's dramatic monologue, which painter does Andrea del Sarto compare himself to? What does he find lacking in his own work in comparison?
(a) Fra Lippo Lippi-Humour
(b) Raphael - Soul
(c) Leonardo da Vinci - Verisimilitude
(d) Botticelli - Liveliness

June 2015

26 Matthew Arnold's 'touchstones' were 'short passages, even single lines' of classic poetry beside which the lines of other poets may be placed in order to detect the presence or absence of high poetic quality. In his 'Study of Poetry' Arnold cited 'touchstones' from such non-English poets as Homer and Dante from the English poets, Shakespeare and Milton. Which English poet did he disapprovingly call 'not one of the great classics' in the list below?
(a) Chaucer (b) Sidney
(c) Spenser (d) Donne

27 Match the following.

List I	List II
A. Christina Rossetti : Goblin Market	1. The tale of a father who inadvertently destroys his son
B. Matthew Arnold: Sohrab and Rustum	2. Gently satiric account of Oxford student on vacation
C. Robert Browing: The Ring and the Book	3. Story of pleasure-seeking Laura and the conventions moral Lizzie who resists temptations
D. Arthur Hugh Clough: The Bothie of Tober-na-Vuolich	4. A sensational 17th century murder presented through multiple dramatic monologues

Codes

	A	B	C	D		A	B	C	D
(a)	3	4	1	2	(b)	2	4	3	1
(c)	3	1	4	2	(d)	4	2	3	1

December 2014

28 Works like The Earthly Paradise, Dante and His Circle, Goblin Market and Other Poems and the journal, The Germ are associated with

(a) the pre-raphaelites
(b) higher criticism
(c) the cavalier poets
(d) the pre-romantics

June 2014

29 Why are Elizabeth Barrett Browning's Sonnets called 'Sonnets from the Portuguese'?

(a) She wrote the whole in Portugal
(b) The sonnets were translated from the Portuguese
(c) She presented it under the guise of a translation from the Portuguese language
(d) The sonnets were narrated by a Portuguese

30 Which of the following is correct?

(a) Aurora Leigh is a poem in 9 books
(b) Aurora Leigh is a collection of sonnets from the Portuguese
(c) Aurora Leigh is a nursery rhyme book
(d) Aurora Leigh is the seeds and fruits of English poetry

31 "She had ...... lilies in her hand and the stars in her hair were ...." (Rossetti's 'The Blessed Damozel')

(a) 7 and 3
(b) 3 and 7
(c) 6 and 4
(d) 4 and 6

ANSWERS

Objective Questions

1. *(d)*	2. *(d)*	3. *(d)*	4. *(a)*	5. *(d)*	6. *(d)*	7. *(c)*	8. *(c)*	9. *(a)*	10. *(b)*
11. *(b)*	12. *(b)*	13. *(d)*	14. *(a)*	15. *(a)*	16. *(a)*	17. *(b)*	18. *(b)*	19. *(d)*	20. *(c)*
21. *(d)*	22. *(a)*	23. *(a)*	24. *(d)*	25. *(c)*	26. *(c)*	27. *(a)*	28. *(d)*	29. *(b)*	30. *(b)*
31. *(b)*	32. *(a)*	33. *(b)*	34. *(c)*	35. *(c)*	36. *(b)*	37. *(d)*	38. *(a)*	39. *(c)*	40. *(a)*
41. *(b)*	42. *(d)*	43. *(d)*	44. *(d)*	45. *(d)*	46. *(d)*	47. *(a)*	48. *(c)*	49. *(c)*	50. *(c)*
51. *(c)*	52. *(a)*	53. *(c)*	54. *(d)*	55. *(b)*	56. *(a)*	57. *(d)*	58. *(b)*	59. *(d)*	60. *(b)*
61. *(a)*	62. *(d)*	63. *(a)*	64. *(a)*	65. *(d)*	66. *(b)*	67. *(c)*	68. *(b)*	69. *(c)*	70. *(c)*
71. *(c)*	72. *(a)*	73. *(d)*	74. *(d)*	75. *(b)*	76. *(a)*	77. *(a)*	78. *(a)*	79. *(a)*	80. *(a)*
81. *(c)*	82. *(b)*	83. *(c)*	84. *(b)*	85. *(d)*	86. *(d)*	87. *(d)*	88. *(d)*	89. *(c)*	90. *(c)*
91. *(b)*	92. *(c)*	93. *(b)*	94. *(a)*	95. *(d)*	96. *(a)*	97. *(d)*	98. *(c)*	99. *(c)*	100. *(c)*
101. *(b)*	102. *(b)*	103. *(a)*	104. *(d)*	105. *(b)*	106. *(a)*	107. *(d)*	108. *(d)*	109. *(d)*	110. *(d)*
111. *(b)*	112. *(c)*	113. *(c)*	114. *(d)*	115. *(c)*	116. *(a)*	117. *(b)*	118. *(c)*	119. *(d)*	120. *(a)*
121. *(c)*	122. *(b)*	123. *(b)*	124. *(d)*	125. *(b)*	126. *(a)*	127. *(a)*	128. *(a)*	129. *(d)*	130. *(c)*
131. *(b)*	132. *(b)*	133. *(c)*	134. *(a)*	135. *(d)*	136. *(c)*	137. *(d)*	138. *(a)*	139. *(a)*	140. *(a)*
141. *(c)*	142. *(d)*	143. *(a)*	144. *(b)*	145. *(c)*	146. *(b)*	147. *(b)*	148. *(c)*	149. *(c)*	150. *(d)*
151. *(a)*	152. *(b)*	153. *(d)*	154. *(b)*	155. *(d)*	156. *(c)*	157. *(b)*	158. *(c)*	159. *(a)*	160. *(c)*

Previous Years' Questions

1. *(d)*	2. *(c)*	3. *(c)*	4. *(b)*	5. *(d)*	6. *(b)*	7. *(d)*	8. *(c)*	9. *(b)*	10. *(d)*
11. *(a)*	12. *(c)*	13. *(c)*	14. *(c)*	15. *(b)*	16. *(b)*	17. *(c)*	18. *(a)*	19. *(a)*	20. *(c)*
21. *(b)*	22. *(a)*	23. *(a)*	24. *(d)*	25. *(b)*	26. *(a)*	27. *(c)*	28. *(a)*	29. *(c)*	30. *(a)*
31. *(b)*									

The Modern, Contemporary Age and American Poetry

Modernist poetry commenced with the appearance of the imagists besides maintaining the previous trends of poetry. WB Yeats and TS Eliot were main poets of the modern age. The contemporary poetry was often written in free verse inviting reader to interpret the poem at his/her own. Ted Hughes and Philip Larkin were the important poets of this era.

Modern Poetry

Modernist poetry in English started in the early years of the 20th century with the appearance of the Imagists. In common with many other modernists, these poets wrote in reaction to the perceived excesses of Victorian poetry, with its emphasis on traditional formalism and ornate diction. In many respects, their criticism echoes what William Wordsworth wrote in *Preface to Lyrical Ballads* to instigate the Romantic movement in British poetry over a century earlier, criticising the gauche and pompous school which then pervaded and seeking to bring poetry to the layman.

Modernists saw themselves as looking back to the best practices of poets in earlier periods and other cultures. Their models included ancient Greek literature, Chinese and Japanese poetry, the troubadours, Dante and the medieval Italian philosophical poets (such as Guido Cavalcanti) and the English metaphysical poets.

Much of early modernist poetry took the form of short, compact lyrics. As it developed, however, longer poems came to the foreground. These represent the modernist movement to the 20th-century English poetic canon. The Modern English poetry emerged in the early years of the 20th century through various schools, styles, and influences.

Modern poetry can be classified into three phases, these are

1. The first phase of the movement, the school of imagism, the style of French symbolist poetry influence of Dome and the dominance of war poetry, these were all different manifestations of modernism in English poetry (AD 1909-16)

In this Chapter

2. During the flowering of Modernist poetry between 1917 and 1929, the 2nd phase of the movement, all these initial manifestations of modernism combined to find a full nature expression in the poetry of TS Eliot, Edith Sitwell and later Yeats, most notable of which is, Eliot's *The Waste Land*, Sitwell's *Gold Coast Customs*, Yeats's *Michael Robartes* and the *Dances*.
3. The 3rd and the final phase of Modernist is largely the decade of the 30s which is marked by the Marxist (Non-Marxist) poets such as Auden, Louis McNiece, C Day Lewis and Stephen Spender.

Chief Characteristics of Modern English Poetry

Characteristics of Modern poetry can be understood under the following heads

Diverse Variety of Themes

Poetry today can be written on almost any subject. The modern poets find inspirations from trains, tramcars, telephones and things of commonplace interest. Modern poets have not accepted the theory of great subjects for poetic composition.

The whole universe is the modern poet's composition. He writes on themes of real life e.g. *The Songs Train* by John Davidson, *Goods Train* of *Night* by Ashley, *Machine Guns* by Richard Aldington, *Listeners* by Walter

Realism

The poetry of the 20th century is marked with a note of realism. Realism in modern poetry was the product of a reaction against the pseudo-romanticism of the last century over and above the influence of science.

The modern poet sees life and paints it as it is with all its wit and ugliness. He tears the veil which the romanticists had clubbed between life and art. Robert Frost, Edmund Blunden and Gibson are the poets of realism in modern poetry.

Love

Love forms the subject of many modern lyrics Robert Bridges has produced fine sonnets of love in *The Growth of Love*. *I Will Not Let Thee Go, When You are Old by WB Yeats.*

Pessimism

There is a note of pessimism and disillusionment in modern poetry. The modern poet has realised the pettiness of human life. The tragedy and suffering of the poor have made him gloomy and sad. Poetry as the expression of the feeling has become autumnal in tone. T Hardy, Huxley and TS Eliot are the poets of pessimism and disillusionment in modern poetry.

Romantic Elements

In spite of the dominance of realism, in modern poetry, the spirit of romance continues to rule the minds of certain poets like Yeats, E Thomas, Masefield etc. The works of these poets have the fact that the spirit of romance is as old as the life itself. Walter De Le Mare's poetry is full of true romantic spirit bordering on supernaturalism. With him, the ghosts and fairies of the old world have come into their own in the 20th century.

Nature

Nature attracts the modern poet no less than the poets of the earlier ages. But for the modern poet, nature is not a mystic. He does not find any spiritual meaning in nature. He feels jolly at the sight of nature's loveliness. He gives a clear picture of birds, clouds landscapes, sea and countryside in his poetry. Masefield, Robert Bridges, Edmund Blunden etc are the great poets of nature in modern poetry.

Humanitarian and Democratic Note

Modern poetry is marked with a note of humanitarianism and democratic feeling. The modern poet, more than Wordsworth (*A Slumber Did My Spirit Seal*), is interested in the life of labourers, workers etc.

He sees, in the daily struggles of these people the same potentialities that the older poets found in those of high rank. Masefield, Gibson, Goldsworthy are mainly interested in the common man and his sufferings.

Religion and Mysticism

The modern age is the age of science, but even in this scientific age, we have poems written on the subject of religion and mysticism. WB Yeats, Francis Thompson, Robert Graves etc are the great poets who have kept alive the flame of religion and mysticism in their poetry.

Diction and Style

Modern poets have a preference for simple and direct expression. Modern poets have chosen to be free in the use of meter. They have followed freedom from trammels of verse. Verse rhythm is replaced by sense rhythm. There is free movement in 20th-century English poetry.

Major Poets of the Modern Age

William Butler Yeats, (1865-1939)

Born in Dublin, Ireland in 1865, WB Yeats was an Irish poet and playwright. He was a driving force behind the Celtic Revival or the Irish Literary Renaissance. Alongwith Lady Gregory, Edward Martyn and others, he founded the Abbey Theatre in December 1904 (also known as the National Theatre of Ireland). The Abbey Theatre became the flagship for leading Irish playwrights and actors. Yeats drew heavily on Irish mythology, history and folklore to create a distinctive national literature. He was the first Irishman to be awarded the Nobel Prize in 1923.

Literary Career and Works

Yeats' first publication, two brief lyrics, appeared in the *Dublin University Review* in 1885. However, the first volume of Yeats' poems The *Wanderings of Oisin and Other Poems,* was published in 1889 and celebrates ancient Irish heroes such as Oisin and St Patrick. His most famous works include *The Tower*, *The Winding Stair and Other Poems, Easter* 1916 and *The Second Coming.*

The most significant influence on Yeats' life and poetry was a beautiful and prominent woman revolutionary devoted to the Irish nationalist cause, Maud Gonne.

She remained his muse, influencing every aspect of his poetry. For Yeats, Gonne represented the ideal of feminine beauty, but a beauty disfigured and wasted by an unsuitable marriage and her involvement in a hopeless political cause, Irish Independence. In his poem *No Second Troy*, Yeats describes Maud Gonne's beauty as exceptional and destructive, similar to Helen of Troy.

With beauty like a tightened bow, a kind
That is not natural in an age like this,
Being high and solitary and most stern?
Why, what could she have done, being what she is?
Was there another Troy for her to burn?

Yeats wrote plays also such as *Masoda* (1886), *Counless Cathleen* (1892), *Deirdre* (1907), *The Resurrection* (1927) and *The Herne's Egg* (1938).

Yeats died in Roquebrune, France, on 28th January, 1939 due to ill health.

Yeats' Contribution to Irish Literary Revival

Yeats was the most prominent member of the Irish Literary Revival and helped to banish the then prevailing sense that British culture was superior to Irish.

Yeats contributed to the formation of the new Irish sense of national identity and to the new sense of confidence, which would induce some to strive for a New Ireland. According to AG Stock, "Yeats's idea of Ireland required a national literature. He wanted Irish writers to be conscious of past; he wanted the native legends and folklore to be known widely enough to be the medium of their image-thinking, which is the wisdom of poetry and the language of a national."

Yeats' writings often depicted the rural Ireland of fable and myth that so captivated him throughout his life. Many of his works drew directly upon the legends of pre-Christian Ireland, such as his poems *The Wanderings of Oisin* and *The Lake Isle of Innisfree*.

In his poem *The Fisherman*, Yeats himself speaks of writing for 'My Own Race' and alludes to the ability and difficulties a poet has in contributing to a sense of national identity.

According to John Frayne, Yeats asserts Irish dignity against the increasingly dominant forms of Anglo-American popular culture. By espousing Irish material and setting in his poetry, he establishes an Irish literary movement for its propagation.

The extract of WB Yeats' The Second Coming is given below. It was from this poem that the African writer Chinua Achebe took the title of his famous novel, Things Fall Apart.

The Second Coming

Turning and turning in the widening gyre
The falcon cannot hear the falconer;
Things fall apart; the centre cannot hold;
Mere anarchy is loosed upon the world,
The blood-dimmed tide is loosed and everywhere
The ceremony of innocence is drowned;
The best lack all conviction, while the worst
Are full of passionate intensity.
some revelation is at hand;
Surely the Second Coming is at hand.
The Second Coming! Hardly are those words out
When a vast image out of Spiritus Mundi
Troubles my sight: a waste of desert sand;
A shape with lion body and the head of a man,
A gaze blank and pitiless as the Sun,
Is moving its slow thighs, while all about it
Wind shadows of the indignant desert birds.
The darkness drops again but now I know
That twenty centuries of stony sleep
Were vexed to nightmare by a rocking cradle,
And what rough beast, its hour come round at last,
Slouches towards Bethlehem to be born?

The Second Coming: Summary

It was published in 1920, *The Second Coming* is an intense, lyrical poem of 22 lines. The poem first appeared in, *The Dial* and *The Nation* in November 1920. Yeats wrote this poem at a time, when he saw great social troubles all around him. Not only was the world trying to recover from the effects of the World War I, but Ireland also reeled under the effects of the Easter Rising.

The Irish Civil War that followed the great war of 1914-1919 and various other events in Europe added to that gloom. The poem is the outcome of a state of mind troubled with ominous forebodings fearful apprehensions. The title of the poem suggests a new manifestation of God to man. The Christian era draws to its close; now that its 'great year' of two thousand years is ending.

The poem begins with the image of a falcon flying out of earshot from its human master. The fixed point, the central belief or idea, around which our civilisation (like a falcon) had revolved (*i.e.,* Christianity) has lost its power. It can no longer hold society in an orderly structure like a wheel around it (a structure which Yeats depicts as a series of gyres or outward-spiraling circles). Instead, things are flying away, falling apart; our civilisation is disintegrating. The poem then shifts into a description of anarchy and an orgy excessive indulgence of violence in which 'the ceremony of innocence is drowned.'

In the second stanza, the speaker asserts, that the world is near a revelation; 'Surely The Second Coming' is at hand.' No sooner does he think of 'The Second Coming,' then he is troubled by "A vast image of the Spiritus Mundi or the collective spirit or soul of the universe. He imagines a sphinx in the desert, 'A shape with lion body and the head of a man, / A gaze as blank and pitiless as the Sun".

Finally, at the end of the poem, the speaker asks a rhetorical question which really amounts to a prophecy that the beast is on its way to Bethlehem, the birthplace of Christ, to be born into the world.

Yeats conceptualised history as a series of interpenetrating gyres. Historical eras overlap, one ending as the next one begins. He believed that these gyres or, eras of history tended to fall into roughly 2000 years' periods. While, one tends to be dominant, the other is always implied and weakly present. He believed that the new 'rough beast' was coming to replace Christianity and that the ideal time to live would be when the two gyres were at the midpoint of change.

William Henry Davies (1871-1940)

WH Davies was a Welsh poet born in Newport, Monmouthshire, Wales in 1871. He was the son of an iron moulder. In November 1874, when William was aged three, his father died. The following year his mother Mary Anne Davies remarried and became Mrs Joseph Hill. She agreed that care of the three children should pass to their paternal grandparents, Francis and Lydia Davies, who ran the nearby Church House Inn at 14, Portland Street. In 1879, the family moved to Raglan Street, then to Upper Lewis Street, from where William attended Temple School. In 1883, he moved to Alexandra Road School and the following year was arrested, as one of a gang of five schoolmates, and charged with stealing handbags. He lost one of his feet during a train accident. In his early age, he did to do many odd jobs to earn his livelihood.

Davies died at Nailsworth, Gloucestershire in 1940.

Literary Career and Works

Davies wrote his first poem entitled *Death*. In his *Poet's Pilgrimage* (1918) Davies recounts the time when, at the age of 14, he was left with orders to sit with his dying grandfather.

Davies's view of his own disability was ambivalent. In his poem *The Fog*, published in the 1913 Foliage, a blind man leads the poet through the fog, showing the reader that one who is handicapped in one domain may well have a considerable advantage in another.

For his poetry Davies drew extensively on his experiences with the seamier side of life, but also on his love of nature. By the time of his prominent place in the Edward Marsh Georgian Poetry series, he was an established figure. He is generally best known for the opening two lines of the poem *Leisure*, first published in *Songs of Joy and Others in 1911*: "What is the life if, full of care/We have no time to stand and stare ....."

His first collection, *The Soul's Destroyer* (1905), established many of the key features of Davies's verse: pastoralism and sympathy for the underdog.

Between 1905 and 1939, he published several volumes of poetry. In 1908, his *Autobiography of a Super-Tramp* was published, which described his experiences of a vagrant life. It was written in bildungsroman mode, Davies begins his autobiography by relating the story of his childhood in Wales, where he was raised by his grandparents after his father died and his mother abandoned her children.

Davies also produced 4 novels, including *The True Traveller* (1912) and *The Adventures of Johnny Walker, Tramp* (1926); other prose works included *Beggars* (1909), *Nature* (1914) and *My Birds and My Garden* (1933). He wrote two poems about his experience. One is called *Sheep*.

The extract from the poem sheep is given below

Sheep

When, I was once in Baltimore,
A man came up to me and cried,
'Come, I have eighteen hundred sheep,
And we sail on Tuesday's tide.'
'If you will sail with me, young man,
I'll pay you fifty shillings down;
These eighteen hundred sheep I take
From Baltimore to Glasgow town.'

Alfred Noyes (1880-1958)

English poet Alfred Noyes was born in Wolverhampton, England on 16th September, 1880. He attended Exeter College, Oxford, where he distinguished himself at rowing, but left without taking his degree because he was visiting his publisher at the time to arrange publication of his first volume of poems, *The Loom of Years* (1902).

Literary Career and Works

Noyes published five more volumes of poetry in the next five years including *Poems* (1904), *The Forest of Wild Thyme* (1905) and *The Flower of Old Japan and Other Poems* (1907). His most famous poem, *The Highwayman* was first published in the August 1906 issue of 'Blackwood's Magazine' and was included the following year in *Forty Singing Seamen and Other Poems*.

Noyes taught English Literature at Princeton University from 1913 to 1923. He also became known for his criticism of modernist writers, particularly James Joyce. One of the significant works in his writing career was the epic *The Torch Bearers*, which was published in three volumes (*Watchers of the Sky*, 1922; *The Book of Earth*, 1925; and *The Last Voyage*, 1930). This was a blank verse trilogy narrating the discoveries of science. Noyes was received into the Roman Catholic Church in 1927 and published a book of theological essays, *The Unknown God*, in 1934. His autobiography *Two Worlds for Memory*, describing his life on both sides of the Atlantic Ocean, was published in 1953.

Noyes died in his 78 years on 28th June, 1958.

Siegfried Sassoon (1886-1967)

One of the war poets of modern age, Siegfried Sassoon was born on 8th September, 1886 in Kent, England. He belonged to a wealthy Jewish family and lived the pastoral life of a young squire: fox-hunting, playing cricket, golfing and writing romantic verses.

Sassoon attended Marlborough College and Cambridge before serving in the British Army during World War I.

Literary Career and Works

Sassoon's first poetry collection, *The Daffodil Murderer* was published in 1913. His experiences of the war led him to express its denunciation in *A Soldier's Declaration*.

This *Declaration* written against the war was prompted by the deaths and suffering of so many of his friends and men under his command, but specifically the death of his great friend David Thomas.

Sassoon's *Declaration* was made 'as an act of wilful defiance of military authority' because he believed that the war was being 'deliberately prolonged' by those who had 'the power to end it'. He also wrote many war poems, which were published in *The Old Huntsman* (1917) and *Counter-Attack* (1918).

Sassoon's semi-autobiographical trilogy *Memoirs of a Fox-hunting Man* (1928), *Memoirs of an Infantry Officer* (1930) and *Sherston's Progress* (1936) was written from the fictional point of view of George Sherston.

In 1957, Sassoon was awarded the Queen's Medal for Poetry. He died on 1st September, 1967.

TE Hulme (1883-1917)

Thomas Ernest Hulme was an English poet and critic. The son of Thomas and Mary Hulme, TE Hulme was born at Gratton Hall, Endon, Staffordshire. He was educated at Newcastle- under-Lyme Grammar school and went to St John's College, Cambridge, but was expelled for rowdy behaviour on Boat Race Night in 1904. He subsequently studied privately in London and Belgium.

Literary Career and Works

Five of Hulme's poems were published in *The New Age* in 1912 as *The Complete Poetical Works of TE Hulme.* In 1913, he translated Henri Bergson's *Introduction to Metaphysics*, which was a major influence on his thought. Hulme joined the army in 1914 and his 'war notes' were published in the *New Age*.

He was killed near Nieuport in 1917. His essays were edited posthumously by Sir Herbert Read, in *Speculations* (1924) and *Notes on Language and Style* (1929).

Edith Sitwell (1887-1964)

British poetess and critic Edith Sitwell was born on 7th September, 1887 in Scarborough, Yorkshire, England. Sitwell had two younger brothers, Osbert (1892-1969) and Sacheverell Sitwell (1897-1988) both distinguished authors. Sitwell's relationship with her parents was not cordial and in 1912, she moved to a small, shabby fourth-floor flat in Pembridge Mansions, Bayswater, with her governess Helen Rootham (1875-1938).

Literary Career and Works

Her first poem, *The Drowned Suns* was published in the *Daily Mirror* in 1913. Her first book, *The Mother and Other Poems*, appeared in 1918. Sitwell also edited the 1916 anthology *Wheels,* an annual poetic anthology.

During World War II, Sitwell retired to Renshaw with her brother Osbert and wrote under the light of oil lamps. The poems she wrote during the war, including *Street Songs* (1942), *The Song of the Cold* (1945) and *The Shadow of Cain* (1947), brought her public acclaim.

She died of cerebral haemorrhage at St Thomas's Hospital on 9th December, 1964 at the age of 77.

Osbert Sitwell (1892-1969)

Osbert Sitwell was born in London on 6th December 1892. He attended private schools in Scarborough and New Barnet. After a year at Aldershot, Sitwell suffered a nervous breakdown and received a transfer to the Grenadier Guards stationed in London. He reluctantly served as an officer and left the army in 1919.

Literary Career and Works

His experiences at the military front filled him with hatred of war. This prompted him to write a pacifist poem *The Winstonburg Line* (1919).

Osbert Sitwell's first work of fiction, *Triple Fugue*, was published in 1924. His first novel, *Before the Bombardment* came out in 1926. His later poetry, *Collected Satires and Poems* (1931); *England Reclaimed* (1927), *Wrack at Tidesend* (1952) and *On the Continent* (1958) have been noted for its elegant wit.

He is best remembered for his five-volume autobiography, *Left Hand, Right Hand!* (1945-50, comprising *Left Hand, Right Hand!; The Scarlet Tree*; *Great Morning; Laughter in the Next Room* and *Noble Essences*). A late addition to his autobiography, *Tales my Father Taught Me*, followed in 1962.

Osbert died on 4th May, 1969, in Italy, at Montegufoni, a castle near Florence.

Thomas Stearns Eliot (1888-1965)

TS Eliot was born in St Louis, Missouri in Midwestern America. Although born in America, Eliot moved to Britain at the age of 25 and eventually attained British citizenship in 1927. He was a famous modern poet, playwright and literary critic. He got his education at Harvard and graduated in philosophy. Eliot was well versed in the knowledge of Latin, French, Greek and German and his works reflects a deep knowledge of the classics.

Literary Career and Works

Eliot met Ezra Pound in 1914. Pound became his literary mentor who got his poems published and aided him in receiving critical acclaim. Eliot's first major poem *The Love Song of J Alfred Prufrock* was published at Pound's insistence in *Poetry: A Magazine of Verse* after Pound persuaded the magazine editor-Harriet Monroe. The poem was later published in a separate book as part of Eliot's first published collection of poetry *Prufrock and Other Observations* in 1917. This famous modernist poem examined the fragmented and tormented psyche, emotionally and physically sterile character of the prototypical modern man. The title of this 'song' comes from Rudyard Kipling's poem *The Love Song of Har Dyal*. Although the title refers to the poem as a 'love song', the poem is actually anti-romantic in tone, reflecting on Prufrock's failure as a lover.

The poem's well known opening lines contain a conceit that compares evening to a patient lying upon the table

> Let us go then, you and I,
> When the evening is spread out against the sky
> Like a patient etherised upon a table;

Eliot's next major work- the 434 line modernist landmark poem *The Wasteland* was first published in *The Criterion*. Eliot dedicated the poem to Pound and referred to him as *il miglior fabbro* or *the better craftsman*. This phrase emphasised Pound's hand in editing and shaping the poem. Although, criticised for being too obscure and complex, *The Wasteland* reflects Eliot's disillusionment with the moral and spiritual decay in post-World War Europe. Apart from writing poetry, Eliot also served as literary editor of the feminist magazine, the *Egoist.*

He was also a notable modern critic known for his essays *Tradition and the Individual Talent* and *Hamlet and His Problems*, both published in 1920.

In *Tradition and Individual Talent*, Eliot defined poetry as 'not a turning loose of emotion, but an escape from emotion; 'not the expression of personality, but an escape from personality'. Eliot's plays *Murder in the Cathedral* (1935), *The Family Reunion* (1939), *The Cocktail Party* (1949), *The Confidential Clerk* (1954), and *The Elder Statesman* (1959) were published in one volume in 1962.

In 1948, he was awarded Nobel Prize in Literature for his pioneer contribution to poetry. He died on 4th January, 1965, in London.

Major Works

Poetry

- *Prufrock and Other Observations (1917)*
- 'The Love song of J Alfred Prufrock
- Portrait of A Lady
- Aunt Helen

Poems (1920)

- Gerontion
- Sweeney Among the Nightingales
- Mr *Eliot's* Sunday Morning Service
- A Cooking Egg
- The Waste Land (1922)
- The Hollow Men (1925)
- Ariel Poems (1927–1954)
- The Journey of the Magi (1927)
- Ash Wednesday (1930)
- Four Quartets (1945)

Plays

- Sweeney Agonistes (published in 1926, first performed in 1934)
- The Rock (1934)
- Murder in the Cathedral (1935)
- The Family Reunion (1939)
- The Cocktail Party (1949)
- The Confidential Clerk (1953)
- The Elder Statesman (first performed in 1958, published in 1959)

Given below is a summary of five sections of The Wasteland, alongwith important lines of each section.

Section I : The Burial of the Dead

This section takes its title from a line in the Anglican burial service. Eliot first depicts the stirring of life in the land with the coming of spring. However, in the contemporary Waste land of Western civilisation, we see only a 'dead land' filled with 'stony rubbish'. This section sets-up the main themes of the poem by establishing the modern city as the real Wasteland of the poem. This section is made up of four vignettes, each from the perspective of a different speaker. The first speaker enters the poem as an unidentified, yet stereotypically modern person who drinks coffee and talks for the specific and artificial time increment of an hour.

The second part of this section launches into a description of a very dry, dusty and desolate world. A girl once known as 'the hyacinth girl' speaks of how she is 'neither living nor dead'. In the third part, Madame Sosostris reads tarot cards and makes predictions that will be fulfilled in later parts of the poem.

The final episode of this section makes mention of the *Unreal City*, the civilisation portrayed in the poem, which has been undone by death. Then a speaker sees a person he knows and cries out after him, asking if the corpse he has planted in his garden has begun to sprout and calling him a hypocrite reader, doppelganger alter ego and brother.

Unreal City

Under the brown fog of a winter dawn,
A crowd flowed over London Bridge, so many,
I had not thought death had undone so many.
Sighs, short and infrequent, were exhaled,
And each man fixed his eyes before his feet.
Flowed up the hill and down King William Street,
To where Saint Mary Woolnoth kept the hours
With a dead sound on the final stroke of nine.
There I saw one I knew and stopped him, crying "Stetson!
"You who were with me in the ships at Mylae!
"That corpse you planted last year in your garden,
"Has it begun to sprout? Will it bloom this year?
"Or has the sudden frost disturbed its bed?
"Oh keep the Dog far hence, that's friend to men,
"Or with his nails he'll dig it up again!
"You! hypocrite lecteur! - mon semblable, - mon frere!"

Section II : A Game of Chess

The title of this section comes from Jacobean playwright Thomas Middleton's two plays *A Game at Chess* and *Women Beware Women*, (which has a scene in which a mother-in-law gets distracted by a game of chess while her daughter-in-law is seduced). This section concentrates on the failure of love/sexuality in the modern world.

This section begins with a description of a woman sitting on a beautiful chair that looks 'like a burnished throne' — a reference to Cleopatra in *Antony and Cleopatra*.

Surrounding the woman at the mirror are other old and withered stories told in paintings. She begins speaking, begging the speaker of the poem to reply, but he or she never replies with words, only silent thoughts. Her day culminates with plans for an excursion and a game of chess.

The second part of this section shifts to a London barroom, where two women discuss a third woman. Between the bartender's repeated calls of 'Hurry Up Please It's Time' (the bar is closing for the night) one of the women recounts a conversation with their friend Lil, whose husband, Albert has just been discharged from the army. Lil is apparently on pills, unhappy in her marriage and childless.

The two women of this section of the poem represent the two sides of modern sexuality, while one side of this sexuality is a dry, barren interchange inseparable from neurosis and self-destruction, the other side of this sexuality is a rampant fecundity productivity associated with a lack of culture and rapid aging.

"My nerves are bad to-night. Yes, bad. Stay with me.
"Speak to me. Why do you never speak. Speak.
"What are you thinking of? What thinking? What?
"I never know what you are thinking. Think."
I think we are in rats' alley
Where the dead men lost their bones.

Section III : Fire Sermon

The title of this section is taken from a sermon given by Buddha in which he persuades his followers to give up Earthly passions and seek spiritual regeneration. Through this section, Eliot showcases the sterility of modern world in which love has been replaced by sex and real emotional connection by meaningless physical intimacy.

The first lines of this section launch directly into a long and vivid description of a litter and rat infested London. The speaker is fishing on banks of the River Thames and musing on his brother and father's death. He is then propositioned by Mr Eugenides, the one-eyed merchant of Madame Sosostris's tarot pack. Eugenides invites the speaker to go with him to a shotel known as a meeting place for homosexual trysts. The speaker introduces himself as Tiresias, a figure from classical mythology that is blind but can 'see' into the future.

Tiresias is 'throbbing between two lives' because Eliot portrays him in this poem as a hermaphrodite, a person who is male and female at the same time. Tiresias is the poet's anti-self who sees all impersonally. Tiresias watches a young female typist and a clerk having sex.

The woman is glad it's over and paces around her room, playing a record on the gramophone. Eliot is diagnosing his London and his world with a disease of the senses, through which sex has replaced love and meaningless physical contact has subdued real emotional connection.

At the violet hour, when the eyes and back
Turn upward from the desk, when the human engine waits
Like a taxi throbbing waiting,
I Tiresias, though blind, throbbing between two lives,
Old man with wrinkled female breasts, can see
At the violet hour, the evening hour that strives
Homeward and brings the sailor home from sea,
The typist home at teatime, clears her breakfast, lights
Her stove and lays out food in tins.
Out of the window perilously spread
Her drying combinations touched by the Sun's last rays,
On the divan are piled (at night her bed)
Stockings, slippers, camisoles and stays.
I Tiresias, old man with wrinkled dugs
Perceived the scene and foretold the rest
I too awaited the expected guest.

Section IV : Death by Water

This section is the shortest of the poem's five sections. It describes Phlebas the Phoenician, who had died by drowning. An echo of the drowned Phoenician that Madame Sosostris displayed in *The Burial of the Dead*, Phlebas is apparently a merchant, judging by the reference to 'the profit and loss'. Eliot emphasises the gravity of his death and claims that, unlike the concepts of Christ's resurrection and the Fisher King, we humans will all meet the fate of Phlebas. The main emphasis of this section is to reject the possibility of any sort of regeneration or renewal.

Phlebas the Phoenician, a fortnight dead,
Forgot the cry of gulls and the deep sea swell
And the profit and loss.
A current under sea
Picked his bones in whispers. As he rose and fell
He passed the stages of his age and youth
Entering the whirlpool.
Gentile or Jew
O you who turn the wheel and look to windward,
Consider Phlebas, who was once handsome and tall as you.

Section V : What the Thunder Said

In the final section of the poem, despite death and destruction, there is emergence of hope and salvation. Although the possibility of redemption has long been discarded, the Fisher King invokes an alternative set of paradigms through which hope can be harnessed. The first three stanzas refer to a desolate and desert setting, in which there is an absence of water and a need for salvation.

The speaker laments the absence of water, thirst imbuing his verse with longing; he imagines the 'drip drop' of water on rocks, but concludes by acknowledging that, alas, 'there is no water.' This setting epitomises Eliot's ideas regarding a physical wasteland and thus emphasises the dire need of society for salvation.

Furthermore the reference to 'falling towers' and 'unreal cities' indicates the destruction of the symbols of materialism and corruption evident within society.

The scene then shifts to the Ganges, half a world away from Europe, where thunder rumbles. The great river Ganges in India is sunken, longing for water. Then the thunder speaks in the manner of a Hindu fable, after a command uttering the single syllable, 'DA.' At the end, a Fisher King type figure is shown on the river shore.

The transition to the setting of the Fisher King allows the parallels between the legend and the 'Wasteland' to become clear and thus offer the readers the hope of salvation. The Fisher King lost the Holy Grail as a result of yielding to desires and after being wounded, he was unable to tend to his land, thus causing it to become a 'Wasteland'. However, despite the moral lesson given by the legend of the Fisher King, an element of hope emerges as it is apparent that through purification and not giving into temptation society can be restored.

> I sat upon the shore
> Fishing, with the arid plain behind me
> Shall I at least set my lands in order?
> London Bridge is falling down falling down falling down
> *Poi s'ascose nel foco che gli affina*
> Quando fiam ceu chelidon - O swallow swallow
> Le Prince d'Aquitaine a la tour abolie
> These fragments I have shored against my ruins
> Why then Ile fit you. Hieronymo's mad againe.
> Datta. Dayadhvam. Damyata.
> Shantih shantih shantih

Richard Aldington (1892-1962)

English poet Richard Aldington was born as Edward Godfree Aldington in Hampshire in 1882. He received his education at Dover College and the University of London.

Literary Career and Works

He is best known as a founding poet of the Imagist movement and as a novelist who conveyed the horror of World War I through his written works. His autobiographical novel *Death of a Hero,* was a psychological study of a young officer in the World War I.

Aldington published several volumes of poetry including *Images 1910-1915*, *Images of War* (1919), *A Fool in the Forest* (1925) and *A Dream in Luxembourg* (1930). He also wrote biographies, writing about his good friend DH Lawrence in *Portrait of a Genius, But...* (1950) and producing a blunt volume about TE Lawrence named *Lawrence of Arabia: A Biographical Enquiry* (1955). Both of these volumes were controversial.

Aldington died in Sury-en-Vaux, Cher, France on 27th July 1962, shortly after being honoured in Moscow on the occasion of his 70th birthday.

Major Works

Poetry

- Images, 1910-1915 (1915)
- Images (1919)
- Images of War (1919)
- Images of Desire (1919)
- War and Love (1919)
- Exile and Other Poems (1923)
- A Fool in' the Forest, a Phantasmagoria (1925)
- The Love of Myrrhine and Konallis and Other Prose
- Poems (1926)
- A Dream in the Luxembourg (1930)
- Love and the Luxembourg (1930)
- Collected Poems, 1915-1923 (1933)
- The Crystal World (1937)
- **An Imagist at War** The Complete War Poems of Richard Aldington (2002)

Novels

- Death of a Hero (1929)
- Heldentod (1930)
- The Colonel's Daughter (1931)
- Stepping Heavenward A Record (1931)
- All Men Are Enemies A Romance (1933)
- Women Must Work (1934)
- Seven against Reeves A Comedy-Farce (1938)
- Reflected Guests (1939)
- Romance of Casanova (1946)

Wystan Hugh Auden (1907-1973)

WH Auden was an Anglo-American poet, born in England in 1907. Although born in England, Auden attained American citizenship in 1946. He got his education from Oxford University. At Oxford, Auden and his fellow undergraduates-Cecil Day Lewis, Louis MacNeice, Christopher Isherwood and Stephen Spender became part of a group known as the Oxford Group or the Auden Generation.

Literary Career and Works

Auden became famous as leader of this group of young intellectual English poets influenced by Modernism, especially by the literary principles of TS Eliot. This group of poets attempted to bring new forms and techniques in English poetry. Auden's first volume of poetry *Poems* was dedicated to Christopher Isherwood and published in 1928. He also collaborated with Isherwood on a number of plays.

Auden's poetry collection *Look, Stranger!* (also called *On This Island*) was dedicated to Erika upon its publication in 1936. In 1939, Auden and Isherwood moved to America.

Auden's poetry is known for its technical virtuosity and deft handling of form and technique. Auden's contemporary Stephen Spender showered praise on him and remarked, "The whole talent, the whole genius of Auden has never been to be a central figure. He's a central figure on the margin."

W H Auden was a Chancellor of The Academy of American Poets from 1954 to 1973 and divided most of the second half of his life between residences in New York City and Austria. He died in Vienna in 1973.

Major Works

- Poems (1930)
- The Operators An English Study (1932, dedicated to Stephen Spender)
- The Dance of Death (1933, play dedicated to Robert Medley and Rupert Doone)
- Poems (1934; contains *Poems* [1933 edition], *The Orators*[1932 edition] and *The Dance of Death*)
- The Dog Beneath the Skin (1935; play with Christopher Isherwood, dedicated to Robert Moody)
- Look, Stranger! (1936, Us Edn. On this Island, 1937) (dedicated to Erika Mann)
- For the Time Being (1944)
- The Age of Anxiety A Baroque Eclogue (1947, dedicated to John Betjeman)
- The Shield of Achilles (1955)
- The Enchfed Flood or The Romantic Iconography of the Sea (1950, dedicated to Alan Ansen)

Stephen Spender (1909-1995)

Stephen Spender was an English poet, essayist and novelist. He was born in London in 1909. He studied at Gresham's School, Holt, University College School, Hampstead and University College, Oxford, where he met W H Auden. Spender's name has frequently been associated with Auden, although the two poets were markedly different in their poetic talent.

They became famous as the Pylon Poets, a group of 1930s, left-wing poets including Louis MacNeice and Cecil Day Lewis, who first translated England's industrial landscape into poetry. The term was popularised by Spender's poem *The Pylons*, which is characteristic of the group's imagery and reflects the political and social concerns of its members. A cursory glance at this poem would demonstrate the industrial imagery used by the Pylon group-roads, skyscrapers, factories etc.

Literary Career and Works

Spender's early poetry, *Poems* (1933) was inspired by themes of social struggle. His poem *Vienna* (1934) was written in praise of the 1934 uprising of Viennese socialists, while *Trial of a Judge* (1938) was an anti-Fascist drama in verse. His autobiography, *World within World* (1951), was a re-creation of the political and social atmosphere of the 1930s. He also tried his hand at novel writing. His first novel *The Temple* was not published until 1988 because of its frank portrayal of homosexuality. Spender also wrote works of literary and social criticism such as *The Destructive Element* (1935), *The Creative Element* (1953), *The Making of a Poem* (1962) and *Love-Hate Relations: English and American Sensibilities* (1974).

He died at the age of 86.

Major Works

- Poems, 1933
- Vienna, 1934
- Trial of a Judge, 1938
- The Edge of Being, 1949
- World within World, 1951
- The Generous Days, 1969
- Love-Hate Relations, 1974
- The Thirties and After, 1978
- Collected Poems 1928-1985, 1985
- Dolphins, 1994

The Pylons

The secret of these hills was stone and cottages
Of that stone made,
And crumbling roads
That turned on sudden hidden villages
Now over these small hills, they have built the concrete
That trails black wire
Pylons, those pillars
Bare like nude giant girls that have no secret.
The valley with its gilt and evening look
And the green chestnut
Of customary root,
Are mocked dry like the parched bed of a brook.
But far above and far as sight endures

Like whips of anger
With lightning's danger
There runs the quick perspective of the future.
This dwarfs our emerald country by its trek
So, tall with prophecy
Dreaming of cities
Where often clouds shall lean their swan-white neck.

Cecil Day Lewis (1904-1972)

Cecil Day Lewis was an Anglo-Irish poet. He was born in Ireland in 1904 but his family moved to England in 1906. He was educated at Sherborne School on a scholarship and was an exhibitioner at Wadham College, Oxford.

Literary Career and Works

He attained recognition as the Poet laureate of England from 1968 until his death in 1972. His early poetry shows a deep influence of communism, though later he renounced his communist leanings.

Day Lewis' first collection of poems, *Beechen Vigil*, appeared in 1925. His collections *Transitional Poem* (1929) From Feathers to Iron (1932), *The Magnetic Mountain* (1933), and *A Time to Dance* (1935) established Day-Lewis's name in the poetic canon.

He also wrote detective stories under the pseudonym Nicholas Blake.

Cecil Day Lewis died from pancreatic cancer on 22nd May, 1972, at the age of 68.

Major Works

Poetry Collections

- Transitional Poem (1929)
- From Feathers to Iron (1932)
- Collected Poems 1929–1933 (1935)
- A Time to Dance And Other Poems (1935)
- Overtures to Death (1938)
- Short Is the Time (1945)
- Pegasus and Other Poems (1957)
- The Whispering Roots and Other Poems (1970)

Novels Written as Nicholas Blake

- A Question of Proof (1935)
- Thou Shell of Death (1936) (also published as Shell of Death)
- There's Trouble Brewing (1937)
- The Beast Must Die (1938)
- Malice in Wonderland (1940)
- The Case of the Abominable Snowman (1941) (also published asThe Corpse in the Snowman)
- The Dreadful Hollow (1953)
- The Widow's Cruise(1959)
- The Worm of Death(1961)
- The Private Wound (1968)

Children's Novels

- Dick Willoughby (1933)
- The Otterbury Incident (1948)

Louis MacNeice (1907-1963)

Louis MacNeice was born in Belfast, Ireland in 1907. He moved to England for his schooling at Sherborne. He was educated at Merton College, Oxford, lectured in classics at Birmingham University from 1930 to 1936 and lectured in Greek at Bedford College for women from 1936 to 1939.

Literary Career and Works

In 1941, he joined the British Broadcasting Company (BBC) as a staff writer and producer. MacNeice found an audience for his work through British radio. Some of his best-known plays, including *Christopher Columbus* (1944) and *The Dark Tower* (1946) were originally written for radio and later published.

His collection *Poems* (1935) helped to establish him as one of the emerging poets of the 1930s. His most significant work was his collaboration with WH Auden on *Letters from Iceland* (1937). This entertaining travel book in prose and verse emerged from a light-hearted summer journey by the two poets in 1936. His later works include *The Roman Smile*, a book of literary criticism a verse translation of the Hippolytus by Euripedes and an autobiographical book.

MacNeice died on 3rd September, 1963, just before the publication of his last book of poems, *The Burning Perch*.

Major Works

Poetry Collections

- Blind Fireworks (1929)
- Poems (1935)
- Letters from Iceland (1937, with WH Auden, poetry and prose)
- The Earth Compels (1938)
- Autumn Journal (1939)
- Prayer Before Birth (1944)
- Holes in the Sky (1948)
- Ten Burnt Offerings (1952)
- Autumn Sequel (1954)
- The Burning Perch (1963)
- Star-gazer (1963)

Plays

- The Agamemnon of Aeschylus (1936, translation)
- Christopher Columbus (1944, radio) and performed at Brighton Dome(2002)
- Goethe's Faust (1949, published 1951, a translation)
- The Mad Islands [1962] and The Administrator [1961] (1964, radio)
- Persons from Porlock [1963] and other plays for radio (1969)
- One for the Grave: A Modern Morality Play (1958)

Non-Fiction

- I Crossed the Minch (1938, travel, prose and verse)
- Modern Poetry: A Personal Essay (1938, criticism)
- Zoo (1938)
- The Poetry of WB Yeats (1941)
- The Strings Are False (1965, autobiography)

Walter de La Mare (1873-1956)

Walter de la Mare was an English poet and short -story writer, best known for his children's verse. He was born in Kent in South of England. He was educated at St Paul's Cathedral School. However, de La Mare left it at the age of 16 and began working in the Anglo-American (Standard) Oil Company, remaining with the firm for 18 years.

Literary Career and Works

His first published story, *Kismet* (1895), appeared in the journal 'Sketch' under the pseudonym Walter Ramal. His first book, a collection of poems called *Songs of Childhood* appeared in 1902: This was regarded as a significant example of children's literature and applauded for its creative imagery and variety of meters. de La Mare eventually devoted himself entirely to writing when he received a Civil List pension in 1908, which enabled him to concentrate on writing. Apart from children's verse, de La *Mare* also wrote ghost stories such as *Eight Tales*, *The Riddle and Other Stories* and supernatural novels like *Henry Brocken* (1904) and *The Return* (1910).

He died in Twickenham, near London, on 22nd June, 1956.

Major Works

Poetry Collections

- Songs of Childhood (1902)
- The Listeners (1912)
- Peacock Pie (1913)
- The Marionettes (1918)
- O Lovely England (1952)

Novels

- Henry Brocken (1904)
- The Three Mulla Mulgars(1910)
- The Return (1910)
- Memoirs of a Midget (1921)
- Mr Bumps and His Monkey (1942)

Short Story Collections

- The Riddle and Other Stories (1923)
- Ding Dong Bell (1924)
- Broomsticks and Other Tales (1925) (children's stories)
- The Connoisseur and Other Stories (1926)
- The Lord Fish (1930) (children's stories)
- Eight Tales (1971)

John Masefield (1878-1967)

John Masefield was born in Ledbury, Herefordshire, to Caroline and George Masefield in 1878.

As a teenager, Masefield worked for some time as a cadet on board the sail-training ship HMS Conway and later went to sea as an apprentice in a square-rigged ship. However, he had to give up dreams of a marine career due to his ill health. In 1897, he returned to England determined to succeed as a writer.

Literary Career and Works

He was British Poet Laureate from 1930 until his death in 1967. He is best remembered for his children's novels. *The Midnight Folk and The Box of Delights.*

Masefield utilised his experiences at sea and poured them into his poetry in collections such as *Salt Water Ballads* (1902). In World War I Masefield served on a hospital ship at Gallipoli. His book *Gallipoli* (1916) is an account of that campaign.

John Masefield died on 12th May, 1967 due to gangrene.

Dylan Thomas (1914-1953)

Welsh poet Dylan Thomas was in Swansea, Glamorgan, Wales on 27th October, 1914. He received his education at Mrs Hole's Dame school, a private school situated few streets away on Mirador Crescent and Swansea Grammar School, in the Mount Pleasant district of the city.

Literary Career and Works

His first poem was published in his school magazine in 1933. He dropped out of school at sixteen to become a junior reporter for the South Wales Daily Post. Later, he left this job and devoted himself entirely to writing. His reputation was established with his first two collections, *Eighteen Poems* (1934) and *Twenty-five Poems* (1936). In 1946, Thomas published his poetry volume, Deaths and Entrances. This book proved to be the turning point in his career.

Dylan Thomas also wrote radio dramas. His play *Under Milk Wood* was first performed in 1953 and published posthumously in 1954. This has been his most famous play translated in many different languages. The play progresses through 'one spring day' in the South Wales seaside town of Llareggub and tells of the dreams and desires of the living and the dead of the town.

Dylan Thomas drank heavily and on one of his lecture tours in New York, he collapsed after drinking at the White Horse Tavern. He was taken to St Vincent's Hospital and died several days later, on 9th November, 1953.

Contemporary Poetry

Contemporary poetry is difficult to define as it is a plane that is being built while in flight, but there are some fundamental characteristics of contemporary poetry that distinguish it from traditional poetry: Contemporary poetry is most often written in free verse (unrhymed lines). The lines follow the natural rhythms of the language and not the strict five stresses per line in iambic pentameter. Contemporary poetry is written in language that is accessible to the common reader. Contemporary poetry suggests ideas rather than overtly stating ideas. Contemporary poetry is brief in comparison to traditional poetry.

Contemporary poetry is grounded in the image. Contemporary poetry invites the reader to complete statements, offer conclusions and extract meaning. The meaning of the contemporary poem exists more in the mind of the reader than in accessing the mind of the poet.

Characteristics of Contemporary Poetry

Some of the important Characteristics of Contemporary poetry are given below

- Contemporary poetry is often written in free verse (unrhymed and with no specific metrical rhythm).
- Readers know and can associate with the language.
- It is brief.
- The poet laces the poem with images using all the senses of the reoder.
- It invites the reader to interpret the poem without yelling from the rooftops the true meaning of the poem.

Poets of the Contemporary Age

Roy Broad Bent Fuller (1912-1991)

He was born in 1912. He became solicitor. In the war period he joined Royal Navy in the middle East. After the war he was elected professor of poetry at Oxford University. His war poetry includes *The Middle of a War* (1942) and *A Lost Season* (1944).

Major Works

Epitaphs and Occasions (1949)

Its disciplined forms and spare language were opposite to the romantic poetry inspired by Dylan Thomas. He was courageous in his experiments and concerned with the condition of people in the contemporary politico- economic atmosphere. On account of his natural sympathy for others, his best poetry describes love.

He died in 1991.

Charles Stanley Causley (1917-2003)

Cornish poet Charles Causley was born in Cornwall in 1917. He was educated at Launceston College. He joined the Royal Navy during World War II.

Major Works

His first collection of poems was published on 1951.

Hands to Dance (1915) and *Forewell, Aggie Weston* (1951) These volumes show lost innocence of youth, country life, social groups and their habits. They have humour.

Johnny Alleluia (1961) and *Modern Folk Ballads* (1966) When he uses ballad rhythm, which is used in folk song his poetry becomes most attractive.

He died in 2003.

Thomas William Gunn (1929-2004)

Thomas William Gunn, born in 1929, was an English poet who was praised for his early verses in England. Both of his parents were journalists. In his youth, he attended University College School in Hampstead, London, then spent two years in the British national service and six months in Paris. Later, he studied English literature at Trinity College, Cambridge and graduated in 1953. He published his first collection of verse, Fighting Terms, the following year.

Major Works

My Sad Captains

In *My Sad Captains*, Gunn portrays the legends of history as the epitomes of determination but without any social inclination or purpose. Like stars in the sky, they continue to shine in the universe of history; but their existence serves no purpose. These sad captains thus thrive in a nihilistic arena where no meaningful role can be attributed to them. They are distant and disinterested as stars. The poem thus verges tends towards on Sartrean existentialism.

The Passages of Joy

The *Passages of Joy* draws it's title from Samuel Johnson's poem *The Vanity of Human Wishes*: *Time hovered o'er*, impatient to destroy/And shuts up all the Passages of Joy. The book ends with a poem about a modern cab driver on a night shift in San Francisco. Gunn is concerned with both the experiences of joy and its loss. A recurrent metaphor in the collection is the childhood game of 'Hide and Seek,' at the end of which, fantastically, all the lost are found.

Other Works

- The Sense of Movement (1957)
- Touch (1967)
- Moly (1971)

Ted Hughes (1930-1998)

Ted Hughes, born in 1930 in Yorkshire, was an English poet and children's writer. Critics frequently rank him as one of the best poets of his generation and one of the twentieth century's greatest writers. He served as Poet Laureate from 1984 until his death in 1998.

Major Works

The Hawk in the Rain (1957)

The *Hawk in the Rain* is a collection of poems by the British poet Ted Hughes published in 1957, it was Hughes's first book of poetry. The book received immediate acclaim in both England and America, where it won the Galbraith Prize. Many of the book's poems imagine the real and symbolic lives of animals, including a fox, a jaguar and the eponymous hawk. Other poems focus on erotic relationships and on stories of the First World War, Hughes's father being a survivor of Gallipoli.

Crow: From the Life and Songs of the Crow (1972)

Crow: From the Life and Songs of the Crow is one of Hunghe's most important works. The book, a collection of poems about the character Crow, borrows extensively from many world mythologies, notably both trickster and Christian mythology. It was his most controversial work: a stylistic experiment which abandoned many of the attractive features of his earlier work, and an ideological challenge to both Christianity and humanism.

Other Works

- Wodwo (1967)
- Birthday Letter (1998)
- The Bull Moses
- The Thought Fox

He was impressed with Yorkshire's local language and traditional oral literature. They gave firmness to his views. He finds power and vitality as necessary principles.

Hugh Mac Diarmid (1892-1978)

His real name was Christopher Murray Grieve. He was born in 1892 in Scotland and died in 1978. He revived the Low Land Scots language, Lallans. He was writing long before the war, but the people did not take him in notice. His use of scientific terms, neo-logisms and foreign phrases made him more difficult. He said that science and Marxism would solve all economic ills. His imaginary passion and comic sense could produce poetry even amid follies.

He edited Northern Numbers, The Voice of Scotland and The Golden Treasury of Scottish Poetry. The nationalist movement inverse was also encouraged by *Modern Scottish Poetry* (1946) and *Scottish verse* (1952).

Major Work

A Drunk Man Looks at the Thistle

A Drunk Man looks at the Thistle is a long poem by Hugh MacDiarmid written in Scots and published in 1926. It is composed as a form of monologue with influences from stream of consciousness genres of writing. A poem of extremes, it ranges between comic and serious modes and examines a wide range of cultural, sexual, political, scientific, existential, metaphysical and cosmic themes, ultimately unified through one consistent central thread, the poet's effectively charged contemplation, looking askance with disapproval or distrust at the condition of Scotland.

Other Works

- Sangschaw (1925)
- In Memoriam James Joyce (1955)
- Acyack Sheaf (1969)

Philip Larkin (1922-1985)

English poet and novelist Philip Arthur Larkin was born on 9th August, 1922 in Coventry.

He was sent to King Henry VIII Grammar School in Coventry. For higher education, he was sent to Oxford University. He passed BA in 1943 in first division. He attended St John's college and made friends with Kingsley Amis who helped him to understand and fulfil his literary objectives. He became famous as a novelist. His first novel *Jill* was published in 1946 and next novel *A Girl in Winter* was published in 1947.

Major Works

The Whitsun Weddings It describes autobiographical elements. He went on a journey from Hull to London for some personal or official reasons. He described the sights and sounds and his reaction to what he saw in the journey.

High Windows This poem is an ironic tribute to the sexual freedom and permissiveness of 1960's. He had admiration for Lawrence's Lady Chatterley's Lover. It may partly explain the plain speaking of certain poems of 'High Windows'. In the opening stanza of the poem, he refers to a love making scene. "When I see a couple of Kids/And guess he's fucking Her and she's taking pills or wearing a diaphragm/I know this is the paradise everyone old has dreamed of all their lives."

Annus Mirabilis This poem's name means the year of miracles. In this poem, an old man sings a ballad, which sees the paper back publication of Lawrence's book as part of a wider shift in popular culture and manners. "Sexual Intercourse began/In 1963 (Which was rather late for me)/Between the end of the Chatterly ban and the Beatles LP"

Afternoons He presents false entertainments cheap fashions, joyless wedding parties, dull refreshment grounds etc of England. He speaks ironically about the husbands standing behind their wives, about an estate of washing and about albums containing wedding photographs and lying near the TV sets.

Toads In this poem, he mocks at the persons, who live on their wits. "Lots of folk live on their wits/Lecturers, lispers/Losels, loblolly men, loute They don't end up as paupers." 'Toad' in the poem is a metaphor for forced work or vocation. The poem is a complaint against something or some kind of work which displeases the poet. Work is compared to a toad that squats on the poet's life.

Church Going In this poem, he goes to the Church without a hat on his head and takes off his cycle-clips before entering it. The poem discusses the futility of going to a church and talks about disintegration of church as a religious institution.

Other Poets of Contemporary Period

Name	Time Period	Major Works
Keidrych Rhys	26th December, 1915-22nd May 1987	The Van Pool (1942) His Wife's Poems (1944)
Alan Ross	6 May, 1922-14th February, 2001	The Derelict Day (1947) Something of the Sea (1954) Tropical Ice (1972) The Taj Express (1973) Poems (2005)
Dylan Marlais Thomas	27th October, 1914-9th November, 1953	18 Poems (1934) Twenty Five Poems (1936) The Map of Love (1939) Entrances (1946) Under Milk Wood (1954)
Laurie Lee	26th June, 1914-3rd May, 1997	The Sun My Monument (1944) The Bloom of Candles (1947) My Many-coated Man (1955)
George Barker	26th February, 1913-27th October, 1991	Eros in Dogma (1944) News of the World (1950) A Vision of the Bests and Gods (1954) The Golden Chains (1968)
David Gascoyne	10th October, 1916-25th, November, 2001	Poems (1943) A Vagrant and Other Poems (1950) Night Thoughts (1956) Sun at Midnight (1970) Early Poems (1980) Five Early Uncollected Poems (1984)
Dennis Joseph Enright	11th March, 1920-31st December, 2002	The Laughing Hyena and Other Poems (1953) Poets of the 1950's (1955) Some Men Are brothers (1960) The Old Adam (1965) Shakespeare And The Students (1970) Sad Ires (1975) Collected Poems (1981) In Search of Lost Time (1992) Telling Tales (1999) Injury Time (2003)
Sir John Betjeman	28th August, 1906-19th May, 1984	Old Lights for New Chancels (1940) Selected Poems (1948) A Few Late Chrysanthemums (1954) Collected Poems (1958) High and Low 1966
Robert Conquest	15th July, 1917-3rd August, 2015	New Lines (1956-1963) Poems (1956) Between Mars and Venus (1962) Arias from a Love Opera, and Other Poems (1969)

Name	Time Period	Major Works
Donald Alfred Davie	17th July, 1922- 18th September, 1995	A Winte Talent (1957) Events & Wisdoms (1964) In the Stopping Train (1977) To Scorch Or Freeze (1988) Church Chapel and the Unitarian Conspiracy (1995) Purity of Diction in English Verse and Articulate Energy (2006)
Vernon Scannell	23rd January, 1922- 16th, November, 2007	Graves and Resurrections (1948) A Mortal Pitch (1957) Epithets of War (1969) Company of Women (1971) The Apple-Raid (1974) Funeral Games (1987) The Black and White Days (1996) Last Post (2007)
Norman Cornthwaite Nicholson	8th January, 1914- 30th May, 1987	Five Rivers (1944) Rock Face (1948) The Pot Geranium (1954) A Local Habitation (1972) Sea to the West (1981)
Kathleen Jessies Raine	14th June, 1908- 6th July, 2003	Stone And Flower (1943) The Pythoness (1949) The Year One (1952) The Hollow Hill (1965) On a Deserted Shore (1973) The Presence (1987) Living with Mystery (1992)
Charles Tomlinson	8th January, 1927- 22th August, 2015	The Necklace (1955) A Peopled Landscape (1963) Penguin Modern Poets (1969) The Shaft (1978) The Return (1987) Cracks in the Universe (2006)
Vernon Phillips Watkins	27th June, 1906- 8 October, 1967	The Ballad of the Mari Lwyd (1941) The Death Bell (1954) Cypress and Acacia (1959) Fidelities (1968)
John Francis Heath Stubbs	9th July, 1918- 26th December, 2006	Wounded Thammuz (1942) A Charm Against the Toothache (1954) Cosmic Poem (1969) The Watchman's Flute (1978) A Partridge in a Pear Tree (1988) Galileo's Salad (1996) Pigs Might Fly (2005)
James Falconer Kirkup	23rd April, 1918- 10th May, 2009	The Drowned Sailor (1947) Thje Descent into the Cave (1957) The Caged Bird in Springtime (1967) The Sand Artist (1978) The House at Night (1988) Pikadon: An Epic Poem (1997) Home Thoughts (2011)
Alexander Comfort	10th February, 1920- 26th March, 2000	A Wreath for the Living (1942) The Song of Lazarus (1945) Haste to the Wedding (1962) A Good Age (1976)

Name	Time Period	Major Works
Elizabeth Joan Jennings	18th July, 1926- 26th October, 2001	A Way of Looking (1955) The Mind has Mountains (1966) Growing Points (1975) Extending the Territory (1985) In the Meantime (1996) Timely Issues (2001)
Jon Silkin	2nd December, 1930- 25th November, 1997	The Portrait and Other Poems (1950) The Re-Ordering of the Stones (1961) Amana Grass (1971) The Psalms and their Spoils (1980) The Lens-Breakers (1992) Making a Republic (2002)
Peter Neville Frederick Porter	16th February, 1929- 23rd April, 2010	Once Bitten Twice Bitten (1961) The Last of England (1970) Fast Forward (1984) Millennial Fables (1994) Afterburner (2004) Better Than God (2009)
Thomas Blackburn	10th February, 1916- 13rd August, 1977	The Outer Darkness (1953) In the Fire (1956) A Smell of Burning (1961)
Patrick Kavanagh	21th October, 1904- 30th November, 1967	Ploughman and Other Poems (1936) The Great Hunger (1942) Come Dance with Kitty Stobling (1960)
Ronald Stuart Thomas	29th March, 1913- 25th September, 2000	The Stone of the Field (1946) Song at the year's Turning (1955) The Bread of Truth (1963) The Way of It (1977) Destinations (1985) To Brave to Dream (2016)

American Poetry

The poetry of the United States, arose first as efforts by colonists to add their voices to English poetry in the 17th century, well before the constitutional unification of the thirteen colonies. Unsurprisingly, most of the early colonists' work relied on contemporary British models of poetic form, diction and theme. However, in the 19th century, a distinctive American idiom began to emerge. By the later part of that century, when Walt Whitman was winning an enthusiastic audience abroad, poets from the United States had begun to take their place at the forefront of the English-language avant-garde.

American Poetry offers a definitive collection of both women and men poets from the beginning of the century to the opening of the twentieth century. The collection begins with early Colonial poems such as John Wilson's *A Song of Thanksgiving for the Lasting Remembrance of God's Wonderful Works* (1603), William Morrell's *New England* (1625) and the complete works of Anne Bradstreet and Edward Taylor. It continues through to early twentieth-century via renowned poets like HW Longfellow, Walt Whitman, Henry David Thoreau, James Russell Lowell, Robert Frost and Sylvia Plath etc.

Poets of American Poetry

HW Longfellow (1807-1882)

He was born at Portland Maine in 1807 in America. He began to publish poetry at the age of 13 years. He resigned from this professorship in 1854. His full name was Henry Wordsworth Longfellow. He worked as a teacher of Modern languages at Harvard University.

Literary Career and Works

He has been called the children's poet. He was a musical poet and a versatile scholar. He wrote both short and long poems. Some of them tell the life of Red Indians. His style is simple. He has used many verse forms.

He wrote sonnets such as *To Shakespeare and the Tides*. We can see a trace of fancy in them. He describes nature here and there in a very delicate and graceful manner.

He describes night as

"Thou layest thy fingers on the lips of care
And they complain no more."

He wrote Italian sonnets, whose rhyme scheme is abba, abba, cde, cde. He wrote novels also. *Hyperion* and *Kavanagh* are his well known novels.

In Kavanagh, he uses wonderful proverbs

- Silence is a great peace maker.
- In youth, all doors open outward, in old age they all open inward.
- When looking for anything lost, begin by looking where you think it is not.

Hyperion is semi autobiographical romance written in 1839. Though he was American, he wrote an Indian epic. *The Song of Hiawatha*. He also wrote about doings of his Puritan forefathers in *Evangeline* and *The Courtship of Miles Standish*. His lyrics have melody and music.

Contemporary writer Edgar Allan Poe criticised Longfellow and accused him of plagiarism. He called Longfellow 'a determined imitator and a dextrous adapter of the ideas of other people'. However, most critics see Poe's accusations as a publicity stunt.

He was a scholar and translator. Through, his works, we can know French, Spanish, German and Italian poets. He loved children. He has been called, the children's poet. He wrote poems such as *Children and Children's Hour. Once, he wrote the following, which can also be said about him.*

'Lives of great men all remind us
We can make our life sublime'
'And departing leave behind us
Foot prints on the sands of time'

In brief, he was a sonneteer, ballad writer versatile scholar, translator, moralist, kind lyricist, who had a gracious personality. He died in 1882.

Major Works

- 'Voices of the Night' (1839).
- 'Pilgrimage Beyond the Sea (1835),
- 'Evangeline' (1847)
- 'The Song of Hiawatha' (1855)
- 'Poems on Slavery (1842).
- 'The Spanish student (1843)
- 'Belfry of Bruges' (1845),
- The Golden Legend' (1851),
- 'Hyperion' and 'Kavanagh'.
- A Psalm of Life (Poem)
- Hymn of the Night
- The Bridge
- The Arrow and the Song
- The Arsenal at Springfield
- The Building of the Ship
- The Village Black Smith
- Morituri Salutamus

John Greenleaf Whittier (1807-1892)

He was born in 1807. He was a greater poet than HW Longfellow. Though in most of his poems, he has no simplicity and tenderness as HW Longfellow's poems, yet they have strength and passionate scorn for the tyrant and the base. If he is given a cause, which touches him, like Anti-slavery or certain aspects of New England life, he gives his best. He died in 1892.

Major Works

- Snow Bound
- Randolph of Roanoke
- Moloch in State Street
- Ichabod
- Maud Muller
- Barbara Frietchie
- The Henchman
- The Barefooted Boy
- Taking the Bees
- Dear Lord and Father of Mankind

Henry David Thoreau (1817-1862)

He was born in 1817. In 1839, soon after he left college, he went on a tour with his brother John. This was a Voyage on the Concord and Merrimac rivers. He was a naturalistic.

Literary Career and Works

He practised Naturalism in Walden Woods in a practical way. He preferred life in woods, observing nature and studying the ways of animals that he loved. His book *Civil Disobedience* influenced Mahatma Gandhi, Father of our nation. He was a worshipper of nature.

He has been called *The Poet Naturalist*. His wonderful phrases are "How can we expect a harvest of thought who have not had a seed-time of character ?", Only he can be trusted with goods who can present a face of Bronze to expectations. His *Walden* influenced WB Yeats, a famous English poet. He died in 1862.

Major Works

- Cape Cod (1865)
- Civil Disobedience (1849)
- Plea for captain John Brown (1859)
- Slavery in Massachusetts (1854)
- Walden (1854)

Walt Whitman (1819-1892)

Walt Whitman was the first powerful poet, who was called the pride of America. He was born on 31st May, 1819 on a small farm at West Hills on Long Island. His father was a farmer and carpenter. His mother had a Quaker background.

He passed his early childbood in the streets of Brooklyn. After the span of ten years his family went to Long Island. He could not get proper education in public schools. He left studies at the age of 11 and began to work as an apprentice to a lawyer. The lawyer was very kind to him and allowed him to read the books from his library. He read Homer, Shakespeare and Walter Scott.

Literary Career and Works

He was a fan of Scott and his writings. He worked for several newspapers. In 1846, he became as editor of *The Daily Eagle* a famous newspaper. He worked as an editor for 2 years. He left the job because of conflict with the owners. He became the editor of the *Daily Crescent* in New Orleans. He began to compose the poems in 1855.

Walt Whitman was an American poet, essayist and journalist. He has been called the 'Bard of Democracy'. Three things impressed him very much. He got from his father the spirit of love for freedom and patriotism. He got from his mother deeply mystic qualities, which made him the poet of the soul. Democracy, the urban people and journalism made him efficient enough to observe things minutely and be genuine and keen onlooker.

In works like *Children of Adam, I Sing the Body Electric* and *Spontaneous Me* alongwith *A Woman Waits for Me,* we see Walt Whitman's treatment of sex. Walt Whitman says 'The sexual life is to be glorified and not to be treated as if it were something shameful'. He also says, 'A man's body is sacred and a woman's body is equally sacred'. He wrote an elegy on the death of Abraham Lincoln, the President of America *O Captain! My Captain!* He was a devotee of nature like Wordsworth. A *Passage to India* celebrates the completion of Suez canal and Transco.

In 1873, he suffered from severe paralytic attack. This year his mother died. He passed his last days at Camden. He died on 26th March, 1892.

Major Works

- Leaves of Grass
- Children of Adam
- Spontaneous Me
- A Woman Waits for Me
- A Passage to India
- Song of Myself
- Drum Taps
- Out of the Cradle Endlessly Rocking
- Answerer
- Sea Drift
- Democratic Vistas written (1871)
- Specimen Days written (1882)

James Russell Lowell (1819-1891)

He was an American romantic poet. He was born in 1819 at Cambridge. He got education at Harvard University. Later on, he became a professor of modern languages there.

Literary Career and Works

His early poetry is full of nature, but later poems are full of patriotism and love for democracy.

He was famous as a literary critic and as a lecturer of English poetry. Besides his poetry, he published *Conversations on Old Poets, Fire Side Travels, Among My Books.* He was greater in prose than in poetry.
He died in 1891

Major Works

- **The Bigelow Papers** (1848)
- **Fable for Critics** This book is on American poets and poetry (1848).
- **Commemoration Ode** and other memorable poems. One ode under the old Elm celebrates the one 100th anniversary of Washington's command of the Revolutionary Army. His patriotism makes his poems, best. They have universal appeal. In prose, he is best in criticism. He has humour. He has no peer in American letters.
- **The Essay on Wordsworth** contains good and admirable matter.
- **The Borderers** is unreal.

Thomas William Parsons (1819-1892)

He was an American poet. He was born in 1819. he was a classical scholar and a student of the classical poet Dante. He died in 1892.

Major Works

- *The first Ten Cantos of the Inferno of Dante* (1843)
- *Poems* (1854).

Bayard Taylor (1825-1878)

He was born in 1825. He was an American poet, literary critic, translator and diplomat. He was a famous traveller. He lived in Germany and Italy and saw their democratic life. He got success in travel letters and was always superior in them and wrote powerful ballads. *Poems of the Orient*, which was written in 1834, is his best work. He wrote many essays. He translated Goethe's Faust, which could not be completed. He wrote an interesting book *Travel Chat*. He will be remembered for these two books.

He died in 1878.

James Ryder Randall (1839-1908)

He was an American poet and journalist born in 1839. He wrote *Maryland, My Maryland* the famous war song of the confederacy. He has been called the 'Poet Laureate of the Lost Cause'. He later became a newspaper editor and correspondent in Washington.
He died in 1908.

Sidney Lanier (1842-1881)

He was born in 1842. He was a versatile genius. He was a musician, soldier, poet and critic. In the American Civil War in 1861, he fought for South America. Since then, he could not forget his painful and horrifying experiences throughout his life and began to remain ill. To cure himself from his ill health, he changed his place. Inspite of changing his climate, he could not restore his health.

He died of TB in North Carolina in 1881. He wrote the *Marshes of Glynn, Sunrise and Corn*. They are famous for their musical flow.

William Bliss Carman (1861-1929)

He was born in 1861 in Canada. He published his first book *Low Tide on Grand Pre* in 1893. He wrote songs and ballads. *His works are Low Tide on Ground Pre* (1893), *Songs from Vagabondia* (1894), *Behind the Arras* (1895), *Ballads of Lost Haven* (1897), *For Horezons* (1925), *Wuld Garden* (1929)
He died in 1929.

Robert Frost (1874-1963)

Robert Frost, the greatest American poet was popular not only in USA, but also in England. He was born in San Francisco, California on 26th March, 1874. His mother Isabelle Moodie was a Scottish lady and poetess. his father was a TB Patient. Robert was a sick child.

He was neurotic. After the death of his father in 1885. His mother started teaching in the village Grammar School. In the beginning, he did not like studies. But later, he took full interest. In 1892, he joined the Dartmonth College. But soon, he left college and started composing poetry. In 1895, he married his school friend Elinor White. He helped his mother in running a private school. He studied at Harvard College for 2 years. He started poultry farm in New Hampshire. In 1912, he sold his land and alongwith his family and wife settled in Beaconsfield, Buking Hamshire, England.

Literary Career and Works

As a poet, he got name and fame. He got rare privilege of living on the campus of various institutions as poet-in residence. He received many honours and awards. He became member of the National Institute of Arts and Letters in 1916 and of the American Academy in 1930. He won Pulitzer Prize four times for poetry. He came back to America in 1915 and became a professor of poetry in Harvard.
He died in January 1963.

Major Works

- Mountain Interval (1916)
- New Hampshire (1923)
- West Running Brook (1928)
- A Further Range (1936)
- A Witness Tree (1942)
- Steeple Bush (1947)
- Complete poems (1949) Alongwith two verse dramas in the end
- A Mosque of Reason (1945) and A Mosque of Mercy (1947)

Adrienne Rich (1929-2012)

She was born in 1929 in Baltimore, Maryland, USA. She is famous for involvement in contemporary women's movement as a poet and theorist. She has published 19 volumes of poetry, three collections of essays and other writings. We find in her work a strong resistance to racism and militarism. Her poem *Aunt Jennifer's Tigers* presents the compulsions of a married woman. She died in 2012.

Her works are *Of Woman Born; Motherhood as Experience and Institution* (1976), *On Lies, Secrets and Silence; Selected Prose* (1979), *A Change of World* (1951), *The Diamond Cutters and Other Poems* (1955), *Midnight Salvage* (1999), *A Human Eye; Essays on Art in Society* (2009).

Sylvia Plath (1932-1963)

She was born on 27th October, 1932 in Massachusetts. She was an American poet, novelist and short story writer. She got name and fame as a professional poet and writer. She married fellow poet Ted Hughes in 1956, having two children together Freida and Nicholas. They lived together first in USA and then in England.

She is credited with advancing the genre of confessional poetry. She is famous for her two collections *The Colossus* and *Other Poems* and *Ariel*. She committed suicide on 11th Feb, 1963 after a long struggle against depression due to marital separation. In 1982, she became the first poet to win a Pulitzer Prize posthumously (after death) for *The Collected Poems*. She had also written a semi-autobiographical novel *The Bell Jar*, which was published shortly before her death.

EXAM BASED QUESTIONS

1 Which age among the following witnessed the World War II?

(a) The Romantic Age (b) The Age of Revival
(c) The Modern Age (d) The Augustan Age

2 Dadaism movement was the result of

(a) French Revolution
(b) insensitivity of Victorian Poets
(c) brutality of World War I
(d) None of the above

3 'Georgian's Poetry' began in which of the following era?

(a) The Neo-classical Age (b) The Modern Age
(c) The Romantic Age (d) None of these

4 What is common to the following poets? Identify the correct description below.

Rupert Brooke
Walter de La Mare
John Drink Water
John Masefield

Codes

(a) All of them wrote in the blank verse
(b) All of them were poets, who were included in The 'Georgian Poetry' edited by Edward Maish
(c All of them were part of 'Pylon Poets'
(d) All of them wrote 'Theatre of the Absurd'

5 Through which among the following, Yeats inherited influence of variety of themes?

(a) A S Collins (b) Father of Blake
(c) Pre-Raphaelite Poets (d) Both 'b' and 'c'

6 In which among the following poems, there is a glimpse of Maud Gonne?

(a) Leda and Swan (b) Second coming
(c) Both 'a' and 'b' (d) None of these

7 Whom did W B Yeats think of as a child in his work, 'Among School Children'?

(a) Lady Gregory (b) Maud Gonne
(c) W H Auden (d) Mrs Elizabeth

8 The poem 'Lapis-Lazuli' was written by

(a) Radcliffe (b) Yeats
(c) Spender (d) Coleridge

9 Which of the following works does not belong to 'WB Yeats'?

(a) The Resurrection
(b) A Dialogue of Self and Soul
(c) The Shadowy Waters
(d) The Hollow Man

10 In the poem 'Sailing to Byzantium' Byzantium is

(a) The Capital of Greece (b) A Modern City
(c) A Mythical King (d) A Mythical City

11 At the end of the poem 'Sailing to Byzantium,' the speaker imagines transformation into

(a) A Mechanical Bird (b) An Auto
(c) A God (d) A Woman

12 In 'Sailing to Byzantium,' the element that death is most associated with

(a) Earth (b) Water
(c) Fire (d) Air

13 'The Tower' is named after Yeats'

(a) Dog (b) Ancestors
(c) Home (d) Son

14 The direction that the spirits would move around the speaker in 'Sailing to Byzantium' is in a

(a) Straight Line (b) Gyre
(c) Circle (d) Zig-Zag

15 In 'A Prayer for my Son,' the speaker's son's name is

(a) Michael (b) John
(c) Patrick (d) George

16 In 'A Prayer for my Son,' the speaker hopes that the ghost may be

(a) alive (b) armed
(c) stitched together (d) friendly

17 In 'Two songs from a Play,' what god does a virgin confront?

(a) Yahweh (b) Juno
(c) Lead (d) Dionysus

18 What does the virgin carry with her in 'Two songs from a Play,'?

(a) Dionysus' Spirit (b) A Lock of Dionysus' Hair
(c) Dionysus' Heart (d) Dionysus' Brain

19 The poem 'Leda and the Swan' describes an act of

(a) Rape (b) Love
(c) Murder (d) Mercy

20 Who was Leda in the poem 'Leda and the Swan'?

(a) Mother of Helen of Troy (b) Wife of Juno
(c) Daughter of Zeus (d) Wife of Mercury

21 Which of the following works was the first book of Edith Sitwell?

(a) The Shadow of Cain
(b) The Songs of the Cold
(c) Street Songs
(d) The Mother and Other Poems

22 Who out of the following enjoyed nature's beauty like Wordsworth?

(a) Lascelles Abercromble (b) Edith Sitwell
(c) WH Davies (d) GB Shaw

23 Which of the following works describes the life of Davies?
(a) Autobiography of a Super-Trump
(b) A Poet's Alphabets
(c) The True Traveller
(d) My Birds and My Garden

24 What is common to the following? Identify to correct description below.
Watchers of the sky
The Book of Earth
The Last Voyage
Codes
(a) All of them are poems by WH Davies
(b) All of these were written by Siegfried Sassoon
(c) All of them are volumes of the epic The Torch Bearers by Alfred Noyes
(d) All of them are works by John Galoworthy

25 Whose theory matches the French critic, 'Remy de Gourmount'?
(a) G B Shaw
(b) T E Hulme
(c) Rudyard Kipling
(d) H G Wells

26 Who among the following wrote poems during the war time and World War I influenced him?
(a) GB Shaw (b) Siegfried Sassoon
(c) CP Snow (d) None of these

27 Which work among the following does not belong to TS Eliot?
(a) The Hollow Man (b) Lake of Innisfree
(c) The Rock (d) Gerontion

28 'The Sacred Wood', 'For Quarters', 'Family Reunion' are the famous works of
(a) WB Yeats (b) TS Eliot
(c) GB Shaw (d) None of these

29 'The Love-Song of Alfred J Prufrock' is a
(a) an ode (b) a lyric
(c) an epic (d) a dramatic monologue

30 'Sweeny Among the Nightingale' was written by
(a) Blake (b) Eliot
(c) Wordsworth (d) Spender

31 'The Waste Land' written by Eliot, appeared first in the quarterly magazine
(a) Blast (b) Life
(c) The Criterion (d) Imagists

32 In its final published version, Eliot's The Waste Land contains a total of
(a) 334 lines (b) 433 lines
(c) 373 lines (d) 423 lines

33 Influence of the Indian Philosophy is seen in the writings of
(a) G B Shaw (b) Noel Coward
(c) Tom Stoppard (d) T S Eliot

34 Which of the following the statements, which does not belong to 'T S Eliot'?
(a) Eliot was born in 1888
(b) He visited French literature and Philosophy
(c) He wrote 'Ideas of Good and Evil'
(d) Murder in the Cathedral is one of the famous work of Eliot

35 Who rapes Philomela in the poem 'The Wasteland'?
(a) Odysseus (b) Zeus
(c) The Typist (d) Tereus

36 Which one of the following modern poems employs Ottava Rima?
(a) Among School Children (b) In Praise of Limestone
(c) The Wild Swans at Coole (d) The Shield of Achilles

37 Which of the following characters from 'Eliot's Waste Land is not correctly mentioned?
(a) The Typist
(b) Madam Sosostris
(c) The Merchant from Eugenides
(d) The Young Man Carbuncular

38 In which of the following scenes of The Waste Land do we have a departure from Standard English?
(a) The typist scene
(b) The pub scene
(c) The hyacinth garden scene
(d) The Chapel Perilous scene

39 The year 1939 proved to be a crucial year for two important writers in England. Identify the correct phrase below
(a) For Yeats who died, for Auden who left England for the US
(b) For Eliot who started publishing verse-drama, for Hardy whose Wessex Poems were published
(c) For Evelyn Waugh and Graham Greene, each for publishing his first novels
(d) For Eliot who won the Nobel Prize and Orwell who published his *Animal Farm*

40 I sit in one of the *dives*
On Fifty Second Street,
Uncertain and afraid
As the clever hopes expire
Of a low dishonest decade.
So beings Auden's 1st September, 1939. What is the meaning of the word in italics?
(a) bench (b) night club
(c) house (d) park

41 Who was the 'miglior fabbro' to whom The Waste Land was dedicated?
(a) Ezra Pound
(b) Vivienne Haigh-Wood Eliot
(c) Samuel Beckett
(d) Coco Chanel

42 Which of these household items is not mentioned in Eliot's The Love Song of J Alfred Prufrock?
(a) Teacups (b) Pillows
(c) Lampshades (d) Coffee spoons

43 From where did Eliot borrow the original title for The Waste Land, He Do the Police in Different Voices?
(a) A popular music hall song
(b) James Joyce's Finnegans Wake
(c) Charles Dickens's Our Mutual Friend
(d) Mark Twain's Huckleberry Finn

44 Which popular nursery rhyme is mentioned at the end of The Waste Land?
(a) Ring-a-roses
(b) London Bridge is Falling Down
(c) Humpty Dumpty
(d) Jack and Jill

45 Which of these is a phrase from Eliot's The Love Song of J Alfred Prufrock?
(a) Do I dare to eat a peach?
(b) Do I presume to pare a plum?
(c) Do I try to swallow a grape?
(d) Do I need to marinade a melon?

46 Which work is sometimes referred to as Eliot's 'conversion poem'?
(a) The Hollow Men (b) Ash Wednesday
(c) The Journey of the Magi (d) Whispers of Immortality

47 In Auden's poem-'Musee des Beaux' Arts', Whose painting of the fall of Icarus Auden refers here?
(a) Raphael (b) Da Vinci
(c) Brughel (d) None of these

48 'The Dog Beneath the Skin' was a collaborative product of a group of friends including Isherwood and
(a) Auden (b) Eliot (c) Coleridge (d) Blake

49 Cecil Day-Lewis volumes of poetry do not include
(a) The Magnetic Mountain (b) The Working Day
(c) Both 'a' and 'b' (d) None of these

50 Who among the poets in England during the 1930 had left-leaning tendencies?
(a) TS Eliot, Ezra Pound, Richard Aldington
(b) Wilfred Owen, Siegfried Sassoon, Rupert Brooke
(c) WH Auden, Louis MacNeice, Cecil Day Lewis
(d) J. Fleckner, WH Davies, Edward Marsh

51 Who among the following invokes supernatural atmosphere in his poems like, The Listeners, Peacock Pie and The Veil?
(a) Walter de La Mare (b) Yeats
(c) Coleridge (d) Spender

52 Which of the work among the following, which does not belong to 'Walter de La Mare'?
(a) Bells and Grass (b) The Age of Anxiety
(c) The Fleeting and Other Poems
(d) Early the Morning

53 'The Window in the Bye Street' has been written by
(a) John Masefield (b) Stephen Spender
(c) Joseph Conrad (d) Arnold Bennett

54 Who among the following understood the plight of the down trodden people and wrote for them?
(a) W H Auden (b) John Masefield
(c) Walter de La Mare (d) None of the above

55 'Sea-Fever' was written by
(a) Yeats (b) Masefield
(c) Coleridge (d) Pound

56 Identify the poem which contains a sinner's confession written by John Masefield?
(a) Enslaved (b) Right Royal
(c) The Everlasting Mercy (d) None of these

57 Identify the work the following which does not belong to 'John Masefield'?
(a) The Coming of Christ (b) End and Beginning
(c) Right Royal (d) The Songs of the Cold

58 Who encouraged Hughes to publish his first collection of poetry?
(a) Sylvia Plath (b) Dylan Thomas
(c) Philip Larkin (d) Seamus Heaney

59 Which of the following verbs is not used to characterise the wind in the poem 'Wind'?
(a) Stampeding (b) Quivering
(c) Floundering (d) Flexing

60 Which of the following is not a symbol in the poem 'Wind'?
(a) The House (b) The Fire
(c) The Wind (d) The Hills

61 What action do the characters perform at the end of the poem 'Wind'?
(a) They Hold Hands (b) They have a Conversation
(c) They Read a Book (d) They Watch a Fire

62 Which word best describes the tone of the poem 'Wind'?
(a) Lethargic (b) Hopeful
(c) Tempestuous (d) Defeated

63 'Wind' was published in which of Hughes' poetry collections?
(a) Tales of Ovid (b) Flowers and Insects
(c) The Hawk and The Rain (d) Birthday Letters

64 Who among the following has been aplty called as 'The Children's Poet'?
(a) Greenleaf (b) Allan
(c) Longfellow (d) None of these

65 'Evangeline' and 'The Courtship of Miles Standish are the famous works of
(a) Greenleaf (b) Longfellow
(c) Whitman (d) Hawthorne

66 Henry, Wordsworth and Longfellow's works include
(a) Voices of the Night (b) The Fireside
(c) The Seaside (d) All of these

67 By whom was written? 'Grapes of Wrath' ....
(a) F Scott Fitzgerald (b) John Steinbeck
(c) Walt Whitman (d) Vikram Seth

68 Which post-war British poet was involved in a disastrous marriage with Sylvia Plath?
(a) Philip Larkin (b) Ted Hughes
(c) Stevie Smith (d) Geoffrey Hill

69 'A Witness Tree', 'A Mosque of Reason', 'Complete Poems' are the works of which writer?
(a) Robert Frost (b) Whitman
(c) Edgar Allan Poe (d) Thoreau

70 Name the author who was awarded the Pulitzer Prize, not one time, but four times is ....
(a) Allan Poe (b) Thoreau
(c) Robert Frost (d) Whitman

71 Who among the following poet said about Ralph Waldo Emerson that he had a "Greek head on right Yankee Shoulders"?
(a) Lowell (b) Whitman
(c) G B Shaw (d) Greenleaf

72 'Biglow Papers' is the famous work of which American writer?
(a) Poe (b) Lowell (c) Longfellow (d) Whitman

73 Which work among the following belongs to 'James Russel Lowell'
(a) The Borderess (b) Essay on Wordsworth
(c) Jane Eyre (d) All of these

74 Which of these do Lanier's works include?
(a) The Marshes of Glynn (b) Corn
(c) Sunrise (d) All of these

75 Which among the following is an elegy on the death of Abraham Lincoln?
(a) I Hear America Singing (b) Stopping by Woods
(c) O Captain! My Captain (d) None of these

76 Eliot considered ...... as a Masterpiece.
(a) Quality Street (b) Dubliners
(c) Ulysses (d) Dear Brutus

77 The Second Coming is a lyrical poem of ....
(a) 44 lines (b) 22 lines
(c) 50 lines (d) 10 lines

78 'The Cocktail Party', 'The Confidential Clerk' are the famous works of ....
(a) Stephen Spender (b) T S Eliot
(c) Lewis (d) WH Auden

79 "Like a ...... etherised upon a ...... TS Eliot, the Love Song of J Alfred Prufrock.
(a) patient, table (b) poet, conceit
(c) doctor, bed (d) family, chair

80 'The Journey of the Magi' is a poem written by TS Eliot, Another piece written by O'Henry is titled ....
(a) The Gift of the Magi
(b) The Magi of the East
(c) The Gifts brought by Magi
(d) None of these

81 'The Poet's Tongue' and 'The Age of Anxiety' are the famous works of ....
(a) TS Eliot (b) GB Shaw
(c) WH Auden (d) None of these

82 'World within World' is the autobiography of ....
(a) Lewis (b) Spender (c) Eliot (d) Coleridge

83 'Vienna', 'The Still Centre' was written by ....
(a) James Barrie (b) Stephen Spender
(c) CP Snow (d) James Joyce

84 .... is known for his work, 'Autumn Journal'.
(a) Virginia Woolf (b) George Gissing
(c) Lovis Macneice (d) E M Forster

85 'Bells and Grass', 'Early One Morning' are the famous works of ....
(a) G B Shaw (b) John Masefield
(c) Ezra Pound (d) Walter de La Mare

86 Which of the statements is true about WB Yeats?
(a) He was not the driving force behind the Irish Literary Renaissance
(b) He did not draw on Irish mythology, history and folklore to create a distinctive national literature
(c) He was the first Irishman to be awarded The Nobel Prize in 1923
(d) Maud Gonne was not the greatest influence on Yeat's life and poetry

87 Which of the following is the wrong statements about TS Eliot?
(a) Eliot has also worked as a critic
(b) Eliot's full name is Thomas Stearns Eliot
(c) Eliot wrote 'Lake of Innisfree'
(d) Eliot was born in 1884

88 Which of the following statements is not correct about 'The Waste Land'?
(a) TS Eliot wrote the poem 'The Waste Land'
(b) The Waste Land has five sections
(c) The Waste Land was published in 1922
(d) 'Death by Water' is not the shortest of the poem's five sections

89 Which of the following statements is not correct about WH Auden?
(a) He was the leader of the Oxford group
(b) He was influenced by the literary principle of JS Eliot
(c) He attempted to bring new forms and techniques in English poetry
(d) He was not a Chancellor of The Academy of American Poets

90 Which of the following statements is incorrect about 'Georgian Poetry'?
(a) It denotes a body of poetry produced between 1912 and 1922
(b) The poets did not constitute a school
(c) The aim was to revive public interest in poetry
(d) Most of them wrote verse which was not lucid in style

91 Which of the following pairs is correctly matched?
(a) WB Yeats : England
(b) WH Davies : Dublin
(c) Alfred Noyes : Wales
(d) TS Eliot : America

92 Which of the following pairs is incorrectly matched?
(a) The Daffodil Murderer : Siegfried Sassoon
(b) The Drowned Suns : Osbert Sitwell
(c) A Fool in the Forest : Richard Aldington
(d) Look, Stranger : WH Auden

93 Which of the following pairs is correctly matched?
(a) Dylan Thomas : 18 Poems
(b) Doris May Lessing : Children of Violence
(c) Charles Tomlinson : The Necklace
(d) Teg Hughes : Laughing Hyena

94 Which of the following pairs is correctly matched?
(a) Ted Hughes : The Hawk in the Rain
(b) Sylvia Plath : The Great Hunger
(c) Philip Larkin : The Bell Jar
(d) Patrick Kavanagh : The Less Deceived

95 Which of the following pairs is correctly matched?
(a) Philip Larkin : Church Going
(b) Ted Hughes : Under the Milkwood
(c) Thomas Black Burn : Hawk Roosting
(d) Dylan Thomas : A Smell of Burning

Directions (Q. Nos. 96-100) *In the questions given below are two statements labelled as Assertion (A) and Reason (R). In the context of the two statements, which one of the following is correct?*

Codes
(a) A is true, but R is false
(b) A is false, but R is true
(c) Both A and R are true, but R is not the correct explanation of A
(d) Both A and R are true and R is the correct explanation of A

96 **Assertion** (A) The Pylon poets first translated England's industrial landscape into poetry.
Reason (R) It is characteristic of the group's imagery and reflects the political and social concerns of its members.

97 **Assertion** (A) The aim of the Georgian poets was to revive public interest in poetry and inaugurate a new poetic age.
Reason (R) They did not write, verse which was lueid in style, deft and delicate.

98 **Assertion** (A) The Oxford group of young, intellectual English poets were not influenced by modernism.
Reason (R) They attempted to bring new forms and techniques in English poetry.

99 **Assertion** (A) Dylan Marlais Thomas was a difficult Poet. He is the poet of the learned like TS Eliot.
Reason (R) His poetry is full of metaphor's, symbolic imagery, Biblical, Freudian or folk image.

100 **Assertion** (A) Barrow poets read their verse in pubs and public places.
Reason (R) They did so because a licence was refused during the festival of Britain.

101 Which of the following works in chronological order as per their publication?
(a) The Canticle of the Rose, Interludes and Poems, Love Poems
(b) Interludes and Poems, Love Poems, The Canticle of the Rose
(c) Love Poems, The Canticle of the Rose, Interludes Poems
(d) Love Poems, Interludes and Poems, The Canticle of the Rose

102 Which of the following in chronological order as per the birth of the author given below?
(a) Walter de La Mare, T S Eliot, W B Yeats
(b) W B Yeats, T S Eliot, Walter de La Mare
(c) Walter de La Mare, W B Yeats, T S Eliot
(d) W B Yeats, Walter de La Mare, T S Eliot

103 Arrange the sections of The Waste Land in the order in which they appear in the poem.
1. The Fire Sermon
2. Death by Water
3. A Game of Chess
4. What the Thunder Said
5. The Burial of the Dead

Codes
(a) 3, 2, 1, 5, 4 (b) 5, 1, 2, 3, 4
(c) 5, 2, 3, 1, 4 (d) 5, 3, 1, 2, 4

104 Which of the following contemporary poems are in correct chronological order?
(a) The Bloom of Candles, Some Men are Brothers, Sun at Midnight, Tropical Ice
(b) Tropical Ice, Sun at Midnight, Some Men are Brothers, The Bloom of Candles
(c) Some Men are Brothers, Tropical Ice, The Bloom of Candles, Sun at Midnight
(d) Sun at Midnight, The Bloom of Candles, Tropical Ice, Some Men are Brothers

105 Which of the following American poets are in correct chronological order?

(a) Sylvia Plath, Robert Frost, Walt Whitman, HW Long Fellow
(b) Robert Frost, HW Long Fellow, Sylvia Plath, Walt Whitman
(c) HW Long Fellow, Walt Whitman, Robert Frost, Sylvia Plath
(d) Walt Whitman, HW Long Fellow, Sylvia Plath, Robert Frost

106 Consider the following statements about Imagism.

1. Was a movemnet in modernist Anglo-American Poetry that originated in 1912.
2. Advocated the use of free verse, common speech patterns and clarity of expression.
3. Used Words that did not contributed the presentation.
4. Did not use direct treatment of the 'thing' whether subjective or objective.

Which of the statements given above are correct?

(a) 1 and 2 (b) 1 and 4
(c) 3 and 2 (d) 3 and 4

107 Consider the following statements about Yeats contribution to Irish Literary Rivival was

1. formation of the new Irish sense of natinal identity.
2. did not help to banish the then prevailing sense that British culture was superior to Irish.
3. did not depict the rural Ireland of fable and myth.
4. drew directly upon the legends, of Pre-Christian Ireland

Which of the statements given above are correct?

(a) 1 and 2 (b) 1 and 4
(c) 3 and 2 (d) 3 and 4

108 Consider the following statements about the Love Song of Alfred Prufrock ....

1. is written by Lascelles Abercrombie.
2. was published in 1917.
3. Examined the fragmented and for mented psyche of the modern man.
4. is romantic in tone.

Which of the statements given above are correct?

(a) 1 and 2 (b) 1 and 4 (c) 3 and 2 (d) 3 and 4

109 What is common to all of these? Identify the correct description below.

The Burival of the Dead
A Game of Chess
Fire Sermon
Death by Water

Codes

(a) All of these are section of the poem The Waste Land by TS Eliot
(b) All of these are poems by Lascelles Abercrombire
(c) All of these are poems written by TE Hulme
(d) All of these are works by Osbert Sitwell

110 Consider the following statements.

1. Philip Larkin was born is 1922.
2. Dylan Thomas died in 1985.
3. Osborne wrote 'Collected Poems'.

Which of the statements given above is/are incorrect?

(a) 1 and 2 (b) 1, 2 and 3
(c) 2 and 3 (d) Only 3

111 Consider the following statements.

1. Philip Larkin wrote 'The Less Deceived'.
2. Doris Lessing was born in 1919.
3. William Golding died in 1930.

Which of the statements given above is/are incorrect?

(a) Only 1 (b) Only 3
(c) 2 and 3 (d) Only 2

112 Consider the following statements about the Barrow poets.

1. During the festival of Britain, the Barrow poets hoped to hawk their verse in the streets.
2. When the licence was refused, they began to read in pubs and public places.
3. This movement not only succeeded, but also encouraged the idea of bringing poetry to the masses.
4. All the great poets of twenties joined this movement.

Which of the statements given above is/are incorrect?

(a) 1 and 2 (b) 2 and 3
(c) 1 and 3 (d) Only 4

113 Philip Larkin's 'The Whitsun Weddings'

1. describes a long train journey.
2. establishes a 'we' voice of collective outlook.
3. traces the disfigurement of a sunny landscape on an advertising poster.
4. give an account of a drug pusher.

The correct combination according to the code is

(a) 1 and 3 (b) 1 and 2 (c) 1 and 4 (d) 2 and 3

114 Consider the following statements for HW Long fellow.

1. He began to publish poetry at the age of 13.
2. He is known as children's poet
3. He wrote the elegy 'O captain, My captain'.
4. He was called the 'Pride of America'.

Which of the above statements is correct For HW Long Fellow?

(a) 1 and 2 (b) 2 and 3 (c) 3 and 4 (d) 2 and 4

115 Consider the following poems by American poets.
1. The Psalm of Life
2. A Woman Waits for Me
3. A Witness Tree
4. Stopping by Woods on a Snowy Evening

Which of the above belong to Robert Frost?

(a) 1 and 2 (b) 2 and 3 (c) 3 and 4 (d) 1 and 4

116 Match the following.

List I (Works)	List II (Authors)
A. Early One Morning	1. T S Eliot
B. Collected Shorter Poems	2. Walter de La Mare
C. The Second Coming	3. W H Auden
D. Four Quartets	4. W B Yeats

Codes

	A	B	C	D		A	B	C	D
(a)	1	2	3	4	(b)	4	3	2	1
(c)	2	3	4	1	(d)	4	2	3	1

117 Match the following.

List I	List II
A. T S Eliot	1. The Orators
B. W H Auden	2. Peacock Pie
C. W B Yeats	3. The Waste Land
D. Walter De La Mare	4. Swan

Codes

	A	B	C	D		A	B	C	D
(a)	1	2	3	4	(b)	3	1	4	2
(c)	4	3	2	1	(d)	1	3	4	2

118 Match the following.

List I (Authors)	List II (Works)
A. Edith Sitwell	1. Biography
B. Osbert Sitwell	2. Wheels
C. Alfred Noyes	3. England Reclaimed
D. John Masefield	4. The Waggon

Codes

	A	B	C	D		A	B	C	D
(a)	2	3	4	1	(b)	1	3	4	2
(c)	1	2	3	4	(d)	4	3	2	1

119 Match the following.

List I (Phrases from Poems)	List II (Titles of Poems)
A. 'Sound of stick upon the floor'	1. 'Byzantium'
B. 'Hade's Bobbin bound in mummy cloth'	2. 'Sailing to Byzantium'
C. 'With beauty like a tightened bow'	3. 'Coole and Ballylee, 1931'
D. 'A tattered coat upon a stick'	4. 'No Second Troy'

Codes

	A	B	C	D		A	B	C	D
(a)	4	1	3	2	(b)	3	2	1	4
(c)	4	3	2	1	(d)	3	1	4	2

120 Match the following modern age poets with their poems.

Modern Age Poet	Poem
1. Osbert Sitwell	A. The Winstonburg Line
2. Richard Aldington	B. War and Love
3. Stephen Spender	C. Vienna
4. Cecil Day Lewis	D. Beechen Vigil

Codes

(a) 1-A, 2-B, 3-C, 4-D (b) 1-D, 2-C, 3-B, 4-A
(c) 1-B, 2-D, 3-A, 4-C (d) 1-C, 2-A, 3-D, 4-B

121 Match the following poems with their contemporary poets.

Poem	Contemporary Age Poet
A. A Lost Season	1. Ted Hughs
B. Modern Folk Ballad	2. Thomas William Gunn
C. My Sad Captains	3. Charles Stanley Causley
D. The Hawk in the Rain	4. Roy Broad Bent Fuller

Codes

(a) 1-A, 2-B, 3-C, 4-D (b) 1-D, 2-C, 3-B, 4-A
(c) 1-B, 2-D, 3-A, 4-C (d) 1-C, 2-A, 3-D, 4-B

122 Match the following American poets with their poems.

American Poet	Poem
A. WH Longfellow	1. Walden
B. Walt Whitman	2. Children and Children's Hour
C. Henry David Thoreau	3. Fountain
D. James Russel Lowell	4. Children of Adam

Codes

(a) 1-A, 2-B, 3-C, 4-D (b) 1-D, 2-C, 3-B, 4-A
(c) 1-B, 2-D, 3-A, 4-C (d) 1-C, 2-A, 3-D, 4-B

123 In the following series, which set of authors and their works is correctly matched?

(a) Samuel Butler-Brave New World; Aldous Huxley-Ulysses; James Joyce-The Shadowy Waters; WB Yeats Odyssey

(b) Samuel Butler-Odyssey; Aldous Huxley-Brave New World; James Joyce-Ulysses; WB Yeats-The Shadowy Waters

(c) Samuel Butler-Ulysses, Aldous Huxley-The Shadowy Waters; James Joyce-Odyssey, WB Yeats-Brave New World

(d) Samuel Butler-The Shadowy Waters; Aldous Huxley-Odyssey; James Joyce-Brave New World; WB Yeats-Odyssey

124 In the given series, which one has all the poems matched correctly with their contemporary age poets?

(a) A Drunk Man Looks at the Thistle-Hugh Mac Diarmid, Annus Mirabilis- Philip Larkin, His wife's Poems-Keidrych Rhys, Under Milk Wood-Dylan Marlais Thomas

(b) A Drunk Man Looks at the Thistle-Philip Larkin, Annur Mirabilis-Keidrych Rhys, His Wife's Poems-Dylan Marlais Thomas, Under Milk Wood-Hugh Mac Diarmid.

(c) A Drunk Man Looks at the Thistle-Keidrych Rhys Annus Mirabilis-Dylan Marlais Thomas, His Wife's Poems-Hugh Mac Diarmid, Under Milk Wood-Philip Larkin.
(d) A Drunk Man Looks at the Thistle-Dylan Marlais Thomas, Annus Mirabilis-Hugh Mac Diarmid, His Wife's Poems-Philip Larkin, Under Milk Wood-Keidrych Rhys.

125 In the given series, which one has all the American poets matched correctly with their poems.
(a) Robert Frost-Ballads of Lost Heaven, Sylvia Plath-Aunt Jennifer's Tigers, William Bliss Carmen-A Mosque of Mercy, Adrienne Rich-Mirror
(b) Robert Frost-Aunt Jennifer's Tigers, Sylvia Plath-A Mosque of Mercy, William Bliss Carmen Mirror, Adriene Rich-Ballads of Lost Heaven
(c) Robert Frost-A Mosque of Mercy, Sylvia Plath Mirror, William Bliss Carmen-Ballads of Lost Heaven, Adrienne Rich-Aunt Jennifer's Tigers
(d) Robert Frost-Mirror, Sylvia Plath-Ballads of Lost Heaven, William Bliss Carmen-Aunt Jennifer's Tigers, Adrienne Rich-A Mosque of Mercy

126 Which famous elegy closes with the following lines?
"In the deserts of the heart
let the healing fountain start
In the prison of his days
Teach the free man how to praise"
(a) In Memoriam
(b) Thyrsis
(c) In Memory of WB Yeats
(d) Verses on the Death of TS eliot

127 "Things fall apart; the centre cannot hold". These are the opening lines of
(a) The Second Coming (b) Vacilation
(c) The Hound of Heaven (d) None of these

128 A Shudder in the loins engenders there the broken wall, "the burning root and tower and Agamennon dead".
This extract have been taken from Yeats
(a) The Tower (b) Leda and the Swan
(c) The Second Coming (d) None of these

129 "Consume my hear away; sick with desire And fastened to a dying animal. It knows not what it is; and gather me. Into the artifice of elirnity". These are the concluding lines of Yeats poem
(a) Lapis Lauli (b) Sailing to Byzantium
(c) The Hound of Heaven (d) None of these

130 The line 'moments of unageing intellect' occurs in Yeat's
(a) Byzantium
(b) Among School Children
(c) Sailing to Byzantium
(d) The Circus Animals Desertion

131 Who among the following used the expression, "We were the last romantic in his work"?
(a) TS Eliot (b) WB Yeats
(c) WH Auden (d) Lady Gregory

132 Who commented on W B Yeats as 'a foreign mind"?
(a) WH Auden (b) Walter de La Mare
(c) T S Eliot (d) None of these

133 Identify the poem that opens with the lines
I walk through the long schoolroom questioning
A kind old nun in a white hood replies;
The children learn to cipher and to sing
(a) Among the School Children
(b) Among School Children
(c) A Man Young and Old
(d) The Man Young and Old

134 "Come away, O human child!
To the waters and the wild
With a faery, hand in hand,
For the world's more full of weeping than you can understand."
Which of the following poets in which of his/her works has used the above lines?
(a) William Butler Yeats, The Collected Poems of WB Yeats
(b) Alfred Noyes, The Highwayman
(c) TS Eliot, Four Quartets
(d) WH Auden, Collected Poems

135 "Had I the heavens' embroidered cloths,
Enwrought with golden and silver light,
The blue and the dim and the dark cloths
Of night and light and the half light,
I would spread the cloths under your feet:
But I, being poor, have only my dreams;
I have spread my dreams under your feet;
Tread softly because you tread on my dreams."
Which of the following poets in which of his/her works has used in the above lines?
(a) William Butler Yeats, The Wind Among the Reeds:
(b) TS Eliot, The Waste Land
(c) W H Auden, The Age of Anxiety: A Baroque Eclogue
(d) Stephen Spender, poems by Stephen spender

136 "Faeries, come take me out of this dull world,
For I would ride with you upon the wind,
Run on the top of the dishevelled tide,
And dance upon the mountains like a flame."
Which of the following poets in which of his/her works has used the above lines?
(a) William Butler Yeats, The Land of Heart's Desire .
(b) TS Eliot, The Love Song of J Alfred Prufrock and Others
(c) Walter de la Mare, Rhymes and Verses: Collected Poems for Young People
(d) John Masefield' Dauber (A poem)

137 "One kiss, my bonny sweetheart; I'm after a prize tonight,
But I shall be back with the yellow gold before the morning light.
Yet if they press me sharply, and harry me through the day,
Then look for me by moonlight,
Watch for me by moonlight,
I'll come to thee by moonlight, though hell should bar the way."

Which of the following poets in which of his/her works has used the above lines?

(a) William Butler Yeats, The Collected Poems of WB Yeats
(b) Alfred Noyes, The Highwayman
(c) TS Eliot, Four Quartets
(d) WH Auden, Collected Poems

138 "For last year's words belong to last year's language
And next year's words await another voice."
Which of the following poets in which of his/her works has used the above lines?

(a) William Butler Yeats, The Collected Poems of WB Yeats
(b) Alfred Noyes, The Highwayman
(c) TS Eliot, Four Quartets .
(d) WH Auden, Collected Poems

139 "April is the cruelest month, breeding
lilacs out of the dead land, mixing
memory and desire, stirring
dull roots with spring rain."

Which of the following poets in which of his/her works has used the above lines?

(a) William Butler Yeats, The Wind Among the Reeds
(b) TS Eliot, The Waste Land
(c) W H Auden, The Age of Anxiety: A Baroque Eclogue
(d) Stephen Spender, poems by stephen Spender

140 "For I have known them all already, known them all
Have known the evenings, mornings, afternoons,
I have measured out my life with coffee spoons."

Which of the following poets in which of his/her works has used the above lines?

(a) William Butler Yeats, The Land of Heart's Desire
(b) TS Eliot, The Love Song of J Alfred Prufrock and Others.
(c) Walter de La Mare, Rhymes and Verses: Collected Poems for Young People
(d) John Masefield' Dauber (A poem)

141 "Between the idea
And the reality
Between the motion
And the act
Falls the Shadow"

Which of the following poets in which of his/her works has used the above lines?

(a) TS Eliot, The Hollow Men .
(b) Dylan Thomas, In Country Sleep, and Other Poems
(c) Ted Hughes, Season Songs
(d) Philip Larkin, High Windows

142 "He was my North, my South, my East and West,
My working week and my Sunday rest,
My noon, my midnight, my talk, my song;
I thought that love would last forever: I was wrong."

Which of the following poets in which of his/her works has used the above lines?

(a) William Butler Yeats, The Collected Poems of WB Yeats
(b) Alfred Noyes, The Highwayman
(c) TS Eliot, Four Quartets
(d) WH Auden, Collected Poems .

143 "We would rather be ruined than changed
We would rather die in our dread
Than climb the cross of the moment
And let our illusions die."

Which of the following poets in which of his/her works has used the above lines?

(a) William Butler Yeats, The Wind Among the Reeds
(b) TS Eliot, The Waste Land
(c) W H Auden, The Age of Anxiety: A Baroque Eclogue
(d) Stephen Spender, poems by stephen spender

144 "Him I delight in accepts joy as joy;
He is richened by sorrow as a river by its bends"

Which of the following poets in which of his/her works has used the above lines?

(a) William Butler Yeats, The Wind Among the Reeds
(b) TS Eliot, The Waste Land
(c) W H Auden, The Age of Anxiety: A Baroque Eclogue
(d) Stephen Spender, poems by stephen Spender

145 "Hi! handsome hunting man
Fire your little gun.
Bang! Now the animal
is dead and dumb and done.
Nevermore to peep again, creep again, leap again,
Eat or sleep or drink again. Oh, what fun!"

Which of the following poets in which of his/her works has used the above lines?

(a) William Butler Yeats, The Land of Heart's Desire
(b) TS Eliot, The Love Song of J Alfred Prufrock and Others
(c) Walter de La Mare, Rhymes and Verses: Collected Poems for Young People
(d) John Masefield' Dauber (A poem)

146 "It's hard not to be able. There, look there!/ I cannot get the movement nor the light;/Sometimes it almost makes a man despair/To try and try and never get it right./Oh, if I could -oh, if I only might/I wouldn't mind what hells I,d have to pass/Not if the whole world called me fool and ass."

Which of the following poets in which of his/her works has used the above lines?
(a) William Butler Yeats, The Land of Heart's Desire
(b) TS Eliot, The Love Song of J Alfred Prufrock and Others
(c) Walter de la Mare, Rhymes and Verses: Collected Poems for Young People
(d) John Masefield' Dauber (A poem) .

147 "Do not go gentle into that good night.
Rage, rage against the dying of the light."
Which of the following poets in which of his/her works has used the above lines?
(a) TS Eliot, The Hollow Men
(b) Dylan Thomas, In Country Sleep, and Other Poems
(c) Ted Hughes, Season Songs
(d) Philip Larkin, High Windows

148 "He could not stand. It was not
That he could not thrive, he was born
With everything but the will
That can be deformed, just like a limb.
Death was more interesting to him.
Life could not get his attention."
Which of the following poets in which of his/her works has used the above lines?
(a) T.S. Eliot, The Hollow Men
(b) Dylan Thomas, In Country Sleep, and Other Poems
(c) Ted Hughes, Season Songs
(d) Philip Larkin, High Windows

149 "Nobody wanted your dance,
Nobody wanted your strange glitter, your floundering
Drowning life and your effort to save yourself,
Treading water, dancing the dark turmoil,
Looking for something to give."
Which of the following poets in which of his/her works has used the above lines?
(a) Ted Hughes, Birthday Letters .
(b) Philip Larkin, The Whitsun Weddings
(c) Henry Wadsworth Longfellow, Ballads and Other Poems
(d) Walt Whitman, Leaves of Grass

150 "They fuck you up, your mum and dad.
They may not mean to, but they do."
Which of the following poets in which of his/her works has used the above lines?
(a) TS Eliot, The Hollow Men
(b) Dylan Thomas, In Country Sleep, and Other Poems
(c) Ted Hughes, Season Songs
(d) Philip Larkin, High Windows

151 "Loneliness clarifies. Here silence stands
Like heat. Here leaves unnoticed thicken,
Hidden weeds flower, neglected waters quicken,
Luminously-peopled air ascends;
And past the poppies bluish neutral distance
Ends the land suddenly beyond a beach
Of shapes and shingle. Here is unfenced existence:
Facing the sun, untalkative, out of reach."
Which of the following poets in which of his/her works has used the above lines?
(a) Ted Hughes, Birthday Letters
(b) Philip Larkin, The Whitsun Weddings
(c) Henry Wadsworth Longfellow, Ballads and Other Poems
(d) Walt Whitman, Leaves of Grass

152 "Morning, noon & bloody night,
Seven sodding days a week,
I slave at filthy WORK, that might
Be done by any book-drunk freak.
This goes on until I kick the bucket.
FUCK IT FUCK IT FUCK IT FUCK IT"
Which of the following poets in which of his/her works has used the above lines?
(a) Philip Larkin, Philip Larkin: Letters to Monica
(b) Robert Frost, Stopping by Woods on a Snowy Evening
(c) Henry Wadsworth Longfellow, Ballads and Other Poem
(d) Walt Whitman, Leaves of Grass

153 "Be still, sad heart! and cease repining;
Behind the clouds is the sun still shining;
Thy fate is the common fate of all,
Into each life some rain must fall"
Which of the following poets in which of his/her works has used the above lines?
(a) Ted Hughes, Birthday Letters
(b) Philip Larkin, The Whitsun Weddings
(c) Henry Wadsworth Longfellow, Ballads and Other Poems.
(d) Walt Whitman, Leaves of Grass

154 "I celebrate myself, and sing myself,
And what I assume you shall assume,
For every atom belonging to me as good belongs to you."
Which of the following poets in which of his/her works has used the above lines?
(a) Ted Hughes, Birthday Letters
(b) Philip Larkin, The Whitsun Weddings
(c) Henry Wadsworth Longfellow, Ballads and Other Poems
(d) Walt Whitman, Leaves of Grass

155 "These woods are lovely, dark and deep,
But I have promises to keep,
And miles to go before I sleep,
And miles to go before I sleep."
Which of the following poets in which of his/her works has used the above lines?
(a) Philip Larkin, Philip Larkin: Letters to Monica
(b) Robert Frost, Stopping by Woods on a Snowy Evening
(c) Henry Wadsworth Longfellow, Ballads and Other Poems
(d) Walt Whitman, Leaves of Grass On the basis of reading of the following poem, answer the questions that follow by choosing the correct option.

Directions (Q. Nos. 156-160) *On the basis of given extract below answer the following questions*

I Build Walls
I build walls:
Walls that protect,
Walls that shield, .
Walls that say I shall not yield
Or reveal
Who I am or how I feel.
I build walls:
Walls that hide,
Walls that cover what's inside,
Walls that stare or smile or look away,
Silent lies,
Walls that even block my eyes
From the tears I might have cried.
I build walls:
Walls that never let me
Truly touch
Those I love so very much.
Walls that need to fall!
Walls meant to be fortresses

156 The poet builds walls because they
(a) Protect him from inclement weather
(b) Don't let any intruder come in
(c) Define the boundary line of his house
(d) Help him in hiding his identity and feelings

157 The walls that the poet makes are made of
(a) Bricks and cement
(b) Green hedge
(c) Wire
(d) Barriers of his own emotions

158 The line that shows that the poet doesn't always think that walls are good is
(a) Walls that say "I shall not yield"
(b) Walls that stare or smile
(c) Walls that need to fall!
(d) Walls that cover what is inside

159 159. The line "Walls that never let me / truly touch / those that I love so very much" means these walls don't let him
(a) Meet his near and dear ones
(b) Express his feelings to his loved ones
(c) Be in touch with his close relatives
(d) Allow his loved ones to come to him

160 The poetic device used for walls in this poem is
(a) Simile (b) Metaphor
(c) Personification (d) Alliteration

PREVIOUS YEARS' QUESTIONS

December 2018

1 This poet was of the Auden generation and was only briefly a member of the communist party. In his poem, 'The Pylons', he averred that the Pylons are "Bare like nude giant girls that have no secrets." This prompted the label, Pylon poets, for the new generation of poets who were happy to use the gas works or pistons of a steam-engine as poetic imagery (Name this poet)
(a) Cecil Day-Lewis (b) Christopher Isherwood
(c) Stephen Spender (d) Louis MacNeice

2 Identify the fireside poets of the US.
(a) William Cullen Byant, HW Longfellow, Oliver Wendell Holmes.
(b) TS Eliot, Wallace Stevens, William Carlos Williams.
(c) Marianne Moore, Elizabeth Bishop, Anne Seaton
(d) Anny Lowell, Emily Dickinson, Phillis Wheatley

3 The following lines are WB Yeats' metaphor for an old man: A tattered coat upon a stick, unless soul clap its hand and sing and louder sing for every tatter is its mortal dress
Here, the aged man is .... , and his 'soul ..... is its mortal dress', is ....
(a) Point Counter Point (b) Tenor, Vehicle
(c) Analogy Analogue (d) Venicle, Tensor

Directions (Q. Nos. 4-7) *Read the following passage and asnwer the questions:*

I have carried the manuscript of these translations about with me for days, reading it in railway trains, or an the top of omnibuses and in restaurants, and I have often had to close it lest some stranger would see how much it moved me. These lyrics-which are in the original, my .... (Indian friends) tell me, full of subtlety of rhythm, of untranslatable delicacies of colour, of material invention-display in though a world I have dreamed of all my life long. The work of a supreme culture, they yet appear as much a growth of the common soil as the grass and the rushes. A tradition, where poetry and religion are the same thing, has passed through the centuries, gathering from learned and unlearned metaphor and emotion, and carried back again to the multitude the thought of the scholar and the noble. If the civilisation of Bengal remains unbroken, if that common mind which-as one divines-runs through all, is not, as with us, broken into a dozen minds that know nothing of each other, something even of what is most subtle in these verses will have come, in a few generations, to the beggar on the roads.

—WB Yeats, from Introduction to Rabindranath Tagore's Gitanjali

4 In this passage, Yeats praises Indian culture primarily because it
(a) is accessible to Westernes though it is rooted in a different religious tradition
(b) has been flexible enough to survive a transition into the modern world
(c) embodies values and gives rise to art that can be shared by people of all classes
(d) reflects a marvellous eclecticism in drawing from many disparate cultures

5 The title of Dylan Thomas's Deaths and Entrances was taken from
(a) William Shakespeare's Macbeth
(b) John Donne's 'Death's Duell'
(c) Rudyard Kipling's 'A Death-Bed'
(d) TS Eliot's Murder in the Cathedral

6 What type of writing Walter Pater define as "the special and opportune art of the modern world"?
(a) The lyric
(b) Comic drama
(c) The novel
(d) Nonfication prose

7 Which post war British poet ends a poem with the line, "get stewed: books are a load of crap"?
(a) Philip Larkin
(b) Ted Hughes
(c) Thom Gunn
(d) Craig Raine

8 The titular figure of Federico Garcia Lorca's elegy "Lament for lgnacio Sanchez Mejias" was
(a) a revolutionary who was associated with Che Guevara
(b) a popular priest and poet
(c) a spy who helped the revolutionaries during the Spanish Civil War
(d) a popular matador and writer

9 What comes 'after great pain' in the famous Emily Dickinson poem?
(a) The letting go
(b) A concrete simplicity
(c) Substantial light
(d) A formal feeling

10 Which of the following poems is quoted as the epigraphy to A Raisin in the Sun by Lorraine Hansberry?
(a) "The Negro Speaks of Rivers"
(b) "Harlem (A Dream Deferred)"
(c) "The Big Sea"
(d) "I, too, Sing America"

July 2018

11 Of whom did WB Yeats say that "We were the last Romantics"?
(a) The Pre-Raphaelite Brotherhood
(b) The Imagiste poets
(c) His Friends in the Irish Literary Revival
(d) Himself and his lady love, Maud Gonne

12 Where, according to T. S. Eliot, are we likely to find "not only the best, but the most individual parts of a poet's work"?
(a) in the poet's juvenilia or rejected drafts
(b) in the best anthologies and scrap-books
(c) in those parts where the dead poets their immortality
(d) in those parts where the living poets depart from their ancestors

13 In 'Gerontion" T S Eliot says
"......... has many cunning passages, contrived corridors/And issues, deceives with whispering ambitions,/ Guides us by vanities"
What is Eliot's Subject
(a) History (b) Politics (c) State (d) Religion

14 Match the following opening lines with their respective titles.

A.	"I leant upon a coppice gate"	1. "Thirteen Blackbirds"
B.	"A Sudden blow the great wings beating still"	2. "Sympathy"
C.	"Among twenty snowy mountains"	3. "The Darkling Thrusts
D.	"I know what the caged bird feels, alas"	4. "Leda and the Swan"

Codes

	A	B	C	D		A	B	C	D
(a)	4	3	2	1	(b)	3	4	1	2
(c)	2	1	3	4	(d)	1	2	4	3

15 Philip Larkin's 'Sas Steps' notices "The way the moon dashes through clouds that blow Loosely as cannon-smoke to stand apart..."
(a) Coleridge's "Dejection : An Ode"
(b) The moonlit scenes in A Midsummer Night's Dream
(c) Philip Sidney's Astrophel and Stella
(d) TS Eliot's Morning at the Window"

November 2017

16 Which of the following poems by WB Yeats repudiates the sensual world in favour of "the artifice of eternity"?
(a) "Under Ben Bulben" (b) "Among School Children"
(c) "Sailing to Byzantium" (d) "After Long Silence"

17 Which of the following images is NOT part of WH Auden's poem "In Memory of W. B. Yeats"?
(a) Mercury sinking in the mouth of the dying day
(b) Wolves running through evergreen forests
(c) Silence invading the suburbs
(d) Memory scattering like beads

18 In which play by Eugene Ionesco do you find the grotesque image of the leg of a corpse thrusting onto the stage, and, which begins to grow larger as the play progresses in a menacing manner?
(a) The Bald Soprano
(b) Amede or How to Get Rid of it
(c) Exit the King
(d) The Lesson

19 "You are your words. Your listeners see
Written on your face the poems they hear
Like letters carved in a tree's bark
The sight and sounds of solitudes endured"
These are lines from a poem by .... on the death of ....
(a) TS Eliot, Robert Frost
(b) Siegfried Sassoon; Wilfred Owen
(c) Stephen Spender; WH Auden
(d) Dylan Thomas; Robert Bridges

January 2017

20 In "Tradition and the Individual Talent" TS Eliot uses the analogy of the catalyst to elucidate his theory of impersonal poetry. He cites the example of a filament of platinum and, in the poetic process this is equivalent to
(a) the language of the poet (b) the mind of the poet
(c) the soul of the poet (d) the life of the poet

21 Which of the following images does not figure in Auden's "Musee des Beaux Arts"?
(a) a boy falling out of the sky
(b) children ... skating on a pond at the edge of wood
(c) ranches of isolation and the busy griefs
(d) the dogs go on with their doggy life

22 "Most blameless is he, centered in the sphere of common duties, decent not to fail in offices of tenderness..."
In these lines from 'Ulysses', what does Ulysses suggest about Telemachus?
(a) He shows heroic qualities
(b) He is patient and selfless
(c) He is very much like his father
(d) He may be too tender-hearted to be king

July 2016.

23 Who among the following is not an imagist?
(a) Ezra Pound (b) WB Yeats
(c) Amy Lowell (d) TE Hulme

24 T. S. Eliot found spiritual support in
(a) Christianity (b) Hinduism (c) Buddhism (d) Judaism

25 In 'Tradition and Individual Talent", according to TS Eliot, the term 'Traditional' usually means
(a) Something positive (b) Something negative
(c) Something historical (d) Something old

26 When was the English ban on James Joyce's Ulysses lifted?
(a) 1924 (b) 1945 (c) 1936 (d) 1962

27 In a poem in memory of Major Robert Gregory, Lady Gregory's son. WB Yeats mentions an Irish writer who had found his inspiration "In a most desolate stony place" that he came "Towards nightfall upon a race/ passionate and simple like his heart." Who is the writer?
(a) JM Barrie (b) JM Synge
(c) Isaac Bickerstaffe (d) Thomas More

28 In his poem "Whispers of Immortality" TS Eliot says that a dramatist "was much possessed by death/And saw the skull beneath the skin" and a poet "knew the anguish of the marrow. The ague of the skeleton "Who are the dramatist and the poet referred to by Eliot?
(a) Christopher Mariowe and Andrew Marvell
(b) John Webster and John Donne
(c) Seneca dnd Homet
(d) Thomas Kyd and Henry Vaughan

29 Which of the following poems by Philip Larkin is best described as a self-elegy, anticipating the poet's death?
(a) 'The Old Fools' (b) 'Aubade'
(c) 'Ambulances' (d) 'Faith Healing'

30 Emily Dickinson's use of open form or free verse is comparable to her contemporary American poet
(a) Anne Bradstreet (b) Robert Lowell
(c) Walt Whitman (d) Sylvia Plath

December 2015

31 Who among the war poets gained notoriety in 1917, when disenchanted with the way the war was being conducted he drafted his letter of 'wilful defiance of the military authority' which captured attention in the Houses of Commons and was forcibly admitted to the war hospital at Craiglockhart, primarily to avoid his being court-martialled?
(a) Rupert Brooke (b) Siegfried Sassoon
(c) Wilfred Owen (d) Issad Rosenberg

32 Who among the following critics discerned in the Shelleyan Lyric the signs 'of adolescence"?
(a) F R Leavis
(b) T S Eliot
(c) Cleanth Brooks
(d) IA Richards

June 2015

33 Who is the author of the collection *The Celtic Twilight*?
(a) JM Synge
(b) Sean O'Casey
(c) WB Yeats
(d) Lady Gregory

34 Which group of the following poets was called the Auden Group because they developed a style and viewpoint similar to what of WH Auden?
(a) Louis MacNiece, CD Lewis, Stephen Spender
(b) John Masefield, Edwin Muir, Normal Mc Caig
(c) MacDiarmid, GM Hopkins, Edwin Muir
(d) WH Davies, Robert Bridges, John Masefield

35 Dylan Thomas's famous poem 'Fern Hill,' is named after ....

(a) a countryside in Austria to which he paid occasional visits
(b) a childhood haunt of the poet's family in Devonshire
(c) the Welsh farmhouse where the poet spent summer holidays as a boy
(d) the Welsh Anglican church to which the young poet used to be taken by his mother

36 "That woman's days were spent
In ignorant good-will,
Her nights in argument
Until her voice grew shrill" (WB Yeats : Easter 1916')
Who is the poet referring to?

(a) Maud Gonne
(b) Lady Augusta Gregory
(c) Kathieen Pilcher
(d) Constance Gore-Booth Markievicz

37 "In the seventeenth century," writes TS Eliot in "The Metaphysical Poets," "a dissociation of sensibility set in, from which we have never recovered; and this dissociation, as is a natural, was aggravated by the influence of the two most powerful poets of the century, ... and ....

(a) Ben Jonnson and Abraham Cowley
(b) George Herbert and Henry Vaughan
(c) John Donne and Andrew Marvell
(d) John Milton and John Dryden

38 In his Introduction to *The Oxford Book of Twentieth-Century English Verse* (1973), Philip Larkin underlines the importance of a native tradition with ...... seen as the major poet of the Modern Period.

(a) William Butler Yeats (b) TS Eliot
(c) Thomas Hardy (d) DH Lawrence

December 2014

39 In which of the following works Yeats developed his theory of 'gyres'?

(a) 'A Vision' (b) 'The Secret Rose'
(c) 'John Sherman and Dhoya' (d) 'The Celtic Twilight'

40 Which of the following is not mentioned as part of the London locale in The *Waste Land*?

(a) St Magnus Martyr (b) King Arthur Street
(c) St Mary Woolnoth (d) Lower Thames Street

41 Who among the following is a working class poet?

(a) John Betjeman (b) Tony Harrison
(c) Thom Gunn (d) Robert Graves

42 And miles to go before I sleep is a line from a poem by

(a) Emily Dickinson (b) Walt Whitman
(c) Ralph Waldo Emerson (d) Robert Frost

43 What common link do you find among
"The Disquieting Muses" by Sylvia Plath
"The Starry Night" by Anne Sexton
"Mourning Picture" by Adrienne Rich and
"Musee des Beaux Arts" by W H Auden?

(a) They inspired paintings
(b) They are confessional poems
(c) They are all inspired by paintings
(d) They are all inspired by Van Gogh's paintings

June 2014

44 The greatness of a poet' Arnold says, "Lies in his powerful and beautiful application of ideas to life". But a critic pointed out it was "not a happy way of putting it, as if ideas were a lotion for the inflamed skin of suffering humanity". Who was this critic?

(a) T S Eliot
(b) F R Leavis
(c) David Lodge
(d) Allen Tate

45 Yeat's 'Sailing to Byzantium' is about

(a) Irish culture
(b) The art and culture of Byzantium in general
(c) Irish revolutionaries
(d) Regenerating the art and culture that existed in Byzantium

46 Which of the following is not true of Imagist poetry

(a) The poet spreads his language across the page as though language were sensation, to reproduce the mental effect of 'image'.
(b) The image is itself an instrument of vision or lens, as well as an expression of imagination.
(c) The imagist like a scientist learns from history and uses it and like a scientist does not deal in emotions.
(d) The new artist as scientist focuses vision through image as against the symbol which resorts to reduction to simplicity.

47 "A sudden blow the great wings beating still Above the staggering girl, her thighs caressed By the dark webs, her nap caught in his bill, He holds her helpless breast upon his breast Who is the author of the above lines?

(a) WB Yeats
(b) TS Eliot
(c) WH Auden
(d) DH Lawrence

48 "Consume my heart away, sick with desire And fastened to a dying animal."
The above lines are taken from

(a) Felix Randal
(b) Sailing to Byzantium
(c) Coole and the Ballylee, 1931
(d) The Second Coming

ANSWERS

Objective Questions

1. *(c)*	2. *(c)*	3. *(b)*	4. *(b)*	5. *(d)*	6. *(a)*	7. *(b)*	8. *(b)*	9. *(d)*	10. *(d)*
11. *(a)*	12. *(c)*	13. *(c)*	14. *(b)*	15. *(a)*	16. *(b)*	17. *(d)*	18. *(c)*	19. *(a)*	20. *(a)*
21. *(d)*	22. *(c)*	23. *(a)*	24. *(c)*	25. *(b)*	26. *(b)*	27. *(b)*	28. *(b)*	29. *(d)*	30. *(b)*
31. *(c)*	32. *(b)*	33. *(d)*	34. *(c)*	35. *(d)*	36. *(a)*	37. *(c)*	38. *(b)*	39. *(a)*	40. *(b)*
41. *(a)*	42. *(c)*	43. *(b)*	44. *(b)*	45. *(a)*	46. *(b)*	47. *(c)*	48. *(a)*	49. *(c)*	50. *(c)*
51. *(a)*	52. *(b)*	53. *(a)*	54. *(b)*	55. *(b)*	56. *(c)*	57. *(d)*	58. *(a)*	59. *(b)*	60. *(d)*
61. *(d)*	62. *(c)*	63. *(c)*	64. *(c)*	65. *(b)*	66. *(d)*	67. *(b)*	68. *(b)*	69. *(a)*	70. *(c)*
71. *(a)*	72. *(b)*	73. *(b)*	74. *(d)*	75. *(c)*	76. *(c)*	77. *(b)*	78. *(b)*	79. *(a)*	80. *(a)*
81. *(c)*	82. *(b)*	83. *(b)*	84. *(c)*	85. *(d)*	86. *(c)*	87. *(c)*	88. *(d)*	89. *(d)*	90. *(d)*
91. *(d)*	92. *(b)*	93. *(d)*	94. *(a)*	95. *(a)*	96. *(c)*	97. *(a)*	98. *(b)*	99. *(d)*	100. *(d)*
101. *(a)*	102. *(b)*	103. *(d)*	104. *(a)*	105. *(c)*	106. *(a)*	107. *(b)*	108. *(c)*	109. *(a)*	110. *(b)*
111. *(c)*	112. *(d)*	113. *(b)*	114. *(a)*	115. *(c)*	116. *(c)*	117. *(b)*	118. *(a)*	119. *(d)*	120. *(a)*
121. *(b)*	122. *(c)*	123. *(b)*	124. *(a)*	125. *(c)*	126. *(c)*	127. *(a)*	128. *(b)*	129. *(b)*	130. *(c)*
131. *(b)*	132. *(c)*	133. *(b)*	134. *(a)*	135. *(a)*	136. *(a)*	137. *(b)*	138. *(c)*	139. *(b)*	140. *(b)*
141. *(a)*	142. *(d)*	143. *(c)*	144. *(d)*	145. *(c)*	146. *(d)*	147. *(b)*	148. *(c)*	149. *(a)*	150. *(d)*
151. *(b)*	152. *(a)*	153. *(c)*	154. *(d)*	155. *(b)*	156. *(d)*	157. *(d)*	158. *(c)*	159. *(b)*	160. *(b)*

Previous Years' Questions

1. *(c)*	2. *(a)*	3. *(b)*	4. *(c)*	5. *(b)*	6. *(d)*	7. *(a)*	8. *(d)*	9. *(d)*	10. *(b)*
11. *(c)*	12. *(c)*	13. *(a)*	14. *(b)*	15. *(c)*	16. *(c)*	17. *(d)*	18. *(b)*	19. *(c)*	20. *(b)*
21. *(c)*	22. *(b)*	23. *(b)*	24. *(a)*	25. *(b)*	26. *(c)*	27. *(b)*	28. *(b)*	29. *(b)*	30. *(c)*
31. *(b)*	32. *(b)*	33. *(c)*	34. *(a)*	35. *(c)*	36. *(c)*	37. *(d)*	38. *(c)*	39. *(a)*	40. *(b)*
41. *(b)*	42. *(d)*	43. *(c)*	44. *(a)*	45. *(b)*	46. *(c)*	47. *(a)*	48. *(b)*		

Pre-Chaucerian to Elizabethan Age

The chapter deals with origin, growth and development of novel and short story. Pre-Chaucerian period refers to the time from the Norman conquests to the middle of the 14th century. The Literature of this period was affected by changes in social, religious and political fields.

Introduction to Fiction

The word 'Fiction' has been derived from Latin word *fictio* which means to form or act of making or moulding. However in literature, it is defined as "literature in the form of prose, especially novels and short stories that describe imaginary events, situations and people." A work of fiction implies act of creating an imaginary world which may or may not exist in reality. A fiction also narrates a story which aims at something bigger like commenting on something significant related to social, political or human related issues.

Fiction may be based on stories of actual historical events. Although fictitious characters are presented in a fictitious setting in stories and novels, they may have some resemblance to real life events and characters. Fiction can inspire us, intrigue us or engage us in new ideas. It can also help us to see ourselves and our world in new and interesting ways.

Objectives of Fiction

The function of fiction is to entertain, to experience new territories, to build hopes and inspire its readers. Literature in general and fiction in particular is capable enough to sweep our emotions and build empathy for others. Fiction gives its reader an experience beyond their daily lives. It provides them an insight into the life of characters, their manners, transformations and events related to them. It is also used to point out the flaws of a character, drawbacks of a society, race or nation in a manner that it does not touch the boundary of stricture or criticism.

In this Chapter

- *Introduction to Fiction*
- *Pre-Chaucerian Period*
- *Age of Chaucer*
- *The Age of Revival*
- *Elizabethan Age*

Types of Fiction

Fiction can be best expressed through the support of short-stories and novels

Short Story

A short story typically takes the form of a brief fictional work, usually written in prose. According to famous short story writer Edgar Allan Poe, a short story is a piece of writing that can be read in one sitting of about half an hour to about two hours. Short stories contain between 1,000 to 20,000 words and typically run not more than 25 to 30 pages. Short stories generally focus on one major plot or storyline with one or two characters.

Origin of Short Story

Though short story always existed as an informal oral tradition, but until the mass middle class literacy of the 19th century arrived in the West, there had been no publishing forum for a piece of short fiction. With the invention of magazine and periodical market to service the new reading public's desires and preferences, writers started their interest in writing short fictions, we can say that short stories developed as a genre in the 19th century. Edgar Allan Poe (1809-1849) is considered the father of the short story.

Growth of Short Story

He perfected the technique of writing short stories and wrote mostly suspense and horror stories. Herman Melville (1819-1891) was another famous short story writer, who established the bench mark for what the short story can attain and allow us to set standards by which all other great writers of this form can be measured. O Henry (1862-1910) was another famous short story writer. He wrote around 300 stories. His trade mark was 'Surprise Ending'.

Development of Short Story

Over the time, genres and writers all around the world have influenced the development of the short story. But the single greatest leap forward in the evolution of a short story in the 19th century is attributed to Anton Chekhov . As 19th century bled into the 20th century, the short story continued to flourish in every corner of the world driven by increasing rate of literacy, the growth of magazines and supplements. In India, modern short story made an appearance almost simultaneously in several languages including Bengali.

Novellas

A novella, in literature is a type of prose fiction which is shorter than full length novels and longer than short stories. It is a well-structured yet a short narrative often satiric or realistic in tone. It usually describes one incident or issue with one or two main characters and it takes place at a single location. Maid difference between novellas and novels is that novellas has fewer subplots, lengths is less and is mostly concerned with personal development of a character.

Origin of Novella

It originated in Italy during middle ages. The individual tales were often gathered into a collection along with anecdotes, legends and romantic tales.

Growth of Novella

Not until late 18th and early 19th century the novella was not developed into a literary genre. The Germans, who were the most active writers of novellas, structured them by precepts and rules and to be written in a realistic mode.

Development of Novella

In late 19th and 20th centuries, a great number of novellas were written by Russian authors. The most famous of them was Leo *Tolstoy's the Death of Ivan Ilyich* (1886) and Fyodar Dostoevsky's "*Notes from the Underground*' (1864). Modern American literature is abounds in novellas from prominent American authors. In late 1800, Henry James authored a number of novellas including '*In the Cage*', and '*The Turn of the Screw*'.

Novel

A novel is a work of fiction that contains over 50,000 words or 120 pages. Novels may have more than one plot or storyline and many well-developed characters. Novels can be as long as their authors want them to be. There is no upper limit to their length. Novel focusses on character development more than plot. It is the study of human psyche.

Origin of Novel

The ancestors of the novel were Elizabethan prose fiction and French heroic romances, which were long narratives about contemporary characters who behaved nobly. The novel came into awareness towards the end of the 1700s, due to growing middle class with more leisure time to read and sufficient money to buy books.

The early English novels were concerned with complex, middle class characters struggling with their morality and circumstances. *Pamela* a series of fictional letters written in 1741 by Samuel Richardson, is considered the first real English novel. Other early novelists include Daniel Defoe, who wrote *Robinson Crusoe* (1719) and *Moll Flanders*. (1722), although his characters were not fully realised enough to be considered full-fledged novels. Jane Austen is the author of *Pride and Prejudice* (1812), and *Emma* (1816), considered the best early English novels of manners.

Growth Development of Novel

The novel became established as the dominant literary form during the reign of Queen Victoria of England (1837-1901). Victorian novelists portrayed middle class, virtuous heroes responding to society and learning wrong from right through a series of human errors. Sir Walter Scott published three volume novels and ingeniously made them affordable to the general public by making them available for purchase in monthly installments. This marketing tactic led to the writing innovation of sub-climaxes as a way to leave readers wanting more each month. Notable Victorian authors include Charles Dickens, considered the best English Victorian novelist, who wrote *A Christmas Carol* (1843) and *Lewis Carroll*, (Charles Ludwidge Dodgson), who wrote *Alice's Adventures in Wonderland* (1864) and *Through the Looking Glass* (1871).

The characters in modern and contemporary novels question the existence of God, the supremacy of the human reason and the nature of reality. Novels from this era reflected great events such as The Great Depression, World War II Hiroshima, the Cold War and Communism.

Famous modern novels include *To The Lighthouse* (1927), by English novelist and essayist Virginia Woolf, *Ulysses* (1921), by Irish novelist and short story writer James Joyce, *All Quiet on the Western Front* (1929), the most famous World War I anti war novel by German novelist and journalist Erich Maria Remarque and *The Sound and the Fury* (1929), by American novelist and short writer William Faulkner, which depicts the decline of the South after the Civil War.

The post-modern novel includes magical realism, metafiction and the graphic novel. It asserts that man is ruled by a higher power and that the universe cannot be explained by reason alone. Modern novels exhibit a playfulness of language, less reliance on tradition values and experimentation with how time is conveyed in the story. Post-modern novels include *The Colour Purple* (1982) by Alice Walker, *In Cold Blood* (1966) by Truman Capote; the non-fiction novel *Roots* (1976) by Alex Haley, *Fear of Flying* (1973) by Erica Jong and the leading magical realist novel, *A Hundred Years of Solitude* (1967) by Gabriel Garcia Marquez.

Elements of Fiction

The Elements of Fiction are described as under

Character

Characters in fiction are people, animals or imaginary creatures that take part in the action of the story. Characters can be conveniently classified as major and minor, static and dynamic. A major character is an important figure at the center of the story's novel's action or theme. The major character is sometimes called a protagonist whose conflict with an antagonist may spark the story's conflict supporting the major character, are one or more secondary or minor characters whose function is partly to illuminate the major characters. Minor characters are often static or unchanging, they remain the same from the beginning of work to the end. Dynamic characters, on the other hand, exhibit some kind of change of attitude, purpose, behaviour, as the story progresses.

Plot

Plot is the action element in fiction it is the arrangement of events that make up a story or novel. Many fictional plots turn on a conflict or struggle between opposing forces, that is usually resolved by the end of the story or novel.

Setting

It is the physical and social context in which the action of a story / novel occurs. The major elements of setting are the time, the place and the social environment that frames the characters. These elements establish the world in which the characters act.

Point of View

It refers to who tells the story or novel and how it is told. The possible ways of telling a story / novel are many, and more than one point of view can be worked into a single story.

Theme

It is the central idea or meaning of a story or novel. Theme in fiction is rarely presented at all; it is abstracted from the details of character and action that compose the story. It provides a unifying point around which the plot, characters, setting, point of view, symbols and other elements of a story are organised.

Style

It is the way a writer chooses words (diction), arranges them in sentences and longer units of discourse (syntax) and exploits their significance.

Pre-Chaucerian Period

Anglo Norman Period (1066-1340)

The Anglo Norman refers to the period from the Norman conquests to the middle of the 14th century. During this period English began to be discarded in favour of French and Latin. During this age, non-fiction prose developed more in form of chronicles and history. No traces of fiction (novels and short stories) were found in this period. Some religious and didactic writings were also found during this period. Bible was also translated but into verse form not in prose form.

Another type of literature that was a combination of signified style of heroic prose and verse narrative also emerged during this period. Romance became a popular literary form, indicating the age to be a chivalric rather than heroic one. Breton Lais were developed by writers like Marie de France and Chretien de Troyes into the form known as romance.

This type of literature was called Medieval Romances. These romances contained stories from aristocratic class, some of the important romances can be classified into three main categories

The Matter of France

It is concerned with war and heroism. Stories from the Matter of France include works such as Otcuel, The Sege of Melayne, Roland and Vernagu, Sir Ferumbras, etc.

The Matter of Britain

The matter of Britain romances are the most famous category of romance. Stories are mainly based on the life of King Arthur and his Knights of the Round Table. Some famous Arthurian Romances include Robert Wace's Geste des Bretons (Deeds of the Britons), Sir Degare, Sir Orfeo, the Knight of the Cart, etc.

The Matter of Rome

It deals with classical stories, The Mighty Exploits of Alexander The Great, the Trojan War, the Siege of Thebes, Adventures of Aeneas, etc.

Age of Chaucer (1340-1400)

Age of Chaucer covers the period from 1340 to 1400. It was a period of transition and turbulance. During this age, remarkable changes occurred in social, religious and political fields. A curious modern note began to be apparent. A sharper spirit of criticism was prevalent and there was a keen interest in man's affairs. The office of the Pope was still extremely powerful and the church was a major social and cultural force of this period. 14th century witnessed 100 years of war with France, Black Death and Peasant's Revolt.

Literature in the Age of Chaucer

14th century witnessed a revival of alliterative poetry but prose writing and fiction were very limited like some tales written in prose in *Chaucer's Canterbury Tales.*

Geoffrey Chaucer (1343-1400)

Geoffrey Chaucer was born around 1343, in the wine merchant's street called Vintry. Chaucer primarily obtained his education at the court and learnt French and Latin.

In 1359, at the age of 19, Chaucer accompanied Lionel, the Duke of Clarence on a military campaign to France, where he was taken as prisoner. English King Edward III (1312-1377) paid a ransom for Chaucer's Release. Later on he was sent by Edward III on diplomatic missions to France, Genoa (Genova) and Florence. His travel exposed him to the work of authors such as Dante, Bocaccio and Froissant.

Literary Career of Works

Chaucer's first work, the Book *Of the Duchess* was written as a memorial poem at the death of Duchess of Lancaster. Though Chaucer is called the father of English poetry but his prologue to *Canterbury Tales* has been no less fiction containing description of so many characters in vivid hues and temperament and from different stratas of life. His prologue to the *Canterbury Tales* has been called The Prologue to Modern Fiction. Its vivid characterisation is one of the hallmarks of fiction. Chaucer's *Troilus and Criseyde* has been called a novel in verse. If he had written this poem in prose style, this poem would have been celebrated as the first English novel.

Chaucer is best known today for his work *The Canterbury Tales*. This is a collection of stories written in English mostly in verse but some are in prose. These stories are the account of different people who were mostly travellers. The Canterbury Tales contains so many miniature novels in itself.

Major Works

The Book of Duchess (1368-69), *The Parliament of Fowls* (1380s), *Troilus and Criseyde* (1378-85), *The Legend of Good Women* (1380s) and *the Canterbury Tales* (1386-95) are his major works. Chaucer's *The Legend of Good Women* is written in prose form and talks about a dream vision. It contains a prologue and nine stories. The prologue of the book cites reason behind Chaucer's collection of stories about good women. Chaucer was accused of defaming women by cupid, *The God of Love*.

He is therefore, instructed to write a book about women who have proved loving and faithful. The book recounts the stories of women from History and Myth who were martyrs to love such as Dido, Thisbe, Medea, Cleopetra, Ariadne, Lucrece, Phillis, Philomela, etc Considered to be an attack on anti-feminism, this book is Chaucer's unfinished work.

The other work of Chaucer *The Canterbury Tales* (1386-95) contains a collection of stories. Its prologue provides the characterisation of the pilgrims. In the general prologue, the narrator speaks in the first person, describing each of the pilgrims as they appeared to him. This account provides the reader with the thoughts as well as actions of the characters.

The two tales which are written in prose are the *Tale of Melibee* and the *Parson's Tale*. Both are written in prose style and focus is on characters. Dame Prudence, the wife of Melibee and in Parson's Tale. There is a long sermon by the Parson on the topic of repentance. Parson has been described as a genuine smart person and a good leader.

The Age of Revival

The Age of Revival started from AD 1400 and lasted till around AD 1550. It witnessed a wide range of political changes with the crowning of Henry V as the king in 1413. A few rebellions took place during this period namely the *Cade's Rebellion* (1450) and *Wars of the Roses* (1455-1485).

During this period, England also saw significant social and economical changes, such as weakening of the old feudal institutions and the strengthening of the landed aristocracy. The merchant class gradually expanded and the middle class slowly increased in strength. The renaissance took place during this period which promoted the rediscovery of the literature and art.

Literature in the Age of Revival

The period following the death of Chaucer was largely a barren period that did not produce any work of note. In the Age of Revival, the focus was more on classical learning. The interest in classical literature presented the growth of native literature.

Mythical romances continued to be translated from the French. Homilies and Saints legends and rhyming chronicles were still being manufactured. So, a lot of writers of this era translated the works of foreign authors in English. These were mainly works of fiction, religious texts and chronicles.

Sir Thomas Malory, William Carton and Thomas More were some of the few well known prose writers of this era.

Writers of Revival Age

Sir Thomas Malory (1415-1471)

Sir Thomas Malory was born around 1415, in an English family. By 1441, he became a Knight and in 1445, he became a member of Parliament for his country. He was leading a prestigious career before he was assailed by a number of charges.

Literary Career and Works

Sir Malory's major work was *The Whole Book of King Arthur* and his noble *Knights of the Round Table*. It was retitled Le Morte d' Arthur. Malory wrote this book during his second imprisonment in London's New Gate Prison and completed it in 1470. It retells the adventures of the Knights of the Round Table in chronological sequence from the birth of Arthur.

Malory's Le Morte d' Arthur

- *Le Morte d'Arthur* is a compilation of tales of romance about King Arthur and his Knights of the Round Table.
- It is the first major work of prose fiction in English.
- It was first published in 1485 by William Caxton.
- It is divided into twenty one books and follows the story from Uther Pendragon's rape of Igraine of Cornwall to the deaths of Launcelot and Guenevere.
- In *Le Morte d'Arthur*, Malory gives a new personality to some of the most striking characters to be found in Arthurian legends: King Arthur himself, the tragic hero; Launcelot, the noblest knight in the world, torn by a conflict of loyalties, which must result in his destruction of all he loves best; Sir Gawain, vengeful and treacherous but steadfast in loyalty to his king; Queen Guinevere, emblem of courtly courtesy, generous, but also fierce and jealous and many more characters.
- Malory's book skillfully blends many genres and narrative styles into a larger whole. Malory's style is fresh and lively and he stands close to the modern English.
- Malory's book inspired writers such as Alfred Tennyson who used it for his the *Idylls of the King* and TH White for his popular fantasy novel *The Once and Future King*.

William Caxton (1422-91)

William Caxton is known as the first English printer. He was born around 1422 in Kent. He was apprenticed to Robert Large, an influential merchant, at the age of 16.

Literary Career and Works

Caxton's first literary effort was his translation of books into English. His first translation was of the popular medieval romance of Troy, *The Recuyell of the Historyes of Troye*, from the French of Raoul le Fèvre, early in 1469.

In the early 1470s, Caxton spent some time in Cologne learning the art of printing. He returned to Bruges in 1472, where he and Colard Mansion, a Flemish calligrapher, set-up a press. His translation of *Fevre's Troy Book* was the first book he printed. His second book, *The Game and Playe of Chesse*, from the *Liber de ludo scacchorum* of Jacobus de Cessolis through the French of Jehan de Vignay, was finished in 1474 and printed soon after; the last book printed by Mansion and Caxton at Bruges was the *Quatre derrenieres choses*, an anonymous treatise usually known as *De quattuor novissimis.*

In 1476, Caxton returned to London and established a press at Westminster, the first printing press in England. The first dated book printed in England was Lord Rivers' translation (revised by Caxton) of *The Dictes or sayengis of the philosophres* (1477).

Literary and Linguistic Importance of Caxton

He was the first English Printer, who as a translator and publisher exerted an important influence on English Literature.

His main contribution is translation of books of other languages in English. He also used print to create new markets for novels and different kinds of writing. He brought the best of English medieval literature to a wide reading public including Chaucer's *Canterbury Tales* and Malory's *Morte d' Arthur, Sayengis of the Philosophres* and *The Book of the Knight in the Town*.

Caxton's direct involvement in the books he printed was not limited to publish his own translations. He was also an editor and publicist who adopted various methods to make the books he printed more attractive and accessible to his audience.

Many of the books he published contain his own prefaces or epilogues, explaining the content or the circumstances that led him to publish them. His own prose made important contribution to the English language, including the introduction of a large number of new words into Lexicon. In all he provided, the first usage of over 1,300 words including nouns such as concussion, fertification, voyager and servitude, etc. Inclusion of these new words certainly helped the future fiction writers in English.

Caxton's role as a printer marks him as a contributor to the English renaissance.

Thomas Moore (1478-1535)

Thomas Moore was an English lawyer, scholar, writer, member of Parliament and chancellor in the reign of Henry VIII. He was born in Milk Street, London on 7th February, 1478, as son of Sir John Moore, a prominent judge.

In 1492, Moore was transferred to Oxford, where he first started Greek studies. It was during this time; he wrote comedies and studied Greek and Latin literature.

Literary Career and Works

One of Moore's first works was an English translation of a Latin biography of the Italian humanist Pico Della Mirandola. It was printed by Wynkyn de Worde in 1510. He was found guilty of treason and was beheaded alongside Bishop Fisher on 6th July, 1535. Moore's final words on the scaffold were: "The King's good servant, but God's First."

Major Works

- Utopia (1516)
- Latin Poems (1518, 1520)
- The Confutation of Tyndale's Answer (1532, 1533)
- Apology (1533)
- The History of King Richard III (1513–1518)
- The Four Last Things (1522)
- Treatise Upon the Passion (1534)
- Treatise on the Blessed Body (1535)
- Instructions and Prayers (1535)
- De Tristitia Christi (1535)

Utopia

Thomas Moore's *Utopia* is his only fully developed work of fiction and as such has attracted literary scholars.

It was originally written in Latin in 1516. The Greek word Utopia translates as no place or nowhere, but in modern parlance, a Utopia has come to signify an ideal place (eu-topia). The book is a work of satire, indirectly criticising Europe's political corruption and religious hypocrisy. It is composed of 2 parts. The first book serves as an introduction and also a commentary on the second. The work depicts what its narrator, Raphael Hythloday, claimed to be an ideal human society, the island of Utopia.

Main features of society at Utopia are elimination of private property, universal labour, moderated pleasure and family as a microcosm of the state. It is the most perfect embodiment of humanist rational ideas.

Elizabethan Age (1550-1625)

Although the Elizabethan age is called The Golden Age of English poetry and drama, it should also be regarded as a glorious age of English prose, for. English prose was set on the track of glory by such great prose writers as Lyly, Greene, Lodge, Nashe, Deloney and Dekker with Sir Philip Sidney on the forefront.

At the outset, the Elizabethan prose turned to be translation of foreign books, especially the Italian Novella or Short romantic stories like *Palace of Pleasure* by William, *Tragical Discourses* by Geoffrey Fenton, *Petite Palace* by George Petite, an original writing published in 1576, was a collection of legendary tales.

The most interesting of the early Elizabethan prose fiction was *The Adventures of Master* FJ by George Gascoigne. It was published in 1573. Of the original prose writers of the Elizabethan age, John Lyly was the most famous. In 1578, the publication of his curious book, *Euphues, the Anatomy of wit* and its sequel entitled Euphues and his England in 1580 created a sensation. Although the books contained love stories with thin plots, they were intended to be read as books of conduct for aristocratic youths.

Through these two books Lyly introduced an inimitable and unique style known as *Euphuism* marks him as a pioneer. The beauty of the style lies in the perfect use of balanced phrases, intricate alliteration, classical allusion, and ornate epithets.

Sir Philip Sidney's, *Arcadia*, the first pastoral romance in English, was modeled on the Spanish pastoral Romance. Sidney's *Arcadia* may better be called a piece of poetry in the form of prose. However, it could exert great influence upon the drama of the age.

In imitation of Lyly, Robert Greene wrote short *Mamillia* (1583). *The Mirror of Modesty* novels and *The Card of Fancy* His most popular romance *Pandosto* provided Shakespeare with the plot of *The Winter's Tale*. *Pandosto* is marked by better narratives, shorter soliloquies and lesser Euphuism than other books. Greene modeled his *Menaphon* (1589) on Sidney's *Arcadia*. Perhaps the best of Greene's Euphuistic romance is *To His Love* published in 1589.

Thomas Lodge became famous for his euphuistic romance Rosalinde, the source of Shakespeare's *As You Like It*. Although Lodge imitated Greene's style of romantic tale, he surpassed his master by introducing masculine material borrowed from Chaucer.

Thomas Dekker was famous for his realistic portrayal of contemporary life. His prose works include *Bellman of London; Lantern and Candlelight; The Seven Deadly Sins of London; News from Hell brought by the Devil's Carrier*, all published between 1606 and 1608. We should note that Dekker's characters are all idealised vagabonds.

Thomas Nashe should be regarded as the first writer of what is called travelogue for his famous book. The *Unfortunate Traveller or The Life* of Jack Wilton. The story relates the life of Jack Wilton, a page in the reign of Henry VIII who becomes an adventurer.

Thomas Deloney is remembered for his famous prose work *Gentle Craft, Jack of Newbery* and *Thomas of Reading*. These books tell the stories of weavers and shoemakers of his time.

Development of Non-Fiction Prose

As the age was intellectually very sound, it inspired a number of scholars to write non-fictional prose. Raphael Holinshed wrote his famous Chronicles which is a compilation of English, Scottish, and Irish history derived from a variety of earlier sources. Thomas North published his scholarly translation of *Plutarch's Lives*. Both the books were the source of Shakespeare's history plays. In this age Richard Hakluyt published his *Principal Navigating, Voyages*, (Traffiques) and *Discoveries of the English Nation*.

There was another great scholar who contributed a great deal to the enrichment of English prose. He was Francis Bacon (1561-1626). He was the first to introduce in English the literary genre, known as the Essay, innovated by the French philosopher Montaigne. Bacon was both a scholar and a creative genius with a unique style of his own. Bacon was the first to introduce the intellectual, impersonal, reflective essays in a style which is inimitable. Brevity is the soul of Bacon's essay. The words chosen by him are crisp and pithy. His sentences though small, speak volumes. It may be said that the Elizabethan intellectual prose finds its culmination in Bacon.

Richard Hooker's masterly work of the *Laws of Ecclesiastical* Policy is one of the greatest of the non-fictional prose works of the Elizabethan age. It began appearing volume by volume in 1594 and continued till the author's death. It was the first book in England which used English for a serious philosophic discussion. Hooker was a Protestant who combined the piety of a saint with the simplicity of a child. His purpose in writing the book was to defend the Church of England and to support certain principles of Church government.

Common Elements of Fiction and Non-Fiction

A basic characteristic common to almost all Elizabethan prose is the nearness of their prose to poetry. It is colourful, blazing, rhythmic, indirect, prolix, and convoluted. The Renaissance spirit of humanism, liberalism and romanticism found full play in the growth and development of English prose in the Elizabethan Age.

The fiction of the age of Elizabeth is generally 'romantic' in nature in the sense that it is of the kind of romance. Many forms of fiction were practiced in the age.

Some important forms and their practitioners are as follows

- The romances of Lyly, Greene and Lodge
- The Pastoral Romance of Sir Philip Sidney
- The Picaresque Novel of Nashe
- The Realistic Novel of Delony.

Fiction Writers of Elizabethan Age

Sir Philip Sydney, Francis Bacon, Raleigh, Raphael Holinshed, Richard Hooker, etc are important prose writers.

Prose was the principal medium in the Elizabethan period and it was attained through treatise, tracts and pamplets. The novel has meagre but significant beginning in Thomas Delorey's work Sydney's *Arcadia* (1590), Lyly's *Euphues, the Anatomy of Wit* (1579), Bacon's *New Atlantis* (1626) and Thomas Nashe's, *The Unfortunate Traveller* (1594).

Thomas Delorey (1543-1600)

Thomas Delorey was an Elizabethan ballad writer and novelist born in 1543. He worked as a silk weaver in Norwich and wrote ballads on contemporary events while working at his trade in Norwich. His earliest venture appear to have been. 'A Declaration made by the Archbishop of Cullen upon the Deeds of his Marriage in 1583'. Delorey died in 1600.

Literary Career and Works

In 1586, Delorey moved to London where he mostly wrote ballads and broad sheets. Two main collections of his ballads are *The Garland of Goodwill* and *Strange Histories of King, Princess, Dukes*.

Delorey's work as a fiction writer includes two novels. *The Pleasant History of John Winchcomb in his Younger Days called Jack of Newbery* and *Thomas of Reading* and a collection of tales, *The Gentle Craft*. All these works derive from his earlier trade as a weaver. Delorey dedicated his novels to the famous cloth workers in England.

John Lyly (1554-1606)

John Lyly was born in Kent in 1554. He studied at Magdalen College, Oxford and went to London about 1576. He is considered to be the first English prose stylist to leave an enduring impression upon the language. John Lyly died in November 1606 in London.

Literary Career and Works

Lyly gained fame with publication of two prose romances Crovd / Euphues. *The Anatomy of Wit* (1578) and *Euphues and His England* (1580).

Euphues: The Anatomy of Wit was received with great appreciation and this novel deals with topics such as religion, love and epistolary style. A prominent defect in this prose style was excessive use of antithesis and alliteration which at times becomes comical rather than becoming impressive.

Major Works

- Campaspe, (1580).
- Sappho and Phao (1584).
- The Triumph of Trophes (1586).
- Pappe with an Hatchet (1589) A Whip for an Ape (1589).
- The Woman in the Moon (1597).
- The Maid's Metamorphosis (1600).

Thomas Lodge

Thomas Lodge was born in 1557 in London. He was the son of Sir Thomas Lodge, who was Lord Mayor of London in 1562. He studied at Merchant Taylor's School and at Trinity College, Oxford. He studied law at Lincoln's Inn, London in 1578.

Literary Career and Works

Lodge was a versatile genius, an accomplished lyricist, dramatist, critic and translator. He also contributed to the early development of the novel and is credited with producing the first formal satire in English. Though Lodge was over-shadowed by other famous writers of his time, his life and works have been examined with renewed interest in the 20th century. Much of his modern literary reputation, rests on his work of Prose-Fiction beginning with the poorly received Forbonios and Prisceria and progressing to his most famous work Rosalynde. Some literary historians consider this work as anticipating novel form.

To escape poverty, Thomas Lodge took several sea Voyages and switched to medicine. Lodge died in 1626 in Brussels.

Major Works

- An Alarum against Usurers (1584)
- Scillaes
- Metamorphosis (1589)
- Rosalynde: Euphues Golden Legacies (1590)
- The Wounds of Civil War (1594)
- A Looking Glasse for London and England (1594) Co-authored with Robert Greene
- A Margarite of America (1596)
- A Treatise of the Plagne (1603)

Thomas Nashe (1567-1601)

Elizabethan Playwright and Satirist Thomas Nashe was born in November 1567 at Lowestoft. His father was initially a clergyman and later became a minister. Thomas Nashe studied at St. John's College Cambridge and gained his bachelor's degree in 1586.

Literary Career and Works

Nashe adopted a pseudonym 'Martin Marprelate' and wrote many pamphelets which criticised and satirised the authoritarianism of the Church of England. Nashe, unfortunately died at a young age of 31 in 1601.

Nashe's most significant work is his picaresque tale. The *Unfortunate Traveller* or *The Life of Jack Wilton* (1594). It is an account of the wild overseas adventures of a youngster called Jack Wilton. This work is considered to be the precursor of the Picaresque novel and is also sometimes known as the first English historical novel.

Major Works

- The Anatomy of Absurdity (1589)
- Preface to Greene's Menaphon (1589)
- An Almond for a Parrot (1590)
- Pierce Penniless (1592)
- Christ's Tears over Jerusalem (1593)
- Terrors of the Night (1594)
- The Unfortunate Traveller (1594)
- Isle of Dogs (1597)

Francis Bacon (1561-1626)

Bacon is known as an English lawyer, statesman, essayist, historian, intellectual reformer, philosopher and champion of modern Science.

He rose high as far as political powers were concerned but was jailed on the charges of bribery for four days. It was after his humiliating experience that he entered a spurt of intellectual activity, published a great number of notable essays and novels and conducted intensive research. Bacon is popularly known as 'the father of empiricism'.

According to empiricism, experience was the source of all human knowledge and not innate ideas. Bacon also believed that if society was to progress, human minds would have to be cleared of their inherent obstructions in order to embrace true learning and knowledge, which was constructive and would help in society's advancement.

Francis Bacon died at High Gate, in The Earl of Arundel's house on 9th April, 1626 due to complications arising from bronchitis.

Bacon also wrote a Utopian Science fiction called *New Atlantis*. The novel, in brief is about a research faculty where in there are teams of specially trained and curious investigators who, after conducting experiments, apply the results of these to create useful inventions for society.

Major Works

- Essays (1597)
- The Elements of Common Law of England (1597)
- Sir Francis Bacon his Apology, in certain impulations concerning the Late Earl of Essex (1604).
- The Proficience and Advancement of Learning (1605)
- De Sapientia Veterum Liber (1609)
- The Wisdom of the Ancients (1619)
- Novum Organum (1620)
- The History of the Reign of King Henry VII (1622)
- The History of Winds (1622)
- Apoph Thegms, New and Old (1625)
- The New Atlantis (1626)

Sir Philip Sidney (1554-86)

Like Lyly, Sidney also prompted a number of imitators. His Arcadia (1590) is the first pastoral romance in English prose, just as Spenser's *The Shepherd's Calendar* is the first verse pastoral romance. All the happenings of the story are envisaged in an imaginary land of idyllic beauty with shepherds, shepherdesses, running brooks, and lush scenery. It tells the story of Basilius, king of Arcadia, who settles in a village with his wife and two daughters named Pamela and Philoclea. Two princes from abroad come to Arcadia and start courting the two girls. One disguises himself as a shepherd and the other as an Amazon. Complications start when both Basilius and his wife fall in love with the 'Amazon', the former taking him to be a real Amazon and the latter, after discovering his real identity. Everything is finally unravelled by Euarchus, king of Macedonia and father of one of the princes. Everything ends happily. This was the first version of the Arcadia, known as the Old Arcadia. In the revised version, Sidney included many complications and also added much symbolism and didacticism which rendered it almost of the nature of The Faerie Queene. In the Arcadia, observes Daiches, "Ideal love, ideal friendship, and the ideal ruler are, directly and indirectly, discussed, suggested, and embodied."

The style of the Arcadia is as artificial and attitudinised as that of Euphues. It is, to quote Daiches again, "highly 'conceited', full of elaborated analogies, balanced parenthetical asides, pathetic fallacies, symmetrically answering clauses and other devices of an immature prose entering suddenly into the world of conscious literary artifice". One of Sidney's constant devices is to take a word and, somewhat like Shakespeare, toss it about till its meaning is sucked dry. As an example of pathetic fallacy consider his reference to the cool wine which seems 'to laugh for joy' as it nears a lady's lips. Similarly, the water drops that slip down the bodies of dainty ladies seem to weep for sorrow. The name that a beautiful lady utters is perfumed by the scent of her breath. When the princesses put on their clothes, the clothes are described as 'glad.' And so forth.

Robert Greene (1560-92)

(Author description given the in unit 1: Drama)

Greene was a patent imitator of Lyly, and later that of Sidney, after he came to know of his *Arcadia*. Though in his actual life he was a debauchee of the worst kind yet in his works he was quite didactic. His several 'novels' include *Pandosto* (1588) which very obviously furnished the plot for Shakespeare's. *A Winter's Tale*. His other important works are *Menopon* (1519), *Mamilla* (1583), and *The Card of Fancy* which was published within a decade of Euphues and, as AC Ward says, "reproduces its mannerisms of style, its elaborately artificial and voluble conversations, its classical embellishments, its images and comparisons from natural history (for Greene, like Lyly, drew upon Pliny), its frequent and lengthy soliloquies." The frequency of letters may have furnished Richardson with a model of epistolary novel. In his *Life and Death of Ned Brown*, a notorious pick-pocket, Greene provides hints for the low-life scenes we meet within the novels of Smollett and Defoe.

EXAM BASED QUESTIONS

1 In literature fiction is described as
(a) an act of making or moulding
(b) to form something new
(c) the form of prose that describes imaginary events, situations and people
(d) work based on facts

2 A fiction may be based on
(a) stories of actual historical events
(b) imaginary situations and settings
(c) with some resemblance to real life events and characters
(d) All of the above

3 The function of a fiction is to give its readers
(a) to take us into a real world
(b) to make us use our logic and analytical abilities
(c) to arouse empathy, sweep emotions and give an insight into the life of the characters
(d) to bring a drastic change in society

4 The advent of short stories was due to
(a) increase in literate readers and start of magazines and periodicles
(b) more free time available to its readers
(c) inventions in printing technology
(d) None of the above

5 Novel was recognised as the dominant literary form during the reign of
(a) Elizabethan Age (b) Age of Revival
(c) Victorian Age (d) Jacobean Period

6 A protagonist in a novel is one
(a) who does not come in the fore-front
(b) around whom the plot of the novel revolves
(c) who does not exhibit any change in altitude or behaviour
(d) a back ground voice

7 What was the change noticed in literature after Battle of Hastings?
(a) Completely new revolution in the field of literature
(b) Completely transformed the sentiments and tastes of English rulers
(c) Innovation of new poems and ballads
(d) New sentiments of French people were introduced

8 The romance stories during Anglo Norman period were influenced by
(a) English and French sources
(b) English and Norman sources
(c) Latin and English sources
(d) Latin and French sources

9 During Anglo Norman period which language began to be discarded in favour of French and Latin
(a) Spanish (b) Greek (c) English (d) Italian

10 Medieval romances had characters which of the following is not a character of them?
(a) Knights (b) Warriors
(c) Beautiful women (d) Religion

11 During the Anglo Norman period the literature that contained stories from aristocratic class was called
(a) chionicles (b) medieval romances
(c) brut (d) histories

12 'The Matter of Rome' talks about
(a) Heroism of Chanson de Roland
(b) Deeds of Alexander and Fall of Troy
(c) Arthur Legends
(d) Knights of Round Table

13 Chaucer's father was a
(a) soldier
(b) wine-merchant
(c) diplomat
(d) owner of leather shoe factory

14 Which work of Chaucer, if written in prose style would have been celebrated as first English novel?
(a) The Parliament of Fowls (b) The House of Fame
(c) Troilus and Criseyde (d) Canterbury Tales

15 In which battle, was Troilus killed?
(a) Battle of Hastings (b) Battle of Atlantic
(c) Falkland War (d) Battle of Achilles

16 What is done by Pandarus in Troilus and Criseyde?
(a) Learn the secrets and bring the young people together
(b) Allows the marriage of Troilus and Criseyde
(c) Fight the war till the last breath
(d) United the two nations and brought peace and harmony

17 Cressida promised to herself that
(a) she will be happily live with her father
(b) she will be true to Troilus
(c) she will be true to Diomede
(d) she will be true to the country

18 Which of the following tales in 'Chaucer's Canterbury Tales' is in prose?
(a) The Parliament of Foules
(b) The Legend of Good Women
(c) The House of Fame (d) The Book of Duchess

19 During which period Chaucer wrote most of his major works?
(a) When he was a soldier
(b) When he became a member of Parliament
(c) When he held the job of customs controller to London
(d) When he held the post of Diplomal

20 In Canterbury tales what is the name of the inn where the pilgrims meet before their journey?
(a) The Tabard (b) The Talbot
(c) The Tivoli (d) The Tolbooth

21 Who was Igraine married to in 'Morte D' Arthur' before she got married to Uther Pendragon?
(a) The Duke of Tintagil (b) Sir Ironside
(c) Sir Uwaine (d) Sir Uriens

22 Which word is applied to denote the whole translation from the middle ages to the modern world, is more correctly applied to the revival of art resulting from the discovery and imitation of classic models in the 14th century?
(a) Renaissance (b) Reformation
(c) Restoration (d) Humanism

23 Which of the following is a prose story by Chaucer?
(a) Tale of Melibens (b) The Parson's Tale
(c) Tale of Knight (d) Both a and b

24 Who among the following is well-known for book Morte d' Arthur?
(a) Malory (b) Kyd
(c) Wycliffe (d) Caxton

25 Why is the Prologue to Canterbury Tales is called the Prologue to Modern Fiction?
(a) Realism (b) Humour
(c) Characterisation (d) Narrative unity

26 The great importance was assigned to intellect, to experience, to scientific experiment. This new out look was known as
(a) humanism (b) revival
(c) renaissance (d) psychology

27 What is the significance of the War of Roses?
(a) England and France had the same national flower-the rose
(b) The war occurred due to roses
(c) The rival faction in the war were symbolised by red and white roses respectively
(d) Rose symbolised the gruesomeners of war

28 The first man to set an independent printing press in England was
(a) Thomas Malory (b) Wycliffe
(c) William Caxton (d) Geoffrey Chaucer

29 Who of the following was responsible for first usage of over 1,300 words in English language?
(a) William Caxton (b) George Peele
(c) Sir Philip Sydney (d) Thomas Malory

30 What is the other name which can be given to 'Utopia'?
(a) The Kingdom of Fools
(b) The World of Imagination
(c) A Strange Island
(d) An Unknown Island

31 What is the narrator's name in Thomas Moore's Utopia?
(a) Knight Christi (b) Raphael Hythloday
(c) Bishop Fisher (d) Thomas Moore

32 Battle of Hastings was fought in the year
(a) 1066 (b) 1056 (c) 1016 (d) 1046

33 The novel Utopia is a work of Satire which criticised
(a) authority of church
(b) dictatorship of the ruler
(c) political corruption of Europe and religious hypocrisy
(d) the rich urban class

34 What was Moore's belief about the goal of the state?
(a) The well being of its citizens
(b) The improvement of international relations
(c) The establishment of efficient tax system
(d) The maintenance of army

35 Thomas Moore did not approve the divorce of which sovereign ?
(a) Henry I (b) Henry III (c) Henry VII (d) Henry VIII

36 The Spanish Armada was defeated under the reign of
(a) Edward III (b) Queen Elizabeth
(c) Queen Mary (d) James I

37 Deloney's prose work 'Jack of Newbery' extolls
(a) the virtues of pope (b) the virtues of weavers
(c) the skills of the poets (d) the authority of the queen

38 Who is known for his work, a prose romance 'Euphues'?
(a) Robert Greene (b) John Lyly
(c) Thomas Kyd (d) Christopher Marlowe

39 John Lyly's works include
(a) Euphues: The Anatomy of Wit, A Whip for an Ape, the Woman in the Moon
(b) Euphues and his England, Jack of Newbery, Utopia
(c) Paraphrase upon the Psalms, A Pathway into the Holy Scriptures, The Pilgrimage
(d) The Alchemist, Two Gentleman of Verona, Shepherd's Garland

40 Whose role as a printer makes him as a contributor to the English Renaissance?
(a) Thomas Lodge (b) Wycliffe
(c) Caxton (d) Tyndale

41 Which literary figure's, works have been examined with renewed interest in the 20th century?
(a) Thomas Lodge (b) John Lyly
(c) Edmund Spenser (d) Thomas Nashe

42 Which work of Thomas Lodge is considered as anticipating novel?
(a) Metamorphosis (b) A Treatise of the Plague
(c) A Looking Glasses for London and England
(d) Rosalynde: Euphues Golden Legacies

43 The Unfortunate Traveller by Thomas Nashe is a typical
(a) pastoral romance (b) revenge play
(c) picaresque novel (d) love tragedy

44 The ballads were meant for
(a) the upper class (b) common people
(c) elite class (d) religious people

45 Who calls Elizabeth age of England as a noble and puissant nation, rising herself, like a strong man after sleep and shaking her insensible locks.
(a) Spenser (b) Johnson (c) Lyly (d) John Milton

46 The great essayist who once said that the vernaculars "would one day play the bankrupt with book." is
(a) Johnson (b) Walter Raleigh
(c) Bacon (d) Steele

47 Who is called the first great stylist in English prose?
(a) John Lyly (b) Thomas Malory
(c) Francis Bacon (d) John Dryden

48 Walter Raleigh wrote his book History of the World while
(a) on exploration (b) in prison
(c) serving queen's army (d) while studying

49 Bacon's novel 'New Atlantis' is an example of
(a) romance fiction (b) mystery fiction
(c) science fiction (d) religious treaty

50 In Bacon's New Atlantis the place where scientists devote themselves to the advancement of knowledge is
(a) Wemberley (b) Solomon's House
(c) The Royal Society (d) Spain

51 In the novel 'The New Atlantis' what famous explorer has a statue in one of the galleries?
(a) Galileo (b) Vasco-de Gama
(c) Columbus (d) None of these

52 Novum organum is a book written by
(a) Thomas Deloney (b) Thomas Watson
(c) Bacon (d) Watson

53 Sir Walter Raleigh's literary works include
(a) fight about the Islet of the Azores
(b) discovery of the Empire of Guiana
(c) the pilgrimage (d) All of these

54 Thomas Deloney dedicated his novels to
(a) Queen Elizabeth
(b) to his family
(c) the famous weavers in England
(d) to religious authorities

55 Jack of Newbury and The Gentle Craft realistically depict contemporary bourgeois life. It was written by
(a) Thomas Nashe (b) Lodge
(c) Robert Greene (d) Thomas Deloney

56 Which among the following literary work was not composed in 1513?
(a) Ballad of Scottish King (b) Canterbury Tales
(c) Translation of Aeneid (d) Utopia

57 The Peasant's revolt occurred in the year
(a) 1521 (b) 1381 (c) 1348 (d) 1415

58 By late 14th century language of court had shifted from Anglo Norman French to which language?
(a) Latin (b) French
(c) Middle English (d) Greek

59 Which poem of Chaucer has been called a novel in verse form?
(a) Prologue to Canterbury Tales
(b) The Parliament of Fowls
(c) Book of the Duchess
(d) Troilus and Criseyde

60 Which of the following is/are from the romance period?
(a) King Arthur (b) The War of Troy
(c) Alexander the Great (d) All of these

61 The Romance 'Cycle of Rome' talks about
(a) Heroism of Chanson de Roland
(b) Deeds of Alexander and Fall of Troy
(c) Arthur Legendary
(d) Knights of Round Table

62 The Black Death resulted into
(a) loss of life and increased wages
(b) betterment of the poor
(c) betterment of the rich
(d) betterment of the government

63 Robert Greene has been called a patent imitator of which of these authors?
(a) Thomas Moore (b) Philip Sydney
(c) John Lyly (d) Both (b) and (c)

64 In which novel was Thomas Moore is the most perfect embodiment of humanist rational ideas?
(a) Utopia
(b) A Messy Zest
(c) The Answer to a Poisoned Book
(d) Treatise on the Blessed Body

65 Who was the first to introduce printing in England?
(a) Gavin Douglas (b) Caxton
(c) Henry V (d) None of these

66 Who was given trade privileges and right to colonise America by Queen Elizabeth I?
(a) John Ford
(b) Beaumont and Fletcher
(c) Walter Raleigh
(d) Richard Hooker

67 Bacon's book 'Advancement of Learning' was first published in which year?
(a) 1575 (b) 1622
(c) 1605 (d) 1623

68 Which humanist writer is believed to have been the first to use the term 'Utopia' in 1516 and wrote a book with the same name?
(a) Thomas Moore (b) Petrarch
(c) Henry VIII (d) Erasmus

69 Whose writing style is fresh, lively and stands close to the modern English during the age of revival?
(a) Hugh Latimore (b) Sir Thomas Malory
(c) John Fisher (d) None of these

70 What was the source of Jhomas Malory's work Morte D' Arthur?
(a) French
(b) English Alliterative poem Morte Arthur
(c) Both (a) and (b)
(d) None of the above

71 Thomas Malory's book 'Morte d' Arthur' inspired which of these writers?
(a) Coleridge (b) Words worth
(c) Tennyson (d) None of these

72 Main features of society at Utopia in Thomas Moore's novel are
(a) elimination of private property
(b) moderated pleasure
(c) universal labour (d) All of these

73 The term ...... was first used by Marx and Engle's to describe their ideal perfect society.
(a) Socialism (b) Utopian Socialism
(c) Communism (d) Marxisim

74 Amalgamation of French and Saxon produced the .... literature.
(a) English (b) Latin (c) French (d) Spanish

75 The common name for factory towns that were built near manufacturing sides and thought to be an attempt of ideal society was
(a) settlement (b) municipality
(c) mill town (d) canton

76 The work 'Troilus and Criseyde' is based on .... work.
(a) Boccacio's (b) Dante's (c) Petrarch's (d) Barboun's

77 .... is a prose story by Geoffrey Chaucer.
(a) The Parson's Tale (b) Tale of Knight
(c) Tale of Melibens (d) Both a and c

78 Chaucer's work ...... contains passages that have been directly taken from Dante.
(a) The Canterbury Tales
(b) The Book of Duchess
(c) The Legend of Good Women
(d) The Parliament of Fowls

79 During the 15th century, Renaissance ideas spread from
(a) Italy to China (b) India to Italy
(c) Italy to Europe (d) Italy to France

80 .... is the first book printed in English.
(a) Morte d' Arthur (b) History of Troy
(c) Philip Sparrow (d) Magnificence

81 .... is a collection of Arthurian romances told in simple and vivid prose.
(a) Thomas Herniot (b) Malory
(c) Morte d' Arthur (d) Tyndale

82 .... said, "I have taken all knowledge for my province."
(a) Ben Johnson (b) John Heywood
(c) Bacon (d) Walter Raleigh

83 Thomas Nashe's Picarseque tale is a book called
(a) Peirce Penniless
(b) The Anatomy of Absurdity
(c) The Unfortunate Traveller
(d) Isle of Dogs

84 Which of the following statements about the Anglo Norman period is incorrect?
(a) English thought was fashioned in the manner of French
(b) The clergy insisted on the use of Latin
(c) A huge number of works appeared in the native tongue
(d) Anglo-Saxon heroic poetry virtually disappeared during this time

85 The following qualities belonged to Morte d' Arthur written by Sir Thomas Malory. Which of the following is an incorrect statement?
(a) It is a store house of medieval legends
(b) It is the first book in England in poetic prose
(c) It inspired Tennyson, Morris, Swinburne and Shakespeare
(d) It was written in the 16th century

86 Which of these about 'Utopia' is correct?
(a) It is written by Thomas Lodge
(b) It was originally written in French in 1516
(c) It is a collection of beast fables
(d) It is composed of two parts

87 Which of the following about 'Utopia' is correct statement?
(a) It was originally written in French.
(b) The Greek word 'Utopia' means nowhere but in modern parlance it signifies an ideal place
(c) It is written in 4 parts
(d) It is written by Thomas Lodge

88 Which of these points is correct about Lais?
(a) Lyrical poems
(b) Written by Anselm
(c) They are usually in octosyllabic couplets
(d) They are intended to be sung

89 Which of the following authors is incorrectly matched with his work?

(a) Eadmer	:	Historia Novorum
(b) Malmesbury	:	Historia Novella
(c) Geoffrey of Monmouth	:	The Bible
(d) Anselm	:	Monologion

90 Which of the following pairs is incorrectly matched?

(a) Matter of France	:	Charlemagne
(b) Matter of Britain	:	King Arthur
(c) Matter of Rome	:	Alexander the Great
(d) Matter of England	:	Adventures of Aeneas

91 Which of these historical events chronology pairs is correctly matched with their period?

(a) Hundred Years' War	:	1337-1453
(b) Edwardian Era War	:	1415-1453
(c) Caroline War	:	1337-1360
(d) Lancastrian War	:	1369-1389

92 Which of these books with their contents is incorrectly matched?

(a) The Book of the Duchess	:	Elegy on the Death of Blanche
(b) The Parliament of Fowls	:	Marriage of King Richard II to Anne
(c) Troilus and Criseyde	:	Trojan War
(d) The House of Fame	:	Pilgrims on their way to a shrine

93 Which of the following pairs is incorrectly matched?

	Work	Author
(a)	Utopia	: Thomas Moore
(b)	Euphues	: Thomas Deloney
(c)	The Maid's Metamorphosis	: John Lyly
(d)	The History of Reign of King Henry VII	: Francis Bacon

94 Which of these personalities and their relation is not correctly matched?

	Personality	Relation
(a)	Troilus	: Son of Priam
(b)	Criseyde	: Lover of Troilus
(c)	Calchas	: Uncle of Criseyde
(d)	Pandarus	: Uncle of Criseyde

Directions (Q. Nos. 95-99) *In the questions given below are two statements labelled as Assertion (A) and Reason (R). In the context of two statements, which one of the following is correct?*

Codes

(a) A is true, but R is false
(b) A is false, but R is true
(c) Both A and R are true, but R is not the correct explanation of A
(d) Both A and R are true, but R is the correct explanation of A

95 **Assertion** (A) Grammar became complicated due to the Norman conquest.
Reason (R) People started finding the simplest way to communicate with people, who did not speak English.

96 **Assertion** (A) French became the language of law and old English became confined to the lower classes.
Reason (R) The Norman conquest brought to power a French speaking ruling class.

97 **Assertion** (A) Canterbury Tales Prologue by Geoffrey Chaucer has been called as Prologue to Modern Fiction.
Reason (R) Its vivid characterisation of varied characters is one of the hall marks of fiction.

98 **Assertion** (A) War of the Roses is a series of civil war between the two royal families.
Reason (R) The breakdown of royal authority during Henry VI's bouts of mental illness led to this war.

99 **Assertion** (A) Elizabethan England saw a significant growth in cultural developments.
Reason (R) The queen herself was a great patron of arts and her actions, image and court atmosphere contributed.

100 Which of the following is in chronological order?

(a) Battle of Hastings, Edward Crowned King of England, Norman Conquest Complete
(b) Edward Crowned King of England, Battle of Hastings, Norman Conquest Complete
(c) Norman Conquest Complete, Edward Crowned King of England, Battle of Hastings
(d) Battle of Hastings, Norman Conquest Complete, Edward Crowned King of England

101 Which of the following is in correct sequence?

(a) Troilus and Criseyde, The Legend of Good Women, The Canterbury Tales
(b) The Canterbury Tales, The Legend of Good Women, Troilus and Criseyde
(c) The Legend of Good Women, Troilus and Criseyde, The Canterbury Tales
(d) Troilus and Criseyde, The Canterbury Tales, The Legend of Good Women

102 Which of the following is in chronological order as per the occurrence of events?

(a) Death of Chaucer, Death of Wycliffe, Death of Edward III
(b) Death of Edward III, Death of Wycliffe, Death of Chaucer
(c) Death of Wycliffe, Death of Edward III, Death of Chaucer
(d) Death of Wycliffe, Death of Chaucer, Death of Edward III

103 Which of the following is in correct sequence per their year of birth?

(a) John Lyly, Thomas Deloney, Thomas Moore
(b) Thomas Moore, Thomas Delorey, John Lyly
(c) Thomas Deloney, Thomas Moore, John Lyly
(d) John Lyly, Thomas Moore, Thomas Deloney

104 Which is the correct sequence of Walter Raleigh's works?

(a) The Discovery of Guiana, Cities, The Sceptic
(b) A Discourse Touching a War with Spain, The History of the World, The Last Fight of the Revenge
(c) A Discourse Touching a War with Spain, The History of the World, The Prerogative of Parliaments
(d) Cities, The Sceptic, Causes of the Magnificency and Opulence of Cities.

105 Consider the following statements.
The influence of the Norman conquest on English language is
1. French became the language of social prestige and status.
2. grammar became complex .
3. pronunciation of English did not change.
4. English gradually disappeared as a written language.

Which of the statements given above is / are correct?
(a) 1 and 2 (b) 1 and 4
(c) 3 and 2 (d) 3 and 4

106 Consider the following statements during Anglo Norman period.
1. More than 10,000 French words found their way into English.
2. English gradually appeared as a written language.
3. Grammer became complicated.
4. Pronunciation of English did not change.

Which of the statements given above is / are correct?
(a) Only 1 (b) Only 4 (c) 1 and 3 (d) 2 and 3

107 Consider the following literary works.
1. The Legend of Good Women
2. The Matter of France
3. The Canterbury Tales
4. The Game and Playe of Chesse

Which of the above works belong to Geoffrey Chaucer?
(a) 1 and 2 (b) 2 and 3 (c) 1 and 3 (d) 1 and 4

108 Consider the following novels.
1. Troilus and Criseyde
2. Jack of Newbery
3. Utopia
4. The History of King Richard III

Which of the above are the novels of Thomas Moore?
(a) 1 and 2 (b) 2 and 3 (c) 3 and 4 (d) 2 and 4

109 Identify the correct description below.
1. The Proficience and Advancement of Learning
2. The History of Winds
3. Apology
4. The New Atlantis

Which are the works of Geoffrey Chaucer?
(a) 1, 4 and 3 (b) 2 , 3 and 4 (c) 1, 2 and 4 (d) 1, 2 and 3

110 Match the authors with the novels.

	List I (Authors)	List II (Novels)
A.	Thomas Moore	1. New Atlantis
B.	Thomas Nashe	2. Thomas of Reading
C.	Francis Bacon	3. Utopia
D.	Thomas Deloney	4. The Unfortunate Traveller

Codes

	A	B	C	D		A	B	C	D
(a)	3	4	1	2	(b)	2	4	3	1
(c)	2	1	4	3	(d)	1	2	3	4

111 The book 'Morte d' Arthur' does not empire which of the following writers?
1. Matthew Arnold 2. William Morris
3. Swin Burne 4. Sir Thomas Malory

Select the correct answer using the codes given below
(a) Only 1 (b) 1 and 2
(c) Only 3 (d) None of these

112 Consider the following works.
1. The Matter of France 2. Morte D' Arthur
3. The Canterbury Tales
4. The Recuyclle of the Historyes of Troye

Which of the above mentioned work is a prose fiction?
(a) 1 and 2 (b) Only 2 (c) 2 and 4 (d) 3 and 4

113 Who was Sir Thomas Malory?
1. This is a book written by Professor Kilteridge.
2. This is a question asked by Professor Kilteridge.

Which of the following statement given above is / are true?
(a) Only 1 (b) Only 2
(c) Both 1 and 2 (d) None of these

114 Consider the following statements
"Utopia is a satirical work about Thomas Moore's own time but it is also a philosophical treatise about an ideal state. In writing this book, Moore clearly pays homage to an ancient Greek philosopher." Who words were these
1. Plato 2. Socrates
3. Cicero

Codes
(a) Only 1 (b) 1 and 2 (c) Only 2 (d) Only 3

115 Match the following works with the authors or which of the given set is correctly matched with their authors?
(a) Thomas Deloney - The Unfortunate Traveller, Thomas Moore - The New Atlantis, Francis Bacon - The Unfortunate Traveller, Thomas Nashe - Utopia
(b) Thomas Deloney - Jack of Newbery, Thomas Moore - Utopia, Francis Bacon - The New Atlantis, Thomas Nashe - The Unfortunate Traveller
(c) Thomas Deloney - Utopia, Francis Bacon- The New Atlantic, Thomas Moore - The Unfortunate Traveller, Thomas Nashe - Jack of Newbery
(d) Thomas Deloney-The New Atlantis, Thomas Moore The Unfortunate Traveller, Francis Bacon - Utopia, Thomas Nashe - Jack of Newbery

116 Which of the following is not in chronological order regarding Bacon ?

(a) Bacon became Attorney General, Advancement of Learning, Broken Heart
(b) John Foxe, Sr Walter Raleigh, Richard Hooker
(c) Richard Hakluyt, Sir Thomas North, Samuel Purchas
(d) The Book of Common Prayer, Book of Martyrs, The Great Lottery

117 In the following series, which one has the correctly matched writers with their works?

(a) Wycliffe - Translated Bible into Vernacular; Chaucer - Piers the Plowman, Langland-Vox Clamantis; John Gower - The Canterbury Tales
(b) Wycliffe - Vox Clamantis; Chaucer Translated Bible into Vernacular: Langland - Piers the Plowman; John Gower The Canterbury Tales
(c) Wycliffe - Translated Bible into Vernacular; Chaucer - The Canterbury Tales; Langland-Piers the Plowman; John Gower - Vox Clamantis
(d) Wycliffe - The Canterbury Tales; Chaucer - Translated Bible into Vernacular; Langland-Piers the Plowman; John Gower - Vox Clamantis

118 In the following series which one has the correctly matched period with the writers?

(a) Bacon - 1478-1535, Deloney - 1561-1626, Watson 1543-1600, Thomas Moore 1515-1592
(b) Bacon - (1561-1626), Deloney - 1543-1600, Watson - 1515-1592, Thomas Moore 1478-1535
(c) Bacon - 1515-1592, Deloney - 1478-1535, Watson 1543-1600, Thomas Moore - 1561-1626
(d) Bacon - 1543-1600 Deloney - 1515-1592, Watson, 1561-1626, Thomas Moore - 1478-1535

119 In the following series which one has correctly matched characters with the novels?

(a) The Priest of Bensalem - Legend of Good Women, Arthur the Great Utopia, Cleopatra - the New Atlantis, Hythloday - Legend of Good Women
(b) The Priest of Bensalem - The New Atlantis, Arthur the Great-Morte d' Arthur, Cleopatra-Legend of Good Women, Hytholoday - Utopia
(c) The Priest of Bensalem - Utopia, Arthur the Great-Legend of Good Women, Cleopatra - The New Atlantis, Hythloday Morte d' Arthur
(d) The Priest of Bensalem - The Legend of Good Women, Arthur the Great - Utopia, Cleopatra - Morte d' Arthur, Hythloday - The New Atlantis

120 How can any be silly enough to think himself better than other people because his clothes are made of finer woolen thread than theirs?
Which of the following novelist in which of his / her works has used these lines?

(a) Thomas Malory - Morte d' Arthur
(b) Parson's Tales - Geoffey Chaucer
(c) Thomas Moore - Utopia
(d) The New Atlantis - Francis Bacon

121 "We gave ourselves for lost men and prepared for death. Yet we did lift up our hearts and voices to God above, who shrweth this wonders in the deep."
Which of the following fiction writers has used these words in which of his / her works?

(a) Walter Raleigh - History of the World
(b) Thomas Nashe - The Unfortunate Traveller
(c) Francis Bacon - The New Atlantis
(d) Thomas Lodge - Rosalynde

122 Which of these writers called Thomas Moore 'A Man for All Seasons'?

(a) Whittington and Erasmus
(b) Francis Bacon
(c) Matthew Arnold (d) Beaumont and Fletcher

123 "Some courtiers to wearie out time woulde tell us further tales of correlius Agirippa, and how when Sir Thomas Moore our countrieman was there, he showed him the whole destruction of Troy in a dreame."
Which of the following fiction writer has used these words in which of his works?

(a) Wycliffe - The Truth of the Sacred Scriptures
(b) The Legend of Good Women - Geoffrey Chaucer
(c) Thomas Nashe - The Unfortunate Traveller
(d) Francis Bacon - The New Atlantis

124 20th century critics in general have tended to perceive this work as a negative commentary.
Whose work done by which author is mentioned here?

(a) The Unfortunate Traveller by Thomas Nashe
(b) Utopia by Thomas Moore
(c) Morte d' Arthur by Malory
(d) The Discovery of Guiana by Walter Raleigh

125 "The very purpose of a knight is to fight on behalf of a lady ...."
Which of the author in which of his works has used this quote?

(a) Thomas Moore - Utopia
(b) Wycliffe - The Truth of the Sacred Scriptures
(c) Thomas Malory - Morte d' Arthur
(d) John Lyly - Eupheus

126 "Is it not for better to abhor sins by the remembrance of others' faults than by repentance of thine own follies."
Which work of which novelist contains these lines?

(a) Utopia - Thomas Moore
(b) Parson's Tale - By Geoffrey Chaucer
(c) Euphues - The Anatomy of Wit by John Lyly
(d) The New Atlantis by Francis Bacon

127 Who said this "Imagination was given to man to compensate him for what he is not, a sense of humour to console him for what he is."

(a) Chaucer (b) Thomas Moore
(c) Walter Raleigh (d) Francis Bacon

128 "Beauty is delicate bait with a deadly hook, a sweet panther with a devouring paunch, a sour poison in a silver pot."
Who is the author who has used these words in which of his works?
(a) Thomas Nashe - The Unfortunate Traveller
(b) Thomas Moore - Utopia
(c) Thomas Malory - Morte d' Arthur
(d) John Lyly - Euphues, the Anatomy of Wit

129 "This way of punishing thieves was neither just-nor good-the severity was too great- the remedy was not effectual."
Which character ulters these words in which fiction during the conversation?
(a) The Priest of Bensalm in the New Atlantis
(b) Raphael Hythloday in Utopia
(c) Arthur the Great in Morte d' Arthur
(d) Cleopetra - The Legend of Good Women

130 Who said "No pleasure is comparable to" the standing upon the vantage ground of truth?
(a) Geoffrey Chaucer (b) Thomas Malory
(c) Francis Bacon (d) John Lyly

131 In whose work of which author would you assign these words. "In misery it is great comfort to have a companion."
(a) The New Atalantis by F Bacon
(b) Utopia by Thomas Moore
(c) Euphues by John Lyly
(d) The Gentlo Craft by Thomas Delorey

132 "I have done to you no treason, for love is free for all men, and though I have loved your lady," She is my lady as well as yours......"
In which work of which author these lines appear?
(a) The Wisdom of the Ancients by Bacon
(b) The Unfortunate Traveller by Thomas Nashe
(c) Utopia by Thomas Moore
(d) Le Morte d' Arthur by Thomas Malory

133 Who said these lines– "Danger will put wit into anie man. Architas anada a wooden done to slie ...... "
(a) The Unfortunate Traveller by Thomas Nashe
(b) Thomas Moore– Utopia
(c) Thomas Delorey– Thomas of Reading
(d) Francis Bacon– Novum Organum

134 Whom would you assign these words? "God sends meat and the Devil sends cooks"
(a) John Lyly (b) Francis Bacon
(c) Thomas Deloney (d) Walter Raleigh

135 "Our taste must always be, more or less, the victim of our limitations, but we should be ware of glorifying in it ...... "
Which author said these words?
(a) John Lyly (b) Thomas Melory
(c) Walter Raleigh (d) Thomas Delorey

136 "I dare not think that any super celestial heaven or what so ever else .... was increate and eternal. And as for the place of God before the world created, the finite wisdom of mortal men hath no perception of it ...."
Which novelist has written these lines in which of his / her works?
(a) Thomas Nashe - The Unfortunate Traveller
(b) Walter Raleigh - History of the World (Part I)
(c) Wycliffe - Lranslation of Bible
(d) Thomas Lodge - An Alarm Against Ususers

137 "Age appears best in four things: old wood to burn, old wine to drink, old friends to trust and old authors to read."
Which authors said this in which of his works?
(a) Thomas Deloney - The Gentle Craft
(b) Thomas Lodge - Rosalynde
(c) Francis Bacon - Essay on Friendship
(d) Thomas Nashe - The Unfortunate Traveller

138 "Wherefore, representing your majesty many times unto my mind and beholding you, not with the inquisitive eye of presumption, to discover that which the scripture telleth me is inscrutable ...."
In which work of Francis Bacon, these lines are spoken?
(a) The Elements of Common Law of England
(b) The Wisdom of the Ancients
(c) The New Atlantis
(d) The Proficience and Advancement of Learning

139 Ruskin speaks of the "Necessity to all high imagination that it should point straight from life."
Whom did he praise in these lines?
(a) Wycliffe (b) Boccacio (c) Dante (d) Chaucer

140 Whom would you assign these words? "A pretty face may be enough to catch a man, but it takes character and good nature to hold him."
(a) Thomas Nashe (b) Thomas Malory
(c) Francis Bacon (d) Thomas Moore

141 "We gave ourselves for lost men and prepared for death. Yet we did lift upon hearts and voices to God above who "Showets his wonders in the deep be seeing him of his mercy ...."
In which work of which author do we find these words?
(a) The Wisdom of the Ancients - Francis Bacon
(b) Utopia - Thomas Moore
(c) Bible Translation - Wycliffe
(d) The New Atlantis - Bacon

142 Who said "He will not tell a story mixed with chaff and wheat."
Which character in Geoffrey Chaucer's Canterbury Tales utters these words?
(a) Knight (b) The Wife of Bath
(c) Parson (d) The Cook

143 "Now I have warned thee of thy vain glory and of thy pride, that thou hast many times erred against thy Maker."

In which Author's which work do these lines appear?

(a) Thomas Nashe the Unfortunate Traveller
(b) Francis Bacon– The New Atlantis
(c) Thomas Moore– Utopia
(d) Thomas Malory– Morte d'Arthur

144 Who said, "Silence is the sleep that nourishes wisdom"?

(a) Geoffrey Chaucer (b) Francis Bacon
(c) John Lyly (d) Philip Sidney

145 Who said, "Either I will find a way or I will make one"?

(a) Thomas Nashe
(b) Robert Greene
(c) Philip Sidney
(d) Francis Bacon

Directions (Q. Nos 146-150) *Read the passage given below and answer the questions that follow.*

"We take cunning for a sinister and crooked wisdom. And certainly there is a great difference between a cunning man and a wise man, not only in point of honesty, but in point of ability. There he that can pack the cards and yet cannot play well; so there are some that are good in canvasses and factions that are otherwise weak men. Again, it is one thing to understand persons, and another thing to understand matters; for many are perfect in men's humours, that are not greatly capable of the real part of business; which is the Constitution of one that hath studied men more than books. Such men are fitter for practice than for counsel; and they are good but in their own alley; turn them to new men and they have lost their aim."

146 This passage talking about cunningness and wisdom is taken from

(a) A novel by Thomas Nashe 'An Unfortunate Traveller'
(b) Chaucer's Canterbury Tales
(c) Bacon's Essay on 'Cunning'
(d) Thomas Moore's novel Utopia

147 What does the phrase 'Crooked Wisdom implies?

(a) Wise men are also cunning
(b) wisdom an dishonesty can go side by side
(c) Wise people also carry many secrets intentionally
(d) Wise people are like open books

148 How according to the author a wise man cannot be perfect to handle business matters?

(a) A wise man may not have the idea of running a business
(b) A wise man may be intelligent enough only to understand the different type of people.
(c) Wise people cannot be great businessman.
(d) Running a business requires a different type of practical intelligence that a wise man may not be equipped with

149 The idiom 'in their own alley' implies

(a) in their own surroundings
(b) ideally suited to one's own interests
(c) to one's own wisdom or taste
(d) one's own province

150 Which of the following description best applies to the above extract?

(a) The author is talking about different types of intelligence
(b) The author wants to differentiate between abilities of a wise man and a cunning man.
(c) A wise man cannot be a good businessman
(d) If some men who are well read can provide guidance to others.

PREVIOUS YEARS' QUESTIONS

December 2018

1 Thomas Nashe's The Unfrotunate Traveller is narrated by

(a) Ben Lyte, a Coase Papist
(b) Jack Wilton, an English Page
(c) Peter Marston, a Sworn Calvinist
(d) Phillip Foxe, an English Highwayman

2 In Thomas More's Utopia (Book 2), the reader is total that in this new world there are few mistakes in marriage because

(a) there is an extensive courtship period preceding the actual wedding
(b) the family Gods invoked before finalising the nuptials
(c) there is a community get together where prospective husband and wives announce wedding plans endorsed by elders.
(d) prospective husbands and wives see one another naked before agreeing to the match.

3 Francis Bacon's New Atlantis is about a Utopian State called

(a) Asgard (b) Avalon
(c) Ben Salem (d) Baltia

January 2017

4 What does the title Morte D' Arthur mean?

(a) Arthur Mortified (b) Death of Arthur
(c) Castle of Arthur (d) Burial of Arthur

November 2017

5 Which of the following is not true of the ideal state in Thomas More's Utopia?

(a) Personal property, money and vice are effectively abolished
(b) The root causes of crime, ambition and political conflict are eliminated
(c) There is only one religion guided by the principle of a benevolent Supreme Being
(d) Its priesthood, which includes some women, is limited in number

6 What work begins thus "It befell in the days of Uther Pendragon, when he was king of all England and so reigned, that there was a mighty duke in Cromwell that held war against him long time"?

(a) Sir Gawain and the Green Knight
(b) Le Morte d'Arthur
(c) Confessio Amantis
(d) Piers Plowman

July 2016

7 In Thomas More's Utopia which of the following leisure past times is not a favourite among Utopians?

(a) Music (b) Public Lectures
(c) Conversation (d) Dicing and Cards

8 Which of the following statements best describe the narrative perspective employed in Thomas More's Utopia?

1. First person narration by Raphael Hythloday
2. Third person narration by a narrators named Thomas More
3. First person narration by a narrator named Thomas More
4. Third person narration by Raphael Hythloday

The right combination according to the codes is

(a) 1 and 3 (b) 2 and 4 (c) 2 and 3 (d) 1 and 2

June 2015

9 Identify the true statements on Thomas More's Utopia.

(a) Utopia is divided into four parts, each dealing with Raphael Hythloday's adventures in the four suburbs of Antwerp.
(b) Utopia is divided in two parts; the first records a conversation between Thomas More and Raphael Hythloday and the second is Hythaloday's discourse on the institution and practices of Utopia.
(c) Utopia is divided into parts; the first is Thomas More's discourse on the institution and practices of Utopia, and the second a conversation between More and Hythloday.
(d) Utopia is divided in four parts; each dealing with the ordered patterns of towns and cities in Antwerp.

December 2014

10 In More's Utopia, the fictional traveller Raphael Hythloday second name in Greek means

(a) Dispenser of Justice (b) Dispenser of Nonsense
(c) Dispenser of Grace (d) Dispenser of Mercy

ANSWERS

Objective Questions

1. (c)	2. (d)	3. (c)	4. (a)	5. (c)	6. (b)	7. (b)	8. (d)	9. (c)	10. (d)
11. (b)	12. (b)	13. (b)	14. (c)	15. (d)	16. (a)	17. (c)	18. (b)	19. (c)	20. (a)
21. (a)	22. (a)	23. (d)	24. (a)	25. (d)	26. (c)	27. (c)	28. (c)	29. (a)	30. (d)
31. (b)	32. (a)	33. (c)	34. (a)	35. (d)	36. (b)	37. (b)	38. (b)	39. (a)	40. (c)
41. (a)	42. (d)	43. (c)	44. (b)	45. (c)	46. (c)	47. (a)	48. (b)	49. (c)	50. (b)
51. (c)	52. (c)	53. (d)	54. (c)	55. (d)	56. (c)	57. (b)	58. (c)	59. (c)	60. (d)
61. (b)	62. (a)	63. (d)	64. (a)	65. (b)	66. (c)	67. (c)	68. (a)	69. (b)	70. (c)
71. (c)	72. (d)	73. (b)	74. (a)	75. (c)	76. (a)	77. (d)	78. (c)	79. (d)	80. (b)
81. (c)	82. (c)	83. (c)	84. (d)	85. (d)	86. (d)	87. (b)	88. (b)	89. (c)	90. (d)
91. (a)	92. (d)	93. (b)	94. (c)	95. (b)	96. (d)	97. (d)	98. (d)	99. (d)	100. (b)
101. (a)	102. (b)	103. (b)	104. (c)	105. (b)	106. (a)	107. (c)	108. (c)	109. (c)	110. (a)
111. (d)	112. (b)	113. (a)	114. (a)	115. (b)	116. (d)	117. (c)	118. (c)	119. (b)	120. (c)
121. (c)	122. (a)	123. (c)	124. (b)	125. (c)	126. (c)	127. (d)	128. (d)	129. (b)	130. (c)
131. (c)	132. (d)	133. (a)	134. (c)	135. (c)	136. (b)	137. (c)	138. (d)	139. (d)	140. (d)
141. (d)	142. (c)	143. (d)	144. (b)	145. (c)	146. (c)	147. (c)	148. (c)	149. (b)	150. (b)

Pervious Years' Questions

1. (b)	2. (d)	3. (c)	4. (b)	5. (c)	6. (b)	7. (d)	8. (a)	9. (b)	10. (b)

Puritan, Restoration and Neo-Classical Age (1625-1798)

This period refers to 17th century Puritan, Restoration and Neo-Classical Age which lasted upto the end of 18th century. Literature of this period was mostly satirical. Novels of this period presented characters in real life events or situations. Literature sensibility focused on feeling of sympathy through which people work together.

Puritan Age

The Puritan Age is named after the rise of the Puritan movement in England in the 17th century. The period from the accession of Charles I in 1625 to the Revolution of 1688 was filled with a mighty struggle. Puritans were a group of English speaking Protestants who were dissatisfied with the religious reformation movement carried out during the reign of Queen Elizabeth. These people wanted a complete purification of Church of England and removal of various rituals of church, clerical vestments and hierarchical leadership.

The Puritans emerged as a strong political force during the English civil war which was a series of conflicts between Charles I's supporters and Parliamentarians or Roundheads on the other hand consisting of Puritan middle class. The war ended in 1651 with the victory of Parliamentarians. The Puritans remained in ascendancy till 1660, When Charles II was restored to the throne. Puritans, though narrow minded and repressive, aimed for religious and civil liberty. According to WH Hudson, The Puritans 'had strict rules regarding life and conduct' and an 'Uncompromising spirit', which sought to confine literature within the circumscribed field of its own particular interests'.

In this Chapter

Literary Trends During the Puritan Age

Literature of Puritan age was characterised by a spirit of somberness, confusion and pensiveness. Some of the literary men had the tendencies to look backward for the old golden age, and some literary figures wanted to look forward for a better world with the throbs of hope and fresh vitality and youth. And in John Milton, the Puritan spirit finds its noblest expression. There was Samuel Daniel, John Donne, George Herbert, Thomas Carew, Robert Herrick, Sir John Suckling, Sir Richard Lovelace, John Bunyan, Robert Burton, Sir Thomas Browne, Thomas Fuller, Izaak Walton, Jeremy Taylor among other important writers of the age.

In keeping with religious ideas and political standards of the Puritans, religious verses, theological tracts and political treatise replaced romantic poetry of the Elizabethan age. Theatres were closed down and an atmosphere of sombreness and intellectual spirit prevailed in literary works of authors and poets.

Prose in Age of Puritans

As Puritans emphasised more on religious beliefs, purity and realism, fiction as such does not find proper place in this period. There is dominance of satire, scepticism, introspection, self-consciousness and self-criticism. Main prose writers during this period wrote personal journals, historical narratives, poetry and biographies and essays. Some essay writers indulged in delineation of character writers like John Earle, Sir Thomas Overbury, Thomas Fuller are all essay writers who deal with different types of characters. But mainly Prose, during Puritan period is dominated by Christian religious writing.

John Milton's prose is remarkable for his use of language. His prose work has significant passages which show the power and harmony of our English speech. Though, Milton is best known for his epic poems like *Paradise Lost, Paradise Regained* and *Samson Agonistes* but his prose work *Areopagitica* (1644), is worth reading as this fiery attack on censorship and call for a free press is written in wonderful prose. Among his prose writings are letters, pamphlets, political tracts and essays such as of Education and Areopagitica and a generous portion of his heretical Christian Doctrine. His prose consists of exemplary, clarity and extraordinary grace; mostly his prose writing come under 'Non Fictional Prose'.

Major Works

- Of Reformation (1641), Of Prelatical Episcopacy (1641).
- Doctrines and Disciplines of Divorce (1643)
- Of Education (1644), Areopagiticia (1644)
- Tetrachordon 1645
- A Treatise of Civil Power 1659
- Brief Notes upon a Late Sermon (1660)
- De Doctrina Christiana (1823) found 148 years after Milton's death, but attributed to Milton

Character Writers

Some other worth mentioning prose writers here are some figures who are called character writers. These character writers also have a close affinity in the satirists in verse like Joseph Hall, John Earle, Thomas Overbury, George Herbert and Thomas Fuller are the greatest of writers in this genre.

John Earle's *Microcosmography* was published in 1628. The book contains 55 characters and each character represents brief humanity at large. In all characters we find an acute observation and a happy humour of expression. It is one of those books which give us a picturesque idea of the manners of our fathers at a period now become remote.

Sir Thomas *Overbury* (1581-1613) He is also known for twenty one prose sketches, 'which he added to the first edition of his poem *The Wife* (1614). Overybury's style is artificial, he sacrifices matter to manner. His style abounds in far-fetched and fantastic conceits and in this way, his concern with manner, pushes out truth with reality.

Another Character-Writer George Herbert (1593-1633) His work *The Country Parson* deals only with one central figure in all thirty seven essays. His work shows the writer's skill in the use of words and a unity of design. There is real life like presentations of life and characters of a parson.

Thomas Fuller (1608-1661) is one of greatest writer who ever touched the character-sketch. His work The *Holy State* and *Profane State* (1641) is one of the greatest book in this genre. The book studies different types of characters. Some are virtuous, some are vicious. The author deals in word play, encompassing a whole wealth of amusing anecdotes.

Richard Baxter was born in Rowton, near Shrewsbury in 1615. Baxter largely remained self-taught. He has written a series of works such as *The Reformed Pastor* (1656) and A *Call to the Unconverted* (1657) which advocated true Catholicism. His autobiography published after his death called *Reliquiae Baxterianae or Mr Richard Baxter's* narrative of the most memorable passages of his life and times. Baxter died on 8th December, 1691.

Restoration Age (1660-1700)

The period from 1660-1700 is known as the Restoration age since monarchy was restored in England with king Charles II coming to the throne in 1660. The restoration of monarchy was accompanied by the re-opening of English theatres and the restoration of the Church of England as the National Church. After Charles II died, his brother James II took over the throne. Afraid of the policies James II right had introduced, William III removed James in 1688 and took over the English throne in 1689. This act is often referred to as the Glorious Revolution because the transfer of power did not involve violence and blood shed.

The start of the Restoration period roughly coincides with the beginning of what is known as the Enlightenment which lasted until the end of the 18th century. There was emphasis on reason and logic, the thinkers of the period helped to develop the modern science that treats the natural world as a testable subject.

Literary Trends of Restoration Period

The restoration marks the beginning of modern prose–an age of intellectualism and rationalism. Many typical literary forms of the modern world including the novel, biography, history, travel writing and journalism– gained confidence during the Restoration period, new scientific discoveries and philosophical concepts as well as new social and economic conditions came into play. There was a great out pouring of pamphlet literature too, much of it was politico-religious.

Rise of Novel in Restoration Period

We can say that novel as a literary genre emerged in the beginning of the 18th century novel developed as a piece of prose fiction due to the people's desire (middle class specially) for reading subjects related to their everyday experience. The novels in this period presented characters in real life events or situations, Daniel Defoe's *Robinson Crusoe* and Henry Fielding's *Tom Jones* are some of early English novels.

The social and intellectual currents of the age were linked for creating something new and different. Those who carried out the action became individualise they were interpreted in and all their complexity and the social pressure on them were minutely detailed. When people wanted to hear stories of those who are not too different from themselves, then novel was born.

Next to Dryden, John Bunyan (1628-1688) was the greatest prose-writer of this period. He is called a pioneer of English novels with two books *The Pilgrim's Progress* and *Grace-Abounding*. Other writers of this period were Lord Halifax, Sir William Temple, Thomas Sprat and George Saville.

Major Writers of Puritan Age

John Bunyan (1628-88)

English writer and preacher John Bunyan was born in Elstow, England in November 1628. He was the son of Thomas Bunyan and his second wife, Margaret Bentley Bunyan. Not much is known about his schooling and Education. At the young age of sixteen, Bunyan had joined the parliamentarian army to fight for the Round heads against the Cavaliers. He married in 1649 and lived in Elstow Until 1655.

Literary Career and Works

Bunyan was arrested for his beliefs during the 'great persecution' of 1660-1690. It was in the prison that Bunyan wrote *The Pilgrim's Progress* (1678) that blends facts with fiction. This was a Christian allegory which traced the life and journey of Christian from the city of Destruction to Salvation. Christian's pilgrimage takes him through the slough of Despond, Vanity Fair and the Delectable Mountains in a succession of adventures that keep the reader turning the pages. Faithful and hopeful he vanquishes many enemies before arriving at the celestial city with the line that still reverberates through the English literary tradition. "So he passed over, and all the trumpets sounded for him on the other side." The novel has a perfect 'arc' and contains unforgettable characters like worldly wiserman, Lord Hategood, Mr Stand Fast and Mr Valiant for Truth. Its unique quality is a robust and engaging sense of humour that appeals to people of all generation.

Major Works

- A Few Signs from Hell or the Groans of a Damned Soul 1658.
- The Holy City or the New Jerusalem (1666)
- Saved by Grace 1675
- The Strait Gate, Great Difficulty of Going to Heaven (1676)
- The Pilgrim's Progress (1678)
- The Life and Death of Mr Badman (1680)
- The Holy War (1682)
- Grace Abounding (1666)
- Bunyan died in 1688 of a Severe Cold.

Aphra Behn (1640-1689)

Aphra Behn is considered to be the first professional woman writer of England. She was born in Wye in 1640. It is believed that Aphra had a Catholic upbringing. She is known as a dramatist, fiction writer and poet and was the first English woman to earn her living by writing. Aphra Behn died on 16th April, 1689 in London.

Literary Career and Works

Aphra wrote a short novel *Oroonoko*. It is about an African Prince Oroonoko, who falls in love with a young woman Imoinda.

When their love is discovered, Imoinda is sold into slavery to Suriname. One day, Oroonoko, who is a slave owner himself, is lured by the captain of an English ship and taken as a slave to Guiana. Here, he is united with his beloved. He tries to attain freedom but is caught and badly beaten. Realising that there is no way out, he kills his love and their unborn child. As soon as he is about to kill himself, he is captured and later executed.

Her novel *Oroonoko* has been termed ground breaking for its depiction of the institution of slavery as cruel and inhuman. Behn has been praised for her characterisation of Oroonoko, a first and decent man who encounters some very cruel traits among his enemies. The other book by Aphra Behn *Love-letters Between a Nobleman and His Sister* is in three volumes. It is a type of epistolary novel. The novel is based loosely on an affair between Ford, Lord Grey of Werke and his wife's sister Lady Henrietta Berkeley, a scandal that broke in London in 1682.

Aphra Behn also wrote two short stories. *The History of the Nun* (1688) and *The Dumb Virgin or The Force of Imagination* (1700). It tells about an anti-heroine Isabella whose reputation for virtuousness and religious devotion ironically becomes her motivation for murder. This short fiction show cases a complicated social psychology and a surprising dark amusing plot.

Another novella—*the Dumb Virgin* tells the story of the sisters and a brother whose defects both in body and fate are engendered by their mother's failure to confirm to the correct paradigm of maternal behaviour. The author's narratives prompt us to rethink the ways in which disability and femininity were both imagined as problems during the 17th century.

Aphra Behn's works unfortunately did not get credit during her life time for her novels. Critics at that time (18th century) regarded Aphra Behn as too romantic. But now what was seen as fault in Aphra Behn can be understood as seasoned professional's creative reworking of fact, fiction memory, imagination and politics. 20th century fiction writer Virginia Woolf has given her due credit for her fictional work.

Major Works

Plays

- The Forced Marriage (1670)
- The Amorous Prince (1671)
- The Dutch Lover (1673)
- Abdelazer (1676)
- The Town Fop (1676)
- The Rover, Part 1 (1677) and Part 2 (1681)
- Sir Patient Fancy (1678)
- The Feigned Courtesans (1679)
- The Young King (1679)
- The Roundheads (1681)
- The City Heiress (1682)
- Like Father, Like Son (1682)
- The Emperor of the Moon (1687)

Novels

- Love-Letters Between a Nobleman and His Sister (1684)
- Oroonoko (1688)
- Short Stories
- The History of the Nun: or, The Fair Vow-Breaker (1688)
- The Dumb Virgin: Or, The Force of imagination (1700)

Poetry

- Poems Upon Several Occasions, With A Voyage to the Island of Love (1684)
- Lycidus: or, The Lover in Fashion (1688)

William Congreve

Main dramatists of this period include William Congreve (1670-1729), William Wycherley, John Vanbrugh and George Etherege, William Congreve was born in Yorkshire England in 1670. His father was an officer in Army. Congreve was educated in Kilkenny and at Trinity College Dublin with Jonathan Swift. Congreve also studied law but was drawn towards Literature and started writing.

Literary Career and Works

At the age of 17, William Congreve along with his famous play *The Way of the World* also wrote a romantic novel *Incognito* (1692). Congreve is more known for his satire, wit and brilliance of language.

In his novel *Incognito*, Congreve seems to have taken its plot from Shakespeare's *Romeo and Juliet, Love's Labour Lost*. The story is somewhat rigid mistaken identity and mass marriage with a Masquerade in between but the pleasure is in the details. This novel is both a valuable and entertaining text.

Major Works

- The Old Bachelor (1693)
- The Double Dealer (1694)
- Love for Love (1695)
- The Mourning Bride (1697)
- The Way of the World (1700)

Neo-Classical Age or Augustan Age (1700-1798)

The 18th century in English Literature is known as 'the Augustan Age', the Neo-Classical Age and the Age of Reason. The term 'Augustan' comes from the parallel between 18th century and the classical Augustan Age of Emperor Augustus Caesar. As the Age of Emperor Augustus was the Golden Age of Roman Empire, similarly 18th century is also seen as the golden period in the history of English Literature. The writers of 18th century imitated the literary forms and themes of the original Augustan writers such as Virgil and Horace.

To a certain extent Neo-classicism represented a reaction against the optimistic, exuberant and enthusiastic renaissance view of man as a being fundamentally good and possessed of an infinite potential for spiritual and intellectual growth. Neo-Classical theorists by contrast saw man as an imperfect being, inherently sinful whose potential was limited. They replaced the renaissance emphasis on the imagination, experimentation and mysticism with an emphasis on order and reason, on restraint on common sense and also on political and economical conservatism. It used reason to scrutinise previously accepted doctrines and traditions.

Social and Economic Background to the Augustan Age

Outlining the socio-economic-political climate of the 18th century Cynthia Stodola Pomerleau states that the 18th century saw the establishment of modern party politics with two opposing parties-Whigs and Tories, the emergence of Britain from isolationism to internationalism, the change in economic policy from mercantilism to laissez-faire capitalism, the growth of the British Empire and the start of the industrial revolution.

Other important changes that took place were, agriculture became market-oriented, rural manufacturing spread capital throughout the population and increased demand led to technical innovation. Between 1700 and 1800, England also experienced a major demographic transformation as its population increased dramatically.

Literacy also grew at a fast rate, while in the 14th century, 80% of English adults couldn't even spell their names, literacy rate reached 62% among the English population of roughly 8 million by 18th century. England became more and more a print-oriented culture in the 18th century.

The proliferation of the printing press, the cheapness of paper and the rise of literacy and economic status meant that many more people could participate in reading. The new readership primarily consisted of the new emerging middle class.

Jeremy Black in his article, 'Newspapers and Politics in the 18th century' states that; "Between 1690 and 1780 the number of newspapers printed annually in England rose from less than a million to 14 million, a growth far in excess of that of the population. The period was the most dramatic in the history of the English press, with the creation of new forms - daily, Sunday and provincial papers and greatly increased freedom of the press, after the lapsing of the Licensing Act in, 1695."

Literature of the Augustan Age

Matthew Arnold called 18th century as 'the age of prose and reason'. As a result of the influence of enlightenment, wit and intellectual conceits, shaped the tone of much Augustan writing. Prose triumphed in this Augustan period. Periodical essays, satires and novels all flourished during this period. Even poetry became prosaic and was used for purpose of criticism or satire.

WJ Long cites reasons for the spread of prose and states, "A multitude of practical interests arising from the new social and political conditions demanded expression, not simply in books, but more especially in pamphlets, magazines and newspapers. Poetry was inadequate for such a task; hence the development of prose, of the 'unfettered word,' as Dante calls it, a development, which astonishes us by its rapidity and excellence. The graceful elegance of Addison's essays, the terse vigour of Swift's satires, the artistic finish of Fielding's novels, the sonorous eloquence of Gibbon's history and of Burke's orations, these have no parallel in the poetry of the age."

Nature was an important influence on Augustan writers. They examined the enduring truths of human nature. By nature, the Augustans meant not external natural world as expressed in the poetry of Romantics, but man and manners of society. In his *Essay on Criticism*, Alexander Pope stated, "First follow nature and your judgement frame by her just standard, which is still i.e. always the same." There was not much drama written in this age. Main important form was the sentimental comedy. Other dramatic forms that reigned during this period were ballad, opera, farce and pantomime.

Literary Characteristics of Augustan Age

Main literary characteristics of Augustan Age can be summed up as follows

- This was an age of new prose forms such as periodicals, criminal biographies, travelogues, political allegories, and romantic tales.
- The predominance of satire is an important literary characteristic of this age.
- Augustan age saw rise of the novel as a genre. It became the most important literary expression of the bourgeoisie and middle class. Defoe, Richardson, Fielding, Smollett were the main exponents of this form.
- The heroic couplet (two lines of rhymed iambic pentameter) was the most important verse form of Augustan age. It suited the spirit of this age because of its epigrammatic quality and terseness.
- Sentimental comedy was a new dramatic form that became popular during this age, but was later burlesqued by writers such as Goldsmith.

Literature of Sensibility

Literature of sensibility refers to a particular type of literature written during the later half of 18th century, which focused on feeling of sympathy and sensibility. By sensibility was meant an ability to emotionally respond to beauty and sublimity. It was a revolt against philosophy of Hobbes and other 17th century empirical philosophers, who viewed human beings as selfish and greedy.

Defining sensibility as an important ideal of 18th century, Charlotte Sussman states that "Sensibility, in contrast posits sympathy as the primary mode through which social beings work together. It contends that people will abide by social rules through mutual respect, even or perhaps especially, those at the top of the social hierarchy." A key text that contributed towards this movement towards sensibility was Adam Smith's *The Theory of Moral Sentiments in* 1759. Smith claimed that even though humans do have a natural tendency to look after their own selves, yet they are also endowed with a natural sympathy as social creatures.

Apart from Smith's philosophical theories, the popularity of the novels of Jean-Jacques Rousseau such as *Julie*, with their emphasis on altruism, refined sensibilities and benevolent feelings, aided the development of an appetite for the literature of sensibility. The novel of sensibility exalted feeling above reason and raised the analysis of emotion to a fine art,

Important examples of the novel of sensibility are Samuel Richardson's *Pamela* (1740) and *Clarissa Harlowe* (1748), Lawrence Sterne's *A Sentimental Journey* (1768) and *Tristram Shandy* (1767) and Henry MacKenzie's *Man of Feeling* (1771). While, sensibility and the discussion of it, is most prominent in the novel, but it is dealt within poetry and drama as well. Plays such as Richard Steele's *The Conscious Lovers* and Cumberland's *The West Indian*, Hannah More's poem *Sensibility* (1782) and Charlotte Smith's *Elegiac Sonnets* (1784) are examples of it.

Major Writers of Augustan Age

Jonathan Swift (1667-1745)

Irish author, clergyman and satirist Jonathan Swift was born in Dublin in 1667. He studied at Kilkenny Grammar School and at Trinity College in Dublin. In 1689, he became Secretary to Sir William Temple, a diplomat and man of Letters. He gained access to his patron's library. He met Esther Johnson who became his lifelong companion and appeared as 'Stella' in his poetry, with his patron's assistance, Swift received an MA degree from Oxford University. In 1701, he was awarded Doctor of Divinity from Trinity College, Dublin,

Literary Career and Works

Swift's first political pamphlet was titled *A Discourse on the Contests and Dissentions in Athens and Rome,* this was followed by his satirical works, *A Tale of A Tub* and *The Battle of the Books* in 1704.

In 1713, Swift was appointed Dean of St Patrick's in Dublin, The same year, he joined with Alexander Pope and others, to form the Scriblerus Literary Club. It was also around this time that he met Esther 'Vanessa' Vanhomrigh (1688-1723), who inspired his poem *Cadenus* and *Vanessa* (1713). In 1728, his 'Stella', Esther Johnson died. Her death moved Swift to write *The Death of Mrs Johnson*.

Swift is known for his Novel *Gulliver's Travels*, a book of fantasy, satire and political allegory, which was published in

1726. The book was a huge success, his pamphlets, *The Grand Question Debated and A Modest Proposal* for preventing the children of poor people from being a burden on their parents or the country and for making them beneficial to the public appeared in 1729. He died in 1745 at the age of 75.

A Tale of A Tub

- Jonathan Swift's *A Tale of A Tub* is a prose satire which was published in 1704,
- The book consists of a tale of three brothers and digressions. The tale is an allegorical story of three brothers - Peter, Martin and Jack. Peter symbolises the Roman Catholic Church; Martin symbolises the Anglican Church (from Martin Luther) and Jack (from John Calvin) symbolises the Dissenters.
- On his deathbed, their father gives each of them a new coat that is guaranteed to last a lifetime, given the proper care. The father represents Christ, the will is the Bible, the coats are Christian faith.
- According to Dr Abigail William, the sons gradually disobey his instruction, finding excuses for adding shoulder knots or gold lace, according to the prevailing fashion. Martin and Jack quarrel with the arrogant Peter (the Reformation) and then with each other (the split between Anglicanism and Puritanism) and then separate.
- The 'tale' presents a consistent satire on religious excess, while the digressions are a series of parodies of contemporary writing in literature, politics, theology, Biblical exegesis and medicine.

The Battle of the Books

- Swift's *The Battle of the Books* was first published with *A Tale of a Tub* in 1704. It is a mock heroic work that depicts a literal battle between books in the King's Library. Swift wrote *The Battle of the Books* primarily to defend the position taken by his patron Sir William Temple in the pamphlet war at the end of the 17th century, regarding the rival claims to greatness of the moderns and the ancients.
- It begins with a note from the bookseller to the reader, telling the reader that it refers to a 'Famous dispute ... about ancient and modern learning.' Sir William Temple had taken the side of the ancients against Charles Boyle, who had praised the ancient writer Phalaris, but Wotton and Bentley had taken Boyle's side. The controversy led to a battle between the books.
- The combat in the 'Battle' is interrupted by the interpolated allegory of the spider and the bee. A bee gets entangled in the web of a spider in the library. Deepak Singh states that Swift compares the spider to the moderns, who spin their scholastic lore out of their own entrails, while the bee is like the ancients who follow nature for their honey.

Gulliver's Travels

- Swift's *Gulliver's Travels* is a work of social and political satire, which was published in 1726. Swift himself claimed that he wrote Gulliver's Travels to vex the world rather than divert it.'
- The protagonist of the novel, Captain Lemuel Gulliver, narrates and speaks directly to the reader from his own experience. Swift uses Gulliver's journey to various lands and the backdrop for his satire. *Gulliver embarks on four distinct journeys* (i) To Lilliput (ii) Brobdingnag (iii) Laputa, Balnibarbi, Luggnagg. Glubbdubdrib and Japan, (iv) To the Country of the Houyhnhnms. The Lilliputians are small, but full of self-importance. They represent the English.
- The Brobdingnagians are physically a lot larger than Gulliver; however they are less threatening than the small Lilliputians. The king is upset at Gulliver's description of Europe, considering Europeans to be violent.
- The Laputans are obsessed with knowledge and spent a great deal of time studying but failed to produce anything productive. The Houyhnhnms represent a successful society, which benefits all of the Houyhnhnms and considers them all equal. On the other hand, the Yahoos represent all i.e. bad with human beings as they are uncivilised, greedy and violent.

A Modest Proposal

- Swifts *Modest Proposal*, published in 1729 in response to worsening conditions in Ireland is among the most severe and scathing of all Swift's pamphlets.
- The complete title of the work is "A Modest Proposal for Preventing the Children of Poor People in Ireland, from Being a Burden on their Parents or Country and for Making them Beneficial to the Public."
- It begins with an account of the impoverished state of the people of Ireland.
- In this work, Swift satirises the English landlords with outrageous humour, proposing that Irish infants be sold as food at age one, when they are plump and healthy to give the Irish a new source of income and the English a new food product to bolster their economy and eliminate a social problem.
- He says his proposal, if adopted, would also result in reduction of the number of Catholics in Ireland, since most Irish infants-almost all of whom were baptised Catholic-would end up in stew and other dishes instead of growing up to go to Catholic churches. Here, he is satirising the prejudice of Protestants towards Catholics.
- The dominant figure of speech in *A Modest Proposal* is verbal irony.

Daniel Defoe (1660-1731)

English writer and journalist Daniel Defoe was born in London in 1660. He studied at Morton's Academy, a school for Dissenters at Newington Green, preparing to become a Presbyterian Minister. However, he changed his mind later and became a hosiery merchant instead. He went bankrupt in 1692 and by 1703, decided to leave the business industry altogether.

Literary Career and Works

He became popular with the publication of his satirical poem, *The True Born Englishman* (1701), which attacked English xenophobia. His ironic pamphlet *The Shortest Way with Dissenters* (1702) demanded the total suppression of dissent and got him imprisoned. In 1703 Robert Harley, Earl of Oxford, a Tory government official, employed Defoe as a spy. With the support of the government, Defoe started the newspaper, 'The review' published between 1704 and 1713, the newspaper appeared three times in a week.

In his later years, Defoe turned to writing fiction. His novels include *Robinson Crusoe* (1719), *Captain Singleton* (1720), *Journal of the Plague Year* (1722), *Captain Jack* (1722), *Moll Flanders* (1722) and *Roxanda* (1724). He died on 24th April, 1731 due to of a stroke and was buried in Bunhill Fields, a cemetery for Dissenters.

Robinson Crusoe

Defoe's novel, *Robinson Crusoe* was based on the true story of a shipwrecked seaman named Alexander Selkirk. Its full title is *The Life and Strange Surprising Adventures of Robinson Crusoe*, of York, Mariner: who lived there for 28 years, all alone in an uninhabited island on the coast of America, near the mouth of the Great River of Oroonoque; Having been cast on shore by Shipwreck, wherein all the men perished, but himself.

- "With an account of how he was at last as strangely delivered by pirates."
- The protagonist of the novel- *Robinson Crusoe* is a young and self-sufficient Englishman, who after several adventures at sea and on land, is cast away on a small, almost uninhabited island. One day, Crusoe is shocked to discover a man's footprint on the beach, which belongs to one of the cannibals said to be living in the region. One of the victims of these cannibals, waiting to be slaughtered, breaks free and runs toward Crusoe's dwelling. Crusoe then protects him and names him Friday. Thereafter, Friday becomes Crusoe's humble and devoted slave.
- In the end, they are finally rescued and taken back to England, Defoe's novel blends the traditions of Puritan spiritual autobiography with an insistent scrutiny of the nature of men and women as social creatures. It also offers a critique of the society as Crusoe creates a utopian environment in the absence of society. Estranged from society and in relationship with nature, Crusoe develops as a spiritual and moral being.

Moll Flanders

It was published in 1722, Defoe's picaresque novel *Moll Flanders* narrates the story of a beautiful and greedy woman who turns to crime. The full title of the novel gives a brief outline of the plot: *The Fortunes and Misfortunes of the Famous Moll Flanders*, who was born in Newgate and during a life of continued variety for threescore years, besides her childhood, was twelve year a whore, five times a wife (whereof once to her own brother), twelve year a thief, eight year a transported felon in Virginia, at last grew rich, liv'd honest and died a penitent written from her own memorandums."

The protagonist of the novel-Moll Flanders is the daughter of a transported convict. She becomes an orphan and begins 'Life at a great disadvantage'. As daughter of a convict, she is thrown into the world with no training in any trade and no prospects other than starvation or the same life of crime as of her parents. Moll is the alias she adopts. She grows into a beautiful teenager and is seduced at an early age. Abandoned by her first lover, she is compelled to marry his younger brother who dies soon. She remarries a draper who soon flees the country as a fugitive from the law.

She marries yet again and moves to America, only to find out that her husband is actually her half-brother. Moll goes through a series of liaisons and marriages, one after the other. After her last husband dies, she squanders in poverty and starts stealing. Eventually. She is caught, imprisoned and sentenced to death. In prison at Newgate, she reunites with her Lancashire husband, who has also been arrested. They both manage to have their sentences reduced and they are transported to the colonies, where they begin a new life as plantation owners. She also gains the inheritance, which her mother had left for her. Finally wealthy, Moll and her husband return to England, where they spend the rest of their lives. Defoe gives a picture of the society of his time where the only options available to women of lower classes were theft or prostitution.

Samuel Richardson (1689-1761)

English writer Samuel Richardson was born in poverty in Derbyshire, England. He only had a basic common school education. His career began as an apprentice to a printer. With his hard work, he was able to set-up a business of his own. Like many printers at that time, he was also a bookseller and publisher. Richardson read widely in order to compensate for having received little formal education.

Literary Career and Works

Richardson started writing in the 1730s. His first known work, published in 1733, was *The Apprentice's Vade Mecum*; or, *Young Man's Pocket Companion*, a conduct book addressed to apprentices. This was followed by *A Seasonable Examination* (1735), a pamphlet supporting a parliamentary bill to regulate the London theaters. He was also commissioned to write a collection of letters that might serve as models for 'country readers,' a volume that has become known as *Familiar Letters on Important Occasions*. During his work on *Familiar Letters on Important Occasions*, Richardson decided to put together a series of letters that would narrate the tribulations of a young servant girl in a country house. He expanded this idea into a novel, which led to the creation of his first novel, *Pamela*: or, *Virtue Rewarded*. The novel received tremendous success.

But also led to a spate of sequels-Fielding's famous *An Apology for the Life of Mrs Shamela Andrews*, a clever and very gross piece of raillery, which appeared in April 1741 and *Pamela's Conduct in High Life* (September 1741), a spurious sequel by John Kelly of the *Universal Spectator*.

To override the unauthorised sequels float in the marketplace, Richardson in his turn produced *Pamela in her Exalted Condition* (1741). His other major works were the novels *Clarissa* (1748) and *Sir Charles Grandison* (1753).

Even after the success of his writing career, Richardson continued with his printing business. After Charles Grandison, he wrote no more novels. He died in London on 4th July, 1761.

Pamela by Samuel Richardson

- Richardson's *Pamela*: or *Virtue Rewarded* is an epistolary novel published in 1740. It narrates the story of the 15 years old Pamela Andrews, who is a servant at an estate in the county of Bedfordshire, England. She becomes a victim of harassment at hands of the master of the estate, Mr B.
- He continually tries to seduce her, abducts her and locks her in one of his estates, but Pamela resists his advances. Mr B proposes to make Pamela his mistress but she refuses his terms and conditions.
- He also tries to get close to Pamela at night by impersonating a drunken maid servant, but she swoons and avoids his advances. Finally, Mr B gets chastened and tries to woo Pamela through love rather than force. Pamela's virtue gets finally rewarded when Mr B proposes to marry her.
- The story ends with both of them getting married and leading a blissful conjugal life. Main themes of the novel include: nature of virtue in a woman, class politics (Pamela is a lower-class female servant- an easy prey for a wealthy master, who has taken a fancy to her and uses his money and power to entice her or sexually harass her) and sexual politics.

Clarissa by Samuel Richardson

- Richardson's *Clarissa*; or, *The History of a Young Lady* is an epistolary novel published in 1748.
- It was published in 7 volumes, 1747-1748,8 years after the appearance of *Pamela*.
- The protagonist of the novel, eighteen years old Clarissa Harlowe is seduced by Richard Lovelace. Lovelace tricks Clarissa into eloping with him.
- Unaware that Lovelace is tricking her, she goes with him to London, where he secures lodgings at Mrs Sinclair's house. Clarissa is unaware that this is a brothel and the women she meets there are whores. Having been involved with (and ruined by) Lovelace in the past, these women are jealous of Clarissa and encourage Lovelace to rape her.
- He eventually rapes an unconscious Clarissa (after Mrs Sinclair has drugged her). However, the rape does not change Clarissa's moral standards and she refuses to compromise with her virtue and marry Lovelace.
- She stops eating and her health gradually deteriorates. She prepares a will and dies.
- The novel is a celebration of virtue and morality in woman, a sort of conduct book for the young ladies of Richardson's time.

Laurence Sterne (1713-1768)

Anglo-Irish novelist Laurence Sterne was born in Clonmel, County Tipperary, Ireland. Sterne studied at Jesus College, Cambridge. He took orders in 1737 and a year later, became the Vicar at Sutton-in-the-Forest, Near York.

Literary Career and Works

In 1747, Sterne published a sermon preached in York titled *The Case of Elijah*. This was followed by The *Abuses of Conscience* in 1750. Few years later, he wrote a sketch on a quarrel between his Dean and a York lawyer, a sort of Swiftian satire of dignitaries of the spiritual courts. Turning his parishes over to a curate, Sterne -began to write **Tristram Shandy**. However, its initial manuscript was rejected by London printers.

Sterne experienced deep bouts of melancholy and it was under such an atmosphere that *Tristram Shandy* was written. Sterne himself states that every word of the novel was 'Written under the greatest heaviness of heart'. The first two volumes of the novel were published by Sterne himself at his own expense. However, after the success of the novel, Sterne obtained a contract for a new volume each year during the rest of his life. .

Between 1759 and 1768, Sterne wrote five instalments of *Tristram*, several volumes of *Sermons of Mr Yorick* and at the end of the period, *A Sentimental Journey*. The last was a comic novel that defies conventional expectations of a travel book. During his late years, Sterne fell in love with Mrs Eliza Draper, the wife of Daniel Draper, an official of the East India Company. His letters to her are collected in *Journal to Eliza*. Sterne was afflicted with tuberculosis and died less than a month after the publication of *A Sentimental Journey*.

Tristram Shandy by Sterne

Tristram Shandy was written between 1759 and 1767. The book was published in five separate instalments, each containing two volumes except the last, which included only the final Volume 9. The text intends to set out the 'autobiography' of Tristram Shandy.

However, the birth of the hero, which the author sets about to discuss on the first page, does not finally occur until Volume IV.

It is a highly unconventional and experimental novel in terms of its style and narrative technique. The book contains several digressions, marbled pages and blank pages. Rabelais's Gargantua and Pantagruel is a major influence on the novel. Each of the characters of the novel has their distinctiveness called hobby-horses. Tristram Shandy's father believed that life should be ordered by a theory while his uncle Toby is obsessed with war and military campaigns.

Henry Fielding (1707-1754)

English novelist and playwright Henry Fielding was born in Sharpham park, England in 1707. He received his education at Eton Cottege and the University of Leiden.

Literary Career and Works

When Fielding returned to England, he started writing theatrical comedies. He also became manager of the Little Theatre in the Haymarket in 1736. *The Author's Farce* and *Rape upon Rape* were some of his famous plays. However, the passing of Theatrical Licensing Act in 1737, put an end to his career as a playwright. He became editor of *The Champion*. He was prompted to turn to **fiction** after reading Richardon's *Pamela*, He not only wrote *Shamela*, a parody of the novel, but followed it up with *Joseph Andrews* in 1742.

In 1743, Fielding published three volumes of *Miscellanies*, which included the famous work, *The Life and Death of Mr Jonathan Wild, the Great*, based on the life of a notorious criminal. His most popular novel, *The History of Tom Jones, A Foundling* established him as leading exponent of the English novel. Fielding had married Charlotte Craddock in 1734, on whom he later modeled the heroines of both Tom Jones and Amelia, Fielding got afflicted with health problems such as asthma, dropsy and severe gout, which forced him to retire in 1754. He also wrote an account of his journey, *The Journal of a Voyage to Lisbon*, in which he chronicled the slowness of travel, the incompetence of doctors and his own courage in overcoming these obstacles. He died in Lisbon in 1754.

Joseph Andrews

- Fielding' novel, *Joseph Andrews* or *The History of the Adventures of Joseph Andrews and of his Friend Mr Abraham Adams* was a response to Richardson's novel, *Pamela*.
- In the preface to this novel, Fielding explains in detail his inauguration of a hybrid genre, the 'comic epic-poem in prose'.
- *Joseph Andrews* is a picaresque novel 'written in imitation of the *Manner of Cervantes*, author of *Don Quixote*. '
- The title character, Joseph Andrews is the brother of Richardson's heroine, Pamela. He is a footman in the household of Sir Thomas Booby and catches the attention of Mr Booby's wife.
- When the Boobys depart for London, Joseph goes along with them. The amorous Lady Booby continues to make advances towards him after her husband's death, but he remains unaffected. Since, he refuses to submit her demands, he is dismissed.
- Thereafter, Joseph sets out for the Booby's country Parish, where he hopes to be reunited with his childhood sweetheart and now fiancee, the illiterate milkmaid Fanny Goodwill. Here, he is engaged in a scuffle with some ruffians.

- He reaches an inn where he meets an old acquaintance Parson Adams. Together, they start on a journey and face a series of hardships, adventures and exploits. They are joined by Fanny. .
- When Lady Booby comes to know that Fanny and Joseph are going to be married, she weaves a plot to sabotage their marriage, but fails in her endeavour.
- At the end, it is revealed that Joseph Andrews was not the son of Andrews, but son of Mr Wilson who had lost him when he was just an infant.
- Both Joseph Andrews and Fanny live happily and their financial problems are solved by Mr Booby's 'unprecedented generosity' in giving Fanny a gift of two thousand pounds.

Tom Jones

- Henry Fielding's third novel *Tom Jones* was published in 1749. Its full title was *The History* of *Tom Jones, A Foundling*.
- Divided into eighteen books, Fielding defines his novel as a 'heroical, historical prosaic poem'. The novel is in part autobiographical and contains aspects of his own life-his love for his first wife and his knowledge of the South-Western part of England.
- The novel narrates the story of the title character from infancy through his marriage to the beautiful and virtuous Sophia Western, the pursuit of whom takes a larger part of the tale. The story begins with Mr Allworthy, a rich and generous country gentleman, finding an abandoned baby in his bed. He names the child Tom Jones and brings him up in his house with Blifil, son of his sister Bridget Blifil and his heir.
- Tom falls in love with his neighbour, the wealthy and beautiful Sophia Western. However, since Tom is an illegitimate child with little money, Sophia's father is opposed to the match.
- Jealous of Tom since childhood, Blifil poisons Allworthy's mind against Tom and because of this, Tom is banished from the house.
- Away from home, Tom encounters a series of adventures. At the end, it is eventually revealed that Tom is the son of Bridget Allworthy, Mr Allworthy's sister.
- Tom and Allworthy are united and Sophia's father also accedes to the marriage.

Tobias Smollett (1721-1771)

Scottish novelist and poet Tobias Smolett was born in Dumbartonshire Scotland in 1721. Smollett was educated at Dumbarton Grammar School and at the University of Glasgow. He served an apprenticeship to surgeons;William Stirling and John Gordon. As a surgeon's mate, he saw active service in the navy, notably during the bloody British defeat at Cartagena in the Caribbean.

Literary Career and Works

On his return to London, he set-up work as a surgeon and occasionally wrote satires. Eight months later in 1748, he came out with his first novel, *Roderick Random*. The novel was a parody based on two satirical picaresque works, Smollett had translated into English: Cervantes's *Don Quixote* (1605-1615) and Alain-Rene Lesage's *Gil Blas* (1715-1747). Roderick Random established Smollett as a literary figure but he still continued his career as a surgeon.

His other works include the picaresque *Peregrine Pickle* (1751) which satirizes English literary and social groups. *The Adventures of Ferdinand Count Fathom* (1753) which satirizes English Gothic fiction and explores Hobbesian determinism and *The Expedition of Humphry Clinker*, an epistolary novel that charts the adventures of a family group travelling through Britain.

In 1755, Smollett translated *Don Quixote*, the source for *The Life and Adventures of Sir Launcelote de Greaves* (1760-61), serialised in his British Magazine. He also wrote *Travels through France and Italy*, a satire on tourists. Smollett died at Leghorn on 21st October, 1771 shortly after the publication of his last book, *The Expedition of Humphry Clinker*.

Oliver Goldsmith (1730-1774)

Oliver Goldsmith was an Irish novelist, playwright and poet who is best known for his novel. *The Vicar of Wakefield* (1766), his pastoral poems and his play. He was born in Ireland in country Longford in 1730. His father was a county vicar, who died at an early age. Goldsmith earned his bachelor of Arts degree in 1749 at Trinity College, Dublin. He studied and coursed through a variety of professions but finally settled for Medicines in 1752. Gold Smith died on 4th April, 1774 after suffering from kidney disease.

Literary Career and Works

For some years Goldsmith worked as hack writer and produced huge quantities of (generally poor) translations and other articles. He was able to attract fame with some more painstakingly work undertaken by him. His career among the intellectual elite is generally regarded to begin with 1759 publication of 'Enquiry into Present State of Polite Learning in Europe' which earned him the admiration of Samuel Johnson who along with Goldsmith and other was a founding member of 'The Club'. Through Johnson's patronage Goldsmith began to publish his first master works including the novel, *the Vicar of Wakefield*.

Major Works

- Enquiry into the present State of Polite Learning in Europe (1759)
- The Citizens of the World 1762
- The Traveller (1764)
- An Elegy on the Death of a Mad Dog (1766)
- The Vicar of Wakefield (1766)
- The Good Natur'd Man (1768)
- The Deserted Village (1770)
- She Stoops To Conquer (1773)

The Vicar of Wakefield

- The only novel written by Goldsmith *The Vicar of Wakefield* was published in 1766. Dr Charles Primrose, the vicar or the title is a kind, generous and an honest man.
- He and his wife Deborah have six children.
- Vicar Primrose refuses to take a salary from his parish and donates all the money to support the poor and the needy on the eve of his son George's marriages to Arabella Wilmot. The vicar loses all his money due to the bankruptcy of his investor. As a result, the marriage is called off.
- George is sent to London to earn a fortune. Family moves to a small parish and vicar is offered management of a small farm on land of Squire Thornhill.
- Squire Thornhill, a notorious womaniser, Seduces vicar's daughter Olivia.
- Meanwhile another character, Mr. Burchell is introduced who meets the Primrose family in an inn.
- He rescues vicar's another daughter Sophia from a flooded river.
- Both Burchell and Sophia fall in love, but Mrs Primrose does not agree to their marriage as Burchell is considered poor. At the end of the story, his true identity is revealed- he is Sir William Thornhill, the Squire's Uncle.
- The novel ends with George marrying Arabella, as he originally intended and Sir William Thornhill marries Sophia.

Another worth mentioning name is Dr Samuel Johnson who was basically English poet, biographer, Critic and Lexicographer. He has written two novellas also.

Dr Samuel Johnson

Dr Samuel Johnson was born in the country town of Lichfield in Staffordshire in 1709. In early childhood, Johnson was plagued by physical difficulties. Johnson found comfort in the written work. Johnson attended Pembroke College, oxford but left in 1731 due to lack of money.

Literary Career and Works

Johnson's first published book was a complete translation of Father Jeronimo Lobo's *Account of Abyssinian*. In May 1738, Johnson's first major work, the poem, *London-Imitation of the Third Satire of Juvenal* was published anonymously. This was followed by his works, *Life of Mr. Richard Savage, The Vanity of Human Wishes* and the play *'Irene'*.

But Johnson's most monumental work, *A Dictionary of the English Language* was begun in 1746 when some publishers approached him and finally in 1755 it was published this work established his literary reputation. Johnson's important works is his satirical novella *Rasselas; Prince of Abissinia, The Life of Ascham, Notes to Shakespeare and the Fountains: A Fairy Tale.*

The History of Rasselas

This book was a little story book, published in April 1759. Johnson describes in this the life of prince Rasselas and Nekayah, his sister, who are kept in a place called the Happy Valley in the land of Abyssinia. The valley is a place free of problems. The constant pleasure does not, however, lead to satisfaction and with the help of a philosopher named Imlac, Rasselas escapes and explores the world. They also witness so many people undergoing suffering in the outside world. They return to Abyssinia but do not wish to return to the state of constant pleasures found in Happy Valley.

This book gained immediate popularity and every year there was a new English edition of the work. This novella was also translated into 5 more languages.

Most famous essayists of this age were Joseph Addison and Richard Steele, who found *The Kitcat Club*, an 18th century English Clubin London with strong literary and political associations. Some other prominent prose writers of this age were Edmund Burke, Edward Gibbon, Thomas Paine. Some philosophers of this age were George Berkeley, David Hartley, David Hume and Adam Smith. All of these writer's work fall under Non-fiction prose.

EXAM BASED QUESTIONS

1 In the 15th and 16th century, which age is known as the awakening of Europe?
(a) The Jacobean Age (b) The Restoration Age
(c) The Elizabethan Age (d) The Puritan Age

2 Historical events often influence literature, which of the following did not occur during the Restoration Period?
(a) Charles II was Restored to the Throne
(b) The French Revolution
(c) The Great Fire of London
(d) the Exclusion Bill Crisis

3 A Civil War broke out in England between charles I's supporter and the Parliament in
(a) 1603 (b) 1642
(c) 1640 (d) 1688

4 Who is responsible for the Puritan spirit and finds its noblest expression?
(a) Burton (b) John Milton
(c) Herbert (d) Donne

5 The Puritans were
(a) a groups of supporter of Charles I
(b) a group of English speaking Protestants
(c) a group of authors and poets
(d) the Roundheads

6 In which age people had strict rules regarding life and conduct
(a) Shakespearean age
(b) The Renaissance period
(c) The Puritans
(d) The Restoration

7 Which of these is not a writer during Puritan Age?
(a) John Milton (b) Thomas Fuller
(c) John Lyle (d) Sir Richard Lovelace

8 Due to whom the name Caroline age came in?
(a) James I (b) Charles I
(c) Edward I (d) Charles II

9 In which year did 'Petition of right come into existence?
(a) 1625 (b) 1626
(c) 1627 (d) 1628

10 The character writers of the early 17th century mostly followed the Greek writer
(a) Theophrastus (b) Homer
(c) Plato (d) None of these

11 The famous theater 'The Globe' was set on fire in the year
(a) 1612 (b) 1613
(c) 1620 (d) 1616

12 The Royalists in the age of Milton are also called as
(a) Cavaliers (b) Protestants
(c) Intellectuals (d) Reformers

13 How 'many characters does George Herbert's 'The Country Parson' deal with in its thirty-seven essays?
(a) Thirty-seven (b) Three
(c) Twenty (d) One

14 Who wrote 'Urn Burial' (1658) inspired by the discovery of some 50 urns in the neighbourhood?
(a) John Milton (b) Izaak Walton
(c) Thomas Browne (d) Thomas Fuller

15 John Milton wrote total 25 pamphlets. How many of them were written in English?
(a) 18 (b) 21 (c) 19 (d) 20

16 Who wrote a series of characters in (1614), which are witty and epigrammatic in form?
(a) Samuel Butler
(b) Izaak Walton
(c) Thomas Overbury
(d) Francis Bacon

17 Thomas Browne's profession was
(a) cobbler (b) doctor
(c) a hunter (d) a pamphleteer

18 Which of these is prose work of John Milton?
(a) The Wife (1614)
(b) A Treatise of Civil Power
(c) Microcosmography
(d) The Pilgrim's Progress

19 Which novel out of the following contains 55 characters representing humanity?
(a) The Wife
(b) The Pilgrim's Progress
(c) Holy State and Profane State
(d) Microcosmography

20 Which of these writers of characters deals with one character in all his essays?
(a) Samuel Butler (b) John Donne
(c) George Herbert (d) Thomas Fuller

21 Who took over the throne in 1689 during Glorious Revolution?
(a) Queen Mary (b) James II
(c) William III (d) None of these

22 Who among the following was the monarch to occupy the throne at the beginning of the Restoration Age?
(a) James II (b) Charles II
(c) William II (d) Queen Elizabeth

23 The Restoration Period also called 'Glorious Revolution' is called so because
(a) transition was very smooth
(b) it did not involve violence and blood shed
(c) advent of reason and logic
(d) reopening of theatres

24 Which period in English literature works the beginning of modern prose?
(a) The Renaissance (b) The Restoration Age
(c) The Puritan (d) The Elizabethan Age

25 Dryden's 'An Essay of Dramatic Poesy' (1668) is written in
(a) poetic form (b) dramatic form
(c) narrative form (d) conversation form

26 Who wrote the book 'Elements of Law' during Puritan age?
(a) Izaak Walton (b) John Milton
(c) Thomas Hobbes (d) Robert Benton

27 Which work of John Dryden established him as verse satirist?
(a) The Indian Emperor
(b) Essay of Heroic Plays
(c) Mac Flecknoe
(d) The Conquest of Granada

28 Dryden lost his laureateship under the rule of
(a) James II (b) William II
(c) William III (d) Charles II

29 What was Daniel Defoe's original surname?
(a) Friend (b) Neighbour
(c) Foe (d) Good

30 Who remarked that restoration makes the birth of our English prose?
(a) TH Long (b) Francis Bacon
(c) Matthew Arnold (d) John Dryden

31 Whose life is an epitome for religious individualism which marked the close of the English reformation?
(a) Bunyan (b) Milton
(c) Herrick (d) Chapman

32 'Holy War' was written by
(a) Bunyan (b) Milton
(c) Burton (d) Robert

33 After reading the book 'The Plainman's Pathway to Heaven' and 'The Practice of Piety' new imagination spread in his life. The book was
(a) The Holy War
(b) Samson Agonistes
(c) The Practice of Piety II
(d) The Pilgrim's Progress

34 When was the novel 'The Pilgrim's Progress' published?
(a) 1678 (b) 1674
(c) 1666 (d) 1670

35 The narrator of 'The Pilgrim's Progress' learns about Christian from
(a) a book
(b) a wise man
(c) a dream
(d) an ancient poem

36 In 'The Pilgrim's Progress', Apollyon's skin is covered with
(a) hair (b) gold
(c) scales (d) leather

37 In 'The Pilgrim's Progress' Christian is able to escape from the Doubting Castle because
(a) he kills Giant Despair
(b) he holds Despair's wife hostage
(c) faithful storms the gates
(d) he remembers he has a key

38 In 'The Pilgrim's Progress' the garden from which Christiana's sons steal fruit belongs to
(a) the devil (b) giant despair
(c) the interpreter (d) great-heart

39 Who is the spiritual guide that shelters Christian in 'The Pilgrim's Progress'?
(a) Prudence (b) The interpreter
(c) Apollyon (d) Faithful

40 In 'The Pilgrim's Progress', which character is executed in the town of Vanity?
(a) Faithful (b) Goodwill
(c) Apollyon (d) Talkative

41 Which character protects Christiana on her pilgrimage in Part II in 'The Pilgrim's Progress'?
(a) Christian (b) Feeble-mind
(c) Piety (d) Great-heart

42 In which work/novel does Congreve take its plot from Shakespeare's play?
(a) The double dealer (b) Incognito
(c) The way of the world (d) The mourning bridge

43 Who among the following are known as 'the fan wheels of novel'?
(a) Gray, Collins, Pope and Sterne
(b) Richardson, Fielding, Smollet and Sterne
(c) Gray, Richardson, Fielding, Collins
(d) Richardson, Fielding, Collins, Blake

44 Which novel contains the famous characters like Mr Worldly Wiseman, Lord Hate-Good, Mr Steadfast etc?
(a) Leviathan
(b) The Pilgrim's Progress
(c) The Life and Death of Mr Badman
(d) Grace Abounding

45 On what type of plantation does the narrator reside in the novel 'Oroonoko'?
(a) Cotton (b) Coffee
(c) Sugar (d) Tobacco

46 The continent from which slaves on the plantation originate is (Oroonako)
(a) Africa (b) South America
(c) Asia (d) Nigeria

47 Who is considered to be the first professional woman writer of England?
(a) Aphra Behn (b) Virginia Woolf
(c) Mrs Jameson (d) None of these

48 Which genre exemplifies Oroonoko?
(a) Chronicle (b) Diary
(c) Novel (d) Fairy Tale

49 The narrative of the novel opens in
(a) England (b) Africa
(c) Suriname (d) Greece

50 The narrator compares the natives in the novel Oroonoko to
(a) Romeo and Juliet (b) Spark and Finn
(c) Adam and Eve (d) Eloisa and Abelard

51 Which of these works are written by Aphra Behn?
(a) The History of the Nun
(b) Love Letters Between a Nobleman and His Sister
(c) The Force of Imagination
(d) All of the above

52 Born in around 1640, this English woman was a popular writer of 'Restoration Era', who is she?
(a) Elizabeth Killigrew
(b) Catherine Pegge
(c) Lucy Walters
(d) Aphra Behn

53 Which work of Congreve takes its Plot I of mistaken identity from Shakespeare?
(a) The Old Bachelor
(b) The Way of the World
(c) Incognito
(d) The Double Dealer

54 In which age the government was divided into two parties?
(a) The Age of Revival (b) The Romantic Age
(c) The Neo-classical Age (d) None of these

55 The word 'nature' in the 18th century literature stands for
(a) nature of writing (b) external nature
(c) the universe (d) human nature

56 With whom Dr Johnson was intimately associated in his personal life?
(a) Boswell (b) Dryden
(c) Alexander Pope (d) Lord Bolingbroke

57 Johnson's 'Dictionary of the English Language' was published in the year
(a) 1710 (b) 1755
(c) 1739 (d) 1759

58 Which 18th century writer was so talented that he crossed the barrier of different genres with poems like 'The Vanity of Human Wishes', fiction like 'Rasselas', and non-fiction like 'A Dictionary of the English Languages' but he retired from writing in his early 50s? Name the writer.
(a) John Gay (b) Samuel Johnson
(c) Sir Richard Steele (d) Christopher Smart

59 Which Augustan writer's epitaph reads: 'One who strove with all his might to champion liberty'?
(a) Alexander Pope
(b) Jonathan Swift
(c) Henry Fielding
(d) Daniel Defoe

60 Which of his voyages, Gulliver discovered mountain like beings?
(a) The land of the Lilliputians
(b) The land of the Brobdingnagians
(c) The land of the Laputans
(d) The land of the Houyhnhnms

61 'Gulliver's Travels' is a satire on
(a) The Scientist and Philosophers
(b) Human Being
(c) Wars and Conquests
(d) All of the above

62 Swift's Modest Proposal is written in the form of a
(a) project on political economy
(b) political allegory
(c) social satire
(d) old-testament history

63 A particular type of literature focused on feelings of sympathy and sensibility in 18th century is called
(a) Classical literature
(b) Literature of sensibility
(c) Epigrammatic literature
(d) Travel stories

64 Tristram Shandy was authored by
(a) Richardson (b) Laurence Sterne
(c) Daniel Defoe (d) Jonathan Swift

65 Who was Stella ?
(a) Swift's wife, Esther Johnson
(b) Swift's mother, Esther Johnson
(c) Swift's lover, Esther Johnson
(d) None of the above

66 JM Coetzee's Foe is postmodern retelling of
(a) Ivanhoe (b) Evelina
(c) Robinson Crusoe (d) The Moonstone

67 Which work of Defoe is based on a true story of a shipwreck named Alexander Selkirk?
(a) Moll Flanders (b) Robinson Crusoe
(c) Captain Singleton (d) Captain Jack

68 Identify the author to whom the credit of writing the first modern novel goes?
(a) James Thomson
(b) James Macpherson
(c) Samuel Richardson
(d) William Blake

69 Which among the following are not the work done by Samuel Richardson?
(a) Virtue Rewarded (b) Families Letters
(c) Moll Flanders (d) Clarissa

70 Which novel of Richardson talks about virtue and morality in woman?
(a) Pamela
(b) Pamela's conduct
(c) Clarissa
(d) Apology for the life of Mrs Shamela Andrews

71 The complete title of Sterne's novel Tristram Shandy is
(a) The Strange and Surprising Adventures of Tristram Shandy, Gentleman
(b) A True Account of The Life of Tristram Shandy, Gentleman
(c) The Life and Opinions of Tristram Shandy, Gentleman
(d) The Strange and Surprising Opinions of Tristram Shandy, Gentleman

72 'Tom Jones' is the famous work of
(a) Lawrence Sterne (b) Tobias Smollett
(c) Samuel Richardson (d) Henry Fielding

73 Which among the following are the works of Henry Fielding?
(a) Amelia (b) Jonathan Wild
(c) Tom Jones (d) All of these

74 'Jonathan Wild the Great', a satirical romance was written by
(a) Lawrence Sterne (b) Tobias Smollett
(c) Henry Fielding (d) Oliver Goldsmith

75 The epithet 'a comic epic in prose' is best applied to
(a) Richardson's Pamela
(b) Sterne's A Sentimental Journey
(c) Fielding's Joseph Andrews
(d) Defore's Robinson Crusoe

76 Which work of Fielding is a response to Richardson's Pamela?
(a) Tom Jones
(b) Shamela
(c) Joseph Andrews
(d) Rape Upon Rape

77 Commodore Trunnion's character belonged to which work of Tobias Smollett?
(a) In Peregrine Pickle
(b) Humphrey Clinker
(c) In Roderick Random
(d) Amelia

78 Which of the following is the last book by Tobias Smollett?
(a) The Adventures of Ferdinant Count
(b) The Expedition of Humphry Clinker
(c) Peregrine Pickle
(d) Travels Through France and Italy

79 The Earliest woman novelist of significance in the 18th century is
(a) Mary Edgeworth (b) Aphra Behn
(c) Mary Russell (d) Mrs Gaskell

80 The work which bought fame to Oliver Goldsmith was ....
(a) The Traveller
(b) The Deserted Village
(c) The Vicar of Wakefield
(d) She Stoops to Conquer

81 The Puritans were a group of English speaking .... who were dissatisfied with the religious reformation movement.
(a) catholics (b) novelists
(c) protestants (d) poets

82 During Puritan age literature, even in love poems an .... replaces the emotions of love and passion.
(a) reasoning
(b) intellectual spirit
(c) adventurous
(d) religious feeling /spirit

83 Lovelace wrote a comedy called ....
(a) The Soldiers (b) To Althea
(c) The Scholars (d) Lucasta

84 The English civil war ended in .... with the victory of parliamentarians.
(a) 1668 (b) 1651
(c) 1660 (d) 1625

85 The novel written by Jonathan Swift shows the .... and wit of English speech.
(a) intellect (b) emotions
(c) fun (d) satire

86 The book 'The Holy State and Profane State is a work of character sketches written by ....
(a) George Herbert (b) Milton
(c) Lovelace (d) Thomas Fuller

87 Restoration age was accompanied with .... and restoration of the Church of England.
(a) reopening of dramas
(b) reopening of theatres
(c) reopening of writing novels
(d) monarch

88 The restoration period is also called an age of intellectualism and ....
(a) romance (b) medieval literature
(c) rationalism (d) religion

89 .... is called a pioneer of English novel with his two books during restoration period.
(a) Dryden
(b) John Bunyan
(c) John Locke
(d) Aphra Behn

90 Oroonoko is a tale of an African prince who falls in love with a lady called ....
(a) Amanda (b) Sophy
(c) Imoinda (d) Jane

91 The novella 'the Dumb Virgin' is a novel about ....
(a) intellect (b) reasoning
(c) disabilities (d) feminity

92 Jonathan's .... was first published with Tale of a Tub in 1704.
(a) Gulliver's Travels
(b) The Battle of the Books
(c) Modest Proposal
(d) The Death of Mrs Johnson

93 Daniel Defoe wrote ...., which is a novel about a true story of a shipwrecked seaman?
(a) Moll Flanders
(b) Sir Charles Grandison
(c) Clarissa
(d) Robinson Crusoe

94 The only novel written by .... is 'The Vicar of Wakefield'.
(a) Daniel Defoe
(b) Laurence Sterne
(c) Oliver Goldsmith (d) Samuel Johnson

95 Satirical novella written by Samuel Johnson is called ....
(a) Rasselas, Prince of Abissinia
(b) the Life of Ascham
(c) The Vanity of Human Wishes
(d) None of the above

96 Which of the following statements is true?
(a) In the 17th century the Puritan Age started
(b) The Puritan Age worked up a rebirth of moral nature of man
(c) Both (a) and (b)
(d) None of the above

97 Which of the following statements is true about the Pilgrim's Progress'?
(a) Next to the Bible, it was the most widely read book
(b) Bible's popularity remains unsurpassed
(c) The Pilgrim's Progress was a short story
(d) The Pilgrim's Progress was the start of proper form of autobiography

98 Which of the following statements about Pamela is correct?
(a) The alternative title is 'Virtue Penalises'
(b) The alternative title is 'Virtue Rewarded'
(c) The novel has two subtitles
(d) The novel has no alternative title

99 Which of the following statements about Clarissa is incorrect?
(a) It is written by Samuel Richardson
(b) It is a historical novel
(c) It was published in 7 volumes
(d) the novel is celebration of virtue and morality in woman.

100 Which of the following statements is incorrect?
(a) Tristram Shandy was written by swift
(b) The initial manuscript of Tristram Shandy was rejected by London printers
(c) Laurence Sterne did not go to school or college
(d) Sterne published all volumes of this novel at his own expense

101 Which of the following authors is incorrectly matched with his work?
(a) Oliver Goldsmith : The Vicar of Wakefield
(b) Aphra Behn : Oroonoko
(c) Daniel Defoe : Gulliver's Travels
(d) Henry Fielding : Tom Jones

102 Which of these book-publication pairs is correctly matched?
(a) 1704 : Gulliver's Travels
(b) 1712 : A Tale of A Tub
(c) 1726 : The Rape of the Lock
(d) 1747 : Clarissa

103 Which of the these author text-pairs is correctly matched?
(a) Alexander Pope : She Stoops to Conquer
(b) William Congreve : The Dumb Virgin
(c) John Milton : A Treatise of Civil Power
(d) Jonathan Swift : Pamela

104 Which of the following statements about Jonathan Swift is not correct?
(a) He was born in Dublin
(b) He was born in 1667
(c) He wrote the 11 Battle of the Book'
(d) He studied in Stanford University.

105 Which of these personalities and their works in which they are portrayed is not correctly matched?
(a) Sophia Western : Tom Jones by Henry Fielding
(b) Robert : Youngest of two brothers in Moll Flanders by D Defoe
(c) Dr. Primrose : Gulliver's Travels
(d) Imoinda Clemene : Oroonoko by Aphra Behn

Directions (Q. Nos. 106-108) *In the question given below are two statements labelled as Assertion (A) and Reason (R). In the context of the two statements, which one of the following is correct?*

Codes
(a) Both A and R are true and R is the correct explanation of A
(b) Both A and R are true, but R is not the correct explanation of A
(c) A is true, but R is false
(d) A is false, but R is true

106 **Assertion** (A) Puritan literature showed no devotion to the crown.

Reason (R) The Monarch ruled in a despotic manner earning the wrath of the masse.

107 **Assertion** (A) When women were censured for taking up writing as a career, Aphra Behn wrote a short novel, 'Oroonoko' besides numerous plays.

Reason (R) It is about an African prince, Oroonoko, who falls in love with a young woman, Imoinda

108 **Assertion** (A) Jonathan Swift's novel 'Gulliver's Travels' is a satire.

Reason (R) It makes fun of human beings and their desire to conquests through was.

Codes
(a) A is true But R is false
(b) A is false But R is true
(c) Both A and R are true and R is the correct explanation of A
(d) Neither A nor R is correct

109 **Assertion** (A) The 18th century has emerged with a new genre known as Novel.

Reason (R) Many issues related to lives of the people were discussed in these novels.
(a) A is true but R is false
(b) A is true but R is not correct explanation of A
(c) A is false but R is true
(d) Both A and R are true and R is the correct explanation of A

110 **Assertion** (A) Henry Fielding has been acclaimed with the 'Father of the English Novel'.

Reason (R) No other author wrote any novel before him.

Codes
(a) A is true and R is correct explanation of A
(b) A is true but R is false
(c) A is false but R is true
(d) Neither A nor R is correct

111 Which of the following novelists are in correct chronological sequence?
(a) Daniel Defoe, Laurence Sterne, Aphra Behn, John Bunyan
(b) John Bunyan, Laurence Sterne, Daniel Defoe, Aphra Behn
(c) John Bunyan, Aphra Behn, Daniel Defoe, Laurence Sterne
(d) Aphra Behn, Laurence Sterne, John Bunyan, Daniel Defoe

112 Which of the following works are in correct chronological order?
(a) Areopagitica, Microcosmography, the History of the Nun, Pilgrim's Progress
(b) Pilgrim's Progress, Areopagitica, Microcosmography, History of the Nun.
(c) Microcosmography, Areopagitica, Pilgrims's Progress, The History of the Nun
(d) The History of the Nun, Areopagitica, Microcosmography, Pilgrim's Progress.

113 Which of the following novelist's sequence is in correct chronological order?
(a) Oliver Goldsmith, Jonathan Swift, Thomas Fuller, Henry Fielding
(b) Thomas Fuller, Jonathan Swift, Henry Fielding, Oliver Goldsmith.
(c) Jonathan Swift, Oliver Goldsmith, Thomas Fuller, Henry Fielding,
(d) Henry Fielding, Oliver Goldsmith, Jonathan Swift, Thomas Fuller

114 Which of the following is in chronological order according of the birth of the novelist?
(a) Jonathan Swift, Daniel Defoe, Samuel Richardson
(b) Daniel Defoe, Jonathan Swift, Samuel Richardson
(c) Jonathan Swift, Samuel Richardson Daniel Defoe
(d) Samuel Richardson, Jonathan Swift, Daniel Defoe

115 Which of the following novel is in chronological order?
(a) Tom Jones, Amelia, Joseph Andrews
(b) Amelia, Tom Jones, Joseph Andrews
(c) Joseph Andrews, Tom Jones, Amelia
(d) Tom Jones, Joseph Andrews, Amelia

116 Which of the following is in chronological order about works as per their publication?
(a) Tristram Shandy, Sir Charles Grandison, Roderick
(b) Roderick, Tristram Shandy, Sir Charles Grandison
(c) Sir Charles Grandison, Tristram Shandy, Roderick
(d) Roderick, Sir Charles Grandison, Tristram Shandy

117 Consider the following novels
1. Pamela
2. Gulliver's Travels
3. The Vicar of Wakefield
4. A Tale of A Tub

Which of the above are works of Jonathan Swift?
(a) Only 1 (b) 2 and 4 (c) 1 and 3 (d) Only 4

118 What is common in the following writers? Identify the correct description below.
1. Daniel Defoe
2. Jonathan Swift
3. Tobias Smollett
4. Samuel Richardson

Codes
I. All were important biographers of Augustan
II. All were famous metaphysical poets
III. All were famous novelists of neo-classical Age
IV. All were famous restoration period essay writers

(a) Only (II) (b) Only (III)
(c) Only (I) and (II) (d) Only (IV)

119 Match of the following

	List I		List II
A.	Joseph Addison	1.	Journal to Steele
B.	Tobias Smollett	2.	The Times
C.	Jonathan Swift	3.	Coffee House Politicians
D.	Charles Churchill	4.	Humphry Clinker

Codes

	A	B	C	D
(a)	1	2	3	4
(b)	3	4	1	2
(c)	4	3	2	1
(d)	1	3	2	4

120 What is common to the following writers
1. Oliver Goldsmith
2. Jonathan Swift
3. Samuel Johnson
4. Tobias Smollett

Codes
(a) All except Milton are prose writers of Puritan age
(b) All are novel writers of Puritan age
(c) All are poets of graveyard poetry
(d) All are expert in characterisation

121 In the following series which one has all the novelists. Correctly matched with their work.
(a) Congreve-A Sentimental Journey, Aphra Behn-Incognito
(b) Congreve-Incognito, Aphra Behn-The History of the Nun, Laurence Sterne-A Sentimental Journey
(c) Congreve-The History of the Nun, Aphra Behn-Incognito, Lawrence Sterne-A Sentimental Journey
(d) Congreve-A History of the Nun, Aphra Behn-The Sentimental Journey, Lawrence Sterne-Incognito

122 In the following series, which one has all the works correctly matched with their composers?
(a) Juvenilia- Richard Lovelace, To Althea- George Wither The Flea- Jeremy Taylor, The Rule and Exercises of Holy Living- John Donne.
(b) Juvenilia- Jeremy Taylor, To Althea- John Donne, The Flea- Richard Lovelace, The Rule and Exercises of Holy Living-George Richard Lovelace, Wither
(c) Juvenilia-George Wither, To Althea-Richard Lovelace, The Flea-Jeremy Taylor, The Rule and Exercises of Holy Living-John Donne
(d) Juvenilia-George Wither, To Althea-Richard Lovelace, The Flea-John Donne, The Rule and Exercises of Holy Living-Jeremy Taylor

123 In the given series which set has all the alternatives matched correctly?
(a) John Bunyan-Roderick Random, Henry Fielding-The Pilgrim's Progress, Daniel Defoe-Robinson Crusoe, Tobias Smollett-Joseph Andrews
(b) John Bunyan-Robinson Crusoe, Henry Fielding-Joseph Andrews, Daniel Defoe-Roderick Random, Tobias Smollett-The Pilgrim's Progress
(c) John Bunyan-The Pilgrim's Progress, Henry Fielding, Joseph Andrews, Daniel Defoe-Robinson Crusoe, Tobias Smollett-Roderick Random.
(d) John Bunyan-Roderick Random, Henry Fielding-Robinson Crusoe, Daniel Defoe-Joseph Andrews, Tobias Smollett-The Pilgrim's Progress.

124 In the following series, which set of work and author is correctly matched?
(a) A Journey to the Western World-Samuel Johnson, The Critic or A Tragedy-Sheridan, Imitations of Horace- Daniel Defoe, Windsor Forest-Alexander Pope
(b) A Journey to the Western World- Daniel Defoe, The Critic or A Tragedy-Sheridan, Imitations of Horace-Alexander Pope, Windsor Forest-Samuel Johnson
(c) A Journey to the Western World- Alexander Pope, The Critic or A Tragedy-Sheridan, Imitations of Horace-Samuel Johnson, Windsor Forest-Daniel Defoe
(d) A Journey to the Western World-Daniel Defoe, The Critic or A Tragedy-Samuel Johnson, Imitations of Horace-Sheridan, Windsor Forest-Alexander Pope

125 In the following series which set of birth place and novelists is correctly matched?
(a) Laurence Sterne-England, Samuel Richards-Scotland, Tobias Smollett-Ireland, Henry Fielding-Derbyshire
(b) Laurence Sterne-Ireland, Samuel Richardson-Derbyshire, Tobias Smollett-Scotland, Henry Fielding-England
(c) Laurence Sterne-Derbyshire, Samuel Richardson-Ireland, Tobias Smollett-England, Henry Fielding-Scotland
(d) Laurence Sterne-Scotland, Samuel Richardson-Ireland, Tobias Smollett-Derbyshire, Henry Fielding-England

126 "But say what you will, "its better to be left than never to have been loved. To pass our youth in dull indifference, to refuse the sweets of life because they once must leave us, is as preposterous as to wish to have been born old, because we one day must be old."

From which work of an author have these lines been taken?

(a) Letterbook, George Etherege
(b) The Plain-Dealer, William Wycherley
(c) The Amorous Prince, Aphra Behn
(d) The Way of the World, William Congreve

127 Which writer of Puritan Age uttered these words

"My lines and life are free; free as the rode."

(a) William blake (b) John Donne
(c) Milton (d) George Herbert

128 Who states in which work "Redemption from sin is greater than redemption from afflictions"?

(a) John Bunyan – The Pilgrim's Progress
(b) Daniel Defoe – Robinson Crusoe
(c) Henry Fielding – Tom Jones
(d) Tobias Smollett – Roderick Random

129 "Give me the liberty to know, to utter and to argue freely according to conscience above all liberties."

Which author in which prose work utters these words?

(a) John Milton – 'Areopagtica'
(b) John Donne – 'The Ecstacy'
(c) Thomas Overbury – 'The Wife'
(d) Thomas Fuller – 'The Holy State and Profane State.

130 Which character in novel The Pilgrim's Progress utters these lines?

"Why, in yonder village there dwells a gentleman whose name is legality, a very judicious man and a man of a very good name that has skill to help men off with such burdens as thine are from their shoulders; ....."

(a) Legality (b) Christian
(c) Mr Worldly Wiseman (d) Apollyon (Monster)

131 Which novelist in which of his work utters these lines?

"People of little understanding are most apt to be angry when their sense's called into question."

(a) John Bunyan The Pilgrim's Progress
(b) Tom Jones Henry Fielding
(c) Samuel Richardson Pamela: Virtue Rewarded
(d) Swift A Tale of A Tub

132 In which work of Jonathan Swift, these lines occur?

"I cannot but conclude the bulk of your natives, to be the most pernicious race of little odious vermin that nature ever suffered to crawl upon the surface of the Earth."

(a) A Tale of A Tub
(b) Gulliver's Travels
(c) Argument against Abolishing Christianity
(d) A Modest Proposal

133 Which author in which of his fiction used these words, "Thus we never see the true state of our condition till it is illustrated to us by its contraries, nor know how to value what we enjoy but by the want of it."

(a) Gulliver's Travels — Jonathan Swift
(b) Tobias Smollett — Roderick Random
(c) Samuel Richardson — Clarissa Harlowe
(d) Daniel Defoe — Robinson Crusoe

134 Who states that, "Fielding made Jane Austen possible by opening the central tradition of English fiction"?

(a) Samuel Richardson (b) FR Leavis
(c) Edward Gibbon (d) Tobias Smollett

135 Which character in Henry Fielding's Tom Jones utters these words?

"I am convinced, My child that you have much goodness, generosity and honour in your temper, if you will add prudence and religion to these, you must be happy for the three former qualities, I admit, make you worthy of happiness but they are the latter only which will put you in possession of it."

(a) Tom Jones (b) Mrs Western
(c) Mr Allworthy (d) Narrator

136 Which Augustan writer's epitaph reads: 'one who strove with all his might to champion liberty'?

(a) Alexander Pope (b) Jonathan Swift
(c) Daniel Defoe (d) Henry Fielding

137 In which author's which work do these lines appear

"Our scored child, a girl, I intended to call after her aunt Grissel; but my wife who during her pregnancy had been reading romances insisted upon her being called Olivia."

(a) Jonathan Swift– A Tale of A Tub
(b) Oliver Goldsmith– The Vicar of Wakefield
(c) Henry Fielding– Tom Jones
(d) Aphra Behn– Oroonoko

138 Which author in which work has said this, "By my soul, I can neither eat, drink nor sleep, nor, what's still worse, love any woman in world but her"

(a) Henry Fielding in Tom Jones
(b) Tobias Smollett in Tristram Shandy
(c) Samuel Richardson in Clarissa
(d) John Bunyan the Pilgrim's Progress

139 Which author spoke these lines "All our discontents about what we want appeared to me to spring from the want of thankfulness for what we have".

(a) Jonathan Swift (b) Daniel Depe
(c) Samuel Richardson (d) Dr. Samuel Johnson

140 "Seek not to know what must not be reveal, for joy only flows where fate is most concealed. A busy person would find their sorrows much more; if future fortunes were known before!"

Whose famous quote is this?

(a) William Congreve
(b) John Bunyan
(e) Aphra Behn
(d) John Dryden

141 "In prayer it is better to have a heart without words than words without a heart.

he that is down, needs fear no fall, He that is low, no pride.

One leak will sink a ship: and one sin will destroy a sinner."

Which Restoration age dramatist's lines are these?

(a) John Bunyan (b) William Congreve
(c) Aphra Behn (d) John Dryden

142 "Music has charms to soothe a savage breast, to soften

rocks, or bend a knotted oak. I've read that things inanimate have moved, and as with living sould, have been inform'd, by magic numbers and persuasive sound."

Which Restoration age writer's lines are these?

(a) John Bunyan (b) William Congreve
(c) Aphra Behn (d) John Dryden

143 Which character in 'Oroonoko' utters these words, "It is not titles make men brave or good or birth that bestows Courage"?

(a) Prince Oroonko (b) Imoinda
(c) The Narrator (d) King of Coramantien

144 "I seek a place that can never be destroyed, one that is pure and that fadeth rot away, and it is laid up in heaven, and safe there, to be given at the time appointed, to them that seek. it with all their heart. Read it so, if you will in my book."

Which writer said this in which of his work?

(a) Jonathan Swift -- A Tale of A Tub
(b) Daniel Defoe — More Flanders
(c) John Bunyan — The Pilgrim's Progress
(d) Oliver Goldsmith — The Vicar of Wakefield

145 Who said, "There are a set of religious or rather moral writers, who teach that virtue is the certain road to happiness and vice to misery, in this world. A very wholesome and comfortable doctrine and to which we have but one objection, namely that it is not true"?

(a) John Bunyan in Pilgrim's Progress
(b) Tobias Smollett in Peregrine Pickle
(c) Henry Fielding in The History of Tom Jones
(d) Joseph Addison in the Spectator.

Directions (Q. Nos. 146-150) *Read the following prose and answer the questions.*

I swam for many hours in the water and I was very tired. Suddenly I realised that the water was not deep any more-my feet touched the ground! I walked a long time and then I came to the beach. It was evening and I was exhausted. I fell asleep on the sand. When I woke up it was morning. I tried to stand up, but I could not move at all. I raised my head a little and I could see ropes around my body. They were tied very tightly. I did not know what had happened to me. Then I saw a very small creature walking along my body. I looked again and I was very surprised to see that this creature was really a tiny man!

Soon there were more of these little men walking on me. There were hundreds of them on the ground near me. They were talking to each other, but I could not understand their language. I shouted very loudly and the little men were afraid. They ran away quickly. Then I tried to free myself and I managed to break the ropes around one of my hands. As soon as I did this, I felt a sharp pain. The little men were shooting arrows at me!The arrows were very small, but they were also very sharp and I decided to lie still. Now the little men constructed a platform near my head. One of them climbed up to the top of the platform. He was standing very close to my ear.

He began to shout into my ear. I could hear what he said, but I did not understand the language he was using. He used signs to communicate with me. He told me that he worked for the Emperor. Then he explained that I was their prisoner. He told me not to be frightened, because they only wanted to take me to see the Emperor.

146 What is the name of the man narrating the story?

(a) Glumdalclitch
(b) Lemuel Gulliver
(c) Grildrig
(d) Lagado

147 The above prose has been taken from

(a) Gulliver's Travels (b) Moll Flanders
(c) Tom Jones (d) Joseph Andrews

148 Which voyage is described in the above prose?

(a) Voyage to Brobdingnag
(b) Voyage to the country of the Houyhnhnms
(c) Voyage to Lilliput
(d) Voyage to Laputa and Balnibarbi

149 What ware the little creatures known as?

(a) The Houyhnhnms (b) The Lilliputians
(c) The Brobdingnagians (d) The Japanese

150 What was the name of the ship that the man was travelling onto?

(a) Hope-Well (b) Adventure
(c) Sea-Sailors (d) Antelope

PREVIOUS YEARS' QUESTIONS

December 2018

1 As a boy growing up in squire Allwrothy's estate, Tom gets one of the following characters into trouble. Identify the character

(a) Partridge (b) Black George
(c) Nightingale (d) Blifil

July 2018

2 Sir Thomas Browne's 'Urn Berial' was prompted by

(a) the discovery of ancient burial urns near Norwich
(b) the contemporary researchers on burial sites in Norway
(c) the death of St Francis of Assissi and his burial
(d) the publication of the English Book of Common Prayer

3 In Tristram Shandy, the Author's preface

(a) is Rawked to the highest bidder
(b) appears in between chapters 13 and 14 in Volume II
(c) is printed in Italics in all editions
(d) appears in between chapters 10 and 11 in Volume 1

4 Gulliver receives the following response when he boasts about his country man: "...... the most pernicious race of little odious vermin that nature even suffered to crawl upon the face of the earth" whose response?

(a) the king of Lilliput's
(b) the king of Brobdingnag's
(c) the Governor of Glubbdubdrib's
(d) the first of the Hayhnhnms he meets

November 2017

5 Aphra Behn's Oroonoko is set in ....

(a) Surinam (b) Abyssinia (c) Egypt (d) Assyria

6 Samuel Richardson named his heroine Pamela after one of the characters in ....

(a) Edmund Spenser's Falrie Queene
(b) Philip Sidney's Arcadia
(c) Venus and Adonis by William Shakespeare
(d) Geoffrey Chaucer's Canterbury Tales

January 2017

7 Which of the following works of Daniel Defoe offered his readers as a collection of 'Strange Surprising Adventures'?

(a) Moll Flanders
(b) Robinson Crusoe
(c) Roxana
(d) Captain Singleton

8 Richardson's Pamela had its origin in

(a) the real case of a woman born to lower middle class parents
(b) an elementary letter-writing manual
(c) the general plight of English women
(d) the suggestion of a friend to defend middle class values

9 In 1692 William Congreve published 'Incognito', a work of fiction which is dubbed a 'novel' on its title page? What is the sub-title?

(a) Love and Duty Reconcil'd
(b) Beauty in Distress
(c) Virtue Rewarded
(d) Love in Excess

10 In Bunyan's Pilgrim's Progress christian and his friend faithful cause a commotion at the vanity fair for many reasons. Which of the following statements is not true of their appearance at the fair?

(a) They are dressed differently than the other fair goers
(b) They speak the language of the Bible at the fair
(c) They sample every entertainment at the fair
(d) They refuse to look at the merchandise at the fair

July 2016

11 In Jonathan Swift's 'Gulliver's Travels', Gulliver refers to William Dampier, the famous writer of the voyages as

(a) master (b) brother
(c) cousin (d) uncle

12 In John Bunyan's Pilgrim's Progress who keeps Christian's head above water in the river of the death?

(a) Hopeful (b) Helpful
(c) Faithful (d) Cheerful

13 By what name is Gulliver known in Brobdingnag?

(a) Grildrig (b) Glumdalclitch
(c) Splacknuck (d) Mannikin

July 2016

14 Why do the Houyhnhnms have so few words in their language

(a) their wants and passions are fewer than human wants and passions and they need fewer words
(b) they consider language to be morally corrupt and prefer to remain silent
(c) they find speech difficult because they are horses
(d) they prefer action to words

15 The narrator or Oroonoko are

1. woman
2. oroonoko
3. a purported eyewitness of the event described
4. trefy

Codes

(a) 1 and 4 (b) 1 and 3
(c) 2 and 3 (d) 2 and 4

16 In John Bunyan's Pilgrim's Progress what is the first obstacle encountered by christi an on his progress

(a) the slough of despond
(b) vanity fair
(c) the River of Death
(d) the Swamp of Despair

December 2015

17 While compiling what sort of book did Samuel Richardson conceive of the idea for his Pamela or Virtue Rewarded.

(a) an account of the plague in London
(b) an instruction manual for manners
(c) A book of devotion
(d) a book of model letters

18 Samuel Johnson's 'Dissertation upon Poetry' is part of which of his following works

(a) the final section of his preface to Shakespeare
(b) a chapter of his novel Rasselas
(c) the epilogue of his lives of Poets
(d) one of his Rambles essays

19 In Tristram Shandy the narrator's presentation of his life and opinion is ....

(a) linear
(b) digressive
(c) chronological
(d) rounded

20 The son of a joiner, he was apprenticed as a printer. He remained a printer throughout his life. He was asked to prepare a series of modern letters for those who could not write for themselves. This humble task taught him the art of expressing himself in letters. Who is the novelist?

(a) Daniel Defoe
(b) Samuel Richardson
(c) Henry Fielding
(d) Tobias Smollett

21 It has been described as novel 'without predecessors', the product of an original mind and became immediately popular. It is a peculiar blend of pathos and humour, though the pathos is sometimes overdone to the point of be coming offensively, sentimental. The novel was published in 1760. What is its name?

(a) Gulliver's Travels (b) The Castle of Otranto
(c) Tristram Shandy (d) A Tender Husband

June 2015

22 After his return from the land of Houyhnhnms Gulliver refused to let his wife and children ....

(a) show disrespect to English horses
(b) ride horse-drawn carriages
(c) touch his bread or drink out of his cup
(d) communicate with him in English tongue

December 2014

23 Laurence Sterne's Tristram Shandy contains

(a) six volumes (b) nine volumes
(c) ten volumes (d) four volumes

24 In Aphra Behn's oroonoko, how does the titular character die

(a) He disembowels himself
(b) He is whipped to death
(c) He is hanged in public square
(d) He is cut to pieces slowly by the executioner

June 2014

25 It has been described as a novel without predecessors' the product of an original mind and became immediately popular. It is a peculiar blend of pathos and humour, though the pathos is sometimes over done to the point of becoming offensively sentimental.

The novel was published in 1760. What is the name of this novel?

(a) Gulliver's Travels (b) The Castle of Otranto
(c) Tristram Shandy (d) A Tender Husband

26 Emotional ties and personal relationships play a minor part in Defoe's works. The following protagonist of Defoe have no family except one who leaves family at an early age. Which is that character?

(a) Moll Flanders (b) Colonol Jacque
(c) Robinson Crusoe (d) Captain Singleton

ANSWERS

Objective Questions

1. (d)	2. (b)	3. (b)	4. (b)	5. (b)	6. (c)	7. (c)	8. (b)	9. (d)	10. (a)
11. (b)	12. (a)	13. (d)	14. (c)	15. (b)	16. (c)	17. (b)	18. (b)	19. (d)	20. (c)
21. (c)	22. (b)	23. (b)	24. (b)	25. (d)	26. (c)	27. (c)	28. (c)	29. (c)	30. (c)
31. (a)	32. (a)	33. (d)	34. (a)	35. (c)	36. (c)	37. (b)	38. (a)	39. (b)	40. (a)
41. (d)	42. (b)	43. (b)	44. (b)	45. (c)	46. (a)	47. (a)	48. (c)	49. (c)	50. (c)
51. (d)	52. (d)	53. (c)	54. (c)	55. (d)	56. (a)	57. (b)	58. (b)	59. (b)	60. (b)
61. (d)	62. (c)	63. (b)	64. (b)	65. (a)	66. (c)	67. (b)	68. (c)	69. (c)	70. (c)
71. (c)	72. (d)	73. (c)	74. (c)	75. (c)	76. (c)	77. (a)	78. (b)	79. (b)	80. (c)
81. (c)	82. (b)	83. (c)	84. (b)	85. (d)	86. (d)	87. (b)	88. (c)	89. (b)	90. (c)
91. (c)	92. (b)	93. (d)	94. (c)	95. (a)	96. (c)	97. (a)	98. (b)	99. (b)	100. (a)
101. (c)	102. (d)	103. (c)	104. (d)	105. (c)	106. (a)	107. (a)	108. (a)	109. (b)	110. (a)
111. (c)	112. (c)	113. (b)	114. (b)	115. (c)	116. (d)	117. (b)	118. (b)	119. (d)	120. (b)
121. (b)	122. (d)	123. (c)	124. (a)	125. (b)	126. (d)	127. (d)	128. (b)	129. (a)	130. (c)
131. (c)	132. (b)	133. (d)	134. (b)	135. (c)	136. (b)	137. (b)	138. (c)	139. (c)	140. (d)
141. (a)	142. (b)	143. (a)	144. (c)	145. (c)	146. (b)	147. (a)	148. (c)	149. (b)	150. (d)

Previous Years' Questions

1. (b)	2. (a)	3. (a)	4. (b)	5. (a)	6. (b)	7. (b)	8. (b)	9. (a)	10. (c)
11. (c)	12. (a)	13. (a)	14. (a)	15. (b)	16. (a)	17. (d)	18. (b)	19. (b)	20. (b)
21. (c)	22. (c)	23. (b)	24. (d)	25. (c)	26. (c)				

The Romantic Age (1798-1837)

This period coincided with French Revolution which was carried against oppression. The literature of this period valued emotions, passion and individuality in place of reason and intellect.

Introduction of Romantic Age

The Romantic period in English literature begins with the publication of William Wordsworth and Samuel Coleridge's *Lyrical Ballads* in 1798 and ends with the accession of Queen Victoria in 1837. Romantic period coincided with the revolution in France and America and therefore it is also known as The Age of Revolution. The French Revolution was a battle to achieve equality and remove oppression incurred by oppressive King Louis XVI. People of France were angered by increased taxation to support their country's involvement in the American Revolution, oppressive feudal system, crop failure and other economic difficulties. The French Revolution began in 1789.

The effect of French Revolution did not confine to France only. It started a revolutionary fervour in England. According to David Cody, "The French Revolution was not only a crucial event considered in the context of Western history, but was also perhaps the single most crucial influence on British, Intellectual, philosophical and political life in the 19th century."

The writers of the Romantic period were inspired by the ideas of the French Revolution and tried to translate these ideas into the realm of literature. The diverse political changes and the triumph of democracy in the period ended with the passage of the Reform Bill in 1832.

Social and Economic Background of the Romantic Age

Towards the end of the 18th century major changes in agriculture, manufacturing, transport and technology took place in England. The first phase of Industrial Revolution was from about 1750 to 1850. Industrial Revolution had its own problems and it also led to social unrest among the working class who were left jobless due to advent of machines.

In this Chapter

- *Introduction of Romantic Age*
- *Gothic Novels in the Romantic Age*
- *The Jacobin Novel in the Romantic Age*
- *Second Stage of Novel Writing in Romantic Age*
- *Novels of Manners*

Literary Background of the Romantic Age

Generally speaking, the Romantic movement in literature is characterised by a shift from the structured, intellectual and reasoned approach of the 1700s to the use of imagination, freedom of thought and expression and idealisation of nature. Romantics valued emotions, passion and individuality in place of logic and reason. Instead of embracing politics as writers of some other eras might have done, the Romantics turned to nature for self fulfilment. They were turning away from the values and ideas of the previous era, embracing new ways of expressing their imagination and feelings.

Though Romantic period consists of two generations of poets like Wordsworth, Coleridge, Blake, Byron, Keats, Shelley. The essence of Romanticism was that literature must reflect all that is spontaneous and unaffected in nature and in man and be free to follow its own fancy in own way. Coleridge and Wordsworth best represent the romantic genius of the age, though Walter Scott had a great literary reputation and Byron and Shelley had larger audience.

The age produced a new type of novel which seems rather restrained now but which in its own day, delighted a large number of audience whose nerves were somewhat excited and who reveled in 'boggey' stories of supernatural terror. These are called Gothic Novels.

Fiction Prose of the Romantic Age

Fiction prose of the Romantic Age grew mainly in the form of novels. The novels of this period can be categorised into three types i.e.

- The Gothic Novel
- The Historical Novel
- The Novel of Manners

Gothic Novel takes its origins from what was the idea of sublime. It is usually set in ancient times and in isolated places like castles or ruins. Terror is a fundamental element in gothic novel and it is the predecessor of horror.

Another fundamental elements is darkness. Furthermore the characters described are exaggerated, they communicate their feelings in an exaggerated manner and there is usually a heroine, a young woman, who is always threatened by a villain and she always runsaway from this villain. There is also a hero that attempts to defend the heroine. This hero is a sensitive man. Another important characteristic is the presence of ghosts, monsters, supernatural beings, vampires. The most important gothic novels are *The Castle of Otranto, The Monk, Frankenstein* that are developed in an epistolary style.

Another type of novel is the historical novel. The most important author is Walter Scott and one of the most important work written by Scott is *Ivanhoe*. The context in which the stories are set always has historical bases. Some characters are invented and other really existed. There is always a very detailed description of the time, society, places: this gave the idea of a true story. The narrator is always in the third person, he is out of the story that is usually told in chronological order but with frequent flashbacks. The narrator wants to compare the past and the present and show how many things they have in common (not much has changed);

The last kind of novel is the Novel of manners that is the development of the so called bourgeois novel because the themes are more or less the same. The most important author is Jane Austen. These novels are set in the upper middle class. There is a distinction between upper middle class and middle class. All the protagonists are really influenced by the rules and manners of the society of that time and all the events are described as occasion for meeting. The main themes in this type of novel are marriage and love (Jane Austen talks about marriage market). Love is always described as complicated. Also friendship is another important theme. Dialogue is very important. Feelings and emotions that are felt by the characters are not directly expressed because in the society described passion and emotions are not considered topics of conversation and often irony is employed.

Gothic Novels in the Romantic Age

Characteristics of the Gothic Novel

According to Lilia Melani, major characteristics of Gothic novel are

- It has a castle where the main action takes place. It may be ruined or intact, haunted or not.
- The settings include dungeons, underground passages, labyrinths, dark corridors, winding stairs, extreme landscapes like thick forests or icy wastes and extreme mountain.
- The plot involves omens and ancestral curses.
- There are elements of magic, supernatural manifestations or the suggestion of the supernatural.
- The gothic novel has a passion-driven wilful villain-hero or villain whose true identity is revealed by the end of the novel.
- It has a curious heroine with a tendency to faint and need to be rescued.

Gothic Novelists

The first Gothic novel was Horace Walpole's *The Castle of Otranto* (1765). After Walpole, the second major exponent of the form was Ann Radcliffe, who produced a half-dozen works, of which the best known is *The Mysteries of Udolpho* (1794). Other examples are Matthew Lewis' **Monk** (1796), Mary Shelley's *Frankenstein* and Polidori's *The Vampyre* (1819).

Horace Walpole (1717-1797)

Horace Walpole, fourth Earl of Oxford was born on 24th September, 1717 in Arlington Street, Westminster, London. Young Walpole spent most of his childhood under the loving eyes of his mother as his father was away most of the time for business purposes. Walpole was tutored at home before he entered Eton College in 1727 and then to King's College. After the death of his mother Horace left the college incomplete and went on a grand tour of the continent. He developed friendship with British Minister to the court of Juscany and Lady Mary Wortley Montagu.

After returning to England, he became member of Parliament. In 1745, Sir Robert Walpole, father of Horace died leaving a large inheritence to his son. He established a printing press at his ancestral estate 'Straw berry Hills'.

This building was incredibly well known and contributed to architectural Gothic revival of the 18th century. He died in March 1797.

Literary Career and Works

Horace Walpole is primarily known for his novel, *The Castle of Otranto* widely considered as the most influential and the first Gothic novel. Walpole claimed that he had a dream while at Strawberry Hill that led to his writing of *The Castle of Otranto* (1764). He also wrote *The Mysterious Mother* (1768) which was not good in literary taste. Horace also wrote volumes on arts and antiques. His other works include the *Three Princes of Serendip, Life and Reign of King Richard III* (1768), *On Modern Gardening* 1780, *A Description of the Villa, Mr Horace Walpole* 1784 etc.

The Castle of Otranto

- *The Castle of Otranto* was published in 1764. The story pivots on Manfred, the tyranical usurper of the Princedom of Otranto. On the day his son Conrad is to marry Isabella, daughter of the Marquis of Vicenza, Conrad is found dead in the courtyard, crushed beneath a giant black plumed helmet that fell from a statue.
- This supernatural occurrence unleashed a train of events that lead to mysterious deaths and hauntings, culminating in the restoration of the rightful heir as ruler of Otranto.
- Manfred wants to marry Isabella in order to produce the heir but Isabella is horrified by the idea and flees from the castle in which she is assisted by handsome young peasant, Theodore.
- Later it was discovered that Theodore was the natural son of father Jerome. Manfred wants to kill Theodore but after giant form of Martyred Prince Alfonso appears, Theodore's right of succession is confirmed.
- After a series of daring rescues and thrilling escapes, the novel concludes with Prince Manfred accidentally murdering his daughter in place of Isabella.
- Theodore marries Isabella in the end and rules Otranto as Prince. Madrid and his wife vow to lead a good religious life thereafter.
- Largely a fantasy set in the chivalric Middle Ages, the novel deals in violent emotions and places its characters in psychological extremes cruelty, tyranny, eroticism, usurpation all become the common points of gothic narratives along with its settings.

Ann Radcliffe (1764-1823)

Considered as the pioneer of the Gothic Novel, Ann Radcliffe was born as Ann Ward in Holborn, London, England in 1764. Not much is known about Radcliffe's life. She is believed to have attended a school run by Harriet and Sophia Lee, who were innovators in the development and writing of Gothic drama and fiction.

Literary Career and Works

At the age of 22, she married to a journalist William Radcliffe, owner and editor of the English Chronicle, in Bath in 1788. The marriage was childless and Radcliffe began writing fiction to amuse herself. Her husband also encouraged her writing. Radcliffe's first two novels *The Castles of Athlin and Dunbayne* (1789) and *A Sicilian Romance* (1790) were published anonymously and received great reviews. Radcliffe finally ascribed her name to her most famous work, *The Mysteries of Udolpho* (1794) and received 500 pounds for it. This novel was the tale of a robber Baron's castle on the Rhine and the dark deeds that haunted it.

Radcliffe's works were extremely popular among the upper class and the growing middle class, especially among young women. She also published a travelogue, *A Journey Through Holland and the Western Frontier of Germany* in 1795. *The Italian* was the last book she published in her lifetime.

Despite the success of her works, Radcliffe led a very quiet life with her husband. It was written of her that "She never appeared in public, nor mingled in private society, but kept herself apart, like the sweet bird that sings its solitary notes, shrouded and unseen. She was more than repaid by the enjoyments, which were fostered in the shade and perhaps few distinguished authors have passed a life, so blameless and so happy...her countenance indicated melancholy. She had been, doubtless, in her youth, beautiful".

During the later years of her life, Ann suffered greatly from asthma. She died on 7th February, 1823 from respiratory problems probably caused by pneumonia and was buried in Saint George's Church, Hanover Square in London.

The Mysteries of Udolpho

- *The Mysteries of Udolpho,* novel by Ann Radcliffe, was published in 1794. It is one of the most famous English Gothic novels.
- The work tells the story of the orphaned Emily St. Aubert, a beautiful and virtuous young woman. She is subjected to cruelties by her guardians, threatened with the loss of her fortune, and imprisoned in a number of castles but finally freed and united with her lover.
- Many strange and fearful events take place in the haunted atmosphere of the solitary castle of Udolpho, set high in the dark and majestic Apennines.
- Like other Gothic novels, The Mysteries of Udolpho contains ruined castles, beautiful countryside, a virtuous heroine and a villain.

Matthew Gregory Lewis (1775-1818)

English Novelist and Dramatist Matthew Gregory Lewis was born in London in 1775. Lewis was educated at Westminster and Christ Church Oxford.

Literary Career and Works

Lewis wrote his popular Gothic novel *The Monk* in 1796. In this, he was influenced by the leading Gothic novelist, Ann Radcliffe and also by contemporary German Gothic literature. The novel narrated the story of a monk who descends into a world of degradation.

Lewis also wrote a popular music drama in the same vein, *The Castle Spectre* (1798). In 1801, he published two sets of poems, *Tales of Wonder* and *Tales of Terror*. He was also successful as a playwright. His melodramatic flair found an appreciative audience in the days of Romantic drama. He died at the age of 42 in the sea during one of his voyages to his estates.

The Monk

- Mathew Lewis's novel *The Monk* (1796) marked a turning point in the history of Gothic literature.
- With its emphasis firmly on the horrific and the shocking, the book moved Gothic away from the gentle terrors of earlier authors and, instead, confronted readers with an onslaught of horror in the form of spectral bleeding nuns, mob violence, murder, sorcery and incest.
- The story is about Ambrosio, the renowned monk who fall victim to sexual temptation with the first woman he meets, which spurs him on the even more wicked acts. The purehearted Agnes is ruthlessly punished by the cruel Prioress; the demon Matilda easily finds a place for herself within the monastery.
- In Lewis' novel, the Catholic emphasis on celibacy creates the very monster it supposedly despises, and Catholic religious belief is equated with base superstition.
- With its twin themes of erotic obsession and the corrupting influence of power, *The Monk* deals with important issues and contains moments of impressive psychological insight. At heart, however, it remains a morality tale about one man's fall from grace through greed, pride and lust.
- *The Monk* was attacked as being too sensational and condemned for its depiction of rape and incest. Coleridge in his critique of the novel stated that "*The Monk* is a romance, which if a parent saw in the hands of a son or daughter, he might reasonably turn pale." Despite that, the novel became so, popular that Lewis was thereafter known as 'Monk' Lewis.

Mary Shelley (1797-1851)

English writer Mary Shelley was born in London in 1797. She had an enviable lineage. Shelley was the daughter of famous political writer William Godwin and the feminist radical Mary Wollstonecraft.

Mary was primarily taught according to Godwin's concept of education at home. Coming from an intellectual background, Mary was surrounded by writers, poets and scientists from an early age.

She and her siblings were exposed almost daily to Godwin's extensive acquaintance among the London intelligentsia, ranging from the poet and philosopher Samuel Taylor Coleridge to scientists like Humphry Davy and her father's bosom friend William Nicholson.

Literary Career and Works

Mary's most important work, her Gothic novel *Frankenstein* or *The Modern Prometheus* was written at the age of 19. After *Frankenstein*, Shelley wrote the novella *Mathilda*, which was never published in her life-time. Shelley's last two novels; *Lodore* (1835) and *Falkner* (1837) were semi-autobiographical. From 1839 onwards, Mary Shelley's health started to decline, preventing her from writing. She died of a brain tumor on 1st February, 1851.

Frankenstein

- Mary Shelley's *Frankenstein* or *The Modern Prometheus* is a Gothic novel which was published in 1818.
- It is dedicated to Mary's father, William Godwin.
- Percy Bysshe Shelley wrote the *Preface* to Mary Shelley's *Frankenstein* in September 1817.
- The novel originated out of a competition proposed by Lord Byron in the summer of 1816, as to who could write the best horror story. The central idea came to Mary in a dream where she saw a student putting together parts of a man's body and working through a big engine to animate it. She first wrote a short story, but Percy Shelley encouraged her to expand it into a novel.
- The novel begins with a series of letters from the explorer Robert Walton to his sister, Margaret Saville. It is Walton, who finds Victor Frankenstein near death, listens to his tale and records it in letters.
- The protagonist of the story is Victor Frankenstein who creates an intelligent, but grotesque monster, from whom he recoils in horror.
- The subtitle of the novel alludes to Frankenstein as a Promethean figure, striving against human limitations to bring light and benefit to mankind. His fall results from his failure and inability to give love to his creature.
- The monster seeks a female mate for him. When Victor refuses to create one, the monster narrates his tragic story. From the time he took birth, he endured rejection from mankind, but never retaliated. As a result, he decides to take revenge on his creator's family to avenge the injury and sorrow he endures from others.
- The monster kills his near and dear ones, even killing his wife on their wedding night.
- Victor Frankenstein vows to devote the rest of his life to finding the monster and exacting his revenge and he soon departs to begin his quest.
- Frankenstein chases the monster through Europe and Russia. He is on the verge of death, when the monster comes to visit him for the last time. The monster mourns for all that he has done, but maintains that he could not have done otherwise, given the magnitude of his suffering.
- At the end of the novel, the monster disappears in the waves and darkness.

The Jacobin Novel in the Romantic Age

The term 'Jacobin Novel' was coined by the critic Gary Kelly in her book, *The English Jacobin Novel* 1780-1805 (1976) refer to a group of novels of the period 1780-1805, which espoused radical ideas. The title was drawn from the *Anti-Jacobin* or *Weekly Examiner*, a conservative journal founded by the Tory politician George Canning, which was published from 20th November, 1797 to 7th July, 1798.

This journal attacked those who questioned the status quo by labelling them as 'Jacobins' the French term for radical revolutionaries and extremist supporters of the revolution. It was originally a term of abuse to discredit their political opponents.

The Jacobin novel was concerned with social and political reform. It was concerned with the reform of institutions such as property, law and marriage. According to Miriam L Wallace in her book, *Revolutionary Subjects in the English Jacobin Novel 1790 - 1805*, "the Jacobin novels engaged with the political and philosophical debates of their times and engaged ideas about the modern state, human nature and abstract civil rights that were associated with the Revolutionary decade and the 'rights of man' and of woman".

They sought to include in their novels, subjects which had hitherto been ignored "property-less men, criminals, women without men and non-Europeans".

Important English Jacobin novels are Mary Wollstonecraft's *Maria* or, *The Wrongs of Woman* (1792), Holcroft's *Anna St Ives* (1792), William Godwin's Caleb Williams (1794), Mary Hay's *The Memoirs of Emma Courtney* (1796) and Robert Bage' *Hermsprong* or *Man As He Is Not* (1796). Holcroft's *Anna St Ives* is usually considered to be first English Jacobin novel.

Jacobin Novelists Thomas Holcroft (1745-1809)

English novelist and dramatist Thomas Holcroft was born in London in 1745. Holcroft was taught to read by his father. During his youth, Holcroft read the Bible the sensational novels popular with the lower classes and pious religious literature. However, he rejected these forms as he grew mature.

Literary Career and Works

He worked for a brief, while as a teacher. He later left this job to join theatre. He acted in various strolling companies until 1778, when he produced *The Crisis*; or, *Love* and *Famine*, at Drury Lane.

Apart from writing around a dozen plays including *The School for Arrogance A Comedy* (1791), *The Road to Ruin: A Comedy* (1792) and *The Deserted Daughter A Comedy* (1795), Holcroft also wrote novels, for which he is primarily known. His first novel *Alwyn* (1780) was an autobiographical account of a strolling comedian. His most popular novels are *Anna St Ives A Novel* (1792), *The Adventures of Hugh Trevor: A Novel* (1794).

In *Anna St Ives*, Holcroft presents utopian notions of social justice through his two main characters Anna, a member of the landed gentry, who supports social reform and equality and her beloved, the poor but honest Frank Henley. Hugh Trevor attacks existing social practices. In both the novels, Holcroft proposes a society based on justice and equality. Both the novels were inspired by the revolutionary ideas of his friend William Godwin. An important part of the Godwin circle, Holcroft was sympathetic to the cause of the French Revolution.

As a result of his activism, Holcroft was indicted for high treason in 1794. He was released later without trial. He responded to this unfair arrest by publishing 'A Narrative of Facts, Relating to a Prosecution for High Treason; including the address to the Jury, which the Court refused to hear, with Letters to the Attorney General, Lord Chief Justice Eyre, Mr Sergent Adair, The Honourable Thomas Erskine, and Vicary Gibbs Esq and the defence the author had prepared, if he had been brought to trial (1795) and A Letter to the Right Honourable William Windham on the intemperance and dangerous tendency of his public conduct (1795). His arrest had an effect on his reputation as a writer. Anti-Jacobins persecuted him and he lived in dire financial straits. Holcroft died on 23rd March, 1809, when he was in the process of completing his memoirs. They were later completed by William Hazlitt.

Elizabeth Inchbald (1753-1821)

English novelist, actress and playwright, Elizabeth Inchbald was born in a small village called Standingfield near Bury St Edmunds in Suffolk, England in 1753. Inchbald went to London in 1772 to seek her fortune on the stage. She struggled to find work because of her speech impediment. She married actor Joseph Inchbald in June 1772 and began working seriously as an actress. She made her first dramatic appearance on 4th September, 1772, as the character Cordelia opposite to her husband's King Lear in Shakespeare's King Lear.

Literary Career and Works

She continued to act after his death in 1779 and also began to adapt plays and write original farces and comedies. Her first play, *A Mogul Tale* was staged in 1784. Her plays, moral and sentimental, include *I'll Tell You What* (1785) and *Wives as They Were* and *Maids as They Are* (1797).

Inchbald is better known for her two novels, *A Simple Story* (1791) and *Nature and Art* (1796) than for her plays. The main protagonist of Inchbald's *A Simple Story*, Miss Milner is an unconventional heroine with both virtues and faults. She is not presented as an ideal character, but as a realistic one. Inchbald's heroine takes the daring step of expressing her desire to marry her guardian, a Catholic priest.

Through her novel, Inchbald also explored the paucity of options available to women. Inchbald's Second Novel, *Nature and Art* holds a central place in the history of the English Jacobin novel. It explores the opposition between the upbringing and actions of Henry Norwynne an unspoiled 'child of nature' (who has been reared without books on an African island) and the corrupt conduct of his aristocratic older cousin, William. In the later years of her life, Inchbald gradually withdrew from London, establishing herself in suburban boarding-houses, often among sisters of charity and devoting her days to the practice of her religion. She died in an obscure Kensington boarding-house, on 1st August, 1821.

William Godwin (1756-1836)

English philosopher and novelist William Godwin was born in Cambridgeshire, England in 1756. He was educated at Hoxton Academy, a liberal Presbyterian college in London. Born into a family of religious Dissenters, Godwin was trained to be a Dissenting minister, but remained in that profession for less than four years. By the end of it, he became a complete atheist.

Literary Career and Works

Godwin moved to London in 1782 and started writing. He completed his first work, *The History of the Life of William Pitt, Earl of Chatham* by 1783. Between 1782 and 1784, Godwin wrote three novels, two political pamphlets, a work on education and a spoof of the critical reviews. He eventually achieved fame and success with his work, *An Enquiry concerning Political Justice,* which appeared in 1793. It was a founding work of philosophical anarchism. In this book Godwin argued that as long as people acted rationally, they could live without laws or institutions. The following year, Godwin's most successful novel *Things as They Are or Caleb Williams* was published. It presented the individual as a victim of society and condemned the power-hungry governments.

Godwin also wrote several works such as *of Population* (1820), a reply to Thomas Malthus's writings on the subject; *Thoughts on Man: His Nature, Production and Discoveries* (1831) and his novel Mandeville (1817). Godwin's final novel, *Deloraine*, appeared in 1833. His last work of philosophical prose was *Thoughts on Man*, published in 1831. In 1833, Godwin was appointed Office Keeper and Yeoman Usher of the Receipt of the Exchequer. He died three years later at the age of 80.

Godwin's Caleb Williams

The full title of Godwin's novel published in 1794, is 'Things As They Are' or The Adventures of Caleb Williams. In the 'Preface' to the novel, Godwin explained his reasons for writing it. The following narrative is intended to answer a purpose more general and important than immediately appears upon the face of it. The question now afloat in the world respecting things as they are, is the most interesting that can be presented to the human mind. While one party pleads for reformation and change, the other extols in the warmest terms the existing Constitution of society. It is, but of late that the inestimable importance of political principles have been adequately apprehended.

The novel described the downfall of Ferdinando Falkland, a British squire and his attempts to ruin and destroy the life of Caleb Williams, a poor, but ambitious young man whom Falkland hires as his personal secretary. Caleb discovers a secret about Falkland that he has murdered someone in the past. Falkland persuades Caleb to remain silent, but cannot bear the fact that a person beneath him in status should hold power over him.

Falkland then starts using various means of unfair trials, imprisonment and pursuit, to make sure that the information of which Caleb is the bearer will never be revealed. Caleb is falsely framed and driven into a nightmare world where good and evil, legitimacy and illegitimacy are confused. To survive, he questions everything he has been raised to believe in. Considered to be the first novel of crime and detection in English literature, Caleb Williams is also a powerful expose of the evils and inequities of the political and social system in 1790s, Britain. The novel examines class distinctions and the misuse of power by the ruling aristocracy.

Mary Wollstonecraft (1759-1797)

British feminist writer Mary Wollstonecraft was born in **Spitalfields, London** in 1759. Wollstonecraft helped her sister Eliza escape from a brutal marriage. Together, the two sisters along with Wollstonecraft's close friend Fanny established a school at Newington Green.

Literary Career and Works

This experience drew Wollstonecraft to write. *Thoughts on the Education of Daughters With Reflections on Female Conduct, is the More Important Duties of Life* (1787).

In 1790, Wollstonecraft produced her *Vindication of the Rights of Man*, the first response to Edmund Burke's *Reflections on the Revolution in France*. She attacked Burke's ideas based on antiquity and tradition. The publication of *A Vindication of the Rights of Man* brought Wollstonecraft to the attention of other radical thinkers such as Tom Paine, John Cartwright, John Horne Tooke, William Godwin and William Blake. Wollstonecraft is best known for her feminist tract, *A Vindication of the Rights of Woman* (1792), which advocated equality of sexes.

Apart from her pamphlets and feminist tracts, Wollstonecraft also wrote two novels, *Mary, A Fiction and Maria: or, The Wrongs of Woman*. She also completed *Original Stories From Real Life; with Conversations*, calculated to Regulate the Affections and *Form the Mind to Truth and Goodness* (1788) and an anthology, *The Female Reader; Miscellaneous Pieces in Prose and Verse; Selected from the Best Writers and Disposed under Proper Heads; For the Improvement of Young Women* (1789), published under the pen name 'Mr. Cresswick, teacher of Elocution'. Wollstonecraft died of an infection on 10th September, 1797, 11 days after the birth of her daughter.

Mary a Fiction or The Wrongs of Woman

Through this novel Wollstonecraft focused her argument that the British legal institution of marriage reduced wives to the same condition as the prisoners in the notorious French prison. The laws governing marriage in England until the late 19th century were based on the fact that wife was the property of the husband.

In this novel, the heroine Mary has to rely on her own resources to establish her independence and intellectual development. In its sequel *Maria: or, The Wrongs of Woman*, Maria fights imprisonment and a loveless marriage to claim her rights.

Maria : or, the Wrongs of a Woman

- Mary Wollstonecraft's Maria or the Wrongs of Woman was her last novel, which was left unfinished at the time of her death in 1797 and published posthumously in 1798 by her husband, William Godwin. The work was considered to be the novelistic sequel to her revolutionary political treatise, *A Vindication of the Rights of Woman.*
- In her '*Preface*' to the novel, Wollstonecraft stated that "in writing this novel, I have rather endeavoured to portray passions than manners". The story is based on an upper-class woman named Maria, a woman imprisoned in an insane asylum by her husband and focuses on the societal rather than the individual wrongs of woman.
- During Her imprisonment, Maria meets and hears the stories of Jemima, the labouring-class woman, who works at the asylum and Henry Darnford, another inmate who has been unfairly incarcerated. The novel criticises the legal system that protected marriage in the 18th century.
- According to Colleen Fenno, "Wollstonecraft emphasises the legal disadvantages of gender by depicting Maria's incarceration as an effect of coverture, which excluded women from owning property."

Mary Hays (1759-1843)

English novelist and feminist Mary Hays was born in Southwark, near London. She was born into a Baptist family to John and Elizabeth Hays. Not much is known about the early years of her life and education.

In 1777, Hays met and fell in love with John Eccles. But, before Hays could attain her love, Eccles died from fever on 23rd August, 1780. Hays had a tough time recovering from this loss and she later devoted herself to reading, writing and corresponding with religious and political reformers.

Literary Career and Works

Robert Robinson, a Baptist preacher became her friend and mentor. He also introduced her to the teachings of the leading Dissenters of her days, such as George Dyer, Joseph Priestley and William Frend. Hays' first literary piece, 'The Hermit, an Oriental Tale' was published in the *Universal Magazine* in 1786. Her first novel *Memoirs of Emma Courtney* was published in 1796. It was an autobiographical novel based on Hays' real life love and pursuit of William Frend.

Frend was her tutor, who had responded to Hays' defence of dissenting worship and appropriately occupied the place of a mentor after Robinson's death. She had misinterpreted his gestures and became romantically attached to him, only to be met with rejection. Hays' frankness about her fictionalised feelings for Frend won her notoriety, despite the preface's insistence that, it was 'calculated to operate as a warning, rather than as an example'. Her second novel *Victim of Prejudice* (1799), dealt with issues of economic and social dependency, sexuality and subjectivity.

We can easily divide the rise of novels in three categories

(i) The Gothic Novels

(ii) Appearance of politically engaged fiction immediately before the French Revolution.

(iii) The rise of women writers to prominence during the late 1750s.

Second Stage of Novel Writing in Romantic Age

The death of Tobias Smollett in 1771 brought an end to the first age period of novel writing in English. The 2nd period and a better one started with Jane Austen's novel sense and sensibility in 1811, follwed by Sir Walter Scott's prose fiction that ranked with the masterpieces of Richardson, Henry Fielding, Lawrence Stern and Tobias Smollett.

There were practical reasons for this 40 years partial eclipse. The war with France made paper expensive, causing publishers in the 1790s and early 1800s to prefer short dense forms such as poetry. It might also be argued in more broadly cultural terms that the comic and realistic qualities of the novel were at odds with the new sensibility of Romanticism. Flourishing as a form of entertainment, the novel, nevertheless underwent several important changes during this period.

Major Novelists of the Second Stage of Romantic Age

Fanny Burney (1752-1840)

English novelist and diarist Fanny Burney was born as Frances Burney in King's Lyn, Norfolk, England in 1752. She was the daughter of Dr Charles Burney, a musical historian and Esther Sleepe. Fanny's mother died, when she was only 9 years old. Her father later married Elizabeth Allen, the wealthy widow of a King's Lynn wine merchant, who proved to be an overbearing step mother.

From the time young Fanny learned her alphabet, she was a writer, composing odes, plays, songs, farces and poems at an early age. However, she burned them all at age 15, most likely under the influence of her stepmother, who did not think it appropriate for women to write. Fanny could not suppress her urge to write and started keeping a diary at the age of 16. It was addressed to 'Miss Nobody', to whom she would reveal 'every thought, every wish of her heart'. Her diary recorded personal and public events from the early reign of George III to the dawn of the Victorian Age.

Literary Career and Works

Fanny's first novel, *Evelina or The History of a Young Lady's Entrance into the World*, was published anonymously in 1778. It was an epistolary novel about an unsure young girl's social development. The novel proved extremely successful.

Her second novel, *Cecilia or Memoirs of an Heiress*, appeared in 1782. In 1793, she produced her *Brief Reflections relative to the Emigrant French Clergy*. Her third novel, *Camilla, or A Picture of Youth* was published in 1796. It proved to be her biggest financial success.

She returned to England from Paris in 1812 and published her last novel, The Wanderer, or Female Difficulties in 1814. Fanny died in London on 6th January, 1840.

The Novel Evelina or the History of a Young Lady's Entrance into the World revealed Fanny Burny as a social commentator with an attentive ear for a dialect and the differentiation of London speech. It concerns the development of a young girl unsure of herself in society and subject to errors of manners and judgement. The plot terminates with Evelina's marriage after the mistakes stemming from her untutored girlhood have been surmounted. A novel treating contemporary manners in an elegant and decorous way and depending for its development of its plot upon the erring and uncertain conduct of the heroine was an innovation that pointed the way for the novels of Jane Austen.

Maria Edgeworth (1768-1849)

Anglo-Irish novelist Maria Edgeworth was born in Blackbourton, Oxfordshire, England in 1768. She was the second child of Richard Lovell Edgeworth and Anna Maria Edgeworth. In Ireland, Edgeworth helped her father in managing the estate and thereby acquired the knowledge of rural economy and Irish peasantry.

Literary Career and Works

Her father encouraged her writing and had an important influence on her works. Her first publication was a plea for female education, *Letters to Literary Ladies* (1795) and her collection of stories known as *The Parent's Assistant* appeared in 1796.

This was her first book of children's literature. Edgeworth's first novel *Castle Rackrent* satirised the conventions of upper-middle class Anglo-Irish landlords and their overall mismanagement of the estates they owned. This novel was written without her father's supervision and appeared anonymously in 1800. It became an immediate success.

Her next work, *Belinda* (1801), a society novel was unfortunately marred by her father's insistence on a happy ending. The novel became controversial for its depiction of an inter-racial marriage between an African servant and an English farm-girl. Edgeworth promotes her heroine's development as a rational, well-educated young woman. Even though she is required to marry well, she is determined to marry on her own terms.

Edgeworth's other works include *Essay on Irish Bulls* (1802), *Leonora* (1806), *Tales of Fashionable Life* (1809 and 1812), *Ennui* (1809), *The Absentee* (1812), *Patronage* (1814) her longest novel about political intrigue and the quest for a universal language and *Ormond* (1817), about pre-revolutionary France. After her father's death in 1817, she edited his memoirs, and extended them with her biographical comments. Her last years were spent working for the relief of the famine-stricken Irish peasants during the Irish Potato Famine (1845-1849). Edgeworth died of a heart attack in Edgeworths town on 22nd May, 1849.

Castle Rackrent

- *Castle Rackrent*, in full 'Castle Rackrent, an Hiberian Tale: Taken from Facts, and from the Manners of the Irish Squires, Before the Year 1782', is a novel by Maria Edgeworth, published in 1800.

- It is viewed as perhaps the first historical novel as well as the first regional novel in the English language. In addition, it is considered the first Angol-Irish novel. A further innovation of Edgeworth's book is its use of an unreliable narrator who observes the Actions he relays rather than participating in them.
- Castle Rackrent is a satire on the Ango-Irish landlords and the way they managed their estates during the time when the Parliament of England and Ireland were attempting to formalise their union through the Acts of Union.
- This is the story of four generation of the Rackrent heirs as told by Thady Quirk their steward. The heirs include the self-absorbed and decadent Sir patrick O'Shaughlin; Sir Murtagh Rackrent, who is prone to taking legal actions; Sir Kit Rackrent, a gambler and cruel husband; and Sir Condy Rackrent, who is shortsighted and thoughtless.
- The narrator's son, Jason Quirk, works to resolve the ongoing estate mismanagement of the others, benefitting from his actions. Following the death of Sir Patrick O'Shaughlin, Thady Quirk, upstanding of character, works for Sir Murtagh at Caste Rackrent Murtagh has a violent temper; his wife, Lady Murtagh is concerned with money, not with the concerns of her tenants or making them happy.
- The next heir to Castle Rackrent in line is Sir Condy Rackrent, a cousin of Sir Kit. Sir Condy is a relatively easygoing master but is not at all thrify when it comes to money. Under his watch, the estate falls more deeply into debt than it has ever been, but he takes no steps to improve conditions.
- Ultimately, Thad's son, Jason, becomes the agent of the estate. As an attorney, he purchases Sir Condy's debts and uses them to force Condy to sign Castle Rackrent over to him. Tenants fear having Jason as their landlord and are sorry over the ruin of Condy. Jason allows Condy to remain on the estate in a hunting lodge.

Walter Scott (1771-1832)

Considered the exponent of the historical novel, Scottish author and poet Walter Scott was born in Edinburg in 1771. Educated first at Edinburgh High School and then at Edinburgh University, he was later apprenticed to his father and called to the bar in 1792.

Literary Career and Works

In 1802-03, Scott's first major work, *Minstrelsy of the Scottish Border,* a collection of ballads appeared. As a novelist, Scott is a creator of a world of events and characters. His novels are pieces of reconstructed history filled with life and flavoured with humanity. Scott is the father of historical novel, a master artist in this form of fiction in English Literature. His first novel was Waverly (1814) which was set during Jacobite uprising of 1745 which sought to restore the Stuart dynasty. For nearly 20 years he published novels in quick succession. These novels were a blend of fact and fiction, history and romance. Scott altered the facts of history and changed the sequence of events in the interest of his art of novel writing.

Major Works

Guy Mannering (1815), the *Heart of Midlothian* (1818), *Rob Roy* (1817), *The Bridge of Lemmermore* (1819), *Ivanhoe* (1820), *Quentin Durward* (1823), *Red Gauntlet* (1824), *The Talisman* (1825) are some of Walter Scott's well known novel.

In 1823, he founded the Bannatyne Club for the publication of old Scottish papers, the club being named for George Bannatyne (1545-1608), a collector of Scottish poems. In 1831, his health deteriorated sharply and he tried a continental tour with a long stay at Naples to aid recovery. But this did not produce any result. Scott was taken home and died in 1832.

Ivanhoe

It was a novel, set in 12th century England, an example of historical fiction. The novel is sometimes given credit for helping to increase popular interest in the Middle Ages in 19th century Europe and America.

It is the story of one of the remaining Saxon noble families at a time when the English nobility was overwhelmingly Norman. It follows the Saxon protagonist Wilfred of Ivanhoe who is out of favour with his father for his allegiance to the Norman king Richard I of England. The story is set in 1194 after the failure of the third crusade. King Richard, who had been captured by the Duke of Saxony, on his way back from crusade, was still supposed to be in the arms of his captors. The legendary Robin Hood, initially under the name of Locksley is also a character in the novel. Other major characters include Ivanhoe's intractable Saxon father, cedrick, a descendant of the Saxon king Harald Godwinson, various knights Templar and Churchmen, the loyal serfs Gurth, the swineherd and the jester Wamba whose observations punctuate much of the action the Jewish moneylender, Isaac of York and his daughter Rebecca.

Novels of Manners
(Major Novelists)

Jane Austen (1775-1817)

English novelist Jane Austen was born at Steventon rectory in Hampshire, England in 1775.

Austen was largely self-educated. She had access to her father's large library and learnt whatever she could from her father and brothers.

Theatricals also constituted a part of Austen's education. From the age of thirteen, Austen's family and close friends staged a series of plays, including Richard Sheridan's *The Rivals* and David Garrick's *Bon Ton*.

Literary Career and Works

It was around 1787 that Austen started writing poems and stories. She wrote a dark satirical comedy *Love and Friendship*, which parodied romantic fiction and *The History of England*, parody of historical writings. Austen also started writing some of her future major works, the first called *Elinor and Marianne*, another story told as a series of letters, which was eventually published as *Sense and Sensibility*.

After, her brief romance with Lefroy, Austen began work on a second novel called 'First Impressions's which would later become 'Pride and Prejudice'.

In the seven and a half years that she lived in the beautiful cottage in Southampton, Austen revised *Sense and Sensibility* and *Pride and Prejudice* and published them, embarking on a period of intense productivity. *Mansfield Park* appeared in 1814, followed by *Emma* in 1816. None of the books published in Austen's life-time had her name on them - they were described as being written 'By a Lady'.

In her late years, Austen contracted Addisons Disease, a tubercular disease of the kidneys. Despite her illness, Austen continued to work on her writings, revising the ending to *The Elliots* (later published as Persuasion) and starting work on *Sanditon*. She died on 8th July, 1817, leaving *Sanditon* unfinished and was buried at the city's famous Cathedral.

Short Summary of Austen's Major Novels

Name	Description
Sense and Sensibility	Austen's first published novel was originally written in 1795, as an epistolary novel (novel in letters) entitled Elinor and Marianne. It is the story of the Dashwood sisters, Elinor and Marianne and their love for Edward Ferrars and Col Brandon respectively.
Pride and Prejudice	Originally titled first impression because the appearances of the characters created the plot of the novel, Austen's second novel narrates the story of the Bennets and their five daughters -Jane, Elizabeth, Mary, Kitty and Lydia. The novel starts off with Mrs Bennet's obsessive desire to get her daughters married. The focus of the story is on the change of emotions of Elizabeth Bennet and Mr Darcy from repulsion to love.
Mansfield Park	This novel is centered on Fanny Price, the poor ward and niece of Sir Thomas and Lady Bertram. She is taken from her parents to be raised by her rich relatives and comes to Mansfield Park as a child of nine. It is a more socially-aware novel than Austen's other works, focusing, as it does on the slave trade and the roots of the British upper-crust's wealth in corruption and exploitation.
Emma	Before beginning this novel, Austen herself had written; "I am going to take a heroine whom no one, but myself will much like". Emma Woodhouse, the heroine of the novel is described as 'rich, clever and handsome'. She is a heiress, who lives with her widowed father at their estate, Hartfield and takes pride in her matchmaking skills.
Northanger Abbey	It is a parody of a Gothic novel. The protagonist of the novel is Catherine Morland-inexperienced country girl, who has never left her home until taken to Bath for a six-week visit by childless neighbours, Mr and Mrs Allen. While. Catherine has read many novels (particularly Gothic novels), she is very inexperienced at reading people. Her naivete about the world and about the motivations of the people she meets is an endless source of confusion and frustration for her.
Persuasion	Austen's last completed novel is a representative mature work. It narrates the story of Anne Elliot (the overlooked middle daughter of the vain Sir Walter Elliot), who breaks off her engagement with Frederick Wentworth because she was persuaded by her mother's great friend and her own trusted confidante, the widow Lady Russell. Lady Russell objects to the match as, Wentworth is a poor naval officer. However, several years later, the situation turns and Wentworth rises to affluence. The novel ends with Anne and Captain Wentworth getting married.

Lamb succumbed to an infection he contracted from a minor cut on his face after having fallen on the street and died at Edmonton, a suburb of London in 1834.

Thomas Love Peacock (1785-1866)

English writer Thomas Love Peacock was born in Dorset England in 1785. His education was cut short due to his father's death. He was raised by his mother at her maternal home. He say taught Greek, Latin, French and Italian.

Literary Career and Works

After a brief experience of business, Peacock determined to devote himself to literature. His poetical works: *Polmyora and other Poems* and *The Monks of St Mark* were published when he was in his late teens.

Today Peacock's reputation rests almost exclusively on the merit of his novels, four of which appeared in quick succession. Peacock's novels record the intellectual, social, economic and literary discussion of early 19th century England. They are in one sense 'Conversational Novels' and many of the characters who take part in various conversations were modelled after the leading personalities of Peacocks's day. Peacock's novels have lost none of their appeal, however, for the subjects they address continue to inform the political and social dialogues.

In the novel Melincourt the author treats subjects such as original versus modern man literary tastes and the education of women but the attention given to other ideas and controversies show that Peacock was not simply rewriting his first novel. Peacock's characters whether they represent serious thinkers who clearly have won their author's approval or buffoons all play part in bringing to life the purpose of the novel which is to expose social flows to show that individuals can and do change.

Peacock remains important today not only because his novels are among the best of their types but because the issues they address are universal.

EXAM BASED QUESTIONS

1 **Which age is also known as Age of Revolution?**
(a) Augustan (b) Neo-classical
(c) Romantic (d) Victorian

2 **The French Revolution was against**
(a) the political parties
(b) against the Monarch's oppresive deeds
(c) crop failiue
(d) economic subversion

3 **The fall of the prison of Bacfille, that marks the beginning of the French Revolution occurred on**
(a) 14th June, 1789 (b) 14th June, 1798
(c) 14th July, 1789 (d) 14th July, 1798

4 **The Romantic Movement in literature is characterised by**
(a) use of imagination and feelings
(b) common man's language
(c) structured and reasoned approach
(d) using classical writers works as their source

5 **Who were the prominent figures of Romantic Age?**
(a) Wordsworth (b) ST Coleridge
(c) Byron (d) All of these

6 **What is the essence of Romanticism?**
(a) Literature must be spontaneous and imaginative
(b) Use of logic and reason
(c) Following certain rules in writing poetry or novel
(d) Writing should be restrained and structured

7 **Prominent features of Gothic novels include**
(a) romance and feelings
(b) mystery and element of supernatural
(c) natural surroundings and beauty
(d) poems and love songs

8 **Who wrote first Gothic novel?**
(a) Anne Radcliffe (b) Mary Shelley
(c) Horace Walpole (d) None of these

9 **In which century did the period known as 'Gothic' begin?**
(a) 19th century (b) 18th century
(c) 17th century (d) 20th century

10 **Which of these is a Gothic novel?**
(a) The Secret Agent
(b) Frankenstein
(c) Othello
(d) The Tales of Huckleberry Fin

11 **Which element Gothic novels do not have?**
(a) heroic male characters
(b) female victims
(c) cursed families
(d) heroic female character

12 **Identify Mary Shelley's most important Gothic novel.**
(a) Ladore (b) Frankenstein
(c) Mathilda (d) Falkner

13 **Many Gothic fiction are set on**
(a) deserts (b) castles
(c) the future (d) other planets

14 **Horace Walpole's 1764 novel, 'The Castle of Otranto', is often credited with being the first Gothic novel. Can you name its villain?**
(a) Wilfred (b) Manfred
(c) Winifred (d) Ruprecht

15 **Identify Radcliffe's most famous Gothic novel.**
(a) The Castle of Athlin and Dunbayne
(b) The Mysteries of Udolpho
(c) Lewis the Monk
(d) The Italian

16 **Mary Shelley's Frankenstein was written as a result of a ghost story competition between friends held on the bank of Lake Geneva in the summer of 1816. Which of her fellow writers was not with her?**
(a) Percy Bysshe Shelley (b) Lord Byron
(c) Sir Walter Scott (d) John William Polidori

17 **Identify Lewis' popular Gothic novel.**
(a) The Castle Spectre
(b) Tales of Wonder
(c) The Monk
(d) Tales of Terror

18 **Jane Austin didn't roll with the Goth crowd yet what kind of book did she write?**
(a) Gothic Parody (b) Gothic love letter
(c) Gothic lyric poem (d) Gothic short story

19 **Who wrote preface to Mary Shelley's Frankenstein?**
(a) Wordsworth (b) Goldwin
(c) P B Shelley (d) Edgeworth

20 **The most sophisticated gothic novels blended which two elements?**
(a) The supernatural and psychological
(b) The old and the new
(c) Violence and machinery
(d) Reason and religion

21 **Who killed Victor Frankenstein's family in Shelley's novel Frankenstein?**
(a) Victor Frankenstein
(b) Robert Walton
(c) Margaret Saville
(d) The Monster Created by Frankenstein

22 The main theme of Godwin's 'Caleb Williams' is
(a) the misuse of power by the ruling aristocracy
(b) class distinctions
(c) Both (a) and (b)
(d) None of the above

23 Which among the following is a tale of the last of the Goths?
(a) Madoc
(b) Roderick
(c) The Curse of Kehama
(d) Kubla Khan

24 Mary Wollstonecraft is best known for
(a) Vindications of the Right of Man
(b) The Wrongs of a Woman
(c) Victim of Prejudice
(d) Calb Williams

25 Who coined the term Jacobin Novel?
(a) Mary Edgeworth (b) Wollstonecraft
(c) Mary Hays (d) Gary Kelly

26 Which is the first English Jacobin novel?
(a) Maria
(b) Caleb Williams
(c) Anna St Ives
(d) The Memoirs of Emma Courtney

27 The first vampire tale in English was written by
(a) MG Lewis (b) John Polidori
(c) Lord Byron (d) Thomas De Quincey

28 Ann Radcliffe's The Mysteries of Udolpho (1794) features the villainous
(a) Valancourt (b) Mantoni
(c) Count De Villefort (d) Milfred

29 In Thomas Holcroft's novel Anna St. Ives, the author proposes a society based on
(a) gender indiscrimination
(b) justice and equality
(c) rich versus poor
(d) capitalism

30 Who wrote the novel 'A Simple Story' in the year 1791?
(a) Ann Radcliffe (b) Thomas Halcroft
(c) Elizabeth Inchbald (d) William Godwin

31 Which was the first completed work of William Godwin ?
(a) Caleb Williams
(b) The History of the Life of William Pitt, Earl of Chatham
(c) Of Population
(d) Thought on Man

32 Which was the first novel by Mary Hays published in 1796?
(a) Victim of Prejudice
(b) Memoirs of Emma Courtney
(c) Maria or the Wrongs of a Woman
(d) The Hermit, an Oriental Tale

33 Identify Fanny Burney's first novel.
(a) Camilla (b) Evelina
(c) Cecilia (d) Belinda

34 Which work of Edgeworth satirises upper middle class Anglo-Irish landlords and their over all mismanagement of Estates they owned?
(a) Belinda (b) Leonara
(c) Castle Reckrent (d) The Absentee

35 Which novel by Fanny Burney was about an unsure young girl and her social development?
(a) The Wanderer
(b) Camilla
(c) The History of a Young Lady's Entrance into the World
(d) Cecilia

36 Young Fanny Burney was fond of composing what from an early age?
(a) Plays (b) Songs
(c) Odes and Poems (d) All of these

37 In the romantic age only there was a partial eclipse of 40 years in novel writing between Gothic and Jacobin novels and novels of late 18th century writers such as Jane Austin and Walter Scott. What was the possible reason?
(a) Paper was expensive
(b) Poetry form was preferred by publishers
(c) Both (a) and (b)
(d) None of the above

38 The first book of children's literature written by Maria Edgeworth is
(a) Letters to Literary Ladies
(b) Belinda
(c) Essay on Irish Bulls
(d) The Parent's Assistant

39 Maria Edgeworth is considered to be the founder of regional novel in English literature because
(a) She portrays national life
(b) She portrays life in a particular locality
(c) Of The Confessions of an English Opium Eater
(d) Of Her Lively Nature

40 Who became the ultimate agent of the estate in Maria Edgeworth's 'Castle Reckrent'?
(a) Sir Condy Reckrent (b) Sir Kit Reckrent
(c) Sir Patrick (d) Jason

41 Who wrote the 'Heart of Midlothian'?
(a) Walter (b) John Gibson
(c) Francis Jeffrey (d) Jane Porter

42 In which novel of Scott the love story is generally pale and feeble, but the strife and passions of big parties are magnificently portrayed?
(a) Old Morality
(b) The Bride of Lammermoor
(c) Marmion
(d) Lady of the Lake

43 **Who was the first novelist in any language to make the scene an essential element in the action?**
(a) Blake (b) Wordsworth
(c) Scott (d) Gibson

44 **In how many volumes was 'Minstrelsy of the Scottish Border' published in 1802-03?**
(a) One (b) Two
(c) Five (d) Three

45 **Who wrote the 'Lady of the Lake'?**
(a) Wordsworth (b) Blake
(c) Walter Scott (d) John Gibson

46 **Who has been credited for pioneering the historical novel?**
(a) Godwin (b) Austen
(c) Southey (d) Scott

47 **Who assists Richard in releasing prisoners in Ivanhae**
(a) Issac (b) Bois Gull bert
(c) Robinhood (d) D' Bracy

48 **Which of the following is not written by Walter Scott?**
(a) Ivanhoe
(b) Lady of the Lake
(c) Heart of Midlothian
(d) The English Mail Coach

49 **Which popular work of Scott showed what a mine of neglected wealth lay just beneath the surface of English history?**
(a) Ivanhoe (b) Kenilworth
(c) Count Robert (d) The Talisman

50 **Who among the following showed Scott's grasp of the romantic side of English Annals?**
(a) Quentin Durward
(b) Peneril
(c) Count Robert
(d) Talisman

51 **Who wrote 'Demonology and Witchcraft'?**
(a) Scott (b) Gibson
(c) Porter (d) Jeffrey

52 **The nobleness of 'Soul of a Scotch Peasant Girl' is shown in**
(a) Lady of the Lake
(b) Marmion
(c) Old Morality
(d) The Heart of Midlothian

53 **Who marked the contrast to extravagant stories with her charming descriptions of every day life?**
(a) Jane Austen
(b) Maria Edgeworth
(c) Mrs Ann Radcliffe
(d) Walter Scott

54 **The year 1814 is significant for two authors in Elizabethan age. Identify the correct phrase below.**
(a) For publication of Austen's Emma and Mary Shelley's Frankenstein
(b) For publication of Keats Odes and Scott's Ivanhoe
(c) For publication of Austen's Mansfield Park and Scott's Waverly
(d) For publication of Shelley's Zastrozzi and Coleridge's Kubla Khan

55 **Which novel by Jane Austen features the character of Sir Walter Elliot?**
(a) Mansfield Park (b) Northanger Abbey
(c) Persuasion (d) Sense and Sensibility

56 **In Northanger Abbey, the heroine, Catherine Morland, enjoys reading what type of novels?**
(a) Gothic (b) Romance Fiction
(c) Science Fiction (d) Western

57 **What is the heroine's name in novel 'Mansfield Park'?**
(a) Fanny Boyce (b) Fanny Brice
(c) Fanny Price (d) Fanny Rice

58 **Jane Austen was born in 1775 at the rectory in Steventon in which English country?**
(a) Derest (b) Hampshire
(c) Somerset (d) Wiltshire

59 **Who are Dashwood sisters in sense and sensibility?**
(a) Elinor and Marianne (b) Cassandra and Joan
(c) Marry and Lydia (d) Amy and Amand

60 **Which among the following is not written by Jane Austen?**
(a) The English Mail Coach
(b) Sense and Sensibility
(c) Emma
(d) Confessions of an English Opium Eater

61 **Thomas Love Peacock is important today because of**
(a) his novels
(b) issues addressed in his novels are universal
(c) Both (a) and (b)
(d) None of the above

62 **Identify which of the following works belong to Peacock?**
(a) Northanger Abbey (b) Camilla
(c) Evelina (d) Nightmare Abbey

63 **Who is the odest single woman in Austen's novels to catch a husband?**
(a) Mr Wood Houses Widow Molter
(b) Miss Taylor
(c) Charlotte Lucas
(d) Anne Elliot

64 Which of the following novels was not completed by Jane Austen?
(a) The Watsons
(b) The Kennedys
(c) First Impression
(d) Love and Friendship

65 Which of the following activities features frequently in novels of Jane Austen?
(a) Singing (b) Playing Football
(c) Swimming (d) Dancing

66 Which novel of Jane Austen has the characters Fitzwilliam Darcy and Elizabeth Bennet?
(a) Sense and Sensibility
(b) Emma
(c) Mansfield Park
(d) Pride and Prejuidice

67 The English writer Thomas Love Peacock was born in England in
(a) 1777 (b) 1785
(c) 1788 (d) 1776

68 What description was used by Jane Austen instead of her name when her novels were published?
(a) George Eliot (b) A Lady
(c) Maid of Honour (d) Ice-Maiden

69 What was Lizzy's first impression of Mr Darcy in the novel Pride and Prejudice?
(a) He was arrogant
(b) He was handsome but proud
(c) He was lazy and unpleasant
(d) He was an introvert

70 Which of Elizabeth's friends never cared much for romance in Pride and Prejudice?
(a) Charlotte Lucas
(b) Georgina Dancy
(c) Maria Lucas
(d) Anne De Bourgh

71 Why does Anne go to Upper Cross instead of Bath with her father and sister in the novel 'Persuasion' by Jane Austen?
(a) As Mrs Smith was going with her family
(b) Because her sister Mary was ill
(c) Because captain Wentworth was going to be in the Uppercross
(d) Because Lady Russell didn't like Bath

72 The short story written by Lamb is
(a) John Worvil
(b) A Tale of Rosamund Gray
(c) Poor Blind Margaret
(d) Both (b) and (c)

73 Peacock's novels are famous today because the issues raised in them are
(a) political (b) equality
(c) universal (d) social flaws

74 Which of the following is a novel by Thomas Peacock?
(a) Ivanhoe (b) The Talisman
(c) Melincourt (d) Victim of Prejudice

75 Jane Austen was .... years old when she died.
(a) 26 years (b) 41 years
(c) 30 years (d) 49 years

76 The Romantic period in English literature began in ...... with publication of ...... by William Wordsworth and Coleridge.
(a) 1775, Cyrical Ballads
(b) 1798, Lyrical Ballads
(c) 1798, French Revolution
(d) 1790, Imaginary Conversations

77 Romantic period coincides with ....
(a) Peasant's Revolution
(b) French Revolution
(c) American Civil War
(d) None of the above

78 The first phase of Industrial Revolution in England was from ...... to ....
(a) 1798 to 1820 (b) 1787 to 1847
(c) 1750 to 1850 (d) 1778 to 1840

79 During romantic age logic and reason were replaced by .... and ....
(a) emotions and individuality
(b) passions and spontaneous
(c) emotions and feelings
(d) imagination and logic both

80 Gothic novels deal with subjects such as ...... and ....
(a) supernatural, depression
(b) female, villains
(c) supernatural, fear
(d) huge, boulders

81 The name of estate inherited by Horace Walpole was ....
(a) Apple Hill (b) Strawberry Hill
(c) Opera House (d) Mansfield

82 The Gothic novel written by Ann Radcliffe in 1794 is ....
(a) The Castle of Otranto
(b) The Mysteries of Udolpho
(c) Monk
(d) A Sicilian Romance

83 The name of the renowned Monk in Matthew Lewis's novel 'The Monk' is ....
(a) Abrosee (b) Ambrosio
(c) Matilda (d) Agnes

84 Mary Shelley's famous Gothic novel Frankenstein begins with a .... from the explorer Robert Walton to his sister.
(a) series of poem (b) narratives
(c) series of letters (d) sermon

85 **The name of the young handsome peasant who helps Isabella in the novel 'The Castle of Otranto' is ....**

(a) Thorndike (b) Theodore
(c) Jerome (d) Manfred

86 **The main character of novel 'The Mysteries of Udolpho' is ....**

(a) An Orphaned Emily Aubert
(b) Emily Jenson
(c) Amelia
(d) Isabella

87 **The character .... in the novel 'Frankenstein' is responsible for creating an intelligent but grotesque monster.**

(a) Wilifred
(b) Victor Frankenstein
(c) Ambrosio
(d) Monk

88 **Jacobin novels refer to a group of novels which espoused ....**

(a) political ideology
(b) spiritual discourse
(c) romantic narratives
(d) radical ideas

89 **The stream of novel concerned with social and political reform in late 18th century were called ....**

(a) Anti Jacobin novels (b) Gothic
(c) Jacobin novels (d) Romantic

90 **Miss Milner, is an unconventional heroine in the novel .... by Elizabeth Inchbald**

(a) Nature and Art
(b) A Mogul Tale
(c) A Simple Story
(d) None of the above

91 **In Pride and Prejudice Darcy proposes to Elizabeth in ....**

(a) Germany
(b) Hunsford Parsonage
(c) The Village Ball
(d) None of the above

92 **Two characters Anna and Frank Henley are present in novel .... written by Thomas Holcroft.**

(a) The Deserted Daughter
(b) Alwyn
(c) Anna St. lves
(d) The Adventures of Hugh Trevor

93 **Which of these about Pride and Prejudice is correct?**

(a) It was originally titled : First Impression
(b) It was originally titled : Last Impression
(c) The present title is the : Original Title
(d) It was originally titled : No Impressions

94 **Which of the following statements about Evelina is correct?**

(a) It is not alternatively titled
(b) It is alternatively titled, 'The History of a Young Lady's Entrance into the World
(c) The alternate title is 'The History of a Young Man's Entrance into the World '
(d) It has a subtitle

95 **Which of these statements about 'Sense and Sensibility' is not true?**

(a) It is written by Jane Austen
(b) It was originally written in 1795
(c) It is an epistolary novel
(d) It is the story of the Bennet sisters

96 **What is common to the following works? Identify the correct description below.**

1. Sense and Sensibility 2. Mansfield Park
3. Emma 4. Persuasion

(a) All of them are Gothic novels
(b) All of them are poems by PB Shelley
(c) All of them are novels by Jane Austen
(d) All of them have been written by Mary Shelley

97 **Consider the following statements.**
According to Lilia Melani, main features of the Gothic novel are

1. It does not have a castle where the main action takes place.
2. It typically does not have ruined buildings.
3. The plot involves omens and ancestral curses.
4. It has a curvaceous heroine with a tendency to faint and a need to be rescued.

Which of the statements given above are correct?

(a) 1 and 4 (b) 1 and 2 (c) 3 and 2 (d) 3 and 4

98 **Consider the following statements.**
The main characteristic of 'Frankenstein' are

1. It is a building in roman.
2. It is dedicated to Mary's father, William Godwin.
3. The novel begins with a series of letters from the explorer Robert Walton to his sister.
4. The protagonist of the story is Robert Walton.

Which of the statements given above are correct?

(a) 1 and 4 (b) 1 and 2 (c) 3 and 4 (d) 3 and 2

99 **Consider the following statements.**
The main characteristics of 'Maria' are

1. It is written by Mary Wollstonecraft
2. It is based on an upper class woman named Maria.
3. It is written by Mary Hays.
4. It is based on the working woman Maria.

Which of the statements given above are correct?

(a) 1 and 4 (b) 1 and 2 (c) 3 and 4 (d) 3 and 2

100 Consider the following statements.
The main characteristic of 'Ivanhoe' by scott was
1. Its plot is based in England
2. Ivanhoe was disinherited by his father
3. It was written by Thomas Love Peacock
4. It was published in 1815

Which of the statements above given is/are correct?

(a) 1and 4 (b) 2 and 4
(c) Only 3 (d) 1 and 2

101 Consider the following statements
The main characteristic of Fanny Barrey was ....
1. She was a writer composing poem and songs from a very early age.
2. Her novel Evelina was published in 1778.
3. She wrote the novel Castle Rackrent.
4. She published her last novel 'Wanderer' in 1812.

Which of the statements above given is/are correct?

(a) Only 1 and 3 (b) 3 and 4
(c) 1, 2 and 4 (d) Only 4

102 Consider the following statements.
The main characteristics of novel 'Melincourt' are
1. It was written by Thomas Love Peacock.
2. It was published in 1817.
3. It was written by Thomas de Quincey
4. It was not published in 1820.

Which of the statements given above are correct?

(a) 1 and 4 (b) 1 and 2
(c) 3 and 4 (d) 3 and 2

103 **Assertion** (A) Gothic novel is devoted to stories of fear, horror and the supernatural.

Reason (R) It represents the dark side of human nature.

(a) A is true, but R is false
(b) A is false, but R is true
(c) Both A and R are true, but R is not the correct explanation of A
(d) Both A and R are true and R is the correct explanation of A

104 **Assertion** (A) The Jacobin novels was not concerned with social and political reform.

Reason (R) It was concerned with the reform of institution such as property, law and marriage.

(a) Both A and R are true and R is the correct explanation of A
(b) Both A and R are true, but R is not the correct explanation of A
(c) A is false, but R is true
(d) A is true, but R is false

105 **Assertion** (A) Walter Scott had contributed a lot to modern literature and he is mainly known for his tales.

Reason (R) He got the talent of story telling from his mother, who was good at story telling.

On the basis of reading the above statements:
Tick the correct option which correctly depicts that Scott was known for his tales.

Codes

(a) Both A and R are true, but R is not the correct explanation of A
(b) Only A is true
(c) Only R is true
(d) Both A and R are true

106 Match the following Gothic novels with their writers (Romantic Age).

Gothic Novels :
1. The Mysteries of Udolpho
2. The Castle of Otranto
3. Frankenstein
4. The Monk

Gothic novel writers of Romantic Age
A. Horace Walpole B. Matthew Lewis
C. Ann Radcliffe D. Marry Shelley

Codes

(a) 1-B, 2-D, 3-A, 4-C (b) 1-C, 2-A, 3-D, 4-B
(c) 1-C, 2-D, 3-A, 4-B (d) 1-A, 2-B, 3-C, 4-D

107 Match the following fiction writers with their works (Romantic Age)

Fiction Writers
1. Jane Austen 2. Walter Scott
3. Thomas Peacock 4. Thomas D Quincey

Romantic Age Works
A. Ivanhoe
B. Confession of Opium Eater
C. Pride and Prejudice
D. Melincourt

Codes

(a) 1-B, 2-D, 3-C, 4-A (b) 1-D, 2-C, 3-B, 4-A
(c) 1-C, 2-A, 3-D, 4-B (d) 1-B, 2-A, 3-C, 4-D

108 Match the following works with their authors

Works
1. Lyrical Ballads
2. A Sicilian Romance
3. Anna St Ives
4. A Simple Story

Authors
A. Ann Radcliffe
B. Thomas Holcroft
C. Wordsworth and Coleridge
D. Elizabeth Inchbald

Codes
(a) 1-A, 2-B, 3-C, 4-D
(b) 1-D, 2-C, 3-B, 4-A
(c) 1-C, 2-B, 3-A, 4-D
(d) 1-C, 2-A, 3-B, 4-D

109 Match the following works with their authors

List I	List II
A. Sense and Sensibility	1. Walter Scott
B. Melincourt	2. Mary Wollstonecraft
C. Ivanhoe	3. Jane Austen
D. Maria: or, the Wrongs of Woman	4. Thomas Love Peacock

Codes

	A	B	C	D		A	B	C	D
(a)	2	3	1	4	(b)	3	4	1	2
(c)	4	3	2	1	(d)	4	3	1	2

110 Match the following.

List I	List II
A. Ann Radcliffe	1. The Monk
B. George Lewis	2. The Mysteries of Udolpho
C. Wallstonecraft	3. Pride and Prejudice
D. Austen	4. Maria or, The Wrongs of Woman

Codes

	A	B	C	D		A	B	C	D
(a)	2	1	4	3	(b)	2	1	3	4
(c)	1	4	3	2	(d)	1	3	4	2

111 In the following series, which set of authors and their works is correctly matched?
(a) Jane Austen-Persuasion; Mary Shelley - Frankenstein; Percy Shelley Ozymandias; George Gordon-Don Juan
(b) Jane Austen Ozymandias; Mary Shelley-Don Juan; Percy Shelley-Persuasion; George Gordon-Frankenstein
(c) Jane Austen Persuasion; Mary Shelley-Don Juan; Percy Shelley-Frankenstein; George Gordon Ozymandias
(d) Jane Austen-Don Juan; Mary Shelley-Persuasion; Percy Shelley-Frankenstein; George Gordon-Ozymandias

112 Which is the right chronology of the following works of publication?
(a) Frankenstein, Persuasion, Exhibition of Rhinoceros and a Zebra
(b) Frankenstein, Exhibition of Rhinoceros and a Zebra, Persuasion
(c) Exhibition of Rhinoceros and a Zebra, Persuasion, Frankenstein
(d) Persuasion, Frankenstein, Exhibition of Rhinoceros and a Zebra

113 Which of the following is in correct sequence? according to the year publication?
(a) Pride and Prejudice, Ivanhoe, Castle Reckrent
(b) Castle Rackrent, Pride and Prejudice, Ivanhoe
(c) Ivanhoe, Pride and Prejudice, Castle Rackrent
(d) Castlc Rackrent, Ivanhoe, Pride and Prejudice

114 Which is the right chronology of the years of publication of the following works?
(a) Lyrical Ballads, The Castle of Otranto, Pride and Prejudice, Melincourt
(b) Pride and Prejudice, Lyrical Ballads, Melincourt, The Castle of Otranto
(c) The Castle of Otranto, Lyrical Ballads, Pride and Prejudice, Melincourt
(d) Melincourt, Lyrical Ballads, The Castle of Otranto, Melincourt

115 Which of the following is in chronological order according to the birth of the writer?
(a) William Godwin, Elizabeth Inchbald, Charles Lamb, Ann Radcliffe
(b) William Godwin, Ann Radcliffe, Elizabeth Inchbald, Charles Lamb
(c) Elizabeth Inchbald, William Godwin, Charles Lamb, Ann Radcliffe
(d) Ann Radcliffe, Elizabeth Inchbald, Charles Lamb, Willian Godwin

116 Consider the following works.
1. Sense and Sensibility
2. Lyrical Ballads
3. Persuasion
4. Ivanhoe

Which of the above given are novels by Jane Austen?
Codes
(a) 1 and 2 (b) 2 and 3 (c) 1 and 3 (d) 2 and 4

117 Consider the following fiction.
1. Dream Children
2. The Three Princes of Serendip
3. The Castle of Athlin and Dunbayne
4. Vindication of the Rights of Man

Which of these works are called Gothic Novels?
(a) 1 and 3 (b) 2 and 4 (c) 1 and 4 (d) 1, 2 and 3

118 Consider the following works.
1. Waverley
2. The Bridge of Lammemoor
3. The Logic of Political Economy
4. Memoirs of Shelley

Which of these works are written by Walter Scott.
(a) 1 and 2 (b) 2 and 4 (c) 2 and 4 (d) 1 and 3

119 Consider the following statements.
1. A belief in individual liberty and sympathy
2. The romantics thought of Nature as permanent
3. A disbelief in individual liberty and sympathy
4. Romantics believed in reason and logic

Which of these statements characterise the Romantics?
(a) 2 and 3 (b) 2 and 4
(c) 1 and 2 (d) 3 and 4

120 What is common to the following works? Identify the correct description below.

1. Sense and Sensibility 2. Mansfield Park
3. Emma 4. Persuasion

Codes

(a) All of them are Gothic novels
(b) All of them are poems by ST Coleridge
(c) All of them are novels by Jane Austen
(d) All of them are essays written by Charles Lamb

121 For whom were these lines written?

"She never appeared in public, nor mingled in private society, but kept herself apart, like the sweet bird that sings its solitary notes, shrouded and unseen."

(a) Jane Austen (b) Mary Shelley
(c) Ann Radcliffe (d) Mary Wollstonecraft

122 Which novel was critiqued by Coleridge in the following words?

"It is a romance, which if a parent saw in the hands, of a son or daughter, he might reasonably turn pale."

(a) Austen's Pride and Prejudice
(b) Lewis the Monk
(c) Holcroft's Anna St Ives
(d) Godwin's Caleb Williams

123 In which novel of which author do these lines occur?

"A well informed mind is the best security against the contagion of folly and vice. The vacant mind is even on the watch for relief and ready to plunge into error to escape from the languor of idleness. Store it with ideas, teach it the pleasure of thinking ...."

(a) Jane Austen in Pride and Prejudice
(b) Charles Lamb in Essay 'Dream Children'
(c) Ann Radcliffe in the Mysteries of Udolpho
(d) Walter Scott in Waverley

124 Which author in which of his novel speaks these lines?

"We are like the herb which flourisheth most when trampled upon."

(a) Jane Austen in Emma
(b) Thomas Love Peacock in Melin Court
(c) Maria Edge Worth in Belinda
(d) Walter Scott in Ivanhoe

125 In Preface, of which novel Wollstonecraft wrote the following Lines?

"In writing this novel, I have rather endeavoured to portray passions than manners."

(a) Original Stories from Real Life
(b) Mary, A Fiction
(c) Maria: or, the Wrong of Woman
(d) the Female Reader

126 According to Colleen Fenno, "Wollstonecraft emphasises the legal disadvantages of gender by depicting protagonist's incarceration as an effect of coverture, which excluded women from owning property."

Which work of Wollstonecraft is talked about in the above lines?

(a) Mary, A Fiction
(b) Maria or the Wrongs of Woman
(c) Thoughts on the Education of Daughters
(d) Vindication of the Rights of Women

127 Which character in Pride and Prejudice of Jane Austen, speaks these words?

"You are perfectly right. You have employed your time much better. No one admitted to the privilege of hearing you; can think anything wanting. We neither of us perform to strangers."

(a) Mr Bennet (b) Mr Darcy
(c) Mrs Bennet (d) Lady Catherine

128 In which Gothic novel of this age do these lines occur?

"The horror of the spectacle; the ignorance of all around how this misfortune happened, and above all, the tremendous phenomenon before him, took away the Prince's speech. Yet his silence lasted longer than even grief could occasion. He fixed his eyes on what he wished in vain to believe a vision; and seemed less, attentive to his loss than buried in meditation on the stupendous object that had occasioned it."

(a) The Myteries of Udolpho
(b) Frankenstein
(c) Caleb Williams
(d) The Castle of Otranto

129 In which work of Sir Walter Scott do these lines appear?

"Revenge is the sweetest morsed to the mouth, that even was cooked in Hell."

(a) Ivanhoe
(b) The Heart of Midlothian
(c) Guy Mannering
(d) The Pride of Lammermoor

130 Jane Austen's Pride and Prejudice starts with the famous statement: "It is a truth universally acknowledged that a single man in possession of a good fortune must be in want of a life."

As we get to read the novel this statement seems to be made from the point of view of

(a) the surrounding families
(b) Mrs Bennet
(c) Mr Bennet
(d) the women of Jane Austen's age and society

131 Who said, "I declare after all there is no enjoyment like reading! How much sooner one time of anything than of a book!...... When I have a house of my own, I shall be miserable if I have not an excellent library"?
(a) Maria Edgeworth in Belinda
(b) Jane Austen in Pride and Prejudice
(c) Fanny Burney in Camilla
(d) Mary Hays in Victim of Prejudice

132 Who said these lines, "I put in no claims either for happiness, for gratification or even for the common comforts of life; yet surely, I had a right to exist"?
(a) Jane Austen
(b) Mary Hays
(c) Maria Edgeworth
(d) William Godwin

133 In which work of Maria Edgeworth do these lines appear?
"What a treasure, to meet anything a new heart .... all hearts nowadays are secondhand at best?"
(a) Castle Rackrent
(b) Patvonage
(c) Belinda
(d) The Absentee

134 In which work of Thomas Love Peacock these lines appear?
"Now I should rather suppose there is no reason for it. It is the fashion to be unhappy. To have a reason for being so would be exceedingly common place: to be so without any is the province of a genius."
(a) Headlong Hall (b) Maid Marian
(c) Nightmare Abbey (d) Melincourt

135 In which famous work of Walter Scott are these lines found?
"Chivalry ...... why maiden, she is the nurse of pure and high affection ...... the stay of the oppressed, the redresser of grievances, the curb of the power of the tyrant ...... Nobility were but an empty name without her, and liberty finds the best protection in her lance and her sword."
(a) Ivanhoe
(b) The Waverly
(c) The Bride of Lemmermoor
(d) Red Gauntlet

136 William, Hazlitt in his essay "The 'Spirit of Age' wrote, He was in the very Zenith of a sultry and unwholesome popularity; he blazed as a sun in the firmament of reputation; no one was more talked of, more looked up to, more sought after and wherever liberty, truth, justice was the theme, his name was not far off now he has sunk below the horizon and enjoys the serene twilight of a doubtful immortality."
About which novelist does Hazlitt talks about in these lines?
(a) William Godwin
(b) Sir Walter Scott
(c) Thomas Love Peacock
(d) Charles Lamb

137 In which work of William Godwin, one of his characters utters these words?
"Strange, that men from age to age should consent to hold their lives at the breath of another, merely that each in his turn may have a power of acting the tyrant according to law! Oh, God give me poverty! shower upon me all the imaginary hardships of human life! ...."
(a) Deloraine
(b) Thought on Man
(c) Caleb Williams
(d) of Population

138 Which character in Fanny Burney's novel 'Evelina' utters these words?
"In all ranks and all stations of life, how strangely do characters and manner differ!
Lord Orville, with a politeness which knows no intermission, and makes no distinction is as unassuming and modest, as if he had never mixed the great, and was totally ignorant of every qualification he possesses; this other lord, though lavish of compliments and fine speeches, seems to me an entire stranger to real good breeding ......"
(a) Mr Villars
(b) Lady Howard
(c) Mrs. Mirvan
(d) Evelina

139 In which novel by which author does this description of a character named Mortimer Delvile appear?
"Mortimer Delville was tall and finely formed, his features, though not handsome, were full of expression, and a noble openness of Manners and address spoke the elegance of his education, and the liberality of his mind."
(a) In Pride and Prejudice by Jane Austen
(b) Cecilia by Fanny Burney
(c) Waverly by Walter Scott
(d) Caleb William by William Godwin

140 In which work of Fanny Burney do these lines appear? "To despite riches, may, indeed be philosophic, but to dispense them worthily, surely must be more beneficial to mankind."
(a) Evelina (b) The Wanderer
(c) Cecilia (d) Camilla

141 About which magazine Scott has said, "No genteel family can pretend to be without it." and Carlyle had remarked that it was "a kind of Delphic Oracle and voice of the inspired for the great majority of what is called the intelligent public?

(a) Edinburgh Review
(b) The London Magazine
(c) Francis's Magazine
(d) The West Minister's Review

142 The following lines are the beginning of which novel by Jane Austen?

"About thirty years age, Miss Maria Ward of Huntingdon, with only Seven thousand pounds had the good luck to capitivate Sir Thomas Bertram ...."

(a) Mansfield Park (b) Emma
(c) Sense and Sensibility (d) Northanger Abbey

143 In whose novels of romantic age does this introductory note appears?

"The title of this work has not been chosen without the grave and solid deliberations, which matters of importance demand from the prudent. Even its first, or general denomination, was the result of no common research or selection, although, according to the example of my predecessors, I had only to seize upon the most sounding and euphonic surname that English history or topography affords ...."

(a) Dream Children by Charles Lamb
(b) Cecilia by Fanny Burney
(c) Belinda by Maria Edgeworth
(d) The Waverly by Walter Scott

144 Which character in Scott's novel Invanhoe utters these words?

"For he that does good having the unlimited power to do evil, deserves praise not only for the good which he performs, but for the evil which he forbears."

(a) Narrator (b) Cedric of Rotherwood
(c) The Black Knight
(d) Wamba

145 Which character in which novel of Jane Austen says these lines?

"I may have lost my heart, but not my self-control '..........' never could I expect to so truly beloved and important, so always first and always right in any man's eyes as I am in my father's.

(a) Marianne Dashwood in Sense and Sensibility
(b) Emma Woodhouse in Emma
(c) Elizabeth Bennet in Pride and Prejudice
(d) Anne Elliot in Persuasion

Directions (Q. Nos. 146-150) *Read the following passage and answer the questions that follow.*

I slept, indeed, but I was disturbed by the wildest dreams. I thought I saw Elizabeth, in the bloom of health, walking on the streets of Ingolstadt. Delighted and surprised, I embraced her, but as I imprinted the first kiss on her lips, they became livid with the hue of death; her features appeared to change and I thought that I help the corpse of my dead mother in my arms; a shroud enveloped her form, and I saw the grave worms crawling in the folds of the flannel. I started from my sleep with horror; a cold dew covered my forehead, my teeth chattered and every limb became convulsed; when, by the dim and yellow light of the moon, as it forced its way through the window shutters, I beheld the wretch the miserable monster whom I had created.

He held up the curtain of the bed; and his eyes, if eyes they may be called, were fixed on me. His jaws opened and he muttered some inarticulate sounds, while a grin wrinkled his cheeks. He might have spoken, but I did not hear; one hand was stretched out, seemingly to detain me, but I escaped and rushed downstairs. I took refuge in the courtyard belonging to the house which I inhabited, where I remained during the rest of the night, walking up and down in the greatest agitation, listening attentively, catching and fearing each sound as if it were to announce the approach of the demoniacal corpse to which I had so miserably given life.

I passed the night wretchedly. Sometimes my pulse beat so quickly and hardly that I felt the palpitation of every artery; at others, I nearly sank to the ground through languor and extreme weakness. Mingled with this horror, I felt the bitterness of disappointment; dreams that had been my food and pleasant rest for so long a space were now become a hell to me; and the change was so rapid, the overthrow so complete!

146 Who created the monster?

(a) Victor Frankenstein
(b) Elizabeth Lavenza
(c) Alphonse Frankenstein
(d) Robert Wolton

147 Why was Victor frightened that night?

(a) The monster wanted to take revenge on him
(b) Victor was alone in the home
(c) He was afraid of dead corpses
(d) None of the above

148 Why does the creature want revenge on Victor?
(a) Victor created him (b) Victor abandoned him
(c) Victor loved him (d) Victor denied creating him

149 What did Mrs. Frankenstein die from?
(a) She died of a broken heart
(b) She was strangled
(c) The news of Elizabeth's death killed her
(d) She contacted scarlet fever

150 Why does the creature decide to be evil?
(a) He doesn't decide; he is naturally evil
(b) He decides the best way to get revenge on Victor is to be evil
(c) He decides that since people immediately thought he was evil, then he would be evil
(d) He has a natural liking for the Dark Side

PREVIOUS YEARS' QUESTIONS

December 2018

1 Evelina was published in 1778
(a) posthumously
(b) using the name Fanny Burney
(c) anonymously
(d) under a pseudonym

2 Which of the following is not indebted to the Gothic genre?
(a) Tobias Smollett's Roderick Random
(b) Ann Radcliffe's the Italian
(c) Matthew Lawis's the Monk
(d) William Beckford's Vathek

3 Which of the two novels of Jane Austen have the Spa Town of Bath as primary location?
1. Emma 2. Pride and Prejudice
3. Northinger Abbey 4. Persuation
Codes
(a) 1 and 4 (b) 2 and 3 (c) 3 and 4 (d) 1 and 2

July 2018

4 Haunted Castles, strange noises and an acceptance of the supernatural with all its trappings mark ....
(a) metafiction (b) fantasy fiction
(c) epistolary fiction (d) Gothric fiction

November 2017

5 In Fanny Burney's novel Evelina, eponymous heroine comes out in society in two locations. They are
1. Both 2. Bristol
3. Leeds 4. London
Right combination according to the codes is
(a) 1 and 2 (b) 2 and 3
(c) 1 and 4 (d) 2 and 4

6 Pick out two Austen heroines from the following who are right-minded but neglected in the beginning but gradually are acknowledged to be correct by characters who have previously looked down on their
1. Elizabeth Bennet 2. Fanny Price
3. Emma Wood house 4. Anne Elliot
The right combination according to the codes is
(a) 1 and 3 (b) 2 and 4
(c) 3 and 4 (d) 1 and 4

7 From among the following who are the Dashwood sisters in Jane Austen's sense and sensibility?
1. Elinor 2. Marianne
3. Mary 4. Amanda
Codes
(a) 1 and 3 (b) 1 and 2 (c) 2 anc 3 (d) 3 and 4

July 2016

8 Which chilling novel of surveillance and entrapment had the alternative title things are they are?
(a) Horace Wolpole's Castle of Otranto
(b) Matthew Gregory Lewis's The Monk
(c) Thomas Love Peacock's Nightmare Abbey
(d) William Godwin's Caleb Williams

December 2015

9 Which of the following works did Walter Scott complete?
(a) The Lay of the Last Minstrel
(b) Marmion
(c) Ivanhoe
(d) The Minstrelsy of Scottish Border

10 The monster in Frankenstein is not responsible for the death of
(a) Clerval (b) Justine
(c) Elizabeth (d) Alphonse Frankenstein

June 2015

11 In The Heart of Midlothian Walter Scott deals with real political and personal details, but notable among his characters is the depiction of ....
(a) Queen Anne (b) Queen Victoria
(c) Queen Caroline (d) Queen Elizabeth

June 2014

12 Who is the author of Mary and the Unfinished 'The Wrongs of Woman'?

(a) Mary Wollstone Craft (b) William Godwin
(c) Mary Hay (d) Elizabeth Inch bald

13 Scolt is known for the creation of mad, irrational witchlike woman characters. From the following list pick the add one out.

(a) Madge Wildfive (b) Meg Murdock Son
(c) Euphemia Deans (d) Meg Merrilees

ANSWERS

Objective Questions

1. (c)	2. (b)	3. (c)	4. (a)	5. (d)	6. (a)	7. (b)	8. (c)	9. (b)	10. (b)
11. (d)	12. (b)	13. (b)	14. (b)	15. (b)	16. (a)	17. (c)	18. (a)	19. (c)	20. (a)
21. (d)	22. (c)	23. (b)	24. (b)	25. (d)	26. (c)	27. (b)	28. (b)	29. (b)	30. (c)
31. (b)	32. (b)	33. (b)	34. (c)	35. (d)	36. (d)	37. (c)	38. (d)	39. (b)	40. (d)
41. (a)	42. (b)	43. (c)	44. (d)	45. (c)	46. (d)	47. (c)	48. (d)	49. (a)	50. (b)
51. (a)	52. (d)	53. (a)	54. (c)	55. (c)	56. (a)	57. (c)	58. (b)	59. (a)	60. (a)
61. (b)	62. (d)	63. (b)	64. (a)	65. (d)	66. (d)	67. (b)	68. (b)	69. (b)	70. (a)
71. (b)	72. (d)	73. (c)	74. (c)	75. (b)	76. (b)	77. (b)	78. (c)	79. (a)	80. (c)
81. (b)	82. (b)	83. (b)	84. (c)	85. (b)	86. (a)	87. (b)	88. (d)	89. (c)	90. (c)
91. (b)	92. (c)	93. (a)	94. (b)	95. (d)	96. (c)	97. (d)	98. (d)	99. (b)	100. (d)
101. (c)	102. (b)	103. (c)	104. (c)	105. (a)	106. (b)	107. (c)	108. (d)	109. (b)	110. (a)
111. (a)	112. (c)	113. (b)	114. (c)	115. (b)	116. (c)	117. (d)	118. (a)	119. (c)	120. (c)
121. (c)	122. (b)	123. (c)	124. (d)	125. (c)	126. (b)	127. (b)	128. (d)	129. (b)	130. (d)
131. (b)	132. (b)	133. (c)	134. (c)	135. (a)	136. (a)	137. (c)	138. (d)	139. (b)	140. (a)
141. (a)	142. (a)	143. (d)	144. (c)	145. (b)	146. (a)	147. (a)	148. (b)	149. (d)	150. (c)

Previous Years' Questions

1. (c)	2. (a)	3. (c)	4. (d)	5. (d)	6. (d)	7. (b)	8. (d)	9. (d)	10. (d)
11. (c)	12. (a)	13. (c)							

The Victorian Age (1837-1901)

The period refers to 19th century Victorian age, which lasted upto the beginning of 20th century. Literature of this period reflects major changes taking place and writers either through poetry or novels dealt on social, economical and intellectual problems which were caused by predominance of industrialisation.

Victorian Age

The Victorian Age is named after the reign of queen Victoria who ruled from 1837 to 1901. She was the first English monarch to see her name given to the period of her reign while still living. It was one of the most prosperous periods in the history of England, a period of industrial development and colonial expansion. Vast social, political and technological changes occurred during this age. It is also sometimes called the Age of Reform as lots of reforms took place during this period.

It was an age of democracy. The major democratic movement in Britain during queen Victoria's reign was directed towards expanding voting population for parliamentary elections. But 1832 Reform Act still failed to extend the voting rights to these individuals who did not have any property in Britain. As a counter attack a Chartist Movement was started in England (1838) which asked or demanded votes for all men, equal electoral payment for MPs, annual general elections and secret ballot. Two Reform Bills (1867) and (1884) achieved further democratisation of British politics and by the end of 19th century universal male suffrage became a reality but women were still not entitled to vote. But it was also an age of triumph of middle class with their belief in progress and moral prudence.

Literary Trends of Victorian Age

The Victorian period was a high point in the history of English literature which produced a number of prominent writers and poets such as Charles Dickens, Thomas Hardy, Tennyson and Browning. Writers of this age were perceptive to numerous changes occurring during this period and reflected upon these in their writings. It was an age when through verse or prose current social, economical and intellectual problems were deflected. It was an age of variegated immense and often self-critical literary activities.

In this Chapter

Though Tennyson and Robert Browing represented the two pillars of Victorian poetry, the Novel became the most chosen form by writers later during the Victorian period. The poet Arthur Hugh Clough attests to this fact when he remarks that, "The modern novel is preferred to the modern poem". As novel was the best means to present a picture of life lived under the stable background of social and moral values of the characters who were like the people encountered by readers. It was the kind of picture of life, the middle class readers wanted to read about. It has been considered as the 'golden age of novel' as novelists portrayed a society in rapid transition besides maintaining realistic approach.

The Victorian period also witnessed tremendous growth in periodicles of all kinds. Many famous novelists published their work in serial instalments in magazines.

Literature for children also developed in Victorian Age as a separate genre. Works of Lewis Carroll (1832-98) *Alice in Wonderland* and *Through the Looking Glass* and also adventure novels such as *Treasure Island*, 1883 and *Dr Jekyll* and *Mr Hyde* by RL Stevenson became well known.

Some literary movements during the Victorian period are worth mentioning. They are Oxford Movement, Aesthetic Movement and Pre-Raphaelite Movement.

Oxford Movement's connection with literature resulted in a series of doctrinal papers called *Tracts*. The Aesthetic Movement was a reaction against utilitarian philosophies and it believed in Art for art's sake. Most important writer of this movement is Oscar Wilde. Pre Raphaelite Movement writers rejected artificial dramatic mannerism and wanted some genuine ideas to express and study nature attributively.

Influence of Victorian Literature

The persistent popular embrace of Victorian literature has had a profound influence on modern literature and media. Writers such as Charles Dickens and the Bronte sisters still sell robustly on most book resellers' lists and are frequently adapted into films and television productions, both directly and in modernised retellings. In addition, many modern novels such as 'A Great and Terrible Beauty' demonstrate that the intricate cultural mode of the Victorian era find a home in modern cultural psyche.

First Generation Victorian Novels

The main features of the first generation novels are as follows

Themes

One of the prominent features, that the novel of the early Victorian era had, was the concern with the 'condition of England question'.

They chose for their themes the specific contemporary problems of the Victorian society caused by the predominance of industrialisation and utilitarianism and wrote about them sometimes as satirists, sometimes as humanists and sometimes as moralists.

Imaginative Rendering of Reality

In spite of the fact that they were conscious of the havoc caused by the industrial revolution, the presence of mass poverty and accumulation of riches in a few hands, yet they believed like the common Victorians that these evils would prove to be temporary and that on the whole, England was growing prosperous, which was evident from the enormous increase in material wealth and there was no reason why this progress should not continue indefinitely.

Characterisation

A significant shift in the English Novel in its movement from the 18th to the 19th century was the change of emphasis from action to character. They gave primacy to the character as opposed to Neo-classical novelists who gave more importance to action.

Loose Plots

The early Victorian novel, unlike both the novel of the preceding era as well as the following novel of the later phase of the Victorian period, was rather formless.

One of the reasons was the new reading public (the masses of middle and lower middle class) for whom they were being written. Like the Elizabethan drama, the novel in the early Victorian phase was written more for any entertainment than for any artistic purpose. But in spite of that, it contained the large purpose of offering a picture and criticism of contemporary life. The second and real cause of the lack of organisation in these novels was that they were serialised in the monthly and weekly magazines. Quite often, a novel took 25 serials to complete in the magazine.

First Generation Novelists

The early Victorian or first generation novelists comprised of Charles Dickens, Anthony Trollope, Mrs Gaskell, Bronte Sisters and William Thackrey etc. Although there were several more novelists of the time, only the ones mentioned here have survived the test of time and are considered representative of the early phase of the Victorian fiction in England.

Second Generation Victorian Novels

The later Victorian novels or the second generation novels were published in 1860s and 70s.

Main features of second generation Victorian novels are as follows

Main Themes

The novelists of the later Victorian era, were not entertainers and reformers as were their elders. Instead, they were more serious composers with greater involvement in the deeper passions of life particularly love.

Moreover, their main concern was with the rural England, which was being destroyed by industry and commerce rather than the city working class and its masters, the mill-owners etc. They depicted the tragedy of transition from the agrarian way of life to the industrial order.

Lack of High Artistic Standard

The second generation Victorian novelists were more 'literary' and less 'popular' than the first generation. They had more academic flavours in their writings and more poetic imagination. They did not have the breadth and variety (with the exception of Middlemarch) of the early novelists but they certainly had greater depth of characterisation and greater intensity of presentation.

Focus on Rural Background

Another change that took place in the English novel around the year 1860, was the shift in its focus from city with its industrialism and utilitarianism to the village with its vision of destruction under the threat of the new scientific rationalism and evolutionism, which started new ethics and human relations inspired by Darwinian concepts of 'struggle for existence' and 'survival of the fittest'.

These new ideas made the novelists look at human society from a new perspective, not as a static Biblical model existing in the dynamic tension between good and evil, but as an evolutionary process of human nature, society and civilisation, growing on the Darwinian principles.

Growth of Intellectualism

Another significant change that took place in the Victorian age, was the shift towards intellectualism. Although Dickens and Thackeray were 'educated' enough to grasp the crosscurrent of ideas in their time, but were not 'learned' in the sense Meredith and other later Victorian novelists were. The novelists of the later Victorian Age were more learned than their predecessors.

Second Generation Novelists

George Eliot, George Meredith, Thomas Hardy, George Butler and RL Stevenson etc were all major novelists of the 2nd generation who started publishing their novels around the end of the 50s or later.

Major Novelists of the Victorian Age

Major novelists of the Victorian Age are Charles Dickens, George Eliot, Elizabeth Gaskell, Charlotte Bronte, Emily Bronte, Anne Bronte, W M Thackerey, Anthony Trollope, George Meredith, Benjamin Disraeli, Charles Kingslay, Wilkie Collins, Samuel Butler, RL Stevenson, George Gissing and Thomas Hardy. *Their brief description is given below*

Charles Dickens (1812-1870)

Victorian novelist Charles Dickens was born in Portsmouth, Hampshire, England on 7th February 1812. He was the second of eight children of John and Elizabeth Dickens. Dickens' father was a clerk in the Naval Pay office, while his mother had been in service to Lord Crew. In 1824, Dickens' father was imprisoned for debt. The entire family, except Dickens, were sent to Marshalsea Prison alongwith their father. Dickens was sent to work in a blacking warehouse, where he pasted labels on bottles for six shillings a week. When his family's position improved, Dickens attended a school in London between 1824 and 1827. Dickens was forced to leave school again in 1827, when his family was evicted from their home in Somers Town for unpaid rent dues. Dickens learned shorthand and began his career as a journalist. He worked as a parliamentary reporter for two London newspapers.

Literary Career and Works

Dickens joined a newspaper *The Morning Chronicle* where he was asked to write a series of sketches about London life. This gave rise to *Sketches by Boze*, his first literary experiment.

Boz was Dickens' family name, which he adopted as a pseudonym. This was followed by his first novel, *The Posthumous Papers of the Pickwick Club* in 1836-37. It was published in serial form in monthly instalments. Dickens was the first person to make serialisation of novels profitable and was able to expand his audience to include those, who could not normally afford such literary works. Dickens married Catherine Hogarth, daughter of the editor of the *Evening Chronicle* on 2nd April, 1836. However, they did not achieve conjugal happiness and got separated many years later.

Dickens' next novels, *Oliver Twist* and *Nicholas Nickleby* established his fame as a novelist. *Oliver Twist* was the story of an orphan, who endures a miserable existence in a workhouse.

This novel was a response to the new Poor Laws of 1834. Dicken's most popular novel are *David Copperfield, Hard Times, A Tale of Two Cities* and *Great Expectations*. He also wrote Christmas stories, the most known of which is a *Christmas Card*.

Dickens has created some of world's most memorable fictional characters and his creative genius has been praised for its realism, comedy, prose styles and social criticism.

Dickens travelled abroad in the 1840s first to America and then through Europe, where he also gave public readings from his works during the travels abroad. During the 1850s Dickens suffered two devastating losses: the death of his daughter and father. He also separated from his wife during this decade. After this period his writing became more serious and expressed a dark world view. Dickens was working on a mystery novel titled *The Mystery of Edwin Drood* at the time of his death. But work remained unfinished as Charles.

Dickens died of a stroke in 1870.

Dickens as Short Story Writer

Dickens also wrote many colourful, sad, funny and witty novellas and short stories of the Victorian era. *Some of his prominent short stories are*

- **A Holiday Romance** Charming four short stories presented through the point of view of four children.
- **A Message From the Sea** It is a story about nautical adventure and mystery story that begins with a message in a bottle.
- **Doctor Mari Gold** A short story about a street peddler who finds happiness with his adopted deaf-mute daughter.
- **Mrs. Lirriper's Legacy** A short story of how Mrs Lirriper and her friend send stories to her son at school.
- **Master Humphrey's Clock** A story of a lonely man who decides to start a club, where the members would read out their stories to others.
- **Mudfog and Other Sketches** Collection of short stories-*Public Life of Mr Tulrumble, The First Meeting of Mudfog, The Pantomime of Life.*
- **Mugby Junction** Collection of short tales revolving around Victorian railway station.
- **Sketches of Young Couples** Collection of short story focusing on couples. A parody of social relations between the sexes.
- **Somebody's Luggage** Story about a waiter who stumbles upon some luggage and tries to identify its owner. Dickens wrote short stories throughout his career, he mixes humour with macabre imagery to create vivid illustrations of the lives of ordinary people. Designed to uncover social injustices and promote reform in his own time, the endearing characterisations and moving situations presented in short stories have appealed to audiences up to the present day.

Major Works

Christmas Books

- A Christmas Carol (1843)
- The Chimes (1844)
- The Cricket on the Hearth (1845)
- The Battle of Life (1846)
- The Haunted Man and the Ghost's Bargain (1848)

Short Story Collections

- Sketches by Boz (1836)
- The Mudfog Papers (1837)
- Reprinted Pieces (1861)
- The Uncommercial Traveller (1860-1869)

Important Characters in Dickens' Novels

Name of Character	Name of Novel
Artful Dodger	Oliver Twist
Abel Magwich	Great Expectations
Bentley Drummle	Great Expectations
Blathers	Oliver Twist
Bumble	Oliver Twist
David Crimple 'Crimp'	Martin Chuzzlewit
Edward Murdstone	David Copperfield
Jaggers	Great Expectations
Kit Nubbles	Old Curiosity Shop
Noddy Boffin	Our Mutual Friend
Quebec Bagnet	Bleak House
Rob the Grinder	Dombey and Son
Sleary	Hard Times
Sloppy	Our Mutual Friend
Stephen Blackpool	Hard Times
Thomas Gradgrind	Hard Times
Uriah Heep	David Copperfield
Harold Skimpole	Bleak House
Mr Wopsle	Great Expectations
Polly Toodle	Dombey and Son
Silas Wegg	Our Mutual Friend
Dick Swiveller	The Old Curiosity Shop
Mr Sowerberry	Oliver Twist
Pumblechook	Great Expectations
Sophia (Sophy) Wackles	The Old Curiosity Shop

Brief Description of Dickens' Novels

Name of the Novel	Description
The Posthumous Papers of the Pickwick Club (1837)	This work was originally commissioned as a series of glorified captions for the work of caricaturist Robert Seymour. The central character of the novel is Samuel Pickwick- founder of the Pickwick club. The novel details the adventures of Samuel Pickwick and his friends.
The Adventures of Oliver Twist (1838)	*Oliver Twist*, subtitled *The Parish Boy's Progress* is Dickens' second novel. It was first published serially in the *Bentley's Miscellany.* It is a rag to riches story of an orphan. Dickens presents the everyday existence of the lowest members of English society. He depicts the experiences of the workhouse, and throws light on London's squalid streets, dark alehouses, and thieves' dens.
The Old Curiosity Shop (1841)	This novel was originally published in *Master Humphrey's Clock* in serial form. It is centred on the thirteen year old Nell Trent and her grandfather, both of whom are residents of Old Curiosity Shop in London. The Old Curiosity Shop is an establishment, where individuals go to purchase precious or antique gifts.
Barnaby Rudge (1841)	This novel was also published in *Master Humphrey's Clock*. It is Dickens' first attempt at a historical novel and is based on the Anti-Catholic protests against the Papists Act 1778, also called the Gordon Riots after the Head of the movement Lord George Gordon.
Dombey and Son (1848)	It is considered Dickens' first artistically mature work and narrates the story of Paul Dombey, powerful head of a shipping company-the House of Dombey. Paul desires a son, who will continue his business.
David Copperfield (1850)	It is the most autobiographical of Dickens' novels. Dickens himself attached a special place to this novel in his oeuvre and wrote," Like many fond parents, I have in my heart of hearts a favourite child. And his name is David Copperfield." The novel is a *bildungsroman*, which traces the life of David Copperfield from the time of his birth to his adulthood. The novel is set in early Victorian England against a backdrop of great social change.
Bleak House (1853)	Out of Dickens' novels, this is the only one to contain a female narrator-Esther Summerson. This novel is Dickens' satire on the English legal system. The central lawsuit of *Bleak House,* Jarndyce and Jarndyce, has been held 'in Chancery' for years.
Hard Times (1854)	The novel is set in Coketown, a northern industrial city. It portrays the exploitation and dehumanisation of honest hard-working factory workers, who have been turned into 'Hands'. Through the characters of Thomas Gradgrind and Josiah Bounderby, Dickens critiques the lifeless utilitarian philosophies of the time.
A Tale of two Cities (1859)	This book is set in London and Paris before and during the time of the French Revolution. It depicts the plight of the French peasants demoralised by the aristocratic class. The book is sympathetic to the overthrow of the French aristocracy, but highly critical of the reign of terror that followed.
Great Expectations (1861)	This novel is a *bildungsroman* that narrates the story of Pip, an orphan, who lives with his sister and his father-in-law Joe. Pip's life takes a turn, when he meets an escaped convict. From then on, Pip suddenly rises from a country labourer to a city gentleman.
Bildungroman	Aliterory genre that focuses on the educational and moral growth of the protagonist.

Many of Charles Dickens novels and stories have been immortalised in famous movies. *Some of these famous movies are as follows*

- A Christmas Carol (1984)
- David Copperfield (1983)
- The Old Curiosity Shop (1975)
- The Pickwick Papers (1952)
- Oliver Twist (1948)
- A Tale of Two Cities (1935)
- Great Expectations (1934)

George Eliot (1819-1880)

Victorian novelist George Eliot was born as Mary Ann Evans at Nuneaton in Warwickshire, England in 1819. She was the youngest daughter of Robert Evans- an estate agent for the Earl of Lonsdale and his second wife Christiana Pearson Evans.

Eliot was unusually educated for a woman of her time. She studied at Miss Latham's School in Attleborough, Mrs Wallington's School in Nuneaton and Miss Franklin's School in Coventry. She was forced to leave school at the age of 16, when her mother died in 1836. However, her father indulged her love of learning, purchased books for her and helped her to learn German and Italian. She also had access to the library of Arbury Hall. After her mother's death, the Eliots shifted to a house near Coventry. The closeness to Coventry society gave Eliot an opportunity to become part of Coventry's intellectual circle where she developed acquaintance with a number of freethinking intellectuals like Charles and Cara Bray. She also met John Chapman, a publisher and bookseller from London.

Literary Career and Works

Eliot's first published work was a poem published in the *Christian Observer* in January 1840, "Knowing That Shortly I Must Put Off This Tabernacle". Her first translation *Life of*

Jesus was published by Chapman in 1846. After the death of her father in 1849, she moved to London and became assistant editor of the *Westminster Review,* a liberal periodical. In 1851, she met the philosopher George Henry Lewes. Lewes was already married, but she spent the next 20 years of her life with him. Eliot's brother, Isaac disowned her due to this relationship. Eliot's rejection by her friends and family over her relationship with Lewes is reflected in her novel, *The Mill on the Floss* (1860).

Mary Anne Evans started using the pen name George Eliot in 1856, when she decided to try her hand at writing novels. *Adam Bede* (1859) was her first full-length novel, which she described as, "A country story-full of the breath of cows and the scent of hay." This novel proved to be a success and raised curiosity about the identity of the author. When Anne Evans was revealed to be the author, she was both criticised and praised.

Adam Bede was followed by *The Lifted Veil* in 1859 and her most popular novel, *The Mill on the Floss* in 1860. Eliot's other works include *Silas Marner* 1861, *Ramola* (1863) *Felix Holt* 1866. *The Spanish Gypsy* 1868, *Middle March* 1871-72, *The Legends of Jubal and other Poems* 1874 and *The Impression of The Ophrastus Such*.

G Eliot's works are known for their realism and psychological insight along with her depiction of rural society.

The death of Eliot's lifelong partner George Henry Lewes after a long illness in 1878 affected her so much that she stopped meeting people. During this time, Eliot met only one person-her business manager John Cross. Cross, 20 years younger to Eliot, proposed marriage to her three times, but met with rejection. Eventually, Eliot gave in and married him on 16th May, 1880. Eliot died just after 7 months of her marriage on 22nd December, 1880.

George Eliot is best known for her novels only and has very few short stories to her credit. She published a short story, *Amos Bartoon*. She also wrote collection of short stories called *Scenes of Clerical Life* (2 volumes 1858) But her main contribution to literature is her novels only.

Major Works

Novels

- Adam Bede (1859)
- The Mill on the Floss (1860)
- Silas Marner (1861)
- Romola (1863)
- Felix Holt, the Radical (1866)
- Middlemarch (1871–72)
- Daniel Deronda (1876)

Poetry

- The Spanish Gypsy (a dramatic poem) (1868)
- Agatha (1869)
- Brother and Sister (1869)
- Armgart (1871)
- The Legend of Jubal (1874)
- Arion (1874)
- A Minor Prophet (1874)
- A College Breakfast Party (1879)
- The Death of Moses (1879)

Short Description of Eliot's Major Works

Name of Novel	Description
Adam Bede	Eliot's first novel, Adam Bede is a pastoral novel set in the rural community of Loamshire, England, in the summer of 1799. The novel revolves around a love triangle between beautiful, but thoughtless Hetty Sorrel, Captain Arthur Donnithorne, the young squire, who seduces her, Adam Bede, her unacknowledged lover and Dinah Morris, Hetty's cousin, a fervent Methodist lay preacher. Eliot took the plot of Adam Bede from the death of Mary Voce, who was executed in 1802 for killing her child. Eliot's aunt Samuel visited Voce in jail and converted her. The character of Adam was inspired by Eliot's own father and the character of Dinah was drawn from her Methodist Aunt Samuel.
The Mill on the Floss' (1860)	It is Eliot's most autobiographical novel. The story of the protagonist, Maggie Tulliver is partially based on Eliot's own life and the character of Tom is based on Eliot's brother, Isaac. Eliot draws on her own experiences with a once-beloved but rigid and controlling brother to depict the relationship between Maggie and her brother Tom.
Silas Marner	Eliot's third novel published in 1861, Silas Marner is a realistic novel centring on a humble weaver-Silas who renounces religion after members of his church blame him for the theft of a pouch of coins.
Romola	Published in 1863, Romola is a historical novel set in Florence during the 1490s Renaissance. It explores late 15th century Florentine religion and politics through the eyes of the beautiful, highly educated Romola and Tito, her witty, cultured and entirely amoral husband.
Felix Holt	Felix Holt is a social and political novel set during the time of the Reform Act of 1832. The action is set in Treby Magna, a town caught up in the transition from the old England of rural farmland associated with a rigid class structure to the new England of manufacturing associated with the breakdown of that structure. It narrates the story of Harold Transome, heir to Transome Court, who comes to claim his inheritance and campaign for a Radical seat in Parliament and Felix Holt, working-class heir to a quack patent medicine business who returns to the town to stir the new electorate to a sense of worth.

Name of Novel	Description
Middlemarch	Subtitled A Study of Provincial Life, Eliot's Middlemarch was first published in 1871 and 1872, as a serial novel in eight parts. It represents the spirit of nineteenth-century England through the common people, and their perspective on change. The heroine of the novel, Dorothea is an excessively religious and pious girl, who marries a man- Mr Casaubon, who cannot satisfy her emotionally or mentally. Virginia Woolf called Middlemarch "The magnificent book, which with all its imperfections, is one of the few English books written for grown-up people".
Daniel Deronda	This novel was Eliot's most controversial novel since it dealt with the position of Jews in British and European society. The novel begins with the meeting of Daniel Deronda and Gwendolen Harleth in the fictional town of Leubronn, Germany.

Elizabeth Gaskell (1810-1865)

British novelist and short story writer Elizabeth Cleghorn Gaskell or Mrs Gaskell was born as Elizabeth Stevenson in Lindsey Row, London in 1810. She was the second surviving child of William Stevenson and his first wife, Elizabeth Holland Stevenson. Her father was a Scottish Unitarian minister at Failsworth, Lancashire. After her mother's early death, Elizabeth was raised in Cheshire, England, where she lived with an aunt in Knutsford. Elizabeth attended Unitarian Sunday school and later 'Avonbank' in Stratford-upon-Avon. After completing her schooling, she was sent to live with her father, who had remarried in 1814. She nursed him until his death on 22nd March, 1829. After her father's death, Elizabeth went to live at the home of Revd William Turner, a relation and a Unitarian minister of Hanover Chapel, Newcastle upon Tyne. He had a lasting impact on Elizabeth's political views.

Literary Career and Works

Elizabeth's first surviving daughter Marianne, was born on 12th September, 1834 and her daughter's first years are recorded in her diary. The death of her only son, William inspired Elizabeth to write her first novel, *Mary Barton*, which was published anonymously in 1848. The novel was concerned with the living conditions of the poor in the industrial towns in Northern England and earned a great deal of interest and praise.

Charles Dickens was so impressed with Elizabeth's first novel that he invited her to contribute to his magazine, *Household Words*, where her next major work, *Cranford*, was serialised beginning in 1851. Elizabeth Gaskell also published stories in *Household Words* including *Traits and Stories of the Huguenots, Morton Hall , My French Master , The Squire's Story , Company Manners , An Accursed Race , Half a Lifetime Ago, The Poor Clare , My Lady Ludlow , The Sin of a Father* and *The Manchester Marriage.*

Elizabeth Gaskell's novels offer a detailed portrait of the lives of many strata of society and is notable for putting local dialects into the mouth of its characters. The Gaskells had moved to Plymouth Grove in Manchester in 1850. This was the place where Elizabeth became part of a literary circle that included Dickens, Charles Eliot Norton, Charlotte Bronte, William and Mary Howett and John Ruskin and where she wrote the rest of her works. Elizabeth's close friendship with Charlotte Bronte inspired her to write a biography on Bronte on the request of Bronte's father. The Life of Charlotte Bronte was published after Charlotte Bronte's death in 1857. *Elizabeth Gaskell's other works are North and South* (1855), *Sylvia's Lovers* (1863) and *Wives and Daughters* (1866). Gaskell died of a heart attack in 1865, leaving her last work, *Wives and Daughters* unfinished at the time of her death.

Major Works

Novels

- Mary Barton (1848)
- Cranford (1851–53)
- Ruth (1853)
- North and South (1854–55)
- Sylvia's Lovers (1863)
- Wives and Daughters: An Everyday Story (1865)

Novellas

- The Moorland Cottage (1850)
- Mr Harrison's Confessions (1851)
- The Old Nurse's Story (1852)
- Lizzie Leigh (1855)
- My Lady Ludlow (1859)
- Round the Sofa (1859)
- Lois the Witch (1861)
- A Dark Night's Work (1863)
- Cousin Phillis (1864)

Short Stories

- Libbie Marsh's Three Eras (1847)
- The Sexton's Hero (1847)
- Christmas Storms and Sunshine (1848)
- Hand and Heart (1849)
- The Well of Pen-Morfa (1850)
- The Heart of John Middleton (1850)
- Disappearances (1851)
- Bessy's Troubles at Home (1852)
- My French Master (1853)
- The Squire's Story (1853)
- Half a Life-time Ago (1855)

- Company Manners (1854)
- The Poor Clare (1856)
- The Doom of the Griffiths (1858)
- Right at Last (1858)
- The Grey Woman (1861)
- The Cage at Cranford (1863)
- Crowley Castle (1863)

Non-Fiction

- An Accursed Race (1855)
- The Life of Charlotte Brontë (1857)
- French Life (1864)

Charlotte Bronte (1816-1855)

Victorian novelist Charlotte Bronte was born in Thornton, Yorkshire in 1816. She was the third child of Rev Patrick Bronte and his wife Maria. Charlotte and her sisters studied at the Clergy Daughters' School at Cowan Bridge. The conditions at this school were so appalling that two of her sisters Maria and Elizabeth, died of consumption. After their deaths, Charlotte was sent back home. She later continued her education at the school at Roe Head, but she left school the following year to teach her sisters at home. She returned to Roe Head School in 1835 as a governess.

Literary Career and Works

In 1846, a collection of poems by Charlotte Bronte and her sisters, Emily and Ann Bronte was published under the male pseudonyms of Currer Bell, Ellis and Acton Bell respectively. Charlotte's first novel, the autobiographical *Jane Eyre* was published in 1847. This novel traced the life and development of the plain, but intelligent Jane Eyre from her traumatic childhood to adulthood. Charlotte herself wrote about the protagonist of the novel, "I will show you a heroine as plain and as small as myself". *Jane Eyre* was followed by *Shirley* in 1848 and *Vilette* in 1853.

Charlotte married her father's curate, Rev Arthur Bell Nicholls in 1854. Though her father was initially opposed to the match, he later agreed to the marriage. Charlotte herself was apathetic towards the match. Shortly after getting married, she became pregnant and was diagnosed with pneumonia. She died of the disease in 1855.

Major Works

- Poems by Currer, Ellis and Acton Bell (1846)
- Jane Eyre (1847)
- Shirley (1849)
- Villette (1853)
- The Professor (her first written novel published posthumously in 1857)

The influence of Charlotte's novels has been immense. Charlottle's combination of romance and satiric realism had been the mark of nearly all the women novelists for a century. Her fruitful innovation were the presentation of a tale through the sensibility of a child or young woman, her lyricism and the picture of love from a woman's stand point.

Jane Eyre

- It was published in 1847, Charlotte Bronte's *Jane Eyre* is a bildungsroman that focuses on the growth and development of Jane Eyre from a rebellious 8 years old orphan to a mature thirty year old married woman.
- The novel is written in first person with the older Jane recalling her life from her childhood.
- The novel is partly based on experiences in Charlotte's own life. Charlotte herself was plain and small like Jane. The death of Helen Burns in the novel recalls the deaths of her sisters at Cowan Bridge. John Reed's decline into alcoholism and dissolution is modelled upon the life of Charlotte Bronte's brother Branwell. Jane's experiences as a governess are based on Charlotte's own years as a governess.
- Charlotte describes five distinct stages in the development of Jane, each linked to a particular place: Jane's childhood at Gateshead, her education at the Lowood School, her time as Adèle's governess at Thornfield, her time with the Rivers family at Morton and at Marsh End (also called Moor House), and her reunion with and marriage to Rochester at Ferndean.
- The novel also contains Gothic elements, focusing on the dark and mysterious. The episode of the Red Room, the madwoman in the attic, the shadowy corridors of Thornfield all add to the Gothic element.
- Bertha Mason, Rochester's first wife, who turns insane, is considered as Jane's double. Richard Juplit states that "Locked away in a hidden room of Thornfield, Bertha's only freedom comes when her keeper falls into a drunken sleep and she can sneak around the house and create havoc. Bertha is locked as tightly in her secluded room as Jane is locked into her subordinate life."
- Coming at the end of the novel, the most famous line in Jane Eyre is 'Reader, I married him.'

Emily Bronte (1818-1848)

One of the three Bronte sisters, Emily was born in Thornton, Yorkshire in 1818. Emily's father was Irish clergyman Patrick Bronte and her mother Maria Barnwell.

Her mother died when she was just three years old. Emily attended the Clergy Daughters' School at Cowan Bridge between 1824 and 1825 but after the death of her elder sisters, Maria and Elizabeth in 1825, she was withdrawn from the school and thereafter educated largely at home by her father, her aunt, her elder sister Charlotte. In 1835, Emily enrolled at Miss Wooler's School at Roe Head, Mirfield where her sister, Charlotte was teaching, but she soon returned home when she became homesick and ill.

There after she worked as a governess at Law Hill Hall in Halifax, West Yorkshire. In 1840 Emily and Charlotte planned to open their own school but did not succeed in their plan.

Literary Career and Works

She wrote under pseudonym Ellis Bell, who wrote poems and produced but one novel *Wuthering Heights* (1847) a highly imaginative work of passion and hate set on the Yorkshire moors. Emily Bronte was perhaps the greatest of three Bronte sisters but the record of her life is extremely meagre and her single novel darkens rather than solves the mystery of her spiritual existence.

Emily's only novel, *Wuthering Heights* was published in 1847. Heathcliff is the main character in the novel, and the whole plot revolves around him from the time when he arrives at Wuthering Heights as a dark and dirty foundling and until he ends his days as a powerful landlord of both Wuthering Heights and Thrushcross Grange. His almost inhuman devotion to Catherine Earnshaw is the moving force in his life. The story of the novel is narrated by Lockwood, a gentleman from London. Emily caught a severe cold at the funeral of her brother, Branwell and died of tuberculosis a year after her novel was published.

Anne Bronte (1820-1849)

The youngest member of the Bronte literary family was also an English novelist and poet. She was born on 17th January, 1820 in Thornton, Yorkshire, England. Soon after her birth, her father Patrick Bronte and family moved to the village of Hawarth where her father was appointed perpetual curate. Anne's mother died of cancer when she was barely one. After her mother's death Anne and her sisters were raised by their aunt Elizabeth Branwell.

Literary Career and Works

Anne's first novel, *Agnes Grey*, a story about the life of a governess, appeared in 1847. It was based on Anne's recollections of her experience with the children of the Ingham family and the Robinson family.

In July, 1848, Thomas Newby marketed Anne's second book, *The Tenant of Wildfell Hall* to an American publisher as the latest work of Currer Bell, affirming that 'to the best of his knowledge' the Bells were one person.

Smith, Elder and Co., who had been promised Currer's next book, were alarmed and furious. Charlotte and Anne saw only one way to prove, beyond doubt, that Currer, Ellis and Acton Bell were separate people. They went to London to reveal their identities to the publishers.

Emily flatly refused to go with them and was adamant that the secret must go no further. *The Tenant of Wildfell* was partially based on Anne's observations of her brother, Branwell. However, even though, Anne's second novel proved a success, her hopes of becoming a renowned writer was darkened by the death of her brother Branwell in September of 1848 and Emily in December of 1848. Anne Bronte was herself diagnosed with tuberculosis and died at Scarborough in 1849.

William Makepeace Thackeray (1811-1863)

English novelist William Makepeace Thackeray was born in Calcutta, India in 1811. He was the son of Richmond Thackeray, an Indian Civil Servant, and his wife Anne. After his father's death in 1815, Thackeray was sent to England. He was educated at a school in Southampton, then Chiswick and later joined Trinity College in 1829. However, he left without taking a degree and went to stay in Germany where he met Johann Wolfgang von Goethe.

After leaving Cambridge, Thackerey travelled on the continent, spending a winter at Weimar which included an introduction to aged Goethe. Thackeray took away from Weimar a command of the language, a knowledge of German Romantic Literature and an increasing Skepticism about religious doctrine.

On his return to England, Thackeray lived the life of a propertied young gentelman, including more gambling, drinking in taverns. After trying his stints at many places. Thackeray started working hard as a journalist. He published ninety magazine pieces and his first book *The Paris Sketch Book*. He became a regular contributor to Fraser's Magazine.

From 1842 to 1851, he was on the staff of Punch, a position that brought in a good income. During his stay at Punch, he wrote *Vanity Fair*, the work which placed him in the first rank of novelists. *Vanity Fair* was followed by *Pendennis, Esmond* and *The Newcomes*, which appeared respectively in 1850, 1852 and 1854. Thackeray died of a cerebral effusion in 1863.

Major Works

- Vanity Fair (1848, novel)
- The Book of Snobs (1848, articles)
- The History of Pendennis (1848–50, novel)
- The History of Henry Esmond, Esq (1852, novel)
- The English Humourists of the 18th Century (1853)
- The Newcomes (1855, novel)
- The Four Georges (1860-61)
- The Rose and the Ring (1855)
- The Memoirs of Barry Lyndon (1844, novel)
- The Virginians (1857–59, novel)
- Lovel the Widower (1860, novel)
- The Adventures of Philip (1862, novel)
- Rebecca and Rowena (1850)

Vanity Fair

It was published serially in London in 1847 and 1848, Thackeray's *Vanity Fair* is subtitled *A Novel Without a Hero.* It is a satirical novel of manners.The title of the novel is derived from John Bunyan's allegorical story *The Pilgrim's Progress,* where Vanity Fair is the name of a stop in a town called Vanity. The heroine of the novel, Rebecca Sharp or Becky is a strong-willed young woman obsessed with status and wealth. Another important character in the novel is Amelia Sedley, who is an exact opposite of Becky.

Amelia's goodness and sweetness is contrasted with Becky's wit and physical charm. While Amelia clings to ideals, Becky is amoral. Vanity Fair follows the fortunes of two contrasting but inter-linked lives: through the retiring Amelia Sedley and the brilliant Becky Sharp, Thackeray examines the position of women in an intensely exploitative male world.

Contemporary reviewers and novelists appreciated the brilliance of the novel. John Forster wrote, "*Vanity Fair* is the work of a mind at once, accomplished and subtle which has enjoyed opportunities of observing many and varied circles of society... his genteel characters ...... have a reality about them."

Anthony Trollope (1815-1882)

Victorian novelist Anthony Trollope was born at Russell Square, London in 1815. His mother Frances Trollope (1780-1863) was the author of many novels. Anthony was a large, awkward shy boy who developed into a burly vigorous even boisterous man. He went to school at Winchester and Harrow but he was a poor student. When he was 19 years old, he went to work in London as a clerk in the post office in 1834. He was transferred to Ireland as a post office surveyer in 1841. In 1844, he married Rose Heseltine; they had two sons.

Literary Career and Works

In 1843, Trollope began work on his first novel *The Macdermots of Ballycloran* (published 1847). He started writing novels to support his income. His Barsetshire novels -*The Warden* (1855), *Barchester Towers* (1857), *Doctor Thorne* (1858), *Framley Parsonage* (1861), *The Small House at Allington* (1864) and *The Last Chronicle of Barset* (1867), depicted in detail the lives of a group of ordinary but interesting people, who live in the county of Barsetshire and was based on English upper middle-class Victorian life.

In his later novels Trollope shifted his interest from the rural scene to urban society and politics. These books include *The Claverings* (1867), *Phineas Finn* (1869), *He Knew He Was Right* (1869), *The Eustace Diamonds* (1873), *The Way We Live Now* (1875), *The Prime Minister* (1876), and *The American Senator* (1877). Trollope died of a paralytic stroke in London in 1882.

Major Works

- The Macdermots of Ballycloran (1847)
- The Kellys and the O'Kellys (1848)
- La Vendée: An Historical Romance (1850)
- The Three Clerks (1858)
- The Bertrams (1859)
- Castle Richmond (1860)
- Orley Farm (1862)
- The Struggles of Brown, Jones and Robinson (1862)
- Rachel Ray (1863)
- Miss Mackenzie (1865)
- The Belton Estate (1866)
- The Claverings (1867)
- Nina Balatka (1867)
- Linda Tressel (1868)
- He Knew He Was Right (1869)
- The Vicar of Bullhampton (1870)
- Sir Harry Hotspur of Humblethwaite (1871)
- Ralph the Heir (1871)
- Doctor Wortle's School (1881)
- The Fixed Period (1882)
- Marion Fay (1882)
- Mr Scarborough's Family (1883)
- The Landleaguers (1883)
- An Old Man's Love (1884)

Barsetshire Series

- The Warden (1855)
- Barchester Towers (1857)
- Doctor Thorne (1858)
- Framley Parsonage (1861)
- The Small House at Allington (1864)
- The Last Chronicle of Barset (1867)

In all Trollope wrote 47 novel in addition to short stories, travel books, hunting sketches, biographies and other volumes.

Trollope's Short Stories

Trollope's work 'selected short stories' is certainly worth reading and it includes a collection of six stories. They are *Histletoe Bough* and *Not If I know It*, *The Parson's Daughter of Oxney Colna*, *Mary Gresley*, *The Spotted Dog* and *The Two Heroines of Plumplington*.

Though during his own time Trollope was criticised by many for his simple didactic novels but his capability as a novelist cannot be ignored.

George Meredith (1828-1909)

English novelist and poet George Meredith was born in Portsmouth, England in 1828. He was the only child of Augustus Urmstone Meredith and Jane Eliza Macnamara. His mother died when he was only 5. A small inheritance from his mother enabled Meredith to attend a superior local seminary and thus very early he assumed the role of a 'young gentleman'. Yet the sensitive boy must gradually have become conscious of the contrast between his role and actual social status. And this reality became more prominent when his father's tailoring shop was declared bankrupt when Meredith was eleven years old. In 1840, a second legacy from his aunt enabled him to go to a boarding school and in 1842 to Movavian school at Neuwied at Rhine river which was to leave its mark upon the remaining of author's life. He was later apprenticed to a London lawyer.

Literary Career and Works

He abandoned law and began work as a freelance journalist. Meredith married a widow, Mary Ellen Nicolls in 1849. His disillusionment with their marriage and his trauma at his wife's sexual betrayal is reflected in his later volume, *Modern Love* (1862), a series of 50 connected poems. He later married Marie Vulliamy in 1863.

Meredith's first book of poetry came out in 1851. His first work of fiction, *The Shaving of Shagpat: an Arabian Entertainment*, appeared in 1855. This was followed by *Farina: a Legend of Cologne* (1857), *The Ordeal of Richard Feverel: a History of Father and Son*(1859), *Evan Harrington* (1860) *and Emilia in England* (1864). His best known work is *The Egoist* (1879). The novel concerns Sir Willoughby Patterne, a highly narcissistic gentleman and his quest to find a socially acceptable wife. Meredith stopped writing novels in his late years, but continued to write poetry. His last collection of poems *A Reading of Life, with Other Poems* was published in 1901. In 1905, he was awarded the Order of Merit. Meredith died at his home in Flint Cottage in 1909.

Meredith was not a good narrator and often it seems he had no hold over his plots. His plots are a medium to hand his dramatic scenes upon. But Meredith was a psychologist novelist as he was interested in the study of mental processes and analysis of motives. His novels are not realistic and have a hard intellectual tone. He was opposed to sentimentalism or softness of every kind.

His novels develop under a comic tone and ridicule folly or stupidity. Meredith's characters both male and female are drawn from aristocratic and upper middle class society. His novels are noted for their sparkling wit and dialogue.

Major Works

The Egoist is perhaps Meredith's best known novel, a tragicomedy. It recounts the story of a self-absorbed Sir Willoughby Patterns and his attempts at marriage. Jilted by his first bride to be, he vacillates between the sentimental Laetitia Dale and the strong willed Clara Middleton. More importantly the novel follows Clara's attempts to escape from her engagement to Sir Willoughby who desires women to serve as mirror for him and consequently cannot understand why she would not want to marry him. It is the combination of wit and poetry in his novels that gives Meredith his special place in the history of English novel.

As an adviser to publishers, Meredith is credited with helping Thomas Hardy start his literary career. Before his death, Meredith was honoured from many quarters. He succeeded 'Lord Tennyson' as president of the Society of Authors. In 1905, he was appointed to the Order of Merit by king Edward VII.

Benjamin Disraeli (1804-1881)

British Prime Minister, parliamentarian and author Benjamin Disraeli was born in London in 1804. He was the son of Isaac Disraeli, author of *Curiosities of Literature* and *Maria Basevi*. Though, Disraeli was born to Italian-Jewish parents, his father baptised his children as Christians in 1817. He studied at Miss Roper's School in Islington and then went to Higham Hall School in Walthamstow between 1817 and 1821.

Literary Career and Works

Disraeli's first novel, *Vivian Grey*, appeared in 1826. The plot of this novel was considered to be retelling of his involvement with John Murray in the publication and failure of a newspaper called *The Representative*. This novel was followed by a series of novels, *The Young Duke* (1831), *Contarini Fleming* (1832), *Alroy* (1833), *Venetia and Henrietta Temple* (1837).

During the same period he had also written *The Revolutionary Epick and three burlesques, Ixion, The Infernal Marriage* and *Popanilla*. Although, Disraeli continued his literary career, he harboured political aspirations. He was elected as Tory candidate for Maidstone in 1837.

His trilogy of novels, *Coningsby* (1844), *Sybil* (1845) and *Tancred* (1847) expounded his political views.

Disraeli served as Chancellor of the Exchequer under Lord Derby as Prime Minister in Conservative governments of 1852, 1858-1859 and 1866-1868. Disraeli formed his first ministry in 1868 on the resignation of Derby on the grounds of ill health. He became Prime Minister for the second time in 1874 at the age of 70. After the 1880 General elections, when William Gladstone became Prime Minister, Disraeli decided to retire from politics. He hoped to spend his retirement writing novels, but soon after the publication of *Endymion* (1880), he became very ill. He died on 19th April, 1881.

Major Works

Novels

- Vivian Grey (1826)
- Popanilla (1828)
- The Voyage of Captain Popanilla (1828)
- The Young Duke (1831)
- Alroy (1833)
- The Rise of Iskander (1833)
- The Infernal Marriage (1834)
- Ixion in Heaven (1834)
- The Revolutionary Epick (1834)
- Henrietta Temple (1837)
- The Tragedy of Count Alarcos (1840)
- Coningsby, or the New Generation (1844)
- Sybil, or The Two Nations (1845)
- Tancred, or the New Crusade (1847)
- Lothair (1870)

Charles Kingsley (1819-1875)

Novelist and historian Charles Kingsley was born at Holne vicarage, Devonshire, England in 1819. He was the son of Rev. Charles Kingsley and his wife Mary Lucas.

Kingsley studied at Helston Grammar School in Cornwall, where the Reverend Derwent Coleridge, Samuel Taylor Coleridge's son, was headmaster. After the family moved to London in 1836, Kingsley entered King's College and Magdalene College, Cambridge in 1838.

Kingsley met Frances (Fanny) Grenfell, with whom he fell almost immediately in love in 1839.

In February 1842, Kingsley left Cambridge to read for Holy Orders and became vicar for Eversley in Hampshire in 1844. He married Frances Grenfell the same year.

Literary Career and Works

Kingsley was a protestant priest who gained prominence in the public arena as an activist for politics and social reform. His commitment to his social agenda manifested itself in his written work not only in his published letters, sermons, scientific essays and lecturers but also as themes of his novels and historical fiction.

An advocate of Christian Socialism, he published several novels about social problems before writing the very successful historical novels *Hypatia* (1853) *Westward Ho* (1855) and *Hereward the Wake* (1866). He was also one of the first clergy to support Charles Darwin's theories and to seek a reconciliation between science and Christian doctrine.

Kingsley's best-known work for children, *The Water-Babies* came out in 1863. The book, written for his youngest son, narrates the story of a young chimney-sweep, who runs away from his brutal employer. During his flight, he falls into a river and is transformed into a water baby.

His last novel, *Hereward the Wake, Last of the English* (1866) appeared serially in 1865 in *Good News*. Kingsley was appointed chaplain to the Queen Victoria in 1859.

From 1860 to 1869, he was professor of modern history at Cambridge. He resigned from this post in 1869 and was appointed canon of Westminster Abbey in 1873.

Kingsley died in 1875 and was buried in St Mary's Churchyard in Eversley.

Major Works

- The Saint's Tragedy (1848)
- Alton Locke, a novel (1849)
- Twenty-five Village Sermons (1849)
- Cheap Clothes and Nasty (1850)
- Yeast, a novel (1851)
- Phaeton, or Loose Thoughts for Loose Thinkers (1852)
- Hypatia, a novel (1853)
- Glaucus, or the Wonders of the Shore (1855)
- Alexandria and her Schools (1854)
- Westward Ho!, a novel (1855)
- Sermons for the Times (1855)
- The Heroes, Greek fairy tales (1856)
- Two Years Ago, a novel (1857)
- Andromeda and other Poems (1858)
- The Good News of God, sermons (1859)
- Miscellanies (1859)

- Limits of Exact Science applied to History (Inaugural lectures, 1860)
- Town and Country Sermons (1861)
- Sermons on the Pentateuch (1863)
- The Water-Babies (1863) (Short Story)
- The Roman and the Teuton (1864)
- David and other Sermons (1866)
- Hereward the Wake: 'Last of the English', a novel (1866)
- The Ancient Régime (Lectures at the Royal Institution, 1867)
- Water of Life and other Sermons (1867)
- The Hermits (1869)
- Madam How and Lady Why (1869)
- At Last: A Christmas in the West Indies (1871)
- Plays and Puritans (1873)
- Health and Education (1874)
- Westminster Sermons (1874)
- Lectures delivered in America (1875)

Kingsley, as a novelist is best remembered for his descriptive faculties. The description of South- American Scenery in *Westward Ho*, Egyptian desert in *Hypatia* and North Devon Society in *Two Years Ago* are brilliant and the American scenery is more vividly described though he has just seen it with his eyes of imagination. His sympathy for children taught him how to secure their interests. His version of the old Greek stories entitled *The Heroes* and *Water Babies* deals with popular natural history and they rank high among books for children.

Wilkie Collins (1824-1889)

English novelist and playwright Wilkie Collins was born in London in 1824. He was the son of the popular landscape painter, William Collins and his wife Harriet Geddes. Collins studied at the Maida Hill Academy and Mr Cole's boarding-school. Later, he entered Lincoln's Inn, London and was called to the bar in 1851. However, he never practised law.

Literary Career and Works

As a student at Lincoln's Inn, Collins met Charles Dickens. Both of them collaborated on short stories such as *The Perils of Certain English Prisoners for Household Words.*

Collins's first play, *The Lighthouse* (1855), was given several performances at Dickens's home, Tavistock House before being professional', produced with great success at the Olympic Theatre. Collins' main income was also derived from numerous contributions he made to Dickens' magazines. Collins' first published book was *The Memoirs of the Life of William Collins, Esq, RA.* His major novel *The Woman in White* was a mystery novel that appeared in 1860. It was published in Dickens new journal, *All the Year Round* from November 1859 to August 1860. This novel was followed by *No Name* (1862), *Armadale* (1866) and *The Moonstone* (1868). *Moonstone* is considered to be the first English detective novel. Wilkie Collins died at his home on Wimpole Street in 1889.

Major Works

- Basil (1852)
- The Woman in White (1860)
- No Thoroughfare (1867), a story and play co-written with Charles Dickens
- Poor Miss Finch (1872), dedicated to Frances Minto Elliot
- The Law and the Lady (1875)
- 'Who Killed Zebedee?' (1881)
- The Black Robe (1881)
- Blind Love (1890-unfinished, completed by Walter Besant)

The Moon Stone (1868) *Man Wife* (1870) *The Fallen Leaves* (1879) *Jezebel's Daughter* (1880) *The Black Rode* (1881) *Heart and Science* (1882-83). Collins works were classified at that time as 'Sensation Novels' a genre seen now a days as the precursor to detective and suspense fiction. He also wrote with an insight on to the plight of the women and on social and domestic issues of his time. Collins published most of his novels as series creating just the right degree of suspense to keep his audience reading from week to week.

Samuel Butler (1835-1902)

English novelist Samuel Butler was born in Nottinghamshire, England in 1835. He was the second of four children in the family of Reverend and Mrs Thomas Butler. He was the grandson of Samuel Butler, headmaster of Shrewsbury School and later bishop of Lichfield. Butler studied at Shrewsbury School and St John's College, Cambridge.

Literary Career and Works

He was intended for the church; but because of his religious doubts, he declined to take the holy orders. After earning an honours degree in classics and mathematics, Butler worked briefly as a lay assistant among the poor in London and studied art. Later, he sailed in 1859 to New Zealand, where he was engaged in sheep farming. During his stay in New Zealand, Butler wrote a few articles for the Christchurch Press including *Darwin among the Machines*, the nucleus of his first satire *Erewhon*.

He also re-read his Scripture, and applied the analytical method he found in Gibbon to the readings of the Resurrection for a pamphlet he would publish in 1866. Butler returned to England in 1864 after a five successfuls 5 years of farming.

Butler's dream to become an artist propelled him after he returned and he got himself enrolled in Heatherley's School of Art and then the Royal Academy School where he exhibited between 1869 and 1876. One of his oil paintings, *Mr Heatherley's Holiday* (1874), is in the Tate Gallery, London, and his *Family Prayers*, in which the ethos of Langar Rectory is satirically conveyed, is at St John's College, Cambridge. Butler's first work, Swiftian satire *Erewhon* appeared in 1872. *Erewhon* is an anagram of `nowhere'. In *Erewhon,* Butler satirises the injustices of Victorian England by means of a utopian society in which all the social mores and laws were the exact opposite of what they were in England. This work was followed by *Erewhon Revisited* in 1900. However, Butler's most famous work is his semi-autobiographical novel *The Way of All Flesh* published after his death. Butler also wrote a popular translation of *The Iliad* in 1898 and of *The Odyssey* in 1900. Butler died of consumption in London on 18th June, 1902.

Major Works

- Alps and Sanctuaries of Piedmont and the Canton Ticino (1881)
- Book of the Machines (1863)
- Erewhon, or Over the Range (1872)
- Erewhon Revisited Twenty Years Later: Both by the Original Discoverer of the Country and by His Son (1901)
- Evolution, Old and New (1879)
- Ex Vot; An Account of the Sacred Monte or New Jerusalem at Verallo-Sessia (1888)
- Shakespeare's Sonnets Reconsidered (1899)
- Unconscious Memory (1890)

The Way of All Flesh

The Way of All Flesh published in 1903, the year after Butler's death as his master piece. It certainly contains much of the quintessence of Butlerism. This largely autobiographical novel tells with ruthless wit, realism and lack of sentiment, the story of Butler's escape from the suffocating moral atmosphere of his home circle. In the novel the character Ernest Pontifer stands for Butler's early self and Overton for his mature self. Towneley and Althea represent 'nice' people who love God. The book was influential at the beginning of the anti-Victorian reaction and helped turn the tide against excessive parental dominance and religious rigidity.

Robert Louis Stevenson (1850-1894)

Scottish novelist, poet and essayist Robert Louis Stevenson was born in Edinburgh, Scotland in 1850. He was the only child of Thomas Stevenson and Margaret Isabella Balfour. Stevenson's father was a civil engineer and pioneering designer of lighthouses.

Stevenson entered Edinburgh University as a science student in 1867. His family expected that he would study engineering and join his father and uncle in the lighthouse business. However, his heart lay elsewhere and he eventually confessed to his father that he wished to pursue writing.

Literary Career and Works

Stevenson's first published book was a travel book called *An Inland Voyage.* It provided an account of his trip from Antwerp to northern France. He wrote other travel books such as *Travels with a Donkey in the Cevennes* (1879) and *In the South Seas* (1893).

In 1876, Stevenson met Frances Vandegrift Osbourne, an American woman nearly ten years senior, at an art colony in France, where he was staying with his cousin Bob. He fell in love with her and married her, after she escaped from a bad marriage and got divorced from her previous husband. His most popular works are his novels *Treasure Island* (1883), *Kidnapped* (1886), *Strange Case of Dr Jekyll and Mr Hyde* (1886) and *The Black Arrow* (1888). *Dr Jekyll and Mr Hyde* is a novel about a man containing both good and evil aspects. Stevenson examines man's relationship with good and evil and comments on the constant conflict between the two.

Stevenson left England after his father's death in 1887 and sailed for America, where he stayed for a year. In 1888, accompanied by his wife, stepson, and mother, he set sail for the South Seas. Several of his later works are about the South Sea Isles, including *The Wrecker* (1892), *Island Nights' Entertainments* (1893), *The Ebb-Tide* (1894) and *In the South Seas* (1896). Stevenson died at home of brain hemorrhage on 3rd December, 1894.

Major Works

- An Inland Voyage (1878)
- Travels with a Donkey in the Cévennes (1879)
- Edinburgh Picturesque Notes (1879)
- The Story of a Lie (1879)
- New Arabian Nights (1882)
- Treasure Island (1882)
- The Black Arrow (1883)
- Kidnapped (1886)
- Dr Jekyll and Mr Hyde (1886)
- The Merry Men (1887)
- The Black Arrow : A Tale of the two Roses (1888)
- The Master of Ballantrae (1889)
- The Misadventures of John Nicholson (1894)
- The Ebb-Tide (1894)
- Weir of Hermiston (1896)
- Songs of Travel and Other Verses (1896)

- St Ives (1897)
- Island Nights' Entertainments (1905)
- Prince Otto: A Romance (1905)
- Lay Morals and Other Papers (1911)
- Records of a Family of Engineers (1916)

Robert Louis Stevenson is not only remarkable for the number of works, he produced in his twenty year literary career, but also the variety of genres he produced like essay, travel writing, short stories, novels and romances as well as poetry, plays and biography. Stevenson wrote some wonderful stuff. Not only have previous generations of young and old thrilled to read his tales but he laid down many of the structures that have gone into making of great popular fiction ever since. Many of todays modern classics are based on elements first popularised by Robert Louis Stevenson.

His four short stories written under the heading *New Arabian Nights* (1882) were fantastic and macabre tales which are considered by many the earliest short stories of note in British literary History.

George Gissing (1857-1903)

English novelist George Gissing was born at Yorkshire, England in 1857. He was the eldest of five children of Thomas Waller Gissing, a pharmaceutical chemist and Margaret née Bedford. After his father's death in 1870, the family suffered financial constraints. Although short of money, Gissing won a scholarship to Owen College. In 1874, he took his BA exam at the University of London where he was placed first in England for both English and Latin and graduated in 1876. Gissing' bright academic career was curtailed and his life almost ruined when he was caught stealing money from the students' cloakroom. The money was intended for Marianne Helen Harrison, or 'Nell'-a young prostitute. He was expelled from university and also ostracised by his family. Gissing eventually married Nell in 1879, though their married life was far from happy.

Literary Career and Works

Gissing earned a living by working as a tutor. Simultaneously, he also worked on his first novel *Workers in the Dawn.* After Nell's death in 1888, Gissing's career soared and he wrote prolifically. *New Grub Street* (1891), his best-known work, depicts the dilemma of the poverty-stricken artist in an alien world. His other works include *Thyrza* (1887), *The Nether World* (1889), *Born in Exile* (1892), *The Whirlpool* (1897), *By the Ionian Sea* (1901) and the partly autobiographical *Private Papers of Henry Ryecroft* (1903). Gissing married another working-class woman, Edith Alice Underwood in 1891, but separated from her in 1897. Gissing died at St Jean Pied de Port, on the Bay of Biscay, on 28th December, 1903.

George Gissing was a prolific writer publishing two dozen novels during his life time as well as an important critical study of Charles Dickens, a somewhat unsentimental look at the sentimental novelist. Gissing's works were a significant contribution to the development of naturalism.

Major Works

- Workers in the Dawn (1880)
- The Unclassed (1884)
- Isabel Clarendon (1885)
- Demos (1886)
- Thyrza (1887)
- A Life's Morning (1888)
- The Nether World (1889)
- The Emancipated (1890)
- New Grub Street (1891)
- Denzil Quarrier (1892)
- Born In Exile (1892)
- The Odd Women (1893)
- In the Year of Jubilee (1894)
- Eve's Ransom (1895)
- The Paying Guest (1895)
- Sleeping Fires (1895)
- The Whirlpool (1897)
- The Town Traveller (1898)
- Charles Dickens:A Critical Study (1898)
- The Crown Of Life (1899)
- By the Ionian Sea (1901)
- Our Friend the Charlatan (1901)
- The Private Papers of Henry Ryecroft (1903)
- Will Warburton (1905)
- Veranilda (1903, unfinished)
- Stories and Sketches (posthumous, 1938)

Lewis Carroll (1832-1898)

Charles Lutwidge Dodgson who wrote with pseudonym Lewis Carroll was born on 27th January, 1832 at Cheshire, England. He was a logician and mathematician. He is especially remembered for *Alice's Adventures in Wonderland* (1865) and its sequel through the *Looking Glass* (1871).

He attended Richmond School, Yorkshire and then proceeded to Rugby School (1846-50). He disliked his four years at public school due to his innate shyness. He also endured several illnesses one of which left him deaf in one ear. After Rugby Lewis spend a further year being tutored by his father, during which time he matriculated at Christ Church, Oxford.

Literary Career and Works

As a boy Caroll excelled in Mathematics and won many academic prizes. Apart from serving as a lecturer in Mathematics, he was an avid photographer and wrote essays, political pamphlets and poetry.

The 'Alice' series of books comprising *Alice's Adventures in wonderland* (1865) and *Through the Looking-Glass and What Alice Found There* (1871) are among the best children's fiction in the world. They are amusing adventure stories of an intelligent little girl. His other works include *The Hunting of the Snark* (1876), *Sylvie and Bruno* (1889), and its second volume, *Sylvie and Bruno Concluded* (1893) and *Symbolic Logic Part I* (1896).

Although he made lasting friendships with many of his young fans and corresponded with several, he never married or had children of his own. In January 1898, he caught violent pneumonia and died at his family home of The Chesnuts, Guildford.

Major Works

- Alice's Adventures in Wonderland (1865)
- An Elementary Treatise on Determinants with their Application to Simultaneous Linear Equations and Algebraical Geometry (1867).
- Phantasmagoria or Rhyme? And Reason? (1869)
- Through the Looking-Glass (1871)
- The Hunting of the Snark (1876)
- Euclid and His Modern Rivals (1879)
- A Tangled Tale (1885)
- Alice's Adventures Under-Ground (1886)
- The Game of Logic (1887)
- Sylvie and Bruno (1893)
- Symbolic Logic : Part (1896)
- Symbolic Logic : Part II (Posthumous)

Thomas Hardy (1840-1928)

Hardy is one of the greatest novelist in the whole range of English Literature. Thomas Hardy united the Victorian (1840-1900) and modern eras and his works act as a bridge between Victorian and modern novels.

Thomas Hardy was born on 2nd June, 1840 in Higher Bockhampton in Dorset England which formed part of the Wessex of his novels and poems. Hardy grew to be a small man over five feet tall. Hardy learned to love books through his mother, Jemina and was able to read before starting school. He was taught by his father, also named Thomas to play the violin. Hardy attended a private school in Stanford. There he studied Latin, Greek, French, Classical Literature and assisted his father in his various building projects.

At the age of sixteen, he left school and was apprenticed to John Hicks, an architect in Dorchester. While, still in Dorchester, Hardy met Horace Moule, a vicar's son, and a student of Queen's College, Cambridge, who became his friend and mentor. In 1862, Hardy moved to London where he found employment in the office of an architect Arthur Blomfied. It was in London that he began attending plays and operas, reading works of Herbert Spencer, Thomas Henry Huxley, John Stuart Mill, John Ruskin and Charles Darwin and started writing poetry. Thomas Hardy breathed his past on 11th January 1928 at Darchester.

Literary Career and Works

In London Hardy continued to write poetry and began sending his poems to publishers who quickly returned them. He kept many of his poems and published in 1898 and afterwards.

Back in Dorchester in 1867 while working for Hicks, he wrote a novel *The Poor Man and The Lady* which he was advised not to publish because it was too critical of Victorian society. His first novel with a plot was *Desperate Remedies* which was published in 1871. But his first commercial success was with the novel *Far From the Madding Crowd* (1874). This novel dealt with the love of Gabriel Oak for the woman farmer Bathsheba Everdene. Hardy's two most famous works are *Tess of Urbevilles* (1891) and *Jude the Obscure* (1896).

Tess of the d'Urbevilles is widely regarded as Hardy's tragic masterpiece. It is the story of Tess, 'simple, sensuous and passionate' country girl whose parents discover their descent from a noble line and send her to seek the assistance of a degenerate relative to whom she finally surrenders. *Jude the Obscure*, on the other hand, is the story of Jude, a poor country boy who aspires to achieve academic glory, escapes from his native village to Chriestminster, but finds his ambitions of joining a university thwarted.

Hardy is the creator of a region called 'Wessex' a small tract of country consisting of six odd counties in South England. Belonging to the rural working class, Hardy was keenly interested in depicting the life of the peasantry and advocating their beliefs and values. Wessex's forests and woodlands have an epic grandeur and his principal characters have the greatness of epic heroes and heroines. Man's predicament in the universe is the theme of Thomas Hardy's novels. It is against the background of vast universe that the drama of human life is enacted in Hardy's novels and the tragedy of heroes and heroines takes place. Hardy presents a picture of the last elemental forces and shows their workings on man's life. His characters are being shaped by the environment around them. Often some natural object or scene directs the movement of the story and guides the actions of characters as is seen in the case of Egdon Heath in the novel.

There can be no doubt about the merit of Hardy's as a novelist, despite certain short comings that it may betray. Conclusively, Hardy occupies an important place in the development of English novel.

Major Works

- Tess of the d'Urbervilles (1891)
- Far From the Madding Crowd (1874)
- The Mayor of Casterbridge (1886)
- Jude the Obscure (1895)
- The Return of the Native (1878)
- Under the Greenwood Tree (1872)
- The Wood Landers (1887)
- A Pair of Blue Eyes (1873)
- The Oxford Book of Gothic Tales
- Great Short Stories-Quick Roads
- Desperate Remedies (1871)
- The Trumpet Major John Love Day (1880)
- Wessex Tales (1888)
- The Fiddlers of the Reels and Other
- A Laodicean : Story of Today (1881)
- The Best Horror Stories
- The Three Strangers and Other Stories
- Towns Men

The Return of the Native

Thomas Hardy was a master of the art of characterisation. Some of his characters are among the immortal figures of Literature. He chose his characters from the lower strata of society. Hardy's female characters are more forceful than his male characters because women are more elemental 'nearer to nature' than men. However his major characters are portrayed with a psychological insight, the minor ones being used only to provide some comic relief.

The plots of Hardy's novels are constructed with great skill and reveal his inventive powers. But they are often marred by elements of improbability, casuality and excessive use of coincidences.

In presenting human life as a tragedy, Hardy may be said to be expressing his pessimism and his gloomy view of life. His disgust at the modern life and civilisation may said to be responsible for his loss of faith and growth of pessimistic outlook.

Hardy as Short Story Writer

Hardy was prolific not only as novelist and poet but also as a writer of short stories. He began publishing short stories in periodicals in 1874 and continued to do so for over thirty years in total over fifty short stories ranging from the brief narratives to the long novellas 'The Romantic Adventures of a Milk Maid'.

He published the main body of his short stories in three volumes *Wessex Tales* (1888), *A Group of Nobel Dames* (1891) and *Life's Little Ironics* (1894). He collected the remaining stories under the title *A Changed Man and other Tales* in 1913. Unlike anything else Hardy wrote *A Group of Noble Dames* is a story cycle in which the speakers forced indoors by inclement weather tell tales of the 18th century Dorset aristocracy.

Hardy's stories are a condensed but more intense version of the novels and as such give a fascinating precis of Hardy's outlook upon and understanding of the world in which psychological factors are prominent.

The continuing popularity of Hardy's novels owes much to their richly varied yet always accessible style and combination of romantic plots and convincingly presented characters. Many of his novels have been adopted also.

EXAM BASED QUESTIONS

1 Queen Victoria ruled in which years?
(a) From 1800 to 1850 (b) From 1798 to 1832
(c) From 1837 to 1901 (d) From 1850 to 1910

2 Why Victorian period is called one of the most prosperous period in history of England?
(a) Industrial revolution
(b) Lots of reforms took place
(c) Because of industrial development and technological changes
(d) None of the above

3 Main purpose of Reform Bills (1867) and (1884) was
(a) to better the condition of women
(b) to increase the vote bank
(c) democratisation of British politics
(d) bring moral prudence

4 Which genre of writing became the most chosen form by writers of Victorian era?
(a) Poetry (b) Novels
(c) Science Fiction (d) Short Stories

5 What was the main theme of the novels of early Victorian era?
(a) Action of the protagonist
(b) Specific contemporary problems prevalent in Victorian society
(c) Super natural element
(d) Rustic life

6 What was the main concern of 2nd generation Victorian novel writers?
(a) Rural England's condition which was being destroyed by industry and commerce
(b) To entertain public
(c) Preach moral values
(d) None of the above

7 When was Darwin's origin of species published?
(a) 1859 (b) 1869
(c) 1879 (d) 1889

8 In which novel of Charles Dickens; the protagonist remembers how he had been "a child's Tom Jones, a harmless creature" in his boyhood?
(a) Great Expectation (b) Hard Times
(c) Pickwick Papers (d) David Copperfield

9 Little Nell is a character in Dickens' novel
(a) Hard Times (b) Oliver Twist
(c) Great Expectations (d) The Old Curiosity Shop

10 Dickens' Pickwick Papers were published in
(a) 1821 (b) 1837
(c) 1834 (d) 1836

11 Which of these Dickens heroes receives a large fortune from a mysterious benefactor?
(a) Eugene Wrayburn (b) Arthur Clennam
(c) Philip Pirrip (Pip) (d) Nicholas Nickleby

12 Which of these Dickens heroines was born and raised in debtor's prison?
(a) Bella Wilful (b) Amy Dorrit
(c) Esther Summerson (d) Estella Havisham

13 In Chapter 9 in the novel David Copperfield, the author writes "I have a memorable birthday", what makes it so memorable?
(a) He is locked up in Salem house
(b) He meets Agnes for the first time
(c) He writes his first short story
(d) His mother and little brother are buried

14 Which of the following is not a reason Hetty goes to Windsor in the novel Adam Bede?
(a) To find captain Donnithorne
(b) Because she is pregnant
(c) To invite Dinah to her wedding
(d) None of the above

15 Charlotte, Emily and Anne Bronte were three sisters each of whom published a novel in 1847. Which novel is not written by any of the sisters?
(a) Jane Eyre (b) Agnes Grey
(c) Villette (d) Wuthering Heights

16 In the novel, 'Middlemarch' George Eliot demonstrates that marriages work best when based on
(a) lust (b) money
(c) compatibility (d) social capital

17 What standard convention in women's novels did Eliot refuse to bow to, in the novel Middlemarch?
(a) A happy ending (b) A marriage plot
(c) A large cast of characters (d) A tragic ending

18 What is the name of the female protagonist in George Eliot's Middlemarch who marries Mr Casaubon?
(a) Dorothea Brooke (b) Anne Vignette
(c) Celia Brooke (d) Mary Garth

19 Elizabeth Gaskell's novel 'Mary Barton' is sub-titled
(a) The Two Nations
(b) A Tale of Manchester Life
(c) A Story of Provincial life (d) The Factory Girl

20 Elizabeth Gaskell wrote a biography of which famous author?
(a) Thomas Hardy (b) Charles Dickens
(c) Charlotte Bronte (d) Jane Austen

21 William Makepeace Thackeray wrote a novel which is a satire of the English society during the 19th century. The title of the novel was borrowed from the allegorical story 'The Pilgrim's Progress'. Name the novel.
(a) The Luck of Bary Lyndon
(b) Vanity Fair
(c) The Virginians
(d) Catherine

22 Which major Victorian author penned "The Mill on the Floss"?
(a) Anthony Trollope (b) Charles Dickens
(c) George Eliot (d) Mrs. Oliphant

23 Which term is used for publishing a work in parts?
(a) Piece work (b) Serialisation
(c) Segmenting (d) Chapters

24 What was the original title of 'North and South'?
(a) East and West (b) North and South
(c) Milton-Northern (d) Margaret Hale

25 After the death of her mother when she was just one year old, Elizabeth Gaskell was brought up by an aunt who lived in the town of Knutsford, Cheshire. What is the name of her novel that is set in a fictional version of that town?
(a) Cranford
(b) The Mayor of Casterbridge
(c) Pendennis
(d) Middlemarch

26 Religion played an important part in Elizabeth Gaskell's life and both her father and her husband were ministers. To which Christian denomination that promotes the idea of God as a single entity did the family belong?
(a) Presbyterianism (b) Calvinism
(c) Baptist (d) Unitarianism

27 Which of Elizabeth Gaskell's novels was left unfinished at the time of her unexpected death following a heart-attack in 1865?
(a) Ruth (b) My Lady Ludlow
(c) Sylvia's Lovers (d) Wives and Daughters

28 Which novel of Charlotte Bronte was published posthumously?
(a) Shirley (b) The Professor
(c) Villette (d) The Good Earth

29 In the novel Shirley, what is the title character's surname?
(a) Keeldar (b) Keelman
(c) Keelrow (d) Kilroy

30 In Jane Eyre, Jane takes up a position at Rochester's home, Thornfield Hall, in what capacity?
(a) Cook (b) Governess
(c) Housekeeper (d) Maid

31 One of the most famous movements of direct address to the reader 'Reader, I married him' occurs in
(a) Henry Fielding's Tom Jones
(b) Charlotte Bronte's Jane Eyre
(c) Laurence Sterne's Tristram Shandy
(d) George Eliot's Middlemarch

32 The 'Madwoman in the attic' is a specific reference to
(a) The narrator of 'Goblin Market'
(b) Augusta Egg's 1858 narrative painting
(c) The Heroine of The Yellow Wallpaper
(d) Bertha Mason of Jane Eyre

33 "I will show you a heroine as plain and as small as myself."
(a) This is Emily Bronte in Wuthering Heights
(b) This is Charlotte Bronte in Jane Eyre
(c) This is George Eliot in Romola
(d) This is Anne Bronte in Agnes Grey

34 Which was the first novel Charlotte wrote, although it wasn't published until after her death?
(a) Jane Eyre (b) Shirley
(c) Villette (d) The Professor

35 In Jane Eyre, who runs the Lowood boarding school that Jane attends?
(a) Mr Brocklebank (b) Mr Brocklehurst
(c) Mr Brocklesby (d) Mr Brockleton

36 In the novel 'Jane Eyre', what is the name of Jane's friend who dies of consumption?
(a) Harriet Burns (b) Hazel Burns
(c) Helen Burns (d) Holly Burns

37 Charlotte's novel Villette is set in which country?
(a) Belgium (b) France
(c) Ireland (d) Switzerland

38 Which of these short story is written by Charles Dickens?
(a) A Message from the sea (b) Mudfog and other sketch
(c) Doctor Marigold (d) All of these

39 The short story by Elizabeth Gaskell 'Company Manners' was written in the year
(a) 1847 (b) 1852 (c) 1854 (d) 1863

40 What is inscribed above the entrance of Wuthering heights by Emily Bronte?
(a) Hindley Earnshaw 1729 (b) 1623
(c) Abandon all hope ye who enter here
(d) Hareton Earnshaw 1501

41 What destination does the young Catherine has in mind when she leaves thrush cross Grange for the 1st time?
(a) Weathering heights
(b) The fairy caves at Penistore Crags
(c) The nearby village
(d) London

42 Over the course of novel which character claims to see Catherine's ghost in the novel 'Wuthering Heights'?
(a) Joseph and Young Catherine
(b) Edgan Linton
(c) Nelly Dean
(d) Lockwood and Heathcliff

43 'The Tenant of Wildfell Hall' is the work by
(a) Charlotte Bronte (b) Emily Bronte
(c) Dickens (d) Anne Bronte

44 In the novel 'Vanity Fair' by Thackeray who convinces Joseph Sedley not to ask Becky to Marry him
(a) William Dobbin (b) Joseph Himself
(c) George Osborne (d) Sir Pitt Crawley

45 Who does Becky marry finally?
(a) George Osborne (b) William Dobbin
(c) Rawdon Crawley (d) Sir Pitt Crawley

46 The novel 'Barchester Towers' is written by
(a) WM Thackeray (b) George Meredith
(c) Anthony Trollope (d) John Ruskin

47 The fictional town where six of Trollope's novels were set was
(a) Yorkshire (b) Dorset
(c) Barchester (d) Sussex

48 The heroine of 'The Eustace Diamonds' who is reminiscent of Becky Sharp in 'Vanity Fair' was
(a) Madame Max (b) Lizzy
(c) Hermione (d) Glencora

49 With what part of the British government did Trollope remain associated while he wrote his novels?
(a) Parliament (b) The Post Office
(c) The Foreign Service (d) Her Majesty's Guard

50 The Times of London was represented in Trollope's novel as
(a) The Sunrise (b) The Logos
(c) The Jupiter (d) The Oracle

51 Which of these short stories is written by Trollope?
(a) Not If I know It (b) Mugby Junction
(c) Round the Sofa (d) Wessex Tales

52 George Meredith's works are
(a) The Egoist (b) Victoria
(c) Rhoda Fleming (d) All of these

53 Which work reflected George Meredith's disastrous marriage to Mary Ellen Nicolls?
(a) A Reading of Earth (b) A Reading of Life
(c) The Empty Purse (d) Modern Love

54 When did George Meredith write 'The Ordeal of Richard Feverel'?
(a) 1862 (b) 1865
(c) 1859 (d) 1871

55 Which was George Meredith's last novel?
(a) Diana of the Crossways (b) The Amazing Marriage
(c) One of Our Conquerors (d) Rhoda Fleming

56 Meredith's characters are drawn from England's
(a) England middle class
(b) Aristocratic society
(c) Upper middle class society
(d) Both (b) and (c)

57 Which novel was the first work of Benjamin Disraeli?
(a) The Young Duke (b) Vivian
(c) Sybil (d) Popanilla

58 In which novel Benjamin Disraeli lampooned publisher John Murray?
(a) Henrietta Temple (b) Coningsby
(c) Vivian Grey (d) Lothair

59 In which novel does Benjamin Disraeli repeats the theme of silver fork?
(a) Popanilla (b) Alroy
(c) Lothair (d) The Young Duke

60 What made Charles Kingsley ahead of his time?
(a) He believed in the power of individuals
(b) Pushed for reforms in education, political system and the sanitation
(c) He held political office to make changes in systems
(d) He believed in rights for women

61 The monk described in novel Hypatia is called
(a) Philip (b) Philammon
(c) Jermin (d) None of these

62 As a novelist Kingsley is best remembered for which quality?
(a) narratives (b) sermons
(c) descriptive faculties (d) characterisation

63 Which famous book for children is written by Charles Kingsley?
(a) Alice in Wonderland
(b) Treasure Island
(c) Arabian Nights
(d) Water Babies

64 What was the original title of the novel Treasure Island?
(a) The Cabin Boy (b) The Hispaniola
(c) The Pirate (d) The Sea Cook

65 In which Stevenson Story is MP Sir Danvers Carew murdered?
(a) The body snatcher
(b) The bottle Imp
(c) The strange case of Dr Jekyll and Mr Hyde
(d) Thrawn Janet

66 'Across the plains' is Stevenson's travel memoir about a train journey 'across which country'?
(a) Australia (b) Canada
(c) The USA (d) South Africa

67 **Which work by George Gissing depicts the dilemma of the poverty stricken artist?**
(a) Born in Exile (b) New Grub Street
(c) Thyrza (d) The Nether world

68 **Where does Mr Widdowson take Monica on their first date in the novel 'The Odd Women' by George Gissing?**
(a) for a horse and trap ride
(b) to the theatre
(c) to an art exhibition
(d) for rowing on the Thames

69 **What is Lewis Carroll's real name?**
(a) William Donald Mcniel
(b) Charles Lutwidge Dodgson
(c) Anthony Jonathan O'Brien
(d) Edgan Allen Poe

70 **What is the name of Alice's Cat in both Alice's books?**
(a) Daphne (b) Diana
(c) Dinah (d) Dorothy

71 **In through the Looking Glass, from whom is Alice rescued by the White Knight?**
(a) The Black Knight
(b) The Dark and Stormy Knight
(c) The Green Knight
(d) The Red Knight

72 **Which novel of Thomas Hardy has a chapter in which a man sells his wife?**
(a) Jude the Obscure
(b) The Mayor of Casterbridge
(c) Tess of the d' Urbervilles
(d) The Return of the Native

73 **What happens to Tess in the novel 'Tess of the d' Urbervilles'?**
(a) She becomes queen
(b) She leaves England
(c) She becomes grandmother
(d) She is hanged

74 **Which county is depicted in the novels of Thomas Hardy?**
(a) Essex (b) Sussex
(c) Surrey (d) Wessex

75 **Who is Jude Fawdey's cousin in Jude the Obscure?**
(a) Mary Chant (b) Tess Durbeyfield
(c) Arabella (d) Sue Bridehead

76 **When was 'Wessex's Tale published?**
(a) 1912 (b) 1914
(c) 1916 (d) 1928

77 **What profession was Thomas Hardy trained for before he became an author?**
(a) Clergy (b) Stonemason
(c) Farmer (d) Architect

78 **In which novel is a suicide and infanticide note found that reads, "Done because we are too many."**
(a) Desperate Remedies
(b) Jude the Obscure
(c) The Return of the Native
(d) Far from the Madding Crowd

79 **Which novel of Thomas Hardy features a school mistress called 'Fancy Day'?**
(a) The Return of the Native
(b) Under the Greenwood Tree
(c) Jude the Obscure
(d) A Pair of Blue Eyes

80 **Which of the Hardy's novels is subtitled 'The Life and Death of a Man of Character'?**
(a) Far from the Madding Crowd
(b) The Mayor of Casterbridge
(c) Desperate Remedies
(d) A Pair of Blue Eyes

81 **The Victorian age is named after .... who ruled from 1837 to 1901.**
(a) queen Elizabeth (b) queen Mary
(c) queen Victoria (d) queen Elizabeth II

82 **......... work of Charles Dickens brought his dignity back.**
(a) Dombey and Son (b) Bleak House
(c) David Copperfield (d) All of these

83 **Dickens novel '.........' is about the injustices of British legal system which persecutes poor debtors.**
(a) Bleak House (b) Little Dorrit
(c) the Princess (d) Nicholas Nickleby

84 **...... worked as an editor of the Cornhill Magazine.**
(a) George Meredith
(b) George Eliot
(c) William Makepeace Thackeray
(d) Thomas Hardy

85 **...... made Anthony Trollope known and it is his masterpiece.**
(a) Phineas Redux (b) Barchester Towers
(c) Doctor Throne (d) The Warden

86 **...... presented solution of social and moral problems with the help of his work.**
(a) Benjamin Disraeli (b) RL Stevenson
(c) John Henry Newman (d) Charles Reade

87 **The Mill on the Floss by George Eliot is looked upon as a**
(a) historical novel (b) regional novel
(c) picaresque novel (d) spiritual autobiography

88 **Dorothea marries .... in the end of the novel Middlemarch.**
(a) Casaubon (b) Lydgate (c) Ladislaw (d) Fredvincy

89 The Egoist by .... has long been most admired for substantial dialogue scenes and tense comedy.
(a) Christina Rossetti
(b) Dante Gabriel Rossetti
(c) Mari Ann Evans
(d) George Meredith

90 Thomas Hardy's novel 'Jude the Obscure' is about a
(a) cleric
(b) a rich boy
(c) a poor country boy
(d) an orphan

91 Which of these statements about Romola is not true?
(a) It is written by George Eliot
(b) It was published in 1863
(c) It is a historical novel set in Florence during the 1490s Renaissance
(d) Tito is Romola's servant in the novel

92 Which of these statements about Middlemarch is not true?
(a) It is written by George Eliot
(b) It is subtitled 'A Study of Provincial Life'
(c) It was first published as a serial novel in eight parts
(d) The heroine of the novel is Maggie Tulliver

93 Which of these statements is correct about Thackeray's Vanity Fair?
(a) It was not published serially in London in 1847 and 1848
(b) It does not have a subtitle
(c) It is a satircal novel of manners
(d) The title of the novel is derived from John Milton's allegorical story

94 Which of these statements is not true about Jane Eyre?
(a) It was written by Charlotte Bronte
(b) It was published in 1847
(c) It is a bildungsroman
(d) The novel does not contain Gothic elements

95 Which of the following statements is not true about Thomas Hardy?
(a) Thomas Hardy depicted the tragic picture of men and women
(b) Arthur Hallam was his close friend
(c) Thomas Hardy wrote novels, poems, short stories
(d) Thomas Hardy died in 1928

96 Which of the following pairs is incorrectly matched?
(a) Alfred Tennyson : In Memoriam
(b) Charles Dickens : Little Dorrit
(c) Anthony Trollope : Manchester Towers
(d) George Eliot : North and South

97 Which of the following pairs is correctly matched?
(a) Alfred Tennyson : Vanity Fair
(b) Emily Brontes : Idylls of the King
(c) WM Thackeray : Wuthering Heights
(d) Charlotte Bronte : Jane Eyre

98 Which of the following pairs is incorrectly matched?
(a) Charlotte Bronte : Jane Eyre
(b) Emily Bronte : Wuthering Heights
(c) WM Thackeray : Vanity Fair
(d) Alfred Tennyson : David Copperfield

99 Which of the following pairs is correctly matched?
(a) 1847 : Jane Eyre
(b) 1850 : The Mill on the Floss
(c) 1853 : David Copperfield
(d) 1860 : Bleak House

100 Which of the following pairs is incorrectly matched?
(a) Charles Dickens : Oliver Twist
(b) Elizabeth Barrett Browning : The Serphim and other Poems
(c) Alfred Tennyson : Morte d' Arthur
(d) WM Thackeray : LAgnes Grey

Directions (Q. Nos. 101-102) *In the questions given below are two statements labelled as Assertion (A) and Reason (R). In context of the two statements, which one of the following is correct?*

Codes
(a) Both A and R are true and R is the correct explanation of A
(b) Both A and R are true, but R is not correct explanation of A
(c) A is true, but R is false
(d) A is false, but R is true

101 **Assertion** (A) Charles Dickens saw his father going through hardships.
Reason (R) Dickens entire family suffered and Dickens had to leave school and work in a factory.

102 **Assertion** (A) Dickens's novels are called 'Newgate Novels'.
Reason (R) They are called so because Dickens adulates in these novels the careers and adventures of criminals.

Directions (Q. Nos. 103-106) *In the questions given below are two statements labelled as Assertion (A) and Reason (R). In context of the two statements, which one of the following is correct?*

Codes
(a) A is true, but R is false
(b) A is false, but R is true
(c) Both A and R are true, but R is not the correct explanation of A
(d) Both A and R are true, and R is the correct explanation of A

103 **Assertion** (A) Darwin's theory of revolution undermined the value of traditional religion and morality.
Reason (R) It revolutionalised man's conception of himself.

104 Assertion (A) Literature of the Victorian Age was marked by the Decadent movement.
Reason (R) The people aspired to set literature and art free from the materialistic pre-occupations of industrialised society.

105 Assertion (A) The Victorian period also witnessed tremendous growth in periodicals of all kinds.
Reason (R) Many famous novelists published their work in serial instalments in magazines.

106 Assertion (A) Wilkie Collins provided such novels which were full of suspense and thrill to the Victorian readers.
Reason (R) Wilkie Collins believed in designing the fantastic characters and well designed plots.

107 Match the following

List I (Novelist)	List II (Works)
A. Anthony Trollope	1. The Women in White
B. Bulwer Lytton	2. Lousin Phillis
C. Mrs Gaskell	3. The Kellys and the O'Kellys
D. Wilkie Collins	4. Eugene Aram

Codes

	A	B	C	D		A	B	C	D
(a)	4	3	1	2	(b)	4	3	2	1
(c)	3	2	4	1	(d)	3	4	2	1

108 Match the following

List I (Works)	List II (Depicts)
A. Oliver Twist	1. Abuses of charity schools and brutal master
B. Little Dorrit	2. Unnecessary degradation and suffering poor
C. Bleak House	3. Injustice persecutes poor debtors
D. Nicholas Nickleby	4. Powerfully drawn figure like Lady Deadlock

Codes

	A	B	C	D		A	B	C	D
(a)	3	2	4	1	(b)	2	1	3	4
(c)	2	3	4	1	(d)	3	1	2	4

109 Match the following

List I (Novelist)	List II (Works)
A. George Eliot	1. The Four Georges
B. Thomas Hardy	2. Romola
C. William Makepeace Thackeray	3. Two on a Tower
D. George Meredith	4. Vittoria

Codes

	A	B	C	D
(a)	3	1	2	4
(b)	2	3	1	4
(c)	3	4	2	1
(d)	4	3	2	1

110 In the given series which one has all the works matched correctly with their publishing years?
(a) Felix Holt the Radical 1857, Adam Bede 1866; Jane Eyre 1847, Hypatia 1853
(b) Felix Holt the Radical 1866, Adam Bede 1859, Jane Eyre 1847, Hypatia 1853
(c) Felix Holt the Radical 1857, Adam Bede 1850, Jane Eyre 1845, Hypatia 1855
(d) Felix Holt the Radical 1857, Adam Bede 1854, Jane Eyre 1849, Hypatia 1856

111 Arrange the following in chronological order as per their publishing year
1. The Spanish Gypsy
2. Felix Holt the Radical
3. Amos Barton
4. Adam Bede

Codes
(a) 4, 3, 2, 1 (b) 3, 4, 2, 1 (c) 3, 2, 4, 1 (d) 2, 3, 4, 1

112 Arrange the following in chronological order as per their date of birth.
1. Benjamin Disraeli
2. George Eliot
3. George Meredith
4. Charles Dickens

Codes
(a) 2, 4, 1, 3 (b) 4, 3, 2, 1
(c) 3, 4, 2, 1 (d) 2, 3, 4, 1

113 Put the following novels by Charles Dickens in a sequential order
1. Great Expectations 2. Hard Times
3. Bleak House 4. Tale of Two Cities

Codes
(a) 3, 2, 4, 1 (b) 2, 4, 3, 1 (c) 1, 2, 4, 3 (d) 4, 2, 1, 3

114 Put the following novels of George Eliot in a sequential order.
1. Middlemarch 2. Daniel Deronda
3. Felix Holt, the Radical 4. Romola

Codes

(a)	1	3	4	2	(b)	2	1	3	4
(c)	4	3	1	2	(d)	4	1	3	2

115 The given series, which one has all the novelists matched correctly with their works?
(a) George Eliot-Hard Times, Charles Dickens-The Four Georges, WM Thackeray-Romola, George Meredith-Vittoria
(b) George Eliot-Romola, Charles Dickens-Hard Times, WM Thackeray-The Four Georges, George Meredith-Vittoria
(c) George Eliot-The Four Georges, Charles Dickens-Vittoria WM Thackeray-Romola, George Meredith-Hard Times
(d) George Eliot-Vittoria, Charles Dickens-Hard Times, WM Thackeray, Romola, George Meredith-The Four Georges

116 Which of the following fictions is in correct chronological order?

(a) Stevenson's Treasure Island, Silas Marner, The Tess of the d' Urbervilles, Sylvia's Lovers
(b) Silas Marner, Tess of d' Urbervilles, Sylvia's Lovers, Stevenson's Treasure Island
(c) Silas Marner, Sylvia's Lovers, Treasure Island, Tess of the d' Urbervilles
(d) Tess of the d' Urbervilles, Sylvia's Lovers, Treasure Island, Silas Marner

117 Consider the following statements
The main characteristics of Adam Bede are

1. It is written by George Eliot and is her first novel.
2. Dinah Morris is not a character in the novel.
3. It is set in the town of Loamshire, England.
4. It is a pastoral novel.

Which of the statements given above are correct?

(a) 1 and 2 (b) 1 and 4 (c) 3 and 2 (d) 3 and 4

118 Consider the following statements Jane Eyre

1. it is written by Emily Bronte.
2. was published in 1847.
3. is a bildungroman.
4. most famous line at the end of the novel is 'Reader, I divorced him'.

Which of the statements given above are correct?

(a) 1 and 2 (b) 1 and 4 (c) 3 and 2 (d) 3 and 4

119 Consider the following statements

1. William Makepeace Thackeray studied law, but later on his thoughts changed about this profession.
2. William Makepeace Thackeray shared his own experience in his work.

Which of the statements given above is/are correct?

(a) Only 1 (b) Only 2
(c) Both 1 and 2 (d) None of the above

120 Consider the following statements
The main characteristics of Wuthering Heights are

1. It is written by Emily Bronte.
2. It was published in 1800.
3. The story of the novel is narrated by Catherine Earnshaw.
4. Heathcliff is the main character in the novel.

Which of the statements given above is/are correct?

(a) 1 and 2 (b) 1 and 4
(c) 3 and 4 (d) 3 and 2

121 Consider the following statements
The main characteristics of Thackeray's Vanity Fair are

1. It is a satirical novel of manners.
2. The heroine of the novel is Rebecca Sharp or Becky.
3. It is not a satricial novel of manners.
4. It does not have a subtitle.

Codes

(a) 1 and 2 (b) 1 and 4 (c) 3 and 2 (d) 3 and 4

122 What is common to the following characters? Identify the correct description below.
Sleary
Stephen Blackpool
Thomas Gradgrind

Codes

(a) All of them are important characters in Dickens novel Hard Times
(b) All of them are immortal characters in Dickens' Oliver Twist
(c) All of them are characters in Dickens' David Copperfield
(d) All of them are poets, who have written ballads

123 Which of these about Middlemarch is correct?

1. It does not have a subtitle
2. It is subtitled : A Study of Town Life
3. It is subtitled : A Study of Provincial Life
4. It has a subtitle : A Study of Country Life

Codes

(a) Only 4 (b) Only 3 (c) Only 1 (d) Only 2

124 "I loved her against reason, against promise, against peace, against hope, against happiness, against all discouragement that could be."

Which novelist has quoted the above lines in which of his/her work?

(a) Charles Dickens, Great Expectations
(b) George Eliot, Romola
(c) Elizabeth Gaskell, Sylvia's Lovers
(d) Charlotte Bronte, Jane Eyre

125 "What greater thing is there for two human souls, than to feel that they are joined for life-to strengthen each other in all labour, to rest on each other in all sorrow, to minister to each other in all pain, to be one with each other in silent unspeakable memories at the moment of the last parting?"

Which novelist has quoted the above lines in which of his/her work?

(a) Charles Dickens, David Copperfield
(b) George Eliot, Adam Bede
(c) Elizabeth Gaskell, Wives and Daughters
(d) Ann Bronte, The Virginians

126 "I care for myself. The more solitary, the more friendless, the more unsustained I am, the more I will respect myself."

Which novelist has quoted the above lines in which of his/her work?

(a) Charles Dickens, Oliver Twist
(b) George Eliot, Middlemarch
(c) Charlotte Bronte, Jane Eyre
(d) Elizabeth Gaskell, Ruth

127 **"He shrank from hearing Margaret's very name mentioned; he, while he blamed her-while he was jealous of her-while he renounced her-he loved her sorely, in spite of himself."**

Which novelist has quoted the above lines in which of his/her work?

(a) Charles Dickens, Our Mutual Friend
(b) George Eliot, The Mill on the Floss
(c) Charlotte Bronte, Shirley
(d) Elizabeth Gaskell, North and South

128 **"Be with me always take any form-drive me mad! only do not leave me in this abyss, where I cannot find you! Oh, God! it is unutterable! I can not live without my life! I can not live without my soul!"**

Which novelist has quoted the above lines in which of his/her work?

(a) Emily Bronte, Wuthering Heights
(b) Charlotte Bronte, The Professor
(c) Anne Bronte, Agnes Grey
(d) WM Thackeray, 'Lovel, the Widower'

129 **If you would have your son to walk honourably through the world, you must not attempt to clear the stones from his path, but teach him to walk firmly over them not insist upon leading him by the hand, but let him learn to go alone.**

Which novelist has quoted the above lines in which of his/her work?

(a) Emily Bronte, Wuthering Heights
(b) Anne Bronte, The Tenant of Wildfell Hall
(c) Charlotte Bronte, Villete
(d) WM Thackeray, The Newcomes

130 **Which character in Vanity Fair by Thackeray utters these words?**
"I am very fond of Amelia, I adore her and that sort of thing. Don't look angry. She is faultless. I know she is. But you see there's no fun in winning a thing unless you play for it.

(a) The narrator
(b) George Osborne
(c) Sir Pitt
(d) Rebecca Sharp

131 **In which work of Thomas Hardy, these lines have been used?**
"Happiness was but the occasional episode in a general drama of pain."

(a) Jude the Obscure
(b) A Pair of Blue Eyes
(c) Wessex Tales
(d) The Mayor of Casterbridge

132 **"She was as one who, in madness, was resolute to throw herself from a precipice, but to whom some remnant of sanity remained which forced her to seek those who would save her from herself."**

Which novelist has quoted the above lines in which of his/her work?

(a) George Meredith, The Tragic Comedians
(b) Benjamin Disraeli, The Tragedy of Court Alarcos
(c) William Makepeace Thackeray, The Rose and the Ring
(d) Anthony Trollope, Can You Forgive Her?

133 **"Why is it that a woman can see from a distance what a man cannot see close?"**

Which fiction writer has quoted the above lines in which of his/her work?

(a)	Benjamin Disraeli	The Tragedy of Count Alarcos
(b)	Thomas Hardy	The Return of the Native
(c)	George Gissing	The Egoist
(d)	Anthony Trollope	The Fixed Period

134 **"They were plighted; they were one eternally; they could not be parted. She listened gravely, conceiving the infinity as a narrow dwelling where a voice droned and ceased not. However, she listened. She became an attentive listener."**

Which novelist has quoted the above lines in which of his/her work?

(a) George Meredith, The Egoist
(b) Benjamin Disraeli, The Infernal Marriage
(c) William Makepeace Thackeray, The Memoirs of Barry Lyndon
(d) Anthony Trollope, The Fixed Period

135 **Which character in which novel of Thomas Hardy quotes these lines?**
"He called her Artemis, Demeter and other fanciful names half-teasingly which she didn't like because she could not understand then."

(a) Tess in Tess of d'Urbervilles
(b) Angel Clare in Tess d' Urbervilles
(c) Lucette Le Sueur the Mayor of Casterbridge
(d) Mrs Yeobright The Return of the Native

136 **Which character in Hardy's the Return of the Native utters these words?**
"Ah, There's too much of that sending to school in these days! It only does harm. Every gate post and born's door you come to is sure to have some bad word or other chalked upon it by the young rascals .... "

(a) Eustacia (b) Wildeve (c) Captain Vye (d) Thomasius

137 **"Let Lady Glyde's maid come in, Louis. Stop! Do her shoes creak?" I was obliged to ask the question. Creaking shoes invariably upset me for the day. I was resigned to see the Young Person, but I was not resigned to let the Young Person's shoes upset me. There is a limit even to my endurance."**

Which novelist has quoted the above lines in which of his/her work?

(a) Samuel Butler, Unconscious Memory
(b) Robert Louis Stevenson, Treasure Island
(c) Charles Kingsley, Alton Locke
(d) Wilkie Collins, The Woman in White

138 "To me it seems that youth is like spring, an overpraised season- delightful if it happen to be a favoured one, but in practice very rarely favoured and more remarkable, as a general rule, for biting east winds than genial breezes. Autumn is the mellower season, and what we lose in flowers we more than gain in fruits."

Which novelist has quoted the above lines in which of his/her work?

(a) Samuel Butler, The Way of All Flesh
(b) Robert Louis Stevenson, The Black Arrow : A Tale of Two Roses
(c) Charles Kingsley, Two Years Ago
(d) Wilkie Collins, Blind Love

139 "The poor are very well off, at least the agricultural poor, very well off indeed. Their incomes are certain, that is a great point, and they have no cares, no anxieties; they always have a resource, they always have the House. People without cares do not require as much food whose life entails anxieties. See how long they live!"

Which novelist has quoted the above lines in which of his/her work?

(a) George Meredith, The Amazing Marriage
(b) Benjamin Disraeli, Sybil, or The Two Nations
(c) William Makepeace Thackeray, The Virginians
(d) Anthony Trollope, An Old Man's Love

140 'Stop!' said the Irishwoman. "I have one more word for you both; for you will both see me again before all is over. Those that wish to be clean, clean they will be; and those that wish to be foul, foul they will be. Remember."

Which novelist has quoted the above lines in which of his/her work?

(a) Samuel Butler, Erewhon
(b) Robert Louis Stevenson, Merry Men
(c) Charles Kingsley, The Water Babies
(d) Wilkie Collins, The Law and the Lady

141 "To know what you prefer instead of humbly saying Amen to what the world tells you, you ought to prefer, is to have kept your soul alive."

Which novelist has quoted the above lines in which of his/her work?

(a) Samuel Butler, Book of the Machines
(b) Robert Louis Stevenson, An Inland Voyage
(c) Charles, Kingsley, Westward Ho!
(d) Wilkie Collins, The Moonstone

142 "Well, I wasn't going to abuse him. I was only going to ask: Is there any quality which distinguishes his work from that of twenty struggling writers one could name? Of course not. He's a clever, prolific man; so are they. But he began with money and friends; he came from Oxford into the thick of advertised people; his name was mentioned in print six times a week before he had written a dozen articles. This kind of thing will become the rule. Men won't succeed in literature that they may get into society, but will get into society that they may succeed in literature."

Which novelist has quoted the above lines in which of his/her work?

(a) Wilkie Collins, The Black Robe
(b) Anthony Trollope, He knew He was right
(c) George Gissing, New Grub Street
(d) RL Stevenson, Travels with a Donkey in the Cevennes

143 "If a had a world of my own, everything would be nonsense. Nothing would be what it is because everything would be what it isn't it ...." ...... and what it wouldn't it would. You see".

Which novelist has quoted the above lines in which of his/her work?

(a) George Gissing - North and South
(b) Wilkie Collins - The Black Robe
(c) Lewis Carrol - Alice's Adventures in Wonderland
(d) George Eliot - Silas Marner

144 "It was silver's voice and before I had heard a dozen words, I would not have shown myself for all the world. I lay there trembling and listening in the extreme of fear and curiosity .... "

Which novelist has quoted these words in which of his/her works?

(a) Wuthering Heights - Emily Bronte
(b) David Copperfield - Charles Dickens
(c) Antony Trollope - The Fixed Period
(d) RL Stevenson - Treasure Island

145 "A man's fate is his own temper; and according to that will be his opinion as to the particular manner in which the courses of events is regulated. A consistent man believes in Destiny, a capricious man in chance."

Which novelist has quoted these words in which of his/her works?

(a) Benjamin Disraeli - Vivian Grey
(b) George Gissing - The Paying Guest
(c) Samuel Butler - The Way of All Flesh
(d) Great Expectations - Charles Dickens

Directions (146-150) *Read the passage and answer the questions that follow.*

"I begin to think," said Estella, in a musing way, after another moment of calm wonder, "that I almost understand how this comes about. If you had brought up your adopted daughter wholly in the dark confinement of these rooms, and had never let her know that there was such a thing as the daylight by which she has never once seen your face-if you had done that, and then, for a purpose, had wanted her to understand the daylight and know all about it, you would have been disappointed and angry?" Miss Havisham, with her head in her hands, sat making a low moaning, and swaying herself on her chair, but gave no answer.

'Or,' said Estella, "-which is a nearer case-if you had taught her, from the dawn of her intelligence, with your utmost energy and might, that there was such a thing as daylight, but that it was made to be her enemy and destroyer, and she must always turn against it, for it had blighted you and would else blight her-if you had done this, and then, for a purpose, had wanted her to take naturally to the daylight and she could not do it, you would have been disappointed and angry?"

Miss Havisham sat listening (or it seemed so, for I could not see her face), but still made no answer. 'So,' said Estella, "I must be taken as I have been made. The success is not mine, the failure is not mine, but the two together make me."

146 Estella is making the point that
(a) Miss Havisham has made her into the person she has become
(b) Miss Havisham has blamed Estella for what are her own shortcomings
(c) Miss Havisham has concealed the truth of Estella's parentage from her
(d) Miss Havisham's mistaken are to be excused by her good intentions

147 Estella argues her point by
(a) posing riddles
(b) drawing an analogy
(c) citing a precedent
(d) appealing to authority

148 The effect of Estella's question at the end of paragraphs 1 and 3 is to ask
(a) What did I do wrong?
(b) How did I hurt you?
(c) What did you expect?
(d) Have you no shame?

149 As used in line 14, 'a nearer case' most nearly means a more
(a) familiar circumstance
(b) likely outcome
(c) immediate concern
(d) relevant instance

150 Why did Miss Havisham raises Estelley to break the heart of men?
(a) She is eccentric
(b) She was a maniac and insane person
(c) As a revenge because she was duped by her fiance minutes before her wedding when she was young
(d) She has become very rich

PREVIOUS YEARS' QUESTIONS

December 2018

1 Which of the following is the most accurate description of Butler English?
(a) A dialect of English spoken by the descendants of Anglo-Indians
(b) A pidgin, also called 'kitchen English' spoken by South Asians in Europe
(c) A minimal pidgin that emerged during colonial times in the Madras Presidency
(d) Any non-grammatical variety of English used by menials in common wealth countries.

2 Identify the character, a black Eyed Dwarf who "Constantly revealed a few discoloured faugs that were yet scattered in his mouth, and gave him the aspect of a panting dog".
(a) Mulberry Hawk in Nicholas Nickleby
(b) Rigand in Little Dorrit
(c) Mr Crook in Bleak House
(d) Daniel Quilp in the Old Curiosity Shop

3 Nicholas Nickleby firmly established Charles Dickens as a dominant novelist of his time and the book as an unvivalled literacy phenomenon. To celebrate the completion of the book, a painter noted that there has been nothing comparable to him since the days of Samuel Richardson. Identify the painter
(a) Leonard Woolf (b) David Wilkie
(c) John Cruick Shank (d) Ernest Dawson

4 .... read Adam Bede with such pleasure that she not only keenly recommended to her relatives but also commissioned two paintings of scenes from the novel
(a) Horace Nightingale (b) George Eliot
(c) Margaret Cavendish (d) Queen Victoria

5 Which of the following Acts were not passed during to Victorian Era?
(a) The married women's Property Rights Act
(b) A Series of Factor Acts
(c) The Custody Act
(d) The Women's Suffrage Act

June 2018

6 Which novel opens thus-"Whether I shall turn out to be the hero of my own life, or whether that station will be held for anyone else, these pages must-show"?
(a) Tristram Shandy (b) Lady Aud ley's Secret
(c) David Copperfield (d) Fitz-Boodle's Confessions

November 2017

7 Charles Dickens' Bleak House is pointed by critical of England's
(a) Privy Council (b) Court of Appeal
(c) Court of Chaucery (d) Military Courts

8 Which novel of Thomas Hardy begins with the Sombre description of Egdon Heath?
(a) Jude The Obscure
(b) The Return of the Native
(c) Far from the Madding Crowd
(d) Under the Greenwood Tree

9 Which 19th century novelist expressed a wish to 'exterminate the race' of Indians following the 1857 Muting in India?
(a) William Makepeace Thackeray
(b) Charles Dickens
(c) George Eliot
(d) Anthony Trollope

January 2017

10 In Charlotte Bronte's Jane Eyre, what does Mr Brockehurst accuse Jane of when he visits Lowood School.
(a) Laziness (b) Stealing (c) Lying (d) Spying

11 The prelude to novel Middlemarch makes a reference to the particular history of a remarkable woman ....
(a) St Agnes (b) St Theresa (c) St Joan (d) St Carmel

12 Which of the following adjectives will not apply to Becky Sharp, a major character in Vanity Fair?
(a) ambitious (b) energetic (c) well born (d) scheming

June 2016

13 Which character in Dickens keeps on hoping that 'Something will turn up'?
(a) Barkis (b) Micawber
(c) Uria Heep (d) Miss Havisham

14 Which of the WM Thackeray's novel's closing sentence is this?
"Which of us is happy in this world? Which of us has his desire? or, having it, is satisfied?"
(a) The History of Henry Esmond
(b) Vanity Fair
(c) The Luck of Barry Lyndom
(d) Pendennis

15 Which of the following is not true of the novels of Charles Dickens?
(a) They deal with the problems of discontents of an urban civilisation
(b) The plots are strikingly tight knit
(c) They share a sense of fun and determining optimism
(d) They incorporate elements of popular contemporary culture

December 2015

16 What did Anthony Trollope seek to criticise through the character Mr Slope?
(a) Methodism (b) Low Churchmen
(c) High Church doctrines (d) Anglicanism

June 2015

17 Like many other novelists, Hardy employed language variation (dialect and standard) with a purpose. In this respect which of the following statements is correct?
(a) His major characters such as Tess and Jude always speak in local dialects as per their social position
(b) His major characters such as Tess and Jude rarely speak in local dialects, in spite of their social position
(c) His major characters such as Tess and Jude rarely speak in standard language in spite of their social position
(d) His major characters such as Tess and Jude rarely speak in a mixture of dialect and standard.

18 Who said, "I am not an angel .... and I will not be one till I die. I will be myself" This is
(a) Maggie Tulliver in Mill on the Floss
(b) Aurora Leigh in the eponymous poem
(c) Jane Eyre in the eponymous novel
(d) Betty Higdon in Our Mutual Friend

19 Chapter III of Oliver Twist opens with a narratorial remark about Oliver being punished for "the commission of the impious and proffane offence of asking for more". What did oliver ask for more?
(a) time to play (b) more food to eat
(c) more books to read (d) more money to spend

June 2014

20 Thomas Hardy's last major novel was
(a) Tess of D'Urbervilles (b) Jude the Obscure
(c) The Return of the Native (d) The Trumpet Major

21 Charles Dickens visit to the United States produced ....
(a) Hard Times (b) Nicholas Nickleby
(c) Martin Chuzzlewit (d) Oliver Twist

22 In which novel does the hero, drives by passion and revenge add a new dimension to the concept of suffering?
(a) Wuthering Heights (b) Jude the Obscure
(c) The Mill on the Floss (d) Hard Times

23 George Meredith's first novel was banned by Mudie's Circulating Library for its supposed moral offence Identify the Novel
(a) The Egoist
(b) Evan Harrington
(c) Diana of the Cross ways
(d) The Ordeal of Richard Feveral

24 Which of the following arrangement is in the correct chronological sequence?

(a) Adam Bede, Wuthering Heights, North and South, Villette
(b) Wuthering Heights, Villette, North and South, Adam Bede
(c) Villette, North and South, Wuthering Heights, Adam Bede
(d) North and South, Wuthering Heights, Adam Bede, Villette

June 2013

25 Which character in Jane Eyre uses religion to justify cruelty?

(a) Blanche Ingram
(b) Mr Brocklehurst
(c) Sir John Rivers
(d) Eliza Reed

26 Little Nell is a character in Dickens'

(a) David Copperfield
(b) The Old Curiosity Shop
(c) Bleak House
(d) Great Expectations

27 In which of Hardy's novels does the character Abel Whittle appear?

(a) Far from the Madding Crowd
(b) The Return of the Native
(c) A Pair of Blue Eyes
(d) The Major of Caster Bridge

28 In Wuthering Heights, Calty appears in a dream beating at a window, wailing, 'Let me in' blood running down her wrist. Who dreams her?

(a) Lock Wood
(b) Health Cliff
(c) Nelly
(d) Edgar Linton

ANSWERS

Objective Questions

1. *(c)*	2. *(c)*	3. *(c)*	4. *(b)*	5. *(b)*	6. *(a)*	7. *(a)*	8. *(b)*	9. *(d)*	10. *(b)*
11. *(c)*	12. *(b)*	13. *(d)*	14. *(c)*	15. *(c)*	16. *(c)*	17. *(b)*	18. *(a)*	19. *(b)*	20. *(c)*
21. *(b)*	22. *(c)*	23. *(b)*	24. *(d)*	25. *(a)*	26. *(d)*	27. *(d)*	28. *(b)*	29. *(a)*	30. *(b)*
31. *(b)*	32. *(d)*	33. *(b)*	34. *(d)*	35. *(b)*	36. *(c)*	37. *(a)*	38. *(d)*	39. *(c)*	40. *(d)*
41. *(b)*	42. *(d)*	43. *(d)*	44. *(c)*	45. *(c)*	46. *(c)*	47. *(c)*	48. *(b)*	49. *(b)*	50. *(c)*
51. *(a)*	52. *(d)*	53. *(d)*	54. *(c)*	55. *(b)*	56. *(d)*	57. *(b)*	58. *(c)*	59. *(d)*	60. *(b)*
61. *(b)*	62. *(c)*	63. *(d)*	64. *(d)*	65. *(c)*	66. *(c)*	67. *(b)*	68. *(d)*	69. *(b)*	70. *(c)*
71. *(d)*	72. *(b)*	73. *(d)*	74. *(d)*	75. *(d)*	76. *(a)*	77. *(d)*	78. *(b)*	79. *(b)*	80. *(b)*
81. *(c)*	82. *(d)*	83. *(b)*	84. *(c)*	85. *(b)*	86. *(b)*	87. *(d)*	88. *(c)*	89. *(d)*	90. *(c)*
91. *(d)*	92. *(d)*	93. *(c)*	94. *(d)*	95. *(b)*	96. *(d)*	97. *(d)*	98. *(d)*	99. *(a)*	100. *(d)*
101. *(a)*	102. *(b)*	103. *(c)*	104. *(c)*	105. *(d)*	106. *(d)*	107. *(d)*	108. *(c)*	109. *(b)*	110. *(b)*
111. *(b)*	112. *(a)*	113. *(a)*	114. *(d)*	115. *(b)*	116. *(c)*	117. *(b)*	118. *(c)*	119. *(c)*	120. *(b)*
121. *(a)*	122. *(a)*	123. *(b)*	124. *(a)*	125. *(b)*	126. *(c)*	127. *(d)*	128. *(a)*	129. *(b)*	130. *(b)*
131. *(d)*	132. *(d)*	133. *(b)*	134. *(a)*	135. *(b)*	136. *(c)*	137. *(d)*	138. *(a)*	139. *(b)*	140. *(c)*
141. *(b)*	142. *(c)*	143. *(c)*	144. *(d)*	145. *(a)*	146. *(a)*	147. *(b)*	148. *(c)*	149. *(d)*	150. *(c)*

Previous Years' Questions

1. *(c)*	2. *(d)*	3. *(b)*	4. *(d)*	5. *(d)*	6. *(c)*	7. *(c)*	8. *(b)*	9. *(b)*	10. *(c)*
11. *(b)*	12. *(c)*	13. *(b)*	14. *(b)*	15. *(b)*	16. *(b)*	17. *(b)*	18. *(c)*	19. *(b)*	20. *(b)*
21. *(c)*	22. *(a)*	23. *(d)*	24. *(b)*	25. *(b)*	26. *(b)*	27. *(d)*	28. *(a)*		

Fiction in Modern Age (1910-1945)

The period referred here is Post World War I. Literature of this period focuses on the inner reality of the human mind in place of external reality. Novels in this age were written on all possible themes and subjects. They deal with characters in a psychological manner. There is no absolute truth, all things are relative.

Introduction of Modern Age

The early decade of the 20th century, especially the period after World War I is known as the Modern Age. The modern period occupied the years shortly after the beginning of the twentieth century through roughly 1945. The period was marked by sudden and unexpected breaks with traditional ways of viewing and interacting with the world. Modernism involved a radical and conscious break with the past, rejection of conventional Victorian morality and inventions of new form of expression.

In the 20th century several social, economic, scientific, cultural and political changes took place that shook the foundations of the existing world order. Developments in the field of science and technology, rise of industrialisation and capitalism, suffragette movement, feminist movement, all these combined to usher in the modern age.

According to Virginia Woolf, "Not only had human character changed but all human relations between masters and servants, husband and wives, parents and children had also shifted."

However, one cataclysmic event around, which the entire modern age centers is the World War I (1914-18). The Great War shattered mankind's belief in the possibility of a stable, peaceful and progressive world. The use of modern warfare in the war, as well as the resultant death and destruction caused by it, revealed a new side to modernity. The war also caused a shift in the nature of power relations and trading patterns.

In this Chapter

Modernist writers felt betrayed by the war, which gave a hard blow to all the traditional institutions they had hitherto believed in. External world no longer provided any answers or meaning and hence writers retreated within. The changing world order necessitated creation of new forms of writing in accordance with the complexity of the Modern Age, thus giving rise to modern literature.

Literary Trends of Modern Age

Imagism

It was a movement in modernist Anglo-American poetry that originated in 1912.

Ezra Pound, Amy Lowell, HD (Hilda Doolittle), Richard Aldington and William Carlos Williams were the main proponents of this movement. The four Imagist anthologies (*Des Imagistes*, 1914; *Some Imagist Poets*, 1915, 1916, 1917) and the magazines *Poetry* (from 1912) and *The Egoist* (from 1914), n the United States and England, respectively, published the vork of a dozen Imagist poets.

Dadaism

t was a literary and artistic movement that emerged in 1916 as a result of disgust with the brutality of World War 1.

Dadaism sought to negate traditional artistic values and deliberately eschewed meaning. It used nonsense and ridicule to mphasise the meaninglessness of the modern world. The novement was short lived and ended in 1923, though it influenced ater movements such as surrealism.

Surrealism

t was a 20th century literary and artistic movement which ained momentum after Dada movement. Surrealists believed n the superiority of the irrational, the unconscious and the nexpected. They revolted against all controls and restraints on reativity through techniques such as automatic writing, elf-induced hallucinations and exploitation of dream/trance tates. They aimed at revolutionising human experience by eeing people from the clutches of false rationality. Apart from reton, other major figures associated with the Surrealist novement were Louis Aragon, Salvador Dali, Paul Eluard and ierre Reverdy.

Characteristics of Modern Literature

Avant–garde is considered to be the hallmark of modern literature. While, in French, it is a military term meaning advance guard, here it refers to the position taken by high modernism. It represents challenging the normative, pushing the boundaries of the status quo and creating new artistic forms. Avant-garde artists reject tradition and undertake to 'make it new'.

- In modern literature, the focus shifts away from external reality to the inner reality of the human mind. There is greater stress on the psychological detailing of the literary character through narrative devices such as the stream of consciousness and interior monologue.
- There is a shift in focus from teleological ways of thinking about, time to time as fluid, discontinuous and non-linear.
- Language becomes condense, plots non-chronological and narrative consciousness shifts away from impersonal omniscient to personal subjective.

Novels in Modern Age

Immense variety and complexity were the salient features of the Modern English novels. The novels by no means are immune to self-conscious reflective impulses of the new century. Modernism introduced a new kind of narration to the novel, one that would fundmentally change the entire essence of novel writing. Novels were written on all possible themes and subjects. They were realistic including all the pleasant and unpleasant facts and represented all aspects of life. There were traditionalists like HG Wells, Arnold Bennett and Galsworthy who proposed new ideas and opened new spheres for human mind but followed Victorian tradition in their techniques.

There were innovators like James Conrad, Henry James, Virginia Woolf who revolutionised the technique of novel writing by entering into the subconscious mind and gave birth to psychological novels. Other than these, biographical novels, war novels, regional and satirical novels, novels of humour and science fiction continued to invade the market.

The modern novel is realistic. It deals with all the facts of contemporary life, the pleasant as well as the unpleasant, the beautiful as well as the ugly and does not present merely a one sided view of life. The novel is pessimistic in tone as it presents the realities of life with all its conflicts and doubts.

The novels of modern age do not tell the full story unlike novels of Victorian age. The characterisation is also superficial as psychologically a true account of a person was not possible. The modern novel is predominantly psychological and impact of the new psychology on plot and character had far-reaching impact on themes of novels. Irony, satire and comparisons are used frequently to illustrate points in regard to society. There is no such thing as absolute truth. All things are relative.

Major Fiction Writers of this Age

Henry James, Rudyard Kipling, HG Wells Arnold Bennett, Dorothy Richardson, William Somerset Maugham, EM Forster, James Joyce, Virginia Woolf, DH Lawrence, AL Huxley, Elizabeth Bowen, George Orwell, Graham Greene, Joseph Conrad, etc. were the Major Fiction Writers of the Modern Age.

Major Novelists of the Modern Age

Joseph Conrad (1857-1924)

Joseph Conrad was a Polish British writer regarded as one of the greatest novelists to write in the English language. He was born on 3rd December, 1857 in Poland. He was the son of a prominent nationalist victim of Russian Repression.

Though Conrad learnt English only in his twenties, he was a master prose-stylist who brought a non-English sensibility to English Literature. He joined the British merchant navy and was naturalised as a British citizen in 1886.

Literary Career and Works

In 1889, Conrad began the critical transition from sailor to writer by starting his first novel Almayer's Folly. Conrad spent around 20 years at the sea. He visited Australia, various islands in the Indian Ocean and the South Pacific, South America and even sailed upto the Congo river in Africa. His experiences on the sea were rendered into his fiction. His characters are drawn from many nations His novel *An Out Cast of the Islands* (1896) was inspired by his own experiences as a mate on board the steamer, The Vigar. His later novel *Heart of Darkness* (1899) was influenced by his own journey to Congo while *Lord Jim* (1900) was based on the actual incident of abandonment of a ship in 1880. The most productive phase of Conrad's career spanned from 1897 to 1911 during which period he wrote *The Nigger of the Narcissus, Youth, Heart of Darkness, Lord Jim, Nostromo The Secret Agent* and *Under Western Eyes*.

His literary work had a profound impact on the Modernist movement. He was a great romantic, yet at the same time a realist. His narrative style and anti-heroic characters have influenced many writers. Conrad was interested in showing psycho-political situations in his novels that drew parallel between the inner lives of single characters and broader sweep of human history.

Conrad's work influenced numerous later 20th century writers from TS Eliot and Graham Greene to Virginia Woolf, Albert Camus and William Faulkner.

Conrad developed an elaborate prose style, which is adventurous in nature and darkly pessimistic. He seems to be interested in the traditional virtues of stead fastness and courage while also concerned with shortcomings that define modern existence and perception. Conrad died of a heart attack in 1924 at the age of 67 in America.

Besides novels Conrad also wrote many short stories such as

- The Lagoon (1897,)
- Tales of Unrest (1898)
- Amy Foster (1901)
- Falka (1901)
- The Secret Sharer (1909)
- Tales of Hearsay (1925)
- The Duel (1908)
- The Informer (1906)
- Gasper Rulz (1906)
- The Inn of the Two Witches (1913)
- Because of the Dollars (1914)

Heart of Darkness

Heart of Darkness first appeared in a three-part series in *Blackwood Magazine* in 1899. It was published as a complete novella in 1904. It is based in part on a trip that Conrad took through modern-day Congo during his years as a sailor. The novella narrates the story of Marlow's job as an ivory transporter down the city of Congo. Through his journey, Marlow develops an intense interest in investigating Kurtz, an ivory-procurement agent and Marlow is shocked upon seeing what the European traders have done to the natives.

Kurtz is one of the main figures of the novel. Kurtz is a petty tyrant, an embodiment of Europe and an assault on European values. He is the unique victim of colonisation; the wilderness captures him and he turns his back on the people and customs that were once a part of him. It is structured as a frame tale, not a first-person narrative. Marlow's story is told by the anonymous narrator who listens to Marlow on the deck of the Nellie.

Conrad's frame narrator, like the reader, learns that his ideas about European imperialism are founded on a number of lies that he wholeheartedly believed. By the end of the novella, Marlow's tale significantly changes the narrator's attitude toward the ships and men of the past. *Heart of Darkness* was one of the first literary texts to provide a critical view of European imperial activities. Conrad's exploration of the darkness potentially inherent in all human hearts inspired the 1979 film, *Apocalypse Now*.

Major Works

- An Out Cast of the Islands (1896)
- Heart of Darkness (1899)
- Lord Jim (1900)
- Nigger of the Narcissus (1897)
- Youth
- Nostromo (1904)
- The Secret Agent (1907)
- Under Western Eyes (1911)
- Typhoon (1903)

HG Wells (1866-1946)

HG Wells, full name Herbert George Wells was born on 21st September, 1866. He was an English novelist, journalist, sociologist and historian best known as father of Science Fiction. At the age of 18, Wells won a scholarship to study biology at the Norman school of science, London where TH Huxley was one of his teachers. He graduated from London University in 1888 and became a science teacher. His first published book was *A Textbook of Biology* (1893).

Literary Career and Works

However, he is best known for his science fiction works as, *The Time Machine* (1895), *The Wonderful Visit* (1895), *The Island of Doctor Moreau* (1896), *The Invisible Man* (1897), *The War of the Worlds*(1898), *The First Men in the Moon* (1901) and *The Food of the Gods* (1904).

He also wrote many short stories which were collected in *The Stolen Bacillus* (1895), *The Plattner Story* (1897) and *Tales of Space and Time* (1899). For a time HG Wells acquired the reputation as a prophet of the future and in the novel *The War in the Air* (1908) he foresaw certain developments in the military use of aircraft. But his imagination flourished at its best not in the manner of the comparatively mechanical anticipations of Jules Verne but in the astronomical fantasies of the *First Men in the Moon* and *The War of the Worlds* also.

Behind Well's inventiveness was a intense concern for humanity and society. According to Andrew Sanders, Wells was one of the few English writers to be 'well read' in both 'modern science and in the scientific method'. In his works, Wells portrayed both the advantages of 'a scientifically planned future' and of 'the anti-humanist bent of certain areas of scientific progress'.

HG Wells, at one stage decided to abandon Science Fiction and wrote some comic novels of lower middle class life, most notably his *Love and Mr Lewiston* (1900) Kipps: *The Story of a Simple Soul* (1905) and *The History of Mr Polly* (1910). Through these novels, he revealed the hopes and frustrations of clerks, shop assistants and underpaid teachers who had rarely been treated in fiction before with such sympathetic understanding.

Inspite of an awareness of possible world catastrophe that underlay much of his earlier work and flared up against in old age, Wells in his lifetime was regarded as the chief literary spokesperson of the optimism that preceded World War I. He lived to see World War II and his advocacy of human rights had a significant role in the formation of the United Nations.

Arnold Bennett (1867-1931)

British novelist, playwright , critic and essayist whose major works form an important link between the English novel and the mainstream of European realism. Arnold was born in Hanley, Staffordshire in 1867. His father was a self made man who had qualified to become a Solicitor. Arnold was educated at the Middle School , New-Castle and later at London University. In 1889, he moved to London and worked as an Assistant Editor of the periodical 'women'.

Literary Career and Works

Bennett's first novel *The Man from the North* was published in 1898. But Bennett is best known for his highly detailed novels of the *Five-Town* the potteries since amalgamated to form the city of Stroke-on-Trents in his native Staffordshire. As a young writer he learned his craft from French realistic novelists who laid emphasis on detailed description of people, scenes and events.

Benett achieved fame as a chronicler of the *Five Towns* as he has used as background for a story. His major novels, *Anna of the Five Towns* (1902) *The Old Wives Tales* (1908) and *Clayhanger* (1910) have their setting in these towns. Bennett wrote 30 novels and even many of the lesser ones display the essential Bennettian values; ironic yet kindly, critical yet with a large tolerance.

During the World War I, Bennett became Director of Propaganda for France at the Ministry of Information. His contribution to the propaganda effort came in the form of a pamphlet, *Liberty: A Statement of the British Case*. Bennett died on 27th March, 1931, at the age of 63.

Contemporary critics like Virginia Woolf perceived weakness in Bennett's work. For them his style was traditional rather than modern which made him an obvious target for those challenging literary conventions. But during 1990, a positive view of his work has been made which made his works widely accepted. The noted English critic John Carey praises him, declaring Bennett to be his 'hero' because his writings represent a systematic dismemberment of the intellectual's case against the masses.

Major Works

- A Man from the North, 1898
- Anna of the Five Towns, 1902
- The Grand Babylon Hotel, 1902
- The Old Wives' Tale, 1908
- Clayhanger, Family 1910
- The Card, 1911
- These Twain, 1915
- Riceyman Steps, 1924
- The Journals of Arnold Bennett, 1932-1933
- Leonara (1903)
- A Great Man (1904)
- Teresa of Watling Street (1904)
- Sacred and Profane Love (1905)
- The Glimpse (1909)
- The Honey Moon (1910)
- The Price of Love (1914)
- The Lions' Share (1916)

Dorothy Richardson (1873-1957)

Dorothy Miller Richardson was a British author and novelist. She was born on 17th May, 1873 in Abingdon, South of Oxford. Her family moved to London, where she attended a progressive school influenced by the ideas of John Ruskin. In London, Dorothy developed acquaintance with members of the Bloomsbury group.

Literary Career and Works

Her writing career began with reviews and essays and journalism in small periodicals. Her first published books, *The Quakers Past and Present* (1914) and *Gleanings from the Work of George Fox* (1915), were non-fiction texts focusing on religious history.

Richardson is considered to be the first writer to use the stream of consciousness narrative technique to illuminate the viewpoint of her protagonist, Miriam in her sequence of 13 novels, *Pilgrimage* (1915-1967.)

It has been viewed as early Modernism's great documentary novel, as daring experimental fiction, as spiritual autobiography and pioneer of cinematographic technique. Richardson also published short stories in a variety of periodicals and a handful of poems.

Although Richardson was an influential modernist and feminist writer, her work has remained forgotten in literary circles. She died penniless and alone in the London suburb of Beckenham, Kent in 1957.

Major Works

- Pointed Roofs (1915)
- Backwater (1916)
- Honeycomb (1917)
- The Tunnel (1919)
- Interim (1920)
- Deadlock (1921)
- Revolving Lights (1923)
- The Trap (1925)
- Oberland (1927)
- Dawn's Left Hand (1931)
- Clear Horizon (1935)
- Pilgrimage (4 vols.) (1938)
- Journey to Paradise : Short Stories and Autobiographical Sketches (1989)

GK Chesterton (1874-1936)

GK Chesterton, his full name Gilbert Keith Chesterton was born on 29th, May 1874 in London, England. He is known as English critic, author of verse, essays, novels and short stories. He is also known for his exuberant personality and rot and figure. He was educated at St. Paul's School and later studied art at the Slade school and literature at University College, London.

Literary Career and Works

After his education, Chesterton began working for the London publisher, 'Redway'. He also worked as a columnist for the Daily News, The Illustrated London News and founded his own paper in 1925, 'GK's Weekly'.

His first two poetry collections, *Greybeards at Play* and *The Wild Knight and Other Poems* appeared in 1900. His first novel *The Napoleon of Notting Hill*, a utopian romance, was published in 1904. His other well-known works are *The Man Who Was Thursday* (1908) and the Father Brown stories. The priest detective Father Brown, who used psychology to put himself in the place of the criminal in order to solve the crime, is one of Chesterton's most enduring creations. Chesterton died on the 14th June, 1936 in Beaconsfield, Buckinghamshire.

He also wrote a loosely knit collection of short stories *The Club of Queer Trades* (1905). He wrote about 200 short stories.

His most successful association of fiction with social judgement is in Chesterton's series on the priest sleuth Father Brown: *The Innocence of Father Brown* (1911) followd by *The Wisdom* (1914), *The Increduility* (1926), *The Secret* (1927) and *The Scandal of Father Brown* (1935).

William Somerset Maugham (1874-1965)

WS Maugham was born on 25th, January in the British Embassy in Paris in 1874. He lost his parents at the age of 10. He was brought up by his uncle and educated at King's School, Canterbury. After a year at Heidelberg, he entered St Thomas's Medical School, London and qualified as doctor in 1897.

Literary Career and Works

His first novel *Liza of Lambeth* became so successful that Maugham gave up medicine and devoted himself entirely to writing. This novel drew from his own experiences as a medical student. It depicts the life and death of Lizen Kemp an 18 year old factory worker living with her ageing mother.

Maugham is primarily known for his four major novels *Of Human Bondage* (1915), a semi-autobiographical account of his time in the medical school; *The Moon and Sixpence* (1919), an exotic tale based on the life of the painter Paul Gauguin; *Cakes and Ale* (1930); a literary satire and *The Razor's Edge* (1944), the story of Larry Darrell- an American pilot traumatised by his experiences of World War I.

These novels bring his interest not only in his country but also in other countries like France, Italy, India and the South seas.

Maugham's short stories have gained popularity as they portray the conflict of Europeans in alien surroundings that provoke strong emotions. Maugham's is skilled in handling plot which is distinguished by economy and suspense.

In his novels, Maugham shows that he is interested in three problems; the problem of renunciation and materialistic craze for possession, the problem of love and the human predicament, the futility and meaninglessness of human life. In his view, renunciation of worldly power is the ultimate solution, love as presented by Maugham presents tragedy than its triumph. Love does not come out successful and happy in his novels.

As a short story writer, some of his most memorable stories are those that deal with the lives of the westerner mostly British colonists in the far East and are typically concerned with the emotional toll that is caused due to isolation. Some of his outstanding works in this genre include *Rain, Footprints in the Jungle, The Outstation.*

Maugham was also an influential travel writer with books such as *On a Chinese Screen* (1922) and *The Gentleman in the Parlour* (1930). Maugham died in Nice, France on 16th December 1965.

Major Works

Novels

- Liza of Lambeth (1897)
- Mrs Craddock (1902)
- The Magician (1908)
- Of Human Bondage (1915)
- The Moon and Sixpence (1919)
- The Painted Veil (1925)
- Cakes and Ale or, the Skeleton in the Cupboard (1930)
- The Razor's Edge (1944)

Travel Books

- The Land of the Blessed Virgin Sketches and Impressions in Andalusia (1905)
- On A Chinese Screen (1922)
- The Gentleman in the Parlour A Record of a Journey From Rangoon to Haiphong (1930)

EM Forster (1879-1970)

EM Forster or Edward Morgan Forster was an English novelist, essayist, short story writer and critic. He was born in London on 1st January, 1879 into an Anglo Irish and Welsh family at Dorset Square, London. He was the only child of his parents and lost his father when he was just 2 years old. He inherited a large sum from his paternal great Aunt. The money was enough to live on and enabled him to become a writer. He attended a day school Tonbridge and then went to King's College, Cambridge.

Literary Career and Works

His works broke the shackles of narrow Victorianism, kept in touch with the changing times and included a strong strain of social comment.

His first novel *Where Angels Fear to Tread* (1905), set in Tuscany, was followed by his *Bildungsroman* novel *The Longest Journey* (1907). Forster is best known for his novels *Howards End* and *A Passage to India*. The epigraph to *Howards End*–'Only Connect' emphasises Forster's humanism. *A Passage to India* is set against the backdrop of Indian Independence movement in 1920s and based on Forster's own experiences in India. He had acted as Secretary to the Maharaja of Dewas Senior.

Forster was also a closet homosexual. He wrote a novel, *Maurice*, in 1914, which was published only after his death due to its overt homosexual theme. Forster died in June, 1970 after a series of strokes.

Major Work

Novels

- Where Angels Fear to Tread (1905)
- The Longest Journey (1907)
- A Room with a View (1908)
- Howards End (1910)
- A Passage to India (1924)
- Maurice (written in 1913-14, published posthumously in 1971)

Short Stories

- The Celestial Omnibus (and other stories) (1911)
- The Eternal Moment and other Stories (1928)
- The Gentleman in the Parlour: A Record of a Journey From Rangoon to Haiphong (1930)

A Passage to India

Forster began writing *A Passage to India* in 1913, just after his first visit to India. Finally published in 1924, *A Passage to India* examines the racial misunderstandings and cultural hypocrisies that characterised the complex interactions between Indians and the English toward the end of the British occupation of India. Forster's narrative centers on Dr Aziz, a young Indian physician whose attempt to establish *friendship* with several British characters has disastrous consequences.

In the course of the novel, Dr Aziz is accused of attempting to rape a young Englishwoman. Aziz's friend Mr Fielding, a British teacher, helps to defend Aziz. Although, the charges against Aziz are dropped during his trial, the gulf between the British and native Indians grows wider than ever and the novel ends on an ambiguous note. The novel is divided into three parts: Mosque, Caves and Temple.

Forsters' novels were described by reviewers as astonishing and brilliantly original. His works have their roots in the Romantic movement. They urge humanity to maintain a close relationship with nature and at the same time to develop the imagination. The values of truthfulness and kindness dominate Forster's lateral thinking. A reconciliation of humanity to the Earth and its own imagination may be the ultimate ideals but according to Forster they are receding in a civilisation devoting itself more and more to technological progress.

In additon to essays, short stories and novels, Forster wrote a biography of his great aunt *Marianne Thornton* in year 1956, a documentary account of his Indian experiences *The Hill of Devi* (1953) and *Alexandria: A History and a Guide*, 1922, 1961.

The majority of Forsters short stories reveal a characteristic i.e. uniting of realism and fantasy. Forster used supernatural in his stories to break free from the restrictions of Edwardian society and to satirise its numerous failings. In some of his mythological stories there is a mythological God of the Woods Pan who symbolises both man's primitive impulses and its formidable power of nature. Forster's concern with salvation is deepened in the stories of the second collection *The Eternal Moment*. His short stories published posthumously, *The Life to Come*, represent a new direction with theme that undeveloped heart is there. In the most highly regarded stories, a Character's Denial of Love reveals the constricting effects of conventional society and leads to his physical, emotional or spiritual death.

Although Forster's short stories have always been appreciated by its readers, they have been overshadowed by his novels.

James Joyce (1882-1942)

He is one of the prominent novelists of 20th century. He was born in Dublin, Ireland on 2nd February, 1882. He was educated at Jesuit School in Dublin. In 1888 he went to Clongeswood College but his father lost his job and James had to withdraw from college.

He graduated in October of 1902 from Royal University. He spent much of his working career as a language instructor. He was said to have known 17 languages.

Literary Career and Works

Joyce's first published book was *Chamber Music*, a collection of 36 love poems. His poetry was noticed by Ezra Pound and TS Eliot and included in Pound's influential *Imagist Anthology* of 1914. His collection of 12 short stories, *Dubliners* drew on his Irish experiences and analysed the stagnation of Dublin society.

Joyce's novels are known for their experimental use of language and modernist forms. In his novels, Joyce used the stream of consciousness technique (a narrative device to render the flow of thoughts and impressions in a character's mind) and the epiphany (a moment of sudden realisation that causes a change in a character's perception/worldview). Joyce's *A Portrait of the Artist as a Young Man* (1916) is a semi-autobiographical novel that describes the formative years of the life of Stephen Dedalus, the protagonist.

His most celebrated novel *Ulysses* chronicles the passage of its protagonist Leopold Bloom on 16th June, 1904. This novel features different narrative styles such as third-person narration, with dialogue and interior monologue interspersed, and first-person narration with distinctive styles.

Different narrative devices obscure the development of the plot and create ambiguity. *Finnegan's Wake* is considered to be Joyce's most incomprehensible work noted for its convoluted language. It deploys a polyglot language composed of words of many different languages. Joyce died in Zürich on 13th January, 1941.

Major Works

- Chamber Music (poems, 1907)
- Dubliners (short-story collection, 1914)
- A Portrait of the Artist as a Young Man (novel, 1916)
- Exiles (play, 1918)
- Ulysses (novel, 1922)
- Pomes Penyeach (poems, 1927)
- Finnegans Wake (novel, 1939)

Ulysses

Joyce first conceived of *Ulysses* as a short story to be included in *Dubliners*, but decided instead to publish it as a long novel, situated as a sort of sequel to *A Portrait of the Artist as a Young Man*. Ulysses picks up Stephen Dedalus's life more than a year after where Portrait leaves off. The novel introduces two new main characters, Leopold and Molly Bloom and takes place on a single day, 16th June, 1904, in Dublin. Leopold Bloom works for a Dublin newspaper.

In *Ulysses*, Joyce uses interior monologue extensively and instead of employing one narrative voice, Joyce radically shifts narrative style with each new episode of the novel. *Ulysses* is an experimental novel in the modernist tradition. It uses parody in its imitation of *The Odyssey*.

The structure of *Ulysses* parallels symbolically the structure of Homer's epic poem, *The Odyssey*. In both works, a man goes on a journey, encountering a variety of people and situations along the way. However, the journey in Homer's work lasts 10 years, whereas the journey in Joyce's work lasts about 18½ hours. The main characters in *Ulysses* also parallel the main characters in *The Odyssey*. Thus, Joyce's Leopold Bloom becomes Homer's *Odysseus* (Roman name, Ulysses); Stephen daedalus becomes Telemachus, the son of Odysseus; Molly Bloom becomes Penelope, the wife of Odysseus.

James Joyce in each of his prose works, used symbols to experience what he called 'epiphany', the revealation of certain special qualities about himself. His early writings reveal individual moods and characters and the plight of Ireland and Irish artists in the 1900s.

Joyce was interested in discovering the truth in his writings and revealing it. He was a good observer of reality which he loved and he always wanted to get at the truth behind the appearance.

As a short story writer Joyce has one collection called *Dubliners* (1914), but it is considered a master achievement in the genre. The collection contains total 15 stories. The stories are examples of Joyce's aesthetic theory of epiphany in fiction. Each is built around a sudden revealation of truth about life inspired by a seemingly trivial incident. The characters in these short stories are all catholic and middle class, although they represent a broad spectrum of ages and occupations.

Scholars also appreciate the fact that short story collection is significant because Joyce introduced a multidimensional narrative method that began revolutionising modern literature.

Virginia Woolf (1882-1941)

Virginia Woolf, modern novelist was born in London on 25th January, 1882. Her full name is Adeline Virginia Stephen. She was the child of ideal Victorian parents. Her father was an eminent literary figure and mother possessed saintly self-sacrifice attitude. She was home-schooled in English classics and Victorian literature. The sudden death of her mother followed by death of her half-sister caused the first of several nervous break downs Virginia had in her lifetime.

However, she was able to collect herself enough to attend courses to study Greek, Latin, German and History at the Ladies' Department of King's College London between 1897 and 1901. In 1904, Virginia's father also died which led to her mental breakdown and she had to be institutionalised. Virginia was also a victim of sexual abuse at the hands of her half-brothers.

Virginia's siblings bought a house at 46 Gordon Square in Bloomsbury, which became a significant place in the history of literature. Here, many literary and artistic friends of Virginia and her siblings formed the Bloomsbury group.

The original members of the group included Virginia and Vanessa, Clive Bell, Leonard Woolf, Adrian and Karin Stephen, Lytton Strachey, Maynard Keynes, Duncan Grant, EM Foster, Saxon Sydney-Turner, Roger Fry, Desmond and Molly MacCarthy.

Literary Career and Works

In 1912, she married Leonard Woolf. The couple collaborated to form the Hogarth Press, which published the works of Virginia and other contemporary writers and artists. Her first novel, *The Voyage Out* was published in 1915.

In 1922, her first experimental novel, *Jacob's Room*, appeared. In 1925, *Mrs Dalloway* was published, followed by *To the Lighthouse* in 1927. Woolf's most experimental novel, *The Waves* consisting of soliloquies spoken by six different characters came out in 1931. These three novels are generally considered to be her greatest claim to fame as a modernist writer. Woolf's involvement with the novelist and poet Vita Sackville-West led to *Orlando* (1928), a *roman à clef* inspired by Vita's life. Two lectures delivered to Women's College at Cambridge in 1928 led to *A Room of One's Own* (1929), a discussion of women's writing and its historical economic and social underpinning.

After Woolf finished the manuscript of her last novel, she was hit by severe depression again. She was unable to work and on 25th March, 1941, she committed suicide by drowning into the River Ouse.

Virginia Woolf became one of the central subjects of the 1970s movement of feminist criticism and her works have since gathered much attention and widespread acclaim for inspiring feminism. Her works have been translated into more than 50 languages.

Virginia Woolf was extremely dissatisfied with the current form of novels as presented by earlier novelists. So in 1908, Virginia decided to 'reform' the novel by creating a holistic form embracing aspects of life, that were 'fugitive' for Victorian novles. Virginia Woolf is best known for her novels *Mrs. Dalloway* (1925) and *To the Lighthouse* (1927) No Element of Story; emergence of an art form, poetisation of the English novel, stream of Consciousness technique, the distinctive nature of reality, artistic sincerity, integrity and feminisation of English novel are the chief characteristics of Woolf's art as a novelist.

Major Works

Novels

- The Voyage Out (1915)
- Night and Day (1919)
- Jacob's Room (1922)
- Mrs Dalloway (1925)
- To the Lighthouse (1927)
- Orlando (1928)
- The Waves (1931)
- The Years (1937)
- Between the Acts (1941)

Biographies

- Flush: A Biography (1933)
- Roger Fry: A Biography (1940)

Non-Fiction Books

- Modern Fiction (1919)
- A Room of One's Own (1929)
- On Being III (1930)
- Three Guineas (1938)

Mrs Dalloway

- *Mrs Dalloway* was published in 1925. The character of Clarissa Dalloway had earlier appeared in a series of short stories, the first of which was titled, *Mrs Dalloway in Bond Street*, published in 1923. This story served as an experimental first chapter to *Mrs Dalloway*.
- *Mrs Dalloway* covers one day from morning to night in one woman's life. Clarissa Dalloway, an upper-class housewife, walks through her London neighbourhood to prepare for the party she will host that evening.
- The action of Mrs Dalloway takes place during a single day in June 1923, in London.
- Clarissa Dalloway's party, which is the culminating event of the book, ties the narrative together by gathering the group of friends, Clarissa thinks about throughout her day. It also concludes the secondary story of the book, the story of Septimus Warren Smith, by having Dr Bradshaw arrive at the party and mention that one of his patients committed suicide that day.
- The book's major competing themes are sanity and insanity, isolation and community or the possibilities and limits of communicativeness.

This novel is embedded with feminism at its core with perfect blend of artistic and emotional values in right proportions with a charismatic approach to characterise the key imaginary character Mrs Clarissa Dalloway . The author has successfully presented the role of Mrs Dalloway in the minds of the readers and there is no confusion at any time though novel toggles between past and present. Woolf has used the character of Clarissa to explore the personal impacts of cultural change from the new technologies of automobiles, airplanes and movies to the new openness of marital and sexual relationships and the beginning of political upheavels.

The influence of Virginia Woolf had been immense, profound and all pervasive and there can be no denying the fact that she is a delicate and subtle artist and novelist. In her short stories Mrs Virginia Woolf focused on minute physical detail and experimented with stream of consciousness technique,interior monologues and symbolism to capture the inner workings of human thoughts. Some of her short stories are lyrical portrayal of varied narrative perspectives through the monologue of the narrator.

Kew Gardens, Monday or Tuesday, 'A Haunted House and other Short Stories', The Mark on the Wall are all short fiction by Mrs Virginia Woolf.

DH Lawrence (1885-1930)

David Herbert Lawrence was born in Eastwood , Nottinghamshire England on 11th September, 1885 . He is known as a novelist, essayist and short story writer. EM Forster called Lawrence the greatest imaginative novelist of his generation. Lawrence belonged to a working class background . Lawrence won a scholarship to Nottingham High School (1898-1901) and left at the age of 16 to earn a living as clerk in a factory . But he had to give up his job after an attack of pneumonia . He became a pupil teacher in Eastwood in 1902 and performed brilliantly in the national examination.

Literary Career and Works

In 1911, Lawrence began his literary career with the publication of his first novel *The White Peacock*.

Lawrence's family background had a significant bearing on his writing. His autobiographical novel *Sons and Lovers* (1913) was sparked by the death of his own mother and examined the influence of his mother on his sexual and psychological development.

His most controversial novel *Lady Chatterley's Lover* (1928) dealt with the sexual frustration of a young married woman Constance or Lady Chatterley whose husband had been paralysed due to a war injury. The unexpurgated edition of this novel was not published until 1960 because of its sexually explicit matter.

Lawrence also wrote poetry and several non-fiction works such as *Movements In European History* (1921), *Psychoanalysis And The Unconscious* (1922) and *Studies In Classic American Literature* (1923). A lifelong sufferer from tuberculosis, Lawrence died in 1930 in France, at the age of 44.

Short stories written by Lawrence make a lasting claim for the greatness of Lawrence. He wrote more than 50 short stories. There is a tremendous variety in the social context and presentation of his characters contain force and reality . These short stories surprise and delight the reader with writings that reveal at first hand Lawrence's insight into human experience.

All of Lawrence's novels are written is a lyrical , sensuous often rhapsodic prose style . He had an extraordinary ability to convey a sense of specific time and place and his writings often reflected his complex personality. Lawrence's work include volumes of stories , poems and essays.

Major Works

Novels

- The White Peacock (1911)
- The Trespasser (1912)
- Sons and Lovers (1913)
- The Rainbow (1915)
- Women in Love (1920)
- Aaron's Rod (1922)
- Lady Chatterley's Lover (1928)

Short Story

- The Prussian Officer and Other Stories (1914)
- England, My England and Other Stories (1922)
- The Fox , The Captain's Doll, The Lady Bird (1923)
- The Virgin and the Gipsy and Other Stories (1930)

Poetry

- Love Poems and Others (1913)
- Amores (1916)
- Look We have Come Through! (1917)
- Pansies (1929)
- Nettles (1930)
- Last Poems (1932)
- The White Horse (1964)

Sons and Lovers

D H Lawrence's third novel *Sons and Lovers* was initially titled *Paul Morel*. It was published in 1913.

Sons and Lovers tells the story of the Morel family and in particular, of Paul Morel. Gertrude and Walter Morel live in a village in the North of England. Gertrude is clever and competent. Walter, her husband, an uneducated coalminer, drinks his money away and is often violent. Divided by class, the two do not understand each other and Gertrude is bitterly unhappy.

The novel is autobiographical. Paul Morel is modeled on the youthful Lawrence, who in his early years, hugely depended upon his mother. Walter Morel is based upon Lawrence's father Arthur Lawrence, while Gertrude Morel is Lawrence's tribute to his own mother. Miriam is based on Jessie Chambers, Lawrence's girlfriend of adolescent years.

Sons and Lovers is also considered the first Freudian novel in English because of its analysis of the Oedipus tie between Paul and Gertrude.

Aldous Leonard Huxley (1894-1963)

English novelist and essayist Aldous Huxley, was born on 26th July, 1894, at Laleham in Godalming, Surrey, England. He belonged to a distinguished scientific family. He was the grandson of the famous zoologist Thomas Henry Huxley, also known as Darwin's Bulldog' for his advocacy of Charles Darwin's theory of evolution. Like his renowned ancestors, Aldous Huxley intended to become a scientist. However, an attack of keratitis punctata at the age of 16 rendered him totally blind for a period of 18 months. Later, he recovered partially and started using special glasses. It was after this that he turned to literature, unable to pursue his chosen career because of his eye ailments.

Literary Career and Works

Huxley was the editor of the magazine *Oxford Poetry*. His first collection of poetry came out in 1916. His first novel *Crome Fellow* (1921) satirised the fads and fashions of the time. Huxley's early comic novels, *Antic Hay Crome Yellon* (1923), *Those Barren Leaves* (1925), and *Point Counter Point* (1928), demonstrate his ability to dramatise intellectual debate in fiction. His most popular work is his dystopian novel *Brave New World* published in 1932. The title of this novel derives from Miranda's speech in William Shakespeare's *The Tempest*. Set in London of AD 2540, this novel depicts a world in which a totalitarian government controlled society by the use of science and technology.

Later in his life, Huxley started to experiment with hallucinogenic drugs such as LSD and mescaline. In 1954, he also published an important study of consciousness expansion through mescaline, *The Doors of Perception.* Huxley died on 22nd November, 1963, in Los Angeles.

Elizabeth Bowen (1899-1973)

Anglo-Irish novelist, Elizabeth Bowen was born on 7th June, 1899 in Dublin. She lived in Ireland until the age of seven, when her family moved to England. After the completion of her education, she returned to Dublin in 1916 to work in a hospital for World War I veterans. Two years later, she moved back to England and enrolled in the London County Council School of Art.

Literary Career and Works

At the age of 20 Bowen started writing short stories . Her first collection of stories , named *Encounters* was published in 1923.

Bowen's early works included the novels *The Hotel* (1927), *The Last September* (1929), *Friends and Relations* (1931) , *The House in Paris* (1935) and her memoir *Bowen's Court* (1942) .However, she is best known for *The Death of the Heart* (1938) and *The Heat of the Day* (1949). *The Death of the Heart* is about an idealistic young girl whose demands for honesty and openness are met with hostile reactions by her family. *The Heat of the Day*, on the other hand, is about an upper-class Irish woman- Stella Rodney's perception of the British Home Front. Her final novel *Eva Trout or Changing Scenes* (1968) won the James Tait Black Memorial Prize in 1969. Elizabeth Bowen died of lung cancer in a London hospital on 22nd February, 1973.

George Orwell (1903-1950)

George Orwell was born as Eric Arthur Blair in Motihari, Bihar, India. Orwell's father worked for the Opium Department of the Civil Service in Motihari. His mother took him to England when he was only one year. Orwell received his education at Eton College, England, After his studies, he began work as an imperial policeman in Burma. However, his tryst with British imperialism and his disgust for it, prompted him to resign from the post and return to England in 1928.

Literary Career and works

His experiences in Burma found expression in his first novel, *Burmese Days*. This novel presented a portrait of the dark side of the British Raj. Orwell's critique of British Imperialism also found an outlet in his essays *A Hanging* and *Shooting an Elephant*.

Orwell was a socialist and his works reflect his beliefs against totalitarianism. In a 1947 essay, he wrote that every line he had written since 1936 had been 'directly or indirectly, against totalitarianism and for democratic socialism.' Orwell's *Animal Farm* (1945) is an allegorical novel that reflects on the events leading up to and during the Stalin era.

It is a satire on Russian Revolution and an indictment of communism. Orwell's second most famous novel, *1984* (1949) is a dystopian novel that depicts a society tyrannised by a totalitarian government. Orwell died at the age of 46 from tuberculosis.

Animal Farm

Animal Farm was published on the heels of World War II, in England in 1945 and in the United States in 1946. He wrote the book during the war as a cautionary fable in order to expose the seriousness of the dangers posed by Stalinism and totalitarian government.

It is George Orwell's satire on equality, where all barnyard animals live free from their human masters' tyranny. Inspired to rebel by Major, an old boar, animals on Mr Jones' Manor Farm embrace animalism and stage a revolution to achieve an idealistic state of justice and progress.

The novel is an allegory, which is a story in which concrete and specific characters and situations stand for other characters and situations, so as to make a point about them. The main action of *Animal Farm* stands for the Russian Revolution of 1917 and the early years of the Soviet Union. Animalism is really communism. Manor Farm is allegorical Russia and the farmer Mr Jones is the Russian Czar. Old Major stands for either Karl Marx or Vladimir Lenin and the pig named Snowball represents the intellectual revolutionary Leon Trotsky. Napoleon stands for Stalin, while the dogs are his secret police.

At first Orwell had difficulty finding a publisher for the small master piece, but the book appeared in 1945, *Animal Farm* made him famous and for the first time prosperous.

Graham Greene (1904-1991)

Henry Graham Greene, an English novelist, short story writer, playwright and journalist was born on 2nd October, 1904 at Berkhamsted, Hertfordshire,England . Greene received his education at Balliol College, Oxford. After finishing his college , Graham converted to Roman Catholicism in 1928, partly through the influence of his future wife , Vivien Dayrell -Browning whom he married in 1927.

Literary Career and Works

Greene briefly worked as a sub- editor at the Nottingham Journal . He later moved to London and worked as a Sub-editor for 'The Times'. His First published work was a book of verse *Babbling April* (1925) and upon the modest success of his first novel , *The Man With in* (1929) he quit 'The Times' and worked as a film-critic and literary editor for 'The Spectator' until 1940. He then travelled widely for much of the next three decades as a freelance journalist , searching out locations for his novels in the process .

Greene's first three novels are held to be of small account. Then a thriller *Stamboul Train* (1930) earned him name. This was first of a string of novels that he termed *Entertainments*, similar to thrillers but which possessed greater moral complexity and depth. The three other novels *A Gun Sole* (1936), *The Confidential Agent* (1939) and The *Ministry of Fear* (1943) were pure entertainments and films were made on all three novels .

But Greene is best known as a novelist for his four major Roman Catholic novels

Brighton Rock (1938), *The Power and the Glory* (1940), *The Heart of the Matter* (1948), *The End of the Affair* (1951).

Catholicism plays a major role in the plot and character of these novels. *Brighton Rock* is a murder thriller set in the 1930s. Catholicism is the religion of the killer here. *The Power and the Glory* tells the story of a Roman Catholic priest in Mexico during the 1930s. In *The Heart of the Matter*, the protagonist Major Scobie is a Catholic police officer and adulterer. The last of the four novels, *The End of the Affair* concerns the story of a married woman and a non-married writer. It goes on for several years during the World War II. The woman finds God halfway through the affair and – beset by a new-found guilt – ends the relationship. Graham Greene also wrote an autobiography- *A Sort of Life* (1971). In this, he stated, "For a writer, success is always temporary. Success is only a delayed failure." Greene died of leukemia at the age of 86 in 1991.

Katherine Mansfield (1888-1923)

Katherine Mansfield , English master of short story, was born on 14th October, 1884 at Willington, New Zealand. After her education in Willington and London , Katherine left New Zealand at the age of 19 to establish herself in England as a writer .

Literary Career and Works

Until 1914 she published stories in *Rhythm* and *The Blue Review*, edited by the critic and essayist John Middletown Murry. *Prelude* (1918) was a series of short stories beautifully evocative of her family memories of New-Zealand. These , with others were collected in *Bliss* (1920) which established her reputation as a short story writer typical of her art.

She studied life objectively and understood characters widely different from herself in temperament and accidents. In her stories, she has tried to present the wearniness and frustration of modern English life. The novels; *The Prelude, To the Bay, The Garden Party, The Fly* represent at its best the subtle psychological art of Katherine Mansfield.

Even though Katherine's career was short, it is widely accepted that Mansfield revolutionised the English short story.

According to the Penguin companion to English Literature "The quiet clarity of detail, the symbolic use of objects and incidents presented with extraordinary physical accuracy, the cunning distillation of atmosphere, are the outstanding features of her stories which have something in common with those of Chekhov."

EXAM BASED QUESTIONS

1 **Which period in history was marked by sudden and expected ways of viewing and interacting the world?**
(a) Neo-Classical Age (b) Romantic Age
(c) Victorian Age (d) Modern Age

2 **Which of the following were prominent features of 20th century or modern age?**
(a) Suffragate movement
(b) Industrialisation capitalism
(c) Feminist movement
(d) All of the above

3 **Who among the following was part of the 'Imagist Movement'?**
(a) GB Shaw (b) GK Chesterton
(c) Ezra Pound (d) Katherine Mansfield

4 **Which of the following phrases best characterise the late 19th century aesthetic movement which widened the breach between artist and reading public?**
(a) Art for intellect's sake (b) Art for God's sake
(c) Art for the masses (d) Art for art's sake

5 **With which enormously influential perspective or practice in the early 20th century was thinker Sigmund Freud associated?**
(a) Phrenology (b) Anarchism
(c) Imagism (d) Psychoanalysis

6 **Which of the following is not associated with high modernism in the novel?**
(a) free indirect style (b) irresolute open endings
(c) the 'mythical methods' (d) narrative realism

7 **Which phrase indicates the interior flow of thought employed in High-modern literature?**
(a) Automatic writing (b) Confused daze
(c) Stream of consciousness (d) Free association

8 **Which novelists from the following proposed new ideas in novels and plays but followed Victorian traditions in their techniques?**
(a) HG Wells (b) Arnold Bennett
(c) Galsworthy (d) All of these

9 **Conrad's Almayer's Folly was published in the year**
(a) 1886 (b) 1895 (c) 1904 (d) 1908

10 **Which of the following novel by Conrad was published in 1907?**
(a) The Nigger of the Narcissus (b) Youth
(c) Heart of Darkness (d) The Secret Agent

11 **Which novel of Conrad is set in Congo?**
(a) Heart of Darkness (b) Youth
(c) The Secret Agent (d) Under Western Eyes

12 **The natives in the novel 'Heart of Darkness' are constantly described in terms of**
(a) animals (b) labourers
(c) insects (d) None of these

13 **Who is the protagonist of the story in the novel Heart of Darkness?**
(a) Aunt (b) Native (c) Marlow (d) Kurtz

14 **Which of the following is not a business prepostion offered to Jim in the novel 'Lord Jim'?**
(a) Guano collecting on the Walpole Reef
(b) Trading post manager in Patusan
(c) Tax collector in Batavia
(d) Water clerk for De-Jongh

15 **Who is known as the father of science fiction?**
(a) Rudyard Kipling (b) DH Lawrence
(c) HG Wells (d) Arnold Bennett

16 **Whose novel Time Machine is set in 802, 701 CE ?**
(a) Issac Asimov (b) HG Wells
(c) Somerset Maugham (d) Arnold Bennett

17 **What is the title of Well's 1897 short story about a man who finds a window into the planet Mars?**
(a) The Crystal Egg (b) The Magic Crystal
(c) The Martian Crystal (d) The Martian Egg

18 **In HG Wells 1896 novel 'The Island of Dr Moreau', what is the name of the evil doctor's assistant?**
(a) Igor (b) Ivan
(c) Montgomery (d) Mortimer

19 **In the novel 'The War of The Worlds' Earth is invaded by aliens from which place?**
(a) Jupiter (b) Mars
(c) The Moon (d) Venus

20 **HG Wells novel Kipps was based on his experiences as what?**
(a) Blacksmith (b) Carpenter
(c) Draper's assistant (d) Journalist

21 **Which event changes Mr Polly's life for the better even through for a short term in novel the History of Mr Polly?**
(a) His mother's death
(b) Friendship with fellow workers
(c) His father dies
(d) He wins a football match

22 What is the name of the future woman who be-friends Time traveller after he saves her life?
(a) Weena (b) Jane (c) Heidi (d) Judy

23 Which work of Arnold Bennett was made into a movie in 1952 starring Alec Guinness and Petula Clark?
(a) Leonara (b) The Card
(c) The Old Wives' Tale (d) The Honeymoon

24 British author Arnold Bennett is perhaps best known for which novel?
(a) The Magnificent Ambersons
(b) The Old Wives' Tales
(c) The Forsyte Saga
(d) The Go-Between

25 Which novelist of 20th century set up home at Trinity Hall Farm near Hockliffe?
(a) Laurie Lee (b) Wilkie Collins
(c) Arnold Bennett (d) George Orwell

26 At the beginning of 'Anna of the Five Towns' Anna's chief responsibility is
(a) maintaining family finances
(b) providing meals for the family
(c) saying daily prayers
(d) being mistress of the house and surrogate mother to her little sister Agnes

27 Which was Bennett's first novel to be published in 1898?
(a) A Great Man (b) The Man From The North
(c) The Grand Babylon Hotels
(d) The Card

28 Which English critic praised Arnold Bennett's works ?
(a) Matthew Arnold (b) John Priestly
(c) John Carey (d) None of these

29 Which novelist developed acquaintance with members of the Bloomsbury Group?
(a) James Joyce (b) Virginia Woolf
(c) Dorothy Richardson (d) HG Wells

30 Who among the following worked on the concept of 'Stream of Consciousness' ?
(a) T E Hulme (b) H G Wells
(c) Dorothy Richardson (d) Both 'a' and 'c'

31 What is the name of the Protagonist in her sequence of 13 novels 'Pilgrimage' by Dorothy Richardson ?
(a) Helen (b) Seneca (c) Miriam (d) Enna

32 In which year was Dorothy Richardson's novel 'Pilgrimage' published ?
(a) 1938 (b) 1925 (c) 1923 (d) 1937

33 Which of the following books did Gilbert Chesterton write in 1908?
(a) Heretics (b) The Defendant
(c) The Man who was Thursday (d) Twelve Types

34 When did GK Chesterton become a Catholic ?
(a) 1914 (b) 1922 (c) 1916 (d) 1918

35 Which character of a detective was Chesterton's creation?
(a) Sherlock Holmes (b) Hercule Poirot
(c) Albert Campion (d) Father Brown

36 Who was the French thief who was first antagonist of Brown and then became a detective ?
(a) Flambeau (b) Vidocq (c) Clouseau (d) Lupin

37 Complete this saying from Chesterton's work The Blue Cross . "The criminal is the creative artist , the detective only the"
(a) critic (b) friend (c) analyst (d) painter

38 Which novel's success led Somerset Maugham towards writing ?
(a) Mrs. Craddock (b) The Magician
(c) The Razor's Edge (d) Liza of Lambeth

39 Which work among the following does not belong to William Somerset Maugham ?
(a) A Man of Honour (b) Quality Street
(c) Salome (d) Both 'b' and 'c'

40 The year 1915 proved to be a crucial year for two important writers. Identify the the correct plan below .
(a) For Somerset Maugham's publication of human Bondage and DH Lawrence's The Rainbow
(b) For Rudyard Kipling and Em Forster, each for publishing his first novels
(c) For John Galsworthy for publishing The Man of Property and TS Eliot the Waste land
(d) For James Joyce's Finnegon's Wake and JB Priestly's The Good Companions

41 In which short story by Maugham a struggling author in Paris spends his whole monthly allowance taking a greedy woman for a meal at an expensive restaurant ?
(a) Miss King
(b) The Three Fat Women of Antibes
(c) Jane
(d) The Luncheon

42 A London governess received a reward when she returns an item of jewellery to its rightful owner. Name the story by Maugham.
(a) Louise (b) The String of Beads
(c) The Round Dozen (d) Mr Know-it -All

43 Who is the central character in 'Of Human Bondage'?
(a) Stephen Carey (b) Harry Carey
(c) Philip Carey (d) Drew Carey

44 In the novel 'The Magician' the character Oliver Haddo is based on which of the following?
(a) Oscar Wilde (b) Houdini
(c) Aleister Crowley (d) Merlin

45 Who is the main character of the novel 'The Razor's Edge'?
(a) Larry Darrel (b) Darryl Lawrence
(c) Houdini (d) TE Lawrence

46 When Somerset Maugham worked as a secret agent for the British Government, what was his code name ?
(a) Baskerville (b) Ashenden
(c) Rasputin (d) Somerville

47 Who out of following has been called the 'Edwardian Novelist' ?
(a) George Gissing (b) E M Forster
(c) Virginia Woolf (d) None of these

48 Forster is best known for his novel
(a) Howards End (b) The Longest Journey
(c) Where Angels Fear to Tread (d) Maurice

49 Which two countries EM Forster deals with in his novel ,'A Passage to India'?
(a) India and Australia (b) India and England
(c) India and Russia (d) India and China

50 Which novel of EM Forster is divided into three parts - mosque, caves and temple?
(a) Howards End (b) The Longest Journey
(c) A Passage to India (d) Maurice

51 Which of the following is an example of homosexual fiction ?
(a) The Well of Loneliness
(b) Maurice
(c) Orlando
(d) The Ballad of the Reading Goal

52 In the novel 'A Passage To India 'what is the main reason Aziz decides not to attend the Bridge Party?
(a) He feels sick
(b) It is his wife's death anniversary
(c) He wants to spend time with his children
(d) He is angry with Major Callendar

53 Whose birth are the Hindus (including Godbole) writing for in the novel 'A Passage to India''?
(a)Shree Krishna (b) Stella Moore's Baby
(c) Jesus (d) Adela's Baby

54 The motto 'Only Connect' is taken from
(a) Joseph Conrad's 'Nostromo'
(b) Rudyard Kipling's 'Kim'
(c) HG Well's 'the History of Mr. Polly'
(d) EM Forster's 'Howards End'

55 What happens to Kuno at the end of the story 'The Machine Stops' by EM Forster ?
(a) He becomes immortal (b) He defeats the machine
(c) He dies (d) He leaves the planet

56 In the story 'Other Kingdom 'what is Mr Beaumont's gift to his wife ?
(a) A kingdom of Elves (b) A necklace
(c) A collection of trees (d) A slave

57 Molly Bloom is a character in James Joyce's .
(a) A Portrait of the Artist as a Young Man
(b) Dubliners
(c) Ulysses (d) Exiles

58 The structure of Ulysses parallels which epic of Homer ?
(a) The Iliad
(b) The Odyssey
(c) Both a and b
(d) None of the above

59 Which public house featured in Ulysses is still allowed to sell drink ?
(a) Davy Byrne's pub (b) John's pub
(c) Both (a) and (b) (d) None of these

60 With whom is Stephen not identified in novel Ulysses ?
(a) Odysseus (b) Telemachus
(c) Hamlet (d) Shakespeare

61 In the novel 'A Portrait of the Artist as a Young Man' at Christmas dinner Stephen witnesses an argument between his father and John Carey on one side and
(a) Dante on the other
(b) His mother on the other side
(c) His brother on the other
(d) Uncle Charles on the other

62 The name 'Dedalus' makes allusion to
(a) the mythological figure who devours his own daughter to prolong his life
(b) The mythological figure who escaped from his island prison by constructing a pair of wings
(c) The mythological figure who solved the riddle of the sphinx
(d) The mythological figure who flew too close to the Sun.

63 'An Epiphany' as used by James Joyce is
(a) an Irish Catholic prayer
(b) a personal moment of clarity
(c) a sub-conscious desire
(d) an Irish marriage ritual

64 The title Araby refers to
(a) the main character's name
(b) a market
(c) the main character's nick name
(d) name of town where story is set

65 Which Irish national figure is celebrated in the novel 'Ivy Day in the Committee Room'?
(a) James Joyce (b) Bono
(c) Charles Stuart Parnell (d) Leopold Bloom

66 In the story 'A Little Cloud' by James Joyce what does the little chandler dream about becoming?
(a) A poet
(b) A newspaper reporter
(c) A legal copier
(d) A weather forecaster

67 **Which are three most experimenting novels of Woolf?**
(a) A Room of One's Own, Mrs. Dalloway, The Waves
(b) The Waves, To the Lighthouse, Mrs. Dalloway
(c) Orlando, A Room of One's Own, The Years
(d) The Waves, Jacob's Room, The Voyage Out

68 **Which was Virginia's last novel?**
(a) Mrs Dalloway (b) The Years
(c) Between the Acts (d) The Waves

69 **Which of the following works of Virginia consists of discussion of women's writing and its historical, economic and social underpinning?**
(a) Orlando (b) The years
(c) Night and Day (d) A Room of One's Own

70 **What event delayed the publication of the 'Voyage out'?**
(a) The Battle of Britain (b) World War I
(c) World War II (d) The Great Depression

71 **What happened to Virginia after completion of a novel?**
(a) She celebrated with champagne
(b) She called Leglton Strachy and boasted
(c) She fell into a deep depression
(d) She went on vacation

72 **The novel Mrs. Dalloway covers how much time?**
(a) One month from May to June
(b) One day from Morning to Night
(c) One year from June 1922
(d) One week from 14th June, 1923 to 20th June, 1923

73 **In which book of DH Lawrence 'Oedipus Complex' has been employed?**
(a) Women in Love (b) Sons and Lovers
(c) Lady Chatterley's Lover (d) The White Peacock

74 **Which novel by Lawrence was his first published novel?**
(a) Sons and Lovers (b) The Trespasser
(c) The White Peacock (d) The Rainbow

75 **What aspects of Lawrence's novels made them controversial during his life time?**
(a) Misogyny (b) Fascist politics
(c) Obscene Language (d) Frank Treatment of Sex

76 **Which of the following novels by DH Lawrence was/were banned during his life time?**
(a) Lady Chatterley's Lover (b) The Rainbow
(c) Sons and Lovers (d) Both (a) and (b)

77 **Who is Mrs. Morel's favourite child until he/she falls ill and dies in the novel Sons and Lovers.**
(a) Annie (b) William (c) Paul (d) Walter

78 **The novel Animal farm relates to what?**
(a) French Revolution
(b) Russian Revolution of 1917
(c) Dictatorship
(d) None of the above

79 **Elizabeth Bowen is best known for**
(a) Encounters (b) Anne Lee's
(c) The Death of Heart (d) The Hotel

80 **Identify the novel in which Aldous Huxley depicts a scientific Utopia of the Wellsian conception**
(a) Eyeless in Gaza (b) Brave New World
(c) Island (d) None of these

81 **The book .... does not belong to Aldous Huxley.**
(a) Time must have a stop (b) Kangaroo
(c) The Burning Wheel (d) Brave New World

82 **.............. believed in the international out look and he always valued personal relationship over everything.**
(a) TE Hulme (b) HG Wells
(c) EM Forster (d) George Gissing

83 **The novel Stamboul Train was written in .... by ....**
(a) 1924, Elizabeth Bowen (b) 1937, EM Forster
(c) 1930 Graham Greene (d) 1925 Aldous Huxley

84 **The concept of Oedipus Complex was introduced by ....**
(a) Aldous Huxley (b) George Orwell
(c) Virginia Woolf (d) DH Lawrence

85 **Virginia Woolf's 'To the Lighthouse' begins in a piece of dialogue "Yes, of course, if it's fine tomorrow", said Mr Ramsay. "But you'll have to be up with lark", she added.**
Present among the listeners of her remark is ....
(a) her father (b) her nephew
(c) her son (d) her driver

86 **The novel Pilgrimage has been written by ....**
(a) Virginia Woolf (b) Elizabeth Bowen
(c) Dorothy Richardson (d) George Orwell

87 **Major Scobie is a character in novel .... by Graham Greene.**
(a) A Sort of Life (b) The Heart of the Matter
(c) The End of the Affair (d) The White Peacock

88 **The stories written by .... were published in the Blue Review edited by John Middletown Murray.**
(a) Elizabeth Bowen
(b) Katherine Mansfield
(c) Dorothy Richardson (d) Graham Greene

89 **The book by .... George Orwell was published in 1945 on the heels of World War II.**
(a) Down and Out in Paris and London
(b) Burmese Days
(c) Animal Farm
(d) None of the above

90 Stella Rodney is an upper class Irish woman in Elizabeth Bowen's novel ....
(a) The Heat of the Day
(b) Encounters
(c) Eva Trout or Changing Scenes
(d) The Death of the Heart

91 Which of the following statements is incorrect about HG Wells?
(a) H G Wells was born in 1866.
(b) He has presented society with different outlook in his works like 'Tono Bungay'.
(c) His works included 'The Man of Property'.
(d) He died in 1946.

92 Which of the following statements about 'EM Forster' is incorrect?
(a) Forster was born in 1879
(b) He belonged to the Edwardian Period (1901-1910)
(c) He wrote for common people and did not write for elite class
(d) His works include 'Autumn Sequel'

93 Which of the following statements is correct?
(a) The novel 'Lady Chatterley's Lover' by DH Lawrence was banned during his life time.
(b) The novel 'A Passage to India' was written by Graham Greene.
(c) Virginia Woolf did not suffer bouts of depression
(d) Joseph Conrad wrote 'Almayer's Folly' in 1900.

94 Which of the following statements about the novelists is incorrect?
(a) Dorothy Richardson used stream of consciousness technique.
(b) James Joyce's 'Ulysses' is a masterpiece.
(c) Arnold Bennett wrote 'Anna of the Five Towns' in 1908.
(d) Priest detective Father Brown was created by GK Chesterton.

95 Which of the following statements is correct?
(a) Joseph Conrad followed Impressionism.
(b) EM Forster was a follower of Liberalism.
(c) Burmese Days by Orwell presented disadvantages of being slave.
(d) 'The Death of The Heart' by Elizabeth Bowen won the James Tait Black Memorial Prize in 1969.

96 Which of the following statements about Mrs. Dalloway is incorrect?
(a) It was published in the year 1930.
(b) The action of the novels takes place in a single day.
(c) Main theme of the book is sanity and insanity, isolation and limits of communication.
(d) Clarissa is the protagonist of Mrs. Dalloway novel.

Directions (Q. Nos. 97-100) *In the questions given below are two statements labelled as Assertion (A) and Reason (R). In context of the two statements, which one of the following is correct?*

Codes
(a) A is true but R is false
(b) A is false but R is true
(c) Both A and R are true but R is not the correct explanation of A
(d) Both A and R are true and R is the correct explanation of A

97 **Assertion** (A) Surrealism was a 20th century literary and artistic movement.
Reason (R) It emerged in Paris as a direct result of the publication of Andre Breton's Manifesto.

98 **Assertion** (A) Avant garde is not considered to be the hall-mark of Modern literature.
Reason (R) It represents challenging the normative pushing the boundaries of the status quo and creating new artistic forms.

99 **Assertion** (A) EM Forster wrote for common people only and didn't write for elite class.
Reason (R) He always valued personal relationship over everything and it is reflected in his work.

100 **Assertion** (A) Virginia Woolf used stream of consciousness technique in her novels.
Reason (R) Virginia Woolf was extremely dissatisfied with Victorian novelists.

101 Stephen Dedalus is a fictional character associated with
1. A Portrait of the Artist as a Young Man
2. Sons and Lovers
3. Ulysses
4. The Heart of Darkness

The correct combination of the above fiction according to codes
(a) 1 and 2 (b) 1, 2 and 3 (c) 3 and 4 (d) 1 and 3

102 Consider the following statements
1. The Brave new world is a dystopian novel.
2. It was published in 1937.
3. The title of this novel derives from Miranda's speech is Shakespeare's the tempest.
4. The novel is set in rural London.

Which of the following statements given above is/are correct?
(a) 1 and 4 (b) 1 and 3
(c) 2 and 4 (d) only 1

103 What is common to the following works? Identify the correct description.
1. Ulysses 2. Mrs Dalloway
3. Pilgrimage 4. To the Light House

(a) All novels use stream of consciousness technique.
(b) All were published in the same year.
(c) All are examples of experimental fiction.
(d) All novelists of these work belong to Victorian period.

104 Consider the following statements about 'The Nigger of the Narcissus' ....

1. It is written by Joseph Conrad.
2. Conrad's Literary work influenced 20th century writers like TS Eliot, Graham Greene etc.
3. The novel has used stream of consciousness technique.
4. The novel was published in 1900.

Which of the statements given above are correct?

(a) 1 and 4 (b) 1 and 3 (c) 2 and 3 (d) 1 and 2

105 Consider the following statements
The novel 'Anna of the Five Towns' is

1. Written by Arnold Bennett in 1902.
2. The book was published after Arnold's death.
3. The book details the constrictions of provincial life among the self made business class.
4. The book has a setting of region called Barchestershire.

Which of the following statements given above is/are correct?

(a) Only 1
(b) 1, 3 and 4
(c) 1 and 3
(d) 2 and 4

106 Consider the following statements about GK Chesterton.

1. Chesterton worked as a columnist for the Daily News.
2. Chesterton wrote 30 novels and many short stories.
3. Chesterton's most enduring creation is priest detective Father-Brown.
4. Chesterton is more recognised as a poet.

Which of the following statements given above are correct?

(a) 1 and 2 (b) 2 and 3 (c) 1 and 3 (d) 1 and 4

107 Consider the following statements.

1. HG Wells is best known for his science fiction.
2. Arnold's main works are based on realism.
3. Forsters works were done with keeping in touch with the changing times.
4. Finnegan's wake by James Joyce is most incomprehensible work.

Which of the following statements are correct?

(a) 1,2 and 4 (b) 1, 3 and 4
(c) 2, 3 and 4 (d) 1 2, and 3

108 Consider the following works.

1. A Portrait of the Artist as a Young Man
2. To the Light House
3. The Waves
4. The Rainbow

Which of the following works are written by Virginia Woolf ?

(a) 1 and 2
(b) 3 and 1
(c) 2 and 3
(d) 2 and 4

109 Which of the following pairs is incorrectly matched?

(a) Joseph Conrad : Heart of Darkness
(b) Thomas Hardy : The Jungle Book
(c) Rudyard Kipling : Kim
(d) HG Wells : The Time Machine

110 Which of the following pairs is incorrectly matched?

(a) Somerset Maugham : Liza of Lambeth
(b) GK Chesterton : The Napoleon of Notting Hill
(c) James Joyce : Mrs. Dalloway
(d) Elizabeth Bowen : The Hotel

111 Which of the following pairs is correctly matched?

(a) DH Lawrence : The Power and the Glory
(b) Virginia Woolf : Mrs Dalloway
(c) James Joyce : Sons and Lovers
(d) Graham Greene : Ulysses

112 Which of the following pairs is incorrectly matched?

(a) Graham Greene : Brighton Rock
(b) Aldous Huxley : Brave New World
(c) Ronald Firbank : Caprince
(d) D H Lawrence : Animal Farm

113 Which of the following pairs is correctly matched?

(a) Graham Greene : Eva Tront
(b) Max Berbohm : The Power and the Glory
(c) George Orwell : Animal Farm
(d) Elizabeth Bowen : A Christmas Garland

114 In the given series which one has all the modern age novelists matched correctly with their year of birth?

(a) DH Lawrence 1894, Graham Greene-1899, Elizabeth Bowen 1885, Aldous Huxley 1883
(b) DH Lawrence 1885, Graham Greene 1904, Elizabeth Bowen-1899, Aldous Huxley 1894
(c) DH Lawrence 1899, Graham Greene 1904, Elizabeth Bowen 1883, Aldous Huxley 1894
(d) DH Lawrence 1883, Graham Greene 1883 Elizabeth Bowen 1894, Aldous Huxley 1885

115 In the following series which set of authors and works is correctly matched?

(a) E M Forster- A Passage to India ; Samuel Butler Odyssey ; D H Lawrence- The Rainbow ; James Joyce Dubliners
(b) E M Forster-The Rainbow- Samuel Butler-A Passage to India ; D H Lawrence- Odyssey ; James Joyce-Dubliners

(c) E M Forster- A Passage to India ; Samuel Butter Dubliners ; DH Lawrence-The Rainbow ; James Joyce-Odyssey
(d) EM Forster-Dubliners ; Samuel Butler-The Rainbow ; DH Lawrence-Odyssey -James Joyce-A Passage to India

116 Which of the following authors as per their death are in chronological order?
(a) DH Lawrence, Virginia Woolf, Graham Greene, H G Well
(b) Louis Macneice, T E Hulme, H G Well, Virginia Woolf
(c) Virginia Woolf, T E Hulme, Louis Macneice, H G Well
(d) DH Lawrence, Virginia Woolf, H G Well, Graham Greene

117 Which of the following works are in their chronological order as per their publication?
(a) Bliss, Mrs. Dalloway, Brave New World, Sons and Lovers.
(b) Mrs. Dalloway, Brave New World, Bliss, Sons and Lovers.
(c) Sons and Lovers, Bliss, Mrs. Dalloway, Brave New World.
(d) Sons and Lovers, Mrs. Dalloway, Brave New World, Bliss.

118 Which of the following is in correct sequence of Virginia Woolf's works?
(a) To the Light House, The Years, Orlando, Night and Day
(b) Night and Day, To the Light House, Orlando, The Years
(c) Orlando, The Years, Night and Day, To the Light House
(d) Orlando, To the Light House, The Years, Night and Day

119 Which of these movements is in correct sequential order?
(a) Imagism, Dadaism, Surrealism
(b) Surrealism, Dadaism, Imagism
(c) Dadaism, Surrealism, Imagism
(d) Imagism, Surrealism, Dadaism

120 Which of these novels is in correct chronological order?
(a) Where Angels Fear to Tread, Time Machine, The Power and Glory, The Napoleon of Notting Hill
(b) The Napoleon of Notting Hill, Time Machine, The Power and Glory, Where Angels Fear to Tread
(c) Time Machine, The Power and Glory, Where Angels Fear to Tread, The Napoleon of Notting Hill
(d) Time Machine, The Napoleon of Notting Hill, Where Angels Fear to Tread, The Power and Glory

121 The extract "The Conquest of the Earth, which mostly means taking it away from those, who have different complexion or slightly flatter noses than ourselves, is not a pretty thing, when you look at yourself too much" .... has been taken from which work of Conrad?
(a) Heart of Darkness (b) The Secret Agent
(c) Under Western Eyes (d) An Outpost of Progress

122 "She walked rapidly in the June Sunlight towards the worst horror of all". These are the conclusive words of the novel
(a) Free Fall
(b) The Last Enemy
(c) Brighton Rock
(d) None of the above

123 The group was linked by what Clive Bell called, "a taste for discussion in pursuit of truth and a contempt for conventional ways of thinking and feeling, contempt for conventional morals if you will."
Which group is being talked about in the above statement?
(a) Auden Generation (b) Bloomsbury Group
(c) Theatre of the Absurd (d) Pylon Poets

124 "He did not care if she was heartless, vicious or vulgar, stupid and grasping, he loved her. He would rather have misery with one than happiness with the other."
These words have been taken from which novel of Somerset Maugham?
(a) The Moon and Six Pence (b) Cakes and Ale
(c) Of Human Bondage (d) The Razor's Edge

125 "I always find it more difficult to say the things I mean than the things I didn't".
These words have been taken from which novel by which author?
(a) 'The Painted Veil' by Somerset Maugham
(b) 'A Passage to India' by EM Forster
(c) 'Ulysses' by James Joyce
(d) 'The Hotel' by Elizabeth Bowen

126 Which author or novelist said, "Literature is a luxury, fiction is a necessity"?
(a) GB Shaw (b) Elizabeth Bowen
(c) GK Chesterton (d) Doris Richardson

127 In which novel of Orwell, do this extract occur, "Flory's main grievance in Burma is his excessive loneliness. This loneliness is ever present and unyielding and he feels it acutely everyday .... ".
(a) Animal Farm
(b) Down and Out in Paris and London
(c) Burmese Days
(d) None of the above

128 "What can you do if you are thirty and turning the corner of your own street, you are overcome, suddenly by a feeling of bliss-absolutely bliss-as though you'd suddenly swallowed a bright piece of that late afternoon Sun ....".
From which work of Katherine Mansfield this extract has been taken?
(a) The Garden Party (b) The Doll's House
(c) A Cup of Tea (d) The Bliss

129 From which novel of Arnold Bennett have these lines been taken?
"The Foundation of England's greatness is that Englishmen hate to look fools."
(a) The Man from the North (b) Anna of Five Towns
(c) Clay Hanger (d) The Card

130 "Good clothes, when put to the test, survive a change in fortune as a Roman arch survives the luxury of departed empire."
This is an extract from which work by Arnold Bennett?
(a) Clay Hanger (b) The Card
(c) These Twain (d) The Old Wives Tale

131 "It isn't possible to love and part you will wish that it was you can transmute love, ignoare it, muddle it, but you can never pull it out of your."
From which work of EM Forster this extract has been taken?
(a) A Passage To India (b) The Longest Journey
(c) A Room with a View (d) Howard's End

132 "One by one they were all becoming shades. Better pass boldly into that other world in the full glory of some passion, than fade and wither dismally with age."
In which collection of short story by James Joyce does this extract occur?
(a) Chamber Music (b) Dubliners
(c) Ulysses (d) Exiles

133 Who said this about James Joyce's Ulysses?
"The work of a queasy Undergraduate scratching his pimples"?
(a) Alfred Tennyson (b) Virginia Woolf
(c) TS Eilot (d) Nicole Krauss

134 Which character in Mrs. Dalloway by Virginia Woolf speaks these words?
"For heaven only knows why one loves it so how one sees it so. Making it up, building it round one, Tumbling it, creating every moment a fresh."
(a) Peter Walsh (b) Richard
(c) Clarissa (d) Clarissa's Mother

135 These both characters feel loneliness, have break roses and love Shakespeare. Name the characters from Mrs. Dalloway.
(a) Peter Walsh and Clarissa
(b) Clarissa and Sally Seton
(c) Clarissa and Richard
(d) Clarissa and Septimus Warren Smith

136 In which work of Virginia Woolf, these lines can be read?
"There was a star riding through clouds one night and I said to the star, consume me."
(a) The Waves (b) Jacob's Room
(c) Mrs. Dalloway (d) Orlando

137 Which character in Sons and Lovers by DH Lawrence makes this statement?
"I don't think I love you as a man ought to love his wife."
(a) Mrs. Morel (b) Narrator (c) Miriam (d) Paul Morel

138 Who said these words in Sons and Lovers?
"Yes (...........) the Photograph of Louie is very striking and I can see she must be attractive ....".
(a) Mrs. Morel (b) Narrator (c) Clara (d) William

139 From which novel by DH Lawrence these lines have been taken
"We've got to live, no matter how many skies have fallen."
(a) The Rainbow (b) The Tresspasser
(c) Lady Chalterley's Lover (d) Women in love

140 "She walked about with the rather fated expression you see in photographs of girls who have subsequently been murdered, but nothing had so far happened to her."
In which work of Elizabeth Bowen have these lines been taken?
(a) The Heat of the Day (b) Friends and Relations
(c) The Hotel (d) The Death of the Heart

141 The novels of Dorothy Richardson were reviewed in a literary Magazine. What was the name of the Magazine?
(a) The Times (b) The Egoist
(c) The Weekly (d) The Guardian

142 In which of the following work by Somerset Maugham the character Isabel Bradley appears.
(a) Liza of Lambeth (b) The Painted Veil
(c) The Magician (d) The Razor's Edge

143 In the novel the Razor's Edge by Somerset Maugham what is the most important thing for Elliott Templeton.
(a) to marry Isabe (b) to find the inner meaning
(c) to be practical
(d) to love his money and positon

144 "Life never gives us what we want at the moment that the we consider appropriate. Adventures do occur, but not punctuality."
In which work of EM forster this extract has been taken
(a) The Longest Journey
(b) Where Angels Fear to Tread
(c) A Room With a View (d) A Passage to India

145 "She was my wife. You are the first English man she has ever come before. Now put her photo graph away."
Which character in A Passage to India Speaks these words?
(a) The Narrator (b) Cyril Fielding
(c) Dr. Ariz (d) Atelier

Directions (Q. Nos. 146-150) *Read the passage given below and answer the questions that follow.*

'Now they have all gone,' said Louis. 'I am alone. They have gone into the house for breakfast, and I am left standing by the wall among the flowers. It is very early, before lessons. Flower after flower is specked on the depths of green. The petals are harlequins. Stalks rise from the black hollows beneath. The flowers swim like fish made of light upon the dark, green waters. I hold a stalk in my hand. I am the stalk. My roots go down to the depths of the world, through earth dry with brick, and damp earth, through veins of lead and silver. I am all fibre. All tremors shake me, and the weight of the earth is pressed to my ribs. Up here my eyes are green leaves, unseeing. I am a boy in grey flannels with a belt fastened by a brass snake up here. Down there my eyes are the lidless eyes of a stone figure in a desert by the Nile. I see women passing with red pitchers to the river; I see camels swaying and men in turbans. I hear tramplings, tremblings, stirrings round me'

"Up here Bernard, Neville, Jinny and Susan (but not Rhoda) skim the flower-beds with their nets. They skim the butterflies from the nodding tops of the flowers. They brush the surface of the world. Their nets are full of fluttering wings. "Louis! Louis! Louis!" they shout. But they cannot see me. I am on the other side of the hedge. There are only little eye-holes among the leaves."

146 The characters Bernard, Neville, Jinny and Susan belong to which novel of Virginia Woolf?
(a) Mrs. Dalloway (b) Jacob's Room
(c) The Waves (d) To the Lighthouse

147 Who cannot be seen?
(a) Bernard (b) Louis
(c) Neville (d) Jinny

148 What does fluttering wings imply?
(a) Butterflies (b) Birds (c) Flowers (d) Net

149 Which place does Rhoda travel after break up with Louis?
(a) India (b) Spain (c) The Opera (d) London

150 What is the major theme of this novel 'The Waves'?
(a) Childhood is the best time
(b) Life's fertility
(c) Transition to inner reality
(d) Death of all characters as they reach adulthood

PREVIOUS YEARS' QUESTIONS

December 2018

1 Match the characters with the work.

Characters	Works
A. Rupert Birkin	1. Sons and Lovers
B. Lydia Lensky	2. Kangaroo
C. Miriam Leivers	3. Women in Love
D. Richard Somers	4. The Rainbow

Codes

	A	B	C	D		A	B	C	D
(a)	1	2	3	4	(b)	3	4	1	2
(c)	2	3	4	1	(d)	4	1	2	3

2 In this novel by Graham Greene, a double agent uses classic works of fiction to encode secret information. "He put Clarissa Harlowe back in the bookcase" is the first clue to his teachery. Then he draws on war and peace and the way we live now as matrices for secretly transmitting information. Identify the novel
(a) The Man Within
(b) Our Man In Havana
(c) The Human Factor
(d) The Confidential Agent

July 2018

3 How does women in Love open?
(a) Rupert Birkin, Lawrence's alter Ego is talking a walk in the English Countryside
(b) The Brangwean sisters, Ursula, and Gudrun, are 'working and taking'
(c) The wedding party gathers at short lands, the criches's home
(d) The last lesson is in progress, "peaceful and still" in Ursula's classroom

November 2017

4 Which of the following lines, by Shakespeare is repeated several times in Virginia Woolf's novel Mrs Dalloway?
(a) "If music be the food of love; play on"
(b) "Fear no more the heat of the sun, nor the furious winter's rages"
(c) "Those are pearls that were his eyes"
(d) "There is a tide in the affairs of man"

5 In Women in Love what is winifred's pekingese dog called?
(a) Bismarck (b) Looloo (c) Lucky (d) Buddy

6 Year before Winton Smith, the protagonist of George Orwell's dystopia, Nineteen-Eighty-Four, got an evidence of the party's dishonesty. What is it?

(a) Emmanuel Goldstein's confession that he is the party operative; not an enemy of the party
(b) O Brien's diary entry hinting at the non-existence of Big Brother
(c) A photograph, which proves that some citizen accused of a crime was out of the country while it was committed
(d) A colleague's revelation that the inner party members have systematically destroyed all historical documents and created false documents.

7 Why does Father Dolan Punish Stephen with the pandybat in Joyce's "Portrait of the Artist as a young Man"?

(a) Stephen is talking to another student to get the answer to a Latin problem
(b) Stephen is not doing his work because his glasses one broken
(c) Stephen is looking out of the window towards the infirmary
(d) Stephen is lost in remembering his mother's farewell and can not hear father Dolan Calling him out

8 Identify the story for which EM Forster wrote the libretto for its opera version.

(a) Heart of Darkness
(b) The Man who would be king
(c) Billy Budd
(d) Death in Venice

9 Which novel by Joseph Conrad presents a young captain who like Coleridge's Ancient Mariner is haunted by the "Vision of a ship drifting in calm and swinging in light airs, with all the crew dying slowly about her decks" and who feels." The sickness of my soul ...... the weight of my sins ...... my sense of unworthiness"?

(a) Under Western Eyes (b) The Shadow Line
(c) Victory (d) The Rescue

January 2017

10 Virginia Woolf's 'To The Light House' has a tripartite structure. The three parts are named the following except

(a) The Sky (b) The Window
(c) Time Passes (d) The Light house

11 In Ulysses, Leopard Bloom works for a Dublin

(a) bar (b) park
(c) newspaper (d) bank

12 "Most blameless is he, centered in the sphere of common duties, decent not to fail in offices of tenderness ...."
In these lines from Ulysses, what does Ulysses suggest about Telemachus?

(a) he shows heroic qualities
(b) he is patient and selfless
(c) he is very much like his father
(d) he may be too tender-hearted to be king

13 The novel 'Maurice' by EM Forster appeared posthumously in 1971. It had a homosexual theme, so forster considered its subject matter too indelicate for publication during his life time. It was influenced by a writer who was a socialist and open homosexual. Identify the writer

(a) Oscar Wilde (b) Edward Carpenter
(c) W. H. Auden (d) EF Benson

14 DH Lawrence's 1926 novel 'The Plumed Serpent' is set in which country?

(a) Egypt (b) South Africa
(c) Mexico (d) Peru

July 2016

15 Who narrates 'Heart of Darkness'?

(a) Marlow (b) Director of Companies
(c) Kurtz (d) An Unnamed Narrator

16 When was the English ban of James Joyce's Ulysses lifted?

(a) 1924 (b) 1945
(c) 1936 (d) 1962

17 Which one of Joseph Conrad's novels expresses the contrast between the solidarity of shipboard life and the profound underlying loneliness of existence Thus "Loneliness impenetrable and transparent, elusive and ever lasting... that surrounds, envelops, clothes every human soul form the cradle to the grave and perhaps beyond?

(a) The Heart of Darkness
(b) The Nigger of Narcissus
(c) Lord Jim
(d) Nostroms

December 2015

18 A remarkable novelist of the English moderest phase who wrote a short book on what the novel is (and why it matters) remarked," Oh dear yes-the novel tells a story" Identify the novelist.

(a) Virginia Woolf
(b) James Joyce
(c) EM Forster
(d) DH Lawrence

19 Virginia Woolf's "To the Light House begins in a piece of dialogue.

"Yes, of course, it is fine tomorrow", said Mrs. Ramsay
"But you'll have to be up with lark", she added.
Present among the listeners of her remark is ....

(a) her father (b) her nephew
(c) her son (d) her driver

20 Her vision was of several caves. She saw herself in one and she was also outside it, watching its entrance, for Aziz to pass in. She failed to locate him. It was the doubt that had often visited her but solid and attractive, like the hills, "I am not" — speech was more difficult than vision. "I am not quite sure".
The above extract from A Passage To India is about Adela's cave experience. Who is questioning Adela?
(a) Mrs Moore (b) Mr Mc Bryde
(c) Fielding (d) Ronney Heaslop

21 Which of these works in 19th Century Russian fiction originated the type of a Superfluous Man?
(a) The Diary of Superfluous Man
(b) A Hero of Our Own Times
(c) Eugene Onegin
(d) Dead Souls

22 Which of the following novels of Joseph Conrad is set in Malay?
(a) Nigger of the Narcissus (b) Lord Jim
(c) Nostromo (d) Heart of Darkness

23 "Yet it is the masculine values that prevail, "observes a famous writer 'speaking cruelly', she continued, 'football and sport are 'important', the worship of fashion, the buying of clothes 'trivial'. Name the author and the text
(a) Mary Wollstonecraft : A Vindication of the Rights of woman
(b) Audre Lorde, "Age, Race, class......"
(c) Virginia Woolf, "A Room of one's own"
(d) Jean Rhys, "After Leaving Mr Mackenzie"

December 2014

24 The first novel written by Graham Greene is
(a) Stambour Train (b) England Made Me
(c) The Heart of the Matter (d) The Man With In

June 2014

25 Which among the following was not written in 1922?
(a) Ulysses (b) Jacob's room
(c) Aaron's Rod (d) A Passage to India

26 DH Lawrence popularised the concept of .... in the novels
(a) realism (b) naturalism
(c) primitivism (d) expressionism

27 In which of the following novels by Conrad do the Gould couple and Decoud appear as characters with Costaguana as the setting?
(a) Victory
(b) Under Western Eyes
(c) Nostromo
(d) The Nigger of the Narcissus

28 In which novel of Virginia Woolf does painter in the act of painting actually figure as a character?
(a) the voyage out (b) the British Empire
(c) Jacob's Room (d) To the Light house

29 The Roman a clef (French for novel with a key) uses contemparary historical figures as its chief character. They are of course given fictional names. One example in Aldous Huxley's 'Point Counter Point'. Its Mark Rampion is modelled on ....
(a) DH Lawrence (b) E M Forster
(c) Wyndham Lewis (d) Arnold Bennett

December 2013

30 Leopold Bloom in Ulysses is
(a) a Great War Veteran
(b) a Dublin bar owner
(c) a Jewish advertising agent
(d) an Irish nationalist

31 Match the following.

	List I (Novels)		List II (Last Line)
A.	Lord Jim	1.	It was done, it was finished yes she through laying down her brush in extreme fatigue. I have had my vision.
B.	To The Light House	2.	April 27 old father, old Artificer, stand me now and ever in good stead
C.	A Passage to India	3.	He feels himself and says often that he is "preparing to leave all this; preparing to leave; while he waves his hand sadly at his butterflies
D.	A Portrait of the artist as a Young Man	4.	'No, Not yet' and the sky said, "No, not there".

Codes

	A	B	C	D		A	B	C	D
(a)	2	4	3	1	(b)	3	2	4	1
(c)	3	1	4	2	(d)	2	3	1	4

32 Which novel of Graham Greene in the following list does not end in some form of suicide by the Protagonist?
(a) The Heart of the Matter (b) England made me
(c) Brighton Rock (d) The Power and the Glory

33 Identify from among the following false statements.
1. Eric Arthur Blair became the famous British novelist George Orwell
2. Orwell was conversant in Hindustani and ford of Indian ford.
3. Young Eric Blair lived in Myanmar's trading town, Katha.
4. This town gave him the model for fictional district of Kyauktada in Burmese days.

Codes
(a) 2 and 4 (b) Only 1 (c) Only 3 (d) All of these

34 Virginia Woolf borrowed the idea of the common reader from Dr Johnson. To which particular work of Johnson's does she remain indebted?
(a) The lives of the Most Eminent English poet; the essay on Milton
(b) The lives of the most eminent English poets; the essay on Gray
(c) Preface to Shakespeare
(d) The Patriol

35 E M Forster's Passage to India begins with a description of the city of Chandrapana. It has an old Indian part and a new part consisting of the British Civil station. Which of the following description of the city is not found in the text.
(a) The streets are mean; the temples in effective
(b) It is a city of gardens
(c) It is a tropical pleasuance washed by a noble river
(d) The new civil station is not sensibly planned and not modern.

June 2013

36 At the end of 'Sons and Lovers', Paul Morel
(a) Sets off in quest of life away from his mother
(b) Considers the option of committing suicide
(c) Joins his elder brother William in London
(d) Embraces a Schoparhauer like Nihilism

37 The book was for many years banned for obscenity in Britain and the US The Central Character is a Catholic Jew in Ireland. The author claimed that the book is meant to make you laugh. Name the book
(a) The Picture of Dorien Gray (b) Herzog
(c) Portnoy's Complaint (d) Ulysses

38 In EM Forster's A passage to India, some of the major symbols are associated with
1. Mountains 2. Tigers
3. Echoes 4. Clouds
Codes
(a) 1 and 2 (b) 1, 2 and 4 (c) 1 and 3 (d) 2 and 4

ANSWERS

Objective Questions

1 *(d)*	2 *(d)*	3 *(c)*	4 *(d)*	5 *(d)*	6 *(d)*	7 *(c)*	8 *(d)*	9 *(b)*	10 *(d)*
11 *(a)*	12 *(a)*	13 *(c)*	14 *(c)*	15 *(c)*	16 *(b)*	17 *(a)*	18 *(c)*	19 *(b)*	20 *(c)*
21 *(c)*	22 *(a)*	23 *(b)*	24 *(b)*	25 *(c)*	26 *(d)*	27 *(b)*	28 *(c)*	29 *(c)*	30 *(d)*
31 *(c)*	32 *(a)*	33 *(c)*	34 *(b)*	35 *(d)*	36 *(a)*	37 *(a)*	38 *(d)*	39 *(d)*	40 *(a)*
41 *(d)*	42 *(b)*	43 *(c)*	44 *(c)*	45 *(a)*	46 *(d)*	47 *(b)*	48 *(a)*	49 *(b)*	50 *(c)*
51 *(b)*	52 *(b)*	53 *(a)*	54 *(d)*	55 *(c)*	56 *(c)*	57 *(c)*	58 *(b)*	59 *(a)*	60 *(d)*
61 *(a)*	62 *(b)*	63 *(b)*	64 *(b)*	65 *(c)*	66 *(a)*	67 *(b)*	68 *(c)*	69 *(d)*	70 *(b)*
71 *(c)*	72 *(b)*	73 *(b)*	74 *(c)*	75 *(d)*	76 *(a)*	77 *(b)*	78 *(b)*	79 *(c)*	80 *(b)*
81 *(b)*	82 *(c)*	83 *(d)*	84 *(d)*	85 *(c)*	86 *(c)*	87 *(b)*	88 *(b)*	89 *(c)*	90 *(a)*
91 *(c)*	92 *(d)*	93 *(a)*	94 *(c)*	95 *(b)*	96 *(a)*	97 *(d)*	98 *(b)*	99 *(c)*	100 *(c)*
101 *(d)*	102 *(b)*	103 *(a)*	104 *(d)*	105 *(c)*	106 *(c)*	107 *(b)*	108 *(c)*	109 *(b)*	110 *(c)*
111 *(b)*	112 *(d)*	113 *(c)*	114 *(b)*	115 *(a)*	116 *(d)*	117 *(c)*	118 *(b)*	119 *(a)*	120 *(d)*
121 *(a)*	122 *(c)*	123 *(b)*	124 *(c)*	125 *(a)*	126 *(c)*	127 *(c)*	128 *(d)*	129 *(b)*	130 *(d)*
131 *(c)*	132 *(b)*	133 *(b)*	134 *(c)*	135 *(d)*	136 *(a)*	137 *(d)*	138 *(a)*	139 *(c)*	140 *(d)*
141 *(b)*	142 *(d)*	143 *(d)*	144 *(c)*	145 *(c)*	146 *(c)*	147 *(b)*	148 *(a)*	149 *(b)*	150 *(d)*

Pervious Years' Questions

1 *(b)*	2 *(c)*	3 *(b)*	4 *(b)*	5 *(b)*	6 *(c)*	7 *(b)*	8 *(c)*	9 *(b)*	10 *(a)*
11 *(b)*	12 *(b)*	13 *(b)*	14 *(c)*	15 *(d)*	16 *(b)*	17 *()*	18 *(c)*	19 *(c)*	20 *(b)*
21 *(c)*	22 *(b)*	23 *(c)*	24 *(d)*	25 *(d)*	26 *(c)*	27 *(c)*	28 *(d)*	29 *(a)*	30 *(c)*
31 *(c)*	32 *(b)*	33 *(d)*	34 *(b)*	35 *(d)*	36 *(a)*	37 *(d)*	38 *(c)*		

Contemporary Period (Post 1945)

The period refers to the time after World War II. In Literature of this period, the writers expressed their discontent with traditional English Society in their works. Post modernism shows a new cultural atmosphere where writer has to make a choice between tradition and experimentation.

Introduction: Contemporary Period

The period after World War II was that of devastation, hopelessness and multitudes of problems of 'displaced persons'. There were millions of displaced persons some had fled willingly, others were deported as undesirable minorities. The Allies did what they could to feed and house the refugees and to reunite families that had been forcibly torn apart but the obstacles were enormous. Most of the countries were in ruins, fields, forests and vineyard were ripped to pieces. Apart from US and Allies such as Canada and Australia, the European powers such as Britain and France had precious little to spare. Britain had largely bankrupted itself fighting the war. Pestilence, war, famine and death-so familiar during the Middle Ages-appeared again in the modern world. War also acted as an agent to accelerate the weakening of European Empire. In many countries social change also sped up with the help of science and technology.

The shared suffering and sacrifice of the war years strengthened the belief in most democracies that government had an obligation to provide basic care for all citizens. The Labour Government in Britain moved rapidly to establish a welfare state. Established political orders-fascist and conservative came under challenge as people looked for new ideas and leaders.

Contemporary English Literature

Literature in the United Kingdom after World War II cannot be generalised under any specific genre. The only clear group is the Angry Young Men, a group of dramatists and novelistists who in the 1950s expressed their discontent with traditional English society in anti-establishment works that have also been described as 'Kitchen Sink Realism'.

In this Chapter

When we talk about contemporary literature and the start date of this label, we have to acknowledge World War II and the surrounding events. The horrors of the war, including bombs, ground wars, genocide and corruption, are the pathways to this type of literature. It is from these real-life themes that we find the beginning of a new period of writing.

Working of contemporary literature reflects a society's social and/or political viewpoints, shown through realistic characters, connections to current events and socio-economic messages. The writers are looking for trends that illuminate societal strengths and weaknesses to remind society of lessons they should learn and questions they should ask. The idea of utopian existence and ideals of modernism were left far behind. Most of the literature in this period is not escapist in nature.

So when we think of contemporary literature, we cannot simply look at a few themes or settings. Since society changes over time, so do the content and messages of this writing.

According to Dr Valerie Morrison, while the modern writer "focused on the objects of his or her culture, contemporary writers and artists are more intent on describing people's emotional states". Contemporary writers believe in lack of order or prevalence of chaos as a defining characteristic of the present world.

Some characteristics of contemporary literature are

- Lack of resolution.
- Focus on the personal, rather than the social.
- Cynicism about the role of art and literature.
- Realistic settings.
- Subversion of traditional gender roles.
- A blurring line between the natural and the artificial/constructed.
- Lack of any possibility for a greater action.

Novel Writing in Contemporary Period

After 1945 when novelists faced the task of explaining the new historical reality and the position of individuals in the post-war order, most novelists realised that this entailed making a choice between traditional literary models and experimental modernist models.

Post modernism or contemporary was born out of this dilemma. Post-modernism can thus said to be a new cultural atmosphere in which the writer is inevitably aware of this open choice between tradition and experimentation. Post-war novelists cannot escape the shadow of either Modernism or Victorianism, so some produced a synthesis which is the real characteristic of post modernistic novel writing. But this synthesis was slow to come.

In the period between 1945-1953, a nostalgic look at the lost pre-war past was combined with a look at the new-reality faced by generation growing up in the 1940s often in provincial surroundings.

In early 1950 brought a new interest in the present possibly as a reaction against the nostalgic backward look at an essentially phoney world from which many, mostly lower middle and working classes, were excluded. In these novels, the margins of culture moved to the centre, expressing, a generalised discontent which was paralleled in the plays of Angry Young Men and also in some poetical works.

Novelists of this period are too many we will discuss them and their works one by one.

Major Contemporary Writers

Charles Percy Snow (1905-1980)

Charles Percy Snow was born on 15th October, 1905 at Leicestershire, England. He graduated from Leicester University and earned a doctorate in physics at the University of Cambridge, where at the age of 25, he became a fellow of Christ's College. After working at Cambridge in molecular physics for some 20 years, he became a University Administrator and with the outbreak of World War II he became a scientific adviser to the British Government. He was Knighted in 1957 and made a Life Peer in 1964. He died in 1980.

Literary Career and Works

In the 1930s Snow began the two volume novel sequence collectively called *Strangers and Brothers* about the academic; public and private life of an Englishman named Lewis Eliot. The novels are a quiet and meticulous analysis of bureaucratic man and the corrupting influence of power. Snow had remained in the public eye through his fiction, book criticism for the Sunday Times and thoughtful pieces for a variety of intellectual weeklies.

His works include his novels: *Stranger and Brothers* (1940), *Time of Hope* (1949), *The Masters* (1951), *The New Men* (1954), *The Conscience of the Rich* (1958) and *Corridores of Power* (1964), *Sleep of Reason* (1968), *The Malcontents* (1972), *In Their Wisdom* (1974), and *A Coat of Varnish* (1978).

His scientific studies and his career in science and technology guided him to praise their qualities and regret the lack of contact between the art and the modern technological age. He put his views in the 1959 Rede Lecture *The Two Cultures* and *The Scientific Revolution*, which irritated FR Leavis to deliver the Richmond Lecture of 1962 in opposition. Snow also described through his novels policy making, governmental decisions, middle class attitudes and the needs of establishment.

As a novelist Snow will be remembered largely for his *Strangers and Brothers Cycle, Its Flat Style, Mirroring its Narrator,* who observed from the inside English society and politics from the World War Ist to Suez.

Evelym Waugh (1903-1966)

Evelym Waugh, his full name; Evelym Arthur St John Waugh, was born on 28th October, 1903 in London. He is regarded as the most brilliant Satirical novelist of his day, Waugh was educated at Lancing College, Sussex and at Hertford College, Oxford.

Literary Career and Works

After short periods as an art student and school master, he devoted himself to solitary observant travel and to the writing of novels.

His main characters in his novels were snobs. One of their main sins was rudeness. His heroes were virtuous, but simple young men, who suffered perplexity and hardship because they were unable to understand many exponents of vice. He treated everything with a lack of seriousness. He did not show any anger at the injustice, which perplexed his characters. His novels were full of merry incidents, gently boiling dialogues by which he ridiculed the class to which he belonged.

Major Works

- **Black Mischief** This novel was written in 1932. It is set in the tattering African Kingdom of Azania.
- **A Handfull of Dust** (1934) This novel explores the painful collapse of the illusions and complacencies of a rural feudalism, represented by Tony Last and exposes the surface values.
- It's cynicism of the thoroughly modern and essentially metropolitan *Bright Young Things*.
- **The Loved One** This novel was written in 1948. It presents his growing seriousness and disillusionment. It is a wild satire on American funeral customs and two-faced wealthy society of that country.
- **Brideshead Revisited** (1945) Waugh had Army experiences. He converted his religion to Roman Catholicism. On account of these two reasons, his later novels had a new feeling of concern. They had wit and scornful comment. In spite on its foolishness, the world had been more joyous and less harmful than the present. The characters were drawn with understanding and developed skillfully. The structure is carefully planned and complex. Charles Ryder is the Narrator and Protagonist in the play.
- **Sword of Honour** (1961) This book contains three novels, *Men at Arms* (1952), *Officers and Gentlemen* (1955) and *Unconditional Surrender* (1961). In these novels, his style is the best.
- They treated the loss of ideals as men were facing war and accompanying views as cruelty, confusion, cynicism and unworthiness. He did not believe in himself or in his class in post-war society. His mood became gloomy but in the end rich comedy kept it away. His other works are *Perenial Philosophy* (1946) and *The Devils of London* (1952).

Lionel Poles Hartley (1895-1972)

Hartley was a British novelist and short story writer. He was born in 1895 at Cambridgeshire, England. He got his degrees at the University of Oxford in 1922. Before that in 1915 during the World War Ist, most of his contemporaries were volunteering for the armed services instead of pursuing University Careers. Hartley also joined the army and in February 1977, he was commissioned as an officer in the Norfolk Regiment. But Hartley never actively did his duty due to weak heart and returned to Oxford to complete his degree.

Literary Career and Works

After his years at Oxford, Hartley worked as a book reviewer in 1924; he met Constance Hultington of GP Putnam, who published his first volume of short stories *Night Fears* and a Novella, *Simonetta Perkins* in 1925. Hartley published his full length novel *The Shrimp and Anemone* only in 1949, though Hartley had written it years before. He wrote of denaturised humanity which was characterised by a sense of loneliness. This feeling was usually produced by refusal of love or frustration of love. He died on 13th December, 1972.

Major Works

- **Eustace and Hilda** This book is a trilogy written between 1944 to 1947. It explores a brother-sister relationship.
- **The Go-Between** The novel was written in 1953. The novelist describes the relationships of children and their attitude to adults without sensibility.
- **The Hireling** (1957) **The Betrayed** (1966) **The Harness Room** (1971) three novels have the same theme. A person, who needed human sympathy most was the one, who was made a victim by those, who seemed to offer affection.

- **Facial Justice** (1960) Hartely described the world, in which the people had spare time to enjoy and money to fulfil their purposes. When he produced his vision of the future, he saw it as a horror, where there was no beauty and a dull moderation prevailed. There was no element of competition. His style was clear. Imagery and symbolism were most important.

Herbert Ernest Bates (1905-1974)

HE Bates was born on 16th May, 1905 at Rushden, Northamptonshire, England. He was an English novelist, short story writer of high reputation and wide popularity.

Bates attended grammar school at Kettering, he qualified for University but did not attend because his family could not afford it. In 1921, at age 16, he joined the Northampton Chronicle as a reporter but he left two months later because he did not like the work. He worked as a clerk in the factory in Rushden, a job he held for 2 years.

Literary Career and Works

His short stories of RAF made him famous such as, *The Greatest People in the World* (1941) and *How Sleep the Brave* (1941), *The Wedding Party* (1965) and *The Four Beauties* (1968). He became the most famous of contemporary short story writers.

He nicely described the relations between people, who were leading limited lives. Often, the story was centred on a young woman, who is placed in wanton situations beyond her full understanding. He wrote about country people in a setting, which was reliable and closely joined with the characters and the mood of the situation.

The Poacher (1935)

The Poacher is a splendid novel, the fifth from the pen of HE Bates, which relates the life of Luke Bishop from about 1880, when he is about 20 years old, to sometime after the end of World War I. There are echoes of Bate's own family history in this novel. The theme of the novel is the imprisonment of the body and spirit by factories, mechanical power, and the suffocating blanket of middle-class respectability.

Fair Stood the Wind for France (1944)

It is a novel written by English author HE Bates. The novel was first published in 1944 and was Bates's first financial success. The title comes from the first line of *Agincourt*, a poem by Michael Drayton (1563-1631). The story concerns John Franklin, the pilot of a Wellington bomber, who badly injures his arms when he crash-lands the aircraft in German-occupied France during the Second World War. He and his crew make their way to an isolated farmhouse and are taken in by the family of a French farmer. Plans are made to smuggle them all back to Britain via Vichy-controlled Marseille but Franklin's condition worsens and he remains at the farm during the hot summer weeks that follow and falls in love with the farmer's daughter Francoise. Eventually they make the hazardous journey together by rowing boat, bicycle and train.

The Jacaranda Tree (1949)

This is HE Bates's acclaimed novel about Burma. During World War II, a small English community are forced to flee when Japanese forces invade Burma. Paterson, the manager of a rice mill, organises the evacuation and takes with him his Burmese mistress and her young brother. The rest of the party takes along their prejudices, their pettiness and their squabbles, and a small enclave of English insularity moves North through Burma. Inevitably, as the journey continues, bitterness, tension and insoluble conflict unfolds. Inspired by Bates's period of service in the Eastern theater of war, The Jacaranda Tree skillfully evokes the atmosphere in Burma during the chaos in invasion.

The Scarlet Sword (1950)

It is a fictional telling of the sacking of St Joseph's Convent in Baramulla, Kashmir by pro-Pakistan Afridi and Pathan tribal soldiers in late October 1947. The novel features a large number of characters including two priests, a journalist, a Hindu dancing girl, a retired Colonel and his wife, a young English woman and her mother, a nurse, tribal soldiers and various other religious, medical and military persons.

The Darling Buds of May (1958)

His most popular creation was the Larkin family in The Darling Buds of May. Pop Larkin and his family were inspired by a colourful character seen in a local shop in Kent by Bates and his family when on holiday.

Malcolm Lowry (1909-1957)

Malcolm Lowry was born in 1909 at Cheshire, England. He is known for his one novel, short stories and poems. He was educated at Leys School, near Cambridge and in rebellion against his conventional bourgeois upbringing he was shipped to China as a cabin boy before going on with his education. At the University of Cambridge, he wrote *Ultramarine*, a novel based on his sea-voyage. He was an alcoholic who saw life as an optical illusion of hallucinations.

Literary Career and Works

Lowry lived in Canada for much of active writing career and is thus also considered a significant figure in Canadian Literature. He won the Governor-General's Award for English Language Fiction in 1961 for his posthumous. collection *Hear US O Lord from Heaven Thy Dwelling Place*.

Under the Volcano (1947). It was to have been part of A largest work, but it remained the only creation of his tormented mind. Its hero has lived through the destruction of Western society and is suffering his private hell. He drives him still further into the sufferings of the hell. He knows the end, but he persists on his course. He denies any thing that may relieve his agonies because he represents man kind, who cannot or will not resist the slow current towards doom. Some critics consider this novel to be one of the greatest of the century. But it has never been fully appreciated. Lowry died in June 1957

Angus Frank Johnstone Wilson (1913-1991)

He was born in 1913 at East Sussex, England Angus was the youngest of six sons born to a upper middle class family who lived a shabby genteel existence in small hotels and boarding houses, chiefly in London. He was educated at West Minster School London and Merton College, Oxford and then worked as a cataloger at the British Museum Reading Room. His mother died when he was 15 years old. He developed a close companionship with his father but after his death Angus realised that he had kept himself in a state of child like innocence about the world and it was necessary to become an adult. He was professor of English Literature at the University of East Anglia (1966-78).

Literary Career and Works

His fiction so many times portrays conflicts in contemporary English Social and intellectual life. *Death Dance* is a collection of early stories which was published in 1969. His first novel Hemlock and After (1952) is regarded by some critics as his best. He died on 31st May, 1991.

Major Works

- **The Wrong Set** (1949) and 'Such Darling Dodos' (1950) He started his literary career with two volumes of these short stories. He described the misfits and neurotics of the middle classes with their decreasing incomes. Their ideas were out mannered in the harsh materialism of Britain after war. Their confidence was declining.
- **Hemlock and After** (1952) Wilson depicts people as a mixture of bodily faults, intellectual weaknesses and fears of insufficiency. He hates foolishness, weak mindedness and pseudo-intellectualism. He can be excessively cruel in exposing the weak points of his society.
- **The Old Man at the Zoo** (1961) This volume is a collection of short stories. They present a horrible dream of the political future.
- **Late Call** (1964) It is a compassionate portrait of an elderly woman who tries to adjust to a new town.
- **The Middle Age of Mrs Eliot** (1958) This novel is most satisfying. It concentrates on a cental figure of Mrs Eliot. It shows her affected reappraisal of herself and a picture of zeal and sympathy which is usually not found in his novels.
- **His Other Novels** *Anglo-Saxon Attitudes* (1956), *No Laughing Matter* (1967), *As If By Magic* (1973), setting *The World On Fire (1980) and drama 'The Mulberry Bush.*

Wilson's discussion of humanism inside his fiction and outside it, is at once profoundly searching and sympathetically generous. His earlier novels were commended for their reintroduction of Victorian festive devices that enabled him to range over very considerable areas of personal, public and social experience.

Colin Henry Wilson (1931-2013)

Colin Wilson, an English novelist and writer on philosophy, sociology, music, literature and the occult, was born on 26th June, 1931. He left school at the age of 16. He subsequently worked as a laboratory assistant, civil servant, labourer, dishwasher and factory worker. For a short while he served in Royal Air Force.

Literary Career and Works

Wilson wrote his first book, *The Outsider* (1956). The book was a study of alienation as glimpsed through the lives and writings of some of the principal intellectual figures of the 20th century. It was at first acclaimed for its brilliance and this initial critical response catapulted Wilson to fame at the age of 24, in the process making *The Outsider* a best seller.

However in subsequent years, literary establishment had changed its opinion of his talent and this negative criticism dogged Wilson until his first novel *Retual in the Dark* (1960) was published. When his second novel *Adrift in Soho* appeared in 1961, Wilson was well on his way to repair his tarnished reputation.

An extremely prolific author, he wrote more than 50 books by the early 1980s. His novels *The World of Violence* (1963) and *Man Without A Shadow* (1963) explain man's refusal to be the victim of either God or chance in a world of violence, sex and crime.

Joyce-Cary (1888-1957)

Anglo-Irish novelist Joyce Cary was born in Ireland in 1888. He studied painting in Edinburg and then in Paris. From 1909 to 1912 he was at Trinity College, Oxford where he studied Law. He joined the Colonial Service in 1914, he served the Nigerian Regiment during World War I. He was wounded while fighting in the cameroons and returned to civil duty in Nigeria in 1917 as a district officer West Africa became the location of his early novels.

Literary Career and Works

His first novel *Aissa Saved* was published in 1932. He also wrote a famous *Trilogy* of novel on art. His novel *Aissa Saved* is the story of an African girl converted to Christianity but still retaining pagan elements in her faith. The famous Triology was *An American Visitor* (1933), *The African Witch* (1936) and *Mister Johnson* (1939). Also a novel about the decline of British Empire *Castle Corner* 1938. Childhood was the theme of his next two novels, his own in *A House of Children* (1941) and that of a Cockney war time evacuee in the country in *Charley is My Darling* (1940). He died in 1957.

Major Works

- **Mister Johnson** His best known novel was inspired by his own career with the Nigerian political service.
- **Trilogy on Art** *Herself Surprised* (1941), *To Be A Pilgrim* (1942) and *The Horse's Mouth* (1944). The last is about a creative artist, who lives an amoral and unorganised life.
- **Prisoner of Grace** (1952) *Except the Lord* (1953) and *Not Honour More* (1955) This trilogy moves slowly and saddens. But it gives a reliable picture of sixty changing years. Alongwith the development of characters, it presents social and political background.
- **The Captive and the Free** (1959) This novel presents his personal convictions in the best possible way.

Keith Spencer Waterhouse (1929-2009)

Keith Spencer was born in February, Leeds, England. He was a British novelist and columnist. He left school at the age of 15 and did various odd jobs before becoming a newspaper man first in Yorkshire and then in London remaining a columnist (for the Daily Mirror and Punch) for most of his life.

Literary Career and Works

Keith is noted for his ability to create comedy and satire out of depressing human predicaments. He wrote plays such as *All Things Bright and Beautiful, Say Who You Are*, filmy plots and television scripts. He died on 4th September, 2009.

Major Works

- **There is a Happy Land** (1957) He wrote this novel in his childhood. It was a recreation through the non-sentimental eyes of a child. He failed to charm the readers.
- **Billy Liar** (1959) It is a novel which was later adopted into a play and a film. This novel shows a young man struggling against the ugliness and tedium of a provincial town and the strict limits of his own abilities by receding into a fantasy world. He has either to ignore reality or join it with his dreams.
- **Jubb** (1963) This novel took escapism into powerless Middle Age, where satisfaction was searched in useless 'good works' pornography and the lonely life.
- **The Bucket Shop** (1969) This novel presents people, who have no talent and the young men, who die so early as they recklessly and angrily try to survive when they have no reason to deserve success.

William Cooper (1910-2002)

He was an English novelist. His real name was Harry Summer Field Hoff. He was born in 1910. He joined Cambridge University for higher education. After taking a degree he joined the Civil Service. Strangely enough, he may be considered as the originator of the Angry young man, who rebels against the system which has tortured him.

Literary Career and Works

Scenes from Provincial Life (1950) and *Scenes from Married Life* (1961) These novels describe the revolt against dull and conventional provincial society, but the rebeller lacks in introductory step. His demand for freedom was little more than a search for a different job, where he could follow the conventions, but make more money. His first novel showed the way to later writers with more violent and shocking ideas of revolt.

The Ever-Interesting Topic (1953) Its theme was progress and tradition in the world. Cooper searched variations on it in *Memoiss of a New Man* (1966) *Love On the Coast* (1973) and *You're not Alone* (1976).

The novel scenes from *Provincial Life* is a wry comedy of manners set in 1939 and constructed as a running report from the coal face of life by Joe-Lunn, a talented but frustrated science teacher at a Midlands Grammar School with its crisp dialogue, shrewd observation and often hilarious set pieces in the book brilliantly captured the faintly stifling atmosphere of the period while at the same time making everyday events seem moving and real. His last novel *Immortality at A Price* (1991) concerns a young biographer.

In total William Cooper wrote 17 novels in all as well as short stories, two plays and a biography of his friend CP Snow. His fictional works were outrightly optimistic as well as comic. He died in 2002.

Kingsley Amis (1922-1995)

Sir Kingsley Amis, an English novelist and critic was born on 16th April, 1922 at London. Amis was educated at the city of London School and at St John's College, Oxford (BA in 1949) his education was interrupted during World War II by his service as Lieutenant in the Royal Corps of Signals. From 1949 to 1961 he taught at Universities in Wales, England and The United States.

Literary Career and Works

He began his literary career by describing an anti-hero who is born in an ordinary family. When he gets a means of rising up, he gives up his unhealthy surroundings. Society disillusions him.

Lucky Jim (1954)

The novel describes a man, who wants little from life except a few simple pleasures, but he likes the material gains which he picks up from rising above himself. Unknowingly he identifies that despite his sneers, he has much in common with the settlement. He cannot face the new environment.

The anti-hero realises that the political and aesthetic values are a fraud. But he has nothing to fill their place. Although he can expose ruin, he cannot create. In the end he gets success. Success gives him self-satisfaction. The success is based on compromise with the system, which he dislikes in different walks of life. This attitude is also seen in, *That Uncertain Feeling* (1955), *I Like It Here* (1958), *Take A Girl Like You* (1960) and *Girl 20* (1971).

One Fat Englishman (1963)

In this novel, Amis described a British visitor's experiences in an American college. While Lucky Jim Dixon was a typical 'Angry Young Man', the Fat Roger Micheldene was the model of the kind of Englishman, who fiercely kept away the difficulties of American way of life. Amis showed the academic ambitions and the academic tensions of the rapidly expanding world of higher education in the period.

The Egyptologists (1965)

The characteristics of Amis's novels are fast movement, wit and some extremely funny incidents. There is no backbiting and pseudo-culture as a man expects in Amis's novel. This novel was written in collaboration with Robert Conquest.

The Anti Death League (1966)

Apart from the characteristics found in his novels, this novel tells of detectives and nuclear warfare, but it is a fierce attack against God because human beings are powerless against the wanton cruelty of death. Any reader may wonder sometimes whether Amis himself dislikes the culture with which his whole life has been associated and that something of his own revolt is shown by his interest in noisy dance and music, James Bond and science fiction as *New Maps of Hell*.

He wrote poetry also. His early poems contested the beliefs of *The Apocalyptic Movement*. *A Look Round the Estate* (1967) is a collection of his poems.

John Braine (1922-1986)

English novelist John Gerrard Braine was born on 13th April (1922) in Yorkshire, England. He is one of so called Angry young men, whose novel *Room At the Top* typifies the concerns of a generation of post World War II British writers. He was much troubled with social conditions of young men in a prosperous society.

Literary Career and Works

Brain wrote 12 novels but he is cheifly remembered today for his first novel *Room At The Top* (1957) and *Life At the Top* (1962).

Room At the Top (1957) and *Life At The Top* (1962) are set in the West Riding. They show that nothing stops in the rat race of material comfort and social status. Yet, when man reaches the top, he has nothing, but everything loses its charm.

Stay With Me Till Morning (1970)

Braine wrote about prosperous families in Yorkshire and complex relationships. There is a need for excitement and search for the excitement in business deals, social gathering and a variety of sexual adventures.

The Crying Game (1968), *The Queen of a Distant Country* (1972) and *Waiting for Sheila* (1976) *The Crying Game* is about a satirical journalist, *The Queen of a Distant Country* is about a commercially successful novelist and *Waiting for Shiela* is about a successful businessman. *The Vodi* (1959) and *The Jealous God* (1964) In,he describes more spiritual problems. But he is less successful and less popular with these themes. He died in 1986.

John Barrington Wain (1925-1944)

English poet and novelist John Barrington Wain was born in Stoke-on-Trent in 1925. He studied at Oxford and later became professor of poetry there. After 1955, he turned to writing full time. He is associated with the Angry Young Man Movement.

Literary Career and Work

Hurry on Down (1953) this novel presents a reliable picture of *Angry Young Man*. This anti-hero hates the society and understands no responsibility towards it. This novel is a farce. He objected to the term *Angry Young Man*.

He wrote many novels such as, *The Contenders* (1958), *A Travelling Woman* (1959), *Strike the Father Dead* (1962) and a collection of short stories *Nuncle* (1960). All of them were amusing, but carefully considered descriptions of young people wildly, sometimes hopelessly trying to find out foundations of some sort. He wrote poetry also, He gave a moral excellence to his poetry as, in *Mixed Feelings* (1951) and *Weep Before God*.

Mr Wain's novels represented the iconoclastic tone of much written fiction in the 1950s. He was called by famous critic Prescott, 'one of the most accomplished and versatile of the younger English writings.' He was also author of a highly respected biography *Samuel Johnson* (1974) and was a prolific journalist, broadcaster and author of radio plays. He died in 1944.

Alan Sillitoe (1928-2010)

Alan Sillitoe was born in March (1928) at Nottingham, England. His father was a Tannery Worker. Sillitoe worked in factories from the age of 14. He left school after having failed the entrance examination to grammar school. He joined the Air Training Corps in 1942 and then the Royal Air Force. He developed tuberculosis and spent 16 months in RAF hospital.

Literary Career and Works

Nottingham is the place around which he set his stories chiefly. He described working people, who are still aware of the great depression though they are living in comparative prosperity. They insist that they are victims of a suppresser system as bureaucrats and capitalists. Their life has become as means of a revenge. Their world is a chaos of violence, incapable suffering, selfishness and unpolished humour. In every way, it is unsafe.

His story the *Loneliness of the Long Distance Runner* was awarded the Hawthornden Pirze.

The various protagonists of Sillitoe's early fiction are generally restless young men from the slum world who oppose the established order of things but who are at the same time affected by Consumerism and Hedonism. Sillitoe moved in his later works beyond this lower class milieu towards analysis of the psychological state of his characters.

Sillitoe also wrote many poems but his work as a novelist and short story writer is acclaimed more than his collection of poem. He died on 25th April, 2010. He was 82.

Major Works

Saturday Night and Sunday Morning (1958) The hero of this novel welcomes danger because it produces excitement, which contemporary society lacks. When there is a danger of order coming into his life, He must create new elements of danger.

The Loneliness of the Long-Distance Runner (1959) This novel blames society for the deficiencies of its members. It looks on anti-social behaviour as a defendable means of the act of revenge.

Short Stories

- The Loneliness of the Long Distance Runner (1957)
- The Ragman's Daughter and Other Stories (1963)
- Guzman, Go Home and Other Stories (1968)
- Men, Women and Children (1973)
- Down to the Bone (1976)

Other Works

Key to the Door (1961)

- The Death of William Posters (1966)
- A Start in Life (1970)
- The Widower's Son (1976)
- The Flame of Life (1974)
- The Story Teller (1979)
- Her Victory (1982)
- The Lost Flying Boat (1983)
- Down From The Hill (1984)
- Life Goes On (1985)

William Gerald Golding (1911-1993)

He was an English novelist. He was born in 1911 at St Columb Minor, near Newuay, Cornwall, England. He was educated at Marlborough Grammar School where his father taught and at Brasenose College, Oxford and graduated in 1935. After working in a Settlement House and in small theatre companies, he became a school master at Bishop Wordsworth's school, Salisbury. He joined the Royal Navy in 1940, took part in the action that saw the sinking of the German battleship Bismarch.

Literary Career and Works

Golding's first published novel was *Lord of the Flies* (1954). He describes man's instinct to destroy any good thing, whether it is material or spiritual. He treats cruelty, selfishness and longing for power. He puts his point of view very clearly. Evil is everywhere and is fought against with difficulty and good is almost impossible to get. Each of his novels is a matchless story for the times, in which symbolism plays an important part. Yet the novels are firmly realistic.

His characters are probable, even though they are compelled by unnatural circumstances into unnatural situations. He won the the Noble Prize in 1983. He died in June in 1993.

Major Works

Lord of the Flies (1954) This book was rejected by 56 publishers. Finally, it was accepted by Faber and Faber.

Now it has been widely hailed and is on the school/college courses in USA, England, India and many other countries. This is his first and most lastingly popular novel. It gives a safer sign of his permanent concern with moral allegory. He set this novel on a desert island on which a marooned (left persons on a desolate place) party of boys from an English Cathedral singing and dancing schools gradually falls away from the elegant civilisation that has so far constructed it. This civilisation cracks and splits under the slightest pressure and declines into dirt, savageness and murder.

The Inheritors (1955) This novel moves back to an anthropological pre-history in which the talented and brutish ancestors of Homo sapiens root out their simpler-minded Neanderthal fore runners. This novel explains more effectively his view that innocence good, happiness were natural before Homo sapiens developed and with him an all-destroying urge to evil.

Pincher Martin (1956) Its plot is brilliantly thought. In this novel, the sailor recasts his complete personal life between the moment of his falling into the sea and his death.

Free Fall (1959) and *The Scorpion God* (1971) These novels are studies of individuals, who on purpose, reject heaven and must sink satisfied into hell like all human beings.

The Spire (1964) The spire shows man clearly getting something that is good yet everything connected with it, is evil, The reader wonders whether mankind can ever get or create anything that is completely good. Joceline, the central character, is the ambitious dean of an unnamed English Cathedral.

Darkness Visible (1979) The novel narrates a struggle between good and evil. It marked Golding's re-emergence as a novelist, eight years after the publication of his previous book, The *Collection* the *Scorpion God*. In the *Darkness Visible*, at the height of the Landon blitz, a naked child steps out of an all-consuming fire. Miraculously saved yet hideously scarred, tormented at school and at work. Matty becomes a wanderea, a seeker after some unknown redemption. Two more lost children await him : twins as exquisite as they are loveless. As Golding weaves their destinies together, as he draws them toward a final firestorm, his book lights up both the inner and outer darkness of our time.

Other Works

Rites of Passage (1980), *Its Sequels Close Quarters* (1987), *Fire Down Below* (1989), *The Paper Man* (1984) and *The Coral Island*. These novels have expanded, what can be seen as an established rhythm of contrasted sea-stories and land stories all of which are concerned with the utmost limit and isolation.

Arthur Koestler (1905-1983)

Arthur Koestler was a Hungarian British author. He was born in 1905 in Hungary. Apart from his school years, he was educated in Austria. He became a journalist for German papers. In the Spanish Civil War, he was arrested by French forces and sentenced to death. After a stampede in the French Confinement Camps, he joined the foreign army.

Literary Career and Works

Arthur Koestler belongs to the class of Western intellectuals in the 1900s who started on the left, landing the Soviet Union and supporting communist cases only to disavow these politics in mid-century. But then he started promoting spirituality and mysticism as alternative to politics.

At the turning point between two extremes was his most famous book, the novel.

Darkness At Noon (1940), this novel represented a terrible picture of corruption and the corrupt use of power. It is the vision of the future where satanist repressive rules are working.

His other novels are *Scum Of The Earth* (1941) and *Thieves In The Night* (1946), *The Age Of Longing* (1951) *The Call Girls* (1972).

He wrote many autobiographical works and non-fiction prose which will be taken in Non-Fiction section. He died in 1983.

Anthony Dymoke Powell (1905-2000)

He was an English novelist who was born in 1905. He was educated at Eton College and Oxford University. After graduation, Powell entered publishing business in London.

Literary Career and Works

He launched his career as a writer in 1931 with the publication of *Afternoon Men* featuring a hero who lacks all ambition and who drifts aimlessly through bohemian circles, finding meaning nowhere. Powell's next novels *From A View to A Death* (1933) *Agents and Patients* 1936 and *What's Become of Waring* deal with variations on the theme of prostituted talent and the will to dominate personal relationship. He died in March 2000.

Major Works

- A Question of Upbringing (1951)
- A Buyer's Market (1952)
- The Acceptance World (1955)
- At Lady Molly's (1957)
- The Valley of Bones (1964)
- The Military Philosophers (1968)
- Temporary Kings (1973)
- Casanova's Chinese Restaurant (1960)
- The Kindly Ones (1962)
- The Solider's Art (1966)
- Hearing Secret Harmonies (1975)

Muriel Sarah Spark (1918-2006)

Scottish novelist Muriel Spark was born in Edinburgh in 1918. She is known for her comic prose and satire with which the serious themes of her novels are presented. She was educated at Edinburgh and later spent some years in Central Africa. This served as the setting for her first volume of short stories *The Go-Away Bird and Other Stories*, (1958).

Literary Career and Works

Until 1957 Spark published only Criticism and Poetry with the publication of *The Comfortors* (1957), however, her talent as a novelist and an ability to create disturbing, compelling characters and a disquieting sense of moral ambiguity was immediately evident.

The Comforters (1957) Her first novel is concerned with a neurotic woman writer Caroline Rose. She has to come to terms with her new found Catholicism with her illusion and with her God like status as a creator.

Curriculum Vitae She wrote an autobiography with this name in 1992. As a Roman Catholic, she accepts the supernatural and understands the power of spirits to influence the course of events. She uses violence if it is necessary for her theme. Her short stories are cleverly written and fall just short of the classic.

She died on 13th April, 2006 in Florence, Italy.

Major Works

- Robinson (1958)
- The Ballad of Peckham Rye (1960)
- A Fairly Honourable Defeat
- The Girls of Slender Means (1963)
- The Abbess of Crewe (1974)
- The Prime of Miss Lean Brodie (1961)
- The Mandelbaum Gate (1965)
- Memento Mori (1959)

Jean Iris Murdoch (1919-1999)

Iris born British author Jean Murdoch was born in 1919 in Dublin and died in 1999. She got education in Oxford University. First she held a post with UNRRA United Nations Relief and Rehabilitation Administration, then she became a deen at Cambridge.

Literary Career and Works

Murdoch published her first novel in 1954 and would go on to publish more than 26 novels. She won a Booker Prize for her novel The Sea, the sea in 2001. She published one of her last novels *The Green Knight* in 1994.

Under The Net (1954) When she was studying at Oxford University, She read Samuel Beckett's *Murphy* and paid homage to it in her first novel *Under The Net*'. It gives an amusing description of the Angry Young Man, who runs after the wealth.

The Flight From the Enchanter (1956) This novel is a study of cruelty, power and the sufferings of a man. Other people cause the sufferings in his life and he can not bear them.

Her other novels are *The Sandcastle* (1957) and *The Bell* (1958). Murdoch was a student of philosophy. She began her literary career with an evaluation of Jean-Paul Sartre. She studied human relations deeply and constructed them tightly. Her characters are unbalanced. She is unable to depict them normally. She combines sorrow with fun. She depends on the symbolism of actions and situations. She does her work intellectually rather than passionately. *A Severed Head* (1961) This novel is the story of a woman, who is engaged in warfare. She is highly intelligent and cruel. She gets victory in the end.

Her characters interchange relationships, sex and sexual symbolism and horror becomes more clear in love and desire. Her other works are *An Unofficial Rose* (1962), *The Unicorn* (1963) *An Accidental Man* (1971), *The Sacred and*

Profane Love Machine (1974), *Bruno's Dream and The Sea, The Sea and The Philosopher's Pupil.* She died in February 1999 after developing *Alzheimer's disease*.

She was awarde the Golden Pen Award for 'a lifetimes distinguish service to literature'.

Doris May Lessing (1919-2013)

British novelist Doris Lessing was born in 1919. She wrote many novels and short stories. She was awarded the David Cohen Prize for a lifetime achievement in British literature in 2001. In 2007 she was awarded Nobel Prize for Literature. In 2008, the popular newspaper *The Times* ranked her fourth on a list of 'The 50 greatest British writers since 1945'.

Literary Career and Works

She is considered a master of the short story and published several collections, including *The Story of a Non-Marrying Man* (1972) and *Stories* (1978). Her African stories are collected in *This Was The Old Chief's Country* (1951) and *The Sun Between Their Feet* (1973).

Lessing also turned to Science Fiction in a five novel sequence titled Canopus in Argos : Archives (1979-1983). The novels; *The Diary Of A Good Neighbour* (1983) and *If The Old Could* (1984) were published under a psudonym.

Her other novels are *The Good Terrorist* (1985), *The Fifth Child* (1988) and *Ben In The World* (2000). *The Sweetest Dream* (2001) is a semi auto biographical novel set primarily in London during the 1960s.

This prolific author left a legacy of more than 55 works that spanned literary genres weaving rich narratives of her personal experiences and political perspectives. She died on 17th November, 2013 in London.

Her style is also seen in *The Four Gated City* (1969) *The Story Of A Non-Marrying Man* (1972), *The Memories of a Survivor* (1975), *Canopus is Argos* (1983), *Briefing for A Descent into Hell, The Good Terrorist and The Left.*

African Stories (1964) She spent most part of her life in African continent. She wrote her experiences in this book. She showed the situation of black people, who were subjected to powerful white men. She suggests that from the application of Marxist doctrines, this problem may be solved.

Children of Violence (1952-1965) This is her five volume sequence, which describes the developing political commitment and the later political disillusion of Martha Quest. The names of the novels are, *The Grass is Singing* (1950) *Children of Violence* (1952) *A Proper Marriage* (1954), *A Ripple From The Storm* (1958) and *Land Locked* (1965).

The Golden Notebook (1962) Though it is very long, yet it is a novel. It is not well organised. It is a summary of her view on all those issues, which have engaged her. The book was widely read and embraced by the growing women's movement. Usually her theme is the dilemma of the new woman, who is still hopes to adapt to conventional ideas of a woman's life inspite of her liberty. Yet her characters are free from the illusion of this life. Love produces loneliness and want of stability.

Anthony Burgess (1917-1993)

English writer Anthony Burgess was born in 1917. He was trained in English literature and phonetics. Burgess taught in the extramural department of Birmingham University (1946-50), also worked for the ministry of Education (1948-50) and was English master at Banbury Grammar School (1950-54). He then served as education officer in Malaya and Borneo (1954-59) where he wrote three novels with a Malaysian setting.

Literary Career and Works

He came back to England and became a full time and prolific professional writer. Under the pseudonym, Anthony Burgess wrote the novels *The Wanting Seed* (1962), and *Honey For The Bears* (1963) were written.

Some other works are *A Clock Work Orange* (1962), *Earthly Power* 1980, *The End of the World News* (1983). *The Kingdom of the Wicked* (1985), *Any Old Iron* (1989) and *A Dead Man in Deptford* 1993.

Burgess novels are a combination of linguistic ability and witty erudition with picaresque plots, bizarre story premises and sharp social satire. 'Although his vision of modern society is pessimistic, his fiction is generally comic. In addition to novels and short stories, he also wrote literary criticism and also wrote television scripts and translation for the stage and wrote some biographies. He died on 22nd November 1993 in London.

Brigid Antonia Brophy (1929-1995)

British novelist and critic Brigid Antonia Brophy was born on 12th June 1929 in London, England.

Her father was a novelist. She started writing at an early age. During World War II, she attended The Abbey School, reading between May 1941 and July 1943. She then attended St Paul's Girls School in London in 1947. She went on a scholarship to Oxford University but left it without a degree.

Literary Career and Works

She began her literary career with witty comments on the weaknesses of modern society such as *Hacken Feller's Ape* (1953) and *The King of a Rainy Country* (1956). She rapidly became one of the most agitated champions of women's liberty.

The Snow Ball (1964)

It is a loud public declaration of womans rights. She wanted to take revenge on Don Juan by demanding sexual satisfaction from all the persons whom she meets. Her other novels are *The Adventures of God in His Search for the Black Girl* (1973) and *Pussyowl* (1976). Her novel *In Transit* (1969) is written in neo-James Joyce Prose.

Edna O'Brien (1930)

Edna O'Brien was born on 15th December, 1930 in Ireland. She is hailed as a novelist, short story writer and screen writer whose works have been noted for her remarkable portrayal of women, evocative description and sexual candour.

Edna received a strict Irish Catholic education and went on to study Pharmacy in Dublin where she received a licence in 1956.

Literary Career and Works

Obrien's popular first novel *The Country Girls* 1960, was the first volume of the *Country Girls Trilogy*.

The place of her birth, Country Clare figures prominently in her works. Brien was a champion of woman's liberty. Her first novel *The Country Girls* discussed sexual matter dealing with women. It is about two Irish country girls-Kate and Baba who are in search of love. The book was banned in Ireland. These three novels constitute a trilogy and trace the two girls' life from their youth to sexual awakening and marriage.

- The Country Girls (1960)
- The Lonely Girl (1962) and
- Girls in their Married Bliss (1964)

August is a Wicked Month (1965) It is about dissatisfied women. She makes sex her weapon. She is frustrated and indifferent. Her other notable works are *Casualties of Peace* (1966) *Night* (1972), *Johnny I Hardly Knew You* (1977), *The High Road* (1988). *House of splendid Isolation* (1994), *Down by the River* (1996), *In the Forest* (2002) and *The Light of Evening* (2006). *The Little Red Chairs* (2015)' was widely praised for its acutely observed characterisation of an Irish villager who had an ill fated affair with a war criminal in hiding.

O'Brien's novels express her despair over the condition of women in contemporary society and in particular, attack women's repressive upbringing. The bleak tone of O'Brien's novels is however broken by flights of lyrical description and by the heroines' attainment of brief periods of happiness.

Collection of Brien's short stories appeared as *The Love Object* (1968), *A Scandalous Woman and Other Stories* (1974), *A Fanatic Heart* (1984), *Lantern Slides* (1990) and *Saints and Sinners* (2011).

Dame Margaret Drabble (1939)

English novelist Margaret Drabble was born in Yorkshire in 1939. She studied at Cambridge and joined the Royal Shakes Pearcan Company at Startfond Avon.

Literary Career and Works

Drabble began writing after leaving the University of Cambridge. The Central character of her novels, although widely different in character and circumstance, are shown in situations of tension and stress, the essentials for this moral growth. Drabble is concerned with the individual's attempt to define the self, but she is also interested in social change. She writes in tradition of such authors as George Eliot, Henry James and Arnold Bennett.

Her first novel, *A Summer Bird Cage* was published in 1963. Her other works are *The Garrick Year* (1964), *The Needle's Eye* (1972) and *The Witch of Exmoor* (1996).

The Ice Age (1977) This novel is based on a series of interlinked relationships all of which humorously suggest something of the shabby and hopeless condition of contemporary England. This is the most suggestive of her novels.

Millstone (1965) This is the story of an unmarried mother who became pregnant after a one night stand, but resolves to bring up the child.

David Mitchell (1969)

David Mitchell was born in 1969 on 12th January at South Part, Lancashire, England. he was raised in a small town in Worcestershire. He attended the University of Kent from which he received a BA in English and American literature and a MA in comparative literature. In 1994, he went to Japan for 8 years where he taught English and dedicated himself to writing.

Literary Career and Works

His first published work was *Ghost Written* (1999) a collection of interconnected narratives that take place in a variety of locations throughout the world. His next book *Number 9 Dream* (2001) also won measured praise from critics. Mitchell's third novel *Cloud Atlas* (2004, Film 2012) was his breakthrough work. It consists of a series of six inter-linked stories written in different styles through which Mitchell explores the seeming progress of the post Industrial Age. The other work are *Black Swan Green* (2006), *The Thousand Autumns of Jacop de Zoet* (2010), a historical novel the *Bone Clocks* (2014) and *Slade House 2015* (a short novel).

Kazuo Ishiguro (1954)

Kazuo Ishiguro was born in Nagasaki Japan on 8th November 1954. He came to Britain in 1960 when his father began research at the National Institute of Oceanography. He studied at grammar school for boys in Surrey.

Literary Career and Works

He has been writing full time since 1982. In 1983, shortly after the publication of his first novel, Kazuo Inshiguro was nominated by Granta Magazine as one of the 20 Best of young British writers.

In 1981, three of his short stories were published in introduction 7 stories by New Writers. His first novel *A Pale View of Hills* (1982) narrated by a Japanese widow living in England, draws on the destruction and rehabilitation of Nagasaki. In 2017 he won the Nobel Prize for Literature. Presently Kazuo lives in London with his family.

Major Works

- An Artist of the Floating World (1986)
- The Remains of the Day (1989)
- The Unconsoled (1995)
- When we were orphans (2000)
- Never Let me Go (2005)
- The Buried Giant (2015)
- Short Story collection–Noctures Five stories of Music and Night Fall (2010)

American Literature

American Literature refers to works of literature in the English language in America. Since America was a set of colonies set up by Britishers, early American literature was colonial literature in form of pamphlets and writings exalting the benefits of the colonies. The 1700 is seen as a revolutionary period for American Literature which saw politically motivated writings. But it was during early 1800s that American Literature began to divide itself from the British roots. Washington Irving and James Fenimone Cooper were the first few writers who helped formulate a distinctly American Literature with American identity and American themes. William Hill Brown wrote the first American novel The *Power of Sympathy* (1789). After this a flood of sentimental novels followed by the end of 19th century. The period from 1820 to the 1860s is known as the Romantic period of American Literature or the American Renaissance. Nathaniel Hawthorn, Herman Melville, Ralph Waldo Emerson, David Thoreau and Walt Whitman were prominent writers of this period. These authors experimented in style and developed themes important to American identity and expression. The Post Civil War period saw writings by Mark Twain and Henry James. This period was considered realistic in its emphasis on truthful depictions. Modern period of American Literature reflected the changing social, political and cultural climates of the American nation. Some of the prominent writers of this period are Robert Frost, Ernest Heming Way, William Faulkner, Carl Sandburg, Edward Albee, Arthur Miller and Tennessee Williams.

Major American Novelists

James Fenimore Cooper (1789-1851)

Cooper was born on 14th September 1789 at Burlington, New Jersey, United States. After private schooling in Albany, Cooper attended Yale from 1803 to 1805. He was the best Latin Scholar of his class.

Literary Career and Works

Cooper published his first fiction *Precaution* in (1820) which was an imitation of Jane Austen's novels of English gentry 'manners'. His second novel *The Spy* 1821 was based on another British model, Sir Walter Scott's *Waverly* novel. But in this novel Cooper broke new ground by using an American Revolutionary War setting. But most renowned novel *The Other Stocking Tales*. *The Pioneers*, (1823) followed and adhered to the successful formula of the *The Spy*, reproducing its basic thematic conflicts and utilising family traditions once again.

The public was fascinated by Cooper's character of the novel *Leather Stocking*. Cooper was encouraged to write a series of sequels in which the entire life of the frontier scout was gradually unfolded. His other novels are *The Last of Mohicans* (1826), *The Prairies* (1827), *The Patha Finder* 1840, *The Deer Slayer* (1841), *The Pilot* 1823 and *The Bravo* (1831).

Some other Novelists of Contemporary Period

Name	Time Period	Major Works
John Wyndham	10th July 1903-11th March 1969	The Day of the Triffids (1951) The Chrysalids (1955),.The Midwich 1957 Chocky (1968)
Henry Green	29th October 1905-13th December 1973	Blindness (1926) (Book) Living (1929) (Novel) Party Going (1939) (Novel) Loving (1945) (Novel) Concluding (1948) (Novel) Nothing; Doting; Blindness (1950) (Novel) Doting (1952) (Novel)
Lawrence George Durrell	27th February 1912-7th November 1990	Novels The Alexandria Quartet Pied Piper of Lovers (1935) White Eagles over Serbia (1957) The Revolt of Aphrodite (1974) Nunquam (1970) The Avignon Quintet (1992)
Frederic Raphael	August 1931-Present	Novels The Earls don Way (1958) The Limit of Love (1960) Darling (1965) Like Men Betrayed (1970) The Glittering Prizes (1976)
Pamela Hansford Johnson	29th May 1912-18th June 1981	This Bed Thy Centre (1935) The Trojan Brothers (1944) The Last Resort (1956) The Humbler Creation (1959) The Survival of the Fittest (1968) The Good Husband (1978) A Bonfire (1981)
Stan Barstow	28th June 1928-1st August 2011	A Kind of Loving (1960) The Watchers on the Shore (1966) A Season with Eros (1971) The Right True End (1976) Next of Kin (1991)
Collin MacInnes	20th August 1914-22th April 1976	City of Spades (1957) Absolute Beginners (1959) Mr Love & Justice (1960) Out of the Garden (1974) Absolute MacInnes : The Best of Colin MacInnes (1985)
Percy Howard Newby	25th June 1918-6th September 1997	A Journey to the Interior (1945) The Snow Pasture (1949) The Retreat (1953) Picnic at Sakkara (1955) A Guest and His Going (1960) A Lot to Ask (1973) Feeling Have Changed (1981) Leaning in the Wind (1986) Something About Women (1995)
John Ronald Reuel Tolkein	3rd January 1892-2nd September 1973	The Hobbit (1937) The Lord of the Rings (1954-1995)
Mervyn Peake	9th July 1911-17th November 1768	Titus Groan (1946) Gormenghast (1950) Titus Alone (1959)
Penelope Ruth Mortimer	19th September 1918-19th October 1999	Johanna (1947) A Villa in Summer (1954) The Bright Prison (1956) The Pumpkin Eater (1962) About Time : An Aspect of Autobiography (1979) The Mandy Man (1983) About Time Too (1993)
Lynne Reid Banks	31th July 1929-Present	One More River (1975) The Farthest-Away Mountain (1976) The Indian in the Cupboard (1980) The Return of the Indian (1985) The L Shaped Room

Nathaniel Hawthorne (1804-1864)

Nathaniel Hawthorne was born in Salem near Boston Massachusetts on 4th July, 1804. He was the son of sea captain. His ancestors belonged to royal family. Later, the family suffered poverty. After the death of Daniel Hawthorne his father in 1808, his mother Elizabeth Manning returned with her three children to Manning House.

In 1816, she went to Raymon Maine. Here, Nathaniel spent three years in the lap of nature in 1819, he was sent to Salem, where he started studying. He arrived Brunswick in 1821 to Domatric. He was among the earliest students at Bodoin college. He passed BA in 1825. He lived for 12 years in Salem and published 44 tales and sketches. He married Sophia who was his neighbour's sister. He worked as a surveyor at Custom House in Salem after marriage. But he left the job for some political reasons.

Literary Career and Works

He was a great symbolist and allegorist and was fond of writing romances. He introduced supernatural elements, in his works. He presented human relations, mystery of life, Puritanism, qualities of sin, value of repentance and redemption etc in his novels. He resembled George Eliot and Thomas Hardy, but he lacked humor and elevation of those writers.

Hawthorne was a prominent part of the transcendentalist movement. His works delve into human nature especially the darker side. Many of his works are set against the somber background of Puritan New England. For example

- Fanshawe (1828)
- Twice Told Tales (1837)

He had a Puritanic spirit. *In The Scarlet Letter, The House of Seven Gabbles* (1851), *The Blithedale Romance* (1852) and the *Marble Faun*, we can see this spirit in a psychological manner.

Hawthorne's *The Scarlet Letter* is about Hester Prynne, a young married woman who has borne an Illegitimate child while living away from her husband in a village in Puritan, New England. The husband Roger Chillingworth arrives in New England to find his wife pilloried and made to wear the letter A (meaning adulteress) in scarlet on her dress as a punishment. Chillingworth becomes obsessed with finding the identity of his wife's former lover. He learns that Hester's paramour is a saintly young minister Arthur Dimmesdale and Chillingworth then proceeds to revenge himself by mentally tormenting the guilt stricken young minister. In the end Chillingworth is morally degraded by his pursuit of revenge and Dimnesdale is broken by his own sense of guilt and publicly confesses his adultery before dying in Hester's arms.

Hawthorne's short stories are also marked by psychological and moral insight seldom equalled by any American writer. His highest regarded short stories include *Mykinsman, Major Molineaux* (1832), *Young Goodman Brown* (1835), *Feather Top* (1852) and *The Minister's Black Veil*. He died on 19th May, 1864 at Plymouth New Hampshire.

Edgar Allan Poe (1809-1849)

He was born on 19th January, 1809 in Boston. His father David Poe was an Irish man. He was irresposible and careless. He was drunkard. He neglected his family. He separated from his wife. After separating from her husband Elizabeth had to earn livelihood for her family by acting in theatre.

Her three children were adopted by other families. Edgar was adopted by John Allan, a merchant. Thus, Edgar got his name Edgar Allan Poe. Allan family went to England. After 5 years, Allan came back to Richmond and Edgar was sent to a local school. He fell in love with Jane Stith Stanard. She was mother of one of his classmates. Poe wrote about this lady in the poem *To Helen*.

He was sent to the University of Virginia in 1826. He began to drink and gamble. To know this, John Allan called him back to Richmond. Edgar wanted to get love and affection from his parents, but John Allan was a practical and realistic man, so he could not get love from him. Soon, he left his house and went to his birth place Boston. He died in 1849.

Literary Career and Works

Edgar Allan Poe's only novel is a classical adventure story with supernatural elements which has fascinated and influenced generation of writers. The inspiration for the novel *The Narrative of Arthur Gordon Pym of Nantucket* was both modern and American. Poe got the idea from a newspaper.

The novel is replete with existential and psychoanalytical fascination. The later part of the 'narrative' explores one of Poe's recurring themes, man's unconscious desire for annihilation. Some stories written by Edgar Allan Poe are *The Murders in the Rue Morgue, The Tell Tale Heart, The Purloined Letter; The Marque of the Red Death, The Imp of The Perverse* and *The Pit and the Pendulum.*

Major Works

- The Raven 1845,
- The Black Cat 1843
- Annabel Lee 1849
- The Gold Bug 1843

Herman Melville (1819-1891)

He was born on 1st August, 1819 in New York. His father Allan Melville was an Scotch Irish, who immigrated to new England. His mother Maria Gansevoort was a Dutch emigrant to New York. He was the second of their eight children.

He attended the Male High School. In 1830 Herman enrolled briefly in Albany Academy but after his father's death, Melville could not continue his education. Herman joined his brother in his father's felt and fur business. Though finances were precarious, Herman attended Albany Classical School in 1835 and became an active member of a local debating society. He died on 28th September 1891.

Literary Career and Works

Young Melville had already started writing. He went on many voyages and his experience in these voyages provided material for his many novels. In his sea adventure stories, he is praised by the native islanders against the *White Civil Man*. According to him, *White Civil Man* is 'the most ferocious animal on the face of the Earth.' Chief glory of his fame rests upon *Moby Dick*.

Moby-Dick; or The Whale

It is a novel about sailor Ishmael's narrative of the obsessive quest of Ahab Captain of the whaling ship PEQUOD for revenge on Moby Dick, the white whale. Moby Dick was published to mixed reviews and its greatness was recognised only in the 20th century. Writers like William Faulkner and DH Lawrence praised the novel immensely and called it "one of the most wonderful books in the world". Its opening sentence, 'Call me Ishmael' is among world literature's most famous sentence.

Major Works

- Typee: A Peep at Polynesian Life (1846)
- Mardi (1848)
- Redburn (1849)
- White Jacket (1850)
- Pierre on the Ambiguities (1852)
- Israel Potter, His 50 Years of Exile (1855)
- The Confidence-Main: A comic masquerade
- Clarel : A poem and Pilgrimage in the Holy Land (1876)
- Billy Budd (1889)
- Omoo (1847)

Mark Twain (1835-1910)

Mark Twain is a pseudonym for Samuel Longborne Clemens who was born on 30th November in Florida, Missouri, US. He was American humorist and novelist who acquired international fame for his travel narratives and adventure stories of boyhood especially *The Adventures of Huckleberry Finn* (1885).

When he was four, his family moved to Hannibal, Missourit, a part town on the Missisippi river that had insipired the fictional town of St Peterburg in the Adventures of Tom Sawyer and Huckleberry Finn. Twain left school after 5th grade to become a printer's apprentice. In 1851, he began working as a type settee, contributing article and humorous sketches to the Hannipal Journal, a newspaper owned by Orion. He died in April 1910.

Literary Career and Works

He is one the most beloved writers of America. His articles and sketches appeared in New York papers and he became the Nevada Correspondent for the San-Fransisco morning call. When the humourist Artremus Ward invited Twain to contribute something for a book of humourous sketches, Twain decided to write up the story, *Jimsmiley and his Jumping Frog*. But as it was a bit late the story was not included in the volume but it was published in the New York Saturday Press in November 1865 and was subsequently reprinted throughout the country.

The Gilded Age was Twain's first attempt at a novel and the experience was apparently congenial enough for him to begin writing *Tom Sawyer*, (1876) which was followed by another great one *The Adventures of Huckleberry Finn* (1885). Mark Twain is also remembered for writing humourous short stories which abound in numbers.

Major Works

- Mark Twain's other works are Innocent Abroad (1869)
- The Prince and the Pauper
- A Connecticut Yankee In King Arthur's Court
- The American Claimant
- Gilded Age
- Horse Tale - a Short Novel
- Mysterious Strangers - a Novel
- Personal Recollection of Joan of Arc
- Those Extraordinary Twins
- Tramp Abroad

Henry James (1843-1916)

Henry James was the second son of Henry James senior and Mary James. He was born on 15th April, 1843 at Washington Place, New York. The family lived in Europe for 5 years. In Switzerland, he studied science. When the family returned to America there was Civil War. In 1861, he was admitted to the Law School, but he left it without completing his graduation.

Literary Career and Works

He met his cousin Mary Temple, who impressed him very much. She was young and zealous. She was fond of reading George Eliot. He portrayed her in many of his works in *The Portrait of a Lady as Isabel Archer, The Wings of the Dove as Milly Theale, The Awkward Age as Nanda* and *The Golden Bowl as Maggie Verver.*

In 1864, the review of Henry James first book appeared in the North American Review. His first story *The Story of a Year* appeared in the Atlantic Monthly in March 1865. In 1866, his story *Poor Richard* was praised by the author William Dean.

He settled in England. In Europe, he met many great writers and artists. In his book *Partial Sketches*, he wrote these experiences. He wrote biography of Nathaniel Hawthorne in 1897. He wrote his first great novel *The Portrait of a Lady* (1881). It got great success. It is called a master piece and is a story of a young, spirited American woman 'affronting her destiny.' The novel is an account of the limits of self-sufficiency which makes it stand as a great American novel and a critique of American exceptionalism." He died of TB in 1870 in the age of 24.

Booker T Washington (1856-1915)

He was born in 1856 in a slave hut to an Afro-American woman on a Virginia plantation. At the age of 9, he began to work in a coal mine. His early life was full of difficulties and hardships.

In a coal mine, he heard about Hampton Norman, an Agricultural Institute. His firm determination carried him to this institute in 1872. He worked there as a caretaker to meet his school expenses.

After graduating from Hampton with honours in 1875, Washington returned to Malden to teach. For eight months, he was a student at Wayland Seminary and institution with a curriculum that was entirely academic. This experience reinforced his belief in an educational system that emphasised practical skills as self-help, in 1879, Washington returned to Hampton to teach in a programme for American Indians.

He died on 14th November 1915, and was buried at Tuskegee Institute.

Literary Career and Works

He wrote almost 40 books which are widely read and highly regarded. Among his work was an autobiography *Up from Slavery* (1901), *Character Building* (1902), *My Larger Education* (1911) and *The Man Farthest Down* 1912. Other works include *The Feature of The American Negro* (1899) and *The Story of My Life and Works* (1900).

William Faulkner (1897-1962)

He is another American novelist and short story writer. He was born on 25th September 1897 at New Albany, Missisippi, United States. He was a reluctant student and left high school without graduating but he devoted himself to the 'undirected reading' first all alone and later under the guidance of 'Philstones' a family friend who combined studies and practice of the law with lively literary interests. He joined British Royal Air Force but soon returned home and enrolled for a few University courses and published some poems.

Literary Career and Works

His first novel *Soliders* Pay (1926) was an impressive achievement and was stylistically ambitious and strongly evocative of the sense of alienation experienced by soldiers, returning from World War I. His 2nd novel *Mosquitoes* (1927) launched a satirical attack on the *New Orleans'* literary scene.

Another novel *The Sound And the Fury* was published in 1929 and after its publication Faulkner established himself as a writer, engaging himself in new themes, new areas of experience and all new technical challenges. The novel contained successive 'stream of consciousness' types monologues of different characters.

Faulkner's next novel *As I Lay Dying* (1930) is a brilliant tragicomedy. It is centred upon the conflicts within the 'poor white' Bundren Family, It is the most systematically multi voiced of Faulkner's novels and marks the culmination of his early post Joycean experimentalism.

Faulkner's success now ensured a large readership and his short stories were placed in popular and paying magazines such as 'Collier's' and Saturday Evening Post.

Another novel which brought fame to Faulkner was *Sanctuary* (1931) a novel about a brutal rape of a Southern College student and it is generally violent.

Another powerful novel. *Light in August* was published in (1932). The novel revolves primarily upon the contrasted careers of Lena Grove, a country woman serenly in present of her biological destiny and Joe Christmas, a dark complexioned orphan uncertain of his parentage.

Other Works

- Absalom Absalom (1936)
- The Town (1957)
- The Reivers (1962)
- The Hamlet (1956)
- The Mansion (1959)

William Faulkner was awarded the Nobel Prize in Literature in 1949, for his powerful and artistically unique contribution to the modern American Novel.

Faulkner wrote more than seventy short stories and six volumes of his short stories were published during his life time. Faulkner's short fiction provides the complete chronological development of yoknapatawpha from the arrival of white man who introduced the concept of private property, upto the 20th century, when the automobile became a common feature in American Society. Faulkner died in 1962.

Gertrude Simmons Burlingham (1876-1938)

She was born in 1876 in America. She was an extraordinarily talented and educated. She struggled and won at that time, when severe prejudice prevailed towards native American culture and women.

Literary Career and Works

Her pen name was Zitkala-Sa. In 1900, she began to publish articles, in which she criticised the Carlisle Indian School. She criticised the principal. Her life as native American woman was dedicated to iliminating the evil of oppression. She died in 1938.

Major Works

- Impressions of an Indian Childhood (1900)
- Schools Days of an Indian Girl (1900)
- An Indian Teacher among Indians (1900)
- Old Indian Legends (1901)
- Why I am a Pagan (1902)

Earnest Hemingway (1899-1961)

Earnest Miller Hemingway was born on 21st July, 1899 in Oak Park, a small town in USA. His father Dr Clarence Edmunds was a famous gynaecologist. His mother Greece Hemingway was fond of singing and painting. His parents were religious. He was highly influenced by his parents. His grandfather Mr Anson Hemingway, who served in the army, introduced him with weapons of violence and war. At school, he participated in various curricular activities actively.

He completed his study in 1917. He went to live with his uncle at Kansas city. He worked as a reporter with Kansas City Star. He wanted to participate in the war. Fortunately, in May 1918, he was made an honourary lieutenant. He wanted to have some adventure in life so he soon was bored with his job of driving the ambulances. Latter, he did the job of carrying mails and chocolates for the soldiers on the front.

After a few days, he was seriously wounded and carried to the Red Cross Hospital. He remained there for three months. He fell in love with Agnes Kurowsky, an American Red Cross nurse. He won many Gallantry Awards for his voluntary series. His beloved Agnes married an Italian major. He was unhappy and returned to USA. From Italy, he married Hadley Richardson in September 1921.

Literary Career and Works

Hemingway has been called one of the most highly attributed authors having written and published ten novels, ten collections of short stories and three autobiographies.

The three main novels of Hemingway are *For Whom The Bell Tolls* (1940), *The Sun Also Rises* (1926) and *The Old Man and The Sea* 1952. *The Sun Also Rises* is about a group of expatriates Americans living in Paris in the twenties.

The novel gave an understandable and clear insight into post war generations. This is considered Hemingway's best work of fiction. The next novel. *For Whom the Bell Tolls*, tells the story of a soldier in the Spanish Civil war their love, their war, their hate and their triumph. The novel was a great success and half a million copies of this were sold in less than two months "Hemingway was also nominated for Pultizer Prize after this novel's success and Hemingway noted it as literary triumph. His last novel *The Old Man And The Sea* was his greatest success. It told the story of an old master fisherman in Cuba and his battle with the largest catch of his life, a giant marlin. No doubts due to Hemingway 'amazing author' reputation, elite; a word just started showering on him. It won the Pulitzer Prize in 1952, the Award of Merit medal for the novel by the American Academy of Arts and Nobel Prize in literature in 1954.

Major Works

Novels

- The Torrents of Spring (1926)
- Fiesta (The Sun Also Rises) (1926)
- A Farewell to Arms (1929)
- To Have and Have Not (1937)
- For Whom The Bell Tolls (1940)
- Across The River and Into the Trees (1950)
- The Old Man and the Sea (1952)
- Island in the Stream (1970)

Stories

- Three Stories and Ten Poems (1923)
- In Our Times (1925)
- Men Without Women (1927)
- Winner Taking Nothing (1933)
- The First Forty-Nine Stories (1938)
- The Snows of Kilimajaro

John Steinbeck (1902-1968)

American writer John Steinbeck was born in 1902 and died in 1968. He won the Nobel Prize for Literature in 1962. His novels deal with the economic problems of rural labour.

Steinbeck attended stanford University California, intermittently between 1920 and 1926 but did not take a degree. Before his books attained success, he spent considerable time supporting himself as a manual labour while writing. His experiences lent authenticity to his depictions of the lines of workers in his stories.

Literary Career and Works

Steinbeck's reputation rests mostly on the naturalistic novels with proletarian themes he wrote in the 1930s. It is in these works that his building of rich symbolic structures and his attempt at conveying mythopoeic and archetypal qualities in his characters are most effective. He died in 1968.

Major Works

- **Cup of Gold** It is a romantic novel. It describes the story of a buccaneer. It was written in 1929.
- **To a God Unknown** (1937) It is the story of a farmer, who commits suicide because it did not rain for a long time and his crops were destroyed. This novel reminds us of the condition of Indian farmers of some states. They depend on rain and their debts force them to commit suicide.
- **Tortilla Flat** It was written in 1935. This humourous novel made him famous.

- **In Dubious Battle** It was written in 1936. This novel describes the life of homeless pickers.
- **Of Mice and Men** It was written in 1937. This novel describes the tragic life of homeless farm hands.
- **The Grapes of Wrath** This novel was written in 1939. It describes the hopeless life of refugeess, who have been uprooted from their homes as a result of exploitation by feudal agrarian system. This is perhaps the greatest novel on the condition of refugees in the world. Government found fault in it saying it was revolutionary or provocative in spirit. John Steinbeck won the Pulitzer Prize and made the way to gain the Nobel prize, which was awarded to him for his fiction work. This novel is the story of Joad family.
- **East of Eden** This novel was written in 1952. This was the most remarkable, in which he describes human struggle against evil symbolically.

Syliva Plath (1932-1963)

She was born on 27th October, 1932 in Massachusetts. She was an American poet, novelist and short story writer. She got name and fame as a professional poet and writer. She married follow poet Ted Hughes in 1956, having two children together Freida and Nicholas. They lived together first in USA and then in England.

Literary Career and Works

She is credited with advancing the genre of confessional poetry. She is famous for her two collections *The Colossus and Other Poems* and *Ariel*. In 1982, she became the first poet to win a Pulitzer Prize posthumously (after death) for *The Collected Poems*. She wrote a semi-autobiographical novel *The Bell* Jar, which was published shortly before her death. Following a long struggle with depression and a marital separation, she committed suicide on 11th February, 1963.

Non-British and Non-American Literature

The non-British and non-American literature mainly comprises the European, Australian, Canadian, Nigerian and African literature. Thus blend of features and characteristics of literature of the above mentioned countries and continents forms the basis of Non-British and Non-American literature.

The history of European literature and of each of its standard periods can be illuminated by comparative consideration of the different literary languages within Europe and of the relationship of European literature to world literature. The global history of literature from the ancient Near East to the present can be divided into five main, overlapping stages. European literature emerges from world literature before the birth of Europe-during antiquity, whose classical languages are the heirs to the complex heritage of the Old World. That legacy is later transmitted by Latin to the various vernaculars. The distinctiveness of this process lies in the gradual displacement of Latin by a system of interavernacular leadership dominated by the Romance languages. An additional unique feature is the global expansion of Western Europe's languages and characteristic literary forms, especially the novel, beginning in the Renaissance. This expansion ultimately issues in the reintegration of European literatrue into world literature, in the creation of today's global literary system. It is in these interrelated trajectories that the specificity of European literature is to be found. The ongoing relationship of European literature to other parts of the world emerges most clearly at the level not of theme or mimesis but of form. One conclusion is that literary history possesses a certain mechanism. Another is that language and literature are not only the products of major historical change but also its agents. Such claims, finally, depend on rejecting the opposition between the general and the specific, between synthetic and local knowledge.

Australian Literature

Australian literature is the written or literary work made in the area or by the people of Australia and its preceding colonies. During its early Western history, Australia was one of many British colonies. Therefore, its literary tradition is linked with English literature. Since 1788, the character of a new continent came into the literature. Themes included aboriginality, companionship, egalitarianism, democracy, migrant and national identity, distance from other Western nations and proximity to Asia, the complexities of urban living and the 'beauty and the terror' of life in the Australian bush.

The literature of Australia characteristically expresses collective values. Even when the literature deals with the experiences of an individual, those experiences are very likely to be estimated in terms of the ordinary, the typical and the representative. It aspires on the whole to represent integration rather than disintegration. It does not favour the heroism of individual action unless it shows dogged perseverance in the face of inevitable defeat. Although it may express a strong ironic disapproval of collective mindlessness, the object of criticism is the mindlessness rather than the conformity.

Canadian Literature

Reflecting the country's dual origin and its official bilingualism, the literature of Canada can be split into two major divisions: English and French. Many writers publishing in the 1960s and 70s subverted the traditional conventions of fiction, shifting from realist to surrealist, self-reflexive, feminist or parodic modes. Although historical events and the investigation of place as an imaginative source remained the most common subject matters, the narrative forms were experimental and playful. During the 1980s and 90s, writers also renegotiated ideas of self and nation and of belonging and loss while breaking down traditional boundaries of both gender and genre.

Although the subject of history exerts a powerful influence on all forms of Canadian writing, the tradition of regional fiction has not lost its momentum.

During the 1980s and 90s, increasing attention was also paid to the plurality and diversity of voices across the country. This period saw the emergence of numerous First Nations, Metis, and Inuit writers. Resisting the imposition of Western concepts of history, land, nation, society and narrative, many of these writers explored their oral traditions, myths, and cultural practices. A recurring theme is the individual's painful trajectory as the individual negotiates between cultures, combats racial prejudice and copes with shattered families and kinship groups; these concerns are also rendered in playful or parodic modes, as protest literature, or as alternatives to frenetic urban consumer cultures. These genres are also a part of the life writing (which also includes biography, bio-fiction, letters and diaries) that dominates the field of Canadian literature and resonates with the tradition of documentary writing.

Other perspectives tackle the experiences of immigrants-their interrogation of the meaning of home and belonging, their feelings of cultural assimilation and estrangement and their intergenerational struggles.

Fuelled by fervent literary nationalism and anti-Americanism, by the expansion of new presses and literary magazines and by the beckoning of avant-garde forms, poetry blossomed after 1960. Prolific, ribald, and iconoclastic, Irving Layton published 48 volumes of poetry celebrating life in memorable lyric lines and lambasting Canadian sexual Puritanism and social and political cowardice.

Nigerian Literature

Nigerian literature is the literature of Nigeria which is written by Nigerians, for Nigerians and addresses Nigerian issues. It is written in English, Igbo, Urhobo, Yoruba, Hausa, and the other languages of the country. The languages used by authors in Nigeria are based in part on geography, with authors in the northern part of the country writing in Hausa. Nigerian authors have won numerous accolades, including the Nobel Prize in Literature and the Man Booker.

African literatures as whole and Nigerian literature in particular was not birthed by the presence of the colonial masters, but rather, existed in myths, folktales, legends, songs and other various forms centuries before Europeans invaded the continent. That period is what is known as the classical period of Nigerian literature.

Literature is a vehicle of ideologies; a composition of language that serves as a cultural representation of a people. Literature, therefore, is more than a imaginative epistle. Nigerian literature before the 19th centuriy was in form of orature. And as is the case in any society, literature comes first in orality and only much later does it metamorphosise into written form and Nigeria is not different.

Ruth Finnegan's book *Oral Literature in Africa* (1970) is an eye opener and states without mincing words that African and Nigerian literature were in vibrant stages before the whites arrived and that Africans had organised and developed replacements for the written form. Songs were sung at wedding; poetry were read to praise gods; tales were performed at town gathering; each family had their own peculiar poetry and stories were told to praise legends. Nigerian Oral literature was a source of entertainment, philosophies and beliefs. Folktales were dramatic replacements for the novel. They are an imaginative form of narrative literature woven around well liked characters, sometimes even animals as they relate with physical world, or sometimes, the supernatural world. In the Eastern and Western part of the country, the tortoise is a star of many such tales. These stories, maybe not written, nonetheless have characters, plot beginning and end, and even epiphanies.

The same applied to myths-which were tales about death, afterlife or creation and the supernatural. Sometimes it looks like an earlier version of today's science fiction. The Europeans brought their own literature, written in books and that combined with the return of Samuel Ajayi Crowther who made Nigerians see the need to record their stories and culture and thus the beginning of Nigerian literature in a written format was initiated and promoted.

Major Non-British and Non-American Writers

Though English Literature has been dominated and influenced by the British composers since the beginning, closely followed by American writers toward the end of 19th century and entire 20th century, yet there has been no dearth of influential writers in and around rest of the world.

The writers from the countries like France, Ireland, Russia, Canada, Nigeria, Italy, Germany and Norway etc. have contributed immensely in the growth and popularity of English literature. Some of the notable non-British non-American writers are William Bliss Carmen, Luigi Pirandello, Pablo Naruda, Umber to ECO, Alphonso Daudet, Selma Largerlof, Ignazio Silone, Leo Tolstoy, Andre Gide and Saul Bellow etc.

Leo-Tolstoy (1828-1910)

Leo Tolstoy was born in Polyana, South of Moscow, Russia in 1828. he began his career as a school teacher, then became an Army officer and later moved to writing. He achieved success with his first novel childhood in 1852.

Literary Career and Works

Count Leo Nikolayevitch Tolstoy is one of the most famous personality in modern Russian literature. His novel *War and Peace* is one of the greatest novels of the world.

Tolstoy's two novels *War and Peace* (1865) *Anna Karenina* (1875) are regarded as among the finest novels ever written, *War and Peace*, in particular seems virtually to define this form for many readers and critics. Among Tolstoy's shorter works *The Death of Ivan Ilyich* (1886) is usually classed among the best examples novella. Tolstoy also achieved world fame as a moral and religious teacher. His doctrine of non-resistance to evil had an important influence on Gandhiji. Mathew Arnold said that "a novel by Tolstoy is not a work of art but a piece of life ...."

Major Works

- Childhood (1852)
- Boyhood (1854)
- Youth (1856)
- The Cossacks (1863)
- War and Peace (1869)
  Anna Karenina (1877)

Alphonse Daudet (1840-1897)

He was born in 1840. He was a French novelist and short story writer. He wrote *The Last Lesson* in the days of the Franco-Prussian war from 1870 to 1871. In this war, Bismark, who was leading Prussian army defeated France. Then Prussia consisted of the nations of Germany, Poland and parts of Austria. In the *Last Lesson*, the French districts of Alsace and Lorraine have passed into Prussian hands. He died in 1897.

His works are *Little Good-for-Nothing* (1885), *Letters from My Mill* (1880), *Tartarin of Tarascon* (1896), *Robert Helmont : The Diary of a Recluse* (1896), *Rose and Nevette* (1892).

Selma Lagerlof (1858-1940)

Swedish author Selma Lagerlof was born in 1858 in Sweden. She wrote many stories, which have been translated into many languages. All of them have a universal theme : a belief that the essential goodness in a human being can be awakened through understanding and love. She won the Nobel Prize in 1909. She died in 1940.

Her works are *The Miracles of the Antichrist, The Wonderful Adventures of Nils.*

William Bliss Carman (1861-1929)

He was born in 1861 in Canada. He published his first book *Low Tide on Grand Pre* in 1893. He wrote songs and ballads, *Behind the Arras* and *Ballads of Lost Heaven*. He died in 1929.

His works are *Low Tide on Ground Pre* (1893), *Songs from Vagabondia* (1894), *Behind the Arras* (1895), *Ballads of Lost Haven* (1897), *For Horezons* (1925), *Wuld Garden* (1929).

Luigi Pirandello (1867-1936)

He was born in 1867 in Italy. He was a great dramatist and novelist. His play are all built upon a pseudo meta-physician theory. He won the Nobel Prize in 1934. He died in 1936. His works are *Six Characters in Search of an Author* (1921), *Enrico IV* (1922), *Seve Pare : A Collection of Dramas* (1925), *Ll fu Mattia Pascal : a Novel* (1904).

Andre Gide (1869-1951)

He was born in 1869. He was a French writer, humanist, moralist. He received the Nobel Prize for literature in 1947. Gide supported individual freedom of impression and action against the claims of morality. He died in 1951.

Major Works

- The Notebooks of Andre Walter (1891)
- Fruits of the Earth (1897)
- Soul (1903)
- The Return of the Prodigal (1907)
- Thesel (1946)

Saul Bellow (1915-2005)

He was born in 1915. He was a great dramatist as well as a novelist. His works were influenced widely by World War II. He was an Italian. Among his most famous characters are Angie March and Moses.

He published short stories translated from Yiddish. He won the Nobel Prize for literature in 1976. He wrote novels and plays. *Humbolt's Gift* won the Pulitzer Prize. He died in 2005.

Major Works

- Dang ling Man (1944)
- The Adventures of Angie March (1953)
- Henderson the Rain king (1959)
- Humbolt's Gift (1975)
- The Victim (1947)

Ignazio Silone (1900-1978)

Ignazio Silone was born on May 1900 at Italy. His real name was Secondino Tranquili and he is known as novelist, short story writer and political leader. He was educated in the town of his birth until he was 15. He managed to finish secondary school and in 1917 he began to work with socialist groups. In 1921, he helped found the Italian Communist Party and in 1922 he became the editor of the party's paper in Trieste II Lavoratore.

Literary Career and Works

Writing under a pseudonym to protect his family, Silone produced his first novel *Fontamara* which was published in Zurich in 1930. The novel became an international sensation and was translated in 14 language. His later novels *Bread and Wine* (1937), *The Seed Beneath The Snow* (1942), portary socialist heroes who try to help the peasants by sharing their suffering in a Christian spirit.

His other works are the *School for Dictators* 1938, *The God that Failed* (1949) *Story Of A Humble Christian* (1968). The stories, written by Silone are *The Abruzzo Cycle*.

Patrick White (1912-1990)

Patrick White, an Australian novelist was born on 28th May, 1912 in London, England. White was born in London while his parents were on a visit to London and he came back to England for his schooling after 12 years in Australia. He worked for some time with his father and then joined King's College Cambridge to study modern languages.

Literary Career and Works

White's first novel *Happy Valley* (1939) was set in New South Wales and showed the influence of DH Lawrence and Thomas Hardy. The material of White's later novels is distinctly Australian but his treatment of it has a largeness of vision not limited to any one country or period. White's conception of Australia reflected in the *Tree of Man* 1955, *Voss* 1957, *Riders in the Chariot* 1961, *The Solid Mandala* 1966 and *Twyborn Affair* 1979. The product of an individual, critical, poetic his style is dense with myth, symbol and isolation and his search for meaning. White also wrote a number of plays and short stories. His short story is titled *Flaws in the Glass* (1981). His incomplete novel, at the time of his death *The Hanging Garden* was published in 2012 which White had hand written in 1981.

White won the nobel prize in literature in 1973 for "An *Epic and Psychological Narrative Art* which has introduced a new continent into literature."

Umberto Eco (Born 1932)

Umberto Eco is a Professor at the University of Bologna in Italy. He acquired a formidable reputation as a scholar for his ideas on semiotics (The study of signs), literary interpretation and medieval aesthetics. Then, he turned to writing fiction, academic texts essays, children's books and newspaper articles. His writings have a wide range.

Literary Career and Works

In 1980, he acquired the equivalent of an intellectual super stardom with the publication of *The Name of the Rose*, which sold more than 10 million copies. The English novelist and academic David Lodge once remarked. "I can't understand how one man can do all the things he (Eco) does". Umberto Eco replied. "May be I give the impression of doing many things. But in the end I am convinced I am always doing the same thing."

Major Works

- The Name of the Rose (1980)
- Foucault's Pendulum (1988)
- The Island of the Day Before (1994)
- Baudolino (2000)

Margaret Atwood (1939)

Margaret Atwood is regarded as one of Canada's finest living writers and she is acclaimed for her novels, story writing along with being a poet and environmental activist. her books have received critical acclaim in the United States, Europe and in Canada. Her books are regularly best sellers and she has won many awards to her credit.

Literary Career and Works

Atwood's interest in women and female experience also emerges clearly in her novels particularly in *The Edible Woman* (1969), *Surfacing* (1972), *Life before Man* (1979), *Bodily Harm* (1981), *The Handmaid's Tale* (1985). Even her later novels such as *The Robber Brido* (1993) and *Alias Grace* (1996) feature female characters defined by their intelligence and complexity.

Her novel *The Blind Assassin*, (2000) won her prestigious Booker Prize. The novel involves multiple story lines interpersed with narrative threads. Her other novels *Oryx and Crape* and *The Year of the Flood* envision a world of fundamental environmental catastrophe.

Isable Allende (1942)

Isabel Allende was bron on 2nd August 1942 at Lima, Peru, she is considered one of the first successful woman novelist from Latin America while living in Chile, Allende finished her secondary studies. She married at an early age. She became a moderately known TV personality, a dramatist and a journalist of feminist magazine.

Literary Career and Works

In 1981, Allende wrote a letter to his dying grand father hoping to thereby keep him alive at least in spirit. Later the letter evolved into a book *The House of the Spirits*, (1982) The book soon ran to more than two dozen editions in Spanish and was translated into a score of languages. The book was a great success. Allende's books are known for vivid story telling and her novels have been translated into more than 30 languages. Allende has won many awards in Chile and around the world and was recently called a 'Literary Legend' by Latino Leaders Magazine.

Major Works

- The Porcelain Fat Lady (1985)
- Of Love and Shadows (1985)
- Eva Luna (1987)
- Two Words (1989)
- The Stories of Eva Luna (1989)
- The Infinite Plan (1991)
- Daughter of Fortune (1999)
- Zorro (2005)
- Forest of the Pygmies (2005)
- Maya's Note book (2011)
- In the Midst of Winter (2017)

Haruki Murakami (1949)

Haruki Murakami is a Japanese novelist, short story writer and essayist. He was born in Kyoto, Japan during the post World war II and was Raised in Shukugawa. His father was the son of a Buddhist priest. Haruki grew up reading a wide range of works by European and American writers.

Literary Career and Works

Murakami began writing fiction at the age of 29. He was inspired to write his first novel *Hear the Wind Sing* (1979) while watching a baseball game. His initial success with this novel encouraged him to continue writing. A year later he published a sequel *Pinball* (1973). In 1982 came the third novel *A Wild Sheep Chase*.

In 1985, another novel *Hard Boiled Wonderland* and *The End of the World* was written which has a dream like fantasy that took magical elements by his work to a new extreme. Musukami achieved a major break-through with the publication of another novel *Norwegian Wood* (1987).

It is a nostalgic story of loss and sexuality. It was a great success and millions of copies were sold in Japan.

Murukami has won many awards for his fiction writing. In 2018, song writer Jason Reeves released the song *Hurukami* as a dedication to the author.

Major Works

- Birthday Girl
- Tony Takitani
- The Wind up Bind and Tuesday's Women
- Samsa in Love
- Dance, Dance, Dance in 1994
- South of the Border, West of the Sun (2000)
- Sputnik Sweet Heart (2001)
- Kafka on the Share (2005)
- After Dark (2007)
- 1Q84 (2011)
- Killing Commendatore (2018)

Roberto Bolano (1953-2003)

He was born in 1953 in Santiago, Chile. He is considred one of the legendary literary figures at the turn of the 21st century. He was an average student and dropped out of high school.

Literary Career and Works

His literary career began when he published a poetry collection while living in Mexico. He turned to fiction writing as it would be more remunerative than Poetry. After producing a series of short stories, he published the novel *The Skating Rink* in 1993. It was followed by *Nazi Literature in Americans* (1996) and *Distant Star* (1996).

Bolano's break-through novel was *The Savage Detectives* (1998) which tells the story of a circle of radical poets known as visceral realists. This novel made Bolano a literary star throughout Latin America and won the prestigious Romulo Gallegos Prize. He wrote with great speed, publishing one book every year.

He died of a liver ailment in 2003 at the age of 50.

Chinua Achebe (1930-2013)

He was a Nigerian novelist, poet, professor and critic. His first novel *Things Fall Apart* (1958) is often considered his best and is most widely read book.

He was born in November 1930 at ogidi, Nigeria. He grew up in the Igbo town. After studying English literature at University of Ibadan, Achebe taught for a short time before joining the staff of the Nigerian Braodcasting corporation in Lagos. Where he served as director of external broadcasting in 1961-66. After an automobile accident in 1990 that left him partially paralyzed, he moved to the US where he taught at Bard college in Annandale on Hudson, New York.

Major Works

- Things Fall Apart 1958
- No Longer At Ease 1960
- Arrow of God 1964
- A Man of the People 1966
- Anthills of the Savannah 1987

Achebe has also published several short stories and Children's book including *How the Leopard Got his Claws* (1973), *Beware Soul Brother* 1971 and *Christmas in Biafra* 1973 are collection of poems.

EXAM BASED QUESTIONS

1 Which most important event has to be acknowledged when we talk about contemporary literature?

(a) French Revolution (b) World War II
(c) World War I (d) Surrealism

2 What was the theme of the contemporary literature?

(a) Nature (b) Imagination
(c) Real life (d) All of these

3 Which literary writing developed most during contemporary period?

(a) Novel (b) Poetry
(c) Drama (d) None of these

4 Which of the following works belongs to CP Snow?

(a) The Wedding Party (b) Farcical Justice
(c) Darkness Visible (d) Time of Hope

5 Which works of CP Snow irritated FR Leavis to deliver lecture in opposition?

(a) Stranger and Brothers, Time of Hope
(b) The Two Cultures, The Scientific Revolution
(c) The New Men, The Masters
(d) Conscience of the Rich, Corridors of Power

6 Waugh's first published book was a biography of which artist and poet?

(a) William Blake
(b) John Donne
(c) Dante Gabriel Rossetti
(d) William Wordsworth

7 Which of the following work of Evelyn takes its title from a poem by TS Eliot?

(a) A Handful of Dust (b) Decline and Full
(c) The Loved One (d) A Little Learning

8 Which novelist wrote of denaturised humanity?

(a) CP Snow (b) LP Hartley
(c) NE Bates (d) JRR Tolkein

9 Which of the following works by Hartley, a trilogy written between 1944 and 1947, explores the brother-sister relationship?

(a) Eustace and Hilda (b) The Go-Between
(c) The Hireling (d) The Betrayed

10 What was HE Bates' pen name for his World War II stories?

(a) Flying Officer X
(b) Top Gun
(c) Lone Wolf
(d) Golden Falcon

11 Which novel of Bates is set in India?

(a) A House of Women
(b) My Uncle Silas
(c) The Scarlet Sword
(d) The Vanished World

12 Which of the following work was the major first commercial success of HE Bates?

(a) Fair Stood The Wind For France
(b) Love for Lyda
(c) The Darling Buds of May
(d) The Jacaranda Tree

13 Malcom Lowry's novel under the volcano is set primarily on what day?

(a) Christmas (b) New Year's Day
(c) Day of the Dead (d) Cinco de-Maya

14 What is the name of the city where 'Under the Volcano' takes place?

(a) Mexico City (b) Tijuana
(c) Quauhnahuac (d) Guadalajara

15 Which collection of short-stories by Angus Wilson presents a horrible dream of the political future?

(a) As If By Magic
(b) Setting the World of Fire
(c) No Laughing Matter
(d) The Old Man at the Zoo

16 Which of the following novel describes a compassionate portrait of an elderly and frustrated woman adjusting to new town life?

(a) Late Call
(b) The Mulberry Bush
(c) Hemlock and After
(d) The Middle Age of Mrs Eliot

17 Which work of Colin Wilson examines the works of important literary figures?

(a) The World of Violence
(b) The Outsider
(c) Man Without a Shadow
(d) Ritual in the Dark

18 Who wrote the novel 'There is a Happy Land' in his childhood and failed to charm the readers?

(a) Keith Waterhouse (b) William Cooper
(c) Anthony Burgess (d) Lawrence Durrell

19 Identify the work by Keith water house which cells the story of a Ferkshirc teenager.

(a) Billy liar (b) Jubb
(c) The Bucket Shop (d) There is a happy land

20 Where did Joyce Cary get material for his first four novels?
(a) Ireland (b) Britain
(c) Africa (d) India

21 Which of the following was the first novel by Joyce Cary?
(a) Aissa Saved (b) Mister Johnson
(c) Trilogy on Art (d) Prisoner of Grace

22 Identify the novels of 'Trilogy of on Art'?
(a) Herself Surprised, To Be A Pilgrim, The Horse's Mouth
(b) Herself Surprised, Prisoner of Grace, Except the Lord
(c) Mister Johnson, Not Honour More, The Captive and the Free
(d) The Horse's Mouth, Except the Lord, Aissa Saved

23 Which author's real name was Harry Summer Field Hoff?
(a) Agnus Wilson (b) Keith Waterhouse
(c) Joyce Cary (d) William Cooper

24 Which novel of Cooper describes the revolt against dull and conventional provincial society?
(a) Love on the Coast
(b) Scenes from Provincial Life
(c) You're Not Alone
(d) Memoiss of a New Man

25 Which work of Kingsley Amis showed the academic ambitions and the academic tensions of the rapidly expanding world of higher education?
(a) Lucky Jim (b) The Egyptologists
(c) One Fat Englishman (d) The Anti Death League

26 Which of the following work does not belong to Amis?
(a) The Crying Game (b) The Egyptologists
(c) I Like It Here (d) Take a Girl Like You

27 Who among the following used his home town as a setting for his novels?
(a) Alan Sillitoe (b) John Braine
(c) Mervyn Peake (d) Percy Howard Newby

28 Clive Lendrick has a loving wife, three beautiful children, a perfect marriage and a nice house in a fashionable Yorkshire village, but feels that something is missing and goes on a search for adventure and excitement. Which novel of Braine deals with the above theme?
(a) The Queen of a Distant Country
(b) The Vodi
(c) Waiting for Sheila
(d) Stay with Me Till Morning

29 Who among the following was associated with Angry Young Man Movement?
(a) John Wain
(b) Kingsley Amis
(c) Henry Green
(d) Anthony Powell

30 In which novel of Wain a reliable picture of angry young man with an anti hero is presented?
(a) Living in the Present (b) The Contenders
(c) Hurry on Down (d) The Young Visitors

31 The Loneliness of a Long Distance Runner is a novel by
(a) Kingsley Amis (b) Alan Sillitoe
(c) John Braine (d) John Osborne

32 Who among the following describes working people as the victims of a suppresser system of bureaucrats and capitalists?
(a) William Golding (b) Patrick White
(c) Alan Sillitoe (d) Arthur Koestler

33 Which of the following is the first novel by Golding?
(a) The Inheritors (b) The Spire
(c) Lord of the Flies (d) Free Fall

34 Which of the following novels of Golding has as its central character, Joceline, the ambitious Dean of an unnamed English Cathedral?
(a) The Spire (b) The Pyramid
(c) Free Fall (d) Darkness Visible

35 Which of the following is the first novel by Arthur Koestler?
(a) Thieves in the Night (b) The Gladiators
(c) Dialogue with Death (d) The Call Girls

36 What is the theme of the novel 'Thieves in the Night'?
(a) Conflicts between Rome and Spain
(b) Conflicts between Arabs and Jewish settlers in the British ruled Palestine
(c) A group of academic scientists struggling to understand the human tendency towards self-destruction
(d) It is about Koestler's first 26 years of life

37 Which novelist started his career in 1931 with publication of a novel 'Afternoon Men'?
(a) Muriel Spank (b) Anthony Powell
(c) Patrick White (d) Golding

38 Whose first novel, 'The Comforters,' is concerned with a woman writer, Caroline Rose, having to come to terms with her new-found Catholicism, with her hallucinations and with God-like status as a creator?
(a) Muriel Spark
(b) Iris Murdoch
(c) Lip Hartley
(d) Agatha Christie

39 Identify Muriel Spark's autobiography from the following
(a) Curriculum Vitae
(b) Memento Mori
(c) A Fairly Honourable
(d) None of the above

40 Who out of the following is the author of philosophical studies such as 'The sovereignty of Good' (1970) and 'Metaphysics as a guide to Morals' (1992)?
(a) Emlie Zola (b) Iris Murdoch
(c) Maupassant (d) None of these

41 In which work of Iris Murdoch, the character Austin sees himself always as a victim of other people and of his own bad luck?
(a) The bell (b) The Sand Castle
(c) The Accidental Man (d) Under the Net

42 Who among the following wrote repulsive aspect of Seneca's Cedipus for Brook's Theatre of Cruelty?
(a) Dorris Lessing (b) William Golding
(c) Ted Hughes (d) Graham Greene

43 Which of the following works of Lessing contains powerful anti-war and anti-stalinist messages?
(a) The Diary of a Good Neighbour
(b) Love, Again
(c) The Fifth Child
(d) The Golden Notebook

44 Which work won Edna O'Brien the Irish Book Award?
(a) August is a Wicked Mouth
(b) The High Road
(c) The Country Girls
(d) Time and Tide

45 Which work of Brien is based on triple homicide?
(a) In the Forest (b) Down by the River
(c) Wild Decembers (d) The Light of Evening

46 Who wrote the novel the wanting seed?
(a) Golding (b) Doris May lessing
(c) Iris Murdoch (d) Anthony Burgess

47 Alex and his friends encounter an old man in the Alley in the novel 'A Clock Work Orange'. How does Alex characterise the unfortunate man?
(a) He is a drunkard (b) A base ball player
(c) He is a banker (d) He is a college professor

48 Which novel by Brophy is a loved public declaration on women's rights?
(a) In Transit
(b) The Snowball
(c) Pusyowl
(d) The King of a Rainy Country

49 Who wrote the Country Girls Trilogy?
(a) David Edgar (b) Edna O Brien
(c) Mary Stewart (d) Lawrence Durrell

50 Which novel of O Brien presents the characterisation of an Irish village woman who had an affair with a war criminal?
(a) A Scandalous Woman (b) Down by the River
(c) The Little Red Chairs (d) The High Road

51 Which contemporary novelist writes in the tradition of George Eliot and Arnold Bennett?
(a) Edna O Brien
(b) David Mitchell
(c) Samuel Beckett
(d) Margaret Drabble

52 In which year was novel 'The Ice Age' published?
(a) 1970 (b) 1975 (c) 1977 (d) 1978

53 Which of these novels is not written by Margaret Drabble?
(a) Lord of the Flies (b) The Needle's Eye
(c) The Witch of Exmoor (d) Millstone

54 Which out of the following is the best known author of high Fantasy works. The Hobbit, The Lord of the Rings, 'The Silmlarillion.'
(a) JRR Tolkien (b) Philip Larkin
(c) Samuel Beckett (d) David Edger

55 What was Adam Ewing's ailment according to Dr Henry Goose? In the novel 'Cloud Atlas'.
(a) Parasite norm
(b) Eucalyptus allergy
(c) Tropical virus
(d) Predatory bacteria

56 In which year did Kazuo Ishiguro get Nobel Prize for Literature?
(a) 1989 (b) 1995
(c) 2017 (d) 2005

57 Identify the work which does not belong to Mary Stewart?
(a) The Stormy Petrel (b) Beloved
(c) My Brother Michael (d) The Last Enchantment

58 Who among the following keenly responded to the idea of creating an avowedly 'Modernist Fiction'?
(a) Lawrence Durrell (b) Beckett
(c) William Golding (d) None of these

59 Identify the writer who was deeply influenced by the American novelist Henry Miller, born in India wrote 'the Black Book'.
(a) Philip Larkin (b) Lawrence Durrell
(c) Samuel Beckett (d) Brecht

60 Which was David Mitchell's first published work?
(a) Black Swan Green
(b) Slade House
(c) Ghost Written
(d) The Bone Clocks

61 On which novel of David Mitchell was a film/movie made in 2012?
(a) Ghost Written
(b) The Thousand Autumns of Jacob de Zoet
(c) Black Swan Green
(d) Cloud Atlas

62 In which novel of Pamela Johnson are two characters Toby Roberts and Ann Thorold?
(a) This Bed Try Centre
(b) The Good Husband
(c) A Bonfire
(d) The Survival of the Fittest

63 Whose 1960s best seller was reissued as a penguin modern classic in 2017?
(a) Penelope Fitzgerald
(b) Penelope Ruth Mortimer
(c) Penelope Lively
(d) None of the above

64 In which room of School does Patrick hide in the novel 'The Indian in the Cupboard' by Lynne Reid Banks?
(a) In Science Lab
(b) In Library
(c) In the Canteen
(d) In the Music Room

65 What is the name of the black man who lives in the room next to Jane's in the novel 'The L Shaped Room'?
(a) Johny (b) Dennis
(c) Murphy (d) John

66 'The Return of the Soldier', 'The Birds Fall Down' are the famous works of
(a) Anthony Powell
(b) Philip Larkin
(c) Rebecca West
(d) None of the above

67 By The American Literature we mean
(a) Work of American in England
(b) Works or writings in English literature in America
(c) Works by non-British writers
(d) None of the above

68 The novel 'Power of Sympathy' was written in which year?
(a) 1778 (b) 1789 (c) 1780 (d) 1784

69 Who among the following is the writer of in modern period of American literature?
(a) Herman Melville
(b) David Thoreau
(c) Mark Twain
(d) William Faulkner

70 Which of the following novels is not a Leatherstoking novel by JF Cooper?
(a) The Prarie (b) Precaution
(c) The Deerslayer (d) The Pathfinder

71 Which of the following novels is not a Sea novel?
(a) The Pilot
(b) The Sea-Lions
(c) The Red Rover
(d) History of the Navy of the United States of America

72 In James Leatherstocking Tales, who is the main figure?
(a) Tonto (b) Chief Warrior
(c) Natty Bumppo (d) Dolly Madison

73 The novel 'The Scarlet Letter' is set where?
(a) England during World War II
(b) Paris during French Revolution
(c) The Middle Ages in Italy
(d) Puritan America

74 In the novel 'The Ambitious Guest' where does the young man say he is going after he settles for the evening at the Lodge?
(a) Salem, Massachusetts
(b) Burlington Vermont
(c) Augusta, Maine
(d) Concord, New Hampshire

75 What is unique about this work of Poe's "The Narrative of Arthur Gordon Pym of Nantucket"?
(a) It is his only novel
(b) It was published after his death
(c) It is his shortest novel
(d) It was his last work

76 In the story 'The Black Cat' by Edgar Poe the narrator's cat was named after which Roman deity?
(a) Pluto (b) Persepine
(c) Ceres (d) Apollo

77 By whom was novel 'White Jacket' written?
(a) Alice Walker
(b) Hawthorne
(c) Herman Melville
(d) Walt Whitman

78 What real city became the prototype of the city from the numerous works written by Mark Twain?
(a) Hannibal (b) Wisconsin
(c) New York (d) Chicago

79 By means of what was Huckleberry Finn going to reduce a want?
(a) a dead cat (b) a live mouse
(c) the frog guts (d) a dog

80 What is the name of Tom Canty's father from the novel, 'The Prince and the Pauper'?
(a) Edward the Eight (b) Bob Canty
(c) Smith Canty (d) John Canty

81 In Moby Dick Captain Ahab falls for his
(a) ignorance (b) pride
(c) courage (d) drunkenness

82 Which author wrote the novel 'The Portrait of a Lady'?
(a) Henry James (b) Mark Wain
(c) Allan Poe (d) Booker T Washington

83 Whose work among the following deals with a young man, while waiting for the coach to take him to the town, where he may essay his fortune, falls asleep in a forest near the highway?
(a) Edgar Allan Poe (b) Nathaniel Hawthome
(c) Henry David Thoerau (d) Whitter

84 Who wrote the novel 'Up from Slavery'?
(a) Edgar Allan Poe (b) N Hawthorne
(c) Henry James (d) Booker T Washington

85 Which of these works is not written by William Faulkner?
(a) Mosquitoes (b) The Sound and The Fury
(c) Soldiers Pay (d) Essay on Wordsworth

86 In which year was Faulkner awarded Nobel Prize in Literature?
(a) 1962 (b) 1947 (c) 1950 (d) 1949

87 The character of Lieutenant Rinaldi appears in which novel?
(a) For whom the Bell Tolls
(b) Farewell To Arms
(c) To Have or Have Not
(d) The First Forty-Nine Stories

88 In which book does Hemingway present sketches of his early life in Paris?
(a) Movable Feast
(b) The Old Man and The Sea
(c) Fiesta
(d) The Torrents of Spring

89 Name the novel which made John Steinbeck known to the people Worldwide.
(a) Tortilla Flat (b) Of Mice and Men
(c) Cup of Gold (d) None of these

90 Which of these works is/are written by Saul Bellow?
(a) Humbolt's Gift
(b) Henderson the Rain King
(c) Dangling Man
(d) All of the above

91 What is the name of the book by Leo Tolstoy that the Secret Police removed from print because it was a threat to its content?
(a) Resurrection (b) What I believe
(c) The Death of Ivan Ilyich (d) War and Peace

92 For whom is the harshest judgement in Leo Tolystoy's next novel War and Peace reserved?
(a) Alexander I (b) Louis XVIII
(c) Napoleon (d) George III

93 93. The novel 'The Last Lesson' was written by
(a) Selnia Lagerlof (b) Alphonse Daudet
(c) William Bliss Carman (d) Luigi Pivandello

94 Carman's first work 'Low Tide on Grand Pre' was published on
(a) 1863 (b) 1893 (c) 1884 (d) 1883

95 Identify the work from the following which does not belong to 'William Bliss Carman'?
(a) Behind the Arras (b) Corn
(c) Sunrise (d) Both (b) and (c)

96 The first work of William Bliss Carman was
(a) Behing the Arras (b) Ballads of Lost Heaven
(c) Low Tide on Grand Pre (d) None of these

97 Which author's pseudonym was Ignanzio Silone?
(a) Clemens (b) William Bliss
(c) Secondo Tranquili (d) None of these

98 Whose first novel in 1939 showed the influence of DH Lawrence and Thomas Hardy?
(a) Leo Tolystoy (b) Saul Bellow
(c) Patrick White (d) William Iennesse

99 The novel 'The Name of the Rose' was written by
(a) Umberto Eco (b) Ignazio Silone
(c) Isabel Allende (d) Haruki Murukami

100 Who is considered one of the first successful woman novelists from Latin America?
(a) Margaret Atwood (b) Isabel Allende
(c) Saul Bellow (d) William Bliss

101 The novel ...... was written in ...... by Malcolm Lowry?
(a) Ultramarine 1920
(b) Death Dance 1969
(c) Under The Volcano 1937
(d) Late Call 1964

102 The book .... does not belong to Angus Wilson.
(a) The Middle Age of Mrs Eliot
(b) The Old Man at the Zoo
(c) Hemlock and After
(d) Ritual in the Dark

103 The novelist ...... served the Nigerian Regiment during World War I
(a) Colin Wilson
(b) Keith Spencer Water House
(c) Joyce-Cary
(d) William Cooper

104 .... is noted for his ability to create comedy and satire out of depressing human predicament.
(a) Joyce Cary
(b) Kingsley Amis
(c) William Cooper
(d) Keith Spencer Water House

105 In the novel by Kingsley Amis the anti hero realises that the political and aesthetic values are a fraud
(a) Take a Girl Like You (b) Lucky Jim
(c) That Uncertain Feeling (d) I Like It Here

106 The novel 'the Crying Game' has been written by
(a) John Barrington Wain (b) Alan Sillitoe
(c) Gerald Golding (d) John Braine

107 William Gerald Golding's first published novel was .... in 1954.

(a) The Inheritors (b) Free Fall
(c) Lord of the Flies (d) The Spire

108 The novelist .... promoted spirituality and mysticism as alternative to politics.

(a) Arthur Koestler (b) Anthony Powell
(c) Muriel Sakah Spark (d) Murdoch

109 The comfortors, The Ballad of Peckham Rye and Curriculum Vital are fictions written by ....

(a) Anthony Powell (b) Margaret Atwood
(c) Muriel Sarah Spark
(d) Steinbeck

110 The novel gives an amusing description of the Angry young man who runs after the meat. It was written by ....

(a) The Girls Slender Means, M Sarah Spark
(b) Under the Net - Jean Iris Murdoch
(c) The Golden Notebook - Doris May Lessing
(d) The Kingdom of the Wicked - Anthony Burgess

111 Which of the following statement/statements about Brigid Antonia Brophy is/are incorrect?

(a) She wrote The Snow Ball in 1964
(b) Novel 'In Transit' is written in Jane Austen's style
(c) She attended St Paul's girls school
(d) She wrote the novel Psy Owl

112 Which of the following statement/statements about Edna O Brien is/are correct?

(a) Her novels express spirituality
(b) Her novels are deeply romantic
(c) O Brien's novels express her despair over the condition of women in society
(d) The novel 'The Little Red Chairs' was written in 1999.

113 Which of the following statement/statements is/are incorrect?

(a) Margaret Drabble's first novel was 'A Summer Bird'
(b) The novel ghost written by David Mitchell was published in 1999
(c) Nathaniel Hawthorne wrote Feather Top
(d) Edgar Allan Poe was only a poet

114 Which of the following statement/statements is/are correct about American novelists

(a) The first American novel was written in 1792
(b) James Fenimore Cooper was born in 1789 in New Jersey, United States in the year
(c) Nathaniel Hawthorne's many works are set against the background of Puritan New England
(d) Herman Melville's sea adventure stories are fake

115 Which of the following is not correct?

(a) 'Up from Slavery' was written by Booker T Washington
(b) 'A Witness Tree' was written by Saul Bellow
(c) William C Douglas wrote 'A Girl with A Basket'
(d) James Allen wrote 'From Poverty to Power'

116 Which of the following statement/statements about Henry James is/are incorrect?

(a) He wrote his first great novel 'The Portraits of a Lady' in 1881
(b) His first story 'The Story of the Year' appeared in the Atlantic monthly in March 1865
(c) Henry James wrote 'Biography of Virginia Woolf'
(d) Henry James was very much impressed by his Cousin Mary Temple

117 Which of the following statement/statements is/are correct?

(a) Faulkner's novel 'The Sound and The Fury' was published in 1950
(b) Faulkner was awarded Nobel Prize in Literature in 1949
(c) Gertrude Simmons Burlingham was born in 1888
(d) 'The Old Man and the Sea' was written by Mark Twain

118 Which statement is incorrect?

(a) Nigerian literature existed in Myths, folk tales, legends, songs etc.
(b) Australia's literary tradition is linked with English literature
(c) The tradition of regional fiction in Canadian literature has lost its momentum
(d) African literature was in Vibrant stages even before the whites arrived there

119 Which of the following statements is/are correct?

1. Leo Tolstoy is one of the most famous personalities in modern Russian literature
2. Selma Lagerlof is an American writer
3. William Bliss Carman was born in 1861 in Canada
4. Margaret Atwood's novels are related with economic class differences

(a) Only 1 (b) 3 and 2
(c) 2 and 4 (d) Only 2

120 Which statement about Haruki Murakami is incorrect?

(a) He is a Japanese novelist
(b) His first novel was 'Hear the Wind Sing'
(c) Haruki published his novel 'Norwegian Wood' in 1989
(d) This novel is a nostalgic story of loss

Directions (Q. Nos.121-124) *Inthe questions given below are two statements labelled as Assertion (A) and Reason (R). In the context of two statements, which one of the following is correct?*

Codes

(a) R is the correct explanation of A
(b) R is not the correct explanation of A
(c) Both A and R are correct
(d) Neither A nor R is correct

121 **Assertion** (A) Margaret Atwood novels abound in depiction of female experiences and women.

Reason (R) Margaret Atwood has won many awards to her credit.

122 **Assertion** (A) William Gerald Golding was awarded the Novel Prize for literature in 1983.

Reason (R) His novels are widely acclaimed as full of symbolism yet firmly realistic.

123 **Assertion** (A) Roberto Bolano, an Latin American novelist first wrote poetry, then shifted to fiction writing.

Reason (R) He found fiction writing more lucrative.

124 **Assertion** (A) John Braine is one of the so called Angry Young Man writers.

Reason (R) His novels show the concerns of generation of post World War II British writers.

125 **Assertion** (A) Edna O Brien had our indomitable spirit and it is reflected in her novels.

Reason (R) Edna O Brien very courageously portrays the oppressive world she had faced in Ireland, in her novels.

Codes

(a) Both A and R are true
(b) Both A and R are true but R is not the correct explanation A
(c) Only R is true
(d) Only A is true

126 **Assertion** (A) Washington Irving and James Fenimore Cooper are said to be pioneers of American Literature.

Reason (R) They wrote literature with American identity and American themes.

Codes

(a) Both A and R are true but R is not the correct explanation of A
(b) Both A and R are true
(c) Only R is true
(d) Neither A nor R are true

127 **Assertion** (A) Anthony Burgess can not be called a prolific writer.

Reason (R) Burgers, not only wrote novels and short stories but also television scripts and translation for the stage.

Codes

(a) R is the correct explanation of A
(b) A is not correct
(c) R is correct but A is not correct
(d) Both A and R are correct

128 **Assertion** (A) Nathaniel Hawthorne was a prominent part of the transcendentalist movement.

Reason (R) Many of his works are set in the background of Puritan New England.

Codes

(a) Both A and R are true but R is not the correct explanation of A
(b) Only R is true
(c) Only A is true
(d) Neither A nor R is true

129 Consider the following works.

1. The Hairy Ape
2. The Farewell to Arms
3. Desire Under the Elms
4. Strange Interlude

Codes

(a) All these are works by Eugene O' Neil
(b) All these are works of Tennesse Williams
(c) All these are works of John Steinbeck
(d) All these are works of Ernest Hemingway

130 Consider the following statements.

1. Herman Melville was born in New York.
2. Herman went on many Yoyages and this experience provided material for his many novel.
3. Herman Melville was awarded Nobel Prize.

Which of the statements given above is/are correct?

(a) Only 1 (b) 1 and 2 (c) Only 3 (d) 1 and 3

131 Consider the following statements.

1. Mark Twain is the pseudonym for Samuel Lang Borne Clemens.
2. He was an English novelist.
3. His stay at port town as a child has inspired the fictional town of St. Petersburg in his two novels.

Which of the statements given above is/are correct?

(a) Only 1 (b) 1 and 2 (c) 1 and 3 (d) Only 3

132 Consider the following statements.

1. Mark Twain was invited by humourist Artremus ward to contribute.
2. But Clemens refused
3. The Adventures of Huckleberry Finn was written by Mark Twain in 1885.

Which of the statements given above is/are correct?

(a) Only 2 (b) 1, 2, and 3
(c) Only 3 (d) 1 and 3

133 Consider the following statements.

1. Booker T Washington started working in a coal mine.
2. In the coal mine he heard about Hampton Norman, an Agricultural Institute.
3. In 1879 Booker T Washington started teaching in a programme for American Indians.

Which of the statements given above is/are correct?

(a) Only 1 (b) 2 and 3
(c) 1, 2 and 3 (d) Only 3

134 1. Earnest Hemingway for sometimes did the job carrying mails and chocolates for the soldiers.
2. The novel 'For Whom the Bell Tolls' is the story of a soldier in the Spanish Civil War
3. Hemingway was awarded the Pulitzer Prize for this novel.

Which of the statements given above are correct?

(a) 1 and 3 (b) 2 and 3
(c) 1 and 3 (d) 1 and 2

135 1. John Steinback was an English writer.
2. Steinback's reputation rests mostly on the naturalistic novels.
3. His novel cup of gold was written in 1929.
4. It is a romantic novel.

Which of the statements given above are/is correct?

(a) Only 1 (b) 2 and 4 (c) 2, 3, and 4 (d) Only 4

136 Match the following fiction writers with their works.

1. Sylvia Plath 2. John Steinbeck
3. Nathaniel Hawthorne 4. Alphonse Daudet
(A) Tortilla Flat (B) Rose and Nevelte
(C) The Bell Jar (D) The Blithedale Romance

Codes

(a) 1-C, 2-D, 3-B, 4-A (b) 1-C, 2-A, 3-D, 4-B
(c) 1-B, 2-A, 3-D, 4-C (d) 1-A, 2-B, 3-C, 4-D

137 Match the following.

List I	List II
A. Pale Fire	1. Thomas Hardy
B. The Sound and the Fury	2. Somerset Maugham
C. Rosencrantz and Guildenstern are Dead	3. William Faulkner
D. Under the Greenwood Tree	4. Tom Stoppard
E. Of Cakes and Ale	5. Vladimir Nabokov

Codes

	A	B	C	D	E
(a)	5	4	3	1	2
(b)	4	5	2	3	1
(c)	5	3	4	1	2
(d)	3	4	5	2	1

138 Match the following

List I	List II
A. David Malouf	1. The Solid Mandala
B. Patrick White	2. Wild Cat Falling
C. Peter Carey	3. Remembering Babylon
D. Colin Johnson	4. True History of the Kelly Gang

Codes

	A	B	C	D
(a)	1	3	2	4
(b)	3	1	4	2
(c)	2	3	1	4
(d)	3	4	2	1

139 Which of the following pairs is correctly matched?

(a) Nathaniel Hawthorne : Poet
(b) Walt Whitman : Critic
(c) Edgar Allan Poe : Novelist
(d) Bayard Taylor : Essayist

140 Which of the following pairs is incorrectly matched?

(a) Selma Lagerlof : 1858-1940
(b) Luigi Pivandello : 1872-1930
(c) Isabella Allende : 1942-......
(d) Penelope Ruth Mortimer : 1918-1999

141 Match the works with their authors and find out which is incorrectly matched?

(a) Henry James : The Victim
(b) Saul Bellow : Herzog
(c) Earnest Hemingway : The Sun Also Rises
(d) Margaret Atwood : The Edible Woman

142 Match the following.

List I	List II
A. John Steinbeck	1. The Glass Menagerie
B. Chinua Achebe	2. In Dubious Battle
C. William Howell	3. A Man of the People
D. Tennessee Williams	4. Indian Summer

Codes

	A	B	C	D
(a)	1	2	3	4
(b)	1	4	3	2
(c)	2	3	4	1
(d)	4	3	2	1

143 Match the following.

List I	List II
A. Chinua Achebe	1. Eatonton
B. James Baldwin	2. Harlem
C. Alice Walker	3. Nigeria
D. Edgar Allan Poe	4. Boston

Codes

	A	B	C	D
(a)	3	2	1	4
(b)	4	3	2	1
(c)	1	2	3	4
(d)	1	3	4	2

144 Which of the following pairs is incorrectly matched?

(a) Henry James : The Ambassador
(b) Edna O Brien : Casualties of Peace
(c) Herman Melville : Moby Dick
(d) Mark Twain : Typee

145 Which character is not correctly matched with the novel in which it appears?

(a) Aunt Polly : Adventure of Tom Sawyer
(b) Roger Micheldene : One Fat Englishman
(c) Charles Lumley : Hurry on Down
(d) Stephen Larke : Key to the Door

146 Which of the following novelists are in the chronological order as per their birth?

(a) Herbert Ernest Bales, Evelyn Waugh, Joyce Carry, Malcolm Lowry
(b) Evelyn Waugh, Malcolm Lowry, Joyce Carey, Herbert Ernest Bales
(c) Joyce Carey, Evelyn Waugh, Herbert Ernest Bales, Malcolm Lowry
(d) Malcolm Lowry, Joyce Carey, Evelyn Waugh, Herbert Ernest Bales

147 Which of the following works are in the chronological order as per their publication?

(a) The Adventures of Huckleberry Finn, To a God Unknown, Soldiers' Pay, The Name of the Rose
(b) The Adventures of Huckleberry Finn, Soldiers' Pay, To a God Unknown, The Name of the Rose
(c) To a God Unknown, The Adventures of Huckleberry Finn, The Name of the Rose, Soldiers' Pay
(d) Soldiers' Pay, The Name of the Rose, To a God Unknown, The Adventures of Huckleberry Finn

148 Which of the following is the right chronology of the following works of publication?

(a) The Handmaid's Tale, Rose and Nevette, The Savage Detectives, 1 Q 84
(b) 1 Q 84, The Handmaid's Tale, Rose and Nevette, The Savage Detectives
(c) The Savage Detectives, The Handmaid's Tale, Rose and Nevette, 1 Q 84
(d) Rose and Nevette, The Handmaid's Tale, The Savage Detectives, 1 Q 84

149 What is the correct chronological order of the birth of these novelists?

(a) Hawthorne, William Faulkner, Margaret Drabble, James Fenimore Cooper
(b) James Fenimore Cooper, Hawthorne, William Faulkner, Margaret Drabble
(c) Margaret Drabble, Nathaniel Hawthorne, James Fenimore Cooper, William Faulkner
(d) Hawthorne, Margaret Drabble, James Fenimore Cooper, William Faulkner

150 In the series given below which one has the literary works (novels, short-stories) matched correctly with their writers?

(a) Pincher Martin - Anthony D Powell, Life Goes On-Joyce Cary, Aissa Saved - WG Golding, Agents and Patients - Alan Sillitoe.
(b) Pincher Martin - Alan Sillitoe, Life Goes On - WG Golding, Aissa Saved - Anthony D. Powell, Agents and Patients - Joyce Cary
(c) Pincher Martin - W. G. Golding, Life Goes On - Alan Sillitoe, Aissa Saved - Joyce Cary, Agents and Patients - Anthony D. Powell
(d) Pincher Martin - Alan Sillitoe, Life Goes On - AD Powell, Aissa Saved - Joyce Cary, Agents and Patients - WG Golding

151 "An engine, an engine
Chuffing me off like a Jew
A Jew to Dachau A suchwitz, Belsen
I began to talk like a Jew,
I think I may well be a Jew."

(a) This is Sylvia Plath in 'Daddy'
(b) This is Saul Bellow in 'Herzog'
(c) This is Nissim Ezekiel in 'The Couple'
(d) This is Robert Frost in 'Mending Walls'

152 Whose words are these, "some thing we miss, not because our eyes are not clear enough ... but because the daylight is too blinding"?

(a) Whitter (b) Longfellow
(c) Hawthorne (d) None of these

153 Whose words are these, "whenever you find yourself on the side of the majority, it is time to reform for pause and reflect?

(a) Hawthorne
(b) Herman Melville
(c) Mark Twain
(d) Allan Poe

154 Which character in which novel of Edgar Allan Poe says these words "Let try heart be still a moment and this mystery explore ......"

(a) Raven in 'The Raven'
(b) Unnamed narrator in 'The Tell Tale Heart'
(c) Mrs Lackobreath in 'Loss of Breath'
(d) Roderick Usher 'The Fall of the House of Usher'

155 "Ralph wept for the end of innocence, the darkness of men's heart and the fall through the air of the true, wise friend called Piggy."

(a) This is Booker T Washington in UP For Slavery
(b) This William G Golding in Lord of the Flies
(c) This is Doris May Lessing in The Golden Notebook
(d) This is Anthony D Powell in Afternoon Men

156 Whose words are these "Life is made up of marble and mud......"

(a) Doris May Lessing
(b) Angus Wilson
(c) Nathaniel Hawthorne
(d) Herman Melville

157 "A writer of story books! what kind of a business in life what made of glorifying God or being serviceable to mankind in his day and generation or ...... may that be? Why the degenerate fellow might as well have been a fiddler ......"

From which novel's introductory section these lines have been taken?

(a) The Birth Mark
(b) The Scarlet Letter
(c) Young Goodman Brown
(d) The Marble Faun

158 "However, as soon as Mrs Hogg stepped into her room she disappeared, she simply disappeared. She had no private life whatsoever. God knows where she went in her privacy......"

In which work of which author do these lines appear?

(a) The flight from the Enchantn by Jean Iris Murdoch
(b) The Grass is singing by Doris May Leasing
(c) The comforters by Muriel Sarah Spark
(d) The kingdom of the wicked by Anthony Burgess

159 "I have never seen or heard of such a fish. But I must kill him. I am glad we do not have to try to kill the stars."
Which character in novel 'The Old Man and The Sea' by of Hemingway utters these words?
(a) Santiago in The Old Man and The Sea
(b) Manolin in The Old Man and The Sea
(c) Perico in The Old Man and The Sea
(d) Joe Di Haggio in The Old Man and The Sea

160 "What's terrible is to pretend that second-rate is the first rate. To pretend that you don't need love when you do, or you like your work when you know quite well you're capable of better."
In which work of which author do these line appear?
(a) The King of a Rainy Country by Brigid A Brophy
(b) August is a wicked month by Edna O' Brien
(c) The Ice Age by Margaret Drabble
(d) The Golden Notebook by Doris May Lessing

161 "In our deepest moments we say the most inadequate things". In which work of Edna O Brien these lines occur?
(a) Girl with Green Eyes
(b) In the Forest
(c) A Fanatic Heart
(d) The Little Red Chairs

162 Who said these lines 'A Half-read book is a half finished love affair'?
(a) David Mitchell in Cloud Atlas
(b) Margaret Drabble in Millstone
(c) William Faulkner - Sanctuary
(d) To A God Unknown - John Steinbeck

163 "But you can live in the most democratic country on earth and if you're lazy, obtuse or servile within yourself, you are not free."
Which author in which novel has uttered these words?
(a) Haruki Murakami in A Wild Sheep Chase
(b) Isabel Allende in Maya's Note book
(c) Patrick White in Voss
(d) Ignazio Silone in novel "Bread and Wine'

164 "What happens when people open their hearts?" 'They get better'
In which novel of Haruki Murakami do these lines appear?
(a) Hard Boiled Wonderland
(b) A Wild Sheep Chase
(c) Pinball
(d) Norwegian Wood

165 "Human relationships are vast as deserts, they demand all daring she seemed to suggest."
(a) Isabel Allende in Evaluna.
(b) Margaret Atwood in the Robber Bride
(c) Patrick White in Voss
(d) Alphonse Daudt in Little Good For Nothing

166 Which fiction writer has quoted the below given lines in which of his/her work?
"There is no death, daughter. People die only when we forget them, "my mother explained shortly before she left me." "If you can remember me, I will be with you always."
(a) Isabel Allende - Eva Luna
(b) Margaret Atwood - Life before Man
(c) Selma Lagerl of - The Wonderful Adventures of Nil
(d) Umberto Eco - The Name of the Rose

167 Which character in novel Anna Karenina match the description given below?
He is passionate and caring towards his lady love but clearly disappointed when he has to give up his dreams of career advancement.
(a) Alexei Karenin
(b) Dmitrich Levin
(c) Stepan Oblonsky
(d) Alexei Vronsky

168 "If every one made war only according to his convictions, there would be no war."
Which character in novel War and Peace Letters these words?
(a) Nikolai Rostov
(b) Prince Bolkonsky
(c) Narrator
(d) None of the above

169 Which literary critic said this, "A novel by Tolstoy is not a work of art but a piece of life ......"
(a) Charles Lamb (b) Samuel Johnson
(c) Matthew Arnold (d) Saul Bellow

170 Whose famous words are these "All happy families are alike; each unhappy family is unhappy in its own way."
(a) Andre Gide (b) William Faulkner
(c) Earnest Hemingway (d) Leo Tolstoy

171 "I had an inheritance from my father, It was the Moon and the Sun.
And though I roam all over the world
The spending of it's never done."
(a) This is William Faulkner in 'Mosquitoes'
(b) This is Earnest Hemingway in 'For Whom The Bell Tolls'
(c) This is Jean Iris Murdoch in 'The Bell'
(d) Anthony D Powell in Agents and Patients

172 "The world breaks everyone and afterward many are strong at the broken places. But those that will not break it kills ......"
In which work of Hemingway these lines appear?
(a) The Old Man And The Sea
(b) For Whom the Bill Tolls
(c) Death in the Afternoon
(d) Farewell to Arms

173 "History had a slow pulse; man counted in years, history in generation."

Which novelist has quoted these wording?

(a) Leo Tolstoy in War and Peace
(b) William Gerald Golding in Pincher Martin
(c) Arthur Koestler in Darkness At Noon
(d) Alan Sillitoe in 'Life Goes On'

174 "Knock your brains out, bust your back, run your feet down to the bone. What for? the man said nothing's promised to you, we know that."

Which fiction writer quotes these words in which of his/her work?

(a) John Barrington Wain in work 'The Contenders
(b) John Braine - Stay With in till morning
(c) Kingsley Amis - Lucky Jim
(d) William Cooper - Immortality At a Price

175 Which novel of Keith Water House presents people who have no talent and the young men, who have no talent and the young men, who die so early as they recklessly and angrily try to survive when they have no reason to deserve success.

(a) Billy Lian (b) Jubb
(c) There is a Happy Land (d) The Bucket Shop

Directions (Q. Nos. 176-180) *Read the passage given below and answer the questions that follow*

Adapted from F Scott Fitzgerald's This Side of Paradise, published in 1920.

Amory Blaine inherited from his mother every trait, except the stray inexpressible few, that made him worth while. His father, an ineffectual, inarticulate man with a taste for Byron and a habit of drowsing over the Encyclopedia Britannica, grew wealthy at thirty through the death of two elder brothers, successful Chicago brokers, and in the first flush of feeling that the world was his, went to Bar Harbour and met Beatrice O'Hara. In consequence, Stephen Blaine handed down to posterity his height of just under six feet and his tendency to waver at crucial moments, these two abstractions appearing in his son Amory. For many years he hovered in the background of his family's life, an unassertive figure with a face half-obliterated by lifeless, silky hair, continually occupied in 'taking care' of his wife, continually harassed by the idea that he didn't and couldn't understand her.

But Beatrice Blaine! There was a woman! Early pictures taken on her father's estate at lake Geneva, Wisconisn, or in Rome at the Sacred Heart Covent-an educational extravagance that in her youth was only for the daughters of the exceptionally wealthy-showed the exquisite delicacy of her features, the consummate art and simplicity of her clothes. A brilliant education she had-her youth passed in renaissance glory, she was versed in the latest gossip of the Older Roman Families; known by name as a fabulously wealthy American girl to Cardinal Vitori and Queen Margherita and more subtle celebrities that one must have had some culture even to have heard of. She learned in England to prefer whiskey and soda to wine, and her small talk was broadened in two senses during a winter in Vienna. All in all Beatrice O'Hara absorbed the sort of education that will be quite impossible ever again; a tutelage measured by the number of things and people one could be contemptuous of and charming about; a culture rich in all arts and traditions, barren of all ideas, in the last of those days when the great gardener clipped the inferior roses to produce one perfect bud.

In her less important moments she returned to America, met Stephen Blaine and married him this almost entirely because she was a little bit weary, a little bit sad. Her only child was carried through a tiresome season and brought into the world on a spring day in ninety-six.

176 In this passage, the underlined word, 'renaissance,' most nearly indicates that Beatrice's education was ....

(a) historical (b) glorious
(c) opulent (d) multifaceted

177 Which of the following words could not describe Beatrice's education?

(a) Pretentious (b) Mundane
(c) Judgmental (d) Superficial

178 As described in the passage, meeting Stephen Blaine is almost .... to Beatrice's life

(a) incidental (b) indispensable
(c) inimical (d) inimitable

179 Which of the following words would not be used to describe Stephen Blaine?

(a) Listless (b) Unconfident
(c) Resolute (d) Incoherent

180 In this passage, the underlined word, 'consummate' most nearly means

(a) somewhat paradoxical (b) antiquate
(c) fault less (d) ornate

Directions (Q. Nos. 181-185) *Read the Passage carefully and answer the questions that follow*

At nine O'clock in the morning, towards the end of November, the Warsaw Train was approaching Petersburg at full speed. It was thawing and so damp and foggy that it was difficult of distinguish anything ten paces from the line to right or left of the carriage windows. Some of the passengers were returning from abroad, but the 3rd class compartments were most crowded, chiefly with people of humble rank, who has come a shorter distance on business. All of course were tired and shivering, their eyes were heavy after the night's journey and all their faces were pale and yellow to match the fog.

In one of the third-class carriages, two passengers had, from early dawn, been sitting facing one another by the window. Both were young men, not very well dressed, and travelling with little luggage; both were of rather striking appearance, and both showed a desire to enter into conversation. If they had both known what was remarkable in one another at that moment, they would have been surprised at the chance which had so strangely brought them opposite one another in a third-class carriage of the Warsaw train. One of them was short man about twenty-seven, with almost black curly hair and small, grey, fiery eyes. He had a broad and flat nose and high cheek bones. His thin lips were continually curved in an insolent, mocking and even with a malicious smile. But the high and well-shaped forehead redeemed the ignoble lines of the lower part of the face. What was particularly striking about the young man's face was its death-like pallor, which gave him a look of exhaustion in spite of his sturdy figure, and at the same time an almost painfully passionate expression, out of keeping with his coarse and insolent smile and the hard and conceited look in his eyes. He was warmly dressed in a full, black, sheepskin-lined overcoat, and had not felt the cold at night, while his shivering neighbour had been exposed to the chill and damp of a Russian November night, for which he was evidently unprepared. He had a fairly thick and full cloak with a big hood.

181 In the passage the third class compartment was the most crowded because

(a) Charges were less
(b) Charges suited the people of humble rank
(c) Both (a) and (b)
(d) None of the above

182 What does the expression 'death like pallor' mean in the passage?

(a) The traveller was perhaps exhausted and sick
(b) The traveller was going to die
(c) The traveller was of pale colour
(d) The traveller had been sleeping

183 Which of the following word would not be used to describe the short man?

(a) He belonged to the aristocratic family
(b) He was unconfident
(c) He was trying to hide his pain
(d) He was determined and resolute

184 The other copassenger did not feel the chill in night as he was

(a) very healthy
(b) he carried a heater with him
(c) dressed in Sheepskin link over coat
(d) he had covered himself with a warm blanket

185 The narrative is set in which century and in which country?

(a) Late 18th century Italy (b) 19th century Russia
(c) Modern Poland (d) Late 20th century Russia

Directions (Q. Nos. 186-190) *Real the Passage carefully and answer the questions that follow*

So, it was In Paris I walked with the policeman and talked with him, and found him everywhere, in shop windows, with big bulging eyes and each eye a wonder to see I saw eyes in Paris bookshop, windows such as I have never seen anywhere, small eyes, big eyes, green eyes, white-feathery eyes, lathery eyes, parroty eyes, pepper eyes and progressive eyes - red eyes for the red and all the world grew into Red beauty - (and, this you will find, in rue Racine) - and green eyes and scarlet eyes, soutane and sepulchre beads and biblical eyes - you find them just behind in smutty shops with big squares and courtyards and bright red geraniums at the bay windows - sooty eyes bespeaking of paradise, yellow eyes Luxembourg, eyes of the young, eyes of children and lovers and of the autumnal falling leaves - everywhere you see eyes in Paris, and they all had colours and I loved them. I lived in rue Servandoni later - and had two eyes there that had needle connection and logic was its palaetiology. For, on the point of the needle, was my love born - and it started stitching my tatterment. Oh, the love-needle, the pertinence, the power, and the purity of the stitching needle. My heart was made into a Hindu sack with prayer-verses on the top as of Benares - and I counted the doubtful beads. I was virtuous and I took on assigned form. The needle stitched and stitched me, and I took on a white and wandlike shape. I became a magician of looks, and I gave eyes to many. I opened a shop of Hindu eyes - I the policeman- and Oh, what a chatter and a clamour was there. God, God is my business, I cried - Hindu Gods. Four annas a hundred tricks - standing on the nose and breathing through the umbilical stitch, practising celibacy through baths and kundalini - etc., etc., - eating milk and nuts to walk in the air, eating bitter neem leaves and sherbet for swallowing nails and toothbrushes and broken glass - for telling the future - motor cars, mansions and marriages, and all, fortunes -I opened such a shop. The trade was good. I did much business. The Municipal Council of Perpignan -for I had moved there by now- voted me a certificate of fine conduct. And all the virgins came to my confessions. I dealt in potions that increased physiological virginity - gave no scratches or itches or leucorrhoea - You touched me and you were cured. It was wonderful. And God was the message they got. I was virtuous and good. And I grew big. I became fashionable. Newspapers spoke of me. I was the policeman of God, and my certificates hung on all my four walls. I was given the Legion d'Honneur. II class, God seemed to speak to me from the heavens every night - and all day all night the logical needle stitched my sores, and when I woke up, I had a good bath and I looked so fresh and young. I could walk the Promenade des Anglais with the agility of a tennis player. They said, here goes the Policeman of God - and later they came and sate me by them in chaiseslongues, and as the sun poured on me tender and golden, I became a legitimate divinity. I had fruits and flowers offered to me, and I was right happy. I was God.

186 The policeman as described in the passage is a symbol of

(a) protection (b) vigilance and duty
(c) corruption (d) None of the above

187 The passage describes the narrator's occupation. What is it?

(a) Policeman (b) Hindu Priest
(c) Businessman (d) Christian Father

188 What does the expression 'God is my business' mean here?

(a) The narrator sells Gods in many forms
(b) The narrator is a priest who prays to God for others and is being paid for this
(c) People come to him for advice
(d) Showing many Yoga tricks

189 The narrator here is simply describing his experiences or is it something else.

(a) a comic narration of events
(b) the prosperity of a priest
(c) satire on fake 'holy man' who makes money by playing with the sentiments of the people
(d) Stupid common folk

190 In the passage the word 'legitimate' most nearly means

(a) some what logical
(b) illegal
(c) permissible
(d) deceptive

PREVIOUS YEARS' QUESTIONS

December 2018

1 Albert Camus borrows the following epigraph to his novel 'The Plague' from
"It is as reasonable to represent one kind of imprisonment by another, as it is to represent anything that really exists by the which exists not".

(a) James Hogg's 'The Confession of a justified Sinner'
(b) Jeremy Bentham's 'The Principles of movals and Legislation
(c) Robert Burton's The Anatomy of Melancholy
(d) Daniel Defoe's Robinson Crusoe

January 2018

2 "Reality is that nothing happens. How many of the events of history have occurred, ask yourselves, for this and for that reason, but for no other reason fundamentally, than the desire to make things happen? I present to you History, the fabrication, the diversion, the reality-obscuring drama."
Which postmodern novel thus subverts the truth claims of traditional historiography?

(a) AS Byatt's possession
(b) John Fowles's The French Lieutenant's Woman
(c) Graham Swift's Waterland
(d) Michael Ondaatje's The English Patient

3 In which of his novels does Italo Calvino construct his narrative through a tarot pack of cards and re-interpret the Western canon providing new versions of Oedipus Rex, Faust, Hamlet, Macbeth and King Lear?

(a) The Castle of Crossed Destinations
(b) Our Ancestors
(c) Invisible Cities
(d) The Path to the Nest of Spiders

4 Anthony Burgess's last novel, published in 1993 is called 'A Dead Man is Deptford'. Who is the central character to whom the title refers?

(a) Sir Walter Raleigh (b) Sir Philip Sydney
(c) Christopher Marlowe (d) Earl of Southampton

5 Identify from among the following list those that cannot be called War Fiction.

1. A Modern Instance 2. Catch-22
3. The Age of Innocence
4. The Naked and the Dead

(a) 1 and 4 (b) 2 and 3 (c) 1 and 3 (d) 2 and 4

6 This novel is dedicated "To the railroad of bones" and has as its epigraph the line,
"I am the woman they give dead women's clothes to" from Christine Gelineau's 'Inheritance'. Identify the novel.

(a) African Psycho by Alain Mabanckou
(b) The Chibok Girls by Helon Habila
(c) The Underground Railroad by Colson Whitehead
(d) The Book of Night Women by Marlon James

7 Which novel by John Banville tells the story of a group of travellers who arrive on a small island and stumble upon the house of Prof. Kreutznaer whose relationship to a painting entitled *The Golden World* by a fictional Dutch artist named Vaublin plays a central role?

(a) Ghosts (b) The Sea
(c) The Ark (d) Eclipse

8 Which novel of Kazuo Ishiguro is narrated by a Japanese widow living in England and draws on the destruction and rehabilitation of Nagasaki?

(a) An Artist of the Floating World
(b) The Unconsoled
(c) A Pale View of Hills
(d) When We Were Orphans

9 Evelyn Waugh once complained that TS Eliot's Poems 1909-1925 was "marvellously good, but very hard to understand." The most pessimistic novel Waugh wrote was called and he owed the title to

(a) Black Mischief - "Sweeney among the Nightingales"
(b) Scoop - "Morning At the Window"
(c) Prancing Nigger - Ash Wednesday
(d) A Handful of Dust - The Waste Land

10 Leo Tolstoy's Anna Karenina's closing lines present

(a) a sad reflection on the unfortunate suicide of Anna which should have been averted
(b) the enlivening freshness of a rain which has been threatening to breakout
(c) Levin's affirmation that whatever happens to him, life is not meaning less but unquestionably meaningful
(d) Vronsky's lament over death of Anna which ends on a positive note

November 2017

11 Who made the comment that, "All modern American Literature comes from one book by Mark Twain called Huckleberry Finn"?

(a) Henry James (b) William Faulkner
(c) Jack London (d) Ernest Hemingway

12 Which of the following novels by Margaret Atwood depicts the historical event of the notorious murders committed in 1843?

(a) The Blind Assassin (b) Alias Grace
(c) Cat's Eye (d) Onyx and Crake

13 Which of the following character in Moby Dick falls over board and turns insane as a result?

(a) Pip (b) Queequeg
(c) Starbuck (d) Tshtego

14 In William Golding's Loard of the Flies which of the following characters is put to death?

(a) Piggy (b) Ralph
(c) Simon (d) Jack

15 Which of the following is not true about Albert Camus's novel, The Plague?

(a) Dr. Rieux describes the phenomenon of dying rats using the metaphors of disease especially the bubonic plague
(b) Paneloux interprets the plague in his first sermon as a sign of the Apocalypse
(c) M Michel is the first victim of the plague
(d) Tarrou thinks that the plague symbolises human in differences.

16 Which one of the Alice Munroe's short stories is about the domestic erosions of Alzheimer's disease?

(a) Dear life (b) Runaway
(c) The Bear Came over the mountain
(d) Dance of the happy shades

17 Why does Father Dolan punish Stephen with the pandy bat in Joyce's Portrait of the Artist as a Young Man?

(a) Stephen is talking to another student to get the answer to a Latin problem
(b) Stephen is not doing his work because his glasses are broken
(c) Stephen is looking out of the window towards the infirmary
(d) Stephen is lost in remembering his mother's farewell and cannot hear Father Dolan calling out his name.

18 Using a non-linear narrative, this American novel expresses the psychic damage to a veteran of World War II and shows how a measure of healing is attained through his acceptance of Laguna myths and rituals. Identify the work ......

(a) Dred (b) Beloved (c) Ceremony (d) End Zone

January 2017

19 Allan Poe's novel 'The Raven' mourns the death of Poe's

(a) lost lenore (b) lost abigail
(c) pet animal (d) lost heritage

20 William Faulkner's 'As I lay Dying' contains one of the shortest chapters in literary history.

Which of these sentences is the chapter in its entirety?

(a) "For the love of God where is my hat"?
(b) "My mother is a fish"
(c) "Addie Bundren was dead to begin with"
(d) "Apricot Jaur is the worst sort of a jaim"

21 Which novel by Patrick white is based on the story of Ludwig Leichhardt, the Prussian naturalist who explored Australia in the mid 1840s in which white's fictional hero says when asked about navigation "The Map? I will first make it"?

(a) The Tree Man (b) Voss
(c) Riders in the Chariot (d) The Solid Mandala

22 Who among the following is not a character in William Golding's Lord of the Flies'?

(a) Ralph (b) Piggy
(c) Peter (d) Jack

23 Who identified "Strangled articulateness' as a theme is Canadian writing?

(a) Margaret Atwood (b) Northrop Frye
(c) Michael Ondaatje (d) Joy Kogawa

24 Which of Kazuo Ishiguro's novels are set mostly in Japan?

1. The Unconsoled
2. The Remains of the Day
3. An artist of the Floating world
4. A Pale view of Hills

Codes

(a) 1 and 3 (b) 2 and 3
(c) 3 and 4 (d) 1 and 4

July 2016

25 Who among the following was born in India?

(a) Paul Scott (b) Lawrence Durrell
(c) EM Forster (d) VS Naipaul

26 What is the name of the boat that rescues Ishmael in Herman Melville's Moby Dick?

(a) Pequod (b) Rachel (c) Hagar (d) Sphnix

27 Identify the first novel written by Patrick White.

(a) The Living And the Dead
(b) The Tree of Man
(c) Happy Valley
(d) The Aunt's Story

28 Which novel of Doris Lessing ends with a projection forward in time after a devastating atomic war?

(a) The Grass is Singing (b) The Golden Note Book
(c) The Four Gated City (d) A Proper Marriage

29 Which novel of Toni Morrison tells the wrenching story of a protagonist who murders her child rather than to allow him/her to live as a slave?

(a) Sula (b) Tar baby
(c) Song of Solomon (d) Beloved

30 By the end of 1950s novelists like Stan Barstow, Sid Chaplin, Alan Sillitoe and David storey were routinely lumped together as representatives of 'Kitchen Sink Realism'. Who in 1954 wrote the article 'The Kitchen Sink' calling attention to the gritty and direct realism?

(a) Martin Harrison (b) Stan Smith
(c) David Sylvester (d) Philip Callow

31 What part of Canada in Alice Munro most famous for depicting?

(a) Vancouver (b) Montreal
(c) Ontario (d) Quebec

32 Who among the following African novelists was a student of philosophy and literature in India?

(a) Nuruddin Farah
(b) Benoki
(c) Helon Habila
(d) Benjamin Kwakye

33 In novel Crime and Punishment which Character speaks the following words. Who/What are they addressed to?
"I waited for you impatiently …… all this blasted psychology is double edged weapon".

(a) Svidrigailov to the pistol with which he shoots himself
(b) Katherine Ivanovna to Marmeladov
(c) Porfiry Petrovich to Raskolinkov
(d) Raskolnikov to the Bible he finds in the prison cell in Siberia

December 2015

34 Patrick White published two novels in the 1950s giving the era of pioneering and exploration in Australian history an epic, ironic and psychological dimension The novel are

1. A Fringe of Leaves
2. The Free of Man
3. Voss
4. The Aunt's Story

Codes

(a) 1 and 2 (b) 2 and 3
(c) 3 and 1 (d) 3 and 4

35 The following is the classical ending of a celebrated novella in English.
"I kept on creeping just the same but I looked at him over my shoulder, "I've got out at last' said, "In spite of you and Jane. And I've pulled off most of the papers, so you can't put me back!"

(a) Yellow woman (Leslie Mormon Silke)
(b) The yellow wallpaper (Charlotte P Gilmau)
(c) Johny Panic and the Bible of Dreams (Sylvia Plath)
(d) Where are you going, where have you been (Joyce c Oates)?

36 Which of the individual is a nihilist from the following?

(a) Pechorin in A Hero of Our Times
(b) Bazarov in Father and Sons
(c) Levin in Anna Karenina
(d) Oblomov in Oblomov

June 2015

37 Margaret Atwood has tried a revisionist writing of a crucial scene in Hamlet Called "Gertrude talks back". The scene in Atwood opens with a reference to the name of an implied listener. Who is this?

(a) Hamlet (b) Ophelia
(c) Polonius (d) Claudius

38 Which of the following is not written by Buchi Emecheta?
(a) The Joys of Motherhood (b) Second Class Citizen
(c) A Question of Power (d) Kehinde

39 Which of the American novelists is associated with the series of five books about Natty Bumppo, an old hunter, also called leather stocking?
(a) Stephen Crane (b) James Fennimore Cooper
(c) Herman Melville (d) Jack London

40 Which of the following novels opens with the description of an accident to a hot air balloon?
(a) John Fowls's The Magus
(b) Ian Mc Ewan's Enduring Love
(c) James Kelman's - How Late it was, How Late
(d) Irvine Welsh's Train spotting

41 Which of the following novels deals with the Biafran war?
(a) July's People
(b) Waiting for the Barbarians
(c) Half of a yellow Sun
(d) Arrow of God

December 2014

42 Which of the following two lists are 'Angry Young Men' of the 1950's British literary Scene?
(a) John Osborne (b) C P Snow
(c) Anthony Powell (d) Kingsley Amis

43 Which of the following novel is not written by Jean Rhys?
(a) After Leaving Mr. Mackenzie
(b) Good Morning, Midnight
(c) The Quiet American
(d) Wide Sargasso Sea

44 Which character in William Golding's Lord of the Flies maintains, "Life is Scientific"?
(a) Simon (b) Piggy
(c) Ralper (d) Jack

45 Who are 'Didi' and Gogo?
(a) They are two characters in End Game
(b) They are nick names respectively for Lucky and Pozzo
(c) They are nicknames respectively for Vladimir and Estragon
(d) They are two character in Breath

46 Which of the following writers writes from Canada?
(a) VS Naipaul (b) Margaret Atwood
(c) Derek Walcott (d) James Joyce

47 Which of the following can not be classified as fantasy fiction?
(a) The Inheritors (William Golding)
(b) The Magus (John Fowls)
(c) The Lord of the Rings (J R R Tolkein)
(d) The History Man (Malcolun Bradbury)

48 Which of the following African writers won the Nobel Prize for Literature?
(a) Chinua Achebe (b) Nadine Gordimer
(c) Ngugi Wa Thiong'o (d) Bessie Head

49 The narrative of this novel is a meticulous present tense account of a woman with a death wish who plots the circumstance of her own violent murder. Identify the novel.
(a) Iris Murdoch's A Fairly Honorable Defeat
(b) Muriel Spark's - The Driver's Seat
(c) Doris Lessing's - Children of Violence
(d) Angela Carter's - The Passion of the New Eve

50 The Kite Runner, a novel by Khalid Hosseini tells the story of ....
(a) Ahmed (b) Nadira (c) Amir (d) Amourah

51 Thomas Babington Macaulay, the writer of the infamous Minute of 1835, finds a mention in Salman Rushdie's ......
(a) Midnight Children (b) Shame
(c) The Moor's Last Sign (d) Fury

52 Who among the following is not an Australian writer?
(a) Morris West (b) Patrick White
(c) Thomas Keneally (d) Bill Pearson

53 All fiction for me is a kind of magic or trickery- 'a confidence trick' The statement has been made by ....
(a) Angus Wilson (b) Anthony Powell
(c) John Fowles (d) George Orwell

54 Which of the following writers did not receive the Nobel Prize for Literature?
(a) Wole Soyinka (b) Chinua Achebe
(c) JM Coetzee (d) Nadine Gordimer

55 The first novel written by Graham Greene is
(a) Stamboul Train (b) England Made Me
(c) The Heart of the Matter (d) The Man Within

June 2014

56 "The artist may be present in his work like God in creation, invisible and almighty, everywhere felt but nowhere seen". Henry James is talking here about the artist's
(a) Impersonality (b) Absence (c) Presence (d) Creativity

57 Identify the incorrect factor in Henry James Theory of the Novel
(a) It should be sentimental (b) It should be objective
(c) It should be realistic
(d) It should be viewed as an artistic form

58 Yasmine Gooneratne's 'The Pleasure of Conquest' termed as a post colonial novel of the 90s is ironically enough set in the tropical island nation of
(a) Sri Lanka (b) Fizi (c) The Caribbean (d) Amnesia

59 George Meredith's first novel was banned by Mudie's circulating Library for its supposed moral offence.

Identify the Novel

(a) The Egoist
(b) Evan Harrington
(c) Diana of the Crossways
(d) The Ordeal of Richard Feveral

60 In which of the following novels by conrad, do the Gould couple and Decoud appear as characters with Costaguana as the setting?

(a) Victory
(b) Under Western Eye
(c) Nortromo
(d) The Nigger of the Narcissus

61 Which of the following statements best apply to Anna Karenina?

1. Among her most prominent qualities are her passionate spirit and determination to live life on her own terms.
2. She accepts the exile to which she has been condemned.
3. She is a victim of Russian Patrichal System
4. Anna is deeply devoted to her family and children.

Codes

(a) 1 and 2 (b) 2 and 3
(c) 1 and 3 (d) 1, 3 and 4

62 Match the following

List I (Authors)	List II (Works)
A. Vladimir Nabakov	1. Germinal
B. Italo Calvino	2. Foucault's Pendulum
C. Umberto Eco	3. If on a writer's Night a Traveller
C. Emile Zola	4. Lolita

Codes

	A	B	C	D
(a)	3	1	4	2
(b)	4	3	2	1
(c)	1	2	3	4
(d)	2	4	1	3

63 In his fiction Mc Ewan more than often suggest the .... of love.

(a) fragility (b) madness
(c) completeness (d) security

64 In one of her novels, Margaret Atwood demonstrated the potentially 'Cannibalistic' nature of human relationships. Identify the novel

(a) Surfacing (b) Lady Oracle
(c) Life before Man (d) The Edible Woman

ANSWERS

Objective Questions

1. (b)	2. (c)	3. (a)	4. (d)	5. (b)	6. (c)	7. (a)	8. (b)	9. (a)	10. (a)
11. (c)	12. (a)	13. (c)	14. (c)	15. (d)	16. (a)	17. (b)	18. (a)	19. (a)	20. (c)
21. (a)	22. (a)	23. (d)	24. (b)	25. (c)	26. (a)	27. (b)	28. (d)	29. (a)	30. (c)
31. (b)	32. (c)	33. (c)	34. (a)	35. (b)	36. (b)	37. (b)	38. (a)	39. (a)	40. (b)
41. (c)	42. (a)	43. (d)	44. (c)	45. (a)	46. (d)	47. (a)	48. (b)	49. (b)	50. (c)
51. (d)	52. (c)	53. (a)	54. (a)	55. (a)	56. (c)	57. (b)	58. (a)	59. (b)	60. (c)
61. (d)	62. (b)	63. (b)	64. (d)	65. (d)	66. (c)	67. (b)	68. (b)	69. (d)	70. (b)
71. (d)	72. (c)	73. (d)	74. (a)	75. (a)	76. (a)	77. (c)	78. (a)	79. (a)	80. (d)
81. (b)	82. (a)	83. (b)	84. (d)	85. (d)	86. (d)	87. (b)	88. (a)	89. (a)	90. (d)
91. (b)	92. (d)	93. (b)	94. (b)	95. (d)	96. (c)	97. (c)	98. (c)	99. (a)	100. (b)
101. (c)	102. (d)	103. (c)	104. (d)	105. (b)	106. (b)	107. (c)	108. (a)	109. (c)	110. (b)
111. (b)	112. (c)	113. (d)	114. (c)	115. (b)	116. (c)	117. (b)	118. (c)	119. (d)	120. (c)
121. (b)	122. (c)	123. (a)	124. (a)	125. (c)	126. (a)	127. (c)	128. (a)	129. (a)	130. (b)
131. (c)	132. (d)	133. (c)	134. (d)	135. (c)	136. (b)	137. (c)	138. (b)	139. (d)	140. (b)
141. (a)	142. (c)	143. (a)	144. (d)	145. (d)	146. (c)	147. (b)	148. (d)	149. (b)	150. (c)
151. (a)	152. (c)	153. (c)	154. (a)	155. (b)	156. (c)	157. (b)	158. (c)	159. (a)	160. (d)
161. (c)	162. (a)	163. (d)	164. (d)	165. (c)	166. (a)	167. (d)	168. (b)	169. (c)	170. (d)
171. (b)	172. (d)	173. (c)	174. (a)	175. (d)	176. (d)	177. (b)	178. (a)	179. (c)	180. (c)
181. (c)	182. (a)	183. (a)	184. (c)	185. (b)	186. (b)	187. (b)	188. (b)	189. (c)	190. (c)

Pervious Years' Questions

1. (d)	2. (c)	3. (a)	4. (c)	5. (c)	6. (d)	7. (a)	8. (c)	9. (d)	10. (c)
11. (d)	12. (b)	13. (a)	14. (c)	15. (b)	16. (c)	17. (b)	18. (c)	19. (a)	20. (b)
21. (b)	22. (c)	23. (b)	24. (c)	25. (b)	26. (a)	27. (b)	28. (c)	29. (d)	30. (c)
31. (c)	32. (a)	33. (c)	34. (a)	35. (b)	36. (b)	37. (a)	38. (c)	39. (c)	40. (b)
41. (c)	42. (c)	43. (c)	44. (b)	45. (c)	46. (b)	47. (d)	48. (b)	49. (b)	50. (c)
51. (c)	52. (d)	53. (a)	54. (b)	55. (d)	56. (a)	57. (a)	58. (d)	59. (d)	60. (c)
61. (d)	62. (b)	63. (a)	64. (d)						

Non-Fiction in Anglo-Norman Period

In this chapter Non-Fiction works of authors from Anglo-Norman period, Chaucerian age upto Revival ages and Elizabethan Age have been dealt with. The literary trends of these periods were to write histories, bruts, chronicles and religious content. Translation of Bible into English was an important event during this period.

Non-Fiction: An Introduction

Non-fiction is the content whose creator, in good faith, assumes responsibility for the truth or accuracy of the events, people, or information presented. In contrast, a story whose creator explicitly leaves open if and how the work refers to reality is usually classified as fiction. Non-fiction, which may be presented either objectively or subjectively, is traditionally one of the two main divisions of narratives (and, specifically, prose writing), the other traditional division being fiction, which contrasts with nonfiction by dealing in information, events, and characters expected to be partly or largely imaginary.

Non-fiction's specific factual assertions and descriptions may or may not be accurate and can give either a true or a false account of the subject in question. However, authors of such accounts genuinely believe or claim them to be truthful at the time of their composition or, atleast, pose them to a convinced audience as historically or empirically factual. Reporting the beliefs of others in a non-fiction format is not necessarily an endorsement of the ultimate veracity of those beliefs, it is simply saying it is true that people believe them (for such topics as mythology). Non-fiction can also be written about fiction, typically known as literary criticism, giving information and analysis on these other works. Non-fiction need not necessarily be written text, since pictures and film can also purport to present a factual account of a subject.

Common literary examples of non-fiction include Expository, Argumentative, Functional, and Opinion pieces; Essays on art or literature; Biographies; Memoirs; Journalism and Historical, Scientific, Technical or Economic writings (including electronic ones).

In this Chapter

Journals, photographs, textbooks, travel books, blueprints and diagrams are also often considered non-fictional. Including information that the author knows to be untrue within any of these works is usually regarded as dishonest. Other works can legitimately be either fiction or non-fiction, such as journals of self-expression, letters, magazine articles, and other expressions of imagination. Though they are mostly either one or the other, it is possible for there to be a blend of both. Some fiction may include non-fictional elements.

Some non-fiction may include elements of unverified supposition, deduction or imagination for the purpose of smoothing out a narrative, but the inclusion of open falsehoods would discredit it as a work of non-fiction. The publishing and bookselling business sometimes uses the phrase literary non-fiction to distinguish works with a more literary or intellectual bent, as opposed to the greater collection of non-fiction subjects.

Types of Non-Fictions

Two subcategories for non-fiction are informational and literary.

Informational non-fiction includes writing with the purpose to describe or express facts. Literary non-fiction also contains facts, but is meant to entertain the reader. In this way, literary non-fiction reads like fiction and has story elements, like character, setting and plot.

Informational Non-Fiction

The writings which are intended to provide their readers with general information of life, society, governance, laws, philosophy and religion etc are called Informational non-fiction. It includes chronicles, religious writings, rule and law books, articles, reports and some essays as well though essays can be literary also. An essay is informational if it carries purely factual content and the same essay can be termed as literary non-fiction if the writer mixes his/her opinion with the given facts.

Literary Non-Fiction

It is a type of prose that employs the literary techniques usually associated with fiction or poetry to report on persons, places, and events in the real world.

The genre of literary non-fiction (also known as creative non-fiction) is broad enough to include travel writing, nature writing, science writing, sports writing, biography, autobiography, memoir,the interview, and both the familiar and personal essay.

"Literary non-fiction puts emphasis on the precise and skilled use of words and tone, and the assumption that the reader is as intelligent as the writer. While information is included, insight about that information, presented with some originality, may predominate. Sometimes the subject of literary non-fiction may not at the onset be of great interest to the reader, but the character of the writing may lure the reader into that subject.

Literary non-fiction appears in books, in some general magazines such as The New Yorker, Harper's, the Atlantic, Commentary, the New York Review of Books, in many small-circulation magazines, in a few newspapers regularly and in some other newspapers from time to time, occasionally in a Sunday supplement, and in book review media.

Some examples of literary non-fiction include personal journals, diaries, memoirs, letters and essays. Personal journals, diaries, memoirs and letters together form a genre termed as 'Autobiographical Non-fiction. Let's look at the characteristics of each of these.

Autobiographical Non-Fiction

Much of literary non-fiction can be described as autobiographical, which is writing from the author's perspective. This type of writing is usually in first person point of view, which means the narrator is a character in the story. Since the author is the narrator, this means the author is the main character in the story. Most autobiographies are novel-length since they cover the subject's entire life. However, there are many shorter works that are still considered autobiographical.

1. **Personal Journal** The first such work is a personal journal, which is a daily written record of personal experiences and observations. This usually consists of short pieces of writing each day. For example, if you were assigned to design an experiment for a science project, you might keep a journal to describe what you did for that experiment every day until the project was due. A journal could be kept for a few weeks or even several years but always has a factual account of experiences of the author.
2. **Diary** Another related autobiographical work is the diary. Similar to journals, diaries contain a daily account of experiences. The difference is diaries include personal thoughts and feelings. While a journal is more based on facts, a diary can have a person's deepest secrets and desires; as such, it is usually not meant to be shared with anyone.
   A great example is the book *The Diary of Anne Frank*. Anne Frank was a real Jewish girl who kept a diary while hiding from the Germans during World War II. She wrote about her personal thoughts and feelings about what was happening to her family. Years later, her diary was found and published by Anne's descendants to showcase the terrors of Nazi Germany.

3. **Memoir** A third type of autobiographical work is the memoir. Memoirs are extremely similar to journals and diaries in these memoirs relate the author's personal experiences. Like diaries, memoirs can also reveal the narrator's personal feelings.

   Memoirs are different because they are not written daily, are meant to be published and shared, and usually focus on one specific event or theme. A well-known memoir is Tuesdays with Morrie. In this book, the author, Mitch Albom, recounts his time spent with his aging sociology professor who is dying from ALS. This memoir is limited to that period of Albom's life. Other events of his life are not shown.
4. **Letter** A final example of an autobiographical work of literary non-fiction is a letter. A letter is a written message addressed to a person or organisation. Letters often contain personal thoughts and opinions, but they are directed at just one person. Letters are never really meant to be published and are usually discarded once the message is received. Emails can be considered a more advanced type of letter.

Characteristics of Non-Fiction

There are several important traits of all non-fiction works

- Most importantly, non-fiction writing must involve real people, places, and events.
- The stories told in non-fiction works must be true. If something in the story is made-up, then it falls under fiction.
- Non-fiction must also contain facts, or information that can be proved to be true.
- With this in mind, a writer can select and organise the facts in a number of ways in order to accomplish his purpose.
- Some facts can be omitted, and others can be shown in a specific light, but overall, facts must be present in the written work.
- Most non-fiction works also have a similar author's purpose, which is the reason the author writes. Most non-fiction is written to express or to inform.
- If the author's purpose is to express, the concepts expressed are always based on true, real-life situations.
- Because of this, one could argue all non-fiction serves to inform the reader.

Nature of Non-Fiction

Non-fictional prose genres cover an almost infinite variety of themes, and they assume many shapes. In quantitative terms, if such could ever be valid in such non measurable matters, they probably include more than half of all that has been written in countries having a literature of their own. Non-fictional prose genres have flourished in nearly all countries with advanced literatures. The genres include political and polemical writings, biographical and autobiographical literature, religious writings and philosophical or moral writings.

After the Renaissance, from the 16th century onward in Europe, a personal manner of writing grew in importance. The author strove for more or less disguised self-revelation and introspective analysis, often in the form of letters, private diaries, and confessions. Also of increasing importance were aphorisms after the style of the ancient Roman philosophers Seneca and Epictetus, imaginary dialogues, and historical narratives and later, journalistic articles and extremely diverse essays.

From the 19th century, writers in Romance and Slavic languages especially and to a far lesser extent British and American writers, developed the attitude that a literature is most truly modern when it acquires a marked degree of self-awareness and obstinately reflects on its purpose and technique. Such writers were not content with imaginative creation alone: they also explained their work and defined their method in prefaces, reflections, essays, self-portraits, and critical articles.

The 19th century French poet Charles Baudelaire asserted that no great poet could ever quite resist the temptation to become a critic also: a critic of others and of himself. Indeed, most modern writers, in lands other than the United States, whether they be poets, novelists, or dramatists, have composed more non-fictional prose than poetry, fiction, or drama. In the instances of such monumental figures of 20th century literature as the poets Ezra Pound, TS Eliot, and William Butler Yeats, or the novelists Thomas Mann and André Gide, that part of their output may well be considered by posterity to be equal in importance to their more imaginative writing.

Elements of Non-Fiction

Obviously, a realm as boundless and diverse as non-fictional prose literature cannot be characterised as having any unity of intent, of technique, or of style. It can be defined, very loosely, only by what it is not. Many exceptions, in such a mass of writings, can always be brought up to contradict any rule or generalisation. No prescriptive treatment is acceptable for the writing of essays, of aphorisms, of literary journalism, of polemical controversy, of travel literature, of memoirs and intimate diaries. No norms are recognised to determine whether a dialogue, a confession, a piece of religious or of scientific writing, is excellent, mediocre, or outright bad, and each author has to be relished, and appraised, chiefly in his own right.

The Only Technique, the English critic FR Leavis wrote in 1957, "is that which compels words to express an intensively personal way of feeling." Intensity is probably useful as a standard; yet it is a variable and often elusive, quality, possessed by polemicists and by ardent essayists to a greater extent than by others who are equally great. 'Loving and taking the liberties of a lover' was Virginia Woolf's characterisation of the 19th century critic William Hazlitt's style: it instilled passion into his critical essays. But other equally significant English essayists of the same century, such as Charles Lamb or Walter Pater, or the French critic Hippolyte Taine, under an impassive mask, loved too, but differently. Still other non-fictional writers have been detached, seemingly aloof, or, like the 17th century French epigrammatist La Rochefoucauld, sarcastic. Their intensity is of another sort.

Features of Non-Fiction

Some of the important features of non-fictions are given below

Reality and Imagination

Prose that is non-fictional is generally supposed to cling to reality more closely than that which invents stories, or frames imaginary plots. Calling it realistic, however, would be a gross distortion.

Since non-fictional prose does not stress inventiveness of themes and of characters independent of the author's self, it appears in the eyes of some moderns to be inferior to works of imagination. In the middle of the 20th century an immensely high evaluation was placed on the imagination, and the adjective imaginative became a grossly abused cliché.

Many modern novels and plays, however, were woefully deficient in imaginative force, and the word may have been bandied about so much out of a desire for what was least possessed. Many readers are engrossed by travel books, by descriptions of exotic animal life, by essays on the psychology of other nations, by Rilke's notebooks or by Samuel Pepys's diary far more than by poetry or by novels that fail to impose any suspension of disbelief. There is much truth in Oscar Wilde's remark that "the highest criticism is more creative than creation and the primary aim of the critic is to see the object as in itself it really is not."

A good deal of imagination has gone not only into criticism but also into the writing of history, of essays, of travel books, and even of the biographies or the confessions that purport to be true to life as it really happened, as it was really experienced. The imagination at work in non-fictional prose, however, would hardly deserve the august name of primary imagination reserved by the 19th century English poet Samuel Taylor Coleridge to creators who come close to possessing semidivine powers.

Rather, imagination is displayed in non-fictional prose in the fanciful invention of decorative details, in digressions practiced as an art and assuming a character of pleasant non-chalance, in establishing a familiar contact with the reader through wit and humour. The variety of themes that may be touched upon in that prose is almost infinite. The treatment of issues may be ponderously didactic and still belong within the literary domain.

For centuries, in many nations, in Asiatic languages, in Medieval Latin, in the writings of the humanists of the Renaissance and in those of the Enlightenment, a considerable part of literature has been didactic. The concept of art for art's sake is a late and rather artificial development in the history of culture, and it did not reign supreme even in the few countries in which it was expounded in the 19th century. The ease with which digressions may be inserted in that type of prose affords non-fictional literature a freedom denied to writing falling within other genres.

The drawback of such a non-descript literature lies in judging it against any standard of perfection, since perfection implies some conformity with implicit rules and the presence, however vague, of standards such as have been formulated for comedy, tragedy, the ode, the short story and even (in this case, more honoured in the breach than the observance) the novel. The compensating grace is that in much non-fictional literature that repudiates or ignores structure the reader is often delighted with an air of ease and of nonchalance and with that rarest of all virtues in the art of writing: naturalness.

Style of Writing

The writing of non-fictional prose should not entail the tension, the monotony, and the self-conscious craft of fiction writing. The search for le mot juste (the precise word) so fanatically pursued by admirers of Flaubert and Maupassant is far less important in non-fictional prose than in the novel and the short story. The English author GK Chesterton (1874–1936), who was himself more successful in his rambling volumes of reflections and of religious apologetics than in his novels, defined literature as that rare, almost miraculous use of language 'by which a man really says what he means.'

In essays, letters, reporting and narratives of travels, the author's aim is often not to overpower his readers by giving them the impression that he knows exactly where he is leading them as a dramatist or a detective-story writer does. Some rambling casualness, apparently irrelevant anecdotes and suggestions of the conclusions that the author wishes his readers to infer are often more effective than extreme terseness.

There is also another manner of writing that is more attentive to the periodic cadences and elegance of prose, in the style of the ancient Roman orator Cicero. The 19th century English essayist William Hazlitt praised the felicities of style and the refinements of the prose of the British statesman Edmund Burke (1729–97) as "that which went the nearest to the verge of poetry and yet never fell over."

A number of English writers have been fond of that harmonious and rhetorical prose, the taste for which may well have been fostered not only by the familiarity with Cicero but also by the profound influence of the authorised version of the Bible (1611).

Martin Luther's translation of the *New Testament* (1522) and of the *Old Testament* (1534) likewise molded much of German prose and German sensibility for centuries.

In the 20th century that type of prose lost favour with American and British readers, who ceased to cherish Latin orators and Biblical prose as their models. In German literature, however, in which harmonious balance and eloquence were more likely to be admired, and in other languages more directly derived from Latin, a musical style, akin to a prolonged poem in prose, was cultivated more assiduously, as exemplified in Italian in the writings of Gabriele D'Annunzio, in French in those by André Gide, and in German in Die Aufzeichnungen des Malte Laurids Brigge (The Notebooks of Malte Laurids Brigge) by the poet Rainer Maria Rilke.

Such an elaborate style appears to be more easily tolerated by the readers in non-fictional writing, with its lack of cumulative continuity and, generally speaking, its more restricted size, than in novels such as Pater's Marius the Epicurean (1885) and occasionally in Thomas Mann's fiction, in which such a style tends to pall on the reader. Similarly, it is easier for the non-fictional prose writer to weave into his style faint suggestions of irony, archaisms, alliterations and even interventions of the author that might prove catastrophic to credibility in fiction.

Critics have argued that essayists, historians, orators and divines often affect a happy-go-lucky ease so as to put them on the same footing with the common reader, but they realise that language and style are vital.

They must know what resources they can draw from vivid sensations, brilliant similes, balanced sentences, or sudden, epigrammatic, effects of surprise.

Presence of Author

The one feature common to most authors of non-fictional prose (a few staid historians and even fewer philosophers excepted) is the marked degree of the author's presence in all they write. That is to be expected in epistolary literature, and, although less inevitably, in the essay, the travel book, journalistic reporting, and polemical or hortatory prose. Although the 17th century French religious philosopher Pascal hinted that 'the ego is hateful,' the author's presence is still strongly felt.

This presence endows their works with a personal and haunting force that challenges, converts, or repels, but hardly ever leaves the reader indifferent.

Saint Paul's epistles owe their impact-perhaps second to none in the history of the Western world-to the self that vehemently expresses itself in them, showing no concern whatever for the niceties of Attic prose. In the treatises, discourses, and philosophical argumentation of the great writers of the Enlightenment, such as Voltaire, Diderot and Rousseau, they frequently resort to the first person singular, which results in a vivid concreteness in the treatment of ideas.

To think the abstract concretely, a precept reminiscent of the 18th century philosophers, was also the aim of the 20th century philosophers Jean-Paul Sartre and Maurice Merleau-Ponty when they naturalised Existentialist thought in France. The growth of personal literature in its myriad shapes is one of the striking features of modern literary evolution.

The very fact that the writer of non-fictional prose does not seek an imaginary projection to impart his vision, his anguish, and his delights to readers also underlines the nature of his intention. A school of critics has vigorously attacked "the intentional fallacy," which leads biographers and some literary historians to ask what an artist intended before evaluating the completed work of art. But in a work of apologetics or of homiletics, in a work of history or of sociology, in a critical or even in a desultory and discursive essay, and certainly in aphorisms or maxims or both, the intention of the author remains omnipresent.

This intention may be disguised under the mask of a parable, under the interlocutors of a philosophical dialogue, or under the admonitions of a prophet, but the reader is never oblivious of the thinker's intent. The reader has a sophisticated enjoyment of one who shares the creator's intent and travels familiarly along with him. He respects and enjoys in those authors the exercise of an intelligence flexible enough to accept even the irrational as such.

Approaches to Write Non-Fiction

In terms of approach, that is, the attitude of the writer as it can be inferred from the writing, the distinguishing features of non-fictional prose writings are the degree of presence of the ego and of the use of a subjective, familiar tone. Such devices are also used, of course, by authors of fiction, but to a lesser extent. Similarly, the basic modes of writing-the descriptive, the narrative, the expository, and the argumentative-are found in both non-fictional literature and in fiction, but in different degrees.

The Descriptive Mode

In non-fictional prose, essayists, moralists, naturalists, and others regularly evoked nature scenes. The most sumptuous masters of prose composed landscapes as elaborately as landscape painters.

The French writer and statesman Chateaubriand (1768–1848), for example, who was not outstandingly successful in inventing plots or in creating characters independent from his own self, was a master of description; his writings influenced the French Romantic poets, who set the impassive splendour of outward nature in contrast to the inner anguish of mortals.

The 19th century English art critic John Ruskin had a more precise gift of observation, as revealed in his descriptions of Alpine mountains and of the humblest flowers or mosses, but his ornate and sonorous prose was the climax of a high-flown manner of writing that later read like the majestic relic of another era.

American non-fictional writers of the same period such as Ralph Waldo Emerson and Henry Thoreau scrupulously described the lessons of organisation, of unity and of moral beauty to be deciphered from the vicissitudes of nature.

Russian essayists vied with novelists in their minute yet rapturous descriptions of the thaw releasing the torrents of spring or the implacable force of the long Northern winters. Writers more inclined to the observation of social life, in satirical sketches of the mechanically polite and artificial habitués of salons, helped the novel of social life come into existence in several Western countries.

Narrative Mode

The narrative element is less conspicuous in writing that does not purport to relate a story than in fictional works, but there is a role for narrative in letters, diaries, autobiographies, and historical writing. Most often, an incident is graphically related by a witness, as in letters or memoirs; an anecdote may serve to illustrate a moral advice in an essay; or an entertaining encounter may be inserted into an essay or a travel sketch. Digression here represents the utmost in art; it provides a relief from the persistent attention required when the author is pursuing his purpose more seriously. Similarly, such writing provides a pleasant contrast to the rigid structure of the majority of novels since the late 19th century.

In historical writing, however, simplicity and clarity of narrative are required, though it may be interspersed with speeches, with portraits, or with moral and polemical allusions. In other forms of non-fictional prose, the meandering fancy of the author may well produce an impression of freedom and of truth to life unattainable by the more carefully wrought novel.

Many writers have confessed to feeling relieved when they ceased to create novels and shifted to impromptu sketches or desultory essays. The surrealist essayists of the 20th century poured their scorn on detective fiction as the most fiercely logical form of writing. In contrast, the author of essays or other non-fictional prose may blend dreams and facts, ventures into the illogical, and delightful eccentricities.

Expository and Argumentative Modes

The rules of old-fashioned rhetoric apply better to expository and argumentative prose than to the other modes. These rules were first set down in ancient Greece by teachers who elicited them from the smooth eloquence of Socrates, the impassioned and balanced reasoning of Demosthenes, and others. The ancient Romans went further still in codifying figures of speech, stylistic devices, and even the gestures of the orator. Such treatises played a significant part in the education of the Renaissance Humanists, of the classical and Augustan prose writers of 17th century England and France, of the leaders of the French Revolution in the 18th century, and even in 19th century historians and statesmen such as Guizot in France and Macaulay and Gladstone in Britain.

But the sophisticated oratory of such 18th-century British orators as Richard Brinsley Sheridan, Edmund Burke, and Charles Fox or, during the 20th century, that of Winston Churchill, hardly seems attuned to audiences in the age of television.

It has been suggested by students of German history that Adolf Hitler, in his vituperative speeches at Nuremberg in the 1930s, fascinated the Germans because they had been unaccustomed, unlike other Western nations, to eloquence in their leaders. If a large part of a population is illiterate, unending flows of eloquence may constitute a convenient means of educating the masses.

Elsewhere, a more familiar and casual type of address from political leaders tends to be preferred in an era of mass media. The gift of a superior orator has been facetiously defined as that of saying as little as possible in as many words as possible. Like sermons, many types of formal address such as lectures, political speeches, and legal pleadings appear to be doomed as documents of literary value, as Burke's or Lincoln's orations and addresses were when they were learned by heart by the younger generations and helped mold the style and contribute to the moral education of men.

Pre Chaucerian to Elizabethan Age

Non-fiction writing has been an important and integral part of the English literature since ages. It started being written as early as the Anglo-Norman Period which is also termed as Pre-Chaucerian Period.

The popular forms of the non-fiction writing prevalent during this era were Chronicles and Bruts.

With the advent of the age of Chaucer, the mode of non-fiction writing moved from chronicles and Bruts to travelogues and religious translations.

Non-fiction of religious fervour continued in the revival age also. At the same time, a new form of non-fiction writing i.e. autobiographies and biographies were also initiated. The Book of Margery Kempe, written around 1436 and first published in 1401, is believed to have been the earliest autobiography in English language. It records the experiences of Margery Kempe (1373-1439), an English religious mystic. Kempe was daughter of a former Mayor of Lynn and the wife of John Kempe.

Elizabethan age witnessed the return of Chronicles and antiquaries besides travelogues as part of non-fictional literature. Literary criticism also began in the Elizabethan age, which can be categorised as non-fictitious work to some extent.

Chronicles in the Anglo-Norman Period

A tradition of writing chronicles became well established in the Anglo-Norman period. These chronicles recorded the history of kings and were written in Anglo-Norman. Chronicles were major source of historical knowledge for medieval people. They contained an extended account in prose or verse of historical events, sometimes including legendary material, presented in chronological order and without authorial interpretation or comment.

In the medieval age, the term 'chronicle' included every kind of history. These histories or chronicles were known in the vernacular as Bruts, after Brutus, the eponymous founder of Britain. They traced the history and legend of the country from the time of the mythical Brutus, descendant of Aeneas and founder of Britain. In the beginning, Anglo-Norman historians restricted themselves to translating earlier historical works such as Anglo-Saxon Chronicle. However, by the end of 12th century, patrons began demanding accounts of their own historical rule to be preserved for posterity. For instance, the biography of William the Marshall, Earl of Pembroke, written around 1226, was commissioned by one of his own sons.

Some of the Anglo-Norman Chroniclers and historians are mentioned below

Simeon of Durham (1090-1129)

Simeon of Durham was an English chronicler and historian. In his youth, he entered the Benedictine monastery at Jarrow, which was later moved to Durham in 1074 and he was professed in 1085 or 1086, subsequently attaining the office of precentor of the church. Simeon's chief work is the *Historia Ecclesiae Dunelmensis*, written between 1104 and 1108. It is a history of the bishopric of Durham from its establishment in 635 at Lindisfarne (Holy Island) to 1096. His *Historia Regum Anglorum et Dacorum* (History of the Kings), consists of two overlapping English histories covering the years 731-957 and 848-1129.

This work was formerly attributed to Simeon. But it is now believed that, he was the author only of the second history: a chronicle for the years 848-1118 (based on the Life of King Alfred by Asser and the Chronicle of Florence of Worcester) and a narrative of the years 1119-1129 (part original, part based on Edmer's history of the church in Canterbury).

Ordericus Vitalis (1075-1142)

Historian Ordericus Vitalis was born at Atcham, near Shrewsbury, in 1075. He was born to an English mother and a French priest, who came over to England with the Normans and received a church at Shrewsbury. At the age of 10, Ordericus was sent over by his father to St Evroult in Southern Normandy and remained for the rest of his life a monk of that abbey. Between 1123 and 1141, he wrote *Historia Ecclesiastica* (The Ecclesiastical History), which mainly dealt with the rule of William the Conqueror.

His history was intended at first to be a chronicle of his abbey, but it developed into a general *Historia Ecclesiastica* in 13 books. *Ordericus* began by transcribing the *Gesta Normannorum Ducum of William* of Jumièges with lengthy interpolations of his own, chiefly relating to the history of Norman families connected with Saint-Évroult. Not later than 1115, at the command of his abbot, he began a history of his own monastery and its patrons, which gradually expanded into a general history of the church and incorporated a chronological outline of events from the birth of Christ, originally intended as a separate work.

Books I and II of *Ordericus' Historia* are an abridged chronicle from the Christian era to 1143; books III-V describe the Norman Conquests of South Italy and England; book VI gives the history of his Abbey. Books VII-XIII consist of his universal history from 751 to 1141, book IX being devoted to the I Crusade. The book is a valuable study of the Normans in England, France and Italy and the history of his own times.

William of Malmesbury (1095-1143)

William of Malmesbury was born in Wiltshire in about 1095. His mother was English while his father was a Norman. At a young age, he was admitted to Malmesbury (Benedictine) Abbey, where he became a monk and later, librarian of the monastery. *Gesta Regum Anglorum* is a compendium of English history in 5 books first published in 1125 and later revised. Gesta pontificum is a compilation of the lives and deeds of English bishops.

Malmesbury's most important work *Historia Novella,* is a sequel to the *Gesta Regum*. This history concerns the period between the death of Henry I (1135) and 1142, about the time of William's death.

The *Historia Novella* is also an important work, which records the major political turmoil that was unflolding during William of Malmesbury's own lifetime the Civil War between King Stephen and the Empress Matilda.

His important works include

- Gesta Regum Anglorum (Deeds of the Kings of England), 449 to 1127
- Gesta Pontificum (Deeds of the Bishops), 1126
- Historia Novella (New History),1128 to 1142

Matthew Paris (1200-1259)

Matthew Paris was an English monk and chronicler, born in about 1200. As a young man, he entered the monastery at St Albans. Matthew was interested in history, so he was given the job of helping Roger of Wendover, the chronicler of the abbey of St Albans. In 1248, he was sent to Norway as the bearer of a message from Louis IX of France to Haakon VI; he made himself, so agreeable to the Norwegian sovereign that he was invited, a little later, to superintend the reformation of the Benedictine monastery of St Benet Holme at Trondhjem. Apart from these missions, his activities were devoted to the composition of history, a pursuit for which the monks of St Albans had long been famous.

Matthew edited the works of Abbot John de Cella and Roger of Wendover, which in their altered form constitute the first part of his most important work, the *Chronica Majora*. It extends from creation until 1259, the year of his death. Paris' work is one of the most valuable sources of knowledge of 13th century life remarkable for its detail, scope and accounts of events in Europe as well as England.

Brut in the Anglo-Norman

Bruts relate to the legendary history of Britain, which tells the story of Brutus, descendant of Aeneas promoting chivalric ideals and celebrating the deeds of knightly heroes, the Brut resembles aristocratic chronicles in content. The story of Brut was first made popular by Geoffrey Monmouth's Historia Regum Britaniae. Anglo-Norman poets Wace and Layamon used material from Monmouth's history and reworked it into French versions.

Wace's Roman de Brut (1155)

Wace was a Norman poet, who was born in Jersey in 1115 and brought up in mainland Normandy. Wace's *Roman de Brut* is an 1155 French verse rendering of Geoffrey of Monmouth's earlier Latin 'history' of Britain, from the time of Brutus, the eponymous founder, to the 7th century. Wace begins his chronicle with an account of the flight of Aeneas and moves quickly to the discovery of the island by Brutus and the division of the land into three kingdoms on his death.

He devotes much of his chronicle, nearly a third of the verses, to Arthur's reign, developing at length his foreign conquests and mentioning, for the first time, the Round Table. Wace uses Geoffrey's stories, such as those of King Lear and King Arthur, with a lively inventiveness and originality, drawing on oral sources and his own knowledge of parts of Britain.

The Roman de Brut became the basis for Layamon's Brut, an alliterative Middle English poem and Piers Langtoft's chronicle. According to Eugene Mason, Wace makes a few additions to Geoffrey's Arthurian history, but "His real contribution to the legend is the new spirit that he has put into it.

In the first place, his vehicle is the swift-moving French octo-syllabic couplet, which alone gives an entirely different tone to the narrative from that of Geoffrey's high-sounding Latin prose."

Mason further adds that apart from matters of style, Wace made other changes to Geoffrey's narrative that are more important for Arthurian romance.

"He wrote the Brut under the patronage of Henry II and if we may trust Layamon's statement, he dedicated it to Queen Eleanor, who was the ardent propagator in England of the courtly ideals of Southern France. Accordingly Wace, perhaps partly because of his own milieu, partly because of his royal patroness, wove into Geoffrey's narrative more pronouncedly chivalric material."

Layamon's Brut (1200)

Layamon was an English poet and a priest, who lived in Worcestershire. Layamon's *Brut* is a poetical paraphrase of the Brut of Wace. It begins with the *Fall of Troy* and proceeds with the story of Brutus, a descendant of Aeneas, who journeys with other Trojans through the Mediterranean Sea until they finally reach the Isle of Avalon, inhabited by giants. The Arthurian passage is the major part of the poem, with some 8000 lines, it makes up to half of the Brut.

However, Layamon extends Wace's poem from 15300 to 32241 verses. Layamon freely adapted the Brut of Wace and added material from other sources. His Anglo-Saxon narrative meter foreshadows the Middle English metrical system. Layamon's additions to Wace are notable, such as his story "Regarding the fairy elves at Arthur's birth and his transportation by them after death in a boat to Avalon, the abode of Argante, their queen".

Layamon's work also shows a marked familiarity with current Welsh tradition. According to Eugene Mason, his "Work has a high value in the vexed question of the origin and growth of Arthurian romance; for it proves the existence of genuine Welsh tradition about Arthur".

The Harley Brut

The anonymous *Harley Brut* consists of 3359 verses composed in Alexandrine monorhymed laisses, it is an extant in five fragments. The 5 portions of the text cover just over a quarter of Geoffrey's *Historia Regum Britaniae*, translating with some gaps from the death of King Lucius upto Arthur's campaign against (coincidentally) the emperor Lucius.

The authorship of this text has been attributed to Claraton, an English writer known to have translated Geoffrey into French verse, but there is no compelling evidence for this. According to Peter Damian-Grint, The Harley author "Shows slightly more interest in the figure of Arthur than in those of Ambrosius, Aurelius and Uther ,to the extent of allowing himself a certain degree of amplification in descriptions of court life. He elaborates on Arthur's crown-wearing in Caerleon after his Northern campaign and provides, when Arthur arrives in France, a long description of his pavilion at Barfleur."

Non-Fiction Writers of the Chaucerian Age

John Mandeville (1300-1371)

John Mandeville was an English prose writer of the Middle Ages. He is known as the author of the travel book, *The Travels of Sir John Mandeville*.

He is believed to have been an English knight, of Saint Albans, a town just North of London. Having left his native country on Michaelmas Day 1322, he spent some 34 years travelling extensively throughout Asia and northern Africa, only ceasing his travels, when the physical infirmities of increasing age finally caught up with him. His world travels thus, ended, Sir John settled in England to write an account of his journeys. He penned down some of his memories from his years abroad.

The Travels of Sir John Mandeville

- One of the most popular of medieval secular texts.
- It was written in approximately 1340s-50s.
- Originally written in Norman French, the work has been translated into English, Latin and other European languages.
- The book is an account of Sir John Mandeville's 30 years odyssey throughout Europe, North Africa, the Far East and Arabia.
- It became a major source for geographical information. **Leonardo da Vinci** and **Christopher Columbus** are believed to have relied upon Mandeville's book.
- Religion is a central focus of the book. Even the descriptions of people are often based on religion.

- The book sees Jerusalem as the centre of the world, believes that the Holy Land belongs to Christendom and sees Muslims as usurpers.
- The narrator reminds its Christian audience of both their rightful claims to the Holy Land and also of their moral failings that stand in the way of that reclamation.
- The narrator also shows interest in wildlife and describes animals in great detail.

John Wyclif/Wycliffe (1330-84)

He was described as 'the morning star of the Reformation', John Wycliffe is best known for his first complete *translation of the Bible* into English. Wycliffe was probably born around 1330 in a Yorkshire village that probably gave him his surname, Wycliffe. Therefore, his name is sometimes spelled as 'Wycliffe.' He was educated at the University of Oxford. Here, he was educated in theology and became prepared for the priesthood. Wycliffe became a regent master in arts at Balliol in 1360 and was appointed master of the college, but he resigned in 1361 to become vicar of Fillingham. He became a bachelor of divinity about 1369 and a doctor of divinity in 1372.

Literary Career and Works

In 1374, King Edward III appointed him rector of Lutterworth and later made him part of a deputation to meet a papal deputation at Brussels. Wycliffe was supposed to negotiate differences between the King and the Pope. About this time, Wycliffe began to argue for a 'dominion founded on grace.' By 'dominion', he meant both the right to exercise authority in church or state and the right to own property. He maintained that these rights were given to men directly from God and that they were not given or continued apart from sanctifying grace. Thus, a man in a state of mortal sin could not lawfully function as an official of church or state, nor could he lawfully own property. He argued that the church had fallen into sin and that it ought therefore to give up all its property and that the clergy should live in complete poverty. This disendowment was to be carried out by the king. In 1376, Wycliffe wrote 'Of Civil Dominion' where he demanded a moral base for church leadership and urged reforms in church.

In 1377, Pope Gregory XI heard about this bold Englishman and issued five papal bulls ordering that Wycliffe be shut up in prison. Because of the support of his friends in England, Wycliffe was not imprisoned, but he was brought to trial in England in 1378. During the trial, Wycliffe openly attacked the authority of the Pope. However, Pope Gregory's death and the rule of a new young king Richard II spread confusion all around and led to the dissolution of the trial.

In 1382, Wycliffe was expelled from Oxford University because of his opposition to traditional church doctrines. After his exclusion, Wycliffe became more determined to translate religious scriptures into English so that common people could understand without the mediation of the priests or church authorities. After his retirement to Lutterworth, Wycliffe became pre-occupied with the translation of the Bible. He was the first person in history to undertake the task of production of a vernacular translation of the Bible. However, he was unable to finish this task. The translation was later completed by Wycliffe's disciples, Nicholas of Hereford and John Purvey.

Wycliffe's health deteriorated in the later years of his life. He probably suffered a stroke around 1384, while he was hearing Mass in his church and three days later he died. He was buried at Lutterworth. However, in 1415, afraid that Wyclif's grave would become a religious shrine, the Council of Constance gave orders that his body should be dug up and thrown into the river. His ashes were thrown in the Swift River in 1428.

Wycliffe's Bible

- In the late 14th century, the Holy Bible was translated from Latin into Middle English by John Wycliffe.
- Though the undertaking was his, the entire Bible was not translated by Wycliffe.
- The translation was carried out under Wycliffe's inspiration and guidance by Nicholas of Hereford and John Purvey.
- The need for the translation arose because Wycliffe saw the Bible as the sole authority for combating the corruption in the church. Also, he believed that each layman ought to know God's Law as codified in the Bible.
- According to Knighton, Wycliffe, by "translating the Bible made it the property of the masses and common to all and more open to the laity and even to women, who were able to read, than formerly, it had been even to the scholarly and most learned of the clergy."

John Wycliffe and the Lollard Movement

Lollardy was a medieval reform movement based on the writings and teachings of the Oxford University theologian, John Wycliffe. Wycliffe's followers were known as 'The Lollards'. It was used as an abusive term and was derived from lollium, which was used early in the 14 century in the sense of a 'hypocrite'. Wycliffe's followers or the Lollards not only attacked many beliefs and practices of the church, but also demanded social reforms.

The main beliefs of the Lollards were

- The pope had no part to play in worldly affairs.
- The church was too worldly.
- Monasticism had drifted from its spiritual foundation.
- The Bible should be available to everyone in their own language.
- 'Dominion is of Grace', that is, true power is God's and attempts to use power for individual gain is therefore wrong.
- As human beings, we are all brothers.

The Lollards preached to the common people in the English language and sowed the seeds for the reformation movement. The initial spread of Wycliffe's views touched all levels of English medieval society; he was supported by nobility and by prominent academics and in many ways became the voice of the lower clergy and the layman. But it was among the lower classes that Lollardy had its most enduring adherents. Though Wycliffe himself died in 1384, Lollardy as a movement lasted until well into the following century.

The Lollard movement naturally blended with the Reformation of the early 16th century. Thomson, in his Later Lollards, says that "by the time the Roman establishment was succeeded by the Anglican, Lollardy was developing into Puritanism." Eventually, these spread into the Covenanters and Non-conformists of Great Britain and America and indeed to every part of the globe.

Major Works

The Truth of the Sacred Scriptures (1378) States that the Bible contains all that is needed for salvation. The Scriptures should be read by all men and not just the clerics.

The Pope's Power (1379) Describes the papacy as an occupation instituted by men and not by God.

Apostasy (1379) Condemns the Roman doctrine of Transubstantiation.

On the Eucharist (1380) Denounces the idea of Christ's real, or corporeal, presence in the Eucharist after consecration. For Wycliffe, the validity depends upon the sanctity of the one receiving it, not on the consecration of the priest.

Trialogus (1382) Calls for a vernacular translation of the Bible for the ordinary people or common man.

Non-Fiction Writers of the Age of Revival

Reginald Peacock (1390-1460)

English prelate and writer, Reginald Peacock has been called "the only great English theologian of the 15th century. He was probably born in Wales in 1390. He received his education at Oriel College, Oxford. He obtained the bishopric of St Asaph in 1444. Peacock was forced to resign his bishopric in January 1459 and his books were publicly burnt because of his inconventional religious views against the power of reason.

Literary Career and Works

Peacock's most important work is *Repressor of Over-much Blaming of the Clergy* (c.1455), which added a new dimension to the Lollard movement. Apart from its religious importance, Peacock's *Repressor* can also be seen as a model of the English of the time, since Peacock was one of the first writers to use the vernacular.

His other works include *The Book of Faith*, a 15th century theological tract and *Donet*, a carefully graded guide to religious knowledge aimed at an educated class of London bourgeois men and women without much formal religious education. After the public recantation of his opinions, Peacock retired to an abbey and died there in 1460.

Sir John Fortescue (1394-1476)

John Fortescue was an English jurist and political theorist active during the reigns of Henry VI and Edward IV. He was born at Norries, in the parish of North Huish, near South Brent, in Devon. He was educated at Exeter College, Oxford and afterwards at Lincoln's Inn.

Literary Career and Works

Fortescue fled to Scotland with the royal family and served as tutor to the young prince Edward. It was there that his book, *De laudibus legum Angliae* (In Praise of English Law) was written in1470 for the prince's instruction.

Fortescue died around 1476 and was buried in the parish church of Ebrington, Gloucestershire.

Fortescue's writing

According to HR Reichel, Fortescue's writings can be divided into three parts. These are

Pamphlets on the Succession

Pamphlets on Lancastrian side were written in Scotland, between 1461 and 1463 and the two most important ones are extant only in Latin. The pamphlets include De titulo Edwardi comitis Marchiae, De Naturâ Legis Naturae and A declaration upon certain writings sent out of Scotland against the King's title to the Realm of England.

Constitutional Writings

Fortescue's reputation rests on his constitutional writings. Two most famous works in this category are

- ***De Laudibus Legum Angliae*** It is the best known of his writings and is in the form of a dialogue between Fortescue and Prince Edward, for whose instruction it was compiled. In this work, Fortescue urges the prince not to neglect the study of law.
- ***The Governance of England,*** also known as 'the difference between an Absolute and a Limited monarchy' is the most mature of his writings. It analyses the reasons for the failure of Lancastrian monarchy.

Miscellaneous Writings

- These include *A Dialogue between Understanding and Faith*, a brief, but touching tract on the miseries produced by the Civil War and two short pieces, *The Commodities of England*, and *The Twenty-two Righteousnesses belonging to a King*.

John Fisher (1469-1535)

English cardinal and Bishop of Rochester, John Fisher was born at Beverley, Yorkshire, England in 1459. He probably received his early education in the school attached to the collegiate church in his native town.

Literary Career and Works

Fisher mostly wrote ascetical or controversial treatises such as *Treatise concernynge...the seven penytencyall Psalms* (1508), *Sermon...agayn ye pernicyous doctrin of Martin Luther* (1521), *Defensio Henrici* VIII (1525), *De Veritate Corporis et Sanguinis Christi in Eucharistia*, *Adversus Johannem Oecolampadium* (1527), *The Ballad of Barry Buttock, a Cautionary Tale* (1529), *De Causa Matrimonii...Henrici VIII cum Catharina Aragonensi* (1530), *The Wayes to Perfect Religion* (1535) and *A Spirituall Consolation written...to hys sister Elizabeth* (1735).

When, it first became known that Henry VIII was planning ways, in which to divorce Catherine of Aragon, Fisher made it clear that he totally opposed such moves. He helped Catherine plan her defense and schooled her in Canon Law. Fisher produced seven publications condemning the impending divorce. Fisher was beheaded on tower hill on the 22nd June, 1535 because he was accused of being a traitor for not acknowledging King Henry VIII as the supreme head of the church.

Hugh Latimer (1485-1555)

English bishop Hugh Latimer is known as one of the chief promoters of the Reformation in England. He was born at Thurcaston, Leicestershire. He joined the likes of Thomas Bilney and Cranmer at the White Horse Tavern where issues on the Lutheran faith were discussed.

Literary Career and Works

He placed great emphasis on the reading of scripture and is thought to be the author of the homily 'A Fruitful Exhortation to the Reading of Holy Scripture,' in the 'First Book of Homilies.' His *Sermon on the Ploughers* and the *Sermons before King Edward VI* are well known. His prose is generally colloquial and direct.

It is simple in construction and composed of short sentences. According to WP Ker, as a preacher, Latimer "has often the aspect of some primitive dramatist on his cart, acting his own tragedy". He was found guilty of heresy because of his reformed views and on 16th October, 1555, was burned at the stake in Oxford.

John Capgrave (1393-1464)

John Capgrave was an English historian, hagiographer and scholastic theologian. He was praised by John Bale as "the most learned of all the Augustinians". Capgrave was born on 21st April, 1393 at Lynn in Norfolk.

Literary Career and Works

Over the course of his career, Capgrave produced voluminous commentaries on parts of the Old Testament and all of the new. Unfortunately, only some of his Latin works have survived: his commentaries on *Genesis, Exodus* and *Acts*; his *De Fidei Symbolis* and a collection of biographies of famous men named Henry. *Liber de Illustribus Henricis, or Book of the Illustrious Henries,* is the only one of his Latin works to have been edited and translated into English. Capgrave is best known for *Nova Legenda Angliae,* the first comprehensive collection of English saints' lives.

Robert Fabyan (1470-1513)

Born in London, Robert Fabyan was an English Chronicler. He belonged to an Essex family.

Fabyan' *Concordance of Histories* begins with Brutus and moves to the death of Richard III. This work is important mainly for its reference to London. Fabyan died on 28th February, 1513.

John Bourchier Second Lord Berners (1467-1533)

John Bourchier, Second Lord Berners was an English soldier, statesman and translator. He was born at Sherfield, Herts and educated at Oxford.

Bourchier has made his name in history as the translator of Froissart. His literary work includes translations such as Froissart's *Chronicles* (1523-25); *Huon of Bordeaux (1534); and The Golden Book of Marcus Aurelius* (1535; from a French version of Guevara's work), The History of Arthur of Lytell Brytaine. Bourchier died at Calais in 1533.

Thomas Cranmer (1489-1556)

Thomas Cranmer was born in 1489. He was the First Protestant Archbishop of Canterbury.

In 1549, Cranmer produced *The Book of Common Prayer*. Cranmer compiled and translated from Latin prayers, which had been in use for generations, rendering them in beautiful and clear prose. During his late years, Cranmer was convicted of heresy and sentenced to death.

Major Works

- An Answer unto a Crafty and Sophistical Cavillation devised by Stephen Gardiner (1551)
- The Answer of Thomas, Archbishop of Canterbury, against the False Calumniations of Doctor Richard Smith. (1551)
- Short Instruction into Christian Religion.
- The Book of Common Prayer Preface to the Great Bible (1539)

George Cavendish (1497-1562)

George Cavendish was an English writer, best known as the biographer of Cardinal Thomas Wolsey. Around 1522, he entered the service of Cardinal Thomas Wolsey as his gentleman usher. This position helped him in writing first hand account of Cardinal's life which he completed in 1557. His important works include Thomas Walsey, Layffe and Deathe Cavendish died in 1562.

George Buchanan (1506-1582)

George Buchanan was a Scottish Historian and humanist Scholar. He was born at Killearn, Stirlingshire, in 1506.

Buchanan incurred the enmity of Cardinal Beaton by his Latin satires on the friars, Somnium (Dream) and Franc- iscantis. Buchanan died in Edinburgh in 1582.

Major Works

- Baptistes sive Calumnia (written before 1544, not published until 1577)
- Jephthes sive Votum (1544)
- The Sphera
- The Art and Science of Government Among the Scots
- De jure Regni apud scotos (1579), History of scotland (1582 posthmaesly)

Thomas Wilson (1524-1581)

Thomas Wilson was an English prose writer. He was born at Stroby in Lincolnshire. He was educated at Eton and in 1541; he became a scholar of King's College, Cambridge.

Wilson's *The Rule of Reason, conteinyng the Arte of Logique* (1551), dedicated to King Edward VI was published in 1551. In his dedication to King Edward, Wilson explained the reasons, which led to its writing and publication. Wilson's most significant work, *Arte of Rhetorique* (1553) was dedicated to John Dudley, Earl of Warwick and Master of Horse.This work explained the principles of eloquence. His other work is Discourse on Usurye (1572). In 1580, Queen Elizabeth appointed Wilson Dean of Durham. He died at St Katherine's Hospital on 16th June, 1581.

Thomas Elyot (1490-1546)

English author and administrator, Thomas Elyot was born in 1490. His father, Richard, was a lawyer and instructor at the Inns of Court, who owned two manors in Wiltshire. From his early life, Elyot was 'continually trained in some daily affairs of the public weal'.

Elyot admits himself that "he was educated in his father's house and not instructed by another teacher from his 12th year, but led by himself into liberal studies and both sorts of philosophy." He also read medicine, but apparently only as an amateur and never practiced.

Literary Career and Works

In 1531, Elyot published his most important and best known work, *The Boke Called the Governor*, dedicated to Henry VIII in this year. This book articulated the values of a successful ruling class and argued that a good classical education was the best way for a youth to prepare for a life of service to the ruler. As a result of this book, Elyot was appointed as an ambassador to Charles V. Following his first diplomatic mission to Charles V Elyot tried to devote himself to his literary works.

Elyot composed the first English dictionary of Classical Latin. He was encouraged by Henry VIII in his endeavours. For his dictionary, Elyot declared his indebtedness to the old collection of words of Festus, Varro, Nonius and Nestor.

He dedicated his new book, *The Defense of Good Women*, to the King's new wife Anne, Elyot served as Member for Cambridge in 1542. He died on 50th March, 1546.

Major Works

- The Boke called the Governor (1531)
- The knowledge, which maketh a Wise Man and Pasquyll the Playne (1533)
- The Bankette of Sapience (1534)
- The Castel of Health (1536)
- Latin Dictionary (1538)
- The Defence of Good Women (1540)
- Preservative Agaynste Deth (1545)

There were two main figures who produced and printed the English version of the Bible for the very first time; they are William Tyndale and Miles Coverdale respectively.

William Tyndale (1494-1536)

Biblical translator and theologian William Tyndale was born on the Welsh border, probably in Gloucestershire, around 1494. He descended from an ancient Northumbrian family. He studied at Oxford, took his MA degree in 1515 and removed to Cambridge, where he was strongly influenced by his professor of Greek language studies, Erasmus, (the first to produce a Greek New Testament). He was ordained to the priesthood in 1521 and soon began to speak of his desire, which eventually became his life's obsession, to translate the Scriptures into English.

Literary Career and Works

Having become attached to the doctrines of the Reformation and devoted himself to the study of the Scriptures, he openly expresses his sentiments in the house of Walsh and had disputes with Roman Catholic dignitaries there. Unable to progress with this translation of Bible in England, Tyndale set out for the continent (about May, 1524) and appears to have visited Hamburg and Wittenberg. The place, where he translated the New Testament, is thought to have been Wittenberg, under the aid of Martin Luther.

In 1525, while living in Wittenberg, Tyndale finished his translation of the New Testament in English. The first printing of William Tyndale's English New Testament was completed in 1526 in Worms, Germany. From there the editions were smuggled into England by hiding them in merchandise, barrels, bales of cotton and sacks of flour. Henry VIII opposed the translation and church officials condemned it.

In the following years, Tyndale continued to make revisions to his translation. In addition to the translation of the Bible, he also produced the following works. His first original composition, *A Pathway into the Holy Scripture*, is a reprint of his *Prologue* to the Quarto edition of his New Testament and had appeared in separate form before 1532; *The Parable of the Wicked Mammon* (1527) and *The Obedience of a Christian Man* (1527-28). In 1530, appeared Tyndale's *Practyse of Prelates* and in 1531 his *Answer to the Dialogue*, his *Exposition of the First Epistle of St John* and the famous *Prologue* to Jonah; in 1532, *An Exposition upon the V VI VII Chapters of Matthew* and in 1536, *A Brief Declaration of the Sacraments* etc., which seems to be a posthumous publication.

In May of 1535, Tyndale was betrayed by a close friend, Henry Phillips. He was arrested by the king's officials and imprisoned in Vilvorde, near modern-day Brussels. There he was tried and convicted of heresy and treason. On the 6th of August 1536, he was strangled at the stake and his body afterwards burnt.

Miles Coverdale (1488-1568)

English translator of the Bible and bishop of Exeter, Miles Coverdale was probably born in that part of the North Riding of Yorkshire called Richmondshire, England. He studied philosophy and theology at Cambridge, was ordained priest at Norwich in 1514. The turning point in Coverdale's life seems to have been a meeting with Sir Thomas More and Thomas Cromwell in 1527, when More urged him to apply himself to sacred learning.

Literary Career and Works

Coverdale turned to the Scriptures and "perceived that the reformation of the church must be effected by the word of God." Shortly afterwards, he met William Tyndale in Hamburg and assisted in his translation of the Pentateuch. In 1534, he published two translations of his own, the first Dulichius's *Vom alten und newen Gott* and the second a *Paraphrase upon the Psalms*.

In 1535, Coverdale secured his place in history forever, by becoming the first person to print an entire Bible in the English language. In 1537, some of his translations were included in the Matthew-Tyndale Bible, the first direct English translation of the complete Bible. In 1538, he was in Paris, superintending the printing of King Henry VIIIs 'Great Bible,' of 1539 and the same year, published, both in London and Paris, an English New Testament. He also edited 'Cranmer's Bible', the 1540 edition of the Great Bible. In 1551, Coverdale was appointed to the Diocese of Exeter. His subsequent life was spent in preaching and reading the scriptures. He died, aged 81, in 1565 and was interred in the church of 'St Bartholomew by the Exchange'.

Elizabethan Chroniclers and Antiquaries

Elizabethan period also witnessed the rise of some notable chroniclers and Antiquaries such as John Foxe, Raphael Holinshed and William Camden, etc. Brief Description of Notable Chroniclers and Antiquaries

John Foxe (1516-1587)

John Foxe was born in Boston, Lincolnshire in 1517. He studied at Brasenose College, Oxford, where he was the pupil of John Harding or Hawarden. A year later, he joined the Magdalen College, from where he did his graduation and masters. In 1539-1540, he became a College Lecturer in logic.

Literary Career and Works

His first surviving literary work, '*Titus et Gesippus*', a Latin comedy based on one of Boccacio's tales was written in 1544. Foxe also found a patron in Mary Fitzroy, Duchess of Richmond, who hired him as a tutor to the orphan children of her brother, Henry Howard, Earl of Surrey. However, when Queen Mary came to the throne, Foxe was deprived of his tutorship. Because of the adverse political and religious climate, he moved with his wife to Strassburg. There, he published a Latin history of the Christian persecutions, which became the first outline of his work *Acts and Monuments*.

Foxe began his famous *Book of Martyrs* in 1552, during the reign of Edward VI. In 1563, he published the first edition of the *Acts and Monuments* (known as Foxe's Book of Martyrs). It was a massive folio volume of about 1800 pages, which covered English church history from Wycliffe until the accession of Elizabeth. Its accuracy was immediately attacked by Catholic writers, notably in the *Dialogi sex* (1566) and by Robert Parsons in *Three Conversions of England* (1570). Foxe died on 18th April, 1587 and was buried at St Giles's, Cripplegate.

Raphael Holinshed (1529-1580)

Raphael Holinshed was born in 1529 to a Cheshire family. Holinshed lived in London and was employed as a translator by Reginald Wolfe, who was preparing a universal history.

Literary Career and Works

After Wolfe's death, Holinshed continued the work started by Wolfe, but reduced the extent of the history to Britain. This historical work appeared in a much shortened version and was published as *Chronicles of England, Scotlande and Irelande* in 1577.

The book was dedicated to Sir William Cecil, Lord Burghley. The book began with a description of Britain from the earliest times and carried on until the reign of Elizabeth. It served as a major source material for many of Shakespeare's plays such as '*Macbeth, King Lear*' and '*Cymbeline*'. Holinshed died in 1580.

William Camden (1551-1623)

William Camden was born in Old Bailey, London in 1551. He was the son of Sampson Camden, a member of the Painter-Stainers guild. He received his education at Christ's Hospital, St Paul's School and Oxford University. At Oxford, Camden befriended Sidney, as well as Richard and George Carew.

Literary Career and Works

In 1575, he began working at Westminster School. It was here that he published the first edition of his *Britannia* in 1586. It was a historical survey of all of Great Britain and Ireland. It was dedicated to William Cecil Lord Burleigh, lord treasurer to Queen Elizabeth. In 1593, Camden became Headmaster of Westminster School and held this post till 1597. In 1597, he was selected for the post of Clarenceaux, King of Arms.

Camden's other important work, *Annales rerum Anglicarum et Hibernicarum regnante Elizabetha* (Annals of affairs in England and Ireland in the reign of Elizabeth) was published in 1615. Camden's later years were spent as an academic. He was appointed as historian of the newly formed Chelsea College. In 1622, he established the Camden Chair of History at Oxford. As Oxford's first lectureship in the field, the endowment helped to shape the university's curriculum and the future study of history. Camden died on 9th November, 1623.

Richard Hakluyt (1552-1616)

Richard Hakluyt was born in Hertfordshire, England, around 1552. He was the second son of a London skinner. Hakluyt's father died, when he was only five and from then on, his cousin became his guardian. Hakluyt's association with his cousin and guardian, Richard Hakluyt (1535-1591), who was a geographer, aroused his interest in geography. Hakluyt studied at Westminster School and at Christ Church, Oxford.

Literary Career and Works

After completing his masters in 1577, he began giving lectures in geography at Oxford. In 1582, he published *Divers Voyages Touching the Discoverie of America* (1582). This was dedicated to Sir Philip Sidney. After its publication, Hakluyt was selected as chaplain and secretary to accompany Edward Stafford, English ambassador at the French court, to Paris in 1583. The information that he collected in Paris was gathered in his work, *'A Particular Discourse Concerninge the Greate Necessitie and Manifolde Commodyties that are Like to Growe to This Realme of Englande by the Westerne Discoueries Lately Attempted, Written in the Yere 1584'*.

In 1589, the first edition of *The Principall Navigations, Voiages and Discoveries of the English Nation* appeared, for which Hakluyt is chiefly known. Hakluyt was appointed as the Rectorin of Wetheringsett-cum-Brockford, Suffolk, by Lady Stafford. He held this position till his death in 1616.

Samuel Purchas (1577-1626)

Samuel Purchas was born at Thaxted, Essex. He studied at St John's College, Cambridge. He was selected as Chaplain to the Archbishop of Canterbury and later became Rector of St Martin's Church, London.

Literary Career and Works

His first acclaimed book, *Purchas His Pilgrimage* (1613) gave a description of different people and places. The work's description of Xanadu inspired Coleridge's poem *'Kubla Khan'*. The success of this book led to his most famous compilation of travel literature, *Hakluytus Posthumus* or *Purchas His Pilgrims* (1625). This was a four-volume collection based on the writings of Richard Hakluyt, the most prominent travel writer of his time. Purchas died in 1626.

Richard Hooker (1554-1600)

Theologian and priest Richard was born in Heavitree, Exeter, Devon in 1554. He was educated at Exeter and later sent to Cropus College, Oxford with Bishop Jewel as his patron.

Literary Career and Works

He served as master of the Temple Church and later served as vicar of churches at Drayton Beauchamp, Bosombe and Bishopsbourne. Hooker's famous 'of the Law of Ecclesiatical Polity' (1593), written in 8 books, formulated key intellectual concepts of Anglicanism. This work defended the threefold authority of the Bible, church tradition and human reason. The first four books of 'The Laws' were published together in 1593, the fifth was published in 1597 and the rest appeared after his death. His other work is 'Learned Discourse of Justification' (1585). Hooker's health began to fail in the year 1600, because of a cold contracted on a journey by water London to Gravesend. He died in the same year.

Major Works

- Of the Laws of Ecclesiatical Plity (1893)
- Learned Discourse of Justification (1595)

Works of Literary Criticism in Elizabethan Age

Many writers worked on the critical analysis of the literature during the Elizabethan period. A few of such significant works have been described in brief below.

George Gascoigne's Certayne Notes of Instruction (1575)

'Gascoigne's *Certayne Notes of Instruction*' first appeared in his work *'The Posies of George Gascoigne, Esquire, corrected, perfected, and augmented by the Author'* in 1575. It is considered to be the first English manual of versification. These notes were written at the request of Master Eduardo Donati. As the intent on the title page indicates, the work concerns "The making of verse or ryme in English". It discusses English verse and meter. Michael Mack states that the book is almost a "Handbook written by a poet for other poets, offering practical advice for keeping audiences entertained". Gascoigne also emphasises ingenuity and invention as qualities of a good poet. Mere rhetorical figures and figures of speech are not enough, unless the poem reflects the poet's originality and invention. He states,

"The first and most necessary point that ever I found need to be considered in making of a delectable poeme is this, to ground it upon some fine invention. For it is not enough to roll in pleasant woordes, nor yet to thunder in Rym, Ram, Ruff, by letter (quoth my master Chaucer) nor yet to abounde in apt vocables, or epythetes, unlesse the Invention have in it also a liquid salis. By this aliquid salis, I meane some good and fine devise, strewing the quicke capacitie of a writer: and where I say some good and fine invention, I meane that I would have it both fine and good."

William Webbe's Discourse of English Poetry (1586)

Webbe's *Discourse of English Poetry Together with the Author's Judgment Touching the Reformation of Our English Verse* was written and published in 1586. The work was dedicated to his patron, Edward Sulyard.

Webbe attempts a historical survey of poetry and also reviews poetry of his day. He also applauds the poetic skills of the lords and gentlemen in the Queen's court. Webbe argues that the scarcity of good English poetry since Chaucer's day was not due to lack of poetic ability; or to the poverty of the language, but to the lack of a proper system of prosody.

He abuses "This tinkerly verse, which we call ryme," as of barbarous origin and comments on the works of his contemporaries, displaying enthusiasm for Spenser's *Shepheardes Calendar* and admiration for Phaer's translation of *Virgil.*

George Puttenham's The Arte of English Poesie (1589)

The Arte of English Poesie was written by English writer and critic George Puttenham in 1589. The book first appeared anonymous and was later ascribed to Puttenham. It was addressed to the Queen, with a publisher's dedication to Lord Burghley. It is considered to be "The most ambitious and comprehensive undertaking in Elizabethan criticism."

According to Charles M Willis, Puttenham had to conceal his name as a writer because his Catholic family was involved in a bitter religious conflict with Protestant and Puritan Church leaders, which reached a climax in 1584 when his Catholic nephew Francis Throckmorton was executed for treason. *The Arte of English Poesie* has been divided into three books. The *First* book contains a history of poetry and discusses diverse kinds of poetry. Puttenham specially mentions Sir Thomas Wyatt and Henry, Earl of Surrey, as 'The first reformers of our English metre and style'. The *second* book discusses prosody and contains an account of five types of English verse structures: the *'Staffe', the 'Measure,' 'Concord or Symphony,' 'Situation'* and *'Figure'*. The *third* book discusses figures of speech.

Philip Sidney's An Apology for Poetry (1595)

Sidney's *An Apology for Poetry* is a spirited defense of poetry against all the charges laid against it. It was originally published under two different titles, *The Defence of Poesie* and *An Apology for Poetry*. The reason for the two titles of this critical treatise derives from its complicated publishing history: three editions in 1595 and a fourth in 1598. The first appearance in 1595 was William Ponsonby's *The Defence of Poesie*; this was followed shortly by Henry Olney's publication of *An Apology for Poetry*.

According to Sidney, poetry is not only the most ancient form of learning, which the earliest thinkers used as a means of introducing difficult ideas to the unlearned, but both philosophers like Plato himself and historians make use of the devices of poetry in order to effectively communicate their message. Sidney's *Apology* is the first serious attempt to apply the classical rules to English poetry.

A third edition was brought out by Ponsonby in 1595 with his title page and fourth edition was brought out by Sidney's sister, who collected his works.

An Apology for Poetry was written partly as a response to Stephen Gosson's *School of Abuse*.

Gosson had stated that a man could employ his time more usefully than in poetry, that it is the 'mother of lies', it is immoral and that Plato was right in banishing poets from his ideal commonwealth.

Thomas Campion's Observations in the Art of English Poesie (1602)

Campion's *Observations in* the Art of English Poesie was published in 1602. The main purpose of the book is set down by Campion on the title page as "Wherein it is demonstratively proved and by example confirmed that the English tongue will receive several kinds of numbers, proper to itself, which are all in this book set forth and were never before this time by any man attempted".

In this work, Campion argued that verse written in English should emulate classical meters. He believed that classical meters fitted the English tongue better than the "Vulgar and unartificial custom of rhyming".

Elise Bickford Jorgens states that Campion offended many lyric poets of the time by declaring that "The facility and popularity of rhyme creates as many poets as a hot summer flies". Most lyric poets of Campion's time were regular users of rhyme. Campion also discussed types of verse forms, which are best suited to English and outlined a method for establishing the number of syllables in lines of English poetry.

Samuel Daniel's A Defence of Rime/Rhyme (1603)

Daniel's *A Defence of Rhyme* was printed in 1603. It was written in reply to Thomas Campion's *Observations on the Art of English Poesie*, which argued that rhyme was not suited to the genius of the English language. Through his work, Daniel wanted to demonstrate that rhyme was 'The fittest harmonie of words that comports with our language'. He argued that rhyme did not check poetic imagination, but imparted an outline to the poet's ideas.

Daniel's prose essay rejected blindly following classical models, emphasised individuality of English mode of writing and plurality of kinds of eloquence. He argued, "All our understandings are not to be built by the square of Greece and Italic. We are the children of nature as well as they. All their Poesie, all their Philosophie is nothing, unless we bring the discerning light of concept with us to apply it to use. It is not bookes, but only that great booke of the world and the all overspreading grace of heaven that makes men truely Judicial."

EXAM BASED QUESTIONS

1 In an autobiography
(a) writer tells someone else's story
(b) writing that is not true
(c) writer tells his own story
(d) gives a description of a topic

2 Non-ficiton
(a) reason for which the author writes
(b) writer tells his own story
(c) writing that is true
(d) writer gives an explanation of ideas

3 Informational non-fiction
(a) intent of informing the reader about a topic
(b) writing that is not true
(c) writer tries to convince the reader
(d) original materials that have not been altered

4 Author's purpose
(a) original materials that have not been altered
(b) reason for which the author writes
(c) short form of literary composition
(d) author tells life story of someone else

5 Literary non-fiction
(a) writer tells his own story
(b) gives description of a particular event
(c) short form of literary compostion
(d) uses literary styles to create a factually accurate narrative

6 In a biography
(a) writer tells his own story
(b) writer tells the story of someone else's life
(c) short form of literary composition
(d) writing gives explanation of ideas

7 Any short work of nonfiction appearing as a part of a magazine, newspaper, or book
(a) article (b) diary
(c) novel (d) blog

8 A type of non-fiction writing that includes personal thoughts and reflections
(a) memoir (b) autobiography
(c) biography (d) expository

9 Which book is believed to have been the earliest autobiography in English language?
(a) The Book of Margery Kempe
(b) La Male Regle
(c) The Lyf of Our Lady
(d) The Example of Vertu

10 'The Paston Letters' is an important work of the 15th century because
(a) of its literary merit
(b) of its valuable and reliable social chronicles
(c) of its innovative style and form
(d) of poverty of the age in prose writing

11 The time period of Samuel Purchas was
(a) 1575-1626 (b) 1552-1616
(c) 1586-1634 (d) 1535-1601

12 In the first edition, Hakluyt describes voyages to
(a) North (b) East
(c) India (d) New world

13 In the second edition Hakluyt describes voyages to
(a) North (b) India
(c) East (d) Both (b) and (c)

14 Non-fiction writers can be divided in to a number of groups like this one
(a) writers of literary criticism
(b) writers of prose
(c) philosophical prose writers
(d) All of the above

15 The most notable achievement in Jacobean prose was
(a) Bacon's Essays
(b) King James translation of the Bible
(c) Robert Burton's Anatomy of Melancholy
(d) None of the above

16 Which Bible is the earliest English version printed with verse divisions?
(a) Tyndale's Translation
(b) The Geneva Bible
(c) The Douay-Rheims Version
(d) King James Version

17 Which of the following is the most important work of Reginald Peacock done in 1455?
(a) The Denet
(b) The Book of Faith
(c) The Poor Man's Mirror
(d) Repressor of Over Much Blaming of the Clergy

18 In which Fortescue praises the Constitution of his country?
(a) Utopia
(b) The Governance of England
(c) De Laudibus Legum
(d) Pastimes of Pleasure

19 Which work of Fortescue is also known as the difference between an absolute and limited monarchy?
(a) The Governance of England
(b) De Laudibus Legum Angliae
(c) The Twenty-Two Righteousness belonging to a Ling
(d) The Commodities of England

20 Who is the author of Defensio Henrici VIII?
(a) John Capgrave (b) Caxton
(c) John Fisher (d) Thomas Elyot

21 What kind of writings did Fisher write?
(a) Controversial treatises
(b) Ballads
(c) Political satire
(d) Religious writings

22 How many publications did Fisher produce condemning the impending divorce of Henry VIII and Catherine of Aragan?
(a) Six (b) Seven (c) Ten (d) Eight

23 Who is the author of the homily 'A Fruitful Exhortation to the Reading of Holy Scripture'?
(a) Sir Thomas Malory (b) Hugh Latimer
(c) Thomas Moore (d) George Buchanan

24 How was the language of the prose written by Latimer?
(a) Colloquial and direct
(b) Complex
(c) Not familiar to common people
(d) None of the above

25 Which of the following works belong to Hugh Latimer?
(a) Morte d' Arthur
(b) In Genesim
(c) Sermons before the King Edward VI
(d) All of the above

26 What is George Cavendish best known for?
(a) Layffe and Deathe
(b) Life of Cardinal Thomas Wolsey
(c) The Laboryouse Journey
(d) None of the above

27 Whom did Thomas Wilson dedicate his 'The Rule of Reason, Conteinyng the Arte of Logique'?
(a) King Edward IV (b) King Richard III
(c) King Henry VIII (d) King Edward VI

28 What is Capgrave best known for?
(a) Nova Legenda Anglie (b) De Fidei Symbolis
(c) Genesis (d) Exodus and Acts

29 Which is only Latin work of Capgrave that is translated into English?
(a) De Fidei Symbolis
(b) Genesis
(c) Liber de Illustribus Henricis
(d) Nova Legenda Angliae

30 Name the Latin, works of Capgrave that have survived.
(a) Genesis, Exodus and Acts, Life of St. Norbert, Life of St. Augustine
(b) Genesis, Exodus and Acts, De Fidei Symbolis, Liber de Illustribus Henricis
(c) Genesis, Life of St. Gilbert, Nova Legenda Angliae, Life of St. Katherine
(d) Exodus and Acts, Liber de Illustribus Henricis, Life of St Katherine, Nova Legenda Angliae

31 Which book is the collection of lives of English saints?
(a) Nova Legenda Anglie
(b) De Fidei Symbolis
(c) Liber de Illustribus Henricis
(d) None of the above

32 Who produced voluminous commentaries on old testament and all of the new?
(a) Hugh Latimer (b) John Capgrave
(c) Thomas More (d) John Fisher

33 Who is the author of 'The History of Arthur of Lytell Brytaine'?
(a) Robert Fabyan (b) John Capgrave
(c) Thomas Cranmer (d) Lord Berners

34 Which of the following is written by Cranmer?
(a) Short Instruction into Christian Religion
(b) Bonner Grindal
(c) Certain Sermons
(d) Skelton

35 'Book of Common Prayer' was written in the year
(a) 1548 (b) 1549 (c) 1550 (d) 1551

36 Who wrote 'Book of Common Prayer'?
(a) John Leland (b) George Cavendish
(c) Thomas Cranmer (d) None of these

37 Which of the following is the first original composition of William Tyndale?
(a) Practyse of Prelates
(b) A Pathway into the Holy Scripture
(c) Answer to the Dialogue
(d) A Brief Declaration of the Sacraments

38 In which of the following work of Tyndale did Coverdale help?
(a) Practyse of Prelates
(b) A Pathway into the Holy Scripture
(c) Pentateuch
(d) None of these

39 Whom did John Bale praised as 'The most learned of all the Augustinians'?
(a) Robert Fabyan (b) Lord Berners
(c) Sir Thomas Malory (d) John Capgrave

40 Who is the writer of "The Boke named the Governor"?
(a) Thomas More (b) Thomas Wilson
(c) Thomas Elyot (d) Thomas Wyatt

41 Whom did Elyot dedicate his 'The Boke named the Governor'?
(a) Charles V (b) Richard III
(c) Edward V (d) Henry VIII

42 Who composed the first English Dictionary of Classical Latin?
(a) George Cavendish (b) Thomas More
(c) John Fisher (d) Thomas Elyot

43 **Which of the following works did Elyot dedicate to Anne?**
(a) Preservative Agaynste Deth
(b) The Boke called the Governor
(c) The Defense of Good Women
(d) The Castell of Health

44 **Which of the following is the earliest version of the great Bible?**
(a) William Tyndale's English New Testament
(b) Wat Tyler's Translation
(c) Cromwell's great Bible, Miles Coverdale's English Bible
(d) King James Authorised Version of the Bible

45 **The first complete printed English Bible was produced by**
(a) William Tyndale (b) William Caxton
(c) Myles Coverdale (d) Roger Ascham

46 **He wanted that even a farmer could read his Bible so he wrote it in simple, lucid, clear, language. Who was he?**
(a) Thomas Matthew (b) Miles Coverdale
(c) William Tyndale (d) Thomas Craninerm

47 **Which of these is not correct for Elizabethan Chronicles and Antiquaries?**
(a) John Foxe (b) Raphael Holinshed
(c) Thomas Nashe (d) William Carden

48 **Who was the best translator of the Elizabethan Age?**
(a) Camden (b) Knox
(c) Hakluyt (d) Thomas North

49 **Which is a collection of critical and literary principles?**
(a) Arcadia (b) Aplogy for poetry
(c) Calendar (d) Needle

50 **The Arte of English Poesie, addressed to the Queen, was written by**
(a) George Puttenham (b) George Gascoigne
(c) William Webbe (d) Thomas Campion

51 **Daniel's A defence of Rhyme was written in reply to**
(a) William Webbe's Discourse of English Poetry
(b) George Gascoigne's cetayne Notes of Instruction
(c) Thomas Campion's Observations in the Art of English Poesie.
(d) Philip Sydney's An Aplogy for Poetry

52 **What do most Christians believe about the Bible?**
(a) God carved the original Bible into stone atop Mount Sinai
(b) God dictated the Bible to Jesus, and Jesus' followers wrote it down
(c) It is inspired by God, but written by various human authors
(d) The New Testament is inspired by God, but the Old Testament is primarily historical background

53 **What else do Christians believe about the Bible?**
(a) It tells the history of God's salvation of His people
(b) It tells the history of the angels
(c) It tells the origins of God
(d) It tells why God created the universe

54 **Which of these is not part of the Bible?**
(a) The teachings of prophets
(b) The teachings of Jesus
(c) The history of the medieval Church
(d) The history of Israel

55 **Which of these is taught by the Bible?**
(a) The true path to prestige and influence
(b) The true path to wealth and personal happiness
(c) How to live in harmony with God and with all of humanity
(d) Techniques of Christian Mysticism

56 **Nearly all the events of the Bible occurred in one region of the world. Which region?**
(a) Northern Europe
(b) Southern Europe
(c) The Middle East
(d) Central Asia

57 **What can be said about the original writings that make up the Bible?**
(a) The complete set of the original documents is stored in the Vatican archives.
(b) The complete set of original documents is stored partly at the Vatican, and partly in museums around the world.
(c) Only a few of the original documents have been preserved to this day.
(d) None of the original documents are known to exist.

58 **The Dead Sea Scrolls were found in caves around the Dead Sea in 1947, and are considered a major source of knowledge about the Bible. What do they contain.?**
(a) The original documents of parts of the Old Testament of the Bible
(b) The original documents of parts of the New Testament of the Bible
(c) The oldest known copies of parts of the Old Testament of the Bible
(d) The oldest known copies of parts of the New Testament of the Bible

59 **In the 4th century Pope Damascus assigned his secretary, Jerome, the task of producing an accurate translation of the Bible in Latin, the language of the Roman Empire. Jerome completed the task in AD 405, and his translation became the standard Bible of Christianity for over 900 years. What was this version called?**
(a) The Geneva Bible
(b) The King James Bible
(c) The Sepuagint
(d) The Vulgate

60 When was the whole Bible first translated into English?
(a) 973 AD (b) 1102 AD (c) 1380 AD (d) 1580 AD

61 Who was responsible for producing the first printed version of the Bible?
(a) Johannes Gutenberg (b) John Wycliffe
(c) King James of England (d) Pope Gregory the Great

62 What is the King James Version?
(a) An English translation from the Latin version of the Bible that was a favourite of James I of England
(b) An English translation commissioned by James I of England and first published in 1611
(c) An English version of the Bible used by the Church of Scotland, but banned in England
(d) The first English translation of the Bible produced in the American colonies, and dedicated to King James of England

63 About how many languages has the Bible been translated into?
(a) 400 (b) 800 (c) 1500 (d) 3000

64 What is the Apocrypha?
(a) A popular book of the Middle Ages that gives fanciful descriptions of heaven and hell.
(b) A group of Christian writings that were included in some early versions of the Bible, but were excluded from the official canon of Christianity
(c) A group of Jewish writings that were included in some versions of Jewish scripture, but were excluded from the official canon of Judaism
(d) A set of heretical writings from the first century that denies the divinity of Jesus

65 What is the difference between Catholic and Protestant Bibles?
(a) Protestant Bibles contain the writings of Martin Luther, but Catholic Bibles do not
(b) The Catholic Bible contains the writings of several popes, but Protestant Bibles do not
(c) The New Testament of the Catholic Bible contains the Gospel of Thomas, but most Protestant Bibles do not
(d) The Old Testament of the Catholic Bible contains the books of the Apocrypha, but most Protestant Bibles do not

66 The Anglo-Norman Period Chronicle 'Chronica Majora' was one of the most valuable sources of knowledge of 13th century life, written by
(a) Matthew Paris (b) William of Malmesbury
(c) Ordericus Vitalis (d) Simeon of Durham

67 The Holy Bible was translated from Latin into Middle English in the late 14th century by ....
(a) John Mandeville (b) John Wycliffe
(c) Sir John Fortescue (d) John Fisher

68 The Governance of England is a constitutional writing by
(a) Reginald Peacock (b) Hugh Latimar
(c) Sir John Fortescue (d) Lord Berners

69 Thomas Cranmer was the writer of a famous religious non-fiction work.
(a) Nova Legenda Angliae
(b) The Ways to Perfect Religion
(c) Sermons on the Ploughers
(d) The Book of Common Prayer

70 .... followed the style of Cicero.
(a) Francis Bacon
(b) Thomas Deloney
(c) Richard Hooker
(d) Thomas Watson

71 Which of the following statements about the English language in Anglo-Norman period is incorrect?
(a) The Norman conquest changed the whole course of English language
(b) English now had around 10000 French words
(c) Pronunciation did not change
(d) Old English spellings changed

72 Which of the following statements is not true for Lollard Movement?
(a) The Pope had no part to play in worldly affairs
(b) The Church was too worldly
(c) Monasticism had drifted from its spiritual foundation
(d) The Bible should not be available to everyone in their language

73 Which of the following pairs is incorrectly matched?
(a) Religious : Malmesbury
(b) Lais : Marie de France
(c) Poetry : Orm (Ormin)
(d) Chronicle : eginald of Canterbury

74 Which of the following pairs is not correctly matched?
(a) John Wycliffe : Lollard Movement
(b) John Mandeville : Canterbury Tales
(c) John Gower : Vox Clamantis
(d) William Langland : Piers Plowman

75 Which of the following pairs is incorrectly matched?
(a) Hugh Latimer : Sermons before King Edward VI
(b) John Fisher : The Ways to Perfect Religion
(c) Caxton : Morte d'Arthur
(d) John Fortescue : The Governance of England

Directions (Q. Nos. 76-78) *In the questions given below are two statements labelled as Assertion (A) and Reason (R). In the context of the two statements, which one of the following is correct?*
(a) Both A and R are true and R is the correct explanation of A
(b) Both A and R are true but R is not the correct explanation of A
(c) A is true but R is false
(d) A is false but R is true

76 **Assertion** (A) Sir John Mandeville spent some 34 years travelling extensively through out Asia and Northern Africa.
Reason (R) He settled in England to write an account of his journey.

77 **Assertion** (A) In 1535, Miles Coverdale secured his place in history for ever by becoming the first person to Print an entire Bible in the English Language.
Reason (R) He also edited John Wycliffe's Bible.

78 **Assertion** (A) 'The Book of Margery Kempe' is an autobiography yet it is written in IIIrd person.
Reason (R) She could not write so she dictated it to two scribes (clerks), who wrote about her in IIIrd person.

79 Identify the one in correct chronological sequence
(a) The Norman conquest – The Death of Geoffrey Chaucer–William Tyndale's New Testament– The Birth of William Shakespeare
(b) The Death of Geoffrey Chaucer–William Tyndale's New Testament–The Birth of William Shakespeare–The Norman Conquest
(c) The Norman Conquest–William Tyndale's New Testament –The Death of Geoffrey Chaucer–The Birth of William Shakespeare
(d) William Tyndale's New Testament–The Norman Conquest–The Death of Geoffrey Chaucer–The Birth of William Shakespeare

80 Arrange the following in chronological order.
1. John Foxe
2. Richard Hooker
3. Sir Walter Raleigh
Codes
(a) 1, 2 and 3
(b) 1, 3 and 2
(c) 2, 1 and 3
(d) 3, 2 and 1

81 Consider the following about Sir John Fortescue:
1. His writing can be divided into three parts, according to HR Reichel.
2. De Laudibus Legum Angliae Falls under the category of Constitutional writings.
3. A Dialogue between understanding and Faith is an example of pamphlets.
4. The Governance of England Falls under the category of miscellaneous writings.
Which of the statements given above are correct?
(a) 1 and 2
(b) 2 and 3
(c) 3 and 4
(d) 1 and 3

82 Consider the following statements about George Buchanan:
1. He was a Scottish Historian and Scholar.
2. He was born at Killearn in 1516.
3. He befriended Cardinal Beaton by his Latin satires on the Friers.
4. Jephthes sive Votum is one of his famous works.
Which of the statements given above are true for him?
(a) 1 and 2 (b) 1 and 4 (c) 2 and 3 (d) 3 and 4

83 Consider the following writers:
1. Mandeville
2. Wycliffe
3. William Tyndale
4. Miles Coverdale
Which of the above given are non-fiction writers of the Age of Revival?
(a) 1 and 2 (b) 2 and 3
(c) 3 and 4 (d) 2 and 4

84 Consider the following non-fictitious works:
1. Acts and Monuments
2. Paraphrase upon the Psalms.
3. Annals of affairs in England and Ireland in the reign of Elizabeth.
4. The Parable of the Wicked Mammon.
Which of the works given above belong to the Elizabethan period?
(a) 1 and 2
(b) 2 and 3
(c) 3 and 4
(d) 1 and 3

85 Consider the following non-fiction writers.
1. John foxe
2. Wiliam Camden
3. Richard Hakluyt
4. Richard Hooker
Which of the writers given above are Elizabethan Chroniclers and antiquariers?
(a) 1 and 2
(b) 2 and 3
(c) 3 and 4
(d) 2 and 4

86 What is common to all of them?
1. Reginald Peacock
2. William Caxton
3. John Fisher
4. Hugh Latimer
Codes
(a) All of them were poets of the Age of Revival
(b) All of them were Romantic poets
(c) All of them wrote in Latin
(d) All of them were important prose writers of the Age of Revival

87 Consider the following statements.
1. Fisher was beheaded for being a traitor.
2. Latimer was found guilty of heresy and was burnt in Oxford.
3. Cranmer was convicted of heresy and sentenced to death.

Which of the following statements given above are correct?
(a) 1 and 3 (b) 2 and 3
(c) 1 and 2 (d) All of these

88 Consider the following statements regarding the 'Book called the Governor'.
1. It was written by Thomas Cranmer.
2. It was dedicated to Henry VIII.
3. As a result of this book, the poet was appointed as an ambassador to Charles V.
4. It is a detailed discussion of how to be a good nobleman and a ruler.

Which of the statements given above is correct?
(a) Only 1 (b) Only 2 (c) Only 3 (d) Only 4

89 Theology is
1. study of Philosophy.
2. study of Religion and God.
3. study of Astronomy.
4. study of Aeronautical sciences.

Which of the statements given above is/are correct?
(a) Only 2
(b) 1 and 2
(c) All of these
(d) None of these

90 Consider the following statements.
1. Richard Hooker in his first book talks about general treatise on law.
2. The second argues that divine law or scripture is not exclusive for its own existence to serve.
3. In the third, he had purpose to make the church an independent identity.

Which of the statements given above are correct?
(a) 1 and 2
(b) 1 and 3
(c) 2 and 3
(d) All of the above

91 Match the following Anglo-Norman chroniclers with their works.

Anglo-Norwah Charoniclers	Works
1. Simeon of Durham	A. Historia Ecclesiae Dunelmensis
2. Ordericus Vitalis	B. The Ecclesiastiacal History
3. William of Malmesbury	C. Historia Novella
4. Matthew Paris	D. Chronica Majora

Codes
(a) 1-A, 2-B, 3-C, 4-D (b) 1-D, 2-C, 3-B, 4-A
(c) 1-B, 2-D, 3-A, 4-C (d) 1-C, 2-A, 3-D, 4-B

92 Match the following work of John Wycliffe with their description.

Works	Description
1. The Truth of the Sacred Scriptures	A. Calls for a vernacular translation of the Bible for the laity.
2. The Pope's Power	B. Condemns the Roman Doctrine of transubstantiation.
3. Apostasy	C. Describes the papacy as an occupation instituted by men and not by God.
4. Trialogus	D. States that the Bibe contains all that is needed for salvation

Codes
(a) 1-A, 2-B, 3-C, 4-D (b) 1-D, 2-C, 3-B, 4-A
(c) 1-B, 2-D, 3-A, 4-C (d) 1-C, 2-A, 3-D, 4-B

93 Match the following non-fiction writers of the Revival Age with their works.

(Non-Fictional Writers of the Revival Age)	(Works)
1. Reginald Peacock	A. Sermons before King Edward VI
2. Sir John Fortescue	B. De Laudibus legum Angliae
3. John Fisher	C. Treatise Concernynge The Seven Penytencyll Psalms
4. Hugh Latimer	D. Repressor of over much Blaming of the clergy

Codes
(a) 1-A, 2-B, 3-C, 4-D (b) 1-D, 2-C, 3-B, 4-A
(c) 1-D, 2-B, 3-C, 4-A (d) 1-B, 2-D, 3-A, 4-C

94 Match the following works with their non-fiction writers of the Elizabethan Age.

(Works)	(Non-Fiction Writer of the Elizabethan Age)
1. Divers Voyages Touching the Discovery of America and the Islands Adjacent.	A. Samuel Purchas
2. Purchas His Pilgrimage	B. Thomas North
3. Of the laws of Ecclesiastical Polity	C. Richard Hakluty
4. The Lives of the Gretians and Romanes Noble.	D. Richard Hooker

Codes
(a) 1-A, 2-B, 3-C, 4-D (b) 1-D, 2-C, 3-B, 4-D
(c) 1-B, 2-D, 3-A, 4-C (d) 1-C, 2-A, 3-D, 4-B

95 Mathc the following.

List I	List II
A. 1138	1. De Amore
B. 1184	2. History of Canterbury
C. 1188	3. Brut
D. 1200	4. History of the Kings of Britain

Codes

	A	B	C	D
(a)	4	3	2	1
(b)	4	1	2	3
(c)	1	3	4	2
(d)	1	2	3	4

96 Match the following.

List I	List II
A. Skelton	1. Love that Doth Reign
B. More	2. Apology
C. Elyot	3. Philip Sparrow
D. Surrey	4. The Boke Called the Governor

Codes

	A	B	C	D		A	B	C	D
(a)	3	2	4	1	(b)	3	4	1	2
(c)	1	2	3	4	(d)	1	4	2	3

97 Match the following.

List I	List II
A. Thomas Cranmer	1. The Boke named the Governor
B. Henry Medwall	2. The Sphera
C. Thomas Elyot	3. Fulgens and Lucrece
D. George Buchanan	4. The Book of Common Prayer

Codes

	A	B	C	D		A	B	C	D
(a)	1	2	3	4	(b)	4	3	1	2
(c)	2	4	3	1	(d)	3	4	1	2

98 In the given series, which one has all the non-fiction writers matched correctly with the kind of writing genre?

(a) Simeon of Durham–Chronicler, Wace- Brut, John Mandeville–Travel Writer, John Wycliffe-Religious non-fiction

(b) Simeon of Durham–Brut, Wace–Travel Writer, John Mandeville–Religious Non-Fiction, John Wycliffe-Chronicler

(c) Simeon of Durham–Travel Writer, Wace–Religious Non-Fiction, John Mandeville–Chronicler, John Wycliffe–Brut

(d) Simeon of Durham–Religious Non-Fiction, Wace–Chronicler, John Mandeville–Brut John Wycliffe–Travel Writer

99 In the given series which all the works matched correctly with their non-fiction writers of the Revival Age?

(a) Concordance of Histories–George Cavendish, The Life and Death of Cardinal Wolsey–Thomas Wilson, The Arte of Rhetorike–Thomas Elyot, The Book of the Governor–Robert Fabyan.

(b) Concordance of Histories–Robert Fabyan, The Life and Death of Cardinal Wolsey–George Cavendish, The Arte of Rhetorike–Thomas Wilson, The Book of the Governor–Thomas Elyot

(c) Concordance of Histories–Thomas Elyot, The Life and Death of Cardinal Wolsey–Robert Fabyan, The Arte of Rhetorike–George Cavendish, The Book of the Governor–Thomas Wilson

(d) Concordance of Histories–Thomas Wilson, The Life and Death of Cardinal Wolsey–George Cavendish, The Arte of Rhetorike–Robert Fabyan, The Book of the Governor–Thomas Elyot.

100 In the given series, which one has all the non-fiction writers of the Elizabethan Age matched correctly with their works?

(a) John Foxe–Britannia, Raphael Holinshed–Learned Discourse of Justification, William Camden–Book of Martyrs, Richard Hooker–Chronicles of England.

(b) John Foxe–Learned Discourse of Justification, Raphael Holinshed–Book of Martyrs, William Camden–Chronicles of England, Richard Hooker–Britannia.

(c) John Foxe–Book of Martyrs, Raphel Holinshed–Chronicles of England, William Camden–Britannia, Richard Hooker–Learned Discourse of Justification.

(d) John Foxe–Chronicles of England, Raphael Holinshed–Britannia, William Camden–Learned Discourse of Justification, Richard Hooker–Book of Martyrs.

101 "O, worldly pomp, how despicable you are when one considers that you are empty and fleeting! You are justly compared to watery bubbles, one moment all swollen up, then suddenly reduced to nothing."

Which of the following writers in which of his/her works has used the above lines?

(a) Ordericus Vitalis, The Ecclesiastical History of England and Normandy, Volume 2

(b) Parris, Parting Shots

(c) John Wycliffe, Wycliffe's Bible

(d) John Mandeville, The Travels of Sir John Mandeville

102 "Indeed cocktail parties are death as I am sure 99 per cent of DS colleagues would agree. Whoever it was who suggested an international treaty banning National Day receptions should be canonised."

Which of the following writers in which of his/her works has used the above lines?

(a) Ordericus Vita lis, The Ecclesiastical History of England and Normandy, Volume 2

(b) Parris, Parting Shots .

(c) John Wycliffe, Wycliffe's Bible

(d) John Mandeville, The Travels of Sir John Mandeville

103 "Be ye renewed [or made new again] in the spirit of your soul; 24 and clothe ye the new man, which is made after God in rightwiseness and (in the) holiness of truth. [and clothe ye the new man, which after God is made of nought (or out of nothing) in rightwiseness and holiness of truth.]"

Which of the following writers in which of his/her works has used the above lines?

(a) Ordericus Vitalis, The Ecclesiastical History of England and Normandy, Volume 2

(b) Parris, Parting Shots

(c) John Wycliffe, Wycliffe's Bible

(d) John Mandeville, The Travels of Sir John Mandeville

104 "Of Paradise I cannot speak properly, for I have not been there; and that I regret."

Which of the following writers in which of his/her works has used the above lines?

(a) Sir John Mandeville, The Travels of Sir John Mandeville
(b) Hugh Latimer, Seventh Sermon before Edward VI (1549)
(c) Henry Cavendish, Biographie Universelle Ancienne et Moderne, Jean-Baptiste Biot as quoted by John Maxson Stillman, The Story of Early Chemistry (1924)
(d) Henry Cavendish, George Wilson, The Life of the Honble Henry Cavendish

105 "We know not whom God loves nor whom He hates."

Which of the following writers in which of his/her works has used the above lines?

(a) Ordericus Vita lis, The Ecclesiastical History of England and Normandy, Volume 2
(b) Parris, Parting Shots
(c) John Wycliffe, Wycliffe's Bible
(d) John Mandeville, The Travels of Sir John Mandeville

106 The drop of rain maketh a hole in the stone, not by violence, but by oft falling.

Which of the following writers in which of his/her works has used the above lines?

(a) Sir John Mandeville, The Travels of Sir John Mandeville
(b) Hugh Latimer, Seventh Sermon before Edward VI (1549)
(c) Henry Cavendish, Biographie Universelle Ancienne et Moderne, Jean-Baptiste Biot as quoted by John Maxson Stillman, The Story of Early Chemistry (1924)
(d) Henry Cavendish, George Wilson, The Life of the Honble Henry Cavendish

107 Be of good comfort, Master Ridley, play the man! We shall this day light such a candle, by God's grace, in England, as I trust shall never be put out.

Which of the following writers in which of his/her works has used the above lines?

(a) Hugh Latimer, The Martyrdom .
(b) William Tyndale, The Writings of A Puritan's Mind Volume 1
(c) John Foxe, Fox's Book of Martyrs Or A History of the Lives, Sufferings, and Triumphant Deaths of the Primitive Protestant Martyrs
(d) Thomas Watson, The Ten Commandments

108 He was the wealthiest of all scholars (savants) and probably also the most scholarly of all the wealthy.

Which of the following writers in which of his/her works has used the above lines?

(a) Sir John Mandeville, The Travels of Sir John Mandeville
(b) Hugh Latimer, Seventh Sermon before Edward VI (1549)
(c) Henry Cavendish, Biographie Universelle Ancienne et Moderne, Jean-Baptiste Biot as quoted by John Maxson Stillman, The Story of Early Chemistrv (1924)
(d) Henry Cavendish, George Wilson, The Life of the Honble Henry Cavendish

109 He could not sing for them a sweet song, or create a 'thing of beauty' which should be 'a joy for ever,' or touch their hearts, or fire their spirits, or deepen their reverence or their fervour. He was not a Poet, a Priest, or a Prophet, but only a cold, clear, Intelligence, raying down pure white light, which brightened everything on which it fell, but warmed nothing-a Star of at least the second, if not of the first magnitude, in the Intellectual Firmament.

Which of the following writers in which of his/her works has used the above lines?

(a) Sir John Mandeville, The Travels of Sir John Mandeville
(b) Hugh Latimer, Seventh Sermon before Edward VI (1549)
(c) Henry Cavendish, Biographie Universelle Ancienne et Moderne, Jean-Baptiste Biot as quoted by John Maxson Stillman, The Story of Early Chemistry (1924)
(d) Henry Cavendish, George Wilson, The Life of the Honble Henry Cavendish

110 "The best thing you can do is get very good at being you."

Which of the following writers in which of his/her works has used the above lines?

(a) Tom Wilson, The Zen of Ziggy .
(b) William Tyndale, The Practice Of Prelates
(c) Miles Coverdale, Author of the Psalms
(d) John Foxe, Foxe's Book of Martyrs

111 The office of a bishop was a room, at the beginning, that no man coveted; and that no man durst take upon him, save he only which loved Christ better than his own life. For as Christ saith, that no man might be his disciple, except that he were ready to forsake life and all; even so might that officer be sure that it would cost him his life at one time or another, for bearing record unto the truth."

Which of the following writers in which of his/her works has used the above lines?

(a) Tom Wilson, The Zen of Ziggy
(b) William Tyndale, The Practice Of Prelates
(c) Miles Coverdale, Author of the Psalms
(d) John Foxe, Foxe's Book of Martyrs

112 "The most clear evidence and assurance of the truth and goodness in these holy things of Christ and the new creature arises out of themselves, as light follows from the body of the Sun, without the contusion or compulsion of an harsh arguments. And by a holy sympathy a regenerate heart entertains with infinite delight these precious and holy truths. Arguments and syllogisms make a great noise in the world. I think they are like that appearance in Horeb to the prophet Elijah when the great and strong wind broke the mountains and broke in pieces all the rocks. But it is said, the Lord was not found in the wind, nor in the earthquake, nor in the fire, but He was in the still, small voice. Lux spiritus santi est lenis luxs, persundens sementibus, the Holy Spirit does gently hover over the soul and brood upon it. Heavenly doctrine falls down upon the spirits of men, not like a mighty violent rain, but like a shower of oil, like a sweet honey-dew."

Which of the following writers in which of his/her works has used the above lines?

(a) Hugh Latimer, The Martyrdom
(b) William Tyndale, The Writings of A Puritan's Mind Volume 1
(c) John Foxe, Fox's Book of Martyrs Or A History of the Lives, Sufferings, and Triumphant Deaths of the Primitive Protestant Martyrs
(d) Thomas Watson, The Ten Commandments

113 "It shall greatly help ye to understand the Scriptures if thou mark not only what is spoken or written, but of whom and to whom, with what words, at what time, where, to what intent, with what circumstances, considering what goeth before and what followeth after."

Which of the following writers in which of his/her works has used the above lines?

(a) Tom Wilson, The Zen of Ziggy
(b) William Tyndale, The Practice Of Prelates
(c) Miles Coverdale, Author of the Psalms
(d) John Foxe, Foxe's Book of Martyrs

114 "The archbishop endeavored to prevail on Mr. Wishart to recant; but he was too firmly fixed in his religious principles and too much enlightened with the truth of the Gospel, to be in the least moved."

Which of the following writers in which of his/her works has used the above lines?

(a) Tom Wilson, The Zen of Ziggy
(b) William Tyndale, The Practice Of Prelates
(c) Miles Coverdale, Author of the Psalms
(d) John Foxe, Foxe's Book of Martyrs

115 "Parsons pulled the straw near to him, and then said to the spectators, "This is God's armor, and now I am a Christian soldier prepared for battle: I look for no mercy but through the merits of Christ;"

Which of the following writers in which of his/her works has used the above lines?

(a) John Foxe, Foxe's Book of Martyrs .
(b) Thomas Watson, The Lord's Supper
(c) Richard Hooker, Of the Laws of Ecclesiastical Polity
(d) Miles Coverdale, Author of the Psalms

116 "Germanicus, a young man, but a true christian, being delivered to the wild beasts on account of his faith, behaved with such astonishing courage, that several pagans became converts to a faith which inspired such fortitude."

Which of the following writers in which of his/her works has used the above lines?

(a) Hugh Latimer, The Martyrdom
(b) William Tyndale, The Writings of A Puritan's Mind Volume 1
(c) John Foxe, Fox's Book of Martyrs Or A History of the Lives, Sufferings, and Triumphant Deaths of the Primitive Protestant Martyrs.
(d) Thomas Watson, The Ten Commandments

117 "Sire-1 have received an order, under your majesty's seal, to put to death all the protestants in my province. I have too much respect for your majesty, not to believe the letter a forgery; but if (which God forbid) the order should be genuine, I have too much respect for your majesty to obey lt."

(a) John Foxe, Fox's Book of Martyrs Or A History of the Lives, Sufferings, and Triumphant Deaths of the Primitive Protestant Martyrs.
(b) Thomas Watson, The Art of Divine Contentment
(c) Richard Hooker, Of the Laws of Ecclesiastical Polity
(d) Miles Coverdale, Author of the Psalms

118 "It is our work to cast care, and it is God's work to take care."

Which of the following writers in which of his/her works has used the above lines?

(a) John Foxe, Fox's Book of Martyrs Or A History of the Lives, Sufferings, and Triumphant Deaths of the Primitive Protestant Martyrs
(b) Thomas Watson, The Art of Divine Contentment .
(c) Richard Hooker, Of the Laws of Ecclesiastical Polity
(d) Miles Coverdale, Author of the Psalms

119 "Ministers can but speak to the ear, the Spirit speaks to the heart."

Which of the following writers in which of his/her works has used the above lines?

(a) Hugh Latimer, The Martyrdom
(b) William Tyndale, The Writings of A Puritan's Mind Volume 1
(c) John Foxe, Fox's Book of Martyrs Or A History of the Lives, Sufferings, and Triumphant Deaths of the Primitive Protestant Martyrs
(d) Thomas Watson, The Ten Commandments

120 Of Law there can be no less acknowledged, than that her seat is the Bosom of God, her voice the harmony of the world: all things in heaven and Earth do her homage, the very least as feeling her care, and the greatest as not exempted from her power.

Which of the following writers in which of his/her works has used the above lines?
(a) John Foxe, Foxe's Book of Martyrs
(b) Thomas Watson, The Lord's Supper
(c) Richard Hooker, Of the Laws of Ecclesiastical Polity
(d) Miles Coverdale, Author of the Psalms

Directions (Q. Nos. 121-125) *Read the given passage carefully and answer the questions that follow.*

Inaugural Address by John F. Kennedy, 20th January, 1961. This is part of the speech that John F. Kennedy gave when he became President of the United States. In your hands, my fellow citizens, more than in mine, will rest the final success or failure of our course. Since this country was founded, each generation of Americans has been summoned to give testimony to its national loyalty. The graves of young Americans who answered the call to service surround the globe.

Now the trumpet summons us again - not as a call to bear arms, though arms we need; not as a call to battle, though embattled we are- but a call to bear the burden of a long twilight struggle, year in and year out, "rejoicing in hope, patient in tribulation"-a struggle against the common enemies of man: tyranny, poverty, disease, and war itself.

Can we forge against these enemies a grand and global alliance, North and South, East and West, that can assure a more fruitful life for all mankind? Will you join in that historic effort?

In the long history of the world, only a few generations have been granted the role of defending freedom in its hour of maximum danger. I do not shank from this responsibility -I welcome it. I do not believe that any of us would exchange places with any other people or any other generation. The energy, the faith, the devotion which we bring to this endeavor will light our country and all who serve it -- and the glow from that fire can truly light the world.

And so, my fellow Americans: ask not what your country can do for you -- ask what you can do for your country. My fellow citizens of the world: ask not what America will do for you, but what together we can do for the freedom of man.

Finally, whether you are citizens of America or citizens of the world, ask of us the same high standards of strength and sacrifice which we ask of you. With a good conscience our only sure reward, with history the final judge of our deeds, let us go forth to lead the land we love, asking His blessing and His help, but knowing that here on Earth God's work must truly be our own.

121 Why does Kennedy start by saying "in your hands"?
(a) Because people need to listen to the speech
(b) To make it clear that people are responsible
(c) So they know what he means in the speech
(d) So they will join hands in the audience

122 Why does Kennedy say "Ask not what your country can do for you"?
(a) Because people need to work for progress
(b) Because he is going to set more taxes
(c) Because the President is the leader of the country
(d) Because he wants people to vote for him

123 What does 'history the final judge mean'?
(a) History books report what happens
(b) In later years people will think about what happens now
(c) When people write histories they tell what people did
(d) People should think about history when they do things

124 Why does he say 'Let us go forth'?
(a) He wants them to leave.
(b) He wants to win the election.
(c) He wants people to save money.
(d) He wants them to work for progress.

125 An inauguration speech is written to inspire people. What is one sentence Kennedy wrote that would inspire people?
(a) Will you join in that historic effort?
(b) The graves of young Americans who answered the call to service surround the globe.
(c) In your hands, my fellow citizens, more than in mine, will rest the final success or failure of our course.
(d) My fellow citizens of the world: ask not what America will do for you, but what together we can do for the freedom of man.

PREVIOUS YEARS' QUESTIONS

December 2018

1 **Adherents of the fourteenth century religious movement associated with vernacular preaching, translation of New Testament into English, and challenges to the authority of priests and bishops were called**

(a) Levellers
(b) Deists
(c) Lollards
(d) Agnostics

2 **The Norman Conquest was a significant landmark in English history. What French did the Normans speak and what was it known as?**

(a) They spoke a dialectical French (also called Anglo-Frisian), somewhat closer to the Parisian.
(b) They spoke Norman French (Anglo-Norman). Theirs was certainly not the standard French.
(c) They spoke standard French (of mainland France). Their French was very sweet and musical.
(d) They spoke normal French, rather distinct from Anglo-Norman, another standard language.

July 2018

3 **During the reign of Norman Kings, it was fashionable to speak .... in upper class circles in England.**

(a) Norse (b) Latin (c) Danish (d) French

4 **......... is the producer of the first complete printed English Bible.**

(a) Jerome (b) William Tyndale
(c) Miles Coverdale (d) Bede

July 2016

5 **Select the right chronological sequence of the date of Bible translations.**

(a) King James Version-Tyndale- Revised Standard Version-Holman Christian Standard Bible
(b) Revised Standard Version-King James Version–Tyndale-Holman Christian Standard Bible
(c) Tyndale-King James Version-Revised Standard Version-Holman Christian Standard Version
(d) Revised Standard Version-Holman Christian Standard Bible-King James Version-Tyndale

ANSWERS

Objective Questions

1. (c)	2. (c)	3. (a)	4. (b)	5. (d)	6. (b)	7. (a)	8. (a)	9. (a)	10. (b)
11. (a)	12. (a)	13. (d)	14. (d)	15. (b)	16. (b)	17. (d)	18. (c)	19. (a)	20. (c)
21. (a)	22. (b)	23. (b)	24. (a)	25. (c)	26. (b)	27. (d)	28. (a)	29. (c)	30. (b)
31. (a)	32. (b)	33. (d)	34. (a)	35. (b)	36. (c)	37. (b)	38. (c)	39. (d)	40. (c)
41. (d)	42. (d)	43. (c)	44. (a)	45. (c)	46. (c)	47. (c)	48. (d)	49. (b)	50. (a)
51. (c)	52. (c)	53. (a)	54. (c)	55. (c)	56. (c)	57. (d)	58. (c)	59. (d)	60. (c)
61. (a)	62. (b)	63. (c)	64. (c)	65. (d)	66. (a)	67. (b)	68. (c)	69. (d)	70. (c)
71. (c)	72. (d)	73. (a)	74. (b)	75. (c)	76. (b)	77. (c)	78. (a)	79. (a)	80. (b)
81. (a)	82. (b)	83. (c)	84. (d)	85. (a)	86. (d)	87. (d)	88. (a)	89. (b)	90. (d)
91. (a)	92. (b)	93. (c)	94. (d)	95. (b)	96. (a)	97. (b)	98. (a)	99. (b)	100. (c)
101. (a)	102. (b)	103. (c)	104. (a)	105. (d)	106. (b)	107. (a)	108. (c)	109. (d)	110. (a)
111. (b)	112. (b)	113. (c)	114. (d)	115. (a)	116. (c)	117. (a)	118. (b)	119. (d)	120. (c)
121. (b)	122. (a)	123. (b)	124. (d)	125. (c)					

Previous Years' Questions

1. (c)	2. (b)	3. (d)	4. (c)	5. (c)

Puritan to the Romantic Age Non-Fiction

The present chapter refers to the non-fiction works of authors from Puritan Age to Romantic Age. The literary trends of this age show heavy reflection of Biblical text during puritan period, diary writing in Restoration Age. During Neo-Classical Age, emphasis was on reason and logic but after this during Romantic Age writers were more concerned with emotional expression rather than appropriate style.

Non-Fiction in Puritan Age

Non-fictional literature of the Puritan age was mainly religious and full of political idealism. Puritans valued realistic writing with an emphasis on religious themes. The Bible played an important role in the daily lives of the Puritans. Families attended church regularly and read the Bible in their homes. Due to this influence, most Puritan writing is based on the styles of the Bible. Puritans compared their own lives to biblical narratives and events and compared themselves to biblical characters to illustrate points.

Among the leading prose writers of the Puritan period, were the translators who produced the classic King James Version of the Bible (1611), to name a few are Jeremy Taylor, Thomas Hobbes and Richard Baxter etc. Writers like Burton, Sir Thomas Browne sought to reconcile the mysteries of religion with the newer mysteries of science. Izaak Walton, author of *The Compleat Anger* (1653), produced a number of graceful biographies of prominent writers. Thomas Hobbes wrote the most influential political treatise of the age, *Leviathan* (1651).

Literary Trends in Non-Fiction Prose during Puritan Age

After the death of James I in 1625, the new monarch Charles I took religious persecution to a new level. He was asked by the Parliament to sign the petition of rights but he continued to show open disregard to Parliament and people.

He also suffered unsuccessful foreign expeditions to France etc. After the Civil War in 1642, there was a division into the Cavaliers or Royalists (Clergy, nobility etc, those in favour of the King) and Roundheads or Parliamentarians (middle class etc those who were in favour of the Parliament).

In this Chapter

- *Non-Fiction in Puritan Age*
- *Major Non-Fiction Writers of the Puritan Age*
- *Non-Fiction in Restoration Age*
- *Major Non-Fiction Writers of the Restoration Age*
- *Diary of the Restoration Age*
- *Non-Fiction Prose Writers of the Neo-Classical Age*
- *Major Philosophers of the Neo-Classical Age*
- *Late 18th Century Non-Fiction Writers of Neo-Classical Age*
- *Non-Fiction in Romantic Age*
- *Major Writers of the Romantic Age*

The Civil War helped the Puritans to set up the Commonwealth. Oliver Cromwell was able to galvanise a military dictatorship during Protectorate up until 1660 when Monarchy was restored. Non-fiction prose of the Puritan Age was also characterised by a spirit of somberness and pensiveness. Some of the important non-fiction prose works of this age are Walton's *The Complete Angler* and Sir Thomas Browne's *Religio Medici*.

Characteristics of Non-Fiction Prose in Puritan Age

Genres

First person narratives were commonplace in the writing of Puritan age especially in the forms of journals and diaries. There were personal accounts of early American colonists depicting tales of travelling to the new lands, immigration, and everyday struggle.

These acted as the bequest to be handed down the generations to come in the future. As many American settlers had left their families back in England, the letter also became a popular form of writing. The main genres of writing included religious sermons, historical narrative, personal journals and poetry.

Themes

The common themes include religious and political idealism. There is also an insistence on practicalism and pragmatism of day to day life. The religious discourse emphasises the concept of predestination and inevitability of sin and a strong sense of guilt and shame. There is heavy usage of symbolism, especially, from the religious scripture.

The age is known for the heavy influence of Biblical text, for example, Old Testament and books like the book of Jeremiah. The genre, known as 'Jeremiads', was split into three portions. The first extolled the faith of the past generations, the second denigrated the sins of the present age and the third make appeals for repentance and contrition. There was an influence of natural phenomena like earthquakes, fires, floods etc as the people of the age were interested in learning about nature and the signs for God's design in nature.

Other thematic works included the idea of reformation or regeneration. Unity and free choice and order were also topical manifestations. The concept of struggle between the world and spirituality was also explored. As most families visited the Church and attended religious sermons, the writing itself reflects the Biblical style of construction. There was also demonisation of the native Indians who were described as followers of Satanism.

Writing Style

The writing style of the Puritan Age was predominantly plain with simple sentences and language. Metaphorical constructions were in limited use and excessive ornamentation or dramatic appeals were discouraged. Symbolism from scriptures was used to make the sermons etc impactful. The main motive was, to tell the truth of Godly existence in a commonly understandable form. Therefore, the use of Greek mythology or forms of classical literature was avoided.

Use of fictional elements was limited to the extent of blasphemy. Puritans believed that literature should not be used for entertainment. It must be used in the service of religious discourse only Puritan writers like Anne Bradstreet and John Winthrop wrote extensively about spirituality. They shared their own spiritual journeys. The aim was to popularise the Puritan beliefs and impose their vision of new social order. They wanted to motivate by creating allusion to that ideal society.

Major Non-Fiction Writers of the Puritan Age

Sir Thomas Browne (1605-1682)

British physician and author Sir Thomas Browne was born in London in 1605. He studied medicine at Broadgates Hall, Oxford. Later, he attended the Universities of Montpellier and Padua and in 1633, received an MD at Leiden.

Literary Career and Works

His most well-known work was the treatise *Religio Medici* which reflected on the nature of God and man. The book not only sets out his spiritual testament, but also gives us his psychological portrait. Describing the work, Coll Monro says, "Variously described as a prose-poem, confession of faith and 'sort of private diary of the soul', the *Religio Medici* (The Religion of a Physician) is hard to categorise."

Although, an exploration of religious thought, it cannot be described as theological nor although, written by a physician, neither it is medical or scientific. Indeed, as Browne explores the central themes of faith and charity, he acknowledges the need to keep religion separate from science for 'many things. The result is an intimate and private expression of his spiritual beliefs ultimately, the nothingness of the world when seen in the perspective of eternity is emphasised. Arguing for a wide and liberal interpretation of Christianity, Browne's tolerant religious philosophy provided the chief interest for contemporary readers. Browne's other works include a book on superstition- *Pseudodoxia Epidemica or Vulgar Errors* and *Hydriotaphia or Urn-Burial*, which is centered on the discovery of a Roman urn burial in Norfolk.

Maojr Works

- Religio Medici (1643)
- Pseudodoxia Epidemica (1646–72)
- Hydriotaphia, Urn Burial (1658)
- The Garden of Cyrus (1658)
- A Letter to a Friend (1656; published post 1690)

Jeremy Taylor (1613-1667)

English bishop and theologian Jeremy Taylor was born at Cambridge in 1613. He was educated at the Perse School, Cambridge before going on to Gonville and Caius College, at Cambridge. Universily After completing his studies at Cambridge and taking holy orders in 1633, Taylor was nominated by Archbishop Laud in 1635 to a fellowship at All Souls College, Oxford.

Literary Career and Works

After the Restoration, in 1661, he became Bishop of Down and Connor in Ireland. Taylor wrote several works on theological and devotional subjects such as *The Rule and Exercises of Holy Living* (1650) and *The Rules and Exercises of Holy Dying* (1651), Taylor died in 1667.

Major Works

- A Discourse of the Liberty of Prophesying (1646), a famous plea for toleration apology for authorised and set forms of Liturgy against the Pretence of the Spirit (1649)
- Great Exemplar ... a History of ... Jesus Christ (1649)
- Twenty-seven Sermons (1651)
- Twenty-five Sermons (1653)
- The Rules and Exercises of Holy Living (1650)
- The Rules and Exercises of Holy Dying (1651)
- A controversial treatise on The Real Presence ... (1654)
- Golden Grove; or a Manual of Daily Prayers and Letanies .... (1655)
- Unum Necessarium (1655), on the Doctrine of Repentance.
- Discourse of the Nature, Offices and Measures of Friendship (1657)
- Ductor Dubitantium, or the Rule of Conscience (1660)

Thomas Hobbes (1588-1679)

English philosopher and writer Thomas Hobbes was born at Westport, adjoining Malmesbury in Wiltshire, on 5th April, 1588. He was born prematurely, when his mother heard of the invasion of The Spanish Armada. As a result, Hobbes later considered that he was born under fear. His father was the Vicar of Charlton and Westport. Hobbes studied at Magdalen College, Oxford.

Literary Career and Works

Hobbes served as tutor to a cousin of his, also called William. It was during this period that Hobbes' philosophy began to take form, and his *Short Tract on First Principles* appeared. This was followed by his other works *Elements of Law* and *De Cive*.

Hobbes was also the mathematics tutor of the Prince of Wales between 1646 and 1648. Left in the company of the exiled royalists, Hobbes' attention turned to political matters and he intended to produce a book to set forth his theory of Civil Government in relation to the political crisis resulting from the civil war of 1642. This resulted in writing of Hobbes' most influential book, *The Leviathan*. It argued that civil peace and social unity are best achieved by the establishment of a commonwealth through social contract. In his late years, Hobbes produced an autobiography in Latin verse, and a complete translation of both *Iliad* and *Odyssey*. He died of a paralytic stroke on 4th December, 1679.

Leviathan

- Thomas Hobbes' *Leviathan* was written during a turbulent time of English history before England had plunged into the Civil War. It was written at a time when Hobbes was living in exile in Paris and feared being put on trial because of his royalist sympathies. He undertook the writing of *Leviathan* to defend the monarchist idea.
  Hobbes' Leviathan is divided into four parts
  (i) of Man,
  (ii) of Commonwealth,
  (iii) of a Christian commonwealth and
  (iv) of the Kingdom of Darkness.
- Hobbes's ideal commonwealth is ruled by a sovereign power responsible for protecting the security of the commonwealth and granted absolute authority to ensure the common defence.
- The commonwealth is depicted as a Leviathan or a sea monster.
- His ideas of the commonwealth are based upon his views of human nature and the state of mankind without government. He believes that men in their natural state without a government are inherently chaotic and constantly at war with each other.

Major Works

- Three of the discourses in the Horae Subsecivae (1620)
- Translation of Thucydides's History of the Peloponnesian War (1629)
- The Elements of Law, Natural and Politic (1640)
- Treatise on Human Nature (1650)
- De Cive (Latin) (1642)
- Philosophical Rudiments concerning Government and Society (English translation of De Cive) (1651)
- Leviathan, or the Matter, Forme and Power of a Commonwealth, Ecclesiasticall and Civil (1651)
- Human Nature or the Fundamental Elements of Policie (1651)
- De Corpore Politico (1651)
- De Corpore (Latin) (1655)
- De Corpore (English translation) (1656)
- De Homine (Latin) (1658)
- Letters upon Liberty and Necessity (1654)
- The Questions concerning Liberty, Necessity and Chance (1656)
- Latin translation of the Leviathan (1668)
- English Translation of Homer's Iliad and Odyssey (1675)

Robert Burton (1577-1640)

English scholar and writer Robert Burton was born in Leicestershire, England in 1577. He entered Brasenose College, Oxford, in 1593, but was transferred to Christ Church. He was also elected as a fellow at Christ Church. Most of Burton's life was spent as a vicar at Oxford.

Literary Career and Works

Burton's Latin comedy *Philosophaster* which exposed charlatanism was performed successfully at Christ Church in 1618. However, he is best known for his monumental work, *The Anatomy of Melancholy*. It was first published in 1621 and contained a pseudoscientific investigation and philosophical discussion of the possibilities of human happiness. Burton described four different temperaments arising from four humours in the human body.

The melancholic would have a preponderance of black bile, the choleric, of yellow bile, the phlegmatic, of phlegm, the sanguine, of blood. With each of these humours was associated a corresponding element, alongwith its qualities as Earth: cold and dry; Fire: hot and dry; Water: cold and humid; Blood: warm and humid: Burton's medical treatise catalogued the many variants, manifestations and causes of the mental 'disease' Melancholy. It is rumoured that Burton hanged himself in his chambers at Christ Church in 1640.

Izaak Walton (1593-1683)

Known as the first professional English biographer, Izaak Walton was born in Stafford, England in 1593. His father, who was an innkeeper, died before his birth. Walton's mother married for a second time.

Walton settled in London where he was apprenticed to an ironmonger. In 1614, he had a shop in Fleet Street, two doors west of Chancery Lane in the parish of St Dunstan's. Around this time, he became acquainted with the Vicar, John Donne. When Donne died, Walton composed *An Elegie* dedicated to him.

Literary Career and Works

After the Royalist defeat at Marston Moor, Walton quit London for the relative security of his native place Staffordshire. He spent his remaining years reading and writing. His most famous work, *The Compleat Angler* was published in 1653. It was a practical guide to the art of angling or fishing. The story consists of three sportsmen: a fisherman (Piscator, who is Walton himself), a huntsman (Venator) and a fowler (Auceps). All of them travel along the river Lea on the first day in May and discuss the relative merits of their favorite pastimes.

Walton was also a noted biographer who wrote *The Life and Death of Dr Donne* (1640), *The Life of Mr Richard Hooker (1665-66), The Life of Mr George Herbert (1670) and The Life of Sir Henry Wotton (1651)*. Walton died in Winchester in 1683.

Thomas Fuller (1608-1661)

English scholar and preacher Thomas Fuller was born at Aldwincle, Northamptonshire in 1608. Fuller's father was the rector of Aldwinkle parish; his mother was Judith Davenant, a sister of John Davenant, who became the bishop of Salisbury. He received his education at Queens' College, Cambridge.

Literary Career and Works

In 1630, Fuller became an Anglican priest. A year later, he published a poem on the subject of David and Bathsheba, titled *David's Heinous Sinne, Heartie Repentance, Heavie Punishment*. He also adhered to the royalist cause during the civil war and the Commonwealth and served briefly as a royal chaplain. In 1646, he wrote *Andronicus, or the Unfortunate Politician*, a satire against Oliver Cromwell. His historical writings include *The Church-History of Britain*, *The History of the University of Cambridge* and *The History of Waltham-Abbey in Essex*. Fuller is best known for his posthumous work, *Worthies of England*, which is considered to be the first attempt at a dictionary of national biography. Fuller died in London in 1661.

Major Works

- Andronicus, or the Unfortunate Politician (1646)
- The Church-History of Britain (1655)
- The History of the University of Cambridge (1655)
- The History of Waltham-Abbey in Essex (1655)
- History of the worthies of England (1662)

Richard Baxter (1615-1691)

English pastor and writer Richard Baxter was born in Rowton, near Shrewsbury, in Shropshire in the year 1615. He was the son of Beatrice Adeney and Richard Baxter, since both his parents did not attach much importance to education, Baxter largely remained self-taught. He studied at a free school, then at royal court, where he became disgusted at what he saw as frivolity and finally left to study divinity.

Literary Career and Works

Baxter became curate at Kidderminster in 1641. He wrote a series of works such as *The Reformed Pastor* (1656) and *A Call for the Unconverted* (1657), which advocated true Catholicism. His autobiography, published after his death is called *Reliquiae Baxterianae* or *Mr Richard Baxter's Narrative of the Most Memorable Passages of His Life and Times*. Baxter died on 8th December, 1691.

Major Works

- The Saints' Everlasting Rest (1650)
- Gildas Salvianus, the Reformed Pastor (1656)
- A Call to the Unconverted (1657)
- Methodus theologiae (1665)
- Reason for the Christian Religion (1667)
- The Christian Directory (1673)
- Catholick Theology (1675)
- A Treatise of Episcopacy (1681)
- Paraphrase of the New Testament (1685)
- Reliquae Baxterianae (1696)

Non-Fiction in Restoration Age

The Restoration age introduced a new genre of non-fiction in the form of diary besides Journals. It also promoted non-fiction, full of intellectualism and rationalism. The work of Francis Bacon helped shape philosophical and scientific method. Robert Burton's *Anatomy of Melancholy* (1621) offers a varied, virtually encyclopedic view of the moral and intellectual preoccupations of the 17th century.

Literary Trends in Non-Fiction Prose during Restoration Age

The Restoration Age was an important era in the development of English prose. It was the period when English prose moved from antiquity to modernity. The prose before the Restoration Age is characterised by word-excess, complexity etc. But prose in and after the Restoration Age, has the modern qualities of clarity, precision and simplicity. With the development of Restoration Age, English prose moves speedily towards being strictly functional. It cuts down all unnecessary ornamentation.

Characteristics of Non-Fiction Prose of the Restoration Age

Transition

With the social change, linguistic change in the Restoration Age also went hand in hand. With the stability in the society, came the stability in language. The period saw a transition from the turbulence of antiquity to stability and balance of the new times. The transition was the sum-total of many complex forces.

Critical Interest

Critical interest in Restoration prose was shown for the first time in the history of English literature. Although, critical interest in the poetry was popular from a much earlier period, interest in prose is visible only in this period. Before this, the rules of English Grammar and syntax were dynamic. In Restoration Age, the need for stabilising the English language was voiced by many eminent writers like Dryden. They expressed the desire to clarity and fix language once and for all.

We find, for the first time in history, writers discussing what is good and what is not. Their new interest starts with Hobbes and the Royal Society. English prose written in Restoration Age favours clarity, simplicity and utility against ornamentation, affection, turgidity etc. One of the best examples is Sprat's History of the Royal Society.

De-Latinisation

The transition from antiquity to modernity in English prose in Restoration Age was a movement towards 'de-Latinisation'. English prose before the Restoration Age was highly Latinised, both in diction (choice of words) and syntax (structure of the sentence). This Latinisation has resulted in complexity of style. The de-Latinisation of English prose around after the Restoration Age meant the simplification and modernisation of English prose. It also implied the bringing written language nearer to the spoken language. In general, we can say that English prose took a great leap forward from antiquity to modernity.

Factors Responsible for the Change

The Royal Society

The most important of the factors for the development of Restoration prose was the establishment of Royal Society in 1662 A D or the promotion of experimental science. It was Charles-II, who granted the establishing of the Society. Courtiers were allowed to have private laboratories of their own. Establishment of Royal Society gave rise to important factors that changed English prose from antiquity to modernity.

The language used by scientists to describe their experiments needed to be clear, unimpassioned and almost mathematical. The plain language, used and recommended by the members of the Royal Society, had much influence upon contemporary men of letters. As a consequence, simplicity in language was adopted by most of the eminent writers of the age.

Sermons

The divines of the age also did as good work as the scientists for the simplicity of the prose. The age is known for the great sermons written during it. Divines drifted themselves from the old style and expressed their sermons ineffective and simple English capable of being understood and appreciated by the common people. They didn't treat their hearers as empty buckets to be pumped into nor did they have a taste for the ornamentation and affection. Tillotson played a major role in affecting the change in English prose. Dryden, one of the greatest masters of English prose, expressed that he had learnt the style chiefly from Tillotson.

Modernisation by Popularisation of Literature

Last but not least, was the modernising influence exerted on English prose by popularisation of the Literature towards the end of 17th century. The expansion of the circle of readers as much responsible for the simplification and stabilisation of English prose. The language employed by the writers, with an eye on common people was naturally simple and clear enough.

Major Non-Fiction Writers of the Restoration Age

John Locke (1632-1704)

English philosopher, theorist and physician John Locke was born in Wrington, Somerset, England in 1632. He had a Puritan upbringing, since both his parents were Puritans. He studied at Westminster School and Christ Church, Oxford. At Oxford, Locke studied medicine. He read and studied with the eminent physicians Robert Boyle and Thomas Sydenham. Sydenham, the major physician of his age, helped bring Locke to prominence and secured him his election to fellow of the Royal Society in 1668. He graduated with a bachelor's of medicine in 1674. After completing his degree in medicine at Oxford, Locke served the Earl of Shaftesbury as a physician and followed him to France in 1675.

Literary Career and Works

It was his ruminations there that formed the basis of one of his most important works, *Essay on Human Understanding*. It was during his period in exile that Locke completed, (but did not yet publish) his *Letter Concerning Toleration*. Locke's *Two Treatises of Civil Government* were published after the Glorious Revolution of 1688, brought William of Orange and Mary to the throne. Three years later, he published his *Thoughts on Education*.

Locke invested a great deal of energy in theology in his later years, and among his works published posthumously are commentaries on the Pauline epistles, a *Discourse on Miracles*, a fragment of the *Fourth Letter for Toleration*, and *An Examination of Father Malebranche's Opinion of Seeing all things in God, Remarks on Some of Mr Norris's Books*.

After his death another chapter of *An Essay Concerning Human Understanding* (was published under the title) *The Conduct of the Understanding*. He died at Oates in Essex on 28th October, 1704. He was buried near Oates by the parish church of High Laver.

An Essay Concerning Human Understanding

- John Locke's *An Essay Concerning Human Understanding* was first published in 1690. It presents a detailed, systematic philosophy of mind and thought. It is structurally divided into four books.
- In his epistle to the reader, which forms a kind of preface to the book, Locke tells us how he became interested in such a subject. It all began in a series of discussions that took place in the company of a small group of friends who had been meeting at regular intervals to exchange with one another, their views on important questions of the day.

- **In Book I**, Locke lays out the three goals of his philosophical project: to discover where our ideas come from, to find out what it means to have these ideas and what an idea essentially is and to examine issues of faith and opinion to determine how we should proceed logically, when our knowledge is limited. He refutes the rationalist notion of innate ideas.
- **In Book II**, Locke describes in detail the process by means of which ideas come to be present in human minds. His fundamental thesis is that experience alone is adequate to account for all the ideas included in anyone's store of knowledge.
- **In Book III**, Locke talks about abstract general ideas. He says that everything that exists in the world is a particular 'thing.' He believes that knowledge does not require a distinct name for every particular; Thing knowledge is enlarged by general views to which things are reduced into sorts.
- **In Book IV**, Locke addresses the nature of knowledge itself, asking what knowledge is and in what areas we can hope to attain it. He defines knowledge as "The perception of the connection of an agreement or disagreement and repugnancy, of any of our ideas."
- Raffaella De Rosa calls Locke's essay as a 'philosophical landmark' and states that the work occupies a prominent position not only among the texts of early modern philosophy but of philosophy of all times.

Major Works

- A Letter Concerning Toleration (1689)
- A Second Letter Concerning Toleration (1690)
- A Third Letter for Toleration (1692)
- Two Treatises of Government (1689)
- An Essay Concerning Human Understanding (1690)
- Some Considerations on the consequences of the Lowering of Interest and the Raising of the Value of Money (1691)
- Some Thoughts Concerning Education (1693)
- The Reasonableness of Christianity, as Delivered in the Scriptures (1695)
- A Vindication of the Reasonableness of Christianity (1695)

John Dryden (1631-1700)

An Essay of Dramatic Poesy

Dryden's *An Essay of Dramatic Poesy* was probably written in 1666 during the closure of London theatres due to plague. It was published in 1688, the essay can be seen as a defence of drama as an art form. The essay is structured as a dialogue/debate between four speakers- Eugenius, Crites, Lisideius and Neander. These stand for William Davenant, Robert Howard, Roger Boyle and Dryden respectively. The essay begins with a reference to a naval battle between the British and Dutch on 3rd June, 1665, in the English Channel.

Four speakers named above observe this battle from a barge floating on Thames. After the battle gets over and the English navy wins, the four speakers begin discussing English drama.

Eugenius literally means 'a well-born genius'. He favours the moderns over the ancients, arguing that the moderns have excelled over the ancients because of having learned and profited from their example.

The name Crites comes from the Greek word 'critic' or one who is able to express a reasoned judgment on something. He argues in favour of the ancients and applauds the observance of the three unities in drama. He considers Ben Jonson as the greatest English playwright because he followed the ancients' example by adhering to the unities.

Lisideius' name is probably based on the royal emblem of France, the fleur-delis. He argues in favour of the modern day French playwrights. He believes that French drama is superior to English drama because of their adherence to the classical unities, because of their focus on one plot and one character, because of their use of narration.

The name Neander literally means 'the new man'. He favours the moderns, but does not disparage the ancients. He states that English are best at 'The lively imitation of nature' (human nature), conceding that while French poesy is beautiful, it is also lifeless like a 'statue'. He critiques 'the barrenness of the French plots' and praises the 'variety and copiousness of the English plays'. Neander also goes on to defend the genre of tragicomedy since it increases the effectiveness of both tragic and comic elements by way of contrast.

He indicates his preference for Shakespeare over Ben Jonson. Shakespeare 'had the largest and most comprehensive soul,' while Jonson was 'The most learned and judicious writer which any theater ever had.' Before Dryden, the English had no native criticism on drama.

Dryden's essay thus breaks new ground and makes serious efforts to develop a theory of drama by discussing ancient, contemporary French and English drama and by comparing the works of various individual English dramatists and the foreign dramatists.

Diary of the Restoration Age

The diary is essentially an autobiographical work, yet different from an autobiography. The diary tries to keep pace with the individuals' Life. In the diary, there is less room for retrospection; the problems and worries of daily life which concern the diarist are past history for the autobiographer. The diary writers have played an important role not only in literary development but also in the recording of historical events. For the recreation of a past age, the diarists are perhaps our richest source of detail. They provide detailed accounts not only of major historical events but also of personalities. They provide information about their social background, manners and morals, contemporary tastes and fashion in recreation, food and dress.

Diaries written in the Restoration age provide us an insight into the day to day life of that period. These diaries were not written with an intention of being read by others. The writers did not wish to make any claim to having produced literature. These are frank and sincere accounts of what actually happened. Diary and memoir writers supplied one of the most remarkable divisions of prose of the seventeenth century. The development of newspapers and the periodicals is also an interesting literary sideline of this era. The civil war undoubtedly stimulated a public appetite for up to the minute news which was supplemented by a new way of living and thinking. The most well known of the diary writers are John Evelyn, Samuel Pepys, and Roger North.

John Evelyn (1620-1706)

Restoration diarist John Evelyn was born in Wotton, Surrey, in 1620. He was the son of a wealthy landowner. Evelyn was educated at Middle Temple, London and Balliol College, Oxford. He joined the Royalist army for a short period, but later went abroad to avoid further involvement in the English Civil War and thereby protecting his brother's estate at Wotton. He returned in 1652 and married Mary, the sole daughter and heir of Sir Rich Browne Knight.

Literary Career and Works

In 1661, he published a book on pollution, *The Inconvenience of the Air and Smoke of London Dissipated*. This was followed by *A Disclosure of Forest Trees* (1664). Evelyn's famous *Diary* was begun, when he was 11 years old and was first published in 1818 under the title *Memoirs Illustrative of the Life and Writings of John Evelyn*. It covered the years between 1641 and 1697. It consisted of descriptions of places and events and is an important historical record of the times. In 1694, Evelyn left residence at Sayes Court to live at Wotton with his brother, whose heir he had become, and whom he actually succeeded in 1699. He spent the rest of his life there. He died on 27th February 1706.

Major Work

- Of Liberty and Servitude (1649), a translation from the French of François de la Mothe le Vayer
- The States of France, as it stood in the IXth year of ... Louis XIII. (1652)
- An Essay on the First Book of T Lucretius Carus de Rerum Natura. (1656)
- The Golden Book of St John Chrysostom, concerning the Education of Children. (1658)
- The French Gardener: instructing how to cultivate all sorts of Fruit-trees (1658)
- A Character of England (1659)
- The Late News from Bruels unmasked and his Majesty Vindicated (1660), in answer to a libellous pamphlet on Charles I by Marchmont Needham;
- Fumifugium, or the inconvenience of the Aer and Smoak of London dissipated (1661)
- Instructions concerning erecting of a Library (1661)
- Tyrannus or the Mode, in a Discourse of Sumptuary Laws (1661)
- Sculpture: or the History and Art of Chalcography and Engraving in Copper (1662)
- Sylva, or a Discourse of Forest Trees ... to which is annexed Pomona (1664)
- A Parallel of the Ancient Architecture with the Modern (1664)
- The History of the three late famous Imposters, *viz.*, Padre Ottomano, Mahomed Bei and Sabatei Sevi (1669)
- Navigation and Commerce, in which his Majesties title to the Dominion of the Sea is asserted against the Novel and later Pretenders (1674)
- A Philosophical Discourse of Earth ... (1676)
- Memoirs Illustrative of the Life and Writings of John Evelyn (1818)

Samuel Pepys (1633-1703)

Diarist Samuel Pepys was born on 23rd February, 1633 in Salisbury Court, London. He was the son of John Pepys, a tailor and Margaret Kite, sister of a Whitechapel butcher. Pepys studied at Huntingdon Free School and St Paul's School. He later attained his education at Trinity College, Cambridge, in 1650, but shortly transferred to Magdalene College, Cambridge. He completed his bachelor's degree in 1654 and entered the service of Edward Montague as his secretary and agent in London. By 1655, Pepys married the 15 years old daughter of a Huguenot exile, Elizabeth St Michel. He became a clerk of the Exchequer, and in 1660, was made Clerk of the King's Ships to the Navy Board.

Literary Career and Works

Pepys began his popular *Diary* in 1660. From 1660 to 1669, Pepys kept an extraordinary diary, with running commentary on his daily rounds, his meals, his health, even his relations with his wife. Pepys never intended the diaries for publication, and he wrote them in unusual shorthand which kept them from being read for many years. When the diaries were published in 1825, they were hailed as an intimate glimpse at life in the Restoration era England. He stopped writing the diary in 1669, when his eyesight started to fail and he feared losing his eyesight completely.

Comparing the diaries of Evelyn and Pepys, AW Ward and AR Waller state that, "Although the two diaries are closely united in popular esteem, they differ greatly in the length of the periods which they cover as well as in the character of their contents. Evelyn's work practically deals with the whole of his life, having been begun at a comparatively early age and continued until a short time before his death, while Pepys's (although of considerably greater length) only occupies a little over nine years of his busy career."

He served as President of the Royal Society from 1684-86, and retired from public service in 1689 at the accession of King William III. Pepys died on 26th May, 1703 in Clapham.

Pepys' Diary

- Covering the years from 1660 to 1669, Pepys in his diary offers a firsthand perspective on the major events during the Restoration, including his own role in helping to bring Charles II back from exile to become king, and his aid in both the Great Plague of 1665 and the Great Fire of 1666.
- He wrote *The Diary of Samuel Pepys* in a cryptic code so that others could not read it. His diary wasn't rediscovered until 1819, more than one hundred fifty years later, at which point the Master of the College had a student decipher Pepys's codes.
- The first edition was edited by Lord Braybrooke and released in an abridged form in 1825 in two volumes. For historians, Pepys' *Diary* is an unparalleled insight into the lives, trends and thoughts of 17th century London.
- According to Arthur Bryant, Pepys's *Diary* "is far more than an ordinary record of its writer's thoughts and actions; it is a supreme work of art, revealing on every page the capacity for selecting the small, as well as the large, essential that conveys the sense of life; and it is probably, after the *Bible* and James Boswell's *Life of Samuel Johnson*, the best bedside book in the English language. One can open it on any page and lose oneself in the life of Charles II's London and of this vigorous, curious, hardworking, pleasure-loving man."

Roger North (1653-1734)

He was the sixth son of Dudley North, 4th Baron North and his wife Anne Montagu and was the brother of Francis North and Dudley North. He was born in Tostock, Suffolk. He attended Bury St Edmunds Grammar School and then ThetFord Grammar School from 1663, followed by Jesus College, Cambridge and the Middle Temple. He became King's Counsel and a Bencher of Middle Temple in 1682. North married Mary, the daughter of Sir Robert Gayer of Stoke Poges, Buckingha- mshire, with whom he had two sons and five daughters.

Literary Career and Works

In 1684, he became Solicitor-General to the Duke of York. After this his career suffered something of a check: Francis' unexpected early death in September 1685 was both a personal loss and a blow to Roger's career, since Francis was replaced as Lord Chancellor by the formidable Lord Jeffreys.

He collected books, and was constantly occupied in writing, but he is best known for his 'Lives of the Norths' published after his death, together with his own autobiography (edition in Bohn's Standard Library, 1890, by Augustus Jessopp), an authority for the period. His comments on musical performace practice, in particular, have proven helpful for musicologists researching the baroque style in England. In addition to his writing on performance practice he wrote on musical aesthetics, on pedagogy, and on tuning and temperament; one of his most important acheivements in this regard, was devising a practical and detailed system for mean-tone tuning in the age before equal temperament. Another well-known work is 'Examen, a defence of Charles II's record as a ruler'. He died at Rougham on 1st March, 1734.

Non-Fiction in Neo-Classical Age

The dawn of the Neo-Classical or Augustan age brought into limelight the periodical essays for the first time. Criminal biographies and travelogues also remained prominent under the genre of non-fiction during the said age. Although, Francis Bacon was the first to have introduced an essay in English Literature during the Renaissance period, its development in England remained rather slow during the 17th century. No doubt, prose made rapid progress during the time of Dryden, the essays remained where Bacon had left it until it was formally and forcefully launched by Joseph Addison and Richard Steele in the 18th century as Periodical Essay.

A periodical is a magazine, with a distinct literary flavour, published at regular intervals, weekly, monthly, quarterly etc. The periodical essay was chiefly the invention of Steele when he started *The Tatler* (1709 AD) thrice a week, the chief aim of which was to expose the false arts of life and to recommend a general simplicity in our dress, our discourse, and our behaviour. Later on, Steele and Addison joined hands and brought the publication of *The Spectator*. It was a daily paper.

Literary Trends in Non-Fiction Prose during Neo-classical Age

Neoclassical literature has been written in a period where social order was undergoing a tremendous change. In the so-called Enlightenment Period, people believed that natural passions aren't necessarily good; natural passions must be subordinated to social needs and be strictly controlled.

Authors believed that reason was the primary basis of authority. They believed that social needs are more important than the individual needs. It is quite contrary to its preceding age, in which emphasis was laid on individualism rather than the socialism.

Characteristics of Neo-Classical Period

Influence of Materialism

When Pope declares the limits of man, he also sets, by implications, the limits for artists

"Know then thyself, presume not God to scan

The proper study of mankind is man!"

But Pope echoes only dominant philosophical thoughts here. After the Renaissance, Platonism and Christian Humanism, we find in the Neo-classical age, the dominance of Materialism and Empirical Science. The ruling thought of the age is shaped by philosophers like Thomas Hobbes, John Locke, and Joseph Butler. The philosophical empiricism of the age propagated through the writings of Bacon, Hobbes and Locke were supported and strengthened by the advancement of empirical science.

Under the influence of empirical philosophy and experimental science, writers of the age narrowed both their vision of man and view of life. The affairs of men, their politics, their morals, and manners became the chief concern. Although the concern with politics was present in the time of Shakespeare also. His and his contemporaries' treatment was ideal and utopian. But the treatment of Neo-classical writers was practical rather than utopian.

Imitation of Classics

One of the most important features of the Neo-classical literature is the imitation of the classics of ancient Greek and Roman literature. Although the Renaissance writers had imitated the classics, whereas Renaissance writers merely derived inspirations from the classics rather than copying the models of the past, the Neo-classical writers strictly adhered to the authority of their models. Thus Neo-classical literature can be called as 'Traditional'.

The Neo-classical writers like Dryden, Pope, Swift, and Johnson were convinced that excellence and perfection in the literary art have been attained by the Roman writers of antiquity, thus they can only copy the models of perfection and excellence.

Concept of Nature

The concept of nature was also an important characteristic of the Neo-classical age. By nature, they never meant the forest nature, but for them, nature meant the general human nature. The general human nature was not what the ordinary men and women felt and thought, but the standard view of human nature as held by Homer and Horace.

Like their static view of the world, the Neo-classical writers thought of human nature also was something static and standard, which is the same in all men and remains the same at all the times. Thus their view of nature as well as of man, world, and genre was static and standard.

Concept of Man

The Neo-classical literature considers man as a limited being, having limited powers. A large number of satires and works of the period attack the man for his pride and advise him to remain content with his limited powers of knowledge. Thus, man in Neo-classical literature remains a being of limited means and powers.

Literary Forms

Among the Neo-classical forms of literature, the most famous were the essays, both in verse and prose. While drama declined and almost disappeared during the later part of the period, Novel made its beginnings. The literature of the age was mostly comic and satiric. An important failure of the age was to produce tragedy.

Age of Reason

Neo-classical Period is often called as the Age of Reason. Thinkers of this age considered reason to be the highest mental faculty and sufficient guide in all areas. Both religious beliefs and morality were grounded on reason. In literature also, the reason is predominant in the Neo-classical age. Emotions and imaginations are also present, but in a controlled way.

The Neo-classical Period in literature brought a sense of decorum and stability to writers. There were rules to be carefully followed. It was a time of careful moral appearance, though appearances were more valued than honesty. However, some England's most brilliant literature can be credited to this era.

The Neo-classical (Augustan) Age Witnessed a new trend in non-fiction Prose. Periodical essays took the centre stage during this period.

Periodical Essay

Periodical essay was a new literary form that emerged during the early part of the 18th century. It was a non-fictional prose form that was published in magazines, newspapers or journals at regular intervals. AR Humphrey had aptly observed that "If any literary form is the particular creation and the particular mirror of the Augustan Age in England, it is the periodical essay."

The term 'Periodical essay' appears to have been first used by George Colman the Elder and Bonnell Thornton in their magazine the *Connoisseur* (1754-56). The rise of the genre began with John Dunton' *Athenian Gazette* on 17th March, 1691.

The Tatler (1709-1711), *The Rambler* (1750-51) and *The Spectator* (1711-1712) were the most successful and influential single-essay periodicals of the 18th century.

Carol Meyers "The periodical essay differed from a newspaper in that the newspaper was concerned with matters of the moment, brought as soon as possible before the public and the essay could proceed on a more leisurely course. Both media used the same format and had essentially the same audience, the middle and upper middle classes. The periodical essays dealt with matters that were contemporary, but not immediate with manners and morals, with tendencies of the time rather than actual events."

"The aim of the literary periodicals of the 18th century was admittedly the analysis and criticism of the contemporary life for a reformatory purpose; men needed to have an instruction and an example in order to know how to act and that example was provided by the periodicals."

Muhammad Naeem gives reasons for the popularity of the periodical essay

- The periodical essay was particularly suited to the genius of the middle classes, who were the new patrons of literature. It gave them what they wanted, pleasure as well as instruction.
- "It was neither too 'literary' to be comprehended and appreciated by the common people nor too journalistic to meet the fate of ephemeral writings. It could be read, appreciated and discussed at the tea-table or in the coffee-house. Its lightness and brevity were its two major popularising features."
- "The periodical essayists, particularly Steele and Addison struck a delicate and rational balance between the strait-jacketed morality of the Puritans and the reckless Bohemianism of the Cavaliers."
- Periodical essays also appealed to women as they paid attention to the interests of the fair sex.
- Most of the periodical essayists used a 'simple and conversational style' so that they could be easily understood and appreciated by their semi-educated or unscholarly readers.

Important Periodicals of the Augustan Age

Name of Periodical	Year	Founder	Published	Aim of Periodical
The Tatler	(1709-1711)	Richard Steele	Published three times a week (Tuesday, Thursday and Saturday).	"to expose the false arts of life, to pull off the disguises of cunningness, vanity and affection and to recommend a general simplicity in our dress, our discourse and our behaviour."
The Spectator	(1711-1712)	Joseph Addison and Richard Steele	Daily publication	"to enliven morality with wit and to temper wit with morality...to bring philosophy out of the closets and libraries, schools and colleges, to dwell in clubs and assemblies, at tea-tables and coffeehouses"
The Rambler	(1750-1752)	Samuel Johnson	Tuesdays and Saturdays	'Join both profit and delight in one' -provide intellectual profit and literary delight to the readers.
The Idler	(1758-1760)	Samuel Johnson	Weekly	

Non-Fiction Prose Writers of the Neo-Classical Age

Joseph Addison (1672-1719)

English essayist, playwright and politician Joseph Addison was born in Milston, Wiltshire in 1672. He studied at Charterhouse, where he was a classmate of Richard Steele and at The Queen's College, Oxford. Two years later, Addison became a Fellow of Magdalen College.

Literary Career and Works

In 1693, Addison addressed a poem to John Dryden, the former Poet Laureate, and his first major work, *An Account of the Greatest English Poets*, a book about the lives of English poets, was published in 1694. This was followed by *An Address to King William* (1695) and a Latin poem entitled *Pax Gulielmi* (1697), on the peace of Ryswick.

Addison rose to fame with *The Campaign* (1704), an epic celebrating the victory of Marlborough at Blenheim. The poem was commissioned by Lord Halifax, and its great success resulted in Addison's appointment in 1705, as undersecretary of state.

Addison is more famous today as an essayist. In 1710, he began contributing essays to *The Tatler,* which Richard Steele had founded in 1709. In 1711, both of them brought out the first number of *The Spectator,* another periodical. In 1713, Addison's *Cato*, a play with political overtones was performed with much success on the stage. Besides these, he also wrote *a Dialogue on Medals* and left unfinished, a work on the evidences of Christianity. Addison died at Holland House on the 17th June, 1719.

Major Works

Pleasures of Imagination

Addison's essay *'Pleasures of the Imagination'* appeared in the periodical *Spectator* Number 416 on 2nd July, 1712. Addison distinguishes pleasures of the imagination into two classes: primary pleasures, which derive from images of objects currently present to sight; and secondary pleasures, which derive from images of objects currently absent from sight and so called up before the mind in some other way. He further divides primary pleasures into three classes: those proceeding from the sight of what is great (or sublime); those proceeding from the sight of what is novel; and those proceeding from the sight of what is beautiful.

An excerpt from the essay is given below for an understanding of Addison's ideas.

"Our sight is the most perfect and most delightful of all our senses. It fills the mind with the largest variety of ideas, converses with its objects at the greatest distance, and continues the longest in action without being tired or satiated with its proper enjoyments.

The sense of feeling can indeed give us a notion of extension, shape and all other ideas that enter at the eye, except colours; but at the same time it is very much straitened and confined in its operations, to the number, bulk and distance of its particular objects. Our sight seems designed to supply all these defects, and may be considered as a more delicate and diffusive kind of touch, that spreads itself over an infinite multitude of bodies, comprehends the largest figures and brings into our reach some of the most remote parts of the universe by the pleasures of the imagination, I mean only such pleasures arise originally from sight and that I divide these pleasures into two kinds, my design being first of all to discourse of those primary pleasures of the imagination which entirely proceed from such objects as are before our eyes; and in the next place to speak of those secondary pleasures of the imagination, which flow from the ideas of visible objects, when the objects are not actually before the eye, but are called up into our memories, or formed into agreeable visions of things that are either absent or fictitious.

A beautiful prospect delights the soul, as much as a demonstration; and a description in Homer has charmed more readers than a chapter in Aristotle. Besides, the pleasures of the imagination have this advantage above those of the understanding, that they are more obvious and more easy to be acquired.

It is but opening the eye and the scene enters. The colours paint themselves on the fancy, with very little attention of thought or application of mind in beholder. We are struck, we know not how, with the symmetry of anything we see, and immediately assent to the beauty of an object, without inquiring into the particular causes and occasions of it. I shall first consider those pleasures of the imagination which arise from the actual view and survey of outward objects; and these, I think, all proceed from the sight of what is great, uncommon, or beautiful."

Richard Steele (1672-1729)

Irish writer and politician Richard Steele was born in Dublin, Ireland in 1672. He studied at Christ Church, Oxford. Steele joined the army and rose to the rank of captain within two years. However, he left it in 1705 to turn his attention towards a career in writing.

Literary Career and Works

In 1701, Steele's *The Christian Hero*, a moralistic tract was published. His first play, the comedy *The Funeral or Grief a-la-mode*, was performed successfully at Drury Lane Theatre in 1701. This play was a satire on the new profession of undertaking. This was followed by *The Lying Lover or The Ladies's Friendship* in 1703. His third comedy, *The Tender Husband or The Accomplished Fools*, produced in 1705, achieved some success.

The 'Dear Prue' is a series of delightful letters which had been addressed to the second wife of Steele, Mary Scurlock, by him. Later he became governor of Drury Lane Theatre, where he produced *The Conscious Lovers* (1723), a popular play. Steele died at Carmarthen, Wales in 1729.

John Arbuthnot (1667-1735)

Satirist and physician Dr John Arbuthnot was born in Inverbervie, Scotland in 1667. After his father's death in 1691, Arbuthnot went to London, where he lived in the house of a learned linen-draper, William Pate and supported himself by teaching mathematics. He received his education at Marischal College, Aberdeen and later took a medical degree at the University of St Andrews, graduating in 1696.

Literary Career and Works

His first work was *Of the Laws of Chance* in 1692, translated from Christian Huygens' *De ratiociniis in ludo aleae*. This was the first work on probability published in English. His other early works were *Essay Towards a Natural History of the Earth and Essay on the Usefulness of Mathematical Learning*.

Arbuthnot's main claim to fame, however, rests on his satirical writings. He became a friend of Jonathan Swift and the two produced satirical political pamphlets. His political allegory, *The History of John Bull* was published as a series of five pamphlets. In 1712, his first pamphlet "Law is a Bottomless Pit, Exemplify'd in the case of the Lord Strutt, John Bull, Nicholas Frog and Lewis Baboon, who spent all they had in a law-suit. Printed from a Manuscript found in the Cabinet of the famous Sir Humphrey Polesworth" appeared. These pamphlets established John Bull as a personification of England.

Arbuthnot was also one of the leading members of the Scriblerus Club, which aimed to satirise bad poetry and pedantry. *The Memoirs of the Extraordinary Life, Works and Discoveries of Martinus Scriblerus* the, main work of this club, was chiefly the work of Arbuthnot.

He also wrote several medical tracts such as *An Argument for Divine Providence*, taken from the constant regularity observed in the births of both sexes (1710); Virgilius Restauratus, printed in the second edition of Pope's *Dunciad* (1729); *An Essay concerning the Effects of Air on Human Bodies* (1733); *An Essay concerning the Nature of Ailments* (1731); and a valuable *Table of Ancient Coins, Weights and Measures* (1727), which is an enlargement of an earlier treatise (1705). He died at his house in Cork Street, in London on 27th February, 1735.

Major Philosophers of the Neo-Classical Age

George Berkeley (1685-1753)

Anglo-Irish philosopher George Berkeley was born in Kilkenny County, Ireland in 1685. He was educated at the Kilkenny School and later entered Trinity College, Dublin. Berkeley completed his Masters degree in 1707 and became a Senior Fellow in 1717. He was ordained as an Anglican priest in 1710. He remained in his college until 1724 working as a tutor and lecturer.

Literary Career and Works

Berkeley's *An Essay towards a New Theory of Vision* appeared in 1709 and *A Treatise concerning the Principles of Human Knowledge* in 1710. The objective of the first was "to show the manner wherein we perceive by sight the distance, magnitude and situation of objects. Also to consider the difference there is between the ideas of sight and touch and whether there is any idea common to both senses" In the second work, Berkeley examined abstract ideas and stated that abstract ideas cannot be formed and are inconsistent. His central principle was that "ideas do not exist outside of a mind perceiving them". He married Anne Foster, daughter of the chief justice of Ireland in 1728 and moved to America. Berkeley devoted this period to study, preached occasionally, and wrote his *Alciphron*, or the *Minute Philosopher*. He died at the age of 67 on 14th January, 1753 in Oxford. Along with John Locke (1632-1704) and David Hume (1711-1776), George Berkeley is considered as one of the most famous Empiricists.

David Hartley (1705-1757)

English philosopher and founder of the Associationist school of psychologists, David Hartley was born in Halifax, Yorkshire in 1705. He was educated at Bradford grammar school and Jesus College, Cambridge. After receiving his BA and MA from Jesus College, Cambridge, Hartley practiced medicine in Bury St Edmunds (1730-35), London (1735-42) and Bath.

Literary Career and Works

Hartley's reputation as one of the founding fathers of the science of psychology rests on his two-volume work, *Observations on Man*, published in 1749. The first volume dealt with the frame of the human body and mind and their mutual connections and influences, the second one with the duty and expectations of mankind.

According to Robert Young in *Complete Dictionary of Scientific Biography, Hartley' Observations* "was the first published work in English to use the term 'psychology' in its modern sense. *Hartley'* principles provided the conceptual framework for the associationist tradition in modern psychology, including learning theory and psychoanalysis'.

He died on 28th August, 1757 at Bath.

David Hume (1711-1776)

Scottish philosopher, economist, and historian David Hume was born at Edinburgh in 1711. He was raised by his mother after his father's death. After an early education at home, Hume entered Edinburgh University where he begun the study of law.

Literary Career and Works

Hume stayed in France for 3 years and worked on his *Treatise of Human Nature.*

He returned to England in 1737 and got published his *Treatise* in 1739. The book's poor reception disappointed Hume. Critics found his views to be heretical and atheistic. Hume then attempted to clarify the *Treatise* with a pamphlet, again published anonymously, and laboriously entitled "An abstract of a late Philosophical Performance, entitled *A Treatise of Human Nature. Wherein the chief Argument and Design of that Book, which has met with such Opposition, and been represented in so terrifying a Light, is further illustrated and explain'd*".

The *Treatise* was followed by his *Essays*, *Moral* and *Political* in 1741 and 1742. Hume's *Philosophical Essays* concerning the human understanding was published in 1748. This was later named as *An Enquiry Concerning Human Understanding* and was a recasting of the first part of the *Treatise* by which he hoped to gain a larger audience.

In 1752, Hume was appointed to the post of librarian at the Advocates's Library. During this period, Hume got a chance to devote himself to his literary activities and proved to be most productive. His Four Dissertations: *The Natural History of Religion, Of the Passions, Of Tragedy, Of the Standard of Taste* was published during this period. Hume died of cancer in 1776.

Adam Smith (1723-1790)

Scottish economist Adam Smith considered as the leading exponent of economic thoughts, was born in a small village in Kirkcaldy, Scotland in 1723. Smith received his elementary schooling in Kirkcaldy and at the age of four, he was said to have been carried off by gypsies but later abandoned by them.

Smith entered the University of Glasgow on scholarship and later attended Balliol College at Oxford. In 1748, he began giving a series of public lectures at the University of Edinburgh.

Literary Career and Works

His first book, *The Theory of Moral Sentiments* was published in 1759. In this work, he argued that our moral ideas and actions are a product of our very nature as social creatures. Smith's most important work however, is *An Inquiry into the Nature and Causes of the Wealth* of Nations (usually shortened to *The Wealth of Nations)* published in 1776, the work analysed the major elements of political economy, from market pricing and the division of labour to monetary, tax, trade and other government policies that affect economic behaviour. Smith died in Edinburgh on 19th July, 1790.

Late 18th Century Non-Fiction Writers of the Neo-Classical Age

Edmund Burke (1729-1797)

English philosopher and statesman Edmund Burke was born in Dublin in 1729. He was the son of a prosperous attorney. After receiving his early education at a Quaker school, Burke entered the University of Dublin in 1744. In February 1748, he graduated in BA and in 1751, took his degree as Master of Arts. After this, he studied law at the Middle Temple in London.

Literary Career and Works

Burke's earliest writings include *A Philosophical Enquiry into the Origin of our Ideas of the Sublime and Beautiful* (1757) and *A Vindication of Natural Society* (1756).

Throughout his term in Parliament, Burke wrote and spoke on the major issues of the day, including constitutional limitations on the power of the crown, taxation and revolution in the American colonies, the problems of Ireland and India, and the French Revolution.

His most famous work, *Reflections on the Revolution in France* (1790) expressed his hostility towards the revolution. However, this opposition cost him the support of his Whig colleagues. Thereafter, he became a largely independent commentator on domestic politics and international affairs with works such as *An Appeal from the New to the Old Whigs* (1791), *Letters on a Regicide Peace* (1795) and *A Letter to a Noble Lord* (1796). Burke died on the 9th July, 1797, at the age of 68.

Major Works

A Philosophical Enquiry into the Origins of Our Idea of the Sublime and the Beautiful

- Edmund Burke's *A Philosophical Enquiry into the Origin of our Ideas of the Sublime and Beautiful* is a treatise on aesthetics, first published in 1757.
- Burke believes that in order to understand the origin of our ideas of the sublime and beautiful, one must examine the experience of pain and pleasure. Pain is not simply the removal of pleasure and pleasure is not simply the removal of pain. Pain may be caused by the removal of pleasure, but pain may also arise in itself. Similarly, pleasure may be caused by the removal of pain, but pleasure may arise in and of itself. Burke makes the opposition of pleasure and pain the source of the two aesthetic categories, deriving beauty from pleasure and sublimity from pain.
- He separates the two categories of the 'beautiful' and the 'sublime'. According to him, beauty is "that quality or those qualities in bodies by which they cause love or some passion similar to it", whereas "Whatever is fitted in any sort to excite the ideas of pain and danger, that is to say, whatever is in any sort terrible, or is conversant about terrible objects, or operates in a manner analogous to terror, is a source of the sublime".
- While beauty has a soothing effect on the body, the sublime, on the other hand, produces a tension within the body.

Reflections on the Revolution in France

- Burke's text, *Reflections on the Revolution in France* (1790), is one of the founding texts of classical conservatism.
- Burke wrote the work in response to a Sermon by the protestant dissenter Richard Price who welcomed the French Revolution.
- Burke reacted against the extremes of the French Revolution, the violence and mayhem which surrounded it.
- He argued that in their espousal of liberty, the French revolutionaries have failed to understand that liberty was only one amongst a range of benefits, all of which were required in mutual connection for a life under civil government that was civilised in the proper sense.
- He believed that ordered liberty resulted in the greatest equality and opportunity.
- Some degree of societal control is necessary since every man acts according to his own selfish interests.
- He claimed that the Revolution disregarded the value of private property.

Edward Gibbon (1737-1794)

English author and historian Edward Gibbon was born in Putney, Surrey, England in 1737. Gibbon's childhood was spent in sickness. Due to his poor health Gibbon could not attain regular formal schooling. He attended Westminster school for a while and was taught by various tutors. After this, he was admitted to Magdalen College, Oxford in 1752.

Literary Career and Works

He also published his first work, written in French, *Essai sur letude de la litterature* (1761; *An Essay on the Study of Literature,* 1764). In 1764, Gibbon visited Rome, where he made an exhaustive study of the antiquities and in October 1764, while musing amid the ruins of the Capitol, was inspired to write of the decline and fall of the city. On the death of his father in 1770, Gibbon came into possession of a comfortable fortune, settled in London and began writing the *Decline and Fall of the Roman Empire,* his best known work. The book traces the trajectory of Western civilisation from the beginning of the Roman Empire to the fall of Byzantium. Gibbon died at London on 6th January, 1794.

Decline and Fall of the Roman Empire

It was first published in 1776, Edward Gibbon's 'The History of the Decline and Fall of the Roman Empire' outlines history of the Roman empire from the end of its golden age to its final political and physical disintegration. Gibbon was inspired to write a history of the Roman Empire and its long fall upon visiting the ruins of the Roman forum in 1764, during his Grand Tour. The whole work was published in six volumes from 1776 to 1788. Gibbon's style throughout the work is full of irony. According to *Kenneth Rexroth*, "The Decline and Fall has a hero-the man of reason. Its thesis is that the life of the man of reason in history is tragic by nature. It has been said again and again that Gibbon's history is the perfect expression and fulfillment of the Age of Reason, the 18th century greater than anything of Voltaire's, greater than Tiepolo or Watteau, greater than any of the noble domestic architecture."

Thomas Paine (1737-1809)

English-American political theorist and writer Thomas Paine was born at Thetford, Norfolk, England in 1737. His poor father wanted to send him to local grammar school but eventually Paine's father was forced to apprentice him to his trade. Later, he began working as an officer of the excise, hunting smugglers, and collecting liquor and tobacco taxes.

Literary Career and Works

During mid 1770's, he got a job as an executive editor of Robert Aitken's brand new Pennsylvania Magazine.

Here, he also witnessed The American Revolution. In 1776, he published his thoughts on American independence in *Common Sense*, a pamphlet that attacked the British Monarchy. During the War of Independence, Paine also volunteered in the Continental Army and started with the writing of his highly influential sixteen American Crisis papers, which he published between 1776 and 1783.

In 1787, Paine returned to England and published his most popular work, *The Rights of Man* in 1791. In this work, Paine argued for the political rights of all men because of their natural equality in the sight of God. It supported the French Revolution and called for a 'bloody revolution.' The book was banned and Paine charged for seditious libel.

It was during imprisonment that Paine published the first part of his *The Age of Reason (The Age of Reason: Being an Investigation of True and Fabulous Theology in full)*, which attacked organised religion. This book again earned him a lot of critics and he was accused of being an atheist.

His last years were marked by poverty, poor health and alcoholism. He was increasingly neglected and ostracised. He died as an outcast in New York on 8th June, 1809.

Major Works

Rights of Man

It is published in 1791, Thomas Paine's book *Rights of Man* was written against Edmund Burke's attack in Reflections *on the Revolution in France* (1790). In this work, Paine attacks the notion of monarchy and privileges. Unlike Burke, who supported hereditary privilege, Paine argues that each generation has the right to establish its own system of government.

Paine uses the example of the American Revolution and the new American constitutional government to demonstrate the superiority of a republican over a monarchical system. He believes that the liberal governments set forth in the French and American Revolutions are the way of the future. These governments establish the three most important rights of man: that man is born free; that he has a right to liberty, property, security and resistance of oppression and that the nation is the source of all sovereignty.

Non-Fiction in Romantic Age

The Romantic Age witnessed non-fiction literature mainly in the form of essays, memoirs and biographical depictions.

Literary Trends in Non-Fiction Prose during Romantic Age

In the eighteenth century, a change had taken place in the prose style. Many eighteenth century prose-writers dependent on the assumptions about the suitability of various prose styles for various purposes, for which they shared with the relatively small, but the sophisticated public. Writers in the Romantic Period were rather concerned more with subject matter and emotional expression than with appropriate style. They wrote for an ever-increasing audience which was less homogeneous in its interest and education than that of their predecessors. The autobiographical exploitation of personality manifests itself in a great variety of ways among writers of the late eighteenth and early nineteenth centuries; it is symptomatic of a significant change in the relation between the writer and the society. There was an indication of a growing distrust of the sharp distinction between matter and manner which was made in the eighteenth century. In the Romantic Period, the tendency was for the writer to draw on his own personality either as illuminating case history or as a gesture of defiance of showmanship or 'alienation' rather than to objectify it in terms of a cause or a system. The growth of the familiar essay, with its highly personal, often whimsical, flaunting of the writer's tastes, prejudices, and idiosyncrasies, represents another aspect of the Romantic exploitation of personality.

Essays have variable shapes and therefore, it is understandable that, though numerous attempts have been made to give a definition to the essay, yet none has met with complete success. Most of such attempts succeeded in covering only a part of the compositions which commonly go under the label of the essay. A comprehensive definition which would cover essays as different as those of Bacon, Addison, Lamb etc. is yet to come. Dr. Johnson's famous definition of the essay is- "The essay is a loose sally (witty) of mind, an irregular, indigested piece, not a regular and orderly composition."

This definition touches only one aspect- though a very important aspect of the essay. Many other writers too, tried to define essay, but they too could explain only one or two aspects of the essay. A definition that covers a vast proportion of essay is- "An essay is a short, incomplete, informal, light, subjective literary composition in prose." also saw significant development. Though essay and criticism, both were not new, criticism had been practiced before by Dryden, Addison, Johnson and Goldsmith; and the personal essay or essay proper, derived from Montaigne (Father of Essay), had attracted Cowley, Addison, Steele, and Goldsmith.

Romantic Prose is not based on love stories, though some of the novels do have a romantic element. Romantic Prose refers to the prose written in Romantic Period.

Characteristics of Non-Fiction Prose in Romantic Age

Following are the main characteristic features of the essay of Romantic Age

Departure from Reason

The Romantic Period came after the Age of Enlightenment, which really had a focus on logic, reason and science and the Romantic Period was a deviation from that. In Romantic literature, we see an emphasis on emotions, imaginations and intuitions-elements of humanity that can defy reason.

Focus on Nature

In Neo-classical Prose, the main focus was on realism, morality and reason, whereas the essay writers of Romantic Age, like Romantic Poets focussed on connecting with the natural world. Thus they tried to escape from troubles of world and quest for the peace of mind in nature.

Elements of Supernaturalism

To further separate itself from the Age of Enlightenment, from logic and reason, there is really no better place to turn than to the supernaturalism. A lot of works like Mary Shelley's Frankenstein or Charlotte Bronte's Jane Eyre contain elements that require the reader to suspend his disbelief to accept what they are reading and go along with something that will defy logic and reason.

Transcendentalism

Transcendentalist Movement was a reaction against the 18th-century rationalism. The movement was based on a fundamental belief in the unity of world and God. Soul was thought to be the world. Thus individual soul was identified with God.

Focus on Individual

A lot of works talked about the rights and freedoms of an individual and their ability to exert their will even against something logical. A lot of these novels have themes of rebellion in the face of oppression. Characters do things that might seem irrational because it is really what they want to do.

Humanitarianism

Like Romantic poets, the Essayists of Romantic Age too showed interest in the common man. The essays of Romantic Age, too like poetry, reflect the feelings of Humanitarianism.

Interest in Past, Primitive and Medieval

Writers of the Neo-classical Age created their works on the basis of reason and morality. The writers of Romantic Age, contrary to them, drew inspirations from the past and justified their statements by experiences of primitive and medieval ages.

Idea of Revolution

Essays of Romantic Age exhibit the idea of Revolution and change.

Major Writers of the Romantic Age

Mary Wollstonecraft (1759-1797)

British feminist writer Mary Wollstonecraft was born in Spitalfields, London in 1759. Her father, Edward John Wollstonecraft, was a tyrannical husband, who bullied his wife, Elizabeth Dixon, into a state of servitude. A weaver by profession, her father left his work, mismanaged his share of family inheritance and engaged in futile attempts to become a gentleman. After her mother's death, Wollstonecraft left home in search of her own livelihood.

Literary Carrer and Works

Together, the two sisters along with Wollstonecraft's close friend Fanny established a school at Newington Green, an experience from which Wollstonecraft drew to write. *Thoughts on the Education of Daughters With Reflections on Female Conduct, in the More Important Duties of Life* (1787). She started work as a lady's companion to a Mrs Dawson, in Bath and later worked as a governess in the family of Lord Kingsborough. Wollstonecraft gradually grew disgusted with the work and returned to London. She became a translator and an adviser to Joseph Johnson, a noted publisher of radical texts.

In 1790, Wollstonecraft produced her *Vindication of the Rights of Man*, the first response to Edmund Burke's *Reflections on the Revolution in France*. She attacked Burke's ideas based on antiquity and tradition. The publication of *A Vindication of the Rights of Man* brought Wollstonecraft to the attention of other radical thinkers such as Tom Paine, John Cartwright, John Horne Tooke, William Godwin and William Blake. Wollstonecraft is best known for her feminist tract, *A Vindication of the Rights of Woman* (1792), which advocated equality of sexes.

Apart from her pamphlets and feminist tracts, Wollstonecraft also wrote two novels, *Mary, A Fiction and Maria: or, The Wrongs of Woman*. She also completed *Original Stories From Real Life; with Conversations,* calculated to Regulate the Affections and *Form the Mind to Truth and Goodness* (1788) and an anthology, *The Female Reader; Miscellaneous Pieces in Prose and Verse; Selected from the Best Writers and Disposed under Proper Heads; For the Improvement of Young Women* (1789), published under the pen name 'Mr. Cresswick, teacher of Elocution'. She married William Godwin, a philosopher in February 1797. Her daughter, Mary Wollstonecraft Godwin (later Mary Shelley, author of *Frankenstein*), was born in August 1797. Wollstonecraft died of an infection on 10th September, 1797, 11 days after the birth of her daughter.

Vindication of the Rights of Women

- Mary Wollstonecraft's *Vindication of the Rights of Woman*, published in 1792, is considered as one of the earliest texts of Western feminism.
- It is partly structured as a response to several works on women education and female conduct written by men during the latter half of the 18th century, among the most significant of these was Jean-Jacques Rousseau's *Emile or On Educations*.
- She states that since childhood, women are taught to believe that they are inferior to men. They are taught to be docile and submissive. Characteristics such as meekness and self-sacrifice are inculcated as feminine virtues, which lead to subjugation of women.
- Wollstonecraft further states that women are denied proper education, which prevents their empowerment. The education given to women only aims at 'acquirement of some corporeal accomplishment' rather than 'the cultivation of the understanding'. It only trains them to get husbands.
- She makes a case for women education and states; "Strengthen the female mind by enlarging it and there will be an end to blind obedience but, as blind obedience is ever sought for by power, tyrants and sensualists are in the right, when they endeavor to keep women in the dark, because the former only want slaves and the latter a play-thing."
- Wollstonecraft argues that both men and women should be treated as rational beings and imagines a social order founded on reason.

Charles Lamb (1775-1834)

Romantic essayist Charles Lamb was born in London in 1775. He was the son of Elizabeth Field and John Lamb. Lamb studied at Christ's Hospital where he formed a lifelong friendship with Samuel Taylor Coleridge. However, he left the school early and did not seek a university career.

After leaving school, Lamb was sent to Hertfordshire where he fell in love with Ann Simmons. He wrote sonnets dedicated to her, which later appeared in Coleridge's Poems.

Literary Career and Works

In 1792, Lamb obtained a position with the British East India Company as an accountant, but he continued to write epigrams, plays, poetry and essays, many printed in such publications as the *The Albion, The Morning Chronicle and The Morning Post*.

When Lamb was 20 years old, he suffered a period of insanity. His sister, Mary Ann Lamb, had similar problems and had murdered her mother in a fit of madness. Mary was confined to an asylum, but was eventually released into the care of her brother. Lamb devoted his life to caring for his sister, Mary, who even collaborated with him on some of his works. They jointly published *Tales from Shakespeare* in 1807.

Lamb was part of a large circle of influential friends such as Percy Bysshe Shelley, William Hazlitt, Henry Brougham, Lord Byron,Thomas Barnes and Leigh Hunt. He and his sister had frequent visitors, their salon evenings consisting of playing cards, eating, drinking, smoking and discussing diverse matters. In 1819, at the age of 44, Lamb, who, because of family commitments, had never married, fell in love with an actress, Fanny Kelly, of Covent Garden and proposed marriage to her.

She refused him and he died a bachelor. Lamb's best known work is the series of essays under his pseudonym Elia, the *Essays of Elia* (1823). The essays first appeared in the *London Magazine*, but were later published in book form in 1823.

The name 'Elia' was taken from a clerk in the South Sea House, where Lamb had worked for some time. Lamb's intimate and conversational tone in these essays captivated the readers.

Lamb's other works are his short story, *A Tale of Rosamund Gray and Poor Blind Margaret* (1798), his play *John Wodvil* (1802), his anthology with critical notes- *Specimens of English Dramatic Poets* who lived about the time of Shakespeare, his ballad *Satan in Search of a Wife* (1831) and *Last Essays of Elia* (1833).

William Hazlitt in his *The Spirit of the Age* remarked that "Mr Lamb has succeeded, not by conforming to the Spirit of the Age, but in opposition to it. He does not march boldly along with the crowd, but steals off the pavement to pick his way in the contrary direction". Lamb succumbed to an infection he contracted from a minor cut on his face after having fallen in the street and died at Edmonton, a suburb of London in 1834.

Major Works

- Blank Verse, poetry (1798)
- A Tale of Rosamund Gray and old blind Margaret (1798)
- John Woodvil, poetic drama (1802)
- Tales from Shakespeare (1807)
- The Adventures of Ulysses (1808)
- Specimens of English Dramatic poets who lived about the time of Shakespeare (1808)
- On the Tragedies of Shakespeare (1811)
- Witches and Other Night Fears (1821)
- The Pawnbroker's Daughter (1825)
- Essays of Elia (1823)
- The Last Essays of Elia (1833)

William Hazlitt (1778-1830)

English writer and critic William Hazlitt was born in Maidstone, Kent, England in 1778. His mother, Grace Loftus, was from a dissenting family in Cambridgeshire, and his father, the Reverend William Hazlitt, was an Irish Unitarian minister. Rev. Hazlitt and his family were forced to leave Kent and live in Ireland because of their support for the American Revolution. However, they returned in 1787 and settled at Wem in Shropshire. Hazlitt was educated at the Unitarian New College at Hackney, but left 2 years later because he did not want to become a Unitarian minister.

Literary Career and Works

Hazlitt went to Paris with the aim of becoming a painter, but gradually convinced himself that he could not excel in this art. He then turned to journalism and literature and came into close association with Wordsworth, Coleridge, Lamb, Hunt and others of the Romantic School.

His first book, *An Essay on the Principles of Human Action*, was published in 1805.

Other works written during this period were *Free Thoughts on Public Affairs* (1806); *An Abridgment of the Light of Nature Revealed, by Abraham Tucker... (1807); The Eloquence of the British Senate...* (2 vols 1807); *A Reply to Maithus, on his Essay on Population* (1807); *A New and Improved Grammar of the English Tongue...* (1810). Hazlitt also wrote several books on literature including *Characters of Shakespeare* (1817), *A View of the English Stage* (1818), *English Poets* (1818) and *English Comic Writers* (1819).

Hazlitt also wrote for *The Times* and in 1808, he married the editor's sister, Sarah Stoddart. The marriage was unhappy and the couple separated several years later in 1823, as a result of an affair with a maid, Sarah Walker.

Hazlitt also wrote an account of this relationship in his book *Liber Amoris*. In 1824, Hazlitt married Isabella Bridgewater, but this relationship only lasted a year. Hazlitt's most well known work; *The Spirit of the Age Contemporary Portraits* (1825), was a collection of character sketches of 25 men he believed to be significant. These included Samuel Taylor Coleridge, William Wordsworth, Robert Southey, William Cobbett, William Godwin, Leigh Hunt, Jeremy Bentham and William Wilberforce. Hazlitt died in poverty on 18th September, 1830.

Thomas De Quincey (1785-1859)

English essayist Thomas de Quincey was born in Manchester in 1785. He was the son of a wealthy linen merchant, Thomas Quincey. After his father's death in 1793, his mother Elizabeth Penson adopted the name 'De Quincey'. His father had left them sufficient financial resources. De Quincey was educated at prestigious schools at Salford, Bath and Winkfield.

In 1801, De Quincey began attending the Manchester Grammar School. He later got bored of it, ran away from this school and wandered around the Wales region, sleeping outdoors in order to stretch his money supply. When he finally had no money left, he returned to London to borrow money. On his reconciliation with his family, he was sent to Oxford, and during this period he began taking opium. By 1813, he was addicted to the drug so much that he consumed ten wine-glasses of the drug each day. He married a farmer's daughter named Margaret Simpson in 1816.

Literary Career and Works

He wrote a few occasional articles to support his family. He was appointed as an editor of a local Tory newspaper, the *Westmoreland Gazette*. However, his first major work was *Confessions of an English Opium Eater*, which appeared in *London Magazine* in 1821.

Apart from this, his other famous works were *On the Knocking at the Gate in Macbeth* (an essay in Shakespearean criticism, which deals with the scene of murder of King Duncan by Macbeth and Lady Macbeth), *On Murder Considered as one of the Fine Arts* (a satirical account of an address made to a club) and *Recollections of the Lake Poets* (a collection of biographical essays of the lake poets-Wordsworth, Coleridge and Southey).

He published *The Logic of the Political Economy* (1844), a dissertation on David Ricardo's economic theory and *Suspiria De Profundis* (1845), the sequel to his *Confessions*, in which he documented his childhood, dreams and fantasies. From 1853 until his death, De Quincey worked with his *Selections Grave and Gay from: Writings Published and Unpublished by* Thomas De Quincey. He died in Edinburgh on the 8th December, 1859.

Major Works

- Confessions of an English Opium-Eater (1822)
- On the Knocking at the Gate in Macbeth (1823)
- On Murder Considered as one of the Fine Arts (1827)
- Klosterheim or The Masque (1832)
- Lake Reminiscences or Recollections of the Lake Poets (1834-40)
- Revolt of the Tartars (1837)
- The Logic of the Political Economy (1844)
- Suspiria de Profundis (1845)
- The English Mail-Coach (1849)
- Autobiographical Sketches (1853)
- California and the Gold Mania (1854)

Thomas Love Peacock (1785-1866)

English writer Thomas Love Peacock was born in Dorset, England in 1785. He was the son of Samuel Peacock and his wife Sarah Love. Peacock's father was a glass merchant, who died three years after his birth. His education was cut short due to his father's death. Thereafter, Peacock was raised by his mother at her maternal home. He taught himself Greek, Latin, French and Italian.

Literary Career and Works

After a brief experience of business, Peacock determined to devote himself to literature. His poetical works; *Palmyra and Other Poems* and *The Monks of St Mark* were published, when he was in his late teens. He served for a short time as secretary to Sir Home Popham at Flushing and paid several visits to Wales. In 1812 he met PB Shelley and formed a close relationship with him. Because of financial constraints, he took a job in 1819 with the East India Company. The following year, he married Jane Gryffydh, daughter of a Welsh rector.

Peacock is best known for his essay *The Four Ages of Poetry* (1820), which provoked Shelley's famous *Defence of Poetry*. It was first published in the journal 'Literary Miscellany' in 1820. In this essay, he wrote about the gradual origin and development of poetry in four ages: Age of Iron; Age of Gold, Age of Silver and Age of Brass. Poetry originated in the Iron Age, in which "Rude bards celebrated in rough numbers the exploits of ruder chiefs, in days when every man was a warrior".

The golden age was the age of the noblest poetic productions, when poetry tended to become retrospective. This was followed by the artificial silver age in which poets re-casted or imitated the poems of the age of gold. The Brass age, was the age, of poetic decay and decline. The current brass era was marked, according to Peacock, by poems of "Verbose and minutely-detailed description of thoughts, passions, actions, persons and things." Peacock in this essay defined the poet as 'a semi-barbarian in a civilised community'.

Apart from this essay, Peacock wrote several other works such as *Recollections of Childhood: The Abbey House* (1837), *Memoirs of Shelley* (1858-62) and novels such as *Melincourt* (1817) and *Nightmare Abbey* (1818). Peacock succeeded James Mill as chief examiner for the East India Company in 1836 and retired on a pension in 1856. He died on the 23rd January, 1866 at Lower Halliford.

Major Works

Essays

- The Four Ages of Poetry (1820)
- Recollections of Childhood: The Abbey House (1837)
- Memoirs of Shelley (1858-62)
- The Last Day of Windsor Forest (1887)

Novels

- Headlong Hall (1815)
- Melincourt (1817)
- Nightmare Abbey (1818)
- Maid Marian (1822)
- The Misfortunes of Elphin (1829)
- Crotchet Castle (1831)
- Gryll Grange (1861)

EXAM BASED QUESTIONS

1 A curious combination of scientific and credulous research in the matter of popular superstition is
(a) Religio Medici (b) Pilgrim's Progress
(c) Vulgar Errors (d) Urn Burial

2 'Vulgar Errors' was written by
(a) Bunyan (b) Browne
(c) Milton (d) Herrick

3 Who was known as a physician and as a learned doctor?
(a) Sir Thomas Browne (b) Sir John Denham
(c) John Bunyan (d) Thomas Fuller

4 Who was called The Shakespeare of Divines?
(a) Jeremy Taylor (b) Thomas Fuller
(c) Robert Burton (d) Richard Baxter

5 'The Saints Everlasting Rest' was written by
(a) Izaak Walton (b) Richard Baxter
(c) Jeremy Taylor (d) Thomas Fuller

6 In Thomas Hobbes book entitled 'Leviathan', the word 'Leviathan' refers to
(a) Leviathan is a monstor
(b) Leviathan is a huge ocean
(c) Leviathan is a huge mammal, created by God
(d) Both (a) and (c)

7 Which out of the following books was written by a busy physician, a supposedly scientific man at that time?
(a) Holy Living
(b) Paradise Lost
(c) Religio Medici
(d) The Compleat Angler

8 Which work is called by Hallam as the first plea for tolerance in religion on a comprehensive basis and on deep seated foundations?
(a) Liberty of Propheysing
(b) The Holy Living and Dying
(c) Saints Everlasting Rest
(d) Pilgrim's Progress

9 In how many parts is 'Leviathan' by Thomas Hobbes divided?
(a) Two (b) Three
(c) Four (d) Five

10 'Elements of Law' is a work by the Puritan age prose writer
(a) Thomas Hobbes
(b) Robert Burton
(c) Izaak Walton
(d) Jeremy Taylor

11 The Puritan age prose writer 'Jeremy Taylor' has written:
(a) The Church--History of Britain
(b) The Rule and Exercises of Holy -Dying
(c) A Call for The Unconverted
(d) The Garden of Cyrus

12 Which of the following is not a kind of idea according to Locke's classification?
(a) Simple (b) Mixed mode
(c) Nominal (d) Abstract general

13 On Locke's account of knowledge, what does all knowledge, ultimately boil down to?
(a) Intuition (b) Demonstration
(c) Belief (d) Innate ideas

14 What is Locke's first target of attack in the Essay?
(a) Skepticism about the external world
(b) Innate prepositions
(c) Innate ideas
(d) Abuses of language

15 On Locke's theory of meaning, to what do words refer?
(a) Objects (b) Real essences
(c) Categories (d) Ideas

16 Which of the following would Locke consider a possible object of knowledge in the strictest sense?
(a) The microstructure of gold
(b) Geometry
(c) Ancient Greek philosophy
(d) The existence of an external world

17 Which of the following is not a method of determining agreement or disagreement between our ideas according to Locke?
(a) Abstraction (b) Relation
(c) Identity and Diversity (d) Reflection

18 According to Locke, a substance is determined by its level of
(a) ontological independence
(b) simplicity
(c) secondary qualities
(d) abstract general ideas

19 Which of the following would not count as a secondary quality according to Locke?
(a) The taste of peanut butter
(b) The faint scent of spring in the air
(c) The perfect roundness of my hoola hoop
(d) Magenta

20 Which of the following does Locke not include among the marks that distinguish sensations from all other ideas?
(a) Vivacity
(b) Passivity
(c) Attendance by pleasure or pain
(d) Transitivity

21 Which of the following would not count as an abstract general idea according to Locke?
(a) Man
(b) Marshmallow
(c) Marriage
(d) Sailboat

22 To which of the following does the pharse 'veil of perception' refer?
(a) The claim that all we are immediately aware of our ideas
(b) The claim that we are aware of everything that is in our own mind
(c) The claim that we cannot know anything for certain
(d) The claim that our words refer to ideas

23 Which of the following would Locke consider the best analogy to the human mind?
(a) A seive (b) Flypaper
(c) Noodles (d) Tabula Rasa

24 Which of the following is not a bee in Locke's bonnet?
(a) Abuses of language
(b) Too much reliance on the senses
(c) Overestimation of our ability to understad the world
(d) Underestimation of our ability to understand the world

25 Which of the following does not state a true fact about Locke's theory of mind?
(a) Everything in the mind is an idea
(b) We are aware of everything that is in our own minds
(c) Thought and consciousness are inseparable
(d) Our thought is guided by certain inborn capacities and dispositions

26 What does the phrase 'transparency of the mental' refer to?
(a) The claim that for something to be in the mind, we must be aware of it
(b) The claim that when we are born, our minds are completely blank
(c) The claim that everybody agrees with certain ethical truths
(d) The claim that everybody knows anything for certain

27 Which of the following does Locke compare color and smell to?
(a) A dream
(b) Exhaustion
(c) Sickness
(d) A piece of wheat

28 Why does Locke invoke the image of an almond being pounded with a pestle?
(a) To demonstrate that we cannot know anything about the external world
(b) To demonstrate that all of our knowledge comes through the senses
(c) To demonstrate that secondary qualities depend on primary qualities
(d) To demonstrate that there are no innate ideas

29 Which of the following ideas does Locke consider to be the likeliest candidate for innateness?
(a) Idea of oneself
(b) Idea of right and wrong
(c) Idea of God
(d) Idea of number

30 Which of the following statements about real essences is true according to Locke?
(a) Real essences pick out nominal essences
(b) Real essences pick out natural kinds
(c) Real essences are based in the hidden micro structures of objects
(d) Real essences were what Aristotle was talking about all along

31 What scientific view did Locke call most plausible in the Essay?
(a) The vortex theory of matter
(b) Newtonian physics
(c) Aristotelian physics
(d) The Corpuscular Hypothesis

32 What best describes Locke's assessment of the notion of a substratum?
(a) Necessary evil (b) Clear and distinct
(c) Long overdue (d) Hopelessly outdated

33 Locke's 'Essay concerning Human Understanding' is a classic statement of ....Philosophy.
(a) aesthetic (b) empiricist
(c) nationalist (d) realist

34 Who is known as the father of literary criticism?
(a) John Dryden (b) Izaak Walton
(c) John Eliot (d) Cromwell

35 Which out of the following is chiefly a biographical record, the first part consisting of numerous historical examples to be imitated?
(a) Vulgar Errors
(b) The Holy War
(c) Worthies
(d) The Holy and Profane State

36 Which poet, critic and translator brought England a modern literature between 1660 and 1700?
(a) Addison (b) Bunyan
(c) Crabbe (d) Dryden

37 Who is known for the complete and bloodless revolution of 1688?
(a) William of Orange
(b) William of Blue
(c) William of Red
(d) William of Black

38 'Law of Freedom' is the book of
(a) George Herbert
(b) Gerrard Winstanley
(c) Thomas Fuller
(d) Jeremy Taylor

39 Samuel Pepys kept his diary from
(a) 1660 to 1669 (b) 1649 to 1660
(c) 1662 to 1689 (d) 1660 to 1689

40 What century is variously called 'The Age of Enlightenment', 'The Age of Sensibility', 'The Augustan Age' and 'The Age of Prose and Reason'?
(a) 16th century (b) 17th century
(c) 18th century (d) 19th century

41 In which age, the government was divided into two parties?
(a) The Age of Revival
(b) The Romantic Age
(c) The Neo-Classical Age
(d) None of the above

42 The Augustan Age is called, so because
(a) King Augustus ruled over England during this period
(b) the English writers imitated the Roman writers during this period
(c) the English King was born in the month of August
(d) This was an age of sensibility

43 The developments that occurred in the 18th century included
(a) social development
(b) intellectual development
(c) industrial development
(d) All of the above

44 The Periodical Essay in the 18th century was introduced by
(a) Churchill (b) Rousseau (c) Tatler (d) Fielding

45 The Rambler appeared every
(a) Tuesday and Saturday
(b) Sunday and Wednesday
(c) Friday and Monday
(d) Thursday and Monday

46 The word 'nature' in the 18th century literature stands for
(a) nature of writing
(b) external nature
(c) human nature
(d) the universe

47 Joseph Addison in his famous work, 'Female Orators' talks about
(a) the talkative nature of women
(b) women's status
(c) the beauty of women
(d) None of the above

48 Which work of Addison celebrates the victory of Marlborough at Blenheim?
(a) Cato
(b) Pleasures of Imagination
(c) An Address to King William
(d) The Campaign

49 Which was the first play of Steele?
(a) The Accomplished Fools (b) The Funeral
(c) The Lying Lover (d) The Conscious Lovers

50 Which work did Steele address to his second wife?
(a) The Conscious Lovers (b) The Lying Lover
(c) The Dear Prue (d) The Tender Husband

51 Which work of Arbuthnot is a political allegory published as a series of five templates?
(a) The History of John Ball
(b) Of the Laws of Chance
(c) Essay Towards a Natural History of Earth
(d) None of the above

52 John Ball is the personification of
(a) Scotland (b) England
(c) France (d) Italy

53 Who is considered as one of the most famous Empiricists?
(a) John Arbuthnot (b) George Berkley
(c) David Hartley (d) Adam Smith

54 Which work gave Hartley a reputation of founding father of Science of Psychology?
(a) Observations on Man (b) Minute Philosophers
(c) Alciphron (d) None of these

55 Which of the following is the most famous work of Burke?
(a) The Wealth of Nations
(b) Treatise
(c) Reflections on the Revolution in France
(d) None of the above

56 Which of the following is the best known work of Gibbon?
(a) Treatise
(b) The Wealth of Nations
(c) Letter to a Noble Lord
(d) Decline and Fall of the Roman Empire

57 Which work of Paine was banned and got him charged for seditious libel?
(a) Common Sense (b) The Rights of Man
(c) Treatise (d) The Life of Ascham

58 Who among the following wrote a book with the title The Age of Reason?

(a) William Godwin (b) Edmund Burke
(c) Thomas Paine (d) Edward Gibbon

59 Which among the following is the oldest and finest specimens of ballad literature, a landmark in the history of the Romantic Movement?

(a) Tale of A Tub
(b) Reliques
(c) Battle of the Books
(d) Rape of the Lock

60 The religious movement Methodism in the 18th century England was founded by

(a) John Tillotson (b) Bishop Butler
(c) Bernard Mandeville (d) John Wesley

61 'Discourse' a famous work done by

(a) Oliver Goldsmith
(b) Alexander Pope
(c) JJ Rousseau
(d) Charles Churchill

62 The 'Condition of England' literature refers to

(a) the literature written by the labour class
(b) the literature of England extolling living conditions
(c) the literature of England depicting the vulnerability of labour classes
(d) the literature of England depicting the imperial projects abroad

63 'Periodical Essays' emerged in the

(a) 18th century (b) 17th century
(c) 16th century (d) None of these

64 'The Guardian' was written by Steele with the help of

(a) Goldsmith (b) Addison (c) Pope (d) Swift

65 'Reflection on the French Revolution' is the great work of

(a) Laurence Sterne (b) Edmund Burke
(c) Joseph Addison (d) Richard Steele

66 Who among the following was not a member of Scriblerus Club?

(a) Thomas Parnel (b) Alexander Pope
(c) Joseph Addison (d) John Gay

67 This periodical had the avowed intention "to enliven morality with wit and to temper wit with morality ...... to bring philosophy out of the closets and libraries, schools and colleges, to dwell in clubs and assemblies, at tea-tables and coffee house." It also promoted family, marriage and courtesy,

The periodical under reference is

(a) The Tatler
(b) The Spectator
(c) The Gentleman's Magazine
(d) The London Magazine

68 This periodical was started in 1709 with a motive "to expose the false arts of life, to pull the disguise of cunning, vanity and affectation, and to recommend a general simplicity in our dress, our discourse and our behaviour". The founder of the periodical wrote under the pseudonym of Isaac Bickerstaff.

The periodical described above is

(a) The Tatler (b) The Spectator
(c) The Critical Review (d) The Rambler

69 The Enlightenment was characterised by

(a) accelerated industrial production and general well-being of the public
(b) a belief in the universal authority of reason and emphasis on scientific experimentation
(c) the protestant work ethic and compliance with christian values of life
(d) an undue faith in predestination and neglect of free will

70 Which among the following is not written by De-Quincey

(a) The English Mail Coach
(b) Suspiria de Profoundis
(c) To Hester
(d) Confession of an English Opium eater

71 In which out of the following we see the creations of Lamb's humour and pathos?

(a) Old China
(b) Dissertation on Roast Rig
(c) A Chapter on Ears
(d) Imperfect Sympathies

72 Which out of the following was the last Essay of Lamb?

(a) Praise of Chimney Sweepers
(b) Dream Children
(c) A Chapter on Ears (d) Grace Before Meat

73 Who wrote Confessions of an 'English Opium Eater'?

(a) Wordsworth (b) Shelley (c) De-Quincey (d) Browne

74 De-Quincey's grotesque humour is realised from which of the following?

(a) Murder considered as one of the fine arts
(b) On the knocking at the gate in Macbeth
(c) Joan of Arc
(d) Suspiria De Profoundis

75 Which of the following is admirably suited to show the man's critical genius?

(a) Murder considered as one of the fine arts
(b) On the knocking at the gate in Macbeth
(c) Joan of Arc
(d) Suspiria De Profoundis

76 'The Tatler' and 'The Spectator' are the famous works of ....

(a) Addison and Swift (b) Addison and Goldsmith
(c) Addison and Steele (d) None of these

77 .... was the first volume published by Gibbon, which made him successful.

(a) History
(b) Memoirs
(c) The Decline and Fall of the Roman Empire
(d) None of the above

78 Four Ages of Poetry is a composition of ....

(a) Coleridge (b) Peacock
(c) Keats (d) Wordsworth

79 .... of the following is the last named essay of De-Quincey.

(a) Joan of Arc
(b) Dream Fugue
(c) The English Mail Coach (d) Revolt of the Tartars

80 Peacock is best known for his essay .... which provoked Shelley's famous defence of Poetry.

(a) Recollections of Childhood
(b) The Four Ages of Poetry
(c) Memoirs of Shelley
(d) The Last Day of Windsor Forest

81 Which of the following statements is true about Thomas Fuller?

(a) Fuller was a person who devoted his life to being a clergy
(b) He was called the Shakespeare of divines
(c) Fuller was known as the busiest man of his age
(d) Fuller was a clergyman and Royalist

82 Which of these statements about the popularity of the 'periodical essay' is correct?

(a) It was not suited to the genius of the middle class, who were the new patrons of literature
(b) It was too literary to be comprehended and appreciated by the common people
(c) They did not appeal to women as they did not pay attention to the interests of the fair sex
(d) The essayists used a simple and conversational style so that they could be easily understood and appreciated

83 Which of the following pairs is correctly matched?

(a) Hobbes : Leviathan
(b) Browne : The Reformed Pastor
(c) Puller : Religion Medici
(d) Baxter : Wortheis of England

84 Which of the following pairs is correctly matched?

Authors		Works
(a) Mary Wollstonecraft	:	A Vindication of the Rights of Woman
(b) Fanny Burny	:	Wavereley
(c) Maria Edgeworth	:	Evelina
(d) Walter Scott	:	Belinda

85 Which of the following pairs is incorrectly matched?

Authors		Works
(a) Thomas Love Peacock	:	Nightmare Abbey
(b) Thomas De-Quincey	:	Confessions of an English Opium, Eater
(c) William Hazlitt	:	A View of the English Stage
(d) Jane Austen	:	Essays of Elia

86 **Assertion (A)** Enlightenment movement advocated scientific rationalism and empirical knowledge

Reason (R) It used reason to scrutinise previously accepted doctrines and traditions.

Codes

(a) A is true, but R is false
(b) A is false, but R is true
(c) Both A and R are true, but R is not the correct explanation of A
(d) Both A and R are true and R is the correct explanation of A

87 Which of the following works are in chronological order?

(a) Leviathan, The Anatomy of Play, Lucasta, Aglaura
(b) The Anatomy of Play, Lucasta, Leviathan, Aglaura
(c) Aglaura, Lucasta, The Anatomy of Play, Leviathan
(d) Lucasta, Aglaura, Leviathan, The Anatomy of Play

88 Which of the following work sequence is in correct chronological order?

(a) Samuel Pepy's 'Diary', Samuel Butler's 'Two letters', John Locke's 'An Essay Concerning Human Understanding John Bunyan's 'The Heavenly Footman'
(b) Samuel Butler's 'Two Letters', Samuel Pepy's 'Diary', John Locke's 'An Essay Concerning Human Understanding, John Bunyan's 'The Heavenly Footman'
(c) John Locke's 'An Essay Concerning Human Understanding' Samuel Pepy's 'Diary', Samuel Butler's 'Two Letters', John Bunyan's 'The Heavenly Footman'
(d) John Bunyan's 'The Heavenly Footman', Samuel Pepy's 'Diary', Samuel Butler's 'Two Letters', John Locke's 'An Essay Concerning Human Understanding'

89 Which of the following is in chronological order of the publication of these works?

(a) The Rambler, The Decline and Fall of the Roman Empire, The Idler
(b) The Decline and Fall of the Roman Empire, The Rambler, The Idler
(c) The Idler, The Rambler, The Decline and Fall of the Roman Empire
(d) The Rambler, The Idler, The Decline and Fall of the Roman Empire

90 Which of the following is in the correct chronological order according to the publication of these works?

(a) The Dunciad, Amelia, The Tatler, The Traveller
(b) Amelia, The Traveller, The Dunciad, The Tatler
(c) The Traveller, Amelia, The Tatler, The Dunciad
(d) The Tatler, The Dunciad, Amelia, The Traveller

91 What is common to the following writers? Identify the correct description below.

1. Robert Burton
2. Thomas Hobbes
3. Izaak Walton
4. Thomas Fuller

Codes

(a) All of them were prose writers of the Puritan Age
(b) All of them wrote lyrics
(c) All of them were romantic poets
(d) All of them wrote poems in blank verse

92 The following writers have composed the works mentioned against their names:

1. Jeremy Taylor–Decorpore
2. Hobbes–Leviathan
3. Walton–The Compleat Angler
4. Fuller–Religio Medici

Which of the following option is/are correct?

Codes

(a) Only 1
(b) 2 and 3
(c) 3 and 4
(d) 1 and 4

93 The following prose writers of the Puritan Age are mentioned with their works against their names:

1. Baxter–Vulgar Errors
2. Taylor–Twenty-seven Sermons
3. Hobbes–Androinicus
4. Browne–Religio Medici

Which of the following options are correct?

(a) 1 and 2
(b) 1 and 3
(c) 2 and 3
(d) 2 and 4

94 A list of the Puritan works is given below:

1. L' Allegro
2. Lycidas
3. A Call to the Unconverted
4. The Reformed Pastor

Which of these is/are the work's of Richard Baxter?

(a) 1 and 3
(b) 1 and 4
(c) Only 3
(d) 3 and 4

95 'Diary' refers to

1. Milton
2. Peppy's
3. Gower
4. Greene

Select the correct answer using the codes given below.

(a) 1 and 4
(b) 1 and 3
(c) Only 2
(d) 2 and 4

96 Consider the following statements correctly. The Romantics were characterised by

1. A belief in individual liberty and sympathy with those who rebelled against tyranny.
2. The Romantics thought of nature as permanent.
3. A disbelief in individual liberty and sympathy with those, who rebelled against tyranny.
4. The Romantics thought of nature as transformative.

Which of the statements given above are correct?

(a) 1 and 2
(b) 1 and 4
(c) 3 and 4
(d) 3 and 2

97 What is common to the following writers? Identify the correct description below

Charles Lamb

William Hazlitt

Thomas de-Quincey

Thomas Love Peacock

Codes

(a) All of them are prose writers of the Romantic Age
(b) All of them are Restoration dramatists
(c) All of them have written Gothic novels
(d) All of them are Lake Poets

98 Consider the following statements about Edmunde Burke.

1. 'Reflections on the Revolution in France' is his most Famous work.
2. He was a Parliamentarian who wrote and spoke on the major issues of the day.
3. He wrote 'Complete Dictionary of Scientific Biography'.
4. He was a Scottish philosopher and economist besides being a writers.

Which of the above given are correct for Edmund Burke?

(a) 1 and 2
(b) 2 and 3
(c) 3 and 4
(d) 2 and 4

99 Consider the following statements about Mary Wollstonecraft:

1. She was a British Feminist writer.
2. 'Rights of Man' was published by her in 1791.
3. She also wrote Maria or 'Wrongs of a Woman'.
4. She applauded Burke's ideas based on antiquity and tradition.

Which of the above given are true for her?

(a) 1 and 2
(b) 1 and 3
(c) 2 and 3
(d) 3 and 4

100 Consider the following works:

1. Vindication of the Rights of Women
2. The History of John Bill
3. Essays of Elia
4. On the Tragedies of Shakespeare

Which of the above given belong to Charles Lamb?

(a) 1 and 2 (b) 2 and 3
(c) 3 and 4 (d) 1 and 4

101 Match the following Rate 18th century Non-Fiction writers with their works.

Late 18th century Non-Fiction Writers

1. Edmund Burke 2. Edward Gibbon
3. Mary Wollstonecraft 4. Thomas Paine

Works

A. Reflections on the Revolution in France
B. Decline and Fall of the Roman Empire
C. The Rights of Man
D. Thoughts on the Education of Daughters with reflections on Female Conduct, in the More Important Duties of Life.

Codes

(a) 1-A, 2-B, 3-C, 4-D
(b) 1-D, 2-C, 3-B, 4-A
(c) 1-B, 2-D, 3-A, 4-C
(d) 1-C, 2-A, 3-D, 4-B

102 Match the following Romantic Age Non-Fiction writers with their works.

Romantic Age Non-Fiction Writers

1. Charles Lamb
2. William Hazlitt
3. Thomas De Quincey
4. Thomas Love Peacock

Works

A. Recollections of Childhood: The Abbey House
B. The Logic of the Political Economy.
C. An Essay on the Principles of Human Action
D. The Last Essay of Elia.

Codes

(a) 1-A, 2-B, 3-C, 4-D
(b) 1-D, 2-C, 3-B, 4-A
(c) 1-B, 2-D, 3-A, 4-C
(d) 1-C, 2-A, 3-D, 4-B

103 Match the following Non-Fiction works with their Restoration Age writers.

Non-Fiction Works

1. An Essay of Dramatic Poesy
2. A Disclosure of Forest Trees
3. Examen
4. An Essay Concerning Human Under standing

Restoration Age Writers

A. Roger North
B. John Dryden
C. John Locke
D. John Evelyn

Codes

(a) 1-A, 2-B, 3-C, 4-D (b) 1-D, 2-C, 3-B, 4-A
(c) 1-B, 2-D, 3-A, 4-C (d) 1-C, 2-A, 3-D, 4-B

104 Match the following.

	List I		List II
A.	Richard Baxter	1.	Church History of Britain
B.	Izaak Walton	2.	The Holy Living and Dying
C.	Jeremy Taylor	3.	The Saints Everlasting Rest
D.	Thomas Fuller	4.	The Compleat Angler

Codes

	A	B	C	D		A	B	C	D
(a)	4	3	1	2	(b)	3	4	2	1
(c)	3	1	4	2	(d)	4	1	3	2

105 Match the following.

	List I		List II
A.	1660	1.	Church of England Restored
B.	1662	2.	England and Scotland Unite
C.	1688	3.	Charles II Restored
D.	1707	4.	Glorious Revolution

Codes

	A	B	C	D		A	B	C	D
(a)	3	1	4	2	(b)	2	3	1	4
(c)	4	1	3	2	(d)	1	2	3	4

106 Match the following.

	List I		List II
A.	Revolt of the Tartars	1.	1897
B.	English Mail Coach	2.	1854
C.	Letters to a Young Man	3.	1823
D.	Joan of Arc	4.	1851

Codes

	A	B	C	D		A	B	C	D
(a)	1	2	3	4	(b)	2	1	3	4
(c)	4	3	2	1	(d)	1	3	4	2

107 Match the following.

	List I		List II
A.	Edinburgh Review	1.	1802
B.	The Spectator	2.	1828
C.	Fraser's Magazine	3.	1830
D.	Blockwood's Magazine	4.	1817

Codes

	A	B	C	D		A	B	C	D
(a)	1	2	3	4	(b)	2	1	3	4
(c)	4	2	1	3	(d)	4	3	2	1

108 **In the following series, which one has all the works matched correctly with their dates of publication?**

(a) Astraea Redux– 1660, Religio Laici–1687, Principia–1682, The Battle of Books–1704
(b) Astraea Redux–1660, Religio Laici–1682, Principia–1687, The Battle of Books–1704
(c) Astraea Redux–1687, Religio Laici–1660, Principia–1704, The Battle of Books–1682
(d) Astraea Redux–1704, Religio Laici–1687, Principia–1682, The Battle of Books–1660

109 **In the given series, which one has non-fiction prose work matched correctly with neo-classical writers?**

(a) The Tatler–Richard Steele, The Rambler–Samuel Johnson, Pleasures of the Imagination–Joseph Addison, An Essay Concerning the Nature of Ailments–John Arbuthnot.
(b) The Tatler–Samuel Johnson, The Rambler–Joseph Addison, Pleasures of the Imagination–John Arbuthnot, An Essay Concerning the Nature of Ailments–Richard Steele
(c) The Tatler–Joseph Addison, The Rambler–John Arbuthnot, Pleasures of the Imagination–Richard Steele, An Essay Concerning the Nature of Ailments–Samuel Johnson
(d) The Tatler–John Arbuthnot, The Rambler–Richard Steele, Pleasures of the Imagination–Samuel Johnson, An Essay Concerning the Nature of Ailments–Joseph Addison.

110 **In the given series, which one has major philosophers of the Augustan Age matched correctly with their non-fiction prose works?**

(a) George Berkeley–The Wealth of Nations, David Hartley–A Treatise of Human Nature, David Hume–Observations on Man, Adam Smith–Alciphron
(b) George Berkeley–Alciphron, David Hartley–Observations on Man, David Hume–A Treatise of Human Nature, Adam Smith–The Wealth of Nations.
(c) George Berkeley–Observations on Man, David Hartley–The Wealth of Nations, David Hume–Alciphron, Adam Smith–A Treatise of Human Nature.
(d) George Berkeley–A Treatise of Human Nature, David Hartley–Alciphron, David Hume–The Wealth of Nations, Adam Smith–Observations on Man.

111 **"He that increaseth wisdom, increaseth sorrow."**

Which of the following non-fiction writers in which of his/her works has used the above lines?

(a) Robert Burton, The Anatomy of Melancholy
(b) Thomas Hobbes, Leviathan
(c) Izaak Walton, The Compleat Angler, or the Contemplative Man's Recreation
(d) Thomas Browne, Religio Medici

112 **"For such is the nature of man, that howsoever they may acknowledge many others to be more witty, or more eloquent, or more learned; Yet they will hardly believe there be many so wise as themselves: For they see their own wit at hand, and other mens at a distance."**

Which of the following non-fiction writers in which of his/her works has used the above lines?

(a) Robert Burton, The Anatomy of Melancholy
(b) Thomas Hobbes, Leviathan
(c) Izaak Walton, The Compleat Angler, or the Contemplative Man's Recreation
(d) Thomas Browne, Religio Medici

113 **"If there be any among those common objects of hatred which I can safely say I doe contemn and laugh at, it is that great enemy of reason, vertue and religion, the multitude, that numerous piece of monstrosity, which taken asunder seeme men, and the reasonable creatures of God; but confused together, make but one great beast, and a monstrosity more prodigious than Hydra; it is no breach of Charity to call these fooles; it is the stile all Holy writers have afforded them, set down by Solomon in canonicall scripture, and a point of our faith to beleeve so."**

Which of the following non-fiction writers in which of his/her works has used the above lines?

(a) Thomas Browne, Religio Medici and Urne-Buriall
(b) Thomas Fuller, A Pisgah Sight of Palestine and the Confines Thereof: With the History of the Old and New Testament Acted Thereon
(c) Jeremy Taylor, Holy Living and Dying
(d) Richard Baxter, The Reformed Pastor

114 **"Passion against Reason, Reason against Faith, Faith against the Devil, and my conscience against all."**

Which of the following non-fiction writers in which of his/her works has used the above lines?

(a) Robert Burton, The Anatomy of Melancholy
(b) Thomas Hobbes, Leviathan
(c) Izaak Walton, The Compleat Angler, or the Contemplative Man's Recreation
(d) Thomas Browne, Religio Medici

115 **"It is said that the darkest hour of the night comes just before the dawn."**

Which of the following non-fiction writers in which of his/her works has used the above lines?

(a) Thomas Browne, Religio Medici and Urne-Buriall
(b) Thomas Fuller, A Pisgah Sight of Palestine and the Confines Thereof: With the History of the Old and New Testament Acted Thereon
(c) Jeremy Taylor, Holy Living and Dying
(d) Richard Baxter, The Reformed Pastor

116 "I acknowledge, dear God, that I have deserved the greatest of thy wrath and indignation; and that, if thou hadst dealt with me according to my deserving, I had now, at this instant, been desperately bewailing my miseries in the sorrows and horrors of a sad eternity. But thy mercy triumphing over thy justice and my sins, thou hast still continued to me life and time of repentance; thou hast opened to me the gates of grace and mercy, and perpetually callest upon me to enter in, and to walk in the paths of a holy life, that I might glorify thee, and be glorified of thee eternally."

Which of the following non-fiction writers in which of his / her works has used the above lines?

(a) Thomas Browne, Religio Medici and Urne-Buriall
(b) Thomas Fuller, A Pisgah Sight of Palestine and the Confines Thereof: With the History of the Old and New Testament Acted Thereon
(c) Jeremy Taylor, Holy Living and Dying
(d) Richard Baxter, The Reformed Pastor

117 "The mind of man possesses a sort of creative power on its own; either in representing at pleasure the images of things in the order and manner in which they were received by the senses, or in combining those images in a new manner, and according to a different order. This power is called imagination."

Which of the following non-fiction writers in which of his / her works has used the above lines?

(a) Edmund Burke, A Philosophical Enquiry into the Origin of our Ideas of the Sublime and Beautiful.
(b) Edward Gibbon, Memoirs of My Life
(c) Thomas Paine, The Age of Reason
(d) George Berkeley, A Treatise Concerning the Principles of Human Knowledge

118 "The theologian may indulge the pleasing task of describing religion as she descended from Heaven, arrayed in her native purity. A more melancholy duty is imposed on the historian. He must discover the inevitable mixture of error and corruption which she contracted in a long residence upon Earth, among a weak and degenerate race of beings."

Which of the following non-fiction writers in which of his / her works has used the above lines?

(a) Richard Baxter, The Saints' Everlasting Rest
(b) John Locke, A Letter Concerning Toleration
(c) Edmund Burke, An Appeal from the New to the Old Whigs, in Consequence of Some Late Discussions in Parliament, Relative to the Reflections on the French Revolution.
(d) Edward Gibbons, The Decline and Fall of the Roman Empire.

119 "To a lover of books the shops and sales in London present irresistible temptations."

Which of the following non-fiction writers in which of his / her works has used the above lines?

(a) Edmund Burke, A Philosophical Enquiry into the Origin of our Ideas of the Sublime and Beautiful
(b) Edward Gibbon, Memoirs of My Life
(c) Thomas Paine, The Age of Reason
(d) George Berkeley, A Treatise Concerning the Principles of Human Knowledge

120 "To live among such excellent helps as our libraries afford, to have so many silent wise companions whenever we please."

Which of the following non-fiction writers in which of his / her works has used the above lines?

(a) Thomas Browne, Religio Medici and Urne-Buriall
(b) Thomas Fuller, A Pisgah Sight of Palestine and the Confines Thereof: With the History of the Old and New Testament Acted Thereon
(c) Jeremy Taylor, Holy Living and Dying
(d) Richard Baxter, The Reformed Pastor

121 "The more they love each other, the more they participate in each other's griefs, and one or the other will be frequently under some sort of suffering."

Which of the following non-fiction writers in which of his / her works has used the above lines?

(a) Thomas Browne, Christian Morals
(b) Richard Baxter, The Godly Home
(c) John Locke, Some Thoughts Concerning Education
(d) John Evelyn, The Diary of John Evelyn

122 "This day came in his Majestie Charles the 2d to London after a sad, and long Exile, and Calamitous Suffering both of the King and Church: being 17 years: This was also his Birthday, and with a Triumph of above 20000 horse and foote, brandishing their swords and shouting with unexpressable joy: The wayes straw'd with flowers, the bells ringing, the streets hung with Tapissry, fountaines running with wine: The Major, Aldermen, all the Companies in their liver[ie]s, Chaines of Gold, banners; Lords and nobles, Cloth of silver, gold and vellvet every body clad in, the windos and balconies all set with Ladys, Trumpets, Musick, and [myriads] of people flocking the streetes and was as far as Rochester, so as they were 7 houres in passing the Citty, even from 2 in the afternoon 'til nine at night: I stood in the strand, and beheld it, and blessed God: And all this without one drop of bloud, and by that very army, which rebell'd against him: but it was the Lords doing, et mirabile in oculis nostris: for such a Restauration was never seene in the mention of any history, antient or modern, since the returne of the Babylonian Captivity, nor so joyfull a day, and so bright, ever seene in this nation: this happening when to expect or effect it, was past all humane policy."

Which of the following non-fiction writers in which of his/her works has used the above lines?

(a) Thomas Browne, Christian Morals
(b) Richard Baxter, The Godly Home
(c) John Locke, Some Thoughts Concerning Education
(d) John Evelyn, The Diary of John Evelyn .

123 "The truth is, I do indulge myself a little the more in pleasure, knowing that this is the proper age of my life to do it; and, out of my observation that most men that do thrive in the world do forget to take pleasure during the time that they are getting their estate, but reserve that till they have got one, and then it is too late for them to enjoy it."

Which of the following non-fiction writers in which of his/her works has used the above lines?

(a) Thomas Browne, The Garden of Cyrus
(b) Richard Baxter, Dying Thoughts
(c) John Locke, Second Treatise of Government
(d) Samuel Pepys, The Diary of Samuel Pepys .

124 "He that sets his home on fire because his fingers are frostbitten can never be a fit instructor in the method of providing our habitations with a cheerful and salutary warmth."

Which of the following non-fiction writers in which of his/her works has used the above lines?

(a) Richard Baxter, The Saints' Everlasting Rest
(b) John Locke, A Letter Concerning Toleration
(c) Edmund Burke, An Appeal from the New to the Old Whigs, in Consequence of Some Late Discussions in Parliament, Relative to the Reflections on the French Revolution. .
(d) Edward Gibbons, The Decline and Fall of the Roman Empire

125 "Independence is my happiness, and I view things as they are, without regard to place or person; my country is the world, and my religion is to do good."

Which of the following non-fiction writers in which of his/her works has used the above lines?

(a) Thomas paine, Rights of Man .
(b) David Hume, Essays on Suicide and the Immortality of the Soul
(c) Adam Smith, The Theory of Moral Sentiments
(d) William Hazlitt, Table-Talk, Essays on Men and Manners

126 "I know what I mean by the term I and myself; and I know this immediately, or intuitively, though I do not perceive it as I perceive a triangle, a colour, or a sound."

Which of the following non-fiction writers in which of his/her works has used the above lines?

(a) John Locke, An Essay Concerning Human Understanding
(b) Edmund Burke, The Works of the Right Honourable Edmund Burke, Vol. 01
(c) Thomas Paine, The American Crisis
(d) George Berkeley, Three Dialogues Between Hylas and Philonous .

127 "Beauty is no quality in things themselves: It exists merely in the mind which contemplates them; and each mind perceives a different beauty."

Which of the following non-fiction writers in which of his/her works has used the above lines?

(a) Thomas Paine, Common Sense
(b) David Hume, Of the Standard of Taste and Other Essays .
(c) Adam Smith, The Theory of Moral Sentiments
(d) William Hazlitt, On the Pleasure of Hating

128 "Generally speaking, the errors in religion are dangerous; those in philosophy only ridiculous."

Which of the following non-fiction writers in which of his/her works has used the above lines?

(a) Thomas Paine, A Letter Addressed to the Abbe Raynal on the Affairs of North America
(b) David Hume, A Treatise of Human Nature .
(c) Adam Smith, The Wealth of Nations
(d) William Hazlitt, The Round Table

129 "Never complain of that of which it is at all times in your power to rid yourself."

Which of the following non-fiction writers in which of his/her works has used the above lines?

(a) Thomas paine, Rights of Man
(b) David Hume, Essays on Suicide and the Immortality of the Soul
(c) Adam Smith, The Theory Of Moral Sentiments .
(d) William Hazlitt, Table-Talk, Essays on Men and Manners

130 "Love turns, with little indulgence, to indifference or disgust: hatred alone is immortal."

Which of the following non-fiction writers in which of his/her works has used the above lines?

(a) Thomas Paine, Common Sense
(b) David Hume, Of the Standard of Taste and Other Essays
(c) Adam Smith, The Theory of Moral Sentiments
(d) William Hazlitt, On the Pleasure of Hating

Directions (Q. Nos. 131-135) *Read the following passage carefully and answer the questions that follow.*

Titanic: The Maiden Journey

1. The titanic, in its watery grave, is a great museum of human history and is at risk of being lost forever because of curious voyagers and treasure hunters, fears Bob Ballard, who first discovered the remains of the iconic ship in 1985. Famous for discovering the great ship, Ballard is a former US Navy Officer and a professor of oceanography.
2. "Titanic is a museum of human history without door and guard. I am deeply concerned about not only the Titanic but all the ancient history that is now at risk. If we cannot save this iconic ship, then there is very little hope we can save ancient ships. The world should realize that you don't have to go down and take everything and you do not have to do a treasure hunt. This is a common heritage of all of us and if we really want to take steps to preserve human history in the ocean, we need to start with Titanic," Ballard said in a telephonic interview from London.
3. Ballard, as part of a tie-up, is presenting a documentary called 'Save the Titanic' on the 100th anniversary of the sinking of the great ship – 15th April, 1912. The ship and her fate continue to fascinate, largely because of the horror that took place that night, with 1,522 passengers and crew losing their lives.
4. Ballard says that despite being on the ocean floor for 100 years, the ship is full of human footprints. "You will find pairs of shoes everywhere. The sea and the life below has claimed everything but they do not know what to do with shoes so you will find a pair of mother's shoes next to her little daughter and that's their gravestone. At her wreckage, we almost felt that we were surrounded by the lifeboats of all the people that were in the water at that spot."
5. Ballard says that the fate of Titanic continues to fascinate so many years after it sank because it is 'irony personified in history'. "The story has all the ingredients to make it timelessly fascinating. You have this revolutionary ship that's unsinkable, and carrying a cross section of people in society. And then, it goes and hits an iceberg and sinks on its maiden journey. It's an irony personified in history."
6. Talking about his discovery, which came after great research and 75 years later, Ballard, says it was a somber moment went they first spotted the boiler of the Titanic. "In the 90s, advanced technology gave us double diving capabilities in the Atlantic Ocean. I knew that the Titanic was sitting at almost 12,000 feet. What led me to her discovery was a simple technique that I followed. We decided to look for the debris trail instead of the ship."
7. Ballard says the ship, if preserved well and not subjected to constant submarine journeys, will last for a long time on the Atlantic floor. "The deep sea, because of its darkness, its cold temperatures and its great pressure, creates a high state of preservation. With a little caution, we can protect the Titanic for future generations to visit."
8. Ballard has also connected to the people of Belfast, who refused to talk about the tragedy "The ship's construction took place at Belfast. After the tragedy, families of the workers refused to talk about it because of the shame and sadness in the loss of life involved."

131 The Titanic sank on
(a) its 100th anniversary
(b) 15th April 1912
(c) an iconic voyage in 1985
(d) leaving the port of Belfast

132 The Titanic continues to attract attention because
(a) it is irony personified in history
(b) its advanced technology gave double diving technologies
(c) it is a treasure hunt
(d) it is a common need

133 Ballard's documentary on the Titanic is titled
(a) museum of human history
(b) the Titanic
(c) save the Titanic
(d) 75 years later

134 Bob Ballard is a
(a) Former US Navy Officer
(b) A professor of oceanography
(c) Both (i) and (ii)
(d) None of the above

135 Which word in the passage means 'very solemn or serious'
(a) maiden
(b) fascinating
(c) heritage
(d) somber

PREVIOUS YEARS' QUESTIONS

December 2018

1 The term 'Digger' is associated with a group of argarian communists who flourished in England in 1649-50 and were led by
(a) Laurence Clarkson
(b) Gerrard Winstanley
(c) George Fox
(d) John Liburne

July 2018

2 Sir Thomas Browne's Urn Burial was prompted by
(a) The Discovery of ancient buial–urns near Norwich
(b) The Contemporary researches on burial rites in Norway
(c) The Death of St. Francis of Assissi and his burial
(d) The Publication of the English Book of Common Prayer

3 "The 18th century practice in 'England of book' selling was midway between direct patronage and impersonal sales. A patron paid half the cost of a book before publication and half on delivery. The author of the book received these payments directly. The patron's name appeared in the preface for the book published in this manner". This practice was known as
(a) subscription (b) contribution
(c) pre-publication (d) remaindering

4 Robert Burton's Anatomy of Melancholy was published in 1621 and expanded and altered in .... subsequent editions.
(a) two (b) four
(c) six (d) five

November 2017

5 Who/Which among the following gave the expression, "a leopard can't change its spot," to English language?
(a) The King James Bible
(b) Geoffrey Chaucer
(c) Shakespeare
(d) The Royal Society

6 The title of Sir Thomas Browne's famous treatise, *Religio Medici* means
(a) Religion of a Doctor
(b) Religion of Magician
(c) Religion of Divinity
(d) Religion of Meditation

7 Identify the correct chronological sequence of the founding of the following 18th century English periodicals.
(a) Tatler–Spectator–The Gentleman's Magazine–Rambler
(b) Speactator–Tatler–The Gentleman's Magazine–Rambler
(c) Rambler–Tatler–Spectator–The Gentleman's Magazine
(d) Tatler–Spectator–Rambler–The Gentleman's Magazine

January 2017

8 Match the author with the work.

	List I		List II
A.	John Locke	1.	A Short View of the Immorality and Profanity of the Stage
B.	William Dampier	2.	Two Treatises on Government
C.	Jeremy Collier	3.	A Short View of Tragedy
D.	Thomas Rhymer	4.	Voyages

Codes

	A	B	C	D		A	B	C	D
(a)	2	1	4	3	(b)	3	4	1	2
(c)	2	4	1	3	(d)	4	3	2	1

9 At the beginning of the Restoration period, there was a seismic shift in the social, political and religious attitudes of the English. Which of the following statement best describes that shift?
(a) England shifted from an aristocratic Catholic monarchy to a parliamentary democracy
(b) England shifted from an atheistic oligarchy to a desistic squirearchy
(c) England shifted form a Republican Puritan Commonwealth to an aristocratic Anglican monarchy
(d) England shifted from a parliamentary democracy to an aristocratic Catholic tyranny

December 2015

10 Who, among the following, advanced the theory that the mind is a tabula rasa at birth and acquires all ideas by experience?
(a) John Locke (b) John Wesley
(c) Isaac Watts (d) Denis Diderot

11 In John Dryden's Essay on Dramatic Poesy Neander defends the English invention of ....
(a) romantic comedy (b) action tragedy
(c) tragi-comedy (d) morality plays

12 In 1688, Dryden wrote *Of Dramaic Poesie:* An Essay which uses...... separate characters to dramatise the conflicting viewpoints which new theatrical activity had produced.

(a) three (b) two (c) four (d) six

13 A significant development in 1662 was the establishment of The Royal Society in England. The main purpose of the society was

(a) to set the rules for the royal court and governance
(b) to guide and promote the development of science and scientific exploration
(c) the set norms for civil society
(d) to promote theatre

14 Choose the right chronological sequence below.

(a) Victorian period, Jacobean period, Tudor period, Restoration Period.
(b) Edwardian period, Tudor period, Jacobean period, Victorian Period
(c) Tudor period, Jacobean period, Restoration period, Edwardian period
(d) Jacobean period, Tudor period, Restoration period, Edwardian period

15 In his 'Epistle to Dr Arbuthnot' Pope tells us that as poet he had benefited from "This saving counsel keep your piece nine years"-which enjoins on writer's patience and great care before they rush to print. Whose 'counsel' is Pope referring to?

(a) Longinus's in On the Sublime
(b) Horace's in Ars Poetica
(c) Quintillian's Institutio Oratoria
(d) Aristotle's Poetics

16 A famous challenge to the Neo-classical tenets of form and reason in aesthetic considerations came from Edmund Burke. His work was titled

(a) an enquiry into the philosophical origin of our ideas of the sublime and the beautiful
(b) philosophical enquiry into the origin of our ideas of the sublime and the beautiful
(c) an enquiry into the philosophical origin of our ideas of the beautiful and the sublime
(d) philosophical enquiry into our original ideas of the beautiful and the sublime

17 The Decline and Fall of the Roman Empire in six volumes was a great achievement by Edward Gibbon. It was published between 1776 and 1788, two significant dates that

(a) signalled the end of the Napoleonic wars and the rise of Feudalism
(b) signalled the American Revolution and the French Revolution
(c) covered the fall of peasantry and the rise of bureaucracy in England
(d) suggest the period of Queen Anne's reign

18 Identify the one erroneous statement on Neo-classicism listed below.

(a) Londovico Castelvetro and Torquato Tasso greatly influenced English writers like Milton and Dryden
(b) Neo-classicism took its final form during the reign of Louis XIV (1638-1715)
(c) Boilean's L'Art poetique influenced Pope's essay on criticism
(d) The English relation to Neo-classicism was one of dialogue. Most literally, this dialogue is effected in Addision's An Essay on Dramatic Poesy

19 The Tatler appeared thrice a week

(a) on Tuesday, Thursday and Saturday
(b) on Sunday, Tuesday and Thursday
(c) on Monday, Wednesday and Friday
(d) on Wednesday, Thursday and Friday

20 Which of the following works is not actually a prose essay?

(a) Essay of Dramatic Poesy
(b) Essay on Man
(c) An Essay Concerning Human Understanding
(d) An Essay Towards a New Theory of Vision

21 Joseph Addison called him 'The Miracle of the present age' and Alexander Pope wrote the epitaph for the monument erected in his memory. Who is he?

(a) John Locke (b) Isaac Newton
(c) Ashey Cooper (d) Christopher Wren

22 'The Decline and Fall of the Roman empire' by Edward Gibbon is significant work in volumes.

(a) 3 (b) 4
(c) 5 (d) 6

ANSWERS

Objective Questions

1. *(c)*	2. *(b)*	3. *(a)*	4. *(a)*	5. *(b)*	6. *(c)*	7. *(c)*	8. *(a)*	9. *(c)*	10. *(a)*
11. *(a)*	12. *(c)*	13. *(a)*	14. *(b)*	15. *(d)*	16. *(b)*	17. *(d)*	18. *(a)*	19. *(c)*	20. *(d)*
21. *(b)*	22. *(a)*	23. *(d)*	24. *(b)*	25. *(d)*	26. *(a)*	27. *(c)*	28. *(c)*	29. *(c)*	30. *(c)*
31. *(d)*	32. *(a)*	33. *(b)*	34. *(a)*	35. *(d)*	36. *(d)*	37. *(a)*	38. *(b)*	39. *(a)*	40. *(c)*
41. *(c)*	42. *(b)*	43. *(d)*	44. *(c)*	45. *(a)*	46. *(c)*	47. *(a)*	48. *(d)*	49. *(b)*	50. *(c)*
51. *(a)*	52. *(b)*	53. *(b)*	54. *(a)*	55. *(c)*	56. *(d)*	57. *(b)*	58. *(c)*	59. *(b)*	60. *(d)*
61. *(c)*	62. *(c)*	63. *(a)*	64. *(b)*	65. *(b)*	66. *(c)*	67. *(b)*	68. *(a)*	69. *(b)*	70. *(c)*
71. *(b)*	72. *(c)*	73. *(c)*	74. *(b)*	75. *(b)*	76. *(c)*	77. *(c)*	78. *(b)*	79. *(a)*	80. *(b)*
81. *(d)*	82. *(d)*	83. *(a)*	84. *(a)*	85. *(d)*	86. *(d)*	87. *(c)*	88. *(a)*	89. *(d)*	90. *(d)*
91. *(a)*	92. *(b)*	93. *(d)*	94. *(d)*	95. *(c)*	96. *(b)*	97. *(a)*	98. *(a)*	99. *(b)*	100. *(c)*
101. *(a)*	102. *(b)*	103. *(c)*	104. *(b)*	105. *(a)*	106. *(a)*	107. *(a)*	108. *(b)*	109. *(a)*	110. *(b)*
111. *(a)*	112. *(b)*	113. *(a)*	114. *(d)*	115. *(b)*	116. *(c)*	117. *(a)*	118. *(d)*	119. *(b)*	120. *(d)*
121. *(b)*	122. *(d)*	123. *(d)*	124. *(c)*	125. *(a)*	126. *(d)*	127. *(b)*	128. *(b)*	129. *(c)*	130. *(d)*
131. *(b)*	132. *(a)*	133. *(c)*	134. *(c)*	135. *(d)*					

Previous Years' Questions

1. *(b)*	2. *(a)*	3. *(a)*	4. *(d)*	5. *(a)*	6. *(a)*	7. *(a)*	8. *(c)*	9. *(c)*	10. *(a)*
11. *(c)*	12. *(c)*	13. *(b)*	14. *(c)*	15. *(b)*	16. *(b)*	17. *(b)*	18. *(d)*	19. *(a)*	20. *(b)*
21. *(b)*	22. *(d)*								

The Victorian and Modern Age Non-Fiction

This chapter refers to writers of non-fiction prose during Victorian and Modern age. The literary trends of Victorian and Modern period were to write treatise or thesis of size and essays of unusual length. The authors also wrote travel accounts, letters, lectures and autobiographies to talk about various socio-cultural issues.

In this Chapter

- *Non-Fiction in Victorian Age*
- *Non-Fiction Prose Writers of the Victorian Age*
- *Non-Fiction Prose in the Modern Age*
- *Non-Fiction Prose Writers of the Modern Age*

Non-Fiction in Victorian Age

Non-fiction in victorian age was unique in its own way and had great impact on the people and the society. Like the other forms of the literature of the Victorian age, namely poetry and novel, the Victorian prose was also inspired by the spirit of realism. While the prose of Romantic Movement was highly imaginative, written for the sole purpose of describing personal experiences, the Victorian prose was not meant for exploring the realms of imaginations alone, but for intellectual debate on contemporary problems of religion, philosophy, politics and arts.

Most of the great or distinguished prose published between the appearance of Macaulay's Essay on Milton in 1825 and the death of Queen Victoria in 1901 reflects the tumult of a very eventful period. More than in any previous era, English literary prose during those years was intimately related to life and thought. It mirrored the rise and fall and transformations of doctrines, ideals, political principles, religious conceptions, scientific theories and cultural change.

Merely to glance through the pages of Carlyle, Ruskin or Arnold is to meet the surge and thunder of conflicting ideas; everywhere there are allusions to the advance of science, the revival of Anglicanism, the growth of democracy, the rapid spread of industrialism, the developing faith in 'progress' and the 'march of mind'.

All the great writers of 'non-fiction' prose were directly or indirectly involved in these conflicting forces. Some of the writers were largely in tune with their age: Macaulay, Mill, Huxley, and Spencer. Others were sharply opposed to some of the most distinctive tendencies of the time: they were self-dedicated 'prophets' and social critics and each offered his own solution for the problems of his bewildered contemporaries.

Carlyle's solution was a religious transcendentalism founded on German literature and philosophy; Newman's answer was a turning to the dogmas of the Roman Catholic Church; Ruskin's early hope was in art, and later in social and economic doctrines derived to some extent from his master, Carlyle; Arnold's message was that of the harmonious and well-rounded culture of the individual and of society and finally, at the end of the century, Pater counselllled a retreat into the world of art and aesthetic sensibility.

Without continuing the list of writers who promoted or reacted against the main tendencies of the age, we can see that any true understanding of them requires some knowledge of the period which produced them. The effort to understand their economic, social, and intellectual background is not without its own rewards, for most of the problems which attacked the Victorians are with us still and many of their suggested solutions have relevance and vitality in our own day. What they wrote constitutes a fascinating chapter in the history of the English mind and also provides a perspective for viewing much that continues to perplex the world.

Above all, a survey of their beliefs and assumptions will illuminate the richness of their prose, a prose which is often highly allusive, sometimes deceptively simple, and always susceptible to fresh and profitable interpretation as the symbol of their thoughts, and the eloquent expression of their convictions.

Salient Features of Victorian Non-Fiction

Some of the important features of Victorian Non-Fiction are mentioned below

Realism

Coming down to the history of English Literature from the Romantic Age of Idealism to the Victorian era of Realism, one experiences the feeling of a return from solitude to society, from nature to industry, from concepts to issues, from spiritualism to pragmatism, from optimism to agnosticism, from lyricism to criticism and from organicism to compromise.

A large part of the complex of change that comes about in English Literature from early 19th century to the later 19th century can be measured from the kind of the change, the images of the ocean undergo when we move from Byron to Arnold. The movement of Realism is generally a minor movement in the later 19th century, which began in France and was later, followed by England.

Compromise

In terms of philosophical ideas, the Victorian period, unlike the earlier periods of literary history in England, was marked by conflicting movement carried on through crusades and counter-crusades, attacks and counter-attacks. The Victorian compromise was a combination of the positive and negative aspects of the Victorian Age.

Whereas, the Romantics could afford to withdraw from the town in the initial stages of the industrialisation, the Victorians, facing the flowering of the Industrial Revolution had no such soft option available to them. Therefore, rather than living in solitude, writers of the Victorian age had to cope with the process of change in which the old agrarian way of life had to make a place for the new individual civilisation.

Utilitarianism

Against the chain of thinkers, including Newman, Arnold, and Ruskin, who were essentially religious, was the formidable force of utilitarian thinkers, continued by JS Mill and agnostic scientists like Darwin, Spencer, Huxley, etc. Although utilitarianism was propounded by Jeremy Bentham, the philosophy came into operation during the Victorian era.

Both the state and the industry came under the heavy influence of this mechanical approach to matters of the human soul. The celebrated principle, "the greatest good for the greatest number" was the governing rule of the utilitarian thought on morals, laws, politics, and administrations.

Agnosticism

Agnosticism is defined as the belief, "that nothing is known or can be known of immaterial things, especially of existence or nature of God." The term 'agnostic' was coined by TH Huxley in 1869 AD. The realisation that God's existence is neither observable nor provable drove society into a state of uncertainty.

People of the Victorian era sought to explore and understand questions about the metaphysical world, but ultimately found no answers and were left in doubt. Agnosticism was a means of identifying the skepticism that stemmed from the inability to logically support the existence of the spiritual beings.

Comprehensive Composition

Like the Victorian novel, the Victorian prose compositions are unusually long. The prose writings of the period are either treatises or thesis of book size or essay of unusual length.

Un-organised Compositions

Like the Victorian novel, the compositions are not formally or even consciously organised, they are held together only by the argument contained therein, not by any formal design or pattern. Ruskin's *Unto This Last* and Mill's *Liberty* are strictly speaking not the works of literature.

However, since they advocate the humane view of life, as against the political, economic or biological, they are allied to literature. Besides, they are written in a language and style, which if not truly literary, approximates the style of literature.

The Victorian age refuses to come out neatly as a clearly marked, well-rounded historical epoch. We cannot apply to it any helpful phrase, like 'the Age of Reason', or 'the Great Awakening'.

This engaging, informative collection of Victorian non-fiction prose juxtaposes classic texts and established writers with more obscure writings and authors in order to illuminate important debates in nineteenth-century Britain–inviting modern readers to see the age anew. The collection represents the voices of a broad scope of women and men on a range of nineteenth-century cultural issues and in various forms—from periodical essays to travel accounts, letters to lectures, and autobiographies to social surveys. Victorian Prose reaches beyond the work of Carlyle, Newman, Mill, Arnold and Ruskin to uncover an array of lesser-known voices of the era. Women writers are given full attention—writings by Mary Prince, Dinah M. Craik, Florence Nightingale, Frances P. Cobbe and Lucie Duff Gordon are among the entries.

Non-Fiction Prose Writers of the Victorian Age

Major non-viction prose writers of the Victorian age are Thomas Carlyle, Thomas Macaulay, John Henry Newman, John Stuart Mill, James Anthony Froude, John Ruskin and Walter Pater. Their brief description is given below.

Thomas Carlyle (1795-1881)

Scottish philosopher, writer and essayist Thomas Carlyle was born in Galloway, Scotland in 1795. He was the eldest son of James Carlyle, a stonemason and Margaret Aitken, the daughter of a bankrupt Dumfriesshire farmer. Carlyle studied at Annan Grammar School and the University of Edinburgh. However, he left without a degree and became a mathematical tutor at Annan Academy in 1814.

In 1816, Carlyle obtained a teaching position at Kirkcaldy where he taught Latin, French, arithmetic, bookkeeping, geometry, navigation and geography. In November 1818, suffering from depression, Carlyle resigned and returned to Edinburgh. In 1823, Carlyle worked as a tutor to Charles and Arthur Buller. In 1826, Carlyle married the writer Jane Welsh.

Literary Career and Works

Carlyle's *Life of Schiller* (1825) first appeared in *London Magazine* in 1823-1824. From 1831-34, he published *Sartor Resartus* (The Tailor Re-Tailored). It was initially published as a series in *Fraser's Magazine*. Subtitled *The Life and Opinions of Herr Teufelsdrockh* ('Mr Devil's Dung', *Sartor Resartus* was published in book form in 1836 in the United States, with a preface by Ralph Waldo Emerson. It is about a fictional editor, who becomes fascinated with a German professor by the name of Professor Teufelsdrockh.

Carlyle's other important works are *The French Revolution* (which discusses the dangers and promise of revolution), *On Heroes, Hero-Worship and the Heroic in History* (stresses the importance of the individual in history, and compares several different kinds of heroes such as Odin, Oliver Cromwell, Napoleon, William Shakespeare, Dante, Samuel Johnson, Jean-Jacques Rousseau, Robert Burns, John Knox, Martin Luther and the Prophet Muhammad) and *Frederick the Great* (a biography of Fredrick the Great of Prussia).

Carlyle was offered the rectorship of Edinburgh University in 1865. He received the Prussian Order of Merit in 1874. Carlyle died on 5th February, 1881 in London, England.

Major Works

- Signs of the Times (1829)
- Sartor Resartus (1831-34)
- The French Revolution (1837)
- Charitism (1840)
- On Heroes and Hero Worship and the Heroic in History (1841)
- Past and Present (1843)
- The Life of John Sterling (1851)
- History of Friedrich II (1858)
- The early kings of Norway (1875)
- Reminiscences of my Irish Journey in 1849 (1882)

Thomas Macaulay (1800-1859)

British historian, essayist and politician Thomas Babington Macaulay was born in Leicestershire, England in 1800. He was the eldest child of Zachary Macaulay, a Scottish Highlander and Selina Zachary, a prominent anti-slavery campaigner. Macaulay was educated privately and at Cambridge, where he became a fellow.

He also studied law and was called to the bar in 1826. However, he did not like the profession and harboured political aspirations. He also became a regular contributor to the *Edinburgh Review*, a journal formed by Whig politician, Henry Brougham. In 1830, Macaulay entered Parliament as member for Calne in Wiltshire. He established his powers as an orator in the Reform Bill debates. He served as Secretary of War in 1839 and Postmaster-General in 1849.

Literary Career and Works

It was during the 1840s that Macaulay got the leisure time to devote himself to writing. His *Lays of Ancient Rome* appeared in 1842 and a collection of *Critical and Historical Essays* in 1843. His major work, *the History of England from the Accession of James II* , was published between 1848 and 1861.

Macaulay was made first Baron, Lord Macaulay of Rothley Temple in 1857. He retired to Holly Lodge, Westminster and died on 28th December, 1859.

John Henry Newman (1801-1890)

One of the important leaders of the Oxford Movement, John Henry Newman was both a Churchman and a scholar. He was born in London in 1801 to a London banker. He was brought up in the Anglican tradition. Newman received his education at Trinity College and Oriel College. He became a fellow and tutor of Oriel College, Oxford. He converted to Catholicism in 1845.

Literary Career and Works

Newman's first book, *The Arians of the Fourth Century* was published in 1832. He also published two novels of conversion, *Loss and Gain* (1848) and *Callista* (1855) and two volumes on ecumenical relations in England, *Lectures on Certain Difficulties felt by Anglicans in submitting to the Catholic Church* (1850) and *Lectures on the Present Position of Catholics in England* (1851).
Newman's most important work is his *Apologia pro Vita Sua* (1864; 'A Defense of His Life'). It was written in answer to the attack upon him by Charles Kingsley and contained an account of his religious life. In this work, Newman describes his gradual conversion to Roman Catholicism.

Newman's other works include *The Idea of University* (1852), a collection of the inaugural lectures for the Catholic University and other academic essays; *An Essay in Aid of a Grammar of Assent* (1870), a treatise on the philosophy of religion. His last major contribution to religious writing was the 1877 *Preface to the Prophetical Office*, now retitled *The Via Media*, in which he detailed the Church's three offices and their interrelations: the prophetic, exercised by theologians; the priestly, by laity; the governing, by Pope and magisterium.

Newman became first honorary fellow of Trinity College in 1878. Pope Leo XIII made him a cardinal in 1879. Newman died at the Oratory House in Edgbaston in 1890. He was beatified by Pope Benedict XVI in Birmingham, England on 19th September, 2010.

Major Works

- The Arians of the Fourth Century (1833)
- Tracts for the Times (1833–1841)
- British Critic (1836–1842)
- On the Prophetical Office of the Church (1837)
- Lectures on Justification (1838)
- Parochial and Plain Sermons (1834–1843)
- Select Treatises of St Athanasius (1842-1844)
- Lives of the English Saints (1843–1844)
- Essays on Miracles (1826, 1843)
- Oxford University Sermons (1843)
- Sermons on Subjects of the Day (1843)
- Essay on the Development of Christian Doctrine (1845)
- Retractation of Anti-Catholic Statements (1845)
- Loss and Gain (novel – 1848)
- Faith and Prejudice and Other Unpublished Sermons (1848–1873)
- Discourses to Mixed Congregations (1849)
- Difficulties of Anglicans (1850)
- The Present Position of Catholics in England (1851)
- The Idea of a University (1852)
- Cathedra Sempiterna (1852)
- Apologia Pro Vita Sua (religious autobiography – 1864)
- Letter to Dr Pusey (1865)
- The Dream of Gerontius (1865)
- An Essay in Aid of a Grammar of Assent (1870)
- Sermons Preached on Various Occasions (1874)
- Letter to the Duke of Norfolk (1875)
- Five Letters (1875)
- Sermon Notes (1849–1878)
- On the Inspiration of Scripture (1884)
- Development of Religious Error (1885)

John Stuart Mill (1806-1873)

English philosopher and economist John Stuart Mill was born in London in 1806. He was the eldest son of James Mill, a utilitarian and Harriet Barrow. John Mill was educated through a rigid system of discipline by his father, who wanted John to follow his own footsteps. He was sent to France to live with Samuel Bentham, the brother of Jeremy Bentham (founder of modern utilitarianism).

In 1823, Mill's father secured him a junior position in the East India Company. He gradually rose to the position of Chief Examiner. Mill suffered an attack of depression in 1826. He felt dissatisfied with his father's Benthamite system of education and believed that this had an adverse impact on his emotional development.

Literary Career and Works

Mill found a cure from this in Wordsworth's poetry. He immersed himself in the writings of a wide variety of thinkers such as John Ruskin, Auguste Comte and Alexis de Tocqueville and edited a new journal that he co-founded with his father and Charles Molesworth, the *London Review.*

In 1830, Mill met Harriet Taylor, who was already married. After the death of Harriet's husband, the two married in 1851. Harriet was of crucial significance to his intellectual and moral development. Mill became Member of Parliament from 1865 to 1868 and strongly advocated the cause of women's suffrage.

Mill's political and economic works include *A System of Logic* (1843), *Principles of Political Economy* (1848), *On Liberty* (1859), *Considerations on Representative Government* (1861) and *Utilitarianism* (1861). He is also known for his feminist essay, *The Subjection of Women*, in which he compares the legal status of women to the status of slaves and argues for equality in marriage and under the law. Mill died in Avignon on 6th May, 1873.

Major Works

- A system of Logic (1843)
- Essays on some Unsettled Questions of Political Economy (1844)
- Principles of Political Economy (1848)
- On Liberty (1859)
- A Few Words on Non-intervention (1859)
- Considerations on Representative Government (1861)
- Utilitarianism (1861)
- The Subjection of Women (1869)
- Autobiography of John Stuart Mill (1871)

James Anthony Froude (1818-1894)

English historian and novelist James Anthony Froude was born in Dartington, Devon in 1818. He was the son of Robert Hurrell Froude and his wife Margaret. Froude studied at Westminster and Oriel colleges, Oxford and was elected fellow of Exeter College, Oxford, in 1842. He joined the High Church movement at Oxford and helped John Henry Newman with his *Lives of the English Saints.*

Literary Career and Works

Froude intended to become a clergyman, but doubts about the doctrines of the Anglican church, published in his scandalous 1849 novel *The Nemesis of Faith,* drove him to abandon his religious career.

He turned to writing history, and his most important work, the twelve volume *History of England from the Fall of Wolsey to the Death of the Spanish Armada* established his repute as 'one of the greatest English prose writers of the 19th century'.

His semi-autobiographical work *Shadows of the Clouds*, was published in 1847 under the pseudonym Zeta. His other works include *The English in Ireland in the 18th Century* (1872-74), *The Life and Letters of Erasmus* (1894), *English Seamen in the 16th Century* (1895) and *Life of Carlyle* (1884).

Froude married Charlotte Grenfell, Charles Kingsley's sister-in-law and daughter of Pascoe Grenfell. The two moved first to Manchester and then to North Wales in 1850, where Froude lived happily, supported by his friends Arthur Hugh Clough and Matthew Arnold.

Froude was appointed regius professor of history at Oxford in 1892. He died on 20th October, 1894 at Kingsbridge, Devonshire.

Major Works

Fiction

- Shadows of the Clouds (1847)
- The Nemesis of Faith (1849)
- The Two Chiefs of Dunboy (1889)

Non-Fiction

- History of England from the Fall of Wolsey to the Defeat of the Spanish Armada (1856-70)
- Short Studies on Great Subjects (1867–82)
- The English in Ireland in the 18th Century (1872–74)
- Caesar: A Sketch (1879)
- Bunyan (1880)
- Thomas Carlyle (1882–84)

- Luther: A Short Biography (1883)
- Oceana, or, England and Her Colonies (1886)
- The English in the West Indies or The Bow of Ulysses (1888)
- Lord Beaconsfield (1890)
- The Divorce of Catherine of Aragon (1891)
- English Sea-Men in the 16th Century (1895)
- Life and Letters of Erasmus (1895)
- My Relations with Carlyle (1903)

John Ruskin (1819-1900)

English writer and critic John Ruskin was born in London in 1819. He was the only child of John James Ruskin, a wine importer and Margaret Cock. Ruskin studied at King's College, London and Christ Church, Oxford University. At Oxford, he won the Newdigate Prize for his poetry.

Literary Career and Works

Ruskin wrote essays and treatises, poetry and lectures, travel guides and manuals, letters and even a fairy tale. Ruskin developed a great passion for the work of J MW Turner. His first major work, *Modern Painters* was written in defence of Turner after reviewers of the annual Royal Academy exhibition savagely treated Turner's works. Ruskin, in this work, claimed that modern landscape painters and especially J MW Turner were far superior to the *Old Masters* of the post-Renaissance period, including Gaspar Poussin, Claude Lorrain, Salvator Rosa and even Michelangelo, whom he depicted as a corrupting influence on art. It was in the Modern Painters that Ruskin coined the term 'pathetic fallacy'.

In *The Seven Lamps of Architecture* (1849) and *The Stones of Venice* (1851), Ruskin treated the fundamentals of architecture. In works such as *Unto the Last* (1862), *Essays on Political Economy* (1862) and *Time and Tide* (1867), Ruskin argued against competition and self-interest and advocated a form of Christian Socialism.

In 1848, Ruskin married Effie Gray and dedicated his novel *The King of the Golden River* to her. However, they later separated in 1854. He fell in love again with Rose la Touche. But after she died, he suffered an attack of mental illness. Despite several bouts of mental illness, Ruskin was able to complete *The Art of England* in 1884. This was followed by *The Storm Cloud of the 19th Century* (1885). He also began work on his autobiography, *Præterita: Outlines of Scenes and Thoughts Perhaps Worthy of Memory in My Past Life.*

Ruskin established the School of Art in Sidney Street, Cambridge, which later became known as Anglia Ruskin University in 1885. He became the first Slade Professor of Fine Arts in 1869 at the Working Men's College, London.

Ruskin spent the last years of his life at a house named Brantwood, located on the shores of Coniston Water, in the Lake District of England. He died of influenza on 20th January, 1900.

Major Works

- Poems (1835–1846)
- The Poetry of Architecture: Cottage, Villa etc. (1837–1838)
- The King of the Golden River, or The Black Brothers (1841)
- Modern Painters (Volumes 1- 9)(1853-1860)
- Review of Lord Lindsay's "Sketches of the History of Christian Art" (1847)
- The Seven Lamps of Architecture (1849)
- Letters to the Times in Defense of Hunt and Millais (1851)
- Architecture and Painting (1854)
- The Elements of Drawing, in Three Letters to Beginners (1857)
- Unto This Last: Four Essays on the First Principles of Political Economy (1860)
- The Flamboyant Architecture of the Somme (1869)
- The Queen of the Air: Being a Study of the Greek Myths of Cloud and Storm (1869)
- Verona and its Rivers (1870)
- Fors Clavigera: Letters to the Workmen and Labourers of Great Britain(Volumes 1- 4)(1871-80)
- Love's Meinie (1873)
- Review of Paintings by James McNeill Whistler (1878)
- Bible of Amiens (1885)
- Proserpina: Studies of Wayside Flowers while the Air was Yet Pure among the Alps and in the Scotland and England, Which My Father Knew (1886)
- Praeterita: Outlines of Scenes and Thoughts Perhaps Worthy of Memory in My Past Life (1885–1889)

Walter Pater (1839-1894)

English essayist and critic Walter Pater was born in London in 1839. He was the son of Richard Glode Pater, (a surgeon) and Maria Hill. Pater's father died when he was only two and his mother died when he was fourteen. His early life was overshadowed by the sudden premature deaths of his parents.

Pater attended King's School in Canterbury and graduated with a BA degree from Queen's College, Oxford. He was elected to a fellowship at Brasenose College and completed his masters there in 1865. At Brasenose, Pater came into contact with Gerard Brown, later to become the first chair of fine arts in the British Isles.

Literary Career and Works

Pater's most significant work, *The Renaissance: Studies in Art and Poetry* was a series of critical essays first published together as a volume in 1873. In this work, Pater defined the role of aesthete to "Distinguish, to analyse, separate from its adjuncts, the virtue by which a (work of art) produce(s)this special impression of beauty or pleasure, to indicate what the source of that impression is and under what conditions it is experienced." His advocacy for Art for Art's sake became a cardinal doctrine of the movement known as 'Aestheticism'.

Oscar Wilde termed *The Renaissance* as his 'golden book,' promoting Pater's works and reputation with his own career. Pater therefore became associated in the public's mind with the aesthetic school and the lives of other decadents, including the poet Algernon Swinburne and Dante Gabrielle Rossetti.

Pater's only novel, *Marius the Epicurean,* was published in 1885. His other works include *Imaginary Portraits* (1887), *Appreciations: With an Essay on Style* (1889) and *Plato and Platonism* (1893).

In 1883, Pater resigned from his post at Brasenose and in 1885 he moved with his sisters to 12 Earl's Terrace Kensington, London, though he lived at Oxford during the academic term. In 1893, he moved back to Oxford, where he lived at 64 S Giles until his death. Pater died at Oxford after a brief illness, on 30th July, 1894.

Major Works

- Coleridge's Writings (1866)
- Notes on Leanardo da Vinci (1869)
- Studies in The History of the Renaissance (1873)
- The Renaissance: Studies in Art and Poetry (Revised edition of the previous Studies, 1877)
- The School of Giorgione (1877)
- Marius the Epicurean (1885)
- Imaginary Portraits (1887)
- Appreciations: With an Essay on Style (1889)
- Plato and Platonism (1893)
- Greek Studies: A series of Essays (1895)

Non-Fiction Prose in the Modern Age

In the modern age, the category of non-fictional prose that probably ranks as the most important, both in the quantity and in the quality of its practitioners is the essay. Journalism, philosophy and politics also formed part of non-fiction prose of the modern age.

Non-fiction prose of the modern age has no other special and specific features unlike the Victorian non-fiction prose. In fact, characteristics of the fictional prose of the modern age apply to non-fiction prose as well.

The major non-fiction writers who made a mark during the modern age are Alfred G. Gardiner, E.V. Lucas, Hilaire Belloc, Max Beerbohm, Gilbert Keith Chesterton, Robert Wilson Lynd, Aldous Leonard Huxley, George Orwell and Graham Greene.

Non-Fiction Prose Writers of the Modern Age

Alfred George Gardiner (1865-1946)

Gardiner was born in Chelmsford, the son of Henry James Gardiner, a cabinet-maker and alcoholic, and his wife, Susanna Taylor. As a boy he worked at the Chelmsford Chronicle and the Bournemouth Directory. He joined the Northern Daily Telegraph in 1887 which had been founded the year before by Thomas Purvis Ritzema. In 1899, he was appointed editor of the Blackburn Weekly Telegraph.

Literary Career and Works

Editor of the Daily News: In 1902 Ritzema was named general manager of the Daily News. Needing an editor, he turned to his young protégé to fill the role. The choice soon proved a great success; under Gardiner's direction, it became one of the leading liberal journals, as he improved its coverage of both the news and literary matters while crusading against social injustices. Yet while circulation rose from 80,000 when he joined the paper to 151,000 in 1907 and 400,000 with the introduction of a Manchester edition in 1909, the paper continued to run at a loss.

Though close to the owner of the Daily News, George Cadbury, Gardiner resigned in 1919 over a disagreement with him over Gardiner's opposition to David Lloyd George.

From 1915 he contributed to The Star under the pseudonym Alpha of the Plough. At the time The Star had several anonymous essayists whose pseudonyms were the names of stars. Invited to choose the name of a star as a pseudonym he chose the name of the brightest (alpha) star in the constellation "the Plough." His essays are uniformly elegant, graceful and humorous.

His uniqueness lay in his ability to teach the basic truths of life in an easy and amusing manner. 'Pillars of Society', 'Pebbles on the Shore', 'Many Furrows' and 'Leaves in the Wind' are some of his best known writings.

Major Works

- Prophets, Priests and Kings (1908)
- Pillars of Society (1913)
- The War Lords (1915)
- Pebbles on the Shore (1916)
- Windfalls (as "Alpha of the Plough") (1920)
- Leaves in the Wind (as "Alpha of the Plough") (1920)
- The Anglo-American Future (1920)
- What I saw in Germany: letters from Germany and Austria (1920)
- Life of George Cadbury (1923)
- The Life of Sir William Harcourt (2 vols.) (1923)
- Many Furrows (as "Alpha of the Plough") (1924)
- John Benn and the Progressive Movement (1925)
- Portraits and Portents (1926)
- Certain People of Importance (as "Alpha of the Plough") (1929)

EV Lucas
(Edward Verrall Lucas) (1868–1938)

British journalist, essayist, travel writer and novelist was born in Eltham, Kent. He received an irregular education before starting work at a bookshop in Brighton where he began to read widely.

Literary Career and Works

After working as a journalist in Sussex and London, he joined the staff of Punch, of which he became assistant editor. *The Open Road* (1899) was followed by well over a hundred titles. His travel writings are principally represented by his *A Wanderer In* ... series, which covered *London* (1904), *Holland* (1905), *Paris* (1909), *Florence* (1912), and other towns and countries in Britain and Europe. His light and urbanely fluent style, which he claimed to have developed by translating Maupassant, was adequate to essays on a remarkable range of subjects; collections of such pieces include *Listener's Lure* (1905), *Old Lamps for New* (1911), and *A Rover I Would Be* (1928). He also published introductory studies of painters, among which are *Vermeer of Delft* (1922) and *John Constable the Painter* (1924). *Over Bemerton's* (1908), the most notable of his numerous novels, draws on his experience of the book trade. He produced the standard edition of The Works of Charles Lamb and Mary Lamb (7 volumes, 1903–5) and wrote the authoritative life of *Charles Lamb* (2 volumes, 1905). *Reading, Writing, and Remembering* (1932) is an autobiography.

Joseph-Hilaire-Pierre-René Belloc, Hilair Belloc (1870-1953)

French-born poet, historian, and essayist who was among the most versatile English writers of the first quarter of the 20th century. He is most remembered for his light verse, particularly for children, and for the lucidity and easy grace of his essays, which could be delightfully about nothing or decisively about some of the key controversies of the Edwardian era.

Belloc was educated at the Oratory School, Birmingham, and then worked as a journalist. After military service, as a French citizen, he entered Balliol College, Oxford, in 1894. He graduated with first-class honours in history, was president of the Union (debating society), and in 1896 married Elodie Hogan (1870–1914) of Napa, Calif. He became a naturalised British subject in 1902 and sat as a member of Parliament for Salford (1906–10), first as a Liberal and then as an Independent.

Literary Career and Works

Verses and Sonnets (1895) and *The Bad Child's Book of Beasts* (1896) launched Belloc on his literary career. *Cautionary Tales*, another book of humorous verse for children, which parodied some Victorian pomposities, appeared in 1907. His *Danton* (1899) and *Robespierre* (1901) proved his lively historical sense and powerful prose style. *Lambkin's Remains* (1900) and *Mr. Burden* (1904) showed his mastery of satire and irony. In *The Path to Rome* (1902) he interspersed his account of a pilgrimage on foot from Toul to Rome with comments on the nature and history of Europe. Born and brought up a Roman Catholic, he showed in almost everything he wrote as an ardent profession of his faith. This coloured with occasional inaccuracy and overemphasis most of his historical writing, which includes *Europe and the Faith* (1920), *History of England*, 4 vol. (1925–31), and a series of biographies ranging in period from *James II* (1928) to *Wolsey* (1930). But he had the power of bringing history to life.

The Four Men (1912) described a walk through Sussex, the county where he made his home, and his love of sailing was vividly illustrated in *The Cruise of the Nona* (1925). In political and economic matters Belloc was a follower of William Cobbett, English author, journalist, and radical influential in the early 19th century. Among Belloc's volumes of lighter verse are *The Modern Traveller* (1898) and the heroic poem in *Praise of Wine* (1932). He also wrote a number of satiric novels, which were illustrated by his close friend, the novelist GK Chesterton.

Belloc engaged in much heated controversy, particularly with HG Wells, whose *Outline of History* he vigorously attacked and with the protestant scholar and historian GC Coulton. Belloc is one of the masters of modern English prose, a good poet and a deeply interesting literary personality.

Max Beerbohm (1872-1956)

English essayist, parodist and caricaturist, Henry Maximilian (Max) Beerbohm was born in London on 24th August, 1872. He was educated at Charterhouse School and Merton College, Oxford. It was at Oxford that Beerbohm became acquainted with Oscar Wilde and became part of the Wilde circle. He even submitted an article on Oscar Wilde to the *Anglo-American Times* under the pen name 'An American' in 1893.

Literary Career and Works

In 1894, the first of Beerbohm's essays, *A Defence of Cosmetics* appeared in *The Yellow Book*. This essay analysed the increase in the use of make-up products and critiqued the use of artifice by women. According to Beerbohm, 'artifice' had become 'the strength of the world' and the 'kingdom' of 'rouge' reigned. In 1896, his first book, *The Works of Max Beerbohm*, was published.. Beerbohm's best known works include *A Christmas Garland* (1912), a parody of literary styles, *Seven Men* (1919), in which he pays homage to the wonderfully eccentric character of a bygone age and *Zuleika Dobson*(1911), his only novel and a satire on undergraduate life in Edwardian Oxford. Beerbohm played the part of a satiric chronicler of his age and received the knighthood in 1939. He died in Rapallo, Italy at the age of 83.

Major Works

- The Works of Max Beerbohm (1896)
- The Happy Hypocrite (1897)
- Zuleika Dobson; or, An Oxford Love Story (1911)
- A Christmas Garland, Woven by Max Beerbohm (1912)
- Seven Men (1919)
- A Peep into the Past (1923)
- Lytton Strachey (1943)
- Mainly on the Air (1946)
- A Peep into the Past and Other Prose Pieces (1972)
- Max Beerbohm and 'The Mirror of the Past' (1982)
- Caricatures of Twenty-five Gentlemen (1896)
- The Poets' Corner (1904)
- Fifty Caricatures (1913)
- A Survey (1921)
- Rossetti and His Circle (1922)
- **Enoch Soames** A Critical Heritage (1997)

GK Chesterton or Gilbert Keith Chesterton (1874-1936)

English novelist, essayist and journalist GK Chesterton was born in London into a middle-class family on 29th May, 1874. He was educated at St Paul's School, before studying art at the Slade School.

Literary Career and Works

After his education, he began working for the London publisher, Redway. Chesterton also worked as a columnist for the *Daily News*, *The Illustrated London News* and his own paper founded in 1925, *GK's Weekly*.

Chesterton wrote a variety of prose. First his social criticism, which was gathered in the work The Defendant (1901), Twelve Types (1902) and Heretics (1905), In it he expressed his proper views in the South African was his second preoccupation was literary criticism. Appreciation and criticism of the works of Charles Dickens (1911) and his prefaces to the individual novels, is among his finest contributions to criticism. This George Bernard Shaw (1909), The Victorian Age in Literature (1913) William Blake (1910) and later monographs William Cobbett 1925 and R.L. Stevenson (1927) have a spontaneity that places him above the works of many academy critics. Chesterton's third major concern was theology and religious agreement. His essays show us his shewed paradoxical irreverence to its ultimate point of real seriousness. He is seen at his best and happiest in such essays as 'On Running After one's Hat' (1908) and "A Defence of Nonsense" (1901) Biographers have identified him as a successor to such victorian authors as Mathew Arnold, Thomas Carlyle, Cardinal John, Henry New Man and John Ruskin. He wrote around 80 looks, several hundred poems, 200 short stories, 4000 essays and several plays. Chesterton died on 14th June, 1936 note

Major Works

- The Wild Knight and Other Poems (1900)
- The Defendant (1901)
- Thomas Carlyle (1902)
- Robert Browning (1903)
- The Club of Queer Trades (1905)
- Heretics (1905)
- Orthodoxy (1908)

Robert Wilson Lynd (1879–1949)

Robert Lynd, an accomplished Irish literary and political essayist, was born in Belfast on 20th April, 1879, the son of Robert John and Sarah Rentoul Lynd, and was educated at the Belfast Academical Institute and at Queen's College. His father was a Presbyterian minister and descendant of a line of ministers, and there were also divines on his mother's side. According to Desmond MacCarthy, his lifelong friend and fellow journalist, there was a family tradition that Lynd's great-grandfather emigrated from Scotland to Ireland because his congregation objected to the lavish display of silver buckle on his shoes. Lynd's father's family also farmed and some of Lynd's more personal essays refer to boyhood days on the farm tending the livestock.

Lynd died in Hampstead in 1949. He is buried in Belfast City Cemetery.

Literary Career and Works

He began as a journalist on The Northern Whig in Belfast. He moved to London in 1901, via Manchester, sharing accommodation with his friend the artist Paul Henry. Firstly he wrote drama criticism, for Today, edited by Jerome K Jerome. He also wrote for the Daily News (later the News Chronicle), being its literary editor 1912-47.

The Lynds were literary hosts, in the group including JB Priestley. They were on good terms also with Hugh Walpole Priestley, Walpole and Sylvia Lynd were founding committee members of the Book Society. Irish guests included James Joyce and James Stephens. On one occasion reported by Victor Gollancz in Reminiscences of Affection, p. 90, Joyce intoned Anna Livia Plurabelle to his own piano accompaniment. He used the pseudonym YY (Ys, or wise) in writing for the New Statesman. According to CH Rolph's Kingsley (1973), Lynd's weekly essay, which ran from 1913-45, was 'irreplaceable'. In 1941, editor Kingsley Martin decided to alternate it with pieces by James Bridie on Ireland, but the experiment was not at all a success.

Political Activism

Lynd's political views were radicalised by his experience of how Ulster and Home Rule developed in the 1912-1914 period. He was appalled at the threat of the use of violence to deliver Ulster from Home Rule and the later decision to postpone the implementation of the Third Home Rule Bill. He later wrote, "Then came August 1914 and England began a war for the freedom of small nations by postponing the freedom of the only small nation in Europe which it was within her power to liberate with the stroke of a pen'. He became a fluent Irish speaker, and Gaelic League member. As a Sinn Féin activist, he used the name Robiard Ó Flionn/Roibeard Ua Flionn.

Major Works

- The Mantle Of The Emperor (1906) with Ladbroke Black
- Irish and English (1908)
- Home Life in Ireland (1909)
- Rambles in Ireland (1912)
- The Book of This and That (1915)
- If the Germans Conquered England (1917)
- Old and New Masters (1919)
- Ireland a Nation (1919)
- The Art of Letters (1920)
- The Passion of Labour (1920) New Statesman articles
- The Pleasures of Ignorance (1921)
- Solomon in All His Glory (1922)
- The Sporting Life and Other Trifles (1922)
- Books and Authors (1922)
- The Blue Lion (1923)
- Selected Essays (1923)
- The Peal of Bells (1924)
- The Money Box (1925)
- The Orange Tree (1926)
- The Little Angel (1926)
- Dr. Johnson and Company (1927)
- The Goldfish (1927)
- The Silver Books of English Sonnets (1927) editor
- The Green Man (1928)
- It's a Fine World (1930)
- Rain, Rain, Go to Spain (1931)
- Great Love Stories of All Nations (1932) editor
- "Y.Y." An Anthology of Essays (1933)
- The Cockleshell (1933)
- Both Sides of the Road (1934)
- I Tremble to Think (1936)
- In Defence of Pink (1937)
- Searchlights and Nightingales (1939)
- An Anthology of Modern Poetry (1939) editor
- Life's Little Oddities (1941) illustrated by Steven Spurrier
- Further Essays of Robert Lynd (1942)
- Things One Hears (1945) illustrated by Claire Oldham
- Essays on Life and Literature (1951)
- Books and Writers (1952)
- Essays by Robert Lynd (1959)
- Galway of the Races – Selected Essays (1990) edited by Sean McMahon
- Without Glasses -abridged

Aldous Leonard Huxley (1894-1963)

English novelist and essayist Aldous Huxley, was born on 26th July, 1894, at Laleham in Godalming, Surrey, England. He belonged to a distinguished scientific family. He was the grandson of the famous zoologist Thomas Henry Huxley, also known as Darwin's Bulldog' for his advocacy of Charles Darwin's theory of evolution. Like his renowned ancestors, Aldous Huxley intended to become a scientist. However, an attack of *keratitis punctata* at the age of 16 rendered him totally blind for a period of 18 months. Later, he recovered partially and started using special glasses. It was after this that he turned to literature, unable to pursue his chosen career because of his eye ailment.

Literary Career and Works

Huxley was the editor of the magazine *Oxford Poetry*. His first collection of poetry came out in 1916. His first novel *Crome Fellow* (1921) satirised the fads and fashions of the time. Huxley's early comic novels, *Antic Hay Crome yellon* (1923), *Those Barren Leaves* (1925), and *Point Counter Point* (1928), demonstrate his ability to dramatise intellectual debate in fiction. His most popular work is his dystopian novel *Brave New World* published in 1932. The title of this novel derives from Miranda's speech in William Shakespeare's *The Tempest*. Set in London of AD 2540, this novel depicts a world in which a totalitarian government controlled society by the use of science and technology.

Later in his life, Huxley started to experiment with hallucinogenic drugs such as LSD and mescaline. In 1954, he also published an important study of consciousness expansion through mescaline, *The Doors of Perception.*

Huxley also wrote and edited non-fiction works on pacifist issues, including "Ends And Means", An Encyclopaedia of Pacifism' and Pacifism and Philosophy. Beginning in 1939 till his death in 1963, Huxley had an extensive association with the Vedanta Society of Southern California, founded and headed by Swami Prabhavananda. In 1944 Huxley wrote the introduction to the 'Bhagvad Gita'; The song of God translated by Swami Prabhavananda, and Christopher Isherwood, which was published by the vedanta society of Southern Colifornia.

Huxley died on 22nd November, 1963 in Los Angles.

Major Works

Essay Collections

- On the Margin (1923)
- Music at Night (1931)
- Ends and Means (1937)
- The Art of Seeing (1942)
- The Perennial Philosophy (1945)
- Science, Liberty and Peace (1946)
- Heaven and Hell (1956)
- Brave New World Revisited (1958)
- Literature and Science (1963)
- Moksha Writings on Psychedelics and the Visionary Experience 1931-63 (1977)

George Orwell (1903-1950)

George Orwell was born as Eric Arthur Blair in Motihari, Bihar, India. Orwell's father worked for the Opium Department of the Civil Service in Motihari. His mother took him to England when he was only one. Orwell received his education at Eton College, England, After his studies, he began work as an imperial policeman in Burma. However, his tryst with British imperialism and his disgust for it, prompted him to resign from the post and return to England in 1928.

Literary Career and Works

He was mainly a novelist but he had written some important non-fictional prose works as well. During his career orwell was best known for his journalism, essays, reviews, columns in newspaper etc.

Orwell's first work, *Down and Out in Paris and London* (1933) was a non-fictional memoir on the theme of poverty that he had experienced in these two cities after leaving Burma.

Major Works

- Down and Out in Paris and London (1933)
- The Road to Wigan Pier (1937)
- Homage to Catalonia (1938)

EXAM BASED QUESTIONS

1 Which work is about a fictional editor, who becomes fascinated with a German professor by the name of professor Teufelsdrockh?
(a) Sartor Resartus
(b) The Life of John Sterling
(c) History of Friedrich II
(d) Past and Present

2 Who, in which of his works, stresses the importance of the individual in history?
(a) Thomas Macaulay, Critical and Historical Essays
(b) JS Mill, 'On Liberty'
(c) Thomas Carlyle, On Heroes and Hero Worship and the Heroic in History
(d) Walter Pater : The Renaissance

3 Which Victorian prose writer received the Prussian order of merit in 1874?
(a) John Henry Newman (b) Thomas Carlyle
(c) James Anthony Froude (d) John Ruskin

4 Who among the following, was a regular contributor to the Edinburgh Review, a journal?
(a) Thomas Carlyle (b) Thomas Macaulay
(c) JS Mill (d) Walter Pater

5 By whom was the journal 'Edinburgh Review' founded?
(a) Thomas Carlyle (b) Thomas Macaulay
(c) John Henry Newman (d) Henry Brougham

6 Which of these is considered to be the most important work of John Henry Newman?
(a) The Ariens of the Fourth Century
(b) Loss and Gain
(c) Apologia Pro Vita Sua
(d) Sermon Notes

7 Which of these works of John Henry Newman was retitled 'The Via Media'?
(a) Preface to the Prophetical Office
(b) Callista
(c) The Idea of A University
(d) Apologia Pro Vita Sua

8 Which of the following Victorian prose writers composed 'The Dream of Gerontius'?
(a) Walter Pater (b) John Henry Newman
(c) Thomas Macaulay (d) James Anthony Froude

9 John Stuart Mill was undeniably influenced by his philosopher father, who treated his young son as an educational experiment, providing him with a broad and deep knowledge of a variety of intellectual topics. What was the name of Mill's father?
(a) James Mill (b) Christopher Mill
(c) Anthony Mill (d) Mark Mill

10 John Stuart Mill came to emulate his father by rising to the position of Chief Examiner in this trading company. Which company was this?
(a) The East India Company
(b) The Virginia Company
(c) The Barbary Company
(d) The London Company

11 The education of John Stuart Mill continued when he was sent to France at the age of 14. This constant study eventually led to a long bout of depression when Mill turned 20, but this was lifted as Mill began to socialise with other young thinkers such as Gustave D'Eichtahl and John Sterling. What other joy is described as being responsible for lifting Mill's depression?
(a) The novels of Charles Dickens
(b) Opium
(c) The poetry of Wordsworth
(d) The music of Mozart

12 In his early twenties, John Stuart Mill was introduced to the woman who could become the love of his life and whom he later married. What was this woman's name?
(a) Simone de Beauvoir
(b) Catherine Thomson
(c) Harriet Taylor
(d) Florence Nightingale

13 Mill rejected the view of philosophers such as Immanuel Kant that there was reality outside of what we could detect using our senses. This aligned him with David Hume and John Locke in this philosophical school of thought. Which school was this?
(a) Stoicism (b) Empiricism
(c) Pragmatism (d) Idealism

14 John Stuart Mill believed in this concept, which holds that the best action to take in any circumstance is that which yields the greatest pleasure for all involved. Which concept, formulated by Jeremy Bentham, is this?
(a) Skepticism (b) Idealism
(c) Pragmatism (d) Utilitarianism

15 John Stuart Mill was a liberal and believed that an individual could do whatever he pleased as long as it did not harm others. In what famous work did Mill outline his liberal beliefs?
(a) The Conscious Mind
(b) Freedom and Resentment
(c) On Liberty
(d) Being and Nothingness

16 Which subject, on which he published an article in 1869, was John Stuart Mill an early supporter of?
(a) Feminism (b) Racial segregation
(c) Marxism (d) Arctic exploration

17 In his 'A System of Logic', John Stuart Mill laid out how logic could (and should) be used to analyse information to come to the most reasonable conclusion. What term is used for this type of reasoning, in which evidence supports the truth of a statement, but does not ensure it?
(a) Definitive reasoning (b) Inductive reasoning
(c) Reductive reasoning (d) Educated guessing

18 John Stuart Mill writes that society can punish people's behaviour when
(a) it contradicts the will of the majority
(b) it undermines social cohesion
(c) it harms other people
(d) All of the above

19 According to John Stuart Mill, education should be
(a) mandated by the state
(b) determined by the wishes of the parent
(c) determined by the wishes of the child
(d) determined by majority opinion

20 If James disagrees with Jessica's private spending habits, JS Mill would say he should
(a) try to pass a law banning that behaviour
(b) ostracize Jessica from all social fuctions
(c) try to prevent her from continuing those habits
(d) none of the above

21 John Stuart Mill tries to justify individual liberty through
(a) showing that it is socially beneficial
(b) showing that it is required by the social contract
(c) showing that it is commanded by God
(d) none of the above

22 A utilitarian is someone who
(a) believes that rights are derived from natural law
(b) ignores the consequences of actions in determining their morality
(c) judges goodness based on whether something promotes social good
(d) says that reason compels people to accept certain universal maxism

23 Liberty is defined by JS Mill in the first chapter of 'On Liberty' as
(a) freedom from captivity
(b) the power to do whatever one wants
(c) a question of whether free will really exists
(d) the nature and limits of the authority society can have over the individual

24 Mill defends freedom of opinion for all of the following reasons except
(a) the popular opinion could be wrong
(b) both opinions might be partly true
(c) debating one's opinions is the only way to really understand them
(d) natural law requires that opinions be seen as sacred

25 John Stuart Mill's requirements for the protection of liberty apply to
(a) Children
(b) Barbarians
(c) Women
(d) None of the above

26 'Unto this Last' is the work of
(a) Elizabeth Barrett Browning
(b) Arthur Hugh Clough
(c) John Ruskin
(d) Charles Dickens

27 Ruskin's ideal social system would include
(a) no capitalist government whatsoever
(b) a government that fosters cooperation, not competition
(c) traditional political structures that have stood the test of time
(d) laborers that constantly offer the best deals on their products to get more work

28 What is Ruskin's primary critique of typical capitalist economies?
(a) Socialism is just more fair
(b) Capitalist art is not good
(c) Capitalist competition produces inferior products/ workers and makes laborers feel alienated
(d) With a rich/poor class division, power becomes too unbalanced

29 According to John Ruskin, why should an artist not work in the studio?
(a) Art that is honest to life is more divine
(b) Truth and beauty are found in nature
(c) It's too mechanical
(d) All of these a, b, c

30 Which of these is the most clear indicator of Romantic influence on Ruskin's thought?
(a) His love of poetry
(b) His love life
(c) His enjoyment of nature and natural drawings
(d) His concept of the role of an artist

31 What caused Ruskin's interest in socio-economic justice?
(a) Studying poor people for one of his books in 1856
(b) A crisis of faith in 1858
(c) The affluence he had growing up
(d) All of these played a part in his developing thoughts on the matter

32 About what subject is John Ruskin's 'The Stones of Venice'?
(a) Architecture
(b) Art criticism
(c) European history
(d) Writing

33 Which of the following is not a style of architecture that John Ruskin considers in 'The Stones of Venice'?
(a) Byzantine (b) Gothic
(c) Renaissance (d) Modernist

34 In 'The Stones of Venice', John Ruskin argues for the superiority of what architectural style?
(a) Byzantine
(b) Gothic
(c) Renaissance
(d) None of the answers are correct

35 What sentiment best expresses what Thomas Carlyle mean by "close the Byron; open thy Goethe"?
(a) Compared to Goethe, Byron didn't write enough about literacy and education
(b) Byron's works are better used as doorstops than as instructive literature
(c) Unlike Byron, Goethe wrote literature that can serve as salutary moral instruction and enlightened, historically self-conscious thinking
(d) In this text, a carefully veiled critique of the monarchy, Byron and Goethe stand in symbolically for Queen Victoria and Charles Darwin respectively

36 What does the phrase 'White Man's Burden', coined by Kipling, refer to?
(a) The British subject's manifest destiny to colonise the world
(b) The distinctly moral responsibility of the British to colonise the world and educate its people
(c) The British need to improve technology and transportation in other parts of the world
(d) The importance of solving economic and social problems in England before tackling the world's problems

37 Which of the following best defines Utilitarianism?
(a) A farming technique aimed at maximizing productivity with the fewest tools
(b) A moral arithmetic, which states that all humans aim to maximise the greatest pleasure to the greatest number
(c) A critical methodology stating that all words have a single meaningful function within a given piece of literature
(d) A philosophy dictating that we should only keep what we use on a daily basis

38 Which of the following discoveries, theories, and events contributed to Victorians feeling less like they were a uniquely special, central species in the universe and more isolated?
(a) geology
(b) evolution
(c) discoveries in astronomy about stellar distances
(d) All of the above

39 Which of the following contributed to the growing awareness in the Late Victorian Period of the immense human, economic, and political costs of running an empire?
(a) The Boer War in the south of Africa
(b) The Jamaica Rebellion in 1865
(c) The Irish Question
(d) All of the above

40 Which of the following authors promoted versions of socialism and revolutionary movements of the working classes to take control of government and industry?
(a) William Morris
(b) John Ruskin
(c) Edward FitzGerald
(d) Both (a) and (b)

41 Which best describes the general feeling expressed in literature during the last decade of the Victorian era?
(a) Melancholic languor and comic self-criticism
(b) Sincere earnestness
(c) Raucous celebration mixed with self-congratulatory sophistication
(d) boredom mixed with a desire for enlivening innovation

42 In which of the following texts is the conception of woman as an 'Angel of the House' most clearly propounded?
(a) Tannyson's The Princess
(b) Jane Austen's Jane Eyre
(c) John Ruskin's Of Queen's Gardens
(d) Oscar Wilde's The Importance of Being Earnest

43 Which of the following Victorian writers regularly published their work in periodicals?
(a) Thomas Carlyle
(b) Matthew Arnold
(c) Elizabeth Barrett Browning
(d) All of the above

44 Which genres seemed particularly amenable to Victorians in instructing the public about social matters and promoting partisan viewpoints?
(a) The novel (b) Non-fiction prose
(c) The short story (d) All of these

45 For what do Matthew Arnold's moral experience of writing non-fiction and Walter Pater's aesthetic preoccupation pave the way?
(a) A renewed secularism in the twentieth century
(b) Modern literary criticism
(c) Late-nineteenth century and early-twentieth-century satirical drama
(d) The surrealist movement

46 Whose pseudonym is 'Alpha of the Plough'?
(a) Robert Lynd (b) Francis Bacon
(c) A.G. Gardiner (d) J.B. Priestley

47 Who was AG Gardiner's fellow-traveller in 'A Fellow Traveller'?
(a) Bird (b) Man (c) Dog (d) Mosquito

48 How did AG Gardiner accuse his fellow-traveller in 'A Fellow Traveller'?
(a) As a vagrant
(b) As a public nuisance
(c) As travelling without a ticket
(d) All of the above

49 Name the writers who continually misquoted the authors they loved.
(a) Pope and Dryden (b) Bacon and Lamb
(c) Hazlitt and Swift (d) Lamb and Hazlitt

50 What does Gardiner feel about the fellow traveller during his journey?
(a) That he has insulted
(b) That he has pleased others
(c) That he has entertained
(d) That he has caused worries

51 How does Gardiner describe his sense of freedom in 'A Fellow Traveller'?
(a) Pleasant
(b) Uneasy
(c) Boring
(d) None of the above

52 According to the author of 'A Fellow Traveller' what can he do when one is alone in the carriage?
(a) Sing and dance
(b) Open and close window
(c) Play golf and even stand on head
(d) All of the above

53 How did the author respond to the behaviour of his fellow traveller?
(a) Kissed him (b) Flicked him off
(c) Prayed with him (d) Danced and sung with him

54 After attacking his fellow traveller with a blow what did the author do?
(a) Lunged him
(b) Jumped on the seat
(c) Adopted tactics of feline cunning
(d) All of the above

55 According to AG Gardiner what are the noblest attributes of man?
(a) Pride and prejudice (b) Anger and rage
(c) Magnanimity and mercy (d) Fear and dilemma

56 Gardiner refers whom to have called the non-human beings as a brother?
(a) St. Francis (b) St Augutus
(c) St. Thomas (d) None of these

57 Gardiner heard a friendly voice in the window who is it?
(a) Station master (b) Engine driver
(c) Guard (d) Friendly porter

58 How did the fellow traveller behave with the author in 'A Fellow Traveller'?
(a) Made a menace
(b) Spoke well and behaved gently
(c) Ignored the author
(d) Sang and slept

59 Why do Bores thrive in the essay 'Bores' by EV Lucas?
(a) Because of people's astuteness
(b) Because of people's eccentricity
(c) Because of people's cunningness
(d) Because of people's cowardice

60 From which collection is the essay 'Bores' taken?
(a) Listener's Lure (b) Cricket all his Life
(c) Events and Embroideries (d) All of the above

61 Who is a true bore in the essay 'Bores' by EV Lucas?
(a) One who is always unconscious of his foolishness
(b) One who is always unconscious of his borishness
(c) One who is always unconscious of his prudishness
(d) None of the above

62 For what feature of them are Bores always known in the essay 'Bores' by EV Lucas?
(a) Cowardice (b) Indolence
(c) Egotism (d) Ingeniousness

63 According to Lucas in the essay 'Bores', What kind of people are seldom bores?
(a) Busy (b) Simple
(c) Kind (d) Poor

64 Why do Bores come out successful in life according to the essay 'Bores' by Lucas?
(a) Because they find a number of ready listeners
(b) Because they find a number of ready speakers
(c) Because they find a number of ready preachers
(d) Because they find a number of ready lecturers

65 What is the only way to get rid of a bore according to Lucas in the essay 'Bores'?
(a) To tell him frankly that he is a nuisance
(b) To tell him frankly that he is a good companion
(c) To tell him frankly that he is a fellow traveller
(d) To tell him frankly that he is a savior

66 Who cannot be shaken off just by gestures or indirect hints in the essay 'Bores'?
(a) Preacher (b) Bores
(c) Lucas (d) A Fellow Traveller

67 To which journal did EV Lucas often contribute articles?
(a) Tatler (b) Spectator
(c) Punch (d) The Hindu

68 Name the word which is used by the Gileadites as a test of detect the fleeing Ephraimites
(a) Bores (b) Shibboleth
(c) Button-holding (d) Stigma

69 What did Greene study at Cambridge?

(a) Geography (b) European Art
(c) Poetry (d) Modern History

70 What was Greene during in 1930s?

(a) Film critic (b) Photographer
(c) Speechwriter (d) Teacher

71 Thomas Carlyle's .... discusses the dangers and promises of the Revolution.

(a) The French Revolution
(b) Signs of the Times
(c) Past and Present
(d) On Heroes, Hero Worship and the Heroic in History

72 .... became a regular contributer to the Edinburgh Review, a journal formed by Whig politician, Henry Brougham.

(a) Thomas Carlyle
(b) Thomas Macaulay
(c) John Henry Newman
(d) John Stuart Mill

73 .... which contained an account of John Henry Newman's Religious Life, was written as an answer to the attack upon him by Charles Kingsley.

(a) Lectures of Justification
(b) Lives of English Saints
(c) Apologia Pro Vita Sua
(d) Retractation of Anti Catholic Statements

74 .... helped JS Mill overcome the adverse impact of Benthamite system of education on his emotional development.

(a) Harriet Taylor, whom J.S. Mill later married
(b) JH Newman's Sermon Notes
(c) Shakespeare's Sonnets
(d) Wordsworth's Poetry

75 .... was written in defence of Turner after reviewers of the annual Royal Academy exhibition savagely treated Turner's works.

(a) John Ruskin's 'Modern Painters'
(b) James Anthony Froude's 'Short Studies on Great Subjects'
(c) Walter Pater's 'Appreciations : With an Essay on Style'
(d) John Stuart Mill's 'A System of Logic'

76 Gardiner feels that he cannot kill his fellow traveller but .... him.

(a) reprieve (b) discharge
(c) dismantle (d) None of the above

77 According to Lucas the one who has a fixed idea to impart is called a ....

(a) flatterer (b) philanthrop
(c) idiosyncratic (d) bore

78 In the essay 'Bores' the most repellent specimen of all the boresis called a .... bore.

(a) blissful (b) eccentric
(c) buttonholing (d) notorious

79 According to E.V. Lucas in his essay 'Bores', unless these weekly papers stop publication, bores are bound to ....

(a) fade (b) demolish (c) flourish (d) cherish

80 .... is a bore's foundation stone in the essay 'Bores'.

(a) Socialism (b) Humour (c) Idealism (d) Egotism

81 Which of the following statements is factually incorrect?

(a) Thomas Carlyle worked as a stonemason before becoming a prose writer
(b) Thomas Macaulay harboured political ambitions and established his powers as an orator in the Reform Bill debates
(c) John Henry Newman was one of the important leadersof the Oxford Movement
(d) JS Mill felt dissatisfied with his father's Benthamite system of education

82 Which of the following is true?

(a) 'The Idea of University' was written by Thomas Macaulay
(b) 'Shadows of the Clouds' is a semi-autobiographical work of James Anthony Froude
(c) 'The Ariens of the Fourth Century' is the last literary work of JH Newman
(d) 'Sermon Notes' is J.S. Mill's most popular work

83 Which of the following statements is not true?

(a) Thomas Carlyle's 'On Heroes, Hero-Worship and the Heroic in History' stresses the importance of the individual in History
(b) The novel 'The Nemesis of Faith' drove James Anthony Froude to abandon his religious career
(c) JS Mill wrote 'Lays of Ancient Rome' in 1842
(d) John Ruskin argued against competition and self interest and dvocated a form of Christian Socialism

84 Which of the following statements is correct?

(a) 'The Early Kings of Norvey' was written by Thomas Macaulay
(b) Thomas Carlyle wrote 'Letter to the Duke of Norfolk' in 1875
(c) 'The London Review' was co-founded by John Henry Newman
(d) The term 'Pathetic Fallacy' was coined by John Ruskin during the course of writing 'the Modern Painters'

85 Which of the following statements is not correct?

(a) 'Frederick the Great', a biography of Frederick the Great of Prussia, was written by Thomas Carlyle
(b) In 'Tracts for the Time' John Henry Newman describes his gradual conversion to Roman Catholicism
(c) In 'The Subjection of Women', J.S. Mill compares the legal status of women to the status of slaves and argues for equality in marriage and under the law
(d) 'The Renaissance : Studies in Art and Poetry' was a series of critical essays by Walter Pater

86 Which of the following pairs is incorrectly matched?

(a) Elizabeth Gaskell : North and South
(b) Charles Darwin : On the Origin of Species
(c) JS Mill : Middlemarch
(d) Matthew Arnold : Culture and Anarchy

87 Which of the following pairs is incorrectly matched?

(a) James Frazer : The Golden Bough
(b) Oscar Wilde : The Importance of Being Earnest
(c) Thomas Hardy : The Mayor of Casterbridge
(d) John Ruskin : The Coral Island

88 Which of the following pairs is correctly matched?

(a) 1837 : Queen Victoria ascends the throne
(b) 1844 : The Great Exhibition is held in London
(c) 1853 : Irish Potato famine
(d) 1851 : Outbreak of Crimean War

89 Which of the following pairs is incorrectly matched?

(a) Sartos Resartus : Thomas Carlyle
(b) Development of Religious Error : Thomas Macaulay
(c) Loss and Gain : John Henry Newman
(d) On Liberty : JS Mill

90 Which of the following is incorrectly matched?

(a) Lays of Ancient Rome : Thomas Macaulay
(b) The Divorce of Catherine of Aragon : James Anthony Froude
(c) Principles of Political Economy : John Ruskin
(d) Marius the Epicurian : Walter Pater

Directions (Q. Nos. 91-95) *In the questions given below are two statements labelled as Assertion (A) and Reason (R). In the context of the two statements, which one of the following is correct?*

Codes

(a) Both A and R are true and R is the correct explanation of A
(b) Both A and R are true, but R is not the correct explanation of A
(c) A is true, but R is false
(d) A is false, but R is true

91 **Assertion** (A) Christianity came under question.

Reason (R) On one side Christianity believed in the existence of God and on the other side, science questioned the very existence of God.

92 **Assertion** (A) Throughout his life Thomas Carlyle kept on fighting with his doubts.

Reason (R) Thomas Carlyle was obsessed with doubt.

93 **Assertion** (A) John Ruskin had a good grasping level and maintained it well.

Reason (R) John Ruskin's mother taught him at the initial stage.

94 **Assertion** (A) JS Mill felt dissatisfied with his father's Benthamite system of education.

Reason (R) Mill found a cure from this in Wordsworth's poetry.

95 **Assertion** (A) Oscar Wilde termed 'The Renaissance' as 'golden book' of Walter Pater.

Reason (R) Walter Pater had composed all his works in similar fashion.

96 Which one of the following is in chronological order?

(a) Macaulay's Essay on Milton, Browning's Pauline, Carlyle's French Revolution
(b) Macaulay's Essay on Milton, Carlyle's French Revolution, Browning's Pauline
(c) Browning's Pauline, Macaulay's Essay on Milton, Carlyle's French Revolution
(d) Browning's Pauline, Carlyle's French Revolution, Macaulay's Essay on Milton

97 Which one of the following statements is in chronological order?

(a) Ruskin's Praterita Began, Stevenson's Treasure Island, Death of Tennyson
(b) Death of Tennyson, Stevenson's Treasure Island, Ruskin's Praterita Began
(c) Stevenson's Treasure Island, Death of Tennyson, Ruskin's Praterita Began
(d) Stevenson's Treasure Island, Ruskin's Praterita Began, Death of Tennyson

98 Which one of the following has the works in correct chronological order of their publication?

(a) Thomas Carlyle's 'The Life of John Sterling', Thomas Macaulay's 'Critical and Historical Essays', Newman's 'Letter to Dr Pursey', JS Mill's 'The Subjection of Women'
(b) Thomas Macaulay's 'Critical and Historical Essays', Thomas Carlyle's 'The Life of John Sterling', 'Newman's 'Letter to Dr Pursey', JS Mill's 'Subjection of Women'
(c) Newman's 'Letter to Dr. Pursey', Thomas Carlyle's 'The Life of John Sterling', Thomas Macaulay's 'Critical and Historical Essays', 'JS Mill's 'Subjection of Women'
(d) JS Mill's 'Subjection of Women', 'Thomas Carlyule's 'the Life of John Sterling', Thomas Macaulay's 'Critical and Historical Essays', Newman's 'Letter to Dr Pursey'

99 Which one of the following has victorian prose writers in correct chronological order as per their birth years?

(a) John Ruskin, Walter Pater, John Stuart Mill, James Anthony Froude
(b) Walter Pater, John Stuart Mill, James Anthony Froude, John Ruskin
(c) John Stuart Mill, James Anthony Froude, John Ruskin
(d) James Anthony Froude, John Stuart Mill, Walter Pater, John Stuart Mill

100 Which one of the following has works of the victorian age in correct chronological order?
(a) Cathedra Sempiterna, Autobiography of John Stuart Mill, Love's Meinie, Lord Beacons Field
(b) Autobiography of John Stuart Mill, Love's Meinie, Lord Beacons Field, Cathedra Sempiterna
(c) Love's Meinie, Lord Beacons Field, Cathedra Sempiterna, Autobiography of John Stuart Mill
(d) Lord Beacons Field, Cathedra Sempiterna, Autobiography of John Stuart Mill

101 Consider the following statements
1. There was a clash between science and religion.
2. The people, who believed in religion were not able to bear the question on religion and the people, who were gaining confidence in science were not ready to maintain faith in religion.

Which of the statements given above is/are correct?
(a) Only 1 (b) Only 2
(c) Both 1 and 2 (d) None of these

102 Consider the following statements.
The litera ture of the Victorian Age
1. did not produce a number of prominent writers.
2. did not have dramatic monologue as the preferred mode of expression.
3. witnessed tremendous growth in periodicals of all kinds.
4. saw the development of children's literature as a separate genre.

Which of the statements given above is/are correct?
(a) 1 and 2 (b) 1 and 4
(c) 3 and 2 (d) 3 and 4

103 Consider the following statements.
1. Literature of Victorian Age represents the political and social life of the period.
2. Power of knowledge came into being and intellectual work was served to the readers.
3. Thinkers, Philosophers, Scientists produced their best works.

Which of the statements given above is/are correct?
(a) Only 1 (b) Only 2
(c) Only 3 (d) All of these

104 Consider the following statements.
John Ruskin in 'Modern Painters'
1. It was written in defence of JMW Turner.
2. Michelangelo and other artists had a corrupting influence on art.
3. did not coin the term 'Pathetic fallacy'.
4. written in 1885.

Which of the statements given above are correct?
(a) 1 and 2 (b) 1 and 4
(c) 3 and 2 (d) 3 and 4

105 The following writers have something in common
Mary Seacole J A Froude
Mary Kingsley Anthony Trollope
What is?
1. They are all Victorians
2. They are all writers of children's fiction
3. They are all members of one literary
4. They are all travel writers
(a) 1 and 2 (b) 3 and 4 (c) 2 and 4 (d) 1 and 4

106 Consider the following statements about Hilaire Belloc.
1. He sat as a member of Parliament for Salford, first as a Liberal and then as an Independent.
2. He reflected his mastery of satire and irony through his works, 'Lambkin's Remains' and 'Mr. Burden'.
3. He had controversy with William Cobbett on political and economic matters.
4. He was one of the pioneers of the victorian age non-fiction.

Which of the statements given above are correct?
(a) 1 and 2 (b) 2 and 3 (c) 3 and 4 (d) 1 and 3

107 Consider the following statements about Max Beerbohm.
1. He was not a part of the Wilde circle.
2. His first essay 'A Defence of Cosmetics' appeared in The Yellow Book.
3. A Christmas Garland, one of his best known works, was a parody of literary styles.
4. He received the Knighthood in 1933.

Which of the above given are correct for Max Beerbohm?
(a) 1 and 2 (b) 2 and 3 (c) 3 and 4 (d) 2 and 4

108 Consider the following statements about Robert Wilson Lynd
1. Desmond Maccarthy was his life long critic.
2. His father, Robert John, was a renowned businessman.
3. He began as a journalist on the Northern Whig in Belfast.
4. He used the pseudonym Y.Y. in writing for the New Statesman.

Which of the above given are correct for Robert Wilson Lynd?
(a) 1 and 2 (b) 2 and 3 (c) 3 and 4 (d) 1 and 3

109 Consider the following statements about Aldous Leonard Huxley
1. He was the editor of the magazine 'Oxford Poetry'.
2. Huxley intended to become a politician.

3. His work 'The Doors of Perception' was an important study of consciousness.
4. He died on 22nd November, 1974.

Which of the above given are true for Aldous Leonard Huxley?

(a) 1 and 2 (b) 2 and 3 (c) 3 and 4 (d) 1 and 3

110 Consider the following works.

1. The End of Affair
2. Ways of Escape
3. Homage to Catalonia
4. Literature and Science

Which of the above given belong to Graham Greene?

(a) 1 and 2 (b) 2 and 3 (c) 3 and 4 (d) 1 and 4

111 Match the following.

List I (Writers)	List II (Works)
A. Thomas Carlyle	1. Catriona
B. RL Stevenson	2. The French Revolution
C. Benjamin Disraeli	3. Tracts for the Times
D. John Henry Newman	4. Vivian Gray

Codes

	A	B	C	D
(a)	3	1	2	4
(b)	3	2	4	1
(c)	2	1	4	3
(d)	4	3	2	1

112 Match the following.

List I (Writers)	List II (Works)
A. RL Stevenson	1. Lays of Ancient Rome
B. TS Macaulay	2. Translation of Rubaiat
C. Edward Fitzgerald	3. Familiar Studies
D. Charles Reade	4. The Cloister and the Health

Codes

	A	B	C	D
(a)	4	3	2	1
(b)	3	1	4	2
(c)	3	2	4	1
(d)	3	1	2	4

113 Match the following

List I (Prose Writers)	List II (Works)
A. Elizabeth Barrett Browning	1. Pickwick Papers
B. Arthur Hugh Clough	2. Sesame and Lilies
C. John Ruskin	3. An Essay on Mind
D. Charles Dickens	4. Sonnets from the Portuguese

Codes

	A	B	C	D
(a)	3	2	4	1
(b)	2	3	4	1
(c)	3	4	2	1
(d)	4	3	2	1

114 In the given series which one has Victorian Prose works matched correctly with their publication year?

(a) The French Revolution-1837, Oxford University Sermons-1843, Bible of Amiens-1885, Plato and Platonism-1893

(b) The French Revolution-1843, Oxford University Sermons-1885, Plato and Platonism-1885, Bible of Amiens-1893

(c) The French Revolution-1885, Oxford University Sermons-1893, Bible of Amiens-1837, Plato and Platonism-1843

(d) The French Revolution-1893, Oxford University Sermons-1837, Bible of Amiens-1843, Plato and Platonism-1885

115 In the given series, which one has victorian prose works matched correctly with their writers

(a) On the Inspiration of Scripture-John Ruskin, A Few Words of Non-Intervention-John Henry Newman, Life and Letters of Erasmus-John Stuart Mill, Verona and Its Rivers-James Anthony Froude

(b) On the Inspiration of Scripture-John Henry Newman, A Few Words of Non-Intervention-John Stuart Mill, Life and Letters of Erasmus-James Anthony Froude, Verona and Its Rivers-John Ruskin

(c) On the Inspiration of Scripture-John Stuart Mill, A Few Words of Non-Intervention-James Anthony Froude, Life and Letters of Erasmus-John Ruskin, Verona and Its Rivers-John Henry Newman

(d) On the Inspiration of Scripture-James Anthony Froude, A Few Words of Non-Intervention-John Ruskin, Life and Letters of Erasmus-John Henry Newman, Verona and Its Rivers-John Stuart Mill

116 In the given series, which one has modern non-fiction prose writers matched correctly with their works?

(a) AG Gardiner-Pillers of Society, E.V. Lucas-The Open Road, Hilaire Belloc-Roberspierre, Max Beerbohm-A Defence of Cosmetics

(b) AG Gardiner-A Defence of Cosmetics, EV Lucas-Robespierre, Hilaire Belloc-The Open Road, Max Beerbohm-Pillers of Society

(c) AG Gardiner-The Open Road, EV Lucas-A Defence of Cosmetics, Hilaire Belloc-Pillers of Society, Max Beerbohm-Robespierre

(d) AG Gardiner-Robespierre, EV Lucas-The Open Road, Hilaire Belloc-A Defence of Cosmetics, Max Beerbohm-Pillers of Society.

117 Match the following non-fiction prose works of AG Gardiner with the year of their publication

Non-Fiction Prose Works of AG Gardiner

1. Prophets, Priests and Kings
2. The War Lords
3. Leaves in the Wind
4. Portraits and Portends

The Year of Publication

A. 1926 B. 1920
C. 1916 D. 1908

Codes

(a) 1-A, 2-B, 3-C, 4-D (b) 1-D, 2-C, 3-B, 4-A
(c) 1-B, 2-D, 3-a, 4-C (d) 1-C, 2-A, 3-D, 4-B

118 Match the following non-fiction prose writers of the Modern Age with their works.

Non-Fiction Prose Works of AG Gardiner

1. Hilaire Belloc 2. Max Beerbohm
3. Gilbert Keith Chesterton
4. Graham Green

Work

A. The Defendant B. The Path of Life
C. A Sort of Life D. A Peep into the Past

Codes

(a) 1-A, 2-B, 3-C, 4-D (b) 1-D, 2-C, 3-B, 4-A
(c) 1-B, 2-D, 3-A, 4-C (d) 1-C, 2-A, 3-D, 4-B

119 Match the following non-fiction prose works with their modern age authors

Non-fiction Prose Works

1. Lambkins Remains 2. The Art of Letters
3. The Art of Seeing 4. The Road to Wigan Pier

Modern Age Authors

A. Robert Wilson Lynd
B. George Orwell
C. Hilaire Belloc
D. Aldous Leonard Huxley

Codes

(a) 1-A, 2-B, 3-C, 4-D (b) 1-D, 2-C, 3-B, 4-A
(c) 1-B, 2-D, 3-C, 4-A (d) 1-C, 2-A, 3-D, 4-B

120 Match the following modern prose works with their authors.

Modern Prose Works

1. Orthodoxy
2. The Book of This and That
3. Brave New World
4. Down and Out in Paris and London

Authors

A. GK Chesterton
B. Robert Wilson Lynd
C. Aldous Leonard Huxley
D. George Orwell

Codes

(a) 1-A, 2-B, 3-C, 4-D (b) 1-D, 2-C, 3-B, 4-A
(c) 1-B, 2-D, 3-A, 4-C (d) 1-C, 2-A, 3-D, 4-B

121 "The lies (Western slander) which well-meaning zeal has heaped round this man (Mumammad) are disgraceful to ourselves only."

Which author, in one of his works, reveals the above lines?

(a) Thomas Carlyle, On Heroes, Hero Worship and the Heroic in History
(b) Thomas Macaulay, History of England from the Accession of James II
(c) John Henry Newman, An Essay in Aid of Grammar of Assent
(d) John Stuart Mill, A System of Logic

122 'Idleness is worst, Idlensss alone is without hope : work earnestly at anything, you will by degrees learn to work at almost all things., There is endless hope in work, were it even work at making money."

Which author, in one of his works, reveals the above lines?

(a) Thomas Macaulay, History of England from the Accession of James II
(b) Thomas Carlyle, Past and Present
(c) John Henry Newman, Development of the Religious Error
(d) John Stuart Mill, Autobiography of John Stuart Mill

123 'Then out spake brave Horatius,
The Captain of the Gate :
To every man upon this Earth
Death cometh soon or late.
And how can man die better
Than facing fearful odds,
For the ashes of his fathers,
And the temples of his Gods'

Which author, in one of his works, reveals the above lines?

(a) John Henry Newman, A Few Words on Non-intervention
(b) Thomas Carlyle, The Life of John Sterling
(c) Thomas Babington Macaulay, Lays of Ancient Rome
(d) John Stuart Mill, Autobiography of John Stuart Mill

124 'What is blessing it is to love books as I love them;-to be able to converse with the dead, and to live amidst the unreal!"

Which author, in one of his works, reveals the above lines.

(a) John Henry Newman, the Idea of a University
(b) Thomas Carlyle, Charitism
(c) John Stuart Mill, Considerations on Representative Government
(d) Thomas Babington Macaulay, The Selected Letters Of Thomas Babington Macaulay

125 'Boys do not fully know what is good and what is evil; they do wrong things at first almost innocently. Novelty hides vice from them; there is no one to warn them or give them rules; and they become slaves of sin, while they are learning what sin is."

Which author, in one of his works, reveals the above lines?

(a) John Henry Newman, Loss and Gain The Story of a Convert
(b) John Stuart Mill, Principles of Political Economy
(c) James Anthony Froude, Shadows of the Clouds
(d) John Ruskin, Bible of Amiens

126 'Ten thousand difficulties do not make one doubt, as I understand the subject; difficulty and doubt are incommensurate."

Which author, in one of his works, reveals the above lines?

(a) Thomas Macaulay, Critical and Historical Essays
(b) John Henry Newman, Apologia Pro Vita Sua
(c) John Stuart Mill, Essays on Some Unsettled Questions of Political Economy
(d) James Anthony Froude, Lord Beaconsfield

127 "A person may cause evil to others not only by his actions but by his inaction, and in either case he is justly accountable 'to them for the injury."

Which author, in one of his works, reveals the above lines?

(a) John Henry Newman, The Dream of Gerontious
(b) James Anthony Froude, Bunyan
(c) John Stuart Mill, On Liberty
(d) John Ruskin, The Seven Lamps of Architecture

128 "The creed which accepts as the foundation of morals, utility or the greatest-happiness, principle, holds that actions are rightin proportion as they tend to promote happiness, wrong as they tend to produce the reverse of happiness. By happiness is intended pleasure, and the absence of pain; by unhappiness, pain, and the privation of pleasure."

Which author, in one of his works, reveals the above lines?

(a) John Ruskin, Verona and its Rivers
(b) John Henry Newman, Five Letters
(c) James Anthony Froude, Luther : A Short Biography
(d) John Stuart Mill, Utilitarianism

129 "Stupidity is much the same all the world over. A stupid person's notions and feelings may confidently be inferred from those which prevail in the circle by which the person is surrounded. Not so with those whose opinions and feelings are an emanation from their own nature and faculties."

Which author, in one of his works, reveals the above lines?

(a) John Stuart Mill, The Subjection of Women
(b) James Anthony Froude, The Divorce of Catherine of Aragon
(c) John Ruskin, Architecture and Painting
(d) Walter Pater, Notes on Leonardo da Vinci

130 "You cannot dream yourself into a character; you must hammer and forge yourself one."

Which author, in one of his works, reveals the above lines?

(a) John Stuart Mill, Utilitarianism
(b) James Anthony Froude, The Nemesis of Faith
(c) John Ruskin, Modern Painters (Volume 1-9)
(d) John Henry Newman, Sermons on Subject of the Day

131 "To banish imperfection is to destroy expression, to check exertion, to paralyze vitality."

Which author, in one of his works, reveals the above lines?

(a) John Henry Newman, Retractation of Anti-Catholic Statements
(b) James Anthony Froude, Life and Letters of Erasmus
(c) John Ruskin, The Stones of Venice
(d) Walte Pater, The School of Giorgione

132 "Let every dawn of morning be to you as the beginning of life, and every setting sun be to you as its close."

Which author, in one of his works, reveals the above lines?

(a) John Henry Newman, Difficulties of Anglicans
(b) James Anthony Froude, My Relations with Carlyle
(c) Walter Pater, Plato and Platonism
(d) John Ruskin, The Two Paths

133 "All books are divisible into two classes : the books of the hours, and the books of all Time."

Which author, in one of his works, reveals the above lines?

(a) John Ruskin, Sesame and Lilies
(b) Walter Pater, Imaginary Portraits
(c) John Henry Newman, On the Inspiration of Scripture
(d) James Anthony Froude, English Sea-Men in the 16th Century

134 "Legions of grotesques sweep under his hand; for has not nature too her grotesques—the rent rock, the distorting lights of evening on lonely roads, the unveiled structure of man in the embryo, or the skeleton?"

Which author, in one of his works, reveals the above lines?

(a) John Ruskin, The Flamboyant Architecture of Somme
(b) Walter Pater, The Renaissance : Studies in Art and Poetry
(c) John Henry Newman, Cathedra Sempiterna
(d) James Anthony Froude, Short Studies on Great Subjects

135 "A book, like a person, has its fortunes with one; is lucky or unlucky in the precise moment of its falling in our way, and often by some happy accident counts with us for something more than its independent value."

Which author, in one of his works, reveals the above lines?

(a) John Henry Newman, Discourses of Mixed Congregations
(b) James Anthony Froude, Oceana or England and Her Colonies
(c) Walter Pater, Marius and Epicurean
(d) John Ruskin, Review of Paintings by James McNeill Whistler

136 "To-day, well Utopia, if everI framed one, would be a land where the laws demanded that people should be vicious. Then one would be able to count at any rate on a little virtue. If no man might live with a woman in any but an irregular union, there would be at once quite a run on honest matrimony and the Law Courts would be full of disperately wicked monogamists; while if every one was expected to steal and swindle, there would soon be a extensive criminal class who respected property."

Which of the following modern non-fiction writers in which of his/her works has used the above lines?

(a) Edward Verrall Lucas, London Lavender
(b) Hillaire Belloc, First and Last
(c) G.K. Chesterton, What's Wrong with the World
(d) Robert Charles Wilson, Julian Comstock : A Story of 22nd-Century America

137 "These are the advantages of travel, that one meets so many men whom one would otherwise never meet, and that one feeds as it were upon the complexity of mankind."

Which of the following modern non-fiction writers in which of his/her works has used the above lines?

(a) Edward Verall Lucas, London Lavender
(b) Hillaire Belloc, First and Last
(c) GK Chesterton, What's Wrong with the World
(d) Robert Charles Wilson, Julian Comstock : A Story of 22nd-Century America

138 "It has been discovered that with a dull urban population, all formed under a mechanical system of State education, a suggestion or command, however senseless and unreasoned, will be obeyed if it be sufficiently repeated."

Which of the following modern non-fiction writers in which of his/her works has used the above lines?

(a) Hilaire Belloc, An Essay on the Restoration of Property
(b) George Orwell, 1984
(c) Graham Greene, The Third Man
(d) Edward Verrall Lucas, London Lavender

139 "The Christian ideal has not been tried and found wanting. It has been found difficult; and left untried."

Which of the following modern non-fiction writers in which of his/her works has used the above lines?

(a) Edward Verrall Lucas, London Lavender
(b) Hillaire Belloc, First and Last
(c) GK Chesterton, What's Wrong with the World
(d) Robert Charles Wilson, Julian Comstock : A Story of 22nd-Century America

140 "Poets have been mysteriously silent on the subject of cheese."

Which of the following modern non-fiction writers in which of his/her works has used the above lines?

(a) Hilaire Belloc, The Path ot Rome
(b) GK Chesterton, Alarms and Discursions
(c) Robert Charles Wilson Spin
(d) Aldous Muxley, Brove New World

141 "You must not take the mistake of thinking that because nothing lasts, nothing matters."

Which of the following modern non-fiction writers in which of his/her works has used the above lines?

(a) Edward Verrall Lucas, London Lavender
(b) Hilaire Belloc, First and Last
(c) GK Chesterton, What's Wrong with the World
(d) Robert Charles Wilson, Julian Comstock : A Story of 22nd-Century America

142 "Actual happiness always looks pretty squalid in comparison with the overcompensations for misery. And, of course, stability isn't nearly so spectacular as instability. And being contented has none of the glamour of a good fight against misfortune, none of the picturesqueness of a struggle with temptation, or a fatal overthrow by passion or doubt. Happiness is never grand."

Which of the following modern non-fiction writers in which of his/her works has used the above lines?

(a) Hilaire belloc, The Path to Rome
(b) GK Chesterton, Alarms and Discursions
(c) Robert Charles Wilson, Spin
(d) Aldous Huxley, Brave New World

143 "Doublethink means the power of holding two contradictory beliefs in one's mind simultaneously, and accepting both of them."

Which of the following modern non-fiction writers in which of his/her works has used the above lines?

(a) Hilaire Belloc, An Essay on the Restoration of Property
(b) George Orwell, 1984
(c) Graham Greene, The Third Man
(d) Edward Verrall Lucas, London Lavender

144 "You know what the fellow said—in Italy, for thirty years under the Borgias, they had warfare, terror, murder and bloodshed, but they produced Michelangelo, Leonardo da Vinci and the Renaissance. In Switzerland, they had brotherly love, they had five hundred years of democracy and peace—and what did that produce? The cuckoo clock."

Which of the following modern non-fiction writers in which of his / her works has used the above lines?
(a) Hilaire Belloc, An Essay on the Restoration of Property
(b) George Orwell, 1984
(c) Graham Greene, The Third Man
(d) Edward Verrall Lucas, London Lavender

145 "The sense of unhappiness is so much easier to convey than that of happiness. In misery we seem aware of our own existence, even though it may be in the form of monostrous egotism : this pain of mine is individual, this nerve that winces belongs to me and to no other. But happiness annihilates us : we lose our identity."
Which of the following modern non-fiction writers in which of his / her works has used the above lines?
(a) G.K. Chesterton, Alarms and Discursions
(b) Robert Charles Wilson, Spin
(c) Aldous Huxley, Brave New World
(d) Graham Greene, The End of the Affair

Directions (Q. Nos. 146-150) *Read the passage given below carefully and answer the questions that follow.*

Vict Leisure is gone—gone where the spinning-wheels are gone, and the pack horses, and the slow waggons, and the pedlars, who brought bargains to the door on sunny afternoons. Ingenious philosophers tell you, perhaps, that the great work of the steam-engine is to create leisure for mankind. Do not believe them : it only creates a vacuum for eager thought to rush in. Even idleness is eager now—eager for amusement : prone to excursion-trains, art-museums, periodical literature, and exciting novels : prone even to scientific theorising, and cursory peeps through microscopes. Old Leisure was quite a different personage : he only read one newspaper, innocent of leaders, and was free from that periodicity of sensations which we call post-time. He was a contemplative, rather stout gentleman, of excellent digestion—of quiet perceptions, undiseased by hypothesis : happy in his inability to know the causes of things, preferring the things themselves. He lived chiefly in the country, among pleasant seats and homesteads, and was fond of sauntering by the fruit-tree wall, and scenting the apricots when they were warmed by the morning sunshine, or of sheltering himself under the orchard boughs at noon, when the summer pears were falling. He knew nothing of weekday services, and thought none the worse of the Sunday sermon if it allowed him to sleep from the text to the blessing—liking the afternoon service best, because the prayers were the shortest, and not ashamed to say so; for he had an easy, jolly conscience, broad-backed like himself, and able to carry a great deal of beer or port-wine, — not being made squeamish by doubts and qualms and lofty aspirations. Life was not a task to him, but a sincecure : he fingered the guineas in his pocket, and ate his dinners, and slept the sleep of the irresponsible; for had he not keept up his charter by going to church on the Sunday afternoons?
Fine old Leisure! Do not be severe upon him, and judge him by our modern standard : he never went to Exeter Hall, or heard a popular preacher, or read Tracts for the Times or Sartor Resartus.

146 The phrases "Even idleness is eager now—eager for amusement" (lines 10-11) exemplify which of the following devices?
I. metaphor
II. personification
III. paradox
Codes
(a) Only III (b) 1 and III
(c) II and III (d) I, II and III

147 The phrase 'innocent of leaders' (line 17-18) can be best said to mean
(a) guiltless of ambition (b) free of editorials
(c) ignorant of competition (d) pure as a commander

148 The point of view in the question "had he not kept up his charter by going to church on the Sunday afternoons?" (lines 48-50) is that of
I. Old Leisure
II. New or modern leisure
III. The narrator of the passage
Codes
(a) Only I (b) Only II
(c) Only III (d) I and III

149 From the whole passage, the reader can infer that the narrator feels
I. some nostalgia for the leisure of the past
II. an awareness of the complacency of the present
III. a concern of the anti-intellectual self-interest of the past
Codes
(a) Only I (b) I and II
(c) I and III (d) I, II and III

150 The tone of the passage is best described as
(a) gently satirical (b) harshly sarcastic
(c) mawkishly sentimental (d) coolly objective

PREVIOUS YEARS' QUESTIONS

December 2018

1 What type of writing Walter Pater define as "the special and opportune art of the modern world"?
(a) The lyric
(b) Comic drama
(c) The novel
(d) Nonfiction prose

2 It was the first narrative on the life of a black woman slave to be published in England in 1831. It has profound influence on the abolition movement in Britain. Identify the book and its author.
(a) Mary Prince—The History of Mary Prince
(b) Mattie Jane Jackson—The Story of Mattie J Jackson
(c) Elizabeth—Memoir of Old Elizabeth, a Coloured Woman
(d) Harriet Jacobs—Incidents in the Life of a Slave Girl

3 The following epitaph was written by Rudyard Kipling during the war of 1914-18.
Hindu Sepoy in France
This man is his own country prayed we know not to what powers.
We pray Them to reward him for his bravery in ours.
'Powers' here refers to ...., 'then' to ...., and 'ours' to ....
(a) The Hindus, the French, the British
(b) The divine, Powers, our country
(c) The military, the Hindu sepoys, Powers
(d) Authorities, his compatriots, our country

4 The 'grammer bullies'-you read them in places like the New York Times and they tell you what is correct.
You must never use "hopefully, we will be going there on Thrusday." That is incorrect and wrong and you are basically an ignorant pig if you say it. This is judgementalism. The game that is being played there is a game of social class. It has nothing do with the morality of writing and speaking and thinking clearly, of which George Orwell, for instance, talked so well.
To which famous essay of Orwell does the author refer here?
(a) "Inside the Whale"
(b) "Politics and the English Language"
(c) "Reflections of Gandhi"
(d) "Why I Write"

Direction (Q. No. 5) *Read the following passage and answer the questions*

I have carried the manuscript to these translations about with me for days, reading it in railway trains, or on the top of omnibuses and in restaurants, and I have often had to close it lest some stranger would see how much it moved me. These lyrics—which are in the original, my ... (Indian friends) tell me, full of subtlety of rhythm, of untranslatable delicacies of colour, of material invention—display in thought a world I have dreamed of all my life long. The work of a supreme culture, they yet appear as much a growth of the common soil as the grass and the rushes. A tradition, where poetry and religion are the samething, has passed through the centuries, gathering from learned and unlearned metaphor and emotion, and carried back again to the multitude the thought of the scholar and the noble. If the civilisation of Bengal remains unbroken, if that common mind which—as one divines—runs through all, is not, as with us, broken into a dozen minds that know nothing of each other, something even of what is most subtle in these verses will have come, in a few generations, to the beggar on the roads.

—W.B. Yeats, from Introduction to Rabindranath Tagore's Gitanjali.

5 In this passage, Yeats praises Indian culture primarily because it
(a) Is accessible to Westerns thought it is rooted in a different religious tradition
(b) Has been flexible enough to survive a transition into the modern world
(c) Embodies values and gives rise to art that can be shared by people of all classes
(d) Reflects a marvellous eclecticism in drawing from many disparate cultures

July 2018

6 In which city did John Ruskin see a paradigm for Victorian Britain?
(a) Vienna (b) Venice
(c) Rome (d) Paris

December 2015

7 Which of the following authors wrote *Studies in the History of the Renaissance*?
(a) Walter Pater
(b) Oscar Wilde
(c) Thomas Carlyle
(d) John Ruskin

ANSWERS

Objective Questions

1. (a)	2. (c)	3. (b)	4. (b)	5. (d)	6. (c)	7. (a)	8. (b)	9. (a)	10. (a)
11. (c)	12. (c)	13. (b)	14. (d)	15. (c)	16. (a)	17. (b)	18. (c)	19. (a)	20. (d)
21. (a)	22. (c)	23. (d)	24. (d)	25. (c)	26. (c)	27. (b)	28. (a)	29. (d)	30. (d)
31. (c)	32. (a)	33. (d)	34. (d)	35. (c)	36. (b)	37. (b)	38. (d)	39. (d)	40. (d)
41. (a)	42. (c)	43. (d)	44. (d)	45. (b)	46. (c)	47. (d)	48. (d)	49. (d)	50. (c)
51. (a)	52. (d)	53. (b)	54. (d)	55. (c)	56. (a)	57. (d)	58. (a)	59. (d)	60. (c)
61. (b)	62. (c)	63. (a)	64. (a)	65. (a)	66. (b)	67. (c)	68. (b)	69. (d)	70. (a)
71. (a)	72. (b)	73. (c)	74. (d)	75. (a)	76. (a)	77. (d)	78. (c)	79. (c)	80. (d)
81. (a)	82. (b)	83. (c)	84. (d)	85. (b)	86. (c)	87. (d)	88. (a)	89. (b)	90. (c)
91. (a)	92. (d)	93. (a)	94. (b)	95. (c)	96. (a)	97. (d)	98. (b)	99. (c)	100. (a)
101. (c)	102. (d)	103. (d)	104. (a)	105. (d)	106. (a)	107. (b)	108. (c)	109. (d)	110. (a)
111. (c)	112. (d)	113. (d)	114. (a)	115. (b)	116. (a)	117. (b)	118. (c)	119. (d)	120. (a)
121. (a)	122. (b)	123. (c)	124. (d)	125. (a)	126. (b)	127. (c)	128. (d)	129. (a)	130. (b)
131. (c)	132. (d)	133. (a)	134. (b)	135. (c)	136. (a)	137. (b)	138. (a)	139. (c)	140. (b)
141. (d)	142. (d)	143. (b)	144. (c)	145. (d)	146. (d)	147. (b)	148. (a)	149. (d)	150. (a)

Previous Years' Questions

1. (d)	2. (a)	3. (b)	4. (b)	5. (c)	6. (b)	7. (a)

Contemporary American and Non-British Non-Fiction

This chapter elaborates about prose non-fiction work of contemporary British, American and Non-British, Non-American writers across the globe. The literary trends of this period was a very indistinct difference between fiction and non-fiction literature. The post modernist literature deals with only interpretations as there are no absolute truths.

Contemporary English Non-Fiction

As we already know, contemporary literature is defined as literature written after World War II through the current time. Before discussing the literary feature, let us look at the historical background. Contemporary history was politically dominated by the Cold War (1945-91) between the United States and Soviet Union. The confrontation ended with the dissolution of the Soviet Union and Warsaw Pact in 1991. The aftermath of Cold War helped in democratising much of Europe, Africa and Latin America. There were changes due to economic boom in the developed countries. By the 1960s, many Western countries began deindustrialising. In their place globalisation led to the emergence of new industrial centres such as Japan, Taiwan and later China which exported consumer goods to developed countries. Science began transforming after 1945, spaceflight, nuclear technology, laser etc. were developed.

Computers were created followed by the internet, beginning the Information Age.

Literary Trends of Contemporary Period

Increased attachment to religion, most commonly characterised literature after World War II. Writers such as Graham Greene, TS Eliot continued powerful merging of thriller plots with studies of moral and psychological ambiguity.

One of the profound changes to have affected serious writing in recent years, has been the spread of fiction and poetry techniques into literary non-fiction : the

In this Chapter

- *Contemporary English Non-Fiction*
- *Major Contemporary Non-Fiction Writers*
- *Contemporary American Non-Fiction*
- *Major Contemporary American Non-Fiction Writers*
- *Non-British Non-American Non-Fiction Writers*

emphasis on 'show, don't tell' requirement or emphasis on concrete sensory details and avoidance of abstraction is on the increase. Morever the narrator loves to talk in the present tense. Now-a-days we cannot very tightly compartmentalise the two genres Fiction and Non-Fiction.

At this moment it is the shifting stance between fiction and non-fiction that compels attention. The danger, as genre-defying or creative non-fiction becomes a genre in its own right—with mix and match poised to become a matter or rote—is that no man's land could become predictably congested.

Fiction and Non-Fiction have been destabilised as categories of late, in favour of view that suggest a more complicated picture of reality and its mediation. New historiographical, novelistic and biographical practices have arisen that drew attention to their resistance to categorisation, flouting past methodology.

Post modernism has played a large part in reducing the barriers between these two genres. Neitzsche is known to have said, "There are no truths, only interpretation." This statement points to a central theme in the post modernist literature—a preoccupation with the problematic nature of truth and falsity. As such we live in an age where it is increasingly difficult to say with authority that a work is definitely fiction or non-fiction.

Still for academic purposes we can consider writers such as, Rebecca West, Graham Greene, Libretto, Stephen Spendor, Louis MacNiece as non-fiction British writers. Essays, memoirs, autobiographies, biographies, travel writing, nature writing, histories—all of these fit under the broad heading of creative non-fiction.

Major Contemporary Non-Fiction Writers

Rose Macaulay (1881-1958)

Rose Macaulay was an English author who wrote several biographies and travel writings. She was born in England on 1st August 1881 in Rugby, Warwickshire. She spent her early years in Vazagge, on the coast near Genoa where she grew up as a Tomboy. In 1894, she was enrolled in the Oxford High School for girls. Later she studied Modern History at Oxford University. She died of a heart attack in 1958.

Literary Career and Works

Her literary career started with the publication of 1st Novel in 1906. After the World War I Rose Macaulay concentrated on Prose and wrote many essays and publisher some of her serious work in two collections : *A Causal Commentary* (1925) and *Catchwards and Claptrap* (1926). Through these works she gained respect and became one of the more prominent *literary figure of her time*. In 1946, she wrote some travel writings : *They Went to Portugal* (1946). It was followed by *Evelyn Waugh* (1946) and *Fabled Shore : From the Pyrenees to Portugal by Road* (1949).

Dame Rebecca West (1892-1983)

Rebecca West, pseudonym of Cicily Isabel Andrews was born on 21st December, 1892 in London, England. She was a British journalist and critic who was perhaps best known for her reports on the *Nuremberg Trials of War Criminals* (1945-46). She was the daughter of an army officer. She was educated at Edinburg.

Literary Career and Works

From 1911 West became involved in journalism, contributed frequently to the left wing press. She made a name for herself as a fighter for woman suffrage. In 1916, she published a critical biography of Henry James that revealed her intellectual curiosity.

On her work as a journalist, she wrote essays and reviews for publication like New York Herald Tribute, The Daily Telegraph, and the New Republic.

Rebecca West loved travelling and her book *Black Lamp and Grey Falcon* (1941) is considered a classic of literature that includes genres of travel, culture and politics.

Her other works of non-fiction included *The Meaning of Treason* (1949), *A Train of Powder* (1955) (reports of criminal trials), *The Court and the Castle* (1958) which examines how political and religious ideas interact in literature.

Rebecca was named Commander of the Order of the British Empire and ten years later became a Dame Commander of the Order. She died of old age in 1983 at the age of 90.

Graham Greene (1904-1991)

Graham Greene is one of the most beloved and prolific writers of the 20th century. He was born on 2nd October, 1904 in Berkhamsted in England. He was very fond of reading right from his childhood. Greene attended prestigious Berkhamsted School. As an undergraduate at Oxford College, Greene studied modern history.

Literary Career and Works

After graduating Greene worked as a journalist in Nottingham and in 1926, he converted to Roman Catholicism. Though Greene is recognised for his novels, he also wrote biographies a memoir, travel stories and children's literature. He contributed to major publications and edited other prominent writers' works as well.

His non-fiction works include partial biography of other works, plays and diaries written by him.

Major Works

- John Aubrey and his Friends (1948)
- Two Plays : The Garden God, The Rest I'll Whistle.
- Some Poets, Artists and A Reference for Mellors 2000.

Diaries

Journals-1982-1986 (1995)

Journals-1987-1989 (1996)

Journals-1990-1920 (1997)

He eventually settled in Switzerland where he died of pneumonia in 1991 at the age of 86.

Antony Beevor (1946)

Sir Antony James Beevor is an English military historian. He was born on 14th December, 1946 in London. He was educated at Winchester and Sandhurst where he studied Military History.

He has published four novels and twelve books of non-fiction.

Major Works

- The Spanish Civil War 1982
- Inside the British Army 1990
- Crete : The Battle and the Resistance 1991
- Paris After the Liberation 1944-1949
- Stalingrad (1998)
- Berlin : The Downfall (2002)
- The Mytery of Olga Chekhova (2004)
- The Battle for Spain : The Spanish Civil War (1936-39)
- The Second World War (2012)
- Amhem : The Battle for the Bridges 1944 (2018)

For his book *Stalingard*, he was awarded the first Samuel Johnson Prize and the Hawthornden Prize for Literature in 1999.

Tony Judt (1948-2010)

Born in 1948 Tony Judt was raised by his Belgian father and mother who had immigrated from Russia. He was sent to a Hebrew School and waded into the world of Israeli politics at the age of 15. He went on to study as a scholarship student at King's College, Cambridge.

Literary Career and Works

Tony Judt had many non-fiction prose writings. He was awarded Pulitzer Prize in general non-fiction finalist 2006.

They are

- Post War : A History of Europe Since 1945 (2005)
- The Memory Chalet (2010)
- Thinking the Twentieth Century (2012)
- Reappraisal : Reflections on the Forgotton 20th Century (2008)
- When the Fact Change : Essays, 1995-2010 (2015)
- A Grand Illusion? An Essay on Europe (1996)
- Past Imperfect : French Intellectuals (1944-56)

Theodore Dalrymple (1949)

Anthony Malcolm Daniels, with pen name Theodore Dalrymple is an English writer and retired prison doctor. He was born in Kensington, London in 1949. His father was a communist businessman and Jewish mother was born in Germany. His work as a doctor took him to Rhodesia, Tanzania, South Africa and Gilbert Island. He returned to England in 1990.

Literary Career and Works

Daniels began sending unsolicited articles to 'The Spectator' in the early 1980s. His first published work, *A Bit of a Myth* appeared in the magazine in August 1983 under the name AM Daniels.

Daniels has written extensively on politics, education, art, culture and medicine.

Life at the Bottom : The World View that Makes the Underclass is a collection of essays which was published in the book form in 2001.

Another collection of essays is *Our Culture, What's left of it: The Mandarins and The Masses* were published in 2005.

Major Works

- Fool or Physician : The Memoirs of a Sceptical Doctor (1987)
- Life at the Bottom : The World View that makes the Underclass (2001)
- Making Bad Decisions : About the way we think of Social Problems (2006)
- In Praise of Prejudice : The Necessity of Preconceived Ideas (2007)
- Not with a Bang but with a Whimper : The Politics and Culture of Decline (2009)
- Spoilt Rotten : The Toxic Cult of Sentimentality (2010)
- The Proper Procedure and Other Stories 2017
- The Knife Went in Real Life Murders and our Culture 2018.

Lisa Jardine (1944-2015)

Lisa Anne Jardine was a British historian of early modern period. She was born on 12th April, 1944 in Oxford. She was an avid reader and attended Newnham College Cambridge and the University of Essex. She was awarded a PhD from the University of Cambridge with a dissertation on Francis Bacon.

Literary Career and Works

Jardine published more than 50 scholarly articles in peer reviewed journals and books and wrote 17 full length books both scholarly and general. Some of her important works include

- 'The Curious Life of Robert Hooke'. The Man who Measured London.
- Ingenious Pursuits : Building the Scientific Revolution
- Biographies of Christopher Wren and Robert Hooke

Among her other books are works on Erasmus, Bacon, she has won many awards including the President's Medal by the British Academy in 2012.

In 2015 Lisa Jardine died of Cancer on October 25th.

Nikolai Tolstoy (1935)

He is an English Russian author who writes under the pseudonym Nikolai Tolstoy. He was born in England in 1935 and is the stepson of the author Patrick O'Brien. He was educated at Wellington College, Sandhurst and Trinity College, Dublin.

Literary Career and Works

Tolstoy has written a number of books about Celtic Mythology. He has also written about World War II and its immediate repercussions.

Major Works

- Victim of Yalta (1977)
- The Half Mad Lord (1978)
- Stalin's Secret War (1981)
- The Tolstoys (1983)
- The Quest for Merlin (1985)
- The Ministers and the Massacres (1986)
- Patrick O'Brian (2004)

AN Wilson (1950)

AN Wilson is a British writer known for his fiction and non-fiction works. He was born on 27th October, 1950 in Staffordshire, England. His parents sent him to Hillstone School, Great Malvern in Worcestershire. He also went to Rugby School and joined the New-college, Oxford from where he completed his MA in 1976.

Literary Career and Works

AN Wilson embarked on a writing career in 1977 with publication of first novel. But in 1980s he forayed into writing biographies and gained a reputation as a frank and entertaining biographer. During this period only, he openly declared that he was an athiest and penned down several works on the themes of religion, spirituality and Atheism. As a newspaper columnist. he has contributed numerous articles on varying topics to 'Daily Mail', 'London Evening Standard', 'Times Literary Supplement', 'New Statesman', 'The Spectator' and 'The Observer'.

In the recent years he has received media attention for his non-fiction works, *Dante in Love* (2011), *The Elizabethans* (2011), *Hitler: A Short Biography* (2011)and *Victoria: A Life* (2014).

His book on Leo Tolstoy won the Whitbread Award for best biography in 1988.

Major Works

- The Laird of Abbotsford : A View of Sir Walter Scott (1980)
- The Life of John Milton : A Biography (1983)
- Hilaire Belloc : A Biography (1985)
- Tolstoy : A Biography (1988)
- Penfriends from Porlock (1988)
- Charles Darwin;Victorian Mythmaker (2017)
- CS Lewis : A Biography (1990)
- Against Religion : Why He should live without It (1991)
- Jesus : A Life (1992), London A Short History (2004)
- The Faber Book of Church and Clergy (1992)
- The Rise and Fall of the House of Windsor (1993)
- Paul : The Mind of the Apostle (1997)
- The Victorians (2002), Our Times (2008)
- Dante in Love (2011), Victoria : A Life (2014)
- The Lampitt Chronicles
- Incline our Hearts (1988)
- A Bottle in the Smoke (1990)
- Daughters of Albion (1991)
- Hearing Voices (1995)
- A Watch in the Night (1996)

Alison Weir

Alison Weir is a British writer of history books and biographies about British Royalty. She was born in Central London on 8th July, 1951. She was educated at city of London school for Girls and North Western Polytechnic and hoped to become a history teacher. Between 1991 and 1997, she ran a school for children with learning difficulties.

Literary Career and Works

In the 1970s, Weir spent four years researching and writing a biography of the *Six Wives of Henry VIII*. The work was initially rejected by publishers as it was deemed very long. A revised version of this biography was later published as her second book.

Weir became a published author in 1989 with the publication of 'Britain's Royal Families'. It was a compilation of genealogical information about the British Royal Family.

Major Works

- The Princess in the Tower (1922)
- Lancaster and York : The War of the Roses (1995)
- The Children of England : The Heirs of King Henry VIII (1996)
- Elizabeth the Queen (1998)
- Eleanor of Aquitaine : By the Wrath of God, Queen of England (1999)
- Henry VIII : The King and His Court (2001)
- Mary, Queen of Scots and the Murder of Lord Darnley (2003)
- Isabella : She Wolf of France, Queen of England (2005)
- The Lady in the Tower : The Fall of Anne Boleyn
- Trailors of the Tower (2010)
- The Ring and the Crown : A History of Royal Weddings (2011)
- Queens of the Conquest (2017)

Contemporary American Non-Fiction

Historical Background

The United States, which emerged from World War II confident and economically strong, entered the cold war in the late 1940s. This conflict with the Soviet Union shaped global politics. The proxy war and threat of nuclear annihilation were some of the influences which shaped American Literature during later half of 20th century. In 1950 and 1960, there were cultural shifts within US due to Civil Rights Movement and the Women's Movement. By the turn of the 21st century, American literature had become a more complex and inclusive story based on a wide-ranging body of past writing.

Literature written by African Americans during the contemporary period was shaped in many ways. Many writers left America repulsed by injustice and discrimination faced by them as black men.

Literary Trends

The contemporary American and non-British literature tend to be influenced by the prosperous life-style that followed World War II.

In contemporary literature the distinction between fiction and non-fiction can be blurred. This is known as Crosses. Fiction writers based stories on real life events and may include authentic material.

On the other hand, non-fiction writers make historical figures come alive by incorporating dialogues and imaginary scenes. Some prominent non-fiction writers of America include, Gore Vidal, Susan Sontag Malcolm Cowley, Alfred Kazin, Irving Howe, Henry Louis Gates, Ralph Ellison, James Baldwin, many American writers involved themselves in distinguished journalism and social commentary for *e.g.*, John Hersey, Lillian Hellman, Frank Conroy, David Foster Wallace, Maya Angelou.

Major Contemporary American Non-Fiction Writers

James Baldwin (1924-1987)

James Arthur Baldwin was an American novelist and non-fiction writer. He was born on 2nd August, 1924 in New York City, United States. He grew up in poverty. From age 14 to 16, he was active during out of the school hours as a preacher. After graduation from high school, he began a restless period of ill-paid jobs, self study and literary apprenticeship in Greenwich village.

Literary Career and Works

In 1955, a Collection of Essays *Notes of a Native Son* was published. In 1957, he lived in US only and took an active part in civil rights struggle that swept the nation. His book of Essays *Nobody Knows My name* (1961), explores black-white relations in the United States. James Baldwin was a uniquely prophetic voice in American letters. His brilliant and provocative essays made him the literary voice of the civil rights era. Baldwin in his essays, fearlessly articulated issues of race and democracy with epigrammatic wit which established him as an essential intellectual voice of his time.

Major Works

- A Talk to Teachers (1963)
- The Fire Next Time (1963)
- The Devil Finds Work (1976)
- The Evidence of Things Not Seen (1985)
- The Price of the Ticket (1985)
- The Cross of Redemption : Uncollected Writings (2010)

Always true to his own convictions, rather than to the tastes of others, Baldwin continued to write what he wanted to write.

Early in December (1987), Baldwin died of stomach Cancer. At the time of Baldwin's death, he had an unfinished manuscript called *Remember This House* which is a memoir of personal recollection of civil rights leaders Medga Evers, Malcolm X and Martin Luther King 'Jr.'

Gore Vidal (1925-2012)

Gore Vidal was pseudonym of Eugene Luther GoreVidal Jr, was born on 3rd October, 1925 at West Point, New York US He was a prolific essayist and novelist. Vidal graduated from Phillips Exeter Academy in New Hampshire in 1941 and also served in the US Army in World War II.

Literary Career and Works

Vidal wrote many novels which made him successful. But it is his essays in which Vidal analysed contemporary American politics and government, and Vidal is well known for his witty and outspoken political opinions with satire.

Major Works

Non-Fictions

- Rocking the Boat (1962)
- Reflections upon a Sinking Ship (1969)
- The Second American Revolution and other Essay (1976-82)
- United States : Essay 1993 (National Book Award)
- Imperial America : Reflections on the United States of Amnesia (2004)

Autobiography

- Palimpsest : A Memoir (1995)
- Point to Point Navigation : A Memoir (2006)
- A Snapshot in History's Glare (2009)
- He died in July 2012 in Los Angeles, California.
- Perhaps contrary to his own wishes, Vidal is more respected as an essayist than novelist.

Susan Sontag (1933-2004)

Susan was an American writer, philosopher, teacher and political activist who mostly wrote essays. She was born in New York city on 16th January, 1933. She had an unhappy childhood with a cold distant mother. She graduated from North Hollywood High school at the age of 15. She studied English literature (MA 1954) and Philosophy (MA 1955) at Harvard University.

Literary Career and Works

During the early 1960s, she wrote a number of essays and reviews which were published in different periodicals such as 'The New York Review of Books'. Her essays are characterised by a serious philosophical approach to various aspects and personalities of modern culture. She first came to national attention in 1964, with an essay entitled *Notes on Camp* in which she discussed the attributes of taste within the gay community.

She has been described as one of the most influential critics of her generation.

Major Works

- Against Interpretation (includes Notes on Camp) (1966)
- Styles of Radical Will (1969)
- Under the Sign of Saturn (1980)
- Where the Stress Falls (2001)
- Regarding the Pain of Others (2003)
- At the Same Time : Essays and Speeches (2007)
- She has written some novels and monographs also.

Allan Bloom (1930-1992)

He is an American writer and philosopher best known for his scholarly volumes of their putative essays and translation of works by Jean Jacques Rousseau and Plato.

He was born on 14th September, 1920 at Indiana Polis, Indiana. Bloom graduated from the University of Chicago with a bachelor's degree at the age of 18. He earned his PhD from the Committee on Social thought in 1955. Bloom died in 1992 at Chicago, Illinois.

Literary Career and Works

Bloom's writing may be placed into two categories : scholarly and popular political commentary. Bloom's translation and essay on *The Republic* is radically different in many important aspects from the previous translations and interpretations of the same work. His first book *The Closing of the American Mind* was published in 1987, five years after Bloom had published an essay in *National Review* about the failure of Universities to serve the needs of the students. The book remained at number one on 'The New York Times Best Seller' list for Non-fiction for four months.

At Closing of the American Mind Bloom's novel was an instant hit as it was a very useful book. It brought into public view the scandal of the Universities which openly taught, there is no principled difference between good and evil. Bloom exposes and denounces the mindless relativism that has exhausted the spirit of the West totally. The book contains some suggestions for the cure.

Major Works

- The Republic of Plato (1968)
- Shakespeare's Politics (1964)
- Jean Jacques Rousseau (1968)
- Introduction to the Reading of Hegel, Cornell (1980)
- Giants and Dwarfs : Essays (1960-1990)
- Love and Friendship (1993)

Joan Didion (1934)

Joan Didion was born in Sacramento, California on December 5, 1934. She received a BA from the University of California, Berkeley in 1956.

Literary Career and Works

Didion is best known for her literary journalism and memoirs. She started working for magazine Vogue in 1956 and continued till 1963, as a copy writer and then as an editor. A collection of magazine columns titled as *Slouching Towards Bethlehem* (1968) established Didion's reputation as an essayist and confirmed her preoccupation with the forces of disorder. In a second collection *The White Album* (1979), Didion continued her analysis of the turbulent 1960s. The inner decay of the establishment is a major theme of the essays constituting the volume *After Henry*.

Her memoir *The Year of Magical Thinking* (2005), Jane Didion recounts her marriage and mourned her husband's death. This memoir won a National Book Award and this was accepted for the stage in 2007.

Major Works

- Blue Night (2011) (a memoir)
- South and West (2017)
- 'Play It As it Lays'
- 'The Centre will not Hold'
- We Tell Ourselves Stories in Order to Live (2006)
- Political Fictions (2001), Miami (1987)
- Salvador (1983)
- Where I was From (2003)

Bill Bryson (1951)

Bill Bryson is an American author of books on travel, the English language, science and other non-fiction topics. He was born and raised in Des Moines, Iowa, on 8th December, 1951. He had an elder brother and a sister. Bryson attended Drake University for two years before dropping out in 1972.

Literary Career and Works

Bryson had dual citizenship of America and Britain. While living in the US in 1990, Bryson wrote a column for a British newspaper for several years. In this he reflected aspects of his repatriation in the United States. These columns were selected and later adopted to turn in a book titled *I'm a Stranger Here Myself*.

After travelling to Appalachian Trail, he wrote a book *A Walk in the Woods* in (2015). Bryson has also written two popular works on the History of English language *The Mother Tongue* and *Made in America*.

Bryson has received many awards and honours for his contribution to writing science books and other books.

Major Works

Down Order In a Sunburned Country US (Travell 1999-2001)

- Bryson's Dictionary of Troublesome Word (2002)
- Walk About (2002)
- Bill Bryson's Africa Diary (2002)
- A Short History of Nearly Everything (2003)
- The Life and Times of the Thunderbold Kid (Memoirs 2006)
- Shakespeare: The World as State (Biography 2007)
- Bryson's Dictionary for Writers and Editors (2008)
- Icons of England (2008)
- One Summer : America (2013)
- The Road to Little Dribbling : More Notes from a Small Island (2015)

Maya Angelou (1928-2014)

Maya Angelou, her original name Marguerite Annie Johnson is an American writer, poet, memoirist and actress whose several volumes of autobiography explore the themes of economic, racial and sexual oppression.

She was born in St. Louis, US on 4th April, 1928. She spent much of her childhood in the care of her paternal grandmother in rural stamps, Arkansan. When she was not yet eight years old, she was raped by her mother's boyfriend. She told about it to her family. After this the man was murdered and the traumatic sequence of events left her almost mute for several years. This early life event is focussed in her, first biographical work *I Know Why the Caged Bird Sings*.

Literary Career and Works

Her first biographical work won her critical acclaim and a National Book Award nomination. Moving to New York city in late 1956s, Angelou found encouragement for her literary talents at the Harlem writers Guild. Angelou received several honors throughout her career; including two NAACP awards in the outstanding literary (non-fiction) category in 2005 and 2009 respectively.

Major Works

- All God's Children Need Travelling Shoes (1986)
- Wouldn't Take Nothing for My Journey Now (1994) (Essay collection)
- A Song Flung up to Heaven (autobiography) (2002)
- Letters to My Daughter (2008) (Essay book)
- A Cook Book named The Welcome Table : A Lifetime of Memories with Recepies (2005)
- Great Food All Day Long (2010)

During her life time Angelou won numerous awards. Due to frail health, she died on 28th May, 2014.

Adam Hochschild (1942)

Adam Hochschild is an American author, journalist, historian and lecturer. He was born on 5th October, 1942 at New York City, US Adam graduated from Harvard in 1963 with a B.A. in History and Literature.

Literary Career and Works

Adam's first book was a memoir *Half the Way Home : A Memoir of Father and Son* (1986). In this book he described the difficult relationship he had with his father. In another book *The Mirror at Midnight : A South African Journey* (1990), he examines the tension of modern South Africa through the prism of the 19th century. In another book *The Unquiet Ghost : Russians Remember Stalin* (1994) Hochschild chronicles, his six months he spent in Russia, travelling to Siberia and the Arctic.

His other work *Finding the Trap Door : Essays*, portraits, Travels (1997) collects his personal essays and shorter pieces of reportage as does the more recent work *Lessons from Dark Time and other Essays* (2018).

Another book *King Leopold's Ghost : A Story of Greed, Terror and Heroism in Colonial Africa* (2006) is a history of the conquest of Congo and it sparked the 20th century's first great international human rights campaign.

Hochschild's book *Bury the Chains : Prophets and Rebels in the Fight to Free an Empire's Staves* (2005) is about the anti slavery movement in the British empire.

Major Works

- To End All Wars : A Story of Loyalty and Rebellion (2011)
- Spain in Our Hearts : Americans in the Spanish Civil War (2016)
- Lessons from a Dark Time and other Essays (2018)
- Adam has won many awards and accolades, and for his book 'Bury The Chains' he was nominated for National Book Award.

Simon Winchester (1944)

Simon is a British-American author and journalist. He was born in London on 28th September, 1944. He attended several boarding schools in Dorset. He spent a year hitch-hiking around the United States. In 1963, he went to St Catherine's college, Oxford to study geology.

Literary Career and Works

He started his career as a writer after giving up his job as geologist. In 1969, Winchester joined the newspaper *The Guardian*. His first book *In Holy Terror* was published by Faber and Faber in 1975. The book drew heavily on the experiences of the turmoil in *Northern Island*. In 1976, another book, titled *American Heart Beat* was published. The author here deals with his travels through the American heart land. Winchester's first truly successful book was *The Professor And The Madman* (1998). Telling the story of the Oxford English Dictionary, the book was a New York Times Best Seller.

Though, Winchester still writes travel books, Winchester has used narrative non-fiction form in writing many more best sellers.

Major Works

- The Map that Changed the World (2001)
- The Meaning of Everything (2003)
- Krakatoa : The Day the World Explolded (2003)
- Simon Winchester's Calcutta (2004)
- A Crack in the Edge of the World : America and The Great California Earthquake (1906)
- The Man who Loved China (2008)
- Atlantic : A Vast Ocean of a Million Stories (2010)
- The Man who United The States : 2013
- When the Earth Shapes : Earthquakes, Volcanoes and Tsunamis (2015)

On 4th July, 2011, Winchester was naturalised as an American citizen. he has won many awards for his outstanding work.

Rebecca Traister (1975)

Rebecca was born in 1975. She was raised on a farm with a Jewish father and baptist mother. She attended Germantown Friends school and North Western University. After college she moved to New York City.

Literary Career and Works

His first book *Big Girls Don't Cry* (2010) was a notable book and it won Emnesta Drinker Book Prize in 2012. Her second book *All The Single Ladies* (2016) has been referred to as a follow up of the first and presents woman's bid for Independence. A third book was published in 2018 titled *Good And Mad : The Revolutionary Power of Women's Anger.* In 2012 Triaster received a Mirror Award for best commentary in Digital Media for two essays that appeared in Salon. She also appears on Cable TV News frequently commenting on feminism and politics.

Non-British, Non-American Non-Fiction Writers

Helen Garner (1942)

Helen Garner is an australian non-fiction writer. She was born in Geelong in 1942. She attended Manifold Heights State School, Ocean Goove State School and The Hermitage in Geolong where she was the head prefect. She studied at University of Melbourne and graduated with majors in English and Fiction.

Literary Career and Works

Though Garner has written many novels, we will here discuss her non-fiction writing. She was fired from her teaching job after publishing *In The Digger* a counter cultural magazine. One of her famous and controversial books is *The First Stone* (1995), an account of a 1992 sexual harassment scandal at Ormond college.

Major Works

Non-Fiction

- True Stories : Selected Non-Fiction (1996)
- The Feel of Steele (2001)
- Joe Cinque's Consolation (2004)
- This House of Grief: The Story of a Murder Trial (2014)
- La Mama : History of Theatre (1988)
- Regions of Thick Ribbed Ice (2015)
- Everywhere I Look (2016)

Essays and Reporting

- Man with the Pearl White Cord (2005)
- Moving Experience (2005)
- Punishing Lawon (2005)
- A Date with Darcy (2013)

She has been awarded many prizes for her fiction and non-fiction writing including Melbourne Prize for Literature in 2006, and in 2019 Australian Council Award for Life Time Achievement in Literature.

Umberto Eco (1932-2016)

Umberto Eco is both a fiction and non-fiction writer. Eco was born in Italy in January, 1932. He attended High School in the city of Alessandria, in northern Italy. Eco received a Salesian education. He joined the University of Turin to take up medieval philosophy and literature.

Literary Career and Works

A group of avant garde artists, painters, musicians and writers whom Umberto had befriended at RAI, became an important part of his writing career. He left RAI in 1959 to become the senior non-fiction editor of the Bompiani Publishing House in Milan, a position he occupied until 1975. Umberto developed ideas on open texts and semiotics and wrote many essays on these subjects.

Major Works

- The Aesthetics of Thomas Aquinas (1988)
- Art and Beauty in the Middle Ages (1985)
- The Open Work (1989)
- Misreading (1993)
- Partial English Translation: Apocalypse Postponed (1994)
- The Middle Ages of James Joyce, The Aesthetics of Chaosman (1989)
- A Theory of Semiotics (1976)
- Six Walks in the Fictional Woods (1994)
- Encounter (1996)
- Belief or Non-Belief : A Dialogue (2000)
- Five Moral Pieces (2001)
- Inventing the Enemy (2012)
- The Book of Legendary Lands (2013)
- Chronicles of a Liquid Society (2017)

Besides non-fiction, Umberto Eco has written many books for children.

Gordon McLauchlan (1942)

Gordon was born in 1942, in Dunedin and lived in New Plymouth, Auckland and Wellington before settling in Auckland. He was educated at Wellington College and spent a year at Victoria University of Wellington before joining as a newspaper reporter.

Literary Career and Works

McLauchlan worked as a journalist, feature writer, sports writer and sub-editor before becoming a freelance journalist/writer in 1973. He became a full time writer in 2000. He has written a number of best sellers including *The Passionless People*. He has been a prolific writer.

Major Works

- Auckland Reed (1978)
- The Acid Test (1981)
- McMeckan: A Biography (1982)
- The Line that Dares: A History of the Union Steam Ship Company (1987)
- A History of New-Zealand Humour (1988)
- The Big Con (1992)
- A Life's Sentences: A Memoir (2004)

Philip Temple (1939)

Philip Temple was born in 1939 in Yorkshire and educated in London. He emigrated to New-Zealand at the age of 18, becoming an explorer, and outdoor educator. His first book reflected this adventurous career and *The World at their Feet* won a Wattie Award in 1970.

Literary Career and Works

Philip became a professional author in 1970. Philip's non-fiction work is wide-ranging from books about exploration and the outdoors to New-Zealand history and electoral reforms. His book about the Wake-field family and the early British settlement of New-Zealand, *A Sort of Conscience* was NZ biography of the year in 2003 and won the Ernest Scott History Prize.

Over the years Philip has been awarded several fellowships, including the Katherine Mansfield Memorial Fellcwship (1979) and 1996 NZ National Liberty Fellowship.

Major Works

- Great Walking Tracks of New Zealand (1977)
- Central (2003)
- High Country (2004)
- The Book of the Kea (1996)
- The Last True Explorer (2002)
- Chance is a Fine Thing (Self Memoir) (2009)
- Presenting New Zealand : An Illustrated History
- The Last True Explorer : Into Darkest New Guinea
- Children's Books
- Articles and Reviews

Sisonke Msimang

Sisonke was born in exile to South African parents. She was raised in Zambia, Kenya and Canada before studying in the US as an undergraduate. Her family returned to South-Africa after apartheid was abolished in the early 1990s.

Literary Career and Works

She is a South African writer, a contributing editor at AIAC. She has written a memoir of exile and home in her book *Always Another Country*. Besides this, she has written many essays and articles.

Major Works

- The Uber Driver and Muhammad Ali
- The Burning
- Africa's First Lady
- Shut down: On the death of Compromise in South Africa
- Africa Day is for Big Men
- The Importance of Reading 'Khwezi' : The Remarkable Story of Fezeka Ntsukla Kuzwayo

'Always Another Country' is a memoir written by Sisonke with a unique perspective on South Africa's history that fundamentally tells the struggle of a deeply torn woman to comprehend a deeply torn country. She has written the story of her youth travelling between continents and cultures, all the while being 'bottle-fed the dream' of a free South Africa by her mother and her exiled father. In this memoir, the author traverses many political issues such as migration, racism and sexual violence. Msimang is also able to throw light on the generation divide in South Africa that has torn away the hopes and aspirations of elder generation. Very humorously she gives a message that the more she distances herself from her parents, the more her own voice can emerge.

Narrative Non-Fiction

Narrative non-fiction also known as creative **non-fiction** or literary non-fiction, is usually defined as a genre which uses the techniques and styles of fiction (character, plot, conflict, scene setting) to tell a true story. Enclosed here is a list of some narrative non-fiction books which guarantee to provide a great reading experience.

Books	Writer
▪ The Immortal Life of Henrietta Lacks	by Rebecca Skloot
▪ Hidden Figures	Margot Lee Shetterly
▪ Packing for Mars	Mary Roach
▪ Leaving Orbit	Margaret Lazarus Dean
▪ Annals of Former World	John McPhee
▪ The Secret Life of Lobsters	Trevor Corson
▪ Night Draws Near	Anthony Shahid
▪ Behind the Beautiful Forevers	Katherine Boo
▪ Mountains Beyond Mountains	Tracy Kidder
▪ Without you, There is No US	Suki Kim
▪ Nothing to Envy	Barbara Demick
▪ Reading Lolita in Tehran	Azar Nafisi
▪ Being Mortal	Atul Gawande
▪ The Secretary	Kim Ghattas
▪ The Lonely War	Nazila Fathi
▪ The Warmth of Other Suns	Isabel Wilkenson
▪ Unbroken	Laura Hillenbrand
▪ The Boys in the Boat	Daniel James Brown
▪ Sin in the Second City	by Karen Abbott
▪ Eighty Days	Matthew Goodman
▪ In the Garden of Beasts	Erik Larson

EXAM BASED QUESTIONS

1 Which out of this does not fall under the category of non-fiction?
(a) Essays (b) Memoirs
(c) Novels (d) Biographies

2 Post modernism is known being skeptical of what kind of narratives?
(a) Grand narratives (b) Complex narratives
(c) Fragmented narratives (d) Odd narratives

3 What characteristic is most often linked with the Cold War?
(a) Guns (b) Carnage
(c) Paranoia (d) Love and hugs

4 What word describes texts that draw attention to themselves as texts?
(a) Mimesis (b) Metafiction
(c) Meta mucil (d) Realism

5 Who ended her highly romantic and impressively wide ranging survey, Pleasure of Ruins (1953) with A Note on New Ruins in which she was fascinated with the 'Catastrophic tipsy chaos' of a British Comb site?
(a) Rose Macaulay (b) Compton Barnelt
(c) Heany (d) Anita Desai

6 When did Rose Macaulay read the essay 'Into Questions and Answers' in 'A Casual Commentary' on BBC Radio?
(a) 1925 (b) 1930
(c) 1928 (d) 1927

7 What does the writer discuss in the essay 'Increasing Daily' in her collection 'A Casual Commentary'?
(a) Population increase
(b) Increase in number of congested cities
(c) Increase in motor vehicles
(d) All of the above

8 Which writer had her/his original name as Cecily Isabel Andrews?
(a) Rose Macaulay (b) Anthony Beevor
(c) Barth (d) Dame Rebecca West

9 In the book 'Black Lamb and Grey Falcon' which journey is described by the author?
(a) Journey to America (b) Journey to Scotland
(c) Journey to Yugoslavia (d) Journey to Australia

10 In which book of Rebecca the trials of Nazi war criminals were described?
(a) Black Lamb and Grey Falcon
(b) The Meaning of Treason
(c) The Court and the Castle
(d) The Nuremberg Trials

11 Which writer described Rebecca as a 'Across between a Charwoman and a Gypsy"?
(a) Elizabeth Bowen (b) Virginia Woolf
(c) Rose Macaulay (d) None of these

12 Graham Greene's book 'A journey without Maps' was the result of his walking tour through
(a) Mexico (b) Sierre Leone (c) Panama (d) Liberia

13 Which work by Antony Beevor is a definitive account of World War II most harrowing battle?
(a) Inside the British army (b) Stalingrad
(c) The Second World War (d) Berlin : The Downfall

14 Sir Antony J Beevor was known as
(a) Journalist (b) Science fiction writer
(c) English military historian (d) T.V. Anchal

15 In which year Beevor's work 'The Spanish Civil War' was published?
(a) 1982 (b) 1985 (c) 1987 (d) 1990

16 Who wrote the famous book 'Past Imperfect'?
(a) Antony Beevor (b) Rebecca West
(c) Tony Judt (d) Theodore Dalyrmple

17 Which book of Tony Judt is nine hundred and sixty pages long?
(a) When the Facts Change
(b) Past Imperfect
(c) Thinking the Twentieth Century
(d) Post War : A History of Europe since 1945

18 Which writer was also known as Anthony Malcolm Daniels?
(a) Theodore Dalyrmple (b) Antony Beevor
(c) Tony Judt (d) Graham Greene

19 Dalyrmple, along with being a writer was also a
(a) historian (b) journalist
(c) prison doctor (Retd.) (d) architect

20 Who wrote the book 'Spoilt Rotten : The Toxic Cult of Sentimentality'?
(a) Tony Judt (b) Antony Beevor
(c) Lisa Jardine (d) Theodore Dalyrmple

21 How many scholarly articles were published in journals by Lisa Jardine?
(a) 50 (b) 45 (c) 115 (d) 40

22 For doing the PhD Lisa Jardine wrote her dissertation on which writer of England?
(a) Geoffrey Chaucer (b) Milton
(c) Francis Bacon (d) None of these

23 Which university appointed Lisa Jardine as professor of Renaissance studies?
(a) Cambridge (b) Oxford
(c) Kunt (d) Queen Mary University

24 Which writer is a descendant of Tolstoy family as well as stepson of Patrick O'Brian?
(a) Leo Tolstoy (b) Nikolai Tolstoy
(c) Lisa Jardine (d) Rose Macaulay

25 In which book by Nikolai Tolstoy, the author talks about forcible repatriation of millions of Soviet citizens?
(a) The Half Mad Lord
(b) Stalin's Secret War
(c) Victims of Yalta
(d) The Ministers and the Massacres

26 In the book 'The Quest for Merlin' by Nikolai Tolstoy who is Merlin?
(a) A painter (b) A biographer
(c) A God (d) A historical figure

27 Who wrote the book 'Tolstoy : A Biography'?
(a) Nikolai Tolstoy (b) Tony Judt
(c) AN Wilson (d) Lisa Zardine

28 Which writer's biography traces the progress of clever child upto his conversion to christianity and the genesis of his writing?
(a) Penfriends from Porlock
(b) The Life of John Milton : A Biography
(c) CS Lewis : A Biography
(d) Hilaire Belloc : A Biography

29 AN Wilson received great media attention for which of his work?
(a) Dante in Love
(b) Daughters of Albion
(c) The Victorians
(d) The Faber Book of Church and Clergy

30 Where did Henry VIII traditionally like to celebrate christmas in the book Henry VIII and his six wives?
(a) Hever Castle (b) Greenwich Palace
(c) Buckingham Palace (d) None of these

31 During her coronation service, to whom was Elizabeth symbolically married?
(a) To her people
(b) To her boyfriend
(c) Prince Henry
(d) No one

32 In Alison Weir's The Lady Elizabeth, why does Henry VIII banish Elizabeth from court?
(a) Elizabeth declared that she would be queen one day
(b) Henry was just in rage over his counsellors
(c) Elizabeth brings Anne Boleyn and says she believed her to be innocent of the crimes
(d) Jane Seymour had just died and he couldn't afford to look at Elizabeth

33 Which prominent cultural shifts could be seen in US between 1950 to 1960?
(a) Civil rights movement (b) Women's movement
(c) Both (a) and (b) (d) None of these

34 What was the effect of cold war which was evident in American literature during 2nd half of 20th century?
(a) Proxy War
(b) World War III
(c) Threat of Nuclear Annihilation
(d) Both (a) and (c)

35 What is known as 'Crosses' in literature?
(a) The blurred distinction between fiction and non-fiction
(b) Stories based on imaginary characters
(c) Presentation of historical figures through narratives
(d) None of the above

36 In which year Baldwin's 'Collection of Essays' published?
(a) 1950 (b) 1955 (c) 1915 (d) 1957

37 Which book by James Baldwin explores black-white relations in the US?
(a) Nobody knows My Name
(b) Notes of a Native Son
(c) The Fire Next Time
(d) The Price of the Ticket

38 Baldwin's collection of essays entitled 'The Evidence of Things Not Seen' concerns the
(a) murders of Medgar Evers, Malcolm and Martin Luther King
(b) Watts riots
(c) Atlanta child murders
(d) early exit of Harlem

39 In 1948, James Baldwin left the United States and moved to which country?
(a) England (b) France
(c) Finland (d) Norway

40 With which opposing intellectuals did Gore Vidal indulge in Television debate?
(a) Richard Wright (b) William F Buckley
(c) Maupin (d) Antony Beevor

41 Which President of US was criticised the most by Vidal Gore?
(a) Richard Nixon (b) George W Bush
(c) Abraham Lincoln (d) Gerald Ford

42 This famous writer's grandfather was a senator. Name the author.
(a) Tony Zudt (b) Gore Vidal
(c) James Baldwin (d) Halcolm Cowley

43 Which author graduated from North Hollywood High School?
(a) Lisa Jardine
(b) Dame Rose Macaulay
(c) Susan Sontag
(d) Gore Vidal

44 Who is the author of the essay, 'Notes on Camp'?
(a) Susan Sontag (b) Dame Rose Macaulay
(c) James Baldwin (d) Malcolm Cowley

45 Which of these adjectives was not used for Susan Sontag?
(a) Original (b) Populist (c) Dull (d) Sybaritic

46 When was her essay collection 'Notes on Camp' published?
(a) 1962 (b) 1964 (c) 1965 (d) 1968

47 Which of these awards were conferred on Susan Sontag?
(a) National Book Critics Circle Award
(b) National Book Award
(c) Mac Arthur Foundation Genius Grant
(d) All of the above

48 Where was Allan Bloom's essay published which was about the failure of Universities?
(a) The Spectator (b) The Guardian
(c) National Review (d) None of these

49 In which book's preface did Allan Bloom said, "his education began with Fi Sigmund Freud and ended with Plato"?
(a) Jean Jacqueas Rousseau
(b) The Republic of Plato
(c) Giants and Dwarfs : Essays
(d) Shakespeare's Politics

50 Along with his friend Werner, Allan Bloom taught which students at the University of Chicago?
(a) Blind students
(b) Dyslexic students
(c) Adult education students
(d) Normal students

51 The book 'Closing of the American Mind' is written by
(a) Joan Didion (b) Susan Sontag
(c) Gore Vidal (d) Allan Bloom

52 In which countries did Allan Bloom teach after graduation?
(a) England (b) Paris
(c) Switzerland (d) Chicago

53 Allan Bloom's which book made him famous and wealthy?
(a) Giants and Dwarfs
(b) Closing of the American Mind
(c) The Republic of Plato
(d) Shakespeare's Politics

54 For which magazine did 'Joan Didion' started working in 1956?
(a) Times (b) Vogue
(c) The Spectator (d) None of these

55 Which book by Didion won her a National Book Award?
(a) The Year of Magical Thinking
(b) South and West
(c) Political Fiction
(d) Blue Night

56 Which University was attended by Bill Bryson?
(a) Chicago University (b) Cornell University
(c) Drake University (d) Cambridge University

57 What is the name of the book which is a collection of Bloom's newspaper columns?
(a) A Wwalk in the Woods
(b) I'm a Stranger here Myself
(c) The Mother Tongue
(d) A Short History of Nearly Everything

58 What does Socrates do with Cephalus' definition of justice in the book 'The Republic of Plato' by Bloom?
(a) Ignore it (b) Incorporate it
(c) Disprove it (d) Promote it

59 In which town in 1951, was Bill Bryson born?
(a) Des Moines, Iowa (b) Reno Nevada
(c) Phoenix Arizona (d) Springfield Missouri

60 What is Maya's original name?
(a) Margaret Johnson
(b) Annie Stephen
(c) Marguerite Annie Johnson
(d) None of the above

61 At what college was Maya named Reynolds professor of American studies?
(a) Harvard (b) Standford
(c) Wake Forest University (d) Cornell University

62 At the age of eight Maya is raped by her mother's boyfriend, Mr Freeman. What happens to him?
(a) He is found dead
(b) He gets hounded out of lawn
(c) He is sent to jail
(d) He gets away with it

63 Why was Bertha Flowers important to Maya?
(a) She was Maya's teacher
(b) She sponsored Maya's education
(c) She was like a mother to her
(d) She was an educated woman who gave her interest in literature

64 What was Maya Angelou's first book?
(a) Just Give Me a Cool Drink of Water before'I die
(b) I Know Why the Caged Bird Sing
(c) On the Pulse of Morning
(d) And I Still Rise

65 Who inspired Maya to write?
(a) Martin Luther King (b) Rosa Parks
(c) Jenifer Lopaz (d) James Baldwin

66 Where did Maya grow up as a child?
(a) Missouri (b) Illinois
(c) California (d) Arkansaw

67 What award was Maya Angelou nominated for in 1972?
(a) Pulitzer (b) Nobel Peace Prize
(c) Grammy (d) Oscar

68 In which book did Adam Hochschild describe his relationship with his father?
(a) The Uniquiet Ghost : Russian Remembers Stalin
(b) Finding the Trap Door : A Secret Trapdoor in An Office
(c) Half the Way Home : A Memoir of Father and Son
(d) The Mirror at Midnight : A South African Journey

69 Which book of Adam Sparked the human right campaign at International level?
(a) To End All Wars—A Story of Loyalty and Rebellion
(b) Spain In Our Hearts
(c) King Leopold's Ghost
(d) A Dark Time and Other Essays

70 Which newspaper did Simon Winchester join in 1969?
(a) The Times Review (b) The Guardian
(c) The Spectator (d) The Washington Post

71 Which book made Simon Winchester famous?
(a) Northern Island (b) In Holy Terror
(c) The Professor and the Madman
(d) The Map that Changed the World

72 England's power grew and it felt embarrassed for not studying its language. Why did citizen want a proper dictionary?
(a) Many wanted to sell them in book stores
(b) Many wanted a dictionary for the English language in its entirely
(c) To help immigrants
(d) More demands on scholars to make a new dictionary

73 Which book by Rebecca Traister won her Emnest a Drinker Book Prize in 2012?
(a) Good and Mad (b) All the Single Ladies
(c) Big Girls don't Cry (d) All of these

74 Rebecca Traistor was born in which year?
(a) 1972 (b) 1974 (c) 1978 (d) 1975

75 To which country the writer Helen Garner belong to?
(a) India (b) South America
(c) Australia (d) New Zealand

76 Which award did Helen get in 2006?
(a) Noble Prize for Literature
(b) National Book Award
(c) Melbourne Prize for Literature
(d) Pulitzer Prize

77 Which has been called Helen's most controversial book?
(a) The First Stone (b) True Stories
(c) The Feel of Steele (d) My Hard Heart

78 Gordon Mclauchlan wrote a book 'Passionless People'. What it is about?
(a) A social critique on New Zealand
(b) A historical account of the country
(c) A realistic account of New Zealanders
(d) An imaginary narrative

79 We can identify Mclauchlan as a
(a) feature writer (b) journalist
(c) sub editor (d) All of these

80 Which book has been written by Philip Temple which has won the Ernest Scott History Prize?
(a) A Sort of Conscience (b) High Country
(c) The Last True Explorer (d) Central

81 Which African author was born in exile to South African parents?
(a) Sisonke Msimang (b) Maya Angelou
(c) Aminatla Forna (d) Ben Okri

82 What is the name of memoir written by Sisonke Msimang?
(a) Africa Day is for big Men
(b) Always Another Country
(c) The Uber Driver and Muhammad Ali
(d) Africa's First Lady

83 The book Fabled Shore : From the Pyreness to Portugal by Road is written by
(a) Lisa Jardine (b) Dame Rose Macaulay
(c) Graham Greene (d) Tony Judt

84 The book .... by Rebecca West is considered a classic literature including genres of travel, culture and politics.
(a) The Meaning of Treason
(b) The Court and The Castle
(c) Black Lamb and Grey Falcon
(d) A Train of Powder

85 Graham Greene is not only a noted novelist but also a .... writer who wrote memoirs, biographies and travel stories.
(a) Prose writer (b) Poet
(c) Dramatist (d) Non-fiction writer

86 The famous book Stalingrad was written by .... in ....
(a) Antony Beevor, 1998
(b) Lisa Jardine, 1990
(c) Sisonke Msimang 1975
(d) Helen Garner 1978

87 The writer .... was sent to a he brew school and waded into .... politics at the age of 15.
(a) Rose Macaulay, British
(b) Tony Judt, Israeli
(c) Theodore Dalrymple, English
(d) Rebecca West, Australian

88 The prose writer .... stayed in US and took part in civil rights struggle.
(a) Gore Vidal (b) Allan Bloom
(c) James Baldwin (d) Susan Santog

89 The book .... was written by Gore Vidal in 1962.
(a) The Second American Revolution
(b) United States : Essay
(c) Rocking the Boat (d) Imperial America

90 The book .... established Joan Didion as an essayist in 1968.
(a) The White Album
(b) Slouching Towards Bethlehem
(c) The Year of Magical Thinking
(d) After Henry

91 The writer Bill Bryson after travelling to Appalachian Trail wrote a book titled .... in 2015.
(a) A Walk in the Woods
(b) I am a Stranger here myself
(c) Walk About
(d) One Summer : America

92 In the book .... the author Simon Winchester deals with his travels through American heartland.
(a) American Heart Beat
(b) In Holy Terror
(c) The Professor and the Madman
(d) The Meaning of Everything

93 In 2012 Rebecca Traistor won .... for best commentary Digital media.
(a) Nobel prize (b) Pulitzer prize
(c) Mirror award (d) Emnesta drinker

94 The author .... has written many texts on Semiotics.
(a) Helen Garder (b) Umberto Eco
(c) Gordon McLauchlan (d) Philip Temple

95 The book Passionless People talks about .... by Gordon McLauchlan.
(a) American heart land (b) New Zealand culture
(c) Royalty of England (d) About India

96 Which of the following statement is incorrect?
(a) The book 'Big Girls don't Cry' was written by Rebecca Traister
(b) Joan Didion was an American non-fiction writer
(c) Philip Temple wrote the book 'South and West' in 2017
(d) James Baldwin wrote an essay book "Nobody Knows my Name"

97 Which of the following statement is correct?
(a) American prose writers made historical figures come alive with the help of imaginary scenes and dialogues
(b) Maya Angelou was not an actress only a prose writer
(c) Vidal discussed nature in his essays
(d) Allan Bloom was a travel writer

98 Which of the following statement is incorrect?
(a) The book 'Closing of the American Mind' became a very successful book
(b) It was written by Allan Bloom in the year 1987
(c) In this book Allan Bloom discusses the failure of American Universities to serve the needs of students
(d) The book won the author Pulitzer Award

99 Which of the following statement is incorrect?
(a) Helen Garner is an Australian novelist and non-fiction writer
(b) She has written the book 'The First Stone'
(c) She got her education at University of Melbourne
(d) She did not write the book 'The Spare Room'

100 Which statement is correct?
(a) Gordon Mclauchlan was born in 1942 in Dunedin, New Zealand
(b) He became a freelance journalist and writer in 1973
(c) He has written the book 'A History of New-Zealand Humour' in 1988
(d) All of the above

101 Which statement is correct?
(a) Sisonke Msimang was raised in Zambia, Kenya and Canada
(b) The book Unbroken is written by Nazila Falhi
(c) The book Last True Explorer was written by Bryson in 1970
(d) The book 'In Holy Terror' was written by Dame Rose Macaulay

102 Which statement is correct?
1. The American writer Susan Sontag is involved as teacher, philosopher, film maker.
2. The title of Sontag's first major work was 'Bill on Campus'.
3. Susan Sontag was born on 16th January, 1933.

Select the correct answer using the codes given below
(a) Only 1 (b) 1 and 3
(c) Only 2 (d) Only 3

103 Consider the following statements.
1. Allan Bloom authored and translated many works during his life time.
2. One of the most famous book by Allan Bloom is 'The Republic of Plato.
3. The famous book by Bloom 'The Closing of the American Mind' was written in 1987.
4. Allan Bloom was a conservative.

Which of the statement(s) given above is/are correct?
(a) 1 and 2 (b) Only 4 (c) 1, 2 and 3 (d) 3 and 4

104 Consider the following statements.
1. Dame Rose Macaulay was an American author.
2. She was born on 1st August, 1881 in Rugby, England.
3. One of her travel book is 'They Went to Portugal'.

Which of the statement(s) given above is/are incorrect?
(a) Only 1 (b) 2 and 3
(c) Only 3 (d) None of these

105 Consider the following statements.
1. The author Lisa Jardine was born in 1944.
2. London University of Queen Mary pinned her down as their professor of Renaissance studies.
3. She wrote about differences of opinion and head on confrontation in her book 'Reading Shakespeare Historically'.

Which of the statement(s) given above is/are correct?

(a) Only 1 (b) 1 and 2
(c) All of these (d) Only 2

106 Consider the following statements.
1. Nikolai Tolstoy was an English Russian author.
2. AN Wilson received media attention for his prose work 'Dante in Love'.
3. Alison Weir wrote the book 'Stalingrad'.

Which of the statement(s) given above is/are incorrect?

(a) Only 3 (b) 1 and 2
(c) Only 1 (d) Only 2

107 In the following questions two statements Assertion (A) and Reason (R) are given. Based on these four codes are given. Find out the correct code.

Assertion (A) Literature written by African-American during the contemporary period was shaped in money map.

Reason (R) These writers were unhappy over injustice and discrimination faced by the blacks in America.

Codes

(a) A is true, but R is false
(b) A is false, but R is true
(c) Both A and R are true and R is the correct explanation of (A)
(d) Both A and R are not true

108 **Assertion** (A) James Baldwin was the literary voice of civil rights.

Reason (R) He wrote brilliant and provocative essays articulating issues of race and democracy.

Codes

(a) A is correct, but R is not correct
(b) Both A and R are correct
(c) R is not the correct explanation of A
(d) Neither A nor R is correct

109 **Assertion** (A) Maya Angelou is an American writer, poet, memoirist and actress.

Reason (R) Her first biographical novel was 'I Know why the Caged Bird Sings'.

Codes

(a) R is the correct explanation of A
(b) A is correct, but R is not the correct explanation of A
(c) Both A and R are correct
(d) Both A and R are not correct

110 **Assertion** (A) Adam Hochschild is an American journalist, historian and lecturer.

Reason (R) His book King Leopold's Ghost is a history of Conquest of Congo.

Codes

(a) A is correct but R is not correct explanation of A
(b) Both A and R are not correct
(c) Both A and R are correct
(d) A is not correct, but R is true

111 What is common to the following works? Identify the correct description below.
1. Post Imperfect : French Intellectuals
2. Our Culture What's Left of It : The Mandarins and The Masses
3. Victims of Yalta
4. Tolstoy : A Biography

Codes

(a) All are works of British contemporary prose writers
(b) All are famous dramatic works of contemporary writers
(c) All are important novels of contemporary age
(d) All are important poetic works

112 What is common to the following writers and authors? Identify the correct description below.
1. James Baldwin 2. Gore Vidal
3. Bill Bryson 4. Maya Angelou

Codes

(a) All were contemporary novelists
(b) All of them wrote essays, biographies and non-fictional writings
(c) All were non-American, non-British authors
(d) All of them worked for T.V. shows

113 What is common to the following works? Identify the correct description below.
1. Always another country
2. The last true explorer
3. A Life's sentences—A Memoir
4. All the single ladies

Codes

(a) All are written by American writers
(b) All works are written by contemporary non-British, non-American prose writers
(c) All works are novels written by non-American authors
(d) All works are memoirs of different authors

114 Consider the following non-fictional prose.
1. The Closing of the American Mind
2. Shakespeare's Politics
3. The Republic of Plato
4. Love and Friendship

Codes

(a) All are works written by Rose Macaulay
(b) All are works written by Maya Angelou
(c) All are works of Allan Bloom
(d) All are works of Bill Bryson

115 **Consider the following authors.**
1. Jane Didion
2. Adam Hochschild
3. Simon Winchester
4. Rebecca Traister

Which of the author(s) is/are British?

(a) Only 1 (b) 2 and 3
(c) Only 4 (d) None of these

116. **Match the following.**

	List I	List II
A.	A Casual Commentary	1. Gordon Mclauchlan
B.	A Walk in the Woods	2. Sisonke Msimang
C.	Auckland Reed	3. Bill Bryson
D.	Always Another Country	4. Dame Rose Macaulay

Codes

	A	B	C	D		A	B	C	D
(a)	1	2	3	4	(b)	2	3	4	1
(c)	4	3	1	2	(d)	3	1	4	2

117 **Match the following.**

	List I	List II
A.	Gore Vidal	1. 1942
B.	Umberto Eco	2. 1944
C.	Simon Winchester	3. 1925
D.	Helen Garner	4. 1932

Codes

	A	B	C	D		A	B	C	D
(a)	1	2	3	4	(b)	3	4	2	1
(c)	4	2	1	3	(d)	2	4	1	3

118 **Match the following.**

	List I	List II
A.	John Aubrey and His Friends	1. 1998
B.	Stalingrad	2. 2004
C.	The Memory Chalet	3. 1948
D.	High Country	4. 2010

Codes

	A	B	C	D		A	B	C	D
(a)	1	2	4	3	(b)	2	3	1	4
(c)	3	1	4	2	(d)	1	4	2	3

119 **Match the following.**

	List I	List II
A.	Paris After the Liberation	1. 1983
B.	Black Lamb and Grey Falcon	2. 1995
C.	When the Facts Change	3. 1944
D.	A Bit of Myth	4. 1941

Codes

	A	B	C	D		A	B	C	D
(a)	4	3	2	1	(b)	1	2	3	4
(c)	3	2	1	4	(d)	3	4	2	1

120 **The period from 1928-2014 belonged to which contemporary author and actor?**

(a) Rose Macaulay
(b) Dame Rebecca West
(c) Antony Beevor
(d) Maya Angelou

121 **Which of the following works is incorrect chronological order as per their publication?**

(a) A Casual Commentary, Berlin : The Downfall, Nobody Knows My Name, The Tolstoys
(b Berlin : The Downfall, Nobody Knows My Name, The Tolstoys, A Casual Commentary
(c) A Casual Commentary, Nobody Knows My Name, The Tolstoys, Berlin : The Downfall
(d) The Tolstoys, Berlin : The Downfall, Nobody Knows My Name, A Casual Commentary

122 **Which of the following chronological order is correct as per the birth of the author given below**

(a) Susan Sontag, Theodore Dalyrmple, Rebecca Traister, Dame Rebecca West
(b) Rebecca Traister, Rebecca West, Theodore Dalyrmple, Susan Sontag
(c) Dame Rebecca West, Susan Sontag, Theodore Dalyrmple, Rebecca Traister
(d) Theodore Dalyrmple, Rebecca Traister, Dame Rebecca West, Susan Sontag

123 **Which of the following work does not belong to Maya Angelou?**

(a) Lamama : History of a Theatre
(b) All God's Children need Travelling Shoes
(c) I Know Why the Caged Bird Sings
(d) Great Food All Day Long

124 **Which of the following pairs is correctly matched?**

(a) Joan Didion : England
(b) Bill Bryson : New Zealand
(c) Gore Vidal : United States
(d) Rebecca West : Australia

125 **'Success is only a delayed failure' who said this?**

(a) Graham Greene in 'A Sort of Life'
(b) Umberto Eco in 'Encounter'
(c) Rose Macaulay 'They Went to Portugal'
(d) Theodore Dalyrmple in 'A Bit of Myth'

126 **"It's the souls duty to be loyal to its own desires. It must abandon itself to its master passion". Who said these lines?**

(a) Maya Angelou (b) Dame Rose Macaulay
(c) Rebecca West (d) AN Wilson

127 **Which author in which work said these lines, "There is no greater agony than bearing an untold story 'Inside You"?**

(a) Antony Beevor in 'Stalingrad'
(b) Tony Judt in 'When the Facts Change'
(c) Maya Angelou in 'I Know why the Caged Bird Sings'
(d) AN Wilson in 'Penfriends from Porlock'

128 Who said these lines, "The extreme paradox arose that one of the most passionate, expressive, humorous and unconventional women who ever lived was paraded before the public as a stiff, pompous little person ..."?
(a) Theodore Dalyrmple in A Bit of Myth
(b) Lisa Jardine in Book on Erasmus
(c) Nikolai Tolstoy in The Ministers and the Massacres
(d) AN Wilson in Victoria A Life

129 Who said this in which book, "It did not do to give your heart to a man so entirely, she thought. Men did not value what they came by easily. Once you loved, you laid yourself open to pain"?
(a) Alison Weir in The Lady Elizabeth
(b) James Baldwin in Nobody Knows My Name
(c) Allan Bloom in Giants and Dwarfs
(d) Bill Bryson in "I am a Stranger here Myself"

130 Who is the author who said this, "I believe that we think much more with the instruments provided by our culture than we do with our bodies and hence the much greater diversity of thought in the world"?
(a) Maya Angelou (b) Susan Sontag
(c) Graham Greene (d) Rebecca Traister

131 "But how true it is that every pleasure has also its reverse side, in brief, its pain or, if not wholly true, how nearly so. Therefore, I have added to most of my pleasures the little flavour of bitterness..."
Whose words in which book are these?
(a) Simon Winchester in Holy Terror
(b) Rose Macaulay in Personal Pleasures (Essay)
(c) Joan Didion in The Year of Magical Thinking
(d) Maya Angelou in Letters to My Daughter

132 Who uttered these words "The willingness to accept responsibility for one's own life is the source from which self-respect springs"?
(a) Philip Temple (b) Bill Bryson
(c) Joan Didion (d) Adam Hochschild

133 Who said these words in which work
"There was a level on which I believed that what had happened remained reversible"?
(a) Joan Didion in The Year of Magical Thinking
(b) Tony Judt in The Memory Chalet
(c) Allan Bloom in the Closing of the American Mind
(d) Umberto Eco in The Name of the Rose

134 "Semiotics is in principle the discipline studying everything which can be used in order to lie."
Who said this in which of his/her work?
(a) Susan Msimang in The Burning
(b) Philip Temple in High Country
(c) Gordon Mclauchlan in The Acid Test
(d) Umberto Eco in A Theory of Semiotics

135 Graca, wife of former South African President Nelson Mandela remarked about which author in these lines
"Brutally and uncompromisingly honest, her beautifully crafted story telling enriches the already extra ordinary pool of young ...... writers of our time"?
(a) Sisonke Msimang (b) Susan Sontag
(c) Nadine Gordimer (d) Sarah Britten

136 Who said this, "People call me a feminist whenever I express sentiments that differentiate me from a doormat or a prostitute"?
(a) Sisonke Msimang (b) Rose Macaulay
(c) Rebecca West (d) Rebecca Traister

137 "When these with violence were burned to death, we wished for our Elizabeth?"
In which work of Alison Weir do these lines appear?
(a) The Wars of the Roses
(b) Boredom, Eleanor of Aquitaine
(c) The Children of Henry VIII
(d) Innocent Traitor

138 Who said this in which work?
"When every benefit received is a right, there is no place for good manners, let alone for gratitude?"
(a) Rebecca West in Black Lamp and Grey Falcon
(b) Theodore Dalrymple in "Life at the Bottom"
(c) Antony Beevor in Stalingrad
(d) Tony Judt in Past Imperfect

139 In whose book do these lines appear?
"The military authorities were concerned that soldiers going home on leave would demoralise the home population with horror stories of the Ostfront."
(a) Graham Greene in Journals 1982
(b) Tony Judt in when the facts change
(c) Antony Beevor in Stalingrad
(d) AN Wilson in Tolstoy, A Biography

140 In which work of Philip Temple, this introduction is found?
"With its rich human heritage and mythology, the ever changing high country is central to the country's psyche and identity."
(a) Great Walking Tracks (b) Central
(c) The Book of the Kea (d) High Country

141 In which work of which author do these lines appear?
'History is never tidy', the past is indeed another country.
(a) The battle for Spain by Antony Beevor
(b) A note on new ruins by Rose Macaulay
(c) The Nuremberg trials by Dame Rebecca West
(d) Post War by Tony Judt

142 Who said these lines in which work?
"I think some men love the idea of a strong independent woman but they don't want to marry a strong independent woman".
(a) James Baldwin in 'The Price of the Ticket'
(b) Rebecca Traister in 'All the Single Ladies'
(c) Rose Macaulay in 'Catch Words and Claptraps'
(d) AN Wilson in 'The Elizabethans'

143 Who said, "Not everything that is faced can be changed but nothing can be changed until it is faced"?
(a) AN Wilson (b) Philip Temple
(c) Graham Greene (d) James Baldwin

144 Who said, "I have never understood the difference between the arts and the sciences or felt the need to choose between them"?
(a) Rose Macaulay (b) Susan Santog
(c) Lisa Jardine (d) Rebecca West

145 Who said, "I prefer to be left alone with my books"?
(a) Umberto Eco (b) Alison Weir
(c) Graham Greene (d) Rebecca West

Directions (Q.Nos. 146-150) *Read the passage given below and answer the questions that follow.*

Aah, now that is more difficult to explain. I have some philosophical interests and I pursue them through my academic work and my novels. Even my books for children are about non-violence and peace...you see, the same bunch of ethical, philosophical interests.

And then I have a secret. Did you know what will happen if you eliminate the empty spaces from the universe, eliminate the empty spaces in all the atoms? The universe will become as big as my fist.

Similarly, we have a lot of empty spaces in our lives. I call them interstices. Say you are coming over to my place. You are in an elevator and while you are coming up, I am waiting for you. This is an interstice, an empty space. I work in empty spaces. While waiting for your elevator to come up from the first to the third floor, I have already written an article! (Laughs).

146 The author in the passage talks about empty spaces. How does he use them?
(a) by taking a small map
(b) an exercising
(c) writing during that period
(d) just relaxing, doing nothing

147 The writer's academic writing style is
(a) very dull and boring
(b) very personalised and interesting
(c) full of extremely complicated language
(d) All of the above

148 How does author uses interstices?
(a) By gainfully using that time
(b) By relaxing for a while
(c) By taking a short nap
(d) Noting down main points of an article

149 What is the word which is similar in meaning to the word 'Eliminate'?
(a) Eradicate (b) Establish
(c) Include (d) Save

150 What is the author's opinion about himself as a writer?
(a) A novelist
(b) Academic scholar
(c) As a freelance journalist
(d) Both 'a' and 'b'

PREVIOUS YEARS' QUESTIONS

2018 July

1 The 1950's saw the rise of backlash against modernism and against New Romanticism that become known as the movement. Which of the following little magazines came to be associated with the movement?
(a) Departure (b) New verse
(c) London Mercury (d) New Pcems

January 2017

2 In his essay from 'work to text' Roland Barthes Soap the following about the text.
1. The text is singular
2. The text can be held in the hand
3. The text is held in language
4. The text is a methodological field

Codes
(a) 1 and 3 (b) 2 and 4 (c) 3 and 4 (d) 3 and 2

July 2016

3 One of the key terms in Michel Foucault's work is discourse. Which is best described as
(a) the power of persuasion in all articulations.
(b) the selective language power people use
(c) conceptual framework which enables some mode of thought and deny or severely constrain certain others
(d) the ability to suggest transcendental levels of meaning is an alternate

December 2015

4 The idea of utterance 'new ethnicities' in post was Britain war advanced by
(a) Donald Hall (b) Stuart Hall
(c) Paul Gilroy (d) Hanif Kureishi

5 FR Leavis and QD Leavis launched a critical journal devoted to the moral centrality of English studies. Name the journal
(a) The English Historical Review
(b) The Criterion
(c) A Scruting
(d) The Edinburgh Review

June 2015

6 One of the most highly revered, scholarly and passionate interpreters of English and world literature, he was appointed the Lord Northcliffe professor of Modern English Literature at University College, London in 1967. Who is the person referred to here?
(a) FR Leavis (b) IA Richards
(c) Frank Kermade (d) David Lodge

7 Who wrote the History of Australian Literature in 1961?
(a) Randolph Stow
(b) H M Green
(c) Handel Richardson
(d) Francis Adams

8 This was a path-breaking feminist essay written in the 1970's which used hybrid terms like 'sext' and chaostros. Identity the author
(a) Luce Irigaray
(b) Helene Cixous
(c) Julia Kristeva (d) Simon de Beauvoir

ANSWERS

Objective Questions

1. (c)	2. (a)	3. (c)	4. (b)	5. (a)	6. (d)	7. (d)	8. (d)	9. (c)	10. (d)
11. (b)	12. (a)	13. (b)	14. (c)	15. (a)	16. (c)	17. (d)	18. (a)	19. (c)	20. (d)
21. (a)	22. (c)	23. (d)	24. (b)	25. (c)	26. (d)	27. (c)	28. (c)	29. (a)	30. (b)
31. (a)	32. (c)	33. (c)	34. (d)	35. (a)	36. (b)	37. (a)	38. (a)	39. (b)	40. (b)
41. (b)	42. (b)	43. (c)	44. (a)	45. (c)	46. (b)	47. (d)	48. (c)	49. (c)	50. (c)
51. (d)	52. (b)	53. (b)	54. (b)	55. (a)	56. (c)	57. (b)	58. (c)	59. (a)	60. (c)
61. (c)	62. (a)	63. (d)	64. (b)	65. (d)	66. (d)	67. (a)	68. (c)	69. (c)	70. (b)
71. (c)	72. (b)	73. (c)	74. (d)	75. (c)	76. (c)	77. (a)	78. (a)	79. (d)	80. (a)
81. (a)	82. (b)	83. (d)	84. (c)	85. (d)	86. (a)	87. (b)	88. (c)	89. (c)	90. (b)
91. (a)	92. (a)	93. (c)	94. (b)	95. (b)	96. (c)	97. (a)	98. (d)	99. (d)	100. (d)
101. (a)	102. (b)	103. (c)	104. (a)	105. (c)	106. (a)	107. (c)	108. (c)	109. (b)	110. (a)
111. (a)	112. (b)	113. (b)	114. (c)	115. (d)	116. (c)	117. (b)	118. (c)	119. (d)	120. (d)
121. (c)	122. (c)	123. (a)	124. (c)	125. (a)	126. (c)	127. (c)	128. (d)	129. (a)	130. (b)
131. (b)	132. (c)	133. (a)	134. (d)	135. (a)	136. (c)	137. (c)	138. (b)	139. (c)	140. (d)
141. (a)	142. (b)	143. (d)	144. (c)	145. (b)	146. (c)	147. (b)	148. (a)	149. (a)	150. (d)

Previous Years' Questions

1. (c)	2. (c)	3. (c)	4. (b)	5. (c)	6. (c)	7. (b)	8. (b)

Language: Basic Concepts, Theories and Pedagogy

The chapter deals with origin and development of language as well as theories of language acquisition. General principles of teaching a foreign language in India have also been discussed.

Language: An Introduction and Definitions

Language is God's special gift to mankind. In the absence of language human civilisation would have remained an impossibility, language is present everywhere. Besides being a means of communication and store house of knowledge, it is an instrument of thinking as well as a source of delight.

Philosophers, logicians, psychologists, literary critics, creative writers, linguistics and many others have been interested in language and have defined it from the point of view of their own discipline. Yet there is no comprehensive definition of language. Since language is studied under the branch of knowledge known as linguistics, we must try to know what language is. We can roughly define language as 'organised noise' used in actual social situations.

The Encyclopedia Britannica defines language as, "A system of conventional, spoken or written symbols by means of which human beings as members of social group and as participants in its culture, communicate."

Below are given some other commonly quoted definitions of language

- Aristotle, "Speech is the representation of the experience of the mind."
- E Sapir, "Language is a primarily human and non instinctive method of communicating ideas, emotions and desires by means of a system of voluntarily produced symbols."
- Henry Sweet, "Language is the expression of ideas by means of speech sounds combined into words."
- Block and Irager, "A Language is a system of arbitrary vocal symbols by means of which a social group cooperates."

In this Chapter

- A H Gardiner, "Language in its widest sense means the sum total of such signs of our thoughts and feelings as are capable of external perceptions and as could be produced and repeated at will."
- Noam Chomsky, "Language is the innate capacity of native speakers to understand and form grammatical sentences."

None of these definitions may be called perfect. Each of them simply hints at certain features of human language.

Features of Language

Some of the important features of language can be understand under the following heads

Means of Communication and Self Expression

Language is the most powerful, convenient and permanent means and form of communication. It is flexible, comprehensive, perfect and extensive. It is the best means of self expression. Human beings express their thoughts, desires, emotions and feelings through language. They also store knowledge, transmit knowledge, messages and experiences from one person to another and from one generation to another through language. Human beings interact and carry on most of the activities through language.

Displacement

Human language has the property of displacement which allows the users of language to talk about things and events not present in the immediate environment. Animal communication lacks this property. Displacement also enables us to talk about things and places whose existence we cannot even be sure of. We can refer to mythical creatures, demons, fairies, angels and superman etc. This property allows the human beings to create fiction and describe possible future worlds.

Arbitrariness

There is no 'natural' connection between linguistic form and its meaning. Linguistic signs have an arbitrary relationship with the object they are used to indicate. They do not in anyway 'fit' these objects. There is no reason why the four legged domestic animals should be called *dog* in English, *Kutta* in Hindi, *Kukkur* in Sanskrit, *hund* in German and *Kalb* in Arabic.

There are of course some words in language as have sounds which seem to echo the sounds of objects or activities. For example, *buzz, hiss, hum hang, cuckoo, cresh* or *slump* in English are called onomatopoeia because they imitate the sounds of their referents. But these words are comparatively few in different languages and differ from one language to another. A dog's bark in English is 'bow bow' but it is 'lol lol' in Tamil. Thus the vast majority of linguistic expressions are in fact arbitrary.

A symbol stands for something else, it serves as a substitute. Language is a system of arbitrary vocal symbols. We use words as symbols for things, objects, concepts and ideas. This symbolism is necessary consequence of the feature of arbitrariness.

Non-Instinctive Conventional

Language comes into being as a result of evolution and convention. Each generation transmits this convention on to the next. Like all human institutions languages also change, grow, expand and die. Language is non-instinctive because it is acquired by human beings from the environment and community in which they live, grow and interact. Every human being however, has been gifted with an innate ability to acquire language.

Thus, human beings do not inherit their language. They acquire it in a culture with other speakers. Cultural transmission of a specific language is crucial in the process of human acquisition.

Duality of Structure

Linguistic symbols are arranged in a particular order. All languages have their system of arrangement. Though symbols in each language are finite, they can be arranged infinitely, that is we can produce an infinite set of sentences by a finite set of symbols.

Language is organised at two levels or layers simultaneously. This quality is called duality. In speech production, we have the physical level at which we can produce individual sounds like: *n*, *b* and *i* when these sounds are produced in a particular combination, as in *bin*, we have another level producing a meaning which is different from the meaning of the combination in *nib*. In this way, at one level we have distinct sound and at another level we have distinct meanings. The duality of levels enables us to produce a large number of sound combinations (e.g. words) with a limited use of distinct sounds.

Every language is a system of systems. All languages have phonological and grammatical systems and within a system there are several sub systems. For example, within the grammatical system we have morphological and syntactic systems, and within these two systems we have several other systems such as those of plural, of mood, of aspect, of tense etc.

Verbal Symbolism

Language is an organisation of sounds of vocal symbols—the sounds produced from the mouth with the help of various organs of speech to convey same meaningful message. It also means that speech is primary to writing. Language is a systematic verbal symbolism. It makes use of verbal elements such as sounds, words and phrases, which are arranged in certain ways to make sentences.

Thus, the use of the vocal auditory channel is a feature of human language which is generated via vocal organs and heard by ears.

Social Phenomenon

Language is a set of conventional communicative signals used by human beings for communication in a community. Language is a possession of a social group. It is a social institution. It exists in society and develops and nourishes culture and establishes human relations. Human beings acquire language as a member of society. Language is thus a social event and can be described only with reference to its speakers.

Human Entity

No species other than human beings have been endowed with language. No animal has such a developed brain and articulatory organs as a human being has. They cannot acquire the complex structure of human language. Human language is open ended, extendable and modifiable whereas the animal language is not.

Creative, Complex, Extendable and Modifiable

Language is a unique phenomenon of this Earth. Each language is unique because each has its peculiarities and distinct traits. Language has creativity and productivity. Novel utterances are continuously being created in all languages. In new situations language users manipulate their linguistic resources to create new expressions and sentences. This points out to the fact that the potential number of utterances in any human language is infinite. This is the productivity (or creativity or open endedness) of human language.

Another characteristic of language is called recursiveness. It enables sentences to be formed inside other sentences. For example, "This is the bull with broken horns that tossed the dog that worried the cat that chased the rat ... can continue to any length."

Language changes according to the need of the society in which it is spoken. With new invention new words are coined to name new objects and concepts. Thus, signals in human language can be combined in a variety of ways.

Structurally Complex

Human language is structurally complex. It differs from region to region and changes with the lapse of time.

Human language has the quality of discreteness. Each sound in the language is treated as discrete. For example, the difference between a P sound and a B sound is not very big (both are plosive, bilabials) but when these sounds are used in language, they lead to a distinction in meaning, e.g. pack and back.

Unlike animal language, a stretch of speech in any human language can be analysed into smaller units and a larger number of meanings can be expressed by means of a limited number of signals. For example, a sentence such as 'Mothers like their daughters' can be analysed into words. Mothers/like/their/daughters. Each word is made up of sounds; for example the word 'like' is made up of *l-ai-k*. The same words can be re-arranged in order to reconstruct another sentence, 'Daughters like their mothers.'

This shows that language is complex as it has two levels of 'structure'. There is a 'primary' level compounding of words and there is a 'secondary' level-compounding of sounds.

Main Components of Language

Learning a language requires four components listening, speaking, reading and writing. This LSRW is the essential way in which any person or a child learns a language.

Listening

When a child is born, he has the innate ability to acquire a language which surrounds him. This language, used by his parents, siblings or any other people around him, is acquired by him through the first process of listening. He/She absorbs the language by only listening at first. Even an adult who wishes to learn a language needs to listen to the new language initially to acquire it.

Speaking

Once the child has absorbed quite a by listening small broken words or phrases are uttered by him which results in his first speech. 'Mama', 'Papa' are constantly repeated and practised till the fluency is achieved and new words added to the vocabulary everyday.

Speech

Human beings developed speech from naturally occurring sounds such a cuckoo and ding dong as well as cries of emotional response such as wow, ugh and opps etc. Speech is often accompanied by physical gestures such as pointing and raising of out-stretched forearm, bent at the elbow. Speech and the accompanying physical actions are characteristic of the interactional function of language. It has to do with how humans use language socially and emotionally; how they indicate friendliness, cooperation or hostility or annoyance, pain or pleasure.

Another major function of language is transaction whereby humans use language to communicate knowledge, skills and information. The transactional function must have developed for the transfer of knowledge from one generation to the next. This transfer function of language remains fairly restricted in time and space as long as it can be realised only in speech. By nature speech is transient. The desire for a more permanent record must have motivated the development of writing.

Reading

Once a command over spoken language is achieved and the child has started communicating with a lot of words himself, he is then introduced to reading. Picture books with words matching the pictures are introduced so that incidental learning takes place and the words can be associated with thier corresponding pictures. The difficulty levels are then increased and so does the ability to read.

Writing

Once the motor skills are developed children are introduced to writing. Jean Piaget's Congintive development theory lists the number of years and what all a child will be able to accomplish in the growing years. To improve the hand, eye coordination and develop the grip of little hands, writing usually starts with a thick crayon and slowly moves to a thinner pencil or pen. Thus writing is introduced and the child learns to communicate through writing as well.

Dialectal variation in speech is a very common and obvious feature, but in writing it is not obvious. Writing often fails the phonology fully and accurately. Accents and tones are generally not captured fully by the systems of writing.

A written form is essentially a representation of a spoken form. But it is very seldom an exact reflection of the spoken form. In English one letter *X* stands for a sequence of sounds *ks* and a sequence of letters *th* sound for one sound *Q*. The sequence 'ough' has many different phonetic values in through, rough, cough, bough, hicough and dough. There are deep differences between a written and spoken form. The differences are found at all levels of structure phonology, morphology, syntax, vocabulary and style.

Written forms are influenced not only by their associated spoken forms but also by other written languages. This often happens in bilingual and multilingual communities. For example, modern Hindi has adopted the punctuation system of English without capitalisation as well as *आ, क, ग, ज, फ* etc to represent foreign sounds.

Linguistic change is another factor influencing the fitness of written and spoken language. But the change in the orthography is relatively much slower than in phonology. It often fades out. Dependence of the written language on the spoken one can be conveniently illustrated by the development of Urdu (written in Persian scripts) in India several new symbols have been devised to represent Hindi sounds.

Relationship Between Speech and Writing

RH Robins clearly points out the relationship between these two forms of language in the following words, "These two modes of linguistic communication speech and writing, virtually exhaust the field. The familiar languages of Europe are written and spoken, that is to say a system of writing and a system of speaking are recognisable and recognised as the same language."

Many languages especially those of relatively small communities are spoken languages whereas some languages are known at the present time only in their written forms, the so called dead languages e.g. (Ancient, Greek, Hittie, Latin, Sanskrit and Pali, etc). Some written styles are virtually unintelligible if read aloud or if used as spoken medium, e.g. the formal languages of legal court act and legislative enactments.

The different writing systems have varying degrees of phonetic accuracy. One extreme is the written symbols of Chinese, which are graphic representation of individual lexical and grammatical items as wholes.

According to Halliday, the central difference between spoken and written languages is that, whereas speech takes place against the background of a situation (*i.e.*, non-linguistic activity), writing has to compensate for the absence of a situation of this kind by supplying equivalent linguistically.

On the basis of the above discussion, we can point out characteristic features of speech and writing

Features of Speech

- Speech is transient and remains restricted in time and space.
- It is confined to the present audience.
- Speech is often accompanied by physical gestures and is more expressive of our feelings and emotions.
- Speech is primary.
- Speech reveals the dialectal features.
- Speech is always marked by accents and tones.
- Speech is personal and subjective.
- Speech is natural and spontaneous.

Features of Writing

- Writing is a more permanent record of knowledge, skill and information.
- It reaches the coming generations spread over a very wide area.
- Writing is without any physical gestures and the reader has to exert himself to interpret the feelings and emotions implied in writing.
- Writing is secondary and a representation of the spoken form.
- Writing is often free from dialectal traits.
- Writing is devoid of these phonological features.
- Writing is impersonal and objective.
- Writing is artificial and one has to learn it with effort.

Basic Concepts : Idiolect, Dialect and Language

Descriptive linguistics deals with the design of the language of a community at a given time. It does not take into consideration and interpersonal and inter-group differences. Synchronic linguistic includes descriptive linguistics and certain other types of investigations, particularly synchronic dialectology which studies the interpersonal and inter group differences of speech habits.

Idiolect

The totality of speech habit of a single person at a given time constitutes an idiolect. It means each individual's language unique and peculiar to himself is called his idiolect.

Language

A language, of course, always belongs to a group of people not to an individual. In the last resort one has to admit that every member of some speech community speaks a slightly different dialect : he has his own idiolect. In this way a language is a collection of more or less similar idiolects. To be more precise a language can be regarded as a constitution of dialects.

Dialect

A dialect is just the same thing, with this difference when both terms are employed in a single context of connatation, the degree of the idiolects in a single dialect is assumed to be greater than that of all the idiolects in the language.

On account of the complexities of topography, settlement, history, inter regional communication and prestige of regional centres, dialect boundaries are often vague, complex and hard to delimit. Dialect are seldom bound to the neat demarcation and classification which one might desire and which an ordinary man sometimes imposes upon them.

If we persue the difference between any two dialects preferably separated by quite a distance, we find that they are of two kinds : phonetic and phonemic differences. *For example* the words pronounced with 'aw' in one dialect area may be pronounced differently as 'ow' in certain other dialect area 't' in Hindi 'toli' 'and 't' in English 'Tory' are not the same, 't' in Hindi 'toli' is unaspirated whereas 't' in English 'Tory' is an aspirated phoneme.

An example of phonetic difference in the pronunciation of 's' used by some speakers of English in dental 's' rather than palatal. In the same way 'r' used by an American is trill 'r' rather than flap.

Language and Dialect

In everyday usage, we generally distinguish between language and dialect. To a linguist a regional dialect or a dialect of a particular social group or class is more than an inferior version of some standard language. In origin, a standard language is simply a dialect, which for historical and linguistically accidental reasons, has acquired political and cultural importance in a particular community.

It has been understood by the linguists, the distinction between languages and dialects is based very largely upon a cultural or political considerations. Many of the so called dialects of Chinese, for instance are more distinct from one another than say Danish and Norwegian or even more markedly, Dutch and Flemish are frequently described as different languages.

Pidgins

In the opinion of Hockelt, pidgins represent the most extreme result of borrowing known so far. As a matter of fact, pidgins are essentially utilitarian trade languages which came into being to serve the communicative needs of buying and selling, loading and unloading etc and which result from process of reciprocal imitation or rudiment of any language learning.

This happened in China trade. The British or the Yankee merchants wanted to be understood. They made a desperate attempt to speak artificial 'broken' English or 'baby-talk' on the mistaken assumption that it was easier for the Chinese to understand. The Chinese too made a desperate attempt to imitate the badly distorted English. Pidgin formed initially Chinese Pidgin. English later confined themselves to English business. Pidgins arise under the pressure of practical circumstances in a bilingual situation,while an artificial language is invented by a scholar sitting severely in his study.

It may, at first seem strange to note that from pidgin emerges an artificial or 'invented' language. A pidgin by definition, a nobody's native language. It is learned by linguistic adults as a second language. The same is true of an artificial language.

When children in some community start speaking pidgin, as their common language, it is called 'creolised'. Creolisation quickly fills out a pidgin with childish and nursery forms Creoles are the artificial languages or the pidgins adopted as a native language by succeeding generations. This is true in case of Esperanto.

Most of the pidgins have had no real life outside the brains of their inventors and a few devotees. But one Esperanto has gone further. To an inventor of an artificial language, the process of invention may seen like a manifestation of habit of speech understanding or misunderstanding of how a language functions. Most of the European languages including Esperanto, are the developed forms of some pidgins or artificial languages. On investigation it would be clear that Esperanto is an aberrant form of Romance and the feature of aberration were an account of pidginisation.

The important thing about pidgin is that it is a language with a life of its own. The English based pidgin speaker would face difficulty in understanding English unless and until the letter is mixed up with the former in grammar and pronunciation on a simplified way. Pidgin is marked by redundancy, loose phonetic system and a small vocabulary, capable of handling the practical situation in business. It has a regular grammar.

Diachronic and Synchronic

Synchrony is the study of a language in a given time, diachrony through time. Synchronic or descriptive linguistics studies a language at one period of time, it investigates the way people speak in a given speech community at a given point in time.

Diachronic, or historical linguistics studies the development of languages through time, for example, the way in which French and Italian have evolved from Latin or Hindi from Sanskrit, it also investigates the changes that take place in language. Saussure says, "Synchronic linguists will be concerned with the logical and psychological relations that bind together successive terms not perceived by the collective mind but substituted for each other without forming a system.' Synchronic linguistics deals with systems, diachronic with units. These are two separate branches of study. Saussure considered synchronic linguistics to be more important: 'The first thing that strikes us when we study the facts of language is that their succession in time does not exist in so far as the speaker is concerned. He is concerned with a state. That is why the linguist who wishes to understate a state, must discard all knowledge of everything that produced it and diachrony.

Saussure has illustrated the difference between synchronic and diachronic linguistics by the difference diagram. In it the axis AB is the synchronic static axis. It can intersect at any point with XY, the moving diachronic axis.

Throughout the nineteenth century, linguistic research was very historical in character. The aim of linguistics was to group languages into families on the basis of their independent development from or common source, or to study change in language. The description of particular languages was made subsidiary to this general aim and there was little interest in the study of the language of a given community without reference to historical considerations. Nevertheless, valid diachronic work has to be based on good synchronic work, because no valid statements about linguistic change can be made unless good descriptions of a language do exist similarly a synchronic statement may well reflect certain historical developments.

Langue and Parole

According to Saussure language (human speech as a whole) consists of langue and parole. Langue is the abstract system of language and parole is its manifestation. It is an individual's speech act and varies from person to person.

The term language includes the entire human potential for speech and writing, both mental and physical. In actual manifestation that we see and hear in terms of individual utterances (i.e. speaking) is called parole. The abstract system behind the manifestation shared by a social group is called langue. The system (langue) together with its manifestation (parole) constitutes speech (i.e. language or tongue). A language system does not exist in the world, it must be constructed from its manifestations.

Langue is the totality (the collective fact) of a language, deducible from an examination of the memories of all the language users. It is a storehouse, 'the sum of word images' in the minds of individual. It is not to be confused with human speech (language) of which it is only a definite part, though certainly an essential one. It is both a social product of the faculty of speech and collection of necessary conventions that have been adopted by social body to permit individuals to exercise that faculty. Langue, therefore, is a corporate, social phenomena. It is homogeneous whereas language is heterogeneous. Langue is grammar + vocabulary + pronunciation system of a community. It includes three basic concepts.

1. **The Language Scheme** (The pure language form defined independently of its social realisation and physical manifestation);
2. **The Language Norm** (The material form defined by its social realisation but independent of particular manifestations);
3. **The Language Custom** (A set of customs accepted by a particular society and defined by observable manifestations).

Ultimately langue has to be related to parole which is the actual usage of individuals, that a community manifests in its everyday speech, the actual concrete act of speaking on the part of the individual, the controlled or controllable psychological activity. Parole is the set of all utterances that have actually been produced, while langue is the set of all possible grammatical sentences in the language. Thus parole is a 'personal, dynamic, social activity, which exists at a particular time and place in a particular situation as opposed to langue which exists apart from any particular manifestation in speech.'

Parole is the only object available for direct observation to the linguist. Utterances are instances of parole. The underline structure in terms of speech we produce them as speakers and understand them as hearers, is the langue and is independent of the physical medium in which it is realised. A langue is not spoken by anybody, but it is a composite body of linguistic phenomena derived from the paroles (personal dialects) of all native speakers. Langue is a social phenomena having reality only as a social institution. It is, therefore, constant, supra-individualistic and generalised. The individual speaker can neither create it nor modify it easily. The main differences between langue and parole are listed below

Langue	Parole
Code	Encoding of a message
Potential	Actualised
Social	Individual
Fixed	Free
Slow-moving	Ephemeral
Psychological	Psycho-physical

Competence and Performance

Chomsky's concept of competence and performance is somewhat similar to Saussure's concept of langue and parole. Competence is the native speaker's knowledge of his language, the system of rules he has mastered, his ability to produce and understand a vast number of new sentences. Competence is the study of the system of rules, performance is the study of actual sentence themselves, of actual use of language in real life situation. The speaker's knowledge of the structure of a language is his linguistic competence and the way in which he uses it, is his linguistic performance.

Competence is an underlying mental system. It underlies actual behaviour, linguistic ability to analyse language, detecting ambiguities, ignoring mistakes, understanding new sentences, producing entirely new sentences. Competence is a set of principles which a speaker masters, performance is what a speaker does. We can find about one's competence only by studying his performance in devious and clever ways. In other words competence is the abstract internal grammar which enables a speaker to utter and understand an infinite number of potential utterances.

This competence is free from the interference of memory span, characteristic errors, lapses of attention etc. Competence in any sphere can be identified with capacity or ability—the ability to produce and understand indefinitely many new sentences, it refers to the native speaker's innate creativity and productivity implicit in the normal use of language.

Although Chomsky's competence/performance dichotomy closely resembles Saussure's langue/parole, yet the main difference is that Saussure stressed the sociological implication of langue, while Chomsky stresses the psychological implications of competence. These distinctions are similar to the distinction between code and message. A code is the pre-arranged signalling system. A message is an actual message sent through that system.

The distinction between competence and performance is crucial for linguistic description since linguistic descriptions are primarily concerned with a language users' knowledge of his language (his linguistic competence). The actual use of language is; on the one hand, controlled by innate properties of the mind and on the other by linguistically irrelevant considerations like shifts in attention, tiredness, boredom, external distractions, memory limitations, lapses in applying the knowledge of the language and such other considerations. The ideal native speaker's competence enables him to generate an infinite number of sentences using a finite set of principles. We can arrive at his finite set of principles only by studying the relationships between sentences and the units in a sentence.

Descriptive and Prescriptive

A grammar is a finite system of rules framed for describing the structure of phrases and sentences which will account for all of the grammatical sequences and rule out all the ungrammatical sequences. In the widest and the traditional sense, grammar is a set of nominative and prescriptive rules in order to set up a standard of 'correct usage'. Until the nineteenth century the grammarian was the law giver. He was concerned with 'linguistic etiquette' that is the identification of the 'proper' or 'best' structures to be used in a language. This is known as the prescriptive approach of the eighteenth century grammarian.

The traditional grammar has a long tradition behind it. It had it origins in the description of languages like Classical, Latin and Greek. Since there were well-established grammatical description of these older languages, it seems appropriate to adopt the existing categories from these descriptions and apply them in the analysis of languages like English. After all, Latin and Greek were the languages of scholarship, religion, philosophy and knowledge so the grammar of these languages was taken to be the best grammar.

The traditional grammar divides words into several classes called the parts of speech. They are noun, pronoun, adjective, article, verb, adverb, preposition, conjunction and interjection. Besides these terms used for parts of speech, traditional grammatical analysis also uses a number of other categories including, 'number', 'person', 'voice', and 'gender. These categories can be discussed in isolation but their role in describing language structure becomes clearer when we consider them in terms of concord or agreement. For example, we say that the verb 'beats' agrees with the noun 'boy' in the following sentences 'The boy beats his sister'. The agreement is partially based on the category of number, that is whether the noun is singular or plural. It is also based on the category of person (the speaker) second person (the hearer) and third person (any other person). The different forms of English persons are usually described in terms of person and number in that we have the first person singular (I), second person singular (you), third person singular (he, she, it) and so on. In the sentence, 'The boy beats his sister', we have a noun boy which is third person singular and the verb 'beats' agrees with the noun.

In addition the form of the verb must also be described in terms of another category, that of tense. In this, the verb is in the present tense which results in a different form the past tense, (*e.g.*, beat). And the sentence is in the active voice, rather than the passive voice, which would take the form 'His sister is beaten by the boy.'

Our final category is that of gender, which is used to describe the agreement between 'boy and his' in our example sentence. In English, we have to describe the relationship in terms of natural gender mainly derived from a biological distinction between male and female. The agreement between boy and his is based on a distinction English makes between reference to male entities (he, his), female entities (she, her) and sexless entities, or animals, when the sex of the animal is irrevelent (it, its).

This type of biological distinction is quite different from the more common distinction found in languages which use grammatical gender. In these languages articles and adjectives take different forms to agree with the gender of the noun. For example, Sanskrit, Greek, Latin, English, German, French, Russian have three genders, Hindi, Punjabi and Rajasthani have two genders. Bengali, Uria, Assami have no distinction of gender. Chinese and Japanese, too, have no genders.

The notion of 'appropriateness' of analytic categories has not always been a consideration. The tables like the following may have some sense in describing a language like Latin but see rather extravagant for English where the forms of the verb are, with one exception, the same.

Tense	Form	Verb
Present tense	First person singular	I love
Active voice	Second person singular	You love
Third person	Singular	He loves
First person	Plural	We love
Second person	Plural	You love
third person	Plural	They love

In Latin the corresponding six forms are : Amo, Amas, Amat, Amamus, Amatis and Amant.

It is one thing to adopt the grammatical labels (*e.g.*, noun, verb) to categorise words in English sentences; it is quite another thing to go on to claim that the structure of English sentences should be like the structure of sentences in Latin. Yet this was the approach taken by some grammarians, mainly in the eighteenth century England. This view of grammar as a set of rules for the proper use of a language is still current. Some examples of this prescriptive approach are as follows

(i) You must not split an infinitive.
(ii) You must not end a sentence with a preposition.

In practice, these rules are often violated and we come across expressions like 'to boldly go' (instead of to go boldly) where the infinitive (to go) is split; or the sentence like what are you looking at? where the preposition **at** comes at the end.

Inadequacies of Prescriptive Grammar

Prescriptive grammar is inadequate and full of shortcomings. Because of its inadequacy so many models of modern grammar have been proposed. The following points deserve special attention

- It is based mainly on Indo-European classical languages, hence it is a poor model for grammars of languages that differ from Greek, Latin, Ṡanskrit, etc.
- It does not adequately distinguish between all linguistic levels—phonetic, morpholological, syntactic and semantic.
- It is normative and prescriptive rather than explicit and descriptive.
- Its rules are illogical, it is inconsistent and inadequate as a description of actual language.
- It neglects the contemporary usage as also the functional and social varieties of language.
- Its approach is diachronic rather than synchronic.
- It tries to study a living language like a dead one.
- Fries calls it 'not in sightful', 'prescientific,', 'prescriptive' and having a 'literary bias'.
- Its definitions are not all inclusive.
- It uses meaning as the primary tool of linguistic analysis. Meaning is a complex entity; it must be based on a formal description of a language.
- It gives priority to the written form of language and ignores the notion that spoken form is prior to the written form.
- It is not a complete grammar, it does not treat all aspects of language adequately; it does not cover even the whole range of the written form of a language, but is restricted to formal literary style.
- It regards grammar as something God-given, neat, holy and does not admit language change and consequent change in grammar.
- It fails to explain all the ambiguities.
- Its methods and notions are unverifiable, inaccurate, incomplete, and inconsistent; its descriptions are inexplicit and intuitive.

The above discussion clearly reveals that a well established grammatical description of Latin is useful guide for studying some languages like Italian or Spanish, is less useful for others like English and may be absolutely misleading if one wants to describe some more European languages. A different approach had to be discovered when linguistic wanted to study North American-Indian languages. Here the analyst collects samples of the languages, he is instructed in and attempts to describe the regular structures of the language as it is used, not according to some view how it should be used. This is called the descriptive approach and it is the basis of most modern attempts to characterise the structure of different languages.

One type of descriptive approach is called structural analysis and its main concern is to investigate the distribution of forms (*e.g.* morphemes) in a language. The method employed involves the use of 'test-frames' which can be sentences with empty slots in them. For example

- The ...... makes a lot of noise.
- I heard a ...... yesterday.

There are a lot of forms which can fit into these slots. To produce good grammatical sentences of English (*e.g.* donkey, car, dog, radio, child etc.). Consequently we can suggest that because all of these fit in the same test frame, they are likely to be examples of the same grammatical category. The table we give to this grammatical category is of course, 'noun'. However there are many forms which do not fit the test frames given in above examples would be Reeta, it, the dog, a cat and so on. For these forms we require different test frames, which could be like this.

- ...... makes a lot of noise.
- I heard ...... yesterday.

Among the forms which fit these test frames are Reeta, Lata, it, the dog, an old car, the professor with the village background and many more. Once again, we can suggest that these forms are likely to be examples of the same grammatical category. The common label for this category is 'noun phrase'. By developing a set of test frames of this type and discovering what forms fit the slots in the test frames we can produce a description of (at least some) aspects of the sentence structures of a language.

This descriptive approach attempts to describe a language as it is used in terms of recurrent elements and recurrent regularities (structure). It insists on purely objective and eschews the mentalistic approach which is based on intuitive analysis of data.

The descriptive or structural approach ignored meaning and insisted that a linguistic should discover various constituents of a language as a botanist discovers the petals of a flower. By structure they mean 'regularities', 'patterns' or 'rules' of language. They first discover 'phonemes' then the 'morphemes' and when a statement of their distribution has been made they proceed on to analyse syntax into constituents and state their relationship in terms of structure. Thus, without any reference to meaning they try to arrive at a abstract synchronic description of the organisation of the language analysed. They developed the system of immediate constituents of analysis.

The characteristics of descriptive approach are attention to structure, study of the spoken language, use of inductive method of scientific analyses and working from form to meaning. This approach is empirical. It insists on exactness of methodology and wants that all definitions be publicly verifiable or reliable. It examines all languages in terms of their phonological and grammatical systems.

The chief weakness of this approach is the neglect of meaning. It reduces the language to a catalogue of items and ignores native speakers intuition and his competence of generating infinite number of sentences from a finite of items. It does not offer explanation for the inter-relations of sentences. It ignores the psychological side of language.

Origin and Development of Language

How did language begin? Words don't leave artifacts behind–writing began long after language did–so theories of language origins have generally been based on hunches. For centuries there had been so much fruitless speculation over the question of how language began that when the Paris Linguistic Society was founded in 1866, its by-laws included a ban on any discussions of it. The early theories are now referred to by the nicknames given to them by language scholars. *Different theories developed thus have been discussed below*

The Bow-Wow Theory

The idea that speech arose from people imitating the sounds that things make: Bow-wow, moo, baa, etc. Not likely, since very few things we talk about have characteristic sounds associated with them and very few of our words sound anything at all like what they mean.

The Pooh-Pooh Theory

The idea that speech comes from the automatic vocal responses to pain, fear, surprise or other emotions: a laugh, a shriek, a gasp. But plenty of animals make these kinds of sounds too, and they didn't end up with language.

The Ding-Dong Theory

The idea that speech reflects some mystical resonance or harmony connected with things in the world. But it remains unclear how one would investigate this.

The Yo-He-Ho Theory

The idea that speech started with the rhythmic chants and grunts people used to coordinate their physical actions when they worked together. There's a pretty big difference between this kind of thing and what we do most of the time with language.

The Ta-Ta Theory

The idea that speech came from the use of tongue and mouth gestures to mimic manual gestures. e.g. saying ta-ta is like waving goodbye with your tongue. But most of the things we talk about do not have characteristic gestures associated with them, much less gestures you can imitate with the tongue and mouth.

The La-La Theory

The idea that speech emerged from the sounds of inspired playfulness, love, poetic sensibility, and song. This one is lovely, and no more or less likely than any of the others.

Gestural Theory

McLane (1996) described gesturing as a means to communicate an experience. While this might encourage a person to speak, there are times where speech just simply cannot be produced e.g. in situations such as taboo topics or situations where the mind does not have words to express what is intended. Based on the research she conducted on trauma patients, McLane suggests that physical and psychological trauma situations are examples in which communication by speech is challenging. As a result, people may turn to gestures as a way of conveying their message.

The gestural theory states that human language was developed from gestures that were a primitive form of communication, as opposed to the vocal signals that might have been adopted by non-human primates. According to Gillespie-Lynch et al (2013), bipedalism might be an influencing factor on gesturing, as walking on two feet allows both hands to be available for gesturing. To date, this theory that hypothesizes that gestures preceded speech in human language remains a popular topic of discussion by both evolutionists and linguists. Numerous anatomical and neuro-physiological data have supported the stance that human language had evolved from gestural communication

Music Theory

Music theory is the keystone of music. It is the 'guts' of music. We hope that our little course can help educate you with maximum effectiveness and minimum confusion. Music theory comprises the rules that make music sound good, and enable music to be written and played by musicians.

- Included in this section are areas of use to beginners, such as basic notation, and jargon. More advanced topics include TAB and key signatures.
- Dictionary explains to the novice some of the common and uncommon vocabulary found within our site and in the world of music.
- Notation includes: how to sight, read the differences between notes, explanations of dynamics and time signatures.
- Intervals discuss the distances between notes.
- Scales and key signatures discuss different scale patterns.
- TAB is a musical notation for guitar players.

Contract Theory

Contract theory is the study of how people and organisations develop legal agreements in situations with uncertain conditions, unknown factors and information asymmetry. Contract theory applies to both multi-party negotiations between a principal and one or more agents and contracts created by a single individual or organisation to specify details of multi-party agreements, such as employee contracts.

Ideally, a contract specifies the responsibilities and requirements of both parties so meticulously that there can be no room for dispute or misunderstanding. However, that ideal may never be achieved, for various reasons. Moral hazard, one model within contract theory, is the risk that one party to a transaction is not acting in good faith. e.g. that party may have withheld important information or provided misleading information or may have undisclosed motivation driving elements of an agreement that are being negotiated. Moral hazard often involves the assumption of risks that disadvantage the party with less information. Other models within contract theory include adverse selection, in which the principal party is not fully informed of the agent's risk factors, and signaling, in which the agent reliably conveys information about itself to the principal, e.g., a job applicant listing qualifications that match the hirer's list of requirements.

Contract theory is a special application of game theory, which is the study of mathematical models of negotiation, conflict and cooperation between individuals, organizations and governments. Central questions of game/contract theory include why an individual makes a particular decision and how the decisions made by one individual affect others.

Learning and Teaching Approaches

An approach is a way of looking at teaching and learning. Underlying any language teaching approach is a theoretical view of what language is, and of how it can be learnt. An approach gives rise to methods, the way of teaching something, which use classroom activities or techniques to help learners learn.

The Communicative Approach or Communicative Language Teaching (CLT)

It is a teaching approach that highlights the importance of real communication for learning to take place. In this post, you'll find definitions, examples and ideas for classroom activities.

In the Communicative Approach, real communication and interaction is not only the objective in learning, but also the means through which it takes place. This approach started in the 70s and became prominent as it proposed an alternative to the then ubiquitous systems-oriented approaches, such as the Audio-lingual method. It means that, instead of focusing on the acquisition of grammar and vocabulary (grammatical/linguistic competence), the Communicative Approach aimed at developing the learner's competence to communicate in the target language (communicative competence), with an enhanced focus on real-life situations.

The communicative approach is based on the idea that learning language successfully comes through having to communicate real meaning. When learners are involved in real communication, their natural strategies for language acquisition will be used, and this will allow them to learn to use the language.

For example: Practice of solving general questions by asking learners to find out personal information about their colleagues is an example of the communicative approach, as it involves meaningful communication.

The Structural Approach

It is a technique in which the structure or pattern is mastered by the learner. The idea is that every phrase, clause, sentence has a valid and proper structure or pattern and if we learn the correct structure or pattern, we can learn the language easily. There can be phonetic, lexical, grammatical, semantic groups and correct pattern of sequencing these groups in a proper structure as declarative sentences with structure of subject + verb + object or complement or interrogative sentences with 'Wh' words or helping verbs or imperative sentences leaving their subjects. So every clause or sentence has to be learnt according to its structure and in this way a language can be learnt or mastered well.

This method sees language as a complex of grammatical rules which are to be learned one at a time in a set order. So for example the verb 'to be' is introduced and practised before the present continuous tense which uses 'to be' as an auxiliary.

The theory underlying this method is that a language can be acquired only when the learner is receptive and has no mental blocks. By various methods it is suggested to the student that the language is easy and in this way the mental blocks to learning are removed.

The Oral Approach or Situational Language Teaching

It is an approach developed by British applied linguists between the 1930s and the 1960s. While it is unknown for many teachers, it had a big influence on language courses till the 1980s.Textbooks such as Streamline English (Hartley and Viney 1979) was designed following the SLT approach principles.

The Oral Approach or Situational Language Teaching is based on a structural view of language. Speech, structures and a focus on a set of basic vocabulary items are seen as the basis of language teaching. This was a view similar to that held by the American structuralists, such as Fries. However, what distinguishes the Situational Language Teaching Approach is its emphasis on the presentation of structures in situations.

Methods of Teaching

A method of teaching is one which a teacher, guide or mentor employs to impart knowledge to its seeker/s for attainment of their goals. Various successful teaching methods are described below.

The Direct Method

In this method, the teaching is done entirely in the target language. The learner is not allowed to use his or her mother tongue. Grammar rules are avoided and there is emphasis on good pronunciation.

Grammar-Translation

Learning is largely by translation to and from the target language. Grammar rules are to be memorized and long lists of vocabulary learned by heart. There is little or no emphasis placed on developing oral ability.

Audio-Lingual

The theory behind this method is that learning a language means acquiring habits. There is much practice of dialogues of every situation. New language is first heard and extensively drilled before being seen in its written form.

Total Physical Response (TPR)

TPR works by having the learner respond to simple commands such as 'Stand up', 'Close your book', 'Go to the window and open it.' The method stresses the importance of aural comprehension.

Communicative Language Teaching (CLT)

The focus of this method is to enable the learner to communicate effectively and appropriately in the various situations she would be likely to find herself in. The content of CLT courses are functions such as inviting, suggesting, complaining or notions such as the expression of time, quantity, location.

The Silent Way

This is so called because the aim of the teacher is to say as little as possible in order that the learner can be in control of what he wants to say. No use is made of the mother tongue.

Community Language Learning

In this method, attempts are made to build strong personal links between the teacher and student so that there are no blocks to learning. There is much talk in the mother tongue which is translated by the teacher for repetition by the student.

Immersion

This corresponds to a great extent to the situation we have at our school. ESL students are immersed in the English language for the whole of the school day and expected to learn math, science, humanities etc through the medium of the target language, English. Immigrant students who attend local schools find themselves in an immersion situation; e.g. refugee children from Bosnia attending German schools, or Puerto Ricans in American schools. .

Task-based Language Learning

The focus of the teaching is on the completion of a task which in itself is interesting to the learners. Learners use the language they already have to complete the task and there is little correction of errors.

This is the predominant method in middle school ESL teaching at Frankfurt International School. The tasks are subsumed in a major topic that is studied for a number of weeks. In the topic of ecology, e.g., students are engaged in a number of tasks culminating in a poster presentation to the rest of the class. The tasks include reading, searching the internet, listening to taped material, selecting important vocabulary to teach other students etc.

The Natural Approach

This approach, propounded by Professor S Krashen, stresses the similarities between learning the first and second languages. There is no correction of mistakes. Learning takes place by the students being exposed to language that is comprehensible or made comprehensible to them.

The Lexical Syllabus

This approach is based on a computer analysis of language which identifies the most common (and hence most useful) words in the language and their various uses. The syllabus teaches these words in broadly the order of their frequency, and great emphasis is placed on the use of authentic materials.

Language Acquisition

Although every aspect of language acquisition is enormously complex, all normal children acquire a reasonable command of their native language without any formal instruction. Descartes has aptly remarked, "There are more so deprived and stupid, without even excepting idiots, that they cannot arrange different words together, forming of them a statement by which they make known their thoughts". Language is a rule governed system and children acquire these rules on the basis of their experience and learn most of the grammar of their native language before the age of five. Children do not have a prediction for a particular language as result of social characteristics; they learn the language of their society.

Two major factors involved in language acquisition are first an innate human potential for the acquisiton of a language and secondly a linguistic environment. Acquisition of language depends upon the interaction between these two factors. Controversy rages as to how much of each *i.e.* innate potential versus environmental conditioning is involved in the process.

Children do not learn all their language all at once. They acquire it by stages and each stage approximates more and more closely to the grammar of the adult language. These stages are almost universal. Some stages last for a short period and others longer. Some stages may overlap for a short period, though the transition between stages has often been observed to be quite sudden.

Before describing the different stages of language development it is useful to differentiate between the child's ability to comprehend speech and his ability to produce it. These skills are usually referred to as the receptive and the expressive language skills. Mcnamara has stated that a child must first know what someone is saying before he can figure out what the words mean. The first step towards acquiring a language is thus the ability to understand and infer what a speaker is talking about. Until the child can do, language learning cannot proceed.

The development of receptive skill begins at birth when the newly born infant is immediately exposed to all kinds of confusing noises. At first he cannot distinguish between one sound and another. After approximately six eight weeks, however, he begins to recognise the difference between the human voice and other noises. By the time the infant is approximately nine months old, he begins to respond to a few simple words. He than analyses these words into phenomes, sounds, words and sentences are components of language which are learned together and interactively. The child starts with meanings and then analyses the speech into words and sounds. It is only for the convenience that we start with the acquisition of the sounds of a language.

Stages of Language Acquisition

Some linguists divide the stages of language acquisition into prelinguistic and linguistic stages. The earliest cries and whimpers of the new born or neonate cannot be considered early language. The development of the expressive language skill is the development of active participation in speech and language. The child's first vocalisation is at birth when the shock of the air in the lungs for the first time produces the reaction which results in noise in larynx. This type of reflex sound, the birth cry, can hardly be considered the beginning of the development of speech. Similarly all sounds made by the child in the first night to twelve weeks are completely stimulus responses or reflexes. The development of speech properly begins when the child can produce sounds at will by conscious effort.

Babbling Stage : Learning the Sound System of a Language

The first stage of the kind of sound production is called babbling and usually begins around the six month period. Between the third and the six month repertoire only a limited number of recognisable speech sounds increase quite rapidly until by the age of about six months he is producing a wide range of sounds and using them in his play. Some of these sounds resemble the sounds of the parents language. When the child utters a sound that resembles a real word, adults react to this utterance with smiles and repeat the word right back. This reinforces the child's response of saying that word and he repeats it again and again. This is called the reduplication stage. The syllabic structure of speech is reinforced during this stage.

Babbling provides the infant with vocal practice. He duplicates syllables consisting of consonant plus vowel, learns to imitate others as well as himself and attempts to echo adults who speak to him. Thus by the end of the babbling period his vocalisation begins to take on the intonation patterns of the parents' language.

Most of the first year of life is devoted to phonetic development and the phonological development takes over predominantly in the second year. The sequence in which speech sounds appear at different periods is fairly regular. During the babbling stages consonants appear in an orderly sequence from back to front, e.g. 'k' and 'g' occur before 'p' and 'm'. For vowels the order is just the opposite; e.g. 'i' and 'e' are usually produced before 'ae' and 'a'. During the second year, when the child's first words normally appear, the order of speech sounds is the reverse of the first year's babbling sequence. Parents reinforce utterances the papa and mama which are likely to occur during this period.

Between the babbling and the first words there is a short period of silence during which the child seems to the attending to individual words he hears rather than merely sounds people make when they speak. With the acquisition of words he begins to discover the rudiments of the phonetic system of his native language. It may be pointed out here the children learn systems of sounds and not how to evaluate individual sounds. This has been proved by the study of bilingual children. They do not make the some pronunciation mistakes in each of their two languages.

Between 10 and 18 months of age the child utters his first words, but has already learned to differentiate himself from others and is learning to interpret the world he lives in. The words which the child invents for himself are called his jargon. The development of jargon is an important stage of the acquisition of language since it is connected with the infant's desire to categorise the world around him and to use symbolic system of reference to it.

Holophrastic Stage : Learning the Syntax and Semantics of a Language

When the child is about 18 months old, he may be using about 20 meaningful words (meaningful in terms of the surrounding adult language) and a great deal of jargon. At this stage his communication with others will still be restricted to single word utterances. In this holophrastic stage these one word sentences are used to communicate a variety of ideas feeling and social awareness. These words are linked with a child's own action or desire for action or are used to convey emotion or serve a naming function. Adults usually interpret what a child means from the social and physical context of his utterances.

During this period of language development children acquire new words at a rapidly accelerating rate. Katherine Nelson has observed that children are able to utter first fifty words in about seven months with the sharpest spurt in the last two months. By twenty four months the average production vocabulary is 180 words and the rate of acquisition accelerate rapidly.

Children's first ten words include the names of animals, food and toys. Children prefer terms applying to manipulate and moving objects rather than to silent and static ones. Single words no matter how aptly chosen, are too ambiguous to represent the many possible meanings children need to express. Parents often expand the children's short utterances. Sometimes when the parents' guess about the child's intention is not correct it provides an added incentive to the child to further elaborate his speech.

The Two-World Stage : Learning the Grammar of a Language

Around the time of their second birthday children beginning to produce two-word utterances. This is the beginning of the grammar in a true sense and the first step towards syntactic competence. The surface structure syntax of these two word utterances confirms to a pivot grammar. All words in the child's lexicon belong to one of the two grammatical classes pivot and open. The pivot class contains a small group of words frequently used/repeated in the form of function words as grammatical operations such as all gone, hi, by-bye and it : the rest are open class or full semantic words.

Pivot words cannot occur alone in an utterance, but open words can. With these two classes of words the following sentence structures are possible.

- pivot + open — all gone milk
- open-pivot — shoe pretty
- open + open — Mommy shoe
- open — Daddy etc.

Those surface structures, however, can represent much more than just four types of sentences. Brown has classified the most common types of two word utterances into two major categories—reference operations and relation operations. When something is said about an object or event, it is called reference operation; e.g. 'that book' may be used to express the message that 'thing over there is a book'. How we can find at least four types of semantic relations such as nomination, notice, reoccurrence and non-existence. Open + open surface structure may represent at least six types of relational operations utterance that describe relations among two objects, events or characteristics. 'Big train' specifies an attribute of train. 'Mommy sock' specifies possession; 'book table' specifies location and so on. Concepts of relation among people and thing, like agent-action, action-object and agent-object can also be inferred from these two-word utterances. But as Lois Bloom argues these pivot grammar are not only incomplete descriptors, but inaccurate as well. Young children cannot be easily understood without reference to the immediate context.

During the two word utterance stage, the child does not use syntactic or morphological markers, that is no inflections for number or person or tense and so on; but these words are not separated by a pause and the intonation contour extends over the whole utterance.

There seems to be no three-word sentences stage but the child may begin to combine the two-word utterances to yield a three-word utterance e.g. mommy drink and drink milk may be combined into mommy drink milk. Slobin has shown that once the child uses three words his sentence has not only a structure but also a hierarchy. Now onwards his sentence may have 2-3 to 3-5 morphemes on the average. However, the small function words such as to, the, can, is and so on are missing from these sentences; they have only the 'context' words.

The child's linguistic competence is never static but is continually changing, and a feature which is absent in his surface structure today may be present tomorrow. As children acquire more and more language, or more closely approximately to the adult grammar, they not only begin to use syntactic or grammatical function words but also acquire the inflectional and derivational morphemes of the language. The child's vocabulary also increases immensely from fifty words at about seventeen months to many thousands by adolescence. With the growth of vocabulary, the word meanings also grow and change. The semantic development is accomplished through differentiation and generalisation.

The child shows a great deal of communicative competence and it can be asserted that by the time he is five or six years old, he has acquired most of the grammatical forms of his native language. This supports the nationalist-innate view of language acquisition.

From the time when the child is about two or two and half years old he uses language to accompany all his activity during play. Everything he does is accompanied by a sort of constant monologue. Language supports the activity to such an extent that it becomes an inextricable part of it and provides the child a kind of language lap practice for the development of his speech. It has been observed that the average output of a four year old child in his walking hours is something like 4000 words per hour.

How is Language Acquired?

As in every other development process physiological-maturational processes play a central role in language development. It has been observed that the brain is particularly well suited for language acquisition between birth and puberty. Although language development is closely related to the child's general neuro-muscular maturation, it is difficult to specify this relationship.

Some aspects of language may be acquired via the relatively simple learning mechanism of classical and operant conditioning but they are not by themselves sufficient for semantic and syntactic development. Adults play an important role in promoting and cajoling the child as well as interpreting and differentiating his utterances by means of adult surface structure. It is not that adults consciously teach the child; it may be more accurate to say that the child learns from the adults rather than they actively teach him. Brown and Hanlon do not find any discernible relations between the syntactic correctness of what the children say and the parental approval. According to them parents rarely correct the syntax of the child's utterances they care more for the truth of what is said.

It is often said that children learn language by imitation, but the sentences produced by children show that they are not imitating adult speech. At best they may imitate a 'rule'. From whom would a child hear a sentence like 'cat stand up table'? Imitation is generally limited by the child's current grammar. He can imitate only those structures which he has already acquired. McNeill has illustrated that trying to correct a child's speech by asking for corrected imitations may be unproductive. A look at the child's pivot grammar shows that imitation plays a subordinate role in the development of these syntactic patterns. In fact, the evidence of some observers suggests that adults imitate children more than children imitate adults.

Nobody teaches grammar to children. They develop a grammar by a process of abstraction from the data with which they are presented and this grammar differs in many respects from the current adult grammar. In the early stages children learn both the present and the past tense forms of the irregular verb such as run, ran, do, did, make, made etc. When they learn the inflection rule for forming past tense forms of the regular verbs by adding d or ed to the verb, they over generalise the rule and use forms like runned, doed and maked. Hence analogy seems to play a major role in language development of children because it is unlikely that a child could develop such forms as a result of imitation. The child's ability to generalise patterns and construct rules is also shown in phonological and semantic development.

Exposure to language in an interpretable context is yet another major factor in language development. R Brown and U Bellugi have shown how parents often interpret and expand their children's telegraphic utterance. Children learn a great deal from these exchanges.

Another way to provide information for children is to speak as adults do. This is called modelling-behaving in ways that we want children to behave.

The young school going child learns the kind of language he uses in his street and play-ground. He learns it mainly from other children; not from adults. Until he goes to school, nursery school or play group, the child is expected to have acquired most of his language from his mother. The mother teaches the child not only his native language but also a way of looking at the world and a way of categorising the experiences the child enjoys, most children love activity and active interaction with people and the world facilitates early language development.

By acquisition of language is meant the process whereby children achieve a fluent control of their native language. The term acquisition is used in place of learning, because learning tends to be employed by psychologists in a more specific sense than is perhaps appropriate. We have described the various stages in language acquisition, but it may be pointed out that the ages given for reaching a particular stage can vary enormously even within what is considered to be the normal range. Neuro-muscular-maturation, conditioning, imitation and exposure to language etc are some of the factors responsible for language development. A child picks up language from his environment and builds up his grammar by a process of abstraction.

Theories of Language Acquisition

It is really an amazing fact that a five year old child masters the intricate system of his native language. Psycho linguistics have, therefore, attempted general theories of language acquisition. Behaviourist psychologist BF Skinner used the concepts and categories of his psychology to describe the behaviour of language. He argues that learning is entirely the product of experience and that our environment affects all of us in the same way. Language is a set of habits acquired by a process of conditioning. This school is known as empiricists or behaviourists. Others have suggested that every body has an innate language. Learning mechanism which determines acquisition of language individually for each of us. This school is known as rationalists or mentalists. *We shall describe behaviourism and mentalism in the paragraphs that follow*

Behaviourism

Behaviourism emphasises the importance of environmental variables in language acquisition. Cambell and Wales assert that "the proper course of adoption in the investigation of language acquisition is to specify first the nature of the linguistic environment and thus identify the possible sources of information available to the child about his language and then to discover, presumably by experimentation, which of these possible sources are used..." Behaviourism, thus, believes that all knowledge is derived from experience. All children start out as 'clean slates'. Language acquisition is getting linguistic habits printed on 'these slates'. Language acquisition is the result of stimulus-response activities. Imitation, repetition, memorisation, reward and reinforcement facilitate this process of language acquisition. Behaviourism believes that learning is controlled by the conditions under which it takes place and that as long as individuals are subjected to the same condition they will learn in the same way. Variations in learning are caused because of the difference in learning experience, difference in the past experience of learning, difference in aptitudes, motivation, memory and age. Thus they seem to apply the general principles of learning to language learning.

According to behavourism, language is a result of stimulus and response. A child should, therefore, learn to make a response in the first place and then the response should be reinforced in a variety of ways. The strength of learning is measured in terms of the number of times that a response has been made and reinforced. So, language learning is a mechanical process of habit formation. Habits are strengthened by reinforcement. Language is a conditioned behaviour which can be learnt only by inducing the child to behave. Repetition plays a vital role in learning a language. Hence, the necessity of mechanical drills and exercises, imitation and repetition are unavailable Moreover behaviourism concentrates on the description of substance and form of the language and continually side-steps meaning.

Mentalism

Mentalism contradicts the above views at almost every point. Children learn a language not because they are subjected to a similar conditioning process, but because they possess an in-born capacity which permits them to acquire a language as a normal maturational process. This capacity is universal. Mentalists have postulated a Language Acquisition Device (LAD), a kind of genetic blue print which determines to some extent the structure of the language systems that are learned by human beings so that language universals are conditioned by what is innate. A child learns a language by exposure to the society and by consciously forming certain hypothesis about language, which he goes on modifying till he comes to the adult model. In other words, he goes on constructing an inner grammar, operating over-generalised rules.

The LAD may consist of a unique capacity or ability that is specialised for language acquisition. It may consist of general cognitive, abilities including sensory, perceptual and social mechanisms. It is subsystem of our cognitive apparatus, which develops a series of grammars as the child matures. These grammars tend to approximate to adult grammar until the final target is not attained i.e. adult language.

Chomsky believes that while learning a language, the child acquires a universal grammar and discovers a deep and abstract theory—a generative grammar of his language. 'The general feature of language structure reflects not so much the course of one's experience, but rather the general character of one's capacity to acquire knowledge.' The child's task is simply to search among the possible grammars and select one that is consistent with the meagre and degenerate data actually available to him. Only human beings can acquire language, but language is not something we know by instinct or inherit from our parents. It is a part of that whole complex of learnt and shared behaviour called culture'. A language is not so much learnt as it is 'selected' from among a set of innately given structures. It is not an imitation but a recreation. Catherine Snow has observed that young children do hear simplified speech. Parents and older children generally simplify their speech to young children. Children infer syntactic rule from his appropriately, simplified and interpretable speech. They do not hear a language full of mistakes, complex sentences and semi sentences. What they hear is 'relatively consistent, organised, simplified and redundant...a set of utterances which in many ways seem quite well-designed as a set of language lessons.'

Thus both schools have said significant things, yet neither is perfect. Language acquisition seems to be a process both of analogy and application, nature and nurture. The difference between the behavioural approach and the mentalistic approach is summarised in the following lines

Behavioural (Empirical) Approach

- Language acquisition is the result of experience.
- It is stimulus-response process.
- Language is a conditioned behaviour.
- Children learn language by imitation and analogy.
- Language learning is based on practice.
- Language learning is mechanical.
- Role of imitation, repetition, reinforcement, memory d motivation is very significant in language learning.
- uage acquisition is the result of nurture.

Mentalistic (Rationalistic) Approach

- It is a result of conditioning.
- It is an innate, in-born process.
- Language is species-specific and species uniform mental process.
- Children learn language by application.
- Language learning is rule based.
- Language learning is analytic, generative and creative.
- Rule of exposure is very significant.
- Language acquisition is the result of nature.

Factors Influencing the Language Acquisition

The nature vs. nurture debate extends to the topic of language acquisition. Today, most researchers acknowledge that both nature and nurture play a role in language acquisition. However, some researchers emphasise the influences of learning on language acquisition, while others emphasize the biological influences.

Receptive Language before Expressive Language

Children's ability to understand language develops faster than their ability to speak it. Receptive language is the ability to understand language and expressive language is the ability to use language to communicate. If a mother tells her fifteen-month-old child to put the toy back in the toy chest, he may follow her instructions even though he can't repeat them himself.

Environmental Influences on Language Acquisition

A major proponent of the idea that language depends largely on environment was the behaviorist BF Skinner. He believed that language is acquired through principles of conditioning, including association, imitation and reinforcement.

According to this view, children learn words by associating sounds with objects, actions and events. They also learn words and syntax by imitating others. Adults enable children to learn words and syntax by reinforcing correct speech. Learning cannot account for the rapid rate at which children acquire language. There can be an infinite number of sentences in a language. All these sentences cannot be learnt by imitation. Children make errors such as over-regularising verbs. e.g. a child may say Billy hitted me, incorrectly adding the usual past tense suffix-ed to hit. Errors like these can't result from imitation, since adults generally use correct verb forms. Children acquire language skills even though adults do not consistently correct their syntax.

Neural Networks

Some cognitive neuroscinetists have created neural networks, or computer models, that can acquire some aspects of language. These neural networks are not preprogrammed with any rules. Instead, they are exposed to many examples of a language. Using these examples, the neural networks have been able to learn the language's statstical structure and accurately make the past tense forms of verbs. The developers of these networks speculate that children may acquire language in a similar way, through exposure to multiple examples.

Biological Influences of Language Acquisition

The main proponent of the view that biological influences bring about language development is the well-known linguist Noam Chomsky. Chomsky argues that human brains have a Language Acquisition Device (LAD), an innate mechanism or process that allows children to develop language skills. According to this view, all children are born with a universal grammar, which makes them receptive to the common geatures of all languages. because of this hard-wired background in grammar, children easily pick upa a language when they are exposed to its particular grammar.

Evidence for an innate human capacity to acquire language skills comes from the following observations:

The stage of language development occur at about the same ages in most children, even though different children experience very different environments.

Children's language development follows a similar pattern across cultures.

Children generally acquire language skills quickly and effortlessly.

Deaf children who have not been exposed to a language may make up their own language. These new languages resemble each other in sentence structure, even when they are created in different cultures.

Biology and Environment

Some researchers have proposed theories that emphasize the importance of both nature and nurture in language acquisition. These theorists believe that humans do have an innate capacity for acquiring the rules of language. However, they believe that children develop language skills through interaction with others rather than acquire the knowledge automatically.

Pedagogy

Pedagogy is a study of teaching methods, including the aims of education and the ways in which such goals may be achieved. The field relies heavily on educational psychology. Which encompasses scientific theories of learning and to some extent on the philosophy of education.

Linguistic Principles of Teaching English

- Language of a system is a symbol. Symbols of a language are vocal. These symbols are meant for speaking, writing is secondary representation of language. Gestures, pictures, signals etc are all meaningful only if there is a language operating.
- Every language is unique in the sense that it has its particular structure, sounds and words. The use of mother tongue can be made to facilitate the learning of a foreign language. Our dependence on mother tongue would obstruct command over the target language.
- Language is a gift of culture. The words and sounds of a particular culture have their value only in their own sphere.
- Language is not static. It grows and undergoes changes. It is dynamic and depends on cultural change. New words, sounds and pronunciation enrich a language.

General Principles of Teaching a Foreign Language

Follow the Natural Way

While teaching a foreign language stress should be laid on the fundamental order of listening, speaking, reading and writing. The learner should be provided with a natural environment in the family and friends in the following ways.

- Encourage learners to exchange views in the target language.
- The teacher should talk to students only in the foreign language
- Arrange language activities and group discussion.
- Students should be provided with opportunities for practical usage.
- Students should be encouraged to immerse themselves in imitation that involves acute and constant observation. There should be regular practice of it.
- Accuracy and correctness should be stressed. Only those words should be used that impart meaning to the context.

Principles of the Formation of Habits

The learner must form the habit of speaking, reading and writing the target language frequently. Language is a subject that depends upon skill and can be picked up easily, if it is made a habit.

Principles of Controlled Vocabulary

- The vocabulary taught and practised should strictly be in the context of real life situations.
- Efforts should be made to bring words from passive vocabulary to a child's active vocabulary.
- When the learner gets the working knowledge of vocabulary, he should be taught the language pattern.

Principles of Selection

The teaching material should be in accordance with the mental age and should have relevance to real life situations. The situation of items of language should be based on the following principles.

- Frequency of language used (How often)
- Range of applicability (Number of situations)
- Coverage
- Availability (items convenient to teach and use)
- Teachability
- Learnability

Principles of Gradation

The first principle is leading from simple to complex. It involves grouping and sequencing.

- Grouping It includes system of a language and its structure *e.g.*, Phonetic grouping, Lexical grouping, Grammatical grouping and Semantic grouping.
- **Sequence** It means what comes after what *e.g.* Lexical sequencing and Semantic sequencing.

Maxims of Language Teaching

The maxims of teaching are universal facts. These help a teacher to proceed systematically. They enable the teacher to find out the way for teaching.

- **Known to Known** It is based on the assumption that students know something. The teacher is surprised to increase the learner's knowledge and widen their outlook. The new knowledge should be interpreted in terms of the old.
- **Concrete to Abstract** The beginners should be taught with concrete things. They being solid can be touched and so they help the learners and they cannot forget the subject matter. The abstract things can only be imagined, so it becomes difficult for the beginners to learn with them.
- **Analysis of Synthesis** Analysis means breaking a long sentence or problem into its convenient parts, while synthesis means grouping of these separate parts into one complete whole. A complex problem can be made simple and easy by dividing it into different parts. Analysis is the approach for understanding and synthesis is the fixation. Analysis of a sentence is taught to the learners. It helps students to understand different parts of a sentence synthesis of sentences should be taught later.
- **Particular to General** The teacher should initially take a particular statement and then on the basis of these particular cases, generalisation should be made.
- **Empirical to Rational** Empirical knowledge is based on observation and first hand experience. It is particular, concrete and simple. It can be felt as well as experienced. Rational is based on our arguments and explanations.
- **Induction to Deduction** Induction means drawing a conclusion from a set of examples. Deduction is just the opposite of it. The teacher should proceed from induction to deduction.
- **Simple to Complex** In the formal classroom teaching, the teacher should proceed from the simple to the complex. The simple learning would create interest in the learner. There after complex material should be introduced gradually. Simple things create motivation and encourage students to learn. This increases students' confidence level and they become receptive for complex matters. Gradually difficult matter can also be introduced.
- **Psychological to Logical** While imparting knowledge to students, the teacher should bear in mind the interest, aptitudes, capacities, development level etc of children while selecting subject matter for them. Then he ought to move on to its logical arrangement. While teaching English, structure should be selected as per the needs and requirements of students. Then it should be arranged in a logical way.
- **Actual to Representative** Actual objects should be shown to learners for effective teaching because they provide them with concrete learning. The learners tend to retain them in their mind for a longer period.
- **Near to Far** Children are able to learn well in the surroundings they belong to. Gradually, they should learn about those things that are far from their immediate surroundings.
- **Whole to Part** The teacher should first acquaint students with the whole lesson and then its different portions can be analysed and studied extensively.
- **Definite to Indefinite** The definite things should be taught first because the learner can have faith in them easily. The knowledge of definite things should be followed by the knowledge of indefinite things. The definite rules of grammar are always helpful.

EXAM BASED QUESTIONS

1 Teaching and learning is a journey from
(a) concrete to abstract
(b) simple to complex
(c) known to unknown
(d) All of the above

2 The method of teaching English adopted at present in school curriculum is
(a) Formative correlation approach
(b) Functional communicative approach
(c) Function corrective approach
(d) Figurative comprehensive approach

3 FCA is in opposition to
(a) Structural approach
(b) Comprehensive approach
(c) Translation and grammar method
(d) Functional approach

4 Communicative Language Teaching replaced basically
(a) Natural language processing
(b) Structural teaching
(c) Situational language teaching
(d) Motivational teaching

5 Direct Method is also known as
(a) Natural method (b) Indirect approach
(c) Inductive approach (d) All these

6 Grammar-Translation Method stresses on
(a) accuracy (b) fluency
(c) appropriateness (d) listening skill

7 Grammar-Translation Method is basically used to teach
(a) grammar
(b) foreign language
(c) rules of any language usage
(d) classical language

8 The objective of Direct Method is
(a) to increase power of comprehension
(b) to increase communicative power
(c) to develop a command over the target language
(d) to develop personality

9 Grammar-Translation Method does not
(a) encourage learning through mother tongue
(b) give importance to grammar
(c) enhance a student's communicative skill
(d) enable the student to use the language fluently

10 Traditional method goes against the
(a) prescriptive grammar (b) simulation
(c) pedagogic principles (d) generalisation

11 The incidental or Correlative Method is known as
(a) inductive (b) deductive
(c) structural (d) reference method

12 Journey from example to generalisation is
(a) inductive (b) deductive
(c) incidental (d) All of these

13 Inductive method proceeds from
(a) heavy materials to light ones
(b) known to unknown
(c) simple to complex
(d) Both (b) and (c)

14 Deductive method proceeds from
(a) law and rule to observation
(b) observation
(c) generalisation to specification
(d) examples and illsutrations

15 One of the principles of materials preparation of language learning is that
(a) complex material should be chosen
(b) grading of materials should be done
(c) any kind of material can be chosen
(d) a small amount of material should be introduced

16 Correct pronunciation of individual sound is related to
(a) accuracy (b) fluency
(c) Both accuracy and fluency
(d) Neither accuracy nor fluency

17 Language acquisition occurs only when
(a) the child is taught the rules of grammar
(b) the child is given a reward
(c) the child has exposure to the language
(d) the child absorbs the language without conscious attention

18 When a child is asked to recite a poem, it can help the teacher to test
(a) knowledge of literature
(b) proficiency of speaking
(c) acting talent
(d) comprehension

19 The structure 'he goes to school' is often produced by learners due to
(a) failure of intelligence
(b) mother tongue interference
(c) over generalisations of rules
(d) wrong teaching

20 For teaching grammar, the best grammar that a teacher can use is
(a) traditional grammar
(b) modern grammar
(c) pedagogic grammar
(d) no grammar is needed

21 A test of listening comprehension is a test of
(a) Receptive skill (b) Productive skill
(c) Hearing skill (d) Phonology skill

22 **Organisation of arguments and ideas in paragraphs is an important aspect of**
(a) writing essays
(b) writing memos
(c) writing stories
(d) writing personal letters

23 **'Brain storming' means**
(a) to collect all kinds of ideas on a topic
(b) to do some mental exercise
(c) to make efforts to understand something
(d) to give some kind of stimulus to the brain

24 **'Interactive' listening is**
(a) listening and responding
(b) listening for mood and tone
(c) listening for word stress and emphasis
(d) listening for finding out speaker's attitude

25 **Which of the following is an incorrect assumption in language teaching?**
(a) Learners acquire language by trying to use it in real situations
(b) Learners' first language plays an important role in learning
(c) Language teaching should have a focus in communicative activities
(d) Language teaching should give importance to writing rather than speech

26 **Reading skill can be developed best by**
(a) writing answers to questions on text
(b) focusing on the use of words from context in the text
(c) doing vocabulary exercises
(d) doing quizzes and playing word games

27 **Mother tongue influence can be effectively minimised in the classroom by**
(a) using the mother tongue more often
(b) giving examples from the mother tongue
(c) giving a lot of exposure in the target language
(d) giving inputs from the target language in a simple, graded manner

28 **Practice of grammatical structures in a controlled manner can be done by**
(a) correcting wrong sentences produced by learners
(b) gap-filling grammar exercises
(c) writing paragraphs and essays
(d) explaining the use of particular structures

29 **A test which is administered at the end of a language course is**
(a) Diagnostic test (b) Placement test
(c) Achievement test (d) Memory test

30 **Study of meaning in a language is known as**
(a) syntax (b) semantics
(c) morphology (d) linguistics

31 **Who has defined speech as the representation of the experience of mind?**
(a) Aristotle (b) Chomsky
(c) Henry Sweet (d) E Sapir

32 **Which of the following is not a direct means of communication?**
(a) Gesture (b) Sneeze (c) Blinking (d) Hearing

33 **The totality of a speech habit of a single person at a given time constitutes his**
(a) dialect (b) ideolect (c) language (d) pidgin

34 **Which of the following are trade languages?**
(a) Jargons (b) Pidgins (c) Dialects (d) Idiolects

35 **According to CL Barber, how many theories explain the genesis of language?**
(a) Five (b) Six (c) Seven (d) Eight

36 **Which of the following is not counted among the dead languages?**
(a) Arabic (b) Ancient Greek
(c) Pali (d) Aramaic

37 **Which of the following is not the characteristic feature of speech?**
(a) Speech is primary
(b) It is impersonal and objective
(c) It is natural and spontaneous
(d) It is confined to the present audience

38 **Which of the following languages have evolved from Latin?**
(a) English and German (b) Greek and Hebrew
(c) French and Italian (d) Pali and Persian

39 **Who says that le langage (human speech as whole) consists of langue and parole?**
(a) Chomsky (b) Halliday
(c) RH Robins (d) Saussure

40 **Which of the following is constant, supra-individualistic and generalised?**
(a) Langue (b) Parole (c) Dialect (d) Idiolect

41 **Which one of the following languages does not have three genders?**
(a) Sanskrit (b) Latin (c) Hindi (d) German

42 **What is the chief weakness of descriptive or structural approach?**
(a) It neglects grammar (b) It neglects meaning
(c) It neglects rules (d) It is very complicated

43 **Which of the following deals with the production of sounds by the organs of speech?**
(a) Auditory phonetics (b) Acoustic phonetics
(c) Phonology (d) Articulatory phonetics

44 **Which of the following is essentially the description of the system and patterns of speech sounds in a language?**
(a) Phonology (b) Phonetics (c) Phonemes (d) Allophones

45 **What is a phoneme?**
(a) It is the biggest unit at the sound level of sound
(b) It is the smallest unit at the sound level of sound
(c) It is the loudest unit at the sound level of sound
(d) All of the above

46 What is a minimal pair?
(a) It is a set of two words which do not differ from each other in one round
(b) It is a set of two words which produce vowel sound
(c) It is a set of two words which differ from each other in one sound
(d) It is a set of two sentences

47 What is the name of the unit which is next in hierarchy to the phoneme?
(a) Allophones (b) Syllable
(c) Morphone (d) Lexical morphene

48 Which of the following words has one syllable?
(a) Come (b) Teacher
(c) Doctor (d) Remember

49 Which of the following is not a behavioural approach?
(a) Language is a conditional behaviour
(b) Language learning is mechanical
(c) Language learning is rule based
(d) Language learning is practice based

50 Which of the following theories states that language arose from instinctive emotional cries, expressive of pain or joy?
(a) The Ding-Dong Theory (b) The Yo He Ho Theory
(c) The Bow-Bow Theory (d) The Pooh-Pooh Theory

51 Give the name of theory that explains that the primitive language was an act of imitation, such as the cries of animals?
(a) The Bow-Bow Theory (b) The Yo-He-Ho Theory
(c) The Ding-Dong Theory (d) The Contact Theory

52 In teaching experienced members guide the immature one's for
(a) spending time (b) qualification
(c) quality of life (d) adjustment of life

53 Which is not the focal point of triangular process of teaching
(a) Teaching method (b) Teacher
(c) Pupil (d) contents

54 The goal of teaching is
(a) to give information
(b) to involve pupils in activities
(c) to impart knowledge
(d) desirable change in behaviour

55 The rules of presenting the contents to make them easy are called
(a) Method of teaching (b) Maxims of teaching
(c) Techniques of teaching (d) Teaching strategies

56 SOLO stands for
(a) System of the Observed Learning Outcome
(b) Structure of the Observed Learingn Output
(c) Structure of the Observed Learning Outcome
(d) System of the Observed Learning Output

57 With reference to solo taxonomy one aspect of a task is understood in
(a) unistructural level (b) multistructural level
(c) rational level (d) extended abstract level

58 Two or more aspects are understood in
(a) unistructural lever (b) multistructural level
(c) rational level (d) extended abstract level

59 Integration is developed between two or more Aspects in
(a) unistructural level (b) multistructural level
(c) rational level (d) extended abstract level

60 To go beyond the given information is
(a) unistructural level (b) multistructural level
(c) rational level (d) extended abstract level

61 SOLO taxonomy was presented by
(a) Bloom (b) Krath whol
(c) Simpson (d) Biggs and collis

62 Students are passive in
(a) Project method (b) Discovery method
(c) Lecture method (d) Inquiry method

63 Symposium is a type of
(a) Discovery method (b) Discussion method
(c) Lecture method (d) Demonstration method

64 Heuristic means
(a) to investigate (b) to show
(c) to do (d) to act

65 Arm-Strong was the exponent of
(a) Problem solving method (b) Project method
(c) Discussion method (d) Heuristic method

66 We move from specific to general in
(a) Inductive method (b) Deductive method
(c) Drill method (d) Discussion method

67 In which method is practice made
(a) Inductive method (b) Deductive method
(c) Drill method (d) Discussion method

68 The Socratic method is known as
(a) Lecture demonstration method
(b) Discussion method (c) Inquiry method
(d) Question- Answer method

69 Which is not true about projects?
(a) It is a purposeful activity
(b) It is proceeded in social environment
(c) It is accomplished in real life
(d) It is teacher centred activity

70 Duration of lessons in macro- lesson plans is
(a) 5-10 min (b) 10-20 min (c) 20-30 min (d) 35-45 min

71 In British approach of lesson planning, more emphasis is on
(a) Activity (b) Teacher
(c) Content presentation
(d) Teacher and content presentation

72 American approach emphasizes
(a) teacher (b) content presentation
(c) learning objectives (d) methods

73 Which one is not the type of lesson plans on the basis of objectives
(a) Micro lesson plan (b) Cognitive lesson plan
(c) Affective lesson plan (d) Psychomotor lesson paln

74 Which is not true about lesson plan?
(a) It is develops confidence
(b) It helps in oderly delivery of contents
(c) It is developed by students
(d) It saves from haphazard teaching

75 Which is not the type of teleconferencing
(a) Audio teleconferencing
(b) Video teleconferencing
(c) TV teleconferencing
(d) Computer teleconferencing

76 Which one is accountable in cooperative learning
(a) Individual (b) Group
(c) Both (a) and (b) (d) None of these

77 Cooperative learning is an alternative to
(a) competitive models (b) teaching models
(c) lesson plans (d) micro teaching

78 The essential characteristic of cooperative learning is
(a) effective learning
(b) positive interdependence
(c) cooperation
(d) division of labour

79 Which is not the advantage of team teaching
(a) Better utilisation of resources
(b) Better planning
(c) Better use of teaching techniques
(d) Better financial benefits of teachers

80 The hypothesis underlying team teaching is
(a) teachers feel bore while working alone
(b) teachers are not competent
(c) the best teachers in schools are shared by more students
(d) the single teacher cannot control the class

81 Example of psychomotor domain is that student
(a) demonstrates awareness to environmental pollution
(b) performs an experiment
(c) can computer results of two experiments
(d) can narrate a story

82 Ability to develop a life style based upon the preferred value system is
(a) responding (b) valuing
(c) organising (d) characterising

83 Example of cognitive domain is
(a) describe a topi(c)
(b) develop an X-ray film
(c) type a letter
(d) take responsibility for tools

84 Student can design a laboratory according to certain specification in which category of objective?
(a) Analysis (b) Synthesis (c) Evaluation (d) Knowledge

85 The highest level of cognitive domain is
(a) synthesis (b) analysis
(c) comprehension (d) evaluation

86 The process of determing the value or worth of anything is
(a) test (b) measurement
(c) assessment (d) evalution

87 Educational objectives have been divided into
(a) two domains (b) three domains
(c) four domains (d) five domains

88 Taxonomy of educational objectives was presented in
(a) 1946 (b) 1956 (c) 1966 (d) 1976

89 The classification of cognitive domain was presented by
(a) Benjamin S Bloom (b) Skinner
(c) Krathwhol (d) Simpson

90 The lowest level of learning in cognitive domain is
(a) comprehension (b) application
(c) knowledge (d) synthesis

91 The right sequence of subgroups cognitive domain is
(a) knowledge, comprehension, application, synthesis, analysis, evaluation
(b) knowledge, comprehension, application, evaluation, analysis, synthesis
(c) knowledge, comprehension, evaluation, application, analysis, syntesis
(d) knowledge, comprehension, application, analysis, synthesis, evaluation

92 To use previous learned material in new situation is
(a) comprehension (b) application
(c) knowledge (d) analysis

93 To break down material into component parts to know its organisational structure is
(a) comprehension (b) application
(c) analysis (d) synthesis

94 The intellectual skills are reflected by
(a) cognitive domain (b) affective domain
(c) psychomotor (d) None of these

95 Attitudes, values and interests are reflected by
(a) cognitive domain (b) affective domain
(c) psychomotor domain (d) None of these

96 Which domain is concerned with physical and motor skills?
(a) cognitive domain (b) affective domain
(c) psychomotor domain (d) None of these

97 **The focus of cognitive domain is**
(a) Physical and Motor skills (b) Intellectual skills
(c) Attitudes and Interests (d) None of these

98 **The lowest level of learning in affective domain is**
(a) responding (b) valuing
(c) attending (d) organisation

99 **Which is placed at the highest level of learning in affective domain?**
(a) Attending (b) Responding
(c) Organisation (d) Characterisation

100 **Right order of sub- groups of affective domain is**
(a) attending, responding, valuing, characterization, organisation
(b) attending, responding, characterization, valuing, organisation
(c) attending, valuing, responding, organization, characterisation
(d) attending, responding, valuing, organization, characterization

101 **The characteristic of behavioural objective is**
(a) observable and immeasurable
(b) non- observable
(c) observable and measurable
(d) None of the above

102 **The right sequence of sub-groups of psychomotor domain is**
(a) perception, set, guided response, mechanism, complex overt response, adaptation, origination
(b) perception, complex over response, set, guided, response, mechanism, adaptation, organisation
(c) set, origination, guided response, mechanism complex overt response, adaptation, perception
(d) guided response, mechanism, perception, set, adaptation, organisation, complex overt response

103 **Objective related to affective domain is**
(a) student can paint a picture
(b) student can draw a graph
(c) student values honesty
(d) student can write a letter

104 **Bring together scientific ideas to form a unique idea is**
(a) application (b) analysis
(c) synthesis (d) evaluation

105 **Students find/explore the information themselves in**
(a) lecture method (b) discovery method
(c) Both (a) and (b) (d) None of these

106 **Role of student is active in**
(a) Discover method (b) Problem solved method
(c) Inquiry method (d) All of these

107 **Micro teaching focuses on the competency over**
(a) method (b) skills
(c) contents (d) None of of these

108 **Which is more suitable in teaching of science?**
(a) lecture method (b) demonstration method
(c) discussion method (d) project method

109 **Which one is a standard for demonstration method?**
(a) Student should observe the demonstration and teacher should not tell important finding
(b) To keep accuracy of results the teacher should dictate the result
(c) Demonstration should be pre- tested to remove the weakness in demonstration
(d) All of the above

110 **What is/are the merits of microteaching?**
(a) Feedback helps in the improvement of method of teaching
(b) Due to shortage of time you divide the lesson plan into small units and thus gain mastery over the content
(c) It helps in self evaluation and teacher build up confidence in them
(d) All of the above

111 **Exhibition of Science fairs promote students ability of**
(a) knowledge order skills
(b) comprehension and application
(c) higher order skills
(d) homer order skills

112 **What is the first step in the project method of teaching?**
(a) Determination of activities
(b) Determination of objectives
(c) Planning (d) Distribution of work

113 **Which one is not the Psychological principle of teaching?**
(a) Proceed from concrete to abstract
(b) Proceed from complex to simple
(c) Proceed from known to unknown
(d) Proceed from simple to difficult

114 **Which is the best method of teaching science at school level?**
(a) Lecture (b) Analytical
(c) Direct (d) Demonstration

115 **Which is not the step of scientific method?**
(a) Observation (b) Experiment
(c) Prediction (d) Interwiew

116 **The word 'Pedagogy' means**
(a) to guide the child (b) to lead the child
(c) to educate the child (d) to understand the child

117 **Pedagogy is the study of**
(a) Education (b) Guiding Students
(c) Learning Process (d) Teaching Methods

118 **Which one of the followings indicates child's physical growth?**
(a) Negative (b) Quantitative
(c) Qualitative (d) Positive

119 **The best method to study growth and development of the child is**

(a) Psychoanalytic method (b) Comparative method
(c) Developmental method (d) Statistical method

120 **What does the term PSRN in development imply?**

(a) Problem solving, reasoning and numeracy
(b) Problem solving relationship and numeracy
(c) Perceptual skill, reasoning and numeracy
(d) Perceptual skill, relationship and numbers

121 **"Individual learns from his own mistakes." This statement is based on which learning theory?**

(a) Instrumental conditioning
(b) Insight
(c) Trial and error
(d) Classical conditioning

122 **What should be the role of teacher in meeting the individual differences?**

(a) Try to know the abilities, interest and aptitude of individuals
(b) Try to adjust the curriculum as per the needs of individuals
(c) Both (a) and (b)
(d) None of the above

123 **Teachers should present information to the students clearly and in interesting way, and relate this new information to the things students**

(a) don't know (b) already know
(c) willing to know (d) not willing to know

124 **Which of the following statements is not true ?**

(a) Growth is a biological process
(b) Development is a quantitative process
(c) Education is a goal-oriented process
(d) Learning is a process of behavioural changes

125 **Which of the following is not the tool for Formative Assessment in sholastic domain?**

(a) Conversation Skill (b) Multiple Choice Question
(c) Projects (d) Oral Questions

126 **Which of the following statement is not true in case of multiple choice questions?**

(a) Even an inexperienced teacher can prepare the questions easily
(b) All choices appear to be plausible
(c) Error-free and quick evaluation is possible by computer
(d) Only one of the choices is the correct answer

127 **According to John Dewey, schools must prepare students for**

(a) research (b) future life
(c) present life (d) entrepreneurship

128 **What type of evaluation identifies learning deficiencies and difficulties of the learners?**

(a) Placement (b) Summative
(c) Continuous (d) Diagnostic

129 **Which from the following should be used to increase correct responses and appropriate behaviour?**

(a) Ignorance (b) Strictness
(c) Reward (d) Praise

130 **At the pre-primary stage reading aloud while writing is given importance. This is based on which theory of learning?**

(a) Trial and Error (b) Conditioning
(c) Insight (d) Imitation

131 **According to Emile, the noblest work in education is to make a/an**

(a) thinker (b) entrepreneur
(c) good citizen (d) reasoning man

132 **Which one of the following is not taken into consideration while preparing the blue-print for a test?**

(a) Topic (b) Instructional objectives
(c) Form of questions (d) Teaching time

133 **The field of study concerned with the construction of thought processes, including remembering, problem solving, and decision-making is called**

(a) Pedagogy (b) Education
(c) Epistemology (d) Cognitive Development

134 **Which is not a factor of motivation?**

(a) Prize (b) Incentive (c) Praise (d) Practice

135 **According to Jean Piaget, children develop abstract logic and reasoning skill during**

(a) Sensory motor stage
(b) Preoperational stage
(c) Formal operational stage
(d) Concrete operational stage

136 **The philosopher who for the first time mentioned the importance of play (or sports) in education was**

(a) Plato (b) Aristotle
(c) Socrates (d) John Locke

137 **Language change takes place ....**

(a) with the lapse of time
(b) according to needs of the society
(c) because of amalgamation of people
(d) due to expansion of business

138 **Dialectical variation in language is ....**

(a) very rare (b) very explicit
(c) very common (d) very vague

139 **Synchrony is the study of a language ....**

(a) in a given time (b) through time
(c) related to past (d) that is deed

140 **Diachronic or historical linguist study the development of languages ....**

(a) that do not exist (b) spoken in orient
(c) spoken in Europe (d) through time

141 Through out the nineteenth century, linguistic research was very ....
(a) political in character (b) religious in character
(c) historical in character (d) social in character

142 According to Saussure, langue is the abstract system of language and parole is its ....
(a) substitute (b) manifestation
(c) opposite (d) another branch

143 Parole is a personal dynamic ...... activity.
(a) cultural (b) political
(c) psychological (d) social

144 The concept of competence and performance refers to
(a) Chomsky (b) Saussure
(c) Bloch and Trager (d) J Whalmough

145 Chomsky's concept of competence and performance is somewhat similar to Saussure's concept of ....
(a) dialect and ideolect
(b) langue and parole
(c) descriptive and prescriptive
(d) appropriateness

146 Allophones are positional variants of
(a) consonant cluster
(b) syllable
(c) morphemes
(d) phonemes

147 Vowel element is essential to the structure of a ....
(a) morphene (b) phoneme
(c) syllable (d) allophone

148 Morphology is the grammar of ....
(a) words (b) phrases
(c) clauses (d) sentences

149 Morphenes are divided into ...... types.
(a) two (b) three
(c) four (d) five

150 All affixes are ...... morphenes.
(a) free (b) loose
(c) fixed (d) bound

151 Ear and brain are examples of ....
(a) acoustic phonetics (b) auditory phonetics
(c) articulatory phonetics (d) None of these

ANSWERS

Objective Questions

1. (d)	2. (b)	3. (a)	4. (b)	5. (a)	6. (a)	7. (d)	8. (c)	9. (c)	10. (c)
11. (a)	12. (a)	13. (d)	14. (a)	15. (b)	16. (a)	17. (c)	18. (d)	19. (c)	20. (c)
21. (a)	22. (a)	23. (a)	24. (a)	25. (d)	26. (b)	27. (d)	28. (b)	29. (a)	30. (a)
31. (a)	32. (d)	33. (c)	34. (b)	35. (c)	36. (a)	37. (b)	38. (c)	39. (d)	40. (a)
41. (c)	42. (b)	43. (d)	44. (a)	45. (b)	46. (c)	47. (b)	48. (a)	49. (c)	50. (d)
51. (a)	52. (d)	53. (a)	54. (d)	55. (b)	56. (c)	57. (a)	58. (b)	59. (c)	60. (d)
61. (d)	62. (c)	63. (b)	64. (a)	65. (d)	66. (c)	67. (c)	68. (d)	69. (d)	70. (d)
71. (d)	72. (c)	73. (a)	74. (c)	75. (c)	76. (c)	77. (a)	78. (b)	79. (d)	80. (c)
81. (b)	82. (d)	83. (a)	84. (b)	85. (d)	86. (d)	87. (b)	88. (b)	89. (a)	90. (c)
91. (a)	92. (b)	93. (c)	94. (a)	95. (b)	96. (c)	97. (b)	98. (c)	99. (d)	100. (d)
101. (c)	102. (a)	103. (c)	104. (c)	105. (b)	106. (d)	107. (b)	108. (d)	109. (c)	110. (d)
111. (b)	112. (d)	113. (b)	114. (d)	115. (d)	116. (b)	117. (d)	118. (b)	119. (c)	120. (c)
121. (c)	122. (c)	123. (b)	124. (b)	125. (c)	126. (a)	127. (c)	128. (d)	129. (d)	130. (b)
131. (c)	132. (d)	133. (d)	134. (d)	135. (c)	136. (b)	137. (b)	138. (c)	139. (a)	140. (d)
141. (c)	142. (b)	143. (d)	144. (a)	145. (b)	146. (d)	147. (c)	148. (a)	149. (a)	150. (d)
151. (b)									

English in India : History, Evolution and Futures

The English language in India has always been of immense importance and has played great role in shaping the future of India. With the arrival of the British in India, its evolution started which went on to flourish through valuable efforts.

Historical Background

Language emerged in the course of human evolution as a means of communication. Different communities developed their own codes with distinctive systems, which had similar universal features in different corners of the world. All human beings have an inherent ability to communicate and are capable of learning one or more languages this brings us to the position of English in India. There is no doubt that English has become the Lingua France of not only India but all countries across the globe. The communication carried out in English is well comprehended and used in all countries. English is one of the six official languages of the UNO. By communication and exchange of cultures English has surely made the world a small, close-knitted place.

The Indian British encounter gave rise to India writing in English and what started as a necessity-the learning of English by Indians for purposes of trade and commerce gradually saw it being used for creative writing as well. English education was introduced with an expectation in early nineteenth century that Indian pens would soon pour out essays, articles, fiction and poetry. In fact Indians had started writing in English much before the formalised English education system began. Much of the initial writing was about social reform and in the form of journalistic articles or treatises especially since English journals and newspapers had also started rolling off the printing presses.

Lord William Bentinck and Raja Ram Mohan Roy first followed by equally meaningful contributions from Rabindranath Tagore, Swami Vivekanand, Bankim Chandra and so on. In the fast shrinking technological world, English has become backbone and need of the hour for the prosperity of not only the individual but also the nation across the globe. Advent of Modern India authors like Arundhati Roy, Amitav Ghosh, Kiran Desai and Chetan Bhagat in India has taken Indian. English from budding stage to the state of blooming flower ready to yield fruits.

In this Chapter

- Historical Background
- Introduction of Indian English Literature
- Indian English Writers

Pre-Colonial Period

The East India Company was set up in 1599 at a meeting attended by leading London merchants and after a century and a half, the company was in a position to dominate the commercial, political and social set up of Bengal and as its power expanded, India as a whole. By 1813, the British had taken up not merely police functions but also the mission of educatiing and 'civilising' Indians. The Charter Act of 1813 brought about a significant change in educational vision as the institutes which offered oriental education were fast being overtaken in popularity and demand by those that offered western education.

The debate between orientatists and anglicists was settled by Macaulay's famous 'Minute'. Raja Rammohan Roy had continuously written letters and articles for the introduction of western education and science through English, which he argued should replace Traditional Sanskrit and Persian.

Thomas Bebington Macaulay was the chairman of the committee formed for deciding the course of action regarding education in India. Macaulay's famous Minute asserted that it was both necessary and possible to "make the natives of this country good English scholars and that to this end our efforts ought to be directed."

On 7th March, 1835, Lord William Bentick resolved that "the great object of the British Government ought to be the promotion of European literature and science among the natives of India, and all funds appropriated for the purpose of education would be best employed on English education alone."

In the beginning, the idea was to promote oriental education and even a grant of one lakh rupees was set aside for it. Printing presses had been printing books in Indian languages as well as in English (grammars, dictionaries, translations) from around the early years of the eighteenth century. Christian Missionaries accelerated the efforts of spreading English as they entered India in 1759, Rev. Schwartz established schools for the teaching of English. The first book published to teach English to the non-Europeans, 'The tutor' come out in 1797, by Johen Miller.

The first English Newspaper in India-Hicky's Bengal Gazette-started in 1780, soon followed by others. Private schools that promoted education in English such as those established in 1717 at Cuddalore near Chennai, in 1718 at Mumbai and 1720 at Kolkata, culminated in the establishment, in 1817, of the Hindu college (Later called Presidency College in 1855) by Raja Rammohan Roy, David Hare and Sir Edward Hyde East.

Colonial Period

Though the stage was set in the Pre-colonial period itself, the actual grip of English began the initial idea of bring English education in India was to create a class of people' 'Indian' in blood and colour but English in taste and opinion. This would inturn create a dominance of the British culture over the Indians and also have a control over the minds of the Indian people through English. It would also serve another purpose of training Indians fit for employment. The British Government proferred Indians with the knowledge of English for the government jobs.

English became the medium of instruction and universities modelled on the University of London were established in Bombay, Calcutta and Madras. Between the years 1835 to 1855 the number of Indians educated in English increased significantly.

The Downward Filtration Theory of Macaulay was being manifested. Macaulay's aim was 'Education was to permeate the masses from above, drop by drop from Himalayas of Indian life and useful information was to trickle downwards, forming in time a broad and stately stream to irrigate the thirsty 'plains'.

As the number of English educated Indians increased, the number of English books sold higher than in Indian languages and the bulk of demand came from educated Indians and not from Englishmen based in India. As distances started to get bridged through the introduction of the railways and the telegraph, a common medium of communication. English started increasing in usage.

In addition, European techniques in science and medicine started making their pusence felt and it was through the English language that they spread among the educated classes.

Once Indians become familiar with the English language as they increasingly used it for utilitarian communication, they started making use of it for creative purposes as well. Essays, speeches, travelogues, letters, biographies, autobiographies, verse, drama, story. All the geners were soon being explored with the result that we now have a large corpus of writing in English that comprises the work of men and women from the subcontinent the freedom fighters generously used English as a tool against the British Raj itself, to make people aware of the atrocities of the British.

Wood's Despatch

Sir Charles Wood played a significant role in spreading English learning and female education in India. In 1854 he sent a despatch to Lord Dalhousie, the then Governor-General of India. It suggested that primary colleges must adopt vernacular languages, high schools must adopt Anglo-vernacular language and on college level English medium for education.

This was called Magna Carta of English Education in India. One of the most favourable steps was to create English class in Indian people to be used as work force in company's administration.

Hunter Commission

Hunter Commission was appointed by Viceroy Lord Ripon with the objectives to look into the complaints of the non-implementation of the Wood's Despatch of 1854; the contemporary status of elementary education in the British territories; and suggest means by which this can be extended and improved. This commission, headed by Sir William Wilson Hunter had submitted its report in 1882. The Hunter Commission brought out the neglect to the primary and secondary education in the country and recommended that the responsibility for the Primary Education must be given to the Local boards and Municipal boards.

Most of its recommendation were accepted by the British Government which resulted in the devolution of elementary education, which significantly reduced the British element in elementary education.

Post Independence

When India broke the shackles of British rule, there was a wave of doing away with all that was British and foreign, the question that was to be dealt with now, was the position of English. The position of first official language was given to Hindi and attempts were made to declare Hindi as the role National language of India. Due to protests from Tamil Nadu and other non-Hindi speaking states, it was decided to temporary retain English for official purposes until 1965. The English Language Amendment Bill declared English to be associate language "until such time as all non-Hindi states had agreed to its being dropped." English was the only means of day-to-day communication between the Central Government and the non Hindi states.

However, it was felt that English was a necessary tool for growth and advancement university education common's opinion on English is that English must continue to be studied. English must continue to be studied. It is a language which is rich in literature humanistic, scientific and technical. English continued to be used as under no circumstances could we sacrifice the many advantages that we have gained by the study of English.

In 1958, The Central Institute of English was started in Hyderabad. Regional institutes were established in Bangalore and Chandigarh, English was studied mainly for education and administration. But because of the revolutionary developments in science, technology, travel, trade, communications and entertainment, English got a new role as the international language of communication. It is now imperative to study all four skills English listening, speaking, reading and writing.

The Government of India also brought out the three languages formula the language Act of 1965 renders : Hindi to be the official language of India. English to be the associate official language for an indefinite period. Regional languages shall be the languages of administration within the respective states.

National Education Commission popularly known as Kothari Commission examined all aspects of the educational sector in India. Formed on 14th July, 1964 under the chairmanship of Daulat Singh Kothari the commission stressed on the importance of English and the role it would play in hipher education as an important library language. A reasonable proficiency in English would make the student qualify for a degree like Master's.

English has thus travelled a long distance to come to be the Lingua Franca, an inseparable part of Indian lives. It is no wonder that now students don't consider it a foreign language anymore.

English became the first language in Indian education and has continued to be taught as the first language upto class 12 as the first language even today in most of the central board schools. The 'modern' leaders of that era in India also supported English language and claimed it to be the main key towards success. Indians who knew good English were seen as the new elite of India. Many new schools were established in which the language of instruction was English. According to the British laws, the language of instruction at university level was English and therefore schools that emphasised English were preferred by ambitious Indians.

Even after India's independence, English remained the main language of India. Officially, it was given a status of an assistant language and was supposed to terminate officially after 15 years of India's independence, but it still remains the important language of India.

Evolution and Development of English in India

The English language came to India in the 17th century with the East India Company. It was formed to conduct trade with India and other countries in the East. Initially, the Britishers tried to learn Indian languages to communicate with Indians. They started special colleges for this purpose. They also took the help of the translators. But when their political powers increased, they created the British Indian provinces like Bengal, Madras and Bombay. So, the English traders gave more importance to English. Some missionary institutions taught English to Indians. The East India Company took the responsibility of the education of the Indians. The Indians were also realising the importance of the English language. English also serves as the communication language among Indians who speak different languages.

Future of English in India

English is very important in some systems like legal, financial, educational or business enterprises in India. People are aware of the importance of English. They are interested in learning the spoken English. As a result, various courses are developed for teaching spoken English. The use of Language Laboratory and Computer Assisted Language Learning (CALL) has created new changes in the teaching of English. The audio cassettes and CDs are being used on a large scale to learn the spoken language. Various softwares of English teaching are developed and used by a growing number of people. There are many private institutions that run the courses of spoken English. Especially in big cities the language trainers are helping the learners to acquire the required proficiency over the communicative skills in general and the spoken skills in particular. Now, Television channels are also working towards improving spoken English.

Even as the goals of English teaching and learning are being continually redefined, we should remember that English would not be taught solely by the native speakers of English in many nations. Some countries like India, Pakistan, Nepal, Bangladesh and several African nations have provided for the teaching of English mainly through their nationals. Some countries like Japan and China open their doors to more number of native speakers of English to teach English.

English has been considered as a major foreign language in India since independence. As the world is getting globalised, there has also been a sense of English as a global language, not just a language of the USA or the UK. Although, English was considered as a major foreign language in India, Indians in different contexts are more likely to have witnessed, or experienced benefits of having more competence than before. These changes in the functions and benefits have brought about change in the status of English from that of a foreign language to a global language. In the of field English language teaching is growing day by day in India because good and dedicated researchers have contributed significantly to English language teaching and moreover number of linguists have made footprint in the field of applied linguistics.

There are three main drivers towards the greater use of English in India

1. **Education** Increasing demand for English-medium schools, widening access to higher education, incorporation of English training in vocational education;
2. **Employment** Many jobs in the organised sector now require good English skills;
3. **Social mobility** English is seen as an access route to the middle classes and geographical mobility within India and beyond.

Inputs Required to Make English Orientation Sustainable

Sustained economic growth requires more English speakers. India's development road-map needs more people to move into the jobs in the organised sector which require English.

Surveys of English proficiency levels are needed. Without knowing more about the English proficiency levels of students and their teachers, it is impossible to make appropriate policy or plan for further training. Without understanding how English skills are distributed in society, it is impossible to estimate the impact of particular interventions. India's language diversity is an important future resource. Schools need to focus on language development in all languages, including lesser used languages and minority languages. The three-language formula as presently implemented does not properly support multilingual development to the desired level. A new approach with special focus on English seems need of the hour as English, without doubt, has future brewing with career and opportunities at home as well as abroad in abundance now and in times to come.

Introduction of Indian English Literature

Indian English Literature specifically refers to works written in English by Indian writers. English as a language was introduced in India during the British rule. Having learned a colonial language, there were few Indian writers, who started writing in English. The first book written by an Indian in English was by Sake Dean Mahomet, titled *Travels of Dean Mahomet*; Mahomet's travel narrative was published in 1793. The first pamphlet written in English by an Indian appeared in 1806. The first play in English, Krishna Mohan Banerjee's *The Persecuted* was published in 1831. The first Indian novel in English, Bankim Chandra Chatterjee's *Rajmohan's Wife* appeared in 1864.

Raja Ram Mohan Roy was one of the early Indian writers, whose works were mostly political in nature. Roy wrote several pamphlets in English espousing the nationalist cause of Indian independence. He also published *Brahmanical Magazine* in English in 1821. Bankim Chandra Chatterjee was another writer credited with writing the first Indian novel in English. His other works in Bengali were also translated into English. After these two writers, the Indian literary scene was dominated by the trio of Raja Rao, Mulk Raj Anand and R K Narayan. According to a critic, William Walsh, it was this trio that established the foundation of Indian novel.

Walsh states, "It is these three writers, who defined the area in which the Indian novel was to operate. They established its assumptions; they sketched its main themes, freed the first models of its characters and elaborated its particular logic. Each of them used an easy, natural idiom which was unaffected by the opacity of a British inheritance. Their language has been free from the foggy taste of Britain and transferred to a wholly new setting of brutal heat and brilliant light".

The 1950s was dominated by writers such as Anita Desai, Khushwant Singh and Arun Joshi. Anita Desai established herself as an eminent Indian woman writer with novels such as *Cry the Peacock* (1965), *Fire on the Mountain* (1977) and *Clear Light of the Day* (1980) in her oeuvre. Khushwant Singh's *Train to Pakistan* and Arun Joshi's *The Apprentice* were other popular books of the period.

Indian Literature in English took a new turn in the 1980s with the publication of Salman Rushdie's *Midnight's Children*. Rushdie's novel traced the history of its protagonist Saleem Sinai born on the eve of Indian Independence. It juxtaposed Saleem's personal life with the history of the Indian nation. The distinct narrative style of the novel, use of magical realism and Indian words in English gave a new definition to Indian literature.

The 1990s and 2000s have witnessed the rise of many important Indian writers, who have taken Indian literature to new heights. These writers include Amitav Ghosh, Vikram Seth, Shashi Tharoor, Shashi Deshpande and Arundhati Roy and Chetan Bhagat. Modern Indian writers have freed English from the baggage of colonial legacy and Indianised it to suit their own cultural needs.

Indian English Writers

Rabindranath Tagore (1861-1941)

'Ekla Chalo, Ekla Chalo, Ekla Chalo Re' and the National Anthem are the most famous songs in West Bengal and also in India. The writer of these songs was Rabindranath Tagore. This great poet of India was born on 7th May, 1861 at Jorasanko in Calcutta. His father was Maharishi Devendranath Tagore, the eldest son of Prince Dwarkanath Tagore, Rabindranath's grandfather. His mother Sarla Devi was a house wife. His grandfather was a close friend of Raja Rammohan Roy, the great thinker, social reformer and founder of the Brahmo Samaj. So, he joined the Brahmo Samaj and read the Upanishads. He worked for religion, culture and social reform.

He was sent to England in 1878. He studied for some time at the University of London under Professor Henry Morley. There, Loken Palil became his life long friend, who always encouraged him. He returned to India in 1881. He learnt Bangla, Sanskrit, English, Science and Music at home. He was much influenced by Kalidas, Dante and Shakespeare. After the death of his mother in 1875, he was looked after by his youngest sister-in-law Kadambari Devi with great care and affection. She was the wife of his elder brother Jyotirindranath Tagore. She was a friend and true companion of the poet. He married Mrinalini Devi on 9th December, 1883. He became the Secretary of Adi Brahmo Samaj and condemned the Hindu Caste System and other orthodox customs. He joined the second session of the Indian National Congress.

Literary Career and Works

He wrote in both Bengali and English. In his childhood he wrote *Banphul*, a narrative poem, which contains 7000 lines. In England, he wrote many poems. Amongst them, *Bhagna Hridaya* is an expression of joys and sorrows. His earliest writing in prose and poetry had begun to be printed in 1875.

His literary career covered more than sixty years. He received the Nobel Prize for his work *Gitanjali*, a collection of short poems in 1913. Mahatma Gandhi called him 'Gurudev'. George V, the British king gave him the title of Knighthood, which he gave up in 1919 in protest against the Jallianwala Bagh Massacre. He was the first Asian, who received the Nobel Prize. He died in 1941 at Shantiniketan, where he had founded the world famous Vishwabharti University in Bolpur, West Bengal. He was a versatile genius. He was a great poet, novelist, dramatist, short story writer, music composer and patriot. His songs are sung as 'Rabindra Sangeet'.

The Gitanjali

Where the mind is without fear and the head is held high;
Where knowledge is free;
Where the world has not been broken up
Into fragments by narrow domestic walls;
Where words comeout from the depth of truth.
Where tireless striving stretches its arms towards perfection;
Where the clear stream of reason has not lost its way into the dreary desert sand of dead habit
Where the mind is led forward by thee
Into ever widening thought and action
Into that heaven of freedom, my father,
Let my country awake.

Major Works

Stories

- Stories from Tagore (1918)
- Mashi and Other Stories (1918)
- The Hungry Stones (1916)
- Selected Short Stories (1991)
- Broken Ties and Other Stories (1925)
- Sentence (1893)
- The Judge (1894)
- Hidden Treasure (1907)
- A Wife's Letter (1914)
- Aparichita (1916)
- The Parrot's Training and Other Stories (1944)
- New Doll (1921)
- The Wrong Heaven (1921)
- The Patriot (1928)
- Ritual and Reform (1928)
- Bolai (1928)
- The Story of a Muslim Woman (1941)

Novels

- Nashtaneer - The Broken Nest (1901)
- Chokher Bali (1901)
- The Wreck (1906)
- Boat Accident (1906)
- Gora (1909)
- Chaturanga (1916)
- The Home and the World (1916)
- Farewell Song (1929)
- Dui Bon - The Two Sisters (1933)
- Malancha - The Arbour (1934)
- Four Chapters (1934)
- Nastanirh (1901)
- Noukadubi (1906)
- Gora (1909)
- Ghare Baire (1916)
- Chaturanga (1916)
- Jogajog (1929)
- Shesher Kabita (1929)

Poetry

- The Crescent Moon (1913 poetry collection)
- Gitanjali (1912 poetry collection)
- The Gardener (1913 poetry collection)
- Fruit-Gathering (1916 poetry collection)
- Stray Birds (1916 poetry collection)
- Crossing (1918)
- Lover's Gift (1918 poetry collection)
- The Fugitive (1921 poetry collection)
- Lipika (1922)
- Fireflies (1928 poetry collection)
- Sheaves (1929 poetry collection)

Drama

- Valmiki-Pratibha (1888)
- The King and the Queen (1889)
- Sacrifice (1890)
- Malini (1896)
- Raja (1910)
- The King of the Dark Chamber (1910)
- The Post Office (1912)
- Chitra (1913)
- The Cycle of Spring (1916)
- Autumn-Festival (1919)
- The Waterfall (1922)
- Sanyasi or The Ascetic (1923)
- Red Oleanders (1924)

Essays

- Sadhana: The Realisation of Life (1913)
- Personality (1917)
- Nationalism (1918)
- The Centre of Indian Culture (1919)
- Thought Relics (1921)
- Cult of the Charkha (1925)
- Crisis in Civilisation (1941)

Lectures

- The Spirit of Japan (1916)
- Creative Unity (1922)
- Man the Artist (1932)
- Greater India (1917)
- The Religion of Man (1931)

Letters

- Glimpses of Bengal - Letters 1885-1895

Memoirs

- My Reminiscences (1912)

Translations

- Songs of Kabir (1915)

Travelogue

- Letters from Russia (1931)

Adaptations

- Kabuliwala
- Ghare Baire
- Dak Ghar
- Teen Kanya
- Charulata
- Jogajog

Swami Vivekanand (1863-1902)

He was born on Monday 12th February, 1863 in Calcutta. His name was Vishveshwar Dutt. His father's name was Babu Vishwanath Dutt. When he was sent to school, his name was changed as Narendranath Dutt.

He passed High School from a famous institute of Calcutta. He passed BA in 1884 from a Christian College in Calcutta.

As a student, he was interested in boxing, swimming, rowing, riding, music and many other activities. He had no faith in God. He became an atheist.

Afterwards, he came in contact with Swami Ramakrishna Paramhansa and became his disciple and saint. After accepting Sanyas, his asceticism the name was changed to Swami Vivekanand. He founded the Ramakrishna Mission.

After the death of his guru in 1886, he began completing his mission. He went on a pilgrimage. After meditating in the Himalayas for six years he went to Tibet. He studied the doctrines of the Buddhism and its various branches deeply. He went to USA in 1893 and took part in the Parliament of Religions at Chicago. He preached the great ideals of Hinduism. Impressed with his personality and address, many foreigners came to India as his disciples. He also preached the doctrines of Hinduism in Japan and England.

Literary Career and Works

He believed in the philosophy, of *Advaitvad*. His main literary works are *Raja Yoga, Karama Yoga* and *Bhakti Yoga, Kali, The Mother*. He tells the men not to be afraid of any trouble because they are immortal souls. He said, "If there is a sin in the world, it is weakness; avoid all weaknesses, weakness is sin, weakness is death." For him, man is a part of divinity. He was a great saint like Maharishi Dayananda. He died in 1902.

The Song of the Free

The wounded snake its hood unfurls,
The flame stirred up doth blaze,
The desert air resounds the calls of heart-struck Lion's rage;
The cloud puts forth its deluge strength
When lightning cleaves its breast,
When the soul is stirred to its in most depth
Great ones unfold their best;
Let eyes grow dim and heart grow faint
And friendship fail and love betray
Let fate its hundred horrors send
And clotted darkness block the way
And nature were one angry frown
To crush you out still know my soul
You are divine, march on and on
Nor right nor left, but to the goal.

Sarojini Naidu (1879-1949)

She was born on 13th February, 1879 in Hyderabad. Her father was Dr Aghorenath Chattopadhayaya, who was a Professor at the Nizam's College. Her mother, Vasada Sundari was talented and cultured like her husband. Her father had leaning in alchemy (a process which turns base metals into gold). Her mother wrote beautiful lyrics. She was sent to Madras, where she passed matric in 1891. She stood first in the entire presidency (divison of a territory).

She fell in love with a young doctor named Govindrajula Naidu. Her parents were disturbed by this unexpected turn of events. They felt she was too young for marriage. So, they sent her away to Madras. After marriage, she was sent to England.

In England, she remained 3 years in touch with two literary figures, Symons and Edmund Gosse. They helped in growing her poetic genius. In 1898, she returned to India. Her parents were impressed and proud of her love.

During the World War I in 1914, she met Mahatma Gandhi. This changed her whole life and career. She became a freedom fighter.

In 1925, she was elected the President of the Indian National Congress. In 1927, she helped in founding the All India Women's Conference. She went to Honolulu as a delegate of the All India Women's Conference and the Pan Pacific Women's Conference in 1928.

In March, 1930, she became the President of the All India Women's Conference. She also took part in Gandhiji's historical Dandi March. After the arrest of Gandhiji and Abbas Tayyabji, she led Gandhiji's Salt Satyagraha at the Dharasana Salt Works in May, 1930 where she was arrested. She went with Gandhiji to 'The Round Table Conference' in London, in September, 1931. She went to the European continent and delivered lectures.

In the World War II in 1939, she was arrested alongwith Gandhiji and other national leaders. Gandhiji started Quit India Movement on 8th August , 1942. She was arrested with Gandhiji on 9th August. Malaria attacked her, so she was released from prison on 21st March, 1943. She became the President of the Asian Relations Conference in New Delhi and delivered a speech on 23rd March, 1947.

India became free on 15th August, 1947. She was declared as the Governor of the United Province (now Uttar Pradesh) in place of BC Roy. Dr BC Roy, resigned the governorship in November, 1947. She died on 10th March, 1949.

Indian Weavers

Weavers weaving at break of day,
Why do you weave a garment so gay?
Blue as wing of a halcyon wild,
We weave the robes of a new-born child.
Weavers weaving at fall of night
Why do you weave a garment so bright?
Like the plumes of a peacock; purple and green,
We weave the marriage veil of a queen.
Weavers weaving solemn and still,
What do you weave in the moon-light chill?
White as a feather and white as a cloud,
We weave a dead man's funeral shroud.

Palanquin Bearers

Lightly, O lightly we bear her along,
She sways like a flower in the wind of our song;
She skims like a bird in foam of a stream,
She floats like a laugh from the lips of a dream.
Gaily, o gaily we glide and we sing,
We bear her along like a pearl on a string
Softly, O softly we bear her along
She hangs like a star in the dew of our song;
She springs like a beam on the brow of the tide,
She falls like a tear from the eyes of a bride.
Lightly, O lightly we glide and we sing,
We bear her along like a pearl on a string.

Literary Career and Works

At the age of 11, she wrote her first poem in 1890. She wrote a long poem, *The Lady of the Lake* consisting of 1300 lines in six days in 1892. She wrote a drama consisting 2000 lines in 1892. Her first major collection of poems of *Golden Threshold*, was published in 1905. It has 40 lyrics on different subjects. Its famous poems are *To India, To a Buddha Seated on a Lotus.*

Her second collection of poems, *The Bird of Time* was published in 1912, in London. It has 46 lyrics with the theme of love. The third collection of poems *The Broken Wing* was published in London, in 1917. It has 61 lyrics. We find an Indian Spirit in them. After her death three collection of poems were published.

The Sectored Flute in 1953, *The Feathers of Dawn* in 1961 and *The Temple*. First collection has three poems and second collection has 37 lyrics. She was called *The Nightingale of India.* Her famous poems are *Indian Weavers*, *The Palanquin Bearers*, *The Gift of India*, *Bangle-Seller*, *The Anthem of Love and Village Song.*

Bankim Chandra Chatterjee (1838-1894)

Bankim Chandra Chatterjee was born on 27th June, 1838 in Kanthanpara, West Bengal. His parents were Jadabchandra Chattopadhyay and Durgadevi. He completed his education from the Presidency College of Kolkata. He was also called Rishi Bankim Chandra Chattopadyay.

Literary Career and Works

At the beginning of his writing career, he wrote in English language as he desired to choose. In this attempt he wrote his first novel titled *Rammohan's Wife*, but he soon felt that he could express his feeling more naturally and clearly in mother tongue. Thus, he produced many of his great works in his mother tongue. *Vande Mataram* is a poem that is mentioned in his novel *Anandamath*, which became the inspirational song for India's freedom struggle and later became the national song of India.

In 1892, he started a Bengali literary magazine under the title *Bangadarshan*. He also served as a Deputy Collector and Deputy Magistrate. He is also called the 'The Father of Bengali Fiction'.

Among the works of Bankim Chandra, *Anandamath* occupies a major position because of its great contribution to India's Freedom struggle through its strong characters and thundering dialogues. Due to ill health, he died on 8th April, 1894.

Major Works

- **Durgeshnandini** This novel is based on history. It was written in 1865.
- **Kapal Kundala** In this novel he wrote about magic, ghost and mystery. It was written in 1866.
- **Mrinalini** This patriotic novel was written in 1869.
- **Anandamath** This patriotic novel was written in 1884 on Bengal Famine. It has the famous song 'Vande Mataram', which became popular in those days among patriotic people and was accepted by the Indian Government as the 'National Song' after Independence. This novel is based on the Sanyasi Revolt of North Bengal in 1773. It draws the fearful and moving picture of Bengal Famine.
- **The Poison Tree** This novel was written in 1884. It is a story of Hindu life in Bengal in the English period.
- **Other Works** *Krishna Kanter's Will* in 1895 and *The Two Rings* in 1897.

Henry Louis Vivian Derozio (1809-1831)

Henry Louis Vivian Derozio was born on 10th April, 1809 in Calcutta. He was both a teacher and poet. He was a lecturer at Hindu College of Calcutta. As a student he widely read French Revolution and deeply studied Robert Burns.

Literary Career and Works

As a lecturer he strongly questioned irrational religious and cultural practices. This drew a large number of student followers, who came to be known as 'Derozians', this led to the creation of a club called Academic Association, which brought a magazine called 'Parthenon'.

The Fakeer of Jungheera is his first long lyrical poem which reflects native Indian stories. This is in Romantic instance and Victorian style and was hailed as a 'competent narrative verse with Byronic echoes'. He developed a great love and respect for Indian society, culture and religion, which can be seen in his short poems. He died in 1831.

The Harp of India

Why hang'st thou lonely on yon withered bough?
Unstrung for ever, must thou there remain,
Thy music once was sweet, who hears it now?
Why doth the breeze sigh over thee in vain?
Silence hath bound thee with her fatal chain;
Neglected, mute and desolate art thou,
Like ruined monument of desert plain:
O! many a hand more worthy far than mine
Once thy harmonious chords to sweetness gave,
And many a wreath for them did Fame entwine
Of flowers still blooming on the minstrel's grave:
Those hands are cold, but if thy notes divine
May be by mortal wakened once again,
Harp of my country, let me strike the strain!

Kashiprasad Ghose (1809-1873)

Kashiprasad Ghose was born on 5th August, 1809. He had a good proficiency in English language at a very young age only. He is considered as the first Indian poet writing in English.

Literary Career and Works

Kashiprasad Ghose alongwith Raja Ram Mohan Roy and Michael Madhusudan Dutt, is called the first Indo-Anglian writer of verse and prose. He was the first Indian to publish a regular volume of English verse.

Ghose wrote an essay under the title *Criticism of Mill's British India* and it was published in the government Gazzette on 14th February, 1828. He also frequently contributed to *Literary Gazzette*, *Sambad Prabhakar* and *Viggan Sebadhi*.

He was a member of Bethune School's Management Board, in 1856. Besides being an honorary Magistrate of Calcutta he also found an English weekly the *Hindu Intelligence* in 1846. He died on 11th Novermber, 1873.

Michael Madhusudan Dutt (1824-1873)

He was born in 1824. He was a Bengali poet and dramatist. He was a Hindu. Later, he became a Christian.

He wrote *The Captive Lady*, Sri Aurobindo said about this poet, *'The God himself took up thy pen and wrote'*. He died in 1873.

- Rizia, the Sultana of Inde
- The Captive Lady
- Vision of the Past
- Sonnets and other Poems

Romesh Chunder Dutt (1848-1909)

Romesh Chander Dutt was born on 13th August, 1848 at Ramnagar in Kolkata. His parents were Isam Chunder Dutt and Thakamani. He was a civil servant by profession, but he was also a writer in Bengali, Economist, Politician and Linguist.

Literary Career and Works

He was famously known as the historical novelist of Bengal. He deeply studied the economic and social conditions of India in 1899, while he was the President of Indian National Congress. During this time, he also wrote books on history and Indian economy highlighting the financial improvement of Indian society under British rule. He has translated Ramayana and Mahabharata into English. Dutt's works *The Economic History, Famines in India and England* depicts high revenue rates, frequent man made and natural calamities, deindustrialisation which were related to government rule in India.

His literary works are *Rajput Jiban Sandhya Maharashtra*, *Jiban Prabhat* and *Madhabi Kankana*. He has translated 'Rig Veda' into the Bengali language. He served as the first President of Bangiya Sahitya Parishad in 1894. He died at the age of 61 in Baroda in 1909.

- Three Years in Europe 1868 to 1871
- The Lake of Palms
- A History of Civilisation in Ancient India, Based on Sanskrit Literature
- The Slave Girl of Agra

Toru Dutt (1856-1877)

Toru Dutt was born in 1856 in Calcutta. She completed her higher French studies in England. Besides, she was proficient in Bengali, English, Hindi and also in Sanskrit. Her father's name was Govind Chunder Dutt.

Literary Career and Works

*Le Journal De Melle Moiselle d'*Arvers was her French novel and her French poetry was A *Sheaf Gleaned* in *French Fields* which was published in 1876. In 1882, her Sanskrit translation of poems entitled *Ancient Ballads and Legends of Hindustan* was published posthumously.

Toru Dutt's, first novel in English entitled *Bianca* or *the Young Spanish Maiden* was published posthumously.

H.A.L Fisher says, "This child of the green valley of the Ganges has by sheer force of native genius earned for herself the right to be enrolled in the great fellowship of English poets."

She was highly influenced by French Romanticism, French language and literature. *Our Casuarina Tree* is a splendid Keatsian poem. She died in 1877 at the very young age of 21 at Calcutta, Bengal, British India. She also wrote some lyrics. Most of her works were published after her death.

- A Sheaf Gleaned in French Fields (won the praise from famous critics)
- Ancient Ballads
- Legends of Hindustan
- Savitri
- Behramji Malabari

Our Casuarina Tree

Like a huge Python, winding round and round
The rugged trunk indented deep with scars
Upto its very summit near the stars,
A creeper climbs in whose embraces bound
No other tree could live. But gallantly
The giant wears the scarf and flowers are hung
In crimson clusters all the boughs among,
Whereon all day are gathered bird and bee;
And oft at night the garden overflows
With one sweet song that seems to have no close,
Sung darkling from our tree, while men repose
When first my casement is wide open thrown
At dawn, my eyes delighted on it rest
Sometimes and most in winter on its crest
A grey baboon sits statue like alone
watching the sunrise while on lower boughs
His puny offspring leap about and play;
And far and near kokilas hail the day
And to their pastures wend our sleepy cows;
And in the shadow, on the broad tank cast
By that hoar tree, so beautiful and vast
The water-lilies spring like snow enmassed.

Manmohan Ghose (1869-1924)

Manmohan Ghose was born on 4th January, 1869. His parents were Dr Krishna Dhan Ghose and Swarnalata Basu. Aurobindo Ghose was his younger brother. He completed his education in Oxford, London. After returning, he worked as a professor of English at Patna College.

Literary Career and Works

While in England Ghose had a friendship with those intellectuals, who impacted his thinking, they were Oscar Wilde, Laurence Binyon, Lionel Johnson and Stephen Philips. *Primavera* was the collection of poems published in England having poems from Ghose, Oscar Wilde and others Oscar Wilde said "The temper of Keats and moods of Matthew Arnold have influenced Mr Ghose and what better influences could a beginner have?"

His poems depict his longing to return to England, one such is 'April', it goes like

Haste, April, upon city streets to blow
Thy purest, warmest breezes, fly beneath
The flower-girls' rags, poor beggary's basket stow
With lordliest gold of daffodils aglow,
I will not love thee, save with sighing breath
On pale, worn cheeks thou waft reprieve of death.

His poems are autobiographical in nature and depict the sorrows of life. His famous poems were published under the title *Songs of Love and Death*. He was an Indian poet, who wrote in English. A critic George Sampson says that "a reader of his poems would readily take them as the work of an English poet trained in the classical tradition." An Indian critic feels that his poetry has no imagery or sentiment that can be termed as Indian. He died on 24th January, 1924.

- Primavera (Poem Collection) 1890
- Songs of Love and Death 1926

Sri Aurobindo (Aurobindo Ghose) (1872-1950)

He was an Indian philosopher, yogi, guru, poet, and nationalist. He joined the Indian movement for independence from British rule, for a while was one of its influential leaders and then became a spiritual reformer, introducing his visions on human progress and spiritual evolution.

Aurobindo studied for the Indian Civil Service at King's College, Cambridge, England. After returning to India he took up various civil service works under the maharaja of the princely state of Baroda and became increasingly involved in nationalist politics and the nascent revolutionary movement in Bengal.

He was arrested in the aftermath of a number of bomb outrages linked to his organisation, but in a highly public trial where he faced charges of treason, Aurobindo could only be convicted and imprisoned for writing articles against British rule in India. He was released when no evidence could be provided, following the murder of a prosecution witness during the trial. During his stay in the jail, he had mystical and spiritual experiences, after which he moved to Pondicherry, leaving politics for spiritual work.

Literary Career and Works

Sri Aurobindo founded a community of spiritual seekers in Pondicherry, which took shape as the Sri Aurobindo Ashram in 1926. The ashram eventually attracted seekers from many countries throughout the world. The evolutionary philosophy underlying Aurobindo's integral yoga is explored in his main prose work, *The Life Divine* (1939). Rejecting the traditional Indian approach of striving for moksha (liberation from the cycle of death and rebirth) as a means of reaching happier, transcendental planes of existence, Aurobindo held that terrestrial life itself, in its higher evolutionary stages, is the real goal of creation.

He believed that the basic principles of matter, life and mind would be succeeded through terrestrial evolution by the principle of super mind as an intermediate power between the two spheres of the infinite and the finite. Such a future consciousness would help to create a joyful life in keeping with the highest goal of creation, expressing values such as love, harmony, unity and knowledge and successfully overcoming the age-old resistance of dark forces. against efforts to manifest the divine on Earth.

Aurobindo's voluminous literary output comprises philosophical speculation, many treatises on yoga and integral yoga, poetry, plays, and other writings. In addition to *The Life Divine*, his major works include *Essays on the Gita* (1922), *Collected Poems and Plays* (1942), *The Synthesis of Yoga* (1948), *The Human Cycle* (1949), *The Ideal of Human Unity* (1949), *Savitri: A Legend and a Symbol* (1950), and *On the Veda* (1956). He died in 1950.

T P Kailasam (1884-1946)

He was a playwright. He was born in 1884 in Karnataka. Kailasam went to London as sponsored by Mysore Maharaja. He had long life of studentship in England.

Literary Career and Works

While, in London he participated in plays. He left the government job as he did not feel inspired and led a bohemian life. Kailasam is famous for his humour plays. He had a short, but sharp speech with wit and humour. His works were satire on society. He contributed lot to the Kannada theatre. He wrote novels in English and Kannada. He also wrote comic plays. He got higher education in London. He died in 1946.

His works are Fulfilment A Monologue, 1933, The Burden 1933 Purpose 1944 and The Brahminos Curse 1946.

Major Works

Poems

- The Dramatist
- Truth Naked
- Mother-Love
- A Monologue
- The Smilin' Seven
- Kaikeyee
- Drona
- Subhadra
- Eternal Cain
- The Lake
- The Sixth Columnist 1943
- The Recipe
- The Artist
- Commiseration (Karna)
- Krishna

Plays

- The Purpose - 1944
- Fulfilment - 1933
- The Burden - 1933
- The Brahmin's Curse - 1946

Dr S Radhakrishnan (1888-1975)

He was born in 1888. He was a great scholar, philosopher and statesman. He served Calcutta University as a professor of philosophy. He served as Professor of Indian religion (Eastern Religion) and Ethics at Oxford University. He became vice chancellor of Banaras Hindu University. He served as an ambassador to the USSR. He became the President of India from 1962 to 1967. He was an impressive speaker, thinker and a famous writer. He died in 1975.

Major Works

- Indian Philosophy
- The Hindu View of Life
- Eastern Religions and Western Thought
- Philosophy of the Upanishads

Jawaharlal Nehru (1889-1964)

He was born in Allahabad on 14th November, 1889. His father, Motilal Nehru was a rich and famous advocate. He got his education at Harrow School and Trinity School at Cambridge, where he studied law in Inner Temple to become a barrister.

He came to India and became a barrister in the High Court of Allahabad. Under the spell of Gandhiji, he came to politics and became a member of the Indian National Congress in 1918. He was sent to jail many times from 1921 to 1928. He was elected the President of the Indian National Congress. He turned down the Cripps offer in 1942. After Independence, he was elected the first Prime Minister of India in 1947. He gave India the Five Year Plans and a policy of Industrialisation. He gave the slogan 'Aram Haram Hai'. He was not only a great leader and statesman but a good writer also. He married Kamla Nehru. His daughter Indira Priyadarshini became the third Prime Minister of India with the name Indira Gandhi. He died in 1964. His works are—*Letters from a Father to His Daughter, Autobiography, The Discovery of India, The Glimpses of World History*.

Nirad C Chaudhari (1897-1999)

Nirad Chandra Chaudhari was born on 23rd November, 1897 in Kishorganj of East Bengal- British India. Though, nothing is known about his mother. His father was a lawyer.

He was very much fond of Western culture and deeply read the life and works of William Shakespeare. He also read widely the Sanskrit classics. His strong admiration of Western culture met with a rejection when he started to live in Oxford where he saw that English were not committed to values of life.

Literary Career and Works

In 1951, his first book *The Autobiography of an Unknown Indian*– a controversial book was released and was dedicated to the memories of British Empire.

In 1987, his last volume of autobiography was published under the title *Thy Hand, Great Anarch*. The essays of his last book were published in 1997 under the title *Three Horsemen of the New Apocalypse*.

Nirad C Chaudhari was famously called 'Last British Imperialist' and last of the 'Brown Sahibs.'

He was awarded by Sahitya Akademi for his work on Max Mueller. He received an honarary docorate in 1990 from the Oxford University and Commander of the order of the British Empire in 1992 from Queen Elizabeth II. He died on 1st August, 1999 at Oxfordshire, England.

Major Works

- Too Long in the West 1951
- The Continent of Circe 1965
- Scholar Extraordinary-Max Mueller 1974
- PC 1974
- Thy Hand, Great Anarch 1987

Harindranath Chattopadhyaya (1898-1990)

He was born in 1898, at Hyderabad in a learned Bengali Brahmin family. His father Aghore Nath Chattopadhyaya was the first DSc of India. They went to Hyderabad from East Bengal and founded the Nizam College. First, he became a professor, then the principal and patron of this college.

Literary Career and Works

Harindranath Chattopadhyay's first collection of poems, The Feast of Youth was published in 1918. The following year, Chattopadhyay married Kamaladevi Dhareshwar, the future pioneer of craft and textile preservation, and moved to London to work as a research scholar. He got admission into Fitzwilliam College and began research on the poet William Blake. While studying in Britain, his poems were published in the Indian Magazine (the journal of the National Indian Association) and Britain and India (the journal of the Theosophical-influenced Britain and India Association).

Chattopadhyay also wrote a play *Tukaram* (1929), based on the poet-saint of Maharashtra, which was performed to critical acclaim and established his name back in India. He had a prolific output in poetry, including the titles The *Magic Tree* (1922), *Poems and Plays* (1927), Strange Journey (1936), The Dark Well (1939), Edgeways and the Saint (1946), Spring in Winter (1956), Masks and Farewells (1951), Virgins and Vineyards (1967) and Life and Myself (1948). He died in 1990.

Major Works

- Abu Hassan in 1918.
- His Poems and Play in 1927
- Siddhartha : Man of Peace in 1956
- The Saint : A Force in 1946
- Kamappan or the Hunter of Kalahasti in 1950
- The Window
- The Parrot
- The Sentry's Lantern
- The Coffin
- The Evening Lamp
- The Sleeper Awakened

Mulk Raj Anand (1905-2004)

He was born in 1905 in Peshawar. His father was a coppersmith, who later became a soldier. His mother was a farmer. He studied at Cambridge University. He was greatly influenced by Premchand and Tagore. He became the Chirman of Lalit Kala Academy. He was surrounded by controversies.

Literary Career and Works

He was also the Secretary of Progressive Writers Association. He wrote more than a dozen novels, about eight short stories and a number of essays. He won the Sahitya Academy Award. He died in 2004.

Untouchable

This is his first novel. It was published in 1935. It begins with scenes of public latrines, dirty bazars, lanes, alleys and gutters. It brought name and fame to him. It was translated into many other languages. Bakha, the hero belongs to the downtrodden race.

Coolie

It was written in 1936. Its hero is Munoo. It is a realistic and picaresque novel. It presents a graphic picture of the Bombay slums. It is a social tragedy in which Munoo's budding youth is crushed by cruel inhuman social forces.

RK Narayan (1906-2001)

He was born in 1906 in a village Rashipuram, in Madras. His father's name was Krishna Swami. He settled down in Mysore. His mother tongue is Tamil, but in Mysore the regional language is Kannada. He writes in English. 'R' in his name represents the name of his village and 'K', the name of his father.

While other brothers and sisters went to Mysore with their parents, he was left behind with his grandmother. After completing his early education, he went to England for Higher education.

He failed in High School examination in 1924 and in Intermediate examination in 1927. He graduated in 1930 from Maharaja College, Mysore. These failures had an adverse effect on his personality. He was fond of reading different type of books and listening stories. He worked as a clerk to support his family. But he was not satisfied. So, he accepted the work of a teacher in a village school.

Literary Career and Works

R K Narayan's literary career began with his short stories, which appeared in 'The Hindu' newspaper. He began to work as the Mysore correspondent of 'Justice', a Madras-based newspaper. When he could not get his first novel 'Swami and Friends' published, a mutual friend showed the draft to Graham Greene who agreed to arrange for its publication.

Narayan played an exceptional role in making India accessible to the outside world through literature. He won numerous awards and adulation during his lifetime. These include the Sahitya Akademi Award in 1958, the Padma Bhushan in 1964,the AC Benson Medal by the Royal Society of Literature in 1980, besides the Padma Vibhushan in 2000. He was nominated to the Rajya Sabha in 1989. This great storyteller passed away on 13th May, 2001 at the age of 94.

Achievements

- He won Sahitya Academy Awards for *The Guide* in 1960.
- He was awarded Padma Bhushan.
- He was awarded Honorary D Literature by the University of Leeds.
- He was awarded Benson Medal.
- He is called a Regional novelist. Malgudi, an imaginary town is located in Mysore state. His immortal characters are Swami Margayya and Raju,Rosie (the hero and heroine of Guide).

Major Works

- The Bachelor of Arts in 1937 - A Novel
- The Dark Room in 1938 - A Novel
- Malgudi Days - A Collection of Short Stories in 1941
- Dodu and Other Stories in 1943
- Cyclone and Other Stories in 1944
- The English Teacher in 1945 - A novel
- An Astrologer and Other Stories
- Mr Sampath - A Novel in 1949. This novel was Filmed in 1951
- The Financial Expert - A novel in 1952
- Waiting for the Mahatma in 1955 - A novel
- The Lawley Road in 1956 - A novel
- The Guide in 1958 - A novel, which was filmed in 1965
- Next Sunday - A Collection of Sketches and Essays in 1960
- My Dateless Diary - An Autobiography in 1960
- The Man Eater of Malgudi in 1962
- God's Demons and Other Stories in 1965
- The Sweet Vendor - A novel in 1967
- A Horse and Two Goats in 1970
- The Painter of Signs in 1974
- My Days - autobiography in 1975 printed by London Chatto and Windus
- The Painter of Sign in 1976
- The Emernal'd Route in 1977
- Malgudi Days in 1982
- A Tiger for Malgudi in 1983
- Talkative Man in 1986
- A Writer's Nightmare

Bhabani Bhattacharya (1906-1988)

Bhabani Bttacharya was born in 1906. He was educated in Patna and in London. His novels and short stories depict the socio, economic and political realities of India.

He was strongly influenced by the writings of Rabindranath Tagore and also the life and works of Gandhiji.

Literary Career and Works

His first novel was published in 1947 entitled *So Many Hungers*, second novel came in 1952 under the title *He who Rides a Tiger* and in 1960 the third novel was published under the title *A Goddess Named Gold*.

The themes dealt in these novels are poverty, hunger and exploitation of farmers during Bengal famine. His last novel was published in 1967 entitled *Shadow from Ladakh*; it won Sahitya Academy Award. He died in 1988.

Major Works

- Some Memorable Yesterdays (1941)
- So Many Hungers! (1947)
- Indian Cavalcade (1948)
- He Who Rides a Tiger (1955)
- The Golden Boat (1956)
- Towards Universal Man (1961)
- Music for Mohini (1964)
- Shadow from Ladakh (1966)
- A Goddess Named Gold (1967)
- Steel Hawk and Other Stories (1968)
- Gandhi the Writer (1969)
- A Dream in Hawaii (1978)
- Socio-Political Currents in Bengal: A Nineteenth Century Perspective (1980)

To The Pupils

Expanding like the petals of young flowers,
I watch the gentle opining of your minds
And the sweet loosening of the spell that binds
Your interlectual energies and powers
That stretch (like young birds in soft summer hours)
Their wings to try their strength. O how the winds
Of circumstances and freshening April showers
Of early knowledge and unnumbered kinds
Of new perceptions shed their influence
And how you worship truth's omnipotence!
What joyance rains upon me when I see
Fame in the mirror of futurity
Weaving the chaplets you have yet to gain
An then I fel, I have not lived in vain.

Raja Rao (1908-2006)

He was born on 19th November, 1908 in the village of Hassana in Mysore. He belonged to an Orthodox South Indian Brahman Family. His father was a Professor in Hyderabad. He received his early education in Hyderabad. After passing matriculation, he went to Aligarh University for higher education. There he came in contact with Professor Dickinson, who inspired him to study French language. He passed BA from Nizam College, Hyderabad. Hyderabad University granted him a government scholarship. He went to France to study French literature. He studied at the university of Mont Pellier. He received PhD at the university of Sorbornne under Professor Cazamian.

He lived in France from 1928 to 1939 and again from 1946 to 1950. There, he married an American actress Katherine. In 1940, he returned to India and went to Banaras in search of a Guru. There he met a great Vedantic scholar, Swami Almanan, who became his guru, guide and adviser. In 1950, he went to America. He was greatly impressed by American culture, Raja Rao said, "America has great splendour once this nation finds itself, it will be truly magnificent."

According to him, America has the great classical civilisation, which will symbolise the true worth and dignity of man.

Literary Career and Works

When he was in France, he wrote his first novel *Kanthapura* in 1938. This novel appeared in a collection of short stories. *The Cow of Barricades* and other stories were also written in French in 1947. His second novel *The Serpent* and *The Rope* was written in France, but its story is based on Indian Culture and Philosophy. It was published in 1960. *The Cat and Shakespeare* was published in, 1965 and *The Police Man* and *The Rose* and Other stories, was published in 1978.

He was influenced by Andre Malraux's novels and aesthetic essays, by Shakespeare's tragedies, Romain Roland's *Jean Christopher* and Mazzini's *Duties of Man*, According to him, Anand Coomaraswamy is the writer, who seems to be the closest to Indian spirit.

He is one of the greatest writers of India. The others are Mulk Raj Anand and R K Narayan. He has great respect for women, once he said, "Woman is the Earth, air, ether, sound, woman is the microcosm of the mind." He won the Sahitya Academy Award for *The Serpent and the Rope*. His name was also considered for the Nobel Prize for literature. The Government of India awarded him the Padma Bhushan.

As a visiting professor he gave lectures at different American Universities on Indian philosophy. After teaching Indian philosophy in the university of Texas, he settled in the USA. He studied the work of Emerson, Thoreau and Walt Whitman, who were all interested in Vedantic philosophy. He died in 2006.

GV Desani (1909-2000)

GV Desani was born in Nairobi, Kenya, on 8th July, 1909. He stayed single throughout his life. He received less formal education, but he was sponsored to self study at national libraries in London. He became well versed in attracting the attention of strangers through conversation and for doing this he also received 5 pounds for each conversation for, which he was called for.

Literary Career and Works

Desai worked as a BBC-sponsored lecturer in London. He also lectured in India on 'India and the Orient' this series was called 'India Invites.'

In 1948, GV Desani's first novel *All About H Halter* was published, which was on the manner of existing social structure, religious instruction, Indianised English and the book became a sensation, which alongwith James Joyce's *Ulysses* helped in shaping post-modern novel. It also made a great influence on Salman Rushdie.

In 1950 Desani's poetic play *Hali* was published. The play was about the spiritual knowledge and Desani's spiritual quest. He collected teachings and yantras, orated mantras by meeting all mystics and gurus all over India. He practised Theravada Buddhism and gave lectures on them, which was tape recorded and later transcribed. He died at the age of 91 in 2000 in Texas.

Major Works

- All About Hotterr (novel) (1948)
- Hali Prose Poem (1952)
- Dozens of signed columns, Illustrated weekly of India (1962-67)
- Mainly or concering Kama and her Immortal Lord (1973)
- Hali and Collected Stories (1991)

Monohar Malgonkar (1913-2010)

Manohar Malgonkar was born on 12th July, 1913. He completed his higher education in Bombay University. He worked as a civil servant. He was also a Lieutenant Colonel, besides, he was a mine owner and a farmer, this shows that he was from a royal family.

Literary Career and Works

His novels have the background of Indian Independence Movement and its results, which are both social and historical with adventure as a spirit *A Bend in the Ganges* is an example of this. It describes the results of partition. The contemporaries of Manohar were Mulk Raj Anand, Khushwant Singh and Kamala Markandeya. RK Narayana called Manohar his 'favourite Indian novelist in English.' Manohar has tried and written both fiction and non-fiction in English language. He died on 14th June, 2010 in Belgaum Karnataka.

Major Works

- Combat of Shadows 1962
- The Princes 1963
- A Bend in the Ganges 1964
- Spy in Amber 1971
- The Devil's Wind 1972
- Distant Drum 1974
- Krishna Shah's Shalimar
- Shalimar: Krishna Shah ke Screenplay par Aadharit Upanyas
- The Men who Killed Gandhi 1978
- The Sea Hawk 1979
- Cue from the Inner Voice: The Choice Before Big Business 1980
- Bandicoot Run· Inside Goa 1982
- Princess: The Autobiography of the Dowager Maharani of Gwalior 1985
- The Garland Keepers 1986
- The Last Maharani of Gwalior: An Autobiography 1987
- Four Graves and Other Stories 1990
- Cactus Country 1992
- Dropping Names1996

Khushwant Singh (Born 1915)

He was born on 2nd February, 1915 at Hadali District Khushab (now district Sargodha) in Pakistan. His father Sir Shobha Singh was a famous builder in Lutyen's Delhi. He was educated at Modern School and then at Government College, Lahore. He was also educated at St Stephens College in Delhi. For higher education, he was sent to King's College in London. He studied Bar at the Inner Temple.

His uncle Sardar Ujjal Singh was ex Governor of Punjab and Tamil Nadu. He edited *Yojana*, an Indian government journal, *The Illustrated Weekly of India*, a news weekly and two major Indian newspapers : *The National Herald* and the Hindustan Times. During his edition, *The Illustrated Weekly became* the best news weekly.

Literary Career and Works

Khushwant Singh's literary contribution to the literature was immense. He entertained his readers with his satirical mode of writing. His work included both fiction and nonfiction. He mainly wrote in English language. Among his major books included *'Train to Pakistan'* (first Published in 1956) which won him international acclaim and Groove Press Award in 1954. The book depicts the partition of India and Pakistan in 1947. His second major work included Essays on India's Emergency by the name *Why I Supported the Emergency* (Published in 2004). His third major work was *Delhi: A Novel*. He also wrote *I shall Not Hear the Nightingale* (Published in 1959). *The Portrait of a Lady: Collected* Stories was in the form of short story collection. He also authored other books such as *Maharaja Ranjit* Singh and Fall of *Sikh Kingdom*.

Apart from these, he wrote and published a classic two-volume book on Sikh History by the name *A history of Sikhs* (Published in 1963). His other famous works included *Truth, Love and A little Malice* in the form of an autobiography and published in 2002, *Sex, Scotch and Scholarship* and *In the Company of Women* (Published in 1999). Significantly, he wrote his last book at the age of 98 titled The Good, *The Bad and the Ridiculous*. Actually, he co-wrote the book with Humra Qureshi. He died on 20th March, 2014, in Sujan Singh Park, Delhi.

Achievements

- He was given the Rockfeller Grant in 1966.
- He was elected a member of Rajya Sabha from 1980 to 1986.
- He was awarded the Padma Bhushan in 1974 for his service to the country, but he returned it after the Siege (Surrounding) of the Golden Temple by the Indian Army in protest.
- In 2007, the Indian government awarded him the Padma Vibhushan, the highest second Civilian Award.
- Sahitya Academy of India gave him Sahitya Academy fellowship in 2010.
- Akhilesh Yadav, the Chief Minister of Uttar Pardesh awarded him all India Minorities Forum Annual Fellowship Award in 2012.
- Train to Pakistan in 1956.
- I shall not Hear the Nightingale in 1959.
- A Sangam City.
- The Company of Women.
- The Portrait of A Lady : Collected Stories.
- Sex, Scotch and Scholarship.
- Celebrating the Best of Urdu Poetry.
- Truth, Love and A Little of Malice.
- A History of The Sikhs 1469-1839.
- A History of The Sikhs 1839-2004.
- Khushwant Singh on Women, Sex, Love and Lust.
- The Sunset Club.
- Sahibs who loved India.
- Delhi : A Novel.
- I Accuse ..... The Anti Sikh Violence of 1984.
- Agnostic Khushwant : There is No God.
- The Free Thinker's Prayer Book.

Amrita Pritam (1919-2005)

Amrita Kaur was born on 31st August, 1919 at Gujranwala, Punjab, which is now in Pakistan. Her father was a poet and a scholar of Brij Bhasha and a school teacher named Kartar Singh Hitkari. After her mother's death in 1930, they went to Lahore.

In 1936, she was married to Pritam Singh to whom she was engaged in childhood. She joined the Progressive Writers movement. In 1944, she was busy in social activities. She also worked at Lahore Radio Station for some time. After partition, she came to India in 1947. She worked in the Punjabi service of All India Radio till 1961.

Literary Career and Works

She was considered the first woman Punjabi poet, writer novelist, essayist and autobiographer. She is equally loved by the Indians as well as Pakistanis. She wrote about hundred books of poetry, fiction, essays, Punjabi folk songs, biographies and autobiographies, which were translated into many Indian and Foreign languages.

Aj Aakhaan Waris Shah Nu (Today I Invoke Waris Shah) is a piercing poem about the 18th century Punjabi poet. It is an expression of her worry over massacres during the partition of India.

Pinjar (The Skeleton) is a famous novel, which was written in 1950, in which she created her memorable character 'Puro'. This is a story of violence against women and massacres during partition. Chandra Prakash Dwivedi made an award winning Hindi film in 2003 based on this novel.

Her first collection of poems *Amrit Lehran* (Immortal Waves) was published in 1936. Between 1936 and 1943, she wrote six collection of poems. *Lok Peed* (People's Anguish) was published in 1944. *Rasidi Ticket* (Revenue Stamp) is an autobiography, which describes her love with Sahir Ludhianvi. *Amrita Imroz : A Love* Story is also an autobiography, which describes the love story of Amrita and Imroz. *Kala Gulab* (Black Rose) in 1968 and *Aksharon Ray Saaye* (Shadows of Words) are also her autobiograpies.

In *Ek Onkar Satnam* and in many books of Osho were written introduction by her Kaal Chetna (Time consciousness) and *Agyat Kay Nimantran* (Call of Unknown) were written on spiritual themes and dreams. *Dharti Sagar te Sippiyan* was filmed 'Radamber' in 1965 and *Unah Di Kahani* was filmed as Daaku in 1976, which was directed by Basu Bhattacharya.

In 1960, she left her husband. She leaned towards Sahir Ludhianvi. When Sudha Malhotra, a singer came in his life, she lived in relationship with Imroz, a famous artist and writer, who designed most of her book covers and made her subject of his many paintings. They lived together for 40 years.

She edited *Nagmani*, a montly literary Magazine in Punjabi for many years, which she ran together with Imroz. Later, she turned to Osho. She died in her sleep on 31st October, 2005 in New Delhi after a long illness and left behind her partner Imroz, daughter Kandlla, son Navraj Kwatra, who was killed in 2012, daughter-in-law Alka and her grand children Taurus, Noor, Aman and Shilpi.

Achievements

- She is the first to receive the Punjab Ratan Award given by Amarinder Singh, the Chief Minister of Punjab.
- She is the first woman, who received Sahitya Academy Award in 1956 for, Suneny (Messages).
- She received the Bhartiya Gyanpeeth Award, India's highest award in 1982 for Kagaj te Canvas (paper and canvas).
- She received Padma Shri in 1969 and Padma Vibhushan, in 2004.
- The Sahitya Academy honoured her with the Sahitya Academy fellowship. India's highest literary award in 2004.
- She received D Litt, the honorary degree from many universities such as Delhi University in 1973, Jabalpur University in 1973 and Vishvabharti in 1987.
- She received international Vaptsarov Award from Republic of Bulgaria in 1979.
- She received degree of officer dens órder dis Arts et des lettres by the French Government in 1987.
- She was nominated as a member of Rajya Sabha from 1986 to 1992.
- She was awarded by Pakistan's Punjabi Academy.
- Punjabi poets of Pakistan sent her a sheet (chadar) from the tombs of Waris Shah and Sufi Mystic poets Bulle Shah and Sultan Bahu.

Nissim Ezekiel (1924-2004)

He was an Indian Jewish poet and critic. He was born in Bombay in 1924. He was born in a Jewish Family. Nissim Ezekiel is considered as the father of post-independence Indian-English verse.

Literary Career and Works

He started modernity in Indian English poetry and became a trend setter in poetry. He studied philosophy at Birbeck College London. After returning in 1952 he brought out his first collection of poems under the title *A Time to Change* and also started to work for the Ilustrated Weekly of India as an editor in 1953.

His poems depicted the existing religious beliefs and communal disharmony of the Indian society. Yet, his poetry shows extreme optimissim of life though life is filled with sorrows and problems. The themes mainly used in his poems are love, loneliness, lust, creativity, human foibles and so on. Ezekiel stresses on simplicity of thought and language in modern poetry. Ezekiel received Sahitya Academy Award in 1983, Padmashree in 1988. He suffered from Alzheimer's disease for long and finally died in Mumbai on 9th January, 2004.

Major Works

Poems

- Time to Change 1952
- Sixty Poems 1953
- The Discovery of India 1956
- The Third 1959
- The Unfinished Man 1960
- The Exact Name 1965
- Snakeskin and Other Poems, translations of the Marathi poet Indira Sant 1974
- Hymns in Darkness 1976
- Latter-Day Psalms 1982
- Collected Poems {1952-88) 1989

Plays

- The Three Plays Kolkata: Writers Workshop, India 1969
- Do Not Call It Suicide Madras: Macmillan India, 1993.

Vijay Tendulkar (1928-2008)

He is one of the four famous dramatists of India. He was born in 1928. As a journalist, he wrote daily columns in newspapers. He started his career as an author by writing short stories. He composed children's plays.

Literary Career and Works

His first major work is *Mames Navache Bet (An Island Called Man)* in 1955. He wrote a number of plays - *Madhlya Bhirti* (The Walls Between) in 1958, *Chimnicha Ghar Hota Menacha (Nest of Wax)* in 1958, *Mee Jinklo Mee Harlo* (I Won, I Lost) in 1963, *Kavalanchi Shala* (School for Crows) in 1963, *Sari Ga Sari* (Rain O Rain) in 1964, *Shantata Court Chalu Ahe* (Silence! The Court is in Session).

This play aroused a general controversy because it describes basic hypocrisy and double standards of the society and harsh social attitudes towards a woman. Ghasiram Kotwal also raised storms in literary and political circles. *Gidhade* (The Vultures) was published in 1970. *Grihastha* (House Holder) was published in 1955. He died in 2008.

Major Works

- Householder (1947)
- The Vultures (1916)
- Silence! The Court is in Session (1967)
- The Cyclist (1991)
- His Fifth Woman (2004)

Jayanta Mahapatra (1928)

He was born in 1928 at Cuttack in Orissa. He wrote a number of books in prose and poetry. He was awarded the Sahitya Academy Award in 1981 for his works. The Government of India honoured him with 'Padma Shri' in 2009. He received his masters in physics from Patna University.

Literary Career and Works

He is the first Indian English poet to receive Sahitya Academy Award for relationship. He is a physicist, bilingual poet and essayist. His poetry depicts the picture of life, rural landscape, mud-houses of rural India through imagination, myth-making and imagery. His famous poems are : *Indian Summer Poem*, *Hunger*, *Dawn of Puri etc*. According to M K Naik Mahapatra's poetry is redolent of the Odisha scene and the Jagannath Temple at Puri figures quite often in it.

Major Works

Poems

- A Rain of Rites
- Life Signs in 1983
- Relationship in 1980.
- The False Start in 1980
- Selected Poems in 1987
- Temple in 1989
- Random Descent in 2005
- Samparka in 2006
- Close the Sky Ten by Ten in 1971
- Dispossessed Nests in 1986
- Burden of Waves and Fruit in 1988
- Swaynmrara and other poems in 1971
- The Lie of Dawns : Poems in 2008
- A Father's Hours
- Waiting in 1979

Prose

- Essay and Memoirs
- The Green Gardener : Short Stories

AK Ramanujan (1929-1993)

Attipate Krishnaswami Ramanujan was an Indian scholar, who wrote in Kannada and English. He was born on 16th March, 1929. He was an author, translator, poet and playwright. He once remarked that his disciplines (i.e., linguistics and anthropology) and his education give him his 'outer form, where as his Indian origin, his first thirty years in India and his knowledge of Kannada and Tamil gave him his inner form. He was awarded 'Padma Sri' by Indian Government. He was also awarded 'Mac Arthur Prize Fellowship' in 1993.

Literary Career and Works

Ramanujan has made a great deal of contribution to the field of Indian literature in English, because of theoretical and aesthetic nature his works explain his ideologies on culture and behaviour, which he calls it as 'context sensitive' thinking. This could be observed in his work 'Is there an Indian way of thinking'.

His ideology of context sensitive thinking could also be seen in his folklore studies namely in the works, *Where Mirrors are Windows* and *Three Hundred Ramayanas* where he discusses the inter textuality of Indian literature. Ramanujan was also a great translator of works in South Indian languages Kannada and Tamil. They are love poems from a classical Tamil anthology, *Speaking of Shiva*, *Hyms for the Drowning* and *A Flowering Tree*. When it comes to his poetry they are almost confessional in style in a jarring realism with varied themes, *e.g. Astronomer*, *Second Sight*, 1986. AK Ramajujan died in Chicago, in July 1993.

Major Works

- The Interior Landscape 1967
- Speaking of Siva 1973
- The Literatures of India 1974
- Hymns for the Drowning 1981
- Poems of Love and War 1985
- Folktales from India 1991
- Is There an Indian Way of Thinking? 1990
- When God Is a Customer 1994
- A Flowering Tree and Other Oral Tales from India 1997

Poetry in English

- The Striders 1966
- Relations 1971
- Selected Poems 1976
- The Collected Poems 1997

Arun Balkrishna Kolatkar (1932-2004)

Arun Balkrishna Kolatkar was born on 1st, November, 1932 in Kolhapur, Maharastra. He completed his education from Sir JJ Institute of Applied Art.

Literary Career and Works

Kolatkar first wrote his poems in English, but was reluctant to publish in English language, though after publishing, it made a great impact on the contemporaries of Arun namely Nizzim Ezekiel and Salman Rushdie. The very first collection of poems was brought under *Jejuri*. Later it also won the Commonwealth Poetry Prize in 1976. Jejuri is a temple in one of towns of Maharastra, the poems are based on a journey to the temple of Khandoba.

His poems bring out the confusions of human beings in modern life. He has also written collection of poems in Marathi under the titles Chirimiri, Bhijki Vahi and Droan. He died due to cancer on 25th September, 2004 in Pune.

Major Works

- Jejuri-Colletion of poems 1976
- A Low Temple-Collection of Poems
- Kala Geltha
- Sarpasatra
- Boatride

VS Naipaul (Born 1932)

Vidhyadhar Suraj Prasad Naipaul was born in 1932. His father was Seepersad Naipaul and mother was Droapatie. He is known as a cosmopolitan writer. He was born in Trinidad, Venezuala. He took a simple degree in English at Oxford.

Literary Career and Works

Naipaul presents wide world of peoples in his novels, which are his travel books. His early novels are comic in stance depicting the life of people in Trinidad. Naipaul dedicated his celebrated novel *A House for Mr Biswas* to his wife Patrica Anu Hale. His first written work was *Miguel Street*, but was not published. In his travel books and documentary works he presents his impressions of the country of his ancestors. Naipaul received the Nobel Prize for Literature in 2001.

Major Works

- The Mystic Masseur in 1957 is a comic novel of Colonial politics. He received the Rhys Memorial, a prestigious prize for it.
- The Suffrage of Elvira in 1958.
- Miguel Street in 1960.
- A House for Mr Biswas in 1961. He became famous for this work.
- Mr Stone and the Knights Companion in 1963.
- The Middle Passage : Impressions of Five Societies - British, French, Dutch in the West Indies and South America in 1963.
- An Area of Darkness in 1964.
- A Flag on the Island in 1967.
- The Mimic Men in 1967 is About an Exiled Carribbean Politician.
- The Loss of El Dorado : A History in 1970.
- In a Free State in 1971.
- The Over Crowded Barracoon and Other Articles in 1972.
- Guerrillas in 1975.
- India : A Wounded Civilisation in 1977.
- The Perfect Tenants and the Mourners in 1977.
- Land in 6 AB the River in 1979.
- The Return of Eva Peron in 1980.
- Acongo Diary in 1980 A Congo
- Among the Believers : An Islamic Journey in 1981
- Finding the Center in 1986.
- A Turn in the South in 1989.
- India : A Million Mutinies Now in 1990.
- Beyond Belief : Islamic Excursions Among the Converted People in 1998.

Ruskin Bond (Born 1934)

He is an Indian author of British descent. He lives with his adopted family in Landour, Mussoorie, India. The Indian Council for Child Education has recognised his role in the growth of children's literature in India. He was awarded the Sahitya Academy Award in 1992 for Our Trees Still Grow in Dehra, his novel in English. He was awarded the Padma Shri in 1999 and the Padma Bhushan in 2014.

Ruskin Bond was born to Edith Clarke and Aubrey Alexander Bond, in Kasauli, Punjab States Agency, British India in 1934. His father taught English to the princesses of Jamnagar palace and Ruskin and his sister Ellen lived there till he was six. Later, Ruskin's father joined the Royal Air Force in 1939 and Ruskin along with his mother and sister went to live at his maternal home at Dehradun.

Shortly after that he was sent to a boarding school in Mussourie. When Bond was eight years old, his mother separated from his father and married a Punjabi Hindu, Hari. His father arranged for Ruskin to be brought to New Delhi where he was posted. He was very close to his father and describes this period with his father as one of the happiest times of his life. When he was ten, his father died of malaria, while he was posted in Calcutta. Ruskin was at his boarding school in Shimla and was informed about this tragedy by his teacher. He was thoroughly heartbroken. Later, he was raised by his mother and stepfather who lived in Dehradun. He did his schooling from Bishop Cotton School in Shimla, from where he graduated in 1950.

Literary Career and Works

He won several writing competitions in the school including the Irwin Divinity Prize and the Hailey Literature Prize. He wrote one of his first short stories, *'Untouchable'*, at the age of sixteen in 1951. Following his high school education he went to his aunt's home in the Channel Islands (UK) in 1951 for better prospects and stayed there for two years. In London, he started writing his first novel, *The Room on the Roof*, the semi-autobiographical story of the orphaned Anglo-Indian boy named Rusty; he did various jobs for a living. It won the John Llewellyn Rhys Prize, (1957) awarded to a British Commonwealth writer under 30. He moved to London and worked in a photo studio while searching for a publisher. After getting it published, Bond used the advance money to pay the sea passage to Bombay and settle in Dehradun.

He worked for a few years freelancing from Delhi and Dehradun. He sustained himself financially by writing short stories and poems for newspapers and magazines. On his youth, he said, "Sometimes I got lucky and some work got selected and I earned a few hundred rupees. Since I was in my 20s and didn't have any responsibilities I was just happy to be doing what I loved doing best." In 1963, he went to live in Mussoorie because besides liking the place, it was close to the editors and publishers in Delhi. He edited a magazine for four years. In the 1980s, Penguin set up in India and approached him to write some books. He had written *Vagrants in the Valley* in 1956, as a sequel to *The Room on the Roof*. These two novels were published in one volume by Penguin India in 1993. The following year a collection of his non-fiction writings, The best Of Ruskin Bond was published by Penguin India.

His interest in supernatural fiction led him to write popular titles such as *Ghost Stories from the Raj*, *A Season of Ghosts*, and *A Face in the Dark and other Hauntings*. Since then he has written over five hundred short stories, essays and novels, including *The Blue Umbrella*, *Funny Side* Up, A *Flight of Pigeons* and more than 50 books for children. He has also published his autobiography: *Scenes from a Writer's Life* describes his formative years growing up in Anglo-India and very recently "*Lone Wolf Dancing*". The Lamp is Lit is a collection of essays and episodes from his journal. His Autobiography, "Lone Fox Dancing", was published in 2017

Kamala Das (1934-2009)

She was born on 31st March, 1934 at Pannayarkulam in the Coastal area of Malabar, Kerala. Poetry was in her blood because her parents were also poets. Her real name was Madhavi Kutty. She was educated mainly at her home. She was married in 1949, at an early age of 15. Her husband believed in sex as a matter of routine, but she was starved of the pleasure of sex. She believed it to be an emotional and spiritual bond. But her husband showed coldness in this matter. She felt dissatisfied. She began to believe in free sex. She changed her love one after another, but she could not get sexual satisfaction. She turned to poetry. She settled in Bombay and has a daughter.

Literary Career and Works

She wrote for journals and magazines. She has also written essays and stories. There is an autobiographical element in all her works. They are the mirror of her life specially in the matter of marriage and sex. She received the Kerala Sahitya Academy Award for her stories in Malyalam. She also received the Asian Pen Anthology for poetry in 1964. She died in 2009.

Major Works

- Summer in Calcutta
- Annette
- A losing Battle
- In love
- Relationship
- The Maggots
- The Suicide
- The Looking Glass
- The Testing of the Sirens
- My Grand Mother's House
- Alphabet of Lust (Novel)
- The Old Playhouse and Other Poems in 1973
- Punishment in Kindergarten
- The Dance of the Eunuchs
- The Descendants
- An Introduction
- Forest Fire
- Krishna
- The Freaks
- The Stone Age
- The Sunshine Cat
- The Winter

My Grandmother's House

There is a house now far away where once
I received love That woman died,
The house withdrew its silence, snakes moved
Among books I was then too young
To read and my blood turned cold like the moon
How often I think of going
There to Keep through blind eyes of windows or
Just listen to the frozen air
Or in wild despair, pick an armful of
Darkness to bring it there to kie
Behind my bedroom door like a brooding
Dog you cannot believe darling
Can you that I lived in such a house and
was proud and loved I who have lost
My way and beg now at strangers doors to
Receive love at least in small change?

Anita Desai (Born 1937)

She was born on 24th June, 1937 in Mussoorie. Her father was a Bengali and her mother was a German. She got her early education in Delhi. She completed her graduation in English literature in 1957, at Delhi University. She was married to Ashwin Desai.

Literary Career and Works

She has written 10 novels and many short stories. She started writing prose at the age of 7. Her stories were published in children's magazines. Her first story *Circus Cat Alley Cot* was published. in 1957. Her second short story *How Gently's The Mist* was published in The Illustrated Weekly of India in 1958. Her collection of stories for children contains *The Peacock Garden, Cat on a House Boat and Village by the Sea.*

Her other novels are *Clear Light of Day* in 1980, *Journey to Ithaca* in 1985, *Feasting Fasting in* 1999.

Desai always tries to show the psychological state of her characters because she thinks that the inner life of man and woman decides his or her character rather than the external condition of life. She is affected by men and women relationship at home. None of her characters are happy.

She uses symbols and images to describe the suffering of mind. She was awarded with Sahitya Academy Award in 1978. She was also listed for the Booker Award.

Major Works

- **Cry the Peacock** This is her first novel published in 1963. Maya is the heroine of the novel. She is a spoiled and stout daughter of a rich Brahmin. She is married to Gautam, who is sensitive, impolite and an intelligent advocate. When she was a child, an astrologer had predicted that after four years of her marriage, she or her husband would die. Due to the fear, she loses her balance of mind. In an insane condition she kills her husband. This novel describes the psychological dilemma of Maya's inner psyche.
- **Voices in the City** This is her second novel published in 1965. The novel describes the miserable condition of Mirode, Monisha and Anita in Calcutta city. Through her personal diary Monisha reveals the mental state, which proves fatal for her.
- **Bye-Bye Black Bird** This is her third novel published in 1975. It describes the condition of Indians, who have settled in London city. Adit and Dev are facing the problems of alienation (the state of being a foreigner) in settling in London.
- **Where Shall We Go This Summer** This is her fourth novel, published in 1975. The novelist is disturbed to see that the people are busy in earning and spending. They have no mission of life. This novel describes the psychological condition of Sita's mind.
- **Fire on the Mountain** This is her fifth novel published in 1977 in London. It reveals Nanda Kaul's motherly feelings, insult and helplessness of alienation (forsaken state).
- **Baum gortner's Bombay** This novel was published in 1988. It is a story of a German Jew, who feels himself as an outsider in his country because he is a Jew. He comes to India, where he is an outsider because he is a firangi.
- **In Custody** This novel was published in 1984. It forces us to think about the decline of Urdu language. Once it was the court language of the Mughals. It ruled over the hearts of the people. But now it is losing its charm. In this novel, Deven Sharma belongs to a middle class family. His father, a school teacher dies in Lucknow. His mother comes to Delhi, Deven becomes a lecturer in Lala Ram Lal College at Mirpore. He is married to an ordinary girl of Haldwani in UP. His dream is to meet Nur Shahjehanabadi, the Urdu poet.

  Murad, his college friend, fulfils his dream by giving him a chance to interview Nur. He is kicked like a football Murad, Safia Begum, Nur Shahjehanabadi and Siddiqui.

Girish Karnad (Born 1938)

He was born at Machheran near Bombay in 1938. He belongs to a Saraswat Konkani family of Mangalore. He lived his early life in Sirssi, a small town. For higher education, he went to England. In 1958 he got scholarship to study in foreign country. He studied at Oxford University from 1960 to 1963. He had been a Bhabha Fellow from 1970 to 1972. As a visiting professor and resident scholar, he acted at the Chicago University. Today he is one of the foremost and most famous dramatists of English language.

Literary Career and Works

He writes in his native language Kannada on original topics and then translates them into English. He wanted to be a poet, but the influence of the theatre made him a dramatist. He himself tells us "I wanted to be a poet, the greatest ambition of my life.

At the age of 22, I realised, "I would not be a poet, but only a playwright."

In his childhood he got a chance with his father to see the performance of the touring drama companies, which were related to Parsi Theatre. He wrote about the influence of these drama companies. After some time he became a film actor. He became a very popular artist on the TV Screen. His four films – Sanskara, Vamsa, Viksha, Tabballyu Nanade won the Presidents Gold Medal. Kadce for which he wrote the Scenerio and directed himself, won the Golden Lotus. Now, he has been working with international film maker, Shyam Benegal. He served as a director of the Central Institute of Film and Television Technology at Pune.

Major Works

- **Yayati** His first play 'Yayati' was published in 1961. It is the story of Hindu myth based on the theme of responsibility. Arnold King wants to exchange his old age with the youth of one of his sons. His two sons refuse to obey him. But the third one agrees to his proposal. This play got a grand success and brought name and fame with wealth.

- **Hayavadana** His second play was published in 1970 and got the Natya Shree Award for the best play in 1971. This story shows a Hindu myth. The woman marries a great learned poet, who has a fast friend. The poet suspects his friend of loving his wife. The two friends sacrifice their heads before the goddess. The woman prays to the goddess to bring them back to life. Her prayer is accepted and she is ordered to put their separated heads on their bodies. In a hurry, the woman changes the heads and put the heads on other's body. The question is "Who is her husband?" The story becomes sensational with the introduction of a boy with a horse's head.
- **Tughlaq** It was first written in Kannada in 1964. After some time on the suggestion of Alyque Padamsee, he translated it into English. It was staged at Bhulabhai Auditorium Bombay successfully. It is a historical play, which has been translated into English as well as many Indian languages. This is the story of Muhammad-bin-Tughlaq.
- **Nagamandal** This latest play is written in English. It is based on the folk-tales of Karnataka.

Shashi Deshpande (Born 1938)

She was born in Dharwad in Karnataka Southern Part of India in 1938. She is the daughter of a famous Kannada and Sanskrit Scholar Aday Rangachar or Sriranga. She read Economics, Law and English and received Diploma in Journalism. She was impressed with many foreign novelists.

Literary Career and Works

Shashi Deshpande completed a course in journalism after which she worked as a journalist for the magazine 'Onlooker'.

After leaving the journalist job Shashi Deshpande published her collection of short stories in the year 1978. She published her first novel in 1980 under the tittle *The Dark Holds no terrors*. In 1999 she published her latest novel named *A Matter of Time* through the feminist press of New York.

She won Sahitya Academy award for her novel *That Long Silence* and Padmashree award in 1990 and 2009 respectively. She has also written four children's books entitled *Writing from the Margin and Other Essays*.

Shashi Deshpande lives in Bangalore with her husband, who is a pathologist. Her recent novel is *Small Remedies* released in 2000.

Major Works

She has published seven novels

- The Dark Holds No Terror in 1980.
- If I Die Today in 1982.
- Come up and Be Dead in 1983.
- Roots and Shadows in 1983.
- That Long Silence in 1988.
- The Bending Vine in 1992.
- A Matter of Time in 1996.

She also wrote four books for children

- A Sum Adventure.
- The Only Witness.
- The Hidden Treasure.
- The Narainpur Incident. The last novel is based on the Quit India Movement and the role of children in it. **The Bending Vine** focuses on the question of rape.

Arun Joshi (1939-1993)

He was an Indian writer born in 1939. He completed his higher education in US and returned to India to become an industrial manager. Arun Joshi deviated his works from everyday attachment yet he did not forget the real existence.

Literary Career and Works

His attempt as a novelist is a great contribution to world literature from Indian literature. Getting self towards transcendental is the technique he adopts in his novels, 'The foreigner' is the best example, where the protagonist returns to Delhi after experiencing life in America.

In his another novel *'The strange case of Billy Biswas'*, Arun Joshi explores how an American educated young boy of India ends up in exploring the tribal life, which is also transcendental and away from every day life. Shri Ram is a biography written with Khushwant Singh. His popular works are *The Foreigner The Apprentice* and *The Strange Case of Belly Biswas*. His novel *The Last Labyrinth* won for him the Sahitya Akademi Award. Arun Joshi died in 1993.

Anees Jung (Born 1944)

Anees Jung was born in 1944 in Hyderabad. She was born in an aristocratic family. Her father Nawab Hosh Yar Jung served as musahib, to the last Nizam of Hyderabad. She completed her higher studies in Sociology and American Studies from Michigan University, US.

Literary Career and Works

She started her career as a journalist; as an editor she worked for Times of India publications. She published her first work in 1987 entitled *Unveiling India*, in which she talks about the problems of women and youth. Once regarding her works she said "My book is not a pretty book, but it addresses the crucial issues like female foeticide, dowry, rape and adolescent problems."

In her another book Beyond the Courtyard Anees has dedicated a chapter to the issue of female foeticide in Punjab. Anees also has focused her writings to show the sufferings of children from deprived background in her book Lost Spring: Stories of Stolen Childhood (2005).

Major Works

- When a Place Becomes a Person 1977
- Flashpoints: Poems in Prose 1981
- Unveiling India 1987
- The Song of India 1990
- Night of the New Moon: Encounters with Muslim Women in India 1993
- Seven Sisters-Among the Women of South Asia 1994
- Breaking the Silence 1997
- Olives from Jericho 1999

Salman Rushdie (Born 1947)

He was born on 19th June, 1947 in Mumbai. He got the Austrian State Prize for European Literature in 1993.

Literary Career and Works

Following his graduation in 1968, Salman Rushdie began working in Pakistani television. Later, he also acted with the Oval House theatre group in Kennington, England, and until 1981, he wrote freelance copy for advertisers Ofilvy and Mather and Charles Barker.

In 1975, Rushdie published his first novel, *Grimus*, a science fiction story inspired by the twelfth century Sufi poem '*The Conference of the Birds*,' was largely ignored by both critics and the public. Rushdie's literary fortunes changed in 1981, when the publication of his second novel, *Midnight's Children*, brought him international fame and acclaim. The story is a comic allegory of Indian history, and tells of the 1001 children born after India's Declaration of Independence, each of whom possesses a magical power. It won the Booker Prize for Fiction, the English-Speaking Union Award, the James Tait Black Memorial Prize (fiction) and an Arts Council Writers' Award. In 1993 and 2008, it was named the 'Booker of Bookers,' acknowledging it as the best recipient of the Booker Prize for Fiction in the award's history.

His third novel, *Shame* (1983), was commonly regarded as a political allegory of Pakistani politics. It used a wealthy family as a metaphor for the country and included characters based on former Prime Minister Zulfikar Ali Bhutto and General Muhammad Zia-ul-Haq. It won the Prix du Meilleur Livre Etranger and made the short list for the Booker Prize. In 1987, Rushdie published a short travel narrative titled *The Jaguar's Smile*.

In 1988, Rushdie became the center of a controversy surrounding the publication of his fourth novel, *The Satanic Verses* which revolves around two Indian actors who struggle with religion, spirituality and nationality. Although the book won the Whitbread Award, Rushdie's free adaptation of Islamic history and theology caused the orthodox Muslim Ayatollah Khomeini of Iran to issue a fatwa, a call for all obedient Muslims to assassinate him. The book was banned and burned in many countries and several people involved with its publication were injured and killed. After the death threat, Rushdie shunned publicity and went into hiding for many years, although he continued to write.

He published a children's book in 1990, titled *Haroun and the Sea of Stories*. It won the Writers' Guild Award (Best Children's Book). He next published a collection of essays, Imaginary Homelands: *Essays and Criticism 1981-1991* (1991), and a collection of short stories, *East, West* (1994). Then came another novel, *The Moor's Last Sigh* (1995), which used a family's history to explore the activities of right-wing Hindu terrorists, and the cultural connections between India and the Iberian peninsula. *The Ground Beneath Her Feet* (1999) was Rushdie's sixth novel, re-imagining the birth of modern rock music. He also published the novel *Fury* in 2001 and *Step Across This Line: Collected Non-fiction 1992-2002* in 2002. His novel '*Shalimar the Clown* published in 2005, was a finalist for the Whitbread Book Awards. In 2012, he published a memoir of his days in hiding, *Joseph Anton*.

Major Works

Novels

- Grimus 1975
- Midnight's Children 1981
- Shame 1983
- The Satanic Verses 1988
- The Moor's Last Sigh 1995
- The Ground Beneath Her Feet 1999
- Fury 2001
- Shalimar the Clown 2005
- The Enchantress of Florence 2008
- Two Years Eight Months and Twenty-Eight Nights 2015
- The Golden House 2017

Collections

- East, West 1994
- Mirrorwork: 50 Years of Indian Writing 1947-1997
- The Best American Short Stories 2008

Children's Books

- Haroun and the Sea of Stories 1990
- Luka and the Fire of Life 2010

Essays and Non-fiction

- The Jaguar Smile: A Nicaraguan Journey 1987
- 'In Good Faith', Granta, 1990
- Imaginary Homelands: Essays and Criticism, 1981-1991 1992
- "The Wizard of Oz: BFI Film Classics", BFI, 1992
- 'Mohandas Gandhi' 1998.
- Step Across This Line: Collected Non-fiction 1992-2002 2002
- 'The East is Blue' 2004
- 'A Fine Pickle' 2009
- 'In the South' -2012

Shobhaa De (Born 1948)

She is one of the famous novelists of India. She was born in 1948. She has written many scripts of TV Serials. She is called a feminist because she shows concern for women's problems. she basically worked as a model and then took to the profession of journalism in 1970.

Literary Career and Works

Nari Hira a magazine published from Mumbai, was edited by Shobha which made her famous. When she used to write for Times of India as a columnist she described the social life of Mumbai and also the lifestyles of celebrities. She is a successful woman as novelist, columnist and a perfect home maker as said by her in her autobiography *SPOUSE*.

Her works are *Shethji* (2012), *Shobhaa at Sixty* (2010), *Sandhya's Secret* (2009), *Spouse, Second Thought* (1996), *Starry Nights* (1989).

Pritish Nandy Borh (1951)

Pritish Nandy was born on 15th January, 1951. In 1982, he became an editor and worked as publishing director of 'The Times of India'. He was also the editor in chief of the Illustrated Weekly of India, he also published the comics title 'Indrajal'. He also conducted shows on television on business.

Literary Career and Works

He is versatile; poet, journalist, politician, animal activist and also a film producer. He was a member of Rajya Sabha in 1998. He also held shows on his paintings. Pritish Nandy was the first to open 'Cyber Cafe' in India. In the 5th Congress of World Poets Nandy was appointed the poet laureate. In 1967 Nandy's first collection of poems was published under the title of *Gods and Olives*. He has received EM Foster Literary Award, in 1976, Padma Shri in 1977 and Homi Bhabha fellowship in 1982.

Rohinton Mistry (Born 1952)

He was born in Bombay in 1952. Mistry completed his BA in philosophy from the university to Toronto. He was from a Parsi family. He is a poet and novelist who received the Encore Prize in 1993.

Literary Career and Works

His first two stories were published in Hart House Review and Canadian Fiction Magazine and won Hart House literary prizes for both. In 1987, his collection of stories was published under the title-*Tales from Firozsha Baag*. His first novel *Such a Long Journey* was published in 1991. His second novel was published in 1995 and it was shortlisted for Booker Prize. His works depict the difficulties of aging, social and economic, life of modern day Indians etc. As he practised zoroastrianism he has also written about it and his works are often regarded as "Indo-nostalgic" he received Neustadt International Prize for Literature in 2012.

Major Works

- Coming Attractions 2- 1984
- Tales from Firozsha Baag-1987
- Such a Long Journey-1991
- A Fine Balance- 1995
- Mistry Pack - 1998
- Family Matters-200l
- Threebies: Rohinton Mistry-2003
- Bookclub in a Box Discusses the Novel Family Matters-2005
- The Scream- 2008

Vikram Seth (Born 1952)

Vikram Seth was born on 20th June, 1952 in Calcutta. Leila was his mother and Prem Seth was his father and spent his childhood in Patna. He went to London in 1957.

Literary Career and Works

Vikram Seth being a polyglot has learnt Welsh, German, French, Mandarin, English, Hindi and Urdu well. All his works, as Vikram Seth himself says, are drawn from real life characters. He also developed an interest in poetry besides learning Chinese in England and went to China to study Classic Chinese poetry.

Though, Vikram Seth has a residence in England, he lives in Delhi with his parents. He has received numerous awards; Common Wealth Poetry Prize-1985, Pravasi Bharatiya Samman-2005, Padmashree in 2007 are some of them. His first successful work was *The Travel Book From Heaven Lake* was published in 1983 was a longest novel in verse form, written in English.

Major Works

Novel

- The Golden Gate–1986
- A Suitable Boy–1993
- An Equal Music– 1999
- A Suitable Girl–2013

Poetry

- Mappings– 1980
- The Humble Administrator's Garden–1985
- All You Who Sleep Tonight–1990
- Beastly Tales–1991
- Three Chinese Poets–1992
- The Frog and the Nightingale–1994
- The Traveller–2008

Amitav Ghosh (Born 1956)

Amitav Ghosh was born on 11th July, 1956 in Kolkata. He completed his masters form Delhi University in 1978 and Doctors in social Anthropology from Oxford University.

Literary Career and Works

Ghosh wrote both fiction and non-fiction. In 1980s, he went to Egypt as an academic researcher where he wrote *In an Antique Land*, which is an account of his travellings in ancient Egyptian village. His novels have complex narrative style which searches for identity.

In 1986 his first novel *The Circle of Reason* was published which is both post colonial in theme and post modern is structure. His second novel was published in 1988 entitled *The Shadow Lines* based on the result of (1947) non-British India.

Major Works

- The Circle of Reason (1986)
- *The Shadow Lines* (1988)
- *The Calcutta Chromosome* (1995)
- *The Glass Palace* (2000)
- *The Hungry Tide* (2004)
- *Sea of Poppies* (2009)
- *River of Smoke* (2011)
- *In an Antique Land* (1992)
- *Dancing in Cambodia* (1998)
- *The Iman and the Indian* (2002)
- *The Incendiary Circumstauces* (2005)

Shashi Tharoor (Born 1956)

He was born in London in 1956. He did B.A from St Stephens Delhi. He took law degree in Tufts University. He worked as Special Assistant to the Under Secretary General for peace. He wrote editorials and short stories. He is the member of parliament from Kerala. In 2009 he served as the minister of external affairs India.

Literary Career and Works

He was 6 years of age when he started writing. His first story was published in the free press Journal when he was 10. When he was of 11 years Operation Bellows was published as his first adventure novel. He was columnist for Gentleman magazine and Indian-Express newspaper. He was under-general secretary of UN till 2007.

Major Works

- The Great Indian Novel- 1989
- The Five-dollar Smile: Fourteen Early Stories and a Farce in Two Acts· The Five Dollar Smile and Other Stories-1990
- Show Business -1992
- India: From Midnight to the Millennium- 1997
- Indien. Zwischen Mythos-2000
- Riot: A Love Story- 2001
- Kerala, God's Own Country Nehru: The Invention of India- 2003
- Bookless in Baghdad- 2005
- Epic India: MF Husain's Mahabharat Project- 2006
- The Elephant, the Tiger, and the Cell Phone: Reflections on India, the Emerging 21st-Century Power- 2007
- India Shadows Across the Playing Field: 60 Years of India-Pakistan Cricket- 2009
- Nehru: A Biography- 2011
- India Shastra: Reflections on the Nation in Our Time-2015
- India: The Future Is Now- 2015
- An Era of Darkness: The British Empire in India- 2016
- India Sutra: Reflections on the World's Largest Democracy in the 21st Century- 2017
- Inglorious Empire- 2017
- Unity, Diversity, and Other Contradictions- 2018
- Why I Am a Hindu-2018
- The Paradoxical Prime Minister- 2018

Arundhati Roy (Born 1961)

She was born on 24th November in 1961 in Bengal. Her full name is Suzanna Arundhati Roy. Her mother's name is Mary Roy, who is a famous social worker. She belongs to Kerala. Her father is a Bengali Hindu, who is a tea-planter. The marriage life of her parents was not successful. Arundhati Roy gave an interview to Sunday Plus and said about her father, "I don't want to discuss my father. I don't know him at all. I have only seen him a couple of times, that is it."

She passed her childhood in miserable conditions in Ayamenam, which is a small town near Kottayam. She left home at the age of 16 to stand on her feet. She lived in a small hut with a tin roof in Firoz Shah Kotla of Delhi. She sold empty beer bottles to earn her livelihood.

She was married to Gerard Da Cunha, who was her friend in Delhi School of Architecture. But her marriage also could not succeed like her parents. After four years of marriage, they were separated. She was soon busy in preparing TV Serials for Doordarshan to divert her attention. She also became busy in social and political issues of the world.

Literary Career and Works

She worked as a Research assistant at the National Institute of Urban Affairs. She did the job so diligently that she was awarded a scholarship to go to Florence, Italy to study the Restoration of monuments and historical urban centres. She began her career as a script writer, "In which Annie gives it those ones' and 'Electric Moon'. Her first novel *The God of Small Things* was published on 4th April, 1997 in Delhi.

It was awarded the Booker Prize in London on 14th October, 1997. *The Cost of Living* was published in 1999, in which she has given her opinion about the Narmada Dam Project and the explosion of India's first Nuclear Bomb.

Major Works

- New Nukes : India, Pakistan and Global Nuclear Disarmament in 2000.
- Power Polities : The Reincarnation of Rumplestiets Kin in 2001.
- 'War is Peace' in Out Look in 2001.
- The Algebra of Infinite Justice 2002.
- Introduction to 13th December, a Reader : The Stranger case of Attack on the Indian Parliament
- The Check Book and the Cruise Missile : Conversations with Arundhati Roy.
- The End of Imagination.
- The Greater Common Good.
- An Ordinary Persons Guide to Empire (2004).
- Public Power in the Age of Empire (2004).
- Soviet Intervention in Afghanistan : Causes, Consequences and India's Responses.
- War Talk (2003).

Arundhati Roy as a Novelist

She wrote a number of articles, interviews and books on various subjects. She is one of the greatest Indian writers in English language with world fame. She has presented problematic issues in her novels. All her books aroused a storm of controversies, which added her fame in the world. She is the first novelist, who has shown general awareness towards social crisis and realities and the burning problems in the modern society.

In the words of Indira Nityanandan, "Arundhati Roy writes in a style truly different from that of other Indo-English novelists, both male and female of the country. She writes differently to a great extent and in doing so breaks many of the accepted rules of language." Her style and technique is praiseworthy.

Kiran Desai (Born 1971)

Kiran Desai is the daughter of Anita Desai, herself short-listed for the Booker Prize on three occasions. She was born in Delhi but spent the early years of her life in Pune and Mumbai. She studied in the Cathedral and John Connon School. She left India at the age of 14 and she and her mother then lived in England for a year and then moved to the United States, where she studied creative writing at Bennington College, Hollins University and Columbia University.

Kiran Desai is an Indian author. Her novel *The Inheritance of Loss* won the 2006 Man Booker Prize and the National Book Critics Circle Fiction Award. In January 2015, The Economic Times, India's leading business publication, listed her as one of 20 'most influential' global Indian women.

Literary Career and Works

Kiran Desai left Columbia for several years to write her first novel, *Hullabaloo in the Guava Orchard* (1998) about a young man in provincial India who abandons an easy post office job and begins living in a guava tree, where he makes oracular pronouncements to locals. Unaware that he knows of their lives from having read their mail, they hail him as a prophet. *Hullabaloo in the Guava Orchard* drew wide critical praise and received a 1998 Betty Trask Prize from the British Society of Authors.

While working on what would become her second novel, Desai lived a peripatetic life that took her from New York to Mexico and India. After more than seven years of work, she published *The Inheritance of Loss* (2006). Set in India in the mid-1980s, the novel has at its centre a Cambridge-educated Indian judge living out his retirement in Kalimpong, near the Himalayas, with his granddaughter until their lives are disrupted by Nepalese insurgents. The novel also interweaves the story of the judge's cook's son as he struggles to survive as an illegal immigrant in the United States. *The Inheritance of Loss* was hailed by critics as a keen, richly descriptive analysis of globalisation, terrorism, and immigration. When she received the Booker Prize for the novel in 2007, Desai became the youngest female writer to win the award.

In 2008 her report on a community to sex workers titled *Night claims the Godavari* was included in AIDS Sutra *Untold Stories from India*. Desai's work has appeared in the International magazines like The New Yorker, Guardian and also in The Vintage Book of Indian Writing.

Chetan Bhagat (1974)

Chetan Bhagat was born in New Delhi, India, on 21st April, 1971. His father was an Army officer and his mother was a government employee in the agricultural department. His younger brother Ketan is also a novelist.

He completed his school years at The Army Public School, Dhaula Kuan in Delhi. He received his undergraduate degree in mechanical engineering from the Indian Institute of Technology Delhi in 1995 and his MBA degree from the Indian Institute of Management Ahmedabad in 1997. Bhagat worked for Goldman Sachs in their Hong Kong office as an investment banker for nearly a decade and wrote *Five Point Someone* while in Hong Kong. He then moved to Mumbai to focus full-time on his writing career while working at Deutsche Bank.

Literary Career and Works

Chetan Bhagat is an Indian author, columnist, screenwriter, television personality and motivational speaker, known for his Indian-English novels about young urban middle class Indians.

Bhagat's novels have sold over seven million copies. He moved to Amazon Publishing on 27th April, 2018 from Rupa Publications as per the news resources, and his first novel with Westland is *The Girl in Room 105*.

Chetan Bhagat is the author of bestselling novels Five *Point Someone* (2004), *One Night @ the Call Center* (2005), *The 3 Mistakes of My Life* (2008), *2 States* (2009), *Revolution 2020* (2011), *What Young India Wants* (2012) (speeches and columns), *Half Girlfriend* (2014), *Making India Awesome* (2015), *One Indian Girl* (2016) and *The Girl in Room* 105(2018).

All the books have remained bestsellers since their release and five have inspired Bollywood films like: Kai Po Che!, 2 States, 3 Idiots, Half Girlfriend and Hello.

In 2008, The New York Times cited Bhagat as "the biggest selling English language novelist in India's history". Time magazine named him as one of the 100 Most Influential People in the World in 2010. Bhagat voices his opinion frequently at leading events. He quit his investment banking career in 2009, to focus on writing. He debuted as a screenplay writer with the 2014 film Kick.

Bhagat also has columns in The Times of India and Hindustan Times And Dainik Jagran... He has featured in Forbes India magazine as one of the top celebrities of India in 2016. He was listed 40th out of 100.

Plagiarising Controversy

Chetan Bhagat was accused of plagiarizing for *One Indian Girl'* a short story written by Anvita Bajpai. The court granted a temporary injunction on sales of the book in April 2017 and vacated it in June 2017 for the legal trial to proceed. The matter is pending before Civil **Court** Bangalore. Bhagat was also accused for plagiarizing *Half Girlfriend*.

Major Works

Novels

- Five Point Someone (2004):
- One Night @ the Call Center (2005)
- The 3 Mistakes of My Life (2008)
- 2 States (2009)
- Revolution 2020 (2011)
- Half Girlfriend (2014)
- One Indian Girl (2015)
- The Girl in Room 105 (2018)

Non-Fiction

- What Young India Wants (2012)
- Making India Awesome (2015)

Awards and Recognition

- Society Young Achiever award in 2004
- Publisher's Recognition award in 2005
- Bhagat in Time magazine's list of World's 100 Most Influential People 2010[24]
- Filmfare Award for Best Screenplay 2014: Kai Po Che
- CNN-IBN Indian of the Year in Entertainment in 2015

EXAM BASED QUESTIONS

1 Name the author of The Gardener, The Fugitive, Chitra Sacrifice, The Post Office.
(a) Rabindranath Tagore
(b) Bankim Chandra
(c) Aurobindo Ghose
(d) Romesh Chunder Dutt

2 What does 'Telling of beads' refer to in the poem 'Leave This Chanting' by Rabindranath Tagore?
(a) Holding beads while reciting prayers
(b) Using beads as a musical accompaniment
(c) Threading beads to make a necklace
(d) None of the above

3 Why is the temple lonely and dark in the poem 'Leave This Chanting' by Rabindranath Tagore?
(a) There are no windows
(b) The lamps are not lit
(c) The doors are shut
(d) The walls are made of stone

4 Where can one find God as per the poem 'Leave This Chanting' by Rabindranath Tagore?
(a) Inside the temple
(b) In the houses of the rich
(c) In heaven
(d) Among the hardworking

5 How should we seek deliverance as per the poem 'Leave This Chanting' by Rabindranath Tagore?
(a) By incessant prayers
(b) By going to the temple regularly
(c) By being pious and righteous-minded
(d) By helping our fellow beings who are in need

6 What should we do to meet God as per the poem 'Leave This Chanting' the Rabindranath Tagore?
(a) Mediate on God
(b) Have true faith in God
(c) Offer flowers and incense
(d) Stand by God 'in toil and in sweat'

7 Name the poet of 'Kali, the Mother'.
(a) Swami Vivekanand
(b) Subramaniam Bharathi
(c) Swami Ramakrishna Paramhans
(d) Sri Aurobindo

8 Who expounded the theory of 'Advaita'?
(a) Ramanujan (b) Sri Shankaracharya
(c) Madhavacharya (d) Swami Vivekananda

9 Arthur Symons wrote about this person, "All the life of the tiny figure seemed to concentrate itself in the eyes: they turned towards beauty as the sunflower turns towards the sun." Who is the person referred to?
(a) Toru Dutt (b) Aru Dutt
(c) Sarojini Naidu (d) Rabindranath Tagore

10 Name Sarojini Naidu's last collection of poems.
(a) The Broken Wing (b) The Golden Threshold
(c) The Bird of Time (d) The Temple

11 Which of the following poems is not composed by Sarojini Naidu?
(a) Palanquin Bearers
(b) Songs of Radha
(c) Fishermen of Coromondel
(d) Indian Philosophy

12 Which of the following works belongs to Sarojini Naidu?
(a) The Temple (b) The Golden Threshold
(c) The Broken Wing (d) The Bird of Time

13 'The Gift of India', 'Bangle-Seller', 'The Autumn of Love', 'Palanquin Bearers'. Identify the author from the following.
(a) Sarojini Naidu (b) Anita Desai
(c) Vikram Seth (d) None of these

14 Who wrote the famous novel 'Anandmath'?
(a) Rabindranath Tagore
(b) Bankim Chandra Chatterjee
(c) Sarat Chandra Chatterjee
(d) None of the above

15 Hal Fisher wrote about this person, "...this child of the green valley of the Ganges has by sheer force of native genius earned for herself the right to be enrolled in the great fellowship of English poets." Who is the poet?
(a) Sarojini Naidu (b) Toru Dutt
(c) Michael Madhusudan (d) Manmohan Ghose

16 Toru Dutt, Romesh Chunder Dutt and Aurobindo, all wrote on one common theme taken out from the Mahabhrata. Identify the story which the three found irresistible.
(a) Kama and Kunti (b) Nal-Damyanti
(c) Savitri (d) Gandhari

17 The Fakir of Jhungheera was written by one of the first Indo-Anglian poets. The poem is often hailed as a "Competent narrative verse with Byronic echoes." Identify the writer.
(a) Toru Dutt
(b) Henry Derozio
(c) Michael Madhusudan Dutt
(d) Hassan Ali

18 Paying a tribute to a Bengali poet who wrote in English also, Sri Aurobindo said, "The God himself took up thy pen and wrote."
Who was he?
(a) Michael Madhusudan Dutt (b) Henry Derozio
(c) Romesh Chunder Dutt (d) Kashiprasad Ghose

19 To whom do we assign following works – The Lake of Palms, A History of Civilisation of Ancient India, The Slave-Girl of Agra?
(a) Manmohan Ghose
(b) Romesh Chunder Dutt
(c) Bankim Chandra Chatterjee
(d) Sharat Chandra Chatterjee

20 Bankim Chandra Chatterjee did not write
(a) Durgesh Nandini (b) Mrinalini
(c) Abu Hassan (d) Anandmath

21 Aurobindo's epic-Savitri contains how many lines?
(a) 21500 (b) 21000 (c) 22000 (d) 24000

22 Which out of the following is the full title of Aurobindo's-Savitri?
(a) Savitri-an Epic
(b) Savitri
(c) Savitri-A poem in Three Parts
(d) Savitri-A Legend and a Symbol

23 Who has written 'Our Casuarina Tree', a splendid Keatsian Poem?
(a) Aurobindo Ghosh
(b) Toru Dutt
(c) RK Narayan
(d) Swami Vivekanand

24 Who out of the following was highly influenced by French Romanticism, French language and literature?
(a) Govind Dutt (b) Toru Dutt
(c) Madhusudan Dutt (d) None of these

25 One of the following works is written by Michael Madhusudan Dutt. Identify which one?
(a) The Shair and Other Poems
(b) The Captive Ladie
(c) Bianca
(d) Lays of Ancient India

26 About an Indian poet writing in English, a critic, George Sampson says that a reader of his poems "Would readily take them as the work of an English poet trained in the classical tradition." An Indian critic feels that his poetry has no imagery or sentiment that can be termed as Indian. Who was this poet?
(a) Michael Madhusudan Dutt
(b) Romesh Chunder Dutt
(c) Aurobindo Ghose
(d) Manmohan Ghose

27 Who wrote Ilion?
(a) Virgil (b) Aurobindo
(c) Homer (d) Rabindranath Tagore

28 The Autobiography of an Unknown Indian' is written by
(a) Vikram Seth (b) VS Naipaul
(c) Nirad C Chaudhuri (d) None of these

29 Which Indian English writer has composed 'A Bunch of Old Letters'?
(a) Namita Gokhle (b) Jeffery Deaver
(c) Jawaharlal Nehru (d) Evelyn Waugh

30 HN Chattopadhaya was an eminent poet and play wright. He did not write
(a) The Window (b) The Two Rings
(c) The Parrot (d) The Coffin

31 The Saint, The Evening Lamp and The Hunter of Kalahasti are written by
(a) John Keats (b) AK Ramanujan
(c) Girish Karnad (d) HN Chattopadhaya

32 Which Indian author wrote the English novel called 'Untouchable'?
(a) Mulk Raj Anand
(b) Munshi Premchand
(c) Girish Karnad
(d) Ruskin Bond

33 Mulk Raj Anand, about one of his female characters say, "Gauri is my tribute to Indian womanhood." In which novel does Gauri appear?
(a) The Road
(b) The Old Woman and The Cow
(c) Untouchable
(d) The Sword and The Sickle

34 We are the men, who will master it?
(a) The Big Heart
(b) The Sword and The Sickle
(c) Two Leaves and a Bud
(d) The Road

35 Who among the following combines anthropology, history and fiction?
(a) Kamala Markandya (b) Mulk Raj Anand
(c) Upmanyu Chatterjee (d) Amitav Ghosh

36 Woman is the Earth, air, ether, sound, woman is the Microcosm of the mind. These lines were written by
(a) Anita Desai (b) Dom Moraes
(c) Arun Joshi (d) Raja Rao

37 Following novels, except one, describe the condition of Indians settled abroad. Mark the one which does not.
(a) The Nowhere Man
(b) Bye-Bye, Blackbird
(c) The Serpent And The Rope
(d) The Guide

38 RK Narayan is one of the most widely read Indian novelists. He wrote for more than fifty years including travelogues, English translations of Indian epics and his memoirs 'My Days'. Which of these is a fictional town created by him?
(a) Alleypey (b) Malgudi
(c) Udipi (d) Coimbatore

39 Who, among the following Indian writers in English, has created an identifiable imagined locale?
(a) Mulk Raj Anand (b) Raja Rao
(c) RK Narayan (d) Anita Desai

40 Who among the following was the first recipient of the Sahitya Academi Award for English Literature?
(a) Raja Rao (b) Mulk Raj Anand
(c) RK Narayan (d) None of these

41 In 'The Guide', we come across a dancer. The name of the dancer is
(a) Rosie (b) Bharti
(c) Savitri (d) None of these

42 Identify the novel in which RK Narayan focuses on family planning?
(a) Mr Sampath (b) The Painter of Signs
(c) The Guide (d) None of these

43 Which novels out of the following does not portray the Gandhian Age and the impact of Gandhi?
(a) The Dark Room (b) Inquilab
(c) In Transit (d) None of these

44 Where is RK Narayan's imaginary town 'Malgudi' located?
(a) In Madras (b) In Cochin (c) In Mysore (d) In Surat

45 Which novel out of the following does not describe the conditions of Westerns living in India?
(a) Coffer Dam (b) The Princess
(c) Heat and Dust (d) None of these

46 Which novel highlights the Bengal famine?
(a) So Many Hungers (b) A Handful of Rice
(c) A Time to be Happy (d) Athawar House

47 Listed below are the works of Bhabani Bhattacharya of which only one is his collection of short stories. Identify it.
(a) So Many Hungers
(b) A Dream in Hawaii
(c) Sea Hawk
(d) Shadow From Ladakh

48 Read the following passage and identify the novel and its author.
"Lago, I am as meek as Moses, but I have just heard that you have been mishandled by that Bhatta Govinda. Whip me, ye devils! Roast me in sulphur! Gall, worse than gall! A rascally Yea-for-smooth knave! Three Judases, each one thrice worse than Judas! Falstaff speaking. I am as subject to heat as butter."
(a) In Custody by Anita Desai
(b) Midnight's Children by Salman Rushdie
(c) All About H Hatterr by GV Desani
(d) Vermillion Boat by Sudhir Ghosh

49 Who is the author of the following novels: A Bend in The Ganges, The Princess, Distant Drums, A Combat of Shadows?
(a) Mulk Raj Anand
(b) Bhabani Bhattacharya
(c) Manohar Malgonkar
(d) Salman Rushdie

50 Identify the author from the following, who has written 'The Devil's Wind' which depicts the events of India's First war of Independence, (1857) Mutiny.
(a) K Subba Rao
(b) Manohar Malgonkar
(c) K S Venkatramani
(d) None of the above

51 Identify the novel, in which Manohar Malgonkar writes the story from the point of view of a Pakistani captain placed in Bangladesh.
(a) Cactus Country
(b) Distant Drums
(c) Combat to Shadow
(d) None of the above

52 'The Crown', 'Into Another Dawn', 'The Lion Cloth' 'My True Faces' are the famous works of
(a) Toru Dutt
(b) Manohar Malgonkar
(c) Anita Desai
(d) Chaman Nihal

53 Who among the following was first Indian poet to have published a regular volume of English verse? He also edited an English weekly, 'The Hindu Intelligence'?
(a) Mohan Lal (b) Kashiprasad Ghosh
(c) RK Narayan (d) None of these

54 Which Indian English writer has composed 'A Bride For The Sahib and Other Stories'?
(a) Khushwant Singh
(b) Surendranath Bandyopadhyay
(c) Ram Mohan Roy
(d) Morarji Bhai Desai

55 The book 'Truth, Love and A Little Malice' is written by
(a) Tarun Tejpal (b) Vikram Seth
(c) Khushwant Singh (d) Nirad C Chaudhuri

56 Who is the author of 'Delhi-A Novel'?
(a) Khushwant Singh
(b) Mulk Raj Anand
(c) Dom Moraes
(d) Arundhati Roy

57 Which of the following is not written by Khushwant Singh?
(a) Sex, Scotch and Scholarship
(b) Truth, Love and Little Malice
(c) The Sunset Club
(d) A Rain of Rites

58 Here is a list of Partition novels,which have 'violence on the woman's body' as a significant theme. Pick the odd one out.
(a) The Pakistani Bride
(b) What the Body Remembers
(c) Train to Pakistan
(d) The Ice-Candy Man

59 In his poem 'A Morning Walk' Nissim Ezekiel talks about a 'Barbaric City sick with slums / Deprived of seasons, blessed with rains / Its hawkers, beggars, iron-lunged / Processions led by frantic drums.' Identify the city.
(a) Kolkata (b) Banaras
(c) Mumbai (d) Agra

60 Which of the following poets wrote the essay 'Naipaul's India and Mine'?
(a) Kamala Das (b) R Parthasarathy
(c) AK Ramanujan (d) Nissim Ezekiel

61 Which among the following is not a typical 'Indian English Poem' by Nissim Ezekiel?
(a) How the English Lessons Ended
(b) The Railway Clerk
(c) Goodbye Party for Miss Pushpa TS
(d) The Patriot

62 Identify the poem from the following, in which we get a moving picture of a mother's suffering, written by 'Ezekiel'.
(a) The Visitor (b) Night of the Scorpion
(c) Philosophy (d) None of these

63 The 'Professor and Philosophy' is a collection of famous poems written by
(a) Pritish Nandy (b) Nissim Ezekiel
(c) Rabindranath Tagore (d) Raja Rao

64 Whose collections of poems are these : A Time to Change, Sixty Poems, The Third, The Unfinished Man?
(a) P Lai (b) Nissim Ezekiel
(c) Kamala Das (d) Bina Aggarwal

65 In Indo-English poet once remarked that his disciplines (i.e., linguistics and anthropology) and his education give him his Outer form, whereas his Indian origin, first thirty years in India and knowledge of Kannada and Tamil give him his inner form. Who said this?
(a) AK Ramanujan
(b) Kamala Das
(c) Gieve Patel
(d) Raja Gopal Parthasarathy

66 Which Indian English writer has composed 'A Bend in The River'?
(a) Ram Mohan Roy
(b) VS Naipaul
(c) Amit Choudhary
(d) Tarashankar Bandopadhyay

67 In which novel does the hero sing the refrain?
"This is the machine age, sons
This is the machine age
Which of the following novels focuses on the question of rape?
(a) The Bending Vine
(b) Voices in The City
(c) Some Inner Fury
(d) A Time to Be Happy

68 Which Indian English writer has composed 'A Childhood in Malabar'?
(a) JK Galbraith
(b) Daniel Patrick Moynihan
(c) Jeffery Deaver
(d) Kamala Das

69 Kamala Das was famous for short poems and stories. Which of the following is not written by her?
(a) A Sangam City (b) The Freaks
(c) Looping Glass (d) The Suicide

70 In Madurai city of temples and poets who sang of water and temples every summer a river dries to a trickle
(a) This is AK Ramanujan in 'A River'
(b) This is Sarojini Naidu in Bangle Sellers
(c) This is Arun Kolatkar in 'Jejure'
(d) This is Jayanta Mahapatra in 'A Father's Hours'

71 Which among the following is not writen by A K Ramanujan?
(a) Breaded Fish
(b) Of Mothers, Among the Things
(c) Poona Train Window
(d) Durgesh Nandini

72 UR Ananthamurthy's Samskara was translated by
(a) Himself
(b) Girish Karnad
(c) HS Shivaprakash
(d) AK Ramanujan

73 Which prestigious price out of the following did VS Naipaul receive?
(a) Commonwealth (b) Rhys Memorial
(c) Booker's (d) None of these

74 Which out of the following is written by VS Naipaul?
(a) The Mystic Masseur (b) In a Free State
(c) The Mimic Men (d) None of these

75 Who among the following is a Sahitya Akademi Award Winner and he loves to write for children?
(a) R K Naryan
(b) Ruskin Bond
(c) Vievekananda
(d) Anita Desai

76 Identify the poet whose first book was 'A Beginning' and he received the Hawthornden Prize the next year and became the youngest poet to get it.

(a) Dom Moraes (b) Frank Moraes
(c) Shiv K Kumar (d) Arun Kolatkar

77 Which among the following was published in 1884?

(a) Durgesh Nandini
(b) Anandmath
(c) Mrinalini
(d) The Poison Tree

78 In which of Anita Desai's novel an insane wife kills her husband?

(a) Voices in The City
(b) In Custody
(c) Cry, The Peacock
(d) Baumgartner's Bombay

79 Baumgartner's Bombay is a novel about a German Jew who remains an outsider all his life, in his country because he is a Jew and in India, where he is a firangi. Who wrote this moving novel?

(a) Vikram Seth
(b) Anita Desai
(c) Nayantara Seghal
(d) Ruth P Jhabvala

80 Which one of the following is a collection of Anita Desai's short stories?

(a) Voices in the City
(b) Games at Twilight
(c) Village by the Sea
(d) Cry, the Peacock

81 What two countries are the settings for 'Fasting and Feasting'?

(a) The United States and Malaysia
(b) India and the United States
(c) The United States and China
(d) The Unites States and Nepal

82 What does Uma spend her life doing in the 'Fasting and Feasting'?

(a) Searching for the perfect husband
(b) Working at a floor loom
(c) Plotting revenge
(d) Being subservient to her parents' demands

83 Where is Arun at the opening of the novel in the novel 'Fasting and Feasting'?

(a) In Italy
(b) In England
(c) In the United States
(d) In India

84 What is Papa's vocation in the novel 'Fasting and Feasting'?

(a) Merchant (b) Lawer (c) Policeman (d) Baker

85 Around what does Mama build her life in the novel 'Fasting and Feasting'?

(a) Meeting Papa's needs
(b) Her religion
(c) Understanding people
(d) Securing her daughter's happiness

86 What does Papa do every day after work in the novel 'Fasting and Feasting'?

(a) Play cricket (b) Call his father
(c) Visit the temple (d) Play tennis

87 What do Mama and Papa do on occasional evenings at the club in the novel 'Fasting and Feasting'?

(a) Play cards (b) Play shuffleboard
(c) Swim (d) Bet or horse races

88 To what kind of life do Uma and Arun resign themselves in the novel 'Fasting and Feasting'?

(a) Religious
(b) Intellectual stimulation but strict
(c) Comfort and boredom
(d) Subservienc

89 This author has been short-listed for the Booker Prize thrice as of 2007 but is yet to win it. however, her daughter won the Booker Prize in 2006 for her second novel. Name this mother-daughter duo.

(a) Sooni and Farida Taraporewala
(b) Kinari and Vidya Sharma
(c) Depa and Rashmi Mehta
(d) Anita and Kiran Desai

90 Which of the following is not a partition novel?

(a) Train to Pakistan
(b) Sunlight on a Broken Column
(c) The Shadow Lines
(d) In Custody

91 Which of the following novels is not a partition novel?

(a) Azadi
(b) Tamas
(c) Clear Light of the Day
(d) That Long Silence

92 Who is the author of the following books : The Foreinger, The Apprentice, The Last Labyrinth, The City and the River?

(a) Ruth P Jhabvala
(b) Amitav Ghosh
(c) Dom Moraes
(d) Arun Joshi

93 Name Salman Rushdie's latest among the given novels.

(a) The Moor's Last Sigh
(b) Fury
(c) The Ground Beneath Her Feet
(d) Satanic Verses

94 Two Indian writers living abroad created furore-one was Vikram Seth who got an unprecedented among as an advance for his novel, the other who came under 'fatwa', for one of his controversial novels, issued by Muslim countries, was
(a) Amitav Ghose
(b) Bharati Mukherjee
(c) Anita Desai
(d) Salman Rushdie

95 What was Aadam Aziz's most prominent feature in the novel 'Midnight's Children'?
(a) His blue eyes
(b) His light hair
(c) His large nose
(d) His dark skin

96 Who is Padma in the novel 'Midnight's Children'?
(a) Saleem's mother
(b) Saleem's nanny
(c) Saleem's wife
(d) Saleem's caretaker

97 Who told Aadam that his nose would always lead him in the right direction in the novel 'Midnight's Children'?
(a) Tai
(b) Naseem
(c) His mother
(d) His father

98 What event coincides with Saleem's birthday in the novel 'Midnight's Children'?
(a) China's independence
(b) Pakistan's independence
(c) Bangladesh's independence
(d) India's independence

99 Which of the following character is one of Saleem's biological parents in the novel 'Midnight's Children'?
(a) William Methwold
(b) Ahmed Sinai
(c) Wee Willie Winkie
(d) Nadir Khan

100 Which of the following characters is one of Shiva's biological parents in the novel 'Midnight's Children'?
(a) Wee Willie Winkie
(b) Amina Sinai
(c) William Methwold
(d) Vanita Winkie

101 Which of the following characters did Saleem consider his mother in the novel 'Midnight's Children'?
(a) Pia (b) Mary Pereira
(c) Padma (d) Reverend mother

102 Which of the following characters represents Western influence in the novel 'Midnight's children'?
(a) Aadam Aziz (b) Tai
(c) Nadir Khan (d) Amed Sinai

103 What phrase does Reverend Mother use repeatedly in the novel 'Midnight's Children'?
(a) What's his name
(b) Who is that
(c) Why are you here
(d) What in the world

104 Which man was Emerald's suitor in the novel 'Midnight's Children'?
(a) Mian Abdullah
(b) Nadir Khan
(c) Ahmed sinai
(d) General Zulfikar

105 What was Mian Abdullah's nickname in the novel 'Midnight's Children'?
(a) Hummingbird (b) Bluebird
(c) Blackbird (d) Songbird

106 Salman Rushdie is a British-Indian author who has won numerous awards including the Booker Prize for Fiction and the Whitbread Novel Award. Which of his books caused Ayatollah Khomeini, the then leader of Iran, to pronounce a fatwa (death sentence) on him?
(a) Midnight's Children
(b) Shalimaar the Clown
(c) The Satanic Verses
(d) The Moor's Last Sigh

107 For which of the following books, Salman Rushdie won the Booker Prize?
(a) Satanic Verses
(b) Midnight's Children
(c) Fury
(d) Shalimaar the Clown

108 Who was Mumtaz's first husband in the novel 'Midnight's Children'?
(a) Nadir Khan (b) Ahmed Sinai
(c) Mian Abdullah (d) Aadam Aziz

109 What name did Ahmed choose for his new wife in the novel 'Midnight's Children'?
(a) Mumtaz (b) Mary
(c) Amina (d) Emerald

110 What terrorist organisation burns down Muslim warehouses in the novel 'Midnight's Children'?
(a) Vishnu (b) Ravana
(c) Shiva (d) Ganesh

111 Who does Amina save from a racist riot in the novel 'Midnight's Children'?
(a) Picture Singh (b) Lafifas Das
(c) Ramram Seth (d) Homi Catrack

112 Who owns the home where the Sinais live in the novel 'Midnight's Children'?
(a) Ibrahim Ibrahim
(b) Wee Willie Winkie
(c) William Methwold
(d) Commander Sabermati

113 What two body parts are significant in Ramram's prophesy in the novel 'Midnight's Children'?
(a) Fingers and toes
(b) Head and shoulders
(c) Eyes and ears
(d) Nose and knees

114 Who among the following writers asserted 'Commonwealth Literature' does not exist?
(a) Amitav Ghosh
(b) Salman Rushdie
(c) VS Naipaul
(d) Nirad Chaudhuri

115 A fatwa was issued in Salman Rushdie's name following the publication of
(a) Midnight's Children
(b) Shame
(c) Satanic Verses
(d) Grimus

116 The literary prize, Booker of Bookers, was awarded to
(a) JM Coetzee
(b) Nadine Gordimer
(c) Martin Amis
(d) Salman Rushdie

117 This author's novels include 'The Hungry Tide', 'The Glass Palace' and 'The Shadow Lines'. He rfused the Eurasian Commonwealth Writers Prize in 2001.
(a) Amitav Ghosh
(b) Suketu Mehra
(c) Vikram Chandra
(d) David Davidar

118 Who is the author of the book 'Shadow Lines'?
(a) Vikram Seth
(b) RK Narayan
(c) Amitav Ghosh
(d) Rohinton Mistry

119 Name this Indo-Canadian writer who has won the Commonwealth Writers Prize twice for 'Such A Long Journey' (1992) and 'A Fine Balance' (1996).
(a) Rohinton Mistry
(b) Kiran Nagarkar
(c) Bapsi Sidhwa
(d) Chitra Bannerjee

120 Name the Indo-English novelist who wrote 'A Suitable Boy'.
(a) Vikram Seth (b) Amitav Ghosh
(c) Upamanyu Chatterjee (d) Anita Desai

121 Who is the author of The Golden Gate?
(a) Shashi Deshpande
(b) Githa Hariharan
(c) Vikram Seth
(d) Siddhartha Dhanwant Sanghvi

122 Shashi Tharoor was in the news when he campaigned to succeed Kofi Annan as the Secretary-General of the United Nations. However, he lost to Ban Ki-moon of South Korea. Which of the following is not a book written by him?
(a) The Great Indian Novel
(b) The Argumentative Indian
(c) Show Business
(d) Riot

123 Identify the verse novel from the following.
(a) Ulysses (b) Golden Gate
(c) Music for Mohini (d) None of these

124 Which among the following is not written by 'Vikram Seth'?
(a) The Golden Gate
(b) Three Chinese Poets
(c) Love Shuffles the Cards
(d) All You Who Sleep Tonight

125 Mistry was from a Parsi Background. He was well aware with the themes like exile, expatriate and sense of being away. Choose among the following which is not written by him?
(a) Such a Long Journey
(b) Swimming Lessons and Other Stories from Firozsha Baag
(c) Rotten English
(d) The Great Indian Novel

126 From the following list, pick out a woman, character, who does not belong to Amitav Ghosh's novels
(a) Ila (b) Urvashi
(c) Sonali (d) Piyali

127 "13th December, a Reader : The Stranger Case of the Attack on the Indian Parliament", is written by
(a) Aundhati Roy (b) Anita Desai
(c) Amrita Pritam (d) Amitav Ghosh

128 Which of the following awards is not given to Indian-English writers?
(a) Th Booker Prize
(b) The Sahitya Akademi Award
(c) Th Gyanpeeth Award
(d) Whitbread Prize

129 In which Year The New York Times Cited Bhagat As 'The Biggest Selling English Language Novelist in India's History'?
(a) 2009 (b) 2010
(c) 2008 (d) 2011

130 "There are times in life you wish dinosaurs weren't extinct and could be whistled to come and gulp you down. I went motionless, fingers in mid-air."

In which of Chetan Bhagat's novels are the above mentioned mood and sentiments expressed?

(a) Five Point Someone.
(b) Half Girlfriend
(c) 2 States : The Story of My Marriage
(d) One Night @ the Call Center

131 Rabindranath Tagore got Nobel Prize for ......

(a) The Ascetic (b) Chitra
(c) Gitanjali (d) The Cycle of Spring

132 ...... among the following is not the work of Ramanujan?

(a) The Striders (b) Mrinalini
(c) Speaking of Siva (d) The Interior Landscape

133 Khushwant Singh earned reputation as a ...... and ......

(a) essayist and writer
(b) writer and journalist
(c) journalist and essayist
(d) journalist and composer

134 ...... among the following is not a work by Pritish Nandy.

(a) On Either Sides of Arrogance
(b) In Secret Anarchy
(c) Poet, Lover, Birdwatcher
(d) From the Outer Bank of the Brahmaputra

135 Salman Rushdie was awarded with the ...... in 1993.

(a) Booker's Prize
(b) Padma Shree
(c) Novel Prize
(d) Booker of Bookers Prize

136 'Indian Philosophy'. 'The Hindu View of Life and Eastern Religious and Western Thoughts' are composed by

(a) Sarvapalli Radhakrishanan
(b) Rabindranath Tagore
(c) Shashi Tharoor
(d) Nissim Ezekiel

137 Untouchable is a creation of

(a) Tagore
(b) Bankim Chandra Chatterjee
(c) Mulk Raj Anand
(d) Prem Chand

138 .... among the following is known for bringing the cultural Revolt?

(a) Rabindranath Tagore
(b) Mulk Raj Anand
(c) Bankim Chandra Chatterjee
(d) Prem Chand

139 'I shall not hear the Nightingale' was published in ......

(a) 1959 (b) 1943 (c) 1976 (d) 1974

140 'The Next Rung', 'Murugan', 'The Tiller and Kandam', 'The Patriot' are the famous works of ......

(a) Shankar Ram (b) K Subba Rao
(c) R K Narayana (d) KS Venkatramani

141 A poem 'The Angle of Misfortune' of about 5000 lines,written by Nagesh Vishwanath Pai. It describes the story of ....

(a) Kamadev (b) King Vikramaditya
(c) Savitri (d) None of these

142 'The Lake of Palms', 'A history of Civilisation of Ancient India', 'The Slave – Girl of Agra' are the famous works of ....

(a) Ramesh Chunder Dutt
(b) Salman Rushdie
(c) Toru Dutt
(d) Hassan Ali

143 'Distant Drums', 'Devil's Wind', 'The Princess'. 'A Combat of Shadows', are the famous works of ....

(a) Salman Rushdie
(b) Manohar Malgonkar
(c) Mulk Raj Anand
(d) Toru Dutt

144 Ramesh Chunder Dutt, Aurobindo Ghosh, Toru Dutt, all wrote on a common theme taken out from the 'Mahabharatha'. The story is based on ......

(a) Nal-Damyanti (b) Savitri
(c) Gandhari (d) None of these

145 'Jejuri', The Commonwealth Poetry Prize Winner work has been written by ....

(a) Arun Kolatkar (b) Anita Desai
(c) A K Ramanujan (d) Kamala Das

146 'The Apprentice', 'The Foreigner', 'The Last Labyrinth', 'The City and the River' are the famous works of

(a) Arun Joshi (b) Dom Moraes
(c) Anita Desai (d) None of these

147 What is common to the following writers? Identify the correct description below.

"A .... of .... is a joy forever."

John Keats, (Endymion.)

(a) Subject, praise (b) Thing, beauty
(c) Nature, sublimity (d) Concept, beauty

148 'The Mimic Men' by V S Naipaul is all about

(a) an expatriate
(b) an exiled Roman King
(c) an Indian living in Trinidad
(d) an exiled Caribbean politician

149 'Love of Dust' is the famous work of

(a) Ruth P Jhabvala (b) Humayun Kabir
(c) Shanker Ram (d) K S Venkataramani

150 Silence ! The Court is in Session is a ...... play translated into English.

(a) Gujarati (b) Bengali (c) Marathi (d) Kannada

151 Examine the following statements and identify one of them which is not correct?

(a) Rudyard Kipling died in the year 1936
(b) He was born in India, but schooled in England
(c) He returned to India as a police constable in Burma
(d) He is the author of Jungle Book and Barrack Room Ballads

152 Which among the following is not correct for Rabindranath Tagore?

(a) The British King George V awarded him Knighthood
(b) He was known as Gurudev
(c) The songs he wrote were selected as National Anthems of India and Bangladesh
(d) After Jallianwala Bagh Massacre he rejected his Knighthood

153 Which of the following statements is not true for Arundhati Roy?

(a) Here full name is Suzanna Arundhati Roy
(b) She is very close to her father who is a Bengali Hindu.
(c) Her first novel is 'The God of Small Things'
(d) She won the Booker Prize for her first novel

154 Which of the following is not correct for Sarojini Naidu?

(a) Her outlook was casual in nature.
(b) She was elected the President of the Indian National Congress in 1925.
(c) She helped in Founding the All India Women's Conference in 1927.
(d) She was called the Nightingale of India.

155 Which of the following statements is not correct for Swami Vivekanand?

(a) His childhood name was Vishweshwar Dutt
(b) He founded Ram Krishna Mission
(c) He was a critic of doctrines of Buddhism
(d) He believed in the philosophy of 'Advaitvad'

156 Which of the following pairs is incorrectly matched?

(a) Michael Madhusudan : The Captive Lady
(b) Manohar Malgonkar : The Crown
(c) Vijay Tendulkar : Ghashiram Kotwal
(d) Anita Desai : The Inheritance of Loss

157 Which of the following pairs is correctly matched?

(a) Jayanta Mahapatra : The Shadow Lines
(b) Kiran Desai : The Inheritance of Lose
(c) Amitav Ghosh : Life Signs
(d) Arun Kolatkar : Jejuri

158 Which of the following pairs is incorrectly matched?

(a) TP Kailasam : Kapalkundala
(b) Ramesh Chunder Dutt : The Baiden
(c) Rohinton Mistry : Such a Long Journey
(d) Bankim Chandra Chatterjee : The Lake of Palms

159 Which of the following pairs is correctly matched?

(a) Amitav Ghosh : All About H Hatterr
(b) Anita Desai : Inheritance of Loss
(c) Shashi Deshpande : A Bend in the Ganges
(d) Salman Rushdie : The Enchantress of Florence

160 Which of the following pairs is incorrectly matched?

(a) Roots and Shadows : 1983
(b) The Mimic Men : 1867
(c) Swami and Friends : 1935
(d) Kala Gulab : 1968

Directions [Q. Nos. 161-165] *In the questions given below are two statements labelled as Assertion (A) and Reason (R). In the context of these two statements, which one of the following is correct?*

Codes

(a) Both A and R are true and R is the correct explanation of A
(b) Both A and R are true, but R is not the correct explanation of A
(c) A is true, but R is false
(d) A is false, but R is true

161 **Assertion** (A) Language plays a very pivotal role in human life.

Reason (R) It is the medium through which views are conveyed from one person to another.

162 **Assertion** (A) Modern Indian literature has been greatly influenced by English Literature.

Reason (R) English has become an important element of contemporary Indian culture.

163 **Assertion** (A) Raja Ram Mohan Roy initiated movements to introduce western scientific education through English.

Reason (R) Lord macaulay was the chairman of the committee which was formed to take a decision regarding replacement of Sanskrit and Persian by English.

164 **Assertion** (A) In 1958, The Central Institute of English was started in Hyderabad. Regional institute were established in Bangalore and Chandigarh.

Reason (R) Officialy, English has the status of main (prime) language in India.

165 **Assertion** (A) English as a language was introduced in India after Independence.

Reason (R) The first book written by an Indian in English was 'Travels of Deah Mahomet by dake Dean Mahomet'.

166 Which is the correct sequence of the novels of VS Naipaul?

(a) The Mystic Masseur, Miguel Street, The Suffrage of Elvira, A House for Mr Biswas
(b) Miguel Street, The Mystic Masseur, A House for Mr Biswas, The Suffrage of Elvira
(c) The Suffrage of Elvira, Miguel Street, The Mystic Masseur, A house for Mr. Biswas
(d) The Mystic Masseur, The Suffrage of Elvira, Miguel Street, A House for Mr Biswas

167 Which among the following in the chronological order?

(a) Abu Hassan, Siddhartha, Man of Peace, Kannappan
(b) Abu Hassan, Kannappan, Siddhartha, Man of Peace
(c) Kannappan, Siddhartha, Man of Peace, Abu Hassan
(d) Kannappan, Abu Hassan, Siddhartha, Man of Peace

168 Which of the following is in chronological order?

(a) Anandmath, The Poison Tree, Durgesh Nandini
(b) Durgesh Nandini, Anandmath, The Poison Tree
(c) Durgesh Nandini, The Poison Tree, Anandmath
(d) The Poison Tree, Durgesh Nandini, Anandmath

169 Which of the following is the correct sequence of their birth?

(a) Sri Aurobindo, Kamala Das, H N Chattopadhaya
(b) Kamala Das, Sri Aurobindo, H N Chattopadhaya
(c) H N Chattopadhaya, Kamala Das, Sri Aurobindo
(d) Sri Aurobindo, H N Chattopadhaya, Kamala Das

170 Which of the following Anita Desai's works is in correct chronological order?

(a) Cry the Peacock, Voices in the City, Bye-Bye Black Bird, In Custody
(b) Voices in the City, Bye-Bye Black Bird, In Custody, Cry the Peacock
(c) Bye-Bye Black Bird, In Custody, Cry the Peacock, Voices in the City
(d) In Custody, Cry the Peacock, Voices in the City, Bye-Bye Black Bird

171 Consider the following statements about Rabindranath Tagore

1. was called Gurudev by Mahatma Gandhi.
2. founded the Viswabharati University.
3. rejected the title of Knighthood in protest against Quit India Movement.
4. was not a poet.

Which of the the statements given above are correct?

(a) 1 and 2 (b) 1 and 4
(c) 3 and 2 (d) 3 and 4

172 Consider the following statement about Sarojini Naidu

1. was called the Nightingale of India.
2. was not a poet, who wrote on different aspects of Indian life.
3. was not in touch with Symons and Edmund Gosse while in England.
4. was a poet and a great lyric writer, who emoted through her poem.

Which of the statements given above are correct?

(a) 1 and 2 (b) 1 and 4
(c) 3 and 2 (d) 3 and 4

173 Consider the following satements about Khushwant Singh

1. did not write political commentary and contemporary satire.
2. did not translate Urdu poetry.
3. column contains message of peace.
4. was elected a member of the Rajya Sabha.

Which of the statements given above are correct?

(a) 1 and 2 (b) 1 and 4
(c) 3 and 2 (d) 3 and 4

174 Consider the following statements about Ruskin Bond

1. was the managing editor of Imprint in Bombay.
2. the Room on the roof was not translated into German.
3. he did not received the Padma Sri Award.
4. he won the John Liewellyn Rhys Prize.

Which of the statements given above is / are correct?

(a) 1 and 2 (b) 1 and 4
(c) 3 and 2 (d) 3 and 4

175 Given below are some of the famous works Tick the one which is not written by Salman Rushdie.

1. The Enchantress of Florence.
2. The Ground Beneath her Feet.
3. Midnight's Children.
4. Nehru : The Invention of India.

Select the correct answer using the codes given below

(a) 1 and 2 (b) Only 4
(c) Only 3 (d) Only 1

176 Consider the following statements.

1. Upamanyu Chatterjee was born in Patna.
2. He graduated in Delhi.
3. He is known for his satirical work.
4. He wrote 'India; A Million Mutinies Now'.

Which of the following statements given above is/are correct?

(a) 1 and 2 (b) Only 3
(c) Only 4 (d) None of these

177 Consider the following statements.

1. R K Narayan was born in Delhi.
2. The Dark Room was published in 1938.
3. R K Narayan got Padma Bhushan in 1964.

Which of the statements given above is/are incorrect?

(a) Only 1 (b) Only 2
(c) 1 and 2 (d) None of these

178 Consider the following statements Raja Rao ...

1. did not come into content with professor Dickinson.
2. did not go to France to study French literature.
3. wrote the novel 'Kanthapura'.
4. was a great philosopher and novelist.

Which of the statements given above are correct?

(a) 1 and 2 (b) 1 and 4
(c) 3 and 2 (d) 3 and 4

179 Consider the following statements Anita Desai

1. always tries to explore the psychological state of her characters.
2. uses symbols and images to describe the suffering of the mind.
3. is not affected by demestic men and woman relationship.
4. thinks that the outer life of man or woman decides his or her character.

Which of the statements given above are correct?

(a) 1 and 2 (b) 1 and 4
(c) 3 and 2 (d) 3 and 4

180 The label 'Diasporic Writer' can be applied to

1. Meena Alexander
2. Arundhati Roy
3. Kiran Desai
4. Shashi Deshpande

Select the correct answer using the codes given below

(a) 1 and 4 (b) 2 and 3
(c) 1, 2 and 4 (d) 1 and 3

181 What is common to the following works? Identify to correct description below.

The Circle of Reason

The Shadow Lines

The Calcutta Chromosome

In an Antique Land

Codes

(a) All these are works by Amitav Ghosh
(b) All these are works by Khushwant Singh
(c) All these are works by Amrita Pritam
(d) All these are works by Shashi Deshpande

182 What is common to the following works? Identify of correct description below.

Malgudi Days,

The Swami and Friends,

The Dark Room, The Guide.

Codes

(a) All these are works by RK Narayan
(b) All these are works by Shashi Deshpande
(c) All these are works by Mulk Raj Anand
(d) All these are works by Raja Rao

183 What is common to the following writers? Identify to correct description below.

The Mystic Masseur Miguel Street

A house for Mr Biswas

The Mimic Men

Codes

(a) All these are works by VS Naipaul
(b) All these are works by RK Narayan
(c) All these have been written by Amitav Ghosh
(d) All these have been written by Pritish Nandy

184 What is common to the following writer? Identify the correct description below.

Jayati
Hayavadana

Tughlaq
Naga Mandal

Codes

(a) All these are plays by Arun Joshi
(b) All these are names of famous folk tales of Karnataka
(c) All these are famous plays of Karnad Girish
(d) All these are characters from contemporary Kannada literature

185 What is common to the following writers? Identify to correct description below.

1. Ruskin Bond 2. RK Narayan
3. Mulk Raj Anand 4. Shashi Deshpande

Codes

(a) They were all awarded the Sahitya Akademi Award
(b) They have all written in Orriya a language
(c) They are all author of Dality literature
(d) They have all written under proudonyms

186 Which of the following is not written by Sri Aurobindo?

1. The Frog and the Nightingale.
2. The Maid in the Mill.
3. The Birth of the Sin.

Select the correct answer using the codes given below.

(a) Only 2 (b) Only 1
(c) Only 3 (d) None of these

187 Who among the following got the Sahitya Akademy Award (1958)?

1. Sarojini Naidu 2. Rabindranath Tagore
3. RK Narayan

Select the correct answer using the codes given below

(a) Only 1 (b) Only 2 (c) 1 and 2 (d) Only 3

188 Which among the following is not a work by Anita Desai?

1. Cry the Peacock 2. Fire on the Mountain
3. God of Small Things

Select the correct answer using the codes given below.

(a) Only 1 (b) Only 2
(c) Only 3 (d) None of these

189 Consider the following works.

1. The Cow of Barricades
2. The Cat and Shakespeare
3. The Suicide
4. The Maggots

Which of the above works belongs to Raja Ras/Rao?

(a) 1 and 2 (b) Only 2 (c) 2 and 4 (d) 1 and 3

190 Consider the following works.

1. The Serpent
2. Alphabet of Lust
3. The Dance of Eunuchs
4. The Rose

Which of the above works belong/s to Kamala Das?

Codes

(a) 1 and 2 (b) 2 and 4
(c) 2 and 3 (d) Only 3

191 Match the following Indian English poets with their poetic works

Indian English Poet	Poetic Work
1. Rabindranath Tagore	A. Gitanjali
2. Sarojini Naidu	B. Indian Weavers
3. Amrita Pritam	C. Immoral Waves
4. Toru Dutt	D. Our Casuarina Tree

Codes

(a) 1-A, 2-B, 3-C, 4-D
(b) 1-D, 2-C, 3-B, 4-A
(c) 1-B, 2-D, 3-A, 4-C
(d) 1-C, 2-A, 3-D, 4-B

192 Match the following Indian English works with their Indian authors

Indian English Work	Indian Author
1. Relationship	A. Khushwant Singh
2. A Sangam City	B. Kamala Das
3. Inheritance of Loss	C. Jayant Mahapatra
4. A rain of Rites	D. Kiran Desai

Codes

(a) 1-A, 2-B, 3-C, 4-D
(b) 1-B, 2-A, 3-D, 4-C
(c) 1-C, 2-D, 3-A, 4-B
(d) 1-D, 2-C, 3-B, 4-A

193 Match the following awards with their recipient Indian Writers.

Awards	Recipient Indian Writer
1. Padma Shri	A. A K Ramanujan
2. Padma Shree	B. Kiran Desai
3. Fiction Award	C. Jayant Mahapatra
4. Asian PEN Anthology Award	D. Kamala Das

Codes

(a) 1-A, 2-B, 3-C, 4-D
(b) 1-D, 2-C, 3-B, 4-A
(c) 1-A, 2-C, 3-B, 4-D
(d) 1-C, 2-A, 3-D, 4-D

194 Match the following Indian English works with the year of their publication.

Indian English Work	The year of Publication
1. A House for Mr Biswas	A. 1971
2. Mr Stone and the Knight Companion	B. 1964
3. An Area of Darkness	C. 1963
4. In a Free State	D. 1961

Codes

(a) 1-A, 2-B, 3-C, 4-D
(b) 1-B, 2-D, 3-A,4-C
(c) 1-C, 2-A, 3-D, 4-B
(d) 1-D, 2-C, 3-B, 4-A

195 Match the following Indian English writers with their works

Indian English Writers	Literary Work
1. HN Chattopadhyaya	A. The Coffin
2. Arundhati Roy	B. The Algebra of Indefinite Justice
3. Anita Desai	C. Fire on the Mountain
4. Amitav Ghosh	D. The Incendiary Circumstances

Codes

(a) 1-A, 2-B, 3-C, 4-D (b) 1-D, 2-C, 3-B, 4-A
(c) 1-B, 2-D, 3-A, 4-C (d) 1-C, 2-A, 3-D, 4-B

196 Match the following.

	List I		List II
A.	KB Vaid	1.	Says Tuka
B.	OV Vijayan	2.	The Diary of a Maid Servant
C.	Dilip Chitre	3.	Samskara
D.	AK Ramanujan	4.	Saga of Dharmapuri

Codes

	A	B	C	D		A	B	C	D
(a)	4	1	2	3	(b)	3	2	1	4
(c)	2	4	1	3	(d)	1	2	3	4

197 Match the following.

	List I		List II
A.	Amitav Ghosh	1.	Cry the Peacock
B.	Amrita Pritam	2.	God of Small Things
C.	Anita Desai	3.	Kagaj te Canvas
D.	Arundhati Roy	4.	The Circle of Reason

Codes

	A	B	C	D		A	B	C	D
(a)	1	2	3	4	(b)	4	3	2	1
(c)	4	3	1	2	(d)	2	3	1	4

198 Match the following.

	List I		List II
A.	A K Ramanujan	1.	The Striders
B.	Bankim Chandra Chatterjee	2.	Durgesh Nandini
C.	Girish Kanad	3.	Yayati
D.	H N Chattopadhaya	4.	Abu Hassan

Codes

	A	B	C	D		A	B	C	D
(a)	4	3	1	2	(b)	2	3	4	1
(c)	3	4	2	1	(d)	1	2	3	4

199 Mach the following.

	List I		List II
A.	The Interior Landscape	1.	1927
B.	Mrinalini	2.	1869
C.	Anandmath	3.	1866
D.	His Poems and Plays	4.	1967

Codes

	A	B	C	D		A	B	C	D
(a)	1	2	3	4	(b)	4	2	1	3
(c)	4	3	2	1	(d)	4	1	3	2

200 Match the following.

	List I		List II
A.	A River	1.	Arundhati Roy
B.	The Cost of Living	2.	A K Ramanujan
C.	The Two Rings	3.	H N Chattopadhaya
D.	The Parrot	4.	Bankim Chandra Chatterjee

Codes

	A	B	C	D
(a)	2	1	4	3
(b)	2	1	3	4
(c)	3	4	1	2
(d)	3	1	2	4

201 Match the following.

	List I		List II
A.	Chandigarh	1.	Kamala Das
B.	Cuttak	2.	Kiran Desai
C.	Peshawar	3.	Jayant Mahapatra
D.	Kerala	4.	Mulk Raj Anand

Codes

	A	B	C	D
(a)	2	3	4	1
(b)	1	2	3	4
(c)	4	3	1	2
(d)	4	1	2	3

202 Match the following.

	List I		List II
A.	Kerala Sahitya Academy	1.	A K Ramanujan
B.	Man Booker Prize	2.	Jayant Mahapatra
C.	Sahitya Academy Award	3.	Kiran Desai
D.	MacArthur Prize Fellowship	4.	Kamala Das

Codes

	A	B	C	D		A	B	C	D
(a)	4	2	1	3	(b)	4	3	2	1
(c)	1	2	3	4	(d)	3	4	1	2

203 Match the following.

	List I		List II
A.	Untouchable	1.	Mulk Raj Anand
B.	Kantapura	2.	Nissim Ezekiel
C.	Collected Poems and Plays	3.	Rabindranath Tagore
D.	Song of Deprivation	4.	Raja Rao

Codes

	A	B	C	D		A	B	C	D
(a)	1	2	3	4	(b)	4	3	2	1
(c)	1	4	2	3	(d)	1	4	3	2

204 Match the following.

	List I		List II
A.	Shobha De	1.	House for Mr Biswas
B.	Shashi Tharoor	2.	The Five Dollar Smile
C.	TP Kailasam	3.	Small Betrayels
D.	V S Naipaul	4.	The Brahmin's Curse

Codes

	A	B	C	D		A	B	C	D
(a)	1	2	3	4	(b)	3	4	2	1
(c)	2	3	4	1	(d)	3	2	4	1

205 Match the following.

List I	List II
A. Jewish Background	1. Mulk Raj Anand
B. Nobel Prize Winner	2. Tagore
C. Padma Shree Award	3. Raja Rao
D. Studied in Cambridge University	4. Nissim Ezekiel

Codes

	A	B	C	D		A	B	C	D
(a)	4	2	3	1	(b)	4	1	2	3
(c)	4	1	3	2	(d)	1	2	3	4

206 In the given series, which one has all the religious texts matched correctly with their Indian English Composers?

(a) The Ramayana–AK Ramanujan, The Bhagvad Gita-Manmathanath Dutt, The Mahabharata-Mohini Chatterjee, Speaking of Shiva-Romesh Chander Dutt

(b) The Ramayana-Romesh Chander Dutt, The Bhagwat Gita-Mohini Chatterjee, The Mahabharata-Manmathanath Dutt, Speaking of Shiva-AK Ramanujan.

(c) The Ramayana-Mohini Chatterjee, The Bhagwat Gita- AK Ramanujan, The Mahashtra-Romesh Chander Dutt, Speaking of Shiva-Manmathanath Dutt

(d) The Ramyana-Manmathanath Dutt, The Mahashtra-Romesh Chander Dutt, The Bhagwat Gita-AK Ramanujan, Speaking of Shiva-Mohini Chatterjee

207 In the given series, which one has all the literary awards/institution matched correctly with the year of their beginning?

(a) Kerala Sahitya Academy-1969, Man Booker Prize-1971, Sahitya Academy Award-1981, Mac Arthur Prize Fellowship-1983

(b) Kerala Sahitya Academy-1983, Man Booker Prize-1981, Sahitya Academy Award-1971, Mac Arthur Prize Fellowship-1969.

(c) Kerala Sahitya Academy-1971, Man Booker Prize-1983, Sahitya Academy Award-1969, Mac Arthur Prize Fellowship-1981

(d) Kerala Sahitya Academy-1981, Man Booker Prize-1969, Sahitya Academy Award-1983, Mac Arthur Prize Fellowship-1971

208 In the given series, which one has all the Indian English authors matched correctly with their mood and style of writing?

(a) VS Naipaul-Memoirist, Vikram Seth-Elizabethan Style, Sri Aurobindo-Pessimistic, TP Kailsam-Humorous Plays

(b) VS Naipaul-Humorous Plays, Vikram Seth-Pessimistic, Sri Aurobindo-Elizabethan Style, TP Kailsam-Memoirist

(c) VS Naipaul-Pessimistic, Vikram Seth-Memoirist, Sri Aurobindo-Elizabethan Style, TP Kailsam-Humorous Plays

(d) VS Naipaul-Elizabethan Style, Vikram Seth-Humorous Plays, Sri Aurobindo-Memoirist, TP Kailsam-Pessimistic

209 In the given series, which one has all the works matched correctly with the year of their publication?

(a) The English Teacher-1935, Swami and Friends-1938, The Guide-1945, The Dark Room-1958.

(b) The English Teacher-1958, Swami and Friends-1945, The Guide-1938, The Dark Room-1935.

(c) The English Teacher-1938, Swami and Friends-1958, The Guide-1935, The Dark Room-1945.

(d) The English Teacher-1945, Swami and Friends-1935, The Guide-1958, The Dark Room-1938.

210 In the given series, which one has all the Indian English writers matched correctly with their works?

(a) Pritish Nandy-Chitra and Sacrifice, Jayant Mahapatra-Father's Hours, Kiran Desai-Hullabaloo in the Guava Orchard, Kamala Das-Love

(b) Pritish Nandy-Love, Jayant Mahapatra-Hullabaloo in the Guava Orchard, Kiran Desai-Father's Hours, Kamala Das-Chitra and Sacrifice

(c) Pritish Nandy-Father's Hours, Jayant Mahapatra-Love, Kiran Desai-Chitra and Sacrifice, Kamala Das-Hullabaloo in the Guava Orchard

(d) Pritish Nandy-Hullabaloo in the Guava Orchard, Jayant Mahapatra-Chitra and Sacrifice, Kiran Desai-Love, Kamala Das-Father's Hours

211 "Clouds come floating into my life, no longer to carry rain or usher storm, but to add colour to my sunset sky."

Which of the Indian writers in which of his/her works has quoted the above lines?

(a) Rabindranath Tagore, Stray Birds
(b) Arundhati Roy, The God of Small Things
(c) Swami Vivekananda, Letters of Swami Vivekananda
(d) Raja Rao, The Cat and Shakespeare

212 "Where the mind is without fear

And the head in held high

where knowledge is free

Where the world has not been broken into fragments by narrow domestic walls."

(a) This is Amrita Pritam in 'Kat Canvas'
(b) This is Rabindranath Tagore in 'Gitanjali'
(c) This is Vikram Seth in 'The Golden Gate'
(d) This is Jayanta Mahapatra in 'Life Signs'

213 "All love is expansion, all selfishness is contraction. Love is therefore the only law of life. He who loves lives, he who is selfish is dying. Therefore love for love's sake, because it is the only law of life, just as you breathe to live."

Which of the Indian writers in which of his/her works has quoted the above lines?

(a) Rabindranath Tagore, Stray Birds
(b) Arundhati Roy, The God of Small Things
(c) Swami Vivekananda, Letters of Swami Vivekananda
(d) Raja Rao, The Cat and Shakespeare

214 **"Was there ever a more horrible blasphemy than the statement that all the knowledge of God is confined to this or that book? How dare men call God infinite, and yet try to compress Him within the covers of a little book!"**

Which of the Indian writers in which of his/her works has quoted the above lines?
(a) Swami Vivekananda, Raja-Yoga
(b) Raja Rao, Kanthapura
(c) Kamala Das, The Descendants
(d) Kamala Suraiyya Das, Wages of Love

215 **"All the life of the tiny figure seemed to concentrate itself in the eyes, they turned towards beauty as the Sunflower turns towards the Sun."**

Identify the person referred here by Arthur Miller.
(a) Aru Dutt (b) Sarojini Naidu
(c) Anita Desai (d) R K Narayan

216 **"Bangle sellers are we, who bear our shining load to, the temple fair, who will buy these delicate, bright rainbow tinted cricles of light? Lusteous token of radiant lives".**
(a) This is Nissim Ezekiel in Night of the scorpion
(b) This is Sarojini Naidu in Bangle Sellers
(c) This is Jayanta Mahapatra in 'Dispossessed Nests'
(d) This is Arun Kolatkar in 'Jejuri'

217 **"Would readily take them as the work of an English poet trained in the classical tradition." Identify the poet about whom George Sampson said these lines?**
(a) Dom Moraes
(b) Manohar Ghosh
(c) Toru Dutt
(d) VS Naipaul

218 **Paying a tribute to a Bengali poet, who wrote in English also, Sri Aurobindo said, "The God himself took up thy pen and wrote." Who was he?**
(a) Henry Derozio (b) Michael Madhusudan
(c) Hassan Ali (d) None of these

219 **"What the mysterious is I do not know. I do not call it God because God has come to mean much that I do not believe in. I find myself incapable of thinking of a deity or of any unknown supreme power in anthropomorphic terms, and the fact that many people think so is continually a source of surprise to me. Any idea of a personal God seems very odd to me."**

Which Indian English author in which of his/her works has used the above lines?
(a) Kamala Das, The Descendants
(b) Anita Desai, Baumgartner's Bombay
(c) Mulk Raj Anand, Untouchable
(d) Jawaharlal Nehru, An Autobiography: Toward Freedom

220 **"The best and noblest gifts of humanity cannot be the monopoly of a particular race or country; its scope may not be limited nor may it be regarded as the miser's hoard buried underground."**

Which Indian English author in which of his/her works has used the above lines?
(a) Anita Desai, Fasting and Feasting
(b) Jawaharlal Nehru, The Descovery of India
(c) Kiran Desai, The Inheritance of Loss
(d) Mulk Raj Anand, Untouchable

221 **"How queer, the Hindus don't feed their cows although they call the cow 'mother'! Bakha thought."**

Which Indian English author in which of his/her works has used the above lines?
(a) Kamala Das, The Descendants
(b) Anita Desai, Baumgartner's Bombay
(c) Mulk Raj Anand, Untouchable
(d) Jawaharlal Nehru, An Autobiography: Toward Freedom

222 **"Gauri is my tribute to my Indian Womanhood."** *In which novel does Mulk Raj Anand depict Gauri?*
(a) The Old Woman and the Cow
(b) Untouchable
(c) Savitri
(d) The Road

223 **"Gandhiji was not born in freedom. All his life, except for a few months. lay within the framework of colonial rule. A good part of that life lay buried in prison cells. Yet he was always the free man, while those who held him imprisoned were the unfree ones."**

Which Indian writers in which of his/her works has quoted the above lines?
(a) Khushwant Singh, The End of India
(b) Salman Rushdie, The Satanic Verses
(c) Bhabani Bhattacharya, Shadow from Ladakh
(d) Ruskin Bond, Scenes From a Writer's Life

224 **"Friendship was another illusion like love, though it did not reach the same mad heights. People pretended that they were friends, when the fact was they were brought together by force of circumstances."**

Which of the Indian writers in which of his/her works has quoted the above lines?

(a) Anita Desai, Fasting, Feasting
(b) Khushwant Singh, Train to Pakistan
(c) VS Naipaul, A Bend in the River
(d) RK Narayan, The Bachelor of Arts

225 "He then explained his new philosophy, which followed the devasting discovery that Love and Friendship were the veriest illusions. He explained that people married because their sexual appetite had to be satisfied and there must be somebody to manage the house. There was nothing deeper than that in any man and woman relationship."

Which of the Indian writers in which of his/her works has quoted the above lines?

(a) Anita Desai, Fire on the Mountain
(b) Khushwant Singh, Delhi: A Novel
(c) VS Naipaul, Miguel Street
(d) RK Narayan, The English Teacher

226 "It is stimulating to live in a society that is not standardised or mechanised, and is free from monotony."

Which of the Indian writers in which of his/her works has quoted the above lines?

(a) Anita Desai, The Village by the Sea
(b) Khushwant Singh, Khushwant Singh on Women, Sex, Love and Lust
(c) RK Narayan, Malgudi Days
(d) Vijay Tendulkar, The Court is in Session

227 "Fortunately there are wars. And rationing is one of the grandest inventions of man. You stamp paper with figures and you feed stomachs on numbers."

Which of the Indian writers in which of his/her works has quoted the above lines?

(a) Rabindranath Tagore, Stray Birds
(b) Arundhati Roy, The God of Small Things
(c) Swami Vivekananda, Letters of Swami Vivekananda
(d) Raja Rao, The Cat and Shakespeare

228 "There is but one force in life and that is Truth, and there is but one love in life and that is love of mankind, and there is but one God in life and that is the God of all."

Which of the Indian writers in which of his/her works has quoted the above lines?

(a) Swami Vivekananda, Raja-Yoga
(b) Raja Rao, Kanthapura
(c) Kamala Das, The Descendants
(d) Kamala Suraiyya Das, Wages of Love

229 "Not forever does the bulbul sing
In balmy shades of bowers,
Not forever lasts the spring
Nor ever blossom the flowers.
Not forever reigneth joy,
Sets the sun on days of bliss,
Friendships not forever last,
They know not life, who know not this."

Which of the Indian writers in which of his/her works has quoted the above lines?

(a) Anita Desai, Fasting and Feasting
(b) Khushwant Singh, Train to Pakistan
(c) VS Naipaul, A Bend in the River
(d) RK Narayan, The Bachelor of Arts

230 "I asked my soul: What is Delhi? She replied: The world is the body and Delhi its life. Mirza Asadullah Khan Ghalib."

Which of the Indian writers in which of his/her works has quoted the above lines?

(a) Anita Desai, Fire on the Mountain
(b) Khushwant Singh, Delhi: A Novel
(c) V.S. Naipaul, Miguel Street
(d) R.K. Narayan, The English Teacher

231 "Oh the gladness of her gladness when she's glad, And the sadness of her sadness when she's sad; But the gladness of her gladness, And the sadness of her sadness, Are as nothing, Charles, To the badness of her badness when she is bad."

Which of the Indian writers in which of his/her works has quoted the above lines?

(a) Anita Desai, The Village by the Sea
(b) Khushwant Singh, Khushwant Singh on Women, Sex, Love and Lust
(c) RK Narayan, Malgudi Days
(d) Vijay Tendulkar, The Court is in Session

232 "So many Gods, so many creeds, so many paths that wind and wind. When just the art of being kind is all that the sad world needs?"

Which of the Indian writers in which of his/her works has quoted the above lines?

(a) Khushwant Singh, The End of India
(b) Salman Rushdie, The Satanic Verses
(c) Bhabani Bhattacharya, Shadow from Ladakh
(d) Ruskin Bond, Scenes from a Writer's Life

233 "There are times when one's life appears to be a stage. People come, people go. They come in order to go and go with no intent of return. When they return, they return as one's past. A past that would make you feel that the present is false."

Which of the Indian writers in which of his/her works has quoted the above lines?

(a) Anita Desai, The Village by the Sea
(b) Khushwant Singh, Khushwant Singh on Women, Sex, Love and Lust
(c) RK Narayan, Malgudi Days
(d) Vijay Tendulkar, The Court is in Session

234 "Greenness hangs, drips and sways from every branch and twig and frond in the surging luxuriance of July."

Which of the Indian writers in which of his/her works has quoted the above lines?

(a) Anita Desai, Fasting and Feasting
(b) Khushwant Singh, Train to Pakistan
(c) VS Naipaul, A Bend in the River
(d) RK Narayan, The Bachelor of Arts

235 "At first she mistook them for sheets of pink crepe paper that someone had crumpled and carelessly flung down the hillside, perhaps after another astonishing party at the club. A moment later she remembered her great-grandmother's words and saw that they were hosts of wild pink zephyranthes that had come up in the night after the first fall of rain."

Which of the Indian writers in which of his/her works has quoted the above lines?

(a) Anita Desai, Fire on the Mountain
(b) Khushwant Singh, Delhi: A Novel
(c) VS Naipaul, Miguel Street
(d) RK Narayan, The English Teacher

236 "The wheel turns and turns and turns: it never stops and stands still."

Which of the Indian writers in which of his/her works has quoted the above lines?

(a) Anita Desai, The Village by the Sea
(b) Khushwant Singh, Khushwant Singh on Women, Sex, Love and Lust
(c) RK Narayan, Malgudi Days
(d) Vijay Tendulkar, The Court is in Session

237 "...People stop, stare. No one stop and stare if one of your own beggars drop dead in street. No just step over him like he is a stone, or a dog turd and go away quickly. But when they see a white man with golden hair lying on the street, everyone stop, everyone cry, "Hai-hai, -poor boy, call doctor, call ambulance. What has happen, Farrokh-bhai?"..."

- Farrokh said to Baumgartner when he wanted to get rid of the reluctant, overly druggd homeless foreigner out of his restaurant."

Which Indian writers in which of his/her works has used the above lines?

(a) Kamala Das, The Descendants
(b) Anita Desai, Baumgartner's Bombay
(c) Mulk Raj Anand, Untouchable
(d) Jawaharlal Nehru, An Autobiography: Toward Freedom

238 "The room rang with her voice, then with silence. In the shaded darkness, silence had the quality of a looming dragon. It seemed to roar and the roar to reverberate, to dominate. To escape from it would require a burst of recklessness, even cruelty."

Which Indian English author in which of his/her works has used the above lines?

(a) Anita Desai, Clear Light of Day
(b) Kiran Desai, Hullabaloo in the Guava Orchard
(c) Kamala Das, The Descendants
(d) Mulk Raj Anand, Untouchable

239 "It was as if the curtains came down on all this, if not entirely obliterated it, when the monsoon rose up in the thunderous clouds from the parched valley below to engulf the hills, invade them with the opaque mist in which a pine tree or a mountain top appeared only intermittently, and then unleashed a downpour that brought Ravi's rambling to a halt and confined him to the house for days at a time, deafened by the rain drumming on the rooftop and cascading down the gutters and through the spouts to rush downhill in torrents."

Which Indian English author in which of his/her works has used the above lines?

(a) Kiran Desai, Hullabaloo in the Guava Orchard
(b) Kamala Das, The Descendants
(c) Mulk Raj Anand, Untouchable
(d) Anita Desai, The Artist of Disappearance

240 "The bougainvillea hung about it, purple and magenta, in livid balloons."

Which Indian English author in which of his/her works has used the above lines?

(a) Kiran Desai, Hullabaloo in the Guava Orchard
(b) Kamala Das, The Descendants
(c) Anita Desai, Games at Twilight
(d) Mulk Raj Anand, Untouchable

241 "The world is what it is; men who are nothing, who allow themselves to become nothing, have no place in it."

Which of the Indian writers in which of his/her works has quoted the above lines?

(a) Anita Desai, Fasting and Feasting
(b) Khushwant Singh, Train to Pakistan
(c) VS Naipaul, A Bend in the River
(d) RK Narayan, The Bachelor of Arts

242 "Look, boys, it ever strike you that the world not real at all? It ever strike you that we have the only mind in the world and you just thinking up everything else? Like me here, having the only mind in the world, and thinking up you people here, thinking up the war and all the houses and the ships and them in the harbour. That ever cross your mind?"

Which of the Indian writers in which of his/her works has quoted the above lines?

(a) Anita Desai, Fire on the Mountain
(b) Khushwant Singh, Delhi: A Novel
(c) VS Naipaul, Miguel Street
(d) RK Narayan, The English Teacher

243 "Love is undying, of that I feel certain. I mean deep, abiding, cherishing love. The love that gives protection even as you, my guardian angel, gave me protection long after you had gone-and continue to give this very day...

A love beyond Death-a love that makes Life alive!"

Which of the Indian writers in which of his/her works has quoted the above lines?

(a) Khushwant Singh, The End of India
(b) Salman Rushdie, The Satanic Verses
(c) Bhabani Bhattacharya, Shadow from Ladakh
(d) Ruskin Bond, Scenes from A Writer's Life

244 "Yesterday, I was sad, tomorrow I may be sad again, but today I know that I am happy. I want to live on and on, delighting like a pagan in all that is physical; and I know that this one lifetime, however long, cannot satisfy my heart."

Which of the Indian writers in which of his/her works has quoted the above lines?

(a) Khushwant Singh, The End of India
(b) Bhabani Bhattacharya, Shadow from Ladakh
(c) Salman Rushdie, Midnight's Children
(d) Ruskin Bond, Delhi is Not Far

245 "At sunset, on the river ban, Krishna
Loved her for the last time and left...
That night in her husband's arms, Radha felt
So dead that he asked, What is wrong,
Do you mind my kisses, love? And she said,
Not not at all, but thought, What is
It to the corpse if the maggots nip?"

Which of the Indian writers in which of his/her works has quoted the above lines?

(a) Swami Vivekananda, Raja-Yoga
(b) Raja Rao, Kanthapura
(c) Kamala Das, The Descendants
(d) Kamala Suraiyya Das, Wages of Love

246 "If wrapping of cloth can impart respectability, the most respctable persons are the Egyptian mummies, all wrapped in layers and layers of gauze."

Which of the Indian writers in which of his/her works has quoted the above lines?

(a) Swami Vivekananda, Raja-Yoga
(b) Raja Rao, Kanthapura
(c) Kamala Das, The Descendants
(d) Kamala Suraiyya Das, Wages of Love

247 "Language is courage: the ability to conceive a thought, to speak it, and by doing so to make it true."

Which of the Indian writers in which of his/her works has quoted the above lines?

(a) Khushwant Singh, The End of India
(b) Salman Rushdie, The Satanic Verses
(c) Bhabani Bhattacharya, Shadow from Ladakh
(d) Ruskin Bond, Scenes from A Writer's Life

248 "I am the sum total of everything that went before me, of all I have been seen done, of everything done-to-me. I am everyone everything whose being-in-the-world affected was affected by mine. I am any that happens after I'm gone which would not have happened if I had not come."

Which of the Indian writers in which of his/her works has quoted the above lines?

(a) Khushwant Singh, The End of India
(b) Bhabani Bhattacharya, Shadow from Ladakh
(c) Salman Rushdie, Midnight's Children
(d) Ruskin Bond, Delhi Is Not Far

249 "She wore flowers in her hair and carried magic secrets in her eyes. She spoke to no one. She spent hours on the riverbank. She smoked cigarettes and had midnight swims..."

Which of the Indian writers in which of his/her works has quoted the above lines?

(a) Rabindranath Tagore, Stray Birds
(b) Arundhati Roy, The God of Small Things
(c) Swami Vivekananda, Letters of Swami Vivekananda
(d) Raja Rao, The Cat and Shakespeare

250 "A man wasn't equal to an animal, not one particle of him. Human life was stinking corrupt, and meanwhile there were beautiful creatures who lived with delicacy on the Earth without doing anyone harm. "We should be dying' the judge almost wept."

Which Indian English authors in which of his/her works has used the above lines?

(a) Anita Desai, Fasting and Feasting
(b) Jawaharlal Nehru, The Discovery of India
(c) Kiran Desai, The Inheritance of Loss
(d) Mulk Raj Anand, Untouchable

251 The Charter Act of 1813 provided how much as the annual expenditure for the revival and promotion of literature in India.?

(a) 1 lakh rupees (b) 2 lakh rupees
(c) 3 lakh rupees (d) 4 lakh rupees

252 Which university was not established during 1854-1858?

(a) Calcutta University
(b) Madras University
(c) Punjab University
(d) Bombay University

253 Macaulay wrote his famous minutes on education policy on ....

(a) 16th February (b) 8th February
(c) 1st February (d) 2nd February

254 Who contributed mainly for the establishment of the University at Pondicherry?

(a) RN Tagore (b) JL Nehru
(c) Sri Aurobindo (d) Vivekananda

255 Consider the following statements

1. It is considered as the Magna Carta of English Education in India.
2. It declared that the aim of the Government's educational policy was the teaching of Western Education.

Which of the above statement(s) is/are correct about Sir Charles Wood's Despatch on Education, 1854?

(a) Only 1 (b) Only 2
(c) Both 1 and 2 (d) Neither 1 nor 2

256 Kolhari Commission was formed under which Education Minister

(a) Abdul Kalam Azad
(b) K L Shrimali
(c) MC Chagala
(d) KC Pant

257 The foundation of Modern Education System in India was laid by

(a) The Charter Act of 1813
(b) Macaulay's Minutes of 1835
(c) The Hunter Commission of 1882
(d) Wood's Despatch of 1854

258 Which of the following commission first decentralised the primary education?

(a) Kothari Commission
(b) Sadler Commission
(c) Hunter Commission
(d) Mudaliar Commission

Directions (Q. Nos. 259-263) *Read the passage given below and answer the questions that follow*

Born on 12th January, 1863 in an affluent Bengali family, Narendra Natha Datta was a precocious child who was what we call nowadays, an all-rounder, excelling in music, studies and athletics. His father Vishwanatha Datta was a well-known attorney. However, he took the spiritual route instead and introduced Hinduism to the world in 1893 when he spoke at the World's Parliament of Religion (probably one of the most epic things any Indian has done abroad!).

The historic speech was given on 11th Sptember, 1893 by Swami Vivekananda. Here's the full text of his opening and closing address.

Sisters and Brothers of America,

It fills my heart with joy unspeakable to rise in response to the warm and cordial welcome which you have given us. I thank you in the name of the most ancient order of monks in the world; I thank you in the name of the mother of religions, and I thank you in the name of millions and millions of Hindu people of all classes and sects.

My thanks, also, to some of the speakers on this platform who, referring to the delegates from the Orient, have told you that these men from far-off nations may well claim the honour of bearing to different lands the idea of toleration. I am proud to belong to a religion which has taught the world both tolerance and universal acceptance.

We believe not only in universal toleration, but we accept all religions as true. I am proud to belong to a nation which has sheltered the persecuted and the refugees of all religions and all nations of the Earth. I am proud to tell you that we have gathered in our bosom the purest remnant of the Israelites, who came to Southern India and took refuge with us in the very year in which their holy temple was shattered to pieces by Roman tyranny. I am proud to belong to the religion which has sheltered and is still fostering the remnant of the grand Zoroastrian nation. I will quote to you, brethren, a few lines from a hymn which I remember to have repeated from my earliest boyhood, which is every day repeated by millions of human beings: "As the different streams having their sources in different paths which men take through different tendencies, various though they appear, crooked or straight, all lead to Thee."

The present convention, which is one of the most August assemblies ever held, is in itself a vindication, a declaration to the world of the wonderful doctrine preached in the Gita: "Whosoever comes to me, through whatsoever form, I reach him; all men are struggling through paths which in the end lead to me." Sectarianism, bigotry, and its horrible descendant, fanaticism, have long possessed this beautiful earth.

259 What was Vishwanatha Datta's profession?

(a) Attorney (b) Spiritual leader
(c) Teacher (d) None of these

260 Who spoke at the World's Parliament of Religion?

(a) Vishwanatha Datta (b) Swami Vivekananda
(c) Both (a) and (b) (d) None of the above

261 Give the opposite of the word 'Occident' from the second passage of the speech.

(a) Delegate (b) Universal
(c) Orient (d) Toleration

262 In the phrase: 'All Lead to Thee', to whom does the word 'Thee' refer?

(a) All religions
(b) The delegates present
(c) Universal brotherhood and peace
(d) God

263 In the phrase: 'I am proud to belong to a nation'— what nation is the speaker referring to?

(a) India (b) Southern India
(c) Rome (d) America

PREVIOUS YEARS' QUESTIONS

December 2018

1 **Braj Kachru has observed a tendency among Indian-English speakers and writers to use hybridised lexical items. One example of this is**
(a) Jugarh (b) Ping-pong
(c) Chaywallah (d) Lathi-charge

2 **Mango Souffle, India's first major gay themed film, is an adaptation of Mahesh Dattani's play**
(a) Do the Needful
(b) Bravely Fought the Queen
(c) Dance like a Man
(d) On a Muggy Night in Mumbai

3 **Which of the following is the most accurate description of Butler English?**
(a) A dialect of English spoken by the descendants of Anglo-Indians.
(b) A pidgin, also called 'Kitchen English' spoken by South Asians in Europe.
(c) A minimal pidgin that emerged during colonial times in the Madras Presidency.
(d) Any non-grammatical variety of English used by menials in Commonwealth countries.

4 **Which of the following statements on Rajmohan's wife is not true?**
(a) Bankin Chandra published it soon after serialization and was elated in seeing its first copy.
(b) The novel was serialized in 1864 in a short-lived magazine in Calcutta.
(c) By common consent, Rajmohan's Wife is the first novel in English published by an Indian.
(d) His vivid descriptions of the routine of Bengali households reveal a lot about the nineteenth century.

5 **1992 demolition of the disputed structure in Ayodhya produced two controversial literary responses. Identify them.**
(a) Out of Place, The Algebra of Infinite Justice
(b) Annals and antiquities, between Sunlight and Shadows
(c) The Moor's Last Sigh, Lajja
(d) Chronicles of a Riot Foretold, Shame

6 **Match the following authors with the novels.**

(Name of Authors)	(Name of Novel)
1. Inheritance	A. Chitra Bamerjee Divakaruni
2. Listening Now	B. Anita Rau Badami
3. Sister of My Heart	C. Anjana Appachana
4. The Hero's Walk	D. Indira Ganesan

Codes
(a) A-1, B-3, C-2, D-4 (b) A-4, B-2, C-1, D-3
(c) A-3, B-4, C-2, D-1 (d) A-4, B-1, C-3, D-2

July 2018

7 **In RK Narayan's *Swami and Friends*, which gave offers Swami the best kind of emotional release from the strains and pressures of disagreeable circumstances?**
(a) Cricket
(b) Football
(c) Tennis
(d) Hockey

8 **In the following series, which one has all the poets correctly matched with their poems?**
(a) Ezekiel, 'Poet, Lover, Birdwatcher'; Ramanujan, 'Small-scale Reflections on a Great House'; Dutt, 'Sunset at Puri'; Mahapatra, 'Our Casuarina Tree'.
(b) Ezekiel, 'Sunset at Puri'; Ramanujan, 'Small-scale Reflections on a Great House'; Dutt, 'Our Casuarina Tree'; Mahapatra, 'Poet, Lover, Birdwatcher'.
(c) Ezekiel, 'Poet, Lover, Birdwatcher'; Ramanujan, 'Sunset at Puri'; Dutt, 'Our Casuarina Tree'; Mahapatra, 'Small-scale Reflections on a Great House'.
(d) Ezekiel, 'Poet, Lover, Birdwatcher'; Ramanujan, 'Small-scale Reflections on a Great House'; Dutt, 'Our Casuarina Tree'; Mahapatra, 'Sunset at Puri'.

9 **Nirad Chaudhuri's Autobiography of an *Unknown Indian* concludes with an essay on the course of Indian history. But in the penultimate chapter Chaudhuri concludes the account of events in his life. How does this narrative end?**
(a) Chaudhuri ties the knot with his childhood sweetheart and moves from Calcutta to Delhi
(b) Chaudhuri obtains a job in the military accounts department and gives it up because he finds it soul-destroying
(c) Chaudhuri joins the editorial team of a Calcutta newspaper and is upset over the drudgery of a reporter's life
(d) Chaudhuri rushes to his ancestral village Bangram on receiving the news of the death of his uncle and recalls his past life

November 2017

10 **The translation of Geeta into English in 1784 called Bhagwat Gita marked, in William Jones's opinion, an "event that made it possible for the first time to have a reliable impression of Indian Literature." Who was the translator?**
(a) Charles Wilkins
(b) HJ Colebrooke
(c) Rammohan Roy
(d) Nathaniel Halhed

11 Who among the following, has translated the classic Malayalam novel, Chemmeen?
(a) AK Ramanujan
(b) Anita Nair
(c) Nandini Nopany
(d) Gita Krishnankutty

12 Who is the narrator in Kamala Markandaya's Nectar in a Sieve?
(a) Premala (b) Saroja
(c) Rukmani (d) Mira

January 2017

13 Identify from the following the work Nirad C. Chaudhuri called "the finest novel in the English language with an Indian theme."
(a) Kim
(b) A Passage to India
(c) Train to Pakistan
(d) Private Life of an Indian Prince

14 In the Story of My Experiments with Truth, MK Gandhi covers the narrative of his life from early childhood through to
(a) 1925 (b) 1929
(c) 1921 (d) 1927

15 Identify the character who is not part of the group of three protagonists in Girish Karnad's Hayavadana.
(a) Padmini (b) Gautama
(c) Kapila (d) Devadatta

16 Aurobindo Ghosh, author of 'Savitri', taught for sometime at Baroda College after his return from England in 1893. Which subject did he teach?
(a) English (b) French
(c) Sanskrit (d) Bengali

17 Who among the following has elaborated on the 'Indianisation' of English?
(a) LM Khubchandani (b) B Kumaravadivelu
(c) BB Kachru (d) Rajendra Singh

18 Match the Novelist with the work.

List I	List II
a. Anita Desai	I. Rich Like Us
b. Nayantara Sahgal	II. The Nowhere Man
c. Arun Joshi	III. In Custody
d. Kamala Markandaya	IV. The Last Labyrinth

Codes

	a	b	c	d
(a)	III	II	IV	I
(b)	III	I	IV	II
(c)	II	I	IV	III
(d)	III	I	IV	II

19 Here is a list of Indian writers who have translated their work into English. Match the writer with his source language.

List I	List II
a. OV Vijayan	I. Kannada
b. Vilas Sarang	II. Malayalam
c. Krishna Baldev Vaid	III. Marathi
d. Girish Karnad	IV. Hindi

Codes

	a	b	c	d
(a)	II	IV	III	I
(b)	I	III	IV	II
(c)	II	III	IV	I
(d)	II	III	I	IV

July 2016

20 Identify the poet, translator, publisher and essayist who founded a press in the 1950s called Writer's Workshop and provided a publishing outlet for Indians writing in English.
(a) P Lal
(b) AK Mehrotra
(c) Vinay Dharwadkar
(d) AK Ramanujan

21 Who among the following bought and renovated the house of the Anglican poet, George Herbert, near Salisbury, England, in 1996?
(a) Daljit Nagra
(b) Vikram Seth
(c) Amitav Kumar
(d) Arundhati Roy

22 Which of the following is not a part of the series of poems called Jejuri, written by Arun Kolatkar?
(a) Yeshwant Rao (b) Chaitanya
(c) The Priest (d) An Old Man

23 The Bhasmasura myth is used in RK Narayan's
(a) The Man-Eater of Malgudi
(b) The Financial Expert
(c) The English Teacher
(d) The World of Nagaraj

24 Which pair of novels by Anita Desai take as their subject the suppression and oppression of Indian women?
I. Whre Shall We Go This Summer?
II. The Zigzag Way
III. Cry, the Peacock
IV. Baumagartner's Bombay

The right combination according to the code is
(a) I and II (b) I and III
(c) II and III (d) III and IV

25 From among the following identify the two Indian English authors who received appreciation and encouragement from their British counterparts:

I. RK Narayan, Graham Greene
II. Nirad C Chaudhuri, Evelyn Waugh
III. Mulk Raj Anand, EM Forster
IV. Raja Rao, Iris Murdoch

The right combination according to the code is

(a) I and II (b) II and IV (c) I and III (d) III and IV

December 2015

26 Which of the following texts of Amitav Ghosh is based on the refugee occupation of an island in the Sundarvans?

(a) Sea of Poppies (b) The Hungry Tide
(c) River of Smoke (d) The Glass Palace

27 Manohar Malgonkar was a hunter, a Lieutenant Colonel in the British army and a tea-planter. He also wrote a memorable novel about the Sepoy Mutiny, especially Peshwa Baji Rao II. What is that novel?

(a) A Distant Drum (b) A Combat of Shadows
(c) A Bend in the Ganges (d) The Devil's Wind

28 Beginning 1996, an Indian publisher commenced the publication of a series of modern Indian novels in English translation. By 2003, it had published 80 novels of repute from almost all Indian languages. Identify the publisher.

(a) Asia Publishing House
(b) Macmillan India
(c) Jaico
(d) Arnold Heinemann

29 In his Poems of Love and War, a collection of classic Indian poems in English translation, A K Ramanujan sought to revive an ancient .... poetic tradition. Choose the right word.

(a) Tamil (b) Sanskrit
(c) Kannada (d) Pali

30 Match the following.

	List I (Indian Texts)		List II (English Translators)
A.	*The Love of Kamarupa and Kamalata*	1.	William Jones
B.	*Ramayana*	2.	Nathaniel Halhed
C.	*Upanishads*	3.	W Franklin
D.	*Abhigyan Sakuntalam*	4.	T H Griffith

Codes

	A	B	C	D
(a)	4	3	2	1
(b)	3	4	2	1
(c)	2	4	3	1
(d)	4	2	3	1

31 Her vision was of several caves. She saw herself in one and she was also outside it, watching its entrance, for Aziz to pass in. She failed to locate him. It was the doubt that had often visited her, but solid and attractive, like the hills, 'I am not-' speech was more difficult than vision. "I am not quite sure."

The above extract from a passage to India is about Adela's cave experience. Who is questioning Adela?

(a) Mrs Moore
(b) Mr McBryde
(c) Fielding
(d) Ronney Heaslop

June 2015

32 To whom did Raja Ram Mohan Roy write in 1823 his letter seeking the introduction of English education in India?

(a) Lord Amherst
(b) Lord Bentinck
(c) Lord Cunningham
(d) Lord Hastings

33 Which of the following is not a feminist novel?

(a) Ashapurna Debi's Subarnalata
(b) Rajam Krishnan's Lamp in the Whirlpool
(c) Chudamani Raghavan's Yamini
(d) Bani Basu's The Enemy Within

34 An Indian English poet once remarked that his discipline and education gave him his 'outer' whereas his Indian origin gave him 'inner' form. Reflecting a part of this claim is a famous essay he called ....

(a) "Is There a Native Way of Thinking?"
(b) "Can the Subaltern Speak?"
(c) "Where Do We Go from Here: Some Speculations?"
(d) "Is There an Indian Way of Thinking?"

35 Match the following.

	List I (Theorists)		List II (Theories)
A.	Bharata	1.	Vakrokti
B.	Kuntaka	2.	Riti
C.	Bhamaha	3.	Dhvani
D.	Anandavardhana	4.	Rasa

Codes

	A	B	C	D
(a)	1	4	2	3
(b)	2	3	1	4
(c)	4	1	2	3
(d)	3	2	4	1

36 Joothan by Om Prakash Valmiki is

(a) a collection of poems
(b) a play
(c) an autobiography
(d) a novel

37 Who of the following has written the novel *The Return*?

(a) Bapsi Sidhwa (b) V S Naipaul
(c) KS Maniam (d) Pankaj Mishra

38 *Flowers* is a short play written by

(a) Mahesh Dattani (b) Asif Currimbhoy
(c) Girish Karnad (d) Paoli Sengupta

39 Which of the following two plays won the Sultan Padamsee Prize for Indian plays in English

1. *Princes*
2. *Where There's a Will*
3. *Larins Sahib*
4. *Doongaji House*

Select the correct answer using the codes given below.

(a) 3 and 4 (b) 1 and 3
(c) 2 and 3 (d) 1 and 4

40 Match the following.

	List I		List II
A.	Mulk Raj Anand	1.	Premashram
B.	Raja Rao	2.	The Cat and Shakespeare
C.	Prem Chand	3.	Coolie
D.	Girish Karnad	4.	Nagamandala

Codes

	A	B	C	D
(a)	3	2	4	1
(b)	2	3	1	4
(c)	3	2	1	4
(d)	4	3	2	1

June 2014

41 Which among the following novels was not written in 1922?

(a) Ulysses
(b) Jacob's Room
(c) Aaron's Rod
(d) A Passage to India

42 Which of the following is not a play by Badal Sircar?

(a) Bhooma (b) Evam Indrajeet
(c) That Other History (d) Agra Bazar

43 Who is the protagonist of Shashi Despande's That Long Silence?

(a) Mohan (b) Jaya
(c) Rati (d) Kamat

44 Why does Girish Karnad base his play Hayavadana on Thomas Mann's Transposed Heads?

(a) It is a mock-heroic transcription of the original Sanskrit tales
(b) It is concerned with materialism
(c) It deals with domestic strife
(d) It deals with ancient times

45 The collected poems of AK Ramanujan has been divided into four sections. Arrange them in their chronological order.

(a) The Striders, The Relations, Second Sight, The Black Hen
(b) The Relations, The Striders, The Black Hen, Second Sight
(c) Second Sight, The Relations, The Black Hen, Striders
(d) The Black Hen, Second Sight, The Striders, The Relations

46 Match the following.

	List I Character		List II Novel
A.	Fakir	1.	The Glass Palace
B.	Tridip	2.	The Hungry Tide
C.	Rajkumar	3.	The Calcutta Chromosome
D.	Murugan	4.	Shadow Lines

Codes

	A	B	C	D
(a)	2	4	1	3
(b)	2	4	3	1
(c)	1	3	2	4
(d)	3	2	4	1

ANSWERS

Objective Questions

1. *(a)*	2. *(a)*	3. *(c)*	4. *(d)*	5. *(d)*	6. *(d)*	7. *(a)*	8. *(b)*	9. *(c)*	10. *(a)*
11. *(d)*	12. *(c)*	13. *(a)*	14. *(b)*	15. *(b)*	16. *(c)*	17. *(b)*	18. *(a)*	19. *(b)*	20. *(c)*
21. *(d)*	22. *(b)*	23. *(b)*	24. *(b)*	25. *(b)*	26. *(d)*	27. *(b)*	28. *(c)*	29. *(c)*	30. *(b)*
31. *(d)*	32. *(a)*	33. *(b)*	34. *(a)*	35. *(b)*	36. *(d)*	37. *(d)*	38. *(b)*	39. *(c)*	40. *(c)*
41. *(a)*	42. *(b)*	43. *(a)*	44. *(c)*	45. *(b)*	46. *(a)*	47. *(c)*	48. *(c)*	49. *(c)*	50. *(b)*
51. *(a)*	52. *(b)*	53. *(b)*	54. *(a)*	55. *(c)*	56. *(a)*	57. *(d)*	58. *(c)*	59. *(c)*	60. *(d)*
61. *(a)*	62. *(b)*	63. *(b)*	64. *(b)*	65. *(a)*	66. *(b)*	67. *(a)*	68. *(d)*	69. *(a)*	70. *(a)*
71. *(d)*	72. *(d)*	73. *(b)*	74. *(a)*	75. *(b)*	76. *(a)*	77. *(d)*	78. *(c)*	79. *(b)*	80. *(a)*
81. *(b)*	82. *(d)*	83. *(c)*	84. *(b)*	85. *(a)*	86. *(d)*	87. *(a)*	88. *(c)*	89. *(d)*	90. *(d)*
91. *(d)*	92. *(d)*	93. *(b)*	94. *(d)*	95. *(c)*	96. *(d)*	97. *(a)*	98. *(d)*	99. *(a)*	100. *(b)*
101. *(b)*	102. *(a)*	103. *(a)*	104. *(d)*	105. *(a)*	106. *(c)*	107. *(b)*	108. *(a)*	109. *(c)*	110. *(b)*
111. *(b)*	112. *(c)*	113. *(d)*	114. *(b)*	115. *(c)*	116. *(d)*	117. *(a)*	118. *(c)*	119. *(a)*	120. *(a)*
121. *(c)*	122. *(b)*	123. *(b)*	124. *(c)*	125. *(d)*	126. *(b)*	127. *(a)*	128. *(c)*	129. *(c)*	130. *(a)*
131. *(c)*	132. *(b)*	133. *(b)*	134. *(c)*	135. *(d)*	136. *(a)*	137. *(c)*	138. *(c)*	139. *(a)*	140. *(d)*
141. *(b)*	142. *(a)*	143. *(b)*	144. *(b)*	145. *(a)*	146. *(a)*	147. *(b)*	148. *(d)*	149. *(c)*	150. *(c)*
151. *(c)*	152. *(d)*	153. *(b)*	154. *(a)*	155. *(c)*	156. *(d)*	157. *(d)*	158. *(c)*	159. *(d)*	160. *(b)*
161. *(a)*	162. *(a)*	163. *(b)*	164. *(c)*	165. *(d)*	166. *(d)*	167. *(b)*	168. *(b)*	169. *(d)*	170. *(a)*
171. *(a)*	172. *(b)*	173. *(d)*	174. *(b)*	175. *(b)*	176. *(c)*	177. *(a)*	178. *(d)*	179. *(a)*	180. *(d)*
181. *(a)*	182. *(a)*	183. *(a)*	184. *(c)*	185. *(a)*	186. *(b)*	187. *(d)*	188. *(d)*	189. *(a)*	190. *(c)*
191. *(a)*	192. *(b)*	193. *(c)*	194. *(d)*	195. *(a)*	196. *(c)*	197. *(c)*	198. *(d)*	199. *(c)*	200. *(a)*
201. *(a)*	202. *(b)*	203. *(d)*	204. *(d)*	205. *(a)*	206. *(b)*	207. *(a)*	208. *(c)*	209. *(d)*	210. *(a)*
211. *(a)*	212. *(b)*	213. *(c)*	214. *(a)*	215. *(b)*	216. *(b)*	217. *(b)*	218. *(b)*	219. *(d)*	220. *(b)*
221. *(c)*	222. *(a)*	223. *(c)*	224. *(d)*	225. *(d)*	226. *(c)*	227. *(d)*	228. *(b)*	229. *(b)*	230. *(b)*
231. *(b)*	232. *(a)*	233. *(d)*	234. *(a)*	235. *(a)*	236. *(a)*	237. *(b)*	238. *(a)*	239. *(d)*	240. *(c)*
241. *(c)*	242. *(c)*	243. *(d)*	244. *(d)*	245. *(c)*	246. *(d)*	247. *(b)*	248. *(c)*	249. *(b)*	250. *(c)*
251. *(a)*	252. *(c)*	253. *(d)*	254. *(c)*	255. *(c)*	256. *(c)*	257. *(b)*	258. *(c)*	259. *(a)*	260. *(b)*
261. *(c)*	262. *(d)*	263. *(a)*							

Previous Years' Questions

1. *(d)*	2. *(d)*	3. *(c)*	4. *(a)*	5. *(c)*	6. *(c)*	7. *(a)*	8. *(d)*	9. *(b)*	10. *(a)*
11. *(b)*	12. *(c)*	13. *(a)*	14. *(c)*	15. *(b)*	16. *(b)*	17. *(c)*	18. *(b)*	19. *(c)*	20. *(a)*
21. *(b)*	22. *(d)*	23. *(a)*	24. *(b)*	25. *(c)*	26. *(b)*	27. *(d)*	28. *(b)*	29. *(a)*	30. *(b)*
31. *(b)*	32. *(a)*	33. *(d)*	34. *(d)*	35. *(c)*	36. *(c)*	37. *(c)*	38. *(c)*	39. *(a)*	40. *(c)*
41. *(d)*	42. *(d)*	43. *(b)*	44. *(a)*	45. *(a)*	46. *(a)*				

Cultural Studies

Literary and cultural studies gives access to historical and emergent traditions of literature, culture and thought. Through critical interpretation and dialogue, we can see how language mediated through texts arranges and allows different ways of knowing and living. In the process you will read some of the greatest wordsmiths and thinkers in the English language.

Introduction of Cultural Studies

'Culture' can quite easily be credited as the source of all art as culture is capable of both influencing and transforming individual everyday experiences, in the private and the public domain. Cultural Studies as an academic discipline, offers to study the ways in which literary texts are theorised and read. This inter-disciplinary field of study offers to investigate and combine politics, political economy, sociology, history, anthropology, philosophy, ethnography, communication and media theories and much more to comprehend the ideological base on which a literary text is built.

Cultural Studies, therefore, is a study of 'a particular way of life, whether of people, or period, or a group,' according to Raymond Williams. Also, it is important to understand that 'Cultural Studies' as an academic discipline is a logical approach to looking at all social practices as 'political' rather than as aesthetic or human.

Thus, like any academic discipline, this field, too, is defined by its

- Object of study- namely culture
- The history of the discipline itself – its origins and evolution
- Assumptions, methods and approaches – the different critical theories

"There is no such thing as a human independent of Culture." --- Clifford Geertz, The Interpretation of Cultures.

The above remark by Clifford Geertz points a certain co-relation between an individual and his contemporary socio-political-economic history which becomes prescriptive in shaping his personal and literary life. "Culture" is the socio-political discourse that dominates the public space and permeates into the private spaces occupied by the individuals and becomes a part of their subconscious identity. Mostly, the literary texts produced by authors are symptomatic of their response/ reaction to the social dynamics of their times, a longing or nostalgia for the period gone by, or a vision of a utopian tomorrow they seek to achieve.

In this Chapter

- *Introduction of Cultural Studies*
- *Feminism*
- *Postcolonialism*
- *Marxism*
- *Poststructuralism*

Origin and Evolution of Cultural Studies

It is very difficult to pin down on a date/ period to mark the origins of 'Cultural Studies' for the study of 'Culture' has always attracted literary and critical scholars as a focal point of their learning of the author and his context. Nonetheless, the tradition could be dated back to the 1860s with Mathew Arnold's 'Culture and Civilisation' which looked at the power of literary texts, especially canonical literature, in shaping individual sensibility.

Origin of Cultural Studies

Cultural Studies as an academic field of study gained currency with the publication of Richard Hoggart's Use of Literacy (1957) and Raymond William's Culture and Society (1958), challenging the privileged aspects of literary traditions and taking into account non-canonical cultural forms.

The stepping stone of Cultural Studies in Britain was the Centre for Contemporary Cultural Studies at the University of Birmingham in 1964 as Richard Hoggart as its first director. Under the directorship of Stuart Hall who joined Hoggart in Birmingham in 1964, the field of British Cultural Studies expanded to concern itself with questions of subjectivity, identity and power-politics.

The scope of the programme widened and its access was shared with a wider audience through the publication of the journal 'Working Papers in Cultural Studies.' By 1978 a series of books were brought out to discuss the approaches within the domain of British Cultural Studies.

Evolution of Cultural Studies

It is important to note that though the discipline of Cultural Studies was primarily framed at Birmingham and the academics there played a key role in its development, the scope of Contemporary Cultural Studies needs to take into account the development of this framework at other sites too, such as in South-East Asia, Australia, Canada, Europe etc.

Also, it is important to comprehend the cultural specificities of those territories or nations to understand Cultural Studies as a global mount. At the same time the various cultural specificities of the places where Cultural Studies developed explain the coming together of wider ideologies of power-politics and identity- politics under the rubric of Cultural Studies, such as the class struggle, feminism, race, caste, nationality and so on.

Theories About Critical Studies

Different thinkers propunded their critical theories. These are

Leavisite Criticism

Deriving from the works of FR Leavis, the Leavisite Criticism focussed on re-distributing social capacities on the basis of access to the canonical traditional literature, popularly known as "the Great Tradition" in the Leavian vocabulary.

It strongly believed that the knowledge of "the Great Tradition" endowed its beneficiaries with social assets. This idea was later termed by Pierre Bourdieu as "Cultural Capital."

Frankfurt School Theory

In contrast to the Leavisite Criticism, the Frankfurt School in the 1930s developed cultural studies stemming from an examination of the popular culture; like popular music, popular literature and magazines. The important theorists of this school, like Adorno and Horkheimer looked at "cultural industries" playing a pivotal role in social cultural theories.

Mass Communication Theory

Recent scholarship is expanding the scope of cultural studies by looking at new vistas like visual studies, cybercultures, new technologies of embodiment and globalisation.

The Politics of the Practising Experts

Cultural studies as a field is constantly fluid and in flux of change for it is a response to the various social changes occurring in the immediate society and world at large. Therefore, the ideological leanings of the practitioners of culture studies have brought within its domain various other ideological theories in reading a text and its context.

Such as Marxism, Feminism, Race, Caste, gender, and so on, which further defines the perception of the given theorist, making his/her work exclusive within an overarching framework.

Major Thinkers of Cultural Studies

Richard Hoggart

Born on 24th September 1918, Richard Hoggart was a British academic with English Literature, Cultural Studies and Sociology as his prime areas of concern. He was born in an impoverished family and lost his parents at a very young age. He was raised by his grandmother. He won a scholarship to read at the University of Leeds and graduated from the University with a First-Class degree. He also served in the Royal Artillery during the Second World War.

Hoggart died at the age of 95 in 2014. He was suffering from dementia.

Literary Career and Works

He served as a Staff Tutor at the University of Hull from 1946 to 1959 and as a Senior Lecturer in English from 1959 to 1962. He also served as a Professor of English at Birmingham University. He founded the Centre for Contemporary Cultural Studies in 1964 and served as its director till 1969. He served as the Assistant director of UNESCO from 1971 to 1975 and as a Warden at University of London from 1976 to 1984.

Hoggart served as a member of various public bodies. He was a key witness in the 1960 British trial of whether DH Lawrence's novel *Lady Chatterly's Lover* was obscene. Later, in 2006, the digital dramatisation of this trial was made for BBC in which actor David Tennant portayed his role.

Major Works

- Auden (1951)
- The Uses of Literacy (1957)
- The Way We Live Now (1995)
- Mass Media in a Mass Society (2004)
- Promises to Keep: Thoughts in Old Age (2005)
- First and Last Things (1999)
- Everyday Language and Everyday Life (2003)
- A Sort of Clowning (1990)
- An Imagined Life (1992)
- A Local Habitation (1989)
- An Idea and its Servants (1978)
- Speaking to Each Other (1970)
- Townscape with Figures (1994)
- An English Temper (1982)
- An Idea of Europe (1987)
- The Tyranny of Relativism (1998)
- Between Two Worlds (2002)
- Liberty and Legislation (1989)
- A Measured Life (1994)
- Contemporary Cultural Studies (1969)
- The Future of Broadcasting The Literary Imagination (1969)
- Continuing Education (1983)
- EM Forster (1982)

Raymond Williams

A Welsh Marxist theorist, novelist and critic, Raymond Henry Williams was born on 31st August, 1921. Widely translated round the globe, Williams' writings on culture and politics were fundamental in understanding the Marxist critique of culture and arts and in the dissemination of Cultural Materialist approach.

Growing up in a non-Welsh neighbourhood, Williams attended King Henry VIII Grammar School in Abergavenny. His political consciousness began to develop fairly early in his life for he was fourteen when the Spanish Civil war broke out and it was the period marked by the rise of Nazism. Also, his membership at a local book club which had leftist leanings kept him in the know-how of the massive changes taking place in the socio-public space. He soon became a supporter of the League of Nations and also bought a copy of the Communist Manifesto by Karl Marx.

While attending College, in Cambridge, he joined the Communist Party of Great Britain. He wrote the Communist Party pamphlet alongside Eric Hobsbawm. In 1940, Raymond Williams joined the British army. However, he stayed back at Cambridge to take his exams; and this was the time when Germany invaded Russia.

In 1946, Williams received his M A from the Trinity College. Soon after, he began to serve as a tutor in adult education at the University of Oxford. In 1946, he also began a journal titled Politics and Letters, which he co-edited with Clifford Collins and Wolf Mankowitz until 1948.

In 1948, inspired by T S Eliot's Notes towards The Definition of Culture, Williams began exploring the concept of culture. His first draft 'The Idea of Culture' resulted in a successful book titled *Culture and Society*, published in 1958. Williams writings were widely acclaimed and interested the New Left.

Major Works

- Culture and Society, 1958
- The Long Revolution, 1961
- The Country and the City, 1973
- Marxism and Literature, 1977
- Politics and Letters: Interviews with the New Left, 1979
- Border Country, 1960
- Culture and Materialism, 1980
- Problems in Materialism, 1980
- Modern Tragedy, 1966
- May Day Manifesto, 1968
- Towards 2000, 1983
- Drama in Performance, 1954
- The English Novel from Dickens to Lawrence, 1970
- Drama from Ibsen to Brecht, 1968
- Writing in Society, 1983
- People of the Black Mountains, 1989
- The Sociology of Culture, 1982
- The Fight for Manod, 1979
- The Volunteers, 1978
- Who Speaks for Wales?
- Loyalties, 1985
- Reading and Criticism, 1950
- Second Generation, 1964

- Communications, 1966
- Orwell, 1971
- Language and Literature, 1981
- The Year 2000, 1983
- Marx on Culture, 2005

Stuart Hall

Born on 3rd February, 1932 Stuart Hall was a Jamaican-born British Marxist sociologist, political and cultural theorist who along with Richard Hoggart and Raymond Williams was the founding member of the Centre for British Cultural Studies in Birmingham. He also founded the influential New Left Review, a bi-monthly journal covering world politics, economy and cultures.

Literary Career and Works

Hall succeeded Hoggart as the director for the Centre for British Cultural Studies in 1968 and served as its director till 1979. He expanded the scope of the curriculum and research base at the centre by incorporating race and gender as allied aspects in the study of culture. He also tried to incorporate new ideas from French theorists such as Michael Foucault.

In 1979, Hall left the post of the director and joined the Open University as a professor of sociology. There, he went on to become the President of the British Sociological Association from 1995-97.

In 1995, Hall was the founding editor of Soundings: A Journal of Politics and Culture. He was also closely associated with the journal, Marxism Today. Hall played a crucial role in the Black Arts Movement. For movie directors, John Akomfrah and Isaac Julien, Hall was a heroic figure.

Hall wrote several influential articles, such as

- Situating Marx: Evaluations and Departures (1972)
- Encoding and Decoding in the Television Discourse (1973)
- Resistance through Rituals (1975)
- Policing the Crisis – A Book – (1978)
- The Hard Road to Renewal (1988)
- Formations of Modernity (1992)
- Questions of Cultural Identity (1996)
- Cultural Representations and Signifying Practices (1997)
- Familiar Stranger: A Life Between Two Islands (2017)

Hall spoke internationally on 'Culture' in a series of lectures in 1983 at the University of Illinois. These lectures were recorded and later became a theoretical base for Cultural Studies 1983: *A Theoretical History* published by Jennifer Slack and Lawrence Grossberg in 2016.

Hall retired from the Open University in 1997. In 2005, he was elected Fellow of the British Academy. In 2008, he received European Cultural Foundations' Princess Margriet Award. At the age of 82, he breathed his last on 10th February, 2014.

His memoir, *Familiar Stranger: A Life Between Two Islands* was posthumously published in 2017.

Key Concepts Related to the Cultural Studies: Hegemony, Power and Ideology

Hegemony

Derived from the Latin word 'hegemonia', hegemony means authority, rule or dominance of one political or economic state over another. Hegemony stands to define the socio-cultural and political dominance of one state or group over the other. Controlled by intricate power relations which could be military, political, economic, religious or social, a given classified group could dominate the culture and values operating in the society and dictating its terms to the sub-ordinate.

As in the case of power relations between the ruling and working class, the coloniser and the colonised, the racial or the gendered superior and the 'other' and so on.

Power

The concept of 'Power' is most fundamental to the shaping of socio-cultural and political spaces, where the dominant hegemonic group maintains a status quo by influencing their socio-economic-politico-cultural order. The dominant is able to influence the beliefs, values and perceptions; and this is done to control the socio-economic resources. Power is mostly authoritative and deeply rooted in the everyday social existence.

Ideology

An ideology is a set of beliefs and ideas held by an individual or a group which becomes a basis for their social, economic or political theory. The term "ideology" was coined by a French philosopher, Antoine Destutt de Tracy in 1796. However, the concept is used much differently today than what Tracy understood it to be.

In the domain of cultural studies, ideology could be understood as clustered patterns of idea determining power relations that steer within a complex social and political space.

Feminism

"One is not born, but rather becomes, a woman."

Simon De Beauvoir's quote from her 1949 book *The Second Sex*, amazingly compresses the whole debate of feminism by highlighting how the cultural machinery operative within any society imposes the idea of performativity on the genders present within the society. A society that privileges the male gender over the female gender believes in ritual repetition of a certain tasks and activities that relegate female gender to a subordinate status. Women, then, even when born with an equal apparatus as their male counterparts, through social conditioning are made to believe and live as inferior grade. Thus 'woman' becomes that category which is socially, politically, economically and in various other ways exploited and these exploitations could be both visible as well as invisible. Various forms of abuses, physical tortures and brutality are various visible forms of violence committed against women. However, there are grave invisible forms of violence that women are subjected to such as being denied their right to education, vote, economic independence, professional opportunities, abortion, right to inheritance and so on.

Feminism or feminisms are a series of movements, ideologies and social activism that seeks to attain social equity for women. It is a discourse that tries to recover those supressed bodies and voices that have been buried by the social and cultural prejudices and these oppressive subjects need not only be the superior gender 'men' but also the female gender that has become patriarchal through centuries of social conditioning that privileges the male gender and believes the discrimination against women to be normative.

It is difficult, nearly impossible, to look at feminism as a uniform body for each society is at a different level of gender-based bias. Also, the feminists in various society seek social equity differently. For instance, in upper class families, the right for women to step out for employment as per their will would be liberating. However, in another class background where both men and women work because of their lower-class status, the working woman does not automatically become an emblem of an empowered woman.

Feminism or feminisms, therefore, are plural and diverse, but at the core, attempt to destabilise the cultural machinery that regards woman as 'the other' or the inferior sex.

Origin and Evolution

The different historical circumstances and the cultural climates of different countries make it difficult to define feminism originating at a given point. However, it is believed that the word 'feminism' was coined in 1837 by a French philosopher Charles Fourier. The word was first used in France and Netherlands in 1872, in Britain in 1890s and in United States in 1910s.

Feminism is diverse and within itself is fragmented based on the different worldviews held by feminists. Yet, broadly the modern western feminism is divided into three waves or phases

1. The first wave of feminism, dating from 1830s to 1920s, is best known for the suffrage movement.
2. The second wave of feminism, dating from 1920s onwards, revolve around women's liberation movement, seeking social equity and various other legal rights for women.
3. The third wave of feminism is more diverse as it stems from the failures of the second wave, attempting to attain the same goals differently.

Besides these three waves of feminism, there is another very important body of feminism, known as the Literary Feminism. The Feminist Literary Criticism was born out of the debates of second wave feminism. It was considered radical and revolutionary as it sought to re-read literature, especially the canonical texts, which before the 1970s were exclusively male authored barring a few exceptions such as Jane Austen, Charlotte Bronte and George Eliot. The canon which so far was considered gender-neutral was attacked by the literary feminists trying to give an explanation for the absence of women writers and women readers from the literary scene. Virginia Woolf's 1929 master piece, *A Room of One's Own* attempts to do that and so begins the era of gender-sensitive reading of the literary texts.

Major Thinkers of Feminism

Elaine Showalter

Believed to be the founding figures of Feminism in the United States academia, Elaine Showalter was born Elaine Cottler in Boston in 1941. She is widely acclaimed for developing the concept and practice of 'gynocritics,' a term denoting the study of women writers. Showalter has widely contributed feminist literary criticism.

Literary Career and Works

She attained her Bachelor's degree from Bryn Mawr College and Master's degree from Brandeis University. She received her PhD in 1970 from the University of California. Soon she started working at Douglass College at Rutgers University. Later she joined Princeton University in 1984 and remained there till she took early retirement in 2003.

Showalter specialised in Victorian literature. Her most important works were on hysteria and madness in women's writing. Her works contributed immensely towards understanding the female literary tradition. She made a pathbreaking contribution in the field by mapping the female tradition going through three phases of feminism.

Showalter was awarded the Guggenheim Fellowship and Rockefelller Humanities fellowship (1981-82).

She also served as the President of the Modern Language Association (MLA). In 2007, she was the chair of judges for the prestigious British literary award, the Man Booker International Prize.

She is credited with coining the term 'gynocritics'. The term values the female perspective in reading of literary works. It is a very important body of work for it rejects the concept that female writing is an answer to sexism or gender-based discrimination. Rather she traces the history of women's writing as a separate body of writing.

Major Works

- A Literature of Their Own, 1977
- The Female Malady, 1985
- A Jury of Her Peers: American Women Writers from Anne Bradstreet to Annie Proulx, 2009
- Hystories: Hysterical Epidemics and Modern Culture, 1997
- Sexual Anarchy, 1990
- Inventing Herself, 2001
- The Vintage Book of American Women Writers, 2001
- Faculty Towers, 2005
- The Civil Wars of Julia Ward Howe: A Biography, 2016
- Sister's Choice, 1991
- Speaking of Gender, 1989
- Women's Liberation and Literature, 1971
- Daughters of Decadence, 1993
- Teaching Literature, 2002

Simone de Beauvoir

Born in January 1908, Simon de Beauvoir was a French feminist, social and political activist, a philosopher and a writer. She significantly contributed to feminist theory and feminist existentialism.

Literary Career and Works

Her most significant contribution is her 1949 treatise, *The Second Sex*, which is one of the foundational texts of the contemporary feminism. She wrote extensively and across genres. She wrote travel diaries, essays, novels and short stories.

1970s onwards, Beauvoir became active in France's women's liberation movement. As a part of the movement she signed a manifesto, that included a list of women who had had an abortion which was then illegal in France.

Simon de Beauvoir had a lifelong relation with Sartre. In La Ceremonie Des Adieux, she wrote the painful account of his last years. After Sartre's death, she published his letters to her.

Both significantly influenced each other's works, though the extent of their influence on each other remains a debatable issue. The other important scholars influencing Beauvoir's works were *Hegel and Leibniz*.

Beauvoir studied Mathematics at the Institute Catholic de Paris, Philosophy at the Sorbonne and literature at Institute Sainte-Marie. She completed her degrees in 1928 and was only the ninth woman to do so, owing to the fact that French women were only recently granted the access to higher education.

She first worked with Maurice Merleau-Ponty and Claude Levi-Strauss. The three of them completed their teaching practice from the same secondary school. From 1929 to 1943, she taught at the Lycee Montgrande, after which she could sustain herself through her writings.

In 1954, de Beauvoir won France's most prestigious literary prize for The Mandarins, in which her lover, Algren, appears as a fictional character.

She died at the age of 76 in 1986 due to pneumonia. She was buried next to Sartre at the Montparnasse Cemetry in Paris. Post her death, De Beauvoir's adopted daughter, Sylvie Le Bon published her letters to both Sartre and Algren.

Major Works

- The Second Sex, 1949
- The Woman Destroyed, 1967
- The Mandarins, 1954
- Memoirs of a Dutiful Daughter, 1958
- She Came to Stay, 1943
- The Ethics of Ambiguity, 1947
- All Men are Mortal, 1946
- Letters to Sartre, 1990
- Adieux: A Farewell to Sartre, 1981
- The Coming of Age, 1970

- The Blood of Others, 1945
- All Said and Done, 1972
- Les Belles Images, 1966
- America Day by Day, 1948
- The Independent Woman
- Diary of a Philosophy Student
- The Long March, 1957
- Must We Burn Sade, 1953
- Pyrrhud and Cineas, 1944
- When Things of the Spirit Come First, 1979
- The Prime of Life, 1961
- After the War: Force of Circumstance, Volume I: 1944-52

Mary Wollstonecraft

Born in 1759, Mary Wollstonecraft was a writer, philosopher and an advocate of women's rights. By the twentieth century, she came to be regarded as one of the founding feminist philosophers; though during her times her unconventional personal relationships received much attention.

Literary Career and Works

For many feminist thinkers, both her life and her works are of prime significance. Her most significant contribution is *A Vindication of the Rights of Woman* (1792) in which she argues that women are not born inferior to men, but turned inferior by being denied the right to education. She goes on to make a plea to the society on behalf of both men and women, as the society as a whole could benefit only by education of both the genders.

During her brief writing career, Wollstonecraft wrote a variety of works, novels, treatises, pamphlets, history books, conduct books and children's literature. After her death in 1797, William Godwin, her widower, published *A Memoir*, revealing her unconventional lifestyle and especially her two affairs with Henry Fuseli and Gilbert Imlay. This *Memoir* more than celebrating her, damaged her reputation.

Wollstonecraft died at the age of 38, soon after giving birth to her second daughter, she grew up to become the great writer Mary Shelley.

Major Works

- A Vindication of the Rights of Men and Women, 1790
- A Vindication of the Rights of Woman, 1792
- Maria: Or the Wrongs of Woman, 1798
- Letters written during a Short Residence in Sweden, Norway and Denmark, 1796
- Thoughts on the Education of Daughters, 1787
- Mary: A Fiction, 1788
- Original Stories from Real Life, 1788
- Mary; Maria, 1991
- Political Writings, 1989
- Posthumous Works of the Author of a Vindication of the Rights of Women
- An Historical and Moral View of the Origin and Progress of the French Revolution and the Effect it has Produced in Europe, 1794
- Collected Letters of Mary Wollstonecraft, 1979
- The Love Letters of Mary Wollstonecraft to Gilbert Imlay, 1879
- The Female Reader, 1789
- Ahead of her Time: A Sampler of Life and Thought of Mary Wollstonecraft
- Moral Conversations and Stories
- The Feminist Papers
- Women and Education

Judith Butler

Born in 1956, Judith Butler is an American philosopher and gender theorist. Her works have significantly contributed to the field of political philosophy, feminist theory, queer and literary theory.

Literary Career and Works

She studied at the Bennington College before going on to study at the Yale University. She received her Bachelor of Arts in 1978 and Doctor of Philosophy in 1984. Since 1993, she has been teaching at the University of California, Berkeley, in the department of Comparative Literature and the Program of Critical Theory. In 2002, she held the Spinoza Chair of Philosophy at the University of Amsterdam. Butler also served on the editorial board of several journals.

Her most notable works are Gender Trouble and Bodies That Matter, in which she puts forth her theory about performativity of gender and challenges the conventional understanding of gendered roles in the society. Butler is a recipient of several awards for her exemplary works.

Major Works

- Gender Trouble, 1990
- Precarious Life, 2004
- Undoing Gender, 2004
- Frames of War: When is Life Grievable?, 2009
- Bodies that Matter, 1993
- The Psychic Life of Power, 1997
- Notes Towards a Performative Theory of Assembly, 2015
- Contingency, Hegemony, Universality, 2000
- Giving an Account of Oneself, 2003
- Senses of the Subject, 2015

- Antigone's Claim: Kinship between Life and Death, 2000
- Parting Ways, 2012
- Subjects of Desire, 1987
- The Power of Religion in the Public Sphere, 2011
- Who Sings the Nation-State, 2007
- Dispossession: The performative in the Political, 2013
- Is Critique Secular, 2009
- Prejudicial Appearances: The Logic of American Antidiscrimination Law, 2000
- Women and Social Transformation, 2003
- What is a People?
- Against Sadomasochism, 1982
- Radical Thinkers, 2016
- The Queer Intersectional in Contemporary Germany, 2018

Julia Kristeva

Julia Kristeva (born on 24th June, 1941) is a Bulgarian-French philosopher, literary critic and a psychoanalyst and feminist.

Literary Career and Works

Kristeva was internationally acclaimed soon after the publication of her very first book, *Semiotike* in 1969. Her entire oeuvre contains works addressing a wide array of subjects, such as intertextuality, semiotics and linguistics, literary theory, psychoanalysis, political and cultural analysis, art histories, feminist approaches and so on. She is popular in the field of structuralism and post-structuralist thought too.

She is believed to be one of the key figures in the school of French feminism along with de Beauvoir, Luce Irigaray and Helen Cixous. Kristeva proposed the idea of multiple identities in her study of feminism. In the feminist circles, her arguments were mostly controversial and therefore her feminist stand was considered ambiguous, yet her famous disambiguation of three types of feminism is a noteworthy contribution.

Kristeva attained her education from several universities in France. She was highly influenced by the works of Michael Bakhtin. She got a chance to read under the tutelage of scholars like Lucien Goldmann and Roland Barthes.

By early 1970s she began to teach at the Columbia University. After her marriage with the novelist, Philippe Sollers Joyaux, she also published a few works under her married name, Julia Joyaux.

Kristeva was the recipient of Holberg International Memorial Prize in 2004.

She won the 2006 Hannah Arendt Prize for Political Thought. She also received among other awards Commander of the Legion of Honor, Commander of the Order of Merit, and the Vaclav Havel Prize.

Kristeva is the founder of the Simon de Beauvoir Prize Committee.

Major Works

- Semiotike, 1969
- Powers of Horror, 1980
- Revolution in Poetic Language, 1974
- Desire in Language, 1969
- The Kristeva Reader, 1986
- New Maladies of the Soul, 1993
- Teresa, My Love: An Imagined Life of the Saint of Avila, 2008
- This Incredible Need to Believe, 2007
- Hatred and Forgiveness, 2005
- Hannah Arendt, 1999
- The Samurai, 1983
- The Severed Head: Capital Visions, 2011
- The Portable Kristeva, 1997
- Language: The Unknown, 1981
- Murder in Byzantium, 2004
- Proust and the Sense of Time, 1993
- The Sense and Non-Sense of Revolt, 2000
- Time and Sense, 1996
- The Old Man and the Wolves, 1991
- In the Beginning was Love, 1987
- Marriage as a Fine Art, 2015
- The Enchanted Clock, 2015
- Colette, 1999
- About Chinese Women, 1974
- Passions of Our Time, 2019
- Nations Without Nationalism, 1993
- Possessions, 1996
- Crisis of the European Subject, 2000
- Intimate Revolt, 2001
- The System and the Speaking Subject, 1975

Luce Irigaray

Born on 3rd May 1930, Luce Irigaray is a Belgian-born French feminist, psychoanalyst, philosopher, linguist and cultural theorist.

Literary Career and Works

Her most notable works are *This Sex Which is not One and Speculum of Other Woman*. Some of her works are imaginary dialogues with eminent Western Philosophers such as Nietzsche and Hiedegger. Also she writes extensively on Hegel, Descartes, Plato, Aristotle, Levinas and Merleau Ponty. She contributes pointedly through her study of language, specifically the difference between the way men and women speak.

Irigaray received her Bachelor's degree from the University of Louvain in 1954 and Masters degree in 1956.

From 1956 to 1959, she taught at a high school in Brussels.

In 1961, she completed her Master's in Psychology from the University of Paris. In 1962, she received a specialist diploma in Psychopathology. In 1968, she completed her doctorate from Paris X Nanterre. She earned a second PhD in 1974. Her second PhD earned her great repute but also led to her suspension from Ecole Freudienne de Paris, directed by Lacan where she attended Lacan's seminars. Her work was not received well by Lacanian and Freudian circles.

Not much is known about Irigaray's personal life for she believed that an interest in her biography would impact the reading of her works and be used against her in the male-dominated society.

Irigaray's works combined various ideologies in putting forth her perspective theory on women/ feminism. She brings together structuralism/ post structuralism, Marxism and psychoanalysis while offering her feminist argument.

Major Works

- This Sex Which is Not One, 1977
- Speculum of the Other Woman, 1974
- Ethics of Sexual Difference, 1982
- In the Beginning She Was, 2012
- Marine Lover of Friedrich Nietzche, 1991
- I Love to You, 1990
- To Be Two, 1994
- The Way of Love, 2002
- Entre Orient et Occident, 1999
- Sharing the World, 2008
- The Irigaray Reader, 1991
- Thinking the Difference for a Peaceful Revolution, 1994
- Forgetting of Air, 1999
- To Be Born: Genesis of a New Human Being, 2017
- Democracy Begins Between Two, 1994
- Elemental Passions: Translated from the French, 1992
- Conversations, 2008
- Everyday Prayers, 2004

Helen Cixous

Born in 1937, Helen Cixous is a French feminist, poet, playwright, philosopher and literary critic. Her most notable work is "The Laugh of the Medusa" which established her as a poststructuralist feminist.

Literary Career and Works

She holds honorary degrees from Universities in Canada, Ireland, UK and USA. From 2008 to 2014, she was at the Cornell University as a Professor.

She attained her Doctorate degree in 1968. Her prime focus during this time was English Literature and the works of James Joyce. She joined the University of Bordeaux in 1962 as an assistant and kept ascending in posts.

During the time of French students riots in 1968, she was charged with the opening of University of Paris VIII, which was believed to have been opened as an alternate to the traditional French academia. In 1974, Cixous opens the Centre for Women's Studies in the University of Paris VIII, the first of its kind in Europe.

In the 1970s, Cixous began writing on the relationship between sexuality and language. Thereon, she has published extensively and on a variety of subjects. Derrida referred to her as "the greatest living writer in the French language."

In 2000, a collection in Cixous' name was created at the Bibliotheque nationale de France to which Cixous donated all her manuscripts.

Major Works

- The Newly Born Woman, 1975
- Stigmata, 1988
- The Book of Promethea, 1983
- Three Steps on the Ladder of Writing, 1993
- Helen Cixous, Rootprints: Memory and Life Writing, 1994
- Coming to Writing and Other Essays
- Writing Notebooks of Helen Cixous, 2004
- Reading with Claice Lispector, 1989
- The Terrible But Unfinished Story of Norodom Sihanouk, King of Cambodia, 1985
- Hyperdream, 2006
- Manhattan, 2002
- First Days of the Year, 1990
- White Ink: Interviews on Sex, Text and Politics, 2008
- Readings: A Novel, 1991
- Dream I Tell You, 2003
- Insister of Jacques Derrida, 2006
- The Laugh of the Medusa, 2010
- Portrait of Jacques Derrida, 2001
- Veils, 2001
- Philippine, 2011
- Death Shall be Dethroned, 2016
- Love Itself: In the Letter Box, 2008
- Zero's Neighbour: Sam Beckett, 2007
- Angst, 1977
- The Day I Wasn't There, 2004
- Inside, 1986

- Abstracts and Brief Chronicles of the Time, 2016
- Eve Escapes, 2012
- Tomb(e), 2014
- So Close, 2007
- Poetry in Painting: Writings on Contemporary Arts and Aesthetics, 2012
- Politics, Ethics and Performance, 2016
- Volleys of Humanity: Essays 1972-2009, 2011
- Twists and Turns in the Heart's Antarctic, 2013
- Neuter, 1972

Postcolonialism

"Things fall apart; the centre cannot hold;
Mere anarchy is loosed upon the world."
(WB Yeats' poem '*The Second Coming*')

The idea of 'anarchy' and things falling apart because the centre cannot hold in a way best describes the traditions of colonialism which the postcolonial corpus of literature, theory and activism challenges. Dating back to the sixteenth century, the colonial and imperial encounter between the West and the non-west has led to historical, political and cultural ramifications often dictating a Eurocentric superiority on the natives who are believed to be inferior, barbaric and uncivilized. The superimposition of the colonial authority along with its culture and civilization have led to the social exclusion and denigration of the native systems, cultures and civilizations.

In an attempt to establish the dominance and pre-eminence of the colonial ruler, the colonizer has often sought to suppress the native systems of culture and civilisation, including their language, ritual practices and other routine life codes by demeaning them as regressive or obsolete. These acts of suppression and oppression, however, were resisted by the natives in order to save their indigenous languages, cultures and lifestyles. Also, at a broader level, there was political resistance to the authority of the colonizer who was considered to be an outsider.

This opposition between the colonizer and the colonized where the colonized attempts to regain its lost power, authority, voice can be understood as postcolonial in history, politics, and literature respectively.

Postcolonialism can therefore be said to be the response of the colonized to the colonial oppression. Postcolonialism is a very important division of cultural studies for it examines the social and political inequalities in order to bring about structural justice. Postcolonialism can be broadly divided into two approaches. The first one being anti-colonial driven by nationalist thinkers and theorists such as Mohandas Gandhi and Frantz Fanon who focus on a practical political mechanism to fight out the colonizer. The other approach, however, concerns itself with the academic discourse in which the theoreticians 'write back' to the 'Empire' sometimes defending the native cultures, while at other times glorifying them. Edward Said and Gayatri Spivak could be associated with this politics of resistance and transformation.

Origin and Evolution

Clearly postcolonialism is to do with the examining of the binary power relations that operate between the colonizer and the colonized. Yet, the prefix 'post' is a cause of a lot of debate in the term postcolonial. The two different traditions within postcolonialism prefer two different terminologies- Post-colonial and postcolonial, respectively. While the first focusses on the history, politics and literature post the colonial rule, in which the date of independence is usually seen as the watershed date; the second usage denotes the years of political and cultural struggles that need not depend on independence to qualify for post-colonial, for they believe their resistance to be postcolonial in thought.

It is difficult to resolve the debate. Yet, it is believed that the nationalist debates after 1945 as well as the intellectual works that were anti-colonialist are both responsible in shaping the postcolonial worldview. In the domain of postcolonial studies, however, Edward Said's publication of Orientalism in 1978 is understood to be the precursor of postcolonial studies. Said non-materialist approach shaped by Foucault's ideas on Power highlights the theory of exclusion and depravation as central to the post-colonial and neo-colonial situations. Other important postcolonial theorists, Spivak and Bhabha, too, used theory to understand the postcolonial situation.

While Spivak offered a Derridean reading, Bhabha offered a Lacanian examination. In the field of postcolonial studies, much was also offered by postcolonial writers of fiction, who were answering back the Empire through their own mechanisms.

Thinkers of Postcolonialism

Elleke Boehmer

Acclaimed as a founding figure in the field of Postcolonial studies, Elleke Boehmer is a Professor of World Literature in English at the University of Oxford and a Governing Body Fellow at Wolfson College. Boehmer was born in 1961 to Dutch parents in Durban, South Africa.

Literary Career and Works

She pursued her studies in English and Modern languages, and also studied medicine, but could not complete it. During this period, Boehmer became influenced by the Black consciousness thought of Steve Biko, an activist. She completed her M. Phil in English literature and her doctoral thesis from St. John's College in the 1980s.

Her first book, 'Colonial and Postcolonial Literature: Migrant Metaphors,' published in 1995 covers a vast expanse, looking at the anglophone literary productions from 1830s, cutting across myriad genres and also examining both the English as well as post-colonial writers. This work is important as it reflects on various processes of identity formation vis-à-vis the lens of nationality, gender, and colonial encounter.

Boehmer worked as the general editor of Oxford University Press for their series in Postcolonial literatures. She is also on editorial boards of many international journals on Postcolonial Writings.

She is also the trustee of the Charlie Perkins Scholarship established in 2010 which funds the study of aboriginal Australian students. She is also a Rhodes Trustee since 2016. In 2014-15, Boehmer served as a judge for the Man Booker International Prize. Boehmer holds several important posts and continues to contriute to her areas of interest.

Major Works

- Colonial and Postcolonial Literature, 1995
- The Shouting in the Dark, 2015
- Stories of Women, 2005
- Indian Arrivals, 1870-1915: Networks of British Empire, 2015
- Nile Baby, 2008
- Postcolonial Poetics, 2018
- Sharmila and Other Portraits, 2010
- Nelson Mandela: A Very Short Introduction, 2008
- Empire, the National, and The Postcolonial, 2002
- Screens Against the Sky, 1990
- An Immaculate Figure, 1993
- Bloodlines, 2000
- Nelson Mandela: The Black Pimpernel, 2013
- The Future of the Postcolonial Past: Beyond Representation, 2017
- Mandela: Introduction and Biography Bundle, 2013

Edward Said

Born in Palestinian America in 1935, Edward Said was a professor of literature at the Columbia University. He is one of the founding figures in the academic domain of postcolonial studies.

Said's father, Wadie Said, was a Palestinian who served as a soldier in the US army. So, Edward Said was born a citizen of the United States. Said received his education at British and American schools. This offered Said a bi-cultural perspective, which he applied to understand the different cultural-politics off the Western and the Eastern worlds, especially the Israeli-Palestinian conflict.

Literary Career and Works

He is a key figure in postcolonial theories offering a critique of the cultural perceptions of the West in their looking down upon the other or "the Orient."

He joined the Columbia University in 1963 as a faculty in the English department and taught there till 2003.

In 1974, he also served as a Visiting Professor of Comparative Literature at Harvard University.

During 1975-76, he was a Fellow of the Centre for Advanced Studies in Behavioural Sciences at the Stanford University. In 1977, he became the professor at the University of Columbia. In 1979, he was a Visiting Professor at John Hopkins University in the department of Humanities.

All in all, he lectured at more than 200 universities in North America, Europe and Middle East. He was awarded at least twenty honorary degrees during the course of his professional life. He was the recipient of the Bowdoin Prize by the Harvard University, Lionel Trilling Book Award, the Wellek Prize of the American Comparative Literature Association, the Spinoza Lens Prize, the Lannan Literary Award for Lifetime achievement, among many others.

His autobiography, Out of the Place (1999) too received three awards. In 2011, BBC published the Representation of the Intellectual, a six-lecture series in which he examined the role of a public intellectual.

He died in September 2003, after enduring leukaemia for about twelve years. Several books were written as a tribute to him and in 2012, the Barenboim-Said Academy was established in Berlin to monumentalise this great critic.

Major Works

- Orientalism, 1978
- Culture and Imperialism, 1993
- The Question of Palestine, 1979
- Covering Islam, 1981
- Out of Place: A Memoir, 1999
- Reflections on Exile and Other Essays, 2000
- On Late Style
- The Edward Said Reader, 2000
- Power, Politics and Culture, 2001
- The World, the Text and the Critic, 1983
- The End of the Peace Process, 2000
- Representations of the Intellectual, 1994
- Peace and its Discontents, 1995
- The Politics of Dispossession, 1994
- Humanism and Democratic Criticism
- Parallels and Paradoxes, 2002
- Freud and the Non-European, 2003
- After the Last Sky, 1986
- Joseph Conrad and the fiction of Autobiography, 1966
- Beginnings: Intention and Method, 1975
- Musical Elaborations, 1991
- Conversations with Edward Said
- Culture and Resistance, 2003
- From Oslo to Iraq
- Music at the Limits
- The Pen and the Sword, 1994
- Yeats and Decolonisation, 1988
- Acts of Aggression, 1999
- Edward Said: Continuing the Conversation, 2006
- Cultural Imperialism, 1993
- The Arabs Today, 1973
- Crimes of Terror: The Legal and Political Implications of Federal Terrorism Prosecutions, 2015 (Posthumous)
- Mona Hatoum, 1993
- The Politics of Anti-Semitism, 2003

Gayatri Spivak

Born in 1942, Gayatri Chakravorty Spivak is one of the most influential figures in the field of postcolonial studies, best known for her essay, *Can the Subaltern Speak*? She is an Indian scholar, literary theorist and postcolonial-feminist critic.

Spivak completed her early education and graduation from Kolkata. In 1961, she joined the graduate program in English at Cornell University. In 1962, she transferred to the department of Comparative Literature and started working under the guidance of Paul de Man. Her thesis was on Yeats. She presented a course on Yeats in Yeats Summer school, Sligo, discussing Yeats' positioning within the postcolonial realm.

Literary Career and Works

In 1965, Spivak joined University of Iowa as professor in the Department of English. She was highly influenced by Marx, Gramsci, Derrida, Mahasweta Devi and Foucault. She translated some of the works of Derrida.

In 1974, she founded the MFA in Translation in the Department of Comparative Literature. Subsequently she started working as a professor and visiting professor at various universities.

She received eleven honorary doctorates from Universities of London, Toronto, Virgili and so on.

In 2012, she received the Kyoto Prize in Arts and Philosophy, being the only Indian recipient in the category. Her name also appears on several advisory boards of academic journals.

Her most significant contribution to the field of postcolonial studies is her idea of marginality and subaltern and the intersection between feminism and postcolonialism. Since 1986, she has preoccupied herself by teaching and training landless illiterates in Bihar, Bengal and Jharkhand.

With the help of the financial aid left to her friend, Lore Metzger, she established the Pares and Sivani Chakravarty Memorial foundation for Rural Education. She also dedicated much of her Kyoto prize money to it, enabling the education and development of the illiterate masses.

Major Works

- In Other Worlds, 1987
- A Critique of Post-colonial Reason, 1999
- The Post-colonial Critic, 1990
- Outside in the Teaching Machine, 1993
- Death of a Discipline, 2003
- The Spivak Reader, 1995
- Other Asias, 2003
- Nationalism and the Imagination, 2010
- An Aesthetic in the Era of Globalisation, 2012
- Can the Subaltern Speak 2008
- Conversations with Gayatri Chakravarty Spivak, 2006
- Readings, 2014
- Who Sings the Nation-state Language, Politics, Belonging (co-edited with Judith Butler), 2007
- Myself Must I Remake: The Life and Poetry of WB Yeats, 1974
- Ethics and Politics in Tagore, Coetzee and Certain Scenes of Teaching, 2018
- Harlem, 2012
- Thinking Academic Freedom in Gendered Post-coloniality, 1992
- Through the Roadblocks: Realities in Raw Motion

Homi K Bhabha

Born in 1949, Homi K. Bhabha is an Indian English scholar and theorist. He was born in Bombay into a Parsi family. He received his early education and Bachelor's degree from the University of Mumbai, and later went to Oxford University

Literary Career and Works

He serves as a Professor of English and American literature and as the Director of the Mahindra Humanities Centre at Harvard University.

He taught at the English Department at the University of Sussex for almost ten years, after which he received a senior fellowship at the Princeton University. He was also a visiting Professor at the University of Pennsylvania and a fellow faculty at Dartmouth College.

Bhabha also served as an Editor of Public Culture, an academic journal by Duke University Press.

In 2012, he was awarded the Padma Bhushan by the Indian Government.

Bhabha is a very important figure in the field of postcolonial studies; he is credited with coining of various important terms in the field of postcolonial studies, such as hybridity, mimicry, difference, ambivalence and so on.

Major Works

- Midnight to the Boom: Painting in India after Independence, 2013
- Mtra Tabrizian: Another Country, 2012
- Our Neighbours, Ourselves: Contemporary Reflections on Survival, 2011
- Raqib Shaw: Absence of God, 2009
- 1000 Names, 1998
- Mary Kelly, 1997
- The Location of Culture, 1994
- Identity: The Real Me, 1987

Marxism

"The class which has the means of material production at its disposal, has control at the same time over the means of mental production, so that thereby, generally speaking, the ideas of those who lack the means of mental production are subject to it."

Karl Marx from The German Ideology

The above statement from Karl Marx, a German political thinker and scientist, believed to be the key figure in putting forth the theory of Marxism, strikingly sums up the crux of his philosophy. Marxism attempts to offer a historical analysis of the socio-economic means of production, thereby offering an understanding of the class relations and social conflicts. According to Marx and his friend and collaborator, Friedrich Engels, an investigation into the structure and the role of economic and productive processes within it is the key to comprehending the contemporary society.

Marxist theorists argue that in capitalist societies, there is a definitive relation between its two major classes, the proletariat and the bourgeoisie, and this relationship comprises mostly of contradictions in the material interests of both. The proletariat or the working class consisting of wage labourers, employed to produce goods and services is exploited by the oppressive bourgeoise or the ruling class that owns the means of production. The bourgeoise would amass and appropriate the surplus produced by the proletariat leading to a more than unequal distribution of the profit, leading to depravation and dissatisfaction among the labour class.

The increasing exploitation of the wage labourers and the growing dissatisfaction among them leads to social crisis which often shoots out a revolution. For Marx this in itself is a process that could finally culminate in the establishment of socialism, a society that is classless and maintains equity among it citizens thereby catering to the needs of all by erasing the boundaries between the bourgeoise and the proletariat, the ruling and the working class.

Marxist Literary theory, drawing its base from economics, moves on to focus on class relations and the market scenario within which the text, the writer and its readers operate. The Marxist critic is able to comprehend not only what the text says but also why it says and what it not says owing to the invisible power relations operative in the society. A Marxist critic, therefore, goes beyond the obvious and tries to understand the underlying ideology of the text and that of its author.

Origin and Evolution

Marxism as a doctrine developed around mid-nineteenth century when Karl Marx and Friedrich Engels put together their concept of historical materialism in order to offer a scientific understanding of the society. The term "Marxism" was popularized by Karl Kautsky who considered himself an orthodox Marxist.

Since Marx and Engels did not put together a systematic theory of Marxism for literary studies, there developed various traditions of Marxism in the later centuries.

The early Marxist literary theory focussed on realism and the realist novel and was believed to be dogmatic. The second phase of Marxist literary theory attempted to challenge the dogmas and offer an extension to the early classical Marxist theory by replacing socialist realism with bourgeoise realism. The Frankfurt School of critics developed their own versions of Marxism depending upon their personal ideological perspectives. Post World War II, the latter half of the twentieth century saw different theories of Marxism blended with psychoanalysis, feminism and media studies.

Karl Marx

Born in Trier, in the German Rhineland in 1818, Karl Marx was a German philosopher, economist, historian, political theoretician and activist. He was born to a Jewish family, who later converted to Christianity. Like his father who pursued a career in law, Marx too studied law in Bonn and Berlin and then completed his PhD thesis in Philosophy in 1841. Marx wanted to pursue an academic career. However, he moved among a group of thinkers considered too radical for the times and this ruined his academic prospects. Soon after Marx concerned himself with political and social issues and took on in the field of journalism.

Literary Career and Works

In 1845, he wrote *The German Ideology*, co-written with Friedrich Engels, in which Marx began to develop the theory of history. In 1848, he returned to Germany to take part in the revolution. As the revolution failed, he came back to London where he spent the rest of his life.

By 1859, he focussed his study entirely on Economics and began to develop his idea of the Political Economy which he published as his *Contributions to the Critique* of the *Political Economy*. This was to become a Preface to his later theory of *Historical Materialism*.

Marx continued to write and publish his ideas on the political economics and historical materialism. He exhausted himself working late into the night, hardly getting enough sleep. This affected his health, leading to his death as a stateless person.

Major Works

- Capital: The Process of Capitalist Production, 1867
- The Communist Manifesto, 1848
- The German Ideology, 1846
- Economic and Philosophic Manuscript of 1844
- A Critique of Political Economy, 1859
- Capital, Volume 1, 1867
- The Eighteenth Brumaire of Louis Napolean, 1852
- Critique of the Gotha Program, 1891
- Theses on Feurbach, 1888
- The Civil War in France, 1871
- The Holy Family, 1845
- Critique of Hegel's Philosophy of Right, 1844
- The Poverty of Philosophy, 1847
- Wage, Labour and Capital, 1849
- The Class Struggles in France 1848-1850
- A World Without Jews, 1844
- Capital, Volume III, 1894
- Value, Price and Profit, 1865
- Theories of Surplus Value
- Capital, Volume II, 1885
- Selected Writings
- Marx/ Engels Gesamtausgabe
- Revolution and Counter-Revolution, 1896
- Collected Works of Karl Marx and Frederick Engels
- An Unfinished Revolution
- Marx-Engels- Werke, 1983
- Marks on Suicide, 1864
- Herr Vogt, 1860
- The Annotated Communist Manifesto, 1848
- On Religion
- Karl Marx on India

Louis Althusser

Born in Algeria in 1918, Louis Pierre Althusser was a French Marxist philosopher. He received his higher education from an establishment called Ecole Norman Superieure in Paris. He spent his life under the influence of Catholic professors and some critics believed his reading of Marxism to be affected by it for Althusser was a big critic of Marxism despite being a key member of the French Communist Party.

Althusser is believed to be a Structural Marxist though his affiliation to French structuralism is not direct and simple and layered with various ideological complexities.

His higher education was deferred due to the second World War. Like many French soldiers serving in the army, Althusser too was held a prisoner in Germany. In prison, Althusser came under the influence of Marxism. The war experience also left an indelible mark on his mental well-being, leaving him depressed for long periods.

However, according to a few critics this period of mental instability played an important role in shaping his philosophical thought.

Literary Career and Works

In 1946, Althusser resumed his studies. Around this period, he came across a series of thinkers and philosophers who influenced and impacted his arguments. Such as Helene Rytmann, Jacques Martin, GWF Hegel, Herman Hesse, and so on. Martin especially cultivated Althusser's interest in reading Jean Cavailles, Georges Canguilhem and Hegel. The combination of Catholicism and Marxism led him to adopt German idealism and Hegelian thought.

Althusser delivered many lectures and conferences at Ecole Norman Superieure in participation with eminent French philosophers such as Lacan and Deleuze. These lectures had a great impact on now well-known French philosophers, who were among his students, like Derrida, Michael Foucault, Pierre Bourdieu, etc.

Later in his life, his bent of mind shifted towards Voltaire, Condorcet, Hobbes and Locke. His study was compiled in book form, released by Francis Matheron in 2006.

In 1980, owing to his growing mental instability, he killed his wife, Helene Rytmann. He was not tried legally because of his mental condition but was sent to an asylum. He did little academic work thereafter and died in 1990.

Major Works

- Lenin and Philosophy and Other Essays, 1970
- Politics and History, 1981
- Sur La Reproduction
- For Marx, 1965
- Philosophy and the Spontaneous Philosophy of the Scientists and the Other Essays, 1974
- Essays on Ideology, 1984
- Montesquieu, Rousseau, Marx, 1972
- How to be a Marxist in Philosophy, 2017
- Essays in Self-criticism, 1974
- The Humanist Controversy and other Writings, 2003

Antonio Gramsci

Antonio Gramsci (1891-1937) was an Italian Marxist, philosopher and communist politician. He is considered a neo-Marxist as he tried to break free from traditional Marxism. He was the founding member of the Communist Party of Italy and was imprisoned by Benito Mussolini's fascist regime. In prison, he wrote about 30 notebooks which significantly contributed to the twentieth century political history.

Gramsci's knowledge base included various thinkers such as Machiavelli, Vilfredo Pareto, Georges Sorel and Benedetto Croce; these were the widely respected Italian intellectuals of his times. His notebooks exhibit a deep understanding of critical theories of these thinkers and cover a wide range of topics like Italian Nationalism, French Revolution, fascism, Fordism, civil society, high and popular culture and so on.

The theory of cultural hegemony could be credited to Gramsci in which he unravels how bourgeoise, that is the state and the ruling class, uses cultural institutions to maintain power in a capitalist society. The bourgeoise develop their ideology which emanated as "common sense" or the belief system which dictates a pattern of cultural norms and values allocating power and resources to the superstructure. The proletariat are left out from this space which becomes elitist.

Literary Career and Works

In 1911, Gramsci won a scholarship to study at the University of Turin. This was a period of great social turmoil as Turin was going through phases of industrialisation kicked off by the setting of fiat and Lancia factories.

In 1913, he joined the Italian Socialist Party and got a chance to observe the Russian Revolution.

In 1914, Gramsci began writing for socialist newspapers and his writings turned him into a respectable journalist.

In 1916, he co-edited Piedmont edition of Avanti, an Italian newspaper, which became the manifesto of the Italian Socialist Party.

For the most part of his life, he kept working for the welfare of the working class. The establishment of the new fascist government under Mussolini and their emergency laws heeded several blows to the socialist parties. Gramsci even served 11 years in jail. His health continued to deteriorate in jail. At the age of 46, he died in the year 1937.

Major Works

- Selections from the Prison Notebooks, 1947
- Prison Notebooks, Volume 2, 1948
- The Antonio Gramsci Reader: Selected Writings 1916-1935, 1937
- The Modern Prince and Other Writings, 1959
- The Southern Question
- Selections from Cultural Writings, 1985
- L'albero del Ricco, 1966
- Selections from Political Writings, 1910-20, 1974
- Pre-prison Writings, 1994
- A Great and Terrible World: The Pre-Prison Letters: 1908-1926, 1992
- Il Materialismo Storico, 1948

Poststructuralism

The term 'Poststructuralism' amidst occurrences of several historical events could be understood as a counter-revolution against the system before it, namely structuralism. Structuralism's premise that human culture could only be comprehended by means of a model, structured on language, was fundamentally challenged by poststructuralists by emphasising the plurality and multiplicity, that is considered as a base by structuralists. The rejection of self-sufficiency offered by the meaning of a given word within a linguistic code is the main premise of the poststructuralists. To both structuralists as well as poststructuralists, language is central. However, one chooses to construct the subject in and with language, while the other questions this very construction of the subject. For this reason, the discourse of the poststructuralists theorists or thinkers is not based on one common doctrine; and is rather based on anti-essentialism.

Origin and Evolution

It is difficult to pin down the origin of poststructuralism to one thinker or one date. However, one can argue that poststructuralism as a philosophical position originated with the disillusionment with the systems in the Post World War II period. More specifically stemming from the disappointments faced from the failure of the Socialist communist politics and the death of the Soviet leader, Joseph Stalin. To rip apart the oppressive Capitalist, socialism was perceived to be necessary. However, dismantling of the bases of the socialist politics was equally pertinent.

Other important events leading to the beginning of the poststructuralist thought were the left-wing protests against the Gaullist party and the students riots in France. This was also the time when the promise of existentialist philosophy of Albert Camus and Jean-Paul Sartre had been exhausted. At this point, emerged several thinkers across the globe, a generation of poststructuralist thinkers such as Roland Barthes, Jacques Derrida, Paul de Man, Michel Foucault, Felix Guattari, Giles Deleuze and Gayatri Spivak. Each of these distinct scholars had their own version of post structural thought, making it difficult to come up with one common definition or school of thought. Yet, all of these challenged the Western metaphysics and its foundational concepts.

Roland Barthes

Born in November 1915, Roland Gerard Barthes was a French literary theorist, critic, philosopher and semiotician. Barthes' ideas developed and influence a wide array of critical theory such as semiotics, structuralism, post-structuralism, and anthropology.

Literary Career and Works

From 1935-39, Barthes studied classical literature. However, his academic periods were plagued by periods of ill health, which prevented him from taking any qualifying examinations. Due to his medical condition, he was also exempted from military service during World War II.

The period between 1939-48 was spent receiving license in grammar and philology. Soon, in the year 1941, he earned an equivalent M.A degree from the University of Paris in Greek Tragedy.

In 1948, Barthes gained various short-term positions at institutes in France, Romania and Egypt. By 1952, he settled at the Centre Nationale de la Recherche Scientifique, where he spent seven years studying sociology and lexicology and contributing to journals and magazines.

In 1957, Barthes began teaching at Middlebury College where he met Richard Howard, who would later become his English translator.

By the 1960s Barthes works had earned him great repute. He was travelling extensively to deliver lectures and attend conferences.

He wrote his best essay in 1967, 'The Death of the Author.' This essay proved an important piece in the study of deconstruction and the structuralist thought. He also contributed to the avant-garde literary magazine, Tel Quel, which was developing similar theoretical premise.

Barthes wrote his autobiography in 1975 titled Roland Barthes. In 1977, Barthes was elected the chair to the Semiotics Department at the College of France. He died in an accident in 1980. His last few works were basically meditations on photographs of his mother who died in 1977.

Major Works

- Mythologies, 1957
- Camera Lucida, 1980
- The Death of the Author, 1967
- A Lover's Discourse, 1977
- S/Z, 1970
- The Pleasure of the Text, 1973
- The Fashion System, 1967
- The Empire of Signs, 1970

- Image-Music-Text, 1977
- Writing Degree Zero, 1953
- Elements of Semiology, 1964
- Mourning Diary, 2009 (Posthumous)
- The Rustle of Language, 1984 (Posthumous)
- A Barthes Reader, 1975
- The Grain of the Voice, 1981 (Posthumous)
- Travels in China
- Critical Essays, 1963
- Criticism and Truth, 1966
- The Semiotic Challenge, 1985 (Posthumous)
- Sade, Fourier, Loyola, 1971
- The Responsibility of Forms
- Sur Racine, 1963
- What is Sport?
- The Eiffel Tower and Other Mythologies, 1979 (Posthumous)
- Introduction to the Structural Analysis of the Narrative, 1966

Jacques Derrida

Born in July 1930, Jacques Derrida was an Algerian-born French philosopher associated with Poststructuralism and Deconstruction. His early education at school was frequently interrupted due to the changing governmental politics implemented at school. However, at the age of 22, he entered the Ecole Normale Superieure where he met and became friends with Louis Althusser. In 1954, he completed his Master's degree in Philosophy on Edmund Husserl.

Literary Career and Works

During 1956-57, Derrida received a grant to study at the Harvard University. He spent the next two years teaching French and English to the children of Algerian soldiers. From 1960-64, Derrida taught philosophy at the Sorbonne. On recommendation of Althusser he earned a permanent teaching position at Ecole Normale Superiere In 1980, Derrida received his first honorary doctorate from the University of Columbia. He was also awarded a state doctorate by the University of Paris.

In 1983, Derrida worked in the film, 'Ghost Dance' depicting his own character. He contributed to the script of the film and worked alongside Ken McMullen in directing it.

In the later years, he received several honorary degrees and awards and worked as a visiting Professor at various universities. He is remembered for his significant contribution to the fields of phenomenology, poststructuralism and postmodernism. He died in 2004 of pancreatic cancer.

Major Works

- Of Grammatology, 1967
- Specters of Marx, 1993
- Archive Fever, 1995
- The Gift of Death, 1992
- Margins of Philosophy, 1972
- The Animal that Therefore I Am, 2002
- Glas, 1974
- The Post Card: From Socrates to Freud and Beyond, 1980
- The Truth in Painting, 1978
- Limited Inc, 1988
- Speech and Phenomena, 1967
- The Work of Mourning, 2001
- The Beast and the Sovereign
- Right to Philosophy, 1990
- Deconstruction in a Nutshell, 1997
- Of Spirit, 1989
- Acts of Literature, 1991
- On Touching- Jean-luc Nancy, 2000
- Spurs, 1978
- El Monolinguismo del Otro, 1996
- Of Hospitality, 1997
- Acts of Religion, 2002
- Rogues: Two Essays on Reason, 2003
- A Derrida Reader, 1991
- Learning to Live Finally
- On Cosmopolitanism and Forgiveness, 2001
- Dar La Muerte, 2004
- Philosophy in a Time of Terror, 2003
- Memoirs of the Blind: The Self-portrait and Other Ruins, 1993
- Deconstruction and Criticism, 1979
- Echographies of Television, 1996
- The Rhetoric of Drugs, 1989
- Voice and Phenomenon: Introduction to the Problem of the Sign Husserl's Phenomenology, 1989
- Sovereignties in Question
- Khora, 1990

Michael Foucault

Born in 1926, Michel Foucault was a French philosopher, historian, social theorist and a literary critic. He is mostly associated with poststructuralist and postmodern thought, though he rejects these labels. His key area of interest, however, laid the relationship between power and knowledge. Foucault received his education at the Lycee Henry IV and Ecole Normale Superiore where he developed an interest in philosophy and came under the influence of Hyppolite and Althusser. He soon began publishing one work after another which brought to fore his structuralist thought. He would, however, distance himself from those ideas a couple of years later.

Literary Career and Works

From 1966 to 1968, Foucault gave lectures at the University of Tunis. In 1968 he returned to France and became the head of the Department of Philosophy at the University of Paris VIII. Around this time, he also became a member of many left-wing groups.

He is notably read by scholars engaged with discussions on feminism, sexuality, historical methodologies and crypto-normativity besides those interested in structuralist and poststructuralist thought processes.

Foucault was extensively read and received several awards. He died in 1984 at the age of 58 due to neurological disorder.

Major Works

- Discipline and Punish, 1975
- The History of Sexuality, 1976
- Madness and Civilisation, 1961
- The Order of Things, 1966
- The Archaeology of Knowledge, 1969
- The Birth of the Clinic, 1963
- What is an Author 1969
- The Birth of Biopolitics, 2004 (Posthumous)
- The Foucault Reader, 1984
- Society Must be Defended, 1992 (Posthumous)
- Security, Territory, Population, 2004 (Posthumous)
- Abnormal, 1999 (Posthumous)
- Power/ Knowledge: Selected Interviews and Other Writings, 1980
- The History of Sexuality: Volume 3, The Care of the Self
- The Hermeneutics of the Subject, 2007 (Posthumous)
- Aesthetics, Method and Epistemology
- Language, Counter-Memory, Practice, 1977
- The Courage of Truth
- This is Not a Pipe, 1973
- Technologies of the Self: A Seminar with Michel Foucault
- Foucault Live
- Death and the Labyrinth, 1963
- The Punitive Society
- Fearless Speech, 2001 (Posthumous)
- The Essential Foucault
- Introduction to Kant's Anthropology
- On the Government of the Living: Lectures at the College de France 1979-1980
- The Foucault Effect: Studies in Governmentality
- Hermeneutics of the Subject

EXAM BASED QUESTIONS

1 What is not true about cultural studies?
(a) Cultural studies is an inter-disciplinary field.
(b) Cultural studies reads the different ways in which texts are read.
(c) Cultural studies is dependent on canonical writers' perspectives.
(d) Cultural studies examines various socio-political and economic factors of the authors as well as the characters of a given text.

2 Which of the following works is written by Clifford Geertz?
(a) Culture and Civilization
(b) The Interpretation of Cultures
(c) Uses of Literacy
(d) Cultural Capital

3 Which of the following is true about Cultural studies? Cultural Studies believes literary texts are symptomatic of
1. The authors' response/ reaction to their social dynamics.
2. The imaginative faculties of their authors.
3. A close reading of the works of canonical writers.
4. A nostalgia for the bygone era/ or a vision for a utopian society.

(a) 1 and 2 (b) 1 and 3
(c) 1 and 4 (d) 2 and 4

4 The antecedents of cultural studies are usually seen in the works of
(a) Richard Hogart
(b) Mathew Arnolds
(c) Raymond Williams
(d) Stephen Greenblatt

5 Which of the following pairs is incorrectly matched?
(a) Mathew Arnolds : Culture and Civilisation
(b) Richard Hoggart : Uses of Literacy
(c) Raymond Williams : Culture and Society
(d) Stuart Hall : Truth and Power

6 The institutionalization of Cultural Studies happened in
(a) Britain in 1964
(b) United States in 1980s
(c) In Britain in 1978
(d) In South Asia in 1980s

7 Who among the following was the first director of the Centre for Contemporary Cultural Studies?
(a) FR Leavis
(b) Mathew Arnolds
(c) Richard Williams
(d) Richard Hoggart

8 The scope of the Cultural studies program widened at the University of Birmingham with the publication of the following journal.
(a) Tel Quel
(b) Working papers in Cultural Studies
(c) Culture and Civilisation
(d) The Interpretation of Cultures

9 Which among the following is not a critical theory in the development of Cultural Studies?
(a) Frankfurt Theory (b) Psychoanalytic Theory
(c) Leavisite Criticism
(d) Mass Communication Theory

10 Who popularized F R Leavis's idea of "The Great Tradition" by terming it as the "Cultural Capital"?
(a) Pierre Macherey (b) Pierre Bourdieu
(c) Robert Browning (d) Louis Althusser

11 In what ways was he Frankfurt school theory different from the Leavisite Criticism?
(a) The Frankfurt school focussed on the examination of the canonical literature.
(b) The Frankfurt school focussed on the examination of the popular culture.
(c) The Frankfurt school focussed on cyberculture.
(d) The Frankfurt school focussed on the political changes taking place in the public space.

12 Under which theory fall the concepts of visual studies cyber cultures, new technologies of embodiment and globalisation?
(a) Mass Communication Theory
(b) Leavisite Criticism Theory
(c) Frankfurt School Theory
(d) The Politics of the Practising Experts Theory

13 Which of these, is not a work by Richard Hoggart?
(a) Liberty and Legislation
(b) A Measured Life
(c) Contemporary Cultural Studies
(d) The Long Revolution

14 Who among the following was a key witness in the British trial of D H Lawrence's novel, "Lady Chatterly's Lover"?
(a) Raymond Williams (b) Stuart Hall
(c) Richard Hoggart (d) Mathew Arnold

15 Which of the following is not true for Richard Hoggart?
(a) He served as a Warden at University of London
(b) He began a journal titled, "Politics and Letters"
(c) He served as the Assistant Director of UNESCO from 1971-75
(d) He was part of the Royal Artillery during the Second World War.

16 The following writer was 14 when the Spanish Civil War broke out. He soon became the supporter of the League of Nations.
(a) Richard Hoggart (b) F R Leavis
(c) Raymond Williams (d) Stuart Hall

17 Besides Raymond Williams, who was the co-author of the pamphlets he wrote for the Communist Party?
(a) Richard Hoggart (b) Eric Hobsbawn
(c) Louis Althusser (d) Antonio Gramsci

18 Which among the following were Raymond Williams' co-editors of "Politics and Letters" started in 1948?
1. Roman Jakobson 2. TS Eliot
3. Clifford Collins 4. Wolf Mankowitz
(a) 1 and 2 (b) 2 and 3 (c) 3 and 4 (d) 1 and 4

19 Which of the following is in the correct order?
(a) Drama in Performance - Modern Tragedy- May Day Manifesto – Writing in Society
(b) Modern Tragedy- May Day Manifesto – Writing in Society - Drama in Performance
(c) May Day Manifesto – Writing in Society - Drama in Performance - Modern Tragedy
(d) Drama in Performance - May Day Manifesto - Modern Tragedy – Writing in Society

20 Match the following works with their Authors.
Works
1. Language and Literature
2. Continuing Education
3. Notes towards The Definition of Culture
4. Situating Marx
Authors
5. Stuart Hall 6. T. S Eliot
7. Richard Hoggart 8. Raymond Williams
(a) 1-8, 2-7, 3-6, 4-5 (b) 1-5, 2-7, 3-6, 4-8
(c) 1-8, 2-5, 3-6, 4-7 (d) 1-6, 2-5, 3-8, 4-7

21 Which among the following is not true for Stuart Hall?
(a) He was the first director for the Centre for British Cultural Studies
(b) He was a Jamaican-born British Marxist.
(c) He founded the "New Left Review", a bi-monthly journal
(d) He played a crucial role in Black Arts Movement.

22 Stuart Hall was not associated with the following journal.
(a) New Left Review
(b) Soundings: A journal of Politics and Culture
(c) Marxism Today
(d) Tel Quel

23 The title of Stuart Hall's memoir was
(a) Kindred (b) Familiar Stranger
(c) The Glass Castle (d) Persepolis

24 What does "hegemony" mean?
(a) Dominance of one political state over another.
(b) Socio-economic disparity
(c) Assimilation between two different cultures
(d) A cluster of patterned ideas determining power relations.

25 Identify the speaker of the following quote: "One is not born, but rather becomes, a woman."
(a) Kate Millet
(b) Julia Kristeva
(c) Elaine Showalter
(d) Simon de Beauvoir

26 By whom was the term 'Ideology' coined?
(a) Simone De Beauvoir
(b) Stuart Hall
(c) Antoine Destutt de Tracy
(d) Richard Hoggard

27 Which of the following is a Memoir by Stuart Hall?
(a) The Hard Road to Renewal
(b) Questions of Cultural Identity
(c) Familiar Stranger: A Life between Two Islands
(d) Resistance Through Rituals

28 The following philosopher coined the term "Feminism."
(a) Helen Cixous
(b) Charles Fourier
(c) Charles Baudelaire
(d) Pierre Bourdieu

29 Who's the author of 1929 essay, "A Room of One's Own"?
(a) Virginia Woolf
(b) Elaine Showalter
(c) Helen Cixous
(d) Sandra Gilbert and Susan Gubar

30 Who among the following is considered to be the founding figures of Feminism in the United States academia?
(a) Virginia Woolf
(b) Elaine Showalter
(c) Helen Cixous
(d) Sandra Gilbert and Susan Gubar

31 Elaine Showalter's prime area of research was
(a) The performativity of gender.
(b) Hysteria and madness in women.
(c) Ecofeminism
(d) Intersection between race and feminism

32 Arrange the following works by Elaine Showalter sequentially.
1. Inventing Herself
2. Speaking of Gender
3. Teaching Literature
4. Sexual Anarchy
(a) 2-4-1-3 (b) 1-3-2-4 (c) 4-3-2-1 (d) 3-4-1-2

33 Who among the following did not exercise an influence on Simon D Beauvoir?

(a) Sartre (b) Hegel
(c) Hoggart (d) Leibniz

34 In the following work by De Beauvoir, her lover, Algren, appears as a fictonal character.

(a) The Second Sex (b) The Mandarins
(c) All Men are Mortal (d) The Coming of Age

35 Which of the following works is not by Simon De Beauvoir?

(a) The Blood of Others
(b) All Said and Done
(c) Sister's Choice
(d) America Day by Day

36 What is not true about Mary Wollstonecraft?

(a) She was a twentieth century advocate of Women's rights.
(b) She was posthumously regarded as a feminist
(c) A Vindication of the Rights of Women is her most notable contribution.
(d) Her daughter was a great writer, Mary Shelley.

37 Published after her death, the memoir that almost damaged her reputation was published by

(a) Mary Shelley (b) William Goldwin
(c) Henry Fuseli (d) Gilbert Imlay

38 Which among the following is in correct sequence?

(a) Thoughts on the Education of Daughter – Mary – A Vindication of the Roghts of Woman – Maria
(b) Thoughts on the Education of Daughter – Maria – A Vindication of the Roghts of Woman – Mary
(c) Mary – A Vindication of the Roghts of Woman – Maria - Thoughts on the Education of Daughter
(d) Thoughts on the Education of Daughter – Maria - Mary – A Vindication of the Roghts of Woman

39 Which of the following is incorrectly paired?

(a) Judith Butler – Undoing Gender
(b) Wollstonecraft – The Feminist Papers
(c) Elaine Showalter – She Came to Stay
(d) Simon De Beauvoir – The Prime of Life

40 Which of the following works is not by Judith Butler?

(a) Giving an Account of Oneself
(b) Subjects of Desire
(c) She Came to Stay
(d) Who sings the Nation-state?

41 Which of these is incorrectly matched?

(a) Julia Kristeva – Bulgarian French philosopher
(b) Judith Butler – American philosopher
(c) Simon De Beauvoir – French philosopher
(d) Luce Irigaray – American philosopher

42 Who among the following did not exercise an influence on Julia Kristeva?

(a) Michael Bakhtin (b) William Goldwin
(c) Lucien Goldmann (d) Roland Barthes

43 Arrange the following works by Julia Kristeva in their correct sequence.

1. Power of Horror
2. Semiotike
3. Revolution in Poetic Language
4. The Samurai

(a) 2-3-1-4 (b) 1-3-2-4
(c) 4-3-2-1 (d) 3-4-1-2

44 What is the central theme of Luce Irigaray's works?

(a) Offering the historical overview of canonical works
(b) Studying the way men and women speak differently
(c) Working towards the education of women
(d) Establishing the class distinctions between different female writers.

45 What is not true about Luce Irigaray?

(a) She had two PhDs.
(b) She was much celebrated in the Freudian and Lacanian circles.
(c) Her second PhD led to her suspension from Ecole de Paris.
(d) She had a Masters degree from the University of Paris.

46 Which among the following is not correctly matched?

(a) This Sex Which is not One : 1966
(b) Ethics of Sexual Difference : 1982
(c) To Be Two : 1994
(d) Forgetting of Air : 1999

47 Helen Cixous researched extensively on the works of

(a) D H Lawrence (b) James Joyce
(c) Charles Baudilire (d) Sigmund Freud

48 Who endowed Helen Cixous with the following title:
"The greatest living writer in the French language"

(a) Noam Chomsky (b) Jacques Derrida
(c) Roland Barthes (d) Elaine Showalter

49 Which among the following is in the chronological order?

(a) The Newly Born Woman – Stigmata – Three Steps on the Ladder of Writing – Dream I Tell You
(b) The Newly Born Woman – Dream I Tell You - Stigmata – Three Steps on the Ladder of Writing
(c) The Newly Born Woman– Three Steps on the Ladder of Writing – Dream I Tell You– Stigmata
(d) Stigmata – Three Steps on the Ladder of Writing – Dream I Tell You - The Newly Born Woman

50 Match the following works with their authors.
Works
1. Angst 2. Everyday Prayers
3. Possessions 4. Parting Ways
Authors
5. Luce Irigaray 6. Helen Cixous
7. Julia Kristeva 8. Judith Butler
(a) 1-6, 2-5, 3-7, 4-8
(b) 1-5, 2-7, 3-6, 4-8
(c) 1-7, 2-5, 3-8, 4-6
(d) 1-6, 2-8, 3-5, 4-7

51 Which among the following texts is considered to be a precursor of postcolonial studies?
(a) Elleke Boehmer's The Shouting in the Dark
(b) Frantz Fanon's The Wretched of the Earth
(c) Edward Said's Orientalism
(d) Gayatri Spivak's Harlem

52 What is the most striking aspect of Elleke Boehmer's very first book, "Colonial and Postcolonial Literature: Migrant Metaphors"?
(a) It is the first book ever written on postcolonialism
(b) It looks at anglophone literary productions from 1830s
(c) It has imaginary dialogues between the colonized and the English writers.
(d) It offers translations of important indigenous texts.

53 Which of the following works is not by Elleke Boehmer?
(a) Nile Baby (b) Stories of Women
(c) After the last sky (d) Bloodlines

54 What is the title of Edward Said's autobiography?
(a) Culture and Imperialism
(b) Nile Baby
(c) Out of the Place
(d) Representations of the Intellectual

55 Arrange the following works by Edward Said in chronological order.
1. Orientalism
2. Culture and Imperialism
3. The Question of Palestine
4. Covering Islam
(a) 1-3-4-2 (b) 1-4-2-3 (c) 1-2-4-3 (d) 1-2-3-4

56 In the Department of Comparative Literature, Gayatri Spivak worked under the guidance of
(a) Edward Said
(b) Mahasweta Devi
(c) Paul de Man
(d) Antonio Gramsci

57 Around 1962, Gayatri Spivak wrote a thesis on
(a) Paul de Man
(b) W. B Yeats
(c) Antonio Gramsci
(d) Mahasweta Devi

58 Who among the following was the only Indian to receive the Kyoto Prize in 2012 in the field of Arts and Philosophy?
(a) Gayatri Spivak (b) Homi Bhabha
(c) Salman Rushdie (d) Vikram Seth

59 Spivak runs a Memorial foundation focussing on the education of illiterates in Bengal, Bihar and Jharkhand with the help of financial aid left to her by her friend,
(a) Homi Bhabha (b) Paul de Man
(c) Lore Metzger (d) Sivani Chakravarty

60 Which of the following works are not by Gayatri Chakravarty?
(a) Death of a Discipline (b) Truth and Power
(c) Other Asias (d) Harlem

61 Match the following works to their dates of publication.
1. In Other Worlds
2. A Critique of Postcolonial Reason
3. Can the Subaltern Speak?
4. The Postcolonial Critic
Dates
5. 2008 6. 1990
7. 1999 8. 1987
(a) 1-8, 2-7, 3-5, 4-6 (b) 1-5, 2-8, 3-7, 4-6
(c) 1-5, 2-6, 3-7, 4-8 (d) 1-7, 2-6, 3-8, 4-5

62 Which of the following pair is incorrect?
(a) Elleke Boehmer – Professor at University of Oxford
(b) Edward Said – Professor at Columbia University
(c) Gayatri Spivak – Professor at Barthes University
(d) Homi Bhabha – Professor at Harvard University

63 In which year was Homi Bhabha awarded the Padma Bhushan by the Indian Government?
(a) 1999 (b) 2000
(c) 2002 (d) 2012

64 Who among the following is credited with the coining of terms like hybridity and mimicry?
(a) Gayatri Spivak (b) Homi Bhabha
(c) Elleke Boehmer (d) Frantz Fanon

65 Which among the following is not a work by Homi Bhabha?
(a) Mary Kelly (b) Maria
(c) Raqib Shaw (d) Mtra Tabrizian

66 Identify the essay from which the following quote has been taken:
"The class which has the means of material production at its disposal, has control at the same time over the means of mental production, so that thereby, generally speaking, the ideas of those who lack the means of mental production are subject to it."
(a) The German Ideology (b) When Goods Get Together
(c) Value, Price and Profit (d) Sur La Reproduction

67 With whom did Karl Marx mostly work in collaboration?

(a) Antonio Gramsci (b) Louis Althusser
(c) Friedrich Engels (d) Jacques Derrida

68 Marxism bases its theory on an inverse relation between

(a) Colonizer and colonized
(b) Bourgeoise and proletariat
(c) Men and women
(d) Imperial and the indigenous

69 **Assertion** In a capitalist society, the proletariat are exploite.
Reason The bourgeoise amasses the surplus production and this leads to unequal distribution of profit.

(a) Both A and R are true.
(b) Both A and R are false.
(c) Both A and R are true, but R is not the correct explanation of (a)
(d) Both A and R are true and R is the correct explanation of (a)

70 According to Marx, the revolution by the exploited classes often leads to the establishment of a

(a) Capitalism (b) Feminism
(c) Republicanism (d) Socialism

71 Who coined the term "Marxism"?

(a) Karl Marx (b) Friedrich Engels
(c) Karl Kautsky (d) Antonio Gramsci

72 The term "historical Materialism" is associated with the following thinker.

(a) Karl Marx (b) Friedrich Engels
(c) Karl Kautsky (d) Antonio Gramsci

73 Which of the following works is not authored by Karl Marx?

(a) The Civil War in France (b) Theses on Feurbach
(c) The Holy Family (d) Essays on Ideology

74 Which of these is in the correct sequence?

(a) The Communist Manifesto– The Civil War in the United States – Karl Marx on India– Notes on James Mill
(b) The Communist Manifesto – Notes on James Mill – The Civil War in the United States – Karl Marx on India
(c) The Communist Manifesto – The Civil War in the United States – Notes on James Mill – Karl Marx on India
(d) Notes on James Mill - The Communist Manifesto – The Civil War in the United States – Karl Marx on India

75 Which of the following is not true for Louis Althusser?

(a) He was a key member of the French Communist Party
(b) He received his higher education from Ecole Norman Superieure
(c) He was critical of Karl Marx
(d) He was sentenced to life imprisonment for killing his wife.

76 Louis Althusser was influenced by a series of thinkers. Who among these does not fit into this list?

(a) Pierre Bourdieu (b) Jean Cavailles
(c) Georges Canguilhem (d) Sergeyevich Solovyov

77 Althusser's research was compiled in book form and released by

(a) Helene Rytmann (b) Francis Matheron
(c) Georges Canguilhem (d) Pierre Bourdieu

78 Which of these is incorrectly paired?

(a) Politics and History – Louis Althusser
(b) On Religion – Karl Marx
(c) Sur La Reproduction – Louis Althusser
(d) Herr Vogt – Louis Althusser

79 Arrange the following works by Louis Althusser in chronological order.

1. How to be a Marxist in Philosophy
2. The Humanist Controversy and Other Writings
3. Essays in Self Criticism
4. Montesquieu, Rousseau, Marx

(a) 1-2-3-4 (b) 4-3-2-1
(c) 2-4-1-3 (d) 1-3-2-4

80 Which among the following is a no-Marxist who is also the founding member of the Communist Party of Italy?

(a) Antonio Gramsci (b) Louis Althusse
(c) Benito Mussolini (d) Bendetto Croce

81 Antonio Gramsci was much influenced by the respected Italian Intellectuals of his times. Who among these is incorrectly placed in the list?

(a) Benito Mussolini
(b) Bendetto Croce
(c) Vilfredo Pareto
(d) Georges Sorel

82 Which of these is not true for Antonio Gramsci?

(a) He was the founding member of the Communist Party of Italy
(b) He was imprisoned during the fascist regime of Adolf Hitler.
(c) He wrote more than 30 notebooks when in prison.
(d) The theory of hegemony is credited to Antonio Gramsci.

83 **Assertion** Gramsci's theory of hegemony reveals that bourgeoise use cultural institutions to maintain their power.
Reason The bourgeoise ideology is emanated as 'common sense' and becomes the belief system in a capitalist economy.

(a) Both A and R are true.
(b) Both A and R are false.
(c) Both A and R are true and R is the correct explanation of A
(d) Both A and R are true but R is not the correct explanation of (a)

84 In 1913, Antonio Gramsci joined the
(a) University of Turin
(b) Italian Socialist Party
(c) The French Socialist Party
(d) Socialist Italian newspaper

85 Antonio Gramsci edited .... , which later became the manifesto of the Italian Socialist Party.
(a) Piedmont edition of Avanti
(b) Piedmont edition of Tel Quel
(c) The literary journal for international studies
(d) The Communist Manifesto of 1848

86 86. Gramsci spent .... years in jail during Mussolini's regime.
(a) Two (b) five
(c) Seven (d) Eleven

87 Which of the following is not a work by Antonio Gramsci?
(a) The Southern Question
(b) Antologia
(c) Selections from Cultural Writings
(d) Spectres of Marx

88 Arrange the following works by Gramsci in chronological order.
1. The Antonio Gramsci Reader: Selected Writings 1916-1935
2. Lettere dal carcere
3. The Modern Prince and Other Writings
4. Selections from the Prison Notebooks
(a) 1-4-3-2 (b) 1-3-2-4 (c) 3-4-2-1 (d) 4-3-1-2

89 Which of the following is not true for poststructuralism?
(a) Post-structuralism critiqued structuralism.
(b) It emphasised the plurality and multiplicity of the meanings in language
(c) It analysed the effects of post war trauma on human brains
(d) It refused to construct a subject within the comprehensibility of language.

90 What possibly led to the development of poststructuralism?
(a) The Communist Manifesto of 1948
(b) The disappointment towards the socialist communist politics
(c) The death of Albert Camus
(d) The increasing interest in the works of Ferdinand De Saussure

91 Which among the following is not true about Roland Barthes?
(a) He served in the military during the World War II.
(b) He died in an accident
(c) He is best known for his essay, "The Death of an Author."
(d) He wrote his autobiography in 1975.

92 Arrange the following works by Roland Barthes in chronological order.
1. Mythologies
2. Camera Lucida
3. The Death of the Author
4. A Lover's Discourse
(a) 1-3-4-2 (b) 1-4-2-3 (c) 3-4-2-1 (d) 2-4-1-3

93 Which of the following works is not by Roland Barthes?
(a) S/Z (b) The Pleasure of the Text
(c) The Fashion System (d) What is an Author?

94 Jacques Derrida completed his Master's degree on the following writer.
(a) Roland Barthes (b) Ferdinand De Saussure
(c) Edmund Husserl (d) Karl Marx

95 Derrida worked in a film in 1983, which was titled
(a) The Life of Jacques Derrida
(b) Ghost Dance
(c) The birth of the Intellect
(d) The Hollow Men

96 Which of the following works is not by Jacques Derrida?
(a) Of Grammatology (b) Specters of Marx
(c) Archive Fever (d) S/Z

97 What was the reason of Derrida's death?
(a) He died in an accident
(b) He died of pancreatic cancer
(c) He died of neurosis
(d) He died of tuberculosis

98 Which of the following is in the correct sequence?
(a) Margins of Philosophy - Glas – The Gift of Death – Archive Fever
(b) Margins of Philosophy - The Gift of Death – Glas – Archive Fever
(c) Margins of Philosophy– The Gift of Death – Archive Fever- Glas
(d) Glas – Margins of Philosophy - The Gift of Death – Archive Fever

99 Match the following works with their authors.
Works
1. S/Z
2. The Beast and the Sovereign
3. The Order of Things
4. Antologia
Authors
5. Antonio Gramsci
6. Michael Foucault
7. Jacques Derrida
8. Roland Barthes
Codes
(a) 1-8, 2-7, 3-6, 4-5 (b) 1-7, 2-8, 3-6, 4-5
(c) 1-6, 2-8, 3-5, 4-7 (d) 1-5, 2-6, 3-7, 4-8

100 In the early years of his writerly career, Foucault was influenced by the following thinkers.

1. Hyppolite
2. Althusser
3. Chomsky
4. Marx

(a) 1 and 2 (b) 2 and 3
(c) 3and 4 (d) 4 and 1

101 Which of these is not a work by Michael Foucault?

(a) Discipline and Punish
(b) The History of Sexuality
(c) The Beast and the Sovereign
(d) Madness and Civilization

102 Arrange the following works chronologically.

1. The Birth of the Clinic
2. What is an Author?
3. The Birth of Biopolitics
4. The Foucault Reader

Codes

(a) 1-2-4-3 (b) 2-1-4-3 (c) 1-4-3-2 (d) 3-1-2-4

103 Which of these is incorrectly paired?

(a) The Birth of Biopolitics - 2014
(b) The Foucault Reader - 1984
(c) Society Must be Defended - 1992
(d) Security, Territory, Population - 2004

104 Arrange the followig works by Richard Hoggart in correct sequence.

1. A Sort of Clowning
2. Promises to Keep: Thoughts in Old Age
3. First and Last Things
4. Everyday Language and Everyday Life

Codes

(a) 1, 3, 4, 2 (b) 1, 3, 2, 4 (c) 2, 3, 4, 1 (d) 4, 3,2, 1

105 **Assertion** Feminism as a discourse tries to recover suppressed bodies and voices, buried by social and cultural prejudices.

Reason They are oppressed by women who are partiarchal and consider suppression of women to be normal.

Codes

(a) Both A and R are true
(b) Both A and R are false
(c) Both A and R are true, but R is not the correct explanation of A
(d) Both A and R are true and R is the correct explanation of A

106 **Assertion** Irrespective of class, women stepping out for work is empowering for women.

Reason It is the woman's right or will if she wishes to seek employment.

Codes

(a) Both A and R are true
(b) Both A and R are false
(c) A is false but R is true
(d) A is true but R is false

107 "The novel is that creation by the woman of the woman, or by the subject who is in the process of becoming woman, of woman under capitalism." Identify the essay from which the above lines have taken.

(a) Juliet Mitchell's 'Femininity, Narrative and Psychoanalysis.'
(b) Michele Barrett's 'Ideology and the Cultural Production of Gender.'
(c) Elaine Showalter's 'The Female Tradition.'
(d) Gauri Viswanathan's 'The Beginnings of English Literary Study in British India.'

108 Match the following thinkers with their key theories/concepts.

	List I		List II
A.	Pierre Bourdieu	1.	Hegemony
B.	Antonio Gramsci	2.	Semiotics
C.	Roland Barthes	3.	Cultural capital
D.	Michel Foucault	4.	Power

Codes

	A	B	C	D		A	B	C	D
(a)	3	2	4	1	(b)	3	1	2	4
(c)	2	3	4	1	(d)	4	1	2	3

109 Essential to the structuralist approach, who coined the term "narratology" in The Grammar of Decameron?

(a) Tzvetan Todorov
(b) Roland Barthes
(c) Gerard Genette
(d) Gerald Prince

110 "All men are intellectuals, one could therefore say; but not all men have in society the function of intellectuals."

Choose the theorist who makes the above statement.

(a) Elaine Showalter
(b) Stuart Hall
(c) Antonio Gramsci
(d) Louis Althusser

111 What was the original title of Elaine Showalter's work, A Literature of Their Own?

(a) When the Goods Get Together
(b) Notes Towards the Definition of a Category
(c) The Female Tradition in the English Novel
(d) Madwoman in the Attic

112 "People know what they do, frequently they know why they do what they do, but what they don't know is what what they do does."

Identify the essay from which this quote from Michel Foucault has been extracte(d)

(a) Madness and Civilization.
(b) Truth and Power.
(c) The Formation of the Intellectuals.
(d) Hegemony and Separation of Powers.

113 Match the following works with their authors.

Works

1. Betty Friedan
2. Bell Hooks
3. Naomi Wolf
4. Audre Lord

Authors

5. The Feminist Mystique
6. The Beauty Myth
7. Sister Outsider
8. Feminism is for Everybody: Passionate Politics

(a) 1-5, 2-6, 3-7, 4-8 (b) 1-5, 2-8, 3-6, 4-7
(c) 2-5, 3-6, 4-7, 1-8 (d) 2-5, 3-7, 4-8, 1-6

114 Consider the point of commonality between the following works?

1. In a Materialist Way
2. The Object of Literature
3. Theory of Literary Production
4. Reading Capital

Codes

(a) These are all works by Pierre Bourdieu
(b) These are all works by Pierre Macherey
(c) These are all works by Umberto Eco
(d) These are all works by Raymond Williams

115 In the context of postcolonial theory, which of the following phrases is ill-placed?

(a) Orientalism (b) Hybridity
(c) Essentialism (d) Gynocriticism

116 We all like to think of ourselves as a standard, and I can see that it is genuinely difficult for the English middle class to suppose that the working class is not desperately anxious to become just like itself. I am afraid this must be unlearned.

Identify the writer of the above-mentioned quote.

(a) Edward Said (b) Julia Kristeva
(c) Raymond Williams (d) V. S. Naipaul

117 In the field of Dalit studies, which of these cannot contribute to theorizing or contextualizing Dalit literature?

(a) Gail Omvedt's Seeking Begumpura
(b) Arjun Dangle's Poisoned Bread
(c) B. R. Ambedkar's The Annihilation of Caste
(d) Raja Rao's Kanthapura

118 "No, we don't believe that any woman should have this choice. No woman should be authorised to stay at home to bring up her children. Society should be totally different. Women should not have that choice, too many women will make that one. It is a way of forcing women in a certain direction."

Identify the speaker of the above lines.

(a) Simon de Beauvoir (b) Julia Kristeva
(c) Elaine Showalter (d) Gayatri Spivack

119 In the following series, which of the set is correctly matched?

(a) Elleke Boehmer – Problems in Current Theories of Colonial Discourse, Ania Loomba – Colonial and Postcolonial Literature, Benita Parry – Colonialism/ Postcolonialism, Homi Bhabha – The Location of Culture
(b) Elleke Boehmer – The Location of Culture, Ania Loomba – Colonialism/ Postcolonialism, Benita Parry – Problems in Current Theories of Colonial Discourse, Homi Bhabha – Colonial and Postcolonial Literature
(c) Elleke Boehmer – Colonial and Postcolonial Literature, Ania Loomba – The Location of Culture, Benita Parry – Problems in Current Theories of Colonial Discourse, Homi Bhabha – Colonialism/ Postcolonialism
(d) Elleke Boehmer – Colonial and Postcolonial Literature, Ania Loomba – Colonialism/ Postcolonialism, Benita Parry – Problems in Current Theories of Colonial Discourse, Homi Bhabha – The Location of Culture

120 .... is associated with the phrase, "Ain't I a Woman"?

(a) Toni Morrison
(b) Maya Angelou
(c) Sojourner Truth
(d) Paul Gilroy

121 Consider the following texts and identify which of these remained unpublished during Karl Marx's lifetime.

1. The German Ideology
2. Theses on Feuerbach
3. On the Jewish Question
4. Critique of the Gotha Program

Codes

(a) 1, and 2 (b) 2 and 3
(c) 3 and 4 (d) 2 and 4

122 The only major work of Simone de Beauvoir, which according to her, Sartre didn't read before its publication was:

(a) Sisterhood is Global
(b) La Vieillesse
(c) When Things of the Spirit Come First
(d) La Ceremonie Des Adieux

123 **Assertion** The Modernist version of hybridity presents culture as still 'bounded.'

Reason There's an attempt that the native culture makes to assimilate with the dominant culture

Codes

(a) Both A and R are true
(b) Both A and R are false
(c) A is true but R is false
(d) A and R are true, but R is not the correct explanation of A

124 Match the following works with their authors

Works

1. Beyond a boundary
2. The Historical Novel
3. Selections from the Prison Notebooks
4. The Civil War in France

Authors

5. George Lukacs 6. CLR James
7. Karl Marx 8. Antonio Gramsci

(a) 1-8, 2-5, 3-6, 4-7 (b) 1-5, 2-6, 3-8, 4-7
(c) 1-6, 2-5, 3-8, 4-7 (d) 1-7, 2-8, 3-6, 4-5

125 Who were the English translators of Helen Cixous' 'The Laugh of the Medusa'?

(a) Lacan and Freud (b) Lacan and Cohen
(c) Derrida and Lacan (d) Paula and Keith Cohen

126 Which of the following texts is not associated with the theories of the gaze?

(a) Ways of seeing
(b) Lisa Harper's The Eyes Accost
(c) Visual Pleasure and Narrative Cinema
(d) The Deconstructive Angel

127 Who among the following is not a post-colonial feminist?

(a) Audre Lord (b) Kate Millet
(c) Jean Rhys (d) Mahashweta Devi

128 Gayatri Spivak coined the term 'strategic essentialism.' What does the term refer to?

(a) A temporary solidarity for social action.
(b) A battle between the sexes.
(c) Activism paraded by Marxists.
(d) The essential marginalization of the subaltern.

129 Frantz Fanon's 'Black Skin, White Masks' is an analysis of ....

(a) Africa in relation to the dualism of Europe and the East.
(b) Psychological effects of colonialism.
(c) Anti-colonial texts.
(d) The processes of decolonization.

130 Gayatri Spivak and her works of 1980s were highly influenced by these two scholars.

(a) Sigmund Freud and Jacques Lacan.
(b) Ranajit Guha and Dipesh Chakraborty.
(c) Edward Said and Stuart Hall.
(d) Dipesh Chakraborty and Edward Sai(d)

131 Which of the following works is not by Claude Levi-Strauss?

(a) The Savage Mind (b) The Raw and the Cooked
(c) Truth and Power (d) Myth and Meaning

132 What is the central theme of Vikram Seth's novels The Golden Gate and A Suitable Boy?

(a) A quest for a companion in life.
(b) A quest for identity
(c) Coming out of the closet
(d) A desire for freedom

133 Homi K. Bhabha's idea that the colonized is that which the colonial occupier is not, is derived from ....

(a) Freud's concept of identity as illusion
(b) Foucault's concept of identity as authority
(c) Lacan's concept of identity as negation
(d) Derrida's concept of identity as a mask

134 "The intellect, as a means for the preservation of the individual, develops its chief power in dissimulation; for its by dissimulation that the feebler, and less robust individuals preserve themselves, since it has been denied them to fight the battle of existence..."
Identify the source of the above-mentioned lines.

(a) Friedrich Nietzche's On Truth and Falsity in their Ultramoral Sense.
(b) Michael Foucault's Truth and Power
(c) David Thoreau's Civil Disobedience
(d) Aijaz Ahmad's Notes Towards the Definition of a Category

135 Which of the following thinkers posed a serious challenge to the structural linguistics of Saussure?

(a) Roman Jakobson (b) Claude Levi Strauss
(c) Jacques Lacan (d) Noam Chomsky

136 Arranging the following works by Stuart Hall in correct sequence.

1. The Popular Arts
2. Without Guarantees
3. Encoding and Decoding
4. Different

Codes

(a) 1, 4, 3, 2 (b) 4, 3, 2, 1 (c) 3, 4, 2, 1 (d) 1, 3, 2, 4

137 Edward Said's 'Orientalism' inspired a host od spin-off and related studies. Which of the following works was not developed as an expansion of Said's thinking?

(a) Ashish Nandy's The Intimate Enemy (1983)
(b) Christopher Miller's Blank Darkness (1985)
(c) Frantz Fanon's The Wretched of the Earth (1961)
(d) Gauri Viswanathan's Masks of Conquest (1989)

138 Which of the following works is not by Booker T. Washington?

(a) Character Building (b) My larger Education
(c) The Negro Problem (d) Physical Geography

139 Which of the following authors criticises the aspects of cultural studies theory by highlighting its strengths and weaknesses in his book titled, 'After Theory'?

(a) Harold Bloom (b) Terry Eagleton
(c) I K Wimsatt (d) Raymond Williams

140 Who coined the term 'translation studies'?

(a) Susan Basnett (b) James S Holmes
(c) Homi Bhabha (d) Loh Dianyang

141 Which of the following texts by Karl Marx was published posthumously?
(a) Communist Manifesto (b) Das Kapital
(c) Theories of Surplus Value
(d) Critique of Political Economy

142 In the following series, which of the set is correctly matched?
(a) Karl Marx – Critique of Political Economy, Theodor Adorno – The Cultural Industry, Terry Eagleton – Marxism and Literary Criticism, Raymond Williams – The Country and the City
(b) Karl Marx – The Cultural Industry, Theodor Adorno – Critique of Political Economy, Terry Eagleton – Marxism and Literary Criticism, Raymond Williams – The Country and the City
(c) Karl Marx – Critique of Political Economy, Theodor Adorno – The Country and the City, Terry Eagleton – The Cultural Industry, Raymond Williams – Marxism and Literary Criticism
(d) Karl Marx – The Country and the City, Theodor Adorno – Critique of Political Economy, Terry Eagleton – Marxism and Literary Criticism, Raymond Williams – The Cultural Industry

143 Match the following works to their authors
Works
A. The Madwoman in the Attic
B. Language and Sexual Difference
C. Simon de Beauvoir: A Re-reading
D. The Second Sex
Authors
1. Susan Gubar and Sandra Gilbert
2. Simone de Beauvoir
3. Judith Okely
4. Susan Sellers
Codes

	A	B	C	D		A	B	C	D
(a)	2	3	4	1	(b)	4	1	2	3
(c)	1	2	3	4	(d)	1	4	3	2

144 A major theory associated with structuralism is ....
(a) Binary opposition (b) Nihilism
(c) Existential crisis (d) Absurdity

145 Jean Rhy's Wide Sargossa Sea challenges the feminist perspective by intersecting it with questions of race. To do this, characters from which canonical novel are given their 'voice'?
(a) George Eliot's Mill on the Floss
(b) Toni Morrison's Beloved
(c) Charlotte Bronte's Jane Eyre
(d) Jane Austen's Pride and Prejudice

146 Identify the pair that had a huge influence on Pierre Macherey.
(a) Spinoza and Hegel (b) Freud and Lacan
(c) Said and Spivak (d) Saussure and Chomsky

147 Which of the following is in correct sequence?
(a) In Search of our Mother's Gardens – Wide Sargossa Sea - Beloved – Sexing the Cherry
(b) Wide Sargossa Sea – Beloved – Sexing the Cherry - In Search of our Mother's Gardens
(c) Wide Sargossa Sea - In Search of our Mother's Gardens – Beloved – Sexing the Cherry
(d) Wide Sargossa Sea - In Search of our Mother's Gardens– Sexing the Cherry– Beloved

148 Which among the following is Pierre Bourdieu's best-known work?
(a) Distinction: A Social Critique of the Judgement of Taste
(b) Marxism and Literature
(c) Barbarians, Philistines and Populace
(d) Sociology of Law

149 Which of the following is true about the 'Two Treatises of Government'?
1. It was published anonymously by John Locke.
2. It was published anonymously by Sir Robert Filmer.
3. It is a treatise stating Filmer's contestations against the paternalistic view of the government.
4. It was published in 1689.
Codes
(a) 1 and 4
(b) 2 and 4
(c) 2 and 3
(d) 1 and 3

150 Derrida uses the phrase "metaphysics" in the context of structuralism. What does this term signify?
(a) A criticism directed at structuralism.
(b) An extension of philosophical thought.
(c) A criticism of metaphysical poets.
(d) A study of subconscious.

151 "The traditional definition of 'hegemony' is political rule or domination, especially in relations between states. Marxism extended the definition of rule or domination to relations between social classes, and especially to definitions of a ruling class."
Identify the essay.
(a) Tradition and Culture
(b) Marxism and Literature
(c) The Formation of the Intellectuals
(d) Ideology and Ideological State Apparatus

152 Which of the following books is considered to be the first sustained structuralist analysis by Barthes?
(a) Criticism and Truth
(b) On Racine
(c) New Imposture
(d) Elements of Semiology

153 Among the following scholars, identify the founders of the Prague Linguistic Circle.

1. Ferdinand de Saussure 2. Roman Jakobson
3. Nikolaii Trubetzkoy 4. Martinet

Codes

(a) 1 and 2 (b) 2 and 3 (c) 3 and 4 (d) 1 and 4

154 Which of the following is in chronological order?

(a) On Racine – S/Z - Structural Analysis of Narratives – The Pleasure of the Text
(b) Structural Analysis of Narratives – S/Z – The Pleasure of the Text - On Racine
(c) On Racine - Structural Analysis of Narratives – S/Z – The Pleasure of the Text
(d) On Racine - Structural Analysis of Narratives –The Pleasure of the Text - S/Z

155 Which of the following is true about Stuart Hall's 'Encoding and Decoding in Television Discourse'?

(a) Semiotics helped to shape a distinctive cultural studies approach to the media.
(b) Semiotics put a constraint on the shaping of cultural studies.
(c) A criticism of allowing agency and complexity to the audience.
(d) Media and film studies hinder the progress of Cultural studies.

156 "In discussing the Negro, it is always to be borne in mind that, unlike all the other inhabitants of America he came here without his own consent; in fact, was compelled to leave his own country and become a part of another through physical force." Identify the essay from which the above-mentioned quote has been taken.

(a) Booker T Washington's The Future of the American Negro
(b) Booker T. Washington's Up from Slavery
(c) WE B Du Bois's The Philadelphia Negro
(d) WE B Du Bois's Black Reconstruction in America

157 Identify the name of the novelist and theorist who headed the publishing team of Tel Quel, founded in 1960.

(a) Julia Kristeva (b) Philippe Sollers
(c) Tzvetan Todorov (d) Gerard Genette

158 Arrange the following texts in the chronological order.

1. Culture and Society 2. The uses of Literacy
3. Mythologies 4. Elements of Semiology

Codes

(a) 1, 2, 3, 4 (b) 2, 1, 4, 3 (c) 4, 3, 2, 1 (d) 3, 2, 4, 1

159 Identify the thinker with whom the term "scopophilia" is associate(d)

(a) Jacques Lacan (b) Sigmund Feud
(c) Laura Mulvey (d) John Berger

160 Who among the following philosophers is a French Structuralist Marxist?

(a) Louis Althusser (b) Antonio Gramsci
(c) Richard Hoggart (d) Roland Barthes

161 "As it seems to be the opinion of some of the gentlemen who compose the committee of Public Instruction that the course which they have hitherto pursued was strictly prescribed by the British Parliament in 1813 and as, if that opinion be correct, a legislative act will be necessary to warrant a change." Identify the writer of these lines.

(a) David Thoreau
(b) Thomas Macaulay
(c) M K Gandhi (d) Edward Said

162 Match the following works with their authors.

Works

A. The Grass is singing B. The Man Died
C. Arrow of God D. Sleep with Me

Authors

1. Wole Soyinka 2. Doris Lessing
3. Hanif Kureishi 4. Chinua Achebe

Codes

	A	B	C	D		A	B	C	D
(a)	2	1	4	3	(b)	1	2	3	4
(c)	1	4	3	2	(d)	4	3	1	2

163 "We must stand on our own feet and fight as best as we can for our rights. So carry on your agitation and organize your forces. Power and prestige will come to you through struggle". Identify the speaker of the above-mentioned lines.

(a) Frantz Fanon (b) B.R Ambedkar
(c) Mahatma Gandhi (d) Wole Soyinka

164 Identify the name of the novel written by Margaret Harkness under the non-de plume, John Hall.

(a) Balzaac (b) City Girl
(c) Crime and Punishment (d) Middlemarch

165 Which of the following is not true about ecofeminism?

(a) Ecofeminists argued that women, nature and the Third World are victims of the exploitative male, capitalist technology.
(b) Eco feminists often used the image of 'web of life."
(c) Ecofeminists were praised by anti-essentialists for equating women with nature.
(d) Ecofeminists believed women had a natural tendency towards pacifism.

166 Identify the writer of the following lines:

"The major critical practitioners simply ignore imperialism. In recently rereading Lionel Trilling's fine little book on E. M Forster, for instance, I was struck that in his otherwise perceptive consideration of Howards End he does not once mention imperialism, which, in my reading of the book, is hard to miss, much less ignore."

(a) Edward Said (b) Raymond Williams
(c) Frantz Fanon (d) Gayatri Spivak

167 In which of the following works of Roland Barthes does his theory of reading come full circle and he passes the creative role from the writer to the reader?

(a) Sur Racine (b) S/Z
(c) The Death of the Author (d) Mythologies

168 Homi Bhabha's reading of Salman Rushdie in The Location of Cultures ensued the concept of ....

(a) Cultural studies (b) Cultural translation
(c) Póstcolonial feminism (d) Ecocriticism

169 Match the following works with their authors.

Works

A. The Mythology of Imperialism
B. Slavery, Imperialism and Freedom
C. Marxism and Imperialism
D. Culture and Society

Authors

1. Jonah Raskin 2. Gordon Lewis
3. VG Kiernan 4. Raymond Williams

Codes

	A	B	C	D		A	B	C	D
(a)	1	2	3	4	(b)	2	4	1	3
(c)	1	4	2	3	(d)	3	4	2	1

170 Consider the following scene and identify its text.

"'God' she said, 'what'm I going to do? I forgot my makeup, he'll kill me."

I studied her: In the twilight her face was grey. "Maybe he won't notice,' I said.

'He'll notice, don't you worry. Not now maybe, it hasn't all rubbed off, but in the morning. He wants me to look like a young chick all the time, if I don't he gets mad."

(a) John Bergers' Ways of Seeing
(b) Margaret Atwood's Surfacing
(c) George Eliot's Middleton
(d) Lisa Harper's The Eyes Accost

171 The concept of sense-to-sense translation is often associated with the following thinker.

(a) Cicero (b) Jerome (c) Herodotus (d) Holmes

172 Identify the book in which Sartre defends realist novel as the only kind of literature capable of addressing ideological controversies.

(a) What is Literature? (b) Writing Degree Zero
(c) Grammar of Decameron (d) Logic of Narrative

173 Identify the pair that accuses Derrida of not paying attention to the social and historical reality by substituting reading for political action?

(a) Sigmund Freud and Jacques Lacan
(b) Edward Said and Terry Eagleton
(c) Raymond Williams and Stuart Hall
(d) Elaine Showalter and Julia Kristeva

174 What makes Juliet Michell's feminist theory different from that of Beauvoir, Millett and Greer.

(a) Juliet Michell advocates Freudian feminist theory.
(b) Juliet Michell critiques Freudian feminist theory.
(c) Juliet Michell advocates Marxist feminist overview of texts.
(d) Juliet Michell disregards Marxist feminist overview of texts.

175 **Assertion (A)** National identity flows in people's bloo(d)

Reason (R) It is acquired from common cultural practices that a society follows, such as reading the same newspaper.

(a) A is true but R is false (b) A is false but R is true
(c) Both A and R are true (d) Both A and R are false

176 Match the following events from Column A to their dates of occurrence in column B.

List I		List II
A. Mussolini came to power	1.	1917
B. The Bolshevik October Revolution	2.	1921
C. Gramsci founded the Communist Party of Italy	3.	1922
D. Gramsci dies in Rome	4.	1937

Codes

	A	B	C	D		A	B	C	D
(a)	3	1	2	4	(b)	4	3	2	1
(c)	2	3	4	1	(d)	1	4	2	3

177 **Assertion (A)** Woman as a speaking "I" does not exist in language.

Reason (R) When a woman says "I" she is talking from the position of a man.

Codes

(a) A is true but R is false (b) A is false but R is true
(c) Both A and R are true (d) Both A and R are false

178 Which of the following statements are correct about Foucault?

1. He joined the French Communist Party in 1948.
2. He often challenges the Marxist ideas about power.
3. He was the founding figure of Ecole Normale Superiere.
4. He attempted suicide and self-mutilation.

Codes

(a) 1, 2 and 3 (b) 1 , 2 and 4
(c) 2 , 3 and 4 (d) 1 , 3 and 4

179 Hind Swaraj or Indian Home Rule is a tract on Indian self-government, originally published in Gandhi's newspaper, titled ....

(a) Indian Opinion on South Africa
(b) Indian Politics in South Africa
(c) Passive Resistance in India
(d) Passive Resistance against British Raj

180 Identify the essay from which the following lines have been taken.

"The study of myths raises a methodological problem, in that it cannot be carried out according to the Cartesian Principle of breaking down the difficulty into as many parts as may be necessary for finding the solution. There is no real end to methodological analysis, no hidden unity to be grasped once the breaking-down process has been completed."

(a) Structure, Sign and Play in the Discourse of the Human Sciences
(b) The Raw and the Cooked
(c) Of Experience
(d) The Savage Mind

181 In the process of systematizing the narrative, Gerard Genette coins new terminology for old concepts. In the new scheme of things, if 'mimesis' stands for scene, 'analepsis' stands for flashback, 'prolepsis' stands for flash-forward; then, what does 'diegesis' stand for?

(a) History (b) Story-telling
(c) Signifier (d) Mood

182 Consider the following works and identify the lectures published posthumously after the death of its author, that form the base of structuralism.

(a) Course in General Linguistics
(b) Tel Quel
(c) Structural Anthropology
(d) Russian Formalism

183 The Russian formalism that influenced the origin of the French structuralism was an offshoot of ....

(a) Noam Chomsky and historical doctrine
(b) Prague School and Polish Structuralism
(c) Prague School and Russian Structuralism
(d) Roman Jacobson and Ferdinand de Saussure.

184 'Equal pay for equal work' is a slogan associated with second-wave of feminism. This type of liberal equality feminism is popularly associated with the following feminist:

(a) Elaine Showalter (b) Kate Millet
(c) Betty Friedan (d) Julia Kristeva

185 Choose two tags to define Mary Daly.

1. French feminist
2. American feminist
3. Ecofeminist
4. Psychoanalyst feminist

Codes

(a) 2 and 3 (b) 2 and 4
(c) 1 and 3 (d) 1 and 4

186 Identify the author of the following quote. "The characteristic feature of contemporary literary radicalism is that it rarely addresses the question of its own determination by the conditions of its production and the class location of its agents. In the rare case where this issue of one's own location— hence of the social determination of one's own practice—"

(a) Karl Marx, Das Kapital
(b) Aijaz Ahmad, In Theory
(c) Antonio Gramsci, The Formation of the I ntellectuals
(d) Michel Foucault, Truth and Power

187 Which of the following is true about Ecriture feminism?

1. Ecriture feminism deconstructs masculine language.
2. Ecriture feminism is political.
3. Ecriture feminism has been a part of the traditional literary canon
4. Ecriture feminism is linear, and authoritative

Codes

(a) 2 and 3 (b) 1 and 2 (c) 1 and 4 (d) 2 and 4

188 Which of the following is considered to be the best-known works of Aijaz Ahmad?

(a) Frontline
(b) In Theory
(c) Orientalism
(d) Passive Resistance and Education

189 "It is the fully articulate and systematic forms which are recognizable as ideology, and there is a corresponding tendency in the analysis of art to look only for similarly fully articulate and systematic expressions of this ideology in the content (base structure) or form (homology) of actual works."

Identify the essay from which the above-mentioned quote has been taken.

(a) Women's Time
(b) What is an author?
(c) From Marxism and Literature
(d) The Work of Art in the Age of Mechanical Reproduction

190 Arrange the following works in chronological order.

1. The Feminine Mystique
2. A Vindication of Rights of Women
3. Gender Trouble
4. The Female Eunuch

Codes

(a) 1, 3, 2, 4 (b) 3, 1, 2, 4 (c) 4, 2, 3, 1 (d) 2, 1, 4, 3

191 **Assertion** (A) According to Edward Said postcolonial resistant writers and readers are contrapuntal.

Reason (R) This is their way of answering back to the colonizer by examining the struggles over meaning taking place in the text of Empire itself.

Codes

(a) Both A and R are true
(b) Both A and R are false
(c) Both A and R are true, but R is not the correct explanation of A
(d) Both A and R are true, and R is the correct explanation of A

192 "History is really a record of every interruption of the even working of the force of love or of the soul."
Identify the speaker of the above quote.

(a) Aijaz Ahmad (b) Vladimir Lenin
(c) Frantz Fanon (d) M K Gandhi

193 Which of the following texts is a collection of essays through which its author refutes the need to support a particular ideology, by negating both black and white stereotypes?

(a) Invisible Man (b) Shadow and Act
(c) The Souls of Black Folks (d) Kindred

194 The term 'semiotics' means ....

(a) A study of interface between different cultural usages of a given language.
(b) A study of signs and symbols and how they are used.
(c) A study of individual-specific usage of language.
(d) A study of language change over a period of time.

195 For many feminists, the work of this following author signals a post-feminist era, when the division between man and woman is finally transcended.

(a) Poetical works of Emily Dickinson
(b) Judith Butler's Gender Trouble
(c) Toril Moi's Sexual/ Textual Politics
(d) Irigaray's This Sex which is not One.

196 Which of the following is in correct sequence?

(a) The Battle of Algiers- A Question of Power- Native Son- My Beautiful Launderette
(b) Native Son- A Question of Power- The Battle of Algiers- My Beautiful Launderette
(c) Native Son- A Question of Power- My Beautiful Launderette- The Battle of Algiers
(d) Native Son- The Battle of Algiers- A Question of Power- My Beautiful Launderette

197 Match the following works to their authors.

Works

A. Unspeakable Things Spoken
B. Criteria of Negro Art
C. Loose Canons
D. Physical Geography

Authors

1. Toni Morrison 2. Henry Louis Gates
3. Immanuel Kant 4. W. E. B. Du Bois

Codes

	A	B	C	D		A	B	C	D
(a)	1	4	2	3	(b)	2	1	3	4
(c)	1	2	4	3	(d)	4	3	2	1

198 "That government is best which governs the least." Identify the speaker of this statement and the essay.

(a) M. K Gandhi, Passive Resistance and Education
(b) David Thoreau, Resistance to Civil Government
(c) Waldo Browne, Man or the State?
(d) Abdel Malik, Orientalism in Crisis

199 **Assertion** Gender is manufactured.

Reason Gender is performed through gendered stylization of the body.

Codes

(a) Both A and R are true
(b) Both A and R are false
(c) Both A and R are true, but R is not the correct explanation of A
(d) Both A and R are true, and R is the correct explanation of A

200 "Men look at women. Women watch themselves being looked at. This determines not only most relations between men and women but also the relation of women to themselves. The surveyor of woman in herself is male: the surveyed female."
Identify the text from which the above-mentioned lines have been taken.

(a) John Bergers' Ways of Seeing
(b) Margaret Atwood's Surfacing
(c) George Eliot's Middleton
(d) Lisa Harper's The Eyes Accost

201 Published as The Autobiography of Malcolm X, who wrote the biography of Malcolm X?

(a) Alex Haley (b) Zora Neal Hurston
(c) Ralph Ellison (d) Octavia Butler

202 Match the following works with their authors.

Works

A. Macaulay's Minute
B. Civil Disobedience
C. On Truth and Falsity in their Ultra moral sense
D. A Room of One's Own

Authors

1. David Thoreau 2. Fredrich Nietzche
3. Virginia Woolf
4. T. B. Macaulay

Codes

	A	B	C	D		A	B	C	D
(a)	2	3	4	1	(b)	3	4	1	2
(c)	1	2	3	4	(d)	4	1	2	3

203 The 'culture and civilization' tradition within English studies stretches back to ....

(a) Matthew Arnold (b) F. R Leavis
(c) Q. D Leavis (d) Stuart Hall

204 "Beckett nicely formulates the theme with which I would like to begin: 'What does it matter who is speaking', someone said, 'What does it matter who is speaking.' In this indifference appears one of the fundamental ethical principles of contemporary writing."

Identify the title of the essay from which the above-mentioned quote has been taken.

(a) Women's Time (b) What is an author?
(c) Of Blindness to the Supplement
(d) The Work of Art in the Age of Mechanical Reproduction

205 Which of the following is in correct sequence?

(a) A Bend in the River- Interpreter of Maladies-The Kite Runner - A Brief Wondrous life of Oscar Wao
(b) A Bend in the River- Interpreter of Maladies— A Brief Wondrous life of Oscar Wao -The Kite Runner
(c) The Kite Runner- A Bend in the River- Interpreter of Maladies—A Brief Wondrous life of Oscar Wao
(d) Interpreter of Maladies— A Brief Wondrous life of Oscar Wao -The Kite Runner- A Bend in the River

206 The story of two telepathic twins from Kerela united over 20 years of separation is the central plot of ....

(a) The Namesake (b) The God of Small Things
(c) A Suitable Boy (d) The Sister of my Heart

207 Match the following works to their authors.

Works

1. The Souls of Black Folks
2. An Appeal to Congress for Impartial Suffrage
3. The Future of American Negro
4. A Question of Power

Authors

5. Bessie Head 6. Booker T. Washington
7. Fredrich Douglas 8. WEB Du Bois

(a) 1-8, 2-7, 3-6, 4-5 (b) 1-5, 2-7, 3-6, 4-8
(c) 1-7, 2-5, 3-8, 4-6 (d) 1-6, 2-7, 3-8, 4-5

208 The following thinker compiled a notebook of Shakespearean idioms and phrases when he was learning English in the 1840s.

(a) Stephen Greenblatt (b) Karl Marx
(c) Michael Bakhtin (d) Raymond Williams

209 Which of the following is not true about Cultural Studies?

(a) It initially developed in Britain as a reaction to liberal Humanism.
(b) It offered cross and interdisciplinary perspectives to reading literary texts.
(c) It privileged canonical literature.
(d) It was concerned with changing whole ways of communicating.

210 Who among the following is the writer of Their Eyes Were Watching God, published in 1937?

(a) Alex Haley (b) Lanston Hughes
(c) Zora Neale Hurston (d) W E B Du Bois

211 **Assertion** The colonizer seeks the colonized to reflect a certain pure image back at him; however, he encounters only an almost sameness, a not-quite otherness.

Reason The colonised even when aspires to remake itself, only slips into hybridization, no matter how subtle.

Codes

(a) Both A and R are true
(b) Both A and R are false
(c) Both A and R are true and R is the correct explanation of A
(d) Both A and R are true but R is not the correct explanation of A

212 Which of the following is true for Jefferson's Notes on the State of Virginia (1787)?

(a) Influenced by the French philosophies, Jefferson believed in racial equity.
(b) Jefferson was concerned with lack of intellectual and spiritual vacuity of the race.
(c) Jefferson believed the racial other to be good at painting, sculpture and particularly in poetry.
(d) Jefferson glorified the aesthetic properties of black bodies.

213 What does Homi Bhabha's concept of 'third space' describe?

(a) An ambivalent cultural interaction of migrant and minority groups with metropolitan cultures.
(b) An unstable intersection between third world, gender and post-war societies.
(c) Untranslatable cultural vocabularies.
(d) A space in which colonized the attempts to replicate the Eurocentric patterns.

214 Arrange the following works chronologically.

1. Treatise of Human Nature
2. On the Different Races of Men
3. Essays on the Nature and Immutability of Truth, in Opposition to Sophistry and Skepticism.
4. Two Treatises of Government

Codes

(a) 4, 1, 3, 2 (b) 1, 3, 2,4 (c) 3, 4, 1, 2 (d) 2, 1, 4,3

215 What is not true about the theoretical base of Gayatri Spivak's works?

(a) Spivak emphasises the different kinds of subject formation within the category of the oppresse(d)
(b) Much like the tendency in texts like Orientalism, Spivak sees colonial oppression as monolithic.
(c) Spivak emphasises specific gendered forms marking out the heterogeneous colonial experience.
(d) Spivak adopts the deconstructive techniques of her mentor, Jacques Derrida.

216 Who said the following lines?
"Let troubles and exploitation go and the kingdom of Bali come."
(a) Iyothee Thass (b) Chokhamela
(c) Jotirao Phule (d) Pandita Ramabai

217 According to Pnina Werbner, a British anthropologist, what is the term used to define final version of multiculturalism?
(a) Transversal Politics
(b) Cyborg Politics
(c) Global Politics
(d) Creolized Politics

218 Which of the following texts is considered as a stepping stone in the field of Theories of gaze?
(a) Ways of seeing
(b) Lisa Harper's The Eyes Accost
(c) Visual Pleasure and Narrative Cinema
(d) Theory of Sexuality

219 Noam Chomsky reformulates the Saussurean distinction between langue and parole by ....
(a) Leaving out the social dimension of language.
(b) Working on the historical evolution of language.
(c) Studying specific genres within literary frameworks.
(d) Drawing a distinction between sign and performance.

220 "If one is a man, still the woman part of his brain must have effect; and a woman also must have intercourse with the man in her. Coleridge perhaps meant this when he said that a great mind is androgynous."
Identify the writer of these lines.
(a) William Wordsworth
(b) Kate Millet
(c) Sigmund Freud
(d) Virginia Woolf

221 Identify the title of the essay from which the following quote has been taken.
"Homosexuality is the law that regulates the socio-cultural order. Homosexuality amounts to the assignment of roles in the economy: some are given the role of producing and exchanging subjects, while others are assigned the role of productive earth and goods."
(a) Truth and Power
(b) When the Goods get Together
(c) Structure, Sign and Play in the Discourse of Human Sciences
(d) Crisis

222 Who among the following is the author of the 1998 publication, "Postcolonial Shakespeares"?
(a) Harold Bloom (b) Ania Loomba
(c) Stephen Greenblatt (d) Suvir Kaul

223 Which of the following texts is not by James Baldwin?
(a) Nobody Knows My Name (b) Giovanni's Room
(c) The Fire Next Time (d) Kindred

224 Which of the following enabled Langston Hughes to publish his first collection of poems?
(a) Paul Lawrence Dunbar (b) Carl Sandburg
(c) Walt Whitman (d) Carl Van Vechten

225 Which among the following is a collection of poems by Chitra Banerjee Divakaruni?
(a) Oleander Girl (b) The Mistress of Spices
(c) Black Candle (d) Queen of Dreams

226 Match the following works to their authors.
Works
A. Imagined Communities
B. Nationalism and the State
C. Nations and Nationalism
D. The Idea of Nationalism
Authors
1. John Breuilly 2. Benedict Anderson
3. Ernest Gellner 4. Hans Kohn
Codes

	A	B	C	D		A	B	C	D
(a)	2	1	3	4	(b)	4	3	2	1
(c)	1	4	2	3	(d)	3	4	1	2

227 An interest in poststructuralism led to the establishment of a colloquium at .... in 1966.
(a) Harvard University (b) John Hopkins University
(c) Ecole Normale Superiore (d) University of Paris IV

228 Who among the following did not collaborate on 1965 book on Marx's Das Kapital?
(a) Louis Althusser (b) Antonio Gramsci
(c) Pierre Macherey (d) Jacques Ranciere

229 Which among the following writers is not the co-author of the 1989 book on postcolonialism, "The Empire writes Back: Theory and Practice in Postcolonial Literature"?
(a) Edward Said (b) Gareth Griffiths
(c) Bill Ashcroft (d) Helen Tiffin

230 The Italian novelist, philosopher and literary critic, Umberto Eco, is widely known for his 1980 novel, titled ....
(a) The Name of the Rose (b) Foucault's Pendulum
(c) The Island of the Day Before (d) The Prague Cemetery

231 What is the term given to a work of fiction in which a prevailing social problem such as gender, race or class is dramatized through the characters in it?
(a) Bildungsroman (b) Fable (c) Protest novel (d) arable

232 The field of 'glossematics' linguistics was developed in 1930s by ....
(a) Ferdinand de Saussure (b) Noam Chomsky
(c) Louis Hjelmslev (d) Roman Jakobson

233 Who among the following is not a Marxist historian?
(a) CLR James (b) Walter Rodney
(c) Max Beer (d) Bill Ashcroft.

234 Which of the following pairs is incorrectly matched?
(a) Rewriting History: The Life and Times of Pandita Ramabai – Uma Chakravarty
(b) The Nation and its Fragments- Partha Chatterjee
(c) Forging Community – Chokhamela
(d) Kabir: The weaver's Song – Vinay Dharwadker

235 "Better than transforming this country into a Hindu country, Hindustan, what is wrong with changing it into Dravidastan, or if the Brahmans could not tolerate this name, into Pakistan, a different name but embodying the same Dravidian ideology?"
Identify the speaker of the above lines.
(a) BR Ambedkar
(b) EV Ramasamy Periyar
(c) Iyothee Thass
(d) M K Gandhi

236 Which of the following does not belong to the category of diasporic fiction?
(a) Shauna Singh Baldwin's We are not in Pakistan
(b) Bharati Mukherjee's Desirable Daughters
(c) Raja Rao's Kanthapura
(d) Chitra Banerjee Divakaruni's Queen of Dreams

237 "Take up the white man's burden
Send forth the best ye breed-
Go bind your sons to exile
To serve your captive's need;
To wait in heavy harness
On fluttered folk and wild-
Your new-caught, sullen peoples,
Half devil and half chil(d)"
What is not true about the above poem?
(a) The poem was written by Rudyard Kipling.
(b) The poet directed it towards the Indian population subject to colonial rule.
(c) The poet discussed in it the troubled state of a culture under siege
(d) The poet aligned himself with the Eurocentric eccentricities.

238 Which of the following pairs is incorrectly matched?
(a) A Fine Balance by Rohinton Mistry
(b) The Inheritance of Loss by Kiran Desai
(c) Red Earth and Pouring Rain by Vikram Chandra
(d) The Glass Palace by Chitra Banerjee Divakaruni

239 The structuralists drew an analogy between.
(a) Language systems and ecosystem.
(b) Language systems and feminism.
(c) Language systems and social systems.
(d) Language systems and historical institutions.

240 Among the list of most prominent Black leaders of the nineteenth and twentieth century, who is incorrectly placed in this category?
(a) Fredrich Douglas (b) Bill Ashcroft
(c) Marcus Garvey (d) Martin Delany

241 Which of the following is not true about postcolonial feminism?
(a) Postcolonial feminism originated in the 1980s.
(b) Postcolonial feminism was a response to feminism focussing entirely on women in the Western cultures.
(c) Postcolonial feminism seeks feminism through the lens of class, race and other socio-political factors.
(d) Postcolonial feminism developed to critique the feminism in under-developed countries.

242 Marxism relies heavily on
(a) A socio-economic analysis of social conflict.
(b) The political doctrine formulated by imperial powers.
(c) Psychoanalytical theory of Freud and Lacan.
(d) Class dynamics operating among the 'other' gender.

243 What is the central theme of Jonathan Lethem's Chronic City?
(a) A coming-out narrative of a Sri Lankan boy.
(b) A narrative illustrating racial prejudices.
(c) A suburban space discussing migrant politics.
(d) A narrative of income inequality.

244 Who among the following is not a diasporic writer?
(a) Hari Kunzru (b) Sunetra Gupta
(c) Baby Kamble (d) Bharati Mukherjee

245 The novel, 'The Gypsy Goddess' is written by the following author.
(a) Vittal Rao (b) Meena Kandysamy
(c) Dilip Chitre (d) Bama Faustina

246 Which among the following works is not a text by Urmila Pawar?
(a) The Weave of my Life (b) The Prisons we Broke
(c) Mother Wit (d) Sixth Finger

247 According to certain critics, an alternative term for post-structuralists could be ....
(a) Existential phenomenology (b) Nihilism
(c) Existential crisis (d) Absurdity

248 Roland Barthes in his work, Elements of Semiology advanced the concept of the ....
(a) Mythologies (b) Cultural artefacts
(c) Metalanguage (d) Theatre of absurd

249 Who among the following authors is associated with the concept of intersectionality?
(a) Bell Hooks (b) Susan Gubar
(c) Kate Millett (d) Gayatri Spivak

250 "Women must write through their bodies, they must invent the impregnable language that will wreck partitions, classes, and rhetorics, regulations and codes, they must submerge, cut through, get beyond the ultimate reverse-discourse, including the one that laughs at the very idea of pronouncing the word 'silence'...In one another we will never be 'lacking.' Identify the writer.
(a) Julia Kristeva (b) Helen Cixous
(c) Luce Irigaray (d) Germaine Greer

251 In the following novel by Toni Morrison, the central female protagonist uses her individuality to bring the entire community together.

(a) Everyday Use (b) Sula
(c) Meridian (d) Alias Grace

252 Match the following novels by Margaret Atwood to their year of publication.

Novels

A. The Blind Assassin
B. Cat's Eye
C. The Handmaid's Tale
D. Oryx and Crake

Year of Publication

1. 1985 2. 2003
3. 2000 4. 1988

Codes

	A	B	C	D		A	B	C	D
(a)	3	4	1	2	(b)	4	2	1	3
(c)	1	2	3	4	(d)	2	1	4	3

253 Which of the following works is not by Frantz Fanon?

(a) Alienation and Freedom
(b) A Dying Colonialism
(c) The Testaments
(d) The Wretched of the Earth

254 The following work by Jean Paul Sartre draws on psychoanalysis and his own radical existentialism to offer a critique of orthodox Marxism.

(a) Surveys from Exile (b) Search for a Method
(c) Marxists on Literature (d) The Cultural Industry

255 Which among the following was the first full-length study of Structuralism in the United States?

(a) Terence Hawkes' Structuralism and Semiotics
(b) Jonathan Culler's Structural Poetics
(c) Tzvetan Todorov's French Literary Theory Today
(d) Mirielle Ribiere's A Beginner's Guide

ANSWERS

Objective Questions

1. *(c)*	2. *(b)*	3. *(c)*	4. *(b)*	5. *(d)*	6. *(a)*	7. *(d)*	8. *(b)*	9. *(b)*	10. *(b)*
11. *(b)*	12. *(a)*	13. *(d)*	14. *(c)*	15. *(b)*	16. *(c)*	17. *(b)*	18. *(c)*	19. *(a)*	20. *(a)*
21. *(a)*	22. *(d)*	23. *(b)*	24. *(a)*	25. *(d)*	26. *(c)*	27. *(c)*	28. *(b)*	29. *(a)*	30. *(b)*
31. *(b)*	32. *(a)*	33. *(c)*	34. *(b)*	35. *(c)*	36. *(a)*	37. *(b)*	38. *(a)*	39. *(c)*	40. *(c)*
41. *(d)*	42. *(b)*	43. *(a)*	44. *(b)*	45. *(b)*	46. *(a)*	47. *(b)*	48. *(b)*	49. *(a)*	50. *(a)*
51. *(c)*	52. *(b)*	53. *(c)*	54. *(c)*	55. *(a)*	56. *(c)*	57. *(b)*	58. *(a)*	59. *(c)*	60. *(b)*
61. *(a)*	62. *(c)*	63. *(d)*	64. *(b)*	65. *(b)*	66. *(a)*	67. *(c)*	68. *(b)*	69. *(d)*	70. *(d)*
71. *(c)*	72. *(a)*	73. *(d)*	74. *(b)*	75. *(d)*	76. *(d)*	77. *(b)*	78. *(d)*	79. *(b)*	80. *(a)*
81. *(a)*	82. *(b)*	83. *(c)*	84. *(b)*	85. *(a)*	86. *(d)*	87. *(d)*	88. *(a)*	89. *(c)*	90. *(b)*
91. *(a)*	92. *(a)*	93. *(d)*	94. *(c)*	95. *(b)*	96. *(d)*	97. *(b)*	98. *(a)*	99. *(a)*	100. *(a)*
101. *(c)*	102. *(a)*	103. *(a)*	104. *(a)*	105. *(c)*	106. *(c)*	107. *(a)*	108. *(b)*	109. *(a)*	110. *(c)*
111. *(c)*	112. *(a)*	113. *(b)*	114. *(b)*	115. *(d)*	116. *(c)*	117. *(d)*	118. *(a)*	119. *(d)*	120. *(c)*
121. *(a)*	122. *(d)*	123. *(c)*	124. *(c)*	125. *(d)*	126. *(d)*	127. *(b)*	128. *(a)*	129. *(b)*	130. *(b)*
131. *(c)*	132. *(a)*	133. *(c)*	134. *(a)*	135. *(d)*	136. *(d)*	137. *(c)*	138. *(d)*	139. *(b)*	140. *(b)*
141. *(c)*	142. *(a)*	143. *(d)*	144. *(a)*	145. *(c)*	146. *(a)*	147. *(c)*	148. *(a)*	149. *(a)*	150. *(a)*
151. *(b)*	152. *(b)*	153. *(b)*	154. *(c)*	155. *(a)*	156. *(a)*	157. *(b)*	158. *(b)*	159. *(b)*	160. *(a)*
161. *(b)*	162. *(a)*	163. *(b)*	164. *(b)*	165. *(c)*	166. *(a)*	167. *(c)*	168. *(b)*	169. *(a)*	170. *(b)*
171. *(b)*	172. *(a)*	173. *(b)*	174. *(a)*	175. *(b)*	176. *(a)*	177. *(c)*	178. *(b)*	179. *(a)*	180. *(b)*
181. *(b)*	182. *(a)*	183. *(b)*	184. *(c)*	185. *(a)*	186. *(b)*	187. *(b)*	188. *(b)*	189. *(c)*	190. *(d)*
191. *(c)*	192. *(d)*	193. *(b)*	194. *(b)*	195. *(b)*	196. *(d)*	197. *(a)*	198. *(b)*	199. *(d)*	200. *(a)*
201. *(a)*	202. *(a)*	203. *(a)*	204. *(b)*	205. *(a)*	206. *(b)*	207. *(a)*	208. *(b)*	209. *(c)*	210. *(c)*
211. *(c)*	212. *(d)*	213. *(a)*	214. *(a)*	215. *(b)*	216. *(c)*	217. *(b)*	218. *(a)*	219. *(d)*	220. *(d)*
221. *(b)*	222. *(b)*	223. *(d)*	224. *(d)*	225. *(c)*	226. *(a)*	227. *(b)*	228. *(b)*	229. *(a)*	230. *(a)*
231. *(c)*	232. *(c)*	233. *(d)*	234. *(c)*	235. *(b)*	236. *(c)*	237. *(d)*	238. *(d)*	239. *(c)*	240. *(b)*
241. *(d)*	242. *(a)*	243. *(d)*	244. *(c)*	245. *(b)*	246. *(b)*	247. *(a)*	248. *(c)*	249. *(a)*	250. *(b)*
251. *(b)*	252. *(a)*	253. *(c)*	254. *(b)*	255. *(b)*					

Nature and Functions of Literary Criticism

Criticism is the play of the mind on a work of literature and its function is to examine its excellencies and defects and finally to evaluate its artistic worth. The chapter refers to literary criticism, its different theories propounded by different writers of different ages. Important critics and their works have also been dealt with.

Criticism: Its Nature and Definition

The study, evaluation and interpretation of literature is known as literary criticism. Etymologically the word 'criticism' is derived from the Greek word meaning 'Judgement', and literary criticism is the exercise of judgement on works of literature. From this it would appear that the nature and function of literary criticism is quiet simple and easy to understand. However, the things are not quite so simple as that. As soon as we proceed to examine the nature and function of criticism in some detail , we are confronted with a host of conflicting views, theories and definitions.

Atkins defines that "Criticism is the play of the mind on the aesthetic qualities of literature , having for its objects an interpretation of literary values."

Victor Hugo said "Is the work good or bad that is the critics domain?"

Saintsbury says, "Criticism busies itself , with the goodness or badness , the success or ill-success , of literature from the purely literary point of view."

Edmund Gosse defines "Criticism is published analysis of qualities and characteristics of a work in literature of fine art."

Matthew Arnold says, "Criticism is a disinterested endeavour to learn and propagate the best that is known and thought in the world."

On the basis of above given definitions it is clear that, "Criticism is the exercise of judgement in the province of art and literature , and the critic is the person who is possessed of the knowledge necessary to enable him to pronounce right judgement upon the merit or worth of such works as come within this province."

In this Chapter

Function of Criticism

According to **SM Schreiber**, "Criticism is the play of mind on a work of literature and it consists in asking and answering rational questions about literature."

The business of the literary critic is, in the first instance to distinguish between a good book and a bad one and that done, to help us to recognise for ourselves, and to get full value out of literary quality when we meet with it. Thus opening for us the whole world of pleasure and imaginative experience and intellectual stimulus which is waiting to be explored but which, without a qualified critic help, we would not discover for ourselves. The ways in which the critic sets about his task are innumerable, ranging from, on the one hand, the most general statement of principles to, a detailed line by line and word by word analysis of one short poem, on the other hand, but the purpose is always the same; to quicken and refine our own and the readers perceptiveness so that, as time goes on, we too may come to share his understanding of and pleasure in, what is best in literature.

Types of Literary Criticism

There are various types of criticism that have flourished from time to time. Brief description of them is given below

Legislative Criticism

In this criticism the critic sought to teach writers how to write and lay down canons, rules, formulae of literary composition. Such legislative criticism claims to teach the poet how to write or how to write better. It is the kind of criticism practised by the Elizabethans and for half a century after Sidney apart, nearly all the Elizabethan critics directed their remarks to the poets rather than the readers of poetry. Their writings, for the most part depressingly uninspired, are the critical equivalent than the recipe-book and they are based on the Master –chef's assumption that any pupil of good intelligence can learn the business, if only he is shown how.

Judicial Criticism

This criticism seeks to pronounce judgement on works of literature on the basis of certain rules. If a work is found to follow these rules, it is good, if not, it is condemned as worthless.Such rules were derived and often wrongly derived, from the ancient Greek and Latin masters, especially Aristotle and Horace. All through the classical era such judicial criticism held sway and Dr Johnson may be regarded as the most powerful exponent of this kind of criticism.

Theoretical Criticism

This kind of criticism deals with literary aesthetics. Attention is focussed not on particular works, but on literature in general. A study is made on the process of creation and the basic principles of artistic beauty and in this way a literary theory is built up. In England, theoretical criticism made its humble beginning in Sidney's *An Apology For Poetry*. In the 17th century, Dryden showed keen interest in literary aesthetics. From this time onwards, interest shifts away from such platonic issues as the nature of poetic truth toward such psychological questions as the nature of creative act.

Evaluative Criticism

It is type of criticism which is concerned with the assessment or evaluation of the worth and significance of a work of art. The work concerned with reference to standards which may be aesthetic, moral or purely personal, and thus an attempt is made to estimate its place and importance. TS Eliot considers moral and ethical standards as necessary to determine the greatness of a work of literature, which cannot be determined merely by literary standards.

Historical Criticism

It views the work of art against the background of the age in which it was written. Every writer is influenced by the age in which he lives and his work cannot properly be estimated without an understanding of the social, economic, religious, political and literary trends which influenced the writer and formed his personality and coloured the very texture of his work. Shakespeare's work cannot be understood without knowledge of the social, and political life of the day, more specially its popular customs and rituals.

Comparative Criticism

This criticism seeks to evaluate a work by comparing it with other works of similar nature, either in one's own language or in other language. This method is foreshadowed in the criticism of Dryden, but Arnold was its first powerful advocate and exponent.

Descriptive Criticism

George Watson points out, "descriptive criticism begins in self-justification with poets discussing their own works, and defending them against hostile attacks as Dryden has done in numerable prefaces. His *Essays of Dramatic Poesy* provides the earlier extent examples of descriptive criticism."

Impressionistic Criticism

It is a type of criticism which seeks merely to record what Anatole France calls, "the adventures of the soul among the masterpiece". Impressionistic criticism is the record of personal responses; it is a record of the critic's own appreciation of aesthetic beauty, untrammelled by any rules and regulations.

The critic does not evaluate a work, he does not call it a good or bad, rather he seeks to convey his own enjoyment of it to his readers. Much of the romantic criticism is individualistic; Walter Pater and other English aesthetes are impressionistic in their criticism. Impressionistic criticism often tends to be wayward, unbalanced and erratic. Hence, it is that in modern times such powerful critics as TS Eliot and other Neo-classics have forcefully and successfully pleaded for greater adherence to tradition and authority on the part of the critic.

Textual or Ontological Criticism

In the modern age, there are a number of dominant trends or approaches to criticism. First and the most important, there is Textual, Formalistic or Ontological Criticism. For the Ontological Critic, the text under consideration is the thing in itself and it is examined and analysed without any consideration of such extrinsic factors as biography, history, sociology, psychology etc. The critic concentrates on the structure of the poem and on the various elements that combine to make up that structure. Words diction, language, image, metre, tone, theme, etc are all closely studied and in this way effort is made to arrive at the true meaning of the writer.

Psychological Criticism

Next in importance comes the modern psychological criticism. The new psychological knowledge, the result of the researches of Freud, Jung, Bergson and others, is harnessed in the service of criticism and new interpretations are provided and hidden significances are discovered. Psychology has provided the critic to study 'the interior life' of the writer and then to study his works with reference to it.

Sociological and Marxist Criticism

Another kind of criticism which enjoys much popularity in the 20th century is the Sociological criticism. It examines a work of art with reference to the social milieu of its author. "Sociological criticism starts with a conviction that art's relations to society are vitally important, and the investigation of these relationships may organise and deepen one's aesthetic response to a work of art.

Wilber Scott says, "Art is not created in a vacuum; it is the work not simply of a person, but of an author fixed in time and space, answering to a community of which he is an important, and articulate part". The sociological critic, therefore, is interested in understanding the social milieu and the extent to which, and the manner in which, the artist responds to it.

Archetypal criticism

Archetypal criticism is a kind of criticism which has attracted considerable attention in recent times. As a matter of fact, it is a branch of psychological criticism which deals with the unconscious, not of the writer or his imagined characters, but of the human race. It is also called the totemic, mythological, or ritualistic criticism. The critic tries to examine literature with the hope of discovering the existence of underlying mythological patterns.

Major Critics and Their Works

Aristotle

Aristotle was the Great Greek philosopher born at Stagira in Macedonia. His father Nichomachus was physician to King Amyntas III, grandfather of Alexander the Great. At the age of 18, Aristotle went to Athens in order to gain admission to Plato's academy. At the academy he created quite a stir among the other students by his unusual manner and qualities.

He showed the mind which was open to many facets of knowledge, politics, drama, physics, medicine, psychology, history, logic, astronomy, ethics, mathematics, rhetoric- these were only some of the branches of knowledge in which he showed a keen interest. Plato is said to have once remarked in a jovial tone that his academy consisted of two parts – the body of his students and the brain of Aristotle.

King Philip, the father of Alexander offered Aristotle the post of tutor to Alexander and Aristotle accepted the offer. However, at the court of King Philip, Alexander began to feel ill at ease because of the atmosphere of vulgarity and ambitious ness by which he found himself surrounded. After a few years, Aristotle returned to Athens, a sadder man but a wise philosopher.

He now decided to devote himself entirely to study and research. He was primarily a teacher, so he established a school in Athens, a rival to the academy. He called the school 'the Lyceum', there he lived for the next twelve years.

It was his habit of pacing up and down that his Lyceum acquired the nickname of 'Peripatetic School' meaning the school of strolling philosophers. To this day, the philosophy of Aristotle is known as the Peripatetic system.

In 323 BC, Alexander the Great, who had been sending money and gifts to Aristotle all these years, died. Aristotle now began to apprehend that he might meet the same fate as Socrates who had been forced by the authorities to drink poison and kill himself because of his perpetual quest for truth.

Accordingly he retired to Euboea, to spend the remaining portion of his life in peace, declaring "Athens must not sin a second time against philosophy." However, Aristotle did not live long after leaving Athens. He passed away only a year after his departure from Athens, at the age of sixty-two.

Aristotle wrote about four hundred books covering almost every aspect of human knowledge and of human activity. Most of his works have however been lost. Of those which are extant, the following are the most famous; *Alexander, The Custom of Barbarians, Organon* or *The Instrument of Correct Thinking, Rhetoric, Logic, Ethics, Physics, Metaphysics, Politics, Poetics.*

Aristotle's Poetics

Aristotle's Poetics seeks to address the different kinds of poetry, the structure of a good poem, and the division of a poem into its component parts. He defines poetry as a 'medium of imitation' that seeks to represent or duplicate life through character, emotion, or action. Aristotle defines poetry very broadly, including epic poetry, tragedy, comedy, dithyrambic poetry, and even some kinds of music.

According to Aristotle, tragedy came from the efforts of poets to present men as 'nobler,' or 'better' than they are in real life. Comedy, on the other hand, shows a 'lower type' of person, and reveals humans to be worse than they are in average. Epic poetry, on the other hand, imitates 'noble' men like tragedy, but only has one type of meter unlike tragedy, which can have several and is narrative in form.

Aristotle's Reply to Plato

The Poetics was most probably intended to be a reply to Plato's condemnation of poetry and poets. Plato, in his description of the ideal republic, had found serious fault with poetry and poets. He was primarily interested in constructing an ideal state. He aimed at making everything, including art and poetry, subservient to morality or to civic virtue and his philosophic ideal or to the pursuit of truth. He found fault with poetry on the ground that it tended to lower the morals of the people.

He attacked poets like Homer and Hesoid on the ground that they misrepresented the Gods and showed them as revengeful, lustful, cruel and as waging war among themselves. Thus poetry according to Plato, told lies about the next world. According to Plato it was not right for poets to describe honoured heroes like Achilles or Priam as indulging in weak lamentations, or as using insolent language, or as being gluttonous, revengeful, or illtempered. Thus, Plato convicted poets of immoral teaching and he condemned the tragedians and comedians for imitating unworthy objects. But Plato did not leave his opposition to poetry there, as a moralist, he disapproved to poetry for being based on falsehood. The artist or the poet, he said, was concerned with appearances only. This world, in which we live and have our being, was according to Plato, an unreal world. The real world in his view was the world of ideas which lay beyond this visible and material world. This world, in other words, was an imitation of the real world or the world of ideas. The artist or the poet imitated the objects of this material and visible world. In doing so, the artist or the poet imitated what was thus the imitation of an imitation.

The artist's work was therefore twice removed from reality. The poet or the artist had therefore no place in Plato's ideal republic. Although Aristotle had been a pupil of Plato, he did not agree with Plato's analysis of art and poetry. He therefore undertook to vindicate the arts including poetry. Aristotle does not, like Plato regard the poet's imitation of this world as a photographic reproduction of this world and its objects.

He does not look upon the arts as a servile or slavish copy of this material world. He interpreted mimesis or imitaton as a representation of the visible world and its objects, a representation which reflected the artist's individual approach to this world. Aristotle's view of imitation was a kind of idealised picture of life and of human beings. As for Plato's charge that poetry weakened human emotions and made people cowardly, Aristotle replied by saying that poetry brought about a Catharsis of emotions and thus provided a certain kind of pleasure to the readers. Poetry did not water or undermine the emotional life of human beings, but served to maintain an emotional balance in their life.

Definition of Tragedy

Tragedy is an imitation of an action that is serious, complete and of a certain magnitude. It is written in language which is embellished with each kind of artistic ornament, the various kind being found in separate parts of the play.

It is written in the form of action or representation, not in the form of narration. Furthermore, tragedy brings about the catharsis of the emotions of pity and fear by arousing these emotions in the audience or the readers.

An Explanation of the Definition

The embellishment of language implies the use of rhythm, harmony, and song. Various kinds of embellishment, being found in separate parts of the play, mean that some parts of the play are rendered through the medium of verse only, while others are rendered with the aid of song. As tragic imitation shows persons acting and doing, it necessarily follows that spectacle will be a part of tragedy.

For the same reason, song and diction will also be its constituent parts, because song and diction are the medium of imitation. Diction means the metrical arrangement of the words. Song is a term which does not need any explanation.

Tragedy is the imitation of an action. An action implies agents or individuals who necessarily possess certain distinctive qualities both of character and thought. Thought and character are the two natural causes from which actions spring and on actions depends all success or failure.

Therefore, the plot of tragedy is the imitation of the action. By plot is meant the arrangement on the incidents. By characters is meant that by virtue of which we attribute certain qualities to the agents or the individual. Thought is required wherever a statement is proved or wherever a general truth is enunciated.

Components of Tragedy

Every tragedy must have six parts. These six parts are: plot, character, diction, thought, spectacle, and song. Two of these (diction and song) constituent the medium of imitation; one of them (spectacle) constituents the manner or mode of imitation and three (plot, character, and thought) are the objects of imitation.

The Supreme Importance of the Plot in Tragedy

The most important of these six elements of the tragedy is the structure of the incidents because tragedy is an imitation not of men, but of an action and life and because life consists of action and its end is a mode of action, not a quality. It is by their action, not by their qualities, that human beings are happy or unhappy. Dramatic action is therefore the most important character.

The incidents and the plot are action of a tragedy, and end is the chief consideration. Without action there cannot be a tragedy; but there may be a tragedy without character. The tragedies written by most poets fail in the rendering of character. If a writer puts together a bunch of speeches expressive of character and well written in respect of diction and thought, he will not produce the essential tragic effect as successfully as by writing a play which has a plot and skilfully constructed incidents but is deficient in respect of characterisation, diction and thought.

It is also noteworthy that the most powerful elements of emotional interest in a tragedy are the reversal of the situation and the recognition scenes, and that these are parts of the plot.

In his definition of tragedy, Aristotle has pointed out that the function of the tragedy is to arouse the feelings of pity and fear for the purgation of such emotions. This he terms as 'Catharsis'. He has used the term catharsis only once and the critics have interpreted it variously. The Greek word Catharsis means purgation, purification and clarification.

All the critics agree that at least on one point tragedy arouses pity and fear, the differences are on the question of its process. Some critics take it as a medical metaphor, denoting a pathological effect on the soul. It has been likened to homeopathic treatment but some others compare it to allopathic method of treatment.

Lucas has rejected both these ideas by saying that the theatre is not a hospital. The sufferings of the hero give free play to these emotions and this is the safest outlet for emotional relief. There is another ethical interpretation that the tragic process is an inner illumination resulting in a more balanced attitude to life and its suffering.

It brings mental equilibrium and rest and thus completes aesthetic gratification. Thus, tragedy makes us realise that a divine law operates in the universe. Humphrey House forcefully advocates the purification theory. He says that purgation means cleansing.

By arousing pity and fear, tragedy trains them and brings back the soul in a balanced state, thus, according to the purification theory, Catharsis implies that emotions are purified of excess and defect and are reduced to intermediate state.

Butcher also agrees with this interpretation of Catharsis. In fact, Aristotle's concept of catharsis is mainly intellectual. It is not a moral doctrine but it is an experience which on one hand encourages them to face such situations more heroically and on the other hand accept their universality.

Longinus

The life of Longinus, the author of the great treatise *On the Sublime*, another Greek document besides Aristotle's *Poetics*, is wrapped in mystery. As the identity of the author and also, the right date of the composition of *On the Sublime* remain unknown and uncertain. It is guessed that he might have been Cassius Longinus of Palmyra, the Counsellor of Queen Zynobia of Syria, who lived in the third century AD. This treatise finds no mention in ancient records and remained almost unknown until Robertello, an Italian critic first presented the work to the modern readers in 1554 but it did not receive sufficient attention until its translation and publication by Boileau in 1674. Thence forth, it achieved miraculous success and came to be regarded as the Bible of the Neo-classicists who despite praising it theoretically did not follow its rules in practice. The title, *On the Sublime*, has been variously translated in English. Thus, Hall (1652) translates it as *Of the Height of Eloquence*; Pulteney (1680) translates it as *A Treatise of the Loftinegs of Elegency of speech*. It is obvious that all these translations are awkward, because there is no word in English which might express the meaning of 'sublime' in its fullness. As Prof. Saintsbury remarks ; "it is well to keep it with a very careful preliminary explanation that the Longinion sublime is not sublimity in its narrower sense, but all that quality, or combination of qualities, which creates, 'enthusiasm' in literature, all that gives consummateness to it, all that deserves the highest critical encomium either in prose or poetry."

Addressing his friend named Terentiannus, Longinus at the very outset of the treatise, tells him about his purpose behind writing the teatise which was that of correcting the mistakes that had crept in Caecilius's essay *On the Sublime* where the author also makes some other important observations besides disclosing the purpose of the treatise.

On the Sublime

After telling the purpose of writing the treatise *On the Sublime*, Longinus endeavours to define and explain sublimity. According to the rhetorician, sublimity is a certain loftiness and excellence of language and it has been possible only through sublimity that the greater poets and writers have derived their eminence and achieved immortality. According to Longinus, sublimity does not only persuade the hearer or the reader but carries him away almost irresistibly. Sublimity reveals itself in the general structure of a literary work of art, as much as, that sometimes even a single phrase, like a flash of lighting, reveals sublimity in it.

Sublimity Can be Taught Through Art

Longinus tells us how some people are mistaken in thinking that sublimity is an inborn endowment of nature to man and has nothing to do with art or artifice. However, Longinus holds the view that a writer can learn when to leave himself totally 'to the direction of genius'. The expression of the sublime often needs the spur, but it also needs the curb which is put by art alone.

Some Enemies of the Sublime

According to Longinus, there are some enemies that spoil the sublime or the loftiness and these enemies are the different shortcomings of the writer's style such as turbidity (vagueness or bombast), purity (triviality), grandiloquence (pompousness) and frigidity (dullness and coldness). Longinus traces the source of all of these shortcomings of style and according to him the common source of all these demerits is the craze for novelty of ideas.

True and False Sublime

After discussing the different enemies of the sublime, i.e. defects of the style, the rhetorician proceeds to distinguish true sublime from the false sublime. According to him, the true sublime always elevates the soul of the hearer. It innates from lofty ideas couched in lofty diction. The hearer derives joy from true sublimity besides elevating his spirits and every time on reading it, he finds entirely new and interesting things in it but it never grows stale, dull or uninteresting. In a word, the true sublime, according to Longinus, "pleases all and pleases always."

On the contrary, the false sublime has only a gaudy or showy exterior concealing inside only the hollowness of it. The language which is used to clothe trivial thoughts is bombastic, affected, showy and artificial. There is also found sometimes the cheap exhibition of passion which is totally superfluous and unnatural.

The Sources of the Sublime

Longinus tells us about the five sources of the sublime which are as follows

Grandeur of Thought

For grandeur of thoughts the writer is required to have the capacity of thinking great conceptions and thoughts. Longinus believes that the great thoughts or ideas always come out from great souls and therefore truly sublime must be free from low and ignoble thoughts, because men with mean and servile thoughts cannot get sublimity. It is only great souls that have the power to produce really great literature. Their words are full of sublimity whose thoughts are full of majesty.

Passionate and Vehement Expressions

After thinking high thoughts, the writer is required to express his high conception or thought vehemently and passionately. According to Longinus skilful and systematic selection of the most important events, emotions and passions and their combination into a single whole also contributes to the sublimity of style.

Correct Use of Figures

Longinus emphasises the correct use of figures and discussing elaborately both

(i) the figures of thoughts and
(ii) the figures of directions.

Noble Diction

The next source of sublime, according to Longinus is noble diction which includes a proper selection and arrangement of words and also proper mastery over the correct use of metaphor and other ornament of language.

Dignified and Elevated Composition

By dignified and elaborate composition, Longinus implies comedy rhythm.

Out of the aforesaid five sources, the first two sources are inborn endowments of a genius while the rest of them are attainable by art.

Amplification

Amplification or increasing strength of sound though the combination of telling details of a subject, has close relation with sublimity. Amplification affords attraction, force and magnitude to style. In the process of amplification, on one impressive point follows another continuously in ascending order. The magnitude of details elevates, uplifts the reader from trivial to sublime and thus gives extension to a subject. The chief difference between amplification and sublimity lies, in the fact that while sublimity may be present even in a single thought but amplification prerequisites certain length and width.

Imitation

The imitation of ancient great poets and writers always leads to sublimity, because these great masters of antiquity serve as standards of excellence and hence their imitation. These antiques are most likely to infuse in the imitator a divine impulse. Elaborating the process of imitation, Longinus tells us that while imitating an antique writer and poet, the imitator should ask himself as to how Homer or Plato would have expressed the idea in question and also as to how the coming ages will judge his composition. Such questions, the rhetorician tells us are most likely to excite the imitating to sublimity.

The Use of Figures

The correct use of vivid figures or images also helps considerably in the creation of sublime effect. For this, a writer should first of all visualise what he describes and afterwards make attempts to create a similar illusion in the minds of his readers or hearers. Longinus clarifies the fact that while the purpose or aim of poetical images is to surprise the reader; the aim of rhetorical images is to afford vividness and clarification.

However, both of them are similar in their effect which is to activate the passions, emotions and feelings of the reader or hearer. These figures, if handed skilfully, contribute considerably to sublime effect, however these figures should be placed in their right places, on the right occasion in the appropriate way. Figures should also be employed in a natural manner, as their artificiality awakens suspicion and sometimes also boredom in the reader or hearer. Artlessness is the greatest art. So, a figure can be said to be at its best only when the very fact that it is a figure escapes the attention of the hearer or the reader.

The Different Figures and Their Right Use

One of the often employed figures is Adjuration or Apostrophe, which is very effective as an appeal or address to a reader or hearer so as to awaken his passions and emotions. The employment of the figures, rhetorical questions and answers makes the language quite impressive, effective, elevated and convincing. But, Longinus cautions us that these questions should emanate from a natural outburst of passion and also should be inspired by the occasion. Therefore, these questions should sound or seem quite natural under the given circumstances. So, if the questions are inspired by a vehement passion, the words become charged and come out of one's lips quite effortlessly or spontaneously, producing a sublime effect. Another figure, suggested by Longinus, is Asyndeton which consists in the omission of connectives between words and sentences and the effect of such omission is one of rush and torrent of passion.

The Combinations of Figure

Combinations of certain figures are particularly effective to impart strength, charm and persuade the diction. So, to produce a powerful emotional effect, figure such as Anaphore (repetition), and Diatyposis (vividness) are generally combined together. Similarly, the figure Hyperbaton gives the effect of violent mental agitation. While speaking passionately a speaker often reverts the logical order and hops from one idea to another with great swiftness. Obviously, this figure imparts a touch of realism to words and produces, eventually the sublime effect.

The Noble Diction

Noble diction i.e the selection of appropriate and endearing words is must for creation of sublime effect because words are bridge through which a writer communicates himself to his readers. 'Beautiful words are devoid of lofty thoughts', on the contrary, inappropriate magnificence of diction as for instance, the choice of petty themes or subjects treated in a grand manner not only marks the sublime effects but also begets genuine anger in the reader or the hearers.

Dignified and Elevated Composition

The dignified and elevated composition is possible only through the harmonious arrangement of words, which is a great source of persuasion and pleasure as well. A dignified composition directly 'reaches our souls' and contributes considerably to loftiness of speech and passion. According to rhetorician, it is the sense of harmony that affords charm and organic unity to a literary work of art, which emanates from harmonious arrangement of words.

On the contrary, broken and agitated movement of language marks dignity and elevation and imparts the composition a semblance of meanness. But too much brevity of expression also tends to soil the sublime effect because, "Deformity instead of grandeur ensures from over compression."

Grandeur of composition is soiled when the thought is pressed into too narrow a compass. In the same way, over-elaboration also makes the composition lifeless. Low or undignified words also disfigure and degrade sublimity. Ill-sounding words or vulgar idioms should always be avoided as they too are inimical for dignified and elevated composition.

A number of critics ascribe the decline of truly great literature in contemporary age to the want of incentive that democracy afforded to the men of genius in the preceeding age. These critics also opine that in contemporary age the growth of lofty genius seems to have stopped.

However, differing altogether from such critics, Longinus thinks that this decline is characteristics of human nature that always seems to find faults with the present. In the view of the rhetorician, the real cause of this decline of eloquence in modern day is the moral degeneration of people at large who think materialistic values to be more important than moral values and who are reluctant to toil save for the sake of admiration, wealth or pleasure.

"Great literature springs from great and lofty soul, and not from those with whom the world is too much."

Horace

Horace whose full name was Quintus Horatius Flaccus, was born at Venusia, modern Venosa in Apulia on 8th December 65 BC and died in Rome on 27th November, 8 BC. Horace himself has told us that his father, though not very well off, was willing to meet all his educational expenses at Rome. After getting his education at the capital, Horace went to Athens for the study of philosophy and for contemporary educational patterns.

He deeply studied their Greek Literature, Greek verses, Greek iambics and Greek lyrics elegiacs. Besides literature, he was also thoroughly conversant with Greek Philosophy. While still a student at Athens, he heard the news of the assassination of Julius Caesar. Being a votary of liberty and republicanism, Horace went back home and joined the army of Brutus, who was a symbol of republican principles to Horace.

However, since the defeat of Republicans at Philippi, Horace threw his sword away and decided to devote himself whole heartedly to the Muse of lyrics. Though not a Republican officially, Horace in his works referred to Cato, the father-in-law of Brutus very praisingly. Late in his life, he had to became a courtier and yet he remained deeply patriotic.

Literary Criticism of Horace

The literary criticism of Horace should be estimated in the light of a primary aims and objectives that he declared to follow himself. His foremost aim was to find at Rome a lofty poetry, serviceable to the state.

He sought to afford this view of poetry to the people because of Augustan era witnessed an awakening of national or patriotic feelings in people at large. In those days people were full of a great enthusiasm and craze for poetry. Horace tells us that, "unlearned and learned alike, we all try our hands writing poems."

The supreme function that a poet could do, according to Horace, has been beautifully summed up by Atkins who averes that " In this newly-found fervour for poets and poetry Horace saw acquisition of strength to the state, for the poet by his way of living and his teaching alike was an inspiration to all. The tender lisping utterance of childhood he gently fashioned, he led youth by kindly precept, he told of noble actions firing men to emulation, he comforted the weak and sorrowful and he intercepted with Gods on behalf of men."

National Needs and the Poet

In the *Epistle to Augustus* he tells us about the purpose of the poet in view of the paramount importance of national requirement. The chief aim of Horace was to give a new lead, a new direction and a new vision to the contemporary period through the creation of a national movement in literature that should be in accordance with the lofty aspiration and noble destiny of the Roman people.

In the view of Horace, literature should be a tool to attain this noble aim because in contemporary period vices like prejudices, pedantry and false standards were going on rampant all around and therefore the task of the poet became doubly serious and important.

The Aim of Poetry

It was, therefore, against this background of national requirements that Horace profounded the conception of the high mission of poetry and gave practical guidance. His chief aim was directed towards solving certain immediate problems sprung from the contemporary literary conditions.

In the *Arts Poetica*, he defines the aim of poetry thus, "The aim of poetry is either to be beneficial or to delight, or in their phrases to combine charm and high applicability to life (a poet should instruct, or please, or both). Whatever you invent for the sake of pleasing, let it be not too distant from truth.

Poetry a Blending of Fiction and Facts

Horace has made a systematic study of poetry, although the treatment is rather brief. He regards poetry to be a mode of imitation.

Horace says, "I would advise the well –instructed imitator to take his model from life and custom and from this derive language faithful to life". But in the view of Horace, poetry is not a statement of absolute truth. It is, in reality, a blending of fiction, facts and fancy. So, if it is fiction, it should be 'composed to please', and 'should be very near the truth'.

Conception of Poetry

In his conception of poetry, Horace is more platonic than Aristotlian, because like Plato, he desires poetry to be the vehicle of truth and morals. In this conception, Horace reminds us also of the stoic philosophers, who adhered themselves faithfully to the continual or didactic view of poetry.

His view sparks of the controversy between 'form' and 'content', and seems inclined to the latter, i.e. content, "Poets desires either to improve or to please or to unite the agreeable and the profitable. Any moral maxim must be brief so that the mind may readily perceive and faithfully retain a pithy sentence; redundant words overflow from a stated mind. Fiction composed to please should be very near the truth, so that the play may demand unlimited belief. You will win every vote if you bind what is improving with what pleases, and at once delights and instructs the reader."

Synthesis Between Plato and Aristotle

Horace's aim is to fold, namely to charm and to be a useful teacher at the same time, "either a poet tries to give good advice, or he tries to be amusing- or he tries to do both.......... Mixture of pleasure and profit appeals to every reader—on equal administration of sermon and tickle." Therefore in his view, poetry worth the name is at once pleasure- giving and morally improving. Herein lies the synthesis between Plato and Aristotle.

Reaffirmation of Emotional Appeal of Poetry

Horace tells us that poets have always played the part of teachers effectively. In ancient times it was the poet, who exercised a humanising and civilising influence upon the barbarians. Horace insists, "It is not enough for poems to have beauty; they must also be pleasing and lead the listener's soul where the soul wishes to.

To illustrate his point that poets are moral teachers. Horace refers to orphans, the great poet and singers, who tamed the savages of the forests with their poetry. They thus civilised even the ferocious tigers and lions. Amphion, the founder of the kingdom of Thebes was capable of moving even the rocks with his songs. In this way, poets were discharging their responsibilities of teaching. Horace, thus, re-affirms the Aristotlian role of emotional appeal of poetry.

According to Horace, a poet should be careful and selective in the choice of words. He has the liberty to use familiar words without waffling and padding. He is equally fear to use new words. He may even coin new words, for "words new and lately coined will win credit if they descend from a Greek source, slightly modified."

So, in the view of Horace, the poet enjoys freedom with certain limitations. Being a conservative critic, Horace always turns wistfully to the glory that is Greece. It is the moral duty of the poet to enrich the vocabulary of the nation. Words have their birth, decay, and death. The words are like forest leaves which change with the autumnal season. "The words perish of old age, the new-born flourish and grow strong in the manner of the young grow. Many expression will be born which now have perished, many will die which now enjoy distinction, if it be so willed by usage, within whose sway rest the arbitrement, and the law, and the standard of speech."

Sir Philip Sidney

Philip Sidney was born at Penshurst on 30th November, 1554. The name of his father was Henry Sidney and mother Lady Mary Dudley, daughter of the Duke of Northumberland. His early education took place at Shrewsbury School. After Shrewsbury School, he went to Christ Church College, Oxford for higher studies in 1568.

In the spring of 1571, he left Oxford without taking a degree and to complete his education. After visiting Paris, Vienna, Venice and Prague, in 1575 he returned home and become a courtier. In 1575, he met for the first time Pendope which became the 'Stella' of his sonnet *Sequence* entitled Astroophil and Stella.

In July, 1578 he was introduced to Gabriel Harvey and Spenser. All the three friends started a literary society called the Areopagus. In 1580, he wrote a letter to the queen disapproving her proposed marriage with the Duke of Anjou and proposing the name of the uncle instead.

This made the queen angry and she dismissed him from the court and he had to go into relinquishment at Wilton where he wrote the *Arcadia* and also perhaps *Apology for Poetrie*. In 1581, he again got the fame of the court and in January, 1583 was knighted. On 21st September, he married Frances Walsingham, the daughter of Elizabeth's Secretary of state.

He was appointed Governor of Flushing but at the Battle of Zutphen in 1586, he died and was buried in St. Paul's Cathedral.

An Apology for Poetrie

It is considered to be landmark in the history of English literary criticism because it is the first treatise to discuss the nature and function of poetry and drama. Sidney has freely expressed his opinion on various aspects and has brought poetry to its honourable place that it enjoyed since antiquity more because the Puritans of that period were denouncing it on various grounds.

During 16th century, lyrics and sonnets were written in abundance so it was the urgent need that some proper poetic theory must be evolved. The Puritans criticised it badly and the most powerful attack was that of Gosson through various articles and pamphlets to which Sidney replied in *An Apology for Poetrie*.

When Sidney started his work, there was no critical background in England. So, the importance of this work has been enhanced all the more. Gosson called the poets as 'pipers and jesters' and poetry 'enemy of good virtues'. In his opinion drama excited popular debauchery because the male played the female parts, which is against the law of the nature. Tragedy shows nothing but cruelty, murder and in comedies there is vulgar love.

Sidney's reply in *An Apology for Poetrie* was eulogised even by the best writer of the day. He performed his task most efficiently because he himself was a poet, a courtier and possessed a large knowledge of the classics. But we should take care that it is not only a reply to the objections by Puritans but presents his originals honourable concept of the poetic profession so much that he had replied to Plato also.

The first thing that Sidney advances in defence of poetry is its antiquity and universality. He says that the poets were the first light bringers to ignorance. It creates a civilising influence. Even the earliest Greek philosophers and historians were basically poets.

His most valuable consideration is his declaration that civilisation sprang from poetry. The Romans honoured the poets so much that they called him Vates, a prophet and a maker. He says 'Nature never set for the earth in so much tapestry as diverse poets have done.' The poet alone can fashion a perfect lover, a perfect friend and a perfectly valiant man even though they are not found in nature.

Sidney includes all imaginative literature in poetry and says that, 'versing and rhyming do not make a poet'. Here, he really grips the main problem of the day. Initially he agrees with Plato that poetry is a 'divine gift', and a result of inspiration. In more than one place, he affirms the working of the divine breath.

But he primarily agrees with Aristotle and says, "Poetry is an art of imitation, for so Aristotle termeth it". Thus, poetry is not merely an art of imitation. The most significant is his declaration that "one may be a poet without versing."

He thinks that it is certainly a fitting medium for poetry but it is not essential. The true test of poetry is to feign noble images of vices and virtues and to impart delightful teaching. Sidney goes a step forward to Aristotle in his definition of poetry and says that imitation is a creative process. The poet does not merely copy but also transmutes the real and the actual and thus attempts an entirely new creation.

However, the creation of the poet is not completely imaginative, rather it is a creation of a perfect ideal world such as exists only in the mind of gods. Poetry thus embodies something of a permanent and universal value. Aristotle believed that the poet arrives at the universal through the particular but Sidney believes that he does so through the contemplation of ideal reality and in both cases poetry is the highest and the noblest. He tells that the poet, in his flight ranges into the divine consideration of what may be and should be and thus creates the world of ideal.

Thus, Sidney's conception of nature of poetry is not gently at variance from that of Aristotle who considered that the poets' material consisted of things as they were and they are. But both of them agree that poetry is something more than mere fancy of a bare transcript of life, both maintain that it embodies elements of the real and the permanent value. Both discern in poetry, the truth of the highest kind.

Regarding the function of poetry, Sidney says " The function of the poetry is to delight and teach and it teaches by moving men to goodness." Sidney contends that the ultimate end of all learning is a virtuous action and to inspire to good life.

Here, he recalls Aristotle that the fruit of learning is not mere knowing but doing. So, with him the final test of value of poetry is not mere conveying of knowledge or ethical teaching but it imparts an elevating influence, an uplifting power which should inspire in men the desire of well doing. It is thus superior both to history and philosophy.

Sidney tells that in the teaching of virtue, both philosophy and history play important part. Philosophy adopts the method of analysis and definition, thus providing "concepts of general validity in their bearing on human conduct."

On the other hand, is concerned with an active rather than a theoretical value. It teaches not by precept but by particular examples from life. But both the methods have their defects. Philosophy deals with abstraction, hence a poor guide for youth and appeals only to the learned. History presents those concrete examples from which general truth emerges confusedly.

The poet alone accomplishes his dual work. He shows a particular virtue pictured most perfectly in someone by whom it has been done. Thus, it teaches the abstract by a particular instance. The philosopher teaches only the learned, the poet teaches all. Even if the philosopher excels the poet in teaching, he cannot move his readers to virtuous action as the poet can.

The poet improves upon the historians also because he gives perfect examples of vices and virtues for human imitation. He makes virtue succeed and vice fall but a historian can seldom do that. The readers imitate the example of perfection presented to him by the poet and thus they are made virtuous.

Thus, poetry is certainly better than any other art or service. This is the gist of Sidney's argument on behalf of poetry. He declares poetry the highest and the noblest form of human wisdom.

Sidney has grouped the Puritans objections into four

1. In the first place it is objected that a man might spend his time more perfectly than by reading poets. He says that poetry is mere rhythm and versification. To this, Sidney says that rhythm is used only as a polish to speech, it regulates verbal harmony and imparts order and proportions to the composition. The sensuous and emotional quality is also added to music as an aid to memory.

   Moreover, poetry teaches us virtuous action by demonstration. Man learns something noble by reading poetry and so it is not useless and wastage of time and energy.

2. Secondly, poetry has been called 'the mother of lies'. The poet talks only of things imaginary and unreal in life and therefore whatever he tells is only falsehood. But Sidney replies to this charge also. He says that it is less likely to tell lies in poetry than other sciences. To lie means the confirmation of what is not true while the poet always presents the highest truth. The historian can lie but not the poet because doesn't deal with what is but with what should be and what should not be. Though the poet offers not facts but fictions, yet his fiction embodies truths of an ideal kind.

3. Then Gosson called poetry 'the nurse of abuse'. It has a corrupting influence and makes man effeminate. This means that poetry misuses and debases the mind of man by turning it to mischief. It is the source of creating evil desires in the heart of man. Sidney replies that the fault of corruption and effeminacy lies not with poet but with the contemporary abuse of poetry should not be condemned. So far as making men effeminate is concerned, this charge applies to all other sciences more than to poetry. In his descriptions, the poet makes men valiant and courageous by presenting such characters.

4. Sidney has also replied to Plato's rejection of poetry. Plato had banished poets from his ideal common wealth. Sidney says, Infact Plato was not against poetry but the abuse of poetry he points out that Plato held poets in high esteem and regarded them as 'sacred things'. Moreover, Plato himself was a born poet and a large part of his dialogues is poetic. He gives high and rightly divine commendation of poetry.

   He speaks of poetry as a divine inspiration. Moreover, Sidney urged that what Plato really objected to were the false conceptions of gods and the superstition which ancient poetry had sustained. So, Plato's objection was directed not against poetry but against the current doctrine.

   Thus, Plato banished the abuse of poetry and not poetry itself. Sidney produced a solution of this much vexing problem. It provided a timely and seasoned reply to the age long denunciation of poetry is the name of Plato and prepared the way of truer appreciation of poetry and the poetic art. In this way, he not only dignified reply to the poet haters in a crushing yet dignified way but a restored poetry once again to its place of honour among the great arts. He claimed it as a serious and fruitful study.

Along with defending poetry form various charges against it Sidney explains the reason of the neglect of poetry in his own times. He says that peaceful years had in reality created a tame and sluggish generations of poets devoid of the ardent and generous spirits necessary for poetic creations. Poetry came to be presented by servile wits, the men uninspired and worldly, in whose company their souls could not range.

They had neither knowledge nor imitation of sound models, nor constant exercise or practice. Moreover, such bastard poets wrote in ignorance of the poetic art, greatly detrimental to poetry, while the true exponents of poetry should be gifted men who wrote well knowingly. Knowing first what they do and how to do it. For the attainment of such skill, he deemed the old classical prescription to be valid, a knowledge of art, imitation of sound models, and constant practice. He also objected to the current state of drama almost for the same reasons.

Turning to lyrical poetry, Sidney has made brief but significant remarks. He laments that we do not have other sorts of poetry and his chief complaint is the futility of the themes of contemporary efforts, adequate in his opinion to inspire true lyrical qualities.

These qualities he finds in Biblical poetry and maintains that the genuine lyrical fire has been kindled in chanting the praises of that ever lasting beauty to be seen by the eyes of the mind. Of the love poetry of the time, he speaks with disapproval, objecting to its insincerity and lack of passion.

He remarks that most of such poems were made up of borrowed and swelling phrases, loosely strung together and ineffective because of their want of genuine force and feeling. The obvious reference here is to the slavish imitation of the Plutarch tradition, but remarkably enough. Sidney himself was not free from it. These poems are of the nature of literary exercise and there is no utterance of actual passion but of sentiments fanciful and unreal. Here, his protest against insincerity in the lyrics is of great significance.

Moreover, he recognises for the first time, the element of personal feeling bound up with the lyrics and advises 'to look in the heart and write'. Thus, Sidney made great contribution to the critical literature in England and established poetry as the noblest kind of art.

He has also extended his opinion regarding diction, style and versification in poetry. He maintains that verse was an ornament of poetry. In matters of diction and style, Sidney found defects even more serious and disturbing. He frequently calls attention to the contemporary craze for fine writing. He asserts that literary expression was tending to become little more than a painted affection, as a result of the use of far-fetched terms, obscure devices like alliteration are used.

He used that these tricks were not confined alone to the versifiers but they coloured prose also, while they formed the part of pulpit as well. He attributes the origin of these vicious practices to the earlier rhetorical studies. He rightly suggests that a better way of acquiring classical style would be to abandon them. We should recapture the methods and spirit of the great classics.

Accordingly, the essence of classical languages was converted into blood and nourishment. Among all these abuses, one more especially claimed Sidney's attention-inordinate use of similes drawn from unnatural history which had already become a fashion. He condemns this Euphuistic style and strongly denounces it everywhere. He be never agreed that "with strange similes, enriched each line", should be observed. Such devices should be used only sparingly.

Similes, in his opinion, contributed not at all to the task of persuasion. They proved nothing but only illustrated, which was often over done to become tedious. To win the credit of the popular ears, plain sensibleness, alone was necessary. He is in favour of simplicity in style and diction.

He is against eloquence which seems like a monster but will always remain stranger to any poor Englishman. He commends that the man who employed the devices should use them carefully.

John Dryden

John Dryden was born on the 9th August, 1631, at Aldwincle, a village in Northamptonshire and both of his parents belonged to the distinguished families of Northamptonshire. His father, Erasmus Dryden was a justice of peace for Northamtonshire and his mother, Mary was the daughter of the Reverend Henrey Pickering.

All Saints first child, the eldest of a family of fourteen of the early life of Dryden only little is known. His father possessed a small property. According to his cousin , Mrs. Breed "Dryden was bred and had his first learning at Titchmarsh." But he received the best part of his education at the Westminster School in 1650 however, Dryden felt Westminster school to enter the Trinity College, Cambridge and matriculated on 16th July of the same year and he won the Westminster scholarship on the second of October, 1650. He passed BA in January 1654.

At the death of his father in June, 1654 he inherited two third of his father's estate which provided him the income of forty pound a year. In 1655, he ceased to be a scholar of the Trinity College, which deprived him of his Master's degree and it was only on the recommendation of King Charles II, later on that he was conferred the MA degree by the Archbishop of Canterbury. Soon after taking his degree, young Dryden went to London.

In 1657, possibly Dryden finally left his college to stay with Sir Gilbert Pickering, his great grandfather from his mother's side.

However, within one year of the Restoration, he had become intimate with Sir Robert Howard, son of the Earl of Berkshire and had free movements in that's circle. His friendship with Sir Robert Howard resulted in Dryden's having been introduced to the theatrical art and he married lady Elizabeth Howard, the sister of Sir Robert Howard, on December 1663. Unfortunately the great plague broke out in London, the theatres had been closed, which could be re-opened only towards the close of 1666 to 1694. At the death of Charles II in 1685, the crown passed to his brother, James, an uncompromising Catholic.

A Nicoll observes "Dryden was searching, as deeply as the spirit of the age, permitted him to search, into the deputes of his heart, endeavouring in a time of flux and of a change, to discover some basis on which he might rear a surer and a more subtle philosophical belief for himself." The sincerity of Dryden's changing the sides from Puritanism to Roman Catholicism was questioned by Lord Macaulay.

However, Prof. Sainsbury define Dryden with these words, "I believe Dryden to have been in the transactions of the year 1685-1687, thoroughly sincere as far as conscious sincerity went, but of a certain amount of unconscious sincerity. I am by no means disposed to acquit him." However, the revolution of 1668 forced James into exile and enthrone William of Orange and Mary. This revolution brought great misfortunes to the follower of Roman Catholic Faith, with the result that Dryden lost his post of Poet Laureate and Historiographer Royal and Dryden silently retired to pursue his literary work.

Some of the finest translations and narrative poems were written by Dryden during this period. During the winter of 1699-1700, Dryden health deteriorated considerably and on 1st May 1700, he breathed his last at his house in Garrard Street and was buried on 13th May, in the poet's corner at Westminster Abbey beside the graves of Chaucer and Cowley.

Among the great English Critics, Dryden holds a very respectable and unique place for he has produced his original views regarding drama and has freed it from the clutches of the ancient writers and theories. He presented his views so freely and fearlessly after a very long time and this is why *An Essay On Dramatic Poesy* was received so enthusiastically.

An Essay on Dramatic Poesy

It was appeared in 1688, it was written in dialogue form. It was an interesting event that was responsible for its origin . In 1663, a French man named Sorbiere came to England and on return to France he published an account of his English journey in which he made derogatory remarks on the English drama. He wrote "these comedies of theirs would not be received so quiet well in France. Their poets play hob with the unity of place and the rule of twenty four hours.Their comic plots run for twenty five years. The first act gives you the marriage of a prince and immediately after wards come the travels and exploits of his son." The responsibility to review the points at issue fell to Dryden's lot.

The *Essay on Dramatic Poesy* is written in the form of the Socratic dialogue, so as to make the discussion delightful. The scene is laid on the Thames-the battle field where on 3rd June, 1665, the English and the Dutch armies fought. There are four talkers of this dialogue. However, these speakers have been identified with actual persons: Eugenius (Lord Buckhurst) Dryden's patson and friend; Crites (Sir Robert Howard) Dryden's brother-in-law; Lisideius (Sir Charles Sedley); and Neander, Dryden himself.

The central theme of the essay is the justification of the merits of English plays. The discussion is focussed chiefly on the propriety of rhyme in plays, the observance of the unities and the controvery between 'Ancient and Moderns'. The talk is confined to the discussion of the drama where in the plus-points of French and English plays, both ancient and modern, are discussed and weighed. The debate refers chiefly to the problem of the proper use of verse-form for dramatic purposes.

Smith and Parks observe that "From each of the arguments come flashes of insight which transcend restoration quibblings and leave us enduring abstracts of the liberal classicism." Among these are the definition of a play, sound judgement on the comparative virtues of regularity and variety of drama, the preference of strongly drawn characters to types and of artful complexity in plot to rule ridden unity and the famous inland critiques on Shakespeare, Beaumont, Fletcher, and Johnson.

The essay has been written in the form of a dialogue among four characters which has been compared by TS Eliot to the dialogue of Plato. However, George Watson observes in this connection that "Dryden cannot possibly be trying to write anything like a platonic dialogue.

He was a professional dramatic and knew how dialogue was written, but there is nothing here remotely like the cut and thrust of a Socratic inequisition, indeed, nothing much like any sort of conversation". The fact that the essay is written into the form of a dialogue where all the four speakers were allowed to represent different point of view is proof of Dryden's tolerant and inquisitive mind.

In the essay, Dryden endeavours to define a play with the remark that "A play ought to be a just and lively image of human nature, representing its passion and humours, and the changes of fortune to which it is subject, for the delight and instruction of mankind." The observations of the ancients were solid and they were faithful imitators and wise observers of that nature which is so torn and ill-represented in our plays.

The merits of these unities of Action, Time and Place, were discussed. The ancient observed the unities and it was argued that "the greatest man of the last age Ben Jonson was willing to give place to them in all things." Therefore, Ben Jonson 'dressed in all the ornaments and colours of the ancient should be accepted as a model'. At this, Engenius remarks that "it is true that the moderns have profited by the rules of the ancients; but you are careful to conceal how much they have excelled them..... We draw not therefore after their lines, but those of Nature, and having the line before us, besides the experiences of all they knew, it is no wonder if he hits some airs and features which they have missed." It was also said in the discussion that ' the unity of place', however it might be practiced by them was never included in their rules; we never find it in Aristotle, Horace or any other ancient, till in our age, the French Poet first made it a precept of the stage.

The unity of Time was not observed even by Terence, while Euripides in limiting himself to one-day has committed an absurdity that will never forgive him.

Lisideius remarks: "if the question had been stated who had written best, the French or English, forty years ago, I should have ....adjudged the honour to our own nation, but since that time we have been all together so bad Englishmen that we had no leisure to be good poets. Beaumont, Fletcher and Johnson who were capable of bringing us to that degree of perfection, were just leaving the world... the muses went to plant in another country and thus Corncille and other Frenchmen, referred their theatre.

Dryden remarks that the French contrive their plots more regularly, and observe the laws of comedy and decorum of the stage, with more exactness than the English; but even then 'neither our faults nor their virtues are considerable enough to place them above us.... It is true, those beautiful of the French poesy are such as will raise perfection higher than where it is.

For instance, Corneille's play 'The Liar' which was cried up in France, when brought upon the English stage, did not receive much praise and it could not stand competition with many plays of Fletcher or Ben Jonson. The plays of Corneille contain little humour, though, of late, Moliere, Quinault and many others have been imitating the graces and turns of the English stage. Dryden emphasises the superiority of the English plays: "if dare to take upon me to find more variety of them in some one play of Ben Jonson's in all together : as he who has seen the *Alchemist*, *The Silent Woman*, or *Bartholomew Fair* cannot but acknowledge with me."

The discussion then turns to the nature of plot of the English and a French play and it is found that the barrenness of the French plot cannot be considered superior to the variety and copiousness of the English poets. French plots are single and carry on only one designs, which is moved forward by all the actors and every scene in the play contributes and moves towards it. On the other hand, English plays, along with the main design have under plots of less considerable persons and intrigues which are carried forward with the motion of the main plot. Further, the variety of English plays, if well ordered, can afford a greater pleasure to the audience.

So, the English plays are not the servile imitation of the French plays, because we have borrowed nothing from them ; our plots are weaved in English looms ; we endeavour therein to follow the variety and greatness of characters which are derived to us from Shakespeare and Fletcher ; the copiousness and well knitting of the intrigues we have from Jonson ; and for the verse itself we have, English precedents of elder date than any of Corneille's plays.

After this, there is a discussion of the property of rhyme in a play. Generally, the critics hold the view that ' rhyme is unnatural in a play', because dialogue there is presented as the effect of sudden thought ; for the play is the imitation of nature ; and since no man, without premeditations speaks in the rhyme, neither ought he to do it on the stage. This hinders not but the fancy may be these elevated to a higher pitch of the thought than it is in ordinary discourse.

For this reason, Aristotle says, "it is best to write tragedy in that kind of verse which is the least such, or which is nearest prose ; and this amongst the Ancients was the Iambic, and with us in blank verse, or the measure of verse kept exactly without rhyme. The number therefore are fittest for a play ; the other for a paper of verses or a poem ; blank verse being as much below them as rhyme is improper for the drama."

Conclusion: To conclude, Atkins sums up the discussion of the essay by telling us about the great critical merits of this discussion: "Such then is the famous essay, which in its loveliness, its shrewd reasoning and urbanity represents a foretaste of what was to be best in Dryden's later critical work".

In its paper French influence may definitely be traced, particularly that of Corneille, whose free play of intellect, his 'Discourse' and 'Examins' found in Dryden a ready response, and this was to remain a distinguishing features of his criticism right on to the end.' It is obvious that the vindication of English plays which is the chief aim of the Essay, has been well achieved and it gives a fitting reply based on facts and reasoning, to the structures passed by Sorbiere on the English plays.

William Wordsworth

Wordsworth was born at Cockermouth, Cumberland, in the Lake District, on 7th April, 1770, the second oldest of five children, of John and Anne Cookson Wordsworth. His father was law agent and rent-collector for Lord Lonsdale and the family was at this period reasonably well off. William attended the Hawkshead Grammar School, near Windermere, until his matriculation at St. John's College, Cambridge.

By this time he was an orphan, under the charge of Guardians. He was an indifferent scholar at Cambridge, and when he graduated had little sense of his future vocation.

In the year after his graduation he went to France (having been there once before, during a summer vacation from Cambridge), where he contracted not only radical republican sympathies but also an affair with one Annette Vallon, to whom his illegitimate daughter, Croline, was born in 1792.

Wordsworth returned to England, where his political sympathies gradually change as the fortunes of liberty in France declined. Supported by a bequest from a friend, he settled with his sister Dorothy near Bristol. It was here that he met Coleridge, and that famous friendship began. In 1798, the two poets published *The Lyrical Ballads* together, and in the same year they visited Germany. In 1799, Wordsworth and his sister settled in the Lake District, in1802, having come into a patrimony long delayed by litigation, he married Mary Hutchinson. In 1813, he was granted the sinecure of distributor of stamps for Westmorland. His life meanwhile was a quite one; the production of editions of his poems was steady and his reputation, especially after 1815, steadily increased. In 1839, he was honoured by Oxford University with the Degree of Doctor of Civil Law, and in 1843, he became poet laureate. For seven years he worked hard till death claimed him in 1850.

Wordsworth Theory of Poetic Diction

In the first edition he stated that the poems in the book were "an experiment to ascertain how far the language of conversation in the middle and lower classes is adapted to the purposes of poetic pleasure." In the second *Preface to the Lyrical Ballads* the poet enunciated the theory of poetic diction in a more comprehensive and categorical form.

He stated, "The principle object proposed in these poems was to choose incidents and situations from common life, and to relate or describe them, throughout, as far as this was possible 'in a selection of language really used by men,' and, at the same time, 'to throw over them a certain colouring of the imagination,' whereby ordinary things should be presented to mind in an unusual aspects and further and above all to make these incidents and situations interesting by tracing in them, truly though not ostentatiously, the primary laws of our nature, chiefly, as far as regarding the manner in which we associate ideas in state of excitement.

The language, too, of these men has been adopted because such men honourly communicate with the best objects from which the best part of language is originally derived." In addition to the comprehensive statement Wordsworth proceeded to a wider generalisation stating that, "It may be safely affirmed that there neither is nor can be, any 'essential' difference between the language of prose and metrical composition. He was endorsed his first statement that 'the real language of men' was the right material. It was to be purified from provincialism and from, all national causes of disgust and dislike." It was to be 'selected' it was to be 'the real language of men in a state of vivid sensation'.

When we examine Wordsworth's statement regarding poetic diction, the following facts clearly catch our attention

1. The language of poetry should be the language really used by men, but it should be 'selection' of such language. All the words used by the people can not be employed in poetry, only selected and chosen words which are used in common parlance can serve the purpose of poetry.
2. It should be the language of men in a state of vivid sensation. It means that language used by the people in a state of animation can form the language of poetry. It should have a certain colouring of imagination. The poet should give the colour of his imagination to the language employed by him in poetic composition.

3. There is no essential difference between the words used in prose and in metrical composition. Words of prose and poetry are not clearly demarcated, so that words which can be used in prose can find place in poetry and vice versa. "What Wordsworth means is that the words in conversation, if they are properly selected, would provide the rough framework of the language of poetry, only the latter is heightened by feeling and emotions."

Through the power of imagination the poet can select words fit for poetic composition. When the poet is truly inspired, his imagination will enable him to select from the "language really used by men", the real and true style of poetry. Wordsworth has democratised the conception of the poet and poetry. According to him, the poet is essentially a man who differs from others men not in kind but only on degree.

He is essentially a man speaking to men and possesses certain gifts in a higher degree than others. His soul is more sensible with a greater power of observation, imagination and communication. He thinks of things long and deep. He has established emotional identification with other men and freely shares the joys and sorrows of common men about whom he must sing. In a way, by his theory of poetic diction and definition of poetry, he became the herald of the Romantic Movement.

He attached the greatest importance to imagination and, as CM Bowra says, "For him, the imagination was the most important gift that the poet can have". It was for the first time that the poetry became the 'spontaneous overflow of powerful feelings recollected in tranquility', with him, imagination became a visualising power that enables the poet to recreate the past. It is considered to be "a great literary landmark which gave a new direction, consciousness and programme to English romanticism."

Another great gift of Wordsworth to literary criticism is his declaration that poetry is the first and last of all knowledge. The poet performs this function by discovering universal laws of human nature and communicating them to his readers and declared that "Every great poet is a teacher." He also established the superiority of poetry to history and science. The scientist studies truth only through intellect while the poet goes down to the inner reality.

So, he is the greater benefactor, a genial friend and companion at the same time, the historical significance of his critical theory is also very great. Instead of artificial phraseology, he stressed on the value of simple and natural language. He emphasised the true nature of poetry as an expression of passion and established a strong foundation for romantic poetry. For him, poetic process is a complex one. Great poetry is not produced on the spur of moment, it is produced only when the original emotion is contemplated in tranquillity. He also argued against the neo-classical morality by saying that the function of poetry was not to instruct but to please.

Inspite of this greatness, there are certainly some deficiencies in his views. He has confined himself exclusively to rustic life and thus has excluded many other important aspects of general human life; which should be included in poetry for its power and effect. In the opinion of Scott James, "he has thus narrowed the range and scope of poetry." Coleridge has highly objected to Wordsworth's theory of poetic diction. Inspite of all this, the credit of democraticising poetry certainly goes to Wordsworth and holds a distinct place in the history of English criticism.

He has established a theory in which imagination is of highest importance and thus paved a new way for imaginative poetry. Rene Wellek says that, "Though Wordsworth left only a small body of criticism, it is rich in survivals, suggestions, anticipation and personal insight."

Coleridge's Criticism of Wordsworth's Theory of Poetic Diction

Wordsworth's theory of poetic diction was disapproved by Coleridge and in the pages of *Biographia Literaria* he found numerous defects in Wordsworth's theory of poetic diction. Coleridge stated that language purged from local and class peculiarities was not different from any other language. Further, the use of metre in poetry necessitate the use of language different from the ordinary language of poetry, still more, the heightened and emotionally worked up state of poet in poems of philosophic import as the *Ode On The Intimation of Immortality from Recollections of Early Childhood* needed a language coloured by emotional fervour and vigorous imagination.

Hence, Wordsworth was mistaken in making a sweeping generalisation for all types of poetic thoughts to be rendered in the language of common speech. Wordsworth's chief error was to extend his theories to include all poetry. No theory, however subtly argued and cogently phrased, can be comprehensive enough to hold good for poetry in general. Again Wordsworth's deductions from the limited scope of his doctrine were rather extravagant.

Herbert Read makes a similar observations when he says, "it is equally true that there are as many poems which contradict the theory as an all inclusive generalisation. The mistake is to imagine that any theory of poetry, which descends to accidentals of diction and metre can be universal in its scope."

Samuel Taylor Coleridge

Coleridge was born in 1772 in Devonshire and was the youngest of the thirteen children of the Vicar of Ottery St Mary. As a child he was extremely precocious. At the age of ten he went to Christ's Hospital and from there he went to Cambridge in 1791. He was there at Jesus College from 1791 to 1794, with an interval in a regiment of Dragons under an assumed name. In 1794, he met Southey and they entered into the Pantisocratic scheme of forming a settlement with community of goods on the Susquehanna River. This plan, which came to nothing, was the result of the revolutionary zeal that had fired him at Cambridge.

In 1795, he married the sister of Southey's wife and in 1796 began his friendship with Wordsworth that resulted in the publication of the epoch-making *Lyrical-Ballads* in 1798. The period from 1797 to 1798 has been called as the Annus Mirabilis (wonderful year) of Coleridge's poetical career by Pater and his best work was produced during this period.

He went through political opinions similar to Wordsworth's and he called *France an Ode* as his 'recantation'. In 1798 he went to Germany and was fascinated by Germany metaphysics that turned the poet Coleridge into Philosopher Coleridge. After returning to England in 1799, he tried journalism and lecturing. The rest of his life was spent in aimless wanderings, in making and re-making plans and schemes and in leading a restless and unhappy life.

He rightly described himself as 'indolence capable of energies', through he possessed a remarkable genius, he was wanting in will-power. Moreover, he was addicted to opium. In 1816, in the hope of conquering his opium addiction, he went to live at Highgate with a surgeon and there he was like an oracle till his death in 1834, for those interested in three genres of literature-poetry, criticism and philosophy. Coleridge was a poet, philosopher and critic rolled into one.

He was a genius whose very versatility became his undoing. His poetry is very scanty in volume and he was left not more than half a dozen poems but of real merits. His prose works in philosophy, politics, criticism, etc are equally fragmentary and unsystematic.

The theories of poetry advanced by the Romantic critic of the early 19th century (Wordsworth, Coleridge, and others) let too many efforts to distinguish between imagination and fancy terms which had formerly been used as virtually synonymous. The word imagination itself already has passed through three stages of meaning in England.

In Renaissance times, it was opposed to reason and regarded as the "means by which poetical and religious conception could be attained and appreciated". Thus, according to Bacon it is one of the three faculties of the rational soul: "History has reference to the memory, poetry to the imagination, and philosophy to the reason; and Shakespeare says that classical period, was the faculty by which images were called up, especially visual images, as explained in Addison's *The Pleasures of Imaginations*, and was related to the process by which 'Imitation of nature' might take place. Because of its tendency to transcend the testimony of the senses, the poet who might draw upon imagination must subject to the check of reason, which should determine its form of presentation. Later, in the 18th century the imagination, opposed to reason, was conceived as so vivid an imaging process that it affected the passion and formed 'a world of beauty of its own', a poetical illusion which served not to affect conduct but to produce immediate pleasure.

The Conception of Imgination of the Romantic Critics

The romantic critics, however, conceived of imagination as a blending and unifying of the powers of the mind which enabled the poet to see inner relationships, such as the identity of truth and beauty. So, Wordsworth says that poets

> Have each his own peculiar faculty,
> Heaven's gift, a sense that fits him to perceive
> Objects unseen before........
> An insight that in some sort he possesses.
> Proceeding from a source of untaught things.

This new conception of imagination necessitated a distinction between it and fancy.

Biographia Literaria

Coleridge in his *Biographia Literaria* especially stressed, though he never fully explained the difference. He called imagination the 'shaping and modifying' power, while fancy as the 'agg regative and associative' power. The imagination 'struggles to idealise and to unify,' while the fancy is merely "a mode of memory emancipated from the order to time and space." To illustrate the distinction Coleridge remarked that Milton had a highly imaginative mind, Cowley a very fanciful one. Leslie Stephen (1879) stated the distinction briefly, "fancy deals with the superficial resemblance, and imagination with the deeper truths that underlie them."

The Views of Coleridge on 'Imagination and Fancy'

The first reference was made by Coleridge to the distinction between imagination and fancy, in the fourth chapter of his *Biographia Literaria*, where Coleridge remarks: "Repeated meditations led me first to suspect and a more intimate analysis of human faculties their appropriate marks, function and effects matured my conjecture into full conviction) that fancy and imagination were two distinct and widely different faculties, instead of being, according to the general belief, either two names with one meaning or at furthest, the lower and higher degree of one and the same power". Coleridge gives examples to illustrate the distinction between imagination and fancy, "to the faculty by which I had characterised Milton, we should confine the term 'imagination'; while the other would be contra distinguished as 'fancy'.

The Functiion of the Primary and Secondary Imagination

In the seventh chapter of his *Biographia Literaria*, Coleridge discuss the functions of the Primary and Secondary Imagiantion: "there are evidently two powers at work which relatively to each other are active and passive and this is not possible without an intermediate faculty which is at once both active and passive. In philosophical language we must denominate this intermediate faculty in all its degree and determinations, the imagination. But in common language and especially on the subject of poetry, we appropriate the name to superior degree of the faculty, joined to a superior voluntary control over it."

The Distinction Between Imagination and Fancy

In the thirteen chapter of *Biographia Literaria*, Coleridge discusses the terms imagination and fancy fully and brings out the distinction between imagination and fancy clearly

Imagination

The imagination I consider either as primary or secondary. The primary imagination I hold to be the living power and prime agent of all human perception and as a repetition in the finite mind of the eternal act of creation in the infinite I am. The secondary imagination I consider as an echo of the former, co-existing with the conscious will, yet still as identical with the primary in the 'Kind' of its agency, and different only in 'degree' and in the 'mode' of its operation.

Fancy

"Fancy, on the contrary, has no other counters to play with, but fixities and definities. The fancy is no other than a mode of memory emancipated from the order of time and space; while it is blended with, and modified by that empirical phenomenon of the will, which we express by the word 'choice'. But equally with the ordinary memory the fancy must receive all its materials readymade from the law of association."

Conclusion

To conclude we can say as Coleridge himself holds that imagination is essentially shaping and creating faulty, "it dissolves, diffuses, dissipates, in order to recreate." On the other hand, fancy is to Coleridge, 'the aggregative and associated power', as "the arbitrary bringing together of things that lie remote and forming them into unity. The materials lie ready formed for the mind and the fancy facts only by a sort of juxtaposition." Though Prof. Rene Wellek maintains that the conception of imagination and fancy had been borrowed by Coleridge from the thinkers of Germany, yet the fact remains Coleridge imagination and fancy is unique and totally original in the domain of literary criticism.

Dr Samuel Johnson

Samuel Johnson was born on 18th September, 1709 in a house which is now preserved in public hands in memory of him. His father Michael Johnson, was a book seller at Lichfield. His mother was Sarah Ford who came of a good yeoman stock. He went to Lichfield Grammar school, and then at the age of fifteen to Stoutbridge.

At both the places he won the regard of fellow students and teacher alike. After leaving Stoutbridge, Johnson spent two years at home in desultory reading. He piled up good knowledge of learning, the result of which was that, then he went up to Oxford, the Master of his college said, he was "the best qualified for the university that he had known ever come there." His college was Pembroke, of which he became a Commoner in 1728.

A lack of funds forced the young Johnson, only after thirteen months residence at Pembroke College, to quit Oxford without a degree in December 1729. In 1732, Johnson went to Brimingham at the invitation of his former school fellow, Edmund Hector. There he translate, from its French version an account of Abyssinia by a Portuguese Jesuit, published in 1735, this was Johnson first book. In Brimingham, he also met a widow, Elizabeth Porter, whom he married in July 1735. The year 1745 proved the literary turning point of Johnson's life. In this year he laid the foundation stone of the authority and the fame he was soon to enjoy.

He published a pamphlet on Shakespeare's *Macbeth*, which won the praise of Warburton, for which Johnson always felt greatful and he began to occupy himself with the idea of preparing an English Dictionary in 1747, he published his *Plan for a Dictionary of the English Language*, addressed to Lord Chasterfield, in which he set out the intented scope and nature of the work.

In 1783, Johnson had a paralytic stroke and he lost his power of speech for some days. His strong will-power enabled him to recover rapidly, but never again did he have ever that modest measure of health which he had once enjoyed. The inevitable loss of friends combined with illness to depress in the last year. The year 1784 opened with a prolonged illness lasting for months. The end came on the 13th December, 1784. He was buried in Westminster Abbey on 20th December. Burke, the President of Royal Society, were among the pall bearers.

Johnson's remarks on Shakespeare dramatic art in his preface bring out clearly his originality as a critic. At the outset he establishes Shakespeare's sound claims to supremacy in literature, not by applying classical or neo-classical rules,but the Longinian test of all great literature, namely 'length of duration and continuance of esteem'. After that he analyses the quality of Shakespeare's art which has given him supremacy over others as the universality of his outlook, the faithful portrayal of the fundamental qualities of human nature common to all ages.

"Nothing can please many and please long", says Johnson, "but just representation of general nature". Shakespeare's greatest quality in his opinion is that he presents those general aspects of human nature which are essential qualities and characteristics of all mankind under all circumstances.

'His characters', he says, 'are not modified by the customs of particular places unpractised by the rest of the world; by the peculiarities of studies or professions, which can operate upon small numbers; or by the accidents of transient fashions or temporary opinions; they are genuine progeny of common humanity such as the world will always supply, and observation will always find."

Shakespeare is always true to life. Shakespeare's characters are real men and women and their dialogues are real speech. While other poets have violated probability and misrepresented life, Shakespeare has uniformly maintained his fidelity to life.
His scenes are occupied by men who act and speak as the reader thinks that he should himself have spoken or acted on the same occasion. He imparts human qualities and human speech even to supernatural agencies. His dramas are 'the mirror of life.'

Shakespeare violated rules, because he sought guidance from life. He wrote with the world open before him. Against the dictates of rules he mixes up comic and tragic sentiments and represents tragic and comic scenes in one and the same play. His plays are neither pure comedies nor pure tragedies but composition of a distinct kind. Johnson, however, defends tragicomedy which is more true to life than either pure tragedy or pure comedy.

It can be objected that tragic and comic scenes and sentiments by counteracting each other mar the effect of tragedy or comedy. To this Johnson's reply is that the interchanges of mingled scenes seldom fail to produce "the intended vicissitudes of passion. Fiction can not move so much, but that the attention may be easily transferred."

Johnson also defends Shakespeare's disregard of unities. Since Shakespeare's histories are neither tragedies nor comedies, they are not subject to the laws of unities. Actions in them is, 'so prepared as to be understood', "the incidents by various and affecting and the characters consistent, natural and distinct. No other unity is intended and therefore none is to be sought." In the other plays, however, Shakespeare observes the unity of action. The plot in them follows the Aristotlian pattern of a beginning, a middle and an end.

Events are well – interconnected and the end is the natural consequence of the preceding events. "There are perhaps some incidents that might be spared", says Johnson, "but the general system makes gradual advances and the end of the play is the end of expectations."

But the unities of time and place Shakespeare shows no regard. Johnson does not regard it necessary to observe these unities. Critics hold that it is impossible to behave that an action of months and year can possibly finish in three hours, the duration of the dramatic performances. But to the critic who puts forth these objections Johnson replies that a dramatic performance is never mistaken for reality.

The spectators are in their senses and know that the stage is only a stage and players only players. Drama is credited only because it is just a picture of real life. Drama is semblance of reality and not reality itself. "Imitation produces pain or pleasure , not because they are mistaken for realities, but because they bring realities to mind."

Johnson praises Shakespeare for his fidelity to life, but he does not defy him. Shakespeare in his opinion, has faults which he does not hesitate to mention. His greatest defect is that "he sacrifices virtue to convenience, and is so much more careful to please than to instruct, that he seems to write without any moral purpose." A writer's duty, according to Johnson, is to instruct and morally improve the world, since Shakespeare neglects the opportunities of moral instruction, he is unsatisfactory as a writer." His precepts and axioms drop casually from him, he makes no just distribution of good or evil, nor is always careful to show in the virtuous a disapprobation of the wicked."

Shakespeare plots are loosely constructed and can be improved with a little consideration. In many of his plays the later part are not well-constructed as the earlier with the result that the catastrophe is either imperfect or improbable. He fails to make an accurate distinction of time or place, and gives to one age or nation the customs, institutions, and opinions of others.

Johnson regards Shakespeare's tragedies as inferior to his comedies. They are labour-things in his opinion and the lack the spontaneity and naturalness of his comedies. The effusion of passion in them are for the most part striking and energetic. But whenever he strains his faculties to invent something new and striking, the result is, "meanness, tediousness and obscurity."

Johnson is among the first of those critics who consider the works of an author in relation to the age to which he belonged. In the Preface he examines Shakespeare's plays in relation to the Elizabethan age, "An author's works to be highly judged", he says, "must be compared with the stage of the age in which he lived and with his own particular opportunities." Literature and language both were developing in the Elizabethan age. Literature was confined to professed scholars and to men and women of high ranks.

The taste of the people was crude and unrefined. Shakespeare plays are crowded with incidents, because it was only through incidents and action that he could hold the attention of his audience. The Elizabethan audience with its undeveloped taste could better appreciate pomps and processions which were visible on the stage, than the poetical language which made it appeal to the ear.

Shakespeare according to Johnson, is an amalgam of excellence and blemishes. Hence, he compares his works not to a garden but to a forest of oak trees in which weeds and brambles grow side by side with myrtles and roses. The wisdom that lies in Shakespeare's plays is not borrowed from books but gathered from life. According to Pope much knowledge is scattered in the works of Shakespeare. But it is knowledge, says Johnson, which books do not supply.

Shakespeare in spite of his shortcomings, is wholly original. He not only developed the English Drama, but even brought it to the verge of perfection in individual scene. Perhaps no poet except Homer invented so much as Shakespeare. The form, the characters, the language, and the shows of the English drama are his," Shakespeare shares with Spenser the praise of having discovered that English language that can be rendered remarkable soft, smooth and harmonious.

Still, according to Johnson, much of the praise and veneration of Shakespeare is due merely to custom. "We fix our eyes upon his graces", he says, "and turn them from his deformities", and endure in him what we should in another loathe and despise." Shakespeare has senses of undoubted excellence, says Johnson, but not even a single play is uniformly fine. Perhaps he did not write according his own idea of perfection, but to please his audience. Perhaps he only aimed at present fame and present popularity, and did not think that his plays were worthy to posterity. That is why he made no collection of his play, or tried to correct the texts of those which were wrongly printed by the publishers of his time. Johnson thinks that it is the duty of Shakespeare's editors to correct the text of his plays as far as possible.

Matthew Arnold

Matthew Arnold was born in Laleham, near Stains in the Middlesex in 1822. He was the eldest son of Thomas Arnold, popularly known as Dr Arnold, the Headmaster of Rugby School. One of the earliest and most abiding influence on Arnold's outlook was that of his father to whom the poet paid most moving tribute in his poem *Rugby Chapel*. His mother, Mary Primrose was a very talented lady and she also exercised a very powerful formative influence upon his personality. He was fortunate enough to enjoy the care, attention and patronage of such gifted parents and so his upbringing from his very early age was very perfect. He got his early education at Laleham and then in Winchester, the old school of Dr. Arnold and after one year he was sent to Rugby, his father's school in 1837 where he remained for four years. It was here that he imbibed the best influence of his reputated father.

He paid a very noble tribute to his father in the immortal poem *The Rugby Chapel*. In 1841, Dr Arnold was appointed Regius Professor of History at Oxford and young Arnold entered Balliol College, Oxford. Here, he distinguished himself by winning several Prizes. He composed a popular poem on Cromwell which brought him Newdigate prize in 1843. In 1845, he was elected fellow of Oriel and he was contracted the noble friendship with Arthur Hugh Clough, whose death in 1861 at Florence, the poet mourned in *Thyrsis* and whose friendship he celebrated in *The Scholar Gipsy*.

He stays at Oxford was the happiest and the most profitable. He was always fashionable in his dress and witty in conversation. He was known to be moving like a 'God among Oxford men'. His principal JC Sharp has given a very interesting account of his life during his undergraduate years in his poem *Ballial Scholar*.

Arnold did graduation from Oxford with honours in classical studies and he now decided to settle himself somewhere in life. For a few months served as a master at Rugby and in 1847 he was appointed as a private secretary to Lord Lansdowne who appointed him in 1851, an Inspector of School under the Government. He held this post for about thirty five years, till almost the end of his life. He married Francis Lucy Wightman, the daughter of a judge in 1851. By this time, Arnold was finally, securely, settled in his occupation. The 1851, proved the most fortunate for Arnold when he was appointed the professor of poetry at Oxford University which office Arnold held very capably for ten years. It is during this period that Arnold wrote his prose works but he could not produce any new poems.

The foundation of his critical principles was laid during this period and he delivered many valuable lectures on criticism, the most famous of them was at Oxford *On Translating Homer*. Arnold's first volume of poetry *The Strayed Reveller* and *Other Poems* was published in 1849. This included poems like *The Forsaken Merman* and *The Sonnet to Shakespeare*. His dramatic poem *Empedocles on Etna* appeared in 1852 and in 1853 came poems, a collection of great poems like *Sohrab and Rustum* and *The Scholar Gipsy*.

In the preface to this volume, Arnold declared that the poetry written in great style must describe an action which is excellent and appeals to the great primary affection. arnold died, suddenly in 1888. At liverpool on 15th April 1888, he ran to catch a tramcar with his wife and died the same moment. At this time, he had gone to meet his elder daughter on her way home from the united states. It ts said that it was a little ironical that arnold, apostle of quite, died of heart failure.

Poetry as Criticism of Life

"poetry is a criticism of life under the conditions fixed for such a criticism by the laws of poetic truth and poetic beauty."

"The future of poetry is worthy of its high destinies, our race, as time goes on, will find an ever surer stay. There is not a creed which is not shaken, not an accredited dogma which is not shown to be questionable, not a received tradition which does not threaten to dissolve. Our religion is materialised itself in the fact, in the supposed fact; it has attached his emotions to the fact and now the fact is failing it. But for poetry the idea is everything; the rest is a world of illusion, of divine illusion. Poetry attaches its emotion to the idea: the idea is the fact. The strongest part of our religion today is its unconscious poetry. " These words of Matthew Arnold put poetry on a very high pedestal, elevating it to the level of philosophy and religion. He predicts a very high destiny for poetry in as much as the belief that it is going to be a true guide and friend to man when he gets lost in the dark paths of life and when his rationalistic philosophy and his spiritual faith have turned totally incapable of helping him.

According to Arnold, poetry is the criticism of life. He means to say that criticism of life presupposes a process of selection and reflection because an artist is also an instinctive critic who knows well how to distinguish between sound and unsound, or only half sound; true and untrue; excellent and inferior; beautiful and ugly. While creating a world of his own, a poet takes best out of the material of life which is available to him. He hides the deformities and magnifies the beautiful and in this manner, he indulges into a criticism of life that helps a lover of poetry to understand and relative those hidden beauties of life and nature, that he himself is capable of understanding and realising because of his inferior sensibility.

Arnold believes that a born poet is instinctively capable of understanding these facts, and as Wordsworth tells us that in the proportion in which a poet possesses this capacity, he is raised above those common people who do not at all possess it. While engaged in the task of criticising life. The poet works only under one obligation, namely, to remain faithful to the conditions that have been fixed for criticism of life by the laws of poetic truth and poetic beauty and if he really remains faithful to these conditions the truth and high seriousness would formatically enter his poetry. As John Keats concludes his *Ode on a Grecian urn* with his oft-quoted lines.

"Beauty is truth, truth beauty-that is all
Ye know on earth, and all ye need to know"

Herein, Keats instinctively realises the existence of a close relationship between truth and beauty, which together form the chief object of a poet's quest.

Poetry is an art and like an artist feels a need for beauty for satisfying the aesthetic sense of man. Primarily, poetry creates awareness of pleasure in beauty. Poetry creates beauty besides other things through poetic truth which is greater to Arnold than historical truth. Arnold's criticism of life is the application of great ideas of life and its problems not under strict scientific laws of truth but under the poetic laws of truth where emphasis is not so much on what actually is as on what should have been. Poetry reveals higher truths and thus performs a function far superior to that of philosophy of religion. According to Arnold, a poetic truth, even though historically bogus, contains higher truth than the bare facts of historical truth.

"History is a record of what was, poetry of what should have been. History deals only with what has actually happened, poetry with that should have happened. Obviously, the application of these great ideas to life are to be applied both logically: It is to be a poetic application."

Arnold's ideal poet is that, "who is able to apply beautiful ideas of life". Arnold feels that "The greatness of a poet lies in his powerful and beautiful application of ideas of life." In his views, the basic question which a poet should answer is: How to live? and true poetry always answers this questions by affording to its readers 'consolation' and 'stay'. "The consolation and stay will be of power of the criticism of life. And the criticism of life will be of power in proportion of the poetry conveying it an excellent rather than inferior, sound rather unsound or half-sound, true rather than untrue or half-true." Arnolds believes that it is only poetry that is certain and reliable guide in almost all departments of human activity.

According to Arnold, "The best poetry is what we want, the best poetry will be found to have a power of forming, sustaining and delighting us, as nothing else can. A clear deeper sense of the best in poetry and of the strength and joy to be drawn from it, is the most precious benefit which we can gather from a poetical collection such as the present."

Arnold's theory of criticism may be illustrated through his criticism of Wordsworth, because according to Arnold, Wordsworth's poetry presents not only a sound criticism of life but it also contains high seriousness which Chaucer and Burns lack so much. According to Arnold, "the purpose of poetry is to console and sustain us as it is in poetry alone that our race will find an ever-surer and surer stays." Arnolds also believes that the poetry of Wordsworth affords us "so much it rest upon, so much which communicates his spirit and engages ours." According to Arnold's great poetry must deal with life with moral ideas precisely because, a poetry of revolt against life. Wordsworth had been regarded by Arnold as a great poet since he deals with life and ideas so powerfully and seriously. Therefore, Arnold judges Wordsworth's place as a poet above poets like Voltaire, Dryden, Pope, Lessing, Schiller etc. Thus, Wordsworth's greatness as a poet lies in the application of ideas to life and in its power to enable and sustain us.

To conclude,. 'High seriousness is as essential to poetry according to Arnold as a grand style. He tells us, "It is a high and excellent seriousness which Aristotle assigns as one of the grand virtues of poetry.

The substance of Chaucer's poetry, his views of things and his criticism of life, has largeness, freedom, shrewdness, benignity, but has not this high seriousness. Homer's Criticism of Life had it. Dante's had it. Shakespeare's has it. It is this chiefly which gives to our spirits what they can rest upon; and with the increasing demands of our modern ages upon poetry, this virtue of giving us what we can rest upon will be more and more highly esteemed."

TS Eliot

Thomas Stearns Eliot, born in 1888 at St. Louis, in the United States, was descended from a family that had long ago resided at East Coker in Somerset, Whence in 1670 his Puritan ancestors emigrated to Massachusetts. He was educated at Harvard, Paris and Oxford. He married in 1915, settled in England, and adopted British citizenship in 1922. After working in Lloyd's Bank for a period, he became a director of the publishing firm of Faber and Faber and held that office till his death.

The collected edition of his poems contains, besides minor and pieces; *Prufrock and Other Observations* (1917), *Ash Wednesday Fragmentary* (1934), *Four Quarters* (1935-40). His important literary criticism is contained in *Selected Essays* (1932) and *On Poetry and Poets* (1957).

Eliot's dramatic production includes; *The Rock, A Pageant Play* (1934), *Murder in the Cathedral* (1935), *The Family Reunion* (1939), *The Cocktail Party* (1950), *The Confidential Clerk* (1954), *The Elder Stateman* (1959). He was invested with the Order of Merit (o.m.) in 1948 and the same year received the Nobel Prize for literature.

Critical Concepts of TS Eliot

One of the greatest English critics of the 20th century, Eliot's criticism marks a total break from the 19th century traditions and gives direction to literary criticism. The pearls of his critical concepts lie scattered throughout his approximately five hundred essays and reviews. Clive Bell correctly eulogises Eliot for his gift of coinage, in prose as well as in poetry. Eliot has coined a member a memorable phrases which are striking and have got wide currency. These phrases of Eliot have made him a great stirrer of thought. For a precise understanding of Eliot's criticism, it will be helpful to examine some of his critical concepts, which are as follows.

1. The term objective correlative was first used by Eliot in his essay on *Hamlet*, to describe a pattern of objects, actions or events, or a situation which can serve effectively to awaken in the reader, the emotional response which the author desires without expressing a direct statement of the emotion, obviously, it is an impersonal or objective means of communicating feeling. Eliot calls the objective correlative 'the only way of expressing emotion in the form of art' and defines it as 'a set of objects, a situation, a chain of events which shall be the formula of that particular emotion, such that when the external facts, which must terminate in sensory experience are given, the emotion is immediately evoked.' The term had wide currency in this sense among contemporary critics. It had been used by Washington Allston in a lecture on art as early as 1850 to describe the process by which the external world produces pleasurable emotion, but Eliot's usage gave it new meaning and made of it a new term. For instance, in *Macbeth*, Shakespeare communicates to the reader the mental grief of Lady Macbeth in the 'sleep walking scene', not through direct description but through an unconscious repletion of her past action. Her mental grief has been so objectified as to be seen through eyes as felt by the heart. Thus, the external situation is sufficient to evoke in the mind of the reader the desired emotion- the grief of lady Macbeth. Thus, instead of communicating the emotions of grief directly to the reader Shakespeare has embodied these emotions in a situation which easily conveys the feelings of grief to the reader.

   Keats has already called the 'Objective correlative as 'Negative capability' to describe the objective and impersonal aspects of Shakespeare, Keats asserted: "A poet has no identity.....he is continually ...... filling some other body." The term has since been applied widely to the qualities in an artist's work which enable him to avoid in the expression of his own personality.

   The term 'Aesthetic Distance' which describes the effect produced when an emotion or an experience is so objectified by the proper use of form that can be understood as being objectively realised, independent of the immediate personal experience of its maker is also closely related to Eliot's 'Objective correlative' and to Keats's 'Negative capability'.

   Different critics have interpreted the term 'Objective correlative' differently. Thus, according to Cleanth Brooks, it means 'organic metaphor', according to sister Mary Cleophas Costello, it means the intensity of meaning structure'. Eliseo Vivas takes it as a 'vehicle of expression for the poet's emotion" while Allan Austin interprets it as 'the poetic content to be conveyed by verbal expression'.

2. The phrases 'Dissociation of Sensibility' and its opposite 'unification of sensibility' were first used by Eliot in his *Essay on the Metaphysical Poets* of the early seventeenth century. In his criticism, the relation between intellect and emotions in art and poetry is of fundamental importance and tne success of artistic performance of the poet or artist depends on the intensity of his sensibility. According to Eliot, a poetical achievement is nothing but the emotional equivalent of the thought. According to TS Eliot, the unification of sensibility means, 'a fusion of thought and feeling,' 'a recreation of thought into feeling', 'a direct sensuous apprehension of thought.' In the view of Eliot such fusion of thought and i feeling is very necessary for good poetry.

   On the other hand, 'dissociation of sensibility' results in bad poetry. Eliot discovers the unification of sensibility in the Metaphysical poets and deplores the setting in of a dissociation of sensibility in the late 17th century, because in the poetry of the aforeside period there was a split between thought and feeling and in the view of Eliot we have hitherto not recovered from his dissociation of sensibility. Eliot believes that the influence of Dryden and Milton has been especially harmful in this connection.

3. In his *Essay on the Metaphysical poets*, TS Eliot tells us about the process of the fusion of thought and feeling. He remarks; "Tennyson and Browning are poets and they think, but they do not feel their thought as immediately as the odour of a rose. A thought to Donne was an experience, it modified his sensibility. When a poet's mind is perfectly equipped for its work, it is constantly amalgamating disparate experiences. The ordinary man's experience is chaotic, irregular, fragmentary.

   Eliot does not consider Browning as a great poet, because, inspite of having ideas, he fails to change his ideas into emotions and sensations, and in his view, merely dry thought or logic do not and cannot make a great poet. Eliot believes that a really great poet has the stamina to experience and feel his thought in the same way as he does odour of a rose, but a bad poet does not possess this capacity.

4. The harmonious working of the creative and critical powers of a poet constitutes another aspect of the unification of sensibility according to Eliot. No doubt a poet creates in the heat of inspiration, but he makes correction in this creation at his

leisure. Therefore, according to Eliot, a poet must not only create but must also bring the critical power to work upon his creation, i.e. he must revise and refine it and in this way give his creation a beautiful shape. According to Eliot, it is urgently necessary for great poet to be a great critic as well, because he must constantly analyse, reject and select.

In his essay *On Tradition*, published in *After Strange Gods*, Eliot maintains ; Tradition is not solely, or even primarily, the maintenance of certain dogmatic beliefs; these beliefs have come to take their living form in the course of information of a tradition.

What I mean by tradition involves all these habitual actions, habits and customs from the most significant religious rites to our conventional way of greeting a stranger, which represent, the blood kinship of ' the same people living in the same place'. It involves a good deal which can be called taboo; that this word is used in our time in exclusively derogatory sense is to me a curiosity of some significance, we become conscious of these items, or conscious of their importance, usually only after they have begun to fall into desuetude, as we all are aware of the leaves of a tree when the autumn wind begins to blow them off when they have separately ceased to be vital.

Energy may be wasted at that point in a frantic endeavour to collect the leaves as they fall and gum from the branches, but the sound tree will put forth new leaves and the dry tree should be put to the axe.

We are always in danger, in enlighting to an old tradition or attempting to re-establish one. Our second danger is to associate tradition with the immovable, to think of it as something hostile to all changes, to aim to return to some previous condition which we imagine as having been capable of preservation in perpetuity, instead of aiming to stimulate the life which produced that condition in its time. It is obvious that Eliot's conception of tradition is a dynamic conception of tradition.

Eliot seems to suggest that a sense of tradition is necessary, because this sense of tradition enables us to realise our kinship with 'the same people living in the same place'. But at the same time we are instructed to bear in mind that the prevailing condition of life that produced a particular tradition is not something immovable, but rather something that constantly grows and becomes different from what it formerly was.

Other Important Critics and their Works

IA Richards (1893-1979)

British literary critic Ivor Armstrong Richards is considered as one of the founders of the school of interpretation known as the New Criticism. He was born in Cheshire in 1893. and educated at Cambridge University's Magdalene College. During his stint as a lecturer at Cambridge, Richards wrote three of his most influential works- *The Meaning of Meaning* (1923; with CK Ogden), a pioneer work on semantics; and *Principles of Literary Criticism* (1924) and *Practical Criticism* (1929).

Alongwith Charles Kay Ogden, Richards also created a simplified language called Basic English, which consisted of a primary vocabulary of 850 words. He believed a universally intelligible language would help to bring about international understanding.

In his book Practical Criticism, Richards analysed the self-reported interpretive work of students. He removed authorial and contextual information from 13th poems, including one by Longfellow and four by decidedly marginal poets. Then he assigned their interpretation to undergraduates at Cambridge University in order to ascertain the most likely impediments to an adequate response. This approach showed how otherwise intelligent college students misread the poems. Richards' concept of practical criticism led in time to the practices of close reading, what is often thought of as the beginning of modern literary criticism. Richards is generally considered as one of the founders of the contemporary study of literature in English. Richards died in 1979, on his return home to Cambridge from a teaching trip to China.

Major Works

- The Foundations of Aesthetics (Co-authored with C K Ogden and James Wood, 1922)
- Principles of Literary Criticism (1924)
- Science and Poetry (1926; revised as Poetries and Sciences, 1970)
- Practical Criticism (1929)
- Mencius on the Mind (1932)
- Coleridge on Imagination (1934)
- The Philosophy of Rhetoric (1936)
- The Meaning of Meaning (co-authored with C K Ogden, 1946)
- Speculative Instruments (1955)
- Beyond (1974)
- Poetries (1974)
- Complementarities (1976)

Irving Babbit (1865-1933)

American academic and literary critic Irving Babbitt was the leader of the American New Humanist critical movement. He was born in Dayton, Ohio, to Edwin Dwight and Augusta Darling Babbitt. He studied at Harvard College in 1885 and obtained a four-years degree in Classics. After completing his graduation, Babbitt took a post as a teacher of Classics at the College of Montana. He was appointed Professor of Romance languages at Williams College, but returned to Harvard to teach French and Comparative literature until his death in 1933.

In his first book, *Literature and the American College* (1908), Babbitt criticised the academic policies of Harvard president Charles William Eliot that allowed students to establish their own courses of study rather than enforce a rigid academic regimen emphasising self-discipline. His second book, *The New Laokoon: An Essay on the Confusion of the Arts* (1910), attacked the 19th century Romantic Movement. Babbitt believed it to be a logical extension of Jean Jacques Rousseau's philosophy of naturalism. According to J David Hoeveler, "Babbitt's humanism defended a dualistic view of human nature, locating in it two opposing forces. On the one hand, human nature possesses an inherently expansionist instinct that seeks release from all constraints and pursues an indefinite liberation of will and imagination. But it also possesses a principle of control, a force for discipline and moderation." Irving Babbitt died in 1933.

Major Works

- Literature and the American College (1908)
- The New Laokoön (1910)
- The Masters of Modern French Criticism (1912)
- Rousseau and Romanticism (1919)
- Democracy and Leadership (1924)
- On Being Creative (1932)
- The Dhammapada (1936)
- Spanish Character, and Other Essays (1940) reprinted as Character and Culture: Essays on East and West
- Representative Writings (1981)

EXAM BASED QUESTIONS

1 What is the meaning of the term 'Hamartia' as used by Aristotle in the 'Theory of Tragedy'?
(a) Tragic end of the Tragedy.
(b) Working of the fate against the hero.
(c) A weak trait in the character of the hero.
(d) A strong quality in the character of the hero.

2 The term Anagnorisis as used by Aristotle mean ....
(a) The hero's recognition of his tragic flow.
(b) The hero's ignorance about his tragic flow.
(c) The hero's recognition of his advisory.
(d) The hero's recognition of his tragic end.

3 Who rejects the pathological theory of Catharsis that 'theatre is not a hospital'?
(a) Humphrey house (b) FL Lucas
(c) Abercrombic (d) IA Richards

4 Aristotle declared that plot is the ....
(a) most essential (b) most useful
(c) soul of the tragedy (d) not necessary

5 Who defines criticism as the play of mind on the aesthetic qualities of literature?
(a) Saintsbury (b) Victor Hugo
(c) Atkins (d) Edmund Gosse

6 What is the first and foremost function of a literary critic?
(a) to get full value out of literary quality
(b) to distinguish between a good book and bad book
(c) to satisfy the readers
(d) to condem the authors and poets

7 What type of men do tragedy and epic represent?
(a) Lowest (b) Villians
(c) Saints (d) Normally good men

8 Which work of Aristotle is the most famous in the history of criticism?
(a) On the sublime (b) The Republic
(c) The poetics (d) Apology for poetry

9 Who was the teacher and most important literary critic before Aristotle?
(a) Plato (b) Horace
(c) Boileau (d) None of these

10 Sydney's 'Apology For Poetry' is an example of
(a) Theoretical Criticism (b) Comparative Criticism
(c) Historical Criticism (d) Evaluative Criticism

11 Who considers poetry to be the mother of lies?
(a) Plato (b) Aristotle
(c) Longinus (d) Sidney

12 How many chapters are there in 'poetics'?
(a) Twenty (b) Twenty six
(c) Thirty four (d) Thirty

13 Who commented that "Even today the Poetics continues to be studied and prescribed as text books in schools and colleges"?
(a) FL Lucas (b) Dr. Johnson
(c) Atkins (d) Dryden

14 What term has Aristotle used for the weakness, error or fault in character of the tragic hero?
(a) Hamartia (b) Pripetia
(c) Catharsis (d) None of these

15 How many formative elements does Aristotle consider for the great tragedy?
(a) Four (b) Six (c) Five (d) Two

16 Who considers Longinus as, "the first comparative critic of literature"?
(a) Abercrombic (b) Scott James
(c) Wimsatt (d) Atkins

17 In whose opinion Longinus "classicism was touched with romance"?
(a) Abercrombic
(b) Scott James
(c) Wimsatt
(d) Atkins

18 Longinus declares that sublime "please all and......".
(a) pleases always (b) pleases everywhere
(c) pleases forever (d) pleases sometimes

19 Longinus says that "Great literature springs from great and....".
(a) lofty souls (b) immortal ideas
(c) high imagination (d) nobility of diction

20 Regarding noble diction, Longinus thinks that "Beautiful words are in truth..... of thought".
(a) the soul (b) the very light
(c) the essence (d) None of them

21 According to Longinus, the chief function of literature is
(a) Aesthetic (b) Entertainment
(c) Compassion (d) Didactic

22 Who has longinus advised to imitate in poetry?
(a) Rules and regulations
(b) Great classical masters
(c) Contemporary literature
(d) Nature and art

23 'On the Sublime' is written in
(a) Dramatic (b) Conversational
(c) Poetic (d) Prose

24 What does Longinus mean by 'puerility'?
(a) Word arrangement (b) Rhythm
(c) Hyperbole (d) Pedantic conceit

25 Who is the friend of Longinus referred to in the beginning of 'on the sublime'?
(a) Caecilus (b) Terentianus
(c) Postumus (d) None of these

26 The two types of sublime are....
(a) excellence and grandeur (b) harmony and rhythm
(c) epic and tragedy (d) true and false

27 In which language has 'on the sublime' been originally composed?
(a) Roman (b) Greek (c) Latin (d) French

28 Longinus borrowed the concept of using metaphor from...
(a) Aristotle (b) Plato
(c) Homer (d) Demosthenes

29 Great utterance is the echo of greatness of....
(a) mind (b) heart (c) soul (d) language

30 In whose opinion has Longinus "turned and tempered them with what is Sanest in Classism"?
(a) Atkins (b) Gibbons
(c) Scott James (d) Saintsbury

31 Complete Longinus declaration that, 'sublimity is a certain loftiness and excellence in ....'.
(a) Poetry (b) Language
(c) Style (d) None of these

32 In which work of Sidney, his theory of poetry has been expressed?
(a) An Apologie for Poetrie (b) Poetic
(c) Essay on Dramatic poesy (d) Critical Essays

33 In which year was An Apologie for poetrie written?
(a) 1580 (b) 1583 (c) 1585 (d) 1590

34 How was it printed?
(a) Posthumously (b) Before his death
(c) In 1585 (d) None of these

35 What is the other title of An Apologie for poetrie given to it by another publisher?
(a) Poetics (b) Essay of Criticism
(c) The Defence of poesie (d) None of these

36 How many version of An Apology for poetrie were published?
(a) Two (b) Three (c) Four (d) Six

37 Who called the poet a Vates?
(a) Greeks (b) Romans
(c) Italians (d) Squamards

38 What is the meaning of Vates in Greek culture?
(a) Maker (b) Prophet
(c) Imagination (d) Singer

39 What type of poetry does Sidney call "the best and most accomplished kind of poetry"?
(a) Lyric (b) Epic
(c) Ode (d) Sonnet

40 Who had objected to the greatness of poetry in the days of Sidney?
(a) Plato (b) Gosson
(c) Sterner (d) Malville

41 Which book had been written by Stephen Gosson?
(a) School of Abuse (b) Evils of Poesy
(c) Corruptor (d) None of these

42 In whose opinion "Sidney wrote not a pedants" encyclopaedia but a gentleman's essay"?
(a) Wimsatt and Brooks (b) Atkins
(c) Dryden (d) Scott James

43 Who says that "Nowhere else do we find the same happy mingling of the ideal and the practical", as an Apologie for Poetrie?
(a) Dr. Johnson (b) Atkins
(c) Scott James (d) Prof. Saintsbury

44 What was the most powerful influence on Sidney?
(a) Greek (b) Latin
(c) French (d) Aristotle

45 Who had banished poetry from ideal commonwealth?
(a) Plato (b) Horace
(c) Gosson (d) Wilson

46 Who composed Arcadia?
(a) Spenser (b) Sidney
(c) Gosson (d) Wilson

47 What was the chief source of Sidney's theory of tragedy?
(a) Plato (b) Horace
(c) Aristotle (d) Longinus

48 Who declared that "the sources of Sidney's defence were classical but the spirit was not very sternly classical"?
(a) Dr. Johnson (b) Atkins
(c) Prof. Saintsbury (d) Wimsatt

49 Complete Sidney's declaration that 'one may be a poet without....'.
(a) singing (c) music
(c) versing (d) knowledge

50 Who said, "The necessity is yet greater than mine"?
(a) Sidney (b) Spanish soldier
(c) Queen (d) Commander

51 How did Sidney die?
(a) Killed (b) Wound of war
(c) Suicide (d) Poisoned

52 What kind of poem is 'Arcadia'?
(a) Lyric (b) Ballad
(c) A prose romance (d) Elegy

53 What is the aim of poetry according to Sidney?
(a) Delight (b) Delightful instruction
(c) Instruction (d) None of these

54 Sidney has rejected English drama because of....
(a) Pure laughter (b) Extreme seriousness
(c) Worthlessness (d) Tragi-comedy

55 The greatest weakness of English drama is its violation of....
(a) three unities (b) unnatural incidents
(c) real characters (d) historical truth

56 Who praised Dryden as the father of English criticism?
(a) Atkins (b) Scott James
(c) Dr. Johnson (d) TS Eliot

57 Which is the most popular critical work of Dryden?
(a) The essay on satire (b) Essay on dramatic poesy
(c) Essay on fables (d) Essay on heroic tragedy

58 Who calls Essay on Fables "the masterpiece in judgement, method and style"?
(a) Atkins (b) Scott James
(c) Dr. Johnson (d) TS Eliot

59 What is the form adopted in Essay of dramatic Poesy?
(a) Two (b) Four
(c) Three (d) Six

60 Which character produces the views of Dryden?
(a) Neander (b) Crites
(c) Lisideius (c) Eugenius

61 Which of the characters favours the greatness of the ancients?
(a) Neander (b) Crites
(c) Lisideius (d) Eugenius

62 In which work has Dryden made the masterly appreciation of Chaucer?
(a) The Spanish Friar (b) Preface to the Fables
(c) The essay on satire (d) Essay on dramatic poesy

63 Which is the perfect modern English play according to Dryden?
(a) Silent woman (b) Duchess of malfi
(c) Macbeth (d) Volpone

64 In whose opinion, Dryden is "the first Englishman to attempt any extended descriptive criticism"?
(a) Saintsbury (b) Dr. Johnson
(c) Watson (d) Pope

65 Who thinks that,"his reputation as a critic rests on sure and lasting foundation"?
(a) TS Eliot (c) FR Leavis (c) Atkins (d) Richards

66 According to Lisideius, the French use rhyme in place of.... .
(a) Poetry (b) Prose
(c) Black verse (d) Dialogue

67 Which English poet has been most praised by Dryden?
(a) Wycliff (b) Milton
(c) Chaucer (d) Spenser

68 What form of drama has been most objected by Lisideius?
(a) Comic (b) Tragic
(c) Tragi-comedy (d) Farce

69 What great achievement has been in the essay of Dramatic Poetry?
(a) Freedom from classical rules
(b) Preference to imaginations
(c) Observing romanticism
(d) Teaching the people

70 The scene of An Essay of Dramatic Poesy has been laid on.....
(a) Hudson (b) Thames
(c) Nile (d) Dover

71 The age of Dryden is known as...... .
(a) Romantic (b) Jacobean
(c) Neo-classical (d) Elizabethan

72 Which form of drama has been most objected by Critics?
(a) Rhyming (b) Black verse
(c) Heroic couplet (d) Prose

73 What is the function of drama according to Dryden?
(a) Delight and instruction
(b) Purgation
(c) Religious teaching
(d) Transport

74 Drama is 'a just and lively image of .....'.
(a) life (b) human nature
(c) nature scene (d) action of man

75 The French drama has been preferred by.....
(a) Neander (b) Crities
(c) Lisideius (d) Eugenius

76 How long was the total literary period of Dryden ?
(a) Thirty years (b) Thirty five years
(c) Forty years (d) Forty two years

77 The central theme of the Essay of Dramatic Poesy is..... .
(a) Justification of English Drama
(b) Rejection of the French Drama
(c) Reject Aristotle
(d) Praise Chaucer

78 Dryden praises Chaucer as….
(a) A superman (b) God's plenty
(c) Uncommon man (d) The greatest poet

79 Who has been symbolised through the character of Critics?
(a) Sir Robert Howard (b) Charles Sackville
(c) Charles Sedley (d) None of these

80 "if he had seen ours, might have changed his mind." Who is 'he' in this remark?
(a) Chaucer (b) Horace
(c) Aristotle (c) Longinus

81 About whom has Dryden remarked, "I admire him but I love Shakespeare" ?
(a) Ben Johnson (b) Homer
(c) Chaucer (d) Shakespeare

82 Who of the following was Dryden's contemporary?
(a) Sir Philip Sydney (b) Thomas Rhymer
(c) Pope (d) Ben Johnson

83 In whose opinion, Dryden's Essay on Fables is 'the best criticism of the world' ?
(a) Dr. Johnson (b) Prof. Saintsbury
(c) Scott James (d) Atkins

84 Dryden declares that 'a bare…will not serve the ends of poetry'.
(a) Entertainment (b) Imitation
(c) Emotion (d) Singing

85 In the opinion of Dryden, which work is the greatest, most noble and most sublime?
(a) Paradise Lost (b) Macbeth
(c) Canterbury Tales (d) Aeneid

86 In his theory of criticism Dryden is very near to….
(a) Plato (b) Aristotle (c) Horace (d) Longinus

87 Dryden is considered to be the first exponent of…. .
(a) Classical criticism (b) Dramatic criticism
(c) Practical criticism (d) None of these

88 Who believes that Dryden "freed from a superstitious regard for the ancients"?
(a) Atkins (b) Prof. Tillyard
(c) Dr. Johnson (d) Watson

89 What was the immediate object of Wordsworth in writing the preface?
(a) Attack on contemporary poet
(b) Defend new poetry
(c) Reject Aristotle
(d) None of these

90 Who first objected to Wordsworth theory of language?
(a) Coleridge (b) Keats
(c) Atkins (d) FW Bateson

91 Who thinks that the preface is against 'positive theory of poetic diction current throughout the 18th century'?
(a) Coleridge (b) Dereck Roper
(c) Atkins (d) FW Bateson

92 Who claimed the preface to be 'half a child of my own brain'?
(a) Gray (b) Collins
(c) Coleridge (d) None of these

93 Which edition of Lyrical Ballads is considered to be a standard critical document?
(a) 1800 (b) 1802
(c) 1815 (d) 1820

94 Who assigns Wordsworth a place equal to Shakespeare and Milton?
(a) Matthew Arnold (b) Atkins
(c) Elton (c) Scott James

95 The preface to the Lyrical Ballad was attached to…. .
(a) 1800 edition (b) 1802 edition
(c) 1815 edition (d) 1820 edition

96 The Lyrical Ballad was first published in….
(a) 1798 (c) 1802 (c) 1815 (d) 1820

97 Who says that for Wordsworth "The plot or situation is not the first thing. It is the feeling that matters"?
(a) CM Bowra (b) Arnold
(c) Scott James (d) Atkins

98 Who declared that for Wordsworth "Imagination was the most important gift that a poet can have"?
(a) CM Bowra (b) Coleridge
(c) Arnold (d) Atkins

99 Wordsworth calls poetry "the breath and finer spirit of….
(a) Humanity (b) All knowledge
(c) Emotions (d) Experiences

100 There neither is, nor can there be, any essential difference between the language of prose and…. .
(a) poetry (b) poetic compositions
(c) verse (d) None of these

101 Who thinks that the preface is not a 'tactful writing'?
(a) Dereck Roper (b) Atkins
(c) Scott James (d) Saintsbury

102 Poetry is the spontaneous overflow of powerful…. .
(a) emotions (b) feelings
(c) passions (d) sentiments

103 For Wordsworth, the chief object of poetry is not to instruct but to give… .
(a) guidance (b) moral teaching
(c) pleasure (d) aesthetic joy

104 Who says that, "Every great poet is a teacher"?
(a) Wordsworth (b) Coleridge
(c) Keats (d) Pope

105 Wordsworth says, "Poetry is born not in the mind but in the heart overflowing with....
(a) emotions (b) thoughts
(c) feelings (d) ideas

106 What is the opinion of Wordsworth enables the poet to recreate the past?
(a) Imagination (b) Knowledge
(c) Learning (d) None of these

107 Who remarks that, "There abide these three: Aristotle, Longinus and Coleridge"?
(a) Saintsbury (b) TS Eliot
(c) Scott James (d) Reve welleck

108 Which is the most suitable language for poetry?
(a) Classical (b) Figurative
(c) Rustic (d) Artificial

109 Wordsworth says that "Poetry is the breath and .... of all knowledge".
(a) soul (b) spirit
(c) emotion (d) passion

110 What, according to Wordsworth is "the worst of all the diseases which have afflicted English poetry"?
(a) Classical imitation
(b) Artificial language
(c) False poetic diction
(d) None of the above

111 In whose opinion, the preface 'marks the beginning of a new age'?
(a) Margret Drabble (b) Scott James
(c) TS Eliot (d) Atkins

112 What is the theme of poetry for Wordsworth?
(a) Town life (b) Rustic life
(c) Nature (c) None of these

113 Which classical critic does Eliot resemble most of all?
(a) Plato (b) Horace
(c) Aristotle (d) Longinus

114 Who considers that the theory of Objective Correlative is " the poetic content to be conveyed by verbal expressions"?
(a) Cleanth Brooks (b) Elises Vevas
(c) Austin (d) None of these

115 In how many parts is the essay 'Tradition and Individual Talent' divided?
(a) Three (b) Two (c) Four (d) One

116 What is Eliot's opinion about Aristotle?
(a) Artificial Ideas (b) Perfect Critics
(c) Theorist (d) None of these

117 In which essay does Eliot explains how the fusion of thought and feeling take place?
(a) On Milton
(b) The Metaphysical poets
(c) The study of Poetry
(d) Tradition and individual talent

118 Who has praised Eliot for his gift of phrasing?
(a) Sampson (b) Atkins
(c) Clive Bell (d) Garrod

119 Eliot says, " poetry is not a turning loose of emotions, but an escape from..".
(a) imagination (b) emotion
(c) intellect (d) surroundings

120 Which work of Eliot is considered to be the manifesto of his critical creed?
(a) On Milton
(b) The metaphysical poets
(c) The study of poetry
(d) Traditional and individual talent

121 Who has criticised most Eliot's theory of objective correlative?
(a) Washington Allston
(b) WB Yeats
(c) Eliseo Vivas
(d) None of the above

122 Which play of Shakespeare does Eliot consider to be an artistic failure?
(a) Macbeth (b) Hamlet
(c) Othello (d) Julius Caesar

123 In which essay has Eliot rejected the poems of Milton and Dryden as artificial?
(a) On Milton
(b) The metaphysical poets
(c) The study of poetry
(d) Traditional and individual talent

124 What is Eliot's most significant contribution to critical analysis and judgement?
(a) Objective Correlative
(b) Association of sensibilities
(c) Dissociation of sensibilities
(d) None of the above

125 In which poet does Eliot find the unification of sensibilities to a greater extent?
(a) Metaphysical poets (b) Romantic poets
(c) Classical poets (d) Modern poets

126 What, according to Eliot is the best scene of objective correlative in Shakespeare's Macbeth?
(a) The Dagger scene (b) The Battle scene
(c) The Sleep Walking scene (d) The Porter scene

127 In which magazine did he work first as editor?
(a) Criterion (b) Egoist
(c) Literary views (c) None of them

128 What was the most important contact of Eliot in London?
(a) Lincoln (b) Churchill
(c) Ezra pound (d) Emerson

129 In which year was Eliot born?
(a) 1888 (b) 1890
(c) 1885 (d) 1880

130 What was the major field of Eliot's study at Howard university?
(a) Metaphysics (b) Philosophy
(c) Painting (d) Politics

131 Where did Eliot desire to be buried after the death?
(a) Westminster Abbey (b) France
(c) East Coker (d) None of these

132 To which part of America did Eliot belongs?
(a) Wales (b) New England
(c) Indiana (d) Panama

133 What was the distinguishing quality of his mother?
(a) A poetess (b) A dramatist
(c) A novelist (d) A journalist

134 What was the name of Eliot's father?
(a) Joseph Eliot (b) Henry Ware Eliot
(c) Charles Eliot (d) Thomas Eliot

135 What was the greatest event of the day he was born?
(a) Outbreak of world war (b) America got freedom
(c) Arnold died (d) None of these

136 Which is the birthplace of Eliot?
(a) USA (b) England
(c) Scotland (d) Ireland

137 Who introduced the term " esmeplastic in agination"?
(a) Wordsworth (b) Coleridge
(c) Shelley (d) TS Eliot

138 Who made the comment that fancy is "the arbitrary to bringing together of things that lie remote and forming them into a unity."?
(a) Dryden
(b) Wordsworth
(c) Coleridge
(d) Arnold

139 Which of the following arrangement of Matthew Arnold's critical works is in the correct chronological sequence?
(a) Preface to the poems – on translating Homer –Essays in criticism (Ist series)- Culture and Anarchy (1869)- Essays in criticism (II series),
(b) On translating Homer-Culture and Anarchy- Essays in criticism (Ist and II series), preface to the poems,
(c) Culture and Anarchy –preface to poems- Essays in criticism (Ist and II series)- on translating Homer.
(d) None of the above.

140 The function of criticism is not merely "judgement in literature" but "a disinterested endeavour to learn and propagate the best that is known and thought in the world, and thus to establish current of fresh and new ideas." Who expressed this opinion?
(a) Ruskin (b) Carlyle
(c) Arnold (d) IA Richards

141 In which essay Arnold defines poetry as "a criticism of life under the conditions fixed for such a criticism by the laws of poetic truth and poetic beauty"?
(a) Wordsworth (b) Shelley
(c) The study of Poetry (d) None of these

142 Which of the following arrangements of TS Eliot's critical works is in the correct chronological order?
(a) The use of poetry and the use of criticism- selected Essays- on poetry and poets- To criticise the critic- the Sacred Wood
(b) The Sacred Wood- on poetry and poets- to Criticise the critic- selected Essays- the use of poetry and the use of criticism
(c) Selected Essays- to criticise the critic- the Sacred Wood- on poetry and poets- the use of poetry and the use of criticism
(d) None of the above

143 In which essay of TS Eliot the phrase "dissociation of sensibility" occurs?
(a) Hamlet and his problems
(b) The metaphysical poets
(c) Tradition and individual talent
(d) None of the above

144 Who, according to TS Eliot, had developed "unified sensibility"?
(a) The Elizabethans and Jacobeans
(b) The Neo-Classicists
(c) The Romantics (d) The Victorians

145 Who among the following is the pioneer of new criticism?
(a) TS Eliot (b) IA Richards
(c) FR Leavis (d) Allan Tate

146 The principles of literary criticism is written by
(a) TS Eliot (b) IA Richards
(c) FR Leavis (d) RP Blackmur

147 Which of the following arrangements of FR Leavis critical works is in the correct chronological order?
(a) The common Pursuit- Revaluation- The Great Tradition- New Bearing in English Poetry
(b) New Bearing in English Poetry- Revaluation- The Great Tradition – The Common Pursuit
(c) Revaluation- The common Pursuit- The Great Tradition- New Bearings in English Poetry
(d) None of the above

148 Who calls FR Leavis "a practical critic"?
(a) Lawrence Lerner (b) George Watson
(c) William K Wimsatt (d) Allen Tate

149 Which of the following books introduced the term new criticism?
(a) IA Richard's the Principles of Literary Criticism
(b) FR Leavis's The Great tradition
(c) TS Eliot The Sacred Wood
(d) John Gowe Ransome's book The New Criticism

150 Identify the correct group consisting of modern critics.
(a) JC Ransome- RP Blackmur – Allen Tate- Robert Pen Warren – William K. Wimsatt
(b) Rene Welleck- William Famson- IA Richards-RS Gane – MC Keon
(c) FR Leavis- IA Richards – Elaine Showalter- David Lodge – Margaret Homan
(d) None of the above

151 Seven types of Ambiguity (1930) is written by
(a) IA Richards (b) JC Ransome
(c) William Empson (d) Austin Warren

152 " A poem should not mean but be" is found in
(a) William Empson's Seven types of Ambiguity
(b) William K. Wimsatt's the Verbal Ieon
(c) MC Beardsley's The International Fallacy
(d) None of the above

153 New criticism is applied to
(a) Anglo- American criticism
(b) Indian-English criticism
(c) Anglo-African criticism
(d) None of these

154 Structuralism was popularised by
(a) Ferdinand De Saussure's book Courses in General Linguistic
(b) IA Richards Meaning of Meaning
(c) Wolfgang Iser's the Reading Process : phenomenological Approach
(d) J Hillis Miller's The Disappearance of God

155 Historically post- structuralism had its origin in
(a) January 1966
(b) October 1966
(c) January 1970
(d) March, 1971

156 A renowned critic enunciated the doctrine of Deconstruction. Who is that critic?
(a) Jacques Derrida
(b) Geoffrey Hartman
(c) JH Miller
(d) MH Abrames

157 Name of critic who enunciated the theory of Deconstruction.
(a) Jacques Derrida (b) Edward Sevid
(c) Nina Baym (d) Stanley Fish

158 Identify the correct group of the exponent of the reader- response theory or the Reception Theory.
(a) ED Hirsch- Stamley Fish- Patrocinia P Schweickart- Janathan Culler
(b) J Hillis Miller- Michel Foucault-Terry Egleton –Stephen Greenbelt
(c) Rene Wellek-Roman Jakabson- Edward Said
(d) None of the above

159 Who was the founder of psychoanalysis and a seminal figure of 20th century thought?
(a) Sir James Frazer
(b) Sigmund Freud
(c) Derrida
(d) TS Eliot

160 What was Dr Johnson's opinion on language of poetry ?
(a) It should be the language of poetry
(b) It should be the language of the learned
(c) It should be a sublime poetic language
(d) None of the above

161 What is meant by rhetoric?
(a) Art of using language effectively or impressively
(b) Using language for exaggeration
(c) Using language musically
(d) Using language metaphorically

162 Who pleaded for 'high-seriousness' in literature?
(a) Matthew Arnold
(b) William Wordsworth
(c) John Dryden
(d) TS Eliot

163 Who said, "The preface to Lyrical Ballads" explains the poetic process of the type of poetry only Wordsworth wrote?
(a) IA Richard (b) FR Leavis
(c) Coleridge (d) Baker

164 Who among the following is also known as a lexicographer?
(a) Webster (c) Golding
(c) Johnson (c) Strene

165 Johnson's phrase, "Fatal Cleopatra", refers to Shakespeare's.....
(a) Neglect of the unities
(b) Fondness of puns
(c) Fondness for similes
(d) Love of allusion

166 The term 'postmodernism' was first used in connection with....
(a) Architecture (b) Painting (c) Literature (d) Music

167 According to Dryden, comedy begets....
(a) Critical pleasure
(b) Divine pleasure
(c) Malicious pleasure
(d) Irresistible pleasure

168 'Wordsworth has not only sight but insight' who said that?
(a) Long (b) Cowley
(c) Southey (d) Keats

169 Who is stated to have said, "Criticism is the art of interpreting art?
(a) Dryden (b) Arnold
(c) Walter Pater (d) Eliot

170 Who is believed to have said, "what Criticism undertakes is the profitable discussion of literature"?
(a) Eliot. (b) FR Leavis
(c) Middleton Murry (d) Chatterton

171 Who said." Language is primarily an auditory system of symbols"?
(a) Bloach (b) Franz Boas
(c) Sapir (d) Whitney

172 The suffragette movement was a movement for....
(a) Social reform
(b) Redness of sufferings
(c) Women's rights
(d) Children's rights

173 Poetry was generally written in "poetic diction" by...
(a) The Elizabethan poets
(b) The Neo-classical poets
(c) The Romantic poets
(d) The Victorian poets

174 Who first used the word 'fancy' and 'imagination' in his history of poetry?
(a) Alexander Pope
(b) William Wordsworth
(c) ST Coleridge
(d) John Dryden

175 DH Lawrence was a pioneer of....
(a) Stream of consciousness novel
(b) Psychoanalytical fiction
(c) Psychological fiction
(c) Imagism fiction

176 DH Lawrence was greatly influenced by ....
(a) Freud (b) Marx
(c) Darwin (d) Aristotle

177 Who wrote, "when a poet's mind is perfectly equipped amalgamating human experience"?
(a) TS Eliot (b) FR Leavis
(c) IA Richards (d) None of these

178 Which of the following was defined by Coleridge as " a mode of memory emancipated from the order of time and space"?
(a) Primary imagination (b) Fancy
(c) Secondary imagination (d) All of these

179 Match the following.

List I	List II
A. Crites	1. English drama
B. Eugenius	2. Classical drama
C. Lisideius	3. Modern drama
D. Neander	4. French drama

Codes

	A	B	C	D		A	B	C	D
(a)	2	3	4	1	(b)	3	4	1	2
(c)	1	2	3	4	(d)	2	4	1	3

180 Match the following.

List I	List II
A. William Wordsworth	1. the study of poetry
B. B, S. T. Coleridge	2. the biographic literia
C. Mathew Arnold	3. the lyrical ballads
D. T. S. Eliot	4. tradition and individual talent

Codes

	A	B	C	D		A	B	C	D
(a)	3	2	1	4	(b)	1	2	3	4
(c)	2	1	3	4	(d)	3	4	2	1

181 Who among the following theorists formulated the concept of the utile dulic, profit combined with delight?
(a) Plato (b) Aristotle
(c) Horace (d) Longinus

182 Who among the following romantic poets ended his life lauded and respected as 'the sage of highgate'?
(a) William Blake (b) PB Shelley
(c) ST Coleridge (d) William Wordsworth

183 "The best poetry will be found to have a power of forming, sustaining and delighting us". This assertion implies:
(a) Poetry is more useful than other arts
(b) All other arts including poetry have their limitations
(c) Poetry has multiple functions to perform
(d) Poetry has no role to play

184 The term "cultural materialism" is associated with....
(a) Stephen Greenblatt (b) Raymond Williams
(c) Matthew Arnold (d) Richard Hoggart

185 IA Richards' famous experiment with poems and his Cambridge students is detailed in practical criticism: a study of literary judgement (1929): Richards was astonished by
(a) The very astute remarks made by his students
(b) The poor quality of his student's stock responses
(c) The non-availability of poems, worthy of class-room attention
(d) The success of his experiment

Directions (Q. Nos. 186-190) *Read the passage carefully and select the right answer from the given alternatives.*

John Dryden in the late seventeenth century defined poetic license as "The liberty which poets have assumed themselves, in all ages, of speaking things in verse which are beyond the severity of prose".

In its most common use the term is confined to diction alone, to justify the poet's departure from the rules and conventions of standard spoken and written prose in matters such as syntax, word order, the use of archaic or newly coined words, and the conventional use of eye-rhymes. The degree and kind of linguistic freedom assumed by poets have varied according to the conventions of each age, but in every case the justification of the freedom lies in the success of the effect.

In a boarder sense, "Poetic License" is applied not only to language, but to all the ways in which poet and other literacy authors are held to be free to violate, for special effects, the ordinary norms not only of common discourse but also of literal and historical truth, including the devices of metre and rhyme, the recourse to literary conventions, and the representation of fictional characters and events.

186 'Poetic License' means
(a) Liberty with diction, alone
(b) Liberty with diction and norms of common discourse
(c) Liberty with historical truth
(d) Liberty with representation of fictional characters

187 'Linguistic freedom' is
(a) Freedom with diction, newly-coined words, syntax
(b) Freedom with the use of colloquial language
(c) Freedom with the use of figurative construction
(d) Freedom with literal truth

188 How do you justify the linguistic freedom taken?
(a) On the basis of scholarship embedded
(b) On the basis of form
(c) On the basis of the success of the effect
(d) On the basis of the thematic grandeur

189 'Diction' means
(a) Severity of prose
(b) Devices of metre and rhyme
(c) Poetic license
(d) Syntax and word order

190 'Poetic License' applies to
(a) poets alone
(b) all literary authors
(c) dramatists only
(d) epic writers only

ANSWERS

1. (c)	2. (a)	3. (b)	4. (b)	5. (c)	6. (b)	7. (d)	8. (c)	9. (a)	10. (a)
11. (a)	12. (b)	13. (a)	14. (a)	15. (b)	16. (a)	17. (b)	18. (a)	19. (a)	20. (b)
21. (a)	22. (c)	23. (b)	24. (d)	25. (b)	26. (d)	27. (b)	28. (a)	29. (c)	30. (c)
31. (b)	32. (a)	33. (c)	34. (a)	35. (c)	36. (a)	37. (b)	38. (a)	39. (b)	40. (b)
41. (a)	42. (a)	43. (b)	44. (b)	45. (a)	46. (b)	47. (c)	48. (b)	49. (c)	50. (a)
51. (b)	52. (c)	53. (b)	54. (d)	55. (c)	56. (c)	57. (b)	58. (a)	59. (b)	60. (a)
61. (b)	62. (b)	63. (a)	64. (c)	65. (a)	66. (c)	67. (c)	68. (c)	69. (a)	70. (b)
71. (c)	72. (a)	73. (a)	74. (b)	75. (c)	76. (c)	77. (a)	78. (b)	79. (a)	80. (c)
81. (a)	82. (b)	83. (b)	84. (b)	85. (a)	86. (d)	87. (c)	88. (b)	89. (b)	90. (a)
91. (d)	92. (c)	93. (b)	94. (a)	95. (b)	96. (a)	97. (b)	98. (a)	99. (b)	100. (c)
101. (a)	102. (b)	103. (c)	104. (a)	105. (a)	106. (a)	107. (a)	108. (c)	109. (b)	110. (c)
111. (a)	112. (b)	113. (c)	114. (c)	115. (a)	116. (b)	117. (b)	118. (c)	119. (b)	120. (d)
121. (c)	122. (b)	123. (a)	124. (c)	125. (a)	126. (c)	127. (b)	128. (c)	129. (a)	130. (b)
131. (c)	132. (b)	133. (a)	134. (b)	135. (c)	136. (a)	137. (b)	138. (c)	139. (a)	140. (c)
141. (c)	142. (a)	143. (b)	144. (a)	145. (b)	146. (b)	147. (b)	148. (a)	149. (d)	150. (a)
151. (c)	152. (a)	153. (a)	154. (a)	155. (b)	156. (a)	157. (a)	158. (a)	159. (b)	160. (d)
161. (a)	162. (a)	163. (a)	164. (c)	165. (b)	166. (b)	167. (c)	168. (a)	169. (c)	170. (b)
171. (c)	172. (c)	173. (b)	174. (d)	175. (a)	176. (a)	177. (a)	178. (b)	179. (a)	180. (a)
181. (c)	182. (c)	183. (c)	184. (b)	185. (b)	186. (b)	187. (a)	188. (c)	189. (d)	190. (b)

UNIT 9

Literary Theory Post World War II

The World War II brought about a change in the perception of people, thinkers and literary artists, critics and theorists alike. It changed many old ways of thinking and offered us new theories and ways of literary criticism. The chapter deals with the term or movement called 'New Criticism', its basic principles and main exponents of this genre including feminist criticism and post colonialism.

Introduction

The period of Post World War II inspired authors, poets, writers, literary critics and theorists involved in each and every genre including poetry, prose, fiction, historical novels, novellas, short stories, fantasy, adventure or the criticism. Inspiring tales of bravery, self-belief and optimism were created in the face of adversities.

The intermediate postwar period separated 'Modernism' from 'Postmodernism' in literature. Literature attained a new maturity and a rich diversity. After the World War II, a new generation arrived, with its different ethnic, regional, and social character. Among the younger writers were children of immigrants, many of them Jews; Africans, only a few generations away from slavery; and eventually, women who, with the rise of feminism, were to speak in a new voice. Though the social climate of the postwar years was conservative, even conformist, some of the most hotly discussed writers were homosexuals or bisexuals.

There was also a desire to renew national prestige and esteem and this was visible in the works. Poetry in the post-war period followed a number of interlinked paths, most notably deriving from surrealism or from philosophical and phenomenological concerns stemming from existentialism, the relationship between poetry and the visual arts and the notions of the limits of language.

Feminism and post-colonialism are two other important issues in post-war English literature. Women writers are not a novelty in English Literature, nor can it be said that they have been systematically discriminated against by literary criticism. However, the rise of 1960s feminism and successive waves (or feminisms) have forced post-war female writers in English to take a position for or against feminism, especially as this has played an important role in academic literary criticism.

In this Chapter

Writers born in the ex-colonies of the British Empire besides writers of other nationalities within the United Kingdom (Welsh, Scottish, Northern Irish) have used English to express the experience of colonisation. New national literatures in English have been born in the post-war period, mainly in Africa, Asia and the Caribbean. The work of migrant writers from the ex-colonies, who now live in Britain, has also forced literary critics to question the meaning of the adjective 'English' in the phrase 'English Literature'.

New Criticism

It emphasises explication, or 'close reading,' of 'the work itself.' It rejects old historicism's attention to biographical and sociological matters. Instead, the objective was the determination as to 'how a piece works' can be found through close focus and analysis, rather than through extraneous and erudite special knowledge. It has long been the pervasive and standard approach to literature in college and high school curricula.

New criticism, incorporating formalism, examines the relationships between a text's ideas and its form, between what a text says and the way it says it. New critics "may find tension, irony, or paradox in this relation, but they usually resolve it into unity and coherence of meaning" (Biddle 100). New criticism attempts to be a science of literature, with a technical vocabulary, some of which we all had to learn in junior high school English classes (third-person, denoument, etc.). Working with patterns of sound, imagery, narrative structure, point of view, and other techniques discernible on close reading of the text, they seek to determine the function and appropriateness of these to the self-contained work.

New Critics, especially American ones in the 1940s and 1950s, attacked the standard notion of 'expressive realism,' the romantic fallacy that literature is the efflux of a noble soul, that *e.g.* love pours out onto the page in 14 iambic pentameter lines rhyming ABABCD etc. The goal then is not the pursuit of sincerity or authenticity, but subtlety, unity, and integrity and these are properties of the text, not the author. The work is not the author's; it was detached at birth. The author's intentions are 'neither available nor desirable' (nor even to be taken at face value when supposedly found in direct statements by authors). Meaning exists on the page. Thus, new critics insist that the meaning of a text is intrinsic and should not be confused with the author's intentions nor the work's affective dimension (its impressionistic effects on the reader). The 'intentional fallacy' is when one confuses the meaning of a work with the author's purported intention (expressed in letters, diaries, interviews, *e.g.*). The 'affective fallacy' is the erroneous practice of interpreting texts according to the psychological or emotional responses of readers, confusing the text with its results.

The new criticism is supposed to be a specifically American movement, but it was pioneered by TS Eliot and I A Richard. Eliot's famous remark that "a poem's existence is somewhere between the writer" and the term new criticism came into general use after the publication of John Crowe Ransom's book *The New Criticism* in 1941 to be applied to a theory and practice that dominated American literary criticism until late in the 1960. It is a revolutionary critical movement which is not concerned with the sociological or historical aspects of the age in which the particular poetry is written. It is a frankly reactionary movement. Famous critics of this school are JC Ransom, RP Blackmur, Allen Tate, Cleanth Brooks, Robert Penn Warren, and William K Wimsatt. In the *Preface to the Anthology Understanding Poetry*, the editors Cleanth Brooks and Robert Penn Warren condemned the use of poetry for all purpose beyond itself, whether historical or moralistic. They asserted that "if poetry is worth teaching at all, it is worth teaching as poetry."

Basic Principles of the New Criticism

- A poem or a work of art should be treated as an object in itself, primarily as poetry and not as any other thing. In analysing and evaluating a work, they usually do not refer to the author's biography, to contemporary social conditions and to its psychological or moral effects on the reader. The literary critic must approach the work with an open mind, ready to study it, 'as it is in itself".
- The new critics are mainly concerned with the study of words, with the structure of poetry. The distinctive procedure of new criticism is explication , or close reading, the detailed and subtle analysis of the complex interrelations and ambiguities of the component elements within a work. The new critics derived their explicative from IA Richards' *Practical Criticism* (1929) and William Empson's *Seven Types of Ambiguity* (1930).
- Poetry is communication and language is the mean of communication. So, the new critics seek to understand the full meaning of a poem through a study of poetic language. The key concepts of this criticism deals with the meaning and interactions of words, figures of speech and symbols. There is a great emphasis on the organic unity of structure and meaning.

- The new critics reacted sharply against the vulgarisation of meaning by the rhetoric of mass communication or privatisation of language. According to Allen Tate, poetry is not mere communication of ideas or attitudes; it is a complex patterning of meaning to be read and appreciated as such JC Ransom draws a distinction between texture and structure of poetry.

Archetypal Criticism

As it applies to literature is a form of criticism "that interprets a text by focusing on recurring myths and archetypes." Rather than looking at the other aspects of the literary work itself, this type of criticism focuses on just the archetypes present. Archetypes are "an original model of a person, ideal example, or a prototype upon which others are copied, patterned, or emulated." With regards to literature, this usually refers to ancient models like those from myths. However, you asked specifically about Carl Jung who was a psychologist. In this case, archetypes are usually referring to a specific behaviour exhibited by a certain type of person rather than a literary example. Archetypal criticism isn't often used as a form of literary criticism now-a-days. It was most popular during the 50's and 60's; this would have been the later part of Jung's lifetime (actual his last remaining years since he died in the early 1960's). His work, along with other psychologist and philosophers created the ideas behind archetypal criticism.

Psychoanalytic Criticism

It adopts the methods of 'reading' employed by Freud and later theorists to interpret texts. It argues that literary texts, like dreams, express the secret unconscious desires and anxieties of the author, that a literary work is a manifestation of the author's own neuroses. One may psychoanalyze a particular character within a literary work, but it is usually assumed that all such characters are projections of the author's psyche.

One interesting facet of this approach is that it validates the importance of literature, as it is built on a literary key for the decoding. Freud himself wrote, "The dream-thoughts which we first come across as we proceed with our analysis often strike us by the unusual form in which they are expressed; they are not clothed in the prosaic language usually employed by our thoughts, but are on the contrary represented symbolically by means of similes and metaphors, in images resembling those of poetic speech".

Like psychoanalysis itself, this critical endeavour seeks evidence of unresolved emotions, psychological conflicts, guilts, ambivalences, and so forth within what may well be a disunified literary work. The author's own childhood traumas, family life, sexual conflicts, fixations, and such will be traceable within the behaviour of the characters in the literary work. But psychological material will be expressed indirectly, disguised, or encoded (as in dreams) through principles such as 'symbolism' (the repressed object represented in disguise), 'condensation' (several thoughts or persons represented in a single image), and 'displacement' (anxiety located onto another image by means of association).

Despite the importance of the author here, psychoanalytic criticism is similar to new criticism in not concerning itself with "what the author intended." But what the author never intended (that is, repressed) is sought. The unconscious material has been distorted by the censoring conscious mind.

Psychoanalytic critics will ask such questions as, "What is Hamlet's problem?" or "Why can't Brontë seem to portray any positive mother figures?"

Sigmund Freud' Psychoanalytic Literary Criticism

The psychoanalytic literary criticism is influenced by psychoanalysis and the tradition began by Sigmund Freud. This approach to literary criticism not only rests on the theories of Freud; it may even be said to have begun with Freud, who wrote literary criticism as well as psychoanalytic theory.

The first aspect of the psychoanalytic criticism begins with the analysis of a particularly interesting character in a work. The fictional characters should be evaluated based on the interpretive process.

The ego balances the primal needs of the identity and the civilising demands of the super-ego. Freud is well-known for his attention to sexual desires as the primary need of the individual. Psychoanalytical theory applies Freud's Oedipus complex to literature by seeking images in the text that reveal the author's unconscious sexual fantasies and desires. These images provide the critic a richer understanding of the writing, as well as insights into the minds of the author and the reader.

Freud "believed that literature could often be interpreted as the reflection of our unconscious life". Psychoanalytical theory works from this belief and seeks images in a text that will provide an illustration of the author's unconscious life."

Literary texts, like dreams, express the secret unconscious desires and anxieties of the author". Even when an author is not writing autobiographically, the speech and behaviour of the author's characters and the descriptions of settings and events are usually imbued with some of the author's personality, desires, and fear.

In analyzing a literary work, the critic discovers clues to his or her own unconscious life by recognizing that the critic's identification and interpretation of the images in a work is informed by the critic's unconscious.

By projecting the author's motivations on the characters of a literary work, sexual ideas may be revealed in the work. Similarly, displacing the author's concerns to a subject in a literary work, or reversing a situation by attributing feelings to the object of those feelings can reveal sexual and other psychological undertones in the work. "An unconscious dynamism ... begins to influence the writer and even often imposes upon him forms of expression which he does not intend to use consciously". The author's unconscious life leads to the more complex inner workings of the human mind, which are a combination of the conscious and the unconscious, and which are populated by the id, the ego, and the superego, and which manifest in projection, displacement, and other literary techniques. Psychoanalytical criticism of literature "focuses on a work of literature as an expression in fictional form of the inner workings of the human mind". By creating a fictional representation, the author is able to explore an array of concepts in a non-threatening venue, and the literary critic is able to sift the original, inner thoughts from the writing.

Oedipus Complex

A concept so important to literary critics is the 'Oedipus complex'. The representation of inner thoughts and ideas often exposes elements of Freud's Oedipus complex in literature. The Oedipus complex is drawn from the famous story of a young man who kills his father and marries his mother, and it represents for Freud the primary inner conflict for any person.

"The complete complex postulates a pre-oedipal desire for both parents which must be transformed in the Oedipus complex in the interest of solid ego formation."

Literary critics using the psychoanalytical theory seek images in texts that reveal the character's or the author's struggle to overcome the urge to remove the same-sex parent in order to form an intimate bond with the other parent. The author may not be aware of his or her Oedipal inclinations, but with attentive close reading, the literary critic is able to uncover hidden truths that may be translated into universal truths about the human condition. By so doing, the critic achieves a deeper understanding of the literary work, of the author's inner thoughts, and of the reader.

Through use of Freud's theories of the unconscious; identification of the elements of the id, ego, and superego; and recognition of the Oedipus complex underlying literary texts; psychoanalytic theory is a useful tool for evaluating literary works to gain a richer understanding of the work, the author, and the reader. The literary critic identifies symbols and images in a literary work that reveal the author's unconscious desires and fears. The struggle of the ego to balance the desires of the id and the superego informs the literary critic about the author's struggle with his or her personal identity and with his or her balancing of primal needs and civilized responsibilities. The psychoanalytical critic is able to reveal the tricks of repression, displacement, isolation, reversal, attribution, and other factors to identify themes, ideas, and messages that are hidden in a literary work. Understanding the psychological messages in a literary work leads to an understanding of the author of that work. This understanding can guide the critic to deeper self-awareness.

Phenomenology/Reader Response Theory

Reading implies some sort of response from the reader. There are various approaches to the response theory in literature. First, the response to a work of art or literature is purely aesthetic. A literary text should be read and purely judges as an aesthetic work, secondly, a literary text should be decoded and interpreted according to the intention, ideology, socio-economic milieu, thirdly a literary text should be interpreted and decoded according to the outlook of the reader, who decipher its meaning from the subjective viewpoint.

Stanley Fish, the American critic of the seventeenth century developed a reader-response perspective called 'affective stylistics'. Like Iser, he concentrates on the adjustment of expectations to be made by readers as they pass along the text, but considers that at the immediately local level of the sentence. He separates his approach very self-consciously from all kinds of formalism (including American New Criticism) by denying literary language any special status; we use the same reading strategies to interpret literary and non-literary sentences. His attention is directed to the developing responses of the readers in relation to the words of sentences as they succeed one another in time. Describing the fallen angels' state of awareness having plummeted from heaven to hell, Milton wrote in *Paradise Lost*: 'nor did they not ever perceive the evil plight'. This cannot be treated as a statement equivalent to 'they perceive the evil plight'. We must attend, argues Fish, to the sequence of words which creates a state of suspension in the reader, who hangs between the two views of the fallen angels' awareness. His point is weakened though not refuted by the fact that Milton was evidently imitating the double negative in the style of classical epic. But the following sentence by Walter Pater receives an especially sensitive analysis by Fish, 'This at least of flame-like, our life has, that it is but the concurrence, renewed from moment to moment, of forces parting sooner or later, on their ways'. He points out that by interrupting 'concurrence of forces' with 'renewed from moment to moment' Pater prevents the readers from establisihing the definite and stable image in the mind, and at each stage in the sentence forces the readers to make an adjustment in expectations and interpretations. The idea of 'concurrence 'is disrupted by 'parting', but then 'sooner or later' leaves the 'parting' temporally uncertain. The reader's expectation of meaning is thus continuously adjusted: the meaning is the total movement of reading. Jonathan Culler has lent general support to Fish's aims, but has criticised him for failing to give us a proper theoretical formulation of his reader criticism. Fish believes that his reading of sentences simply follow the natural practice of informed readers. In his views, a reader is someone who possesses a 'linguistic competence', has internalised the syntactic and semantic knowledge required for reading. The 'informed reader' of literary texts has also acquired a specifically 'literary competence'. *Culler makes two trenchant criticisms of Fish's position*

- He fails to theorise the conventions of reading; that is, he fails to ask the question 'What conventions do readers follow when they read?'
- His claim to read sentences word by word in a temporal sequence is misleading: there is no reason to believe that readers actually do take in sentences in such a piecemeal and gradual way. Why does he assume, for example, that the reader, faced with Milton's 'Nor did they not perceive', will experience a sense of being suspended between two views?

There is something factitious about Fish's continual willingness to be surprised by the next word in the sequence. Also, Fish himself admits that his approach tends to privilege those texts which proceed in the self-undermining way. Elizabeth Freund points out that in order to sustain his reader orientation Fish has to suppress the fact that the actual experience of reading is not the same thing as the verbal rendering of that experience. By treating his own reading experience as itself an act of interpretation he is ignoring the gap between experience and the understanding of an experience. What Fish gives us, therefore, is not a definitive account of the nature of reading but Fish's understanding of his own reading experience.

In *Is There a text in This class?* (1980) Fish acknowledges that his earlier work treated his own experience of reading as the norm, and goes on to justify this position by introducing the idea of 'interpretative communities'. This meant that he was trying to persuade readers to adopt 'a set of community assumptions so that when they read they would do what I did'. Of course, there may be many different groups of readers who adopt particular kinds of reading strategies, but in this later phase of his work the strategies of a particular interpretative community determine the entire process of reading-the stylistic facts of the text and the experience of reading them. If we accept the category of interpretative communities, we no longer need to choose between asking questions about the text or about the reader, the whole problem of subject and objects disappears. However, the price that must be paid for this solution is high; by reducing the whole process of meaning-production to the already existing conventions of the interpretative community, Fish seems to abandon all possibility of deviant interpretations and resistance to the norms which governs the act of interpretation. As Elizabeth Freund points out; 'The appeal to the imperialism of agreement can chill the spines of readers whose experience of the community is less happily benign than Fish assumes'.

Phenomenology

A modern philosophical tendency which stresses the perceiver's central role in determining meaning is known as 'phenomenology'. According to Edmund Husserl, the proper object of philosophical investigation is the contents of our consciousness and not objects in the world. Consciousness is always of something, and it is the 'something' which appears to our consciousness which is truly real to us. In addition, argued Husserl, we discover in the things which appear in consciousness ('phenomena' Greek, meaning 'things appearing') their universal or essential qualities. Phenomenology claims to show us the underlying nature both of human consciousness and 'phenomena'.

This was an attempt to revive the idea (eclipsed since the romantics) that the individual human mind is the centre and origin of all meaning. In literary theory this approach did not encourage the purely subjective concerns for the critic's mental structure but a type of criticism which tries to enter into the world of writer's works and to arrive at an understanding of the underlying nature or essence of the writings as they appear to the critic's consciousness.

The early work of J. Hillis Miller, the American critic was influenced by the phenomenological theories of the so-called 'Geneva School' of critics, who included Georges Poulet and Jean Starobinski. *e.g.* Miller's first study of Thomas Hardy, *Thomas Hardy-Distance and Desire* (1970, he wrote further 'deconstructive' studies later) uncovers the novels pervasive mental structures, namely 'distance' and 'desire'. The act of interpretation is possible because the text allows the reader access to the author's consciousness, which, says Poulet, 'is open to me, welcomes me, lets me look deep inside itself, and ... allows me... to think what it thinks and to feel what it feels'. Derrida would consider this kind of thinking 'logocentric' for supposing that the meaning is centered on a 'transcendental subject' (the author) and can be recentred on another such subject (the reader).

Shift Towards Reader Oriented Theory

The shift towards the reader-oriented theory is prefigured in the rejection of Husserl's 'objective' view by his pupil Martin Heidegger. The latter argued that what is distinctive about human existence is its Dasein (givenness); our consciousness both projects the things of the world and at the same time is subjected to the world by the very nature of existence in the world. We find ourselves 'flung down', into a time and place we did not choose, but simultaneously it is our world in so far as our consciousness projects it. We can never adopt an attitude of detached contemplation, looking down upon the world as if from a mountain top.

We are inevitably merged with the very object of our consciousness. Our thinking is always in a situation and is therefore always historical, although this history is not external and social but personal and inward. It was Hans-Georg Gadamer who, in *Truth and Method* (1975), applied Heidegger's situational approach to literary theory. Gadamer argued that the literary work does not pop into the world as the finished and neatly parcelled bundle of meaning, rather meaning depends on the historical situation of the interpreter. Gadamer influenced 'reception theory'.

Cultural Materialism

Cultural studies is a new discipline. In literature, it has created a new branch of literary criticism, known as cultural criticism, which considers culture as a source of literature. It is not just a representation of art and literature. For a thorough comprehension of a literary work we must understand those forces of culture that have formed language and specific patterns.

Cultural materialism is a term used by the Marxist critic Raymond Williams, which has been adopted by a number of British Scholars to indicate the Marxist orientation of their mode of new historicism. They insist that, whatever the 'textuality' of history, a culture and its literary products are always to an important degree conditioned by the real material forces and relations of production in their historical era. They are particularly interested in the political significance, and especially the subversive aspects and effects, of a literary text, not only in its own time, but also in later versions of the text in the theatre and in the cinema, and in its altering interpretation and treatment by later literary critics. Cultural materialists stress that their criticism is itself oriented towards political intervention. In their own era, in an express 'commitment,' as Jonathan Dollimore and Alan Sinfield have put it, "to the transformation of a social order, which exploits people on grounds of race, gender and class." Similar views are expressed by those American exponents of the new literary history who are political activists; indeed, some of them claim that if new historicists limit themselves to describing social domination and exploitation in literary texts of the past, but stop short of a commitment to remark the present social order, they have been co-opted into complying with the politically aloof formalism of the types of literary criticism that they set out of displace.

It is one of the major anthropological perspectives for analyzing human societies. It incorporates ideas from Marxism, cultural evolution, and cultural ecology. Materialism contends that the physical world impacts and sets constraints on human behaviour. The materialists believe that human behaviour is part of nature and therefore, it can be understood by using the methods of natural science. Materialists do not necessarily assume that material reality is more important than mental reality. However, they give priority to the material world over the world of the mind when they explain human societies. This doctrine of materialism started and developed from the work of Karl Marx and Friedrich Engels. Marx and Engels presented an evolutionary model of societies based on the materialist perspective. They argued that societies go through the several stages, from tribalism to feudalism to capitalism to communism. Their work drew little attention from anthropology in the early twentieth-century. However, since the late 1920s, anthropologists have increasingly come to depend on materialist explanations for analyzing societal development and some inherent problems of capitalist societies. Anthropologists who heavily rely on the insights of Marx and Engels include neo-evolutionists, neo-materialists, feminists, and postmodernists.

Cultural materialists identify three levels of social systems that constitute a universal pattern

1. Infrastructure 2. Structure and 3. Superstructure. Infrastructure is the basis for all other levels and includes how basic needs are met and how it interacts with the local environment. Structure refers to a society's economic, social, and political organisation, while superstructure is related to ideology and symbolism. Cultural materialists like Marvin Harris contend that the infrastructure is the most critical aspect as it is here where the interaction between culture and environment occurs. All three of the levels are interrelated so that changes in the infrastructure results in changes in the structure and superstructure, although the changes might not be immediate. While this appears to be environmental determinism, cultural materialists do not disclaim that change in the structure and superstructure cannot occur without first change in the infrastructure. They do however claim that if change in those structures is not compatible with the existing infrastructure the change is not likely to become set within the culture.

Cultural materialism is a Marxist-based approach to objective anthropological interpretation, which differs from traditional Marxism by expanding the view of dialectical materialism to include specific cultural, environmental, and other influences — and therefore outcomes — that would be neither universal nor historically inevitable. As in Marxism, cultural materialism proposes three primary influences on cultural change — infrastructure (technology, economics, demographics), structure (cultural and kinship systems), and superstructure (ideology, religion) — but regards culture more as evolutionary than determined, with infrastructure, especially reproduction, operating as the primary variable in determining cultural development. Marvin Harris is largely credited with the development of cultural materialism. As a research method, cultural materialism emphasizes the scientific method and objective analysis over the less demonstrable claims of structuralism or the relativism of postmodernism.

Orientalism

Edward Said points out Orientalism occupies three overlapping domains. It designates firstly the 4000-year history of and cultural relations between Europe and Asia: secondly the scientific discipline producing specialists in oriental languages and culture from the early nineteenth century; and thirdly the long-term images, stereotypes and general ideology about the 'Orient' as the 'Other', constructed by generations of Western scholars, which produce myths about the laziness, deceit and irrationality of Oriental as well as their reproduction and rebuttal in current debates on the Arab-Islamic worlds and its exchanges, particularly, within the United States. 'Orientalism' depends, in all these aspects, on a culturally constructed distinction between 'the Occident' and 'the Orient' and is inescapably political, as is its study. This then raises the crucial issue for postcolonialism of the position of the critic; as Said puts it in *Orientalism Reconsidered* (1986), of 'how knowledge that is non-dominative and non-coercive can be produced in a setting that is deeply inscribed with the politics, the considerations, the positions and the strategies of powers'.

Said rejects any assumption of a free point outside the object of analysis and rejects, too, the assumptions of Western historicism which has homogenised world history from a privileged and supposedly culminating Eurocentricity. Said's work draws upon Marxism, Adorno's 'negative dialectics', and more markedly, as we have noted, on Foucault's analysis of discourse as power, to elucidate the function of cultural representations in the construction and maintenance of 'first /third-world' relations. Analysis, he says, must be understood as in the fullest sense being against the grain, deconstructive, Utopian'.

He calls for a critical 'decentred consciousness' and for interdisciplinary work committed to the collective libertarians aim of dismantling systems of domination. At the same time he warns against the obstacle to this goal of 'possessive exclusivism'; the danger that anti-dominant critiques will demarcate separatist areas of resistance and struggle. The critic's credentials do not reside in the presumed authenticity of ethnic or sexual identity or experience, or in any purity of method, but elsewhere. Where and what this else-where is, is the major problem of postcolonial criticism, and of other differently directed forms of radical ideology critique. Said's own *Orientalism* has been criticised in this respect or its under-theorised and under-problematic appeal to humanist values; but while the stronger echoes of deconstruction in Said's late writing help to answer this charge, deconstruction in itself does not ground the kinds of political practice and change Said wishes to see.

Relevance of Orientalism

Orientalism is a very important book that has had a wide influence, both in universities and in politics. It is a key text in postcolonial studies and was considered revolutionary when it first appeared in 1978. Said shows how academic writing can be deeply connected to the politics and workings of colonialism, and how the one fed the other in order to justify the West's self-imposed status as a superior culture. According to Said, colonialism wasn't just the act of colonising a particular place, it was an all-encompassing way of understanding the world.

Orientalism laid out its arguments in an interdisciplinary way, breaking down boundaries between academic disciplines. In setting out his arguments, Said covered everything from painting and literature to travel and political writing. In this way, the book influenced many areas of study across the humanities and social sciences. As well as bringing a brand new perspective to studies of colonialism, Said's book also challenged academics to look at their own ways of working. For these important reasons, Orientalism is still an extremely relevant book, and continues to influence and direct scholarly work that looks to understand society and culture.

Marxist Theories

Marxist criticism has the longest history. Marx himself made important general statement about culture and society in the 1850s. Even, so it is correct to think of Marxist criticism as a twentieth century phenomenon. The basic tenets of Marxism are no easier to summarise than the essential doctrines of Christianity, but two well-known statements by Marx provide a sufficient point of departure:

- It is not the consciousness of men that determines their being, but, on the contrary, their social that determines their consciousness.
- The philosophers have only interpreted the world in various ways; the point is to change it.

Both statement were intentionally provocative. By contradicting widely accepted doctrines, Marx was trying to put people's thought into reverse gear. First, Philosophy has been merely airy contemplation; it is time that is engaged with the real world. Secondly, Hegel and his followers in German philosophy have persuaded us that the world is governed by thought, that the process of history is the gradual dialectical unfolding of the laws of Reason, and that material existence is the expression of an immaterial spiritual essence. People have been led to believe that their ideas, their cultural life, their legal system, and their religions were the creations of human and divine reason, which should be regarded as the unquestioned guides to human life. Marx reverses this formulation and argues that all mental systems are the products of real social and economic existence. The material interests of the dominant social class determine how people see human existence, individual and collective. Legal systems, for example, are not the pure manifestations of human or divine reason, but ultimately reflects the interests of the dominant class in particular historical periods.

In one account, Marx described this view in terms of an architectural metaphor: the 'superstructure'. To say 'rests upon' is not quite the same as saying 'is caused by'. Marx was arguing that what we call 'culture' is not an independent reality but is inseparable from the historical conditions in which human beings create their material lives; the relations of exploitations and dominations which govern the social and economic order of a particular phase of human history will in some sense 'determine' the whole cultural life of the society. In its crudest formulations, the theory is evidently far too mechanical. For example, in *The German Ideology* (1846) Marx and Engels talk about morality, religion and philosophy as 'phantoms formed in the brains of men', which are the 'reflexes and echoes' of 'real life processes'.

In a famous series of letters written in the 1890s Engels insists that, while he and Marx always regarded the economic aspects of society as the ultimate determinent of other aspects, they also recognised that art, philosophy and other forms of consciousness are relatively autonomous and possess an independent ability to alter men's exisence. After all, how else do Marxists expect to alter people's awareness except by political discourse? Were we to examine the novels of the eighteenth century in Europe, we would recognise, if we were Marxists, that these writings arose at particular phases in the development of early capitalist society. The conflict of social classes establishes the social ground upon which ideological sphere, but possess a relationship to ideology which is often less direct even than is found in the case of religious, legal and philosophical systems.

The special status of literature is recognised by Marx in a celebrated passage in his *Grundrisse*, in which the problem of an apparent discrepancy between economic and artistic development is discussed. Greek tragedy is considered a peak of literary development and yet it coincides with a social system and a form of ideology which are no longer valid for modern society. The problem for Marx was to explain how an art and literature produced in a long-obsolete social organisation can still give us aesthetic pleasure and be regarded as 'a standard and unattainable ideal'. He seems to be accepting reluctantly a certain 'timelessness' and 'universality' in literature and art; reluctantly, because this would be a major concession to one of bourgeois ideology's premises. However, it is now possible to see that Marx was simply falling back on received ways of thinking about literature and art. Our discussion of Mukarovasky established what can now be regarded as a Marxist view; that canons of great literature are socially generated. The 'greatness' of Greek tragedy is not a universal and unchanging fact of existence, but a value must be reproduced from generation to generation.

Even if we reject a privileged status for literature, there remains the question of how far literature's historical development is independent of historical development in general. In his attack on the Russian Formalists in *Literature and Revolution*, Trotsky, conceded that literature had its own principles and rules. 'Artistic creations', he admits, is 'a changing and transformation of reality in accordance with the peculiar laws of art'. He still insists that the 'reality' remains the crucial factor and not the formal games which writers play. Nevertheless, his remarks point forward to a continuing debate in Marxist criticism about the relative importance of literary form and ideological contents in literary works.

Feminist Criticism

As a self-aware and concerted approach to literature, feminist criticism was not inaugurated until late in the 1960s. Behind it, however lie two centuries for struggle for women's rights, marked by such books as Mary Wollstonecraft's *A Vindication of the Rights of Woman* (1792), John Stuart Mill's *The Subjection of Woman* (1869), and the American Margaret Fuller's *Woman in the Nineteenth century* (1845). Feminist literary criticism continues in our time to be closely interrelated with the movement by political feminist for social, economic and cultural freedom and equality.

An important precursor in feminist criticism was Virginia Woolf, who, in addition to her fiction, wrote *A Room Of One's Own* (1929) and numerous other essays on woman authors and on the cultural, economic and educational disabilities within what she called a 'patriarchal' society that have hindered or prevented women from realising their creative possibilities. A much more radical critical mode was launched in France by Simone De Beauvoir's *The Second Sex* (1949), a wide ranging critique of the cultural identification of women as merely the negative object, or 'other', to man as the defining and dominating 'subject' who is assumed to represent humanity in general; the book dealt also with 'the great collective myths' of woman in the work of many male writers.

Modern Feminist Criticism

In America, modern feminist criticism began with Mary Eliman's defts and witty discussion in *Thinking About Woman* (1968), about the derogatory stereotypes of woman in literature written by men, and also about the alternative and subversive points of view in some writing by women. Even more influential was Kate Millett's polemical and hard-hitting *Sexual Politics*, published the following year. By 'politics' Millett's refers to the mechanism that express and enforce the relations of power in society; she represent Western social arrangements and institutions as covert ways of manipulating power so as to establish and perpetuate the dominance of man and the subordination of women. In her books, she attacks the male bias in Freud's psychoanalytic theory, and also analyses selected passages by DH Lawrence, Henry Miller, Norman Mailer, and Jean Genet as revealing the ways in which their authors, in fictional fantasy, aggrandise their aggressive phallic selves and degrade women as submissive sexual objects.

Since 1969 there has been an explosion of feminist writings without close parallel in the previous of critical innovations, in a movement that, as Elaine Showalter has remarked, displays the urgency and excitement of a religious awakening. This current criticism, in America, England, France, and other countries, is not a unitary theory or procedure. It manifests, among those who practise it, great variety of critical vantage points and procedures including adaptations of psychoanalytic, Marxist and diverse post-structuralist theories and its vitality is signalised by the vigour of the debates within the ranks of professed feminist themselves. The various feminisms, however, share some assumptions and concepts that constitute the common ground for the diverse ways that individual critic explores the factor of sexual difference and privilege in the production, the form of content, the reception and the critical analysis and evaluation of works of literature;

- The basic view is that Western civilization is pervasively patriarchal (ruled by the father)- that is, it is male-centered and controlled, and is organised and conducted in such a way as to subordinate women to men in all cultural domains: familial, religious, political, economic, social, legal, and artistic. From the Hebrew Bible and Greek philosophy to the present, the female tends to be defined by negative reference to the male as the human norm, hence as an Other, or kind of non-man, by her lack of the identifying male organ, of male powers, and of the male character traits that are presumed, in the patriarchal view, to have achieved the most important inventions and works of civilization and culture. Women themselves are taught in the process of their being socialised, to internalise the reigning patriarchal ideology, and so are conditioned to derogate their own sex and to cooperate in their own subordination.
- It is widely held that while one's sex is determined by anatomy, the prevailing concepts of gender-of the traits that constitute what is masculine and what is feminine-are largely, if not entirely, cultural constructs that were generated by the omnipresent patriarchal biases of our civilization. As Simon De Beauvoir put it, "One is not born, but rather becomes, a woman... it is

civilization as a whole that produces this creature ... which is described as feminine." In this way, the masculine in our culture has come to be identified as active, dominating, adventurous, rational, creative, the feminine, by systematic opposition to such traits, has come to be identified as passive, acquiescent, timid, emotional, and conventional.

- The further claim is that this patriarchal (or 'masculinist', or 'androcentric') idealogy pervades those writings which have been considered great literature and which until recently have been written almost entirely by men for men. Typically, the most highly regarded literary works focus on male protagonists- *Oedipus, Ulysses, Hamlet, Tom Jones, Captain Ahab, Huck Finn*- who embody masculine traits and ways of feeling and pursue masculine interests in masculine fields of action. To these males, the female characters, when they play any role, are marginal and subordinate, and are represented either as complementary to or in opposition to masculine desires and enterprises.
- Such works, lacking autonomous female role models and implicitly addressed to male readers, either leave the women reader an alien outsider or else solicit her to identify against herself by taking up the position of the male subject and so assuming male values and ways of perceiving, feeling, and acting. It is often held, in addition, that the traditional aesthetic categories and criteria for analysing and appraising literary works, although represented in standard critical theory as objective, disinterested, and universal, are in fact infused with masculine assumptions, interests and way reasoning, so that the standard rankings, and also the critical treatments, or literary works have in fact been tacitly but thoroughly gender-biased.

Main Focus of Feminist Critics

A major interest of feminist critics in English-speaking countries has been to reconstitute all the ways we deal with literature so as to do justice to female points of views, concerns, and values. One emphasis has been to alter the way a woman reads the literature of the past so as to make her not an acquiescent, but *The Resisting Reader*; that is, one who resists the author's intentions and designs in order, by a 'revisionary rereading', to bring to light and to counter the covert sexual basis written into a literary work. Another prominent procedure has been to identify recurrent 'images of woman' especially in novels and poems written by men, these often represented as falling into two aesthetic patterns. On the one side we find idealised projections of men's desires (the Madonna, the Muse of the arts, Dante's Beatrice, the Pure and Innocent Virgin, the 'Angel in the House' that was represented by the Victorian poet Coventry Patmore); on the other side are demonic projections of men's sexual resentments and terrors (Eve and Pandora as the sources of all evils, destructive sensual temptresses such as Delilah and Circe, the malign witch, the castrating mother). While many feminist critics have decried the literature written by men for its depiction of women as marginal, docile, and subservient to men's interests and emotional needs ad fears, some of them have also identified male writers who, in their view, have managed to rise above the sexual prejudices of their time sufficiently to understand and represent the cultural pressures that have shaped the characters of women and forced upon them their negative and subsidiary roles; the latter class is said to include, in selected works, such authors as Chaucer, Shakespeare, Samuel Richardson, Henrik Ibsen and George Bernard Shaw.

Gynocriticism

A number of feminists have concentrated, not on the women as reader, but on what Eliane Showalter calls gynocriticism-that is, a criticism which concerns itself with developing a especially female framework for dealing with works written by women, in all aspects of their production, motivation, analysis, and interpretation, and in all literary forms, including journals and letters. Notable books in this mode include Patricia Meyer Spacks, *The Female Imagination* (1975), on English and American novels of the past three hundred years; Ellen Moers, *Literary Woman* (1976), on major women novelists and poets in England, America, and France; Elaine Showalter, *A Literature of Their Own, British Woman Novelists from Bonte to Lessing* (1977); and Sandra Gilbert and Susan Gubar, *The Madwoman in the Attic* (1979). This last book stresses especially the psychodynamics of women writers in the nineteenth century. Its authors propose that the 'anxiety of authorship' that resulted from the stereotype that literary creativity is an exclusively male prerogative, effected in women writers a psychological duplicity that projected the monstrous counter figure to the heroine, typed by Bertha Rochester, the madwoman in Charlotte Bronte's Jane Eyre; such a figure is 'usually in some sense the author's double, an image of her own society and rage'.

One concern of gynocritics is to identify what are taken to be the distinctively feminine subjects matters in literature written by woman-the world of domesticity, for example, or the special experience of gestation, giving birth, and nurturing, or mother-daughter and woman-woman relations in which personal and affectional issues, and not external activism, are the primary interests. Another concern is to uncover in literary history a female tradition, expressed by a sub-community of woman writers who were aware of, emulated, and found supported in earlier woman writers, and who in turn provide models and emotional support to their own readers and successors. A third undertaking is to show that there is a distinctive feminine mode of experience, or 'subjectivity' in thinking, feeling, valuing and perceiving oneself and the outer world. Related to this is the attempt to specify the trait of a 'woman language' or distinctively feminine style of speech and writing, in sentence structure, type of relations between the elments of a discourse, and characteristics figures and imagery.

Some feminists have turned their critical attention to the great number of women's domestic and 'sentimental' novels, which are noted perfunctorily and in derogatory fashion in standard literary history yet which dominated the market for fiction in the nineteenth century and produced most of the best sellers of the time; instances of this last critical enterprise are Eliane Showalter's *A Literature of Their Own* (1977), on British writers, and Nina Baym's *Woman's Fiction: A Guide to Novels by and Woman in America,1820-1870* (1978). Sandra Gilbert and Susan Gubar have written the later history of woman's writing in *No Man's Land: The Phase of the Woman Writer in the Twentieth century*.

Helene Cixous posits the existence of an incipient 'feminine writing' which has its source in the mother, in that stage of the mother-child relations before the child acquires the male-centered verbal language. Thereafter, in her view, this prelinguistic potentiality in the unconscious manifests itself in those written texts which, abolishing all repressions, undermine and subvert the fixed signification, the logic, and the 'closure' of our phallocentric language and open out into a joyous freeplay of meanings. Alternately, Luce Irigaray posits, 'woman's writing' which evades the male monopoly and the risk of appropriation into the existing system by establishing as its generative principle, in place of the monolithic phallus, the diversity, fluidity, and multiple possibilities inherent in the structure and erotic functioning of the female sexual organs and in the distinctive nature of female sexual experiences. Julia Kristeva posits a 'chora' or prelinguistic, pre-Oedipal, and unsystematised signifying process, centered on the mother, that she labels 'semiotic'. This process is repressed as we acquire the father-controlled, syntactically ordered, and logical language that she calls 'symbolic'. The semiotic process, however, can break out in a revolutionary way –her prime example is avant-garde poetry, whether written by women or by men –as a 'heterogeneous destructive causality' that disrupts and disperses the authoritarian 'subject' and strikes free of the oppressive order and rationality of our standard discourse which, as the product of the 'law of the Father' consigns women to a negative and marginal status.

In recent years a number of feminists have used poststructuralist positions and techniques to question the founding concepts of feminism itself. They point out the existence of differences and adversarial strands within the supposedly monolithic history of patriarchal discourse, and they emphasise the inherent linguistic instability in the basic conceptions of 'women' or 'the feminism' as well as the diversities within these supposedly universal and uniform female identities that results from differences in race, class, nationality, and historical situation. Barbara Johnson, *A World of Difference* (1987); Rita Felski, *Beyond Feminist Aesthetics; Feminist Literature and Social Change* (1989); and the essays in *Feminism/Postmodernism*, ed. Linda J. Nicholson (1990) are noted works of Feminist Post-structuralism.

Russian Formalism

A type of literary theory and analysis which is originated in Moscow and Petrograd in the second decade of this century. At first, opponents of the movement applied the term formalism derogatorily, because of this focus on the formal patterns and technical devices of literature to the exclusion of its subject matter and social values; later, however, it became simply a natural designation. Among the leading representatives of the movement were Boris Eichenbaum, Victor Shklovsky, and Roman Jacobson. When this critical mode was suppressed by the soviets in the early 1930s, the center of the formalist study of literature moved to Czechoslovakia, where it was continued especially by members of the Prague Linguistic Circle, which included Roman Jacobson (who had migrated from Russia), Jan Mukarovsky, and Rene Wellek, Beginning in the 1940s both Jacobson and Wellek continued their influential work as professors at American Universities.

Formalism views literature primarily as a specialised mode of language, and proposes a fundamental opposition between the literary use of language and the ordinary, 'practical' use of language. It conceives the central function of ordinary language to be the communication to auditors of a message, or information, by references to the world existing outside of language. In contrast, it conceives literary language to be self-focused, in that its function is not to make extrinsic references, but to offer us a special mode of experience by drawing attention to its own 'formal' features-that is, to interrelationship among the linguistic signs themselves. The linguistics of literature differs from the linguistics of practical discourse, because its laws are oriented toward producing the distinctive features that formalists calls literariness. As Roman Jacobson wrote in

1921: "The object of study in literary science is not the literature but 'literariness', that is, what makes a given work a literary work."

The Literariness of a work, as Jan Mukarovsky described it in the 1920s, consists "in the maximum of foregrounding in the utterance," that is, the foregrounding of "the act of expression, the act of speech itself." (To 'foregrounding' is to bring something into the highest prominence, to make it dominant in perception.) By 'backgrounding' the referential aspect and the logical connections in language, poetry makes the words themselves 'palpable' as phonic signs. The primary aim of literature in thus foregrounding its linguistic medium, as Victor Shklovsky puts it in an influential formulation, is to estrange, or defamiliarise; that is, by disrupting the mode of ordinary linguistic discourse, literature 'makes strange' the world of everyday perception and renews the readers' lost capacity for fresh sensation. In the *Biographia Literaria,* 1817, Samuel Taylor Coleridge had long before described the 'prime merit' of a literary genius as the representation of 'familiar objects' so as to evoke 'freshness of sensation'; but whereas the romantic critic had stressed the authors' ability to communicate his fresh mode of experiencing the world, the formalists stressed the function of purely literary devices to produce the effect of freshness in the readers sensation. The foregrounded properties or 'artistic devices', which estrange poetic language often described as 'deviations' from ordinary language.

Such deviations, which are analysed most fully in the writings of Roman Jacobson, consist primarily in setting up and violating patterns in the sound and syntax of poetic language-including patterns of speech sounds, grammatically constructions, rhythm, rhymes; and stanza forms- and also in setting up prominent recurrences of key word or images.

Some of most fruitful works of Jacobson and others, valid outside the formalist perspective, have been in the analysis of meter and the repetitions of sounds in alliteration and rhyme; these features of poetry they regard not as supplementary adornments of the meaning, but as effecting a reorganisation of language on the semantic as well as the phonic and syntactic levels. Formalists have also made the influential contributions to the theory of prose fiction. With respect to this genre, the central formalists distinction is that between the 'story' (the simple enumeration of a chronological sequence of events) and a plot. An author is said to transform the raw material of a story into a literary plot by the use of a variety of devices that violate sequence and defamiliarise the story elements; the effects is to foreground the narrative medium and devices themselves, and in this way to disrupt what had been our standard responses to the subject matter.

Semiotics

At the end of the nineteenth century Charles Sanders Peirce, the American philosopher, founded a study that he called 'semiotic' and in his *Course In General Linguistics* (1915) the Swiss linguistic Ferdinand De Saussure independently proposed a science which he called 'semiology'. Since then semiotics and semiology have become alternative names for a general science of signs, as these function in all areas of human experience. The considerations of signs is not limited to explicit systems of communication such as language. The Morse code, and traffic signs and signals; a great diversities of other human activities and productions-our bodily postures and gestures, the social rituals we perform, the clothes we wear, the meals we serve, the buildings we inhabit, the objects we deal with-convey common 'meanings' to members to participate in a particular culture, and so can be analysed as signs which function in diverse kinds of signifying systems. Although the study of language (the use of specifically verbal signs) is regarded as itself only one branch of the general signs of semiotics, linguistics, the highly developed signs of language, in fact supplies the basic concepts and methods that a semiotician applies to the study of other social sign-systems.

CS Peirce distinguished three classes of signs, defined in terms of the kind of relation between the signifying items and that which it signifies;

- An icon functions as a sign by means of inherent similarities, or shared features, with what it signifies; examples are the similarity of a portrait to the person it depicts, or the similarity of a map to the geographical area it stands for.
- An index is a sign which bears a natural relation of cause or effects to what it signifies; thus, smoke is a sign indicating fire, and pointing weathervane indicates the direction of the wind.
- In the symbol (or in a less ambiguous term, the 'sign proper'), the relation between the signifying item and what it signifies is not a natural one, but entirely a matter of social convention. The gesture of shaking hands, for example, in some cultures is a conventional sign of greeting or parting, and a red traffic light conventionally signifies 'stop!'. The major and most complex example of this third type is purely conventional sign, however, are the words that constitute a language.

Saussure introduced many of the terms and concepts exploited by current semioticians. Most important are the following

- A sign consists of two inseparable components or aspects, the signifier (in language, a set of speech sounds, or a marks on a page) and the signified (the concept or idea, which is the meaning of the sign).
- A verbal sign, in Saussure's term, is 'arbitrary'. That is, with the minor exception of onomatopoeia (words which we perceive as similar to the sounds they signify), there is no inherent, or natural connection between a verbal signifier and what it signifies.
- The identity of all elements of a language, including its words, their component speech sounds, and the concepts the words signify, are not determined by 'positive qualities', or objective features in these elements themselves, but by differences, or a network of relationships, consisting of distinctions and oppositions from other speech sounds, other words, and other signified that obtain only within a particular linguistic system.
- The aim of linguistics, or of any other semiotic enterprise, is to regard the 'parole' as only a manifestation of the langue (that is the general system of implicit differentiations and rules of combination which underlie and make possible a particular use of signs). The focus of semiotic interest, accordingly, is not on a particular parole, but on the general system of the 'langue' that the parole manifests.

Modern semiotics, like structuralism, has develop in France under the aegis of Saussure, so that many semioticians are also structuralists. They deal with any set of social phenomenon or production as 'texts'; that is, as constituted by self-sufficient, self-ordering, hierarchical structures of differentially determined signs, of codes, and of rules of combination and transformation which make them 'meaningful' to members of a particular society who are competent in that signifying systems. Claude Levi-Strauss, in the 1960s and later, inaugurated the application of semiotics to cultural anthropology, and also established the foundations of French structuralism in general, by using Saussure's linguistics as a model for analysing, in primitive societies, a great variety of phenomena and practices, which he treated as quasi-languages that manifest the structures of an underlying systems. These include kinship systems, totemic systems, ways of preparing food, myths and prelogical modes of interpreting the world.

Jacques Lacan has applied semiotics to Freudian psychoanalysis- interpreting the unconscious, for example, as a structure of signs. Michel Foucault developed a mode of semiotic analysis to deal with the changing medical interpretations of symptoms of disease; the diverse ways of identifying, classifying and treating insanity; and the altering conceptions of human sexuality. Roland Barthes explicitly applying Saussurean principles and methods, has written semiotic analysis of the constituents and codes of the differential signs systems advertisement; which describe and promote women's fashions, as well as analysis of many 'bourgeois myths' about the world which, he claims, are exemplified in such social signs-systems as professional wrestling matches, children's toy, cookery and the, striptease. Barthes was also in his earlier writings a major exponent of structuralist criticism , which deals with a literary text as 'a second-order semiotic system'; that is, it views a literary text as employing the first-order semiotic systems of language to form a higher level semiotic structure, in accordance with a especially literary system of differential elements, conventions, and codes.

Deconstruction

Derrida's paper structure, sign, and play in the Discourse of the Human Sciences, given at a symposium at John Hopkins University in 1966, virtually inaugurated a new critical movement in the United States known as deconstruction. Its argument put in question the basic metaphysical assumption of western philosophy since Plato. The notion of 'structure', he argues, even in, 'structuralist' theory has always presupposed a 'centre' of meaning of some sort. This 'centre' governs the structure but itself not subject to structural analysis.

People desire a centre because it guarantees being as presence. For example, we think of our mental and physical life as centred on an 'I'; this personality is the principle of unity which underlies the structure of all that goes on in this space. Freud's theories completely undermine this metaphysical certainty by revealing a division in the self between conscious and unconscious. Western thought has developed innumerable terms which operate as centring principles; being, essence, substance, truth, form, beginning, end, purpose, consciousness, man, God, and so on. It is important to note that Derrida does not assert the possibility of thinking outside such terms; any attempt to undo a particular concept is to become caught up in the term that the concept depends on. For example, if we try to undo the centring concept of 'consciousness' by asserting the disruptive counterforce of the 'unconscious', we are in danger of introducing a new centre, because we cannot choose but enter the conceptual system (conscious/unconscious) we are trying to dislodge. All we can do is to refuse to allow either pole in a system (body/soul, good/bad, serious/unserious) to become the centre and guarantor of presence.

Logocentrism

This desire for centre is called 'logocentrism' in Derrida's classic work, *Of Grammatology*. 'Logos' (Greek for 'word') is a term which in the New Testament carries the greatest possible concentration of presence: 'In the beginning was the word.' Being the origin of all things, the 'word' underwrites the full presence of the world; everything is the effect of this one cause. Even though, the Bible is written God's word is essentially spoken. A spoken word is emitted from a living body appears to be closer to an originating thought than a written word. Derrida argues that this privileging of speech over writing (he calls it 'phonocentrism') is a classic feature of Logocentrism.

What prevents the sign from being a full présence? Derrida invents the term 'differance' to convey the divided nature of the sign. In French the 'a' in 'differance' is not heard so we hear only 'difference'. The ambiguity is perceptible only in writing; the verb 'differ' means both 'to differ' and 'to defer'.' To differ' is a spatial concept: the sign emerges from a system of differences which are spaced out within the system. 'To defer' is temporal: signifiers enforce an endless postponement of 'presence'. 'Phonocentric' thought ignores 'difference' and insists upon the self-presence of the spoken word. Phonocentrism treats writing as a contaminated form of speech. Speech seems nearer to originating thought. When we hear speech we attribute to it a 'presence' which we take to be lacking in writing. The speech of the great actor, orator, or politician is thought to possess 'presence'; it incarnates, so to speak, the speaker's soul. Writing seems relatively impure and obtrudes its own system in physical marks which have a relative permanence; writing can be repeated (printed, reprinted, and so on) and this repetition invites interpretation and reinterpretation. Even when a speech is subjected to interpretation it is usually in written form. Writing does not need the writer's presence, but speech always implies an immediate presence.

The sounds made by a speaker evaporate in the air and leave no trace (unless recorded), and therefore, do not appear to contaminate the originating thought as in writing. Philosophers have often expressed their dislike of writing; they fear that it will destroy the authority of philosophic truth. This truth depends upon pure thought (logic, ideas, propositions) which risk contamination when written. Francis Bacon believed that one of the main obstacle to scientific advance was the love of eloquence: 'men began to hunt more after words than matter; and more after .... Tropes and figures, than after the weight of matter.. soundness of argument.' However, as the word 'eloquence' suggests the qualities in writing to which he objected are those originally developed by orators. Thus, those very features of elaboration in writing which threaten to cloud the purity of thought originally cultivated for speech.

This coupling of 'writing' and 'speech' is an example of what Derrida calls a 'violet hierarchy'. Speech has full presence, while writing is secondary and threatens to contaminate speech with its materiality. Western philosophy has supported this ranking in order to preserve presence. But, as the Bacon example shows, the hierarchy can easily be undone and reversed. We begin to see that both speech and writing share certain writerly features; both are signifying processes which lack presence. To complete the reversal of the hierarchy, we can now say that speech is a species of writing. This reversal is the first stage of a Derridean 'deconstruction'.

Derrida uses the term 'supplement' to convey the unstable relationship between couplets such as speech/writing. For Rousseau writing is merely a supplement to speech; it adds something inessential. In French 'suppleer' also means 'to substitute' (to take the place of), and Derrida shows that writing not only supplement but also takes the place of speech, because speech is always already written. All human activity involves this supplementarity (addition-substitution). When we say that 'nature' preceded 'civilisation', we are asserting another violent hierarchy in which a pure presence lauds itself over a mere supplement. However, if we look closely, we find that nature is always already contaminated with civilization, there is no 'original' nature, only a myth which we desire to promote.

Consider another example, Milton's *Paradise Lost* may be said to rest on the distinction between good and evil. Good has the original fullness of being. It originated with God. Evil is a second comer, a supplement, which contaminates his original unity of being. However, if we look more closely, we begin to see reversal taking place. For example, if we seek a time when good was without evil, we find ourselves caught in an abysmal regression. Was it before the Fall? Before Satan's? What caused Satan's Fall? Pride. Who created pride? God, who created angels and human free to sin. We never reach an original moment of pure goodness. We may reverse the hierarchy and say that there are no 'good' acts by humans until after the Fall. Adam's first act of sacrifice is an expression of love for the fallen Eve. This 'goodness' comes only after evil. God's prohibition itself presupposes evil.

In *Areopagitica* Milton opposed the licencing of books because he believed that we can be virtuous only if we are given the opportunity to struggle against evil; 'that which purifies us is trial and trial is by what is contrary'. Thus, good comes after evil. There are many critical and theological strategies which can sort out this mess, but there remains a basis for deconstruction. Such a reading begins by noting the hierarchy, proceeds to reverse it, and finally resists the assertion of a new hierarchy by displacing the second term from a position of superiority too. Blake believed that Milton was on Satan's side in his great epic, and Shelley thought that Satan was morally superior to God. They simply reverse the hierarchy, substituting evil for good. A deconstructive reading would go on to recognise that the couplet cannot be hierarchised in either direction without 'violence'. Evil is both addition and substitution. Deconstruction can begin when we locate the moment when a text transgresses the laws it appears to set up for itself. At this point texts go to pieces, so to speak.

Characteristics of Writing

In 'Signature Event Context' Derrida gives writing three characteristics

1. A written sign is a mark which can be repeated in the absence not only of the subject who emitted it in a specific context but also of a specific addressee.
2. The written sign can break its 'real context' and can be read in a diferent context regardless of what its writer intended. Any chain of signs can be, 'grafted' into a discourse in another context.
3. The written sign is subject to 'spacing' (espacement) in two senses: firstly, it is separated from other signs in particular chain; secondly, it is separated from 'present reference' (that is, it can refer only to something not actually present in it.)

These characteristics appear to distinguish writing from speech. Writing involves the certain irresponsibility, because if signs are repeatable out of context, then what authority can they possess? Derrida proceed to deconstruct the hierarchy by, for example, pointing out that when we interpret oral signs, we have to recognise certain stable and identical forms (signifiers), whatever accent, tone or distortion may be involved in the utterance. It appears that we have to exclude the accidental phonic (sound) substance and recover a pure form. This form is the repeatable signifier, which we had thought characteristics of writing. Once again, we conclude that speech is species of writing.

JL Austin's theory of 'speech acts' was developed to supersede the old logical-positivist view of language which assumed that the only meaningful statements are those which describe a state of affairs in the world. All other sorts of statements are not real ones but 'pseudo-statement'. Austin uses the term 'constative' to cover the first (referential-statements), and 'performative' to cover those utterances which actually perform the action they describe, ('We swear to tell the whole truth and nothing but the truth' performs an oath). Derrida acknowledges that this makes a break with logocentric thought by recognising that speech does not have to represent something to have a meaning. However, Austin also distinguishes between degrees of linguistic force. To make a merely linguistic utterance (say to speak an English sentence) is a locutionary act. A speech act which has illocutionary force involves performing the act, (to promise, to swear, to argue, to affirm and so on). Austin requires that speech acts must have contexts. An oath can occur only in a court within the appropriate judicial framework or in other situations in which oaths are conventionally performed. Derrida questions this by suggesting that the repeatability (iterability) of the speech act is more fundamental than its attachment to a context.

Austin remarks in passing that to be performative, a statement must be spoken 'seriously' and not be a joke or used in a play or poem. An oath in a Hollywood court scene is 'parasitic' upon a real-life oath. John Searle's reply to Derrida, *Reiterating the Differences*, defend's Austin's view and argues that a 'serious' discourse is logically prior to fictional, 'parasitic' citations of it. Derrida probes this and neatly demonstrates that a 'serious' performative cannot occur unless , it is a repeatable sign-sequence (what Barthes called the 'always-already-written'). A real courtroom oath is just as the special case of the game people play in film and books. What Austin's pure performative and the impure, parasitic versions have in commons that they involve repetition and citation, which are typical of the 'written'.

The power of the deconstructive movement can be gauged by the fact that many other major intellectual traditions have been forced into radical reassessments. For example, a rapprochement between deconstructive philosophy and modern Marxism is impressively undertaken by Michael Ryan in his *Marxism and Deconstruction* (1982), in which he shows how both have encouraged 'plurality' rather than 'authoritarian unity', criticism rather than obedience, 'difference' rather than 'identity' and a general scepticism about absolute or totalising systems.

Post-Colonialism

A further movement which draws on the more radical implications of poststructuralism is the study of colonial discourse, or what is usually termed 'postcolonial criticism' – although we should offer a caveat about settling too neatly on a name for this internally diverse cluster of writers and writings. Analysis of the cultural dimension of colonialism/imperialism is as old as the struggle against it; such work has been a staple of anti-colonial movements everywhere. It entered the agenda of metropolitan intellectuals and academics as a reflex of a new consciousness attendant on Indian Independence (1947) and as part of a general leftist reorientation to the 'Third-World' struggles (above all in Algeria) from the 1950s onwards. Frantz Fanon's *The Wretched of the Earth* (1961) was and remains an inspirational key text (it had an important preface by the metropolitan 'convert', Jean Paul Sartre). Thereafter, 'postcolonial-criticism' overtook the troublesome ideological category of 'Common-wealth literature' to emerge in the 1980s as a set of concerns marked by the indeterminacies and decentredness otherwise associated, philosophically, with poststructuralism and particularly deconstruction.

The appearance of postcolonial criticism has therefore overlapped with the debates on postmodernism, though it brings, too, an awareness of power relations between Western and 'Third-World' cultures which the more playful and parodic, or aestheticising, postmodernism has neglected or been slow to develop. From a postcolonial perspective, Western values and traditions of thought and literature, including versions of postmodernism, are guilty of a repressive ethnocentrism. Models of Western thought (derived, for example, from Aristotle, Descartes, Kant, Marx, Nietzsche and Freud) or of literature (Homer, Dante, Flaubert, TS Eliot) have dominated world culture, marginalising or excluding non-Western traditions and forms of cultural life and expression.

Jacques Derrida has described Western metaphysics as 'the white mythology' which reassembles and reflects the culture of the West: the white man takes his own, mythology, Indo-European mythology, his own logos, that is, the 'mythos' of this idiom, for the universal form of that he must still wish to call 'Reason', and the methods of deconstruction has proved a major inspiration for postcolonial critics. Some of the other theoretical arguments discussed elsewhere in this book-derived, for example, from Bakhtin's dialogics, Gramsci's concept of hegemony and Foucault's writings on power and knowledge- have also been relevant to post or anti-colonial ways of thinking and reading, and Lyotard's 'postmodern' critique of the universalising historical narratives and strategies of Western rationality has clearly been influential too. The fact these models find their source in Western intellectual traditions, however, makes them somewhat problematical. In Lyotard's case, for example, there is ironically a totalising thrust to his 'war on totality' and to his 'incredulity towards master narratives' and, for some, an arrogance all too characteristics of the blindnesses of Western avant-gardist paradigms.

Linda Hutcheon attempts to clarify some of these matters by drawing a distinction between respective aims and political agendas. Thus, postmodernism and poststructuralism direct their critique at the unified humanist subject, while postcolonialism seeks to undermine the imperialist subject. The first, she says, must 'be put on hold' in order for postcolonial and feminist discourses 'first to assert and affirm a denied or alienated subjectivity'. But this is to commit non-western cultures (as it commits women) to a form of subjectivity', and a 'repressed' narrative of individual and national self-legitimation characterising Western liberal-humanism.

The danger, evidently, is that 'colonial subjects' are confirmed in their subjection to Western ideological modes, which are themselves confirmed at the same time in their controlling centrality. This is the perspective of 'Orientalism' explored and exposed by Edward Said (*Orientalism*, 1978), a principle influence upon post-colonial criticism, whose work is motivated by his political commitment to the Palestinian cause. Foucault's most distinguished American disciple, Said is attracted to his mentor's Nietzschean version of poststructuralism because it allows him to link the theory of discourse with real social and political struggles. By challenging Western discourse, Said follows the logic of Foucault's theories: no discourse is fixed for all time: it is both a cause and an effect. It is not only wields power but also stimulates oppositions.

New Historicism

Since the early 1980s, has been the accepted name for a mode of literary study that its proponents oppose to the formalism they attribute both to the New Criticism and to the critical deconstruction that followed it. In place of dealing with the text in isolation from its historical context, new historicists attend primarily to the historical and cultural conditions of its production, and also of its later critical interpretations and evaluations. This is not simply a return to an earlier kind of literary scholarship, for the views and the practices of the new historicist differ markedly from those of former scholars who had used political and intellectual history as a 'background' to account for the characteristic subject matter of literature at a particular time and place.

What is more distinctive in the new mode of historical study, marking it as poststructural, is mainly the result of concepts and procedures that it has assimilated from various recent theories of literary and other writings.

Prominent Influences

Especially prominent influences are

- The views of the revisionist Marxist thinker, Louis Althusser, that ideology manifests itself in different ways in the discourse of each of the semi-autonomous institution of an era, and also that ideology operates to position its readers as the 'subject' in the discourse, in a way that is fact, 'subjects' them- that is, subordinates them- to the interests of the ruling classes.
- Michael Foucault's theory that a pattern of power-relations at any given era in a society constitute the concepts, oppositions, and hierarchies of its discourse, and in this way determine what will be accounted knowledge and truth, as well as what will be considered humanly normal and serve to define and exclude what, in that era, is accounted to be criminal, insane, or sexually deviant.
- The central concept in deconstruction criticism that all texts involve modes of signification that war against each other, merged with Mikhail Bakhtin's concept of the Dialogic nature of many literary texts, in the sense that they present a number of independent often conflicting voices.
- Recent developments in cultural anthropology, especially Clifford Geertz's view that a culture is constituted by distinctive sets of signifying system, and his use of what he calls thick descriptions- the close analysis or 'reading', of a particular social production or event so as to recover the meanings it had for the peoples involved in it, as well as to discover the patterns of conventions, codes, and modes of thinking that invests the cultural item with those meanings.

New historians acknowledge that they themselves, like all authors, are 'subjectivities' that have been shaped and informed by the circumstances and discourses specific to their era, hence that their own critical writings construct, rather than discover ready-made, the textual meanings they describe and the literary and cultural histories they narrate. To mitigate the risk that they will unquestioningly appropriate texts written in the past, they tend to assess that the course of history between the past and present is not coherent, but exhibits discontinuities, breaks and ruptures; by doing so, they hope to 'distance' and 'estrange' an earlier text and so sharpen their ability to detect its differences from their present ideological assumptions.

A number of historicists present their readings of texts written in the past as (in their favoured metaphor) 'negotiations' between past and present. In this two-way relationship, the features of a cultural products, which are identifiable only relatively to their differences from the historicists's own subject-position, in return make possible some degree of in sight into the power-configurations –especially in the aspects of class, gender, race and ethnicity- that prevail in the historicist's present culture.

Stephen Greenblatt inaugurated the currency of the label 'new historicism' in his introduction to a special issue of *Genre* (1982), he prefers, however, to call his own critical enterprise cultural poetics, in order to highlight his concerns with literature and the arts as integral with other social practices that, in their complex interactions, make up the general culture of an era. In his writings on the renaissance, one of Greenblatt's recurrent critical tactics to inaugurate his essays by telling an anecdote, or by referring to a text or cultural objects that seems remote from literature, to subject the selected items to a close reading (Clifford Geertz's term, a 'thick descriptions') designed to bring out the beliefs, norms and rhetorical plays of power that are implicit in it. To apply that analysis so as to reveal similar cultural elements and configurations in literary text of the same period. For example, in an essay called *Invisible Bullets* Greenblatt reads a selection from Thomas Harriotts *A Belief and True Report of the New Found Land of Virginia*, written in 1588, as a representative discourse of the English colonizers of America which, without its author's awareness, serves to confirm 'the Machiavellian hypothesis of the origin of princely power in force and Fraud', yet nonetheless draws its 'audience irresistibly toward the celebration of that power'.

Greenblatt also asserts that Harriott tests the English power-structure that he attests by recording in his *Report* the counter-voices of the American Indians who are being appropriated and oppressed by that power. Greenblatt then identifies similar modes of power discourse and counter-discourse in the dialogues in Shakespeare's *Tempest* between Prospero, the appropriator and Caliban, the expropriated native of island, and goes on surprisingly, to find similar discursive configurations in the texts of Shakespeare's *Henry IV, 1 and 2* and *Henry V*. In Greenblatt's reading, the dialogue and the events of the Henry plays reveal the degree to which princely power is based on predation, calculation, deceit and hypocrisy at the same time, the plays do not scruple to record the dissonant and subversive voices of Falstaff and various other representatives of Elizabethan sub-cultures.

These counter-establishment revelations in Shakespeare's plays, however, serve to maneuver their audience to accept and even glorify the power-structure to which that audience is itself subjected. Greenblatts general thesis is that, in order to some degree allows, but actively fosters subversive elements and forces, yet in such a way is more effectively to 'contain' such challenges to forces of subversion has been criticised as 'pessimistic' and 'quietest' by new historicists who insists on the capacity of subversive ideas and practices-including those manifested in their own critical writings- to effect drastic social changes.

Ransom and Brooks

An early, founding essay in the self-identification of New Criticism is John Crowe Ransom's *Criticism Inc* (1937). His book on Eliot, Richards and others, entitled *The New Criticism*, 1941, gave the movement its name. Ransom, one of the 'Fugitives' and editor of the *Kenyon Review* 1939-59, here lays down the ground rules: *Criticism Inc* is the 'business' of professionals –professors of the literature in the universities in particular; criticism should become more scientific, or precise and systematic; students should study literature, and not merely about literature as 'imperfect in objectivity, or 'aesthetic-distance'; criticism is not ethical, linguistic or historical studies, which are merely 'aids'. The critic significantly titled *The Well-Wrought Urn: Studies in the Structure of Poetry* (1947), is in our view the best exemplification, explicitly and implicitly, of New Critical practices one could hope to find.

Brooks at once quotes the opening of MacLeish's *Ars Poetica*; refers to Eliot and his notion of the 'objective correlative' rejects the relevance of biography: reiterates throughout the terms 'dramatic propriety', 'irony', 'paradox' (repeatedly) and 'organic context'; performs a bravura reading of the poem which leaves its 'sententious' final dictum as a dramatically organic element of the whole; constantly admires the poem's 'history' above the 'actual' histories of 'war and peace' of 'our time-ridden minds', of 'meaningless' 'accumulations of facts' of 'the scientific and the philosophical' generalisation which dominates our world; explicitly praises the poems insight into essential truth; and confirms the poem's value to us, (in 1942, in the midst of the nightmare of wartime history) precisely because like Keats's urn, 'it is all breathing human passion far above' thus stressing the ironic fact that all human passion does leave one cloyed, hence the superiority of art.

The Intentional and Affective Fallacies: Wimsatt and Beardsley

As New Criticism is, by definition, a praxis, much of its 'theory' occurs along the way in more specifically practical essays and not as theoretical writing. But there are two New Critical essays in particular which are overtly theoretical and which have become influential texts more generally in modern critical discourse: *The Intentional Fallacy* (1946) and *The Affective Fallacy* (1949) written by WK Wimsatt- a professor of English at Yale University and author of the symptomatically titled book, *The Verbal Icon: Studies in The Meaning of Poetry* (1954) in collaboration with Monroe C. Beardsley, a philosopher of aesthetics. Both essays, influenced by Eliot and Richard engage with the 'addresser' (writer) –'message' (text)- 'addressee' (reader) nexus outlined in the Introduction, in the pursuit of an 'objective' criticism which abjures both the personal input of the writer ('intention') and the emotional effect on the reader (affect) in order purely to study the 'words on the page' and how the artefact 'works'. The first essay argues that 'the design or intention of the author is neither available nor desirable as a standard' for judging the success of a work of literary art; that a poem 'goes about the world beyond [the author's] power to intend about it or control it' –it 'belongs to the public'; that it should be understood in terms of the 'dramatic speaker', of the text, not the author; and be judged only by whether it 'works' or not. Much critical debate has since raged about the place of intention in criticism, and continues to do so: Wimsatt and Beardsley's position strikes a chord, for example, with poststructuralist notions of the 'death of the author' and with deconstruction's freeing of the text from 'presence' and 'meaning'. But there the resemblance ends, for the New Criticism still basically insist that there is a determinate possible. This runs quite counter to deconstruction's notion of the 'iterability' of a text in its 'multiplex' 'positioned' rereadings.

This difference becomes very much clearer in the second essay, which argues that the 'affective fallacy' represents 'a confusion between the poem and its results': 'trying to derive the standard of criticism from the psychological effects of the poem... ends in impressionism and relativism'. Opposing the 'classical objectivity' of New Criticism to 'romantic reader psychology', it asserts that the outcome of both fallacies is that 'the poem itself, as an object of specifically critical judgment, tends to disappear'. And the importance of a poem in classic New Critical terms is that by 'fixing emotions and making them more permanently perceptible', by the 'survival' of 'its clear and nicely interrelated meanings its completeness, balance and tension', it represent the most precise emotive report on customs': In short though cultures have changed, poems remains and explain'. Poems, in other words, are our cultural heritage, permanent and valuable artefacts; and therein lies the crucial difference from more contemporary theoretical positions.

The Chicago School: Rhetoric of Fiction

As a footnote to the New Criticism, however, and before we turn to Leavis, it is worth mentioning another American 'movement' of mid-century which was especially influential in the study of fiction: the so-called 'Chicago school' of 'Neo-Aristotelians'. Theoretically offering a challenge to the New Critics but in fact often seen as only a new critical 'heresy' in their analysis of formal structure and in their belief, with TS Eliot, that criticism should study 'poetry as poetry and not another thing', the 'Neo-Aristotelian' were centred, form the later 1930s through the 1940s and 1950s, on RS Crane at the University of Chicago. Establishing a theoretical basis derived principally from Aristotle's Rhetoric and Poetics, Crane and his group sought to emulate the logic, lucidity and scrupulous concern with evidence found there; were worried by the limitations of New Critical practice (its rejection of historical analysis, its tendency to present subjective judgements as though they were objective, its concern primarily with poetry); and attempted therefore to develop a more inclusive and catholic criticism which would cover all genres and draw for its techniques, on a 'pluralistic and instrumentalist' basis, from whatever method seemed appropriate to a particular case. The anthology *Critics and Criticism: Ancient and Modern* (1952; abridged edition with preface by Crane, 1957) contains many examples of their approach, including Crane's own exemplary reading of Fielding's *Tom Jones, The Concept of Plot and the Plot of Tom Jones*.

Chicago School of Neo-Aristotelians

A reaction against the new critics began under the leadership of Ronald S. Crane in the late thirties. This group of critics is known as Chicago School of neo-Aristotelians who, according to George Watson, employed "a more formidable scholarship and a less popular style, insisted upon a return to questions of design and structure by whatever method and upon whatever assumption seemed appropriate to the particular case." The Chicago view according to the Crane himself was 'pluralistic and instrumentalist' insisting that "we must accord to critics the right of free choice as between different basic methods".

The Chicago critics are so called because they all worked at the University of Chicago and formed a homogenous group with little difference in their views and critical methods. The main characteristics of this school may be summed up as pluralism and neo-Aristotlerianism. The most explicit statements of their pluralism are contained in Mc Keon's *The Philosophic basis of Art and Criticism*, Geson's *An Outline of Poetic Theory* and Crane's *The Language of Criticism and Structure of Poetry*. They took special interest in Aristotle's Poetics, commenting on the method of Chicago critics, Pritchard writes: "Far from proclaiming a new critical panacea, the Chicago critics urged the application to literature of varied critical procedures. Their purpose being to understand the work of art, they being to bear upon it whatever they believe will serve to elucidate it, no matter whence it may be derived. Critical principles ... are simply instrument of injury and analysis."

Moral Formalism: FR Leavis

Despite, or rather because of, the fact that FR Leavis (and 'Leavisite criticism' more generally, flowing from the journal *Scrutiny* [1932-53]) became the major single target for the New Critical theory of the 1970s and beyond in the British context at least, both Raymond Williams in *Politics and Letters* (1979) and Terry Eagleton in *Literary Theory: An Introduction* (1983) bear witness to his enormous, ubiquitous influence of English studies from the 1930s onwards. Apropos of Leavis's *The Great Tradition* 1948, Williams remark that by the early 1970s, in relation to the English novel, Leavis had completely won. I mean if you talked to anyone about (it), including people who were hostile to Leavis, they were in fact reproducing his sense of the shape of its history'. And more generally, Eagleton writes: Whatever the 'failure' or 'success' of scrutiny... the fact means that English students in England today [1983] are 'Leavisites' whether they know it is not, irremediably altered by that Historic intervention.'

Leavis, profoundly influenced by Matthew Arnold and by TS Eliot (Leavis's *New Bearings in English Poetry*, 1932 in effect first taught the English how to 'read' *The Waste Land*), was, like Richards and Empson, one of the new academics in Cambridge in the late 1920s and early 1930s who turned the English syllabus away from the bellettrism of Sir Arthur Quiller Couch and others, and put it at the centre of arts education in the university. His *Education and the University* (1943), in part made up of essays published earlier, including the widely influential *A sketch for an 'English' school* and *Mass Civilization and Minority Culture* – bears witness- as do later works like *English Literature in Our Time and The University*, 1969, *The Living Principle: English as a Discipline of Thoughts*, 1975, and *Thought, Word and Creativity*, (1976), to the fact that Leavis was an educator as much he was a critic and to the practical and empirical, strategically anti-theoretical nature of his work. In a famous exchange with the American critic Rene Wellek, *e.g.* he defends his refusal to theorise his work by saying that criticism and philosophy are quite separate activities and that the business of the critic is to 'attain a peculiar completeness of response (in order) to enter into possession of the given poem .....in its concrete fullness'.

In addition to editing *Scrutiny*, to teaching generations of students- many of whom themselves became teachers and writers-and to being a informing presence, behind, for example, the widely selling, ostensibly neutral but evidently Leavisite *Pelican Guide to English Literature* (1954-61), edited by Boris Ford in seven volumes, Leavis produced many volumes of criticism and cultural commentary; all of which are indelibly imbued with his 'theory'.

Just as Leavis 's moral fervour distinguishing him from the more abstract or aesthetic formalism of the new critics, so, too, does his emphatically sociological and historical sense. Literature is a weapon in the battle of cultural politics, and much of the great literature of the past (as for Eliot-especially but not exclusively –from the 'pre-dissociation of sensibility' seventeenth century) bears witness to the 'organic' strength of pre-industrial cultures. The past and past literature, as for Arnold and Eliot once more, act as a measure of the 'wasteland' of the present age-although the work of the 'great' moderns (Eliot and DH Lawrence, for example) in its 'necessary' difficulty, complexity and commitment to cultural values, is also mobilised on 'Life's' behalf in the inimical world of the twentieth century.

As for the New Critics too, great works of literature are vessels in which humane values survive, but for Leavis they are also to be actively deployed in an ethico-sociological cultural politics. Paradoxically then, and precisely because of this, Leavis's project is both elitist, and culturally pessimistic. It is perhaps not surprising therefore, that in the twentieth century it became so profoundly popular and influential; had indeed until quite recently become naturalised as *Literary Studies*. (In this context see Perry Anderson's critique of Leavisism in *Components of the National Culture* 1968, in which he asserts that Leavisian literary criticism, in mid-century Britain, filled the vaccum left by the failure to develop a British Marxism or Sociology.) Hence, the absence of theory, not being a theory, but merely 'true judgement' and common sense based on lived experience.

Structuralism and Post-Structuralism

We have discussed that the New critics are mainly concerned with the study of words and the structure of poetry. There is a great emphasis on the organic unity of structure and meaning. According to David Lodge 'Structuralism is or was a movement in what the continental Europeans call the human sciences which sought to explain and understand cultural phenomenon(from poems to menus, from primitive myths to modern advertisements) as manifestations of underlying system of significations, of which the exemplary model is verbal language itself , especially as elucidated by the Swiss linguist , Ferdinand De Saussure."

The literary theorists have widened the scope of literary criticism by borrowing its terms and concepts very largely from other disciplines-linguistics, philosophy, Marxism and psychoanalysis. So, literary criticism has become a powerful source of interdisciplinary approach and expansion of knowledge. The varied interpretation of literary texts are derived from the minute analysis of the texture and structure, of various works in the light of different theories. So, a literary work is a liable to varied interpretations, which the writer, perhaps, never intended. David Lodge points out that in "our era criticism is not merely a library of secondary aids to a understanding and appreciation of literary texts, but also a rapidly increasing body of knowledge in its own right."

Structuralism is a school of literary criticism which flourished during 1960s. Ferdinand De Saussure's book *Courses in General Linguistics* (1916) popularised structuralism and introduced Structural Linguistics, which attaches importance to signs, that is, the black marks: 'C-a-t' rather than the object called 'Cat'. It is an attempt to apply this linguistic theory to objects and activities other than language itself. According to Eagleton in structuralism the Poetics detaches or dislocates the sign from the object and, thus, the usual relation between sign and referent is disturbed. It is the referent which invests the sign with "a certain independence as an object of value in itself." The theory of structuralism, which considers the text of a literary work as an integrated verbal entity and ignores the content, the writer, the society and the reader response, distances itself from any suggestion of value judgement. It could no longer influence the literary scenario of twentieth century. It found only a limited number of followers and in course of time it was rejected. It was followed by post-structuralism, which found its staunch exponent in Jacques Derrida who enunciated the theory of Deconstruction.

Julia Kristeva: Language and Revolution

Kristeva's most important work on literary meaning is *La revolution du language poetique* (1974). Unlike that of Barthes her theory is based upon a particular system of ideas: psychoanalysis. The book attempts to explore the process by which what is ordered and rationally accepted is continually being threatened by the 'heterogeneous' and the 'irrational'.

Kristeva gives us a complex psychological account of the relationship between the 'normal' and the 'poetic'. Human beings are from the beginning a space across which physical and psychic impulses flow rhythmically. This indefinite flux of impulses is gradually regulated by the constraints of family and society (potty-training, gender-identification, separation of public and private, and so on). At the earliest, pre-Oedipal stage, the flow of impulses centres on the mother, and allows not the formulation of a personality but only a rough demarcation of parts of body and their relations. A disorganised prelinguistic flux of movements, gestures, sounds and rhythms lays a foundation of semiotic material which remains active beneath the mature linguistic performance of the adult. She calls this material 'semiotic' because it works like an unorganised signifying process. We become aware of this activity in dreams in which images are processed in 'illogical' ways.

In the poetry of Mallarme and Lautreamont these primary processes of rhythm and sound patterns are liberated from the unconscious (according to Lacan, they are the unconscious). Kristeva relates the use of sound in poetry to primary sexual impulses. The opposition Mama and Papa sets nasal 'm' against plosive 'p'. The 'm' transmits the maternal 'orality', which the 'p' relates to male 'anality'.

As the semiotic becomes regulated, the beaten pathways become the logic, coherent syntax and rationality of the adult, which Kristeva calls the 'symbolic'. The symbolic works with the substance of the semiotic and achieves a certain mastery over it, but can never produce its own signifying substance. The symbolic places subjects in their positions and makes it possible for them to have identities. Kristeva adopts Lacan's Freudian explanation of the emergence of this phase.

The word 'revolution' in Kristeva's title is not simply metaphoric. The possibility of radical social change is, in her view, bound up with the disruption of authoritarians discourses. Poetic language introduces the subversive openness of the semiotic 'across' society's 'closed' symbolic order: 'What the theory of the unconscious seeks, poetic language practices, within and against the social order.' Sometimes she considers that modernist poetry actually prefigures a social revolution which in the distant future will come about when society has evolved a more complex form. However, at other times she fears that bourgeois ideology will simply recuperate this poetic revolution by treating it as a safety value for the repressed impulses it denies in society. Kristeva's view of the revolutionary potential of women writers in society is just as ambivalent.

Deleuze and Guattari: Schizoanalysis

Gilles Deleuze and Felix Guattari, in *Anti-Oedipus: Capitalism and Schizophrenia* (1972) and *Kafka: Pour une litterature mineure* (1975) offer at once a radical critique of psychoanalysis-drawing on, but going beyond, Lacan- and a close textual method for the reading of texts which they term 'Schizoanalysis'. Their attack on schizoanalysis primarily targets its representation of desire as based in lack or need, which Deleuze and Guattari see as a capitalist device that deforms the unconscious: the Oedipus complex, hijacked as an internalised set of power relations, is the result of repression by capitalism within the family. Schizoanalysis would, conversely, construct an unconscious in which desire constitutes an untrammelled 'flow' –an energy which is not contained by Oedipal 'anxiety' but is a positive source of new beginning: 'schizoanalysis' means the liberation of desire where paranoiac unconscious desire 'territorializes',- in terms of nation, family, church, school, etc- a schizophrenic one 'deterritorializes', offering a subversion of these (capitalist) totalities. In this sense, as Elizabeth Wright has said, Deleuze and Guattari's 'material psychiatry' becomes a political factor in its attempts to realise the libidinal flow from what they see as oppressions rather than repression.

The relationship of schizophrenia to literature is that the latter too can subvert, and free itself from the system. But the author texts also needs a 'desire-liberating reader', a 'schizoanalyst', to activate its potentially revolutionary discourses. Deleuze and Guattari's analysis of Kafka, whom they find particularly suited, to their project (his work in a favourite concepts of theirs is a 'rhizome'-'a fertile tuber that sprouts unexpected plants out a concealment'. [Wright]), is a bravura close, textual, entirely anti-New-critical, out-deconstructing-deconstruction analysis of his work, which exposes the 'gaps' and tensions in the text, the continuously fluid combinations of images, and the subversion of 'normal' notions of representations, symbol and text within both psychoanalytic and other literary critical discourse. In practice of the 'revolutionary' schizoanalytic' reader/writer will 'deterritorialize' any given representation: in this case of 'Kafka' hence accounting for his 'revolutionary' force by exposing the unconscious discourses of desire as more powerful than those of family and state. Nevertheless, as for Kristeva, the paradox of Deleuze and Guattari's promotion of schizoanalysis is that the domain of literature and literary criticism can only ever be a displacement of their revolutionary political potential.

The Sources of the Movement

In a strict sense, the term 'new criticism' is applied to the criticism written by John Crowe Ransom, Allen Tate, RP Blackmur, Robert Penn Warren, and Cleanth Brooks. It is derived from Ransom's book, *The New Criticism*, published in 1941, which discussed a movement in America in 1930s which paralleled movement in England led by critics like TS Eliot, IA Richard and William Empson. Generally, the term is applied, however, to the whole body of contemporary criticism which centres its attention in the work of art as an object in itself; finds in it a special kind of language opposed to-or at least different from the language of science or philosophy and examines it through the process of close analysis. The new critics constitute the school in contemporary criticism which most completely employs the objective theory of art.

The movement has varied sources, among which are IA Richard's *The Principles of Literary Criticism* (1924), William Empson's *Seven Types of Ambiguity* (1930), the work of Remy de Gourmont, *The Anti-Romanticism of TE Hulme*, the French *Explication de Texte*, the psychological theories of the Archetype, the concepts of order and tradition of the *Southern Agrarians*, and the work of Ezra Pound and TS Eliot.

Joel Spingarn

He laid the foundation of new criticism through his lecture in 1910 at Columbia University. IA Richards had a great regard for him. He was very learned, well versed in the theory of literary criticism and he rejected the convectional approaches which, in his opinion, were outdated and futile.

His approach to criticism had its roots in anti-historicism and declared that the critic should closely study the work concerned, find out the intention of the author and then try to examine how much he has succeeded in achieving it. In his opinion criticism "should hold a mirror to literature as literature holds it up to nature."

The main concern of the critic is to find out what the poet has tried to express and how has he expressed it. He considered learning as essential for the critic. But he was against both judicial criticism and impressionistic criticism and advocated that the critic should concentrate all his attention upon the work of art and study it objectively.

This iconoclastic address demolished the old critical traditions and paved the way for the rise of the New Criticism. He has attacked dogmatic criticism and is critical of the three prevalent American approaches that literature is a moral force. He rejected the notion that literature should be judged on the basis of morals. He said that the artists conviction about moral and social organisation does not provide the entire content of his work.

The critic must seek an aesthetic in the artist and all else is secondary. He also made a forceful plea for wide scholarship and a cosmopolitan outlook and thus tried to counter the narrow nationalism which had distorted the American criticism in the years immediately following World War I.

Kenneth Burke

Burke has acquired a great eminence among the group of new critics particularly because he was profoundly influenced by Eliot and Freud. His major books are *Counter Statement* and *The Philosophy of Literary Form*. He had full faith that an artist must concentrate on the form and that form, content, structure and meaning are inseparable from it.

However, he differs from Eliot and Freud both in certain important aspects. His other important essays are *Psychology and Form*, *The Status of Art and Programme*. He, like the others of New Criticism believed that the artist must concentrate on the form, for it is the form which carries his meaning. But the text of the excellence of the form lies in the satisfaction which it imparts to the readers.

He took *Hamlet* for his text and developed the proposition that form refers to the creation and satisfying of an appetite in the reader's mind so that proper form in a work is equivalent to the psychology of the audience. He objected that Freudians had focussed their research upon the artists' possible neurosis which is wrong to furnish information about literature.

He tells that in this scientific age, the form in literature has been supplanted by information and it is incorrect to think of psychology as information rather than an artistic effects. Science lays emphasis upon information, analysing the psychology of the hero without studying its effects.

Thus, his stress on psychology makes him different from the basic tenets of the New Criticism that the work of art is a thing in itself and should be studied as such so he has been blamed for the affective fallacy against which Eliot has so carefully warned.

John Crowe Ransom

He is the most eminent and influenced among the New Critics. He was the founder of *Kenyon Review*. *The World's Body* and *The New Criticism* are his most powerful critical works. He was a man of wide learning in literature and philosophy and his approach to literary criticism is generally formalistic. He stressed chiefly on verbal and textual analysis. In his earlier works, he has differentiated between science and poetry and points out that the scientist regards the myths as lies and considers it an incorrect attempt to explain natural phenomena while the poet see myth as symbolic representation of particular truths. Science depends on general principles but ignores the particular matters which are necessary for poetry. Poetry sees objects as natural wholes while science sees them as specimen type.

The scientist is satisfied merely by externals but the poet wants to know the object as it is in itself without any desire to put it to practical use. He contemplates the objects both with his sights and imaginations and so his knowledge is more thorough and real. Science has only surface knowledge but poetry contemplates the inner essence. The poet expresses himself in artistically beautiful form which imparts aesthetic satisfaction to his readers. Thus, Ransom is very much concerned with poetry as an art and a poet should care only for artistic effects without any moral consideration.

Ransom also proves that Modern poetry is much superior to the Victorian poetry. In his opinion, the older poetry was a poetry of ideas which expressed the ideas and beliefs of the poet and of his age. Man naturally recollects and dreams of those things which he has deserted.

As such art is an expression of such dreams and recollection and has the pleasure of recognition. So imagination, through recollection enables the poet to imagine the objects which he may not be contemplating at that moment. Such images constitute the texture of a poem. He has evolved the dual concept of structure and texture and believed that they form the texture of a poem. He thinks that the concept of structure is more comprehensive and includes the development of theme in a poem. Ransom advises that the critic must first study the structural properties of a poem and then move on to an appreciation and judgement of its texture.

As he proceeds, various other details are added to the poetic texture and metaphor is on such detail which is a type of second poem. He says, "Poetry thus often transcends its ostensible argument by adding an ambiguity or analogy.... The critic must devote his most careful attention to texture, realising that he is analysing an ontology, an order of existence....." this is why, he has criticised a number of practioners of the new school. In his opinion, Eliot is simply an academic scholar who is concerned only with tradition which prevents him from the correct evaluation of the work of art.

He is also critical of Cleanth Brooks because he is excessively verbal and fails to perceive the beauty of the poem as a whole. He entirely ignores the synthesis like other New Critics and so he fails to establish a satisfactory unifying basis for the poem. Ransom advised that the New Critics must also consider the use and the motive of the poetry.

Thus, he makes the forceful plea for the use of modern psychology by the critics as well as for the usefulness of the prose paraphrase for understanding the meaning of the poet. He favours the liberal and comprehensive outlook. Slowly Ransom widened his critical outlook. He told that at a lower level, the critic examines such matters like language but at the higher level, he speculate and inquires into the final cause.

He further enlarged the scope of criticism by expressing the view that linguistic analysis developed for poetry applies also to the style of fiction. He, thus, occupies an important place as a theorist at the new school of criticism, enlarged its scope and corrected its excesses.

Allen Tate

Among the most important pioneers of the New Criticism, Allen Tate stands only second to Ransom. His important critical works are *Reactionary Essays in Poetry* and *Ideas and Reason in Madness* and *The Forlorn Demon*. He is opposed to the theories which connect literature with history, sociology and with other sciences and the literature is used as propaganda. The critic should concentrate his attention on the poem and should remember that the purpose of the poem is not to confirm any theory.

The theory that poetry had some moral and social end is not poetic but philosophical. He is more receptive to ideas. There are certain ideas and beliefs which are the common heritage of the people and the poets and if they are used by the poets, they would be left free to concentrate on the structure of the poem.

Like Eliot, he also believes in tradition that poet should make use of tradition and traditional beliefs but they also modify it. In this way, in the work of a great poet, there is always a tension between tradition and experiment. He has also developed a kinetic explanation of the poem. He strongly stands against historical criticism and moral estimate.

He believes that the critic must deliver a total judgement about the work of art as a whole. Social and historical consideration takes him away from real human experience and the spiritual and emotional part of life and this obstruct his right approach to literary criticism. He considers both the literary genre and the entire individuality of the work. He examines past authors, works in the light of the formal objectivity.

William Empson

Among the prominent English critics of the modern criticism, Empson has made the most formative contribution. He was, in a way, disciple of Richards and was chiefly inspired by him in all his theories and declarations. His first and most important work is *Seven Type of Ambiguity* and his fame as a critic rest on this single work. He has pointed out seven ambiguities in the way of proper judgement of a work of art. The first arises when a word or a grammatical structure is effective in several ways at the same time.

Another difficulty arises when two or more meanings are added to the single idea by the author. Sometimes, there are two ideas in the act of writing and does not have it completely in his mind as often happens with the use of similes. This difficulity arises when a statement is contradictory or irrelevant and the reader is forced to invent of his own. In the given context, they possess an opposing meaning. Then it becomes difficult for the reader to follow the real and true meaning of the work. Watson praises him that, "Empson did not invent the technique of verbal analysis .... But he was the first to systematise it....."

Deconstruction

"A school of criticism, or approach to reading literature which owes its development mainly to the writings of Jacques Derrida (1930). His papers *Structure, Sign and Play* (1966) inaugurated a new critical movement in the United States especially at Yale University."

Clarifying this term in the critical differences, Barbara Johnson writes that, "Deconstruction is not synonymous with destruction.... It is in fact much closer to the original meaning of the word 'analysis' ..... A deconstructive reading is reading which analysis the specificity of a text's critical difference from itself."

Derrida's new concept of writing is based on three complex words-difference, trace and arche-writing. Difference means two actions- differing and deferring. Differing is one not being another. Deferring is something being delayed or postponed. According to Derrida, each sign performs double functions – differing and deferring. Hence, the structure of the sign is conditioned by these two factors and not by signifier or signified. This means that each sign is something that is unlike other sign. Each sign differs from other sign.

This sign has no fixed meaning for its meaning is contextual. All that a sign can do is to urge upon us to search for what is lacking and remind us what is not. The deconstructive have made a division of criticism into two types- metaphysical and deconstructive. The metaphysical criticism pre-supposes that the text has a fixed meaning which the critic is supposed to explain whereas the business of deconstructionism is not to deconstruct the text but to show how the text has deconstructed itself. Derrida's theory has given rise to reactions to the fields of literary criticism. Deconstructive criticism believes in the determination of meaning. In fact, "deconstruction is not dismantling of the structure of a text but a demonstration that it has already dismantled itself".

In short, deconstruction is the name given to a radical and wide ranging development in the human sciences especially philosophy and literary criticism. Derrida, the French philosopher had undoubtedly initiated it in a series of highly influential books published in late 1960s. These books of Derrida focuses chiefly on language. He contends that the traditional and metaphysical way of reading makes a number of false assumptions about the nature of text.

A traditional reader believes that language is capable of expressing ideas without changing them and that is the hierarchy of language, writing is secondary to speech and that, the author of a text is a source of its meaning. Derrida constructive style of reading subverts these assumptions and challenges of the ideas that the text has an unchanging, unified meaning. Western culture has tended to assume that speech is a clear and direct way to communicate but Derrida questions this assumptions. As a result, the author's intention in speaking can not be unconditionally accepted. This multiplies the number of facts of a text.

Psychoanalytical Criticism

The Psycho Analytical School of criticism has exercised a powerful influence on the creative literature of the 20th century in England and America both. Although this approach to literature is not new but it has been popularised and recognised so commonly in the recent years. Freud is the father of this school and Jung also contributed a lot.

Though he was the follower of Freud to a large extent, he disagreed with him in certain aspects. Later, the French writer Lacan came forward with his own concept and thus many interpretation were made but Freud still remains the most powerful influence.

His potential influence can be judged easily if we examine the contemporary literature- the novel and poetry equally. Everywhere we found a stamp of these psychological concepts on various works. In his theory of psychology, Freud was chiefly interested in the unconscious and attempts scientifically the relationship between the unconscious impulses and the conscious mind which led him to literature.

In their imaginative writing, great writers found an outlet to their repressed erotic impulses and great literature presents the desire of their unconscious mind transformed and distanced. According to him, the most powerful impulse in man was his tendency to make love to his mother for which he treats his father as his rival. This feeling has been termed as Oedipus Complex.

The man or woman may not be conscious of this impulse as Oedipus himself was unaware, but literature realise it because it is common to all. This theory of Freud has certain impact on works like *Sons and Lovers* by DH Lawrence and he must have had Freud in his mind. There is undoubtedly no definite link between the two and that it was merely Freud's influence to depict his theory in this work. Lawrence shows the love of Paul to his mother just like that of lover to his beloved.

He sleeps with her and caresses her which naturally results in his enmity with his father who ill treats her. It is this emotional attachment that he fails to establish relations with any other woman. Even his mother is suffering from the same instinct and does not tolerate his relation with any other girl. The behaviour of moral himself has posed a serious psychological problem.

The discoveries in the field of psycho analysis have made a very significance and powerful impact on literature. They insist upon primeval human emotions which are buried within him.

This forms one of the major themes of modern literature. A psycho analyst regards human personality as a vital and dynamic phenomenon. He treats the human personality as a battle field where there is an endless struggle between his instinct and impulses.

Psycho analytical critical literature can be divided mainly in different categories for the purpose of analysis. Most of the psycho analytical criticism in literature is of two types which are quite limited. The process of psycho analysis of an author is a quite different work which creates some criticism for itself as the author's work itself.

The psycho analytical criticism of the content of the characters and their motivation has a limited value due to their respective circumstances which they face in their life while producing a particular work. Freud's own works were based only on these two types of criticism. His essays either depict the author's psycho analytical ability to express himself or the symptoms of the unconscious in art. In both these cases, the importance of art is valued.

Two important critics Kenneth Burke and Harold Bloom are deeply indebted to Freud. Bloom actually rewrites the literary history in Oedipus Complex form. He says that the meaning of a poem can be expressed by the way of another poem, hence we can say that the poem itself is the cause of generation of another poem.

Bloom is a far sighted critic with the creative mind because he reads a historic work as a heroic battle or just as a drama based on psychology. Almost all the psycho analytical critics-Freud, Hegel and Lacan particularly have been instrumental in describing the language structure in the formation of interpretation of the subject as well as the interdiction or repudiation of otherness.

Lacan has emphasised language as the means through which the subjective identity, social reality and the Freudian unconscious are structured and negotiated. Moreover, although classical psycho analytical discourse tends to emphasise the sexual difference over and above other varieties of differences, it maintains the significant relations to Post Colonial theory. No humanists theory which neglect the values of jealousy, guilt and aggression can be widely accepted by the human as modern. Thus, psycho analytical trend has become a very important branch of Modern Critical theories.

Structuralism

The present linguistics have posed an important question whether criticism is being called upon to organise its structuralist vocation in structural method. In fact, literature is primarily a work of language and structuralism is pre-eminently a linguistic method. Sound, form, words and sentences constitute the common object of the linguistic. However, the word 'structure' used in different meanings in different fields, is applied in literature only to the structure of language.

It is a system of arrangement in totality and the structuralist generally observes the analytical method. "Their stance is still the traditional stance of objectivity, their goal of traditional goal of truths". Culler has explained structuralism in very great detail. He tells that Barthes once defined structuralism as the 'most specialised' and 'consequently most relevant version'.

He considered it a method for the study of cultural artefacts derived from the method of contemporary linguistics. There are two possible ways of using linguistics methods in the study of literature.

The first would be to describe in linguistic terms the language of literary texts. There is second approach and it is take linguistics as a model which indicates how one might go about constructing a poetics which stands to literature as linguistic stands to language. For this kind of structuralism only a few fundamental principles of linguistics are directly relevant.

The structural study of poetic language and of the form of literary expression in general cannot, in fact, reject the analysis relations between code and message. The structuralism is not confined to counting feet and to observing the repetition of phonemes, it must also attack semantic phenomena which constitute the essence of poetic language and more generally the problems of literary semiology.

In fact, structuralism and its close relation with semiology are based on two fundamental insights. The first is that social and cultural phenomena do not have essence but are defined by a network of relations, both internal and external. Structuralism studies the structure or systems of relations by which cultural objects are defined and distinguished from one another, semiology studies cultural objects are signs that carry the meanings. But it is extremely important not to make the distinction, not to try to separate the two enterprises since one entails the other where a profitable study of literature is concerned.

Structuralism as a method is based on the study of structures wherever they occur. Structuralism ought to be on its own ground. Moving from language to literature, we find an analogous situation if one has no knowledge of literature and indeed no acquaintance with the concept of literature. If presented with a poem, he would be quite baffled. He would understand word and sentences but he would not know what this strange thing was. Just as the task of linguistic is to make explicit the system of a language which make linguistic communication possible, so in the case of literature, a structuralist poetic must enquire what knowledge must be postulated to account for our ability to read and understand literary works. Structuralism leads us to think of the poem not as a self- contained but as a sequence which has meaning only in relation to literary system, or rather to the institution of literature which guides the reader. The sense of a poem's completeness is a function of the totality of the interpretive process. We should also take care of the conventions which are assumed by the writer.

The French psychologist Lacan, while defining the human consciousness, has given us significant structuralist notation that has influenced the structuralist activity of our time. In fact, in his opinion, structuralist is the outcome of linguistic foundation and Culler's essay *Structuralism and Literature* is the most comprehensive discussion on this problem and mode of literature.

EXAM BASED QUESTIONS

1 Who wrote 'The New Criticism', giving the movement its name?

(a) John Crowe Ransom (b) Manrve C Beardsley
(c) Aristotle (d) Spenser

2 What do Wimsatt and Beardsley rail against in 'The Intentional Fallacy'?

(a) The idea that authors are the ultimate source of meaning.
(b) Close reading
(c) Reading poems as poems
(d) Watching movie adaptations of novels

3 According to the title of his well-known work, what was William Empson analysing?

(a) 13 ways of looking at a blackbird
(b) Seven types of ambiguity
(c) Sixteen candles
(d) Hundreds of soap operas

4 In which work would you learn about 'the heresy of paraphrase'?

(a) Cleanth Brook's 'The Well Wrought urn'
(b) Yvor Winters' Poetry
(c) James Joyce's Ulysses
(d) William Empson's 'Seven Types of Ambiguity'

5 What major work of New Criticism became a standard textbook?

(a) Understanding poetry, by Cleanth Brooks and Robert Penn Warson
(b) The new criticism by John Crowe Ransom
(c) Miss Emily and the bibliographer by Allen tate
(d) The Intentional Fallacy by Wimsatt and Beardsley

6 What method is closely associated with New Criticism?

(a) Close reading
(b) Analysing how texts reflects their historical moment
(c) Exposing power relations
(d) Over-reading

7 What were New Criticism reacting against?

(a) Feminist readings of texts
(b) Marxism
(c) Historical and biographical readings of texts
(d) Oprah's book club

8 Which genre of the new critics must enjoy analysing?

(a) Novels (b) Poetry (c) Essays (d) Romance novels

9 If you are reading like a new critic, what sort of things are you looking for?

(a) Ambiguity, tension, irony, paradox, technique, form
(b) Clues to the author's love life, dreams and relationship to his/her parents
(c) Hints about the author's politics
(d) Evidence for what life was like back in the days

10 What essay title sounds most like a New Critic writing?

(a) How victorian readers 'responded to marriage plots'
(b) Ambiguity and irony in William Carlos William poetry
(c) Sewers and Dumpsters Modern waste collection
(d) Live in the Elizabeth court: poetic clues to the queen's preference

11 The linguistic generally associated with the initiation of 'structuralism' as a movement is:

(a) Ferdinand de Sassure (b) Simon Blackburn
(c) Noam Chomsky (d) Levi-Starus

12 Structuralism originated in

(a) 1890s (b) 1900s
(c) 1960s (d) 1970s

13 The observation that structuralism is 'belief that the phenomenon of human life are not intelligible except though their interrelations' was made by-

(a) Jacques Derrida (b) Simon Blackmur
(c) Vladmir Propp (d) Claude Levi-Strauss

14 France saw a particular rise in structuralism in:

(a) 1960s (b) 1900s (c) 1970s (d) 1930s

15 Consider the following statements about structuralism:

1. **Structuralism got spread all over the world following a rise in its importance in France**
2. **Structuralism is related to criticism in all fields of literature and painting**
3. **Structuralism began in 1960s**
4. **Structuralism tries to identify some already tentum structures in all new creations**

Codes

(a) 1, 2 and 3 (b) 1, 3 and 4
(c) 3 and 4 (d) 1 and 4

16 Which of the following critics is not considered to have deart basically with structuralism?

(a) Jacques Derrida (b) Vladmir Propp
(c) Claude Levi-Strauss (d) Roman Jacobson

17 The literary movement that began in response to structuralism was

(a) Romanticism
(b) Colonialism
(c) Post-structuralism
(d) Post-colonialism

18 Post-structuralism particularly observes the following short-coming in structuralism.

(a) The structure it considered were not credible
(b) The structure it includes are not self-sufficient
(c) It overlooked a number of basic structures
(d) The theory of structure of itself was not credible

19 Which of the following critics is associated with post-structuralism rather than structuralism?

(a) Michel Foucault (b) Vladmir Propp
(c) Jacques Lacan (d) Roman Jacobson

20 Consider the following statements about structuralism.

1. It was a movement concerned to intellect
2. It believed in identifying the structures in products like texts
3. It was used in number of fields like linguistics, psychology, anthropology etc
4. It came into prominence with the works of Jacque Derrida

Codes

(a) 1, 2 and 3 (b) 1, 2, 3 and 4
(c) 3 and 4 (d) 2, 3 and 4

21 The 'Gang of Four' regarding structuralism did not include:

(a) Levi-Strauss (b) Lacan (c) Barthes (d) Prop

22 Feminism has been defined as asking new questions of old texts by

(a) Lois Tyson (b) Lisa Tursle
(c) Margarate Fuller (d) George Eliot

23 'The madwoman in the Attic' (1979) is written by

(a) Sandra Gilbert and Susan Gubar
(b) Sandra Gilbert and George Eliot
(c) Susan Gubar
(d) Susan Gubar and Lisa Tursle

24 Which of these is not a phase suggested by showalter regarding women's writing?

(a) The Feminist Phase (b) The Feminism phase
(c) The female phase (d) The feminine phase

25 The Mad-women in Attic is

(a) Barthes Jenkins (b) Jane Eyre
(c) Thomfield (d) Charlotte Brante

26 The Madwomen thesis generally suggests that

(a) Women are considered mad by men
(b) The frustration felt by women due to gender discrimination make them feel like being mad
(c) The suppression of their creation power by society in a subversive manner
(d) In the past, the only way for women to fight gender discrimination had been to behave like mad women

27 Consider the following sentences regarding feminism.

1. Feminism believe that women are not familiar to English language as men are.
2. Feminism believes that the way women writers used language was different than the way male writers did.
3. Feminism believes that women use language in a comparatively degressive manner
4. Feminism believes that language of women writers gives full expression to their ego.

Codes

(a) 1 and 4 (b) 1, 2 and 3
(c) 2 and 3 (d) All of these

28 The most obvious connection that feminism has observed between myth and women's social condition is

(a) Myth has contributed in establishing social names tha could help men to dominate women
(b) Myth has lent support to women in fighting against th gender discrimination
(c) Change in myth has been the biggest support to wome for changing their status in the society
(d) Myth has always been indifferent to discriminatio faced by women at the hands of men.

29 Who is associated to the famous lecture 'The classical Feminist Tradition'?

(a) Elaine showlater (b) Germaine Greer
(c) Kate millet (d) Paul Fry

30 The female Eunuch was published in

(a) 1970s (b) 1960s (c) 1965 (d) 1975

31 Identify the proper chronological order of the following works concerned to feminism

(a) Thinking about women; sexual politics, The Fema Eunuch; A Literature of their own
(b) Sexual politics; Thinking about women; The fema Eunuch The literature of their own
(c) Thinking about women; The Female Eunuch; literature of their own; sexual politics
(d) The Female Eunuch; A literature of their ow Thinking about women; Sexual Politics

32 The concept of gynocriticism is believed to be pioneered by which of the following works?

(a) The Female Eunuch (b) A Literature of their ow
(c) Thinking about women (d) Sexual politics

33 'A Literature of their own', was published in

(a) 1970s (b) 1980s
(c) 1986 (d) 1977

34 Which of the following has not been particularly part of Feminism as a literary movement of any stage?

(a) Treatment of female characters by male writers
(b) Treatment of female characters by female writers
(c) Role played by women in the publishing industry
(d) The influence of male writers on the work of fema writers

35 EO Wilson's term 'biophilia' means

(a) A love of life (b) Fear of death
(c) Rejection of nature (d) Appreciation of boom

36 Ecocriticism

(a) Is sometimes called "green cultural studies"
(b) Is criticism concentrating on the relationship betwee literature and natural environment
(c) Is one of the fastest growing critical approach
(d) All of the above

37 The inventor of the 'dialectic'
(a) Karl Marx
(b) George Wilhelm Friedrich Hegel
(c) Michel Foucault (d) Theodore Dreiser

38 The leading literary Darwinist today is
(a) E.O. Wilson (b) Joseph Carroll
(c) Tim Harvath (d) Colleen McCruise

39 Literary Darwinism is opposed to
(a) Poststructuralism (b) Ecofeminism
(c) Deconstruction (d) Both (a) and (b)

40 "Hegemony" as defined by Antonio Gramsci
(a) Means how dominant groups maintain their power
(b) Can be imposed by those in in power in such a way as to make those beneath them feel they have free choice
(c) Reflects a socialist worldwide
(d) Both (a) and (b)

41 Who composes the behaviour of apes to characters in a Shakespeare play?
(a) Ian McEwan (b) Joseph Carroll
(c) Daniel Nettle (d) Charles Darwin

42 What is the difference between old 'historicism' and 'New historicism'?
(a) They are essentially the same
(b) The 'old historicism' concerns itself only with high culture
(c) 'Old historicism' is merely background and context, literature only reflecting only history, while 'new historicism' argues that literature and history influence each other
(d) The new historicism reflects everything about the 'old historicism'

43 George Lukacs preferred literature that
(a) Reflected social realism
(b) Employed modernist technique such as stream-of-consciousness narration
(c) Was intended as 'art for art's sake'
(d) Presented only characters trapped in the social order

44 Who was it, influenced by Mathew Arnold, who sought to remake the British education system so that literary knowledge could be distributed more widely, especially in the working classes?
(a) FR Leavis (b) Karl Marx
(c) Raymond Williams (d) Louis Althussis

45 Who is the critic most interested in how those in power in his books Discipline and punish: The birth of the prism and the history of sexuality'?
(a) Michel Foucault (b) Stephen Greenblatt
(c) Jacques Lacan (d) Antonio Gramsci

46 Like literary Darwinists, ecocritics propose-
(a) Their approach as the essential matrix for all literary study
(b) T locate human values in nature
(c) An end to literary criticism
(d) Both (a) and (b)

47 Some critics are suspicious of literary Darwinism because
(a) Darwinism was reinterpreted along racial lines by Herbert Spencer
(b) It calls up such evil as genetic determinism and eugenics
(c) It reduces art of genetics
(d) All of the above

48 The ideas of the 'political unconscious' and 'subject position' are those of
(a) Pierre Bourdieu (b) Antonio Gramsci
(c) Raymond William (d) Frederic Jameson

49 Foucault's 'episteme' is
(a) The universal meaning of a symbol
(b) The board 'totalizing' function of culture observation in literary texts
(c) A fragment of history (d) An unusual phoneme

50 Literary Darwinist argue that
(a) Evaluation precedes, and to some extent, explains discourse
(b) Literature has an adaptive function for evolutionary fitness, including sexual competition
(c) All human beings share the need to create cognitive order
(d) All of the above

51 British cultural materialism claims that
(a) Culture is the property of the working class as well as the upper class
(b) Culture is the needless abstraction
(c) Only those with proper education have culture
(d) Culture is the opiate of the masses

52 The 'commodity fetish' according to Marx, is:
(a) The desire for luxury goods
(b) A rejection of consumerism
(c) When exchange value takes on a power of its own
(d) Restricted to upper classes

53 The concept of 'consilience' or 'the unity of knowledge' was the idea of:
(a) Joseph Carroll
(b) David P. Barash
(c) Charles Darwin
(d) EO Wilson

54 Archetypal criticism.
(a) Deals with the similarities od patterns in the literature of widely diverse culture
(b) Focuses on a reader active engagement with a piece of print or non-print
(c) Examines how differing religious beliefs ethnicities, identifications, political beliefs and individual view points affects how text are created and interpreted
(d) Focuses between relationships between genders

55 Who introduced the term 'New criticism'?
(a) FR Leavis (b) IA Richard
(c) John Crowe Ransom (d) TS Eliot

56 The word archetype means
(a) A recurrent symbol or motif in literature
(b) A widely heard but fixed and oversimplified image or idea of a particular type of person or thing
(c) A type of arc
(d) Having distinctive qualities of a particular type of person or thing

57 A person might use archetypal criticism when reading stories from different
(a) Cultures (b) Environment
(c) Myth (d) Motif

58 Choose an answer that might be a motif in different archetypal writings motif- a recurring word, characters, object or idea in literary works.
1. A heroes journey
2. The evil-step mother
3. A wicked witch of the west
4. The mystical cave

Codes
(a) 1 and 2
(b) 1, 2 and 3
(c) Only 1
(d) None of the above

59 What would be an example of archetypal criticism in movies?
(a) The story of the guy getting the girl
(b) The story of a guy stuck in the maze
(c) The story of a sibling getting stuck in their closet
(d) The story of a whale that eats people

60 The literary movement, according to Eagleton, "brought structuralist and post-structuralist criticism to birth in the first place"?
(a) Post-modernism (b) Modernism
(c) Romanticism (d) Surrcalism

61 In American deconstruction, why does literary criticism became an 'ironic', uneasy business?
(a) Because it lays bare the physicality of meaning
(b) Because it lays bare the illusoriness of meaning
(c) Because it lays bare the permanence of meaning
(d) Because it lays bare the temporality of meaning

62 Eagleton argues that for Stanley fish, what a 'text' does to us is a matter of what we do to what?
(a) To the author (b) To the reader
(c) To the text (d) To the critics

63 For Eagleton, what are the two ways in which literary theory can have a distinct purpose and identity?
(a) It can define itself in terms of methods of inquiry and the manner of enquiry
(b) It can define itself in terms of methods of inquiry or the object being required into
(c) It can define itself in terms of other methods of inquiry
(d) It can define itself in terms of inquiry or the object being required into

64 In psychoanalytic treatment, what happens during transference?
(a) The analyst 'transfers' on to the patient the diagnosis
(b) The patient 'transfers' on to the analyst feelings she or he experiences
(c) The patient 'transfers' on to the analyst the conflicts she or he experiences
(d) The analyst 'transfers' on to the patient the conflict he or she suffers from

65 According to Eagleton, what is the disadvantage of claiming literature as more valuable and rewarding than other texts?
(a) Because it is no longer true
(b) Because it is untrue
(c) Because it is true
(d) Because it is partly true

66 According to Eagleton, structuralism has proved that there is nothing .... about codes.
(a) Progressive (b) Evaluation
(c) Innocent (d) Guilty

67 According to Eagleton, why is Shakespeare considered great literature?
(a) Because masses constitute him as a great literature
(b) Because the literary institution constitute him as great literature
(c) Because he is better than other literature
(d) Because he is great literature

68 According to Eagleton, Stanley Fish model excludes the possibility that there is a .... of interpretations.
(a) Dominance (b) Acceptance
(c) Struggle (d) Rejection

69 In structuralism, the relationship between the sign and what it refers to is what?
(a) Opposite (b) Necessary (c) Arbitrary (d) Identica

70 What is the name of the American hermeneuticist E. D. Hirsch Jr's famous 1967 books?
(a) Meaning or method (b) Feminist
(c) Post-structuralist (d) De-constructive

71 The German philosopher Edmund Husserl argued that object can be regarded as things .... by consciousness
(a) Understood (b) Realized
(c) Evaluated (d) Intended

72 According to Eagleton, in the romantic aestheti theory the meaning of the word literature became what?
(a) Psychology (b) Realism
(c) Communism (d) Ideology

73 What is the name Edmund Husseal gave to his philosophical method ?
(a) Reception theory (b) Phenomenology
(c) Hermeneutics (d) New criticism

74 Eagleton argues that reading literature in a new critical way was a recipe for
(a) Political progress (b) Political ambition
(c) Political consciousness (d) Political inertia

75 Why do feminist embrace the work of Jacques Lacan despite the fact that he was contemporary of the women's movement?
(a) Because lacan embraced Freudianism
(b) Because lacan taught Freudianism
(c) Because lacan re-write Freudianism
(d) Because lacan rejects Freudianism

76 What are Northrop Frye's three re-current patterns of symbolism in literature?
(a) Apocalyptic, demonic, analogical
(b) Tragic, comic, romantic
(c) Analogical, demonic, tragic
(d) Comic, apocalyptic, roamantic

77 What is the name of the author whose story "Sarrasine" Roland Barthes examines in
(a) Balzae (b) Tolstoy (c) Nobokov (d) Eliot

78 "New criticism" was the idealogy of an ...., ... intelligentsia who reinvented in literature that is not at the same time a record of barbarism?
(a) Aggressive, violent (b) Educated, grounded
(c) Uprooted, defensive (d) Apathetic, placid

79 Who said, "there is no cultural document that is not at the same time record of barbarism"?
(a) Karl Marx (b) Michel Faucault
(c) Walter Benjamin (d) Julia Kristeva

80 According to Eagleton, what is the oldest form of literary criticism?
(a) Religion (b) Rhetoric
(c) Sociology (d) Philosophy

81 According to Eagleton, structuralism is a .... of inquiry, whereas semiotics is a .... of study?
(a) Method, field (b) Manner, field
(c) Type, manner (d) Field, type

82 Concept of cultural materialism was given by Marvin Harris in ....?
(a) 1968, 1979 (b) 1958, 1965
(c) 1969, 1971 (d) 1966, 1970

83 In the following statement, what foes the word "Panoptic", means.
Michel Faucault's pervasive image of the state is that of 'panoptic'?
(a) All knowing (b) All-mighty
(c) All-seeing (d) All hearing

84 .... read major works from an eccentric point of view and extend the application of concepts to area other than the natural world
(a) Ecofeminists (b) Ecocentrists
(c) Ecocritics (d) Ecologists

85 According to "psychoanalytic criticism" many of Sigmund Freud's ideas concern aspects of
(a) Death (b) Sexuality
(c) Conservation (d) Humanity

86 Who was the major theorist of postmodernism and French writer of the book 'simulations'?
(a) Jean Francis Lyolard (b) Jean Baudrillard
(c) Andre Gide (d) Stephen Mallame

87 According to post-modernism 'the modern began with the"
(a) Enlightment (b) Innocence
(c) Reason (d) Mythology

88 The British Critics .... described cultural materialism as 'a politicized form of historiography'.
(a) W. Samerset Maugham (b) Charles de Lint
(c) Robertson Davies (d) Graham Halderners

89 "stylistics" states that the stop-start quality can be renamed and cohesion achievers by what linguistic call 'pronominalization' using
(a) Adjectives (b) Verbs
(c) Pronoun (d) nouns

90 Author Peter Barry claimed to properly inaugurated post-colonial criticism was Edward Said ...., which Was a specific exposure of the Eurocentric universalism.
(a) Existentalism (b) Pre-Eurocentric
(c) Phallocentricism (d) Orientalism

91 Psychoanalytic criticism discussed that the use by the conscious of these linguistic means of self-expression in part of .... evidence for the claim that unconscious is structured like a language.
(a) Lacan (b) Washington
(c) Murray (d) Barry

92 Which of the following terms best fit the following definition: a form of literary criticism which uses same of the techniques of psychoanalysis in the interpretation of literature?
(a) Applied criticism
(b) Psychoanalytical criticism
(c) Practical criticism
(d) Impressionistic criticism

93 Jean Baudrillard was associated with what is usually known as
(a) The loss of the real
(b) The forfeut of the real
(c) The gain of the real
(d) The knowledge of the real

94 Another term for ecocriticism is
(a) Green studies (b) Earth studies
(c) Wind studies (d) Water studies

95 Ecocritics emphasizes writers who highlight as their subject matter.
(a) Animals (b) Children
(c) Nature (d) Feminists

96 Feminists criticism informs the reader that "for her notion of the basic opposition between semiotic and the symbolic 'kristeva' was indebted to Jacques lacan and his distinction between two realms, the .... and the ....
(a) Story, discourse
(b) Syntagm, sytagmatic
(c) Imagery, symbolisc
(d) Reference, referent

97 Which of the following terms is about 'lexical items' (words) which cross the boundaries between sentences, binding them into a single continues utterance even though they are grammatically separate sentances?
(a) Cohesicm (b) Trope
(c) Syntax (d) Trace

98 According to Plato, 'a state of language anterior to the word' is called
(a) Semiotic (b) Organic forms
(c) Surrealism (d) Chora

99 .... is a co-founder of ecocriticism with Harold Fromna that developed in the early 1990's in the USA.
(a) Frank Herbert (b) Cheryll Glotfelty
(c) Robert Heinlein (d) George Orwell

100 Which of the following people broke away from feminism and made new allegiances, in particular with gay men rather than with other women?
(a) Muriel Spark (b) Paulina Palmer
(c) Anne Koedt (d) Bonnie Zimmerman

101 According to the 'Marxist criticism', what was the name of the group that had flourished in the 1920s until disbanded by the party even though their work was not strictly Marxist in spirit.
(a) Russian Formalists (b) German Formalists
(c) Irish Formalists (d) Korean Formalists

102 According to 'Narratology', ... focalization is classic narration called omniscient narration.
(a) Internal (b) External
(c) Spiritual (d) Zero

103 Which of the following works of S Eliot was a collage of juxtaposed, incomplete stories or fragments of stories, according to post-modernism.
(a) Prufrock and other observation
(b) The waste land
(c) The use of poetry and the use of criticism
(d) Essays ancient and modern

Directions (Q. Nos. 104-108) *Read the following passage given below and answer the questions that follow.*

It would be more accurate to say that discourse, rather than language, plays a crucial part in structuring our experience. The whole idea of 'language' is something of a fiction: what we normally refer to as 'language' can more realistically be seen as heterogeneous collection of discourses. Each of us has access to a range of discourses, and it is these different discourses which gives us access to, or enable us to perform, different 'selves'. A discourse can be conceptualised as a "system of statements which cohere around common meaning and values". So *e.g.* in contemporary Britain there are discourses which can be labelled 'conservative'- *i.e.* discourses emphasise values and meanings where the status quo is cherished and there are discourses which can be labelled 'Patriarchal'- that is discourse which emphasis meanings and values which assume the superiority of males. Dominant discourses such as these appear 'natural': they are powerful precisely because they are able to make invisible the fact that they are just one among many different discourses.

Theorising language in this way is still new in linguistic (to the extent that many linguists would not regard analysis in terms of discourses as being part of linguistics). One of the advantages is talking about discourses rather than about language is that the concept 'discourse' acknowledges the value-laden nature of language. There is no neutral discourse: whenever we speak we have to choose in between different systems of meaning, different sets of values. This process allows us to show how language is implicated in our construction of different 'shelves': different discourses position us in a different way in relation to the world.

104 Which of the following is true in the light of passage?
(a) Language is inaccurate
(b) Discourse is accurate
(c) Language comprises discourse
(d) Discourse comprises language

105 What words/phrases suggest the plurality of discourse in this passage?
1. Different shelves
2. Range
3. System of statements
4. Heterogeneous collection

Codes
(a) 1 and 4 (b) 2 and 3 (c) 3 and 4 (d) Only 1

106 Having called language 'something of a fiction', how does the author suggest its opposite? By using the phrase
(a) Conceptualised as a system (b) More accurate to say
(c) Range of discourse
(d) More realistically be seen

107 Which among the following statements is not true?
(a) Conservative discourses plead for the status quo
(b) Patriarchal discourses privilege male values
(c) Dominant discourses are natural
(d) Dominant discourses seem natural

108 What does this passage plead for?
(a) Theorising language in a new way
(b) Theorising language in terms of discourses
(c) Studying language as discourse
(d) Studying discourse as a language

ANSWERS

Objective Questions

1. (a)	2. (a)	3. (b)	4. (a)	5. (b)	6. (a)	7. (d)	8. (b)	9. (a)	10. (b)
11. (a)	12. (c)	13. (b)	14. (a)	15. (d)	16. (a)	17. (c)	18. (d)	19. (a)	20. (a)
21. (d)	22. (b)	23. (a)	24. (a)	25. (a)	26. (c)	27. (c)	28. (a)	29. (d)	30. (a)
31. (a)	32. (b)	33. (d)	34. (c)	35. (a)	36. (d)	37. (b)	38. (b)	39. (d)	40. (d)
41. (c)	42. (c)	43. (a)	44. (a)	45. (a)	46. (d)	47. (d)	48. (d)	49. (b)	50. (d)
51. (a)	52. (c)	53. (d)	54. (a)	55. (c)	56. (a)	57. (a)	58. (a)	59. (a)	60. (b)
61. (b)	62. (c)	63. (d)	64. (c)	65. (b)	66. (c)	67. (b)	68. (c)	69. (c)	70. (d)
71. (d)	72. (d)	73. (b)	74. (d)	75. (c)	76. (a)	77. (b)	78. (c)	79. (c)	80. (b)
81. (a)	82. (a)	83. (c)	84. (c)	85. (b)	86. (b)	87. (a)	88. (d)	89. (c)	90. (d)
91. (a)	92. (b)	93. (a)	94. (a)	95. (c)	96. (c)	97. (a)	98. (d)	99. (b)	100. (b)
101. (a)	102. (b)	103. (b)	104. (d)	105. (a)	106. (d)	107. (d)	108. (b)		

Research Methods and Materials in English

Research topics could be from any subject. It is a means of addressing one's curiosity. To begin research, one needs to have a problem, or an issue that sparks off the curiosity and can be turned into a question. This could be achieved from observing the world, professional literature or research done in the concerned area.

Meaning of Research

The English noun 'research' comes from the Middle French 'recerche' (16th century) which goes back to the Latin 'circare' (to go around, to wander, ...). Research is an investigation conducted with an aim to solve a problem. It is similar to the Science projects one conducts in Schools, wherein one attempts to learn something by way of experimenting. In order to start a research, one must have a question, a need to find an answer to something. As defined by Cambridge Dictionary, "a detailed study of a subject, especially in order to discover new information or reach a (new) understanding".

Research is a careful and detailed study into a specific problem, concern, or issue using the scientific method.

Research is undertaken within most professions. More than a set of skills, research is a way of thinking: examining critically the various aspects of your day-to-day professional work; understanding and formulating guiding principles that govern a particular procedure; and developing and testing new theories that contribute to the advancement of your practice and profession. It is a habit of questioning what you do, and a systematic examination of clinical observations to explain and find answers for what you perceive, with a view to instituting appropriate changes for a more effective professional service.

Very little research in the field is pure in nature. *i.e.*, very few people do research in research methodology person. Most research is applied research, which has wide application in many disciplines. Every profession uses research methods in varying amounts in many areas. They use the methods and procedures developed by research methodologists in order to increase understanding in their own profession

In this Chapter

- *Meaning of Research*
- *Literary Research*
- *Research Material*

and to advance the professional knowledge base. It is through the application of research methodology that they strengthen and advance their own profession. Examine your own field. You will find that its professional practice follows procedures and practices tested and developed by others over a long period of time.

It is in this testing process that you need research skills, the developments of which fall in the category of pure research. As a matter of fact, the validity of your findings entirely depends upon the soundness of the research methods and procedures adopted by you. Within any profession, where you directly or indirectly provide a service, such as health (nursing, occupational therapy, physiotherapy, community health, health promotion and public health), education, psychology or social work, the application of research can be viewed from four different perspectives:

Research is one of the ways to find answers to your questions. When you say that you are undertaking a research study to find out answers to a question, you are implying that the process being applied:

- is being undertaken within a framework of a set of philosophies;
- uses procedures, methods and techniques that have been tested for their validity and reliability;
- is designed to be unbiased and objective.

Types of Research

If you examine a research endeavour from the perspective of its application, there are two broad categories: pure research and applied research.

Pure Research It involves developing and testing theories and hypotheses that are intellectually challenging to the researcher but may or may not have practical application at the present time or in the future. Thus such work often involves the testing of hypotheses containing very abstract and specialised concepts. Pure research is also concerned with the development, examination, verification and refinement of research methods, procedures, techniques and tools that form the body of research methodology.

Examples of pure research include developing a sampling technique that can be applied to a particular situation; developing a methodology to assess the validity of a procedure; developing an instrument, say, to measure the stress level in people; and finding the best way of measuring people's attitudes.

Applied Research The knowledge produced through pure research is sought in order to add to the existing body of knowledge of research methods to give rise to the Applied research. In other words, the research techniques, procedures and methods that form the body of research methodology are applied to the collection of information about various aspects of a situation, issue, problem or phenomenon so that the information gathered can be used in other ways – such as for policy formulation, administration and the enhancement of understanding of a phenomenon.

Characteristics of Research

Philosophical orientation may stem from one of the several paradigms and approaches in research – positivist, interpretive, phenomenology, action or participatory, feminist, qualitative, quantitative – and the academic discipline in which one has been trained. Chief characteristics of a research can be summarised as the following:

Validity It can be applied to any aspect of the research process. It ensures that in a research study correct procedures have been applied to find answers to a question.

Reliability It refers to the quality of a measurement procedure that provides repeatability and accuracy.

Unbiased and Objective It means that you have taken each step in an unbiased manner and drawn each conclusion to the best of your ability and without introducing your own vested interest. The author makes a distinction between bias and subjectivity.

Subjectivity It is an integral part of your way of thinking that is 'conditioned' by your educational background, discipline, philosophy, experience and skills. *e.g.* a psychologist may look at a piece of information differently from the way in which an anthropologist or a historian looks at it. Bias, on the other hand, is a deliberate attempt to either conceal or highlight something.

Controlled The concept of control implies that, in exploring causality in relation to two variables, you set up your study in a way that minimises the effects of other factors affecting the relationship.

Rigorous You must be scrupulous in ensuring that the procedures followed to find answers to questions are relevant, appropriate and justified.

Systematic This implies that the procedures adopted to undertake an investigation follow a certain logical sequence. The different steps cannot be taken in a haphazard way. Some procedures must follow others.

Verifiable This concept implies that whatever you conclude on the basis of your findings is correct and can be verified by you and others.

Empirical This means that any conclusions drawn are based upon hard evidence gathered from information collected from real-life experiences or observations.

Critical Critical scrutiny of the procedures used and the methods employed is crucial to a research enquiry. The process of investigation must be foolproof and free from any drawbacks. The process adopted and the procedures used must be able to withstand critical scrutiny.

Objectives of Research

The objective of any research is 'to expand human knowledge'. It helps in giving direction for the research work. This involves basic steps such as exploring, investigating, describing, measuring, etc. If one narrows down this, one finds that research aims to address the question concerned. In other words, it is making a small beginning to something with much larger ending.

Objectives of Research in Research Methodology

The purpose of research is to discover answers to questions through the application of scientific procedures. The main aim of research is to find out the truth which is hidden and which has not been discovered as yet. Though each research study has its own specific purpose, yet these objectives can broadly be summarised as the following

- To gain familiarity with a phenomenon or to achieve new insights into it
- To portray accurately the characteristics of a particular individual, situation or a group
- To determine the frequency with which something occurs or with which it is associated with something else
- To test a hypothesis of a causal relationship between variables

The objectives of any research should always be SMART i.e.

Specific focused and target oriented.

Measurable easy to calculate or count upon pros and cons.

Achievable as per one's means and aspirations.

Realistic as per one's capabilities and limitations.

Timed to be realised in the fixed time frame.

Levels	Nature of Objective	Description
1	Assessment	To observe the situation and infer results
2	Exploration	To discover the truth behind a problem
3	Evaluation	To measure the level of existence
4	Examination	To test the existence
5	Comparison	To compare and contrast between given variables
6	Estimation	To project probable level of happening
7	Propagation	To declare a concept, theory, system or model

To sum up, the objective of research is a systematic investigation of a phenomenon which involves answering questions such as

Why?

How?

What?

When?

Who?

Where?

Research Approaches

Research approach means, 'a systematic plan or strategies that one uses to achieve particular objectives'. It is based on the nature of the research problem.

On the Basis of Mode of Enquiry Perspective

Another perspective in our typology of research concerns the process you adopt to find answers to your research questions. Broadly, there are two approaches to enquiry

1. The structured approach;
2. The unstructured approach.

Structured Approach In the structured approach everything that forms the research process – objectives, design, sample, and the questions that you plan to ask of respondents – is predetermined.

The unstructured approach, by contrast, allows flexibility in all these aspects of the process. The structured approach is more appropriate to determine the extent of a problem, issue or phenomenon, whereas the unstructured approach is predominantly used to explore its nature, in other words, variation/diversity per se in a phenomenon, issue, problem or attitude towards an issue. *e.g.* if you want to research the different perspectives of an issue, the problems experienced by people living in a community or the different views people hold towards an issue, then these are better explored using unstructured enquiries.

Unstructured Approach To find out how many people have a particular perspective, how many people have a particular problem, or how many people hold a particular view, you need to have a structured approach to enquiry. Before undertaking a structured enquiry, in the author's opinion, an unstructured enquiry must be undertaken to ascertain the diversity in a phenomenon which can then be quantified through the structured enquiry.

Both approaches have their place in research. Both have their strengths and weaknesses. Therefore, you should not 'lock' yourself solely into a structured or unstructured approach.

On the Basis of Objectives Perspective

If you examine a research study from the perspective of its objectives, broadly a research endeavour can be classified as descriptive, correlational, explanatory or exploratory.

Descriptive Approach A research study classified as a descriptive study attempts to describe systematically a situation, problem, phenomenon, service or programme, or provides information about, say, the living conditions of a community, or describes attitudes towards an issue. *e.g.* it may attempt to describe the types of service provided by an organisation, the administrative structure of an organisation, the living conditions of Aboriginal people in the outback, the needs of a community, what it means to go through a divorce, how a child feels living in a house with domestic violence, or the attitudes of employees towards management.

The main purpose of such studies is to describe what is prevalent with respect to the issue/problem under study.

Correlational Approach The main emphasis in a correlational study is to discover or establish the existence of a relationship/association/interdependence between two or more aspects of a situation. What is the impact of an advertising campaign on the sale of a product? What is the relationship between stressful living and the incidence of heart attack? What is the relationship between fertility and mortality? What is the relationship between technology and unemployment? What is the relationship between a particular literary work and the generation of its readers? What is the effect of a health service on the control of a disease, or the home environment on educational achievement?

These studies examine whether there is a relationship between two or more aspects of a situation or phenomenon and, therefore, are called correlational studies.

Explanatory Approach Explanatory research attempts to clarify why and how there is a relationship between two aspects of a situation or phenomenon. This type of research attempts to explain, e.g. why stressful living results in heart attacks; why a decline in mortality is followed by a fertility decline; or how the home environment affects children's level of academic achievement.

Exploratory Approach The fourth type of research, from the viewpoint of the objectives of a study, is called exploratory research. This is when a study is undertaken with the objective either to explore an area where little is known or to investigate the possibilities of undertaking a particular research study. When a study is carried out to determine its feasibility it is also called a feasibility study or a pilot study. It is usually carried out when a researcher wants to explore areas about which s/he has little or no knowledge. A small-scale study is undertaken to decide if it is worth carrying out a detailed investigation.

On the basis of the assessment made during the exploratory study, a full study may eventuate. Exploratory studies are also conducted to develop, refine and/or test measurement tools and procedures. Although, theoretically, a research study can be classified in one of the above objectives–perspective categories, in practice, most studies are a combination of the first three; that is, they contain elements of descriptive, correlational and explanatory research.

Significance of Research

Research is undertaken to satisfy one's curiosity. It may be done to prove a theory and contribute to further the existing knowledge in a field of study.

Following points highlight the significance of research

- To facilitate learning and add on to the existing knowledge.
- To raise public awareness and to understand various issues
- To aid in business success.
- To support truths and prove the lies.
- To find and seize opportunities.
- To inculcate love for reading, writing, analyzing and sharing valuable information
- To nourish and exercise the mind

Research holds a different meaning to different people. For some, it is a task to be 'avoided' while there are those who would do it to secure a job or a promotion. Yet, there are some who like to learn, even though they may be ordinary people with no connection to the academics; for them research is not just important, but a need.

Research Process

Research process contains a series of closely related activities which has to carry out by a researcher. Research process requires patients. There is no measure that shows your research is the best. It is an art rather than a science.

You will generally find that you will not usually follow the process stage by stage, but will often move continually back and forth between the elements, or carry out two or more of the elements concurrently, especially if you are undertaking a more interactive, creative or qualitative study. Although different models of the research process exist, each containing different numbers of stages, most include the same general elements.

It is important to remember that these are not isolated, discrete stages, but are actually part of one overall process. As we said earlier, it may also be the case that for certain methodological approaches the order of the stages may be somewhat different; *e.g.* a qualitative research project may involve a continual integration of reviewing the literature and data collection. Alternatively, a grounded approach will generally involve data collection at a much earlier stage, before the theoretical and conceptual frameworks have been fully developed. Thus, you should be prepared to be flexible, depending upon the nature of the research being undertaken. Whatever approach you take, however, it is important that you maintain a sense of coherence within the overall research project, or what some refer to as a 'golden thread', or 'vertical thread'.

This thread should be the research question, and everything within the research process should be related to answering that question.

Following are the main steps in social or business research process.

- Selection of Research Problem
- Extensive Literature Survey
- Making Hypothesis
- Preparing the Research Design
- Sampling
- Data Collection
- Data Analysis
- Hypothesis Testing
- Generalisation and Interpretation
- Preparation of Report

Selection of Research Problem

The selection of topic for research is a difficult job. When we select a title or research statement, then other activities would be easy to perform. So, for the understanding thoroughly the problem it must have to discuss with colleagues, friend, experts and teachers. The research topic or problem should be practical, relatively important, feasible, ethically and politically acceptable.

Literature Review or Extensive Literature Survey

After the selection of research problem, the second step is that of literature mostly connected with the topics. The availability of the literature may bring ease in the research. For this purpose academic journals, conference and government reports and library must be studied.

Making Hypothesis

The development of hypothesis is a technical work depends on the researcher experience. The hypothesis is to draw the positive and negative cause and effect aspects of a problem. Hypothesis narrows down the area of a research and keep a researcher on the right path.

Preparing the Research Design

After the formulation of the problem and creating hypothesis for it, research design is to prepare by the researcher. It may draw the conceptual structure of the problem. Any type of research design may be made, depend on the nature and purpose of the study. Daring R. Design the information about sources, skill, time and finance is taken into consideration.

Sampling

The researcher must design a sample. It is a plan for taking its respondents from a specific areas or universe. *The sample may be of two types*

1. Probability Sampling
2. Non-probability Sampling

Data Collection

Data collection is the most important work, is researcher. The collection of information must be containing on facts which is from the following two types of researcher.

1. **Primary Data Collection** Primary data may be from the following.
   - Experiment
   - Questionnaire
   - Observation
   - Interview
2. **Secondary Data Collection** it has the following categories:
   - Review of literature
   - Official and non-official reports
   - Library approach

Data Analysis

When data is collected, it is forwarded for analysis which is the most technical job. Data analysis may be divided into two main categories.

1. **Data Processing** it is sub-divided into the following; Data editing, Data coding, Data classification, Data tabulation, Data presentation, Data measurement.
2. **Data Exposition** Date Exposition has the following sub-categories; description, explanation, narration, conclusion/findings, recommendations/suggestions.

Hypothesis Testing

Research data is then forwarded to test the hypothesis. Do the hypothesis are related to the facts or not? To find the answer the process of testing hypothesis is undertaken which may result in accepting or rejecting the hypothesis.

Generalisation and Interpretation

The acceptable hypothesis is possible for researcher to arrival at the process of generalisation or to make and theory. Some types of research has no hypothesis for which researcher depends upon on theory which is known as interpretation.

Preparation of Report

A researcher should prepare a report for which he has done is his work. He must keep in his mind the following points:

- Report Design in Primary Stages: The report should carry a title, brief introduction of the problem and background followed by acknowledgement. There should be a table of contents, grapes and charts.
- Main Text of the Report: It should contain objectives, hypothesis, explanations and methodology of the research. It must be divided into chapters and every chapter explains separate title in which summary of the findings should be enlisted. The last section would be clearly of conclusions to show the main theme of the R-study.
- Closing the Report: After the preparation of report, the last step in business research process contains of bibliography, references, appendices, index and maps or charts for illustration. For this purpose the information should more clearer.

Terms used in Context of Footnotes and Reference Writing

Ibid It is the abbreviation for the Latin term Ibidem, meaning, the same. It refers to the same author and source (e.g., book and journal) in the immediately preceding reference.

Op,cit. It is the abbreviation for the Latin opus citatum, meaning the work is cited. It refers to the reference listed earlier by the same author.

Loc.cit. It is of Latin origin and abbreviation for loco citato, meaning in the place cited. It is a footnote or endnote term used to repeat the title and page number for a given work.

etal. It refers to, and others; it is used when referring to a number of people.

Method Vs Approach

Approach	Method
Axiomatic	Procedural
A set of correlative assumptions	An overall plane
Within Approach, there can be many methods, for example in linguistics, behaviorism is an approach.	Within Behaviorism, AUDIO LINGUAL METHOD is a method.

Important Terms used in Research Method

Theory

A theory is a scientist's interpretation of the observations about a phenomenon. A theory begins as an educated guess, known formally as a hypothesis. Scientists continue to do research studies to test the hypothesis. However, scientific theories can be tested through research and found to be supported or rejected.

Concept Vs Construct

A concept is an idea that can be generalised or agreed-upon by many people. Examples are satisfaction and risk. A construct is a statement of a concept in a way that is useful for scientific theorising. It is more specific and less abstract than a concept has to be.

Field Study Vs Field Survey

Field Study It includes small sample size with a greater depth of study.

Field Survey It includes a large sample size with a lesser depth of study.

ANOVA

Analysis of variance (ANOVA) is a statistical technique that is used to check if the means of two or more groups are significantly different from each other. ANOVA checks the impact of one or more factors by comparing the means of different samples

Paper

An essay or dissertation read at a seminar or published in a journal is called a 'Paper'. It is either a result of research effort or an intellectual exercise. It includes all the steps of a research process such as literature review, data collection, etc. It usually follows the journal's editorial policy.

Article

Articles are usually informative in nature. They typically address the topic in a general scope as a means of introduction. They may appear in newspaper, magazine, consumer or industry publication.

Meeting

A meeting is an assembly of people whether it is a symposium, workshop, conference or so on. In a very remote sort of a way, all of them convey the same meaning – that is, people coming together for a purpose.

Symposium

It is usually a formal meeting at which specialists deliver addresses on a topic or on related topic and then answer the questions relating to these topics. It is essentially one in which the participants form an audience and make presentation.

Colloquium

It is usually a formal meeting at which specialists deliver addresses on a topic or on related topic and then answer the questions relating to these topics. A colloquium is targeted to a well-educated but not specialized audience.

Conference

A conference is a meeting of people who confer about a topic. It is a meeting where people come for discussion.

Webinar or Web Conference

They refer to presentations that involve an audio and video component.

Seminar

The word seminar is derived from the Latin word seminarium meaning seed plot. It is a formal presentation by one or more experts to a small group of audience. It can be conducted on recurring or regular basis, monthly or even weekly; there is an invited speaker, and audience is much more technically versed or specific in nature. Seminar focuses on some particular subject in which everyone present is requested to actively participate: Colloquia and seminar both happen in an academic setting.

Workshop

Workshops tend to be smaller and more intense than seminars. This format often involves students practicing their new skills during the event under the watchful eye of an instructor.

Hands-on workshops typically involve participants doing work on a particular issue during the program. The promise is that when they leave, they'll have at least a rough plan or tools in place to address the challenge.

Impact Factor

The impact factor of an academic journal is a measure reflecting the average number of citations to recent articles published in the journal. It reflects the relative importance of a journal within its field. The journals with high impact factors are deemed to be more important than those with lower ones. The h-index is an index that attempts to measure both – the productivity and the impact of the published work of a scientist or a scholar. The g-index is like h-index; it has an averaged citation count.

Literary Research

When you think of research, do you picture scientists in lab coats with test tubes and experimental rats? That is a common. But, as a student, you may have been asked to do literary research, and are probably confused about what that means and how to get started. Well, here we go!

The first thing to think about is that 'literary' relates to literature. Research usually means finding something new: a substance, a formula, or an invention. So, literary research means finding something new within a literary work. It really is that simple. Just like a lab scientist, you are being asked to take what is already there and find a new way to interpret the information, and then discuss it.

The first thing to do is get familiar with what research articles and papers look like. You can find many articles online by simply searching for the title of a work and adding 'academic articles' to your search terms. The research librarian at your school or public library should also be an excellent source for help. This might seem time consuming, but you can't expect to write something if you have no idea what the finished product should look like.

Literary Research is of four kinds

1. Bibliography and Textual Criticism

Textual research is concerned with the establishment of an authoritative text, correction of past editions, chronology, authenticity and attribution. No reader can appreciate a text which is full of errors. Secondly, he/she must know that the text he/she is reading is a genuine one. In modern times, definitive editions are prepared in the personal supervision of the author but in the past it was not so. If we study the editions from 16th to even 19th century editions, we will find striking variations.

In modern times this kind of research has gained more importance. Now, we know the difference between Shakespeare's bad quarto and good folio, the forgeries of the 19th century and the pirated editions of Charles Dickens.

2. Biographical

This type of research though neglected in India, is of first importance in the understanding of an author's mind and art. The task of the biographer is really very difficult. All biographers are not fortunate. A biographer has to collect material from different sources, study the author's published works and unpublished works as well, interview him, meet and collect information from the people close to him, distinguish fact from fiction and after that present the life story, laying more emphasis on the literary side by correlating the important events of his life and time and his works, systematically, chronologically and interestingly.

3. Theoretical

This kind of research can be compared to the basic research in natural and social sciences. Its aim is to propound a theory of literature or modify and improve an already existing one. Coleridge and Wordsworth were the first to propound a theory of literature ably followed by Mathew Arnold. In the 20th century, advances in psychology, linguistics and sociology have forced people to look at literature from quite different angles. The modern critics have defined their approach, methods and technique and analysed literary texts on the basis of theories they have formulated after a wide range of study.

4. Interpretive

This kind of research can be equaled to the applied research in sciences. It analyses, interprets and evaluates a literary text of an author by applying the principles of a particular theory what is important in this kind of research is the systematic approach in the use of principles and use of both inductive and deductive methods. A literary text is original. It can not be replica of the other. As a result the researcher has to modify his methods and techniques occasionally and sometimes to revise the theory he has adopted.

All these kinds of research are complimentary to each other and anyone of them can not be neglected. A literary research is a composite whole and a researcher must know all its aspects. It is only when he chooses a special field that he indulges in any one of these kinds of researches.

Aims and Objectives and Literary Research

Literary Research has four main objectives

Advancement of Knowledge

As Research means going from the known to the unknown. It is essential that the researcher should have a thorough knowledge of what has been done in the past and what is the present status of knowledge in the field of investigation. For example if he wants to do research on Milton, he must study not only all the works of the poet but also the views of different critics from time of Milton to the present day. It also includes the discovery of new facts and a fresh interpretation of the known facts. If we simply describe or repeat what other people have done, we will never be able to do research. In our research of literature, we must refer to both the positive and negative points of our predecessors, correct their ideas and advance our own explanation of the facts that were either overlooked or wrongly observed. It is only the genuineness and originality of interpretation which makes our research a contribution to the total body of knowledge.

Broadening the Mind and Sharpening the Critical Insight of the Researcher

A critical insight can be developed through wide reading and participation in seminars and symposia. A creative writer wields all the knowledge he has gained in his imaginative work. So, a researcher cannot develop a critical insight unless and until he has an elementary knowledge of the natural sciences, social sciences, philosophy, history and religion, moreover a young researcher must be able to make distinction between a good text and a bad text. For example most of the bazaar editions of Shakespeare are full of errors. It will be a good idea to compare bazaar editions with the critical editions. Another thing a researcher should keep in mind is to develop the ability to evaluate and judge the general reliability of published research.

Creation of Genuine and Intelligent Interest in Literature

Research is something more than earning a qualification or fame. Therefore, the aim of literary research is to create in the young researcher a genuine interest in literature. An average reader will not bother why one literary text is superior to other but a researcher, through his understanding and ability to appreciate, is able to explain. For example why George Eliot is superior to Somerset Maugham. He is confident in his analysis because he has read literature with genuine interest, developed his critical insight and analysed both the novelists systematically.

Research Creates a Sense of Belongingness to a Collaborative Community

Research is a collective responsibility shared by all researchers. It is also not limited to any time period. There are thousands of scholars in literature who all belong to a community which is dedicated to the enrichment of culture, to better understanding of man's feelings, emotions and problems through literature.

We can conclude in the words of Dr FR Leavis, "Research should be able to generate in the University a centre of human consciousness, perception, knowledge, judgement and responsibility .... Research must aim at establishing a creative front and doing creative work on the contemporary intellectual frontier."

Qualitative Approach

In Humanities the research methods are generally of Qualitative approach. Some of them are explained below

Archival Methods

This type of research uses archives (a collection of historical documents or records providing information about a place, institution, or group of people) as a primary source of data. It could be quantitative or qualitative. It involves seeking out and extracting evidence from the archival records.

Advantages

- Unobtrusive, Trustworthy Material, Detailing of events;
- A good Archive saves great deal of time and energy.

Disadvantages

- The culture of documentation could be problematic sometimes.
- Archives remain closed for thirty to fifty years.
- Reality is presented as it is perceived by one side.

Autobiographical Methods

The biographical research, a Qualitative method, focuses on biographical identity. It assumes that the link between social structure and individuals could only be understood sufficiently by analyzing the development of the individual's personality in the life course. Biography is understood in terms of a social construct.

This approach is strongly linked to phenomenology and A. Schütz's work. The core idea is that during the life course individuals accumulate diverse biographical experiences into a coherent description of their life course. These experiences are present in our knowledge we use in everyday life, biographical decision-making as well as in the story we present in an interview-situation. Our self-representations or biographical stories are linked to these experiences they are not totally free from our past. The link into the past gives us the possibility to do research on the past life history and the development of the today's self out of the present perspective.

Against this background the research tries to assess the difference between experienced life history (our past experiences) and narrated life story (how we interpret our life from the current point of view) in order to show how their current biography or self-description is determined by the past experiences.

The material for analysis consists of interviews, video recordings, photographs, and a diversity of sources. Prominent influences associated with this method are Alfred Schütz, Peter L. Berger, and Thomas Luckmann and Harold Garfinkel. It is important method used in 'German Sociology'.

The Research Committee of Biography and Society of the International Sociological Association (ISA) was created in 1984 and is dedicated "to help develop a better understanding of the relations between individual lives, the social structures and historical processes within which they take shape and which they contribute to shape, and the individual accounts of biographical experience "(such as life stories or autobiographies)".

Types of Narrative Research

Autobiographies	Biographies	Life Writings
Personal Accounts	Personal Narratives	Narrative Interviews
Personal Documents	Documents of Life	Life Stories and Histories
Ethnohistories	Ethnographies	Autoethnographies
Ethnopsychologies	Person-centred Ethnographies	Popular Memories

Oral History

Oral history is one of the oldest, best known and most often used methods in qualitative research. Oral historians ask people to talk about their overall life experiences or to discuss specific experiences and events in a narrative form, recording this information with either audio or video equipment.

It is defined as "the collection, preservation and dissemination of historical data obtained through planned in-depth, life history interviews." Hubert H Bancroft, the California publisher and historian, deserves credit for taking a big step; he had his assistants interview a number of people who contributed to building the nation including men who'd built the Central Pacific Railroad).

His interviewers took shorthand and their transcripts were deposited in the Bancroft Library (now at the University of California in Berkeley); the immediate purpose was to provide material for Bancroft's multi volume history of western America. In 1948, Allan Nevins, the Columbian University historian, further developed and popularized the idea for the overall benefit of the scholars. He collected spoken reminiscences of political leaders, statesmen and academic scholars for "future historians, for research and as a tool for orally based biography". Nevins recorded and archived historical data often not found in traditional written records. He did this by collecting spoken data with a tape recorder and producing near-verbatim transcripts that preserved the resulting narratives.

Since then the idea has grown and has been adopted by various Institutions nationally and Internationally. Advocates of Oral history method regard it not only as a method of primary source documentation but also as a process for constructing and transmitting history from oral sources.

Visual Methodologies

Visual methodologies are a collection of methods used to understand and interpret images. Visual data can fall into two categories: visual images produced by others and studied by the researcher, and visual representations generated by the researcher.

These methods have been used for a long time in anthropology and sociology; however, they are a relatively new way to research for the majority of disciplines. It is a qualitative research methodology. The images could be in the form of photographs, drawings, paintings, sculptors, cartoons, posters, etc or another form of visual representation.

It can also include three-dimensional objects – material culture. The discipline of cultural studies provides diverse examples of research on both images and material culture.

The origins of image based sociological research are found in the discipline of anthropology at the end of the nineteenth century. Photography was used to provide visual information that could be used to categorise human races, with the data being used to explore theories of physical and social evolution. People such as Australian indigenous groups were studied and classified in research that now seems wholly dated, not to say racist. The technique languished somewhat in the early twentieth century, until social anthropologists including Gregory Bateson and Margaret Mead showed the potential of visual ethnography in their study of culture and social organisation, in their book *Balinese Character*.

Visual methods enhance the richness of data by discovering additional layers of meaning, adding validity and depth, and creating knowledge. They add to traditional methods by capturing more detail and a different kind of data than verbal and written methods. Visual methodologies can be used on almost any population by allowing participants to express their ideas in a nonverbal way but have been under utilised in health research.

Visual methods result in increased trustworthiness of the findings through member checking. We can conclude by saying that an image is never a 'mere' reflection of reality, but rather a multi-layered text that can be used in tandem with other sources of data to obtain a more complex view of the subject of the research.

Discourse Analysis

The word discourse means 'written or spoken communication or debate'. The study and analysis of the use of naturally occurring language in any social context is discourse analysis, and it makes use of various qualitative methods to increase our understanding of human experience. Some of the objects of discourse analysis are discourse, writing, conversation, communicative event. Text linguistics is a closely related field.

The essential difference between discourse analysis and text linguistics is that discourse analysis aims at revealing socio-psychological characteristics of a person/persons rather than text structure. The term first came into general use following the publication of a series of papers by Zellig Harris from 1952 reporting on work from which he developed transformational grammar in the late 1930s.

In the late 1960s and 1970s, a variety of other approaches to a new cross-discipline of Discourse Analysis began to develop in most of the humanities and social sciences concurrently with, and related to, other disciplines, such as semiotics, psycholinguistics, sociolinguistics and pragmatics. Many of these approaches, especially those influenced by the social sciences, favour a more dynamic study of oral talk-in-interaction.

An example is 'conversational analysis', which was influenced by the Sociologist Harold Garfinkel, the founder of Ethnomethodology (a method of sociological analysis that examines how individuals use everyday conversation to construct a common-sense view of the world).

Michel Foucault became one of the key theorists of the subject, especially of discourse, and wrote The Archaeology of Knowledge. In this context, the term 'discourse' no longer refers to formal linguistic aspects, but to institutionalized patterns of knowledge that become manifest in disciplinary structures and operate by the connection of knowledge and power. Since the 1970s, Foucault's works have had an increasing impact especially on discourse analysis in the social sciences. Thus, in English Studies, Michael Foucault is a key figure in developing of this method.

The Uses of Ethnographic Methods in English Studies

Ethnography is a methodology with more than one hundred years of history. It arose in the Western world as a particular form of knowledge about distant cultures (typically non-Western ones) which were impenetrable to analysis consisting only of fleeting contact or brief conversations. After having entered several disciplines of social sciences (anthropology, sociology and psychology), in recent times ethnography has become an important tool also in English Studies as part of interpretive methodologies and research.

The word 'ethnography' is derived from the Greek (ethnos), meaning 'a company, later a people, nation' and -graphy, meaning 'writing'. Herodotus, known as the father of history, had significant works on the cultures of various peoples beyond the Hellenic realm such as the Scythians, which earned him the title 'philobarbarian', and may be said to have produced the first works of ethnography.

Gerhard Friedrich Müller developed the concept of ethnography as a separate discipline whilst participating in the Second Kamchatka Expedition (1733–43) as a professor of history and geography. Whilst involved in the expedition, he differentiated Völker-Beschreibung as a distinct area of study. This became known as 'ethnography,' following the introduction of the Greek neologism ethnographia by Johann Friedrich Schöpperlin and the German variant by AF Thilo in 1767.
August Ludwig von Schlözer and Christoph Wilhelm Jacob Gatterer of the University of Göttingen introduced the term into the academic discourse in an attempt to reform the contemporary understanding of world history.
The ethnographer finds out about other cultures, or features of a culture (for English Studies, this may relate to the cultural dimensions of literature or language) by undertaking prolonged periods in the 'field', participating and observing in all or certain relevant aspects of social life.
Ethnography is 'multimedia research'. It could be both – Qualitative and Quantitative In context of English Studies, it questions how to read and interpret ethnographic texts.
The subject-areas where ethnographic research technique are effectively and broadly classified into two categories

1. **Travel Writings** Within this, it can further be in the form of travelogues, the autobiographical novel, the journalistic narration and the scientific report. Participant observation, a key method of this research method plays a vital role in producing travel accounts.
2. **Reading Groups** There has been a rise in the reading groups and they too offer an insight for research.
3. **Audience Response Criticism** This refers to the audience research in theatre, cinema or at a performance site such as literature festivals. They might be conducted utilising ethnographic methods to create 'micro-ethnographies'. Study of narrowly defined groups is known as Micro-ethnographies. For example, Boa-tribe members. Thus, ethnography refers to both to a process of research and to the research account, the ethnographic report that is compiled from the research. In short, it is both a 'method of study and a result of such study'. Thus both are important – the research process and the research text.

Numbers and Words: Quantitative Methods for Scholars of Texts

In literature the qualitative analysis methods have received more attention than the quantitative methods. This is partly due to the value attached to words and numbers – viewing the former as subjective and the latter as objective.

Number can be used both as interpretive tool and as a means of conveying sets of information not readily producible in another form. In particular, computational methods for calculating frequency with which certain words occur and the context in which they are set; this can be a useful tool for interpreting the meaning of a text and for the purposes of authorship attribution.

Also, statistical methods can be used for displaying information about texts, audiences, the production and consumption of texts and so on. Numerical information needs to be understood as partial and as productive of very specific kinds of information. Thus, in English Studies, quantitative methods can be used to interpret information and the interpretations produced.

Examples of quantitative analysis in English studies

- Detailing of wealth in the 18th century novels
- Use of dates in literary texts and in connection with authors
- Frequency of occurrence of words, phrases or imagery

Quantitative analysis has not had much impact on traditional literary studies. Its practitioners bear some of the responsibility for this lack of impact because all too often quantitative studies fail to address problems of real literary significance, ignore the subject-specific background, or concentrate too heavily on technology or software.

Recently, there has been an increased interest in archives within literary criticism which will almost necessarily lead to the introduction of quantitative methods to help critics cope with the huge amount of electronic text now becoming available. Some quantitative studies have also begun to appear in mainstream literary journals, a sure sign of their growing acceptance. The increasing frequency of collaborations between literary scholars and practitioners of quantitative methods of many kinds also promises to produce more research that strikes an appropriate balance between good methodology and significant results. Prospects for the emergence of quantitative approaches as a respected, if not central, branch of literary studies seem bright.

Textual Analysis

Textual analysis refers to the close reading of a text (including artifacts). It is a staple point of English Studies research. It takes into account the background research into the context of the cultural artifact under scrutiny, the context of its production, its content and its consumption. One must consult the original sources rather than rely on second-hand accounts in this process since all will import certain biases into the material.

Understanding the meaning making differently understood in different historical periods and by different theoreticians, is key to undertaking textual analyses. Meaning-making is a relational process, between cultural artifacts and consumer and between consumers (viewers, readers) and those to whom consumers communicate the meanings they have established for a given artifact. When we perform textual analysis on a text, we make an educated guess at some of the most likely interpretations that might be made of that text.

There is no such thing as a single, 'correct' interpretation of any text. There are large numbers of possible interpretations, some of which will be more likely than others in particular circumstances.

There are five types of texts in content analysis

1. Written text, such as books and papers
2. Oral text, such as speech and theatrical performance
3. Iconic text, such as drawings, paintings, and icons
4. Audio-visual text, such as TV programs, movies, and videos
5. Hypertexts, which are texts found on the Internet

Computers are increasingly used in content analysis to automate the labeling (or coding) of documents. Simple computational techniques can provide descriptive data such as word frequencies and document lengths. Machine learning classifiers can greatly increase the number of texts that can be labeled, but the scientific utility of doing so is a matter of debate.

Interviewing

Interview requires a series of practical skills, a clear understanding of the different kinds of interview one might conduct and their underlying assumptions, knowledge of the different ways in which interviews can be transcribed and how these constitute and influence interpretations of interview material. An interview is a conversation where questions are asked to extract information. Usually, the interviewer is a professional or paid researcher, who may be trained; he/she poses questions to the interviewee, in an alternating series of usually brief questions and answers.

They can be contrasted with focus groups in which an interviewer questions a group of people and observes the resulting conversation between interviewees or surveys which are more anonymous and limit respondents to a range of predetermined answer choices. In phenomenological or ethnographic research, interviews are used to uncover the meanings of central themes in the life world of the subjects from their own point of view.

There are three types of interviews

1. **Structured Interviews** These are interviews that take place with few, if any, interview questions. They often progress in the manner a normal conversation would, however it concerns the research topic under review
2. **Semi-structured Interviews** These type of interviews contain the components of both, structured and unstructured interviews. In semi-structured interviews, interviewer prepares a set of same questions to be answered by all interviewees. At the same time, additional questions might be asked during interviews to clarify and/or further expand certain issues.
3. **Unstructured Interviews** These are usually the least reliable from research viewpoint, because no questions are prepared prior to the interview and data collection is conducted in an informal manner. Unstructured interviews can be associated with a high level of bias and comparison of answers given by different respondents tends to be difficult due to the differences in formulation of questions.

Interviewing as a qualitative research method often combines with or is part of, other research methods, including auto-biographical methods, ethnographic methods, oral history and indeed, textual analysis or discourse analysis at the point where the interview material is interpreted. It thus forms a central plank of many research processes.

Creative Writing as a Research Method

This has been relatively a new method of research in English Studies. Creative writing is an important element within English departments, which represents the invention and generation of ideas, images and performances where these lead to new or substantially improved insights. The 2001 RAE (Research

Assessment Exercise) panel saw creative writing 'as an important element within English departments', which was 'assessed in accordance' with the provision in RAE.

In 2008 RAE (Research Assessment Exercise, UK) report, creative writing and applied, practice-based and pedagogical research in English featured as part of the domain of English, no longer requiring extended explanations and thus demonstrating a certain embeddedness in contemporary understandings of the discipline. In context of public funding bodies, defining creative writing is a difficult task. There have been debates across the creative arts platform – creative writing to fine arts, music, film, video, digital work, dance and performance - about the assessment of creative work as research. Creative work is often required to be accompanied by theoretical writing that provides detail about the research dimensions of the creative work. This would then qualify it as a research work.

The articulation at meta-discursive level of how the research process underpinning creative work is embedded within it constitutes one way of establishing creative work as research. There is a debate about considering Creative writing as a research method and opinions are divided on this. A distinction emerges between the work of language and the work of a writer, resulting in creative writing as 'a mode of research into the nature of literary form and language'. This insight is linked into the practice of re-writing as the process of discovery at every draft. Thus this process can be related to the need for reading as the activity which informs writing as discovery of both content and form. These inter-related processes and activities can be documented and critically analysed – that is, a meta-narrative about the research process informing creative activity can be derived from these – is an important contribution to the question of how to understand creative writing as a research method.

English Research Methods and the Digital Humanities

Digital humanities research methods in English Studies are a relatively recent phenomenon, to date still carried out mainly by specialist researchers in particular fields of textual analysis and in linguistics.

However, the advent of more and more computer software and hardware, which is also becoming easier to use, has greatly enhanced opportunities for researchers in literary studies to work on literary and other texts. Digital Humanities can be defined as an academic field concerned with the application of computational tools and methods to traditional humanities disciplines such as literature, history, and philosophy. It can be explained as the critical study of how digital technologies and methods intersect with humanities scholarship and scholarly communication. It investigates the use of digital tools and software for interpretation and analysis of humanities research questions and how digital methodologies can be used to enhance various disciplines such as art history, classical studies, history, literature, music and many others.

Digital Humanities allows scholars to approach old problems with new means, or to ask new questions that could not have been asked with the traditional means of humanistic enquiry. Whatever the approach chosen, Digital Humanities remains grounded in humanities research and interests.

History of Digital Humanities

Digital humanities descends from the field of humanities computing, whose origins reach back to the 1930s and 1940s in the pioneering work of English professor Josephine Miles and Jesuit scholar Roberto Busa and the women they employed. In collaboration with IBM, they created a computer-generated concordance to Thomas Aquinas' writings known as the Index Thomisticus. Other scholars began using mainframe computers to automate tasks like word-searching, sorting and counting, which was much faster than processing information from texts with handwritten or typed index cards. In the decades which followed archaeologists, classicists, historians, literary scholars and a broad array of humanities researchers in other disciplines applied emerging computational methods to transform humanities scholarship.

The first specialised journal in the digital humanities was Computers and the Humanities, which debuted in 1966. The Association for Literary and Linguistic Computing (ALLC) and the Association for Computers and the Humanities (ACH) were then founded in 1977 and 1978, respectively.

Though this field also has issues that need to be addressed; it needs to be seen for the role it will play in future of Research in English Studies.

Research Material

What can be the tools and materials of the research 'A research student of literature may ask. In science materials are the objects of nature and the tools are scientific instruments. Can we adopt the same types of methods in literary research? Yes, we can. Literary Research is equally systematic, methodical and objective, hence scientific; it has specific materials for investigation and scientific tools for arriving at a conclusion.

The Materials of literary research are Manuscripts and Printed Books. These two include all the texts, letters, diaries, journals, memoirs and reviews and critical comments and criticism by the author.

Manuscripts can be divided into two broad divisions : hand written manuscripts before the introduction of the printing machine in England second is manuscripts after spellings were modernised in the 18th century.

- Manuscripts of old English pose a few problems such as spelling of old English words are strikingly different from those of New English words.
- Some of old English words have become obsolete.
- The syntax of middle English is also different in many cases.
- New English manuscripts pose little problems except these two
- A large number of manuscripts are unsigned.
- The writing is illegible when the writer is in a hurry or tired.

The printing machine was set up by Caxton in 1476. The press made the work easier and more accurate. However, printed editions are not always reliable and pose before the research student the following problems

- There is a considerable difference between a manuscript and a printed edition.
- The number of edition or reprint is rerely recorded.
- The year of publication is rarely recorded.
- Polemical articles do not bear the author's names.
- There are pirated editions and forged manuscripts.

Paper

The paper of a text is also a part of the materials of research. the study of the paper is important for determining the date of a text and ascertain its genuineness. A paper expert can tell the age of a paper by examining its quality and water mark. In this way a forged manuscript can be cross checked for its authenticity.

Ink

Ink is third important part of the materials. We can find out the period by analysing the kinds of ink which were used in different ages.

Finding Material

The nature of finding materials depends on the topic. If we have to edit a text, e.g. Shakespeare's *Othello*, we have to look for the manuscript, the different editions, critical commentaries and relevant criticism. But if we are writing a dissertation on WB Yeats's use of myths, we need not consult the manuscripts. We have to study books on Irish mythology the books discussing myths in general and all works of yeats and critical works on the author.

The complex nature and size of materials has made literary research a really difficult and also interesting form of investigation for the discovery of truth.

The libraries of national importance maintain the manuscripts of old authors. For the living authors, the best source is authors themselves or their trustees.

Tools of Research in Literature

The basic tools, observation and experiment are common to all kinds of research. But there are some exclusive tools that are used in literary research. *They are*

- Bibliography
- Scientific tools
- Note System
- Textual Analysis

Bibliography

The word 'bibliography' means a list of books and articles on a given subject or an author. In literary research the term means 'the science of books'.

The historical bibliography can help a researcher in finding the history of writing, printing, binding, illustration, publishing and selling. This helps in determining the date of a text. It can also help a researcher in locating the library where the respective books will be found. Enumerative Bibliography helps the research student to know the books he actually needs. Practical Bibliography is concerned with the methods of work of student and author reading, compilation of notes and bibliography, preparation of manuscript, typing of the research paper or the thesis.

Notes System

They provide facts for future reference Note taking helps students concentrate or pay attention during lectures and study of books.

Scientific Tools

Some new digital tools are available for researchers where a researcher can find relevant and reliable sources for a literature review. Some of them are Google scholar, Pubpeer, Pubchase, Reference Management, Zoterato, Mendeley, Read Cube, End Note etc.

Textual Analysis

It is the method or tool, a researcher uses to describe and interpret the characteristics of a recorded or visual message. The purpose of textual analysis is to describe the content, structure and functions of the messages contained in text.

EXAM BASED QUESTIONS

1 A hypothesis is a

(a) Law (b) Canon
(c) Postulate (d) Supposition

2 The essential qualities of a researcher are

(a) Spirit of enquiry
(b) Reliance on observation and evidence
(c) Systematization or theorizing of knowledge
(d) All of the above

3 In the process of conducting research 'Formulation of Hypothesis' is followed by

(a) Statement of objectives
(b) Analysis of data
(c) Selection of research tools
(d) Collection of data

4 Einstein gave the Theory of Relativity. This research is categorized as

(a) Descriptive Research (b) Sample Survey
(c) Fundamental research (d) Applied research

5 A research paper is a brief report of research work which is based on

(a) Primary data
(b) Secondary data only
(c) Both Primary and Secondary Data
(d) None of the above

6 Ex Post Facto research means

(a) The research is carried out after the incident
(b) The research is carried out before the incident
(c) The research is carried out during the happening of an incident
(d) The research is carried out keeping in mind the possibilities of an incident

7 The research that aims at immediate application is

(a) Action research (b) Historical research
(c) Conceptual research (d).Fundamental research

8 A researcher conducts a research on finding out which leadership style contributes more to institutional effectiveness. This will be an example of

(a) Basic research (b) Action research
(c) Applied research (d) None of these

9 Which of the following is the first step in starting a research process?

(a) Searching sources of information to locate problem
(b) Survey of related literature
(c) Identification of problem
(d) Searching for solutions to the problem

10 Research is

(a) Searching again and again
(b) Finding solution to any problem
(c) Working in a scientific way to search for truth of any problem
(d) None of the above

11 A good piece of research is a product of

(a) collective scholarship (b) a good library
(c) an analytical mind (d) a touch of genius

12 Which one of the following is a research tool?

(a) Graph
(b) Pictures
(c) Open ended Questionnaire
(d) Diagram

13 The condition of 'controlled group' is applied in

(a) Survey research (b) Historical research
(c) Experimental research (d) All of these

14 Which of the following is classified as in the category of the developmental research?

(a) Philosophical research (b) Action research
(c) Descriptive research (d) Historical research

15 In Experimental Research, which process is not required ?

(a) Close observation (b) Manipulation
(c) Controlling (d) Content analysis

16 Research problem is selected from the standpoint of

(a) interest of the researcher
(b) funding party
(c) social relevance
(d) availability of relevant literature

17 Formulation of hypothesis is a condition that may not be required in

(a) Survey method (b) Historical studies
(c) Experimental studies (d) None of these

18 Research is always

(a) verifying the old knowledge
(b) exploring new knowledge
(c) Both (a) and (b)
(d) None of the above

19 In this research, the field study applies the laws to draw more and more clear ideas about the problem. Identify this research.

(a) Applied research
(b) Action research
(c) Philosophical research
(d) All of the above

20 The work of a biographer is to
(a) distinguish fact from fiction
(b) collect all the information about the concerned person
(c) write spontaneously at the moment
(d) Both (a) and (b)

21 The objectivity of the research can be enhanced
(a) through its impartiality (b) through its reliability
(c) Both of the above (d) None of these

22 Literary Research studies
(a) Literary text
(b) Literary writers
(c) Both Literary text and writer
(d) None of the above

23 What is textual Research
(a) Establishment of an authoritative text
(b) Corrections of past edition
(c) Genuineness of the text
(d) All of the above

24 What is the authenticity of a research finding?
(a) Originality (b) Validity
(c) Objectivity (d) All of these

25 What are the main characteristics of a scientific finding?
(a) Empirical (b) Theoretical
(c) Experimental (d) All of these

26 The technical term for a generalized conclusion on the basis of a sample is known as
(a) Data analysis and interpretation
(b) Statistical inference
(c) All of the above
(d) None of the above

27 An investigator attempts to trace an effect. This type of study is known as:
(a) Survey research (b) 'Ex-post Facto' Research
(c) Historical Research (d) None of these

28 Which of the following does a researcher uses to test null hypothesis?
(a) T test (b) ANOVA
(c) Chi square test (d) Factorial analysis

29 Which of the following expressions is used when two or more successive footnotes refer to the same work ?
(a) Et.al (b) Ob.cit: (c) Loc.cit. (d) Ibid

30 Ten year old girls are taller than eight year old boys. This is an example of a reference drawn from
(a) Vertical study (b) Cross-sectional study
(c) Time series study (d) Philosophical study

31 The conferences are aimed at which of the following?
(a) Discussions about relevant current topics
(b) Sharing information of the results of a new research
(c) Multiple target groups
(d) All of the above

32 When is a research problem feasible?
(a) It has utility and relevance
(b) It is researchable
(c) None of the above
(d) Both (a) and (b)

33 Fundamental research reflects the ability to
(a) Present new principles
(b) Combine new ideals
(c) Analyse the existing material in the concerned area
(d) Study of the existing literature

34 Who can conduct a research?
(a) A hard working person.
(b) Somebody with a Post graduate degree
(c) One who has a reasoning ability
(d) One who is a doctor

35 Which of the following is a parameter for judging the depth of any research?
(a) Funding of the research
(b) Time period of the research
(c) Aims and objectives of the research
(d) Heading of the research

36 Identify the correct statement.
(a) Validity is ensured by reliability
(b) Reliability is ensured by validity
(c) Reliability depends on Objectivity
(d) Both Reliability and validity are independent of each other

37 Identify the one which is not a method of research?
(a) Observation (b) Historical
(c) Survey (d) Analysis

38 Which of the following is a classification of research?
(a) Pure and Fundamental
(b) Qualitative and Quantitative
(c) Applied and Action
(d) All of the above

39 Which is the first step of research
(a) Selecting a problem (b) Searching a problem
(c) Finding a problem (d) Identifying a problem

40 The qualities of a researcher are
(a) a specialist rather than a generalist
(b) diligent and determined in his study
(c) Both (a) and (b)
(d) None of the above

41 Sin qua non of a good research is
(a) Null Hypothesis
(b) Research supervisor who is good
(c) Well stocked library
(d) A good funding organization

42 Which of the following is not a quality of the researcher?
(a) A union of his aim and what he seeks
(b) Alert mind
(c) Sharp acumen in analysis
(d) Deep commitment to go beyond the evidence

43 What are the different types of Literary Researcher?
(a) Biographical
(b) Theoretical
(c) Interpretive
(d) All of the above

44 Main objective of Literary Research is
(a) sharpening the critical insight of the researcher
(b) advancement of knowledge
(c) create an intelligent interest in literature
(d) All of the above

45 Which of the following statements is correct?
(a) Research objectives are defined in the beginning of the thesis
(b) A scholar with an analytical and penetrating mind.
(c) None of the above
(d) Both (a) and (b)

46 What does objectivity in research mean?
(a) Discovering the truth
(b) Having consistent outcomes
(c) Inter-researcher agreement
(d) Sophisticated Methods

47 Pre-requisites of a researcher in subjects of Humanities and Social Sciences are
(a) Archives, Supervisor, Topic, Knowledge
(b) Patience, Critical Analysis, Topic, Supervisor
(c) Flexible Thinking, Records, Topic, Supervisor
(d) Good Behaviour, Honesty, Supervisor, Topic, Biased Assumptions

48 In a Scientific method of research, which one of the following is an aim?
(a) To remove false relations
(b) To enhance interpretation of data
(c) To introduce new data
(d) To confirm triangulation

49 In the field of academics, a researcher should consider himself as
(a) Have an open mind
(b) Totally dependent on the supervisor
(c) Extremely knowledgeable
(d) A status-quo maintainer

50 Which of the following statements is incorrect? while conducting a literary Research involves
(a) the concerned person can work randomly
(b) Researcher must have a thorough knowledge about the work and critical reviews about the concerned author
(c) the discovery of new facts and fresh interpretation
(d) advancing one's explanation of facts which were previously overlooked.

51 The main aim of interdisciplinary research is
(a) to reduce the importance of single subject in research domain
(b) to make the research problem more simple
(c) to give a new direction to research methodology
(d) to bring out integrated approach to research

52 What does the bibliography given in a research report indicate?
(a) Aids other scholars
(b) Is irrelevant to research
(c) Reveals the knowledge of the researcher
(d) None of the above

53 The meaning of research as a process is best described by the phrase
(a) Objective Observation
(b) Systematic Activity
(c) Trial and Error
(d) Problem Solving

54 Assumptions are formulated on the basis of
(a) cultural background
(b) specific characteristics of the groups
(c) None of the above
(d) Both (a) and (b)

55 The term 'phenomenology' is related to the process of
(a) ANOVA or Analysis of Variance
(b) probability sampling
(c) qualitative research
(d) None of the above

56 Research is not considered ethical if
(a) it attempts to prove a particular point
(b) it reveals the identity of the respondent
(c) it does not investigate the data scientifically
(d) is not of a very high standard

57 In research, a common test demands priority on
(a) reliability
(b) validity
(c) objectivity
(d) All of these

58 A team of experts in a specific area of knowledge collected at a place and prepared a study contents for a new stream. This may be termed as
(a) seminar
(b) conference
(c) symposium
(d) workshop

59 The materials of literary Research will include
(a) Manuscripts
(b) Printed looks
(c) Both of these
(d) None of these

60 Research ethics do not include
(a) honesty
(b) subjectivity
(c) integrity
(d) objectivity

61 Archival method of research involves
(a) study of history
(b) quantitative methods
(c) seeking information from historical documents or records.
(d) None of the above

62 The oldest and best known and most often used method of qualitative research is
(a) oral History
(b) interview method
(c) creative writing
(d) visual Methodologies

63 The term Discourse means
(a) Sexual intercourse (b) Academic course
(c) Chat on a subject (d) Decrease

64 Alfred Schütz Austrian philosopher and social phenomenologist is associated with
(a) Digital humanities (b) Archival methods
(c) Auto-biographical methods (d) Textual analysis

65 Visual data excludes which of the following:
(a) Images (b) Photographs
(c) Posters (d) All of these

66 "Frequency of occurrence of words, phrases or imagery" is an example of
(a) Discourse Analysis
(b) Quantitative Analysis in English Studies
(c) Textual Analysis
(d) Ethnography studies

67 Identify the correct statement.
(a) Textual analysis takes into account the 'context'.
(b) There is no such thing as a single, 'correct' interpretation of any text.
(c) Close-reading of a text, including artifacts, is termed as Textual analysis.
(d) All of the above

68 An Interview
(a) is a conversation where questions are asked to extract information.
(b) requires a series of practical skills
(c) Both the above
(d) None of the above

69 Ethnography is 'multimedia research'. It could be
(a) quantitative (b) qualitative
(c) Both of these (d) None of these

70 Interviews could be
(a) unstructured (b) semi structured
(c) structured (d) All of these

71 Travel writings could be in the form of
(a) Travelogues (b) Scientific reports
(c) Stories (d) None of these

72 An academic field concerned with the application of computational tools and methods to traditional humanities is called
(a) Digitization (b) Digital Research
(c) Digital Humanities (d) None of these

73 Josephine Miles and Roberto Busa, English Professors did pioneering work in this field. Identify the field.
(a) Archival Method (b) Digital Humanities
(c) Ethnography (d) Textual Analysis

74 Identify the correct statement.
(a) 'Computers and the Humanities' is the first specialized journal in digital humanities in 1966.
(b) Association for Literary and Linguistic Computing was founded in 1977.
(c) Association for Computers and the Humanities (ACH) was founded in 1978.
(d) All of the above

75 An interviewer is a ....
(a) professional researcher (b) paid researcher
(c) Both of these (d) None of these

76 An interviewee is ....
(a) the same as an interviewer
(b) the person who is being interviewed
(c) a female interviewer
(d) a female who is being interviewed

77 The iconic texts can be ....
(a) Drawings (b) Paintings
(c) Icons (d) All of these

78 Micro-ethnography is ....
(a) study of ethnographic groups
(b) study of narrowly defined groups
(c) study of small groups
(d) study of little groups

79 Audience response criticism refers to ....
(a) the way the Audience offers criticism
(b) the way spectators offers their opinions
(c) the audience research in audio-visual mediums.
(d) the audience research in drama.

80 The word 'ethnography' is derived from the Greek word ....
(a) ethnos (b) ethos
(c) ethose (d) ethono

81 The audio-visual text include ....
(a) TV Programs (b) Movies
(c) Videos (d) All of these

82 Analysing the development of the individual personality in the life course can be termed as ....
(a) oral history research (b) auto-biographical research
(c) ethnographical research (d) interviewing

83 Archival Methods of research is a ....
(a) quantitative method (b) qualitative method
(c) Both of these (d) None of these

84 Some of the material for analysis, in the Auto-biographical research, consists of
(a) interviews (b) video recordings
(c) photographs (d) All of these

85 The collection, preservation, and dissemination of historical data obtained through planned in-depth, life history interviews can be termed as
(a) ethnographical research
(b) auto-biographical research
(c) oral history method of research
(d) None of the above

86 Hubert H Bancroft is associated with
(a) oral history method (b) discourse analysis
(c) textual analysis (d) visual methodologies

87 **Visual Data can fall into two categories:**
(a) Visual images produced by others
(b) Visual representations generated by the researcher
(c) Both of these
(d) None of these

88 **Discourse means**
(a) written or spoken communication
(b) written or spoken debate
(c) Both of these
(d) None of these

89 **Identify the correct statement:**
(a) Discourse analysis and text linguistics is the same.
(b) Discourse analysis and text linguistics is different
(c) Both of the above
(d) Discourse analysis and Text linguistics are different but closely related.

90 **Ethnomethodology is a method of**
(a) Sociological analysis (b) Ethnographic studies
(c) Both these (d) None of the above

91 **The advent of the new cross-discipline of Discourse Analysis began during**
(a) Twentieth century
(b) Nineteenth century
(c) Later half of the twentieth century
(d) Later half of the Nineteenth century

92 **In English Studies,**
(a) Only qualitative methods are used
(b) Only quantitative methods are used
(c) Both qualitative and quantitative methods are used
(d) None of the above mentioned methods are used

93 **August Ludwig von Schlözer and Christoph Wilhelm Jacob Gatterer of the University of Gottingen introduced this term in the academic discourse. Identify this term.**
(a) Ethnography (b) Discourse
(c) Digital humanities (d) None of these

94 **Identify the correct statement.**
(a) Zellig Harris published a series of papers from 1952.
(b) These papers reported on work from which he developed transformational grammar in the late 1930's.
(c) The term discourse analysis first came into general use following the publication of these papers by Zellig Harris.
(d) All of the above

95 **Ethnography is an important methodology used in disciplines such as**
(a) social science (b) anthropology
(c) psychology (d) sociology

96 **The archaeology of knowledge, influential work by Michael Foucault contains the theories on**
(a) Discourse
(b) Digital Humanities
(c) Quantitative Methods of research in English Studies
(d) Creative Writing

97 **Use of dates in literary texts in connection with authors would be a part of which kind of research? Choose the most suitable method.**
(a) Archival method (b) Historical method
(c) Quantitative methods (d) All of these

98 **In the Auto-biographical method of research, Biography is understood in terms of**
(a) social construct
(b) physical construct
(c) scientific construct
(d) emotional construct

99 **Interview is a ....**
(a) type of test for a selection
(b) a screening step for a job
(c) a conversation where questions are asked to extract information
(d) All of the above

100 **Michael Foucault is a key theorist in the subject of**
(a) Auto-biographical research
(b) Discourse analysis
(c) Visual methodologies of research
(d) None of the above

101 **Identify the correct statement:**
(a) Interviewing is a quantitative research method
(b) Interviewing includes other research methods like oral history and auto-biographical methods
(c) Interviewing does not include ethnographic methods
(d) All of the above

102 **Digital Humanities originated in**
(a) Twenty first century
(b) Twentieth century
(c) First half of the twentieth century
(d) Early Twenty First century

103 **Defining creative writing is a difficult task in context of**
(a) Society
(b) Individuality
(c) Public funding bodies
(d) None of the above

104 **Digital Humanities descends from the field of**
(a) Humanities
(b) Computing
(c) Humanities Computing
(d) None of the above

105 **In the context of English studies, what does ethnography questions?**
(a) how to read and interpret English texts
(b) how to read English texts
(c) how to interpret English texts
(d) how to read and interpret ethnographic texts

106 **Hypertexts are the**
(a) The texts that are over-rated
(b) The texts found on the Internet
(c) Both of the above
(d) None of the above

107 Ethograph in English studies finds out
(a) other cultures
(b) other text books
(c) cultural dimensions of literature of language
(d) None of the above

108 Josephine Miles and Robert Busa are English professors who did pioneering work in the first half of twentieth century in the field of Digital Humanities. Which company did they collaborate with in this?
(a) IBM (b) Microsoft
(c) Hewlett Packard (d) Intel

109 The first specialized journal in the Digital Humanities was
(a) Computers and the Humanities
(b) Humanities and Computers
(c) Digi Humanities
(d) Digital Humanities

110 Visual images is a form of
(a) mixed data (b) visual data
(c) photographs (d) pictures

111 Which of the following are methods of research used in English Literature?
(a) Archival Methods, Oral History, Visual Methodologies,
(b) Ethnographic Studies, Discourse Analysis, Textual Analysis
(c) Interviewing, Autobiographical Methods
(d) All of the above

112 Identify the term used for studies which portrays the characteristics of a particular situation or groups or individuals in an accurate manner
(a) Descriptive (b) Experimental
(c) Exploratory (d) None of these

113 Reference and Bibliography are different in what ways?
(a) The references contain the minute details in order to verify them.
(b) The references have the surname of the person on its first priority.
(c) The references have the actual page number.
(d) All of the above

114 Research proposal is also called
(a) abstract (b) methodology
(c) synopsis (d) summary

115 The research method used to investigate cultures and population subgroups and which seeks to describe and explain cultural behaviour is
(a) phenomenology (b) action research
(c) ethnography (d) grounded research

116 Who prepares the research papers?
(a) The scientists
(b) The research supervisors
(c) The research scholars
(d) All of the above

117 The main aim of a Seminar is
(a) adding to the existing knowledge
(b) sharing the research outcomes
(c) Both of the above
(d) None of the above

118 Symposium is
(a) method of taking decisions
(b) reaching a certain conclusion using discussion
(c) a group which is well organized and has a large audience and less speakers.
(d) All of the above

119 Research is an ethical process. Ethics here means
(a) Abiding by the research values
(b) Beauty of the research report
(c) The research content
(d) All of the above

120 Identify the true statement about Allan Nevins.
(a) He was a Columbian University Historian
(b) He was born in India
(c) He was adopted by Afro-American parents
(d) None of the above

121 Image is never a 'mere' reflection of reality, but rather a multi-layered text. This statement can be rewritten as
(a) Image is a reflection of reality
(b) Image is a speaking picture
(c) Image is sometimes a reflection of reality
(d) None of the above

122 Conversational analysis is a type of
(a) archival analysis method
(b) creative writing analysis method
(c) quantitative method of analysis
(d) discourse analysis

123 Ethnographic research technique can be categorized into categories such as
(a) travel writings
(b) reading groups
(c) audience response criticism
(d) All of the above

124 The least reliable interview type from research viewpoint is
(a) Structured Interviews (b) Unstructured Interviews
(c) Semi-structured Interviews
(d) None of the above

125 Discourse analysis and text linguistics are closely related with an essential difference.
(a) True (b) False
(c) Partially True (d) Partially False

126 Textual analysis on a text means making an educated guess at some of the most likely interpretations that might be made of that text.
(a) True (b) False
(c) Partly false (d) Partly true

127 Which of the following statements is correct?
(a) Objectives should be stated clearly
(b) Variables can also be termed as problem
(c) Objectives should be stated in question form
(d) None of the above

128 Herodotus is believed to have produced
(a) the first works of history
(b) the first works of ethnography
(c) Both of the above
(d) None of the above

129 Creative writing
(a) Is an important element within English department
(b) Represents the invention and generation of ideas, images and performances
(c) Both of the above
(d) None of the above

130 Digital humanities research methods in English studies are carried out mainly by specialist researchers in particular fields of
(a) textual analysis (b) linguistics
(c) Both of these (d) None of these

131 Ethnography refers to
(a) method of study (b) result of such study
(c) None of these (d) Both of these

132 Research is conducted
1. to generate new knowledge
2. to develop a theory
3. not to obtain research degree
4. reinterpret existing knowledge

Which of the above is correct?
(a) 1, 3, and 2 (b) 3, 2 and 4
(c) 2, 1 and 3 (d) 1, 2 and 4

133 The review of Research reports should be done in context of
1. investigator bias
2. cultural context
3. methodological factors

Which one of the following is correct?
(a) 1 and 3 (b) Only 1
(c) Only 3 (d) 1, 2 and 3

134 Which of the following options are the main tasks of research in modern society?
1. To add on to the existing knowledge.
2. To explore new facts.
3. To conduct a systematic examination and analyse the data collected in an objective manner.
4. To evaluate the earlier writings

Which of the following options is correct?
(a) 1, 2 and 3 (b) 4, 2 and 3
(c) 2 and 3 (d) 2, 3 and 4

135 Which of the following statements are true?
1. Interviewing is a part of auto-biographical methods
2. Interviewing is a part of ethnographic methods
3. Interviewing is a part of textual analysis

Select the correct answer using the codes given below
(a) Only 1 (b) 2 and 3 (c) 1, 2 and 3 (d) 1 and 2

136 Select the most suitable option.
A. Discourse analysis and text linguistics have an essential difference.
B. Discourse analysis aims at revealing the socio-psychological characteristics of a person rather than text structure.

Codes
(a) Both A and B are correct. (b) Both A and B are false.
(c) Only A is correct. (d) Only B is correct.

137 Match the following

	List I		List II
1.	Allan Nevins	A.	Visual Methodology
2.	George Bateson	B.	Oral History
3.	Zellig Harris	C.	Ethnography
4.	Gerhard Friedrich Müller	D.	Discourse Analysis

Codes

	1	2	3	4		1	2	3	4
(a)	C	A	D	B	(b)	B	A	D	C
(c)	A	B	C	D	(d)	D	B	A	C

138 **Assertion** (A) Literature is different from natural sciences

Reason (R) Literary Research has to study both the text as well as the writer
(a) A is true but R is not correct
(b) R is true but A is not correct
(c) Both A and R are true and R is the correct explanation of
(d) None of them is correct

139 **Assertion** (A) Questionnaire can be used in literary research.

Reason (R) Questionnaire is a tool for data collection so it can be used for English research also
(a) A is true but R is not correct
(b) R is true but A is not correct
(c) A is not true and R is not correct explanation
(d) A is true and R is correct explanation of A

140 **Assertion** (A) Literature Research requires research materials

Reason (R) The materials of Literary Research are manuscripts and printed books.
(a) A is true but R is correct
(b) R is true but A is not correct
(c) A is not correct and R is not correct explanation of A
(d) A is correct and R is correct explanation of it

ANSWERS

Objective Questions

1. *(d)*	2. *(d)*	3. *(d)*	4. *(c)*	5. *(c)*	6. *(a)*	7. *(a)*	8. *(c)*	9. *(c)*	10. *(c)*
11. *(c)*	12. *(d)*	13. *(c)*	14. *(b)*	15. *(b)*	16. *(a)*	17. *(b)*	18. *(c)*	19. *(a)*	20. *(d)*
21. *(c)*	22. *(c)*	23. *(d)*	24. *(d)*	25. *(d)*	26. *(c)*	27. *(c)*	28. *(b)*	29. *(d)*	30. *(a)*
31. *(d)*	32. *(d)*	33. *(a)*	34. *(c)*	35. *(c)*	36. *(d)*	37. *(b)*	38. *(d)*	39. *(d)*	40. *(c)*
41. *(b)*	42. *(d)*	43. *(d)*	44. *(d)*	45. *(d)*	46. *(c)*	47. *(b)*	48. *(a)*	49. *(a)*	50. *(a)*
51. *(d)*	52. *(c)*	53. *(a)*	54. *(d)*	55. *(c)*	56. *(c)*	57. *(d)*	58. *(d)*	59. *(c)*	60. *(b)*
61. *(c)*	62. *(a)*	63. *(c)*	64. *(d)*	65. *(d)*	66. *(b)*	67. *(d)*	68. *(c)*	69. *(c)*	70. *(d)*
71. *(a)*	72. *(c)*	73. *(b)*	74. *(d)*	75. *(c)*	76. *(b)*	77. *(d)*	78. *(b)*	79. *(c)*	80. *(a)*
81. *(d)*	82. *(b)*	83. *(c)*	84. *(d)*	85. *(c)*	86. *(a)*	87. *(c)*	88. *(c)*	89. *(d)*	90. *(c)*
91. *(c)*	92. *(c)*	93. *(a)*	94. *(d)*	95. *(a)*	96. *(a)*	97. *(d)*	98. *(a)*	99. *(d)*	100. *(b)*
101. *(b)*	102. *(c)*	103. *(c)*	104. *(c)*	105. *(d)*	106. *(b)*	107. *(c)*	108. *(a)*	109. *(a)*	110. *(b)*
111. *(d)*	112. *(d)*	113. *(d)*	114. *(c)*	115. *(c)*	116. *(d)*	117. *(a)*	118. *(d)*	119. *(a)*	120. *(a)*
121. *(b)*	122. *(d)*	123. *(d)*	124. *(b)*	125. *(a)*	126. *(a)*	127. *(a)*	128. *(c)*	129. *(c)*	130. *(c)*
131. *(d)*	132. *(d)*	133. *(c)*	134. *(c)*	135. *(c)*	136. *(a)*	137. *(b)*	138. *(c)*	139. *(d)*	140. *(d)*

ENGLISH

Model Paper-1

General Instructions

1. There are total one hundred questions in this paper. Each question carries 2 marks.
2. All questions are compulsory.

---

1 Identify the term among the following which does not relate to a movement in art or literature?

(a) Cubism (b) Empiricism
(c) Expressionism (d) Realism

2 Name the famous Dutch Scholar, who is known for Wolloquis and in Praise of Folly

(a) Shakespeare (b) Erasmus
(c) John Marston (d) Boccacio

3 Which poem written in form of eight syllabled couplets, containing 30,000 lines, relates the history of the world as recorded in the old and new Testaments.

(a) Cursor Mundi
(b) The Owl and the Nightingale
(c) Roman de Troie
(d) Livre des Creatures

4 What does it mean if women are called 'surplus' or 'redundant' in the Victorian era?

(a) They remained unmarried due to a population imbalance between the sexes
(b) The unfair labor conditions resulted in a surplus of textiles causing them to drop in price
(c) They were women writers who wrote frequently about similar topics
(d) They prostituted themselves as a way to make money in a market economy that didn't provide extensive job opportunities to women

5 While in America, Brecht wrote the screenplay for a film directed by Fritz Lang. Can you name it?

(a) The Hangman Must Die
(b) American Guerrilla in the Philippines
(c) Hangmen Also Die!
(d) American Werewolf

6 Who wrote a series of characters in (1614), which are witty and epigrammatic inform?

(a) Samuel Butler (b) Izaak Walton
(c) Thomas Overbury (d) Francis Bacon

7 The Romantic period in English literature began in which year with publication of which work by William Wordsworth and Coleridge.

(a) 1775, Cynical Ballads
(b) 1798, Lyrical Ballads
(c) 1798, French Revolution
(d) 1790, Imaginary Conversation

8 Which phrase indicates the interior flow of thought employed in High-modern literature?

(a) Automatic writing
(b) Confused daze
(c) Stream of consciousness
(d) Free association

9 "A man is not a bird to come and go with the springtime." Which character makes this statement in the play 'The Death of a Salesman'?

(a) Charley (b) Biff (c) Linda (d) Happy

10 Which play of Osborne focuses on the life and marital struggles of an intelligent and educated but dissatisfied young man of working class origin, Jimmy Porter, and his equally competent yet impassive upper middle class wife Alison? It takes inspiration from John's personal life experiences.

(a) The Devil Inside Him (b) Look Back in Anger
(c) Under Plain Cover (d) Watch It Come Down

11 In the 4th century Pope Damascus assigned his secretary, Jerome, the task of producing an accurate translation of the Bible in Latin, the language of the Roman Empire. Jerome completed the task in AD 405, and his translation became the standard Bible of Christianity for over 900 years. What was this version called?

(a) The Geneva Bible (b) The King James Bible
(c) The Septuagint (d) the Vulgate

12 Match the following Indian English poet with their poetic works

Indian English Poet	Poetic Work
1. Rabindranath Tagore	A. Gitanjali
2. Sarojini Naidu	B. Indian Weavers
3. Amrita Pritam	C. Immoral Waves
4. Toru Dutt	D. Our Casuarina Tree

Codes

(a) 1-A, 2-B, 3-C, 4-D (b) 1-D, 2-C, 3-B, 4-A
(c) 1-B, 2-D, 3-A, 4-C (d) 1-C, 2-A, 3-D, 4-B

13 In Indo-English poet once remarked that his disciplines (i.e. linguistics and anthropology) and his education give him his outer form, whereas his Indian origin, first thirty years in India and knowledge of Kannada and Tamil give him his inner form. Who said this?

(a) AK Ramanujan (b) Kamala Das
(c) Gieve Patel
(d) Raja Gopal Parthasarathy

14 .... is associated with the phrase, 'Ain't I a woman'?

(a) Toni Morrison (b) Maya Angelou
(c) Sojourner Truth (d) Paul Gilroy

15 "Human beings and especially human beings as an integral part of a social organisation are regarded as primary subject matter of literature".

This assertion implies

(a) Human being alone can be subject matter of literature
(b) Human are social beings are the nucleus of all literary exercise
(c) Literature transcend the human and non-human
(d) All beings animal and human contribute towards the creation of literature

16 'On the Sublime' is written in .... style.

(a) dramatic
(b) conversational
(c) poetic
(d) prose

17 Which of the following statements is not true?

(a) Growth is a biological process
(b) Development is a quantitative process
(c) Education is a goal-oriented process
(d) Learning is a process of behavioural changes

18 Which of the following statements is incorrect while conducting a literary research involves

(a) the concerned person can work randomly
(b) researcher must have a through knowledge about the work and critical reviews about the concerned author
(c) the discovery of new facts and fresh interpretation
(d) advancing one's explanation of facts which were previously overlooked

19 "And while they were in the same place, there came a great mist about them and a darkness, so that they could not know what way they were going, and they heard the noise of a rider coming towards them. 'It would be a great grief to us,' said Conn, to be brought away into a strange country."

Which of the following dramatists in which of his/her works has had the above lines?

(a) Henrik Ibsen, A Doll's House
(b) Lady Augusta Gregory, Gods and Fighting Men
(c) George Bernard Shaw, Man and Superman
(d) JM Barrie, Peter Pan

20 Thrice rung the Bell, the Slipper knock'd the Ground And the press'd Watch return'd a silver sound, Belinda still her downy Pillow prest, her guardian Sylph proln'gd the balmy rest. Twas he had summon'd to her silent Bed The Morning Dream that hover'd o'er her Head'. Name the poem and the poet of the above line.

(a) Poem on the Last Day, Edward Young
(b) The Rape of the Lock, Alexander Pope
(c) The Season, James Thomson
(d) The Vanity of Human Wishes, Samuel Johnson

21 Match the following poems with their contemporary poets.

Poem	Contemporary Age Poet
A. A Lost Season	1. Ted Hughs
B. Modern Folk Ballad	2. Thomas William Gunn
C. My Sad Captains	3. Charles Stanley Causley
D. The Hawk in The Rain	4. Roy Broad Bent Fuller

Codes

(a) 1-A, 2-B, 3-C, 4-D
(b) 1D-, 2-C, 3-B, 4-A
(c) 1-B, 2-D, 3-A, 4-C
(d) 1-C, 2-A, 3-D, 4-B

22 "An engine, an engine
Chuffing me off like a Jew
A Jew to Dachau A suchwitz, Belsen
I began to talk like a Jew,
I think I may well be a Jew."
(a) This is Sylvia Plath in 'Daddy'
(b) This is Saul Bellow in 'Herzog'
(c) This is Nissim Ezekiel in 'The Couple'
(d) This is Robert Frost in 'Mending Walls'

23 Barabbas is ruined by Christians. He plans a revenge by resorting to incredible cruelties until he falls into a cauldron of boiling water prepared for his enemies. This is in short, the story of a play by Marlowe. Identify the play.
(a) Edward II (b) The Jew of Malta
(c) The Massacre of Paris (d) Dido

24 "But you can live in the most democratic country on Earth and if you're lazy, obtuse or servile within yourself, you are not free."
Which author in which novel has uttered these words?
(a) Haruki Murakami in A Wild Sheep Chase
(b) Isabel Allende in Maya's Note book
(c) Patrick White in Voss
(d) Ignazio Silone in novel 'Bread and Wine'

25 Who among the following is also known as a lexicographer?
(a) Webster (b) Golding (c) Johnson (d) Strene

26 Consider the following statements.
The main characteristics of 'Maria' are
1. It is written by Mary Wollstonecraft.
2. It is based on an upper class woman named Maria.
3. It is written by Mary Hays.
4. It is based on the working class woman Maria.

Which of the statements given above are correct?
(a) 1 and 4 (b) 1 and 2
(c) 3 and 4 (d) 3 and 2

27 Match the following works with their authors correctly.

List I	List II
A. Phineas Fletcher	1. Coopers Hills
B. Edmund Waller	2. Poetical Blossoms
C. Sir John Denham	3. Go Lovely Rose
D. Abraham Cowley	4. The Locusts

Codes

	A	B	C	D		A	B	C	D
(a)	4	1	2	3	(b)	1	2	4	3
(c)	3	2	4	1	(d)	4	3	1	2

28 In whose opinion Longinus "classicism was touched with romance"?
(a) Abercrombic (b) Scott James
(c) Wimsatt (d) Atkins

29 The tramp in Pinter's first big hit, the care taker often travels under an assumed name. It is
(a) Bernard Jenkins (b) Roly Jenkins
(c) Jack Jenkins (d) Peter Jenkins

30 The novel has a scene where African American students are made to compete and fight with each other as they rush for gold coins tossed on an electric blanket. Identify the novel
(a) Richard Wright : Native Son
(b) James Baldwur : Another Country
(c) Ralph Ellison : Invisible Man
(d) Toni Morrison : Bluest Eye

31 **Assertion** (A) Literature Research requires research materials.
Reason (R) The materials of literary research are manuscripts and printed books.
(a) A is true but R is correct
(b) R is true but A is not correct
(c) A is not correct and R is not correct explanation of A
(d) A is correct and R is correct explanation of it

32 Morphology is the grammar of ....
(a) words (b) phrases
(c) clauses (d) sentences

33 Which of the following is not true for Richard Hoggart?
(a) He served as a Warden at University of London.
(b) He began a journal titled, 'Politics and Letters'
(c) He served as the Assistant Director of UNESCO from 1971-75
(d) He was part of the Royal Artillery during the Second World War.

34 Match the following

List I	List II
A. William Wordsworth	1. the study of poetry
B. BST Coleridge	2. the biographic literia
C. Matthew Arnold	3. the lyrical ballads
D. TS Eliot	4. tradition and individual talent

Codes

	A	B	C	D		A	B	C	D
(a)	3	2	1	4	(b)	1	2	3	4
(c)	2	1	3	4	(d)	3	4	2	1

35 The Suffragette movement's purpose was ....
(a) social reform
(b) women's rights
(c) democratic reforms
(d) children's rights

36 Paying a tribute to a Bengali poet who wrote in English also, Sri Aurobindo said, "The God himself took up thy pen and wrote." Who was he?
(a) Michael Madhusudan Dutt
(b) Henry Derozio
(c) Romesh Chandra Dutt
(d) Kashiprasad Ghose

37 What tone will be best suited to the following poem.

And, by the incantation of this verse,
Scatter, as from an
Un extinguished hearth
Ashes and Sparks, my words
among mankind!
Be through my lips to
Unawakened' Earth
The trumphet of a prophecy! O wind
If winter comes, can spring be far behind?

(a) regret
(b) exultation
(c) optimism
(d) gloomy

38 Match the following

	List I		List II
A.	John Steinbeck	1.	The Glass Menagerie
B.	Chinua Achebe	2.	In Dubious Battle
C.	William Howell	3.	A Man of the People
D.	Tennessee Williams	4.	Indian Summer

Codes

	A	B	C	D		A	B	C	D
(a)	1	2	3	4	(b)	1	4	3	2
(c)	2	3	4	1	(d)	4	3	2	1

39 The Romance stories during Anglo-Norman period were influenced by

(a) English and French sources
(b) English and Norman sources
(c) Latin and English sources
(d) Latin and French sources

40 "A curious modern note begins to be apparent at this period. There is a sharper spirit of criticism, a more searching interest in men's affairs and a less child like whin and a less complacent acceptance, of the established order. The vogue of the romance, though it has by no means gone, is being superseded by the more acute spirit of drama, which even at this early time is faintly foreshadowed.

Another more modern feature that at one strikes the observer is that the age of anonymity is passing away. Though many of the tests still lack named authors, the greater number of books can be definitely ascribed. Moreover, we have for the first time a figure of outstanding literary importance, who gives to the age the form and pressure of his genius."

The above extract is said by whom and for whom?

(a) Edward Albert for Chaucer
(b) Edward Spenser for Chaucerian Age
(c) Edward Albert for Chaucerian Age
(d) William Langland for Chaucer

41 In the given series, which one has characters, matched correctly with their plays

(a) Caludius-Rosencrantz and Guildenstern Are Dead, Bernard-The Death of a Salesman, Joey-The Home-Coming, Lulu-The Birthday Party.
(b) Claudius-The Death of a Salesman, Bernard-The Home-Coming, Joey-The Birthday Party, Lulu-Rosencrantz and Guildenstern Are Dead.
(c) Claudius-The Home-Coming, Bernard-The Birthday Party, Joey-Rosencrantz and Guidlenstren Are Dead, Lulu-The Death of a Salesman.
(d) Claudius-The Birthday Party, Bernard-Rosencrantz and Guildenstern Are Dead, Joey-The Death of a Salesman, Lulu-The Home-Coming.

42 .... is noted for his ability to create comedy and satire out of depressing human predicament.

(a) Joyce Cary
(b) Kingsley Amis
(c) William Cooper
(d) Keith Spencer Waterhouse

43 In Madurai city of temples and poets who sang of water and temples every summer a river dries to a trickle

(a) This is AK Ramanujan in 'A River'
(b) This is Sarojini Naidu in 'Bangle Sellers'
(c) This is Arun Kolatkar in 'Jejure'
(d) This is Jayanta Mahapatra in 'A Father's Hours'

44 "The world is what it is; men who are nothing, who allow themselves to become nothing, have no place in it."

Which of the Indian writers in which of his/her works has quoted the above lines?

(a) Anita Desai, Fasting and Feasting
(b) Khushwant Singh, Train to Pakistan
(c) VS Naipaul, A Bend in the River
(d) RK Narayan, The Bachelor of Arts

45 Which of the following statements best describe an example of the influence of an affective factor on second language acquisition?

(a) A second language learner makes educated guesses about meanings of words in a text.
(b) A second language learner uses familiar vocabulary to form sentences mentally before speaking.
(c) An adult second language learner finds it impossible to form second language sounds that do not occur in Ist language.
(d) A second language learner employs several words from the first language while speaking but not in wirting.

46 Who among the following characters in Thomas More's Utopia did not correspond in biographical background to an actual historic person

(a) Morton
(b) Hythloday
(c) Giles
(d) More

47 Who among the following writers describes novels as "not form which you see but emotion which you feel"?
(a) DH Lawrence (b) Jean Rhys
(c) Virginia Woolf (d) Joseph Conrad

48 Locke's Essay concerning Human Understanding is a classic statement of .... philosophy.
(a) aesthetic (b) empiricist
(c) nationalist (d) None of these

49 "Things fall apart; the centre cannot hold". These are the opening lines of
(a) The Second Coming (b) Vacillation
(c) The Hound of Heaven (d) None of these

50 In the given series, which one has all the American poets matched correctly with their poems.
(a) Robert Frost-Ballads of Lost Heaven, Sylvia Plath-Aunt Jennifer's Tigers, William Bliss Carmen-A Mosque of Mercy, Adrienne Rich-Mirror
(b) Robert Frost-Aunt Jennifer's Tigers, Sylvia Plath-A Mosque of Mercy, William Bliss Carmen-Mirror, Adrienne Rich-Ballads of Lost Heaven
(c) Robert Frost-A Mosque of Mercy, Sylvia Plath-Mirror, William Bliss Carmen-Ballads of Lost Heaven, Adrienne Rich-Aunt Jennifer's Tigers
(d) Robert Frost-Mirror, Sylvia plath-Ballads of Lost Heaven, William Bliss Carmen-Aunt Jennifer's Tigers, Adrienne Rich-A Mosque of Mercy

51 "But pleasures are like poppies spread,
You seize the flower, it's bloom is shed;
Or, like the snow-fall in the river,
A moment white, then melts forever."
Which of the following poets in which of his/her works has used the above lines?
(a) William Blake, 'Barren Blossom'
(b) Robert Burns, Tam O'Shanter
(c) Alexander Pope, An Essay on Criticism
(d) William Cowper, The Poetical Works Of William Cowper

52 Which among the following is a fragment, which seems to have planned as the story of a pure young girl, who fell under the spell of a sorcerer, in the shape of a woman Geraldine?
(a) Day Dream (b) The Devil Thought
(c) Christabel (d) Kubla Khan

53 How would you describe George Meredith's Modern Love (1862)?
(a) A ballad (b) A lyric travelogue
(c) A verse romance (d) A sonnet sequence

54 Choices of linguistic forms in using a language or how a language in actually spoken/written, especially one that differs from its prescribed grammar, is called
(a) utterance (b) use
(c) usage (d) deviation

55 Consider the following statements about structuralism which of these are correct
1. Structuralism got spread all over the world following a rise in its importance in France.
2. Structuralism is related to criticism in all fields of literature and painting.
3. Structuralism began in 1960s.
4. Structuralism tries to identify some already tentum structures in all new creations.

Codes
(a) 1, 2 and 3 (b) 1, 3 and 4 (c) 3 and 4 (d) 1 and 4

56 Match the following

List I	List II
1. Allan Nevins	A. Visual Methodology
2. George Bateson	B. Oral History
3. Zellig Harris	C. Ethnography
4. Gerhard Friedrich Muller	D. Discourse Analysis

Codes

	1	2	3	4
(a)	C	A	D	B
(b)	B	A	D	C
(c)	A	B	C	D
(d)	D	B	A	C

57 "The intellect, as a means for the preservation of the individual, develops its chief power in dissimulation; for its by dissimulation that the feebler, and less robust individuals preserve themselves, since it has been denied them to fight the battle of existence..."
Identify the source of the above-mentioned lines.
(a) Friedrich Nietzsche's On Truth and Falsity in an Ultramoral Sense
(b) Michael Foucault's Truth and Power
(c) David Thoreau's Civil Disobedience
(d) Aijaz Ahmed's Notes Towards the Definition of a Category

58 Which of the following has Scottish Chaucerians in the correct chronological order?
(a) Sir David Lindsay, William Dunbar, Robert Henryson, James I
(b) James I, William Dunbar, Robert Henryson, Sir David Lindsay
(c) James I, Robert Henryson, William Dunbar, Sir David Lindsay
(d) William Dunbar, Robert Henryson, Sir David Lindsay, James I

59 "Perhaps my best years are gone. When there was a chance of happiness. But I wouldn't want them back. Not with the fire in me now. No, I wouldn't want them back."
Which of the following dramatists in which of his/her works has had the above lines?
(a) John Galsworthy, Flowering Wilderness
(b) Samuel Beckett, Krapp's Last Tape and Embers
(c) Noel Coward, Blithe Spirit
(d) Eugene Ionesco, The Bald Soprano

60 Match the following

List I	List II
A. Thomas Cranmer	1. The Boke Called the Governor
B. Henry Medwall	2. The Sphera
C. Thomas Elyot	3. Fulgens and Lucrece
D. George Buchanan	4. The Book of Common Prayer

Codes

	A	B	C	D
(a)	1	2	3	4
(b)	4	3	1	2
(c)	2	4	3	1
(d)	3	4	1	2

61 **Assertion** (A) Gender is manufactured.
Reason (R) Gender is performed through gendered stylisation of the body.

(a) Both A and R are true
(b) Both A and R are false
(c) Both A and R are true, but R is not the correct explanation of A
(d) Both A and R are true, and R is the correct explanation of A

62 "Men look at women. Women watch themselves being looked at. This determines not only most relations between men and women but also the relation of women to themselves. The surveyor of woman in herself is male : the surveyed female." Identify the text from which the above-mentioned lines have been taken.

(a) John Bergers' Ways of Seeing
(b) Margaret Atwood's Surfacing
(c) George Eliot's Middleton
(d) Lisa Harper's The Eyes Accost

Direction (Q. Nos. 63) *In the questions given below are two statements labelled as Assertion (A) and Reason (R). In context of the two statements, which one of the following is correct?*

Codes

(a) Both A and R are true and R is the correct explanation of A
(b) Both A and R are true, but R is not correct explanation of A
(c) A is true, but R is false
(d) A is false, but R is true

63 **Assertion** (A) Charles Dickens saw his father going through hardships.
Reason (R) Dickens entire family suffered and Dickens had to leave school and work in a factory.

64 Dorothea marries .... in the end of the novel Middle march.

(a) Casaubon (b) Lydgate
(c) Ladislaw (d) Fredvincy

65 The function of criticism is not merely 'judgement in literature' but "a disinterested endeavour to learn and propagate the bast that is known and thought in the world, and thus to establish current of fresh and new ideas." Who expressed this opinion?

(a) Ruskin (b) Carlyle
(c) Arnold (d) IA Richards

66 Match the following poets with their poems.

List I (Poet)	List II (Poem)
A. Edmund Spenser	1. The Shepheardes Calender
B. Philip Sidney	2. Astrophell and Stella
C. Michael Drayton	3. Endymion and Phoebe
D. Fulke Greville	4. The Phoenix Nest

Codes

	A	B	C	D		A	B	C	D
(a)	1	2	3	4	(b)	4	3	2	1
(c)	3	1	4	2	(d)	2	4	1	3

67 Consider the following statements about Fulke Greville.

1. He sailed with Sir Francis Drake in his expedition to the Spanish West Indies in 1585.
2. He joined the Earl of Leicester against the wishes of Queen Elizabeth in 1586.
3. He wrote an elegy 'The Phoenix Nest' on the death of Philip Sydney.
4. He wrote a biography of his friend 'Life of the Renowned Sir Philip Sydney.

Which of the statements given above are correct?

(a) 1 and 2 (b) 2 and 3
(c) 1 and 4 (d) 3 and 4

68 "Be still, sad heart! and cease repining;
Behind the clouds is the sun still shining;
Thy fate is the common fate of all,
Into each life some rain must fall"

Which of the following poets in which of his/her works has used the above lines?

(a) Ted Hughes, Birthday Letters
(b) Philip Larkin, The Whitsun Weddings
(c) Henry Wadsworth Longfellow, Ballads and Other Poems.
(d) Walt Whitman, Leaves of Grass

69 Consider the following statements for HW Longfellow.

1. He began to publish poetry at the age of 13.
2. He is known as children's poet.
3. He wrote the elegy 'O captain, My captain'.
4. He was called the 'Pride of America.'

Which of the statements given above is correct For HW Long Fellow?

(a) 1 and 2 (b) 2 and 3 (c) 3 and 4 (d) 2 and 4

70 **Dadaism movement was the result of**
(a) French Revolution
(b) Insensitivity of Victorian Poets
(c) The Modern Age (d) The Augustan Age

71 **Which work of Fortescue is also known as the difference between an absolute and limited monarchy?**
(a) The Governance of England
(b) De Laudibus Legum Angliae
(c) The Twenty-Two Righteousness belonging to a Ling
(d) The Commodities of England

72 **"Ministers can but speak to the ear, the Spirit speaks to the heart."**
Which of the following writers in which of his/her works has used the above lines?
(a) Hugh Latimer, The Martyrdom
(b) William Tyndale, The Writings of A Puritan's Mind Volume 1
(c) John Foxe, Fox's Book of Martyrs Or A History of the Lives, Sufferings, and Triumphant Deaths of the Primitive Protestant Martyrs
(d) Thomas Watson, The Ten Commandments

73 **Assertion (A) Modern Indian literature has been greatly influenced by English Literature. Reason (R) English has become an important element of contemporary Indian culture.**
Codes
(a) Both A and R are true and R is the correct explanation of A
(b) Both A and R are true, but R is not correct explanation of A
(c) A is true, but R is false
(d) A is false, bur R is true

74 **Which of the following pairs is in correctly matched?**
(a) Jayanta Mahapatra : Life Signs
(b) Kiran Desai : The Inheritance of Loss
(c) Amitav Ghosh : In Custody
(d) Arun Kolatkar : Jejuri

75 **For teaching grammar, the best grammar that a teacher can use is**
(a) traditional grammar (b) modern grammar
(c) pedagogic grammar (d) no grammar is needed

76 **Match the following Indian English writers with literary works**

Indian English Writers	Literary Works
1. HN Chattopadhyaya	A. The Coffin
2. Arundhati Roy	B. The Algebra of Indefinite Justice
3. Anita Desai	C. Fire on the Mountain
4. Amitav Ghosh	D. The Incendiary Circumstances

Codes
(a) 1-A, 2-B, 3-C, 4-D (b) 1-D, 2-C, 3-B, 4-A
(c) 1-B, 2-D, 3-A, 4-C (d) 1-C, 2-A, 3-D, 4-B

77 **Assertion** (A) When women were censured for taking up writing as a career, Aphra Behn wrote a short novel, Oroonoko besides numerous plays. **Reason** (R) It is about an African prince, Oroonoko, who falls in love with a young woman, Imoinda.
Codes
(a) Both A and R are true and R is the correct explanation of A
(b) Both A and R are true, but R is not correct explanation of A
(c) A is true, but R is false
(d) A is false, bur R is true

78 **"All is not gold that glitters,**
Pleasure seems sweet, but proves a glass of bitters"
Which of the following dramatists in which of his/her works has used the above lines?
(a) Oliver Goldsmith, She Stoops to Conquer
(b) Oliver Glodsmith, The Good-Natured Man
(c) Joseph Addison, Cato
(d) Richard Steele, The Lying Lover

79 **"DAISY : I never knew you were such a realist-I thought you were more poetic. Where's your imagination? There are many sides to reality. Choose the one that's best for you. Escape into the world of imagination."**
Which of the following dramatists in which of his/her works has had the above lines?
(a) John Galsworthy, The White Monkey
(b) Sean O'Casey, Red Roses for Me
(c) Eugene Ionesco, Rhinoceros
(d) Samuel Becket, Waiting for Godot

80 **In this research, the field study applies the laws to draw more and more clear ideas about the problem. Identify this research.**
(a) Applied research (b) Action research
(c) Philosophical research (d) All of these

81 **Who said, "The preface to Lyrical Ballads explains the poetic process of the type of poetry only Wordsworth wrote?**
(a) IA Richard (b) FR Leavis (c) Coleridge (c) Baker

82 **If you arc reading like a new critic, what sort of things are you looking for?**
(a) Ambiguity, tension, irony, paradox, technique, form
(b) Clues to the author's love life, dreams and relationship to his/her parents
(c) Hints about the author's politics
(d) Evidence for what life was like back in the days

83 **"Doublethink means the power of holding two contradictory beliefs in one's mind simultaneously, and accepting both of them." Which of the following modern non-fiction writers in which of his/her works has used the above lines?**

(a) Hilaire Belloc, An Essay on the Restoration of Property
(b) George Orwell, 1984
(c) Graham Greene, The Third Man
(d) Edward Verrall Lucas, London Lavender

84 Major Scobie is a character in novel .... by Graham Greene.
(a) A Sort of Life
(b) The Heart of the Matter
(c) The End of the Affair
(d) The White Peacock

85 Virginia Woolf's 'To the Lighthouse' begins in a piece of dialogue "Yes, of course, if it's fine tomorrow", said Mr Ramsay. "But you'll have to be up with lark", she added.
Present among the listeners of her remark is ....
(a) her father (b) her nephew
(c) her son (d) her driver

86 Graca, wife of former South African President Nelson Mandela remarked about which author in these lines
"Brutally and uncompromisingly honest, her beautifully crafted story telling enriches the already extra ordinary pool of young ...... writers of our time"?
(a) Sisonke Msimang (b) Susan Sontag
(c) Nadine Gordimer (d) Sarah Britten

87 "Loneliness clarifies. Here silence stands like heat. Here leaves unnoticed thicken, Hidden weeds flower, neglected waters quicken,
Luminously-peopled air ascends;
And past the poppies bluish neutral distance
Ends the land suddenly beyond a beach of shapes and shingle. Here is unfenced existence.
Facing the sun, untalkative, out of reach."
Which of the following poets in which of his/her works has used the above lines?
(a) Ted Hughes, Birthday Letters
(b) Philip Larkin, The Whitsun Weddings
(c) Henry Wadsworth Longfellow, Ballads and Other Poems
(d) Walt Whitman, Leaves of Grass

88 Who was the childhood friend of Helena in 'A Midsummer Night's Dream'?
(a) Thesus (b) Hermia (c) Lysander (d) Demetrius

89 The first printed collection of William Shakespeare's plays was brought out by Heming and Condell who asserted that they did the work "in order to keep the memory of so worthy a friend and fellow alive," What is this first edition now called?
(a) Heming and Condell's Edition
(b) Everyman's Shakespeare
(c) First Folio (d) Authentic Shakespeare

90 Which of these is correct about the Spanish Tragedy?
(a) It is not example of revenge tragedy
(b) It was modelled on Spenser's revenge tragedies
(c) The play did not introduce a new kind of character obsessive, blooding and mistrustful plotter
(d) It was not written between 1582 and 1589

91 What method is closely associated with New Criticism?
(a) Close reading
(b) Analysing how texts reflect their historical moment
(c) Exposing power relations
(d) Over-reading

92 The main aim of inter-disciplinary research is
(a) to reduce the importance of single subject in research domain
(b) to make the research problem more simple
(c) to give a new direction to research methodology
(d) to bring out integrated approach to research

93 Select the most suitable option.
A. Discourse analysis and text linguistics have an essential difference.
B. Discourse analysis aims at revealing the socio-psychological characteristics of a person rather than text structure.

Codes
(a) Both A and B are correct (b) Both A and B are false
(c) Only A is correct (d) Only B correct

94 The right sequence of subgroups cognitive domain is
(a) knowledge, comprehension, application, synthesis, analysis, evaluation
(b) knowledge, comprehension, application, evaluation, analysis, synthesis
(c) knowledge, comprehension, evaluation, application, analysis, synthesis
(d) knowledge, comprehension, application, analysis, synthesis, evaluation

95 Which word is applied to denote the whole translation from the Middle Ages to the modern world, is more correctly applied to the revival of art resulting from the discovery and imitation of classic models in the 14th century?
(a) Renaissance (b) Reformation
(c) Restoration (d) Humanism

Directions (Q.Nos. 96-100) *Read the Passage carefully and answer the questions that follow. Adapted from 'The Cask of Amontillado' by Edgar Allan Poe (1846)*

The thousand injuries of Fortunato to I had borne as I best could, but when he ventured upon insult I vowed revenge. You, who so well know the nature of my soul, will not suppose, however, that I gave utterance to a threat. At length I would be avenged; this was a point definitively settled-but the very definitiveness with which it was resolved precluded-the idea of risk. I must not only punish but punish with impunity. A wrong is unredressed when retribution overtakes its redresser. It is equally unredressed when the avenger fails to make himself felt as such to him who has done the wrong. It must be understood that neither by word nor deed had I given Fortunato cause to doubt my good will. I continued as was my wont, to smile in his face, and he did not perceive that my smile now was at the thought of his immolation.

He had a weak point - this Fortunato - although in other regards he was a man to be respected and even feared. He prided himself upon his connoisseurship in wine. Few Italians have the true virtuoso spirit. For the most part their enthusiasm is adopted to suit the time and opportunity to practice imposture upon the British and Austrian Millionaires. In painting and gemmary, Fortunato, like his countrymen, was a quack, but in the matter of old wines he was sincere. In this respect I did not differ from him materially; - I was skilful in the Italian vintages myself, and bought largely whenever I could.

It was about dusk, one evening during the supreme madness of the carnival season, that I encountered my friend. He accosted me with excessive warmth, for he had been drinking much. The man wore motley. He had on a tight-fitting parti-striped dress, and his head was surmounted by the conical cap and bells. I was so pleased to see him that I thought I should never have done wringing his hand.

I said to him - "My dear Fortunato, you are luckily met. How remarkably well you are looking to-day. But I have received a pipe of what passes for Amontillado, and I have my doubts."

"How?" said he. "Amontillado? A pipe? Impossible? And in the middle of the carnival"

"I have my doubts," I replied; and I was silly enough to pay the full Amontillado price without consulting you in the matter. You were not to be found, and I was fearful of losing a bargain."

"Amontillado!"

"I have my doubts."

"Amontillado!"

"And I must satisfy them."

"Amontillado!"

"As you are engaged, I am on my way to Luchesi. If anyone has a critical turn it is he. He will tell me."

"Luchesi cannot tell Amontillado from Sherry."

"And yet some fools will have it that his taste is a match for your own."

"Come, let us go."

"Whither?"

"To your vaults."

96 **"A wrong is equally unredressed when the avenger fails to make himself felt as such to him who has done the wrong" In this line, the narrator indicates that he wants what to happen?**

(a) He wants to avenge a harm done to Fortunato
(b) He wants Fortunato to know why he is being punished
(c) He wants to understand how Fortunato feels about having offended him
(d) He wants to make Fortunato apologise

97 **In the line "I continued, as was my wont, to smile in his face, and he did not perceive that my smile now was at the thought of his immolation," the word immolation is closest in meaning to what?**

(a) Sacrifice (b) Punishment
(c) Chastisement (d) Burning oneself

98 **In the line, "I must not only punish but punish with impunity," the word "impunity" is closest in meaning to what?**

(a) freedom from punishment or consequences
(b) disputation of the truth
(c) the taking on of responsibility for something
(d) exemption from lesssgal action

99 **In the line, "I continued, as was my wont, to smile in his face, and he did not perceive that my smile now was at the thought of his immolation," the word wont is closest in meaning to what?**

(a) A habitual way of doing something
(b) A desire for something
(c) A distaste for something (d) A need for something

100 **According to the first line, what causes the narrator to decide to vow revenge on Fortunato?**

(a) Fortunato has injured him in a thousand ways.
(b) Fortunato has become friends with Luchesi.
(c) Fortunato has claimed to be a connoisseur of wine.
(d) Fortunato has insulted him somehow.

ANSWERS

1. (b)	2. (b)	3. (a)	4. (c)	5. (c)	6. (c)	7. (c)	8. (c)	9. (c)	10. (b)
11. (d)	12. (a)	13. (a)	14. (c)	15. (b)	16. (b)	17. (b)	18. (a)	19. (b)	20. (b)
21. (b)	22. (a)	23. (b)	24. (d)	25. (a)	26. (b)	27. (d)	28. (b)	29. (a)	30. (c)
31. (d)	32. (a)	33. (a)	34. (a)	35. (b)	36. (a)	37. (c)	38. (c)	39. (d)	40. (c)
41. (a)	42. (d)	43. (a)	44. (c)	45. (b)	46. (b)	47. (c)	48. (b)	49. (a)	50. (c)
51. (b)	52. (c)	53. (d)	54. (c)	55. (d)	56. (b)	57. (a)	58. (c)	59. (c)	60. (b)
61. (d)	62. (a)	63. (a)	64. (c)	65. (c)	66. (a)	67. (d)	68. (d)	69. (a)	70. (c)
71. (a)	72. (d)	73. (a)	74. (c)	75. (c)	76. (a)	77. (b)	78. (a)	79. (c)	80. (a)
81. (a)	82. (a)	83. (b)	84. (b)	85. (c)	86. (a)	87. (b)	88. (b)	89. (c)	90. (b)
91. (a)	92. (d)	93. (a)	94. (a)	95. (a)	96. (a)	97. (d)	98. (a)	99. (d)	100. (a)

ENGLISH
Model Paper-2

General Instructions

1. There are total one hundred questions in this paper. Each question carries 2 marks.
2. All questions are compulsory.

---

1 In Ben Johnson's Volpone, the animal imagery includes
1. the fox and the vulture
2. the fly and the cockroach
3. the fly, the crow and the raven
4. the fox, the vulture and the goat

Codes
(a) 1 and 2 (b) Only 4
(c) 2 and 4 (d) 1 and 3

2 Which is the only epic preserved in the Anglo-Norman script in the British Museum
(a) Ipomedon
(b) Pelerinage de Charlemagne
(c) Romance of Horn
(d) None of these

3 Name the British poet, who was the successor of Chaucer, but predecessor of Spenser.
(a) Robert Henryson
(b) William Dunbar
(c) James I of Scotland
(d) Criseyde

4 What is the name of playlet Hamlet stages for Claudius?
(a) Slings and Arrows
(b) Vice of Kings
(c) The Murder of Gonzago
(d) The Slaying of Lucianus

5 When was John Webster's 'The White Devil' published?
(a) 1601 (b) 1609 (c) 1599 (d) 1612

6 The Fakir of Jhungheera was written by one of the first Indo-Anglian poets. The poem is often hailed as a "Competent narrative verse with Byronic echoes." Identify the writer.
(a) Toru Dutt
(b) Henry Derozio
(c) Michael Madhusudan Dutt
(d) Hassan Ali

7 Which Indian English writer has composed 'A Bend in The River'?
(a) Ram Mohan Roy
(b) VS Naipaul
(c) Amit Choudhary
(d) Tarashankar Bandopadhyay

8 Who composed the first English Dictionary?
(a) George Cavendish (b) Thomas More
(c) Johan Fisher (d) Thomas Elyot

9 Which novel out of the following contains 55 characters representing humanity?
(a) The Wife (b) The Pilgrim's Progress
(c) Holy State and Profane State
(d) Microsomography

10 What is the chief weakness of descriptive or structural approach?
(a) It neglects grammar (b) It neglects meaning
(c) It neglects rules (d) It is very complicated

11 Which of the following critics is not considered to have dealt basically with structuralism?
(a) Jacques Derrida (b) Vladmir Propp
(c) Claude Levi-Strauss (d) Roman Jacobson

12 When Keats writes about the beakerfull of the blissful Hippocrene?
'The Hippocrene' is
(a) the fountain for the horse
(b) A spring scared to the muse
(c) Mount Helicon produced from a blow of Pegasus.
(d) Both A and B

13 Match the following works with their authors

List I	List II
A. Sense and Sensibility	1. Walter Scott
B. Melincourt	2. Mary Wollstonecraft
C. Ivanhoe	3. Jane Austen
D. Maria or the Wrongs of Woman	4. Thomas Love Peacock

Codes

	A	B	C	D		A	B	C	D
(a)	2	3	1	4	(b)	3	4	1	2
(c)	4	3	2	1	(d)	4	3	1	2

14 "But how true it is that every pleasure has also its reverse side, in brief, its pain or, if not wholly true, how nearly so. Therefore, I have added to most of my pleasures the little flavour of bitterness..."
Whose words in which book are these?
(a) Simon Winchester in Holy Terror
(b) Rose Macaulay in Personal Pleasures (Essay)
(c) Joan Didion in The Year of Magical Thinking
(d) Maya Angelou in Letters to My Daughter

15 Sin qua non of a good research is
(a) Null Hypothesis
(b) Research supervisor who is good
(c) Well stocked library
(d) A good funding organisation

16 **Assertion** (A) Questionnaire can be used in literary research.
Reason (R) Questionnaire is a tool for data collection so it can be used for English research also.
(a) A is true but R is not correct
(b) R is true but A is not correct
(c) A is not true and R is not correct explanation
(d) A is true and R is correct explanation of A

17 The institutionalisation of Cultural Studies happened in
(a) Britain in 1964
(b) United States in 1980s
(c) In Britain in 1978
(d) In South Asia in 1980s

18 Which of the following pairs in incorrectly matched?
(a) Matthew Arnolds : Culture and Civilisation
(b) Richard Hoggart : Uses of Literacy
(c) Raymond Williams : Culture and Society
(d) Stuart Hall : Truth and Power

19 Ecocriticism.
(a) Is sometimes called 'green cultural studies'
(b) Is criticism concentration on the relationship between literature and natural environment
(c) Is one of the fastest growing critical approach
(d) All of the above

20 Who among the following is a Sahitya Akademi Award Winner and he loves to write for children?
(a) R K Naryan (b) Ruskin Bond
(c) Vievekananda (d) Anita Desai

21 Which of these historical events chronology pairs is correctly matched with their period?
(a) Hundred Years' War 1337-1453
(b) Edwardian Era War 1415-1453
(c) Caroline War 1337-1360
(d) Lancastrian War 1369-1389

22 **Assertion** (A) Grammar became complicated due to the Norman conquest.
Reason (R) People started finding the simplest way to communicate with people, who did not speak English.
Codes
(a) A is true, but R is false
(b) A is false, but R is true
(c) Both A and R are true, but R is not the correct explanation of A
(d) Both A and R are true, but R is the correct explanation of A

23 Which is not true about projects?
(a) It is a purposeful activity
(b) It is proceeded in social environment
(c) It is accomplished in real life
(d) It is teacher centred activity

24 The right sequence of sub-groups of psychomotor domain is
(a) perception, set, guided response, mechanism, complex overt response, adaptation, origination
(b) perception, complex over response, set, guided response, mechanism, adaptation, organisation
(c) set, origination, guided response, mechanism complex overt response, adaptation, perception
(d) guided response, mechanism, perception, set, adaptation, organisation, complex over response

25 According to Tai-Won-Kim, 'With its primary focus on magnificence's financial mismanagement and the political and economic consequences of his willful conduct, his play calls for a royal balance between extravagance and parsimony and thereby links the arts of political and personal government."
Who wrote the above mentioned play 'Magnificence'?
(a) William Caxton (b) Erasmus
(c) Skelton (d) Heywood

26 Consider the following statements regarding 'Second Shepherd's Play'.
1. It was written in late 15th century.
2. It is a part of Wakefield's cycle of mystery plays.
3. An angle arrives and tells the Shepherd that a child is born in Bethlehem.
4. But the child is not born.

Which of the statements given above is correct?
(a) Only 1 (b) Only 2 (c) Only 3 (d) Only 4

27 Name the earliest example of debate poetry in the Middle English Ages.
(a) Cursor Mundi (b) Roman de Troie
(c) The Owl and the Nightingale
(d) The legends of St Malchus

28 Match the following poems with their category of nature.

Poem	Category of Nature
1. The Owl and the Nightingale	A. Religious and Didactic
2. Lanval	B. Romance
3. Sir Degare	C. Lais
4. Love Rune	D. Debate

Codes

	A	B	C	D		A	B	C	D
(a)	1	2	3	4	(b)	4	3	2	1
(c)	3	1	4	2	(d)	2	4	3	1

29 The term Ecological imperialism was coined by
(a) Vandana Shiva (b) Lawrence Buell
(c) Paulo Freire (d) Alfred Crosby

30 "Count no man happy until he dies, free of pain at last" is the last line of
(a) Oedipus at Colonus
(b) Agamemmon
(c) Oedipus the King
(d) Orestes

31 ...... Every other stone
is God or Cousin
there is no crop
other than God
and God is harvested here
around the year'
This extract is from
(a) Jayant Mahapatra's Konark
(b) Arun Kolatkar's Jejuri
(c) P Lal's being very simple, God
(d) R. Parthasarthy's 'Under Another Sky'

32 The term 'cultural materialism' is associated with ......
(a) Stephen Greenblatt
(b) Raymond Williams
(c) Matthew Arnold
(d) Richard Hoggart

33 33. Match the following.

List I	List II
A. Crites	1. English drama
B. Eugenius	2. Classical drama
C. Lisideius	3. Modern drama
D. Neander	4. French drama

Codes

	A	B	C	D		A	B	C	D
(a)	2	3	4	1	(b)	3	4	1	2
(c)	1	2	3	4	(d)	2	4	1	3

34 According to 'Narratology', ... focalisation is classic narration called omniscient narration.
(a) Internal (b) External
(c) Spiritual (d) Zero

35 Identify the correct statements.
(a) Interviewing is a quantitative research method
(b) Interviewing includes other research methods like oral history and auto-biographical methods
(c) Interviewing does not include ethnographic methods
(d) All of the above

36 Frantz Fanon's 'Black Skin, White Masks' is an analysis of...
(a) Africa in relation to the dualism of Europe and the East
(b) Psychological effects of colonialism
(c) Anti-colonial texts
(d) The processess of decolonisation

37 **Assertion** (A) Arms and the man was GB Shaw's first commercial success.
Reason (R) It debunks romantic Recorism associated with war and deals with the futility of war.
Codes
(a) A is true, but R is false
(b) A is false, but R is true
(c) Both A and R are true, but R is not the correct explanation of A
(d) Both A and R are true and R is the correct explanation of A

38 'Jejuri', The Commonwealth Poetry Prize Winner work has been written by......
(a) Arun Kolatkar (b) Anita Desai
(c) A K Ramanujan (d) Kamala Das

39 Which of the following is not correct for Sarojini Naidu?
(a) Her outlook was casual in nature
(b) She was elected the President of the Indian National Congress in 1925
(c) She helped in Founding the All India Women's Conference in 1927
(d) She was called the Nightingale of India

40 Match of the following.

List I		List II	
A.	Joseph Addison	1.	Journal to Steel
B.	Tobias Smollett	2.	The Times
C.	Jonathan Swift	3.	Coffee House Politicians
D.	Charles Churchill	4.	Humphry Clinker

Codes

	A	B	C	D		A	B	C	D
(a)	1	2	3	4	(b)	3	4	1	2
(c)	4	3	2	1	(d)	1	3	2	4

41 Daniel Defoe wrote ……, which is a novel about a true story of a shipwrecked seaman?

(a) Moll Flanders (b) Sir Charles Grandison
(c) Clarissa (d) Robinson Crusoe

42 "O Lady! We receive but we give,
And in our life alone does Nature live:
Ours is her wedding garment, ours her shroud!
And would we ought behold, of higher work,
Than that inanimate cold world allowed"
The above extract has been taken from Coleridge's………

(a) Christabel
(b) Kubla Khan
(c) The Dejection Ode
(d) The Ancient Mariner

43 The scene of An Essay of Dramatic Poesy has been laid on……

(a) Hudson (b) Thames (c) Nile (d) Dover

44 Which of the following works of TS Eliot was a collage of juxtaposed, incomplete stories or fragments of stories, according to post-modernism?

(a) Prufrock and other observation
(b) The waste land
(c) The use of poetry and the use of criticism
(d) Essays ancient and modern

45 Which of the following arrangement of Matthew Arnold's critical works is in the correct chronological sequence?

(a) Preface to the poems– On translating Homer–Essays in criticism (1st series)–Culture and Anarchy (1869)–Essays in criticism (II series)
(b) On translating Homer–Culture and Anarchy–Essays in criticism (Ist and II series), Preface to the poems
(c) Culture and Anarchy–Preface to poems–Essays in criticism (Ist and II series) On translating Homer.
(d) None of the above

46 "I don't want realism. I want magic! Yes, yes, magic! I try to give that to people. I misrepresent things to them. I don't tell the truth, I tell what ought to be the truth. And it that's sinful, then let me be damned for it!"

Which of the following dramatists in which of his/her works has had the above lines?

(a) Harold Pinter, No Man's Land
(b) Arthur Miller, The Crucible
(c) Tennessee Williams, A Streetcar named Desire
(d) Eugene O'Neill, The Iceman Cometh

47 The given series, which one has all the novelists matched correctly with their works?

(a) George Eliot-Hard Times, Charles Dickens-The Four Georges, WM Thackeray-Romola, George Meredith-Vittoria
(b) George Eliot-Romola, Charles Dicknes-Hard Times, WM Thackeray-The Four Georges, George Meredith-Vittoria
(c) George Eliot-The Four Georges, Charles Dicknes-Vittoria WM Thackeray-Romola, George Meredith-Hard Times
(d) George Eliot-Vittoria, Charles Dickens-Hard Times, WM Thackeray, Romola, George Meredith-The Four Georges

48 Which of these statements is correct about Thackeray's Vanity Fair?

(a) It was not published serially in London in 1847 and 1848
(b) It does not have a subtitle
(c) It is a satirical novel of manners
(d) The title of the novel is derived from John Milton's allegorical story

49 The objective of Direct Method is

(a) to increase power of comprehension
(b) to increase communicative power
(c) to develop a command over the target language
(d) to develop personality

50 "Clouds come floating into my life, no longer to carry rain or usher storm, but to add colour to my sunset sky."

Which of the Indian writers in which of his/her works has quoted the above lines?

(a) Rabindranath Tagore – Stray Birds
(b) Arundhati Roy – The God of Small Things
(c) Swami Vivekananda – Letters of Swami Vivekananda
(d) Raja Rao – The Cat and Shakespeare: A Tale of India

51 Consider the following statements

1. Arthur Miller is considered one of the greatest American Dramatists.
2. He belonged to a prosperous family of high class.
3. 'His first play 'Honours at Dawn' won him the University's Avery Hopwood Award'.
4. 'Summer and Smoke' was written by him.

Which of the statements given above are correct?

(a) 1 and 2 (b) 2 and 3 (c) 1 and 3 (d) 3 and 4

52 **Assertion** (A) Literature is different from natural sciences.
Reason (R) Literary Research has to study both the text as well as the writer.
(a) A is true but R is not correct
(b) R is true but A is not correct
(c) Both A and R are true and R is the correct explanation of A
(d) None of them is correct

53 The term 'semiotics' means……
(a) A study of interface between different cultural usages of a given language
(b) A study of sings and symbols and how they are used
(c) A study of individual-specific usage of language
(d) A study of language change over a period of time

54 The field of study concerned with the construction of thought processes, including remembering, problem solving, and decision-making is called
(a) Pedagogy (b) Education
(c) Epistemology (d) Cognitive Development

55 John Stuart Mill was a liberal and believed that an individual could do whatever he pleased as long as it did not harm others. In what famous work did Mill outline his liberal beliefs?
(a) The Conscious Mind
(b) Freedom and Resentment
(c) On Liberty
(d) Being and Nothingness

56 Match the following non-fiction writers of the Revival Age with their works.

Non-Fictional Writers of the Revivial Age	Works
A. Reginald Peacock	1. Sermons before King Edward VI
B. Sir John Fortescue	2. De Laudibus legum Angliae
C. John Fisher	3. Treatise Concernynge The Seven Penytencyll Psalms
D. Hugh Latimer	4. Repressor of over much Blaming of the clergy

Codes

	A	B	C	D		A	B	C	D
(a)	1	2	3	4	(b)	4	3	2	1
(c)	4	2	3	1	(d)	3	1	2	4

57 "Ralph wept for the end of innocence, the darkness of men's heart and the fall through the air of the true, wise friend called Piggy."
(a) This is Booker T Washington in UP for Slavery
(b) This William G Golding in Lord of the Flies
(c) This is Doris May Lessing in The Golden Notebook
(d) This is Anthony D Powell in Afternoon Men

58 What is the correct chronological order of the birth of these novelists?
(a) Hawthorne, William Faulkner, Margaret Drabble, James Fenimore Cooper
(b) James Fenimore Cooper, Hawthorne, William Faulkner, Margaret Drabble
(c) Margaret Drabble, Hawthorne, James Fenimore Copper, William Faulkner
(d) Hawthorne, Margaret Drabble, James Fenimore Cooper, William Faulkner

59 "One kiss, my bonny sweetheart; I'm after a prize tonight.
But I shall be back with the yellow gold before the morning light.
Yet if they press me sharply, and harry me through the day,
Then look for me by moonlight,
Watch for me by moonlight,
I'll come to thee by moonlight, though hell should bar the way."
Which of the following poets in which of his/her works has used the above lines?
(a) William Butler Yeats, The Collected Poems of WB Yeats
(b) Alfred Noyes, The Highwayman
(c) TS Eliot, Four Quartets
(d) WH Auden, Collected Poems

60 What were New Criticism reacting against?
(a) Feminist readings of texts
(b) Marxism
(c) Historical and biographical readings of texts
(d) Oprah's book club

61 Elizabeth Barrett's poem 'the Cry of the Children' is concerned with which major issue on the Time of Troubles during the 1830s and 1840s?
(a) Women's rights and suffrage
(b) Child labour
(c) Chartism
(d) The prudishness and old-fashioned ideals of her fellow victorians

62 Fill in the blanks from Tennyson's The Princess.
Man for the field and woman for the….
Man for the sword and women for the …… she.
Man with the head and woman with the…… .
Man to command and woman to …… .
(a) crop: scabbard; foo; agree
(b) throne; scepter; soul; decree
(c) school; scalpel; pen; set free
(d) hearth: needle: heart; obey

63 Which of these statements about 'Dramatic' Monologue is incorrect?
(a) A single person, who is clearly not the poet utters the speech
(b) The person addresses and interacts with one or more people
(c) The main purpose of the lyric is to reveal the speaker's temperament and character
(d) The dramatic monologue as a poetic form achieved its first distinction in the works of Tennyson

64 RK Narayan is one of the most widely read Indian novelists. He wrote for more than fifty years including travelogues, English translations of Indian epics and his memoirs 'My Days.' Which of these is a fictional town created by him?
(a) Alleypey (b) Malgudi
(c) Udipi (d) Coimbatore

65 **Assertion** (A) Raja Ram Mohan Roy initiated movments to introduce Western scientific education through English.
Reason (R) Lord Macaulay was the chairman of the committee which was formed to take a decision regarding replacement of Sanskrit and Persian by English.
Codes
(a) Both A and R are true and R is the correct explanation of A
(b) Both A and R are true, but R is not the correct explanation of A
(c) A is true, but R is false
(d) A is false, but R is true

66 Which of the following pairs is correctly matched?

(a)	Amitav Ghosh	All About H Hatterr
(b)	Anita Desai	Inheritance of Loss
(c)	Shashi Deshpande	A Bend in the Ganges
(d)	Salman Rushdie	The Enchantress of Florence

67 Yasmine Gooneratne's 'The Pleasures of conquest termed as a post colonial novel of the 90s is ironically set in the tropical island nation of
(a) Sri Lanka (b) Fizi
(c) The Caribbean (d) Amnesia

68 Joseph Addison called him, 'The Miracle of the Present Age' and Alexander Pope wrote the epitaph for the monument erected in his memory. Who is the person?
(a) John Locke (b) Issac Newton
(c) Ashley Cooper (d) Christopher Wren

69 Which of the following statements best applies to Anna Karenina?
1. Among her most prominent qualities are her passionate spirit and determination to give life on her own terms
2. She accepts the exile to which she been condemned
3. She is a victim of Russian Patriarchal system
4. Anna is deeply devoted to her family and children

Codes
(a) 1 and 2 (b) 2 and 3 (c) 1 and 3 (d) 1, 3 and 4

70 Match the following.

List I (Novles)	**List II** (Major Symbols)
A. Dombey and Son	1. Fog
B. The Return of the Native	2. Train
C. Bleak House	3. Health
D. Tess of D' Urbervilles	4. Mist

Codes

	A	B	C	D		A	B	C	D
(a)	2	3	1	4	(b)	4	2	3	1
(c)	2	3	4	1	(d)	1	3	4	1

71 The following is an exchange between two characters husband and wife, in a famous play. The lines appear at the very end of an emotionally changed sequence of the last scene.
"...... I've stopped believing in miracldes."
But I'll believe tell me! Transform ourselves to the point that......"?
"That on living together could be a true marriage." She goes out of the hall.
Which play? name the characters.
(a) Othello, Desdemona and Othello
(b) Sure Thing, BiII and Betty
(c) A Doll's House, Helmer and Nora
(d) Death of a Salesman, Willy and Linda

72 Virginia Woolf borrowed the idea of the common reader from Dr Johson To which particular work of Johnson's does she remain indebted?
(a) The Lives of the most eminent English Poets, The essay on Milton
(b) The Lives of the most Eminent English Poets, the essay on Gray
(c) Preface to Shakespeare
(d) The Patriot

73 Identify the post Apartheid novel by Nadine Gordimer.
(a) The Conservationist (b) The House of Gun
(c) The Lying Days (d) Burger's Daughter

74 William Wordsworth had a deep influence on Thomas Hardy. 'According to Hardy' a particular peom by Wordsworth was his best cure for despair. Name the poem.
(a) Michael
(b) Tintern Abbey Revisited
(c) The Idiot Boy
(d) The Leech Gatherer

75 I sit in one of the *dives*
On Fifty Second Street,
Uncertain and afraid
As the clever hopes expire
Of a low dishonest decade.
So beings Auden's 1st September, 1939. What is the meaning of the word in itatlics
(a) bench (b) night club
(c) house (d) park

76 Which of the following is not a product of learning?
(a) Skill (b) Knowledge
(c) Maturation (d) Physical Structure

77 Which of the following second language learner would most likely acquire the second language more easily?
(a) A high school student who has been enrolled in mandatory classess in the second language from elementary level
(b) A visitor to a country where 2nd language is spoken
(c) A business person for whom fuency in the second language may lead to carreer advancement
(d) An immigrant living in a country where the second language is spoken he feels accepted by speakers of the second language

78 **Assertion** (A) In 1958, The Central Institute of English was stated in Hyderabad. Regional institutes were established in Bangalore and Chandigarh.
Reason (R) Officialy, English has the status of main (prime) language in India.
Codes
(a) Both A and R are true and R is the correct explanation of A
(b) Both A and R are true but R is not the correct explanation of A
(c) A is true but R is false
(d) A is false but R is true

79 Considered to be the first professional woman writer, Aphra Behn's first play,...... appeared in 1670.
(a) The Amorous Prince
(b) Abdelazer
(c) The Rover
(d) The Forc'd Marriage

80 George, the eldest son, was in love with the daughter of a neighbouring gentleman. As their fortunes were well-suited, the match was certain to take place in the play 'The Vicar of Wakefield.' What was the name of the lovely young lady?
(a) Miss Rosamund Carteret (b) Miss Catherine Spriggs
(c) Miss Elizabeth Darby (d) Miss Arabella Wilmot

81 Match the following.

List I (Novles)	List II (Major Symbols)
A. The Mourning Bride	1. William Wycherley
B. The Gentleman Dancing Master	2. Thomas Otway
C. The Sullen Lovers	3. William Congreve
D. Don Carlos	4. Thomas Shadwell

Codes

	A	B	C	D		A	B	C	D
(a)	1	2	3	4	(b)	2	3	1	4
(c)	3	1	4	2	(d)	3	2	1	4

82 In the given series, which one has all the Indian English authors matched correctly with their mood and style of writing?
(a) VS Naipaul-Memoirist, Vikram Seth-Elizabethan Style, Sri Aurobindo-Pessimistic, TP Kailasam-Humorous Plays
(b) VS Naipaul-Humorous Plays, Vikram Seth Pessimistic, Sri Aurobindo-Elizabethan Style, TP Kailsam-Memoirist
(c) VS Naipaul-Pessimistic, Vikram Seth-Memoirist, Sri Aurobindo-Elizabethan Style, TP Kailsam-Humorous Plays
(d) VS Naipaul- Elizabethan Style, Vikram Seth-Humorous Plays– Sri Aurobindo- Memoirist, TP Kailasam Pessimistic

83 Which of the following options are the main tasks of research in modern society?
1. To add on to the existing knowledge.
2. To explore new facts.
3. To conduct a systematic examination and analyse the data collected in an objective manner.
4. To evaluate the earlier writings

Which of the following options are correct?
(a) 1, 2 and 3 (b) 4, 2 and 3
(c) 2 and 3 (d) 2, 3 and 4

84 Who is stated to have said, "Criticism is the art of interpreting art"?
(a) Dryden (b) M Arnold
(c) Water Pater (d) TS Eliot

85 Match the following works with their authors

Works	Authors
A. Das Kapital	1. Jacques Derrida
B. Of Grammatology	2. Elanie Showalter
C. A Literature of their own	3. Luce Irigaray
D. This Sex which is not one	4. Karl Marx

Codes

	A	B	C	D		A	B	C	D
(a)	4	1	2	3	(b)	1	2	3	4
(c)	2	1	4	3	(d)	1	3	2	4

86 A major theory associated with structuralism is ......
(a) Binary opposition (b) Nihilism
(c) Existential crisis (d) Absurdity

87 Match the following works with the authors or which of the given set is correctly matched with their authors?
(a) Thomas Delorey- The Unfortunate Traveller, Thomas Moore- The New Atlantis, Francis Bacon- The Unfortunate Traveller, Thomas Nashe-Utopia
(b) Thomas Delorey- Jack of Newbery, Thomas Moore-Utopia, Francis Bacon- The New Atlantis, Thomas Nashe- The Unfortunate Traveller

(c) Thomas Delorey-Utopia, Francis Bacon- The New Atlantic, Thomas Moore-The Unfortunate Traveller, Thomas Nashe- Jack of Newbery
(d) Thomas Delorey- The New Atlantis, Thomas Moore-The Unfortunate Traveller, Francis Bacon- Utopia, Thomas Nashe- Jack of Newbery

88 **Which of the following about 'Utopia' is correct statement?**
(a) It was originally written in French
(b) The Greek word 'Utopia' means nowhere but in modern parlance it signifies an ideal place
(c) It is written in four parts
(d) It is written by Thomas Lodge

89 **Who said, "Silence is the sleep that nourishes wisdom"?**
(a) Francis Bacon (b) Geoffrey Chaucer
(c) John Lyly (d) Philip Sydney

90 **Which of these books with their contents is incorrectly matched?**

(a)	The Book of the Duchess	Elegy on the Death of Blanche
(b)	The Parliament of Fowls	Marraige of King Richard II to Anne
(c)	Troilus and Criseyde	Trojan War
(d)	The House of Fame	Pilgrims on their Way to a Shrine

91 **A lovyere and a lusty bacheler,**
With lokkes crulle as they were leyd in presse.
Of twenty year of age he was, I gesse.
Of his stature he was of evene lengthe,
And wonderly deliver and greet of strengthe.
And he had been somtyme in chivachye.
In Flaundres, in Artoys and Pycardie,
And born hym wel, as of so litel space,
In hope to stonden in his lady grace.
Embrouded was he, as it were a meede
Al full of fresshe floures, whyte and rede.
Which pilgrim of Chaucer's Canterbury Tales is described in the above extract?
(a) The Squire (b) The Friar
(c) The Merchant (d) The Yeoman

92 **...... in 'A Midsummer Night's Dream' is a young man of Athens in love with Hermia?**
(a) Thesus (b) Oboneron (c) Titania (d) Lysander

93 **Match the following**

	List I		List II
A.	Every Man in His Humour	1.	1605
B.	The poetasters	2.	1610
C.	Volpone, The Fox	3.	1598
D.	The Alchemist	4.	1602

Codes

	A	B	C	D		A	B	C	D
(a)	3	4	2	1	(b)	3	4	1	2
(c)	4	3	2	1	(d)	2	1	4	3

94 **Which book of Tony Judt is nine hundred and sixty pages long?**
(a) When the facts change
(b) Past imperfect
(c) Thinking the twentieth century
(d) Post War: A History of Europe since 1945

95 **What is the name of memoir written by Sisonke Msimang?**
(a) Africa Day is for big Men
(b) Always Another Country
(c) The Uber Driver and Muhammad Ali
(d) Africa's Frist lady

96 **In whose book do these lines appear 'The military authorities' were concerned that soldiers going home on leave would demoralise the home population with horror stories of the Ostfront."**
(a) Graham Greene in Journals 1982
(b) Tony Judt in When the Facts Change
(c) Antony Beevor in Stalingrad
(d) AN Wilson in Tolstoy, A Biography

Directions (Q. Nos. 97-101) *Read the given poem and answer the questions that follow.*

A Bird Came Down.
A Bird, came down the Walk
He did not know I saw
He bit an Angle Worm in halves
And ate the fellow, raw,
And then he drank a dew
From a convenient grass
And then hopped sidewise to the wall
To let a Beele pass
He glanced with rapid eyes,
That hurried all abroad
They looked like frightened Beads, I thought,
He stirred his Velvet Head
Like one in danger, Cautious,
I offered him a Crumb,
And he unrolled his feathers,
And rowed him softer Home
Than Oars divide the Ocean,
Too silver for a seam
Or Butterflies off Banks of Noon,
Leap Plashless as they swim.

97 **What is the poem about?**
(a) A normal occurrence in nature of a bird searching for its food and its interaction with a human
(b) A fight between a bird and a poet
(c) A bird eating a beetle
(d) A bird teaching others how to eat a worm

98 **Why has the poet called the grass convenient?**
(a) Because the bird could see the beetle in the grass
(b) Because grass is greener on the other side
(c) Because it was easy for the bird to have dew from it.
(d) Because the bird could see the worm in the grass

99 How do you explain the 'plashless' in the last line?

(a) The poet tells us that the bird cannot swim
(b) Since the bird does not have oars it could not splash in the water
(c) Since dew was on the grass the bird did not make a splash
(d) The poet compares the flight of the bird as though it was a 'swim' in the air without the accompanying splashes on water

100 The bird did not do which of the following?

(a) Cook the worm and eat it
(b) Let the beetle pass
(c) Unroll his feathers
(d) Glance with rapid eyes

101 How does the poet descirbe the eyes of the bird?

(a) Watery like dew
(b) Like grass
(c) Like frightened beads
(d) Like butterflies

ANSWERS

1. (d)	2. (b)	3. (b)	4. (c)	5. (d)	6. (b)	7. (b)	8. (d)	9. (d)	10. (b)
11. (a)	12. (d)	13. (b)	14. (b)	15. (b)	16. (d)	17. (a)	18. (c)	19. (d)	20. (b)
21. (a)	22. (b)	23. (d)	24. (a)	25. (c)	26. (d)	27. (c)	28. (b)	29. (d)	30. (c)
31. (b)	32. (b)	33. (a)	34. (b)	35. (b)	36. (b)	37. (d)	38. (a)	39. (a)	40. (d)
41. (d)	42. (c)	43. (b)	44. (b)	45. (a)	46. (c)	47. (b)	48. (c)	49. (c)	50. (a)
51. (c)	52. (c)	53. (b)	54. (d)	55. (a)	56. (c)	57. (b)	58. (b)	59. (b)	60. (d)
61. (b)	62. (d)	63. (d)	64. (b)	65. (b)	66. (d)	67. (d)	68. (b)	69. (d)	70. (a)
71. (c)	72. (b)	73. (b)	74. (a)	75. (b)	76. (d)	77. (d)	78. (c)	79. (d)	80. (d)
81. (c)	82. (c)	83. (c)	84. (c)	85. (a)	86. (a)	87. (b)	88. (b)	89. (a)	90. (d)
91. (a)	92. (d)	93. (b)	94. (d)	95. (b)	96. (c)	97. (a)	98. (c)	99. (d)	100. (a)
101. (c)									

ENGLISH

Model Paper-3

General Instructions

1. There are total one hundred questions in this paper. Each question carries 2 marks.
2. All questions are compulsory.

---

1 Arthur Symons wrote about this person, "All the life of the tiny figure seemed to concentrate itself in the eyes they turned towards beauty as the sunflower turns towards the sun." Who is the person referred to?

(a) Toru Dutt
(b) Aru Dutt
(c) Sarojini Naidu
(d) Rabindranath Tagore

2 Which of these writers of characters deals with one character in all his essays?

(a) Samuel Butler (b) John Donne
(c) George Herbert (d) Thomas Fuller

3 Which of the following statements about the genres during Anglo-Norman period is incorrect?

(a) Chronicles recorded the history of kings
(b) Works of early writers were mostly romances
(c) Religious writing portrayed the religious life of women
(d) Romances dealt with marvel filled adventures

4 Where did a new literature arise in the world, the first modern literature?

(a) Italy (b) Germany
(c) France (d) All of these

5 Who expounded the theory of 'Advaita'?

(a) Ramanujan (b) Sri Shankaracharya
(c) Madhavacharya (d) Swami Vivekananda

6 Which novel contains the famous characters like Mr Worldly Wiseman, Lord Hate-Good, Mr Steadfast etc?

(a) Leviathan
(b) The Pilgrim's Progress
(c) The Life and Death of Mr Badman
(d) Grace Abounding

7 Which is the most important work by John Locke, which is structurally divided into four books?

(a) Two Treatises of Government
(b) Some Thoughts Concerning Education
(c) Essay on Human Understanding
(d) None of the above

8 Whose collections of poems are these: A Time to Change, Sixty Poems, The Third, The Unfinished Man?

(a) P Lai (b) Nissim Ezekiel
(c) Kamala Das (d) Bina Aggarwal

9 A test of listening comprehension is a test of

(a) Receptive skill (b) Productive skill
(c) Hearing skill (d) Phonology skill

10 Who among the following was the first director of the Centre for Contemporary Cultural Studies?

(a) FR Leavis (b) Matthew Arnolds
(c) Richard Williams (d) Richard Hoggart

11 The scope of the Cultural studies program widened at the University of Birmingham with the publication of the following journal.
(a) Tel Quel
(b) Working Papers in Cultural Studies
(c) Culture and Civilisation
(d) The Interpretation of Cultures

12 ....read major works from an eccentric point of view and extend the application of concepts to area other than the natural world.
(a) Ecofeminists (b) Ecocentrists
(c) Ecocritics (d) Ecologists

13 Which of the following is incorrectly matched?

(a)	Samson Agonistes	John Milton
(b)	Mac Flecknoe	John Dryden
(c)	On a Girdle	William Davenante
(d)	Hudibras	Samuel Butler

14 **Assertion** (A) Very little theatrical activity was seen in England during the Puritan Age.
Reason (R) With the outbreak of the Civil War, theatres were closed down.
(a) A is true, but R is false
(b) A is false, but R is true
(c) Both A and R are true, but R is not the correct explanation of A
(d) Both A and R are true and R is the correct explanation of A

15 Mary Shelley's famous Gothic novel Frankenstein begins with a ....from the explorer Robert Walton to his sister.
(a) series of poem (b) narratives
(c) series of letters (d) sermon

16 Which character is Fanny Burney's novel Evelina utters these words?
"In all ranks and all stations of life, how strangely do characters and manner differ! Lord Orville, with a politeness which knows no intermission and makes no distinctions is as unassuming and modest as if he had never mixed the great and was totally ignorant of every qualification he possesses, this other lord, through lavish of compliments and fine speeches seems to me an entire stranger to real good breeding........".
(a) Mr Villars (b) Lady Howard
(c) Mrs Mirvan (d) Evelina

17 Post-structuralism particularly observes the following short-coming in structuralism.
(a) The structured it considered were not credible
(b) The structure it includes are not self-sufficient
(c) It over looked a number of basic structures
(d) The theory of structure of itself was not credible

18 Research is conducted
1. to generate new knowledge
2. to develop a theory
3. not to obtain research degree
4. reinterpret existing knowledge

Which of the above is correct?
(a) 1, 3, and 2
(b) 3, 2 and 4
(c) 2, 1 and 3
(d) 1, 2 and 4

19 The review of research reports should be done in context of
1. investigator bias
2. cultural context
3. methodological factors

Which of the following statements given above is/are correct?
(a) 1 and 3 (b) Only 1
(c) Only 3 (d) 1, 2, and 3

20 Who rejects the pathological theory of Catharsis that 'theatre is not a hospital'?
(a) Humphrey house
(b) FL Lucas
(c) Abercrombic
(d) IA Richards

21 Which of the following works of Tennyson are in correct chronological order?
(a) Poems; Chiefly Lyrical, The Princess, Maud and Other Poems, Idylls of the King
(b) The Princess, Idylls of the King, Maud and Other Poems, Poems; Chiefly Lyrical
(c) Idylls of the King, The Princess, Maud and the Other Poems, Poems, Chiefly Lyrical
(d) Maud and the Other Poems, Poems; Chiefly Lyrical, Idylls of the King, The Princess

22 "Sometimes I said: It is an empty name
I long for; to a name why should I give
The peace of all the days I have to live
Yet gave it all the same.
Alas, thou foolish one! alike unfit
For healthy joy and salutary pain:
Thou knowest the chase useless, and again
Turnest to follow it."

Which of the following poets in which of his/her works has used the above lines?
(a) Elizabeth Barrett Browning, Aurora Leigh and Other Poems
(b) Dante Gabriel Rossetti, Pre-Raphaelite Poetry: An Anthology
(c) Christina Rossetti, A Pause for Thought, Complete Poems
(d) Algernon Charles Swinburne, The Garden of Proserpine

23 Match the following works with their non-fiction writers of the Elizabethan Age:

Works	Non-Fiction Writer of the Elizabethan Age
1. Divers Voyages Touching the Discovery of America and the Islands Adjacent	A. Samuel Purchas
2. Purchas His Pilgrimage	B. Thomas North
3. Of the laws of Eccelesiastical Polity	C. Richard Hakluty
4. The Lives of the Gretians and Romanes Noble	D. Richard Hooker

Codes
(a) 1-A, 2-B, 3-C, 4-D
(b) 1-D, 2-C, 3-B, 4-D
(c) 1-B, 2-D, 3-A, 4-C
(d) 1-C, 2-A, 3-D, 4-B

24 Which author in which work said these lines, "There is no greater agony than bearing an untold story Inside You"?
(a) Antony Beevor is 'Stalingrad'
(b) Tony Judt in 'When the Facts Change'
(c) Maya Angelou in 'I Know why the Caged Bird Sings'
(d) AN Wilson in 'Penfriends from Porlock'

25 One of the principles of material preparation for language learning is that ....
(a) complex material should be chosen
(b) graded material should be chosen
(c) any kind of material can be chosen
(d) a small amount of material should be chosen

26 Which of the following is an incorrect assumption in language teaching?
(a) Learner's acquire language by trying to use it in real situations
(b) Learner's first language plays an important role in learning
(c) Language teaching should have a focus in communication activities
(d) Language teaching should emphasis on writing rather than speech.

27 Which of the following statements is incorrect about GB Shaw?
(a) He wrote 'Arms and the Man'
(b) He won the Nobel Prize in Literature
(c) He won an Oscar for adaptation of his play 'Pygmalion'
(d) He was a successful novelist

28 The play 'Waiting for Godot' established................ as a leading figure of the Theatre of Absurd.
(a) Sean O' Casey
(b) Noel Coward
(c) Eugene lonesco
(d) Samuel Beckett

29 Match the following.

List I	List II
A. David Malouf	1. The Solid Mandala
B. Patrick White	2. Wild Cat Falling
C. Peter Carey	3. Remembering Babylon
D. Colin Johnson	4. True History of the Kelly Gang

Codes

	A	B	C	D		A	B	C	D
(a)	1	3	2	4	(b)	3	1	4	2
(c)	2	3	1	4	(d)	3	4	2	1

30 The Poem 'Leda and the Swan' describes an act of
(a) Rape (b) Love (c) Murder (d) Mercy

31 What term has Aristotle used for the weaknesses error of fault in character of the tragic hero?
(a) Hamartia (b) Pripetia
(c) Cathasis (d) None of these

32 Which of the following novelists are in the chronological order as per their birth?
(a) Herbert Ernest Bales, Evelyn Waugh, Joyce Carry, Malcolm Lowry
(b) Evelyn Waugh, Malcolm Lowry, Joyce Carey, Herbert Ernest Bales
(c) Joyce Carey, Evelyn Waugh, Herbert Ernest Bales, Malcolm Lowry
(d) Malcolm Lowry, Joyce Carey, Evelym Waugh, Herbert Ernest Bales

33 "They fuck you up, your mum and dad. They may not mean to , but they do."
Which of the following poets in which of his/her works has used the above lines?
(a) TS Eliot, The Hollow Men
(b) Dylan Thomas, In Country Sleep, and Other Poems
(c) Ted Hughes, Season Songs
(d) Philip Larkin, High Windows

34 'Garmond of Gude Ladies' is written by
(a) Lyndsay (b) Henryson
(c) Lydgate (d) None of these

35 Which character is not correctly matched with the novel in which it appears?

(a)	Anut Polly	:	Adventure of Tom Sawyer
(b)	Roger Micheldene	:	One Fat Englishman
(c)	Charles Lumley	:	Hurry on Down
(d)	Stephen Larke	:	Key to the Door

36 **Assertion** (A) Jonathan Swift's novel 'Gulliver's Travels' is a satire.
Reason (R) It makes fun of human beings and their desire to conquests through was.
Codes
(a) A is true But R is false
(b) A is false But R is true
(c) Both A and R are true and R is the correct explanation of A
(d) Neither A nor R is correct.

37 "Nobody wanted your dance,
Nobody wanted your strange glitter, your floundering
Drowning life and your effort to save yourself,
Treading water, dancing the dark turmoil,
Looking for something to give."
Which of the following poets in which of his/her works has used the above lines?
(a) Ted Hughes, Birthday Letters
(b) Philip Larkin, The Whitsun Weddings
(c) Henry Wadsworth Longfellow, Ballads and Other Poems
(d) Walt Whitman, Leaves of Grass

38 Which of the following pairs is correctly matched?

(a)	Nathaniel Hawthorne	:	Poet
(b)	Walt Whitman	:	Critic
(c)	Edgar Allan Poe	:	Novelist
(d)	Bayard Taylor	:	Essayist

39 According to the 'Marxist criticism', what was the name of the group that had flourished in the 1920s until disbanded by the party even though their work was not strictly Marxist in spirit.
(a) Russian Formalists (b) German Formalists
(c) Irish Formalists (d) Korean Formalists

40 Arrange the following works by Richard Hoggarts in correct sequence.
1. A Sort of Clowning
2. Promises to Keep: Thoughts in Old age
3. First and Last Things
4. Everyday Language and Everyday life
(a) 1-3-4-2 (b) 1-3-2-4
(c) 2-3-4-1 (d) 4-3-2-1

41 **Assertion** (A) The coloniser seeks the colonised to reflect a certain pure image back at him; however, he encounters only an almost sameness, a non-quite otherness.
Reason (B) The colonised even when aspires to remake itself, only slips into hybridisation, no matter how subtle.
(a) Both A and R are true
(b) Both A and R are false
(c) Both A and R are true and R is the correct explanation of A
(d) Both A and R are true but R is not the correct explanation of A

42 During Anglo Norman period which language began to be discarded in favour of French and Latin.
(a) Spanish (b) Greek (c) English (d) Italian

43 Which of the following statements is correct about Eugene lonesco?
(a) He was one of the play wright of the 'Theatre of the Absurd'.
(b) His plays have not been characterised as 'anti-plays'.
(c) His plays do not beak the conventions of naturalistic theatre.
(d) His plays do not present parodies of human conditions.

44 In the context of English studies, what does ethnography questions?
(a) how to read and interpret English texts
(b) how to read English texts
(c) how to interpret English texts
(d) how to read and interpret ethnographic texts

45 Friendship is a disinterested commerce between equals; love, an abject intercourse between tyrants and slaves.
Which of the following dramatists in which of his/her works has used the above lines?
(a) Oliver Goldsmith, She Stoops to Conquer
(b) Oliver Goldsmith, The Good-Natured Man
(c) Joseph Addison, Cato
(d) Richard Steele, The Lying Lover

46 In which book of Rebecca the trials of Nazi war criminals were described?
(a) Black Lamb and Grey Falcon
(b) The Meaning of Treason
(c) The Court and the Castle
(d) The Nuremberg Trials

47 Match the following.

List I	List II
A. Jewish Background	1. Mulk Raj Anand
B. Nobel Prize Winner	2. Tagore
C. Padma Shree Award	3. Raja Rao
D. Studied in Cambridge University	4. Nissim Ezekiel

Codes

	A	B	C	D		A	B	C	D
(a)	4	2	3	1	(b)	4	1	2	3
(c)	4	1	3	2	(d)	1	2	3	4

48 "Gauri is my tribute to my Indian Womanhood." In which novel does Mulk Raj Anand depict Gauri?
(a) The Old Woman and the Cow
(b) Untouchable
(c) Savitri
(d) The Road

49 In the first three plays of Marlowe each of the heroes is consumed by a burning passion which leads to his doom. In The Jew of Malta, it is the greed for riches, in Dr Faustus it is inordinate thirst for knowledge. Which passing is depicted in his Tamburlaine?
(a) Thirst for bloodshed
(b) Homicidal instinct
(c) Lust
(d) Thirst for power

50 Who is the author of 'Delhi-A Novel'?
(a) Khushwant Singh (b) Mulk Raj Anand
(c) Dom Moraes (d) Arundhati Roy

51 Whichof the following statement is not true in case of multiple choice questions?

(a) Even an inexperienced teacher can prepare the questions easily.
(b) All choices appear to be plausible.
(c) Error-free and quick evaluation is possible by computer.
(d) Only one of the choices is the correct answer.

52 Which of the following statements are true?

1. Interviewing is a part of auto-biographical methods
2. Interviewing is a part of ethnographic methods
3. Interviewing is a part of textual analysis

Select the correct answer using the codes given below.

(a) Only 1 (b) 2 and 3
(c) 1, 2 and 3 (d) 1 and 2

53 The structure 'he goes to school' is often produced by learners due to

(a) failure of intelligence
(b) mother tongue interference
(c) over generalisations of rules
(d) wrong teaching

54 Which of the following is not written by Khushwant Singh?

(a) Sex, Scotch and Scholarship
(b) Truth, Love and Little Malice
(c) The Sunset Club
(d) A Rain of Rites

55 According to John Dewey, schools must prepare students for

(a) research (b) future life
(c) present life (d) entrepreneurship

56 Johnson's phrase, 'Fatal Cleopatra', refers to Shakespeare's....

(a) Neglect of the unities
(b) Fondness of puns
(c) Fondness for similes
(d) Love of allusion

57 In the given series, which one has all the religious texts matched correctly with their Indian English Composers?

(a) The Ramayana-AK Ramanujan, The Bhagwad Gita-Manmathanath Dutt, The Mahabharata-Mohini Chatterjee, Speaking of Shiva-Romesh Chauder Dutt
(b) The Ramayana-Romesh Chauder Dutt, The Bhagwat Gita-Mohini Chatterjee, The Mahabharata-Manmathanath Dutt, Speaking of Shiva-AK Ramanujan.
(c) The Ramayana-Mohni Chatterjee, The Bhagwat Gita-Ak Ramanujan, The Mahashtra-Romesh Chauder Dutt, Speaking of Shiva-Manmathanath Dutt
(d) The Ramyana-Manmathanath Dutt, The Mahashtra-Romesh Chauder Dutt, The Bhagwat Gita-AK Ramanujan, Speaking of Shiva-Mohini Chatterjee

58 Structuralism was popularised by

(a) Ferdinand De Saussure's book Courses in General Linguistic
(b) IA Richards Meaning of Meaning
(c) Wolfgang Iser's the Reading Process: Phenomenological Approach
(d) J Hillis Miller's The Disappearance of God

59 "All love is expansion, all selfishness is contraction. Love is therefore the only law of life. He who loves lives, he who is selfish is dying. Therefore love for love's sake, because it is the only law of life, just as you breathe to live."

Which of the Indian writers in which of his/her works has quoted the above lines?

(a) Rabindarnath Tagore – Stray Birds'.
(b) Arundhati Roy – 'The God of Small Things'.
(c) Swami Vivekananda – 'Letters of Swami Vivekananda'.
(d) Raja Roy – The Cat and Shakespeare: A Tale of India

60 Match the following Victorian poets with their poems.

Victorian Poet
1. Alfred Lord Tennyson
2. Robert Browning
3. Matthew Arnold
4. Elizabeth Barrett Browning

Poem
A. Charge of the Light Brigade
B. Porphyria's Lover
C. The Strayed Reveller and other Poems
D. The Battle of Marathon

Codes
(a) 1-A, 2-B, 3-C, 4-D (b) 1-D, 2-C, 3-B, 4-A
(c) 1-B, 2-D, 3-A, 4-C (d) 1-C, 2-A, 3-D, 4-B

61 "But love me for love's sake, that ever more Thou may'st love on through love' eternity". Which of the following poets in which on his/her works has used the above lines?

(a) Alfred Lord Tennyson, In Memoriam
(b) Robert Browning Men and Women and Other Poems
(c) Matthew Arnold, Dover Beach and Other Poems
(d) Elizabeth Barrett Browning Sonnets from the Portuguese

62 In the given series, which one has all the literary awards/institution matched correctly with the year of their beginning?

(a) Kerala Sahitya Academy-1969, Man Booker Prize-1971, Sahitya Academy Award-1981, Mac Arthur Prize Fellowship-1983
(b) Kerala Sahitya Academy-1983, Man Booker Prize-1981, Sahitya Academy Award -1971, Mac Arthur Prize Fellowship-1969
(c) Kerala Sahitya Academy-1971, Man Booker Prize-1983, Sahitya Academy Award-1969, Mac Arthur Prize Fellowship-1981
(d) Kerala Sahitya Academy-1981, Man Booker Prize-1969, Sahitya Academy Award-1983, Mac Arthur Prize Fellowship-1971

63 **Assertion** (A) Dickens's novels are called 'Newgate Novels'.
Reason (R) They are called so because Dickens adulates in these novels the careers and adventures of criminals.
Codes
(a) A is true, but R is false
(b) A is false, but R is true
(c) Both A and R are true, but R is not the correct explanation of A
(d) Both A and R are true, and R is the correct explanation of A

64 Baldwin's collection of essays entitled 'The Evidence of Things Not Seen' concerns the
(a) Murders of Medgar Evers, Malcolm and Martin Luther King
(b) Watts Riots
(c) Atlanta Child Murders
(d) Early Exit of Harlem

65 "That tendency.........to he awake between the hours of two and four, when the chrysalis of faint misgiving becomes so readily the butterfly of panic".
Which of the following dramatists in the which of his/her works has had the above lines?
(a) George Bernard Shaw-Major Barbara
(b) JM Barrie-Peter Pan
(c) John Galsworthy-The White Monkey
(d) Sean O' Casey-The Shadow of a Gunman

66 What is the other name which can be given to 'Utopia'?
(a) The Kingdom of Fools
(b) The World of Imagination
(c) A Strange Island
(d) An Unknown Islands

67 Match the following characters with their plays.

List I (Character)	**List II** (Play)
1. Nora	A. Hedda Gabler
2. Tesman	B. A Enemy of the People
3. Regina	C. A Doll's House
4. Dr Thomas Stockman	D. Ghosts

Codes
(a) 1-A, 2-B, 3-C, 4-D
(b) 1-D, 2-C, 3-B, 4-A
(c) 1-C, 2-A, 3-D, 4-B
(d) 1-A, 2-C, 3-B, 4-D

68 What type of evaluation identifies learning deficiencies and difficulties of the learners?
(a) Placement
(b) Summative
(c) Continuous
(d) Diagnostic

69 The romance stories during Anglo-Norman period were influenced by
(a) English and French sources
(b) English and Norman sources
(c) Latin and English sources
(d) Latin and French Sources

70 **Assertion** (A) Dylan Marlais Thomas was a difficult poet. He is the poet of the learned like TS Eliot.
Reason (R) His poetry is full of metaphor's, symbolic imagery, biblical, freudian or folk image.
Codes
(a) A is true, but R is false
(b) A is false, but R is true
(c) Both A and R are true, but R is not the correct explanation of A
(d) Both A and R are true and R is the correct explanation of A

71 "Beauties in vain their pretty eyes may roll; Charms strike the sight, but merit wins the soul."
Which of the following poets in which of his /her works has used the above lines?
(a) Alexander Pope, The Rape of the Lock.
(b) Edward Young, Night Thoughts: Or, The Complaint and The Consolation
(c) John Gay, The Beggar's Opera
(d) James Thomson, The City of Dreadful Night

72 Which work of Thomas Lodge is considered as anticipating novel?
(a) Metamorphosis
(b) A Teatise of the Plague
(c) A Looking Glasses for London and England
(d) Rosalynde: Euphues Golden Legacies

73 In the given series, which one has all the Indian English writers matched correctly with their works?
(a) Pritish Nandy-Chitra and Sacrifice, Jayant Mahapatra-Father's Hours, Krian Desai-Hullabaloo in the Guava Orchard, Kamala Das-Love
(b) Pritish Nandy-Love Jayant Mahaparta-Hullabaloo in the Guava Orchard, Krian Desai-Father's Hours, Kamala Das-Chitra and Sacrifice
(c) Pritish Nandy-Father's Hours, Jayant Mahapatra-Love, Kiran Desai-Chitra and Sacrifice, Kamala Das-Hullabaloo in the Guava Orchard
(d) Pritish Nandy-Hullabaloo in the Guava Orchard, Jayant Mahapatra-Chitra and Sacrifice, Kiran Desai-Love, Kamala Das-Father's Hours

74 **Assertion** (A) Darwin's theory of revolution undermined the value of traditional religion and morality.
Reason (R) It revolutionalised man's conception of himself.
codes
(a) A is true, but R is false
(b) Both A and R are true
(c) Both A and R are true but R is not correct explanation of A
(d) Both A and R are false

75 "Semiotics is in principle the discipline studying everything which can be used in order to lie." Who said this is which of his/her work?

(a) Susan Msimang in the Burning
(b) Philip Temple in High Country
(c) Gordon Mclauchalan in the Acid Test
(d) Umberto Eco in a Theory of Semiotics

76 IA Richards' famous experiment with poems and his Cambridge students is detailed in practical criticism: a study of literary judgement (1929). Richards was astonished by

(a) The very astute remarks made by his students
(b) The poor quality of his student's stock responses
(c) The non availability of poems, worthy of classroom attention
(d) The success of his experiment

77 Who said these words in which work. "There was a level on which I believed that what had happened remained reversible"?

(a) Joan Didion in the Year of Magical Thinking
(b) Tony Judt in the Memory Chalet
(c) Allan Bloom in the Closing of the American Mind
(d) Umberto Eco in the Name of the Rose

78 The book.........was written by Gore Vidal in 1962.

(a) The Second American Revolution
(b) United States: Essay
(c) Rocking the Boat
(d) Imperial America

79 ....modeled his lyrical drama 'Atlanta in Calydon'.

(a) William Morris
(b) AC Swinburne
(c) John Ruskin
(d) DG Rossetti

80 Who asked Pope to write a comic poem about the historical incident between Arabella Fermor and Lord Petre in order to reconcile their families?

(a) Joseph Addison
(b) John Caryll
(c) Henry St. John Lord Bolingbroke
(d) Jonathan Swift

81 "Well, I wasn't going to abuse him. I was only going to ask: Is there any quality which distinguishes his work from that of twenty struggling writers one could name? Of course not. He's a clever, prolific man; so are they. But he began with money and friends; he came from Oxford into the thick of advertised people; his name was mentioned in print six times a week before he had written a dozen articles. This kind of thing will become the rule. Men won't succeed in literature that they may get into society, but will get into society that they may succeed in literature."

Which novelist has quoted the above lines in which of his/her work?

(a) Wilkie Collins – The Black Robe
(b) Anthony Trollope – He knew he was right
(c) George Gissing – New Grub Street
(d) RL Stevenson – Trevels with a Donkey in Cevennes

82 'The Mimic Men' by V S Naipaul is all about

(a) an expatriate
(b) an exiled Roman King
(c) an Indian living in Trinidad
(d) an exiled Caribbean politician

83 Which of the following has not been particularly part of Feminism as a literary movement of any stage?

(a) Treatment of female characters by male writers
(b) Treatment of female characters by female writers
(c) Role played by women in the publishing industry
(d) The influence of male writers on the work of female writers

84 "If a had a world of my own, everything would be nonsense. Nothing would be what it is because everything would be what it isn't it ......" "........and what is wouldn't it would. You see".

Which novelist has quoted the above lines in which of his/her work?

(a)	George Gissing	North and South
(b)	Wilkie Collins	The Black Robe
(c)	Lewis Carrol	Alice's Adventures in Wonderland
(d)	George Eliot	Silas Marner

85 "The reason birds can fly and we can't is simply because they have perfect faith, for to have faith is to have wings."

Which of the following dramatists in which of his/her works has had the above lines?

(a) Henrik Ibsen - An Enemy of the People
(b) George Bernard Shaw - Back to Methuselah
(c) JM Barrie - The Little White Bird
(d) John Galsworthy - The Forsyte Saga

86 In the given series, which one has all the works matched correctly with the year of their publication ?

(a) The English Teacher-1935, Swami and Friends-1938, The Guide-1945, The Dark Room-1958.
(b) The English Teacher-1958, Swami and Friends-1945, The Guide-1938, The Dark Room-1935.
(c) The English Teacher-1938, Swami and Friends-1958, The Guide-1935, The Dark Room-1945
(d) The English Teacher-1945, Swami and Friends-1935, The Guide-1958, The Dark Room-1938

87 Which of these statements about 'In Memoriam' is true?

(a) It is not an elegiac tribute to Arthur Henry Hallam
(b) It is not written by Lord Tennyson
(c) The poem was written over the course of 20 years
(d) The poem concludes with an epithalamion

88 Assertion (A) According to Edward said postcolonial resistant writers and readers are contrapuntal.

Reason (R) This is their way of answering back to the coloniser by examining the struggles over meaning taking place in the text of Empire itself.

(a) Both A and R are true
(b) Both A and R are false
(c) Both A and R are true, but R is not the correct explanation of A
(d) Both A and R are true, and R is the correct explanation of A

89 Match the authors with the novels.

List I (Authors)	List II (Novels)
A. Thomas Moore	1. New Atlantis
B. Thomas Nashe	2. Thomas of Reading
C. Francis Bacon	3. Utopia
D. Thomas Deloney	4. The Unfortunate Traveller

Codes

	A	B	C	D
(a)	3	4	1	2
(b)	2	4	3	1
(c)	2	1	4	3
(d)	1	2	3	4

90 "Where the mind is without Rear
And the head in held high
Where knowledge is free
Where the world has not been broken into fragments by narrow domestic walls."

(a) This is Amrita Pritam is 'Kat Canvas'
(b) This is Rabindranath Tagore in 'Gitanjali '
(c) This is Vikram Seth is 'The Golden Gate'
(d) This is Jayanta Mahapatra in 'Life Signs'

91 EO Wilson's term 'biophilia' means

(a) A Love of Life
(b) Fear of Death
(c) Rejection of Nature
(d) Appreciation of Boom

92 Reference and Bibliography are different in what ways?

(a) The references contain the minute details in order to verify them.
(b) The references have the surname of the person on its first priority.
(c) The references have the actual page number.
(d) All of the above

93 Archetypal criticism.

(a) Deals with the similarities of patterns in the literature of widely diverse culture
(b) Focuses on a reader active engagement with a piece of print or non-print
(c) Examines how differing religious beliefs ethnicities, identifications, political beliefs and individual view points affects how text are created and interpreted
(d) Focuses between relationships between genders

94 "He sat beside me pleasantly and played his sweet music to me, and in the end he foretold things that put drunkenness on my wits".

Which of the following dramatists in which of his/her works has had the above lines?

(a) Ibsen Henrik – Ghosts
(b) Lady Augusta Gregory – Gods and Fighting Men
(c) George Bernard Shaw – Mrs. Warren's Profession
(d) JM Barrie – The Little Minister

95 Which event changes Mr Polly's life for the better even through for a short term in novel the' History of Mr Polly'?

(a) His mother's death
(b) Friendship with fellow workers
(c) His father dies
(d) He wins a football match

Directions (Q Nos. 96-100) *Read the passage given below and answer the questions that follow.*

'Now they have all gone,' said Louis, 'I am alone'. They have gone into the house for breakfast, and I am left standing by the wall among the flowers.

It is very early, before lessons. Flower after flower is specked on the depths of green. The petals are harlequins. Stalks rise from the black hollows beneath. The flowers swim like fish made of light upon the dark, green waters. I hold a stalk in my hand. I am the stalk. My roots go down to the depths of the world, through earth dry with brick, and damp earth, through veins of lead and silver. I am all fibre. All tremors shake me, and the wight of the earth is pressed to my ribs. Up here my eyes are green leaves, unseeing. I am a boy in grey flannels with a belt fastened by a brass snake up here. Down there my eyes are the lidless eyes of a stone figure in a desert by the Nile. I see women passing with red pitchers to the river; I see camels swaying and men in turbans. I hear tramplings, tremblings, stirrings round me'. "Up here Bernard, Neville, Jinny and Susan (but not Rhoda) skim the flower-beds with their nets. They skim the butterflies from the nodding tops of the flowers. They brush the surface of the world.Their nets are full of fluttering wings. 'Louis! Louis! Louis!' they shout. But they cannot see me. I am on the other side of the hedge. There are only little eye-holes among the leaves".

96 The characters Bernard, Neville, Jinny and Susan belong to which novel of 'Virginia Woolf'?

(a) Mrs. Dalloway
(b) Jacob's Room
(c) The Waves
(d) To The Lighthouse

97 Who cannot be seen?

(a) Bernard
(b) Louis
(c) Neville
(d) Jinny

98 What does fluttering wings imply?

(a) Butterflies
(b) Birds
(c) Flowers
(d) Net

99 Which place does Rhoda travel after break up with Louis?

(a) India
(b) Spain
(c) The Opera
(d) London

100 What is the major theme of this novel 'The Waves'?

(a) Childhood is the best time
(b) Life's fertility
(c) Transition to inner reality
(d) Death of all characters as they reach adulthood

ANSWERS

1. (c)	2. (c)	3. (b)	4. (c)	5. (b)	6. (b)	7. (c)	8. (b)	9. (a)	10. (b)
11. (b)	12. (c)	13. (c)	14. (c)	15. (c)	16. (d)	17. (d)	18. (d)	19. (c)	20. (b)
21. (a)	22. (c)	23. (d)	24. (c)	25. (b)	26. (d)	27. (d)	28. (d)	29. (b)	30. (a)
31. (a)	32. (c)	33. (d)	34. (b)	35. (d)	36. (c)	37. (a)	38. (d)	39. (a)	40. (a)
41. (c)	42. (c)	43. (a)	44. (d)	45. (c)	46. (d)	47. (a)	48. (a)	49. (d)	50. (d)
51. (a)	52. (c)	53. (c)	54. (d)	55. (c)	56. (b)	57. (b)	58. (a)	59. (c)	60. (a)
61. (d)	62. (a)	63. (b)	64. (a)	65. (c)	66. (d)	67. (c)	68. (d)	69. (d)	70. (d)
71. (a)	72. (d)	73. (a)	74. (c)	75. (d)	76. (b)	77. (a)	78. (c)	79. (b)	80. (b)
81. (c)	82. (d)	83. (c)	84. (c)	85. (c)	86. (d)	87. (d)	88. (c)	89. (a)	90. (b)
91. (a)	92. (d)	93. (a)	94. (b)	95. (c)	96. (c)	97. (b)	98. (a)	99. (b)	100. (d)